ISBN 978-1-5282-2950-0
PIBN 10939393

1 MONTH OF
FREE
READING

at
www.ForgottenBooks.com

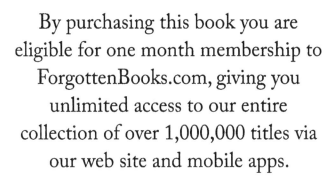

By purchasing this book you are eligible for one month membership to ForgottenBooks.com, giving you unlimited access to our entire collection of over 1,000,000 titles via our web site and mobile apps.

To claim your free month visit:

www.forgottenbooks.com/free939393

English
Français
Deutsche
Italiano
Español
Português

www.forgottenbooks.com

Mythology Photography **Fiction**
Fishing Christianity **Art** Cooking
Essays Buddhism Freemasonry
Medicine **Biology** Music **Ancient
Egypt** Evolution Carpentry Physics
Dance Geology **Mathematics** Fitness
Shakespeare **Folklore** Yoga Marketing
Confidence Immortality Biographies
Poetry **Psychology** Witchcraft
Electronics Chemistry History **Law**
Accounting **Philosophy** Anthropology
Alchemy Drama Quantum Mechanics
Atheism Sexual Health **Ancient History**
Entrepreneurship Languages Sport
Paleontology Needlework Islam
Metaphysics Investment Archaeology
Parenting Statistics Criminology
Motivational

ANNALS

OF

THE CONGRESS OF THE UNITED STATES.

FOURTEENTH CONGRESS.—FIRST SESSION.

THE

DEBATES AND PROCEEDINGS

IN THE

CONGRESS OF THE UNITED STATES;

WITH

AN APPENDIX,

CONTAINING

IMPORTANT STATE PAPERS AND PUBLIC DOCUMENTS,

AND ALL

THE LAWS OF A PUBLIC NATURE;

WITH A COPIOUS INDEX.

FOURTEENTH CONGRESS—FIRST SESSION:

COMPRISING THE PERIOD FROM DECEMBER 4, 1815, TO APRIL 30, 1816, INCLUSIVE.

COMPILED FROM AUTHENTIC MATERIALS.

WASHINGTON:

PRINTED AND PUBLISHED BY GALES AND SEATON.

1854.

PROCEEDINGS AND DEBATES

OF

THE SENATE OF THE UNITED STATES,

AT THE FIRST SESSION OF THE FOURTEENTH CONGRESS, BEGUN AT THE CITY OF WASHINGTON, MONDAY, DECEMBER 4, 1815.

MONDAY, December 4, 1815.

The first session of the Fourteenth Congress, conformably to the Constitution of the United States, commenced this day at the City of Washington; and the Senate assembled.

PRESENT:

JOSEPH B. VARNUM, from the State of Massachusetts.

WILLIAM HUNTER and JEREMIAH B. HOWELL, from Rhode Island.

DUDLEY CHACE and ISAAC TICHENOR, from Vermont.

DAVID DAGGETT, from Connecticut.

NATHAN SANFORD, from New York.

JAMES J. WILSON, from New Jersey.

ABNER LACOCK and JONATHAN ROBERTS, from Pennsylvania.

OUTERBRIDGE HORSEY, from Delaware.

JAMES BARBOUR, from Virginia.

JOHN GAILLARD, from South Carolina.

CHARLES TAIT, from Georgia.

GEORGE W. CAMPBELL and JOHN WILLIAMS, from Tennessee.

BENJAMIN RUGGLES, from Ohio.

JAMES BROWN and ELIGIUS FROMENTIN, from Louisiana.

JOHN GAILLARD, President pro tempore, resumed the Chair.

ISAAC TICHENOR, appointed a Senator by the Legislature of the State of Vermont, for the term of six years, commencing on the 4th day of March last; NATHAN SANFORD, appointed a Senator by the Legislature of the State of New York for the term of six years, commencing on the 4th day of March last; JAMES J. WILSON, appointed a Senator by the Legislature of the State of New Jersey, for the term of six years, commencing on the 4th day of March last; JAMES BARBOUR, appointed a Senator by the Legislature of the State of Virginia, for the term of six years, commencing on the 4th day of March last; GEORGE W. CAMPBELL, appointed a Senator by the Legislature of the State of Tennessee, for the term of six years, commencing on the 4th day of March last; JOHN WILLIAMS, appointed a Senator by the Legislature of the State of Tennessee, for the term of two years, in place of George W. Campbell, resigned; BENJAMIN RUGGLES, appointed a Senator by the Legislature of the State of Ohio, for the term of six years, commencing on the 4th day of March last; respectively produced their credentials, which were read, and the oath prescribed by law was administered to them, and they took their seats in the Senate.

The oath was also administered to Messrs. HUNTER, ROBERTS, and HORSEY; their credentials having been read and filed during the last session.

Ordered, That the Secretary acquaint the House of Representatives that a quorum of the Senate is assembled, and ready to proceed to business.

Messrs. VARNUM and HUNTER were appointed a committee on the part of the Senate, together with such committee as may be appointed by the House of Representatives, on their part, to wait on the President of the United States, and notify him, that a quorum of the two Houses is assembled and ready to receive any communications that he may be pleased to make to them; and the Secretary was directed to notify the House of Representatives accordingly.

The PRESIDENT communicated a letter from the committee in behalf of the gentlemen concerned in erecting the new building on the Capitol Hill for the accommodation of Congress, offering the same to Congress until the Capitol may be ready for their reception; which was read.

Whereupon, on motion, by Mr. HORSEY,

Resolved, That a committee be appointed on the part of the Senate, to join such committee as may be appointed on the part of the House of Representatives, to inquire and report upon the state of the new building on Capitol Hill offered to Congress by letter addressed to the President of the Senate of this day, by a committee on their part, of the gentlemen concerned in erecting the same; and that the said joint committee be instructed to inquire and ascertain upon what terms and conditions the use of the said building for the accommodation of Congress may be obtained, until the Capitol may be ready for their reception.

Resolved, That Messrs. HORSEY, LACOCK. and FROMENTIN, be the committee on the part of the Senate.

On motion, by Mr. VARNUM,

Resolved, That each Senator be supplied, during the present session, with three such newspapers, printed in any of the States, as he may choose; provided the same be furnished at the usual rate for the annual charge of such papers; and provided, also, that if any Senator shall choose to take any newspapers other than daily papers; he shall be supplied with as many such papers, as shall not exceed the price of three daily papers.

On motion, by Mr. LACOCK, a committee was appointed agreeably to the forty-second rule for conducting business in the Senate; and Messrs. LACOCK, HOWELL, and DAGGETT, were appointed the committee.

On motion, by Mr. FROMENTIN, a committee was appointed agreeably to the twenty-second rule for conducting business in the Senate; and Messrs. FROMENTIN, SANFORD, and TICHENOR, were appointed the committee.

Mr. FROMENTIN submitted the following motion for consideration, which was read, and ordered to the second reading:

Resolved, That a committee of three members be appointed, who, with three members of the House of Representatives, to be appointed by that House, shall have the direction of the money appropriated to the purchase of books and maps, for the use of the two Houses of Congress.

On motion, by Mr. LACOCK, it was read a second time by unanimous consent, and considered as in Committee of the Whole, and no amendment having been proposed, the President reported it to the House accordingly; and on the question, "Shall this resolution be engrossed and read a third time?" it was determined in the affirmative. It was then read a third time by unanimous consent, and passed; and Messrs. FROMENTIN, HUNTER, and GOLDSBOROUGH, were appointed the committee.

Mr. HOWELL submitted a motion for the appointment of two Chaplains, of different denominations, to Congress, during the present session, one by each House, who shall interchange weekly; which was read, and passed to the second reading.

Mr. LACOCK submitted the following motion for consideration, which was read:

Resolved, That Mountjoy Bayly, Doorkeeper and Sergeant-at-Arms to the Senate, be, and he hereby is, authorized to employ one assistant and two horses, for the purpose of performing such services as are usually required by the Doorkeeper of the Senate; which expense shall be paid out of the contingent fund.

Ordered, That it pass to the second reading.

TUESDAY, December 5.

WILLIAM W. BIBB, from the State of Georgia, took his seat in the Senate.

A message from the House of Representatives informed the Senate, that a quorum of the House of Representatives is assembled, and have elected HENRY CLAY, one of the Representatives for the State of Kentucky, their Speaker, and THOMAS DOUGHERTY, their Clerk, and are ready to proceed to business. They have appointed a committee on their part, to join the committee appointed on the part of the Senate, to wait on the President of the United States, and inform him that a quorum of the two Houses is assembled, and ready to receive any communications he may be pleased to make to them. They concur in the resolution of the Senate for the appointment of a joint committee on the arrangements for the library, and have appointed a committee on their part. They also concur in the resolution of the Senate for the appointment of a joint committee, to inquire and report of the state of the new building on Capitol Hill, offered for the accommodation of Congress, and have appointed a committee on their part.

Mr. VARNUM reported, from the joint committee, that they had waited on the President of the United States, and that the President informed the committee, that he would make a communication to the two Houses this day at 12 o'clock.

PRESIDENT'S MESSAGE.

The following Message was received from the PRESIDENT OF THE UNITED STATES:

Fellow-citizens of the Senate
    and House of Representatives:

I have the satisfaction, on our present meeting, of being able to communicate to you the successful termination of the war which had been commenced against the United States by the Regency of Algiers. The squadron in advance on that service, under Commodore Decatur, lost not a moment after its arrival in the Mediterranean, in seeking the naval force of the enemy then cruising in that sea, and succeeded in capturing two of his ships, one of them the principal ship, commanded by the Algerine Admiral. The high character of the American commander was brilliantly sustained on the occasion, which brought his own ship into close action with that of his adversary, as was the accustomed gallantry of all the officers and men actually engaged. Having prepared the way by this demonstration of American skill and prowess, he hastened to the port of Algiers, where peace was promptly yielded to his victorious force. In the terms stipulated, the rights and honor of the United States were particularly consulted, by a perpetual relinquishment, on the part of the Dey, of all pretensions to tribute from them. The impressions which have thus been made, strengthened as they will have been, by subsequent transactions with the Regencies of Tunis and of Tripoli, by the appearance of the larger force which followed under Commodore Bainbridge, the chief in command of the expedition, and by the judicious precautionary arrangements left by him in that quarter, afford a reasonable prospect of future security, for the valuable portion of our commerce which passes within reach of the Barbary cruisers.

It is another source of satisfaction that the Treaty of Peace with Great Britain has been succeeded by a Convention on the subject of commerce, concluded by the Plenipotentiaries of the two countries. In this result a disposition is manifested on the part of that nation, corresponding with the disposition of the United States, which, it may be hoped, will be improved into liberal arrangements on other subjects, on which the parties have mutual interests, or which might endanger their future harmony. Congress will decide on the expediency of promoting such a sequel, by giving effect to the measure of confining the American navigation to American seamen; a measure which, at the same time that it might have that conciliatory tendency, would have the further advantage of increasing the independence of our navigation, and the resources for our maritime defence.

In conformity with the articles in the Treaty of Ghent, relating to the Indians, as well as with a view to the tranquillity of our Western and Northern frontiers, measures were taken to establish an immediate peace with the several tribes who had been engaged in hostilities against the United States. Such of them as were invited to Detroit acceded readily to a renewal of the former treaties of friendship. Of the other tribes who were invited to a station on the Mississippi, the greatest number have also accepted the peace offered to them. The residue, consisting of the more distant tribes, or parts of tribes, remain to be brought over by further explanations, or by such other means as may be adapted to the dispositions they may finally disclose.

The Indian tribes within, and bordering on the Southern frontier, whom a cruel war on their part had compelled us to chastise into peace, have latterly shown a restlessness, which has called for preparatory measures for repressing it, and for protecting the Commissioners engaged in carrying the terms of peace into execution.

The execution of the act for fixing the Military Peace Establishment, has been attended with difficulties which even now can only be overcome by Legislative aid. The selection of officers; the payment and discharge of the troops enlisted for the war; the payment of the retained troops, and their re-union from detached and distant stations; the collection and security of the public property in the Quartermaster, Commissary, and Ordnance Departments; and the constant medical assistance required in hospitals and garrisons, rendered a complete execution of the act impracticable on the first of May, the period more immediately contemplated. As soon, however, as circumstances would permit, and as far as it has been practicable, consistently with the public interests, the reduction of the Army has been accomplished; but the appropriations for its pay and for other branches of the military service, having proved inadequate, the earliest attention to that subject will be necessary; and the expediency of continuing, upon the Peace Establishment, the staff officers who have hitherto been provisionally retained, is also recommended to the consideration of Congress.

In the performance of the Executive duty upon this occasion, there has not been wanting a just sensibility to the merits of the American Army during the late war: but the obvious policy and design in fixing an efficient Military Peace Establishment did not afford an opportunity to distinguish the aged and infirm, on account of their past services; nor the wounded and disabled, on account of their present sufferings. The extent of the reduction, indeed, unavoidably involved the exclusion of many meritorious officers of every rank from the service of their country; and so equal, as well as so numerous, were the claims to attention, that a

decision by the standard of comparative merit could seldom be attained. Judged, however, in candor, by a general standard of positive merit, the Army register will, it is believed, do honor to the establishment; while the case of those officers, whose names are not included in it, devolves, with the strongest interest, upon the Legislative authority, for such provision as shall be deemed the best calculated to give support and solace to the veteran and the invalid; to display the beneficence, as well as the justice, of the Government; and to inspire a martial zeal for the public service upon every future emergency.

Although the embarrassments arising from the want of an uniform National currency have not been diminished since the adjournment of Congress, great satisfaction has been derived in contemplating the revival of the public credit, and the efficiency of the public resources. The receipts into the Treasury, from the various branches of revenue, during the nine months ending on the 30th of September last, have been estimated at twelve millions and a half of dollars; the issues of Treasury notes of every denomination, during the same period, amounted to the sum of fourteen millions of dollars; and there was also obtained upon loan, during the same period, a sum of nine millions of dollars; of which the sum of six millions of dollars was subscribed in cash, and the sum of three millions of dollars in Treasury notes. With these means, added to the sum of one million and a half of dollars, being the balance of money in the Treasury on the first of January, there has been paid, between the first of January and the first of October, on account of the appropriations of the preceding and of the present year, (exclusively of the amount of the Treasury notes subscribed to the loan, and of the amount redeemed in the payment of duties and taxes,) the aggregate sum of thirty-three millions and a half of dollars, leaving a balance then in the Treasury estimated at the sum of three millions of dollars. Independent, however, of the arrearages due for military services and supplies, it is presumed that a further sum of five millions of dollars, including the interest on the public debt payable on the first of January next, will be demanded at the Treasury to complete the expenditure of the present year, and for which the existing ways and means will sufficiently provide.

The National debt, as it was ascertained on the first of October last, amounted in the whole to the sum of one hundred and twenty millions of dollars, consisting of the unredeemed balance of the debt contracted before the late war, (thirty-nine millions of dollars,) the amount of the funded debt contracted in consequence of the war, (sixty-four millions of dollars,) and the amount of the unfunded and floating debt, (including the various issues of Treasury notes,) seventeen millions of dollars, which is in a gradual course of payment. There will, probably, be some addition to the public debt, upon the liquidation of various claims, which are depending; and a conciliatory disposition on the part of Congress may lead honorably and advantageously to an equitable arrangement of the militia expenses incurred by the several States, without the previous sanction or authority of the Government of the United States; but when it is considered that the new, as well as the old portion of the debt has been contracted in the assertion of the national rights and independence; and when it is recollected that the public expenditures, not being exclusively bestowed upon subjects of a transient nature, will long be visible in the number and equipments of the American navy, in the military works for the defence of our harbors and our frontiers, and in the supplies of our arsenals and magazines, the amount will bear a gratifying comparison with the objects which have been attained, as well as with the resources of the country.

The arrangements of the finances, with a view to the receipts and expenditures of a permanent Peace Establishment, will necessarily enter into the deliberations of Congress during the present session. It is true that the improved condition of the public revenue will not afford the means of maintaining the faith of the Government with its creditors inviolate, and of prosecuting, successfully, the measures of the most liberal policy, but will also justify an immediate alleviation of the burdens imposed by the necessities of the war. It is, however, essential to every modification of the finances, that the benefits of an uniform National currency should be restored to the community. The absence of the precious metals will, it is believed, be a temporary evil; but, until they can again be rendered the general medium of exchange, it devolves on the wisdom of Congress to provide a substitute, which shall equally engage the confidence, and accommodate the wants of the citizens throughout the Union. If the operation of the State banks cannot produce this result, the probable operation of a National Bank will merit consideration; and if neither of these expedients be deemed effectual, it may become necessary to ascertain the terms upon which the notes of the Government (no longer required as an instrument of credit) shall be issued, upon motives of general policy, as a common medium of circulation.

Notwithstanding the security for future repose, which the United States ought to find in their love of peace, and their constant respect for the rights of other nations, the character of the times particularly inculcates the lesson, that, whether to prevent or repel danger, we ought not to be unprepared for it. This consideration will sufficiently recommend to Congress a liberal provision for the immediate extension and gradual completion of the works of defence, both fixed and floating, on our maritime frontier, and an adequate provision for guarding our inland frontier against dangers to which certain portions of it may continue to be exposed.

As an improvement in our Military Establishment, it will deserve the consideration of Congress, whether a corps of invalids might not be so organized and employed, as at once to aid in the support of meritorious individuals, excluded by age or infirmities from the existing establishment, and to procure to the public the benefit of their stationary services, and of their exemplary discipline. I recommend, also, an enlargement of the Military Academy, already established, and the establishment of others in other sections of the Union. And I cannot press too much on the attention of Congress, such a classification and organization of the militia as will most effectually render it the safeguard of a free State. If experience has shown, in the recent splendid achievements of militia, the value of this resource for the public defence, it has shown also the importance of that skill in the use of arms, and that familiarity with the essential rules of discipline, which cannot be expected from the regulations now in force. With this subject is intimately connected the necessity of accommodating the laws, in every respect, to the great object of enabling the political authority of the Union to employ, promptly and effectu-

ally, the physical power of the Union in the cases designated by the Constitution.

The signal services which have been rendered by our Navy, and the capacities it has developed for successful co-operation in the national defence, will give to that portion of the public force its full value in the eyes of Congress, at an epoch which calls for the constant vigilance of all Governments. To preserve the ships now in a sound state; to complete those already contemplated; to provide amply the imperishable materials for prompt augmentations, and to improve the existing arrangements into more advantageous establishments, for the construction, the repairs, and the security of the vessels of war, is dictated by the soundest policy.

In adjusting the duties on imports, to the object of revenue, the influence of the tariff on manufactures will necessarily present itself for consideration. However wise the theory may be, which leaves to the sagacity and interest of individuals the application of their industry and resources, there are in this, as in other cases, exceptions to the general rule. Besides the condition which the theory itself implies, of a reciprocal adoption by other nations, experience teaches that so many circumstances must concur in introducing and maturing manufacturing establishments, especially of the more complicated kinds, that a country may remain long without them, although sufficiently advanced, and, in some respects, even peculiarly fitted for carrying them on with success. Under circumstances giving a powerful impulse to manufacturing industry, it has made among us a progress, and exhibited an efficiency, which justify the belief that, with a protection not more than is due to the enterprising citizens whose interests are now at stake, it will become, at an early day, not only safe against occasional competitions from abroad, but a source of domestic wealth, and even of external commerce. In selecting the branches more especially entitled to the public patronage, a preference is obviously claimed by such as will relieve the United States from a dependence on foreign supplies, ever subject to casual failures, for articles necessary for the public defence, or connected with the primary wants of individuals. It will be an additional recommendation of particular manufactures, where the materials for them are extensively drawn from our agriculture, and consequently impart and insure to that great fund of national prosperity and independence an encouragement which cannot fail to be rewarded.

Among the means of advancing the public interest, the occasion is a proper one for recalling the attention of Congress to the great importance of establishing throughout our country the roads and canals which can be best executed, under the national authority. No objects within the circle of political economy so richly repay the expense bestowed on them; there are none, the utility of which is more universally ascertained and acknowledged; none that do more honor to the Governments whose wise and enlarged patriotism duly appreciates them. Nor is there any country which presents a field, where nature invites more the art of man, to complete her own work, for his accommodation and benefit. These considerations are strengthened, moreover, by the political effect of these facilities for intercommunication, in bringing and binding more closely together the various parts of our extended confederacy. Whilst the States, individually, with a laudable enterprise and emulation, avail themselves of their local advantages, by new roads, by navigable canals, and by improving the streams susceptible of navigation, the General Government is the more urged to similar undertakings, requiring a national jurisdiction, and national means, by the prospect of thus systematically completing so inestimable a work. And it is a happy reflection, that any defect of Constitutional authority, which may be encountered, can be supplied in a mode which the Constitution itself has providently pointed out.

The present is a favorable season also for bringing again into view the establishment of a National seminary of learning within the District of Columbia, and with means drawn from the property therein subject to the authority of the General Government. Such an institution claims the patronage of Congress, as a monument of their solicitude for the advancement of knowledge, without which the blessings of liberty cannot be fully enjoyed, or long preserved; as a model, instructive in the formation of other seminaries; as a nursery of enlightened preceptors; and, as a central resort of youth and genius from every part of their country, diffusing, on their return, examples of those national feelings, those liberal sentiments, and those congenial manners, which contribute cement to our union and strength to the great political fabric, of which that is the foundation.

In closing this communication, I ought not to repress a sensibility, in which you will unite, to the happy lot of our country, and to the goodness of a superintending Providence, to which we are indebted for it. Whilst other portions of mankind are laboring under the distresses of war, or struggling with adversity in other forms, the United States are in the tranquil enjoyment of prosperous and honorable peace. In reviewing the scenes through which it has been attained, we can rejoice in the proofs given, that our political institutions, founded in human rights, and framed for their preservation, are equal to the severest trials of war, as well as adapted to the ordinary periods of repose. As fruits of this experience, and of the reputation acquired by the American arms, on the land and on the water, the nation finds itself possessed of a growing respect abroad, and of a just confidence in itself, which are among the best pledges for its peaceful career. Under other aspects of our country, the strongest features of its flourishing condition are seen, in a population rapidly increasing, on a territory as productive as it is extensive; in a general industry and fertile ingenuity, which find their ample rewards; and in an affluent revenue, which admits of a reduction of the public burdens, without withdrawing the means of sustaining the public credit, of gradually discharging the public debt, of providing for the necessary defensive and precautionary establishments, and of patronizing, in every authorized mode, undertakings conducive to the aggregate wealth and individual comfort of our citizens.

It remains for the guardians of the public welfare, to persevere in that justice and good will towards other nations, which invite a return of these sentiments towards the United States; to cherish institutions which guarantee their safety and their liberties, civil and religious; and to combine, with a liberal system of foreign commerce, an improvement of the national advantages, and a protection and extension of the independent resources of our highly favored and happy country.

In all measures having such objects, my faithful co-operation will be afforded.   JAMES MADISON.

WASHINGTON, *December* 5, 1815.

The Message was read, and one thousand and fifty copies thereof ordered to be printed for the use of the Senate.

The resolution, authorizing Mountjoy Bayly to employ one assistant and two horses, was read the second time, and considered as in Committee of the Whole; and no amendment having been proposed, the President reported it to the House accordingly; and the resolution was ordered to be engrossed, and read a third time.

The resolution, for the appointment of Chaplains, was read the second time, and considered as in Committee of the Whole; and no amendment having been proposed, the President reported it to the House accordingly; and the resolution was ordered to be engrossed, and read a third time.

WEDNESDAY, December 6.

JAMES TURNER, from the State of North Carolina, and JOHN CONDIT, from the State of New Jersey, respectively took their seats in the Senate.

Mr. ROBERTS presented the petition of Joseph C. Morgan, attorney in fact for Xaverio Nandi, late Chargé d'Affaires at Tripoli, stating that difficulties had arisen which prevented the settlement of said Xaverio Nandi's account, and praying that the proper officer of the Government may be authorized to settle and discharge the same; and the petition was read, and referred to a select committee, to consider and report thereon by bill or otherwise; and Messrs. ROBERTS, SANFORD, and HORSEY, were appointed the committee.

Mr. HUNTER presented the petition of Jacob Babbit, merchant, of the port of Bristol, in the State of Rhode Island, praying the remission of duties secured to be paid on a large quantity of sugar, which was totally destroyed by the unprecedented storm on the 23d of September last, as therein stated; and the petition was read, and referred to a select committee, to consider and report thereon by bill or otherwise; and Messrs. HUNTER, BIBB, and HOWELL, were appointed the committee.

The resolution for the appointment of Chaplains, was read the third time, and passed as follows:

Resolved, That two Chaplains, of different denominations, be appointed to Congress, during the present session, one by each House, who shall interchange weekly.

The resolution authorizing Mountjoy Bayly to employ one assistant and two horses, was read a third time and passed.

THURSDAY, December 7.

SAMUEL W. DANA, appointed a Senator by the Legislature of the State of Connecticut, for the term of six years, commencing on the 4th day of March last, produced his credentials, was qualified, and he took his seat in the Senate.

JEREMIAH MORROW, from the State of Ohio, also took his seat in the Senate.

Mr. HORSEY, from the joint committee appointed to inquire into the state of the new building on Capital Hill, offered by the proprietors for the accommodation of Congress, and upon what terms the said building could be obtained until the Capitol may be ready for their reception, made a report which was read.

Mr. HORSEY also asked and obtained leave to report a bill to authorize the President of the United States to lease, for the term therein mentioned, the new building on Capitol Hill, with appurtenances, for the better accommodation of Congress; and the bill was read, and passed to the second reading.

The PRESIDENT communicated the memorial of the Legislative Council and House of Representatives of the Mississippi Territory, praying further time to complete the payments on public lands; which was read and referred to a select committee, to consist of five members, and Messrs. BROWN, MORROW, CHACE, TAIT, and BARBOUR, were appointed the committee.

A message from the House of Representatives informed the Senate that the House have passed a bill, entitled "An act to authorize the President of the United States to lease, for the term therein mentioned, the new building on Capitol Hill, with the appurtenances, for the better accommodation of Congress; in which bill they request the concurrence of the Senate.

The bill last mentioned was read three times by unanimous consent, and passed.

FRIDAY, December 8.

The PRESIDENT communicated a report of the Secretary for the Department of the Treasury, prepared in obedience to the act, "to establish the Treasury Department, and the act supplementary thereto," and the report was read.

The Senate proceeded to the appointment of a Chaplain on their part, and, on the ballots having been counted, it appeared that the Reverend JOHN GLENDIS had a majority, and was elected.

PRESIDENT'S MESSAGE.

Mr. BIBB submitted the following motions for consideration:

Resolved, That so much of the Message of the President of the United States as relates to Foreign Affairs, be referred to a select committee, with leave to report by bill or otherwise.

Resolved, That so much of the Message of the President of the United States as relates to the Militia, be referred to a select committee, with leave to report by bill or otherwise.

Resolved, That so much of the Message of the President of the United States as relates to Military Affairs, be referred to a select committee, with leave to report by bill ortherwise.

Resolved, That so much of the Message of the President of the United States as relates to Naval Affairs, be referred to a select committee, with leave to report by bill or otherwise.

Resolved, That so much of the Message of the President of the United States as relates to Finance, and an Uniform National Currency, be referred to a select committee, with leave to report by bill or otherwise.

Resolved, That so much of the Message of the President of the United States as relates to Manufactures, be referred to a select committee, with leave to report by bill or otherwise.

Resolved, That so much of the Message of the President of the United States as relates to Roads and Canals, be referred to a select committee, with leave to report by bill or otherwise.

Resolved, That so much of the Message of the President of the United States as relates to a National Seminary of Learning within the District of Columbia, be referred to a select committee, with leave to report by bill or otherwise.

MONDAY, December 11.

ROBERT H. GOLDSBOROUGH, from the State of Maryland, took his seat in the Senate.

The PRESIDENT communicated the report of the Secretary for the Department of War, made conformably to the act of the 3d of March, 1809, entitled "An act further to amend the several acts for the establishment and regulation of the Treasury, War, and Navy Departments;" and the report was read.

The Senate resumed the motion made the 8th instant, for the appointment of a Committee on so much of the Message of the President of the United States, as relates to Foreign Affairs, and agreed thereto; and Messrs. BIBB, DANA, TAYLOR, BARRY, and KING, were appointed the committee.

The Senate resumed the motion made the 8th instant, for the appointment of a Committee on so much of the Message of the President of the United States, as relates to the Militia, and agreed thereto; and Messrs. VARNUM, LACOCK, WILSON, TICHENOR, and TURNER, were appointed the committee.

The Senate resumed the motion made the 8th instant, for the appointment of a Committee on so much of the Message of the President of the United States, as relates to Military Affairs, and agreed thereto; and Messrs. BARBOUR, WILLIAMS, RUGGLES, GOLDSBOROUGH, and CONDIT, were appointed the committee.

The Senate resumed the motion made the 8th instant, for the appointment of a Committee on so much of the Message of the President of the United States, as relates to Naval Affairs, and agreed thereto; and Messrs. TAIT, DAGGETT, SANFORD, FROMENTIN, and HOWELL, were appointed the committee.

The Senate resumed the motion made the 8th instant, for the appointment of a Committee on so much of the Message of the President of the United States, as relates to Finance and an Uniform National Currency, and agreed thereto; and Messrs. CAMPBELL, CHACE, BIBB, KING, and MASON, were appointed the committee.

The Senate resumed the motion made the 8th instant, for the appointment of a Committee on so much of the Message of the President of the United States, as relates to Manufactures, and agreed thereto; and Messrs. HUNTER, ROBERTS, TALBOT, CONDIT, and THOMPSON, were appointed the committee.

The Senate resumed the motion made the 8th instant, for the appointment of a Committee on so much of the Message of the President of the United States, as relates to Roads and Canals, and agreed thereto; and Messrs. MORROW, BROWN, HORSEY, WILSON, and GORE, were appointed the committee.

The Senate also resumed the motion made the 8th instant, on so much of the Message of the President of the United States, as relates to a National Seminary of Learning within the District of Columbia, and agreed thereto; and Messrs. BROWN, FROMENTIN, SANFORD, DANA, and HUNTER, were appointed the committee.

Mr. DAGGETT presented the petition of Cyprian Nichols, and others, manufacturers of mould candles of tallow, praying a reduction of the duty of three cents per pound, laid on at the last session of Congress, for reasons stated in the petition; which was read, and referred to the Committee this day appointed, on so much of the Message of the President of the United States as relates to Manufactures.

Mr. BARBOUR submitted the following motion for consideration:

Resolved, That each member of the Senate be annually furnished with a copy of the Register of the Officers of the Army and Navy of the United States.

Mr. ROBERTS presented the memorial of Thos. Leiper and others, tobacco, cigar, and snuff manufacturers, of the city and county of Philadelphia, praying the repeal of a duty of twenty per centum, ad valorem, imposed upon such articles manufactured or made for sale within the United States, or Territories thereof, by an act of Congress, passed the 18th of January, 1815, for reasons stated at large in the memorial; which was read, and referred to the Committee this day appointed, on so much of the Message of the President of the United States as relates to Manufactures.

Mr. ROBERTS presented the petition of Dawson and Monison, and others, brewers of malt liquors, of the city of Philadelphia, representing their grievances from the operation of the excise law, passed by Congress at their last session, and praying relief for reasons stated in the petition; which was read, and referred to the Committee last mentioned.

On motion by Mr. DAGGETT,

Resolved, That when the Senate adjourn, they adjourn to meet on Wednesday next, in the new building on Capitol Hill.

The PRESIDENT communicated reports of the Secretary for the Department of Navy, made in obedience to the resolutions of the Senate of the 28th of January, and the 28th of February, 1815, upon the several subjects thereof; which were read.

WEDNESDAY, December 13.

RUFUS KING, from the State of New York, and JOHN TAYLOR, from the State of South Carolina, respectively took their seats in the Senate.

NATHANIEL MACON, appointed a Senator by the Legislature of the State of North Carolina, in place of Francis Locke, resigned, produced his credentials, was qualified, and he took his seat in the Senate.

Mr. ROBERTS presented the memorial of Edmund Kinsey and others, manufacturers of saddlery, in the city of Philadelphia, praying a repeal of the taxes on domestic manufactures, for reasons stated at large in the memorial; which was read, and referred to the Committee, appointed the 11th instant, on so much of the Message of the President of the United States as relates to Manufactures.

Mr. ROBERTS also presented the memorial of Lewis Ryan and others, manufacturers of boots and bootees, in the city of Philadelphia, praying the repeal of taxes upon all domestic manufactures, for reasons stated at large in the memorial; which was read, and referred to the committee last mentioned.

Mr. DAGGETT presented the petition of Abel Bissell and others, manufacturers of cotton fabrics, representing their peculiar situation, and praying the interposition of Congress, for protection and relief, as stated in the petition; which was read, and referred to the committee last mentioned.

Mr. WILSON presented the petition of John Duckworth, jr., and others, praying the establishment of a post route from Pittstown, in the county of Hunterdon, in the State of New Jersey, to the village of Harmony, in the county of Sussex, for reasons stated in the petition; which was read, and referred to a select committee; and Messrs. WILSON, CONDIT, and ROBERTS, were appointed the committee.

Mr. RUGGLES presented the petition of the Reverend Joseph Anderson, praying that the sum of $323 68, the first instalment paid by him, on a quarter section of land in Ohio, and forfeited in consequence of non-payment, may be placed to his credit on a subsequent purchase, for reasons stated at large in the petition; which was read, and referred to the committee to whom was referred, the 7th instant, the memorial of the Legislative Council, and House of Representatives of the Mississippi Territory.

The Senate resumed the consideration of the motion submitted on the 11th instant, by Mr. BARBOUR; which, on his motion, was amended and agreed to, as follows:

Resolved, That the Secretary of War and the Secretary of the Navy be requested to furnish annually, on the first of January, each member of the Senate with a copy of the Register of the Officers of the Army and Navy of the United States.

THURSDAY, December 14.

Mr. ROBERTS presented the petition of John Thompson, praying interest may be allowed him on an old claim for Revolutionary services, for reasons stated in the petition; which was read, and referred to a select committee; and Messrs. ROBERTS, MACON, and SANFORD, were appointed the committee.

Mr. FROMENTIN presented the petition of Denis de la Ronde, of New Orleans, in the State of Louisiana, praying compensation for the destruction of certain property by order of General Coffee, in the defence of New Orleans, as is stated in the petition; which was read, and referred to the Committee, appointed the 11th instant, on so much of the Message of the President of the United States as relates to Military Affairs.

Mr. FROMENTIN presented the petition of a number of citizens of the State of Louisiana, in behalf of John de Lassize, praying indemnification for property destroyed by the British on the invasion of New Orleans, as stated in the petition; which was read, and referred to the committee last mentioned.

Mr. FROMENTIN also presented the petition of a number of citizens of New Orleans, and landholders in the State of Louisiana, in behalf of Jumonville de Villiers and others, praying compensation for property destroyed during the late invasion of that city, as stated in the petition; which was read, and referred to the last mentioned committee.

Mr. FROMENTIN also presented the petition of the Mayor, Aldermen, and inhabitants of the city of New Orleans, praying the public squares in said city, occupied for the arsenal, military hospital, and barracks, may be sold, and the said buildings removed without the suburbs of the city, for reasons stated at large in the petition; which was read, and referred to a select committee, to consist of five members; and Messrs. FROMENTIN, BROWN, TAYLOR, WILLIAMS, and MORROW, were appointed the committee.

On motion, by Mr. CAMPBELL, the annual report of the Secretary of the Treasury, upon the state of the finances of the United States, made the 8th instant, was referred to the Committee, appointed the 11th instant, on so much of the Message of the President of the United States as relates to Finance, and an Uniform National Currency.

FRIDAY, December 15.

The PRESIDENT laid before the Senate a communication from William Lambert, made in pursuance of a resolution of the House of Representatives of the United States, of the 18th of February last, comprehending abstracts of such calculations relative to the longitude of the Capitol, in the City of Washington, as were made before the passage of that resolution, with the data on which they are founded; which was read.

Mr. BROWN presented the petition of the heirs and executors of Ignace Delino, late of the State of Louisiana, praying compensation for certain property destroyed by order of General Jackson, during the invasion of that State by the British, as is stated in the petition; which was read, and referred to the Committee, appointed the 11th instant, on so much of the Message of the President of the United States as relates to Military Affairs.

Mr. BARBOUR, from the Committee on Military Affairs, reported, in part, a bill for the relief of disbanded soldiers, in certain cases therein mentioned; and the bill was twice read by unanimous consent, considered as in Committee of the Whole, and the further consideration thereof postponed to Monday next.

Mr. FROMENTIN presented the memorial of the President and Directors of the New Orleans Navigation Company, praying a further appropriation to enable them to complete their intended canal, and a confirmation of their title to a certain tract of land, as particularly mentioned in the memorial; which was read, and referred to the committee to whom was referred, the 14th instant, the memorial of the Mayor, Aldermen, and inhabitants of the city of New Orleans.

MONDAY, December 18.

The oath prescribed by law was administered to CHRISTOPHER GORE, his credentials having been read and filed during the last session, and he took his seat in the Senate.

WILLIAM T. BARRY, from the State of Kentucky, also took his seat in the Senate.

Mr. ROBERTS presented the petition of the Board of Trustees of the Orphan Asylum of the City of Washington, praying a donation for a site for the building, and to aid in its erection, as stated in the petition; which was read, and referred to a select committee, to consist of five members, to consider and report thereon by bill or otherwise; and Messrs. ROBERTS, GOLDSBOROUGH, BARBOUR, HUNTER, and WILLIAMS, were appointed the committee.

Mr. BROWN presented the petition of Thomas I. Allen, brother and administrator of William H. Allen, late commander of the United States' brig Argus, and in behalf of the surviving officers and crew of that vessel, and the heirs and representatives of her other officers, and those of her crew, deceased, praying remuneration for a number of British vessels, with their cargoes, captured in the Irish Channel, which were destroyed according to orders, as stated in the petition; which was read, and referred to the Committee to whom was referred, the 11th instant, so much of the Message of the President of the United States as relates to Naval Affairs.

Mr. LACOCK presented the petition of Solomon Parke, and others, watchmakers in the city of Philadelphia, praying that the duties on imported watches and parts of watches may be diminished, for reasons stated in the petition; which was read, and referred to the Committee, appointed the 11th instant, on Manufactures.

Mr. VARNUM presented the petition of John Frothingham and of Arthur Tappan, merchants of Boston, stating that they are native citizens of the United States, and were residing at Montreal, for the purposes of trade, at the time war was declared between the United States and Great Britain; at which time they returned to the United States, and removed a part of their merchandise, and praying to be relieved from penalties incurred by the violation of the non-importation laws, in consequence of their withdrawing their effects from Canada; and the petitions were read, and respectively referred to the Committee, appointed the 11th instant, on Foreign Relations.

Mr. FROMENTIN submitted the following motions for consideration:

Resolved, That such papers as may be ordered to be printed by order of the Senate, under an injunction of secrecy, be printed in such number as may be sufficient, eventually, to supply the members of both Houses of Congress with a copy of the same; and that the same be deposited with the Secretary of the Senate, and be bound with the other documents delivered annually to the members of both Houses, after the injunction of secrecy may have been removed.

Resolved further, That there be prefixed to the said documents a title page and an index.

A message from the House of Representatives informed the Senate that the House have passed a bill, entitled "An act making additional appropriations to defray the expenses of the army and militia, during the late war;" in which bill they request the concurrence of the Senate.

The bill last mentioned was twice read, by unanimous consent, and referred to the Committee, appointed the 11th instant, on Finance, and an Uniform National Currency.

The Senate resumed, as in Committee of the Whole, the consideration of the bill for the relief of disbanded soldiers, in certain cases therein mentioned; and, on motion by Mr. BARBOUR, the consideration thereof was postponed until to-morrow.

TUESDAY, December 19.

THOMAS W. THOMPSON, from the State of New Hampshire, took his seat in the Senate.

Mr. ROBERTS presented the memorial of John Redman Coxe, praying remission of the duties on a collection of minerals and philosophical apparatus, imported at his individual expense to aid him in the discharge of his duties as Professor of Chemistry in the University of Pennsylvania, as is stated in the memorial; which was read, and referred to the Committee, appointed the 11th instant, on Finance, and an Uniform National Currency.

Mr. BARBOUR submitted the following motion for consideration:

Resolved, That a committee be appointed, whose duty it shall be to inquire into the justice and expediency of extending relief to the officers and soldiers of Virginia, of the Revolutionary war, both on the State and Continental Establishment, to whom the faith of the State was pledged before the transfer, by Virginia, of the lands northwest of the river Ohio to the United States, and to whom, in redemption of that pledge, warrants for their bounty in lands had been granted, but which, from such transfer, cannot be carried into effect: and that the said committee do also inquire into the means which, in their opinion, will be best calculated to establish, on equitable principles, the line of demarcation between the lands reserved by Virginia, northwest of the river Ohio, and those granted the United States; and that they have leave to report by bill or otherwise.

The Senate resumed the consideration of the motions submitted the 18th instant, relative to such papers as may be ordered to be printed by order of the Senate, under an injunction of secrecy; and agreed thereto.

The Senate resumed, as in Committee of the Whole, the consideration of the bill for the relief of disbanded soldiers in certain cases therein mentioned; and the bill having been amended, the President reported it to the House accordingly; and, on the question, "Shall this bill be engrossed and read a third time?" it was determined in the negative.

Mr. LACOCK presented the petition of a number of the inhabitants of Beaver county, in the State of Pennsylvania, remonstrating against the transportation and opening of the mail on the Sabbath; and the petition was read.

WEDNESDAY, December 20.

Mr. TAIT, submitted the following motion for consideration, which was read, and passed to the second reading.

Resolved, That the Committee of Accounts be instructed to cause such alterations to be made in the Senate Chamber as may be deemed necessary for the better accommodation of the Senate; and that the expenses, necessarily incurred, be paid out of the contingent fund.

Mr. HUNTER presented the petition of John Dennis, of Newport, in the State of Rhode Island, praying the remission of duties paid, and secured to be paid, on a quantity of coffee, which was destroyed by the storm on the 23d of September last, as is stated in the petition; which was read, and referred to the committee to whom was referred, the 6th instant, the petition of Jacob Babbit.

The Senate resumed the consideration of the motion, made the 19th instant, for the appointment of a committee, to inquire into the justice and expediency of extending relief to the officers and soldiers of Virginia, of the Revolutionary war, &c; and agreed thereto; and Messrs. BARBOUR, MORROW, KING, CHACE, and MACON, were appointed the committee.

Mr. BARBOUR communicated the resolution of the Legislature of the Commonwealth of Virginia, proposing to cede to the United States the territory northwest of the river Ohio, together with sundry other documents in relation to that subject; which were read, and referred to the committee last mentioned, to consider and report thereon.

Mr. CAMPBELL, from the committee on so much of the Message of the President of the United States, as relates to Finance, and an Uniform National Currency, to whom was referred the bill, entitled "An act making additional appropriations to defray the expenses of the Army and militia, during the late war," reported it with an amendment, which was considered as in Committee of the Whole; and having been agreed to, the President reported the bill to the House amended accordingly; and on the question—

"Shall the amendment be engrossed, and the bill read a third time as amended?" it was determined in the affirmative.

The amendment to the last mentioned bill, having been reported to the Committee correctly engrossed, the bill was read a third time, as amended, by unanimous consent, and passed.

On motion, the title was amended, by adding thereto " with Great Britain."

Mr. CAMPBELL, from the Committee on Finance, and an Uniform National Currency, communicated sundry documents, which were read.

Mr. DANA gave notice, that at the next sitting of the Senate, he should ask leave to bring in a bill relative to evidence in cases of naturalization.

The PRESIDENT communicated a report of the Secretary of the Treasury, comprehending the annual statement of the duties of customs, for the year 1814; and of the sales of public lands, for the year ending on the 30th of September, 1815; also the statements relating to the internal duties, and direct tax, required by the 33d section of the act of Congress, of the 22d of July, 1813; which were read.

THURSDAY, December 21.

Mr. DANA asked and obtained leave to bring in a bill relative to evidence in cases of naturalization; and the bill was read, and passed to the second reading.

On motion by Mr. BARBOUR,

Resolved, That the Secretary of the Naval Department be directed to communicate to the Senate, whether any, and, if any, what steps have been taken during the recess, to ascertain the most convenient harbors in the waters of the Chesapeake Bay for the reception of ships of war; and that he also be directed to communicate, whether the middle ground between the Capes of the said Bay has been explored with a view to that object, and the result of such examination.

Mr. BROWN presented the memorial of the Legislative Council and House of Representatives of the Mississippi Territory, praying the appointment of an additional judge for that part of the Territory lying east of Pearl River, for reasons stated in the memorial; which was read, and referred to a select committee, and Messrs. BROWN, WILLIAMS, and CAMPBELL, were appointed the committee.

The PRESIDENT communicated the report of the Secretary for the Department of Navy, in relation to the moneys transferred during the last recess of Congress, from certain appropriations for particular branches of expenditure, to other branches of expenditure in that Department, made in obedience to the first section of the act passed the 3d of March 1809, entitled "An act further to amend the several acts for the establishment and regulation of the Treasury, War and Navy Departments;" and the report was read.

Mr. SANFORD submitted the following motion for consideration:

Resolved, That so much of the Message of the President of the United States as relates to the measure of confining the American navigation to American seamen, be referred to a select committee, with leave to report by bill or otherwise.

The resolution to authorize the Committee of Accounts to cause certain alterations to be made in the Senate Chamber, was read a second time, and considered as in Committee of the Whole; and no amendment having been proposed, the President reported it to the House accordingly; and on the question, "Shall this resolution be engrossed and read a third time?" it was determined in the affirmative; and it was then read a third time by unanimous consent, and passed.

A message from the House of Representatives informed the Senate that they have passed a bill entitled "An act for the relief of Jabez Hull;" also a bill entitled "An act for the relief of Jonathan B. Eastman;" in which bills they request the concurrence of the Senate.

The two bills last mentioned were read, and passed to the second reading.

FRIDAY, December 22.

Mr. DAGGETT presented the petition of John A. Thomas, late a captain in the 25th regiment United States infantry, praying an allowance of six hundred and fifty dollars, which were stolen from him while in the discharge of his duty as recruiting officer, as is stated in the petition; which was read, and referred to the Committee on Military Affairs.

Mr. LACOCK presented the petition of a number of the inhabitants of Beaver county, in the State of Pennsylvania, remonstrating against the transportation and opening of the mail on the Sabbath; and the petition was read, and, together with a similar petition presented the 19th instant, severally referred to a select committee; and Messrs. LACOCK, DAGGETT, and DANA, were appointed the committee.

Mr. DAGGETT submitted the following resolution, which was read, and passed to the second reading:

Resolved, by the Senate and House of Representatives of the United States of America in Congress assembled, That, for the purpose of procuring some alterations in the Hall of Congress, for the better accommodation of the two Houses, the President of the Senate and the Speaker of the House of Representatives be authorized to adjourn their respective Houses from the 22d of December, instant, to the second day of January next.

On the question—"Shall this resolution be now read the second time?" it was objected to by Mr. VARNUM, as against the rule.

Mr. HUNTER presented the petition of James Burrell, jun., and others, a committee acting for, and in behalf of the cotton manufacturers in Providence, and its vicinity, praying that a law may be passed, prohibiting the importation of all cotton goods, (nankeens excepted,) the production of places beyond the Cape of Good Hope, and laying such duty on those of a coarse texture imported from other countries, as shall give to them protection and relief, for reasons stated at large in the petition; which was read, and referred to the committee appointed the 11th instant, on so much of the Message of the President of the United States as relates to manufactures.

On motion by Mr. BARBOUR, it was agreed, that when the Senate adjourn, it be to Tuesday next.

The Senate resumed the consideration of the motion, for the appointment of a committee on so much of the Message of the President of the United States, as relates to the measure of confining the American navigation to American seamen; and, on motion by Mr. LACOCK, the further consideration thereof was postponed.

The bill relative to evidence in cases of naturalization, was read the second time, and referred to a select committee, to consider and report thereon; and Messrs. DANA, SANFORD, and LACOCK, were appointed the committee.

The bill entitled "An act for the relief of Jabez Hull," was read the second time, and referred to the Committee on Military Affairs, to consider and report thereon.

The bill entitled "An act for the relief of Jonathan B. Eastman," was read the second time, and referred to the Committee on Military Affairs.

TUESDAY, December 26.

The PRESIDENT communicated a report of the Secretary for the Department of Navy, on the expenditure and application of moneys drawn from the Treasury, from the first of October, 1814, to the 30th of September, 1815, inclusive, and of the unexpended balances of former appropriations remaining in the Treasury, on the first of October, 1814; and the report was read.

The following Message was received from the PRESIDENT OF THE UNITED STATES:

To the Senate and House of
Representatives of the United States:

I lay before Congress, copies of a Proclamation, notifying the Convention concluded with Great Britain, on the 3d day of July last, and that the same has been duly ratified; and I recommend to Congress such Legislative provisions, as the Convention may call for on the part of the United States.

JAMES MADISON.

DECEMBER 23, 1815.

The Message was read, and referred to the Committee appointed the 11th instant, on Foreign Relations.

Mr. ROBERTS presented the memorial of Thomas Murray, an inhabitant of the City of Washington, praying compensation as head cooper of the Navy Yard at that place, for reasons stated in the memorial; which was read, and referred to a select committee; and Messrs. ROBERTS, TAIT, and MACON, were appointed the committee.

Mr. TAYLOR presented the petition of Walter Sims, of the city of Philadelphia, praying further time to file his release to the United States, of his title to land in the Mississippi Territory, to enable him to receive the indemnification to which he will thereby be entitled, as stated in the petition; which was read, and referred to a select committee; and Messrs. TAYLOR, HUNTER, and MORROW, were appointed the committee.

Mr. ROBERTS presented the memorial of John McKinney and others, the President and Directors of the Merchants' Bank of Alexandria, in behalf of themselves, and the stockholders thereof, praying an act of incorporation, for reasons stated in the memorial; which was read.

Mr. RUGGLES presented the memorial of William Farris, sen., praying the renewal of his patent right to certain improvements in propelling vessels and land carriages, as stated in the memorial; which was read, and referred to a select committee; and Messrs. RUGGLES, BROWN, and DANA, were appointed the committee.

Mr. ROBERTS presented the memorial of Alexander Cook, and others, tallow chandlers, of the city of Philadelphia, praying a repeal of the duty on mould candles, manufactured within the United States, for reasons stated in the memorial; which was read, and referred to the Committee, appointed the 11th instant, on Manufactures.

Mr. SANFORD had leave to withdraw the motion made the 21st instant, for appointing a committee on so much of the Message of the President of the United States as relates to the measure of confining the American navigation to American seamen.

On motion by Mr. TAIT, the report of the Secretary for the Department of the Navy, made the 11th instant, in relation to the permanent increase of the Navy, was referred to the Committee on Naval Affairs.

On motion by Mr. DAGGETT, the further consideration of the resolution, authorizing the President of the Senate, and Speaker of the House of Representatives, to adjourn the respective Houses from the 22d of December, instant, to the second day of January next, was postponed to the first Wednesday in January next.

On motion by Mr. LACOCK, it was agreed, that when the Senate adjourn, it be to Friday next.

FRIDAY, December 29.

ISHAM TALBOT, from the State of Kentucky, arrived on the 27th, and attended this day.

Mr. TALBOT presented the memorial of John Bate, praying a renewal of his lease of a saline, belonging to the United States, in the Illinois Territory, for reasons stated in the memorial; which was read, and referred to the committee to whom was referred, the 7th instant, the memorial of the Legislative Council and House of Representatives of the Mississippi Territory, to consider and report thereon, by bill or otherwise.

On motion by Mr. BROWN, it was agreed, that when the Senate adjourn, it be to Tuesday next.

TUESDAY, January 2, 1816.

Mr. DAGGETT presented the petition of David Kimberly and others, manufacturers in the city and county of New Haven, praying a repeal of the laws imposing duties on domestic manufactures, for reasons stated in the petition; which was read, and referred to the Committee, appointed the 11th December, on Manufactures.

Mr. ROBERTS presented the petition of Thomas Reilly and others, a committee of the manufacturers of cotton and wool in the city of Philadelphia, and its vicinity, praying the protection of Congress, by imposing adequate duties upon the importation of foreign articles, as stated in the petition; which was read, and referred to the committee last mentioned.

The PRESIDENT communicated the memorial of the Legislative Council and House of Representatives of Indiana Territory, stating that their population entitles them, under existing laws, to be admitted into the Union, on an equal footing with the original States, and praying a convention may be authorized to determine on its expediency; and praying also the donation of certain sections of land in said Territory, for purposes therein expressed; and the memorial was read, and referred to a select committee; and Messrs. MORROW, BARRY, and BROWN, were appointed the committee.

The PRESIDENT also communicated another memorial of the Legislative Council and House of Representatives of the Indiana Territory, praying suspension of prosecutions under the law laying a tax on articles manufactured within the United States, for reasons stated in the memorial; which was read, and referred to the Committee, appointed the 11th December, on Finance, and an Uniform National Currency.

Mr. TAYLOR presented the petition of the stockholders of the Columbian Insurance Company of Alexandria, praying an act of incorporation, for reasons stated in the petition; which was read, and referred to the committee last mentioned.

Mr. CAMPBELL presented the petition of the President and Directors of the Bank of the Metropolis, praying an act of incorporation, for reasons stated in the petition; which was read, and referred to the same committee.

Mr. BROWN presented the petition of David Porter, a Captain in the Navy of the United States, praying the exclusive privilege of navigating, for a limited time, the waters contiguous to the District of Columbia, by vessels of his invention, worked by animal power, as stated in the petition; which was read, and referred to a select committee; and Messrs. BROWN, DAGGETT, and TAIT, were appointed the committee.

Mr. BROWN, from the committee to whom the subject was referred, reported a bill for the relief of Joseph Anderson; and the bill was read, and passed to the second reading.

Mr. VARNUM presented the petition of Sarah Jarvis and others, praying payment of the balance which may be found due to Leonard Jarvis, deceased, for services during the Revolutionary war, as stated in the petition; which was read, and referred to a select committee; and Messrs. VARNUM, MACON, and CAMPBELL, were appointed the committee.

Mr. CHACE presented the petition of Robert White, praying a pension, in consideration of wounds received in the service of his country

during the late war, as stated in the petition; which was read, and referred to a select committee; and Messrs. CHACE, MACON, and RUGGLES, were appointed the committee.

Mr. HORSEY presented the petition of William Young and others, engaged in manufactories on the Brandywine, and its vicinity, praying the interposition of Congress, for the support of the manufactures of the United States, as stated in the petition; which was read, and referred to the Committee, appointed the 11th December, on Manufactures.

WEDNESDAY, January 3.

The PRESIDENT communicated a report from the Secretary of the Department of the Navy, comprehending a statement of the contracts made by that Department, during the year 1815, prepared in obedience to the act of the 3d of March, 1809, entitled "An act further to amend the several acts, for the establishment and regulation of the Treasury, War, and Navy Departments;" and the report was read.

The PRESIDENT also communicated a letter from the Secretary for the Department of War, accompanied by a corrected register of the army, for each member of the Senate, conformably to a resolution of the Senate of December 13, 1815; which was read.

Mr. TAYLOR presented the petition of John Longden and others, the committee of the Mechanics' Relief Society of Alexandria, praying a law may be passed authorizing them to raise, by lottery or lotteries, a sum not exceeding twenty thousand dollars, to be applied to the objects of their constitution, as stated in the petition; which was read, and referred to a select committee; and Messrs. TAYLOR, TALBOT, and DAGGETT, were appointed the committee.

Mr. VARNUM presented the petition of Thomas Cutts, jun., of Massachusetts, praying the reimbursement of money paid by him, for a part of a vessel sold for the benefit of the United States, on the ground of a decision of the supreme judicial court of Massachusetts district, that no title vested by said sale in the petitioner; and the petition was read, and referred to the Committee, appointed the 11th December, on Finance, and an Uniform National Currency.

A message from the House of Representatives informed the Senate that the House have passed a bill, entitled "An act for the relief of Thomas and John Clifford, Elisha Fisher, and Company, Thomas Clifford, and Thomas Clifford and Son;" a bill entitled "An act to authorize the payment for property lost, captured, or destroyed by the enemy, while in the military service of the United States;" a bill entitled "An act for the relief of Charles Markin;" also, a bill entitled "An act to enlarge the time for ascertaining the annual transfers, and changes of property subject to the direct tax, and for other purposes;" in which bills they request the concurrence of the Senate.

The four bills last mentioned were read, and passed to the second reading.

Mr. WILLIAMS submitted the following motion for consideration:

Resolved, That a committee be appointed to inquire into the expediency of selling a lot, the property of the United States, situated in the town of Knoxville; and that said committee have leave to report by bill or otherwise

The bill for the relief of Joseph Anderson was read the second time, and considered as in Committee of the Whole; and, having been amended, the PRESIDENT reported it to the House accordingly; and on the question, "Shall this bill be engrossed and read a third time?" it was determined in the affirmative.

Mr. MORROW submitted the following motion for consideration:

Resolved, That the Committee on Military Affairs be instructed to inquire and report the aggregate quantity of lands due for bounties to the soldiers enlisted into the army during the late war; and in case it shall appear that a deficiency exists, either in the quantity or quality of the lands already designated and appropriated for that purpose, that the said committee report, by bill or otherwise, the provisions necessary for the full, and speedy allotment of lands engaged to be granted to the said soldiers.

THURSDAY, January 4.

The PRESIDENT communicated a report of the Secretary for the Department of War, comprehending statements of the expenditure and application of such sums of money as have been drawn from the Treasury of the United States for the use of the Military Department, from the 1st of October, 1814, to 30th September, 1815, inclusive, conformably to the act further to amend the several acts for the establishment and regulation of the Treasury, War, and Navy Departments, passed March 3, 1809; and the report was read.

Mr. DANA, from the committee to whom was referred the bill relative to evidence, in cases of naturalization, reported it with amendments; which were read.

Mr. ROBERTS presented the petition of Edward Barry, sailingmaster, and George Hodge, boatswain, in the Navy Yard of the United States at Washington, praying indemnification for the loss of household furniture, books, and instruments of navigation, destroyed by fire on the 24th of August, 1814, as is stated in the petition; which was read, and referred to the committee to whom was referred, the 26th of December, the petition of Thomas Murray.

The Senate resumed the consideration of the motion made the 3d instant, for the appointment of a committee to inquire into the expediency of selling a lot, the property of the United States, situated in the town of Knoxville, and agreed thereto; and Messrs. WILLIAMS, HUNTER, and RUGGLES, were appointed the committee.

The bill entitled "An act, for the relief of Charles Markin," was read the second time, and referred to the committee, to whom was referred the 7th December, the memorial of the Legisla-

14th CON. 1st SESS.—2

tive Council and House of Representatives of the Mississippi Territory.

Mr. BROWN presented the petition of Thomas Sloo, register of the land office, and John Caldwell, receiver of public moneys, at Shawneetown, praying an increase of compensation, for reasons stated in the petition; which was read, and referred to the committee last mentioned.

The bill entitled "An act, to enlarge the time for ascertaining the annual transfers and changes of property, subject to the direct tax, and for other purposes," was read the second time, and referred to the Committee, appointed the 11th December, on Finance, and an Uniform National Currency.

The bill entitled "An act, for the relief of Thomas and John Clifford, Elisha Fisher and Company, and Thomas Clifford and Son," was read the second time, and referred to the committee last mentioned.

The bill entitled "An act, to authorize the payment for property lost, captured, or destroyed by the enemy, while in the military service of the United States," was read the second time, and referred to the Committee on Military Affairs.

The Senate resumed the consideration of the motion, made the third instant, for instructing the Committee on Military Affairs, in relation to lands due for bounties to the soldiers, enlisted into the army during the late war, and agreed thereto.

The bill for the relief of Joseph Anderson was read the third time, and passed.

FRIDAY, January 5.

Mr. ROBERTS presented the petition of John McMullin, and others, goldsmiths, silversmiths, and jewellers, of the city of Philadelphia, praying a repeal or modification of the law imposing duties on domestic manufactures, for reasons stated in the petition; which was read, and referred to the Committee, appointed the 11th December, on Manufactures.

Mr. TAIT from the Committee on Naval Affairs, communicated a letter from the Secretary for the Department of Navy, together with a statement exhibiting the names, rates, and stations of the respective vessels in the Navy of the United States.

Mr. ROBERTS presented the petition of John L. Pierson, late Lieutenant Colonel of Pennsylvania militia, in the service of the United States, praying to be reimbursed, a certain sum of money recovered of him by a judgment of court, for rations obtained and used by the regiment under his command, while in the actual service of the United States, as is stated in the petition; which was read, and referred to a select committee; and Messrs. ROBERTS, BARRY, and TURNER, were appointed the committee.

The Senate adjourned to Monday.

MONDAY, January 8.

JEREMIAH MASON, from the State of New Hampshire, took his seat in the Senate.

Mr. FROMENTIN, from the committee to whom

the subject was referred, reported a bill confirming to the Navigation Company of New Orleans the use and possession of a lot in said city; and the bill was read, and passed to the second reading.

Mr. TAYLOR presented the petition of John Longden and others, a committee in behalf of the Mechanic Relief Society of Alexandria, praying an act of incorporation; which was read, and referred to the committee appointed the second instant, on the petition of the same persons.

Mr. LACOCK presented the petition of a large number of the inhabitants of Armstrong county, in the State of Pennsylvania, praying the discontinuance of the carrying and opening the mail on the Sabbath; and the petition was read, and referred to the committee to whom was referred, on the 22d December, the petitions on the same subject.

Mr. ROBERTS presented the memorial of Stephen Girard, and others, of Philadelphia, praying the passage of a law prohibiting the exportation of specie, for a period not less than twelve months, for reasons stated in the memorial; which was read, and referred to the Committee, appointed the 11th December, on Finance, and an Uniform National Currency.

Mr. FROMENTIN submitted the following motion for consideration:

Resolved, That a committee be appointed to inquire into the propriety of increasing, by law, the salaries of the officers of the Senate, with power to report by bill or otherwise.

The Senate resumed, as in Committee of the Whole, the consideration of the bill relative to evidence in cases of naturalization, together with the amendments reported thereto by the select committee; and on motion, by Mr. ROBERTS, the further consideration thereof was postponed until to-morrow.

The following Message was received from the PRESIDENT OF THE UNITED STATES:

To the Senate and House of
 Representatives of the United States :

I communicate, for the information of Congress, the report of the Director of the Mint, of the operation of that establishment, during the last year.

JAMES MADISON.
JANUARY 8, 1813.

The Message was read.

A message from the House of Representatives informed the Senate that the House have passed a bill, entitled "An act for the relief of William Morrissett;" a bill entitled "An act for the relief of Henry Fanning;" also a bill entitled "An act for the relief of Martin Cole, John Pollock, George Westner, and Abraham Welty;" in which bills they request the concurrence of the Senate.

The three bills last mentioned were read, and passed to the second reading.

────────

TUESDAY, January 9.

The Senate resumed the consideration of the motion made the 8th instant, for the appointment of a committee to inquire into the propriety of increasing, by law, the salaries of the officers of

the Senate, and agreed thereto: and Messrs. FROMENTIN, LACOCK, and BIBB, were appointed the committee.

The bill, entitled "An act for the relief of William Morrissett, was read the second time, and referred to the Committee, appointed the 11th of December, on Finance, and an Uniform National Currency.

The bill, entitled "An act for the relief of Henry Fanning," was read the second time, and referred to a select committee; and Messrs. WILSON, KING, and BROWN, were appointed the committee.

The bill, entitled "An act for the relief of Martin Cole, John Pollock, John Westner, and Abraham Welty," was read the second time, and referred to the committee appointed the 7th of December, on the memorial of the Legislature of the Mississippi Territory.

Mr. MORROW presented the memorial of John Holker, formerly Consul General of France, praying the renewal of certain loan-office certificates destroyed by fire, as stated in the memorial, which was read, and referred to the Secretary for the Department of Treasury.

The bill confirming to the Navigation Company of New Orleans the use and possession of a lot in the said city; was read the second time.

The Senate resumed, as in Committee of the Whole, the consideration of the bill relative to evidence in cases of naturalization, together with the amendments reported thereto by the select committee; and the amendments having been agreed to, and the blanks filled with the word "five," the President reported the bill to the House accordingly.

On the question, "Shall this bill be engrossed, and read a third time?" it was determined in the affirmative.

The PRESIDENT communicated a letter from the Commissioner of the General Land Office, accompanied by two reports, on claims for land in the State of Louisiana; which were read, and referred to the committee appointed the 7th of December, on the memorial of the Legislature of the Mississippi Territory.

Mr. WILSON submitted the following motion for consideration:

Resolved, That a committee be appointed to inquire into the expediency of revising and digesting the several acts of Congress on the subject of naturalization; or, of compiling and publishing the said acts, and distributing the same to the officers of the several courts authorized to issue certificates of naturalization.

Mr. BIBB, from the Committee on Foreign Relations, to whom the subject was referred, reported a bill concerning the Convention to regulate the commerce between the territories of the United States and His Britannic Majesty; and the bill was read, and passed to the second reading. The bill is as follows:

A bill concerning the Convention to regulate the commerce between the territories of the United States and His Britannic Majesty.

Be it enacted, &c., That so much of any act or acts as is contrary to the provisions of the Convention between the United States and His Britannic Majesty, the ratifications whereof were mutually exchanged, the twenty-second day of December, one thousand eight hundred and fifteen, shall be deemed and taken to be of no force or effect.

COMPENSATION FOR HORSES LOST.

Mr. TALBOT presented the memorial of the Legislature of the State of Kentucky, praying compensation for horses lost by the citizens of that State, during the late war, while in the service of the United States, as stated in the memorial; which was read, and referred to the Committee, appointed the 11th December, on Military Affairs. The memorial is as follows:

To the honorable the Senate and House of Representatives of the United States of America, in Congress assembled:

The memorial of the Legislature of the State of Kentucky would respectfully call the attention of Congress to a subject of considerable importance to many of their citizens, who unfortunately lost their horses during the various campaigns carried on from this State, in the late war with the British and their savage allies, particularly on the Northwestern frontier, where the losses sustained were peculiarly severe, owing to many circumstances which we will detail, and which at the time demanded every sacrifice.

The extensive wilderness bordering upon our Northwestern frontier, every part of which was infested by a cruel and savage enemy, made it necessary that large bodies of mounted riflemen should be employed in order to meet the various attacks of an insidious foe, and to comply with which the people of the Western country never hesitated, or inquired what compensation was to be made them. They relied upon the justice of their country, which, they believed, would never be withheld from the soldier who had risked his life in defence of his country's rights.

The Legislature are aware of the provision made by act of Congress for the use and risk of horses lost by mounted men previous to the declaration of war, and they have no doubt there are some cases which have not as great claims upon the Government as others. Yet, when the situation of the State of Kentucky is taken into consideration, it will be found that the claims of her citizens to compensation for horses lost during the war will be found not inferior to any other section of the Union. Placed at a considerable distance from the scene of military operations, the calls for men by the Government were generally made at a time when the greatest despatch and energy were required.

In the Summer of 1812, the surrender of General Hull, the fall of Detroit, Mackinac, and Chicago, and the consequent siege of Forts Wayne and Harrison, called aloud for all the patriotism of the State of Kentucky.

The emergency could only be met by mounted men, who, in a few days, were found filling up the ranks of Generals Harrison and Hopkins; the remaining forts were saved, the frontiers protected, a savage enemy checked in his bloody career, and destruction and retribution carried back into his own country; and the various tribes of hostile Indians, flushed with their recent success, were driven to seek refuge under the cannon of their British friends.

In aid of which important services, the regiment of dragoons under the command of Colonel Simrall, the volunteer company of Captain Smith, and the twelve months' volunteers with Captain Garrard, contributed their full portion of zeal and patriotism at the battle of Mississinewa in the midst of winter, besides many other important services, which lost to them many horses besides those killed in battle. These are cases which richly deserve the notice of a grateful country.

Early in the year 1813 a regiment of mounted riflemen, under the command of Col. Richard M. Johnson, was hurried into service to relieve Fort Meigs and protect the frontiers of the State of Ohio. This regiment was usefully employed, and it is believed fully answered the expectation of their country. Previous to the second investiture of Fort Meigs, they penetrated far into the enemy's country, and by forced marches reached that important post at a critical period, and were employed by the Commanding General to procure intelligence of the enemy's movements near Malden; by which means General Harrison was enabled to carry on his operations in security. These, and subsequent marches of unusual celerity, had a tendency to break down and destroy many of the best horses belonging to that corps.

Again, when it was found, late in the month of July, 1813, that the contemplated force of regular troops could not be collected, the Commanding General of the Northwestern Army was compelled to call upon the Governor of Kentucky for an additional militia force.

The lateness of the season, the necessity of the times, the importance of the service required, as well as the critical period which had arrived, in which the hopes of a desponding country were to be realised or again blasted—all combined to point out to the Executive of this State that mounted men could alone meet the approaching crisis, and render that service so loudly called for by every friend to his country. With these views, it is well known that between three and four thousand mounted men rallied round the standard of their country, which had been erected by the venerable Shelby, many of whom had to travel between two and three hundred miles before they reached the point of rendezvous. With these troops, without delaying a single day unnecessarily, the Governor of Kentucky moved on to the headquarters of the Northwestern army, where his arrival was as critical as it was important, and absolutely necessary to meet the views of General Harrison. Forced marches were required and performed; our citizens did not linger on the road, or suffer their spirits to be depressed; for many, after losing their horses by fatigue, would keep up with the army on foot, to the astonishment as well as pride of their country and fellow-soldiers.

We cannot avoid further stating to your honorable body that, in order to take advantage of Commodore Perry's success upon Lake Erie, and carry the war into the enemy's country, it was necessary to leave the horses of the troops enclosed in the peninsula formed by the Sandusky Bay and Portage river, where they subsisted in the forest upwards of one month, which much reduced them, and consequently produced many serious and unavoidable losses on the homeward march, as a sufficiency of forage could not be procured at that place. An important victory was gained, and the most sanguine anticipations of the Government realized. And will the nation now, on the return of peace, refuse to remunerate our citizens, many of whom are poor, and some of whom have lost their only horse? We trust not, and therefore earnestly solicit the attention of Congress to this subject, which, though of small moment to the nation at large, yet is important to individuals.

We would also include the cases of horses lost during the Fall of 1814, under Major P. Dudley, who served with General McArthur, in Upper Canada, who, we believe, rendered important services to our country in cutting off the supplies of the enemy, and which would have been most severely felt by them in case another campaign had opened in that quarter.

Nor can her citizens have less claim on the justice of their country to remunerate them for lost property, who, during an inclement season, and through a country peopled by savage enemies only, encountered every danger and difficulty in the wagon department, transporting provisions, forage, and camp equipage for the army and garrisons of the Northwest; many of whom were induced to embark in that dangerous employ more from a desire to serve their country than from the prospect of gain. Nor were the services rendered their country by the detachment of Kentucky troops under the command of Colonel William Russell, on the Wabash river, less meritorious, nor the losses sustained by them less just to remunerate.

We therefore most seriously request that the cases of lost horses alluded to in this memorial be attended to, and that our citizens be fully compensated, as far as the justice of their several cases may require; and, for the purpose of bringing this subject before Congress, be it

Resolved by the General Assembly of the Commonwealth of Kentucky, That the Governor of this State be requested to transmit a copy of the foregoing memorial to each of our Senators and Representatives in Congress, with a request that they immediately lay the same before that body, and that they use their best influence to have the same complied with as soon as the nature of the case will admit.

JOHN J. CRITTENDEN,
Speaker of the House of Representatives.
R. HICKMAN,
Speaker of the Senate.
Approved : December 21, 1815.
ISAAC SHELBY.

———

WEDNESDAY, January 10.

WILLIAM H. WELLS, from the State of Delaware, took his seat in the Senate.

The PRESIDENT communicated a report of the Secretary of the Treasury, exhibiting the sums respectively paid to each clerk in the several offices of that Department, for services rendered during the year 1815, made in obedience to the provisions of the act of April 21, 1806, to regulate and fix the compensation of clerks; and the report was read.

Mr. BROWN presented the petition of Thomas Ap Catesby Jones, a lieutenant in the Navy of the United States, for himself, and in behalf of the officers and crews of the division of gunboats, lately under his command near Ship Island, which was, on the 14th of December, 1814, attacked and captured by a detachment from the fleet under the command of Admiral Sir Alexander Cochrane, praying compensation for their clothing and other property which they lost, as

is stated in the petition; which was read, and referred to the Committee on Naval Affairs.

The Senate resumed the consideration of the motion made the 9th instant, for the appointment of a committee to inquire into the expediency of revising and digesting the several acts of Congress, on the subject of naturalization, and agreed thereto; and Messrs. DANA, WILSON, and LACOCK, were appointed the committee.

Mr. BARBOUR, from the Committee on Military Affairs, to whom was referred the bill, entitled "An act for the relief of Jonathan B. Eastman," reported it without amendment; and the bill was considered as in Committee of the Whole; and passed to the second reading.

Mr. FROMENTIN, from the committee, reported the bill concerning evidence in cases of naturalization, correctly engrossed; and on motion, by Mr. TALBOT, the further consideration thereof was postponed until to-morrow.

The bill concerning the convention, to regulate the commerce between the territories of the United States and His Britannic Majesty, was read the second time, and considered as in Committee of the Whole; and on motion, by Mr. SANFORD, the bill having been amended, the President reported it to the House accordingly.

On the question, " Shall the bill be engrossed, and read a third time ? it was determined in the affirmative.

The bill was then read a third time, by unanimous consent, and passed.

A message from the House of Representatives informed the Senate that the House have passed a bill, entitled "An act to authorize the discharge of James Jewett, from his imprisonment;" also a bill, entitled "An act for the relief of George S. Wise," in which bills they request the concurrence of the Senate.

The two bills last mentioned were read, and passed to the second reading.

———

THURSDAY, January 11.

The PRESIDENT communicated the memorial of the Legislature of the Indiana Territory, praying that David Floyd, and his associates, may be authorized to open and work a certain salt-spring in the said Territory, as is stated in the memorial; which was read, and referred to the committee appointed the 7th of December on the memorial of the Legislature of the Mississippi Territory.

Mr. HORSEY presented the petition of James Tilton, late Physician and Surgeon General of the Army of of the United States, praying an allowance for rations, forage, quarters, postage, &c., while in the service of the United States, and an annual benevolence that may sustain him above want and dependence, in consideration of his long and faithful public services, as stated in the petition; which was read, and referred to a select committee; and Messrs. HORSEY, CONDIT, and TAIT, were appointed the committee.

Mr. TAIT, from the Committee on Naval Affairs, communicated sundry documents relative to the operations of the squadron under command of Commodore Decatur, against the Barbary Powers; which were read.

Mr. TAYLOR presented the petition of John Cannon, and others, claimants of public lands, praying provision may be made by law for their indemnification, as stated in the petition; which was read, and referred to the committee to whom was referred, on the 26th December, the petition of Walter Sims.

The bill, entitled "An act to authorize the discharge of James Jewett from his imprisonment," was read the second time, and referred to a select committee; and Messrs. VARNUM, DAGGETT, and MACON, were appointed the committee.

The bill, entitled "An act for the relief of George S. Wise," was read the second time, and referred to the Committee on Military Affairs.

Mr. BIBB, from the Committee on Finance, and an Uniform National Currency, to whom was referred the bill, entitled "An act to enlarge the time for ascertaining the annual transfers and changes of property subject to the direct tax, and for other purposes," reported it without amendment.

Mr. WILSON, from the committee to whom was referred the bill, entitled "An act for the relief of Henry Fanning," reported it without amendment.

The engrossed bill, relative to evidence in cases of naturalization, was read a third time, and passed.

The bill, entitled "An act for the relief of John B. Eastman," was read a third time, and passed.

Mr. FROMENTIN, from the committee to whom the subject was referred, reported a bill to fix the compensations of the officers of the Senate therein mentioned, and the bill was read, and passed to the second reading.

The Senate resumed, as in Committee of the Whole, the consideration of the bill confirming to the Navigation Company of New Orleans the use and possession of a lot in the said city; and on motion, by Mr. FROMENTIN, the bill having been amended, the President reported it to the House accordingly.

On the question, "Shall this bill be engrossed and read a third time?" it was determined in the affirmative.

Mr. TAIT, from the Committee on Naval Affairs, reported, in part, a bill authorizing the appointment of certain Naval officers therein named; and the bill was read, and passed to the second reading.

FRIDAY, January 12.

The PRESIDENT communicated a report of the Postmaster General, relative to the salaries of the clerks of that Department for the year 1815; which was read.

The PRESIDENT also communicated the petition of a number of the inhabitants of the county of Clermont, in the State of Ohio, praying the discontinuance of the carrying and opening of the mail on the Sabbath; and the petition was read, and referred to the committee to whom were referred, on the 22d December, the petitions of sundry inhabitants of Beaver county, in the State of Pennsylvania, on the same subject.

On motion, by Mr. VARNUM, the committee to whom was referred the petition of Sarah Jervis, and others, were discharged from the further consideration thereof, and it was referred to the Secretary for the Department of Treasury.

Mr. WILSON presented the petition of Jacob Wrighter, of Trenton, in the State of New Jersey, praying a pension, in consideration of wounds received while in the service of the United States, during the late war, as stated in the petition; which was read, and referred to the committee to whom was referred, on the second instant, the petition of Robert White.

Mr. HORSEY presented the petition of Charles King, and others, members of the congregation of Trinity Church in Georgetown, praying authority to raise by lottery a sum sufficient to enlarge their church, for reasons stated in the petition; which was read, and referred to a select committee; and Messrs. HORSEY, VARNUM, and BARBOUR, were appointed the committee.

The bill confirming to the Navigation Company of New Orleans the use and possession of a lot in said city, was read a third time, and passed.

The bill authorizing the appointment of certain Naval officers therein named, was read the second time and considered as in Committee of the Whole; and on motion, by Mr. TAIT, the further consideration thereof was postponed until Monday next.

The bill to fix the compensations of the officers of the Senate therein mentioned, was read the second time, and taken up as in Committee of the Whole; and on motion, by Mr. FROMENTIN, the further consideration thereof was postponed until Monday next.

The Senate resumed, as in Committee of the Whole, the consideration of the bill entitled "An act for the relief of Henry Fanning;" and it passed to a third reading.

The Senate resumed, as in Committee of the Whole, the consideration of the bill entitled "An act to enlarge the time for ascertaining the annual transfers and changes of property subject to the direct tax, and for other purposes;" and it passed to a third reading.

Adjourned to Monday next.

MONDAY, January 15.

Mr. HOWELL presented the petition of James D'Wolf, of Bristol, in the State of Rhode Island, praying the patronage of Congress to the cotton manufactures of the United States, for reasons stated in the petition; which was read, and referred to the Committee on Manufactures.

Mr. WILLIAMS presented the petition of William Lawrence, Lieutenant Colonel in the Army of the United States, in behalf of himself and the officers and non-commissioned officers and privates, composing the garrison of Fort Bowyer in the Summer of the year 1814, praying payment for certain vessels and cargoes, captured and destroyed, belonging to the enemy of the United States, as stated in the petition; which was read, and referred to the Committee on Naval Affairs.

Mr. GOLDSBOROUGH presented the petition of Isaac Burneston, and others, a committee appointed by the cotton manufacturers in the city of Baltimore, praying the patronage and guardianship of Congress, as stated in the petition; which was read, and referred to the committee last mentioned.

On motion by Mr. HORSEY,

Ordered, That eight hundred copies of the following papers, relative to the public roads and canals, be printed for the use of both Houses of Congress, viz:

A resolution of the Senate of the 2d March, 1807.

A letter from the Secretary of the Treasury.

A report of the same.

Mr. Latrobe's communication, marked E.

Mr. Fulton's letter, marked F.

Mr. BARBOUR presented the memorial of the Levy Court of the county of Washington, in the District of Columbia, praying the establishment of a penitentiary, for reasons stated in the memorial; which was read, and referred to a select committee; and Messrs. BARBOUR, GOLDSBOROUGH, and HORSEY, were appointed the committee.

Mr. TAIT, from the Committee on Naval Affairs, communicated a letter from the Secretary for the Department of Navy, containing estimates of the expense of building and equipping one seventy-four, two forty-fours, and two sloops of war; which were read.

The bill entitled "An act to enlarge the time for ascertaining the annual transfers and changes of property subject to the direct tax, and for other purposes," was read a third time, and passed.

The bill entitled "An act for the relief of Henry Fanning" was read a third time, and passed.

The Senate resumed the consideration of the bill authorizing the appointment of certain Naval officers therein named.

On the question, "Shall this bill be engrossed and read a third time?" it was determined in the affirmative.

A message from the House of Representatives informed the Senate that the House have passed a bill, entitled "An act to regulate the commerce between the United States and the territories of His Britannic Majesty, according to the Convention concluded on the 3d day of July, 1815; and the ratifications of which were exchanged on the 22d day of December, 1815," in which they request the concurrence of the Senate.

The bill last mentioned was read, and passed to the second reading.

The Senate resumed, as in Committee of the Whole, the consideration of the bill to fix the compensations of the officers of the Senate therein mentioned; and after progress, on motion by Mr. DAGGETT, the further consideration thereof was postponed until Wednesday next.

Mr. DANA submitted the following motion for consideration:

Resolved, That a committee be appointed, to inquire whether any provision is necessary for authorizing the proper officers, from time to time, to make payment of the sums which the Senators and Representatives in Congress are entitled by law to receive from the Treasury of the United States, in compensation for their services.

Mr. WILLIAMS, from the committee appointed to consider the subject, reported a bill authorizing the sale of public lands; and the bill was read, and passed to the second reading.

TUESDAY, January 16.

Mr. TAYLOR presented the memorial of the City Council of Charleston, South Carolina, on the subject of a marine hospital for that port; which was read, and referred to a select committee; and Messrs. TAYLOR, BIBB, and DAGGETT, were appointed the committee.

The bill entitled "An act to regulate the commerce between the United States and the territories of His Britannic Majesty, according to the convention concluded on the 3d day of July, 1815, and the ratifications of which were exchanged on the 22d day of December, 1815," was read the second time, and referred to the Committee on Foreign Relations.

The bill authorizing the sale of public lands was read the second time, and considered as in Committee of the Whole; and, on the question, "Shall this bill be engrossed, and read a third time?" it was determined in the affirmative.

The bill authorizing the appointment of certain Naval officers therein named, was read the third time.

Resolved, That this bill pass, and that the title thereof be, "An act authorizing the appointment of Admirals."

The Senate resumed the consideration of the motion, made the 15th instant, for the appointment of a committee to inquire whether any provision is necessary for authorizing the payment of the sums which the Senators and Representatives are entitled to receive in compensation for their services; and, on motion by Mr. ROBERTS, the further consideration thereof was postponed until Tuesday next.

Mr. VARNUM, from the committee to whom was referred the bill entitled "An act to authorize the discharge of James Jewett from his imprisonment," reported it with an amendment, which was read, and taken up as in Committee of the Whole; and, on motion, the further consideration thereof was postponed until to-morrow.

WEDNESDAY, January 17.

The PRESIDENT communicated a report of the Postmaster General, containing a list of contracts made in the year 1815, which was read.

Mr. TURNER presented the petition of William O'Neale and Robert Taylor, of the City of Washington, praying compensation for a schooner, chartered to the United States to attend the flotilla under the command of Commodore Barney, in June, 1814, which was sunk in the river Patuxent, to prevent her and the property on board from falling into the hands of the enemy, as stated in the petition; which was read, and referred to the Committee on Military Affairs.

Mr. TAIT, from the Committee on Naval Affairs, to whom was referred the bill entitled "An act for the relief of George S. Wise," reported it without amendment.

Mr. TAIT, from the Committee on Naval Affairs, to whom was referred the petition of Thos. I. Allen, on the subject, reported a bill to reward the officers and crew of the late United States' brig Argus; and the bill was read, and passed to the second reading.

Mr. FROMENTIN, from the committee, reported the bill authorizing the sale of public lands, correctly engrossed; and, on motion of Mr. MORROW, it was referred to a select committee; and Messrs. WILLIAMS, HUNTER, and RUGGLES, were appointed the committee.

Mr. BIBB, from the committee to whom was referred the bill entitled "An act to regulate the commerce between the United States and the territories of His Britannic Majesty, according to the convention concluded the 3d day of July, 1815, and the ratifications of which were exchanged on the 22d day of December, 1815," reported it without amendment.

The Senate resumed, as in Committee of the Whole, the consideration of the bill, entitled "An act authorizing the discharge of William Jewett from his imprisonment," together with the amendment reported thereto by the select committee; and the further consideration thereof was postponed until Monday next.

On motion, by Mr. TAYLOR, the petition of James Jewett, together with the accompanying documents, were referred to the Secretary of the Treasury.

The Senate resumed, as in Committee of the Whole, the consideration of the bill to fix the compensations of the officers of the Senate therein mentioned; and, on motion of Mr. TAIT, it was recommitted to a select committee, further to consider and report thereon; and Messrs. LACOCK, WILSON, and VARNUM, were appointed the committee.

Mr. HORSEY, from the committee to whom was referred the petition of Charles King, and others, reported a bill to authorize a lottery in Georgetown, District of Columbia; and the bill was read, and passed to the second reading.

Mr. KING presented the petition of Cornelia Livingston and Peter V. B. Livingston, of the city of New York, in behalf of themselves and of the infant children of Philip Livingston, deceased, and the heirs of his father, praying further time may be allowed them for protecting their titles and establishing their claims to certain lands in the Mississippi Territory, as stated in the petition; which was read, and referred to the committee appointed the 7th of December, on the memorial of the Legislative Council and House of Representatives of the Mississippi Territory.

THURSDAY, January 18.

Mr. TAYLOR presented the memorial of James Levins, of South Carolia, praying compensation for vanquishing and bringing into the United States, as prisoners of war, one midshipman and four seamen, of the navy of Great Britain, alone and unassisted, as stated in the memorial; which was read, and referred to the Committee on Naval Affairs.

Mr. LACOCK, from the committee to whom was recommitted the bill fixing the compensations of the officers of the Senate therein mentioned, reported it with an amendment.

The bill to reward the officers and crew of the United States' brig Argus, was read a second time.

The bill to authorize a lottery in Georgetown, District of Columbia, was read the second time.

COMMERCE WITH GREAT BRITAIN.

The Senate resumed, as in Committee of the Whole, the consideration of the bill entitled "An act to regulate the commerce between the United States and the territories of His Britannic Majesty, according to the convention concluded the 3d day of July, 1815, and the ratifications of which were exchanged, on the 22d day of December, 1815;" and no amendment having been proposed thereto, the President reported the bill to the House: and, on the question, "Shall this bill be read a third time?"

Mr. JAMES BARBOUR rose and addressed the Chair as follows: Mr. President, as it seems to be the wish of the Senate to pass upon this subject without debate, it adds to the reluctance I always feel when compelled, even by a sense of duty, to intrude on their attention. Yet, as I feel myself obliged, under the solemn responsibility attached to the station I hold here, to vote against the bill under consideration—as I think, also, it is but a due respect to the other branch of the Legislature, from whom it is my misfortune to differ, and but an act of justice to myself to state the grounds of my opinion, I must be pardoned for departing from the course which seemed to be desired by the Senate.

In the exercise of this privilege, with a view to promote the wishes of the Senate as far as a sense of duty will permit, I will confine myself to a succinct view of the most prominent objections which lie against its passage, rather than indulge in the extensive range of which the subject is susceptible. Before I enter into the discussion of the merits of the question, I beg leave to call the attention of the Senate to the course which was adopted by us in relation to this subject. A bill, brought in by the Committee on Foreign Relations, passed the Senate unanimously, declaring that all laws in opposition to the convention between the United States and Great Britain, concluded on the 3d July last, should be held as null and void. The principle on which this body acted, was, that the treaty, upon the exchange of its ratification, did, of itself, repeal any commercial regulation, incompatible with its provisions, existing in our municipal code; it being by us believed at the time that such a bill was not necessary, but by a declaratory act, it was supposed, all doubts and difficulties, should any exist, might be removed. This bill is sent to the House of Representatives, who, without acting thereon, send us the one under consideration, but differing materially from ours. Far from pretending an intimate knowledge of the course of business pursued by the two Houses, I do not say that the mode adopted in this particular case is irregular, but if it has not the sanction of precedent, it appears to me to be wanting in that courtesy which should be perpetually cherished between the two Houses. It would have been more decorous to have acted on our bill; to have agreed to it if it were approved; to reject or amend it. In the latter case, upon its being returned to the Senate, the views of the other body would have been contrasted with our own, and we might then have regularly passed upon the subject. A different course, however, has been adopted; and if a regard to etiquette had been the only obstacle to my support to the bill, it would have been readily given; for it is the substance, and not the shadow, which weighs with me. The difference between the two bills is rendered important by its involving a Constitutional question.

It is my misfortune, for such I certainly esteem it, to differ from the other branch of the Legislature on that question; were it a difference of opinion on the expediency of a measure, it might readily be obviated, as being entirely free, or at least I hope so, from pride of opinion. My disposition is to meet, by mutual concession, those with whom I am in the habit of acting; but when a principle of the Constitution is involved, concession and compromise are out of the question. With one eye on the sacred charter of our liberties, and the other on the solemn sanction under which I act here, I surrender myself to the dictates of my best judgment, (weak enough God knows,) and fearlessly pursue the course pointed out by these guides. My regret is certainly greatly lessened by the reflection that there is no difference of opinion with any one on the propriety of executing the treaty with good faith—we differ only as to the manner in which our common purpose shall be effected.

The difference between the friends of the bill, and those opposed to it is, as I understand it, this: the former contend, that the law of Congress, discriminating between American and British tonnage, is not abrogated by the treaty, although its provisions conflict with the treaty, but that to effect its repeal, the bill in question, a mere echo of the treaty, must pass; the latter, among whom I wish to be considered, on the contrary say, that the law above alluded to was annulled upon the ratification of the treaty. I hope I have succeeded in stating the question fairly, for that certainly was my wish, and it is also my determination to discuss it in the same spirit.

This, then, is the issue which is made up between the friends and the opponents of the bill; and although in its practical effects I cannot believe it would be of consequence which way it is

decided, yet, as the just interpretation of the Constitution is the pivot on which it turns, from that consideration alone the question becomes an interesting one.

Fortunately for us we have a written Constitution to recur to, dictated with the utmost precision of which our language is susceptible—it being the work of whatsoever of wisdom, of experience, and of foresight, united America possessed.

To a just understanding of this instrument, it will be essential to recur to the object of its adoption; in this there can be no difference of opinion. The old band of union had been literally dissolved in its own imbecility; to remedy this serious evil, an increase of the powers of the General Government was indispensable.

To draw the line of demarcation between the powers thus granted to the General Government, and those retained by the States, was the primary and predominating object. In conformity with this view, we find a general enumeration of the powers assigned the former, of which Congress is made the depository; which powers, although granted to Congress in the first instance, are, in the same instrument, subsequently distributed among the other branches of the Government. Various examples might be adduced in support of this position. The following for the present will suffice: Art. 1, sec. 1, of the Constitution declares, that "all legislative powers herein grant-' ed shall be vested in a Congress of the United ' States, which shall consist of a Senate and ' House of Representatives." Yet we find, by the seventh section of the same article, the President invested with a large share of legislative power, and, in fact, constituting an integral branch of the Legislature; in addition to this, I will here barely add, that the grant of the very power to regulate the exercise of which gave birth to this bill, furnishes, by the admission of the friends of the bill, another evidence of the truth of this position, as I shall show hereafter; and, therefore, to comprehend the true meaning of the Constitution, an isolated view of a particular clause or section will involve you in error, while a comprehensive one, both of its spirit and letter, will conduct you to a just result; when apparent collisions will be removed, and vigor and effect will be given to every part of the instrument. With this principle as our guide, I come directly to that part of the Constitution which recognises the treaty-making power. In the 2d clause, 2d sec., 2d art., are the following plain and emphatic words: "He (the President) shall have power, ' by and with the advice and consent of the Sen-' ate, to make treaties, provided two-thirds of the ' Senators present concur." Two considerations here irresistibly present themselves—first, there is no limitation to the exercise of the power, save such restrictions as arise from the Constitution, as to the subjects on which it is to act; nor is there any participation of the power, with any other branch of the Government, in any way alluded to.

Am I borne out in this declaration by the clause

referred to? That I am, seems to me susceptible of demonstration. To the President and Senate has been imparted the power of making treaties. Well, what is a treaty? If a word have a known signification by the common consent of mankind, and it be used without any qualification in a law, constitution, or otherwise, the fair inference is that the received import of such word is intended to be conveyed. If so, the extent of the power intended to be granted admits of no difficulty. It reaches to those acts of courtesy and kindness, which philanthropy has established in the intercourse of nations, as well as to treaties of commerce, of boundaries, and, in fine, to every international subject whatsoever. This exposition is supported by such unequivocal authority, that it is believed it will not be questioned. I, therefore, infer that it will be readily yielded, that in regard to the treaty, in aid of which this bill is exhibited, the treaty-making power has not exceeded its just limits. So far we have proceeded on sure ground; we now come to the pith of the question. Is the legislative sanction necessary to give it effect? I answer in the negative. Why? Because, by the second clause of the sixth article of the Constitution, it is declared that all treaties made or which shall be made, under the authority of the United States, shall be the supreme law of the land. If this clause means anything, it is conclusive of the question.

If the treaty be a supreme law, then whatsoever municipal regulation comes within its provisions must *ipso facto* be annulled—unless gentlemen contend, there can be at the same time two supreme laws, emanating from the same authority, conflicting with each other, and still both in full vigor and effect. This would indeed produce a state of things without a parallel in human affairs, unless indeed its like might be found in the history of the Popes. In one instance, we are told, there were three at one time roaming over the Christian world, all claiming infallibility, and denouncing their anathemas against all who failed to yield implicit obedience to their respective mandates, when to comply with the one was to disobey the other. A result like this, so monstrous in its aspect, excludes the interpretation which produces it. It is a safe course in attempting to ascertain the meaning of a law or constitution to connect different clauses (no matter how detached) upon the same subject together. Let us do it in this case. The President shall have power, by and with the advice and consent of the Senate, to make treaties, which treaties shall be the supreme law of the land. I seek to gain no surreptitious advantage from the word supreme, because I frankly admit that it is used in the Constitution, in relation to the laws and constitutions of the States; but I appeal to it merely to ascertain the high authority intended to be imparted by the framers of the Constitution to a ratified treaty. It is classed in point of dignity with the laws of the United States. We ask for no superiority, but equality; and as the last law made annuls a former one, where they conflict, so we contend that a subsequent treaty, as in the present case,

revokes a former law in opposition thereto. But the other side contend, that it is inferior to the law in point of authority, which continues in full force despite of a treaty, and to its repeal the assent of the whole Legislature is necessary. Our claims rest on the expressed words of the Constitution—the opposite on implication; and if the latter be just, I cannot forbear to say that the framers of the Constitution would but ill deserve what I have heretofore thought a just tribute to their meritorious services. If they really designed to produce the effect contended for, instead of so declaring by a positive provision, they have used a language which, to my mind, operates conclusively against it. Under what clause of the Constitution is the right to exercise this power set up? The reply is, the 3d clause of 8th section 1st article—Congress shall have power to regulate commerce with foreign nations, &c. I immediately inquire to what extent does the authority of Congress, in relation to commercial treaties, reach? Is the aid of the Legislature necessary in all cases whatsoever, to give effect to a commercial treaty? It is readily admitted that it is not. That a treaty, whose influence is extra territorial, becomes obligatory the instant of its ratification. That, as the aid of the Legislature is not necessary to its execution, the Legislature have no right to interpose. It is then admitted that while a general power on the subject of commerce is given to Congress, that yet important commercial regulations may be adopted by treaty, without the co-operation of the Legislature, notwithstanding the generality of the grant of power on commercial subjects to Congress. If it be true that the President and Senate have, in their treaty-making power, an exclusive control over part and not over the whole, I demand to know at what point that exclusive control ceases? In the clause relied upon, there is no limitation. The fact is, sir, none exists. The treaty-making power over commerce is supreme. No legislative sanction is necessary, if the treaty be capable of self-execution, and when a legislative sanction is necessary, as I shall more at large hereafter show, such sanction, when given, adds nothing to the validity of the treaty, but enables the proper authority to execute it; and when the Legislature do act in this regard, it is under such obligation as the necessity of fulfilling a moral contract imposes.

If it be inquired of me what I understand by the clause in question, in answer I refer to the principle with which I set out; that this was a grant of power to the General Government of which Congress was in the first instance merely the depository, which power, had not a portion thereof been transferred to another branch of the Government, would have been exclusively exercised by Congress, but that a distribution of this power has been made by the Constitution; as a portion thereof has been given to the treaty-making power, and that which is not transferred is left in the possession of Congress. Hence, to Congress it is competent to act in this grant in its proper character by establishing municipal regulations. The President and the Senate, on the other hand, have the same power within their sphere, that is, by a treaty or convention with a foreign nation, to establish such regulations in regard to commerce, as to them may seem friendly to the public interest. Thus each department moves in its own proper orbit, nor do they come in collision with each other. If they have exercised their respective powers on the same subject, the last act, whether by the Legislature or the treaty-making power, abrogates a former one. The Legislature of the nation may, if a cause exist in their judgment sufficient to justify it, abrogate a treaty, as has been done; so the President and Senate by a treaty may abrogate a preexisting law containing interfering provisions, as has been done heretofore, (without the right being questioned,) and as we say in the very case under consideration. I will endeavor to make myself understood by examples; Congress has power, under the clause in question, to lay embargoes, to pass non-intercourse or non-importation or countervailing laws, and this power they have frequently exercised. On the other hand, if the nation against whom one of those laws is intended to operate, is made sensible of her injustice and tenders reparation, the President and Senate have power by treaty to restore the amicable relations between the two nations, and the law directing otherwise, upon the ratification of the treaty, is forthwith annulled. Again, if Congress should be of opinion that the offending nation had not complied with their engagements, they might by law revoke the treaty, and place the relation between the two nations upon such footing as they approved. Where is the collision here? I see none. This view of the subject presents an aspect as innocent as that which is produced when a subsequent law repeals a former one. By this interpretation you reconcile one part of the Constitution with another, giving to each a proper effect, a result always desirable, and in rules of construction claiming a precedence to all others. Indeed, sir, I do not see how the power in question could have been otherwise arranged. The power which has been assigned to Congress was indispensable; without it we should have been at the mercy of a foreign Government, who, knowing the incompetency of Congress to act, would have subjected our commerce to the most injurious regulations, as was actually the case before the adoption of the Constitution, when it was managed by the States, by whom no regular system could be established; indeed we all know this very subject was among the most prominent of the causes which produced the Constitution. Had this state of things continued, no nation which could profit by a contrary course would have treated. On the other hand, had not a power been given to some branch of the Government to treat, whatever might have been the friendly dispositions of other Powers, or however desirous to reciprocate beneficial arrangements, they could not, without a treaty-making power lodged somewhere, be realized. I therefore contend, that although to Congress a power is given in the clause alluded to,

to regulate commerce, yet this power is in part, as I have before endeavored to show, given to the President and Senate in their treaty-making capacity—the truth of which position is admitted by the friends of the bill to a certain extent. The fact is, that the only difference between us is to ascertain the precise point where legislative aid is necessary to the execution of the treaty, and where not. To fix this point is to settle the question. After the most mature reflection which I have been able to give this subject, my mind has been brought to the following results: Whenever the President and Senate, within the acknowledged range of their treaty-making power, ratify a treaty upon extra territorial subjects, then it is binding without any auxiliary law. Again, if from the nature of the treaty it is self-executory, no legislative aid is necessary. If, on the contrary, the treaty from its nature cannot be carried into effect but by the agency of the Legislature, that is, if some municipal regulation be necessary, then the Legislature must act not as participating in the treaty-making power, but in its proper character as a legislative body. Examples will serve to illustrate more satisfactorily the view I wish to present. If for an equivalent we had agreed by treaty that our vessels should not pass the Cape of Good Hope or the Straits of Magellan, this being extra territorial, then no law would have been necessary; this I understand is conceded by all parties.

Secondly. If by treaty we agree to surrender prisoners of war, or property taken from the enemy, or, as in the very case under consideration, that for an equivalent we will forbear to exact a higher tonnage duty on British than American ships, then the treaty, as it needs not legislative aid, is self-executory; and, finally, if we had agreed in the last convention that, if the British Government would abstain from impressment, no British sailors should be employed on board American ships, and that those who should offend therein should be obnoxious to a penalty, then the Legislature must act to fix the amount of such penalty, to prescribe the manner in which it should be prosecuted, and to fix the tribunal which should have cognizance of the case. I have thus, as explicitly as it is possible for me, given you my view of the just pretensions of the treaty-making power, on the one hand, and of the legislative on the other. This construction, so palpable to my mind, and so irrefragable, instead of being met by argument, conducted with moderation, and addressed to the understanding, has been assailed elsewhere with every epithet of opprobrium, as leading to a concentration of power in the hands of the President and Senate. If such reveries deserved to be noticed, I will state, with a view to quiet the alarmed, that this now dreaded power was exercised with less security to the nation by the old Congress. There, without the security arising from the approbation of the President, that body enjoyed the treaty-making power to the same extent as it is now exercised. And although this existed in the most disastrous period of the Republic, I have never heard it intimated that the power was abused. Indeed, sir, if the Constitution itself does not form the horizon of my view, and I am at liberty to look to the reasons which influenced the authors of the Constitution to place the treaty-making power where they did, I cannot help believing, that independent of the consideration of a greater degree of secrecy, despatch, &c., which was expected of the Senate, that the elements of which the body is composed, the immediate representatives of the States, in their sovereign capacity, had great weight in the arrangement. The consideration, too, that the small States would be equally represented here with the largest, would not be without its weight. And it is a singular fact, that although a treaty should be ratified by the consent of fourteen States, the representatives from four of the largest States in the Union, in the other branch, could arrest its execution, if that branch of the Government were to participate in the treaty-making power. As I have already taken the liberty, so I must ask for a continuance of the privilege to notice what I have heard said elsewhere, relative to the subject under consideration. It is urged by some, that the control of the sword and the purse is granted to Congress in no other way than their power to regulate commerce; and that if the President and Senate can act independently of the Legislature in one case, so they may in all. Far be from me such an opinion. I unhesitatingly say, that the purse and the sword have been placed under the safeguard of the national will; that any attempt on the part of the President and Senate to exclude the House of Representatives from their share of this trust, would be unconstitutional; and that it would not only be their right, but their duty to oppose it; in this opinion, I feel warranted both by the letter and genius of the Constitution. It is especially declared, by the 6th clause of the 9th section, that no money shall be drawn from the Treasury but in consequence of appropriations made by law; if by a treaty, therefore, it is covenanted that money shall be paid, Congress alone is competent to appropriate it, as was done in regard to Jay's Treaty, and that of Louisiana. As to the power of declaring war, it is surely placed in the Congress. This arrangement, which transfers this great attribute of sovereignty from the Executive department of the Government, where with all other nations it is lodged, to the Legislature, is one of the most striking features of our happy form of Government. I will not consent to discuss this question on the contracted scale of a special pleader. In forming my opinion, I shall consult the spirit of the Constitution; it is republican; its foundations rest on the unalienable rights of man; its acts flow directly from the will of the people. Where can the power over the sword and the purse reside with so much safety as in the National Legislature? There it has been placed; had it been otherwise, your Government would have been anything but republican. I pass from this view to that taken by the other side, which admits that the President and Senate have a right to abrogate the declaration of war without the aid of

Congress, because to Congress is not given the power to make peace. It is to me most wonderful that gentlemen, instead of relying on the just theory of the Constitution, as ascertained through an enlarged view of the spirit and general organization of that instrument, should be content to rest their opinion on so fallacious a construction; for, were it true, Congress could never repeal a tax or disband an army, however unnecessary they might be esteemed, because no express power to do so had been given them. The true principle is, that Congress alone can declare war. The President and Senate, in their treaty-making capacity, can terminate it; and when peace is established by treaty, an auxiliary law of the Legislature, being unnecessary, is never passed.

The friends of the bill seek to avail themselves of precedents furnished by the British Government, where it is contended treaties are always laid before Parliament to receive their sanction before they become obligatory. I protest against them. The difference between the treaty-making power there and here, is as great as that which separates wisdom from folly, or purity from corruption. There the sole power of making treaties is lodged in an hereditary and irresponsible Chief Magistrate, who may have been placed by accident or crime on the throne, and who may be the most unfit man in the kingdom for any office. His weakness subjects him to the control of secret advisers, who, playing the part of chief jugglers behind the scene, exhibit him as the mere punch of the puppet-show. In a nation having the least pretension to freedom, the official acts of such an officer should be subject to control; unfortunately none substantially exists. I say substantially, for although in point of fact treaties may be carried down to Parliament, it is but matter of form, for we all know that body has long since become an appendage of the Ministry; that they are as obedient to his nod as the needle to the pole. The British Government, in its best form, was but a wretched piece of patch-work—the result of fraud, of accident, or of force. Whatever liberty it might once have possessed is, I fear, forever gone. The anodyne drug of corruption has been administered to the high and the low, till all orders have become contaminated, and the nation is ripening for that inevitable doom which alike awaits nations and individuals. What resemblance exists between that Government and ours in regard to the organization of the power under consideration? Here a Chief Magistrate, called to office by the unbiassed suffrages of millions of freemen, responsible for his acts, and shortly to return to the mass of his fellow-citizens, aided by the direct representatives of the States in their sovereign capacity, two-thirds of whom must concur to give a validity to a treaty. The security against the abuse of power here, is as great as human ingenuity can devise; there as feeble. I therefore renew my protest against precedents drawn from such a source.

I find, sir, I have already exceeded the limits I had prescribed to myself, and I fear taxed your patience to an unreasonable degree. Yet, there are many things still on my mind, to which I wish to give utterance, but I will come to a close. You will perceive, I have discussed the Constitution as it is, not as it should be; that is a question *coram non judice.* Yet I will say, that for myself, I should feel no kind of solicitude as to the result, were the other House permitted to participate in the treaty-making power. I entirely confide in their patriotism and wisdom. I have no doubt that any treaty which should receive the sanction of the President and two thirds of the Senate, would also meet with the approbation of the House of Representatives. Indeed, sir, when the question was first stirred, I wished to be persuaded, that the other branch had a Constitutional claim to the power they were exercising. All my feelings were in that direction, for they are with me a favorite branch of the Government. Whenever my attention here can be dispensed with, I hasten to the House of Representatives; I hear with rapture their eloquence, I devour with a greedy ear the oracles of their wisdom, and I hope am edified by the lessons of their experience. With those sentiments and feelings I listened to the discussion on this subject, with a wish to be convinced, but I listened in vain. My judgment, after listening attentively to a very long debate, pronounced against their pretensions, and hence I am constrained to give the vote which I shall pronounce; nor shall I fear any of the consequences which have been foretold as likely to arise from this determination, one of which is, that the House of Representatives will dwindle into the contemptible condition of merely registering our edicts. The power they possess, I should imagine, is enough to satisfy the utmost reach of an honorable ambition. But, be that as it may, the people of whom we are both the servants, have prescribed limits to our respective authority. To each, it looks for the preservation of that portion confided to its guardianship. To the Senate, I speak in the spirit of the Constitution, has been confided the solemn trust, not only of guarding the rights of the States, but also, to resist on the one hand the silent current of Executive influence, and on the other, to tell the proud man of popular pretension, thus far you may advance and no farther. It is an awful trust, and wo to him who betrays it. For one, I will place myself on the utmost verge of our authority, and maintain it unimpaired, or, if it be the will of Providence otherwise to direct, to meet my fate, whatever it may be, with fortitude. I hope, sir, in the decision which I am about to pronounce, I have been entirely exempt from the spirit of the corps. Power, for its own sake, has no charm for me. The part I have taken will by all be placed to no other motive than a sense of duty. The unostentatious discharge of one's duty, is like alms given in secret; the reward of both is found in an approving conscience. One other remark, and I am done; it is to repel the insinuation, that with the construction of the treaty-making power, as I contend for it, corruption may find its way to the President and Senate, who may barter away the liberties of the country. If so disastrous a time should ever arrive, as that the President of the United States and two thirds of this body should have become so base as barter their inestimable birthright and that of the nation for a mess of pottage, is it to be believed that the other branch will have escaped the general contagion? If fortunately they have, such an act of the treaty-making power would be as futile as it would be wicked; but, if, which is more probable, the extreme case supposed should occur, corruption will not be confined to this branch, it will have embraced the nation. When that shall be the case, the phraseology of the Constitution, or the arrangement of its powers, will not weigh of the dust of the balance; it will be torn by the rude hand of violence and its fragments given to the wind. These to me are idle fears, and reasoning, if indeed it can be so called, on them, must be fallacious. To reason against the exercise of power, upon the possibility of its abuse, is to oppose at once all delegated authority, and to subvert the Constitution, which rests on a certain portion of morality and patriotism. This security, with the restrictions imposed by the Constitution, the deep interest we all have in common with our fellow-citizens, our accountability to our constituents, but above all the energy of freedom, a devotion to which is interwoven with every ligament of an American bosom, are sufficient guarantees, that in this country power will not be abused, or, if it be, its duration will be short. I say, sir, it is an idle fear, that has no other foundation than the anticipated corruption of the Senate and President. The mode of their election is ample security against the possibility of such a consequence, and I thank my God, that my mind is not able to conceive what shape the temptation would assume that could seduce us from our duty, and still less as it regards the President. He occupies the highest pinnacle of human elevation, which mankind can bestow or man receive. What value could he attach to a diadem or a purple reeking in the gore of his country, when weighed against the spontaneous preference of millions of freemen? And how terrible would be the change of his condition? He now presses his pillow in peace, hushed to repose by the soft whispers of an approving conscience; then, should he even succeed in his wicked attempts, he would be doomed to watch his ill-gotten power "with the sleepless eye of disquieting ambition," and be devoted to the curses of mankind, as the destroyer of the liberty of his country.

I have very imperfectly, I am sure, stated my opinions and the reasons producing them; and I have also endeavored to repel the objections which have been urged on the opposite side. A short recapitulation will close the discussion on my part. I have endeavored to show, that the assignment of power to the General Government, in opposition to that retained by the States, was the important object with the framers of the Constitution. That Congress was made merely the depository in the first instance, of such powers, which were afterwards to be distributed by subsequent provisions in the Constitution among the different branches. I furnished examples in support of this theory, to which I may here add the clause giving to Congress the power of a uniform rule of naturalization, which has been acted upon by the treaty-making power, as in the cases furnished as well by Jay's as the Louisiana Treaty; that as it regards the power in question, namely, that relative to commerce, it is fairly within the range of the treaty-making power. That when this branch of Government acts, it is to a particular extent independent of the Legislature; and when a treaty is *self*-executory, as in the case under consideration, that no legislative aid is necessary, and that therefore, to say the least of it, this bill is a supererogation; I have also endeavored to fix with precision where legislative aid is necessary; I have surrendered without difficulty the real emblems of sovereignty, the control of the sword and the purse, to the safeguard of the national will; I have endeavored to relieve our construction from the difficulties urged against it, and have endeavored to show that it gives vigor and effect to every part of the Constitution, and obviates all collision; and I have finally endeavored to dispel the fears which have been permitted to arise from the abuse of the power confided to the President and the Senate, by showing that their fidelity is guarantied by every security which human nature can furnish. I will conclude by returning my unfeigned thanks for the marked attention with which I have been favored.

When Mr. B. had concluded—

Mr. FROMENTIN rose and spoke as follows:

Mr. President, I regret that I cannot subscribe to the doctrine laid down by the honorable gentleman from Connecticut, (Mr. DAGGETT,) and by the honorable gentleman from New Hampshire, (Mr. MASON.) It is true, that the bill which was sent by the Senate to the House of Representatives on the subject of the Treaty, was received by the House whilst they were engaged in the discussion of a bill on the same subject, and before that bill had been finally agreed to by them; but, sir, it is equally true, that the House of Representatives originated the bill which they have since sent to the Senate, before a bill on the same subject had been thought of in this House. Can it be contended, that either House shall have the right to put an end to the proceedings of the other, by legislating on the same subjects on which they are apprized the other House is actually engaged, and by passing a bill in a hurry, on a motion to dispense with the ordinary rules prescribed for our deliberations; thus actually to prevent the legislative deliberations of another independent body? Sir, I am tenacious of the rights appertaining to this body, not from the motives which have been on more occasions than one illiberally attributed to the Senate, not from the *esprit de corps*, but because of those rights being delegated to us by the Constitution, I deem it a sacred duty to preserve them inviolate, and to transmit them unimpaired to our successors. The very same reason, sir, makes me not less tenacious of the

rights of the other House; and it matters not to me whence the assault proceeds which is directed against the Constitution; as long as I have the honor of a seat in this body, I will, to the utmost of my power, resist every attack against Constitutional rights, whether the attack be directed against this body, or whether it originates in this body against what I conceive to be the Constitutional rights of the other branches of the Government. I cannot, sir, sanction this unwarrantable usurpation of the legislative ground. I said that I regretted that I could not, consistently with my respect for the rights of the other House, agree to the course proposed to be pursued by the two honorable gentlemen who preceded me, and I do most sincerely regret it. Could we pursue that course, and could we anticipate that the House of Representatives, operated upon by similar motives, should treat the bill we have sent them as it is proposed to treat their bill, I should rejoice that both bills should remain inoperative; for, sir, I do not like the bill passed by the Senate much better than the bill passed by the House of Representatives. Both bills, in one respect, are, in my opinion, radically defective. Both bills enact provisions evidently useless; and I hold it, Mr. President, that whatever is useless in legislation, without referring in this particular instance to the risk of establishing a precedent, is never unaccompanied with danger. I would rejoice, sir, if I could devise any possible way of avoiding a discussion upon the subject of the bill on your table. But I know of no way of avoiding it; and at the same time that both the importance of the subject, and our respect for the other House, preclude the idea of either passing or rejecting this bill, *sub silentio*, it is a matter of congratulation that the principles upon which we are called upon to pronounce are so simple and evident, and the practice which has till now prevailed under them so fully established, that but little need to be said to satisfy the Senate that the bill on your table ought to be rejected.

Mr. President, so much has been said already on this subject, both in the other House and out of doors, that every member of the Senate may be said to be in possession of almost all the arguments for and against the provisions of the bill on your table. In the few observations which I propose making, I will sedulously avoid repeating any of the arguments which I have heard urged upon the subject. The sixth article of the Constitution is as follows: " This Constitution, and ' the laws of the United States which shall be ' made in pursuance thereof, and all treaties made, ' or which shall be made under the authority of ' the United States, shall be the supreme law of ' the land."

A treaty then is a law; it is not to become a law when an act shall have been passed by Congress to make it so, otherwise the word treaties would have been useless in the article quoted— treaties then being necessarily included under the general term, laws of the United States; it is so, *ipso facto*. From the moment it has been ratified by the President, by and with the advice and consent of the Senate, the Constitution declares that it is the supreme law of the land. Can a law—can what the Constitution declares to be a law—need any further assistance to become so? Can it need the enaction of another law to make it so? Where will this process end? A treaty and an act of Congress are, by the Constitution, put upon the same footing; both are declared to be laws; there cannot be two definitions of a law. If the law, as it results from a treaty, wants the super-enactment of an act of Congress, I can devise no reason why an act of Congress should not require another act of Congress, too, before the first act can be considered as a law. I see no end to this enactment and re-enactment. It has been contended that, admitting the treaty to be a law, still it cannot, unless the provisions of the treaty be re-enacted by Congress, repeal a former law, which is in contradiction to the new law, as it results from the treaty. If this doctrine was true, Mr. President, how is it that Congress did not think it necessary to re-enact the articles of the Treaty of Peace lately concluded with Great Britain? Did not the Treaty of Peace repeal the act of Congress by which war had been declared against Great Britain? Or, will gentlemen contend that this act is not yet repealed—that it is still in force? Are we, then, I ask, still at war with Great Britain? And if we are not—if we are at peace with Great Britain—is not the act declaring war against Great Britain actually repealed; and if it be repealed, is it not repealed by the Treaty of Peace; and if it be repealed by the Treaty of Peace, can it be questioned that a treaty, constitutionally ratified, does actually repeal every law anterior to that treaty, which is in opposition to the provisions of that treaty? Sir, it is a settled principle—a principle which, as far as I am informed, has never been contradicted—that the last law repeals the former law so far as the provisions of the former law are irreconcilable with the provisions of the latter; and if the practice had not obtained of inserting a repealing clause in such of our acts as are in contradiction with former acts on the same subject, those former acts, thus in contradiction, should, nevertheless, be repealed. The repealing clause in our acts is, it is true, the declaration of the repeal; but the repeal is actually produced by the enactment of the provisions of the law at war with the preceding law. The preceding law is actually repealed by the law imposing obligations, or prescribing duties incompatible with the obligations imposed, or the duties prescribed by a former law. For instance, take the act of Congress admitting the State of Louisiana into the Union; that act does not contain any clause to repeal the acts formerly passed by Congress for the government of the portion of territory now known by the name of the State of Louisiana. Will it be contended that these acts are not repealed, quite as much repealed, as if a repealing clause had been inserted in the act for the admission of Louisiana; and if those acts be repealed, is it not because their provisions are irreconcilable with the provisions of the late act; and does

not that example, among many others which I might have selected, establish fully the principle which I contend for, that, without the superfluous provisions of a repealing clause, such provisions of any law. incompatible with the provisions of a later law, are necessarily and *ipso facto* repealed by the provisions of the later law; and if this be undeniable with respect to one description of laws, is it not so with respect to laws of every other description? If it be true with respect to the acts of Congress, is it not true with respect to laws resulting from a treaty made under the authority of the United States? Sir, this House cannot get rid of the dilemma; either you cannot repeal former laws by the enactment of later laws in contradiction of the former, without a repealing clause—and I have proved that you did it—or what you may do by the enactment of one of the description of laws known to our Constitution, without a repealing clause, may be done by another description of laws equally known to our Constitution, without the assistance of a repealing clause.

Mr. President, can it be apprehended that this clause in the Constitution, "under the authority of the United States," will be construed to include, by implication, very far-fetched implication indeed, the House of Representatives, which truly does constitute a no inconsiderable share of the authority of the United States? but can no more, on that account, consider itself as constituting an essential indispensable part of every power necessary for all the acts which are to be done under the authority of the United States. Sir, these words, "the authority of the United States," are very broad; they cover an immense ground. But can they ever be supposed to mean, that every authority in the United States is to be consulted before any act can have validity which is to be done under the authority of the United States? Extensive, no doubt, and very properly so, but not unlimited, are the rights of the House of Representatives; and, like every other branch of the Government, in this our Government of checks, thus far, to wit: as far as the Constitution has vested the right in the House of Representatives. Thus far has she a right to go, but no farther; and it is the bounden duty of the Senate to resist, on the part of the House, as well as on the part of the Executive, any attempt at an encroachment of rights which, by the Constitution, are vested in the Senate. Sir, if the words, "under the Constitution of the United States," did, in the present instance, necessarily include the House of Representatives, it is difficult to conceive why the Convention, instead of using the words, "authority of the United States," did not use the words, "authority of Congress." The clause where these words are to be found, is not the clause of the Constitution by which the power of making or ratifying treaties is delegated, but an annunciation only of what in future the people of the United States declare they will consider as a treaty binding upon them; it will be a treaty made under the authority of the United States; that is, a treaty

HISTORY OF CONGRESS.

Commerce with Great Britain.

made by that authority in the United States to which the power has been delegated by the Constitution to make treaties, which shall be binding upon the people of the United States. Give me leave to add here, by way of rendering every obstacle which might be attempted to be erected on the forced construction of these words, that their insertion in the article of the Constitution, where they are to be found, originated in the necessity of discriminating between treaties made under the authority of the United States, and treaties made under the authority of some individual State. Every body who is conversant with the history of the United States at the time the Constitution was framed, knows that several States had been making treaties; some treaties were in fact pending between some States, and some nations of Indians, at the time the Constitution was adopted. The United States, by adopting the clause, "under the authority of the United States," gave public notice that they should not consider themselves as bound by any treaty made by individual States; but by such only as should be made under the authority of the United States; that is, by the President of the United States, by and with the advice and consent of the Senate, which, according to the Constitution, are, as far as respects the power of making treaties, binding on this nation—the authority of the United States. Sir, the President and the Senate of the United States are the attorneys, in fact, of the people of the United States, to make, in their name, with a foreign nation, every contract which they conceive to be demanded for the interest of the people of the United States. Suppose I gave you a power of attorney to sell for me, and in my name, a tract of land on certain stipulated conditions, to be fulfilled by the purchaser. On the fulfilment of those conditions, you have agreed, under the authority which I had vested in you by the letter of attorney, that I should convey the land. The conditions have been fulfilled on the part of the purchaser, and he applies to me to convey the land accordingly. Could I, Mr. President, under these circumstances, be admitted to plead that there was too much danger in the exercise of the power by me delegated to an individual thus to bind me; and would not the court compel me to fulfil all the engagements entered into by the attorney, in fact, to whom I should have delegated the power to bind me: provided he had not, in that respect, exceeded the powers expressed in the letter of attorney? Sir, if the President and Senate have not, in the making of a treaty, exceeded the powers given to them by the Constitution, it is the duty of Congress not to re-enact its provisions, to give it a validity which may be supposed to be wanting; but to pass such laws as may be necessary to give it effect, which laws are to be built upon, and made conformable to the provisions of the treaty, because that instrument is valid, and in full force from the moment of its ratification, according to the Constitution.

Having thus endeavored, Mr. President, to demonstrate, from the plain, unsophisticated exposition of the words of the Constitution, the mean-ing, the only meaning which they appear to me to be susceptible of, I will add a few words to show that the practice, till now, under our Constitution, comes in aid of the construction I have contended for. I have already mentioned the Treaty of Peace lately concluded with Great Britain, as a satisfactory proof that the House of Representatives did not, at that time, deem it necessary that the provisions of a treaty should be re-enacted by Congress to repeal any law in existence prior to the conclusion of that treaty. I could refer, in support of the same doctrine, to the numberless treaties which have been made with the Indians since the organization of our Government. But, sir, I mean to be very short, and I come at once to a treaty which not only bore upon our commercial regulations, but which appropriated an immense sum of money, a larger sum of money than was ever appropriated by any other law; and, sir, I hope to be able to demonstrate that a claim was set up at that time, by the House of Representatives, for the exercise of the high pretensions which they have now, for the first time, manifested. If I should succeed in establishing this fact, I think I shall have proved, satisfactorily, both that the letter of the Constitution, and that the practice of the Government under it, repel the idea that the consent of the House of Representatives is necessary to give validity to a treaty, or, which is the same thing, to repeal any law which should be irreconcilable with that treaty; for, sir, I cannot conceive of the existence of two contradictory laws being in force at the same time, in the same country, on the same subject; and it must follow, of course, as attempted to be established before, that the latter repeals the former law.

The treaty I allude to, sir, is the treaty concluded at Paris on the 30th of April, 1803, between the United States and France. This treaty and the several conventions signed at the same date, annexed to the said treaty, approved, ratified, and exchanged, in the same form, at the same time, and jointly with the said treaty, and as much a part of the said treaty as if the clauses in the two conventions had been inserted in the said treaty, stipulated certain commercial regulations, and contained provisions for the payment of a sum of fifteen millions of dollars. What was the conduct of Congress at that time? Did the House of Representatives of those days, which have been very often mentioned as the golden age of pure, unadulterated republicanism in this country—did the House of Representatives contend, that the treaty could not be carried into effect, until the provisions of the treaty had been by them re-enacted in the shape of an act of Congress? No, sir, such doctrine was not dreamt of then. The House of Representatives considered the treaty as the supreme law of the land. They did not question the right, nor did they indulge in speculations upon the possible corruption of a future President and Senate. They took the treaty to be the supreme law of the land. They did, with respect to the treaty, what the first Congress, which assembled under our present form of

Government did, with respect to the Constitution. They did not re-enact the provisions of the treaty, as the first Congress did not re-enact the articles of the Constitution. But, as, in compliance with the articles of the Constitution, the first Congress enacted the necessary laws to carry that Constitution into effect; so did the eighth Congress, in compliance with the articles of the Treaty of Paris, concluded on the 30th of April, 1803, pass the necessary laws to carry that treaty into effect. Accordingly, sir, we find that on the 31st of October, 1803, the Congress of the United States passed an act, a very short act, sir, only two sections, to enable the President of the United States to take possession of the territories ceded by France to the United States, by the treaty concluded at Paris on the 30th of April last, and for the temporary government thereof. This act, as I before said, is very short; give me leave to read it. [The act was read.] As you see sir, this act does not contain any such provisions as are contained in the act on your table. Not one of the articles of the treaty is mentioned in that act. No section is to be found in it making an appropriation for fifteen millions of dollars; no section to extend the rights of American citizens to the inhabitants of the ceded territories; no section to alter our commercial relations, with respect to France and Spain, so far as relates to the privileges to be granted to the vessels of those two countries, in the ports of the ceded territories. No, sir, not one word is whispered about these mighty and most important points; and yet, sir, the treaty which contains all these important stipulations is a law. The House of Representatives, who either originated or gave their assent to the act which I read—I know not which, nor can I now ascertain—but it is quite immaterial—the House of Representatives, I say, by passing that act, proclaimed to the world, not only that the treaty, without their approbation, was the supreme law of the land, but that they themselves considered it so. As far as the doctrine of precedents may go, the House of Representatives are concluded upon this point.

Will it be said, sir, that laws were passed afterwards by Congress for the creation of stock, for the payment of claims of citizens of the United States on the Government of France, and for other purposes, some of which, not all, sir, are the same, as some of the purposes intended to be effected by the treaty? This objection may postpone the decision of the question, by necessitating a further answer. It cannot alter that decision. Give me leave, Mr. President, to answer this objection by putting a question myself to the advocates of the claims of the House of Representatives on this floor. Can an instrument of writing be a treaty, and no treaty, at the same time? Can the House of Representatives, admitting them to have the right to refuse to pass such laws as may be necessary to carry into effect a treaty, duly and constitutionally approved and ratified by the President—by and with the advice and consent of the Senate—can, I say, the House of Representatives pass laws to give effect to certain stipula-

tions of a treaty, without, at the same time, admitting that such other stipulations of the same treaty, without which, the particular article for the giving effect to which, they have passed laws, should not have been agreed to, are as binding as the particular article to which they have given effect by a law? And how, sir, can those other stipulations be binding unless they be a law? In the treaty to which I have referred, there are two prominent stipulations, to wit: a cession of the province of Louisiana by France to the United States, and a promise, by the United States, to pay fifteen millions of dollars to France. By the act of the 31st of October, 1803, the President of the United States is authorized to take possession of Louisiana; but the United States are not bound by the same act to pay France fifteen millions of dollars; yet Congress knew very well, when they passed the act authorizing the President to take possession of Louisiana, that there had been contracted for on the part of the United States, an obligation to pay fifteen millions of dollars for that purpose. Possession could not be taken without providing for the payment; yet not a word is said about making provision for the payment, and possession is ordered to be taken. Sir, provision was made for the payment. The House then considered the obligation to pay the fifteen millions of dollars stipulated to be paid by the President and the Senate as complete, as binding, as beyond their control; they knew, they confessed, that the treaty was the supreme law of the land; they knew that they could not add to, or detract from the obligations of a treaty by any act of theirs; they said nothing, sir. It is true that they passed afterwards the necessary laws to carry into effect the provisions of the treaty; and, among others, the provisions which had stipulated the payment and mode of payment of the fifteen millions of dollars. But, sir, the passing of those several acts, even according to the doctrine of the most strenuous advocates for the claims of the House of Representatives, does not alter the position I maintain. The passing of those acts was forced upon them. After carrying into effect one article of the treaty, they were bound to carry every other article into effect. These acts, sir, posterior to the 31st of October, 1803, do not re-enact the articles of the treaty. They do not contract the obligation; they provide for the fulfilment of the obligations contracted by the paramount law. They are handmaids to the law resulting from the treaty. The treaty then was law before the enactment of those acts; and so, sir, is the treaty lately concluded, without any of the enactments in the bill on your table. During the time which elapsed, after passing the act of the 31st of October, 1803, until the time when the several acts were passed, which provided for the carrying into effect other articles of the treaty, those articles were certainly the law of the land; and if they were, they were so, not because re-enacted by Congress, since it is confessed on all hands that they had not then been re-enacted—they were so then only because they were inserted in the treaty. The treaty then was a law, without the re-enactment of the articles it contained by Congress.

One word more, Mr. President, and I have done. By the treaty of the 30th of April, 1803, the rights and privileges of American citizens were extended to all the inhabitants of the territory ceded by that treaty to the United States. Not only has no act been passed by Congress re-enacting the article of the treaty which confers those rights and privileges on the people of the ceded territory; but, sir, it is not improper to remark, that the treaty, so far as relates to the granting of those rights and privileges, operates as a repealing clause of the several statutes passed by Congress prescribing the mode by which foreigners are to be naturalized. How, I ask, how could this have taken place, if the eighth Congress had not considered that the treaty was a law, and not only that it was a law, but that it was a law repealing *ipso facto* all the acts of Congress which were in opposition to the treaty? From this view of the subject, I cannot hesitate a moment in voting for the rejection of the bill on your table.

When Mr. F. had taken his seat—

Mr. ROBERTS addressed the Chair as follows:

Mr. President: Seeing no one about to occupy the floor, I rise, though ill prepared, to offer my opinion. I should do it under any circumstances with great diffidence. Having been under an impression there was no disposition to enter into a discussion of this bill, I had too much neglected turning my thoughts to its provisions, until gentlemen, holding different opinions from those I am compelled to form, had invited discussion, and almost made it unavoidable. I yesterday moved an adjournment, with a view to a better consideration of the subject; and have since devoted to it some attention. I have found it one of the most serious character, as it goes to fix a high and important construction of the Constitutional law. The ultimate effects of the decision which may be now made, if it results in a rejection of the bill, must be momentous, however light its immediate ones may be esteemed. Gentlemen who have preceded me on the other side of the question, have the advantage of being familiarized with this sort of discussion, from their professional pursuits. [Mr. BARBOUR disclaimed being of that character.] The gentleman from Virginia, said Mr. R., disclaims the professional character. I beg his pardon; the other gentlemen I apprehend are of that character, at least.

This question, Mr. President, presents nothing beyond the comprehension of a plain mind, and ordinary application.

Several exceptions been taken to this bill. It has been objected to on the point of etiquette. It is said it is materially variant from the one passed on the same subject by this body, after solemn and deliberate consideration; and that consistency demands of us its rejection. Lastly, it is objected, that it is unnecessary, and must, if passed, be of evil consequences. This last objection, if found valid, must be fatal. I proceed to show it is not.

The gentleman from Virginia (Mr. BARBOUR) has laid down the question now before us. "Does a treaty repeal a law that has had the sanction of Congress, without its consent?" I should rather state it—" Does a treaty, ratified by two-thirds of the Senate and President, become a law without legislative sanction?" I contend it cannot constitutionally. In adducing proof of this, I shall not recur to precedents, often inapplicable, and never satisfactory in the settlement of just principles of legal construction. The Constitution is the only safe authority to which an appeal can be made, in order to ascertain what powers are possessed by any branch of Government. In referring to this instrument, it is worthy of remark, that it is a specimen almost without parallel of concise and comprehensive diction. It contains few redundant words, and forming a whole, which must be kept in view, to a just construction of its parts.

The first section of the first article declares, "all legislative power shall be vested in a Congress of the United States, which shall consist of a Senate and House of Representatives." This short clause, Mr. President, will be found to have a predominating influence through the whole instrument. The language is so strong, and so comprehensive, that nothing can impair its force but a modification of its meaning, express and palpable. No construction by implication, however strong, can be adequate. All power of making laws shall be vested in a Congress: it must be worse than absurdity to say, then, that a treaty can become a law of the land, without its approbation. The following sections provide for organizing the Senate and House of Representatives, and defining the powers of each: In the eighth section, we find what Congress have power to do. This section closes with a clause of especial importance in our present inquiry. We find here that, "Congress shall have power to make all laws necessary and proper for carrying into execution the foregoing powers, and all other powers, vested by this Constitution in the Government of the United States, or in any department thereof." In coming at a correct construction of a law, much depends on a correct interpretation of words. Those passages show that all powers to make laws, for carrying into execution every power vested in the Government, or any department thereof, (most obviously the treaty-making power is here included,) is by the Constitution vested in Congress. Here is an especial reference, not only to foregoing powers, but all other powers, subsequent as well as precedent. A legislative power is a power to give laws. All legislative power is given to Congress, and no other department of the Government can exercise it. If a treaty be a law, to any affirmative effect, it can only become so when it has been sanctioned by the Senate and House of Representatives. That the treaty-making power is not a law-making power, I consider as already established, by the most certain construction of the Constitution. But, by pursuing the examination of its other provisions, we shall find in them confirmation strong to demonstration. The ninth section contains exceptions out of, and limitations on the legislative power, and every other power in the Government. It does not only say they shall not legislate on the subjects enumerated, but no power in the Government shall infringe upon them. The delegated authorities are severally and collectively inhibited from any interference with them. One of the exceptions is, "that no tax or duty shall be laid on articles exported from any State." Another is, "no money shall be drawn from the Treasury, but in consequence of appropriations made by law." It will be admitted by all, that the meaning of the word law, as used here, is a rule prescribed by Congress. A treaty, then, the provisions of which require appropriations to carry them into effect, cannot become an operative law, though ratified by two-thirds of the Senate and President, till Congress have by law appropriated money to carry it into execution. The ratification of a treaty, then, is obviously a very different authority from that of passing laws to execute it. But, it has been said, a treaty when ratified becomes a law, imposing on Congress the duty to make appropriations, without option. This conclusion must be incorrect—first, because it goes to make the President and Senate the legislative authority, and the Senate and House of Representatives, the Executive authority—second, because legislation must of necessity be an act of free will, from motives of expediency—and third, if the Legislature refuse to appropriate, there can be no coercive remedy. If a treaty, when ratified, becomes a law, it must be a law adequate to appropriating money, subject to be drawn from the Treasury, without the consent of Congress. The argument leads to this conclusion, or it means nothing. It would not have been more obviously improper, to have stipulated with Britain, in the convention this bill is intended to carry into execution, for the levy of a duty on articles exported into the United States, equal to the existing duty on British exports. This seems to be the unavoidable, embarrassing construction that arises from attempting to build up a sovereign and little limited power, on an insulated phrase of the Constitution, without reference to the context.

"Congress," Mr. President, "have power to ' raise and support armies, but no appropriation ' of money to that use shall be for a longer term ' than two years." Now, if the treaty-making power can make a law, as is contended by the objectors to this bill, that imposes on Congress the duty of appropriating money, on the same principle they can certainly make a law, by treaty, to raise and support armies. Having reference to the usages of nations, nothing is more common in treaties of alliance than stipulations for keeping up a standing military force. The Constitution has, however, in this Government, intrusted the power of raising armies, to Congress alone. Nay—the House of Representatives are made the especial guardians against the misuse of this high trust. The appropria-

tions are limited to two years. A new House of Representatives must assent to their longer continuance. What becomes of this important check if the treaty-making power is magnified into a high and sovereign legislative authority? But some gentlemen have confined it to internationa concerns. But their objection to this bill extend it to concerns that are national. They conten the treaty is a law, without the consent of Con gress; if so, it goes to impair the revenue, by very considerable diminution of the duties o imports and tonnage. My friend from Sout Carolina, (Mr. TAYLOR,) yesterday justly re marked, that we had heard much about legisla tive pledges of faith to the public creditors; an he had been taught to believe, that when mad by both Houses of Congress, they could not b violated, but by consent of both. Reject this bill and the Senate withdraw the pledge, withou the consent of the House, and have no power t originate a substitute. If then the doctrine, tha the treaty-making power is a paramount powe exclusively vested in the President and Senate with no other limit than their discretion, as t what are fit objects for it to act upon, and tha their ratification binds the nation, as gentlemen have contended, all the limitations on the legis lative power in the Constitution are frivolous, t say no more, and nugatory. If treaties, when ratified merely, are the supreme law of the land the amendatory clause in the Constitution is o little value. When a treaty is made a law, by sanction of the authority of the United States whatever that authority may be found to be, i becomes a pact, binding on this nation as a con tracting party, till the other party infracts th covenant, or it is done by us by act equivalent t that of war. These may be of lasting effect, an thus the President and Senate may even preclud the benefit of amendment. Thus too must b opened, if gentlemen's construction is true, broad and extensive field for gradual and dan gerous encroachments on the liberties of thi people.

In the second article, Mr. President, we find i provided, that "the Executive power shall b vested in a President of the United States o America;" all power to make laws, to carry int effect any powers vested in the Government, o any department thereof, is vested in Congress Executive power is a power that has "the qual ity of performing active, not deliberative, not le gislative." No two powers can be in their natur more distinct; nay, even more opposite. In th Constitutional allotment of the Executive dutie this distinctness is preserved with great precision "The President shall be Commander-in-Chief o the Army and Navy, and of the militia whe called into actual service;" but, "Congress shal pass laws for calling out the militia, governing,' &c. The duty of the President is strictly execu tive. He shall have power, by and with the ad vice and consent of the Senate, two-thirds of th Senators concurring, to make treaties; and h shall nominate, and by and with the advice an consent of the Senate appoint ambassadors; and shall take care the laws be faithfully executed. I cannot find, by the remotest implication, any authority, either in the general grant, or in the enumeration of Executive powers given to the President, or conjointly to him and the Senate, anything like Legislative authority, except, indeed, it be drawn from the cabalistic words *make treaties*. On the simple verb *to make*, gentlemen rest their construction to deprive the House of Representatives, the most confidential branch of the Government, of their voice in making laws of the land. As well might it be said the appointment of an ambassador had the effect of law, and his outfit and salary followed as matter of course. *Make*, we understand, is equivalent to, "to form of materials." As soon, then, as the elements of a treaty are embodied, the stimulus of ratification is to give life and activity to the instrument, beyond the control of the people's representatives, though ever so subversive of their rights. But gentlemen attempt to extend their ground of construction, by referring to the sixth article, which reads, "this Constitution, and the 'laws of the United States, which shall be made 'in pursuance thereof, and all treaties which shall 'be made under the authority of the United States, 'shall be the supreme law of the land, and the 'judges in every State shall be bound thereby." The words "under the authority of the United States," have been conveniently passed over, or slightly noticed. They are not surplusage—their meaning is important—a treaty not made under the authority of the United States shall not be the law of the land. Here it is plain and palpable the legislative authority is included, else why all the checks and limitations on that authority?

The judicial power is to extend to "all cases in law and equity arising under the Constitution, the laws of the United States, and treaties which shall be made under their authority." Thus, twice is enumerated, in what order the Constitution, the laws, and treaties made under the authority of the United States, shall stand. In both cases it is precisely the same, treaties are in the third place. To make them obligatory on the State judges, they must be sanctioned by the authority of the United States. The House of Representatives have by solemn and deliberate act emphatically declared, in their opinion, the commercial convention with Great Britain will not have been made a law of the land under the authority of the United States, without the consent of the Senate and House of Representatives in their legislative capacity. This at least proves the competency of the treaty-making power doubtful—where doubts exist, it is the safer way to remove them, when it can be done. If the most numerous, and not the less enlightened branch of the Legislature doubt, may not the State judges doubt, and thus a case arise where one authority conflicts with another about what is law? The remedy for this evil is easy, is safe; render to the legislative authority what is its due.

We have been told, Mr. President, the treaty-making power is the highest power exercised in any community; that it is a sovereign power. I

apprehend this language is much too strong, unless it is meant to say it has no limits but in the discretion of those who exercise it. If, as we are told, this power, when exercised by the proper authority, binds the nation, and that proper authority comes from the words *make treaties*, then will I admit it is a sovereign power indeed. Happily, however, I find by the Constitution a treaty law has no peculiar preference to a statute law. The former has the third place, and the same power can abrogate either. But treaty-making is not the highest act of power in this community—levying war and taxes, and regulating justice, are powers of a higher character, and equally sovereign. But, gentlemen have admitted this power must be applied to a fit subject to bind the nation. The other branch of the Legislature says, the treaty in question goes to regulate commerce with foreign nations, and Congress can only do this by law. Here then is not a fit subject, and I apprehend few will be found that do not require the assent of the House of Representatives to make a law.

The treaty-making power, we are told, cannot touch the sword and the purse—these are guarantied to the national will. This leaves little to contend about. The treaty-making power, if it even be a substantive power, will have limited exercise if it touches not the sword and the purse. I do not know if I can enumerate the catalogue of treaty topics. There are treaties of peace, of amity and commerce, of alliance, offensive and defensive, of limits, of cession, and of subsidy. Which of these can be touched without contact with the power of the purse and the sword? I see none but a treaty of peace; it wants no affirmation. I contend, however, that no treaty which has any operative or active character, can have the effect of law without interfering with the authority vested in Congress, as much as those relating to the purse and the sword. The gentleman from New Hampshire (Mr. MASON) asks, was the power of making a treaty in the President and Senate when the commercial convention with Britain was made? and adds, they have it, or it is nowhere granted. I think I have proved it is granted, and that they have it not. The gentleman thinks the treaty-making power does not interfere with the power of Congress to regulate commerce with foreign nations. If treaty regulations made by the President and Senate be law, they not only repeal statutes and supersede the power of legislation for the time being, but during the existence of the treaty. This is a construction of the legislative power to regulate commerce, without the consent of the most important branch of Congress. In this case it will be against their expressed will. The legislative is a grand power, says the gentleman; the treaty-making authority is a special one. How is a special incidental power, let me ask, by any sound rule of construction, to obliterate a grand leading power, such as that of legislation? This disposition to aggrandize the treaty-making power on the ruins of legislative authority, results in perpetual absurdity. Better to leave the treaty making power, the gentleman tells us, where the people have placed it; it is there I wish it to remain, and the legislative power also. It is not as to who are constitutionally authorized to make treaties we differ, but to whom it is given to make them law? It is an Executive power in its nature, says the gentleman, and every wise nation has placed it there. So far as negotiation is concerned, it is Executive; so far as ratification is concerned, it is Executive; but the Executive cannot make it a law without usurpation of the Legislative authority. When the Executive proceeds to make laws he becomes a legislator, and we arrive at the absurdity of despotism by making his will the law of the land. The gentleman from New Hampshire (Mr. Mason) says the "law of the land" is a common law term; but are we thence to go to common law legislation to learn how the Executive can make treaties the law of the land? A judicial decision cannot make treaties the law of the land, contrary to the will of the Legislature, without usurpation.

Gentlemen recur to the era of our Government to show it was designed to strengthen the Federal authority; and tell us power is parcelled out to the different departments. This affords a good rule by which to construe the Constitution. It contains provisions for a due and distinct exercise of all necessary powers for the administration of a just and free Government—on the one hand, strong enough to secure social security and happiness; and on the other, restrained from invading either by a due division and definement of authority. A desire to invest one authority with increased power by construction, must destroy the symmetry of the system, if not the system itself. The high powers of legislation are checked by two co-ordinate branches, and an Executive negative, and they ought never to be exercised in any other manner. There cannot, then, be two laws at once; there can be no conflict, no doubt, no difficulty. All laws will then emanate from the same source, as the sages who framed our Government intended. The House of Representatives have invited us to this course by their bill.

The gentleman from Virginia (Mr. Barbour) seems disposed to resolve the question into one of great and small States. He conceives four States might, on a treaty question in the House of Representatives, control fourteen. He recalled the statement, but his error, in point of numbers, was small; one vote, added to those of the four largest States, would make a quorum of that House. But, in point of fact, I think he is in error—no evil can arise from this circumstance—no treaty can be ratified without passing as much within the power of the small States as the large ones, nor go before the House. The House will reject no treaty but on strong grounds. The welfare of the small States cannot be more deeply staked in a treaty than that of the large ones in the event of its passage or rejection. If the President and Senate can make treaties *laws of the land* by their ratification, who shall conserve the rights of the large States, when numbers are so much against them?

The gentleman from Virginia (Mr. Barbour) has contended, that the Congress have power to establish a uniform rule of naturalization; it has been ceded, by Jay's Treaty, that the treaty-making power can, under its legitimate exercise, reciprocally naturalize the natives of the United States, and of the country of the other contracting party. An appeal to that treaty will not warrant such a construction. It is drawn up with the strictest care not to encroach on the power of Congress to establish a uniform rule of naturalization. With the indulgence of the Senate, I will read the article: "Such settlers and traders 'as shall continue to reside within the boundary 'lines, shall not be compelled to become citizens 'of the United States, or to take any oath of allegiance to the Government thereof, but they shall 'be at full liberty so to do if they think proper 'and they shall make and declare their election 'in one year after the evacuation aforesaid. And 'all persons who shall continue there after the 'expiration of the said year, without having declared their intention of remaining subjects of 'His Britannic Majesty, shall be considered as 'having elected to become citizens of the United 'States." It is unnecessary to remark, that all this stipulation provides for, is the option to become, or not to become, citizens. It merely engages for the United States, that no law shall be passed to prevent such as do not elect to remain British subjects, to take an oath of allegiance and become citizens of the United States. The gentleman from Louisiana (Mr. Fromentin) has referred to the treaty ceding that country to the United States, to show that it trenched upon the powers of Congress, in respect to naturalization and regulating commerce. The article of the treaty which provides for the admission of that territory into the Union as States, is expressly worded so as not to infract the Constitution. So much did the President believe the sanction of Congress necessary to carry that treaty into execution, that, immediately on its ratification, he sent a message to Congress, pressing the speedy enactment of laws to give it effect. But I cannot find the slightest evidence of the President, as a negotiator, showing any disposition to act under a construction of exercising a sovereign power. In page eighteen of the Executive papers of the second session of the twelfth Congress, we find these instructions: "As an inducement to Great 'Britain to discontinue the practice of impressment from American vessels, you may give 'assurance that a law will be passed (to be reciprocal) to prohibit the employment of British seamen in the public or commercial service of the United States." Mr. Russell explains to the British Minister, that this assurance is given, under the sense of the Federal Constitution; that is, that it involved the assent of Congress, over whom the Executive had no control. Our Commissioners, in negotiating the convention in question, referred to a law of last session to show the sense of the legislative authority, and to give assurance of their concurrence in stipulations to equivalent effect. This law had been forwarded as instruction, no doubt.

The gentleman from Virginia (Mr. BARBOUR) seems aware that his construction may be thought to vest a dangerous power in the President and Senate; two-thirds of the Senate, says he, must ratify a treaty, they are elected by the Legislatures of the States, and are men who have gone through the ordeal of State office. The President, he adds, is elected by the people, and must be a man distinguished for his virtue and services. But, Mr. President, however the mode of constituting the Executive and the Senate may promise the obtainment of good men, it is obvious and palpable, that they are not the favorite depositories of high discretionary trust in the Constitution. The House of Representatives only can originate revenue bills. The House of Representatives are to check the appropriations for the support of armies once in two years. While the gentleman is talking about the confidence due to the Senate, we all remember, at the era our Government was established, opinions were held by some not very partial to free Government. Such opinions are still held. We can all remember with what feelings the first Senate assembled; what questions were discussed, and what projects were contemplated. Public opinion has made these feelings in some degree disappear; but, in the nature of things, we may look for more here than in the House of Representatives. If we look to the powers, the paucity of numbers, the period of office, or the mode of election, for this body; are they calculated most to allay or excite jealousy? The plain letter of the Constitution gives the President and Senate power enough, without extending it by constructive authority, raised on vague implication.

We are not to look for the destruction of the liberties of this people, from a single stride of authority, but by one branch arrogating to itself power with the concurrence of another, to the disparagement of a third. It must be by artful and gradual encroachment, under cover of forced construction, and by a cautious application of power thus obtained. Hence, we are taught to fear the effect of the precedent the rejection of this bill might establish, more especially as it would set at naught the solemn opinion of the House of Representatives.

The gentleman from Virginia remarks, he has endeavored to discuss the question as he finds the Constitution; were a proposition to amend it before us, he could have no difficulty. I request him to examine it anew; I think, fairly interpreted, it is what he could wish it. Let us leave law-making and treaty-making where the people have placed it. Then, indeed, shall we have done justice to the wisdom of those sages who formed the Constitution. We are asked, if the President and Senate become corrupt, what will there be to preserve the House of Representatives? I answer, *frequent election,* and greater numbers.

Need I now remark, Mr. President, that I think this bill necessary; all I have said goes to prove

it. I had thought yesterday to offer an amendment, not very dissimilar to the bill we have sent to the House of Representatives—I had prepared it. Better reflection convinces me this bill is necessary. Its enactments are precisely correspondent with the provisions of the commercial convention with Great Britain. It will not be enough that the courts shall look to that instrument for the law, the statute ought also to be before them.

On the subject of etiquette, it ill becomes us to be very punctilious. The bill passed by this body was not, on my part, a very deliberate act; nor was it to be looked for, that it should have arrested the House on the passage of their own bill, from the time of its arrival on their table.

It has been my desire, Mr. President, to preserve that coolness in the delivery of my sentiments which is due to this body, and the dignity of the subject. Declamation and rhetorical flourish has been made to give place to sober examination, and a desire only to justify what I find to be my duty, in the vote I am to give. My conviction is clear, the bill ought to pass.

When Mr. ROBERTS sat down—

Mr. MACON, of North Carolina, said, as the reading of the bill which had passed the Senate twice on the same day, had been noticed, and that too with reference to a rule which made it necessary for the second reading to be by the unanimous consent of the House, he felt it his duty to state, that when it was read the second time, it was not on his table, and that while it was reading the third time, it was laid on it wet, not in time to be read before the bill was passed. He did not object to the third reading, because he had but a few days before taken his seat, and did not like so very soon to be the only objecting member, to that which appeared to be the general wish of the Senate. He did not blame any one for the reading of the bill twice on the same day that it passed; if blame attached to any person, it was to himself. He had frankly stated the grounds on which he acted; perhaps it might be a sort of false delicacy. He considered it due to the Senate to say that, when, on the next day, he objected to the reading of a bill a second time on the same day, it was done under the painful recollection of what had taken place the day before, and with no view to delay the public business, or to thwart the inclination of the Senate.

Mr. M. said, as he was now up, he should give some of the reasons which would induce him to vote for the bill from the House of Representatives—in doing which he promised to be very short. He agreed with the gentleman who differed with him as to the propriety of passing the bill, that the Constitution should be so construed as to give to every part its full effect, and to every department of the Government the power allotted to it, and that no department should attempt to encroach on the power delegated to another. If one should unfortunately make the attempt, he would add that it ought to be immediately resisted. With respect to what had been said about the House of Representatives, he would only observe that he had been a member of it, and never witnessed an attempt to encroach on the powers delegated to others; nor did he believe a case could be found which would establish the fact that the attempt had been made. The time of their service forbids it. The attempt will never be made by either House, unless there shall be much of what is called the spirit of the corps among the members, and two years is too short time for much to be acquired. Certainly a great deal more may be acquired in six; nor can it be supposed that the numbers of that House can so readily acquire it as the few of this. The time of service is as one to three, and the number of members somewhere about five to one. The time of service is two years shorter than that of the President, and that of the Senate two years longer; it would, therefore, seem that if any two of the legislative departments were to combine (he spoke only of the qualified legislative character of the President) to encroach on the powers delegated to the other, that the time of service would be a great consideration in forming the combination, and that would be sufficient to prevent the House of Representatives from being one.

If the treaty-making power be as great as has been contended for, it appeared to him that the House of Representatives had but two powers which might not be taken away by it, neither of which were of the most pleasant kind—one to impeach, the other to originate revenue bills. The last mentioned, the late treaty has slightly and indirectly touched. If the assent of the House be not necessary to repeal the law imposing higher duties on foreign ships, and goods imported in them, than on American ships, and goods imported in them, the treaty does not originate a revenue bill, but it lessens the tax on foreign ships, and goods imported in them, according to the opinion of those who oppose the bill, and that too pledged for the payment of the public debt. To lessen a tax, seems to be about the same thing as to repeal a higher and lay a lower tax on the same article. If the President and Senate can lessen one tax by treaty, they most assuredly can every one. Of what value, then, is the power to originate revenue bills, or legislative pledges for the payment of the debt, if the two departments of the Government which cannot originate a revenue bill, nor of themselves pledge the revenue, can, by treaty with a foreign Power, reduce the taxes, and, to the amount reduced, do away the pledge. To make such a power work well, it ought to have the authority to originate revenue bills, pass and pledge them, or to compel the House of Representatives to give their aid to carry their measures into execution. The House of Representatives, like every deliberative assembly, cannot act under compulsion, but must act, to act rightly, according to its own judgment and discretion. If a treaty can reduce a tax without the consent of the House of Representatives, why not raise one? Nothing seems more clear than that it ought to require the same power to do either of the acts. But to make this, if possible,

more plain, he would ask what would have been thought of the Constitution at the time it was considered and debated in the State conventions which adopted it, if, at the end of the article which delegates legislative power to Congress not to the President and Senate, a clause had been added to this effect, that the President and Senate might, by a treaty with a foreign Government, repeal whatever acts Congress might pass? If they can repeal one, they may every one; and if they can reduce the tax beforementioned, they can undoubtedly repeal it; and if the treaty making power can of itself rightfully act on one of the powers delegated to Congress, it can on all. If the construction which the friends of the bill oppose be the true one, then the Constitution would not have been changed by the supposed additional clause. The gentleman from Virginia will pardon me for saying, that no clause can be found in the Constitution which secures to the House of Representatives, or to Congress, the sword and the purse, if the power to lay and collect duties and imposts, and to regulate trade, is not. Every power delegated to Congress is in the same article. There is no exception in favor of the sword or purse; if the treaty-making power includes one, it must all, for all are granted alike. The late treaty touches the purse to the amount of the tax reduced.

If the assent of Congress be not necessary to equalize the duties on foreign and American ships and goods imported in them, why pass the act of the last session, which contains the principle of the bill, and ought to be considered as settling the question? The bill ought now to pass, or the act, to say the least of it, was useless; because the treaty-making power could do of itself that which the act proposed to foreign Governments. According to his construction, which gave to every part of the Constitution its full effect, and to every department of the Government the power granted to it, the reason was obvious; it was one of the subjects, the power over which had been granted to Congress; it was therefore necessary that Congress should act, as it ough always, in every such case; nor was there any just cause to apprehend a difficulty in making treaties under this construction; indeed, he thought the chairman of the committee (Mr Bibb) to whom the bill had been referred had satisfactorily shown, that, in practice, the construction he contended for had been adopted, and that no inconvenience had been discovered by experience. Suppose the Constitution to be of more doubtful construction than it really is, and the practice not settled, ought not that construction and that practice to be adopted which would best accord with its principles, and of course be best calculated to promote the general welfare; and would not such construction and such practice recommend the passing of the bill? The question is not however one of expediency, but whether the construction makes the bill necessary. It is my endeavor to show that it does. The construction contended for is warranted by that great principle which characterizes all the

American Governments—that the majority shall govern; the ratification of a treaty by two-thirds of the Senate under the present Constitution, and by nine States under the old Confederation, as well as the provision for the adoption of the Constitution by nine States, he believed, were all bottomed on that principle. This he thought would satisfactorily appear by attending to the number of Representatives apportioned to the States. By the Convention which framed the present Constitution, the whole number was sixty-five, of which Massachusetts had eight, New York six, Pennsylvania eight, and Virginia ten; this supports the opinion advanced, that any nine States under the Confederation were supposed to contain a majority of the people; hence, under that Government it required nine of the thirteen States to ratify a treaty; and this also accounts for the two-thirds in the Senate. The fixing on this number was doubtless to secure the same principle when the new States should be admitted into the Union, and the few cases in which the House of Representatives were not to act; but not to alter or change the power granted to any department of the Government; certainly not to give the treaty-making power an authority over the revenue, because, from the rule by which Representatives was apportioned, and the admission of new States into the Union, it would readily have occurred that this might give the whole power delegated to the Government to a minority. Such an oversight will not be imputed to the Convention. In fact, if a treaty can do away a law, which it required Congress to pass, it follows, that a minority of the nation, by their Senators and the President, can undo that which a majority by their Representatives in every department of the Government had done. To be convinced of this, it is only necessary to attend to the rule by which Electors to vote for the President are apportioned among the States; and to the fact, that two-thirds of the States, the smallest certainly, have not a majority of the people. Any construction which gives this power to a minority, is a departure from the great American principle before stated, that a majority shall govern. Is it possible, Mr. President, that the wise and good men who formed the Constitution intended that a minority should govern, and that, too, by the treaty-making power?

Every Government treating with another, is supposed to understand the treaty-making power of the Government with which it treats, no matter where lodged, whether in the Executive alone, or in the Executive and Legislature jointly. In England, when the King, by treaty, promises to pay money, every Government in Europe knows that he cannot pay it without the consent of Parliament, and that he must apply to that body for it, whether an article be in the treaty or not for such application. So well established is the rule, and so well do Governments understand the power of each other, that France never complained after she had made treaties with the old Congress, in the year 1778, that Congress had no Constitutional authority to make or execute

treaties. There was no doubt of the fact, because the articles of Confederation were not adopted by the States till the year 1781.

If in every case a treaty is law as soon as it is ratified by the President, the word law must have two different and distinct meanings in the Constitution, or money may be drawn from the Treasury by a treaty appropriation. The words are, no money shall be drawn from the Treasury but in consequence of appropriations made by law; not by acts of Congress or treaties, but law; and acts and treaties are both law. Then both may appropriate and both draw money from the Treasury; this construction gives the treaty-making power in the United States more authority than it has in England. The late treaty will prevent money from going into the Treasury; it might with as much propriety have drawn money out of it; if he was mistaken, the treaty-making power was only limited by the Constitution; it might treat on any and every power delegated to the General Government; it might make and execute a treaty of subsidy; in fact, it might put the nation in a state of war, which Congress alone have the power to declare; and according to treaty law, a part of the difficulty on this important and interesting question has no doubt been produced by an improper construction of that part of the Constitution which delegates power to Congress to declare war; under this power, Congress had passed a law to declare war, whereas, according to his understanding, it only required a statement made, after the manner of the civilised world, of the causes which produced the declaration; to a war thus declared, a Treaty of Peace properly put an end; there would be no law to prevent it.

Mr. Jefferson's letters, when Secretary of State, on the Treaty of Peace of 1783 with Great Britain, had been introduced to show that he understood that treaty to be the law of the land, and that it was so understood in the nation, and that under Mr. Jay's treaty the people at Detroit held land. With respect to the Treaty of 1783, it is only necessary to observe, that the old Congress had power to make treaties, but none to execute them; the execution depended entirely on the governments of the States, who did as they pleased. He thought no argument could be drawn from any fact connected with that treaty against the bill. The treaty of Mr. Jay, so far as it related to the people at Detroit, and everything which has since been done touching the boundary line; ought to be considered, as it certainly was, a continuation of the Treaty of Peace in the year 1783, with the intent to its full and fair execution. The people at Detroit were, at the time of that treaty, in the same situation that the people of the other parts of the nation were in the year 1783. The Whigs, with their property, remained in the United States, and the Tories, with theirs, left them. A foreigner holding land under Mr. Jay's treaty, held against State laws, and not against the laws of the United States. This is provided for in the Constitution; it has not, therefore, any bearing on the point in debate. The case of Louisiana has also been mentioned, with the intention to show the opinion of Mr. Jefferson and the then Congress; it was only necessary to add, to what had been said by the gentleman from Georgia, that whoever would be at the trouble to examine the Message of Mr. Jefferson, communicated to the House of Representatives with the treaty by which the country was acquired, will see the reason why both the acts noticed were not passed at the same time, and that he expressly calls for legislative aid to carry it into execution. A similar call was made in the case of the British Treaty finished under his Administration. It is confidently believed that neither of the cases show his or the opinion of Congress to be against the construction for which the friends of the bill contend; but, on the contrary, that both support it.

He agreed with the gentleman from South Carolina, (Mr. TAYLOR,) that ours is a Government of suspicion; every election proves it; the power to impeach proves it; the history of Cæsar, of Cromwell, and Bonaparte, proves that it ought to be so to remain free. He promised to be short, and would sit down.

Mr. CAMPBELL, of Tennessee, said, this subject had assumed a degree of importance, from the course the debate had taken, to which, at first, it did not appear entitled. As he differed in opinion from some of the gentlemen who spoke on each side of the question, he deemed it a duty, though it had not been in his power, from a cause known to gentlemen, to give the subject that consideration to which it was entitled, to lay before the Senate a brief view of the grounds on which he should act.

It may be proper, said Mr. C., to inquire, in the first place, what the subject is on which we are called to legislate. A treaty has been made by the proper authorities, containing provisions relating to commerce, which affect your fiscal regulations, and may diminish your revenue; the Chief Magistrate of the nation, under whose instructions it was negotiated, and to whom is intrusted, by the Constitution, the "faithful execution" of the laws, lays it before you, and "recommends such legislative provisions as it may call for on the part of the United States." On the one side it is contended, that no legislative enactment is necessary; that the treaty is complete, and may be executed by the proper officers and tribunals of Government; and some have gone so far as to assert, that not only this, but every other treaty, constitutionally made, is complete without the aid of a law; and repeals all laws opposed to its provisions. On the other it is insisted, that this treaty cannot be executed without a law to carry its provisions into effect; and on this side some have contended, that no treaty affecting existing laws is complete without the sanction of a legislative act, at least repealing those laws opposed to its provisions. He could not, Mr. C. said, agree to the doctrine advocated on either side of this question, carried to the extent contended for. A fair construction of the several clauses of the Constitution, relating to this subject, would not, in his opinion, support it.

It may be proper here, said Mr. C., in order to a more distinct understanding of the question under discussion, to inquire:

1. What a treaty is, independent of the character given it by the Constitution? and,

2. What it becomes in virtue of that character?

1. A treaty, independent of the character given it by the Constitution, may be stated to be, a compact between two or more independent States, mutually binding on, and pledging the faith of each, for the performance of the stipulations it contains. The manner in which these stipulations shall be carried into effect, must depend on the nature of the governments of the respective States. If the Executive and Legislative powers are vested in the same person, as in the case of a despotic Government, the promulgation alone of the treaty may be considered as at once giving it all the binding force requisite to the full execution of its provisions; the fiat of the despot carrying with it Legislative as well as Executive sanction. In such a case, the power that negotiates a treaty executes it; and the question now before you cannot arise. But it is otherwise with Governments differently organized. Where the Legislative power is vested in a branch of the Government distinct from that exercising the Executive power, a treaty made by the latter requiring legislative provisions for its fulfilment, can only pledge the faith of the nation that its Legislature will enact the laws requisite for that purpose; and in such case it must rest on the will of the Legislature, whether the treaty shall be carried into effect or not. Thus, in England, no treaty, containing stipulations, materially affecting the interests of the nation, is carried into effect, without being laid before Parliament for its sanction, and for such legislative enactments as its provisions may require.

This difference, in the manner of executing the provisions of a treaty by different Governments, according to the organization of each, is not necessarily productive of any injurious consequences. At the time a treaty is formed, the nature of the Governments, parties to it, is known; and the confidence reposed in the fulfilment of its stipulations, must depend on the reliance placed in the national faith which is pledged by it. Each party agrees to it, with a distinct understanding, that its full execution depends upon the concurrence of the proper departments in each Government, in adopting the requisite legal provisions for carrying its stipulations into effect; and knowing at the same time, that if one party fails to execute its provisions, the others are no longer bound thereby. From this view of a treaty, considered independent of the Constitutional provision, it does not seem to possess the power ascribed to it, of repealing existing laws opposed to its provisions, or of going into operation in all cases, without the aid of legislative enactment.

He would next, Mr. C. said, inquire,

2. What a treaty became in virtue of the character given to it by the Constitution?

That instrument declares, that "all treaties made, or which shall be made, under the author-

' ity of the United States, shall be the supreme
' law of the land; and the judges in every State
' shall be bound thereby; anything in the consti-
' tution or laws of any State to the contrary not-
' withstanding."

On the one hand it is contended, (said Mr. C.,)
that by this provision a treaty is made paramount
to all existing laws of the United States, as well
as to the laws and constitutions of the several
States, and at once repeals, or at least removes
out of its way, such as are opposed to its stipulations; on the other, that it is paramount only to
the constitutions and laws of the respective States,
and cannot, without the sanction of the National
Legislature, control a law of the General Government.

I cannot, said Mr. C., agree with the arguments
advanced on either side of this question, carried
to their full extent. It would seem sufficiently
clear that, by this provision, a treaty acquired the
character of a law of the United States, at least
for some purposes; and the only important inquiry appears to be, whether it does so for all purposes, and in regard to all subjects to which it
may relate; and if not, for what purposes, and in
regard to what subjects it requires that character?
The solution of this inquiry involves the giving
a correct construction to the Constitutional provision in question. To enable us to do this, it
will be necessary to refer to such other clauses of
that instrument as relate to the same subject;
and, by comparing them together, see how far
they control or explain each other. For the same
rules of construction that are adopted in regard
to other instruments of the like kind, as statute
laws, will equally apply to this; and it is believed that, by a due observance of these rules,
most of the difficulties which have arisen in this
discussion may be remedied. It is laid down as
a rule that, in the construction of one part of a
statute, every other part ought to be taken into
consideration, and one part construed by another;
also, that a statute should be so construed, that no
clause, sentence, or word, should be superfluous
or void; and further, the general words in one
clause of a statute may be restrained by the particular words in a subsequent clause in the same
statute. Apply those rules to the case before us.
The first clause in the Constitution declares,
"that all legislative powers therein granted shall
be vested in a Congress of the United States,
which shall consist of a Senate and House of
Representatives." If this clause be considered
alone, and unconnected with the subsequent provisions of that instrument, relating to the same
subject, it would go a great way to support the
doctrine contended for, that a law being considered the offspring of legislative power, can only
emanate from the National Legislature, thus constituted the sole depository of all such powers.
And an honorable gentleman from Massachusetts
(Mr. VARNUM) has, with considerable force, stated
that, as by this provision of the Constitution, all
legislative powers were vested in Congress, he
could not perceive how any such power could be
considered as vested in any other department of

the Government, or how a treaty, made by the
President and Senate alone, could be viewed as a
law. But when we consider this clause in connexion with the subsequent provisions of that instrument, relating to the same subject, the force
of this argument will be found to be greatly diminished, if not entirely done away. By one of
those provisions it is declared, that "he (the Pres-
' ident) shall have power, by and with the advice
' and consent of the Senate, to make treaties;
' provided two-thirds of the Senators present con-
' cur;" and by another, being that first referred to,
such treaty, when so made, is declared to "be the
supreme law of the land." Thus the President
and Senate are, in express terms, authorized to
make a treaty, which is pronounced, in terms
equally clear, a law of the United States, on the
same footing with the other laws, made pursuant
to the Constitution. They must, therefore, be
considered as vested with some portion of legislative power; and if so, the general expression,
"all legislative powers," used in the first clause
of the Constitution, cannot be construed according to the literal meaning of the words, but must
be considered as restrained by the express terms
of the subsequent provisions already referred to,
and as only vesting those general powers, subject
to the modifications thus imposed. This construction is supported by the rules already noticed, and
will be further strengthened by another view
which may be taken of the subject. If those several provisions were construed according to the
literal import of the words used in each, they
would be inconsistent with each other, and some
of the expressions or words would become superfluous or void; but this is contrary to one of the
clearest rules of construction, by which every
clause, expression, and word, is, if possible, to
have some meaning—some operative effect—and
all to be reconciled and rendered consistent with
each other. In the construction of instruments
of this kind, we should likewise keep in view the
particular subject to which each provision immediately relates; construe the words used with a
particular reference to that subject, and endeavor
to ascertain the intention of the makers, rather
than be guided solely by the literal import of
the words; and here the maxim, "*qui hæret in
litera, hæret in cortice,*" might well apply. The
framers of the Constitution, when adopting the
first clause, must have had in view the distribution of the general powers of the Government among the several departments thereof.
That clause relates exclusively to Congress as
the great depository of general legislative powers, and should be construed with a particular
reference to the functions they are to perform.
For the purposes of internal legislation, no doubt,
all legislative powers are vested in them, in exclusion to the other departments of the Government. But it does not follow, as a necessary
consequence, that those powers carried with them
the authority to direct and control the management of our foreign relations. That subject was
not then taken into view; it was considered in a
subsequent part of the Constitution; and as it

the intention to show the opinion of Mr. Jefferson and the then Congress; it was only necessary to add, to what had been said by the gentleman from Georgia, that whoever would be at the trouble to examine the Message of Mr. Jefferson, communicated to the House of Representatives with the treaty by which the country was acquired, will see the reason why both the acts noticed were not passed at the same time, and that he expressly calls for legislative aid to carry it into execution. A similar call was made in the case of the British Treaty finished under his Administration. It is confidently believed that neither of the cases show his or the opinion of Congress to be against the construction for which the friends of the bill contend; but, on the contrary, that both support it.

He agreed with the gentleman from South Carolina, (Mr. TAYLOR,) that ours is a Government of suspicion; every election proves it; the power to impeach proves it; the history of Cæsar, of Cromwell, and Bonaparte, proves that it ought to be so to remain free. He promised to be short, and would sit down.

Mr. CAMPBELL, of Tennessee, said, this subject had assumed a degree of importance, from the course the debate had taken, to which, at first, it did not appear entitled. As he differed in opinion from some of the gentlemen who spoke on each side of the question, he deemed it a duty, though it had not been in his power, from a cause known to gentlemen, to give the subject that consideration to which it was entitled, to lay before the Senate a brief view of the grounds on which he should act.

It may be proper, said Mr. C., to inquire, in the first place, what the subject is on which we are called to legislate. A treaty has been made by the proper authorities, containing provisions relating to commerce, which affect your fiscal regulations, and may diminish your revenue; the Chief Magistrate of the nation, under whose instructions it was negotiated, and to whom is intrusted, by the Constitution, the " faithful execution" of the laws, lays it before you, and " recommends such legislative provisions as it may call for on the part of the United States." On the one side it is contended, that no legislative enactment is necessary; that the treaty is complete, and may be executed by the proper officers and tribunals of Government; and some have gone so far as to assert, that not only this, but every other treaty, constitutionally made, is complete without the aid of a law; and repeals all laws opposed to its provisions. On the other it is insisted, that this treaty cannot be executed without a law to carry its provisions into effect; and on this side some have contended, that no treaty affecting existing laws is complete without the sanction of a legislative act, at least repealing those laws opposed to its provisions. He could not, Mr. C. said, agree to the doctrine advocated on either side of this question, carried to the extent contended for. A fair construction of the several clauses of the Constitution, relating to this subject, would not, in his opinion, support it.

It may be proper here, said Mr. C., in order a more distinct understanding of the question under discussion, to inquire:

1. What a treaty is, independent of the character given it by the Constitution ? and,

2. What it becomes in virtue of that character

1. A treaty, independent of the character given it by the Constitution, may be stated to be, a compact between two or more independent State mutually binding on, and pledging the faith each, for the performance of the stipulations contains. The manner in which these stipulations shall be carried into effect, must depend the nature of the governments of the respectiv States. If the Executive and Legislative power are vested in the same person, as in the case of despotic Government, the promulgation alone the treaty may be considered as at once giving all the binding force requisite to the full exec tion of its provisions; the fiat of the despot carrying with it Legislative as well as Executiv sanction. In such a case, the power that negot ates a treaty executes it; and the question no before you cannot arise. But it is otherwise wit Governments differently organized. Where th Legislative power is vested in a branch of th Government distinct from that exercising th Executive power, a treaty made by the latter r quiring legislative provisions for its fulfilmen can only pledge the faith of the nation that i Legislature will enact the laws requisite for th purpose; and in such case it must rest on the wi of the Legislature, whether the treaty shall b carried into effect or not. Thus, in England, treaty, containing stipulations, materially affectin the interests of the nation, is carried into effec without being laid before Parliament for its sanc tion, and for such legislative enactments as i provisions may require.

This difference, in the manner of executing th provisions of a treaty by different Government according to the organization of each, is not ne cessarily productive of any injurious consequen ces. At the time a treaty is formed, the natur of the Governments, parties to it, is known; an the confidence reposed in the fulfilment of i stipulations, must depend on the reliance place in the national faith which is pledged by i Each party agrees to it, with a distinct unde standing, that its full execution depends upon th concurrence of the proper departments in eac Government, in adopting the requisite legal pr visions for carrying its stipulations into effec and knowing at the same time, that if one part fails to execute its provisions, the others are n longer bound thereby. From this view of a treat considered independent of the Constitutional pr vision, it does not seem to possess the power a cribed to it, of repealing existing laws opposed t its provisions, or of going into operation in a cases, without the aid of legislative enactment.

He would next, Mr. C. said, inquire,

2. What a treaty became in virtue of the cha acter given to it by the Constitution ?

That instrument declares, that " all treatie 'made, or which shall be made, under the autho

' ity of the United States, shall be the supreme
' law of the land; and the judges in every State
' shall be bound thereby; anything in the consti-
' tution or laws of any State to the contrary not-
' withstanding."

On the one hand it is contended, (said Mr. C.,) that by this provision a treaty is made paramount to all existing laws of the United States, as well as to the laws and constitutions of the several States, and at once repeals, or at least removes out of its way, such as are opposed to its stipulations; on the other, that it is paramount only to the constitutions and laws of the respective States, and cannot, without the sanction of the National Legislature, control a law of the General Government.

I cannot, said Mr. C., agree with the arguments advanced on either side of this question, carried to their full extent. It would seem sufficiently clear that, by this provision, a treaty acquired the character of a law of the United States, at least for some purposes; and the only important inquiry appears to be, whether it does so for all purposes, and in regard to all subjects to which it may relate; and if not, for what purposes, and in regard to what subjects it acquires that character? The solution of this inquiry involves the giving a correct construction to the Constitutional provision in question. To enable us to do this, it will be necessary to refer to such other clauses of that instrument as relate to the same subject; and, by comparing them together, see how far they control or explain each other. For the same rules of construction that are adopted in regard to other instruments of the like kind, as statute laws, will equally apply to this; and it is believed that, by a due observance of these rules, most of the difficulties which have arisen in this discussion may be remedied. It is laid down as a rule that, in the construction of one part of a statute, every other part ought to be taken into consideration, and one part construed by another; also, that a statute should be so construed, that no clause, sentence, or word, should be superfluous or void; and further, the general words in one clause of a statute may be restrained by the particular words in a subsequent clause in the same statute. Apply those rules to the case before us. The first clause in the Constitution declares, "that all legislative powers therein granted shall be vested in a Congress of the United States, which shall consist of a Senate and House of Representatives." If this clause be considered alone, and unconnected with the subsequent provisions of that instrument, relating to the same subject, it would go a great way to support the doctrine contended for, that a law being considered the offspring of legislative power, can only emanate from the National Legislature, thus constituted the sole depository of all such powers. And an honorable gentleman from Massachusetts (Mr. VARNUM) has, with considerable force, stated that, as by this provision of the Constitution, all legislative powers were vested in Congress, he could not perceive how any such power could be considered as vested in any other department of the Government, or how a treaty, made by the President and Senate alone, could be viewed as a law. But when we consider this clause in connexion with the subsequent provisions of that instrument, relating to the same subject, the force of this argument will be found to be greatly diminished, if not entirely done away. By one of those provisions it is declared, that " he (the Pres-
' ident) shall have power, by and with the advice
' and consent of the Senate, to make treaties;
' provided two-thirds of the Senators present con-
' cur;" and by another, being that first referred to, such treaty, when so made, is declared to " be the supreme law of the land." Thus the President and Senate are, in express terms, authorized to make a treaty, which is pronounced, in terms equally clear, a law of the United States, on the same footing with the other laws, made pursuant to the Constitution. They must, therefore, be considered as vested with some portion of legislative power; and if so, the general expression, "all legislative powers," used in the first clause of the Constitution, cannot be construed according to the literal meaning of the words, but must be considered as restrained by the express terms of the subsequent provisions already referred to, and as only vesting those general powers, subject to the modifications thus imposed. This construction is supported by the rules already noticed, and will be further strengthened by another view which may be taken of the subject. If those several provisions were construed according to the literal import of the words used in each, they would be inconsistent with each other, and some of the expressions or words would become superfluous or void; but this is contrary to one of the clearest rules of construction, by which every clause, expression, and word, is, if possible, to have some meaning—some operative effect—and all to be reconciled and rendered consistent with each other. In the construction of instruments of this kind, we should likewise keep in view the particular subject to which each provision immediately relates; construe the words used with a particular reference to that subject, and endeavor to ascertain the intention of the makers, rather than be guided solely by the literal import of the words; and here the maxim, "qui hæret in litera, hæret in cortice," might well apply. The framers of the Constitution, when adopting the first clause, must have had in view the distribution of the general powers of the Government among the several departments thereof. That clause relates exclusively to Congress as the great depository of general legislative powers, and should be construed with a particular reference to the functions they are to perform. For the purposes of internal legislation, no doubt, all legislative powers are vested in them, in exclusion to the other departments of the Government. But it does not follow, as a necessary consequence, that those powers carried with them the authority to direct and control the management of our foreign relations. That subject was not then taken into view; it was considered in a subsequent part of the Constitution; and as it

divided? And is not this circumstance itself sufficient ground to legislate on the subject, that your public functionaries may have some unerring guide to direct their conduct? But it has been alleged this would be sanctioning an encroachment on the powers of the Senate, a violation of the Constitution, which we are bound to support. If the measure appeared to him in this light, he would, Mr. C. said, unite with gentlemen in opposing it. He admitted each department should move within the sphere assigned it. He had, however, heard no argument that convinced him this would be a violation of the Constitution; and he was unable to perceive how it could be so considered.

He did not consider the power of the Senate in making treaties so important—so transcendent, as they had been represented. How is a treaty negotiated? (said Mr. C.) The instructions for the purpose are given by the President, without consulting this body, (not being required to do so by the Constitution;) the treaty is formed without your knowledge; and the only agency you have in the business, is, when laid before you for ratification, to disapprove or approve its provisions, with or without amendment, and advise accordingly, amounting to little more than a mere negative. Is there anything in this to justify the Senate in considering a treaty so peculiarly its own offspring, as in no case to allow the other House any agency in having its provisions carried into effect?

It may here be asked whether it be competent to the House of Representatives, in cases requiring legislative aid for executing the provisions of a treaty, to decide on the policy of such treaty; and in case of disapproving it, prevent its going into effect by refusing the aid required? This is a question which once agitated the great political parties in this country, but which it may not be necessary to discuss on the present occasion, as no difference of opinion appears to exist respecting the policy of carrying this treaty into effect. As the subject, however, had been referred to, he would (Mr. C. said) very briefly state the view in which it appeared to him. When a treaty is concluded requiring legislative aid to execute its provisions, the House of Representatives is undoubtedly bound to afford that aid by all the obligations which the pledged faith of the nation can impose, as well as by the considerations arising from the importance to the national character of having the public faith, so pledged, preserved inviolate; but, on the other hand, the members of that body must take into consideration the Constitution under which they act, and which they are bound to support; the great interests of the nation, and how far they may be affected by the treaty in question; and weighing all these considerations, must have the right, subject only to the responsibility they impose, to act as free agents, to exercise their free will, and grant or refuse the aid required according to the best judgment, guided by a single view to the public good, they are able to form on the subject. If their assent be necessary to give effect to, and ex-

ecute a treaty, they must have the power, the right to grant or refuse that assent. If they have no right in any case to deliberate on the laws requisite to execute a treaty, they can no longer be viewed as the representatives of a free people delegated to express their will, or as the guardians of their rights, but only as the instruments of the treaty-making power, the mere registers of its edicts. But is there any danger to be apprehended to the Government, to the public interest, from the view which has been taken of this subject? Is it not consistent with the plan, the spirit of the Constitution, which makes the different departments of Government operate as checks on the conduct of each other, and thus guard against a dangerous preponderance being acquired by either?

Some gentlemen seem to consider the Senate as the peculiar guardian of the Constitution, the shield of the Government against the innovating spirit of the popular branch. On what ground is this claim set up? On that of its superior stability arising from its permanent character, the longer term of service of its members, and deriving their authority from the State Legislatures instead of immediately from the people. He conceived (Mr. C. said) more importance was attached to these circumstances, than they would, on examination, be found to possess. From the nature of its organization, and the limited number of which it consisted, the changes it underwent would be found nearly, if not quite equal to those that occurred in the other House; and as to the mode in which its members were chosen, there was but one step between them and the people and that did not, in his opinion, much diminish their dependence on them. The members of the Legislature being elected by the people, and immediately responsible to them, would generally in choosing a Senator, consult their will, and be governed as much thereby in this, as in other acts of their political conduct. Though, therefore this body, in its organization, partook of the federative character, and thereby tended to equalize the relative weight of the States in the National Legislature, yet, deriving its origin in part, in the manner just stated, from the will of the people, it was substantially dependent on them as well as the other House. And why should it not? This is a Government formed by the people, (not by the States, as such,) deriving all its authority from them, and having no existence separate from their will; consisting only of a few of themselves selected for a time to guide the vessel of State, in which all are equally embarked; and having performed the duties assigned them, retiring again into the walks of private life, to mingle with their fellow citizens, from whom they had emerged by the mere force of public opinion. While, therefore, on the one hand, there appeared no sufficient reason for the apprehended encroachments on the privileges of the other House, and the rights of the people, by the treaty-making power, on the other, he could not perceive any ground to justify the dangers apprehended for the stability of the Government from encroachments by the other House on the Constitutional powers of this.

HISTORY OF CONGRESS.

The safety, however, of the Constitution, and of public liberty, (said Mr. C.) rests on foundations more solid than the permanent character and stability of this, or the political honesty of the other House ; it rests on the sound sense, intelligence, and public virtue of the people. So long as these remain in their full vigor, so long will liberty triumph over all attempts to subvert it ; but should the people become enervated, ignorant, and corrupt, from the very organization of your Government not only the members of the Legislature, but your Executive and other officers, and all engaged in the management of public affairs, if they do not lead the way in, must partake of the same degeneracy, and the subversion of liberty, the decline and final ruin of the Republic, inevitably follow.

When Mr. CAMPBELL had concluded—

On motion, by Mr. ROBERTS, it was agreed to take the question by yeas and nays. And then the Senate adjourned.

FRIDAY, January 19.

Mr. WILLIAMS presented the petition of William Garrett, of the State of Tennessee, praying payment for a quantity of beef and pork lost on its passage, in the Mississippi, to New Orleans, for the use of the Navy of the United States, as stated in the petition; which was read, and referred to the Secretary for the Department of Navy.

A message from the House of Representatives informed the Senate that they have passed a bill, entitled "An act for the relief of John Redman Coxe ;" a bill, entitled "An act for the relief of the heirs of George Nebinger ;" a bill, entitled "An act for the relief of Jonathan White ;" a bill, entitled "An act for the relief of John G. Camp ;" also, a bill, entitled "An act for the relief of Jonathan Rogers, junior, of Waterford, in the State of Connecticut ;" in which bills they request the concurrence of the Senate.

The five bills last mentioned were read, and passed to the second reading.

The Senate resumed the bill, entitled "An act to regulate the commerce between the United States and the territories of His Britannic Majesty, according to the convention concluded the third day of July, 1815; and the ratifications of which were exchanged on the 22d day of December, 1815."

And the question recurring, "Shall this bill be read a third time ?" it was determined in the negative—yeas 10, nays 21. as follows:

YEAS—Messrs. Bibb, Condit, Lacock, Macon, Morrow, Roberts, Ruggles, Taylor, Varnum, and Wilson.

NAYS—Messrs. Barbour, Barry, Brown, Chace, Daggett, Dana, Fromentin, Gaillard, Goldsborough, Hersey, Howell, Hunter, King, Mason of New Hampshire, Talbot, Tait, Thompson, Tichenor, Turner, Wells, and Williams.

Mr. WILLIAMS, from the committee to whom was recommitted the bill authorizing the sale of public lands, reported it with an amendment.

The PRESIDENT communicated a letter from the Commissioner of the General Land Office,

transmitting a report of the commissioners appointed for the purpose of ascertaining and adjusting claims to land in the western district of the late Territory of Orleans, now State of Louisiana; and the letter and report were read, and referred to the committee last mentioned.

The following Message was received from the PRESIDENT OF THE UNITED STATES:

To the Senate and House of
Representatives of the United States :

The accompanying extract from the occurrences at Fort Jackson, in August, 1814, during the negotiation of a treaty with the Indians, shows that the friendly Creeks, wishing to give to General Jackson, Benjamin Hawkins, and others, a national mark of their gratitude and regard, conveyed to them, respectively, a donation of land, with a request that the grant might be duly confirmed by the Government of the United States.

Taking into consideration the peculiar circumstances of the case—the expediency of indulging the Indians in wishes which they associated with the treaty signed by them, and that the case involves an inviting opportunity for bestowing on an officer, who has rendered such illustrious services to his country, a token of its sensibility to them—the inducement to which cannot be diminished by the delicacy and disinterestedness of his proposal to transfer the benefit from himself: I recommend to Congress that provision be made for carrying into effect the wishes and request of the Indians, as expressed by them.   J. MADISON.

JANUARY 18, 1816.

The Message, and accompanying extract, were read, and referred to the committee appointed, the 7th of December, on the memorial of the Legislative Council and House of Representatives of the Mississippi Territory.

The Senate resumed, as in Committee of the Whole, the consideration of the bill to reward the officers and crew of the late United States' brig Argus; and on motion, by Mr. TAIT, the further consideration thereof was postponed until the first Monday in February next.

The Senate resumed, as in Committee of the Whole, the consideration of a bill to authorize a lottery in Georgetown, District of Columbia ; and on the question, "Shall this bill be engrossed and read a third time ?" it was determined in the negative.

The Senate resumed, as in Committee of the Whole, the consideration of the bill, entitled "An act for the relief of George S. Wise," and the further consideration thereof was postponed until Monday next.

The Senate resumed, as in Committee of the Whole, the consideration of the bill to fix the compensations of the officers of the Senate therein mentioned; together with the amendment reported thereto by the select committee; and on motion, by Mr. LACOCK, the further consideration thereof was postponed until Monday next.

The Senate adjourned to Monday.

MONDAY, January 22.

ARMISTEAD T. MASON, appointed a Senator by the Legislature of the Commonwealth of Virginia, in place of William B. Giles, resigned, arrived on the 20th instant, and this day produced his credentials; which were read, and the oath prescribed by law was administered to him, and he took his seat in the Senate.

Mr. TALBOT called up the petition of Nicholas Boilevin, presented on the 7th of February, 1815, praying reimbursement for certain property destroyed by the Indians, as stated in the petition; which was referred to the Committee on Military Affairs.

The bill entitled "An act for the relief of John Redman Coxe," was read the second time, and referred to the Committee on so much of the Message of the President of the United States as relates to Finance and an Uniform National Currency.

The bill entitled "An act for the relief of the heirs of George Nebinger," was read the second time.

The bill entitled "An act for the relief of Jonathan White," was read the second time, and referred to the committee appointed, the 7th of December, on the memorial of the Legislature of the Mississippi Territory.

The bill entitled "An act for the relief of John G. Camp," was read the second time, and referred to a select committee; and Messrs. BARBOUR, WILSON, and ROBERTS, were appointed the committee.

The bill entitled "An act for the relief of Jonathan Rogers, junior, of Waterford in the State of Connecticut," was read the second time, and referred to a select committee; and Messrs. DAGGETT, VARNUM, and ROBERTS, were appointed the committee.

The Senate resumed, as in Committee of the Whole, the consideration of the bill entitled "An act to authorize the discharge of James Jewett from his imprisonment," together with the amendment reported thereto, by the select committee; and on motion, by Mr. VARNUM, the further consideration thereof was postponed until Wednesday next.

The Senate resumed, as in Committee of the Whole, the consideration of the bill, authorizing the sale of public lands, together with the amendment reported thereto by the select committee; and the amendment having been agreed to with an amendment, the President reported the bill to the House accordingly.

On the question, "Shall this bill be engrossed, and read a third time?" it was determined in the affirmative.

The Senate resumed, as in Committee of the Whole, the consideration of the bill to fix the compensations of the officers of the Senate therein mentioned, together with the amendment reported thereto by the select committee; and on motion by Mr. LACOCK, the further consideration thereof was postponed until to-morrow.

TUESDAY, January 23.

The PRESIDENT communicated a letter from Gabriel Moore, Speaker of the House of Representatives of the Mississippi Territory, enclosing the proceedings in relation to the nomination of two persons, one of whom to be commissioned to fill the vacancy in the Legislative Council, occasioned by the resignation of Thomas Barnes which was read.

The PRESIDENT also communicated the memorial of Daniel C. Lane, and Patrick Shields, associate judges of the court of Harrison county in the Indiana Territory, in behalf of themselves and the said county, praying an additional member may be given to the said county, should the Territory be authorized to elect delegates to meet in convention, for reasons stated in the memorial; which was read, and referred to the committee appointed the 2d instant, on the memorial of the Legislative Council and House of Representatives of the Indiana Territory.

The Senate resumed, as in Committee of the Whole, the consideration of the bill to fix the compensations of the officers of the Senate therein mentioned, together with the amendment reported thereto by the select committee; and on motion, by Mr. FROMENTIN, the bill was recommitted to a select committee, to consist of five members, with instructions to inquire into the expediency of increasing the salaries of all the officers of Government, and report thereon; and Messrs. FROMENTIN, LACOCK, MACON, DAGGETT and VARNUM, were appointed the committee.

The Senate resumed the consideration of the motion made the 15th instant, for the appointment of a committee to inquire whether any provision is necessary for authorizing the payment of the sums which the Senators and Representatives are entitled to receive, in compensation of their services; and, on motion, by Mr. DANA, the further consideration thereof was postponed to the first Monday in December next.

The bill authorizing the sale of public lands was read a third time.

Resolved, That this bill pass, and that the title thereof be, "An act authorizing the sale of a lot of ground belonging to the United States, situated in the town of Knoxville, and State of Tennessee."

The Senate resumed, as in Committee of the Whole, the bill entitled "An act for the relief of the heirs of George Nebinger."

On motion, by Mr. WILSON, it was referred to a select committee; and Messrs. ROBERTS, WILSON, and MACON, were appointed the committee.

The Senate resumed, as in Committee of the Whole, the consideration of the bill entitled "An act for the relief of George S. Wise;" and on motion by Mr. MASON, of New Hampshire, it was recommitted to the Committee on Naval Affairs, with instructions to inquire into the expediency of making some general provisions by law for similar cases, and report thereon.

Mr. CHACE, from the committee appointed on the subject, reported a bill to increase the pensions of Robert White, and Jacob Wrighter; and the bill was read, and passed to a second reading.

And on motion, the Senate adjourned until to-morrow.

WEDNESDAY, January 24.

The PRESIDENT communicated a report of the Secretary of the Treasury, on the petition of James Jewett, referred to him the 17th instant; and the report was read; and on motion of Mr. ROBERTS, that it be printed for the use of the Senate, it was determined in the negative.

Mr. WILLIAMS presented the petition of Matthew W. McClellan, late second lieutenant in the 39th regiment, praying to be released from accounting for four hundred and forty-eight dollars, alleged to have been stolen from him, as stated in the petition; which was read, and referred to the Committee on Military Affairs.

Mr. ROBERTS, from the committee to whom was referred the petition of Joseph C. Morgan, attorney in fact of Xaverio Nandi, late Consular agent of the United States at Tripoli, made a report, which was read.

Mr. ROBERTS also reported a bill for the relief of Xaverio Nandi; and the bill was read, and passed to the second reading.

Mr. ROBERTS, from the committee to whom the subject was referred, reported a bill for the relief of Edward Barry and George Hodge; and the bill was read, and passed to a second reading.

The bill to increase the pensions of Robert White and Jacob Wrighter, was read the second time, and considered as in Committee of the Whole; and on the question, "Shall this bill be engrossed, and read a third time?" it was determined in the affirmative.

The Senate resumed, as in Committee of the Whole, the consideration of the bill entitled "An act to authorize the discharge of James Jewett from his imprisonment," together with the amendment reported thereto by the select committee; and the amendment having been rejected, the President reported the bill to the House: and on the question, "Shall this bill be read a third time?" it was determined in the negative.

Mr. BIBB presented the petition of Thomas Law and others, inhabitants of the City of Washington, praying the division and sale of certain open squares in said city, as stated in the petition; which was read, and referred to a select committee; and Messrs. BIBB, MASON of Virginia, and GOLDSBOROUGH, were appointed the committee.

THURSDAY, January 25.

Mr. VARNUM presented the memorial of Thos. B. Wait, William S. Wait, and Silas L. Wait, of Boston, proposing to publish an improved edition of the State Papers of the United States, and praying the patronage of Congress, as stated in the memorial; which was read, and referred to a select committee, with instructions to inquire into the expediency of publishing documents, which have heretofore been deemed confidential; and to report thereon, by bill or otherwise.

Ordered, That Messrs. KING, VARNUM, and FROMENTIN, be the committee.

The PRESIDENT communicated a report of the Secretary for the Department of War, comprehending contracts made by him in the year 1815, and those made by the purchasing and ordnance departments, for the same period, in compliance with "An act, concerning public contracts," passed the 21st of April, 1808; and the report was read.

The PRESIDENT also communicated a report of the Secretary of the Navy Department, in relation to the most convenient harbors in the waters of the Chesapeake bay for the reception of ships of war, made in obedience to a resolution of the Senate of the 21st of December, 1815; and the report was read.

Mr. BIBB submitted the following motion for consideration:

Resolved, by the Senate and House of Representatives of the United States of America in Congress assembled, That the following amendment to the Constitution of the United States be proposed to the Legislatures of the several States, which, when ratified by the Legislatures of three-fourths of the States, shall be valid, to all intents and purposes, as part of the said Constitution:

The Senators of the United States shall be chosen for three years.

Mr. TAIT presented the petition of David Geissinger, late of the United State's sloop of war the Wasp, now a lieutenant in the Navy, praying that compensation may be granted to the officers and crew, and their legal representatives, of the late United States' sloop of war Wasp, in consideration of the distinguished and eminent services rendered to the country, by the late Captain Blakely, his officers, and crew, as stated in the petition; which was read, and referred to the Committee on Naval Affairs.

A message from the House of Representatives informed the Senate that the House have passed a bill, entitled "An act to continue in force the act, entitled 'An act for imposing additional duties upon all goods, wares, and merchandise, imported from any foreign port or place, and for other purposes;" a bill, entitled "An act to continue in force an act, entitled 'An act laying a duty on imported salt, granting a bounty on pickled fish exported, and allowances to certain vessels employed in the fisheries;" a bill, entitled "An act to repeal so much of an act, passed on the 23d of December, 1814, as imposes additional duties on postage;" also a bill, entitled "An act continuing in force certain acts laying duties on bank notes, refined sugars, and for other purposes;" in which bills they request the concurrence of the Senate.

The four bills last mentioned were read, and passed to the second reading.

Mr. FROMENTIN, from the committee, reported the bill to increase the pensions of Robert White and Jacob Wrighter, correctly engrossed; and, on motion by Mr. TICHENOR, it was recommitted to a select committee, further to consider and report thereon; and Messrs. CHACE, BARBOUR, and MACON, were appointed the committee.

Mr. VARNUM presented the memorial of Francis Le Barron, praying a grant of the privilege of opening and working any copper mine which he may discover, or cause to be discovered, on or near the southern shores of Lake Superior, and on the islands thereof, within the limits of the United States, for a certain number of years, for reasons stated in in the memorial; which was read, and referred to a select committee; and Messrs. Varnum, Mason of Virginia, and Daggett, were appointed the committee.

Mr. Roberts presented the memorial of George Mony and others, stockholders in the manufacturing company of Lancaster, in the State of Pennsylvania, praying the protection of Congress, as stated in the petition; which was read, and referred to the Committee on so much of the Message of the President of the United States as relates to Manufactures.

Mr. Lacock presented the memorial of Charles Stewart, on behalf of himself, the officers, and crew, of the United States' ship Constitution, praying compensation for the prize-ship Levant, which was forcibly taken possession of by the enemy, and carried from out the harbor of Port Praya, within the neutral waters of the Prince Regent of Portugal, as stated in the memorial; which was read, and referred to the Committee on Naval Affairs.

Mr. Morrow presented the memorial of the Illinois and Wabash Land Companies, by Solomon Eitting, their agent, praying relief from Congress, as stated in the memorial; which was read, and referred to the committee appointed the 7th of December, on the memorial of the Legislative Council and House of Representatives of the Mississippi Territory.

Mr. Barbour, from the Committee on Military Affairs, to whom was referred the petition of John A. Thomas, made a report thereon.

Mr. B., from the same committee, to whom was referred the bill, entitled "An act to authorize the payment for property lost, captured, or destroyed, by the enemy, while in the military service of the United States," reported it with amendments.

Mr. Roberts presented the memorial of Catharine Robertson, praying compensation for services rendered by her former husband, Jacob Ritter, during the Revolutionary war, as stated in the memorial; which was read, and referred to the Committee on Military Affairs.

Mr. R. also presented the petition of Daniel Renner and Nathaniel H. Heath, praying remuneration for their ropewalk and materials, burnt by the enemy, during their invasion of the City of Washington, as stated in the petition; which was read, and referred to the Committee on Military Affairs.

The bill for the relief of Xaverio Nandi was read the second time; and the further consideration thereof was postponed until Monday next.

The bill for the relief of Edward Barry and George Hodge was read the second time, and the further consideration thereof was postponed.

Friday, January 26.

Mr. Daggett, from the committee to whom was referred the bill, entitled "An act for the

relief of Jonathan Rogers, jr., of Waterford, i the State of Connecticut," reported it without amendment.

Mr. D. also presented the memorial of Rober Sewall, praying compensation for the loss an destruction of his property in the City of Wash ington, by the enemy, which was occasioned b having his house converted into a military fo tress, as is stated in the memorial; which wa read, and referred to the Committee on Militar Affairs.

On motion, by Mr. Macon,

Resolved, That the Secretary of the Treasur be directed to lay before the Senate, a statemer exhibiting the amount of duty paid on salt, fro the establishment of the present Government distinguishing, as far as may be practicable, th amount paid in each State, and the amount bounty and allowance also paid in lieu of draw back in each State.

On motion of Mr. Morrow,

Resolved, That a committee be appointed inquire whether any and what provision is n cessary to to be made for the payment of per sions in the States wherein the office of Con missioner of Loans is not established, and also the several Territories, and that they have lea to report by by bill or otherwise.

Ordered, That Messrs. Morrow, Talbot, an Barry, be the committee.

Mr. Chace, from the committee, to whom wa recommitted the bill to increase the pensions Robert White and Jacob Wrighter, reported with amendments.

The bill, entitled "An act to continue in forc the act, entitled 'An act for imposing addition duties upon all goods, wares, and merchandis imported from any foreign port or place, and f other purposes;" was read the second time, an referred to the committee appointed on so muc of the Message of the President of the Unite States as relates to Finance and a Uniform N tional Currency.

The bill entitled "An act to continue in forc 'An act laying a duty on imported salt, grantin a bounty on pickled fish exported, and allowanc to certain vessels employed in the fisheries," w read the second time, and referred to the com mittee last mentioned.

The bill entitled "An act to repeal so much an act, passed on the 23d day of December, 181 as imposes additional duties on postage," w read a second time, and referred to the same com mittee.

The bill entitled "An act continuing in forc certain acts, laying duties on bank notes, refine sugars, and for other purposes," was read the se ond time, and referred to the same committee.

Mr. Barbour, from the committee to who was referred the bill, entitled "An act for the r lief of John G. Camp," reported it without amen ment; and the bill was considered as in Commi tee of the Whole, and passed to the third readin;

Mr. Fromentin, from the Joint Library Con mittee, made a report; which was read.

Mr. Fromentin, from the same committee, r

ported a bill, further providing for the Library of Congress; and the bill was read, and passed to the second reading.

The Senate resumed the consideration of the report of the select committee, to whom was referred the petition of John A. Thomas; whereupon,

Resolved, That the petition of John A. Thomas be rejected.

The resolution submitted the 25th instant, for a proposed amendment to the Constitution of the United States, was read the second time; and, on motion by Mr. BIBB, the further consideration thereof was postponed to, and made the order of the day for, the first Monday in February next.

The Senate resumed, as in Committee of the Whole, the consideration of the bill, entitled "An act to authorize the payment for property lost, captured, or destroyed by the enemy, while in the military service of the United States," together with the amendments reported thereto by the select committee; and, on motion by Mr. TALBOT, the further consideration thereof was postponed until Monday next.

The Senate adjourned to Monday.

MONDAY, January 29.

Mr. TAIT, from the Committee on Naval Affairs, communicated a letter from the Secretary of the Navy Department, with several statements, containing the estimates of expenses necessary to keep in service, for one year, a 74, a 44, and a 22 gun ship, respectively; which were read.

Mr. MORROW presented the petition of A. Johnston and others, inhabitants of Coshocton county, in the State of Ohio, praying compensation for horses, wagons, and camp equipage, for the use of *militia* in the service of the United States, as *stated* in the petition; which was read.

Mr. ROBERTS presented the memorial of George Roberts and others, merchants of the city and county of Philadelphia, praying provision may be made for the continuation of the present rate of duties, for a certain length of time; or for the establishment of a new tariff, at the time when the increased duties shall cease by the existing law, for reasons stated in the memorial; which was read, and referred to the committee appointed on so much of the Message of the President of the United States as relates to Finance, and an Uniform National Currency.

Mr. ROBERTS also presented the memorial of Richard Caton and others, praying a duty may be laid on alum and copperas imported into the United States, for reasons stated in the memorial; which was read, and referred to the committee last mentioned.

Mr. MASON, of New Hampshire, submitted the following resolution for consideration; which was read, and passed to the second reading:

Resolved, by the Senate and House of Representatives of the United States of America in Congress assembled, That of the two hundred copies of the documents ordered to be printed by a resolve of the Senate and House of Representatives of the 27th of December, 1813, the Secretary of State be, and he is hereby, authorized to take one copy for each of the Judges of the Supreme Court of the United States, to be transmitted to said Judges, according to the provisions of the act of Congress of the 18th of April, 1814.

Mr. WILSON submitted the following motion for consideration:

Resolved, That the President of the United States be requested to cause to be laid before Congress a statement of the actual number of officers, non-commissioned officers, musicians, and privates, now composing the Military Establishment of the United States, to what posts they are distributed, and the number at each post, respectively.

The bill further providing for the Library of Congress was read the second time.

The Senate resumed, as in Committee of the Whole, the consideration of the bill for the relief of Xaverio Nandi; and, the bill having been amended, the PRESIDENT reported it to the House accordingly; and on the question, "Shall this bill be engrossed and read a third time?" it was determined in the affirmative.

The Senate resumed, as in Committee of the Whole, the consideration of the bill for the relief of Edward Barry and George Hodge; and, the bill having been amended, the PRESIDENT reported it to the House accordingly; and on the question, "Shall this bill be engrossed and read a third time?" it was determined in the affirmative.

The Senate resumed, as in Committee of the Whole, the consideration of the bill to increase the pensions of Robert White and Jacob Wrighter, together with the amendments reported thereto by the select committee; and the amendments having been agreed to, in part, the PRESIDENT reported the bill to the House accordingly; and on the question, "Shall this bill be engrossed and read a third time?" it was determined in the affirmative.

The Senate resumed, as in Committee of the Whole, the consideration of the bill, entitled "An act for the relief of Jonathan Rogers, jun., of Waterford, in the State of Connecticut;" and, on motion by Mr. DAGGETT, it was recommitted to a select committee, further to consider and report thereon; and Messrs. DAGGETT, ROBERTS, and VARNUM, were appointed the committee.

Mr. CAMPBELL, from the committee appointed on so much of the Message of the President of the United States as relates to Finance, and an Uniform National Currency, to whom was referred the bill, entitled "An act to continue in force the act, entitled 'An act for imposing additional duties upon all goods, wares, and merchandise, imported from any foreign port or place, and for other purposes,'" reported it with amendments; which were read.

Mr. CAMPBELL, from the same committee, to whom was referred the bill, entitled "An act to continue in force an act entitled 'An act laying a duty on imported salt, granting a bounty on pickled fish exported, and allowances to certain vessels employed in the fisheries," reported it without amendment.

Mr. CAMPBELL, from the committee to whom was referred the bill, entitled "An act to repeal so much of an act, passed on the 23d day of December, 1814, as imposes additional duties on postage," reported it without amendment.

Mr. CAMPBELL, from the same committee, to whom was referred the bill, entitled "An act continuing in force certain acts laying duties on bank notes, refined sugars, and for other purposes," also reported it without amendment.

The bill, entitled "An act for the relief of John G. Camp," was read a third time, and passed.

The Senate resumed, as in Committee of the Whole, the consideration of the bill, entitled "An act to authorize the payment for property lost, captured, or destroyed by the enemy, while in the military service of the United States," together with the amendments reported thereto by the select committee; and, on motion by Mr. LACOCK, the further consideration thereof was postponed until Wednesday next.

Mr. KING presented the memorial of Walter Willis and others, merchants of New York, praying the continuance of the double duties on importations, to the 31st of December next, and representing the partial operation of the Stamp act; and the memorial was read, and referred to the committee appointed on so much of the Message of the President of the United States as relates to Finance and an Uniform National Currency.

TUESDAY, January 30.

The PRESIDENT communicated a letter from T. Worthington, Governor of Ohio, with a copy of resolutions passed by the Legislature of that State, disapproving of the amendments to the Constitution of the United States, proposed by the Legislatures of the States of Massachusetts and Connecticut; which were read.

Mr. KING presented the memorial of the Mayor, Aldermen, and Common Council of the City of New York, praying the reimbursement of certain sums advanced and expended in the defence of the Third Military District, as stated in the memorial; which was read, and referred to a select committee; and Messrs. KING, VARNUM, and TAIT, were appointed the committee.

Mr. WILLIAMS presented the memorial of Joseph Hart and others, of Blount county, in the State of Tennessee, remonstrating against the transportation and opening the mail on the Sabbath; and the memorial was read, and referred to the committee, to whom were referred, on the 22d of December, the petition of sundry inhabitants of Beaver county, in the State of Pennsylvania, on the same subject.

Mr. WILLIAMS also presented the petition of Richard Mitchell, of the county of Hawkins, in the State of Tennessee, praying remission of certain judgments obtained against him, by the United States, in the circuit court at Knoxville, in the State of Tennessee, for reasons therein stated at large; and the petition was read, and referred to a select committee; and Messrs. WILLIAMS,

TALBOT, and MACON, were appointed the com mittee.

Mr. WELLS presented the petition of Isaa Briggs, praying relief in the settlement of his ac counts, as surveyor of the lands of the Unite States south of the State of Tennessee; and com pensation for exploring and ascertaining the t(pography of a post route from Washington Cit to New Orleans, as stated in the petition; whic was read, and referred to a select committee; an Messrs. WELLS, MACON, and CHACE, were ap pointed the committee.

Mr. GOLDSBOROUGH presented the memorial (Robert Gilmore and Sons, and others, citizens an merchants of Baltimore, praying a continuanc of the double duties on importations to the 30t of November next, for reasons stated in the m(morial; which was read, and referred to the Con mittee appointed on so much of the Message (the President of the United States as relates t Finance and an Uniform National Currency.

Mr. DAGGETT presented the petition of Talco Wolcott, of Hartford, in the State of Connecticu praying relief for an alleged violation of the no! importation laws, as stated in the petition; whic was read, and referred to the committee last me1 tioned.

Mr. DANA presented the memorial of D. L' man, in behalf of the woollen manufacturers Massachusetts, Connecticut, and Rhode Islan praying the protection of Congress, as stated 1 the memorial; which was read, and referred the Committee appointed on so much of the Me sage of the President of the United States as r lates to Manufactures.

The Senate resumed the consideration of th motion made the 29th instant, by Mr. WILSO! which was amended, and agreed to, as follows:

Resolved, That the President of the United Stat be requested to cause to be laid before the Senate statement of the actual number of officers, non-co! missioned officers, musicians, and privates, now co posing the Military Establishment of the United Stat(to what posts they are distributed, and the number each post, respectively.

The resolution directing a copy of the doc ments, printed by a resolve of Congress of t! 27th of December, 1813, to be transmitted to ea of the Judges of the Supreme Court, was read t! second time, and considered as in Committee the Whole; and on the question, "Shall this r(olution be engrossed and read a third time?" was determined in the affirmative.

The Senate resumed, as in Committee of t Whole, the consideration of the bill further p1 viding for the Library of Congress; and on m tion, by Mr. ROBERTS, the further consideratic thereof was postponed until Friday next.

The Senate resumed, as in Committee of t Whole, the consideration of the bill, entitled "/ act to continue in force the act entitled 'An a for imposing additional duties upon all goo wares, and merchandise imported from any f(eign port or place, and for other purposes,'" gether with the amendments reported thereto 1 the select committee; and the amendments havi been agreed to, the PRESIDENT reported the bill to the House accordingly.

On motion, by Mr. GOLDSBOROUGH, to strike out the first section of the bill, it was determined in the negative—yeas 4, nays 27, as follows:

YEAS—Messrs. Dana, Goldsborough, Mason of New Hampshire, and Thompson.

NAYS—Messrs. Barbour, Barry, Bibb, Brown, Chace, Condit, Daggett, Fromentin, Gaillard, Howell, Hunter, King, Lacock, Macon, Mason of Virginia, Morrow, Roberts, Ruggles, Talbot, Tait, Taylor, Tichenor, Turner, Varnum, Wells, Williams, and Wilson.

On the question, "Shall the amendments be engrossed, and the bill read a third time as amended ?" it was determined in the affirmative.

The Senate resumed, as in Committee of the Whole, the consideration of the bill, entitled "An act to repeal so much of an act, passed on the 23d of December, 1814, as imposes additional duties on postage ;" and no amendment having been proposed thereto, the bill passed to a third reading.

The Senate resumed, as in Committee of the Whole, the consideration of the bill, entitled "An act continuing in force certain acts laying duties on bank notes, refined sugars, and for other purposes ;" and no amendment having been proposed thereto, the bill passed to a third reading.

The Senate resumed, as in Committee of the Whole, the consideration of the bill, entitled "An act to continue in force an act, entitled 'An act laying a duty on imported salt, granting a bounty on pickled fish exported, and allowances to certain vessels employed in the fisheries."

On motion, by Mr. MACON, the further consideration thereof was postponed until Thursday next.

The bill to increase the pensions of Robert White and Jacob Wrighter was read a third time, and the blanks filled with the word "twenty."

Resolved, That this bill pass, and that the title thereof be "An act to increase the pensions of Robert White and Jacob Wrighter."

The bill for the relief of Edward Barry and George Hodge was read a third time, and passed.

The bill for the relief of Xaverio Nandi was read a third time, and passed.

Mr. BROWN, from the committee appointed on the memorial of the Legislature of the Mississippi Territory, to whom was referred the bill entitled "An act for the relief of Jonathan White," reported it without amendment.

Mr. BROWN, from the same committee, to whom was referred the bill, entitled "An act for the relief of Martin Cole, John Pollock, George Westner, and Abraham Welty," reported it without amendment.

Mr. BROWN, from the same committee, to whom was referred the bill entitled "An act for the relief of Charles Markin," reported it without amendment.

WEDNESDAY, January 31.

The PRESIDENT communicated a report of the Secretary of the Navy Department, on the petition of William Garrett, referred to him on the 19th instant; and the report was read and referred, together with the petition and the accompanying papers, to the Committee on Naval Affairs.

Mr. RUGGLES presented the petition of Edward Wilson, of Belmont county, in the State of Ohio, praying the privilege of applying the amount of two payments he has made on a quarter section of land, purchased of the United States, to the payment of any other unlocated land in the State which he may think proper to enter, for reasons stated in the petition; which was read, and referred to the committee appointed the 7th of December, on the memorial of the Legislative Council and House of Representatives of the Mississippi Territory.

Mr. SANFORD presented the petition of Harman Hendricks, merchant of New York, praying restitution of moneys illegally exacted from him by the collector of New York, as duties on copper of a certain description, as stated in the petition; which was read, and referred to a select committee; and Messrs. SANFORD, BROWN, and CHACE, were appointed the committee.

The engrossed resolution directing a copy of the documents printed by a resolve of Congress, of the 27th December, 1813, to be transmitted to each of the Judges of the Supreme Court, was read a third time, and passed.

The Senate resumed, as in Committee of the Whole, the consideration of the bill, entitled "An act for the relief of Martin Cole, John Pollock, George Westner, and Abraham Welty ;" and no amendment having been proposed thereto, the bill passed to a third reading.

The bill entitled "An act, continuing in force certain acts laying duties on bank notes, refined sugars, and for other purposes," was read a third time ; and amended by unanimous consent.

Resolved, That this bill pass with amendment.

The bill entitled "An act to repeal so much of an act passed on the 23d of December, 1814, as imposes additional duties on postage ;" was read a third time, and passed.

The amendments to the bill entitled "An act to continue in force the act, entitled 'An act for imposing additional duties upon all goods, wares, and merchandise, imported from any foreign port or place, and for other purposes," was read a third time as amended ; and on the question "Shall this bill pass as amended ?" it was determined in the affirmative—yeas 25, nays 5, as follows:

YEAS—Messrs. Barbour, Barry, Bibb, Brown, Chace, Condit, Fromentin, Gaillard, Howell, Hunter, Lacock, Mason of New Hampshire, Mason of Virginia, Morrow, Roberts, Ruggles, Sanford, Talbot, Tait, Taylor, Turner, Varnum, Wells, Williams, and Wilson.

NAYS—Messrs. Dana, Goldsborough, Horsey, Thompson, and Tichenor.

So it was *Resolved*, That this bill pass with amendments.

A message from the House of Representatives informed the Senate that the House have passed a bill, entitled "An act to alter and amend the law of costs ;" in which they request the concurrence of the Senate.

The bill last mentioned was read, and passed to the second reading.

The Senate resumed, as in Committee of the Whole, the consideration of the bill, entitled "An act to authorize the payment for property lost, captured or destroyed by the enemy, while in the military service of the United States," together with the amendments reported thereto by the select committee; and Mr. VARNUM was requested to take the Chair.

On motion by Mr. LACOCK, to amend the proposed fifth section, by inserting the word "or" before the word "consumed," in the fifth line; and to strike out the words "or injured," in the same line; it was determined in the affirmative—yeas 22, nays 9, as follows:

YEAS—Messrs. Barbour, Barry, Bibb, Chace, Condit, Daggett, Dana, Horsey, Howell, Lacock, Mason of New Hampshire, Morrow, Roberts, Talbot, Tait, Taylor, Thompson, Tichenor, Turner, Varnum, Williams, and Wilson.

NAYS—Messrs. Brown, Fromentin, Goldsborough, Hunter, King, Mason of Virginia, Ruggles, Sanford, and Wells.

On motion, by Mr. BARBOUR, the bill was recommitted to the Committee on Military Affairs, further to consider and report thereon.

The Senate resumed, as in Committee of the Whole, the consideration of the bill, entitled "An act for the relief of Jonathan White;" and no amendment having been proposed thereto, the bill passed to a third reading.

The Senate resumed, as in Committee of the Whole, the consideration of the bill, entitled "An act for the relief of Charles Markin;" and no amendment having been proposed thereto, the bill passed to a third reading.

Mr. BARRY presented the memorial of the Legislature of the State of Kentucky, praying an allowance, in money or land, may be made by Congress to the widows and orphans of volunteers of that State, who may have died in the military service of the United States; and the memorial was read, and referred to the Committee on Military Affairs.

THURSDAY, February 1.

Mr. SANFORD presented the petition of James P. Watson, of New York, praying to be placed on the pension list, as a lieutenant of the Navy of the United States, for reasons stated in the petition; which was read, and referred to the Committee on Naval Affairs, to consider and report thereon, by bill or otherwise.

The bill entitled "An act to alter and amend the law of costs," was read the second time, and referred to a select committee; and Messrs. ROBERTS, DAGGETT, and RUGGLES, were appointed the committee.

The bill entitled "An act for the relief of Martin Cole, John Pollock, George Westner, and Abraham Welty," was read a third time, and passed.

The bill entitled "An act for the relief of Jonathan White," was read a third time, and passed.

The bill entitled "An act for the relief of Charles Markin," was read a third time, and passed.

FRIDAY, February 2.

The PRESIDENT communicated a letter from the Commissioner of the General Land Office, with a supplementary report of the commissioners appointed to ascertain and adjust claims for land in the late Territory of Orleans, now State of Louisiana; which was read, and referred to the committee appointed the 7th of December, on the memorial of the Legislature of the Mississippi Territory.

Mr. DAGGETT presented the petition of William S. Hotchkiss and others, citizens of Newburn, in the State of Connecticut, concerned in the business of rope-making, praying a law may be passed granting a suitable drawback of the duties on foreign hemp manufactured into cordage in the United States, and thence exported, or some other relief, for reasons stated in the petition; which was read, and referred to the Committee appointed on so much of the Message of the President of the United States as relates to Manufactures.

On motion, by Mr. SANFORD, the committee to whom was referred the petition of Harmon Hendricks was discharged from the further consideration thereof, and it was referred to the Committee appointed on so much of the Message of the President of the United States as relates to Finance and an Uniform National Currency.

The Senate resumed, as in Committee of the Whole, the consideration of the bill further providing for the Library of Congress, and Mr. VARNUM was requested to take the Chair; and

Mr. ROBERTS moved to strike out the 4th, 5th, 6th, and 7th sections of the bill, and proposed for consideration sundry new sections to be inserted in lieu thereof; which were read, and, on motion by Mr. BARBOUR, the further consideration of the bill and amendments were postponed until Monday next.

Mr. KING, from the committee to whom was referred the memorial of Thomas B. Wait and Sons, praying for encouragement in the printing of a second and improved edition of the public documents, to be comprised in nine volumes, reported the following resolution; which was read and passed to the second reading.

Resolved, That five hundred copies of the State papers and public documents proposed to be printed by T. B. Wait and Sons, be taken for the use of Congress and the several Executive departments; T. B. Wait and Sons engaging to deliver the same at the Department of State, in well bound volumes, at two dollars and a quarter for each volume.

The Senate adjourned to Monday.

MONDAY, February 5.

ROBERT G. HARPER, appointed a Senator by the Legislature of the State of Maryland, from the 29th of January, 1816, to the 3d of March, 1821, produced his credentials, which were read and the oath prescribed by law was administered to him, and he took his seat in the Senate.

The PRESIDENT communicated a report of the Secretary of the Treasury, made in obedience to the resolution of the Senate of the 26th of January, 1816, exhibiting the amount of duties received on imported salt, from the commencement of the present Government, to the 31st of December, 1814, and the bounty paid on the exportation of pickled fish and salted provisions; and the report was read.

Mr. TAIT, from the Committee on Naval Affairs, to whom was referred the report of the Secretary of the Navy, on the petition of William Garratt, reported the following resolution; which was read:

Resolved, That the prayer of the petitioner is unreasonable, and ought not to be granted.

Mr. SANFORD presented the petition of Lathrop Thompson and others, of Southold, in the State of New York, remonstrating against the transportation and opening the mail on the Sabbath; and the petition was read, and, on motion by Mr. SANFORD, referred to the committee to whom were referred on the 22d of December, the petitions of sundry inhabitants of Beaver county, in the State of Pennsylvania, on the same subject.

Mr. CONDIT presented the petition of a number of widows, orphans, and females, of New Manchester, in the State of New Jersey, praying the encouragement of domestic manufactures, for reasons stated in the petition; which was read, and referred to the Committee on Manufactures.

Mr. SANFORD gave notice that, to-morrow, he should ask leave to bring in a bill concerning certain courts of the United States, in the State of New York.

Mr. LACOCK communicated a resolution of the *Legislature of the Commonwealth of Pennsylvania,* instructing the Senators, and requesting the Representatives of that State, in Congress, to use their endeavors to procure the passage of a law dividing the State of Pennsylvania into two districts, and establishing a district and circuit court of the United States, at Pittsburg, in the county of Alleghany.

Whereupon, on motion by Mr. LACOCK,

Resolved, That a committee be appointed to inquire into the expediency of dividing the State of Pennsylvania into two districts; and establishing a district and circuit court of the United States at Pittsburg, in the county of Alleghany.

Ordered, That Messrs. LACOCK, ROBERTS, and CHACE, be the committee.

The resolution for purchasing five hundred copies of the State papers and public documents, proposed to be printed by T. B. Wait and Sons, was amended and read, and passed to the second reading.

The Senate resumed, as in Committee of the Whole, the consideration of the bill to reward the officers and crew of the late United States' brig *Argus*; and, on motion by Mr. TAIT, the further consideration thereof was postponed until to-morrow.

The Senate resumed, as in Committee of the Whole, the consideration of the resolution for a proposed amendment to the Constitution of the United States, that the Senators of the United States shall be chosen for three years; and, on motion by Mr. BIBB, the further consideration thereof was postponed until Monday next.

A message from the House of Representatives informed the Senate that the House have passed a bill, entitled "An act to repeal the duties on certain articles manufactured within the United States;" in which bill they request the concurrence of the Senate.

The bill last mentioned was read, and passed to the second reading.

The Senate resumed, as in Committee of the Whole, the consideration of the bill further providing for the Library of Congress, together with the amendments proposed thereto; and, on motion by Mr. TAYLOR, the bill was referred to a select committee, further to consider and report thereon; and Messrs. FROMENTIN, TAYLOR, and GOLDSBOROUGH, were appointed the committee.

The Senate resumed, as in Committee of the Whole, the consideration of the bill, entitled "An act to continue in force an act, entitled 'An act laying a duty on imported salt, granting a bounty on pickled fish exported, and allowances to certain vessels employed in the fisheries; and, on motion by Mr. DAGGETT, the further consideration thereof was postponed until to-morrow.

TUESDAY, February 6.

Mr. FROMENTIN, from the committee to whom was referred the bill further providing for the Library of Congress, reported it amended.

Mr. VARNUM, from the committee to whom was referred the memorial of Francis Le Barron, reported a bill, authorizing the opening and working copper mines on Lake Superior, and for other purposes; and the bill was read, and passed to the second reading.

Mr. TAIT, from the Committee on Naval Affairs, to whom was referred the petition of James P. Watson, reported the following resolution; which was read:

Resolved, That it is inexpedient at this time to grant the prayer of the petitioner, and that he have leave to withdraw his petition.

Agreeably to notice given, Mr. SANFORD asked and obtained leave to bring in a bill, concerning certain courts of the United States, in the State of New York; and the bill was read, and passed to the second reading.

The Senate resumed the consideration of the report of the Naval Committee, to whom was referred the petition of William Garratt. Whereupon,

Resolved, That the prayer of the petitioner is unreasonable, and ought not to be granted.

The Senate resumed the consideration of the resolution, authorizing the purchase of five hundred copies of State papers, proposed to be published by T. B. Wait and Sons, which was amended and agreed to as follows:

Resolved, That five hundred copies of the State

papers and public documents, proposed to be printed by T. B. Wait and Sons, be taken for the use of Congress, and the several Executive departments; T. B. Wait and Sons, engaging to deliver the same at the Department of State in well bound volumes, at two dollars and a quarter for each volume.

Whereupon, on motion by Mr. VARNUM, the said resolution was recommitted to Messrs. KING, VARNUM, and FROMENTIN, with instructions to report a bill accordingly.

The following Message was received from the PRESIDENT OF THE UNITED STATES:

To the Senate and House of
Representatives of the United States:

It is represented, that the lands in the Michigan Territory, designated by law towards satisfying land bounties promised the soldiers of the late army, are so covered with swamps and lakes, or otherwise unfit for cultivation, that a very inconsiderable proportion can be applied to the intended grants. I recommend, therefore, that other lands be designated by Congress, for the purpose of supplying the deficiency.

JAMES MADISON.

FEBRUARY 6, 1816.

The Message was read, and referred to the Committee on Military Affairs.

The bill, entitled "An act to repeal the duties on certain articles manufactured within the United States," was read the second time, and referred to the Committee appointed on so much of the Message of the President of the United States as relates to Finance and an Uniform National Currency.

The Senate resumed, as in Committee of the Whole, the consideration of the bill, entitled "An act to continue in force an act, entitled 'An act laying a duty on imported salt, granting a bounty on pickled fish exported, and allowances to certain vessels employed in the fisheries;" and on the question, "Shall this bill be read a third time?" it was determined in the affirmative—yeas 23, nays 6, as follows:

YEAS—Messrs. Barry, Bibb, Brown, Campbell, Chase, Condit, Gaillard, Horsey, Howell, Hunter, King, Lacock, Mason of New Hampshire, Mason of Virginia, Morrow, Ruggles, Sanford, Tait, Talbot, Taylor, Wells, Williams, and Wilson.

NAYS—Messrs. Goldsborough, Macon, Thompson, Tichenor, Turner, and Varnum.

The Senate resumed, as in Committee of the Whole, the consideration of the bill, to reward the officers and crew of the United States' brig Argus; and on motion, by Mr. TAIT, the further consideration thereof was postponed until Thursday next.

INTERNAL IMPROVEMENTS.

Mr. MORROW, from the committee appointed on so much of the Message of the President of the United States, as relates to roads and canals, made a report in part, which was read, together with a bill, making appropriation for the construction of roads and canals; and the bill was read, and passed to the second reading.

The report and bill are as follows:

That a view of the extent of territory, the number and magnitude of navigable lakes, rivers, and bays; the variety of climate, and consequent diversity of productions embraced by the United States, cannot fail to impose the conviction, that a capacity exists in the country to maintain an extensive internal commerce. The variety of productions peculiar to the several parts invites to the prosecution of a commerce of the most interesting kind. A commerce internal, subject solely to the regulations of the country, not dependent on, or materially affected by the vicissitudes of foreign competition or collisions; the profits on which will rest in the country, and make an addition to the wealth of the nation. Such a commerce will, in its natural tendency, create interests and feelings, consonant with the great interests of the community. Any practicable scheme, therefore, for improvement of roads and inland navigation, having for its object the encouragement and extension of a commerce so beneficial, has strong claims to the attention and aid of Government, constituted to promote the general welfare.

Such improvements, executed on an extensive scale, would unquestionably contribute to the general interest and increase of wealth in the nation, for, whatever tend to accelerate the progress of industry, in its various and particular branches, or to remove the obstacles to its full exertion, must, in the result, produce that effect. The contemplated improvement in roads and canals, by extending the communication for commercial and personal intercourse, to the interior and distant parts of the Union, would bestow common benefits, and give an enlarged faculty to the great branches of national industry, whether agricultural, commercial, or manufacturing.

The agricultural products, which at present, from inconvenient distance, their weight, or bulk, are unportable, could then be carried to a distant market: the reduction on the charge for transportation would become an addition to the price; and a ready market and increased price, enhance the value of the land from which the products were drawn.

The general commerce of the country would thereby receive a proportional advantage from the increase of the quantity of articles for exportation, the facility and extension to the vending of imported commodities, and also from a more general consumption arising from an increased ability in the community to purchase such commodities. To manufacturers a reduction on the charge for transportation of the raw material, and wrought commodity, would be highly beneficial. The beneficial effects on individual interests, and the general wealth in society, arising from a system of cheap conveyance, by artificial roads and canals, does not rest on speculative opinion or abstract reasoning for confirmation; all doubts as to the advantages, have been removed by the test of experience in every country, where such improvements have been executed on a liberal scale.

To insure to the pursuits of useful industry in a nation, a state of the greatest prosperity, it is only necessary to protect their interests from foreign aggression, to leave them unrestrained by artificial provisions, to remove, or ameliorate, the natural obstacles to their exertion, by public works, rendering conveyance practicable and cheap.

Such public works, while they are calculated to subserve the pecuniary interests of every industrious class of the community, are highly important in a political point of view. The citizens, in the most remote parts would be brought into close connexion, by a facility to commercial and personal intercourse. The common interests and identity of feelings thence arising, would, as a cement to the parts, bind together the whole, with the strong bond of interest and affection, giving stability and perpetuity to the Union; and, as a means of security, tend to increase our capacity for resistance to foreign aggressions, by rendering less expensive, and more effective, our military operations. The disadvantages experienced and heavy charges incurred during the late war, for want of inland navigation along the seacoast, connecting the great points of defence, are of too recent date, and decisive a character, to require any other demonstration that a facility in inland communication constitutes a principal means of national defence.

It is believed that improvements so important to the political and general interest of society, stand strongly recommended to the attention of the National Legislature. The General Government alone possess the means and resources to give direction to works calculated for general advantage, and to insure their complete execution.

The particular objects of this kind, to which public aid should be given, the means to be employed, and the mode of applying the public moneys remain to be considered.

The objects are, such artificial roads and canals as are practicable of execution, and which promise a general or extensive advantage to the community; others, of minor importance, that are local in their nature, and will produce only local benefits, will, more properly, be left for execution to the means and enterprise of individuals, or to the exertions of particular States. It is, indeed, a political maxim, well attested by experience, that wherever private interests are competent to the provision and application of their own instruments and means, such provision and means should be left to themselves.

The great works which are calculated for national advantage, either in a military or commercial view, their execution must depend (at least for aid) on the General Government. Wherever great obstacles are to be overcome, great power and means must be employed. To such works the means of associated individuals are incompetent, and the particular States may not have a sufficient interest in the execution of works of the most essential advantage to other parts of the community. In other cases, where interest might be sufficiently operative, the means or the power may not be possessed, their territorial jurisdiction being limited short of the whole extent of the work.

Among many other objects of improvement in inland navigation and roads, coming within the above description, the following appears to be recommended by their importance to the attention of Congress: 1st. Canals opening an inland navigation along the Atlantic seacoast. 2d. A great turnpike road from North to South. 3d. Turnpike roads forming communications between the Atlantic and Western rivers. 4th. Military roads communicating with the frontier posts; and, 5th. A canal around the Falls of Ohio, or opening the bed of the river at that place.

The present state of the national finances, and the effect which engaging in many expensive works at the same time would produce, in raising the price of labor, seems to point out the policy of applying the public means to one, or only a few of these objects, in the first instance.

The difficulty and delicacy of selecting a particular object from among many others of acknowledged importance and great interest, is sensibly felt. In making the decision, general interests must be kept in view, and be held superior to local considerations. It appears proper, that when the Government authorize the expenditure and application of public moneys, to one of these objects, they should at the same time adopt a system, calculated to insure, in due time, the execution of other works requiring their aid.

After due consideration, and that examination which the committee have been able to give to the subject, they respectfully recommend to the first attention of Congress, "the Chesapeake and Delaware Canal," being in their opinion of the first importance, and requiring the aid of the General Government. It forms the central link in that great chain of inland navigation along the seacoast, proposed to be opened. It is believed, from the best evidence, to be practicable of execution, and of itself, unconnected with other improvements, will afford the most extensive advantages. On this the committee will make a special report.

Of the different modes which might be devised of applying public moneys to objects of internal improvements, that of authorizing subscriptions for a limited number of shares of the stock of companies incorporated for the purpose, appears, on every consideration, to be the most eligible. By limiting the number of shares to be subscribed, to a third, or less than one half, of the whole stock, there is more security that the Government shall not become engaged in impracticable projects for improvements, and also for the economical expenditure of the funds, than would be, on the plan of a direct application by Government, of the public moneys.

The committee, in order to ascertain what funds may be made applicable to the objects of internal improvement, with due regard to the state of the finances, and demands on the Treasury, requested information from the Treasury Department. The information obtained accompanies this report. It will be observed that the surplus revenue applicable to these objects is hypothetically stated in the Secretary's letter, as necessarily it must be, in the present state of the revenue laws.

It appears, however, under any contemplated change in the existing system, that the revenue would be sufficient to supply, after the present year, and during a state of peace, an annual appropriation of $600,000 for the purpose of internal improvement. That sum would constitute a fund capable of effecting many valuable objects of that kind; and, under prosperous circumstances, the fund might be gradually augmented in the proportion of the decrease of the public debt. But, if it shall enter into the policy of Government to authorize expenditures in execution of the works calculated for public advantage and general convenience, the same policy will direct to the provision of the means. For it cannot be doubted that the resources of the nation are amply sufficient, when brought in aid of private means, to effect every object of improvement on roads and canals, that are of an extensive nature, and of national concern.

The committee respectfully propose, that an annual appropriation be made, to constitute a fund for making roads and opening canals; that the fund shall be under the direction of the Secretary of the Treasury, who shall, whenever authorized by Congress, subscribe for shares in the stock of companies incorporated for making artificial roads or opening canals, and shall pay out of the aforesaid fund the instalments as they become due on such shares; that any dividends thence arising, when any work shall be completed, shall be paid into and become a part of said fund, and the Secretary shall report, at each session, to Congress, all expenditures, and the general state of the fund, as well as the state of the works in which the Government are concerned.

The committee have directed a bill to be reported embracing the above provisions.

The bill is as follows:

Be it enacted, &c., That the annual sum of —— dollars be, and the same is hereby, appropriated for the purpose of constituting a fund, for making artificial roads, and opening canals; which annual sum shall be set apart, and invariably pledged, as a fund for the purpose aforesaid, and for no other use or purpose whatsoever; and the same shall be placed, and held under the special charge and direction of the Secretary of the Treasury, for the time being: *Provided,* That nothing herein contained shall be construed to prevent Congress from suspending this appropriation during a state of war with any foreign Power, in which the United States may be engaged.

SEC. 2. *And be it further enacted,* That whenever Congress shall, by law, authorize subscription to be made for shares of the stock of any company incorporated, for making artificial roads or canals, and a subscription conformable thereto shall have been made on behalf of the United States, all moneys which shall become due according to the provisions of such acts, on the shares of stock holden by the United States, shall be paid out of the aforesaid fund.

SEC. 3. *And be it further enacted,* That all dividends or profits which shall accrue from the shares of stock holden by the United States, shall be received by the said Secretary, and shall by him be paid into the said fund, and become a part thereof.

SEC. 4. *And be it further enacted,* That it shall be the further duty of the said Secretary, to make to Congress, at each session, a report on the state of the said fund, with the expenditures and receipts, together with the state of the work on all roads and canals, in the construction of which the United States have become concerned in the manner aforesaid.

CHESAPEAKE AND DELAWARE CANAL.

Mr. MORROW, from the same committee, made the following report, in part, together with a bill to authorize the Secretary of the Treasury to subscribe, in behalf of the United States, for —— shares in the capital stock of the Chesapeake and Delaware Canal Company; and the bill was read and passed to a second reading.

The committee, to whom was referred so much of the President's Message as relates to roads and canals, having, in their general report, recommended to Congress the Chesapeake and Delaware canal as an object of first importance requiring the aid of the General Government, beg leave to make a separate report concerning the same.

The Chesapeake and Delaware canal, as an object of high national importance, has for many years claimed the attention of Congress. It was first presented to their consideration in the year 1806, by a memorial of the president and directors, dated the 1st of December, 1805; and, by a report subsequently made, on the 21st of March, 1806, it appears that an enlightened committee of the Senate recommended that aid should be granted to the memorialists. The report of this committee was finally adopted, and one or more bills passed

the Senate authorizing a grant of land to the company, not exceeding two hundred thousand acres, to be exchanged for the stock of the company. These bills, however, were postponed by the House of Representatives, owing, it is believed, to the peculiar embarrassments of the country at the periods they were sent for concurrence.

In June, 1813, the subject of the Chesapeake and Delaware canal was again brought forward before the Senate, and, on the 13th of July, a committee reported that it would not be expedient to act upon the subject at so late a period of the session, but at the time earnestly recommended it to the early and attentive consideration of the Senate at the next meeting of Congress. But then, unfortunately, the war and the financial embarrassments of the country forbade an attempt to revive the subject. Now, however, all the pre-existing obstacles would seem to be happily removed, and the present moment appears to your committee highly auspicious for Congress to interpose, and to grant its prompt and efficient aid to the company.

For a full and able exposition of the history of the Chesapeake and Delaware canal, of its utility, of its practicable and easy execution, of the progress and state of the work, of the probable expense, and of the causes which compelled the company to suspend their operations, your committee beg leave to refer the Senate to the said memorial of the president and directors, with their observations accompanying the same; to the report of the Senate, made thereupon, of the 21st of March, 1806, and also to the report of the Secretary of the Treasury on roads and canals, made in pursuance of a resolution of the Senate of the 2d of March, 1807; and pray that the same may be taken as a part of this their report.

After this general reference, your committee deem it unnecessary to go into a full discussion of the merits and utility of the Chesapeake and Delaware canal. They will, however, glance at one or two of the most important considerations.

The Chesapeake and Delaware canal may with justice be considered as of first-rate importance in the great proposed line of inland navigation along the Atlantic seaboard from North to South, and its execution as assuring the opening of that great communication at no very distant period.

It embraces within itself a wide extended range of interests from North Carolina, including all the towns and landings on the rivers and waters of that State, emptying into the Albemarle and Pamlico sounds, as well as that of the numerous rivers of Virginia and Maryland, which empty into the Chesapeake Bay, for a distance of six hundred miles, to Trenton, on the Delaware.

But this is not the most interesting view of this subject. The Chesapeake and Delaware canal is especially calculated to subserve and promote the great interests of the nation. As a military work, it offers facilities of the highest importance.

From the extent and exposure of the Atlantic States to an enemy possessed of a naval superiority, how important is it to have an interior navigation along and near the frontier, which will admit of the transportation of an army, with its artillery, &c., in safety, from point to point, with a celerity of movement equal to that of the enemy.

During the Revolutionary war, it is stated that General WASHINGTON often lamented the want of a navi-

HISTORY OF CONGRESS.

gable canal from the Chesapeake to the Delaware. His supplies for the most part were drawn from the Chesapeake, and the difficulties he experienced in procuring the means for transporting them across the isthmus are said to have been inconceivably great.

But what he most lamented was the dangerous and vexatious detention to which he was inevitably subjected, when he arrived at the isthmus on his march to the South, for the want of wagons to transport his stores and heavy artillery from one bay to the other. This detention, at a juncture so critical, under circumstances less favorable, might have proved fatal to him and to his army.

The inconveniences felt and incalculable expense incurred by individuals as well as the public, during the late war, in the vast and heavy transportations across the isthmus, must be fresh in the recollection of every one. So great was the carriage, during this period, of goods, tobacco, flour, cotton, and other bulky articles across the peninsula, that it became necessary to use four distinct lines of transportation from different points of the Chesapeake to corresponding points of the Delaware, at an expense of wagonage estimated for one year at not less than four hundred and fourteen thousand dollars, nearly one-half of the estimated cost of the canal.

The committee further remark that, if it is at any time to enter into the liberal policy of Congress to aid the Chesapeake and Delaware canal, there are reasons in reference to the particular state of the work itself why that aid should be speedily afforded.

For the want of funds the operations of the company have stood suspended for ten years and upwards; and that important and difficult part of the work, the feeder, (nearly completed,) with its several embankments, culverts, and bridges, is exposed to daily injury, and in danger of great dilapidation, if not ruin. Besides, the company not having been able to comply with certain contracts for lands and water rights for the use of the canal, suits have been brought and judgments obtained by the proprietors against them; so that the lands and water rights so purchased are in danger of being sold, and the money actually paid in part for said lands and water rights, amounting to large sums, is in danger of being actually lost.

One other remark the committee have deemed worthy of notice. The Chesapeake and Delaware canal necessarily passes through the extremities of two States, without being so central to either as to command the general interests of either government. Its peculiar local situation would, therefore seem to recommend it to the aid and patronage of the General Government, especially in connexion with its acknowledged local and general utility.

The whole expense of the canal is estimated
at - - - - - - - - - - $850,000
Of which has been paid by the stockholders,
and expended on the work - - 100,000
Yet wanted to complete the canal - 750,000
To raise this sum, the committee
propose that Congress should
authorize a subscription for
2,000 shares of the stock of the
company, at $200 per share,
making - - - - $400,000
There remains to be paid in, on
the stock subscribed and not
forfeited - - - - 100,000 — 500,000
Leaving a deficit of - - - $250,000

which, it is presumed, will be made up by additional individual and other subscriptions.

In fixing upon the sum of $400,000, the committee have had regard to the embarrassments of the company, the magnitude of the work, and the disposition heretofore manifested by the Senate to grant lands to the company equal in value to the sum now proposed.

Upon due consideration, the committee are of opinion that the sum of $400,000 ought to be appropriated, to be applied by way of subscription for the stock of the Chesapeake and Delaware Canal Company, and have accordingly submitted a bill with this report for that purpose.

Observations respecting the Chesapeake and Delaware Canal.

The Committee of the President and Directors of the Chesapeake and Delaware Canal Company, appointed to present their memorial, and solicit the aid and patronage of Congress, beg leave respectfully to offer to the members of the Senate and House of Representatives the following facts and observations relative to the said canal, as the ground and reasons for their application:

The utility of canals in every country where they have been introduced is proved by the example of so many great nations, both ancient and modern, that at this period it seems almost unnecessary to enter into an investigation of their general utility, or of their history. In order, however, to show their application to the United States with more force, and to prove the greatness of their importance, a short sketch of their introduction, and subsequent improvement by many distinguished nations, may revive the recollection of the members to numerous facts and principles which must have occurred to them in their general studies.

At a very early period of society, the Egyptians bestowed immense advantages on their country by the canals they executed along the river Nile, and from the Mediterranean to the Red Sea, through the isthmus of Suez, by which means the commerce of India and all the maritime parts of Asia was opened to Europe and the countries communicating with the Mediterranean, and was the source of all their great improvements in the arts and power. The accounts of several modern travellers, and particularly the researches of the French and British, who lately visited that country, afford ample testimony of the existence, operation, and advantages of these canals.

From sources no less authentic, and particularly from the late embassy of Lord Macartney, we learn the immense extent and utility of the canals of China, which bring the products of that vast Empire from its most distant provinces, interchange those of one region and climate with another, and establish a profound system of political economy through the country.

The Greeks and Romans attempted to intersect the Isthmus of Corinth, and several other important passes; but, partly from their ignorance of lock navigation, and partly from their genius being less devoted to commerce and manufactures than to war and the luxury of the fine arts, few works of this kind remain in the countries they governed.

No sooner, however, had the spirit of commerce revived, after the barbarous ages, than the nations of Europe began extensive works of this kind; since which, the improvement of those works has continually increased with the civilization of the countries which have adopted them, and has been the chief means of introducing and nourishing their commerce, their manufactures, and those useful arts which have changed the condition of mankind, and promoted the happiness of the people more than all other circumstances.

Some of the first modern canals were undertaken and executed by the free republics of Italy, where lock navigation, which forms an important era in the history of canals, was first used.

France, under her ancient Kings, early engaged in enterprises of so much value to the nation; Henry IV. constructed the canal of Briare, and designed many others, which have since been executed. Louis XIV. began and completed the great canal of Languedoc, which, extending from the Mediterranean to Toulouse, opened the communication from that sea to the Bay of Biscay, and has at once furnished incalculable advantages, by saving a circuit of near two thousand miles of sea navigation, and established a monument of his greatness more durable than all the other transactions of his reign; succeeding Kings, in the same manner, added numerous works of the kind; and the nation, both while a Republic and under its present Emperor, amidst all the wars and calamities it has suffered, has unceasingly devoted itself to the construction of canals.

In Holland and Flanders, still more attention has been bestowed to this important subject. The former nation may, indeed, be said to owe its political origin and existence to canals, since they not only drain the country, but intersect it so much in every direction as to form the universal means of communication.

In Flanders so numerous are canals, that few of its cities are without them; and the admirable agriculture and manufactures of those provinces have been formed and brought to maturity by the aid which water conveyance affords them.

But the island of Great Britain furnishes a proof of the advantages of canals beyond any other country. That nation has now become the maritime rival, and almost the controller, of every commercial people; her superiority has arisen from her unbounded commerce, and the vast wealth it has introduced, the basis of which wealth is her immense manufactures, which supply the wants of a large portion of the earth; the foundation of these manufactures has again been formed by her internal improvements, and particularly her canals, which, since their introduction by the Duke of Bridgewater, scarce fifty years ago, have been so rapidly extended as to traverse the kingdom in every direction. By these means her mines of coal, iron, limestone, and every other raw material, have been opened and dispersed for the purpose of manufacture; while the products of agriculture have been conveyed from province to province, and the demands of one place supplied the resources of another; hence, by her immense inland navigation, universal industry and employment have been everywhere diffused; first, to supply her own wants, and, secondly, to furnish a vast supply for export, to obtain the wealth of other countries.

The United States, both from their present political and natural situation, demand from their Government every aid it can furnish, which renders it dubious whether there is any object which can more highly merit the attention of their rulers. Their soil and the industry of the people have, in a few years, carried their agriculture to an immense extent; and their enterprise has created, with the means it furnishes, a commerce which now vies with the oldest nations of Europe. But her rapid increase in prosperity has already drawn upon her the envy, the jealousy, and the hostility of other nations, which alone can be countered acted by improving her internal strength, supplying he wants, as far as possible, by her own produce and man ufactures, and extending her agriculture, so as to gain from its surplus the wealth of other nations, and fur nish her own Government with the support it may re quire in every exigency.

For all these purposes her want of population, and the allurements held out by her unsettled territory, form the only obstacle. The price of labor retards her agricultural improvements, and prevents the more rapid increase of her manufactures; and the difficulty of communication from one part of her territory to another, adds immensely to these disadvantages. It must be obvious, therefore, that whatever mechanical or other arts can lessen or supply the want of manual labor, or whatever improvements can accelerate internal communication, are of infinitely more importance in the present situation of the country than at a future one, and form at this moment the fairest objects for private exertion and public encouragement.

It is only necessary to examine the produce of the different States, to be convinced how much that produce may be so disposed as to form an incalculable increase of internal resource and foreign wealth.

The Southern States furnish abundance of materials, which, if cheaply conveyed to the Middle and Northern States, would encourage manufactures. Coal, which is the basis of almost every manufacture, abounds on the navigable waters of James river, in Virginia, and is wanted not only in the maritime cities, and along the whole seacoast, but in those interior situations where means exist for forming mills and waterworks; wheat, flour, and corn, are produced in the Middle States, and wanted both to the southward and eastward; tobacco is the growth only of a few States, and is wanted in the rest; fish, oil, lumber, and a variety of other articles, are produced to the northward, and are all in demand to the southward; in the interior of all the States there are vast quantities of limestone, iron, copper, lead, and other materials, which are accessible to navigation, and will not bear a carriage by land, but which may be universally diffused by means of interior canals, uniting with a general one through the Union.

The advantages, and indeed the necessity of canals, may be proved by a few simple facts. A ton of goods, by weight or measurement, (of forty cubic feet,) is frequently brought from Europe, a distance of three thousand miles, for forty shillings sterling, or about nine dollars; this rate admits of salt, coal, stone, lumber, and the most bulky articles, being imported from beyond the seas cheaper than they can be conveyed for a very short distance by land, since a ton of goods cannot be carried on good roads for the same price more than thirty miles. Hence the charges of conveyance through the United States are very great, even for fine and valuable articles; but on the bulky products of agriculture, and on mineral productions, they operate as a total exclusion. In England, wherever coal is discovered, it immediately becomes the basis of manufactures, as the materials to be worked into use; such as iron, copper, clay for earthenware, glass, &c., are either conveyed to it, or the coal itself is brought to the places where these articles abound; this can only be effected by canals. A coal mine may, therefore, exist in the United States not more than ten miles from valuable ores of iron and other materials, and both of them be useless until a canal is established between them, as the price of land carriage is too great to be borne by either.

Nor does the conveyance of produce coastwise by sea lessen the expense in any manner proportioned to that of canals, or even of foreign vessels, for which the following reasons may be assigned: first, the coasting trade is chiefly carried on in vessels which take their produce from, and deliver it into, small ports; these vessels are therefore generally small, and are navigated at a far greater expense in proportion than large vessels; secondly, the danger of coasting voyages is greater, which proportionably increases the risk and prices of insurance; thirdly, the delays of delivery, accident, &c., port charges, repairs, and other expenses, are accumulated on small vessels. Hence goods are frequently brought from Europe nearly as low as they can be conveyed by sea from Baltimore to Philadelphia—cities which by land are not more than one hundred miles from each other. This is remarkably the case with respect to coal, which is brought into most of our maritime cities from Liverpool, and sold as cheap as it can be brought to them from James river, which is not one-sixth of the distance.

But canals obviate all these inconveniences; they avoid the risk of a stormy coasting navigation, and render the charge of insurance little or nothing; they reduce the number of hands employed in conveyance, as upon the canals themselves one horse saves the labor of many men; and where river navigation is connected with them, their superior safety and ease require in no degree the expense of coasting vessels; the navigation is also never impeded by winds or tides, but vessels pass on at all times with entire certainty, except from frosts alone; and the arrival of produce to a market may be calculated on with a great degree of exactness; all which circumstances far overbalance the tolls which are paid upon them. By proceeding through the country, also, they open a variety of markets, both for the sale of their produce, and to obtain some other in return. A vessel, for instance, loaded with produce in the Chesapeake bay, would have the advantage of calling at Baltimore, or of proceeding directly on through Delaware to Philadelphia, and from thence to New York, Albany, or Boston, in a direct course, with a choice of all these markets, and the certainty of providing, at some of these, articles in return; a kind of voyage which it would be nearly impossible to perform coastwise.

Upon a survey of any map of the United States, it will appear that the distance from the head of Chesapeake bay, round by sea, to Philadelphia, is nearly five hundred miles, which is saved by a canal of twenty-one miles; the distance again from Trenton, on the Delaware, to New York, or Brunswick, on the Raritan, is near three hundred miles, and will be saved by a canal of twenty-seven miles: such is the saving in point of distance. With respect to time, it may be reckoned as follows:

From New York to Brunswick is a customary passage of one tide - - - - - - - -	7 hours.	
From Brunswick to Trenton, by a canal, at the rate of four miles an hour, is	-	7 "
From Trenton to Philadelphia, is -	-	10 "
		24 "

This voyage is performed in this time nearly with certainty, whereas coastwise it requires a week, and often longer.

The passage from Philadelphia to the mouth of the intended canal, near Wilmington, is   - 12 hours.

From thence to the end of the canal	-	5 hours.
From the end of the canal, on Elk river, according to the usual time of the packet boats, to Baltimore - - - -	-	9 "
		26 '

This voyage requires, on an average, from a week to ten days by sea; indeed, the inconvenience is so great that it is rarely attempted.

Other calculations might be adduced to prove still further advantages; for instance, from Newport, in Rhode Island, and from Albany to New York, is nearly an equal distance of about 180 miles, and the passage from either is made to New York in about 36 hours; so that, adding them to the distance from New York to Baltimore, a passage would be made of 358 miles, nearly with certainty, in about 90 hours.

The Chesapeake and Delaware canal is intended to be made of the depth of seven feet six inches, which will accommodate all the vessels usually plying on the Chesapeake and Delaware, and is such as all vessels employed in the whole interior navigation of the United States may be easily conformed to. When that canal is opened, the communication will be complete from Norfolk or the Capes of Virginia, and from all the towns and landings on the Chesapeake, and its numerous waters, for a distance of near four hundred miles, to Trenton, on the Delaware; and should the Jersey canal be opened, this distance will be extended 250 miles further, if to Albany, and nearly 300, if to Newport and Providence.

It is easy, however, to see, by examining any map of the United States, that this extent may be carried much further. To the southward, the canal through the Dismal Swamp, now in execution, will open the communication to the waters of Albemarle Sound, and from thence, through the inlets, to South Carolina and Georgia. To the northward a communication is now nearly opened from Albany, up the Mohawk river, to Lake Ontario, and all the upper lakes; if a similar one be made from the Hudson river to Lake Champlain, it will extend the navigation to Quebec; and to the eastward, if the pass from Buzzard's to Boston bay be opened, which has been contemplated, it will, in like manner, extend it to Boston and all the coasts of Massachusetts.

Thus, with opening only a few short passes, of which the Chesapeake and Delaware canal is the great and preliminary one, a communication may be made nearly free from all the dangers of the ocean along the whole coast of the United States.

This communication will derive immense advantages, and in turn impart them to the local situations through which it passes in the several States; its general course, particularly from the Chesapeake to New York, will be nearly Northeast and Southwest, by which the navigation will be aided by the most prevailing winds, especially through the Spring and Summer; it will either intersect or be blended with all the rivers which lead into the interior of the several States; hence, its shores will form an immediate deposite for all their produce; it will also visit numberless smaller streams on which manufactories are or may be established, supply them with materials, and in turn carry from them their produce.

Such are the advantages of this communication, at all times, whether in peace or war; but, in the latter state, which the country has already, and may again experience, these advantages are increased to an incalculable degree. The principal advantage which the British derived in the Revolutionary war, arose from the command they possessed of the sea and of our coast by their navy; this advantage may be again obtained for some time, and forms the chief means by which an enemy can injure us, as it requires a considerable navy to guard our extensive coast. The consequences of these advantages were, first, in blocking up our harbors and seizing our seaports, the trade of which being destroyed, the sufferings of all those districts which depended on them for a market and supply of foreign articles became very great; secondly, our trade abroad being destroyed, supplies, though often obtained in abundance at various parts of our extensive seacoast, in defiance of the vigilance of an enemy, were but very partially dispersed through the country; and, thirdly, by the rapidity with which a naval force could move along our seacoast, their armies were easily conveyed from one port to another, to attack us in numerous points at once, to make incursions, and do great injury before our armies could move against them by land with the necessary baggage, artillery, and stores. Hence, several armies became necessary, and, even with these, the difficulty of communication rendered it by no means easy to form an adequate defence of our extensive country.

But if the communication in question be formed, our defence becomes comparatively easy. In the course of the late war, even in Europe, canals were an immense advantage to the armies who possessed them. In France, Flanders, and Holland, they formed a great and powerful aid; and one instance in Ireland will show the advantages derived from them here. In one of the invasions of that country, when the French had landed on the western counties, upon the intelligence reaching Dublin, an army of 10,000 men, completely equipped, with all their artillery and baggage, embarked on the canal, and, by attaching the cavalry horses to the boats, the whole was conveyed, ready for action, sixty miles in ten hours—a distance which would otherwise have required three or four days, with all the disadvantages arising from the fatigues of a march.

By these means, if an army were stationed in the vicinity of either of the canals in Delaware or Jersey, both of which are central to the United States, they might be conveyed from the Chesapeake to New York, or still further eastward or southward, with as much expedition as an enemy could sail along the coast.

Our late excellent President and Commander-in-Chief, General Washington, was known often to have expressed and lamented the disadvantages which he sustained for want of such a communication, especially from the Delaware to the Chesapeake, as not only by far the greatest proportion of the supplies for the army at all times were drawn from the Chesapeake, to such an extent as to require four hundred wagons nearly in constant employ, but, in his march to the southward, the baggage, stores, and heavy artillery were conveyed by water, and upwards of one hundred river-craft employed for the purpose, from Philadelphia to Christiana bridge, and again on the Chesapeake. Yet such was the difficulty of procuring wagons to convey them across the isthmus that he experienced inconceivable delay in going to the Southern army; and if the enemy had embarked again for New York or Jersey, those countries must have been completely invested before he could have returned to their assistance.

As a military work, a canal is in itself of that nature that, while it affords the utmost advantage to army of the country, it can be of no use to an invading enemy, being a deep ditch; especially when the size intended to be constructed from the Chesapeake to the Delaware, it presents a strong front against attack, capable of being defended by batteries and passable only with the same difficulties as rivers and streams, the possession of which is always an object of consequence in defence. If an enemy be likely to gain possession of it, the withdrawing the boats and letting off the water, which are easily to be accomplished in a retreat, would render it useless to them while all the injury they could do it could be easily repaired, when it became again in possession of the country. This fact was verified in the attack made the British army upon Ostend, in 1798, expressly the purpose of destroying one of the finest canals Flanders, which had been of great use to the French army in defence of that country; but though the landed and succeeded in destroying the basin a principal works at the entrance of the canal, yet, having no boats to pass into the interior, that army was soon overcome, and the canal in a few weeks completely restored to use.

So sensible are the English nation of the immense benefit of canals as works of defence, that, in addition to the numbers they now possess, they have devoted part of their army to form another, expressly as a protection against invasion. This canal is intended to extend from London to the coast of Kent, near Romney, by which means troops from the metropolis and all the interior of the country may be immediately conveyed to that part of the coast most favorable the landing of an enemy, while, by strengthening the banks of the canal with forts, a succession of posts would be kept up to annoy and retard the march of any army which should land, and to secure the retreat of their own.

In this view, the situation of the Chesapeake and Delaware canal is one of the most admirable that occurs in the United States, or could be desired in any country. It is placed at a great distance from the ocean. The river Delaware may be easily made defensible below the mouth of the canal by batteries, small navy, and other means which have already formed an admirable defence of that river. The Chesapeake Bay could also be defended by a naval force far less than would be adequate to protect the coast; but if an enemy should force its passage up either bay, or land below, and march to possess themselves of the canal, time would be given to prepare for defence; the facility of communication in the interior would concentrate the forces of the country, and the position of the neighboring grounds would enable them to make a bold and successful stand.

This position is indeed at once so strong and so central that it is highly probable that, in any future attack of the country, it would be selected as the station of an army of defence for the Middle States. Along the northwest line of the canal the eminences of Iron hill and Gray's hill form high, bold, insulated points, capable of being fortified against any attack commanding the whole course of the canal within sight, and but a few miles distant from both the Chesapeake and Delaware bays; while in their rear they have the interior of the upper part of Maryland, Delaware, and Pennsylvania, for drawing supplies, and affording one of the strongest countries for retreat.

The distance of this position is also nearly equal from the State of New York and from Virginia; to either of which an army could be conveyed in a few hours, by the means already pointed out, should an attack be made against them.

The practicability of forming canals is at this period no longer a matter of doubt or speculation. In Europe, every obstacle of nature has been overcome in order to accomplish them; where mountains or hills interpose, they are either ascended and descended again by locks, or they are perforated, and the canals carried through them, often for many miles; valleys are crossed by embankments or by aqueducts; streams and rivers by bridges of masonry, differing from common ones only in their superior strength; morasses are drained or filled up; and, in short, the execution of the numerous works which have been made, or are now making, furnishes at once proofs and models of every kind of work which can occur in effecting canal navigation; so that, at this moment, they do not remain an object of invention, but simply of imitation and perseverance.

The communication over the isthmus of the Chesapeake and Delaware is of that nature to have invited the attention of all men who had just ideas of the important objects of canal navigation, from the earliest settlement of the country. No sooner had the genius of the Duke of Bridgewater planned his great improvements in England than the spirit and enterprise of the country, even when so young in the arts and feeble in its means, was excited to imitate them. So long ago as the years 1769 and 1770, a committee of the Philosophical Society, consisting of Dr. Franklin, Mr. Rittenhouse, Mr. Hollingsworth, Mr. Thomas Gilpin, and several others, were appointed to survey this country, and they ascertained, in the fullest manner, not only the ease, but the practicability of a canal. The ability of the country, however, was at that period inadequate to undertake it; and, the war occurring soon after, the task of performing it was reserved for the present age, with the immense advantages it possesses in means, and in the numerous examples furnished by other nations.

The operations and surveys which have been made by the company now formed, within the last three years, will appear by the reports they have published, (which will be presented herewith,) and will furnish the fullest confirmation of those formerly made, with a variety of other facts, which the superior knowledge and ability of engineers at the present period enable them to make.

The course of the canal, as now marked out and decided upon, from Welch Point, on Elk river, where vessels of any size may approach it, to bold navigable water on the Christiana, near the Delaware, is twenty-one miles. All this course is over a country wholly unimpeded by hills, rocks, morasses, or any material difficulty whatever. The canal is intended to be supplied by water from Elk river and White Clay creek, taken at positions on each of them sufficient to give the necessary elevation, and conducted by feeders, or canals of supply, to the main canal itself. These feeders are constructed on a smaller scale than the main canal, but are also made sufficient for barge navigation, and promise to afford a considerable augmentation to the profits of the work, as they extend northward nearly to the boundaries of Maryland and Delaware with Pennsylvania, countries affording stone, lime, timber, and many mineral productions in great demand in the Southern States, and numerous mill-seats, which may be converted into manufactories by the aid the canal will give them.

As the supply of the canal with water was the basis of its navigation, when completed, and afforded great advantages to all the operations of the work itself, by furnishing water carriage for removing the earth, stone, and other necessary materials, the company have been engaged, thus far, in completing the canal of supply from Elk river, which was found to furnish sufficient water for opening the canal, and for navigation upon it. The ground through which this feeder has been constructed presented many difficulties not occurring in the main canal itself, as, in passing upwards to the course of the feeder, it enters a hilly country abounding with ridges of stone, deep valleys, and many other objects of labor; none, however, of more difficulty than yielded to a moderate degree of perseverance; and the board feel a great degree of satisfaction that, in nearly completing it, as they have done, they have had time and opportunity to form and mature a system for their operations, to gain considerable experience, to collect a body of excellent workmen, and, by encountering their greatest difficulties in their outset, to be prepared to enter upon the work of the main canal itself with superior confidence and advantage. The course of the feeder which has already been opened is about five miles, which is completed, except a few short spaces, and the construction of the necessary bridges and other masonry. The work of a few months, therefore, will render this part of the undertaking complete, and confine the future operations of the company to the main canal itself.

As some estimate of the expense of this undertaking may be required, the committee have only to mention that, in all works, whether of a public or private nature, and even in those of the most simple and customary construction, difficulties occur in forming just estimates, and still more in confining the expenditure to them when made. This observation, they are sensible, must forcibly apply to a work nearly new in its kind in these States, and of a nature more complicated than usual; but, in the present instance, the board possess the advantage of considerable experience, which they trust they can apply, with some confidence, to an estimate of their future work; they, therefore, with as much certainty as can be expected in an undertaking of the kind, calculate that the completion of the main canal will not exceed $25,000 per mile, or $550,000 altogether.

In the commencement of this undertaking, the private subscriptions amounted to near $400,000, of which about one-fourth has been received and expended in purchases of the water-rights and land, and in the preparations necessary to collect and accommodate a large body of workmen, and to supply them with tools and materials, and in the operations of the feeder. From the subscriptions, also, some deduction must be made for losses by bankruptcy, deceased persons, and those casualties which attend the collection of money. After all these are deducted, there remains a large sum of efficient funds for the purpose of continuing the work.

The chief difficulty, however, which the board have experienced, which offers itself as the obstacle to their progress, and forms the basis of their application to Congress, is the despondency of the private subscribers, many of whom are persons of small or moderate fortunes, to whom the amount of their subscriptions is of considerable consequence, and who, therefore, are actuated by fears, and feel the deprivation of capital and interest, for a few years, until the canal can be completed, more forcibly than the just and reasonable hopes that, when completed, the canal, in addition to its great public utility, will afford a large private emolument.

The calculations which have been formed upon this head have been founded upon the knowledge obtained by the board of the vast trade at all times carried on across the peninsula, even under the great inconvenience of carriage by land, a just appreciation of the increase of this trade, and the numerous advantages otherwise offered by the canal.

It, therefore, appears essentially necessary to the completion of this work that the patronage and support of it should be taken up by the public, and that the hopes of individuals should rest upon something beyond private exertion. In the present moment, it may be considered as one of those children of the public which is struggling for existence, and demanding that aid which may confirm its strength and enable it to advance to maturity. If deprived of this support, it will probably perish, and not only become an object of great public injury and regret, in itself, but, in its example, protract the undertaking of all great works, or load them with despondency if begun. The aid of the Legislature of the United States would completely revive the spirit and hopes of the subscribers, bring forth their exertions, and give to the company that confidence which would enable them to draw resources from their own means, as the subscriptions of the individuals would be immediately obtained whenever a small degree of public protection and support is given them.

Of the advantage of this protection and support, the history of the political economy of all countries furnishes the most ample proof. Every nation has found it necessary, in its first attempts to establish manufactures, roads, canals, and even commerce itself, whether foreign or internal, absolutely to begin them at the public expense, or to cherish the efforts which the enterprise and public spirit of individuals prompt them to make. The States of Holland and of the Low Countries first made, and have ever since supported, their canals with the public money. Henry IV constructed the canal of Briare, and several others, by the same means. Lous XIV not only introduced the manufactures of France by his own institutions, but paid the expense of the canal of Languedoc, and afterwards gave it to Mr. Riquet, the engineer, forever: and the whole history of the English nation, and of every session of its Parliament, is replete with donations and acts for granting the public aid and protection to every work which is calculated to promote the general system of political economy; from whence has arisen that enterprise in individuals which attempts every improvement, from the confidence created by so many successful examples, and by the certainty that the Government will, in some way, lend its support where private means are not sufficient.

The Chesapeake and Delaware canal, though so admirable in its natural situation, and of such immense importance, has some difficulties of a political nature to encounter, which particularly places it under the protection of Congress. It passes through the extremities of two States, viz: Delaware and Maryland, and near to that of another, (Pennsylvania,) without being so central to either as to command the general interests

of either Government, especially as both Maryland and Pennsylvania have so many objects of a similar kind in the interior of their own States; and Delaware is possessed of means too limited to give the necessary encouragement. Hence, though the advantages to all those States are undoubtedly great, its importance as a national work, and as an undertaking which one State relies on the other to attempt, prevents its receiving the full support of either, and compels it to look to Congress for aid and protection as a national work.

Of what nature or in what way it may appear expedient for the Federal Legislature to grant its aid to this undertaking, it is by no means proper, or within the province or abilities of the committee to point out; whether in subscribing to a number of shares, or in a specific grant, such as has been given to harbors, roads, light-houses, and works of a similar nature, or in any other manner, must be left wholly to the superior knowledge and discretion of the Legislature. All that the committee wish to impress on the members to whom they respectfully offer these observations is, the immense importance of the undertaking itself; the necessity of public support to insure its progress or save it from ruin; and the certainty that even a very moderate aid will increase its private support, and insure the execution of a work, great, indeed, in its own importance, but still greater as the basis and example of all others which the improvement of our country may require, or the genius and enterprise of its citizens undertake for the general benefit of the Union, detached from the objects of particular States, of which the wisdom of Congress will always form the best judgment and discrimination.

KENSEY JOHNS,
JOSHUA GILPIN,
ROBT. H. GOLDSBOROUGH.

DECEMBER 1, 1805.

On motion. by Mr. MORROW, the memorial of the President and Directors of the Chesapeake and Delaware Canal Company, presented the 28th of January, 1806, with the observations accompanying the same, together with the report of the Senate thereupon, of the 21st of March, 1806, were ordered to be printed for the use of the Senate.

WEDNESDAY, February 7.

Mr. BARBOUR, from the Committee on Military Affairs, to whom was referred the bill, entitled "An act to authorize the payment for property lost, captured, or destroyed by the enemy, while in the military service of the United States," reported it with amendments.

Mr. DAGGETT presented the petition of Horatio Aldin & Co., and others, citizens of Connecticut, praying compensation for a number of vessels destroyed by the enemy, in Connecticut river, on the 8th of April, 1814, as stated in the petition; which was read, and referred to the Committee on Military Affairs.

Mr. CAMPBELL, from the Committee on Finance and an Uniform National Currency, to whom was referred the bill, entitled "An act for the relief of William Morrissett," reported it with an amendment.

Mr. WILLIAMS, from the committee to whom

was referred the petition of Richard Mitchell, made a report, which was read, together with a bill for the relief of Richard Mitchell; and the bill was read, and passed to a second reading.

Mr. TAYLOR presented the memorial of Abner Landrum, engaged in the manufacture of stone ware to a considerable extent, praying the protection of Congress in regulating the tariff of duties, as stated in the memorial; which was read, and referred to the Committee on Finance and an Uniform National Currency.

Mr. CAMPBELL, from the Committee on Finance and an Uniform and National Currency, submitted the following motion for consideration:

Resolved, That the Secretary of the Treasury be, and he is hereby, directed to ascertain, and cause to be laid before the Senate, a statement exhibiting the actual condition of the several incorporated banks within the District of Columbia, on the first day of January, 1816, specifying the actual and authorized amount of their capital stock, the amount of specie, and the amount of the bills or notes of other banks in their vaults; the amount of debts due to, and of notes or bills in circulation of each bank.

Mr. TAIT presented the petition of Sarah Goelet, widow of James F. Goelet, deceased, formerly Sailingmaster in the Navy of the United States, praying that the pension allowed her late husband may be extended to her, during her life, for reasons stated in the memorial; which was read, and referred to the Committee on Naval Affairs.

Mr. SANFORD presented the petition of Hunting Miller, and others, inhabitants of East Hampton, in the State of New York, praying the establishment of a post office in that place, for reasons stated in the petition; which was read, and referred to the committee on the petition of John Duckworth, jr., and others.

Mr. KING, from the committee to whom the subject was referred, reported a bill, authorizing a subscription for the printing of a second edition of the public documents; and the bill was read, and passed to a second reading.

The bill, entitled "An act to continue in force an act, entitled 'An act laying a duty on imported salt, granting a bounty on pickled fish exported, and allowances to certain vessels employed in the fisheries," was read a third time, and passed— yeas 22, nays 6, as follows:

YEAS—Messrs. Barbour, Barry, Bibb, Brown, Campbell, Chace, Condit, Daggett, Fromentin, Gaillard, Hunter, King, Mason of New Hampshire, Morrow, Roberts, Ruggles, Sanford, Tait, Talbot, Taylor, Wells, and Wilson.

NAYS—Messrs. Goldsborough, Macon, Thompson, Tichenor, Turner, and Varnum.

The Senate resumed the consideration of the report of the Naval Committee, on the petition of James P. Watson: Whereupon,

Resolved, That it is inexpedient at this time to grant the prayer of the petitioner, and that he have leave to withdraw his petition.

The bill concerning certain courts of the United States, in the State of New York, was read the second time and considered as in Committee of the Whole, and ordered to be engrossed and read a third time.

The bill authorizing the opening and working copper mines on Lake Superior, and for other purposes, was read the second time, and taken up as in Committee of the Whole; and the further consideration thereof postponed until Monday next.

The bill making appropriation for the construction of roads and canals, was read the second time, and taken up as in Committee of the Whole; and the further consideration thereof postponed until Friday next.

The bill to authorize the Secretary of the Treasury to subscribe in behalf of the United States for —— shares, in the capital stock of the Chesapeake and Delaware Canal Company, was read the second time, and taken up as in Committee of the Whole; and the further consideration postponed until Friday next.

The Senate resumed, as in Committee of the Whole, the consideration of the bill further providing for the Library of Congress, together with the amendments reported thereto by the select committee. Mr. VARNUM was requested to take the Chair, and the bill having been amended, the President resumed the Chair, and Mr. VARNUM reported the bill accordingly; and it was ordered to be engrossed, and read a third time.

A message from the House of Representatives informed the Senate that the House have passed the bill which originated in the Senate, entitled "An act concerning the convention to regulate the commerce between the territories of the United States and His Britannic Majesty," with amendments; in which they request the concurrence of the Senate.

The Senate proceeded to consider the amendments of the House of Representatives to the bill last mentioned; and, on motion by Mr. BIBB, they were referred to the Committee on Foreign Relations, to consider and report thereon.

Mr. GOLDSBOROUGH submitted the following motion for consideration:

Resolved, That the Secretary of the Navy be instructed to lay before the Senate copies of all the correspondence he may have had with the prize agent, the navy agent at New York, and other persons, relative to the ship Cyane, captured by the United States frigate Constitution; and that he furnish copies of certificates of the valuation of the different prizes brought into the United States, by the ships of war, and taken into the service of the United States; with a statement of their actual force when captured.

The PRESIDENT communicated a report of the Commissioners of the Sinking Fund, stating that the measures which have been authorized by the Board, subsequent to their last report of the 6th of February, 1815, so far as the same have been completed, are fully detailed in the report of the Secretary of the Treasury to this Board, dated the 6th day of the present month, and in the statements therein referred to, which are herewith transmitted, and prayed to be received as a part of this report; which was read.

Mr. LACOCK presented the petition of Walter

Jones, jr., and others, inhabitants of the District of Columbia, praying the passage of a law relating to slaves held by persons residing therein; and the petition was read. and referred to a select committee; and Messrs. LACOCK, BARBOUR, and GOLDSBOROUGH, were appointed the committee.

Mr. CHACE called up the petition of Henry Dishbron and James Chittenden, of the Michigan Territory, presented the 12th of January, 1812, praying compensation for property taken and destroyed by the Indians and British, as stated in the petition; which was read, and referred to the Committee on Military Affairs.

THURSDAY, February 8.

The PRESIDENT communicated a letter from the Commissioners of the Navy Pension Fund, transmitting their annual statement respecting the operation of their trust; showing the amount of the fund, the number of the pensioners, and the amount of disbursements; which were read, and referred to the Committee on Naval Affairs.

The bill for the relief of Richard Mitchell was read the second time.

The bill authorizing a subscription for the printing of a second edition of the public documents was read the second time, and considered as in Committee of the Whole; and ordered to be engrossed and read a third time.

The Senate resumed the consideration of the motion made the 7th instant, for directing the Secretary of the Navy to lay before the Senate certain information relative to the ship Cyane, and other prizes brought into the United States, and taken into the service thereof, and agreed thereto.

The bill further providing for the Library of Congress, having been reported by the committee correctly engrossed, was read the third time, and the blank filled with "one thousand."

Resolved, That this bill pass, and that the title thereof be "An act providing for the settlement of certain accounts against the Library of Congress, and for establishing the salary of the Librarian.

The bill concerning certain courts of the United States, in the State of New York, was read a third time, and passed.

Resolved, That this bill pass, and that the title thereof be, "An act concerning certain courts of the United States, in the State of New York."

On motion, by Mr. SANFORD, the Committee on Naval Affairs were instructed to inquire into the expediency of providing by law for the appointment of one or more Judge Advocates in the Navy.

On motion, by Mr. VARNUM, the committee to whom was referred that part of the Message of the President of the United States which relates to Finance and an Uniform National Currency, were instructed to inquire into the expediency of confining the payment of all taxes, and other moneys due the United States, to specie Treasury notes, and the notes of such banks as are in the practice of redeeming their notes with specie.

On motion, by Mr. HORSEY, the committee to whom was referred the petition of James Tilton, late Physician and Surgeon General of the Army of the United States, were discharged from the further consideration thereof, and it was referred to the Secretary for the Department of War, to consider and report thereon to the Senate.

The Senate resumed, as in Committee of the Whole, the consideration of the bill entitled "An act to authorize the payment for property lost, captured, or destroyed by the enemy, while in the military service of the United States," together with the amendments reported thereto by the select committee, and Mr. VARNUM by request took the Chair; and the bill having been amended, on motion by Mr. MASON, of New Hampshire, the further consideration thereof was postponed until Monday next.

Mr. BIBB, from the Committee on Foreign Relations, to whom were referred the amendments of the House of Representatives to the bill, entitled "An act concerning the convention to regulate the commerce between the territories of the United States, and His Britannic Majesty," together with the bill, reported them without amendment; and, on motion by Mr. BIBB, the consideration thereof was postponed to, and made the order of the day for, to-morrow.

Mr. CAMPBELL, from the Committee on Finance and an Uniform National Currency, to whom was referred the bill, entitled "An act to repeal the duties on certain articles manufactured within the United States," reported it without amendment.

Mr. CAMPBELL, from the same committee, to whom was referred the bill, entitled "An act for the relief of John Redman Coxe," reported it with an amendment.

Mr. TAYLOR, from the committee to whom the subject was referred, reported a bill further supplementary to an act, entitled "An act providing for the indemnification of certain claimants of public lands, in the Mississippi Territory;" and the bill was read, and passed to the second reading.

The Senate resumed the consideration of the motion made the 7th instant, for directing the Secretary of the Treasury to cause to be laid before the Senate a statement; exhibiting the actual condition of the several incorporated banks within the District of Columbia, on the first day of January, 1816, and agreed thereto.

The Senate resumed, as in Committee of the Whole, the consideration of the bill, to reward the officers and crew of the late United States' brig Argus; and on motion, by Mr. DAGGETT, the consideration thereof was further postponed, until to-morrow.

The Senate resumed, as in Committee of the Whole, the consideration of the bill entitled "An act, for the relief of William Morrissett," together with the amendment reported thereto by the select committee, and the amendment having been agreed to, the PRESIDENT reported the bill to the House accordingly; and on the question "Shall the amendments be engrossed, and the bill read a third time as amended?" it was determined in the affirmative.

FRIDAY, February, 9.

The Senate resumed, as in Committee of the Whole, the consideration of the bill, to reward the officers and crew of the late United States' brig Argus; and on motion, by Mr. TAIT, that the further consideration thereof be postponed until the first Monday in July next, it was determined in the affirmative—yeas 18, nays 14, as follows:

YEAS—Messrs. Bibb, Gaillard, King, Lacock, Macon, Mason of New Hampshire, Morrow, Roberts, Ruggles, Talbot, Tait, Taylor, Thompson, Turner, Varnum, Wells, Williams, and Wilson.

NAYS—Messrs. Barry, Brown, Chace Condit, Daggett, Dana, Fromentin, Goldsborough, Harper, Horsey, Howell, Mason of Virginia, Sanford, and Tichenor.

The Senate resumed the consideration of the amendments of the House of Representatives to the bill, entitled "An act concerning the convention to regulate the commerce between the territories of the United States and His Britannic Majesty."

On motion, by Mr. KING, that the further consideration thereof, together with the bill, be postponed until the first Monday in July next, it was determined in the negative—yeas 17, nays 18, as follows:

YEAS—Messrs. Barbour, Brown, Chace, Daggett, Fromentin, Gaillard, Goldsborough, Horsey, Howell, Hunter, King, Mason of New Hampshire, Sanford, Talbot, Thompson, Tichenor, and Turner.

NAYS—Messrs. Barry, Bibb, Campbell, Condit, Dana, Harper, Lacock, Macon, Mason of Virginia, Morrow, Roberts, Ruggles, Tait, Taylor, Varnum, Wells, Williams, and Wilson.

On motion, by Mr. BIBB, the further consideration thereof was postponed until to-morrow.

The Senate adjourned to Monday.

MONDAY, February 12.

Mr. WILLIAMS presented the petition of Alfred M. Carter, of Tennessee, on behalf of himself and the other heirs of his deceased father, Landon Carter, praying payment for an unliquidated loan office certificate, for five hundred dollars, as stated in the petition; which was read, and referred to the Committee on Finance and an Uniform National Currency.

Mr. ROBERTS presented the petition of Robert Jones and others, who were attached to the United States' brig Jefferson, on Lake Ontario, in the late war, and embarked on board the schooner Surprise, for Baltimore, to join the United States ship Erie, and were cast away on their passage, and lost all their clothing and other effects, and praying compensation for the same, as stated in the petition; which was read, and referred to the Committee on Naval Affairs.

Mr. ROBERTS also presented the petition of Joseph Henry and others, who were attached to the flotilla, in the Patuxent, under the command

14th CON. 1st SESS.—5

of Commodore Barney, in the late war, during the invasion of the enemy, praying compensation for their clothing, which was destroyed by blowing up the said flotilla, as stated in the petition; which was read, and referred to the Committee on Naval Affairs.

On motion, by Mr. CAMPBELL, the Committee on Finance and an Uniform National Currency, to whom were referred the memorial of Walter Willis, and others, of New York, and the memorial of George Roberts and others, of the city and county of Philadelphia, were discharged from the further consideration thereof, respectively.

On motion, by Mr. ROBERTS, the committee to whom was referred the bill, entitled "An act for the relief of the heirs of George Nebinger, were discharged from the further consideration thereof; and it was referred to the committee appointed on so much of the Message of the President of the United States as relates to Finance and an Uniform National Currency.

Mr. GOLDSBOROUGH presented the memorial of James Kemp, President of the Bible Society of Baltimore, praying that the Secretary of the Treasury may be authorized by law to remit the duties on the importation of certain stereotype plates, as stated in the memorial; which was read, and referred to the Committee on Finance and an Uniform National Currency.

The bill further supplementary to the act, entitled "An act providing for the indemnification of certain claimants of public lands in the Mississippi Territory," was read the second time.

COMMERCE WITH GREAT BRITAIN.

The Senate resumed the consideration of the amendments of the House of Representatives, to the bill, entitled "An act concerning the convention to regulate the commerce between the territories of the United States and His Britannic Majesty."

On motion, by Mr. BIBB, to agree to the first amendment, to wit: line one, strike out the words, "and declared," it was determined in the negative—yeas 15, nays 19, as follows:

YEAS—Messrs. Bibb, Campbell, Condit, Dana, Lacock, Macon, Mason of Virginia, Morrow, Roberts, Ruggles, Tait, Taylor, Varnum, Williams, and Wilson.

NAYS—Messrs. Barbour, Barry, Brown, Chace, Daggett, Fromentin, Gaillard, Goldsborough, Harper, Horsey, Howell, Hunter, King, Mason of New Hampshire, Talbot, Thompson, Tichenor, Turner, and Wells.

On motion, by Mr. BIBB, to agree to the other amendment, to wit; line 2, after the word "assembled," strike out the residue of the bill, and in lieu thereof, insert as follows:

"That the same duties be, and the same are hereby, imposed on articles of the growth, produce, or manufacture, of His Britannic Majesty's territories in Europe, imported into the United States in British vessels, as are, or shall be imposed on the importation of the like articles in American vessels.

SEC. 2. *And be it further enacted*, That the same tonnage, and other duties and charges, are hereby imposed on British vessels in any of the ports of the

United States, as are, or may be payable in the same ports, by vessels of the United States, except such British vessels, as shall come from the West Indies or the dominions of His Britannic Majesty in North America.

SEC. 3. *And be it further enacted,* That the same bounty shall be allowed on the exportation of any article, the growth, produce, or manufacture of the United States, to His Britannic Majesty's territories in Europe, when such exportation shall be in British vessels as are, or may be allowed when such exportation is, or may be in vessels of the United States.

SEC. 4. *And be it further enacted,* That in all cases where drawbacks are, or may be allowed on the re-exportation of any goods, the growth, produce, or manufactures of the territories of His Britannic Majesty, the same drawback shall be allowed on such re-exportation, where the original importation of the same may have been in British vessels, as are, or may be allowed on such re-exportation, where the original importation may have been in vessels of the United States.

SEC. 5. *And be it further enacted,* That so much of each and every act of Congress as is inconsistent with the provisions of this act be, and the same is hereby, repealed.

SEC. 6. *And be it further enacted,* That this act shall take effect from and after the 22d day of December, 1815, and continue in force until the 3d day of July, 1819, and no longer."

It was determined in the negative—yeas 11, nays 23, as follows:

YEAS—Messrs. Bibb, Campbell, Condit, Lacock, Macon, Mason of Virginia, Morrow, Roberts, Ruggles, Varnum, and Wilson.

NAYS—Messrs. Barbour, Barry, Brown, Chace, Daggett, Dana, Fromentin, Gaillard, Goldsborough, Harper, Horsey, Howell, Hunter, King, Mason of New Hampshire, Tait, Talbot, Taylor, Thompson, Tichenor, Turner, Wells, and Williams.

So it was, *Resolved,* That the Senate disagree to the amendments of the House of Representatives to the bill last mentioned.

TUESDAY, February 13.

The PRESIDENT communicated a report of the Secretary of the Treasury, made in obedience to the resolution of the House of Representatives, of the 23d of February, 1815, on the subject of a general tariff of duties, proper to be imposed on imported goods, wares, and merchandise; and the report was read, and two hundred additional copies thereof ordered to be printed for the use of the Senate.

Mr. TAIT, from the Committee on Naval Affairs, to whom the subject was referred, reported a bill for the relief of Lieutenant Colonel William Lawrence, of the Army of the United States, and of the officers, non-commissioned officers, and privates, composing the garrison of Fort Bowyer, in the Summer of the year 1814; and the bill was read, and passed to the second reading.

Mr. TAIT, from the Committee on Naval Affairs, to whom was referred the petition of Sarah Goelet, reported the following resolution, which was read:

Resolved, That it would be inexpedient to grant the prayer of the petitioner, and that she have leave to withdraw her petition.

Mr. TAIT, from the Committee on Naval Affairs, to whom was recommitted the bill, entitled "An act for the relief of George S. Wise," with instructions to inquire into the expediency of making some general provisions by law for similar cases, reported it without amendment, together with the following resolution, which was read:

Resolved, That it is inexpedient to make any general provisions on the subject.

Mr. CAMPBELL laid before the Senate the resolutions of the Legislature of the State of Tennessee, rejecting the amendments proposed by the States of Massachusetts and Connecticut, to the Constitution of the United States; which were read.

Mr. C. also communicated the instructions of the Legislature of the State of Tennessee to their Senators in Congress, to lay before the General Government the expediency of delaying the collection of the direct tax, either in whole or in part; also, to use their best exertions to effect the passage of a law exonerating part of the citizens of White county from the payment of any more direct tax, until they are placed on an equality with the other citizens of the State; which were read.

The bill, entitled "An act for the relief of William Morrissett," was read a third time, as amended, and passed.

The engrossed bill, authorizing a subscription for the printing of a second edition of the public documents, was read a third time, and passed.

The PRESIDENT communicated resolutions of the Legislature of the State of Ohio, instructing their Senators in Congress, and requesting their Representatives to use their endeavors to procure the passage of a law "providing for the organization, arming, and disciplining the militia, and for governing such part of them as may be employed in the service of the United States, and also providing more effectually for calling them forth to execute the laws of the United States, suppress insurrections, and repel invasions; which were read, and referred to the committee appointed on so much of the Message of the President of the United States as relates to the militia.

The Senate resumed, as in Committee of the Whole, the consideration of the resolution for a proposed amendment to the Constitution of the United States, that the Senators of the United States shall be chosen for three years: and Mr. VARNUM was requested to take the Chair. And, after debate, on motion by Mr. LACOCK, the further consideration thereof was postponed until Tuesday next.

Mr. BARBOUR, from the committee to whom was referred the resolution relating to the claims of the officers and soldiers of the Virginia line, on State and Continental Establishment, for bounty lands, reported a bill to ascertain and establish the western boundary of the tract reserved for satisfying the military bounties allowed to the officers and soldiers of the Virginia line, on Continental Establishment. And the bill was read, and passed to the second reading.

Mr. BARBOUR, from the same committee, further made report, together with the following resolution:

Resolved, That provision should be made by law for satisfying the claims for land bounty of the officers and soldiers of the said State, on her own establishment.

And the report and resolution were read, and the further consideration thereof postponed to, and made the order of the day for, Tuesday next.

Mr. BARBOUR, from the Committee on Military Affairs, to whom was referred the memorial of the Legislature of Kentucky, relative to the widows and orphans of the militia, who died in the service of the United States, made a report; which was read.

A message from the House of Representatives informed the Senate that the House have passed a resolution to indemnify the sureties of Commodore John Rodgers, in which they request the concurrence of the Senate.

The Senate resumed, as in Committee of the Whole, the consideration of the bill, entitled "An act to authorize the payment for property lost, captured, or destroyed by the enemy, while in the military service of the United States."

Mr. MASON, of New Hampshire, proposed to insert in the bill the following amendment:

"That the President of the United States be and he is hereby authorized to appoint so many commissioners as he shall deem necessary for the purposes hereinafter mentioned, who shall be respectively sworn faithfully to perform their trusts. All testimony to be admitted in support of any claim against the United States, within the provisions of this act, shall be taken on oath before some one of such commissioners. And it shall be the duty of the said commissioners carefully to examine all witnesses produced before them, on such interrogatories, and according to such instructions as shall be prescribed by the Secretary of the Treasury, touching the following claims, to wit:"

Considerable discussion took place on this amendment, in which Messrs. BARBOUR and TALBOT opposed, and Mr. MASON, of New Hampshire, supported the motion. Before the question was taken, the subject was laid, for the present, on the table, and the Senate proceeded to the consideration of Executive business.

WEDNESDAY, February 14.

The resolution to indemnify the sureties of Commodore John Rodgers was twice read, by unanimous consent, and considered as in Committee of the Whole, and passed to a third reading.

Mr. BARBOUR, from the Committee on Military Affairs, to whom was referred the petition of Daniel Renner and Nathaniel H. Heath, praying compensation for losses sustained by the depredation of the enemy, during their barbarous irruption into the District of Columbia, made a report, together with the following resolution, which was read:

Resolved, That the petition of Daniel Renner and Nathaniel H. Heath, is unreasonable, and ought not to be granted, and that they have leave to withdraw their petition.

Mr. BARBOUR, from the Committee on Military Affairs, to whom was referred the petition of Ignace Delino, made a report, together with the following resolutions; which were read:

Resolved, That the petition of Ignace Delino is reasonable, and ought to be granted.

Resolved, That provision should be made for ascertaining, with precision, the amount of losses sustained by the said Ignace Delino.

Mr. BARBOUR, from the Committee on Military Affairs, to whom was referred the memorial of Catharine Robertson, made a report, together with the following resolution; which was read:

Resolved, That the petition of Catharine Robertson be rejected.

Mr. HUNTER, from the committee to whom the subject was referred, reported the bill for the relief of Jacob Babbitt and John Dennis; and the bill was read, and passed to the second reading.

The bill for the relief of Lieutenant Colonel William Lawrence, of the Army of the United States, and of the officers, non-commissioned officers, and privates, composing the garrison of Fort Bowyer, in the Summer of the year 1814, was read the second time.

The Senate resumed the consideration of the report of the Committee on Naval Affairs, to whom was referred the petition of Sarah Goelet: Whereupon,

Resolved, That it would be inexpedient to grant the prayer of the petitioner, and that she have leave to withdraw her petition.

The Senate resumed the consideration of the report of the Committee on Naval Affairs, to whom was recommitted the bill, entitled "An act for the relief of George S. Wise," with instructions to inquire into the expediency of making some general provisions by law, for similar cases: Whereupon,

Resolved, That it is inexpedient to make any general provisions on the subject.

Mr. CAMPBELL communicated the instructions of the Legislature of the State of Tennessee, to their Senators in Congress, to use their best endeavors to have provision made for the payment of arms impressed and lost, or destroyed, in the service of the United States; which were read.

A message from the House of Representatives informed the Senate that the House *insist* on their amendments to the bill, entitled "An act concerning the convention to regulate the commerce between the territories of the United States and His Britannic Majesty." They ask a conference upon the subject of the disagreeing votes of the two Houses, and have appointed managers on their part.

They have passed a bill, entitled "An act to reduce the amount of direct tax upon the United States, and the District of Columbia, for the year 1816; and to repeal, in part, the act, entitled 'An act to provide additional revenue for defraying the expenses of Government, and maintaining the public credit, by laying a direct tax upon the United States, and to provide for assessing and collecting the same;" and also the act, entitled "An act to provide additional revenue for defraying the expenses of Government, and maintaining the public credit, by laying a direct tax upon the District of Columbia;" a bill, entitled "An act making appropriations for ordnance and ordnance stores, for the year 1816;" a bill, entitled "An act rewarding the officers and crew of the sloop of war Hornet, for the capture and destruction of the British sloop of war Penguin;" a " resolution requesting the President to present medals to Captain Stewart, and the officers of the frigate Constitution;" also, a "resolution requesting the President to present medals to Captain James Biddle, and the officers of the sloop of war Hornet;" in which bills and resolutions they request the concurrence of the Senate.

BRITISH DEPREDATIONS.

Mr. BARBOUR, from the Committee on Military Affairs, to whom were referred the petitions of Nicholas Boilevin, of John de Lassize, and of Jumonville de Villiers and others, praying compensation for losses sustained by the depredations of the enemy in the late war, made an adverse report thereon; which was read, and is as follows:

That no doubt exists on the minds of the committee as to the truth of the facts disclosed in the petitions; the losses complained of, resulting from a barbarous warfare carried on by the ferocious inhabitants of the wilds, as well as by the regular forces of His Britannic Majesty, have been most severe on the unfortunate petitioners. Whether it becomes the magnanimity of a Government whose only object should be the protection and prosperity of all its citizens to dispense relief in cases like these, and thereby to cause the war to fall equally on all, is a question which the committee believe is placed beyond their cognizance, in consequence of the course heretofore pursued by Congress in regard to losses sustained during the war—a course which seems to inculcate that indemnity is due to all those whose losses have arisen from the acts of our own Government, or those acting under its authority; while losses produced by the conduct of the enemy are to be classed among the unavoidable calamities of war, and do not entitle the sufferers to indemnification by the Government. The losses of the petitioners belong to the latter class, and therefore the committee, yielding to what is believed to be the settled purpose of Congress, have agreed to the following resolution:

Resolved, That the petitions of Nicholas Boilevin, John de Lassize, and Jumonville de Villiers, and others, are unreasonable, and ought not to be granted.

THURSDAY, February 15.

On motion by Mr. BARRY, a committee was appointed to inquire into the expediency of extending, by law, to all settlers on the public lands of the United States, who have settled thereon since the 1st day of January, 1808, the same privilege extended to each settled prior to that day, by the second section of the act of Congress, passed

March 3d, 1807; and that they have leave to report by bill or otherwise; and Messrs. BARRY, MORROW, and BROWN, were appointed the committee.

On motion by Mr. KING,

Ordered, That the Secretary of the Senate procure for their use four copies of Brice's Selection of the Commercial Laws of the United States; also four copies of Graydon's Digest of the Laws of the United States; and also four copies of Pitkin's Statistical View of the Commerce of the United States.

Mr. GOLDSBOROUGH presented the petition of E. R. Dupont, and others, manufacturers of gunpowder, praying an increase of duty on foreign gunpowder, and also to exempt it from the benefit of a drawback of duties on its re-exportation, as stated in the petition; which was read, and referred to the Committee on Finance and an Uniform National Currency.

Mr. CONDIT presented the petition of Israel Crane, and others, manufacturers of cotton, in West Bloomfield, in the State of New Jersey, praying the protection of Congress, for reasons stated in the petition; which was read, and referred to the committee last mentioned.

The three bills and two resolutions brought up yesterday for concurrence, were read, and passed to the second reading.

On motion by Mr. BIBB,

Resolved, That the Senate *insist* on their disagreement to the amendments of the House of Representatives to the bill, entitled "An act concerning the convention to regulate the commerce between the territories of the United States and His Britannic Majesty," and agree to the conference proposed thereon.

Ordered, That Messrs. KING, BARBOUR, and BIBB, be the managers on the part of the Senate.

The resolution to indemnify the sureties of Commodore Rodgers, was read a third time, and passed—yeas 22, nays 5, as follows:

YEAS—Messrs. Barbour, Barry, Bibb, Brown, Chace, Condit, Daggett, Gaillard, Goldsborough, Harper, Howell, Hunter, Mason of New Hampshire, Mason of Virginia, Roberts, Ruggles, Talbot, Tait, Tichenor, Turner, Williams, and Wilson.

NAYS—Messrs. King, Macon, Morrow, Thompson, and Varnum.

Mr. DAGGETT, from the committee to whom was recommitted the bill, entitled "An act for the relief of Jonathan Rogers, jun., of Waterford, in the State of Connecticut," reported it without amendment.

Mr. HARPER gave notice that he should ask leave to bring in a bill to establish a law library at the Seat of Government, for the use of the Supreme Court of the United States; and also a bill to limit the right of appeal and writ of error from the circuit court of the United States, to cases amounting to —— dollars, or upwards.

On motion by Mr. BIBB, the Committee on Foreign Relations, to whom were referred the petitions of Arthur Tappan and John Frothingham, were discharged from the further consideration thereof, respectively.

The Senate resumed the consideration of the report of the Committee on Military Affairs, to whom was referred the petitions of Nicholas Boilevin, of John de Lassize, and of Jumonville de Villiers, and others.

On the question to agree thereto, it was determined in the affirmative—yeas 26, nays 3, as follows:

YEAS—Messrs. Barbour, Barry, Bibb, Condit, Daggett, Gaillard, Harper, Howell, Hunter, King, Lacock, Macon, Mason of New Hampshire, Mason of Virginia, Morrow, Roberts, Ruggles, Talbot, Tait, Taylor, Thompson, Tichenor, Turner, Varnum, Williams, and Wilson.

NAYS—Messrs. Brown, Fromentin, Goldsborough.

So it was *Resolved*, That the petitions of Nicholas Boilevin, John de Lassize, and Jumonville de Villiers, and others, are unreasonable, and ought not to be granted.

The Senate resumed the consideration of the report of the Committee on Military Affairs, on the petition of Daniel Renner, and Nathaniel H. Heath. Whereupon,

Resolved, That the petition of Daniel Renner and Nathaniel H. Heath is unreasonable, and ought not to be granted; and that they have leave to withdraw their petition.

The Senate resumed the consideration of the report of the Committee on Military Affairs on the memorial of Catharine Robertson; and the further consideration thereof was postponed until Saturday next.

The Senate resumed the consideration of the report of the Committee on Military Affairs, on the petition of the representatives of Ignace Delino; and the further consideration thereof was postponed until Wednesday next.

The bill for the relief of Jacob Babbit and John Dennis, was read the second time.

The bill to ascertain and establish the boundary of the tract reserved to satisfy the military bounties allowed to the officers and soldiers of the Virginia line, on Continental Establishment, was read the second time.

FRIDAY, February 16.

The PRESIDENT communicated a report of the Secretary of the Treasury, on the petition of Sarah Jarvis and others, prepared in obedience to the resolution of the Senate of the 12th instant; and the report was read.

The resolution requesting the President of the United States to present medals to Captain Chas. Stewart, and the officers of the frigate Constitution, was read the second time.

The resolution requesting the President of the United States to present medals to Captain James Biddle, and the officers of the sloop of war Hornet, was read the second time.

The bill, entitled "An act to reduce the amount of direct tax upon the United States, and the District of Columbia, for the year 1816; and to repeal in part the act, entitled 'An act to provide additional revenue for defraying the expenses of Government, and maintaining the public credit, by laying a direct tax upon the United States, and to provide for assessing and collecting the same;" and also the act, entitled "An act to provide additional revenue for defraying the expenses of Government, and maintaining the public credit, by laying a direct tax upon the District of Columbia;" was read the second time, and referred to the Committee on Finance and an Uniform National Currency.

The bill entitled "An act making appropriations for ordnance and ordnance stores, for the year 1816," was read the second time, and referred to the committee last mentioned.

The bill, entitled "An act rewarding the officers and crew of the sloop of war Hornet, for the capture and destruction of the British sloop of war Penguin;" was read the second time, and referred to the Committee on Naval Affairs.

The Senate resumed, as in Committee of the Whole, the consideration of the bill for the relief of Richard Mitchell; and the further consideration thereof was postponed until Monday next.

A message from the House of Representatives informed the Senate that the House have passed the bill, entitled "An act to increase the pensions of Robert White and Jacob Wrighter," with amendments; in which they request the concurrence of the Senate.

On motion, by Mr. VARNUM, the amendments of the House of Representatives to the bill last mentioned, together with the bill, was referred to the Committee on Military Affairs.

The Senate resumed the consideration of the bill authorizing the opening and working copper mines on Lake Superior, and for other purposes; and, on the question, Shall this bill be engrossed and read a third time? it was determined in the negative.

The Senate resumed, as in Committee of the Whole, the bill making appropriations for the construction of roads and canals; and the further consideration thereof was postponed to, and made the order of the day for, Monday next.

The bill to authorize the Secretary of the Treasury to subscribe, in behalf of the United States, for —— shares in the capital stock of the Chesapeake and Delaware Canal Company, was resumed as in Committee of the Whole; and the further consideration thereof was postponed to, and made the order of the day for, Monday next.

The Senate resumed, as in Committee of the Whole, the consideration of the bill, entitled "An act to repeal the duties on certain articles manufactured within the United States;" and the further consideration thereof was postponed until Monday next.

The Senate resumed, as in Committee of the Whole, the consideration of the bill further supplementary to the act, entitled "An act providing for the indemnification of certain claimants of public land in the Mississippi Territory;" and the further consideration thereof was postponed to, and made the order of the day for, Tuesday next.

The Senate resumed, as in Committee of the Whole, the consideration of the bill, entitled "An act for the relief of George S. Wise;" and the further consideration thereof was postponed until the first Monday in July next.

The Senate resumed, as in Committee of the Whole, the consideration of the bill for the relief of Lieutenant Colonel William Lawrence, of the Army of the United States, and of the officers, non-commissioned officers, and privates, composing the garrison of Fort Bowyer, in the Summer of the year 1814; and the further consideration thereof was postponed until Monday next.

The Senate resumed, as in Committee of the Whole, the consideration of the bill, for the relief of Jacob Babbitt and John Dennis; and, after debate, the further consideration thereof was postponed until Wednesday next.

The Senate resumed, as in Committee of the Whole, the consideration of the bill, entitled "An act for the relief of Jonathan Rogers, junior, of Waterford, in the State of Connecticut," and Mr. VARNUM was requested to take the Chair; and no amendment having been proposed thereto, the PRESIDENT resumed the Chair, and Mr. VARNUM reported the bill to the Senate; and it passed to a third reading.

The Senate resumed, as in Committee of the Whole, the bill, entitled "An act for the relief of John Redman Coxe," together with the amendment reported thereto by the select committee; and the amendment having been agreed to, the PRESIDENT reported the bill to the House accordingly; and on the question, "Shall the amendment be engrossed, and the bill read a third time as amended?" it was determined in the affirmative.

Mr. KING presented the petition of B. E. Verjon, praying a patent right may be granted to him for certain improvements in refining sugar, notwithstanding his non-residence in the United States for the term required by law; and the petition was read, and referred to a select committee; and Messrs. KING, BROWN, and HUNTER, were appointed the committee.

Mr. HARPER asked and obtained leave to bring in a bill to establish a law library, at the Seat of Government, for the use of the Supreme Court of the United States; and the bill was read, and passed to the second reading.

Mr. HARPER also asked and obtained leave to bring in a bill to limit the right of appeal from the circuit court of the United States for the District of Columbia; and the bill was read, and passed to the second reading.

Mr. BARRY, from the committee appointed to consider the subject, reported a bill relating to settlers on the lands of the United States; and the bill was read, and passed to a second reading.

Adjourned to Monday.

MONDAY, February 19.

The PRESIDENT communicated a report of the Secretary of the Treasury, exhibiting the actual condition of the several incorporated banks within the District of Columbia, on the 1st day of January, 1816, as reported by the cashiers, to that Department, made in compliance with the resolution of the Senate of the 8th instant, and the report was read.

Mr. TAYLOR presented the petition of John Philip Wilhelmi, a citizen of the United States, praying permission to bring into the United States certain slaves from the island of Saint Thomas, as stated and described in the petition; which was read, and referred to a select committee; and Messrs. TAYLOR, VARNUM, and BIBB, were appointed the committee.

Mr. ROBERTS, from the committee to whom was referred the petition of John L. Pearson, made a report, which was read.—Whereupon,

Resolved, That the petitioner have leave to withdraw his petition.

Mr. HORSEY presented the memorial of David Rymes, and others, citizens of the borough of Wilmington, in the State of Delaware; and also the memorial of the burgesses and borough council of the said borough, praying protection to the manufacturing establishments in the United States, for reasons stated in the memorials; which were read, and referred to the Committee on Manufactures.

Mr. HUNTER gave notice, that to-morrow he should ask leave to bring in a bill providing for the publication of the decisions of the Supreme Court of the United States.

The bill relating to settlers on the lands of the United States, was read the second time.

The bill to limit the right of appeal from the circuit court of the United States for the District of Columbia, was read the second time.

The bill to establish a law library at the Seat of Government, for the use of the Supreme Court of the United States, was read the second time.

The Senate resumed, as in Committee of the Whole, the consideration of the bill making appropriation for the construction of roads and canals, and Mr. VARNUM was requested to take the Chair; and the bill having been amended, the further consideration thereof was postponed to, and made the order of the day for, Monday next.

The Senate resumed, as in Committee of the Whole, the consideration of the bill to authorize the Secretary of the Treasury to subscribe, in behalf of the United States, for —— shares in the capital stock of the Chesapeake and Delaware Canal Company; and the further consideration thereof was postponed to, and made the order of the day for, Monday next.

The bill entitled "An act for the relief of Jonathan Rogers, jr., of Waterford, in the State of Connecticut," was read a third time, and passed.

Mr. KING, from the committee to whom the subject was referred, reported a bill to extend certain privileges, as therein mentioned, to Bernard Edme Verjon; and the bill was read, and passed to the second reading.

The Senate resumed, as in Committee of the Whole, the consideration of the bill entitled "An act to authorize the payment for property lost, captured, or destroyed, by the enemy, while in the military service of the United States," and Mr. TALBOT proposed sundry amendments thereto; and, on motion by Mr. T., the further consideration of the bill. together with the several amendments proposed thereto, was postponed to, and made the order of the day for, to-morow.

The Senate resumed, as in Committee of the Whole, the bill for the relief of Richard Mitchell; and the further consideration thereof was postponed until to-morrow.

The Senate resumed, as in Committee of the Whole, the consideration of the bill entitled "An act to repeal the duties on certain articles manufactured within the United States;" and it passed to a third reading.

The amendment to the bill entitled "An act for the relief of John Redman Coxe," was read a third time as amended, and passed.

Mr. Fromentin presented the memorial of John Jones, and others, interested in lands in the State of Louisiana, held under Spanish grants, praying a confirmation thereof, as stated in the memorial; which was read, and referred to the committee on the memorial of the Legislature of the Mississippi Territory.

A message from the House of Representatives informed the Senate that the House have passed a resolution for the appointment of a joint committee to examine into the proceedings of a former Congress, on the lamented death of the late George Washington, and to take into consideration what further measures it may be expedient to adopt at the present time, in relation to that solemn and interesting subject, in which they request the concurrence of the Senate.

· The resolution last mentioned was read three times by unanimous consent, and concurred in.

Ordered, That Messrs. King, Varnum, and Barbour, be the committee on their part.

The Senate resumed, as in Committee of the Whole, the consideration of the bill for the relief of Lieutenant Colonel William Lawrence, of the Army of the United States, and of the officers, non-commissioned officers, and privates, composing the garrison of Fort Bowyer, in the Summer of the year 1814; and, no amendment having been proposed thereto, on the question, "Shall this bill be engrossed and read a third time?" it was determined in the affirmative.

The Senate resumed, as in Committee of the Whole, the bill to ascertain and establish the western boundary of the tract reserved for satisfying the military bounties allowed to the officers and soldiers of the Virginia line on Continental Establishment; and the further consideration thereof was postponed until to-morrow.

The Senate resumed, as in Committee of the Whole, the consideration of the resolution requesting the President of the United States to present medals to Captain Charles Stewart, and the officers of the frigate Constitution; and, no amendment having been proposed thereto, it passed to a third reading.

The Senate resumed the consideration of the report of the Committee on Military Affairs, on the petition of Catharine Robertson; and the further consideration thereof was postponed until the third Monday in March next.

The Senate resumed, as in Committee of the Whole, the consideration of the resolution requesting the President of the United States to present medals to Captain James Biddle, and the officers of the sloop of war Hornet; and, no amendment having been proposed thereto, it passed to a third reading.

Mr. Tait, from the Committee on Naval Affairs, to whom was referred the bill entitled "An act rewarding the officers and crew of the sloop of war Hornet, for the capture and destruction of the British sloop of war Penguin," reported it without amendment.

Mr. Hunter asked and obtained leave to bring in a bill providing for the publication of the decisions of the Supreme Court of the United States; and the bill was read, and passed to the second reading.

The resolution requesting the President of the United States to present medals to Capt. Charles Stewart, and the officers of the frigate Constitution, was read a third time.

Resolved, unanimously, That this resolution pass.

The resolution requesting the President of the United States to present medals to Captain James Biddle, and the officers of the sloop of war Hornet, was read the third time.

Resolved, unanimously, That this resolution pass.

The bill for the relief of Lieutenant Colonel William Lawrence, of the Army of the United States, and of the officers, non-commissioned officers, and privates, composing the garrison of Fort Bowyer, in the Summer of the year 1814, was read the third time, and passed.

The bill entitled "An act to repeal the duties on certain articles manufactured within the United States," was read the third time, and passed.

The Senate resumed, as in Committee of the Whole, the consideration of the bill further supplementary to the act, entitled "An act providing for the indemnification of certain claimants of public lands in the Mississippi Territory;" and, no amendment having been proposed thereto, on the question, "Shall this bill be engrossed, and read a third time?" it was determined in the affirmative.

The bill to extend certain privileges, as therein mentioned, to Bernard Edme Verjon, was read the second time, and considered as in Committee of the Whole; and, having been amended, the President reported it to the House accordingly; and on the question, "Shall this bill be engrossed and read a third time?" it was determined in the affirmative.

The bill was then read a third time by unanimous consent, and passed.

Mr. Barbour, from the Committee on Military Affairs, to whom was referred the amendments of the House of Representatives to the bill entitled "An act to increase the pensions of Robert White and Jacob Wrighter," reported that the Senate agree thereto, with amendments.

The Senate resumed, as in Committee of the Whole, the consideration of the bill entitled "An act to authorize the payment for property lost, captured, or destroyed, by the enemy, while in the military service of the United States, together with the amendments proposed thereto;" and, on motion by Mr. TALBOT, the further consideration thereof was postponed to, and made the order of the day for, to-morrow.

The Senate resumed, as in Committee of the Whole, the resolution for a proposed amendment to the Constitution of the United States, that the Senators shall be chosen for three years; and on motion by Mr TAYLOR, the further consideration thereof was postponed until Monday next.

The Senate resumed, as in Committee of the Whole, the consideration of the bill, to limit the right of appeal from the circuit court of the United States, for the District of Columbia; and on the question, "Shall this bill be engrossed, and read a third time?" it was determined in the affirmative.

The Senate resumed, as in Committee of the Whole, the bill for the relief of Richard Mitchell; and the further consideration thereof was postponed until to-morrow.

The Senate resumed, as in Committee of the Whole, the bill to ascertain and establish the western boundary of the tract reserved for satisfying the military bounties, allowed to the officers and soldiers of the Virginia line, on Continental Establishment; and the further consideration thereof was postponed until to-morrow.

The Senate resumed, as in Committee of the Whole, the consideration of the bill, to establish a law library at the Seat of Government, for the use of the Supreme Court of the United States.

On motion by Mr. TALBOT, it was referred to a select committee, to consider and report thereon; and Mr. TALBOT, Mr. HARPER, and Mr. HUNTER, were appointed the committee.

The Senate resumed, as in Committee of the Whole, the consideration of the bill, relating to settlers on the lands of the United States; and the bill having been amended, on motion by Mr. BIBB, it was recommitted to Mr. BARRY, Mr. MORROW, and Mr. BROWN, further to consider, and report thereon.

PETITION OF THOMAS CUTTS.

Mr. CAMPBELL, from the Committee on Finance and an Uniform National Currency, to whom was referred the petition of Thomas Cutts, of Biddeford, in the State of Massachusetts, made a report, which was read, as follows:

· That a judgment was recovered in favor of the United States against Tristram Hooper, Moses Lowell, and Benjamin Chandler, on a revenue bond; an execution issued thereon against their property, and was levied by the deputy marshal for the District of Maine, on three-eighth parts of the schooner Catharine, at the sale of which, on the 19th January, 1806, the petitioner, Thomas Cutts, became the purchaser, at four hundred and twenty-five dollars. A claim was afterwards set up to the said three-eighths of said schooner by Asa Stephens, founded on an attachment previously levied

thereon; and in an action brought against the petitioner, it appears the title of the said Stephens to three-fourth parts of said three-eighth parts of said schooner was established; and it was of course decided, that no right to the said three-fourth parts vested in the petitioner by his purchase at said marshal's sale. The petitioner alleges that, besides the loss of the three-fourths of said three-eighths of this vessel, he has been put to great expense and trouble in defending his supposed title, derived from said marshal's sale, and prays such relief as Congress may deem just and equitable.

The committee cannot perceive anything in this case to distinguish it from the ordinary case of a sale under an execution, in which the plaintiff cannot be considered as warranting the title to the property. The purchaser buys at his own risk, and must judge for himself, from the best information he can obtain, whether the title of defendant in the execution be good or not; and it is believed he generally regulates the price he offers according to the opinion he forms on this point. The committee are therefore of opinion the petitioner is not entitled to relief, and recommend to the Senate the following resolution:

Resolved, That the prayer of the petitioner ought not to be granted.

WEDNESDAY, February 21.

The Senate resumed the consideration of the amendments of the House of Representatives to the bill entitled "An act to increase the pensions of Robert White and Jacob Wrighter," together with the report of the Committee on Military Affairs thereon; and the report having been disagreed to,

Resolved, That they agree to the amendments of the House of Representatives to this bill.

Mr. VARNUM, from the Committee on the Militia of the United States, reported, in part, a bill concerning field officers of the militia; and the bill was read, and passed to the second reading

On motion by Mr. HARPER, the further consideration of the engrossed bill to limit the right of appeal from the circuit court of the United States for the District of Columbia, was postponed until Wednesday next.

The Senate resumed, agreeably to special order, the consideration of the report of the committee to whom was referred the resolution relating to the claims of the officers and soldiers of the Virginia line, on State and Continental Establishment for bounty lands, which recommends that provision should be made by law, for satisfying the claims for land bounty of the officers and soldiers of the said State, on her own establishment; and after debate, on motion by Mr. MASON, of New Hampshire, the further consideration thereof was postponed to the first Monday in March next.

On motion by Mr. MASON of New Hampshire, the further consideration of the bill to ascertain and establish the western boundary of the tract reserved for satisfying the military bounties allowed the officers and soldiers of the Virginia line, on Continental Establishment, was postponed to the first Monday in March next.

Mr. FROMENTIN, from the committee, reported the bill further supplementary to the act entitled

"An act providing for the indemnification of certain claimants of public land in the Mississippi Territory," correctly engrossed; and, on motion by Mr. TAYLOR, it was recommitted to Mr. TAYLOR, Mr. HUNTER, and Mr. MORROW, further to consider and report thereon.

A message from the House of Representatives informed the Senate that they have passed a bill entitled "An act granting bounties in land and extra pay to certain Canadian volunteers;" in which bill they request the concurrence of the Senate.

The bill last mentioned was read, and passed to the second reading.

Mr. MASON, of Virginia, presented the petition of the President, Directors, and Company of the Central Bank of Georgetown and Washington, praying a charter of incorporation, for reasons stated in the petition; which was read, and referred to the Committee on Finance and an Uniform National Currency.

The Senate resumed, as in Committee of the Whole, the consideration of the bill, entitled "An act to authorize the payment for property lost, captured, or destroyed, by the enemy, while in the military service of the United States," together with the several amendments proposed thereto; and, on motion by Mr. BARRY, the further consideration thereof was postponed until to-morrow.

The Senate resumed, as in Committee of the Whole, the bill for the relief of Jacob Babbitt and John Dennis; and, on motion by Mr. VARNUM, the further consideration thereof was postponed until Friday next.

The Senate resumed the consideration of the report of the Committee on Military Affairs, on the petition of the representatives of Ignace Delino; and, on motion by Mr. BARBOUR, the further consideration thereof was postponed to the first Wednesday in March next.

The Senate resumed, as in Committee of the Whole, the consideration of the bill entitled "An act rewarding the officers and crew of the sloop of war Hornet, for the capture and destruction of the British sloop of war Penguin;" and, no amendment having been proposed thereto, it passed to a third reading.

The Senate resumed the bill for the relief of Richard Mitchell, and the further consideration thereof was postponed until to-morrow.

THURSDAY, February 22.

The bill entitled "An act granting bounties in land and extra pay to certain Canadian volunteers," was read the second time, and referred to the Committee on Military Affairs.

Mr. TAYLOR presented the petition of Dominique Diron, of Charleston, in the State of South Carolina, praying compensation for a certain vessel burnt in the port of Savannah, in Georgia, in November 1811, as stated in the petition; which was read, and referred to the Secretary for the Department of State.

Mr. LACOCK, from the committee to whom was referred the memorial of Walter Jones, jun., and others, reported a bill concerning the District of Columbia; and the bill was read, and passed to the second reading.

The bill concerning field officers of the militia was read the second time.

The bill entitled "An act rewarding the officers and crew of the sloop of war Hornet, for the capture and destruction of the British sloop of war Penguin," was read a third time, and passed.

The Senate resumed, as in Committee of the Whole, the bill for the relief of Richard Mitchell; and, on motion by Mr. DAGGETT, the further consideration thereof was postponed until Monday next.

The Senate resumed, as in Committee of the Whole, the consideration of the bill providing for the publication of the decisions of the Supreme Court of the United States.

On motion by Mr. HUNTER, it was referred to a select committee, to consider and report thereon; and Messrs. HUNTER, MASON of New Hampshire, and TALBOT, were appointed the committee.

The Senate resumed the report of the Committee on Finance, on the petition of Thomas Cutts; and, on motion by Mr. CHASE, the further consideration thereof was postponed until Thursday next.

The Senate resumed, as in Committee of the Whole, the bill, entitled "An act to authorize the payment for property lost, captured, or destroyed by the enemy, while in the military service of the United States," together with the several amendments proposed thereto; and, on motion by Mr. FROMENTIN, the further consideration thereof was postponed until to-morrow.

Mr. CAMPBELL, from the Committee on Finance and an Uniform National Currency, to whom was referred the bill, entitled "An act to reduce the amount of direct tax upon the United States and the District of Columbia, for the year 1816; and to repeal, in part, the act entitled 'An act to provide additional revenue for defraying the expenses of Government, and maintaining the public credit, by laying a direct tax upon the United States, and to provide for assessing and collecting the same;" and also the act entitled "An act to provide additional revenue for defraying the expenses of Government, and maintaining the public credit, by laying a direct tax upon the District of Columbia;" reported it with amendments.

A message from the House of Representatives announced to the Senate the death of the honorable ELIJAH BRIGHAM, late a member of the House of Representatives, from the State of Massachusetts, and that his funeral will take place to-morrow, at 12 o'clock.

On motion by Mr. VARNUM,

Resolved unanimously, That the Senate will attend the funeral of the honorable ELIJAH BRIGHAM, late a member of the House of Representatives, from the State of Massachusetts, to-morrow at 12 o'clock; and, as a testimony of respect for the memory of the deceased, they will go into mourning, and wear a black crape round the left arm, for thirty days.

147   HISTORY OF CONGRESS.   148

FRIDAY, February 23.

The Senate assembled and adjourned to Monday.

MONDAY, February 26.

The PRESIDENT communicated a letter from the Secretary of the Treasury, accompanied with a statement of emoluments of the officers employed in the collection of the customs, for the year 1815; which were read.

On motion by Mr. TAIT, the Committee on Naval Affairs, to whom was referred the memorial of Thomas Ap Catesby Jones, a lieutenant in the Navy, of Robert Jones and others, and of Joseph Henry and others, were discharged from the further consideration thereof respectively; and they had leave to withdraw their memorials.

Mr. ROBERTS presented the petition of the Mayor, Aldermen, and Common Council of the City of Washington, representing that great delay and injury is experienced, from not having a port of entry therein; and the petition was read, and referred to the Committee on Finance and an Uniform National Currency.

Mr. ROBERTS presented the memorial of the Bible Society of Philadelphia, praying that provision may be made to exempt from duty, certain stereotype editions of the sacred scriptures, and bibles and testaments in foreign languages, as may be hereafter imported by bible societies, for reasons stated in the memorial; which was read, and referred to the committee last mentioned.

Mr. ROBERTS, also presented the memorial of the American Convention for promoting the abolition of Slavery, recommending the adoption of certain measures for the promotion of the interests of that unhappy class of their fellow beings, involved in the thraldom of slavery, as stated in the memorial; which was read, and referred to a select committee, to consist of five members; and Messrs. ROBERTS, KING, RUGGLES, MASON, of Virginia, and CHACE, were appointed the committee.

Mr. HORSEY presented the petition of John Rudolph, of the borough of Wilmington, in the State of Delaware, praying remuneration for losses sustained as contractor for supplying rations to troops in the service of the United States, during the late war, as stated in the petition; which was read, and referred to the Committee on Military Affairs.

Mr. CHACE presented the petition of Robert Lovewell, of St. Albans, in the State of Vermont, praying a pension, in consideration of a wound received while in the service of the United States, during the late war, as stated in the petition; which was read, and referred to the Committee on Military Affairs.

Mr. CHACE also presented the petition of Benjamin Putnam, of Windsor county, in the State of Vermont, praying some compensation in consideration of his sufferings, during his captivity, and remuneration for sacrifices he made to regain his liberty, having been captured by the enemy during the late war, as is stated in the petition;

which was read, and referred to the Committee on Military Affairs.

Mr. LACOCK, from the committee to whom the subject was referred, reported a bill dividing the State of Pennsylvania into two judicial districts; and the bill was read, and passed to the second reading.

On motion by Mr. KING, a member was added to the committee on the proceedings on the lamented death of the late GEORGE WASHINGTON, in place of Mr. BARBOUR; and Mr. MASON, of Virginia, was elected.

Mr. BROWN, from the committee to whom the subject was referred, reported a bill for the relief of Edward Wilson; and the bill was read, and passed to the second reading.

The bill concerning the District of Columbia was read the second time.

Agreeably to special order the Senate resumed, as in Committee of the Whole, the consideration of the bill making appropriation for the construction of roads and canals; and on the question, "Shall this bill be engrossed and read a third time?" it was determined in the affirmative.

The Senate resumed, as in Committee of the Whole, the bill to authorize the Secretary of the Treasury to subscribe, in behalf of the United States, for —— shares in the capital stock of the Chesapeake and Delaware Canal Company; and, on motion by Mr. MORROW, the consideration thereof was further postponed, and made the order of the day for to-morrow.

The Senate resumed, as in Committee of the Whole, the bill entitled "An act to authorize the payment for property lost, captured, or destroyed by the enemy, while in the military service of the United States," together with the amendments proposed thereto; and, on motion by Mr. DAGGETT, the consideration thereof was further postponed until to-morrow.

The Senate resumed, as in Committee of the Whole, the consideration of the bill concerning field officers of the militia; and, the bill having been amended, the PRESIDENT reported it to the Senate accordingly; and on the question, "Shall this bill be engrossed and read a third time?" it was determined in the affirmative.

The Senate resumed, as in Committee of the Whole the consideration of the bill for the relief of Jacob Babbitt and John Dennis; and on the question, "Shall this bill be engrossed and read a third time?" it was determined in the affirmative.

Mr. TAIT gave notice that to-morrow he should ask leave to bring in a bill to increase the pension of William Munday.

The Senate resumed the consideration of the resolution for a proposed amendment to the Constitution of the United States, for choosing the Senators thereof; and, on motion by Mr. WILSON, the consideration thereof was further postponed to, and made the order of the day for, to-morrow.

Mr. HORSEY submitted the following motion for consideration:

Resolved, That a committee be appointed to inquire

whether it would be expedient and proper to prohibit by law the formation of private banking associations, in future, within the District of Columbia; and also to consider and inquire whether it would be expedient and proper to prohibit by law the emission and circulation of the notes of all unchartered banks within the said District, which shall not have obtained charters on or before the —— day of —— next.

A message from the House of Representatives informed the Senate that the House have concurred in the report of the committee of conference, on the disagreeing votes of the two Houses. upon the amendments proposed by the House of Representatives to the bill, entitled "An act concerning the convention to regulate the commerce between the territories of the United States and His Britannic Majesty;" and that the bill be amended accordingly. They have passed a bill, entitled "An act making further provision for military services during the late war, and for other purposes;" in which they request the concurrence of the Senate.

The bill last mentioned was read, and passed to the second reading.

ROBERT FULTON'S HEIRS.

Mr. KING presented the petition of Harriet Fulton, widow and executrix of the late Robert Fulton, praying the extension of his patent, as inventor of a method of navigating vessels by the agency of fire and steam, for reasons stated in the petition; which was read, and referred to a select committee to consist of five members; and Messrs. KING, DAGGETT, MASON of Virginia, MORROW, and CHACE, were appointed the committee.

The memorial is as follows:

To the honorable the Congress of the United States:

The petition of Harriet Fulton, widow and executrix of the late Robert Fulton, humbly represents:

That the said Robert Fulton, on the 11th day of February, 1809, and on the 9th day of February, 1811, obtained two patents from the President of the United States, as the inventor of a method of navigating vessels by the agency of fire and steam; and departed this life on the 23d day of February last, leaving your petitioner and four young children dependant on his said invention for support, and a large debt, which arose from his unwearied and expensive efforts in prosecuting and perfecting this great improvement.

That notwithstanding various attempts have been made to propel vessels by the power of steam, yet he was the first person who established its practical effects in navigation. It is unnecessary to expatiate on the advantages of this important discovery; they are particularly felt and acknowledged in all parts of the civilised world. America, peculiarly favored in the number, magnitude, extent, and importance of her navigable waters, must look for her highest prosperity in her internal communication and trade; and it is now undeniably established that steam vessels can surmount difficulties heretofore considered insuperable; that neither tide, nor wind, nor current, can arrest their course; and that for velocity of progress, economy of transportation, and facility of communication, they are superior to all competition.

It is well known to your honorable body that all great improvements in human affairs are the result of patient investigation and elaborate industry; that, in their origin, their progress, and final perfection, application must be associated with genius; and, particularly in those beneficial inventions which are connected with combinations of mechanical powers, not only extraordinary faculties are required, but heavy expenses must be incurred, great risks must be sustained, and much time must be consumed, before they are brought to any perfection. The greatest benefactors of the human race have generally done but little for themselves; and, after having devoted their lives with indefatigable labor and with disinterested zeal to the general good, they have left no legacy to their posterity but an illustrious reputation.

Your petitioner is fully sensible of the delicacy of her situation; she is conscious that she may expose herself to the imputation of vanity; but surely the partiality of a wife will be pardoned, and the tender affections of a parent consulting the welfare of her children will be an apology. In order to support their cause, it is necessary to speak of their father, and, alas! all her recollections of his worth are imbittered by affliction for her loss.

After the husband of your petitioner had obtained a patent for his invention, several years necessarily elapsed before he derived any revenue from it, and in the intervening time he was exposed to enormous expense. He, in consequence, left a debt exceeding $150,000, which was incurred to raise the capital required for this complicated and expensive operation; neither was he, in his lifetime, able to derive any profit from the sale of his patent right, but incurred great expense in defending it against charges and imputations that the same had not been regularly obtained, or that some formal requisite had been omitted; when, without his enthusiasm, industry, and talents, this great improvement would, probably, have been lost to the world.

If the patronage of Government ought to be in proportion to the benefits diffused, then your petitioner can, without arrogance, appear before you, and solicit, in behalf of herself and her children, a liberal extension of his patent; for, without this indulgence, it will be impossible to derive any essential benefit from it.

It has been the policy of enlightened Governments in modern times to encourage the efforts of genius, and to hasten the progress of discovery, by exclusive privileges for definite periods; a limitation of time is, of course, prescribed as a rule of general application, during which it is presumed that the patentee will obtain a sufficient remuneration for his expenses, and for the benefits he has rendered to society; but, on extraordinary occasions, justice and expediency unite in favor of extending the time of the grant, and cases have frequently occurred where this indulgence has been obtained.

In Great Britain a patent for fourteen years was granted to James Watt for a newly invented method of lessening the consumption of steam and fuel in fire engines; an act of Parliament was, six years thereafter, passed, extending the privileges given by the patent to twenty-five years. Thus Mr. Watt, for an improvement in steam engines, received from the munificence of the British Government exclusive privileges for thirty-one years. The case of Oliver Evans is well known; he obtained a patent for an improvement in the machinery of mills, and Congress afterwards passed a law extending the patent seven years; and, notwithstanding the acknowledged utility of those inventions, no one will contend that they ought to be placed on an equal footing with steam vessels.

But your petitioner's husband did not confine his views to this subject alone. The public defence occupied his utmost attention, and engaged his most anxious solicitude. During the late war he devised a steam frigate for the better protection of our cities and harbors. While superintending the execution of this impregnable fortress, he laid the foundation of the disease which terminated his life in a short period. And ought not the widow and the offspring of the man who has planned the means of protecting his country against its enemies to be placed above the pressure of embarrassment and the humiliation of dependence? For such services he never sought, or intended to receive, any remuneration from the Government.

Your petitioner thus confidently appeals to the justice and the bounty of your honorable body in behalf of the children of a man who died while zealously employed in the service of his country, and who has conferred the most extensive benefits upon the world. Let not the widow and the orphan plead to you in vain.

And your petitioner will ever pray, &c.
         HARRIET FULTON.
NEW YORK, *January,* 1816.

SENATE CHAMBER, *March* 14, 1816.

DEAR SIR: An application has been made to Congress, in behalf of the widow and children of the late Mr. Fulton, for an extension of his patents for steamboats. As a popular opinion has existed that Mr. Fulton, before his death, had derived great profits from the privileges secured to him by these patents, and that his family will be likely to derive therefrom further and great emolument during the unexpired term of the patents, I am directed by a committee of the Senate to which the petition from Mr. Fulton's family is referred, to obtain such information as is within our reach respecting the situation of the pecuniary affairs or estate of Mr. Fulton. If Mr. Fulton's family already possess, or are likely to acquire, during the residue of the term of the patents, a liberal remuneration for his invention, there would seem to be no sufficient reason in favor of an extension of the patents; while, on the other hand, if such remuneration has not been, or is not likely to be received, during the unexpired term of the patents, such is the very great public utility of the steamboats which have been brought into use by Mr. Fulton, that a strong motive would be found to exist for a prolonging of the patents for the benefit of Mr. Fulton's family.

As Mr. Fulton lived in New York, the city of your residence, and was well known by you, it has occurred to me that it may be in your power to give to the committee some information on this subject.

With very great respect, I have the honor to be, dear sir, your most obedient servant,
         RUFUS KING.
BROCKHOLST LIVINGSTON.

WASHINGTON, *March* 14, 1816.

DEAR SIR: Your favor of this date has just been delivered to me. I have no doubt that the opinion which prevails in respect to the profits made by Mr. Fulton out of his privileges secured by the steamboat patents, however general it may have become, is incorrect; at the same time, it is not at all extraordinary that such

an impression should have gone abroad, as the gross receipts of the boats in which he was concerned were very large, and well calculated to excite such a belief. But those who make these calculations are not always competent to make them, and sometimes neglect or are unwilling to take into the computation the very large expenses attending such establishments. I should not have been able to form on this subject a more accurate estimate than others, had it not been for information derived from Mr. Fulton himself a very few weeks before his death. In a conversation with him on this subject, he assured me, and with very considerable emotion, that, notwithstanding the fortune which he was supposed to have made from his concern in steamboats, he had not yet paid for his share of them, but, on the contrary, was involved in so large a debt as to be induced to dispose of a great part of his interest in these patents, although I have since understood that a contract which he had entered into for that purpose had not been carried into effect at the time of his death. This statement has since been confirmed by Captain Bunker, who commanded the steamboat Fulton, who was very well acquainted with his affairs, and who has assured me that that gentleman died insolvent, which is now the general opinion in New York.

Considering the expense of building a steamboat of any size, as well as that of running her, it is not very probable that Mrs. Fulton will derive any great emolument under the present patents, during the residue of their term. Prudent men will hardly be willing to incur so great an expense, when the privilege will so soon expire, and their profits be exposed to considerable diminution. Mrs. Fulton's friends have therefore reason to fear that, unless the extension now contemplated be obtained, but little profit will be made by her during the term yet unexpired of these patents.

With very great respect, I have the honor to be, dear sir, your most obedient servant,
         B. LIVINGSTON.
Hon. RUFUS KING.

LOST CERTIFICATES.

The PRESIDENT communicated a report of the Secretary of the Treasury, on the petition of John Holker, made in obedience to the resolution of the Senate, of the 9th ultimo; and the report was read. It is as follows:

In obedience to a resolution of the 9th of January, 1816, the Secretary of the Treasury has considered the memorial of John Holker, formerly Consul General of France referred to him by the Senate, and he has now the honor to submit the following report:

The material facts involved in the consideration of the memorial are the following:

That, on the 2d of January, 1780, the memorialist was possessed of loan office certificates to the amount of $426,800; part of them, to the amount of $405,100, issued from the loan office of Pennsylvania; part of them, to the amount of $7,900, issued from the loan office of Massachusetts; part of them, to the amount of $300, issued from the loan office of New Hampshire; part of them, to the amount of $800, issued from the loan office of Rhode Island; part of them, to the amount of $1,200, issued from the loan office of New York; and part of them, to the amount of $11,500, issued from the loan office of Georgia.

That, on the 2d of January, 1780, the house of the memorialist in the city of Philadelphia was burnt, and the loan office certificates above mentioned, with other valuable effects, were consumed.

That the loss of the loan office certificates was made known to Congress, as well as to the Superintendent of Finance, soon after the accident, and a renewal of the certificates claimed.

That, at the time of the accident, no provision had been made by law for the renewal of lost certificates; but, on the 10th of May, 1780, Congress passed a resolution authorizing a renewal upon certain conditions; of which these material on the present occasion were: 1st. That the certificates destroyed should be advertised immediately in the newspapers of the State where the accident happened; and, if they have been taken out of the loan office of a different State, in the newspapers of such State also. 2d. That a copy of the advertisement shall be lodged in the loan office whence the certificates issued, together with the evidence of loss. 3d. That a bond should be given, with a condition to indemnify the United States.

That the memorialist, by an advertisement dated the 8th of August, 1780, which appears in the "Pennsylvania Journal," published in the city of Philadelphia on the 9th of August, 1780, and at several subsequent dates, gave notice of the loss of the loan office certificates, and particularly described each of them.

That, on the 2d of May, 1787, the Board of Treasury considered the above advertisement as a compliance, in that respect, with the terms of the resolution of Congress of the 10th of May, 1780, and directed the loan office of Pennsylvania to renew the certificates which had been issued in that State to the amount of $405,100, upon receiving a bond from the memorialist to indemnify the United States against any future claim. These certificates were accordingly renewed.

That the memorialist, by an advertisement dated the 4th of October, 1789, which appears in the "Massachusetts Centinel," published in Boston on the — of November, 1789, and at several subsequent dates, gave notice of the loss of such of the certificates as had been issued at the loan office of Massachusetts, and particularly decribed them.

That the memorialist, by an advertisement dated the 26th of July, 1790, which appears in the "New York Journal," published in New York on the 6th of August 1790, and at several subsequent dates, gave notice of the loss of such certificates as has been issued at the loan office of New York, and particularly described them.

That the memorialist alleges that he caused like advertisements to be published in the States of New Hampshire, Rhode Island, and Georgia, giving notice of the loss of such certificates as had been issued at the loan offices of those States, respectively; but the newspapers in which the advertisements were published do not accompany the memorial.

That, on the 19th of February, 1792, the memorialist again formally applied to the Secretary of the Treasury for a renewal of the certificates, and was answered on the 20th of June following, that, "as the thing then appeared to the Secretary he saw no chance for the memorialist but in the final winding up of the arrangements concerning the public debt, when the existence or non-existence of the certificates would be ascertained." And this answer was accompanied with a note from the Comptroller of the Treasury, stating that "the memorialist did not comply with the resolution of Congress in advertising the certificates *immediately*; that, in some cases, no proper evidence

was adduced that the certificates were advertised at all in the States in which they were issued; and that, in his opinion, this claim should be suspended until an arrangement of all the certificates had been completed."

That, on the 21st of April, in the year 1794, an act was passed, limiting the time for presenting claims for destroyed certificates of certain descriptions, in which it was declared "all claims for renewal of certificates of the unsubscribed debt of the United States, of the description commonly called 'loan office certificates,' or 'final settlements,' which may have been accidentally destroyed, shall be forever barred and precluded from settlement or allowance, unless the same shall be presented at the Treasury on or before the 1st day of June, in the year 1795." And the act adds, "that no claim shall be allowed for the renewal of loan office certificates destroyed before the 4th day of March, 1789, unless the destruction of the same was advertised, according to the resolution of Congress of the 10th of May, 1780, or before that time was notified to the office from which the same was issued; nor shall any claims be allowed for the renewal of loan office certificates destroyed on or after the 4th day of March, 1789, nor of final settlement certificates destroyed at any time, unless the destruction of the same was so far made public as to be known to at least two credible witnesses soon after it happened, and shall have been, before the presentation of the claim to the Auditor of the Treasury, advertised for at least six weeks, successively, in some one of the newspapers of the State in which the destruction happened, and also in some one of the newspapers of the State in which the certificates issued, if that was another State, &c.

That the memorialist's claim for a renewal of the certificates was presented, with the evidence in support of it, to the Auditor of the Treasury, on the 7th October, 1794; but the Auditor did not deem the claim admissible by him under the act of the 21st of April, 1794, and returned the papers to the memorialist on the 7th of May, 1814.

That the memorialist has made repeated applications to Congress for relief, and the applications have been referred to the Committee of Claims, and to the Department of the Treasury, but it does not appear that any report or decision has been made upon the case.

That it appears, from the records of the Treasury, that the certificates alleged by the memorialist to have been destroyed by fire on the 2d of January, 1780, were actually issued from the several loan offices mentioned in the claim of the memorialist; that none of them have ever been subscribed to the funding system; that the renewal of the certificates issued at the loan office of New York, amounting to $1,200, was claimed on the 25th of May, 1795, for Henry Bass and Ann Martin, under the act of the 21st of April, 1794, but the claim was rejected by the Auditor, because "no proof of destruction was given, nor were the certificates advertised as required by the resolution of the 10th of May, 1780; and, also, because they were claimed by the memorialist;" and that for the rest of the certificates there has been no claim, nor have they in any manner been presented at the Treasury by any other person than by the memorialist.

Under these circumstances, the memorialist prays that Congress will interpose for his relief; and the compliance with his prayer may probably depend upon the following considerations: 1st. Whether the existence, possession, and destruction of the loan office certificates are satisfactorily proved; 2d. Whether the essential forms of the law have been observed in making public the destruction of the certificates; and 3d. Whether the claim to a renewal of the certificates is barred by the positive provisions of the act of the 21st of April, 1794.

1st. The existence of the certificates is proved by the public records. The possession of the certificates by the memorialist, when his house was burnt, is proved by the best evidence of which the case is susceptible. Even upon the strict rules of evidence, in a court of common law, the testimony of the interested party is, from necessity, allowed to prove the loss of written instruments, as a foundation for introducing a copy, or for proving the contents of the original. The oath of the memorialist is direct and explicit on the subject. The burning of his house on the 2d of January, 1780, was an occurrence of public notoriety; and it is, moreover, proved upon oath, independent of the oath of the memorialist. The fact that the certificates were then consumed was made known to Congress, and probably produced the act of the 10th of May, 1780. The certificates were publicly advertised in detail, at the place where they were consumed, on the 9th of August, 1780; and from that day until the present day, a period of more than thirty-five years, the memorialist has constantly urged his claim, and no counter-pretension has ever been presented, except in the instance which has been mentioned. The public records show that the United States are still indebted for the whole amount of the lost certificates.

The claim of Bass and Martin to the renewal of the certificates issued from the loan office of New York appears at the Treasury under very extraordinary circumstances, on the 25th of May, 1795, a few days before the expiration of the statute to bar it, about fifteen years after the memorialist had advertised their loss in Philadelphia, and about five years after he had advertised their loss in New York. From the 25th of May, 1795, until the present time, Bass and Martin have ceased to claim; and it is represented that the memorialist, uniformly declaring the claim to be unfounded, has suggested that the description of the certificates was fraudulently taken from his advertisement in the newspapers of New York.

It is believed, upon this view of the case, that the existence, possession, and destruction of the certificates claimed by the memorialist are satisfactorily established.

2d. On the 2d of January, 1780, when the certificates were destroyed, there existed no law prescribing the form for making the loss public, and for obtaining a renewal. Subsequent regulations ought, therefore, to be applied to the case, upon the most liberal construction, in favor of a claimant.

The act of the 10th of May, 1780, established regulations upon the subject, for the first time providing,

1. That all certificates destroyed through accident should be advertised immediately in the newspapers of the State where the accident happened, but this rule for an immediate advertisement could not apply to the case of certificates which had been burnt four months previously; and, accordingly, the Board of Treasury allowed that an advertisement three months subsequently, on the 9th of August, 1810, with respect to the certificates issued at the loan office of Pennsylvania, was a compliance with the act of Congress in point of time.

2. That if the certificates had been taken out of the loan office of a State, different from the State in which they were destroyed, they should be advertised in such State also, and the claim and evidence left with the loan officers. The advertisement is proved to have been made in the years 1789 and 1790, in the States of Massachusetts and New York, as to the certificates issued in those States, respectively, and it is alleged to have been made about the same time in the States of New Hampshire and Georgia. The reasons assigned for not making an advertisement in those States at the time that it was made in Pennsylvania, are, principally, that the act of Congress was not deemed to apply strictly to the case, and that the then hostile possession of the country by the British troops rendered the measure impracticable.

It seems, indeed, to have been the sense of the Secretary and Comptroller of the Treasury, in 1792, that nothing had occurred up to that time which was fatal to the claim of the memorialist; but that the claim ought to be suspended until the general arrangement of the certificates had been completed under the funding system, when the existence or non-existence of the particular certificates in question would be ascertained. The arrangement has been long completed, and the lapse of more than twenty-five years strips the case of all reasonable doubt upon the non-existence of the certificates, whatever may have been the failure of advertising their loss in strict form.

3d. The act of the 31st of April, 1794, barred all claims for the renewal of loan office certificates which were accidentally destroyed, unless they were presented at the Treasury on or before the 1st of June, 1795. But the claim of the memorialist was presented on the 7th of October, 1794, and, therefore, it is not barred by the lapse of time.

The act further declares, however, that no claim shall be allowed for the renewal of loan office certificates destroyed before the 4th of March, 1789, unless the destruction of the same was advertised according to the resolution of Congress of the 10th of May, 1780, or, before that time, was notified to the office from which the same was issued. But the certificates in question were destroyed before the 4th of March, 1789; and they were advertised in the manner, at the times, and under the circumstances, which have been already stated.

Upon the whole, the Secretary of the Treasury has the honor to conclude this performance of the duty which the Senate has assigned to him with these propositions:

1. That the loan office certificates constitute a debt of record, which the United States have never paid or satisfied.

2. That the debt has not been barred by the act of limitations, in consequence of the lapse of time prescribed for claiming it at the Treasury.

3. That the debt has, nevertheless, been disallowed by the Auditor, because the destruction of the certificates was not advertised and notified in the strict form prescribed by the resolution of the 10th of May, 1780.

4. But that, under all the circumstances of a contemporaneous, constant, and public claim, the memorialist is entitled to the relief solicited from the Legislature, upon giving a bond of indemnity.

All which is respectfully submitted.

A. J. DALLAS,
Secretary of the Treasury.

TREASURY DEPARTMENT, *Feb. 20, 1816.*

TUESDAY, February 27.

The PRESIDENT communicated a letter from the Secretary of the Navy Department, transmitting the information required by the resolution of the Senate of the 8th instant, relative to the ship Cyane, &c.; and the letter and accompanying documents were read.

Mr. VARNUM, from the Committee on the Militia of the United States, reported, in part, a bill for calling forth the militia to execute the laws of the Union, suppress insurrection, and repel invasion, and to repeal the laws heretofore passed for those purposes; and the bill was read, and passed to the second reading.

The bill entitled "An act making further provision for military services during the late war, and for other purposes," was read the second time, and referred to the Committee on Military Affairs.

The bill dividing the State of Pennsylvania into two judicial districts, was read the second time.

The bill for the relief of Edward Wilson was read the second time.

The Senate resumed the motion made the 26th instant, relative to unchartered banks within the District of Columbia; and, on motion by Mr. HORSEY, the further consideration thereof was postponed until Thursday next.

On motion by Mr. MORROW, the memorial of John Holker, together with the report of the Secretary of the Treasury thereon, made the 26th instant, was referred to a select committee, to consider and report thereon by bill or otherwise; and Messrs. MORROW, MACON, and HORSEY, were appointed the committee.

Mr. MASON, of New Hampshire, presented the petition of Jemima Swett, praying the assistance of Government, in consideration of the loss of her son, (who was her only support,) on board the United States sloop of war Wasp, as stated in the petition.

The petition was read, and referred to the Committee on Naval Affairs, to consider and report thereon by bill or otherwise.

Mr. CONDIT presented the memorial of John Stevens, of New Jersey, praying the extension of his patent right for improvements in propelling vessels by steam, for reasons stated in the memorial; which was read, and referred to the committee to whom was referred on the 26th instant, the petition of Harriet Fulton.

Mr. TAIT asked and obtained leave to bring in a bill to increase the pension of William Munday; and the bill was read.

Ordered, That it pass to the second reading.

Agreeably to special order, the Senate resumed, as in Committee of the Whole, the consideration of the bill to authorize the Secretary of the Treasury to subscribe, in behalf of the United States, for —— shares in the capital stock of the Chesapeake and Delaware Canal Company, and, on motion by Mr. CAMPBELL, the consideration thereof was further postponed to, and made the order of the day for to-morrow.

AMENDMENT TO THE CONSTITUTION.

Mr. VARNUM laid before the Senate the instructions of the Legislature of the Commonwealth of Massachusetts, to their Senators in Congress, to endeavor to obtain an amendment to the Constitution of the United States. Whereupon, Mr. V. submitted the following resolution for consideration; which was read, and passed to the second reading:

Resolved by the Senate and House of Representatives of the United States of America, in Congress assembled, two-thirds of both Houses concurring, That the following be proposed to the Legislatures of the several States, as an amendment to the Constitution of the United States; which, when ratified by three-fourths of the said Legislatures, to be valid, to all intents and purposes, as part of the said Constitution, viz:

"That, for the purpose of choosing Representatives in the Congress of the United States, each State shall, by its Legislature, be divided into a number of districts, equal to the number of Representatives to which such State may be entitled.

"Those districts shall be formed of contiguous territory, and contain, as nearly as may be, an equal number of inhabitants, entitled, by the Constitution, to be represented. In each district the qualified voters shall elect one Representative, and no more.

"That, for the purpose of appointing electors of President and Vice President of the United States, each State shall, by its Legislature, be divided into a number of districts, equal to the number of electors to which such State may be entitled. Those districts shall be composed of contiguous territory, and contain, as nearly as may be, an equal number of inhabitants entitled, by the Constitution, to representation. In each district the persons qualified to vote for Representatives shall appoint one elector and no more. The electors, when convened, shall have power, in case any of those appointed as above described shall fail to attend for the purposes of their said appointment, on the day prescribed for giving their votes for President and Vice President of the United States, to appoint another or others to act in the place of him or them so failing to attend.

"Neither the districts for choosing Representatives, nor those for appointing electors, shall be altered in any State until a census, and apportionment of Representatives under it, subsequent to a division of the State into districts, shall be made. The division of States into districts, hereby provided for, shall take place immediately after this amendment shall be adopted and ratified as a part of the Constitution of the United States; and successively, immediately afterwards, whenever a census, and apportionment of Representatives under it, shall be made. The division of such State into districts, for the purposes both of choosing Representatives and of appointing electors, shall be altered agreeable to the provisions of this amendment, and on no other occasion."

REVENUE BILLS.

On motion by Mr. CAMPBELL, the Senate resumed, as in Committee of the Whole, the consideration of the bill entitled "An act to reduce the amount of direct tax upon the United States and the District of Columbia, for the year 1816; and to repeal in part the act entitled 'An act to provide additional revenue for defraying the expenses of Government, and maintaining the public credit, by laying a direct tax upon the United States, and to provide for assessing and collecting the same;" and also the act entitled "An act to provide additional revenue for defraying the expenses of Government, and maintaining the public credit, by laying a direct tax upon the District of Columbia," together with the amendments reported thereto, by the Committee on Finance; and Mr. VARNUM was requested to take the Chair.

On the question to agree to the first amendment proposed, as follows:

Sec. 1, line 2, after the word "that," strike out the rest of the section, and insert, in lieu thereof, "instead of the direct tax of six millions of dollars annually laid upon the United States, by the act entitled "An act to provide additional revenues for defraying the expenses of Government, and maintaining the public credit, by laying a direct tax upon the United States and to provide for assessing and collecting the same," passed the 9th of January, 1815, a direct tax of three millions of dollars be, and the same is hereby annually laid upon the United States, and apportioned to the States respectively, in the manner and according to the sums prescribed by the first section of an act entitled "An act to lay and collect a direct tax within the United States," passed the 2d day of August, 1813, and all the provisions of the act first above named, passed the 9th of January, 1815, except so far as the same have been varied by subsequent acts, and are varied by this act, shall be held to apply to the assessment and collection of the direct tax of three millions of dollars hereby laid upon the United States; which said tax shall be and remain pledged for the same purposes and in the same manner as the said tax of six millions of dollars was, in and by the said last-mentioned act.

A division of the question was called for by Mr. DANA; and it was taken on striking out, and determined in the negative—yeas 12, nays 20, as follows:

YEAS—Messrs. Brown, Chace, Daggett, Fromentin, Gaillard, Gore, Hunter, King, Lacock, Mason of New Hampshire, Roberts, and Taylor.

NAYS—Messrs. Barry, Bibb, Campbell, Condit, Dana, Goldsborough, Horsey, Howell, Macon, Mason of Virginia, Morrow, Ruggles, Talbot, Tait, Thompson, Turner, Varnum, Wells, Williams, and Wilson.

On motion by Mr. MASON, of New Hampshire, to strike out the second section of the bill, as follows:

SEC. 2. *And be it further enacted,* That the direct tax of three millions of dollars be, and the same is hereby laid upon the United States, for the year 1816, and apportioned to the States respectively in the manner and according to the sums prescribed by the first section of an act, entitled "An act to lay and collect a direct tax within the United States," and all the provisions of the act entitled "An act to provide additional revenues for defraying the expenses of Government, and maintaining the public credit, by laying a direct tax upon the United States, and to provide for assessing and collecting the same," passed on the 9th of January, 1815, except so far as the same have been varied by subsequent acts, and excepting the first section of the said act, shall be held to apply to the as-

sessment and collection of the direct tax of three millions of dollars hereby laid upon the United States.

It was determined in the negative—yeas 16, nays 16, as follows:

YEAS—Messrs. Daggett, Dana, Fromentin, Goldsborough, Gore, Horsey, Hunter, King, Lacock, Macon, Mason of New Hampshire, Talbot, Thompson, Turner, Varnum, and Wells.

NAYS—Messrs. Barry, Bibb, Brown, Campbell, Chace, Condit, Gaillard, Howell, Mason of Virginia, Morrow, Roberts, Ruggles, Tait, Taylor, Williams, and Wilson.

On motion by Mr MASON, of New Hampshire, the further consideration of the bill was postponed until to-morrow.

COMMERCE WITH GREAT BRITAIN.

Mr. KING, from the managers at the conference, on the subject of the disagreeing votes of the two Houses upon the bill entitled "An act concerning the convention to regulate the commerce between the territories of the United States and His Britannic Majesty," made the following report:

That the conferees of the House of Representatives commenced the conference by stating, that of the treaties made in pursuance of the Constitution, while some might not, others may, require the enactment of laws to carry them into execution; and, considering the convention with England as a treaty of the latter kind, the conferees of the House of Representatives made the following objections to the bill passed by the Senate:

1st. That by the addition of the word "declared" to the usual formula, instead of a bill of positive enactment, it assumes the form of a declaratory law.

2d. That the bill is defective, because its commencement is uncertain.

3d. That it is defective, because its duration is uncertain.

4th. That it is furthermore defective in respect to the equalization of duties; it being uncertain whether, for this purpose, the native duties are to be raised, or the alien duties abolished.

The conferees of the Senate did not contest, but admitted the doctrine, that of treaties made in pursuance of the Constitution, some may not, and that others may, call for legislative provisions to secure their execution, which provision Congress, in all such cases, is bound to make. But they did contend, that the convention under consideration requires no such legislative provisions, because it does no more than suspend the alien disability of British subjects in commercial affairs, in return for the like suspension in favor of American citizens; that such matter of alien disability falls within the peculiar province of the treaty-power to adjust; that it cannot be securely adjusted in any other way, and that a treaty duly made, and adjusting the same, is conclusive, and by its own authority suspends or removes antecedent laws that are contrary to its provisions.

That even a declaratory law to this effect is matter of mere expediency, adding nothing to the efficacy of the treaty, and serving only to remove doubts wherever they exist.

The conferees of the Senate therefore insisted on retaining the word "declared," in addition to the usual formula of enactment, because it imparts to the bill passed by the Senate the character of a declaratory law; a quality without which any law would, in this case, be inadmissible.

A law that declares to be of no force or effect so much of all laws as are contrary to the provisions of the convention, recognises the existence and authority of that convention; the date and limitations of which must ascertain the commencement and duration of the law, while its stipulations place the people of the two nations on a footing of commercial equality by the abolition of discriminating duties on both sides.

Thus the bill passed by the Senate does not appear to be defective in the particulars referred to by the conferees of the House of Representatives: nevertheless, as doubts were expressed on this subject, the conferees of the Senate proposed certain amendments for the purpose of removing these doubts, and confirming the intentions and meaning of the bill.

The conferees of the Senate, therefore, recommend to the Senate, to insist on their disagreement to the amendments made to the bill by the House of Representatives, and to agree to the following amendments to the bill, which have been mutually agreed to by the conferees of the two Houses:

Line 2, after the word "act," strike out the words "or acts as are," and insert these words, "as imposes a higher duty of tonnage or of impost on vessels and articles imported in vessels of Great Britain than on vessels and articles imported in vessels of the United States."

Line 4. Strike out the word "shall," and after the word "be" insert these words, "from and after the date of the ratification of the said convention, and during the continuance thereof."

Whereupon, *Resolved*, That the Senate concur in the report, and that the bill be amended accordingly.

WEDNESDAY, February 28.

Mr. WILLIAMS, from the Committee on Military Affairs, to whom was referred the bill, entitled "An act granting bounties in land and extra pay to certain Canadian volunteers," reported it without amendment.

Mr. WILLIAMS, from the same committee to whom was referred the bill, entitled "An act making further provision for military services during the late war, and for other purposes," reported it without amendment.

The bill to increase the pension of William Munday, was read the second time, and referred to the Committee on Naval Affairs.

The resolution proposing an amendment to the Constitution, to regulate the mode of choosing Representatives in Congress, and Electors for President and Vice President of the United States, was read the second time.

The bill concerning field officers of the militia was read a third time, and passed.

The bill for the relief of Jacob Babbitt and John Dennis was read the third time, and passed.

On motion, by Mr. DAGGETT, the consideration of the engrossed bill, to limit the right of appeal from the circuit court of the United States, for the District of Columbia, was further postponed until Monday next.

14th CON. 1st SESS.—6

The bill making appropriation for the construction of roads and canals, having been reported by the committee correctly engrossed, on motion, by Mr. FROMENTIN, that the consideration thereof be postponed until the fourth day of July next, it was determined in the negative—yeas 10, nays 22, as follows:

YEAS—Messrs. Daggett, Fromentin, Gore, King, Macon, Mason of New Hampshire, Taylor, Thompson, Turner, and Varnum.

NAYS—Messrs. Barry, Bibb, Brown, Campbell, Chace, Condit, Dana, Gaillard, Goldsborough, Horsey, Howell, Hunter, Lacock, Mason of Virginia, Morrow, Roberts, Ruggles, Talbot, Tait, Wells, Williams, and Wilson.

On motion, by Mr. MORROW, the further consideration thereof was postponed until Wednesday next.

The Senate resumed, as in Committee of the Whole the bill, entitled "An act to reduce the amount of direct tax upon the United States and the District of Columbia, for the year 1816; and to repeal in part the act, entitled 'An act to provide additional revenue for defraying the expenses of Government, and maintaining the public credit, by laying a direct tax upon the United States, and to provide for assessing and collecting the same; and also the act, entitled 'An act to provide additional revenue for defraying the expenses of Government, and maintaining the public credit, by laying a direct tax upon the District of Columbia;" and the bill having been amended, on motion, by Mr. ROBERTS, the further consideration thereof was postponed until Friday next.

Mr. GORE presented the petition of the treasurer and assistant treasurer of the Massachusetts Bible Society, praying to be allowed the benefit of drawback on a number of bibles exported by them, as stated in the petition; which was read, and referred the Committee on Finance and an Uniform National Currency.

THURSDAY, February 29.

The bill for calling forth the militia to execute the laws of the Union, suppress insurrection, and repel invasion, and to repeal the laws heretofore passed for those purposes, was read the second time.

Mr. KING, from the committee to whom the subject was referred, reported a bill for the benefit of the widow and children of Robert Fulton, deceased; and the bill was read, and passed to the second reading.

Mr. SANFORD presented the petition of Willet Coles, of the city of New York, praying to be discharged from his imprisonment, for reasons stated in the petition; which was read, and referred to the Committee on Finance and an Uniform National Currency.

The Senate resumed the consideration of the motion made the 26th instant, relative to unchartered banks within the District of Columbia, which, having been amended, was agreed to as follows:

Resolved, That a committee be appointed to

163   HISTORY OF CONGRESS.   164

SENATE.   *Proceedings.*   MARCH, 1816.

inquire whether it would be expedient and proper to prohibit by law the formation of private banking associations, in future, within the District of Columbia, and also to consider and inquire whether it would be expedient and proper to prohibit by law the emission and circulation of the notes of all unchartered banks within the said District, with leave to report by bill or otherwise.

Ordered, That Messrs. HORSEY, MASON of New Hampshire, and TAIT, be the committee.

The Senate resumed, as in Committee of the Whole, the consideration of the bill to authorize the Secretary of the Treasury to subscribe, in behalf of the United States, for —— shares in the capital stock of the Chesapeake and Delaware Canal Company.

On motion, by Mr. MASON, of New Hampshire, the further consideration thereof was postponed until the third Monday in March next.

The Senate resumed, as in Committee of the Whole, the consideration of the resolution for a proposed amendment to the Constitution of the United States, that the Senators shall be chosen for three years; and on the question, "Shall this resolution be engrossed and read a third time? it was determined in the negative—yeas 7, nays 24, as follows:

YEAS—Messrs. Bibb, Lacock, Mason, Roberts, Sanford, Taylor, and Turner.

NAYS—Messrs. Barry, Brown, Campbell, Chace, Condit, Daggett, Dana, Fromentin, Gaillard, Goldsborough, Horsey, Howell, Hunter, King, Mason of New Hampshire, Morrow, Ruggles, Talbot, Tait, Thompson, Tichenor, Varnum, Williams, and Wilson.

The Senate resumed the bill, entitled "An act to authorize the payment for property lost, captured, or destroyed, by the enemy, while in the military service of the United States;" and, on motion by Mr. TURNER, the consideration thereof was further postponed until to-morrow.

The Senate resumed, as in Committee of the Whole, the consideration of the bill for the relief of Richard Mitchell; and, on the question, "Shall this bill be engrossed and read a third time?" it was determined in the affirmative.

The Senate resumed, as in Committee of the Whole, the consideration of the bill concerning the District of Columbia; and, on motion by Mr. LACOCK, the further consideration thereof was postponed until Thursday next.

The Senate resumed, as in Committee of the Whole, the consideration of the bill dividing the State of Pennsylvania into two judicial districts; and, on motion by Mr. LACOCK, the further consideration thereof was postponed until Thursday next.

The Senate resumed, as in Committee of the Whole, the consideration of the bill, entitled "An act granting bounties in land and extra pay to certain Canadian volunteers;" and no amendment having been proposed thereto, it passed to a third reading.

The Senate resumed, as in Committee of the Whole, the bill, entitled "An act making further provision for military services during the late war,

and for other purposes;" and, on motion by Mr. WILLIAMS, the further consideration thereof was postponed until to-morrow.

The Senate resumed the resolution proposing an amendment to the Constitution, to regulate the mode of choosing Representatives in Congress, and Electors for President and Vice President of the United States;" and, on motion by Mr. VARNUM, the further consideration thereof was postponed until to-morrow.

The Senate resumed the bill for the relief of Edward Wilson; and the further consideration thereof was postponed until to-morrow.

Mr. BARRY, from the committee to whom was recommitted the bill relating to settlers on the lands of the United States, reported it without amendment.

FRIDAY, March 1.

Mr. SANFORD presented the petition of George Rossier and others, of the city of New York, praying the renewal of certain Treasury notes miscarried or lost in the public mail, as stated in the petition; which was read, and referred to a select committee, to consider and report thereon by bill or otherwise; and Mr. SANFORD, Mr. BIBB, and Mr. CAMPBELL, were appointed the committee.

Mr. CAMPBELL, from the Committee on Finance and an Uniform National Currency, to whom was referred the petition of Alfred M. Carter, for himself, and the heirs of Landon Carter, made a report thereon, together with the following resolution, which was read:

Resolved, That the prayer of the petitioner ought not to be granted.

Mr. CAMPBELL, from the Committee on Finance and an Uniform National Currency, to whom was referred the bill, entitled "An act making appropriations for ordnance and ordnance stores for the year 1816," reported it with amendments.

Mr. ROBERTS, from the committee to whom was referred the bill, entitled "An act for the relief of the heirs of George Nebinger," reported it without amendment.

Mr. TAIT, from the Committee on Naval Affairs, to whom was referred the bill to increase the pension of William Munday, reported it without amendment.

Mr. TAIT, from the Committee on Naval Affairs, to whom the subject was referred, reported a bill, in addition to an act, entitled "An act in relation to the Navy Pension Fund;" and the bill was read, and passed to the second reading.

The Senate resumed, as in Committee of the Whole, the consideration of the resolution proposing an amendment to the Constitution, to regulate the mode of choosing Representatives in Congress, and Electors for President and Vice President of the United States; and, on motion by Mr. VARNUM, it was referred to a select committee, to consist of five members, to consider and report thereon; and Mr. VARNUM, Mr. KING, Mr. FROMENTIN, Mr. MACON, and Mr. LACOCK, were appointed the committee.

The bill for the relief of the widow and children of Robert Falton, deceased, was read the second time.

The Senate resumed the bill, entitled "An act to authorize the payment for property lost, captured or destroyed by the enemy, while in the military service of the United States;" and, on motion by Mr. MASON, of Virginia, the consideration thereof was further postponed until Friday, the 15th instant.

The Senate resumed, as in Committee of the Whole, the bill, entitled "An act making further provision for military services during the late war, and for other purposes;" and, on motion by Mr. WILLIAMS, the further consideration thereof was postponed until Monday next.

Mr. KING, from the committee to whom the subject was referred, reported a bill concerning certain advances made for the public service by the city of New York; and the bill was read, and passed to the second reading.

The Senate resumed the consideration of the report of the Committee on Finance and an Uniform National Currency, on the petition of Thomas Cutts, of Biddeford, in the State of Massachusetts. Whereupon,

Resolved, That the prayer of the petitioner ought not to be granted.

The bill for the relief of Richard Mitchell was read a third time, and passed.

The bill, entitled "An act granting bounties in land, and extra pay to certain Canadian volunteers," was read a third time, and passed.

REVENUE BILL.

The Senate resumed the consideration of the bill, entitled "An act to reduce the amount of direct tax upon the United States, and the District of Columbia, for the year 1816; and to repeal in part the act, entitled 'An act to provide additional revenue for defraying the expenses of Government, and maintaining the public credit, by laying a direct tax upon the United States, and to provide for assessing and collecting the same;' and also the act, entitled 'An act to provide additional revenue for defraying the expenses of Government, and maintaining the public credit, by laying a direct tax upon the District of Columbia.'"

On motion by Mr. GOLDSBOROUGH, that the bill be recommitted to the Committee on Finance and an Uniform National Currency, with instructions to provide for the collection of all arrearages of the direct tax for past years, and to repeal the act, " to provide additional revenue for defraying the expenses of Government, and maintaining the public credit, by laying a direct tax upon the United States, and to provide for assessing and collecting the same," passed on the 9th January, 1815,—it was determined in the negative—yeas 12, nays 20, as follows:

YEAS—Messrs. Daggett, Dana, Goldsborough, Gore, Hunter, King, Macon, Mason of N. Hampshire, Thompson, Turner, Varnum, and Wells.

NAYS—Messrs. Barry, Bibb, Brown, Campbell, Chace, Condit, Gaillard, Harper, Howell, Lacock, Mason of Virginia, Morrow, Roberts, Ruggles, Sanford, Tait, Taylor, Tichenor, Williams, and Wilson.

On motion by Mr. ROBERTS, that the Senate agree to the first amendment proposed by the Committee on Finance, which was negatived as in Committee of the Whole, as follows:

Section 1, line 2, after the word "that," strike out the rest of the section, and insert in lieu thereof, "instead of the direct tax of six millions of dollars annually laid upon the United States by the act, entitled 'An act to provide additional revenue for defraying the expenses of Government and maintaining the public credit, by laying a direct tax upon the United States, and to provide for assessing and collecting the same,' passed the 9th January, 1815, a direct tax of three millions of dollars be and the same is hereby annually laid upon the United States, and apportioned to the States respectively, in the manner and according to the sums prescribed by the first section of an act, entitled 'An act to lay and collect a direct tax within the United States,' passed the 2d day of August, 1813; and all the provisions of the act first above-named, passed the 9th January, 1815, except so far as the same have been varied by subsequent acts, and are varied by this act, shall be held to apply to the assessment and collection of the direct tax of three millions of dollars, hereby laid upon the United States; which said tax shall be and remain pledged for the same purposes and in the same manner as the said tax of six millions of dollars was, in and by the said last-mentioned act:"

It was determined in the negative—yeas 16, nays 18, as follows:

YEAS—Messrs. Brown, Chace, Fromentin, Gaillard, Gore, Harper, Hunter, King, Lacock, Mason of New Hampshire, Morrow, Roberts, Sanford, Tait, Taylor, and Tichenor.

NAYS—Messrs. Barry, Bibb, Campbell, Condit, Daggett, Dana, Goldsborough, Howell, Macon, Mason of Virginia, Ruggles, Talbot, Thompson, Turner, Varnum, Wells, Williams, and Wilson,

On motion, by Mr. HARPER, to amend the said proposed amendment, by inserting in line 10, after "States," the words "for five years;" so as to continue the tax annually laid upon the United States, for that term; it was determined in the negative—yeas 10, nays 24, as follows:

YEAS—Messrs. Chace, Fromentin, Gaillard, Harper, Hunter, Lacock, Roberts, Sanford, Tait, and Taylor.

NAYS—Messrs. Barry, Bibb, Brown, Campbell, Condit, Daggett, Dana, Goldsborough, Gore, Howell, King, Macon, Mason of New Hampshire, Mason of Virginia, Morrow, Ruggles, Talbot, Thompson, Tichenor, Turner, Varnum, Wells, Williams, and Wilson.

On motion, by Mr. WELLS, to strike out the second section of the bill, it was determined in the negative—yeas 16, nays 18, as follows:

YEAS—Messrs. Daggett, Dana, Goldsborough, Gore, Harper, Hunter, King, Lacock, Macon, Mason of New Hampshire, Talbot, Thompson, Tichenor, Turner, Varnum, and Wells.

NAYS—Messrs. Barry, Bibb, Brown, Campbell, Chace, Condit, Fromentin, Gaillard, Howell, Mason of Virginia, Morrow, Roberts, Ruggles, Sanford, Tait, Taylor, Williams, and Wilson.

On the question "Shall the amendment be engrossed, and the bill be read a third time as amended?" it was determined in the affirmative

SATURDAY, March 2.

Mr. TALBOT, from the committee to whom was referred the bill to establish a law library at the Seat of Government, for the use of the Supreme Court of the United States, reported it with amendments, which were read.

Mr. ROBERTS, from the committee to whom the subject was referred, reported a bill for the relief of John Thompson; and the bill was read, and passed to the second reading.

Mr. BIBB presented the memorial of John P. Van Ness, and others, original proprietors of the City of Washington, stating, that on laying out the said city, certain open squares were reserved for public buildings, for which they received a compensation per acre; and praying that if those squares are now appropriated to a different use, and sold for the purpose of building thereon, they may receive the same compensation to which they would have been entitled if that had been the original determination; for reasons stated in the memorial; which was read, and referred to the committee to whom was referred, on the 24th January, the petition of Thomas Law, and others, inhabitants of the City of Washington, praying the division and sale of certain open squares in said city.

The Senate resumed the consideration of the report of the Committee on Finance on the petition of Alfred M. Carter; and on motion, by Mr. WELLS, it was recommitted to a select committee, to consider and report thereon; and Messrs. TALBOT and WELLS were appointed the committee.

The bill concerning certain advances made for the public service by the city of New York, was read a second time.

The bill in addition to an act entitled "An act in relation to the Navy Pension Fund," was read the second time.

The Senate resumed, as in Committee of the Whole, the consideration of the bill for the relief of Edward Wilson; and on the question "Shall this bill be engrossed and read a third time?" it was determined in the affirmative.

Mr. KING submitted the following motion for consideration:

Resolved, That a committee be appointed to confer with the person appointed to superintend the re-construction and repairs of the Capitol, and to suggest such alterations of the Senate Chamber, and the connected offices thereof, as shall provide greater accommodation for the Senate and its officers, than the former distribution afforded.

The amendment to the bill entitled "An act to reduce the amount of direct tax upon the United States and the District of Columbia, for the year 1816; and to repeal in part the act entitled 'An act to provide additional revenue for defraying the expenses of Government, and maintaining the public credit, by laying a direct tax upon the United States, and to provide for assessing and collecting the same;' and also the act entitled 'An act to provide additional revenue for defraying the expenses of Government, and maintaining the public credit, by laying a direct tax upon the

District of Columbia," having been reported by the committee correctly engrossed, the bill was read a third time as amended; and on the question "Shall this bill pass as amended?" it was determined in the affirmative—yeas 18, nays 11, as follows:

YEAS—Messrs. Bibb, Brown, Campbell, Condit, Gaillard, Howell, Macon, Morrow, Roberts, Ruggles, Sanford, Talbot, Tait, Taylor, Turner, Wells, Williams, and Wilson.

NAYS—Messrs. Daggett, Dana, Fromentin, Goldsborough, Hunter, King, Lacock, Mason of New Hampshire, Thompson, Tichenor, and Varnum.

So it was *Resolved,* That this bill pass with an amendment.

MONDAY, March 4.

Mr. TAYLOR, from the committee to whom was recommitted the bill further supplementary to the act entitled "An act providing for the indemnification of certain claimants of public land in the Mississippi Territory," reported it with an amendment; which was read.

Mr. SANFORD, from the committee to whom the subject was referred, reported a bill for the relief of George Rossier and others; and the bill was read, and passed to the second reading.

The bill for the relief of John Thompson was read the second time.

The Senate resumed the consideration of the motion made the second instant, in relation to the re-construction and repairs of the Capitol, and on motion, by Mr. KING, it was amended and agreed to as follows:

Resolved, That a committee be appointed for the purpose of suggesting to the person appointed to superintend the re-construction and repairs of the Capitol, such alterations of the Senate Chamber, and connected offices thereof, as shall provide greater accommodation for the Senate and its officers than the former distribution afforded.

Ordered, That Messrs. KING, HUNTER, and MACON, be the committee.

The Senate resumed, as in Committee of the Whole, the consideration of the bill to increase the pension of William Munday, and the bill having been amended, the PRESIDENT reported it to the House accordingly; and, on the question, "Shall this bill be engrossed and read a third time?" it was determined in the affirmative.

The Senate resumed, as in Committee of the Whole, the consideration of the bill, entitled "An act for the relief of George Nebinger;" and on motion, by Mr. ROBERTS, it was referred to the committee to whom was recommitted the report of the Committee on Finance, on the petition of Alfred M. Carter, to consider and report thereon.

The Senate resumed, as in Committee of the Whole, the consideration of the bill relating to settlers on the lands of the United States; and the bill having been amended, the PRESIDENT reported it to the House accordingly; and on motion, by Mr. BARRY, the further consideration thereof was postponed to, and made the order of the day for, to-morrow.

The Senate resumed, as in Committee of the Whole, the bill for calling forth the militia to execute the laws of the Union, suppress insurrection, and repel invasion, and to repeal the laws heretofore passed for those purposes ; and on motion, by Mr. VARNUM, the further consideration thereof was postponed until to-morrow.

The Senate resumed, as in Committee of the Whole, the consideration of the bill for the relief of the widow and children of Robert Fulton, deceased ; and after debate thereon, on motion, by Mr. TAYLOR, the further consideration thereof was postponed until to-morrow.

The Senate resumed, as in Committee of the Whole, the consideration of the bill entitled "An act making appropriations for ordnance and ordnance stores for the year 1816, together with the amendments reported by the Committee on Finance and an Uniform National Currency, and the amendments having been agreed to, in part, with further amendments, the PRESIDENT reported the bill to the House accordingly.

On the question, "Shall the amendments be engrossed, and the bill read a third time, as amended?" it was determined in the affirmative.

A message from the House of Representatives informed the Senate that they have passed a bill, entitled "An act for the relief of John M. Forbes," in which bill they request the concurrence of the Senate.

The bill last mentioned was read, and passed to the second reading.

TUESDAY, March 5.

The bill for the relief of George Rossier, and others, was read the second time.

The bill, entitled "An act for the relief of John M. Forbes," was read the second time, and referred to a select committee to consider and report thereon ; and Messrs. SANFORD, HUNTER, and HOWELL, were appointed the committee.

The engrossed bill for the relief of Edward Wilson was read a third time, and passed.

The engrossed bill to increase the pension of William Munday was read a third time and passed.

The amendments to the bill, entitled "An act making appropriations for ordnance and ordnance stores, for the year 1816," was read a third time as amended, and passed.

The Senate resumed the consideration of the bill relating to settlers on the lands of the United States and, after debate, adjourned.

WEDNESDAY, March 6.

Mr. DAGGETT gave notice that to-morrow he should ask leave to bring in a bill further extending the time for issuing and locating military land warrants.

Mr. VARNUM having proposed an amendment thereto, on motion, by Mr. MASON, of Virginia, the further consideration of the bill, together with the proposed amendment, was postponed until Thursday, the 14th instant.

The Senate resumed, as in Committee of the Whole, the consideration of the bill for calling forth the militia to execute the laws of the Union, suppress insurrections, and repel invasion, and to repeal the laws heretofore passed for those purposes.

The engrossed bill making appropriation for the construction of roads and canals was read a third time ; and on motion, by Mr. MASON, of New Hampshire, the consideration thereof was postponed until the first Monday in April next.

The Senate resumed the consideration of the bill relating to settlers on the lands of the United States ; and on the question "Shall this bill be engrossed and read a third time ?" it was determined in the affirmative—yeas 21, nays 13, as follows :

YEAS—Messrs. Barry, Bibb, Brown, Campbell, Chace, Condit, Fromentin, Gaillard, Howell, Lacock, Mason of Virginia, Morrow, Roberts, Ruggles, Sanford, Talbot, Tait, Taylor, Wells, Williams, and Wilson.

NAYS—Messrs. Daggett, Dana, Goldsborough, Gore, Horsey, Hunter, King, Macon, Mason of New Hampshire, Thompson, Tichenor, Turner, and Varnum.

Mr. DANA submitted the following motion for consideration :

Resolved, That a committee be appointed to inquire into the propriety of making further provision concerning the application of moneys appropriated for arming and equipping the body of the militia.

On motion, by Mr. MORROW, the committee to whom was referred the petition of John Holker, together with the report of the Secretary of the Treasury thereon, were discharged from the further consideration thereof, and they were referred to the committee to whom was recommitted the report of the Committee on Finance and an Uniform National Currency, on the petition of Alfred M. Carter.

Mr. SANFORD, from the committee to whom was referred the bill entitled "An act for the relief of John M. Forbes," reported it without amendment.

THURSDAY, March 7.

Mr. DAGGETT asked and obtained leave to bring in a bill further extending the time for issuing and locating military land warrants, and for other purposes ; and the bill was read, and passed to the second reading.

The PRESIDENT communicated a report of the Postmaster General, of unproductive post routes, for the year 1815, which was read.

Mr. SANFORD submitted the following resolution ; which was read, and passed to a second reading :

Resolved, by the Senate and House of Representatives of the United States of America in Congress assembled, two-thirds of both Houses concurring, That the following article be proposed to the Legislatures of the several States, as an amendment to the Constitution of the United States ; which, when ratified by three-fourths of the said Legislatures, shall be valid as part of the said Constitution, to wit :

The Judges of all the Courts of the United States shall be subject to removal from office, by the President and both Houses of Congress, when, in their opinion, the public good will be promoted by removal; but, in such cases, two-thirds of both Houses shall concur with the President in the removal.

The Senate proceeded to the consideration of the bill, in addition to an act, entitled "An act in relation to the Navy Pension Fund." [This bill provides for the better regulation of this fund, the manner in which moneys accruing thereto shall be accounted for by the officers of the United States in the several judicial districts of the United States; and also contains a provision for allowing to officers, seamen, and marines, disabled in the service, in cases of extreme disability, such an increase of pension, where the Commissioners of the Fund may deem it necessary, as shall be competent to their necessary subsistence; provided the whole pension shall in no instance exceed the full amount of monthly pay which the disabled person was by law entitled to in the said service.]

The objects of the bill having been explained by Mr. TAIT, the chairman of the committee who reported it; the bill was ordered to be engrossed for a third reading, without opposition.

A message from the House of Representatives informed the Senate that the House have passed a bill, entitled "An act in addition to an act to regulate the Post Office Establishment;" also, a bill, entitled "An act authorizing and requiring the Secretary of State to issue letters patent to Andrew Kurtz;" in which bills they request the concurrence of the Senate.

The two bills last mentioned were read, and passed to the second reading.

The Senate resumed the consideration of the motion made the 6th instant, for the appointment of a committee to inquire into the propriety of making further provision concerning the application of moneys appropriated for arming and equipping the body of the militia; and, having agreed thereto, Messrs. DANA, VARNUM, and MACON, were appointed the committee.

The Senate resumed, as in Committee of the Whole, the consideration of the bill for the benefit of the widow and children of Robert Fulton, deceased; and, on motion by Mr. KING, the further consideration thereof was postponed until Monday next.

The bill relating to settlers on the lands of the United States was read a third time, and passed.

The PRESIDENT communicated a letter from the Secretary for the Department of War, transmitting the information called for by the resolution of the Senate of the 30th of January last; and the letter and accompanying papers were read.

CITY OF NEW YORK.

The bill for refunding to the Corporation of New York certain moneys expended by them in the erection of breastworks, or defences, near that city, during the late war, was taken up. A motion to postpone it until to-morrow week gave rise to a wide discussion.

The motion for postponement was supported by Messrs. TALBOT, ROBERTS, LACOCK, TAYLOR, VARNUM, and BARRY, on various grounds, reducible, however, to two points; first, that the expense thus incurred was unauthorized by the United States, and ought to be subjected to a rigid scrutiny; secondly, that, if the claim was equitable, it ought not to be separated from the general class of cases of equal merit, some of which were included in a bill lying on the table of the Senate, &c.; that it was improper to legislate on a principle of favoritism on a particular case.

The motion to postpone was opposed by Messrs. TAIT, DAGGETT, KING, SANFORD, and HARPER, on the ground of the merits of the claim, as exhibited in the accompanying documents, and the impossibility and, indeed, inexpediency of including, in any general provision, the mass of incongruous cases of indemnity and compensation claimed from various parts of the United States, growing out of the late war.

The motion to postpone until to-morrow week was negatived; but, subsequently, by general consent, on motion of Mr. BARRY, the bill was postponed to Thursday next.

On motion, by Mr. LACOCK, the memorial of the Mayor, Aldermen, and Common Council, of the city of New York, praying the reimbursement of certain sums advanced and expended in the defence of the third military district, together with the accompanying documents, were referred to the Secretary for the Department of War, to consider and report thereon to the Senate.

AMERICAN NAVIGATION.

Mr. BIBB, from the Committee on Foreign Affairs, made a report on the subject of a system of navigation for the United States, and the report was read.

Mr. B., from the committee, also reported a bill to establish a system of navigation for the United States; and the bill was read, and passed to the second reading. The report is as follows:

The attention of the committee has been drawn to the policy of "confining the American navigation to American seamen" by the Message of the President of the United States. Two considerations, distinct in their character, are suggested in behalf of the measure —1st. As it might have a conciliatory tendency towards foreign nations; and, 2dly. As it would increase the independence of our navigation and the resources of our maritime defence.

"An act for the regulation of the seamen on board the public and private vessels of the United States," passed the 3d day of March, 1813, prohibits the employment, as seamen, of the subjects or citizens of any foreign nation which shall prohibit the like employment of citizens of the United States. That act furnishes indisputable evidence of the conciliatory spirit of the national councils; and a corresponding disposition on the part of other Governments only is wanting to give it effect. The committee, however, deem it expedient to advance the independence of the navigation and resources of maritime defence of the United States, and for that purpose submit a bill to the consideration of the Senate. That the nature and extent of its provisions may be the more readily understood, the following outline of the existing regulations concerning commercial vessels, and of the proposed modifications, is presented.

Commercial vessels which are registered or enrolled according to the existing laws are denominated ships or vessels of the United States. For carrying on trade with foreign countries, they are registered. For the coasting trade or fisheries of the United States, they are enrolled and licensed.

Ships or vessels built within the United States, or captured and condemned as prize, or adjudged forfeited for breach of law, and belonging wholly to citizens of the United States, may be registered or enrolled, if they are commanded by citizens either native or naturalized. Such vessels are regarded as belonging to the ports at or nearest to which the managing owners reside. And they are registered or enrolled in the offices of the customs for the districts which comprehend the respective ports.

When a vessel is registered, the ownership, name, description, and tonnage, being legally ascertained, are stated distinctly, with the name of the master, and entered in some proper book for a record or registry to be kept by the collector of the customs. A certificate of such registry is issued as evidence of ownership to accompany the vessel. In addition to the seal and signature of the Register of the Treasury of the United States, it is attested under the seal of the collector with his signature, and is countersigned by the naval officer or surveyor, where there is such an officer, for the port to which the vessel belongs. And a copy is transmitted to the Register of the Treasury.

The certificate of registry for a vessel to be employed in foreign voyages may continue in force so long as the ownership continues the same. On a change of property, if purchased by any citizen of the United States, the vessel is registered anew. When the master is changed, the collector of the customs is authorized to endorse a memorandum of such change on the certificate of registry.

The requisites for this important document are prescribed in the act of the 31st of December, 1792, entitled "An act concerning the registering and recording of ships or vessels." And various provisions in the same act were adapted to guard the interest of shipbuilders and ship-owners of the United States against the intrusions or impositions of foreigners.

In relation to vessels of twenty tons or upwards which may be enrolled, the same qualifications and requisites are prescribed, and similar guards against abuses are provided in the act of the 18th February, 1793, entitled "An act for enrolling and licensing ships or vessels to be employed in the coasting trade and fisheries, and for regulating the same." A certificate of enrolment, which is issued for a coasting or fishing vessel of the United States, is strictly analogous to the certificate of registry for a merchant vessel. The documents contain similar statements respecting the vessels and the titles of the owners, and are authenticated in the same manner.

Vessels of less than twenty tons are licensed, without being enrolled, according to the act of the 18th of February, 1793. And the duty of tonnage on a licensed vessel is payable once in a year. A license is issued from the office of the customs for the vessel to be employed in the coasting trade or the whale fishery or cod fishery. It may be in force for one year, and is given under the hand and seal of the collector, who is required to make a record of such licenses, and

transmit copies to the Register of the Treasury. That the privileges appertaining to ships or vessels of the United States in the coasting trade or fisheries may be fully enjoyed, the same law requires enrolled vessels to have licenses.

As the act of the thirty-first of December, seventeen hundred and ninety-two, has provided that the privileges appertaining to registered ships or vessels of the United States shall not continue to be enjoyed longer than they continue to be commanded by citizens of the United States, it has, in effect, required every such vessel to have one citizen on board as master or commander. And the same requisite is included in the act of the eighteenth of February, seventeen hundred and ninety-three, for enrolling or licensing ships or vessels. These acts contain the principal regulations for commercial shipping. There are no laws in operation which require any more of the citizens to be employed for navigating the vessels in foreign trade or in the coasting trade or fisheries. There is no act of Congress which requires the subordinate officers, or any part of the crew on board any vessel whatever, to be citizens of the United States.

On examination it appears that systematic regulations, concerning the ownership of vessels, were established by the registering act of December, 1792, and the enrolling and licensing act of February, 1793. But the United States have remained to this day without a navigation act for each branch of their commerce.

As it concerns the maritime interests of the United States, therefore, it is of importance to establish a policy requiring the commercial vessels of the United States to be navigated principally by mariners of the country. With this view, it is considered proper to allow the privileges of American character to none but vessels navigated by American mariners as the law may require; to provide for ascertaining who shall be regarded as such mariners; and to make it requisite for vessels of the United States to have documents on board as evidence of being so navigated.

That the policy may be carried into effect without inconvenience, various particulars in a system of navigation must correspond to existing laws respecting the collection of duties, the ownership of vessels, or the government of persons in the merchant service or fisheries. Several regulations similar to those already in force are proposed to be incorporated.

The documents for vessels sailing on foreign voyages may supersede the use of any other certificates of citizenship for persons employed in navigating them. And it is proposed to repeal the section of the act of May, 1796, which has authorized the collectors to deliver certificates to individual mariners. Abuses which are known to have prevailed in relation to such certificates may be avoided by requiring proper documents to accompany the vessels.

Statement of the whole number of *seamen annually registered as American*, under the act of the 28th of May, 1796; being an "abstract of seamen registered in the several custom-houses of the United States, according to returns made to the Department of State," as contained in a report made to the Senate, dated the 19th of February, 1813.

For the three last quar.

ters of the year	-	1796	- - 4,849
For the years	- -	1797	- - 9,021
		1798	- - 7,031

For the years			1799	-	-	6,514
			1800	-	-	3,390
			1801	-	-	6,917
			1802	-	-	891
			1803	-	-	10,734
			1804	-	-	6,623
			1805	-	-	10,722
			1806	-	-	9,900
			1807	-	-	7,937
			1808	-	-	1,121
			1809	-	-	9,170
			1810	-	-	3,668
			1811	-	-	4,836
			1812	-	-	3,252

Whole number returned as registered 106,787

Remark.—The report of the 19th of February, 1813, from the Secretary of State, contains the following remark: "It may be proper to observe, that from the deficiency of returns it is to be reasonably inferred that the number of seamen actually unregistered in the United States, during the period embraced by this report, exceeds that now stated by one-third."

Statement of the number of *naturalized persons annually registered as American seamen*, under the act of the 28th of May, 1796, according to a report from the Secretary of State to the Senate, dated the 6th of January, 1813.

For the three last quarters						
of the year	-	-	1796	-	-	70
For the years	-	-	1797	-	-	185
			1798	-	-	111
			1799	-	-	95
			1800	-	-	54
			1801	-	-	48
			1802	-	-	26
			1803	-	-	140
			1804	-	-	124
			1805	-	-	68
			1806	-	-	70
			1807	-	-	71
			1808	-	-	55
			1809	-	-	214
			1810	-	-	147
			1811	-	-	39
			1812	-	-	33

Number returned as naturalized - 1,530

Remark.—In relation to the returns of persons born in foreign countries who have been legally naturalized in the United States, and registered as American seamen, in the report of the 6th of January, 1813, it is observed: "Those for 1811 and 1812, above stated, are not complete."

TREASURY DEPARTMENT, *Jan. 28, 1816.*

SIR: Permit me to answer your inquiries, relative to the amount of American tonnage, and the number of seamen, Americans and foreigners, employed in the merchant service, by communicating a copy of the letter, which I have addressed to the Chairman of the Committee of Foreign Relations of the House of Representatives, upon the same subject. I have, &c.

A. J. DALLAS.

Hon. W. W. BIBB,
Chairman Com. Foreign Relations.

TREASURY DEPARTMENT, *Jan. 26, 1816.*

SIR: I have the honor to acknowledge the receipt of your letter, requesting, on behalf of the Committee of Foreign Relations, information upon the following subjects:

1. The amount of American tonnage.

2. The number of seamen required for the navigation of American vessels.

3. The number of American seamen, either native or naturalized.

4. The number of foreign seamen now employed in the merchant service of the United States.

I. The annual statement of the amount of American tonnage, on the 31st of December, 1814, which was recently laid before Congress, exhibits an aggregate of 1,159,208 80-95 tons, as included in the returns made to this Department, by the collectors of the customs; but for the reasons assigned in the letter of the Register of the Treasury, accompanying that statement, the actual amount ought not to be estimated, on the 30th of December, 1814, at more than 1,029,281 85-95 tons.

By an estimate formed from the returns of the collectors, to the 30th of September, 1815, the aggregate amount of the tonnage, included in the returns, will be 1,363,758 62-95 tons; but this amount is liable to a deduction, similar to that abovementioned, and the tonnage of American vessels actually employed, at the last period, may be estimated at about 1,217,000 tons, divided in the following manner:

American tonnage employed in foreign trade, about	-	-	-	-	-	840,000
Do. in the coasting trade, about		-	-	-		350,000
Do. in the fisheries	-	-	-	-	-	27,000
		Tons	-	-	-	1,217,000

II. The number of seamen required for the navigation of American vessels may be computed from the crews which they usually ship, including officers and boys, at an average of nearly six for every hundred tons employed in the foreign and coasting trade, and of about eight for every hundred tons employed in the fisheries. This computation will place the whole number of seamen, required for the navigation of American vessels, at about 70,000.

III and IV. The number of American seamen, native or naturalized citizens, and the number of foreign seamen, who are employed in the merchant service of the United States, cannot be ascertained from any documents in the Treasury Department. It is believed, indeed, that there does not exist, anywhere, the means of classing the seamen according to that discrimination; nor of ascertaining their number, except in the general mode of computation, which has been adopted upon the present occasion. The acts for the relief and protection of American seamen provide that the collector of every district shall keep a book, in which, at the request of any seaman, being a citizen of the United States, and producing proof of his citizenship authenticated in a manner which the act has omitted to define, he shall enter the name of the applicant; and that each collector shall return a list of the seamen so registered, once every three months, to the Secretary of State, who is required to lay before Congress an annual statement of the returns. It is also provided that, before a clearance be granted to any vessel bound on a foreign voyage, the master shall deliver to the collector of the customs a list containing, as far as he can ascertain, the names, places of birth, and residence, and a description of the persons who compose his ship's company, for whom he is bound to account upon his return to the United States. But experience has shown that neither the register, which only includes the names of citizens who themselves request to be registered, nor the crew lists furnished by the masters of vessels employed in the foreign trade, upon general information, afford a satisfactory test to distinguish the native from the naturalized seaman, nor even to distinguish the citizen from the alien; and that neither can be relied on to establish the aggregate number of seamen employed in the merchant service. In the year 1807 an attempt was made to estimate the proportion of foreign to American seamen on board of American vessels; but the basis of the estimate was too unsettled and hypothetical to command confidence in the result. It was then supposed that nearly the sixth of the whole number of seamen employed in navigating American vessels were foreign seamen, and more particularly, that of the number of seamen employed in the foreign trade, at least one-fourth were foreigners. There are reasons to presume that the proportion of foreign to American seamen is less at this time than it was in the year 1807, and that it will become less still, as the nations of Europe, in consequence of the general peace, become more and more the carriers of their own imports and exports.

I have the honor to be, &c.
A. J. DALLAS.

FRIDAY, March 8.

Mr. VARNUM, from the committee to whom was referred the resolution to amend the Constitution of the United States so as to regulate the mode of choosing Representatives in Congress and Electors of President and Vice President thereof, reported it with amendments, which were read.

Mr. ROBERTS, from the committee to whom the subject was referred, reported a bill incorporating the subscribers to the Orphan Asylum of the City of Washington; and the bill was read and passed to the second reading.

The bill further extending the time for issuing and locating military land warrants, and for other purposes, was read the second time, and referred to the committee on the memorial of the Legislative Council and House of Representatives of the Mississippi Territory.

The resolution to amend the Constitution of the United States, so as to subject to removal from office the judges of all the courts thereof, was read the second time.

The bill to amend the act for regulating the Post Office Establishment, respecting the compensation of postmasters, and to allow the members of Congress the privilege of franking during the recess, was read a second time, and referred to a select committee; and Messrs. WILSON, ROBERTS, MORROW, CHACE, and THOMPSON, were appointed the committee.

The bill, entitled "An act authorizing and requiring the Secretary of State to issue letters patent to Andrew Kurtz, was read the second time, and referred to a select committee, to consider and report thereon; and Messrs. ROBERTS, WILSON, and BROWN, were appointed the committee.

Mr. GOLDSBOROUGH submitted the following motion for consideration:

Resolved, That it be referred to the consideration of the Naval Committee, whether it is expedient and proper to instruct the Secretary of the Navy to cause a fair valuation to be made of the ship of war, "The Cyane," her tackle, apparel, and stores, (according to the customary mode in such cases,) and to pay to the captors the whole amount of such valuation; and that they make report thereon.

Mr. HUNTER, from the committee to whom was referred the bill providing for the publication of the decisions of the Supreme Court of the United States, reported it with amendments; which were read.

The Senate resumed, as in Committee of the Whole, the consideration of the bill, entitled "An act making further provision for military services during the late war, and for other purposes;" and, on motion by Mr. WILLIAMS, the further consideration thereof was postponed until Monday next.

The Senate then proceeded to the consideration of a bill to provide a law library for the use of the Judges of the Supreme Court.

[This bill proposes the appropriation of five thousand dollars, for the purchase of law books to compose a library for the use of the Supreme Court.]

After some desultory debate on the modification of the details of this bill, between Messrs. TALBOT, SANFORD, MASON of New Hampshire, and WILSON, the bill was postponed to Monday.

The bill, in addition to an act, entitled "An act in relation to the Navy Pension Fund," was read a third time, and the blank having been filled with "three hundred," the bill was amended by unanimous consent.

Resolved, That this bill pass, and that the title thereof be "An act in addition to an act entitled 'An act in relation to the Navy Pension Fund."

On motion, by Mr. MORROW, the further consideration of the bill to ascertain and establish the western boundary of the tract reserved for satisfying the military bounties allowed to the officers and soldiers of the Virginia line, on Continental Establishment, was postponed until Thursday next.

On motion, by Mr. MORROW the further consideration of the report of the committee to whom was referred the resolution relating to the claims of the officers and soldiers of the Virginia line, on State and Continental Establishment, for bounty lands, was also postponed until Thursday next.

The Senate resumed the consideration of the bill supplementary to the act for the indemnification of certain claimants to lands in the Mississippi Territory.

This bill proposes, in its first section, to extend the time for filing releases by claimants; and in the second regulates the manner in which the claims of the representatives of deceased persons shall be substantiated, &c.

The latter section was struck out, in pursuance of the recommendation of the select committee, the ground of which recommendation was explained by Mr. TAYLOR, to be the interference of this provision with the peculiar powers of State governments and courts, in relation to descents and the distribution of estates.

Thus amended, the bill was, without opposition, ordered to be engrossed for a third reading.

CASE OF GEORGE ROSSIER.

The bill for the relief of George Rossier was then taken up. The bill proposes to indemnify the above named person for the loss of two Treasury notes of a thousand dollars transmitted by mail, on the exhibition of sufficient evidence that the same have not been paid or funded, and on giving security to indemnify the United States from loss from their future appearance.

Messrs. SANFORD and DAGGETT supported this bill. Mr. ROBERTS suggested, as a ground of opposition to the bill, that this was a case standing on the same footing as other cases of losses by the mail, for which the United States could not be expected to be liable. To which Mr. SANFORD replied, showing the distinction, and adducing analogous cases to show not only the equity, but the precedents of such a course as that proposed by the bill.

For the purpose of further consideration, the bill was postponed to Tuesday.

CLAIM OF COLONEL THOMPSON.

The Senate took up the bill, reported by a select committee, for the relief of John Thompson. The bill proposes to allow to Colonel Thompson interest on a claim for Revolutionary services, the principal of which was granted to him by an act of Congress in 1812.

Some investigation took place on the merit of the claim, which was supported by Messrs. ROBERTS and FROMENTIN, and was opposed by Messrs. VARNUM, TURNER, DAGGETT, MACON, KING, MASON of New Hampshire, and TAYLOR.

If the claim was just, as Congress had heretofore decided, it was said, it ought to be allowed in full; and such, it was argued, was the intention of the Congress, but not the construction at the Treasury, in the act which did pass. On the other hand it was said, that an allowance by any Congress to any claimant, ought to be considered as in full, and conclusive of what was justly due; and in this case it was moreover said, that the claim itself had been of a doubtful character, having been rejected more than once before it at last succeeded. To which it was replied, besides defending the justice of the claim, that the former decision of Congress in its favor precluded that question.

The question was taken, after much debate, on ordering the bill to be engrossed for a third reading, and decided in the negative—yeas 5, nays 15, as follows:

YEAS—Messrs. Chace, Morrow, Roberts, Sanford, and Tait.

NAYS—Messrs. Condit, Daggett, Dana, Gaillard, Goldsborough, Hunter, King, Macon, Mason of New Hampshire, Ruggles, Taylor, Tichenor, Turner, Varnum, Wells, Williams, and Wilson.

MONDAY, March 11.

Mr. ROBERTS presented the memorial of Ferdinando Fairfax, of the City of Washington, opposing the extension of the patent of the late Robert Fulton, as the inventor of a method of navigating vessels by the agency of fire and steam, as prayed for by Harriet Fulton, for reasons stated in the memorial; which was read.

Mr. SANFORD presented the petition of William Radcliff and others, of the city of New York, praying the payment of certain debentures, which has been suspended by order of the Treasury Department of the United States, as stated in the petition; which was read, and referred to a select committee to consider and report thereon by bill or otherwise; and Messrs. SANFORD, BROWN, and DANA, were appointed the committee.

Mr. DAGGETT presented the memorial of the President and Directors of the Patriotic Bank of Washington, praying a charter of incorporation, for reasons stated in the memorial; which was read, and referred to the Committee on Finance and an Uniform National Currency.

Mr. RUGGLES submitted the following motion for consideration:

Resolved, That a committee be appointed to inquire into the expediency of making provision for altering the location of the road laid out from the foot of the rapids of the Miami river of Lake Erie to the western boundary of the Connecticut Reserve, so that the said road may pass through the reservation of two miles square on the Sandusky river; and also, whether any and what further provisions are necessary to be made for the surveying and sale of the public lands adjoining on the aforesaid road.

The bill incorporating the subscribers to the Orphan Asylum of the City of Washington, was read the second time.

A message from the House of Representatives informed the Senate that the House have passed a bill entitled "An act to change the mode of compensation to the members of the Senate and House of Representatives, and the Delegates from Territories;" also, a bill entitled "An act for the relief of Gustavus Loomis;" in which bills they request the concurrence of the Senate.

The two bills last mentioned were read, and passed to the second reading.

The following Message was received from the PRESIDENT OF THE UNITED STATES:

To the Senate and House of
    Representatives of the United States:

I lay before Congress a statement of the militia of the United States, according to the latest returns received by the Department of War.

                JAMES MADISON.
MARCH 9, 1816.

The Message and statement were read.

The bill from the House of Representatives for making further provision for military services during the late war, was taken up; and, the question being about to be put whether it should be read a third time—

Mr. WILSON announced his intention to move an amendment to the bill, by introducing a provision which he understood had failed in the House of Representatives, but which, in his opinion, public justice, gratitude, and feeling required to be adopted. He then read the sketch of a new section to allow donations of land, in proportion to their rank, to the officers deranged by the late reduction of the Army. To ascertain whether the Senate would be willing to receive an amendment of this character, he moved to postpone the bill till to-morrow. The postponement was agreed to.

The Senate next took up the bill to establish a Law Library at the Seat of Government, for the use of the Supreme Court of the United States. There was some debate on this subject, not in opposition to the provision of law books for the purpose designated as well as for the use of Congress, but on a motion of Mr. WILSON to amend the bill by striking out so much thereof as proposes to place the law books to be purchased in an apartment separate from the general library; which was negatived, 13 to 8.

The bill was ordered to a third reading. [The appropriation proposed in the bill to be applied to its object at this time is five thousand dollars.]

The bill for the relief of John M. Forbes, which came from the Representative Hall, was next considered; and after a due explanation by Mr. HUNTER of its object, (to authorize a settlement of Mr. Forbes's account for interest and difference of exchange of money paid in Europe for the support of distressed seamen) the bill was ordered to be read a third time.

The bill concerning the District of Columbia (respecting the introduction of slaves from adjoining States) was, on motion of Mr. LACOCK, postponed to Friday.

The Senate resumed the consideration of the report of the Committee on Military Affairs, on the petition of the representatives of Ignace Delino; and on motion, by Mr. WILLIAMS, the further consideration thereof was postponed until Monday next.

The PRESIDENT communicated a report of the Secretary for the Department of War, made in obedience to the resolution of the Senate of the 7th instant, on the memorial of the Mayor and Common Council of the city of New York; and the report was read.

The bill providing for the publication of the decisions in the Supreme Court of the United States, was considered, amended, and ordered to be engrossed for a third reading. [The bill proposes to allow to a Reporter of the decisions of the Supreme Court, one thousand dollars per annum, provided the said decisions be published within six months after the adjournment each year, and fifty copies thereof delivered free of charge to the Secretary of State, to be distributed as prescribed by the bill.]

The Senate resumed, as in Committee of the Whole, the bill dividing the State of Pennsylvania into two judicial districts; and, on motion by Mr. LACOCK, the consideration thereof was further postponed until Friday next.

The Senate resumed, as in Committee of the Whole, the consideration of the resolution to amend the Constitution of the United States, that the judges of all the courts thereof shall be subject to removal from office; and, on motion by Mr. LACOCK, on the further consideration thereof was postponed to, and made the order of the day for Monday next.

YAZOO CLAIMS.

The bill further supplementary to the act entitled "An act providing for the indemnification of certain claimants of public lands in the Mississippi Territory," was read a third time.

The blank for the day to which the time for filing releases is extended, was, on motion by Mr. TAYLOR, filled with the first Monday in December next.

The blank for the additional compensation to each of the commissioners appointed to adjust these claims, and to the secretary of the board, in consideration of the further services required of them, was next to be filled.

Mr. TAYLOR, after a compliment to the talent, assiduity, and integrity of the board, as calling for a compensation larger than they had hitherto been allowed, and more adequate to the services rendered by them, moved to fill the blank with $1,500; which was agreed to without a division.

And thus amended, the bill was passed and sent to the House of Representatives.

FULTON'S PATENT.

The bill for the benefit of the widow and children of Robert Fulton, deceased, was next taken up:

Mr. KING proposed to postpone it to Wednesday; Mr. ROBERTS to recommit it.

In the little debate which took place, Mr. ROBERTS referred to the memorial this morning presented, as affording a reason why the bill should not pass, or at least should receive reconsideration in committee; he also incidentally remarked that there was no such evidence of cost in perfecting the invention, or want of profit from the use of it, as would support the claim for an extension of the patent, &c. To which Mr. KING replied, that the question of the validity of the original patent was one wholly of a judicial nature; it was one in regard to which Congress could neither take away or confer privileges—the bill could extend no rights not vested by the patent, &c., and all questions arising out of the priority of invention, &c. belonged and must remain with the courts of justice. Mr. WILSON favored commitment, though favorable to the extension of the patent.

Mr. KING having withdrawn his motion for postponement, the bill was recommitted to Messrs. KING, MORROW, DAGGETT, CHACE, and ROBERTS.

AMENDMENT TO THE CONSTITUTION.

The amendment proposed to the Constitution, requiring the election of Electors and Representatives of Congress to be made in all the States by districts, was taken up; and the question stated on ordering it to a third reading.

Mr. LACOCK expressed his surprise that a proposition for amending the Constitution should be so lightly treated as not to have had a day assigned for its discussion. He thought it required more deliberation; and therefore moved to postpone it and make it the order of the day for Monday.

Mr. DANA professed his readiness to vote on the question at once, with the hope that the proposition would be rejected. It seemed to him to be introducing a sort of bed of Procrustes, to declare that, because it was convenient for one State to elect its Electors and Representatives by districts, all the other States, convenient or not, should be compelled to do the same.

Without further debate, the postponement was agreed to.

TUESDAY, March 12.

Mr. TAIT, from the Committee on Naval Affairs, to whom the subject was referred, reported a bill respecting the late officers and crew of the sloop of war Wasp; and the bill was read and passed to the second reading.

The Senate resumed the consideration of the following resolution, yesterday moved by Mr. RUGGLES:

Resolved, That a committee be appointed to inquire into the expediency of making provision for altering the location of the road laid out from the foot of the rapids of the Miami river and Lake Erie to the western boundary of the Connecticut Reserve, so that the said road may pass through the reservation of two miles square on the Sandusky river; and also whether any and what further provisions are necessary to be made for the surveying and sale of the public lands adjoining on the aforesaid road.

This question gave rise to some discussion. Mr. KING moved to refer the resolve to the Commissioner of the General Land Office, to consider and report thereon. This motion was supported by himself, and opposed by Messrs. RUGGLES, MORROW, TAIT, and TAYLOR; the field of debate of course very limited, the question being only as to the mode of making an inquiry. The motion of Mr. KING was negatived.

The resolve, as above, was agreed to; and Messrs. RUGGLES, KING, and MORROW, appointed a committee accordingly.

The bill entitled "An act for the relief of Gustavus Loomis," was read the second time, and referred to the Committee on Military Affairs.

The bill entitled "An act for the relief of John M. Forbes," was read a third time, and passed.

On motion, by Mr. ROBERTS, the memorial of Ferdinando Fairfax, presented the 11th instant, was referred to the committee to whom was referred the bill for the benefit of the widow and children of Robert Fulton, deceased, to consider and report thereon by bill or otherwise.

A message from the House of Representatives informed the Senate that the House have passed the bill entitled "An act to extend certain privileges, as therein mentioned, to Bernard Edme Verjon," with amendments; in which they request the concurrence of the Senate; and that they have also passed a bill entitled "An act

for the relief of John T. Wirt;" in which they request the concurrence of the Senate.

The bill last mentioned was read, and passed to the second reading.

Mr. WILLIAMS, from the committee to whom the subject was referred, reported a bill for the relief of John Holker, formerly Consul General of France to the United States; and the bill was read, and passed to the second reading.

On motion, the Senate proceeded to consider the amendments of the House of Representatives to the bill entitled "An act to extend certain privileges, as therein mentioned, to Bernard Edme Verjon." Whereupon,

Resolved, That they concur therein.

The Senate resumed the consideration of the bill entitled "An act making further provision for military services during the late war, and for other purposes; and on motion, by Mr. RUGGLES, the further consideration thereof was postponed until Monday next.

The bill to establish a law library at the seat of Government, for the use of the Supreme Court of the United States, was read a third time, and the blank filled with "two thousand."

Resolved, That this bill pass, and that the title thereof be "An act concerning the library of Congress."

The bill providing for the publication of the decisions of the Supreme Court of the United States was read a third time, and passed.

The bill for the relief of M. Rossier (in the case of lost Treasury notes) was further considered, and ordered to a third reading, after debate, by a vote of 15 to 11.

The bill to incorporate the subscribers to the Female Orphan Asylum of the City of Washington, was taken up. Its benevolent objects were explained, its utility warmly anticipated, and the motives of its institutors justly viewed by Mr. ROBERTS. No further debate took place, except a question by Mr. WILSON as to the number of children now fostered by it; to which Mr. ROBERTS replied that the present number was seven.

On the question to engross the bill for a third reading, there were for the bill 12, against it 12. The President (Mr. GAILLARD) voting in the affirmative, the bill was ordered to be engrossed for a third reading.

COMPENSATION BILL.

The bill from the House of Representatives, to change the mode of compensation of the Senators, Delegates, and Representatives in Congress, was read the second time.

Mr. TAYLOR moved to refer the bill to the Committee of Finance.

Mr. BIBB opposed the reference. The principles embraced in the bill were not, he said, of a complicated nature, but such as might be determined without the formality of a reference to a committee. He confessed, that the bill was not exactly in the shape which he should prefer; but, as he thought it had decided advantages over the present system and rate of compensation, he should vote for it as it stood, and against any amendment which should be proposed. He should vote against any amendment, he said, because of the peculiar delicacy of the subject; and considering that the bill had been proposed by the House of Representatives, so much the most numerous branch of the Legislature, he was unwilling to have any controversy with that House about it. Amendments might hereafter be made by a supplementary bill, if found necessary in the course of the operation of the system.

Mr. TAYLOR said, that the course which he had proposed, was not different from that generally given to every bill coming from the House. It was the proper course to be pursued, for a variety of reasons: Suppose the salaries of other officers of the Government should be thought incompetent, the Committee of Finance might propose amendments to the bill calculated also to include them; for, he intimated, the passage of a bill to compensate ourselves alone, seemed to be too close an observance of the old but pithy adage, charity begins at home. Our foreign Ministers, he said, received, besides their outfit, a salary of nine thousand dollars, to enable them to make a display abroad: it would seem, by the distinction in favor of foreign Ministers, in this respect, as if Congress did not care what appearance our great officers of the Government exhibited at home, under our own eyes. Mr. T. said, he was not opposed to the increase of compensation of the members of the Legislature, and should vote for this bill, if so altered as to make the compensation compatible with the reasons upon which the proposed increase was obviously founded. In order to let the people know that their interests were consulted as much, where we are concerned, said he, as in other cases, I wish the bill to take the usual course of reference to a select committee.

Mr. DANA said, there was certainly something due to the delicacy of sentiment of the gentleman from South Carolina, which had induced him to make this motion. It being at all times a matter of delicacy to act on questions concerning our own compensation, Mr. D. said, he did not wonder that, in his anxiety to avoid error on the one side, he should bend over too far in the other direction. In reference to the laws heretofore passed on these subjects, he said, he found it had not been thought at all necessary to combine the compensation of Executive and Legislative officers; nor did he see why the members of Congress should measure their compensation by that of other officers of the Government. This question was one separate and distinct; it was a question of its own character, he said, and ought to stand alone. He was, therefore, opposed to commitment in order to amend the bill.

Mr. CAMPBELL said, as a member of the Committee of Finance, he was not aware that that Committee could give any information to the Senate on the subject of this bill, which would enable it to act better than they could without it. The principle of the bill, he said, was a naked one, whether the compensation of the members should or should not be increased; the question in relation to the manner of compensation was also a single question. Mr. C. said, he felt in so great a degree the delicacy which had been adverted to, that he would not say much on this subject. As to the argument that the salaries of some other officers of Government require an increase, he was not disposed to deny the fact; but, in addition to the reply that it was not necessary to connect that question with the one now before the Senate, he said, the salaries of those officers had been raised since the compensation of the members of Congress had been fixed. Mr. C did not profess himself to be an advocate for the manner of compensation proposed by this bill; he had serious doubts on the subject; but he thought proper to state, that this measure, having been adopted by the other House, which is considered generally as immediately responsible to the people for its acts, and the members of which pride themselves on being the purse-holders of the nation, it appeared to him that this House was relieved from the necessity of probing the subject as closely as it might otherwise be proper. Not, he said, that he thought that the Senate was at all bound by their vote, but in this respect the other House was at least as responsible as this. The present compensation to the members of Congress, he was convinced, was entirely too low, if it was intended that they should have a compensation anything like competent to pay their necessary expenses. He was opposed to the reference altogether; if committed, he hoped it would be to another committee than that which had been named.

Mr. DAGGETT said, the question embraced by this bill was one which he should be always disposed to leave with the other house. He would not interfere, he said, to prevent that compensation which they should deem adequate to their services. He felt no reluctance in contending, and contending earnestly, with the House of Representatives, on questions such as that of the extent of the treaty-making power, the expediency and amount of a land-tax; indeed, on any question of a general nature; but, he said, there was an innate delicacy in the Senate's undertaking to say that the House of Representatives should not have a sort of control over questions like this. He was, therefore, disposed to take a bill of this nature, and pass it as soon as, according to the forms of the House, it could be done, and to have little said about it. If they had even increased the compensation still further, or if they had thought fit to diminish it, he should not have thought it necessary, for his part, to say a word about it.

Mr. MACON did not consider this as a question of compensation. The question now to be considered was, whether the bill was calculated to carry itself into execution. In this view it was necessary to commit it, rather than with a view to any facts or principles connected with it. The details of the bill ought to be examined, in order to see whether any rule could be devised which would suit better than that embraced by the bill. Gentlemen who considered this bill so perfect that it ought not to be touched, so plain that he who runs may read, would of course vote against commitment. He confessed that he had not himself that distinct view of it. What relates to ourselves, he said, ought more than anything else be made so plain, that no doubt could attend it. He should, therefore, vote to commit this bill, believing it might be improved. As to the rights of the two Houses, Mr. M. said, they were equal. Each House had on such a subject the same rights as the other. The presumption was, and on that ground they ought to proceed, that if this House should make a bill from the other House better than as it came from them, the House of Representatives would concur in the amendment. This was the general practice; and, in adhering to it, he did not see how the Senate could be placed in a delicate situation in relation to the other House.

Mr. CHACE was also in favor of the commitment of this bill. He did not see, he said, why gentlemen should be ready to throw the burden of this measure (if a burden it was) on the shoulders of the House of Representatives. As regards the rate of compensation generally, every man must act on it, he said, from his own conviction. Mr. C. was himself clearly of opinion that this bill wanted considerable amendment. It had been yet but a short time under consideration. He asked, whether it was a fair way of legislation, when a bill was manifestly imperfect, to insist on passing it, with a view of perfecting it by a supplementary bill, as had been intimated? Was it not best, he asked, to make the bill perfect at first? Why afraid, he asked, to approach a bill of this character? Why regard it as a measure bearing the injunction *noli me tangere?* The Constitution and rules of proceeding, he admitted, did seem to give to the other House the power of originating money bills; but, on a question of this kind, he did not see why this House should not be under the same obligation as the other to examine critically bills of this kind.

Mr. SANFORD said, in the course of a few remarks on this subject, that this bill should be treated as all other bills were. It was almost a matter of course on all bills to refer the subject thereof, on the motion of a member, to a committee for examination. He wished to know, as regarded his vote, what would be the effect of this bill; whether it would increase the rate of compensation of members, as well as change the mode? He wished, in short, to see this bill take the course of all other bills.

Mr. DANA again rose, and showed, that though the practice was to refer bills on their second reading, it was to examine the bearings of the bills. This bill, he said, embraced principles, the extent of which could be seen with a single cast of the eye. It had no complex details; it repealed no former acts requiring a comparison and examination of existing laws, &c. He did not, for these and other reasons, deem it necessary to commit the bill.

The question on commitment was decided in the negative—yeas 9, nays 22, as follows:

YEAS—Messrs. Chace, King, Macon, Morrow, Ruggles, Sanford, Taylor, Varnum, and Wilson.

NAYS—Messrs. Barry, Bibb, Brown, Campbell, Condit, Daggett, Dana, Gaillard, Gore, Horsey, Howell, Hunter, Lacock, Mason of New Hampshire, Roberts, Talbot, Tait, Thompson, Tichenor, Turner, Wells, and Williams.

And then, on motion, the Senate adjourned until to-morrow.

WEDNESDAY, March 13.

The bill to establish a system of navigation for the United States, was read the second time, and on motion, by Mr. DANA, the further consideration thereof was postponed to, and made the order of the day for Monday, the 25th instant.

The bill respecting the late officers and crew of the sloop-of-war WASP was read the second time.

The bill for the relief of John Holker, formerly Consul General of France to the United States, was read the second time.

The bill entitled "An act for the relief of John T. Wirt," was read the second time, and on motion, by Mr. ROBERTS, referred to the Committee on Military Affairs.

Mr. WILLIAMS, from the Committee on Military Affairs, to whom was referred the bill entitled "An act for the relief of Gustavus Loomis," reported it without amendment.

Mr. ROBERTS, from the committee to whom was referred the bill entitled "An act authorizing and requiring the Secretary of State to issue letters patent to Andrew Kurtz," reported it without amendment.

The following Message was received from the PRESIDENT OF THE UNITED STATES:

To the Senate and House of Representatives of the United States:

I lay before Congress a report of the Secretary of the Treasury, containing a statement of proceedings under the act to regulate the laying out and making a road from Cumberland, in the State of Maryland, to the State of Ohio, with a statement of past appropriations, and an estimate of required appropriations.

JAMES MADISON.

MARCH 12, 1816.

The Message and statements therein referred to were read.

The Senate resumed the consideration of the motion made the 18th instant, for referring to the consideration of the Naval Committee the expediency of causing a fair valuation to be made of the old ship of war "The Cyane," and to pay to the captors the amount of such valuation; and agreed thereto.

The bill for the relief of George Rossier and others was read a third time, and passed.

On motion by Mr. HARPER, the bill to limit the right of appeal from the circuit court of the United States for the District of Columbia, was referred to a select committee, to consider and report thereon; and Mr. HARPER, Mr. TALBOT, and Mr. GOLDSBOROUGH, were appointed the committee.

189   HISTORY OF CONGRESS.   190

MARCH, 1816.   *Female Orphan Asylum—Compensation Bill.*   SENATE.

WASHINGTON FEMALE ORPHAN ASYLUM.

The engrossed bill to incorporate the subscribers to the Washington Female Orphan Asylum was read a third time.

Mr. HARPER assigned the reasons why he should vote against the bill. If he were to judge of this question by the respectability of the names connected with it, or by the objects of the institution embraced in the bill, he certainly should vote for the bill; but it would be such a variation from the whole course and scope of our laws, that he was obliged to vote against it. Nothing, he said, could be more laudable than such associations, but he submitted whether their incorporation by law was at all necessary to enable them to perfect their object. Was this strange anomaly in law, of a body politic composed of married women, at all necessary to the objects of the institution? He could not see it. If the object was to enable the institution to acquire real property, it could be accomplished, he said, without an act of incorporation: a simple deed of trust would answer the purpose very well, &c.

Mr. ROBERTS sustained the bill. If a person were to die and leave property to the institution, unless in a corporate form, it could not inherit it. This charter, he said, was a grant of but little magnitude: it was such a privilege as, in many of the States, the courts were authorized to grant, under proper restrictions. As to the alleged novelty of the proposition, it might be new in regard to this District, because the legislation of Congress for it had been very limited; but similar acts were to be found on the statute books of some of the States. The charter would give no privilege nor sanction any abuse. It would enable the trustees of a praiseworthy institution to secure, in the most eligible and favorable manner, the application of such means as may be given by benevolent persons to the benevolent objects of the association, &c.

Mr. CAMPBELL also assigned a few reasons in favor of the bill.

The question on the passage of the bill was decided in the negative—yeas 16, nays 17, as follows:

YEAS—Messrs. Brown, Campbell, Chace, Dana, Gaillard, Howell, Hunter, Lacock, Roberts, Sanford, Tait, Thompson, Tichenor, Turner, Williams, and Wilson.

NAYS—Messrs. Barry, Bibb, Condit, Daggett, Goldsborough, Gore, Harper, Horsey, King, Macon, Mason of New Hampshire, Morrow, Ruggles, Talbot, Taylor, Varnum, and Wells.

So the bill was rejected.

COMPENSATION BILL.

The Senate proceeded to the consideration, in Committee of the Whole, of the bill to change the mode of compensation of the Senators, Representatives and Delegates in Congress.

[This bill proposes to change the rate and mode of compensation, from six dollars per day during attendance to one thousand five hundred per annum.]

Mr. TAYLOR, in proposing an amendment to the bill, said, he was left, from the absence of reasons assigned in favor of the bill, to presume the motive of it to be, that there would be a greater despatch in the public business, if members were paid by the job than if they were paid by the day. He doubted the correctness of this inference. If, for six dollars a day, the sessions of Congress are spun out to an inconvenient length, and public business delayed by the desire of members to increase the amount of their pay, (supposing them the immoral agents which the adoption of this system presupposes)—would they not, he asked, be induced by the change in the mode of compensation, in order to curtail their expenses and increase their profits, to go home before the public business is finished, or so urge the public business as to leave it in an imperfect form? He thought, as he said yesterday, that the amount of the present allowance was incompetent; that the sacrifice was too great, to come here for nothing, and in many instances, at a certain loss. He felt a desire, however, that an alteration should be made in this bill, to lessen the inducement which it appeared to him to hold out to the members to hurry over or neglect the public business, &c. With such views, he moved to strike out three thousand (the compensation, double that allowed to the members, of the President of the Senate and Speaker of the other House) and in lieu thereof to insert two thousand dollars; with a view to reduce the compensation of the members from one thousand five hundred to one thousand, and to add a new section, for allowing, besides, three dollars per day to the members for each day they actually attend in Congress. This amendment, he said, would bring into play the principle of paying by the job, and would prevent the public work from being done in a slovenly manner, by paying a daily compensation adequate, or nearly so, to the daily expenses of the members.

Mr. MACON also moved to amend the bill so as to strike out the salary feature altogether, and in lieu thereof to insert a provision that the compensation should be hereafter —— dollars per day—intending that the blank might be filled with such sum as the Senate should prefer. He was opposed to the idea of a salary for legislative services; such a rule of compensation was not known under any of the governments of the States, &c.

Mr. DAGGETT opposed all amendments of this nature to the bill; considering it better to take it in its present shape. The increase of compensation, he estimated, according to an average computation, would not be greater than as one hundred to seventy-one, &c. Was it worth while for this small object to enter into a controversy with the other House? He showed, besides, that the salaries of all the officers of Government (judges excepted, to his regret) had been increased since the compensation of the members was fixed, &c.

Both the amendments above stated were negatived without a division.

Mr. TAYLOR then proposed an amendment to the detail of the bill, which he considered very defective. The amendment was as follows:

" That in case any Senator, Representative, or Delegate, shall not attend in his place at the day on which Congress shall convene, or shall absent himself before the close of the session, a deduction shall be made from the sum which would otherwise be allowed to him, in proportion to the time of his absence,"

And to insert in lieu thereof the following:

" That in case any Senator, Representative, or Delegate, shall not attend in his place every day in which Congress shall be in session, within any year, deduction shall be made of his annual allowance, proportioned to the time he shall be absent, when compared to the whole time in which Congress shall be in session within the said year."

This motion gave rise to considerable debate, chiefly of a critical nature, in which Messrs. TAYLOR, DANA, CHACE, HARPER, DAGGETT, and TALBOT, took part. The motion was negatived, 26 to 7, as follows:

YEAS—Messrs. Chace, Macon, Ruggles, Sanford, Taylor, Varnum, and Wilson.

NAYS—Messrs. Barry, Bibb, Brown, Campbell, Condit, Daggett, Dana, Gaillard, Goldsborough, Gore, Harper, Horsey, Howell, Hunter, King, Lacock, Mason of New Hampshire, Morrow, Roberts, Talbot, Tait, Thompson, Tichenor, Turner, Wells, and Williams.

Mr. WILSON observed, that he would not detain the Senate long, as he saw they were impatient for the question; but he felt it a duty to the prudent and economical State which he in part represented, to state his objections to the bill now before the Senate. This he should do as briefly as possible.

In the first place, he disliked its retrospective operation, in going back more than a year to give an additional reward for services already rendered, and in many instances paid for. This principle he thought objectionable in itself, and dangerous as a precedent.

The time at which the bill was brought forward, was another serious objection. Just at the close of a very expensive war, when many of the internal taxes and high impost duties are yet continued, to enable the Government to meet the demands upon the Treasury—while numerous and extensive claims for articles furnished, and services rendered, are yet unpaid and unliquidated—and while our revenue system is unsettled, and its productiveness unknown—he could not believe this to be the proper period for increasing salaries, either of ourselves or others. We ought at least to wait until those taxes are repealed, those claims discharged, and that revenue ascertained, before we thought of augmenting the compensation of members of Congress or officers of the Government.

He was also, Mr. W. said, displeased with the mode adopted in this bill. An annual salary to legislators, who sometimes sat longer, and sometimes shorter, was a novel principle, and its effects very doubtful. It might produce an injurious haste in the transaction of business—it might shorten the term, or lessen the frequency of the sessions of Congress—and, on the whole, appeared to him less safe than the per diem provision.

The amount contemplated by the bill he deemed too large. It would nearly or quite double the allowance which former Congresses had deemed sufficient, and under which present members had accepted their seats. It was a greater sum than many important officers under the General Government received for incessant service—and more than many of the States give to their principal officers. In New Jersey, not a single officer, excepting only the Governor, received a salary to this amount. The Judges of the Supreme Court, selected for their talents, experience and integrity, from amongst our best and wisest citizens, and engaged, with little intermission, during the whole year in their arduous and important duties, received far less compensation than is here provided for members of Congress, who are employed in public business less than half the year.

The precedent, Mr. W. said, he regarded as a very pernicious one. Raising our own pay, will be but an entering wedge to increasing the compensation of officers of the Government generally, civil, judicial, military, and naval. Though our charity begins at home, it will not be permitted to end here. This consequence he should deprecate. He did not consider high salaries consistent with the principles or safety of our Republican institutions—inasmuch as they tended to introduce, or to increase, ambition, intrigue, and corruption.

The manner in which the bill was hurried through, was not, he said, in his opinion, less exceptionable than the bill itself. In the other House (if he might be permitted to allude to its course there) it was introduced one day, read and considered the next, and passed the third. In the Senate, postponement, commitment, and amendment, are all refused; and it is to be pushed through, by main strength, with a haste altogether unusual in cases so doubtful in their character, and so important in their consequences.

On the whole, Mr. W. said, he did most earnestly hope, for these and other reasons which might be enumerated, that the Senate would reject this bill.

No amendment having been agreed to, the President resumed the Chair, and the bill was reported to the Senate.

On motion, by Mr. SANFORD, to strike out of line 9, " three thousand," and of line 11, " fifteen hundred," it was determined in the negative—yeas 10, nays 23, as follows:

YEAS—Messrs. Chace, King, Macon, Ruggles, Sanford, Taylor, Tichenor, Turner, Varnum, and Wilson.

NAYS—Messrs. Barry, Bibb, Brown, Campbell, Condit, Daggett, Dana, Gaillard, Goldsborough, Gore, Harper, Horsey, Howell, Hunter, Lacock, Mason of New Hampshire, Morrow, Roberts, Talbot, Tait, Thompson, Wells, and Williams.

On the question Shall this bill be read a third time?" it was determined in the affirmative—yeas 22, nays 11, as follows:

YEAS—Messrs. Barry, Bibb, Brown, Campbell, Condit, Daggett, Dana, Gaillard, Gore, Harper, Horsey, Howell, Hunter, Lacock, Morrow, Roberts, Talbot, Tait, Thompson, Turner, Wells, and Williams.

NAYS—Messrs. Chace, Goldsborough, King, Macon, Mason of New Hampshire, Ruggles, Sanford, Taylor, Tichenor, Varnum, and Wilson.

THURSDAY, March 14.

Mr. ROBERTS presented the memorial of Mathew McConnell, and others, a committee on behalf of the surviving officers of the Pennsylvania line of the Revolutionary army, praying remuneration for their services, by which the independence and sovereignty of the United States were achieved and established, as stated in the memorial; which was read, and referred to the Committee on Military Affairs.

Mr. HARPER, from the committee to whom was referred the bill to limit the right of appeal from the Circuit Court of the United States for the District of Columbia, reported it with amendments, which were read.

The Senate proceeded to the consideration of the bill, reported by a committee of the Senate, for the relief of John Holker. [The bill is to allow him the amount of certain loan office certificates destroyed by fire.] Mr. ROBERTS suggested grounds of opposition to the bill, on its merits and the importance of the precedent it might afford for claims to an indefinite amount. Mr. WILLIAMS sustained the claim on its merits as deduced from the evidence, and the expediency of allowing a claim manifestly just, which would have been allowed without the intervention of Congress, but for a mere formality which had been omitted, &c.

This bill was postponed to Monday next, on motion of Mr. ROBERTS, after some conversation between Messrs. ROBERTS, WILLIAMS, WELLS, DAGGETT, TALBOT, and HARPER—in the course of which no decided opposition was manifested by any gentleman to the bill.

Mr. DAGGETT submitted the following motion for consideration:

Resolved, That the committee appointed on so much of the Message of the President of the United States as relates to Finance and an Uniform National Currency, be instructed to inquire into the expediency of providing by law for an augmentation of the salaries of the Judges of the Supreme Court of the United States.

The Senate resumed, as in Committee of the Whole, the consideration of the bill concerning certain advances made for the public service by the city of New York; and on motion, by Mr. SANFORD, the further consideration thereof was postponed until Thursday next.

The Senate resumed, as in Committee of the Whole, the consideration of the bill for calling forth the militia to execute the laws of the Union, suppress insurrection, and repel invasion, and to repeal the laws heretofore passed for those purposes; and on motion, by Mr. VARNUM, the further consideration thereof was postponed to, and made the order of the day for, Monday next.

The Senate resumed, as in Committee of the Whole, the consideration of the bill to ascertain and establish the western boundary of the tract

14th CON. 1st SESS.—7

reserved for satisfying the military bounties allowed to the officers and soldiers of the Virginia line, on Continental Establishment; and on motion, by Mr. MASON. of Virginia, the consideration thereof was further postponed to, and made the order of the day for, Tuesday next.

On motion by Mr. MASON, of Virginia, the further consideration of the report of the committee to whom was referred the resolution relating to the claims of the officers and soldiers of the Virginia line, on State establishment, for bounty lands, was also postponed to, and made the order of the day for, Tuesday next.

The Senate resumed, as in Committee of the Whole, the consideration of the bill entitled "An act for the relief of Gustavus Loomis;" and it passed to a third reading.

The Senate resumed, as in Committee of the Whole, the consideration of the bill entitled "An act authorizing and requiring the Secretary of State to issue letters patent to Andrew Kurtz," and on motion by Mr. ROBERTS, the further consideration thereof was postponed until Wednesday next.

On motion by Mr. CAMPBELL, the Committee on Finance and an Uniform National Currency, to whom was referred the petition of the Legislative Council and House of Representatives of the Indiana Territory, praying the suspension of prosecutions under the law laying a tax on domestic manufactures; and the memorial of John Redman Coxe, professor of chemistry in the University of Pennsylvania, were discharged from the further consideration thereof respectively.

The bill respecting the late officers and crew of the sloop of war Wasp, was taken up. [This bill proposes to allow twelve months' pay to the relatives of the officers and crew of the lost sloop of war, and also authorizes the distribution of fifty thousand dollars among the same, as a reward for the capture of the British sloops of war Reindeer and Avon.] The bill was amended, and ordered to be read a third time.

INDIAN AFFAIRS.

The PRESIDENT communicated a report of the Secretary for the Department of War, made in obedience to the resolution of the Senate of the 2d of March, 1815, in relation to Indian affairs, and the report was read, and is as follows:

DEPARTMENT OF WAR, *March* 13, 1816.

In obedience to the resolution of the Senate, of the 2d of March, 1815, I have the honor to transmit the enclosed documents, which exhibit the general expenses of the Indian department, embracing annuities and presents; and the general and particular views of the Indian trade, called for by the resolution.

Nos. 1, 2 and 3, exhibit the amount of annuities due and payable, and the sums actually paid to the several Indian tribes within our limits; the presents made to them, and the general expenses of the Indian department, during the four years preceding the 3d of March, 1815.

In the sum exhibited as presents, is included a great quantity of provisions furnished the friendly tribes during the war, who, on account of their attachment to the United States, were compelled to abandon their country, and take refuge within our settlements. The same cause prevented their engaging in the chase, the principal source of their supplies in times of peace. The embarrassments produced by a state of war, prevented the regular payment of the moneyed part of their annuities, and in many cases rendered it impossible to discharge that portion which was payable in merchandise. This circumstance presented a strong inducement to furnish them liberally with those supplies which we had at command, and which were even more necessary to them than the merchandise which we were bound to furnish. It is, however, believed that these supplies have been swelled to an unreasonable amount, by extensive impositions, which have been practised upon the Government, in the issue of provisions to them, which renders it necessary to discontinue the practice, or to devise new and suitable checks to guard against their repetition.

The statements marked from A to Z, exhibit the state of the fund set apart for Indian trade, during the four years preceding the 31st of March, 1815. It appears from these statements, that from the commencement of the trade, to the 31st December, 1809, a loss of $44,538 36 had been incurred, and that during the period designated in the resolution, the sum of $15,906 45 had been gained, notwithstanding the loss of $43,369 61 from the capture of several of the trading posts by the enemy, during the war. These two items, forming the aggregate sum of $59,276 06, may be considered as the commercial profit of the establishment, during that period, which would give an annual profit of nearly $15,000. But the annual expenses paid out of the Treasury, in support of the establishment, exceed $20,000, which presents a specific loss of more than $5,000 annually. The difference in the result of the management of this fund antecedent to the 31st of December, 1809, from that which is exhibited in these statements, during the four years preceding the 31st March, 1815, is no doubt, in great degree, the effect of the experience acquired by the prosecution of the trade. It is probable, that a more intimate acquaintance with the nature of the commerce, a more skilful selection of the goods, and of the agents employed in vending them, and a considerable increase of the capital invested in it, will in a short time produce a small and gradually increasing profit, after defraying all the expenses incident to the establishment, which are now payable out of the public Treasury. Under the most skilful management, the profits cannot be an inducement for continuing the system now in operation. That inducement, if it exists at all, must be found in the influence which it gives the Government over the Indian tribes within our limits, by administering to their wants, increasing their conforts, and promoting their happiness. The most obvious effect of that influence, is the preservation of peace with them, and among themselves. The exclusion of all intercourse between them and the whites, except those who have the permission of the Government, and over whose conduct a direct control is exercised, has insensibly contributed to this desirable object.

The amelioration in their condition, desired by the Government, has continued to advance, but in so slight a degree as to be perceptible only after a lapse of years. If the civilization of the Indian tribes is considered an object of primary importance, and superior to that of rapidly extinguishing their titles, and settling their lands by the whites, the expediency of continuing the system now in operation, under such modifications as have been suggested by the experience already acquired, appears to be manifest. The success of such an experiment requires the exercise of all the influence which the annual distribution of annuities and presents, aided by that which must flow from a judicious supply of all their wants, in exchange for those articles which the chase, and the increasing surplus of their stock of domestic animals, will enable them to procure. This influence, skilfully directed for a series of years, cannot fail to introduce among them distinct ideas of separate property. These ideas must necessarily precede any considerable advancement in the arts of civilization, and pre-suppose the institution of laws to secure the owner in the enjoyment of this individual property ; because, no man will exert himself to procure the comforts of life, unless his right to enjoy them is exclusive.

The idea of separate property in things personal, universally precedes the same idea in relation to lands. This results no less from the intrinsic difference between the two kinds of property, than from the different effects produced by human industry and ingenuity exerted upon them. The facility of removing personal property from place to place, according to the will or convenience of the owner, gives to this species of property, in the estimation of the huntsman, a value superior to property in lands, which his wants, as well as his habits, compel him annually to desert for a considerable portion of the year. To succeed perfectly in the attempt to civilise the aborigines of this country, the Government ought to direct their attention to the improvement of their habitations, and the multiplication of distinct settlements. As an inducement to this end, the different agents should be instructed to give them assurances, that in any treaty for the purchase of lands from their respective tribes, one mile square, including every separate settlement, should be reserved to the settler, which should become a fee simple estate, after the expiration of a certain number of years of actual residence upon, and cultivation of it. Perhaps an additional reservation of a quarter or half section of land to each member of such family, would add to the inducements, not only to make such separate settlements, but to the raising of a family. If measures of this kind were adopted by the Government, and steadily pursued for a series of years, while, at the same time, a spirit of liberality was exhibited in the commerce which we carry on with them, success, the most complete, might be confidently expected. But commerce with our Indian neighbors, prosecuted only upon a contracted scale, and upon the principles of commercial profit, would tend not only to diminish the influence of the Government with them, but would not fail entirely to alienate their affection from it. A period has arrived when the trade must be greatly extended, or entirely abandoned to individual enterprise. To reserve the trade in the hands of the Government, whilst the wants of the Indians are but partly supplied, would be to make them feel its influence only in their privations and wretchedness.

The right of the British Northwest Company to participate in this trade, independent of the will of the Government, is now at an end. The settlements of the lands ceded by the Creeks, in 1814, will exclude the Southern tribes from all intercourse with the Spanish ports in the Gulf of Florida. The preservation of peace with those tribes, as well as the execution of the plans which may be devised for their civilization, require that this intercourse should not be renewed. The great distance of some of the tribes in the Northwest Territory, and in the northern regions of Louisiana, from the settled parts of the United States, will probably make it necessary to permit the British merchant, from Canada, to participate in the commerce of these tribes, until more accurate information is obtained as to their situation and numbers, their wants, and their capacity to pay for articles of the first necessity. As this knowledge is gradually acquired, and the mode of conducting the trade better understood, the exclusion of foreigners from all participation in it may be safely effected. If the trade is to be continued in the hands of the Government, the capital ought to be increased to $500,000. The exclusion from all commercial intercourse with the ports in the Gulf of Florida, and the necessity of extending our trading establishments further to the West and the North, with a view to the ultimate exclusion of foreign participation in it, forcibly suggest the propriety of such an increase. This capital will probably be found greatly below what is necessary to supply the wants of the various tribes within our limits. The deficiency, it is believed, will be supplied by the Northwest Company, and by individual enterprise. At present, the Governors of our Territories are compelled to give licenses to trade with the Indians, to every person who can give security. The power of rejecting the application, on account of the character of the applicant, appears to be necessary. If the licensed traders were compelled to take an oath to observe the laws regulating Indian trade, it might aid in correcting the abuses, especially in vending spirituous liquors, which have too generally been practised by them. It is deemed expedient to establish a depot of merchandise at St. Lewis, or its vicinity, under the direction of a deputy superintendent, who should have power, in addition to supplying the regular and established trading houses, to deliver to persons of good moral character, who should be able to give security, any quantity of goods not exceeding $10,000, for which peltries, and other articles of Indian commerce, should be received in payment at a fair price and at fixed periods; or, that they should be sold by the Superintendent, on account of the purchaser. In the latter case, a premium, equal to the use and the risk of the capital, should be added to the price of the goods. This, as well as several other important ideas, are more fully developed in the communication of Governor Edwards, and of the Superintendent of Indian Trade, which are herewith communicated, marked R. and Z. Z.

In compliance with that part of the resolution which requires my opinion of the expediency of vesting the general management of Indian affairs in a separate and independent department, I have the honor to state, that an arrangement of that nature appears to me to be highly proper, if the commerce of those nations is to be retained in the hands of the Government. The only rational principle upon which it is considered necessary to place the Indian trade under the control of the War Department, is the necessity of relying upon it for the small military force which has hitherto been stationed at the different trading posts which have been established. This countenance and support could be given to the department to which it might be confided, with the same facility as if it still remained subordinate to the Department of War. The accounts of the Superintendent of Indian Trade are now returned to the Treasury Department, to which, so far, the Superintendent is accountable. The accounts of the agents of the Government for the several tribes in amity with us, are still returned, and settled in the War Depart-

ment. From the payment of annuities to the various Indian tribes within the United States, a new species of jurisprudence has sprung up, which operates as a heavy tax upon the time of the Secretary of War.

All losses of property by American citizens, from the robberies, thefts, and depredations of those tribes, are to be remunerated out of the annuities payable to them. The evidence in all these cases is extra-judicial, and requires the examination and approbation of the Secretary before remuneration can be made. The presents which are made to them, the allowances to artificers settled among them by the Government, in fact, every disbursement of money connected with the Indian departments, except in the prosecution of trade with them, has to receive the special sanction of the Head of this Department. The duties incumbent on this officer, resulting from the control of the Indian department, are so multifarious, so impossible to be reduced within general regulations, that a considerable portion of his time is necessarily devoted to them.

The organization of the accountant's office is such as to render it impossible for that officer, by any human exertion, promptly to despatch the business which has been accumulating from year to year, until the mass has become so imposing as to render the legislative aid indispensably necessary to correct the evil.

The creation of a separate and independent department, to which all the Indian accounts, including those which are still settled in the accountant's office, will not supersede the necessity of modifications in the organization of that office. The changes which are deemed necessary to insure the prompt settlement of the accounts of the War Department, are respectfully submitted to the Senate, in paper marked A 2.

If a new department be formed, much of the miscellaneous duties now belonging to the Department of State ought to be transferred to it. The changes which ought to be made, in this regard, will obtrude themselves upon the attention of the Senate whenever the subject shall be considered.

It is believed that, at the present moment, no plan can be devised for carrying on the Indian trade that will be equally advantageous to the Indians, although it may be more economical to the public. This opinion is founded, in a considerable degree, upon the fact that those who have a competent knowledge of the manner in which this trade must be prosecuted, to be successful, are destitute of the capital necessary for the prosecution to the extent demanded by the wants of the Indians. The capital of those parts of the Union where those persons are to be found, is not sufficient for the purposes of commerce among themselves. It is exposed to no risks, and the profit is great; consequently, it will not be employed in commerce with the Indians. The risks to which capital will be subject, when placed in the hands of these enterprising traders, as well from their casual want of integrity as from the robberies and thefts of the Indians, will prevent the capitalists of the commercial cities from supplying them with the means of engaging in this commerce. The proposition to establish a depot at some point about the mouth of Missouri, for the purpose of supplying those who will be able to give sufficient security with such an amount of goods as will enable them to prosecute the trade to advantage, will, in a series of years, produce a number of persons skilled in the manner of carrying it on successfully, and create a capital in their hands, which will be probably continued in that channel, and eventually justify the Government in leaving it under judicious regulations, which experience will not fail to suggest, entirely to individual enterprise.

These views are substantially founded upon the conviction, that it is the true policy and earnest desire of the Government to draw its savage neighbors within the pale of civilization. If I am mistaken in this point—if the primary object of the Government is to extinguish the Indian title, and settle their lands as rapidly as possible, then commerce with them ought to be entirely abandoned to individual enterprise, and without regulation. The result would be continual warfare, attended by the extermination or expulsion of the aboriginal inhabitants of the country to more distant and less hospitable regions. The correctness of this policy cannot, for a moment, be admitted. The utter extinction of the Indian race must be abhorrent to the feelings of an enlightened and benevolent nation. The idea is directly opposed to every act of the Government, from the declaration of independence to the present day. If the system already devised has not produced all the effects which were expected from it, new experiments ought to be made. When every effort to introduce among them ideas of separate property, as well in things real as personal, shall fail, let intermarriages between them and the whites be encouraged by the Government. This cannot fail to preserve the race, with the modifications necessary to the enjoyment of civil liberty and social happiness. It is believed, that the principles of humanity, in this instance, are in harmonious concert with the true interests of the nation. It will redound more to the national honor to incorporate, by a humane and benevolent policy, the natives of our forests in the great American family of freemen, than to receive, with open arms, the fugitives of the old world, whether their flight has been the effect of their crimes or their virtues.

I have the honor to be, &c.
WM. H. CRAWFORD.
Hon. JOHN GAILLARD,
  President pro tem. of the Senate.

THE COMPENSATION BILL.

The bill to change the mode of compensation of the Senators, Representatives, and Delegates in Congress, was read a third time.

Mr. MASON, of Virginia, said he was ever reluctant to differ in opinion from the majority of the Senate—for such a difference of opinion seldom failed to impress him with doubts of the correctness of that which he entertained. But on this occasion he was compelled to oppose the measure under consideration. He regretted that he was not in his place to have stated his objection to this bill at an earlier stage of its progress, for he was aware that, to oppose it at this time, when the sense of the Senate had been fully ascertained and expressed—when its fate was to all appearance determined and known, and when no opposition to it could be availing, would expose him to the imputation of vanity or affectation, or perhaps to the suspicion of unworthy motives. But this consideration should not deter him from the discharge of his duty. He felt conscious of the rectitude and purity of his motives, and he believed other gentlemen to be actuated by similar motives.

He would prefer several modifications of the bill, but he had only one insuperable objection to it, which was that it was retrospective, and immediate in its operation. He considered it improper or indelicate (without meaning the least reflection upon any gentleman who advocated it) to vote money out of the Treasury into our own pockets. For all useful public purposes he was willing to impose taxes, and to vote money as liberally as any gentleman. But he considered the object of this bill to be of too mixed and doubtful a character to exempt its advocates entirely from the suspicion of interested and selfish motives. He was very far from imputing such motives to them. But it was not enough to do right. The Representatives of the people should so conduct themselves as to be above the suspicion of unworthy motives. He was no Jacobin, and he would never act or speak with a single eye to popular approbation and favor. But he respected the opinion of the people, as every public agent should do; and although he would not do wrong to obtain their good opinion, yet he would always act as far as he could, consistently with his duty, in such a way as to meet their approbation. For, in a Government like ours, particularly, it was in vain to pretend to despise or disregard public opinion. It was not only the tenure by which we held our places, but it was the basis of the Government itself. Take from the Government that support, and what was now order and beauty would become despotism, or anarchy and chaos. He should, therefore, always respect the opinion of the people, and endeavor to obtain their approbation, as far as he could without a sacrifice of public duty. He admitted that the compensation of the members ought to be increased. He thought it ought to bear the same proportion to the expenses to which members are now exposed that it did to their expenses when the law fixing the present rate of compensation passed; and he had no doubt that the people would approve such an increase, for he had great confidence in their liberality and good sense. But he could not vote for the bill to take effect immediately. He would move to amend it, so as to postpone its operation until the expiration of the term of the present Congress; but he understood that such a motion had already been made, and rejected. And, as he could not obtain that modification of the bill, he was compelled to vote against it all together.

Mr. CHACE also opposed the passage of the bill, on the grounds already taken against it. He could not consent to legislate in this manner. No person, he believed, had yet computed that the compensation hereafter to be given to the members of Congress would be less than ten dollars per day, while Mr. C. computed that it would amount at a fair average estimate to seventeen dollars and a half per day, for each day they attended. This Government had been many years in operation, and it was not till very lately that complaints had been made that the compensation of the members was insufficient. This, he said, was an unfortunate time for the discovery, while the public debt was unliquidated, millions of public accounts yet unsettled, many of the patriot soldiers yet unpaid, and taxes continued—was this the proper time to increase the pay of the members to so extravagant a height? Mr. C. was of the opinion that compensation of members ought to be increased, but it ought to be done with prudence and with reference to the justice of the case, &c. The passage of such a bill as this would be justly disapproved by the people. Mr. C. also objected to the bill because defective in its details. That the subject might be maturely considered, he moved to postpone the bill to Monday.

Mr. HARPER opposed the postponement, because it was not alleged that information was desired, or that the details of the bill were such as required a long examination to understand it. The subject of the bill was as well understood as it could be by a postponement of any length.

Mr. DANA also opposed the postponement. The only argument against it, he believed, was, that the passage of the bill would be unsatisfactory to the people. If the bill was proper in itself, and there was anything in this terror of the popular disapprobation, it was a strong reason why they should not pause so long as was proposed; for, if once seized with a panic on this question, the terror might perhaps by delay become extreme. If this bill were justly dissatisfactory to the people, he said, it might be a reason to pause; but, for his part, he should not like to return and tell his constituents that he was afraid to vote for this bill, lest it should be dissatisfactory to them. His constituents, he said, were not opulent, nor yet afflicted by poverty; they lived at less expense than gentlemen could here; but, he said, he should manifest no respect for their discernment, if he were to suppose they could not see why members incurred greater expenses here than were necessary at home. He should show little respect for their disposition, if he supposed that they wished that the men whom they chose to represent them here should degrade themselves in order to live upon the compensation allowed, or should sacrifice their private property in serving the public. It might be expected of the public agents to make sacrifices in times of great emergency and national difficulty; but it would be idle, in ordinary times, to call on public men to be patriotic to their own loss and injury. Although, he said, the people of the State which he represented were not as wealthy as they were in some other parts of the country, he trusted they were not afflicted with that poorness of spirit that they would deny their Representatives a due compensation for their services. He had no hesitation in saying, that the proposed rate of compensation was not too much for any man who was fit to represent the people and State whom he had the honor, in part, to represent; and, however delicate the inquiry, he would not enter into a contest with his constituents about the correctness of their selection in sending him here. On the whole, he said, he concluded that it was not only proper to increase the compensation of the members, but, being proper, that it would be popular to vote for the bill. In regard to Mr. MASON's objection that the compensation was to take place immediately, he said it would forever exist in regard to this body, some of whom must, whenever a question of change of compensation is agitated, vote on a question affecting their own emoluments. But, he proceeded to show, this was a question on which the people had themselves decided. The Constitution of the United States, when first submitted to the people, contained an article providing that no law varying the compensation of the members of Congress should take effect until an election should intervene; thus presenting the question now raised by the gentleman from Virginia, in relation to this bill. This question was thus presented in solemn form to the people. They did not accept the article, said Mr. D. It is therefore decided by the people, that the Congress may correctly increase the compensation of its members during the time for which they are elected, &c.

Mr. MASON said, in reply to one of Mr. DANA's observations, that he wished to put off the operation of this bill to the 5th day of March next, when at least a part of the Senate and the whole of the House of Representatives would have returned to the people, and would not, without re-election, derive any benefit from the bill, &c. As for those of the Senate who will remain in office beyond the 4th of March next, he suggested that those who chose might avoid voting on the question, under the rule which authorizes any member of the Senate to be excused from voting on a question in which he is personally interested, &c.

Mr. CRACE complained that his arguments on this subject had not been fairly met and answered, but that gentlemen had flown off to incidental or irrelevant points, &c. The gentleman from Connecticut had intimated that the people of his State were high-minded men; Mr. C. said they were also a people of steady habits; and he asked whether they would have ever consented to give to their public officers a compensation at the rate of seventeen and a half dollars per day?—at a rate of salary which, during the time of their actual service, would exceed that of the Vice President of the United States—which he computed thus: Congress would meet on the first Monday in December next, and tarry until the 4th day of March. The utmost term of that session would be three months, and it might be less. The compensation for that year would then exceed seventeen dollars per day. Would the people relish this? he asked; for, he added, when we legislate in our own behalf, we ought to have due reference to the opinion of the people, as far as connected with the principles of justice and reason. He had no objection to making the compensation somewhat greater, but he wished it to be clearly defined, and not larger, relatively, than the present compensation was when first fixed. On this bill, if it passed, he further said, would be founded demands for an increase of compensation from every person in public office within the United States—from every clerk, &c., at the Seat of Government. In this and other views he regarded the bill, in its present shape, highly inexpedient.

Mr. ROBERTS rose to defend his vote from the

arguments of those opposed to the bill. He was duly sensible, he hoped, of the situation in which members of this House stood in relation to public opinion; but he knew not, on this subject, what public opinion was. This question was presented to him for decision without that light. There had been a feeling generally prevalent, as far as his information extended, that the present compensation of the members was not sufficient. It had been his conviction that it was better not to agitate this question at the present time; but the proposition had originated in the other House, which was at least as responsible to public opinion as this; and, believing it not objectionable in principle, he felt it his duty to vote for it. If it were an unpopular act, he said, its weight would fall on the shoulders of those who voted for it—it might occasion their removal from the public councils, by which it might be that the public interest might be promoted: if so, he was willing to make the sacrifice. The proposed amount of compensation was perhaps too large; with the ideas of this subject arising from his humble situation in life, had he had the direction of this question, he should not perhaps have fixed it so high; but, he considered the two Houses, on this question, like a jury much divided on the subject before them, but obliged to decide upon something. On the ground of abstract right, however, without regard to the House of Representatives, he considered it expedient to pass the bill: it might be improved perhaps in detail, but the principle he considered as correct. Whatever appealed to the honorable feelings of the members of Congress could not fail of exciting them to a more earnest discharge of their duty, than a rule of compensation which pays them for each day they attend the public service. As to the plea of the extravagance of the proposed compensation, he denied the fairness of the view in which it had been presented, as well as the correctness of the computation as to the length of the sessions. But not only the mere time of attendance in this House ought to be taken into view, but the interference of the duties of the station with their domestic occupations and arrangements. Mr. R. said he should contradict the character his habits and mode of life had given him, if he were to become an advocate for extravagance; but, on the other hand, he did not, nor did the people, desire to see members living here in a state of privation and suffering. If his views of this subject should be disapproved by the people, he was willing to retire from their service, &c.

The question was then taken on postponement, and negatived.

Mr. MASON, of Virginia, then moved to recommit the bill with a view to amend it.—Negatived, yeas 9.

The question was then taken on the passage of the bill, and decided in the affirmative—yeas 21, nays 11, as follows:

YEAS—Messrs. Barry, Bibb, Brown, Campbell, Condit, Daggett, Dana, Gaillard, Harper, Horsey, Howell, Hunter, Lacock, Morrow, Roberts, Talbot, Tait, Thompson, Turner, Wells, and Williams.

NAYS—Messrs. Chace, King, Macon, Mason of New Hampshire, Mason of Virginia, Ruggles, Sanford, Taylor, Tichenor, Varnum, and Wilson.

The question being then on the title of the bill, to change the mode of compensation of the members, &c.,

Mr. VARNUM suggested that the title of the bill would be advantageously amended by making it "a bill to double the compensation," &c.

Mr. DANA said, if the gentleman desired to move the amendment, that it was a legal opinion that the title of an act need not necessarily correspond with its contents.

No amendment being moved to the title, it was agreed to.

FRIDAY, March 15.

Mr. ROBERTS presented the petition of Ferdinando Fairfax, of the City of Washington, in behalf of himself and others, praying the renewal or extension of certain patents granted to William Thornton, for inventions in and applicable to steam navigation, for reasons stated in the petition; which was read, and referred to the committee to whom was referred, on the 11th instant, the bill for the relief of the widow and children of Robert Fulton, deceased; to consider and report thereon by bill or otherwise.

Mr. WILSON submitted the following motion for consideration:

Resolved, That the report of the Secretary at War of the 7th instant, made in compliance with the resolution of the Senate, of the 30th of January last, be referred to the Committee on Military Affairs, with instructions to inquire into the expediency of authorizing, by law, the filling up and preserving complete, by enlistment, the Military Peace Establishment of the United States, as now fixed by law.

The Senate resumed, as in Committee of the Whole, the consideration of the bill to limit the right of appeal from the circuit court of the United States for the District of Columbia, together with the amendments reported thereto by the select committee, and having agreed to the amendments, the PRESIDENT reported it to the House accordingly, and on the question, "Shall this bill be engrossed and read a third time?" it was determined in the affirmative.

The Senate resumed, as in Committee of the Whole, the consideration of the bill dividing the State of Pennsylvania into two judicial districts; and, on motion by Mr. ROBERTS, the consideration thereof was further postponed to Tuesday next.

The bill entitled, "An act for the relief of Gustavus Loomis," was read a third time, and passed.

A message from the House of Representatives informed the Senate that the House have passed a bill entitled "An act to incorporate the subscribers to the Bank of the United States," in which they request the concurrence of the Senate.

The bill was read, and passed to the second reading.

On motion by Mr. BIBB, the bill was read the second time, by unanimous consent, and referred to the Committee on Finance and an Uniform National Currency.

Mr. Brown, from the committee to whom was referred the bill further extending the time for issuing and locating military land warrants, and for other purposes, reported it with amendments.

The Senate resumed, as in Committee of the Whole, the consideration of the bill concerning the District of Columbia; and, on motion by Mr. Roberts, the consideration thereof was postponed to Thursday next.

THE JUDICIARY.

The Senate then proceeded to the consideration of the following resolution, submitted yesterday by Mr. Daggett, viz:

Resolved, That a committee be appointed to inquire into the expediency of providing by law for an augmentation of the salaries of the Judges of the Supreme Court of the United States.

On this subject there was some discussion as to the proper mode of procedure; in which Messrs. Roberts, Daggett, Talbot, Mason, of New Hampshire, Bibb, Lacock, and Brown, took part.

On motion of Mr. Mason of New Hampshire, the District Judges were added to this motion.

Mr. Roberts moved to amend the resolve, by adding also "the Attorney General of the United States."

Mr. Talbot desired to embrace also the Heads of Departments and Foreign Ministers, whom he thought still more inadequately compensated than the judges, &c.

In the course of the debate, the expediency of increasing the salaries of the judges, and also of the great officers of Government, was not distinctly questioned, but rather generally admitted. It appeared, however, that a committee had been appointed, some time ago, to inquire into the expediency of increasing the salaries of the officers of the Government generally. It having been suggested that the committee already appointed had this subject before them—

On motion of Mr. Daggett, the further consideration of the resolve was postponed to Monday week.

PAYMENT FOR PROPERTY LOST, &c.

The Senate then proceeded to the consideration of the bill from the House of Representatives, authorizing the payment for property lost, captured or destroyed in the service of the United States.

The bill has been much amended, and indeed essentially changed in all its features, since it came into the Senate.

As it was last reported from a select committee it proposes the appointment of a board of commissioners, at the Seat of Government, to sit on and finally decide all claims of the character embraced by the bill.

An amendment moved by Mr. Mason of Virginia, to appoint commissioners to collect evidence, arrange and report it to Congress (but not to decide upon it) was debated at considerable

length; being zealously opposed by Mr. Talbot, and also by Messrs. Taylor, Daggett, and Fromentin, and supported by Messrs. Mason, of New Hampshire, and Dana. It was finally negatived.

The bill was further considered, and the amendments first above described were agreed to. The time for exhibiting claims is limited to two years.

The bill provides for cases of losses of property under contracts with the Government, as well as by impressment, &c.

Mr. Mason, of New Hampshire, moved to strike out the word "contract."

This motion gave rise to some debate. It was supported by the mover, Messrs. Roberts, and Daggett, on the ground that it would subject the United States to pay for losses the risk of which every individual in making contracts must have taken into consideration, and regulated his contract accordingly. The motion was opposed by Messrs. Brown, Barry, Lacock, and Talbot, on the ground that there were many cases in which wagons, teams, boats, &c. are employed in services, the nature and danger and risk of which the commanding officer of an army would be criminal in making public, &c. And in such cases, where the United States imposed conditions not understood or anticipated, equitable remuneration for loss ought to be made, &c.

Before the decision of this question, it was superseded by a motion to strike out the whole section in which it stood.

The further consideration of the bill was then postponed to Monday, to which day the Senate adjourned.

MONDAY, March 18.

Mr. Wilson presented the petition of John Johnson, and others, owners of an establishment for the manufacturing of woollen cloth in the State of New Jersey, praying the patronage and protection of Government, for reasons stated in the petition; which was read, and referred to the Committee on Manufactures.

Mr. Wilson submitted the following motion for consideration:

Resolved, That the Message of the President of the United States, of the 9th instant, transmitting a statement of the militia of the United States, according to the latest returns, be referred to the Militia Committee, with instructions to devise and report such provisions as may be necessary and expedient to insure the annual returns of the militia of the several States, now required by law, to be made by their respective Adjutant Generals, to the War Department of the United States.

A message from the House of Representatives informed the Senate that the House have passed a bill entitled "An act for the relief of certain claimants to lands in the district of Vincennes;" a bill entitled "An act for the relief of Erastus Loomis;" also a bill entitled "An act to alter the times of holding the circuit and district courts of the United States for the district of Vermont;" in which bills they request the concurrence of the Senate. They have also passed the bill, which originated in the Senate, entitled "An act relative to evidence in cases of naturalization," with amendments, in which they request the concurrence of the Senate.

The Senate proceeded to consider the amendments to the bill last mentioned; and, on motion by Mr. HORSEY, the further consideration thereof was postponed until to-morrow.

The three bills last brought up for concurrence were read, and passed to the second reading.

The bill to limit the right of appeal from the circuit court of the United States for the District of Columbia, was read a third time, and passed.

The engrossed bill respecting the late officers and crew of the sloop of war Wasp, was read a third time, and passed.

The Senate resumed the motion made the 15th instant, for referring the report of the Secretary of War of the 7th instant, to the Committee on Military Affairs; and, on motion by Mr. WILSON, the further consideration thereof was postponed until to-morrow.

The bill to provide for the indemnification for private losses of property employed in the public service, in its amended shape, (going to constitute a board of commissioners to audit and settle claims of this description,) was further amended, and at length ordered, with its various amendments, to be read a third time.

The Senate resumed as in Committee of the Whole, the consideration of the bill for calling forth the militia to execute the laws of the Union, suppress insurrection, and repel invasion, and to repeal the laws heretofore passed for those purposes, together with the proposed amendment; and on motion, by Mr. WILSON, the consideration thereof was further postponed until to-morrow.

The Senate resumed the consideration of the bill entitled "An act making further provision for military services during the late war, and for other purposes," and on motion, by Mr. TALBOT, the consideration thereof was further postponed until to-morrow.

The Senate resumed, as in Committee of the Whole, the consideration of the bill for the relief of John Holker, formerly Consul General of France to the United States; and on motion, by Mr. ROBERTS, the consideration thereof was further postponed until Thursday next.

The Senate resumed the consideration of the report of the Committee on Military Affairs on the petition of the representatives of Ignace Delino; and on motion, by Mr. BARBOUR, the consideration thereof was further postponed to this day fortnight.

On motion, by Mr. CHACE, the bill entitled, "An act to alter the times of holding circuit and district courts of the United States, for the district of Vermont," was read the second time, by unanimous consent, and considered as in Committee of the Whole; and passed to the third reading.

On motion, by Mr. MORROW, the committee appointed on the memorial of the Legislature of the Mississippi Territory, was instructed to inquire into the propriety of authorizing the Legislature of the State of Ohio to dispose of so much of the reservation of six miles square, in the county of Jackson and State aforesaid, as may be necessary for a site to a town convenient for a seat of justice in the said county; with leave to report by bill or otherwise.

The Senate resumed, as in Committee of the Whole, the consideration of the bill further extending the time for issuing and locating military land warrants, and for other purposes; together with the amendments reported thereto by the select committee; and the amendments having been agreed to, the PRESIDENT reported the bill to the House accordingly; and on the question "Shall this bill be engrossed and read a third time?" it was determined in the affirmative.

The Senate resumed the consideration of the resolution to amend the Constitution of the United States, so as to regulate the mode of choosing Representatives in Congress, and Electors of President and Vice President thereof; and on motion, by Mr. WILSON, the consideration thereof was further postponed until Wednesday next.

Mr. HORSEY submitted the following motion for consideration:

Resolved, That the committee appointed on the resolution of the Senate of the 29th ultimo, relative to private banking associations in the District of Columbia, be instructed to inquire whether it be expedient and proper to provide for the more effectual payment of specie by the several banks in the said District.

On motion, by Mr. LACOCK, the committee to whom was referred so much of the Message of the President of the United States as relates to roads and canals, was instructed to inquire into the expediency of laying out a national or military road from the town of Washington in Pennsylvania, to Sandusky Bay, passing through Charlestown in Virginia, Cadiz, New Philadelphia, and Wooster in the State of Ohio.

THE JUDICIARY.

The Senate resumed the consideration of the resolve proposed by Mr. SANFORD, embracing an amendment to the Constitution, to make the judges removable from office on the vote of two-thirds of both Houses of Congress, with the consent of the President, &c.

Mr. SANFORD proposed to refer the resolve to a select committee; but, subsequently, Mr. DAGGETT moved to postpone it to Wednesday.

In the conversation respecting the mode of disposing of this business, some general remarks were made, of a decided character, by Mr. KING, against the object of the resolve, on the ground of its proposing to invade the independence of the Judiciary, so all-important and sacred a part of our Constitution, that the Legislature ought not even to propose to disturb it. Mr. ROBERTS and Mr. SANFORD, in reply, took ground against Mr. KING's doctrine, which they argued placed the judges on an eminence more exalted than was consistent with the genius of our Government or the extent of our Constitution, &c. This debate incidentally arose, and may be considered as merely breaking ground preliminary to the discussion which may take place on this question, if it is discussed at all. Mr. FROMENTIN also strongly protested against interfering with the Judiciary, forcibly remarking that blood followed from every the slightest wound inflicted on that valuable institution, &c.

The further consideration of the subject was postponed to Monday.

TUESDAY, March 19.

The bill entitled "An act for the relief of Erastus Loomis," was read the second time, and referred to the Committee on Naval Affairs.

The bill entitled "An act for the relief of certain claimants to lands in the district of Vincennes," was read the second time, and referred to the committee appointed the 7th December, on the memorial of the Legislature of the Mississippi Territory.

The motion made the 15th instant, by Mr. WILSON, referring the report of the Secretary of War, of the 7th instant, to the Committee on Military Affairs, was withdrawn.

The Senate resumed the consideration of the motion, made the 18th instant, for referring the Message of the President of the United States, of the 9th instant, transmitting a statement of the militia of the United States, to the Militia Committee; and agreed thereto.

The Senate resumed the consideration of the motion for instructing the committee appointed on the 29th ultimo to inquire whether it be expedient and proper to provide for the more effectual payment of specie by the several banks in the District of Columbia; and agreed thereto.

The bill, entitled "An act to alter the times for holding the circuit and district courts of the United States, for the district of Vermont," was read a third time, and passed.

The Senate resumed, as in Committee of the Whole, the consideration of the bill to ascertain and establish the western boundary of the tract reserved for satisfying the military bounties allowed to the officers and soldiers of the Virginia line, on Continental Establishment; and, on motion, by Mr. BARBOUR, the consideration thereof was further postponed until Thursday next.

On motion, by Mr. BARBOUR, the consideration of the report of the committee to whom was referred the resolution relating to the claims of the officers and soldiers of the Virginia line on State and Continental Establishment, for bounty lands, was further postponed until Thursday next.

The Senate resumed the consideration of the amendments of the House of Representatives to the bill, entitled "An act relative to evidence in cases of naturalization."—Whereupon,

Resolved, That they concur therein.

The bill further extending the time for issuing and locating military land warrants, and for other purposes, was read a third time, and passed.

The amendments to the bill, entitled "An act to authorize the payment for property lost, captured, or destroyed by the enemy, while in the military service of the United States," having been reported by the committee correctly engrossed, the bill was read the third time, as amended, and the blank filled.

Resolved, That this bill pass with amendments.

On motion, the title was amended by adding thereto " and for other purposes."

The Senate resumed, as in Committee of the Whole, the bill for calling forth the militia to execute the laws of the Union, suppress insurrection, and repel invasion, and to repeal the laws heretofore passed for those purposes, together with the proposed amendment; and, on motion, by Mr. LACOCK, the consideration was further postponed until Thursday next.

The Senate resumed, as in Committee of the Whole, the bill dividing the State of Pennsylvania, into two judicial districts; and on motion, by Mr. LACOCK, the consideration thereof was further postponed until Thursday next.

MILITARY SERVICES.

The bill from the House of Representatives making further provision for military services during the late war, and for other purposes, being taken up,

Mr. WILSON offered the following amendment as a fourth section to the bill:

Be it further enacted, That donations of land be granted to all the officers of the regular army who have been disbanded as supernumeraries, either in consolidating regiments or corps during the late war, or in reducing the army conformably to the act of March the third, one thousand eight hundred and fifteen, as follows, to wit: to each major general, one thousand two hundred and eighty acres; to each brigadier general, one thousand one hundred and twenty acres; to each colonel and lieutenant colonel, nine hundred and sixty acres; to each major, eight hundred acres; to each captain, six hundred and forty acres; to each subaltern, four hundred and eighty acres; and to officers of the medical and other staff, who have no rank, in proportion to their pay, according to the scale aforesaid.

The amendment being read,

Mr. WILSON observed that, on a subject which had so long been the theme of reflection and discussion, he did not intend to take up much of the time of the Senate. He would merely observe that he thought the allowance contemplated by this amendment to the disbanded officers of the late Army, was required by justice, inasmuch as their pay was, at best, insufficient to meet the extra expenses to which they had been subjected during the late war, in travelling from one post to another, and in living on the frontiers. As their pay had been often long delayed, and payment, at length, frequently made in depreciated currency, that good policy demanded this allowance, as it would, in a considerable degree, satisfy a very numerous meritorious class of men, who now thought their services and sacrifices had been poorly rewarded by their country; as it would have a beneficial effect, in case of a future war, upon the young and enterprising who might be inclined to enter the military service—who would see that they would not be turned off at the close of the war without any acknowledgment or reward; as it would be the means of forming a military barrier on our frontiers, against the incursions of the savages, and against invasions by the Mississippi or the Lakes; and as it would induce many of the soldiers to retain and settle their bounty lands under the auspices of these officers. That this gratuity was sanctioned by precedents furnished at the close of the Revolutionary war, and on the disbandment of the Army in 1800; and that public opinion, so far as it could be collected, called for this, or some other expression of the national gratitude to the disbanded officers, &c.

Mr. BROWN declared himself in favor of the principle of the amendment, but thought a discrimination ought to be made between those officers who had rendered essential service, and such as had done little or nothing. Some, he observed, had been in service many years, and were now turned out, with habits which prevented them from resorting to any kind of business for a support; while others had never seen an enemy, nor made sacrifices of any kind. He did not think it would be just to put all on the same footing; and, to allow time to make a discrimination, he moved a postponement of the bill.

Mr. TALBOT was against a postponement. The bill contained provision for the widows and orphans of militiamen, which it was highly important should pass with as little delay as possible; and he did not think it would be right to postpone the bill to introduce a provision incongruous with the provisions already contained in it.

Mr. WILSON replied that if the gentleman had read the bill through, he would have seen that the amendment offered was not incongruous with its provisions, as a part of the bill related to land bounties granted to soldiers of the regular army; and it could not be incongruous to introduce a provision concerning officers of the same establishment.

Mr. TALBOT explained, but declared himself still opposed to the postponement.

Mr. BROWN again spoke in favor of an allowance to such officers as had devoted their lives to the service of their country, and moved a postponement, to afford an opportunity of modifying the amendment so as to meet his views.

Mr. BARBOUR advocated the postponement. He could not vote for the amendment as it now stood, but was in favor of a liberal provision for those whose heads had been bleached in their country's service. If he were allowed time to prepare it, he would offer a section to provide for such as he deemed entitled to the munificence of the nation.

The bill was then postponed until to-morrow, without deciding on Mr. WILSON's motion.

WEDNESDAY, March 20.

Mr. TAIT, from the Committee on Naval Affairs to whom was referred the bill entitled "An act for the relief of Erastus Loomis," reported it without amendment."

Mr. SANFORD presented the petition of John

G. Gootsberger, of the city of New York, praying the allowance of the drawback of duties on certain goods and merchandise, as stated in the petition; which was read, and referred to the Committee on Finance and an Uniform National Currency.

Mr. WILSON, from the committee to whom was referred the bill entitled "An act in addition to an act to regulate the Post Office Establishment," reported it with amendments; which were read.

A message from the House of Representatives informed the Senate that the House have passed a bill, entitled "An act making further provision for settling claims to land in the Territory of Illinois;" also a bill, entitled "An act to abolish the existing duties on spirits distilled within the United States, and to lay other duties in lieu of those at present imposed on licenses to distillers of spirituous liquors;" in which they request the concurrence of the Senate. They have also passed a resolution appointing a committee on their part, to join such committee as may be appointed by the Senate, to consider and report what business will demand the attention of Congress prior to adjournment; in which they request the concurrence of the Senate.

The two bills, and the resolution last brought up for concurrence, were read, and passed to the second reading.

The Senate resumed, as in Committee of the Whole, the consideration of the resolution to amend the Constitution of the United States, so as to subject the judges of all the courts thereof to removal from office; and on motion, by Mr. LACOCK, the further consideration thereof was postponed until Monday next.

The Senate resumed, as in Committee of the Whole, the consideration of the bill entitled "An act authorizing and requiring the Secretary of State to issue letters patent to Andrew Kurtz;" and on motion, by Mr. ROBERTS, the further consideration thereof was postponed until Monday next.

Mr. CAMPBELL, from the Committee on Finance and an Uniform National Currency, to whom the subject was referred, reported a bill for the relief of the Baltimore and Massachusetts Bible Societies; and the bill was read, and passed to the second reading.

MILITARY SERVICES.

The Senate resumed the consideration of the bill entitled "An act making further provision for military services during the late war, and for other purposes," together with the amendment proposed thereto, by Mr. WILSON, and on motion, the question to agree to the said amendment, as follows:

"SEC. — *Be it further enacted,* That donations of land be granted to all the officers of the regular army who have been disbanded as supernumeraries, either in consolidating regiments or corps during the late war, or in reducing the Army conformably to the act of March the third 1815, as follows to wit: to each Major General, one thousand two hundred and eighty acres; to each Brigadier General, one thousand one

hundred and twenty acres; to each Colonel and Lieutenant Colonel, nine hundred and sixty acres; to each
Major, eight hundred acres; to each Captain, six hundred and forty acres; to each subaltern, four hundred
and eighty acres; and to officers of the medical and
other staff, who have no rank, in proportion to their pay,
according to the scale aforesaid:"

It was determined in the negative—yeas 10,
nays 15, as follows:

YEAS—Messrs. Barry, Brown, Chace, Condit, Fromentin, Lacock, Macon, Ruggles, Sanford, and Wilson.

NAYS—Messrs. Barbour, Bibb, Daggett, Gaillard,
King, Mason of New Hampshire, Morrow, Roberts,
Talbot, Tait, Thompson, Tichenor, Turner, Varnum,
and Wells.

Mr. BARBOUR then moved a new section to the
bill, embracing a land bounty to disbanded officers
of a certain class, (having intimated his intention,
previous to the last vote, to move it.)

The bill was then postponed till to-morrow,
without deciding on Mr. BARBOUR'S motion.

AMENDMENT TO THE CONSTITUTION.

The Senate resumed the consideration of the
resolution to amend the Constitution of the United States, so as to regulate the mode of choosing
Representatives in Congress, and Electors of President and Vice President of the United States.

On motion, by Mr. LACOCK

" That it be referred to a select committee, with instructions to inquire into the expediency of proposing
an amendment to the Constitution of the United States,
providing for the election of President and Vice President by the Electors of each State qualified to vote for
the most numerous branch of the State Legislature:"

Mr. BARBOUR having stated his idea of a marked
difference in principle between the two objects of
electing Electors and Representatives; in which
view he was seconded by Mr. LACOCK, and Mr.
MASON of New Hampshire having remarked
thereon—

Mr. BARBOUR said, that it was essential to the
character of a pure representation, that the Representative should have a common feeling with
his constituents; that he should know their wants
and be possessed of their sentiments. Residence
is part of the proper character of a Representative,
who ought not to be placed at such a distance
from his constituents that he can know neither
their wants nor their feelings. The case is different with respect to the election of Electors, in
respect to whom that personal knowledge is not
necessary to their constituents. Not, Mr. B. said,
that he would take the power of electing a President of the United States out of the hands of the
people. God forbid, said he, that the power of
electing a President of the United States should
be lodged in any other hands than those of the
people themselves. The whole Congress united,
dictating a nomination, would weigh no more
than a feather in the balance against the public
will; any dictation in opposition to the public
sentiment, would be considered as an outrage on
the rights of the people, and justly scouted by
them. The man who is chosen an Elector knows
the sentiments, which he is bound to carry with

him into the Electoral College, and which only
it is his duty to express. The people emphatically elect the President; but those selected to
express their will, may be chosen by general ticket
without violating the representative principle.
Mr. B. was, therefore, opposed to that part of the
proposition before the Senate which embraced
the Electors of President and Vice President. In
regard to the inconvenience of laying out States
into districts for electing Representatives, he said,
he could not see the inconveniences suggested
by the gentleman from New Hampshire, (Mr.
MASON,) as it would occur but once in ten years.
The advantages of an uniformity in the mode of
election, he said, was obvious in regard to Representatives. It would put down all that ma-
nœuvring which would repress the sentiments
of the people by a juggle, which, he said, was an
inconvenience much greater than the labor of
designating the metes and bounds of a district.
In consequence of the elections by districts in the
large States, and by general ticket in the small
States, an undue preponderance had heretofore
been given, Mr. B. said, to the small States in
the councils of the nation. The general ticket
for Electors had its origin in one of the Eastern
States, to which we are indebted for many political
ideas; it had been received with great opposition
indeed, but, from self-defence, the Southern States
had been most of them obliged to follow the example. Under the district system, Pennsylvania
exhibited a melancholy spectacle; whilst the small
Eastern States gave each many votes, the weight
of Pennsylvania, great as she is, dwindled down
to a solitary vote. Pennsylvania, which should
have loomed in the horizon as large as any State
in the Union, became invisible in consequence
of the general ticket being resorted to. To regain
her station in the Union, she was compelled to
follow the example. Virginia, also, obliged by
inevitable necessity, arising from the principle of
self-preservation requiring her to counterpoise that
system which had made its appearance in another
quarter of the Union, reluctantly resorted to it.
After some further illustrative remarks, Mr. B.
said, in every point of view, he was now opposed
to the districting the State for the election of
Electors; whilst he considered the remainder of
the proposition before the Senate as a recurrence
to the true principles of the Constitution, which
required that Representatives should be uniformly
elected by districts. The representative body
would then be that pure organ of the popular will
in the National Councils, which the spirit of the
Constitution intends it.

Mr. MASON, of New Hampshire, said, he had
no disposition to enter into the controversy respecting great States and small States. He
never had understood, however, that any State
south of Virginia, had led Virginia into a change
of the mode of election of Electors. According
to history, as he had read it, Mr. M. said, Virginia
was the first State that changed its mode of election; he knew of no State which had previously
changed it. The Eastern States had made no
change at all in that respect, having been uniform

in adhering to one system. It was not of much importance, he said, who led and who followed; the question is, what shall be the remedy in future for the want of uniformity now felt? The gentleman from Virginia was desirous that the small States should be districted for the election of their Representatives—for what? That the people may express their will. Mr. M. admitted there was substance in this argument as to the great States, but not as to the small ones, in which every man proposed to their suffrage, by general ticket, was almost equally well known to his constituents, as if they were elected by districts. As to the election of Electors, and the observation that the voice of the whole Congress, united in favor of any man, would be but as a feather in the scale, Mr. M. said it was a feather which always had turned, and always would turn, the balance. He spoke not with reference to any particular transaction; but, let the Congress continue to make their nomination, the State Legislatures their nominations of Electors, and these two together would forever give a President to the United States. All the arguments of the gentleman in favor of electing Representatives by districts apply, but with much greater force, to the election of Electors; for here is the great pressure of danger; in this point, may it always be expected that an influence will be exerted over the people, which he said he knew no way of counteracting, but by putting each Elector within the sphere of the personal knowledge of those who are to choose him. With this view only did Mr. M. incline to favor this part of the proposition to amend the Constitution, which, if adopted, would make it more difficult that anything like dictation should be practised in the case of the election of Electors. The election of Electors by districts, would tend to take the power of appointing the head, the sole depository of the power of the nation, out of hands in which the Constitution endeavored to prevent its ever being placed. He was, therefore, favorable to that part of the motion before the Senate which related to the election of Electors. In the other clause of the proposed Constitutional amendment (relating to the election of Representatives) he saw no great advantage; he wished the practical evil under the present system to be pointed out. The States electing by general ticket, he said, were not more populous than some of those districts in the States choosing by districts, in which two, three and four members were for convenience elected. As long, Mr. M. said, as the States exercised the power they now possess (of selecting the mode of election) in a manner satisfactory to themselves, it would be unwise to interfere with it. Preferring himself to leave it where it was, he was opposed to that part of the amendment.

Mr. KING said that, so far as regarded the manner and time of choosing Representatives and Senators to Congress, a majority of the Congress may by law now establish the very manner of choosing Representatives, which was now proposed to be erected into a Constitutional rule. It seemed to him, therefore, unnecessary to alter the Constitution by imposing a rule, when, according to the Constitution, a competent power can now make the same regulation by law. Not so with that part of the amendment before the Senate, which the gentleman from Virginia proposed to strike out. The States may now severally direct the manner of choosing their own Electors; it is proposed that the manner shall be prescribed by the Constitution. This, Mr. K. thought would be an important change, and the only change suggested in the Constitution which he deemed an improvement. He thought he might venture to say, that if there was any part of the Constitution deemed by its framers and advocates to be better secured than any other against the enterprises which have since occurred, it was the very provision on the subject of elections to the Presidency. The idea was, that the action of that particular agency which has since controlled it, was as much displaced by the Constitutional plan of election of President and Vice President, as could possibly be devised. The opinion had been that all undue agency or influence was entirely guarded against; that the men selected by the people from their own body would give their votes in such a manner as that no opportunity would be afforded for a combination, to change the freedom and popular character which naturally belonged to the electoral bodies. Such had been the idea of the nation at the time of the adoption of the Constitution. We all know, said he, the course which this thing has taken. The election of a President of the United States is no longer that process which the Constitution contemplated. In conformity with the original view of the authors of that instrument, I would restore, as thoroughly as possible, the freedom of election to the people: I would make the mode of election uniform through the country, by throwing the whole nation into as many districts as there are Electors, and let the people of each district choose one Elector. One idea on this subject, he thought worth more than all the arguments against this course; that then all the people of the country would stand precisely on the same footing; and no particular addresses could be made to the special interests and particular views of particular men or particular sections of the country. The course now pursued in this respect, Mr. K. said, was not entitled to that high distinction. On the contrary, those who reflected on it could not help seeing that our progress in Government was not for the better; that it was not likely hereafter to be in favor of popular rights. It was with the people the Constitution meant to place the election of the Chief Magistrate, that being the source least liable to be corrupt. But if, under the name of the liberty of the people, said Mr. K., we put this power into other hands, with different interests, we place it in a situation in which the rights of the people are violated. In this point of view, to him (he said) this particular clause of the proposed amendment to the Constitution was of great value. Let the question of the mode of election of Senators and Representatives rest where it is; if Congress choose to interpose, let them. The other part of the proposition was in favor of the rights of the people, of the freedom of the country ; for, with regard to these rights and freedom, no man could name a matter so important as the choice of the President of the nation. It is an infirmity in our natures that we look for chiefs and rulers, either for their superior virtue, or their supposed subserviency to the views of those in subordinate situations. It was against the evil of the latter principle, Mr. K. desired to guard. The liberties of the people, repeated he, of which we speak much, are more affected by the choice of President than by any other ordinary political act. In this point they are vulnerable ; here ought the rights of the people and of the States to be guarded. Our existence and the passions of the present day are ephemeral ; public liberty should be immortal. Considering that this body should be to the people and the States not only the safe guardians of their rights but the protectors of their liberty, he hoped they would adopt a provision he considered so nearly connected with the perpetuation of both.

Mr. BARBOUR said, he was not unaware that it was competent to Congress by law to regulate the mode of electing Representatives ; but it seemed to him to be one of those important political principles which ought not to depend on the will of Congress. The Representative ought not, it appeared to him, to be the depositary of the power of regulating the mode of electing his successor. In regard to the Presidential election, which the gentleman from New York regarded as of paramount importance—our limited Magistracy, Mr. B. said, was not in his view in any degree formidable to the liberties of the people. The President must execute the public sentiment ; when he departs from it, he from that moment dates his continuance in office. There was, Mr. B. said, a case on record in which a President had sought to carry on an administration in opposition to the public sentiment ; he reaped his reward—one which, Mr. B. said, he hoped would attend all who should make the like attempt. All wise Governments look with more caution to those who represent the public will than those who execute it. It was a desideratum, Mr. B. said, that the purity and uniformity of their election should be fixed immutably as a part of the Constitution, beyond the control of the Legislature. The proposition of an amendment of this sort is an appeal to public opinion which may be safely made. Whatever may be the corruption (which God forbid !) which shall at any time pervade the Congress, they will always be restrained by an express provision of the Constitution ; and, if this amendment be adopted, they will not have the power of regulating the mode of their own election according to their will or caprice. It was wonderful to him, Mr. B. said, that so important a question should ever have been left to the decision of those who were interested in it ; and could be accounted for only by viewing it in the light of an experiment. He desired to see it placed on a surer foundation. In reply to Mr. MASON, who denied

the force of the distinction in principle between the election of Electors and Representatives by a general ticket, he said, that in elections of Representatives by general ticket, men were frequently elected to Congress in that mode, who would not have been permitted by the people to represent the district for which they are elected. The Elector, on the other hand, is the mere organ of public sentiment, on a question in regard to which there is no sort of difficulty in ascertaining the will of the people. Mr. B. next spoke in reply to Mr. KING's remarks, in reference to the Presidential election. I would ask every member of the Senate, said he, whether any other sentiment has been expressed, or anticipation formed, in regard to this question than that the will of the people should be the rule of its decision ? Will any gentleman undertake to say that any man could be elected Chief Magistrate of this nation who was not the choice of the people ? The gentleman has suggested that it was intended, by the manner in which the Constitution is organized, that the Electors should come up to the Electoral College without any bias on their minds as to the character for whom their suffrage is to be given. Did the gentleman, as one of the makers of that Constitution, suppose that the minds of men, chosen for the purpose, would be wholly uninfluenced at the time they were called on to give their electoral vote ? Is it possible or ought it to be, that their minds should be free from preference until the moment they are called on to put their ballot in the box ? Such an idea is perfectly illusory and impracticable. The question must be decided by the people, (who are in this case the Grand Inquest,) who are the fit men to compete for this high station. If the Electors are to decide that question, after they enter on the performance of the electoral duty, they become the only source of election, and wholly deprive the people of this, which the gentleman conceives their most important right. The truth is, and must be so obvious as to be indisputable, that the Electors are only the organs of that public sentiment which has been long and unequivocally made up. Let us suppose the time ever to arrive, when an attempt shall be made to take from the people the election of their Chief Magistrate—could it succeed ? Take the Congress and the State Legislatures, and throw all their weight together in one scale, and the will of the people in the other ; those who oppose the people's will, at once will kick the beam. Why is it that the constituted authorities seem to have any agency now in nominating candidates for the Presidency ? It is in homage to that popular sentiment of which they have the knowledge. Mr. B. said, he did not believe that all the Congress united, and all the Legislatures of all the States combined, could succeed against public opinion. There was, therefore, no danger to the liberties of the people from the present mode of electing a President of the United States. An important reason why a different rule of selection prevails in the case of Electors and Representatives, he said, was, that in the choice of the Representatives the people merely are represented; in the choice of Electors, the people and the sovereignty of a State are represented. If Electors were uniformly chosen by districts, a State—Virginia for instance—might have twenty-five Electors, and give but one vote; whilst Delaware, entitled only to three Electors, would, in the same election, give three votes—having an influence in the election, inversely proportioned to its comparative population, of three to one. It followed, he said, that unless the principle of a general ticket prevailed in the election of Electors, a State, possessing infinitely the greatest number of Electors, might, by a manœuvre or juggle, be deprived of its franchise on this great question.

Mr. MACON said, there was nothing more certain to his mind, than that the mode of election of Electors ought to be uniform throughout the United States; because, if it were otherwise, it was possible that a minority might elect the great officers of the United States. A small State, unanimous for one candidate, might by general ticket counterbalance the weight of two large States voting by districts. There was no way but by uniform district election, he said, to obtain with certainty the sense of the people. We have seen, in the history of this Government, the mode of election in some States change more than once. We must take people as we find them; and expect that they will change their mode of election when it is necessary to secure them their just weight in the Union. To guard against these changes in self-defence, or from political views, the only mode was to provide for an uniformity of election by districts. The difficulty in regard to districting States was not so great as had been represented. The State which he represented had, until lately, been in the habit of forming two sets of districts—the one for Representatives, and the other for Electors, and had not experienced much difficulty in it. Was it not better to surmount this small difficulty than to have different principles of election in different States? Of all the elections affecting the nation, none, he said, so nearly touched its great interests as the election of the great office of President; and if in any case the public voice should be heard more distinctly than another, it was in that election. What, he asked, had been recently done at this place, alluding to the nomination lately made? Do what we can, said he, we cannot get clear of this, which Mr. M. admitted to be an evil. But what had been the practice in States where the general ticket system prevails? A year before the election, frequently, do not these same States make a nomination of Electors? This is the consequence of the general ticket system, adopted from choice by some States, and followed by necessity from others. Although it were true, as had been stated, that Congress could regulate the mode of choosing Representatives, it was to put it out of the power of any party to change the mode of election to answer any particular purpose, that he would make an amendment to the Constitution in this respect, to prevent such changes as the States had made in

the mode of electing their Electors. When parties are nearly balanced, they must be expected to calculate, so long as the power is with them, whether the change in this or that way will not give them the majority. Mr. M. said he had much rather see the question settled, and parties no longer geographical, as they would always be, if the system of general election continued to prevail. There were some States in the Union which had never changed the mode of electing Electors or Representatives. What, he asked, had been the consequence? No state of the country, no conduct of the Government, had produced in those States the least apparent change in their political complexion. The best interests of the country, in the opinion of Mr. M., required that both clauses of the proposed amendment to the Constitution should be agreed to; which would, as much as possible, put it in the power of the people to elect the men whom they prefer. A fair canvass never had taken place, nor ever could take place, in voting by general ticket, where the people, instead of having a personal knowledge of those for whom they vote, must take their characters on trust. Another reason for fixing an uniform mode of election by the Constitution, was, that at present doubts are entertained of the constitutionality of both modes of election, in the quarters of the country where they respectively occur, &c.

Mr. LACOCK remarked, that, from what had been said, there appeared to be a general opinion that there would be an advantage in bringing the question nearer to the people. Why was it thought necessary that the people should have some knowledge of him whom they elect? That they might know him to be a faithful man, who would vote for the candidate whom they preferred. Now, Mr. L. said, he could see no reason why these agents should be employed between the people and their votes. If they were dispensed with, and the people in each State were to give in their votes, (as they do in several States for their Governors,) these votes to be returned to the State Executives, and by them to the General Government, there would be no occasion for the machinery of electoral colleges, and of course no difficulty in fixing an uniform mode of election. In this popular mode of election, Mr. L. said, there could be no fear of corruption. He knew, he said, that it would be objected that this mode of election would produce popular fermentation; but he denied it. Depend upon it, said he, that if ferment exists on this question, it will be excited by the officers of Government, and those connected with them; the people at home will remain unmoved, and on the day of election will, at their respective polls, soberly and dispassionately decide the question. Mr. L. then moved to recommit the resolution with instructions to report an amendment to provide for the election of President and Vice President by the Electors of each State qualified to vote for the most numerous branch of the State Legislatures.

Mr. HARPER said, as he might be called away by other business before this question was decided, he would take this opportunity of expressing his opinion, and his hope that the motion last made would not prevail, because it seemed to him that the principle it embraced was infinitely less expedient than that now on the table. It would have a tendency to produce more anomalies than now exist in the Constitution; to refer the election of President to a less certain rule than we have at present. It would induce a great deal of unnecessary trouble and vexation, and would at last come to the same result, as in the more simple and less embarrassing mode by the choice of Electors. As to the main proposition before the Senate, Mr. H. said, he was decidedly in favor of it, for this general reason; that its adoption would tend to make the elections of President less a matter of juggle and intrigue than they now are. He would not say that it would have the effect of wholly excluding intrigue, of placing this great election on the footing on which the great men who framed the Constitution vainly imagined they were placing it, of a free, unbiassed expression of the public will; but he thought it would bring it nearer than at present. Party arrangements and bargains would not be so easy. Bargains could not be so readily struck with one State for this great office, with another for that—he would not say as had been done, but certainly as may be done, according to the present mode of election. Districting the States for Electors, Mr. H. said, would, in his judgment, have a tendency to render the Presidential election more free and independent; to remove it more from the grasp of party arrangements; to prevent bargains between profligate agents, and the selling of the nation for offices to the highest bidder. He was, therefore, decidedly opposed to striking out that part of the proposition before the Senate.

On suggestion of Mr. DANA, Mr. LACOCK having so modified his motion as to divest it of its peremptory character, and make it a motion for inquiry merely—

Mr. DANA said, in that shape, he should vote for the proposition of the gentleman from Pennsylvania. He acknowledged that if Electors are to be pledged absolutely that they will give their votes for a particular person, he could perceive nothing but a solemn formality in the election of Electors, perfectly unnecessary. He knew not why these men should be interposed between the people and the candidates, that they may have an opportunity, not (under the practical construction of their office) of exercising their judgment in selecting the fittest men, but of playing some trick on the people. This was a subject, Mr. D. said, on which he had his doubts. As the views of the Convention on this subject had been mentioned, he said he would state, that he once had permission to examine the original journals of the Convention in the office of State; and it appeared that, in regard to the election of President, almost every possible mode had been tried and rejected. It was proposed at first that the election should be made by the National Legislature. This was agreed to, but afterwards reconsidered. It was then proposed that the President should be chosen by Electors elected by the several States: this was rejected. It was then proposed, and rejected also, that he should be chosen by the people. The real fact was, the Convention, in forming a government of which there was no model in history, had great difficulties to surmount. Projects of all kinds were tried, and none could succeed to their satisfaction, on this particular point. At length, after many fruitless votes on different propositions, a grand committee was appointed to consider the subject. They ultimately adopted the compound ratio which now exists, and added the feature of Vice Presidency to the system. In regard to the latter office, by way of illustrating its inutility, and the manner and motives by which it was disposed of, he referred to a historical fact from Grecian history. On an occasion in which a dispute arose among the allied Generals who had fought best on a certain campaign, and they could not agree—the question was decided by ballot, on which two names were to be inscribed; each General put his own name first, and all put that of Themistocles as second best. Since the amendment to the Constitution in regard to that office, Mr. D. said, he had considered the Vice Presidency as merely an item in the general market of intrigue. The person to fill it is always chosen, because he may otherwise be a formidable rival, or because he will be subservient to the views of those who hold the Presidency. Those who wield a party can, by means of that office, say to a powerful State, "here is your change; we will give you a Vice President if you will vote our ticket for President." Whilst this was the character of that office, Mr. D. said, he would have none of it: he would not give as much compensation to a Vice President as to a President pro tempore of the Senate; for, in point of character, he considered it as one of the most trifling offices in the Government. So far as regarded the most certain mode of guarding against cabal and intrigue, the very circumstance of districting a State for ten years at a time, is that which would enable men to intrigue with certainty to a particular point. To guard with certainty against intrigue, the mode of election should be left uncertain. The whole plan of districting the United States, he said, was more completely adapted to the purposes of intrigue, bribery, and corruption, than any that had ever been devised. Believing thus, he must vote against it, not taking it for granted himself that mere change will prove a remedy to existing difficulties. The distinction between the two parties which formerly existed, Mr. D. took occasion to say, was now, or soon would be, merely nominal. Where was the difference between them now, he asked, except that those on one side had gone beyond the others, and the others had fallen a little back? There might be a nominal artificial distinction, but there was, in fact, but very little real difference. The general violence and error of party, he said, was purity itself, compared with the personal corruption that we have to guard against—the difficulty of preventing which will be increased rather than diminished by electing wholly

Electors, when convened, shall have power, in case any of those appointed as above prescribed shall fail to attend for the purposes of their said appointment, on the day prescribed for giving their votes for President and Vice President of the United States, to appoint another or others to act in the place of him or them so failing to attend."

It was determined in the negative—yeas 12, nays 20, as follows:

YEAS—Messrs. Barbour, Barry, Bibb, Dana, Gaillard, Lacock, Mason of Virginia, Roberts, Ruggles, Sanford, Tait, and Wilson.

NAYS—Messrs. Brown, Chace, Condit, Daggett, Fromentin, Goldsborough, Horsey, Howell, Hunter, King, Macon, Mason of New Hampshire, Morrow, Talbot, Thompson, Tichenor, Turner, Varnum, Wells, and Williams.

On motion, by Mr. BARBOUR, that the further consideration of the resolution be postponed to the first Monday in July next, it was determined in the affirmative—yeas 18, nays 14, as follows:

YEAS—Messrs. Barbour, Barry, Bibb, Daggett, Dana, Gaillard, Horsey, Howell, Hunter, Lacock, Mason of Virginia, Roberts, Ruggles, Sanford, Talbot, Tait, Wells, and Wilson.

NAYS—Messrs. Brown, Chace, Condit, Fromentin, Goldsborough, King, Macon, Mason of New Hampshire, Morrow, Thompson, Tichenor, Turner, Varnum, and Williams.

THURSDAY, March 21.

The bill, entitled "An act to abolish the existing duties on spirits distilled within the United States, and to lay other duties, in lieu of those at present imposed on licenses to distillers of spirituous liquors," was read the second time, and referred to the Committee on Finance and an Uniform National Currency.

The bill, entitled "An act making further provision for settling claims to land in the Territory of Illinois," was read the second time, and referred to the committee on the memorial of the Legislature of the Mississippi Territory.

The resolution from the House of Representatives, for the appointment of a joint committee on the subject of an adjournment of Congress, was read the second time.

The bill for the relief of the Baltimore and Massachusetts Bible Societies, was read the second time.

The Senate resumed the consideration of the bill entitled "An act making further provision for military services during the late war, and for other purposes," together with the amendment proposed thereto; and on motion, by Mr. TALBOT, the further consideration thereof was postponed until to-morrow.

The Senate proceeded to the consideration of the bill " for calling forth the militia to execute the laws of the Union, suppress insurrections, and repel invasions." This bill, in addition to the enactments contained in former laws, provides that in cases of neglect or refusal of the Governors or Commanders-in-Chief in each State, to call forth the militia, when legally required, the Pre-

sident of the United States shall be authorized to call upon any officer or officers having command in the militia, who shall forthwith comply with the requisition, and detach the men under their command.

After several unsuccessful motions to amend and postpone the bill indefinitely, Mr. MASON, of Virginia, submitted amendments for consideration, and the bill was postponed until Monday next.

A message from the House of Representatives informed the Senate that the House have passed a bill, entitled "An act for the liquidation of certain claims, and for other purposes;" also, a bill, entitled "An act to repeal the act, entitled 'An act to provide additional revenues for defraying the expenses of Government and maintaining public credit, by laying duties on household furniture, and on gold and silver watches," in which bills they request the concurrence of the Senate.

The two bills last mentioned were read, and passed to the second reading.

POST OFFICE ESTABLISHMENT.

The Senate resumed, as in Committee of the Whole, the consideration of the bill entitled "An act in addition to an act to regulate the Post Office Establishment," together with the amendments reported thereto by the select committee. Mr. VARNUM was requested to take the Chair:

And on the question to agree to the 4th amendment reported, to strike out the whole of the 3d section, as follows:

" SEC. 3. *And be it further enacted,* That letters and packets to and from any member of the Senate, or member or delegate of the House of Representatives of the Congress of the United States, the Secretary of the Senate, and Clerk of the House of Representatives, shall be conveyed free of postage from the commencement of every Congress until the termination thereof, and for thirty days thereafter: *Provided always,* That no letter or packet shall exceed two ounces in weight."

It was determined in the affirmative—yeas 22, nays 11, as follows:

YEAS—Messrs. Barry, Brown, Campbell, Chace, Condit, Daggett, Gaillard, Howell, Lacock Macon, Mason of Virginia, Morrow, Roberts, Ruggles, Talbot, Tait, Thompson, Tichenor, Turner, Varnum, Williams, and Wilson.

NAYS—Messrs. Dana, Fromentin, Goldsborough, Gore, Horsey, Hunter, King, Mason of New Hampshire, Sanford, Taylor, and Wells.

On motion, by Mr. FROMENTIN, to substitute the following in lieu of the 3d section stricken out :

" SEC. 3. *And be it further enacted,* That letters and packets to any member of the Senate, or member or delegate of the House of Representatives of the Congress of the United States, the Secretary of the Senate, and Clerk of the House of Representatives, shall be conveyed free of postage from the commencement of every Congress until the termination thereof, and for thirty days thereafter: *Provided always,* That no letter or packet shall exceed two ounces in weight."

It was determined in the negative—yeas 9, nays 24, as follows:

YEAS—Messrs. Daggett, Dana, Fromentin, Goldsborough, Gore, Hunter, King, Sanford, and Tait.

NAYS—Messrs. Barry, Brown, Campbell, Chace, Condit, Gaillard, Horsey, Howell, Lacock, Macon, Mason of New Hampshire, Mason of Virginia, Morrrw, Roberts, Ruggles, Talbot, Taylor, Thompson, Tichenor, Turner, Varnum, Wells, Williams, and Wilson.

The bill having been amended the President resumed the Chair, and Mr. VARNUM reported it to the House accordingly.

FRIDAY, March 22.

Mr. THOMPSON presented the memorial of the proprietors of the Middlesex Canal, in the Commonwealth of Massachusetts, praying the patronage and protection of Congress, for reasons stated at large in the memorial; which was read, and referred to the Committee appointed on so much of the Message of the President of the United States as relates to roads and canals, to consider and report thereon by bill or otherwise.

Mr. HARPER presented the petition of William Patterson and Robert Patterson, owners of certain lands in the vicinity of Baltimore, which during the late war were injured by the erection of batteries, intrenchments, and other works, for defensive operations thereon, and praying remuneration for the loss and injury by them sustained, as stated in the petition; which was read, and referred to the Committee on Military Affairs.

Mr. THOMPSON presented the petitions of sundry inhabitants of the State of New Hampshire, against the transportation of the mail on the Sabbath; and the petitions were read, and referred to the committee appointed the 22d of December on similar petitions from Pennsylvania, to consider and report thereon by bill or otherwise.

The bill entitled "An act for the liquidation of certain claims, and for other purposes," was read the second time, and referred to the Committee on Military Affairs to consider and report thereon.

The bill entitled "An act to repeal the act entitled 'An act to provide additional revenues for defraying the expenses of Government, and maintaining the public credit, by laying duties on household furniture, and on gold and silver watches," was read the second time, and referred to the Committee on Finance and an Uniform National Currency.

Mr. BROWN gave notice that to-morrow he should ask leave to bring in a bill establishing a port of delivery at the town of Bayou St. John.

Mr. RUGGLES, from the committee to whom the subject was referred, reported a bill to authorize the President of the United States to alter the road laid out from the foot of the rapids of the river Miami of Lake Erie, to the western line of the Connecticut Reserve; and the bill was read, and passed to the second reading.

Mr. BROWN, from the committee to whom the subject was referred, reported a bill to authorize the Legislature of the State of Ohio to sell a certain part of a tract of land reserved for the use of that State; and the bill was read, and passed to the second reading.

The Senate resumed the bill, entitled "An act making further provision for military services during the late war, and for other purposes," together with the amendment proposed thereto; and on motion, by Mr. TALBOT, the consideration thereof was further postponed until Monday next.

The Senate resumed the consideration of the resolution from the House of Representatives for the appointment of a joint committee on the subject of an adjournment; and it passed to a third reading.

On motion, by Mr. SANFORD, the resolution last mentioned was read a third time by unanimous consent, and concurred in.

Ordered, That Messrs. DAGGETT, HORSEY, and MACON, be the committee on their part.

The Senate resumed, as in Committee of the Whole, the consideration of the bill, entitled "An act for the relief of Erastus Loomis;" and it passed to a third reading.

On motion, by Mr. TAIT, the bill was read a third time by unanimous consent, and passed.

On motion, by Mr. MASON, of Virginia, the consideration of the bill to ascertain and establish the western boundary of the tract reserved for satisfying the military bounties allowed the officers and soldiers of the Virginia line on Continental Establishment, was further postponed until Monday next.

On his motion, the consideration of the report of the committee relating to the claims of the officers and soldiers of the Virginia line, on State and Continental Establishment, for bounty lands, was also further postponed until Monday next.

On motion, by Mr. SANFORD, the consideration of the bill concerning certain advances made for the public service by the city of New York, was further postponed until Monday next.

The Senate resumed, as in Committee of the Whole, the consideration of the bill for the relief of John Holker, formerly Consul General of France to the United States; and on the question, "Shall this bill be engrossed and read a third time?" it was determined in the affirmative.

On motion, by Mr. ROBERTS, the consideration of the bill dividing the State of Pennsylvania into two judicial districts, was further postponed until Tuesday next.

On motion, by Mr. ROBERTS, the consideration of the bill concerning the District of Columbia, was further postponed until Monday next.

The Senate resumed, as in Committee of the Whole, the consideration of the bill for the relief of the Baltimore and Massachusetts Bible Societies," and on the question, "Shall this bill be engrossed and read a third time?" it was determined in the affirmative.

Mr. WILSON presented the memorial of William Gamble, praying additional compensation for his services as inspector of the customs in the district of Niagara, for reasons stated in the memorial; which was read, and referred to the Secretary of the Treasury, to consider and report thereon to the Senate.

Mr. VARNUM presented the memorial of Joseph

Marquand, collector of the revenue for the district of Newburyport, praying an increase of compensation for his services, as stated in the memorial; which was read, and referred to the Committee on Finance and an Uniform National Currency.

Mr. Dana submitted the following motion for consideration:

Resolved, That the President of the United States be requested to cause information to be laid before the Senate in relation to such proceedings as have been had for completing an accurate chart of the coasts within the extent of twenty leagues from any part of the shores of the United States, and in relation to such examinations and observations as may have been made with respect to St. George's Bank, and any other bank or shoal, and the soundings and currents beyond such distance to the Gulf Stream, in pursuance of the act of the 10th of February, 1807, entitled "An Act to provide for surveying the coasts of the United States."

Mr. Campbell, from the Committee on Finance and an Uniform National Currency, to whom was referred the bill, entitled "An Act to incorporate the subscribers to the Bank of the United States," reported it without amendment; and, on motion by Mr. Campbell, the further consideration thereof was postponed to, and made the order of the day for, Monday next.

Mr. Horsey, from a select committee, reported a bill to provide more effectually for the payment of specie to the several banks within the District of Columbia.

[This bill provides that if any bank or banking company in the District of Columbia shall refuse, after the first day of January next, to pay its notes or checks with specie, the same may be obtained against them by the holder, with twelve per cent. interest from the time of such failure or refusal, to pay such notes in specie, &c. But this remedy shall not be used by any bank, or bank agent, as a remedy against another bank.]

INCREASE OF SALARIES.

Mr. Fromentin, from the committee to whom the subject was referred, reported a bill providing for the increase of the salaries of the officers of Government therein mentioned, and the bill was read, and passed to the second reading.

The report and bill are as follows:

The committee appointed to inquire into the expediency of increasing the salaries of all the officers of Government, beg leave to report—

That, from the most thorough investigation by them bestowed on the subject referred to them, they can have no hesitation in recommending an increase of salary to all the officers of Government mentioned in the bill which accompanies, and which they pray may be considered as part of this report. By contrasting the prices of all the necessaries of life at the time at which the salaries of the officers of Government were first fixed with the prices now to be given for the same necessary articles, your committee are satisfied that the expenses of living have been increased in a proportion much greater than the increase contemplated in the bill now submitted to the Senate. At the same time, therefore, that they were persuaded an addition was to

be made to the salaries of the officers of Government, they entertained doubts as to the amount of augmentation which it might be proper for them to recommend, having a due regard both to the necessities of the officers to be provided for, and to the principles of a wise and prudent economy. From these doubts your committee feel themselves relieved by the principle of augmentation established in the act lately passed to change the mode of compensating the members of Congress.

From the year 1790, when the Government first went into operation, to the end of the thirteenth Congress, it appears, by a reference to the journals, that Congress have been in session four thousand one hundred and forty-eight days; which number of days, divided by twenty-six, the whole number of years which have elapsed from the beginning of the first to the end of the thirteenth Congress, gives for each year an average number of one hundred and fifty-nine days and a fraction during which Congress have been in session, without making any mention of the additional number of days during which the Senate have been occasionally called upon to sit on Executive business.

Had the compensation of members of Congress then been, as it now is, at the rate of $1,500 per annum, instead of six dollars per day, they would have received nine dollars and a fraction, making the increase to their salary, as fixed by the act to change the mode of compensating the members of Congress, about fifty per cent. over the sum at which it was originally fixed in the year 1790; an increase, however, still reduced somewhat below fifty per cent., as no alteration has taken place in the mileage.

Fifty per cent., then, being about the increase made by Congress to the compensation of their own members, may be fairly considered as the standard by which the salaries of the officers of Government ought to be now regulated; and the committee would have reported to you a resolution to that effect, had there been no occasional increase of salary to some of the officers whose compensation was originally fixed in the year 1790, and had there not been several offices created since with rather more adequate salaries.

These circumstances preclude, on the part of the committee, the possibility of a compliance with a strict adherence to the principle of increase in every case in absolutely the same exact proportion. Your committee were further induced to sacrifice unimportant fractions to the advantage resulting from adopting a mode of compensation amounting to a round sum. With this view of the subject referred to them, and without losing altogether sight of the principle adopted by Congress in the act providing for the increase of their own compensation, your committee beg leave to add that, except in a few cases, where, from the considerations above mentioned, they have reported below the increase of fifty per cent., they have rather generally gone beyond than remained below the principle of an increase of fifty per cent. to the salaries as they were originally fixed in the year 1790.

A Bill providing for the increase of the salaries of the officers of Government therein mentioned.

Be it enacted, by the Senate and House of Representatives of the United States of America in Congress assembled, That, in lieu of the salaries formerly allowed to the officers of Government mentioned in this act, there shall be allowed to them from the 1st day of January, 1816, the following annual salaries, payable quarterly, at the Treasury of the United States, to wit:

To the Secretary of State - - - $5,000
To the Secretary of the Treasury - - 6,000
To the Secretary of War - - - 6,000
To the Secretary of the Navy - - 6,000
To the Attorney General - - - 4,000
To the Comptroller - - - - 4,000
To the Postmaster General - - - 4,000
To the Auditor - - - - - 3,500
To the Treasurer - - - - - 3,500
To the Commissioner of the General Land
  Office - - - - - - - 3,500
To the Commissioner of the Revenue - 3,500
To the Register - - - - - 3,500
To the Accountant of War - - - 3,000
To the Accountant of the Navy - - 3,000
To the Paymaster of the Army - - 3,000
To the Governors of the several Territories - 2,500
To the Secretaries of the several Territories - 1,500
To a Minister Plenipotentiary and Envoy Ex-
  traordinary to the Courts of Paris, London,
  and St. Petersburg - - - - 12,000
To a Minister Plenipotentiary and Envoy Ex-
  traordinary to any other Court - - 9,000
To a Minister resident - - - - 7,600
To a Chargé des Affaires - - - 5,500
To a Secretary of Legation - - - 2,500
To the Chief Justice of the United States - 6,000
To the Associate Justices of the Supreme Court 5,000
To the Chief Justice of the District of Colum-
  bia - - - - - - - 3,000
To the associate justices of the District of Co-
  lumbia - - - - - - 2,500
To the district judge for the district of Maine 1,500
To the district judge for New Hampshire - 1,500
To the district judge for Vermont - - 1,500
To the district judge for Massachusetts - 2,000
To the district judge for Rhode Island - 1,500
To the district judge for Connecticut - 1,500
To the district judges for New York, each - 2,000
To the district judge for New Jersey - 1,500
To the district judge for Pennsylvania - 2,000
To the district judge for Delaware - 1,500
To the district judge for Maryland - 2,000
To the district judge for Virginia - 2,000
To the district judge for Kentucky - 2,000
To the district judge for Tennessee - 2,000
To the district judge for Ohio - - 1,500
To the district judge for North Carolina - 2,000
To the district judge for South Carolina - 2,000
To the district judge for Georgia - - 2,000
To the district judge for Louisiana - 3,500
To the judges of the several Territories, each - 1,500
To the Secretary of the Senate - - 2,500
To the Clerk of the House of Representatives 2,500
To the principal clerk in the office of the Secre-
  tary of the Senate - - - - 1,750
To each of the engrossing clerks in the office
  of the Secretary of the Senate - - 1,500
To the principal clerk in the office of the Clerk
  of the House of Representatives - - 1,750
To each of the engrossing clerks in the office
  of the Clerk of the House of Representatives 1,500
To the Chaplain to the Senate, at the rate of
  $1,000 per annum.
To the Chaplain to the House of Representa-
  tives, at the rate of $1,000 per annum.

POST OFFICE ESTABLISHMENT.

The Senate resumed the consideration of the bill, entitled "An act in addition to an act to regulate the Post Office Establishment."

On the question to agree to the following, as a substitute for the third section, stricken out:

SEC. 3. *And be it further enacted,* That letters and packets to and from any member of the Senate, or member or delegate of the House of Representatives of the United States, the Secretary of the Senate, and Clerk of the House of Representatives, shall be conveyed free of postage for thirty days previous to each session of Congress, and for thirty days after the termination thereof: *Provided always,* That no letter or packet shall exceed two ounces in weight; and in case of excess of weight, that excess alone shall be paid for.

It was determined in the affirmative—yeas 19, nays 6, as follows:

YEAS—Messrs. Brown, Daggett, Dana, Fromentin, Gaillard, Goldsborough, Harper, Horsey, Hunter, Mason of Virginia, Morrow, Ruggles, Sanford, Talbot, Tait, Taylor, Thompson, Wells, and Williams.

NAYS—Messrs. Condit, Macon, Roberts, Turner, Varnum, and Wilson.

Sundry other amendments having been agreed to, on motion, by Mr. MACON, the bill was recommitted to Messrs. WILSON, ROBERTS, MORROW, CHACE, and THOMPSON, further to consider and report thereon.

MONDAY, March 25.

Mr. CAMPBELL, from the Committee on Finance and an Uniform National Currency, to whom was referred the petition of Willet Coles, made report thereon, together with the following resolution:

Resolved, That the petitioner have leave to withdraw his petition.

The report and resolution were read.

Mr. BROWN asked and obtained leave to bring in a bill establishing a port of delivery at the town of Bayou St. John; and the bill was read, and passed to the second reading.

Mr. CHACE, from the Committee on Finance and an Uniform National Currency, to whom was referred the bill, entitled "An act for the relief of Thomas and John Clifford, Elisha Fisher and Company, Thomas Clifford and Son," reported it without amendment. He also made a report in relation thereto, which was read.

The Senate resumed the consideration of the motion made the 14th instant, for instructing the Financial Committee to inquire into the expediency of providing by law for the augmentation of the salaries of the Judges of the Supreme Court of the United States; and on motion, the further consideration thereof was postponed until the first Monday in July next.

The bill to authorize the President of the United States to alter the road laid out from the foot of the rapids of the river Miami of Lake Erie, to the western line of the Connecticut Reserve, was read the second time.

The bill to authorize the Legislature of the

State of Ohio to sell a certain part of a tract of land reserved for the use of that State, was read the second time.

The bill providing for the increase of the salaries of the officers of Government therein mentioned, was read the second time.

The bill to provide more effectually for the payment of specie by the several banks within the District of Columbia, was read the second time.

Mr. BARBOUR presented the petition of James Stubblefield and Roswell Lee, superintendents of the armories of the United States established at Harper's Ferry, in the State of Virginia, and at Springfield, in the State of Massachusetts, praying an increase of compensation as stated in the petition; which was read, and referred to the Committee on Military Affairs.

A message from the House of Representatives informed the Senate that the House have passed a bill, entitled "An act placing certain persons on the list of navy pensioners;" also, a bill entitled "An act for organizing the general staff, and making further provision for the Army of the United States;" in which bills they request the concurrence of the Senate. They have passed the bill which originated in the Senate, entitled "An act to limit the right of appeal from the circuit court of the United States for the District of Columbia," with an amendment, in which they request the concurrence of the Senate.

The Senate proceeded to consider the amendment of the House of Representatives to the bill last mentioned, and concurred thereon.

The two bills last brought up for concurrence were read, and passed to the second reading.

The bill for the relief of the Baltimore and Massachusetts Bible Societies, was read a third time, and passed.

The bill for the relief of John Holker, formerly Consul General of France to the United States, was read a third time, and passed.

The Senate resumed, as in Committee of the Whole, the consideration of the bill to establish a system of navigation for the United States, and on motion by Mr. BIBB, the further consideration thereof was postponed until to-morrow.

THE NATIONAL BANK BILL.

The bill from the House of Representatives to incorporate the subscribers to the Bank of the United States, was taken up as in Committee of the Whole. The first section having been read—

Mr. CAMPBELL stated, as chairman of the Committee of Finance, that whilst this bill was before that committee, amendments had been proposed to it, but, though a majority of the committee had been of opinion that the bill required amendment, as they did not entirely concur as to the nature of the amendments, they had determined to report the bill without amendment. He was one, he said, who considered the bill defective. It had been his intention to have this day submitted his views of the bill, and to have moved amendments to it accordingly; but the state of his health would not permit him at this time to perform that duty. He should therefore leave the bill to be disposed of by the Senate in such way as the Senate might think proper, reserving to himself the right at some future moment to give his views of the bill, &c.

Mr. MASON, of New Hampshire, moved to strike out five, the proportion of specie to be paid in at the time of subscription, and in lieu thereof to insert ten; the effect of which motion would be to make the whole amount of specie paid in at the time of subscription $2,800,000, instead of $1,400,000. The two great objects proposed by the friends of this bill, he said, were—1st, to release the country from the mass of spurious paper which was said to be the circulating medium; 2dly, to aid the Government in its finances. To effect the first object, the bank must commence its operations in specie. To enable it to do this, he proceeded to show, that in his view a larger proportion of specie was necessary to the first payment. The United States stock subscribable and payable at the same time, to the amount of seven millions, would, he said, be no more aid to the bank in discounting with a view to redeeming its notes with specie, than would so many bank bills. The amount of $1,400,000 in specie, divided among the different branches which he presumed would be immediately established, would, he argued, be insufficient for any operation whatever. Let the bank issue paper sufficient to produce any effect, and the specie in its vaults would be instantly withdrawn from them; twenty-five days would be sufficient for that purpose. In Baltimore, Philadelphia, and the District of Columbia, he said, the notes of the bank would be seized on by every individual who has any occasion for specie, &c.—the bank, then, to be safe, would be able to issue no more paper than to the amount of its specie paid in. Would such an issue, he asked, serve to reform the currency, or give the Government any aid in its finances? It might be said, the bank would commence operations slowly and with caution; but, Mr. M. said any man acquainted with the institution of banks knows that the sum first paid in is nearly all that the stockholders ever pay. The bank would continue in operation forever, he said, without taking from the stockholders any considerable sum more than the first instalment; for, as far as the bank discounted, the second instalment would be paid into the bank with specie of the first instalment, &c. This was a position so fully supported by all experience. that he presumed it would not be denied. For its specie capital, then, the bank must depend principally on the amount first paid in: the bank might sell some stock, &c., to obtain specie, but the direct bringing in of specie would not be much after the first instalment. The sum of $2,800,000 was not a large instalment to be first paid in on a capital of thirty-five millions, and, according to the statements of gentlemen, there would be no difficulty in obtaining the necessary amount of specie to make the first payment. He concluded by saying that his motion, if adopted, would essentially aid the bank in commencing its operations, and increase its effect in reforming the circulation of the country, as far as this bill can have that effect.

Mr. KING, of New York, supported this motion. Before he proceeded to make any remarks on the motion, he touched upon a question preliminary in its character, and which he regarded as of great importance, inasmuch as it superseded all detail, and, if decided affirmatively, rendered it utterly unless to discuss the details of the bill. Advert- ing to the discussion which had taken place in this House on late occasions in regard to public opinion, he said that public opinion, well defined and understood, the well considered judgment of the majority of the nation, no one doubted, was entitled to profound respect from this House. Public opinion, he said, was not so embodied, not cast into such a shape, that much confidence could be placed in that argument on the subject of the establishment of a National Bank. Yet, he said, public opinion does exist; and where it is relative to Constitutional questions of great municipal law, it may be relied on as authority. The Legislative power of the nation was placed in two separate branches; public opinion in favor of this distribution of it was so general and strong that no educated man in the nation could doubt it. It was, therefore, not only a provision of the Constitution, but unquestionably the decision of public opinion, that, upon any measure fit to be made a law, the discussion on all its provisions ought to be subjected to separate examination in the separate branches of the Legislature, and that the decision of one branch should not operate to preclude a re-examination by the other; that each branch of the Legislature should deliberate on any measure which has passed the other branch, with the same freedom as if the bill had originated in that House. The subject now under considera- tion, Mr. K. went on to say, was a most important measure, and had passed the other branch of the Legislature. Those very considerations, rather than forbidding, demanded a peculiar and cir- cumspect examination of the bill in this branch of the Legislature. It may, for example, have fortuitously passed the other House. Care ought to be taken that it do not in like manner fortu- itously pass the Senate. The smallness of the majority in the other House, the possibility of its varying, &c., instead of being reasons for hurry- ing over this bill, were reasons why it should be examined more freely. If this reasoning were not true, the Constitution and public opinion were equally wrong; the Legislature should con- sist of but one branch. He was not, therefore, permitted to doubt, he said, that the Senate, dis- regarding the suggestion, that possibly the bill might fail on being again brought before the other House by amendments from this House, would decide according to the obligations of their stations here, and with an unbiassed regard to their fitness on such amendments as should be proposed; leaving the responsibility for the con- sequences of a performance of their duty, where, by the Constitution, it ought to rest. These sug- gestions flowed from an apprehension on the

part of Mr. K., that, although the question was surrounded with difficulties, the Senate would be urged to pass the bill without amendment, lest, on its return to the House, if the Senate did its duty by amending it, the bill would fail. Mr. K. then turned his attention to the bill, which, he said, was imperfect in its provisions in the view which any gentleman might take of it, as could be easily shown. The particular proposition now before the Senate though important, he said, was not as much so as other points in the bill. But the gentleman from New Hampshire had con- clusively shown that one and a half millions was the greatest extent to which, as it now stood, the bank could safely issue on a specie system. Illus- trating his view of the subject by a detailed state- ment of the process, he said, that the first dis- counts of the bank being necessarily to those most pressed by the State banks, the proceeds of the discounts would immediately find their way into the vaults of the State banks, &c. Under this view, a million and a half of dollars would be a sum entirely too small wherewith to enter into competition with the existing banks. If the is- sues of the bank exceeded the specie paid in, the first process would be, immediately to transfer the specie from the general bank to the local banks; if the bank confined its discounts within that sum, its agency would be very limited in- deed, &c. Connected with this subject, Mr. K. said, was another idea, which perhaps it would be premature now to enlarge on; which was, that according to the provisions of this bill, as he un- derstood them, the bank need not, may not, will not, be a specie bank; the very circumstances already suggested would compel the bank to be- come a paper bank, to issue a paper that will not command specie. This, then, should be an ad- ditional motive to the Senate to increase the amount of the specie payment, that the bank may be enabled to avoid such a state of its affairs as would compel it to become a paper bank, &c. With these views Mr. K. hoped the Senate would agree to the amendment proposed.

Mr. BIBB, of Georgia, rose to oppose the amend- ment. Feeble as he was, he said, nothing less than the most imperious obligations of public duty could have brought him to the Senate. But, believing, as he did, that the adoption of any amendment whatever to the bill would certainly endanger or defeat its passage, and that upon its fate depended, more than on any other measure to which the attention of Congress could be drawn at this moment, the welfare and prosperity of the country, he felt bound, unmindful of the conse- quences, to make a great effort to aid, with his vote at least, the progress of the bill. He regret- ted exceedingly the physical incapacity which would prevent him from laying before the Senate at large his views of the question, which, how- ever, he proceeded to assign as far as he was able. It appeared to him, he said, impossible for a states- man, in the habit of contemplating national ques- tions, and considering cause and effect, not to look at the present condition of the country with apprehension and alarm. By a combination of circumstances not necessary to be enumerated, one of the leading objects of the adoption of the Federal Constitution was at this moment lost to the nation. Whether it should be finally lost to the nation, or should be recovered, would depend, in all human probability, on the conduct of the Senate on this occasion. To enable the Government to fulfil its engagements to the public creditors, to restore confidence among the citizens of the country in regard to pecuniary transactions, to prevent anything but gold and silver from being a legal tender, to maintain the obligation of contracts, were, he said, the leading objects which produced the adoption of the Constitution. The regulation of the general currency of the country, without which the attainment of these great objects is impracticable, is, said Mr. B., at this moment wrested from the hands of the Government by petty corporations and swindling individuals throughout the community. This, he said, is the abject condition of our affairs. Could any honorable Senator reconcile it to his conscience to leave his seat at the present session, without making an effort, a great effort, to reform the national currency, to regain the power over it which we have lost? The country was rich in resources, its people in individual means; and yet both the country, and individuals, were unequal to meet their engagements honestly and faithfully; and, not only so, but the Government was compelled to legalize that species of swindling by which the important, necessary power of sovereignty, the regulation of the currency of the country was taken from the Government. It was unnecessary, he said, to recapitulate the cause which had produced this state of things, but he did verily believe, that, unless the present Congress should take some efficient measure to compel the resumption of payment of specie, it was extremely doubtful whether it ever would be done. He called the attention of the Senate to the acts of the State governments; scarcely a session passed in which bank charters were not granted by them to the amount of millions—and, as the influence of these State banks increased, so did the difficulty of legislating on this subject. Mr. B. then considered the subject in other points of view. At the present moment, he said, the people in the Eastern States pay the revenue to the United States in Treasury notes; but the Secretary of the Treasury was making a great effort to call in that species of paper. When that object was accomplished, what would be the situation of the Eastern States? Whilst other quarters of the country were paying their taxes in paper, those banks must either pay in paper as valuable as specie, or in specie itself; the inevitable consequence must be, that the banks of that part of the country must follow the example of all the other banks. All the banks in the country would then be united against a return to specie payment. So far as he had heard, Mr. B. said that the opinion of a large majority of the Senate was, that some course of measures should be adopted for the remedy of the evil; the only question was as to the mode. He had heard but two modes proposed; the one, to declare by law that after a certain day the paper of those banks refusing to pay specie should not be receivable in dues to the Government; the other, to establish a National Bank. The first plan, he said, was impracticable; the people cannot pay what they cannot get—besides, that such a measure would cause a combination of the banks, too strong for the Government to overpower. Mr. B. said he would go further; he believed a large majority of the Senate had declared themselves in favor of a National Bank; that they had made up their minds that it was the best possible means of restoring the country to the old state of things. Now, he asked, whether, on a question of mere detail, they ought to risk the loss of an object so important as this bill? Mr. B. asserted to the Senate, and he said he would justify the ground, that, although this bill might not be perfect, he should vote against every amendment of every character; justified in so doing by the importance of the passage of the bill. The honorable gentleman from New York had strongly inveighed against such a course. Mr. B. intimated that it was precisely the course the gentleman himself had taken on the question of the Direct Tax at a former session. It had been then admitted that amendments proposed would make the bill more perfect; but their rejection was justified on the ground of the importance of the bill, and the probability that an agreement to the amendments might occasion the rejection of the bill on its return to the other House. That was a correct course, Mr. B. said, and that course he should now pursue. He also referred to a precedent of higher authority—the recommendation of the Convention who framed the Constitution, to the people, that, although susceptible of amendment to advantage, the Constitution should be accepted as it stood, lest, by the collision of opinion on amendments, it should be lost. The Constitution had been accordingly so accepted, and subsequently amended by adding to it new sections. Mr. B. was against all amendments to the bill. In regard to this particular feature of the bill, it could not, in any view, be of sufficient importance to justify endangering the bill. He denied the justice of the intimation that this was not to be a specie bank. Substantially, he said, it possessed all the features of the old Bank of the United States, the plan of which gentlemen had so highly approved; with the addition of several important checks not contained in the plan of that bank, the nature of which Mr. B. explained. He vindicated some of the principal features of this bill, to which, on either hand, objections had been made, particularly that which gave the appointment of five of the directors to the Government—which was due to the interest of the Government in the bank, as well on account of its stock, as of the necessary attention to the security of its deposites. As to its not being a specie bank, if the control of the Government was as powerful as he considered it, it would be the fault of the Government alone if it were not a specie bank. We must suppose the Government and the people themselves corrupted, before you suppose that it will not be a specie bank. With the aid of all the Eastern banks, being, besides, the depository of the revenue of the United States, and thus having all the State banks debtors to it, how could the State banks destroy it? Congress might additionally provide that, at some distant day, the notes of banks not paying specie, should cease to be received in payment of dues to the Government, &c.—at some distant day, he said, for he was not for destroying or injuring the State banks, &c. Mr. B. concluded his speech by expressing his hope that the Senate would not agree to any amendment to the bill.

Mr. BARBOUR, of Virginia, next took the floor, and opposed the proposed amendment in a speech of considerable length, of which what follows is but an outline. He, too, like the gentleman from Georgia, considered the question of bank or no bank as the most important that could be presented to the National Legislature at this session. The rejection of this bill, he believed, would expose us to a continuation of all the inconveniences experienced in every quarter of the Union from the present state of the circulating medium, causing a fluctuation and uncertainty in the value of property and products greatly to be deprecated, and bringing with it a train of evils it would be almost impossible to enumerate. On the other hand, he said, he had such confidence in the efficacy of a National Bank, in correcting the evils of the mass of paper afloat, in enabling the Government and individuals to fulfil their engagements, that he had brought his mind to the conclusion that the establishment of a National Bank would be an epoch in the affairs of the nation; that, instead of the cloud which darkens the horizon, it will usher in a new day of prosperity, replete with benefits to the nation, &c. With the gentleman from New York, (Mr. KING,) Mr. B. said, he entirely coincided in sentiment as to the respect due to public opinion, when distinctly expressed and well understood; but why that sentiment was recurred to at the present time, he did not precisely understand; for sure he was, that on this occasion it had been audibly and distinctly expressed from every part of the United States, as well as from the Executive authority, in favor of this measure: and above all, it had been recently declared from an unequivocal source, the House of Representatives, who are the mirror in which the sentiments of the people are reflected, and whose decision on such a topic is a pillar of light, the pursuit of which will never involve us in difficulty. Mr. B. agreed, also, with the gentleman in his views of the independent duty of this House, in reviewing the proceedings of the other branch of the Legislature, so far as regarded the absolute right of the Senate to decide, according to their own impressions of the fitness of things, on measures presented to them by the other House; but if the gentleman meant that it was a reason for jealousy in regard to any measure that it had passed that House, Mr. B. differed from him *toto cœlo*. On the contrary, he said, that circumstance would be, with him, a persuasive argument in favor of any measure; for, though

he would surrender to them no part of the rights of this body, he should perpetually recur to that body as an oracle from which true responses may be drawn as to the public will. It may err; when it did, in his opinion, he should not feel himself bound by its views, &c.

Mr. B. then proceeded to the consideration of the great subject before the House. The Constitution, he said, had imparted to the Congress, among other great attributes, the power of regulating the coin of the United States. How had Congress acquitted themselves of this duty? Where and of what effect were these regulations? Where was the uniformity of currency? Mr. B. described the variety and fluctuation of value of the paper in circulation, not only in various States, but in contiguous towns and counties, &c. This was a great evil, deprecated on all hands. The power intended by the Constitution to have been lodged in the hands of the General Government, was, by the failure of the Government to make use of it, exercised by every State in the Union, frequently by individuals, &c. Hence arose an excess of paper issues, causing depreciation to an extent which could scarcely be estimated—an evil which called for a remedy in a language not to be misunderstood. Where was the antidote which the Executive, in this only the organ of the public sentiment, had called on Congress to interpose? The patient, said Mr. B., is sick, from the crown of his head to the sole of his foot; he asks for oil and wine to be poured into his wounds, which would be otherwise fatal. Where is the man who will propose any other antidote than that now before us? Where is the adventurous knight who will suggest another remedy? If there be a Don Quixote in politics, let him appear. No, Mr. B. said, not even a nostrum had been tendered to substitute this plan. If no other remedy was offered, ought they, he asked, to higgle about details, to split hairs on the question? Mr. B. then spoke of the necessity of mutual concession among legislators; without which, he said, the idea of legislation was the most vague and illusory that ever entered the human mind. It was necessary, Mr. B. then argued, for the present diseased paper medium, since specie had fled the country, or was scattered in the bowels of the earth, to substitute a medium impressed with the seal of the nation. If an institution were established to issue a paper of that description, we should have, he said, in lieu of a medium, the value of which will not live ten, fifteen, or twenty miles from the spot where we receive it, a paper which will embrace the Union in its grasp. It would also be a great financial instrument, necessary to the fulfilment of the national duties in this respect. On this head, the experience of the last war spoke a language which incredulity itself could not doubt. In the dark and gloomy period of the last Winter, when this subject was discussed, no doubt had been entertained that this was the only means of remedying an evil from which so much was apprehended. That time, he rejoiced, had passed by; but he hoped the lessons of experience would not be permitted to pass away with the urgency of the occasion.

In regard to the details of this bill, he said, he did not see the necessity of amending them. It had been stated that this would be a paper bank, and in order to prevent that, an increase of the specie payments was suggested. Mr. B. believed such an amendment was unnecessary. Being not necessary, what, he asked, would be its effect? It would be to place the bank wholly in the hands of a few fortunate individuals or banks who had specie in their possession. The smaller the first payment in specie was made, within the limits of necessity to the object, in his opinion, the wiser would be the plan. The establishment of a bank, or any other system, could not be expected to afford an instant remedy to the existing evil, any more than a dose of medicine would restore to instant health and pristine vigor the man who had been wasting by long sickness. The effect of this amendment, without accelerating the operations of the bank, would be to favor the monopolist of specie, &c., he who had had the caution or forecast to board up the dollars and cents. The bulk of the specie to be paid into this bank, Mr. B. had no doubt, ought and must be drawn from abroad. In regard to the argument, that the sum was too small to enable the bank to commence its operations with safety, &c., Mr. B. contended that money was too sharp-sighted, too lynx-eyed in its vigilance to be (using a common saying) caught napping. There was no fear, he said, of the banks being ruined, by lending money to men pressed from other quarters; the board of direction of a bank formed a barometer in which the responsibility of every man passing before it was as correctly graduated as the weather is by the instrument so called; they would take care, as they always did, not to part with their dollars to accommodate an unfortunate debtor, &c. In answer to the argument of Mr. KING, who, he said, had discovered that this was to be a paper and not a specie bank, and was to aggravate the evils it was intended to cure, Mr. B. referred to the regulations by which it was to be governed to show that this apprehension was unfounded. Besides, he said, the bank would not disregard its interest, which required it to continue specie payments. You need not fence in the interests of this institution, said he; you might as well pass a law to compel your Secretary to receive his salary; interest is the strongest security which man can give to man. As the needle acknowledges the principle of polarity, so does the human heart always point to its interest. That objection against this bill, therefore, seemed to Mr. B. to be a chimera from which nothing was to be apprehended.

It was no question now, he said, whether banking should exist—that being beyond the control of Congress; but whether it was proper that a portion of it should be placed under the authority of the General Government, instead of its being wholly under the control of the States, who establish banks not only in their populous towns, but even in the dreary wilderness. This being

the only question, he solemnly appealed to gentlemen, whether there could be two opinions on that point. Ought this great attribute of sovereignty to be surrendered by this Government to the authority of the State Legislatures? This question he answered in the negative. The existing evil, he then argued, would be remedied by the establishment of a bank, whose influence was ramified into every part of the United States. The State banks had nothing to fear, if they would conduct themselves properly, from such an institution. If any of them, on the other hand, should violate their trust, and show a centrifugal quality, it would be in the power of this great orb to restore them to their stations. If any of the State banks do not fulfil their engagements, Mr. B. said, if they do not meet the occasion, their paper will sink into disrepute. This bank will be the silent and efficient remedy; it will move on almost imperceptibly, gradual in its approach, but certain in its effects. Mr. B. took this occasion to vindicate the banks in the Commonwealth of Virginia from the charge it had been fashionable to make against the State banks, of improvidence in their administration. Those banks resisted to the utmost the attempts to procure loans from them; that which they had, with great reluctance, from a sense of duty refused to the Government, their patriotism at length induced them to grant to the wants of thousands of men surrounding their capital, who but for their relief would have greatly suffered, &c. Where banks had wantonly abused their privileges, he cared not what was said of them, but he felt no disposition to put those under the ban of the empire who had acted thus correctly, &c.

In regard to objections he had heard to the influence of the Government over this bank, Mr. B. said, his objection was, that it had not interest enough in it; but in this respect, as in others, he was willing, to obtain a great object, to concede some part of his views. He recurred to the experience of his own State to show that no evils had been experienced from the existence of such a control to a much greater extent than proposed in this bill, &c. No banks, he believed, had been better conducted, or stood higher in the public opinion, than those of Virginia. If the bank were a faithful one, it had no fear to apprehend from the appointment by the Government of one-fifth of its directors, to which proportion the Government was entitled by the interest it would have with the bank.

Having thus briefly touched on all the objections he had heard to the bank, Mr. B. concluded by recapitulating his arguments, and expressing his hope that the only remedy as he believed, for a great evil, would be agreed to.

Mr. MASON, of New Hampshire, spoke in support of his motion to amend the bill. He certainly had entertained no expectation, he said, when he submitted the motion, that it would have drawn the bill into so general discussion. Whenever a National Bank had been proposed, he said, he had always supported it with such modifications as he thought correct. He did believe a well regulated institution of this kind would be useful to the Government; and, though the Government had at a certain period declined the exercise of its power in this respect, he felt no inclination to prevent them from again occupying the ground of the old United States Bank. He was, he said, now willing to give his aid in establishing a bank on proper principles; but he never could assent to this or any other measure on the ground taken by the gentlemen from Georgia and Virginia. The bill was, according to the forms of the Senate, read section by section for the purpose of amendment; and yet gentlemen declared they would not listen to any proposition to amend the bill, but take it as it stood. [Mr. BIBB explained, that his remark was confined to unessential amendments.] It might, Mr. M. said, be difficult to define what makes an amendment important; for him it was sufficient reason for an amendment, that the bill would be better with than without it. He could not, he said, see the force of the objection to sending this bill back to the House of Representatives better than it came from them; gentlemen must certainly conclude that that House was greatly in love with a bad bill. It always had been held irregular to suggest in one branch of the Legislature what might have passed in debate in the co-ordinate branch; it was certainly, Mr. M. said, more improper to go into a wide field of conjecture to find out what would happen there. Although there might be good reasons for concession and accommodation to the views of the other House, Mr. M. said, they had not yet arrived at that stage of the business when it was necessary, which was not until the House should refuse to accept the amendments of the Senate. It was a dangerous ground to assume, Mr. M. added, that the House of Representatives would vary their ground on this question. Although he had as much respect for them as he ought, he also remarked, he should not take public opinion from the Representatives of the people. The Constitution prescribed to the Senate no such practice. The course of taking measures from the popular branch of the Legislature, believing them proper because it has adopted them, precludes all legislation, &c., and is therefore inconsistent with the principles of our Government.

Mr. M. agreed that the public suffered much inconvenience from what was termed the state of the public medium; it was not very material whether it was produced by what the gentleman from Georgia had termed swindling, or what the gentleman from Virginia had called the patriotic conduct of the banks. Mr. M. replied to other arguments used by the gentlemen who had opposed his motion. In regard to the operation of interest on moneyed institutions, he said, he believed that principle was felt as much by the State banks as by that which it was now proposed to incorporate. Any bank, guided by other motives, would depart from the objects of the institution. Mr. M. attached no sort of consequence to the idea of the passage of this bill, in order to exercise the power of the Government to regulate the coin of the country. The laws of the United

States, he said, had already regulated it, he knew of no law which authorized any officer of the Government to receive any part of this spurious money which the gentleman said was in circulation. The laws were already perfect on this subject. If the Executive officers had received other moneys in payment than those authorized by law, Mr. M. said, they had acted without law—without right. What necessity there might have been for their doing so, he would not now examine. Cases might arise, in which the officers of the Government may take upon themselves the responsibility of neglecting the execution of a law, &c. That an evil existed, he said, all agree, and all suppose that the bank to be incorporated by this bill will in a greater or less degree lessen the evil, or entirely correct it. The object of his motion was to give the bank the greatest possible power to effect these purposes. It had been said, that the bank would at first move slowly. But, Mr. M. said, he had no sanguine anticipation that this amendment, or any other, or the prudence of the directors, would be able wholly to cure the evil. What had been the cause of the evil? The banks themselves; banks incorporated under the same restrictions as this bill contained, issue now the very rags which had been described. The remedy now proposed, was, Mr. M. thought, something like Sangrado's practice: more bank paper of the same sort—more hot water for the same evil. In regard to the impossibility of this bank's doing anything but a specie business, Mr. M. undertook to assert, that the charter, in its present shape, gave the bank the power to issue notes, without even promising payment of specie. The clause which authorizes the bank to issue notes did, in fact, for the want of due restrictions, authorize the bank to issue notes payable when it pleased; none but notes payable on demand were indeed receivable in payment of taxes to the Government—but they might be issued payable two years after date for other purposes, and would probably circulate quite as well as the notes of New York, Philadelphia, and Baltimore. He should imagine, he said, that, as the bank was now constituted, sensible men, having the management of it, would not attempt to do business without taking that course. Mr. M. pointed out other defects, as he viewed them, of the bill.

There was no provision for a forfeiture of the charter of the bank, or for annulment on failure of its going promptly into operation. However, it would be idle, he said, to discuss the bill, if the opinions of the gentlemen from Georgia and Virginia were to prevail with the majority of the Senate, that it would be dangerous to amend the bill, lest it should fail thereby. If this was the opinion of the Senate, the sooner they came to that determination the better; it would save them labor, and perhaps character, to decide the question at once. The same argument might be urged, he said, with as much propriety every day, and on every subject, as had been principally urged against the amendment.

Mr. DANA, of Connecticut, said he did not expect to vote for the bank bill in its present form, but notwithstanding, he did not think it would be proper to adopt this amendment; one-twentieth part of the whole capital, appeared to him to be as large a proportion as ought to be called for in specie at the time of subscription. If danger were anticipated from the smallness of the amount of specie, it would perhaps be better to introduce into the bill a provision, that the bank should not issue paper until it had a sufficient quantity of coin to justify it in so doing. Though he should not vote for the bank, he should regret to see its first issues to individuals who were connected with the institution; indeed, he should rather suppose, the great demand for discounts from the bank, would be to enable the merchants to pay bonds, constantly falling due to the Government for customs. These merchants, for their notes, will obtain credits at the bank, to the amount of perhaps, seven, eight, or ten millions in the course of the year. The United States will be the only power that can call for it; and, Mr. D. presumed, there would be no danger of a run on the bank from the Government, &c.

Mr. TAYLOR, of South Carolina, said he should have liked to have heard the amendment argued on its own merits, because the force of the argument against would perhaps be weakened by connecting it with other considerations which had been brought into debate. If he approved of the amendment, he would vote for it, though he would say, that for a small or inconsiderable alteration, he would not jeopardize a great principle or a great measure, such as he conceived this bill. With respect to the proposed amendment, considering the state of the currency of the country, and the known fact that specie abounds in parts of the country, whilst in others it is not to be obtained at all—to carry the gentleman's amendment more directly to what would be its absolute result, he ought first to have provided for confining the opening of the books of subscription to that part of the country where specie is in a state of circulation. Without designing it, for he would not certainly impute such a design to the gentleman, the adoption of this amendment would be giving a complete monopoly to the Eastern country. Believing it desirable that the benefits of this institution should be extended to every part of the country, he was therefore opposed to the amendment. The restoration of specie payments, Mr. T. said, was not the work of a moment. The power to sell two millions of its stock in the first year, of which the bank would no doubt avail itself, and the deposites of the Government, together with the specie paid in on the subscription, would, he said, enable the bank to operate to as great an extent as was advisable. This amendment, besides being unnecessary, would, he believed, produce an undue monopoly to one section of the country, and to the hoarders where specie was not current. It is calculated to reward those whose conduct has had a tendency to bring about the very evil now proposed to be remedied. The amendment would also throw advantages into the hands of the cap-

italists of Charleston, &c., which it would deny to those of the middle country; for it so happened, in the course of trade, that specie was reduced in value there to about two and a half to five per cent. above the current paper of that State, not more than in ordinary times used to be given for specie in quantities. For these general reasons, Mr. T. was opposed to the amendments.

Mr. MASON, of New Hampshire, remarked that specie was not confined to the Eastern or Southern States; the banks in the Middle States still retain as much specie as they ever had. If the bank might sell stock for specie, why might not individuals do the same, in the first instance, and pay it into the bank? United States' stock would at a certain price command specie anywhere.

Mr. SANFORD spoke in support of the proposed amendment, denying the correctness of the doctrine on which opposition was made to any amendment of this bill. It was a subject, he said, which particularly required caution and circumspection in deciding upon it. He considered the amendment before the Senate as presenting this question: With what sum shall the bank commence its operations? This being intended to be a specie bank, Mr. S. said, every proposition tending more certainly to make it more so, was worthy of favorable consideration. The bill as it stood contemplated $1,400,000 in specie as a sufficient basis for the bank to begin upon. Mr. S. said, he could not but think, with Mr. MASON, that this sum was too small. There was nothing in the bill to prevent the bank from issuing $35,000,000 on this amount of specie paid in, if they thought proper to do so. Those who were called on to pay the second instalment in specie would, he said, go to the bank with its bills, and drain it at once of every dollar. The bill was, Mr. S. thought, in other respects, deficient in detail, as he showed by reference to its provisions. The bank would get no specie but what it received in the first payment, unless the course of exchange should become more favorable, or the state of things generally should essentially vary. The rational and prudent course, he thought, would be, to require as much specie as possible in the first instance. Without amendments to regulate the paper issues of the bank, &c., this would be a mere paper bank, he said, like those which already exist. The amendment appeared to him extremely proper, and therefore he should vote for it.

Mr. TAYLOR replied to Mr. SANFORD, and quoted the provisions of the bank to show, that the bank dare not issue one dollar more paper than it had a reasonable prospect of being able to honor with gold or silver. The bank had the power to do otherwise, it was true; and so have we power to cut our own throats—but the bank is no more likely than we are to commit a *felo de se.* As to the second instalment being paid with the specie of the first, Mr. T. said, it was impossible to pay $2,800,000, (the amount of the second instalment,) with $1,400,000, (the amount of the first,) and the worst, therefore, only one-half of the second instalment could be drawn from the vaults of the bank.

The Senate then adjourned, leaving the pending question undecided.

TUESDAY, March 26.

Mr. DANA presented the petition of Nehemiah Hubbard, and others, inhabitants of the collection district of Middletown, in the State of Connecticut, praying that the port of Middletown may be constituted a port of entry, for reasons stated in the petition; which was read, and referred to a select committee; and Messrs. DANA, SANFORD, and DAGGETT, were appointed the committee.

Mr. WILSON, from the committee to whom was recommitted the bill entitled "An act in addition to 'An act to regulate the Post Office Establishment,'" reported it with amendments, which were read and considered as in Committee of the Whole; and the amendments having been agreed to, with a further amendment, the President reported the bill to the House accordingly; and on the question, "Shall the amendments be engrossed, and the bill read a third time as amended?" it was determined in the affirmative.

Mr. BARBOUR, from the Committee on Military Affairs, to whom was referred the bill, entitled "An act for the relief of John T. Wirt," reported it without amendment.

The bill establishing a port of delivery at the Bayou St. John, was read the second time.

The bill, entitled "An act placing certain persons on the list of navy pensioners," was read the second time, and referred to the Committee on Naval Affairs, to consider and report thereon.

The bill, entitled "An act for organizing the general staff, and making further provision for the Army of the United States," was read the second time, and referred to the Committee on Military Affairs.

The Senate resumed the consideration of the motion made the 22d instant, for information in relation to the proceedings which have been had in pursuance of the act of the 10th of February, 1807, entitled "An act to provide for surveying the coasts of the United States," and agreed thereto.

The Senate resumed the consideration of the report of the Committee on Finance and an Uniform National Currency, to whom was referred the petition of Willet Coles. Whereupon, the petitioner had leave to withdraw his petition.

BANK OF THE UNITED STATES.

The Senate resumed, as in Committee of the Whole, the consideration of the bill, entitled "An act to incorporate the subscribers to the Bank of the United States."

Mr. MASON, of New Hampshire, having withdrawn the motion made the 25th instant, to amend the third section, proposed the following proviso to be added to the 12th rule:

"*Provided,* That all bills or notes so to be issued by said corporation, shall be made payable on demand, other than bills or notes for the payment of a sum not

less than —— dollars each, and payable to the order of some person or persons, which bills or notes it shall be lawful for said corporation to make payable at any time not exceeding —— days from the date thereof."

This motion gave rise to considerable debate between those who thought such a restriction necessary and those of a different opinion. It was at length agreed to by yeas and nays.

On the question to agree thereto, it was determined in the affirmative—yeas 20, nays 14, as follows:

YEAS—Messrs. Brown, Daggett, Dana, Fromentin, Gaillard, Goldsborough, Gore, Horsey, Hunter, King, Macon, Mason of New Hampshire, Mason of Virginia, Sanford, Taylor, Thompson, Tichenor, Wells, Williams, and Wilson.

NAYS—Messrs. Barbour, Barry, Bibb, Campbell, Chace, Condit, Howell, Lacock, Morrow, Roberts, Ruggles, Tait, Turner, and Varnum.

This decision in favor of one amendment opened the door to the proposition of a great number of amendments which have been or will be proposed to the bill.

The discussion of one or two that were proposed occupied the Senate until the hour of adjournment.

WEDNESDAY, March 27.

Mr. DAGGETT presented the petition of Daniel Carroll, of Duddington, and others, citizens of Washington, praying an act to incorporate a company to continue a turnpike road leading from Calvert's mills, from the District line, to the Eastern Branch bridge, as stated in the petition; which was read, and referred to a select committee; and Messrs. DAGGETT, HORSEY, and MASON of Virginia, were appointed the committee.

Mr. TAIT, from the Committee on Naval Affairs, to whom was referred the bill, entitled "An act placing certain persons on the list of navy pensioners," reported it without amendment; and the bill having been considered as in Committee of the Whole, it passed to a third reading.

Mr. TAIT, from the Committee on Naval Affairs, to whom the subject was referred, reported a bill to reward the officers and crew of the United States frigate Constitution; and the bill was read, and passed to the second reading.

The Senate resumed, as in Committee of the Whole, the consideration of the bill, entitled "An act authorizing and requiring the Secretary of State to issue letters patent to Andrew Kurtz;" and it passed to a third reading.

The Senate resumed, as in Committee of the Whole, the consideration of the bill to authorize the Legislature of the State of Ohio to sell a certain part of a tract of land reserved for the use of that State; and on the question, "Shall this bill be engrossed and read a third time?" it was determined in the affirmative.

Mr. LACOCK submitted the following motion for consideration:

Resolved, That the Committee on Military Affairs be instructed to inquire into the propriety of granting bounty lands to such of the disbanded officers of our late Army as have been disabled by wounds while in the public service.

Mr. DAGGETT, from the joint committee appointed to examine the business on the tables of the two Houses, to ascertain what portion required to be acted on this session, and to fix on a period for its close, made a report, together with the following resolution:

Resolved, That the President of the Senate and Speaker of the House of Representatives be authorised to close this session, by the adjournment of their respective Houses, on the 22d day of April, 1816.

The report and resolution were read, and passed to the second reading.

BANK OF THE UNITED STATES.

The Senate resumed the Bank bill. The consideration of amendments progressed. An amendment was adopted, among others, to postpone the opening of the books from the 1st day of June to the 1st day of July.

Mr. MASON, of New Hampshire, then moved another amendment, by way of a new section, to declare the act null and void, if the bank is not put into operation within one year after its date.

Mr. BIBB moved to amend this amendment so as to make it reserve to Congress the right to annul the charter, at any time within twelve months after the 1st day of February next, if the bank be not put in operation before that day.

These motions gave rise to much desultory debate, as indeed did all the amendments proposed.

Mr. BIBB's motion was agreed to; and Mr. MASON's proposition, so modified, was agreed to.

Mr. CAMPBELL then moved to amend that part of the bill which directs books to be opened at certain places, so as to assign to each State a certain proportion of the stock to be subscribed, to remain there for a certain time, to allow it to be subscribed in the States respectively, in proportion to their representation—intending to follow up this amendment by a motion to introduce a provision that the bank should be compelled, on the request of the Legislature of any State, to establish a branch of the bank therein.

In support of this motion, Mr. C. made a speech of some length on the general principles of the bill.

This amendment was in the end negatived by a vote of 20 to 11.

Late in the day, the consideration of the bill was further postponed till to-morrow.

THURSDAY, March 28.

The bill to reward the officers and crew of the United States frigate Constitution, was read the second time.

Mr. KING, from the committee to whom was recommitted the bill for the benefit of the widow and children of Robert Fulton, deceased, reported it with an amendment, which was read.

The Senate resumed, as in Committee of the Whole, the consideration of the bill to authorize the President of the United States to alter the road laid out from the foot of the rapids of the river Miami of Lake Erie, to the western line of the Connecticut Reserve; and no amendment having been proposed thereto, on the question, "Shall this bill be engrossed and read a third time?" it was determined in the affirmative.

The Senate resumed, as in Committee of the Whole, the consideration of the bill establishing a port of delivery at the town of Bayou St. John; and the bill having been amended, the PRESIDENT reported it to the House accordingly; and on the question, "Shall this bill be engrossed and read a third time?" it was determined in the affirmative.

The Senate resumed, as in Committee of the Whole, the consideration of the bill entitled "An act for the relief of John T. Wirt," and it passed to a third reading.

The bill entitled "An act in addition to an act to regulate the Post Office Establishment," was read a third time as amended, and was further amended by unanimous consent, and passed with amendments.

The bill entitled "An act authorizing and requiring the Secretary of State to issue letters patent to Andrew Kurtz," was read a third time and passed.

The bill entitled "An act placing certain persons on the list of navy pensioners," was read a third time, and passed.

Mr. CAMPBELL, from the Committee on Finance and an Uniform National Currency, to whom was referred the bill entitled "An act to repeal the act entitled 'An act to provide additional revenues for defraying the expenses of Government, and maintaining the public credit, by laying duties on household furniture, and on gold and silver watches," reported it without amendment.

The Senate resumed, as in Committee of the Whole, the consideration of the bill entitled "An act to incorporate the subscribers to the Bank of the United States."

Mr. FROMENTIN withdrew his proposed amendment.

Sundry amendments having been agreed to, and further amendments proposed, on motion by Mr. WILLIAMS, the further consideration of the bill, together with the proposed amendments, was postponed until to-morrow.

FRIDAY, March 29.

Mr. DAGGETT, from the committee to whom the subject was referred, reported a bill supplementary to an act entitled "An act to incorporate a company for making certain turnpike roads within the District of Columbia," and the bill was read, and passed to the second reading.

The Senate resumed the consideration of the motion made the 27th instant, relative to bounty lands, which was amended and agreed to as follows:

Resolved, That the Committee on Military Affairs be instructed to inquire into the propriety of granting bounty lands to such of the disbanded officers of our late army as have been disabled by wounds while in the public service, and of granting the same quantity of land to each soldier who has served during the late war, and been honorably discharged.

On motion by Mr. ROBERTS, the bill entitled "An act making further provision for military services during the late war, and for other purposes," was recommitted to the Committee on Military Affairs, further to consider and report thereon.

Mr. BARBOUR, from the Committee on Military Affairs, to whom was referred the bill entitled "An act for organizing the general staff, and making further provision for the Army of the United States," reported it without amendment.

Mr. BARBOUR, from the Committee on Military Affairs, reported a resolution directing medals to be struck, and, together with the thanks of Congress, presented to Major General Harrison and Governor Shelby, and for other purposes;" and the resolution was read, and passed to the second reading.

The joint resolution, authorizing the President of the Senate and Speaker of the House of Representatives to adjourn their respective Houses on the 22d day of April, 1816, was read the second time.

Mr. WELLS, from the committee to whom the subject was referred, reported a bill for the relief of Isaac Briggs; and the bill was read, and passed to the second reading.

The Senate resumed, as in Committee of the Whole, the consideration of the bill to reward the officers and crew of the United States frigate Constitution; and no amendment having been agreed to on, the question, "Shall this bill be engrossed and read a third time?" it was determined in the affirmative.

The engrossed bill to authorize the Legislature of the State of Ohio to sell a certain part of a tract of land reserved for the use of that State, was read a third time, and passed.

The bill to authorize the President of the United States to alter the road laid out from the foot of the rapids of the river Miami of Lake Erie, to the western line of the Connecticut Reserve, was read a third time, and passed.

The bill establishing a port of delivery at the town of Bayou St. John was read a third time, and passed.

The bill entitled "An act for the relief of John T. Wirt," was read a third time, and passed.

Mr. FROMENTIN gave notice that to-morrow he should ask leave to bring in a bill to erect a light-house at the mouth of the Mississippi river.

BANK OF THE UNITED STATES.

The Senate resumed, as in Committee of the Whole, the consideration of the bill entitled "An act to incorporate the subscribers to the Bank of the United States," together with the proposed amendments.

On motion by Mr. MASON, of New Hampshire, to insert at the end of the 17th section the following:

"And if the said corporation shall at any time sus-

pend or refuse payment, in gold or silver, of its notes, bills, obligations, or other debts, to such an amount, and for such length of time as Congress may deem injurious to the United States, in such case Congress may repeal this act, and abolish the said corporation, and make such regulations and provisions for the settlement of the affairs and payment of the debts of said corporation, and for distributing its remaining property among the stockholders, as shall be deemed just and proper."

It was determined in the negative, yeas 14, nays 17, as follows:

YEAS—Messrs. Barbour, Bibb, Daggett, Goldsborough, Gore, Horsey, King, Mason of New Hampshire, Mason of Virginia, Sanford, Talbot, Taylor, Thompson, and Turner.

NAYS—Messrs. Barry, Brown, Campbell, Chace, Condit, Dana, Fromentin, Howell, Hunter, Macon, Morrow, Roberts, Tait, Varnum, Wells, Williams, and Wilson.

The bill having been further amended, on motion by Mr. WELLS, the further consideration thereof was postponed until to-morrow.

SATURDAY, March 30.

On motion by Mr. WILSON,

Resolved, That the Secretary be directed to inform the House of Representatives that an omission has taken place in engrossing the amendments made by the Senate to the bill from the House of Representatives, entitled "An act in addition to an act to regulate the Post Office Establishment," and request that the House will return the said bill and amendments to the Senate, with a view that the said omission may be supplied.

Mr. MASON, of Virginia, submitted the following motion for consideration:

Resolved, That the Committee on Roads and Canals be instructed to inquire into the expediency of authorizing the Secretary of the Treasury to subscribe fifty thousand dollars to the Great Coastwise Canal and River Navigation Company, incorporated by the Legislature of Virginia, for the purpose of cutting a canal from the port of Norfolk, through the Eastern Branch of Elizabeth River, to the channel of Currituck Sound, on the terms and conditions proposed by the president and directors of the said Great Coastwise Canal and River Navigation Company.

The bill supplementary to an act entitled "An act to incorporate a company for making certain turnpike roads within the District of Columbia," was read the second time.

The resolution directing medals to be struck, and, together with the thanks of Congress, presented to Major General Harrison and Governor Shelby, and for other purposes, was read the second time.

The bill for the relief of Isaac Briggs was read the second time.

A message from the House of Representatives informed the Senate that the House have returned to the Senate the bill, entitled "An act in addition to an act to regulate the Post Office Establishment," together with the amendments thereto;

and that the House have passed a bill, entitled "An act to enable the people of the Indiana Territory to form a constitution and State government, and for the admission of such State into the Union on an equal footing with the original States;" a bill, entitled "An act for the relief of certain purchasers of public lands in the Mississippi Territory;" a bill, entitled "An act authorizing the President of the United States to lease the Saline, near the Wabash river, for a term not exceeding seven years;" a bill, entitled "An act to amend an act, entitled 'An act for the relief of Edward Hallowell;" a bill, entitled "An act supplemental to the act, entitled 'An act regulating and defining the duties of the judges of the Territory of Illinois, and for vesting in the courts of the Territory of Indiana a jurisdiction in chancery cases arising in the said Territory;" a bill, entitled "An act for the relief of Henry Malcolm;" a bill, entitled "An act directing the discharge of Ebenezer Keeler and John Francis from imprisonment;" a bill, entitled "An act directing the discharge of Moses Lewis from imprisonment;" a bill, entitled "An act for the remission of certain duties on the importation of books for the use of Harvard College, and on the carriage and personal baggage of his Excellency William Gore, Governor of the British province of Upper Canada;" a bill, entitled "An act for the relief of Robert Kidd;" and also a bill, entitled "An act supplementary to the act to provide additional revenues for defraying the expenses of Government and maintaining the public credit, by laying a direct tax upon the United States, and to provide for assessing and collecting the same;" in which bills they request the concurrence of the Senate.

BANK OF THE UNITED STATES.

The Senate resumed, as in Committee of the Whole, the consideration of the bill, entitled "An act to incorporate the subscribers to the Bank of the United States."

On motion by Mr. KING, to strike out of section 8, after the word "directors," in the 3d line, the following: "five of whom, being stockholders, shall be annually appointed by the President of the United States, by and with the advice and consent of the Senate, not more than three of whom shall be residents of any one State."

On this motion a debate ensued, which continued until about three o'clock, and in which Messrs. KING and GORE advocated, and Messrs. BIBB, BARBOUR, ROBERTS, and CAMPBELL, opposed the motion.

The amendment was finally negatived—yeas 14, nays 21, as follows:

YEAS—Messrs. Daggett, Dana, Goldsborough, Gore, Harper, Horsey, Hunter, King, Macon, Mason of New Hampshire, Sanford, Thompson, Tichenor, and Wells.

NAYS—Messrs. Barbour, Barry, Bibb, Brown, Campbell, Chace, Condit, Fromentin, Gaillard, Howell, Mason of Virginia, Morrow, Roberts, Ruggles, Tait, Talbot, Taylor, Turner, Varnum, Williams, and Wilson.

A new section was then offered, by Mr. GOLDSBOROUGH, in the following words:

"*And be it enacted,* That if, at any time, the United States shall cease to hold stock in this bank, the five Directors on the part of the United States, and the power herein given to the President, by and with the advice and consent of the Senate, to appoint directors, shall immediately cease; and that, for every million four hundred thousand dollars of said stock which the United States may part with, there shall be an abridgement of the power of appointing one of the five directors hereinbefore provided for."

On this amendment a debate took place, in which Messrs. GOLDSBOROUGH, KING, HARPER, MACON, and FROMENTIN, supported, and Messrs. BIBB, CAMPBELL, TAIT, TAYLOR, and CHACE, opposed it.

About half past four the Senate adjourned, without having taken the question.

MONDAY, April 1.

The PRESIDENT communicated the general account of the Treasurer of the United States from the first of October, 1814, to the first of April, 1815, as also the accounts of the War and Navy Departments, from the first of October, 1814, to the first of October, 1815, together with the reports of the accounting officers of the Treasury thereon; which was read.

Mr. ROBERTS, from the committee to whom was referred the bill, entitled "An act to alter and amend the law of costs," reported it without amendment.

Mr. VARNUM presented the petition of John Otis, attorney of William Otis, late collector of the customs for the district of Barnstable, praying relief for expenses incurred by him for carrying into execution the embargo laws, as stated in the petition; which was read, and referred to the Committee on Foreign Relations.

Mr. BROWN, from the committee to whom was referred the bill, entitled "An act for the relief of certain claimants to lands in the district of Vincennes," reported it without amendment.

Mr. SANFORD presented the memorial of Jesse Torrey, jun., representing that he has it in contemplation to undertake the establishment, in the City of Washington, of a garden or general repository of living American plants, shrubs, and trees, particularly such as are supposed or known to contain medicinal properties, and praying the patronage of Congress, as stated in the memorial; which was read, and referred to the committee appointed on so much of the Message of the President of the United States as relates to a National Seminary of Learning within the District of Columbia, to consider and report thereon by bill or otherwise.

The eleven bills last brought up for concurrence were read, and severally passed to the second reading.

The Senate resumed, as in Committee of the Whole, the consideration of the bill, entitled "An act to repeal the act, entitled 'An act to provide additional revenues for defraying the expenses of

Government, and maintaining the public credit, by laying duties on household furniture, and on gold and silver watches;" and it passed to the third reading.

The Senate resumed the consideration of the motion made the 30th ultimo, instructing the Committee on Roads and Canals to inquire into the expediency of authorizing the Secretary of the Treasury to subscribe fifty thousand dollars to the Great Coastwise Canal and River Navigation Company, and agreed thereto.

Mr. WILLIAMS, from the committee to whom was referred the bill, entitled "An act for the relief of the heirs of George Nebinger," reported it with an amendment, which was read.

Mr. FROMENTIN asked and obtained leave to bring in a bill to erect a light-house at the mouth of the Mississippi river; and the bill was read, and passed to the second reading.

The Senate resumed, as in Committee of the Whole, the consideration of the bill, supplementary to an act, entitled "An act to incorporate a company for making certain turnpike roads within the District of Columbia," and on the question, " Shall this bill be engrossed and read a third time ?" it was determined in the affirmative.

A message from the House of Representatives informed the Senate that the House have passed a bill, entitled "An act to enable the people of the Mississippi Territory to form a constitution and State government, and for the admission of such State into the Union on an equal footing with the original States ;" in which bill they request the concurrence of the Senate. They have concurred in the amendments of the Senate to the bill, entitled "An act to authorize the payment for property lost, captured, or destroyed by the enemy, while in the military service of the United States," with amendments, in which they request the concurrence of the Senate.

The Senate proceeded to consider the amendments of the House of Representatives to their amendments to the bill last mentioned, and concurred therein.

The bill last brought up for concurrence was read, and passed to the second reading.

The bill to reward the officers and crew of the United States frigate Constitution was read a third time, and passed.

Mr. FROMENTIN, from the committee, reported that they had re-examined the amendments to the bill, entitled "An act in addition to an act to regulate the Post Office Establishment," and that they were correctly engrossed.

Ordered, That the Secretary return the bills, together with the amendments, to the House of Representatives.

On motion by Mr. BARBOUR, the consideration of the bill making appropriation for the construction of roads and canals, was further postponed until to-morrow.

BANK OF THE UNITED STATES.

The Senate resumed the consideration, in Committee, of the bill from the House, to incorporate the subscribers to the Bank of the United States,

the amendment offered by Mr. GOLDSBOROUGH on Saturday still before the Committee.

Messrs. MASON, of Virginia, BIBB, and TAYLOR, spoke against the amendment, and Mr. GOLDSBOROUGH in its favor; when the question was taken, and the motion negatived—yeas 16, nays 18, as follows:

YEAS—Messrs. Daggett, Dana, Fromentin, Gaillard, Goldsborough, Harper, Horsey, Hunter, King, Macon, Mason of New Hampshire, Sanford, Thompson, Tichenor, Turner, and Wells.

NAYS—Messrs. Barbour, Barry, Bibb, Brown, Campbell, Chace, Condit, Howell, Mason of Virginia, Morrow, Roberts, Ruggles, Talbot, Tait, Taylor, Varnum, Williams, and Wilson.

Mr. HARPER moved an amendment, limiting the selection of directors by the President to such as held stock to the amount of —— dollars, (ten thousand was named by the mover,) and that they should cease to be directors when they ceased to hold stock to that amount.

This motion was supported by Messrs. HARPER, DANA, and TAYLOR, and opposed by Messrs. ROBERTS, BARBOUR, MACON, CAMPBELL, and FROMENTIN, and negatived—ayes 9, noes 10.

Mr. KING moved an amendment, preventing directors appointed by the Government from acting as agents or proxies of any stockholders.

Mr. KING spoke in favor of, and Messrs. ROBERTS and CAMPBELL against, this amendment; which was negatived without a division.

On motion of Mr. BIBB, an amendment was adopted, requiring that there should not be more than thirteen nor less than seven directors, to each Branch Bank.

Mr. TAYLOR proposed an amendment, making the stock of the United States unalienable ; Mr. CAMPBELL spoke against it ; negatived—ayes 10, noes 18.

Mr. BROWN offered an amendment, excluding the United States as a stockholder from being represented in the choice of directors, &c. ; agreed to.

Mr. WELLS rose and addressed the Chair, as follows :

Mr. President, the Senate having gone through the different amendments which have been before them, and it not being probable that there are many more, if any other, intended to be brought forward, the proper period for submitting a proposition, which will fairly bring into notice the general views of this subject, has, perhaps, now arrived. In support, then, of the proposition of postponement, to the first Monday in December next, of the further consideration of this bill, which I purpose to move you, I beg the indulgence of the Senate, while I endeavor to show, first, that it transcends the Constitutional power of Congress to pass a bill containing the provisions which this does ; secondly, the inexpediency of enacting such a law as this, even if we possess the Constitutional power to do it ; and thirdly, that our true policy is to avoid, at this time, legislating upon the subject—to pass no law, at the present session, incorporating a banking company.

That which has heretofore been the occasion of so much heated controversy, was simply a question relating to the existence or non-existence of a power in Congress to incorporate a company for establishing a bank. That question is now at rest, nor do I propose to disturb it. The sole inquiry we now have to make is, as to the true character and just extent of this authority, that we may not, in the exercise of it, carry it beyond its proper limits.

The power that is granted is a power to establish a bank for a particular end, and, of course, constitutes only a part of the general power, in relation to the establishment of banks that previously existed in the States. For this reason it is a power of a minor character to that of the States, and is to be exercised always with a steady and distinct view to the end for which it is created. So far as it goes, it is a lawful power, and has a right to pursue its prescribed course. It may keep company with the State authority, but has no right to quarrel and slay its companion on the road. Every application, then, of this power, by the United States, which has a tendency to embarrass or impair the free exercise of the power reserved to the States, is unwarranted, and if done by us with a view to such a purpose, is the affair of arrogance and usurpation.

This is not a primary, expressed, original power. In vain, as such, do we seek for it in the Constitution. It is only a secondary, an implied, derivative power, if such may be properly termed the means of executing an expressly delegated power. Here it may fairly be asked, Why was this power left to implication? Did it escape notice? Was it overlooked? Was it too unimportant for enumeration? Every view of this subject, and every relation in which it can be placed, to the other authorities, affords an inference not easily resisted, that a grant of this power was not intended to be applied. If the express grant of such a power was moved, the silence of the Constitution, as to that power, proves that it must have been rejected. I understand that it was moved in that body, and was rejected. If this was actually the case, (as I am persuaded it was,) it certainly requires the utmost effort of ingenuity to prove that this power was left to implication, in order that the subordinacy of its character might be the more clearly established, and the arrogance of its pretensions the more easily repressed. This is all, if it be not a great deal more than any fair mode of interpreting the Constitution, as we have it, will warrant. We cannot, for a moment, suppose that the great men, who formed this frame of government, were unacquainted with, or unmindful of, the imposing character of this power, or of its history here or abroad. Did they not know that a proposition to incorporate a banking company, by the old Congress, had been, by that body, rejected? And furthermore, could those grave and learned men been unaware (if they intended this power to be inferred as a means of executing another power) of the arduous, perhaps I might be permitted to say, the odious character of the task

they devolved upon implication? Did not that enlightened body know that grants of specially enumerated authorities would not warrant the exercise of a power as a means for carrying into effect another power, where the means itself is, in character and importance, entitled to rank with some one of the enumerated authorities? That such is the real character of the means in question, in relation to some of those authorities, even limited and circumscribed as it may be, I am obliged to admit there is too much reason for insisting. That I have a doubt, therefore, on my mind, on this point, I am free to confess. It is possible, perhaps it is probable, if the vote I am to give upon this bill demanded of me, in respect to that difficulty, a decision, that further deliberation, aided by the authorities which, I am told, support the opposite opinion, might remove that doubt.

Sir, I confidently rely upon the cheerfulness with which honorable gentlemen who have heretofore so strenuously denied the existence of the power in question in this Government, will accompany me in the inquiry respecting the extent of this power. It is agreed, on all hands, to be (not an original, substantive, but) a derivative, incidental power. What, then, is the specially enumerated power to which it is incident, as one of the "necessary and proper" means for its execution?

Is it an incident to the power to "promote the general welfare?" The capacious character of this provision, if it is to be viewed simply as a grant of power, would render the subsequent enumeration of special powers a matter of supererogation. The terms "general welfare," when used in the Constitution, can only be considered as having themselves reference to one of the great objects for the promotion of which this Government was established, and for the accomplishment of which the special powers, contained in the Constitution, have been delegated.

Is this authority to establish a bank an incident to the power of Congress "to borrow money on the credit of the United States," by reason of its correlative tendency in procuring a faculty to lend? If this be the source from which it is lawfully derived, we need look no further for the origin of this or of any other authority. If this be its fountain-head, we have here a never-failing spring of power, abundantly sufficient for all the purposes, lawful or unlawful, of this or of any other Government upon earth. I turn away from it, therefore, without further investigation.

Is this power derived from that of coining money, regulating its value and that of foreign coin? Is the right to establish a National Bank, on account of its tendency in our hands to operate upon what is called the currency of the country, derived from this or any other specially delegated authority? There are two provisions in the Constitution which have some bearing upon this point. That to which I have just referred respecting coin, and that which prohibits the States the issue of "bills of credit, and the declaring of anything but gold and silver a lawful tender in the payment of debts." It cannot be necessary to argue that a power to make a bank distinctly with a view to its putting into circulation promissory notes that shall have the faculty of mixing and keeping company with the currency of the country, and of becoming something like paper money, is not a necessary and proper auxiliary to the power in this Government of making a metallic medium; that a power, in short, to make a metallic money has not incident to it, as a. " necessary and proper" means for its execution, the power to make a paper money. Nor need any time be spent in resisting an inference, drawn from a restraint imposed upon a particular power in the State governments, which affects to communicate to, and to set up in, this Government a faculty co-ordinate with another power, which is left in those governments, free and unshackled. So far, then, as honorable gentlemen say this measure is intended or calculated, whether with a view to regulation or improvement, or under any other pretence, to operate upon what is called the national currency; or, in other words, to restrain the States from establishing similar institutions, and impair the free exercise of the franchises of those already incorporated, it is warranted by no part of the Constitution.

I come now, sir, to that part of the Constitution where alone can be found, if anywhere, the lawful source of the authority of this Government to incorporate a banking company. We have the power "to lay and collect taxes, duties, imposts, and excises," for certain great national purposes. It is now admitted, by most of the former opponents of this doctrine, that the establishment of a National Bank is nothing more than the employment of a " necessary and proper" means for carrying " into execution" the power to which I have just referred. The correctness of this doctrine, I have before declared it to be not my purpose to call into question. This part of my argument is entirely predicated upon its admission, and is designed solely to be confined to those views of the subject which will show the true character and just extent of this authority, and enable us to determine whether we are not carrying it, by the provisions of the bill now on our tables, further than is warranted by the Constitution. This, then, being the power to which the authority to establish a bank is incident, as a "necessary and proper" means for its execution, we cannot have much difficulty in the definition of its limits. Its effect upon this power must be in relation to the collection, the safe-keeping and transmission of the public revenue. The notes which a bank issues may (but, by the by, the affairs of a bank may be mismanaged and they may not) provide the people with an equal medium for the payment of their public dues to this Government. This is, to a certain extent, to operate upon the currency; it is not merely to afford the people, in their relations with the Government, something more portable and convenient to procure, and pay, than metallic money, but it is to provide them with a medium of contribution, at a time when the metallic medium shall disappear from circulation. Here provision, in relation to the currency generally, would seem at first, to be intended for an event like that of the disappearance of the metallic medium; but we must always remember that our power, in relation to the medium of circulation, refers solely to a metallic medium; and of course excludes the other—*expressio unius est exclusio alterius.* If it be not questioned how far, in this point of view, as connected with the currency (a subject, as beforementioned, expressly legislated upon) there is a power to procure for the people these kind of facilities, for the payment of their taxes; surely the power must, in this respect, confine itself directly to this end. What then is the capital necessary for constituting a bank to answer this purpose? This ought to have been shown us. Those who have no warrant to employ this power, but distinctly with a view to the attainment of a particular end, must have known that the purposes for which alone it can be lawfully used, prescribe the limitations to its exercise. The moral obligation imposed upon them not to exceed those limits, requires, likewise, that they should ascertain where they were placed. If there has been an inquiry made upon this head, what principles have guided that inquiry; and which of them have been presented to the Senate? What calculations have been submitted to us, to show that, in respect to the capital, we are not exceeding the pale of our authority? The hazard of excess must not be incurred, while there are any means at our command of ascertaining how it may be avoided. It is not for those of us who think it, at this time, inexpedient to establish a bank, to show where the excess is. It is incumbent upon the friends of this bill, who call upon us for our votes, who desire that we should keep them company, to prove to us that they are going no further than they ought to go. This they have not done. It has not been affirmatively proven to us that a capital to this amount is necessary; and, for one, I think it can be demonstrated that a capital of thirty-five millions, is larger than is required, for the purposes for which we are to establish a bank. A capital much lower than even twenty millions would be adequate to the establishment of a bank, in each State in the Union; and the objects of safe-keeping, and easy transmission of the public revenue accomplished. The capital of this bank, with a view to the effect of its notes, in affording an equal medium for the payment by the people, and the receipt by the Government, of the public dues, is not to be inquired into, with a view to any given state of things. The charter is to last for twenty years. If this capital, during that period, should be likely to become too small, the power to raise it by our own, or other subscriptions, may be reserved. If we have a view, in ascertaining the proper extent of this capital, to periods when the preservative of a metallic medium shall be withdrawn from the paper circulation, then this capital (if the bank is to be what its advocates insist upon to be their intention to render it, a specie paying bank,) is unnecessarily large. Its issues, in such times, must be limited, not by the amount of the public revenue, but by that of the specie in its vaults. If our attention, however, is principally directed, as to me it seems it ought to be, to the usual and natural state of things, when the presence of the metallic medium will afford to the paper currency a free and uninterrupted circulation, then a much smaller capital than that of thirty-five millions, in such a state of things, would enable the bank, by the successive issues and returns of its paper, to afford to the people and to the Government the desired facilities. The process between the Government and the people, is that of payment and disbursement; and the steady and uniform succession of these operations, which can never be disturbed, communicates to a paper medium, even in a higher degree, the well known faculty belonging to a metallic medium, of transacting a large amount of business, with a small amount of money. In this view of the subject, can there be a question whether a much smaller capital would not afford every lawful facility that the revenue operations of this Government require? A capital of ten millions successfully accomplished this object, and with the aid of three or four millions of other banking capital, conjointly with the metallic medium, circulated the whole business of the Government and the country. Surely, then, a national banking capital of twenty millions, with the banking capital of the States, will be now amply sufficient for the same purposes; however high may be our estimate of the increased activity and expansion of the industry and enterprise of the country. If I am well founded in these remarks, I have sustained and established one Constitutional objection to this bill; by showing that the capital of this bank is larger than is necessary for the accomplishment of the objects we are required to keep in view, in the establishment of this institution.

There is another and a more interesting point of view which it remains to notice, and which goes to show that this bill does not merely, in respect to capital, exceed our Constitutional authority. I refer to that provision which authorizes the appointment of a certain proportion of the directors of this bank by the Government. Every control and authority over this great moneyed institution, so intimately connected as it is with the great interests of society, beyond what is requisite for the promotion of the limited objects we are bound to keep in view, communicates to the Government an influence and patronage which it has no right to possess. It is proper that I should circumscribe, within narrow limits, what I have to say in respect to the just character of that influence, after the able view of it which must have been presented by the honorable member from New York (Mr. KING) in support of his motion to strike out this part of the bill. The honorable chairman (Mr. BIBB) who reported this bill, in reply to that argument, insisted that there was incident to the power to establish a bank, that of prescribing the regulations which are necessary to guard the country

against the mischief it might otherwise do. Sir, I deny not the truth of this position; but still it equally remains to be shown that the regulation in question, which invests the Government with an influence of such magnitude, is "necessary and proper" to prevent a greater mischief than the one which the regulation itself introduces. The honorable gentleman from Virginia (Mr. BARBOUR) contends for the salutary effect of this regulation, and insists that it communicates to the Government an influence too unimportant to justify any serious apprehension. He considers these directors merely as sentinels on the watch tower, and that the smallness of their number can never give to the Government a dangerous ascendency in the management of this institution. Let us for a moment inquire into the character of these directors. If they are sentinels on the watch tower; if they are to be enlisted into our service, what bounty are we to give them; what pay are they to receive from us? They are to perform for us an important service; they are to apprize us of the earliest approaches of danger. The board of directors will be daily assembled, and these our sentinels must mount guard as often; they are to have a full share of trouble in the superintendence of this institution, and they are to do all this, not for the good of the concern, in which they have no participation, but for our advantage solely, that we may know, in time to take care of ourselves, when this company is likely to go astray from its duty to the stockholders, the country, or the Government. These are services, I admit, of great value, and to be performed, no doubt, by able and virtuous men; and yet, for all this, you pay nothing; and why so? Are we to calculate upon a degree of patriotism and disinterestedness, to which we make no claim ourselves? The truth is, we do not expect these services to be performed for us without remuneration; but the anomaly consists in our not paying for them ourselves. These spies are to be in *our* service, and to labor for *us*, on account of the pay they receive from *others*. In imitation of the Napoleon model, these gentlemen are to be maintained by those whom they are set over to guard. Their posts will be places in request at all times—in peace as well as in war. In times of peace, of public repose, when the business of the country is undisturbed, and the Government in no need of loans from the bank, these directorships will be entirely useless, for any lawful purpose, to the United States. During this period, the men who hold these appointments, and their numerous friends, will be but as vultures fattening on the institution. During this period you obtain a patronage for the Administration, through the medium of these directors, and their retainers, without the performance of any lawful service. In this respect, then, the provision is unconstitutional; and the influence for which you oblige others to pay, is as unjust as it is unconstitutional. But when the season of difficulty arrives; when war shall disturb and break up the regular course of business; when public and private credit shall be shaken; when the good of the country shall imperiously require the affairs of this institution to be conducted with even more than the usual prudence and circumspection, then will be the time that the pernicious agency of this directorship, co-operating with other active influences, will wield this great moneyed corporation, at the will and pleasure of the Government. It is no answer to tell us of the smallness of the number of these directors. The Hercules is in the system—in the power that the Government possesses of continuing or withholding its deposites. These directors are but the club with which you arm him. The smallness of their number is no security. The principle upon which they are introduced is unsound, is corrupt, is contagious, and its natural tendency will be to spread itself. These five directors, (whom the Government then will take care to keep in their own pay,) themselves the absolute creatures of those from whom they have derived their authority, will be sure to find at the board, when the spirit of party in the country runs high, others become as subservient as themselves; and cannot fail, in a season of difficulty and embarrassment, with their united influence, to accomplish, through the fears and the hopes of the rest, whatever shall be demanded of the bank, as the price of the continuance of the Governmental favor. By this process, will loan upon loan be rivetted upon the bank, until this great debtor will become its lord and master. Surely these apprehensions cannot justly be called the offspring of distempered imaginations. Honorable gentlemen certainly who, themselves, have painted in such glowing tints the terrors of this influence—not of the influence of such a body politic as this, in which it is organized, and directly set up and established, and openly avowed to the world, but of one where it was sedulously guarded against—surely such will not insist that there is no foundation for alarm. Formerly it was said, give this new power, this lever, but a fulcrum, a point to rest upon, and, like another Archimedes, it will move the political world as it pleases. Afford it but an opportunity to act upon the States, and there will be nothing in their sovereignties or the people beyond its purchase. Formerly it was calculated, in its mildest form, to destroy the responsibility between the Government and the people; and leading to extravagance, to corruption, and to wicked and ruinous wars, to overturn the liberties of this nation. If these representations of danger were somewhat surcharged in respect to the former institution, how just are they with respect to the present! To me it seems that now is the time that we ought most sedulously to guard against a power of this kind in the Government, while the young, the enterprising, the ambitious, and the military character of this country is developing itself. I say the military character of this nation, because it is but too apparent that the events of the late "glorious war" (as it is not unfrequently triumphantly termed) have had no tendency to increase our fondness for the pursuits of peace. That there was glory in that war. I am proud to

acknowledge; but speaking of the war generally, and the situation of the country during its continuance, of its causes, and its errors, I may be permitted to say, if there was glory—and I repeat again I am proud to acknowledge it—it was only "gloom in glory dressed." Much, sir, I fear that this happy country, once so fond of peace, when sufficiently practised upon, is to become as deeply enamored of war and valorous enterprise as La Mancha's Knight, and, with him, is to be made to exclaim, "armor is our dress and battles our repose." I shall press this objection no farther. We are permitted by the Constitution to incorporate a banking company to facilitate the collection and disbursement of our revenue. It has been shown that this power must be exercised with a view to its proper objects, and that every regulation that looks further than the attainment of these objects is unwarranted; and in relation to this directorship, I think it must be apparent, that it is entirely foreign to these objects; or, if in a slight degree incidentally connected with them, that its main bearing is upon other points, and that its general tendency, by the concurring testimony of all parties, is to communicate an influence to the Government of the United States of an extremely dangerous character. The bill, therefore, in this respect, is unconstitutional.

The remaining Constitutional objection to this bill arises from its interference with the concurrent power of the States. It is to operate upon the State banks, "peaceably if it can, forcibly if it must." With this object in view, the bill no doubt has been formed to have due effect. Indeed, with the controlling influence of the Government, it cannot fail to accomplish its object, whenever the necessary impulse for that purpose shall be given. If a faculty is communicated to a power in this Government to regulate a concurrent power in the State goverments, there is an end at once of the co-ordinacy of these powers; one of them instantly becomes only the humble dependant upon the other, and must even cease its existence whenever the will and pleasure of its superior shall be known. How extraordinary has been the course of opinions upon this subject!

The friends of a bank formerly required for this Government the exercise only of an equal and concurrent power, even not so much; they are now obliged to argue against honorable gentlemen who refused that power, and who now, in effect, contend for the exercise of a superior and exclusive power. If such, then, is intended to be the effect of this bill, and if its provisions are calculated for the attainment of that end, it is most indubitably unconstitutional. If what is termed implication, is to become the lawful proprietor of what she is only permitted to use for a special purpose, and is to bear off, too, what she has no pretence for asking to borrow, all our paper regulations are idle. With an encroaching and restless agency of this kind in the Constitution, there is no limit to the power of this Government. I shall press no further Constitutional objections to this bill, but will now proceed, with the further indulgence of the Senate, to examine the general policy of this measure.

This bill came out of the hands of the Administration ostensibly for the purpose of correcting the diseased state of our paper currency, by restraining and curtailing the over issue of banking paper; and yet it came prepared to inflict upon us the same evil; being itself nothing more than simply a paper-making machine, and constituting in this respect a scheme of policy about as wise, in point of precaution, as the contrivance of one of Rabelais' heroes, who hid himself in water for fear of rain. The disease, it is said, under which the people labor, is the banking fever of the States; and this is to be cured by giving them the banking fever of the United States. To my mind, the real evil consists not so much in a superabundance of paper, as in a scarcity of specie. The paper currency does not exceed what is required to circulate the business of the country; it only wants the accrediting, the quickening, the vivifying principle which it requires a certain proportion of specie to communicate to it. But this bill is to supply that want; it is to be our alchemist, and is to effect for us even the transmutation of paper into gold. How this matter is to be conducted, we have not been told. It is admitted that the great desideratum will not be afforded all at once. The process, we are informed, requires time; but we are assured that, in the end, it will not disappoint our hopes. For one, sir, I am not willing to trust to a scheme of this sort. Not only it is not shown how its professed object is to be accomplished, but the fallacy of its pretensions is susceptible of demonstration. This is to be a specie, or a paper-paying bank. Take either hypothesis—suppose it the former—will it increase the quantity of specie in the country; will it restore to circulation that which is in the country; or will it put into circulation anything that will answer the purpose of specie? That it will increase the quantity of specie, powerful as may be its alchemy, none will pretend. Will it emancipate from restraint what is already in the country? That the quantity of specie in the United States is diminished, is acknowledged, and it will not be denied that a much larger proportion of specie, than formerly was sufficient to maintain the free circulation of bank paper, will be required to revive and establish public confidence in that currency as a steady and certain representative of gold and silver. Those banks, therefore, that have now the precious metals locked up in their vaults, not only will but ought to keep them there, until the necessary addition is made by the course of trade; more especially ought they to do so, at this time, when the course of that trade has thrown the exchange so much against us, that every dollar they paid out would be exported. If this bank is to be a specie bank, will it put into and keep in circulation anything that will answer the purpose of specie? Who are to borrow of this bank, and what will be their inducements to borrow? Those who obtain discounts will receive paper equal in value to gold and silver; and their debts must be paid off, when

they become due, not in the notes of other banks, but in the notes of this bank, or in gold and silver. If they borrow for the purpose of obtaining a more equal and unvarying medium, than any other bank paper will afford them, of remittance to any part of the United States, or with a view to purchase cheaper anything they may want to buy, their object is accomplished. But when the time arrives for them to pay off their debts to the bank, they must purchase up the paper of this bank, or gold and silver, with other banking paper, and with the same or a greater loss. What will they then have gained by the transaction? Pay their debts they must, when they become due; and, cost what it will, they must procure the paper of the same bank, or gold and silver. They have gained, say ten per cent. in their remittance, or their purchase, and they must give it up again to obtain the means of paying these debts; and, moreover, run, without any advantage, the risk of being disappointed in procuring those means. There will be, likewise, accompanying this, another operation. Those who borrow (if any under such circumstances, will borrow) must have a view to purchase, or remittance to some other part of the Union; and, in that mode, the paper of this bank will get into the hands of persons who have no debts to pay to the bank. What will they do with this paper? Will it come into their possession so utterly untainted with suspicion, with such all-inspiring confidence, as to make the holders of it prefer it to gold and silver? Certainly not. The recollection of recent events, the infirm condition of the other banking paper, will prompt the holders of it to demand immediately in exchange that which they know is immutable in its value. And, moreover, there may be a sudden fluctuation in the rate of foreign exchange, which may communicate to gold and silver a temporary appreciation over the paper currency, without sensibly (if at all) depressing contemporaneously its value in relation to anything else it may command. When this takes place, the holder of the gold and silver obtained from this bank in exchange for its paper, will find a profit between the value at which he received the paper, and the gold which he has obtained for it, sufficient to induce him to part with it for the currency of the other banks; and which profit he can, by investment and purchase, render certain before the impulse of appreciation can be communicated to what he finally obtains. While, therefore, the exchange against the country is progressing, this process will accompany it, and effect the removal abroad of our specie. To emancipate specie from the restraints now imposed upon it, is to permit it to pursue its own course; and that course (in the present state of foreign exchanges) leads it out of the United States; and thus the immediate and inevitable effect of our legislation for restoring specie to circulation, is to send what we have remaining of it out of the country. If in this state of things, then, this bank is to be a specie bank, it can issue paper only to the amount of its specie. It cannot issue paper even to that amount, because there will be no inducement to borrow, upon the terms upon which a specie bank can now alone lend; and even if it could lend out, on these terms, paper to the amount of its specie, it would effect nothing in value towards the great object of this policy. It would be only amusing itself, like Diogenes, who set himself about rolling his tub, rather than be idle while all others were employed. But allow me here, sir, to ask, what is to be done, if this bank, in which we as stockholders are to have so deep an interest, should, as it probably pretty soon will, wade out of its depth; should exhaust its specie, (as it inevitably must do if it issues paper to an amount exceeding, even in a very limited degree, its specie capital,) and become unable to pay its paper? When that happens, as happen it must if there is not a considerable addition to the specie capital of the country, the urgency of the case will make its own law; and it will either be the law of public opinion, of public necessity, and public interest—the same law under which the State banks now operate—or it will be a law of our own enactment, striking off the shackles we are now riveting upon this institution. No, sir, this bill cannot restore the specie in the country to circulation, nor can it dissolve the powerful spell which fear, and suspicion, and even prudence, have placed upon it. Of our capacity to increase its quantity by this bill, we have about as good evidence as the facetious writer before referred to had of his royal descent; he had, he tells us, "a marvellous desire to be a king himself;" we have " a marvellous desire," I admit, to increase the quantity of specie, and we have no other better way of showing the specie-making tendency of this bill.

I beg leave, sir, to remark upon the distinctly avowed coercive policy in which this bill originated, with a view to considerations that are foreign to the Constitutional question. This bank has an immense capital; and when the state of things in this country shall be better settled; when a favorable course of trade shall have brought us the necessary supplies of specie, the operations of this, and other banks, will be conducted as formerly. This, then, will become a paper making bank, as well as the others; but the excess of all will be guarded against by the necessity which will be imposed of maintaining the principle of convertibility. This new bank, with its branches, will have afforded it by governmental deposites, and the receipt by the United States of the public revenue, in its paper, the means of extending its discounts, and increasing its issues in proportion to its capital, greatly beyond what the other banks can venture to do; and particularly must the operations of the State banks continue very limited and circumscribed, until the first hostile impulse communicated to this institution has ceased to operate, and until due confidence can be inspired that the same vindictive spirit will not again be aroused and inflamed. In this state of things the banking capital you now create will firmly establish itself, and eventually take the place of so much of the capital of the State banks. You create a banking capital beyond what is requisite for the attainment of the lawful ends of this Government, no one having disproved, indeed all seeming to admit, the existence already in the country of a sufficient banking capital. Why, then, is this injustice done, of supplanting one species of banking capital with another? Can we forget that a large proportion of the State banks is the offspring of our own policy? We refused the reincorporation of the old Bank of the United States; we declined altogether the exercise of the authority to establish these institutions, and mainly upon the ground that the power to organize them was exclusively vested in the State governments. This opinion was adopted, and zealously and perseveringly asserted by the most potent States in the Union; and subscribed to, and openly maintained by the most enlightened, the most intelligent, and influential supporters of the present order of things. Hence the origin of a great many of the State banks. The subscribers to those banks, relying upon the soundness, or at least, the permanency of this opinion, purchased their charters of the States; and the public money of those governments has been invested to a large amount in those banks. What, then, can warrant, in a renunciation of former sentiments, the extension of the capital of this bank beyond the proper objects of such a bank? It is equally forbidden by the Constitution, and by the plain principles of common justice. Let the conduct of these institutions (generally speaking) be examined; let it be exposed to the severest scrutiny, and there will be nothing found to justify the severity of this measure. Even if it be admitted that the course of these bodies, set free from the restraints which usually oblige them to revolve in their proper orbits, has been somewhat erratic—what then? Has their course been that of public calamity, and private distress? You must judge of them by the good as well as the evil they have done. They have been the nerve and spring of your industry; they have been the spirit which has animated your enterprise; and if they have been a fountain which has sent out bitter waters, they have sent out sweet waters too. What would have been your condition—what would be our condition this moment, without them? Have they banished the specie from the country? That was the affair of our achievement. This useful friend we lost ourselves; and they have, to the best of their ability, supplied its place. Is it for us to bestow upon them unqualified censure; for us, whose measures annihilated the restraints, and withdrew from them the great security of steadiness and uniformity? Is it for us to condemn them in mass, who were the first to seize with avidity, and to profit to the fullest extent of our influence over them, of the opportunity made by ourselves to lead them astray? Then our conduct to them was "as soft as the tips of our ears;" but now that our purpose is served, "our gorge rises" at them, and, in the time of their need, we unhesitatingly devote them to destruction.

I have said, sir, that the evil was not in a superabundance of paper, but in a scarcity of specie; for I think every view taken of the operations of the bank will show, with but few exceptions, that they have not exceeded their proper limits. The first effect of loosening their restraints was not to send them a heedless, headlong course. The influence of habit continued after the necessity which gave it birth had ceased. They went on the same path, and might have been so expected to do for some time by their own momentum. These banks were generally under the direction of able and honest men; not of such as were incapable of appreciating the difficulty and delicacy of their situation, but of men whose prudence, foreseeing the embarrassments they would have to contend with, immediately replaced the restraints which necessity had imposed and maintained. The particular instances of excess which have been referred to are those of exception; and, even in those cases, the business of the banks has fallen below what specie times have witnessed and will warrant; and still further below what this bank, with its paper circulating capacity, will do in such times. What course, different from that which they have taken, would we have had them to pursue in the situation in which they were placed? Ought they, in a time of public and private calamity and distress, have called upon their debtors? Ought their paper to have disappeared in the proportion that specie was withdrawn? And if this ought to have been done, how was the business of the country to have been transacted in the absence of both specie and paper? If these banks had called in their paper as the specie disappeared, and as the necessary demand for it increased—at a time, too, when public confidence, accompanied by public necessity and public convenience, tendered herself ready to perform for this circulation every office of specie—to reanimate it—to breathe into it a new and efficient principle of vitality; if such, under such circumstances, had been the conduct of these banks, we should have been, ourselves, among the loudest to complain. They did then, sir, what they ought to have done. Like wise and prudent men, instead of resisting an evil they could not avert, they did all that was left for them to do; they applied to it the best and only remedy that remained; one which, if it has not cured the disease, has at least alleviated its affliction.

I do not know that there is much hope of effecting the postponement of this measure; yet every consideration belonging to it, every view which can be taken of it, seems to me to require of us the utmost deliberation and circumspection. I know that there is a loose and vague notion afloat in the public mind, of one great uniform national currency. I will not dignify this notion by calling it public opinion. I know, sir, that we are looked to, as were, in other times, "the baker and the baker's son;" but surely the cool and intelligent and enlightened men of our country, who have reflected seriously upon the existing state of things, do not expect relief, in this matter, from our legislation. They know full well how much easier it is to legislate a country into difficulties, than it is to legislate it out of them. They understand the nature of the disease—its cause, and its remedy. They look not to us for health, who have medicined them into sickness. All they ask of us is to desist, "to let them alone." Time is their physician. They want time to recover from us—he has "healing upon his wings," we have none upon ours. Those who know not the cause of our disease—who have been blind to the natural tendency, to this state of things, of the measures which have been pursued for several years back, who know not the agencies which have withdrawn the specie from our country, and who cannot comprehend the influences which have given such activity and effect to those agencies, may have a notion that we can relieve them; and it cannot be expected that the deep responsibility, which is involved by the measures which have led to the present difficulties, should take much pains to dissipate the delusion. If we are to profit by this delusion, which conceals the past from public view, let us not go still further into error. The step we are going to take, we should remember, with the honorable gentleman from New York, (Mr. SANFORD,) is not one which we can retrace. In common cases, if we commit an error, subsequent legislation can remedy it. Not so here. An error committed, in the passage of this law, is beyond our power to correct. And furthermore, let us specially remember the magnitude of the power which we propose to regulate. It is not merely the banking power of this institution, but the banking power of the States. What is to be the bearing of our legislation upon great interests like these, so closely interwoven as they are with the pursuits of the people, it is incumbent upon us well and maturely to consider. The science of banking, connected as it is, in peace and in war, with the circulating medium, with the various operations of Government, with the different great interests of society in general, with the individual industry and enterprise of the citizens, with the value of other capital, and with the moral character of the people, is a science, like all others, of progressive improvement; and is, perhaps even at this time, but very imperfectly understood by those who have devoted most time to its study. Could, sir, this science now call to her aid, him who wrote upon this subject, "as with a sunbeam"—the justly celebrated author of the "Wealth of Nations"—even this, her favorite son, would be obliged to confess that much of his theory, which the world has so long adopted, was but like "the clouds that gather 'round the setting sun, and seeming only to form 'a part of the brightness, by which they are illu-'mined." Who then, among "us," is entitled to hold the "lamp of truth" to this subject? None of us, it is true, can be blind to the causes of the evil complained of. We know now too well the effect of the bold experiments we have tried upon the people. Tremendous as they were, it required but little skill to make them. But to build up anew what we have broken down, to repair what we have wasted, is an achievement of another sort. Peace, and the uninterrupted pursuits of industry and enterprise spread their blessings around us. Restrictive regulations and war have snatched many of them from us. The price the country has paid for our experiments is gone. If it has not made us wiser, we have nothing in return. What we have lost must be replaced as it was gained. Legislation is the medicament which has made us sick, but it has no charm to restore us to health. One great interest in our country, from sad experience of our measures, has long since learned to look to the period of assembling the National Councils as to the period of national calamity. What Thucydides says of the speech of Alcibiades, turning against his own country and explaining to her enemies her vulnerable positions, "while he speaks she totters," may justly be remarked of too many of our measures—while we legislate the country totters. The great body of our merchants have, in a special manner, cause to tremble at our legislation; that great body of men, whom the swooping denunciation of an honorable member on this floor has this day placed in the most degraded and the most worthless ranks of society. The honorable member makes exceptions, which serve, however, only to set in stronger view the estimate he forms of the rest. Sir, when honorable members of this House, and from great and potent States in the Union, entertain these sentiments, and express them upon this floor, it manifests a hostility to commerce, which justifies all the apprehensions of her friends. It is full time for the merchants—the Morrises and the Fitzsimmonses to take their seats among us, to assert their own character and maintain their own interests. Were they here they would find occasions to tell us, that it is not the farmer, or the country gentleman, the fleeces of whose flocks grow too slow for our Walpoles—that we have repaired to their "altars," not to worship there, but to shut up their "Bible," and bear off their "God;" that the seat of Commerce is not to be found "in the midst of the secret and solitary hill, not her voice to be heard in the murmur of the mountain stream."

Upon a subject, sir, like that now before us, of a complex and intricate character, having the closest relations to the strongest interests in society; with no special illumination ourselves; in the absence of all practical information; uninspired with much of confidence in our own skill by the success of our former experiments on political economy; is it wise to act at all; but, most especially, upon a subject of this character, is it possible, in the nature of things, for a general legislation, which commits itself to the strong impulse of one given pressure, to pursue the proper course? In circumstances like the present, it is circumspection, it is deliberation which is required, and not action. There are situations of peril in which the soldier halts. There are crises of difficulty and embarrassment in which the statesman pauses. It is folly, it is rashness, and not wisdom, not courage, that marches blindfold upon danger. "It is no inconsiderable part of wisdom to understand how much of an evil is to be endured;" and particularly so, when there is

reason to hope that the evil will remedy itself. The existing laws which authorize the issue of Treasury notes, will remove all sectional difficulties, and afford to the people a safe and equal medium for the payment of their taxes.

I rely upon the indulgence of the Senate to excuse my having so long trespassed upon their time. I do not flatter myself with the expectation that my humble views of this subject will have much weight; they are such as have presented themselves to my mind; and, imperfect as they may be, I have obeyed only the sense of duty, in submitting them to the Senate. It remains, sir, to move you, which I now do, that the further consideration of the bill upon your table should be postponed to the first Monday in December next.

When Mr. W. had concluded—

Mr. DANA made a brief reply; after which the question was taken on the motion, and negatived —yeas 6, nays 29, as follows:

YEAS—Messrs. Gaillard, Goldsborough, Horsey, Macon, Sanford, and Wells.

NAYS—Messrs. Barbour, Barry, Bibb, Brown, Campbell, Chace, Condit, Daggett, Dana, Fromentin, Gore, Harper, Howell, Hunter, King, Mason of New Hampshire, Mason of Virginia, Morrow, Roberts, Ruggles, Talbot, Tait, Taylor, Thompson, Tichenor, Turner, Varnum, Williams, and Wilson.

On motion of Mr. CAMPBELL, the time for taking the subscriptions was extended from six to twenty days.

On motion of Mr. CAMPBELL, another amendment was adopted, relative to the establishment of branches in the several States.

Mr. DAGGETT gave notice that he should here. after submit an amendment to the Senate; after which the bill was reported to the Senate, and the amendments were ordered to be printed.

TUESDAY, April 2.

The bill entitled "An act to enable the people of the Mississippi Territory to form a constitution and State government, and for the admission of such State into the Union on an equal footing with the original States," was read the second time, and referred to the committee on the memorial of the Legislature of the Mississippi Territory.

The bill entitled "An act to enable the people of the Indiana Territory to form a constitution and State government, and for the admission of such State into the Union on an equal footing with the original States," was read the second time, and referred to the committee last mentioned.

The bill entitled "An act, supplementary to the act to provide additional revenues for defraying the expenses of Government, and maintaining the public credit, by laying a direct tax upon the United States, and to provide for assessing and collecting the same," was read the second time, and referred to the Committee on Finance and an Uniform National Currency.

The bill entitled "An act to amend an act, entitled 'An act for the relief of Edward Hallowell," was read the second time, and referred to the committee last mentioned.

The bill entitled "An act for the relief of Henry Malcolm," was read the second time, and referred to the same committee.

The bill entitled "An act for the relief of Robert Kidd," was read the second time, and referred to the same committee.

The bill entitled "An act authorizing the President of the United States to lease the Saline, near the Wabash river, for a term not exceeding seven years," was read the second time, and referred to the committee on the memorial of the Legislature of the Mississippi Territory.

The bill entitled "An act for the relief of certain purchasers of public lands in the Mississippi Territory," was read the second time, and referred to the same committee.

The bill entitled "An act for the remission of certain duties on the importation of books for the use of Harvard College, and on the carriage and personal baggage of his Excellency William Gore, Governor of the British Province of Upper Canada," was read the second time, and considered as in Committee of the Whole; and it passed to a third reading.

The bill to erect a light-house at the mouth of the Mississippi river, was read the second time.

Mr. DANA, from the committee to whom the subject was referred, reported a bill, concerning the entry of vessels at the port of Middletown; and the bill was read, and passed to the second reading.

Mr. DANA, from the committee to whom the subject was referred, reported a resolution for printing the laws relative to naturalization; and the resolution was read, and passed to the second reading.

The bill entitled "An act supplemental to the act, entitled 'An act regulating and defining the duties of the Judges of the Territory of Illinois, and for vesting in the courts of the Territory of Indiana a jurisdiction in chancery cases arising in the said Territory," was read the second time, and referred to a select committee; and Messrs. RUGGLES, MORROW, and DAGGETT, were appointed the committee.

The bill entitled "An act directing the discharge of Ebenezer Keeler and John Francis from imprisonment," was read the second time. and referred to a select committee; and Messrs. ROBERTS, SANFORD, and DAGGETT, were appointed the committee.

The bill entitled "An act directing the discharge of Moses Lewis from imprisonment," was read the second time, and referred to the committee last mentioned.

A message from the House of Representatives informed the Senate that the House of Representatives have passed a bill, entitled "An act making appropriations for the support of the Military Establishment of the United States, for the year 1816;" a bill entitled "An act making appropriations for the support of the Navy of the United States, for the year 1816;" also, a bill en-

titled "An act continuing the salaries of certain officers of Government;" in which bills they request the concurrence of the Senate. They have concurred in the amendments of the Senate to the bill, entitled "An act in addition to an act to regulate the Post Office Establishment," with an amendment, in which they request the concurrence of the Senate.

Mr. DAGGETT submitted the following motion for consideration:

Resolved, That the committee to whom are referred the bills for the admission of the Indiana and Mississippi Territories into the Union, as new States, be, and hereby are instructed to ascertain, and report to the Senate, the actual number of inhabitants in the said Territories respectively; distinguishing the number of free persons, from the number of all other persons.

BANK OF THE UNITED STATES.

The Senate resumed the consideration of the bill, entitled " An act to incorporate the subscribers to the Bank of the United States," and the amendments agreed to as in Committee of the Whole, having been concurred in with an amendment, Mr. MASON, of New Hampshire, renewed his motion to add to the seventeenth section the following proviso:

"And if the said corporation shall at any time suspend or refuse payment, in gold or silver, of its notes, bills, obligations, or other debts, to such an amount, and for such length of time, as Congress may deem injurious to the United States, in such case Congress may repeal this act and abolish the said corporation, and make such regulations and provisions for the settlement of the affairs and payment of the debts of said corporation, and for distributing its remaining property among the stockholders, as shall be deemed just and proper."

On the question to agree thereto, it was determined in the negative—yeas 14, nays 22, as follows:

YEAS—Messrs. Barbour, Daggett, Gaillard, Goldsborough, Gore, Horsey, King, Mason of New Hampshire, Mason of Virginia, Sanford, Talbot, Thompson, Tichenor, and Turner.

NAYS—Messrs. Barry, Bibb, Brown, Campbell, Chace, Condit, Dana, Fromentin, Harper, Howell, Hunter, Lacock, Macon, Morrow, Roberts, Ruggles, Tait, Taylor, Varnum, Wells, Williams, and Wilson.

On motion of Mr. DAGGETT, to add to the bill the following section:

" SEC. 23. *And be it further enacted,* That it shall at all times be lawful for a committee of either House of Congress, appointed for that purpose, to inspect the books, and to examine into the proceedings of the corporation hereby created, and to report whether the provisions of this charter have been, by the same, violated or not, and whenever any committee as aforesaid shall find and report, or the President of the United States shall have reason to believe that the charter has been violated, it may be lawful for Congress to direct, or the President to order a scire facias to be sued out of the circuit court of the district of Pennsylvania, in the name of the United States, (which shall be executed upon the president of the said corporation for the time being, at least fifteen days before the commencement of the term of said court,) calling on the said corporation to show cause wherefore the charter hereby granted shall not be declared forfeited; and it shall be lawful for the said court, upon the return of the said scire facias, to examine into the truth of the alleged violation; and if such violation be made appear, then to pronounce and adjudge that the said charter is forfeited and annulled: *Provided, however,* every issue of fact which may be joined between the United States and the corporation aforesaid shall be tried by jury. And it shall be lawful for the court aforesaid to require the production of such of the books of the said corporation as it may deem necessary for the ascertainment of the controverted facts; and the final judgment of the court aforesaid shall be examinable in the Supreme Court of the United States, by writ of error, and may be there reversed or affirmed according to the usages of law."

It was determined in the affirmative—yeas 27, nays 8, as follows:

YEAS—Messrs. Barry, Brown, Chace, Daggett, Dana, Fromentin, Gaillard, Goldsborough, Gore, Harper, Horsey, Howell, Hunter, King, Macon, Mason of New Hampshire, Mason of Virginia, Sanford, Talbot, Tait, Taylor, Thompson, Tichenor, Turner, Wells, Williams, and Wilson.

NAYS—Messrs. Barbour, Bibb, Campbell, Condit, Lacock, Morrow, Roberts, and Varnum.

On motion by Mr. HARPER, to strike out of section 11, after "hold," in the seventh line, the following: "in the proportions following, that ' is to say, for one share, and not more than two ' shares, one vote; for every two shares above ' two and not exceeding ten, one vote; for every ' four shares above ten and not exceeding thirty, ' one vote; for every six shares above thirty and ' not exceeding sixty, one vote; for every eight ' shares above sixty and not exceeding one hun- ' dred, one vote; and for every ten shares above ' one hundred, one vote; and no person, copart- ' nership, or body politic, shall be entitled to a ' greater number than thirty votes."

It was determined in the negative—yeas 7, nays 23, as follows:

YEAS—Messrs. Daggett, Fromentin, Goldsborough, Harper, Horsey, Mason of New Hampshire, and Wells.

NAYS—Messrs. Barbour, Barry, Bibb, Brown, Campbell, Chace, Condit, Dana, Gaillard, Howell, Hunter, Lacock, Macon, Mason of Virginia, Morrow, Roberts, Sanford, Talbot, Tait, Tichenor, Turner, Varnum, Williams, and Wilson.

The bill having been further amended, on the question, "Shall the amendments be engrossed and the bill read a third time as amended?" it was determined in the affirmative—yeas 23, nays 10, as follows:

YEAS—Messrs. Barbour, Barry, Bibb, Brown, Campbell, Chace, Condit, Daggett, Fromentin, Harper, Horsey, Howell, Hunter, Mason of Virginia, Morrow, Roberts, Talbot, Tait, Taylor, Turner, Varnum, and Williams.

NAYS—Messrs. Dana, Gaillard, Goldsborough, Macon, Mason of New Hampshire, Sanford, Thompson, Tichenor, Wells, and Wilson.

On motion, the Senate adjourned.

WEDNESDAY, April 3.

A message from the House of Representatives informed the Senate that the House have passed a bill, entitled "An act to increase the pensions of invalids in certain cases, for the relief of invalids of the militia, and for the appointment of pension agents in those States where there is no commissioner of loans;" also, a bill, entitled "An act making appropriations for the support of Government for the year 1816." They have also passed a resolution for the appointment of a joint committee to inquire into the expediency of making certain alterations in the mode of transacting the business of Congress, and have appointed a committee on their part; in which bills and resolution they request the concurrence of the Senate.

The resolution last mentioned was read three times, by unanimous consent, and concurred in; and Messrs. VARNUM, BARBOUR, and DAGGETT, were appointed the committee on the part of the Senate.

The five bills last brought up for concurrence were read, and severally passed to the second reading.

On motion, by Mr. MORROW,

Ordered, That the committee to whom was referred the bill, entitled "An act to enable the people of the Indiana Territory to form a constitution and State government, and for the admission of such State into the Union on an equal footing with the original States," be discharged from the further consideration thereof, and that it be referred to the committee appointed the 2d of January, on the memorial of the Legislative Council and House of Representatives of the Indiana Territory, to consider and report thereon.

Mr. BARBOUR, from the Committee on Military Affairs, to whom the subject was referred, reported a bill to increase the compensation of the superintendents of the manufactories of arms at Springfield and Harper's Ferry; and the bill was read, and passed to the second reading.

Mr. BARBOUR, from the Committee on Military Affairs, to whom was referred the bill, entitled "An act for the liquidation of certain claims, and for other purposes," reported it with an amendment, which was read.

Mr. ROBERTS presented the memorial of manufacturers of shot, in the city of Philadelphia, praying a duty of three cents per pound may be imposed on shot imported into the United States, for reasons stated in the memorial; which was read, and referred to the Committee on Manufactures.

Mr. DANA, from the committee to whom the subject was referred, reported a bill, concerning the annual sum appropriated for arming and equipping the Militia; and the bill was read, and passed to the second reading.

The bill concerning the entry of vessels at the port of Middletown, was read the second time.

The bill entitled "An act to repeal the act, entitled 'An act to provide additional revenues for defraying the expenses of Government and maintaining the public credit, by laying duties on household furniture, and on gold and silver watches," was read a third time, and passed.

The Senate proceeded to consider the amendment of the House of Representatives to the amendments of the Senate to the bill, entitled "An act in addition to an act to regulate the Post Office Establishment," and concurred therein.

The bill entitled "An act for the remission of certain duties on the importation of books, for the use of Harvard College, and on the carriage and personal baggage of his Excellency William Gore, Governor of the British Province of Upper Canada," was read a third time, and passed.

The bill supplementary to an act, entitled "An act to incorporate a company for making certain turnpike roads within the District of Columbia," was read a third time, and passed.

On motion by Mr. MORROW, the consideration of the engrossed bill, making appropriation for the construction of roads and canals, was further postponed until Monday next.

The Senate resumed, as in Committee of the Whole, the consideration of the bill to establish a system of navigation for the United States; and, on motion by Mr. DANA, the further consideration thereof was postponed until to-morrow.

The Senate resumed. as in Committee of the Whole, the consideration of the bill for calling forth the militia to execute the laws of the Union, suppress insurrection, and repel invasion, and to repeal the laws heretofore passed for those purposes, together with the proposed amendments; and, on motion by Mr. MASON, of Virginia, the further consideration thereof was postponed until to-morrow.

On motion by Mr. DANA,

Resolved, That the Secretary for the Department of War be directed to lay before the Senate a statement of the sums expended for the purchase or manufacture of arms and military equipments for the militia, in pursuance of the act of the 23d of April, 1808, entitled "An act making provision for arming and equipping the whole body of the militia of the United States;" and also a statement of the arms and military equipments which have been so provided, and of the distribution thereof, in execution of the same act.

The Senate resumed, as in Committee of the Whole, the consideration of the bill to ascertain and establish the western boundary of the tract reserved for satisfying the military bounties allowed to the officers and soldiers of the Virginia line on Continental Establishment; and, on motion by Mr. BARBOUR, the further consideration thereof was postponed until Friday next.

The Senate resumed the consideration of the report of the committee, to whom was referred the resolution relating to the claims of the officers and soldiers of the Virginia line on State and Continental Establishment, for bounty lands; and, on motion by Mr. BARBOUR, the further consideration thereof was postponed until to-morrow.

The Senate resumed, as in Committee of the Whole, the consideration of the bill to authorize the Secretary of the Treasury to subscribe, in behalf of the United States, for —— shares in the capital stock of the Chesapeake and Delaware Canal Company; and, on motion by Mr. HORSEY, the further consideration thereof was postponed until Monday next.

The Senate resumed the consideration of the report of the Committee on Military Affairs, on the petition of Catharine Robertson; and, on motion by Mr. ROBERTS, the further consideration thereof was postponed until the first Monday in June next.

Mr. BARBOUR, from the Committee on Military Affairs, to whom was referred the bill entitled "An act making further provision for military services during the late war, and for other purposes," reported it with amendments; which were read.

The Senate resumed the consideration of the motion made on the 2d instant, relative to the number of the inhabitants of the Mississippi and Indiana Territories; which was amended, and agreed to as follows:

Resolved, That the committees to whom are referred the bills for the admission of the Indiana and Mississippi Territories into the Union as new States, be, and hereby are, instructed to ascertain and report to the Senate the actual number of inhabitants in the said Territories respectively, distinguishing the number of free persons from the number of all other persons, and the number of persons on the east side of the Tombigbee river, in the Mississippi Territory, from those on the west side of the river.

Mr. CAMPBELL, from the Committee on Finance and an Uniform National Currency, to whom was referred the bill entitled "An act for the relief of Robert Kidd," reported it without amendment.

Mr. CAMPBELL, from the same committee, to whom was referred the bill, entitled "An act for the relief of Henry Malcolm," reported it without amendment.

Mr. CAMPBELL, from the same committee, to whom was referred the bill, entitled "An act to amend an act, entitled 'An act for the relief of Edward Hallowell," reported it without amendment.

Mr. KING, from the committee appointed on the subject, submitted the following motion for consideration:

Resolved, That the Senate approve of the alterations suggested for the enlargement of the Senate room, and the better arrangement of the offices of the Senate; and that the plan of the proposed alterations drawn by the surveyor of the public buildings, together with a copy of this resolution, be transmitted to the President of the United States.

BANK OF THE UNITED STATES.

The amendments to the bill, entitled "An act to incorporate the subscribers to the Bank of the United States," having been reported by the committee correctly engrossed, the bill was read a third time, as amended; and, the blanks having been filled, the bill was further amended by unanimous consent.

On the question, "Shall this bill pass, as

amended ?" it was determined in the affirmative —yeas 22, nays 12, as follows:

YEAS—Messrs. Barbour, Barry, Brown, Campbell, Chace, Condit, Daggett, Fromentin, Harper, Horsey, Howell, Hunter, Lacock, Mason of Virginia, Morrow, Roberts, Talbot, Tait, Taylor, Turner, Varnum, and Williams.

NAYS—Messrs. Dana, Gaillard, Goldsborough, Gore, King, Macon, Mason of New Hampshire, Ruggles, Sanford, Tichenor, Wells, and Wilson.

Resolved, That this bill pass, with amendments. [Messrs. BIBB and THOMPSON, the only absentees, are understood to have been detained from the Senate by ill health; the former of these gentlemen being seriously indisposed.]

THURSDAY, April 4.

Mr. BROWN, from the committee to whom the subject was referred, reported a bill for adjusting the claims to land, and establishing a land office for the districts of land lying east of the Mississippi river, and island of New Orleans; and the bill was read, and passed to the second reading.

Mr. CAMPBELL, from the Committee on Finance and an Uniform National Currency, to whom was referred the bill entitled "An act to abolish the existing duties on spirits distilled within the United States, and to lay other duties in lieu of those at present imposed on licenses to distillers of spirituous liquors," reported it with an amendment.

The bill entitled "An act making appropriations for the support of Government for the year 1816," was read the second time, and referred to a select committee; and Messrs. LACOCK, DAGGETT, and MORROW, were appointed the committee.

The bill entitled "An act continuing the salaries of certain officers of Government," was read the second time, and referred to the committee last mentioned.

The bill entitled "An act making appropriations for the support of the Military Establishment of the United States, for the year 1816," was read the second time, and referred to the Committee on Military Affairs.

The bill entitled "An act making appropriations for the support of the Navy of the United States, for the year 1816," was read the second time, and referred to the Committee on Naval Affairs.

The bill entitled "An act to increase the pensions of invalids in certain cases, for the relief of invalids of the militia, and for the appointment of pension agents in those States where there is no commissioner of loans," was read the second time, and referred to the Committee on the Militia of the United States.

The bill to increase the compensation of the superintendents of the manufactories of arms at Springfield and Harper's Ferry, was read the second time.

The bill concerning the annual sum appropriated for arming and equipping the militia, was read the second time.

Mr. MORROW, from the committee to whom was referred the bill, entitled "An act to enable the people of the Indiana Territory to form a constitution and State government, and for the admission of such State into the Union on an equal footing with the original States," reported it with amendments; which were read.

Mr. MORROW, from the same committee, communicated a certified statement of the census of the Indiana Territory.

The following Message was received from the PRESIDENT OF THE UNITED STATES:

To the Senate of the United States:

I transmit to the Senate a report from the Secretary of the Treasury, complying with their resolutions of the 26th March last.

JAMES MADISON.

APRIL 4, 1816.

The Message and report, therein mentioned, were read.

The Senate resumed, as in Committee of the Whole, the consideration of the bill for calling forth the militia to execute the laws of the Union, suppress insurrection, and repel invasion, and to repeal the laws heretofore passed for those purposes, together with the proposed amendments; and, after progress, on motion by Mr. BROWN, the further consideration thereof was postponed until the fourth Monday in July next.

The Senate resumed the report of the select committee, relating to the claims of the officers and soldiers of the Virginia line, on State and Continental Establishment, for bounty lands; and on motion, by Mr. BARBOUR, the consideration thereof was further postponed until this day fortnight.

The Senate resumed, as in Committee of the Whole, the consideration of the bill concerning certain advances made for the public service by the city of New York; and on motion, by Mr. BARBOUR, it was referred to the Committee on Military Affairs, "with instructions to inquire whether any, and, if any, what provisions ought to be made by law for payment of damages sustained by persons on whose lands military works have been constructed during the late war, either under the authority of any officer of the United States, or that of any State, corporation, or otherwise, not hitherto provided for."

The Senate resumed, as in Committee of the Whole, the consideration of the bill concerning the District of Columbia; and on motion, by Mr. DAGGETT, the further consideration thereof was postponed until Tuesday next.

The Senate resumed, as in Committee of the Whole, the consideration of the bill dividing the State of Pennsylvania into two judicial districts.

On motion by Mr. MASON, of New Hampshire, to strike out the first section of the bill, the question was lost, the Senate being equally divided yeas 15, nays 15, as follows:

YEAS—Messrs. Daggett, Goldsborough, Gore, Harper, Hunter, King, Macon, Mason, of New Hampshire, Talbot, Taylor, Thompson, Tichenor, Turner, Varnum, and Wells.

NAYS—Messrs. Barbour, Barry, Brown, Chace, Condit, Gaillard, Lacock, Mason, of Virginia, Morrow, Roberts, Ruggles, Sanford, Tait, Williams, and Wilson.

NAVIGATION SYSTEM.

The bill "to establish a navigation system for the United States" being under consideration, Mr. HARPER moved to recommit it to the Committee of Foreign Relations, and to refer to the same committee the following resolutions, which he read in his place, and laid on the table, viz:

Resolved, That provision ought to be made by law for excluding gradually from the naval and merchant service of the United States all persons other than native citizens, or citizens heretofore naturalized.

Resolved, That provision ought to be made by law for compelling merchant vessels of the United States to have on board a number of apprentices, in proportion to the tonnage of such vessels, respectively.

Mr. HARPER said, his object in moving this recommitment was to prevail on the Senate, if possible, to remould the bill, so as to incorporate into it the new ideas contained in these resolutions—new, he meant, as respected that bill, though no doubt very familiar within these walls, and to well-informed and reflecting men throughout the country. And as the motion, should it prevail, would give a new shape to the bill, and a new character to our whole maritime system—a character which he deemed it of the highest importance to impart to that great branch of our policy —he thought it incumbent on him to state, somewhat at large, the leading considerations which, in his opinion, recommended this measure. He was sensible that neither those considerations nor the measure itself were new to that House or to the nation. They had often no doubt been the subject of reflection and discussion abroad, and sometimes of deliberation within those walls; but as he—not having then the honor of a seat in that body—had no part in those deliberations, he might perhaps be more readily excused, for occupying some portion of its time with his ideas concerning the great interests involved in the question.

These resolutions, Mr. H. said, (and especially the first, which contained by far the most important principle,) had two distinct objects; each recommended by considerations peculiar to itself, and both tending to the same great end—the honor, safety, and prosperity of the nation. The first was to preserve peace, as far as its preservation might depend on us, by excluding all foreign seamen from our merchant ships, and thus preventing those collisions with the maritime Powers of the world which must of necessity arise from conflicting claims on the ocean to allegiance. The second, to prepare for war, by accelerating the production of a numerous class of native seamen; the most effectual mode of doing which, was to confine the navigation of our ships of war and merchant vessels—as these resolutions proposed to confine it—to our native citizens, and those heretofore naturalized among us. Such, he said, was the twofold object of his motion—to avoid contests with other nations, and especially with that between which and us, from similarity of language, appearance, and pursuits, they were most likely to arise; and to make timely and effectual preparation for maintaining our rights against all nations, and especially that great maritime Power with which, in all probability, we could not long avoid serious collisions, if we would; and perhaps—judging from the temper of a large part of this nation—would not, if we could. From these collisions the resolutions which he had submitted would, in his opinion, have a tendency to save us. So far their operation would be admitted, he presumed, to be highly beneficial. Every measure must be so, that tended, by fair and honorable means, to narrow the ground and diminish the occasions of serious misunderstandings with other Powers. The effect, indeed, would be not complete. Neither this measure nor any other could save us entirely from contests with a Power between which and this country so many fruitful and perennial sources of discord existed; but, it was doing much to diminish the number of those sources, and to dry up one of the most fruitful. This, he believed, would be effected by the resolutions under consideration. How they would produce that effect he would next proceed to consider.

Every honorable gentleman who heard him, knew how the two nations—the United States and Great Britain—stood towards each other, in relation to their maritime policy and pretensions. The United States asserted it as a right, and had established it as a habit, to incorporate foreigners by naturalization into their political association —into the nation—and thus to withdraw them from their allegiance to their native Governments. This practice extended to all the European States, but affected Great Britain more than any other nation, from obvious and well known causes. We went a step further—we had laid it down as a maxim in our laws and foreign policy that protection is due on the ocean to these naturalized foreigners, against their original Governments, to the same extent as to our native citizens; and this protection we had repeatedly, and in various forms, promised to afford. We had held out to the subjects of every Power—to the people of all nations—a promise of protection against their native Governments, on the ocean as well as on the land, provided they would conform to our laws of naturalization. Thus the matter stood on our part.

The foreign Powers, on the other hand, and particularly Great Britain, had, from time immemorial, adopted it as a maxim of their laws and constitutions, essential, in their opinions, to the preservation of government and civil society, that allegiance is perpetual and unalienable, so far as relates to the mere act of the person who owes it; that every member of the community contracts by his birth obligations of obedience to the laws, and of service and fidelity to the State, from which he cannot withdraw, without the consent of the Sovereign. In fine, that this contract, like all others, can only be dissolved by the consent of both parties—one of whom is the indi-

285   HISTORY OF CONGRESS.   286

APRIL, 1816.   *Navigation System.*   SENATE.

vidual or subject, and the other the Sovereign representing the community or State. He would not, he said, now inquire whether, as an abstract principle, this doctrine was correct. The inquiry was unnecessary for his present purpose. Should it ever become necessary, he was prepared to meet the question, and entertained opinions concerning it which he should be ready to avow and maintain. It was sufficient for the present purpose, and must be known by all who heard him, that the Government to which he alluded, and over whose conduct or opinions we had no control, did hold and always had held this doctrine, and had always manifested a fixed determination not to recede from it, or to relinquish the rights to which it gave birth. It was equally well known that many other Governments—nay, he might say *all* the Governments of the world, except our own; all those at least which belonged to the European system, and with which we had any connexion—held the same principle, and from time to time asserted it, as might happen to suit their interest or their policy. How far we might hereafter find it necessary to adopt and assert this principle ourselves, he deemed it unnecessary now to inquire; though he had a very distinct opinion on that subject, which, on every proper occasion, he should be ready to avow and support. It was enough for us, at present, that Great Britain *did* assert this principle of perpetual, indissoluble allegiance, and had manifested, on all occasions, a determination to support it, at every hazard.

Knowing then, he said, as we did, this determination, this fixed purpose of that nation, to assert, at every hazard, the right which she thus claimed to the services of all her people whom she could find in merchant ships on the ocean, or in her own territory; knowing, also, the importance which she attached to this right, regarded by her as essential to her prosperity, her safety, and even her existence; the question for us to solve, laying aside all consideration of the soundness of her doctrine, of the abstract right of the case, and looking only to the practical consequences, was this: how far would it be wise in us to engage in a contest with that nation on grounds considered as so doubtful, on principles not acknowledged by any other Power; where the universal opinion of mankind, out of our own country, would be against us, and opinions at home might be very much divided. It was a point on which such a division must be expected; a point on which the most enlightened and patriotic men might entertain, and in fact did entertain, the most opposite opinions; for it was well known that a very large portion of the American people, including many individuals of the highest character for virtue, knowledge, and love of country, were of opinion that one nation had no right, by its naturalization laws or any other means, to withdraw the subjects of another from their allegiance. He did not now intend to inquire into the correctness of this opinion, but merely to advert to the fact that such an opinion was entertained by a very numerous and highly respectable class of our citizens, whose feelings and opinions

it was of the highest importance to consult, in order to obtain their zealous co-operation in any struggle that might ensue. Good citizens would always obey the laws; but unless they approved the ground of a war, mere obedience was all that could be expected from them. Zeal, devotedness, voluntary services, and sacrifices of person and property, could only be expected, from men of honorable minds, in a cause which they approved; and there were great numbers of the most honorable and virtuous men of this country who would not and could not approve of any quarrel entered into for the mere purpose, not of vindicating any rights, or redressing any injuries of our own citizens, of the native sons of our soil, but of asserting a right in this country to acquire new citizens, of whom we had no need, by withdrawing foreigners from the power of their own Governments; to confer favors on foreigners, at the expense of the country and its native inhabitants. There were, Mr. H. said, certain principles, affecting the rights of our native citizens, in defence of which he was at all times ready to incur every risk, and brave every danger. Those rights were sacred, and whenever openly assailed must be defended at every hazard. Questions might indeed arise about the nature and extent of some of those rights; but there were others of a nature too clear to be disputed, and too sacred to be touched; which, when openly assailed, must be defended at every hazard, and even when incidentally infringed, through inadvertency, accident, or mistake, claimed the jealous attention and ready interposition of the Government. Without entering into any exact definition of these high and sacred rights, which he did not conceive to be now necessary, it might be remarked that the right of personal liberty, of exemption from compulsory service to a foreign Government, under any form whatever, was among the most undeniable of the number; and there never was a time when he was not ready to resist, to every extremity, any such claim to the service of native American citizens, had such a claim been made by any Government whatever. The claim, however, which was now under consideration, the claim of the British Government to the services of its own subjects, whenever it could find them in merchant ships on the ocean, or in its own ports, was by no means of this description; and the right asserted by this country to protect British subjects and other foreigners, on the ocean, against the claims of their own Governments, was not a right in which our native citizens, the sons of our soil, had any interest. It was a claim for the benefit of foreigners, not always of the most desirable class, who often come to us because they found it inconvenient to remain in their own country; whom we wished to adopt, for their benefit, and not for our own, into our family, and to extend to them not only the privileges but the protection due only to our native sons. It was from the collisions arising out of such a policy that he wished to save the country; collisions dangerous to its peace, not useful to its interests, nor conducive to its honor. He wished, by the measure now proposed, to avoid contests on such grounds; in which we could neither have the approbation and countenance of other nations, nor be united among ourselves. The public opinion of the world was of itself of great importance, and he would sacrifice much to gain it to our cause, in every conflict in which we might be compelled to engage. It was a great moral power, which no wise Government would neglect. But great as it was, he thought it very inconsiderable in comparison with union among ourselves. It was on that union that the force of every nation, and especially of this, living, as we did, under a government of consent which rested wholly on public opinion, must in a most material degree depend. No sacrifices, except those of primary and essential rights, were too great for attaining so desirable an object. The right of which he now proposed to divest ourselves was of a most doubtful character; whether we regarded the right itself, or the expediency of its exercise; and as, notwithstanding all our care, it might not be in our power to avoid serious contests with other nations, and chiefly with that to which he had so often alluded, he wished to put all doubtful causes out of the conflicts to which we might be destined, and so to choose our ground, that all the differences of opinion among ourselves might hereafter be confined to the time of beginning the contest, and the manner of conducting it, but not extend to the right itself for which we were to contend.

There was another view of the subject, Mr. H. said, in which this measure strongly recommended itself to his mind. A new state of things had arisen; we were about to enter on a new career, and before we began it he wished to get entirely rid of this cause of collision with foreign Powers, arising from our claim of right to protect those on the ocean whom they assert a right to consider and treat as their subjects. He called this a new career because, for more than twenty years, a state of things had existed in the world totally different from that at which we now had fortunately arrived. When you and I, sir, said Mr. H., came into life, as public men, we saw the commencement of that state of things which has now passed away, and which gave rise, while it continued, to political systems, views, and opinions, not applicable to the present condition of the world. At the beginning of the period to which I allude, we saw a new and mighty Power struggling into existence, and displaying even then, under the pretence of establishing freedom at home and promoting it abroad, a spirit of gigantic and unprincipled ambition, which soon rendered it the scourge and terror of all surrounding nations. It assailed them all, in turn, with all the weapons of fraud and force, while it loudly stigmatized, as combinations against liberty and national independence, those leagues which its aggressions had compelled them to form for their own defence. This new Power, after pursuing for a while, with wild and revolutionary fury, a plan of universal dominion, but ill concealed though not distinctly avowed, settled down into

a military despotism, the most formidable in its means and profligate in its principles that the world has ever seen; which boldly, openly, and steadily, pushed forward the scheme of conquest and universal empire originated by its predecessors; and, after crushing or humbling every Power but one, which alone had the courage and strength to maintain the conflict, bent at length all its vast and accumulated force against that Power, the only remaining obstacle, which alone stood in the breach, struggling to keep up the mound, and to save itself, and with itself, us and the rest of the world, from the torrent which equally threatened all.

In this state of things, Mr. H. said, there was no room for deliberation, no freedom of choice, no course of conduct but one; and that was, to abstain from every act, however proper in other times, that could then tend to weaken the arm uplifted in the common cause; that might diminish the power exerted for the common defence; or tend to break down or undermine the mound which restrained the mighty torrent, and preserved it from sweeping us and the rest of the world into one common ruin. In such a state of things it was not for nations to act as in ordinary times, or on maxims of ordinary policy. Injuries which in ordinary times were to be vigorously repelled, were then to be patiently borne, on account of the infinitely greater evils which the attempt to repel them might introduce. The utmost indulgence was to be exercised. Every encroachment, that could be made to wear the appearance of right, that did not assume the character of open and direct aggression, was to be borne, rather than to run the risk of weakening those exertions, on which such mighty interests depended.

Now the state of things, he said, was changed. That tremendous power was overthrown, the Government that wielded it had been annihilated, and the nation which supplied its means of power was reduced below its usual and proper level. If danger still existed, it was on the other side. We were no longer called on to bear or forbear; nor to judge of injuries or encroachments by distinct or collateral circumstances. We might now estimate them by their intrinsic nature, and act concerning them upon the ordinary maxims of political wisdom. Those maxims enjoin it on a nation like this, rising rapidly into power and importance, to watch over its rights with a jealous and vigilant care; to regard its honor as inseparably connected with its true interests, and as making a part of its dearest rights; to consider justice as the first of its duties; to advance no claims which were not clear and incontrovertible, and to maintain those with inflexible constancy. This view of things had induced him to regard the nation as entering on a new career, as at the commencement of a new era, and he thought it of the utmost importance that in this state of things we should take no false steps, and assume no questionable ground; that we should so act as to cause it to be distinctly understood, that while the United States would submit to no intentional injury, nor suffer even any accidental trespass to pass without notice, and if need be redress, they would carefully avoid all interference with the rights of others, and assert no claims but such as were clear and important. This was the position which he wished this country to take, and to maintain, in the commencement of the new era now opening before them. Here in his opinion they ought to plant their foot; and having chosen well their ground, with a view to the rights and feeling of other nations as well as their own, to stand on it immoveably, prepared for every consequence. On such ground the resolutions which he had moved would in his opinion place them. By excluding the subjects of other Powers from our ships of war and merchant vessels, we would avoid all collision with them on the ocean, upon this delicate point; all interference with a claim of allegiance, to which they attach so much importance, and have displayed so firm a determination to maintain. Having done this we shall stand perfectly free, with the world and ourselves, to resist steadily and effectually any encroachments which they may attempt, on our acknowledged and important rights, and all such encroachments be for one should be always ready to resist, to the utmost extremity, in whatever quarter they may be attempted.

While we took this view, Mr. H. said, of the very doubtful right of withdrawing foreigners from their allegiance to their Governments, and protecting them on the ocean against claims arising out of that allegiance; a right, in his opinion, not only extremely doubtful but very unimportant; he wished distinctly to mark out two classes of emigrants, as exceptions from his motion and his reasoning.

The first class was that of foreigners heretofore naturalized. Whatever might be, in point of abstract principle, the correctness or incorrectness of our conduct, in passing those laws under which foreigners had been incorporated into our nation, by which they had in effect been invited and encouraged to come among us, we could not now suffer it as to them to be made a question. Those laws had operated as an invitation to emigrants, and as a promise of protection against their native governments. Perhaps they were intended so to operate; but however that might be, such undoubtedly had been their effect. We had invited these strangers, whether wisely or properly was not now the question, to take sanctuary in our land, and promised them protection on board of our ships. We could not now abandon them without dishonor. Our word was out, and we must protect them at all events. We must redeem our pledge; and Mr. H. said that he was ready at any moment to draw the sword in defence of this class of citizens, the citizens heretofore naturalized, whose rights he would never suffer to be drawn into question. He would say, in the commencement of any negotiation, "This ground is sacred and must not be touched. Our faith is pledged, and must be redeemed." He had accordingly provided in the first resolution for this class of citizens.

The second class, he said, need hardly be men-

tioned; so obvious were the principles by which it was protected. It consisted of those foreigners, whether naturalized or not, who remained within our territory. They were protected by our territory while they so remained, because within our territory no foreign Power could exercise any jurisdiction, or exert any act of authority whatever. We therefore extend protection to such persons, in the usual exercise of our rights of sovereignty, and as a necessary consequence of those rights, while they reside in our country, and remain on our soil. When they choose to depart, the protection ceases. The general proposition, therefore was to be understood as subject to those two exceptions; one of which indeed was incorporated into the resolutions themselves, and the other was so obvious, that nothing but a desire to avoid all possibility of being misunderstood, in a matter of so much delicacy, would have induced him to advert to it thus particularly. Indeed, it might be remarked that this principle of public law was of such universal operation, that persons guilty of the greatest crimes, murder for instance, and even treason, if they could escape from the country where those crimes were committed, into a foreign territory, found protection and immunity; and nothing but special provisions by treaty could control the operation of this general law. This doctrine was exemplified in the history of every country and every age.

Mr. H. then proceeded to the second division of the subject, which he observed was by far the most important. He had hitherto considered the resolutions in their tendency to preserve us in peace, by removing one great ground of controversy with foreign Powers, and especially with Great Britain, and to unite us at home in such conflicts or other grounds as we might be unable to avoid. He would now consider them in their tendency to prepare us effectually for war. It would, he presumed, be admitted by all, that we ought to make betimes the most efficient preparations for those great conflicts with other Powers to which we were called by our destiny. The United States could not expect to remain always at peace. Perhaps they ought not to desire it; for long-continued peace enervates, corrupts, and debases a nation, and prepares it for subjugation, by rendering it too timid, too avaricious, and too effeminate to defend itself. Be that, however, as it may, continual peace was not in our power, and therefore we ought to look to frequent wars, and prepare for them. They would grow out of our habits, our pursuits, our character, our form of government, and our situation with respect to the great maritime Powers of the world. Our people were too enterprising, too active, too eager in the pursuit of commercial gain, to remain quietly at home. Inhabiting a most extensive seacoast, bred and almost born on the ocean, they were naturally impelled to maritime enterprise. Their free institutions gave them a bold and adventurous spirit. Their equality of civil and political rights rendered them eager for the acquisition of wealth, because that acquisition placed them on a footing of absolute equality with those who possessed the greatest advantages. Commerce and maritime adventure opened to them, to all that numerous part of them at least that dwelt on the Atlantic shore, the nearest and most flattering prospect of wealth. All these causes impelled us to the ocean, and sent us in quest of gain through every sea and to the remotest shores. Our free Government, while it generated and fostered a spirit of restless and daring adventure, left us unrestrained to the bent of our character and inclinations; for it had no power, except under very particular circumstances of rare occurrence, to mould and direct the industry and pursuits of the nation. It received its tone and character from public sentiment, which, instead of leading it, must generally follow. Hence arose maritime and commercial pursuits of unexampled activity, ardor, and extent; and while we spread our ships over every sea, and eagerly sought every market which afforded even a distant prospect of gain, we were necessarily and frequently brought into contest and collision with other nations engaged in similar pursuits, especially that nation whose character and situation in these respects were so much like our own. With that nation, therefore, we must at every turn cross and clash. And to these inherent causes of difference many others might be added, of a peculiar nature, which need not be enumerated, because they would readily occur to every reflecting mind. Some of them were minute and even trivial, though well suited to produce irritation. Others lay much deeper, and being intimately connected with the great and essential interests of the two nations, real or supposed, could hardly fail to produce the most serious contests, capable of being adjusted only by the sword. Many of the maritime pretensions of that great Power were of this description. They need not be named, because they were in every one's recollection; but it might safely be said that they were of a nature to which this country, in the ordinary state of the world, which was its actual state, never would or could submit. This nation was too proud, too ambitious, too enterprising, either to consent that its people should be kept at home, or that their intercourse with other countries should be controlled, restrained, or regulated by any power whatever. Judging from what has happened, and from the principles which we know to be held and asserted by the great Power to which he had alluded, we could not but know that attempts at this restraint and control will be made. Thus we should be driven into the conflict, whatever care we might take to avoid it. Perhaps we ought not to wish to avoid it, for peace is not always the best thing for a nation; but whatever might be our wishes, it would not be long in our power. Collisions would take place, explanations and reparations would be demanded, perhaps not always in the most conciliatory and moderate tone. They would sometimes be given, as often happens, in such a manner as to make matters worse. Resort would then be had to arms, and thus we should soon be driven or

drawn into every quarrel among the great maritime Powers. We should be impelled to join the weaker side, because on that side our alliance would be courted, our principles acknowledged, and our pride flattered. It would also be our interest to unite with the weaker maritime Powers in their efforts to check and restrain the lofty pretensions and overbearing domination of the strongest. This, he said, was the natural and constant course of things, which had been for a long time suspended by the extraordinary state of the world, but had now returned to its usual channel; and thus, by a destiny which we could not control, we should become parties in every contest among the maritime Powers. From being parties, we should gradually become principals, and find ourselves at length at the head of the league.

Since then, he said, it was our destiny to fight, it became us to consider in time how we might fight most advantageously, and best prepare for the struggles which we could not avoid. He had no doubt that our true policy and the character of our people led us to the ocean, as the proper field of contest, which was equally pointed out by the nature and genius of our Government. That was the natural and most efficacious direction of our force. It was there that the character of the country had been most nobly sustained; that the most brilliant triumphs had been achieved; that the fairest presages of future glory had been given. The mistakes of rulers might sometimes send our brave sons to perish, in fruitless expeditions by land, among the snows and damp and dreary forests of the North, or in the pestilential swamps and morasses of the South, but the irresistible force of circumstances would soon correct their errors, and recall us to the ocean, as the true scene of our power and glory.

Since it was on maritime power, therefore, that we must rely, to maritime exertions that we should be irresistibly impelled, it behooved us to consider what were the best and most efficient means of maritime force, what was its most solid basis. Was it ships? No. Money? No. What then? He would answer, that it was a brave, hardy, and numerous class of native and patriotic seamen, bound to us by the ties of birth, education, early habit; impelled by the feelings of patriotism and the love of glory; a class of men without which ships are useless, and which money cannot buy. And can you, he asked, rely on foreigners for this all-important aid? On men attracted to your service by the mere desire of wages or of gain, connected with you by no common interests or feelings, united to you by no ties of kindred or affection, mere birds of passage, which flock to your shores in the summer of peace and prosperity, and fly from you when the storm begins to howl? Danger scares them away. These men, thrown on our shores in time of peace by their own Governments who wish to get rid of the expense of maintaining them, enticed to us by the hope of high wages and easy service, when we happen to be neutral, and their own Governments at war, fly when danger approaches, and leave us defenceless, as far as our defence may depend on them. On whom, then, can the country rely? To whom must it look in the hour of danger? I answer to our native citizens, attached to us by birth, education, habit, and domestic ties. These are our sure dependence. They will not leave us in the time of trial, for their affections are with us, their hearts are with us, their parents and their children are with us. On them we may rely in our greatest extremity.

It was the object of his motion, Mr. H. said, to foster the growth of this inestimable class of men, and thus to make the best, the most effectual, and extensive preparation for supporting our rights on the ocean, where alone they would be effectually asserted. He wished to encourage the manufacture of native American seamen, the only production which he was willing to force, by any species of what is called protecting duty. Since there was a sort of rage for encouraging manufactures, he wished to give it a right direction by encouraging the growth, not of woolcarders and cotton-spinners, of deformed, feeble, and diseased laborers in work-shops and factories, but of hardy, gallant, and active seamen, to man our navy; and, by protecting our commerce on the ocean, to enable us to import from other countries those articles which could not be produced among ourselves, without forcing them by oppressive taxes on nine-tenths of the community for the benefit of the other tenth. This, in his opinion, was the true way of encouraging industry and promoting the solid and lasting prosperity of the country; to protect all, and leave all to seek the most profitable modes of employing their skill, labor, and capital. This protection could only be afforded by a powerful marine, which would enable our commerce to seek the most profitable markets for our own productions, and to supply us on the best terms with those of other countries. Every branch of industry would then find and preserve its proper level. To the formation of such a marine, a sufficient supply of native American freemen was essential, and that supply it was the object of his motion to secure. An object in his opinion of the greatest importance in every point of view, which would, he hoped, be deemed a sufficient apology on his part for having occupied so much of the time of that honorable body in this feeble, and, he feared, ineffectual attempt to procure the adoption of the measure under consideration.

With respect to the manner of carrying this measure into effect, so as to obtain the object ultimately, and in the shortest practicable time, without producing derangement in our commercial operations, or serious embarrassment to our ship owners, which he was sensible must be the consequence of precipitation, in every measure of this sort, he considered this as matter of detail, into which he did not intend then to enter. It would be proper and even necessary in the future stages of the business.

All that he now desired was to refer the propo- sition to the committee, which had reported the bill then before the Senate, and had long had this whole subject under consideration. Here the measure would undergo a full examination with a view both to its practicability, its expediency, and the details of its execution. A report on the subject would then bring the whole matter again before the Senate, with all the facts and explanations necessary for a proper decision.

On the second resolution, for requiring merchant ships to have apprentices on board, he observed that little need now be said. Its object was the same with the first, to provide in time the means of naval power, by promoting the growth of native seamen; and it would be found, he believed, powerfully conducive to that end. It was a measure sanctioned by long experience, in other maritime countries, and especially in Great Britain; in whose practice and institutions we might expect to find the most useful lessons in the act of advancing naval power. The only points therefore for the consideration of the Committee, should his motion of recommitment and reference prevail, would be to what extent, and under what modifications, the measure of requiring apprentices ought to be adopted, and what were the best means of insuring its success, consistently with the state of the country, and the nature of our institutions.

Mr. HARPER then concluded with moving that the bill "to establish a system of navigation for the United States be recommitted to the Committee of Foreign Relations; and that the resolutions, which he had laid on the table, be referred to the same committee, for consideration and report."

In the debate which ensued on this motion, Mr. KING adverted in terms of very strong disapprobation to that part of the British practice of impressment which constitutes their naval officers, and frequently those of very inferior rank, judges in the last resort, on the question whether a seaman claiming to be a native American citizen was so or not; which enables this petty officer, frequently little better than the commander of a press-gang, to decide without evidence, without inquiry, and without appeal, on the dearest rights which belong to a freeman—his right of personal liberty; and to condemn him without a hearing to a rigorous confinement and most irksome servitude on board of a foreign ship of war. This practice Mr. K. censured in terms of severe and just reprehension, declaring that it was intolerable in principle, and had been to a great extent abused in practice, though not so great as had sometimes been stated, by impressing and detaining native American citizens, under pretence of their being British subjects. From the general cast of Mr. K.'s observations on this point, he appeared to be under the impression that Mr. HARPER considered this part of the British practice of impressment as correct, or at least as proper to be tolerated.

Mr. HARPER in explanation observed, that he was very sorry to find himself misunderstood in such a point by the honorable gentleman from

New York, for whose opinions he felt the highest deference and respect. He had not deemed it necessary, from the general course of his observations in support of his motion, to enlarge particularly on the subject alluded to by the honorable gentleman, but he had supposed that his ideas on that point were clearly conveyed by strong and necessary implication from the general tenor of his arguments. Since that however appeared not to be the fact, he would ask leave of the Senate to explain himself more fully, for it was a point on which of all others he was least willing to be misunderstood. He therefore stated distinctly what he had thought sufficiently clear, that he entirely concurred with the honorable gentleman from New York, in the opinions and feelings which he had so forcibly expressed, concerning the British practice in question—the practice of erecting their inferior naval officers, or any of their officers however high in rank, into judges upon the dearest and most sacred rights of American citizens, the rights of personal freedom, with power to decide in the last resort, without evidence and without a hearing, and to carry their own unjust sentences into immediate execution, by dragging the unhappy victims into compulsory service on board of a foreign ship of war, perhaps the enemy of this country. This practice, he agreed with the honorable gentleman, ought to be resisted at every hazard and to the last extremity; and to put ourselves in a condition to resist it effectually, was one great object of the resolutions which he had submitted. It was only, in his opinion, after having excluded British subjects from our merchant ships, that we could correctly and effectually resist their claim, of a right to come on board those ships in search of their subjects. If we chose to receive their subjects on board, and then told them that we would protect all who were on board, or all but those whom we or the commanders of our merchant ships might think fit to acknowledge to be British subjects, and to give up as such, it was obvious that we should do exactly what we so justly complained of in them. We should take upon ourselves, or confer on the commanders of our merchant vessels, the power of deciding in the last resort, with or without evidence, and with or without a hearing, who were to be considered as British subjects, and to execute the sentences, by withholding from the power and service of their own Government all those British subjects whom such judges might think fit to declare American citizens. To such a course of proceeding the British Government could not be expected to submit. They would resist it, and thus we should be involved in a quarrel, on grounds, to say the least of them, exceedingly doubtful, which it was most desirable to avoid. But if his measure were adopted, and all British subjects not heretofore naturalized were excluded from our ships, we should be in a situation to resist their whole practice of impressment, as applicable to our ships, on the most clear and solid grounds; and thus cut up the evil by the roots. We shall be able to say to them "we have none of your

'subjects on board of our ships, no persons to 'whose service you can claim a right, and there-'fore on board of our ships you must not come." We shall then have drawn a clear line of demarcation which we shall be able and I trust ever willing to defend. I can assure the honorable gentleman that I for one will go as far and stand as long in its defence as any one who hears me. Let us once exclude British subjects not already naturalized from our ships, and thus deprive that Government of all fair pretence for sending their officers on board, and I for one will join in resisting to every extremity this practice, which will then assume the character of an undisguised attack on our rights, and even on our independence. But it cannot have that character, while we receive their subjects into our merchant vessels, however liable it may be to occasional abuse. I wish in this particular, as in every other, to put ourselves perfectly on the right side, so as to avoid the contest if we can, and if we cannot, to begin it with justice clearly on our side; and this, Mr. President, I consider as one of the best effects of my motion, and perhaps its strongest recommendation.

When Mr. HARPER had concluded, the Senate adjourned.

FRIDAY, April 5.

Mr. FROMENTIN presented the memorial of William Garrard, and others, land commissioners, in the western district of the Territory of Orleans, now State of Louisiana, praying compensation for their services, as stated in the memorial; which was read, and referred to a select committee.

Messrs. FROMENTIN, BROWN, and MORROW, were appointed the committee.

Mr. ROBERTS presented the memorial of a large number of manufacturers and mechanics of the city of Philadelphia, praying the tariff of duties recommended by the Secretary of the Treasury may be imposed for the encouragement and protection of domestic manufactures, for reasons stated in the memorial; which was read, and referred to the Committee on Manufactures.

Mr. TAIT, from the Committee on Naval Affairs, to whom was referred the bill entitled "An act making appropriations for the support of the Navy of the United States for the year 1816," reported it without amendment.

Mr. VARNUM, from the Militia Committee, to whom was referred the bill entitled "An act to increase the pensions of invalids in certain cases, for the relief of invalids of the militia, and for the appointment of pension agents in those States where there is no commissioner of loans," reported it without amendment.

Mr. ROBERTS, from the committee to whom was referred the bill entitled "An act directing the discharge of Moses Lewis from imprisonment," reported it without amendment.

The Senate resumed the consideration of the resolution submitted the 3d instant, approving the alterations suggested for the enlargement of the Senate room, and the better arrangement of offices of the Senate; and agreed thereto.

The bill for adjusting the claims to land and establishing a land office for the district of lands lying east of the Mississippi river, and island of New Orleans, was read the second time.

The Senate resumed the bill to ascertain and establish the western boundary of the tract reserved for satisfying the military bounties allowed to the officers and soldiers of the Virginia line, on Continental Establishment; and, on motion by Mr. MORROW, the consideration thereof was further postponed until Thursday the 18th instant.

Mr. BROWN, from the committee to whom was referred the bill entitled "An act for the relief of certain purchasers of public lands in the Mississippi Territory," reported it without amendment.

Mr. CAMPBELL, from the committee appointed on so much of the Message of the President of the United States as relates to Finance and an Uniform National Currency, to whom was referred the memorial of the Bible Society of Philadelphia, made a report, together with the following resolution:

Resolved, That the prayer of the memorialists ought not to be granted.

The report and resolution were read.

Mr. CAMPBELL, from the same committee, to whom was referred the petition of John G. Gottsberger, of the city of New York, made a report, together with the following resolution:

Resolved, That the petitioner have leave to withdraw his petition.

The report and resolution were read.

The Senate resumed the consideration of the bill for establishing a system of navigation for the United States; and on the question, "Shall this bill be engrossed and read a third time?" it was determined in the affirmative.

The Senate resumed, as in Committee of the Whole, the consideration of the bill providing for the increase of the salaries of certain officers of the Government; and on motion, by Mr. TALBOT, the further consideration thereof was postponed until Thursday next.

The Senate resumed, as in Committee of the Whole, the consideration of the bill entitled "An act for the benefit of the widow and children of Robert Fulton, deceased," together with the amendment reported thereto by the select committee, and the amendment having been agreed to with further amendments, the PRESIDENT reported the bill to the House accordingly; and the amendments having been concurred in, on the question, "Shall this bill be engrossed and read a third time?" it was determined in the affirmative.

Mr. HARPER withdrew the motion, submitted the 4th instant, for excluding foreigners from the naval and merchant service of the United States, and for compelling merchant vessels of the United States to have on board a certain number of apprentices.

The Senate resumed, as in Committee of the Whole, the consideration of the bill to provide more effectually for the payment of specie by the several banks within the District of Columbia; and the consideration thereof was further postponed until to-morrow.

The Senate resumed, as in Committee of the Whole, the consideration of the resolution for a proposed amendment to the Constitution of the United States, for the removal of the judges.

On motion, by Mr. MASON, of New Hampshire, that the further consideration thereof be postponed until the first Monday in July next, it was determined in the affirmative—yeas 19, nays 7, as follows:

YEAS—Messrs. Barbour, Barry, Brown, Campbell, Daggett, Dana, Fromentin, Gaillard, Goldsborough, Hunter, King, Mason of New Hampshire, Morrow, Ruggles, Talbot, Tait, Thompson, Varnum, and Williams.

NAYS—Messrs. Chace, Condit, Lacock, Macon, Roberts, Sanford, and Turner.

SATURDAY, April 6.

On motion, by Mr. TALBOT, the committee to whom were referred the petitions of John Longdon, and others, members of the Mechanics' Relief Society of Alexandria, were discharged from the further consideration thereof respectively.

The Senate resumed the consideration of the report of the committee to whom was referred the memorial of the Bible Society of Philadelphia. Whereupon,

Resolved, That the prayer of the memorialists ought not to be granted.

The Senate resumed the consideration of the report of the committee to whom was referred the petition of John G. Gottsberger, of the city of New York. Whereupon,

Resolved, That the petitioner have leave to withdraw his petition.

The Senate resumed, as in Committee of the Whole, the consideration of the bill for dividing the State of Pennsylvania into two judicial districts; and on motion, by Mr. LACOCK, it was recommitted to a select committee, further to consider and report thereon, and Messrs. LACOCK, MASON, of New Hampshire, and DAGGETT, were appointed the committee.

The Senate resumed, as in Committee of the Whole, the consideration of the joint resolution authorizing the President of the Senate and Speaker of the House of Representatives to adjourn their respective Houses, on the 22d day of April, 1816; and, on motion, by Mr. LACOCK, the further consideration thereof was postponed until Saturday next.

The Senate resumed, as in Committee of the Whole, the consideration of the bill entitled "An act for organizing the general staff, and making further provision for the Army of the United States; and on motion, by Mr. TICHENOR, the further consideration thereof was postponed until Tuesday next.

The Senate resumed, as in Committee of the Whole, the consideration of the joint resolution, directing medals to be struck, and, together with the thanks of Congress, presented to Major General Harrison and Governor Shelby, and for other purposes; and on motion, by Mr. BARBOUR, the further consideration thereof was postponed to, and made the order of the day for Saturday next.

The bill for the benefit of the widow and children of Robert Fulton, deceased, was read a third time; and on the question, "Shall this bill pass?" it was determined in the affirmative—yeas 16, nays 6, as follows:

YEAS—Messrs. Barbour, Condit, Daggett, Dana, Gaillard, Goldsborough, Gore, Horsey, King, Macon, Morrow, Roberts, Sanford, Tichenor, Turner, and Williams.

NAYS—Messrs. Barry, Lacock, Talbot, Thompson, Varnum, and Wilson.

The bill to establish a system of navigation for the United States, was read a third time, and passed.

The PRESIDENT communicated a letter from the Commissioner of the General Land Office, relating to a report of the commissioners on claims for lands in the western land district of the State of Louisiana, transmitted to the House of Representatives; and the letter was read.

MONDAY, April 8.

MR. ROBERTS presented the memorial and remonstrance of Thomas M. Longstreth and others, manufacturers of paper-hangings in the city of Philadelphia, praying that in lieu of the duty of one cent per pound on whiting, as proposed in the contemplated tariff, a moderate ad valorem duty may be imposed, if any impost on that article shall be deemed expedient; for reasons stated in the memorial; which was read, and referred to a committee.

The Senate resumed, as in Committee of the Whole, the bill to provide more effectually for the payment of specie by the several banks within the District of Columbia; and on motion, by Mr. ROBERTS, the further consideration thereof was postponed until Monday next.

The Senate resumed the consideration of the report of the Committee on Military Affairs, to whom was referred the petition of the representatives of Ignace Delino. Whereupon,

Resolved, That the petition of the representatives of Ignace Delino is reasonable, and ought to be granted.

Resolved, That provision should be made for ascertaining with precision the amount of losses sustained by the said Ignace Delino.

The Senate resumed, as in Committee of the Whole, the consideration of the bill entitled "An act for the relief of the heirs of George Nebinger," together with the amendments reported thereto by the select committee; and the amendments having been agreed to, the PRESIDENT reported the bill to the House accordingly, and the amendments were concurred in, and on the question, "Shall the amendments be engrossed, and the bill read a third time as amended?" it was determined in the affirmative.

Mr. LACOCK, from the committee to whom was referred the bill entitled "An act making appropriations for the support of Government for the year 1816," reported it with amendments, which were read.

The engrossed bill, making appropriation for the construction of roads and canals, was read a third time.

On motion, by Mr. MASON, of New Hampshire, that the further consideration thereof be postponed until the first Monday in July next, it was determined in the affirmative—yeas 18, nays 9, as follows:

YEAS—Messrs. Barry, Chace, Condit, Daggett, Gaillard, Gore, Hunter, King, Macon, Mason of New Hampshire, Roberts, Sanford, Talbot, Tait, Thompson, Turner, Varnum, and Williams.

NAYS—Messrs. Barbour, Brown, Dana, Fromentin, Horsey, Lacock, Morrow, Ruggles, and Wilson.

Mr. FROMENTIN, from the committee to whom the subject was referred, reported a bill for settling the compensation of the commissioners, clerk, and translator of the board for land claims in the western district of the Territory of Orleans, now State of Louisiana; and the bill was read, and passed to the second reading.

The Senate resumed, as in Committee of the Whole, the bill entitled "An act to alter and amend the law of costs;" and, on motion by Mr. TALBOT, the further consideration thereof was postponed until the first Monday in July next.

Mr. FROMENTIN, from the committee to whom the subject was referred, reported a bill authorizing the sale of lots owned by the United States, in the city of New Orleans, and for other purposes; and the bill was read, and passed to the second reading.

The Senate resumed, as in Committee of the Whole, the consideration of the bill entitled "An act for the relief of Thomas and John Clifford, Elisha Fisher, and Company, Thomas Clifford, and Thomas Clifford and Son;" and the bill having been amended, the PRESIDENT reported it to the House accordingly; and the amendment having been concurred in, on the question, "Shall the amendment be engrossed, and the bill read a third time as amended?" it was determined in the negative.

Mr. CAMPBELL, from the committee appointed on so much of the Message of the President of the United States as relates to Finance and an Uniform National Currency, to whom was referred the bill entitled "An act supplementary to the act to provide additional revenues for defraying the expenses of Government and maintaining the public credit, by laying a direct tax upon the United States, and to provide for assessing and collecting the same," reported it with amendments, which were read.

A message from the House of Representatives informed the Senate that the House have passed a resolution requesting the honorable Nathan Sanford, a member of the Senate, may be permitted to attend before the committee of the House of Representatives, appointed to inquire into the official conduct of Judge Tallmadge, to be examined touching the subjects contained in a report relating to the alledged misconduct of Judge Tallmadge, in his office, as one of the Judges of the District Court for the State of New York. They have passed a bill entitled "An act to regulate the duties on imports and tonnage;" in which they request the concurrence of the Senate.

The bill last brought up for concurrence was read, and passed to the second reading.

The PRESIDENT communicated a report of the Secretary for the Department of War, made in obedience to the resolution of the Senate of the third instant, directing him to lay before the Senate a statement of the sums expended in the purchase or manufacture of arms and military equipments for the militia, in pursuance of the act of the 23d of April, 1808, entitled "An act making provision for arming and equipping the whole body of the militia of the United States;" and also a statement of the arms and military equipments, which have been so provided, and of the distribution thereof. And the report was read.

Mr. TICHENOR submitted the following motion for consideration:

Resolved, That the Secretary of the War Department be directed to lay before the Senate, with as little delay as possible, a statement of the Military Establishment of the United States for the year 1796, therein distinguishing the general staff, with the expense of the said staff the whole year; and a like statement for the years 1791, 1794, 1798, 1808, 1809, 1813, and 1815, respectively.

The Senate resumed, as in Committee of the Whole, the consideration of the bill for the relief of Isaac Briggs; and, on motion by Mr. TALBOT, the further consideration thereof was postponed until Monday next.

TUESDAY, April 9.

Mr. BARBOUR, from the Committee on Military Affairs, to whom the subject was referred, reported a bill for the relief of the legal representatives of Ignace Chalmet Delino, deceased; and the bill was read, and passed to the second reading.

Mr. VARNUM, from the joint committee of the Senate and House of Representatives, appointed to inquire into the expediency of making certain alterations in the mode of transacting the business of Congress, recommend the following resolutions:

Resolved, That, on the adjournment of any Congress, the unfinished business, to wit, bills, resolutions, and reports of committees, shall remain at the next session of the same Congress in the same situation they were at the time of the adjournment.

Resolved, That it shall be the duty of the Clerks of the respective Houses to keep a docket of the business in the order in which it is presented; and to preserve all the documents and papers in relation to it; and it shall be the duty of the proper officers to preserve for the use of the Houses, and left upon the tables of the members, so that they may be ready for re-delivery and use at the ensuing session of the same Congress.

The bill entitled "An act to regulate the duties on imports and tonnage," was read the second time, and referred to the Committee on Finance and an Uniform National Currency.

The Senate proceeded to consider the resolution of the House of Representatives requesting the attendance of the honorable Nathan Sanford, a member of the Senate, before the committee of that House, for the purpose of giving his testimony in the matter under examination of the said committee, concerning the alledged misconduct of Matthias B. Tallmadge, one of the Judges of the District Court for the State of New York.

Whereupon, Mr. KING submitted the following motion for consideration:

Resolved, That the Senate, in compliance with the resolution of the House of Representatives of yesterday, do allow the attendance of the honorable Nathan Sanford, a member of this House, before the committee of the House of Representatives, for the purpose of giving his testimony in the matter under examination of the said committee, concerning the alledged misconduct of Matthias B. Tallmadge, one of the Judges of the District Court for the State of New York.

Mr. LACOCK, from the committee to whom the subject was referred, reported a bill relative to the transportation and opening of the mail, in certain cases; and the bill was read; and on the question, "Shall this bill be read the second time?" it was determined in the negative.

The amendments to the bill entitled "An act for the relief of the heirs of George Nebinger," having been reported by the committee correctly engrossed, the bill was read a third time as amended.

Resolved, That this bill pass with amendments.

The title was amended by adding thereto, " and of Landon Carter."

The Senate resumed, as in Committee of the Whole, the consideration of the bill entitled "An act making appropriations for the support of Government for the year 1816," together with the amendments reported thereto by the select committee; and the amendments having been agreed to, with amendments, the PRESIDENT reported the bill to the House accordingly; and the amendments having been concurred in, on the question, " Shall the amendments be engrossed, and the bill read a third time, as amended?" it was determined in the affirmative.

A message from the House of Representatives informed the Senate that the House have passed a bill entitled "An act for the more convenient arrangement of the times and places of holding the circuit courts of the United States for the districts of South Carolina and Georgia;" in which bill they request the concurrence of the Senate.

The bill last mentioned was read, and passed to the second reading.

Mr. CAMPBELL, from the committee appointed on so much of the Message of the President of the United States as relates to Finance and an Uniform National Currency, to whom was referred the petition of Talcott Wolcott, made a report, together with the following resolution:

Resolved, That the prayer of the petitioner ought not to be granted.

The Senate resumed, as in Committee of the Whole, the consideration of the bill to authorize the Secretary of the Treasury to subscribe, in behalf of the United States, for —— shares in the capital stock of the Chesapeake and Delaware Canal Company; and, on motion by Mr. VARNUM, the further consideration thereof was postponed until the first Monday in July next.

The Senate resumed the consideration of the motion made the 8th instant, directing the Secretary of the War Department to lay before the Senate a statement of the Military Establishment of the United States, for the years 1788, 1791, 1794, 1798, 1803, 1809, 1813, and 1815, respectively; and agreed thereto.

Mr. VARNUM communicated sundry documents to be filed with the petition of Sarah Jarvis, and others, praying payment of the balance which may be found due to Leonard Jarvis, deceased, for services during the Revolutionary war.

The Senate resumed, as in Committee of the Whole, the consideration of the bill concerning the District of Columbia; and on the question, "Shall this bill be engrossed and read a third time?" it was determined in the affirmative.

The Senate resumed, as in Committee of the Whole, the consideration of the bill, entitled "An act for the relief of certain claimants to lands in the district of Vincennes," and it passed to a third reading.

Mr. CAMPBELL gave notice that he should ask leave to bring in a bill to authorize the State of Tennessee to issue grants and perfect titles on certain entries and locations of lands therein described.

Mr. DANA gave notice that he should ask leave to bring in a bill concerning the maritime precincts of the United States.

The Senate resumed, as in Committee of the Whole, the consideration of the bill concerning the entry of vessels at the port of Middletown; and on the question, "Shall this bill be engrossed and read a third time?" it was determined in the affirmative."

The Senate resumed, as in Committee of the Whole, the consideration of the resolution for printing the laws relative to naturalization; and on the question, "Shall this resolution be engrossed and read a third time?" it was determined in the affirmative.

A message from the House of Representatives announced to the Senate the death of the Hon. RICHARD STANFORD, a member of the House of Representatives from the State of North Carolina, and that his funeral will take place to-morrow at 12 o'clock. Whereupon, on motion by Mr. MACON,

Resolved, unanimously, That the Senate will attend the funeral of the Hon. RICHARD STANFORD, late a member of the House of Representatives from the State of North Carolina, to-morrow at 12 o'clock; and, as a testimony of respect for the memory of the deceased, they will go into mourning, and wear a black crape round the left arm for thirty days.

MILITARY SERVICES.

The Senate resumed, as in Committee of the Whole, the consideration of the bill, entitled "An act making further provision for military services during the late war, and for other purposes," together with the amendments reported thereto by the select committee.

On the question to agree to the first amendment proposed, amended as follows:

Be it further enacted, That donations of land be granted to all the officers of the regular army who were in service, and who have been disbanded in reducing the army conformably to the act of third March, 1815, and who shall not have been reinstated in the army by the seventeenth of May next, to wit: to each Major General, one thousand two hundred and eighty acres; to each Brigadier General, one thousand one hundred and twenty acres; to each Colonel and Lieutenant Colonel, nine hundred and sixty acres; to each Major, eight hundred acres; to each Captain, six hundred and forty acres; to each subaltern, four hundred and eighty acres; and to officers of the medical and other staff, who have no rank, in proportion to their pay according to the scale aforesaid.

It was determined in the negative—yeas 10, nays 12, as follows:

YEAS—Messrs. Barry, Brown, Chace, Condit, Fromentin, Gaillard, Lacock, Macon, Ruggles, and Turner.

NAYS—Messrs. Barbour, Daggett, Dana, Gore, Horsey, Hunter, King, Mason of New Hampshire, Morrow, Talbot, Tait, and Varnum.

WEDNESDAY, April 10.

The Senate assembled, and adjourned to 11 o'clock to-morrow morning.

THURSDAY, April 11.

The bill for settling the compensation of the commissioners, clerk, and translator, of the board for land claims in the western district of the Territory of Orleans, now State of Louisiana, was read the second time.

The bill authorizing the sale of lots owned by the United States, in the city of New Orleans, and for other purposes, was read the second time.

The bill for the relief of the legal representatives of Ignace Chalmet Delino, deceased, was read the second time.

The resolutions reported from the joint committee appointed to inquire into the expediency of making certain alterations in the mode of transacting the business of Congress, were read the second time.

The Senate resumed the consideration of the report of the committee, to whom was referred the petition of Talcott Wolcott; whereupon,

Resolved, That the prayer of the petitioner ought not to be granted.

The bill entitled "An act for the more convenient arrangement of the times and places of holding the circuit courts of the United States for the districts of South Carolina and Georgia," was read the second time.

Mr. BROWN, from the committee to whom was

referred the bill, entitled "An act making further provision for settling claims to land in the Territory of Illinois," reported it with amendments; which were read.

Mr. BARBOUR, from the Committee on Military Affairs, to whom was referred the bill, entitled "An act making appropriations for the support of the Military Establishment of the United States, for the year 1816," reported it with an amendment; which was read.

Mr. RUGGLES, from the committee to whom was referred the bill, entitled "An act supplemental to the act, entitled 'An act regulating and defining the duties of the Judges of the Territory of Illinois, and for vesting in the courts of the Territory of Indiana a jurisdiction in chancery cases arising in the said Territory," reported it with amendments; which were read.

A message from the House of Representatives informed the Senate that the House have passed a bill, entitled "An act for the relief of Charles Ross and Samuel Breck, surviving executors of John Ross, deceased;" a bill, entitled "An act for the relief of William Hamon;" a bill, entitled "An act for the relief of Joseph Wheaton;" the bill, entitled "An act for the relief of the widow and minor children of Zacquill Morgan, late a Captain in the United States Army;" a bill, entitled "An act for the relief of Manassah Miner;" a bill, entitled "An act for the relief of a company of the twentieth brigade of Virginia militia, commanded by Captain Jonathan Walmsley;" a bill, entitled "An act for the relief of Thomas B. Farish;" a bill, entitled "An act for the relief of Charles Todd;" a bill, entitled "An act for the relief of William Flood;" a bill, entitled "An act for the relief of Peter Audrain;" a bill, entitled "An act for the relief of Ephraim Shaler;" a bill, entitled "An act for the relief of Patrick O'Flyng, Abigail O'Flyng, and Edmund O'Flyng;" a bill, entitled "An act for the relief of Joseph Wilson;" a bill, entitled "An act to authorize the sale of lands forfeited to the United States, in the district of Jeffersonville, at the land office in said district;" a bill, entitled "An act for the relief of Thomas Farrer, William Young, William Moseley, and William Leech;" a bill, entitled "An act for the payment of the Militia in the case therein mentioned;" a bill, entitled "An act for the relief of Joseph Wilson;" a bill, entitled "An act for the relief of Paul D. Butler;" a bill, entitled "An act authorizing the payment for the court-house of Hamilton, in the State of Ohio;" a bill, entitled "An act for the relief of Rufus S. Reed, and Daniel Dobbins;" a bill, entitled "An act for the relief of the President and Directors of the Washington Bridge Company;" a bill, entitled "An act to fix the commissions of the collectors of the direct tax and internal duties, and to revive and continue in force 'An act further to provide for the collection of duties on imports and tonnage;" a bill, entitled "An act for the relief of Asher Palmer;" a bill, entitled "An act for the relief of the supervisors of the county of Clinton, in the State of New York;" a bill, entitled "An act for the relief of John Crosby, and

John Crosby, jun.;" a bill, entitled "An act for the relief of Taylor & McNeal, Evans & McNeal, and Henry and John McLeister;" a bill, entitled "An act for the relief of certain owners of goods entered at Hampden, in the District of Maine;" a bill, entitled "An act declaring the consent of Congress to acts of the State of South Carolina, authorizing the City Council of Charleston to impose and collect a duty on the tonnage of vessels from foreign ports, and to acts of the State of Georgia, authorizing the imposition and collection of a duty on the tonnage of vessels in the ports of Savannah and St. Mary's;" a bill, entitled "An act to increase the compensations now allowed by law to inspectors, measurers, weighers, and gaugers, employed in the collection of the customs;" a bill, entitled "An act declaring the assent of Congress to an act of the General Assembly of the State of Virginia;" also, a "Resolution requiring the Secretary of State to compile and print, once in every two years, a register of all officers and agents, civil, military, and naval, in the service of the United States;" in which bills and resolution they request the concurrence of the Senate.

The thirty bills, and the resolution last brought up for concurrence, were read, and severally passed to the second reading.

The bill entitled "An act for the relief of certain claimants to lands in the district of Vincennes," was read a third time, and passed.

The bill concerning the District of Columbia having been reported by the committee correctly engrossed, on motion, by Mr. DAGGETT, the further consideration thereof was postponed until to-morrow.

The bill concerning the entry of vessels at the port of Middletown, was read a third time, and passed.

The resolution for printing the laws relative to naturalization, was read a third time, and passed.

The amendments to the bill, entitled "An act making appropriations for the support of Government for the year 1816," having been reported by the committee correctly engrossed, the bill was read a third time, and the blank filled.

Resolved, That this bill pass with amendments.

Mr. LACOCK gave notice that he should ask leave to bring in a bill making an appropriation for the compensation of the commissioner and clerk, authorized by an act, entitled "An act to authorize the payment for property lost, captured, or destroyed by the enemy, while in the military service of the United States, and for other purposes."

The following Message was received from the PRESIDENT OF THE UNITED STATES:

To the Senate and House of
　　Representatives of the United States:

With a view to the more convenient arrangement of the important and growing business connected with the grant of exclusive rights to inventors and authors, I recommend the establishment of a distinct office within the Department of State, to be charged therewith, under a director, with a salary adequate to his services, and with the privilege of franking communications by mail from and to the office. I recommend, also, that further restraints be imposed on the issue of patents to wrongful claimants, and further guards provided against fraudulent exactions of fees by persons possessed of patents.

JAMES MADISON.

APRIL 11, 1816.

The Message was read.

Mr. DANA asked and obtained leave to bring in a bill concerning the maritime precincts of the United States; and the bill was read, and passed to the second reading.

Mr. CAMPBELL asked and obtained leave to bring in a bill to authorize the State of Tennessee to issue grants and perfect titles on certain entries and locations of lands therein described; and the bill was read, and passed to the second reading.

The PRESIDENT communicated a report of the Secretary for the Department of War, exhibiting the names of the clerks employed in the several offices attached to that Department, and the sums given to each for the year 1815; and the report was read.

The Senate resumed, as in Committee of the Whole, the consideration of the bill, entitled "An act making further provision for military services during the last war, and for other purposes, together with the amendments reported thereto by the select committee; and the amendments having been disagreed to, the PRESIDENT reported the bill to the House; and on the question, "Shall this bill be read a third time?" it was determined in the affirmative—yeas 15, nays 9, as follows:

YEAS—Messrs. Barbour, Barry, Brown, Condit, Fromentin, Lacock, Macon, Mason of Virginia, Morrow, Roberts, Ruggles, Sanford, Talbot, Turner, and Williams.

NAYS—Messrs. Daggett, Gaillard, Goldsborough, Hunter, Tait, Thompson, Tichenor, Varnum, and Wells.

INCREASE OF SALARIES.

The Senate resumed, as in Committe of the Whole, the consideration of the bill providing for the increase of the salaries of the officers of Government therein mentioned.

On motion, by Mr. TALBOT, to strike out from line 37 to line 79, of the bill, comprehending all the judges, it was determined in the negative—yeas 5, nays 20, as follows:

YEAS—Messrs. Barbour, Barry, Mason of Virginia, Talbot, and Turner.

NAYS—Messrs. Brown, Chace, Condit, Daggett, Dana, Fromentin, Gaillard, Goldsborough, Hunter, Lacock, Macon, Morrow, Roberts, Ruggles, Sanford, Tait, Thompson, Varnum, Wells, and Williams.

The bill having been amended, the PRESIDENT resumed the Chair, and Mr. BARRY reported the bill to the House accordingly; and on the question, "Shall this bill be engrossed and read a third time?" it was determined in the negative—yeas 12, nays 14, as follows:

YEAS—Messrs. Barry, Brown, Daggett, Fromentin, Hunter, Lacock, Macon, Morrow, Roberts, Tait, Turner, and Williams.

NAYS—Messrs. Barbour, Chace, Condit, Dana, Gaillard, Goldsborough, Mason of New Hampshire, Mason of Virginia, Ruggles, Sanford, Talbot, Thompson, Varnum, and Wells.

FRIDAY, April 12.

Mr. GOLDSBOROUGH presented the petition of Bernard O'Neil, and also the petition of William F. Abbott and others, praying compensation for the loss of property destroyed by the enemy during the late war, as stated in the petitions, which were read, and referred to the Committee on Military Affairs.

The bill entitled "An act authorizing the payment for the court-house of Hamilton, in the State of Ohio," was read the second time, and referred to the Committee on Military Affairs.

The bill entitled "An act for the payment of the militia in the case therein mentioned," was read the second time, and referred to the committee last mentioned.

The bill entitled "An act for the relief of the supervisors of the county of Clinton, in the State of New York," was read the second time, and referred to the same committee.

The bill entitled "An act for the relief of a company of the twentieth brigade of Virginia militia, commanded by Captain Jonathan Walmsley," was read the second time, and referred to the same committee.

The bill entitled "An act for the relief of Patrick O'Flyng, and Abigail O'Flyng, and Edmund O'Flyng," was read the second time, and referred to the same committee.

The bill entitled "An act for the relief of William Flood," was read the second time, and referred to the same committee.

The bill entitled "An act for the relief of Joseph Wilson," was read the second time, and referred to the same committee.

The bill entitled "An act for the relief of the President and Directors of the Washington Bridge Company," was read the second time, and referred to the same committee.

The bill entitled "An act for the relief of Thomas Ap Catesby Jones," was read the second time, and referred to the Committee on Naval Affairs.

The bill entitled "An act for the relief of Rufus S. Reed and Daniel Dobbins," was read the second time, and referred to the committee last mentioned.

The bill entitled "An act for the relief of Taylor & McNeal, Evans & McNeal, and Henry and John McLeister," was read the second time, and referred to the same committee.

The bill entitled "An act for the relief of John Crosby and John Crosby, jr.," was read the second time, and referred to the same committee.

The bill entitled "An act for the relief of Asher Palmer," was read the second time, and referred to the same committee.

The bill entitled "An act to authorize the sale of lands forfeited to the United States in the district of Jeffersonville, at the land office in said district," was read the second time, and referred to the committee on the memorial of the Legislative Council and House of Representatives of the Mississippi Territory.

The bill entitled "An act for the relief of Peter Audrain," was read the second time, and referred to the committee last mentioned.

The bill entitled "An act to increase the commissions now allowed by law to inspectors, measurers, weighers, and gaugers, employed in the collection of the customs," was read the second time, and referred to the Committee on Finance and an Uniform National Currency.

The bill entitled "An act to fix the commissions of the collectors of the direct tax and internal duties, and to revive and continue in force 'An act further to provide for the collection of duties on imports and tonnage,'" was read the second time, and referred to the committee last mentioned.

The bill entitled "An act declaring the assent of Congress to an act of the General Assembly of the State of Virginia," was read the second time, and referred to the Committee on Roads and Canals.

The bill entitled "An act for the relief of Joseph Wheaton," was read the second time, and referred to a select committee; and Messrs. DAGGETT, SANFORD, and GOLDSBOROUGH, were appointed the committee.

The bill entitled "An act for the relief of William Hamon," was read the second time, and referred to the committee last mentioned.

The bill entitled "An act for the relief of the widow and minor children of Zacquill Morgan, late a captain in the United States' Army," was read the second time, and referred to the same committee.

The bill entitled "An act for the relief of Charles Ross and Samuel Brook, surviving executors of John Ross, deceased," was read the second time, and referred to the same committee.

The bill entitled "An act for the relief of Manasseh Miner," was read the second time, and referred to the same committee.

The bill entitled "An act for the relief of Thomas B. Farish," was read the second time, and referred to the same committee.

The bill entitled "An act for the relief of Charles Todd," was read the second time, and referred to the same committee.

The bill entitled "An act for the relief of Ephraim Shaler," was read the second time, and referred to the same committee.

The bill entitled "An act for the relief of Thomas Farrer, William Young, William Moseley, and William Leech," was read the second time, and referred to the same committee.

The bill entitled "An act for the relief of Paul D. Butler," was read the second time, and referred to the same committee.

The bill entitled "An act declaring the consent of Congress to acts of the State of South Carolina, authorizing the City Council of Charleston o impose and collect a duty on the tonnage of essels from foreign ports; and to acts of the

State of Georgia, authorizing the imposition and collection of a duty on the tonnage of vessels in the ports of Savannah and St. Mary's," was read the second time, and referred to the same committee.

The bill entitled "An act for the relief of certain owners of goods entered at Hampden, in the District of Maine," was read the second time, and referred to the same committee.

The resolution requiring the Secretary of State to compile and print, once in every two years, a register of all officers and agents, civil, military, and naval, in the service of the United States, was read the second time.

The bill concerning the maritime precincts of the United States, was read the second time.

The Senate resumed the consideration of the motion submitted the 9th instant, by Mr. KING, which was amended and agreed to as follows:

Resolved, That the Senate, in compliance with the resolution of the House of Representatives of the 8th instant, do allow the attendance of the honorable NATHAN SANFORD, a member of this House, before the committee of the House of Representatives, for the purpose of giving his testimony in the matter under examination of the said committee concerning the alleged misconduct of Matthias B. Tallmadge, one of the judges of the district court for the State of New York.

The bill concerning the District of Columbia, (authorizing the introduction of slaves into the District of Columbia, the property of persons coming to reside here,) was read a third time; and on the question, "Shall this bill pass?" it was determined in the negative—yeas 13, nays 16, as follows:

YEAS—Messrs. Barbour, Barry, Brown, Fromentin, Gaillard, Goldsborough, Lacock, Macon, Mason of Virginia, Roberts, Tait, Turner, and Williams.

NAYS—Messrs. Condit, Daggett, Dana, Gore, Horsey, Hunter, Mason of New Hampshire, Morrow, Ruggles, Sanford, Talbot, Thompson, Tichenor, Varnum, Wells, and Wilson.

The bill entitled "An act making further provision for military services during the late war, and for other purposes," was read a third time; and on the question, "Shall this bill pass?" it was determined in the negative—yeas 12, nays 13, as follows:

YEAS—Messrs. Barbour, Barry, Condit, Fromentin, Lacock, Macon, Morrow, Sanford, Talbot, Turner, Williams, and Wilson.

NAYS—Messrs. Daggett, Gaillard, Goldsborough, Gore, Horsey, Hunter, Mason of New Hampshire, Roberts, Tait, Thompson, Tichenor, Varnum, and Wells.

On motion of Mr. WELLS, to reconsider the vote on the passage of the bill last mentioned, it was determined in the affirmative—yeas 18, nays 12, as follows:

YEAS—Messrs. Barbour, Barry, Campbell, Chace, Condit, Fromentin, Gaillard, Lacock, Macon, Mason of Virginia, Morrow, Ruggles, Sanford, Talbot, Turner, Wells, Williams, and Wilson.

NAYS—Messrs. Daggett, Goldsborough, Gore, Horsey, Hunter, King, Mason of New Hampshire, Roberts, Tait, Thompson, Tichenor, and Varnum.

The question recurring, "Shall this bill pass?" it was determined in the affirmative—yeas 17, nays 14, as follows:

YEAS—Messrs. Barbour, Barry, Brown, Campbell, Chace, Condit, Fromentin, Lacock, Macon, Mason of Virginia, Morrow, Ruggles, Sanford, Talbot, Turner, Williams, and Wilson.

NAYS—Messrs. Daggett, Gaillard, Goldsborough, Gore, Horsey, Hunter, King, Mason of New Hampshire, Roberts, Tait, Thompson, Tichenor, Varnum, and Wells.

So it was *Resolved*, That this bill pass.

Mr. CAMPBELL, from the committee to whom was referred the bill, entitled "An act to regulate the duties on imports and tonnage," reported it with amendments, which were read.

A message from the House of Representatives informed the Senate that the House have passed a bill, entitled "An act for the relief of William Crawford, Frederick Bates, and William Garrard;" a bill, entitled "An act authorizing the payment of a sum of money to James Levins;" a bill, entitled "An act for the free importation of stereotype plates, and to encourage the printing and gratuitous distribution of the Scriptures by the Bible Societies within the United States;" a bill, entitled "An act for the relief of the heirs of Alexander Roxburgh;" a bill, entitled "An act providing for the sale of the tract of land at the British fort at the Miami of the Lake, at the foot of the Rapids, and for other purposes;" a bill, entitled "An act providing for the sale of the tract of land at the lower rapids of Sandusky river;" a bill, entitled "An act providing for the distribution of one hundred thousand dollars among the captors of the Algerine vessels captured and restored to the Dey of Algiers;" a bill, entitled "An act to alter certain parts of the act providing for the government of the Territory of Missouri;" a bill, entitled "An act for the relief of Samuel Dick, William Bruce, and Asa Kitchell;" also, a bill, entitled "An act to increase the pension of William Munday;" with an amendment;—in which bills they request the concurrence of the Senate. They concur in the amendments of the Senate to the bill, entitled "An act making appropriations for the support of Government for the year 1816," except that which proposes to insert a new section to the bill, to which they disagree.

The Senate proceeded to consider their amendment to the bill last mentioned, disagreed to by the House of Representatives. Whereupon,

Resolved, That they recede therefrom.

The Senate proceeded to consider the amendment of the House of Representatives to the bill, entitled "An act to increase the pension of William Munday." Whereupon,

Resolved, That they disagree thereto.

Mr. LACOCK asked and obtained leave to bring in a bill making further appropriations for the year 1816; and the bill was read, and passed to the second reading.

The nine bills last brought up for concurrence were read, and severally passed to the second reading.

The Senate resumed, as in Committee of the

Whole, the consideration of the bill, entitled "An act to abolish the existing duties on spirits distilled within the United States, and to lay other duties in lieu of those at present imposed on licenses to distillers of spirituous liquors," together with the amendment reported thereto by the select committee. Mr. VARNUM was requested to take the Chair.

On motion by Mr. CAMPBELL, to strike out of section 4, line 7, the word *four*, and insert in lieu thereof *three*, it was determined in the negative— yeas 9, nays 20, as follows:

YEAS—Messrs. Barry, Campbell, Chace, Goldsborough, Macon, Morrow, Ruggles, Talbot, Williams.

NAYS—Messrs. Barbour, Brown, Condit, Daggett, Dana, Fromentin, Gaillard, Gore, Horsey, Hunter, King, Lacock, Mason of New Hampshire, Roberts, Tait, Thompson, Tichenor, Turner, Varnum, Wells.

The bill having been amended, the PRESIDENT resumed the Chair, and Mr. VARNUM reported it to the House, accordingly. And, on the question, "Shall the amendment be engrossed, and the bill read a third time as amended?" it was determined in the affirmative.

The Senate resumed, as in Committee of the Whole, the consideration of the bill, entitled "An act to enable the people of the Indiana Territory to form a constitution and State government, and for the admission of such State into the Union on an equal footing with the original States," together with the amendments reported thereto by the select committee; and the bill having been amended, the PRESIDENT reported it to the House, accordingly.

On motion by Mr. GOLDSBOROUGH, to strike out of section 3, lines 4 and 5, after the word "election," "and shall have paid a county or territorial tax," it was determined in the negative— yeas 9, nays 13, as follows:

YEAS—Messrs. Barry, Chace, Gaillard, Goldsborough, Macon, Talbot, Turner, Varnum, Williams.

NAYS—Messrs. Barbour, Brown, Campbell, Condit, Fromentin, Horsey, Hunter, Mason of New Hampshire, Morrow, Roberts, Ruggles, Tait, and Tichenor.

The amendments having been concurred in, on the question, "Shall the amendments be engrossed, and the bill read a third time as amended?" it was determined in the affirmative.

SATURDAY, April 13.

Mr. GORE presented the petition of Samuel Upton and Thomas Adams, praying to be discharged from the payment of certain bonds given for duties on the goods found in the stores at Castine, in the State of Massachusetts, upon the re-occupation of that place by the United States, under the Treaty of Peace, as stated in the petition; which was read, and referred to the Committee on Finance and an Uniform National Currency.

Mr. BARBOUR, from the Committee on Military Affairs, to whom was referred the bill, entitled "An act for the relief of Patrick and Abigail O'Flyng, and Edmund O'Flyng," reported it without amendment.

Mr. BROWN, from the committee to whom was referred the bill, entitled "An act authorizing the President of the United States to lease the Saline, near the Wabash river, for a term not exceeding seven years," reported it without amendment.

Mr. BARBOUR, from the committee to whom was referred the bill, entitled "An act for the relief of the President and Directors of the Washington Bridge Company," reported it with an amendment, which was read.

Mr. BARBOUR, from the same committee, to whom was referred the bill, entitled "An act for the relief of William Flood," reported it with an amendment, which was read.

Mr. BARBOUR, from the same committee, to whom was referred the bill, entitled "An act for the relief of Joseph Wilson," reported it with an amendment, which was read.

Mr. BARBOUR, from the same committee, to whom was referred the bill for the relief of a company of the 20th brigade of Virginia militia, commanded by Captain Jonathan Walmsley," reported it without amendment.

Mr. BARBOUR, from the same committee, to whom was referred the bill, entitled "An act authorizing the payment for the county court-house of Hamilton, in the State of Ohio," reported it with an amendment, which was read.

Mr. BARBOUR, from the same committee, to whom was referred the bill, entitled "An act for the relief of the supervisors of the county of Clinton, in the State of New York," reported it with an amendment, which was read.

Mr. DAGGETT, from the committee to whom was referred the bill, entitled "An act for the relief of the widow and minor children of Zacquill Morgan, late a captain in the United States' Army," reported it without amendment.

Mr. DAGGETT, from the same committee, to whom was referred the bill, entitled "An act for the relief of Joseph Wheaton," reported it without amendment.

Mr. DAGGETT, from the same committee, to whom was referred the bill, entitled "An act for the relief of Thomas Farrer, William Young, William Moseley, and William Leech," reported it with an amendment, which was read.

Mr. DAGGETT, from the same committee, to whom was referred the bill, entitled "An act for the relief of William Hamon," reported it without amendment.

Mr. DAGGETT, from the same committee, to whom was referred the bill, entitled "An act for the relief of Charles Ross and Samuel Breck, surviving executors of John Ross, deceased," reported it with amendments, which were read.

Mr. DAGGETT, from the committee to whom was referred the bill, entitled "An act for the relief of Manassah Miner," reported it with an amendment, which was read.

Mr. DAGGETT, from the same committee, to whom was referred the bill, entitled "An act for the relief of Paul D. Butler," reported it with an amendment, which was read.

Mr. DAGGETT, from the same committee, to whom was referred the bill, entitled "An act for the relief of Ephraim Shaler," reported it without amendment.

On motion by Mr. BARBOUR, the Committee on Military Affairs, to whom was referred the petition of William and Robert Patterson, of Baltimore, were discharged from the further consideration thereof.

The PRESIDENT communicated the memorial of Joseph Nourse, Register of the Treasury of the United States, praying an increase of compensation, as stated in the memorial, which was read, and referred to the committee to whom was referred, on the 12th instant, the bill, entitled "An act for the relief of Joseph Wheaton," to consider and report thereon by bill or otherwise.

The bill, entitled "An act to authorize the State of Tennessee to issue grants and perfect titles on certain entries and locations of lands therein described," was read the second time, and referred to the committee on the memorial of the Legislative Council and House of Representatives of the Mississippi Territory.

The bill making further appropriations for the year 1816, was read the second time.

The bill, entitled "An act to alter certain parts of the act providing for the government of the Missouri Territory," was read the second time, and referred to a select committee; and Messrs. MORROW, RUGGLES, and MASON of New Hampshire, were appointed the committee.

The bill, entitled "An act authorizing the payment of a sum of money to James Levins," was read the second time, and referred to the Committee on Naval Affairs.

The bill, entitled "An act providing for the distribution of one hundred thousand dollars among the captors of the Algerine vessels captured and restored to the Dey of Algiers," was read the second time, and referred to the committee last mentioned.

The bill, entitled "An act for the relief of William Crawford, Frederick Bates, and William Garrard," was read the second time, and referred to the committee on the memorial of the Legislative Council and House of Representatives of the Mississippi Territory.

The bill, entitled "An act providing for the sale of the tract of land at the Lower Rapids of Sandusky river," was read the second time, and referred to the committee last mentioned.

The bill, entitled "An act providing for the sale of a tract of land at the British fort at the Miami of the Lake, at the foot of the Rapids, and for other purposes," was read the second time, and referred to the same committee.

The bill, entitled "An act for the relief of Samuel Dick, William Bruce, and Asa Kitchell," was read the second time, and referred to the same committee.

The bill, entitled "An act for the relief of the heirs of Alexander Roxburgh," was read the second time, and referred to the committee to whom was referred the bill, entitled "An act for the relief of Joseph Wheaton," to consider and report thereon.

The bill, entitled "An act for the free importation of stereotype plates, and to encourage the printing and gratuitous distribution of the Scriptures by the Bible Societies within the United States," was read the second time, and referred to the Committee on Finance and an Uniform National Currency, to consider and report thereon.

The amendments to the bill, entitled "An act to enable the people of the Indiana Territory to form a constitution and State government, and for the admission of such State into the Union on an equal footing with the original States," having been reported by the committee correctly engrossed, the bill was read a third time as amended.

Resolved, That this bill pass with amendments.

The amendment to the bill, entitled "An act to abolish the existing duties on spirits distilled within the United States, and to lay other duties in lieu of those at present imposed on licenses to distillers of spirituous liquors," having been reported by the committee correctly engrossed, the bill was read a third time as amended.

Resolved, That this bill pass with an amendment.

Mr. BROWN, from the committee to whom the subject was referred, reported a bill to authorize the issuing of a grant to Major General Jackson for a tract of land; and the bill was read, and passed to the second reading.

A message from the House of Representatives informed the Senate that the House have passed a bill, entitled "An act authorizing the Comptroller of the Treasury to cancel certain export bonds executed by Caspar C. Schutte;" a bill, entitled "An act confirming the titles of certain purchasers of land who purchased from the Board of Trustees of the Vincennes University," a bill, entitled "An act for the relief of Thomas H. Boyle;" a bill, entitled "An act for the relief of Young King, a chief of the Seneca tribe of Indians;" a bill, entitled "An act granting to Amos Spafford the right of pre-emption;" a bill, entitled "An act rewarding the officers and crew of the Constitution for the capture of the British sloop of war Levant," a bill, entitled "An act concerning Pharaoh Farrow and others," the bill, entitled "An act for the relief of the widow and children of Charles Dolph, deceased;" a bill, entitled "An act authorizing the payment of a sum of money to John T. Courtney and Samuel Harrison, or their legal representatives;" and a bill, entitled "An act for the relief of Charles Levaux Trudeau;" in which bills they request the concurrence of the Senate. They have passed the bill, entitled "An act providing for the settlement of certain accounts against the Library of Congress, and for other purposes," with amendments, in which they request the concurrence of the Senate.

The ten bills last brought up for concurrence were read, and severally passed to the second reading.

On motion, by Mr. CAMPBELL, it was agreed that the consideration of the bill, entitled "An act to regulate the duties on imports and tonnage," together with the amendments reported thereto by the select committee, be made the order of the day for Monday next.

The Senate resumed, as in Committee of the Whole, the consideration of the joint resolution directing medals to be struck, and, together with the thanks of Congress, presented to Major General Harrison and Governor Shelby, and for other purposes.—Mr. VARNUM was requested to take the Chair.

On motion, by Mr. LACOCK, to amend the resolution by striking out therefrom "Major General William Henry Harrison," it was determined in the affirmative—yeas 13, nays 11, as follows:

YEAS—Messrs. Dana, Gaillard, Gore, Hunter, King, Lacock, Mason of New Hampshire, Roberts, Tait, Thompson, Tichenor, Turner, and Varnum.

NAYS—Messrs. Barbour, Barry, Condit, Horsey, Macon, Morrow, Ruggles, Talbot, Wells, Williams, and Wilson.

The resolution having been amended, on motion, by Mr. ROBERTS, the further consideration thereof was postponed until Monday next.

The Senate resumed, as in Committee of the Whole, the consideration of the joint resolution authorizing the President of the Senate and Speaker of the House of Representatives to adjourn their respective Houses on the 22d day of April, 1816, and on motion, by Mr. KING, the further consideration thereof was postponed until Saturday next.

The Senate resumed, as in Committee of the Whole, the consideration of the bill entitled "An act for organizing the general staff, and making further provision for the Army of the United States," and the bill having been amended the PRESIDENT reported it to the House accordingly; and on motion, by Mr. LACOCK, the further consideration thereof was postponed until Monday next.

The Senate resumed, as in Committee of the Whole, the consideration of the bill, entitled "An act for the liquidation of certain claims and for other purposes," together with the amendments reported thereto by the select committee; and the bill having been amended, the PRESIDENT reported it to the House accordingly.

On motion, by Mr. ROBERTS, to concur in the first amendment proposed, as amended as follows:

"Section 1, line 7, after 'casualty,' insert 'and in all cases where officers or agents of the militia, whether in the line or staff, may have accounts to settle with the Government of the United States, and difficulties shall arise under existing laws from loss of vouchers, or from unavoidable casualty."

It was determined in the negative—yeas 9, nays 18, as follows:

YEAS—Messrs. Barbour, Barry, Brown, Fromentin, Lacock, Morrow, Roberts, Talbot, and Williams.

NAYS—Messrs. Campbell, Chace, Condit, Daggett, Dana, Gaillard, Gore, Horsey, King, Macon, Mason of New Hampshire, Ruggles, Sanford, Tait, Thompson, Tichenor, Turner, and Varnum.

The other amendments having been concurred in, on the question "Shall the amendments be engrossed, and the bill read a third time as amended ?" it was determined in the negative.

DIRECT TAX.

The Senate resumed, as in Committee of the Whole, the consideration of the bill, entitled "An act supplementary to the act to provide additional revenues for defraying the expenses of Government, and maintaining the public credit, by laying a direct tax upon the United States, and to provide for assessing and collecting the same," together with the amendments reported thereto by the select committee; and the amendments having been agreed to, the President reported the bill to the House accordingly.

On the question to concur in the following amendment proposed.—Add to the end of the bill the following section:

"Sec. —. *Provided always and be it further enacted,* That the equalization and apportionment of the direct tax made in the year 1815, by the board of principal assessors for the State of Delaware, in virtue of the before recited act, entitled "An act, to provide additional revenues for defraying the expenses of Government and maintaining the public credit by laying a direct tax upon the United States, and to provide for the assessing and collecting the same," shall not be in force or have any effect as it relates to that State's quota of the direct tax imposed by the act of Congress passed the fifth day of March, 1816, or that shall be imposed by any subsequent act of Congress; and it shall be the duty of the said board of principal assessors again to convene in general meeting, on the —— day of —— next, at —— in the said State, and then and there diligently and carefully re-consider and re-examine the several lists of valuation for the direct tax for the said State, for the year 1814, and they shall have power to revise, alter, re-adjust, and equalize the several lists of valuation aforesaid for the counties of the said State respectively, by adding thereto or deducting therefrom such a rate per centum as shall render the valuation of the said counties relatively equal, according to the present actual ready-money value of the property assessed and contained in the said lists of valuation; and shall thereupon apportion to each county in the said State, a quota of the tax, bearing the same proportion to the whole direct tax imposed on the State, as the aggregate valuation of each county bears to the aggregate valuation of the State; and the valuation, equalization, and apportionment so made by the board of principal assessors aforesaid, shall be in full force and operation, and remain unchanged, subject only to the exceptions contained in the first section of this act; and the said board of principal assessors shall, within twenty days after their meeting as hereinbefore directed, complete the said revision, equalization, and apportionment, and shall record the same, and in all respects not herein otherwise directed, shall conform to the provisions contained in the act in this section first-above recited:"

It was determined in the affirmative—yeas 16, nays 6, as follows:

Yeas—Messrs. Barry, Brown, Campbell, Chace, Gaillard, Gore, Horsey, Hunter, King, Morrow, Ruggles, Sanford, Talbot, Thompson, Wells, and Williams.

Nays—Messrs. Condit, Macon, Mason of New Hampshire, Roberts, Turner, and Varnum.

The amendments having been concurred in,

on the question "Shall the amendments be engrossed and the bill read a third time ?" it was determined in the affirmative.

Monday, April 15.

Mr. Tait, from the Committee on Naval Affairs, to whom was referred the bill entitled "An act for the relief of Thomas Ap Catesby Jones," reported it without amendment.

Mr. Tait, from the same committee, to whom was referred the bill, entitled "An act for the relief of Rufus S. Reed and Daniel Dobbins," reported it without amendment.

Mr. Tait, from the same committee, to whom was referred the bill, entitled "An act for the relief of Asher Palmer," reported it without amendment.

Mr. Tait, from the same committee, to whom was referred the bill, entitled "An act for the relief of John Crosby and John Crosby, jr." reported it without amendment.

Mr. Tait, from the same committee, to whom was referred the bill, entitled "An act for the relief of Taylor and McNeal, Evan and McNeal, and Henry and John McLeister," reported it without amendment.

Mr. Daggett, from the committee to whom was referred the bill, entitled "An act for the relief of certain owners of goods entered at Hampden, in the District of Maine," reported it without amendment.

Mr. Morrow, from the committee to whom was referred the bill, entitled "An act declaring the assent of Congress to an act of the General Assembly of Virginia therein named," reported it without amendment.

On motion, by Mr. Morrow,

Ordered, That the committee appointed on so much of the Message of the President of the United States as relates to roads and canals, to whom were referred the resolution of the Senate of the 18th of March, instructing them to inquire into the expediency of laying out a national or military road from the town of Washington, in Pennsylvania, to Sandusky Bay; and the resolution of the 1st instant instructing them to inquire into the expediency of authorizing the Secretary of the Treasury to subscribe fifty thousand dollars to the Great Coastwise Canal and River Navigation Company; and also the memorial of the President and Directors of the Middlesex Canal, in the State of Massachusetts, be respectively discharged from the further consideration thereof.

The amendments to the bill, entitled "An act supplementary to the act to provide additional revenues for defraying the expenses of Government, and maintaining the public credit, by laying a direct tax upon the United States, and to provide for assessing and collecting the same," having been reported by the committee correctly engrossed, the bill was read a third time as amended, and the blanks were filled.

Resolved, That this bill pass with amendments.

The Senate proceeded to consider the amendments of the House of Representatives to the bill,

HISTORY OF CONGRESS.

Proceedings.

entitled "An act providing for the settlement of certain accounts against the Library of Congress, and for establishing the salary of the Librarian."
Whereupon,

Resolved, That they concur therein, and that the title be amended by inserting after the word "Congress," "for extending the privilege of using the books therein."

Mr. ROBERTS, from the committee to whom was referred the bill, entitled "An act directing the discharge of Ebenezer Keeler and John Francis from imprisonment," reported it without amendment.

The bill entitled "An act authorizing the Comptroller of the Treasury to cancel certain export bonds executed by Caspar C. Schuttle," was read the second time, and referred to the Committee on Finance and an Uniform National Currency.

The bill entitled "An act for the relief of Young King, a chief of the Seneca tribe of Indians," was read the second time, and referred to the Committee on Military Affairs.

The bill, entitled "An act for the relief of Thomas H. Boyle," was read the second time, and referred to the committee on the memorial of the Legislature of the Mississippi Territory.

The bill, entitled "An act for the relief of Charles Levaux Trudeau," was read the second time, and referred to the committee last mentioned.

The bill, entitled "An act confirming the titles of certain purchasers of land who purchased from the Board of Trustees of the Vincennes University," was read the second time, and referred to the same committee.

The bill, entitled "An act granting to Amos Spafford the right of pre-emption," was read the second time, and referred to the same committee.

The bill, entitled "An act authorizing the payment of a sum of money to John T. Courtney and Samuel Harrison, or their legal representatives," was read the second time, and referred to the Committee on Naval Affairs.

The bill, entitled "An act rewarding the officers and crew of the Constitution for the capture of the British sloop-of-war Levant," was read the second time, and referred to the committee last mentioned.

The bill, entitled "An act concerning Pharaoh Farrow and others," was read the second time, and referred to the same committee.

The bill, entitled "An act for the relief of the widow and children of Charles Dolph, deceased," was read the second time, and referred to Messrs. DAGGETT, SANFORD, and GOLDSBOROUGH, to consider and report thereon.

Mr. ROBERTS presented the memorial of Robert Waln and others, merchants of the city of Philadelphia, praying Congress to except from the operation of the new tariff certain cotton goods as shall be imported from India under certain circumstances, as stated in the memorial; which was read.

Mr. GORE presented the petition of Levi Thaxter and others, inhabitants of Boston and its vicinity, praying that the importation of sheep's wool may be free of duty, for reasons stated in the petition; which was read.

Mr. KING presented the memorial of the Mayor, Aldermen, and Commonalty of the city of New York, in Common Council convened, praying Congress to repeal the present duty on coal, and leave the article free from taxation altogether, for reasons stated in the memorial; which was read.

Mr. CAMPBELL, from the committee to whom was referred the bill, entitled "An act to fix the commissions of the collectors of the direct tax and internal duties, and to revive and continue in force "An act further to provide for the collection of duties on imports and tonnage," reported it without amendment.

Mr. CAMPBELL, from the same committee, to whom was referred the bill, entitled "An act to increase the compensations now allowed by law to inspectors, measurers, weighers, and gaugers, employed in the collection of the customs," reported it without amendment.

Mr. CAMPBELL, from the same committee, to whom was referred the bill, entitled "An act for the free importation of stereotype plates, and to encourage the printing and gratuitous distribution of the Scriptures by the Bible Societies within the United States," reported it without amendment.

On motion by Mr. CAMPBELL, the Committee on Finance and an Uniform National Currency, to whom was referred the petition of Harman Hendricks, of New York, were discharged from the further consideration thereof, and the petitioner had leave to withdraw his petition and papers.

A message from the House of Representatives informed the Senate that the House have passed a bill, entitled "An act for the relief of Elizabeth Hamilton;" a bill, entitled "An act supplementary to the act passed the 30th of March, 1802, to regulate trade and intercourse with the Indian tribes and to preserve peace on the frontiers;" a bill, entitled "An act providing for the sale of certain lands in the State of Ohio, formerly set apart for refugees from Canada and Nova Scotia;" also a bill, entitled "An act for the gradual increase of the Navy of the United States;" and a "Resolution to indemnify Jabez Mowry and others:" in which bills and resolution they request the concurrence of the Senate.

The four bills and resolution last brought up for concurrence were read, and severally passed to the second reading.

Mr. DAGGETT, from the committee to whom was referred the bill, entitled "An act for the relief of the heirs of Alexander Roxburgh," reported it without amendment.

On motion by Mr. TALBOT, to reconsider the vote on passing to a third reading the bill, entitled "An act for the liquidation of certain claims, and for other purposes," it was determined in the negative—yeas 11, nays 18, as follows:

YEAS—Messrs. Barbour, Barry, Chace, Dana, Lacock, Morrow, Roberts, Ruggles, Talbot, Turner, and Williams.

NAYS—Messrs. Brown, Campbell, Condit, Daggett,

Gaillard, Gore, Horsey, Hunter, King, Macon, Mason of New Hampshire, Sanford, Tait, Thompson, Tichenor, Varnum, Wells, and Wilson.

On motion by Mr. ROBERTS,

Resolved, That the Message of the President of the United States of the 11th instant, recommending the establishment of a distinct office within the Department of State, to be charged with the business connected with the grant of exclusive rights to inventors and authors, be referred to a select committee, to consider and report thereon, by bill or otherwise.

Ordered, That Messrs. ROBERTS, MACON, and KING, be the committee.

A message from the House of Representatives informed the Senate that the House have passed a resolution that the President of the Senate and Speaker of the House of Representatives be authorized to close this session by the adjournment of their respective Houses, on Saturday the 20th day of April instant; in which they request the concurrence of the Senate.

The Senate resumed, as in Committee of the Whole, the consideration of the bill, entitled "An act to regulate the duties on imports and tonnage," together with the amendments reported thereto by the select committee; and Mr. VARNUM was requested to take the Chair.

On the question to agree to the following proposed amendments, to wit:

"Line 180, strike out the whole line. Line 181, strike out the whole line, except *Madeira.*"

It was determined in the affirmative—yeas 15, nays 14, as follows:

YEAS—Messrs. Barbour, Chace, Daggett, Fromentin, Gaillard, Goldsborough, Gore, Horsey, Hunter, King, Mason of New Hampshire, Sanford, Tichenor, Varnum, and Wells.

NAYS—Messrs. Barry, Brown, Campbell, Condit, Dana, Macon, Morrow, Roberts, Ruggles, Talbot, Thompson, Turner, Williams, and Wilson.

The bill having been amended, on motion, the Senate adjourned.

TUESDAY, April 16.

Mr. BROWN, from the committee appointed on the memorial of the Legislature of the Mississippi Territory, to whom was referred the bill, entitled "An act confirming the titles of certain purchasers of land who purchased from the Board of Trustees for the Vincennes University," reported it without amendment.

Mr. BROWN, from the same committee, to whom was referred the bill, entitled "An act to authorize the sale of lands forfeited to the United States in the district of Jeffersonville, at the land office in said district," reported it without amendment.

Mr. BROWN, from the committee to whom was referred the bill, entitled "An act providing for the sale of the tract of land at the lower rapids of the Sandusky river," reported it without amendment.

Mr. BROWN, from the same committee, to whom was referred the bill, entitled "An act providing for the sale of the tract of land at the British fort

14th CON. 1st SESS.—11

at the Miami of the Lake, at the foot of the rapids, and for other purposes," reported it without amendment.

Mr. BROWN, from the same committee, to whom was referred the bill, entitled "An act for the relief of Samuel Dick, William Bruce, and Asa Kitchell," reported it without amendment.

Mr. BROWN, from the same committee, to whom was referred the bill, entitled "An act for the relief of Thomas H. Boyle," reported it without amendment.

Mr. BROWN, from the same committee, to whom was referred the bill, entitled "An act granting to Amos Spafford the right of pre-emption," reported it without amendment.

Mr. BROWN, from the same committee, to whom was referred the bill, entitled "An act for the relief of Charles Levaux Trudeau," reported it with an amendment; which was read.

Mr. BROWN, from the same committee, to whom was referred the bill, entitled "An act for the relief of William Crawford, Frederick Bates, and William Garrard," reported it with amendments; which were read.

Mr. TAIT, from the Committee on Naval Affairs, to whom was referred the bill, entitled "An act authorizing the payment of a sum of money to John T. Courtney and Samuel Harrison, or their legal representatives," reported it without amendment.

Mr. TAIT, from the same committee, to whom was referred the bill, entitled "An act rewarding the officers and crew of the Constitution for the capture of the sloop-of-war Levant," reported it without amendment.

Mr. TAIT, from the same committee, to whom was referred the bill, entitled "An act concerning Pharaoh Farrow," reported it without amendment.

Mr. TAIT, from the same committee, to whom was referred the bill, entitled "An act providing for the distribution of one hundred thousand dollars among the captors of the Algerine vessels captured and restored to the Dey of Algiers, reported it without amendment.

Mr. TAIT, from the same committee, to whom was referred the bill, entitled "An act authorizing the payment of a sum of money to James Levins," reported it without amendment.

Mr. DAGGETT, from the committee to whom the subject was referred, reported a bill to increase the salary of the Register of the Treasury, and to allow him a compensation for his agency in countersigning and issuing Treasury notes; and the bill was read, and passed to the second reading.

Mr. DAGGETT, from the committee to whom was referred the bill entitled "An act for the relief of the widow and children of Charles Dolph, deceased," reported it without amendment.

Mr. BARBOUR, from the Committee on Military Affairs, to whom was referred the bill entitled "An act for the relief of Young King, a chief of the Seneca tribe of Indians," reported it without amendment.

Mr. DAGGETT, from the committee to whom

was referred the bill entitled "An act declaring the assent of Congress to acts of the State of South Carolina, authorizing the City Council of Charleston to impose and collect a duty on the tonnage of vessels from foreign ports, and to acts of the State of Georgia, authorizing the imposition and collection of a duty on tonnage of vessels in the ports of Savannah and St. Mary's," reported it with an amendment; which was read.

The bill to authorize the issuing of a grant to Major General Andrew Jackson for a tract of land, was read the second time.

The resolution last brought up for concurrence was read, and passed to the second reading.

On motion, by Mr. WILSON,

Resolved, That the resolution requiring the Secretary of State to compile and print once in every two years, a register of all officers and agents, civil, military, and naval, in the service of the United States, be referred to a select committee to consider and report thereon.

Ordered, That Messrs. WILSON, MACON, and SANFORD, be the committee.

The bill, entitled "An act supplementary to the act passed the 30th of March, 1802, to regulate trade and intercourse with the Indian tribes, and to preserve peace on the frontiers," was read the second time, and referred to a select committee. Messrs. MORROW, VARNUM, and BARRY, were appointed the committee.

The resolution to indemnify Jabez Mowry, and others, was read the second time, and referred to the Committee on Foreign Relations.

The bill, entitled "An act for the gradual increase of the Navy of the United States," was read the second time, and referred to the Committee on Naval Affairs.

The bill, entitled "An act providing for the sale of certain lands in the State of Ohio formerly set apart for the refugees from Canada and Nova Scotia," was read the second time, and referred to the committee on the memorial of the Legislature of the Mississippi Territory.

The bill, entitled "An act for the relief of Elizabeth Hamilton," was read the second time, and referred to the Committee on Military Affairs.

A message from the House of Representatives informed the Senate that the House have passed a bill, entitled "An act to establish post roads;" a bill, entitled "An act supplementary to an act entitled 'An act granting bounties in lands and extra pay to certain Canadian volunteers;" a bill, entitled "An act for the benefit of John P. Maxwell and Hugh H. Maxwell;" a bill, entitled "An act regulating the currency within the United States of the gold and silver coins of Great Britain, France, Portugal, and Spain, and the crowns of France, and five franc pieces;" a bill, entitled "An act for the confirmation of certain claims to land in the western district of the State of Louisiana;" a bill, entitled "An act to provide for the appointment of a surveyor of the public lands in the Territories of Illinois and Missouri;" also, a bill, entitled "An act fixing the compensation of the Secretary of the Senate and Clerk of the House of Representatives, and making a tempo-

rary provision for the clerks employed in their offices;" in which bills they request the concurrence of the Senate.

They have passed the bill which originated in the Senate, entitled "An act respecting the late officers and crew of the sloop of war Wasp," with amendments, in which they request the concurrence of the Senate; the bill entitled "An act for the relief of Edward Wilson," with amendments, in which they request the concurrence of the Senate; also, the bill entitled "An act further supplementary to the act entitled 'An act providing for the indemnification of certain claimants of public lands in the Mississippi Territory," with amendments, in which they request the concurrence of the Senate.

The seven bills last brought up for concurrence were read, and severally passed to the second reading.

The following Message was received from the PRESIDENT OF THE UNITED STATES:

To the Senate and House of
    Representatives of the United States:

I lay before Congress copies of a convention concluded between the United States and the Cherokee Indians, on the second day of March last, as the same has been duly ratified and proclaimed. And I recommend that such provision be made by Congress as the stipulations therein contained may require.

               JAMES MADISON.

APRIL 16, 1816.

The Message was read.

The Senate resumed, as in Committee of the Whole, the consideration of the bill, entitled "An act to regulate the duties on imports and tonnage;" and Mr. VARNUM was requested to take the Chair.

On motion by Mr. ROBERTS, to strike out of line 130, "forty-five," it was determined in the negative—yeas 14, nays 18, as follows:

YEAS—Messrs. Barry, Brown, Campbell, Chace, Condit, Fromentin, Lacock, Morrow, Roberts, Ruggles, Sanford, Talbot, Tichenor, and Wilson.

NAYS—Messrs. Barbour, Daggett, Dana, Gaillard, Goldsborough, Gore, Harper, Horsey, Hunter, King, Macon, Mason of New Hampshire, Tait, Thompson, Turner, Varnum, Wells, and Williams.

On motion, by Mr. TALBOT, to insert at the end of line 146, "and all other materials," it was determined in the negative—yeas 11, nays 20, as follows:

YEAS—Messrs. Barry, Brown, Chace, Condit, Fromentin, Lacock, Roberts, Ruggles, Talbot, Williams, and Wilson.

NAYS—Messrs. Barbour, Daggett, Dana, Gaillard, Goldsborough, Gore, Harper, Horsey, Hunter, King, Macon, Mason of New Hampshire, Morrow, Sanford, Tait, Thompson, Tichenor, Turner, Varnum, and Wells.

On motion, by Mr. MASON, of New Hampshire, the further consideration of the bill was postponed until to-morrow.

The Senate proceeded to consider the amendments of the House of Representatives to the bill, entitled "An act for the relief of Edward Wilson." Whereupon,

Resolved, That they concur therein.

The Senate proceeded to consider the amendments to the bill entitled "An act respecting the late officers and crew of the sloop-of-war Wasp." Whereupon,

Resolved, That they concur therein.

The Senate proceeded to consider the amendments of the House of Representatives to the bill, entitled "An act further supplementary to the act entitled 'An act providing for the indemnification of certain claimants of public lands in the Mississippi Territory." Whereupon,

Resolved, That they concur therein.

Mr. BROWN, from the committee to whom was referred the bill, entitled "An act to enable the people of the Mississippi Territory to form a constitution and State government, and for the admission of such State into the Union on an equal footing with the original States," reported it without amendment. He also made a report on the subject; which was read.

The bill, entitled "An act to establish post roads," was read the second time by unanimous consent, and referred to the committee to whom was referred, on the 13th of December, the petition of John Duckworth and others.

WEDNESDAY, April, 17.

A message from the House of Representatives informed the Senate that the House have passed a bill, entitled "An act for the relief of Moses Turner;" a bill, entitled "An act for the relief of Samuel Manac;" a bill, entitled "An act to authorize the building of three light-houses, viz: one on Race Point, one on Point Gammon, and one on the island of Petite Manon, in the State of Massachusetts;" also a bill, entitled "An act making appropriations for rebuilding light-houses, and for completing the plan of lighting them according to the improvements of Winslow Lewis; for placing beacons and buoys; for preserving Little Gull Island; and for surveying the coast of the United States;" in which bills they request the concurrence of the Senate.

The four bills last brought up for concurrence were read, and severally passed to the second reading.

Mr. DANA, from the Committee on Foreign Relations, to whom was referred the resolution from the House of Representatives to indemnify Jabez Mowry and others, reported it with amendments, which were read.

Mr. TAIT, from the Committee on Naval Affairs, to whom was referred the bill, entitled "An act for the gradual increase of the Navy of the United States," reported it with an amendment, which was read.

Mr. DAGGETT, from the committee to whom was referred the bill, entitled "An act for the relief of Charles Todd," reported it without amendment.

Mr. DAGGETT, from the committee to whom was referred the bill, entitled "An act for the relief of Thomas B. Farrish," reported it without amendment.

On motion by Mr. ROBERTS, the committee to

whom was referred the memorial of James Milnor, in behalf of the American Convention for promoting the abolition of Slavery were discharged from the further consideration thereof.

The bill, entitled "An act fixing the compensation of the Secretary of the Senate and Clerk of the House of Representatives, and making a temporary provision for the clerks employed in their offices," was read the second time, and referred to a select committee, to consider and report thereon; and Messrs. WILLIAMS, LACOCK, and MACON, were appointed the committee.

The bill, entitled "An act supplementary to an act, entitled 'An act granting bounties in lands and extra pay to certain Canadian volunteers," was read the second time, and referred to the Committee on Military Affairs.

The bill, entitled "An act regulating the currency within the United States of the gold coins of Great Britain, France, Portugal, and Spain, and the crowns of France, and five franc pieces," was read the second time, and referred to the Committee on Finance and an Uniform National Currency.

The bill, entitled "An act for the benefit of John P. Maxwell, and Hugh H. Maxwell," was read the second time, and referred to the committee on the memorial of the Legislature of the Mississippi Territory.

The bill, entitled "An act for the confirmation of certain claims to land in the western district of the State of Louisiana," was read the second time, and referred to the committee last mentioned.

The bill, entitled "An act to provide for the appointment of a surveyor of the public lands in the Territories of Illinois and Missouri," was read the second time, and referred to the same committee.

The resolution authorizing the President of the Senate and Speaker of the House of Representatives to adjourn their respective Houses on the 30th day of April instant, was read the second time.

DUTIES ON IMPORTS.

The Senate resumed, as in Committee of the Whole, the consideration of the bill, entitled "An act to regulate the duties on imports and tonnage." Mr. VARNUM was requested to take the Chair.

Mr. BARBOUR moved to strike out of line thirty-one "five," and on his motion, it was agreed to take the question by yeas and nays.

On motion by Mr. HARPER, that the further consideration of the bill be postponed until the first day of August next, it was determined in the negative—yeas 3, nays 27, as follows:

YEAS—Messrs. Goldsborough, Harper, and Macon.

NAYS—Messrs. Barbour, Barry, Brown, Campbell, Chace, Condit, Daggett, Dana, Fromentin, Gaillard, Gore, Horsey, Hunter, King, Lacock, Morrow, Roberts, Ruggles, Sanford, Talbot, Tait, Thompson, Tichenor, Turner, Varnum, Wells, and Williams.

On the question to agree to the motion by Mr. BARBOUR, to strike out of line thirty-one, "five," to reduce the duty on woollen manufactures from twenty-five to twenty per cent. ad valorem, it was determined in the negative—yeas 9, nays 20, as follows:

YEAS—Messrs. Barbour, Campbell, Gaillard, Goldsborough, Harper, Macon, Roberts, Tait, and Turner.

NAYS—Messrs. Barry, Brown, Chace, Condit, Daggett, Dana, Gore, Horsey, Hunter, King, Lacock, Morrow, Ruggles, Sanford, Talbot, Thompson, Tichenor, Varnum, Wells, and Williams.

On motion by Mr. BARBOUR, to strike out of line thirty-six and thirty-seven, "nineteen," and insert in lieu thereof "seventeen," to limit the maximum duty on woollen manufactures to one, instead of three years, it was determined in the negative—yeas 9, nays 20, as follows:

YEAS—Messrs. Barbour, Campbell, Gaillard, Goldsborough, Macon, Roberts, Tait, Turner, and Williams.

NAYS—Messrs. Barry, Brown, Chace, Condit, Daggett, Dana, Gore, Harper, Horsey, Hunter, King, Lacock, Morrow, Ruggles, Sanford, Talbot, Thompson, Tichenor, Varnum, and Wells.

On motion by Mr. MACON, to strike out of line one hundred and forty-four "twenty," and insert in lieu thereof "twelve and a half," with a view to reduce the duty on salt per bushel seven and an half cents, it was determined in the negative—yeas 13, nays 15, as follows:

YEAS—Messrs. Barbour, Brown, Dana, Fromentin, Goldsborough, Hunter, Macon, Roberts, Tait, Thompson, Tichenor, Turner, and Varnum.

NAYS—Messrs. Barry, Campbell, Chace, Condit, Daggett, Gore, Harper, Horsey, King, Lacock, Morrow, Ruggles, Sanford, Wells, and Williams.

THURSDAY, April 18.

The PRESIDENT communicated the petition of Benjamin G. Bowen, and others, messengers in the several public departments, praying an increase of compensation as stated in the petition; which was read, and referred to the committee to whom was referred the bill, entitled "An act fixing the compensation of the Secretary of the Senate and Clerk of the House of Representatives," &c.

Mr. RUGGLES presented the petition of John Coffee, junior, and others, of Belmont county, in the State of Ohio, praying a post office in said county, as stated in the petition; which was read, and referred to the committee on the petition of John Duckworth, junior, and others.

Mr. CHACE presented the memorial of Willis Hall, junior, and others, praying the grant of a large body of land on the Illinois river, for a reasonable pecuniary consideration, as an inducement to emigrate to that country for the purpose of forming a barrier to the present frontier settlement against the hostile savages, as stated in the memorial; which was read, and referred to the committee on the memorial of the Legislature of the Mississippi Territory.

The bill, entitled "An act making appropriations for rebuilding light-houses and for completing the plan of lighting them according to the improvements of Winslow Lewis; for placing beacons and buoys; for preserving Little Gull Island; and for surveying the coast of the United States," was read the second time, and referred to the committee last mentioned.

The bill, entitled "An act to authorize the building of three light-houses, viz: one on Race Point; one on Point Gammon; and one on the island of Petite Manon, in the State of Massachusetts," was read the second time, and referred to the Committee on Naval Affairs.

The bill, entitled "An act for the relief of Moses Turner," was read the second time, and referred to a select committee; and Messrs. CHACE, DAGGETT, and MACON, were appointed the committee.

The bill, entitled "An act for the relief of Samuel Manac," was read the second time, and referred to the Committee on Military Affairs.

Mr. MORROW, from the committee to whom was referred the bill, entitled "An act to alter certain parts of the act providing for the government of the Territory of Missouri," reported it without amendment.

Mr. MORROW, from the same committee, to whom was referred the bill, entitled "An act supplementary to the act passed the 30th of March, 1802, to regulate trade and intercourse with the Indian tribes, and to preserve peace on the frontiers," reported it without amendment.

The bill to increase the salary of the Register of the Treasury, and to allow him a compensation for his agency in countersigning and issuing Treasury notes, was read the second time.

On motion by Mr. SANFORD, the committee to whom was referred the petition of William Radcliff and others, of the city of New York, were discharged from the further consideration thereof.

A message from the House of Representatives informed the Senate that the House have passed a bill, entitled "An act for the relief of David Coffin, Samuel and William Rodman, and Samuel Rodman, jun.;" a bill, entitled "An act providing for cases of lost military land warrants, and discharges for faithful services;" also a bill, entitled "An act concerning the owners, officers, and crew of the privateer Roger;" in which bills they request the concurrence of the Senate.

A message from the House of Representatives informed the Senate that the House have passed a bill, entitled "An act to establish a land district in the Illinois Territory, north of the district of Kaskaskia," in which bill they request the concurrence of the Senate.

DUTIES ON IMPORTS.

The Senate resumed, as in Committee of the Whole, the consideration of the bill, entitled "An act to regulate the duties on imports and tonnage." Mr. VARNUM was requested to take the Chair; and the bill having been further amended, the PRESIDENT resumed the Chair, and Mr. VARNUM reported the bill accordingly.

On the question to concur in the amendment agreed to in Committee of the Whole, to wit:

"Line 160, strike out the whole line."

"Line 161, strike out the whole line except *Madeira*."

It was determined in the negative—yeas 14, nays 16, as follows:

YEAS—Messrs. Barbour, Brown, Gaillard, Goldsborough, Gore, Harper, Horsey, Hunter, King, Mason of New Hampshire, Sanford, Tichenor, Varnum, and Wells.

NAYS—Messrs. Barry, Campbell, Chace, Condit, Dana, Lacock, Macon, Morrow, Roberts, Ruggles, Talbot, Tait, Thompson, Turner, Williams, and Wilson.

On motion by Mr. KING, to amend the bill so as to read, "on Madeira, Burgundy, Champaign, Rhenish, and Tokay, one dollar per gallon," it was determined in the affirmative—yeas 20, nays 11, as follows:

YEAS—Messrs. Barbour, Barry, Brown, Fromentin, Gaillard, Goldsborough, Gore, Harper, Horsey, Hunter, King, Mason of New Hampshire, Morrow, Sanford, Talbot, Tait, Thompson, Tichenor, Varnum, and Wells.

NAYS—Messrs. Campbell, Chace, Condit, Dana, Lacock, Macon, Roberts, Ruggles, Turner, Williams, and Wilson.

On motion of Mr. WILSON, to strike out of line 130, "forty-five," and insert, in lieu thereof, "sixty," to increase the duty on iron in bars and bolts, a division of the question was called for by Mr. THOMPSON, and it was taken on striking out, and determined in the negative—yeas 14, nays 16, as follows:

YEAS—Messrs. Barry, Brown, Campbell, Chace, Condit, Lacock, Roberts, Ruggles, Sanford, Talbot, Tichenor, Wells, Williams, and Wilson.

NAYS—Messrs. Barbour, Dana, Fromentin, Gaillard, Goldsborough, Gore, Harper, Horsey, Hunter, King, Macon, Mason of New Hampshire, Tait, Thompson, Turner, and Varnum.

On motion by Mr. BARBOUR, to amend the bill by striking out, of line 144, the duty on salt, it was determined in the negative—yeas 14, nays 17, as follows:

YEAS—Messrs. Barbour, Brown, Dana, Fromentin, Gaillard, Goldsborough, Hunter, Macon, Tait, Thompson, Tichenor, Turner, Varnum, and Wells.

NAYS—Messrs. Barry, Campbell, Chace, Condit, Gore, Harper, Horsey, King, Lacock, Mason of New Hampshire, Morrow, Roberts, Ruggles, Sanford, Talbot, Wells, and Wilson.

FRIDAY, April 19.

Mr. WILLIAMS, from the committee to whom was referred the bill, entitled "An act fixing the compensation of the Secretary of the Senate and Clerk of the House of Representatives, and making a temporary provision for the Clerks employed in their offices," reported it with amendments, which were read.

Mr. TAIT, from the Committee on Naval Affairs, to whom was referred the bill, entitled "An act to authorize the building of three lighthouses, viz: one on Race Point, one on Point Gammon, and one on the island of Petite Manon, in the State of Massachusetts," reported it without amendment.

Mr. TAIT, from the same committee, to whom was referred the bill, entitled "An act making appropriations for rebuilding light-houses, and for completing the plan of lighting them according to the improvements of Winslow Lewis; for placing beacons and buoys; for preserving Little Gull Island; and for surveying the coast of the United States," reported it without amendment.

Mr. MASON, of Virginia, submitted the following motion for consideration:

Resolved, That the Secretaries of War and of the Navy be directed to inquire into the expediency of authorizing the Secretary of the Treasury to subscribe fifty thousand dollars to the Great Coastwise Canal and River Navigation Company, incorporated by the Legislature of Virginia for the purpose of cutting a canal from the port of Norfolk through the eastern branch of Elizabeth river to the channel of Currituck Sound, on the terms and conditions proposed by the President and Directors of the said Great Coastwise Canal and River Navigation Company, and that the said Secretaries be also directed to report their opinions on this subject to Congress at the commencement of its next session.

The four bills brought up yesterday for concurrence were read, and severally passed to the second reading.

On motion by Mr. ROBERTS, the committee to whom was referred the memorial of Thomas Murray, were discharged from the further consideration thereof, and the memorialist had leave to withdraw his memorial.

A message from the House of Representatives informed the Senate that the House have passed a bill, entitled "An act making an appropriation for enclosing and improving the public square near the Capitol, and to abolish the office of Commissioners of the Public Buildings, and of Superintendent, and for the appointment of one Commissioner for the Public Buildings;" a bill, entitled "An act providing an additional compensation to the district judge of the southern district of New York;" a bill, entitled "An act to enable the levy court of the county of Alexandria to lay a tax for the purpose of defraying the expense of erecting a jail and court-house;" and also a bill, entitled "An act to authorize the survey of two millions of acres of the public lands, in lieu of that quantity heretofore authorized to be surveyed in the Territory of Michigan, as military bounty lands;" in which bills they request the concurrence of the Senate.

DUTIES ON IMPORTS.

The Senate resumed the consideration of the bill, entitled "An act to regulate the duties on imports and tonnage."

On motion by Mr. MASON, of New Hampshire, to strike out of line 50 the word "five," it was determined in the negative—yeas 12, nays 15, as follows:

YEAS—Messrs. Barbour, Gaillard, Goldsborough, Gore, Macon, Mason of New Hampshire, Mason of Virginia, Tait, Thompson, Tichenor, Turner, and Williams.

NAYS—Messrs. Barry, Chace, Condit, Daggett, Dana, Horsey, Hunter, King, Lacock, Morrow, Roberts, Ruggles, Talbot, Varnum, and Wilson.

On motion by Mr. HARPER, to strike out the following proviso:

" *Provided,* That all cotton cloths, or cloths of which cotton is the material of chief value, (excepting nankeens imported directly from China,) the original cost of which at the place whence imported, with the addition of twenty per cent., if imported from the Cape of Good Hope, or from places beyond it, and of ten per cent. if imported from any other place, shall be less than twenty-five cents per square yard, shall, with such addition, be taken and deemed to have cost twenty-five cents per square yard, and shall be charged with duty accordingly;"

It was determined in the negative—yeas 10, nays 22, as follows:

YEAS—Messrs. Barbour, Gaillard, Goldsborough, Gore, Harper, Macon, Mason of New Hampshire, Tait, Turner, and Williams.

NAYS—Messrs. Barry, Brown, Campbell, Chace, Condit, Daggett, Fromentin, Horsey, Hunter, King, Lacock, Mason of Virginia, Morrow, Roberts, Ruggles, Sanford, Talbot, Thompson, Tichenor, Varnum, Wells, and Wilson.

On motion by Mr. DANA, to strike out the following section:

" SEC. 3. *And be it further enacted,* That the act passed the 3d day of March, 1815, entitled 'An act to repeal so much of the several acts imposing duties on the tonnage of ships and vessels, and on goods, wares, and merchandise imported into the United States, as imposes a discriminating duty on tonnage between foreign vessels and vessels of the United States, and between goods imported into the United States in foreign vessels and vessels of the United States,' shall apply and be in full force as to the discriminating duties established by this act on the tonnage of foreign vessels, and the goods, wares, and merchandise therein imported;"

It was determined in the negative—yeas 14, nays 19, as follows:

YEAS—Messrs. Daggett, Dana, Fromentin, Gaillard, Gore, Hunter, King, Macon, Mason of New Hampshire, Roberts, Sanford, Thompson, Tichenor, and Wells.

NAYS—Messrs. Barbour, Barry, Brown, Campbell, Chace, Condit, Goldsborough, Harper, Horsey, Lacock, Mason of Virginia, Morrow, Ruggles, Talbot, Tait, Turner, Varnum, Williams, and Wilson.

On the question—" Shall the amendments be engrossed, and the bill read a third time as amended?" it was determined in the affirmative—yeas 25, nays 7, as follows:

YEAS—Messrs. Barry, Brown, Campbell, Chace, Condit, Daggett, Fromentin, Gaillard, Horsey, Hunter, King, Lacock, Mason of Virginia, Morrow, Roberts, Ruggles, Sanford, Talbot, Tait, Thompson, Tichenor, Varnum, Wells, Williams, and Wilson.

NAYS—Messrs. Barbour, Goldsborough, Gore, Harper, Macon, Mason of New Hampshire, and Turner.

SATURDAY, April 20.

On motion by Mr. BROWN, the committee to whom was referred the memorial of Willis Hall, junior, and others, were discharged from the further consideration thereof.

On motion by Mr. MACON,

Resolved, That the Secretaries of the Departments be directed to report jointly to the Senate, in the first week of the next session of Congress, a plan to insure the annual settlement of the public accounts, and a more certain accountability of the public expenditure, in their respective departments.

The Senate resumed the consideration of the motion made the 19th instant, which was amended, and agreed to, as follows:

Resolved, That the Secretaries of War and of the Navy be directed to inquire into the expediency of authorizing the Secretary of the Treasury to subscribe fifty thousand dollars to the Great Coastwise Canal and River Navigation Company, incorporated by the Legislature of Virginia, for the purpose of cutting a canal from the port of Norfolk through the eastern branch of Elizabeth river to the channel of Currituck Sound, on the terms and conditions proposed by the President and Directors of the said Great Coastwise Canal and River Navigation Company, and that the said Secretaries be also directed to report their opinions on this subject to Congress at the commencement of its next session; and also to report their opinions of the comparative public advantages to be derived from that canal, and the canal through the Dismal Swamp, mentioned by the Secretary of the Treasury in his report on the subject of roads and canals, made in pursuance of a resolution of the Senate of March 2, 1807.

Mr. BARBOUR, from the Committee on Military Affairs, to whom was referred the bill, entitled "An act for the relief of Samuel Manac," reported it without amendment.

Mr. WILSON, from the committee to whom was referred the " resolution requiring the Secretary of State to compile and print, once in every two years, a register of all officers and agents, civil, military, and naval, in the service of the United States," reported it without amendment.

Mr. WILSON, from the committee to whom was referred the bill, entitled "An act to establish post roads," reported it with amendments, which were read.

The four bills brought up yesterday for concurrence were read, and severally passed to the second reading.

The bill, entitled "An act making an appropriation for enclosing and improving the public square near the Capitol, and to abolish the office of Commissioners of the Public Buildings, and of Superintendent, and for the appointment of one Commissioner for the Public Buildings," was read the second time, by unanimous consent, and referred to a select committee; and Messrs. LACOCK, MACON, and DAGGETT, were appointed the committee.

The bill, entitled "An act providing an additional compensation to the district judge of the southern district of New York," was read the second time, by unanimous consent, and referred to Messrs. DAGGETT, SANFORD, and GOLDSBOROUGH, to consider and report thereon.

The bill, entitled "An act to enable the levy court of the county of Alexandria to lay a tax for the purpose of defraying the expense of erecting a jail and court-house," was read the second time, by unanimous consent, and referred to the committee last mentioned.

The bill, entitled "An act to authorize the survey of two millions of acres of the public lands, in lieu of that quantity heretofore authorized to be surveyed, in the Territory of Michigan, as military bounty lands," was read the second time, by unanimous consent, and referred to the committee on the memorial of the Legislature of the Mississippi Territory.

The bill, entitled "An act for the relief of David Coffin, Samuel and William Rodman, and Samuel Rodman, junior," was read the second time, and referred to the Committee on Finance and an Uniform National Currency.

The bill, entitled "An act providing for cases of lost military land warrants, and discharges for faithful services." was read the second time, and referred to the Committee on Military Affairs.

The bill, entitled "An act to establish a land district in the Illinois Territory, north of the district of Kaskaskia," was read the second time, and referred to the committee on the memorial of the Legislature of the Mississippi Territory.

The bill, entitled "An act concerning the owners, officers, and crew of the privateer Roger," was read the second time, and referred to the Committee on Naval Affairs.

The Senate resumed, as in Committee of the Whole, the consideration of the resolution reported from the joint committee, authorizing the President of the Senate and Speaker of the House of Representatives to adjourn their respective Houses on the 22d day of April instant; and on motion, by Mr. CAMPBELL, the further consideration thereof was postponed until the first Monday in June next.

On motion by Mr. CAMPBELL, the further consideration of the resolution from the House of Representatives, authorizing the President of the Senate and Speaker of the House of Representatives to adjourn their respective Houses on the 20th day of April instant, was postponed until Wednesday next.

The Senate resumed the consideration of the bill, entitled "An act for organizing the general staff, and making further provision for the Army of the United States."

On the question to concur in the following amendment, agreed to, as in Committee of the Whole: Insert as 2d section,

"*Be it further enacted,* That the President be, and he is hereby authorized, by and with the advice and consent of the Senate, to appoint, in addition to the officers of the Corps of Engineers already authorized by law, two Brigadier Generals, to be attached to that corps, who shall receive the same pay, forage, rations, and other emoluments, as the officers of the same grade of the present Military Establishment;"

It was determined in the negative—yeas 15, nays 16, as follows:

YEAS—Messrs. Barbour, Barry, Brown, Chace, Fromentin, Gaillard, Hunter, Lacock, Mason of Virginia, Morrow, Ruggles, Talbot, Tait, Turner, and Williams.

NAYS—Messrs. Condit, Daggett, Goldsborough, Gore, Harper, Horsey, King, Macon, Mason of New Hampshire, Roberts, Sanford, Thompson, Tichenor, Varnum, Wells, and Wilson.

The other amendment having been concurred in, on the question, "Shall the amendments be engrossed, and the bill read a third time as amended?" it was determined in the affirmative.

The Senate resumed, as in Committee of the Whole, the consideration of the resolution directing medals to be struck, and, together with the thanks of Congress, presented to Major General Harrison, and Governor Shelby, and for other purposes. Mr. VARNUM was requested to take the Chair; and the resolution having been amended, the PRESIDENT resumed the Chair, and Mr. VARNUM reported it accordingly.

On the question to concur in the amendment agreed to, as in Committee of the Whole, to strike out "Major General William Henry Harrison," it was determined in the negative—yeas 13, nays 14, as follows:

YEAS—Messrs. Campbell, Daggett, Gaillard, Gore, King, Lacock, Mason of New Hampshire, Mason of Virginia, Roberts, Tait, Tichenor, Turner, and Varnum.

NAYS—Messrs. Barbour, Barry, Chase, Condit, Harper, Horsey, Macon, Morrow, Ruggles, Sanford, Talbot, Wells, Williams, and Wilson.

On motion by Mr. HORSEY, the resolution was recommitted to the Committee on Military Affairs, further to consider and report thereon.

Mr. CAMPBELL, from the committee to whom was referred the bill, entitled "An act regulating the currency, within the United States, of the gold and silver coins of Great Britain, France, Portugal, and Spain, and the crowns of France, and five franc pieces," reported it without amendment.

The amendments to the bill, entitled "An act to regulate the duties on imports and tonnage," having been reported by the committee correctly engrossed, the bill was read a third time as amended.

Resolved, That this bill pass with amendments.

The Senate resumed, as in Committee of the Whole, the consideration of the bill to provide more effectually for the payment of specie by the several banks within the District of Columbia; and, on motion by Mr. TAIT, the further consideration thereof was postponed until the first Monday in June next.

The Senate resumed, as in Committee of the Whole, the consideration of the bill to erect a light-house at the mouth of the Mississippi river; and, on motion by Mr. FROMENTIN, the further consideration thereof was postponed until the first Monday in June next.

The Senate resumed, as in Committee of the Whole, the consideration of the bill for the relief of Isaac Briggs; and, on motion by Mr. DAGGETT, the further consideration thereof was postponed until the first Monday in June next.

The Senate resumed, as in Committee of the Whole, the consideration of the bill, entitled "An act for the relief of Henry Malcolm," and on the question, "Shall this bill be read a third time?" it was determined in the negative. So the bill was lost.

The Senate resumed, as in Committee of the Whole, the consideration of the bill concerning the annual sum appropriated for arming and equipping the militia; and on the question, "Shall this bill be engrossed, and read a third time?" it was determined in the affirmative.

The Senate resumed, as in Committee of the Whole, the consideration of the bill to increase the compensation of the superintendents of the manufactories of arms at Springfield and Harper's Ferry; and on the question, "Shall this bill be engrossed, and read a third time?" it was determined in the affirmative.

Mr. BROWN, from the committee to whom was referred the bill, entitled "An act to provide for the appointment of a surveyor of the public lands in the Territories of Illinois and Missouri," reported it with amendments, which were read.

MONDAY, April 22.

Mr. TAIT, from the Committee on Naval Affairs, to whom was referred the bill, entitled "An act concerning the owners, officers, and crew of the privateer Roger," reported it without amendment.

Mr. BROWN, from the committee to whom was referred the bill, entitled "An act providing for the sale of certain lands in the State of Ohio, formerly set apart for refugees from Canada and Nova Scotia," reported it without amendment.

Mr. BROWN, from the committee to whom was referred the bill, entitled "An act to establish a land district in the Illinois Territory, north of the district of Kaskaskia," reported it without amendment.

Mr. BARBOUR, from the Committee on Military Affairs, to whom was referred the bill, entitled "An act for the relief of Elizabeth Hamilton," reported it without amendment.

Mr. BARBOUR, from the same committee, to whom was referred the bill, entitled "An act supplementary to an act entitled 'An act granting bounties in lands and extra pay to certain Canadian volunteers," reported it without amendment.

Mr. BARBOUR, from the same committee, to whom was referred the bill, entitled "An act providing for cases of lost military land warrants and discharges for faithful services," reported it without amendment.

The Senate resumed, as in Committee of the Whole, the consideration of the bill, entitled "An act for the relief of Robert Kidd;" and on the question, "Shall this bill be read a third time?" it was determined in the negative. So the bill was lost.

The Senate resumed, as in Committee of the Whole, the consideration of the bill, entitled "An act to amend an act entitled 'An act for the relief of Edward Hallowell;'" and it passed to a third reading.

The bill to increase the compensation of the superintendents of the manufactories of arms at Springfield and Harper's Ferry, was read a third time, and passed.

The bill concerning the annual sum appropriated for arming and equipping the militia, was read a third time, and passed.

The amendments to the bill entitled "An act for organizing the general staff, and making further provision for the Army of the United States," having been reported by the committee correctly engrossed, the bill was read a third time as amended.

On the question, "Shall this bill pass as amended?" it was determined in the affirmative—yeas 15, nays 11, as follows:

YEAS—Messrs. Barbour, Barry, Brown, Condit, Fromentin, Gaillard, Howell, Lacock, Mason of Virginia, Morrow, Roberts, Sanford, Tait, Turner, and Williams.

NAYS—Messrs. Daggett, Goldsborough, Horsey, King, Macon, Mason of New Hampshire, Thompson, Tichenor, Varnum, Wells, and Wilson.

So it was *Resolved,* That this bill pass with amendments.

The Senate resumed, as in Committee of the Whole, the consideration of the bill "for adjusting the claims to land and establishing a land office for the districts of lands lying east of the Mississippi river and island of New Orleans;" and the bill having been amended, the PRESIDENT reported it to the House accordingly.

On the question to concur in the following amendment, agreed to as in Committee of the Whole, to be added at the end of the second section:

"*Provided, always,* That nothing in this act contained shall be construed, deemed, or taken, to affect or impair the right or rights of any person or persons claiming any of the lands aforesaid;"

It was determined in the affirmative—yeas 16, nays 9, as follows:

YEAS—Messrs. Barbour, Condit, Daggett, Dana, Gaillard, Goldsborough, Horsey, King, Mason of New Hampshire, Roberts, Sanford, Tait, Thompson, Tichenor, Wells, and Wilson.

NAYS—Messrs. Brown, Fromentin, Howell, Macon, Mason of Virginia, Morrow, Turner, Varnum, and Williams.

The bill having been further amended, on the question, "Shall this bill be engrossed, and read a third time?" it was determined in the affirmative.

Mr. DAGGETT, from the committee to whom was referred the bill, entitled "An act to enable the levy court of the county of Alexandria to lay a tax for the purpose of defraying the expense of erecting a jail and court-house," reported it without amendment.

Mr. DAGGETT, from the same committee, to whom was referred the bill, entitled "An act providing an additional compensation to the district judge of the southern district of New York," reported it without amendment.

Mr. BARBOUR communicated a resolution of the Legislature of the State of Virginia, adopting the amendment to the Constitution of the United States, proposed by the Legislature of North Carolina, for dividing each State into districts for the purpose of choosing Representatives in the Congress, and of appointing Electors of President and Vice President of the United States.

The resolution and proposed amendment were read.

Mr. MASON, of Virginia, communicated a resolution of the Legislature of the State of Virginia, rejecting the amendments to the Constitution of the United States, proposed by the Legislatures of Connecticut and Massachusetts.

The resolution and proposed amendments were read.

The Senate resumed, as in Committee of the Whole, the consideration of the bill, entitled "An act for the relief of certain purchasers of public lands in the Mississippi Territory," and it passed to a third reading.

The Senate resumed, as in Committee of the Whole, the consideration of the bill, entitled "An act to increase the pensions of invalids in certain cases, for the relief of invalids of the militia, and for the appointment of pension agents in those States where there is no commissioner of loans;" and it passed to a third reading.

The Senate resumed, as in Committee of the Whole, the consideration of the bill, entitled "An act making appropriations for the support of the Military Establishment of the United States, for the year 1816," together with the amendment reported thereto by the select committee. Mr. BARRY was requested to take the Chair, and the amendment having been disagreed to, the PRESIDENT resumed the Chair, and Mr. BARRY reported the bill to the House; and on motion, by Mr. BARBOUR, the further consideration thereof was postponed until to-morrow.

The Senate resumed, as in Committee of the Whole, the consideration of the bill, entitled "An act supplemental to the act entitled 'An act regulating and defining the duties of the judges of the Territory of Illinois, and for vesting in the courts of the Territory of Indiana a jurisdiction in chancery cases, arising in the said Territory;" and the bill having been amended, the PRESIDENT reported it to the House accordingly.

On the question, "Shall the amendments be engrossed, and the bill read a third time as amended?" it was determined in the affirmative.

The Senate resumed, as in Committee of the Whole, the bill, entitled "An act for the more convenient arrangement of the times and places of holding the circuit courts of the United States for the districts of South Carolina and Georgia," and it passed to a third reading.

On motion by Mr. TURNER, the bill last mentioned was read a third time by unanimous consent, and passed.

The Senate resumed, as in Committee of the Whole, the consideration of the bill, entitled "An act for the relief of Patrick and Abigail O'Flyng, and Edmund O. Flyng," and it passed to a third reading.

The bill last mentioned was read a third time by unanimous consent, and passed.

A message from the House of Representatives informed the Senate that they have passed a bill,

entitled "An act making appropriations for repairing certain roads therein described;" a bill, entitled "An act to authorize the surveying and making a road in the Territory of Illinois;" a bill, entitled "An act appropriating the sum of two thousand five hundred dollars, for the purposes therein mentioned;" a bill, entitled "An act authorizing the payment of a sum of money to John Rodgers, and others;" a bill, entitled "An act for the relief of Joseph S. Newell;" a bill, entitled "An act authorizing the payment of a sum of money to Joseph Stewart, and others;" a bill, entitled "An act authorizing the judges of the circuit court for the District of Columbia to prepare a code of jurisprudence for the said District;" a bill, entitled "An act allowing pay to certain persons made prisoners with the revenue cutter Surveyor;" a bill, entitled "An act concerning preemption rights given in the purchase of lands to certain settlers in the State of Louisiana, and in the Territories of Missouri and Illinois;" also, a bill, entitled "An act for reducing the duties on licenses to retailers of wine, spirituous liquors, and foreign merchandise;" in which bills they request the concurrence of the Senate. They have passed the bill from the Senate, entitled "An act establishing a port of delivery at the town of Bayou St. John," also, the bill, entitled "An act concerning the entry of vessels at the port of Middletown;" with amendments, in which they request the concurrence of the Senate.

The Senate proceeded to consider the amendments of the House of Representatives to the bill last mentioned.—Whereupon,

Resolved, That they concur therein.

The ten bills last brought up for concurrence were read, and severally passed to the second reading.

The Senate resumed, as in Committee of the Whole, the consideration of the bill, entitled "An act making further provision for settling claims to land in the Territory of Illinois," together with the amendments reported thereto by the select committee, and the bill having been amended, the PRESIDENT reported it to the House accordingly; and the amendments having been concurred in, on the question, "Shall the amendments be engrossed, and the bill read a third time, as amended?" it was determined in the affirmative.

Mr. CAMPBELL, from the committee to whom was referred the bill, entitled "An act for the relief of David Coffie, Samuel and William Rodman, and Samuel Rodman, junior," reported it with an amendment, which was read.

On motion by Mr. CAMPBELL, the committee to whom was referred the petition of Samuel Upton, and Thomas Adams were discharged from the further consideration thereof.

The Senate resumed, as in Committee of the Whole, the consideration of the bill for settling the compensation of the commissioners, clerk, and translator of the board for land claims, in the western district of the Territory of Orleans, now State of Louisiana; and the bill having been amended, the PRESIDENT reported it to the House accordingly; and on the question, "Shall this bill be engrossed and read a third time?" it was determined in the affirmative.

The Senate resumed, as in Committee of the Whole, the consideration of the bill authorizing the sale of lots owned by the United States in the city of New Orleans, and for other purposes; and on the question, "Shall this bill be engrossed and read a third time?" it was determined in the affirmative.

The Senate resumed, as in Committee of the Whole, the consideration of the bill for the relief of the legal representatives of Ignace Chalmet Delino, deceased; and on the question, "Shall this bill be engrossed and read a third time?" it was determined in the affirmative.

The Senate resumed, as in Committee of the Whole, the consideration of the resolutions reported from the joint committee, to inquire into the expediency of making certain alterations in the mode of transacting the business of Congress; and, on motion by Mr. TAIT, the further consideration thereof was postponed until the first Monday in June next.

The Senate resumed, as in Committee of the Whole, the consideration of the bill concerning the maritime precincts of the United States; and, on motion by Mr. DANA, the further consideration thereof was postponed until Friday next.

The Senate resumed, as in Committee of the Whole, the consideration of the bill making further appropriations for the year 1816; and, on motion by Mr. DAGGETT, the further consideration thereof was postponed until Wednesday next.

The Senate resumed, as in Committee of the Whole, the bill, entitled "An act authorizing the President of the United States to lease the Saline, near the Wabash river, for a term not exceeding seven years;" and it passed to a third reading.

The Senate resumed, as in Committee of the Whole, the consideration of the bill, entitled "An act for the relief of William Flood," together with the amendment reported thereto by the select committee; and the amendment having been disagreed to, the PRESIDENT reported the bill to the House; and on the question, "Shall this bill be read a third time?" it was determined in the affirmative—yeas 27, nays 2, as follows:

YEAS—Messrs. Barbour, Barry, Brown, Chace, Condit, Daggett, Fromentin, Gaillard, Goldsborough, Gore, Harper, Horsey, Howell, King, Mason of New Hampshire, Mason of Virginia, Morrow, Ruggles, Sanford, Tait, Thompson, Tichenor, Turner, Varnum, Wells, Williams, and Wilson.

NAYS—Messrs. Macon and Roberts.

A message from the House of Representatives informed the Senate that the House disagree to some, and agree to other amendments of the Senate to the bill, entitled "An act supplementary to the act to provide additional revenues for defraying the expenses of Government and maintaining the public credit, by laying a direct tax upon the United States, and to provide for assessing and collecting the same."

The Senate resumed, as in Committee of the Whole, the consideration of the bill, entitled "An act for the relief of Joseph Wilson," together with the amendment reported thereto by the select committee; and the amendment having been agreed to, the PRESIDENT reported the bill to the House accordingly; and on the question, "Shall the amendment be engrossed, and the bill read a third time, as amended?" it was determined in the affirmative.

The Senate resumed, as in Committee of the Whole, the consideration of the bill, entitled "An act for the relief of the President and Directors of the Washington Bridge Company," together with the amendment reported thereto by the select committee; and the amendment having been agreed to, the PRESIDENT reported the bill to the House accordingly; and on the question, "Shall the amendment be engrossed, and the bill read a third time as amended?" it was determined in the affirmative.

TUESDAY, April 23.

Mr. CHACE, from the committee to whom was referred the bill, entitled "An act for the relief of Moses Turner," reported it without amendment.

The bill, entitled "An act appropriating the sum of two thousand five hundred dollars, for the purpose therein mentioned," was read the second time, and referred to the Committee on Naval Affairs.

The bill, entitled "An act authorizing the payment of a sum of money to Joseph Stewart and others," was read the second time, and referred to the committee last mentioned.

The bill, entitled "An act allowing pay to certain persons made prisoners with the revenue cutter Surveyor," was read the second time, and referred to the same committee.

The bill, entitled "An act for the relief of Joseph S. Newell," was read the second time, and referred to the committee on the memorial of the Legislature of the Mississippi Territory.

The bill, entitled "An act concerning pre-emption rights given in the purchase of lands to certain settlers in the State of Louisiana, and in the Territories of Missouri and Illinois," was read the second time, and referred to the committee last mentioned.

The bill, entitled "An act making appropriations for repairing certain roads therein described," was read the second time, and referred to the Committee on Roads and Canals.

The bill, entitled "An act to authorize the surveying and making a road in the Territory of Illinois," was read the second time, and referred to the committee last mentioned.

The bill, entitled "An act for reducing the duties on licenses to retailers of wines, spirituous liquors, and foreign merchandise," was read the second time, and referred to the Committee on Finance and an Uniform National Currency.

The bill, entitled "An act authorizing the payment of a sum of money to John Rodgers and others," was read the second time, and referred to Mr. DAGGETT, Mr. SANFORD, and Mr. GOLDSBOROUGH, to consider and report thereon.

The bill, entitled "An act authorizing the judges of the circuit court for the District of Columbia to prepare a code of jurisprudence for the said District," was read the second time.

The Senate resumed the consideration of the bill, entitled "An act making appropriations for the support of the Navy of the United States for the year 1816."

On motion of Mr. LACOCK, to insert at the end of the first section, "For building and completing vessels of war on the Lakes, two hundred thousand dollars," it was determined in the negative —yeas 10, nays 17, as follows:

YEAS—Messrs. Barry, Chace, Lacock, Mason of Virginia, Morrow, Roberts, Ruggles, Tichenor, Turner, and Varnum.

NAYS—Messrs. Barbour, Brown, Condit, Daggett, Dana, Gaillard, Goldsborough, Gore, Horsey, King, Macon, Mason of New Hampshire, Tait, Thompson, Wells, Williams, and Wilson.

And no amendment having been agreed to, it passed to the third reading.

On motion, the bill last mentioned was read a third time, by unanimous consent, and passed.

Mr. LACOCK submitted the accounts of expenditures on the building now occupied by Congress, showing the amount of the cost thereof to the proprietors.

The Senate resumed, as in Committee of the Whole, the consideration of the bill, entitled "An act directing the discharge of Moses Lewis from imprisonment."

On motion by Mr. VARNUM, that the further consideration thereof be postponed until the first Monday in June next, it was determined in the negative—yeas 12, nays 16, as follows:

YEAS—Messrs. Barbour, Barry, Chace, Condit, Howell, Macon, Mason of Virginia, Morrow, Roberts, Turner, Varnum, and Wilson.

NAYS—Messrs. Brown, Daggett, Gaillard, Goldsborough, Gore, Harper, Horsey, King, Lacock, Mason of New Hampshire, Ruggles, Tait, Thompson, Tichenor, Wells, and Williams.

Ordered, That it pass to a third reading.

The Senate resumed the consideration of the bill, entitled "An act making appropriations for the support of the Military Establishment of the United States, for the year 1816."

On motion by Mr. BARBOUR, that the Senate agree to the following amendment:

Section 1, line 36, after " dollars," insert " For defraying the expenses incurred by calling out the militia during the war, in addition to the sums heretofore appropriated by law to that object, one million two hundred and fifty thousand dollars:

It was determined in the affirmative—yeas 17, nays 16, as follows:

YEAS—Messrs. Barbour, Barry, Bibb, Brown, Condit, Fromentin, Horsey, Howell, Lacock, Macon, Mason of Virginia, Roberts, Tait, Turner, Wells, Williams, and Wilson.

NAYS—Messrs. Campbell, Chace, Daggett, Dana, Gaillard, Goldsborough, Gore, Harper, King, Mason of New Hampshire, Morrow, Ruggles, Sanford, Thompson, Tichenor, and Varnum.

On the question, "Shall the amendments be engrossed, and the bill read a third time, as amended?" it was determined in the affirmative.

The Senate proceeded to consider their amendments disagreed to by the House of Representatives to the bill, entitled "An act supplementary to the act to provide additional revenues for defraying the expenses of Government and maintaining the public credit, by laying a direct tax upon the United States, and to provide for assessing and collecting the same." Whereupon,

Resolved, That they recede therefrom.

The bill, entitled "An act for the relief of certain purchasers of public lands in the Mississippi Territory," was read a third time, and passed.

The bill, entitled "An act to amend an act entitled 'An act for the relief of Edward Hallowell," was read a third time, and passed.

The bill, entitled "An act to increase the pensions of invalids in certain cases, for the relief of invalids of the militia, and for the appointment of pension agents in those States where there is no commissioner of loans," was read a third time, and passed.

The bill, entitled "An act authorizing the President of the United States to lease the Saline, near the Wabash river, for a term not exceeding seven years," was read a third time, and passed.

The bill, entitled "An act for the relief of William Flood," was read a third time, and passed.

The bill for adjusting claims to land and establishing a land office for the districts of lands lying east of the Mississippi river and Island of New Orleans, was read a third time, and passed.

The bill authorizing the sale of lots owned by the United States, in the city of New Orleans, and for other purposes, was read a third time, and passed.

The bill for settling the compensation of the commissioners, clerk, and translator of the board for land claims in the western district of the Territory of Orleans, now State of Louisiana, having been reported by the committee correctly engrossed, was read a third time, and passed.

The bill entitled "An act for the relief of the legal representatives of Ignace Chalmet Delino, deceased," was read a third time, and passed.

The amendments to the bill, entitled "An act supplemental to the act, entitled 'An act regulating and defining the duties of the judges of the Territory of Illinois, and for vesting in the courts of the Territory of Indiana, a jurisdiction in chancery cases, arising in the said Territory," having been reported by the committee correctly engrossed, was read a third time as amended.

Resolved, That this bill pass with amendments.

The amendments to the bill entitled "An act making further provision for settling claims to land in the Territory of Illinois," having been reported by the committee correctly engrossed, the bill was read a third time as amended.

Resolved, That this bill pass with amendments.

The amendment to the bill entitled "An act for the relief of the President and Directors of the Washington Bridge Company," having been reported by the committee correctly engrossed, the bill was read a third time as amended.

Resolved, That this bill pass with an amendment.

The amendment to the bill entitled "An act for the relief of Joseph Wilson," having been reported by the committee correctly engrossed, the bill was read a third time as amended.

Resolved, That this bill pass with an amendment.

The Senate resumed, as in Committee of the Whole, the consideration of the bill, entitled "An act for the relief of a company of the twentieth brigade of Virginia militia, commanded by Captain Jonathan Walmsley." Mr. VARNUM was requested to take the Chair; and no amendment having been proposed, the PRESIDENT resumed the Chair, and the bill was reported to the House, and it passed to a third reading.

Mr. LACOCK, from the committee to whom was referred the bill, entitled "An act making an appropriation for enclosing and improving the public square near the Capitol, and to abolish the office of Commissioners of the Public Buildings, and of Superintendent, and for the appointment of one Commissioner of the Public Buildings," reported it with amendments, which were read.

The Senate resumed, as in Committee of the Whole, the consideration of the bill, entitled "An act for the relief of the supervisors of the county of Clinton, in the State of New York," together with the amendment reported thereto by the select committee; and the amendment having been agreed to, the PRESIDENT reported the bill to the House accordingly; and on the question, "Shall the amendment be engrossed, and the bill read a third time as amended?" it was determined in the affirmative.

The Senate resumed, as in Committee of the Whole, the consideration of the bill, entitled "An act authorizing the payment for the court-house of Hamilton, in the State of Ohio," together with the amendment reported thereto by the select committee; and the amendment having been agreed to, the PRESIDENT reported the bill to the House accordingly; and on the question, "Shall the amendment be engrossed, and the bill read a third time as amended?" it was determined in the affirmative.

Mr. BROWN, from the committee to whom was referred the bill, entitled "An act for the confirmation of certain claims to land in the western district of the State of Louisiana," reported it with amendments, which were read.

WEDNESDAY, April 24.

The PRESIDENT communicated a report of the Secretary of the Treasury, relative to the memorial of William Gamble; and the report was read.

Mr. BROWN, from the committee to whom was referred the bill, entitled "An act concerning preemption rights given in the purchase of lands to certain settlers in the State of Louisiana, and in the Territories of Missouri and Illinois," reported it without amendment.

Mr. BROWN, from the committee to whom was

referred the bill, entitled "An act for the relief of Joseph S. Newell," reported it without amendment.

Mr. DAGGETT, from the committee to whom was referred the bill, entitled "An act authorizing the payment of a sum of money to John Rodgers and others," reported it without amendment.

Mr. MORROW, from the committee to whom was referred the bill, entitled "An act to authorize the surveying and making a road in the Territory of Illinois," reported it without amendment.

Mr. MORROW, from the committee to whom was referred the bill, entitled "An act making appropriation for repairing certain roads therein described," reported it without amendment.

Mr. BARBOUR, from the Committee on Military Affairs, to whom was referred the bill, entitled "An act for the payment of the militia therein mentioned," reported it without amendment.

The Senate resumed, as in Committee of the Whole, the consideration of the bill making further appropriations for the year 1816; and, on motion by Mr. LACOCK, the further consideration thereof was postponed until Friday next.

The Senate resumed, as in Committee of the Whole, the consideration of the bill, entitled "An act for the relief of the widow and minor children of Zacquill Morgan, late a captain in the United States Army," and, on motion by Mr. DAGGETT, the further consideration thereof was postponed until the first Monday in July next.

The Senate resumed, as in Committee of the Whole, the consideration of the bill, entitled "An act for the relief of Joseph Wheaton," and it passed to a third reading.

Mr. BARBOUR submitted the following motion for consideration:

Resolved, by the Senate and House of Representatives of the United States of America in Congress assembled, That the President of the United States be, and he is hereby, authorized to employ, in addition to the corps of engineers as now established, a skilful assistant, whose compensation shall not exceed the pay, forage, rations, and other emoluments of Brigadier General.

The Senate resumed, as in Committee of the Whole, the consideration of the bill, entitled "An act for the relief of William Hamon," and it passed to a third reading.

The Senate resumed, as in Committee of the Whole, the consideration of the bill, entitled "An act for the relief of Thomas Farrer, William Young, William Moseley, and William Leech," together with the amendment reported thereto by the select committee; and the amendment having been agreed to, the PRESIDENT reported it to the House accordingly; and on the question, "Shall the amendment be engrossed, and the bill read a third time as amended?" it was determined in the affirmative.

The Senate resumed, as in Committee of the Whole the consideration of the bill, entitled "An act for the relief of Manasseh Miner," together with the amendment reported thereto by the select committee; and the bill having been amended, the PRESIDENT reported it to the House accordingly; and on the question, "Shall the amendment be engrossed, and the bill read a third time as amended?" it was determined in the affirmative.

The Senate resumed, as in Committee of the Whole, the consideration of the bill, entitled "An act for the relief of Charles Ross and Samuel Breck, surviving executors of John Ross, deceased," together with the amendments reported thereto by the select committee; and the amendments having been agreed to, the PRESIDENT reported the bill to the House accordingly; and on the question, "Shall the amendments be engrossed, and the bill read a third time as amended?" it was determined in the affirmative.

The Senate resumed, as in Committee of the Whole, the consideration of the bill, entitled "An act for the relief of Ephraim Shaler."

On motion, by Mr. BARBOUR, to strike out the whole of the bill after the enacting clause, and insert in lieu thereof the following:

"That in all cases during the late war with Great Britain, where difficulties may arise in settling the claims of officers and soldiers, of the regular army, and the militia, on account of death, captivity, loss of papers by the destruction of the enemy, or any other unavoidable casualty, the proper officers of the War Department, under the supervision of the Secretary of War, shall be authorised to settle said accounts, upon principles of equity, by resorting to the affidavits of the parties and citizens, or other circumstances entitled to credit, corroborating or contravening the justice of such claims: *Provided always,* That the authority aforesaid shall only be exercised in those cases where the loss of papers or deficiency of vouchers, or evidence, shall be proved, to the satisfaction of the proper departments, to have arisen from death, capture, or destruction of the enemy, or any other unavoidable casualty, as aforesaid: *And provided also,* That such proof be exhibited within two years from and after the passing of this act: *And provided also,* That the party's own oath shall not of itself be deemed sufficient proof of the loss of papers; but may be received, and shall in all cases be required in connexion with other proof or circumstances."

It was determined in the negative—yeas 12, nays 14, as follows:

YEAS—Messrs. Barbour, Barry, Chace, Fromentin, Howell, Lacock, Mason of Virginia, Morrow, Roberts, Ruggles, Turner, and Williams.

NAYS—Messrs. Condit, Daggett, Dana, Gaillard, Goldsborough, Gore, Mason of New Hampshire, Sanford, Tait, Thompson, Tichenor, Varnum, Wells, and Wilson.

And no amendment having been agreed to, the bill passed to a third reading.

The Senate resumed, as in Committee of the Whole, the consideration of the bill, entitled "An act for the relief of Paul D. Butler," together with the amendment reported thereto by the select committee; and, the amendment having been agreed to, the PRESIDENT reported the bill to the House accordingly; and on the question, "Shall the amendment be engrossed, and the bill read a third time as amended?" it was determined in the affirmative.

The Senate resumed, as in Committee of the Whole, the consideration of the bill, entitled "An act directing the discharge of Ebenezer Keeler and John Francis, from imprisonment," and it passed to a third reading.

The Senate resumed, as in Committee of the Whole, the consideration of the resolution requiring the Secretary of State to compile and print, once in every two years, a register of all officers and agents, civil, military and naval, in the service of the United States," and it passed to a third reading.

The bill entitled "An act directing the discharge of Moses Lewis from imprisonment," was read a third time.

The bill entitled "An act for the relief of a company of the 20th brigade of Virginia militia, commanded by Captain Jonathan Walmsley," was read a third time; and on the question, "Shall this bill pass?" it was determined in the affirmative—yeas 23, nays 5, as follows:

YEAS—Messrs. Barbour, Barry, Chace, Condit, Daggett, Gaillard, Harper, Horsey, Howell, Lacock, Macon, Mason of New Hampshire, Mason of Virginia, Morrow, Roberts, Ruggles, Sanford, Tait, Thompson, Wells, Williams, and Wilson.

NAYS—Messrs. Goldsborough, Gore, Tichenor, Turner, and Varnum.

So it was *Resolved,* That this bill pass.

The amendment to the bill, entitled "An act making further appropriations for the support of the Military Establishment for the year 1816," having been reported by the committee correctly engrossed, the bill was read a third time as amended.

Resolved, That this bill pass with an amendment.

The amendment to the bill, entitled "An act authorizing the payment for the county court-house of Hamilton, in the State of Ohio," having been reported by the committee correctly engrossed, the bill was read a third time as amended.

Resolved, That this bill pass with an amendment.

The bill entitled "An act for the relief of the supervisors of the county of Clinton, in the State of New York," having been reported by the committee correctly engrossed, the bill was read a third time as amended.

Resolved, That this bill pass with an amendment.

The Senate resumed, as in Committee of the Whole, the consideration of the bill, entitled "An act to increase the compensations now allowed by law to inspectors, measurers, weighers, and gaugers, employed in the collection of the customs," and it passed to a third reading.

The Senate resumed, as in Committee of the Whole, the consideration of the bill, entitled "An act for the free importation of stereotype plates, and to encourage the printing and gratuitous distribution of the Scriptures by the Bible Societies within the United States," and it passed to a third reading.

The Senate resumed, as in Committee of the Whole, the consideration of the bill, entitled "An act for the relief of the heirs of Alexander Rox-burgh," and it passed to a third reading.

Mr. LACOCK, from the committee to whom was referred the bill, entitled "An act continuing the salaries of certain officers of Government," reported it without amendment.

A message from the House of Representatives informed the Senate that the House have passed a bill, entitled "An act concerning invalid pensioners;" a bill, entitled "An act for the relief of George T. Ross, Daniel T. Patterson, and the officers and men lately under their command;" also, a resolution requesting the President of the United States to cause further observation to be made, with a view of ascertaining the longitude of the Capitol, in the City of Washington; in which bills and resolution they request the concurrence of the Senate. They have agreed to the amendments to the bill entitled "An act for the relief of the President and Directors of the Washington Bridge Company," with an amendment, in which they request the concurrence of the Senate. They have disagreed to the amendments of the Senate to the bill, entitled "An act supplemental to the act, entitled 'An act regulating and defining the duties of the judges of the Territory of Illinois, and for vesting in the courts of the Territory of Indiana, a jurisdiction in chancery cases arising in the said Territory."

The Senate proceeded to consider their amendments, disagreed to by the House of Representatives, to the bill last mentioned. Whereupon,

Resolved, That they recede therefrom.

The Senate proceeded to consider the amendment of the House of Representatives to their amendment to the bill, entitled "An act for the relief of the President and Directors of the Washington Bridge Company." Whereupon,

Resolved, That they concur therein.

The two bills and resolution last brought up for concurrence were read, and severally passed to the second reading.

The Senate resumed, as in Committee of the Whole, the consideration of the resolution from the House of Representatives, authorizing the President of the Senate and Speaker of the House of Representatives to adjourn their respective Houses on the 20th day of April instant, and the resolution having been amended by striking out "20th," on motion, by Mr. BARBOUR, to fill the blank with "27," it was determined in the affirmative—yeas 16, nays 15, as follows:

YEAS—Messrs. Barbour, Barry, Daggett, Goldsborough, Harper, Horsey, Howell, Mason of New Hampshire, Mason of Virginia, Roberts, Ruggles, Sanford, Thompson, Tichenor, Wells, and Wilson.

NAYS—Messrs. Brown, Chace, Condit, Dana, Fromentin, Gaillard, Gore, King, Lacock, Macon, Morrow, Tait, Turner, Varnum, and Williams.

The resolution having been amended, the PRESIDENT reported it to the House accordingly; and on the question to concur in the amendment agreed to as in Committee of the Whole, filling the blank with "27," it was determined in the negative—yeas 15, nays 16, as follows:

YEAS—Messrs. Barbour, Barry, Daggett, Golds-

borough, Horsey, Howell, Mason of New Hampshire, Mason of Virginia, Roberts, Ruggles, Sanford, Thompson, Tichenor, Wells, and Wilson.

NAYS—Messrs. Brown, Campbell, Chace, Condit, Dana, Fromentin, Gaillard, Gore, King, Lacock, Macon, Morrow, Tait, Turner, Varnum, and Williams.

On motion, to strike out "Saturday, the —— day of April, instant," and insert "Wednesday, the first day of May next," it was determined in the affirmative—yeas 16, nays 15, as follows:

YEAS—Messrs. Barry, Campbell, Condit, Dana, Fromentin, Goldsborough, Gore, King, Lacock, Mason of Virginia, Morrow, Roberts, Ruggles, Tait, Varnum, and Wells.

NAYS—Messrs. Barbour, Brown, Chace, Daggett Gaillard, Horsey, Howell, Macon, Mason of New Hampshire, Sanford, Thompson, Tichenor, Turner Williams, and Wilson.

On the question, "Shall the amendment be engrossed, and the resolution read a third time as amended?" it was determined in the affirmative.

Mr. TAIT, from the Committee on Naval Affairs, to whom was referred the bill, entitled "An act authorizing the payment of a sum of money to Joseph Stewart, and others," reported it without amendment.

The Senate resumed, as in Committee of th Whole, the consideration of the bill, entitled "An act to fix the commissions of the collectors of the direct tax and internal duties, and to revive and continue in force "An act further to provide for the collection of duties on imports and tonnage."

On motion, by Mr. MASON, of New Hampshire, to strike out the third section of the bill, as fol lows:

SEC. 3. *And be it further enacted,* That the act en titled "An act further to provide for the collection o duties on imports and tonnage," passed on the day of March, 1815, be, and the same is, hereby vived and made of force: *Provided however,* Th nothing in the eighth section thereof shall be constru to affect the duration of the act so revived, but the said act shall be of force without limitation as to time.

It was determined in the negative—yeas 8 nays 12, as follows:

YEAS—Messrs. Daggett, Gaillard, Goldsborough Gore, Harper, Macon, Mason of New Hampshire, an Thompson.

NAYS—Messrs. Campbell, Chace, Condit, Howell Mason of Virginia, Morrow, Roberts, Ruggles, Tai Turner, Varnum, and Wilson.

On motion, by Mr. HARPER, the bill havin; been amended, the PRESIDENT reported it to th House accordingly; and on the question, "Shal the amendments be engrossed, and the bill read third time as amended?" it was determined i the affirmative.

The Senate resumed, as in Committee of th Whole, the consideration of the bill, entitled "A act for the relief of Thomas Ap Catesby Jones, and it passed to a third reading.

The Senate resumed, as in Committee of th Whole, the consideration of the bill, entitled "A act for the relief of Rufus S. Reed and Danie Dobbins," and it passed to a third reading.

The Senate resumed, as in Committee of th

Whole, the consideration of the bill, entitled "An act for the relief of Asher Palmer," and it passed to a third reading.

The Senate resumed, as in Committee of the Whole, the consideration of the bill, entitled "An act for the relief of John Crosby and John Crosby, junior," and it passed to a third reading.

The Senate resumed, as in Committee of the Whole, the consideration of the bill, entitled "An act for the relief of Taylor and McNeal, and Henry and John McLeister," and it passed to a third reading.

The Senate resumed, as in Committee of the Whole, the consideration of the bill, entitled "An act for the relief of certain owners of goods entered at Hampden, in the District of Maine." Mr. VARNUM was requested to take the Chair, and no amendment having been agreed to, the PRESIDENT resumed the Chair, and the bill was reported to the House; and it passed to a third reading.

The Senate resumed, as in Committee of the Whole, the consideration of the bill, entitled "An act supplementary to an act granting bounties in lands and extra pay to certain Canadian volunteers," and it passed to the third reading.

On motion, the bill last mentioned was read a third time by unanimous consent, and passed.

The Senate resumed, as in Committee of the Whole. the consideration of the bill, entitled "An act declaring the assent of Congress to an act of the General Assembly of Virginia therein named," and it passed to a third reading.

The Senate resumed, as in Committee of the Whole, the consideration of the bill, entitled "An act confirming the titles of certain purchasers of land, who purchased from the Board of Trustees for the Vincennes University," and it passed to a third reading.

The Senate resumed, as in Committee of the Whole, the consideration of the bill, entitled "An act to authorize the sale of lands forfeited to the United States, in the district of Jeffersonville, at the land office in said district," and it passed to a third reading.

The Senate resumed, as in Committee of the Whole, the consideration of the bill, entitled "An act providing for the sale of the tract of land at the British fort, at the Miami of the Lake, at the foot of the Rapids, and for other purposes," and it passed to a third reading.

The Senate resumed, as in Committee of the Whole, the consideration of the bill, entitled "An act providing for the sale of the tract of land at the lower rapids of the Sandusky river," and it passed to a third reading.

The Senate resumed, as in Committee of the Whole, the consideration of the bill, entitled "An act for the relief of Samuel Dick, William Bruce, and Asa Kitchell," and it passed to a third reading.

The Senate resumed, as in Committee of the Whole, the consideration of the bill, entitled "An act for the relief of Thomas H. Boyle," and it passed to a third reading.

The Senate resumed, as in Committee of the

Whole, the consideration of the bill, entitled "An act granting to Amos Spafford the right of pre-emption," and it passed to a third reading.

The Senate resumed, as in Committee of the Whole, the consideration of the bill, entitled "An act for the relief of Charles Levaux Trudeau," together with the amendment reported thereto by the select committee; and the amendment having been agreed to, the PRESIDENT reported the bill to the House accordingly; and on the question, "Shall the amendment be engrossed, and the bill read a third time. as amended?" it was determined in the affirmative.

The Senate resumed, as in Committee of the Whole, the consideration of the bill, entitled "An act for the relief of William Crawford, Frederick Bates, and William Garrard," together with the amendments reported thereto by the select committee; and the amendments having been agreed to, the PRESIDENT reported the bill to the House accordingly; and on the question, "Shall the amendments be engrossed, and the bill read a third time as amended?" it was determined in the affirmative.

The Senate resumed, as in Committee of the Whole, the consideration of the bill entitled "An act authorizing the payment of a sum to John T. Courtney and Samuel Harrison, or their legal representatives," and it passed to a third reading.

The Senate resumed, as in Committee of the Whole. the consideration of the bill, entitled "An act rewarding the officers and crew of the Constitution for the capture of the British sloop-of-war Levant;" and on the question, "Shall the bill be read a third time?" it was determined in the affirmative—yeas 19, nays 6, as follows:

YEAS—Messrs. Barry, Brown, Campbell, Chace, Condit, Daggett, Gaillard, Goldsborough, Gore, Harper, Howell, Lacock, Ruggles, Sanford, Tait, Thompson, Tichenor, Williams, and Wilson.

NAYS—Messrs. Barbour, Bibb, Macon, Mason of Virginia, Turner, and Varnum.

Mr. CAMPBELL, from the committee to whom was referred the bill, entitled "An act for reducing the duties on licenses to retailers of wines, spirituous liquors, and foreign merchandise," reported it without amendment.

The Senate resumed, as in Committee of the Whole, the consideration of the bill, entitled "An act concerning Pharaoh Farrow and others;" and it passed to a third reading.

The Senate resumed, as in Committee of the Whole, the consideration of the bill, entitled "An act authorizing the payment of a sum of money to James Levings;" and it passed to a third reading.

The Senate resumed, as in Committee of the Whole, the consideration of the bill, entitled "An act for the relief of the widow and children of Charles Dolph;" and it passed to a third reading.

The Senate resumed, as in Committee of the Whole, the consideration of the bill, entitled "An act for the relief of Young King, a chief of the Seneca tribe of Indians;" and it passed to a third reading.

The Senate resumed, as in Committee of the Whole, the consideration of the bill, entitled "An act providing for the distribution of one hundred thousand dollars among the captors of the Algerine vessels, captured and restored to the Dey of Algiers;" and it passed to a third reading.

The Senate resumed, as in Committee of the Whole, the consideration of the bill to authorize the issuing of a grant to Major General Andrew Jackson for a tract of land. Mr. VARNUM was requested to take the Chair.

On motion, by Mr. LACOCK, that the further consideration thereof be postponed until the first Monday in July next, it was determined in the affirmative—yeas 17, nays 12, as follows:

YEAS—Messrs. Barry, Daggett, Dana, Gaillard, Goldsborough, Gore, King, Lacock, Macon, Mason of New Hampshire, Morrow, Roberts, Ruggles, Thompson, Turner, Wells, and Wilson.

NAYS—Messrs. Barbour, Brown, Campbell, Chace, Condit, Fromentin, Harper, Howell, Mason of Virginia, Sanford, Tait, and Varnum.

THURSDAY, April 25.

Mr. TAIT, from the Committee on Naval Affairs, to whom was referred the bill, entitled "An act appropriating the sum of two thousand five hundred dollars, for the purpose therein mentioned;" reported it without amendment, and the bill was considered as in Committee of the Whole, and passed to a third reading.

Mr. TAIT, from the same committee, to whom was referred the bill, entitled "An act allowing pay to certain persons made prisoners with the revenue cutter Surveyor," reported it without amendment; and the bill was considered as in Committee of the Whole, and passed to a third reading.

On motion, by Mr. KING, the committee to whom was referred the memorial of John Stevens, of New Jersey, were discharged from the further consideration thereof.

On motion, by Mr. RUGGLES, the committee to whom was referred the petition of William Faris, were discharged from the further consideration thereof.

The resolution authorizing the employment of a skilful assistant, in addition to the corps of engineers, was read the second time, and considered as in Committee of the Whole, and having been amended, the PRESIDENT reported it to the House accordingly; and on the question, "Shall this resolution be engrossed and read a third time?" it was determined in the affirmative.

The "Resolution requesting the President of the United States to cause further observations to be made, with a view of ascertaining the longitude of the Capitol, in the City of Washington," was read the second time.

The bill entitled "An act for the relief of George T. Ross, Daniel T. Patterson, and the officers and men lately under their command," was read the second time, and referred to the Committee on Naval Affairs.

The bill entitled "An act concerning invalid pensioners," was read the second time, and referred to a select committee; and Messrs. LACOCK, MORROW, and VARNUM, were appointed the committee.

Mr. WILSON presented the petition of Titus V. Sliter and others, praying pensions, as stated in the petition; which was read, and referred to the committee last mentioned.

The Senate resumed, as in Committee of the Whole, the consideration of the bill, entitled "An act to enable the people of the Mississippi Territory to form a constitution and State government, and for the admission of such State into the Union on an equal footing with the original States."

On motion, by Mr. BARBOUR, the further consideration thereof was postponed until the first Monday in July next.

The bill entitled "An act for the relief of Joseph Wheaton," was read a third time, and passed.

The bill entitled "An act for the relief of William Hamon," was read a third time, and passed.

The bill entitled "An act for the relief of Ephraim Shaler," was read a third time, and passed.

The bill entitled "An act directing the discharge of Ebenezer Keeler and John Francis from imprisonment," was read a third time, and passed.

The bill to increase the compensation now allowed by law to inspectors, measurers, weighers, and gaugers, employed in the collection of the customs, was read a third time, and passed.

The bill entitled "An act for the free importation of stereotype plates, and to encourage the printing and gratuitous distribution of the Scriptures by the Bible Societies within the United States," was read a third time, and passed.

The bill entitled "An act for the relief of Young King, a chief of the Seneca tribe of Indians," was read a third time, and passed.

The bill entitled "An act for the relief of the widow and children of Charles Dolph, deceased," was read a third time, and passed.

The bill entitled "An act authorizing the payment of a sum of money to James Levins," was read a third time, and passed.

The bill entitled "An act providing for the distribution of one hundred thousand dollars among the captors of the Algerine vessels, captured and restored to the Dey of Algiers," was read a third time, and passed.

The bill entitled "An act concerning Pharaoh Farrow," was read a third time, and passed.

The bill entitled "An act rewarding the officers and crew of the Constitution for the capture of the British sloop-of-war Levant," was read a third time, and passed.

The bill entitled "An act authorizing the payment of a sum to John T. Courtney and Samuel Harrison, or their legal representatives," was read a third time, and passed.

The bill entitled "An act granting to Amos Spafford the right of pre-emption," was read a third time, and passed.

The bill entitled "An act for the relief of Sam-

HISTORY OF CONGRESS.

Proceedings.

nel Dick, William Bruce, and Asa Kitchell," was read a third time, and passed.

The bill entitled "An act for the relief of Thos. H. Boyle," was read a third time, and passed.

The bill entitled "An act providing for the sale of the tract of land at the lower rapids of Sandusky river," was read a third time, and passed.

The bill entitled "An act providing for the sale of the tract of land at the British fort, at the Miami of the Lake, at the foot of the rapids, and for other purposes," was read a third time, and passed.

The bill entitled "An act to authorize the sale of lands forfeited to the United States, in the district of Jeffersonville, at the land office in said district," was read a third time, and passed.

The bill entitled "An act confirming the titles of certain purchasers of land who purchased from the Board of Trustees for the Vincennes University," was read a third time, and passed.

The bill entitled "An act declaring the assent of Congress to an act of the General Assembly of Virginia, therein named," was read a third time, and passed.

The bill entitled "An act for the relief of certain owners of goods entered at Hampden, in the district of Maine," was read a third time, and passed.

The bill entitled "An act for the relief of Taylor and McNeal, Evans and McNeal, and Henry and John McLeister," was read a third time, and passed.

The bill entitled "An act for the relief of John Crosby and John Crosby, jr.," was read a third time, and passed.

The bill entitled "An act for the relief of Asher Palmer," was read a third time, and passed.

The bill entitled "An act for the relief of Rufus S. Reed and Daniel Dobbins," was read a third time, and passed.

The bill entitled "An act for the relief of Thomas Ap Catesby Jones," was read a third time, and passed.

The bill entitled "An act for the relief of the heirs of Alexander Roxburgh," was read a third time, and passed.

The amendment to the bill, entitled "An act for the relief of Thomas Farrer, William Young, William Moseley, and William Leech," having been reported by the committee correctly engrossed, the bill was read a third time as amended, and passed.

The amendments to the bill, entitled "An act for the relief of Charles Ross and Samuel Breck, surviving executors of John Ross, deceased," having been reported by the committee correctly engrossed, the bill was read a third time as amended.

The amendments to the bill, entitled "An act for the relief of Manassah Miner," having been reported by the committee correctly engrossed," the bill was read a third time as amended.

Resolved, That this bill pass with amendments.

The amendment to the bill, entitled "An act to fix the commissions of the collectors of the direct tax and internal duties, and to revive and con-

tinue in force 'An act further to provide for the collection of duties on imports and tonnage," having been reported by the committee correctly engrossed, the bill was read a third time as amended.

Resolved, That this bill pass with an amendment.

The amendment to the bill, entitled "An act for the relief of Charles Levaux Trudeau," having been reported by the committee correctly engrossed, the bill was read a third time as amended.

Resolved, That this bill pass with an amendment.

The amendments to the bill, entitled "An act for the relief of William Crawford, Frederick Bates, and William Garrard," having been reported by the committee correctly engrossed, the bill was read a third time as amended.

Resolved, That this bill pass with amendments.

The amendment to the "Resolution authorizing the President of the Senate and Speaker of the House of Representatives to adjourn their respective Houses," having been reported by the committee correctly engrossed, on motion by Mr. TAIT, the further consideration of the resolution was postponed until to-morrow.

The amendments to the bill, entitled "An act for the relief of Paul D. Butler," having been reported by the committee correctly engrossed, the bill was read a third time as amended.

Resolved, That this bill pass with amendments.

The "Resolution requiring the Secretary of State to compile and print, once in every two years, a register of all officers and agents, civil, military, and naval, in the service of the United States," was read a third time, and passed.

The Senate resumed, as in Committee of the Whole, the consideration of the "Resolution to indemnify Jabez Mowry and others," together with the amendments reported thereto by the select committee; and the amendments having been agreed to, the PRESIDENT reported the resolution to the House accordingly; and on the question, "Shall the amendments be engrossed, and the resolution read a third time as amended?" it was determined in the affirmative.

The Senate resumed, as in Committee of the Whole, the consideration of the bill, entitled "An act for the gradual increase of the Navy of the United States," together with the amendment reported thereto by the select committee; and the amendment having been agreed to, the PRESIDENT reported the bill to the House accordingly; and on the question, "Shall the amendment be engrossed, and the bill read a third time as amended?" it was determined in the affirmative.

Mr. BROWN, from the committee to whom was referred the bill, entitled "An act for the relief of Peter Audrain," reported it with an amendment, which was read, and considered as in Committee of the Whole, and agreed to, and the PRESIDENT reported the bill to the House accordingly; and on the question, "Shall the amendment be engrossed, and the bill read a third time as amended?" it was determined in the affirmative.

The Senate resumed, as in Committee of the Whole, the consideration of the bill, entitled "An act for the relief of Charles Todd ;" and on the question, "Shall this bill be read a third time? it was determined in the affirmative—yeas 15, nays 14, as follows:

YEAS—Messrs. Barbour, Barry, Brown, Campbell, Daggett, Gaillard, Goldsborough, Harper, Horsey, Howell, Mason of Virginia, Sanford, Tichenor, Turner, and Williams.

NAYS—Messrs. Bibb, Chace, Condit, Dana, King, Lacock, Macon, Roberts, Ruggles, Tait, Thompson, Varnum, Wells, and Wilson.

Mr. BROWN, from the committee to whom was referred the bill, entitled "An act for the benefit of John P. Maxwell and Hugh H. Maxwell." reported it without amendment, and the bill was considered as in Committee of the Whole, and passed to a third reading.

Mr. BROWN, from the committee to whom was referred the bill, entitled "An act to authorize the survey of two millions of acres of the public lands, in lieu of that quantity heretofore authorized to be surveyed, in the Territory of Michigan, as military bounty lands," reported it without amendment.

The Senate resumed, as in Committee of the Whole, the consideration of the bill, entitled "An act supplementary to the act passed the 30th of March, 1802, to regulate trade and intercourse with the Indian tribes, and to preserve peace on the frontiers ;" and it passed to a third reading.

The Senate resumed, as in Committee of the Whole, the consideration of the bill, entitled "An act to alter certain parts of the act providing for the government of the Territory of Missouri ;" and it passed to a third reading.

The Senate resumed, as in Committee of the Whole, the consideration of the bill, entitled "An act for the relief of Thomas B. Farish ;" and on motion by Mr. VARNUM, the further consideration thereof was postponed until the first Monday in July next.

The Senate resumed, as in Committee of the Whole, the consideration of the bill to ascertain and establish the western boundary of the tract reserved for satisfying the military bounties allowed to the officers and soldiers of the Virginia line, on State and Continental Establishment; and on motion by Mr. MASON, of New Hampshire, the further consideration thereof was postponed until the first Monday in July next, and

Ordered, That the further consideration of the report of the committee to whom was referred the resolution relating to the claims of the officers and soldiers of the Virginia line, on State and Continental establishment, for bounty lands, be also postponed until the first Monday in July next.

The Senate resumed, as in Committee of the Whole, the consideration of the bill to increase the salary of the Register of the Treasury, and to allow him a compensation for his agency in countersigning and issuing Treasury notes; and on the question, "Shall this bill be engrossed and read a third time ?" it was determined in the affirmative—yeas 21, nays 7, as follows:

YEAS—Messrs. Barbour, Barry, Chace, Condit, Daggett, Dana, Gaillard, Goldsborough, Harper, Horsey, Howell, King, Mason of New Hampshire, Morrow, Ruggles, Sanford, Tait, Thompson, Tichenor, Varnum, and Williams.

NAYS—Messrs. Bibb, Lacock, Macon, Roberts, Turner, Wells, and Wilson.

The Senate resumed, as in Committee of the Whole, the consideration of the bill, entitled "An act to authorize the building of three light-houses, viz: one on Race Point, one on Point Gammon, and one on the island of Petite Manon, in the State of Massachusetts," and it passed to a third reading.

The Senate resumed, as in Committee of the Whole, the consideration of the bill, entitled "An act making appropriations for rebuilding lighthouses, and for completing the plan of lighting them according to the improvements of Winslow Lewis, for placing beacons and buoys, for preserving Little Gull Island, and for surveying the coast of the United States," and it passed to a third reading.

Mr. VARNUM gave notice that he should ask leave to bring in a bill to increase the salary of Chaplains to Congress.

The Senate resumed, as in Committee of the Whole, the consideration of the bill, entitled "An act for the relief of Samuel Manac," and it passed to a third reading.

The Senate resumed, as in Committee of the Whole, the consideration of the bill, entitled "An act making an appropriation for enclosing and improving the public square, near the Capitol, and to abolish the office of Commissioners of the Public Buildings, and of Superintendent, and for the appointment of one Commissioner for the Public Buildings," together with the amendments reported thereto by the select committee ; and the amendments having been agreed to, with further amendment, the PRESIDENT reported the bill to the House accordingly ; and on the question, "Shall the amendments be engrossed and the bill read a third time as amended ?" it was determined in the affirmative.

The Senate resumed, as in Committee of the Whole, the consideration of the bill, entitled "An act to establish post roads," together with the amendments reported thereto by the select committee. Mr. VARNUM was requested to take the Chair, and the amendments having been agreed to, the PRESIDENT resumed the Chair, and the bill was reported accordingly ; and on the question, "Shall the amendments be engrossed, and the bill read a third time as amended ?" it was determined in the affirmative.

The Senate resumed, as in Committee of the Whole, the consideration of the bill, entitled "An act regulating the currency within the United States, of the gold coins of Great Britain, France, Portugal, and Spain, and the crowns of France, and five franc pieces," and it passed to a third reading.

The Senate resumed, as in Committee of the Whole, the consideration of the bill, entitled "An act to provide for the appointment of a surveyor of the public lands, in the Territories of Illinois and Missouri," together with the amendments reported thereto by the select committee; and the amendments having been agreed to, the PRESIDENT reported the bill to the House accordingly; and on the question, "Shall the amendments be engrossed, and the bill read a third time as amended?" it was determined in the affirmative.

The Senate resumed, as in Committee of the Whole, the consideration of the bill, entitled "An act concerning the owners, officers, and crew of the privateer Roger," and the bill having been amended, the PRESIDENT reported it to the House accordingly; and on the question, "Shall the amendments be engrossed, and the bill read a third time as amended?" it was determined in the affirmative.

The Senate resumed, as in Committee of the Whole, the consideration of the bill, entitled "An act providing for the sale of certain lands in the State of Ohio, formerly set apart for refugees from Canada and Nova Scotia," and it passed to a third reading.

The Senate resumed, as in Committee of the Whole, the consideration of the bill, entitled "An act to establish a land district in the Illinois Territory, north of the district of Kaskaskia," and it passed to a third reading.

The Senate resumed, as in Committee of the Whole, the consideration of the bill, entitled "An act for the relief of Elizabeth Hamilton," and on the question, "Shall this bill be read a third time?" it was determined in the negative—yeas 20, nays 6, as follows:

YEAS—Messrs. Barbour, Barry, Brown, Chace, Daggett, Gaillard, Goldsborough, Gore, Horsey, Howell, King, Lacock, Mason of New Hampshire, Mason of Virginia, Morrow, Ruggles, Sanford, Thompson, Tichenor, and Williams.

NAYS—Messrs. Condit, Macon, Roberts, Turner, Varnum, and Wilson.

The Senate resumed, as in Committee of the Whole, the consideration of the bill, entitled "An act providing for cases of lost military land warrants, and discharges for faithful services," and it passed to the third reading.

The Senate resumed, as in Committee of the Whole, the consideration of the bill, entitled "An act to enable the Levy Court in the county of Alexandria to lay a tax for the purpose of defraying the expense of erecting a jail and courthouse," and it passed to a third reading.

The Senate resumed, as in Committee of the Whole, the consideration of the bill, entitled "An act providing for an additional compensation to the district judge of the southern district of New York," and it passed to a third reading.

The Senate resumed, as in Committee of the Whole, the consideration of the bill, entitled "An act for the relief of David Coffin, Samuel and William Rodman, and Samuel Rodman, junior," together with the amendment reported thereto by

the select committee; and the amendment having been agreed to, the PRESIDENT reported the bill to the House accordingly; and on the question, "Shall the amendment be engrossed, and the bill read a third time as amended?" it was determined in the affirmative.

The Senate resumed, as in Committee of the Whole, the consideration of the bill entitled "An act for the confirmation of certain claims to land in the western district of the State of Louisiana," together with the amendments reported thereto by the select committee; and the amendments having been agreed to, the PRESIDENT reported the bill to the House accordingly; and on the question, "Shall the amendments be engrossed, and the bill read a third time as amended?" it was determined in the affirmative.

The Senate resumed, as in Committee of the Whole, the consideration of the bill, entitled "An act authorizing the judges of the circuit court for the District of Columbia to prepare a code of jurisprudence for the said District," and the bill having been amended, the PRESIDENT reported it to the House accordingly; and on the question, "Shall the amendment be engrossed, and the bill read a third time as amended?" it was determined in the affirmative.

The Senate resumed, as in Committee of the Whole, the consideration of the bill, entitled "An act for the relief of Moses Turner," and it passed to a third reading.

The Senate resumed, as in Committee of the Whole, the consideration of the bill, entitled "An act concerning pre-emption rights given in the purchase of lands to settlers in the State of Louisiana, and in the Territories of Missouri and Illinois," and it passed to a third reading.

The Senate resumed, as in Committee of the Whole, the consideration of the bill, entitled "An act for the payment of the militia in the case therein mentioned," and it passed to a third reading.

The Senate resumed, as in Committee of the Whole, the consideration of the bill, entitled "An act for the relief of Joseph S. Newell," and it passed to a third reading.

The Senate resumed, as in Committee of the Whole, the consideration of the bill, entitled "An act continuing the salaries of certain officers of Government," and it passed to a third reading.

The Senate resumed, as in Committee of the Whole, the consideration of the bill, entitled "An act to authorize the surveying and making a road in the Territory of Illinois," and it passed to a third reading.

The Senate resumed, as in Committee of the Whole, the consideration of the bill, entitled "An act making an appropriation for repairing certain roads therein described," and it passed to a third reading.

The Senate resumed, as in Committee of the Whole, the consideration of the bill, entitled "An act authorizing the payment of a sum of money to John Rodgers and others," and it passed to a third reading.

The Senate resumed, as in Committee of the

Whole, the consideration of the bill, entitled "An act authorizing the payment of a sum of money to Joseph Stewart and others," and it passed to a third reading.

SALARIES OF SECRETARY AND CLERK.

The Senate resumed, as in Committee of the Whole, the consideration of the bill, entitled "An act fixing the compensation of the Secretary of the Senate and Clerk of the House of Representatives, and making a temporary provision for the clerks employed in their offices," together with the amendments reported thereto by the select committee; and on the question to agree to the first amendment, to wit : "Section 1, line 6, strike out 'three thousand,' and insert 'two thousand five hundred," it was determined in the negative—yeas 10, nays 18, as follows :

YEAS—Messrs. Condit, Gaillard, Gore, Lacock, Macon, Morrow, Roberts, Ruggles, Varnum, and Wilson.

NAYS—Messrs. Barbour, Barry, Brown, Campbell, Chace, Daggett, Fromentin, Goldsborough, Harper, Horsey, Howell, King, Mason of New Hampshire, Mason of Virginia, Sanford, Tait, Tichenor, and Williams.

The second amendment having been agreed to, the bill was further amended, and on motion by Mr. LACOCK, that the further consideration of the bill be postponed until the first Monday in June next, it was determined in the negative—yeas 5, nays 23, as follows :

YEAS—Messrs. Lacock, Macon, Roberts, Varnum, and Wilson.

NAYS—Messrs. Barbour, Barry, Brown, Campbell, Chace, Condit, Daggett, Fromentin, Gaillard, Goldsborough, Gore, Harper, Horsey, Howell, King, Mason of New Hampshire, Mason of Virginia, Morrow, Ruggles, Sanford, Tait, Tichenor, and Williams.

No further amendment having been agreed to, the PRESIDENT reported the bill to the House; and on the question to concur in the amendment agreed to as in Committee of the Whole, to wit : Section 3, line 1, strike out " for the present year only," it was determined in the affirmative—yeas 19, nays 7, as follows :

YEAS—Messrs. Barbour, Barry, Brown, Chace, Daggett, Fromentin, Gaillard, Goldsborough, Gore, Harper, Horsey, Howell, King, Mason of New Hampshire, Mason of Virginia, Sanford, Tait, Tichenor, and Williams.

NAYS—Messrs. Condit, Lacock, Macon, Morrow, Roberts, Varnum, and Wilson.

On motion by Mr. VARNUM, to add a new section as follows:

"*And be it further enacted,* That for the present year there be allowed and paid two hundred dollars to each of the clerks in the offices of the several Departments of the Government, whose compensation has not heretofore exceeded thirteen hundred dollars, in addition to their usual compensation, and the sum of ninety dollars to each of the messengers and assistant messengers attached to the Departments of the Government."

It was determined in the negative—yeas 7, nays 21, as follows :

YEAS—Messrs. Condit, Lacock, Roberts, Ruggles, Tait, Varnum, and Williams.

NAYS—Messrs. Barbour, Barry, Brown, Campbell, Chace, Daggett, Fromentin, Gaillard, Goldsborough, Gore, Harper, Horsey, Howell, King, Macon, Mason of New Hampshire, Mason of Virginia, Morrow, Tichenor, Turner, and Wilson.

On motion of Mr. LACOCK, to insert the following section :

"*And be it further enacted,* That to all clerks employed in the several Departments of the Government, who receive less than eight hundred dollars, there shall be allowed an addition of twenty-five per centum for the present year ; to all clerks who receive above eight hundred dollars and not exceeding one thousand two hundred and fifty dollars, twenty per centum ; and to all clerks who receive above one thousand two hundred and fifty dollars and not exceeding one thousand five hundred dollars, fifteen per centum ; and to the several messengers employed in the public offices, there shall be allowed to them respectively, an addition of twenty per cent."

It was determined in the negative—yeas 13, nays 18, as follows :

YEAS—Messrs. Condit, Daggett, Gaillard, Howell, Lacock, Morrow, Roberts, Ruggles, Sanford, Tait, Turner, Varnum, and Williams.

NAYS—Messrs. Barbour, Barry, Brown, Campbell, Chace, Dana, Fromentin, Goldsborough, Gore, Harper, Horsey, King, Macon, Mason of New Hampshire, Mason of Virginia, Thompson, Tichenor, and Wilson.

On motion by Mr. VARNUM, to add the following section :

" *And be it further enacted,* That the Chaplains of the two Houses of Congress shall be entitled to receive, as compensation for their services, at the rate of one thousand dollars per annum each, to commence with the present session of Congress."

It was determined in the negative—yeas 13, nays 17, as follows :

YEAS—Messrs. Condit, Dana, Gaillard, Howell, Morrow, Roberts, Ruggles, Tait, Thompson, Tichenor, Turner, Varnum, and Wilson.

NAYS—Messrs. Barbour, Barry, Brown, Campbell, Chace, Daggett, Goldsborough, Gore, Harper, Horsey, King, Lacock, Macon, Mason of New Hampshire, Mason of Virginia, Sanford, and Williams.

On the question, " Shall the amendments be engrossed, and read a third time as amended ?" it was determined in the affirmative.

FRIDAY, April 26.

Mr. TAIT, from the Committee on Naval Affairs, to whom was referred the bill, entitled "An act for the relief of George T. Ross, Daniel T. Patterson, and the officers and men lately under their command," reported it without amendment, and the bill was considered as in Committee of the Whole, and it passed to a third reading.

The bill last mentioned was read a third time, by unanimous consent, and passed.

On motion by Mr. SANFORD, it was agreed that Harman Hendricks have leave to withdraw his petition and papers.

The Senate resumed, as in Committee of the Whole, the consideration of the bill, entitled "An act declaring the consent of Congress to acts of the State of South Carolina, authorizing the City Council of Charleston to impose and collect a duty on the tonnage of vessels from foreign ports; and to acts of the State of Georgia, authorizing the imposition and collection of a duty on the tonnage of vessels in the ports of Savannah and St. Mary's," together with the amendment reported thereto by the select committee; and the amendment having been disagreed to, the bill was reported to the House, and ordered to a third reading.

On motion, the bill last mentioned was read a third time by unanimous consent, and passed.

Mr. VARNUM asked and obtained leave to bring in a bill fixing the compensation of the Chaplains of Congress; and the bill was read, and passed to the second reading.

The Senate resumed, as in Committee of the Whole, the consideration of the resolution to ascertain the longitude of the Capitol, in the City of Washington; and on the question, " Shall this resolution be read a third time ?" it was determined in the negative. So the resolution was lost.

The bill authorizing the payment of a sum of money to John Rodgers and others," was read a third time, and passed.

The bill entitled "An act making an appropriation for repairing certain roads therein described," was read a third time, and passed.

The bill entitled "An act to authorize the surveying and making a road in the Territory of Illinois," was read a third time, and passed.

The bill entitled "An act continuing the salaries of certain officers of Government," was read a third time, and passed.

The bill entitled "An act for the relief of Joseph S. Newell," was read a third time, and passed.

The bill entitled "An act for the payment of the militia, in the case therein mentioned," was read a third time, and passed.

The bill entitled "An act concerning pre-emption rights given in the purchase of lands to certain settlers in the State of Louisiana, and in the Territories of Missouri and Illinois," was read a third time, and passed.

The bill entitled "An act for the relief of Moses Turner," was read a third time, and passed.

The bill entitled "An act providing an additional compensation to the district judge of the southern district of New York," was read a third time, and passed.

The bill entitled "An act to enable the Levy Court of the county of Alexandria to lay a tax for the purpose of defraying the expense of erecting a jail and court-house," was read a third time, and passed.

The bill entitled "An act providing for cases of lost military land warrants, and discharges for faithful services," was read a third time, and passed.

Seth Hamilton," was read a third time, and passed.

The bill entitled "An act for the relief of Eliza-

The bill entitled "An act to establish a land district in the Illinois Territory, north of the dis-

trict of Kaskaskia," was read a third time, and passed.

The bill entitled "An act providing for the sale of certain lands in the State of Ohio, formerly set apart for refugees from Canada and Nova Scotia," was read a third time, and passed.

The bill entitled "An act regulating the currency within the United States of the gold coins of Great Britain, France, Portugal, and Spain, and the crowns of France, and five franc pieces," was read a third time, and passed.

The bill entitled "An act for the relief of Samuel Manac," was read a third time, and passed.

The bill entitled "An act making appropriations for rebuilding light-houses, and for completing the plan of lighting them according to the improvements of Winslow Lewis; for placing beacons and buoys; for preserving Little Gull Island; and for surveying the coast of the United States," was read a third time, and passed.

The bill entitled "An act to authorize the building of three light-houses, viz: one on Race Point, one on Point Gammon, and one on the Island of Petite Manon, in the State of Massachusetts," was read a third time, and passed.

The bill entitled "An act to alter certain parts of the act providing for the government of the Territory of Missouri," was read a third time and passed.

The bill entitled "An act supplementary to the act passed the 30th of March, 1802, to regulate the trade and intercourse with the Indian tribes, and to preserve peace on the frontiers," was read a third time, and passed.

The bill entitled "An act allowing pay to certain persons made prisoners with the revenue cutter Surveyor," was read a third time, and passed.

The bill entitled "An act authorizing the payment of a sum of money to Joseph Stewart and others," was read a third time, and passed.

The bill entitled "An act for the benefit of John P. Maxwell and Hugh H. Maxwell," was read a third time, and passed.

The bill entitled "An act for the relief of Charles Todd," was read a third time, and passed.

The bill entitled "An act appropriating the sum of two thousand five hundred dollars, for the purpose therein mentioned," was read a third time, and on the question, " Shall this bill pass ?" it was determined in the negative—yeas 9, nays 15, as follows:

YEAS—Messrs. Barry, Brown, Daggett, Goldsborough, Horsey, Howell, Sanford, Tait, and Wells.

NAYS—Messrs. Bibb, Campbell, Condit, Gaillard, Gore, King, Lacock, Macon, Morrow, Roberts, Tichenor, Turner, Varnum, Williams, and Wilson.

So the bill was lost.

The bill to increase the salary of the Register of the Treasury, and to allow him a compensation for his agency in countersigning and issuing Treasury notes, was read a third time and passed.

The resolution authorizing the President of the United States to employ a skilful assistant in the corps of engineers, was read a third time and passed.

The amendments to the resolution to indemnify Jabez Mowry and others, having been reported by the committee correctly engrossed, the resolution was read a third time as amended.

Resolved, That this resolution pass with amendments.

The amendments to the bill entitled "An act to provide for the appointment of a surveyor of the public lands in the Territories of Illinois and Missouri," having been reported by the committee correctly engrossed, the bill was read a third time as amended.

Resolved, That this bill pass with amendments.

The amendments to the bill entitled "An act for the gradual increase of the navy of the United States," having been reported by the committee correctly engrossed, the bill was read a third time as amended.

Resolved, That this bill pass with an amendment.

The amendments to the bill entitled "An act concerning the owners, officers, and crew of the privateer Roger," having been reported by the committee correctly engrossed, the bill was read a third time as amended.

Resolved, That this bill pass with amendments.

The amendment to the bill entitled "An act for the relief of David Coffin, Samuel and William Rodman, and Samuel Rodman, junior," having been reported by the committee correctly engrossed, the bill was read a third time as amended.

Resolved, That this bill pass with an amendment.

The amendment to the bill entitled "An act for the relief of Peter Audrain," having been reported by the committee correctly engrossed, the bill was read a third time as amended.

Resolved, That this bill pass with an amendment.

The amendments to the bill entitled "An act fixing the compensation of the Secretary of the Senate and Clerk of the House of Representatives, and making a temporary provision for the Clerks employed in their offices," having been reported by the committee correctly engrossed, the bill was read a third time as amended.

Resolved, That this bill pass with amendments.

The bill entitled "An act making an appropriation for enclosing and improving the public square near the Capitol, and to abolish the office of Commissioners of the Public Buildings, and of Superintendent, and for the appointment of one Commissioner of the Public Buildings," was read a third time as amended.

Resolved, That this bill pass with amendments.

The amendments to the bill entitled "An act for the confirmation of certain claims to land in the western district of the State of Louisiana," having been reported by the committee correctly engrossed, the bill was read a third time as amended.

Resolved, That this bill pass with amendments.

The amendments to the bill entitled "An act to establish post roads," having been reported by the committee correctly engrossed, the bill was read a third time as amended.

Resolved, That this bill pass with amendments.

The amendment to the bill entitled "An act authorizing the judges of the circuit court of the District of Columbia, to prepare a code of jurisprudence for the said District," having been reported by the committee correctly engrossed, the bill was read a third time as amended.

Resolved, That this bill pass with an amendment.

On motion by Mr. CAMPBELL,

Ordered, That the Committee on Finance and an Uniform National Currency, to whom were referred the following petitions and memorials, to wit: the memorial of Richard Caton and others; the memorial of Abner Landrum; the memorial of Thomas, George, and Thomas, and others; the petition of the President and Directors of the Central Bank of Georgetown and Washington; the memorial of Stephen Girard and others; the petition of Joseph Marquand; the petition of the President and Directors of the Bank of the Metropolis; the petition of the Columbian Fire Insurance Company of Alexandria; and the memorial of the President and Directors of the Patriotic Bank of Washington, be discharged from the further consideration thereof, respectively.

On motion by Mr. BARBOUR,

Ordered, That the Committee on Military Affairs, to whom were referred the following petitions and memorials, to wit: the petition of Benjamin Putnam; the petition of Mathew W. M'Lellan; the petition of Horatio Aldin and Company; the petition of John Rudolph; the petition of Robert Lovewell; the petition of Bernard O'Neal; the memorial of Mathew M'Connel and others; the petition of Robert Sewall; the petition of Nicholas Boilevin; the petition of John de Lassize; and the petition of Henry Dishbron and James Chittenden, be discharged from the further consideration thereof, respectively.

The Senate resumed, as in Committee of the Whole, the consideration of the bill, entitled "An act to authorize the survey of two millions of acres of the public lands, in lieu of that quantity heretofore authorized to be surveyed, in the Territory of Michigan, as military bounty lands," and it passed to a third reading.

The bill last mentioned was read a third time by unanimous consent, and passed.

The Senate resumed, as in Committee of the Whole, the consideration of the bill, entitled "An act for reducing the duties on licenses to retailers of wines, spirituous liquors, and foreign merchandise," and it passed to a third reading.

The bill last mentioned was read a third time by unanimous consent, and passed.

Mr. CAMPBELL, from the committee to whom was referred the bill, entitled "An act authorizing the Comptroller of the Treasury to cancel certain export bonds executed by Casper C. Schutte," reported it without amendment.

On motion by Mr. TAIT, it was agreed to reconsider the vote on the resolution from the House of Representatives relative to the adjournment of the present session of Congress, and it was determined to strike out "Wednesday, the first day of May next," and insert "Tuesday, the 30th day of April, instant;" and on the question, "Shall the amendment be engrossed and the resolution read a third time as amended?" it was determined in the affirmative.

On motion that the resolution be now read a third time, it was objected to by Mr. VARNUM, as against the rule.

Mr. LACOCK presented the petition of Edmund Stephenson, praying for an increase of pension, as stated in the petition, which was read and referred to the committee to whom was referred the bill, entitled "An act concerning invalid pensioners," to consider and report thereon.

A message from the House of Representatives informed the Senate that the House have passed a resolution relative to the more effectual collection of the public revenue, in which they request the concurrence of the Senate.

The resolution last mentioned was read the first and second time by unanimous consent, and referred to the Committee on Finance and an Uniform National Currency, to consider and report thereon.

SATURDAY, April 27.

On motion by Mr. BROWN,

Ordered, That the committee, to whom were referred the following memorials and petitions, viz: the memorial of Jesse Torrey, junior; the memorial of the Legislative Council and House of Representatives of the Mississippi Territory; the petition of Cornelia Livingston and P. V. B. Livingston, of the city of New York; and the petition of John Jones and others, be discharged from the further consideration thereof, respectively.

On motion by Mr. WILLIAMS,

Ordered, That the committee to whom was referred the petition of Benjamin G. Bowen, and others, messengers of the Public Departments, be discharged from the further consideration thereof.

Mr. FROMENTIN laid before the Senate the resolution of the Legislature of the State of Louisiana, disagreeing to the amendment of the Constitution of the United States, limiting the term of service for Senators of the United States to four years, as proposed by the Legislature of the State of Georgia.

The resolution and proposed amendment were read.

Mr. FROMENTIN also laid before the Senate the resolution of the Legislature of the State of Louisiana, disapproving and rejecting the amendments to the Constitution of the United States by the States of Massachusetts and Connecticut.

The resolution and proposed amendments were read.

A message from the House of Representatives informed the Senate that they disagree to the amendments of the Senate to the bill, entitled "An act fixing the compensation of the Secretary of the Senate and Clerk of the House of Representatives, and making temporary provision for the clerks in their offices. They have concurred in the amendments of the Senate to the bill, entitled "An act to establish post roads," except the third, to which they disagree.

The bill fixing the compensation of the Chaplains of Congress was read a second time, and considered as in Committee of the Whole; and the blank having been filled with "five hundred," on the question, "Shall this bill be engrossed and read a third time?" it was determined in the affirmative.

The amendment to the resolution from the House of Representatives, relating to the adjournment of the present session of Congress, having been reported by the Committee correctly engrossed, the resolution was read a third time as amended.

Resolved, That this resolution pass with an amendment.

The Senate resumed, as in Committee of the Whole, the consideration of the bill, entitled "An act authorizing the Comptroller of the Treasury to cancel certain bonds executed by Casper C. Schutte;" and it passed to a third reading.

The bill last mentioned was read a third time, by unanimous consent, and passed.

The Senate proceeded to consider their amendments to the bill, entitled "An act fixing the compensation of the Secretary of the Senate and Clerk of the House of Representatives, and making a temporary provision for the clerks employed in their offices." disagreed to by the House of Representatives. Whereupon,

Resolved, That they insist thereon.

On motion by Mr. LACOCK, the committee to whom was recommitted the bill dividing the State of Pennsylvania into two judicial districts were discharged from the further consideration thereof.

A message from the House of Representatives informed the Senate that the House insist on their disagreement to the first and second amendments of the Senate to the bill, entitled "An act fixing the compensation of the Secretary of the Senate and Clerk of the House of Representatives, and making a temporary provision for the clerks employed in their offices." They have passed a bill, entitled "An act to allow a drawback of duties on spirits distilled and sugar refined within the United States;" a bill, entitled "An act making appropriations for carrying into effect a treaty between the United States and the Cherokee tribe of Indians, concluded at Washington on the 22d day of March, 1816;" also a bill, entitled "An act supplementary to an act making alterations in the Treasury and War|Departments, passed the 8th day of May, 1792;"—in which bills they request the concurrence of the Senate.

The bill entitled "An act to allow a drawback of duties on spirits distilled and sugar refined within the United States" was read the second time, by unanimous consent, and referred to the Committee on Finance and an Uniform National Currency, to consider and report thereon.

The bill entitled "An act making appropriations for carrying into effect a treaty between the United States and the Cherokee tribe of Indians, concluded at Washington on the 22d day of March, 1816," was read the second time by unanimous consent, and referred to the Committee on Military Affairs.

Mr. BARBOUR, from the Committee on Military Affairs, to whom the bill last mentioned was referred, reported it without amendment, and the bill was considered as in Committee of the Whole, and passed to a third reading; and the bill was read a third time by unanimous consent, and passed.

The Senate proceeded to consider their first and third amendments, disagreed to by the House of Representatives, to the bill, entitled "An act fixing the compensation of the Secretary of the Senate and Clerk of the House of Representatives, and making a temporary provision for the clerks employed in their offices." Whereupon, on motion by Mr. KING,

Resolved, That they do further insist on their first and third amendments, and ask a conference on the disagreeing votes of the two Houses.

Ordered, That Mr. KING, Mr. WILLIAMS, and Mr. MASON of New Hampshire, be the managers of the same on the part of the Senate.

The bill entitled "An act supplementary to an act making alterations in the Treasury and War Departments, passed the 8th day of May, 1792," was read the second time by unanimous consent, and considered as in Committee of the Whole, and passed to a third reading. It was read a third time by unanimous consent, and passed.

Mr. CAMPBELL, from the committee to whom was referred the resolution relative to the more effectual collection of the public revenue, reported it with an amendment, which was read, and considered as in Committee of the Whole; and Mr. DANA having submitted a further amendment, on motion by Mr. MASON, the further consideration of the resolution, together with the amendments, was postponed until Monday next.

A message from the House of Representatives informed the Senate that the House further insist on their disagreement to the first and third amendments of the Senate to the bill, entitled "An act fixing the compensation of the Secretary of the Senate and Clerk of the House of Representatives, and making a temporary provision for the clerks in their offices." They agree to the conference proposed on the subject, and have appointed managers on their part.

MONDAY, April 29.

On motion by Mr. FROMENTIN, Dennis de la Rondi, of New Orleans, in the State of Louisiana; the petitioners, by a number of citizens of the State of Louisiana, in behalf of John de Lassize, of New Orleans; and also the petitioners in behalf of Jumonville de Villiers and others; had leave to withdraw their petitions and papers, respectively.

On motion by Mr. ROBERTS, the committee to whom was referred the Message from the Presi-dent of the United States, recommending the creation of a distinct department for the issuing of patents, were discharged from the further consideration thereof.

The Senate proceeded to consider the amendments of the House of Representatives to the bill entitled "An act to increase the salary of the Register of the Treasury, and to allow him a compensation for his agency in countersigning and issuing Treasury notes."—Whereupon,

Resolved, That they concur therein.

On motion, by Mr. FROMENTIN, the heirs and representatives of Ignace Delino had leave to withdraw their petition and papers.

Mr. LACOCK, from the committee to whom was referred the bill, entitled "An act concerning invalid pensioners," reported it with amendments; which were read, and considered as in Committee of the Whole, and the amendments having been agreed to, the bill was further amended, and the PRESIDENT reported it to the House accordingly; and on the question, "Shall the amendments be engrossed, and the bill read a third time as amended?" it was determined in the affirmative.

The amendments having been reported by the committee correctly engrossed, the bill was read a third time as amended, by unanimous consent.

Resolved, That this bill pass with amendments.

The Senate resumed, as in Committee of the Whole, the consideration of the bill making further appropriations for the year 1816; and the bill having been amended, the PRESIDENT reported it to the House accordingly; and on the question, "Shall this bill be engrossed, and the bill read a third time?" it was determined in the affirmative.

The bill was read a third time by unanimous consent, and passed.

Mr. BIBB, from the committee to whom was referred the bill, entitled "An act to allow a drawback of duties on spirits distilled and sugar refined within the United States," reported it with amendments; which were read, and considered as in Committee of the Whole, and the amendments having been agreed to, the PRESIDENT reported the bill to the House accordingly; and on the question, "Shall the amendments be engrossed, and the bill read a third time, as amended?" it was determined in the affirmative.

The amendments having been reported by the committee correctly engrossed, the bill was read a third time as amended, by unanimous consent.

Resolved, That this bill pass with amendments.

The engrossed bill, fixing the compensation of the Chaplains of Congress, was read a third time, and passed.

The Senate proceeded to consider their amendment to the bill, entitled "An act to establish post roads;" disagreed to by the House of Representatives. Whereupon,

Resolved, That they recede therefrom.

Mr. KING, from the managers on the part of the Senate, at the conference on the amendments of the Senate, disagreed to by the House of Representatives, to the bill, entitled "An act fixing compensation of the Secretary of the Senate and Clerk of the House of Representatives, and making a temporary provision for the clerks employed in their offices," reported that the Senate insist on their first and third amendments, and that the bill be further amended by adding, after the word "effect," in the last line, the words, "and continue in force for two years."

The Senate proceeded to consider the report last mentioned. Whereupon,

Resolved, That they concur therein, and that the bill be amended accordingly.

Mr. LACOCK submitted the following resolution; which was read, and passed to the second reading:

Resolved, That Robert Tweedy, Tobias Simpson, and George Hicks, Assistants to the Sergeant-at-Arms and Doorkeeper of the Senate, be paid, out of the contingent fund, two dollars a day for each day they may have attended the Senate during the present session of Congress; and that Charles Tims be allowed one hundred dollars for his attendance during the present session.

The resolution was read the second time by unanimous consent, and considered as in Committee of the Whole; and on the question, "Shall this resolution be engrossed, and read a third time?" it was determined in the affirmative.

The resolution was then read a third time by unanimous consent, and passed.

A message from the House of Representatives informed the Senate that the House have passed the bill sent from the Senate, entitled "An act to increase the salary of the Register of the Treasury, and to allow him a compensation for his agency in countersigning and issuing Treasury notes," with amendments, in which they request the concurrence of the Senate. They have concurred in the report of the committee of conference on the disagreeing votes of the two Houses on the bill, entitled "An act fixing the compensation of the Secretary of the Senate and Clerk of the House of Representatives, and making a temporary provision for the clerks in their offices," and that the bill be amended accordingly.

COLLECTION OF THE REVENUE.

The Senate resumed, as in Committee of the Whole, the consideration of the resolution relative to the more effectual collection of the public revenue, together with the amendments proposed thereto.

The resolution was in the following words:

Resolved, by the Senate and House of Representatives of the United States of America in Congress assembled, That the Secretary of the Treasury be, and he hereby is, required and directed to adopt such measures as he may deem necessary, to cause, as soon as may be, all duties, taxes, debts, or sums of money accruing or becoming payable to the United States, to be collected and paid in the legal currency of the United States, or Treasury notes, or notes of the Bank of the United States, as by law provided and declared; and that, from and after the twentieth day of February next, no such duties, taxes, debts, or sums of money accruing or becoming payable to the United States as aforesaid, ought to be collected or received otherwise than in the legal currency of the United States, or Treasury notes, or notes of the Bank of the United States.

On motion by Mr. BARBOUR, that the further consideration thereof be postponed until the first Monday in July next, it was determined in the negative—yeas 9, nays 21, as follows:

YEAS—Messrs. Barbour, Goldsborough, Lacock, Mason of Virginia, Morrow, Roberts, Ruggles, Wells, and Wilson.

NAYS—Messrs. Barry, Bibb, Campbell, Chace, Condit, Daggett, Dana, Fromentin, Gaillard, Gore, Harper, Howell, King, Macon, Mason of New Hampshire, Sanford, Tait, Tichenor, Turner, Varnum, and Williams.

On the question to agree to the following amendment reported by the select committee:

Strike out all the resolution after the word "assembled," in the enacting clause, and insert in lieu thereof the following:

That all duties, taxes, debts, or sums of money accruing or becoming due to the United States, ought to be collected and received in the lawful money of the United States, or in Treasury notes, or in notes of the Bank of the United States, as by law provided and declared.

And resolved further, That, from and after the —— day of —— next, no such duties, taxes, debts, or sums of money accruing or becoming payable to the United States as aforesaid, ought to be collected or received otherwise than in the lawful money of the United States, or in Treasury notes, or notes of the Bank of the United States, as aforesaid: *Provided, nevertheless,* That, until the —— day of —— next, it shall be lawful for the Secretary of the Treasury to cause the said duties, taxes, debts, or sums of money so accruing and becoming payable, to be collected and received in the notes of any bank established by authority of the United States, or of any of them, which shall be equal in value to the Treasury notes, bearing an interest of five and two-fifths per cent. per annum. And in case the notes of any of the said banks shall be of less value than the Treasury notes aforesaid, the same may be received at a discount equal to the difference in value between such notes and the aforesaid Treasury notes, at the time the same shall be so received. And that it shall be lawful for the Secretary of the Treasury, from time to time, to ascertain the difference aforesaid, and to issue instructions directing the rates of discount at which such notes shall respectively be so received.

And resolved further, That whenever the notes of any of the aforesaid banks, which shall be of less value than the aforesaid Treasury notes, shall be paid in satisfaction of any debt or sum of money due from the United States, the same shall be paid at a discount equal to the difference in value between such notes and the aforesaid Treasury notes at the time of such payment.

It was determined in the negative—yeas 11, nays 19, as follows:

YEAS—Messrs. Chace, Daggett, Dana, Fromentin, Gore, Howell, King, Mason of New Hampshire, Sanford, Tichenor, and Turner.

NAYS—Messrs. Barbour, Barry, Bibb, Campbell, Condit, Gaillard, Goldsborough, Harper, Lacock, Macon, Mason of Virginia, Morrow, Roberts, Ruggles, Tait, Varnum, Wells, Williams, and Wilson.

On the question to agree to the following motion, proposed by Mr. DANA:

"And that bank bills or notes, which may be received in payment of sums due to the United States, in any one district of the customs, shall be equally

371

HISTORY OF CONGRESS.

372

SENATE.

Adjournment.

APRIL, 1816.

receivable in payment of like duties within every other district;"

It was determined in the negative—yeas 3, nays 27, as follows:

YEAS—Messrs. Dana, Macon, and Turner.

NAYS—Messrs. Barbour, Barry, Bibb, Campbell, Chace, Condit, Daggett, Fromentin, Gaillard, Goldsborough, Gore, Harper, Howell, King, Lacock, Mason of New Hampshire, Mason of Virginia, Morrow, Roberts, Ruggles, Sanford, Tait, Tichenor, Varnum, Wells, Williams, and Wilson.

Mr. CAMPBELL moved to add a clause (substantially) to include, in the receivable paper, the notes of all banks which shall pay their notes on demand in the legal currency of the United States; which was agreed to.

On the question, "Shall the amendments be engrossed, and the resolution read a third time as amended?" it was determined in the affirmative—yeas 19, nays 11, as follows:

YEAS—Messrs. Barry, Bibb, Campbell, Chace, Condit, Daggett, Dana, Fromentin, Gaillard, Harper, Howell, Macon, Mason of Virginia, Sanford, Tait, Tichenor, Turner, Varnum, and Williams.

NAYS—Messrs. Barbour, Goldsborough, Gore, King, Lacock, Mason of New Hampshire, Morrow, Roberts, Ruggles, Wells, and Wilson.

The amendments having been reported by the committee correctly engrossed, the resolution was read a third time, as amended, by unanimous consent.

Resolved, That this resolution pass with amendments.

TUESDAY, April 30.

A message from the House of Representatives informed the Senate that they have passed the bill from the Senate, entitled "An act making further appropriations for the year 1816," with an amendment, in which they request the concurrence of the Senate.

Mr. LACOCK submitted the following resolution:

Resolved, That there be paid out of the contingent fund of this House to Robert Tweedy, Tobias Simpson, and George Hicks, the extra sum of one hundred dollars each, as a gratuity for their uniform good conduct.

And the resolution was three times read by unanimous consent and passed.

The Senate proceeded to consider the amendment of the House of Representatives to the bill last mentioned, and concurred therein.

Mr. VARNUM and Mr. ROBERTS were appointed a committee on the part of the Senate, jointly with such committee as may be appointed on the part of the House of Representatives, to wait on the President of the United States, and notify him that, unless he may have any further communication to make to the two Houses of Congress, they are ready to adjourn.

Mr. LACOCK submitted the following resolution:

Resolved, That there be paid to the Sergeant-at-Arms and Doorkeeper of the Senate, sixty-one dollars and fifty cents, out of the contingent fund, for furnishing an extra horse for forty-one days at the present session.

And the resolution was three times read and passed.

Mr. VARNUM reported from the joint committee that they had waited on the President of the United States, who informed them that he had no further communication to make to the two Houses of Congress.

A message from the House of Representatives informed the Senate that the House, having finished the business before them, are about to adjourn.

Ordered, That the Secretary inform the House of Representatives that the Senate, having finished the Legislative business before them, are about to adjourn.

Whereupon, the PRESIDENT adjourned the Senate *sine die.*

PROCEEDINGS AND DEBATES

HOUSE OF REPRESENTATIVES OF THE UNITED STATES,

AT THE FIRST SESSION OF THE FOURTEENTH CONGRESS, BEGUN AT THE CITY OF WASHINGTON, MONDAY, DECEMBER 4, 1815.

MONDAY, December 4, 1815.

This being the day appointed by the Constitution of the United States for the meeting of Congress, the following members of the House of Representatives appeared, produced their credentials, and took their seats, to wit:

From New Hampshire—Charles H. Atherton, Bradbury Cilley, Roger Vose, and Jeduthun Wilcox.

From Massachusetts—William Baylies, George Bradbury, Elijah Brigham, Benjamin Brown, Samuel S. Conner, John W. Hulbert, Cyrus King, Jeremiah Nelson, Albion K. Parris, Timothy Pickering, John Reed, Thomas Rice, Nathaniel Ruggles, and Solomon Strong.

From Rhode Island—John L. Boss, junior.

From Connecticut—Epaphroditus Champion, John Davenport, jun., Lyman Law, Jonathan O. Moseley, and Lewis B. Sturges.

From Vermont—Daniel Chipman, Luther Jewett, Chauncey Langdon, Asa Lyon, Charles Marsh, and John Noyes.

From New York—Samuel R. Betts, James Birdsall, Micah Brooks, Oliver C. Comstock, Henry Crocheron, Thomas R. Gold, Jabez D. Hammond, John Lovett, Hosea Moffit, John Savage, Abraham H. Schenck, John W. Taylor, Enos T. Throop, George Townsend, Jonathan Ward, and James W. Wilkin.

From New Jersey—Ezra Baker, Ephraim Bateman, and Henry Southard.

From Pennsylvania—William Crawford, William Darlington, John Hahn, Joseph Heister, Joseph Hopkinson, Samuel D. Ingham, Aaron Lyle, William Maclay, William Milnor, William Piper, Thomas Smith, James Wallace, John Whiteside, Thomas Wilson, and William Wilson.

From Delaware—Thomas Cooper.

From Maryland—John C. Herbert, Philip Stuart, and Robert Wright.

From Virginia—Philip P. Barbour, James Breckenridge, William A. Burwell, Thomas Gholson, Peterson Goodwyn, Aylett Hawes, John P. Hungerford, Joseph Lewis, jun., William McCoy, Hugh Nelson, Thomas Newton, James Pleasants, jun., William H. Roane, Ballard Smith, Magnus Tate, and Henry St. George Tucker.

From North Carolina—Joseph H. Bryan, James W. Clarke, John Culpeper, Nathaniel Macon, William H. Murfree, Richard Stanford, Lewis Williams, and Bartlett Yancey.

From South Carolina—John C. Calhoun, John J. Chappell, William Lowndes, William Mayrant, Henry Middleton, Thomas Moore, John Taylor, and William Woodward.

From Georgia—John Forsyth, Bolling Hall, Wilson Lumpkin, and Richard Henry Wilde.

From Kentucky—James Clark, Henry Clay, Joseph Desha, Richard M. Johnson, Alney McLean, Stephen Ormsby, Solomon P. Sharpe, and Micah Taul.

From Tennessee—Newton Cannon, Bennett H. Henderson, Samuel Powell, James B. Reynolds, and Isaac Thomas.

From Ohio—John Alexander, James Caldwell, David Clendenin, William Creighton, jun., and John McLean.

From Louisiana—Thomas B. Robertson.

A quorum, consisting of a majority of the whole number of members, being present, the House proceeded, by ballot, to the choice of a Speaker, and, upon examining the ballots, it appeared that HENRY CLAY, one of the Representatives for the State of Kentucky, was duly elected; Whereupon, Mr. CLAY was conducted to the Speaker's Chair, and the oath to support the Constitution of the United States, as prescribed by the act, entitled "An act to regulate the time and manner of administering certain oaths," was administered to him by Mr. WRIGHT, one of the members for the State of Maryland; after which he made his acknowledgments to the House in the following words:

"GENTLEMEN: It is not merely in compliance with a respectful usage, but from the most profound gratitude, that I thank you for the honor which you have just conferred on me. I shall find, in the discharge of the arduous duties of the Chair, considerable alleviation, from the natural progress of the system of order, and from the improvement which it has received under the able presidency of my predecessor. But, gentlemen, it is chiefly upon your liberal co-operation and support that I place my reliance. Under the expectation of receiving this, I shall proceed, with all the impartiality of which I am capable, to the execution of the duties which you have assigned me, soliciting your

375   HISTORY OF CONGRESS.   376

H. of R.   *Standing Committees—President's Message.*   December, 1815.

indulgence for unintentional error, and soliciting it particularly during my present indisposition."

The oath or affirmation to support the Constitution of the United States, as prescribed by the act above mentioned, was then administered, by the Speaker, to all the other members present.

William Lattimore, from the Mississippi Territory; Jonathan Jennings, from the Indiana Territory; and Benjamin Stephenson, from the Illinois Territory, having also appeared and produced their credentials as delegates to represent the said Territories in the fourteenth Congress, the said oath was administered to them by the Speaker, when they took their seats.

The House proceeded to elect a Clerk, when it appeared that of one hundred and twenty-two votes, Thomas Dougherty, Esq., had one hundred and fourteen, and was, therefore, duly elected.

The Speaker laid before the House a letter from Joseph Wheaton, offering himself as a candidate for Sergeant-at-Arms.

On motion of Mr. Wright, after some little discussion, it was

Resolved, That Thomas Dunn be appointed Sergeant at Arms; Thomas Claxton, Doorkeeper; and Benjamin Burch, Assistant Doorkeeper to this House.

The several resolutions passed by the Senate were received, read, and concurred in.

Messrs. Wright and Hopkinson, were appointed the committee on the part of this House to wait on the President of the United States.

Messrs. Lowndes, Forsyth, and Champion, were appointed to inquire into the state of the new building prepared by the citizens for Congress.

The usual orders as to rules, &c., were adopted.

Tuesday, December 5.

Several other members, to wit: from Pennsylvania, Jared Irwin; from Maryland, George Baer; from Virginia, James Johnson, John Kerr, and Daniel Sheffey; and from North Carolina, William Gaston, and Daniel M. Forney, appeared, produced their credentials, were qualified, and took their seats.

Mr. Wright, from the joint committee appointed yesterday to wait on the President of the United States, reported that the committee had performed that service, and that the President answered that he would make a communication to the two Houses to-day, at twelve o'clock.

A Message was then received from the President of the United States, which was read, and referred to the Committee of the Whole on the state of the Union. [For this Message see Senate proceedings of this date, *ante* page 12.]

Wednesday, December 6.

Several other members, to wit: from New Jersey, Lewis Condict; from Pennsylvania, John Sergeant; and from North Carolina, William C. Love, appeared, produced their credentials, were qualified, and repaired to their seats.

Ordered, That the petition of the Legislature of the Mississippi Territory, for an admission into the Union, as an independent State, presented on the 21st of January, 1815, be referred to Messrs. Lattimore, Robertson, Cannon, McLean, of Kentucky, Strong, Noyes, and Lumpkin.

A message was received from the Senate, proposing the usual appointment of two Chaplains of different religious denominations, to interchange weekly between the two Houses.

This proposition was concurred in, with some dissenting voices, and to-morrow assigned for the election of the Chaplain on the part of this House.

STANDING COMMITTEES.

On motion of Mr. Taylor, of New York, the Standing Committees were ordered to be appointed, pursuant to the rules and orders of the House. They are as follows:

Committee of Elections—Mr. Taylor, of New York, Mr. Piper, Mr. Sharpe, Mr. Pickering, Mr. Vose, Mr. Barbour, and Mr. Law.

Committee of Ways and Means—Mr. Lowndes, Mr. Burwell, Mr. Taylor, of New York, Mr. Moseley, Mr. Robertson, Mr. Ingham, and Mr. Gaston.

Committee of Commerce and Manufactures—Mr. Newton, Mr. Musfree, Mr. Baylies, Mr. Parris, Mr. Chappell, Mr. Boss, and Mr. Sergeant.

Committee of Claims—Mr. Yancey, Mr. Alexander, Mr. Goodwyn, Mr. Davenport, Mr. Lyle, Mr. Stanford, and Mr. Chipman.

Committee on the Public Lands—Mr. Robertson, Mr. Creighton, Mr. Clark, of Kentucky, Mr. Hall, Mr. King, of Massachusetts, Mr. McCoy, and Mr. Sturges.

Committee for the District of Columbia—Mr. Tucker, Mr. Lewis, Mr. Irwin, of Pennsylvania, Mr. Savage, Mr. Herbert, Mr. Taylor, of South Carolina, and Mr. Brigham.

Committee on the Post Office and Post Roads—Mr. Ingham, Mr. Cannon, Mr. Breckenridge, Mr. Throop, Mr. Conner, Mr. Caldwell, and Mr. Langdon.

Committee on Pensions and Revolutionary Claims—Mr. Chappell, Mr. Comstock, Mr. Stuart, Mr. Milnor, Mr. Southard, Mr. Henderson, and Mr. Wilcox.

Committee on the Judiciary—Mr. Nelson, of Virginia, Mr. Ormsby, Mr. Cooper, Mr. Wright, Mr. Wilde, Mr. Gold, and Mr. Sergeant.

Committee on Public Expenditures—Mr. Murfree, Mr. Gholson, Mr. Champion, Mr. Thomas Wilson, Mr. Hammond, Mr. Nelson, of Massachusetts, and Mr. Wallace.

Committee of Accounts—Mr. McLean, of Ohio, Mr. Rudd, and Mr. Betts.

Committee of Revisal and Unfinished Business—Mr. Condict, Mr. Bradbury, and Mr. Maclay.

PRESIDENT'S MESSAGE.

On motion of Mr. Taylor, of New York, the House having resolved itself into a Committee of the Whole on the state of the Union, Mr. Condict in the Chair, the Message of the President was read. Whereupon, on motion of Mr. Tay-

Lon, of New York, the following resolutions were adopted, viz:

1. *Resolved*, That so much of the Message of the President of the United States as relates to Foreign Affairs, be referred to a select committee.

2. That so much as relates to the Military Peace Establishment, to the organization of a Corps of Invalids, to Fortifications, to the protection of the Inland Frontier, and to the Military Academies, be referred to a select committee.

3. That so much as relates to our Naval Affairs, be referred to a select committee.

4. That so much as relates to an Uniform National Currency, be referred to a select committee.

5. That so much as relates to Roads and Canals, be referred to a select committee.

6. That so much as relates to a National Seminary of Learning within the District of Columbia, be referred to a select committee.

7. That so much as relates to the classification and organization of the Militia, be referred to a select committee;

8. That so much as relates to an alleviation of the burdens imposed by the necessities of the War, and the general subject of the Revenue, be referred to the Committee of Ways and Means.

9. That so much as relates to Manufactures, be referred to the Committee of Commerce and Manufactures.

10. That the said committees have leave to report by bill or otherwise.

These resolutions having been reported by the Committee to the House, were all concurred in.

Mr. Forsyth, Mr. Macon, Mr. Wilkin, Mr. Gholson, Mr. Atherton, Mr. Sheffey, and Mr. Sharpe, were appointed a committee pursuant to the first resolution.

Mr. Johnson, of Kentucky, Mr. Barbour, Mr. Moore, of South Carolina, Mr. Forsyth, Mr. Desha, Mr. Champion, and Mr. Hulbert, were appointed a committee pursuant to the second resolution.

Mr. Pleasants, Mr. Middleton, Mr. Cooper, Mr. Parris, Mr. Hammond, Mr. Boss, and Mr. McLean, of Kentucky, were appointed a committee pursuant to the third resolution.

Mr. Calhoun, Mr. Macon, Mr. Pleasants, Mr. Hopkinson, Mr. Robertson, Mr. Tucker, and Mr. Pickering, were appointed a committee pursuant to the fourth resolution.

Mr. Creighton, Mr. Lowndes, Mr. Cooper, Mr. Ingham, Mr. Condict, Mr. Lovett, and Mr. Alexander, were appointed a committee, pursuant to the fifth resolution.

Mr. Wilde, Mr. Sergeant, Mr. Calhoun, Mr. Sheffey, Mr. Herbert, Mr. Savage, and Mr. Ormsby, were appointed a committee pursuant to the sixth resolution.

Mr. Clark, of Kentucky, Mr. Taylor, of New York, Mr. Kerr, of Virginia, Mr. Piper, Mr. Moore, of South Carolina, Mr. Breckenridge, and Mr. Forney, were appointed a committee pursuant to the seventh resolution.

Mr. Gholson suggested a doubt whether these resolutions embraced a subject of very great importance, which was recommended by the President to their attention. He referred to the au-

thority which, in the view of the President, ought to be given to the Executive of the United States efficiently to command the services of the militia in the cases contemplated by the Constitution.

Mr. Taylor referred to the Message to show that, by necessary connexion, this topic was included in the general terms of the resolution (as above) which relates to the organization of the militia. It was therefore in his opinion already committed. If at any future day an express instruction on that head to the committee should be found to be necessary, it could then be given.

Mr. Wright said there was another very important subject adverted to by the President which was not embraced, he believed, in the resolutions just adopted; though he was not certain it was not, because he could not distinctly understand them by casually hearing them read and decided on without previous notice. He referred to the recommendation to provide for the payment of the militia called into service during the late war, without the authority of the United States. This was a subject he had much at heart, not only as respected the State he represented, but other parts of the Union, whose militia had promptly turned out to meet the enemy before the authority of the United States could be put in motion to guide their zeal. It was due to the militia who fought for the country that they should be paid; it was due to the magnanimity of the nation that it should make the payment from the National Treasury. In the part of the State which he represented, all the military duties during the war had been performed at the instance of the militia officers, the country being so cut off by the bay from the seats of both the State and General Governments, as to prevent prompt communication with them. The recommendation on this subject contained in the Message was one which, he said, did great credit to the head and heart of the Executive, and he hoped the House would not overlook or slight it, &c.

Mr. Taylor, of New York, observed that he thought it would be better to defer the examination of this subject until brought before the Congress in some shape by the parties concerned. If these separate exertions of patriotism required compensation, they would be brought before Congress in the form of memorials, from the States or individuals who had made them. Thus brought before Congress, the subject might be referred to a committee and generally and fully examined.

Mr. Wright, after some further remarks, submitted the following motion:

"That so much of the President's Message as relates to the arrangement of the militia expenses, incurred by the several State Governments, without the previous sanction or authority of the Government of the United States, be referred to a select committee."

This motion was agreed to, *nem. con.*; and Messrs. Wright, Barbour, Rice, Powell, Smith of Pennsylvania, Lyon, and Cilley, were appointed the committee.

Mr. P. Barbour, of Virginia, said there was another subject of importance referred to in the Message, which he wished to bring to the view of the House, that, if not included in the references already made, it might be referred to a committee. He meant the payment of the expenses of the militia called out regularly under the authority of the United States, who had not yet been paid, in consequence of the deficiency in the amount of appropriations for that object. He had actual knowledge of the fact of many militia thus situated, remaining unpaid, and seriously suffering for the want of what was justly due them. From the correspondence between the Pay Department and the Militia Officers, which he had seen published, the delay of payment was produced by the exhaustion of the appropriations of the last session. This defect, if existing, should be immediately supplied. To bring this question before the House, he moved—

"That the Committee of Ways and Means be instructed to inquire whether the appropriation of money made at the last session of Congress, for defraying the expenses of the militia called into the service of the United States, under the authority of the several States, be sufficient; and, if not, what is the amount of the deficiency."

Mr. LOWNDES suggested that the Committee of Ways and Means, when appointed, would not have it in their power to act on the subject proposed to be referred to them, until the report of the Secretary of the Treasury should be received. That report, which would probably afford all the information the gentleman desired, might be expected in a few days; and, upon that report it would of course become the duty of the Committee of Ways and Means to act, without a particular reference.

Mr. BARBOUR, then, observing that he had but desired to bring this subject directly to the view of the House, waived his motion for the present.

THURSDAY, December 7.

Several other members, to wit: from Massachusetts, SAMUEL TAGGART and LABAN WHEATON; from New York, ASA ADGATE; and from Pennsylvania, HUGH GLASGOW, appeared, produced their credentials, were qualified, and took their seats.

Mr. TAYLOR, of New York, presented a petition of Westel Willoughby, junior, praying to be admitted to a seat in the House, in the place of William S. Smith, returned as one of the members for the State of New York, whom he alleges to have been unduly returned.—Referred to the Committee on Elections.

THE NEW BUILDING.

Mr. LOWNDES, from the committee on the subject, delivered in the following report:

"The committee appointed on the part of the House of Representatives to inquire, in conjunction with a committee on the part of the Senate, into the state of the new building on Capitol Hill, offered by the proprietors for the accommodation of Congress, upon what terms the said building could be obtained until the Capitol may be ready for their reception, report; That, having examined the building in question, they con-

sider it much better adapted to the convenience of both Houses of Congress than that they at present occupy. The committee appointed by the owners of the building, have represented it as having cost (with the land attached to it) thirty thousand dollars, five of which has been expended on objects necessary for the accommodation of Congress, which will become useless when they shall leave the building. This committee have stated that the proprietors will be fully satisfied to enter into a contract with the United States under which they shall receive $5,000, with an annual rent of $1,650, (being an interest upon their capital of six per cent., with the addition of the price of insurance,) making the lease determinable at the pleasure of Congress. Should these terms be acceded to by Congress, the committee believe that the building will be ready for their reception on Monday next. The terms appear to the committee of both Houses to be equitable, and they have submitted a bill to carry them into effect."

Mr. LOWNDES then reported a bill to authorize the President of the United States to lease, on the terms therein mentioned, " the new building on Capitol Hill, with the appurtenances, for the better accommodation of Congress;" which was twice read, referred to a Committee of the Whole; passed through a Committee of the Whole, engrossed, and read a third time, and sent to the Senate for concurrence.

ADDITIONAL COMMITTEES.

Mr. WILDE offered the following resolution, as an amendment to the rules and orders of the House, which was read, and ordered to lie on the table:

Resolved, That in addition to the standing committees heretofore authorized by the rules and orders of this House, the following standing committees be authorized and appointed:

A Military Committee;
A Naval Committee;
A Committee on Foreign Affairs;
A Committee on the Militia;
A Committee on Roads and Canals;
A Committee of Ordnance, Fortifications, Arsenals, and Harbor Defence;
To consist of seven members each.

That it shall be the duty of the said Military Committee to take into consideration all such reports from the War Department, petitions, matters, and things relating to the Army of the United States, as shall be presented, or shall, or may come in question, and be referred to them by the House, and to report, from time to time, their opinion thereon:

That it shall be the duty of the said Naval Committee to take into consideration all such reports from the Secretary of the Navy, or the Commissioners of the Navy Board, petitions, and other matters and things respecting the Navy of the United States, as shall be presented, or shall, or may come in question and be referred to them by the House, and to report, from time to time, their opinion thereon.

That it shall be the duty of the said Committee on Foreign Affairs to take into consideration all such reports from the Department of State, messages, or parts of messages, petitions, and other matters and things respecting the intercourse and relations of the United States with foreign nations, as shall be presented, or shall, or may come in question, and be referred to them by the House, and to report their opinion thereon.

That it shall be the duty of the said Committee on the Militia to take into consideration all such reports, petitions, and other matters and things respecting the militia of the United States, as shall be presented, or shall, or may come in question, and be referred to them by the House, and to report, from time to time, their opinion thereon.

That it shall be the duty of the said Committee on Roads and Canals to take into consideration all such reports, petitions, and other matters and things relating to the construction, preservation, and extension of roads and canals, in the United States, and the improvement of river navigation, as shall be presented, or shall, or may come in question, and be referred to them by the House, and to report, from time to time, their opinion thereon.

That it shall be the duty of the said Committee of Ordnance, Fortifications, Arsenals, and Harbor Defence, to take into consideration all such reports, petitions, and other matters and things, relating to the ordnance, fortifications, arsenals, armories, and works of defence, both fixed and floating, on the harbors, on the coasts, or on the inland frontier of the United States, as shall be presented, or shall or may come in question, and be referred to them by the House, and to report, from time to time, their opinion thereon.

The House then proceeded to ballot for a Chaplain on its part to serve during the session; when, after several ballotings, the Rev. SPENCER H. CONE, having a majority of votes, was declared to be duly elected.

The SPEAKER laid before the House a letter from the Secretary of the Treasury, transmitting his annual report on the state of the finances of the United States, which was read, and referred to the Committee of Ways and Means, except so much thereof as relates to a national currency, which was referred to the committee to whom that subject was referred on yesterday.

A message from the Senate informed the House that the Senate have passed the bill " to authorize the President of the United States to lease, for the term therein mentioned, the new building on Capitol Hill, with the appurtenances, for the better accommodation of Congress."

The House adjourned until Monday morning.

MONDAY, December 11.

Several other members, to wit: from New York, PETER B. PORTER; from Pennsylvania, THOMAS BURNSIDE; from Maryland, STEVENSON ARCHER; from Virginia, JOHN CLOPTON; from North Carolina, WILLIAM R. KING and ISRAEL PICKENS; from South Carolina, BENJAMIN HUGER; and from Georgia, ALFRED CUTHBERT and THOMAS TELFAIR, appeared, produced their credentials, were qualified, and took their seats.

RUFUS EASTON, also, appeared and took his seat, as the delegate for the Territory of Missouri.

Mr. HOPKINSON and Mr. SERGEANT, respectively, presented a petition of a committee of sundry citizens of Philadelphia, concerned in various manufacturing establishments, praying that a standing committee may be appointed, "whose province and duty it shall be to watch over the interests of our manufacturing citizens, there not appearing to the memorialists any propriety in the reference of the subjects of Commerce and Manufactures to the same committee."—Referred to a Committee of the Whole to-morrow.

Mr. GOLD presented a petition of the " Auburn Manufacturing Company," in the State of New York, concerned in the manufacturing of cotton fabrics, in behalf of themselves and others interested in their ultimate success, praying that the importation from foreign countries of cotton fabrics, of a coarse texture, may be absolutely or virtually prohibited.—Referred to the Committee of Commerce and Manufactures.

Mr. LATTIMORE presented a petition of the Legislature of the Mississippi Territory, praying that further time may be given to purchasers of public lands in said Territory to complete their payments, and that the interest claimed on payments not punctually paid at the time they became due, may be remitted.

The SPEAKER laid before the House a letter from the Secretary of War, transmitting statements showing the application of moneys which have been transferred by order of the President, from several of the appropriations to other appropriations, for the support of the Military Establishment, since the last session of Congress; which were referred to the Committee of Ways and Means.

On motion of Mr. JOHNSON, of Kentucky,

Resolved, That the Committee of Claims be directed to inquire into the expediency of liquidating the claims of citizens against the United States, for the loss of property whilst in the public service during the late war.

Mr. REYNOLDS submitted the following resolution, which was read and ordered to lie on the table:

Resolved, That the Committee on the Public Lands be instructed to inquire into the expediency of appropriating all that tract of land, known by the name of the "Congressional Reservation," lying in the counties of Maury and Giles, in the State of Tennessee, for the extinguishment of the Gerieme land warrants, issued by the State of North Carolina; and that the actual occupants within the bounds of said tract, who have been living on said land since the 1st day of January last past, shall have a preference to perfect titles thereto: *Provided,* No one shall be permitted to appropriate more than six hundred and forty acres, nor less than fifty acres of land.

On motion of Mr. THOMAS,

Resolved, That the Committee on Military Affairs be instructed to inquire into the expediency of providing by law for the relief of the widows and children of all such non-commissioned officers, musicians, and privates, as have been killed in battle, died of wounds received in the public service, or died in service, in any of the corps composing the Army of the United States during the late war.

Mr. TAYLOR, of New York, from the Committee of Elections, made a report on the petition of Westel Willoughby, jr., contesting the election of WILLIAM S. SMITH, a member returned to serve in this House from the State of New York. The report states it to be ascertained to the satisfaction of the committee, that the whole number of votes given in the district, which is composed of the counties of Madison and Herkimer, was 5,292; of which 2,540 were returned for WILLIAM S. SMITH, 2,466 for Westel Willoughby, jr., 309 for Westel Willoughby, and seven scattering votes; that it is proved, the error of the omission of the word "junior," to a part of the returns, was committed by the returning officers, the votes having in fact been given for Westel Willoughby, junior. The committee recommend that Mr. SMITH's seat be vacated, and that Mr. WILLOUGHBY be declared entitled to his seat.

The report was referred to a Committee of the Whole.

TUESDAY, December 12.

Several other members, to wit: from New York, DANIEL CADY; from Maryland, CHARLES GOLDSBOROUGH; from Virginia, BURWELL BASSETT; and from Kentucky, BENJAMIN HARDIN, appeared, were qualified, and took their seats.

Mr. SHEFFEY presented a petition of Robert Porterfield, praying to be admitted to a seat in the House, as one of the Representatives for the State of Virginia, in the place of WILLIAM MCCOY, whom he alleges to have been unduly elected and returned.—Referred to the Committee of Elections.

Mr. WRIGHT submitted the following resolution:

Resolved, That each member of the Senate and of the House of Representatives be annually furnished with a copy of the Registers of the officers of the Army and Navy of the United States, with the State or nation of their nativity.

The resolution was then read, and referred to Messrs. PICKERING, WRIGHT, and BASSETT.

Mr. YANCEY submitted the following resolution, which was read, and ordered to lie on the table:

Resolved, That so much of the rule affecting stenographers, as requires them to be placed in the galleries, be repealed; and that the Speaker be authorized to assign them such station in the House as he shall deem convenient and proper.

The House resolved itself into a Committee of the Whole on the report of the Committee of Elections, on the petition of Westel Willoughby, jr., contesting the election of William S. Smith; and after some time spent thereon, Mr. SPEAKER resumed the Chair, and Mr. LEWIS reported the concurrence of the Committee of the Whole, in the resolutions contained in the said report, to wit:

1. *Resolved,* That William S. Smith is *not* entitled to a seat in this House.

2. *Resolved,* That Westel Willoughby, jr., *is* entitled to a seat in this House.

The House proceeded to consider the report of the Committee of the Whole, and the resolutions being again read, were severally concurred in by the House.

WEDNESDAY, December 13.

Several other members, to wit: from Massachusetts, ELIJAH H. MILLS; from New York, MOSS KENT; from Delaware, THOMAS CLAYTON; and from Pennsylvania, ISAAC GRIFFIN, appeared, produced their credentials, were qualified, and took their seats.

WESTEL WILLOUGHBY, jr., from New York, who was, on yesterday, declared duly elected a member of this House, in the place of William S. Smith, also appeared, was qualified, and took his seat.

The SPEAKER laid before the House the following letter from Mr. MACON, of North Carolina:

To the Speaker of the House of Representatives:

SIR: I deem it my duty to inform you and the members of the House, that I have this day, by letter to the Governor of North Carolina, resigned my seat in the House of Representatives.

I cannot withdraw from those with whom I have been associated for years without expressing the grateful sense I entertain of their uniform kindness, and assuring them that it will be remembered with pleasure during my life.

I am, sir, your obedient servant,

NATH. MACON.

WASHINGTON, *Dec.* 12, 1815.

Ordered, That Mr. PICKENS be appointed of the Committee of Foreign Relations, in the place of Mr. Macon, resigned.

Ordered, That Mr. ARCHER be appointed of the Committee upon the subject of an Uniform National Currency, in the place of Mr. Macon, resigned.

On motion of Mr. CANNON,

Resolved, That a committee be appointed to inquire into the expediency of providing for the widows and orphans of the officers, non-commissioned officers, musicians, and privates of the volunteers and militia who have been killed in battle, died in service, or of wounds received while in the service of the United States during the war, by allowing them donations in land or otherwise; and that they have leave to report by bill or otherwise.

Messrs. CANNON, KING of North Carolina, HARDIN, HUGER, HAWES, STURGES, and BURNSIDE, were appointed a committee pursuant to the said resolution.

On motion of Mr. YANCEY, the House proceeded to consider the resolution submitted by him yesterday, relating to stenographers, and the same being again read, was concurred in by the House.

On motion of Mr. WILDE, the House proceeded to consider the resolution submitted by him on the seventh instant, proposing to amend the standing rules and orders of the House, by the appointment of several additional standing committees, and the same being again read, was ordered to lie on the table.

On motion of Mr. STANFORD, a committee was appointed to revise the standing rules and orders of the House.

Messrs. STANFORD, BASSETT, SERGEANT, GOLD

Desha, Crawford, and Telfair, were appointed the committee.

On motion of Mr. Stanford, the resolution of Mr. Wilde, proposing the appointment of several additional standing committees, was referred to the committee last appointed.

On motion of Mr. Sergeant, the Committee of the whole House were discharged from the further consideration of the petitions of sundry manufacturers in the city of Philadelphia, presented and referred on the 11th instant; and they were referred to the committee last mentioned.

On motion of Mr. Tucker, the Committee for the District of Columbia were instructed to inquire into the expediency of authorizing the Secretary of State, on the part of the United States, to subscribe for a certain number of copies of an edition of the laws, exclusively relating to the District of Columbia, proposed to be published by J. B. Colvin of the said District.

On motion of Mr. McLean, of Ohio, the Committee on the Judiciary were instructed to inquire whether any, and, if any, what amendments are necessary to a law passed at the last session of Congress, entitled "An act regulating and defining the duties of the United States' judges, for the Territory of Illinois;" and, also, what amendments are necessary to the act passed at the last session of Congress, regulating the General Court of the Territory of Indiana.

On motion of Mr. Tucker, the Committee for the District of Columbia were instructed to inquire into the expediency of providing, by law, for the enclosure and improvement of the public square, near the Capitol, in the said District.

On motion of Mr. Wilde, the Committee on the Judiciary were instructed to inquire whether any, and, if any, what additional provisions are necessary to be made for the more effectual awarding, granting, issuing, and returning writs of *habeas corpus* by the courts of the United States.

SETTLERS IN MISSOURI.

Mr. Easton moved the following resolution:

Resolved, That the Committee on the Public Lands be instructed to inquire whether any, and, if any, what alterations and amendments are necessary to be made in the law giving the right of pre-emption to settlers on the public lands in the Territory of Missouri.

A motion was made by another gentleman to amend the same by adding thereto the words, "and also in the Territories of Illinois and Indiana." Upon which motion

Mr. Easton observed, that the law giving the right of pre-emption to the settlers on the public lands in the Illinois Territory had been amended at the last session. He was not, however, opposed to the proposed inquiry; that the object of the resolution offered by him was to place those settlers on the public lands in the Missouri Territory upon a similar footing to such settlers on the Illinois Territory; that the law of Congress of April 12, 1814, gave to the settlers on the public lands, in the Territory of Missouri, the right of pre-emption in the purchase thereof upon the

same terms as is granted to settlers of the like description in the Illinois Territory, by the act of the 5th of February, 1813, which had been amended at the last session of Congress. By a reference to the last mentioned act of Congress, it would be found that no person can purchase, under the provision of the act, more than one quarter section of land, and that to be bounded by the sectional and quarter sectional lines; that by those acts of Congress, no provision has been made in favor of settlers upon fractional sections, of less quantity than one hundred and sixty acres, and fractional quarter sections; that by the general provisions made by law, the officers of the land offices are prohibited to sell lands in less quantity than tracts of one hundred and sixty acres; that in the Indiana Territory the lands had been surveyed, and the settlers then located themselves within certain known boundaries; that it was not so in Missouri Territory, where the private claims to land had been adjusting for more than twelve years, and the public lands are not yet surveyed; many persons had settled under Spanish grants, some of which had been annulled by the Government; that among the numerous private claims there would be found a great many fractional sections and fractional quarters of less quantity than one hundred and sixty acres, upon which persons are settled; and the object of the resolution offered by him was to secure to each settler on the public lands his improvement in that Territory.

The amendment was adopted and the resolution agreed to.

THURSDAY, December 14.

Mr. Hopkinson presented petitions of sundry inhabitants of the city of Philadelphia, praying that an act may be passed establishing a National Bank, with branches, founded on such a capital, and regulated by such principles as shall secure public and private confidence.—Referred to the Committee on the subject of an Uniform National Currency.

Mr. Lattimore presented petitions from sundry inhabitants of the Mississippi Territory, east of Pearl river, praying that provision may be made for taking a census of the inhabitants of the said Territory, and that the Territory may be erected into an independent State.—Referred.

Mr. Speaker laid before the House a letter from William Lambert, of the City of Washington, enclosing abstracts of such calculations relative to the longitude of the Capitol, in the City of Washington, as were made by him before the passage of the resolution of this House, of the 18th of February last, upon this subject; which were ordered to lie on the table.

On motion of Mr. Lewis, the Committee for the District of Columbia were instructed to inquire into the expediency of completing the Capitol, by erecting a centre building, according to the original plan.

On motion of Mr. Thomas, the Committee on the Public Lands were instructed to inquire into the expediency of granting rights of occupancy and pre-emption, at two dollars per acre, to all such persons as shall be actually seated, on the first day of October, 1816, upon any section of land obtained by treaty or conquest from the Creek nation of Indians during the late war.

Friday, December 15.

Another member, to wit: from Virginia, John G. Jackson, appeared, produced his credentials, was qualified, and took his seat.

Mr. Speaker presented a petition of the Legislature of the Mississippi Territory, praying that the titles to lands in said Territory, granted by the former Spanish Government, which had previously been granted by the British Government, may be confirmed to the holders under the Spanish grant.

Mr. Lattimore presented a similar petition from sundry inhabitants of the Mississippi Territory.—Referred to the Committee on the Public Lands.

Mr. Lowndes, from the Committee of Ways and Means, reported a bill making additional appropriations to defray the expenses of the army and militia during the years 1814 and 1815; which was read twice, and committed to a Committee of the Whole.

Mr. Speaker laid before the House a letter from the Secretary of the Navy, transmitting a statement of the application of the moneys drawn from the Treasury for the use of the Navy Department, for one year, ending on the 30th of September, 1815.—Referred to the Committee on Naval Affairs.

On motion of Mr. Forsyth, the Library Committee were instructed to inquire into the expediency of increasing the sum appropriated for the salary of the Librarian of Congress; and for the contingent expenses of the Library, and of allowing additional compensation to the Librarian for services performed since the last session of Congress.

Adjourned to Monday.

Monday, December 18.

Several other members, to wit: from the State of New York, Thomas P. Grosvenor and John B. Yates, and from the State of Pennsylvania, John Ross; appeared, produced their credentials, were qualified, and took their seats.

Mr. King, of Massachusetts, presented a petition of sundry inhabitants of different parts of the District of Maine, praying that one of the terms of the district court of the United States for the district of Maine, may be removed from Wiscasset to Portland.—Referred to the Committee on Judiciary.

Mr. Forsyth presented a petition of the Board of Trustees of the Orphan Asylum of the City of Washington, praying for an act of incorporation, and for a donation of certain public lots in the City of Washington.

Mr. Johnson, of Kentucky, presented a petition of sundry inhabitants of the Territory of Illinois, praying for pre-emption rights to the lands on which they reside.

Mr. Johnson, of Kentucky, also presented a petition of the Legislature of the Illinois Territory, praying that the claims of certain inhabitants of said Territory to pre-emption rights to lands, may be confirmed, and that some further provisions may be made relating to the selection of lands in said Territory, for the use of seminaries of learning.

On motion of Mr. Robertson, the committee on the rules and orders of the House were instructed to inquire into the expediency of appointing clerks to the standing committees, with leave to report by bill or otherwise.

On motion of Mr. Jennings, a committee was appointed to inquire into the expediency of changing the western limit of the Territory of Indiana, with leave to report by bill or otherwise; and Messrs. Jennings, Reynolds, Hardin, Hungerford, and Baer, were appointed the committee.

On motion of Mr. Easton, the Committee on the Public Lands were instructed to inquire, if any, what, further provisions by law are expedient to be made for ratifying the unconfirmed claims to land in the Territory of Missouri, and to provide for their location.

Resolved, That the Committee on the Public Lands be instructed to inquire, if any, what alterations or amendments are necessary to be made in the act, entitled "An act for the final adjustment of land titles in the State of Louisiana and Territory of Missouri."

The following resolution was submitted by Mr. Easton, which was read, and ordered to lie on the table:

Resolved, That the Committee on the Public Lands be instructed to inquire into the expediency of regulating by law the leasing and working the public lead mines in the Territory of Missouri, in such manner as to secure the lessees in the quiet enjoyment of their leases, and to enable the Government to collect its rents.

On motion of Mr. McLean, of Ohio, the Committee on Pensions and Revolutionary Claims were instructed to inquire into the expediency of authorizing by law the appointment of suitable persons for the payment of military pensions, within those States where Commissioners of Loans are not appointed.

DISTRICT JUDGES.

Mr. Gold offered for consideration the following resolution:

Resolved, That the Committee on the Judiciary be instructed to inquire as to the judicial duties of the respective district judges of the United States, whether the same have been in certain districts greatly increased since the establishment of the salaries of the judges therein; and whether the compensation at present allowed by law be adequate to the discharge of the duties enjoined upon the judges.

Mr. Gold remarked, in support of this motion, that when the compensation of the district judges had been fixed, it was no doubt adequate to the services that they then had to perform; but it was very notorious that the duties had increased in some districts in a fourfold degree. Such had been the increase of the business of the district judge in New York State, that it had been found necessary by Congress to divide the State into two districts. The act for that purpose, however, contained a provision that in case the judge of one of those districts should be unable to attend to the duties of his office, the judge of the remaining district should perform the duties of both. Now, the fact was, that the judge of one of those districts had been wholly unable to attend his judicial duties; in consequence of which the duties of that district had devolved on the judge of the other. He was, by this circumstance, obliged to travel two thousand miles a year, at an expense which nearly absorbed, in necessary travelling expenses, the whole amount of his salary. As there might be other districts in the same situation, he had couched the motion in terms so general as would embrace all.

The resolution was agreed to.

ADDITIONAL MILITARY APPROPRIATIONS.

On motion of Mr. LOWNDES, the House resolved itself into a Committee of the Whole on the bill making additional appropriations for defraying the expenses of the army and militia during the years 1814 and 1815.

Mr. LOWNDES explained briefly the object of the bill. The deficiency in the present year's appropriations, arose from the error in estimating the expense at four millions only, barely enough for the support of ten thousand men, when, in fact, for the principal part of the first two quarters of the year more than four times that number ought to have been provided for. The deficiency of preceding years, it was well known, was caused by the heavy expenses of large detachments of militia, exceeding the estimate which had been made, &c. Mr. L. handed to the Chair, for the information of the House, the following letter from the Paymaster of the Army to the Secretary of War, which was read:

ARMY PAY OFFICE,
CITY OF WASHINGTON, *Dec.* 16, 1815.

SIR: From the best calculations I have been able to make, the deficiency of appropriations for the regular Military Establishment for the year 1814, may be estimated at eight hundred thousand dollars, namely:

On account of pay - - - - - $615,000
On account of subsistence of officers, including their private servants - 85,000
On account of retained bounties to recruits 100,000

$800,000

And for the year 1815, at one million seven hundred thousand dollars, namely:

On account of pay - - - - - $1,250,000
On account of the subsistence of officers, including their private servants - 150,000
On account of retained bounties to recruits 300,000

$1,700,000

Forming an aggregate arrearage for these two years of two million five hundred thousand dollars, viz:

On account of pay - - - - - $1,865,000
On account of the subsistence of officers, including their private servants - - 235,000
On account of retained bounties to recruits 400,000

$2,500,000

A further sum of three million five hundred thousand dollars is also estimated to meet, in part, the outstanding claims of militia, volunteers, and Indian warriors, heretofore called into the service of the United States, exclusive, however, of the claims of certain States for expenditures upon their militia, which are not yet duly recognised on the part of the United States. It may be classed as follows:

On account of pay - - - - - $3,095,000
On account of the subsistence of officers, including their private servants - - 265,000
On account of forage, of the horses of officers only - - - - - 60,000
On account of the clothing of officers' private servants - - - - 80,000

$3,500,000

To give you a more condensed view of the preceding statements, the following recapitulation is submitted:

Pay of regular troops - -	1,865,000	
Pay of militia, &c - -	3,095,000	
		4,960,000
Subsistence of regular troops -	235,000	
Subsistence of militia, &c.	265,000	
		500,000
Forage of militia, &c. - -	60,000	
Clothing of militia, &c. - -	80,000	
Retained bounties to recruits for the regular service - - - -		400,000
		$6,000,000

I am, very respectfully, sir, your most obedient servant,

ROBERT BRENT,
Paymaster U. S. Army.

Hon. WM. H. CRAWFORD,
Secretary of War.

On motion of Mr. LOWNDES, the blanks in the bill were so filled as to embrace the following appropriations:

For the Quartermaster's department - $950,000
For the pay of the army and militia - 5,617,000
For the subsistence of the army and militia 2,310,373
For forage - - - - - 60,000
For clothing - - - - - 106,000
For bounties and premiums - - 400,000
For the Medical and Hospital departments 100,000
For fortifications - - - - 200,000
For the Ordnance department - - 140,000

Mr. SHARPE moved to strike out of the bill the words "during the years 1814 and 1815," on the ground that the insertion of these years would exclude claims of prior date, which he knew to be yet unsatisfied, though recognised by the Government as just; among these, he particularly mentioned the case of the men who served in General Hopkins's expedition. He presumed it to be the intention of the bill to include all claims remaining unpaid; with which object the language of the bill did not correspond.

Mr. LOWNDES disavowed any intention to exclude any just claims from payment; nor did he think such would be the effect of the present phraseology. The accounts of the department were kept under a general head for each item, without making any discrimination as to the date of its becoming due. These appropriations would of course go to the general heads, and be equally subject to all claims, of whatever date.

Mr. SHARPE replied, but his motion was overruled by the House by a majority of two.

The bill having been reported to the House, Mr. SHARPE moved to lay the bill on the table, to give an opportunity to ascertain from the War Department the fact in relation to outstanding claims prior to 1814; but after some conversation this motion was withdrawn; and,

By consent of Mr. LOWNDES, the bill was so amended by the House as to read, "during the late war," instead of "during the years 1814 and 1815."

The bill was then ordered to be engrossed, and read a third time; and was subsequently read a third time, and passed.

TUESDAY, December 19.

Mr. NEWTON, from the Committee of Commerce and Manufactures, reported a bill for the relief of Thomas and John Clifford, Elisha Fisher & Co., Thomas Clifford, and Thomas Clifford and Son; which was read twice and committed to a Committee of the Whole on Thursday next.

Mr. YANCEY, from the Committee of Claims, made a detailed report on the petition of Jonathan B. Eastman, which was read; when Mr. Y. reported a bill for the relief of Jonathan B. Eastman, which was read twice, and committed to a Committee of the Whole.

Mr. YANCEY made a report in detail upon the petition of Jabez Hull, which was read, when Mr. Y. also reported a bill for the relief of Jabez Hull, which was read twice, together with the report last aforesaid, and committed to a Committee of the Whole.

Mr. YANCEY also reported a bill to authorize the payment for property lost, captured, or destroyed by the enemy while in the military service of the United States; which was read twice, and committed to a Committee of the Whole to-morrow.

Mr. REYNOLDS submitted the following resolution, which was read and rejected by the House:

Resolved, That the Committee on Public Lands be instructed to inquire into the expediency of reducing the price of public lands, and report by bill or otherwise.

On motion by Mr. EASTON, the House proceeded to consider the resolution submitted by him yesterday, and the same being again read, was modified and agreed to, as follows:

Resolved, That the Committee on the Public Lands be instructed to inquire into the expediency of providing, by law, for better regulating the leasing and working the public lead mines and salt springs belonging to the United States, in such manner as to protect the lessees in the quiet enjoyment of their leases, and to enable the Government to collect its rents.

WEDNESDAY, December 20.

Two other members, to wit: from New York, VICTORY BIRDSEYE, and from Kentucky, SAMUEL McKEE, appeared, produced their credentials, were qualified, and took their seats.

Mr. HULBERT presented a petition of the manufacturers of cotton goods in the county of Berkshire, and State of Massachusetts, praying that measures may be adopted to preserve and encourage the cotton manufacturing establishments within the United States.—Referred to the Committee of Commerce and Manufactures.

Mr. JOHNSON, of Kentucky, from the Committee on Military Affairs, reported a bill for the relief of the infirm, disabled, and superannuated officers and soldiers of the Revolutionary war, the late war, and the army of the United States, for the time being; which was read twice, and committed to a Committee of the Whole House on Monday next.

The House resolved itself into a Committee of the Whole on the bill for the relief of Jona. B. Eastman; which was passed through the committee and ordered to be engrossed for a third reading.

The bill for the relief of Jabez Hull took the same course, after some debate on a fruitless attempt of Mr. TAYLOR to obtain a recommitment of the bill, with a view to make it more comprehensive.

THURSDAY, December 21.

Two members, to wit: from Rhode Island, JAMES B. MASON, and from New York, PETER H. WENDOVER, appeared, produced their credentials, were qualified, and took their seats.

Mr. HULBERT presented a petition of a committee appointed by the breeders of Merino sheep, and manufacturers of fine woollen cloths, residing in the county of Berkshire, and State of Massachusetts, praying that such measures may be adopted as will afford security and encouragement to the enterprise in which they are engaged.—Referred to the Committee of Commerce and Manufactures.

Mr. HOPKINSON presented a petition of sundry inhabitants of Philadelphia, praying for the establishment of a National Bank.—Referred to the Committee on the subject of an Uniform National Currency.

A message from the Senate informed the House that the Senate have passed the bill "making additional appropriations to defray the expenses of the army and militia of the United States during the late war," with amendments, in which they ask the concurrence of this House.

HISTORY OF CONGRESS.

Congressional Reservation.

The said amendments were then read and concurred in by the House.

Mr. YANCEY, from the Committee of Claims, made a report on the petition of Caleb Earl and John Keen, of Philadelphia, who pray indemnification from the Government for the loss of a vessel; which, having been embargoed, fell into the hands of the enemy at Alexandria. The report recommended that "the prayer of the petitioners ought not to be granted;" and was concurred in.

Mr. YANCEY also made a report on the petition of John Armstrong, of Tennessee, who prays to be allowed certain commissions on internal revenue collected. The report is adverse to his prayer, and was concurred in.

Mr. YANCEY also made report on the petition of Mr. John King, of the Northern Neck of Virginia, who prayed that his house, wantonly destroyed by the enemy in one of their predatory incursions during the late war, (at the same time that he was kidnapped and carried off to Halifax,) may be rebuilt by Government. The report is wholly adverse, on principle, to the prayer of the petition, and was concurred in.

The SPEAKER laid before the House a letter from the Secretary of the Treasury, transmitting an annual statement of the duties and customs for the year 1814, and of the sales of public lands for the year ending the 30th of September, 1815; and also a statement of the proceeds of the internal duties and direct tax, stating the amount due, and the amount paid, and the expenses of collection, in each collection district within the United States; which documents were, on motion of Mr. MILNOR, all ordered to be printed.

A letter was received from the Secretary of the Navy, enclosing a statement of moneys transferred from certain specific appropriations to other objects of expenditure, &c.

Both the above documents were referred to the Committee of Ways and Means.

The engrossed bill for the relief of Jonathan B. Eastman, and the engrossed bill for the relief of Jabez Hull, were read a third time and passed.

The bill for the relief of Thomas and John Clifford, and others, of Philadelphia, was taken up in Committee of the Whole. This case, as stated by Mr. NEWTON, is one in which the Messrs. Clifford have paid a certain sum in duties on articles which the Supreme Court has since decided were not dutiable under the existing laws. This bill is to enable them to withdraw from the Treasury the moneys thus erroneously paid. The bill was ordered to be engrossed for a third reading.

CONGRESSIONAL RESERVATION.

On motion of Mr. REYNOLDS, the House proceeded to the consideration of the following resolve, submitted by him a few days ago:

Resolved, That the Committee on Public Lands be instructed to inquire into the expediency of appropriating all that tract of land known by the name of the "Congressional Reservation," lying in the counties of Maury and Giles, in the State of Tennessee, for the extinguishment of the Gerieme land warrants issued by the State of North Carolina, and that the actual occupants within the bounds of said tract, who have been living on said land on the first day of January last past shall have a preference to perfect titles thereto: *Provided,* No one shall be permitted to appropriate more than six hundred and forty acres, nor less than fifty acres, of land.

This motion Mr. YANCEY proposed to amend, by striking out the whole, except the word "*Resolved*," and inserting the following, in lieu thereof:

"That the Committee on Public Lands be instructed to inquire into the expediency of appropriating so much of the land lying in the State of Tennessee, known by the name of the 'Congressional Reservation,' as may be sufficient to extinguish the claims under land warrants issued by the State of North Carolina, agreeably to the third section of an act of Congress of the 18th of April, 1806, entitled 'An act to authorize the State of Tennessee to issue grants and perfect titles to certain lands therein described, and to settle claims to the vacant and unappropriated land within the same.'"

Mr. YANCEY supported his motion, by showing how the interest of North Carolina would be injuriously affected by the passage of the resolution in its present shape.

Mr. REYNOLDS said he had no objection to the amendment, except his anxiety that those persons who had settled on these lands seven or eight years, and to this day been undisturbed by the Government, should have the preference in purchasing. He had their case much at heart. If ever there were people in the Union entitled to the right of pre-emption, it was those people. They formed the barrier of that country. They were a part of the brave men that defeated the Creek Indians; and even partook in the glory of the defence of Louisiana, when their country required their services. Such men deserved attention from Government. But being also anxious for the other object of his motion, and there appearing to be an objection to connecting them, he should consent to the amendment now proposed.

Mr. GASTON took a view of the successive laws of North Carolina, Tennessee, and the United States, on the subject of these land claims. The State of North Carolina, in parting with her rights to the United States, in 1803 or 1804, had done it on certain conditions; one of which was, that, in obtaining titles, no preference should be given to the citizens of Tennessee over those of any other State. It was therefore immaterial, he said, what were the particular merits of the individuals to whom the gentleman from Tennessee desired to secure the right of pre-emption. If the hands of Congress were tied up by the terms of the act of cession of North Carolina, the merits of these settlers on the lands would not avail to establish their claim to pre-emption rights.

Mr. ROBERTSON thought the discussion of the claims of actual settlers to rights of pre-emption to be at this time premature, as not properly before the House. He saw no objection to the resolution now proposed to be amended.

Mr. Pickens spoke in favor of the amendment. The State of North Carolina had made a grant of her rights in an act containing certain conditions, and requiring the assent of Congress as a preliminary. The assent contained in the act of Congress in 1806, in the opinion of North Carolina, was not sufficient to satisfy her previous act; and, in consequence of this insufficiency, she had repealed her first act. The question, whether this repeal was valid would depend on the question whether the act of Congress of 1806 contained the reservations in favor of North Carolina, which she required as the conditions of the surrender of her rights. The last clause of the original resolution, which the gentleman from Tennessee had so much at heart, embraced a principle on which, in his opinion, the Congress had no right to act, North Carolina having expressly stipulated against it.

The amendment proposed by Mr. Yancey was agreed to; and, thus agreed to, the resolution was passed.

ROADS AND CANALS.

Mr. Darlington offered for consideration the following resolution:

Resolved, That the committee appointed on so much of the President's Message as relates to Roads and Canals be instructed to inquire into the expediency of extending prompt and efficient aid, on the part of the General Government, to the company incorporated for the purpose of cutting a canal from the waters of the Chesapeake to those of the Delaware, commonly called the Chesapeake and Delaware Canal.

Mr. Darlington said, he flattered himself that the House would not only agree to the resolution, but act effectually on the subject of it. It was fashionable, he added, to call ourselves an enlightened people. He was not disposed to controvert this principle, but he hoped we should, by our acts, substantiate our claim to this character. The members of the Government had, he believed, been made sensible, by the course and events of the war, of the importance of inland communication, and he hoped they would, during peace, profit by their experience, and give it all the aid in their power.

The motion of Mr. D. was agreed to.

Friday, December 22.

Mr. Condict presented a petition from the Manufacturing Association of New Jersey, praying that the importation of cotton fabrics of a coarse texture may be absolutely or virtually prohibited.—Referred to the Committee on Commerce and Manufactures.

Mr. Archer presented sundry documents in relation to the election and return of George Baer as one of the members of this House for the State of Maryland, which were referred to the Committee of Elections.

Mr. Taylor, of New York, presented a petition of Erastus Root, praying that the seat of John Adams, whom he alleges has been unduly returned as one of the members of this House for the State of New York, may be vacated; and that he may be admitted to a seat in the House in the place of the said John Adams.—Referred to the Committee of Elections.

The Speaker laid before the House a letter from the Commissioner of the General Land Office, transmitting a letter from the Register of the Land Office and Receiver of Public Moneys at Kaskaskia, accompanied with a list of persons who have had less than four hundred acres confirmed to them, and a statement of claims for donations as heads of families, improvement rights, and militia rights, which were referred to the Committee on the Public Lands.

Mr. Yancey offered for consideration the following resolution. It appeared to him, he said, that such a measure as it embraced, if adopted, would be productive of much good to the nation and to the House, and could not involve any violation of the rights of individuals:

Resolved, That the committee to whom has been referred the revision and amendment of the rules and orders of the House, be instructed to inquire into the expediency of adopting a rule to the following effect: That after a claim has been heard upon its merits, and rejected by the House, it shall not be referred to a committee, unless the member presenting it shall state that it is supported by additional testimony, which in his opinion would produce a different decision of the House.

The motion was agreed to.

PUBLIC LANDS.

Mr. Henderson, of Tennessee, submitted the following resolution for consideration:

Resolved, That the Committee on Public Lands be instructed to inquire into the expediency of allowing to those persons claiming public lands in the Mississippi Territory under an act of the Legislature of Georgia, passed January 7, 1795, who have failed to compromise and make a settlement of their claims in conformity with the provisions of an act of Congress, entitled, an act for the indemnification of certain claimants of public lands in the Mississippi Territory, within the time therein limited, a further time to obtain the benefit of said mentioned act.

The resolution was agreed to.

Mr. Robertson, from the Committee on Public Lands, made an unfavorable report on the petition of John W. Winn; which was read and concurred in.

Mr. Robertson, also, from the same committee, made a favorable report on the petition of C. Markle, accompanied by a bill for his relief; which was twice read and committed.

Mr. Robertson, from the same committee, made the following report:

The Committee on the Public Lands, who were instructed by a resolution of the House to inquire into the expediency of granting rights of occupancy and pre-emption at two dollars per acre to all such persons as shall be actually seated, on the 1st day of October 1816, upon any section of land obtained by treaty or conquest from the Creek nation of Indians during the late war:

Report, That, from the year 1785 to the present time, laws to prevent unauthorized individuals from settling on the public and unappropriated lands of the United

397   HISTORY OF CONGRESS.   398

DECEMBER, 1815.   *Western Roads—Private Losses in Service.*   H. OF R.

States have been in constant operation; that intrusions on Indian lands have been equally forbidden; that the policy and wisdom of such laws appear to be undeniable. If those by whom they have been violated have in some instances been vested with the rights of pre-emption, yet it seems clearly impolitic to hold out invitations to a further disregard of them. The committee are not aware that the system in this respect requires alteration or amendment. They therefore respectfully submit the following resolution:

Resolved, That it is inexpedient to grant rights of occupancy or pre-emption to such persons as shall settle on the public lands which have been obtained by treaty or conquest from the Creek Indians during the late war.

This report being under consideration—

Mr. THOMAS opposed the report with much zeal, as well on the ground of the expediency of establishing an uniformity in the price of the public lands, as on that of the propriety of favoring those whose enterprise and spirit first should penetrate the wilderness by useful settlements. These points he illustrated by various arguments, and particularly dwelt on the importance of an early settlement of that frontier country, &c.

Mr. ROBERTSON replied in defence of the report, on the ground of the impolicy and absurdity of adopting measures that should encourage the violation of the existing laws which prohibit unlicensed settlements on the public lands. The question of changing the mode of disposing of the public lands, he said, was yet before the committee, and not, therefore, properly before the House, though it soon would be. Mr. R. made some remarks going to prove the anxiety of the Government to throw this land into market, &c. (with a view to its early settlement,) as evinced by the progress already made in preparing it for that purpose, in preference to other lands that had been much longer in possession of the United States, &c.

WESTERN ROADS.

Mr. EASTON, after a number of remarks going to show the importance of the object he had in view and the difficulty, if not impossibility, of its being executed in any other way than under the authority of the Government, moved the following instruction to the Committee on Roads and Canals:

Resolved, That the Committee on Roads and Canals be instructed to inquire into the expediency of opening roads, to wit: from Shawneetown to Kaskaskias, in Illinois; from the town of Hamilton in Ohio to Vincennes in Indiana, thence to the town of St. Louis in Missouri, thence by the way of Arkansas to the northern boundary line of the State of Louisiana.

The motion was agreed to.

[The following is the plan proposed by Mr. EASTON, in his observations for opening and improving roads: The President of the United States to be authorized to appoint a suitable number of commissioners to survey, mark, and lay out the said roads, and to designate the places where it will be necessary and proper that persons should settle, for the purpose of keeping houses of entertainment for accommodation of travellers; that

the Governors or Secretaries of the respective Territories be authorized to lease to an inhabitant who will settle at those places, a tract of land not exceeding six hundred and forty acres, nor less than three hundred and thirty acres, on condition of their opening and keeping in repair the road for the distance allotted to them for the term of ten years, which allotments shall be next adjoining the lands so leased to them respectively; and at the expiration of the leases, the lessees, their heirs or assigns, upon satisfying the President of the United States for the time being, that they have fulfilled the conditions of the leases, respectively, shall be entitled to receive a patent for the lands so leased from the Government: *Provided,* That no one lessee shall be required to keep the road in repair for more than five miles for a tract of three hundred and twenty acres, nor more than ten miles for a tract of six hundred and forty acres; and the commissioners in laying out and marking said roads, shall report to the Governors or Secretaries the several allotments specially, specifying in what allotments the lessees ought to be entitled to six hundred and forty acres, and in what allotments they will be entitled to a less quantity of land, and to what amount; which said allotments shall respectively be numbered, and laid down upon a plat of the said roads, to be platted by the surveyors to be employed to run the same; one copy whereof shall be deposited with the Governor of the Territory in which the road shall be, and other copies of the plats of said roads to be deposited in the office of the Commissioner of the General Land Office.]

PRIVATE LOSSES IN SERVICE, &c.

On motion of Mr. YANCEY, the House resolved itself into a Committee of the Whole, on the bill authorizing the payment for private property lost, captured, or destroyed, whilst in the service of the United States, during the late war.

Various amendments of a verbal nature were made to the bill, on which considerable discussion took place.

The most earnest discussion took place on motions successively made by Messrs. DESHA, THOMAS, WILDE, and CLAY, to amend the bill so as to include the case of the horses belonging to those militia who captured Proctor's army, that were lost in consequence of their riders being separated from, and crossing the lake without their horses, which were left in the care of the United States' officers.

These motions were advocated by the above gentlemen, and others, and opposed by Mr. YANCEY and others. The main objection of them was, that the daily allowance (by the act of 1795) to mounted volunteers and militia, for the use of their horses, was intended to cover all risks, except those incident to battle; and that the accidents of breaking loose, getting mired, &c., by which the horses in question were lost, were such as were intended to be covered by the liberal allowance of forty cents per day for the use and risk of horses. On the other hand, it was contended, with force, that the United States, having separated the rider from his horse, and assumed the care of it, was liable for accidents which occurred, generally, in consequence of the absence of the care and attention bestowed on the animal by his proprietor.

No one of the amendments on this subject prevailed, all of them being negatived. by 20 or 30 majority.

The following are Mr. Desha's remarks on the above bill:

Mr. Desha said, his object in rising was to move that so much of the amendment, proposed by the chairman of the Committee of Claims, to the bill under consideration, as relates to a deduction of forty cents per day, allowed by the act of 1795, for the use and risk of horses, should be struck out. He flattered himself, that before he sat down, he should be able to convince the honorable gentleman, that the bill with his amendment, unless the part that relates to the deduction of forty cents per day should be erased, was partial in its provisions, and manifestly unjust, particularly as related to Governor Shelby's volunteers, who were separated from their horses on Lake Erie, in the Fall of 1813. The bill, as it now stands, makes provision for paying for horses lost, in consequence of the failure, on the part of Government, to furnish a sufficiency of forage, without any deduction—neither ought there to be any. This is just; but how does it stand in relation to horses lost in consequence of the owners being separated from them by order of the commanding General, as was the case with Governor Shelby's men, who, under the order of the commanding officer, left their horses on the peninsula, between Sandusky and Portage river, crossed the lake where it was forty miles wide, principally in open boats, pursued the enemy upwards of a hundred miles into the interior of Canada, overtook them, and with the aid of a regiment of volunteers, commanded by my worthy colleague, captured Proctor's army, and defeated, with considerable slaughter, hosts of the savage allies of Britain. And can it be said that these men did not render as important services as those who lost their horses for want of forage. Then why this deduction of forty cents per day, from the commencement of the service? It is partiality in the extreme. I have no hesitation in saying, that Government is bound, in justice, to pay for all horses lost at Portage, by accident or otherwise. The horses, for upwards of four weeks, were virtually and indeed actually in possession of the Government, by order of its agent, during which time the owners had no control over them; men were left to take care of them, and to prevent them from breaking over the fence made across the peninsula. Then I say, in law, equity and justice, that all losses sustained during this time, the Government is bound to pay for; and to refuse, I have no hesitation in saying, is manifest injustice.

What was the situation on your borders at the time the volunteers tendered their services? Hull had surrendered up an army. Winchester had been defeated at the river Raisin. Dudley's regiment was cut up at the Rapids. The blood of the frontier inhabitants was flowing under the tomahawk and scalping knife. Dismay hovered on your borders. Such was the situation when the aged and patriotic Shelby, Governor of Kentucky, beat up for volunteers. After it was known that he would head them in person and lead them against the enemy, a short notice produced at the place of rendezvous, thirty-five or six hundred volunteers prepared to follow their patriotic leader into Canada, or anywhere else where they might be serviceable to their country. Pay was scarcely a consideration with them; yet they could not believe that their country would be ungrateful. The understanding was, that if their horses were lost, Government would pay for them. The quartermaster general, by the order, and under the eye of the Governor, had the horses valued by disinterested persons, and entered in a book for that purpose, copies of which, I believe, are deposited in the War Department. Under these circumstances, had not the volunteers a right to expect remuneration in case of losses, where such losses were not occasioned through any neglect on their part—and will Government act ungratefully towards her patriotic sons of the West, who, with other exertions, captured a whole army, with the aid of my colleague's regiment, and wrested, as it were, the tomahawk and scalping knife from the hands of hordes of savages, by giving peace to the frontiers, by deducting forty cents per day from the hard-earned wages of men who rendered important services, and in doing which they had the misfortune to lose their horses? Will we by this act verify what has been so often said by the enemies of free Governments, that Republics are always ungrateful?

Mr. Desha had no hesitation in believing, that, if every horse belonging to Governor Shelby's volunteers had been lost—and the number lost was inconsiderable—and had to be paid for by Government—it was still a saving business to them; particularly when the expense of transportation of baggage is taken into consideration, together with the importance of the service rendered, as well as the immense amount of property taken from the enemy on the Thames. The men convened at the place of rendezvous at a short notice. It would have taken considerable time to have procured wagons and teams for the transportation of the baggage. It would have taken weeks in marching the men on foot upwards of three hundred miles to the lake, and much difficulty and time to have gotten the baggage wagons there, through a country that abounds in swamps and marshes. Before the army could have arrived, under all these difficulties, the windy season, which commences periodically on the Lakes, must have set in, which would have rendered it impossible for the army to have crossed over in the kind of craft they had to cross in. The failure of the expedition would have been the inevitable consequence, and the expense would have been nearly equal to what it is now, when success attended our arms. The desperate devastations and massacres of the savage enemy would have continued another season on our borders. The Government would have had to have sent more men, and been subjected to the expense of another campaign, the success of which, independent of the expense, would have been more doubtful, as the enemy would have gotten over the panic, and been in all probability better prepared for your reception. Add to this the amount of property taken from the enemy, supposed to be considerable—upwards of a million of dollars in value—in munitions of war; ordnance, military stores, and other property.

Mr. D. said, when all these things were considered, together with the almost incalculable difficulties, toils, hardships, and starvations, that had to be encountered and surmounted on the expedition, Government ought not to hesitate in doing justice, if they were not disposed to remunerate liberally. But, what astonished him more than anything else, was the extraordinary opposition of the chairman of the Committee of Claims, who reported this bill, to granting pay for lost horses, and the want of his usual liberality in construing the act of 1795, which allows forty cents a day for the use and risk of horses. In this instance, the honorable gentleman appears not to have taken the use of horses into consideration, or certainly he would not be so anxious for the deduction, as contemplated in his amendment, from the commencement of the service. It is certainly a laudable principle, that of holding fast the public purse-strings; but this ought not to be the first consideration with a politician: justice ought to be deemed paramount to every other consideration. The honorable gentleman does not feel as I do on this occasion; and I have no doubt but he has a full share of philanthropy in his composition. It must be ascribed to the circumstance of the gentleman having been sitting at home at his ease; heard the account of our success, and no doubt was highly pleased with it; and probably heard of some of the difficulties we had to encounter; but it slipped by like the passing wind, and left no lasting impression. If the gentleman had been present, and witnessed the toils and difficulties that had been encountered, he perhaps would feel the same sympathies that I feel, and would think with me, that the part of his amendment that relates to a reduction of forty cents per day ought to be stricken out; and that justice demands, and sound policy dictates, that Government should pay for the horses lost, without any deduction of pay.

The bill was reported to the House with several amendments, and ordered to lie on the table.

Adjourned to Tuesday next.

Tuesday, December 26.

Another member to wit: from Connecticut, Benjamin Tallmadge, appeared, produced his credentials, was qualified, and took his seat.

Mr. Bradbury, presented a petition of sundry merchants in the District of Maine, praying for he establishment of a National Bank; and Mr.

Hopkinson presented similar petitions from sundry inhabitants of the city of Philadelphia.—Referred to the Committee on an Uniform National Currency.

Mr. Mason presented a petition of a committee appointed by, and acting for and in behalf of the cotton manufacturers residing in Providence and its vicinity, in the State of Rhode Island, praying that the importation of all cotton goods, (nankeens excepted,) the production of places beyond the Cape of Good Hope, may be prohibited; and that such additional duties may be laid on cotton goods of a coarse texture, imported from other countries, as will give to the petitioners the necessary protection and encouragement.

Mr. Hopkinson presented a petition of a committee of the manufacturers of cotton and woollen goods in the city of Philadelphia and its vicinity, praying that additional duties may be imposed on the importation of woollen manufactures, and that a duty of twenty-five per centum ad valorem may be imposed on the importation of cotton goods from foreign countries.—Referred to the Committee of Commerce and Manufactures.

A Message was received from the President of the United States, transmitting copies of a proclamation notifying the Convention concluded with Great Britain on the 3d day of July last, recommending to Congress such legislative provisions as the Convention may call for on the part of the United States.—Referred to the Committee on Foreign Affairs.

An engrossed bill entitled "An act for the relief of Thomas and John Clifford, Elisha Fisher and Company, Thomas Clifford, and Thomas Clifford and Son," was read the third time and passed.

On motion of Mr. Ross,

Resolved, That the Secretary of State be directed to communicate to the House, if anything, and what, has been done in pursuance of the act of Congress, of the 18th of April, 1814, entitled "An act authorizing a subscription to the laws of the United States, and for the distribution thereof," and if anything has occurred to delay or prevent the preparation, execution, or distribution of the work, to whom, or to what cause, it is attributable.

MILITARY ACADEMIES.

Mr. Johnson, of Kentucky, from the Committee on Military Affairs, reported a bill "making provision for three additional Military Academies."

[This bill proposes that there shall be established three additional Military Academies; one within the District of Columbia; one at Mount Dearborn, in South Carolina; and one in the vicinity of Newport, at the junction of the Ohio and Licking rivers, in the State of Kentucky, with the same establishment of officers, and under the same regulations generally as the present Military Academy; the number of cadets in the several Military Academies never to exceed in the whole, the number of eight hundred.]

The bill was twice read and committed.

403   HISTORY OF CONGRESS.   404

H. of R.   *Private Losses in Service.*   December, 1815.

CONTESTED ELECTION.

Mr. TAYLOR of New York, from the Committee of Elections, made a report on the petition of Erastus Root, contesting the election of John Adams, a member returned to serve in this House.

The report states, that Mr. Adams was returned in consequence of the error committed by the deputy clerk of Green county, (one of the two composing that Congressional district,) who, in copying the polls, spelt the name *Rott* instead of *Root*, whereby 576 of his votes were vitiated, which left a majority to Mr. Adams, who was therefore returned. The committee report that Mr. Root had in fact the majority of votes, as appeared by evidence before them, and was admitted by Mr. Adams. The committee recommend the adoption of the following resolutions:

"*Resolved,* That John Adams is *not* entitled to a seat in this House.

"*Resolved,* That Erastus Root *is* entitled to a seat in this House."

The report was further explained by Mr. TAYLOR, and no objection having been made to it on any part, it was agreed to, *nem. con.*

Mr. ROOT appeared, was qualified, and took his seat.

WEDNESDAY, December 27.

Mr. KING, of Massachusetts, presented a petition of the York Cotton Factory Company, in the State of Massachusetts, praying that such protection and encouragement may be extended to the manufacturing establishments within the United States, as may, in the wisdom of Congress, seem meet and proper.—Referred to the Committee of Commerce and Manufactures.

Mr. ROSS presented petitions of sundry inhabitants of the county of Lehigh, in the State of Pennsylvania, praying that the several acts imposing duties on distilleries, on domestic manufactures, and on retailers, may be repealed, and that the direct tax may be augmented.

Mr. PLEASANTS from the Committee on Naval Affairs, reported a resolution requesting the President of the United States to present medals to Captain James Biddle, and the officers of the sloop-of-war Hornet; which was read twice, and committed to a Committee of the Whole on Friday next.

Mr. PLEASANTS also reported a bill rewarding the officers and crew of the sloop-of-war Hornet, for the capture and destruction of the British sloop-of-war Penguin; which was read twice, and committed to a Committee of the Whole on Friday next.

Mr. THOMAS, after stating that a distinction not intended by the Government, now existed in the laws between soldiers of the usual military age, and those enlisted above and below it, under a law passed at a late period in the war, moved the following resolution:

Resolved, That the Committee on Military Affairs be instructed to inquire into the expediency of granting donations of an hundred and sixty acres of land to all persons under the age of eighteen, and over that of forty-five years, enlisted as regular soldiers in the Army of the United States to serve for five years, or during the late war, and who have or shall receive an honorable discharge.

The motion was agreed to.

On motion of Mr. THOMAS,

Resolved, That the Committee on Military Affairs, be instructed to inquire into the expediency of providing by law for the equitable liquidation of all claims against the Quartermaster's department, for rations and forage furnished to any of the troops of the United States, either volunteers, militia, or regulars, by a citizen whose accounts or vouchers are informal.

PRIVATE LOSSES IN SERVICE, &c.

The House resumed the consideration of the amendments reported by the Committee of the Whole to the bill making compensation for property lost, captured, or destroyed while in the military service of the United States; and the said amendments being again read, were concurred in by the House.

A motion was then made, by Mr. YANCEY, further to amend the said bill by inserting the following section:

SEC. 2. *And be it further enacted,* That any person, whether of cavalry, mounted militia, or volunteers, who, in the late war aforesaid, has sustained damage by the loss of a horse, in consequence of the owner being dismounted, or separated and detached from the same, by order of the commanding officer, or in consequence of the rider being killed or wounded in battle, shall be allowed and paid the value of such horse, at the time he was received into the public service; deducting therefrom the amount which has been paid, or may be claimed, for the use and risk of the same, while in the service aforesaid.

Mr. DESHA moved to strike out the latter clause of this proposed amendment, which he considered unjust as well as ungenerous.

Mr. JOHNSON said, the character of the men, immediately interested in this subject, had the strongest claim upon the justice of Congress. The farmers and mechanics, and men who, generally speaking, gained a livelihood by labor; men who had lived in domestic ease, quiet, and happiness, until called upon to defend the soil and the rights of their country; men in moderate circumstances, and many of them really poor, flocked to your standard—virtuous, valiant, and patriotic. They never aimed at power, and authority, and distinction, save that which has arisen from the glory they have acquired from their valiant deeds, and having by their toils and sufferings elevated the character of the nation to the highest pinnacle, are satisfied to retire to private life to enjoy, under the shade of the vine and the fig tree, rights and privileges which they have, with others, defended. These are the men who must be affected by the decision of this question; these are the men who ask for justice, not charity, although they believe, that, upon this principle, an appeal would not be vain. This bill makes unjust distinctions. Cases of hardships are omitted. Horses lost in battle, from unavoidable casualty, should be classed with horses killed in battle. No reason can be given why the distinction should be made. It is a distinction without difference. Justice discards any such rule. Why pay for horses killed in battle ?—because the risk is no ordinary one, but extraordinary. The same reason will embrace horses lost in battle. In each case Congress is bound in justice and good policy to remunerate the sufferers.

Again, the bill provides for the payment of horses lost for want of forage ; this is a very important provision, founded in justice, arising from an implied obligation on the part of the United States to pay damages resulting from a failure on the part of the Government to furnish forage, which was one condition upon which the mounted volunteer undertook to serve his country ; and if it was impracticable to comply with this positive stipulation, and that is admitted, the misfortune should not rest upon the citizen soldiers, but on Government. But, Mr. J. said, a case as strong as either of the others, presented itself for consideration, the payment for horses lost where the rider was dismounted by order of the commanding General. Take the memorable case of Governor Shelby and his gallant corps. Here again the principles of policy and justice plead for remuneration ; the reason is obvious, an act of Government produced the result. The horses were in this case lost by an order of the commanding General, without any fault or negligence in the mounted volunteer. Can there be a stronger case ? It may be strengthened, it may be placed, not only on the order of the commander, but on the intrinsic merit of that order. What causes produced this order ? The impossibility of riding over the waters of Lake Erie, and the necessity of pursuing the enemy. If the President and his Cabinet had been there, would the order have been sanctioned ? If Congress had been there, would Congress have sanctioned the order ? These inquiries need no answer. Then, upon what principle can these claims be rejected, and all similar claims ? for the argument will apply to all other cases. But the case may yet be strengthened. In the result of the measure—in the destruction of the enemy in that quarter—compare the labors of these men with the paltry sum which will be expended in paying for a few lost horses. A provision has been reported to give these men pay for their horses, after deducting forty cents per day, which the law gave them. The proposition contains a most manifest injustice. The value of the horse, and the ordinary risk of the horse, were worth forty cents per day ; and, notwithstanding, it is proposed to take away that which Government contracted to give the mounted volunteer. Did the Government have to use coercion ? No, thousands flocked to the standard of their country in the hour of peril, not doubting in times of peace they should meet with at least justice if not liberality. Such was the confidence of the American people. It is to be hoped that this confidence was well founded ; that this just expectation will be realized. But, Mr. J. said, members seemed to want correct information as to the services and

value of the horse of a mounted volunteer. It dispensed with all the expensive train of baggage wagons and provision escorts. It saved thousands to the United States, at the moment that it enabled the commanding officer to protect invaded frontiers, to pursue the enemy, and force him to battle or surrender.

In many parts no other force would have done ; the forces never disappointed expectation, and Congress should not hesitate on this occasion to be just if not liberal.

The feelings of gratitude and justice should be towards those people ; they demand no indemnity for the common calamities of war ; by the wanton destruction of private property by the enemy, the sacking of towns, burning of houses;—no such claims are set up; the Government had no agency in these injuries. These barbarities were not produced by any official act of the Government. The nation cannot forget the sorrows of these men, and the nation will demand good cause for a refusal on our part to pay them. A few days ago the merit of these men was presented strongly to the affections of this nation. Their services will not be forgotten ; their sufferings were great and their separation from their horses produced much hardship, and was the cause of the loss of their property, and Government cannot refuse remuneration.

Mr. SMITH of Virginia, spoke at length, as well as Mr. DESHA, in favor of the first part of the proposed new section, and against the proviso.

The motion of Mr. DESHA was opposed by Mr. YANCEY, who said, if it were adopted, he should be compelled to vote against his own amendment.

The question on Mr. DESHA's motion was decided by yeas and nays, as follows: For his amendment 54, against it 83, as follows:

YEAS—Messrs. Adgate, Baer, Baker, Barbour, Bassett, Birdseye, Brooks, Burnside, Caldwell, Chappell, Clarke of North Carolina, Clendennin, Clopton, Comstock, Creighton, Darlington, Desha, Forney, Griffin, Hahn, Heister, Henderson, Hungerford, Irwin of Pennsylvania, Jackson, Johnson of Virginia, Johnson of Kentucky, Kerr of Virginia, Love, McCoy, McKee, McLean of Kentucky, McLean of Ohio, Moore of South Carolina, Newton, Parris, Powell, Reynolds, Roane, Robertson, Ross, Schenck, Smith of Virginia, Southard, Taul, Taylor of South Carolina, Thomas, Townsend, Wallace, Ward of New Jersey, Wendover, Whiteside, Willoughby, and Thomas Wilson.

NAYS—Messrs. Alexander, Archer, Atherton, Baylies, Betts, Birdsall, Boss, Bradbury, Breckenridge, Brigham, Brown, Burwell, Cady, Calhoun, Champion, Chipman, Clayton, Condict, Cooper, Crawford, Cuthbert, Davenport, Forsyth, Gaston, Gholson, Gold, Grosvenor, Hall, Hammond, Hawes, Herbert, Hopkinson, Hulbert, Ingham, Jewett, Kent, King of Massachusetts, King of North Carolina, Langdon, Law, Lovett, Lowndes, Lumpkin, Lyle, Lyon, Maclay, Marsh, Mason, Mayrant, Mills, Milnor, Moffit, Nelson of Massachusetts, Noyes, Pickens, Piper, Pleasants, Reed, Rice, Root, Ruggles, Sergeant, Savage, Sheffey, Smith of Pennsylvania, Stanford, Strong, Stuart, Sturges, Taggart, Tallmadge, Tate, Telfair, Vose, Wheaton, Wilcox, Wilde, Wilkin, Williams, William Wilson, Woodward, Yancey, and Yates.

ceive will merely be a compensation for services rendered. The bill, therefore, is more of a military than charitable character, and is not meant as a substitute for the pension system.

Mr. WILDE moved an amendment to the bill, the object of which was to afford the benefit of its provisions to such of the militia of the United States as have actually served in war, and who have incurred disability by wounds or diseases contracted during their term of service. This motion he supported by arguments drawn from the merits of the militia thus disabled, and the injustice of making a discrimination in favor of regulars.

This amendment was agreed to.

The Committee of the Whole rose and reported the bill to the House. No opposition was made to any of the amendments to the bill, except the one last mentioned, which was opposed by Mr. HUGER, who drew a distinction between the regulars and militia, whom, he said, he had rather see provided for in any other way. The amendment was defended by Mr. WILDE and Mr. JOHNSON, and was agreed to.

On the question whether the bill should pass to a third reading,

Mr. CONNER said he felt it his duty to rise on this occasion. He coincided with the sentiments of the gentleman from South Carolina, that the amendment proposed by the gentleman from Georgia was an improper amendment; that its effect was to mix corps which should be kept distinct, or destroy that *esprit du corps* which should ever prevail in an army. However, as the evil effects of the amendment in operation might not be very great, he would vote for the bill in its present shape rather than it should not pass. Mr. C. said, he believed the passage of that bill depended on whether motives of humanity, policy, and justice, should prevail over those of a merely pecuniary nature, and he trusted that that point would not for a moment remain doubtful in this honorable body. It was humane, and coincident with the dictates of the wisest policy, that hospitals be erected in the vicinity of the operations of armies, for the reception of the wounded. Certainly the same humanity and wisdom dictated that corps of invalids or hospitals for invalids be organized for the protection of those brave men who had been crippled in their country's service, and who have thus been disabled from application, or procuring the means of support. In his opinion the Government would be equally censurable for the neglect of the one as a General would be for the wanton abandonment of the other. This bill, while it provided for that object, would have the further highly beneficial effect of rendering disposable, for active operations in the field, a force of nearly the amount contemplated by the bill, which would otherwise be employed in garrison duty. A variety of considerations might be urged which would go to demonstrate that this subject is intimately connected with the interests of the Army, with creating a martial spirit, and affording inducements and means of a rapid augmentation of our Military

Establishment in times of danger and emergency. The Duke of Sully had recorded, as one of the finest strokes of policy, and as one of the greatest evidences of the masterly mind and benevolent heart of Henry IV, his establishment of a hospital for invalids. But Mr. C. forbore from urging such considerations, because he apprehended that arguments which had for their object the interest, or tended to demonstrate the efficiency of regular armies, would have but little weight with the honorable body of which he was a member. Last Winter, indeed, when danger was imminent, when the Constitution was tottering on its base, when the great central power which holds together these federative bodies was so far weakened, that there was danger and expectation of some of them being hurled from their respective orbits, it was considered that the national arm should be invigorated; that militia was inefficient but for the purpose of internal defence; that we should have system and organization; that in peace we should be prepared for war. Such, said Mr. C., were popular sentiments in that honorable body when the storm was at its height. But suddenly it was hushed; there was a calm; all apprehension of danger or disquiet had vanished; there were to be no more "wars or rumors of wars;" eternal sunshine was seen to gleam through the vista of futurity. He confessed that he was not a convert to the faith of this political millenium. He saw it not in our extended domain, which embraced every clime, nor in our rich commerce, which covered every sea, and excited the jealousy and cupidity of modern Europe. And he thought he discovered more than "a speck of war" than he beheld a nation, powerful in finance and in arms, a natural rival, with strong incentives to hostility, and wedded to war, hanging like a dark and threatening cloud on our North and West. In short, his limited knowledge of human nature, and the annals of past times, led him to conclude, that with brighter auspices, indeed with towering auspices, we were destined to the same collisions as other nations, to contests protracted and severe. But whatever might be the views of that honorable body as to the design of this measure, either as it regarded the Army or the general interests of the country, he hoped at least that justice would prevail. He hoped by the passage of the bill that they would bind up the soldier's wounds. That honorable gentleman from Kentucky, (pointing to Colonel JOHNSON,) who had received severe wounds while in the service of his country, well knew, that although to the soldier's mind death is divested of his terrors in the field, yet the reflection of being a maimed and crippled object, without the means of application or support, unhonored, forgot, or known only as an object of contumely, that calls forth indignation or affected pity, that excites disgust, was a terrible consideration. The noblest feelings of the heart are trampled on; wounds, which should be badges of honor, become monuments of disgrace. Let us, said Mr. C., by the passage of this bill, divest the mind of such humiliating fears, and inspire the defender of his country's rights while encountering disease, hardship, and danger in the field, with this consoling assurance, that, if killed, he would receive the benediction of his God; if wounded, he would be cheered with the smiles of his Government and country.

The bill was ordered to be engrossed for a third reading.

FRIDAY, December 29.

Another member, to wit: from Maryland, ALEXANDER C. HANSON, appeared, produced his credentials, was qualified, and took his seat.

The SPEAKER presented a memorial of the Legislature of the Mississippi Territory, praying that the fractional sections of public land in that Territory may be subdivided.—Referred to the Committee on the Public Lands.

The SPEAKER also presented a petition of the Legislature of the Mississippi Territory, praying that the officers and men who served under Lieutenant Colonel Nixon and Major Hinds may receive payment for their services.—Referred to the Committee on Arrangements of Militia Expenses incurred by States without authority of the General Government.

The SPEAKER also presented another petition of the Legislature aforesaid, praying that the said Territory may be erected into a State government, and that such State may be admitted into the Union.—Ordered to lie on the table.

The SPEAKER presented another petition of the Legislature of the Territory aforesaid, praying that such inhabitants of their Territory as may have suffered losses by the hostile Indians, may be remunerated by grants of land out of the tracts lately ceded to the United States by the said Indians.—Referred to the committee appointed on the 14th instant, on a similar petition from the said Legislature.

Mr. YANCEY, from the Committee of Claims, made a report on the petition of William Morrissett, which was read; when Mr. Y. reported a bill for his relief; which was read twice, and referred to a Committee of the Whole.

Mr. STANFORD, from the committee appointed to revise the rules and orders of the House, made a report, which was read, and committed to a Committee of the Whole on Monday next.

Mr. BIRDSALL, from the committee appointed on the petition of Henry Fanning, by leave of the House reported a bill for the relief of Henry Fanning; which was read twice, and committed to a Committee of the Whole on Friday next.

An engrossed bill entitled "An act for the relief of the infirm, disabled, and superannuated officers and soldiers of the Revolutionary war, the late war, and the Army of the United States, for the time being," was read the third time, and ordered to lie on the table.

On motion of Mr. THROOP, the Committee on Pensions and Revolutionary Claims were instructed to inquire into the expediency of increasing the rate of pensions to officers and soldiers disabled in the service of the United States during the late war with Great Britain; and also into the expediency of amending the law relative to the proof required from officers and privates in the militia to establish their claims to a pension.

On motion of Mr. PARRIS, the Committee on Military Affairs were instructed to inquire into the expediency of providing by law for the equitable liquidation of all claims for wages due the estates of such non-commissioned officers, musicians, and privates, as have died while in the service of the United States during the late war, upon the best evidence it may be in the power of the person or persons making application therefor, considering the nature of the claims respectively, to produce.

The bill reported by the Committee of Ways and Means, for enlarging the time for ascertaining transfers and changes of property affected by the act for laying a direct tax, passed through a Committee of the Whole, and was ordered to be engrossed for a third reading; as also was the bill for the relief of Charles Markle, giving him permission to change his entry of a purchase of public lands.

Mr. REYNOLDS, adverting to the decision of the House the other day against his motion for inquiring into the expediency of reducing the price of the public lands, said he hoped he should be more fortunate in another attempt to favor those disposed to settle and cultivate the public lands. The Government had just issued a proclamation for driving from the public land those who had actually settled on it. This was doubtless an unpleasant task to the Government, but it appeared that it had been thought a just policy. He now wished to give an opportunity to every man who wanted land to purchase ground enough to settle on. With this view he moved the following resolution:

Resolved, That the Committee on Public Lands be instructed to inquire into the expediency of sub-dividing quarter sections of land offered for sale, and also into the expediency of allowing a greater discount for the prompt payment of the purchase money.

The question to agree to this proposed resolution was decided in the negative, 53 to 40.

PETITION OF ANDREW MONTGOMERY.

A report on the petition of Andrew Montgomery, of the Mississippi Territory, an officer in the military service of the United States, who prayed compensation for a slave of his own who attended him as a servant, was brought up by Mr. YANCEY, from the Committee of Claims. The report was read, and was found to recommend a rejection of the claim.

On the question that the House do concur in the resolution of the committee,

Mr. WRIGHT rose, and, after giving it as his opinion that it would be unjust to reject the claim, moved that the consideration of the subject should be postponed.

Mr. YANCEY said, that it would be better to refer it to a Committee of the whole House, and moved to that effect; but the motion was lost.

Mr. Y. then, adverting to what had fallen from

Mr. Wright, said that no difference in the color of men engaged as servants could operate to exclude the claim of compensation; but there *was* a difference between a *free* man and a *slave* taken as an attendant on an officer. The object of the petition was to obtain compensation for the value of the slave. If an officer, being allowed a waiter, gets a freeman to attend him, and that freeman were killed or disabled, would it enter into the contemplation of Congress, or of any man, to pay the value of that freeman? Wages were regularly allowed for the services of such attendants. But this petition asks for the wages for those services, and compensation for the value of the negro also. He considered the report as founded on just principles, and it would be confirmed.

Mr. Wright entered at large into the discussion of the case. It being considered degrading and humiliating to military officers to do the drudgery of servitude about their persons, it had been the custom to allow them to take such a servant out of the ranks; in which situation, the man was as much exposed as if he were a soldier. His not being obliged to fight was no shield to him. And if the officer, by substituting a slave of his own, gave a man to the service, it was unjust that he should suffer the loss of so much property by the slave's falling in the course of his duty. Had the servant been a freeman, his representatives or relatives would be allowed compensation; and why should not the owner of a slave lost in the same way? Mr. W. disavowed any expectation that the petitioner should be allowed the *whole* value of the slave; but, that he ought to have some part of it, was in his opinion undeniable.

Mr. Reynolds, of Tennessee, reminded the House that they had just passed a bill to compensate owners for losses sustained in horses, mules, oxen, boats, and *every* kind of property; and yet a committee now told them that they ought to make an exception of this case, on no other grounds than the property lost being the slave of the officer. He insisted that it was no less incumbent on the House to pay for this than for a cart or a horse, unless it could be shown that a law existed declaring that loss of slaves should not be entitled to compensation.

Mr. Yancey again spoke, and was answered by Mr. Wright.

Mr. Pickering put this question: If a white man were hired and killed, would they pay his widow the price of a man? He believed not. As to compensation to the wounded and maimed, Mr. P. observed they were granted, not because the men were wounded or maimed, but because they were rendered thereby incapable of supporting themselves; for, if they were killed, they got nothing.

Mr. Huger thought it important that the principle involved in this case should be settled, and therefore suggested that the resolution should lie on the table, in order that gentlemen might revolve it in their minds. It was therefore proposed to let it lie till Tuesday, but refused.

Mr. H. then proceeded to observe, that he did not so much regard the interest of the owners as of the public, in what he was suggesting. With a view to the future, it was impolitic to discourage officers of the Southern States from bringing their own servants along with them into the field. The House should recollect, that, if a white man be employed as a servant, it detracts so much from the military force—it by so much lessens the army—and that it is besides a great advantage to have the slave brought, because he is had at a less expense. But no officer, he said, would venture his property in that way, if compensation be refused in this instance. For, if the slave be left at home, he is sure to bring in a handsome revenue to his owner, without any other than the ordinary risks of his life.

The question of concurrence was put, and passed in the affirmative.

ADMISSION OF MISSISSIPPI.

Mr. Lattimore, from the committee appointed on the 6th instant on a petition of the Legislature of the Mississippi Territory, and to whom was referred a petition of the inhabitants of said Territory respecting a census, made a detailed report, which was read; when Mr. L. reported a bill to enable the people of the Mississippi Territory to form a constitution and State government, and for the admission of such State into the Union, on an equal footing with the original States; which was read twice, and committed to a Committee of the Whole on Tuesday next.

The report is as follows:

By the articles of agreement and cession between the United States and the State of Georgia, it is provided "that the territory thus ceded [now Mississippi Territory] shall form a State, and be admitted as such into the Union, as soon as it shall contain sixty thousand free inhabitants, or at an earlier period, if Congress shall think it expedient, on the same conditions and restrictions, with the same privileges, and in the same manner, as is provided in the ordinance of Congress of the 13th of July, 1787, for the government of the Western Territory of the United States; which ordinance shall, in all its parts, extend to the territory contained in the present act of cession, that article only excepted which forbids slavery."

The memorialists, after stating the number of persons taken under the last general census, which was forty thousand three hundred and fifty-two of all descriptions, and adverting to the accession of population produced by the annexation of a part of West Florida, and by subsequent emigrations, conclude that the Territory contained at that time (December, 1814) the number required by the agreement referred to above to entitle it to admission on an equal footing with the original States. As this, however, was a matter of conjecture and uncertainty, they solicit admission as an act of courtesy on the part of the United States.

Your committee possess no means of forming anything like a satisfactory estimate of the present population of the Territory in question; but they conceive that, unless it be the determination of Congress to defer its admission until it can be claimed in strict conformity to the compact with Georgia, there is no good reason for a further delay on the score of a deficiency of numbers, as such deficiency, if not now questionable, will not probably much longer exist. Without taking into consideration the recent settlers, who are subject to the late proclamation under the "act to prevent settlement being made," &c., the presumption is not unreasonable that, if any considerable part of the lands obtained from the Creeks be prepared for a legal settlement within the time contemplated, the Territory will contain more than the number required before it can be finally erected into a State.

It is known to your committee that the consent of Georgia to a division of this Territory has been asked, and obtained; and, should it be divided before it is admitted, the admission of either part would, from a want of numbers, be subject to additional objection and further delay. But doubts may be entertained whether the Territory can, with strict propriety, be divided without the consent of its inhabitants, as well as that of Georgia and of the United States. Although the people of the Territory had no agency in the agreement above granted they were the object of it, and as such became a third party to it, and vested by it of a right which is explicitly defined. This agreement provides "that the Territory thus ceded shall form a State, [not one or more States,] and shall be admitted as such into the Union, as soon as it shall contain sixty thousand free inhabitants." If, then, admission shall be deferred in consequence of division, the expectation of the inhabitants will be disappointed, and their right impaired. It is chiefly to avoid such a result that your committee have declined recommending a division of the Territory, which otherwise might be expedient to lessen the inconveniences which, with or without division, the local Government will, for a long time at least, have to sustain.

In relation to the simple question of admission, as presented by the memorialists, precedents are not wanting, either to encourage their application or to grant their request. The State of Ohio was admitted before it possessed the number which the ordinance required, and Louisiana did not come in, as to time or numbers, in virtue of a strict and insuperable claim. It is not improbable that the Mississippi Territory may contain at this time a greater population than either of these States did when they were admitted; and it is believed that its state of political minority and probation has been of longer duration than that of any of the adopted States. If, then, after fifteen years of restraint, the people of this country should evince even an impatient desire for enlargement, it is but just to ascribe it to that sense of independence which is common to the nation, and which should be rather encouraged than depressed. It is a policy worthy of a Government which is constituted and maintained by the public will to foster throughout the Union those feelings which give energy to the national character, and to extend to every portion of it those rights which conduce to the general good. Nor could a period more propitious to these ends be selected than the present, when all American citizens have new cause to approve of their principles, to confide in their institutions, and to be proud of their name.

So far your committee have considered this subject as though an immediate admission of the Territory was desired by all of its inhabitants; but they are not prepared to say that such is the fact. While it is true that such admission has been repeatedly solicited for a succession of years, it is also true that, about four years ago, a small minority of the representative branch of the Territorial Legislature protested against it, and that, about a year thereafter, a considerable number of the people themselves petitioned that all

proceedings in Congress on the subject might be postponed. It was on these two occasions only, as your committee believe, that any indisposition to a State government has been expressed to the National Legislature by any of the people of the Territory, or of their representatives in their behalf. Nor is it understood or believed that the reluctance manifested by a portion of these people arose from a want of a due and equal appreciation of the rights and advantages of an independent State. The causes of opposition, so far as any opposition has been shown, seem to have been, in part, an unwillingness to incur additional expense in supporting a State Government while under a peculiar pressure from the war; but chiefly an apprehension that a State Government, with its inseparable appendage, a federal district court, would be immediately followed by a great number of expensive and dangerous, if not ruinous, lawsuits for lands, which would grow out of (what are called) the Yazoo and British claims. The war, however, is now at an end, and the Yazoo claims may be considered as quieted; but the British claims still exist, and constitute the subject of several petitions now before Congress, on which it is not the province of your committee to speak.

The petitions of sundry inhabitants east of Pearl river, in the same Territory, which also have been referred to your committee as having relation to the question which has been considered, state that the eastern parts of said Territory have not an equal share of representation with the western in the Territorial Legislature; suggest an apprehension that such inequality may continue under a State Government; and pray that provision may be made for taking a census of the people of the Territory, for the purpose of securing to all a representation according to numbers and equal rights. If the interposition of Congress be necessary to effect what the petitioners seem to have principally in view, namely, a fair representation in the convention which will be elected to form a constitution, some general provision to this end will properly belong to the act authorizing the convention to be chosen; and should it nevertheless afterwards appear to the satisfaction of Congress that any part of the Territory has not had its due proportion of representation in such convention, they will no doubt use the corrective which they possess, in rejecting the constitution which may be formed.

Upon a full view of the whole subject which has been referred to the consideration of your committee, they are of opinion that it is expedient to admit the Mississippi Territory into the Union as prayed for by the memorialists, and have prepared a bill for this purpose, which they ask leave to report.

MILITARY ACADEMIES.

The House resolved itself into a Committee of the Whole on the bill for establishing three additional Military Academies.

Mr. CAMPBELL proposed to change the location of the Southern Academy from Mount Dearborn to Columbia, on account of the superior advantages of that place over Mount Dearborn, and the eligibility of its situation for such an institution.

Mr. PICKENS was in favor of a more upland site than either of those mentioned, and gave a decided preference of the two to Mount Dearborn over Columbia. He proposed a point in Buncombe county.

Some further debate took place on this motion, which was strenuously advocated by Mr. Chappell, and opposed by Mr. Pickens and Mr. Holbert.

The motion was negatived by a large majority.

Mr. Pickens then moved to substitute "Ashville, in Buncombe county, North Carolina," in lieu of "Mount Dearborn, South Carolina;" which motion was also negatived by a considerable majority.

Mr. Burnside moved to amend the bill, so as to establish an academy at Carlisle, Pennsylvania, in addition to the three named in the bill. He thought it due to the extent and population of Pennsylvania, to establish one in that State; and Carlisle, he said, was peculiarly fitted for the location of a Military Academy, by its salubrity, the military establishment of the United States already there, &c.

This motion was also negatived by a large majority.

Mr. Pickens then moved to amend the bill so as to limit the number of additional academies to two, one within the District of Columbia, and one at Ashville, in Buncombe county, the advantages of which situation he explained to the House.

This motion was opposed by Mr. Johnson of Kentucky. When he concluded—

On motion of Mr. Pickens, the Committee rose, reported progress, and obtained leave to sit again.

COMMERCE WITH GREAT BRITAIN.

Mr. Forsyth, from the Committee of Foreign Relations, reported the following bill:

A bill to regulate the commerce between the territories of the United States and of His Britannic Majesty, according to the Convention concluded the third day of July, 1815.

Be it enacted, &c., That the same duties be, and the same are hereby, imposed on articles of the growth, produce, or manufacture, of His Britannic Majesty's territories in Europe, imported into the United States in British vessels, as are or shall be imposed on the importation of the like articles in American vessels.

SEC. 2. *And be it further enacted,* That the same tonnage and other duties and charges are hereby imposed on British vessels, in any ports of the United States, as are or may be payable in the same ports by vessels of the United States, except such British vessels as shall come from the East or West Indies or the dominions of His Britannic Majesty in North America.

SEC. 3. *And be it further enacted,* That the same bounty shall be allowed on the exportation of any article, the growth, produce, or manufacture, of the United States, to His Britannic Majesty's territories in Europe, when such exportation shall be in British vessels, as are, or may be allowed, when such exportation is or may be in vessels of the United States.

SEC. 4. *And be it further enacted,* That in all cases where drawbacks are or may be allowed on the re-exportation of any goods, the growth, produce, or manufacture of the territories of His Britannic Majesty, the same drawbacks shall be allowed on such re-exportation, where the original importation of the same may have been in British vessels, as are or may be allowed on such re-exportation where the original importation may have been in vessels of the United States.

SEC. 5. *And be it further enacted,* That so much of each and every act of Congress as is inconsistent with the provisions of this act be, and the same is hereby, repealed.

SEC. 6. *And be it further enacted,* That this act shall continue in force until the 3d day of July, 1819, and no longer.

The bill was twice read and referred to a Committee of the Whole.

The House adjourned, to meet again on Tuesday next.

TUESDAY, January 2, 1816.

Mr. Parris presented a petition of a committee on behalf of the non-commissioned officers and soldiers of the 21st regiment of infantry, of the United States, praying that they may have the privilege of locating the land to which they, and those who may have left the said regiment, are entitled, in one entire body.—Referred to the Committee on Military Affairs.

Mr. King, of Massachusetts, presented a petition of sundry manufacturers of cotton and woollen goods in the town of Brunswick, and District of Maine, praying that the importation of all cotton goods from India may be prohibited, and that additional duties may be imposed on cotton goods imported from other countries; also, that the importation of coarse woollen goods may be prohibited.

Mr. Clayton presented a similar petition from sundry manufacturing establishments on the Brandywine river and its vicinity, in the State of Delaware, in behalf of themselves and others interested in similar establishments.—Referred to the Committee of Commerce and Manufactures.

Mr. Clayton presented a petition of Allen McLane, one of the surviving officers of the Revolutionary army, praying that the half pay for life, which was solemnly promised to him by the Congress of 1780, may now be granted to him, substantially, to commence from the time of the reduction of that army.—Referred to the Committee on Pensions and Revolutionary Claims.

Mr. Lewis presented a petition of the members of a masonic society in Alexandria, in the District of Columbia, under the name of the Alexandria Washington Lodge, No. 22, praying that they may be authorized, by lottery, to raise a sum of money, to be applied to the building of a house for the use of a public museum.

Mr. Robertson presented a petition of David Porter, a Captain in the Navy of the United States, praying that he may be allowed the exclusive privilege of navigating, for a limited time, the waters of the District of Columbia with vessels built on his plan, and worked by animal power.—Referred to the Committee for the District of Columbia.

Mr. Robertson, from the Committee on the Public Lands, made a report on the petition of the President and Commissioners of the town of Mobile, which was read, and the resolution therein contained was concurred in by the House as follows:

Resolved, That the petitioners have leave to withdraw their petition.

Mr. STEVENSON presented a petition of the Legislature of the Territory of Illinois, praying that certain evils existing in the judicial system of the said Territory may be remedied, and that they may be empowered in future to pass laws regulating the courts of said Territory.—Referred to the Committee on the Judiciary.

Mr. ROBERTSON also made a report on the petition of James Horne, and Joshua Horne, which was concurred in by the House.

Mr. WRIGHT from the committee on that part of the President's Message which relates to an arrangement of the militia expenses incurred by States without the sanction of the General Government, reported a bill to authorize the settlement and payment of certain claims for the services of the militia, which was read twice, and committed to a Committee of the Whole on Tuesday next.

Mr. BRADBURY, from the committee appointed on the petition of James Jewett, reported a bill to authorize the discharge of James Jewett from his imprisonment, which was read twice, and committed to a Committee of the Whole.

The SPEAKER laid before the House a letter from the Secretary of State, communicating such particulars as are known to the Department of State concerning the publication of a new edition of the laws of the United States, in obedience to a resolution of the 26th ultimo, which was ordered to lie on the table.

An engrossed bill, entitled "An act for the relief of Charles Markin," was read a third time, and passed.

An engrossed bill, entitled "An act to enlarge the time for ascertaining the annual transfers and changes of property subject to the direct tax, and for other purposes," was read the third time, and passed.

MILITARY ACADEMIES.

The House, according to the order of the day, again resolved itself into a Committee of the Whole on the bill for establishing three additional Military Academies.

The amendment on the table at the former sitting on this subject, (viz: on motion of Mr. PICKENS to limit the increase to two academies, one within the District of Columbia and one at Ashville, Buncombe county, North Carolina,) was taken up, and rejected.

Mr. WILDE then proposed to amend the bill so as to establish one additional academy only, and that one within the District of Columbia. This motion he supported by arguments going to show the expediency of such an institution being as much as possible of a national character, and under the eye of the Government. His object was not to diminish the number of cadets, but to give to the institution of the Military Academies, as far as possible, a national character, which, he thought, would be assisted by depriving them of local or sectional features, &c.

Mr. PICKERING was in favor of so much of the proposed amendment as went to limit the number of additional academies to one, but opposed to the location of that one in the District of Columbia. He preferred that it should be located at Harper's Ferry, a point which he appeared to consider as invested with great advantages, from its being already the site of an armory, from its situation being very healthy, and in the midst of a country fertile in all the necessaries of life.

Mr. SHEFFEY required a division of the question, so as to place the question simply before the House, whether the additional number of academies should be one or three.

Mr. CUTHBERT said he was in favor of both branches of the amendment which had been proposed by his colleague, (Mr. WILDE.) War, he said, was a subject which came within the direction of the General Government only, having relation exclusively to foreign Powers. Unquestionably, therefore, the preparations for war, whether of one kind or another, whether relating to military education or the collection of the munitions of war, should be exclusively under the control of the General Government, and have no relation to the States. It should be an object to prevent the military system from having anything in it peculiar to the States, and to make it purely national. What would produce this most effectually in regard to the Military Academies? To have one in one State and one in another, or to have one only, and that in the District, which belongs to the United States, under the eyes of the Government? Certainly the latter. What could be more dangerous to the tranquillity of the nation, than a military rivalship among the States? What ought we to be more anxious to prevent—what could be more dangerous to the prosperity of the Government—what could more threaten that disunion of the States which we ought most to dread and guard against, than this sort of military rivalship? There would be a danger, he argued, from establishing separate Military Academies at different points, of a rivalship, amounting to animosity, arising between the officers educated in the different academies, and propagating and diffusing itself among the mass of the people. The establishment of a single Military Academy at this point, he thought, would have a directly opposite tendency. Young men from different States associating together, and liberalizing each other, would imbibe and carry with them to their homes that national character which alone can be the cement of the Union. The object of Congress, then, should be to establish an academy of this kind, where our youth should become attached, not to the particular interests of particular States, but to the dignity and splendor of the nation; where they should acquire, not State feelings, but patriotic sentiments. Men thus educated would attach more closely the interests of all the States, instead of promoting jealousy among them. The objection to the situation within this District, that it would be too near a populous city, was not valid, inasmuch as the character of the institution depended not so much on its peculiar situation as on the regulations by which it was governed. Every Military Academy was in some respects a military monastery, and under its rigid regulations the students in an academy in or near this city would be as much cut off from intercourse with it, as if the academy were three thousand miles distant from it. This was, in another view, a peculiarly proper position for a Military Academy. Being the Seat of Government, besides the place of assemblage of the legislators from different parts of the Union, which would enable parents to keep up intercourse with their children, it was also the resort of all foreigners of information who visit the country, and would afford to the institution all the benefit of their experience, as well as that of the intelligence of our own country. The great objection to multiplying Military Academies was this: that when they are once established, they cannot be abolished, however inexpedient they may be found. Restricting the number now, there would be no difficulty in increasing them hereafter. But establish an academy in Carolina and one in Kentucky, and by any attempt hereafter to abolish either of them, the State will consider itself as insulted, and oppose it accordingly. He was in favor, therefore, of establishing only one at present. Perhaps the plan contained in the bill was not complete; perhaps there ought to be one large and several subordinate academies. If so, let there be established one principal academy here, and harmonious subordinate institutions elsewhere. In any point of view, he approved of the amendment proposed by his colleague.

Mr. Johnson, of Kentucky, opposed the motion, as calculated to destroy the bill. The object of making us one people, he said, was one dear to his heart; so sacred that he would oppose no Constitutional measures calculated to promote it. But if it was now contended that a great national Military Academy was to aid effectually in that important object, by collecting at one point and amalgamating the military spirit of the nation, this proposition did not go far enough. It ought also to propose to abolish the Academy at West Point, so as to leave but the one new proposed to be established here. Mr. J. could not assent to the idea of rivalship between the States in consequence of multiplying the Military Academies. What, he asked, in this view, had been the effect of the institution at West Point? Had any local jealousy or rivalship been produced by it? On the contrary, it was admitted on all hands that it had produced very beneficial effects without any such alloy. If a great military institution could be established at this place, calculated to effect the object the gentleman had at heart, he should not perhaps object to it; but the objections which had been made to establishing other academies applied with equal force to West Point as to those now proposed to be established at other points. Mr. J. made some observations going to establish the great advantages to be derived from these Military Academies compared with the expense of them. The people of every section of our country, he said, had spirit to vin-

dicate their rights, if they were instructed in the mode of doing it. Officers only were wanted to lead them on, and impart to them the benefit of the instruction which they have received; and no method of forming officers could be compared, for efficacy and economy, to that by Military Academies. The expense of all the academies now proposed, including the pay of professors, support of cadets, &c., he showed, by a statement from the proper authority, would not exceed $400,000 annually—a small sum indeed compared to the object. He concluded by saying that he was opposed to any modification of the bill whatever.

Mr. Hulbert also spoke against the proposed amendment. He was opposed to it, because he believed the adoption of it would be the destruction of the bill. He had belonged to the committee which had reported the bill, and had given it in its present shape his hearty assent. He believed it necessary that the institution of the Military Academies should be enlarged in some shape or other. If the one at West Point could be sufficiently enlarged, he had no objection to that course; but within his recollection, he said, attempts had been made to remove that at West Point and establish it here. To that plan he was utterly opposed; and, should the present motion succeed, he believed it would put an end to the idea of enlarging the Military Academy at all. Mr. H. appeared to be satisfied that the establishment of one additional academy only, and that one in this District, could not succeed. He was decidedly of opinion that we ought to have more cadets than we now have at military schools, gaining that instruction in military science, for the want of which we failed so greatly in the opening of the late war. The disgraces we have suffered, and costs we have incurred, during that war, for the want of this instruction, form a strong argument in favor of multiplying the means of obtaining it. When the army went into the field at the commencement of the late war, its officers had just been selected from civil life, without reference to their military science or experience—defeat and disgrace were the consequences. He adverted to the maxim, that an army of hares, commanded by a lion, were better than an army of lions, commanded by a hare. In the spirit of this maxim, Mr. H. contended that, to prepare the nation for war, we ought not to have a large Military Establishment in time of peace, but men of science in every part of the nation ready to take the field in time of danger. If a war be considered just, said he, there will never be any difficulty in raising an army in this country; the people will turn out en masse, if they have officers qualified to command them. If, by means of Military Academies, eight hundred cadets are constantly in a course of instruction, there will be no difficulty in finding proper persons to command an army of any extent we may ever want. It might be said that eight hundred cadets would be too many—he did not believe it. We have seven millions of people, and if we are again involved in war and have to select some thousand officers, we should not find too many cadets to choose from. He denied the probability of jealousy or rivalship between the States from the establishment of several academies; on the contrary, the effect of the establishment at this place of one only, would be to excite that very jealousy that gentlemen dreaded. Alluding to the distance of some of the Southern and Western States, Louisiana particularly, from West Point, and even from the District of Columbia, he said, there ought to be an academy south of this place. The committee had recommended only three in addition to that at West Point. The people of the North, he believed, would be perfectly satisfied with that one. They had already been more than once alarmed with the idea of removing that academy. He hoped that their alarm never would be realized, but that the academy would remain at West Point as long as the rock on which it is built. The committee had agreed to establish one here and one in South Carolina; and objections having been made from the West to this distribution, the committee had agreed to recommend one there also. The Western country, he said, was increasing with unexampled rapidity—he wished it was not increasing quite so fast—but the territory beyond the Alleghany, he believed, would soon contain a majority of the people of the United States; and their claim, therefore, could not be denied to a participation in the benefits of this institution. Mr. H. said, he was satisfied the locations in the bill were as good as could be made. He knew very well it was the opinion of some of the leading members of the Administration that we should have but one academy, and that that one ought to be here; but that this was not the proper place for it, he thought, was very evident. He wished the bill to pass as it now stood. He was pleased in the opportunity of giving his assent to this recommendation of the President. He rejoiced, he said, to see such recommendations from that quarter; they reminded him of the good old times when WASHINGTON, and those who followed his maxims and principles, ruled the nation. He was glad to see these recommendations, founded on good old principles, proceed from one who had been a little *estranged* heretofore. He hoped that the bill would pass without the proposed amendment.

Mr. WILDE replied to some of the objections which had been made to his motion. As to the academy at West Point, he said, if it were now for the first time proposed to establish an academy there, he should oppose it with all his powers, even were he a Representative from the State of New York. He objected to the separation of the academy into several parts in different States, not so much on the score of jealousy or rivalship which it would create among the States, as on the score of his radical objection to the tendency of such a course to increase the dependence of the General Government on the State Governments. Wherever national establishments were proposed, even now, it would appear as if those States which have the greatest political influence must have some gratification conferred on them, before they

would consent to measures which could not be carried without their consent. It would be found to be so, when the question of navy yards, of a national university, or any other question of a national character, became the subject of discussion. None, Mr. W. said, was more convinced than he' was of the value of having good commanders in an army; and the necessity of proper qualifications for that purpose by military education was too trite a remark to require elucidation; nor was it less doubtful that our arms had occasionally failed during the late war from the want of proper commanders. A few months, or even weeks, were all that was required to form soldiers for the field, but time was required to form accomplished commanders. He was therefore fully impressed with the utility of Military Academies; but he was in favor of such an establishment being purely national, and therefore located at or near the Seat of Government; in which proposition he hoped to unite all those who, having no local feeling or predilections to gratify, looked only to the necessity of having this institution under the eyes of the Government, and within its control. The state of the times was an objection heretofore made to this measure, which no longer existed. We have found, from experience, that the present Military Establishment, though comparatively small, has furnished us with some of the best officers for our Army, and have every reason to expect proportionate benefits from it, if enlarged on a liberal scale, and in such a manner as shall give it an entirely national instead of local character.

Mr. WRIGHT advocated the general objects of the bill at some length. He illustrated the necessity of education for military men, by reasons drawn from analogy. For instance, said he, would you trust a physician to bleed you without a certainty that he possessed some skill in the surgical art? Surely not; and will you commit the liberties of the country to those who know nothing of their duty? Mr. W. was in favor of establishing as many academies as would accommodate eight hundred students, but against locating one immediately at the Seat of Government, thinking it would be more expedient to establish it higher up the Potomac. Otherwise the places designated in the bill were as geographically correct as they could possibly be. As to the idea of exciting jealousy or undue rivalship, by dividing the academies, he said he hoped there always would be a proper rivalship—a rivalship of merit and services among those educated at one or the other of these academies. He thought the disposition of the four academies, at different points, was an argument in favor of the bill instead of against it, because it would bring academies nearer to those who desired to send their children to them, &c.

Mr. CLAY, (Speaker,) in reference to the argument in support of the amendment, that the moral effect of establishing three additional academies, instead of one only, and that at the Seat of Government, would be injurious to the Union, as tending to create sectional feeling, &c., said that all arguments, founded upon the supposition of danger to the Union, deserved great consideration; but, whilst he applauded the motives of gentlemen in urging these arguments, he was obliged totally to differ from them in their conclusions. The moral effect of establishing several, instead of one institution of this kind, would be to increase the affection of the people for the Union. If the bond of union was to be strengthened by the measures of the Government, what ought to be the character of them? What ought to be the policy of the Government? To distribute benefits; to afford to every man in the Union an obvious, palpable evidence of the benefits afforded to him by the Government under which he lives. If the proposition were to establish four or five turnpike roads in different parts of the Union, he said he should suppose the argument of the danger of creating a sectional influence would as much apply to that measure as to a proposition for the diffusion through the nation of that knowledge—the want of which during the late war we had but too much reason, from fatal experience, to regret. It would be by making the Government strong without, and furnishing motives of affection to every bosom within, that they would inculcate the sentiments which the advocates of this amendment were so desirous to inspire. Mr. C. said, he would afford the means of instruction, as far as possible, to every man bound to raise an arm in defence of his country. With what sentiments would such a policy inspire the bosom of the citizen? Would it excite sectional feelings? No; the bosom turns with thankfulness to the source of benefits received, as unerringly as the needle to the pole. The individual receiving the advantages afforded by these institutions would not look to any particular State, but would trace his obligation to the fountain-head, and to the support and strength of the Union all his exertions would be directed. Whatever may be the destination of the student, whether to civil or military life, if the principles of human nature govern him, he will always reflect, that to the parental care and beneficence of the Government he is indebted for the advantages he has received, and to the support of that Government his best exertions will be given. If gentlemen were right in their argument, Mr. C. said, we ought to commence anew; we should abolish the academy already existing at West Point, and let there be but one, and that one within the District of Columbia. Mr. C. said he, with the gentleman from Massachusetts, (Mr. Hulbert,) approved of the recommendations in the President's Message on this and other subjects, whether they were the doctrines of *new* or of *old* times. From that quarter of the Union, however, (the West,) which that gentleman had so feelingly regretted was growing too fast—a regret in which, Mr. C. said, the gentleman would excuse him from participating—he did not believe there was one student in the present Military Academy. The remark equally applied to the South; and yet in those sections of the country there were, perhaps, thousands of young men who would be peculiarly

happy in obtaining the benefits of such an institution, if brought within their reach. He would, therefore, establish academies in the different sections of the Union. The effort was as vain to disguise as to forget that there are various sections of our country; gentlemen might argue in vain against a fact, which the geography of the country most clearly established. We must take our natural boundaries as they are, since we cannot alter or abolish them. Mr. C. said, in conclusion, he would not take from other sections the benefits of this institution to consolidate and locate it within this District, on account of its supposed unhealthiness and for other reasons. He would not alter the present features of the bill because of objections to them, which he considered fanciful and visionary. The distribution of the academies he thought might have been more advantageously made, particularly as regarded the one in the Western country; but he would not, therefore, deprive any section of the country of the great advantages which he hoped this institution would diffuse throughout the Union.

Mr. Cuthbert rose to correct an error into which he said the gentleman had fallen in regard to the education at West Point being confined entirely to Northern youth. If nothing else proved it an error, the name of McRee was sufficient, who was from a Southern State. He instanced other cases within his knowledge of students from the South. Let it be recollected, said Mr. C., that we have been long in a state of peace; during which time the attention of the country was not turned to military affairs; and it could not be expected that many would then desire to send their children to such a seminary. But would any one argue, he said, that our notions on military affairs were the same now that they were three or four years ago? No; the glory reaped by our army, its utility as proved by the events of the war, had changed the general opinions on this subject; and, consequently, there were now many applications for admission into the Military Academy. The argument which likened the case of the establishment of academies, to that of turnpike roads, afforded its own refutation. Those very roads, by promoting general intercourse, were a part of the means most conducive to the object of Mr. C. in fixing the academy at the Seat of Government, which was the promotion of a nationality of sentiment. This argument therefore would not stand. The gentleman from Kentucky had said that cadets would always look to the hand which supported them. Mr. C. was for bringing them in closer contact with that hand, so that their attention could not be diverted from it by local feelings, &c.

Mr. Forsyth said he was of the committee which reported the bill now before the House, and coincided in opposition to the proposed amendment. It was conceded on all hands, he said, that the institution of West Point had been of great service to the community, and that its beneficial effects had not been lessened by its sectional situation. It appeared to be admitted, Mr. F. said, that there ought to be an increase of the number of cadets; and the only question was, whether it should be by the addition of one or three schools. The committee had been of opinion that two hundred youths in one place were as many as could be conveniently attended to by the few officers employed at each academy; he had not changed his opinion on that subject, and was therefore opposed to the proposed amendment. The motive of the proposed amendment, he said, was laudable: proceeding from a desire to obviate the possibility of local jealousies. Was there anything, he asked, in the nationality of the District of Columbia, to prevent the operation of these feelings? Do we not know, said he, that if these local feelings are felt in any portion of the United States, they are felt in a still stronger degree within this District; there was, he said, nothing in the nationality of the spot to destroy them. The benefit which might arise from the academy being placed immediately " under the eyes of the Government" appeared not to be denied. Cast your eyes, (said Mr. F.,) around the District of Columbia; are there any proofs of its having derived any particularly great benefits from having been under the exclusive care of the General Government? No; on the contrary, though it has been constantly under the eyes of Congress, it has as constantly been neglected. Look at the statute book, said he. Congress has the exclusive legislation over this District; and how has Congress legislated for it? I had occasion the other day to turn to the laws on this subject, and I am almost ashamed to state the result of my inquiry. Half a dozen statutes of little importance embrace all that this Legislature has done for the District for near twenty years that it has been under its eyes and exclusive care. The laws of the District were not even uniform in its various parts. Crimes in one part of the District are punished in one way, and in another part differently. Whilst the condition of the citizens of Maryland and Virginia were experiencing a daily amelioration of their condition, by the improvement of their jurisprudence, the system of laws by which this District was governed remained stationary, as they existed when the District formed a part of those two States. If the District of Columbia had not flourished or improved under the care of Congress, what evidence was there that the Military Academy, under similar circumstances, would derive any advantage from such a location? Mr. F. said, for his part, he believed the Military Academy placed here would enjoy just the same advantage that had accrued to this District from the care of Congress; and, if the old Academy had been placed here, he believed it never would have produced the same results as had been experienced from it. His colleague (Mr. CUTHBERT) and others appeared to be very anxious to destroy State feelings and jealousy and pride—Mr. F. said they ought to be destroyed. But why fight the shadow, and let the substance pass? These feelings of local animosity, he said, were cherished by other causes than such as that supposed by his colleague; of these he would refer to but one; the constant practice of selecting

Ministers and great officers of the Government from local considerations; of taking, for instance, a man of inferior merit from one State, because there happens to be already one in service from the State from whence a better might have been selected. To such practices as these, he said, we must look for the nourishment of local feelings and State jealousies. The object of the diffusion of these institutions was not the benefit or convenience of the States, but of the people, and their convenience was consulted by the distribution of academies at different points. In regard to the argument of brotherly affection among the cadets being promoted by collecting them all together at one point, Mr. F. said there was no magical effect in the location within the ten miles square. Every object in this respect might be accomplished by their collection at any one point, wherever it may be, by a provision, legislative or otherwise, that the youth of the South should be placed in an academy in the North, and *vice versa*, or by having them intermingled in the academies, in due proportion from every section, one among another. All the benefits argued as likely to proceed from concentration, may thus be secured. Mr. F. was, therefore, wholly against the amendment.

Mr. CALHOUN said, the only question really before the House at this time appeared to be, what was the best mode to produce a national spirit. That policy, he said, which creates the best political system; which promotes the national prosperity; which provides efficiently for the national security; that policy, by the effect of which every part of the country feels itself secure, whilst commerce is prosperous, and agriculture and manufactures are protected; that, he said, was the policy which would certainly create a true national feeling. Everything in opposition to such a policy would end in sectional feelings. Applying these general remarks to the present question, what, he asked, was the object of the bill? To establish a military school. What was the object of this school? To contribute to the national security; by the diffusion of military knowledge. Whether one great central school was better calculated to produce this effect, than several separate schools, was the question. Mr. C. said he believed it would not. If we had a central great school, as now proposed, it would principally be filled with the sons of wealthy men; of great and influential men, others would not have the means of sending their sons abroad for education; for here, certainly, the allowance by the Government would not cover the expenses of the young men. Where, in this country, shall we look for genius and talent? Most indubitably in the middle ranks; in the lower ranks in preference to the higher: not that these classes actually contain a greater portion of talent, but that they have stronger stimulants to its exertion. Rich men, being already at the top of the ladder, have no further motive to climb. It is that class of the community who find it necessary to strive for elevation, that furnishes you with officers. Look, said Mr. C., at the officers who distinguished themselves in service during the late war. Were there among them the sons of wealthy men or great men? If there were any such, Mr. C. said, he knew of none. The rule he applied was a general one. If the school were established here, the means of support afforded by the Government to the cadets would not cover their expenses; men in moderate circumstances would be unable to send their sons, and the country would be deprived of their valuable services. The academy would be in a great measure filled by the sons of the wealthy and influential men within four hundred miles of this place. Mr. C. said he believed the provisions of this bill were more important than any yet on the table of the House, and as important as any that would come before the House at the present session. The way to render the nation secure, is not by maintaining a large foreign army, very expensive and a little dangerous; it is not thus you will keep up a proper military spirit; but by military education. Upon the officers of armies in a great measure depends, particularly in a free Government, the success of war. Free Governments always afford materials for soldiers. Of the celebrated brigade of Scott, Mr. C. said, three-fourths of the privates had not been in service more than six months. All that was wanted to make soldiers among us was education, which the private can soon acquire; but the making of officers is the work of time, particularly in the present state of the science of war—and it was proper, therefore, to provide amply for that object. In time of war, Mr. C. said, we ought to get soldiers speedily, we ought to come into the population at once, by the measure so much reprobated at the last session from the other side of the House. Mr. C. was in favor of establishing more than one additional military school, in order to diffuse, as far as possible, military science. This, he said would secure us against invasion from abroad, and, by making the militia formidable against despotism at home. It was in this way that militia would be made more efficient than in any other. At present, the number of academies proposed to be established might be sufficient; but he hoped that they would be progressively increased, and that it would not be long before we should have one in every considerable State in the Union. Mr. C. compared the feelings of the House now and previous to the war. Now, he said, we see everywhere a nationality of feeling; we hear sentiments from every part of the House in favor of union, and against a sectional spirit. What had produced this change? The glory acquired by the late war, and the prosperity which had followed it. Let us direct our attention, then, said he, to the objects calculated to accomplish the prosperity and greatness of the nation, and we shall certainly create a national spirit.

Mr. Tucker, after some general remarks on the utility of institutions of this desciption, spoke on the particular question before the House. If we were to have but one or even two academies, and that one or two confined to a particular section of the Union, what would be the effect of this arrangement? To make officers only for that part of the country where the schools were established. In the event of war, where were the officers to be found whom this institution is to create? If military instruction were confined to one section, so, necessarily, must be the selection of officers for your armies; and thus sectional feelings will inevitably be created. By such a course, moreover, we should make one part of the country strong, and another relatively weak. The whole argument in favor of this bill—and without the argument the bill was nothing—was, that it was calculated to create military power by giving military science. The very argument on which the whole bill depended, was a sufficient argument in favor of its being general in its scope, embracing every section of the Union. The argument of the advantage of associating young men from every part of the country together, was not as forcible as the considerations which opposed the proposed limitation of the number of academies. If we were to have one only, he was, although friendly to the interest of this District, opposed to its being placed here. If, instead of the mild and amiable man at the head of our Government, we had an ambitious individual there, what would be ask more of you, than to put all the military officers under his influence, and thus subject them wholly to his control? He hoped the House would decide that the number proposed was few enough, though there might be better locations perhaps selected, &c.—for there certainly ought not to be an academy established at any place, from which, for the safety of the cadets, it would be necessary at any season of the year to remove.

Mr. Robertson, of Louisiana, was in favor of the amendment. It would be so expensive travelling, that the constituents of gentlemen from Virginia and Kentucky would not bring their children to the school. What did they think of the situation of the people of the State which he represented? Travelling from Carolina or Kentucky to the Seat of Government might be expensive; but the trouble of going from Louisiana to Carolina, or the mouth of the Kentucky river, was infinitely more so. Yet, on the part of the people of Louisiana, whose interests were thus affected, he felt no hesitation in saying that the influence of the general principles ought to outweigh these considerations; and he should prove his conviction in this respect by voting for the amendment. Ideas had been broached this day, which, he said, were new to him. How long since we had been taught to look for the preservation of the Union to a military spirit? In such a spirit generally pervading the militia, he agreed, the liberties of the nation found a safe protection; but, instead of allowing that spirit to pervade the community, the favorite object of some gentlemen was to erect it into a separate and distinct establishment. Instead of one of the most important, he considered this bill as one of the most unimportant bills which could come before the House of a general nature during the present session. We had during the war but one military school; and now, in a state of peace, gentlemen had suddenly discovered the necessity of establishing four military schools. As one, Mr. R. said, he saw no necessity for it. He preferred to have but one academy, and that at the Seat of Government. No local considerations produced this preference on his mind, but it arose from the general impression that, next to travelling through the country, and examining the habits and customs of its different parts, the best way of extinguishing State jealousies and local feelings, was to associate the youths of the different parts of the country as much as possible. Let us establish then, he said, institutions for the civil and military education of youth within this District—a District belonging not peculiarly to any part of the country, but having more than any other an interest in the prosperity of every part of it. Let us, said Mr. R., lay aside sectional feelings; let us consider ourselves, in this hall, as members of the General Government; let us promote the general interest, and, my word for it, said he, the States will take care of themselves. If a national influence be produced by the establishment of a military school, would not the effect be much more general if the institution were established at the Seat of Government, than if at any other point? He thought it would; he was satisfied that the youth of the country ought to come here for their education, whence communications could be readily made to every part of the country; where their education and general welfare could be superintended by those who annually reside some time at the Seat of Government from the respective States, and where the mode of education could be generally known and properly appreciated. In order to prevent, as far as possible, the creation of a military spirit distinct from the general interest, and to give all possible advantage, utility, and economy to the establishment, he was in favor of the amendment.

Mr. SEROSANT was in favor of the amendment, because he considered one academy as sufficient, in addition to the one now in existence; but he was opposed to placing the new academy within the District of Columbia. He considered this institution as a school for soldiers. If the course of education should consume four years, under the plan proposed by this bill, there would be annually discharged from the academy (having completed their military education) about two hundred young men. The present Army Establishment, Mr. S. said, embraced about five hundred officers, he believed. The number, therefore, who would annually complete their military education, would be much greater than could be employed in the Army, which was the object of their instruction at the public expense. It had been said, that they would make officers for the militia; but, after coming out of the schools, if they were not put into the Army, they must betake themselves to other occupations, and would soon lose in other pursuits the military knowledge they had gained; the soldier would be sunk in the citizen. Allow ten years to elapse after the conclusion of his education, before his talents are put to use, and

the cadet will be but little superior in military capacity to the general mass of the community. It appeared to him, Mr. S. said, that this bill was calculated to give an unreasonable extension to the idea of military education, though he approved of a reasonable increase of the present system. If four academies were established in different sections of the country, other sections would come forward and put in their claims; and Congress would be constantly pressed, by the strong motive of gratifying particular sections of the country, to increase the number, without a deliberate regard to the actual wants of the country. The argument of the gentleman from Massachusetts, (Mr. HULBERT,) in favor of the number of three, was, that it was difficult to produce a consentaneous sentiment in favor of one place; it was, in substance, that we must have four, because we ought to have two. Mr. S. said, he had heard nothing going to show that the establishment at West Point could not be sufficiently extended; and for his part, he said, he should prefer that course. A great deal had been said of national spirit and national feelings, which would be cultivated, it was argued, by the establishment of the additional academy at this place. If he were to hazard an opinion on this subject, it would be, that this was the worst place in the Union to establish an academy. If political or party dissension inflames any part of the country, is not this the place in which it burns with intense heat? It must, from the necessity of the case, be so. How, then, can you expect young men, assembled here, to escape its contagion? He placed the question in another view. He said that the separation of the youth from their homes and from society, and placing them at a distance, where they are all equally strangers, and where there are no lines of distinction, would make them as brothers, would give to them all a common interest and common object. He should, in this view, consider West Point or Harper's Ferry as a better situation for the academy than any populous city. At those points, the young men assembled would become citizens of the United States. Mr. S. acknowledged the force of the argument, that you do a great deal towards creating a national feeling, by giving us something worthy of our respect. Make our country strong, and you make men proud of it. Apply the argument. Would this effect, he asked, be produced by dividing the military talent we possess among different institutions? No, the object would be defeated, unless men who excel in the different branches of science could be found for instructors; and he much doubted whether there could be obtained, with the inducements offered by this bill, men of proper abilities and attainments for four Military Academies. He would greatly prefer to extend the Academy at West Point. The distance from some sections of the Union was not so great an object as was represented. It mattered nothing to the young soldier whether he was an hundred or a thousand miles from home. He who takes to that occupation knows beforehand it is one of privation and hardship, and he

435   HISTORY OF CONGRESS.   436

H of R.   *Money Lost by a Purser—Military Academies.*   JANUARY, 1816.

expects to meet with both from the moment he takes the sword in hand. The distance from his home is to him of no consequence. In bringing young men all together at one place, Congress would do something, he said, towards promoting that national feeling and harmony of sentiment which is so often spoken of. If it could be shown that one institution would not educate as many young men as were necessary to be instructed, then the ground would be fairly laid for increasing the number. Unless it should be, he should vote against the number proposed.

The question was then taken on striking out three, and inserting one, and decided in the affirmative—yeas 91.

The question to make the corresponding amendment in the section, viz: to strike out all respecting the location of the academies, except what relates to the one proposed to be established in the District of Columbia, was also decided in the affirmative.

Mr. PICKERING then moved to strike out the words "within the District of Columbia," and insert, "at or near Harper's Ferry, on the Potomac."

On suggestion of Mr. CLAY, Mr. PICKERING varied his motion so as to confine it to striking out the District of Columbia, leaving a blank to be filled as the House might think proper.

The motion, so varied, was decided in the affirmative by a large majority. So the District was put out of the question.

Mr. CLAY then moved to fill the blank in the section with the words "Pittsburg, at the junction of the Alleghany and Monongahela rivers."

This motion being under consideration, the Committee rose, and obtained leave to sit again.

WEDNESDAY, January 3.

Mr. SERGEANT presented a petition of Charles Stewart, late commander of the frigate Constitution, on behalf of himself, and the officers and crew of the said frigate, setting forth that, during the late war with Great Britain, he captured the British ship the Levant, and sent her into a port under the jurisdiction of the Government of Portugal, from whence she was forcibly retaken by the British forces; and praying that the value of said ship may be paid to himself, his officers, and men, as prize money.

Mr. INGHAM presented a petition of John Mc-Cauly, prize agent to the officers and crew of brig Syren, praying to be paid for a vessel captured by the said brig, during the late war with the Bey and Regency of Tripoli, which was afterwards taken into the Naval service of the United States.—Referred to the Committee on Naval Affairs.

Mr. TUCKER, from the Committee for the District of Columbia, reported a bill authorizing a subscription for an edition of such of the laws of the United States as relate exclusively to the District of Columbia; which was read twice, and committed to a Committee of the Whole.

On motion of Mr. DESHA, the Committee of

Commerce and Manufactures were instructed to inquire into the expediency of establishing, by law, a port of entry at Maysville, in the State of Kentucky.

MONEY LOST BY A PURSER.

Mr. YANCEY, from the Committee of Claims, made a report on the petition of William F. Rodgers, which was read, and the resolution therein contained was concurred in by the House.

The report is as follows:

That the petitioner was purser of the United States ship Adams, which was destroyed at Penobscot to prevent her falling into the hands of the enemy; that the petitioner states that he was directed by the captain of the Adams, about the 30th August, 1814, to obtain from the navy agent at Portland, money to pay the crew, which he did to the amount of about $1,800; that, before he had an opportunity of paying the same over to the crew, the enemy appeared in great force on the river, and that he deemed it prudent and safe to deposite the money for safe-keeping with General Crosby, who was then acting as agent of the ship.

It appears to the committee, from the affidavit of General Crosby, that the petitioner, at the time of the attack on the Adams, handed to him a check on the Portland Bank for $800, and a bundle of paper money, which General Crosby did not count, but which the petitioner has since stated to him contained $1,000; that the check and bundle of money which were given to him were deposited in a small trunk; and that, on the near approach of the enemy, the General directed his little son to carry the trunk into the adjacent wood, and that he, being alarmed by the firing, dropped it and fled. The trunk was afterwards found, and was plundered, and one of the persons suspected of the plunder pursued and detected with the check and $400 in his possession. The petitioner states that he has been able to get only $300 of that and the check. He prays of Congress that an act may be passed, giving him a credit in his account with the United States of $800.

The committee are of opinion, from a full consideration of all the circumstances of this case, that the petitioner is not entitled to relief, and therefore recommend to the House the following resolution:

Resolved, That the prayer of the petitioner ought not to be allowed.

Mr. YANCEY also reported a bill for the relief of George S. Wise, which was read twice, and committed to a Committee of the whole House to-morrow.

MILITARY ACADEMIES.

The House resolved itself into a Committee of the Whole, on the bill for the establishment of Military Academies.

Mr. CLAY (Speaker) withdrew the motion he had yesterday made to place the only academy remaining on the bill at Pittsburg; and in lieu thereof moved to establish it at or near the mouth of Licking River on the Ohio, not as a point he preferred, because he thought better situations than that might be selected, but because the Committee on Military Affairs had originally decided in favor of that site. Mr. C. urged various arguments in favor of this location of the additional academy.

The question on this motion was decided in the negative—68 to 56.

A motion of Mr. Cannon, to insert Nashville in the State of Tennessee, met with no better success, there being only about fifty votes in favor of it.

Mr. Lewis then moved to insert in the blank Harper's Ferry, in the State of Virginia.

This motion was opposed at some length by Mr. Wright, who preferred the original proposition to establish three additional Military Academies; but if only one were to be established, he would wish to see it established further South.

Mr. Lewis's proposition met with no favor, there being but 15 or 16 votes in the affirmative.

Mr. Burnside then moved to insert Carlisle, in the State of Pennsylvania.—This proposition received about the same number of votes as the last.

Mr. Barbour had preferred greatly the District of Columbia, if only one additional academy was to be established; but, as the House had departed from the District, he thought the position of the academy ought to be determined by geographical considerations, having reference to the one already established. Under the impression that this was a point which combined geographical with local advantages, he moved Abingdon, in the State of Virginia.

Mr. Sheffey, the Representative from that district, stated the precise bearings of Abingdon, and the advantages which recommend it to the attention of the House.

Mr. Cannon spoke in favor of Knoxville, in Tennessee, in preference to Abingdon; in which idea he was supported by Mr. Wright.

Mr. Barbour having withdrawn his motion, to allow the question to be taken on Knoxville, there appeared to be in favor of that place 84 votes; against it 63.

So the House decided to insert Knoxville, in Tennessee.

Mr. Wilde then moved to strike out the whole of the first section, except the enacting clause, and in lieu thereof to insert a provision authorizing the establishment by the Executive of one or more Military Academies, not exceeding three, at such places as the President of the United States shall prescribe.

Mr. Calhoun moved to amend the amendment by striking out the words one or more, and inserting three.—Negatived.

After some debate, Mr. Wilde's motion was rejected by a large majority.

Mr. Root, after some prefatory observations and subsequent illustrations, founded on what he conceived the abuse of the benefits of these institutions, by their being diverted to the purposes of general education of their sons by those wealthy or influential men who gained their sons admission there, moved the following amendment to the bill:

"That no candidate for a cadet (except as hereinafter provided) shall be admitted into any of the academies aforesaid, who shall not be under the age of twenty-one years, nor until after he shall have been examined by the said professors and teachers, or a majority of them, and found to be well versed in the Latin, Greek, French and Spanish languages; in history and geography, in the various branches of the mathematics, including trigonometry, geometry, and in moral, natural and experimental philosophy and astronomy, and shall then, with approbation in writing of his father, mother, or guardian, as the case may require, engage, by a regular engagement, to serve for the term of five years, unless sooner promoted or discharged; and in case he shall absent himself without leave, or be discharged for any other cause than lasting debility of body or mind, or in case of promotion shall refuse or neglect to accept thereof, or shall resign within three years thereafter, for any other cause than as above-mentioned, the father, mother, or guardian, as the case may require, shall forfeit and pay to the United States, the full amount of the pay and emoluments of such cadet, during his continuance at any of the said academies: *Provided, nevertheless,* That whenever it shall appear to the President that any young man, of natural abilities, is desirous of entering as a cadet into any of the said academies, and it shall be certified in writing, by his parent or guardian, that he or she is unable to educate his or her son or ward, and the verity of such certificate shall be satisfactorily established, it shall be lawful for the President to authorize his admission into any of the said academies, upon the terms heretofore in practice at the Military Academy at West Point; and provided, also, that any number of cadets above the age of fourteen, and under the age of twenty-one years, exceeding the number limited in and by this act, may be admitted into any of the said academies, and discharged on the request of their respective parents or guardians, on clothing and subsisting themselves, and without receiving pay or rations from the United States."

This amendment was negatived by a considerable majority.

The question being on the Committee's rising and reporting the bill as amended—

Mr. King, of Massachusetts, said, that had he been satisfied with the course of this debate, or could have hoped for such a decision on this bill as he could acquiesce in, he should not have troubled the House with any observations thereon. Gentlemen appeared to take many things for granted on this occasion, which, for one, he was not disposed to concede; particularly the power of Congress to pass the bill in its present form, and the expediency of doing it. In what part of the Constitution do we find, said he, the power for establishing these academies, or indeed any seminaries of learning? But I pray you, sir, let me not be misunderstood upon this subject; let it not be supposed that I wish to close any door of information which it is possible for us to keep open. No, sir; but I could have wished that much of our treasure which has been wasted in useless objects, could have been devoted to the cause of science; but this power does not appear to have been delegated to us by the people. Their money is not to be bestowed by us on any individual, unless for services rendered. It may be supposed by many, that this bill is similar in its provisions to that establishing the present Military Academy at West Point; but they vary totally in principle and features. By the 26th section of that act which passed in March, 1802, soon after Mr. Jefferson came into office, and was for fixing the Military Peace Establishment, the President was authorized to organize a corps of engineers, to consist of one principal engineer, six assistant engineers, and ten cadets, with power of promotion—but at no time to exceed twenty officers and cadets; by the 27th section they were stationed at West Point, and were to constitute a Military Academy, but were subject, at all times to do duty in such places, and on such service as the President might direct. Thus they were, to every extent, a part of the Military Peace Establishment, and were organized as other troops are; not so the establishments contemplated by this bill; which goes to alter the present Establishment, and to convert the whole into seminaries of learning, and the cadets into students in the various arts and sciences—without any services to be rendered to the public for the expense which must be incurred in their education. And at the end of three or five years, they are thrown back upon society, with nothing but their swords to carve their way to fortune and to power. It is not consistent, sir, with the principles of our institutions, with the genius of our Republican Government, to form and cherish a body of this kind; mere soldiers of fortune. Gentlemen say that they are to be educated to form officers for our standing army, and for the militia. I thought, sir, at the last session, when you fixed your Military Establishment—your standing army in time of peace—at ten thousand men, three times the number of your Peace Establishment under Washington and Adams, and four thousand more than was first voted in this House—the principal argument in favor of so large an establishment was, that it would afford us a sufficient number of well instructed officers, should we again be involved in war. But, sir, how are these cadets to be incorporated as officers into your present Army? Do you intend they shall supersede the veteran officers of the line? Will that promote harmony in the ranks, or reward merit in your officers? Let them answer the question.

In what part of our Constitution then, sir, do we find our power to establish academies on the principle contemplated by this bill? I shall probably be pointed to our power "to raise and support armies." But do these cadets form any portion of our Army? Is it even intended, were they capable, that they should do duty as soldiers? Not at all. Sir, I do not like this mode of legislating the people out of their rights and their property, by degrees; you first pass a law, organizing a corps of engineers and cadets, provide for their instruction, for an equivalent in duty and service to be rendered by them, and place them in a Military Academy; you now convert this Military Academy into a seminary of learning generally, take away the equivalent, and educate the young men who may be so fortunate as to gain admission there, at the public expense. If you can thus constitutionally educate eight hundred young men, why not eight thousand—why

not, indeed, all the youth of the country?—there would, indeed, be some equality in this latter case, as all the people would then be equally benefited.

Granting, however, for the argument, that you have the power to pass this bill—where is the necessity or the expediency of doing it? As I before remarked, and as was on a former occasion contended by all those who now advocate this bill, will not your standing army of ten thousand men afford you officers sufficient—better instructed and accustomed to command? Nor, sir, is the expense of this establishment to be overlooked. Rid yourselves of the arrearages of the late war, before you make too many preparations for another. Revive public credit; replenish your Treasury; do justice to the Army and Navy, which have fought your battles, and preserved you in the hour of peril—as far, I mean, as the Government put it in their power to serve their country. Pay the veteran soldier and seaman, who have survived the storm of war, the pittance that is due to them. Pay their pensions to the maimed and halt, for the legs and arms which you have caused, by your war, to be severed from them; and, "if you can administer to a mind diseased," comfort and bind up the broken hearts of the widow and fatherless.

But, sir, plausible as the reasons are which have been urged by some in favor of this bill, harmless as some of its features may appear, I am persuaded that what is thus shown to the public are only the ostensible purposes for which it is recommended. For the real purposes, we must go to the dark recesses of the palace, or the still more dark recesses of the mind of the President, or of his declared successor. We must go to the Message of the President at the opening of the session, for the origin and purpose of this bill. And I agree with my honorable friend from Massachusetts, (Mr. Hulbert,) that a good measure is not to be rejected because offered by a person whom we distrust; and when such a measure is offered, let it be by what hand it may, I will go as far as that honorable gentleman in support of it, if it has for its object the interest of the people or the welfare of our country. But confidence is said to be a plant of slow growth, and the honorable gentleman will pardon me, if I cannot go with him from the highest distrust of, to the greatest confidence in, the intentions and views of the present Chief Magistrate. Look at the tenth and eleventh pages of the Message. He there, first, recommends, as an improvement in our Military Establishment, the organization of a corps of invalids. A bill for this purpose has been acted upon by the House. Next an enlargement of the Military Academy, and the establishment of others in other sections of the Union. This is attempted by the present bill. He goes on: "And I cannot press too much on ' the attention of Congress such a classification ' and organization of the militia as will most ef- ' fectually render it the safeguard of a free State." Free State, indeed! How long would any country remain free with the whole physical force thereof in the hands of the Chief Magistrate?

We well understand, sir, what this mild term *classification* means. It was urged upon us, pressed upon us, at the last session, in the odious form of a French conscription. Yes, sir; the sons of America, the hopes of their country and of their families, were to be torn from the arms of their parents and harnessed to the chariots of war. Yes, sir; this virtuous measure was, indeed, pressed upon us by the then Secretary of War, now Secretary of State, and heir apparent of the Presidency. "With this subject," says your President, "is intimately connected the necessity of accommodating the laws, in every respect, to the great object of enabling the political authority of the Union," (meaning himself,) " to employ promptly and effectually," (yes, without any control of the States,) "the physical power of the Union," (that is, the bayonets,) "in the cases designated by the Constitution;" that is, to execute conscription and embargo laws; to suppress insurrections which his own tyranny and oppression may have caused; and to repel invasions which his own rashness and folly, as in the late war, invited. Grant the power, by this short paragraph of the Message requested with so much earnestness, and elevate an ambitious bloodthirsty villain to the Presidency, and the liberties of this country would not survive a year of his Administration. And if the people, or their representatives, do grant this power, and thereby raise the sword to their throats, it is to be hoped that our then master would, in mercy, even end our miseries with our lives. But, sir, your President is not to have this power, though he seek it with tears; he has not made that correct use of the power which he now unfortunately possesses, that we should feel perfectly safe in surrendering our liberties into his hands.

But, sir, the real object of this bill is Executive patronage. Patronage is written in every feature of it. The President is not to organize this corps as other military corps are, but he is to appoint the eight hundred cadets. A fine opportunity to provide for the young fry of the Administration, the mere underbrush of the Government, and the royal cousins of the Palace. He, besure, had it in his power to provide for the old birds of the Administration, and, to do them justice, they have well feathered their nests, and their gaping, unfledged offspring will now be fed from the bill of the Government. Sir, this is not mere suspicion. This bill puts it in the power of the President to indulge the most odious favoritism, and, from what has been done on other occasions, there is no doubt this power will be abused. The honorable gentleman from the State of New York (Mr. ROOT) has proved that abuses have crept into the institution at West Point—that none but the sons of the rich and the powerful can gain admittance there. And the most odious partiality is manifested in some of the appointments in the Navy, particularly of midshipmen. Mere children, of the favored few, have been appointed, who never were on board a ship of war, and have nothing of the seaman about them except the anchor on their buttons; and this, too, to the ex-

clusion of many brave and deserving sailors, masters, and mates, whom your restrictive acts drove from the merchants' employ. I know of many improper appointments of this kind; some in this very city. However, they belonged to the royal cousins. It is a shame, sir, that the brave Navy of this country should suffer by such gross partiality. Many, able and willing to serve on board our gallant Navy, dear to their friends and an ornament to their country, despairing of obtaining better service, have been compelled by the pressure of the war, to seek employ and support on board your private armed vessels; and in too many cases their lives have been a forfeit to their necessities. And, sir, what will be the consequences of these abusive appointments in your Navy? These boys, always thus thrown in at the cabin-windows, will, from the dates of their commissions as midshipmen, be preferred to the hardy seaman who has weathered many a gale at sea, escaped the perils of the ocean, and survived the shock of battle. This must not, nay, shall not be. The Navy is the darling of the people. They will protect it.

The friends of this bill have introduced many things into the debate which have no connexion with the subject. An honorable gentleman from South Carolina, (Mr. CALHOUN,) whose intelligence and acuteness we often have occasion to admire, congratulates himself and the House on the expression of national feeling and patriotism, which he thinks he can discover in the country, and which he is pleased to ascribe to what he is pleased to call, *the glory and success of the war.* Glory and success of the war! Where in the name of God does he discover this glory and success? I have often read this language in party prints, devoted to the powers that are, and it may have been attended with success in taverns and grog-shops—not that I would insinuate that the honorable gentleman gains his intelligence from these corrupt sources—his spirit and independence are above them. I say, sir, this language may have issued from these corrupt sources, but I never expected to hear it on this floor. Where, let me ask the honorable gentleman, are we to look for this glory and success—where will foreign nations look for it? When you declared the late war; when this House published their far-famed manifesto, which I believe that honorable gentleman himself had a hand in composing, (and it was an honor to the head, whatever it might be to the heart that drew it,) you proclaimed to the world the wrongs and the insults you had suffered, and intimated that the sword you drew was not to be sheathed until they were redressed, and future aggressions provided against. Let me ask, then, sir, have you obtained a single object for which you drew the sword? Look at your declaration—your causes of war—and see if you find one of them provided for in your Treaty of Peace. Injuries which you declared must be redressed, or this would cease to be an independent nation—they are not only not provided for, but abandoned, surrendered, given up to your enemy. Sir, had this been a conquered country, our Ministers on their knees before their haughty conqueror, with his drawn sword at their throats, terms more humiliating could not have been dictated. You give up your sailors—ay, "free trade and sailors' rights," and all—give up definition of blockade—give up violated neutral rights, and leave a portion of your own country (Moose Island) in the possession of the enemy, till they shall be pleased to decide whether your own country does or not belong to you. Glory and success, indeed! But do not for a moment imagine, sir, that I would in the least detract from the well-earned fame of your gallant Navy, and certain individuals and corps of your Army; but this exclusively belongs to them. Sir, the more meritorious, as they were so miserably seconded by the Government. The very name of your Navy animates the patriot's bosom. The constellation of her heroes shall "shine as the brightness of the firmament, and as the stars forever and ever."

Sir, your Government is not yet identified with the Navy, nor the individuals of the Administration with those heroes who are encircled with glory. Will you, sir, attempt to strip the garland from the brow of a Hull, a Decatur, nay, all our gallant sailors, to decorate the prolific head of the miserable projector of contemptible gunboats; or tear by the roots, from a Ripley, a Scott, a Jackson, and a Brown, if you please, and their brave companions in arms, their well-earned laurels, to adorn the brows of the heroes of the ruined Capitol, or to transplant them in the barren fields of Bladensburg? Believe me, sir, their brows cannot bear the weight of such glory any more than the individuals can acquire it. Will such blasted fields yield the fruit of honor? Foreign nations, sir, and impartial posterity, will do justice to them all. This is not a subject of my calling up; it affords no pleasure to me to enumerate the faults of the Government, or the distress and disgrace of my country. It is the love I bear that country, interwoven as it is with every sensation of the heart, which makes me grieve for the misfortunes which the rashness and folly of her rulers by the late war have brought upon her; millions of treasure wasted, and thousands of lives of American citizens, each as valuable as that of your President, sacrificed, in a ruinous, unnecessary, and inexpedient war. Let the friends and promoters of that war, in future, maintain that humble silence thereon which its solemnity demands.

Mr. HULBERT said he begged the indulgence of the Committee a few minutes. He wished to reply to some observations which had fallen from his honorable colleague, (Mr. KING.)

He said he was surprised to hear the objection that Congress have no Constitutional right to establish Military Academies. He believed it was the first time the objection had ever been made. If, as his colleague contended, the establishment of Military Academies was unconstitutional, it was not a little surprising that no one had ever before made the discovery. Several laws in relation to the institution at West Point had been passed under Administrations of very different political character; but whatever might have been thought of the expediency of those laws, he was confident no one had ever questioned their constitutionality. The Constitution of the United States says, "Congress shall have power to raise and support armies." This he thought a clear and ample authority to pass the bill before us. His honorable colleague had asserted that this was the first time the terms "Military Academy" had ever been used in our laws. This was a great mistake. If the gentleman had looked into the laws of 1802, he would have found the very terms which now appear to him so novel. His colleague had also asserted that the Military Academy formed no part of the Peace Establishment. Here he was equally erroneous. The corps of engineers constitutes the Academy at West Point, and that corps had been constantly preserved since its first organization, and the act of 1815, fixing the present Peace Establishment, expressly declares that that corps shall be retained. Mr. H. thought the point too plain to admit of a doubt.

The honorable gentleman had urged, as a very serious objection against this bill, that we had no money to spare for the proposed appropriation. Mr. H. said he knew that the Treasury had been drained, had been completely exhausted; but a deep and rapid current of revenue was now pouring into it, and he hoped it would soon be replenished. The sum proposed for the erection of three new academies was only two hundred thousand dollars, and even that sum could now be considerably lessened, as it had been determined to establish but one additional school. He hoped he was fully aware of the necessity and importance of economy; but it was not economy to refuse to give small sums of money for great and important benefits, and such he believed would be the fruits of this measure. His colleague would, he was confident, agree with him, that the age of calculators was as much to be dreaded as the age of spendthrifts.

My honorable colleague, continued Mr. HULBERT, says he strongly suspects that the real object of this bill is not disclosed. He fears that some mischief lurks behind the curtain. This may, be says, be a part of a plan of the present Administration to get the military power under their control, and thereby destroy the liberties of the country. Mr. H. said he belonged to the committee who reported this bill. He thought it a plain and simple proposition to enlarge the present establishment of the Military Academy. He saw in the measure none of those frightful evils so strongly apprehended by the gentleman. He hoped his honorable colleague would not be too much alarmed; would not be too suspicious. He said he had, when young, often been cautioned not to be looking out for bears; for they always appeared to those who expected to see them. This caution he recommended to the attention of his honorable colleague.

My colleague, said Mr. H., has strenuously urged that the appointment of so great a number of cadets, as is contemplated by the bill, would give to the President an improper and dangerous patronage. To whom would the gentleman give the power of appointment? Might it not be made a system of favoritism by any other man, or body of men, as well as by the President? The President has by the Constitution the power of appointing all officers of the Army, by and with the advice and consent of the Senate. But since the Senate cannot with convenience be consulted on the selection of each cadet, why not give the authority to the President alone? Mr. H. said he was one of those who never believed that Executive patronage was too great in this country. He would rather see it increased than lessened. All grants of power might be abused, but that was not a sufficient argument against the grant. As to the story of children strutting in the dress of midshipmen, Mr. H. said he strongly suspected that his colleague here had seen another bear; that he had been deceived by some mock military exhibition of the school boys of this city, which he had himself sometimes seen here and elsewhere on holydays.

His honorable friend and others had contended that the number of cadets proposed was too great; that there would be more than could be commissioned by the Government. Mr. H. said it was not expected that all of the cadets would be employed as officers in time of peace. The very object of this military institution was to be prepared for war. Undoubtedly many of the cadets, after having finished their military education, would willingly return to their homes and engage in the pursuits of civil life. But in time of war, in the day of peril and danger, in the hour that should try men's souls, they would come forth at the call of their Government, and lead the hardy freemen of their country to victory and to glory. Let gentlemen calculate how many commissioned officers are employed in the present Peace Establishment, and then reflect that the time may come when we may have an army of sixty or a hundred thousand men to be officered, and surely they will not think the proposed number of cadets too large.

It had been said that the plan proposed for our adoption was calculated to excite a military spirit in our country, which would perpetually urge us to war with other nations, and might, in the end, destroy our own liberties. Were such, said Mr. H., the effects of that military spirit and military science so eminently displayed in our Revolutionary war? No; but directly the reverse. That spirit and that science gave us the very liberty and independence which we now enjoy.

Mr. H. said he had anxiously hoped that the distressing calamities, the defeat and foul disgrace which we had experienced in the beginning of the late war, had awakened the nation to a just sense of the importance of military science and preparation for a state of hostilities. Who did not shrink from such calamity and disgrace! He remembered them with shame and with horror. He had seen the face of the nation turn pale—the coldness of death had seized upon the extremities of the empire, and was creeping toward the heart—nay, it had reached the heart! It was to prevent the recurrence of such scenes, the repetition of such disasters, that he anxiously wished the passage of this bill.

To excite opposition to this bill, his colleague had poured forth a torrent of indignation against the late war. Mr. H. said no one more deeply lamented, nor more sincerely censured, the declaration of that war than he did. He considered it a rash and desperate measure. But the storm had passed over, and it was time to repair the ruins it had made. He had already declared, and he took this opportunity to repeat the declaration, that he esteemed the late message of the President as the harbinger of better times; the measures it recommended, and the spirit of conciliation it displayed, were worthy of the Chief Magistrate of a great and enlightened people. This, Mr. H. said, was one of the measures so recommended; and he would cheerfully give it his support, because he thought it calculated to promote the best interests and glory of his country.

Mr. JOHNSON said it had been his duty to address the House so frequently on this interesting subject, that it was with reluctance that he now had to answer some remarks which had fallen from two gentlemen from Massachusetts, (Messrs. KING and HULBERT.) He had been very much pleased with the greater part of the observations of the gentleman last up, (Mr. HULBERT.) He said he reciprocated many sentiments which had been expressed, many he admired, and many had a direct tendency to enlighten; in fact, strong evidence had been given of a liberal support of the bill, and enlarged views of the beneficial results of military instruction. The same magnanimous course might have induced an omission of expressions calculated to excite party feelings and recrimination. He said he had indulged in a hope that the observations of yesterday would have been verified, viz: that nationality of sentiment prevailed in this House, and that on this occasion there would be an amalgamation of feeling and a union of sentiment; but the strong language of the gentleman to-day had lessened that hope, for the gentleman is pleased to say that he holds in the greatest abhorrence and detestation the declaration of war against Great Britain; and Mr. J. said he must declare with equal sincerity that he recollected with equal abhorrence and detestation the violent opposition to that war, and that disaffection to the Constitution which prevailed in many parts of the United States, and in none to a more criminal extent than that in which the gentleman resided. It cannot be denied that the want of a proper system of military instruction previous to the war, as proposed by this system, was the cause of some of our difficulties, and this argument in favor of the bill is entitled to consideration; but disunion was the chief cause of those calamities and disasters which afflicted the nation, and to which the gentleman alludes. No necessity existed, if time allowed, to bring to the recollection of the

House the example of Spain in her resistance of
imperial France, and the example of France in
submitting to the invasion of the allies. The
history of the United States would furnish memorable examples of the glorious achievements of
a manly, vigorous, and united resistance, and the
evils of faction and a division of sentiment which
relied upon the magnanimity of a most implacable enemy; it was this mean, submitting spirit,
united to an incessant opposition to the Administration, the object of which was power, that the
most of the disasters and evils of the war may be
attributed; these facts cannot be disguised, they
are known to the people, and they think accordingly. This was not a proper occasion to detain
the House upon the subject of the war, but as
great anxiety had been manifested to invite a discussion of that subject, whenever the proper time
should arrive, it would not be improper to examine the conduct and merit of those who declared
the war and supported it, and those who opposed
it and made use of every exertion in the councils
of the nation, and out of it, to prevent a glorious
termination of the war. Such inquiry would be
useful in affording the people a better opportunity in the hour of calm reflection to decide the
merit of the two parties in the nation. But the
same gentleman had made use of another expression which deserved notice, viz: that at a certain
period of the war good men of all parties looked
pale, and in fact the sleep of death had seized the
extremities of the nation. It is not denied that
this remark may apply to that part of the Union
which that gentleman represents; he may have
seen and felt this gripe of death, and this may
have been the efficient cause why the arm of the
Government was so feeble in that quarter as to
prevent the hardy yeomanry of Maine from driving the enemy from Castine. But Mr. J. said
he hoped he should be excused in stating that no
such alarm existed in the West; no pale faces
were seen, nor did the gripe of death seize that
part of the Union. The people felt indignant,
but no alarm nor disappointment at the savage
and barbarous conduct of the enemy; those who
lived during the Revolution, or had read in history, expected such conduct from Great Britain
as soon as war was declared; but this consideration could have no other effect than to unite the
friends of liberty and those who loved their country. The declaration of war involved many calamities; this was known to every reflecting mind,
and the patriot considered these a lesser evil than
further submission to foreign encroachment.
The murder of the wounded soldier, the profana-
tion of the temples of religion, and the destruction
of many villages, only proved the greater necessity there was to oppose that nation which
threatened our existence as an independent Government. On most occasions, Mr. J. said, the
other gentleman (Mr. KING) had indulged in ascribing hidden and ambitious views to the President of the United States. It was not necessary
to account for such deadly hostility or personal
hatred to a man whose public services had identified him with every wise measure of the Gov-

ernment for upwards of thirty years, whose talents had always been the pride of his country,
whose integrity could not be impeached, and
whose moral character had gained the veneration
and respect of all who knew him well; but it
may be necessary to say, that on this occasion
motives and hidden views had been most unnecessarily brought forward against the committee,
and also against the President who had publicly
recommended this measure. Mr. J. said he was
convinced that no gentleman, upon reflection,
who felt the strength of virtue in his own bosom,
could indulge in——[Here Mr. KING explained,
and Mr. J. declined to say anything more.]

The Committee then rose and reported the bill.
The question being on the number of cadets to
be attached to the Military Academy or Corps of
Engineers—

Mr. PICKERING opposed the number of eight
hundred, which was proposed by the Military
Committee.

Mr. FORSYTH was opposed to a reduction of
the number. He was in favor of making such
preparations as if we calculated on the recurrence
of war. Was it not known, he asked, that the
nation with whom we were lately at war—with
whom we should, in all probability, before very
long be again at war—was strengthening its frontier by repairing its old fortifications and building new ones? Was it not known that that nation had more than fourteen thousand regular
troops on the frontier? What could be the object of this preparation? It might be merely
defensive; he hoped it was so. Believing it to
be the intention of the Government of this nation to preserve peace, he trusted we should have
it in our power. But the object of the British
Government may be different, and these preparations may have an offensive object. Our motions should be regulated by theirs; and, if the
nature of our institutions forbids a large Military
Establishment, preparations should be made in
another way. On all hands it was admitted
that the measure proposed by this bill, was the
most efficient practical mode of adding to our
military strength; and he hoped the bill would
not be limited in its scope to a smaller number
than was proposed. In reply to the argument of
the gentleman from Pennsylvania, that the youth
educated at the academy would be fit for nothing
but the military service of the country, he said,
they would be as well fitted for entering into the
walks of civil life, as those who had been educated in a different manner—and gentlemen could
not seriously imagine any danger from turning
out into the community two or three hundred
well educated young men. As their services
might be necessary for military purposes, and the
knowledge they acquire would not in any event
be lost to the country, he hoped the number would
not be diminished.

Mr. CALHOUN also opposed the reduction of
the number of cadets; because, if the present
number were retained, it would afford ample
room for a proper selection of officers. In another
point of view, he thought it materially necessary

to retain the proposed number. The whole population of the United States is composed of men, active, vigorous, and spirited. With good officers to lead them, you may at any time make out of any portion of them active, good soldiers. What is requisite to make our militia efficient? Military knowledge, only, said Mr. C. The cadets will many of them return to the body of the people, and become a part of the militia. Suppose a renewal of the struggle between us and the nation with whom we were recently at war; suppose she should put forth her whole strength to crush this young country; we shall then find the use of having men qualified to lead our citizens to meet her invading foe. The whole population of the country becomes an efficient force, because it has among it men properly educated and qualified to lead an army into the field. Every citizen of a free country, and of course of this country, said Mr. C., has two duties to perform; the duty of defending his country by arms if necessary, and the duty of voting, and thus participating in the management of the affairs of his country. Every young man of ardent feeling will desire to qualify himself for their proper performance. These are duties which every citizen ought zealously to perform, and from which, if the people ever shrink, our nation will not long have existence. Mr. C. appealed to the history of Republics, which had so often lost their liberties from the indisposition of the citizens to perform their share of military duty. It ought to be the object of a wise Government to resist a tendency towards apathy in the people; to diffuse military science. The dependence on regular force merely was a contracted idea, which he hoped this House would not give into. The Army, Mr. C. said, was, and ought always to be, a respectable part of the military force of the nation; but a well organised Militia is its bulwark—and they are but a rabble without discipline. Hence the necessity for the free diffusion of military science. He hoped, therefore, the largest number of cadets proposed to be authorized, would be agreed to.

The amendments, which go to limit the additional academies to one, to be established at Knoxville, Tennessee, were agreed to without a division.

Mr. TAYLOR then moved an amendment, directing that the cadets should be admitted into the academies, from the several States and Territories, in numbers proportionate to the militia returns thereof, and that the Secretary of War should make an annual return of the names and residence of the cadets at these academies, the time of their admission, and their respective places of residence.

The motion was agreed to.

Some diversity of opinion, and some animated debate, took place on the number of cadets to be authorized by the bill. It ended in a motion, by Mr. TAYLOR, of New York, to strike out eight hundred, the number proposed by the bill, so as to leave it blank, to be filled according as a majority might then decide. For this motion, there were

79 votes; against it, 55. So the motion was carried.

The question being taken on filling the blank with six hundred, it was decided in the affirmative—yeas 77.

Mr. ROOT then moved to amend the bill, so as to extend the period of encampment required by this bill from six weeks to three months; which, after debate, was negatived.

After the rejection of a proposition, by Mr. PICKERING, to amend the bill so as to bind the cadets more certainly to the military service, after having been educated in the academy—

On motion of Mr. HULBERT, the bill was recommitted to the Military Committee, to adjust its details to the principles already decided on.

ESTIMATE OF EXPENSES.

The SPEAKER laid before the House the estimates from the Treasury of the expenses of the Government for the ensuing year; which were referred to the Committee of Ways and Means.

The letter is as follows:

TREASURY DEPARTMENT, *Jan.* 2, 1816.

SIR: I have the honor to transmit, herewith, for the information of the House of Representatives, an estimate of the appropriations proposed for the service of the year 1816, amounting in the whole to the sum of nineteen millions nine hundred and fifteen thousand four hundred and thirty-one dollars and forty-five cents. There having been already appropriated, by the act of the 21st of December last, the sum of nine millions eight hundred and eighty-five thousand three hundred and seventy-two dollars, for certain military expenses, there will be left the sum of ten millions and thirty thousand and fifty-nine dollars forty-five cents, under the following heads, viz:

For the civil list - - - -	961,812 34
For miscellaneous expenses - -	573,071 11
For the expenses of intercourse with foreign nations - - - -	261,000 00
For the Military Establishment, including the Indian department - - - 14,541,677	
From which, deducting the amount appropriated by the act of the 21st December, 1815 - - - 9,885,372	
There is left the sum of - - -	4,656,305 00
For the Naval Establishment, including the Marine Corps - - -	3,638,071 00
	$10,030,059 45

The funds out of which the appropriations for the year 1816 may be discharged, are the following:

1. The sum of six hundred thousand dollars, annually reserved by the act of the 4th of August, 1790, out of the duties of customs, towards the expenses of Government.

2. The proceeds of the stamp duties, and the duty on sugar refined within the United States.

3. The surplus which may remain of the customs, the direct tax, and the internal duties, (other than those on refined sugar and on stamps,) after satisfying the payments for which they are pledged and appropriated.

4. The proceeds of such loans as may be made un-

der the unexecuted authority, contained in the acts of the 14th of March, 1812; the 24th of March and 15th November, 1814; and the 3d of March, 1815; and of the issues of Treasury notes, under the unexecuted authority contained in the act of the 24th of February, 1815.

5. Any other unappropriated moneys which may come into the Treasury during the year 1816.

I have the honor to be, &c.   A. J. DALLAS.

Hon. Speaker
Of the House of Representatives.

Thursday, January 4.

Mr. Baylies presented a petition of the manufacturers of cotton goods, in the county of Plymouth, in the State of Massachusetts, praying that such measures may be adopted as will afford security and encouragement to the cotton manufactories within the United States.—Referred to the Committee of Commerce and Manufactures.

Mr. Lewis presented a petition of sundry inhabitants of the county of Alexandria, praying that a court-house, a jail, and sundry public offices, for the use of the county of Alexandria, may be erected at the expense of the General Government.

Mr. L. also presented a petition of the Mechanic Relief Society of Alexandria, praying that they may be authorized, by lottery, to raise money for the purpose of erecting a school-house for the education of the children of the mechanics of said town.

Mr. L. also presented a petition of the Trustees of the Alexandria Academy, praying that the banks in Alexandria, who have applied, or may hereafter apply, for charters, or extension of charters, may be compelled to subscribe ten thousand dollars each in the stock of said academy.—Referred to the Committee for the District of Columbia.

Mr. Clark, of Kentucky, presented a petition of the Kentucky Abolition Society, praying that a tract of vacant and unappropriated lands may be set apart for the residence of free negroes and mulattoes, and that they may be transported to the said lands at the public expense.—Referred to the Committee on the Public Lands.

Mr. Robertson, from the Committee on the Public Lands, reported a bill for the relief of Martin Cole, John Pollock, George Westner, and Abraham Welty; which was read twice, and ordered to be engrossed and read a third time to-morrow.

Mr. Newton, from the Committee of Commerce and Manufactures, reported a bill for the relief of John Redman Coxe; which was read twice, and committed to a Committee of the Whole.

Mr. Cannon, from the committee appointed on the 14th ultimo, reported a bill to provide for the widows and orphans of the officers, non-commissioned officers, musicians, and privates, of the volunteers and militia, who have been killed in battle, died in service, or of wounds received while in the service of the United States during the late war; which was read twice, and committed

to a Committee of the whole House on Monday next.

A message from the Senate informed the House that the Senate have passed a bill "for the relief of Joseph Anderson," in which they ask the concurrence of this House.

The bill was read twice, and referred to the Committee on the Public Lands.

The Speaker laid before the House a letter from the Secretary of War, transmitting statements of the expenditure and application of such sums as have been drawn from the Treasury for the Military Department, from the 1st of October, 1814, to the 30th of September, 1815, which were referred to the Committee of Ways and Means.

On motion of Mr. Easton, the Committee on the Public Lands were instructed to inquire into the expediency of providing, by law, for the establishment of a land office, for the sale of the public lands, at the town of Arkansas, in the county of Arkansas; and a land office at the town of Jackson, in the county of Cape Girardeau, in the Territory of Missouri.

On motion of Mr. Stanford, the Committee of the Whole were discharged from a further consideration of the report of the committee appointed to revise the rules and orders; and it was recommitted to Messrs. Stanford, Bassett, Sergeant, Gold, Desha, and Telfair.

Mr. Pleasants, in offering the following motion, remarked, that he had no wish to produce any sensation in the House, nor to agitate, at present, any question relating to the unfortunate affair of Dartmoor prison, but he was desirous to be placed in possession of any official documents in relation to it which may be in the hands of the Executive department; with that view, he moved—

"That the President of the United States be requested to cause to be laid before this House, if in his opinion it will not be inconsistent with the public welfare, any communications which may have passed between this Government and the Government of Great Britain, in relation to the transactions at Dartmoor prison, in the month of April last, so far as the American prisoners of war, there confined, were affected by them."

On the suggestion of Mr. Jackson, of Virginia, that there might be documents in the possession of the Government, relating to this subject, not connected with the correspondence with the British Government, the resolution was modified so as to embrace such documents; and, thus modified, the motion was agreed to, and a committee ordered to be appointed to lay the same before the President.

The bill for the relief of Henry Fanning, and the bill for the relief of William Morrisett, passed through Committees of the Whole, and were ordered to be engrossed for a third reading.

SETTLERS ON THE PUBLIC LANDS.

Mr. Jennings rose and observed, that he wished to call the attention of the House to a subject growing out of a late proclamation of the President of the United States, ordering all settlers on the public lands to be removed after an early

453   HISTORY OF CONGRESS.   454

January, 1816.   *Bankruptcy—Commerce with Great Britain.*   H. of R.

day in March next. By an act of Congress, dated the 3d of March, 1807, the President of the United States was authorized so to do; but, by the second section of the same act, a provision was made, that any such settlers who were actually settled on the public lands prior to the passage of that act, might continue to reside thereon; provided such settlers should, prior to the 1st of January, 1808, apply to the proper officers of the land offices, and obtain a permission to reside thereon, conditioned to deliver up possession whenever required by a purchaser of the United States, and conditioned, likewise, to commit no waste or damages while residing thereon.

Mr. J. observed, that he was not personally acquainted with the views of the Congress of the United States, in passing the act referred to, but, if he was correctly informed, the object was to bear materially on the settlers who had settled on the disputed tract of country, commonly called the Yazoo purchase, although the act has a general operation. Those persons who had settled on the public land, lying within the Territory of Indiana, before the war, had sat down on the lands last purchased of the Indians, and remained there, and still remain. These persons, said Mr. J., have suffered greatly by their exposed situation to the attacks of the savages, and have been of great advantage in defending the frontier during the late hostility of the Northwest Indians. They, or a very great portion of them, he said, were now prepared with money to purchase so soon as those lands shall be exposed to sale by the Government. By these persons the operation of the proclamation will be severely felt, indeed; inasmuch as the sales of those lands will not, probably, take place before May next, and those settlers, in the mean time, must leave their homes and firesides, only to seek a residence for a few months. He thought it extremely hard now to remove them after they had been suffered to remain undisturbed before and during the war; whereas, if they were permitted to remain a few months longer, the sales of those lands would, in a great degree, render the measure unnecessary, and greatly limit the unpleasant effects which its execution will certainly produce. He therefore submitted the following resolution:

Resolved, That the Committee on the Public Lands be instructed to inquire into the expediency of extending, by law, to all settlers on the public lands of the United States, who have settled thereon since the 1st day of January, 1808, the same privilege extended to such settlers prior to that day, by the second section of the act of Congress, passed March 3, 1807.

The resolution was agreed to without debate, by a majority of twenty or thirty votes.

SYSTEM OF BANKRUPTCY.

Mr. King, of Massachusetts, offered for consideration the following resolutions:

Resolved, That the situation of the unfortunate merchants and traders, reduced, by misfortunes and circumstances beyond their control, from competence to want, now demand that Congress should exercise the power vested in them by the people for the relief of the unfortunate debtor, by the establishment of a uniform system of bankruptcy throughout the United States.

Resolved, That the Committee on the Judiciary be instructed to prepare and report a bill to establish a uniform system of bankruptcy throughout the United States.

Mr. K. said, that as a bill on this subject would require much labor in perfecting its details, he thought it would not be worth while to put this burden on any committee, unless the House should show a disposition to adopt the principle. He had, therefore, thrown his motion into an imperative form. The power to establish such a system was expressly given in the Constitution, and, being given, Mr. K. contended, was not intended by the framers of the Constitution to lie dormant there, but to be exercised for the benefit of the people. Mr. K. cited, as evidence of the popular sentiment on this head, the acts of the Legislatures of several of the States on the subject, some of which had been declared by the judges unconstitutional, inasmuch as the Constitution had expressly given the power to the General Government. This was a strong reason why Congress ought to act on the subject. Mr. K. called the attention of the House to the situation of the merchants, whose fortunes had for some years been as fluctuating as the waves; and to the operation on the mercantile community of the restrictive system, of so little importance against an enemy, and so cruel an operation to them. Every motive, in short, which ought to actuate legislators or gentlemen, Mr. K. remarked, ought to induce the House to grant the relief desired to the suffering merchant and tradesman.

Mr. Wright, in a few observations on this subject, denied the right of State judges to decide against the validity of insolvent laws, passed by the States.

Mr. Throop moved that the resolution be laid on the table, and be ordered to be printed.

Mr. Jackson required a division of the question on this motion.

Mr. Taylor, of New York, expressed his views on this subject, which were, substantially, that he was willing, and he presumed there would be no objection to vote for an inquiry into this subject; though he was unwilling, without investigation, to decide in favor of a general bankrupt law. He thought if the proposition were for an inquiry into the subject merely, that there would be no objection to it.

Mr. King then withdrew his motion, with a view to accommodate the wishes of gentlemen friendly to the object, and, in lieu thereof, substituted the following:

Resolved, That the Committee on the Judiciary be instructed to inquire into the expediency of establishing an uniform system of bankruptcy throughout the United States.

This proposition was agreed to without a division.

COMMERCE WITH GREAT BRITAIN.

The House resolved itself into a Committee of the Whole, on the bill to carry into effect the stipulations of the Treaty of Commerce, lately concluded with Great Britain. The first section of the bill having been read—

Mr. Forsyth (the chairman of the Committee of Foreign Relations) stated the general object of the bill, and the nature of its provisions. The bill, he said, was intended to carry into effect those parts of the treaty which require legislative interposition; which he enumerated, and compared the provisions of the bill in this respect, with the provisions of the treaty. He then stated to the House the present discriminating duties on tonnage and on importation, and showed that the bill went to conform them to the provisions of the treaty, and placed British merchants in that respect on the same footing with ours. He next adverted to the British tariff, and showed the British discriminating duties, and the great advantages which would be derived to the United States by their abolition, in pursuance of the treaty, &c.

Two or three amendments to the bill were then moved by Mr. F., and agreed to, one of which went to give this act a retrospective effect, and to make its provisions take effect from the date of the ratification of the treaty; and another to confine the repeal of our discriminating duty to goods coming directly from the territories of Great Britain in Europe.

Mr. Clay (Speaker) said, he did not rise on this occasion to enter into a discussion of the general merits of the instrument brought incidentally before the House by the present bill, particularly as there appeared to be no wish on any side of the House to enter on that subject. He rose to make some explanations relative to the third article, which perhaps might not be considered unnecessary. It would be perceived, he said, that the third article of the convention, which opens the trade to the British East Indies, restricted us to certain enumerated ports. This was a restriction not contained in the Treaty of 1794, nor in that negotiated by Messrs. Monroe and Pinkney, commonly called the rejected treaty. The reason was, that upon the expiration of the charter of the East India Company, which took place three or four years ago, the question so long agitated in Great Britain had again come up, whether the monopoly of the trade to India should remain with the company, as it had done. On that occasion, it had been thought proper by the British Government to deviate to a certain extent from its former policy, and open the trade to British subjects, generally, under some restrictions. By the act which then passed, the British subjects were limited to these specified ports; and it had been thought right by Great Britain, especially as it was in her opinion a grant to us without an equivalent, to limit our citizens to the same ports. That act of Parliament, Mr. C. said, was a new era in the trade to British India; and it was impossible to estimate the value of the concession to us, without taking into consideration that important change. When the trade was wholly in the hands of the company, they had been found incompetent to supply India with the specie necessary for circulation; and the trade had been

opened to us, and other foreign Powers, to make up the deficit. Now that British subjects were let into the trade, it remained to be ascertained by experience whether they could not furnish the requisite supply of specie without the aid of foreigners. If they could, the opening of the trade to foreign Powers operates as an advantage in their favor, and to the prejudice of the British merchant, to the whole amount of the profits derived by such foreign Powers. These suggestions, Mr. C. said, he had thought proper to make to the Committee. inasmuch as some gentlemen might not have adverted to the change of the laws by which that trade was regulated.

Mr. Gaston said, that believing the convention, since its ratification in due form, had become a law of the land, and unable to perceive wherein it needed the help of an act of Congress to give it operation, he had viewed the bill before the Committee as nugatory and unmeaning. Although he had thought it strange that gentlemen who had abjured so many of the errors of their predecessors, should thus, by construction, retain and perhaps extend a most inconvenient error in regard to the effect of treaties, he was willing, without interruption on his part, to indulge them in their course. But regarding himself as having no agency in relation to this convention, he had not entertained the most remote thought of examining into its merits or demerits. He was induced, however, to say a word in relation to the third article of the convention, in consequence of the observations made on it by the honorable Speaker. This gentleman had stated, with a view to form an estimate of the value of the limited East India trade therein conceded, as compared with the more general grant on the same subject in the Treaty of Mr. Jay, that, subsequent to the date of that treaty, Great Britain had opened this trade to her own subjects, not of the East India Company, and therefore needed not so much the assistance of foreign merchants to bring supplies of bullion. If this formed an item for raising the value of the concession, it was proper to state another fact which would go to the opposite side of the account, and serve to adjust the balance. Since Mr. Jay's Treaty, (he believed in 1797,) the British Parliament had opened this same trade to the subjects of all friendly foreign Powers, and to this day without treaty it remained open to them all; the fact was, that the British East India possessions were valuable more for revenue than commerce. This revenue required a free importation of bullion from whatever quarter it could be had, and a free exportation of their commodities to foreign countries; it was, besides, desirable that this exportation should be made to distant regions, where they were not likely to come into direct competition with the manufactures of the parent kingdom.

Whether the East India trade was at all desirable to this country, was a question on which enlightened statesmen greatly differed; our table was groaning under the weight of petitions for prohibiting the great mass of importations from that quarter, and there had been a long and loud complaint against the perpetual drain of specie to it. However this might be, it was very certain that the only concession made by the third article was of a trade already open to us by a general law, and which was so desirable to them that they might find it their interest to pay us a bounty not to abandon it. Great Britain and her rulers well understood the spirit of traffic, and we might rely on it they had not in this instance given us a "*quid*" without a "*quo*" in return for it.

Mr. CLAY said, that the gentleman from North Carolina and himself were at issue on the fact. Mr. C. denied that the trade to the British East Indies was open to us by act of Parliament. By the regulations of the local authority of those countries, the trade might be open to us; but the difference between such regulations and the stipulations of a treaty was, that if there were any value in the trade to the British East India possessions, the treaty stipulation prevents us from being deprived of it by a repeal of those regulations during the continuance of the treaty. The benefit of the trade itself was another question; if not beneficial, the treaty did not force it on us. Mr. C. added, that he was not disposed to enter into a discussion of the treaty-making power. It might be sufficient for him to say that, at the worst, according to the opinions of gentlemen on the other side, the act would be harmless; whilst, in the opinion of gentlemen on this side, it was entirely necessary.

Mr. GASTON rejoined a few words, rather in acquiescence in the idea of this bill being harmless. As to the East India trade, he said, it was not to be presumed that the trade which the Government of Great Britain held out to every foreign Power without an equivalent, could itself be of any great use. As to the stipulation on this head, in the treaty, supposed to be so favorable to us, Mr. G. said, that Great Britain was not in the habit of giving advantages without equivalents.

[In reply to a previous remark of Mr. GASTON, that it was entirely an error to suppose a law necessary to give effect to a treaty, which, being the supreme law of the land, is paramount to existing laws—]

Mr. FORSYTH said, he had no disposition to enter into the discussion of this question; but it might be necessary that he should say, that the passage of this bill was not merely harmless but indispensable; because the power of legislation was vested in Congress, and could be exercised by no other authority. This doctrine was not only correct and Constitutional, but had been acted on by all Administrations and in all times. The provisions of the treaty being general, it was, independent of the general question of the effect of a treaty on existing laws, necessary to declare in what manner the act should be carried into effect.

Some further observations passed on this subject between Mr. GASTON and Mr. FORSYTH, which were afterwards more amply stated by them in debate.

The Committee having risen, and reported the bill and amendments, an objection was made by Mr. MILNOR to an amendment going to limit the operation in the bill to British vessels coming directly from the British territories in Europe. On this question, some debate took place—Mr. FORSYTH contending, though he considered the amendment as of no great importance, that it was according to the letter and spirit of the treaty.

On motion of Mr. MILNOR, the House adjourned without deciding this question.

<hr>

FRIDAY, January 5.

Mr. WHEATON presented a petition of a committee of sundry manufacturers of cotton goods, in Bristol county, in Massachusetts, praying that all cotton goods, (nankeens excepted,) imported from places beyond the Cape of Good Hope, may be prohibited, and that additional duties may be imposed on goods of that description imported from other countries.—Referred.

Mr. SOUTHARD presented a similar petition from the manufacturers of cotton goods in Somerset county, New Jersey.—Referred.

Mr. SERGEANT presented a petition of sundry inhabitants of Philadelphia, praying that the several acts imposing duties on domestic manufactures may be repealed.

Mr. SERGEANT also presented a petition of the goldsmiths, silversmiths, and jewellers, of the city of Philadelphia, praying that the act imposing duties on gold and silver plate and jewelry may be repealed.

Mr. SHARPE presented a petition of sundry inhabitants of Barren county, in the State of Kentucky, praying that the act imposing duties on domestic manufactures may be repealed, and that the duty on spirits may also be repealed.

Mr. ROBERTSON presented a petition of the sugar planters, in the State of Louisiana, praying that the duties laid during the late war with Great Britain, on foreign sugar, rum, and molasses, may be made permanent.—Referred to the Committee of Ways and Means.

Mr. PICKERING, from the committee appointed on the 12th ultimo, reported resolutions requiring the Secretary of State to compile and print, once in every two years, a register of all officers and agents, civil, military, and naval, in the service of the United States; which was read twice, and committed to a Committee of the Whole on Tuesday next.

On motion, of Mr. EASTON, the Committee on Military Affairs were instructed to inquire into the expediency of providing, by law, for the printing and distribution among the militia officers of the several States and Territories, a suitable number of copies of the militia laws of the United States, the rules and articles of war, and the discipline adopted by the United States.

An engrossed bill, entitled "An act for the relief of William Morrissett," was read the third time, and passed.

An engrossed bill, entitled "An act for the relief of Henry Fanning," was read the third time, and passed.

An engrossed bill, entitled "An act for the re-

459   HISTORY OF CONGRESS.   460

H. of R.   *Vessel Lost in Flotilla Service—Admission of Indiana.*   JANUARY, 1816.

lief of Martin Cole, John Pollock, George Westner, and Abraham Welty," was read the third time, and passed.

The bill for the relief of George S. Wise, and the bill to authorize the discharge of James Jewett from his imprisonment, were ordered to a third reading.

The bill authorizing the payment for property lost, captured, or destroyed in the service of the United States, during the war. was, on motion of Mr. FORSYTH, postponed to Friday next.

The SPEAKER laid before the House a letter from the Commissioner of the General Land Office, transmitting the report of the land commissioner for the district east of Pearl river; and the report of James D. Cooley, commissioner for the district west of Pearl river.

VESSEL LOST IN FLOTILLA SERVICE.

Mr. YANCEY, from the Committee of Claims, made a report on the petition of William O'Neale and Robert Taylor, which was read, and the resolution therein contained was concurred in by the House. The report is as follows:

That the petitioners are owners of the schooner Islet, which, in the month of June, 1814, then lying in the river Patuxent, they chartered to the United States as a store-ship to the flotilla commanded by Commodore Barney, upon the following terms: The petitioners were to find a sufficient number of seamen to navigate the vessel, the captain of the vessel to be under the orders of the commander of the flotilla, to carry such quantity of naval stores as was agreed on, and her safety, in every respect, to be at the *risk* of the owners: for which services and *risk* the United States agreed to give to the petitioners the sum of ten dollars per day; that, on the approach of the enemy, in August, 1814, it was deemed prudent by the commanding officer of the flotilla to blow it up, to prevent its falling into the hands of the enemy, but the schooner Islet, which was left to the care and management of Captain Taylor, one of the petitioners, was run up the river and sunk by him, to prevent the vessel and stores from falling into the hands of the enemy; the vessel has not been raised. The petitioners pray of Congress a compensation equal to the value of the vessel, and such further relief as may be just.

The committee are of opinion that the petitioners, having undertaken in their contract to be at all *risks* of the vessel, and the vessel having been sunk by its commander, who is one of the petitioners, are entitled to no relief.

They therefore recommend to the House the following resolution:

Resolved, That the prayer of the petitioners ought not to be granted.

ADMISSION OF INDIANA.

Mr. JENNINGS, from the committee appointed on the 28th ultimo, on the petition of the Legislature of the Territory of Indiana, made a detailed report, which was read; when, Mr. J. reported a bill to enable the people of the Indiana Territory to form a constitution and State government, and for the admission of such State into the Union, on an equal footing with the original States; which was read twice, and committed to a Committee of the Whole to-morrow.

The report is as follows:

That the said Territory is bounded on the east by the State of Ohio; on the south by the State of Kentucky; on the west by the river Wabash, from its mouth to a point opposite the town of Vincennes, and from thence by a due north line until it intersects a due east and west line which shall touch the southern extreme of Lake Michigan; and on the north by the line last described; that the said Territory is a portion of the Territory northwest of the river Ohio, which, by the ordinance for the government thereof, was ordained to constitute not less than three nor more than five States; that the ordinance aforesaid, whenever the Territory of Indiana shall possess sixty thousand free inhabitants, guaranties to those inhabitants the benefit of being admitted into the Union upon an equal footing with the original States; that the ordinance aforesaid not having declared under what authority the population of the said Territory should be ascertained, to complete their title to an admission into the Union, the Legislature thereof, after having, by actual census, ascertained that the Territory of Indiana possesses a population of upwards of sixty thousand free inhabitants, have deemed it the most prudent and respectful to submit to Congress the result of that census, and ask the passage of a law to enable the people of said Territory to form a constitution and State Government.

Your committee, believing the said Territory to possess a population of sixty thousand free inhabitants, at least, deem it unnecessary to offer any further reasons in support of the expediency of granting the principal prayer of the memorialists; and therefore beg leave to report a bill to enable the people of the Territory of Indiana to form a constitution and State government, on conditions not less advantageous and similar to those heretofore granted to other Territories of the United States.

CORYDON, *February* 24, 1816.

DEAR SIR: Agreeably to your request, I embrace the first moment within my power to send you a certified statement of the census of the Indiana Territory, taken from the official returns of the listers, certified by the clerks of the various counties, and forwarded to the House of Representatives of the said Territory, at their session which commenced on the 4th day of December, 1815, to wit:

Counties.	White males of 21 and upwards.	Total No.
Wayne,	1,295	6,407
Franklin,	1,430	7,370
Dearborn,	902	4,424
Switzerland,	377	1,832
Jefferson,	874	4,270
Clark,	1,387	7,150
Washington,	1,420	7,317
Harrison,	1,056	6,975
Knox,	1,391	8,068
Gibson,	1,100	5,330
Posey,	320	1,619
Warrick,	280	1,415
Perry,	350	1,720*
		63,897

---

* From the county of Perry, no lister's book had been received from the clerk, but the representative of that county says he had the number above stated from good authority.

461   HISTORY OF CONGRESS.   462

JANUARY, 1816.   *Uniformity of Elections—Commerce with Great Britain.*   H. OF R.

I, William Hendricks, Clerk of the House of Representatives, do hereby certify that the within statement is correct. Given under my hand the day above written.

W. HENDRICKS, *Clerk of the House of Representatives.*

UNIFORMITY OF ELECTION.

Mr. PICKENS, of North Carolina, rose to make a motion on a subject which he had for some time considered of great importance to the national interest. Although he had heretofore in vain pressed it on the consideration of the House, he thought the change of the circumstances of the nation, and the harmonious relations of political parties, at present, justified the hope that he should now meet with better success. The proposition he was about to submit had at different times been supported by the unanimous vote of both branches of the Legislature of North Carolina; and under the sanction of this respectable authority, he thought it his duty again to offer it to the consideration of the House, which he did in the following shape:

Resolved, by the Senate and House of Representatives of the United States of America in Congress assembled, two thirds of both Houses concurring therein, That the following amendment to the Constitution of the United States, be proposed to the Legislatures of the several States, which, when ratified by the Legislatures of three fourths of the said States, shall be valid to all intents and purposes as a part of the said Constitution.

For the purpose of choosing Representatives in the Congress of the United States, each State shall be divided, by its Legislature, into a number of districts equal to the number of Representatives to which the State may be entitled.

Each district shall contain, as nearly as may be, equal numbers, which shall be determined by adding to the whole number of free persons, including those bound to service for a term of years, and excluding Indians not taxed, three fifths of all other persons.

In each district the qualified voters shall elect one Representative.

For the purpose of choosing Electors of President and Vice President of the United States, each State shall be districted, by its Legislature, into a number of districts equal to the number of Electors to which the State may be entitled. Each district shall contain, as nearly as may be, equal numbers ; which shall be determined by adding to the whole number of free persons, including those bound to serve for a term of years, and excluding Indians not taxed, three-fifths of all other persons. In each district the persons qualified to vote for Representatives in the Congress of the United States, shall choose one Elector ; the Legislature of each State shall have power to regulate the manner of holding elections, and making returns of the Electors chosen. In case all the Electors shall not meet at the time and place appointed for giving their votes, a majority of the Electors met shall have power, and proceed to supply the vacancy.

A division of the States into districts, for choosing Representatives in the Congress of the United States, and into districts for choosing Electors of President and Vice President of the United States, shall take place as soon as conveniently may be, after each enumeration and apportionment of Representatives shall be made, which districts shall remain unaltered, until after the succeeding enumeration and apportionment of Representatives.

The resolution was twice read, and referred to a Committee of the Whole.

COMMERCE WITH GREAT BRITAIN.

The House resumed the consideration of the report of the Committee of the Whole on the bill carrying into effect the commercial convention with Great Britain.

The question being on the agreement to the amendments reported by the Committee of the Whole.

Mr. FORSYTH defended the amendment. He was of opinion that that construction and no other ought to be put on the treaty, which was embraced by the amendment. In the construction of any part of an instrument, reference must be made to its object. The whole object of the treaty was, to regulate the direct commerce between the United States and the territories of Great Britain in Europe. The exception in respect to the East India trade proved the rule, and excluded the idea of other exceptions. The correctness of this construction, he said, was further evinced by the correspondence between our Ministers and the British negotiators, &c., as he proceeded to show, by reference to the published correspondence, &c.

Mr. ROBERTSON, after remarking that no inference could be drawn from papers not before the House, (as the correspondence of our Ministers was not,) proceeded to observe, that he could not see the necessity of the amendment. It did not belong to the treaty, any more than to the interests of the United States. That treaty gave privileges, of which this amendment, if adopted, would deprive us. The amendment went to cut off a trade which it *is* of importance to us to preserve. The terms of the instrument to be carried into effect by the bill, did not, as far as he could understand, authorize the construction that British vessels, coming from other than British ports, are to be subject to higher duties than if they came direct from a port of Great Britain. The terms of the treaty and the interests of commerce equally forbade such a construction. Appreciating the capability and enterprise of this as a navigating and ship-building people, he was perfectly ready to enter the lists with any or all commercial nations, on the fair and liberal principles belonging to commerce, unaffected by commercial restrictions. He desired no more, in this respect, than that we should be placed on an equal footing with other Powers, not doubting but we should gain profit from the competition. He referred to the act of the last Congress, hypothetically repealing the discriminating duties, as evidence of the intention of Congress to hold out an invitation to all nations to do away their discriminating duties, on a pledge that we would do the same. The treaty, he said, was merely an echo of the principles of that law. Then why should not the most liberal interpretation be given to the treaty ? He could, he said, readily conceive that a commerce carried on circuitously by Great Britain, under such a construction, would be of but little importance to her, because of the relative situation of her and our ports. But there were many cases occurring in the course of commercial transactions, when the privilege would be highly advantageous to us, as in the case of clearing out to one port, and desiring to seek further for a market, &c., a case daily occurring. For the construction of a treaty we ought to resort nowhere but to the instrument itself; and he did not think the amendment could be supported on it.

Mr. TUCKER said, that he feared he should incur the imputation of presumption, in venturing upon a discussion involving commercial considerations, with which he could not pretend to be familiar. Convinced, however, of the impropriety of such of the amendments reported by the Committee of the whole House, as had a tendency to discriminate between the *direct* and *indirect* trade with the British dominions in Europe, he rose very respectfully to suggest to his friend, at the head of the Committee of Foreign Affairs, the propriety of waiving those amendments; and, at the same time, to offer to the House the reasons which had induced such a suggestion.

It appears to me, continued Mr. T., that in legislating on this convention, we should confine ourselves to the terms of the instrument itself, without attempting, by any superadded phraseology, to give it a construction which we may suppose it will bear. The terms of the law ought strictly to correspond with those of the treaty, lest by departing from it we should hazard a breach of faith, the imputation of which we should be solicitous to avoid. Whether we regard the convention as so plain as not to be susceptible of a twofold meaning, or not, it is equally evident that it would be unwise to depart from its phraseology in framing the act under consideration. For, if it be not susceptible of more than one meaning, why shall we attempt to explain what requires no explanation? If, on the contrary, it does admit of a double construction, what right have we, as one of the contracting parties, to pronounce upon the true interpretation of the instrument, which may not equally be claimed by the other party to the convention? By such a course of proceeding, the treaty itself would be the source of most serious collisions. But if, on the contrary, we should pass this act in the terms of the treaty, and leave to the Executives of the two nations to settle and adjust any ambiguity it may contain, no evil can ensue. If it be attempted, in the two countries, to settle the meaning of the instrument by legislative provision, it is probable the parties will soon be at issue, as no means can be devised for mutual explanations between them, in a legislative character. But, if the adjustment be left with the Executive, such mutual explanations can and will take place, and every unpleasant collision may be avoided.

But let us inquire for a moment, whether the evils likely to be incurred by the United States, in case the provisions of the treaty are confined to the direct trade, are of so serious a nature, as to tempt us, even for a moment, to put at hazard our reputation for good faith. So far from believing that we shall suffer by such a construction, I feel perfectly satisfied that we should be the gainers; and, though I am conscious that I approach a subject on which commercial men ought chiefly to be consulted, yet, I will solicit the attention of the House, whilst I distinctly state the reasons of this opinion.

Pursuing the latitude which has been taken by others, I shall embrace in my remarks both the amendments which contemplate a distinction between the direct and indirect trade. There are two clauses of the treaty which are affected by these amendments. The first relates to the equalization of the tonnage, or duties and charges of the vessel, and provides that " no higher or other ' duty or charges shall be imposed in any of the ' ports of the United States on British vessels, than ' those payable in the same ports by vessels of the ' United States," with a correspondent provision in favor of the United States. If this provision be confined to the direct trade between the United States and Great Britain, according to the terms of the bill, as amended by the committee. British vessels, it is true, could not enter into a competition with an American vessel, in carrying British articles from the continent of Europe or other foreign ports to America, because the additional tonnage would give a preference to the American bottom. But it must be recollected that a reciprocal disadvantage is incurred by American bottoms in a like trade from the Continent to Great Britain, in American articles; and that, according to the narrow and limited construction contended for, an American vessel could not enter into a competition with a British vessel in the carriage from the Continent to Great Britain. But what will be the operation of the convention? To permit American vessels to compete on equal terms with British vessels, in the carriage of American produce from the Continent and elsewhere, to Great Britain, or in any other trade which is now permitted, or may be hereafter suffered to be carried on in foreign ships at all; and to give a correspondent privilege to British vessels in the trade to the United States of America. Which then is likely to derive the greatest advantage from the regulation? That which is most likely to avail itself extensively of the privileges of the convention. And which is most likely to avail itself extensively of these privileges? The American ship owner, I presume, since the proximity of the ports between which he will generally trade, will make the pursuit more convenient and more profitable than that in which the British ship owner can be employed, under the same provisions of the convention. It seems manifest, for instance, that it would be much more convenient for an American to enter into the trade between Portugal and England, distant from each other only a few days' sail, than for an Englishman to engage in the trade between Portugal and the United States, separated as they are by an ocean of 3,000 miles; if so, more of our ship owners than of the British, are likely to avail themselves of the privileges of the treaty, and of course we shall gain more than we can lose by its stipulations, in relation to tonnage, according to the construction for which I contend.

So much then for the provision in relation to the tonnage. Let us next see what is the operation of the next clause.

It provides that " the same duties shall be paid ' on the importation into the United States of ' any articles, the growth, produce, or manufacture ' of His Britannic Majesty's territories in Europe, ' whether such importation be in American or ' British vessels," with a correspondent provision in favor of American articles. The remarks already made in relation to the former clause apply with the same force to this. There is, it is true, but little probability of either of the two nations engaging in an indirect trade, so long as this convention lasts, by which the direct trade is permitted on such advantageous terms. In the nature of things, every merchant will prefer the direct to the roundabout trade. The importation into the United States, of British articles from foreign ports other than those of Great Britain, will, therefore, rarely take place, and will, I presume, be confined to cases where the British goods do not find a ready sale in the foreign market, and are sent to America from thence, as affording a better prospect of mercantile advantage. So, too, the importation into the ports of Great Britain, from continental ports, of American merchandise, will only occur when the American merchant, after reaching the foreign port, finds it to his advantage to change his market, and sends his cargo from its first port of destination to Great Britain. Which of these cases is likely to occur most frequently ? Is it more probable that the exporter of manufactures from Great Britain will find it necessary to change his market, and send his goods from the continent of Europe or other foreign ports to the United States, or that the American exporter of tobacco and cotton will, on his arrival at a continental port, find his advantage in looking for a better market in London or Liverpool? The latter, without doubt. The former must rarely happen—the latter, as my friend from Louisiana has already intimated, occurs very frequently. Great disadvantage in such cases would, of course, be experienced, if the American merchant should, in the foreign port, when he wished to change his market, encounter additional tonnage and additional imports, in case he made use of an American vessel for the transportation. In truth, no American vessel could enter into the competition with British bottoms under such unpropitious circumstances. Yet would this be precisely the state of things if the treaty be confined to the direct trade. On the other hand, if it applies also to the indirect trade, the tobacco and cotton, and other bulky articles, of American export, may change their market without its being necessary to seek for British vessels, to the exclusion of those of the United States ; and American vessels would thus monopolize very soon the freight from which they are now excluded.

I cannot, therefore, but believe, that it is our interest to contend, that the convention, according to the true construction of it, comprehends the indirect as well as the direct trade. That such was the intention of the American commissioners, and the wish of the American Government, is indeed strongly inferrible from the existence of the act of Congress, read by the gentleman from Louisiana, in which the most general terms are used, equally comprehensive with those in the convention, and equally embracing indirect as well as direct trade. With this strong and decisive expression of the legislative will, the Executive have concluded this convention. They seem to have followed the expressions of the act, nor could they or the commissioners be justly censured, if the provisions were really disadvantageous. Believing the contrary, as I do, I cannot give my assent to an amendment which would exclude us from a fair advantage gained by the treaty ; and, even if my impressions on this subject were different, I should think it improper to attempt a legislative exposition of the instrument. As I have already intimated, it seems to me that it would be most advisable to leave the construction, if doubtful, to be settled between the Executives of the two nations, without hazarding collision or a breach of faith, by introducing into the law our own interpretation.

Mr. GASTON said, that he had yesterday, in Committee of the Whole, expressed an opinion in relation to this bill, which subsequent reflection had convinced him was erroneous. He had remarked, that although the bill was in his judgment unnecessary, it was nevertheless harmless. He was now satisfied that the bill was not only unnecessary, but of a pernicious character ; and while he owed it to the House to retract his error, he owed to himself an apology for adopting it. The fact was, that believing the House of Representatives could have no agency in executing the commercial convention between the United States and Great Britain, and having his attention much occupied with public business of a different character, he had thought very little of the convention itself, or of the bill which had been introduced for carrying it into effect. And when it was remarked by a member of the House, that a law re-enacting what he (Mr. G.) supposed to be already law, was at worst but a superfluous act of legislation, and could not therefore do harm ; the remark seemed plausible, and commanded his assent for the moment. Perfectly persuaded, however, that this impression was incorrect, and that any legislation by the House was full of mischief, he would submit a motion calculated to try the principle of the bill. He therefore moved its indefinite postponement.

In making this motion, he assured the House, that he was not actuated by anything like a spirit of opposition. He had come into Congress with a perfect disposition to co-operate with his associates of whatever political party, in any measures which might promote the public weal. And he indulged the hope, that now, when the troubled night of war had departed, and the day-

467   HISTORY OF CONGRESS.   468

H. of R.   *Commerce with Great Britain.*   January, 1816.

star of peace again beamed on our land, there would be at least a short interval of calm and sunshine, in which all could work cheerfully and harmoniously together.

In attempting to show the impropriety of the bill, Mr. G. would endeavor, if possible, not to tread upon the ground consecrated by party prejudice. He believed it was not necessary for his argument to lay down any principles in relation to the effect of a treaty constitutionally made, that might not be conceded as correct by the ancient champions of the party which now held the government of the Union. It would no doubt be recollected, that a vehement contest about the efficacy of the British Treaty had taken place in the House of Representatives, at an early period of our Federal Government. He could not undertake to speak confidently of the opinions of all who took part in that controversy, (for it was a long while since he had read the debate,) but he believed the great point in contestation, was the nature of the obligation on the House of Representatives to make appropriations in conformity to the treaty. One class of politicians (and he believed them right,) considered it as a moral obligation which could only yield to obligations of a paramount kind. The other class of politicians viewed it as an obligation of discretion only, which left the House a full right to judge of the expediency or inexpediency of the treaty. There could not have been a serious difference of opinion among the wise and able men of either side, whether a treaty constitutionally made, upon a subject fit for a treaty, was or was not a law; to be executed by the Executive, expounded by the Judiciary, as other laws made in other forms, prescribed by the Constitution. The words of that instrument were too precise to admit of rational doubt. "This Constitution, and ' the laws of the United States, which shall be ' made in pursuance thereof, and all treaties made, ' or which shall be made under the authority of ' the United States, shall be the supreme law of ' the land."—Art. 6, part 2d. "He the (President) ' shall take care that the laws be faithfully exe- ' cuted."—Art. 2d, sec. 3d. "The judicial power ' shall extend to all cases in law and equity aris- ' ing under this Constitution, the laws of the ' United States, and the treaties made, or which ' shall be made, under their authority."—Art. 3, ' sec. 2.

That it was never supposed necessary to impart a legislative sanction to a treaty, in order to vest it with every attribute of a law, was further evinced by the uniform practice of our Government under different Administrations. Notwithstanding the British Treaty contained various provisions of a commercial character, no act of Congress was passed to carry them into effect. The sole legislation which took place was an act making appropriations for the pay of the Commissioners to be appointed under the treaty. This was done precisely upon the same principles as an appropriation is made to defray the expenses attending the execution of other laws; not because the treaty or the laws require such sanction to give them validity, but because, by the Constitution, public revenue can only be disbursed in consequence of regular appropriations. But there was a later precedent, directly in point, and which some gentlemen might be disposed to regard with greater reverence. In the convention which was concluded between the United States and the First Consul of the French Republic, there was an article stipulating that captures made on either side should be restored. The French ship Berceau had been captured by us long before, and by the laws of the land had become the absolute property of the nation. No act of Congress was passed, none was supposed necessary, to enable the President to transfer this property of the nation to the French Republic. The treaty was deemed law sufficient for that purpose, and the then President (Mr. Jefferson) caused the Berceau to be restored according to the treaty.

Mr. G. was perfectly aware that treaties, like other laws, might be so made as to require the aid of supplemental legislation. Such, however, was not the case with the convention referred to in this bill. A remark was yesterday made by a gentleman from Georgia, (Mr. Forsyth,) designed to show that this convention needed such auxiliary legislation; but, on reflection, he was satisfied that the remark was not well founded. The gentleman observed that the convention stipulated only for an equality of duties in certain cases, upon importations in British and American vessels, without specifying whether this equality was to be produced by raising the rates on American vessels, or depressing those on British vessels. It will be found, however, said Mr. G., that the treaty, in this respect, executes itself. We have laws fixing the rate of tonnage on American vessels, and the duties on importations in them. Other laws prescribe that additional rates and duties shall be imposed in the case of foreign vessels. A treaty is then made with Great Britain prescribing that her vessels shall be subject to the same rates and duties as are levied on American ships. As this treaty is a law of the land, it should be construed precisely as any other law. Suppose the stipulations were contained in an act of Congress, then, upon the principle that the subsequent acts repeal so much of the prior acts as is inconsistent with them, the effect assuredly is to except British ships from the operation of the laws affecting foreign vessels generally. Whatever your duties may be in regard to American bottoms, the same duties are, by the treaty, made to apply to British ships.

Mr. G. said that these observations were designed to prove, and, in his judgment, did prove, that the bill was unnecessary. This, however, was but introductory to the position which he had advanced, that the bill was of a dangerous and injurious character. In a Government of laws, it was always to be desired that those who were called on to obey, and those who were appointed to expound the national will, should not be perplexed and embarrassed by superfluous regulations. But there were prominent and especial evils following from an unnecessary legislation in regard to treaties. The power of making them, said Mr. G., is, by the Constitution, vested in the President, calling to his aid the counsel of the Senate. If this power be so exercised that the treaty can execute itself, what is the effect of an unnecessary law enacted for its execution? To the thoughtless and superficial it might seem merely an encroachment upon the prerogative of the Executive, and this might not be deemed an evil very much to be dreaded by the friends of political freedom. But, in fact, it is not a diminution of the power of the Executive; it is a diminution only of his responsibility. The law confers no additional validity on the treaty; it is altogether inoperative, except as an implied sanction of the terms of the treaty. The President is answerable for making a bad compact; but, under the form and pretence of enlarging legislative power, a shield is to be interposed between him and the public censure.

Besides, if the precedent be established that a treaty must be legislated into validity, an obligation is imposed upon the Legislature, and every branch of it, to make the provisions of the law conform strictly to the stipulations of the treaty. In other words, the Legislature must expound the treaty. It is easy to point out some striking absurdities which would result from this doctrine, though it is difficult to imagine all that will arise from it. Let us suppose a complex treaty, in the exposition of parts of which there is an honest and important difference of opinion between the two branches of the Legislature. What is to be done? Ordinary difference of opinion which cannot be removed, and where co-operation is necessary, may be adjusted by compromise. But on this subject compromise is impracticable. The sacrifices required to be mutually made are not of opinion on a question of expediency, but of conscience on a matter of right. Each is bound by the highest of obligations to expound the treaty according to the design of its framers. If, in this exposition, they cannot agree, the treaty cannot be expounded, the legislative sanction cannot be given, and the plighted faith of the nation must be broken.

Again, it must be admitted, for the Constitution is, on this particular, clear and imperative, that the judicial power shall apply to all cases arising under a treaty, and of necessity in its application to such cases must expound the treaty. How is this judicial power to be exercised when the courts who are invested with it shall not agree to the correctness of your exposition? Are they to be bound by your exposition? If so, then their power is not applied to cases as they arise under the treaty, but as they arise under your statute. If they are not bound by your exposition, then your act, instead of vivifying the treaty, is itself a dead letter. If they sacrifice their consciences to adopt your construction, they do not exercise judicial power on the treaty; if they do not make this sacrifice, but exercise the judicial power which the Constitution gives them, then you have a law, and a Constitutional law, which your own tribunals have a Constitutional right to disregard.

But one would suppose that a stronger argument to prove the danger of this legislative enactment of a treaty could not be afforded, than is to be found by attending to the course which has been pursued on this bill. Not to dwell upon the singular absurdity of one of the amendments which it has been thought necessary to incorporate into it; an amendment which declares this bill a law twenty days before it is or can become a law under the Constitution, the House is perplexed in discussing the meaning of various passages in the treaty admitted to be ambiguous, and for the correct interpretation of them is referred by the chairman of the Committee of Foreign Relations—to what? To information officially laid before it? To authentic documents in its possession? No; the House is referred to a correspondence between the negotiators of the two nations, which the gentleman (Mr. FORSYTH) tells us has been laid before the Senate; and a part of which he reads from a paper printed (as he also informs us) for the use of the Senate. For what purpose was this correspondence laid before the Senate? Assuredly it must have been to aid them in understanding the treaty before they should give advice as to its ratification. But the House of Representatives, although bound to aid in legislating the treaty into operation, and in framing a law which shall conform to its precise meaning; and though greatly embarrassed to divine his meaning in consequence of the vagueness of the treaty, is left to act without the benefit of this necessary information, except it be of such fragments as may be doled out by the bounty of the Senate, or picked up by the industry or good fortune of its members. If this House have to expound the treaty, it is entitled to the possession of every document which can throw light upon its meaning. It cannot be called on to act, and be denied the means to act with intelligence. These means, there is but one authentic and Constitutional mode of laying before us. They must be officially communicated, or the House, in respecting them, will show a want of respect for itself.

Mr. G. concluded, by remarking that if the House should concur with him in the opinion that the convention was complete in itself, and needed no legislative aid to carry it into effect, they ought to be exceedingly cautious in setting a precedent which was calculated to mislead and embarrass. Although no immediate injury might result from the act in this case, other than the delay and the difficulty of getting at the meaning of this treaty, yet immense inconveniences might flow from following such a precedent, in cases of more complexity. As the bill was a departure from the established usage of the Government—unnecessary, and likely as a precedent to be productive of mischief hereafter—he believed the wise and safe course was to decline acting further upon it.

Mr. WRIGHT said, he hoped and trusted the amendment proposed to this bill would not be adopted. The bill had for its object, he said, the establishment of an uniformity of the impost and tonnage, as well as of the drawbacks on articles the growth, produce, or manufacture of His Britannic Majesty's territories in Europe, imported into any of the ports of the United States. The amendment proposes to limit the importations by adding, " directly from the territories aforesaid." The treaty, in its terms, may include the indirect as well as the direct trade, and has been ratified by the President, by and with the advice and consent of the Senate, and has become the supreme law of the land. This treaty is a compact between Great Britain and the United States. The British Parliament has no power but to pass laws to carry treaties into effect—the King has the sole power of making them; and here the President and Senate have the power of the King, from whence results the impropriety of our attempting, in a law to carry the treaty into effect, any additions to the treaty. We have no diplomatic power. If there is any ambiguity in any article, we, who represent only one of the parties, have no power to bind the other party by any act or construction; that can be effected only by an explanatory article made by the agents of both parties. Sir, in any contestation about the treaty and its true import, this amendment, if adopted, could not be considered as part of the instrument. The treaty is a record, and like all others, can be tried only by itself. I ask, if the Judiciary, in expounding this treaty, were to be of opinion that it included the indirect as well as the direct trade, what would be the operation of the proposed amendment, if adopted? It certainly would be considered as the act of but one party, as having no operation in the case, a work therefore, of supererogation.

Mr. GASTON having moved to postpone the further consideration of the bill indefinitely—

The bill was, on motion by Mr. TUCKER, laid on the table.

LAWS OF THE DISTRICT OF COLUMBIA.

The House resolved itself into a Committee of the Whole, on the bill to authorize a subscription to such laws of the United States as relate exclusively to the District of Columbia.

The bill was zealously supported by Mr. TUCKER, and opposed by Mr. WRIGHT and others.

On motion of Mr. CANNON, the number of copies proposed to be subscribed for (one thousand) was reduced to three hundred.

The bill having been reported to the House, some further discussion took place on it.

On the question of ordering the bill to be read a third time, there were, for the bill 44, against it 64.

So the bill was rejected.

Mr. PICKENS then adverted to the miserable system of jurisprudence, by which this territory was ruled, composed of the laws of Virginia on one side, and Maryland on the other side of the river, as they stood fifteen or twenty years ago, the people of the District being deprived of the advantages of subsequent amendments made by these States; and, after remarking on the inability of Congress to devote time from more

weighty occupations to examine and reform the judicial system of the District, moved, in substance,

" That the Committee on the District of Columbia be instructed to inquire into the expediency of employing a suitable person to prepare a code of jurisprudence for the District of Columbia, to be laid before Congress for their adoption."

Mr. TUCKER moved that the Judiciary Committee be substituted for the District Committee, as well because he desired the aid of other talents on this subject than of the chairman of the District Committee, (meaning himself,) as because that committee had already as much business before them as they would be able to despatch, especially if they met with no better encouragement from the House than had attended his exertions this day.

Mr. TUCKER's motion to amend was agreed to by a small majority; and, thus amended, the motion of Mr. PICKENS was agreed to.

MONDAY, January 8.

Several other members, to wit: from Maryland, WILLIAM PINKNEY; from Virginia, JOHN RANDOLPH; and from Tennessee, WILLIAM G. BLOUNT, appeared, produced their credentials, were qualified, and took their seats.

Mr. HULBERT presented a petition of the proprietors of the Boston Glass Manufactory, praying that such measures may be adopted as will afford to the manufacturers of glass, the security and encouragement necessary to the continuance of their manufactures.

Mr. MILLS presented a petition of the manufacturers of cotton and woollen cloth, in the counties of Hampshire, Franklin, and Hampden, in the State of Massachusetts, praying that the duties at present imposed on all cotton and woollen fabrics imported from foreign countries may be increased; that the importation of cotton goods from places beyond the Cape of Good Hope may be prohibited; that American cotton and woollen fabrics may be exclusively used for the Army and Navy; that the existing duty on foreign indigo and olive oil may be repealed; and that a National Bank may be established.

Mr. LAW presented a similar petition from sundry manufacturers of cotton goods in the State of Connecticut.

Mr. JOHNSON, of Kentucky, presented a petition of the Lexington White Lead Manufacturing Company, praying that a duty of six cents per pound may be imposed on white lead imported from foreign countries.

Ordered, That the said petitions be referred to the Committee of Commerce and Manufactures.

Mr. WENDOVER presented a petition of the manufacturers of tobacco, in the city of New York, praying that the act laying duties on manufactured tobacco may be repealed, and that the bonds which they have entered into may be returned to them.

Mr. KING, of North Carolina, presented a petition of Thomas Cowan, and others, manufacturers of salt on the seacoast of North Carolina, praying that the direct tax imposed upon their establishments may be remitted, as their works have been destroyed by high water, and that the duty on a quantity of salt which was also destroyed, may be also remitted.—Referred to the Committee of Ways and Means.

Mr. MURFREE presented a resolution of the Legislature of the State of North Carolina, requesting the Senators and Representatives in Congress, from that State, to use their best endeavours to prevail on the General Government to open a direct outlet to the ocean for the waters of the Albemarle Sound.—Referred to the Committee on Roads and Canals.

On motion of Mr. GOLDSBOROUGH, the Committee on the Post Office and Post Roads was instructed to inquire into the expediency of repealing the 4th and 6th sections of an act passed at the last session of Congress, entitled "An act in addition to the act regulating the Post Office establishment," or of exempting from the operation of the said sections, vessels whose business is confined to the bays and rivers of the United States and the Territories thereof, and are not employed in the carriage of the mail.

COMMERCE WITH GREAT BRITAIN.

The House resumed the consideration of the bill to regulate the commerce of the United States, according to the Convention of Commerce with Great Britain—the question being on the motion of Mr. GASTON to postpone the bill indefinitely.

Mr. FORSYTH said that the motion for an indefinite postponement of the bill, made by the gentleman from North Carolina, (Mr. GASTON,) rested upon the ground that it was not necessary to legislate upon the subject of the convention. Mr. F. presumed that it was not the intention of gentlemen to enter into the investigation of the extent of the treaty-making power, or of the nature of the obligation imposed by a treaty when made. He could not suppose it was intended to rake up the ashes of the dispute on that question in the year 1796. The Constitutional principle had been settled so far as it depended upon the Representatives of the people at that period on the first treaty with a foreign Government which had been concluded after the adoption of the Constitution. By referring to the journals of the proceedings of Congress, it would be found, that the principle established was, "that when a treaty stipulates regulations 'on any of the subjects submitted by the Consti' tution to the power of Congress, it must depend ' for its execution, as to such stipulations, on a law ' or laws, to be passed by Congress." The recollection of the gentleman from North Carolina was, therefore, not faithful, when he supposed the doctrine of that day confined the power of Congress, in the execution of treaties, to cases of appropriation only. The rule was general, and applied to all cases, without distinction, over which power was specially given by the Constitution to the legislative department. This general rule, since that period, has been uniformly

and consistently observed. In the execution of the British Treaty, no law was passed at the period of the memorable dispute already alluded to, but one appropriating money; but the cause might be discovered by referring to the treaty itself. None of its provisions were inconsistent with the existing laws. Subsequently, however, it was found necessary to provide by law for the faithful execution of the 19th article. By this article it was stipulated, that when one party was a belligerent, and the other a neutral Power, to prevent injury to the property, &c., of the neutral upon the ocean, from the improper conduct of the captains and crews of private armed vessels, the owner and master should give bond and security in the sum of fifteen hundred or three thousand pounds, according to the size of the vessel and the number of her crew, to answer for the injuries which might be sustained by such misconduct. When the *quasi* war was authorized against France, the President was empowered to grant commissions to private armed vessels; the stipulation of the treaty was embodied in the act of Congress. The same provision was made in nearly the same words, in the war against Tripoli. The conduct of the Government had been regulated by the same rule in their legislative acts to carry into effect the treaty with Spain. An appropriation law was passed to pay the necessary expenses. This was all that was then deemed necessary. But the 10th article of the treaty intended to provide for the case of vessels of either nation, forced by distress into the ports of the other. The condition of the treaty was dictated both by policy and humanity. It was, that the goods thus forced under the protection of either of the contracting parties should, if landed, be reloaded and carried away, without the payment of the customary duty either on the vessel or cargo. No act was passed until the case actually occurred. Sometime during or before the year 1804, the Spanish brigantine Nancy came into Norfolk in distress. In order to give to her owners the benefit of the treaty stipulation, it was deemed necessary to pass an act remitting the duties in that particular instance, and providing that they should not be payable in similar instances in future. The treaty with France in 1801 had been alluded to by the gentleman from North Carolina, (Mr. GASTON.) By referring to the appropriation act, passed in consequence of the ratification of that treaty, it will be found to contain a declaration of the obligation to return vessels captured during the war, according to the condition of the convention. Mr. F. presumed that this was supposed a sufficient authority for the delivery of the Berceau by the President, in performance of the conditions of the treaty. The statute book was full of examples, but none were more decisive than those founded upon the cession of Louisiana to the United States by France in 1803. Although France ceded it to the United States, and of course governed by their laws, so far as they were applicable to its situation, at that time it was deemed most expedient to pass an act to lay and collect duties on imports and tonnage within the said territory. In this act provision was made to secure to French and Spanish ships the commercial advantages which were promised as one of the conditions of the cession. But this was not all: In the year 1800, an act was passed, allowing drawback of duties on goods exported from the United States to New Orleans, being a foreign port. Although the reason of this act had ceased, and it might have been considered repealed by the transfer of this port to the United States, it was supposed necessary to repeal the act by an act of Congress, passed in 1803.

Louisiana, too, was admitted into the Union, not by treaty stipulation, but by an act of Congress, in performance of the obligation imposed by it.

Mr. F. said that no difference was made by the Constitution between treaties with foreign Powers, and treaties made with the Indians within the territorial limits of the United States. The rule had been extended to them. Without enumerating the particular cases, he could refer to an arrangement which had been made with all the Indian tribes with whom we had entered into compacts—that crimes committed by whites upon Indians, within the Indian territory, should be punished in the same manner as if the same offence had been committed upon a citizen of the United States, within the jurisdiction of some district of the United States. This engagement had been complied with, so far as it could be complied with, by the Government. Prosecutions had been instituted against those who had been accused of such offences. Mr. F. did not remember of any punishments; but this was not the fault of the Government. These prosecutions were, however, commenced, not upon the treaty, but upon the law, made in consequence of the treaty engagement. These remarks, Mr. F. trusted, would satisfy the House, that the course proposed to be pursued, in relation to the late convention with Great Britain, was perfectly in unison with the practice in all former cases, and justified by the rule upon which that practice had been founded. The only difference between the present and former cases was, that in this case the convention stipulates advantages to British vessels, which cannot be enjoyed without an alteration of the system of revenue, and repeal of existing laws. Some gentlemen had imagined that the law of the last session, on the subject of discriminating duties, contained all the necessary provisions to meet this contract between the two countries. This was a mistaken opinion. The law of the last session repealed our discriminating duties on tonnage, &c., of foreign vessels, and on goods imported in foreign vessels, upon a condition which has not happened, that is: that an abolition of *all* the discriminating duties, so far as they were injurious to the commerce of the United States, should have taken place in that foreign nation to which the vessels and goods should belong. The treaty between this country and Great Britain stipulates an abolition of discriminating duties *only* in the ports of His Britannic Majesty's European dominions. Mr. F. said it was somewhat extraordinary that it should be doubted in this country whether the House of Representatives were authorized to act upon a subject which, in England, would have required the interposition of the House of Commons. He did not intend to draw any argument from the resemblance of the two Governments; the Executive power, including its authority to make treaties, was more limited than in Great Britain. Yet in Great Britain, this very treaty will require an act of Parliament before it can be carried completely into effect; an act which some of us will live long enough to see. This was the ordinary course in that country. At some of the most remarkable periods in British history, instances had occurred. A commercial treaty was negotiated between France and England, after the peace of Utrecht; it was not carried into effect, because the House of Commons rejected the bill introduced by the Ministry to alter the commercial and revenue laws according to the compact between the two nations. In the year 1786, a treaty of commerce between those nations, was carried into effect by an act of Parliament, framed according to its stipulations. Mr. F. said, that the Order in Council of the 17th August, 1815, which he had taken occasion to read to the House a day or two before, was founded upon an act of Parliament, passed, as he had understood, for the express purpose of enabling the Prince Regent to conform the existing regulations of commerce to the treaty which might be made by the Ministers of the United States and Great Britain, and in the discussion of the principles of which they were then engaged. The Order in Council, like the act upon which it was founded, was to continue in force until six weeks after the next session of Parliament. Within these six weeks after the meeting of Parliament, the necessary provision will, no doubt, be made by the competent authority in the ordinary mode.

The gentleman from North Carolina (Mr. Gaston) had advanced a singular opinion, that by exercising the power of passing laws to give effect to treaties, you diminish the responsibility without diminishing the power of the President and Senate. Mr. F. could not conceive how a check upon the exercise of any authority could diminish the responsibility of the person to whom it was granted. It was certainly true, when Congress passed acts according to the provision of a treaty, they declared to the people, it was better to perform the stipulations it contained, than to violate the faith of the nation, which had been pledged by the Constitutional authority. But if Congress, from a conviction that the rights of the people had been wantonly surrendered or the national honor tarnished by treaty, should refuse to pass the laws necessary for its execution, the President and Senate would feel, what they can feel in no other way, the responsibility under which their power is exercised.

It had been said, that treaties are the law of the land. It is so printed in the margin of the

477　　　　　　HISTORY OF CONGRESS.　　　　　　478

JANUARY, 1816.　　　　Commerce with Great Britain.　　　　H. OF R.

article of the Constitution to which the gentleman (Mr. GASTON) had referred, and it seemed to be taken for granted, that law and treaty were convertible terms. If this idea is correct, the distinction taken between acts of appropriation to pay the expenses of treaties, and other legislative acts to carry them into effect, is unnecessary. The Constitution says, that money shall not be drawn out of the Treasury unless appropriations are previously made by law. But a treaty being a law, an appropriation may be made by treaty. But, Mr. F. said, the object of that part of the Constitution was, to declare the supremacy of the Constitution, acts made in pursuance thereof, and treaties made or to be made under the authority of the United States, over the constitutions and laws of the States. The relative force or effects of treaties and laws was to be collected from the whole charter; from the nature and dependence of its parts—from the objects over which treaties and laws severally operated—and from the intention of the people by whom the power of making them were granted, and for whose benefit they are to be exercised. But, Mr. F. said, the examination of these topics would require him to enter further into the Constitutional question than he wished or intended to go. For the present he would content himself with the expression of the general proposition upon the basis of which the bill had been reported. Whenever a treaty contains anything contrary to the Constitution, it is void; whenever it contains anything contrary to existing laws, the laws must be repealed by Congress before the engagement can be complied with; because the Constitution can be altered only by the Constitional mode of amendment. A law can be repealed only by the authority which enacted it.

Mr. F. said, although the question respecting the propriety of the amendments made in Committee of the whole House, was superseded by the motion of indefinite postponement, he hoped to be indulged with a few observations in reply to some suggestions of the gentleman from Louisiana, (Mr. ROBERTSON;) from Virginia, (Mr. TUCKER;) and from North Carolina, (Mr. GASTON.) He was not conscious of having committed any impropriety in referring to documents printed by order of the Senate. He did not suppose information was less valuable in one form than in another. He had not taken his construction of the treaty from the correspondence he had quoted, but from the instrument itself, and he could not see the irrationality or irregularity of referring to such documents for the confirmation of an opinion previously formed. From the gentleman from North Carolina (Mr. GASTON) he certainly did not expect observations of the character which had dropped from him, as he had been informed that they agreed in opinion, upon the construction of that article of the convention which had been the source of discussion.

Mr. F. said, he was not induced to offer the amendments to the Committee, by a belief that such a construction was advantageous to the United States, but simply because he believed it to

have been the intention of the parties. If the calculation of advantages was to govern the construction, the amendments ought not to prevail. It had been suggested by the gentlemen from Virginia and Louisiana, that vessels of the United States, bound to France and Spain, might reach the port of destination, and finding a bad market might choose to go to England in search of a better. Gentlemen asked if such vessels were to be deprived of the benefits of this treaty. Mr. F. said, he was not able to speak with precision and certainty on this subject, but, according to his present impressions, he believed that a vessel under such circumstances would be considered as engaged in the trade between France or Spain and Great Britain, and not in the trade between the United States and Great Britain. Mr. F. apologized for this digression from the question, and concluded by reserving to himself the privilege of entering more fully into the examination of the treaty-making power, if it should be made necessary by the discussion, which had been so unprofitably and unnecessarily commenced.

Mr. BARBOUR said, the bill now before the House proposed to regulate the commerce between the United States and Great Britain, according to the convention concluded on 3d July, 1815; a motion had been made for its indefinite postponement; and the reason assigned for that motion was, that the convention itself was conclusive upon the subject, without the aid of any legislative act.

The question then, said he, which this motion presents, is, whether legislation upon the subject, be or be not an act of supererogation; it will be my endeavor to prove that it is not; in other words, I shall attempt to maintain this proposition, that whenever a treaty operates upon a subject, which, like the present, is amongst the enumerated powers of legislation, delegated by the Constitution to Congress—that in such case, the assent and co-operation of Congress are necessary to give effect to such treaty, by the passage of a law, in compliance with its stipulations.

The correctness of this proposition depends upon the proper construction of the Constitution of the United States, in relation to the legislative and treaty-making powers. It is from this source mainly, that both the opposers and the advocates of this bill attempt to derive support.

If I understand the argument of its opposers, it amounts in substance, to this—the Constitution, say they, gives to the President and Senate the right of making treaties, provided two-thirds of the Senators present concur; and it declares, that treaties when thus made shall be the supreme law of the land. Now this treaty has been ratified in the mode prescribed; it is therefore the supreme law of the land, and what is already the supreme law, can derive no additional validity from any other law.

But, sir, in what does this supremacy consist? Is it in a superiority over the Constitution and laws of the United States? The Constitution itself answers to this question, that it is not; for it will be seen that the same clause which declares treaties the supreme law of the land, associates with them the Constitution and laws of the United States; it throws the three into one class, and declares that the whole class, to wit: the Constitution of the United States, the laws of the United States, and treaties made under their authority, shall be the supreme law of the land—supreme over what? The next paragraph answers the question, by declaring, that the judges of every State shall be bound thereby, anything in the constitution or law of any State to the contrary, notwithstanding. It is obvious, that the supremacy is a term of relation to the States; the United States, and its Constitution, laws and treaties, are put in competition with the States and their constitutions and laws; and as it respects the latter, the former are declared to be supreme; but there is no graduation of superiority between the Constitution, laws, and treaties of the United States as amongst themselves. This doctrine of supremacy, then, has no influence upon the present question.

But gentlemen who oppose the bill, contend, that the power of making treaties is given in general terms; there is no exception of the subject-matter of this treaty, therefore it is included; and consequently, that the treaty-making power is competent, of itself, to give complete effect to treaty stipulations upon the subject of commerce, without legislative aid.

If there were no other part of the Constitution which had a bearing upon this question, there would be more solidity in the argument; but there are other important provisions of the Constitution, which have direct relation to the question; and it is indispensable to a just construction of that instrument that, they be taken together. Sir, this is the universal rule for the construction of all instruments, that, to arrive at a just interpretation of their meaning, you must not take isolated parts, but the whole instrument together.

The propriety of this rule of construction, so reasonable in itself, will be proven, I think, beyond question, by the comparison which I am about to make between that part of the Constitution which confers the treaty-making power, and those parts of the same instrument which relate to the legislative power; from this comparison, it seems to me necessarily to result—that the grant of legislative power, *quo ad* the subject granted, must operate some limitation, some check upon the treaty-making power; or otherwise, the partition between the different branches of the Government will be broken down; the whole character of the Government will be essentially changed; and the treaty-making power, like Aaron's serpent, will swallow up the rest. Having made these general remarks, in relation to the limitations and checks upon the treaty-making power, I will now beg leave to apply them to the immediate bill before us.

The Constitution declares, that all legislative power herein granted shall be vested in Congress; but Congress have heretofore passed laws regulating the commerce between the United States and Great Britain. The treaty stipulates an alteration, a repeal of those regulations; now if the treaty be construed to be conclusive upon the subject, without any act on the part of Congress, must it not be seen, that here is at once legislative power exercised by a branch of the Government other than Congress? This proposition cannot be denied, unless it be contended that the repeal of a law is not an act of legislation; I apprehend it cannot be necessary to prove this proposition. But let us apply this doctrine more closely to the question before us. The Constitution, after depositing with Congress the Legislative power therein granted, proceeds to define that power; among other parts of the enumeration is this: " Congress shall have power to regulate commerce with foreign nations." Now, sir, this bill, both in its provisions and its title, professes to regulate, and does regulate the commerce between the United States and Great Britain. Here, then, is a power expressly given to Congress; and yet, according to the doctrine now contended for, it may be exercised by the President and two-thirds of the Senators who may be present, without the aid of Congress. Mark the difference. Congress is composed of a Senate and House of Representatives; the treaty-making power of the President and two-thirds of the Senators present; take from Congress the regulation of commerce and give it to the treaty-making power, and you entirely exclude from that important power all that branch of the Government which represents the people directly. Can this construction be correct? If it be, it must be upon the principle, that one part of the Constitution alone is to be consulted, whilst other parts of the same instrument are to be disregarded; for, take them together, and if there be any meaning in words, it is, that as to commerce, Congress shall have power to regulate it; which cannot be, if another branch of Government have power to change that regulation, without consulting or needing the co-operation of that body.

See, sir, to what consequences this doctrine will lead; if the treaty-making power may regulate commerce without the sanction of Congress, then the same Power may declare war without the sanction of Congress; because the very same Constitution which gives Congress the one power gives them the other; and if they may be deprived of one, by parity of reason, they may be deprived of the other. And yet, sir, I believe no gentleman has met this part of the argument by affirming that the nation can be involved in war by treaty; they have seen that such a doctrine would carry them too far; that it would go to the extent of justifying a treaty of alliance offensive and defensive, which might involve us in all the calamities of war, by entangling us in European contests; when it is distinctly understood to have been the intention of the Constitution, that this nation should never be involved in war, but by the voice of the immediate Representatives of the people: this is the great, the safe guarantee, that war will never be undertaken but for some great national object, when, and when only, the people will go with their Representatives. But this doctrine, if true, does not stop here; it goes further, it will justify a treaty stipulation to supply a subsidy, and will thus violate that part of the Constitution which declares that no money shall be drawn from the Treasury, but by an appropriation made by law. Sir, it goes one step further yet; it would justify the subsidy of which I have just spoken, without limitation as to time, though the Constitution expressly declares, that even Congress shall not make an appropriation for the support of armies for more than two years.

Now, sir, the criterion by which to test a position is, to trace it to its consequences; if it leads directly to such, as even its author cannot defend, there is no principle in logic clearer than that such a position, though it may be specious, is not solid. I am persuaded that no member will go the length of maintaining the position, which I have been examining, in the consequences to which I have pursued it; by this rule, then, they must give up the position itself.

It seems to me to be shown, then, that although the grant of the treaty-making power, is in words not limited in themselves, yet, a just construction of the Constitution affixes to it these two kinds of limitation; first, that nothing can be done by treaty, which the Constitution declares shall not be done; secondly, that whenever the subject of a treaty is one of the powers delegated to Congress, that then the assent and co-operation of Congress are necessary to give it effect, by passing a law in conformity with its stipulations. And this, sir, is the doctrine for which I contend, whilst as a member of the House of Representatives I disclaim all participation in the negotiating and making a treaty.

The member from Georgia has shown, by a minute research into the practice of the Government, that it accords with the construction for which I have contended; I rely upon this, as a strong additional proof of the propriety of that construction.

A reference has been made in the course of the argument to the practice under the British constitution. I know, sir, that this constitution is in itself but a succession of precedents; I know that there are many predominant differences between the British and American constitutions; but there are also some points of analogy: and perhaps few stronger than that in the treaty-making power; in each country, it is confided to the Chief Executive Magistrate, with this difference, that in the United States the Senate are associated with the President. Notwithstanding, however, the treaty-making power in Great Britain resides in the King, yet it appears from the various instances cited by the member from Georgia, to which I will add the Treaty of Peace of 1783, between that country and the United States, that even in Great Britain, the treaty-making power is so far limited as to make it necessary to lay treaties before Parliament, and to ask their aid in making appropriations for carrying them into execution; but if this results in Great Britain, from the power which the House of Commons, without any writ-

14th CON. 1st SESS.—16

ten constitution, have claimed and established, of holding the purse of the nation, the argument certainly applies with increased force here, where, by the express provision of a written constitution, the subject upon which this treaty operates is amongst the powers delegated to Congress.

I will now beg leave to answer one argument, which seems to be so much relied on, on the other side, as to be considered in itself almost decisive of the question in their favor. It is said, that we have conceded, that the President, with the consent of the Senate, may, without that of Congress, make a Treaty of Peace, and that this is in effect giving up the argument; because, as it requires a law of Congress to declare war, and a Treaty of Peace, upon our own concession, may terminate that war, here is at once an example of a treaty repealing a law. The answer, sir, is this: the Constitution gives to Congress the power to declare war, but it does not give them the power to make peace; it would have been idle to have given such a power. To put this idea in a strong light, let us see what would be the language of a law, enacting peace. Be it enacted, &c., that there shall be peace between the United States and Great Britain. But the enemy, I will suppose, does not choose to be at peace, notwithstanding our law; therefore, the war would continue. It is thus out of our power alone to make peace; but, it is not out of our power to regulate commerce; it is true, that we could not regulate it in British ports; but we could regulate it in our own ports, both as to American and British vessels without their consent. The difference then between a Treaty of Peace and a Treaty of Commerce, is this: the one touches a subject which can only be operated on by treaty; the other embraces a subject which may be regulated without treaty.

This question, sir, occurred in the discussion upon the British treaty, in 1795; it was then very ably discussed; I have no doubt that, in the ideas I have thrown out, I have glided into some of those urged on that occasion; my apology is, that, upon the recurrence of the same question, it is impossible not to fall in some degree into the same train of argument. I conclude, by expressing my hope that the motion for indefinite postponement will not prevail.

Mr. GOLD commenced, with congratulating the House upon the favorable auspices under which the highly important Constitutional question, involved in the passage of the bill under consideration, was presented for determination. The angry passions of war had subsided; party feelings in a great degree hushed to silence, and the public mind in a state of tranquillity, propitious to fair inquiry. He added, the question is not embarrassed with any difficulty or diversity of opinion on the point, whether the treaty is to be carried into effect, for as to that all concurred, and hence, the mere principle, under the Constitution, is presented to the judgment of the House. But, although the treaty in question is not to be affected by this determination, a more important question, in its effect upon the foreign relations of the

United States, upon the peace of the country, upon the character of the Government, has hardly arisen under the Constitution. Mr. G. asked, what is the object of the bill? what the evil to be remedied? A mere direction to the custom-house to conform the impost on British tonnage to the rate on American vessels and cargoes. Such is the object, an object which may be attained by the provision of a single paragraph of three lines; and yet, sir, what is the form of the bill before the House for this purpose? It contains all the provisions of the treaty, embodied in the form of an act of Congress. Is it possible to mistake the object of the bill in this form, a form so much broader than the professed end to be attained, than the evil to be remedied? Is it not seen that the bill submits to the House the whole terms, the entire merits of the treaty, and necessarily imposes on the House a consideration of the whole scope and merits of the instrument, the whole field of the negotiation, in the same manner as if it were a common subject of legislation? For this it is confidently submitted, that no precedent will be found either in the memorable treaty with the same nation, negotiated by Mr. Jay, or in any other act in the history of the Government. If an appropriation be required to carry into effect a treaty; if a direction to the custom-house be intended, why not give it, and there stay your hand? Do not embody the treaty in an act of Congress for a solemn precedent, bearing to the world the conclusion that it is not the treaty, but an act of Congress, that creates the law with foreign nations, and fixes the measure of obedience. It cannot be mistaken, he repeated, that the bill, in the form adopted, submits to this House, for its judgment, the merits of the treaty; to approve or disapprove, to give or withhold assent, upon the exercise of legislative discretion, as on ordinary acts of Congress, to the treaty's going into effect. Certainly, the authors of this bill do not present it to Congress, sitting as a Parliament of Paris, to act an humble ministerial part, to become a mere instrument of registry. No, sir, such an appeal would degrade the body, would destroy its attributes, and reduce it from the elevated station assigned it by the Constitution. The positions of the honorable member from Georgia, (Mr. Forsyth,) who reported and here defends the bill, the authorities he cites in his support, all go to show that the treaty is submitted, by the bill, to the discretion of Congress. That honorable gentleman cites, for authority, examples in the British Parliament, of treaties being defeated, by the refusal of the Commons to concur in the requisite acts to carry them into effect, founded on the ground of disapprobation of the merits of the treaty. Mr. G. added, that he deprecated the influence of such examples upon the proceedings of a Government founded on a written Constitution, of distinct departments and divided powers, and he should be wanting to his duty, if he did not enter his solemn protest against the doctrine thus pressed upon the House. For what, sir, is to be the consequence, but a submission of the treaty-making power, and uproot-

ing the first principles of the Constitution? The measure may not, from the uninteresting provisions of the treaty and general acquiescence, produce immediate evil, and for that cause does not awaken alarm; but the precedent, in other times and under different circumstances, cannot fail to produce consequences most pernicious to the peace and welfare of the United States. Who does not discern the signs of the times? who is so indifferent to what is passing before his eyes, as not to see which are the weaker departments of the Government, and from which encroachments are to be apprehended?

"Treaties shall be the supreme law of the land," is the language of the Constitution. This language is strong and emphatic; and how it is to be satisfied by the construction or rule of the advocates of the bill, has not been shown. On the very face of this measure, we perceive that the treaty can only become a law when united and combined with an act of Congress.

It has been denied, that the Constitution makes a treaty, standing disjunctively and alone, the law of the land, because the sentence includes with treaties the Constitution and acts of Congress. The terms are, "this Constitution, and the laws ' of the United States, which shall be made in ' pursuance thereof; and all treaties made, or ' which shall be made, under the authority of the ' United States, shall be the supreme law of the ' land;" adding, what resulted necessarily from the provision, that State judges should be bound thereby. This provision presents three distinct and independent sources of law—the Constitution, acts of Congress, and treaties—each standing on its own Constitutional ground, single and alone, unaided by the other; a treaty requiring no more the aid of an act of Congress to its validity, than an act of Congress does that of a treaty. If in any case, certainly not the present, an act of Congress be required in execution of a treaty, not to its validity, the duty is imperative on Congress as much as it is the duty of the Judiciary department to hear and give judgment on an act, and of the Executive to cause the sentence to be executed.

It has been said by an honorable gentleman from Virginia, (Mr. Barbour,) that the operation of the above provision is on the constitutions and laws of the separate States, in making a treaty a law in relation to them, but not so as to the legislative power of Congress. I can perceive nothing in the Constitution to justify this partial and strange construction, and it is not a little difficult to conceive how a treaty can become a law in one place and not another; how it can bind the States severally as a law, and not the United States. The same honorable gentleman attempted to sustain the authority of Congress to interfere with commercial treaties, on the provision in the Constitution which gives to Congress the general power to regulate commerce, insisting that this power could not be infringed or impaired by the treaty-making power.

If this be the Constitution, we are poor, indeed, in the authority of the President and Senate, in the treaty department; for commerce is the great field in the foreign relations of the Government; and at no remote period it may well be imagined, that that field will be so occupied by legislative regulations, as to leave little, very little, for a commercial treaty to operate upon. But, as the rule was applied by the honorable gentleman, the legislative power may supersede the stipulations of a subsisting treaty on the subject, under the power of regulating commerce, because it is a Constitutional power, and not subject to treaty stipulations; and although an act confirmatory of the treaty may have been passed, the same body, in the exercise of this unalienable power of the Constitution, may repeal it.

In the application of this principle, the honorable member insists that an act of Congress is necessary to reduce the impost on British tonnage to that of American tonnage, conformably to the treaty; that an act cannot be abrogated or annulled, without a repealing act for the purpose. If this be so, what has become of the most important act this Government ever passed—the act declaring war against Great Britain, passed in June, 1812? Is it yet in force for want of a statute repeal, or did it not fall under the operation of the treaty-making power? The case leaves no escape; the power to declare war is exclusively in Congress; the act for that purpose most eventful, and its abrogation by the treaty without question.

Is it, then, any longer to be doubted, but that the treaty in question is competent to modify the tonnage duty on British shipping? If it be not, Mr. G. said, he looked in vain for any operation or effect of the treaty power; the very provision is subverted, and the terms, "supreme law of the land," a dead letter. For, Mr. Speaker, the very definition of "law," as "a rule of action," as assigning to each and every member of the community his duty, cannot, in its necessary application under the treaty, fail to reach and fix the duty of the custom-house officer on the point in question. If it fall short of this, the provisions of the treaty are no more than propositions or projects for Congress to adopt or reject, at discretion.

Mr. HOPKINSON said, that not anticipating that this bill, which was laid upon the table but yesterday, would so soon be called up for discussion, he had not given that reflection to it, which was necessary for an argument on its principles. Such thoughts and suggestions, however, as had occurred to him on the moment, he would offer to the House with all possible brevity, and a sincere wish that he had been able to give more consideration to their matter, and a better shape to their manner. The gentlemen who press the passage of this bill, said he, seem to take a range of observation far wider than the subject, and to travel over ground not necessary now to be explored. The subject itself offers matter enough for consideration, and of sufficient importance too to deserve the undivided attention of the House. Their ingenuity has been exerted, and their imagination put into action, to create and combine

cases of supposed treaties, which would require the aid of the House to carry them into effect, and which must be submitted to its power and control. That cases may occur, and surely that cases may be imagined, in which this House might find itself exceedingly embarrassed by a treaty made by the President and Senate, cannot be denied; but is the case now before us of that description? Does anybody feel the least reluctance to have the convention go into operation? Does anybody say its provisions are of a kind to require any aid from us to carry them into execution, as where money is required, or some collateral assistance, before the treaty can be consummated by 'performance? Why, then, shall we fret and embarrass ourselves with possible cases of difficulty, when we are called upon only to decide one, in which there is no difficulty? The cases put are all of an extreme kind, from which it is seldom safe to draw an argument. When, however, they shall occur, they will be met by the House with proper firmness and discretion; on a full view of all its rights and duties, as regulated by the Constitution, conscientiously performing the latter, and assuming no more of the former than it is entitled to. But let us leave those cases until they do occur: "Sufficient unto the day is the evil thereof."

The question now before the House is, "Shall this bill be indefinitely postponed?" and I would presume, that if it can be shown that it is utterly unnecessary and useless; that it can produce no sensible effect; that, when passed, it will leave its subject-matter precisely as it found it, there is reason enough shown why it should not be passed. It is surely unbecoming the wisdom and dignity of this body to be gravely enacting nugatory laws; or, as some of the gentlemen have termed this, *harmless* law. The enactment of a law can never be without consequences, for if the law itself means nothing and does nothing as a law, it must injure the reputation of the body enacting it. This brings me then directly to the question, do the gentlemen who insist upon this bill believe that it is, in any manner, necessary to the validity of the convention to which it refers? Does that convention require such a law to give it force and effect? Are we to put the finishing hand to it, without which it is a dead letter? It asks no appropriation of money; it requires no collateral or extrinsic act to be done to enable it to live, and move, and execute its functions. If it be the supreme law of the land, it does of itself all that is necessary for its full consummation; and if it be not the law of the land, what is it? If it be *anything* it is *everything.* This treaty has been made, ratified, and exchanged by the President and Senate, in the manner directed by the Constitution. Are gentlemen willing to say, that, notwithstanding this, it still requires our concurrence or confirmation to give it life and validity. Is it no longer a treaty if we shall refuse our concurrence?—for it is manifest that if our refusal will not destroy it, our concurrence cannot help it. It is one indivisible act, and its consequences are equally indivisible. I have an insuperable objection to following gentlemen in the discussion of points not necessary to the full understanding and fair decision of the matter before us, and which necessarily lead us into heated controversies and angry questions. When the aid of this House, by money or otherwise, is called for, in order to carry into execution the provisions, or some of them, of a treaty, which it shall think injurious to the important interests of the country, and it shall be put to us to say, whether we will grant the required assistance, or meet the consequences of a refusal, the House will doubtless take its course with that sound discretion and deliberate judgment which the high, the awful responsibility of the act will demand. They will endeavor to reconcile their Constitutional obligations with the safety and interests of the State. A case of this appalling shape and magnitude may be trusted, and must be trusted with the consciences of those who may be called upon to decide it. Happily, such is not the case we are now acting upon. I, therefore, confidently bring back the question to the gentlemen, and wait their answer, how and in what manner and degree this convention is to be affected by the adoption or rejection of this bill? What influence will it have upon the validity of a contract thus made and concluded, ratified, and exchanged? That the subject-matter of the treaty is within the treaty-making power, can scarcely be denied. Nothing is affected by it but the rate of duties to be paid by the respective parties in their respective ports—as fair and usual a subject of national contracts, or treaties, as can be imagined. If the President and Senate have not power to make treaties of this kind, their power is a mockery; a name without a substance; an authority with nothing upon which it can ever act or be exercised. It is contended by the gentleman from Georgia, that a treaty which affects existing laws upon a subject within the peculiar power of Congress, cannot be carried into operation without the concurrent act of this House; and therefore, that, inasmuch as the imposing or removing of duties is given by the Constitution expressly to Congress, a treaty cannot change a law regulating duties without the aid or concurrence of Congress in its ordinary mode of legislation. But this proposition is doubtless much too broad, and most general propositions are. What is more clearly, decidedly, and exclusively in the power of Congress than the right of declaring war? This must be done by a law of Congress, and can be done in no other way. Yet this law of Congress, made on a subject thus within its exclusive power, may be repealed, and has been repealed, by a Treaty of Peace made by the President and Senate, in the manner prescribed by the Constitution, without any reference to the will or pleasure of this House, any dependence on its authority, or any concurrence of its laws. The treaty is duly made and ratified—peace follows—the war is terminated—the act of Congress declaring war, and all other acts in relation to it repealed, without the least interference of this House, or its opinion upon the

subject being even asked or attended to. A treaty must be considered, as it really is, a compact or bargain between two parties, which, once made and concluded in the manner both have agreed to be binding, is no longer in the power of either. If, therefore, this convention has received its ratification in the manner and by the authority prescribed by our Constitution or form of Government, it is at this moment a valid and binding bargain between the two nations, and no longer rightfully in the power of either. If this convention has not been so ratified; that is, if it has not been done in the proper manner and by the proper authority, it is neither a treaty nor a contract, nor anything else; and yet we find the President has exchanged it with the other Power, as a thing done and ratified in due form and with competent authority; and we find he has proclaimed it to the American people and to the world, as a treaty made and ratified, and as the law of the land to be hereafter observed and obeyed. Has the President been premature in all this, and exceeded the Constitutional limits of his authority? Let it be remembered, too, that the public promulgation of this convention as a thing done and concluded, as a bargain made and ratified, as the Constitutional law of the land, was the first knowledge or intimation of its nature or contents received by this House. It came to us in the same manner and at the same time it came to every other citizen of the United States. It was communicated to the Senate, together with all the correspondence and documents relating to it, in secret; it was examined, discussed and decided upon in the Senate in secret; the doors of the chamber were closed upon us; we might have knocked, but should have had no admittance. Does this look like an act requiring our confirmation or aid, or on which we are to be required to pass any judgment? Call first upon the President to furnish you with the necessary information; demand of him to send you the correspondence between the Ministers on this subject, which we are now to pass our vote upon. All this he did for the Senate; and if he has overlooked us, let us remind him of it before we proceed any further. But can a treaty annul an act of Congress? Can it repeal a law? Why not? If a treaty be, as the Constitution expressly declares, a law of the land, and a supreme law, is there anything strange or inconsistent in its repealing another and a prior law? But the prior law, say the gentlemen, was passed and enacted by the three branches of the Government; and this treaty has been made but by two. And what of this, if the same authority, the same Constitution, which gives the three branches power to make a law in general cases, gives the two branches power to make it in this case. If the Constitution declares it to be the law, it must have all the effect of law, by whomsoever made. In the nature of things there cannot exist at the same time, under the same authority, two contradictory, inconsistent laws, or rules of action. One or other must give way; both cannot be obeyed; and if, in this case, the treaty has no Constitutional supremacy over an ordinary act of legislation, it at least has the admitted advantage of being earlier in point of time, of being the last Constitutional expression of the will of the nation on this subject. It is worthy of remark, that the general power of legislation is given to Congress in one part of the Constitution; the special power of making treaties to the President and Senate in another part; and then the acts of both, if constitutionally done, are declared, in the same sentence, in another part of the Constitution, to be the supreme law of the land, and placed precisely upon the same footing of authority. I conclude these hasty undigested remarks, with repeating, that if gentlemen believe, and I have not heard it denied, that the convention will go into operation, and is indeed now in operation, without the aid of the law proposed, it is a sufficient reason why the law should not be passed.

The question on postponement was decided in the negative—yeas 60, nays 81.

The question recurred on agreeing to the amendments made in Committee of the Whole, on which a debate took place the other day. The object of the amendments was to except from the equalization of duties all such British vessels as do not come direct from Europe. The amendments were negatived without a division.

Some other amendments were proposed, one of which was agreed to, viz: to strike out the East Indies from the number of exceptions to the operation of the act.

The question then having been stated, "Shall the bill be engrossed for a third reading?"

Mr. GASTON remarked, that perceiving the general wish to come to a conclusion, on this bill, he had abstained from answering many remarks which had been made in opposition to his motion for indefinite postponement. But as the controversy was revived on the question for engrossing the bill, he would avail himself of the opportunity to rescue his opinions from misconception, and defend them against the most important of the arguments by which they had been assailed. In ascribing to the convention the power of repealing so much of the acts of Congress on the subject of discriminating duties as was opposed to its provisions, he was supposed by gentlemen to contend for a supremacy of the power to make treaties over the power to enact laws. Some seem even to have imagined, that he exalted this power of framing treaties over the Constitution itself. His opinions were founded on no such erroneous principle. He regarded acts of Congress formed on subjects within the jurisdiction of Congress, and treaties formed on subjects proper for treaties, as being equally laws of the nation, and he claimed for neither a superiority over the other. The Constitution vests all the legislative powers which it grants in one organ of the national will, the Congress of the United States. It vests the whole of the power of making treaties in another organ of the national will, the President acting with the concurrence of two thirds of the Senate of the United States. It defines what are the legislative powers granted, because such a definition was necessary to distinguish between those delegated to

the General Government and such as were retained by the States. It does not limit the power of making treaties, because no part of this power was to be retained by the States. The entire power therefore on the subject of treaties, which sovereign States, according to the usages and laws of nations, may exercise, unless where it is restricted by specific prohibitions in the Constitution, is vested under this general grant in the proper depository. The Constitution then imparts to proper acts of the legislative authority, and also of the treaty-making power, the character and attributes of "laws," that is, of rules of action prescribed by the sovereign power. They both derive their efficacy from being Constitutional expressions of the will of the nation; and where there are two expressions of that will, which cannot stand together, the last necessarily abrogates the first. A law may repeal a treaty. This was done in the case of the Treaty of 1778, with France, distinctly repealed by an act of Congress. And a treaty for the same reason may also repeal a precedent act of Congress, as must be admitted to be the case of the treaties of peace with Great Britain and the Regency of Algiers, repealing the acts declaring war against those nations.

The idea that, because the legislative power granted to Congress is restricted to certain subjects, therefore the power to make treaties cannot operate on these subjects without legislative aid, seemed to him neither sound logic, nor a construction permitting the treaty power to have any useful effect. Neither a treaty of peace, of alliance, or of commerce, can well be made without affecting some of these subjects. The first usually contains stipulations in regard to captures made or to be made, and indemnities for wrongs suffered. The last must apply directly to the right of regulating commerce with foreign nations; and treaties of alliance specify the aids of men and money to be afforded in the cases prescribed. The power therefore to make treaties, which the Constitution confides exclusively to the President, concurring with two-thirds of the Senate, is essentially annulled by a construction that requires a legislative assent, wherever these treaties operate upon subjects which are the usual well known and legitimate subjects of treaty. For certainly the discretionary power of assenting to or dissenting from any instrument, and thereby giving or refusing it efficacy, is essentially the power to make it. And if this construction obtain, treaties may be said to be prepared by the President and Senate, but they can be made only by Congress.

Mr. G. did not conceive that the opinions he had expressed were liable, when properly understood, to the criticism which had been made by the gentleman from Virginia, (Mr. BARBOUR;) they did not involve the inconsistency of permitting an act of the entire Legislature to be repealed by the will of a part only of that Legislature. The nation, either in the enactment of laws or in the making of treaties, is always the agent. It is the will of the nation which operates in both instances—though the expression of this will is made through distinct organs to which the functions are respectively confided. Perhaps, too, it will be found that there are salutary checks provided against an erroneous expression of this will, in the one case, as in the other. To acts of legislation, the concurrence of the President is not indispensable. Two-thirds of the Senate and House of Representatives can make laws without his aid. In the formation of treaties he must act, and his act must have the sanction of two-thirds of the Senate. The power of making treaties and that of making laws, and the depositories of these powers should be considered as perfectly distinct from each other, as if the individuals who acted in the one case never had an agency in the other.

It did not follow, however, from his doctrine in regard to the efficacy of treaties, that they necessarily changed or repealed legislative acts, with which they did not entirely accord. The stipulations of a treaty might amount, and often did amount, to no more than a pledge to alter or abrogate these acts, or to make legislative regulations conformable to such stipulations. Where the treaty was of this nature—that is to say, executory merely, legislative aid was necessary. But where it could execute itself, there it needed no aid. What was the nature of the obligation to carry a treaty of the former kind into effect, it was not necessary now to examine. When, however, he stated, on a former occasion, that he viewed this obligation as morally binding on this House, as a branch of the legislative authority, he did not think that he uttered a sentiment which, in the language of the gentleman from Massachusetts, (Mr. KING,) degraded the House of Representatives into a mere chamber for registering the edicts of the President and Senate. He viewed it as a fundamental principle of our Government, that every man, and every body of men in it, owed obedience to the laws of the land. The House of Representatives cannot claim an exemption from this duty. They may aid in repealing laws—but so long as the laws exist, whether they have derived their origin from a legislative or a treaty declaration of the will of the sovereign power, the House of Representatives, the Senate, the President, are bound by them. The obligation to appropriate for treaties, was just as binding as the obligation to appropriate for the objects of existing laws. If the gentleman considered this moral restraint as unfriendly either to personal liberty or to the political freedom of this body, he (Mr. G.) neither wished for himself, or those who were dear to him, a liberty superior to law.

In regard to the practice of Government on similar occasions, the gentleman from Georgia (Mr. FORSYTH) had cited instances which he was not then prepared to examine. Such an examination required a deliberate review of the treaties and acts referred to, which demanded time and books that could not now be commanded. It was possible that some of the cases did prove an unnecessary legislation on subjects which treaties had adequately provided for. But what was the answer to the two prominent and marked cases

which Mr. G. had before noticed, viz: the British treaty of 1795, and the convention with the French Republic. In the first there were stipulations abolishing discriminating duties on importations from Canada, yet no act of Congress was passed to give efficacy to these stipulations—the treaty made them law. In the French convention there was a provision for a mutual restriction of captures. Congress, it is said by the gentleman from Georgia, did pass an act in regard to this provision. They indeed did, and this act was the strongest illustration of their entire concurrence in the opinions he had expressed. This act makes an appropriation of money to authorize payment for such of the property as could *not* be restored in kind; but it pretended not to command such restoration where it was practicable. If the construction of the gentleman had prevailed, the last was necessary. But neither the Congress gave such direction, nor did the President wait for it. He restored the Berceau. According to the exposition which he (Mr. G.) had adopted, the appropriation of money was necessary, because the Constitution prohibits the payment of money without an appropriation.

Mr. G. forbore from going further into the discussion, from a conviction that the House was anxious for the question.

Mr. THROOP said that he did not rise for the purpose of entering into a detailed argument on the question submitted to the House, but merely to state the reasons for the vote he should give; this he deemed due to his friends in this House, because he found himself opposed to the opinions of a majority of them. He should vote against the bill because he thought it unnecessary to pass such a law. The act in question did nothing more than put into the form of a law the several provisions of the treaty regulating the commerce between the two countries, which were of themselves the supreme law of the land. These provisions did not require a construction, nor any aid by law to carry them into execution. If the object was merely to instruct the revenue officers, he would prefer its being done by the President, or the Secretary of the Treasury, whose duty he conceived it to be, and whose competency could not be doubted. He did not know that the passage of this law, following the provisions of the treaty, would do any great mischief, but he was opposed to the principles on which it was attempted to be supported, and feared that it would at some future period form a dangerous precedent. The treaty-making power was lodged by the Constitution in the President and Senate, and their act became obligatory on the nation, without the interference of this House, by that section of the Constitution, which declares that, "this Constitution 'and the laws of the United States which shall 'be made in pursuance thereof, and all treaties 'made, or which shall be made, under the au- 'thority of the United States, shall be the su- 'preme law of the land." An argument has been attempted to be drawn from the fact that the Constitution, laws, and treaties, are classed together in the same sentence, and are all declared to be the law of the land. He said he did not know that he understood what the conclusion was; but if it was as he apprehended it to be, that, being all classed together, and in one sentence declared to be the supreme law, that then a treaty was of no greater force than a law, he did conceive that the same argument would prove that the Constitution was not paramount to a law, and if that construction prevailed, Congress might by law repeal the Constitution. But grant that the treaty had no greater efficacy than a law, and could repeal and be repealed by a law, then the act under consideration was unnecessary, as the treaty, being subsequent to the law creating discriminating duties, repealed that law; and when a new tariff of duties was created it might be made to conform to the treaty. But it is said the treaty is a compact; hence, it is no law to be observed by the people, but only a direction to Congress to pass a law. He said, because it is a compact it is superior to the law. An individual may prescribe to himself a rule of conduct, by which he will be governed, but he may depart from that rule whenever he pleases; it is a law to himself, and the power which enacts may repeal. But if he stipulates with another a rule of conduct to be observed by himself, it is a compact, and he cannot depart from it without a violation of his plighted faith, and the rights of that other. This is the distinction between a treaty and a law, and which renders a treaty paramount to the law; the law prescribes a rule of conduct to the citizens of the State, by which they are to be governed, and may be repealed at any time; but a treaty is a compact between two sovereign States, which cannot be departed from by one without violating the faith of that State, and the rights of the other. He said, that an answer to the argument that the treaty is only a direction to Congress to pass a law, was to be found in the concluding part of the same section of the Constitution, which, after stating that treaties, &c. shall be the supreme law of the land, adds: "and the judges in each State shall be bound thereby." Here was a direction not to Congress, but to the courts of law, to construe and enforce the treaty, which they were bound to do without reference to any construction which might be put upon it by an act of this body. He trusted he should not be told that this direction was to the judges of the State courts, and not to the judiciary of the United States, and that a treaty might be enforced in the State courts, but would require a law to enforce it in the courts of the United States. For, according to that construction it might produce this absurdity, that the treaty would operate upon the States individually, and Congress might refuse to pass a law whereby it could not be treated as a law by the United States' courts. He said, that he could not sanction the idea that this House had any control over the treaty-making power, to ratify or annul their acts, unless it was in cases where the treaty could not execute itself, but

required for that purpose provision to be made by law, such as raising money, &c. Some gentlemen seem alarmed lest the President and Senate, by an assumption of power, should at length claim the right of making war, which they could do by stipulating for war in a treaty. He said, should the right of declaring war exist in one branch of the Legislature independent of the others, he could not but see but it might as safely be lodged with the President and Senate, as with this House. The right here claimed of supervising the treaty, would lead to that result. War has ceased; we are at peace with Great Britain, by treaty; but if this House, in the plenitude of their wisdom, had not thought proper to ratify the treaty, the war is renewed; we must resume our arms, which would effectually vest this branch of the Legislature with the power of making war. He said he did not believe that it entered into the views of the framers of the Constitution to vest this House with the power of rejecting or ratifying a treaty; if it did, they would not have left a power so important to be gathered from inference. They would have made express provision for it. It would have been easy for them, and they would have declared that the power of making treaties should be vested in the President of the United States and Congress.

The bill was further opposed by Mr. PICKERING, and Mr. MILLS, and advocated by Mr. KING of Massachusetts, and Mr. LOWNDES.

The yeas and nays having been required by Mr. ROOT, on motion, the subject was further postponed until to-morrow.

BANK OF THE UNITED STATES.

Mr. CALHOUN, from the committee on that part of the President's Message which relates to an Uniform National Currency, reported a bill to incorporate the subscribers to the Bank of the United States; which was read twice and committed to a Committee of the Whole on Monday next.

The bill is as follows:

A Bill to incorporate the Subscribers to the Bank of the United States.

Be it enacted, by the Senate and House of Representatives of the United States of America in Congress assembled, That a Bank of the United States of America shall be established, with a capital of thirty-five millions of dollars, divided into three hundred and fifty thousand shares, of one hundred dollars each share; but Congress may, at any time hereafter, augment the capital of the said bank, to a sum not exceeding fifty millions of dollars, in such manner as shall be by law provided. Seventy thousand shares, amounting to the sum of seven millions of dollars, part of the capital of the said bank, shall be subscribed, and paid for by the United States, in the manner hereinafter specified; and two hundred and eighty thousand shares, amounting to the sum of twenty-eight millions of dollars, shall be subscribed and paid for, by individuals, companies, or corporations, in the manner hereinafter specified.

SEC. 2. *And be it further enacted,* That subscriptions for the sum of twenty-eight millions of dollars, towards constituting the capital of the said bank,

491   HISTORY OF CONGRESS.   492

H. of R.   *Commerce with Great Britain.*   January, 1816.

tions are respectively confided. Perhaps, too, it will be found that there are salutary checks provided against an erroneous expression of this will, in the one case, as in the other. To acts of legislation, the concurrence of the President is not indispensable. Two-thirds of the Senate and House of Representatives can make laws without his aid. In the formation of treaties he must act, and his act must have the sanction of two-thirds of the Senate. The power of making treaties and that of making laws, and the depositories of these powers should be considered as perfectly distinct from each other, as if the individuals who acted in the one case never had an agency in the other.

It did not follow, however, from his doctrine in regard to the efficacy of treaties, that they necessarily changed or repealed legislative acts, with which they did not entirely accord. The stipulations of a treaty might amount, and often did amount, to no more than a pledge to alter or abrogate these acts, or to make legislative regulations conformable to such stipulations. Where the treaty was of this nature—that is to say, executory merely, legislative aid was necessary. But where it could execute itself, there it needed no aid. What was the nature of the obligation to carry a treaty of the former kind into effect, it was not necessary now to examine. When, however, he stated, on a former occasion, that he viewed this obligation as morally binding on this House, as a branch of the legislative authority, he did not think that he uttered a sentiment which, in the language of the gentleman from Massachusetts, (Mr. King,) degraded the House of Representatives into a mere chamber for registering the edicts of the President and Senate. He viewed it as a fundamental principle of our Government, that every man, and every body of men in it, owed obedience to the laws of the land. The House of Representatives cannot claim an exemption from this duty. They may aid in repealing laws—but so long as the laws exist, whether they have derived their origin from a legislative or a treaty declaration of the will of the sovereign power, the House of Representatives, the Senate, the President, are bound by them. The obligation to appropriate for treaties, was just as binding as the obligation to appropriate for the objects of existing laws. If the gentleman considered this moral restraint as unfriendly either to personal liberty or to the political freedom of this body, he (Mr. G.) neither wished for himself, or those who were dear to him, a liberty superior to law.

In regard to the practice of Government on similar occasions, the gentleman from Georgia (Mr. Forsyth) had cited instances which he was not then prepared to examine. Such an examination required a deliberate review of the treaties and acts referred to, which demanded time and books that could not now be commanded. It was possible that some of the cases did prove an unnecessary legislation on subjects which treaties had adequately provided for. But what was the answer to the two prominent and marked cases

which Mr. G. had before noticed, viz: the British treaty of 1795, and the convention with the French Republic. In the first there were stipulations abolishing discriminating duties on importations from Canada, yet no act of Congress was passed to give efficacy to these stipulations—the treaty made them law. In the French convention there was a provision for a mutual restriction of captures. Congress, it is said by the gentleman from Georgia, did pass an act in regard to this provision. They indeed did, and this act was the strongest illustration of their entire concurrence in the opinions he had expressed. This act makes an appropriation of money to authorize payment for such of the property as could *not* be restored in kind; but it pretended not to command such restoration where it was practicable. If the construction of the gentleman had prevailed, the last was necessary. But neither the Congress gave such direction, nor did the President wait for it. He restored the Berceau. According to the exposition which he (Mr. G.) had adopted, the appropriation of money was necessary, because the Constitution prohibits the payment of money without an appropriation.

Mr. G. forbore from going further into the discussion, from a conviction that the House was anxious for the question.

Mr. Throop said that he did not rise for the purpose of entering into a detailed argument on the question submitted to the House, but merely to state the reasons for the vote he should give; this he deemed due to his friends in this House, because he found himself opposed to the opinions of a majority of them. He should vote against the bill because he thought it unnecessary to pass such a law. The act in question did nothing more than put into the form of a law the several provisions of the treaty regulating the commerce between the two countries, which were of themselves the supreme law of the land. These provisions did not require a construction, nor any aid by law to carry them into execution. If the object was merely to instruct the revenue officers, he would prefer its being done by the President, or the Secretary of the Treasury, whose duty he conceived it to be, and whose competency could not be doubted. He did not know that the passage of this law, following the provisions of the treaty, would do any great mischief, but he was opposed to the principles on which it was attempted to be supported, and feared that it would at some future period form a dangerous precedent. The treaty-making power was lodged by the Constitution in the President and Senate, and their act became obligatory on the nation, without the interference of this House, by that section of the Constitution, which declares that, "this Constitution 'and the laws of the United States which shall 'be made in pursuance thereof, and all treaties 'made, or which shall be made, under the au- 'thority of the United States, shall be the su- 'preme law of the land." An argument has been attempted to be drawn from the fact that the Constitution, laws, and treaties, are classed together in the same sentence, and are all declared to be the law of the land. He said he did not know that he understood what the conclusion was; but if it was as he apprehended it to be, that, being all classed together, and in one sentence declared to be the supreme law, that then a treaty was of no greater force than a law, he did conceive that the same argument would prove that the Constitution was not paramount to a law, and if that construction prevailed, Congress might by law repeal the Constitution. But grant that the treaty had no greater efficacy than a law, and could repeal and be repealed by a law, then the act under consideration was unnecessary, as the treaty, being subsequent to the law creating discriminating duties, repealed that law; and when a new tariff of duties was created it might be made to conform to the treaty. But it is said the treaty is a compact; hence, it is no law to be observed by the people, but only a direction to Congress to pass a law. He said, because it is a compact it is superior to the law. An individual may prescribe to himself a rule of conduct, by which he will be governed, but he may depart from that rule whenever he pleases; it is a law to himself, and the power which enacts may repeal. But if he stipulates with another a rule of conduct to be observed by himself, it is a compact, and he cannot depart from it without a violation of his plighted faith, and the rights of that other. This is the distinction between a treaty and a law, and which renders a treaty paramount to the law; the law prescribes a rule of conduct to the citizens of the State, by which they are to be governed, and may be repealed at any time; but a treaty is a compact between two sovereign States, which cannot be departed from by one without violating the faith of that State, and the rights of the other. He said, that an answer to the argument that the treaty is only a direction to Congress to pass a law, was to be found in the concluding part of the same section of the Constitution, which, after stating that treaties, &c. shall be the supreme law of the land, adds: "and the judges in each State shall be bound thereby." Here was a direction not to Congress, but to the courts of law, to construe and enforce the treaty, which they were bound to do without reference to any construction which might be put upon it by an act of this body. He trusted he should not be told that this direction was to the judges of the State courts, and not to the judiciary of the United States, and that a treaty might be enforced in the State courts, but would require a law to enforce it in the courts of the United States. For, according to that construction it might produce this absurdity, that the treaty would operate upon the States individually, and Congress might refuse to pass a law whereby it could not be treated as a law by the United States' courts. He said, that he could not sanction the idea that this House had any control over the treaty-making power, to ratify or annul their acts, unless it was in cases where the treaty could not execute itself, but

required for that purpose provision to be made by law, such as raising money, &c. Some gentlemen seem alarmed lest the President and Senate, by an assumption of power, should at length claim the right of making war, which they could do by stipulating for war in a treaty. He said, should the right of declaring war exist in one branch of the Legislature independent of the others, he could not but see but it might as safely be lodged with the President and Senate, as with this House. The right here claimed of supervising the treaty, would lead to that result. War has ceased; we are at peace with Great Britain, by treaty; but if this House, in the plenitude of their wisdom, had not thought proper to ratify the treaty, the war is renewed; we must resume our arms, which would effectually vest this branch of the Legislature with the power of making war. He said he did not believe that it entered into the views of the framers of the Constitution to vest this House with the power of rejecting or ratifying a treaty; if it did, they would not have left a power so important to be gathered from inference. They would have made express provision for it. It would have been easy for them, and they would have declared that the power of making treaties should be vested in the President of the United States and Congress.

The bill was further opposed by Mr. PICKERING, and Mr. MILLS, and advocated by Mr. KING of Massachusetts, and Mr. LOWNDES.

The yeas and nays having been required by Mr. ROOT, on motion, the subject was further postponed until to-morrow.

BANK OF THE UNITED STATES.

Mr. CALHOUN, from the committee on that part of the President's Message which relates to an Uniform National Currency, reported a bill to, incorporate the subscribers to the Bank of the United States; which was read twice and committed to a Committee of the Whole on Monday next.

The bill is as follows:

A Bill to incorporate the Subscribers to the Bank of the United States.

Be it enacted, by the Senate and House of Representatives of the United States of America in Congress assembled, That a Bank of the United States of America shall be established, with a capital of thirty-five millions of dollars, divided into three hundred and fifty millions shares, of one hundred dollars each share; but Congress may, at any time hereafter, augment the capital of the said bank, to a sum not exceeding fifty millions of dollars, in such manner as shall be by law provided. Seventy thousand shares, amounting to the sum of seven millions of dollars, part of the capital of the said bank, shall be subscribed, and paid for by the United States, in the manner hereinafter specified; and two hundred and eighty thousand shares, amounting to the sum of twenty-eight millions of dollars, shall be subscribed and paid for, by individuals, companies, or corporations, in the manner hereinafter specified.

SEC. 2. *And be it further enacted,* That subscriptions for the sum of twenty-eight millions of dollars, towards constituting the capital of the said bank, shall be opened on the first Monday in June next, at the following places, that is to say: at Portsmouth, in the State of New Hampshire; at Boston, in the State of Massachusetts; at Providence, in the State of Rhode Island; at New Haven, in the State of Connecticut; at Burlington, in the State of Vermont; at New York, in the State of New York; at ——, in the State of New Jersey; at Philadelphia, in the State of Pennsylvania; at Wilmington, in the State of Delaware; at Baltimore, in the State of Maryland; at Richmond, in the State of Virginia; at Lexington, in the State of Kentucky; at ——, in the State of Ohio; at Raleigh, in the State of North Carolina; at Nashville, in the State of Tennessee; at Charleston, in the State of South Carolina; at Augusta, in the State of Georgia; at New Orleans, in the State of Louisiana; and at Washington, in the District of Columbia. And the said subscriptions shall be opened under the superintendence of three commissioners, to be appointed at, and for, each of the said places, by the President of the United States, (who is hereby authorised to make such appointments,) and shall continue open every day, from the time of opening the same, between the hours of ten o'clock in the forenoon, and four o'clock in the afternoon, until the Saturday following, at four o'clock in the afternoon, when the same shall be closed; and immediately thereafter, the commissioners, or any two of them, at the respective places aforesaid, shall cause two transcripts or copies of such subscriptions to be made, one of which they shall send to the Secretary of the Treasury, one they shall retain, and the original they shall transmit, within seven days from the closing of the subscriptions as aforesaid, to the commissioners at Philadelphia aforesaid. And on the receipt of the said original subscriptions, or of either of the said copies thereof, if the original be lost, mislaid, or detained, the commissioners at Philadelphia aforesaid, or a majority of them, shall immediately thereafter convene, and proceed to take an account of the said subscriptions. And if more than the amount of twenty-eight millions of dollars shall have been subscribed, then the said last mentioned commissioners shall apportion the same among the several subscribers, according to their several respective subscriptions, allowing and apportioning to each subscriber at least one share. And in case the aggregate amount of the said subscriptions shall exceed twenty-eight millions of dollars, the said last mentioned commissioners, after having apportioned the same as aforesaid, shall cause lists of the said apportioned subscriptions to be made out, including in each list the apportioned subscription for the place where the original subscription was made, one of which lists they shall transmit to the commissioners, or one of them, under whose superintendence such subscriptions were originally made, that the subscribers may thereby ascertain the number of shares to them respectively apportioned as aforesaid. And in case the aggregate amount of the said subscriptions made, during the period aforesaid, at all the places aforesaid, shall not amount to twenty-eight millions of dollars, the subscriptions to complete the said sum shall be, and remain open, at Philadelphia aforesaid, under the superintendence of the commissioners appointed for that place; and the subscriptions may be then made by any individual, company, or corporation, for any number of shares, not exceeding in the whole the amount required to complete the said sum of twenty-eight millions of dollars.

Sec. 3. *And be it further enacted,* That it shall be lawful for any individual, company, or corporation, when the subscriptions shall be opened, as herein before directed, to subscribe for any number of shares of the capital of the said bank, not exceeding three thousand shares; and the sums so subscribed shall be payable, and paid in the manner following, that is to say: seven millions of dollars thereof in gold or silver coin of the United States, or in foreign gold or silver coin, at the value thereof, as heretofore established by an act, entitled "An act regulating the currency of foreign coins," passed the tenth day of April, in the year one thousand eight hundred and six; and twenty-one millions of dollars thereof in like gold or silver coin, or in the funded debt of the United States, contracted at the time of the subscriptions respectively. And the payments made in the funded debt of the United States shall be paid and received at the following rates, that is to say: the funded debt, bearing an interest of six per centum per annum, at the nominal or par value thereof; the funded debt bearing an interest of three per centum per annum, at the rate of sixty-five dollars for every sum of one hundred dollars of the nominal amount thereof; and the funded debt, bearing an interest of seven per centum per annum, at the rate of one hundred and six dollars and fifty-one cents, for every sum of one hundred dollars of the nominal amount thereof; together with the amount of the interest accrued on the said several denominations of funded debt, to be computed and allowed to the time of subscribing the same to the capital of the said bank as aforesaid. And the payments of the said subscriptions shall be made and completed by the subscribers, respectively, at the times and in the manner following, that is to say: at the time of subscribing, there shall be paid five dollars on each share, in gold or silver coin as aforesaid, and twenty-five dollars more, in coin as aforesaid, or in funded debt as aforesaid; at the expiration of six calendar months after the time of subscribing, there shall be paid the further sum of five dollars on each share, in gold or silver coin as aforesaid, and twenty-five dollars more, in coin as aforesaid, or in funded debt as aforesaid; at the expiration of twelve calendar months from the time of subscribing, there shall be paid the further sum of five dollars on each share, in gold or silver coin as aforesaid, and twenty-five dollars more, in coin as aforesaid, or in funded debt as aforesaid; and at the expiration of eighteen calendar months, there shall be paid the further sum of ten dollars in gold or silver coin as aforesaid.

Sec. 4. *And be it further enacted,* That, at the time of subscribing to the capital of the said bank as aforesaid, each and every subscriber shall deliver to the commissioners, at the place of subscribing, as well the amount of their subscriptions, respectively, in coin as aforesaid, as the certificates of funded debt, for the funded debt proportion of their respective subscriptions, together with a power of attorney, authorizing the said commissioners, or a majority of them, to transfer the said stock in due form of law, to "the president, directors, and company, of the Bank of the United States of America," as soon as the said bank shall be organized. *Provided, always,* That if, in consequence of the apportionment of the shares in the capital of the said bank among the subscribers, in the case and in the manner hereinbefore provided, any subscriber shall have delivered to the commissioners, at the time of subscribing, a greater amount of gold or silver coin and funded debt, than shall be necessary to complete the payments for the share or shares to such subscribers, apportioned as aforesaid, the commissioners shall only retain so much of the said gold or silver coin, and funded debt, as shall be necessary to complete such payments, and shall forthwith return the surplus thereof, on application for the same, to the subscribers lawfully entitled thereto. And the commissioners, respectively, shall deposite the gold and silver coin, and certificates of public debt, by them respectively received as aforesaid, from the subscribers to the capital of the said bank, in some place of secure and safe keeping, so that the same may, and shall be specifically delivered and transferred, as the same were by them respectively received, to the president, directors, and company of the Bank of the United States of America, or to their order, as soon as shall be required after the organization of the said bank. And the said commissioners, appointed to superintend the subscriptions to the capital of the said bank as aforesaid, shall receive a reasonable compensation for their services, respectively, and shall be allowed all reasonable charges and expenses incurred in the execution of their trust, to be paid by the president, directors, and company of the bank, out of the funds thereof.

SEC. 5. *And be it further enacted,* That it shall be lawful for the United States to pay and redeem the funded debt subscribed to the capital of the said bank, at the rates aforesaid, in such sums and at such times as shall be deemed expedient, anything in any act or acts of Congress to the contrary thereof, notwithstanding. And it shall also be lawful for the president, directors, and company, of the said bank, to sell and transfer, for gold and silver coin or bullion, the funded debt subscribed to the capital of the said bank as aforesaid: *Provided, always,* That they shall not sell more thereof than the sum of two millions of dollars in any one year; nor sell any part thereof at any time within the United States, without previously giving notice of their intention, to the Secretary of the Treasury, and offering the same to the United States at the current price, not exceeding the rates aforesaid.

SEC. 6. *And be it further enacted,* That, at the opening of the subscription to the capital stock of the said bank, the Secretary of the Treasury shall subscribe, or cause to be subscribed, on behalf of the United States, the said number of seven thousand shares, amounting to seven millions of dollars, as aforesaid, to be paid in gold or silver coin, or Treasury notes, or in stock of the United States, bearing interest at the rate of six per centum per annum, in seven equal annual payments of one million of dollars each, the first whereof shall be made at, or as nearly as conveniently may be after, the opening of the said subscriptions: *Provided, always,.* That it shall be lawful for the Secretary of the Treasury, with the approbation of the President of the United States, and the consent of the president, directors, and company of the said bank, to anticipate and pay in advance, all or any of the said annual payments, at such times, and in such manner, as shall be mutually stipulated and agreed.

SEC. 7. *And be it further enacted,* That the Secretary of the Treasury, with the approbation of the President of the United States, shall, from time to time, select and designate the mode of paying for the said subscription of the United States, to the capital of the said bank as aforesaid. And if payment thereof, or of any part thereof, be made in public stock, bearing interest at the rate of six per centum per annum, as aforesaid, the said interest shall be payable quarterly, to commence from the time of making such payment

on account of the said subscriptions, and the principal of the said stock shall be redeemable in any sums, and at any periods which the Government shall deem fit. And the Secretary of the Treasury shall, from time to time, cause the certificates of such public stock to be prepared, and made in the usual form, and shall pay and deliver the same to the president, directors, and company of the said bank, at or as soon as conveniently may be after, the time and times, hereinbefore prescribed for the payment of the said subscription of the United States, to the capital of the said bank as aforesaid; or at such other time and times as may be agreed upon in pursuance of the authority hereinbefore given, to anticipate the payments of the said subscription as aforesaid. And if payment of the said subscription of the United States to the capital of the said bank as aforesaid, or of any part thereof, shall be made in Treasury notes, such Treasury notes shall not bear interest, but shall pass by endorsement, or by delivery, for such sum, to be specified on the face thereof, respectively, as the Secretary of the Treasury, with the approbation of the President of the United States, shall direct; and shall be receivable in all payments to the United States, and in all payments to the president, directors, and company, of the said bank. And the Secretary of the Treasury shall, from time to time, cause the said Treasury notes to be prepared, and shall pay and deliver the same to the president, directors, and company, of the said bank, at or as soon as conveniently may be after, the time and times hereinbefore prescribed, for the payment of the said subscription of the United States, to the capital of the said bank as aforesaid; or at such other time and times as may be agreed upon, in pursuance of the authority hereinbefore given, to anticipate the payments of the said subscription as aforesaid. And it shall be lawful for the Secretary of the Treasury, or for the president, directors, and company, of the said bank, to issue, and reissue, at their par value, such of the said Treasury notes as shall be received in payments by the United States, or by the said bank, respectively, as aforesaid: *Provided, always,* That the United States may at any time redeem and cancel the said Treasury notes, or any part thereof, while the same shall be in the possession of the said bank as the property thereof: *And provided, also,* That it shall be the duty of the Secretary of the Treasury, out of the said Treasury notes received in payments to the United States, as aforesaid, to cause a portion thereof to be cancelled yearly, and every year, so that the whole amount issued may be redeemed and cancelled on or before the expiration of eight years from the time of opening the subscription to the capital of the said bank as aforesaid.

SEC. 8. *And be it further enacted,* That if any person shall falsely make, forge, or counterfeit, or cause or procure to be falsely made, forged, or counterfeited, or willingly aid or assist in falsely making, forging, or counterfeiting, any note in imitation of, or purporting to be a Treasury note as aforesaid; or shall falsely alter, or cause or procure to be falsely altered, or willingly aid or assist in falsely altering, any Treasury note issued as aforesaid; or shall pass, utter, or publish as true, any false, forged, or counterfeit note, purporting to be a Treasury note as aforesaid, knowing the same to be falsely made, forged, or counterfeited; or shall pass, utter, or publish, or attempt to pass, utter, or publish as true, any falsely altered Treasury note issued as aforesaid, knowing the same to be falsely altered; or shall be, directly or indirectly, knowingly concerned in any of the offences aforesaid, every such person shall be deemed and adjudged guilty of felony; and being thereof convicted by due course of law, shall be sentenced to be imprisoned, and kept to hard labor, for a period not less than three years, nor more than ten years, and be fined in a sum not exceeding five thousand dollars.

SEC. 9. *And be it further enacted,* That the subscribers to the said Bank of the United States of America, their successors and assigns, shall be, and are hereby, created a corporation and body politic, by the name and style of "The President, Directors, and Company, of the Bank of the United States," and shall so continue until the third day of March, in the year one thousand eight hundred and thirty-six, and by that name shall be, and are hereby, made able and capable, in law, to have, purchase, receive, possess, enjoy, and retain, to them and their successors, lands, rents, tenements, hereditaments, goods, chattels, and effects, of whatsoever kind, nature, and quality, to an amount not exceeding, in the whole, fifty-five millions of dollars, including the amount of the capital stock aforesaid; and the same to sell, grant, demise, alien or dispose of; to sue and be sued, plead and be impleaded, answer and be answered, defend and be defended, in all courts and places whatsoever; and also to make, have, and use a common seal, and the same to break, alter, and renew, at their pleasure; and also to ordain, establish, and put in execution such by-laws and ordinances and regulations as they shall deem necessary and convenient for the government of the said corporation, not being contrary to the Constitution and laws of the United States; and generally to do and execute all and singular the acts, matters, and things which to them it shall or may appertain to do; subject, nevertheless, to the rules, regulations, restrictions, limitations, and provisions, hereinafter prescribed and declared.

SEC. 10. *And be it further enacted,* That, for the management of the affairs of the said corporation, there shall be twenty-five directors, five of whom shall be annually appointed by the President of the United States, by and with the advice and consent of the Senate, and twenty of whom shall be annually elected at the banking house in the city of Philadelphia, on the first Monday of January, in each year, by the qualified stockholders of the capital of the said bank, and by a plurality of votes then and there actually given, according to the scale of voting hereinafter prescribed. And the directors, so duly appointed and elected, shall be capable of serving, by virtue of such appointment and choice, from the first Monday in the month of January of each year, until the end and expiration of the first Monday in the month of January of the year next ensuing the time of each annual election to be held by the stockholders as aforesaid. And the board of directors, annually, at the first meeting after their election in each and every year, shall proceed to elect one of the five directors appointed by the President of the United States, to be president of the corporation, who shall hold the said office during the same period for which the directors are appointed and elected as aforesaid: *Provided, always,* That the first appointment and election of the directors and president of the said bank shall be at the time and for the period hereinafter declared: *And provided, also,* That in case it should at any time happen that an appointment or election of directors, or an election of the president of the said bank, should not be so made as to take effect on any day when, in pursuance of this act, they ought to take effect, the said corporation shall not, for that cause, be deemed to be dissolved; but it shall be lawful, at any other time, to make such appointments, and to hold such elections, (as the case may be,) and the manner of holding the elections shall be regulated by the by-laws and ordinances of the said corporation; and until such appointments or elections be made, the directors and president of the said bank, for the time being, shall continue in office: *And provided, also,* That in case of the death, resignation, or removal of the president of the said corporation, the directors shall proceed to elect another president from the directors appointed by the President of the United States as aforesaid; and in case of the death, resignation, or absence from the United States, or removal, of a director from office, the vacancy shall be supplied by the President of the United States, or by the stockholders, as the case may be. But the President of the United States alone shall have power to remove the president of the bank, or any of the directors appointed by him as aforesaid.

SEC. 11. *And be it further enacted,* That as soon as the sum of eight millions four hundred thousand dollars, in gold and silver coin, and in the public debt, shall have been actually received on account of the subscriptions to the capital of the said bank, (exclusively of the subscription aforesaid, on the part of the United States,) notice thereof shall be given by the persons under whose superintendence the subscriptions shall have been made at the city of Philadelphia, in at least two newspapers printed in each of the places, (if so many be printed at such places respectively,) where subscriptions shall have been made, and the said persons shall, at the same time, and in like manner, notify a time and place within the said city of Philadelphia, at the distance of at least thirty days from the time of such notification, for proceeding to the election of twenty directors as aforesaid, and it shall be lawful for such election to be then and there made. And the President of the United States is hereby authorized, during the present session of Congress, to nominate, and, by and with the advice and consent of the Senate, to appoint five directors of the said bank; and the persons who shall be elected and appointed as aforesaid, shall be the first directors of the said bank, and shall proceed to elect one of the five directors appointed by the President of the United States as aforesaid, to be president of the said bank; and the directors and president of the said bank, so appointed and elected as aforesaid, shall be capable of serving in their respective offices, by virtue thereof, until the end and expiration of the first Monday of the month of January next ensuing the said appointments and elections; and they shall then and thenceforth commence and continue the operations of the said bank, at the city of Philadelphia.

SEC. 12. *And be it further enacted,* That the directors for the time being shall have power to appoint such officers, clerks, and servants under them, as shall be necessary for executing the business of the said corporation, and to allow them such compensation for their services, respectively, as shall be reasonable; and shall be capable of exercising such other powers and authorities, for the well governing and ordering of the officers of the said corporation, as shall be prescribed, fixed, and determined by the laws, regulations, and ordinances of the same.

SEC. 13. *And be it further enacted,* That the following rules, restrictions, limitations, and provisions shall form and be fundamental articles of the constitution of the said corporation, to wit:

1. The number of votes to which the stockholders shall be entitled, in voting for directors, shall be according to the number of shares he, she, or they, respectively, shall hold, in the proportions following, that is to say: for one share, and not more than two shares, one vote; for every two shares above two, and not exceeding ten, one vote; for every four shares above ten, and not exceeding thirty, one vote; for every six shares above thirty, and not exceeding sixty, one vote; for every eight shares above sixty, and not exceeding one hundred, one vote; and for every ten shares above one hundred, one vote; but no person, copartnership, or body politic, shall be entitled to a greater number than thirty votes; and after the first election no share or shares shall confer a right of voting, which shall not have been holden three calendar months previous to the day of election. And stockholders actually resident within the United States, and none other, may vote in elections by proxy. But no person shall give, in the whole, a greater number of votes, as proxy, and in his own right, than he would be entitled to give in his own right only, according to the proportion of voting hereinafter prescribed.

2. Not more than three-fourths of the directors elected by the stockholders, and not more than four-fifths of the directors appointed by the President of the United States, who shall be in office at the time of an annual election, shall be elected or appointed for the next succeeding year; but the director who shall be the president at the time of an election may always be reappointed by the President of the United States, and be re-elected president of the bank by the directors thereof.

3. None but a resident citizen of the United States shall be a director, nor shall a director be entitled to any emolument, but the stockholders may make such compensation to the president, for his extraordinary attendance at the bank, as shall appear to them reasonable.

4. Not less than seven directors shall constitute a board for the transaction of business, of whom the president shall always be one, except in case of sickness or necessary absence, in which case his place may be supplied by any other director whom he, by writing, under his hand, shall depute for that purpose. And the director so deputed may do and transact all the necessary business belonging to the office of the president of the said corporation, during the continuance of the sickness or necessary absence of the president.

5. A number of stockholders, not less than sixty, who, together, shall be proprietors of one thousand shares or upwards, shall have power at any time to call a general meeting of the stockholders, for purposes relative to the institution, giving at least ten weeks' notice in two public newspapers of the place where the bank is seated, and specifying in such notice the object or objects of such meeting.

6. Each cashier or treasurer, before he enters upon the duties of his office, shall be required to give bond, with two or more sureties, to the satisfaction of the directors, in a sum not less than fifty thousand dollars, with a condition for his good behaviour, and the faithful performance of his duties to the corporation.

7. The lands, tenements, and hereditaments, which it shall be lawful for the said corporation to hold, shall be only such as shall be requisite for its immediate accommodation in relation to the convenient transacting of its business, and such as shall have been *bona fide* mortgaged to it by way of security, or conveyed to it in satisfaction of debts previously contracted in the course of its dealings, or purchased at sales, upon judgments which shall have been obtained for such debts.

8. The total amount of debts which the said corporation shall at any time owe, whether by bond, bill, note, or other contract, over and above the debt or debts due for money deposited in the bank, shall not exceed the sum of fifty millions of dollars, unless the contracting of any greater debt shall have been previously authorised by a law of the United States. In case of excess, the directors under whose administration it shall happen, shall be liable for the same in their natural and private capacities; and an action of debt may in such case be brought against them, or any of them, their or any of their heirs, executors, or administrators, in any court of record of the United States, or either of them, by any creditor or creditors of the said corporation, and may be prosecuted to judgment and execution, any condition, covenant, or agreement to the contrary notwithstanding. But this provision shall not be construed to exempt the said corporation, or the lands, tenements, goods, or chattels of the same, from being also liable for, and chargeable with, the said excess.

Such of the said directors, who may have been absent when the said excess was contracted or created, or who may have dissented from the resolution or act whereby the same was so contracted or created, may respectively exonerate themselves from being so liable, by forthwith giving notice of the fact, and of their absence or dissent, to the President of the United States, and to the stockholders, at a general meeting, which they shall have power to call for that purpose.

9. The said corporation shall not, directly or indirectly, deal or trade in anything except bills of exchange, gold or silver bullion, or in the sale of goods really and truly pledged for money lent and not redeemed in due time, or goods which shall be the proceeds of its lands. It shall not be at liberty to purchase any public debt whatsoever; nor shall it take more than at the rate of six per centum per annum for or upon its loans or discounts.

10. No loan shall be made by the said corporation for the use or on account of the Government of the United States, to an amount exceeding five hundred thousand dollars, or of any particular State to an amount exceeding fifty thousand dollars, or of any foreign prince or State, unless previously authorized by a law of the United States.

11. The stock of the said corporation shall be assignable and transferable according to such rules as shall be instituted in that behalf, by the laws and ordinances of the same.

12. The bills obligatory and of credit, under the seal of the said corporation, which shall be made to any person or persons, shall be assignable by endorsement thereupon, under the hand or hands of such person or persons, and his, her, or their executors or administrators, and of his or their assignee or assignees, and so as absolutely to transfer and vest the property thereof in each and every assignee or assignees successively, and to enable such assignee or assignees, and his, her, or their executors or administrators, to maintain an action thereupon in his, her, or their own name or names. And the bills or notes which may be issued by order of the said corporation, signed by the president, and countersigned by the principal cashier or treasurer thereof, promising the payment of

money to any person or persons, his, her, or their order, or to bearer, although not under the seal of the said corporation, shall be binding and obligatory upon the same, in like manner, and with like force and effect, as upon any private person or persons, if issued by him, her, or them, in his, her, or their private or natural capacity or capacities, and shall be assignable and negotiable in like manner as if they were so issued by such private person or persons, that is to say: those which shall be payable to any person or persons, his, her, or their order, shall be assignable by endorsement, in like manner, and with the like effect as foreign bills of exchange now are; and those which are payable to bearer shall be assignable and negotiable by delivery only.

13. Half yearly dividends shall be made of so much of the profits of the bank as shall appear to the directors advisable; and once in every three years the directors shall lay before the stockholders, at a general meeting, for their information, an exact and particular statement of the debts which shall have remained unpaid, after the expiration of the original credit, for a period of treble the term of that credit, and of the surplus of the profits, if any, after deducting losses and dividends. If there shall be a failure in the payment of any part of any sum subscribed to the capital of the said bank, by any person, copartnership, or body politic, the party failing shall lose the benefit of any dividend which may have accured prior to the time for making such payment, and during the delay of the same.

14. The directors of the said corporation shall establish a competent office of discount and deposite in the District of Columbia, whenever any law of the United States shall require such an establishment; and it shall be lawful for the directors of the said corporation to establish offices wheresoever they shall think fit, within the United States or the Territories thereof, and to commit the management of the said offices, and the business thereof, respectively, to such persons, and under such regulations, as they shall deem proper, not being contrary to law or the constitution of the bank. Or, instead of establishing such offices, it shall be lawful for the directors of the said corporation, from time to time to employ any other bank or banks, to be first approved by the Secretary of the Treasury, at any place or places that they may deem safe and proper, to manage and transact the business proposed, as aforesaid, to be managed and transacted by such offices, under such agreements, and subject to such regulations as they shall deem just and proper. Thirteen managers or directors, of every office established as aforesaid, shall be annually appointed by the directors of the bank, to serve one year; they shall choose a president from their own number, each of them shall be a citizen of the United States, and not more than three-fourths of the said managers or directors, in office at the time of an annual appointment, shall be reappointed for the next succeeding year; but the president may be always reappointed.

15. The officer at the head of the Treasury Department of the United States shall be furnished, from time to time, as often as he may require, not exceeding once a week, with statements of the amount of the capital stock of the said corporation, and of the debts due to the same; of the moneys deposited therein; of the notes in circulation; and of the specie in hand; and shall have a right to inspect such general accounts in the books of the bank as shall relate to the said statement: *Provided,* That this shall not be construed to imply a right of inspecting the account of any private individual or individuals with the bank.

Sec. 14. *And be it further enacted,* That if the said corporation, or any person or persons, for, or to the use of the same, shall deal or trade in buying or selling goods, wares, merchandise, or commodities, whatsoever, contrary to the provisions of this act, all and every person and persons, by whom any order or direction for so dealing or trading, shall have been given; and all and every person and persons who shall have been concerned as parties or agents therein, shall forfeit and lose treble the value of the goods, wares, merchandises, and commodities, in which such dealing and trade shall have been, one-half thereof to the use of the informer, and the other half thereof to the use of the United States, to be recovered in any action of law, with costs of suit.

Sec. 15. *And be it further enacted,* That if the said corporation shall advance, or lend any sum of money, for the use, or on account of the Government of the United States, to an amount exceeding five hundred thousand dollars; or of any particular State, to an amount exceeding fifty thousand dollars; or of any foreign prince or State, (unless previously authorized thereto by a law of the United States,) all and every person and persons, by and with whose order, agreement, consent, approbation, and connivance, such unlawful advance or loan shall have been made, upon conviction thereof, shall forfeit and pay, for every such offence, treble the value or amount of the sum or sums which have been so unlawfully advanced or lent, one-fifth thereof to the use of the informer, and the residue thereof to the use of the United States.

Sec. 16. *And be it further enacted,* That the bills or notes of the said corporation, originally made payable, or which shall have become payable, on demand, shall be receivable in all payments to the United States, unless otherwise directed by act of Congress.

Sec. 17. *And be it further enacted,* That during the continuance of this act, and whenever required by the Secretary of the Treasury, the said corporation shall give the necessary facilities for transferring the public funds from place to place, and for distributing the same in payment of the public creditors, without charging commissions, or claiming allowance, on account of difference of exchange, and shall also do and perform the several and respective duties of the commissioners of loans for the several States, or of any one or more of them, at the times, in the manner, and upon the terms, prescribed by the Secretary of the Treasury.

Sec. 18. *And be it further enacted,* That the said corporation shall not, at any time, suspend, or refuse to pay, the notes thereof, in gold or silver coin, upon demand, according to the contract and promise of such notes: *Provided always, nevertheless,* That upon the representation of the said corporation, Congress shall have power to authorise the suspension or refusal aforesaid, for a time to be limited by law; and that during the recess of Congress it shall be lawful for the President of the United States, upon a like representation, to authorise such suspension for a term which shall not exceed six weeks after the opening of the next ensuing session of Congress.

Sec. 19. *And be it further enacted,* That in consideration of the exclusive privileges and benefits conferred by this act, upon the said bank, the President

Directors, and Company thereof, shall pay to the United States, out of the corporate funds thereof, the sum of one million and five hundred thousand dollars, in three equal payments, that is to say: five hundred thousand dollars at the expiration of two years, five hundred thousand dollars at the expiration of three years, and five hundred thousand dollars at the expiration of four years, after the said bank shall be organized and commence its operations, in the manner hereinbefore provided.

SEC. 20. *And be it further enacted,* That no other bank shall be established by any future law of the United States, during the continuance of the corporation hereby created, for which the faith of the United States is hereby pledged: *Provided,* Congress may renew existing charters for banks in the District of Columbia, not increasing the capital thereof; and may grant charters, if they deem it expedient, to any banking associations now in operation in the said District, and renew the same, not increasing the capital thereof. And, notwithstanding the expiration of the term for which the said corporation is created, it shall be lawful to use the corporate name, style, and capacity, for the purpose of suits, for the final settlement and liquidation of the affairs and accounts of the corporation, and for the sale and disposition of their estate, real, personal, and mixed; but not for any other purpose, or in any other manner whatsoever, nor for a period exceeding two years after the expiration of the said term of incorporation.

Accompanying the bill was the following letter, and plan of a National Bank, from the Secretary of the Treasury:

TREASURY DEPARTMENT, *Dec.* 24, 1815.

SIR: I have the honor to acknowledge the receipt of your letter, dated the 23d instant, informing me "that the committee on so much of the President's Message as relates to the national currency had determined that a National Bank is the most certain means of restoring to the nation a specie circulation," and had directed you to obtain the opinion of this Department on the following points:

1st. The amount and composition of the capital of the bank.

2d. The government of the bank.

3d. The privileges and duties of the bank.

4th. The organization and operation of the bank.

5th. The bonus to be required for the charter of the bank.

6th. The measures which may aid the bank in commencing and maintaining its operations in specie.

It affords much satisfaction to find that the policy of establishing a National Bank has received the sanction of the committee, and the decision, in this respect, renders it unnecessary to enter into a comparative examination of the superior advantages of such an institution for the attainment of the objects contemplated by the Legislature. Referring, therefore, to the outline of a National Bank, which is subjoined to this letter, as the result of an attentive consideration bestowed upon the subjects of your inquiry, I proceed, with deference and respect, to offer some explanation of the principles upon which the system is founded.

I. It is proposed that, under a charter for twenty years, the capital of the National Bank shall amount to $35,000,000; that Congress shall retain the power to raise it to $50,000,000, and that it shall consist three-quarters of public stock, and one-quarter of gold and silver.

1st. *With respect to the amount of the capital—* The services to be performed by the capital of the bank are important, various, and extensive. They will be required through a period almost as long as is usually assigned to a generation. They will be required for the accommodation of the Government, in the collection and distribution of its revenue, as well as for the uses of commerce, agriculture, manufactures, and the arts, throughout the Union. They will be required to restore and maintain the national currency; and, in short, they will be required, under every change of circumstances, in a season of war, as well as in the season of peace, for the circulation of the national wealth, which augments with a rapidity beyond the reach of ordinary calculation.

In the performance of these national services the local and incidental co-operation of the State banks may undoubtedly be expected; but it is the object of the present measure to create an independent, though not a discordant, institution; and while the Government is granting a monopoly for twenty years, it would seem to be improvident and dangerous to rely upon gratuitous or casual aids for the enjoyment of those benefits, which can be effectually secured by positive stipulation.

Nor is it believed that any public inconvenience can possibly arise from the proposed amount of the capital of the bank with its augmentable quality. The amount may, indeed, be a clog upon the profits of the institution, but it can never be employed for any injurious purpose, (not even for the purpose of discount accommodation beyond the fair demand,) without an abuse of trust, which cannot, in candor, be anticipated, or which, if anticipated, may be made an object of penal responsibility.

The competition which exists at present among the State banks will, it is true, be extended to the National Bank; but competition does not imply hostility. The commercial interests and the personal associations of the stockholders will generally be the same in the State banks and in the National Bank. The directors of both institutions will naturally be taken from the same class of citizens. And experience has shown not only the policy, but the existence of those sympathies by which the intercourse of a National Bank and the State banks has been, and always ought to be, regulated, for their common credit and security. At the present crisis it will be peculiarly incumbent upon the National Bank, as well as the Treasury, to conciliate the State banks; to confide to them, liberally, a participation in the deposites of public revenue, and to encourage them in every reasonable effort to resume the payment of their notes in coin. But, independent of these considerations, it is to be recollected that when portions of the capital of the National Bank shall be transferred to its branches, the amount invested in each branch will not, probably, exceed the amount of the capital of any of the principal State banks, and will certainly be less than the amount of the combined capital of the State banks, operating in any of the principal commercial cities. The whole number of the banking establishments in the United States may be stated at two hundred and sixty, and the aggregate amount of their capitals may be estimated at eighty millions of dollars; but the services of the National Bank are also required in every State and Territory, and the capital proposed is thirty-five millions, of which only one-fourth part will consist of gold and silver.

2d. *With respect to the composition of the capital of the bank.*—There does not prevail much diversity of opinion upon the proposition to form a compound capital for the National Bank, partly of public stock, and partly of coin. The proportions now suggested appear also to be free from any important objections. Under all the regulations of the charter, it is believed that the amount of gold and silver required will afford an adequate supply for commencing and continuing the payments of the bank in current coin; while the power which the bank will possess to convert its stock portion of capital into bullion or coin, from time to time, is calculated to provide for any probable augmentation of the demand. This object being sufficiently secured, the capital of the bank is next to be employed, in perfect consistency with the general interests and safety of the institution, to raise the value of the public securities, by withdrawing almost one-fifth of the amount from the ordinary stock market. Nor will the bank be allowed to expose the public to the danger of a depreciation, by returning any part of the stock to the market, until it has been offered, at the current price, to the Commissioners of the Sinking Fund; and it is not an inconsiderable advantage, in the growing state of the public revenue, that the stock subscribed to the capital of the bank will become redeemable at the pleasure of the Government.

The subscription to the capital of the bank is opened to every species of funded stock. The estimate that the revenues of 1816 and 1817 will enable the Treasury to discharge the whole of the Treasury note debt, furnishes the only reason for omitting to authorize a subscription in that species of debt. Thus,

The old and new six per cent. stocks are receivable at par.

The seven per cent. stock, upon a valuation referring to the 30th of September, 1816, is receivable at 106.51 dollars per cent.

The three per cent. stock, which can only be redeemed for its nominal or certificate value, may be estimated, under all circumstances, to be worth about sixty-two per cent. when the six per cent. stock is at par; but as it is desirable to accomplish the redemption of this stock upon equitable terms, it is made receivable at sixty-five per cent., the rate sanctioned by the Government, and in part accepted by the stockholders in the year 1807.

Of the instalments for paying the subscriptions, it is only necessary to observe that they are regulated by a desire to reconcile an early commencement of the operations of the bank with the existing difficulties in the currency, and with the convenience of the subscribers. In one of the modes proposed for discharging the subscription of the Government, it is particularly contemplated to aid the bank with a medium which cannot fail to alleviate the first pressure for payments in coin.

II. It is proposed that the National Bank shall be governed by twenty-five directors, and each of its branches by thirteen directors; that the President of the United States, with the advice and consent of the Senate, shall appoint five of the directors of the bank, one of whom shall be chosen as president of the bank by the board of directors; that the resident stockholders shall elect twenty of the directors of the National Bank, who shall be resident citizens of the United States, and that the National Bank shall appoint the directors of each branch, (being resident citizens of the United States,) one of whom shall be designated by the Secretary of the Treasury, with the approbation of the President of the United States, to be president of the branch bank.

The participation of the President and Senate of the United States in the appointment of directors, appears to be the only feature in the proposition for the Government of the National Bank which requires an explanatory remark.

Upon general principles, wherever a pecuniary interest is to be effected by the operations of a public institution, a representative authority ought to be recognised. The United States will be the proprietors of one-fifth of the capital of the bank, and in that proportion, upon general principles, they should be represented in the direction. But an apprehension has sometimes been expressed lest the power of the Government thus inserted into the administration of the affairs of the bank should be employed eventually to alienate the funds, and to destroy the credit of the institution. Whatever may have been the fate of banks in other countries, subject to forms of Government essentially different, there can be no reasonable cause for apprehension here. Independent of the obvious improbability of the attempt, the Government of the United States cannot, by any legislative or executive act, impair the rights, or multiply the obligations of a corporation constitutionally established, as long as the independence and integrity of the judicial power shall be maintained. Whatever accommodation the Treasury may have occasion to ask from the bank, can only be asked under the license of a law; and whatever accommodation shall be obtained must be obtained from the voluntary assent of the directors, acting under the responsibility of their trust.

Nor can it be doubted that the department of the Government, which is invested with the power of appointment to all the important offices of the State, is a proper department to exercise the power of appointment in relation to a national trust of incalculable magnitude. The National Bank ought not to be regarded simply as a commercial bank. It will not operate upon the funds of the stockholders alone, but much more upon the funds of the nation. Its conduct, good or bad, will not affect the corporate credit and resources alone, but much more the credit and resources of the Government. In fine, it is not an institution created for the purposes of commerce and profit alone, but much more for the purposes of national policy, as an auxiliary in the exercise of some of the highest powers of the Government. Under such circumstances the public interests cannot be too cautiously guarded, and the guards proposed can never be injurious to the commercial interests of the institution. The right to inspect the general accounts of the bank may be employed to detect the evils of a mal-administration; but an interior agency in the direction of its affairs will best serve to prevent them.

III. It is proposed that, in addition to the usual privileges of a corporation, the notes of the National Bank shall be received in all payments to the United States, unless Congress shall hereafter otherwise provide by law; and that, in addition to the duties usually required from a corporation of this description, the National Bank shall be employed to receive, transfer, and distribute, the public revenue, under the directions of the proper department.

The reservation of a legislative power on the subject of accepting the notes of the National Bank in payments to the Government, is the only new stipulation in the present proposition. It is designed not merely as one of the securities for the general conduct of the bank, but as the means of preserving entire the sovereign authority of Congress relative to the coin and currency of the United States. Recent occurrences inculcate the expediency of such a reservation, but it may be confidently hoped that an occasion to enforce it will never arise.

It is not proposed to stipulate that the bank shall in any case be bound to make loans to the Government; but, in that respect, whenever a loan is authorized by law, the Government will act upon the ordinary footing of an applicant for pecuniary accommodation.

IV. It is proposed that the organization of the National Bank shall be effected with as little delay as possible; and that its operations shall commence and continue upon the basis of payments in the current coin of the United States, with a qualified power under the authority of the Government to suspend such payments.

The proposition now submitted necessarily implies an opinion that it is practicable to commence the operations of the National Bank upon a circulation of gold and silver coin; and, in support of the opinion, a few remarks are respectfully offered to the consideration of the committee:

1. The actual receipts of the bank, at the opening of the subscription, will amount to the sum of $8,400,000; of which the sum of $1,400,000 will consist of gold and silver, and the sum of $7,000,000 will consist of public stock convertible by sale into gold and silver. But the actual receipts of the bank, at the expiration of six months from the opening of the subscription, will amount to the sum of $16,800,000; of which the sum of $2,800,000 will be in gold and silver, and the sum of $14,000,000 will be in public stock convertible by sale into gold and silver. To the fund thus possessed by the bank, the accumulations of the public revenue and the deposites of individuals being added, there can be little doubt, from past experience and observation in reference to similar establishments, that a sufficient foundation will exist for a gradual and judicious issue of bank notes payable on demand in the current coin; unless, contrary to all probability, public confidence should be withheld from the institution, or sinister combinations should be formed to defeat its operations, or the demands of an unfavorable balance of trade should press upon its metallic resources.

2. The public confidence cannot be withheld from the institution. The resources of the nation will be intimately connected with the resources of the bank. The notes of the bank are accredited in every payment to the Government, and must become familiar in every pecuniary negotiation. Unless, therefore, a state of things exist in which gold and silver only can command the public confidence, the National Bank must command it. But the expression of the public sentiment does not, even at this period, leave the question exposed to difficulty and doubt; it is well known that the wealth of opulent and commercial nations requires for its circulation something more than a medium composed of the precious metals. The incompetency of the existing paper substitutes to furnish a national currency is also well known. Hence, throughout the United States, the public hope seems to rest, at this crisis, upon the establishment of a National Bank; and every citizen, upon private or upon patriotic motives, will be prepared to support the institution.

3. Sinister combinations to defeat the operations of a National Bank, ought not to be presumed, and need

not be feared. It is true that the influence of the State banks is extensively diffused; but the State banks, and the patrons of the State banks, partake of the existing evils; they must be conscious of the inadequacy of State institutions to restore and maintain the national currency; they will perceive that there is sufficient space in the commercial sphere for the movement of the State banks and the National Bank; and, upon the whole, they will be ready to act upon the impulse of a common duty, and a common interest. If, however, most unexpectedly, a different course should be pursued, the concurring powers of the National Treasury and the National Bank will be sufficient to avert the danger.

4. The demand of an unfavorable balance of trade appears to be much overrated. It is not practicable, at this time, to ascertain either the value of the goods imported since the peace, or the value of the property employed to pay for them. But when it is considered that a great proportion of the importations arose from investments of American funds previously in Europe; that a great proportion of the price has been paid by American exports; that a great proportion has been paid by remittances in American stocks; and that a great proportion remains upon credit to be paid by gradual remittances of goods, as well as in coin; it cannot be justly concluded, that the balance of trade has hitherto materially affected the national stock of the precious metals. So far as an opportunity has occurred for observation, the demand for gold and silver to export appears rather to have arisen from the expectation of obtaining a higher price in a part of Europe, and from the revival of commerce with the countries beyond the Cape of Good Hope, than from any necessity to provide for the payment of the recent importations of goods into the United States. The former of these causes will probably soon cease to operate, and the operation of the latter may, if necessary, be restrained by law.

The proposition now under consideration further provides for a suspension of the bank payments in coin upon any future emergency. This is merely a matter of precaution; but, if the emergency should arise, it must be agreed on all hands that the power of suspension ought rather to be confided to the Government than to the directors of the institution.

V. It is proposed that a bonus be paid to the Government by the subscribers to the National Bank, in consideration of the emoluments to be derived from an exclusive charter, during a period of twenty years.

Independent of the bonus here proposed to be exacted, there are undoubtedly many public advantages to be drawn from the establishment of the National Bank; but these are generally of an incidental kind, and (as in the case of the deposites and distribution of the revenue) may be regarded in the light of equivalents, not for the monopoly of the charter, but for the reciprocal advantages of a fiscal connexion with the public Treasury.

The amount of the bonus should be in proportion to the value of the charter grant; or, in other words, to the net profits which the subscribers will probably make, in consequence of their incorporation. The average rate of the dividends of the State banks, before the suspension of payments in coin, was about eight per cent. per annum. It appears by a report from this department to the House of Representatives, dated the 3d of April, 1810, that the annual dividends of the late Bank of the United States, averaged, throughout

time to pay for lands purchased of the United States, which was read: When Mr. ROBERTSON reported a bill for the relief of certain purchasers of public lands in the Mississippi Territory, which was read twice and committed to a Committee of the Whole, on Friday next.

Mr. STANFORD, from the committee to whom was recommitted the report upon the subject of a revision of the rules and orders of the House, reported the same with amendment; and the said report was committed to a Committee of the Whole to-morrow.

Mr. JOHNSON, of Kentucky, from the Committee on Military Affairs, reported a bill making provision for an additional Military Academy, which was read twice and committed to a Committee of the Whole on Thursday next.

Ordered, That the said bill be read a third time to-morrow.

An engrossed bill, entitled "An act for the relief of George S. Wise," was read the third time and passed.

An engrossed bill, entitled "An act to authorize the discharge of James Jewett from his imprisonment," was read the third time and passed.

A Message from the President of the United States received yesterday, was read, transmitting the report of the Director of the Mint, of the operations of that establishment, during the last year.

The SPEAKER laid before the House a letter, from the Secretary of the Navy, transmitting the annual report of the Commissioners of the Navy Pension Fund; which were ordered to lie on the table.

On motion of Mr. BIRDSEYE, the Committee on Foreign Relations were instructed to inquire into the expediency of prohibiting, by law, all commercial intercourse between the citizens or subjects of any foreign Power and the Indians within the United States, or Territories belonging to the United States.

EXTENSION OF A PATENT RIGHT.

Mr. MARSH, from a select committee, made a report on the petition of John Tyler and Benjamin Tyler which was read: When Mr. MARSH, reported a bill to extend to Benjamin Tyler and John Tyler, of the State of New Hampshire, the patent right to certain improvements in the construction of corn and other mills; which was read twice and committed to a Committee of the Whole on Friday next.—The report is as follows:

That the petitioners represent that, prior to the year 1800, one Benjamin Tyler had invented a new and useful improvement in the construction of flour and other mills; that on that day he obtained a patent, according to law, for the exclusive right of using the said improvement for the term of fourteen years from that date; that afterwards he made an assignment of the said patent to the petitioners in due form. They further represent that several persons interfered with and invaded the right of using the said improvement thus secured to them by the said patent and assignment, by introducing the same into mills without their license; that, in the year 1804, they instituted a suit against one of the persons thus intrenching on their exclusive right to the said improvement; that the defendant in the said suit, by means of combinations of various interested individuals, protracted the pendency of said suit until the year 1810; that the court then arrested the verdict found in the said cause for the plaintiffs, on account of some supposed defect in the declaration; that the petitioners, in the prosecution of the said suit, were put to great expense and trouble, and though by the said verdict they established their right to the exclusive use of the said improvement, yet they lost the benefit of the damages and cost awarded to them by the said verdict; and that, by means of the pendency of the said suit during the space of six years, their said improvement was brought into discredit, and they deprived of the benefit and profit of selling the right to others of using the said improvement, while the time for which the same had been patented to them had in some measure expired.

They pray Congress to pass an act granting to them the exclusive right of using, and vending to others to be used, the said improvement for another term of fourteen years after the expiration of their said patent.

The committee report that they find the facts stated in the said petition supported by sufficient testimony, and that the said invention is a new and useful improvement in the construction of mills, and that the prayer of the petitioner ought to be granted. They recommend to Congress the following resolution:

Resolved, That the prayer of the petitioners ought to be granted; and that the exclusive right of using the said improvement be extended to the said petitioners for the term of seven years from this time.

REVENUE SYSTEM REVISED.

Mr. LOWNDES, from the Committee of Ways and Means, to whom have been referred that part of the President's Message which relates to the revenue, and the annual report of the Secretary of the Treasury, and that part which relates to the establishment of a National Bank, made a report; which was read, and referred to a Committee of the Whole on Friday next.—The report is as follows:

The Committee of Ways and Means, to whom have been committed that part of the President's Message which relates to the revenue, and the annual report of the Secretary of the Treasury, excepting that part which relates to the establishment of a bank, ask leave to explain the general views which have induced them to submit to the House the propositions with which they shall conclude their report:

" The arrangement of the finances, with a view to the receipts and expenditures of a permanent Peace Establishment," has been the first subject, after providing for the deficiency in the appropriations of 1815, which has engaged the attention of the committee. Whilst they recognise, with unmixed satisfaction, "that improvement in the condition of the public revenue, which will allow an immediate alleviation of the burdens imposed by the necessities of the war," they well know that such an alleviation can only be expected and wished to an extent "which shall leave to the Government the means of maintaining its faith inviolate, and of prosecuting successfully the measures of a liberal" and provident policy.

In forming an opinion upon the expenditures of a permanent Peace Establishment, they have supposed it right that their attention should be directed, not only to the resources of the United States, but to the condition of other Powers. In the perplexed system of European policy the United States can have no disposition to interpose ; but their conduct must necessarily be affected by views connected with the military or financial resources of those States with which their relations are most interesting. It is impossible not to see that Europe is more military than ever, and that, accustomed by twenty years of war to exertions that were once thought impracticable, her Governments have acquired a power which makes preparation more difficult and more necessary on the part of every State exposed to the chance of their hostility. It must be doubtful what precise increase of expenditure these considerations of foreign policy or views of internal improvement may induce Congress eventually to authorize; but even the measures now before them appear to require a considerable addition to the estimates of the annual peace expenditure.

The only preparation against the dangers of foreign aggression, which it falls within the duties of the Committee of Ways and Means to recommend, is that of a revenue; which, in supplying the wants of the Government, shall not burden unnecessarily the industry of the citizen; which shall be capable of repairing, by an expansion of the powers of some of its parts, the injuries which war may inflict in others; and, above all, shall be disencumbered from debt as soon as the resources of the country and the conditions of its contracts will permit. Public debts have, indeed, sometimes been considered as giving stability and order to a State, but the committee can never believe that a Government which secures every civil and political right to the great body of the people, can want that security which would be afforded by the distribution of any amount of annual interest upon its debt, which, to be received by the few, must be paid by the many. It may be true that a public debt only makes a different distribution of the income of society, but it pays the stockholder what would be reserved for supporting the seaman and the soldier. That Government, indeed, does well, which, when forced into war, brings into the contest every resource which credit or revenue can furnish; but it neglects one of its first duties when it allows the season of peace to pass away without an adequate provision for removing every encumbrance upon its effective revenue. The committee accordingly consider it as an indispensable requisite in any arrangement of revenue and expenditure in peace, that it shall provide for the rapid extinguishment of the public debt.

To attain this object a considerable revenue will be required. In selecting the taxes which should compose it, the duties upon imported articles may be expected to furnish the principal supply. Cheap and easy in their collection, paid like all indirect taxes, when it is convenient to pay them, they will be found, under a system of prudent moderation, to discourage no branch of national industry. Duties, indeed, either upon importation or exportation, seem to be the natural resource of countries thinly peopled, which, exporting a large amount of their agricultural productions, receive in return the manufactures of older States. The distance, too, of the States from which our importations are made, renders it more difficult to evade the payment of duties here than in countries which are separated from active and enterprising neighbors by a river or a conventional line. But as our

agriculture obtains markets at home, as wealth spreads itself over inland countries, where commerce can but imperfectly follow, our imports as well as our exports must bear a continually lessening proportion to the wealth of the country.

And even now, while the principal source of ordinary revenue in peace must be furnished by the customs, it is probable that they could not be continued or increased to an amount which the interest and reimbursement of our debt and the provisions for our security require, without increasing too far the temptation to illicit importation. The objections, too, to an entire reliance upon them, have been too fully developed by recent experience to allow the committee to recommend that they should constitute the whole income of the country. The liberal provision which they are capable of making in peace, disappears in the moment when war requires larger contributions. The Government which is left at such a time to explore new systems of internal taxation, to discover and draw into the public service the men who are capable of filling the different departments of the revenue, is reduced to a condition in which the zeal, and bravery, and resources of the nation can produce their natural effects but imperfectly. The committee, therefore, concur fully with the Secretary of the Treasury in the opinion which he has expressed, "that the establishment of a revenue system, which shall not be exclusively dependent upon the supplies of foreign commerce, appears, at this juncture, to claim particular attention."

As a result of these general views the committee, with deference to the House, recommend the adoption of the plan of revenue contained in the report of the Secretary of the Treasury, with the exception of that part of it which proposes to continue the additional duties upon postage, and to repeal the additional duties on licenses to retailers of wines, spirituous liquors, and foreign merchandise, imposed by the act of December, 1814. The communication of intelligence between the different parts of the country, it appears to the committee to be the just policy of our Government to facilitate and encourage; and, although it might have been right to exact a revenue from it, under circumstances which made it necessary to apply every resource to the defence of the State, the present situation of the Treasury may well allow of its repeal. The duties on licenses to retailers admit, in the opinion of the committee, of a modification, which, by proportioning the price of the license in some degree to the business of the retailer, shall render them as productive as the new rates, and less oppressive than the old ones. But as such modification could only apply to licenses for 1817, the committee propose to make it the subject of a future report.

The permanent laws now in force may be expected, after the expiration of temporary duties, to produce a net annual revenue of $25,278,640.

The direct tax, a net amount of - -		$5,600,000
The sale of public lands - -		1,000,000
Licenses to distillers, gross amount - - -	$1,205,000	
Carriages - - -	175,000	
Licenses to retailers - -	900,000	
Auctions - - - -	400,000	
	2,675,000	2,514,500
Duties on furniture and watches - -	300,000	

On manufactures	-	1,311,000	
Excise on distilled spirits	-	2,500,000	
		4,111,000	3,864,340
Postage	- - - -	-	300,000
Customs	- - - -	-	12,000,000
			$25,278,840

Such is the estimate of the annual revenue which, by law, is declared to be pledged "to provide for the payment of the expenses of the Government, for the punctual payment of the public debt, and for creating an adequate sinking fund." If the recommendation contained in the report of the Secretary, with the modifications proposed by the committee, shall be carried into effect, there will be deducted from this revenue of - - - - - $25,278,840
The net amount of duties on furniture and watches, on manufactures and distilled spirits - $3,864,340
The postage duty   300,000
And from the net product of the land tax - 2,900,000
                      7,064,340
But there will be added to the revenue—
By the additional duty on stills - $1,200,000
Duty on stamps - 400,000
On refined sugar   150,000
On salt - 500,000

Gross amount - 2,256,000
Net amount - 2,115,000
By an addition to the customs, equal to the product of an average addition of 42 per cent. to the rates of permanent duty - 5,040,000
                      7,155,000
Making the excess of revenue added, above that deducted - - - - 90,660
And the annual revenue - - 25,369,500

In the report of the Secretary of the Treasury, which has been referred to the committee—
The amount of the annual civil, diplomatic, and miscellaneous expenses is estimated at - $1,800,000
The annual military expenses at - 5,112,155
The annual naval expense at - 2,716,510
The interest in the funded debt, at about 6,150,000
                      15,778,669

To this estimate of annual expenditure might be added the amount of about $1,850,000, appropriated to the payment of the principal of the public debt; which, with the $6,150,000 applicable to the payment of the interest, constitutes the sinking fund of $8,000,000. But perhaps an easier view of the subject may be afforded by stating separately the whole sum which it is proposed to apply to the payment of the principal of the public debt, exclusively of the interest.

If the annual revenue, under the law proposed, be $25,369,500, and the ordinary annual expense be $15,778,669, there will be a balance of $9,590,831, which may be applied, as Congress shall direct, to national defence, to internal improvement, and to the extinguishment of the public debt. The considerations which have been already adverted to as enjoining the policy of providing for the extinguishment of the public debt as soon as the resources of the country and the condition of its contracts will permit, induce the committee to propose that to that object may be annually appropriated seven millions, after the year 1816; which, added to the sum appropriated to the payment of interest, will form a sinking fund of $13,150,000, and extinguish the public debt in less than twelve years. This appropriation would still leave an excess of annual revenue above the estimates of ordinary expenditure furnished by the Secretary of the Treasury of upwards of two millions and a half, to be applied to any other branch of the public service.

The committee have confined their observations to the receipts and expenditures of a permanent Peace Establishment. The modification of the plan of the Secretary of the Treasury which they have proposed, will produce too small an effect upon the receipts of 1816 to require a distinct exposition of them, and the deficiency in the receipts of 1816, (which is suggested in the Treasury report,) cannot disturb the calculations which have been submitted of the receipts and expenditures of succeeding years, since the estimated deficiency is less than seven millions, and the outstanding revenue on the 1st of January 1817, will be about twenty millions. If, however, the demands upon the Treasury in 1817, in consequence of Congress assuming the payment of expenses incurred during the war, which it has not yet sanctioned, or from any other cause, shall be increased beyond the present estimates, or beyond an amount for which the unappropriated revenue may provide, the sinking fund may be charged for the year 1817 with the payment of the Treasury notes which may be issued under the laws now in force. In preventing an addition of new funded debt, it will perform its office as usefully as in extinguishing the old debt.

1. *Resolved,* That it is expedient to continue in force, until the 30th day of July next, and until an act shall be passed establishing a new tariff of duties, the act entitled "An act for imposing additional duties upon all goods, wares, and merchandise, imported from any foreign port or place, and for other purposes;" passed on the 1st July, 1812.

2. *Resolved,* That it is expedient to continue in force the act, entitled "An act laying a duty on imported salt, granting a bounty on pickled fish exported, and allowance to certain vessels employed in the fisheries;" passed on the 29th July, 1813.

3. *Resolved,* That it is expedient to continue in force the act, entitled "An act laying duties on sugar refined within the United States;" passed July 24, 1813.

4. *Resolved,* That it is expedient to continue in force the act, entitled "An act laying duties on notes of banks, bankers, and certain companies; on notes, bonds, and obligations, discounted by banks, bankers, and certain companies; and on bills of exchange of certain descriptions;" passed on the 2d of August, 1813, also the act supplementary thereto, passed on the 10th day of December, 1814.

5. *Resolved,* That it is expedient to repeal, from the —— day of —— next, so much of the act, entitled

521

HISTORY OF CONGRESS.

522

JANUARY, 1816.

Commerce with Great Britain.

H. OF R.

"An act to provide additional revenues for defraying the expenses of Government and maintaining the public credit, by duties on sales at auction, and on licenses to retail wines, spirituous liquors, and foreign merchandise, and for increasing the rates of postage," passed on the 23d of December, 1814, as imposes additional duties on postage.

6. *Resolved,* That it is expedient so to amend the act, entitled "An act to provide additional revenues for defraying the expenses of Government, and maintaining the public credit, by laying a direct tax upon the United States, and to provide for assessing and collecting the same," passed on the 9th January, 1815, as to reduce the direct tax to be levied, for the year 1816, and succeeding years, to three millions; and also so to amend the act, entitled "An act to provide additional revenues for defraying the expenses of Government and maintaining the public credit, by laying a direct tax upon the District of Columbia," passed on the 27th of February, 1815, as to reduce the direct tax to be levied therein, annually, to $9,999 20.

7. *Resolved,* That it is expedient to repeal the act, entitled "An act to provide additional revenues for defraying the expenses of Government and maintaining the public credit, by laying duties on spirits distilled within the United States and Territories thereof, and by amending the act laying duties on licenses to distillers of spirituous liquors," passed on the 21st of December, 1814, excepting only the 16th, 18th, 19th, and 24th sections thereof, from and after the 1st of April next, and from the same day to add one hundred per cent. to the amount of the duty which all stills now subject to duty are liable to pay.

8. *Resolved,* That it is expedient to repeal, from and after the 18th day of April next, the act, entitled "An act to provide additional revenues for defraying the expenses of Government and maintaining the public credit, by laying duties on various goods, wares, and merchandise, manufactured within the United States," passed on the 18th of January, 1815; and also the act, entitled "An act to provide additional revenues for defraying the expenses of Government and maintaining the public credit, by laying a duty on gold, silver, and plated ware, and jewelry, and paste work, manufactured within the United States," passed on the 27th of February, 1815, from the same day.

9. *Resolved.* That it is expedient to repeal the act, entitled "An act to provide additional revenues for defraying the expenses of Government and maintaining the public credit, by laying duties on household furniture, and on gold and silver watches," passed on the 18th of January, 1815.

10. *Resolved,* That it is expedient so to amend the rates of duties upon imported articles, after the 30th of June next, as that they shall be estimated to produce an amount equal to that which would be produced by an average addition of forty-two per cent. to the permanent rates of duties.

11. *Resolved,* That the deficiency arising from the reduction or abolition of any of the duties heretofore pledged by law for the support of the Government, for the payment of the public debt, and the establishment of a sinking fund, shall be supplied by appropriating to those objects a sufficient amount from the product of the taxes or duties proposed to be continued or increased.

12. *Resolved,* That it is expedient that, from and after the year 1816, an addition shall be made to the sum of $8,000,000, now annually appropriated for the pay-

ment of the interest and principal of the public debt, so as to make the whole sum to be appropriated annually to that purpose, $13,500,000.

Ordered, That the Committee of Ways and Means be discharged from a further consideration of the several petitions referred to them, which relate to the subjects embraced in the last mentioned report.

COMMERCE WITH GREAT BRITAIN.

The House, according to the order of the day, resumed the consideration of the bill for carrying into effect the Convention of Commerce between the United States and Great Britain—the question being on ordering the bill to be engrossed for a third reading.

Mr. GHOLSON said, that being a member of the committee who had reported the bill then before the House, he had considered it especially his duty to give to it the most thorough investigation. He regretted that, owing to his personal indisposition, it had been out of his power to bestow on the subject that attention, which its importance most undoubtedly merited. He, however, had listened patiently to the arguments which had been offered by gentlemen on the other side of the House, in opposition to the bill. These arguments had produced no conviction to his mind. So far from it, (said Mr. G.) I am fully satisfied, that if the doctrines which have been contended for by gentlemen of distinction and eminent abilities, in the opposition, were reduced to practice, then indeed would the great and essential powers of the Government be transferred exclusively to the President and Senate, and this House would become almost a cypher—but little more than a mere tribunal of registry.

Two of the chief and principal objects of the federal compact were, the provision of an adequate national revenue, and the regulation of commerce with foreign nations. Jurisdiction over both these subjects is given by the Constitution, in clear and explicit terms, to the Congress of the United States. The Constitution expressly grants to Congress the power "to lay and collect taxes, duties, imposts, and excises;" and, moreover, "to regulate commerce with foreign nations, and among the several States, and with the Indian tribes."

But if the affairs of revenue from imposts, and of commerce, can be finally and conclusively arranged by the treaty-making authority, without the aid of legislation, it is perfectly obvious, that the grants of power just recited can be nullified and extinguished at the mere pleasure of the President and Senate, who alone exercise the treaty-making authority; that powers which are bestowed on them and on this House conjointly, can be exercised by them exclusively.

Now, sir, to prove that the treaty, to effectuate which the present bill is proposed, does, in fact, take cognizance both of the subject of taxation and of commerce, it is only necessary to look at the treaty itself. The treaty, in almost its whole aim and purport, relates to these subjects. It not only regulates our commerce with a foreign nation, but expressly undertakes to repeal a tax. By the existing law, British ships pay higher duties in our ports than American ships. The treaty provides, that in certain cases, embracing the principal trade between the two countries, British ships shall pay no higher duties than American. Thus the law of the land, providing for a public revenue, is so far attempted to be revoked by the treaty in question.

If, then, the self sufficiency of this treaty, for its own execution, without the agency of legislative provisions, can, according to the argument of the gentlemen from Pennsylvania and Massachusetts, (Messrs. Hopkinson and Pickering,) be maintained, it must be upon the ground, that the treaty-making power can either repeal a tax or regulate foreign commerce, independently of this House. Let us examine the subject in this aspect of it.

If it be admitted, that the treaty-making power can repeal a tax, it will, I apprehend, scarcely be denied, that the same power can, in like manner, impose a tax. Suppose, then, the President and Senate were, by convention with Great Britain, to stipulate for one hundred per cent. increase of duties on all merchandises imported into the United States from all foreign places, except from the British possessions, alleging that this exemption, in favor of Great Britain, was in consideration of the India trade, for which, it is said, no equivalent has been given by us. This would be an enormous tax on the people; and a tax, too, levied witout the consent of their representatives. But, sir, where did the idea originate of the imposition of a tax in a free country, without the concurrence of the immediate representatives of the people? The idea is preposterous, and one against which I enter my solemn protestation! I deny that there is any power on earth that can tax my constituents one cent, without their approbation, freely given, through their representative on this floor.

But still it is insisted that although the treaty contains provisions repealing the discriminating duties on British vessels and on goods imported in them, it is nevertheless a valid instrument. Suppose, sir, this repealing power had been exercised on another subject. Suppose the President and Senate had undertaken by treaty stipulation wholly to repeal the tax on foreign spirits. The amount of the tax repealed cannot vary the principle—if they can repeal a tax for one dollar, they can repeal one imposing millions. Yet I apprehend that the repeal by the treaty-making power, of the tax last mentioned, would be considered so outrageous an usurpation of the legislative authority, that it would not be submitted to for one moment.

Further, sir, according to the same reasoning, even the direct tax might be reduced or repealed by the treaty-making power. If by that tax agriculture were supposed to be oppressed, the doctrine contended for, would enable the President and Senate (the United States receiving an equivalent) to remove the tax in order to encourage the production of such articles as Great Britain

might want from this country, and to supply her with them in greater abundance, and on better terms. The articles, for instance, of cotton, tobacco, and flour.

These cases all demonstrate the absurdity of claiming for the treaty-making power, in this country, any control whatever over the public revenue. The truth is, that except as a part of the Legislature, it possesses none; and from the very structure of our Government, cannot possess any.

The claim, sir, of the same power to regulate, at its pleasure, our foreign commerce, without the interference of this House, will be found to rest on no better grounds.

If with a view to a better understanding, and a closer connexion with Great Britain, the President and Senate were to agree by convention with that nation, to prohibit the exportation of cotton and woollen manufactures from the United States, for the next thirty years; or were to stipulate that the United States should not clear any vessel direct from other ports to France, Spain, Holland, or any other European country, except to Great Britain, such convention would, on the face of it, appear to be a complete and perfect act, and requiring, therefore, agreeably to the arguments of the gentlemen on the other side, no legislative sanction; all that would be necessary would be instructions from the Secretary of the Treasury to the collectors of the customs. If, as it has been contended, the treaty-making authority possesses absolute control over our foreign commerce, there can exist no doubt of its competency to enter into these engagements. Yet the very attempt to control them would be considered monstrous, and would no doubt be universally resisted. The doctrine, sir, proves too much, and therefore proves nothing.

Again: suppose the treaty-making power were, as was once contemplated by the British Government, to engage that during any European war in which Great Britain might be a party, all American vessels bound to the ports of any nation in hostility with Great Britain, should first call or touch at some *British port*, and there pay a *tax*, and take a *license* for the benefit of prosecuting their voyages! Let me ask if such an engagement would not be considered as a most daring usurpation? Yes, sir, it would be viewed as an alarming encroachment upon the rights of this House, and of the nation, and would be repelled with indignation? And still this and all the cases of treaty stipulation which I have supposed would come fully within the rule laid down by gentlemen on the other side of the question, as the limit of the treaty-making power, namely, that whenever a treaty can, according to its own terms, execute itself, it requires no legislative sanction. I trust I have already sufficiently shown the fallacy of this position.

But some gentlemen have recurred to another ground of argument. They say that treaties are themselves the supreme law of the land, and can, therefore, require no legislation to give to them additional validity. This idea was strenuously enforced by a gentleman from Massachusetts, (Mr. MILLS.)

In considering the remarks of gentlemen on this branch of the subject, it will be perceived how necessary it is that positions in debate should be laid down with accuracy and precision. Gentlemen may be astonished, perhaps, when I announce to them my dissent from the position which they have so triumphantly advanced, in relation to the supremacy of treaties. Now, I deny, sir, the correctness of the proposition that treaties are the supreme law of the land. I very readily admit that treaties, made under the authority of the United States, that is, Constitutional treaties, are the supreme law of the land. But the broad, unqualified assertion, that treaties generally, (whether violative of the Constitution or not,) partake of that high and sacred character, is manifestly untenable. Here, then, the very gist of the question is, whether the Constitution does in fact confer the right to make such a treaty as the one before us, without the sanction of this House?

Having endeavored to show that such right has not been conferred, I will decline repeating the arguments which I have already had the honor of addressing to the House; especially after the luminous exposition of the subject with which we have been favored by the honorable gentleman from South Carolina, (Mr. LOWNDES.) Nor will I detain you respecting the definitions that have been given with regard to the extent of the treaty-making power. As to that, I will observe, that, subject to the limitations of the Constitution, I should conceive the treaty-making authority in this country as large and as comprehensive as the same authority in any other civilized State. After conceding to this House the privileges for which it contends, and which are evidently guarantied to it by the Constitution, there would still be left to the treaty-making authority a wide range of powers. For instance, the entire subject of belligerent regulations, including the most important topic of impressment; the question of search, the subject of boundaries, and many others which it would be useless perhaps to enumerate.

I cannot perceive, sir, the advantage of resorting, as gentlemen have done, to the British Government for precedents on this occasion. The analogies between that Government and ours, are in general too weak to authorize the deduction therefrom of any principle that can be safely depended on. It is understood, however, that the practice even of the British Government has always been in accordance with the principles which are maintained by the advocates of this bill.

It results, therefore, from every view of the subject, of which I conceive it is fairly susceptible, that the bill now before us is not only not an useless one, as it has been said to be, but that it is absolutely indispensable; indispensable, in order to the fulfilment of the stipulations of the treaty, and because it relates to powers which cannot be exercised without the concurrence of this House.

Mr. CALHOUN observed, that the votes on this bill had been ordered to be recorded; and that the House would see, in his peculiar situation, a sufficient apology for his offering his reasons for the rejection of the bill. He had no disposition to speak on this bill, as he felt contented to let it take that course which, in the opinion of the majority, it ought, until the members were called on by the order of the House to record their votes.

The question presented for consideration is perfectly simple, and easily understood—Is this bill necessary to give validity to the late treaty with Great Britain? It appeared to him that this question is susceptible of a decision, without considering whether a treaty can in any case set aside a law; or, to be more particular, whether the treaty which this bill purposes to carry into effect does repeal the discriminating duties. The House will remember that a law was passed at the close of the last session conditionally repealing those duties. That act proposed to repeal them in relation to any nation which would on its part agree to repeal similar duties as to this country. On the contingency happening the law became positive. It has happened, and has been announced to the country that England has agreed to repeal. The President, in proclaiming the treaty, has notified the fact to the House and country. Why then propose to do that by this bill which has already been done by a previous act? He knew it had been said in conversation that the provisions of the act were not as broad as the treaty. It did not strike him so. They appeared to him to be commensurate. He would also reason from the appearance of this House that they were not very deeply impressed with the necessity of this bill. He never, on any important occasion, saw it so indifferent. Whence could this arise? From the want of importance? If, indeed, the existence of the treaty depended on the passage of this bill, nothing scarcely could be more interesting. It would be calculated to excite strong feelings. We all know how the country was agitated when Jay's Treaty was before this House. The question was on an appropriation to carry it into effect—a power acknowledged by all to belong to the House—and on the exercise of which the existence of the treaty was felt to depend. The feelings manifested corresponded with this conviction. Not so on this occasion. Further: the treaty has already assumed the form of law. It is so proclaimed to the community; the words of the proclamation are not material; it speaks for itself; and if it means anything, it announces the treaty as a rule of public conduct, as a law exacting the obedience of the people. Were he of the opposite side, if he indeed believed this treaty to be a dead letter until it had received the sanction of Congress, he would lay the bill on the table and move an inquiry into the fact why the treaty has been proclaimed as a law before it had received the proper sanction. It is true, the Executive has transmitted a copy of the treaty to the House; but has he sent the negotiation?

Has he given any light to judge why it should receive the sanction of this body? Do gentlemen mean to say that information is not needed; that though we have the right to pass laws to give validity to treaties, yet we are bound by a moral obligation to pass such laws? To talk of the right of this House to sanction treaties, and at the same time to assert that it is under a moral obligation not to withhold that sanction, is a solecism. No sound mind that understands the terms can possibly assent to it. He would caution the House, while it was extending its powers to cases which he believed did not belong to it, to take care lest it should lose its substantial and undoubted power. He would put it on its guard against the dangerous doctrine that it can in any case become a mere registering body. Another fact in regard to this treaty. It does not stipulate that a law should pass to repeal the duties proposed to be repealed by this bill, which would be its proper form, if in the opinion of the negotiators a law was necessary; but it stipulates in positive terms for their repeal without consulting or regarding us.

Mr. C. here concluded this part of the discussion, by stating that it appeared to him, from the whole complexion of the case, that the bill before the House was mere form, and not supposed to be necessary to the validity of the treaty. It would be proper however, he observed, to reply to the arguments which have been urged on the general nature of the treaty-making power, and, as it was a subject of great importance, he solicited the attentive hearing of the House. It is not denied, he believed, that the President with the concurrence of two thirds of the Senate have a right to make commercial treaties; it is not asserted that this treaty is couched in such general terms as to require a law to carry the details into execution. Why then is this bill necessary? Because, say gentlemen, that the treaty of itself, without the aid of this bill, cannot exempt British tonnage and goods imported in their bottoms, from the operation of the law laying additional duties on foreign tonnage and goods imported in foreign vessels; or, giving the question a more general form, because a treaty cannot annul a law. The gentleman from Virginia, (Mr. Barbour,) who argued this point very distinctly, though not satisfactorily, took as his general position, that to repeal a law is a legislative act, and can only be done by law; that, in the distribution of the legislative treaty-making power, the right to repeal a law fell exclusively under the former. How does this comport with the admission immediately made by him, that the Treaty of Peace repealed the act declaring war? If he admits the fact in a single case, what becomes of his exclusive legislative right? He indeed felt that his rule failed him, and in explanation assumed a position entirely new; for he admitted that when the treaty did that which was not authorized to be done by law, it did not require the sanction of Congress, and might in its operation repeal a law inconsistent with it. He said, Congress is not authorized to make peace; and for

this reason a Treaty of Peace repeals the act declaring war. In this position, he understood his colleague substantially to concur. He hoped to make it appear that, in taking this ground, they have both yielded the point in discussion. He would establish, he trusted, to the satisfaction of the House, that the treaty-making power, when it was legitimately exercised, always did that which could not be done by law; and that the reasons advanced to prove that the Treaty of Peace repealed the act making war, so far from being peculiar to that case, apply to all treaties. They do not form an exception, but in fact constitute the rule. Why then, he asked, cannot Congress make peace? They have the power to declare war. All acknowledge this power. Peace and war are the opposites. They are the positive and negative terms of the same proposition; and what rule of construction more clear, than that when a power is given to do an act, the power is also given to repeal it? By what right do you repeal taxes, reduce your Army, lay up your Navy, or repeal any law, but by the force of this plain rule of construction? Why cannot Congress then repeal the act declaring war? He acknowledged with the gentleman, they cannot, consistently with reason. The solution of this question explained the whole difficulty. The reason is plain; one Power may make war; it requires two to make peace. It is a state of mutual amity succeeding mutual hostility; it is a state that cannot be created but with the consent of both parties. It required a contract or a treaty between the nations at war. Is this peculiar to a Treaty of Peace? No, it is common to all treaties. It rises out of their nature, and not from any accidental circumstance attaching itself to a particular class. It is no more or less than that Congress cannot make a contract with a foreign nation. Let us apply it to a treaty of commerce—to this very case. Can Congress do what this treaty has done? It has repealed the discriminating duties between this country and England. Either could by law repeal its own. But by law they could go no farther; and for the same reason that peace cannot be made by law. Whenever, then, an ordinary subject of legislation can only be regulated by contract, it passes from the sphere of the ordinary power of making laws, and attaches itself to that of making treaties, wherever it is lodged. All acknowledge the truth of this conclusion, where the subject on which the treaty operates is not expressly given to Congress. But in other cases they consider the two powers as concurrent; and conclude, from the nature of such powers, that such treaties must be confirmed by law. Will they acknowledge the opposite, that laws on such subjects must be confirmed by treaties? And if, as they state, a law can repeal a treaty when concurrent, why not a treaty a law? Into such absurdities do false doctrines lead. The truth is, the legislative and treaty-making power, are never in the strict sense concurrent. They both may have the same subject, as in this case commerce; but they discharge functions as different in relation to it in their nature, as their subject is alike.

When we speak of concurrent powers, we mean when both can do the same thing; but he contended, that when the two powers under discussion were confined to their proper sphere, not only the law could not do what could be done by treaty, but the reverse was true; that is, they never are nor can be concurrent powers. It is only when we reason on this subject that we mistake; in all other cases the common sense of the House and country decide correctly. It is proposed to establish some regulation of commerce; we immediately inquire, does it depend on our will; can we make the desired regulation without the concurrence of any foreign Power. If so, it belongs to Congress, and any one would feel it to be absurd to attempt to effect it by treaty. On the contrary, does it require the consent of a foreign Power; is it proposed to grant a favor, to repeal discriminating duties on both sides? It is equally felt to belong to the treaty power; and he would be thought insane who would propose to abolish the discriminating duties in any case, by an act of the American Congress. It is calculated, he felt, almost to insult the good sense of the House, to dwell on a point apparently so clear. What then would he infer from what had been advanced? That, according to the argument of gentlemen, treaties, producing a state of things inconsistent with the provisions of an existing law, annul such provisions. But as he did not agree with them in the view which they took, he would here present his own for consideration. Why then has a treaty the force which he attributed to it? Because it is an act in its own nature paramount to laws made by the common legislative powers of the country. It is in fact a law and something more, a law established by contract between independent nations. To analogise it to private life, law has the same relations to treaty, as the resolution taken by an individual to his contract. An individual may make the most deliberate promise—he may swear it in the most solemn form—that he would not sell his house or any other property he may have; yet, if he would afterwards sell, the sale would be valid in law; he would not be admitted in a court of justice to plead his oath against his contract. Take a case of Government in its simple form, where it was purely despotic, that is, all power lodged in the hands of a single individual. Would not his treaties repeal inconsistent edicts?

Let us now ascend from the instances cited, to illustrate the nature of the two powers, to the *principle* on which the paramount character of a treaty rests. A treaty always affects the interests of two; a law, only that of a single nation. It is an established principle of politics and morality, that the interest of the many is paramount to that of the few. In fact, it is a principle so radical, that without it no system of morality, no rational scheme of Government, could exist. It is for this reason that contracts, or that treaties, which are only the contracts of independent nations, or, to express both in two words, that plighted faith has in all ages and nations been considered so solemn. But it is said, in opposition to this

position, that a subsequent law can repeal a treaty; and to this proposition, he understood that the member from North Carolina (Mr. GASTON) assented. Strictly speaking, he denied the fact. He knew that a law might assume the appearance of repealing a treaty; but he insisted it was only in appearance, and that, in point of fact, it was not a repeal. Whenever a law was proposed, declaring a treaty void, he considered that the House acted not as a legislative body, but judicially. He would illustrate his ideas? If the House is a moral body, that is, if it is governed by reason and virtue, which it must always be presumed to be, the only question that ever could occupy its attention whenever a treaty is to be declared void, is whether, under all of the circumstances of the case, the treaty is not already destroyed, by being violated by the nation with whom it is made, or by the existence of some other circumstance, if other there can be. The House determines this question. Is the country any longer bound by the treaty? Has it not ceased to exist? The nation passes in judgment on its own contract; and this, from the necessity of the case, as it admits no superior power to which it can refer for decision. If any other consideration moves the House to repeal a treaty, it can be considered only in the light of a violation of a contract acknowledged to be binding on the country. A nation may, it is true, violate its contract; they may even do this under the form of law; but he was not considering what might be done, but what might be rightfully done. It is not a question of power, but of right. Why are not these positions, in themselves so clear, universally assented to? Gentlemen are alarmed at imaginary consequences. They argue not as if seeking for the meaning of the Constitution, but as if deliberating on the subject of making one; not as members of the Legislature, and acting under a Constitution already established, but as that of a convention about to frame one. For his part, he had always regarded the Constitution as a work of great wisdom, and, being the instrument under which we existed as a body, it was our duty to bow to its enactments, whatever they may be, with submission. We ought scarcely to indulge a wish that its provisions should be different from what they in fact are. The consequences, however, which appear to work with so much terror on the minds of the gentlemen, he considered to be without any just foundation. The treaty-making power has many and powerful limits; and it will be found, when he came to discuss what those limits are, that it cannot destroy the Constitution, our personal liberty, involve us without the assent of this House in war, or grant away our money. The limits he proposed to this power are not the same, it is true, but they appeared to him much more rational and powerful than those which were supposed to present effectual guards to its abuse. Let us now consider what they are? The grant of the power to make treaties is couched in the most general terms. The words of the Constitution are, that the President shall have power, by and with the advice and consent of the Senate, to make treaties, provided two-thirds of the Senators present concur. In a subsequent part of the Constitution, treaties are declared to be the supreme law of the land. Whatever limits are imposed on those general terms ought to be the result of the sound construction of the instrument. There appeared to him but two restrictions on its exercise; the one derived from the nature of our Government, and the other from that of the power itself. Most certainly all grants of power under the Constitution must be controlled by that instrument; for, having their existence from it, they must of necessity assume that form which the Constitution has imposed. This is acknowledged to be true of the legislative power, and it is doubtless equally so of the power to make treaties. The limits of the former are exactly marked; it was necessary to prevent collision with similar co-existing State powers. This country is divided into many distinct sovereignties. Exact enumeration here is necessary to prevent the most dangerous consequences. The enumeration of legislative powers in the Constitution has relation then, not to the treaty-power, but to the powers of the State. In our relation to the rest of the world the case is reversed. Here the States disappear. Divided within, we present the exterior of undivided sovereignty. The wisdom of the Constitution appears conspicuous. When enumeration was needed, there we find the powers enumerated and exactly defined; when not, we do not find what would be vain and pernicious. Whatever, then, concerns our foreign relations; whatever requires the consent of another nation, belongs to the treaty power; can only be regulated by it; and it is competent to regulate all such subjects; provided, and here are its true limits, such regulations are not inconsistent with the Constitution. If so they are void. No treaty can alter the fabric of our Government, nor can it do that which the Constitution has expressly forbid to be done; nor can it do that differently which is directed to be done in a given mode, and all other modes prohibited. For instance, the Constitution of the United States says, no money "shall be drawn out of the Treasury but by an appropriation made by law." Of course no subsidy can be granted without an act of law, and a treaty of alliance could not involve the country in war without the consent of this House. With this limitation it is easy to explain the case put by my colleague, who said that, according to one limitation, a treaty might have prohibited the introduction of a certain description of persons before the year 1808, notwithstanding the clause in the Constitution to the contrary. Mr. C. said that he would speak plainly on this point; it was the intention of the Constitution that the slave trade should be tolerated till the time mentioned. It covered him with confusion to name it here. He felt ashamed of such a tolerance, and took a large part of the disgrace, as he represented a part of the Union by whose influence it might be supposed to have been introduced. Though Congress alone is prohibited by the words of th

clause from inhibiting that odious traffic, yet his colleague would admit that it was intended to be a general prohibition on the Government of the Union. He perceived his colleague indicated his dissent. It will be necessary to be more explicit. Here Mr. C. read that part of the Constitution, and showed that the word "Congress" might be left out, in conformity to other parts of the Constitution, without injury to the sense of the clause; and he insisted that the plain meaning of the parties to the Constitution, was, that the trade should continue till 1808, and that a prohibition by treaty would be equally against the spirit of the instrument. Besides these Constitutional limits, the treaty power, like all powers, has others derived from its object and nature. It has for its object contracts with foreign nations, as the powers of Congress have for their object whatever can be done in relation to the powers delegated to it without the consent of foreign nations. Each in its proper sphere operates with general influence; but when they became erratic, then they were portentous and dangerous. A treaty never can legitimately do that which can be done by law; and the converse is also true. Suppose the discriminating duties repealed on both sides by law, yet what is effected by this treaty would not even then be done; the plighted faith would be wanting. Either side might repeal its law without breach of contract. It appeared to him that gentlemen are too much influenced on the subject by the example of Great Britain. Instead of looking to the nature of our Government, they have been swayed in their opinion by the practice of that Government to which we are but too much in the habit of looking for precedents. Much anxiety has recently been evinced to be independent of English broadcloths and muslins. He hoped it indicated the approach of a period when we should also throw off the thraldom of thought. The truth is, but little analogy exists between this and any other Government. It is the pride of ours to be founded in reason and equity; all others have originated more or less in fraud, violence, or accident. The right to make treaties in England can only be determined by the practice of that Government, as she has no written Constitution. Her practice may be wise in regard to her Government, when it would be very imprudent here. Admitting the fact to be, then, that the King refers all commercial treaties affecting the municipal regulations of the country to Parliament, for its sanction, the ground would be very feeble to prove that to be the intention of our Constitution. Strong difference exists between the forms of the two Governments. The King is hereditary; he alone, without the participation of either House of Parliament, negotiates and makes treaties; they have no Constitution emanating from the people, alike superior to the Legislature and the King. Not so here. The President is elected for a short period; he is amenable to the public opinion; he is liable to be impeached for corruption; he cannot make treaties without the concurrence of two-thirds of the Senate, a fact very material to be remembered, which body is in like manner responsible to the people at periods not very remote; above all, as the laws and Constitution are here perfectly distinct, and the latter is alike superior to laws and treaties, the treaty power cannot change the form of Government, or encroach on the liberties of the country, without encroaching on that instrument, which, so long as the people are free, will be watched with vigilance.

Mr. RANDOLPH said, when he took his seat yesterday, or rather before he was qualified to take his seat, he had considered the bill then and now under discussion as one of perhaps as trivial a nature as ever engaged the attention of this House, or of any legislative body. But, of this bill, it might be said, *vires acquirit eundo;* and of this perhaps he was about to afford the House some proof, by adding his little rill to swell the torrent of debate to which this bill had given rise. Certainly—and he knew with what suspicions such declarations were generally received, but he spoke it *bona fide*—he had no intention to utter one word on the subject until he heard doctrines against which he felt himself bound to enter his solemn protest. He might say of this bill, as of some disease, the danger was in the mode of treatment, in the doctor, and not in the disease. He hoped the gentleman from South Carolina would pardon him when he had heard doctrines from him this day, against which he felt it his solemn and bounden duty to enter his protest. There was nothing in this, he knew, to alarm the gentleman, for it was the protest of a feeble isolated individual, but of an individual who would discharge his duty off this floor and on this floor, with the same zeal and perseverance as if he commanded a majority of the House at his beck. If he understood the gentleman, Mr. R. said, he had declared that a treaty, being of the nature of a compact, touching the interests of other nations than our own, it therefore followed, that the treaty-making power, so long as it confined itself to its own sphere, that of contract; so long as it received equivalents for what it gave, whether real or nominal, according to the gentleman's doctrine no matter—they are not to be crippled up, not to be examined; that inasmuch as the interest of two nations instead of one, were concerned in all treaties; therefore the treaty-making power is paramount to the legislative power—did he or did he not understand the gentleman? It was impossible to misunderstand him; for, Mr. R. said, he had stated his positions with a precision and clearness which left no room for doubt—yes, that treaties, being paramount, of course repealed the law of the land, so far as the law of the land came into collision with any article of a treaty which was confined to the legitimate objects of a treaty, viz: to contracts with another nation. But the honorable gentleman from South Carolina had, with peculiar infelicity of illustration, drawn examples from despotic Governments. Would a treaty made by a Sultan of Constantinople or an Emperor of France go to repeal a law of the Turkish or French empire? Certainly it would. For what are the laws of a despotic monarchy but the breath of the sovereign, call him what you will? And was that an analogy on which to found a construction of our Constitution, on which the gentleman had bestowed so high but not undeserved an eulogium? No; it was because a treaty made by a despotic Power will repeal the law of the land there, that a treaty made by Presidential authority will not repeal the law of the land here. To come to the gentleman's *experimentem crucis*, and try the strength of his argument, that a treaty is paramount to the law of the land. Suppose the Treaty of Peace had contained a provision for ceding away a part or the whole of South Carolina, as an equivalent for Jamaica, for territory in India, or for Ireland. Would the gentleman consider such a stipulation, although in the nature of a contract, as amounting to a law of the land? But, perhaps, he said, he should be told that that which is paramount to the law of the land, is not paramount to the Constitution, and that the Constitution prohibits the cession of a State or part of a State to a foreign Power. It was unquestionably true, whatever might be his opinion, that such is not the universal opinion; although it might perhaps be proved by the event, that as the United States had heretofore acquired territory by treaty, we have also parted with territory by treaty—as in the instance of Moose Island, and it may be, in the instance of the new boundary line to be run between us and Canada, that it may be so run as to take off part of the territory which was a part of the United States—yes, a part of the good old thirteen United States.

But, the gentleman had said something of the effect of a contract of an individual on an oath previously taken. What analogy, Mr. R. asked, was there between the absurd and preposterous conduct of an individual who attempts to tie himself up by an oath from imprudence, from the gambling-table, from the bottle, from squandering his estate, &c., and the acts of Government, especially as those acts are affected by the acts of two branches of the Government farthest removed from the people, who do not speak their sense as much as we do? Mr. R. here expressed a doubt whether, from having been out of the habit of speaking and having overstrained his voice, he had been able to make himself understood. He then adverted to the observation of the gentleman from South Carolina, that the President and Senate have an unquestionable right to put an end to the calamities of war by making a Treaty of Peace, over which this House could have no control. Mr. R. agreed with that gentleman, that the exercise of the power to put an end to the calamities of war, was the most important ever granted by a free people, except the exercise of the power to declare war. He agreed also with the gentleman, after Congress had declared war, the President and Senate might by treaty restore the state of peace; but he could not agree with the gentleman, that a treaty, although it should confine itself to what the gentleman called a contract, was paramount to law, and competent to repeal existing laws. Suppose that the Treaty of Peace had been a treaty of alliance, and had stipulated that the United States should levy an 'army of an hundred thousand men, and that they should be sent to the Continent to aid the British, Prussian, and Austrian arms on the plains of Waterloo—would this House have been bound to raise the men? Would Congress have been bound to provide the means of maintaining them? Certainly not.

In the declaration of war, it had been argued, by the gentleman from South Carolina, that the House had acted in a judicial capacity. In a judicial capacity! exclaimed Mr. R. He had heard it, he said, in and out of this House, questioned whether this House acted *judiciously* in declaring war, but he never heard it before suggested whether or not they had acted *judicially* on that occasion. He had never before heard it doubted, whether the Congress in passing any act, acted judicially or legislatively. [Mr. Calhoun here made a brief explanation and statement of the extent of his position.] Mr. R. expressed his obligation to the gentleman for having stated his argument exactly as he had at first understood it. He would put it to this House, to the nation, to every man, woman, and child in the nation. Suppose the Treaty of London had been unsuspended by the truce of Amiens, would the declaration of war with Great Britain have put an end to that treaty? It would;—and would that act have been a judicial act, when the consent of the President and Senate was necessary to our acting at all? Did the gentleman mean to say, continued Mr. R., that when the Treaty with France was repealed by an act making war, during Mr. Adams's administration, it was repealed by a judicial act? Was it possible? Was there a man wide awake who could advance such an opinion? This House, he said, acted judicially when it decided on the qualifications of a member; the Senate when it tried an impeachment. But how could that be a judicial act which reads—*Be it enacted by the Senate and House of Representatives, &c.* Go to the Secretary of State's office, said Mr. R., if the rolls be still in existence, and see in what that act differs from any other—the title is as plain, the parchment as smooth. This act, which repealed an existing treaty, which treaty could not be revived after peace, unless renewed and again ratified, differs in no respect of form or solemnity from the simplest law ever made for the relief of a petitioner before this House. It does not differ from any other legislative act; and you have no judicial power, as far as my recollection now supplies me, beyond the right to try the title to a member's seat, and the right to expel a refractory and disorderly member.

Mr. R. said he did not mean to enter into the comparison between the constitution of Great Britain and that of the United States, considering it irrelevant. Mr. R. agreed that our Constitution was to be found in the charter, and in the practice under the Constitution, whether legislative or judicial, provided the precedents are taken from good Constitutional times—for he would never take precedents under any administration during times of great turbulence or excitement, when the best of us are under temptations, to which most of us yield, of carrying our passions and prejudices into public life. With all due submission to the gentleman from South Carolina, and to this House, Mr. R. said he did declare that the President and Senate did not and never had possessed the power, by any contract with a foreign Power, of repealing any law of the land, or enacting any law in its stead. This he said, was his opinion of this great Constitutional question; he had expressed it in this hasty way, under the excitement of the abhorrence—he hoped the gentleman would pardon him; it had nothing personal in it—of the abhorrence he felt at the doctrine which the gentleman had uttered on this floor—a doctrine which there was a time when it would have been called highly federal doctrine; and certainly not the less objectionable to Mr. R. on that account, either at that time or this—the doctrine that, so long as they could find another power to contract with, the President and Senate might exercise a power paramount to all law, though not to the Constitution. This was too dangerous a power to be given to the President and Senate under such a sweeping clause. If this bill had passed through this House *sub silentio*, if it had been carried or rejected, he should never have thought much of it; for it would never have assumed to him that aspect, which it had done since this morning—since the gentleman had asserted, that so long as they confined themselves to the legitimate sphere of contract, the President and Senate might exercise a power superior to all law whatever.

Mr. R. said, he was happy to find, however, that the gentleman had, in a degree, dissipated the horrid phantom which had so much alarmed not his imagination but his judgment. The gentleman had admitted, that there was a certain influence—a certain Constitutional check on the President and Senate of the United States—for example, impeachment as regarded the President, and public opinion as regarded the Senate—and that the spirit of the Constitution would at all times meliorate the power which, in the gentleman's opinion, the President and Senate possessed of violating every law of the land. Mr. R. granted that this was the case, and that the first reflection on it had caused Mr. R. himself to depreciate this bill below its actual importance—for he really had thought the House was making a great deal out of nothing, swelling a molehill into a mountain—until he heard the debate, when he became convinced, in so far as the power of the House of Representatives was important in the Constitution of the United States, so far as it behooves the House of Representatives to hold the power which had been conferred on them, for the nation's good, by the nation; that, so far, this was a question of importance. That the time should ever come when the President of the United States should dare to negotiate a treaty which would meet with the decided reprobation of the people of the country and their Representatives, was another question; that the time should ever come when the House of Representatives would ever have the incivility to refuse to pass laws to carry into effect such a treaty, is also another question. I do not believe, said he, (addressing the Speaker,) that either of these periods will happen in my life time, or in yours; because I believe, sir—I hope I am not mistaken—that the good sense of the people of the United States, if it please God to permit us to remain in peace—that their good sense will, in spite of all the efforts to swell up great standing armies, mighty navies, heavy taxes, and to advance the glory (as it is called) of the Government under which I live, in the blood and misery of the people—that they will put an end, as they have once before put an end to such projects, the same in kind but differing in degree—differing indeed, because infinitely below what I have seen for some time past agitated. And whether the House of Representatives declare with the honorable gentlemen on the other side of the House, that we have the power, or with my friend from North Carolina, that we have not the power or the right to pass this bill—during your life-time and mine, the Constitution will not be violated. This bill, Mr. R. repeated, was not of much importance in its matter, but in the manner of its discussion. By way of pinning the honorable gentleman down, said he, let me conclude the few crude remarks I have to make, by this question; suppose that a part of the contract by the late treaty had been, that each party should burn, sink, or dismantle an equal number of ships-of-the-line, frigates, and so on—that provision would require no appropriation;—or, suppose the treaty had contained a stipulation to destroy all our fleet, provided Great Britain would destroy an equal number of hers—this would have required no appropriation; it would have been within the legitimate sphere of contracts; it would have been a bargain; it would have even had reciprocity; it would have kept the word of promise to the ear, but broke it to the hope. But then, said Mr. R., comes in the power of impeachment—the great remedy; I have no idea of it—it has been tried and found wanting, in the case of a member of the other House, and in the case of a high judicial officer. The power of impeachment, he said, appeared to him to be not the daily bread, but the extreme medicine of the Constitution. He had no faith in it—he had no faith in a course of mercury, to restore health and vigor to that constitution which was broken down by disease—nor did he believe, if such a stipulation as he had represented had been found in a treaty, that a majority of this House could have been found to vote for an impeachment. Impeachment, Mr. R. said, extends to loss of office, to disqualification; that may be a terrible punishment to the young and aspiring; but to those who are retiring from the political theatre, amidst the plaudits of a great part of the nation over which they preside, such a punishment had no terrors. Mr. R. concluded by saying, he believed he had trespassed

on the House too long; he could not, however, repress the expression of his horror at the doctrines which had been advanced—doctrines, if they prevailed, subversive not only of the Constitution of the United States, but of all free government whatever.

Mr. KING, of Massachusetts, spoke as follows:

Mr. Speaker, as the vote which I shall give upon this bill, will differ from those which will be given by those friends with whom I have the pleasure generally to act, I owe it to them and to myself to explain, as briefly as possible, the reasons of that vote, leaving the general argument to others more able and willing to discuss it. When this subject was first started in the House; when this bill was first introduced, and it was observed by many gentlemen that no bill was necessary, that the convention was already the law of the land, without much reflection I inclined to that opinion; concluding that what was already the law of the land, could not, by any act of ours, be more the law of the land. But, sir, when, in the course of debate, I heard my honorable friend from North Carolina (Mr. GASTON) speak of the moral obligation which this House was under to appropriate money to carry any treaty stipulation into effect, which might require the aid of Congress, and of the awful responsibility we should incur, were we to refuse to make such appropriation, he appeared to acknowledge a case where a treaty was not complete without legislative aid, and that the House might incur the responsibility of refusing such aid; my first impression I therefore thought wrong, and with the treaty, the bill, and the Constitution, before me, I was determined to investigate the subject attentively on its merits, with such light, however dim, as the Supreme bestower of every good gift had seen fit to impart to me. Of the opinion out of doors and of the times, I know nothing; to confess to you the truth, sir, I was afraid to recur to opinions of other times, lest they should have been produced by an excitement unfavorable to correct conclusions in politics. The result of my investigation on this subject is: that whenever a treaty or convention does, by any of its provisions, encroach upon any of the enumerated powers vested by the Constitution in the Congress of the United States, or any of the laws by them enacted in execution of those powers, such treaty or convention, after being ratified, must be laid before Congress, and such provisions cannot be carried into effect without an act of Congress. For instance, whenever a treaty affected duties on imports, enlarging or diminishing them, as the present one did to diminish; whenever a treaty went to regulate commerce with foreign nations, as that expressly did with one, as the power to lay duties and the power to regulate commerce are expressly given to Congress, such provisions of such treaty must receive the sanction of Congress before they can be considered as obligatory and as part of the municipal law of this country. And this construction is strengthened by a part of the general power given to Congress, following the enumerated powers, "to make all laws which shall be

'necessary and proper, for carrying into execu-
'tion the foregoing powers, and all other powers
'vested by the Constitution in the Government
'of the United States, or in any department or
'office thereof." In other words, for carrying
into execution the treaty-making power (that being among the other powers) in all cases where
it has been exercised on subjects, placed by the
Constitution within the control of the legislative
department. This construction is further strengthened by the concession of honorable gentlemen,
in one case, that where appropriations of money
are necessary for carrying the provisions of any
treaty into effect, there legislative provision is
necessary. Now, sir, to concede that the sanction of Congress is necessary in one case of enumerated and specified power, is to concede it in
all such cases. Nor, sir, can any serious inconvenience arise from this construction. As to negotiations with foreign Powers, our Ministers will
always know the peculiar structure of our Government; nor can foreign Ministers, who may
ever be sent to treat with us, be ignorant thereof.
Besides, the distinction, as to the several kinds of
treaties, is well known,; some, respecting solely
our external relations, or the intercourse between
our Government and that of a foreign Power,
will execute themselves, or are perfect without
any legislative aid; and it can instantly be determined, from the nature of the provisions, when
legislative aid is necessary. Further, sir, your
Government has well understood this distinction.
Some treaties they, by their proclamations, merely ratify and confirm, where legislative aid is necessary, as in the present case; others, they not
only ratify and confirm, but enjoin an observance
thereof upon all our citizens, as will be seen by
turning to the ratification, by Mr. Jefferson, of
several treaties published in the seventh volume
United States laws. The fear that the President
and Senate (they must both, or two-thirds of the
latter, concur) will agree with the House in passing an improper law on the subject of a treaty
which they had before ratified, cannot be well
founded. There is much more reason to fear
that they may be induced to ratify a treaty requiring legislative provision, which the House
ought to refuse. Should a case of that kind occur,
while I have the honor to be one of the Representatives of the people, I shall have no hesitation, with my brethren, to interpose ourselves
between the Executive and the people, in the defence of their rights, or the freedom of our country. Far, then, from shrinking from what my
honorable friend is pleased to call an awful responsibility, I should think it a sacred duty to
meet the crisis, resist the encroachment, and leave
the consequences with God. I never will consent
that the House of Representatives of the people
shall become a mere Parliament of Paris, to register the edicts of the President. I shall vote for
the bill.

Mr. Mills said, nothing had been further from
his intention than to take a part in the present
debate. But although he had bestowed but little
attention to the subject, he begged the indulgence

of the House for a moment to the few remarks
which the discussion had suggested to his mind,
and which had not been noticed by those who
had preceded him in the debate. Crude and in-
digested as these remarks may appear, he could
venture to engage they would have at least the
merit of brevity. Mr. M. said, he was opposed
to the passage of the bill; not because he felt the
least disposition to impede the execution of the
treaty, lame and imbecile as it is, to which it relates, but because he foresaw the danger of embarrassing the other branches of the Government
by this interference, and because he believed, as
well from the structure of the Government, as
from the express provisions of the Constitution,
we could not interpose our authority in the way
contemplated by this bill, without attempting an
unwarrantable exercise of power not delegated to
this House by the Constitution. It would be not
merely an act of useless legislation, but of down-
right usurpation. Gentlemen had indulged themselves at great length in search of arguments to
prove the inexpediency of vesting the absolute
and uncontrolled power of making treaties, in the
President and Senate, and had taxed their imaginations for proof of the mischiefs which might
result from the exercise of this power. Sir, we
are not at liberty to go into that inquiry. The
question is not, where ought this important prerogative of sovereignty to be lodged? But, where
is it deposited by the Constitution? We are not
sitting as a convention to make such a distribution of powers as we think best calculated to secure the preservation of liberty, but we are called
upon to exercise those powers already vested in
us by the instrument which we have solemnly
sworn to support.

The practice of other Governments is equally
irrelevant to the present inquiry, and especially
of those Governments whose forms of proceeding,
and the distributions of whose powers, bear but a
remote analogy to our own. Ours is a federative
Government, composed of distinct and separate
sovereignties, and clothed with no powers, excepting those which are expressly delegated by
the Constitution, or which necessarily result from
them. It is an anomaly among existing Governments, and from the manner in which it was
formed, Mr. M. said, he thought it might easily
be shown, that it was never the intention of the
convention to vest the House of Representatives
with any participation in the treaty-making
power.

Thirteen independent States, each possessing
all the attributes of sovereignty—the power of
making treaties among the rest—varying in size,
in population, in wealth, and in strength, of different habits, interests, and pursuits, assemble to
form a Constitution for their mutual protection
and defence. The wise men to whom the accomplishment of this great object was intrusted
had to contend with the prejudices of the people,
and the jealousies of the States, to reconcile interests at variance with each other, and so to
combine and shape them as not to sacrifice those
of one section of country to the supposed advan-

tage of others. It was, of course, a system of compromise and conciliation—each surrendering something for the good of all.

It was, therefore, for the purpose of protecting the interests and guarding the rights of the States that the Constitution requires the assent of two-thirds of the members of the Senate to the ratification of a treaty. It is not because the Senate are a co-ordinate branch of the Legislature that they are called upon to advise the President upon this subject, but because they represent the sovereignty of the States; and in requiring the assent of two-thirds of the Senate, it was believed that no treaty would ever be ratified unless it was for the interest of two-thirds of the States. But, said Mr. M., adopt the doctrine contended for by the gentlemen on the other side—admit this House to a participation of this power, and what would be the consequence? Why, sir, it would be in the power of four States only, out of the eighteen, now composing the Union, to defeat the ratification of a treaty which had received the sanction of the President and two-thirds of the Senate. Yes, sir, although the Senate, representing the respective States, might have given their unanimous advice to the President, it would still be in the power of the Representatives of Massachusetts, New York, Pennsylvania, and Virginia, to prevent its being carried into effect. Where, sir, are the rights of the respective States, so sedulously guarded by the Constitution; where is the security of the small States; or, where the interests of the commercial ones, if a treaty made for the protection of those great objects is liable to be defeated by a combination of this sort? The supposition is monstrous. No, sir, the House of Representatives have no more right to interfere than they would have if the Constitution had required the advice of two-thirds of the Governors of the respective States to the confirmation of a treaty. It is the assent of the States, and not of the people numerically, which was intended to be secured.

Mr. M. said, the remarks he had already made were founded principally upon the structure of our Government, and what must have been the intention of its founders. But from an examination of the Constitution itself, and a comparison of its various parts, he had been astonished that any difference of opinion should exist upon this subject. He should not, however, detain the House with a labored argument upon this part of the case, inasmuch as the reasoning of the honorable gentleman from Pennsylvania, (Mr. HOPKINSON,) and those who had preceded him upon the same side, must have produced a conviction upon the minds of all over whom he could hope to have any influence, and must be, in his apprehension, conclusive upon all who take the Constitution for their guide. That instrument declares, that "all treaties made or to be made under the authority of the United States shall be the supreme law of the land." It expressly vests in the "President, by and with the advice and consent of the Senate, provided two-thirds of the members present concur, the power to make

treaties." The treaty with Great Britain, now under consideration, has been made and ratified precisely in the form thus prescribed. The inference is, therefore, irresistible: It is the supreme law of the land; and no power on earth can render it more obligatory. It is a compact entered into between two sovereign independent nations, acting under their respective lawful authorities; it is perfect and complete in all its parts, has received the sanction of each party, and is proclaimed to the world by your President, acting under the same instrument by which we hold our seats, not as an inchoate and incomplete act, requiring any further ceremony to render it valid, but as made and concluded, and already binding each party to its respective stipulations.

The inconsistencies arising out of the construction of the Constitution, contended for by the advocates of this bill, Mr. M. said, were numerous and palpable. He would instance but one or two: By the bill, the House undertake to put a construction upon the treaty. We pass the bill and send it to the Senate. That body, upon the ground that our construction is not correct, refuse, by a majority of one, to pass a bill for carrying into effect a treaty to which two-thirds have already given their deliberate consent—what would be the result? Would the treaty cease to operate, and lose its binding efficacy? Again, suppose the bill passes both the Senate and House, and your President refuses his sanction on the very ground that you are trenching upon his legitimate authority, and assuming a power not delegated to Congress. Where is then your treaty; and how stand your relations with Great Britain? A doctrine so replete with absurdity cannot be correct. Let us not, sir, employ our time in the vain effort to legislate where we have no power and can produce no effect. Let each department of the Government confine itself to the sphere in which the Constitution has placed it. Employment enough may be found in the rightful exercise of authority, while nothing but disorder and confusion will result from its abuse.

Mr. M. said, it would be easy to show that the practice of our Government under the Constitution, had been conformable to the principles for which he contended; but as the hour of adjournment had arrived, and he had already trespassed upon the patience of the House longer than he intended, he would detain them no further.

Mr. REYNOLDS said he rose with some diffidence to express his opinion on the great question now before the House, particularly after the great display made by the gentlemen from South Carolina, (Mr. CALHOUN,) and from Virginia, (Mr. RANDOLPH,) who had just sat down. But whenever a great Constitutional question is involved, Mr. R. said, he would always take the liberty to deliver his sentiments while he had the honor of a seat in this House. He did not mean, however, to enter into the general discussion, which the question now assumed by the eloquence of the honorable gentleman from Virginia, (Mr. RANDOLPH,) at this late hour, but merely to state the grounds on which his opinion rested. Mr. R. said it was time enough to meet the extreme case put by the honorable gentleman, when it should really and absolutely occur. And whenever Ministers, who were appointed to negotiate a treaty with a foreign Power, would cede a State, or part of a State, or any territory whatever, and that sanctioned by the President and two-thirds of the Senate, he hoped to God there would always be found a redeeming spirit in this House, to check at once a course so enormous and unconstitutional. Mr. R. admitted, that there are, and may be treaties which this House may be bound to register, if you please to call it, and adopt as the supreme law of the land; and those, in his opinion, are exclusively treaties of peace, that do not require any act of legislation to carry the same into effect. But, he insisted, that all treaties of commerce and alliance, or those which required this House to appropriate the money of their constituents, did, and ought to have the sanction of Congress before they could be viewed as complete, or "the supreme law of the land." And it was on this ground, Mr. R. said, he was opposed in toto to the doctrines advanced by the gentleman from South Carolina, (Mr. Calhoun,) in favor of the treaty-making power. But, said the gentleman, with some degree of triumph, the President of the United States has already considered the commercial treaty as complete, because he has published the same to the world as the law of the land, and has merely transmitted a copy of it to this House without any documents to act upon. Sir, said Mr. R., this Message is the strongest evidence that can be adduced in favor of the position I have taken. The President of the United States knew well what he was about, and the course he has taken speaks volumes on the subject. What does the Message say, Mr. Speaker? It announces to us that the treaty has been duly ratified, and recommends to this House to pass such laws as may be required to carry the same into effect. Sir, this is a treaty regulating commerce between this country and Great Britain. The Constitution has confided the regulation of foreign commerce to the Congress of the United States. It is a municipal law, over which this House has a right to act. I shall therefore, sir, vote for the bill on your table, although I do not deem it of much importance as to the validity of the treaty now under consideration, or that its passage is absolutely necessary on the present occasion, but for the purpose of recording my vote in support of the great Constitutional authority of this House.

Mr. Hardin appealed to the plain common sense and intelligence of the House, whether the bill upon which they were lavishing so much of their time and exertions, was not entirely superfluous and nugatory. Here was a treaty, a contract fairly, and with full deliberation, concluded between the lawful sovereignties of this country and Great Britain, ratified as the Constitutional law of the country directed, by the President, with the advice of two-thirds of the Senate, and by the President proclaimed to the people as the law of the land, with an injunction for the due

observance of it—containing nothing that interfered with the municipal laws of the country—no regulation that might not be carried into immediate effect without legislative interference—involving no call whatsoever for money, and yet tenaciously held up as an object of legislation, and made the subject of a bill which did little more than re-echo it. He was as much aware as the gentlemen who supported the measure, that the treaty-making power could not, by a treaty, lawfully make war or impose taxes or encroach upon those powers which the Constitution had deposited in Congress; but it was no less true that the Constitution declares in unequivocal terms that the President may make treaties, and that no restriction or limitation whatsoever, to his power in that respect, is specified in that instrument, which is sufficiently declaratory of the extent of the power, inasmuch as it says that treaties made in the form and with the authorities already mentioned shall be the law of the land. Some of those honorable gentlemen, by way of smoothing the passage of the bill through the House, had argued that it was so far at least unobjectionable, that it could do no hurt, that if it did no good it could do no harm; but Mr. H. reminded the House of the eminence on which it stood; that it was composed of the assembled representatives of the nation, sent there to deliberate and to resolve upon its most important concerns, and he therefore deprecated, as it would be a dereliction of the high character of such an august assembly, their gravely deliberating upon nothing. He respected the dignity of the body too much to give his assent to their entertaining a measure, for no better reason, than because it was harmless. Besides, that act which now appeared so harmless, might, ultimately, turn out to be very mischievous, as a precedent; and this violation of the Constitution, in a thing no matter how trifling, might, hereafter, be made the ground of a more daring encroachment. On this point, he warned the House to be cautious, to guard, not only the main body, but the out-posts; and to reflect in due time, that some twenty or thirty years to come, this precedent might be brought forward, to the incalculable injury, perhaps the ruin of the Constitution.

Gentlemen had said, that, on a commercial subject, no treaty could be obligatory, because the Constitution had assigned to Congress the regulation of commerce. Where then, said he, will gentlemen stop? To Congress, say they, is delegated the exclusive jurisdiction over everything. According to their construction, therefore, the treaty-making power was impotent, a nullity, it could do nothing; it could not make peace, because peace repeals war, the right of making which is delegated to Congress: and it could not form alliances, for the same reason. But gentlemen, he observed, seemed not to recollect the old logical maxim, that he who proves too much, proves nothing. The President, say they, cannot repeal the excise!—no; but the President can make a peace without the concurrence of that House, and fortunate it was, that he could do so.

We now, said Mr. H., feel the happy effects of that power, and conceive that a treaty of peace has been accomplished without any encroachments, or pretended encroachments on our Congressional acts. The power to treat generally, he said, was vested in the President by the Constitution—but to the law of nations it was left, to determine the limitations of that power. If it be true, said Mr. H., that by the terms of the Constitution of the United States, this treaty is already the law of the land, then is the treaty guarantied by that Constitution; and yet gentlemen insist that it is not valid, and that this House ought to be consulted. By the Constitution we are forbidden to be heard in the subject, yet they will have it otherwise, and by this species of indirection, this left-handed course, bring the treaty under our legislative cognizance. Sir, I say we cannot do indirectly that which we are forbidden to do directly. Treaties might be made, no doubt, he said, for the execution of which it might be necessary to call upon the House to make laws; offensive and defensive treaties for instance, which could not otherwise be carried into effect; but when, as in the present case, the treaty was complete, and capable of executing itself, nothing of the kind was necessary.

As to the instances which had been adduced of Congress being called upon to enact laws for carrying treaties into effect, he believed that there was not one of them similar to this. The case of Jay's Treaty was not. The Federalists supported that on two grounds: one that it was a good treaty; the other that, whether good or bad, it would not be consistent with the honor of the country to reject it; but it never was brought forward as this is, a re-echo of itself in the shape of a bill. And as to the cases taken from the proceedings of the British records, the organization of that Government was in all respects so different from that of ours, that it was impossible to argue fairly or conclusively from the one, to the other.

The question was taken on ordering the bill to a third reading, about three o'clock, and decided in the affirmative—yeas 86, nays 69, as follows:

YEAS—Messrs. Alexander, Archer, Baker, Barbour, Bassett, Bateman, Birdseye, Blount, Brooks, Bryan, Burnside, Burwell, Caldwell, Cannon, Clendenin, Clopton, Comstock, Condict, Conner, Crawford, Creighton, Cuthbert, Darlington, Desha, Forsyth, Ghelson, Glasgow, Griffin, Hahn, Hall, Hammond, Hawes, Haister, Henderson, Hungerford, Ingham, Irwin of Pennsylvania, Jackson, Johnson of Virginia, Johnson of Kentucky, Kerr, King of Massachusetts, Lowndes, Lumpkin, Lyle, Maclay, Mayrant, McCoy, McLean of Kentucky, McLean of Ohio, Middleton, Murfree, Newton, Parris, Pickens, Piper, Pleasants, Powell, Randolph, Reynolds, Roane, Robertson, Root, Ross, Savage, Schenck, Sharpe, Sheffey, Smith of Virginia, Southard, Taul, Taylor of New York, Taylor of South Carolina, Telfair, Townsend, Tucker, Wallace, Wendover, Whiteside, Wilde, Wilkin, Williams, Willoughby, Thomas Wilson, William Wilson, and Yancey.

NAYS—Messrs. Atherton, Baer, Baylies, Betts, Boss, Bradbury, Breckenridge, Brown, Cady, Calhoun, Champion, Chipman, Cilley, Clark of Kentucky,

Clayton, Cooper, Culpeper, Davenport, Forney, Gaston, Gold, Goldsborough, Grosvenor, Hanson, Hardin, Herbert, Hopkinson, Huger, Jewett, Kent, King of North Carolina, Langdon, Law, Lewis, Lovett, Lyon, Marsh, Mason, McKee, Mills, Milnor, Moffit, Moore of South Carolina, Moseley, Nelson of Massachusetts, Noyes, Ormsby, Pickering, Pinkney, Reed, Rice, Ruggles, Sergeant, Smith of Pennsylv'a, Stanford, Strong, Sturges, Taggart, Tallmadge, Thomas, Throop, Vose, Wheaton, Wilcox, Woodward, Wright, and Yates.

WEDNESDAY, January 10.

Mr. LANGDON presented a petition of Jones, Guernsey, & Co., and Billy Todd & Co., manufacturers of woollen cloths, in the State of Vermont, praying that woollen goods (superfine broad cloths excepted) may be prohibited from being imported into the United States from foreign countries, or that additional duties may be imposed upon their importation.

Mr. PINKNEY presented a petition of the cotton manufacturers in the city of Baltimore, praying that the importation of all cotton goods from places beyond the Cape of Good Hope, and those of European manufacture, interfering with those manufactured within the United States, may be prohibited, or that additional duties may be laid on the importation of said articles.—Referred to the Committee of Commerce and Manufactures.

Mr. PINKNEY presented a petition of sundry inhabitants of the State of Maryland, who were severally wounded while in the military service of the United States, during the late war with Great Britain, praying for pensions, or such other relief as Congress may think proper to grant.—Referred to the Committee on Pensions and Revolutionary Claims.

Mr. McKEE, from a select committee, reported a bill authorizing the President of the United States to renew the lease of John Bate to the saline near the Wabash river, for a term not exceeding seven years; which was read twice, and committed to a Committee of the Whole.

Mr. PLEASANTS, from the Committee on Naval Affairs, reported a resolution requesting the President of the United States to present medals to Captain Charles Stewart and the officers of the frigate Constitution; which was read twice, and committed to a Committee of the Whole on the resolution requesting the President of the United States to present a gold medal to Captain James Biddle and the officers of the Hornet.

A message from the Senate informed the House that the Senate have passed a bill, "concerning the convention to regulate the commerce between the territories of the United States and His Britannic Majesty," in which they ask the concurrence of this House.

COMMERCE WITH GREAT BRITAIN.

The engrossed bill to regulate the commerce of the United States, according to the Convention of Commerce concluded with Great Britain on the 3d day of July last, was read the third time, and the question was stated "Shall the bill pass?"

Mr. EASTON said, he had intended yesterday to

deliver his sentiments in relation to the subject-matter of the bill upon which the vote of the House was about to pass; not having then been so fortunate as to gain the floor, he now had risen to advocate its passage, and, for that purpose, begged the indulgence of the House; he asked not only the indulgence but the attention of the House to the arguments he was about to urge upon the occasion. He considered the passage of the bill very important, as it regarded the powers, under the Constitution, delegated to Congress; the powers delegated to the President and Senate; the powers delegated to the courts of justice; and highly important as it regarded the rights and liberties of the people of this nation.

He apprehended very injurious consequences might, at some future period, result to the nation by a contrary course. The convention being reciprocal and beneficial, it was the avowed intention and desire of all parties to carry it into effect. It had been said, by gentlemen on both sides of the House, that the convention was, of itself, the supreme law of the land, while a majority had inclined to the opinion that legislative provisions are necessary to give it force and efficiency, though some doubted as to the expediency of legislating at all upon the subject. I am of opinion, said Mr. E., that it is not à treaty until it shall have been sanctioned by the Congress of the United States, by a legislative act, to carry it into effect.

The precedent about to be established, on the present occasion, was, of all others, the most favorable to the security, or pernicious in the extreme to the future liberties of the American people.

What are the powers, by the Constitution, delegated to Congress? And what are those delegated to the treaty-making power? In adverting to the Constitution, it will be found that "all legislative powers are vested in a Congress of the United States, which shall consist of a Senate and House of Representatives." "The Congress shall have power to regulate commerce with foreign nations." Surely, then, this power is not granted to any other authority. It cannot be given to two separate, distinct, and independent authorities. If it is given to Congress, it is not given to the treaty-making power, to the exclusion of Congress; it may be given to both to act in concert; it is not given to the one, to act to the exclusion of the other. This is a Government of laws; it is not a Government by compacts, by conventions, or by treaties concluded independent of the powers of Congress, in violation of the Constitution, and beyond the control of the supreme authority of the land, the sovereignty of this nation. What is the present convention? It is "a convention to regulate commerce between the territories of the United States and his Britannic Majesty;" it is then an agreement, upon the face of it, "to regulate commerce with a foreign nation." The President "has power, by and with the advice and consent of the Senate, to make treaties, provided two-thirds of the Senators present concur." It is not ordained, in this clause of the Constitution, that such trea-

ties are made "under the authority" of the United States, nor that a treaty thus made, shall "be the supreme law of the land." It would be, indeed, extraordinary, if the destinies and liberties of this nation were to rest upon the will of the treaty-forming power; I say treaty-forming power, because it is but another expression to convey a correct idea.

A power composed (as the case might happen) of the Executive and thirteen Senators, a less number by far than a majority of that honorable body; a power specially given to one authority, under the Constitution, cannot be construed to be given to another; such a construction would introduce into the Government an irregularity and an inconsistency fatal to its harmony, and destructive in its consequences. The President has a qualified negative upon the laws of Congress; the Senate are a part of Congress. Is not the regulation of commerce trusted to the proper authority? Is it not in safe hands? Will you, can you, treat the authority given to Congress by the Constitution, "to regulate commerce," as a dead letter?

If this construction prevails, is the treaty made without the concurrence of the President and Senate? If it be binding without the assent of Congress? If that assent is given, it is a treaty made under the authority of the United States. If it is withheld, it is a treaty made under the authority of the President and Senate, and not a treaty made under the authority of the United States. I should regret, and who are they that would not regret, to see the authority and destinies of this nation placed in the hands of an Executive and a Senate.

If the treaty-making power possess the authority to make commercial and other regulations, they may go on regulating until they will have regulated this branch of the Government (the House of Representatives) out of its whole weight of influence upon the councils of the nation; their authority will become a mere *carte blanche*, to be filled up as the treaty-making power may think proper to dictate or direct. Congress may regulate commerce in one manner; the President and Senate, at their pleasure, change that regulation.

It is a correct principle, that subsequent laws, inconsistent with former laws, repeal such former laws, and is a rule which cannot be controverted. It is principle as sound and potent as the eternal principles of justice. But the question to be decided is, when does a treaty become a law, when has it efficacy as such, and when shall it be binding as the supreme authority of the nation? Two separate and distinct legislative authorities, independent of each other, possessing equal power, cannot, in one and the same Government, exist together. That is, if the Executive and Senate alone can legislate, it is perfectly idle to vest the legislative authority in Congress. "A house divided against itself cannot stand." Congress divided against itself must fall. Congress have power, or they have not power, to legislate. If they do possess the whole powers of legislation granted under the Constitution, of which there cannot be a question, it follows, as a certain and incontrovertible conclusion, that the President and Senate alone, forming only two branches of the legislative authority of this Government, acting in their Executive capacities, as necessarily they must do in negotiating treaties, do not possess authority to legislate independent of the House of Representatives, the immediate representatives of the people—the people have not granted such power.

It would be admitted, he presumed, that ours is the best Constitution and Government " here below;" that it is the best to be found among the nations of the earth. It may emphatically be styled a Constitution of checks and balances; the Senate, in its legislative capacity, is a check upon the House of Representatives; the President upon the Congress. There must be a concurrence, according to the provisions of the Constitution, to form a law, and laws must be made before they can be executed. On the Executive and treaty-making capacity of the President and Senate, the House of Representatives, with the Constitution in their hand, hold a check; a treaty cannot become the supreme law of the land, which is inconsistent with the Constitution, or the powers delegated to Congress by the Constitution.

"The President shall nominate, and, by and with the advice of the Senate, shall appoint Ambassadors, other public Ministers and Consuls." Suppose they should appoint " swarms of officers," needless and unnecessary. The appointments are complete, the officers are made; they hold the seals of office under the authority of the Constitution; they are officers to all intents and purposes, they are commissioned under the authority of the United States, their appointments do not infringe any right or trespass upon any authority delegated to Congress, and yet, in my humble opinion, Congress would not be bound in honor, or otherwise, to sanction such a procedure by originating an appropriation bill for the outfits and expenditures of such officers. Congress are not bound, nor is the nation bound, nor are the courts of justice bound, to consider a treaty as the law of the land, until that law has been made under the authority only competent to make laws for the people of this nation, to wit: the Congress of the United States.

It has been contended that the treaty repeals the discriminating duties, and it being concerning affairs wholly international, that the legislative acts of this Government operate wholly internally, and cannot reach or affect the domestic or internal regulations of the foreign nation; that the convention therefore is a compact, and its subject-matter a contract to which the legislative authority of this country cannot extend. I admit, said Mr. E., that all treaties when completed and carried into effect by the supreme authority of a State or Kingdom, are compacts, and form a part of the law of nations, but this nation is not bound by a contract to which it has not given its assent; the Senate do not go abroad, nor do they negotiate the terms of a treaty at

home; to an honorable and beneficial treaty, the assent of Congress and of this honorable House is as easily obtained as that of the Senate; in ordinary legislation committees report bills, they go to different readings, according to the rules prescribed by the different branches of the Legislature, are rejected, or finally, with the approbation of the President, pass into laws, and become binding on the nation. The President has no legislative authority, strictly so speaking, and yet no bill can become a law without his assent, but by the consent of two-thirds of both Houses of Congress.

There is no expression in the Constitution that authorizes the Senate to ratify a treaty; the phrase used by the Constitution is, to make treaties. The question is, when shall a treaty be said to be made? Ministers and Envoys Extraordinary are appointed and commissioned to agree upon the terms of a treaty; they meet the foreign embassy in convention; they conclude a treaty. The convention with Great Britain was concluded on the third day of July, one thousand eight hundred and fifteen; it was then moulded. It was not then made, although in common *parlance* it is said to have been made. It was like dough unbaked. It will not be bread till it is baked. The treaty is forwarded to the President; if he disapproves of it, he returns it to those who framed it; if he likes it, he submits it to the Senate; if they approve of it, it is ratified; it is then said to be made. But it is not yet completed under the authority of the United States; it is only a treaty *sub modo;* it is not a treaty in effect. It does not become the property of the nation till it shall have received the sanction of the national consent, through the organs of the national will. The Constitution does not declare that a treaty made, by and with the advice and consent of the Senate, shall be the supreme law of the land. It does not say that a treaty so concluded, so ratified, so made, or whatsoever you may please to term it, is made under the authority of the United States. It cannot be a treaty till it shall have received the sanction of the national authority under the Constitution; when it shall have received that sanction, it is then, and not till then, a treaty made under the Constitution and under the laws of the United States, and such a treaty made under their authority, to which the judicial power shall extend. They are treaties only made under the authority of the United States, which are declared to be the supreme law of the land by the Constitution, and which the judges in every State are bound to obey. For example: It might be said that a piece of parchment in printed form of a commission, filled out with the name of the incumbent, and sign manual of the Executive subscribed to it, is a commission; and yet it is not a commission under the authority of the United States until the proper seal shall be thereto set and affixed in due form of law.

Sir, the present convention is a commercial regulation, which interferes with the powers expressly delegated to the legislative authority, and therefore must receive the legislative sanction,

551   HISTORY OF CONGRESS.   552

H. of R.   *Commerce with Great Britain.*   January, 1816.

the confirmation of Congress, before it can be binding on the people of this nation; and without which it is not competent to the President and Senate, or to the judicial authority, to enforce.

The Constitution expressly ordains, that "Congress shall have power to make all laws which shall be necessary and proper for carrying into execution all powers vested by the Constitution in the Government of the United States, or in any department or office thereof." No department or officer coming in contact with the powers delegated to Congress by the Constitution have authority under the Government, and it would be a solecism to say we have a Government under the Constitution independent of Congress. This construction can do no injury to our Republican institutions; it may be productive of much good: it is placing it beyond the reach of the treaty-making power. To repeal this treaty by making another, no inconvenience will result, as two-thirds of the Senate have concurred in approving of it; and I should presume there can be no obstacle to the passage of the bill in that honorable body.

I perceive, sir, said Mr. E., by a bill now on the table, that the Senate propose to declare by act of Congress, "that so much of any act or acts as is contrary to the provisions of the convention shall be deemed and taken to be of no force or effect." If the treaty is a law, and, as such, binding upon the nation, the passage of such a bill is wholly unnecessary, upon the principle that subsequent laws repeal former laws in all cases where they are inconsistent with each other. And why are two-thirds of the Senate required to make a treaty? It would appear to me that as this House have not the power to negotiate a treaty, it would be scarcely proper that it should be called upon to discuss one, that two-thirds of the Senate present would not deem beneficial and honorable to the country. If a contrary construction shall prevail, and it shall be determined that a treaty made and approved by the President and Senate is of itself the supreme law of the land, then indeed can they legislate, and then indeed can they regulate commerce; and the supreme authority will be placed in the hands of the Executive, the Senate, and the courts of justice, who may also legislate without the aid, and beyond the control of Congress, make contracts, and carry into effect treaties, however odious they may be to the people, or to their immediate Representatives. This may be, I do not say it will be, the effect of this monstrous treaty-making power.

Congress may declare war; no authority is expressly given by the Constitution to make peace. If any treaty would be binding, made independent of the legislative authority, he was inclined to believe it would be a treaty of peace, and yet this would only form one exception; it would be a treaty not against the provisions of any article of the Constitution, as the power is not delegated to any other branch of the Government; it becomes the exclusive province of the treaty-making power, and does not require a law to give it validity, or to carry it into effect; it is a treaty made under

the authority of the United States. The great objects in going to war are the protection of the national rights, and to secure an honorable peace. Such a peace would be acquiesced in by common consent; and the power to make peace is not a dangerous power; it is suited to the trust of the Executive alone, who would have authority, being the Commander-in-Chief of the whole military, to carry it into effect. But it is perfectly idle to talk of authority to do this, that, or the other thing, under our Constitution and form of Government, without power to carry that authority into effect. The power to act under the Constitution, is evidence of a right to act, and to act with effect. The Constitution should be construed to harmonize all its parts, and the construction which he had given would produce such harmony. It is unnecessary, and would be improper in Congress to legislate upon the treaty, to give it a construction that belongs to another authority, to the courts of judicature; any construction Congress might give it would not be binding upon the courts; yet every member who legislates upon a treaty must, in making up his opinion, whether to carry it into effect or not, give it his own construction, in order to form such opinion correctly.

In the sixth article of the Constitution it is declared, that the "Constitution, and the laws of the United States, which shall be made in pursuance thereof, and all treaties which shall be made under the authority of the United States, shall be the supreme law of the land, and the judges in every State shall be bound thereby." What is the authority of the United States? The Constitution and will of the people expressed through their Representatives in the Congress of the United States; the legislative authority of the nation is that authority without which no law or treaty can become the supreme law of the land. An individual officer, a judge, a marshal, or a justice of the peace, may act under the authority of the United States, so long as he keeps himself within the pale of the Constitutional limits, and the laws of the United States enjoining the duties to be by him performed. The Constitution is the paramount law, but without the aid of Congress it becomes inoperative. A person may possess the faculty to play upon an organ, but if he has not that instrument he does not possess either the power or the means to play upon it. The President, by the Constitution, shall be Commander-in-Chief of the Army and Navy, when called into the service of the United States; but he cannot command, if there shall not be any Army or Navy called into the service of the United States.

"The judicial power shall extend to all cases in law and equity, arising under the Constitution, the laws of the United States, and the treaties which shall be made under their authority." If the words "under their authority" had been omitted, their powers would not have been construed to extend to foreign treaties. Hence the judicial power cannot carry into effect a treaty not made under the authority of the Constitution and laws of the United States; a law is as necessary to the validity of a treaty as the Constitution itself.

He did not wish to be understood, that a law is necessary in all cases to the validity of a treaty; he meant to extend it only to cases where a treaty would contravene the powers delegated to Congress. If the Constitution itself gives authority to make the treaty, the treaty thus made becomes the supreme law of the land; the judges in every State shall be bound thereby, and the judicial power of the United States shall extend to it; but a treaty not thus made cannot be carried into execution by the judicial authority; they certainly would not adjudge a treaty to be made under the authority of the United States, when the treaty is made in derogation of that authority. He spoke of the authority expressly delegated to Congress.

Suppose a treaty made on a subject not prohibited nor permitted by the Constitution, as in the case of the treaty for the purchase of the province of Louisiana;—that power is not expressly delegated to any authority under the Constitution, nor is it forbidden; the Constitution is silent; one of the conditions of the compact is for the payment of $15,000,000 to France; the convention is ratified; the money is not paid; is it then a treaty? It is not. It becomes a nullity if the money is withheld; but, according to the argument of some gentlemen, it is a treaty, and the supreme law of the land; and yet it is not a treaty; and so, it is a treaty, and it is not a treaty. Suppose the money paid, it is then a treaty, and not till then has it received the sanction of the legislative authority, under the Constitution, and becomes the supreme law. The treaty contains a stipulation that the inhabitants shall be admitted into the Union. It is the supreme law of the land; and the courts are not enabled to carry that clause of the treaty into effect; it requires farther legislative provisions.

It has been said, sir, that the President has ratified the convention by Great Britain, that it has been approved of by the Senate, and sent forth to the public by a proclamation as a treaty; and if it is not a treaty the President knows not what he is about. Sir, said Mr. E., the President does know what he is about; that wise, intelligent, and upright Chief Magistrate, who has long enjoyed the confidence of this nation, was a member of the convention which framed the Constitution, and understands the subject correctly. In his communication of the treaty to the Senate and House of Representatives, on the 23d day of December last, he says: "I lay before Congress copies 'of a proclamation notifying the convention con- 'cluded with Great Britain, on the 3d day of 'July last, and that the same has been duly rati- 'fied; and I recommend to Congress such legis- 'lative provisions as the convention may call for 'on the part of the United States."

He who helped to make the Constitution recommends to Congress legislative provisions in relation to this treaty, and such as it may call for, on the part of the United States.

The principles for which I contend, Mr. Speaker, said Mr. E., are briefly these : A treaty though made has not force, and cannot be said to be made under the national authority, without a law of Congress giving it that authority, or to carry it into effect; that is, in all cases where the treaty in its provisions interferes with, or contravenes any of the powers expressly delegated to the legislative authority, or where from the nature of the treaty itself it requires legislative provision; but if the treaty is not contrary to the provisions of the Constitution, and does not contravene any of the powers delegated to Congress, and is of the description that it can be carried into effect by the President alone, or by the President and Senate, or by the judicial authority, without the aid of Congress, legislation in such cases becomes wholly useless; treaties thus made are the supreme law of the land, which every citizen is bound to respect and to obey.

Mr. CUTHBERT.—From the temper discovered by the House, at the introduction of this bill, I had expected but little discussion. This expectation has been disappointed. Discussion has been opened and extended. Those who advocate the principles which make the bill necessary, can no longer withhold themselves from the debate. When my friend from South Carolina (Mr. CALHOUN) yesterday resumed his seat, I felt myself under the influence of a strong impulse to reply, but restrained, because I participated in the general anxiety to listen to a gentleman who has recently appeared in this hall. I now rise for the purpose of such reply, which I shall enter upon without preamble, and accomplish with brevity. First, then, I demand that which cannot well be refused to me, and which being granted, all that I desire to establish must of necessity follow. What, then, do I demand? It is this: Are the principles of our Republican Constitution of Government founded in the reason and nature of things, necessary to the conservation of public liberty, the safeguard of the general interests, and the security of the equal rights of the citizen? Has it been the result of a spirit of liberty, chastened by sober wisdom, and a sober wisdom animated by the spirit of liberty; that all our Constitution and law rests upon this principle.—"All legislative power shall be vested in a Congress, consisting of a Senate and House of Representatives?" Is this structure of Government, this intrustment of the powers of legislation that, without which we can form no idea of civil and political liberty, and a safe guardianship of the general interests? Yes, with confidence, I demand if there be any in this House who will question these principles. Certainly none! How strange, wild, and contradictory then does it appear, that having acknowledged that our republican constitution of Government, founded on the reason of things and the nature of man, can allow only one plan of legislation to be consistent with the liberties and interests of the people, any one should immediately add, that this same constitution provides another and entirely different mode of legislating. Yes, I say, it does appear absurd and contradictory, that it being necessarily granted that our Constitution has vested all the liberties of the citizen and the interests of the community on this principle, that all legislative power shall be vested in a Congress composed of one popular branch, the immediate representatives of the people, styled the House of Representatives, and another branch representing the same sovereignties, under the style of the Senate—it should be added, that this same Constitution provides the making of laws by the Chief Magistrate and the Senate, without reference to the immediate Representatives of the people. For such are the claims for the treaty-making power, made by those who advocate its extent in this debate. As what may not become the subject of a treaty; commercial regulation, the raising of armies and of navies, extension of the rights of citizenship? What, then, are there to be no grand and fixed principles of liberty, which, settling on their foundations, from day to day, shall acquire with the progress of time an immoveable firmness! No grand principles, which, incorporating themselves with the soul of the American citizen, shall make a part of his very nature, and revolting into strong action, on violation, shall thus become the sanction of their own preservation? May that plan of policy which ought to be believed to have cast its roots so deeply, and taken so strong a hold, be torn up thus easily, I had almost said, thus wantonly? In fine, may a treaty with a foreign despot, petty or mighty, subvert to its base the legislative authority on which depends the entire scheme of our polity and liberty?

For what is there that may not become (as has been said) the subject of a treaty; commercial regulation, the raising of money, of armies, and of fleets, the franchises of citizenship, and whatever properly belongs to, and is most interesting in legislation? My friend from South Carolina, clear, rapid, ardent, and impatient in his intellectual operations, is, perhaps, carried too strongly towards metaphysical subtlety and the soundness and completeness of theory. If from this cause he has here erred, I would beg leave to remind him, that wretched indeed would be the condition of the human race could the great principles of Government be understood only by a few minds, subtle, refined, and comprehensive. Wretched, indeed, would be the condition of the human race, did the public liberty rest only in the refined subtleties of metaphysics. My friend, with the higher and more solid attributes of genius, is not without some of its shining defects. Fertile in the invention of topics to sustain the cause he advocates, he is inclined to select those which do not readily present themselves to common apprehension. Recommended as they are to himself by the beauty and freshness of novelty, he is aware that they carry the minds of those to whom he addresses himself by a kind of surprise, producing a quick and lively impression. But such reasoning should be regarded with suspicion. Thus, then, we are told, that a treaty being a contract to which two nations are parties, must be of higher and more solemn obligation than a law which is the act of one nation. Such a treaty contract, it is said, being of a higher nature, and more binding force than a law, may repeal a law, cannot require the sanction of a law, or by a law be invalidated. How fallacious this reasoning! Who in this country, I ask, is the party concerned as principal in a treaty contract? The people. Who their agent? The treaty-making power. Where are the instructions of the agent to be found? In the Constitution. And can a contract be considered as complete and of binding force, that has not received the sanction which, according to its character, is required by the instructions of the principal. What inferior contract can dissolve, or in any manner affect the conditions of that imperial contract, the constitution of republican Government, in which the citizens by a solemn act engage themselves to each other, and prescribe limits to those who administer their affairs? It is this contract on which rests all Government, which gives force to all laws and life and validity to all other contracts.

But the faith of the nation we are told is pledged by a treaty. Ah! that is the question in discussion. Is the faith of the nation pledged? Certainly, the faith of the nation is not pledged where a treaty requires the sanction of a law, until that sanction is afforded. It is the seal manual that stamps the hitherto incomplete engagement. Foreign nations are bound to understand the constitution of the Government of the people with whom they treat. Our Constitution is the credentials borne in hand by our negotiators.

The error (as it appears to me) of those who deny the necessity of a law of Congress to give full force to treaties which embrace subjects properly of legislation, has its commencement in this: that they do not comprehend in their view of the Constitution its different parts, but, seizing on the treaty-making power alone, carry it to an irrational extent, and with a violent invasion over all the rest which are forced to yield. The Constitution is then rightly construed when its several principles, all set in operation, are properly adjusted, balanced, and harmonized. Each must receive its due weight and force according to its weight and relation to others.

With regard to the law under consideration, the members of this House may be divided into several classes. To those (of whom I am one) who believe the sanction of a law in this case necessary, no persuasion need be addressed. There is another class who believe that in cases where treaties affect internal regulations, their legislative interposition is demanded. Let such consider that it would be extremely difficult if not impossible to deny that character to this treaty, and that it is the less hazardous course to act on that presumption. There are others again who regard the passage of a law in many of these cases as a matter of form. Let such reflect that forms are not unfrequently the best protection to what is substantiated.

I conclude with a doctrine which may excite objection and clamor, but which, I with confidence predict, will become the doctrine of the nation. What is the doctrine? It is this: this House is the grand inquest of the nation, and in public discussion upon bills must examine whether the Constitution has been preserved in its integrity, and the honor of the nation unviolated in treaties.

Mr. Tucker said that he should not have risen to offer to the House any remarks on the subject before it, if he had not conceived that there were some important considerations that had not yet been presented to its view. Gentlemen, he said, have so eagerly entered upon the discussion of the general question in relation to the treaty-making power, a question of the greatest magnitude and interest, that their attention seems to have been in a great measure withdrawn from the bill under consideration. Let us remember, however, that whatever may be our respective opinions on the subject of the powers of the several branches of Government, the passage of this bill may in the present state of things become absolutely necessary; let us reflect, that upon our decision on this occasion, the execution of the treaty on our part in the spirit of good faith, may essentially depend, and whilst we look to the question of Constitutional power, let us not entirely forget the peculiar character of this treaty, and the provisions of this bill.

Before I call the attention of the House to the treaty itself, and endeavor to explain the necessity of legislative interference on this occasion, let me touch for a moment on the subject of the treaty-making power; without pretending, however, to a comprehensive investigation of the Constitutional doctrines in relation to it, as such an attempt would lead to too wide a discussion, and might prove both tedious and uninteresting.

I concede, without hesitation, that the treaty-making power is vested in the President and Senate; but, so far from assenting to the proposition that Congress have in no case a right to interfere, I contend that it may be of the very essence of a treaty to engage on the part of the United States that Congress will, or will not do an act, or will, or will not, pass a law.

I understand a treaty made by the Executive to be an engagement entered into by the President and Senate on the part of the United States, with a foreign Power, by which something may be engaged to be done or omitted on the part of this nation. It is rather a contract by which the parties undertake that something shall be done, than an act by which it is done. The stipulations of the instrument which the nation by its Executive undertakes to perform, are also of various characters, and separate and distinct natures. Some may be Executive merely, some Legislative; and indeed, from the treaty made under the old Confederation whereby it was stipulated that the creditors of the two nations should meet with no impediment in the recovery of their debts, it seems, that the engagements of the contracting Powers may on some occasions be referable to the Judi-

ciary department of the Government. In either case, the treaty entered into by the President and Senate, can be regarded in no other light than as an engagement on the part of this nation, that the stipulations of the contract shall be carried into effect by that department of the Government within whose province they may respectively fall. Thus, if it be agreed, that an Executive act shall be done, the Executive alone may carry the treaty into full and complete operation. If it be agreed that something shall be done, which falls within the province of the legislative power, then the legislative aid become necessary, because, though the President and Senate may make a treaty, the Constitution nowhere empowers them to make a law. These principles are not only clear and palpable, I conceive, but they have been acted on, and are admitted in effect by the course of argument which has been pursued. Thus, if it be engaged that peace shall be made and armies withdrawn, the Executive, by its mandate, proclaims peace, or commands the retreat of its forces; yet, however solemn and obligatory a treaty from the moment of its signature becomes upon that department on which it binds, until that department acts, it is no rule of action for those under its control. If a treaty of peace for example be made, yet if the Executive fail to promulgate it, if they refuse to proclaim it, if they refuse to give orders to their armies, and their commanders to suspend hostilities, no commander, no officer would be justified in acting under it until his orders were received, unless he did so upon his own responsibility. So too in the case of the treaty under consideration. However conclusive and plain the treaty may be, who will pretend that every collector and deputy collector in the Union may, without orders from any department of the Government, consider the treaty as the supreme law, as his supreme rule of conduct, and act accordingly? If not, then some other act is necessary to carry this treaty into operation, whether Executive or Legislative, I will not now stop to inquire. The treaty, then, does not execute itself. If it not (without anything further) the supreme law or rule of conduct for every individual, for, if it be, then every individual is justified in acting at once without waiting Executive instruction; nay, after receiving such instruction, they would in conscience be bound to follow the treaty (thus become the law of the land) rather than the instruction of the President and his Secretaries.

These considerations prove, sufficiently, I conceive, that even where stipulations are made which are fully within the province of the Executive power, a treaty does not, cannot, execute itself; that it is in truth a contract to do something, not an act by which it is done.

This distinction, Mr. Speaker, becomes yet more plain, when we come to apply it to a treaty containing stipulations by which the nation engages to do something that falls within the sphere of legislative power. I will not stop to prove, by laborious reasoning, that cases may occur in which the legislative body must be called on to execute the provisions of a treaty; I will not fatigue the

House with an effort to show that there are cases in which the treaty can neither operate as a law, nor the Executive enforce its provisions without a law. It would be useless, for the position has always been admitted, has often been acted on, and is now most amply conceded. Such, sir, is the case of a treaty, the stipulations of which, calling upon the treasures of the country, require an appropriation. Such, too, the case of a cession of territory spoken of in the debate, if we could dream of such a power existing anywhere in the Federal Government. Such, too, the case of the stipulations in the convention by which Louisiana was ceded to the United States, whereby on certain terms she was to be admitted into the Union. Let us pause for a moment and ask ourselves, whether such treaties can be regarded as executing themselves; whether they can have operation without legislative aid? Can a treaty lay a tax; can a treaty make an appropriation; can a treaty, *ipso facto,* cede territory; can a treaty erect a Territory into a State? Can these things be done by the treaty alone, or by the aid and instrumentality of the Executive without Legislative assistance? It is admitted on all hands they cannot. Even the most zealous supporters of the treaty-making power acknowledge, that they must in such cases look to the Legislature, though they contend that this body is bound to pass the necessary laws. I will not stop at this time to examine this principle, but ask, whether it is not palpable from these admissions, that in all such cases a treaty does not actually make or change the law, but only engages on the part of the United States that it shall be made or changed? If so, I am not incorrect in supposing, that a treaty is merely an engagement that certain acts shall be done by that department of the Government within whose province they may fall; and that it does not operate in cases falling within the sphere of the Legislative power, without the aid of that branch of the Government.

If it were otherwise, if we were indeed to give into the monstrous construction, that a treaty of itself is to be regarded a a law; that it can repeal a solemn act of the Legislature, and operate directly upon the community without the agency of that branch of the Government, in cases exclusively within the legitimate sphere; to what fatal lengths shall we not be led. If treaties have this effect in one case, why not in all? If in taking off a duty, why not in making an appropriation; if in repealing one law, why not in passing another; why not in laying taxes, granting subsidies, making cessions of territory, and even paying tribute to an Algerine Dey without consent of Congress, if indeed our gallant seamen had not procured more honorable terms for us in the late negotiation? Can gentlemen draw the line of discrimination? Can they point out that part of the Constitution, which, in the supposed concession to the treaty-making power of the legislative authority, says to the former, "thus far shall thou go and no farther?" And if they cannot, this independence of the Legislature must exist in all cases or none. It is admitted that it does not ex-

ist in all (as in the cases of appropriation, &c.) and I therefore conclude it exists in none.

But if the legislative authority be necessary, is it true that we are bound to act in a particular way? Is it true that we must pass the laws which the treaty-making power engages we shall pass? Impossible! When our aid is called for, we must have the power to deliberate; if to deliberate, we must have a discretion to pass or to reject; since without it deliberation is a mockery and legislative solemnities a fair subject of derision and contempt.

There is another point of view, Mr. Speaker, in which I would present this subject to the House. To whom has the Constitutional charter given the legislative power? I answer, in the explicit language of the instrument in its commencing clause, "to a Congress of the United States, which shall consist of a Senate, and House of Representatives." Is this ample grant restricted by any subsequent part of the instrument? We are referred by gentlemen to the treaty-making power, and to the clause which, as they contend, declares that "treaties shall be made the supreme law of the land." If indeed by any fair construction this clause can be deemed to declare that treaties shall be superior to the laws, then our adversaries may claim the victory; otherwise they must yield it. But does it so? It declares the Constitution and the laws of Congress, and the treaties, to be the supreme law.—Superior to what? To the laws of the States; as we perceive by the conclusion; "anything in the constitution or laws of any State to the contrary notwithstanding." It declares all three to be supreme; it does not attempt to graduate the respective authority of each, nor can it be predicated of either, that under this clause it is superior to the others. Even the Constitution itself would have no claims to superiority, if it looked only to this passage for its title to supremacy.

If then the legislative power be vested in Congress, and if by this clause it be not taken away or subject to the control of the treaty-making power, I presume it remains unimpaired in the representatives of the nation. If so, their concurrence is not only essential to carry into effect a treaty touching upon legislative powers, but, in acting upon it, they must deliberate with the freedom of independent legislators.

It is contended, however, by the gentleman from South Carolina, (Mr. CALHOUN,) that a treaty is superior to the law, because it is a contract between our nation and another Power. I am ready to admit, Mr. Speaker, the ingenuity of the gentleman in drawing this distinction. It is what may well be expected from his ingenious and active mind. But I think it will appear that it is more ingenious than solid, more true than applicable to the subject.

I admit that where a contract has been entered into and completed by all the necessary powers under our Constitution, it is binding upon the nation. But the question still recurs, when is it complete? In the case of a treaty containing stipulations merely Executive, it is complete when

561   HISTORY OF CONGRESS.   562

JANUARY, 1816.   Commerce with Great Britain.   H. OF R.

the ratifications are exchanged. In the case of a treaty which requires a legislative act to give it operation, we contend that the legislative sanction must be given before it is complete. Until then it is not a binding contract, and the rights of the third party (the foreign Power) do not exist. Is it not the *petitio principii*, or (if the gentleman will permit me to use the vulgar translation) is it not begging the question to contend, that before the legislative sanction the contract is binding, when the very question between us is, whether that sanction be necessary to make it binding?

Let it not be said that foreign nations know nothing of these Constitutional niceties. My friend from South Carolina (Mr. LOWNDES) has already given the proper answer to such a suggestion. The foreign Power which contracts with us is bound to look to the Constitutional charter to see that they contract with the proper authority. Suppose the treaty were ratified by the President without the assent of the Senate. Could the foreign Power complain of broken faith because we should refuse to abide by it? Could it allege that it knew nothing of the Senatorial ratification; that it was not versed in the mysteries of our Constitution? By no means. If a foreign Power contracts without looking to the authority and Constitutional extent of powers of those who undertake to treat with them, the loss be upon them—we are not to be the sufferers. So, if, as we contend, all treaties involving legislative power require legislative sanction, foreign Powers must look to it; and seeing that the Executive are not omnipotent, and have no power to bind us absolutely in such cases, they must act accordingly.

Let us, in testing the correctness of the principle contended for on the other side of the House, examine, moreover, whether it does not lead to inevitable inconsistency. It is asserted that a treaty is superior to a law in conflict with its provisions, and repeals a prior legislative act which is at variance with its stipulations. Here then the treaty-making power is superior to the law. Yet it is admitted that Congress can declare war, a prior treaty to the contrary notwithstanding, and by the act of war annul and abrogate a treaty. Here then the law is superior to the treaty-making power. Can it at the same time be both superior and inferior? Can it be true that whilst the President and Senate can repeal pre-existing laws, the same power which made those pre-existing laws, can in its turn become superior, and abrogate the act of the President and Senate? Impossible! it is an inconsistency that cannot be admitted; it is a construction that would beget unutterable confusion.

But it is said by the gentleman from South Carolina, (Mr. CALHOUN,) that the act of declaring war is rather a judicial than a legislative act. I understand the gentleman's idea and admit the ingenuity of the distinction, though it cannot avail him in answer to the difficulty I have suggested. I suppose the gentleman to mean, that in passing an act declaring war, the Congress of the United States express their opinion or judg-

ment on the state of the relations between this country and its adversary, pronouncing that in their judgment subsisting treaties are broken, and that such an act is not to be regarded as mere ordinary legislation in which the interest and advantage of the nation are the chief objects in view. Should we admit this subtle distinction, does it avoid the difficulty? Is not the Congress if possessed of the power of declaring war, whatever be the nature of the act, superior to the treaty-making power whose contracts it thereby abrogates? And does not the question still recur, whether it can be both superior and inferior—whether the legislative and the treaty-making power can reciprocally and *ad infinitum* repeal the acts of each other?

Such, Mr. Speaker, are some of the considerations on the subject of the treaty-making power which have presented themselves to my mind; and though it would not be difficult to take a much more excursive range on this interesting subject, yet I shall leave to others to do so, and proceed to the second inquiry I proposed to myself—Does the treaty under consideration require legislative aid to effect its provisions? If it does, gentlemen on all sides of the House should concur in voting for the bill. We should do so, because we all believe it advisable to carry the treaty into effect; those on the other side should do so peculiarly, because, according to their doctrines, they are morally bound to legislate where the treaty requires legislative aid. All should be solicitous to avoid the slightest imputation on the faith of the nation.

If ever there was a treaty in which legislative aid was necessary, this appears to me peculiarly to require it. Its stipulations not only comprehend subjects within the sphere of the legislative power, but those subjects of legislation which are more peculiarly the province of this branch of the Government. Whether we consider the question in relation to the peculiar powers of this House in relation to taxation, to the pledge of the duties in question to the public creditors, or the particular provisions of the instrument, I can perceive no Constitutional means of carrying the convention into effect without legislative co-operation.

Is there, I will ask, any subject of legislation, Mr. Speaker, in which this House has greater interest or greater Constitutional control than that which is in anywise connected with taxation and revenue? Can gentlemen point out anything more important, and more interwoven with all our feelings than the question, "on what articles shall taxes be laid; from what subjects shall the necessary revenues of the Government be raised?" What has produced in this House more sensation than whether the revenues shall be raised from whiskey, from salt, from merchandise, or land? The objects of taxation are equally important and interesting with the quantum to be raised, or the appropriation of it after it has been raised; and if gentlemen admit that an appropriation by this House is necessary to effectuate the provisions of a treaty, which engages that such an appropria-

encroachment on the legislative rights of Congress.

I am one of those who view the bill upon the table as declaring that it is not within that capacity, as looking down upon the convention as the still-born progeny of arrogated power, as offering to it the paternity of Congress, and affecting by that paternity to give to it life and strength; and as I think that the convention does not stand in need of any such filiation, to make it either strong or legitimate, that it is already all that it can become, and that useless legislation upon such a subject is vicious legislation, I shall vote against the bill. The correctness of these opinions is what I propose to establish.

I lay it down as an incontrovertible truth, that the Constitution has assumed (and, indeed, how could it do otherwise?) that the Government of the United States might and would have occasion, like the other Governments of the civilized world, to enter into treaties with foreign Powers, upon the various subjects involved in their mutual relations; and further, that it might be, and was, proper, to designate the department of the Government in which the capacity to make such treaties should be lodged. It has said, accordingly, that the President, with the concurrence of the Senate, shall possess this portion of the national sovereignty. It has, furthermore, given to the same Magistrate, with the same concurrence, the exclusive creation and control of the whole machinery of diplomacy. He only, with the approbation of the Senate, can appoint a negotiator, or can make any step towards negotiation. The Constitution does not, in any part of it, even intimate that any other department shall possess either a constant or an occasional right to interpose in the preparation of any treaty, or in the final perfection of it. The President and Senate are explicitly pointed out as the sole actors in that sort of transaction. The prescribed concurrence of the Senate, and that, too, by a majority greater than the ordinary legislative majority, plainly excludes the necessity of Congressional concurrence. If the consent of Congress to any treaty had been intended, the Constitution would not have been guilty of the absurdity of first putting a treaty for ratification to the President and Senate exclusively, and again, to the same President and Senate as portions of the Legislature. It would have submitted the whole matter at once to Congress, and the more especially, as the ratification of a treaty by the Senate, as a branch of the Legislature, may be by a smaller number than a ratification of it by the same body, as a branch of the Executive government. If the ratification of any treaty by the President, with the advice and consent of the Senate, must be followed by a legislative ratification, it is a mere nonentity. It is good for all purposes, or for none. And if it be nothing in effect, it is a mockery by which nobody would be bound. The President and Senate would not themselves be bound by it; and the ratification would at last depend, not upon the will of the President and two-thirds of the

Senate, but upon the will of a bare majority of the two branches of the Legislature, subject to the qualified legislative control of the President.

Upon the power of the President and Senate, therefore, there can be no doubt. The only question is, as to the extent of it, or, in other words, as to the subject upon which it may be exerted. The effect of the power, when exerted within its lawful sphere, is beyond the reach of controversy. The Constitution has declared, that whatsoever amounts to a treaty, made under the authority of the United States, shall immediately be supreme law. It has contradistinguished a treaty as a law, from an act of Congress as a law. It has erected treaties, so contradistinguished, into a binding judicial rule. It has given them to our courts of justice, in defining their jurisdiction, as a portion of the *lex terræ,* which they are to interpret and enforce. In a word, it has communicated to them, if ratified by the department which it has specially provided for the making of them, the rank of law, or it has spoken without meaning. And if it has elevated them to that rank, it is idle to attempt to raise them to it by ordinary legislation.

Upon the extent of the power, or the subjects upon which it may act, there is as little room for controversy. The power is to make treaties. The word treaties is *nomen generalissimum,* and will comprehend commercial treaties, unless there be a limit upon it by which they are excluded. It is the appellative, which will take in the whole species, if there be nothing to narrow its scope. There is no such limit. There is not a syllable in the context of the clause to restrict the natural import of its phraseology. The power is left to the force of the generic term, and is therefore as wide as a treaty-making power can be. It embraces all the varieties which it could be supposed this Government could find it necessary or proper to make, or it embraces none. It covers the whole treaty-making ground which this Government could be expected to occupy, or not an inch of it.

It is a just presumption, that it was designed to be coextensive with all the exigencies of our affairs. Usage sanctions that presumption—expediency does the same. The omission of any exception to the power, the omission of the designation of a mode, by which a treaty, not intended to be included within it, might otherwise be made, confirms it. That a commercial treaty was, above all others, in the contemplation of the Constitution, is manifest. The immemorial practice of Europe, and particularly of the nation from which we emigrated, the consonance of enlightened theory to that practice, prove it. It may be said, indeed, that at the epoch of the birth of our Constitution, the necessity for a power to make commercial treaties was scarcely visible, for that our trade was then in its infancy. It was so; but it was the infancy of another Hercules, promising, not, indeed, a victory over the lion of Nemæa, or the boar of Erymanthus, but the peaceful conquest of every sea which could be subjected to the dominion of commercial enterprise. It was then as apparent as it is now, that the destinies of this great nation were irrevocably commercial;

that the ocean would be whitened by our sails, and the "*ultima thule*" of the world compelled to witness the more than Phœnician spirit and intelligence of our merchants. With this glorious anticipation dawning upon them; with this resplendent Aurora gilding the prospect of the future; nay, with the risen orb of trade illuminating the vast horizon of American greatness, it cannot be supposed that the framers of the Constitution did not look to the time when we should be called upon to make commercial conventions.

It needs not the aid of the imagination to reject this disparaging and monstrous supposition. Dullness itself, throwing aside the lethargy of its character, and rising for a passing moment to the rapture of enthusiasm, will disclaim it with indignation.

It is said, however, that the Constitution has given to Congress the power to regulate commerce with foreign nations, and that, since it would be inconsistent with that power, that the President, with the consent of the Senate, should do the same thing, it follows that this power of Congress is an exception out of the treaty-making power. Never were premises, as it appears to my understanding, less suited to the conclusion. The power of Congress to regulate our foreign trade, is a power of municipal legislation, and was designed to operate as far, as upon such a subject, municipal legislation can reach. Without such a power, the Government would be wholly inadequate to the ends for which it was instituted. A power to regulate commerce by treaty alone would touch only a portion of the subject. A wider and more general power was therefore indispensable, and it was properly devolved upon Congress, as the Legislature of the Union.

On the other hand, a power of mere municipal legislation, acting upon views exclusively our own, having no reference to a reciprocation of advantages by arrangements with a foreign State, would also fall short of the ends of Government in a country, of which the commercial relations are complex and extensive, and liable to be embarrassed by conflicts between its own interests and those of other nations. That the power of Congress is simply legislative in the strictest sense, and calculated for ordinary domestic regulations only, is plain from the language in which it is communicated. There is nothing in that language which indicates regulation, by compact or compromise, nothing which points to the co-operation of a foreign Power, nothing which designates a treaty-making faculty. It is not connected with any of the necessary accompaniments of that faculty, it is not furnished with any of those means, without which it is impossible to make the smallest progress towards a treaty.

It is self-evident that a capacity to regulate commerce by treaty was intended by the Constitution to be lodged somewhere. It is just as evident that the legislative capacity of Congress does not amount to it, and cannot be exerted to produce a treaty. It can produce only a statute, with which a foreign State cannot be made to

concur, and which will not yield to any modifications which a foreign State may desire to impress upon it for suitable equivalents. There is no way in which Congress, as such, can mould its laws into treaties, if it respects the Constitution. It may legislate and counter-legislate; but it must forever be beyond its capacity to combine in a law, emanating from its separate domestic authority, its own views with those of other Governments, and to produce a harmonious reconciliation of those jarring purposes and discordant elements, which it is the business of negotiation to adjust.

I reason thus, then, upon this part of the subject. It is clear that the power of Congress, as to foreign commerce, is only what it professes to be in the Constitution, a legislative power, to be exerted municipally without consultation or agreement with those with whom we have an intercourse of trade; it is undeniable that the Constitution meant to provide for the exercise of another power relative to commerce, which should exert itself in concert with the analogous power in other countries, and should bring about its results, not by statute enacted by itself, but by an international compact called a treaty; that it is manifest that this other power is vested by the Constitution in the President and Senate, the only department of the Government which it authorizes to make any treaty, and which it enables to make all treaties; that if it be so vested, its regular exercise must result in that which, as far as it reaches, is law in itself, and consequently repeals such municipal regulations as stand in its way, since it is expressly declared by the Constitution that treaties regularly made shall have, as they ought to have, the force of law. In all this I perceive nothing to perplex or alarm us. It exhibits a well-digested and uniform plan of Government, worthy of the excellent men by whom it was formed. The ordinary power to regulate commerce by statutory enactments could only be devolved upon Congress, possessing all the other legislative powers of the Government. The extraordinary power to regulate it by treaty could not be devolved upon Congress, because, from its composition and the absence of all those authorities and functions which are essential to the activity and effect of a treaty-making power, it was not calculated to be the depository of it. It was wise and consistent to place the extraordinary power to regulate commerce by treaty, where the residue of the treaty-making power was placed, where only the means of negotiation could be found, and the skilful and beneficial use of them could reasonably be expected. That Congress legislates upon commerce subject to the treaty-making power, is a position perfectly intelligible; but the under-standing is in some degree confounded by the other proposition, that the legislative power of Congress is an exception out of the treaty-making power. It introduces into the Constitution a strange anomaly—a commercial State, with a written Constitution and no power in it to regulate its trade, in conjunction with other States, in the universal mode of convention.

It will be in vain to urge that this anomaly is merely imaginary, for that the President and Senate may make a treaty of commerce for the consideration of Congress. The answer is, that the treaties which the President and Senate are entitled to make, are such as, when made, become law; that it is no part of their functions simply to initiate treaties, but conclusively to make them; and that where they have no power to make them, there is no provision in the Constitution how or by whom they shall be made.

That there is nothing new in the idea of a separation of the legislative and conventional powers upon commercial subjects, and of the necessary control of the former by the latter, is known to all who are acquainted with the constitution of England. The Parliament of that country enacts the statutes by which its trade is regulated municipally. The Crown modifies them by a treaty. It has been imagined, indeed, that the Parliament is in the practice of confirming such treaties; but the fact is undoubtedly otherwise. Commercial treaties are laid before Parliament because the King's Ministers are responsible for their advice in the making of them, and because the vast range and complication of the English laws of trade and revenue render legislation unavoidable, not for the ratification, but the execution of their commercial treaties.

It is suggested, again, that the treaty-making power (unless we are tenants in common of it with the President and Senate, to the extent at least of our legislative rights) is a pestilent monster, pregnant with all sorts of disasters! It teems with "gorgons, and hydras, and chimeras dire!" At any rate I may take for granted that the case before us does not justify this array of metaphor and fable, since we are all agreed that the convention with England is not only harmless, but salutary. To put this particular case, however, out of the argument, what have we to do with considerations like these? Are we here to form or to submit to the Constitution, as it has been given to us for a rule by those who are our masters? Can we take upon ourselves the office of political casuists, and, because we think that a power ought to be less than it is, compel it to shrink to our standard? Are we to bow with reverence before the national will as the Constitution displays it, or to fashion it to our own; to quarrel with that charter, without which we ourselves are nothing, or to take it as a guide which we cannot desert with innocence or safety? But why is the treaty-making power, lodged, as I contend it is, in the President and Senate, likely to disaster us, as we are required to apprehend it will? Sufficient checks have not, as it seems, been provided, either by the Constitution or the nature of things, to prevent the abuse of it. It is in the House of Representatives alone that the amulet which bids defiance to the approaches of political disease, or cures it when it has commenced, can in all vicissitudes be found. I hold that the checks are sufficient, without the charm of our legislative agency, for all these occasions which wisdom is bound to foresee and to guard against; and that, as to the rest, (the eccentricities and portents which no ordinary checks can deal with,) the occasions must provide for themselves.

It is natural, here, to ask of gentlemen, what security they would have? They cannot take a *bond of fate*, and they have every pledge which is short of it. Have they not, as respects the President, all the security upon which they rely from day to day for the discreet and upright discharge of the whole of his other duties, many and various as they are? What security have they that he will not appoint to office the *refuse* of the world; that he will not pollute the sanctuary of justice by calling vagabonds to its holy ministry, instead of adorning it with men like those who now give to the bench more dignity than they receive from it; that he will not enter into a treaty of amnesty with every conspirator against law and order, and pardon culprits from mere enmity to virtue? The security for all this, and infinitely more, is found in the Constitution and in the order of nature; and we are all satisfied with it. One should think that the same security, which thus far time has so discredited, might be sufficient to tranquillize us upon the score of the power which we are now considering.

We talk of ourselves as if we only were the Representatives of the people. But the First Magistrate of this country is also the representative of the people, the creature of their sovereignty, the administrator of their power, their steward and servant, as you are. He comes from the people—is lifted by them into place and authority—and after a short time returns to them for censure or applause. There is no analogy between such a magistrate and the hereditary monarchs of Europe. He is not born to the inheritance of office; he cannot even be elected until he has reached an age at which he must pass for what he is—until his habits have been formed, his integrity tried, his capacity ascertained, his character discussed and probed for a series of years by a press which knows none of the restraints of European policy. He acts, as you do, in the full view of his constituents, and under the consciousness that, on account of the singleness of his station, all eyes are upon him. He knows too, as well as you can know, the temper and intelligence of those for whom he acts, and to whom he is amenable. He cannot hope that they will be blind to the vices of his administration, on subjects of high concernment and vital interest; and, in proportion as he acts upon his own responsibility, unrelieved and undiluted by the infusion of ours, is the danger of ill-advised conduct likely to be present to his mind.

Of all the powers which have been intrusted to him, there is none to which the temptations to abuse belong so little as to the treaty-making power, in all its branches—none which can boast such mighty safeguards in the feelings and views and passions which even a misanthrope could attribute to the foremost citizen of this Republic. He can have no motive to paralyze by a commercial or any other treaty the prosperity of his country. Setting apart the restraints of honor and patriotism, which are characteristic of public men in a nation habitually free, could he do so without subjecting himself as a member of the community—to say nothing of his immediate connexions—to the evils of his own work? A commercial treaty, too, is always a conspicuous measure; it speaks for itself; it cannot take the garb of hypocrisy, and shelter itself from the scrutiny of a vigilant and well-instructed population. If it be bad, it will be condemned; and if dishonestly made, be execrated. The pride of country, moreover, which animates even the lowest of mankind, is here a peculiar pledge for the provident and wholesome exercise of power. There is not a consideration by which a chord in the human breast can be made to vibrate that is not in this case the ally of duty. Every hope, either lofty or humble, that springs forward to the future; even the vanity which looks not beyond the moment; the dread of shame and the love of glory; the instinct of ambition; the domestic affections; the cold pondering of prudence; and the ardent instigations of sentiment and passion,—are all on the side of duty. It is in the exercise of this power, that responsibility to public opinion, which even Despotism feels and truckles to, is of gigantic force. If it were possible—as I am sure it is not —that an American citizen, raised upon the credit of a long life of virtue to a station so full of honor, could feel a disposition to mingle the little interests of a perverted ambition with the great concerns of his country, as embraced by a commercial treaty, and to sacrifice her happiness and power by the stipulations of that treaty, to flatter or aggrandize a foreign State, he would still be saved from the perdition of such a course, not only by Constitutional checks, but by the irresistible efficacy of responsibility to public opinion, in a nation whose public opinion wears no mask, and will not be silenced. He would remember that his political career is but the thing of an hour, and that, when it has passed, he must descend to the private station from which he rose, the object either of love and veneration, or of scorn and horror. If we cast a glance at England, we shall not fail to see the influence of public opinion upon a hereditary King, an hereditary nobility, and a House of Commons, elected in a great degree by rotten boroughs, and overflowing with placemen. And if this influence is potent there against all the efforts of independent power and widespread corruption, it must in this country be omnipotent.

But, the treaty-making power of the President is further checked by the necessity of the concurrence of two-thirds of the Senate, consisting of men selected by the Legislatures of the States, themselves elected by the people. They too must have passed through the probation of time before they can be chosen, and must bring with them every title to confidence. The duration of their office is that of a few years; their numbers are considerable; their Constitutional responsibility as great as it can be; and their moral responsibility beyond all calculation.

The power of impeachment has been mentioned as a check upon the President, in the exercise of the treaty-making capacity. I rely upon it less than upon others of, as I think, a better class; but, as the Constitution places some reliance upon it, so do I. It has been said, that impeachment has been tried and found wanting. Two impeachments have failed, as I have understood, (that of a Judge was one,) but they may have failed for reasons consistent with the general efficacy of such a proceeding. I know nothing of their merits, but I am justified in supposing that the evidence was defective, or that the parties were innocent, as they were pronounced to be. Of this, however, I feel assured, that if it should ever happen that the President is found to deserve the punishment which impeachment seeks to inflict—even for making a treaty to which his judges have become parties—and this body should accuse him in a Constitutional way, he will not easily escape. But, be that as it may, I ask if it is nothing that you have power to arraign him as a culprit? Is it nothing that you can bring him to the bar, expose his misconduct to the world, and bring down the indignation of the public upon him, and those who dare to acquit him?

If there be any power explicitly granted by the Constitution to Congress, it is that of declaring war; and if there be any exercise of human legislation more solemn and important than another, it is a declaration of war. For expansion it is the largest; for effect the most awful of all the enactments to which Congress is competent; and it always is, or ought to be, preceded by grave and anxious deliberation. This power, too, is connected with, or virtually involves, others of high import and efficacy; among which may be ranked the power of granting letters of marque and reprisal, of regulating captures, or prohibiting intercourse with, or the acceptance of protections or licenses from, the enemy. Yet farther: a power to declare war implies, with peculiar emphasis, a negative upon all power, in any other branch of the Government, inconsistent with the full and continuing effect of it. A power to make peace in any other branch of the Government is utterly inconsistent with that full and continuing effect. It may even prevent it from having any effect at all, since peace may follow almost immediately (although it rarely does so follow) the commencement of a war. If, therefore, it be undeniable that the President, with the advice and consent of the Senate, has power to make a treaty of peace available *ipso jure*, it is undeniable that he has power to repeal, by the mere operation of such a treaty, the highest acts of Congressional legislation. And it will not be questioned that this repealing power is, from the eminent nature of the war-declaring power, less fit to be made out by inference than the power of modifying by treaty the laws which regulate our foreign trade. Now, the President, with the advice and consent of the Senate, has an incontestable and uncontested right to make a treaty of peace of absolute inherent efficacy, and that, too, in virtue of the very same general provision in the Constitution which the refinements of political speculation, rather than any known rules of construction, have led some of us to suppose excludes a treaty of commerce.

By what process of reasoning will you be able to extract from the wide field of that general provision the obnoxious case of a commercial treaty, without forcing along with it the case of a treaty of peace, and along with that again the case of every possible treaty? Will you rest your distinction upon the favorite idea that a treaty cannot repeal laws competently enacted; or, as it is sometimes expressed, cannot trench upon the legislative rights of Congress? Such a distinction not only seems to be reproached by all the theories, numerous as they are, to which this bill has given birth, but is against notorious fact and recent experience. We have lately witnessed the operation in this respect of a treaty of peace, and could not fail to draw from it this lesson: that no sooner does the President exert, with the consent of the Senate, his power to make such a treaty, than your war-denouncing law, your act for letters of marque, your prohibitory statutes as to intercourse and licenses, and all the other concomitant and dependent statutes, so far as they affect the national relations with a foreign enemy, pass away as a dream, and in a moment are "with years beyond the flood." Your auxiliary agency was not required in the production of this effect; and I have not heard that you even tendered it. You saw your laws departing as it were from the statute book, expelled from the stronghold of supremacy by the single force of a treaty of peace, and you did not attempt to stay them; you did not bid them to linger until you should bid them go; you neither put your shoulders to the wheel of expulsion, nor made an effort to retard it. In a word, you did nothing. You suffered them to flee as a shadow, and you know that they were reduced to shadow, not by the necromancy of usurpation, but by the energy of Constitutional power. Yet you had every reason for interference then, which you can have now. The power to make a treaty of peace stands upon the same Constitutional footing with the power to make a commercial treaty. It is given by the same words. It is exerted in the same manner. It produces the same conflict with municipal legislation. The ingenuity of man cannot urge a consideration, whether upon the letter or the spirit of the Constitution, against the existence of a power in the President and Senate to make a valid commercial treaty, which will not, if it be correct and sound, drive us to the denegation of the power exercised by the President and Senate, with universal approbation, to make a valid treaty of peace.

Nay, the whole treaty-making power will be blotted from the Constitution, and a new one, alien to its theory and practice, be made to supplant it, if sanction and scope be given to the principles of this bill. The bill may, indeed, be considered as the first of many assaults, not now intended, perhaps, but not therefore the less likely to happen, by which the treaty-making power, as

created and lodged by the Constitution, will be pushed from its place, and compelled to abide with the power of ordinary legislation. The example of this bill is beyond its ostensible limits. The pernicious principle, of which it is at once the child and the apostle, must work onward, and to the right and the left, until it has exhausted itself; and it never can exhaust itself until it has gathered into the vortex of the legislative powers of Congress the whole treaty-making capacity of the Government. For if, notwithstanding the directness and precision with which the Constitution has marked out the department of the Government by which it wills that treaties shall be made, and has declared that treaties so made shall have the force and dignity of law, the House of Representatives can insist upon some participation in that high faculty, upon the simple suggestion that they are sharers in legislative power upon the subjects embraced by any given treaty, what remains to be done, for the transfer to Congress of the entire treaty-making faculty, as it appears in the Constitution, but to show that Congress have legislative power direct or indirect upon every matter which a treaty can touch? And what are the matters within the practicable range of a treaty which your laws cannot either mould, or qualify, or influence? Imagination has been tasked for examples by which this question might be answered. It is admitted that they must be few, and we have been told, as I think, of no more than one. It is the case of contraband of war. This case has, it seems, the double recommendation of being what is called an international case, and a case beyond the utmost grasp of Congressional legislation. I remark upon it, that it is no more an international case than any matter of collision incident to the trade of two nations with each other. I remark further, that a treaty upon the point of contraband of war may interfere as well as any other treaty with an act of Congress. A law encouraging, by a bounty or otherwise, the exportation of certain commodities, would be counteracted by an insertion into the list of contraband of war, in a treaty with England or France, any one of those commodities. The treaty would look one way, the law another. And various modes might readily be suggested in which Congress might so legislate as to lay the foundation of repugnancy between its laws and the treaties of the President and Senate with reference to contraband. I deceive myself greatly if a subject can be named upon which a like repugnancy might not occur. But even if it should be practicable to furnish, after laborious inquiry and meditation, a meagre and scanty inventory of some half dozen topics to which domestic legislation cannot be made to extend, will it be pretended that such was the insignificant and narrow domain designed by the Constitution for the treaty-making power? It would appear that there is with some gentlemen a willingness to distinguish between the legislative power expressly granted to Congress and that which is merely implicit, and to admit that a treaty may control the results of the latter. I reply to those gentlemen, that one legislative power is exactly equivalent to another; and that, moreover, the whole legislative power of Congress may justly be said to be expressly granted by the Constitution, although the Constitution does not enumerate every variety of its exercise, or indicate all the ramifications into which it may diverge to suit the exigencies of the times. I reply, besides, that even with the qualification of this vague distinction, whatever may be its value or effect, the principle of the bill leaves no adequate sphere for the treaty-making power. I reply, finally, that the acknowledged operation of a treaty of peace in repealing laws of singular strength and unbending character, enacted in virtue of powers communicated *in terminis* to Congress, gives the distinction to the winds.

And now that I have again adverted to the example of a treaty of peace, let me call upon you to reflect on the answer which that example affords to all the warnings we have received in this debate against the mighty danger of intrusting to the only department of the Government, which the Constitution supposes can make a treaty, the incidental prerogative of a repealing Legislature. It is inconsistent, we are desired to believe, with the genius of the Constitution, and must be fatal to all that is dear to freemen, that an Executive Magistrate and a Senate, who are not immediately elected by the people, should possess this authority. We hear from one quarter that if it be so the public liberty is already in the grave, and from another, that the public interest and honor are upon the verge of it. But do you not perceive that this picture of calamity and shame is the mere figment of excited fancy, disavowed by the Constitution as hysterical and erroneous in the case of a treaty of peace? Do you not see that if there be anything in this high-colored peril it is a treaty of peace that must realize it? Can we in this view compare with the power to make such a treaty that of making a treaty of commerce? Are we unable to conjecture, while we are thus brooding over anticipated evils which can never happen, that the lofty character of our country (which is but another name for strength and power) may be made to droop by a mere treaty of peace; that the national pride may be humbled; the just hopes of the people blasted; their courage tamed and broken; their prosperity struck to the heart; their foreign rivals encouraged into arrogance and tutored into encroachment by a mere treaty of peace? I confidently trust that, as this never has been so, it never will be so; but surely it is just as possible as that a treaty of commerce should ever be made to shackle the freedom of this nation, or check its march to the greatness and glory that await it. I know not, indeed, how it can seriously be thought that our liberties are in hazard from the small witchery of a treaty of commerce, and yet in none from the potent enchantments by which a treaty of peace may strive to enthral them. I am at a loss to conceive by what form of words, by what hitherto unheard-of stipulations, a commercial treaty

is to barter away the freedom of united America, or of any the smallest portion of it. I cannot figure to myself the possibility that such a project can ever find its way into the head or heart of any man or set of men whom this nation may select as the depositaries of its power; but I am quite sure that an attempt to excite such a project in a commercial treaty, or in any other treaty, or in any other mode, could work no other effect than the destruction of those who should venture to be parties to it, no matter whether a President, Senate, or a whole Congress. Many extreme cases have been put for illustration in this debate; and this is one of them; and I take the occasion which it offers to mention, that to argue from extreme cases is seldom logical, and, upon a question of interpretation, never is. We can only bring back the means of delusion, if we wander in the regions of fiction and explore the wilds of bare possibility in search of rules for real life and actual ordinary cases. By arguing from the possible abuse of power against the use or existence of it, you may and must come to the conclusion, that there ought not to be, and is not, any Government in this country or in the world. Disorganization and anarchy are the sole consequences that can be deduced from such reasoning. Who is it that may not abuse the power that has been confided to him? May not we, as well as the other branches of the Government? And, if we may, does not the argument from extreme cases prove that we ought to have no power, and that we have no power? And does it not, therefore, after having served for an instant the purposes of this bill, turn short upon and condemn its whole theory, which attributes to us, not merely the power which is our own, but inordinate power, to be gained only by wresting it from others? Our Constitutional and moral security against the abuses of the power of the Executive Government have already been explained. I will only add that a great and manifest abuse of the delegated authority to make treaties would create no obligation anywhere. If ever it should occur, as I confidently believe it never will, the evil must find its corrective in the wisdom and firmness, not of this body only, but of the whole body of the people co-operating with it. It is after all in the people, upon whose Atlantean shoulders our whole Republican system reposes, that you must expect that recuperative power, that redeeming and regenerating spirit, by which the Constitution is to be purified and redintegrated when extravagant abuse has cankered it.

In addition to the example of a treaty of peace which I have just been considering, let me put another, of which none of us can question the reality. The President may exercise the power of pardoning, save only in the case of impeachments. The power of pardoning is not communicated by words more precise or comprehensive than the power to make treaties. But to what does it amount? Is not every pardon *pro hac vice* a repeal of the penal law against which it gives protection? Does it not ride over the law, resist its command, and extinguish its effect? Does it not even control the combined force of judicature and legislation? Yet, have we ever heard that your legislative rights were an exception out of the prerogative of mercy? Who has ever pretended that this faculty cannot, if regularly exerted, wrestle with the strongest of your statutes? I may be told, that the pardoning power necessarily imports a control over the penal code, if it be exercised in the form of a pardon. I answer, the power to make treaties equally imports a power to put out of the way such parts of the civil code as interfere with its operation, if that power be exerted in the form of a treaty. There is no difference in their essence. You legislate in both cases subject to the power. And this instance furnishes another answer, as I have already intimated, to the predictions of abuse with which, on this occasion, it has been endeavored to appal us. The pardoning power is in the President alone; he is not even checked by the necessity of Senatorial concurrence. He may, by his single *fiat*, extract the sting from your proudest enactments, and save from their vengeance a convicted offender.

Sir, you have my general notions upon the bill before you. They have no claim to novelty. I imbibed them from some of the heroes and sages who survived the storm of the contest to which America was summoned in her cradle. I imbibed them from the Father of his Country. My understanding approved them, with the full concurrence of my heart, when I was much younger than I am now; and I feel no disposition to discard them now that age and feebleness are about to overtake me. I could say more—much more—upon this high question; but I want health and strength. It is perhaps fortunate for the House that I do, as it prevents me from fatiguing them as much as I am fatigued myself.

Mr. RANDOLPH rose.—He said he was certainly very far from being among those, if any there were, who rejoiced in the personal indisposition which deprived the House of the very ingenious, correct, and, he might add, able argument with which they had just been entertained. On the contrary, Mr. R. said, he had listened to it with very great pleasure, as a specimen of the powers of the human mind which he was not often accustomed to witness, even in this honorable House. But notwithstanding this display of eloquence, he was disposed to return to an opinion, which he had entertained when he first took his seat on Monday last, that this question was swoln by the strange, not to say injudicious management of it, to an importance which its real merits do not deserve. I give up to the gentleman from Maryland, said Mr. R.—I am told he is from Maryland—to his utmost fury and indignation, those fanciful and fine-spun theories which seem to interdict the Executive of the United States from negotiating a commercial treaty, or any other treaty whatsoever with any foreign Power. On this point, sir, I agree with the gentleman altogether. I go with him the whole length, that it is competent to the President and Senate to negotiate a treaty of commerce, alliance, and subsidy, with any foreign Power, from the greatest potentate in Europe down to a Chickasaw chief. The honorable gentleman will excuse me when I rise to declare that, howsoever I have been gratified in the display which he has made of his abilities, in one respect he certainly has disappointed me. The honorable gentleman will excuse me when I say he has not met the question. The question, said Mr. R., is not the competency of the Executive to negotiate commercial or other treaties, but its competency, in doing so, to repeal existing laws of the land, and enact other laws in their stead; in other words, the question is, the competency of the Executive to do by treaty that which can be done, as we contend, only by legislative acts. That is the question. If he understood the gentleman, Mr. R. said, he had declared that the bill before the House was not in execution of the treaty; that it contained no auxiliary enactments; that it was not necessary that the bill should pass at all; that it was a twin-brother of the treaty. If the gentleman had pursued his analogy with respect to laws and treaties, he would have found this second twin-brother worthy of being nurtured and brought to man's estate, instead of being treated as illegitimate and stifled in its birth; that this poor little twin, which came second best in the world, had not that fair division of the patrimonial estate which our laws provide; that it was, in short, to be put out of the way, that the Presidential heir may inherit and enjoy the whole estate. If this bill were necessary, then, the gentleman had said that the President and Senate had been guilty of a tremendous usurpation. How far this view of the question might bear on the ultimate vote of the House, Mr. R. said, he could not say; but it would bear very hard upon the President, if the vote should be to-day as it was yesterday. If the argument of the gentleman from Maryland were correct, unless his representations on this head should materially affect the vote of the House, that decision would bear hard on the President and Senate. But a few minutes before the gentleman had delivered his sentiments, the Senate themselves had in open court plead guilty to the charge of usurpation; for they had sent down to this House a bill, either something or nothing, which, if anything, had pronounced their usurpation. If the treaty were what the gentleman contended, *ipso facto* the law of the land, the bill which the Senate had sent down was mere surplusage. We do not deny, said Mr. R., that a treaty, the ratifications being exchanged, has existence without the sanction of this House—at least I do not deny it—and I am responsible for no man's opinions but my own, glad enough at times if I were irresponsible for them—but I do contend that a treaty does not deprive this House of one jot, one tittle of its legislative and Constitutional authority. I am not, in the language of the learned doctor of laws in Padua, to Shylock, "take thou the pound of flesh, but not one jot of blood;" I am not for giving to the President and Senate the treaty-making power, and then denying to them the use of it;

581   HISTORY OF CONGRESS.   582

JANUARY, 1816.   *Commerce with Great Britain.*   H. OF R.

but I am for giving to them all the power, and all the influence which they ought to have in the Government. Whilst the gentleman from Maryland was thinking on the responsibility of the President and Senate, why did he not reflect on our own? Go we not back to be pressed—I hope not to be oppressed—by laws of our own enaction. If the President and Senate go back to the community, to receive their approbation or condemnation—I speak of the theory, of which I may say *odi et arceo;* for I have long lost my faith in theories, and in theorists too. If the President and Senate feel their accountability to the people, how much more are we amenable to them, when we return with the same responsibility, and at shorter periods, to our constituents? If there be any truth in the old adage, that short accounts make long friends, we shall stand on as good footing with our neighbors as some Presidents who have retired to private life. Our responsibility is greater than that of the President and Senate. What is the responsibility of a man who is to retire after a service of eight or ten years, to palaces which he has built with the plunder of his country; of a man who has enriched his relatives by a species of nepotism, and surrounded himself with a society of his own; who can be content to sit down with infamy in private life, provided his bags are swelled to distention, and his appetite pampered with delicacies which habit has made necessary to his enjoyments? But, granting the argument of the gentleman from Maryland, deeming of the responsibility of the President as he deems, we would make assurance doubly sure, and take a bond of fate for the correct discharge of the Executive functions in this respect. The gentleman from Maryland had said, that if the doctrine supported by the friends of this bill were sound, this Constitution was an anomaly in Government. It is so, Mr. R. said, and he was surprised to hear it found out to-day as if for the first time. It is an anomaly; happy for us that it is, and long might it continue so!

The gentleman from Maryland had said, if the sanction of this House became necessary to carry a treaty into effect, it was not only in their power, but it was their duty to pass a bill for that purpose. Mr. R. said he would grant the gentleman his position with a small modification; he would grant it if the gentleman would add a proviso, that the provision of said treaty did not betray the great interests, liberties, or rights of the nation. The gentleman had put the case of a definition of contraband by treaty, as being paramount to a law of Congress encouraging the culture of the article declared to be contraband; a case which would, according to his humble judgment, Mr. R. said, better suit a court of admiralty than a legislative hall. But he ought, he added, to be obliged to the honorable gentleman for having taken into his argument an idea which Mr. R. had yesterday endeavored to imbody in his own; for, he said, taking the very case the gentleman had put, there could not be a stronger selected to prove that his general argument was untenable. Suppose the Executive were to make a treaty, in

which tobacco, rice, and cotton, were declared contraband of war, to which he might add breadstuffs, butter, salt beef, onions, and notions of all sorts; would not this treaty require legislative enactment to carry it into effect; or would it, like a treaty of peace, require no intervention on the part of this House? It would have that effect, perhaps, in a British court of vice-admiralty at Halifax, Providence, or Bermuda; but did the gentleman in his heart believe that such a treaty could become the law of the land on the instant of its promulgation? It could not stand; the breath, the tempest of public indignation, would in an instant sweep it to eternity; it would go to the tomb of the Capulets. The gentleman demands of us, said Mr. R., to exorcise the treaty; to question it, whether it brings with it "airs from Heaven or blasts from Hell;" whether its "intents be wicked or charitable." The treaty, Mr. R. said, came to him in a most agreeable shape; he was disposed to ratify it by legislation; and, if legislative enactment were not necessary, whence the bill which had passed to its third reading in this House; and whence the bill from the Senate? If a treaty were of that pervading force, that, like mercury, it searches the remotest parts of the constitution, why the bill which in this House had progressed so far, and which he hoped would pass to the Senate, whatever imputation, according to the gentleman's argument, it might cast on the Executive of rank and tremendous usurpation.

For his part, Mr. R. said, he was extremely sorry that this should happen to be the only occasion, which had come within his cognizance lately, in which, according to the illustration of the honorable gentleman from Maryland, the House had refused, like the clerk in the church, to make the appointed responses to the minister. Mr. R. said he was not one of those who would construe this occurrence into any imputation on the majority, any more than on the minority of the House; for it happened to be a two-edged sword—it cut as much upon the right hand as upon the left, and as much upon the left hand as upon the right. One side, he said, maintained its consistency, because it cost them nothing, and the other side of the House maintained theirs for the same reason. We are each and all of us, said he, maintaining our consistency, and on the best possible terms—for it costs us nothing. The bill before us gives no power; it takes none away—it bestows no praise. it conveys no censure, except what may be inferred from the argument of the honorable gentleman. Mr. R. wished, he said, that in the future progress of their deliberations, the consistency of one side of the House might be equally maintained; he wished that the spirit of the Administration of Thomas Jefferson, of the first Congress assembled under his Administration, might be maintained by the majority of this House of the present day—even if the minority should, for the sake of consistency, be obliged to take the other side, and load the country with debts, taxes, armies, and navies, and all the constituent elements of Federalism, under the name of Democracy.

Yes, Mr. R. said, he wished that the consistency of one side might be maintained, even at the expense of consistency of the other—but, he believed he was travelling a little out of the record. To return to the question.

Mr. R. said, he would suppose that this commercial treaty had stipulated that a duty, not exceeding a certain amount, should be imposed by the two contracting parties on certain manufactures, peculiar to ourselves only, and operating therefore on us exclusively. Could there be a doubt that this House would refuse to carry that treaty into effect by passing laws laying the necessary taxes, and would leave it to Great Britain, if she chose, to make it a cause of war with us? Have not this House the power, and would they not use it, of carrying such a treaty into effect; or, if it seems good to them, to refuse to carry it into effect, leaving it to the option of the other party to make it a cause of war or not? But, the gentleman had said, grant these doctrines to be correct, and we are the most unfortunate people under the sun—we could have no treaties! Was there any fear, Mr. R. asked—was the theory of our Government so little understood, and the practice so much forgottten, that it could be supposed there would ever be wanting in this House a proper degree of deference (he would not say an improper degree of deference) to the wisdom and counsels of the Executive? Let us suppose it possible, however, said Mr. R., that we should be placed in this unfortunate situation; that it should not be in our power to make a commercial treaty with any people under the sun—I believe the sun would still shine as bright, and the grass grow as green as ever. Are we, sir, to suppose, in this young country, that all diplomatic skill resides with us—and go abroad a treaty-making as Hudibras and Don Quixotte in quest of adventures, expecting to gain all the advantages and receive no blows in return? No two knights, Mr. R. said, were ever more wofully mistaken; but not more than we should be, entertaining notions equally absurd. No, said Mr. R., if we make a treaty with any people under the sun, we must give a *quid pro quo*, and must always expect to give more than we get. It had been, he said, a maxim in Great Britain before the separation of the United States from that Government, and it was a maxim yet, that whatever she had acquired by the valor of her arms, she had lost by negotiation. The last treaty of Paris might form an exception to the general rule, but, like all exceptions, it would only prove the rule. The circumstance he had referred to grew out 'of the form of the Government of Great Britain. As the form of our Government is more popular than hers, our proceedings more public, and as we are equally liable to that state of faction which is the shadow of liberty, and proves the substance to exist, until it shall be put down by the strong arm of military despotism—whatever we get abroad we may expect to pay for. We must pay, and dearly too, Mr. R. said, for any advantages we should obtain from those wily Kings and Ministers abroad, who glory in diplomacy, which is but another name for duplicity. After the treaty of 1783, he said, we sent Ministers abroad a treaty-making with every Power that would treat with us, by way of trying our manhood—we had just come of age, taken our affairs into our own hands—he had known many young heirs try their skill in making bargains with their more wary neighbors, until they bargained away their whole estate. To such perhaps, it would be no injurious restraint if they were debarred the treaty-making power until arrived at years of discretion. We shall get nothing at all from these foreign nations, he assured the House, without giving therefor a full equivalent.

The honorable gentleman from Maryland had stated, that if the President and Senate had not the power to make a commercial treaty, and that treaty when made did not instantly become the law of the land, then the President and Senate have the power to make no treaty—and yet the gentleman had furnished in the course of his own argument an instance in direct contradiction of this position—that is, a treaty of peace, which did not in any shape require the sanction of this House. The Treaty of Peace, then, is an exception to the necessity of the intervention of this House to carry treaties into effect; and it might be said that a naked treaty of peace—"let there be peace, and there was peace"—was almost the only treaty which could be negotiated, that did not require the consent of this House. Under the old Confederation, however, it was said Congress had made an alliance with France. This, Mr. R. observed, was a strong case for the gentleman's argument—for it might be said, if the old Congress, confessedly inferior in power, possessed the right to make a treaty of alliance which had been near involving us in the vortex of the French revolution, *a fortiori* the President and Senate now ought to have the power. He agreed to the force of this argument, if for President and Senate the Government was substituted. This brought him, he said, to the old opprobrium of legislation, that the question started is seldom the question run down—the question was, do the President and Senate possess the power, exclusive and independent of the legislative power, to bind the people in all cases whatsoever, and to make treaties paramount to all law? That was the point—that was the gist of the question—there the argument rubbed.

If, instead of a treaty of commerce, the treaty now under consideration had been a treaty of alliance and subsidy, could the troops have been raised or taxes levied without the intervention of the legislative authority of this House? Mr. R. said they could not; and he had understood the gentleman also to admit this. What, then, was the amount of the difference between the gentleman and himself? It was this: that Mr. R. contended this treaty, being, in his opinion, one requiring legislative enactment to carry it into effect, this House was to exercise its legislative power in this respect under a sound discretion, and a high responsibility for the public good. It was not, in Mr. R.'s opinion, a sound construction, because it was competent to the President and Senate to make a treaty of peace, that they could repeal or modify a law laying a tax. Miserable indeed would be the condition of humanity, if the power to put an end to the calamities of war could not be intrusted to them; and, by the way, Mr. R. said he had no hesitation in saying, that with all the pride, and consequence, and airs that the Government had given to itself, even in this Treaty of Peace, in that simple agreement, "let the conflict cease," our adversary had got a fair and full equivalent, for she got full as much as she gave.

The President and Senate may restore the relations of peace, it had been argued. Might they therefore, Mr. R. asked, repeal all the laws of the land by treaty? But it seemed the President and Senate were controlled by public opinion, and that was a sufficient check—alluding, he supposed, to the press, the great battery of public opinion. Why, then, had it not been said in the Constitution, let there be a public opinion, and all is safe; it is enough for us if the acts of our rulers may be freely canvassed. I believe, said Mr. R., that our rights and liberties are safe, but in a very different repository from that referred to—in the State Legislatures, in the bosom of the free yeomanry of the country, asserted by their muskets and their rifles, and never yielded unless cautiously and warily attacked, unless the ground be broken at a vast distance from the sentinels of public liberty, and the approach secretly made.

Was the sanction of the House necessary to carry this treaty into effect? It was, or it was not; if it was, the President and Senate had been guilty, it was said, of gross usurpation. But the gentleman from Maryland had acknowledged that as there are treaties which are self-executory, there are others which require legislative enactment, and which the aid of the House is required to carry into effect. A treaty of peace, by merely restoring the relations of peace and amity, Mr. R. said, did execute itself. But was it so with a treaty stipulating that duties should be taken off or laid on, or both? The analogy between a treaty restoring the relations of peace between this country and another, and other treaties, cannot be brought in aid of a treaty which is not self-executory, which does require legislative enactment to carry it into effect, as proven by the vote of this House yesterday, and the vote of the Senate to-day, [referring to the bill passed by the Senate declaring the effect of the treaty.] Mr. R. said he could conceive a case in which even a treaty restoring the relations of peace and amity between the United States and another nation, might be received in this House as a breach of national confidence, which the House would not endure. As he liked to bring every case which he presented to this House as near the reality as could be, to liken it to something which had happened, or was very likely to happen, he would take a case which might have happened between the United States and France. It was well known, Mr. R.

said, that a very large description of people in the United States, at the breaking out of the French revolution, had been anxious to plunge the United States into a war with Great Britain and her allies; and it was contended that the public faith was pledged to guarantee the safety of the French West India Islands, &c. The demand of our aid had been made in a much more sacred name than that of a sugar island—in the name of the imprescriptable rights of mankind; the liberty of the world was said to be in jeopardy; the tyrants of the world, it was said, had conspired against liberty, and we ought no longer to withhold our aid. Mr. R. said he hoped no member of this House, nor the most worthless scribbler out of it, would understand him as imputing censure to those who felt thus ardently. By the wisdom of that man who alone, at that juncture, could have held the reins of empire, who alone could have reined in the public madness, by his wisdom we had been saved from being involved in the vortex of that tremendous comet, which

——From his horrid hair
Shook pestilence and war.

Every patriot, not the pseudo patriot, not he who wishes to ride on the surface of the billow, inflated by his own breath—every real patriot approved and honored his conduct. Suppose, instead of standing in opposition to the feelings of the day, reversing the old adage, *Quicquid delirant reges, plectuntur Achivi*—suppose General Washington had let slip the dogs of war, hallooed them on, and engaged in that war, which was terminated by the truce of Amiens—or suppose General Washington, as was the fact not long after, had been removed from the councils of his country, and succeeded by a gentleman of different political opinions, and that the first act of the new President had been to patch up a treaty of alliance with the allies, Great Britain particularly; such a treaty as would inevitably, whilst it kept peace with England, have produced war with France; would the people of America have endured this? Mr. R. did not think they would. Such was his opinion of the public sentiment of hatred to Great Britain and predilection to republican France, which then existed, that he believed this House, instead of carrying the treaty into effect, would have been made the means of compelling peace with France, and renewing the war with Great Britain. He would take another precedent, however, from a Government, the constitution of which was not anomalous—a case anterior to the Revolution which, according to the fond idea of British jurists, had fixed the liberty of England on an imperishable foundation; he would take a case from the most corrupt reign of the most corrupt family that perhaps God ever permitted to afflict the world—a case from the days of the Stuarts. He averred it as a fact, and all history, he said, would bear him out in it, that the last of the Stuarts lost his throne in consequence of his subserviency to a foreign Power, which foreign Power was the

587 HISTORY OF CONGRESS. 588

H. of R. *Commerce with Great Britain.* January, 1816.

object of the suspicion, deadly hatred, and fear of the nation he governed. He did aver that the Dutch wars of Charles II—that base and rotten policy laid open more than a century after that wily man thought the evidence of it buried below the caverns of the deep, would have lost him his crown, if he had continued to reign. James II was little else than the successor in form of Charles II; and James II lost his crown as Charles II would, in the end, have lost his, by making treaties against the wishes of the people, with a foreign Power most obnoxious and hateful to the British nation, &c. If such was the case in England, how much more strong is the argument that in this country the President and Senate should never make any treaty, particularly one which requires legislative enactment to carry it into effect, without the previous or subsequent consent of this body.

Mr. R. said, he would trespass on the Committee only by a few other remarks. He was, he hoped it was unnecessary to say, no drawcansir. He was for peace and good will among men. He understood the honorable gentleman from Maryland, when dwelling on the effect of the power of impeachment, which he (Mr. R.) believed would have as much effect on great delinquents as a feather or a flake of snow on the impenetrable hide of a rhinoceros—he understood the gentleman to say, in allusion to a remark that the power of impeachment had been tried and found wanting, that the fact did not necessarily imply—as the honorable gentleman on whom it was tried would have said, it was a *non sequitur* to urge, that the power of impeachment was nugatory. I grant it, said Mr. R. As little versed as I am in dialectics, as little of a logician or methodist in argument as I am, I am willing to admit that it does not follow, because a felon is acquitted, the law is inefficient, because the acquittal may have arisen from a defect in the evidence, in the law, or in the administration of the law; it may have arisen from another cause, which I would be the meanest and basest of mankind to admit, or it might have arisen from the defect of talent in the prosecuting attorney; and that is one of the crying sins of this nation, which calls loudly for reform. Daily and hourly are felons acquitted because they can give heavy fees to lawyers of great abilities, who know how to make the worst appear the better reason, in the courts at least; while the Commonwealth is content to have its business let out to the lowest bidder, and its judicial business is managed, I will not say in the same manner, but not always well. I do aver that I should be wanting in respect for the gentlemen with whom I was associated on that occasion if I admitted that the inuendo, if I am to understand it as such, of the honorable gentleman had any application to them. I have not the slightest indisposition to admit that it may have application to one, but I believe I see in my eye a much more substantial reason for the acquittal in the case alluded to than the want of ability with which the prosecution was conducted. Mr. R. saw in the ability of the defence

of the accused at least as probable a cause of the acquittal as the one which had been mentioned. But, it was really paying to the highest court in this nation a very poor compliment. What, sir! our most potent, grave, and reverend seniors—our very noble and approved good masters—if the doctrine of the gentleman be correct, that what they approve we must ratify—what, sir! the Senate, on the evidence of at least fifty witnesses not capable of making up an opinion on a question presented to them! The acquittal in that case was referable, not to the want of ability on the part of some of the gentlemen at least. Let us look back, said he; one of those gentlemen has since filled the office of Secretary of the Treasury. What, sir! a man placed at the head of the Treasury not capable of conducting an ordinary prosecution in a court of justice. I will never admit an insinuation of that sort to wound the fame of one of my colleagues on that occasion. Another one is now a judge of the Supreme Court, civil and criminal, of the State of Maryland. Was he not capable of summing up the law and evidence in such a case? I will not admit it. Another of the managers of the impeachment has since illustrated the government of Georgia. He has displayed an independence which does him honor with all feeling and independent men. Was he not capable of speaking to an ordinary case before a court? I cannot admit it. No; the acquittal took place, because the Constitution requires, and wisely, as in the case of a treaty, the assent of two-thirds of the court to the condemnation of the accused; and the assent of that two-thirds was not found in the case of impeachment alluded to, while it never has been and never will be found wanting to the ratification of any treaty which the President may negotiate. Mr. R. said, he had received a lesson on that subject which it was not necessary now to repeat. He meant not to tell the secrets of his prison-house. In the year 1800, he received a lesson, which if he was not better, he trusted he should be wiser for to his dying day, touching the nature of the initiatory and ratifying branches in relation to treaties.

One word more, Mr. R. said, and he had done. He wished he had followed the example of the honorable gentleman from Maryland in one respect, incapable as he was of following him in any other. He wished that he too had taken his leave, and sat down when he found his strength exhausted. He had thought it better, however, to finish what he had to say at once, and then to dinner, with what appetite we may. The gentleman had made one statement he wished to notice; that the treaty was a treaty or no treaty; that the ratifications being exchanged, it was law or not law. It is a law in those respects not requiring the intervention of Congress, but it requires legislative provisions, because it requires duties to be lowered or raised, which is equivalent to requiring an appropriation or the imposition of taxes, powers acknowledged to belong exclusively to Congress. What faith, the gentleman asked, could be put by foreign Powers in compacts with this Government, if a treaty may be rendered void after its ratifications are exchanged by the refusal of this House to act on it? There was the widest difference between the possession of a power, and the expediency of exercising it. Suppose a treaty should have received every possible sanction—that of this House included—we still have at any time a right to break it off, without consulting the other party, and go to war. A nation puts faith in other nations, not because of this or that form of Government, this or that check, or this or that balance in the operations of a Government, but according to its conviction of the disposition of other nations to maintain their faith. By that criterion, by that standard of character, ours is at least as good as sterling, and, he believed, a carat better. Great Britain put faith in us for the same reason we put faith in her—tempering our faith—for though scepticism be damnable heresy in religion, it is sometimes otherwise in politics—tempering it with a proper degree of distrust on both sides. If we put faith in a single individual at the head of a Government, as in the case of treaties with European Powers, how much more reason have they to put faith in the guarantee afforded by the pledge of every branch of a Government like ours, representing the whole people of the United States? Before the Prince Regent in England can violate a treaty, and make war, he must be supported by a vote of credit from the House of Commons; this is some restraint on him; but we have made treaties with the despots of every clime and color, from the lily and rose of the North to the jet black of Africa; and yet we are under no sort of doubt that these high contracting parties will adhere to their faith so long as they feel it their interest to do so. It, then, at last turned out, that foreign nations had nothing at all to do with this question; that whether the ratifications are exchanged properly or improperly, was an affair between us at home, with which foreign Powers could not be permitted to meddle; and, Mr. R. said, if he was asked for a just cause of war, he could figure to himself none better than an attempt by any foreign Power at intervention in our affairs. This treaty of commerce gave us leave to trade to the East Indies, and to touch at St. Helena. In that shape it came to the United States, and was ratified here by both Governments—how? In the shape in which it came? No. The very lowest grade of diplomatic functionary, he spoke of his office only—put his finger on one article, and said, beware of St. Helena. A Minister of Great Britain can take a treaty, and make a nose of wax, or any thing else he pleases of it; but the House of Representatives of the United States are to have no word in it. He asked, whether it was competent to a British Minister after a treaty had been solemnly signed under the eye of his own master, materially to alter the provisions of a treaty?— and the alteration was a material one, because the comfort and refreshment of touching at St. Helena was a matter of some consequence in an East India voyage. It was of little consequence,

he said, to us, who should be soon dismissed to a good hotel and smoking table; but to the poor scorbutic seaworn sailor, it was of great value. Was it safer for this House to exercise a controlling power on the acts of the President and Senate, so as to meet the coming disease; or that it should be entirely restrained from interfering, and the President and Senate go on making treaties until an extreme case, when the people would interfere and correct the procedure. Mr. R. said, he was no Jacobin; he hoped it was unnecessary to say that. He was no man for a Government of mobs, but of order, law, and religion; but, he said, there are points beyond which the people cannot be restrained; or should we rather let the President and Senate go on, provided they can find a Dey of Algiers to treat with; provided they can find a place to stand on until they make this sweeping treaty-making power a fulcrum to move the Constitution from its orbit? Mr. R. concluded by observing that the Senate had sent a bill to this House; a bill which he considered as yielding the question, and on which it would perhaps be best to act in preference to that now before the House.

Mr. PINKNEY rose to explain—to make a few observations which he said he should have made before, but that he had understood the gentleman to wish not to be interrupted. Mr. P. said that he thought he need not state to the House that his language had not been liable to the exception which the gentleman from Virginia had shown a disposition to take to it. The gentleman had said that impeachment had been tried and found wanting; in reference to which remark he (Mr. P.) had said that the example to which the gentleman had referred was not conclusive in support of that position; that impeachment might fail from various reasons; that the party impeached might be innocent—into which question he had not entered. Mr. P. said he was almost wholly unacquainted with the nature of either of the cases. His language was not liable to the imputation of having sought to reprehend the conduct of the gentlemen who conducted either.

The gentleman had said, that he is no drawcansir. Neither am I, sir. I should not have desired to reflect on the gentleman from Virginia; far from it; I am always disposed to speak in his praise; he has given such proofs of his genius as command my respect. But if I had a desire, which I had not, to cast a reflection on him, what reason was there to suppose I had a desire to do so on those, some of whose names I do not know? I supposed that the House of Representatives had selected men of the first ability, always as competent as any lawyer, to conduct the impeachment. I take it for granted that the impeachment was managed with the utmost dexterity and talent. All I meant to say was, that the failure of that impeachment did not prove that impeachment would always be found wanting. In the case expressly alluded to (that of Judge Chase) I presumed the innocence of the party. This explanation is due not only to the honora-

Militia Claims—Claim for Half Pay.

ble gentleman to whom my remarks apply, but to my own honor and character.

Mr. Randolph expressed his happiness at hearing the remarks of the gentleman from Maryland. The gentleman, he said, had misunderstood him in supposing him not to be disposed to allow the gentleman to explain; from his not having done so, Mr. R. confessed he had considered him as sustaining the inuendo. He reciprocated the sentiments of respect, &c., which the gentleman had expressed, &c.

During the discussion, the bill was received from the Senate, which is noticed above.

Mr. Forsyth stated the reasons why he hoped, notwithstanding the receipt of the bill from the Senate, that the bill now before the House would pass, as, according to his view, the Senate had, by passing that bill, attempted to evade the question before the House.

The question was about to be put, when Mr. Stanford having intimated his desire to speak on the question, on motion, the House adjourned.

Thursday, January 11.

Mr. Betts presented a petition of Christopher Colles, of the city of New York, engineer, stating that he has invented a new and useful species of telegraph, and praying, on his relinquishing his patent right therein to Congress, that he may receive in lieu thereof a commission for life—such as they may judge the importance of the subject deserves.—Referred to the Committee on Military Affairs.

Mr. Chappell reported a bill for the relief of the heirs of George Nebinger; which was read twice, and committed to a Committee of the Whole.

Mr. Chappell also reported a bill for the relief of Jonathan White; which was read twice, and committed to a Committee of the Whole.

On motion of Mr. Newton,

Ordered, That the Clerk procure, for the use of this House, and also of the Committees thereof, twenty-five copies of Graydon's Digest of the Laws of the United States.

Mr. King, of North Carolina, submitted the following resolution; which was read, and ordered to lie on the table for one day:

Resolved, That the rules of this House be so amended, that the Commissioners of the Navy Board shall be admitted to seats within the hall of this House.

A message from the Senate informed the House that the Senate have passed a bill "relative to cases of naturalization," in which they ask the concurrence of this House. They have also passed a bill "for the relief of Jonathan B. Eastman."

MILITIA CLAIMS.

Mr. Wright, from the committee on that part of the President's Message which relates to an arrangement of the expenses of militia incurred by States without the authority of the General Government, made a report on the petition of P. Andrews and others, and on the petition of the Legislature of the Mississippi Territory, relating to the pay of Nixon and Hind's cavalry; which was read. Whereupon the said petitions and report were referred to the Secretary of War. —The report is as follows:

That, although they are satisfied that the cases so referred to them are not within the purview of the original reference, yet they have taken the same under their consideration, and have come to the conclusion that no legislative act is necessary for the relief of the petitioners.

In the first case, the committee were satisfied that the muster-rolls of the militia, by their own officers, was legal evidence of their claims, particularly when remote from any regular corps; in which opinion they were confirmed, by an inquiry of the Secretary of War, who informed the chairman of the committee, that the regulation requiring the militia being mustered by a regular officer, proceeded from an order of the Secretary of War, which had been recently superseded; and that the necessary order had been given to effect the payment of these militia, on their muster-rolls by their own officers; whereby the benefits required will be had without an act of Congress for that purpose.

The committee were also of opinion that the militia of a Territory, called out as sanctioned by the Executive authority of a Territory, were to be considered as acting under the authority of the United States, and that the laws sufficiently provided for their payment, on the requisite evidence of their services; in which opinion, also, they were confirmed by the concurrent opinion of the Secretary of War.

On the last case, to wit: the propriety of paying the holders of the due bills or certificates of soldiers' claims, to their assignees, the Legislature of Mississippi admits the wisdom of the policy that interdicted it, in the case of the regulars, but suggests the different characters of the militia and regulars as a principle to induce the excepting the case of the militia out of the law. The committee are not sufficiently impressed with the suggestion of the memorialists to induce them to concur in that opinion, but are satisfied that if it was a wise policy in the case of the regulars, it can be fraught with but little mischief in the case of the militia. That it will introduce different rules of evidence in the case of the claims of the militia and regulars, inconsistent with the equanimity of sound legislation, and contrary to the opinion of the Secretary of War.

All which is submitted, &c.

CLAIM FOR HALF PAY.

Mr. Chappell made a report on the petition of Allen McLane; which was read, and ordered to lie on the table.—The report is as follows:

That the petitioner was a highly meritorious officer of the Revolutionary army, attached to Colonel Harry Lee's legionary corps, and served until November, 1781, when, by the permission of General Washington, he retired on half-pay for life. He states that, some time after he left the army, he applied at the office of the Auditor of Accounts for his half-pay, when he was informed that Colonel Lee had commuted it, and that, consequently, he was not entitled to it, and that he must take a certificate of five years' full pay in lieu thereof. He denied Colonel Lee's authority to commute for him, and alleges that he never did commute. He, however, admits that, being indebted and hard pressed for money, and finding that he could not obtain a settlement of his account for half-pay, he did, under these circumstances of necessity, accept a certificate for five years' full pay, protesting, at the same time, against its legality. He also admits that he received from Congress a warrant for three hundred acres of land, and states that he was compelled to part with both his certificate and warrant for very small sums. He prays that Congress will now allow him his half-pay for life, deducting therefrom the amount of the certificate which he received.

The committee would be gratified if they could, consistently with duty, recommend the relief prayed for; but they feel that it would be both contrary to law and to policy. The case is barred by the statute of limitations, even if it had never been settled; it is also, according to legal construction, barred by the act of the petitioner himself. The acceptance of the certificate for five years' full pay discharged the obligation of the Government to him. He, however, appeals to the magnanimity and liberality of Congress, and urges that the payments, which were made in depreciated paper, ought not to be considered as a fulfilment of the promise made by the old Congress in their resolve of the 22d of March, 1783; but in this the committee are of a different opinion. The certificate was such as Congress had promised; it was such as the other public creditors received; it was all the Government could give; and, however much it is to be regretted that the public securities of that time suffered a depreciation, yet the petitioner is not more entitled to indemnity for that depreciation than the number of other persons who received Government securities. His case is not different from theirs, and, therefore, proves the impolicy of any measure which shall, at this late period, attempt such indemnity.

He alludes to the acts of some of the States, by which the depreciation of their pay was made up to the officers and soldiers, and grants of land given them, and, therefore, thinks his claim on Congress is strengthened. These the committee suppose were acts of justice or generosity on the part of such States, and are certainly highly honorable to them; but neither the generosity nor justice of any State can impose an obligation on Congress. Congress has fulfilled its promises to the petitioner; and if he has any claim, it is not here, but on that Government which, from past experience, will be ready to reward his merits. They, therefore, feel bound to decide against his claim, but, wishing not to prejudice it, recommend the adoption of the following resolution:

Resolved, That the petitioner have leave to withdraw his petition.

COMMERCE WITH GREAT BRITAIN.

The bill from the Senate concerning the Convention between the United States and Great Britain, ratified on the 23d day of December last, was taken up, and read the first time.

The question being stated, "Shall the bill be read a second time?"—

Mr. FORSYTH briefly stated the grounds of his hostility to the bill. He considered it as an attempt on the part of the Senate to evade the question now before the House. Evasion, he said, was sometimes said to be admissible in diplomacy, when dangerous or difficult questions were presented for consideration; but it was never proper in legislation. The bill before the House, he said,

was, moreover, not an act to repeal certain acts or parts of acts, but a mere declaration that the laws which contravene the Treaty are of no effect; it was in effect a declaration that a convention between this country and a foreign country does *ipso facto* repeal the laws of the land. He therefore moved that the bill be rejected.

The question being stated from the Chair: "Shall the bill be rejected?"

Mr. STANFORD expressed his dissent to this proposition, and his impression that the bill from the Senate was in effect the same as the bill now before this House. The fifth section of the latter bill was in nearly the same terms as the bill from the Senate. He was therefore opposed to a rejection of the bill, and moved that it lie on the table.

Mr. FORSYTH hoped the motion to lay the bill on the table would not prevail. There was none of that similarity between the two bills which was supposed by the gentleman from North Carolina. The bill from the Senate proposed a declaration by Congress merely as to the effect of the Treaty on existing statutes; whilst the bill under debate in this House proposed by law to repeal those statutes. Mr. F. wished to throw on the Senate, instead of taking upon the members of this House, the responsibility of rejecting the bill of this House, &c.

The question to lay the bill on the table was decided in the negative, 70 to 62.

Mr. GOLD opposed the proposition to reject the bill, and could not conceive the grounds on which the charge of evasion against the Senate could be sustained. The bill from the Senate being decorous in its form, did it contemplate a proper and legitimate end? It did, he said, and therefore excluded the grounds of the imputation thrown on the Senate by the gentleman from Georgia. Such an imputation ought not to stand on slight ground. It touched considerations of courtesy, decorum, and harmony, between different parts of the Government. When they were once trespassed on, no one could safely say where the controversy would end. If the bill from the Senate contained anything improper or disrespectful to this House, the course now proposed might be proper; but the motion was a strong one, and went to preclude the consideration and amendment of the bill, should it require it, and, in his opinion, would hardly comport with the respect due from one House to the other.

Mr. PICKERING said, he had voted against the bill's lying on the table, and he should vote for the rejection; and yet he preferred it to the bill now before the House. He should vote for the rejection of the bill, he said, because he conceived it not necessary for the execution of the Treaty. He preferred it greatly to the other bill, because, being only declaratory of the Treaty, it was an admission that the Treaty was valid, and could be carried into effect without the intervention of this House. He was in favor of rejecting the bill, however, for another reason than that it was unnecessary; not because he did not feel towards the Senate all the respect due to them; but that he hoped, if the bill were rejected, the Senate

HISTORY OF CONGRESS.

would, without hesitation, reject the bill of this House, as an interference with their exclusive power to make treaties.

Mr. Root said, he did not see in the bill from the Senate, any disposition to evade the great question lately under debate in this House; but he did discover a direct determination of the subject-matter of debate—a declaration, that a treaty is capable of annulling our statute laws. It is a declaratory act throughout, in its terms as well as in effect: the bill runs, "Be it enacted and declared," &c. The Senate by their bill had, he said,,declared, that a treaty, after being ratified, and its ratifications exchanged, does repeal the statute laws of the country. The body which had ratified the Treaty had pronounced that their act was paramount to all existing laws; this, Mr. R. said, was contrary to his opinion, and he should therefore vote for the rejection of their bill.

Mr. Robertson wished to have again tried the question of laying the bill from the Senate on the table, but the Speaker decided such a motion not now to be in order. Mr. R. then remarked, that this was a question of much importance, and he hoped no passion would intermingle in its discussion, or influence the decision of it, which, whatever it might be, ought to be the result of cool, deliberate consideration. He did not consider the act of the Senate, in sending this bill to the House, as indecorous, but as a proper exercise of their powers. However, it again brought up the whole question, and, with the permission of the House, he would concisely examine it. I was delighted, said Mr. R., with the eloquence of the gentleman from Maryland, (Mr. Pinkney.) I was pleased with his lucid and fair manner of meeting the question, but I was shocked with his principles. I never did hear, I never did expect to hear, within these walls, principles so dangerous as those to which the gentleman has boldly, I was about to say daringly, given utterance. The treaty-making power, according to his doctrine, is without limit; it is without restraint; prostrates before it all the rights of this House, and tramples under foot opinions heretofore held sacred. Whatever treaty, of whatever kind, fall within the powers of any civilized Government, it is competent to our President and Senate to form; if the instrument be in itself complete, if it merely annul and abrogate laws, this House cannot interfere; thus the whole of our statutes, the entire code of our laws, lies at their mercy, and may, with the aid of any foreign sovereign who will unite in the scheme, be forever annihilated. Such is the doctrine of the gentleman from Maryland. Whence does it spring; how has it been supported? Let us probe it to the bottom—let us examine it with deliberation. Where is the legislative power in this Government vested by the Constitution? This is the sole and simple question; if it be not the only point in controversy, then my lips are closed—I have nothing more to say. If the President and Senate can make treaties, without repealing existing laws or making new ones, why let them do so—let them treat, and treat, and treat; they will

not alarm my fears; I shall feel no concern. There may be, for anything I know to the contrary, many treaties which do not necessarily include legislation; there are treaties of alliance, triple and quadruple, treaties of neutrality, partition, family compacts, &c.; give them up these; on these, and such as these, they may exercise their treaty-making power. But let them not legislate. There are bounds to this authority, as claimed for them. The legislation of Congress is defined and limited by the Constitution, but treaty legislation has no bounds. The President and Senate, with the aid of a few commissioners and a foreign sovereign, an Emperor or a King of France, a Lord Castlereagh, or any other despot, may govern this people without check, or control, or responsibility. They may—the gentleman from Maryland says they can. They can legislate, although all legislative power is vested in Congress, consisting of a House of Representatives, Senate, and President. They may regulate commerce, although the right to regulate commerce is given to Congress; they may draw money from the Treasury by law, for a treaty is a law. Look to the general powers of Congress; look to the specified; look to the limitations imposed upon that body; leave out this House, substitute a foreign Government; their general powers are usurped; their specified powers taken from them; the limitations imposed for the good of the people utterly disregarded. The President and Senate—let them not, legislate; it is the proudest, it is the only prerogative of republicanism. Legislation and representation in free Governments go hand in hand. They are not representatives—they are not responsible. The gentleman from Maryland says they are more responsible than members of this House. How stands the fact? The President is elected for four years, the members of this House for two; but as, under the practice of the Constitution, the Chief Executive Magistrate serves but two terms, the last is without a shadow of responsibility; he does not present himself at the bar of the public, to receive sentence of approval or condemnation. But the President is liable to impeachment. Indeed! impeachment? Yes, to be tried by that very body who advised the ratification of the instrument; to be tried by his accomplices! I ask the gentleman from Maryland if he would make himself laughed at by every man, woman, and child in the community, by bringing about so futile and farcical an exhibition? We see, then, the responsibility of the President; let us examine that of his compeers. The Senators are appointed for six years; not by the people, but by some dozens of individuals who form the State Legislatures; they are not impeachable, if that were in this case of any importance, neither are they amenable to censure, because they transact their Executive business with closed doors; they act in private. No one knows how any Senator votes, he is the sole depositary of his own secret —he votes and speaks as his caprice, his interests, or his judgment dictates—he fears no punishment, for his course is hidden; his Executive powers are exerted in conclave—mark the word, *Execu-*

tive powers—would it be believed, that in the United States of America laws were repealed and enacted in the exercise of Executive business? Why, what an anomaly is this Executive-legislative management!

The gentleman from Maryland goes the full length. If the treaty merely repeals laws, if it require not the aid of this House, the instrument is complete—the deed is done; but if, and according to his doctrine it can never happen, it requires some act of ours; then we have no discretion, we receive orders and must obey, if, after the stabs inflicted on this body, animation still exist. The gentleman tells you to raise your suicidal arm and perpetrate self-murder! worse, your parricidal arm, and plunge a dagger in the bosom of your country, for the Republic no more survives! It contains not one single feature to distinguish it from the despotisms of Europe. If this doctrine prevail, and that equally abominable principle which authorizes the judges to declare the little remnant of your legislation null and void, because, in their opinion, unconstitutionally exercised; hemmed in thus by the Executive and the Judiciary, there is no further use for this assembly. If the Legislature, the pre-eminent authority in all free Governments, be thus blocked up, thus circumvented, and that, too, by comparatively insignificant departments—departments inferior, subordinate, ministerial, then I have no hesitation in saying, that I should not regret the flames that blazed around that once splendid edifice now in view, nor that a similar fate should befall this humble building in which we this day are met; for one, I would not disgrace myself by holding a seat in this degraded and miserable body.

The gentleman from Maryland contends, that whatever treaty may be made by any Power on earth may be made by our President and Senate; that when made it becomes the law of the land; that in this respect their power is universal and unlimited. In what respect? In making treaties which are the laws of the land: in other words, that the President and Senate can make laws of the land on all subjects, and that, too, without limitation. Surely nothing more is necessary than to state such doctrines to make them universally abhorred. But to deny their truth, is, according to the gentleman, to produce the most extravagant anomaly imaginable in the Constitution. Is it not rendering the Constitution of the United States a more extravagant anomaly to strip the Legislature of the right to legislate, and transfer the law-making power to the Executive? If one must yield; if the President and Senate must be retrenched in their treaty-making power, or Congress deprived of the right to legislate, then is there no room for hesitation. Difficulties in regard to intercourse with foreign Governments can only embroil us with them; but an interference with the rights and duties of Congress prostrates the only barrier between the people and despotism, and embroils them with each other. Let us preserve the Union, the Constitution, principles of republicanism, and the privileges of this House; let us guard against the introduction of slavish and European notions of Executive supremacy, and we have nothing to fear from the hostility of a world in arms. But who are they whom we behold in array, supporting the extravagant pretensions of the Senate of the United States? What a singular phenomenon they exhibit: we find them ranged against the body of which they form a part; we find them voluntarily surrendering up the essential principle of their existence, and that, too, in favor of a jealous and a rival department; while the Executive Magistrate, in all Governments sufficiently disposed to claim the full measure of his prerogative, himself admits the power properly to belong to those by whom it is thus so unaccountably abandoned. I assert, that the President of the United States does not believe, with the gentleman from Maryland, that a treaty can repeal or enact a law, and I proceed now to prove it. In a letter dated July 27, 1812, from Mr. Monroe, then Secretary of State, to Mr. Russell, we find the following remarks: "As an inducement to 'the British Government to discontinue the prac- 'tice of impressment from our vessels, by which 'alone our seamen can be made secure, you are 'authorized to stipulate a prohibition, by law, to 'be reciprocal, of the employment of British sea- 'men in the public or commercial service of the 'United States. A stipulation to prohibit by law 'the employment of British seamen in the ser- 'vice of the United States, is to be understood in 'the sense and spirit of our Constitution. The 'passage of such a law must depend of course on 'Congress, who it might reasonably be presumed 'would give effect to it." Can language be more explicit; the renunciation of the power ascribed to the Executive more full? Compare it with the language of the gentleman from Maryland? According to him the treaty might have itself repealed, instead of stipulating that Congress should repeal the law in question. There are many other instances of a similar kind; but one, as clear and complete as the present, is of as much value as one thousand. Let it be observed, too, that this is not strictly a commercial affair; and how, if it were not competent to the treaty-making power to act independently of Congress in this case, shall it be contended it can act independently of that body, in commercial questions, notwithstanding the Constitution gives to Congress the power to regulate commerce? The doctrine of the gentleman, properly understood, amounts to what I have already stated—an exclusive right in the President and Senate to legislate for this nation in all cases; it is neither more nor less, nor can ingenuity give to it any other meaning. And why should this enormous this overwhelming power be yielded? Cannot the provision of any treaty be declared by law? Will not reciprocal legislation between independent nations supply the place of treaties? Might not a law contain all the provisions of the convention which has given rise to this debate? Might it not, do I say? Look at the law passed at the last session by the proper authority, it is merely re-echoed by this treaty; a law of the

British Government meeting that of ours, would have answered precisely the purposes of their instrument; and the same may be said of all treaties. Why, if Congress cannot regulate commerce, was the power given? Why acted upon? Why the act to which I have referred? The conduct of this House may be accounted for easily enough. We deem the subject placed in part under our control; but why did the Senate legislate? Why did they originate the act? Did they then think that commerce could not be regulated but by the three branches? Was the act an usurpation of the treaty-making power? It commenced with themselves. Was it superfluous, or insufficient? Surely that body will make no such admission.

The House of Representatives contends for no exclusive authority; it contends for such a participation in the Government as is assigned to it by the Constitution. Treaties may be made by legislation; but legislation must not exist through treaties. The right which we assert cannot be productive of irremediable inconvenience. The power contended for by the Senate, and their advocates, subverts the very foundation of the Government—totally changes its character, and establishes rank and unqualified despotism.

The debate now took the general form of that which had occupied the House for several days.

The passage of the bill which originated in this House was successively advocated by Mr. ROBERTSON, Mr. ROSS, and Mr. SHARPE, in speeches of considerable length and strength of argument; and the other side of the question was in like manner sustained by Mr. WRIGHT.

Mr. WRIGHT spoke as follows: Mr. Speaker, I must beg the indulgence of the House, while I deliver my opinion on the bill now under consideration; not, sir, because of the effect of the bill—for it effects nothing but the affectation of continuing a treaty already proclaimed the supreme law of the land—but because I feel it my duty to endeavor to keep the respective departments of the Government within the limits prescribed to them by the Constitution; nor could I suffer even my own impressions of expediency, much less that of others, to operate on my mind in the consideration of a Constitutional question. Sir, we are not sitting to frame, but to execute the instrument, agreeably to the true intent and meaning of the framers of it, by which every honorable man must feel himself bound as in the construction of any other compact.

Sir, this Constitution must be considered, as it was made, a compact among the several States, and its various provisions, as they may operate in favor of the larger or smaller States, as mutual concessions and compromises, for the vast advantages gained by the whole United States by their confederation in one Government.

It is an instrument that has passed the Rubicon, and been ordealed by the scrupulous investigation of its merits in the convention of the States that ratified it; and, sir, could I believe in political inspiration, I should readily ascribe its perfections to that influence. By the second article

second section of the Constitution, "the President shall have power, by and with the advice 'and consent of the Senate, to make treaties, provided two-thirds of the Senators present concur," and he shall nominate, and by and with the advice and consent of the Senate, appoint Ambassadors, &c. By virtue of this power, the President, by and with the advice and consent of the Senate, two-thirds of the Senators present concurring, made and ratified this treaty between Great Britain and the United States, and the President has caused the same to be promulgated by proclamation; after which, it is now proposed to be confirmed by the bill under consideration. And it is contended by gentlemen on this floor, that, as by the first article, eighth section, it is provided, "that Congress shall have power to regulate commerce with foreign nations, and among the several States, and with the Indian tribes;" that, therefore, they have a controlling power over any treaty relating to commerce with foreign nations.

Sir, the treaty-making power is a sovereign power; in Europe their Kings enjoy it without control; here it is vested in the President and Senate. The Senate represented the sovereignty of the States; and the sovereignty of the States, like all sovereignties, are equal, and, of course, correctly equally represented. The renowned Emperor of Russia possesses no greater degree of sovereignty over his vast extended empire, than the ruler of the most petty Power of Europe over his dominions. This equality of power in the States in the Senate, was intended to secure the sovereign rights of the smaller States from the oppression of the larger, and was one of the compromises before alluded to; and I have no doubt the vote on this question will test the necessity of provision, and the justness of the jealousy of the small States, and the propriety of guarding them in the Senate, from the overwhelming power of the large States on this floor, where four States can control the Union, and who are now endeavoring to invest themselves with a concurrent power with the Senate in the formation of commercial treaties.

Sir, while I shall advocate the exclusive power of the President and Senate to make commercial treaties in manner and form, as they have in this case exercised it, I shall not deny to Congress the power to regulate commerce with foreign nations, among the several States, and with the Indian tribes. The treaty-making power relates to international subjects. Treaties are compacts between Sovereign and Sovereign, relying for their execution on the good faith of the contracting Powers. Laws are rules of conduct prescribed by the legislative power for the government of the citizen—are national acts, to be enforced by pains and penalties, and executed by municipal authority. The treaty-making power then necessarily relates to the interest of two Powers, and must relate to international subjects. The legislative power can relate only to subjects national and municipal, and be executed by the officers of the Government, whose jurisdiction is bounded by all the United States; hence results the impracticability of legislating internationally, or of treating nationally. No nation can treat with itself, or legislate for another nation. Congress cannot appoint Ministers to treat, nor can she treat as a Congress; but Congress can and must regulate commerce, by fixing the tariff of imposts, the rate of tonnage, and the allowance for drawbacks. This they have done, and this they alone have the power of doing. The treaty-making power have the right, by treaty, to stipulate with a foreign Power, that the same regulations of impost and tonnage, and of drawbacks, which Congress have or may impose on ships and goods, the property of the citizens of the United States, coming into our ports, should be imposed on the ships and goods of the subjects of Great Britain, if they shall enter the ports of the United States, provided they will make the like stipulations in favor of our ships and goods, entering the ports of Great Britain. If there be no commercial treaty with the Power, whose ships and goods shall enter the ports of the United States, the regulations of imposts and tonnage, made by Congress, must be the rule by which such ships and goods must be governed, and be collected by the officers of the United States, appointed for that purpose. But, if a compact, international, is made, giving to each other the right to import into the ports of each other, upon the same terms that their own ships and goods enjoy, and that compact be made by the treaty-making Power, giving a reciprocal benefit to the contracting parties, it must be obligatory, or there can be no power to treat. I ask, if the treaty-making power agrees with Great Britain, that the same impost and tonnage which Great Britain imposes on her own ships and tonnage, coming within the ports of Great Britain, shall also be imposed on the ships and goods of the United States, entering British ports; whether that treaty is not binding on the United States, and whether Congress can, by any law, interfere with such compact, and whether such international act was ever intended to be considered as one of the powers of Congress to regulate commerce with foreign nations; and can it be that the treaty-making power can make such compact with England, clearly within the exclusive treaty-making power; and not be authorized to give the like privilege to British ships and goods, as the remuneration for their grant in the treaty to our ships and goods? Can it be that the framers of the Constitution intended to authorize the treaty-making power to make a compact with a foreign Power, for commercial benefits, and restrain the treaty-making power from remunerating such Power for such benefits? I presume not, and if the stipulation shall be, that the same exact commercial advantages shall be enjoyed by Great Britain in America, as Great Britain extends to America in England, can any man doubt that such compact is just, Constitutional, and conclusive? Can it be that the right to stipulate what should be the international regulation of the imposts and tonnage

on American ships and goods, in Great Britain, should be given to the treaty-making power, and the right to fix the remuneration should be given to the legislative power? I presume no man will ascribe to the framers of that instrument so improbable an intention, that one power be intrusted with fixing the *quid*, and the other power with fixing the *quo*—such a distribution of power would be contrary to all manner of experience. I cannot conceive that any honorable man can entertain such opinions, unless he has made up his mind to prostrate the treaty-making power at the shrine of the Legislature. It has been shown that the treaty-making power has been expressly given to the President and Senate, and it will be found in that profound and enlightened treatise in the Constitution, *The Federalist*, 2d vol. p. 201, "that the power to 'make treaties is an important one, especially as 'it relates to war, peace, and commerce, and that 'it is expressly given to the President, by and 'with the advice and consent of the Senate;" and in 2d vol. p. 276, "that the House of Representatives ought to have no power in the formation of treaties." Then the instrument was before the people, and then, with these explanations of the intent of the instrument, it was submitted to the convention of the States, and ratified understandingly, with this exposition, proving affirmatively, that the President and Senate had the power to make treaties and negotiate; that the House of Representatives had nothing to do with treaties. Sir, however plausible the arguments of gentlemen contending for this legislative power may seem to be, yet I trust, when the exposition of the Constitution, which I have had the honor to submit, comes to be clearly considered, and the treaty-making power, and the legislative power, duly examined and compared, they will be found perfectly consistent with each other, and each to revolve on its own Constitutional axis, and within its own orbit, without crossing in any manner the orbit of the other.

Yet, sir, notwithstanding this plain exposition of the powers to legislate and to treat, and the distinct demarcation of their Constitutional limits, the impracticability of treating on legislative subjects, or of legislating on the subjects of treaties, we are called on by the honorable gentleman from Kentucky (Mr. SHARPE) to recollect that we are treading on hallowed ground, that we had recently taken our oath to preserve the Constitution, which the exercise of the treaty-making power by the President and Senate, without the concurrence of Congress will, in his judgment, violate.

Sir, without intending in any manner to question that honorable gentleman's regard to that instrument, or to arraign him for its violations, but only to rescue myself from his unkind imputation, I hope I shall be excused in citing the opinions of that patriot General WASHINGTON on this subject, who presided in the convention that framed the instrument, and witnessed every act taken in that body to perfect it, and perfectly understood the true intent and meaning of every provision and section of it. He, sir. as President, having sworn to preserve this Constitution, at the time of Jay's memorable treaty, almost contemporaneously with the making of the Constitution, and when the subject must have been fresh on his recollection, expressly refused to furnish the House of Representatives with the papers developing the merits of that treaty, over which, he alleged, they had no control, and in which they had no Constitutional agency; whose opinion on this Constitutional question I quote with as perfect confidence of its constitutionality, as I should quote Coke Littleton in a court of common law on a common law question. Yes, sir, and was I to be arraigned even in Heaven, on the charge of the gentleman from Kentucky for violating this instrument, was it admissible to produce the opinion of that virtuous and enlightened statesman, I could have no doubt that it would be highly respected there, where I confidently hope his spirit is a sainted inhabitant.

The gentleman from Virginia (Mr. Randolph) has expressed great surprise that the gentleman from South Carolina (Mr. Calhoun) should have said, "that the act repealing the treaty with France was a judicial act." It certainly was a judgment entered up by Congress against France, " that she had violated that treaty, and that thereby the United States were absolved and discharged from all its obligations." It related to a foreign Power, was international in its object, and not legislative in its character. He repeatedly asked, what? a "judicial act"—a "judicial act!" He said he had never before heard that act called a judicial act, but quaintly remarked that he had frequently heard the act declaring the late war said to be not a "judicious act." Of that, sir, I have no doubt, although the very rumor of that war produced the repeal of the Orders in Council, and the war itself liberated all our impressed seamen, and restored thousands of the native sons of America to the bosom of their country and their friends, who, by impressment, had been long laboring under the most ignominious bondage. Nor, sir, have I a doubt, that if the honorable gentleman will trace the gentry whom he has heard making that declaration back to the war of our glorious Revolution, he will find many of them or their progenitors who declared even that war not a judicious act, although it effected the emancipation of a nation; and, by the establishment of the rights of man on the true basis, the sovereignty of the people, will, it is devoutly to be hoped, effect the emancipation of a world.

The same gentleman, in reply to my honorable colleague, (Mr. Pinkney,) when speaking of the security the power of impeachment had given, that the Senate should not corruptly violate the rights and interests of the nation, when in the exercise of the treaty-making power, treats the power of impeachment with great levity indeed; that it had been tried in case of Mr. Chase and Mr. Blount, and had been found wanting, and had convinced him that there was

no security in the trial by impeachment, and of its perfect inutility.

Sir, I had the honor of being a Senator at that time, and although I was one of the judges, who differed in opinion with my associates, who acquitted Mr. Chase, I am, in justice to that body, bound to declare, that it was the most dignified tribunal I had ever beheld, although a constant attendant on courts of justice for more than thirty years. The awful solemnity of that trial has been universally admitted, and has acquired for that body lasting fame; and I very strongly incline to believe that although Mr. Chase was acquitted, that the awfulness of that trial has been a panacæ to all future judicial irregularities. Sir, although I voted on several of the articles of impeachment against Mr. Chase, and that most conscientiously, I never for a moment doubted that my judicial associates who voted that Mr. Chase was "not guilty," were as much under the influence of a pure conscience as myself, nor was I for a moment dissatisfied with my honorable associates who acquitted him. And I had always supposed that after Mr. Chase had been declared by that tribunal, on so full and fair a trial, " not guilty," that that record would imply the absolute verity of his innocence, and that all disinterested men would feel a gratification that Mr. Chase, who had been appointed to that high office by a Washington, to which his legal talents had so pre-eminently entitled him, had been acquitted, particularly when they recollected that Mr. Chase had been one of the most distinguished patriots of the American Revolution.

But the honorable gentleman from Virginia, and myself, in that trial, acted different parts; I, that of a judge who, with my associates, was bound to decide the question on the evidence in the case, agreeably to the rules prescribed by the Constitution, and to respect the decision as the act of that high court of impeachment, in the discharge of a most solemn duty. He acted the part of a prosecutor, although not less honorable to himself, yet calculated to produce different feelings, particularly as he introduced the charges against Mr. Chase, he felt himself in a certain degree responsible for their verification; and my votes on the several articles of impeachment are his surest guarantee that I have never felt the slightest disapprobation of his conduct in the institution of that prosecution, although I cannot approbate his present persecution.

Mr. Lowndes then rose, not to enter into the general question, which had been so fully debated, but to express his views of the question before the House. He had great objection, he said, to the proposed rejection of the bill from the Senate. He scarcely could conceive a case, he said, in which the rejection of a bill without consideration would be proper. If rejected, that decision might be the result of calm and deliberate consideration, but such would not be the public impression. The Senate might also in turn reject our bill. In what aspect would this present itself to the public eye? The impression might be erroneous; but it certainly would be, that temper rather than judgment had caused these decisions. Suppose an opposite course to be taken. Suppose that the bill now under consideration should be postponed; and that the House should calmly, temperately, and therefore firmly—for he scarcely ever had known a proper firmness unconnected with some degree of temper—suppose they should thus, after having examined and discussed it, pass the bill originally reported in this House, and that our fears should be realized by the Senate's rejecting it. Suppose this House, uninfluenced by any hasty passion, spleen, or false delicacy, should then take up the Senate's bill, amend it so as to resemble the other one, again offer it to the Senate as, in the opinion of this House, that sort of bill which a sound exposition of the Constitution requires us to pass: suppose, even the worst, that the Senate also reject this bill. The double rejection would then be theirs; and no blame of haste or passion could be attached to this House: the question would stand on its own merits. With these and others views, Mr. L. moved to postpone the bill for one week.

Mr. FORSYTH said he found himself somewhat embarrassed by the observations of the gentleman from South Carolina. He professed, he said, in having made this motion, the most perfect respect for the Senate; it was not profession merely, but his real feeling. The motion he had made to reject the bill had proceeded, not from any splenetic emotion, but from a perfect conviction that the bill under consideration in this House ought to pass. Mr. F. then stated various difficulties which would result from sending the bill of this House to the Senate, whilst the Senate's bill was undecided on. The gentleman from South Carolina and himself, Mr. F. said, had the same object. Mr. F. had no desire that the House should be governed by prejudices or hasty emotions; he had a desire, that, when it acted, it should act decisively.

Mr. CALHOUN said he was certainly anxious that the bill which originated in this House should not pass; but he was equally anxious that no decision should take place without deliberation and full conviction. As he wished to give a fair opportunity of directly meeting the question which had been debated, he should vote to lay the Senate's bill on the table.

Mr. HANSON intimated an intention to move that the bill should be indefinitely postponed; and said that he purposed to do so, not because he considered (as he certainly did) that the House, in the measures they were pursuing with respect to the British convention, were deliberating on an act of usurpation—not that, in the motion he should offer, or in the vote he might give, he intended to reflect upon the Senate—but because he was convinced that the House possessed no Constitutional power to legislate upon the instrument under consideration. And, whatever deficiency there might be in the remarks he had to offer, he promised that there was one thing, at least, they should not want—brevity.

Mr. H. said, that he did not consider the subject before the House as one of those which afforded gentlemen an opportunity of festooning their eloquence, embroidering it with rhetorical flourishes, or swelling it beyond its natural dimensions, with extraneous and inapplicable matter. On the contrary, he expected that, as it had been *pressed* before the House, he should find it met in the way that great Constitutional lawyers meet great Constitutional questions.

Taking the business then in this way, it was first for their consideration whether that House constituted a part of the treaty-making power; when they had decided that, as inevitably they must, in the negative, the next question, was the most simple imaginable—namely, where the treaty-making power was in effect lodged—not where it ought to be lodged;—and, on this point, they might be at once relieved from all further trouble of investigation by casting their eyes upon the Constitution, which vests the power in the President, by and with the consent of the Senate, and cautiously and providently guards it by a provision that two-thirds of the Senators present should concur. And this clause, he said, contained the only limitation that was to be found attached to it in that instrument. It was impossible, he said, for language to be more precise or express in conveying the purposes of the human mind, or for words to be more unsusceptible of doubt or misconstruction, than those in which this clause was written: ' Shall have power to *make.*'' What, said he, can be understood by " to make," but entirely and wholly to accomplish— to render perfect and complete—to leave no part of it undone? If the treaty, then, wanted any part of the process appointed by the framers of the Constitution, even for its completion, it could not be made. But, when it went through the Whole, and obtained the last finishing—namely, the concurrence of two-thirds of the Senate— then it was *made;* and it would be an absurdity, in terms, to say that more was necessary to its perfection. This concurrence of two-thirds of the Senate was the safeguard erected by the Constitution, who thought it sufficient to preserve it against every abuse; and this construction of it is testified by innumerable contemporaneous authorities, of different political parties and sentiments. This was the construction of President WASHINGTON, and this was the construction of the several authors of *The Federalist.*

Gentlemen say that the laws of Congress are superior to this power. Mr. H. emphatically dissented from this position. The Constitution created the two distinct branches of power, at one and the same time, and by one and the same instrument—made them co-ordinate and co-existent. By the law of the land, therefore, the treaty-making power was made equal in these points—indeed, even paramount to the other—for it imparts to it the power to repeal it. " All treaties (says the Constitution) are the supreme law of the land." From the moment of its ratification and promulgation, therefore, and according to President WASHINGTON's construction, this treaty became the supreme law of the land at once.

And permit me to say, sir, continued Mr. H., that so it was considered, and this by the Executive of the United States, which may be readily demonstrated by the development of a fact—of which I have been informed, which I do firmly believe to be true, and with which in all probability many people, perhaps even here, are acquainted—and that is, that circular letters of instruction were actually printed and prepared to be sent off to the custom-house officers all over the Union, directing them to conform to the new laws and regulations created by the treaty. In this country we have received intelligence that, under this conviction, the tonnage on American vessels had been reduced in Great Britain; that, by an Order in Council, that benefit has been attached in England to our commerce; and that, in the confidence placed in our fidelity, our trade was without delay exempted from duties, so that there a vested right has been created by the provisions of the treaty. In this country we were equally bound by it as the supreme law of the land, insomuch that it may be questioned whether, from the moment of the promulgation of the ratified treaty by the President, any merchant could be bound to pay the late duties.

Sir, "this strange confusion,"—this bootless embarrassment—like many other difficulties, arises from gentlemen carrying their party feelings, their prejudices, and their passions, home to the Constitution. That great palladium of our independence had been compared to that miniature representation of the planetary system called an *Orrery*, in which each planet runs its own little orbit distinct from those of the others, and yet the whole is harmonious and exact. I fear, sir, that the experiments which it seems to be so much the temper of the times to make, will ere long crack this harmony, introduce discord in its stead, and, under that celebrated delusion of the day, invented by Mr. *Redheffer*—a more just object of comparison than Lord *Orrery's* miniature plan of the solar system.

Gentlemen complain that the Executive, by this act, trenches upon the Legislative branch of the Constitution. And see, sir, what at the same time they themselves aim at doing! Under the power vested in them by the Constitution, the President and Senate make a treaty; and because appropriations may be requisite, not so much to execute it, as in consequence of its execution, they would take upon them, by a bare majority of this House—perhaps of but one—to defeat that whole Constitutional branch, (the treaty-making power,) assuming, on patriotic pretences, to elevate themselves above it. Would it not be a gross anomaly, sir, if the Constitutional act of the President and the Senate—that, too, not of the Senate voting as in ordinary by a bare majority of perhaps one, but by two-thirds of the Senate against the other third—should be annulled by this branch of the Legislature? Shall it be said, that, because the execution of this treaty might require an appropriation of money—suppose to pay their salaries to the commissioners employed to run our new British line, and gentlemen should

take it in their heads to dislike that provision—that therefore this House can, on that miserable pretext, nullify the treaty-making power, and thereby strip our Government of the most essential article of self-preservation—I say, sir, *self-preservation*, because, what *has* been done may be done again? And suppose England, liberated from her European struggles, and again at war with us; her hordes of soldiers landed on our shore; our Capitol taken and burnt; our cities sacked, beggared, and in possession of the enemy; our once opulent people, and the repositories of their wealth—the banks—not on the verge merely, but tumbling into the very gulf of bankruptcy—to what refuge should our Government resort to save all that was not already in the enemy's hands, when that sacred part of our Government, the power of treating, was destroyed, or lodged *nowhere*? Or, suppose all that portion of the country included between Massachusetts and the British possessions were in the hands of the enemy, and by our Ministers at Ghent treating on the basis of the *uti possidetis* so much of our country was shifted over to Britain by treaty, would this House be competent to legislate for Castine? No. We might declare war against and endeavor to fight for it, if we could, but we could not legislate away the treaty.

Sir, the radical error in this measure, and all the difficulties that hang over the proceeding, arise from a fond indulgence of the fancy in extreme cases—cases that can never, without a violation of the ordinary course of things, exist—from supposing the Executive capable of acts compounded with madness, folly, and baseness; and from supposing it and two-thirds of the Senate rank, corrupt, and profligate beyond example. But, sir, if these things even *did* occur, the national occasion would provide for itself. On the whole, sir, I consider the interference of this House with the treaty-making power an usurpation; that it would be unjustifiable in us to legislate upon it; that the treaty is capable of executing itself; and that there is no necessity for any law whatever to be enacted in respect to it.

On these grounds, sir, I move that the bill be postponed indefinitely.

Mr. LOWNDES, having further expressed his anxiety to avoid a direct rejection of the Senate's bill, varied his motion so as to supersede Mr. HANSON's, moving to lay the bill on the table.

Which motion was then decided in the affirmative without a division.

The House then resumed the consideration of their bill on the subject, being a bill "to regulate the commerce of the United States according to the Convention of Commerce," &c.; and the question still being "Shall the bill pass?"

Mr. STANFORD said, he would beg leave to make his acknowledgments to the House, if the adjournment of yesterday evening was to afford him the opportunity of making the few remarks he had intended to make before the question was taken. He, however, had no wish to consume but a few minutes of the time of the House, and hoped that he would not then do it.

He said, he was an old member, and on the question before the House, as gentlemen debated it, stood committed as to the course he should take, and, under like circumstances, should still feel it his duty to take; but in his judgment the bill before them did not involve the old question, whether this House had, or had not the power, in certain cases, to give effect to a treaty. Such cases might exist, and might well be supposed to exist, where appropriations were called for, or where regulations became necessary, growing out of legislative power to give effect to a treaty, as in the case of acquiring territory—or where the treaty itself should stipulate for some legislative provision in fulfilment of its views. In such cases he held it, he said, that the House had not only the power to legislate to give effect to such treaty, under its own discretion, but, under the same discretion, to refuse to legislate, and defeat the ends of such treaty. Any other doctrine, he contended, would lead to the absurdity of legislation, without the right to deliberate; or to that of voting without the right to judge whether the measure was, or was not, for the public good.

Although, therefore, he did not believe the Constitution gave, or was intended to give any direct share in the treaty-making power, to the House of Representatives, yet that it held an indirect control over a certain class of treaties, he could not be brought to doubt. He meant, to be sure, such treaties, and such only, as those to whose provisions legislation became indispensable—as without the passage of some law of Congress, they could not go into effect; of this description, he conceived those to be, of which he had spoken.

As the most of our treaties, however, were not of such description, but such as were sufficiently full in their details, and went plainly and obviously to their intended objects, it would seem equally absurd to attempt to legislate them into effect—or, in the language of the gentleman from Maryland, (Mr. Pinkney,) by a law to re-echo the very words of a treaty, thereby to seem to give it effect. Mr. S. said, if his views were correct, and he must own he felt the fullest confidence in them himself, he could not see how gentlemen could press the necessity of the present law, to give effect to or regulate anything in the late commercial treaty with Great Britain. It is certainly a treaty of the latter description, plain and simple in its details, and one which calls for no appropriation, no authoritative law, nor regulation of any kind. Already has the President sent it out with his proclamation, and he must have considered it as having effect from the time, or he ought not to have proclaimed it.

This question came up between the two Houses, under the former British treaty, for the first time, upon a call for an appropriation to carry it into effect. Again, a few years after, under the foreign intercourse bill, when the House claimed the exercise of some discretion in voting for or against the salaries of certain Ministers whom the President and Senate had appointed on missions abroad, which the House did not approve, and thought

proper to oppose. In both these instances, the appropriations were made, notwithstanding the opposition; but, in the third instance, an appropriation was called for, and refused, to carry into effect an Indian treaty in the Yazoo country. The reason for this refusal is well known, but the difficulty being removed at a subsequent period, the money was voted, and the treaty carried into effect. Mr. S. said, in the case of the acquisition of Louisiana, legislation became necessary, not only to appropriate money, but to extend government to the citizens of that Territory, and no question or difficulty was made about it, and he felt persuaded it was a rightful claim on our part, to exercise a sound discretion in all such cases.

But how gentlemen brought up the question under the present treaty, he could not perceive. The treaty called for no money, no regulation, no law, as a *sine qua non* to its existence. As well might we be called upon to pass laws to give effect to the various Indian treaties, which are now going out before the public under the President's proclamation. So far as I know, no one thinks of any law, as necessary to their entire effect.

He would ask, he said, how came it to pass that no law was thought necessary to give effect to the treaty with France, which terminated the kind of war which Mr. Adams had gone into with that nation in defence of our maritime rights? It is not sufficient to say that the friends of his Administration did not pretend to think any law necessary. The fact is, that although the treaty was negotiated and concluded by Mr. Adams, it was at the very close of his Administration, and was of course carried into effect by Mr. Jefferson and his friends, and they never seemed to think any act of Congress necessary to give it effect. So far from it, Mr. Jefferson, without any other law, or rule of construction to guide him, except the treaty itself, took it upon himself to repair the Berceau at the cost of more than thirty thousand dollars, and to restore her thus equipped to France, and he was defended on the ground that it was nothing more than a fair and liberal construction of the treaty, which stipulated the surrender of captures on both sides.

But a case still more recent presents itself. He cited the Treaty of Peace so lately concluded with Great Britain. That treaty went into immediate effect under the President's proclamation, and one of the effects of the treaty was to surrender to the British the islands in the Passamaquoddy with all their population, customs, and laws, and all this by virtue of the treaty, without any law—nor was it even suggested that that House had to legislate about it. Or, are we to understand that all our municipal laws are still in force about Moose Island? That our revenue cutters are still under orders to ply about that island, and guard the United States against smuggling and smugglers from that quarter? Our revenue laws remain unrepealed, and people are bound by them unless the treaty has superseded them; and that it has so superseded them, it is difficult even to make a question. We know that our laws are not there regarded.

Mr. S. then concluded his remarks with observing, that if the arguments of gentlemen be correct, it would seem to him they ought to assume the ground of legislating all treaties into effect as well as this; and if they did not intend to go so far as that, he thought they might well have dispensed with legislating in the present instance. For his part he could not see that it was necessary, and should vote against the bill.

Mr. PICKERING rising to speak, the House adjourned.

FRIDAY, January 12.

Another member, to wit: from Connecticut, TIMOTHY PITKIN, appeared, produced his credentials, was qualified, and took his seat.

Mr. HULBERT presented a petition of sundry manufacturers of domestic goods, in Berkshire county and State of Massachusetts, praying that the existing duties on the various domestic manufactures may be abolished.—Referred to the Committee of Ways and Means.

Mr. HOPKINSON presented a petition of Daniel Pettibone, praying compensation for the use, in the armories of the United States, of a machine, invented by him, for the boring of gun barrels.—Referred to the Committee of Claims.

Ordered, That the petition of the Legislature of the Mississippi Territory, presented on the 29th ultimo, be referred to the Committee of the Whole on the bill to enable the people of the Mississippi Territory, to form a constitution and State government, and for admission of such State into the Union, on an equal footing with the original States.

On motion of Mr. PICKERING, the Clerk of this House was directed to purchase, for the use of the House, five copies of the Laws of the United States.

A motion was made, by Mr. PICKERING, that the House rescind the order of yesterday for the purchase of twenty-five copies of Graydon's Digest; and the question being taken thereon, it was determined in the negative.

The House proceeded to consider the resolution submitted yesterday, by Mr. KING, of North Carolina, to amend the rules, so as to admit within the Hall of Congress the Commissioners of the Navy Board; and the same being again read, was concurred in by the House.

On motion of Mr. MARSH, the Committee on the Judiciary were instructed to inquire into the expediency of altering the times of holding the circuit and district courts of the United States, in the district of Vermont.

A message from the Senate informed the House that the Senate have passed a bill "confirming to the Navigation Company of New Orleans, the use and possession of a lot in the said city," in which they ask the concurrence of this House.

COMMERCE WITH GREAT BRITAIN.

The House resumed the consideration of the bill for regulating the commerce of the United States according to the late convention with Great Britain—the question still being on the passage of the bill—

Mr. PICKERING said, that after so long a discussion of the question before the House, he would not have risen had not some lights, in which it should be viewed, passed unobserved.

In this country, said he, we hold that all the powers of Government originate with the People. Those powers the people might distribute in any manner they pleased. They might have vested all legislative power in one man; in a President, or in a President and Senate, or in a President, Senate, and House of Representatives. To see how they have in fact distributed the powers of Government, we must look to the Constitution, which they have framed for that purpose.

The first clause in the Constitution reads thus: "All legislative powers herein granted, shall be vested in a Congress of the United States, which shall consist of a Senate and House of Representatives." And the inference of gentlemen on the other side of the House is, that whatever powers are expressly granted to Congress, are exclusively granted; or, if any other branches of the Government act upon the subjects of those powers, the concurrence of this House is necessary to render their acts valid. But if gentlemen will turn to the seventh section of the first article of the Constitution, they will see an important restriction on the sweeping legislative power apparently granted to the Senate and House in the first section: "Every bill which shall have passed the House of Representatives and the Senate, shall, before it shall become a law, be presented to the President of the United States," for his approbation; without which it will not become a law, unless, on a reconsideration of it, with the President's objections, it shall be approved by two-thirds of each House. Here, then, is one exception to the sweeping legislative powers granted to Congress, as composed of the Senate and House of Representatives, that is, of bare majorities of the two Houses; and a special legislative power is created, and vested in two-thirds of the two Houses, whose concurrence is, in such case, necessary to make a law.

In like manner, is complete legislative power vested in the President and Senate. For we see, in the passage of the Constitution so often recited, that all treaties made under the authority of the United States, are declared to be the law of the land; and the President and Senate are exclusively vested with the power to make treaties, two-thirds of the Senators present concurring.[*]

---

[*] When it is declared, that "this Constitution, and the laws of the United States which shall be made in pursuance thereof, and all treaties made, or which shall be made, under the authority of the United States, shall be the supreme law of the land;" no more is meant, than they are supreme in relation to the constitution and laws of the individual States; and hence, after declaring what shall be the supreme law of the land, the Constitution adds, "and the judges in every State shall be bound thereby; anything in the constitution or laws of any State to the contrary notwithstanding." In one other sense, indeed, the Constitution is the supreme law, because it is the act of the people in their sovereign capacity, in the several

But it is said, that among the various powers granted to Congress, one is " to regulate commerce with foreign nations;" and that if such regulation of commerce be made the subject of a treaty, an act of Congress, including the concurrence of this House, is requisite to make it the law of the land. Here the negotiating of a treaty and the making of a treaty are compounded, although they are perfectly distinct. When a Minister, or other Executive agent, has negotiated a treaty, it is, by the President, laid before the Senate; and when, with their advice and consent, it is ratified by the President, it is made—it is complete; and no act of the House of Representatives can add anything to its validity. The word *made* is equally applicable to laws and to treaties. "This Constitution, and the laws of the United States made in pursuance-thereof, and all treaties made, or which shall be made, under the authority of the United States, shall be the supreme law of the land."

As to the subjects of treaties: When the framers of the Constitution gave to the President and Senate power to make them, without specifying or limiting the subjects to which they should be confined, it is plain the term treaties was intended to embrace the usual subjects of these contracts between nations. At the time when the Constitution was ordained, we had four commercial treaties—with France, Holland, Prussia, and Sweden; and a treaty of alliance, and a convention or treaty relating to consuls, with France. All these subjects, then, it is certain, are within the treaty-making power of the President and Senate. The convention with Great Britain, to which the bill before us refers, embraces but two of them—commerce and consuls.

But, seeing that Congress have power to regulate commerce with foreign nations, why should it be made the subject of treaties? The answer is, to give stability and security to commerce. Suppose the United States and Great Britain, merely by laws of the two countries, had equalized the duties on American and British vessels and their cargoes, in the manner provided by the commercial convention, and suppose that, in expectation of the permanency of those laws, the growers of cotton and tobacco in the United States; and cannot be changed but by a like act of sovereignty. Hence the laws enacted by Congress are required to be made in pursuance of the Constitution. And although no such restriction is laid on treaties, because treaties embrace some subjects not mentioned in the Constitution, (such as the making of peace and forming alliances with foreign nations,) yet a treaty, no more than an act of Congress, which should contain any provision violating the Constitution, would be of any validity. For the treaty-making power of the President and Senate, as well as the legislative power of Congress, being derived from the Constitution, every exertion of that power in repugnance to it, or involving the abrogation of any of its provisions, must necessarily be void. To maintain the contrary, would be equally absurd as to say, that a superstructure could stand when its foundation was removed, or that a branch could retain life when the root was dead.

States were to ship those articles in vessels of the United States to Great Britain, and, pending the voyage, the Government of that country should deem it expedient to repeal her equalizing laws, and restore the discriminating duties of tonnage and impost on American vessels and their cargoes; this would bring a very serious loss on those owners. But a treaty would prevent such repeal, and consequent injury.

To a just understanding of the question before the House, another distinction should be taken; that is, between the validity and the execution of a treaty. While gentlemen on the other side (with a single exception) admit that some treaties made by the President and Senate are valid, without any act to be done on the part of this House, such as simple treaties of peace, and even of alliance; seeing no special power is granted to Congress by the Constitution, to make peace and form alliances; yet it is said, that when the intervention of this House is necessary, as in providing and making appropriations of money to carry treaties into execution, then the sanction of this House is requisite to give them a binding force. But let it be supposed that the Constitution, instead of vesting the whole treaty-making power in the President and Senate, had ordained that no treaty should be valid, unless approved by the House of Representatives; and suppose, also, that all the three branches of Government concurring, a treaty of commerce and limits were made, such as that with Spain, in 1795, no one would then question its validity; and yet, unless the President and Senate appointed commissioners to run the boundary lines, to mark the limits of the respective territories, and unless the House of Representatives, concurring with the President and Senate, appropriated money to defray the expense thereof, the treaty would remain unexecuted.

According to the doctrine maintained by the framer and advocates of the bill before us, there have never been any valid treaties between the United States and foreign nations, since the organization of our Government; for no law of Congress has re-enacted their articles, (as is attempted by the present bill,) or by a general enactment pronounced them to be the law of the land. Take up any of those treaties; for instance, the treaties of 1795 with Great Britain and Spain, where the appointment of commissioners and appropriations of money were necessary to their execution. Congress passed laws making such appropriations; not to give validity to the treaties, but simply, in the language of those laws, to carry them into effect.

But shall treaties operate a repeal of a law of the United States? Yes, because treaties being, equally with acts of Congress, the law of the land, they must repeal all the provisions of prior laws contravening their stipulations—according to the well-known maxim, that the latter laws repeal all antecedent laws containing contravening provisions; and so long as treaties exist, so long the Government and nation are bound to observe them, and the decisions of the judges must conform to their stipulations. But as treaties may thus annul the laws of Congress, so may these laws annul treaties; and when Congress shall, by a formal act, declare a treaty no longer obligatory on the United States, the judges must abandon the treaty, and obey the law. And why? Because the whole authority, on our part, which gave existence and force to the treaty, is withdrawn by the annulling act. Such is the effect of a law of Congress declaring war against a nation between whom and the United States any treaties had been made. Take for example the case of France, with whom we had a treaty of amity and commerce, a treaty of alliance, and a consular convention. These treaties having been repeatedly violated on the part of the French Government, and the just claims of the United States for reparation of the injuries so committed having been refused; and their attempts to negotiate an amicable adjustment of all complaints between the two nations having been repelled with indignity; and as the French persisted in their system of predatory violence, infracting those treaties, and hostile to the rights of a free and independent nation; for these causes explicitly, Congress, in July, 1798, passed a law, enacting that those treaties should not thenceforth be regarded as legally obligatory on the Government or citizens of the United States; and two days afterwards Congress passed another law, authorizing the capture of all French armed vessels, to which the commerce of the United States long had been, and continued to be, the prey. And as in this, so in every other case in which Congress shall judge there existed good and sufficient cause for declaring a treaty void, they will so pronounce, either because they intend to declare war, or because they are willing the United States should meet a war, to be declared on the other side, as less injurious to the country than an adherence to the treaty. But should Congress, without adequate cause, declare a treaty no longer obligatory, they must be prepared to meet the reproach of perfidy, besides exposing the United States to the evils of war, should the offended nation think fit to avenge the wrong, by making war upon them.

A gentleman from Virginia, (Mr. Randolph,) among other reasons why this House should claim, and exercise as a right, the giving of its formal sanction to a treaty, said, that foreign nations would place more confidence in treaties so sanctioned. Mr. P. held the contrary opinion. Foreign nations, he remarked, with whom we should negotiate treaties, would look into our Constitution, to see where the power to make treaties was lodged; and finding it vested in the President and Senate exclusively; if they saw that, in practice, the House of Representatives interposed its pretensions, that the assent of that House also was necessary; and if they saw the President and Senate yielding to such pretensions—to such a manifest encroachment on their exclusive powers—instead of increasing, it would diminish their confidence in the acts of the Government. For confidence is inspired and best secured by the stability of a Government, and the adherence of all its branches to their respective rights.

Mr. P. concluded his observations in saying, that the Senate would feel it its duty to maintain its Constitutional rights. That, having acted with the President in making the Commercial Treaty with Great Britain, which had thus become the law of the land, it was not to be expected that the Senate would adopt the bill before the House, and thus re-enact the articles it had so recently enacted; and in the last article expressly declared to be binding and obligatory on the United States. It would be better, therefore, not to send the bill to the Senate.

Mr. Taylor, of New York, spoke as follows:

Mr. Speaker, I have listened to the remarks of the honorable member from Massachusetts (Mr. Pickering) with the attention due to age and experience. The important offices he has held under this Government, and the extended period of his political life, claim for his opinions particular respect. But the tribute of respect is all I can pay. I cannot assent to his construction of the Constitution, as it applies either to the legislative or the treaty-making power. In my judgment these powers, under the Constitution of the United States, are perfectly distinct in relation both to the authority exercising them, and the subjects upon which they can definitively act. A treaty is a compact of accommodation between independent States, relating to their public affairs. It derives all its efficacy from the consent and agreement of the parties; it operates upon the willing only; it is obeyed by the parties no longer than obedience is voluntary. If its engagements are violated, there is no tribunal competent to afford redress; recompense can be found only in the provisions of a new compact, equally voluntary to the first, or in a resort to the *ultima ratio regum.* The proper subjects of treaty arrangement are, those to which legislative power cannot reach by reason of its limited jurisdiction. Were it not for this, no treaty would, or indeed could, be made; there could be no parties capable of contracting. Freedom of will would be wanting, for it is of the nature of legislative power to impose upon all persons, subject to its jurisdiction, an obligation to conform themselves to the rule it prescribes. It possesses within itself a capacity of making all laws necessary to carry its enactments into complete execution; all other power is inferior and subject to its control. It is restrained only by the Constitution of the Government under which it acts, and limited only by its territorial jurisdiction: "The idea 'of law necessarily comprehends that of a pen-'alty, consequent upon its violation, of a tribunal 'which determines the penalty, and a physical 'force to put it in execution." In a Government where the will of a despot is the supreme law, it is immaterial to the subject whether that will be expressed in the annunciation of a treaty or an edict; but in a Government where the law-making power is vested in three departments, and the treaty-making or bargaining power in two of them, it may become vastly important to national liberty, that these two departments should not be permitted, in the form of treaties, to exercise the sovereign power of enacting and repealing laws. Does, then, the Constitution give to the President of the United States the power, by and with the advice and consent of the Senate, in the form of a treaty, to legislate for the people of this country, by repealing the laws of Congress and enacting others in their stead? The question is important; it should be discussed with temperance, and decided with firmness. I agree with my honorable colleague (Mr. Gold) that the present occasion is auspicious for both.

It is admitted on both sides of the House that the treaty now under consideration is well advised, and ought to be carried into full execution on the part of the United States. But it is denied by the honorable member from Massachusetts, (Mr. Pickering,) and by most of those who, on this occasion, vote with him, that a law of Congress is necessary to give it effect, because the Constitution declares that the President shall have power, by and with the advice and consent of the Senate, to make treaties, provided two-thirds of the Senators present concur; and that all treaties made, or to be made, under the authority of the United States, shall be the supreme law of the land.

Let it be remembered, that municipal law maintains its obligation over all those subjects which are within its jurisdiction, and that a treaty law enforces its agreements or compacts only on public international affairs which municipal law cannot reach. A law of Congress compels obedience to its enactments on all subjects over which legislative power is granted to that body by the Constitution; but what power is more clearly granted than that of regulating commerce? And what law is more purely municipal than that which prescribes the sum of money to be paid on the importation into a territory of a particular article of trade or commerce? It enters into considerations of domestic policy, equally important and various. The wants of the citizens of a State, both in peace and war; the encouragement of their home manufactures, and generally their whole domestic concerns, are affected by it. It is, therefore, a fit subject of municipal legislation. By whom then is such legislation to be exercised? The Constitution, in the first section of its first article, gives the answer: "All legislative powers herein granted shall be vested in a Congress of the United States, which shall consist of a Senate and House of Representatives." The eighth section of the same article, which grants to Congress the power of declaring war, raising and supporting armies, and coining money, grants, in terms equally strong and definite, the power also of laying duties and regulating commerce. But it is contended, that as a treaty is the supreme law of the land, so it attaches to itself the essential quality of all other law, that of repealing former laws contradicting its enactments; and gentlemen have attempted to illustrate this position by calling our attention to the Treaty of Peace, and

asking whether it did not repeal the law declaring war? I answer the inquiry in the negative. The act of declaring war is, in most limited Governments, purely executive. The Constitution vests the exercise of that power in Congress, and in exerting it Congress acts rather executively than legislatively. An act declaring the relations of amity which had existed between two nations, to be terminated, may be prefaced with a recital, that the offending nation had committed acts of hostility against the other, and, therefore, that a state of war existed, as was done at the last session of Congress, in passing the act for protecting the commerce of the United States against the Algerine cruisers; or, omitting a recital in the law, it may simply enact, that a state of war is declared to exist between the two countries, leaving the publication of its causes to a report or manifesto, as was done in declaring war against Great Britain. In either case the law is purely declaratory. It presupposes hostile acts to have been committed, and does nothing more than promulgate, in an official form, the existing relations between the Governments concerned. An act declaring war is in its nature also of limited duration. The only legitimate end of war is peace. Surely it is the only end contemplated by the Constitution of the United States. It is to continue in force until relations of amity shall be restored, in the manner pointed out by the Constitution, and no longer. Whenever that event happens, the law becomes inapplicable, and expires by its own limitation. A treaty of peace, therefore, does not repeal an act declaring war.

Neither is a treaty the supreme law of the land, in the same sense that either the Constitution or an act of Congress is supreme. The second paragraph of the sixth article of the Constitution declares: "This Constitution, and the 'laws of the United States which shall be made 'in pursuance thereof, and all treaties made, or 'which shall be made, under the authority of the 'United States, shall be the supreme law of the 'land, and the judges in every State shall be 'bound thereby; anything in the constitution or 'laws of any State to the contrary notwithstanding."

First, then, the Constitution is supreme, as being the charter of liberty proposed to the people of the United States, by their convention on the 17th of September, 1787, and afterwards ratified by the people of all the States, which cannot be altered by act of Congress, nor by treaty; nor in any other manner than that prescribed by the Constitution itself. It is therefore superior in dignity and authority to every other law. Second, laws of the United States, made in pursuance of the Constitution; and third, treaties made under the authority of the United States, although inferior to the Constitution, are, within their respective powers of making laws concerning the internal, and making compacts relative to the external affairs of the country, supreme in comparison of the Constitution and laws of any State, and binding upon the judges thereof. This construction of the Constitution preserves the harmony of all its parts. It leaves each department to act within its own sphere, and conforms to the rule that, in expounding an instrument, such construction shall be adopted, that all its parts may stand together, and effect be given to each. But the construction, advocated by those who oppose the passage of this bill, on the ground that legislative interference is unnecessary, is in manifest contradiction of the Constitution itself, and the acknowledged powers of this House. If the words "supreme law" are to be applied in precisely the same sense to the Constitution, to acts of Congress, and to treaties, it follows that a treaty is of equal dignity and binding obligation to the Constitution. And, as a posterior law repeals all of a prior date which contradict its enactments, a treaty may alter, amend, or repeal, the Constitution itself. But the President and thirteen Senators may make a treaty—therefore they may, in the form of a treaty, make amendments to the Constitution which cannot be made without the consent of three-fourths of the States in the Union. Their construction is in manifest violation also of the acknowledged powers of Congress. It is admitted by all that if a treaty contain a stipulation, on the part of the United States, to make a payment of money, that it cannot be carried into effect without the passage of a law by Congress making an appropriation for that purpose—why not? Will gentlemen inform me? The Constitution does not say that an appropriation law shall be passed by the Senate and House of Representatives. No, sir; it only says, "no money shall be drawn from the Treasury but in consequence of appropriation made by law." But if a treaty is the supreme law of the land, capable of altering, amending, or repealing, the laws of Congress, money drawn from the Treasury in consequence of an appropriation contained in a treaty, would be drawn, not only legally, but in pursuance of the supreme law itself. A conclusion, fraught with such monstrous absurdity, has not yet found an advocate on this floor; but such is the inevitable consequence of the construction for which gentlemen in the Opposition contend.

Mr. Speaker, it has been asked, whether the treaty will not be executed even if Congress refuse to pass a law for that purpose. I answer in the negative. By the existing laws, goods imported into the United States from Great Britain in American vessels pay a certain duty, and goods imported in British vessels pay a different duty. By the treaty it is agreed that, in both cases, they shall be charged with the same duty; the treaty does not, neither could it, determine what that duty should be; whether it should be the higher or lower rate, or a modification of both; that could only be decided by municipal law; to make that decision the bill under discussion is introduced; legislation on the subject is thought necessary by the President himself. In his Message communicating the treaty, he says, "I recommend to Congress such legislative provisions as the convention may call for on the part of the United States." Such is not the form in which treaties

capable of executing themselves are communicated. For a proof of this I refer gentlemen to the President's Message at the last session of Congress, announcing the Treaty of Peace with Great Britain.

We have already seen that the Constitution, in its first article, contains a declaration that all legislative power shall be vested in Congress. The eighth section of the same article proceeds to enumerate the subjects over which that power may be exercised. "The Congress shall have power to lay and collect taxes, duties, imposts, and excises." But of what avail is this power if the President and thirteen Senators can, by treaty, abolish a tax or duty laid by Congress, and establish another? If they can vary a tariff of duties in any particular, they can abolish it altogether. They can agree that all goods, the growth, produce, or manufacture, of the British dominions, shall be admitted into the United States free of duty, in consideration that the British Government will extend the same privilege to American produce imported into Great Britain; or in consideration that the British Government will grant to the United States the provinces of Upper and Lower Canada, to be governed as the President and Senate, or as the President alone, or as any other individual may direct; or in consideration that the British Government would pay to the President of the Senate, or to the Paymaster General of the Army of the United States, an annuity of ten millions of dollars, to be disbursed by the President of the United States, or for any other consideration which they might think proper to accept.

"To borrow money on the credit of the United States."

But of what avail is this power if the President and Senate can repeal the revenue laws of Congress, enacted with a view to pay the interest and repay the principal of money so borrowed; or if they can, by treaty, borrow money themselves and pledge the public faith, or mortgage the public lands, for its reimbursement?

"To regulate commerce with foreign nations."

But of what avail is this power, if the President and Senate can definitively agree, by treaty, with a foreign nation, what articles of commerce shall be admitted into the United States, and what excluded; what duties shall be paid, and what remitted; and, generally, upon all subjects relating to both foreign and domestic commercial transactions?

"To establish a uniform rule of naturalization."

But of what avail is this power, if the President and Senate can, by treaty, stipulate that the subjects of a foreign Government, either shall not be admitted into the United States, or, being admitted, shall not be naturalized, or if they can repeal the naturalization laws enacted by Congress, and establish others contradictory thereto?

"To declare war."

Even this exalted attribute of sovereignty is of little importance to Congress, if the President and Senate can, by a treaty of alliance, bind the United States to commit an act of hostility against a nation with which we are at peace, thereby producing a state of actual war as effectually as if declared by the Constitutional organ of the Government.

"To raise and support armies."

But this grant of power may be rendered useless, if the President and Senate can, by treaty stipulation, fix the number of men to be retained on the Military Establishment of this and another country, with a view to the mutual security of both; or, by a treaty of alliance, determine the contingent of force to be furnished by the United States and the amount of subsidy to be received therefor.

"To provide and maintain a Navy."

This power also is annihilated, if the President and Senate can agree with the Government of another nation, what amount of naval force shall be retained in service by the respective countries.

The Constitutional power of Congress over the militia, if the construction advocated on a former occasion by the gentleman from Massachusetts, (Mr. PICKERING,) and his political friends, be correct, (which construction has been sanctioned too by the Government of more than one State in the Union,) is too contemptible to justify a single remark in regard to its possession.

In fine, there is no legislative power granted to Congress by the Constitution which the President and Senate may not usurp, nay, which they cannot lawfully exercise under the construction given to that instrument by the gentleman from Massachusetts, except perhaps the power of exercising "exclusive" legislation over the District of Columbia.

Against such enormous political heresy, I am constrained to enter my solemn protest; if it ever receives the sanction of this House, the charter of American liberty will not be worth preserving; the rights, dignity, and power of this House, derived not from sovereign States, but from a more noble right—the people themselves, whose Representatives we are, whose wants and wishes the Constitution presumes us better to know than any other branch of the Government, and to whom we are amenable for the exercise of the power confided to us, those rights will be abandoned, this dignity sullied, and our power of standing between the people and oppression will be gone forever. The President and Senate, uniting legislative authority to Executive patronage, will manage the concerns of the Government in their own way, not responsible to any earthly tribunal.

Gentlemen, however, have told us not to be alarmed, all is well, there is no danger, the President and Senators are honorable men, good men and true, acting under a high responsibility, with wisdom to discern, and virtue to pursue the best interests of the country. All this may be true, but what security have you, Mr. Speaker, that their seats will always be occupied by men of equal merits? Kings have been bribed and Senates corrupted; what has happened to the Chief Magistrates and Senators of other ages and nations may possibly happen hereafter in our own country.

God grant that it may not, at least, that neither we nor our children to the hundredth generation may see the evil. But should it be the misfortune of the American people to have the administration of their Government committed to corrupt hands, what incalculable mischief would not follow the doctrines of Presidential and Senatorial legislative supremacy! If a treaty should be made, combining in its provisions all the usurpation which I have supposed possible, accompanied with circumstances indicating the most unhallowed ambition, even the poor satisfaction of punishing the offenders would be denied to the people. The Senate is the sole judge of its own members, who are not liable to impeachment in any case whatever, and the President, if impeached, would be tried by judges equally criminal with himself; who, in their Senatorial capacity, advised the very act, for doing which the President would be arraigned at the bar of their House. The absurdity of such a trial is too manifest to require comment.

But it is asked, is this House infallible? Is it proof against corrupt and ambitious influence? Is its patriotism above all price? I answer, that its numerous members, elected for a short period by the people themselves, are at least equally unlikely to indulge projects of ambition dangerous to the liberties of their fellow-citizens, as the members of the Senate, which in practice is almost, and in theory altogether, a permanent body. The people have therefore some additional security in the public virtue of this House for at least honest legislation, which would be entirely withdrawn by the construction of the Constitution against which I protest. And if it happen contrary to my expectation that the Senate shall reject this bill, which I trust we shall shortly send to them for their concurrence, the period will already have arrived when every barrier which this House can erect will be required at our hands to guard the rights of the people against the tyranny of Senatorial usurpation.

But we are again told to quiet our fears, for "there is no danger." Mr. Speaker, it was one of the first lessons taught me by my parents, not to believe in the doctrine of "no danger." I remember to have read in a good old-fashioned book, that it was the doctrine successfully preached by the Serpent to "the mother of mankind." It was in substance the language used by Joab, who too was an honorable man, a chief and a captain over the host, while he was preparing to plunge his murderous weapon into the side of Abner, the son of Ner; and, in fine, it was the language of the Tories in the Revolutionary war. But it never was the language of a Revolutionary Whig. When the British Government imposed a three-penny tea tax upon the people of this country, the Tories, or as they called themselves, the Loyalists, said, "no danger," it is an honorable Government, and the power will not be abused. But what said the Whigs? It is, said they, the principle, and not the sum against which we contend. If we abandon the principle, there is no stopping point; we shall be chained together like manacled slaves, and driven wherever our masters please to drive us. Such too was the language of Republican Whigs in 1798. And it will be the language of Whig principles to the end of the world; examine the page of all history, and you will find the no danger creed recommended by the Catilines, Arnolds, and Leonards of all nations, and resisted by their Franklins, Browns, and Jacksons. We, Mr. Speaker, are the people's watchmen; their sentinels. It is our duty to be vigilant, to guard their liberties, and to sound an alarm at every approach of danger; and, while I have the honor to occupy this place, not one jot nor one tittle of their rights, nor of the Constitutional power of this House, shall be usurped by the Senate, or any other department of the Government, by my consent.

Mr. WILDE said he little thought, when this debate commenced, that it would have been continued so long, and thought as little that, in the course of it, he should have troubled the House with any remarks. Till now, indeed, he had been a mute, as far as he could be, a patient, and he hoped not altogether inattentive, listener. Had his views of the subject been presented to the House by any other gentleman, he should still have remained so, content to prefer, however ignoble the choice, the safety of silence to the hazards of debate. As they had not, he would venture to intrude them as briefly as he could, that at least they might not tire those whom they did not please.

He desired previously, however, to offer a word or two in answer to some arguments which had been urged in the course of this discussion. It had been said by the gentleman from South Carolina, (Mr. CALHOUN,) that the bill upon your table is unnecessary, because an act was passed at the last session repealing our discriminating duties as to all nations who should repeal their discriminating duties as to us. Now, sir, asked Mr. W., what evidence have we that Great Britain has repealed her discriminating duties as to us? The treaty, indeed, provides that she shall do so, and there is no doubt it will be done. But at present, sir, they are merely suspended by the Order in Council of the 17th of August, which we have seen in the newspapers, and which does not refer either to the words or the date of the treaty, and can as little be connected with the law of the last session. On the contrary, its duration is limited to six weeks after the commencement of the next session of Parliament, pointing evidently to a repeal of those duties by act of Parliament before the expiration of that period; and, by and by, we shall see the act repealing those duties, which it is necessary should be abolished before the law of the last session can operate effectually. Farther, sir, a strict examination of that law will show that, however it might have been intended, its words fairly interpreted, reach only to goods, wares, and merchandise, the growth or produce of the foreign nation, and not to the ships or vessels in which they may be imported; whilst the convention stipulates that all discrimination as to both shall be at an end. The law of the last session, therefore, is not co-extensive with the stipulations of the convention, and cannot supersede the necessity of the present bill. But the passage of that very law, sir, furnishes an argument against the doctrines of the gentlemen who have alluded to it, so far as any argument can be drawn from the practice and opinions of the last Congress. If they believed, as the gentlemen do, that the President and Senate had the power of making a treaty which should have the force of a law in repealing those duties, why was it necessary to pass a law providing for their repeal? Evidently, sir, it would not have been thought necessary; for, according to such a supposition, they must have believed the President and Senate had this power independent of all law. Their passing this law, therefore, is the strongest proof they could have given us of their belief that the President and Senate had not this power.

Mr. W. said, if he understood the gentleman from Massachusetts (Mr. PICKERING) correctly, he undertook to show, by the uniform practice of this Government since the adoption of the Constitution, that laws had not been passed to carry treaties into effect, except where an appropriation of money was required, and he thence inferred, that laws for that purpose had not been deemed necessary. Mr. W. declared he had examined all the treaties which had been made, and the laws which have been passed regarding them, in conjunction with his friend and colleague who reported this bill to the House, and who gave a brief statement of the nature of the treaties made and the laws passed, and of the evident reasons why, in certain cases, laws had not been thought necessary. His colleague certainly did not go into details, because with such subjects every member of the House was presumed to be acquainted; but the result of their examination was a conviction in them both, that whenever laws had not been passed in conformity with the stipulations of a treaty, it was generally, if not universally, because those stipulations did not touch any of the objects committed exclusively to the jurisdiction of Congress; or, in other words, did not require the enactment of any new, or the change of any old, municipal regulation. To enter into an examination and comparison of those laws and treaties now, would, Mr. W. observed, be to inflict more upon the patience of the House than it would be willing to endure. If, however, a positive precedent upon his part was demanded, he would lay his hand upon it at once; and it was not the less welcome, to him at least, on account of its having been established during the administration of Mr. Jefferson, a period of what he had been accustomed to consider as correct principles. It was the stronger, because Mr. Jefferson, when Secretary of State, is said to have maintained the opinion now supported by the gentlemen on the opposite side of the House. The Louisiana convention, Mr. W. said, was open before him, and he found there a stipulation upon the very same subject, and in form not very unlike that of the treaty now under discussion.

That stipulation provided for the admission of French and Spanish vessels into the port of New Orleans for twelve years, upon the same footing as American vessels; the law which was passed on that occasion did contain a provision to the same effect. [Here Mr. WILDE read the law and the convention.]

The bill before you, Mr. W. remarked, has been called "the echo of the treaty, its reflected image, its twin brother." He would ask, if this law and the article in the Louisiana convention are not at least of the same family, and as like one another as Sebastian and Viola?

Having made this reply to some of the arguments of others, Mr. W. said he would now proceed to offer a few of his own.

If he had not misconceived some of the remarks of the gentleman from Maryland, (Mr. PINKNEY,) it was admitted, that a treaty might be either self-executory, or might require a law to carry it into effect. He agreed perfectly in that opinion. but no rules had been furnished for deciding what treaties were self-executory, and what required laws to assist their operation; without such rules, it would be impossible to determine the present question, which is, to what class does this treaty belong?

What the hand of a master neglected to perform, either because his eye was fixed upon greater objects, or because he deemed it unworthy of his genius, the hand of a novice might venture to attempt; for, if he failed, he forfeited nothing but a reputation which is not worth preserving, while if he succeed, he acquires all he can ever hope for—the praise of being useful. The rule which he would offer was probably not such a one as the gentleman himself would have given; certainly not as good an one, possibly little better than no rule at all. He offered it not without hesitation, and it was simply this:

That where the stipulations of a treaty relate entirely to objects purely international or extra-territorial, then they are self-executory, or at most require nothing more than an exertion of the Executive or judicial powers to carry them into effect. But that where they relate solely to objects intra-territorial, objects purely of municipal legislative jurisdiction, there they require the exertion of the municipal legislative authority to assist their operation.

To the first class belonged conventions regulating the reciprocal rights and duties of nations, when one of them shall be belligerent and the other neutral, including the definition of blockade, of contraband of war, of enemy's property, of the right of search, and of all other questions coming within the jurisdiction of the admiralty or maritime courts of either nation, sitting under and professing, at least, to decide according to the authority of national law. In the same class were included all treaties merely of peace. As to these the President and Senate ratify the treaty. The President, as Commander-in-Chief, can suspend hostilities, and the tribunals of prize are competent to do the rest.

To the second class he would refer all treaties,

conventions, and agreements, having solely for their object a change, either reciprocal or otherwise, of any regulations merely municipal, in one or both countries. If the change was to be reciprocal, according to his idea, it would require the interposition of the Legislature of each country respectively; if it is not to be reciprocal, it would require the interposition of the Legislature of that country only in which the change was to be effected.

Further, sir, said Mr. W. treaties may be mixed or compounded of stipulations, relating to objects, some of which belong to one class and some to the other.

Of this description are treaties of guarantee, of alliance, of subsidy, of cession, of boundaries, and many others which I will not attempt to enumerate. So far as these relate to objects purely international, they are self-executory, or, at all events, may be executed without the aid of the legislative power. But so far as they concern objects solely of municipal legislation, so far they require the aid of the legislative authority to carry them into effect. If the terms are reciprocal, they will require reciprocal legislation in each country. respectively, so far as they relate to the latter class of objects. If they are not reciprocal, they will require legislation in that country only where municipal regulations are to be altered or affected.

Thus a treaty merely of guarantee or alliance, between two nations, both of whom are at peace, is self-executory; it is perfected by the exchange of ratifications. Its objects are purely international, and require no legislation, because they require no new municipal regulations, neither do they require the change of any already in existence.

But if such a treaty stipulate that one or both parties shall raise and keep up a certain number of troops, this stipulation, if it be reciprocal, must be legislated upon in both countries; if not reciprocal, it must be legislated upon in that country which is to keep up the troops, because as to that country the object of the treaty is a municipal regulation.

As to a treaty of subsidy, that too would require legislation in the country paying the subsidy, because the appropriation of money is a municipal regulation.

With regard to treaties of alliance, with a nation already engaged in a war, as well as to treaties of cession and boundary, they are required to be considered as with relation to the extent of the power vested in the authority making them, as with relation to the objects of the treaties themselves. If the same authority which is invested with the power of making treaties, possesses also the power of declaring war, then that authority may make a treaty of alliance with a nation actually engaged in a war. But if the power of making treaties and of declaring war is not lodged in the same hands, then the authority of the treaty-making power does not extend to such a case; because to make a treaty of alliance with a nation engaged in war, is to make war on the enemy of that nation. Even if the treaty-making power is also invested with the power of declaring war, still all the stipulations of any treaty of alliance which it may make with a belligerent nation, so far as the same relates to raising troops, paying money, or to other objects of municipal regulation, so far will the stipulations of such a treaty require legislative interposition to carry them into effect. On the other hand, so far as such stipulations concern objects merely international and extra territorial, so far they are self-executory, or, at all events, may be executed by the executive and judicial powers, without any legislative assistance.

With reference to treaties of boundary and cession, he would say, that if the treaty-making power of a nation is constitutionally authorized to fix its boundaries or cede any part of its territory by treaty, and does by treaty contract its boundaries or cede a part of its territory, such treaty is self-executory. If by a treaty of cession or boundary it extends the limits of the nation, or acquires new territories, such a treaty, so far as it relates to objects merely municipal, will require legislation; your laws, civil and criminal, cannot be extended over it merely by treaty.

To decide how far any treaty, and particularly the treaty before us, requires legislative assistance to carry it into effect, we must ascertain first, the Constitutional extent of the treaty-making power over the objects of that treaty; and secondly, how far the treaty stipulations concern such objects as are purely international, and are for this reason self-executory; and how far these stipulations relate to objects municipal and intra-territorial, and therefore cannot execute themselves or be executed without legislative interposition.

The President and Senate have power to make treaties; this is said to mean all treaties—treaties of commerce as well as the rest. Granted. Still this does not decide the question. These treaties when made may be either self-executory, or they may require the aid of laws to carry them into execution. Of which class is this treaty? What are the objects of some of its stipulations? Are they purely international or municipal? Extra or intra-territorial? They relate to the equalization of duties. Can anything, he asked, be so entirely an object of municipal regulation? Can anything be more completely intra-territorial?

Let us consider, said Mr. W. the nature of the treaty-making power. Is it a power to pledge the faith of the nation, to anything or to everything; possible or impossible? Evidently not. It is a power to pledge the faith of the nation for the performance of such things only as are naturally and constitutionally possible. Is it a power to pledge the faith of the nation absolutely and without qualification in all cases? Or only absolutely in some cases and qualified in others? Certainly the latter. And this seemed to him the distinction. The treaty-making power is authorized to pledge the faith of the nation absolutely for the performance of all stipulations purely international or extra-territorial, because these are either self-executory, and are in fact partly

executed by the exchange of ratifications, as in a treaty of peace; or they depend for their execution on the executive and judicial powers, which are sufficient for that purpose, as in the restoration of prizes captured after the cessation of hostilities; as in the decision of contraband, enemy's property, blockade, the right of search, the change of property, and all other questions of maritime jurisdiction. But as to all objects of mere municipal regulation, it is not authorized to pledge the faith of the nation absolutely and without qualification, because these are to be effected only by laws, and cannot make laws, though it can make treaties. But this treaty is a law, and the supreme law. The answer was easy—it had been given a dozen times. If the President and Senate could legislate by treaty upon one object, purely municipal and intra-territorial, they could legislate by treaty upon all objects purely municipal and intra-territorial. They could lay taxes by treaty, raise troops by treaty, in short, exercise the whole legislative authority of the country by treaty. What then became of the distinction that has been taken between treaties self-executory and treaties which require laws to carry them into execution? One or the other ground must be abandoned. Either treaties operate as laws upon all objects purely municipal and intra-territorial, or upon none. If upon all, every treaty is self-executory. If upon none, then every treaty operating upon such objects requires a law to give it effect. But no object can be more completely municipal and intra-territorial, than the objects of this treaty. What can be more entirely an object of municipal regulation than the imposition of duties? What more completely intra-territorial than the execution of those duties in our own ports? Surely then a law is necessary.

In support of the position that a treaty is a law of the land, and a supreme law, an article of the Constitution had been quoted, and some stress laid upon the argument. If that article is accurately examined, it would be found to refer only to the States. "The judges in every State shall be bound thereby, anything in the Constitution and laws of any State to the contrary notwithstanding." If the framers of the Constitution had intended that a treaty should control acts of Congress, would they not have added "anything contained in any act of Congress to the contrary notwithstanding?" Could anything be more obvious? But it had been said, also, that a treaty could repeal a law, and the Treaty of Peace was triumphantly appealed to as evidence of the fact. It is asked, Did not the Treaty of Peace repeal the law declaring war? Mr. W. answered, if it did, still it would not affect his position, which was, that no treaty could repeal any regulation merely municipal. Was war a mere municipal regulation? According to what law is it to be declared and waged? By what law is it regulated? Certainly the law of nations. Can any object be merely municipal which is regulated entirely by the law of nations? Certainly not. There were writers on national laws whose works were confined to a consideration of the

629　　　　　HISTORY OF CONGRESS.　　　　　630

January, 1816.　　　　　Commerce with Great Britain.　　　　　H. of R.

rights of war and peace. Mr. W. admitted that raising troops and money to wage war, were mere municipal regulations, but raising troops was not waging war. It was true also that war may be either extra or intra-territorial. Still he would inquire by what law was it regulated? Was it an international or municipal object? But he did not by any means admit that the Treaty of Peace repealed the law declaring war. He held that a law could be repealed only by a law. He said that the law declaring war expired by its own limitation, as soon as peace was concluded. What was the meaning of the law declaring war? He spoke not of its words, but its effects. Simply this: "War is hereby declared against Great Britain, and shall be waged and continue until peace is made?" Would it admit any other meaning? But if, as gentlemen suppose, the Treaty of Peace operated by repealing the act declaring war, then nothing more was necessary than to repeal that act, in order to be at peace. He once indeed had heard a great peace advocate jocularly maintain this opinion. But he imagined it would not be gravely asserted. No, undoubtedly, would be the reply; for the consent of a foreign nation would be wanting. Well, then, Mr. W. would say, even with the consent of that foreign nation, a repeal of the law declaring war, would not make peace, because that would be to transfer the power of making peace from the President and two-thirds of the Senate to the President and a bare majority of both Houses. If, then, repealing the law declaring war, even with the consent of the foreign nation to make peace, would not have placed us in a state of peace, how could it be said that the Treaty of Peace operated by repealing the act declaring war?

Mr. W. said there was one view taken of this subject by the gentleman from Virginia, (Mr. Tucker)—he would call him his friend, if their intimacy admitted the expression, for he should think himself honored by the friendship of the gentleman—which he would attempt to enlarge.

If a duty might be repealed by treaty, the whole of our duties might be so repealed. The commissioners who made this treaty, had their instructions admitted, might have stipulated that all American vessels and goods should be duty free in England; all English vessels and goods duty free in the United States. Here would have been twelve or thirteen millions of your revenue swept away at once; and as that revenue is pledged, you would have been compelled to provide other funds for the payment of the public creditor.

Having answered several, Mr. W. said, he would in turn ask one question of the gentlemen on the opposite side. A distinction had been taken between treaties requiring an appropriation of money, and others, because the article in the Constitution is restrictive: "No money shall be drawn from the Treasury, but in consequence of appropriations made by law." Whenever money was wanted, therefore, it seemed to be conceded a law must be passed; whereas the article rela-

ting to commerce being merely permissive, no law was thought necessary. Now the power to regulate commerce and to make war were given to Congress in the same form of words. Congress shall have power to regulate commerce; Congress shall have power to declare war. Their powers over these objects must be coextensive. He would ask if the President and Senate, under the general treaty-making power, were authorized to enter into a treaty of alliance, offensive and defensive, with a foreign nation actually engaged in war? If they were, then all the most essential powers of the Government belonged to them; they could make war by treaty; they could make peace by treaty; they could raise and keep up troops by treaty; they could lay and collect taxes by treaty, and repeal them by treaty; provide for calling out the militia by treaty; and when gentlemen prided themselves in the cheek that they could not appropriate money by treaty, they had forgotten that they could borrow money on the credit of the United States by treaty.

For his own part, Mr. W. did not think they could do any of those things, and he should be sorry if they could; and he did not think so because he believed the sound, the true, the safe, and honest interpretation of the Constitution to be, that whatever any branch of the Government could not constitutionally do directly, it could not do indirectly; and as the President and Senate could not make war directly, or regulate commerce directly, they could not make war by treaty, nor regulate commerce (so far as it was municipal and intra-territorial) by treaty.

The power of Congress to regulate commerce, had been called a residuary power, a power to regulate such parts of commerce as have not been regulated by treaty. He had no objection to the term residuary power. He would admit it to be a residuary power, but he said it was a power to regulate such parts of commerce as could not be effectually regulated by treaty. Such parts as require other sanctions than those of the law of nations to enforce them. The President and Senate, Mr. W. said, had power to regulate commerce by treaty, so far as it was purely international and extra-territorial. Congress had power to regulate commerce by law, so far as it was purely municipal and intra-territorial.

The President and Senate could not lay or repeal duties by treaty. Congress could not extend or limit the right of search, or the definition of blockade, or contraband, by law. Thus each had its proper objects, and over those objects the authority of each was complete.

But the treaty-making power necessarily includes the power of pledging the national faith qualifiedly, that certain acts shall be done which its own authority is not of itself competent to do. If it does so pledge the national faith for the performance of such acts, then it was for that power whose aid is required to effect them, to say how far it will redeem the pledge. The form of the stipulation, Mr. W. contended, makes no difference. Foreign nations treat with us with a knowledge of our Constitution, and the stipulations of a treaty are understood with reference to Constitutional powers. The pledge given by a treaty is understood to be a pledge to do all which the treaty-making power can, of itself, perform, and to cause to be done, if possible, by the other departments of the Government, whatever its own power is not competent to do.

A treaty, to be sure, had been said to repeal a law, and, therefore, it would be said that the treaty-making power has in this instance stipulated for nothing more than it was competent of itself to perform. If a treaty could repeal one law, it can repeal another; if it could repeal some, it can repeal all; for he called upon gentlemen to recollect what was so clearly and forcibly demonstrated by the gentleman from South Carolina, (Mr. Lowndes,) that the restrictions contained in the Constitution were restrictions on the power of Congress, not restrictions on the treaty-making power.

He would add nothing further. He had promised not to tire the House; and yet, though he had only thrown out hints rather than arguments, he was afraid that promise was already broken.

Mr. Sharpe said, he was persuaded that the House was already fatigued with the protracted discussion which this subject had undergone. He should, therefore, in delivering his sentiments, be as brief as was in his power. It was most unquestionably true, as had been stated, that the inquiry which it behooved the House to make, was not what ought to be the proper distinction of the powers of the Constitution, but what they really are. If the comprehensive and almost unlimited power contended for, was exclusively vested in the President and Senate, it became the duty of the House, in obedience to the supreme will, to yield a ready acquiescence. But he thought it not unreasonable to contend, that unless that power was clearly granted, and in terms wholly unequivocal, a different course ought to be adopted. If there was a rational doubt, or an apparent conflict in the different parts of the Constitution, as it respects the subject before the House, that construction ought to be given which best comports with the spirit and genius of the Government, and preserves the salutary checks which have been provided against the abuse of power.

The leading features of this Constitution, said Mr. S., are strongly and distinctly marked. Its principal characteristics consist in a distribution of its powers to different departments, and in such an organization of each as tends to check abuses. The legislative, executive, and judicial powers are confided to different public agents, who, in the exercise of their respective functions, act as checks upon each other. The legislative power is so organized as to afford great security against the adoption of improper measures. In the ordinary course of legislation, no act is binding on the nation until it has received the assent of a majority of the Representatives of the people and of the States; and, likewise, the assent of the President, the representative of both. Surely,

then, it is not unreasonable to contend (in the absence of any positive provision) that a treaty, made by the President and Senate, embracing the same subjects, confided to the Legislature in distinct terms, ought not to have the force of a law, which has received the approbation of all the constituent branches of the legislative power.

Before he proceeded further, Mr. S. said, he wished to be distinctly understood. He did not mean to contend that the House of Representatives had any agency in making treaties, or that a direct vote of ratification was necessary or proper, but he meant to contend that a treaty did not operate as an absolute repeal of an existing law in conflict with it; and that, when it contained affirmative stipulations, in relation to subjects expressly confided to Congress, a law was necessary to give it effect. This construction will make every part of the Constitution consistent with its own principles, and with the spirit which pervades the whole.

In the distribution of its powers, the Constitution has expressly provided that all legislative power therein granted shall be vested in the Congress of the United States. In a subsequent part, the objects to which it shall extend are specially enumerated. No concurrent special authority, in relation to these objects, is granted to any other department of the Government. But a general power is given to the President and Senate to make treaties, which I admit means all treaties usually among nations. The question then is, does this general power to make treaties, so far as it is exercised, operate to the utter destruction of the special power of legislation; or, shall both have their effect? Among the rules which are adopted, in the construction of the instrument, none seems to be better settled, than that general powers cannot destroy those specially granted; but that when there is a conflict, the former must yield to the latter; and a rule equally correct is, that every part of an instrument shall have its due effect, if possible. Can it then be correctly contended, that the power to make treaties, conferred in general terms, annihilates (so far as the provisions of a treaty extend) the power to make laws, specially granted? Is it not more correct to adopt a construction which will equally preserve the power to make treaties, and the power to make laws, which will give to the President and Senate the exclusive authority to make all treaties, and leave to the House of Representatives a concurrent power in the execution of such as embrace subjects expressly granted by the Constitution to Congress? A very extensive field for the operation of the treaty-making power will still exist. Every treaty of peace, of limits—all treaties regulating the conduct of the contracting nations, when either shall be at war—designating what shall be contraband, or what shall be a legal blockade—regulating the right of search, and many others, will fall within its exclusive jurisdiction; and as it respects those treaties, embracing legislative objects, it will possess the right to form them, in the first instance, and also a concurrent voice in their execution.

633   **HISTORY OF CONGRESS.**   634

JANUARY, 1816.   *Commerce with Great Britain.*   H. OF R.

A consideration of the comparative character of the legislative and treaty-making powers tends strongly to support this construction, and to prove, in a manner perfectly satisfactory to myself, that the latter is not superior, not equal, to the former. That which is called sovereign power in every Government, is the power to make laws. In Great Britain, it is clothed with the character of omnipotence, because, as to the objects which it embraces, it is superior to any other human power, and annuls all that come in collision with it. The Executive and Judicial powers are under its control, and subject to its direction. In this Government, the power of legislation is confined to certain objects; but, as it respects these objects, its sovereignty is complete. unless restricted by the spirit or letter of the Constitution. Hence I contend, that as to all legislative subjects, the sovereign or supreme power has been confided to Congress, and that the treaty-making power, (being an Executive power,) so far as it acts on those subjects, is inferior, and subordinate to it.

But it is said, that a treaty, though the act of the Executive department is elevated to an equality, if not superiority, with an act of Congress, by an express provision of the Constitution, in which it is declared, that the "Constitution and laws made in pursuance thereof, and all treaties made, or hereafter to be made, shall be the supreme law of the land." Let us examine this subject. Let us look into the existing state of things when this Constitution was framed. The State sovereignties then existed, and were to be preserved to a certain extent. The powers of the General Government, in their operation, must frequently and necessarily act on the same subjects over which the States retained some authority, and, consequently, produce collision. As it respected treaties, there was another consideration, which made it highly necessary that their relative character should be established. It is well known that much discussion had taken place, and a variety of sentiments entertained as to the force and effect of the Treaty of Peace of 1783. It was contended, (and I think some of the States so construed it,) that the stipulation contained in that treaty, conflicting with the laws of the States, merely municipal, did not repeal those laws. In order, then, that these collisions might be prevented, and a due subordination secured to the authority confided to the United States, it became indispensable to declare it supreme in relation to the States. Hence it has provided, that the Constitution, laws, and treaties, "should be the supreme law of the land, anything in the Constitution or laws of any State to the contrary notwithstanding."

That the Constitution did not intend to declare what should be the effect of treaties, in relation to the laws of the United States; that it did not intend to elevate an Executive act so as to make it equal or superior to an act of the sovereign or legislative power, but leave it possessed of its natural character, is susceptible of other illustrations. In the European States, where the whole power of the Government is vested in a single individual or in a single body of men, treaties are equal to laws, because they contain a manifestation of the will of the whole sovereign power, in which laws themselves consist. In the Government of Great Britain, however, where the treaty-making power and the legislative power are lodged in different hands, (and in that respect is like our own,) a treaty, embracing legislative subjects, is not equal to an act of Parliament; but depends, so far as these subjects are concerned, for its execution, on the legislature. With the British constitution before their eyes, (and that they had it steadily in view, the distribution of power and the phrases employed sufficiently attest,) can it be supposed that the framers of the Constitution, if they intended to give to treaties the extraordinary effect now contended for, would not have declared so in express terms? I say extraordinary effect, because in the only Government similar, as it respects this question, to our own, treaties, embracing legislative subjects, are not equal to laws. In the clause which declares the Constitution, laws made in pursuance thereof, and treaties made under the authority of the United States, the relative character of each is not designated; and it may be as readily contended that treaties are equal to the Constitution, as that they are equal to laws. If they are equal to the Constitution, then, according to the doctrine on the other side, being last in point of time, they must repeal and supersede whatever comes in conflict with it. In relation to treaties, it is not even declared that, in order to become the supreme law, they shall be made " in pursuance to the Constitution." This, to my mind, proves satisfactorily, that the clause in question did not intend to fix the relative quality of the Constitution, laws, and treaties; but to leave it to that construction which the nature of these acts and the character of the Government would readily suggest.

Permit me now to examine the extent to which the doctrines advanced on the other side would lead us. It has been said that the cases which have been suggested in argument to show the vast and almost unlimited power conferred on the President and Senate by the construction contended for in opposition to the bill, are extreme, and ought therefore to be rejected. But to me it appears obvious, that to test the correctness of any principle, you ought to look to the consequences to which it will lead. One honorable member (Mr. CALHOUN) has contended, that treaties are superior to acts of Congress, and another, (Mr. PINKNEY,) that they are equal; though there is a difference in the force of these opinions, in substance they are the same. They amount to this, that a treaty repeals all laws opposed to it, and that it executes itself. The latter gentleman has indeed admitted that it may sometimes be necessary to pass a law to execute a treaty, but not because there is a defect of power on the part of those who make the treaty, but because its stipulations may not be sufficiently definite. These opinions tend to the utter subversion of the legislative power, at least so far as it is vested in this House. Let us see their tendency. The Constitution has confided in Congress the power to regulate commerce with foreign nations. On this subject, so highly interesting to the people, their Representatives are invested with the right to judge and determine what particular regulations are most conducive to their prosperity. But the opinions stated on this floor authorize the interposition of the President and Senate at any time to supersede this right, partially or entirely, at their discretion; partially, by making treaties of commerce with some nations; entirely, by making treaties with all who have any commercial intercourse with us.

According to the honorable member from Maryland, (Mr. PINKNEY,) if this House should refuse to raise a large military force required by the President, he may accomplish this object by negotiating a treaty with some foreign Power, in which the raising of such force shall be made a stipulation. It is only necessary to make the treaty sufficiently definite; to stipulate the number of regiments, the number of companies in each, and the number and quality of the officers to be employed, and the force, with the consent of two-thirds of the Senate, will be immediately raised; the treaty will execute itself. Should money be wanting to accomplish the object, it may be obtained in the same way by treaty—a thing not unusual among other nations.

Let me pursue the subject. The Constitution has granted to Congress the power to declare war. In the exercise of a power in which everything dear to the people is involved, which causes their blood to flow and their hard earnings to be wrested from them, the co-operation of the Representatives was wisely required. But a treaty may make war without their consent, if we admit the construction contended for. A treaty with a foreign Power may stipulate that we shall make common cause with her against her enemy; the public force will be employed accordingly, and the country thus brought into an actual state of war. The same construction will authorize the President and Senate to lay and collect taxes, duties, imposts, and excises. Many cases might be supposed illustrative of this position. I will beg leave to state one only. Suppose, in the treaty of commerce with Great Britain, it had been stipulated that British cottons and woollens should pay a duty of ten or fifteen per cent. ad valorem, in the ports of the United States, and that French goods of a similar description should pay forty, fifty, or sixty per cent. Here it is most obvious that the duty which the people of the United States would pay, above the ordinary duty imposed by law, would be levied on them without the consent of their Representatives, though the Constitution expressly provides, not only that their assent shall be necessary, but that all bills for raising revenue shall originate with them.

Congress are authorized by the Constitution to establish an uniform rule of naturalization. In pursuance of which, they have passed laws for the purpose of admitting foreigners to the rights of citizens, on certain conditions: among other things, a residence of five years is required. But if a treaty is equal or superior to an act of Congress, a whole foreign nation may be naturalized by treaty.

The Constitution has committed to Congress the duty of defending the country against foreign and domestic violence, and for that purpose has given them power "to raise and support armies, and to provide and maintain a navy." Suppose a treaty should be made with a foreign nation, in which it should be stipulated that our army should be disbanded, and our navy dismantled, and that no other similar force should be substituted; would the treaty disband the army and dismantle the navy without any legislative provision? If so, then the President and Senate have the entire control of the public defence, and may lay wholly prostrate a most important power belonging to this House.

The construction contended for will authorize the President and Senate to incorporate a foreign territory as a member of this Union. By the Constitution, Congress are empowered to admit new States; but if a treaty supersedes legislation, then it most unquestionably follows, that, by a compact with a foreign nation, foreign territory may be ceded and admitted into the Union, invested with all the privileges of a State.

From a candid and serious consideration of the extent to which we should be led by the high-toned doctrines which have been advanced, I cannot for a moment admit their correctness. Can it be possible that it could ever have been in the contemplation of those for whom this Government was formed, that the powers of their Representatives should be superseded whenever it should please the President and Senate to dispense with them? Is it rational to suppose that the Constitution, which recognises the sovereignty of the people, should intend that a foreign nation, nay, (as has been justly remarked,) a Chickasaw chief, might be substituted for this House, and, as to all the powers given by the Constitution, act in its stead? I think it far more consistent, more reasonable to insist, that all legislative acts, designated as such in the Constitution, must receive the assent of all the constituent branches of the Legislature.

It has been conceded by some gentlemen, in the course of this discussion, that an act of Congress is necessary to execute a treaty which provides for the expenditure of public money; but that this is the only case. I can see no reason for this distinction; the Treaty with Great Britain, now before the House, stipulates, that the discriminating duties, as it respects British vessels, shall be abolished; in consequence of which, our revenue will be considerably diminished. Is there any substantial difference between drawing money from the Treasury, and preventing an equal annual amount from coming into it? If the President and Senate can impose taxes and duties on the people, why not exercise a power far inferior, and apply their proceeds to such objects as they think proper? If a treaty in every other respect is equal at least to an act of Congress, why not in this? Why may not money be appropriated by treaty, when, according to the sentiments of gentlemen, it is the law of the land? It has been said, that the powers of this House are operative only in ordinary cases, where no treaty provides for the same object. With equal propriety may it be said, that the clause of the Constitution which directs, that "no money shall be drawn from the Treasury but in consequence of appropriations made by law," applies only to ordinary cases of expenditure, and not when a treaty stipulates for the payment of money.

It has been strongly urged, that because a treaty of peace puts an end to the war, without the concurrence of this House, it follows that a treaty repeals an act of Congress, as the war must have been declared by that body. But I do not consider a declaration of war as a legislative act, it is not so deemed in Great Britain; and there is nothing in its nature which gives it that character. Among civilized nations, it has long been usual, as well to apprize the adversary nation that in future she will be treated as an enemy, as to manifest a direct respect for the opinions of mankind, to state in a public manifesto the reasons which had provoked a resort to arms. In imitation of this practice, the Constitution had authorized Congress to declare war; but the effect of a declaration of war is nothing more than that those who have the direction of the public force become authorized to employ it against the declared enemy. It establishes no new law. During the continuance of the war, the public law of nations must regulate the conduct and the rights of the parties. To put an end to such a state of things, municipal legislation is not competent; it can only be effected by mutual compact between the contending nations.

It will be readily perceived, that if a declaration of war is not a legislative act, then it is not subject to be repealed, as such acts ordinarily are: and the only way in which an end can be put to it is that already mentioned. According to the understanding of all, to declare war is a distinct substantive act; and to make peace is another. We never heard of peace being made by annulling a declaration of war; hence I conclude, that to make peace is not among the delegated powers of Congress, either express or implied; and that, therefore, a treaty of peace neither repeals a legislative act, nor interferes with any of the powers belonging to this House.

An honorable member from North Carolina (Mr. GASTON) has said, that our co-operation is wholly unnecessary; that the President will execute the treaty in question, by giving instructions to the collectors of the customs to conform their conduct to the stipulations of the treaty. This appears to me entirely erroneous. The collectors are not the agents of the President, but the officers of the law. They derive their existence from it, and their duty is prescribed by it. They cannot justify themselves in their obedience to the mere instructions of the President. It must first appear that the act of Congress imposing discriminating duties is repealed, before they can omit to collect them. Whether the treaty effects this is the question before the House.

The honorable gentleman from Maryland (Mr. PINKNEY) stated, the other day, that Congress have not the power to make any compact with a foreign Government; that if the President and Senate have not the exclusive power to bind the nation, in all cases, by treaty, then there is no power in this Government to make treaties of commerce and other treaties, embracing any of the subjects delegated to Congress. But it will be observed, that the power on the part of the President and Senate to make all treaties, is not denied; the question is, after they are so made, what is their effect? The principle has been very correctly and ably stated by my honorable friend from Virginia, (Mr. TUCKER.) Treaties embracing subjects not confided to Congress, depend for their execution on no other power than that which made them; as to those treaties which embrace such subjects, their execution belongs to the Legislature. In the one case the stipulation is complete; in the other it is only a promise that those who have the power shall make it so.

The honorable gentleman, however, is mistaken in his opinion, that Congress can enter into no compact with a foreign nation; at least the practice of this Government is against him. We all recollect the act of the first of May, 1810, which enabled France, (to use the language of a gentleman from Tennessee, formerly a member of this House,) to twist the cord about our necks which was first scorched by the flames of Moscow, and finally cut asunder by the hands of the Allies at Leipsic and Waterloo. By that act it was stipulated, that if Great Britain or France should revoke their injurious edicts against our commerce, certain acts should be done by this Government. France pretended to accept this overture, and a compact was said to be thus formed, from the effect of which we have just escaped. Last year another law passed, which provided that the discriminating duties should cease in relation to all nations who should adopt a like liberality towards our navigation; in consequence of which, some of the stipulations in the present treaty with Great Britain were adopted. In these cases the President acts as the agent of the law, and not in virtue of his character as superintending our foreign relations.

It has been said that there is greater security in the treaty-making power being exclusively exercised by the President and Senate in all cases, than if the opinions of those friendly to the present bill should be adopted. And the honorable gentleman from Maryland entered into a course of reasoning to show the superior responsibility which attaches particularly to the President, calculated to secure a more wise and more correct exercise of the power. This argument proves too much. It tends to establish, that all the power of this Government ought to be vested in the President, because of his superior wisdom and the superior responsibility of his situation. The gentleman has said much of the influence of public opinion on those who stand in high responsible situations, and has referred us to Great Britain, where he says public opinion is very powerful. I agree with him, that what is called public opinion has great effect on the administration of the Government. It is the unbiassed sentiment of the sound and sensible part of the community, who have not committed themselves to support any set of measures, because they have not participated in the creation of the public functionaries, the King and the Lords being hereditary, and the Commons elected by a very few. But in this country there is very little expression of public opinion, distinct from that which is manifested by election; every person thinks himself pledged in some degree to support the conduct of those on whom he has bestowed his suffrage, and the abuses of power must be extreme before the current of public opinion will set against those who are at the head of a predominant party.

If the construction contended for on the other side should receive the assent of this House, I hesitate not to say, that there will be less security, less responsibility, than in Great Britain. On one subject there has always been great jealousy there; I mean the introduction of foreign troops. It is a settled maxim of their constitution, that they cannot be introduced without the consent of Parliament; but in this country there would be no such security. Should we refuse to gratify an ambitious President who designed to subvert the liberties of this country with a large army, he may negotiate with a foreign Power, and, with the assent of two-thirds of the Senate, introduce foreign troops. I cannot believe that the people ever did intend to confer power thus tending to jeopardize those liberties for the preservation of which this Constitution was adopted.

Mr. Hopkinson spoke as follows:

Mr. Speaker, I am indeed sincere, when I assure you and this honorable House, that I am most reluctant, at this late hour of the day, the usual time of adjournment, to solicit your attention to some remarks upon the bill now offered for your sanction, and which must now receive that sanction or a decisive rejection. In an early stage of this business, I gave to your consideration a few observations in opposition to the bill, which were the offspring of the moment, having neither the maturity of reflection, nor the strength of arrangement. Since then, however, the bill has assumed a shape of greater magnitude; and the discussion of it has developed principles so interesting and important; discriminations so various and minute; and positions so novel and contradictory, that I should feel myself wanting in duty, were I to refuse the only opportunity I can ever have of bearing my voice and testimony against them. Before, however, I presume to hope for your indulgent attention at so late a stage of the debate, that every member was looking for the question to be put; and so late an hour of the day, that we are all weary of these walls, I beg leave to remind you that the debate on this bill was not

renewed by the minority; after it was ordered to be engrossed for a third reading by a very considerable majority, as far as I know, no further attempts would have been made to arrest or impede its progress, because no rational hope existed of finally preventing its enactment. The victorious majority, however, were not satisfied to let this matter go to rest in this way; for I beg you to recollect that, when the bill was presented to the House for its passage into a law, three gentlemen of the majority thought it necessary to address the House in support of it, before a word was uttered from us to impeach it. Was it not natural, then, that this over anxiety about the fate of a bill, sanctioned already by so large a vote, this renewed exertion to support that which was already so strongly supported, should excite in us a suspicion that a weakness was felt somewhere, which it was our duty to seek for and expose; that some vital defect existed in the cause or the argument which gave this alarm, and called for additional aid? Or was it, Mr. Speaker, that the majority, not content with the triumph of success, not satisfied with the prostration of the adversary, would thus pursue and assault him, defeated and overthrown? If this was the feeling which stimulated the honorable gentlemen to a renewal of the conflict, surely we may be pardoned for repelling the attack with all our powers, and rousing our energies to the utmost exertion of resistance. If, then, there has been waste of time, and fatigue of spirits in the continuance of this debate, surely we stand acquitted of the fault and its consequences. This, however, of itself, I confess, would not be a sufficient apology for my intrusion upon your attention again; unless I may add to it the belief, that I may still present the case in some aspects, in which it has not yet been presented. I will assuredly not recur to the ground taken by me in my first address.

Let me entreat the House to bring back their attention to the true and single question to be decided on; and to that instrument by which that decision must be governed and directed. We are not now sitting in convention to frame a constitution for the United States; but in Congress, to pass a law under a Constitution already framed. This law we must conform to that Constitution; and we are bound to submit to the distribution of power as made by the Constitution, whatever our opinions may be of its wisdom, its expediency, or its consistency with the rights or claims of the popular branch of the Government. We must inquire what the Constitution is, and not what honorable gentlemen may wish it to be. After, therefore listening, with due respect and terror too, if you please, to all the doubts and dangers, suspicions and jealousies, forebodings of ruin, and execrations of sectional power, which ingenuity may suggest, or imagination give birth or shape to, we must at last lay down all this extravagance, dismiss all these phantoms, and soberly take up this little book, the Constitution; examine what it commands to be done, and make up our minds to submit to it. We must not amuse or deceive ourselves with large estimations of our own power and importance, claiming, as some gentlemen have done, the sovereignty of the people to reside in us, but calmly consider ourselves as acting under a delegated, limited, distributed authority, which gives to us all we have, and marks the extent of it; and which, with equal right and independence, gives to the other branches of this confederated Government their powers and their limits also. To this great authority, this charter of our powers and our duties, we must all submit; and I cannot question that every member of this House has a ready and willing disposition to conform himself and his vote to the directions here given; I confidently believe that I have but to satisfy them of the truth of the construction we contend for, to be secure of their acquiescence in it.

How stands the question, then, under and by the Constitution? How do the principles and arguments of the supporters of the bill abide this test? I state the question to be, "whether a treaty, constitutionally made, does or does not repeal a law, inconsistent with it, also made constitutionally?" This puts the case fairly and simply before the House. A treaty, admitted to be on a subject within the treaty-making power, not in conflict with any of the provisions of the Constitution, nor overstepping any of the marked boundaries therein set; and concluded, ratified, and exchanged, in the manner, by the authorities and under the forms prescribed by the Constitution; is in opposition or contradiction to a municipal law enacted by Congress, in the ordinary course of legislation; and the question is, whether a treaty thus made subsequently to the law, does not, of itself, repeal the law; or must the authority of the House be called in aid of the treaty to repeal and remove the law in conflict with it? I will now, sir, state, with equal precision, the position I mean to maintain in the argument of this question. It is this: that there is no possible case, real or imagined, in which the vote or sanction of this House is necessary, or can be effectual, either to confirm or destroy a treaty thus made. There is no case under the Constitution in which this House ever can have a direct control, an affirmative or negative vote on the validity or invalidity of a treaty. A treaty may fail to have effect; its execution may be prevented; but its validity as a contract, legal and binding, cannot be touched by this House. It may be a broken, a violated contract, but it is still a contract. When something is necessary for the execution of the provisions of a treaty, or some of them, which something is exclusively within the power of this House, it may indeed be refused; but this affects not the nature of the contract, which received its character, its Constitutional efficacy and obligation from the hands of the President and the Senate, who have been intrusted by the people with the power thus to bind them. This House may, in the exercise of their power over some collateral matter, as money, for instance, interfere with, and perhaps prevent, the fulfilment or execution of a treaty; but they do it by a violation of the public faith, and not by invalidating

14th CON. 1st SESS.—21

the treaty which bound it. They may refuse to grant the means necessary to the performance of the contract, but they cannot decree it to be no contract. The same thing, sir, may happen in private life, in the common transactions of men. One may solemnly make a contract, and daringly refuse to fulfil it; but is it, therefore, no contract? He may, indeed, be unable to perform it, but can he, therefore, say he was never bound? Believing it to be in my power to obtain a certain tract of land, or a quantity of stock, I bind myself, for a good consideration, to sell and deliver it to another. I afterwards find I cannot induce the holder of the land to part with it, or cannot procure the stock. Shall I, therefore, say to the disappointed and abused party with whom I made this engagement, that I am no longer bound by it; nay, that it never was a contract at all, because I made a bad calculation of my means to perform it, although I made no such restriction, reservation, or condition, with him? Assuredly, not. So, when the Republic, by her Constitutional organs, which is in fact, by herself, has made, concluded, ratified, and exchanged a treaty with a foreign Power, shall she nullify and avoid it, *ab initio*, by declaring her inability to induce another branch of her power to furnish the means necessary to its execution? With what indignation and contempt would such a pretence be received by the other party, and by the world? But, it is asked, what is a contract that cannot be enforced; a treaty that cannot be carried into effect? I answer, sir, that, in the case of the individual, the courts of justice would punish this hardihood of fraud; and, in the case of nations, there being no such common arbiter to do and compel justice to be done between the parties, the faithless one must stand ready to defend her breach of faith with the sword of her citizens and the waste of her treasures, amidst the scorn of the world. She must look to the "*ultima ratio regum*" for her justification and support; and she must abide this solemn appeal with a bad conscience, in a bad cause. But, sir, before this appeal, and during the appeal, and after it, be its result what it may, the original soundness and validity of the contract remains unimpaired and unimpairable, by the chances or the issue of an unjust contest, in defence of a violated faith.

Permit me, sir, to recall your attention to the circumstances of the British Treaty of 1794, which has been resorted to as a text of argument on both sides of the House. That treaty was negotiated by a Minister duly authorized, and was afterwards, with all Constitutional form and ceremony, ratified and exchanged by the President, by and with the advice and consent of the Senate. The merits and provisions of the treaty were afterwards examined and discussed with unusual animation, not to say violence, in the House of Representatives. But how was this done? Was the treaty ever laid formally before them, for their concurrence or opinion? Was the advice of the House asked, as to the expediency or inexpediency of any of its provisions? Was the question, treaty or no treaty—ratify or not ratify—

ever placed before the House, in terms or in substance? Did any member, the most abhorrent of the measure, ever dream of propounding such questions for the decision of the House? And yet such would, and ought to have been the case, if any had imagined this House had a voice in affirming or rejecting a treaty, or a control over the President and Senate in making one. But it happened that something was wanted, not to consummate the validity of this treaty, or give it a legal existence, and a binding force, but to carry some of its provisions into effect. And what was that something? Not the assent, the confirmation, the fiat of this House, but its money. It is worthy of remark, that the objectionable parts of the treaty were not those that required this money; but its opponents could come at the provisions they disliked, but which required no appropriation of money, only through parts they did not dislike, but which did require such appropriation. Why, then, in this sideway, this indirect assault, did the enemies of that treaty endeavor to overthrow it, or rather those parts of it to which they are hostile, if they had a Constitutional right to make a direct attack upon it; to withhold their confirmation, without which it could have no binding operation; to impose their veto, by which the whole would perish? But, sir, neither the treaty, nor any of its provisions, was ever distinctly before them; no resolution or bill, either to affirm or reject it, was ever propounded or offered to the House. Why did not those gentlemen, with the Constitution in their hands, march boldly up to the attack, and assert directly their right to pass upon a treaty, as such, and to grant or refuse it the force and obligation of a law and a contract? An attempt so extravagant never was made or hinted at; after a struggle of extraordinary pertinacity, at last the House of Representatives did, as I trust they will always do, yielded to their Constitutional duty, and gave the money required. But, sir, to bring the principle now in controversy to a test, suppose that the House had refused the money, would the treaty have been no longer a treaty, or rather did it wait the assent of that House before it became one—before it had the character and obligations of a national compact? Assuredly not; for I fear no contradiction when I assert, that if the House had so refused, and the President could have procured competent persons to perform the duties of the commissioners, to be appointed under the treaty, and for whose compensation the money was wanted, without compensation, he might have done so. He ought to have gone on to execute and fulfil the stipulations of the treaty, and the whole would have been binding on us all, as the "supreme law of the land." Will any gentleman deny this; and, if admitted, does it not decide the question—I mean the general right of the President and Senate to make a treaty, uncontrolled by the power of this House? And if a treaty be well made and fully consummated, under the authority of the President and Senate, it becomes, by the express words of the Constitution, the supreme law of the land; and, being the law,

it must necessarily have the most obvious and essential effect of a law; that is, to repeal or renew all prior laws inconsistent with it. The last declaration of the will of the nation, if properly made, must, by an obvious necessity, abrogate a former declaration in contradiction to it; and thus, to return to the question originally proposed for discussion—a treaty, constitutionally made, may repeal a prior law also constitutionally made. To say it is a law, but that it has no power to repeal a law, is to deny it the first and most essential principle and quality of a law; is, in truth, a contradiction in terms utterly irreconcileable and incomprehensible.

But gentlemen had labored their ingenuity and inflamed their imagination, to suppose a variety of extreme cases, in which the President and Senate might possibly make treaties, destructive of the first rights and interests of the country. They might make a treaty which would impose a different rate of excise or impost on different parts of the United States, although the Constitution declares they shall be uniform; or imposing a duty on exports; or ceding a part of the territory of the United States; and in order to give the last supposed case a most formidable aspect, a whole State—the State of South Carolina—has been supposed to be the victim of this Executive power. And it is asked, shall not the House of Representatives, in such cases, avert the tremendous mischief, by refusing to ratify the treaty, and making it void? I answer, unhesitatingly, no; nor is it necessary they should. I recur to my first proposition; this House can neither make nor add to the obligation of a good treaty, or annul a bad one. In the cases put the treaty is void, *ab initio*, by the force of the Constitution; or, to speak more properly, it never was a treaty, and therefore cannot be annulled. A contract of this sort attempted to be made is not binding on the nation, and never was so for an instant. But it is not the power of this House by which it is overthrown; but by that great original power, the Constitution, which has given bounds to the treaty-makers as well as to this House; and when either pass over those bounds, whatever is done is a mere nullity. In a case like this, the assent of this House, uniting with the act of the President and Senate, the whole combined could not give the act a binding force on the people, whose delegated authority has been transcended. This House, then, is equally powerless, either to raise up or destroy a treaty contrary to the express provisions of the Constitution —and here, it will be seen, I differ from some of the honorable gentlemen who join me in opposing the bill; I cannot consider the treaty-makers as universal and omnipotent as they do. No part of the territory of Pennsylvania can be granted from her by the treaty-making power, or any other power in the United States. An absolute dominion of the soil is the first and most essential right of sovereignty, and with this the States have never parted in their grant to the United States. When we cannot make a law to regulate the course of descents of real estate in the several

States, or to direct the mode and form of making conveyances, will it be pretended we can bargain away the soil itself? Besides, what becomes of the guarantee of a republican form of government to every State, if any one of them may be ceded and delivered over to an Emperor or despot? I need not to detain the House by explaining how a part of the country held by an enemy, by the right of conquest, at the close of the war, and when the preservation of the whole may render a peace indispensable, may introduce other considerations and results; I give no opinion on such a case.

An honorable gentleman from Virginia (Mr. SHEFFEY) had said much about the sovereign power of this House. He considers this to be the temple of the sovereignty of the people; that this sovereignty is deposited with us, to be held and wielded at our pleasure only; and as the making of a treaty is an exercise of the sovereign power, he thence infers that it belongs here, or, at least, cannot be exercised without our assent and agency. The error of this reasoning lies in not considering the peculiar nature of our Government; and we are constantly falling into mistakes, by drawing arguments and conclusions from the principles and practice of Governments of a construction so different as to admit no analogy. The sovereign power of the people of America, sir, is not in this House, nor in the President and Senate, nor in all of them combined; it is not in the Government of the United States—it remains in and with the several States, who have delegated and distributed certain portions of it to the General or Federal Government, in the instrument we call the Constitution; and, therefore, when we would decide whether a particular power belongs to this or that branch of the General Government, we must not deduce from general principles, or the nature and attributes of sovereignty, but look to that instrument, in and by which the only sovereign power in this country—the people of the respective States—have declared to whom they have imparted and intrusted the particular power in question. Let us, then, lay aside the empty boast of sovereignty, and be content to take our station as appointed by the Constitution, and use the powers there given. As to all the cases of supposed possible treaties which have been put and multiplied upon us in the course of this discussion, violating the express stipulations of the Constitution, and overthrowing the primary, essential rights of the people, I repeat, that we need not fear them, nor look to the patriotism of this House for protection against them; we have a better, a sure protection in the Constitution, which strangles such an effort even in its birth, and requires no aid from this House in performing the work.

I regret, sir, that so much of the argument in support of this bill has been directly and avowedly founded on suspicions and jealousies of the power of the Senate. The basis of every Government, of ours most especially, nay, of all the dealings and transactions of men, is a fair and honorable confidence in each other. Without this, neither the public nor private business can

go along for a moment; if distrust is to be the order of the day, if we are to fear treachery and ambuscade at every step, the consequence is that we must stand still. I find, sir, it is a favorite sentiment with some gentlemen who have spoken on this occasion, that this House may claim a superiority of trust and confidence over the Senate on account of our closer proximity to the people. It is true, we are the last birth of the sovereign will, but some few months old, and the Senate is a stout boy of six years. We may, indeed, be the pet of the mother, as the last and most spoiled child usually is, especially if she have a little caprice in her temper, which cannot be denied to ours. But, sir, I am far from believing that the experience of the Senate is any disadvantage to their wisdom; or that they feel themselves so elevated as no longer to respect or regard the source of all their power and importance. I have no such apprehensions of them; but, if I had, may I interpose my fears between them and their Constitutional rights? Shall I blast their powers with any suspicions? "Beware of jealousy." If the time shall ever come when the different branches of this Government shall cease to have a just and honorable confidence in each other; when they shall cease to know that they emanate from the same power; are created by the same breath; when they shall cease to feel that they represent the same interests; are bound by the same duties, and are responsible to the same authority, then is the day of confusion and calamity come upon us; and in the unrighteous struggle all legitimate power will be lost. But "there is no such thing." Such suggestions are made here to point an argument or turn a phrase, but no man seriously fears or believes them. A gentleman from Louisiana (Mr. ROBERTSON) has said that, with the Senate and President claiming to repeal laws by treaties on the one hand, and the judiciary to declare them unconstitutional on the other, the power of this House is reduced to nothing. We are, says he, trenched on all sides, and can move and act in no direction. True, sir, we have our limits, our measured bounds, beyond which we may not move or act. But the gentleman is in an error in ascribing the restraint either to the President and Senate on the one side, or the judiciary on the other. It is the Constitution in both, that encumbers both us and them. They are but the organs, the instruments declaring and enforcing the high commands, the sovereign will of the people, as manifested and declared in the Constitution; they are sworn to do this, and this they must do, whomsoever they may offend. If this House overstep the prescribed bounds, it is the duty of the judiciary to call it back; or, at least, in administering the law to the citizen, to execute that law which is supreme, rather than that which is subordinate and limited, when they come in conflict. Is the judge, who passes the sentence of the law on a convicted culprit, guilty of murder; or is he guilty of usurpation, when he passes the sentence of the Constitution, on an unconstitutional law? Are the President and Senate to be charged with usurpation, in obeying the mandates of the Constitution, and executing its trusts and powers? No, sir, in both cases they are but the organs, and not the makers of the law; the instruments, not the source of the power.

If we look to the convention itself, what do we find there as to the authority which is necessary to consummate its obligations, and give them a binding force on the people of the United States. In the fifth article it is expressly and unequivocally declared, that "this convention, when the 'same shall have been duly ratified by the Presi- 'dent, by and with the advice and consent of the 'Senate, and by His Britannic Majesty, and the 'respective ratifications mutually exchanged, shall 'be binding and obligatory on the said United 'States and His Majesty for four years from the 'date of its signature; and the ratifications shall 'be exchanged in six months from this time, or 'sooner, if possible." Now, all this has been fully and duly done. The President and Senate have ratified the act, and the ratifications have been mutually exchanged, and doubtless the agent of the British Government has transmitted to his Court our ratification as the consummation of the contract; and yet, after all this, we are told that the assent of this House is still required to give force and effect to the convention, and make it binding on the United States. What a solemn mockery have we been practising; what a deliberate deception have we passed upon the other contracting Power! Mr. Speaker, I see your honorable name to this instrument, and to this article. You, sir, have personally and officially assured the British Commissioners that the compact you made with them should be binding on your country, if ratified by the President and Senate. Had you at that time a mental reservation, a concealed proviso in favor of the controlling power of this House over the deed; did you believe and conceal from them that the sanction of this House was also requisite? No, sir, I am sure you did not; you told them explicitly, and you told them truly, that when your act should be confirmed by the President and Senate, it would be the law of our land, binding on the United States. The British Commissioners knew they were negotiating with the most distinguished citizens of their country, whose public situation had peculiarly qualified them to know, what indeed every citizen should know, the Constitution of their own Government. What will be their surprise, then, to learn that our three Commissioners were either unacquainted with the law of their country on the very business they were transacting, or that, knowing it, they had concealed or omitted to disclose a highly important circumstance in relation to the authority under which they acted; nay, that they have actually signed an article which, by every rule of fair and candid construction, negatives the existence of that circumstance; negatives the idea that the sanction of this House must be added to that of the President and Senate to give a binding force to this inchoate compact. Why, sir, did you not tell those gentlemen, fairly and openly, that you

had at home a certain body, called the House of Representatives, very jealous of all power but its own, whose good will must also be conciliated in the business, and without whose approbation the convention could never live in our atmosphere? It was because it never entered your mind that any such approbation was or could be necessary. Such an idea did not ever pass in your dreams; besides, you have undertaken that the "ratifications shall be exchanged in six months, or sooner." How could you do this, if you thought this House was to act on them; when the usual term of meeting would not arrive for four months after the date of the instrument, and you could not say how long we might choose to debate about it. For the President and Senate, such an agreement might be safely made.

The honorable gentleman from Georgia (Mr. Forsyth) has drawn an argument from the Message of the President, which accompanied the convention, in support of the bill in question. To my mind, this message furnishes a result directly contrary, at least so far as to show that the President considers no law from us necessary to give validity to the treaty. What does he say? "I lay before Congress"—what? The convention for their consideration and approbation? No; but "copies of a proclamation notifying the convention concluded," &c., "and that the same has been duly ratified;" that is, having by a proclamation previously given notice to our citizens and the world, of the convention that had been duly concluded and duly ratified, he pays us the compliment of giving us a sort of special notice of the fact, by laying before us copies of the same proclamation he had previously laid before the public. He then recommends such legislative provisions as the convention may (not does) call for on the part of the United States. That is, there may be some matters of debate in your custom-houses or elsewhere; it may be, you will choose to equalize the duties, either by raising both to the British standard, or lowering both to the American, and upon such matters exercise your discretion. But surely this is a very different thing from requiring or expecting of us to re-enact the whole convention in the form of a law, in order to give it a binding force on the United States. Now, assuredly, so far as we may respect the personal authority of any man on this question, there is no one more entitled to consideration than the high personage alluded to. He was a distinguished agent in making the Constitution; and afterwards a distinguished champion in defending and expounding it, both by his eloquence and his pen; and we may and ought to place much confidence in his constructions of its intent and meaning.

The friends of this bill rest their argument, almost wholly, on the eighth section of the first article of the Constitution, in which the powers of Congress are specially enumerated, among which we find the power to "regulate commerce with foreign nations," expressly granted. Now there is surely nothing unwise, or inexpedient, or inconsistent, in giving this general power to Congress; and afterwards granting to another branch of the Government the special right to regulate commerce in a given special case, that is, in the case of a treaty or compact with another nation on this subject. And here I would admit and apply the rule of construction given us by the gentleman from Virginia, (Mr. SHEFFEY,) that is, that the special power must always be an exception from a limitation of the general power, which is the only means by which both can have operation and effect. But, sir, it seems to me a very essential error has been indulged in this part of the argument. It has been asserted that this section of the Constitution was intended to delineate and prescribe the powers of Congress, that is, of the general legislative power, in contradistinction to the executive or judicial power, or to mark the boundaries between the different branches of the General Government. Nothing can be more mistaken. The sole object is, to mark and establish the line or boundary between the General or Federal Government, and the State governments. The word Congress is not here used in its strict Constitutional meaning, but rather as designating the federal power. This is obvious from the least attention to the subject. By the first section of the first article, the Congress of the United States is declared to consist of the Senate and House of Representatives. If, then, in the eighth section, the term Congress is to be taken in its strict Constitutional sense, it would follow that the Senate and House of Representatives have, without recourse to any other authority, the power to lay and collect taxes, borrow money, regulate commerce, &c., when in fact we know that they have not this power without the assent of the President, unless indeed by two-thirds of each body. This is sufficient to show the danger of fastening our eyes upon any one clause or page of the Constitution to decide its meaning, and the propriety of taking the whole together in order to fix the construction of any part.

We find in this eighth section that Congress may exercise the powers there enumerated, but we find in another place, that the President must concur, and we must take both together as the law of the Constitution. So, in this eighth section we find that Congress has the power to regulate commerce; but in another place we also find a power given to the President and Senate to make treaties, which from their very nature must in many and most instances have relation to commerce, and of consequence so far a power is also given to the President and Senate to regulate commerce. It must be remarked, that in the grant to Congress there are no exclusive words from which it may be inferred, that in no case any other branch of the Government shall interfere with the regulation of commerce; and this answers the question so frequently put to us in the course of this debate, why may not a treaty draw money directly from the Treasury, which is a right given to Congress in the same section which grants the right to regulate commerce. The phraseology is wholly different in the two cases. In case of money, it is declared that "no money shall be drawn from

the Treasury, but in consequence of appropriations made by law."

We have urged the undisputed case of a treaty of peace repealing a law declaring war; to which no satisfactory explanation or answer has been made. The honorable gentleman from South Carolina (Mr. LOWNDES) has attempted one, which is utterly insufficient, and founded on the most palpable error. He says this is all right, because the power of making peace is not among the enumerated powers of Congress. Why, by the same reasoning, then, we may by this treaty remove the discriminating duties, for the taking off a duty is also not among the enumerated powers of Congress. But the right of removing flows necessarily from the right of imposing a duty; and so the right of making peace would flow from the right of making war, were it not for another reason. The Convention intended to confer on Congress, meaning as I contend in this place, the Federal Government, the power to do those things which a Government may and can do of itself, by its own single authority, and without any dependence upon, or reference to, the will of another nation. Of this sort is every enumerated power. But to make peace, requires the concurrence of the nation with whom you are at war; and is necessarily a subject of negotiation, of treaty, of compact, and not of legislation. It would have been little less than an absurdity for the Convention to have said that the Congress, or any other department of the Government, should have power to make peace. It does not pretend to confer this power on the President and Senate; but merely authorizes them to make treaties, which treaties may obtain peace.

I will offer, sir, one further remark, and then detain you no longer. By the sixth article of the Constitution, it is declared that "this Constitution, ' and the laws of the United States which shall ' be made in pursuance thereof, and all treaties ' made, or which shall be made, under the author- ' ity of the United States, shall be the supreme law ' of the land." Here we see three classifications of this supreme law; not three grades, as the gentleman from Pennsylvania (Mr. ROSS) has remarked, for I cannot comprehend any grades of supremacy. We have three classes, all put on the same footing of authority; and treaties are declared to be as much the supreme law of the land, as laws made in pursuance of the Constitution. Now, the third classification, to wit, "treaties made under the authority of the United States," would be wholly superfluous and unnecessary, on the construction contended for by our opponents; for if a treaty becomes a law of the land, and derives its binding force and effect, not from its own intrinsic power, but by and under the authority of a law of Congress, then are treaties included in the second classification of supreme laws, to wit, "laws made in pursuance of the Constitution," and it was worse than nugatory to say anything more about them. It has, however, been contended that the treaty must be made "under the authority of the United States;" and assumed that this can only be done by the Congress of the

United States, in which that authority resides. It is obvious that this argument, or rather assertion, takes for granted the whole matter of dispute; and should, therefore, be proved before it is so much relied on. But is not a treaty made "under the authority of the United States," if it be made by the department of the Government in which the Constitution of the United States has confided the power to make treaties? The authority of the United States is in the Constitution, to be used and exercised according to the distribution there made of it, and every branch acting in its proper sphere acts with the whole authority of the United States. It should also be observed that this clause of the Constitution relates to treaties made, or which shall be made, under the authority of the United States, meaning perhaps to include any treaties or conventions which might have been made, at any period, by any of the individual States.

I am so grateful for the indulgent attention of the House, at this late hour, that I will detain them no longer with thanks and apologies.

When Mr. H. had concluded, the House adjourned.

Saturday, January 13.

Mr. Wendover presented petitions of sundry inhabitants of the United States, praying Congress to take into consideration the present situation of the cotton manufactories of the country, and enact such laws and regulations as may be deemed expedient for the interests of those concerned therein, as well as for the interest of the public in general.—Referred to the Committee on Commerce and Manufactures.

Mr. Porter presented a petition of sundry inhabitants of the county of Niagara, in the State of New York, praying compensation for losses occasioned by the invasion of that frontier by the British forces, during the late war, in which invasion the villages of Buffalo, Black Rock, Manchester, and Lewiston, were totally destroyed.—Referred to Messrs. Porter, Throop, Bassett, Herbert, Chipman, Wilkin, and Murfree.

Mr. Savage presented a petition of Thomas Williams, lately one of the chiefs of Iroquois tribe of Indians, in the dominions of Great Britain, but now a resident of the State of New York, praying remuneration for losses sustained by him in consequence of his abandoning the British dominions and joining the American forces, during the late war with Great Britain.—Referred to the Secretary of War.

Mr. Yancey, from the Committee of Claims, made a report on the petition of John G. Camp, which was read; when Mr. Y. reported a bill for the relief of John G. Camp; which was read twice, and committed to a Committee of the Whole.

On motion of Mr. Porter, the Committee on Pensions and Revolutionary Claims were instructed to inquire into the expediency of placing the following officers and private soldiers of the New York militia on the pension list, on the ground of wounds and disabilities received while in the service of the United States, namely: Captain John Huie, Sergeant John Maxon; privates, Ptolemy Sheldon, John B. Williams, Erastus Disbrow, Jabez Fisk, and Jonathan D. Carrier.

Mr. P. also presented sundry documents in support of the claims to pensions of the officers and soldiers named in the foregoing resolution, which were referred to the Committee on Pensions and Revolutionary Claims.

Mr. Ingham, from the Committee of Ways and Means, reported a bill to amend an act, entitled "An act for the relief of Edward Hallowell;" which was read twice, and committed to a Committee of the Whole.

Mr. Law, from a select committee, reported a bill for the relief of Jonathan Rogers, junior, of Waterford, in the State of Connecticut; which was read, and committed to a Committee of the Whole.

COMMERCE WITH GREAT BRITAIN.

The House resumed the consideration of the question depending yesterday at the time of the adjournment, to wit: Shall the engrossed bill "to regulate the commerce between the territories of the United States and of His Britannic Majesty, according to the convention concluded on the 3d day of July, 1815," pass?

Mr. Forsyth rose and spoke as follows: I am extremely reluctant, Mr. Speaker, to protract the decision of this question; and if I believed the few observations I propose to make would delay it beyond the present day, I should certainly remain silent, notwithstanding the strong inducements I have to address you. My purpose is to vindicate the bill before you, and its advocates, from charges which have been repeated by almost every gentleman who has pretended to examine the principles of the one or the motives of the other.

The bill has been represented as contradicting and belying all the doctrines heretofore established on this subject; as a dangerous and unprecedented novelty; as assuming for its basis a principle that legislative aid is necessary to the validity of all treaties which can be made by the Constitutional authority. Is it necessary for me again to refer to the laws heretofore passed in the execution of treaties to prove how utterly unfounded is the first accusation? Will the honorable gentlemen who have in such forcible terms condemned the introduction of this novelty turn over the statute book and examine with accuracy the provisions made for the execution of the treaties of Great Britain,* Spain, and France? Sir,

---

* In a former address to the House on this subject, Mr. Forsyth was under the impression that no laws had been passed, or were necessary, in execution of the Treaty of 1794. A subsequent examination of that treaty, and of the acts of Congress, has enabled him to correct this mistake. It was agreed by the third article of the treaty, that merchandise imported into the United States from the British territories in North America, by land or inland navigation, should be subject to no

they will find that the statutes passed in the execution of these instruments are twin brothers, echoes, reflected images. However they may be disposed to condemn this useless legislation, it will be necessary to found their condemnation upon something more substantial than a vague declamation against novelties, precedents for which are to be found in every treaty made since the establishment of the Government of the United States.

The basis of the bill is not the principle stated, that legislative aid is necessary to the validity of treaties. Gentlemen have exhausted their ingenuity, their time, and their eloquence, in the discussion of a doctrine utterly denied by the bill and those who advocate it. The doctrine contended for is, that in certain cases specified by the Constitution, legislative aid is necessary to the execution of treaties. Is there no difference between the two propositions? On the contrary, is not the distinction apparent to the eye and obvious to the touch? The distinction between the validity of an instrument and the execution of its provisions, between the obligation of contract and the performance of that obligation? We are not disposed to call in question the propriety of this name which has been given to this instrument, or to baptize it by any other than that which it properly derives from its godfather and godmother, the President and the Senate; we insist not that it is the figment or shadow of a treaty, but that it shall be neither more nor less than a treaty, valid and obligatory as such as a contract, but not having the force of law in its operation upon the municipal concerns of this people without legislative enactment. And where, sir, is the danger to arise; not from the establishment, but from the continuance of this Constitu-

higher duties than would be payable if imported in American vessels into the Atlantic ports of the said States. A provision perfectly similar, so far as respected the intercourse by land with Canada, to that introduced in the late convention, with respect to the intercourse with the European British territories, and which was equally inconsistent with the existing revenue laws, which then as now imposed an additional duty of ten per cent. on the duty imposed on merchandise imported in American vessels. When the importation was made in foreign vessels, the same article contained also several other provisions, either inconsistent with the existing laws, or embracing objects within the sphere of the legislative powers of Congress—such as the exemption of duty on peltries, on goods belonging to the Indians, and on merchandise carried over the portages; the regulation of the rates of tonnage; the general permission to import all goods not altogether prohibited, &c. The Western posts were not delivered up until 1797, and it was only in 1799 that revenue districts and custom-houses were established by law on Lakes Ontario, Erie, and Huron. The same act which established those, "the act to regulate the collection of duties on imports and tonnage, passed the 2d of March, 1799," contains several sections enacted for the purpose of conforming the act to the stipulations of the treaty above mentioned; those sections are the 104th and 105th, (4th vol. Laws of the United States, pages 440 and 441,) and embrace all the provisions of the third article alluded to.

tional practice? Can it be supposed that it will be necessary, convenient, or proper, for the President and Senate to make treaties, to the execution of which Congress will refuse its aid? Can it be expected, after the national faith has been pledged by the competent authority, that any department of the Government will refuse to do the acts necessary for the redemption of the pledge? May not the same causes which operated to produce the acquiescence of the President, and the recommendation of two-thirds of the Senate, be at all times trusted to procure a bare majority of this branch of Congress for the fulfilment of its part of the national obligation? Every treaty ratified imposes upon the Government, in all its departments, the obligation to fulfil it. The extent of that obligation is a question not now necessary to be examined or discussed. So far as relates to the late convention with Great Britain, no disposition is felt in any part of the House to avoid the discharge of all the duties which are imposed by its ratification. The advocates of this doctrine have been accused of a desire to encroach upon the Constitutional power of the other body. This House has been called the pet child of an over-indulgent mother, and warned not to assume rights, presuming upon that indulgence, which are exclusively vested in another child of the same family. The propriety of this warning is to be tested by the truth of the principle it assumes, that the legislative right is vested in the other and less favored child. How far the honorable gentleman from Pennsylvania (Mr. HOPKINSON) has succeeded in establishing this truth the House will judge. I beg leave, however, to remind him, that in the execution of this duty he proposed one question and argued a different one. The question whether a treaty subsequently made, repeals an existing law contrary to its stipulations, was the one proposed to be considered, and the one now before the House. This is to be determined by what the Constitution is, and not what it ought to be. This was the groundwork of his argument; but instead of raising it upon this basis, he abandons it at the first stroke of his trowel, and builds his whole superstructure upon a distinct and undisputed foundation: that there is no supposable case in which the vote of this House is necessary to give validity to a treaty. Sir, we are in the exercise of our Constitutional powers, and performing the duties of our station, in opposing principles never before contended for; ruinous in their consequences to the security of public happiness, destructive of the ends of the Constitution. We are the guardians of the rights of the people, placed as sentinels to watch the avenues of power, to prevent the encroachments of all the other departments of the Government, and to scan with inquisitorial scrutiny the motives which govern their conduct. In all the discussions and warmth which has heretofore been excited by the supposed conflict between the powers of the two Houses, an attempt never was before made to prevent the passage of an act to carry a treaty into effect, on the ground that the treaty itself becomes a law, notwithstanding the existence of a contradictory statute. The uniform practice, and the doctrines heretofore held, are equally in contradiction to this novel and unprecedented attempt.

In the long, animated, and lucid discussion of the treaty-making power in the year 1796, it was contended by the Federal minority, 1st. That a treaty once ratified was binding on the nation, and that Congress was as much bound to pass the laws necessary to carry such treaty into effect, as the President and Courts were to execute its provisions; 2dly. That if there was any discretion in Congress, it was limited to the special act required of them—to the propriety of making appropriations, of regulating duties, &c., and that they had no right to take into consideration, as a motive of dissent, other parts of the treaty which avowedly required no legislative sanction. The determination of the Representatives of the people at that period—I mean the Republican majority—was still more clearly contradictory to this new doctrine. Upon what, sir, is the reliance for its establishment at this late day? Literally upon a marginal note of the printer of the Constitution, which says treaties are laws of the land. I will not repeat what I had already occasion to remark, and what has been so much more fully illustrated by other gentlemen, that the text of this part of the Constitution has no bearing upon this question, it was adopted for a purpose explained sufficiently by reference to the article itself, to ascertain the supremacy of the Constitution, laws, and treaties of the United States over State constitutions and State laws. Is reliance placed upon the article which authorizes the President, by and with the advice and consent of two-thirds of the Senate, to make treaties? The making the contract, and the effect of it, are totally different things. The ascertainment of what department of the Government is authorized to make treaties, does nothing towards the establishment of the doubtful question of the extent and effect of them when made. It is upon the article which extends the judicial power to all cases in law and equity arising under the Government and laws of the United States, and the treaties made, or which shall be made, under their authority. This is not sufficient, for this provision is necessary to the perfection of the Constitution, whether treaties are of themselves sufficient or require legislative enactment. Cases would arise under treaties which avowedly require no legislative provision, and to those cases it was necessary to extend the judicial power of the General Government. These are all the clauses of the Constitution on the subject, and not one of them separated from the residue authorizes the conclusion which had been drawn from them. Nor is this conclusion justified by any possible combination or analysis of them. An attempt, however, is made to supply this defect in the letter of the Constitution, by a course of reasoning upon the nature of treaties and the necessity which exists for giving such a construction in order to perfect the grant of power

to the President and Senate, to enable the Executive to exercise it in such a manner as to produce the end intended to be accomplished by the grant. It is said, also, that a treaty being a contract between nations, operating upon the parties to it, is superior to a law which operates only upon the citizens or subjects of either of the parties. I deny the correctness of the data and the arguments founded upon them. It is necessary from the nature of the treaty power that its object should not be defined, but the necessity of limiting the effect of the exercise of the power is the same, is indeed infinitely greater than the necessity of limiting the exercise of legislative power, the more especially in a Government constituted like ours, where the legislative power is bridled by its division into separate branches. Unless, indeed, it should be shown that there is greater danger to be apprehended from the combination and corruption of two bodies dissimilarly constituted in the same State, than from the corruption of one of them, and its combination with a foreign Power—a position, whose falsehood is demonstrated both by theory and experience. What is the end to be accomplished? The preservation of the national faith by a faithful discharge of the contract. Is the mode of fulfilling it important to this end? Is not the national faith sacredly complied with, either by the enactment of laws in execution of the treaty, or by considering the treaty as law in itself? It is true, sir, that it is more convenient for those who exercise this power that it should not be thus clogged, the more especially if it is sought to be exerted in doubtful or desperate cases; but the foreign Government with whom your engagement is formed, has no more concern with the manner in which it is to be executed than with any other internal regulation. It is, however, said to be all-powerful, because it is a contract. This, permit me to say, is the first time I have heard the doctrine advanced that a law which commands is inferior to a contract which promises; that the act of performance is inferior to the word of promise. The very contrary is the doctrine I hold; the law is superior because the treaty is but the promise, the contract, which can be redeemed or fulfilled only by subsequent enactment. The inferiority of the treaty to the legislative power is obvious from the nature of the two powers and the manner in which they are to operate; the first is granted from necessity, the second for convenience; the first is essential to the existence of society, the second adventitious; the first operates within the State, the latter is granted from its possible connexion with, and effect upon, the objects for which the first was delegated. But, sir, the effect resulting from the establishment of this monstrous pretension, requires to be examined. The people who framed the Constitution imagined that they had secured all their rights from violation by the checks and guards. They believed at least that no laws could be passed without the consent of their Representatives biennially responsible to them for the wisdom and purity of their conduct.

In order to preserve within its proper sphere the Congress of which these Representatives were a constituent part, they fixed certain boundaries within which they should be permitted freely to act, and within which they fondly imagined no other authority could be permitted to interfere with the exercise of their powers. Inadvertently, however, they have authorized the President and Senate to make treaties, and this general permission is made the instrument of wresting from their Representatives their share in the management of the national interest. A foreign Power or Indian tribe is substituted for the Representatives of the people, and the President and Senate with this extra Constitutional assistance is omnipotent; their word is good against the world. They may lay taxes, borrow money, regulate commerce, establish uniform rules of bankruptcy, coin money, declare war, raise armies, and change your Constitution ad libitum. We are told that these are extreme cases, not to be supposed; the Senate are too pure to act thus; that the Constitution limits their power by declaring that no money shall be taken from the Treasury except by appropriations previously made by law; and some have adopted the ground that the power of the purse and the sword is with the Congress, and cannot be affected by treaty. We are informed, too, that it is not a fair mode of reasoning, to put extreme cases. Doubtful principles are always to be tested by considering the consequences deducible from them. If they are fairly deduced, and are manifestly absurd, however apparently correct the premises may be, however difficult to detect their fallacy, we may conclude with unerring certainty that they are false. In this case gentlemen refuse to examine because they dare not face the consequences of the principles they recommend. If there is anything in their argument of the purity and wisdom of the Senate, the argument is equally applicable to ourselves, and we and those who succeed us, I hope, may be as safely trusted as the present or any other Senate which may assist in the management of the national concerns. Admitting the present purity and wisdom of the Senate, have you a bond that they are to remain so? It will be remembered that the descendants of the Senators who died on their chairs when Rome was sacked by the Goths, were the vilest parasites and panderers of imperial power. What is the boasted restriction imposed by the section that "no money shall be drawn from the Treasury but in consequence of appropriations made by law?" It is true that most important acts of power require the expenditure of money. Many, however deadly to the public interest and security, may be effected without its aid.

An honorable gentleman from Pennsylvania (Mr. HOPKINSON) who warned us "to beware of jealousy," has shown us how easily this section may be evaded. He has told us that a treaty may be carried into execution without appropriations, if the President can procure the required service to be performed without compensation. From this it follows, as an irresistible corollary, that, if the money necessary can be procured in any other way, the treaty may be executed. If, for example, the foreign Power should prefer to pay the money rather than lose the advantages of the contract. This position, taken in connexion with his solemn warning, like the conduct and the voice of Iago, is calculated to awaken and stimulate that passion against whose influence he bids us "beware." But whence arises this squeamish distinction between appropriation laws and other laws? Is a treaty a law to some purposes and not a law for others? From what source is this distinction drawn? Why will gentlemen after swallowing the hemlock refuse the necessary means to give it immediate effect? Can they hope to escape the deadly influence of the poisonous draught? They indeed prolong for a short period a miserable existence; they may render the mortal agony more intense by protracting the moment of dissolution; but, sir, their fate is sealed, and no human power can sever them from death. What is the efficacy of this limitation, supposing it to be beyond evasion and dispute? What is its potent efficacy, if, by your President and Senate, a band of five hundred thousand armed banditti are admitted into the centre of your territory? Constitutional limitations, without any power of enforcement but the people, neither forewarned nor forearmed by their representatives, (for, if our aid is not necessary, the first intimation we may have will be the landing of these hordes upon our shores,)—what are they against fixed bayonets and ruthless ambition? It is in vain to say this will not, cannot happen. Sir, I know it cannot, will not happen, if we are true to our own trust; but if this unlimited authority is granted to the President and Senate, who will say that in the next century it may not occur? The honorable advocates of this doctrine rely for the fidelity of the execution of the power upon the mode of selecting the Senators, upon their honorable desire to live in history, to be recorded to after times as virtuous and patriotic—upon the omnipotent influence of public opinion. I am not disposed to call in question the correctness of the mode of selection adopted by the Constitution, but if this is the only safeguard, Heaven help us, for we are beyond the reach of earthly assistance. Let any man who believes in the unerring wisdom which has been exhibited in the choice of Senators, enter the Senate House at any period since the establishment of the Government; he would have found intelligence, virtue, and patriotism, but he would have found also, by their side, stupidity, vice, and selfishness. Brawling ignorance has more than once occupied the chair which ought to have been filled by unassuming merit; and sacrifices have been offered on the altars of treason, erected in the very centre of the Senate Chamber. Will it be insisted that these, at present partial evils, may not become, in the gradual progress of society, universal corruption? That the body at present visited by occasional blotches may not hereafter be covered with leprosy, against whose contagion the Constitution intended to

659   HISTORY OF CONGRESS.   660

H. of R.   *Commerce with Great Britain.*   January, 1816.

guard? If this is not sufficient, how much more inefficient is the confidence reposed in their desire to live recorded for their virtues in after times. History has been justly styled the record of human turpitude, and he who wishes to occupy a conspicuous place on the roll, will most surely succeed if his life is distinguished by successful villainy. To be virtuous, to perform with fidelity the duties of life, to be honest and incorruptible in private and in public stations, will secure to the man his portion of happiness in this life, and a reward in that to come; but to acquire that species of immortality which is conferred by the pen of the historian, he must possess very different qualities, and exercise them for very different purposes. It is, indeed, the fortunate lot of some individuals to be conspicuous in their opposition to the crimes of others, but they owe their place in the temple of history to the criminality of their opponents. The name of WASHINGTON never would have survived the first century after his death but for the oppressions of England, and the consequent Revolutionary contest. William Tell would have died unnoticed and unknown, an humble and virtuous peasant of the canton of Uri, but for the villainy of Gesler, and the ambition of Austria. Public opinion, then, is to be the efficient guard. And what is it? In the pursuit of our duty virtue teaches us to disregard it. Of its influence, corruption renders us insensible. Admitting it to be thus omnipotent upon unsuccessful crime—for history teaches us that the failure or success of a project but too often fixes its character—how does it operate? Not on the crime, but on the criminal; it permits him to perfect the injury, but visits him afterwards with its punishment. The Constitution knows no such guards. It was framed with a view, if I may adopt the phrase, to preventive, not vindictive justice. It intended to prevent the commission of the offence, not to punish the criminal.

I will not occupy your time by an examination of the strange doctrine that the power of the purse and sword being with us, the treaty-making power is sufficiently limited. This, if it does anything, gives up the whole ground. The power over the sword, to make war, depends upon the same terms as the power to regulate commerce, and all the other powers granted to Congress. No man whose head is not strangely confused, or whose forehead is not covered with Corinthian brass, can pretend to make a distinction between them. If one is exclusive, so are the rest.

I have said, Mr. Speaker, that the President and Senate may alter your Constitution by treaty if these doctrines are correct. The Constitution provides that amendments may be made by two-thirds of the State Legislatures, and two-thirds of the Congress. It says, in the clause already mentioned, that commerce may be regulated, and money coined, and war made by Congress. If, then, the treaty-making power is paramount to the power of Congress, is it not paramount to the authority of Congress and the States?

If a foreign Government can be substituted in the place of the Representatives of the people, what forbids the same substitution in the place of Congress and the States? The same argument applicable to the first set of powers is applicable to the last. It will not, I presume, be contended, in these days of modern improvement in the law of nations, that a foreign Power cannot by treaty make any regulations in the Government of a neighboring State or people. I would, before I conclude, bring to the recollection of the House an argument urged by a gentleman from Virginia, (Mr. SHEFFEY,) and the answer given to it by a gentleman from Pennsylvania, (Mr. HOPKINSON.) It was this: That the powers given to Congress are definite in their terms, and appropriate to their objects, while the power given to the President and Senate to make treaties is given in general and unrestricted terms. It was asked, and as I shall show no satisfactory answer was given to the question, by what rule of construction a power primarily and specially given to a body can be assumed and exercised by another to which, in a subsequent clause, a mere general authority is given. Upon every acknowledged principle of construction the specific power would clearly, in such case, be deemed a reservation and exception out of the general grant. In answer, what was urged? Not that the conclusion was incorrect; not that the principle was false; but its force was evaded by what I must call a sophism, and that not distinguished by its ingenuity. The answer was, that the Constitution gives to Congress a general power over commerce, but to the President and Senate a special power over commerce. From a general grant, broad and undefined as it could be made, a power to make treaties a special power to regulate commerce, is deduced by argument. This special power, depending upon the correctness of the deduction, is made an exception out of the specific grant of power to Congress, of legislating exclusively upon the same subject. Thus a special power, derived by argument from a general grant, is made to destroy a special power expressly granted. Such, sir, are the resources to which one of the ablest of the supporters of this new doctrine is driven in its defence.

The same gentleman sought to rest the claim of the power of the Senate upon the notion, that the powers of Congress and the treaty-making power were concurrent. This idea, admitting it to be correct, does not obviate the difficulty. If these powers are exercised upon the same objects to produce the same effects, there is no contradiction or difficulty; but if they operate in opposite directions, which is paramount, which is inferior? The vexed question necessarily recurs. It has been suggested, that the one last exercised is to prevail, inasmuch as the last act always repeals the preceding act. This suggestion is not entitled to the weight which has been given to it. It rests upon a fallacy easily detected. It proceeds upon another proposition, that the last exertion of the same authority is superior to, and sets aside the former act. Here, however, the act of one power constitutionally exerted, is repealed by the act of another differently constituted. This position is, attempted to be enforced by another still more refined and indefensible: That Congress have ordinary, and the President and Senate extraordinary, legislative powers; the one proceeding by acts, and the other by treaties. I do not understand how gentlemen obviate the difficulty thrown in their way by the first article of the Constitution, which declares, that all legislative powers herein granted, shall be vested in a Congress of the United States. Not all ordinary, but all legislative power shall be exercised by Congress. Where, then, is the part of the Constitution which contains this extraordinary grant of extraordinary legislation?

Sir, what an extraordinary spectacle our Government would exhibit to the world, if these positions are true. To-day the President and Senate, without our assistance, can do nothing affecting the happiness or security of this people. In a matter highly interesting and important, deeply affecting the national interest—the national honor—the President and Senate, in their legislative capacity, are desirous a particular system should be adopted; this House refuses its concurrence—the system necessarily fails. To-morrow a Constitutional juggle is played off, and the system is fixed eternally upon us. A foreign Government or Indian tribe makes a contract or treaty (the terms are convertible) with the President; he sends it by his Secretary to the Senate; the doors are closed; the Eleusinian mysteries are celebrated; and, after the requisite sacrifices in the temple of secrecy, the contract is ushered into the world. To borrow the metaphorical language of the gentleman from Maryland, it starts into life the supreme law of the land; either establishing a new system obnoxious to, and rejected by, the Representatives of the people, or overturning all the systems heretofore established with their concurrence. The Constitution of the United States, so much the object of our admiration, and the praise of other nations, does not deserve the eulogiums bestowed upon it, if such practices are consistent with its principles. At one moment the Senate is but a co-equal and co-ordinate branch of the legislative authority; at the next its will is supreme and irresistible. To-day, in the hands of the President, it is powerless as the staff of the Israelite; to-morrow, it is converted, by his assistance, into a serpent, active and devouring, swallowing up everything within the range of the Constitution. To-day it is powerless as a fevered Cæsar, crying "bring me some drink, Tytinius, like a sick girl;" to-morrow it is Cæsar imperial, at "whose nod we must bend our bodies," with reverence and submission.

Mr. Speaker, I have much more to say on this subject, but the persons in conversation behind me, warn me that I must not continue my remarks, without a contest for the attention of the House. It will not be considered as unpardonable on my part, to abandon a conflict so useless and ungrateful, and to leave them the undisputed masters of the field.

Mr. JACKSON said he regretted that he had consulted his feelings more than his judgment, when he last evening expressed a wish to submit some remarks upon the question before the House; a wish, prompted by the impulse of the moment, after hearing the ingenious argument of the gentleman from Pennsylvania, which seemed to him to require a reply from those who thought, as Mr. J. did, that this bill was indispensably necessary to carry into effect, with good faith, the provisions of the treaty. Mr. J. remarked, he was the more reluctant now to occupy their time, after the arguments just delivered by his friend from Georgia, (Mr. FORSYTH,) in reply to the gentleman from Pennsylvania; but as he had given a pledge to the House, he would proceed briefly to redeem it, with the express reservation, that if, in the course of his remarks, any manifestation of impatience occurred, he would instantly terminate them. I differ, said Mr. J., from gentlemen who conceive that the question before us, in consequence of the coincidence of opinion in regard to the treaty, possesses no interest in reality, or in the view of those who are called upon to decide it. It is true, and it is not less fortunate than true, that thus far the discussion has been conducted upon liberal principles, involving only the consideration of what is a just interpretation of the Constitution, without the baneful influence of party animosities; yet it cannot be doubted that the question is really and intrinsically of vast importance, as has been amply developed by this discussion. And I consider the decision which shall be pronounced now, as calculated to fix, perhaps for ages, the interpretation of the Constitution in relation to one of its most important provisions; it will not only try the opinions formerly advanced, by an unerring test, but being given in the same age which gave birth to the Constitution, will possess all the weight of a precedent established almost contemporaneously with the charter. It is now too late to deny the influence of precedents in a free Government. Perhaps, whatever exists of value in the British Constitution is the authority of precedent; an authority so highly esteemed, as to give rise to the legal maxim, that "*communis error facit jus ;*" that it is better to acquiesce in an erroneous interpretation, long settled and become a rule of decision, than that the rights of society should be put at hazard by a disregard of all former opinions by the expounders of the laws and the Constitution.

I regard this as a striking illustration of the idea, that the powers of genius and eloquence are so transcendant as to set all the sober maxims of reason at naught, and by the magic of their influence "make the wrong appear the better reason." And although I listened with constant attention to the fine specimens we have had of that high prerogative, I will not say I attended with pleasure to the splendid exhibition of talents by the gentlemen on the other side of the question; for in proportion to their strength are their arguments dangerous—hurtful. The wound inflicted by a gilded dagger is ofttimes more mortal than that produced by a leaden bullet. This is the age of reason; and the politician who seeks for fame must address himself to the judgment of the community; he must convince by his arguments, rather than delight by his oratory; and he that gives a wrong bias to public opinion by the display of extraordinary abilities, is more to be dreaded than the man who rails against the principles of the Government, and openly endeavors to subvert it. In all Governments having a written constitution much, very much depends upon its faithful interpretation; and yet, unfortunately, the interpretation which is given almost always partakes of the predilections of those by whom the instrument is expounded. Some good men think that a main defect of our system consists in the inadequacy of the powers of the Executive, and hence, on all questions involving their consideration, they give a construction calculated to increase rather than to restrict them. And to this cause alone do I ascribe it, that we hear doctrines avowed which render all the great powers of legislation a nullity, and which bind the nation hand and foot to the car of the Executive, and the counsellors of the Executive, in the exercise of the treaty-making power.

In order to arrive at a just conclusion, the proper mode is to regard the Constitution as obligatory upon us—to indulge in no speculative theories as to what it ought to be; "*ita lex scripta est*," and as it is written so let it be expounded. Perhaps it is due to candor that I should state my opinions upon the extent of the Executive power also, in order that the rule I am applying to others may have its proper weight in estimating my arguments; with that view alone, I declare my firm conviction to be, that the Executive authority is already strong enough—it wants not the aids or props of construction; and if the question under discussion were as to the competency of the Executive authority upon a motion to amend the Constitution in that particular, instead of being a question as to its extent merely, I believe it would be decided again that no principle of public liberty required any addition to the grant of power already defined by that instrument.

I say, sir, that the doctrines advocated do annihilate the legislative powers of Congress, and convert us into a mere registering body. Let me state some of the positions advanced, and see if I am not justified in this opinion. It is said—

1st. That the treaty-making power is unrestricted, and exceptions to it are by construction merely.

2d. That it is a complete power independently of the Legislature, and where its fulfilment requires legislative enactments, they are compelled by the treaty to preserve our faith, as the payment of a debt, or the conveyance of land, when stipulated for by a competent authority.

3d. That this treaty requires no further sanction to give it validity.

4th. That it was promulgated by the President as a valid and obligatory instrument, requiring no legislative aid.

5th. That this is not a bill auxiliary to, or giving effect to the treaty, and is therefore useless.

6th. And that the security we have against the abuse of this vast power is in the public opinion, which, it is said, is an ample security.

I will examine each of these propositions in the order now presented.

The first is, that the treaty-making power is unrestricted, &c. Regarding the Constitution as an entire instrument, in which every provision was intended to have effect and harmonize with all the others, and that no superfluous terms or phrases were used by its framers, I perceive a restriction on this power in the grant itself, which relates to treaties, and defines their force when made, viz: The President shall have power to make treaties; "and all treaties made, or which shall be made, under the authority of the United States, shall be the supreme law," &c. The term "under," is synonymous here with pursuant to, in obedience, or in conformity with; for if it had been designed to be without limitation, other words, less significant in their meaning, would have been employed—but waiving this suggestion, which may be objected to as a mere criticism, I will say, it is restricted by many prominent provisions of the Constitution, namely: in all the instances where the exercise of a general power is prohibited to the United States, as in the cases enumerated by the 9th section of the 1st article, which declares that no tax shall be laid on exports, &c., and it is restricted also by other provisions, whereby an express power over other specified objects is given to the Congress of the United States; and it is wholly incompatible with the plainest rules of construction, that a power expressly granted, can be annihilated by inference and interpretation merely, which would be the effect of permitting the treaty-making department to supersede the legislative authority in all the cases enumerated in the 8th section.

In this section it is declared Congress shall have power to declare war, to raise armies, to provide a navy, &c. If, however, the President and Senate shall approve a treaty of offensive and defensive alliance, they may thereby involve us in war, and stipulate that our contingent shall be an army of twenty or fifty thousand men; several ships-of-the line; a subsidy of many millions, and whatever else they shall conceive conducive to the attainment of the objects of the treaty—a consequence to which the doctrines avowed will indubitably lead us, and which will as clearly usurp all the great legislative powers of the Federal Government. An argument is urged by the advocates of this construction, which depends for its correctness upon the influence and extent of the provision which declares that treaties shall be the supreme law of the land. It is said there are no grades in supremacy, and a supreme implies a subordinate power; that the treaty power being supreme, the legislative power must yield to it, or if the powers be equal, the treaty repeals all laws, theretofore in force, conflicting with its stipulations.

The fallacy of this reasoning is demonstrated by referring it to the test relied on, viz: the provision in the Constitution declaring the effect of treaties, &c. Its language is, " this Constitution, ' and the laws of the United States, which shall ' be made in pursuance thereof, and all treaties ' made, or which shall be made under the author- ' ity of the United States, shall be the supreme ' law of the land." It is not treaties merely which are declared to be the supreme law of the land, but the Constitution and the laws of the United States also. The Constitution is first named: It shall be the supreme law; it is supreme- mest of these supremes, and fully establishes the reverse of the proposition that there are no grades in supremacy; for example, it is admitted that a treaty stipulation directly repugnant to an ex- press prohibition, is void, unless it is because the Constitutional charter is paramount to treaties conflicting with it. And how are these supreme laws marshalled? I answer, according to their grades of supremacy: 1st. The Constitution; 2d. The laws of the United States; and 3d. The treaties—according to a familiar maxim, "*qui prior est tempore potior est jure;*" if the laws conflict with the Constitution, they are *ipso facto* void; if treaties contravene existing laws, they are invalid, until the laws are repealed. It is said, as the power to make commercial treaties is not withheld, it constitutes a portion of the gen- eral grant "to make treaties." It is not denied by the advocates of this bill, that this position is a sound one; on the contrary, we admit its truth; we say it exists as all other subjects with- in the legitimate objects of conventional agree- ments, subject to the limitations or controlling power defined in the Constitution. To illustrate my opinion, the President and Senate may, by treaty, agree to regulate our commerce with a foreign nation, because its regulation comes with- in the scope of the treaty-making power, sub- ject, nevertheless, to the subsequent sanction of Congress, without which it is invalid, because "Congress shall have power to regulate com- merce with foreign nations." The direct power is given to Congress, in positive terms—the indi- rect subordinate power is given to the President and Senate, by inference only! Here the rule of construction I have referred to, comes in aid of our doctrine, that an express grant shall not be defeated by implication, if the intention of the grantor is unequivocally manifested in its favor.

I admit we cannot have a treaty unless it is through the Executive agency. What I contend for is, that when the treaty embraces a subject requiring legislation, either by a promise to pay money, or that a law shall cease to operate, in all cases Congress must act to render the treaty effec- tual; that, to repeal a law is as much an act of legislation as to pass a law appropriating money, or for raising taxes, &c.; and that you cannot legislate by treaty, because it is declared by the Constitution that all legislative powers therein granted shall be vested in Congress.

It is said that the act declaring war was repealed

by treaty, and hence it is contended every other law may in like manner be repealed. This case, if it were in point, has not the force that prece- dents are entitled to, because it was not discussed; and it has not the sanction of age, without which, as one of them, no case is considered as of bind- ing validity. But, the case is not an analogous one. The act of war was, first, declaratory that the relations of peace no longer existed with Great Britain; and, second, it authorized the President to employ the national forces in its prosecution.

War is, indeed, as was eloquently remarked by the gentleman from Maryland, (Mr. PINKNEY,) a great prerogative; it is the highest attribute of sovereignty; the greatest scourge of nations. The good and the wise resort to war only when it be- comes the lesser of great evils, between which they are compelled, by the wickedness and folly of their enemies, to make a choice. The laws of war are essentially humane and liberal, and every civilized nation that respects the opinions of the world, and the faithful award of posterity, will keep them sacred. By these laws, the commander of an army may agree to an armistice. The Pre- sident, who is the Commander-in-Chief, may alone suspend hostilities, and with his Constitu- tional advisers (the Senate) may terminate them. And this is from the necessity of the case, *inter arma silent leges.* And, when the calamities of war can be honorably ended, the construction should be liberal, if a rigid rule rendered the power doubtful. In the next place, the Treaty of Peace was a complete act; it abridged no power, it vio- lated no right, and required no legislation. It was the exclusive attribute of the treaty power, for it is not enumerated among those granted in the Constitution. Again, the treaty was self- executory; and in fine, it did nothing more than promise that the President, to whom, by the dec- claration of war, was given the power to wage it, would forbear to prosecute it any longer. How different in all respects is this Commercial Treaty! It is to be in constant prospective operation, and violates daily the express injunctions of a statute which declares that the British vessels shall pay a duty in our ports, from which the treaty ex- empts them. The treaty, then, exercises all the functions of legislation—it repeals an act of Con- gress. But, in order to establish the similarity further, it is proper to remark that we co-operated in giving our sanction to the Treaty of Peace by disbanding the Army, and changing the aspect of all our external relations. If, indeed, as has been contended, the power to make treaties is limited, and when made, the treaties are instantly valid, without the agency of Congress, and exceptions to this power are by construction merely,—then it may be said of our Constitution, as has been asserted of Republicanism, that "it means any- thing or nothing," and the wisdom and precaution of its framers and adopters have been vain and fruitless.

I come now to the second point in the order of my arrangement, viz.: that the treaty-making power is complete, and independent, &c. In my answer to it, I will ask, what is meant by the terms so frequently used, "Congress shall have *power?*" And what is intended by the phrase *power* there employed? I suppose it is synonymous with *right* or *discretion*, and means a legislative *control* over the subject delegated, and does not imply *compulsion, obligation*. And yet we are told, if the fulfilment of the treaty requires legislative enactments, they are compelled by the treaty. I do not speak of a physical compulsion, but a moral obligation; for, if our honor binds us to make the grant, no one pretends that it should be withheld for a moment. The argument on this point was illustrated by supposing two cases—the one where a debt was contracted by a competent agent; the other where an agent sold land in behalf of his principal, under a power which did not authorize the sale. Although in the latter case it was admitted the principal was not bound, yet it was contended there was nevertheless a valid contract. In the first case it was said the debt must be paid, and in the second, you must convey the land to save the agent harmless. Sir, these cases are not apposite. Here the contract is inchoate; the debt is not yet contracted; we gave no power to sell the farm; and are not bound to make good the engagements of one that transcended his powers. But, foreign nations, it is said, regard us as bound, and our faith as pledged to them, whenever a treaty is ratified. This consideration will always render the question an extremely delicate and highly responsible one, and no doubt will have due weight in determining the House of Representatives as to the propriety of passing the necessary laws. I cannot, however, admit, that any civilized nation is so ignorant of our institutions as to suppose that a treaty, when ratified by the President, with the advice of the Senate—no matter what are its provisions—is *ipso facto* obligatory, and that a refusal by Congress to carry it into effect would violate the national faith. After the refusal of the British Government to ratify the Erskine arrangement, for making which so much praise was bestowed on the President, until it was ascertained that His Majesty did not approve of it, it will be recollected that the Opposition partly changed their tone from praise to censure, and excused the British for a non-compliance, because the Minister had not obeyed his instructions, and condemned the President for treating with him without requiring the production of his *patent powers*. Our treaty powers are *patent*; they are defined by the Constitution; they are limited in it. The agent who contracts for his principal, producing his powers, binds him only as far as they go; beyond them he appeals to the discretion of the principal alone; there is no contract, and the party trusting to it has no right to complain if the agreement shall be rejected. It is a well-known rule, that where an agent contracts for the Government, he is not individually liable if he had authority to contract, and it falls within the same principle that he is not liable if he produce the power under which he makes an agreement, and signs it as agent. In the first case, the Government is bound by a valid contract; in the second

case, the Government is not bound, as it gave no power, and the individual is not, because he suppressed no fact, he suggested no falsehood, he annexed his letter of attorney to the agreement, and signed it as agent.

If the Congress are bound on all treaty questions in the extraordinary intercourse among nations, and must legislate to give them effect, we are a mere registering body; we ought to go home, and no longer presume to be a deliberative assembly. The complaint which led to the Revolution was the assertion by the King and Parliament of "a right to bind us in all cases whatsoever;" and, after a glorious and successful resistance, we have gained but little, if it shall be once established, that the Representatives of the people have no rights under this Government, and that in derogation of State rights, and in violation of express prohibitions, the treaty-making power can "bind us in all cases." In support of this dangerous power, it is urged that, in establishing the opposite doctrine, we palsy the Executive arm of the Government. And if this consequence were to follow, I pray you whether it would not be a better evil than to annihilate the legislative body? But, say the gentlemen, we admit you have a right to regulate commerce; yet it is by adopting municipal regulations only. How is it, if this distinction be correct, that the Constitution declares we shall have power to regulate commerce with foreign nations? One gentleman (Mr. Pickering) has attempted an answer; he says it relates only to such nations as will not enter into a treaty of commerce with us. To this explanation I reply, the clause contains no such limitation; and if a foreign nation will not treat with the Executive, I should despair of success by sending the whole Congress abroad for that purpose. If the ships of a foreign nation come within our limits for the purposes of traffic, our regulations, by which they are bound, are municipal, and none of them can be termed a regulation of commerce with such foreign nation. The admission, however, of those that contend our power is municipal only, is fatal to their argument. What is the obvious meaning of the term municipal? Not a regulation of commerce in the body of a State between its citizens, for we have no such power; nor a regulation of commerce "among the States," for that is granted by a separate clause; but its regulation in the ports and harbors of the United States—the very office which it is contended this treaty performs in defiance of the law in your statute book. It is argued that a treaty may, without legislative aid, regulate our foreign trade by defining what shall be deemed contraband of war, and by prohibiting exports of such articles. I admit that the treaty power may stipulate as to what articles shall be contraband, and yet I deny the right of that power to prohibit their exportation. The law of nations designates certain articles as contraband of war; these have been particularly defined by conventional agreements, and that between Russia and England is the most liberal. In these articles you shall not trade with a nation at war, because such a nation, converting them to the purposes of war, is thereby enabled to annoy its adversary, and being neutral yourself, it is your duty to preserve an inviolable impartiality between the belligerents; yet a trade in those articles is not unlawful, provided it is carried on with a Power at peace, and consequently it being a belligerent restriction, it ceases entirely to have effect in time of peace, and in time of war is confined to the parties at war. It follows as a necessary consequence that the exportation cannot be interdicted, but the destination merely.

The third position assumed is, that the treaty requires no sanction; because, says the gentleman from Pennsylvania, (Mr. HOPKINSON,) all prior conflicting laws are repealed by the treaty. The repeal of a law, as has been shown, is a legislative act, and all legislative powers are vested in Congress. The conclusion is, therefore, irresistible, that the argument is erroneous. Another remark is, that there is no instance of the question being put, whether a treaty or no treaty; that in 1795 this House only claimed the right to withhold or grant money to carry the treaty into effect. So in this case we say as it proposes to regulate commerce by repealing the discriminating duties, we have the right to decide upon such repeal, and do not decide the question of treaty or no treaty either. And this for a plain and obvious reason : it does not comport with the practice of the House, or rules of legislation, to decide an abstract proposition. The only departure from this rule, that I recollect, was when, in consequence of the outrageous edicts of Great Britain and France, this House solemnly declared, by the votes of all the members except two, (and these two opposed the declaration on the ground that it was an irregular course,) that the United States could no longer submit to those edicts without a sacrifice of their rights, honor, and independence. It is said, also, that when the treaty power is violated, the check is not here, but in the Constitution. Certainly, sir, it cannot be denied that if we permit the Constitutional powers of the Legislature to be usurped, without an effort to maintain them, we cannot answer for our conduct to our consciences or to our country. We stand here as the sentinels of the people to challenge all hostile attempts to invade their liberties, all hostile attacks subversive of the Constitution.

The gentleman (Mr. HOPKINSON) told us the argument in support of the bill was built upon the supposed impropriety of the conduct of the Senate. How, wherein, I pray you ? By asserting our rights; in performing our duties ? We claim to participate in acts of legislation; we cannot, if we would, permit the Senate to legislate; if there be any inference of impropriety, the fault lies in the Constitution in creating two branches of the Legislature, and not in performing our functions as one of them. We were called the spoiled child of the Constitution, and were solemnly admonished to beware of jealousy. Sir, we are the favorites of the Constitution, the great agent of all political operations; the money of

the people has been confided to us; the purse-strings of the nation have been given into our hands, and, until we loosen them, not a dollar can be drawn from their pockets. But wherein, I ask, do we manifest this jealousy ? If by the term it be meant that nice sense of propriety which induces the world, in speaking of a high-minded gentleman, to say that he is jealous of his honor, I accept the application; but if it be meant that we manifest a distrust of the virtue or patriotism of the Senate, I disavow it. Our ground is elevated above the atmosphere in which jealousy of that kind finds its aliment; it is the ground of faithful interpretation and not of expediency; and I will ask the gentleman, in his own language, if the assertion was not used to point an argument or to round a period ?

If the view already presented be a correct one, not only does the treaty require the sanction of a law, but it cannot be executed without an act of the Legislature. It was remarked that this construction would violate the assurances of our Ministers, as they told the British the treaty would be complete on being ratified, and the fifth article was read in support of the assertion. Suppose that such was indeed their opinion in form; it proves nothing more than the discussion now proves, that many distinguished able men take up a similar opinion; the true question is, which opinion is the correct one.

And this brings me to the consideration of the 4th point, viz : that the treaty was promulgated by the President as a valid and binding instrument requiring no legislation. I wish it to be understood that I disclaim entirely the binding influence of any opinions from any quarter; the weight they ought to have is always proportioned to their inherent correctness, and the distinguished talents of those by whom they are pronounced. I always pay due respect to such authority, for the same reason that I would in a court of law to the judgments of Lord Ellenborough. But the President has not expressed the opinion, according to my view, that the gentlemen ascribe to him, but the reverse. I have been led to compare the language of the proclamation promulgating this treaty with that used in the cases of the declaration of war issued on the 19th of June, 1812, of the Treaty of Peace dated the 18th of February, 1815, and I find a marked difference between them. [Here Mr. J. read the proclamations alluded to, which after announcing the facts, " enjoins all persons to be vigilant and zealous in discharging their duties and faithfully to observe and fulfil the treaty." whilst the proclamation touching the convention declares merely that it has been " accepted, ratified and confirmed."] Why, I ask you, this material difference in the proclamations? The Treaty of Peace proclaims the fact to which it relates and "specially enjoins a faithful observance and fulfilment of the treaty." The convention is simply accompanied by a notice that it has been accepted and ratified. Sir, the answer is to be found in the Message of the President dated the 22d of December, in which he "recommends to Congress such legislative provisions as the convention may call for on the part of the United States." Wherefore this Message, if the President did not believe that legislative aid was necessary? The gentleman from Pennsylvania, (Mr. Hopkinson,) in discussing this point, adverted to the Message and criticised its language. The President, said he, has not used the term *does* call for; but *may* call for. The word *may* is synonymous with *shall* or *will*, and to my mind conveys the same idea with *does*, the word selected by the gentlemen. And can it be supposed that the President intended this evasion? Why recommend to us legislative provisions at all, if none were necessary, and he considered them unnecessary?

The 6th and last point to be noticed is, that the security we have against the abuse of the vast power contended for by the opponents of this bill, is in the public opinion. I differ with my friend from Georgia in regard to public opinion, according to the acceptation of his remarks, though I believe we do not essentially differ. I bow to the public opinion, revere it, and the politician who defies its mandates will sooner or later be prostrated by them. The *vox populi* is emphatically the *vox dei*. Not the spurious opinion of a faction that lives upon the breath of a demagogue, and which passes by me as the idle wind which I regard not. But that sober deliberate opinion which is slow to censure and reluctant to condemn, until reason and truth come in aid of rumor, and stamp their impression upon its award. Which, although like the pendulum of a clock it may by winding up the wheels oscillate to and fro until the impetus which propels it is exhausted, at last stands still at that central point where its influence is unbounded, and its power is irresistible. Yet for that very reason that it is slow to operate, is it improper to rely on it as the only safeguard. Why a written Constitution at all, why not abolish the instrument and declare at once that the whole reliance is on public opinion? Sir, if our Henry had been told of this as the security, by the advocates for the Constitution, in the Convention of which he was a member; the lightning of his eloquence, vivid, lasting, piercing as it was when thus elicited, would have been poured out in such a resistless stream, that the parchment, like the oak of the forest when riven by the bolts of Heaven, would have been torn to pieces and scattered in countless fragments to the four winds of the earth. We have a security against the abuse of power which is ample, if it be only vigilantly guarded and faithfully observed. It lies—

1st. In the Constitution itself;

2d. In the oaths of those who have sworn to support it;

3d. In the moral sense of the public agents;

4th. In their responsibility to the people; and

5th. In the force of the public opinion.

By a due exercise of all their proper functions by all, we shall hand down this Constitution unimpaired to our posterity, and they to theirs, with the holy exclamation of *esto perpetua!*

Mr. Huger rose, he assured the House, not to take a part in the debate, nor to offer any arguments of his own. It would be unpardonable in him to do so at that late hour, when the patience of the House must be so nearly exhausted, and the subject had been discussed so ably, so fully, and, as it appeared to him, so unanswerably, on that side of the question, which he should support by his vote. Yet, as it had escaped all those who had preceded him, he could not refuse to himself the gratification, before the yeas and nays were taken, of directing the attention of the House to an authority which (if the arguments already adduced had not produced conviction on every mind) could not fail to decide the point at issue, and under the shadow of which he should at all events be most happy to record his name. Gentlemen themselves, he was well satisfied, would feel indebted to him, late as the hour was, for offering to their consideration, before the final vote was taken, the extracts he was about to read from the book he had in his hand, when he informed them that they were from the pen of the immortal Washington.

Without further preface, therefore, he begged leave to refer gentlemen to the journals of the 4th Congress, page 193, in which they would find recorded President Washington's Message accompanying the Treaty with Great Britain, or, as it is usually called, Jay's Treaty of '94–'5, in the following words:

"*Gentlemen of the Senate*
    and House of Representatives:

"The Treaty of Amity, Commerce, and Navigation between the United States of America and His Britannic Majesty, having been duly ratified, and the ratifications having been exchanged at London the 28th of October, 1795, I have directed the same to be promulgated, and transmit a copy hereof for the information of Congress.

"G. WASHINGTON.

"March 6, 1796."

Such, then, was the Message of President Washington, which accompanied the copy of the Treaty of '94–'95, transmitted to the House of Representatives for the information of Congress, but asking no legislative aid, sanction or co-operation whatsoever, although the Treaty had (in that precisely as in the present instance) been exchanged, ratified, and directed by him to be promulgated.

But it will be further recollected, that in the course of the discussion which afterwards took place on the subject of the treaty, grounds were taken similar to those now contended for, and a resolution was passed requiring the President to lay before the House of Representatives copies of certain papers which it was presumed might throw a light upon the merits of the treaty. In answer to this resolution, or request, the President returned a written Message on the 30th March, which would be found in the journals, page 292. Mr. H. observed he would not take up the time of the House by reading the whole Message at length, but he earnestly requested, and felt himself authorized to claim, the undivided attention of gentlemen to such extracts as had a particular bearing on the question now about to be decided, and which he should proceed to submit to them.

" The course which the debate has taken on the resolution of the House, leads to some observations on the mode of making treaties under the Constitution of the United States.

" Having been a member of the General Assembly, and knowing the principles on which the Constitution was formed, I have ever entertained but one opinion on this subject; and from the first establishment of the Government to this moment, my conduct has exemplified that opinion; that the power of making treaties is exclusively vested in the President, by and with the advice and consent of the Senate; and that every treaty so made and promulgated thenceforward became the law of the land.

" It is thus the treaty-making power has been understood by foreign nations; and in all the treaties made with them, we have declared, and they have believed, that when ratified by the President, with the advice and consent of the Senate, they became obligatory. In this construction of the Constitution, every House of Representatives has heretofore acquiesced, and until the present time not a doubt or suspicion has appeared, to my knowledge, that this construction was not the true one; nay, they have more than acquiesced, for till now, without controverting the obligation of such treaties, they have made all the requisite provisions for carrying them into effect.

" There is also reason to believe that this construction agrees with the opinions entertained by the State conventions when they were deliberating on the Constitution, especially by those who objected to it, because there was not required, in commercial treaties, the consent of two-thirds of the whole number of the members of the Senate, instead of two-thirds of the Senators present, and because in treaties respecting territorial and certain other rights and claims, the concurrence of three-fourths of the whole number of the members of both Houses, respectively, was not made necessary.

" It is a fact declared by the General Convention, and universally understood, that the Constitution of the United States was the result of a spirit of amity and mutual concession; and it is well known that under this influence the smaller States were admitted into an equal representation in the Senate with the larger States; and that this branch of the Government was invested with great powers, for on the equal participation of those powers the sovereignty and political situation of the smaller States were deemed essentially to depend.

" If other proofs than these, and the plain letter of the Constitution itself be necessary to ascertain the point under consideration, they may be found in the journals of the General Convention which I have deposited in the office of the Department of State. In those journals it will appear that a proposition was made that no treaty should be binding on the United States, which was not ratified by a law, and that the proposition was explicitly rejected.

" As, therefore, it is perfectly clear to my understanding that the consent of the House of Representatives is not necessary to the validity of the treaty, &c., a just regard to the Constitution, and to the duty of my office, &c., forbid a compliance with your request.
                 " G. WASHINGTON.

" MARCH 30, 1796."

14th CON. 1st SESS.—22

Mr. HUGER said he would not venture to add a single word more on the subject, but resume his seat, lest, perchance, some observation of his might draw the attention of the House from the extracts he had just read, or weaken the effect of the opinion in regard to the point at issue between honorable gentlemen, so unequivocally given by that immortal man, who was by all acknowledged to have been equally the founder of this great Republic, and the father of that Constitution they were about to interpret.

Mr. RANDOLPH and Mr. WRIGHT followed in some remarks; when the question on the passage of the bill was taken, and decided in the affirmative—yeas 86, nays 71, as follows:

YEAS—Messrs. Adgate, Alexander, Baker, Barbour, Bassett, Bateman, Birdsall, Birdseye, Blount, Brooks, Bryan, Burnside, Burwell, Caldwell, Cannon, Clarke of North Carolina, Clendennin, Clopton, Comstock, Condict, Conner, Crawford, Creighton, Cuthbert, Darlington, Desha, Forsyth, Griffin, Hahn, Hall, Hammond, Hawes, Heister, Henderson, Hungerford, Ingham, Jackson, Johnson of Virginia, Johnson of Kentucky, Kerr of Virginia, King of Massachusetts, Lowndes, Lumpkin, Lyle, Maclay, Mayrant, McCoy, McLean of Kentucky, McLean of Ohio, Middleton, Murfree, Nelson of Virginia, Newton, Parris, Pickens, Piper, Pleasants, Powell, Randolph, Reynolds, Roane, Robertson, Root, Ross, Savage, Schenck, Sharpe, Sheffey, Smith of Virginia, Southard, Taul, Taylor of New York, Taylor of South Carolina, Telfair, Townsend, Tucker, Wallace, Wendover, Whiteside, Wilde, Wilkin, Williams, Willoughby, Thomas Wilson, William Wilson, and Yancey.

NAYS—Messrs. Atherton, Baylies, Betts, Boss, Bradbury, Breckenridge, Brigham, Brown, Cady, Calhoun, Champion, Chappell, Chipman, Cilley, Clark of Kentucky, Clayton, Culpeper, Davenport, Forney, Gaston, Gold, Goldsborough, Grosvenor, Hanson, Hardin, Herbert, Hopkinson, Huger, Hulbert, Jewett, Kent, King of North Carolina, Langdon, Law, Lewis, Love, Lovett, Lyon, Marsh, Mason, McKee, Mills, Milnor, Moffit, Moore of South Carolina, Moseley, Nelson of Massachusetts, Noyes, Ormsby, Pickering, Pitkin, Reed, Rice, Ruggles, Sergeant, Smith of Pennsylvania, Stanford, Strong, Stuart, Sturges, Taggart, Tallmadge, Thomas, Throop, Vose, Ward of New York, Wheaton, Wilcox, Woodward, Wright, and Yates.

Ordered, That the title be "An act to regulate the commerce between the United States and the territories of His Britannic Majesty, according to the convention concluded on the 3d day of July, 1815, and the ratifications of which were exchanged on the 22d day of December, 1815."

MONDAY, January 15.

Several other members, to wit: from New Hampshire, WILLIAM HALE; from Massachusetts, ASAHEL STEARNS and ARTEMAS WARD; and from New Jersey, BENJAMIN BENNETT, appeared produced their credentials, were qualified, and took their seats.

Mr. GROSVENOR presented a petition of the Columbian Manufacturing Society, in the State of New York, praying that additional duties may be imposed on cotton goods imported from foreign countries.—Referred to the Committee on Commerce and Manufactures.

Mr. GOLD presented a petition of Elizabeth Hamilton, widow of the late General Alexander Hamilton, deceased, praying that the commutation of half pay, due for the services of her said husband, as an officer of the Revolutionary Army, may be paid to his representatives.—Referred to the Committee on Pensions and Revolutionary Claims.

Mr. TUCKER, from the District Committee, made an unfavorable report on the petition of the Masonic Lodge in Alexandria, called Washington Lodge, No 22, who pray for authority to raise money by way of lottery for certain purposes. The report is adverse to the petition, on the general ground of hostility to lotteries. The report was ordered to lie on the table.

On motion of Mr. EASTON, the Committee of Ways and Means were instructed to inquire into the expediency of making an appropriation, by law, sufficient to discharge and satisfy the claims of such individuals as are entitled to compensation on account of depredations committed by the Osage Indians.

The bill from the Senate "relative to evidence in cases of naturalization," was read twice, and referred to Messrs. JOHNSON of Kentucky, PITKIN, THOMAS WILSON, WENDOVER, and BAYLIES.

The bill from the Senate "confirming to the Navigation Company of New Orleans, the use and possession of a lot in said city ;" was read the first time.

THE REVENUE.

The House, on motion of Mr. LOWNDES, resolved itself into a Committee of the Whole, on the report of the Committee of Ways and Means on so much of the President's Message, and the annual Treasury report, as relates to the revenue.

The first resolution having been read, in the following words, viz :

Resolved, That it is expedient to continue in force, until the 30th day of June next, and until an act shall be passed establishing a new tariff of duties, the act, entitled "An act for imposing additional duties upon all goods, wares and merchandise, imported from any foreign port or place, and for other purposes ;" passed on the 1st of July, 1812.

Mr. LOWNDES gave a general explanation of the views of the committee in regard to this resolution ; referring, for the grounds of it, to the instruction given to the Secretary of the Treasury to report a tariff of duties, and the implied intention of the Congress to act on that subject at the present session.

Mr. SERGEANT explained the grounds of his hostility to the present form of this resolution. The period to which it was proposed to extend the double duties, and the terms in which it was conveyed, he considered very objectionable, as well on account of the mercantile as of the manufacturing interest. As to the one, it would introduce an uncertainty prejudicial to their business ; and, as to the manufacturers, he apprehended the effect of the resolution would be to alarm the whole manufacturing interest, which was now looking up to the Government for additional support, instead of expecting an early reduction of the existing duties. Mr. S., under these impressions, moved to strike out of the resolution the words, "the 30th day of June next, and until an act shall be passed, establishing a new tariff of duties," and, in lieu thereof, to insert "the first day of January next."

Mr. HUGER opposed this motion, on the ground that it proposed to collect heavy taxes from the agricultural part of the community, the consumers, in order to accommodate the merchant, who happened to have unexecuted orders abroad. Mr. H. though friendly, as he remarked in the course of his speech, to commerce and manufactures, could not consent to tax his constituents, during peace, for the benefit of the merchants, to the same extent as was thought necessary under all the pressure and exigencies of the war.

Mr. WRIGHT went still farther than Mr. HUGER in his opposition to the continuation of the double duties. He was opposed to continuing them a single day beyond the time already fixed for the expiration of the law. He was opposed to taxing the great body of the agricultural community in any way that could possibly be avoided, merely for the benefit of merchants or manufacturers. He was opposed to heavy taxes, proposed to be continued, in any shape, because he did not consider it necessary for any valuable purpose ; and he appeared to be very positive in his opinion, that the interest of the merchant and manufacturer were not a sufficient motive for perpetuating oppressive taxes on the landed interest, &c.

The question, on Mr. SERGEANT's motion was decided in the negative, without a division.

The first resolution, in the words above, was then agreed to without a division.

The second resolution, in the following words, being under consideration, viz :

Resolved, That it is expedient to continue in force the act, entitled "An act laying a duty on imported salt ; granting a bounty on pickled fish exported, and allowances to certain vessels employed in the fisheries ;" passed the 29th of July, 1813.

This resolution was agreed to by a majority of more than three to one.

The third resolution, in the following words, was then read :

Resolved, That it is expedient to continue in force the act, entitled "An act laying duties on sugar, refined, within the United States ;" passed on the 24th of July, 1813.

Mr. HUGER moved to reject this resolution. Sugar, in some countries a luxury, had become in the United States, he said, a necessary of life ; besides which, it had become one of the principal manufactures of the nation. But this was not all ; by the effects of embargoes and war for some years, and now, by our exclusion of our ships from the West India islands, sugar had become so dear as to be obtained with difficulty ; and refined sugar in particular, so scarce, that it could not be had sometimes for money. At Charleston, he had sought at one time for some refined sugar, and found that there was not a loaf to be had in that city, while in Philadelphia the sugar refiners, he understood, had given up their work.

Mr. LOWNDES said, that the expenditure of the Union on refined sugar did not exceed $150,000 a year. Such a sum, paid too generally by the opulent, could not, he said, be oppressive.

The resolution was agreed to by a large majority.

The fourth resolution, for continuing the present stamp duties on bank notes, &c., came next under consideration.

This resolve was opposed by Messrs. STRONG, WRIGHT, and MILNOR, on account of the insignificance of the proceeds thereof, when contrasted with the inconvenience to which it puts the community, and the partiality of its operations. To which arguments, Mr. SOUTHARD, as well as Mr. LOWNDES, replied, denying the justice of the character given to the tax, and asserting its facility of collection, and operation on wealthy or moneyed men, as giving it a preference to almost any other tax embraced in the system.

Mr. BURNSIDE moved to amend the resolution so as to confine the continuation of duties to those on the notes of banks, bankers, and certain companies, (excluding notes discounted, and on bills of exchange.) This motion was supported by himself and Mr. MILNOR; and opposed by Mr. LOWNDES. It was negatived by a decided majority.

The resolution itself was then agreed to by a large majority.

The fifth resolve, which proposes to abolish the additional duty on postage, was then taken up and agreed to by a large majority.

Mr. LOWNDES suggested that the Committee should rise and report these resolutions to the House, before acting on the remainder of the report. The resolutions already agreed to, applied to laws which will expire on the 18th of February, and he wished them to be referred to the Committee of Ways and Means, in order to report bills conformably thereto.

Mr. SERGEANT endeavored to prevent the Committee's rising, in order to bring before the House the resolution for repealing the duties on manufactures, &c.; a speedy decision of which he considered of great importance.

Mr. LOWNDES opposed this course, because of certain information on the subject thereof, required by the Committee, which was not yet ready.

The motion for the Committee to rise was agreed to; and the question was about to be put on concurring with the Committee of the Whole in their agreement to the first resolution.

Mr. RANDOLPH rose, and commenced a speech in a rather desultory but pointed manner, on the general character of the report of the Committ e of Ways and Means, which he condemned. H°e had not spoken long, when the SPEAKER intimated that he had digressed too far from the subject of debate.

An appeal was taken by Mr. HANSON from the Speaker's decision on this point; which, after much acrimonious and some argumentative debate, was affirmed by the House, by a vote of 79 to 59.

Mr. RANDOLPH resumed his discourse, which he concluded just before sun-set.

Mr. GOLDSBOROUGH then moved to amend the said first resolution, by striking out all that part of it which refers to a "new tariff." Whereupon, the House adjourned.

TUESDAY, January 16.

Mr. WARD, of Massachusetts, presented a petition of Jane A. Blakely, of Boston, in the State of Massachusetts, stating her fears for the loss of her husband, Captain Johnston Blakeley, of the United States ship-of-war "Wasp," and praying that measures may be adopted for the support of herself and the daughter of the said Captain Blakeley.—Referred to Messrs. WARD of Massachusetts, CONNER, NELSON of Massachusetts, PARRIS, and BIRDSEYE.

Mr. NELSON, of Massachusetts, presented a similar petition from the wives and mothers of sundry petty officers and seamen on board the said ship; which was referred to the committee last appointed.

Mr. WARD, of Massachusetts, presented a petition of sundry manufacturers of cotton goods, in the State of Massachusetts, praying that such measures may be adopted by the General Government as will afford security and encouragement to the manufacturing establishments within the United States.

Mr. WARD also presented a petition of the master hatters in Boston, praying that the tax imposed on hats manufactured within the United States may be repealed.

Mr. WARD also presented a petition of the Vermont Mineral Factory Company, praying that a duty may be imposed on copperas imported into the United States from foreign countries.

Mr. STEARNS presented a petition of Samuel Kidder, junior, and others, engaged in a chemical establishment, praying that duties may be imposed on oil of vitriol, aqua fortis, spirits of nitre fortis, muriatic acid, alum, ink powder, sugar of lead, vermillion, flour of sulphur, red precipitate, corrosive sublimate, calomel, sal soda, and lunar caustic, imported from foreign countries.

Mr. STEARNS also presented a petition of Hyde Winship & Company, manufacturers of candles, praying that the duty imposed on mould tallow candles may be repealed.

Ordered, That the said petitions be referred to the Committee of Commerce and Manufactures.

Mr. WARD, of Massachusetts, presented a petition of sundry distillers in Boston, praying that the tax on spirits distilled from foreign materials may be repealed.

Mr. WARD also presented a petition of sundry auctioneers in Boston, praying that the duties imposed upon sales at auction may be reduced.

Mr. WARD also presented a petition of sundry

merchants in Boston, praying that a new tariff of duties may take effect on the 17th of February next, or that the double duties may continue until the 1st day of January, 1817.

Mr. STEARNS presented a petition of sundry manufacturers of tallow candles, in the county of Middlesex and State of Massachusetts, praying that the duty imposed upon mould tallow candles may be repealed.

Mr. PITKIN presented a petition of the master hatters in Hartford county, and State of Connecticut, praying that the tax imposed upon hats manufactured within the United States may be repealed.

Ordered, That the said petitions be referred to the Committee of the Whole, on the report of the Committee of Ways and Means of the 9th instant, upon the subject of revenue.

Mr. WARD, of Massachusetts, presented a petition of Jonathan Merry, praying compensation for sundry vessels, captured by French cruisers in the years 1796, 1797, and 1799, out of the moneys reserved by the Government of the United States in the purchase of Louisiana.—Referred to the Committee of Claims.

Mr. WARD also presented a petition of the Convention of Congregational Ministers, in the State of Massachusetts, praying that the mails may not be opened or transported on Sundays.—Referred to the Post Office Committee.

Mr. LYLE presented a petition of sundry inhabitants of Washington and Alleghany counties, in Pennsylvania, praying that the mails may not be opened or transported on Sundays.

Mr. LOWNDES laid before the House a letter from the Secretary of the Treasury, and a letter from the Commissioner of the Revenue, addressed to him as Chairman of the Committee of Ways and Means, containing estimates of the probable amount of the internal duties which have accrued, and will accrue for the year 1815; which were read, and referred to the Committee of the Whole on the report of the Committee of Ways and Means, of the 9th instant, upon the subject of revenue.

Mr. NEWTON, from the Committee of Commerce and Manufactures, made a report on the petition of William Hamon, which was read; when Mr. N. reported a bill for the relief of William Hamon; which was read twice, and committed to a Committee of the Whole.

Mr. NELSON, of Virginia, from the Committee on the Judiciary, reported a bill supplementary to the act, entitled "An act regulating and defining the duties of the judges of the Territory of Illinois," and for vesting in the courts of the Territory of Indiana a jurisdiction in chancery cases arising in that Territory; which was read twice, and committed to a Committee of the Whole.

Mr. NELSON also reported a bill providing an additional compensation to the district judge of the southern district of New York, for performing the duties of judge of the northern district thereof; which was read twice, and committed to a Committee of the Whole.

Mr. JOHNSON, of Kentucky, from the Committee on Military Affairs, reported a bill making further provision for military services during the late war, and for other purposes; which was read twice, and committed to the Committee of the Whole on the bill making provision for an additional military academy.

Mr. JOHNSON also reported a bill for the liquidation of certain claims, and for other purposes; which was read twice, and committed to the Committee of the Whole last mentioned.

The bill from the Senate, "confirming to the Navigation Company of New Orleans the use and possession of a lot in said city," was read the second time, and referred to the Committee on the Public Lands.

On motion of Mr. PITKIN,

Resolved, That the correspondence between the American and British Commissioners, on the subject of the Commercial Treaty, lately negotiated between the United States and Great Britain, which have been printed by order of the Senate, and now made public, together with a tariff of duties on lumber imported into Great Britain, which was printed with said correspondence, be printed for the use of the House.

On motion of Mr. MARSH, the Committee on the Judiciary were instructed to inquire into the expediency of so altering the law of the United States, in relation to costs in the courts thereof, as to allow full costs in all cases in which the said courts have exclusive jurisdiction, notwithstanding the plaintiff shall not recover, in damages, the sum of five hundred dollars.

A message from the Senate informed the House that the Senate have passed a bill "authorizing the appointment of admirals;" in which they ask the concurrence of this House.

THE REVENUE.

The House resumed the consideration of the report of the Committee of the Whole, on a part of the propositions of the Committee of Ways and Means, respecting the revenue.

The question before the House was (as on the adjournment yesterday) on an amendment moved by Mr. GOLDSBOROUGH to the resolution proposing the continuance of the double duties until June next. This amendment of Mr. GOLDSBOROUGH proposed to strike out so much as proposes to continue the double duties until a new tariff shall be established by law.

After a few remarks from Mr. GASTON and Mr. GOLDSBOROUGH, respecting this amendment—

Mr. RANDOLPH, after stating that he had a motion to offer, said that he was induced to believe that it was through inattention the very extraordinary proceeding of yesterday was suffered to pass *sub silentio*—he meant that of the Committee of the House going through a part only of the report of the Committee of Ways and Means—sending it back to be reported in the shape of bills, and leaving the rest of it behind to be separately acted upon; for he would venture to affirm, that it was the first time a committee of that or of any other legislative assembly had ever made a report in part. There were twelve resolutions—five of those had been detached, to be served upon again, when done, in the shape of bills, while the remaining seven were left behind to employ the House. It was not, however, on the point of Parliamentary incorrectness that he founded his motion, but on still more important grounds.

It was proposed to levy what he called grievously heavy burdens, though perhaps what other gentlemen would denominate only necessary supplies. By the good old rules of the House—which seemed to him to have shared the fate of the poet's old silk stockings in the anecdote, and to have been so often darned, and altered, and cobbled, that it was doubtful whether any part of the original texture remained behind—every bill for laying taxes was required to be discussed in a Committee of the Whole. But in the present case, he said, that would not have been done. It might have been recommitted, but gentlemen did not choose to discuss it in a Committee of the Whole, and may say that when the bills upon the resolutions are reported, they may then be discussed. But what security was there, that when they were reported they would not be grasped with the same strong hand as before, and as they had been refused discussion in the Committee, be again proceeded upon without discussion; for gentlemen might as well order them to be engrossed, as do what they had already done with them. The rules of the House, he repeated, were that every measure of the kind should be fully discussed in a Committee of the House. On these grounds he intended to move (and he desired the House to observe that he asked no favor, nothing but the established law, sheer law,) that these resolutions be recommitted to a Committee of the Whole, in order that the measure might proceed, and the taxes be laid in the true spirit of the Government; or, is it come to that with us, exclaimed Mr. R., that we dare take upon us to double all the taxes upon the people of this country, with as little concern or ceremony as we order a petition to go to this or to that committee.

Mr. Randolph added, that he moved the recommitment on two grounds.

The first of those grounds, he said, was the conduct of the House in reporting a part of the resolutions, and not discharging the committee from the rest.

The second, because there had been no discussion of the report in the Committee; and that, on the contrary, all discussion had, by a solemn decision, been stifled.

Mr. Ingham endeavored to justify the conduct of the Committee, by a precedent from the proceedings of the last Congress, in laying these very taxes.

Mr. Stanford replied to Mr. Ingham; after which, the question was put and negatived—yeas 59, nays 91, as follows:

Yeas—Messrs. Baer, Baylies, Boss, Bradbury, Breckenridge, Brigham, Chipman, Cilley, Clopton, Cooper, Culpeper, Davenport, Gaston, Goldsborough, Grosvenor, Hale, Hanson, Hardin, Herbert, Hopkinson, Hunger, Hulbert, Kent, King of Massachusetts, King of North Carolina, Law, Lewis, Lovett, Lyon, Marsh, Mason, McKee, McLean of Ohio, Mills, Milnor, Moore of South Carolina, Moseley, Nelson of Massachusetts, Noyes, Pickering, Pitkin, Randolph, Reed, Reynolds, Rice, Roane, Ruggles, Sergeant, Sheffey, Smith of Pennsylvania, Stanford, Strong, Stuart, Sturges, Tallmadge, Vose, Wilcox, Williams, and Wright.

Nays—Messrs. Adgate, Alexander, Baker, Barbour, Bassett, Bateman, Bennett, Betts, Birdsall, Birdseye, Blount, Brooks, Bryan, Burwell, Cady, Caldwell, Calhoun, Cannon, Chappell, Clarke of North Carolina, Clark of Kentucky, Clayton, Clendennin, Comstock, Condict, Conner, Crawford, Creighton, Cuthbert, Darlington, Desha, Forney, Forsyth, Gold, Griffin, Hahn, Hawes, Heister, Henderson, Hungerford, Ingham, Irwin of Pennsylvania, Jewett, Johnson of Virginia, Johnson of Kentucky, Kerr of Virginia, Love, Lowndes, Lumpkin, Lyle, Maclay, Mayrant, McCoy, McLean of Kentucky, Middleton, Moffit, Murfree, Nelson of Virginia, Newton, Ormsby, Parris, Pickens, Piper, Pleasants, Powell, Root, Savage, Schenck, Sharpe, Smith of Virginia, Southard, Taul, Taylor of New York, Taylor of South Carolina, Telfair, Thomas, Throop, Townsend, Tucker, Wallace, Ward of New York, Wendover, Whiteside, Wilde, Wilkin, Willoughby, Thomas Wilson, William Wilson, Woodward, Yancey and Yates.

The question then recurred upon Mr. Goldsborough's amendment.

Mr. Wright, of Maryland, spoke as follows:

Mr. Speaker, I wish to remind the House, that we are legislating for the nation, and not for the merchants and manufacturers exclusively, and that the good of the whole ought to be the pole star to guide us. I hope the time proposed for the extension of the double duties will not obtain; but the 17th of February next, the time fixed by the provisions of the law, which does not only fix the time to one year after the termination of the year, but expressly declares it shall continue "no longer," whereby the faith of the nation has been pledged to the American people that the double duties shall then cease. There is no doubt a portion of the people near the Canada line, who have been engaged in smuggling, who would make it perpetual, and thereby pocket the double duties; as the great inundation of tin-carts during the war, filled with goods from Canada, will attest. But I should hope that honorable gentlemen on this floor, would not countenance the continuance of so impious a practice. The merchants of Boston, with the highly respectable Mr. William Gray at their head, petition for the discontinuance of the double duties on the 17th of February, agreeably to the plighted faith of the nation, as they had directed their importations, so that they might arrive after the expiration of the law imposing them. Sir, I am prepared to adopt a sound corrected tariff of duties, but not prepared to continue, one hour, the double duties, in violation of the nation's faith. Sir, permit me here to present-briefly my objection to the system of taxes now proposed; I wish, therefore, to be permitted to call gentlemen back to the year 1795, when the public debt amounted to seventy millions, and when, under General Washington's Administration, it was provided, by the Sinking Fund, to sink the debt in twenty-eight years; then, sir,

683   HISTORY OF CONGRESS.   684

H. of R.   *The Revenue.*   January, 1816.

twenty-eight years was thought a sufficient time to sink seventy millions, but now, sir, after a glorious war, which has greatly distressed the American people, especially when the enemy pressed them—and I can speak from experience, for Kent Island, twenty-one miles by seven, a part of the county where I reside, was a long time in their possession, and our militia were constantly out; nor was the Western Shore less oppressed, as my colleague, General Stuart, can attest—we are called on to pay, on the heels of the war, one hundred and twenty millions in twelve years. Sir, have we forgot the *quasi* war, and the taxes imposed for its prosecution, and the consequences? I hope not; and I hope neither we nor the nation will ever forget, that, at the commencement of Jefferson's republican Administration, we repealed all the internal taxes as unnecessary, unless some untoward circumstances should occur —such as war. We then dismissed the sixteen midnight judges, as they were called. Gentlemen well recollect my devotion to the prosecution of the war, and my readiness to impose the necessary taxes for that purpose; but, above all, the readiness of the people to pay those taxes; and that they had covered the nation with glory, and themselves with imperishable laurels, so as justly to claim at our hands as much indulgence as had been granted the people under Washington's Administration. If, then, twenty-eight years was allowed for the payment of seventy millions, can it now be just to compel our people to pay one hundred and twenty millions in twelve years, the time proposed by the plan before us? Sir, we can, after the establishment of a correct tariff of duties, dismiss the internal taxes as well now as in 1812, and in my judgment with the same propriety; and it is now necessary for the ease of the people. Sir, the public debt in 1802, when compared with the revenue of that day, and the demands of the Treasury, was as great as it is now, when compared with the increased population; and the consequent increase of the revenue from imposts and tonnage, and the sale of the public lands, and the surplus revenue arising from those sources, will effect a sinking fund sufficient to sink the present debt of one hundred and twenty millions as rapidly as the debt of seventy millions was provided to be sunk in 1795. I therefore invoke gentlemen to consider well the measures now under consideration, and not act a hasty or imprudent part; although I never considered a national debt a national blessing, I cannot consent to its extinguishment by oppression.

Mr. Grosvenor and Mr. Huger spoke in favor of the amendment, and Mr. Taylor and Mr. Lowndes against it.

It was contended, by the advocates of this amendment, that to retain the clause referring to a new tariff, would introduce a looseness and vagueness in our laws, and produce an uncertainty as to the intentions of Congress, which would be prejudicial as well to individual as to public interest. By the opponents of the amendment it was contended that the present phraseology would mislead the public mind, and deceive interested individuals as to the views of Congress, which, unquestionably, favored the establishment of a new tariff; and would besides prejudice the public interest, inasmuch as a concurrence of circumstances, such as long discussion, clashing opinions on the details, &c., might protract the adoption of a new tariff of duties beyond the 30th of June, the time prescribed in this resolve for the expiration of the double duties.

Mr. Sergeant spoke at considerable length, and with much zeal, in behalf of the manufacturers, whose interests he evinced much anxiety to guard; but he said he would vote against the proposed amendment, because he was disposed to extend the limitation of time to January next.

Mr. Randolph asked the Speaker, if the question were not on striking out of the resolution the words "and until an act shall be passed establishing a new tariff?"—and on the Speaker answering in the affirmative—so I thought, said Mr. R., and yet I could not help doubting my understanding on the case. This is a limitation I have never before known or heard of. A law to remain in force, not to a particular time, but until a particular contingency shall have happened; until another law now in contemplation shall have passed! This, sir, is such a curiosity in legislation as I have not only never witnessed or heard of but, never so much as imagined; and as not only myself, but, I do most potently believe, no man living, or that ever lived, did hear of. This question, sir, has been an old bone of contention between the two parties which divide this country, almost from the establishing of the Constitution. It was always a principle obstinately maintained by the Federalists, that the power of taxing extended beyond this House, and that taxes might be imposed permanently; while the opposite party as obstinately contended that the power over taxation, could not, constitutionally, be let out of the hands of the Representatives; or, in other words, that the makers of the Constitution never intended to impart to the Senate or the President any right to impose taxes on the people. To every gentleman who knows the history of our Government, and to every member who has been familiar with this House and its proceedings, for any considerable length of time, it is well known to have been the constant subject of controversy, or, as I said before, a never failing bone of contention, as much so at least as any other subject; and the point being now voluntarily surrendered by the very men who had ranged themselves on the side of those who maintained the exclusive right of this House to taxation, is to me a proof, additional to the many I have long had, that the time is come when the system of Mr. Jefferson, though it was the ladder by which the present Administration mounted into power, is to be departed from, both in practice and theory, in the conduct of public affairs, and that the great principles which governed the policy of Mr. Jefferson are to be entirely renounced. It is true of all free Governments—and it is still more true of that of the United States than any other in the world— that the House in which the people are represented should never yield to any other, in the slightest extent, the power over the purse. This, sir, is a Government of compromise, in the settling of which, we, the great States, stipulated, as the terms of the compromise, that the smallest of those States should be of equal weight with ourselves in the Senate, and in the election of a President greater than in proportion to their strength—a fact the House should never lose sight of. Let the Senate then do their duty, let them make those acts which by the Constitution they are authorized to do—but let them not originate any money bills—never give that staff out of your own hands to be voted away by that body. I have infinitely less jealousy of the President, (I do not speak personally of him who now fills that office, I speak of the Chief Magistrate of the United States, whoever and whenever he may be,) than I have of the Senate. It is in human nature, sir; not having lawfully the power to originate money bills, on money bills they will be most likely to make attempts to evince their power; like all other bodies they will be animated by the impulse of the *esprit de corps*, and will exercise it if you give them an opportunity. The question is, then, shall we give them that opportunity? We hear much said about taxes, about our funds being pledged to the public creditors; and about the national faith being violated with respect to those creditors if we should repeal the double taxes, oppressive as they are to the people. To this I answer that the public faith never was broken when I had a share in the councils of the country—and yet we did repeal an entire system of taxation, though the whole of it was pledged for the public debt; and here, sir, we have another proof that the present Government have renounced the true Republican principles of Jefferson's Administration on which they raised themselves into power, and that they have taken up, in their stead, those of John Adams. At that time—I mean when we repealed that system of taxation—the Federalists were against the repeal, as these men are now, and, like these, insisted that the taxes were pledged to the public creditors. This, sir, is another plain indication that they have changed the principle by their pretences to which they have gulled the people, and obtained their ascendency, and that, as I have somewhere else remarked, their principle now is old Federalism, vamped up into a something bearing the superficial appearance of Republicanism. Yes, we repealed those taxes upon the ground that so long as the nation should punctually pay the public creditor his due, the latter had no right to inquire out of what fund it came. Suppose, sir, I borrow a sum of money and promise to pay my creditor out of the sales of my next crop of cotton, and that I should think fit to raise corn enough to pay him, and choose to reserve my cotton in store for a more advantageous market—will any man be absurd enough to say that I violate the faith I had pledged to that creditor, if I do not sell my cotton? The Federalists at that time said, that we had violated the public faith—while we, on the other hand, contended that so long as the creditor

was paid his just demand, he had no right to ask where we got the means; whether we drew them, like the Federalists, from internal taxes, or, like the Republicans of that day, from our import duties, and the funds of the custom-house. But, sir, Jefferson had other funds—funds of his own—funds out of the reach, as it should seem, of our present financiers; his ways and means were the very reverse of theirs; his was economy, retrenchment; he put the country out of the reach of its creditors by retrenching the public expenditure to the amount of the debts to be paid. By these ways and means, the Treasury overflowed with wealth, and a committee was appointed, not to raise double taxes, or, by wholesale vote, to continue in force those already raised, but to dispose of the surplus revenue that flowed into the Treasury. Thus, he was accustomed to have lying by, in the Bank of the United States, from five to seven millions of dollars more than the expenses of the Government and the disbursements of the sinking fund, though he was all the time redeeming the public debt. That, sir, was the result of practising as well as preaching. That was the result of really acting upon the Republican principles he professed, instead of professing one principle and practising another—professing Republicanism and practising old Federalism. Can the House pass a more severe sentence on Mr. Jefferson, than in saying that the repeal of the internal taxes was a violation of the national faith? But, let us go to the proof—At the time I allude to, the six per cent. stocks were above par, payments being made, too, in good hard dollars; not rags, but silver, or, if you chose it, gold. What is the price now? you are at peace, and yet your stocks are at ninety-eight; and what is the value of the stuff you get for it, the rags?—why, thirteen per cent. under par, so that you get just eighty-five out of each hundred of your stock. But then there was a pledge to the people, who it seems are in a state of pupillacy and want guardians—(poor little things! I apprehend that in the administration of their affairs, the executorship is much better than the heirship,) a pledge to establish a sinking fund to redeem the debts incurred by the mismanagement of the executors. You promised that if the minor would elect you his guardian, you would pay off the encumbrances on his estate. Did you do so? No; the ward was robbed, and his property was lavished away upon war feasts in Canada, and upon tilts, and shows, and tournaments.

My honorable colleague (Mr. Sheffey) has said, that the case of the manufacturers is not fairly before the House. True! it is not fairly before the House. It never can be fairly before the House; whenever it comes before us, it must come unfairly, not as "a spirit of health—but a goblin damned"—not "bringing with it airs from Heaven, but blasts from Hell"—it ought to be exorcised out of the House: for, what do the principles about which such a contest is maintained amount to, but a system of bounties to manufacturers, in order to encourage them to do that which, if it be advantageous to do at all, they will do, of course, for their own sakes; a largess to men to exercise their own customary callings, for their own emolument; and Government devising plans, and bestowing premiums out of the pockets of the hard working cultivator of the soil, to mould the productive labor of the country into a thousand fantastic shapes; barring up, all the time, for that perverted purpose, the great, deep, rich stream of our prosperous industry. Such a case, sir, I agree with the honorable gentleman, cannot be fairly brought before the House. It eventuates in this: whether you, as a planter will consent to be taxed, in order to hire another man to go to work in a shoemaker's shop, or to set up a spinning jenny. For my part I will not agree to it, even though they should, by way of return, agree to be taxed to help us to plant tobacco; much less will I agree to pay all, and receive nothing for it. No, I will buy where I can get manufactures cheapest; I will not agree to lay a duty on the cultivators of the soil to encourage exotic manufactures; because, after all, we should only get much worse things at a much higher price, and we, the cultivators of the country, would in the end pay for all. Why do not gentlemen ask us to grant a bounty for the encouragement of making flour?—the reason is too plain for me to repeat it; then why pay a man much more than the value for it, to work up our own cotton into clothing, when, by selling my raw material, I can get my clothing much better and cheaper from Dacca.

Sir, I am convinced that it would be impolitic, as well as unjust, to aggravate the burdens of the people, for the purpose of favoring the manufacturers; for this Government created and gave power to Congress, to regulate commerce and equalize duties on the whole of the United States, and not to lay a duty but with a steady eye to revenue. With my good will, sir, there should be none but an ad valorem duty on all articles, which would prevent the possibility of one interest in the country being sacrificed, by the management of taxation, to another. What is there in those objects of the honorable gentleman's solicitude, to give them a claim to be supported by the earnings of the others? The agriculturists bear the whole brunt of the war and taxation, and remain poor, while the others run in the ring of pleasure, and fatten upon them. The agriculturists not only pay all, but fight all, while the others run. The manufacturer is the citizen of no place, or any place; the agriculturist has his property, his lands, his all, his household gods to defend; and, like that meek drudge, the ox, who does the labor, and ploughs the ground, and then, for his reward, takes the refuse of the farm yard, the blighted blades and the mouldy straw, and the mildewed shocks of corn for his support;—while the commercial speculators live in opulence, whirling in coaches, and indulging in palaces; to use the words of Dr. Johnson, coaches, which fly like meteors, and palaces, which rise like exhalations. Even without your aid, the agriculturists are no match for them. Alert, vigilant, enterprising, and active, the manufacturing interest are collected in masses, and ready to associate at

a moment's warning, for any purpose of general interest to their body. Do but ring the fire bell, and you can assemble all the manufacturing interest of Philadelphia, in fifteen minutes. Nay, for matter of that, they are always assembled, they are always on the Rialto; and Shylock and Antonio meet there every day, as friends, and compare notes, and lay plans, and possess in trick and intelligence, what, in the goodness of God to them, the others can never possess. It is the choicest bounty to the ox, that he cannot play the fox or the tiger. So it is to one of the body of agriculturists, that he cannot skip into a coffee-house, and shave a note with one hand, while with the other he signs a petition to Congress, portraying the wrongs, and grievances, and sufferings he endures, and begging them to relieve him; yes, to relieve him out of the pockets of those whose labors have fed and enriched, and whose valor has defended them. The cultivators, the patient drudges of the other orders of society, are now waiting for your resolution. For, on you it depends, whether they shall be left further unhurt, or be, like those in Europe reduced, *gradatim*, and subjected to another squeeze from the hard grasp of power. Sir, I have done.

Mr. SHEFFEY, and others, regarded the expression respecting the tariff as paving the way, if not absolutely providing for an indefinite continuation of the double duties.

The motion of Mr. GOLDSBOROUGH was finally agreed to, by a majority of about ten votes.

Mr. SERGEANT then moved to strike out the "thirtieth June," (the day to which the continuation of the double duties is limited in the resolve,) and in lieu thereof to insert the "first day of January next."

Mr. KING was opposed to this motion; because, as he conceived, the national faith was pledged that the duties should expire on the 18th of next month.

Mr. SERGEANT earnestly and at large supported his motion.

The motion was negatived, however—77 to 56.

WEDNESDAY, January 17.

Mr. HAMMOND presented a petition of sundry inhabitants of the United States, praying that such measures may be adopted as will encourage and promote the interests of the cotton manufacturing establishments within the United States.

Mr. MIDDLETON presented a petition of the City Council of Charleston, in South Carolina, praying to be repaid the moneys expended by the said corporation in the support and maintenance of seamen confined by sickness in the marine hospital in that city, and that additional funds may be provided for the use of the said hospital.—Referred to the Committee of Commerce and Manufactures.

Mr. GASTON presented a petition of the Legislature of the Territory of Missouri, praying that a tract of land may be granted to the commissioners of the county of Laurence, on which they propose to authorize the erection of a town and court-house, and other public buildings.—Referred to the Committee on Public Lands.

Mr. TUCKER presented a petition of the Levy Court of the county of Washington, in the District of Columbia, praying that the powers granted to the said court, by an act authorizing them to erect a penitentiary, may be enlarged and extended.—Referred to the Committee on the Judiciary.

On motion of Mr. JOHNSON, the Military Committee were discharged from the further consideration of the petition of the officers and soldiers of the twenty-third regiment of United States' infantry, praying for permission to locate their lands in one body; and the petitioners had leave to withdraw their memorial.

The bill from the Senate "authorizing the appointment of Admirals" was read twice, and referred to the Committee on Naval Affairs.

THE REVENUE.

The House resumed the consideration of the first five propositions of the Committee of Ways and Means respecting the revenue.

The first resolution, for continuing in force the double duties on imports and tonnage until the 30th day of June next, being still under consideration—

Mr. MACLAY moved a reconsideration of yesterday's vote, whereby the House refused to strike out of said resolve the 30th June, and insert the 1st January.

The House having agreed to reconsider the said question—66 to 63—the question again presented itself to strike out the 30th day of June, and insert the 1st day of January, so as to prolong the double duties to the latter day.

On this question, the whole ground of debate occupied yesterday and the preceding day was again travelled over. The advocates of this motion maintained that its adoption was necessary to secure the manufacturers from loss, and almost ruin, as well as to enable the merchants to lay their course intelligently in the business of the approaching season. On the other hand, it was contended by some that the extension of these duties would be an unnecessary and grievous tax on the consumers for the benefit of the manufacturers, and the convenience of the merchants; and by other gentlemen the broad ground was taken that the faith of the Government being pledged to discontinue the duties at the end of one year after the expiration of the war, it would of course be more unjust to protract their cessation to a more distant day, than to that already proposed in the resolve.

Many topics not directly applicable to the subject were brought into the question, and complained of by some of the gentlemen who mingled in debate, who said that the interests of manufacturers did not belong to this question, nor perhaps the interests of the merchants; that it was a question of national policy, which ought to stand on its own merits. And some of those who spoke and voted against the extension to January, did so on the ground that such a course would be equally adverse to the interests of the manufacturer and merchant, as to those of the community generally.

The gentlemen who spoke on the affirmative side of this question were, Messrs. SERGEANT and BURNSIDE; and those on the negative side. Messrs. LOWNDES, ROSS, GROSVENOR, PITKIN, WRIGHT, KING, GASTON, MILLS, PICKERING, and RANDOLPH.

The question on this motion was at length decided, late in the day, by the following vote:

YEAS—Messrs. Betts, Birdseye, Blount, Brooks, Bryan, Burnside, Cannon, Clendennin, Clopton, Conner, Creighton, Darlington, Desha, Hahn, Hawes, Heister, Henderson, Hopkinson, Ingham, Johnson of Kentucky, Kerr of Virginia, Lyle, Maclay, Mayrant, McCoy, McLean of Kentucky, McLean of Ohio, Milnor, Nelson of Virginia, Newton, Piper, Powell, Reynolds, Root, Sergeant, Strong, Taul, Taylor of New-York, Thomas, Throop, Wallace, Ward of N. York, Wendover, Whiteside, Williams, Thomas Wilson, and William Wilson—47.

NAYS—Messrs. Adgate, Alexander, Atherton, Barr, Baker, Barbour, Bassett, Bateman, Baylies, Bennett, Boss, Bradbury, Breckenridge, Brigham, Burwell, Cady, Caldwell, Calhoun, Chappell, Chipman, Cilley, Clarke of North Carolina, Clark of Kentucky, Clayton, Comstock, Condict, Cooper, Crawford, Culpeper, Cuthbert, Davenport, Forney, Forsyth, Gaston, Gold, Goldsborough, Griffin, Grosvenor, Hale, Hall, Hammond, Hanson, Hardin, Herbert, Huger, Hungerford, Irwin of Pennsylvania, Jewett, Johnson of Virginia, Kent, King of Massachusetts, King of North Carolina, Langdon, Law, Lewis, Love, Lovett, Lowndes, Lumpkin, Lyon, Marsh, McKee, Middleton, Mills, Moore, Moore of South Carolina, Moseley, Murfree, Nelson of Massachusetts, Noyes, Ormsby, Parris, Pickens, Pickering, Pitkin, Pleasants, Randolph, Reed, Roane, Robertson, Ross, Ruggles, Savage, Schenck, Sharpe, Sheffey, Smith of Pennsylvania, Smith of Virginia, Stanford, Stearns, Stuart, Sturges, Tallmadge, Taylor of South Carolina, Telfair, Townsend, Tucker, Vose, Ward of Massachusetts, Wilcox, Wilde, Willoughby, Wright, Yancey, and Yates—105.

So the motion to extend the continuance of double duties to the first day of January was negatived, and the House adjourned.

THURSDAY, January 18.

Mr. CILLEY presented a petition of the Exeter and Rockingham Cotton Manufacturing Companies, in the State of New Hampshire, praying that the importation from foreign countries of all cotton goods of a coarse texture may be prohibited.—Referred to the Committee of Commerce and Manufactures.

The following bills passed through Committees of the Whole, and were ordered to be engrossed for a third reading: the bill for the relief of the heirs of George Nebinger; the bill for the relief of Jonathan White; the bill for the relief of John G. Camp; the bill for the relief of Jonathan Rogers, jun., of Waterford, Connecticut; the bill for the relief of John Redman Coxe; and the bill for the relief of Joseph Anderson.

The bill for the relief of the widows and orphans of militia killed, or who have died of wounds re-

691   HISTORY OF CONGRESS.   692

H. of R.   *Colonization of Negroes—The Revenue.*   JANUARY, 1816.

ceived during the late war, was some time before a Committee of the Whole. The Committee rose, and the bill was referred to the Committee of the Whole on the bill making further provision for military services during the late war, and for other purposes.

Mr. HULBERT presented a petition of Ann Gerry, widow of Elbridge Gerry, deceased, late Vice President of the United States, praying that the salary which would have been paid to the deceased, had he lived to the end of the term for which he was elected, may be given to her, for the support of herself and children.—Referred to Messrs. HULBERT, CONNER, and GASTON.

Mr. ROBERTSON, from the Committee on the Public Lands, made a report on the petition of the Legislature of the Illinois Territory, referred on the 18th ult. and 9th instant, and on the petition of sundry inhabitants of the said Territory, referred on the 18th ult., which was read; when Mr. R. reported a bill, making further provision for settling the claims to land in the Territory of Illinois; which was read twice, and committed to a Committee of the Whole.

Mr. ROBERTSON also made a report on the petition of Antoine Drouet and Dillas, which was read; when Mr. R. reported a bill for the relief of certain claimants to land in the district of Vincennes; which was read twice, and committed to a Committee of the Whole.

Mr. ROBERTSON also made a report on the petition of sundry inhabitants of the Territories of Indiana and Illinois, referred on the 14th and 15th ult. and 16th inst.; which was read, and the resolution therein contained was concurred in by the House, as follows:

Resolved, That the prayer of the petitioners ought not to be granted.

COLONIZATION OF NEGROES.

Mr. ROBERTSON made a report on the petition of the Kentucky Abolition Society; which was read, and the resolution therein contained was concurred in by the House.

The report is as follows:

That, according to the petition, great numbers of slaves have been emancipated in different parts of the United States; that the number may be expected to increase daily; that they are not allowed the privileges of free citizens when they are emancipated, and are prohibited by law from emigrating to many of the other States and Territories; in consequence of all this, and, to use the words of the petition, as they are suffering many privations for the want of room and opportunities for the expansion of genius and encouragement to industry, they pray that a suitable territory may be laid off as an asylum for all negroes and mulattoes emancipated or to be emancipated within the United States; and that such donations, allowances, encouragement, and assistance, be afforded them as may be necessary for conveying them thither, and settling them therein. The committee beg leave to observe, that the Government is not in the habit of granting such advantages to white citizens, nor can they well perceive why they should be expected in favor of those of any other color. The public lands of the United States are sold or earned by services rendered to the country; and all those who

wish to reside on them have heretofore (as most probably they must continue to do) paid their own travelling expenses. The committee, too, cannot but believe that there is no part of our highly favored country where industry and economy will not insure to those who practise them an easy and independent support. The committee can see no cause for the interference of the Government on this subject; they have, consequently, prepared a resolution, which is respectfully submitted.

Resolved, That the prayer of the petition ought not to be granted.

The honorable the Speaker and Representatives of the United States of America in Congress assembled, the petition of the Kentucky Abolition Society, at their annual meeting, holden in Franklin county, near Frankfort, Kentucky, October 18 and 19, 1815, respectfully showeth:

That, whereas great numbers of slaves have been emancipated in different parts of these United States, and it may be expected, from the genius of our Government, and from a spirit of benevolence that seems to be taking place among all classes of citizens, that the number will be daily increasing: and whereas they are not allowed the privileges of free citizens where they are emancipated, and most of the States and Territories have passed laws to prevent this class of human beings from emigrating to them; and, from their poor and degraded situation where they at present reside, they are suffering many privations for the want of room and opportunities for the expansion of genius and encouragement to industry: and whereas there are vast tracts of unappropriated lands within the boundaries of the United States, and as we now enjoy a time of peace and prosperity, opening the way, and inviting the Government to so benevolent a project, we do therefore (and we make no doubt but we substantially speak the language of thousands of our fellow-citizens) most earnestly petition your honorable body, that you cause a suitable territory of lands to be laid off as an asylum for all those negroes and mulattoes who have been, and those who may hereafter be, emancipated within the United States; and that such donations, allowances, encouragement, and assistance be afforded them, as may be necessary for conveying them thither, and settling them therein; and that they be under such regulations and government, in all respects, as your wisdom shall dictate.

The friendly attention of your honorable body to this, our humble address, will ever be remembered with gratitude by your petitioners.

Signed by order of the Society, in annual meeting, as above written.

DAVID BARROW, *Pres't.*

Attest:

Moses MARTIN, *Sec'ry.*

THE REVENUE.

The House resumed the consideration of the unfinished business of yesterday, to wit: the 1st, 2d, 3d, 4th, and 5th resolutions attached to the report of the Committee of Ways and Means, of the 9th instant, upon the subject of Revenue; to which resolutions the Committee of the Whole have reported their agreement. Whereupon the House concurred with the Committee of the Whole in their agreement to the said first resolution, amended to read as follows:

1. *Resolved*, That it is expedient to continue in force, until the 30th day of June next, the act, entitled "An act for imposing additional duties upon all goods, wares, and merchandise, imported from any foreign port or place, and for other purposes," passed on the 1st July, 1812.

The question was then taken to concur, in like manner, in the second resolution, which is in the following words:

2. *Resolved*, That it is expedient to continue in force the act, entitled "An act laying a duty on imported salt, granting a bounty on pickled fish exported, and allowances to certain vessels employed in the fisheries," passed on the 29th July, 1813.

And it passed in the affirmative—yeas 90, nays 43, as follows:

YEAS—Messrs. Alexander, Baker, Barbour, Bassett, Bateman, Baylies, Bennett, Betts, Birdsall, Birdseye, Blount, Boss, Bradbury, Brooks, Bryan, Burnside, Caldwell, Calhoun, Cannon, Chappell, Clark of Kentucky, Clayton, Comstock, Condict, Conner, Creighton, Cuthbert, Desha, Forsyth, Glasgow, Gold, Griffin, Grosvenor, Hahn, Hammond, Hanson, Hardin, Hawes, Henderson, Hopkinson, Hulbert, Ingham, Kent, King of North Carolina, Law, Lowndes, Lyle, Maclay, Maykrant, McKee, McLean of Kentucky, McLean of Ohio, Middleton, Milnor, Moseley, Newton, Pickering, Pleasants, Powell, Reed, Reynolds, Root, Ross, Ruggles, Sergeant, Schenck, Smith of Pennsylvania, Smith of Virginia, Stearns, Sturges, Tallmadge, Taul, Taylor of New York, Taylor of South Carolina, Telfair, Thomas, Throop, Townsend, Tucker, Ward of Mass., Ward of New York, Wendover, Wheaton, Wilde, Wilkin, Willoughby, William Wilson, Woodward, Yancey, and Yates.

NAYS—Messrs. Atherton, Breckenridge, Brigham, Burwell, Cady, Chipman, Cilley, Clarke of North Carolina, Clopton, Culpeper, Gaston, Goldsborough, Hall, Herbert, Hungerford, Jewett, Johnson of Virginia, Kerr of Virginia, King of Massachusetts, Langdon, Love, Lovett, Lumpkin, Lyon, Marsh, McCoy, Mills, Moffit, Moore of South Carolina, Nelson of Mass., Nelson of Virginia, Noyes, Rice, Roane, Savage, Sheffey, Stanford, Strong, Stuart, Vose, Wilcox, Williams, and Wright.

The third, fourth, and fifth resolutions were then again read and concurred in by the House; which said resolutions are as follows:

3. *Resolved*, That it is expedient to keep in force the act, entitled "An act laying duties on sugar refined within the United States," passed on the 24th July, 1813.

4. *Resolved*, That it is expedient to continue in force the act, entitled "An act laying duties on notes of banks, bankers, and certain companies; on notes, bonds, and obligations, discounted by banks, bankers, and certain companies; and on bills of exchange of certain descriptions," passed the 2d of August, 1813; and also the act supplementary thereto, passed on the 10th day of December, 1814.

5. *Resolved*, That it is expedient to repeal, from the 3d day of March next, so much of the act, entitled "An act to provide additional revenues for defraying the expenses of Government, and maintaining the public credit, by duties on sales at auction, and on licenses to retail wines, spirituous liquors, and foreign merchandise, and for increasing the rates of postage," passed

on the 23d of December, 1814, as imposes additional duties on postage.

Ordered, That the said first, second, third, fourth, and fifth resolutions be recommitted to the Committee of Ways and Means, with instruction to report bills conformably thereto.

FRIDAY, January 19.

Mr. LOWNDES, from the Committee of Ways and Means, reported a bill to continue in force the act, entitled "An act for imposing additional duties upon all goods, wares, and merchandise, imported from any port or place, and for other purposes;" which was read twice, and committed to a Committee of the Whole.

Mr. LOWNDES, from the same committee, also reported a bill to continue in force an act, entitled "An act laying a duty on imported salt, granting a bounty on pickled fish exported, and allowances to certain vessels employed in the fisheries;" which was read twice, and committed to the Committee of the Whole.

Mr. LOWNDES, from the same committee, also reported a bill to repeal so much of an act, passed on the 23d of December, 1814, as imposes additional duties on postage; which was read twice, and committed to the Committee of the Whole last appointed.

Mr. LOWNDES, from the same committee, also reported a bill to continue in force certain acts therein mentioned; which was read twice, and committed to the Committee of the Whole last appointed.

On motion of Mr. EASTON, the Committee on Military Affairs were instructed to inquire into the expediency of allowing the non-commissioned officers and privates of the militia, army, and the several companies of rangers who served during the late war, interest on the respective sums due to them from the time they ought to have been paid until they shall be actually paid.

The following engrossed bills were read a third time and passed: A bill for the relief of George Nebinger; a bill for the relief of Jonathan White; the bill for the relief of John G. Camp; the bill for the relief of Jonathan Rogers, junior, of Waterford, Connecticut; the bill for the relief of Joseph Anderson; the bill for the relief of John Redman Coxe. The bills were all sent to the Senate for concurrence, except that for the relief of Joseph Anderson, which had previously passed that body.

COPPER COINS, &c.

Mr. ROOT, in offering a motion on this subject, said that the want of a national circulating medium had been a topic of much complaint. This subject had been referred to a committee, and that committee had reported a bill for establishing a National Bank as the means of producing the desired uniformity in the national currency, as regarded the circulation and exchange between different sections of the Union. But the evil of the absence of small change, Mr. R. said, was as generally felt by all classes of the community, as the difficulty of remittance of large sums. For a premium you can anywhere get from a broker such large money as will circulate; but not so with the small change that is in circulation, which, such as it is, will scarcely pass a stone's throw from the place where one receives it, and will scarcely be accepted by the servants at the taverns. How was this evil to be remedied? By the act establishing the Mint, Congress had enacted that the copper coin should be of a weight below what was the real value of the metal in bolts, bars, or sheets. The copper coin originally weighed eleven pennyweights; by a subsequent act of Congress in 1792, it was ordered that the cent should weigh 208 grains, or 8 pennyweights, 16 grains. By a subsequent act the President was authorized to reduce the weight of the cent, by proclamation, whenever he should think fit, two pennyweights.

Such a proclamation never had been issued, Mr. R. believed, and the weight of the cent therefore remained eight pennyweight sixteen grains. A pound avoirdupois, therefore, contained thirty-three cents and six and a half mills; whilst copper had frequently been much higher, and during the war double as much per pound; the price, however, being now reduced, was probably about par with cents. Owing to the high price of copper, the coinage of copper coin at the Mint had ceased for some time. It now appeared, from the report of the Director of the Mint, that the Mint was about to recommence the coinage of copper, of which it was estimated they could turn out about fifty tons in the course of a year. The coins, Mr. R. said, would, according to law, be distributed among the respective States, according to their population; they would be distributed in quantities, in casks, and there remained for sale as an article of merchandise, until the price of copper should be so much higher than the value of the cents as shall afford a sufficient profit on the sale of them, for the purpose of being melted up for sheets, bolts, or stills, &c. Mr. R. said he presumed the Director of the Mint was mistaken in supposing the cents already coined remained in the United States, unless in the form of bolts, &c. The copper coin of the United States had never been made a legal tender, because being worth more generally than the nominal value, people were glad enough to take them. There never had been any punishment enacted for counterfeiting it, because, for the same reason, there was no motive for the offence. If the weight should be diminished, however, both these measures might become necessary. He therefore moved,

"That the weight of the copper coin ought to be reduced to four pennyweights the cent.

"That the copper coin of the United States ought to be made a legal tender to the amount of one dollar.

"That provision ought to be made by law for the punishment of counterfeiting the copper coin of the United States."

On motion of Mr. CALHOUN, these propositions were referred to a select committee.

STANDING RULES AND ORDERS.

The House resolved itself into a Committee of the Whole, on the report of the Committee on the Rules and Orders of the House. After several amendments to the rules had been proposed and agreed to, Mr. STANFORD moved to expunge from them that which related to "the previous question." He said he owed it to himself and to the oath, which, as a member of that House, he had taken, to get rid, if possible, of a rule under which the most tyrannical control might be exercised over the House, and the debates of that assembly be deprived of their freedom, and by which the majority might exercise the most complete despotism, shutting out the Representatives of the people from the free Constitutional privilege of expressing their opinions and maintaining the rights of their constituents. He expressed his regret that such an abominable badge of slavery should have found its way into the regulations of any free deliberative assembly; gave a succinct history of its rise and progress in that House, and portrayed the pernicious effects of it, as shutting up, at the will and pleasure of the majority, the current of deliberation, and enabling them to get rid, when they pleased, of a discussion that was disagreeable to them, and of a decision that might be deemed hostile to their party or their purposes. The last mischievous construction of the rule—the last twist of the screw, he observed, was fastened upon them in a moment of excitement, partly in resentment at a resistance made to their measures, and perhaps partly for the despatch of business during the war. But now when, not only the war had ceased, but much of the asperities which existed at that time had vanished—when we were "all Federalists, all Republicans"—and there could no longer be a pretext for exercising it—when, in short, it could no longer be pretended to be wanting—he hoped it would be expunged, or suspended, and that as the House had got rid of the excitement, they would also get rid of the rule. If the minority had no right in debate, but what they were to owe to the courtesy of the majority, it was no longer a free deliberative assembly; nor could the country for which they were assembled to legislate be free. The right to deliver their sentiments in Congress they possessed from the people, and no majority in that House had a right to take it from them. He had seen the time when it would be resisted in that House, and he hoped he should see the time come again when such tyrannical rules would be disabled of their force, and chased out of the rules of Congress; the majority had no rights to give, and they could have none that he would receive at their hands.

Mr. RANDOLPH said he seconded Mr. STANFORD's motion with pleasure. He never rose with more satisfaction, and he hoped the rule would be modified so as to reinstate it, as it was in the Administration of Thomas Jefferson, during which period it was the same that it had been in the time of his predecessor. Mr. R. declared that he had listened to Mr. STANFORD with delight; his sentiments were of the good old times; they were worthy of the school in which he had been bred.

Mr. R. then entered into a history of the rule so obnoxious to every lover of freedom—a history in itself very curious and interesting, and rendered much more so by the felicitous manner in which he exhibited it. He brought the genealogy of the previous question down from a very remote period, and that, too, one of the worst of the British history; but he showed that though bearing the same name the present one differed from its ancestors, and differed very much for the worse. If it was to stain the rules and orders it ought to have a new name, and be called the *gag law*. What the Federalists called "the sedition law," he said his party called the *gag law*, and so ought this to be called. Not but that he owned the sedition law itself was good in many respects, the objection to it was that it assumed the exercise of a power which did not belong to Congress over the press, and insidiously usurped a jurisdiction denied by the Constitution; yet in comparison with the previous question, he said the sedition law was as white as wool—was indeed innocence itself.

Mr. R. then proceeded to carry on his history of the rule from its first entrance into the business of that House until it had arrived, upon a late occasion, to the highest degree of malignity and oppressiveness in its exercise; the most outrageous despotism over the counsels of the representative body. He could not depict it, he said, in stronger colors than by giving a simple statement of the fact, that the previous question was called while a member was addressing the Chair.

Mr. R. said that a member of that House who was so deprived of the freedom of speech that he could not at any time stand up and defend the invaded rights of his constituents was a *nuisance*—the slightest abuse of liberty seldom failed to end in slavery—and the liberty which the people of the United States did enjoy would be lost by this abuse. Yet, however, the nation's liberty was not entirely lost—it was "not less than Archangel ruined"—it was yet open to the House to preserve it. He then drew a picture of the mischiefs attending the application of the previous question in the hands of corrupt men, and said that, instead of being what every rule of that House ought to be—an instrument for the advancement and protection of the freedom of debate—it was perverted into an engine to intercept fair discussion, and prevent the sense of the House from being taken. If an amendment which startled the leaders of the majority were moved, instead of meeting it with reason, and letting it go for the sense of the House, one of the party had but to move the previous question, and the amendment instantly disappeared, as if it had sunk through a trap-door or fallen through a broken place in a bridge, and not a vestige was ever more heard of it—no, not so much as would serve to justify the member that offered it to his constituents, or to inform them what he had been endeavoring in vain to do for their interests. For example: if a member moved to propose twenty cents a bushel tax upon salt, and he (Mr. R.) taking into consideration that it would come too heavy on his constituents to tax so highly one of the most essential articles of life—one of the sacred emblems of hospitality—should propose to amend the resolution by substituting ten for twenty, the majority not finding it convenient to argue the case, or being unable to reason, and therefore like Falstaff, "if reasons were as plenty as blackberries," resolute not to give a reason on compulsion, should call for the previous question, the amendment would disappear; the unsuspecting, confiding people would be deceived, and would never hear that the amendment was moved, or that the Representative to whom they had confided their interests had done his duty; but on the contrary would conclude that he had voted for imposing on them that oppressive tax.

Thus, he said, amendments fell dead in that House, and with them the right of free discussion. There were other members of those rules, he said, which might well content those gentlemen, whatever their appetite might be for despotism. Some that might satisfy the grand inquisitor himself. The motion to reconsider was one of those—that simple rule might satisfy the most lynx-eyed duenna, anxious to restrain the wanton excursions of debate. There was another, too, always at hand, which was still superior to the previous question—*the call to order.* On this subject Mr. R. was very pointed and powerful. He showed from the rules of the British House of Commons, laid down by Mr. Hatsell, that no instance ever was known in that body of a member's being prevented from discussing any proposition, either immediately, *sub judice*, or that he wished to bring before them; and that the only interruption allowable in it, was confined to cases where anything touching the royal authority was introduced, which by the constitution were forbidden to be discussed in it. Not only Mr. Hatsell, but Mr. Onslow, who so long presided in that body, never saw a member of the minority or opposition bench refused a hearing—they would as soon think of stopping the vollied lightning of heaven, as of stopping the elder Pitt. No; in the British House of Commons debate was free.

After expatiating on better parts of the subject, as well as on several topics incidental and auxiliary to the train of his reasoning, Mr. R. declared it to be his conviction that if this rule continued on the books, it would sooner or later be resisted if put in practice; but whether resisted or not, it ought to be resisted, and at every or any hazard. He had ever been a Whig—a warm and sincere friend to the Revolution—but when he compared the tax upon tea, with this pernicious rule "the previous question," he doubted which struck most deeply at the personal rights of the people of America, or at the independence of the country.

Mr. CLAY rose in reply to Mr. RANDOLPH, and endeavored to justify the previous question—partly on the grounds of the Constitutional right of the House to make it—the majority had the power to make it, and therefore were right in making it; partly on the expediency—it was certainly expedient for the same reason; besides which, he thought the public interest required it. He said Mr. Randolph's history of the order had itself shown that the previous question was not resorted to until the abuse of debate rendered it expedient, and in illustrating this he reminded the House of the very remarkable circumstance of a certain gentleman having, for the purpose of delay, spoken four and twenty hours without stopping. He said that the House must adapt their rules to experience, until the objects of its institution were fulfilled.

He did not think it necessary to go to Great Britain for precedents; but if they did, he could show the superior freedom of our House, taking all the rules of the British House of Commons together. They had there, he said, a previous question for stopping members, peculiar to themselves—that was, making a noise to drown the voice of the person who endeavored to speak. Another was, that there was no protracting a debate beyond the rising of the House. Here, said Mr. C., have we not had a question debating for six or seven weeks? Mr. C. then adverted to the personal invectives in the British Parliament, contrary to all example in the American House of Representatives. He had himself, in the short time he was in London, heard a British Minister, high in office, charge a member with wishing to produce a revolution in the country; and he had heard that member retort upon the Minister the charge of bribery and corruption, and tell him that he ought to lose his head.

What would be the situation of the House, Mr. C. asked, without such a rule as the previous question; and what was it more than a declaration of the House that they had heard enough, and would proceed to decide; and that the majority were not to be controlled by the minority?

Mr. Gaston rose and spoke as follows:

Mr. Chairman, the proposition which has been made by my worthy friend and colleague (Mr. Stanford) to expunge from the rules of this House what is there called "the previous question," brings distinctly forward for consideration a subject which has the most imperious claims on the attention of every individual of this honorable body. It vitally concerns the rights of the members of this House, and the essential interests of the people whom they represent. From the moment, sir, I have been able to comprehend what, from that chair and on this floor, has been expounded to be "the previous question," I have believed it hostile to every principle of our Government, inconsistent with all notions of correct legislation, and without a precedent in the annals of any free deliberative assembly. At different periods of the last Congress I had thought of attempting to procure some amendment of this arbitrary rule, but I was prevented from prosecuting my purpose by a conviction that the party feelings which had grown out of the

war, and which had then reached their highest state of excitement, forbade all hope of that deliberate consideration which was indispensable to a correct decision. The present Congress, I have flattered myself, afforded a fit opportunity for a revision of this rule. With the return of peace to our land had returned also a spirit of mutual forbearance between the political parties of the House. Now, it might be practicable to discuss and decide a great question upon its intrinsic merits, and not simply with a view to its influence on the interests or purposes of faction. Indulging this hope, it was my fixed determination not to permit the present sessions to pass away without an effort to rescue my own rights, and the rights of those whom I represent, from the further oppression of this instrument of tyranny. I have been anticipated by my colleague, and I rejoice that I have been thus anticipated. From none could the call upon this honorable House to emancipate itself from the thraldom of "the previous question," proceed with more authority and propriety than from its oldest surviving son; from him who has witnessed the growth of this rule from its first intrusion here *to its present all-controlling domination.* And, sir, I rejoice equally at the opposition which the motion of my colleague has encountered. If this hideous rule could have been vindicated, we should have received that vindication from the gentleman who has just resumed his seat, (Mr. Clay.) If his ingenuity and zeal combined could form for the previous question no other defence than that which we have heard, the previous question cannot be defended. If beneath his shield it finds so slight a shelter, it must fall a victim to the just, though long delayed, vengeance of awakened and indignant freedom. If Hector cannot protect his Troy, the doom of Troy is fixed by fate.

It is indispensable, before we proceed further in the consideration of this subject, that we should perfectly understand what is our previous question. Gentlemen may incautiously suppose that it is the same with what has been called the previous question elsewhere. This would be a most fatal mistake. Our previous question is altogether "*sui generis,*" the only one of its kind; and to know it, we must consider not merely what is written of it in our code, but what it has been rendered by exposition and construction.

Our previous question "can only be admitted when demanded by a majority of the members present." It is a question "whether the question under debate shall now be put"—on the previous question "there shall be no debate." "Until it is decided, it shall preclude all amendment and debate of the main question." If it be decided negatively, viz: that the main question shall not now be put, the main question is of course superseded; but if it be decided affirmatively that the main question shall now be put, the main question is to be put instantaneously, and no member can be allowed to amend or discuss it. The previous question is entitled to precedence over motions to amend, commit, or postpone the main question, and therefore when admitted puts these entirely aside. This, according to the latest improvement, is now our rule of the previous question; and certainly in your Patent Office there is no model of a machine better fitted for its purposes than this instrument for the ends of tyranny. It is a power vested in the majority to forbid, at their sovereign will and pleasure, every member, not of that majority, from making known either his own sentiments or the wishes or complaints of his constituents, in relation to any subject under consideration, or from attempting to amend what is proposed as a law for the government of the whole nation.

It is a fundamental principle of civil liberty, that no citizen shall be affected in his rights without an opportunity of being heard in support of them. Our Constitution provides "that no citizen shall be deprived of life, liberty, or property, without due process of law." Every freeman is recognised by our Constitution as possessing also the right, either by himself or peaceably assembled with others, to petition the Government for a redress of grievances. The peculiar duties of the Representatives of freemen delegated with authority to bind their constituents by law, constitute these Representatives the agents of the people, to make known their grievances, their wants, and their wishes; that thus, by mutual and free intercommunication, rules of action may be framed fitted "to promote the general welfare." To refuse to receive the petition of the poorest and meanest member of society, alleging a grievance, and applying to the competent authority for redress, is an act of tyranny prohibited by the Constitution. To impair, by a judicial sentence, any one of his rights, or restrain him in the exercise of his freedom—to touch either his purse or his person, until after regular process to apprize him of the charge brought against him, and a full hearing of any defence he may urge by himself or his counsel, is confessedly iniquitous and unconstitutional. Yet by this detested rule, he, his neighbors, the whole community, may be mulcted with taxes to an indefinite amount, and subjected to obligatory rules of action, involving consequences fatal to liberty, property, and life, and their recognised agents, their Constitutional counsel, their Representatives, not suffered to allege a grievance or offer a defence! No individual can be condemned unheard—no individual can be refused a hearing of his petition. But thousands petitioning through their Representatives may be commanded into silence, and a whole country sentenced without a trial. The people are to be allowed Representatives in the great national council, who are forbidden to make known their wants—they are indulged with agents who are refused a hearing!

Sir, such absurdities will not bear examination. They cannot be tolerated by thinking and dispassionate men. It is vain to allege, in the language of the Speaker, that as the House is permitted by the Constitution "to determine the rules of its proceeding," it has a perfect right to forbid discussion, when, and as it pleases. It cannot (rightfully cannot) so regulate its proceedings as to annihilate the Constitutional franchise, either of a member or his constituents. They have a right to be heard before their money is voted, or their liberty restrained, and he is their delegated agent. The whole Congress cannot, by law, deprive them of their Constitutional franchise, to petition for redress of grievances; and this House is not competent to close the mouth through which the petitioners speak. Under the pretence of determining the rules of its proceedings, the House has no more authority to deny to any portion of the people the fair agency of their Representatives, than a court of justice under a plea of preserving decorum, to forbid a criminal the assistance of counsel. The power in either case is given for the preservation and more effectual enjoyment of the rights of which it is the guardian. It may regulate, but it cannot destroy them. It may prevent their abuse, but it cannot forbid their exercise. The court is not obliged to hear counsel as often as they may wish to speak, nor to tolerate impertinence or contempt. The House may not allow debate on a motion for adjournment, or a question whether language be indecorous, but if either forbid the duly constituted agent from performing his regular and proper functions, it is then usurpation, not right; it is abuse of power, not regulation. The privilege of the Representative to declare the will, to explain the views, to make known the grievances, and to advance the interests of his constituents, was so precious, in the estimation of the authors of our Constitution, that they have secured to him an irresponsibility elsewhere, for whatever may be uttered by him in this House; "for any speech or debate in either House, they (the Senators and Representatives) shall not be questioned in any other place." The liberty of speech is fenced round with a bulwark, which renders it secure from external injury—here is its citadel—its impregnable fortress. Yet here, even here, it is to be strangled by the bowstring of the previous question. In vain may its enemies assail it from without; but within, the mutes of despotism can murder it with impunity!

The existence of this arbitrary rule is incompatible with the independence which belongs to the character of a Representative. Called by the voice of a great and free people to the high (and I had almost said sacred) office of making laws for their government, we should all of us feel that our functions and the privileges essential to their discharge, are delegations of sovereignty, not the revocable precarious grants of a courteous majority of our own body; legislating for freemen we should ourselves be free. But what pretensions can he advance to freedom, who is indebted for the exercise of his supposed rights to the grace and favor of his associates? Our English ancestors considered those tenures free which were independent of another's will. To hold by the will of another was the tenure of a "villain"—a slave. And has the Constitutional right of a Representative of the people, in the freest of all free countries, become nothing more than a species of privileged villanage—of splendid servitude? Instead of the legislator being independent of all, but God and his country, in the exercise of his functions, is he to receive as a favor the permission of his fellows to take a part in legislation? The degradation is not the less, because those on whom he depends are equally degraded with himself. Each may be regarded as a slave, in an association of slaves, of which the majority are tyrants. Can it be, that to such a body, and so composed, the people of the United States designed, by their great Constitutional charter, to confide the mighty trust "of securing the blessings of liberty to themselves and their posterity?" Can it be that they should select as guardians of their rights those who should have no right to assert them? That never can be called a right which owes its existence to favor.

This rule of the previous question, instead of being sanctioned by the Constitutional authority which the House possesses of making rules to govern its proceedings, is at variance with the very object, for the attainment of which this power was delegated. The great purpose of rules in every community is to protect the weak against the tyranny of the strong. The end of regulations in a society where a majority governs, is to limit the power of the majority, and to secure the few from the oppressions of the many. The celebrated Arthur Onslow (who held the office of Speaker of the English House of Commons for more than three and thirty years, and discharged its duties with an ability and impartiality which have never been surpassed) used to remark, that "nothing tended more to throw 'power into the hands of Administration, and 'of a majority of the House of Commons, than a 'neglect of, or departure from, its rules; that the 'forms of proceeding, as instituted by their ances'tors, operated as a check and control on the ac'tions of ministers, and were a shelter and pro'tection to a minority against the attempts of 'those in power." And the accurate and judicious Hatsell, who has recorded this memorable observation, very properly remarks that it is founded in good sense, for that "it is always in the power 'of the majority, by their numbers, to stop any 'improper measures proposed on the part of their 'opponents;" but "the only weapons by which 'the minority can defend themselves against sim'ilar attempts from those in power are the rules 'of proceeding, by a strict adherence to which 'the weaker party can only be protected from 'those irregularities and abuses which these 'forms were intended to check, and which the 'wantonness of power is but too often apt to 'suggest to large and successful majorities."

Now, sir, it must be admitted, that the ordinary and correct course of legislation is, to afford a fair opportunity for a free interchange of opinions. "*Dieu deliberandum quod semel est statuendum*" is the old maxim, which, in Hakewell's quaint but expressive language, is thus paraphrased: "That which is to bear the stamp of a 'law must be a long time moulding; there must 'be previous debates, bandings of arguments, and

'clashings of opinions, pro and con, go before; 'for as we find that fire issueth forth from the 'concussion of flint and iron, so truth comes 'forth out of the eventillations and clashings of 'several opinions." It cannot be denied, too, that it is in the regular order of all deliberations to weigh and dispose of amendments before a final decision on the main subject. Yet the express end and aim of our previous question rule is, to prevent an interchange of opinions and to forbid amendments. Its purpose is to reverse everything like correct legislation, and to enable a "successful majority" in the "wantonness of power," unchecked "by forms of proceeding," unopposed by "the legitimate weapons of defence," to deprive the minority of every right, and to make its capricious will stand for reason, its passion for law. Surely strange notions have been broached at this inventive spot. It is right to subject the majority to the restraint of parliamentary rules, except when it chooses to be free from them! The majority shall not be permitted to oppress the minority, unless it have the inclination! Thus, also, a national bank is unconstitutional in good times, and oaths are registered in Heaven, but if the Government needs a bank, and the times prompt to a usurpation of power, then the Constitution accommodates itself to the exigency, and oaths are no longer troublesome. Constitutions and rules of proceeding are binding so long as there is no temptation to transgress them.

I have said, sir, that there is no precedent to be found in the annals of any free deliberative body for such a rule as our " previous question," and although I feel almost as great a repugnance to pledges as has been expressed by my eloquent friend from Virginia, (Mr. Randolph,) yet I pledge myself to maintain this position. In the English House of Commons the previous question has been known as a form of proceeding for more than two centuries, but it differs radically and essentially from our detested rule, which bears the same name. In England it can never be used so as to deprive any member of his right to discuss or to amend the question under debate. Ours is used avowedly for these purposes.

The origin of the previous question in the English House of Commons is hidden in obscurity. In Grey's Parliamentary Debates it is remarked by Sir Thomas Littleton, that Sir Henry Vane was the first that ever proposed putting a question " whether the question should be now put;" in consequence of which, the Speaker, Mr. Seymour (afterwards Sir Edward Seymour) observes: " No man can find any precedent of Sir ' Henry Vane's question. By that question we ' can never come to an end in any business. The ' question in being may be the next day put, and ' so you usher in an impossibility of bringing ' things to a period;" and Sir Robert Howard adds, in the spirit of prophecy, " This question is like the image of the inventor, a perpetual disturbance." The debate which gave rise to these remarks (March, 1672) turned upon the question whether a bill of supply should be engrossed before certain grievances were redressed. There is a debate (January, 1674) recorded in the same volume, wherein the previous question was used, and which respected the inquiry whether the House should proceed to the consideration of the King's speech, before it should ascertain by an address to the Crown whether, by the peace mentioned in the speech, is intended a separate or a joint peace. From these it would seem that an early, perhaps the first, use of the previous question was to postpone one subject in order to take up another. But whatever might have been its original use, it was early discovered to be susceptible of a service very convenient to ministers and their adherents, and to which they have since frequently applied it—that of getting rid of an unpleasant motion which it was not convenient to reject. The first instance I have seen of this application of the previous question, was in the case of this very Mr. Speaker Seymour, in October, 1673, who, probably afterwards, entertained a more favorable opinion of the previous question than what he had expressed about eighteen months before. Sir Thomas Littleton submits a motion to remove the Speaker and appoint a Speaker *pro tempore*, on the ground that the Speaker holds an office incompatible with the faithful discharge of his duties to the House—the office of privy counsellor to the King. This motion is supported by others on a different, and, what was then perhaps deemed a delicate ground, that the Speaker "exposed the honor of the House in resorting to gaming houses with foreigners as well as Englishmen, and to ill places." The last is treated by the Speaker's friends (fashionable men and courtiers) as a trivial objection, and the first is resisted by precedents. Upon the whole, however, it is found expedient to get rid of the motion by the previous question, and therefore "on the question being propounded that Mr. Speaker do leave the Chair, a Speaker *pro tempore* be appointed, the question being put 'that the question be now put,' it passed in the negative." It will be observed that in the instances cited of the use of the previous question, and in all others which may be resorted to, it never prevented full debate of the main question. The ancient practice was, as we learn from Hakewell, "if the matter moved to receive a debate, 'pro and contra, in that debate, none may speak 'more than once to the matter. And after some 'time spent in the debate, the Speaker, collecting 'the sense of the House upon the debate, is to re-'duce the same into a question, which he is to 'propound; to the end, that the House in the de-'bate afterwards may be kept up to the matter of 'that question, if the same be approved by the 'House to contain the substance of the former 'debate." It was the right of every member to speak once, if he wished it, to the matter moved, and of this right he could not be deprived by any use of the previous question. Hakewell proceeds to state: "If upon a debate it be much contro-'verted, and much be said against the question, 'any member may move that the question may be 'first made whether that question shall be put or

14th CON. 1st SESS.—23

'shall be now put, which usually is admitted at 'the instance of any member, especially if it be 'seconded and insisted on; and if that question 'being put pass in the affirmative, then the main 'question is to be put immediately, and no man 'may speak any further to it, either to add or 'alter. But before the question whether the 'question shall be put, any person who hath not 'formerly spoken to the main question, hath lib-'erty to speak for it or against it, because else 'he shall be precluded from speaking at all to it." The previous question was simply a demand that when the main question should be ripe for decision, the House should first pronounce whether it was then expedient to decide it. It was no matter at what period of the debate on the main question this demand was made, the previous question could only be put when the main question was about to be put, and the main question could not be demanded while any person who had not spoken wished to speak upon it. "It is 'a great mistake," says Sir Thomas Lee, "that 'the previous question, if asked, must necessarily 'be put, for you may do it all at one time, and 'not at another." In fact, when the previous question was demanded, there were two questions before the House—the one whether the main question should be decided, the other what should be the decision on it. If the first were determined negatively, it of course precluded the necessity of determining the other; but if the first were answered affirmatively, the other was to follow immediately. Before, however, either branch of this double question was put, every member had a perfect right to be heard. In later times the previous question has been frequently resorted to, but never to destroy this right of speaking to the main question. For instance, let us take the debate on the motion of Sir James Lowther, (November 3, 1775,) "that the introducing of Hano-'verian troops into any part of the dominions be-'longing to the Crown of Great Britain, without 'the consent of the Parliament first had and ob-'tained, is contrary to law." The affirmative of this proposition was maintained by Gov. Johnson, Mr. Sergeant Adair, and others, and the negative by Lord Barrington and Mr. Stanly; when Mr. Gordon declared his opinion to be that the measure was illegal, but well meant and highly expedient, moved the previous question. Then it was that the Solicitor General, Mr. Wedderburne, entered fully upon the subject. In opposition to the main question, he contended for the legality of the practice, and stated numerous precedents by which it was sanctioned; and in support of the previous question he entered into a variety of circumstances and arguments to show the propriety of the measure. He was followed by Mr. Burke, Lord North, and others, expressing their sentiments fully, as well in relation to the original motion, as to the previous question demanded on it. The advantage which the ministry gained in this instance by the previous question, was not to silence the minority and prevent a discussion of the main question, but to rally round their standard those who would desert them if compelled to vote directly on the main question. They sought by this measure to strengthen their main body of well-trained troops, by the accession of the irregular militia who could not be relied on in a desperate charge. Take, for another instance, Mr. Burke's motion for leave to bring in his famous bill "for composing the present troubles and for quieting the minds of His Majesty's subjects in America." After the previous question is moved, the whole subject opened by the motion is debated by the great champions on either side who entered on the controversy.

I believe, sir, that some confusion has been thrown on the subject of the previous question (a confusion, from which even the luminous mind of the compiler of our Manual, Mr. Jefferson, was not thoroughly free) by supposing it designed to suppress unpleasant discussions, instead of unpleasant decisions. The fact is, that formerly the discussions in the English House of Commons were not designed at all for the public ear, but solely for the members of the House. There are various orders, collected by Hatsell, forbidding the Clerk and his assistants from taking notes, or permitting copies to go forth, of any arguments or speeches made in the House. And we know that when Dr. Johnson first published those specimens of British Parliamentary eloquence, which spread its fame through the world, he was compelled to throw over his design the veil of fiction. They were announced as the debates of "the Senate of Lilliput," and the speakers were designated by the most barbarous appellations. To this day a publication of speeches made in either House of Parliament is, in strictness, regarded as a contempt, and may be punished as such. In a body, whose discussions were not designed for the public, and whose proceedings were known only by their final votes and orders, composed of men who had ever some grievances to allege, who claimed the privilege of free speaking, so essential for the exercise of that right, and whose plain habits of discourse were free from the fastidious delicacy of latter days; all subjects, from which the fear of royal indignation did not restrain them, were freely bandied to and fro, until the House was ready to act or to declare its determination not to act upon them. The previous question could not be used to prevent the discussion of an unpleasant subject. For, whether the previous question was called or not, every member had a right to be heard once on the main question.

The previous question in the English House of Commons deprived no member of the right to amend the main question. It has indeed been made a doubt whether an amendment could be received, if offered after the previous question had been moved and seconded, and proposed from the Chair. Among the arguments by which this doubt was repelled, it has been observed that to refuse the amendment because not before offered, would be to put it "in the power of any 'two members by moving and seconding the pre-'vious question, immediately after the main ques-'tion is proposed, to deprive the House of that

'power which they ought to have in all in-'stances of amending and altering any question 'proposed to them." On the other hand, those who entertained this doubt answered, "no incon-'venience can arise from the doctrine; for, if before the previous question is proposed from the Chair, though it should have been moved and seconded, any member should inform the House that he wished to make amendments to 'the main question, he will then certainly be at 'liberty to do it, and the Speaker, supported by 'the House, will give that priority to the motion 'for amending, to the motion for the previous 'question, which common sense requires." However this doubt may be decided, all concur in declaring that in the English House of Commons the previous question cannot preclude the exercise of the undoubted right "in all instances of amending and altering any question proposed to them," nor can it supersede that "priority for amendments" which "common sense requires." No, sir, it was reserved for us in this age of illumination, and in this freest of all free Governments, to adopt a rule which sets common sense at defiance, and prohibits the exercise of undoubted Parliamentary right. It was reserved for us to declare that the previous question shall have priority of a motion to amend.

If we can find no sanction for our rule in the previous question of the British Parliament, let us examine how far it is founded on American precedents. Here we shall discover an early departure from the European management of the previous question; but a departure strictly consistent with the legitimate purpose of such a question, and which far from shackling legislative freedom, simplified the rule, while it afforded full latitude for discussion and amendment. If we will examine the journals of the Continental Congress, we shall perceive their practice to have been to regard the previous question, as a motion to set aside the main question, which was of course a distinct proposition, and open like all others for free debate. To this proposition the debate was confined. If the main question was set aside, the debate proceeded no further. If the motion to set aside the main question did not prevail, it was then before the House unaffected by this motion, and necessarily in a situation to receive such a disposition as the House thought proper to give it. Postponement, amendment, debate, were then as completely in order, as before the unsuccessful motion had been made. This was truly an improvement of the old rule; an American graft upon the British stock. Simplicity of debate was promoted by confining the controversy, in the first instance, to the propriety of taking the main question—not only unpleasant decisions, but unpleasant and unnecessary discussions might be thus prevented. If on the preliminary inquiry, the subject was pronounced a proper one for the decision of Congress, there was then scope for the exercise of their unshackled wisdom in regard to it. Two instances will be sufficient to show this American usage of the previous question, in the Continental Congress. "A motion was made to resolve that the members of this House keep secret from all but the members of this House, under like obligations of secrecy, such information as may be derived from an inspection of the papers of the committee of secret correspondence, or from hearing the same read." After debate, the previous question was moved by Mr. DUNN—ten States voted in the affirmative, "and so it was resolved in the affirmative, and the main question was set aside." Again, on Friday, July 25th, 1788, "the following proposition being under debate, viz : that the Secretary at War direct the detachment of troops marching to the westward, to rendezvous at Easton in Pennsylvania, and from thence into the county of Luzerne, for quelling the disturbances in that county, provided the Executive Council of Pennsylvania, shall find the assistance of those troops necessary, and provided that the said troops shall not be delayed in their march to the Ohio, more than two weeks; the previous question was moved by the State of Virginia, and seconded by the State of Massachusetts, viz : 'that the main question be not now put,' and on the question to agree to the previous question, the question was lost—on the question to agree to the main question, it was resolved in the affirmative."

In the year following, Congress convened under the present Constitution. In the House of Representatives one of the first acts was to establish rules of proceeding; and the committee on whom this duty was imposed, consisted of gentlemen, many of whom had served their country in the Continental Congress, and among whom, with high claims to distinction, was the present Chief Magistrate of the United States. It is manifest that this committee and the House regarded the previous question precisely as it had been viewed in the Old Congress, as a preliminary inquiry into the propriety of the main question, which, if decided favorably to a hearing of that main question, left it perfectly free to the sound discretion of the House. They, indeed, altered the form of putting the previous question, from the negative to the affirmative style of interrogation. "The previous question shall be in this form, Shall the main question be now put?" They also required that five members should concur in asking for it. "It shall only be admitted when demanded by five members." They limited the debate on this preliminary inquiry: "On a previous question, no member shall speak more than once without leave," whereas, on other questions, he had a right to speak twice; but, in the full spirit of the established American practice, they confined the debate to the previous question until that was decided, and only until then—"Until the previous question is decided, it shall preclude all amendment and further debate of the main question"— unequivocally evincing that "amendment and further debate of the main question," might take place *after* decision of the previous question. And this, sir, was the clear, settled, undeviating exposition of this rule, for upwards of twenty years after its adoption by this House. I will prove this position by irrefragable testimony. In the sec-

ond session of the Third Congress a resolution was moved, "that the President of the United States be requested to cause an ascertainment to be made of the losses sustained by the officers of Government, and other citizens, on their property, (in consequence of their exertions in support of the laws,) by the insurgents in the western counties of Pennsylvania." Upon this resolution "the previous question was called for by five 'members, to wit, Shall the main question to 'agree to the said resolution be now put? It was 'resolved in the affirmative—yeas 52, nays 31. 'The said resolution was then amended at the 'Clerk's table; and the main question being put 'that the House do agree to the said resolution, 'amended to read as followeth: 'Resolved, That 'the President of the United States be requested 'to cause an ascertainment to be made of the 'losses sustained by the officers of Government, 'and other citizens, by the actual destruction of 'their property (in consequence of their exertions 'in support of the laws) by the insurgents in the 'western counties of Pennsylvania, together with 'a representation of the particular condition of 'the respective sufferers in relation to their ability to prosecute their several claims, and recover 'at law satisfaction from the insurgent aggressors.' It was resolved in the affirmative." Here was amendment after a decision that the main question should now be put. We had no Sir Henry Vane then to explain to us this emphatic *now.* In the second session of the Fifth Congress, (Thursday, 5th April, 1798,) a motion was made, "that the instructions and despatches from the 'Envoys Extraordinary to the French Republic, 'communicated on the 3d instant by the Presi- 'dent of the United States, be published." The motion was referred to the Committee of the whole House on the state of the Union, who reported a disagreement to the proposition. The report being under consideration, a motion was made and seconded, that the House concur with a Committee of the Whole. Whereupon the previous question was called for by five members, to wit: "Shall the main question, to agree to the 'said motion, be now put? It was decided in the 'affirmative. And then, *debate* arising on the said 'main question, an adjournment was called for; 'whereupon the several orders of the day were 'postponed, and the House adjourned." On the succeeding day, "the House resumed the consideration of the said main question; whereupon 'ordered, that the further consideration be post- 'poned until this day week." Here the main question was not only debated, but postponed, after a decision that it should now be put. This, sir, was in 1798, in the days which have been falsely called "the days of terror;" but which I feel a pride in showing were the days of correct principles. We had not then discovered how to construe away the rights of the people or their representatives, by a verbal criticism on the adverb "now." This illustrious discovery was reserved for the genius of modern republicanism.

The first attempt that was ever made to destroy the freedom of debate by a perversion of the previous question, was *resisted* as it should be—I speak it to the honor of this House—was resisted by a solemn and almost unanimous protest. It was on the 15th December, 1807, when the Speaker's chair was occupied by a gentleman from Massachusetts, who perhaps on that account claimed to be regarded as the lineal successor of Sir Henry Vane, and therefore the best expositor of his invention. On a motion for referring the memorial of sundry merchants of Philadelphia to a Committee of the whole House, the previous question was called for, and on being taken in the form prescribed, "Shall the main question be now put?" it was resolved in the affirmative. The main question on the reference of the memorial then occurring, "Mr. Ely, one of the members 'from Massachusetts, addressed the Chair, and 'was proceeding in some remarks touching the 'merits of the said main question, when Mr. 'Speaker called the member from Massachusetts 'to order, and decided, as the opinion of the Chair, 'that after the previous question is called for and 'answered in the affirmative, it precludes all de-'bate on the main question; whereupon an ap-'peal to the House, from the decision of the 'Chair, was made by Mr. Randolph, seconded by 'Mr. Bibb;" and the said decision being again stated, "that after the previous question is called 'for, and determined in the affirmative, it pre-'cludes all debate on the main question," the question was taken thereon, to wit: "Is the said decision of the Chair correct?" and passed in the negative by yeas and nays—yeas 14, nays 103. The principle of freedom asserted in this decision, was reasserted with equal solemnity and union of opinion in the next session of Congress. On the 1st December, 1808, a resolution was pending in the following words. "*Resolved*, That the 'United States cannot, without a sacrifice of their 'rights, honor, and independence, submit to the 'late edicts of Great Britain."

"On motion of Mr. Gardenier the previous 'question thereon was demanded by five mem-'bers, to wit: Shall the main question be now 'put? and the said previous question being taken, 'it was resolved in the affirmative. A question 'of order being then called for, to wit: Is the main 'question open to farther debate? Mr. Speaker 'declared that, conformably to the determination 'of the House on the fifteenth of December last, 'it did not preclude debate on the main question. 'From which decision of the Chair an appeal 'was made to the House by Mr. David R. Wil-'liams, and, the same being seconded, the ques-'tion was stated by Mr. Speaker, to wit: Is the 'decision of the Chair correct? and, debate aris-'ing thereon, the House adjourned." On the next day the House resumed the consideration of the question of appeal, and the decision of the Chair being again read, the question was put "Is the said decision of the Chair correct? it was resolved in the affirmative by yeas and nays—yeas 101, nays 18." It was impossible that any rule should be more completely settled, both by uninterrupted usage and solemn deliberate adjudications, than was the rule of the previous question in this

House. It was a rule perfectly consistent with good sense, with the requisite independence of the members of the House, and with the right of the free people whom they represented. It preserved decorum; it had a tendency to prevent unnecessary discussions; it superseded improper questions, while it left perfectly untouched the fundamental principles of parliamentary and political freedom. Thus, sir, it continued the more firm, for the impotent attempts which had been made to pervert it—and the better understood, from the blunders which its examination had exposed. Such was the state of things when, on the memorable night of the 27th February, 1811, the monster, which we now call the previous question, was ushered into existence, and utterly supplanted the harmless, useful being, whose name it usurped.

Sir, of the proceedings of that night I have no personal knowledge. The Journals, however, record them with a fidelity which, however to be lamented on other accounts, is essential to the interests of truth. The House, after a busy day, and a short recess for dinner, met at six o'clock in the evening; they then resumed the consideration of certain amendments, reported by a Committee of the Whole to a supplemental bill prohibiting commercial intercourse with Great Britain, and the question recurred to concur with the last amendments reported by the Committee. "Debate arising, 'the previous question was called for by Mr. Ghol-'son, and, being demanded by five members, was 'taken in the form prescribed by the rules and 'orders of the House, to wit: 'Shall the main 'question be now put?' and resolved in the affirm-'ative. After which Mr. Gardenier, one of the 'members from the State of New York, was pro-'ceeding to state the main question, when a mem-'ber from Virginia (Mr. Gholson) objected to 'the right of the member from New York to de-'bate the main question, after the previous ques-'tion had been demanded by five members, taken 'and decided in the affirmative; on which Mr. 'Speaker decided that, according to the practice 'of the House, it was in order to debate the main 'question after the previous question had been 'taken. From which decision of the Chair an 'appeal was made to the House by Mr. Gholson, 'seconded by two members; and debate arising 'on the appeal, a question of order was moved by 'Mr. P. B. Porter, whether the said appeal could 'be debated? on which Mr. Speaker decided that, 'conformable to the practice of the House, it was 'in order to debate the said appeal. From which 'decision of the Chair an appeal was made to the 'House by Mr. P. B. Porter, and seconded by two 'members. And on the question, 'Is the said de-'cision of the Chair correct?' it was determined 'in the negative—yeas 13, nays 66. The ques-'tion recurred on the appeal first stated; and on 'the question, 'Is the said decision of the Chair 'correct?' it was determined in the negative. 'The main question was then taken, to concur 'with the Committee of the Whole in their last 'amendment, and resolved in the affirmative."

The Journal then proceeds to state, that two

713   HISTORY OF CONGRESS.   714

JANUARY, 1816.   Standing Rules and Orders.   H. OF R.

successive amendments were moved by Mr. Gardenier, on which, on motion of Mr. Ringgold, the previous question was immediately called, debate prohibited, and the amendments rejected. A motion was then made by Mr. Ringgold that the bill be engrossed and read a third time; on which motion the previous question was called by Mr. P. B. Porter, and resolved in the affirmative, and the bill forced to a third reading instantly. On the third reading, on motion of Mr. Ringgold, the previous question was again demanded, and, being decided in the affirmative, the bill was passed. Here we have the great precedent which has furnished the rule for the subsequent use of the previous question; a precedent which nothing could induce me to examine and lay bare to the public inspection, short of an overruling sense of duty; a precedent stamped with every mark of error, oppression, and abuse of power. It is perfectly apparent that this night session was holden for the purpose of carrying this supplemental non-intercourse bill through all its stages. This was the holy end that was to sanctify the requisite means. "Debate arising," on agreeing to an amendment reported by the Committee, "the previous question was called for by Mr. Gholson." Now, sir, it is a settled principle in parliamentary practice, that the previous question cannot be put on an amendment. The very question on an amendment is, whether "certain words shall be inserted into, or remain part of a question." The decision of the amendment "determines that they shall or shall not stand in a particular place, and has, therefore, all the effect of a previous question." So says Mr. Jefferson in his manual—"Suppose a motion to postpone, commit, or amend 'the main question, and that it be moved to sup-'press that motion by putting the previous ques-'tion on it. This is not allowed, because it would 'embarrass questions too much to allow them to 'be piled on one another several stories high, and 'because the same result may be had in a more 'simple way, by deciding against the postpone-'ment, commitment, or amendment." A previous question on an amendment is an absurdity. It is a previous question mounted on a previous question. But parliamentary usage was of no consequence. "Debate" had arisen on the amendment, and this debate was to be put down, or the bill might not be passed that night. The previous question was therefore called. It being decided that the question on the amendment was to be put as the main question, debate was proceeding on this main question; but this did not consist with the will of the majority, and debate was objected to as out of order. The Speaker declared it in order, for he had received too impressive a lesson on this point, to commit again the error which had been so solemnly corrected. It was expedient, however, to overrule this decision. An appeal was therefore taken. On this appeal a debate arose, and the Speaker was called on to pronounce whether debate on an appeal was in order. To such a question he could return but one answer; he knew, every man in the House knew, debate was in order. The rule is unequivocal and ex-

press, "on an appeal no member shall speak more than once without leave of the House." But debate was inconvenient, and, rule or no rule, debate should not be tolerated. A second appeal was then taken. Without a reason urged it was decided, in the face of a known and positive rule, there could be no debate on an appeal. It was next decided, without argument, in opposition to twenty-two years of uninterrupted usage, confirmed by the most solemn decisions made after a full hearing and on deliberation, that there could be no debate on the main question. Thus liberated from every restraint, and armed with the newly forged weapon of the previous question, a mad majority, in the wantonness of power, at midnight, when all that was not passion was stupor, proceeded in their career of legislation. The call of "previous question" negatived amendment; a second cry of "previous question" engrossed the bill; a third shout made it a law. Yet this is the precedent on which our present exposition of the previous question rests for its basis! True, we reject every part of it, but that which the majority now finds an interest in retaining. We deny its propriety in forbidding debate on an appeal, for three days have not passed since we solemnly debated an appeal from the Speaker's decision. We hold it erroneous in applying the previous question to an amendment, and cause it to take effect on the bill or resolution itself, stepping over the amendment. But we follow it as a guide for prohibiting discussion on the main question. It is, sir, a well known rule of evidence founded on common sense, that if a witness manifest a disregard for truth in any part of his testimony, the whole of what he says is discredited. You can, in such a case, have no security that he relates the truth at all. And by the same reason, when a precedent is cited for the exposition of a rule of action, which bears on its face a violation of rule, it should be thrown aside altogether.

Full well do I remember the first instance in which I witnessed the use of this newly expounded previous question, and never shall I forget the feelings which it then excited in my bosom. It was at the first session of last Congress, and on a bill to impose a direct tax of three millions of dollars on the people of the United States. In that bill we had undertaken to assess, without any valuation, the precise sums which were to be paid by the several counties in each State. To remedy the injustice which this hap-hazard assessment must necessarily produce, a gentleman from Tennessee, of great influence in the House, (Mr. GRUNDY,) moved an amendment, restricted in its terms to the State of Tennessee, authorizing a correction of such injustice by the board of assessors after a valuation. The amendment was about to be adopted by an almost unanimous voice, when some gentleman moved to amend it, so as to extend its application to another State. This was agreed to by the House. It was then moved to amend it further, by extending its provisions to the parent State of Tennessee, to North Carolina. Sir, the previous question was called and carried. The main question was ordered to be put; the amendment first proposed—the amendment to it, which was accepted, and the further amendment to it, when the previous question was called, were declared to be swept away by this besom of destruction; and without debate, without an opportunity of amendment, the bill was engrossed. Such a mode of laying taxes was so abhorrent from all my notions of freedom, that new as I was here—an unfledged member—I dared to join in an appeal to the House from the decision of the Chair, and vainly, yet zealously, exerted all my powers to reverse it. Use, sir, has rendered the previous question more familiar to me, but it has not diminished my abhorrence of it. On the contrary, use has but the more fully explained the detested ends which it can be made to answer. Six times at least was the previous question used in the last session to put down discussion, and the exercise of representative freedom. Once on a bill giving arbitrary powers to the deputies of collectors; twice in relation to the conscription project; three times upon the mammoth bank bill. Thank God! it once recoiled with salutary violence on those who used it. The last stupendous scheme of political folly and wickedness, (such I deemed it,) owed its failure to the use of the previous question. Many gentlemen on both sides of the House know this to be the fact.

By what argument is this innovation—this outrage on parliamentary law—thus hostile to the spirit, if not the letter of the Constitution, to the rights of the people, to the independence of their representatives, to the very purpose for which law is needed—by what argument is its justification attempted? They may be all comprised in one word—"necessity." Necessity! the excuse for every folly, the pretext for every crime. Necessity! which the miserable culprit, who steals a loaf to feed a starving family, pleads in vain at the bar of your criminal courts, but which successful tyrants in every age have made the apology of their usurpations on freedom—necessity requires this previous question. I deny it, sir! Centuries have rolled away in England since the forms of free debate belonged to their Parliament, yet the necessity of a resort to this instrument of coercion never has been there discovered. Our Continental Congress managed the momentous affairs of this nation during many years of war and revolution, and they found not this necessity. Twenty-two years had passed under our present form of Government before the necessity was pretended. No instance can be shown of a fair exercise of legislative power being prevented by the want of an unlimited authority to silence discussion. And unquestionably before a forfeiture is decreed, of the fairest and best privilege belonging to the people and their Representatives, one offence, at least, ought to be clearly proven. "But a case may be imagined, in which it might ' be necessary to have this supreme control over ' the right of speech. Suppose the last day of the ' session, and a law highly salutary about to be ' enacted, which a few obstinate members are re- ' solved to defeat by protracted debate, it would ' be necessary in this case to silence them." Sir,

there is no species of political empiricism more dangerous than to make rules of ordinary application, with a view to extreme and barely possible cases. It is, in the language of the immortal Burke, " to make the medicine of the Constitution its daily bread." Extreme cases carry their remedies with them. But I see no such necessity in the case supposed. If the law be essential the next Congress may pass it; and, if the ordinary delay be injurious, it may be immediately convened. But, then, "laws cannot be enacted with convenient despatch." Let us not indulge the chimerical hope of a Government exempt from every political inconvenience, more than of an animal existence free from the infirmities of nature. The ponderous strength of the elephant, and the swiftness of the greyhound, are not found united. The vigor and promptitude of despotism accord not with the freedom and public virtue of republican Governments. While we enjoy the invaluable blessing of liberty, let us not murmur at the trivial price we pay. Despatch, in law-making, is inconsistent with deliberative freedom. Fortunately it is not in itself a quality of great value. Despatch is essential in the execution of laws, but salutary caution should preside in the making of them. Five times in the course of the last session this "necessity" for speedy legislation forced the previous question on the bank and conscription bills; yet so purely imaginary was this "necessity," that no legislation took place upon them—none were enacted into laws. An intelligent individual is now scarcely to be found in the United States who will not admit that the non-intercourse project, to establish which, with convenient expedition, was the justifying end of the first outrage on free debate, was beyond measure silly and mischievous. Legislate in haste, and you are sure to repent at leisure. But it is "necessary there should be a power to correct abuses of the right of speech." I admit you have the legitimate power to correct abuses, but you have none to abolish the right. You may correct them, if it is found expedient, by restricting still more the frequency of speeches; by permitting wide and general discussions only on subjects which fitly bring into view the state of the nation; by admonition from the Chair against casual wanderings; by the censure of the House for obstinate and contemptuous abuses of its patience; by assigning specific days for specific business, and continuing the session until the business be done; and, above all, by the most powerful of all correctives—by marked inattention to the effusions of vanity and folly. The two last remedies which I have mentioned, have been found all-sufficient in the British House of Commons. A debate there, on an interesting subject, takes place at the appointed day, and is scarcely ever adjourned over. If the prolongation of debate here, *from day to day*, be injurious to the public business, why do we adjourn it *from day to day?* Say not that you put down freedom of speech from "necessity," when you are governed merely by the fear of a cold dinner. Inattention to vanity and folly I hold also to be a justifiable and an effectual remedy. Not that I would consent to put down a speaker by conversation, rude noises, or any such indecent expressions of dissatisfaction, but when the love of talking evidently got the better of modesty and good sense, and this superiority was often manifested, the orator should declaim to empty benches. Every man has a right to speak, but every man has also an imprescriptible right to rescue his ears and his brain from the invasion of nonsense. This remedy might not produce an instantaneous cure, but it would prove efficacious in the end; at least as efficacious as most remedies for the disorders which infest a political community. It is not more essential to the well-being of this body to prevent abuses of the freedom of speech, than to the well-being of the State to prevent abuses of the freedom of action. Because crimes occasionally escape unpunished from defects, either "in the evidence in the law, or the application of the law," does it therefore become "necessary" to abolish civil liberty through the land? So with all your correctives there will be occasional trespasses on decorum, by unnecessary and tedious harangues. But is it on that account necessary to put the House under martial tyranny? Will you cure a wen by cutting off the head? Redress abuse by annihilating right?

"But the majority have a right to govern. It is for them to say when discussion shall end and action begin." If by right, sir, he meant power, the assertion is correct. Or, if by government be meant only regulation within the compact of association, it is equally correct. But that a numerical majority of any society has a perfect right to do as it pleases, is the most impious of political heresies; and a majority, acting on such an assumption, is the most dreadful of all despotisms. The primary object of law is an association, of equals, the fundamental principle of the compact is to restrict the physical sovereignty within moral limits. In a Republican Government this is done by Constitutional charters, by specific delegations of power to distinct and accountable agents, by oaths, by the influence of patriotism, and love of fame. In Governments not republican, it is effected by creating a political distinct from the physical sovereignty, by vesting the power of the Government in a king or an aristocracy. Sir, a majority uncontrolled by rule—unlimited in power—unembarrassed by impediments to action—find it where you may, in a nation, in a village, in a deliberative body—is misrule, tyranny, oppression, caprice, cruelty and confusion; anything but free government. The majority here, like majorities elsewhere, where civil and political liberty prevails, have a right to govern according to the prescribed rule; and when a rule is about to be formed for limiting their action, it should be a rule which may indeed protect the rights of which it affects to have a care. Not a nominal rule, which imposes no restraint. Not a rule which leaves every right to the mercy of unlimited sway. "Strike," said the illustrious Athenian to his commander, "but hear me." The first may be your right, the second is mine.

Such is the language to the majority. It is your privilege to decide, but the minority have a right to be heard.

Mr. Chairman, it is a maxim in the bill of rights of the Constitution of that State, to which you, (Mr. YANCEY) and myself, have the honor to belong, that "a frequent recurrence to fundamental principles is necessary to the preservation of political liberty." In the bustle of incessant action, in the animated contests of parties, goading and goaded by each other, in the paroxysms of political fever, these principles will be forgotten. It is prudence, it is duty, to avail ourselves of a season when passion is lulled and reason is free to act, when the preternatural excitement has abated; to review past errors and guard against their recurrence. The rule in question ought not to exist. No majority should be trusted with it. A majority never can be found who will use it discreetly. The day you make a man a slave, it has been said, you deprive him of half his virtue. The day you make him a despot you rob him of all. Human nature cannot endure unlimited power, and bodies of men are not more discreet in their tyranny than individual tyrants. This rule is not needed for any legitimate purpose. Every one of its fair objects may be answered either by a motion to postpone to a day certain, or by the motion for indefinite postponement. I speak in this respect from experience. Ten years since, on a revisal of the rules of order in the most numerous branch of the Legislature of North Carolina, the previous question was expunged. It has never since been known there, nor has any subsequent Legislature experienced inconvenience from the want of it.

This moment is peculiarly favorable for an impartial decision on the proposition before us. The return of peace has brought about a new order of things, which must be followed by modifications of parties impossible to be distinctly foreseen. Interests which have been heretofore opposed will be found acting in concert; and jealousies and enmities, which a common feeling has suppressed, will be roused into activity. There are few, perhaps there is no intelligent member of this body, in whose theories and maxims of political philosophy, the changes and trials though which we have passed, have not produced some alteration. Besides, an event approaches, which in every free country is necessarily accompanied by party mutations; the Executive power is about to change hands. At this moment no one can confidently pronounce whether before this Congress closes he will be found among the majority or minority of the House. This then is the auspicious moment for putting down, with one consent, this odious tyranny. The victims of oppression should disdain to become its instruments; the possessors of arbitrary power know not how soon they may be compelled to feel its injustice.

The Committee rose, without coming to any decision on the question; and the House adjourned.

SATURDAY, January 20.

Mr. ATHERTON presented a petition of the owners of six cotton spinning mills, in the towns of New Ipswich and Mason in the State of New Hampshire, praying that the importation of cotton goods from places beyond the Cape of Good Hope may be prohibited, and that additional duties may be imposed on cotton goods imported from other places.—Referred to the Committee of Commerce and Manufactures.

Mr. BURWELL presented a memorial of Dr. James Smith, the agent appointed in pursuance of the act of the 27th of February, 1813, " to encourage vaccination," containing such representations as he believes will induce Congress to give that further and more ample encouragement to vaccination which the welfare and happiness of our country so imperiously demand, accompanied with the outlines of a plan for the more effectual encouragement of vaccination in the United States; which was referred to Messrs. BURWELL, CONDICT, CRAWFORD, GOLDSBOROUGH, and HANSON.

Mr. CONDICT, from the Committee of Revisal and Unfinished Business, made a report, which was ordered to lie on the table.

Mr. SPEAKER laid before the House a letter from the Commissioner of the General Land Office, transmitting a report of the land commissioners for the western district of the late Territory of Orleans, now State of Louisiana; which was referred to the Committee on the Public Lands.

A Message received yesterday from the PRESIDENT, was opened and read. It transmits a statement of occurrences at Fort Jackson, in 1814, during the negotiation of a treaty with the Indians, and recommends a compliance with the wishes of the friendly Indians, in granting certain lands to General Jackson and others. The Message was referred to the Committee on Public Lands.

A message from the Senate informed the House that the Senate disagree to the bill from this House, entitled "An act to regulate the commerce between the United States and the territories of His Britannic Majesty, according to the convention concluded the 3d day of July 1815, and the ratifications of which were exchanged on the 22d day of December, 1815.

On motion of Mr. RANDOLPH, the Secretary of the Treasury was required to lay before the House an account of the receipts and expenditures of the Treasury, (distinguishing the duties on imports and tonnage, and the sales of public lands, from the other sources of revenue; and distinguishing the expenditures on account of the Army, of the Indian Department, of the Navy, and of Foreign Intercourse,) from the 3d day of March, 1789, up to the last accounts made up at the Treasury.

The House resumed the consideration of the bill from the Senate respecting the convention to regulate commerce between the territories of the United States and Great Britain, which bill Mr. FORSYTH had moved to reject, Mr. HANSON

had moved to postpone indefinitely, and which was finally ordered to lie on the table.

The question on Mr. HANSON's motion was decided in the negative; Mr. FORSYTH withdrew his motion; and the bill was twice read, and referred to a Committee of the Whole.

THE REVENUE.

The House, on motion of Mr. LOWNDES, again resolved itself into a Committee of the Whole, on the remainder of the report of the Committee of Ways and Means, embracing sundry propositions in respect to the revenue.

The resolve first in order having been read, in the following words:

Resolved, That is expedient so to amend the act, entitled "An act to provide additional revenues for defraying the expenses of Government and maintaining the public credit, by laying a direct tax upon the United States, and to provide for assessing and collecting the same," passed on the 9th January, 1815, as to reduce the direct tax to be levied for the year 1816, and succeeding years, to three millions; and, also, so to amend the act, entitled "An act to provide additional revenues for defraying the expenses of Government and maintaining the public credit, by laying a direct tax upon the District of Columbia," passed on the 27th of February, 1815, as to reduce the direct tax to be levied therein, annually, to $9,999 20.

Mr. LOWNDES entered into a defence of the measure; the effect of which, he said, was nothing else than to take away certain taxes of the people, and to substitute in their stead others that would be less severely felt. In answer to an assertion made by Mr. RANDOLPH on a former day, that the permanent duties would be sufficient for the public exigencies without resorting to double ones, he begged the House to recollect that, in the year 1818, the demands upon the public Treasury would be ten millions and a half, for the Naval and Military Establishments, while the revenue from imposts could be estimated at no more than twelve millions—so that there would remain only one million and a half to answer the other expenditures of the Government.

Mr. LOWNDES, in the course of his speech, but much of which was intended as a reply to Mr. RANDOLPH's late speech, which indisposition compelled him to make much shorter than he originally intended, ascribed to Mr. RANDOLPH a change of opinion respecting the expediency of paying off the public debt.

Mr. RANDOLPH denied the change of opinion imputed to him; he held the same opinions respecting public debts, and the application of the public funds, that he ever had done; but the benefits of experience would be lost upon him if he did not know that whenever a Ministry, no matter whether it was the Ministry of an elective President or an hereditary King, chose to supply the deficiencies created by their own incapacity or profusion, they were never at a loss to conjure up pretences for laying their hands on the public money. So far from objecting to the payment of the public debt, he would wish to pay it up to the very day, for he thought that neither a nation with a great public debt, nor a nation that had a great overgrown revenue to be collected, could possibly be free. The facility of borrowing, rendered Ministers profuse, and enabled them to involve their nation in inextricable embarrassments, by obtaining more money than could be drawn from the fair resources of the country, and he mentioned the case of Britain as one in point. That nation, he said, was once considered by some statesmen as likely to sink under the weight of its debt; how came it, then, that she was since able to increase that debt so enormously, and that after that, she was able to keep on foot a navy the most numerous and powerful in the world, and an army of eight hundred thousand men; and that she was not only able to maintain all this, but to subsidize all the nations of Europe whom she could prevail upon to fight against France? For his part, he could not but look with affright and abhorrence at the debt created by the war, yet he would vote to pay it to the last cent; but what a picture of waste and prodigality must that be which rendered the proposed system of taxation necessary! It was not, he said, in the power of any argument of his to place the mismanagement of public affairs in so strong a light as was afforded by the simple fact, that the old impost and tonnage duties were not sufficient to defray the public expenses without internal taxes to a commensurate amount. If the honorable gentleman would apply all the revenues from the impost and tonnage to the liquidation of the public debt, and more should be found wanting, Mr. R. said he would go any length to pay whatever more should be wanting; but he was averse to tax the people for an enormous Peace Establishment, which he thought not only unnecessary, but mischievous. Respecting the payment of the debt, he was not disposed to draw favorable inferences from the past. If in twenty-three years they had not been able to pay seventy millions, in what time could they hope to pay one hundred and many odd millions; and what probability was there that peace would last long enough to make an impression of any consequence on the public debt, while the country was loaded with such expensive establishments?

He was averse to so vast a Military Establishment, not only on account of the expense, but of the danger. If Ministers wanted war, there were no means so likely to procure it for them as an overgrown Military Establishment. Military men were fond of glory, the constituent elements of which were blood and taxes; and if Government were ambitious of a second Punic war, their Military Establishment was the direct road to it; he would therefore, he said, apply the whole of their resources to the extinguishment of the national debt. And here he remarked, that Mr. LOWNDES's calculation of twelve millions, being the amount of the impost duties, must be a mistake. The reports from the New York custom-house put down that estimate. Such an estimate might, indeed, answer the purpose of inducing them to adopt the system of internal taxation, which he considered as the introduction of certain ruin to the country. Much as he had deprecated the war, if

it was made a pretext to saddle the country with internal taxation—if it was only a device to make the people take the yoke more kindly, and to fill the country with a host of excisemen, vermin the most noxious to the eyes of freemen—he said his opinion of the war would be changed, and changed much for the worse. The House had been tried with internal taxation before the war, but were restive and would not take to it; so to make them fall into it kindly, war was declared—for, was it not known that the war was defended on that very principle?

Well, war was declared; the coast of the country was ravaged by the enemy; and the majority swallowed the physic, bitter as it was, for the sake of the war; but still it was on the condition that when the war should cease, the physic should be changed. The war had ceased, and was the bitter potion changed? No! *Haustus repetendus*—the draught was to be repeated, and it was now held to their lips. This however was, he feared, but the beginning; the colt was too young yet awhile to carry full weight at the first backing; he might grow restive if they put on twenty stone till he was a little better broke in; but if the House bore this, they would soon hear of more being necessary. Before another three and twenty years should elapse, there would be another harvest of glory to be reaped; and the same song would be sung over and over again, till at last it would fare with the United States as it fared with Great Britain, who was saddled with a debt which sent her laborers at night supperless to bed.

Mr. R. pointed out the dangerous bearing of a great public debt upon republican institutions, and dwelt particularly on the ascendency which the handling of public money gave to individuals; to collect money, he said, was power; wisdom, happiness, influence, everything. The possession of that influence had ever been fatal to nations, and what exemption had we from it? It was about the period of the Revolutionary war, that one of the most splendid of English writers gave this definition of monarchy: speaking of that anomaly presented by the Government of Rome under the second Emperor, Augustus, when the forms of the old Roman commonwealth were preserved, and there were tribunes and consuls, as well as in the time of Scipio, he says, that "every Government in which a single magistrate, by whatever ' title he may be called, is intrusted with the exe- ' cution of the laws, the command of the military, ' and the distribution of the public revenues, is a ' monarchy." It remained, then, for the House to determine whether they would abandon the principles contended for at the Revolution, and make this measure the corner-stone, upon which they would build up a system of taxation which would send the American as well as the British did the European laborer, supperless to bed.

Mr. R. declared, that his opinions of men had undergone no radical change; he had the same faith in sinking funds as ever—but very little when in the hands of that being which a philosopher had defined to be a two-legged unfeathered animal. He had great respect for religion; but that respect was not drawn from inquisitions, nor from the sanguinary zeal of Queen Mary, nor from the disposition of every sect to persecute all others. So it was with regard to sinking funds; he knew their history from the time of Sir Robert Walpole down to the present incumbent of the Treasury, and he knew that they were always perverted from their just destination to answer the purposes of every Minister, when necessity required it. When the prodigality or incapacity of Ministers rendered a supply expedient, the sinking fund was resorted to, and necessity was the plea. Were money wished for, and no plausible necessity were immediately at hand, why then create a necessity. He must be a very bungler in his trade who could not do that. That physician must be a botch, indeed, who could not keep the patient in bed. Provided the money be desired, this necessity never will be wanting; for never was there a being in the shape of a Minister so contemptible as not to be able to find or to create it. Mr. R. concluded with saying, that the honorable gentleman's estimating the annual produce of the impost and tonnage at twelve millions must be a mistake, since it was as much as that fifteen years ago. The country had in that time doubled in population, and more than doubled in wealth. And if they who held the reins of Government would only dispense with over regulation, instead of being obliged to lay new taxes for resources, they would have had a considerable overplus in the Treasury.

The question being about to be put on the first resolution—

Mr. CLAY said, he approved of the general system contained in this report, and, with some modifications, should give it his support; but he thought it was susceptible of amendment. He thought the amount of the land tax too high for the ordinary season of peace. It was not necessary to go into an inquiry at this moment, whether the land does not eventually pay all taxes, in whatever shape levied or collected; but he laid down the general principle, that in time of peace we should look to foreign importations as the chief source of revenue; and in war, when they are cut off, that it was time enough to draw deeply on our internal resources. Mr. C. said, he thought we ought to reduce the land tax still lower than proposed, and also some other of the taxes which appeared most burdensome in their nature; retaining enough to keep the system of internal taxation so organized, as that an addition to the existing taxes only would be necessary to produce immediately such an accession to the revenue as should make it adequate to the necessities of the country. Mr. C.'s plan was to make up for his proposed decrease of the direct tax, by an increase of the duties on imports. He wished to reduce the direct tax to two millions, or to a million and a half; and when that proposition was decided on, he was desirous of proposing another, that the tax should be limited to one year, so as to make it a tax from year to year, instead of a tax without limitation.

Mr. HARDIN desired to strike out the whole amount proposed, so as to leave the sum *blank;* which blank he should be opposed to filling at all. He was opposed to any direct tax for the purpose of expensive Military and Naval Establishments; and said he should offer some day next week, if no other member would, a motion that the Army Establishment be reduced.

Mr. CLAY so varied his motion, to accommodate his colleague, as to move to strike out the sum entirely, and leave in the resolution a blank, to be filled as the House should think proper.

Mr. RANDOLPH was opposed to the motion to reduce the direct tax. Although opposed to any part of the system, he preferred the direct tax to the excise,—because, every man then knew and felt what he had to pay. He was in favor of making the direct tax an annual bill, as proposed by the Speaker, but expressed his surprise at the Speaker's opinion that, in peace, we should rely on the imposts for revenue, and, in war, on internal taxation, &c.

Mr. DESHA spoke in favor of a repeal of the direct tax, and, in support of it, urged some arguments not distinctly heard by the reporter.

Mr. CLAY made a few remarks in reply to Mr. RANDOLPH and Mr. HARDIN, and went on to remark:—It had been said, that this was a time of profound peace. It was true, we were happily at peace with all the world; but who knew how long it would be our good fortune to remain so? What was the present state of our relations to Old Spain? Who could now say, with certainty, how far it might be proper to aid the people of South America in regard to the establishment of their independence? He did not know how other people thought on those subjects, but they made a serious impression on his mind. We have recently heard, said he, and I believe the information came from the Minister himself, that a demand has been made by the Minister of the Spanish Government of the surrender of a part of the soil of the country; he meant that part of the country formerly known by the name of West Florida, which lies west of the Perdido, and part of which is now incorporated in the State of Louisiana. Mr. C. said, he would not speak, in the terms in which he might be authorized to speak, of the impudence of such a demand; but he considered it indicative of the general disposition of the Government which that Minister represented. Besides, he asked, was the state of Europe settled? Every one had heard of the proceedings of the Congress of European potentates at Vienna; we heard, too, that their ideas of legitimate government were carried to an extent destructive of every principle of liberty; we have seen these doctrines applied to create and overthrow dynasties at will. Do we know, said he, whether we shall escape their influence? Do we not know, though no such intention may exist at present, we shall, by adopting that policy which recommends a reduction of the Army and Navy, invite their attention to our weakness? Mr. C. said, he was for preserving the system of internal revenue, on a reduced scale. He wanted to see

Europe settled ; to see the relations between this country and Spain placed on a footing which would insure tranquillity on our borders. Until he saw these things, he was not for exhausting the purse of the country of the funds necessary to enable it to vindicate its rights at home, or, if necessary, to aid in the cause of liberty in South America.

Mr. McKEE said he was in favor of leaving the resolution blank as to the amount of direct tax. He perfectly concurred with his colleague, (Mr. HARDIN,) that unless a disposition should be manifested in Congress, different from anything indicated either by the proceedings of this body, or by conversations out of the House, he should be opposed to filling the blank at all. Let me, said he, ask the Speaker (Mr. CLAY) whether we should have dared in 1812 to have laid a direct tax of three millions of dollars, or any tax at all, for the purpose of supporting the Peace Establishment we now have? When particular circumstances in 1812 demanded an increase of our Army, and of the resources necessary to support it, what was the course which the National Legislature resorted to, to render those measures palatable ? Did we not say, those measures should exist only during war? Did we not say that, within one year after the return of peace, the nation should be relieved from taxation ? Now that peace was restored, ideal dangers were to be conjured up, to justify the maintenance of large establishments ; and where was the Government that could not at any time conjure up reasons such as these ? Against the doctrines which his colleague (Mr. CLAY) had expressed, and no doubt candidly and honestly entertained, Mr. McKEE said he as sincerely and candidly and honestly entered his protest, as he (Mr. CLAY) had against the opinions of his colleague (Mr. HARDIN.) The doctrines of this report, Mr. McKEE said, occupied the very ground which was taken in Great Britain a century ago, and would certainly produce the same effects here as they had done there, if like causes produce like effects. Show me the nation, said he, with large expenditures of money, large taxes to support it, and I will show you a people who have no substantial freedom, whose liberty is a mere phantom, and has no substance in it. Would any one say that the liberties of the people of Great Britain were not as well secured now as they were a century ago ? Their rights exist with the same guarantees ; they have the freedom of press and of speech: why then do we say, and truly say, the people of Great Britain are the subjects of an unrelenting tyranny ? Because they are oppressed by a system of taxation, taking from the mouth of labor its bread, and depressing the industry of the country. Like causes would produce like effects in this country. Were gentlemen not now hunting up causes of alarm as motives for maintaining those expensive establishments ? Had any individual in the House proposed to reduce the national expenditure? He had expected the Financial Committee would have began its operations by promising to lop off some of those excrescences

which have grown up out of the necessity of the times. There is not a tax on the statute book for which, Mr. McK. said, he did not vote ; but he did so to meet the occasion which demanded them. He did not vote for taxes or for Military Establishments at those times to saddle the American people with them forever. They had now answered the occasion for which it was said they were created, and he was for repealing them ; though he agreed with the gentleman from Virginia, if any internal tax was to be retained, it ought to be the land tax. It was a preferable tax, because it comes home to the feelings of the poor and the rich, every man feels it ; it does not slip unnoticed through society. But, if it were continued, with other taxes, unless better reasons were assigned for them than had been, Mr. McK. said he was much mistaken if gentlemen would not soon hear of it in a manner infinitely more authoritative than any argument he could urge.

Mr. RANDOLPH moved that the Committee should rise ; because, he said, a fact had fallen from the Speaker (Mr. CLAY) which would have much weight on the proceedings of the House when it came properly before them. According to the genius of this Government, none of its Ministers had seats on the floor of this House, and consequently those members become the medium of communicating its sentiments who stand high in the confidence of the Executive. Who should stand high in its confidence if the Speaker of this House did not ?—and he had made a declaration, with a view to influence the vote of the House, on a money bill too, involving matter of deep and high import. Mr. R. said, he did not wish that the opinion and influence of the Speaker should have that effect on the deliberations of this House, which it ought not to have in case the negotiation, if there was one pending, between us and Spain, should be in a better state than that of which the gentleman had spoken. If such were the relations between us and Spain as he had represented, Mr. R. said it might have, and perhaps he might say, ought to have, considerable weight on the great questions now pending. For his part, however, Mr. R. said, he, like the gentleman from Kentucky, (Mr. McKEE,) could not be frightened with the raw head and bloody bones of Old Spain. He believed that General Andrew Jackson and the Tennessee militia would give a good account of all the Spaniards who will ever show themselves west of the Perdido, and their red brethren the Creeks, the Choctaws, and Seminoles, to boot. — [Here Mr. CLAY rose to explain, and Mr. RANDOLPH gave way for the purpose.]

Mr. CLAY said that, when up before, he had not said nor intimated, nor did he intend to be understood, as communicating any fact which the Executive was in possession of in relation to the views of Spain. He had had no conversation with any member of the Administration on the subject. He alluded to a rumor, equally he presumed, in the possession of the gentleman from Virginia as of himself ; he had heard it as coming from the Minister himself at a public entertainment. Mr. C. denied that he had any relation with the Executive, the Cabinet, or any of its members, other than any other member of the House had or might have. He had not now, nor ever had, any other relation. Whilst up, if the gentleman would permit, he would make a single remark on that part of the gentleman's argument. The gentleman had shown, by the latter part of his remarks, that this motion was wholly unnecessary; for, though the gentleman had commenced by saying that a fact had been communicated which would have an important bearing on the question before the House, he had ended by saying that, if the fact were true, he would trust to General Jackson and the Tennessee militia to drive all intruders from the soil in that quarter. Mr. C. said he believed the bravery, the heroism of those citizens would be a safe reliance; but he was disposed, if necessary, to afford them auxiliary aid, &c., without drawing too largely on their patriotism.

Mr. RANDOLPH resumed the floor. Although the fact communicated by the honorable Speaker to this House might not have come from any member of the Cabinet, nothing could be more natural than for Mr. R. to suppose it might; for, he said, when he was intimate with the members of the Cabinet, he had been let into their secrets, and perhaps too deeply into them. Although this rumor, which had come, as the honorable Speaker had told them, from the Spanish Minister, might not have any influence on his vote, he doubted whether it would not have considerable influence on the votes of other gentlemen. It was not logical—in the fashionable phrase it was a *non sequitur*, to say, that because the rumor did not affect him, it might not affect the opinions of others; for perhaps the honorable Speaker will allow, said Mr. R., that I am impregnable to arguments of such a nature. With respect to this rumor, Mr. R. said he was at the first of it. He never had had any communication with any Minister, domestic or foreign, but at his instance; he never had, nor ever would he. He was now, he repeated, at the first of this rumor. Stated as this rumor had been, was it no cause why the Committee should rise? He thought it was—he knew that the Speaker had not intimated that he had obtained his information from this or that source; that, Mr. R. said, was an inference of his own—but, as far as language can convey ideas, he was both deaf and stupid if the Speaker had not intimated that the state of our relations with Spain, combined with the reported demand of the Spanish Minister, would influence his opinion on the subject before the House. As for South America, Mr. R. said, he was not going a tilting for the liberties of the people of Spanish America—they came not to our aid—let us mind our own business; let not our people be taxed for the liberties of the people of Spanish America. Above all, Mr. R. said, he did not mean to pour out the blood and treasure of his constituents for the sake of the people of Caraccas and Mexico. In fact he did not want to go in the track of Aaron Burr or Jonathan Dayton—he did not want any of the territories in that region by conquest, purchase,

or voluntary cession. If they established an independent government, he would maintain with these people, as with all other nations, the relations of peace and amity. This struggle for liberty in South America, Mr. R. said, would turn out in the end something like the French liberty, a detestable despotism. You cannot make liberty, he said, out of Spanish matter—you might as well try to build a seventy-four out of pine saplings. What ideas, he asked, had the Spaniards of rational liberty; of the trial by jury; of the right of *habeas corpus;* of the slow process by which this House moves and acts? None—no, said he, none; expediency, necessity, the previous question, the inquisition—these were among the engines belonging to their ideas of government. The honorable Speaker Mr. R. said, had told the House on a late occasion, that he saw instances of this or that in the British House of Commons; the honorable gentleman had been sent on a late occasion by our Government to Europe—he had been near the field of Waterloo—Mr. R. said he was afraid, the gentleman had caught the infection; that he had snuffed the carnage—and when a man once catches that infection, like that of ambition or avarice, whether taken in the natural way or by inoculation, the consequences are permanent. What! said Mr. R., increase our standing army in time of peace on the suggestion that we are to go on a crusade in South America? Do I not understand the gentleman? [The SPEAKER here intimated a negative to this question.] I am sorry I do not, said Mr. R. I labor under two great misfortunes—one is, that I can never understand the honorable Speaker; the other is, that he can never understand me—on such terms an argument cannot be maintained between us—therefore, for his share, Mr. R. said, he should put an end to it.

Mr. CLAY then rose, and said, that he did not know how the gentleman could possibly have understood him as desiring to augment the Army at this time, or as desiring to undertake a crusade to South America? [Mr. R. intimated across the House, that he had inferred his views, and not quoted his language.] Mr. C. said as the question was for the Committee to rise, he was precluded from going into the general argument, which he deferred till a proper opportunity.

Mr. CALHOUN was in favor of the motion for the Committee to rise; because, he said, this was a question involving momentous considerations. On the ways and means depended every measure of the Government. On the decision of the questions now before the Committee depended the question whether a liberal and enlightened policy should characterize the measures of the Government. Gentlemen ought therefore to proceed with caution. If gentlemen were of opinion that our navy ought not to be gradually improved; that internal improvements should not be prosecuted; if these were their sentiments, they were right in desiring to abolish all taxes. If they thought otherwise, it was absurd, it was preposterous to say, that we should not lay taxes on the people. Mr. C. said gentlemen ought not to give into the contracted idea, that taxes were so much money taken from the people; properly applied, the money proceeding from taxes was money put out to the best possible interest for the people. He wished, he said, to see the nation free from external danger and internal difficulty. With such views, he could not see the expediency of abolishing the system of finance established with so much labor and difficulty. It was a subject which ought to be approached seriously and deliberately. The broad question was now before the House, whether this Government should act on an enlarged policy; whether it would avail itself of the experience of the last war; whether it would be benefitted by the mass of knowledge acquired within the few last years; or whether we should go on in the old imbecile mode, contributing by our measures nothing to the honor, nothing to the reputation of the country. Such would not be his course. He believed this great people, daily acquiring character and strength, would excite the jealousy of foreign Powers. He had no hostility to the Power to which he had particular reference; but he had a friendship for his own country. He thought it due to the wisdom of its councils, and to its security, that it should be well prepared against possible assaults from abroad. If danger should come, we shall then be ready to meet it. If it never come, we shall derive a sufficient consolation from a knowledge of our security. In this view of the magnitude of this topic, and to give gentlemen on every side an opportunity of speaking on the question which is now opened, which is to decide whether we are to travel downward, or to raise the nation to that elevation to which it ought to aspire, he should vote for the Committee's rising.

Mr. CLAY intimated that, under similar considerations, he also should vote for the Committee to rise.

Mr. LOWNDES expressed his wish that the Committee should not rise; and Mr. SERGEANT spoke in favor of its rising in order to obtain some official information which he deemed necessary to a correct decision of the question before the House.

Mr. JOHNSON, of Kentucky, spoke strongly against the Committee's rising, on account of the great time already consumed in debate on other topics, the rapid progress of the session, and the multitude of topics demanding the attention of the House, &c., which required that less time should be consumed in debate.

Mr. HARDIN said he wished also to express his sentiments on this subject, as well as other members, who had perhaps consumed less of the time of the House in debate than the gentleman from Kentucky, (Mr. JOHNSON.) He wished to know, he said, what the gentleman from South Carolina meant by national glory? Whether he meant by it large standing armies and navies, and tens of millions of debt and taxes? He wished to ascertain these and other things. [The Chairman here reminded Mr. H. that the question for the Committee to rise did not admit a

debate on the merits of the main question; and that his observations were not in order.] Mr. H. said, being a new member, he knew little of what was called *order* in the House, and did not mean to violate it; he had heard a great deal about it, but seen very little of it since he took his seat. He concluded by saying he was in favor of the Committee's rising, to afford an opportunity for a free debate on the subject.

The Committee rose, and the House adjourned.

MONDAY, January 22.

Another member, to wit, from New York, WILLIAM IRVING, appeared, produced his credentials, was qualified, and took his seat.

Mr. TUCKER presented a petition of the commissioners appointed at a meeting of sundry inhabitants of the town of Alexandria, in the District of Columbia, for the establishment of a bank in said town, to be called "The Real Estate Bank of the United States," praying that the said bank may be incorporated by an act of Congress.—Referred to the Committee for the District of Columbia.

Mr. TUCKER, from the Committee on the District of Columbia, made a report on the petition of the Mechanic Relief Society of Alexandria, praying to be authorized to raise money by lottery for the purposes of the society. The report recommends, on the ground of hostility to lotteries, that the prayer of the petition be not granted.

This report was opposed by Messrs. LEWIS and WRIGHT, on the ground of justice to the District, the people of which, they contended, ought, in self-defence, against the inundation of tickets from other States, to be permitted to raise money for public purposes, as was permitted for many purposes by the States. To this argument Mr. TUCKER replied, that, being under the conviction (as no doubt a majority of the House was) that lotteries were a species of gambling of the most extravagant and injurious kind, he could not consent to do what he considered a positive evil to produce a possible good, and therefore did not consider the argument as of any force against the report, &c.

The report was concurred in without a division.

Mr. TUCKER reported a bill to authorize the President and Directors of the Potomac Company to acquire certain lands by purchase, and to dispose of water rights; which was read twice, and committed to a Committee of the whole House to-morrow.

On motion of Mr. LOWNDES, the Committee of the whole House, to whom is committed the bills reported by the Committee of Ways and Means on the 19th instant, were discharged from a further consideration thereof, and they were committed to the Committee of the whole House on the report of the Committee of Ways and Means of the 9th instant upon the subject of revenue.

Mr. YANCEY, from the Committee of Claims,

made a report on the petition of John T. David; which was read; when Mr. Y. reported a bill for the relief of John T. David; which was read twice, and committed to a Committee of the Whole.

Mr. YANCEY also made a report on the petition of Joseph Wheaton; which was read; when Mr. Y. reported a bill for the relief of Joseph Wheaton; which was read twice, and committed to a Committee of the Whole.

On motion of Mr. JENNINGS, the Committee on the Public Lands were instructed to inquire into the expediency of authorizing the officers of the land office for the district of Jeffersonville to expose to public sale, at the said land office, such tract or tracts of land as have or may become forfeited to the United States for nonpayment.

On motion of Mr. NELSON, of Massachusetts, the Committee of Commerce and Manufactures were instructed to inquire into the expediency of providing by law for the repairs and support of piers situated in the harbor of Newburyport, in the State of Massachusetts.

On motion of Mr. WRIGHT, the Committee on Military Affairs were instructed to inquire into the reduction of the Army as directed by law, and when the Peace Establishment was completed; and also, whether the officers of the Peace Establishment retained are out of those in office during the war, or appointed since the peace, and report the list of officers, if any, appointed since the peace, that are retained, and the State or Territory of their residence.

On motion of Mr. ATHERTON, the Secretary of the Treasury was directed to lay before this House a statement of the amount of the valuation of real estate and slaves in the several States, made by virtue of the act of the 22d day of July, 1813, for the assessment and collection of direct taxes, separately designating in such statement the amount of the valuation of the buildings, lands, and slaves, in each State.

The following letter, received on Saturday by the SPEAKER, was now laid by him before the House:

GENERAL POST OFFICE, *Jan.* 20, 1816.

SIR: Having this morning heard that reports were in circulation unfavorable to the character of this Department, in relation to its fiscal concerns, I respectfully request that a committee of the honorable House may be appointed to investigate these concerns.

Respectfully, I am your obedient servant,

R. J. MEIGS, *Postmaster General.*

Hon. HENRY CLAY, *Speaker H. R.*

The letter was referred to the Committee on the Post Office and Post Roads.

DUTIES ON MERCHANDISE.

Mr. LOWNDES presented to the House a letter from the Secretary of the Treasury to the Chairman of the Committee of Ways and Means, containing an estimate of the whole amount of duties on merchandise which accrued in the year 1815.—Referred to the Committee of the Whole on the report of the Committee of Ways and Means upon the subject of revenue.

The letter is as follows:

TREASURY DEPARTMENT, *Jan.* 20, 1816.

SIR: I have received your note, requesting a statement of the whole amount of bonds given for duties on importations which accrued in 1815. The portion of the duties on merchandise imported, for which no bonds are given, is probably not more than one per cent. of the whole amount, and cannot, without difficulty, be distinguished from that portion for which bonds are given. It is so small that I have not thought it necessary to make any separate estimate of it, and shall, therefore, give in answer to your note an estimate of the whole amount of duties on merchandise imported, which accrued in the year 1815.

The estimate contained in the annual report was made in the month of November, before returns for any part of the fourth quarter of the year, except from the smallest and most inconsiderable districts, had been received, and before the large importations of that quarter were known at the Treasury to have taken place. At the present moment the returns from the larger districts, for the third quarter of the year, are not complete, and for the fourth quarter of the year are still more deficient. The great pressure of business in the custom-house has, doubtless, occasioned this unusual delay. The consequence is, that it is only for the first and second quarters of the year 1815, that a correct statement can be given. For the third quarter an estimate can be given nearly correct; but for the fourth quarter it can be formed only by comparison with the preceding, the returns of bonds taken being deficient from some of the most considerable districts for the whole quarter, and from nearly all the most considerable districts for the two last months of the quarter.

After making this explanation, I have to state, that the amount of duties on merchandise, imported during the first quarter of the year 1815, amounted to—

	$862,845 27
And during the second quarter of the same year to	10,434,275 56
From the returns received, it is believed that the duties for the third quarter of the year will somewhat exceed those for the second. They are, therefore, estimated at	10,700,000 00
The returns for the fourth quarter are so imperfect as to afford little or no means of estimating the total amount. It is known generally that the importations in the month of November were large, and that in the months of October and December they were less considerable. It is supposed that for the whole quarter the duties will equal those of the third quarter, say	10,700,000 00
Estimated amount of duties on merchandise imported during the whole year	32,697,120 83

The tonnage duties, light money, and duties on passports and clearances amounted, during the first and second quarters of the year 1315 to	251,136 99
During the third and fourth quarters, as fewer foreign vessels were employed in our commerce, these branches will be proportionally less productive, and are estimated at	300,000 00
	551,136 99

Gross proceeds of the customs, as estimated for the year 1815   -   - 33,346,257 82

The drawbacks, bounties, allowances,
and expenses of collection, are to be
deducted from this sum in order to
ascertain the net amount which will
be receivable into the Treasury.
The debentures for drawbacks issued
during the first quarter of the year
1815, amounted to -   -   -   -   76,274 41
And during the second quarter of that
year, to -   -   -   -   -   -   323,086 39
During that period the re-exportations
were very small, compared with those
which took place during the third and
fourth quarters.
As the markets became glutted with
foreign merchandise, the quantity
sent abroad for better prices would
naturally increase. It is believed that
the drawback on the portions thus
re-exported, during the third and
fourth quarters of 1815, will amount
to the sum of -   -   -   -   -   3,500,000 00
The bounties and allowances actually
payable during the year 1815, will
be small, probably not exceeding   -   100,000 00
The expenses of collection will be augmented by the cost of several new
revenue cutters, to replace those lost
during the war. The whole amount
may be estimated at   -   -   -   900,000 00
                                           _____
                                           4,899,360 80

And will leave for the net amount of
the revenue of customs, accruing in
the year 1815, the sum of   -   - 28,346,897 02

This exceeds the sum stated in the annual report
by an amount of $3,348,897 02; an excess produced
by the extraordinary importations during the fourth
quarter of the year, beyond what had been anticipated; and in relation to which it may not be improper to remark, that, as those importations have surcharged the market with many articles, a proportionate
diminution in the importation of those articles, and
consequently of the duties upon such importations
during the ensuing year may be expected.
It ought also to be observed, that this excess will be
wholly absorbed by the deficit, as stated in the annual
report of the moneys receivable into the Treasury during the year 1816; and, indeed, will be insufficient to
meet the whole of that deficit. But it will relieve the
Treasury from the necessity of borrowing money, or
of issuing Treasury notes, or of leaving Treasury
notes already issued in circulation, for making good
that deficit to an extent equal to the sum of $3,348,897
02, above stated.
I have the honor to be, very respectfully, &c.
                                           A. J. DALLAS.
Hon. WILLIAM LOWNDES, *Chairman, &c.*

THE REVENUE.

The House again resolved itself into a Committee of the Whole on the report of the Committee of Ways and Means upon the subject of
revenue; as also on the bill " to continue in force

the act for imposing additional duties upon all
goods, wares, and merchandise, imported from
any foreign port or place ;" also, on the bill " to
continue in force the act laying a duty on imported salt, granting a bounty on pickled fish, exported, and allowances to certain vessels employed in the fisheries;" also, on the bill "to repeal
so much of the act passed on the 23d of December, 1814, as imposes additional duties on postage ;" also, on the bill "to continue in force certain acts therein mentioned ;" and on sundry
petitions.
The bill for continuing the present rates of duties (that is, what are commonly called the double
duties) to the 30th day of June next, was first
taken up ; and having been read—
Mr. LOWNDES proposed to amend the bill by
adding thereto a new section, enacting, that from
and after the 30th June next, there shall be laid,
levied, and collected, in the manner now proposed
by law for the collection of duties on foreign
goods, wares, and merchandise, forty-two per
cent. on the amount of duties then existing, until
a new tariff of duties shall be established by law.
Mr. CLAY, (Speaker,) desirous to increase this
rate of duty, in order to allow the diminution of
the direct tax, when that question should come up,
moved to strike out of this section the words forty-
two, and in lieu thereof to insert fifty per cent.—
which addition of eight per cent. to the proposed
amount, he calculated, would produce an additional million of dollars to the revenue, and allow
a diminution by so much of the amount of the
proposed direct tax.
Considerable debate took place on this motion ;
in the course of which the comparative expense
of the mode of collection of this amount of tax
in one way or the other was discussed.
The motion was opposed on the principle of
preference of the direct tax, in its proposed extent, to increasing the duties on imports, by
Messrs. LOWNDES, SERGEANT, HUGER, and MIL-
NOR ; and supported on the opposite ground by
Messrs. CLAY and DESHA.
Mr. CLAY's motion was negatived, 80 to 64.
Mr. RANDOLPH moved to strike out of the section proposed by Mr. LOWNDES, the words referring to a new tariff to be established, considering
them as mere surplusage ; in which view he was
supported by Mr. GOLDSBOROUGH. The motion
was objected to by Mr. LOWNDES, who vindicated them on the ground of their holding forth
to those concerned an indication that these duties
were not to be permanent, but limited in their
continuance. The motion was negatived by a
large majority.
The question on adding the new section (above
described) was decided in the affirmative—yeas 85.
On motion of Mr. THROOP, a new section was
added to the bill, calculated to give greater security to the collection of the duties established by
the bill.
Mr. REED moved to amend the bill so as that
the rate of duties proposed to be established to
take effect after the 30th June, shall take effect
from and after the 18th day of February next.

This motion was negatived by a considerable majority.

The bill for continuing the duty of twenty cents per bushel on salt was then taken up.

Mr. RANDOLPH moved to strike out a vital part of the bill; which was, in effect, a motion to reject it.

This motion was supported with much earnestness by Messrs. WRIGHT, PICKENS, JEWETT, RANDOLPH, and STANFORD. and opposed by Messrs. PICKERING and HARDIN.

The debate, so far as it applied to the question actually before the House, embraced the arguments which have been repeatedly urged on the floor of Congress pro and con. this tax.

The motion to destroy the bill was negatived.

Mr. RANDOLPH then made three successive attempts to amend the bill: 1st, so as to limit its duration to one year; 2d, so as to reduce it to the old rate of twelve and a half cents per bushel; 3d, so as to add to the bill a provision for an additional duty of five cents per bushel on imported coal, with a view to encourage the home trade in that article.

These several motions were supported by Mr. RANDOLPH, but all rejected; the first by a vote of 76 to 46, the others by considerable majorities.

The Committee then rose and reported the bills to the House; and had leave to report to sit again upon the remainder of the subjects above specified.

TUESDAY, January 23.

Mr. SOUTHARD presented a petition of sundry freeholders and inhabitants of the State of New Jersey, praying for the establishment of a National Bank.

Mr. JACKSON presented a petition of Robert Lowe Stobie, praying that he may be permitted to take out a patent for a ship's rudder, and a pump for extracting foul air from the holds of vessels, of which he is the inventor, as at present he is unable to do so, because of his not being a citizen of the United States.—Referred to Messrs. JACKSON, ROSS, and WARD of Massachusetts.

Ordered, That the letter from William Lambert, with abstracts of calculations relative to the establishment of a first meridian at the Seat of the General Government, received on the 14th ult.; together with the memorial of the said Lambert heretofore presented, and the accompanying papers upon the subject of the establishment of a first meridian, be referred to Messrs. NELSON of Virginia, MIDDLETON, RANDOLPH, PITKIN, and IRVING of New York.

Mr. LEWIS presented a petition of sundry inhabitants of the State of Virginia, praying that the Merchants' Bank of Alexandria may be incorporated by Congress.—Referred to the Committee for the District of Columbia.

Mr. NELSON, of Virginia, presented a petition of William Tatham, setting forth the services he has rendered the nation in laying the foundation of a topographical establishment, and praying that justice and equity may be administered in his case, that his materials may be purchased at a fair price, and that his remaining years and experience may be employed in such pursuits as the President may direct for the public good.—Referred to the Secretary of War.

Mr. ROBERTSON, from the Committee on the Public Lands, reported the bill from the Senate "confirming to the Navigation Company at New Orleans the use and possession of a lot in the said city," without amendment; and the bill was committed to a Committee of the Whole.

Mr. ROBERTSON, from the Committee on the Public Lands, made a report on the petition of the Legislature of the Mississippi Territory, presented on the 29th December last, upon the subject of fractional sections of land; which was read, and the resolution therein contained was concurred in by the House, as follows:

Resolved, That the prayer of the petitioners ought *not* to be granted.

Mr. CHAPPELL, from the Committee on Pensions and Revolutionary Claims, made a report on the petition of Matthew and Elizabeth Roxburgh; which was read; when Mr. C. reported a bill for the relief of the heirs of Alexander Roxburgh; which was read twice, and committed to a Committee of the Whole.

The Committee for the District of Columbia were discharged from a further consideration of that part of the petition of Captain David Porter, which relates to the practicability and probable advantage to the United States of the horse marine battery, proposed to be erected by him; and it was referred to the Committee on Naval Affairs.

Mr. LANGDON, from a select committee, made a report on the petition of Moses Turner; which was read; when Mr. L. reported a bill for the relief of Moses Turner; which was read twice, and committed to a Committee of the Whole.

The SPEAKER laid before the House a letter from Peter B. Porter, informing that he has transmitted to the Executive of the State of New York, a resignation of his seat in the House of Representatives as one of the members for the State of New York.

On motion of Mr. COMSTOCK, the Committee on Pensions and Revolutionary Claims were instructed to inquire into the propriety of calculating the pensions of the invalid soldiers of the late war, from the time at which the disability of such soldiers was respectively incurred, or such soldiers were discharged from the Army in consequence thereof.

On motion of Mr. WENDOVER, the Committee of Commerce and Manufacturers were instructed to inquire into the expediency of providing, by law, more effectually to prevent the introduction and use of false invoices for goods imported into the United States from foreign ports.

On motion of Mr. LEWIS, the Committee for the District of Columbia were instructed to inquire into the expediency of equalizing the laws respecting the removal of slaves from the State of Virginia and Maryland, into the District of Columbia.

A message from the Senate informed the House

that the Senate have passed a bill, "authorizing the sale of a lot of ground belonging to the United States, situated in the town of Knoxville, in the State of Tennessee," in which they ask the concurrence of this House.

THE REVENUE.

The House resumed the consideration of the amendments reported by the Committee of the Whole, to the bill to continue in force the act for imposing additional duties upon all goods, wares, and merchandise, imported from any foreign port or place; and the said amendments being again read, the first thereof was concurred in by the House.

The question was then stated to concur in the second amendment, which proposes to insert the following section as the second in the bill:

"SEC. 2. *And be it further enacted,* That, from and after the 30th day of June next, there shall be laid, levied, and collected, in the manner now prescribed by law, for the collection of duties on foreign goods, wares, and merchandise, the sum of 42 per cent. on the amount of the duties which shall then exist on foreign goods, wares, and merchandise, until a new tariff of duties shall be established by law."

A motion was made by Mr. GROSVENOR to amend the said amendment, by striking out these words: "a new tariff of duties shall be established by law," and inserting "the first day of February, 1817, unless a new tariff of duties shall, before that time, be established by law."

This motion was supported by Mr. GROSVENOR, opposed by Mr. LOWNDES, and negatived—ayes 57, noes 87.

A motion was then made, by Mr. DESHA, to amend the said amendment, by striking out the words "forty-two," and inserting "fifty;" and the question being taken, was determined in the negative—yeas 68, nays 80, as follows:

YEAS—Messrs. Adgate, Alexander, Baker, Bassett, Bennett, Birdsall, Blount, Brooks, Bryan, Burnside, Burwell, Caldwell, Cannon, Chipman, Clarke of North Carolina, Clopton, Condict, Creighton, Darlington, Desha, Forney, Hahn, Hall, Hardin, Hawes, Heister, Henderson, Hulbert, Ingham, Jackson, Johnson of Virginia, Johnson of Kentucky, Kerr of Virginia, King of North Carolina, Love, Lumpkin, Lyle, Lyon, Maclay, Mayrant, McCoy, McKee, McLean of Kentucky, Nelson of Virginia, Newton, Ormsby, Parris, Pickens, Piper, Powell, Reynolds, Roane, Root, Savage, Sharpe, Smith of Virginia, Southard, Taul, Thomas, Townsend, Wallace, Ward of New York, Wheaton, Whiteside, Williams, Willoughby, William Wilson, and Yancey.

NAYS—Messrs. Archer, Atherton, Bateman, Baylies, Betts, Birdseye, Boss, Bradbury, Breckenridge, Brigham, Cady, Champion, Cilley, Clayton, Clendennin, Comstock, Crawford, Culpeper, Cuthbert, Davenport, Forsyth, Gaston, Gold, Griffin, Grosvenor, Hale, Hanson, Hopkinson, Huger, Irwin of Pennsylvania, Jewett, Kent, King of Massachusetts, Langdon, Law, Lewis, Lovett, Lowndes, Middleton, Mills, Moffit, Moore of South Carolina, Moseley, Murfree, Nelson of Massachusetts, Noyes, Pickering, Pitkin, Pleasants, Reed, Rice, Robertson, Ross, Ruggles, Sergeant, Schenck, Shaffey, Stanford, Strong, Stuart,

14th CON. 1st SESS.—24

Sturges, Taggart, Tallmadge, Tate, Taylor of New York, Taylor of South Carolina, Telfair, Throop, Vose, Ward of Massachusetts, Wendover, Wilcox, Wilde, Wilkin, Thomas Wilson, Woodward, Wright, and Yates.

Mr. REED renewed the motion he made yesterday, as stated before; which motion was again negatived.

The amendments made in Committee of the Whole having been agreed to, the bill was ordered to be engrossed for a third reading.

The bill for continuing the duty on imported salt, was next taken up. An amendment was proposed, by Mr. BRIGHAM, to commute the duty to fifteen cents on every fifty-six pounds of salt, but was negatived. The bill was then ordered to be engrossed for a third reading.

The House then resolved itself into a Committee of the Whole, on the revenue subject.

The bill first taken up, was the bill to continue in force the acts therein mentioned, being those embracing the duties which the House had determined by resolution to continue, viz: the duty on stamps, and that on sugar refined within the United States.

Mr. BURNSIDE moved to amend the bill in that part embracing the continuation of the duty on stamps, so as to exempt from taxation discounted notes and bills of exchange. This motion was supported by Messrs. BURNSIDE and MILNOR, opposed by Mr. INGHAM, and negatived by a large majority.

The other bill, for repealing so much of an act laying certain duties as relates to the additional duties on postage, was next taken up. A proposition was made to amend the bill, by Mr. WARD, so as to include a modification of the duty on sales at auction; which was negatived.

The Committee then rose, and reported the bills to the House.

The engrossed bill to continue the double duties on imports, was read a third time, and passed without a division.

The bill to continue in force the bill laying a duty on imported salt, was read a third time. The yeas and nays on its passage having been required by Mr. STANFORD—a debate arose on its passage, which was opposed by Messrs. Ross, STANFORD, RANDOLPH, BRIGHAM, and C. KING.

The opposition to the bill was on various grounds, but the debate turned principally on the liability to abuse of the privilege of drawback to those vessels employed in the fisheries. The tax was also opposed as oppressive, and as being one of the war taxes, which it was said ought not to be continued. The field of debate was entirely relinquished to the opponents of the bill, except by those who defended the bounty to fishermen, &c.

Mr. STANFORD declared that he considered it the most iniquitously unequal tax that ever was imposed. The Western country, he said, paid none; and one State paid nearly one hundred and fifty thousand dollars, while the whole produce of the tax was fixed at five hundred thousand; so that that one State paid almost a third of the whole tax; and, in the fishing countries, they smuggled the salt they used, and yet received a drawback or bounty equal to the amount of the tax upon it.

Mr. PICKERING said, the gentleman from Carolina labored under a mistake. He wished the honorable gentleman would produce his evidence of the charge. Smuggling salt was, from the very nature of the thing, so improbable that the idea of it was ridiculous. The fishing vessels were small, and the owners knew what salt was required, and took enough to sea to cure their fish; they were not so foolish as to depend upon a precarious supply—none of them would run the risk of defeating their voyage, by going out upon the bare chance of meeting a vessel from abroad laden with salt. He said that every encouragement was now, more than ever, necessary to fishermen; the town of Marblehead was almost destroyed by the effects of the war. A hundred fishing vessels sailed out of it, carrying about a thousand men, before the war; but now there were but thirty-three; at the same time the people were so impoverished that they were not able to build vessels, and their right to fish on the coast of Labrador, Newfoundland, and the Gulf of St. Lawrence, was taken from them in consequence of the war.

Mr. RANDOLPH said, it was stated by a late Secretary of the Treasury, that the allowance paid to the fisheries in lieu of drawback, surpassed the duty accruing from the tax upon the salt they used; the reason was, that the fishermen received salt from vessels at sea, and sold their drawback debentures to purchase rum and other articles. He went much at length into this abuse, an account of which he had received that very morning, from a very respectable and intelligent informant.

Mr. REED observed, he rose principally to correct some errors which the honorable gentleman from North Carolina, (Mr. STANFORD,) and the honorable gentleman from Virginia, (Mr. RANDOLPH,) had fallen into, in relation to the drawback on the salt duty, allowed to persons engaged in the fisheries.

I approve, said he, of the bill now under discussion, and hope I may be indulged a few minutes in offering some reasons in favor of the vote I shall give.

We are deeply in debt, and need considerable amount of revenue to meet our engagements and support our credit. From what sources shall we obtain the revenue we need? A duty on salt was imposed at the commencement of the Administration of WASHINGTON, and was twice increased during the first nine years of the Federal Government. This duty was continued until 1806. Can we have a stronger expression of the opinion of former legislatures on the subject?

It is true the salt tax falls on all classes of men, but it is also true (with the provisions of this bill) it oppresses none.

It is a tax which operates, in many respects, justly. Salt is so bulky, and comparatively of so small value, that it cannot be smuggled. The

honest man pays no more than the dishonest and dishonorable. But we have been informed by an honorable gentleman from Vermont, (Mr. JEWETT,) that salt is smuggled into Vermont from Canada, and he mentions the fact as a reason against imposing a duty on salt.

Sir, to me, this information was truly surprising. I never before heard of smuggling salt. If the information be correct, and it comes from such a source that I do not doubt it, on what article of importation shall we impose a tax? I have long been of opinion that the great difficulty in smuggling salt, and evading the duty, was a sound reason for imposing it, and so far from being persuaded to change my opinion by the statement of the honorable gentleman, I am more than ever convinced of the expediency of the duty. No doubt, great changes have of late taken place in this country, in relation to the payment of duties. I fear many are not influenced by those honorable and honest principles which ought to govern any man. If we cannot collect a duty on salt, on account of smuggling, on what, I ask gentlemen, can we collect revenue? Can we collect it from a duty on silks and broadcloths? Can we collect it from valuable goods of small bulk?

But the bill is opposed because it operates unequally. The land tax is probably most equal in its operation, yet many gentlemen, perhaps a majority, are dissatisfied with it. I beg gentlemen who complain of the inequality of this duty, to examine for a moment the report of the Secretary of the Treasury, as it respects the comparative amount of the internal duties paid by different States. I hold the report in my hand. The State of Massachusetts paid of the carriage tax $33,995 24; Vermont paid of the same tax $2,890 24. The whole tax amounted to the sum of $225,179 47. Massachusetts paid of the auction tax $35,350 04; Vermont paid $14 25; New Hampshire paid $776 67; North Carolina paid $1,237 62; Virginia paid $4,079 37. I will proceed no further. It must be manifest to all, that any one of the above taxes operates extremely unequal. Some press harder on one place and class of people, and some on another. We ought as far as possible so to impose taxes as to operate equally on all, and oppressively on none. The high price of salt in some places is not owing to the duty, but to the expense of transportation.

It has been observed by some gentlemen in the course of this debate, that the inhabitants on the seacoast pay much heavier taxes than those in the interior of the country. Most of such persons are seamen, or engaged in commerce. They cannot raise their own wool and flax, and manufacture their own clothes, nor can they live almost wholly on the produce of their farms. They live principally on imported articles, as coffee, tea, sugar, molasses, &c., which can hardly be dispensed with at sea. From their situation and circumstances, therefore, they use much more of foreign and imported articles than those who live in the interior of the country on farms, and they of course pay much more of the double duties.

Some gentlemen seem to speak as if salt were the only necessary of life, and the salt duty the only tax felt by the poor. This, I think, a mistake. Most of the taxes imposed fall on the poor as well as the rich. The poor must be fed and clothed. They will use many imported articles which we may consider necessaries; on all these articles heavy duties are imposed.

Sir, notwithstanding all I have heard against manufacturers, in my opinion they merit our attention. I would not encourage them to the injury of any other interest. We ought to consult the real interest of all—of the farmer or planter —of the mechanic or manufacturer—and of the merchant. What was the situation of the United States and of New England during the Revolutionary war? Did not the inhabitants of this country, at that time, suffer for the want of many necessary manufactories? The price of salt at that time in New England, on the seacoast, was four or five dollars. After the duty on salt was imposed and continued a number of years, some of our citizens, believing the duty would be continued, erected salt-works, at great labor and expense, vats and covers to make salt or sea water by evaporation. It has been considered as a manufactory highly useful. It has been encouraged by the Legislature of Massachusetts, and, no doubt, all purchasers have derived an advantage from the competition and consequent reduction of the price of salt. When the law imposing a duty on salt was repealed, in 1806, the manufacturers suffered extremely. What has been the effect of the salt manufactories during the late war in Massachusetts? Salt has been sold in their neighborhood for less than one dollar per bushel. Similar salt-works may be erected almost anywhere, where there is salt water. Some who complain of the salt duty have probably derived an advantage already from the manufactory, greater than all the duty they have ever paid.

The amount of drawback, mentioned by the honorable gentleman from North Carolina, (Mr. Stanford,) paid some years ago, probably includes the drawback then allowed on salted provisions, on which a drawback is not now allowed. If not, it has not been proved that the drawback at that time exceeded the duty paid on salt actually used in the fisheries.

The sum of four dollars per ton allowed to fishing vessels, which have been employed four months, in lieu of a drawback, may, in some instances, exceed the duty on salt used; but, I do not believe, on the whole, it is an equivalent.

In the year 1792, a number of petitions were presented to Congress on the subject of the fisheries. They were referred to Thomas Jefferson, then Secretary of State. He examined the subject, and gave a detailed report. The result of his investigation is, that no nation was ever able to carry on the fisheries without supporting them from the Treasury; but is of opinion that the advantage of our situation " would place our ' fisheries on a ground somewhat higher; such ' as to relieve our Treasury from that necessity,

' but not to permit it to draw support from them. ' nor to dispense the Government from the obli- ' gation of effectuating free markets for them." What was his opinion as to the importance of the fisheries? What has been the opinion of European nations, and of the wise men of our own? " If (said he) our fisheries be suffered to ' decay, the loss of seamen, unnoticed, would be ' followed by other losses in a long train. If we ' have no seamen, our ships will be useless, con- ' sequently our ship timber, iron, hemp, and ship- ' building be at an end; ship carpenters go over ' to other nations; our young men have no call ' to the sea; our produce be carried in foreign ' bottoms, be saddled with war freight and insu- ' rance in time of war, and history will prove ' that the nation which would be our carrier has, ' for one hundred years past, had three years of ' war for four years of peace."

I am desirous to answer the honorable gentleman from North Carolina, (Mr. Stanford,) and the honorable gentleman from Virginia, (Mr. Randolph,) because I think their statements erroneous, and yet I am at a loss how to reply. Their charges consist of surmises and suspicions. They say they have been informed that vessels frequently go to sea, on a fishing voyage, without salt, expecting to meet vessels at sea loaded with salt, and there supply themselves and evade the duty.

The gentlemen are totally mistaken. I have been, for some years, well acquainted with a number of men engaged in the fisheries, and I never, until this day, heard it suggested. I believe gentlemen in an error, for the reason offered by my honorable colleague, (Mr. Pickering.) What rational man would ever act so unwisely? Go a thousand miles to sea with a vessel and seven or eight men after fish without salt? Without salt they could do nothing. What man, in his senses, would run such a hazard to defraud the Government of $40? I assure gentlemen they have no occasion to apprehend any danger from the case mentioned. I hope their honor and honesty would be sufficient security, if not, their interest certainly will.

We are told by the honorable gentleman from Virginia, (Mr. Randolph,) that he has been informed by a respectable and intelligent man that the fishing business failed after the repeal of the salt duty; that, perhaps, the debenture certificate might be very convenient for those poor men, engaged in the fisheries, to purchase whatever they might need for the voyage, or for their families.

In the first place, it is not a fact, that, on the whole, the fisheries declined, in consequence of the repeal of the salt duty.

There were more vessels engaged in the fishing business in 1807 than at any former period. Since that period other causes have destroyed the fisheries. But had the honorable gentleman been correct in his information on the subject, he himself in the close of his statement offered a sufficient reason for their decline, to wit, that poor men engaged in the fisheries wanted ready money, which was obtained by their debentures during the continuance of the duty on salt, and not as has been intimated that the drawback exceeded the duty. Indeed from what I have been able to learn on the subject from men engaged in the business, I do not believe the drawback exceeds the duty. I believe those engaged in the fisheries have paid this year as much duty on salt over and above the drawback as farmers who possess property of equal value.

I feel happy to agree with the honorable gentleman from North Carolina, (Mr. Stanford,) respecting the character and importance of this class of citizens. I fully concur with him in opinion that the fisheries, as a nursery of hardy, intrepid, good seamen, are of vastly more consequence to this nation than military academies.

It seems now, by the consent and approbation of all, we are to have a navy. Indeed the result of our late wars has demonstrated its utility. It then behooves us to act wisely, and foster the fisheries, that, should war unfortunately again happen, these fishermen (wholly without employment in time of war) may enter on board our armed ships, and do as they always have done, bravely fight in defence of their country. During the Revolutionary war and late war, they have suffered more than any other class of citizens; still they expect no favors. They now pay heavy taxes unknown to others, such as duties on books and lines. duck, cordage, naval stores, and tonnage.

I am not disposed to comment upon the late war with Great Britain, or the late treaty. I trust, however, it will not be improper on this occasion to state, that previous to the late war, we enjoyed important privileges which are now lost. I particularly allude to the privilege of taking fish at Newfoundland, and also on the coasts, bays, and creeks of all other of His Britannic Majesty's dominions in America, and to dry and cure fish in any of the unsettled bays, harbors, and creeks of Nova Scotia, Magdalen Island, and Cape Labrador, so long as the same shall remain unsettled. This nation once esteemed it an important privilege. After our Revolutionary war, our Ambassadors absolutely *insisted* on the right of the fisheries. They would not sign even a treaty of peace unless that right was secured. It deserves to be noticed that our privilege to the fisheries was secured by the 3d article of the Treaty of Peace. It also constitutes the 3d article of the definitive treaty of 1783.

I forbear at this time to go into considerations of the value of the privilege we have lost, because I trust we are now treating for it. I hope it will yet be obtained, that we may be placed in as favorable a situation as we were previous to the late war with Great Britain.

Mr. King expressed his disbelief of the information given to Mr. Randolph. No man, he said, would go to sea on the bare hope of meeting a vessel from Turks Island casually sailing with a cargo of salt.

Mr. Randolph said that if large vessels sailed from the New England ports to the West Indies, and men ventured in them three thousand miles without a compass. rather than go to the expense of one, they would feel no difficulty to go to sea on the *hope* of getting salt, particularly if they calculated upon the salt vessels from Turks Island, running purposely in the track of the fishing vessels.

A motion made by Mr. Stanford to postpone the bill to Monday, was negatived.

The question was then taken by yeas and nays, on the passing of the bill, and carried, at a late hour.—Yeas 89, nays 52, as follows:

Yeas—Messrs. Alexander, Archer, Baker, Bassett, Bateman, Baylies, Bennett, Betts, Birdsall, Birdseye, Blount, Boss, Bradbury, Brooks, Caldwell, Calhoun, Cannon, Chappell, Clark of Kentucky, Clayton, Comstock, Condict, Crawford, Creighton, Cuthbert, Darlington, Davenport, Desha, Forsyth, Gold, Griffin, Grosvenor, Hammond, Hanson, Hardin, Hawes, Henderson, Hopkinson, Hulbert, Ingham, Jackson, Johnson of Kentucky, Kent, King of North Carolina, Law, Lowndes, Lyle, Maclay, Mason, Mayrant, McLean of Kentucky, Middleton, Mills, Milnor, Moseley, Murfree, Newton, Ormsby, Pickering, Pitkin, Pleasants, Powell, Reed, Reynolds, Robertson, Root, Ruggles, Sergeant, Sharpe, Smith of Virginia, Stearns, Sturges, Tallmadge, Taul, Taylor of New York, Taylor of South Carolina, Telfair, Thomas, Throop, Tucker, Wallace, Ward of Massachusetts, Wendover, Wilde, Willoughby, Thomas Wilson, Woodward, Yancey, and Yates.

Nays—Messrs. Atherton, Breckenridge, Brigham, Burnside, Burwell, Cady, Chipman, Cilley, Clark of North Carolina, Clopton, Culpeper, Gaston, Goldsborough, Hahn, Hall, Heister, Hungerford, Irwin of Pennsylvania, Jewett, Johnson of Virginia, King of Massachusetts, Langdon, Lewis, Lovett, Lumpkin, Lyon, McCoy, Moffit, Moore of South Carolina, Nelson of Massachusetts, Nelson of Virginia, Noyes, Parris, Pickens, Piper, Randolph, Rice, Roane, Ross, Savage, Southard, Stanford, Strong, Taggart, Tate, Voss, Whiteside, Wilcox, Williams, William Wilson, and Wright.

Wednesday, January 24.

A message from the Senate informed the House that the Senate have disagreed to the bill from this House, entitled "An act authorizing the discharge of James Jewett from his imprisonment."

The bill from the Senate "authorizing the sale of a lot of ground belonging to the United States, situated in the town of Knoxville and State of Tennessee," was read twice, and committed to the Committee on the Public Lands.

Mr. Taylor, from the Committee of Elections, made a report on the credentials of the members of this House, declaring them sufficient, &c.; which was read.

CANADIAN REFUGEES.

Mr. Throop, from the select committee to whom was referred the petition of Abraham Markle and Gideon Frisbie and their associates, reported a bill for the relief of certain Canadian refugees, who joined the American Army during the late war with Great Britain; which was read twice, and committed.—The report is as follows:

That, on due consideration of the memorial, and of the evidence of the facts therein contained, they are satisfied that the memorialists and their associates were residents in Upper Canada at the commencement of the late war between the United States and Great Britain, to which they had migrated from the United States; that, unwilling to take up arms against their native country, being attached to the principles and forms of its Government, and encouraged by the hopes of success and protection held out to them by the commanders of the several American armies which appeared on their frontier and invaded their province, they abandoned their families and their fortunes, and joined the American standard; that these acts incurred a forfeiture of their estates to the British Government, which were seized to the use of that Government by its officers, in pursuance of laws passed for that purpose. It further appeared to your committee that the memorialists and their associates joined the American Army at a period when their services were much wanted, and that they were with the Army in all its important actions and operations on the Niagara, during the campaign of 1814, under General Brown, and contributed much to its success by their bravery, their acquaintance with the inhabitants of the Canadas, and the knowledge they imparted of the local situation of the country; that, in consequence of their adherence to the American cause, some of them were reduced from opulence, and all of them to want.

Your committee are therefore of opinion that the case of the memorialists and their associates presents a strong claim on the equity of this Government, and have instructed their chairman to present a bill for their relief.

RELATIONS WITH SPAIN.

Mr. ROBERTSON offered for consideration a resolution to this effect:

Resolved, That the President of the United States be requested to lay before this House such information as he may possess, which he may not think it improper to communicate, relative to the demands said to have been made by the Government of Spain for the cession of a part of Louisiana.

Mr. R. said, he felt it his duty to make this motion, in consequence of the reports with which the papers in various parts of the nation teemed in respect to this subject. If it was a topic highly interesting to the people of the United States generally, it was particularly so to the people of the State which he represented, (Louisiana.) They had been sufficiently annoyed and vexed, for the last fifteen years, by frequent changes and rumors of changes of their form of Government; and whether this report were true or not, it was proper that the minds of his constituents should be quieted in regard to it. The immense distance at which they were situated from the Seat of Government would make them more anxious to know the truth on this head; and he should feel that he neglected their interests if he failed to make the effort which he had done, to remove all doubts from their minds on the subject.

The motion was agreed to without debate, and without a division; and Messrs. ROBERTSON and CLAYTON appointed a committee to lay the same before the President.

THE REVENUE.

The engrossed bill to continue in force the acts therein mentioned—the act laying a duty on bank notes and notes discounted, and the bill laying a duty on sugar refined within the United States—was read a third time. The question on the passage of the bill was decided in the affirmative—Mr. RANDOLPH having required the yeas and nays thereon, in order, as he said, to record his vote against it. For the bill 103, against it 43, as follows:

YEAS—Messrs. Adgate, Alexander, Archer, Atherton, Baker, Bassett, Bateman, Bennett, Betts, Birdseye, Blount, Boss, Breckenridge, Brooks, Burnside, Burwell, Cady, Caldwell, Calhoun, Cannon, Chappell, Chipman, Clarke of N. Carolina, Clark of Kentucky, Clendennin, Condict, Conner, Crawford, Creighton, Cuthbert, Darlington, Desha, Forney, Forsyth, Gaston, Griffin, Grosvenor, Hahn, Hall, Hammond, Hardin, Hawes, Henderson, Huger, Hungerford, Ingham, Irving of New York, Irwin of Pennsylvania, Jackson, Johnson of Virginia, Johnson of Kentucky, Kerr of Virginia, King of N. Carolina, Lewis, Love, Lowndes, Lumpkin, Lyle, Maclay, Mayrant, McCoy, McKee, McLean of Ohio, Middleton, Moore of South Carolina, Nelson of Virginia, Newton, Ormsby, Parris, Pickens, Pleasants, Powell, Reynolds, Roane, Robertson, Root, Ross, Savage, Schenck, Sharp, Sheffey, Smith of Virginia, Southard, Taul, Taylor of New York, Taylor of South Carolina, Telfair, Thomas, Throop, Townsend, Tucker, Wallace, Ward of New York, Wendover, Whiteside, Wilde, Wilkin, Williams, Thomas Wilson, William Wilson, Woodward, Yancey, and Yates.

NAYS—Messrs. Baylies, Bradbury, Brigham, Brown, Champion, Cilley, Clayton, Culpeper, Davenport, Gold, Goldsborough, Hale, Hopkinson, Jewett, King of Massachusetts, Langdon, Law, Lovett, Lyon, Mason, Mills, Milnor, Moffit, Moseley, Nelson of Massachusetts, Noyes, Pickering, Pitkin, Randolph, Reed, Ruggles, Sergeant, Stanford, Stearns, Strong, Stuart, Sturges, Taggart, Tate, Vose, Ward of Massachusetts, Wilcox, and Wright.

Ordered, That the title be "An act continuing in force certain acts laying duties on bank notes, refined sugars, and for other purposes."

An engrossed bill entitled "An act to repeal so much of an act, passed on the 23d of December, 1814, as imposes additional duties on postage," was read a third time, and passed.

The House again resolved itself into a Committee of the Whole, on the remainder of the report of the Committee of Ways and Means.

The question before the House on the last adjournment, and which now recurs, was on a motion of Mr. CLAY to strike out *three millions,* the amount of the direct tax proposed to be levied annually on the United States.

Mr. CLAY, considering the decision of the House yesterday, in regard to a proposed increase of the duties on imports, as decisive against his object, which was to substitute for a part of the proposed direct tax a small additional duty on imports, calculated to produce the same amount—withdrew his motion. He then moved to amend the resolve respecting the direct tax, so as to limit it to one year, with a view to place it annually under the control of this House. This motion was agreed to by a large majority.

Mr. HARDIN then moved to amend the resolve, so as to declare it expedient to repeal the direct tax laws altogether, except so much as is necessary to enforce the collection of the tax already due.

Mr. HARDIN said that, on Saturday last, he had notified the House that, in some shape or other, he intended to bring the question before them as to the expediency of repealing the direct tax; that on that day, he had made one or two efforts to bring the question directly before the House when in Committee of the Whole, but .every attempt failed, because, as alleged by the Chair, it was not in order. It ought not to have been a matter of importance to the Chair, in his endeavors on that day to present the question for consideration, whether he was or was not exactly in trim order; because if a man be entitled to admission, his bowing at the door like a Frenchman or an Englishman, a beau or a clown, as long as he behaved decently, did not add to nor diminish his right. Nor did he believe that this want of a little of the ceremony deemed important by the Chair, ought to have prevented him from being heard upon a great national question, when he was solicitous to address the House on the subject; or that because he had had at that time the complaint so common to some gentlemen in this House, to wit: the speech-making fever. Mr. H. said that the amendment to the resolution of the Committee of Ways and Means having been offered by him, it laid him under some obligations to the House to assign the reasons which had induced him to do it. Mr. H. said he approached the subject with great diffidence and reluctance; diffident he was, because he distrusted his own capacity to do the subject justice; and reluctant he was, because, to his great regret, he had witnessed in that House an unconquerable indisposition to alter, change, or modify anything reported by any one of the Standing Committees of the House. He said the manner in which the legislative business was conducted destroyed the freedom of legislation altogether. The President signifiyd his will to the Heads of Departments— they made their annual report to the House, recommending the adoption of certain measures; it was pretty well understood that what they recommended was the will of the Executive; the reports of the Heads of Departments were referred to the Standing Committees, a majority of whom were followers of the Executive; they kept in secret conclave for a month or two, until the House became all anxiety, and solicitude was on tiptoe. Each day an inquiry would be made when they would report? Not ready yet, would be the answer. The members of the committee looked grave, pensive, and melancholy, as if oppressed with a mighty weight of thought. At last they would burst upon the House with their report; and what was it when made? A mere echo, a mere response to Executive will, with small and immaterial variations, intended for the purpose of inducing the House to believe that

they had matured the subject well, when, perhaps, they had never thought about it; pre-determined, from the first, to re-echo back in substance Presidential will; and when the report thus made finds its way into the House, it is fixed. Right or wrong, it must not be altered. Each member of the committee adheres to it, each hanger-on supports it, and all, as the poet says, "Who live and never think," support it. Mr. H. said that independent of the disadvantages he labored under as above stated, he also felt a little chagrined at the manner in which these questions respecting the taxes, direct and indirect, are brought before the House. Each item of taxation being separately discussed, each wheel of the machinery is separately presented, and we are admonished not to touch it, because the whole work will be stopped if you touch one of the wheels. I have heard of many manœuvres in military and naval tactics. This, sir, may, for what I know, be a system of legislative manœuvre, and it is a most admirable one to answer the object intended for. I know of many who would gladly make alterations in the system, but do not attempt it for fear of breaking up its foundation. The committee have had it under consideration for a month or two, and we ought not to meddle with it. Mr. H. said the task was too Herculean for him to believe that he could effect and procure the adoption of the amendment proposed by him. Hence arises, said Mr. H., my reluctance, Mr. Chairman, to address at this time this honorable committee; but as I pledged myself to the House on Saturday last I would make this effort to repeal the direct tax, I now proceed to redeem that pledge—to perform that promise.

It is contended by those in favor of the continuation of the direct tax, among whom I am sorry to see my colleague, the honorable Speaker, first, that the direct tax is necessary, in aid of the present and prospective receipts of the Treasury, to enable the Government to meet the demands against her, which consist of the necessary expenditures for the civil, diplomatic, and miscellaneous expenses; the Military and Naval Establishments; the interest on the national debt contracted before the war, and so much of the interest as we are bound to pay annually, and also the interest on the debt contracted since the war. It is furthermore contended, even should the sum proposed to be raised by the continuance of the direct tax be not actually wanting for the purposes and objects above alluded to, yet, that the system itself ought to be preserved, and ought never hereafter to be abolished, because it will enable Government to extend her internal improvements, add a large sum to the Sinking Fund, and, also, by preserving the system, the machine can readily be put in motion, whenever another war, or the energies of Government may demand.

The first point which I shall endeavor to prove, Mr. Chairman, will be, that the sum contemplated to be raised by the direct tax for the purposes mentioned by those who are in favor of the tax, is not necessary to effectuate those objects. Secondly, even if it should be necessary, sooner than the tax should continue, it would be better to reduce the standing army from ten to six thousand, which reduction would relieve the Treasury from an annual demand to the amount of nearly the net proceeds of the direct tax. I shall also endeavor to show that if the tax be not necessary to enable the Government to meet the demands against her, that it ought to be repealed as an unwise, an odious tax; one oppressive in its collection to the Government, and oppressive to the people. I shall, in discussing the several points, in passing along, notice such observations as occur to me, and I deem materially pertinent to the point, which were made in opposition to the doctrine I now contend for. And lastly, as we have in this House heard much of national glory, and in what it consists, particularly from the gentleman from South Carolina, I shall give, as briefly as I can, what constitutes the national glory of a republican Government. As to the first point I propose to establish, permit me, before I enter into an enumeration of facts relating to the demands against the Government, and which she will be bound annually to pay, and also of the probable receipts of the Treasury, to inform this House that I have no data to make my calculations from except those furnished by the Secretary of the Treasury; and I am induced to believe that his statement of facts, so far as I rely upon them, to prove the points I contend for, will not be doubted, for when he makes his estimates from conjecture, they are made, it is evident, as unfavorable to my side of the question as he could possibly make them. For, turning your attention, Mr. Chairman, to the report of the Secretary of the Treasury, and to the system of revenue he proposes, his object and that of the President cannot be misunderstood; that is, internal taxes, direct and indirect; large standing armies in time of peace, with a continual outcry of danger where none exists; large sums of money to be disbursed in a variety of chimerical projects, to increase instead of lessen the demands against the Government. All this for the purpose of enhancing their own ideal glory, continuing and extending public patronage, and running the road of power in the same way that President Adams did, except to attempt and succeed in those measures which Adams, when most invested with power never dreamed of, measures calculated to oppress the people and destroy the republican form of Government.

According to the report of the Secretary of the Treasury, the amount of the national debt, contracted before the war. was. on the last of September, 1815, $39.135,484 96; the interest and annual reimbursement of that debt, as much as we are bound to pay by contract, is $3,460,000; the amount of the funded debt since the war, as liquidated and funded up to the last of September, 1815, is $70,000,000; the interest which Government is bound annually to pay on that debt, is $4,200,000; the amount of the civil, diplomatic and miscellaneous expenses, is estimated at the sum of $1.800.000; for the Military Establishment, at ten thousand men, $5,112,159; for the

Naval Establishment, including $200,000, annually appropriated to the increase of the Navy, $2,716 510; the total amount for all the expenditures, as estimated by the Secretary, is $17,288,669. These estimates are all made upon a predication that the Army will always have their complement of men and officers, and no one lacking; and what is somewhat astonishing, and would be more so, if in these days there was not so many strange things to wonder at, that the civil list of next year, in times of peace, is estimated at $540,000 more than was the estimate for 1812. So much for dexterity in working hard to waste public money! But, Mr. Chairman, it is only one item in my proofs going to show that the Secretary of the Treasury, to effectuate the great administration system of public patronage, arising from taxes, armies, navies, &c. extended his estimates higher than was necessary. Let us now examine the supposed receipts of the Treasury, given by the Secretary, bottomed upon the principle that the double duties are to be continued until June, 1816, and the system of indirect taxation adopted as recommended. The greater part of the bills have either passed, or the House, by resolutions, has already expressed its determination to pass them. As to the amount arising from tonnage and customs, after the double duties cease, and forty-two per centum is added to the old duties, as is contemplated, the receipts of the Treasury will be $17,000,000; internal duties, as estimated, $4,500,000; sales of public lands, $1,000,000; postage, and incidental receipts, $400,000; making in the whole, exclusive of the direct tax, $22,900,000: leaving in the Treasury, after paying off every demand against Government, a surplus of $5 611,331 annually. But it is contended, that the receipts of the Government are precarious, and may fall short of what they are estimated at. I do not believe that will be the case, but, instead of falling short, will greatly exceed what they are estimated at; for I do verily believe, they are estimated too low—and if I was to say by design, perhaps I would not say too much; for. when I am speaking of design, it will be remembered by this House, that in the annual report of the Secretary. he informed us that the sum received and receivable into the Treasury for last year, from duties, was only $25,000,000; but when, by a resolution of this House yesterday, calling on the Secretary to state, specifically, the amount of each quarter, he this morning sent to the House this report, which I hold in my hand, in which he is compelled to acknowledge his mistake, and, no doubt to his unspeakable regret, further to acknowledge that the receipts of the Treasury, instead of $25,000,000, as stated, is $28,848,897. In passing along, the House must pardon these little digressions; for I cannot omit pointing out those little inaccuracies in the report, by way of showing that the whole soul and energies of the Executive and his Ministers are devoted to this favorite system of taxation, standing armies, &c. The net amount of our revenue, arising from tonnage and customs, after the double duties, and forty-two per centum is added to the old duties, is estimated, as I have said before, at $17,000,000; that is a sum sufficient to establish the position I set out to prove. But it is contended, that the estimation is too high. To prove it too low, in the years 1807 and 1808, when our trade was embarrassed by the restrictive system, the amount of tonnage and customs were somewhere about $15,000,000. Now, if our trade in imports and tonnage only equals either of these years, when you add forty-two per centum thereto, instead of customs and tonnage netting $17,000,000, as estimated, it will net upwards of $20,000,000. This estimate which I have made is fortified by this additional circumstance: in 1815, with the double duties on, the tonnage and customs amounted to $28,348,897. Take off the double duties, and in lieu thereof add forty-two per centum, and if our imports and tonnage for years to come only equal last year, it will bring into the Treasury $20,127,-717. But it is said we have lost the carrying trade, and all the tonnage employed in it, and the amount of duties arising in consequence of some goods being obliged to be landed here to enable the vessels to clear from our ports. It is also alleged we have lost some of our tonnage in being restricted, limited, and circumscribed, in our fisheries, (one of the acquisitions obtained by the war.) I am not, Mr. Chairman, acquainted with those branches of trade, and, therefore do not know what will be the probable loss the revenue will sustain on account of the causes before mentioned; but I have conversed with gentlemen who are, and they inform me that the probable loss on account of the loss of the carrying trade and part of the fisheries, will not exceed more than two millions per annum. But admit it to be two, nay, three millions, do you not believe that the increase of population and wealth in this country, since 1807 and 1808, more than equals those partial losses to our revenue, and also the additional loss the revenue may sustain by the demand for goods being to a small extent supplied by home manufacture? The sales of public lands are estimated at $1,000,000, because the receipts from that source last year amounted to that sum. But I am informed by a member of this House, that the amount of sales last year, was upwards of $2,000,000; and this House must know, Mr. Chairman, that now the Indian war is over, what a vast population is now, and will be for years, rolling from the East to the West—so much so, that I should not be astonished, if the sales of land, instead of one, are three or four millions per annum. This House will not, I trust, forget this further particular, that each year the demands against the Government will be diminished to the amount of the interest upon each instalment of principal that is paid, and the sources of revenue will increase, and surely it would be wise and sound policy, that if the first year we were only able to meet the demands against Government, seeing that the second year we will have a surplus, which will increase each succeeding year, to ease the people from the burden of taxation, as much as possible; for they have already suffered in various ways greatly, in consequence of the war. But it is also alleged, that the taxes should be continued to put into our coffers large sums of money, to be appropriated to the Sinking Fund, to extinguish the principal of the new debt when it becomes payable, which I believe is in 1825, 1826, 1827? To that course of argument I answer that long before that time the old national debt will be extinguished, which will leave a surplus of money in the Sinking Fund, and which can be supplied to the extinguishment of the principal of the new debt as it becomes due; and also, the surplus that will remain from the revenue without the direct tax. These two several items can usefully be applied to the total extinction of the principal of the new debt, when it becomes due and payable. Mr. H. said, that he would remind this House, that when our revenue, in 1814, amounted only to $11,826,907, that the domestic debt, independent of the foreign debt, which was several million, amounted, after the purchase of Louisiana, to $80,691,120, and then it was not deemed necessary by the President and Congress to have either a direct or indirect tax; and which debt, both domestic and foreign, was by the last of September, 1815, all paid off but $39,000,000; and now we must have both direct and indirect taxes to a great amount, and forty-two per centum added to the duties and tonnage—all for what purpose? because we want it now? no, but to apply it now to a sinking fund, there to remain until the first of the debt becomes due in 1825. To get the money, Mr. Chairman, into the public coffers is the object; to apply it to the Sinking Fund is the pretext for getting it; thus the real object in collecting the money may be three or four fold. First, to have money at command to squander it away upon flatterers and favorites: secondly, to keep up the system of taxation to strengthen the Executive by the additional means of distributing offices, and perhaps added to these reasons there may be some little reluctance at seeing some favorites go out of office who are now in, and who must be turned out should this law be repealed; or peradventure, though the idea I acknowledge is somewhat romantic, to give the heir apparent, when he fills the Presidential Chair—for you all know who I mean by the heir apparent, (Mr. Monroe)—the popularity attendant upon the repeal of such odious laws, which will be the means of insuring his re-election. But we are told, Mr. Chairman, that this resolution, to which I propose the amendment, is only for one year; this is only sugaring the pill to make us take the medicine the better—if it be necessary for one year it is necessary for years to come. It will be recollected by the House, that on account of the peace the receipts of the Treasury for 1815 were upwards of $13,000,000 more than the demands against the Government, and also the receipts which will accrue before the double duties expire, which is in June, 1816, will bring such a sum into the Treasury as will enable the Government to meet the extraordinary demands against her, which demands consist in the appropriations this session to pay off the demands due the Army, and the Treasury notes now in circulation. The

Secretary, in his report, says that it is not necessary to legislate for one year only; that the Treasury is competent to meet all the extraordinary demands against it this year.

But, if it were otherwise, and it was necessary to reduce our expenses within the income from duties on commerce, Mr. H. said, he would reduce the Army. He was aware that, in approaching this subject, he touched a hornet's nest, and perhaps should be stung. The Army, which in 1802 was deemed so hurtful, was now the favorite, because by its means our friends can get into office, and we must have an army of 10,000 men, that is, on paper; it was not cared whether we had the men, so that we have the officers, and the surgeons, contractors, &c.; so that we have the hulk of this mammoth, we care little for the blood and sinews. No, Mr. H. said, the ranks of the Army are not filled. During the late war, though we had sixty thousand men on paper, we had at no time twenty-five thousand in the field. We had plenty of officers, so many of them, that he had heard a suggestion, that they ought to be reduced and organized so as to assist to fill the vacant ranks. He was, he said, for reducing the Army to six thousand men. But the House was told, the Army must not be reduced; that the defence of the nation ought to be regarded as a primary object. Certainly; but was it to depend upon a standing army? Let me remark, said he, that this argument is inconsistent with the genius of our Government, which requires us to depend on the militia for our defence; for that object every citizen is a soldier. Whenever this people cannot defend their liberties, then has the body politic become rotten, then may we bid farewell to liberty. But it is said these ten thousand men are necessary for garrison service. Where, he asked, were garrisons necessary? If they were necessary for the whole country from the District of Maine to the mouth of the Mississippi, there ought to be a hundred thousand instead of ten thousand men. What are three or four hundred men in this or that spot for the purposes of defence against an invading enemy? Mr. H. said he should like to see a garrison at New Orleans, and at one or two posts on the frontier. But of what account would be a few at one place, and a few at another? There was a regiment at *Prairie du Chien*—of what account are they? These Indians have no dread of permanent garrisons, but of mounted riflemen. What could a few decrepid men do against a horde of active and vigorous Indians? But we are to have not only this force, but the Executive project of an invalid corps of two thousand men, to be used for garrison service; and we are to put these one-legged and one-armed men to watch the Indians on the Wabash, who flit about like ghosts—here to-day, there to-morrow—who can travel an hundred miles in a night on an emergency; who have an open frontier, if they wish to come, to which garrisons at two hundred miles apart afford but little protection. These Indians dread a contest with the United States; they know the people of the West only wish an opportunity to crush them; and that

they have the ability to do it. Where, then, said Mr. H., are we to employ our ten thousand men? Against Spain, says the Speaker; for, somewhere or other, either at a ball, party, sleighing match, or in a hack, the Spanish Minister had signified something about the Floridas. What did he say, or where did he say it, no one knows. The story about this talk of the Spanish Minister's, put him in mind of the preacher who gave notice that he should begin at such a point on Kentucky river, and preach all the way down, from day to day; and the particulars of the story about the Spanish Minister were about as well defined. But, if it were true, was this to be held up as an object of terror to us? Proclaim, said Mr. H., to the people, that Mexico is free spoil; that the land on Red river will be theirs if they conquer it, and the Western people will swarm upon it like the locusts upon Egypt. These ten thousand regulars are not wanted for that purpose; the Spaniards would not be a breakfast for us. But these men are to be kept up. Why? Because the Spanish people have rebelled against their own Government in the provinces? What have we to do with that? The Government of Old Spain being opposed in the provinces, the very circumstance of the rebellion is the strongest reason why Spain should be friendly towards us. She knows, if the United States were to march its forces there, the standard of liberty would be everywhere erected. This, then, is no reason for keeping up the Army. But, it is said, the affairs of Europe are unsettled. When were they ever more settled? When the Army was reduced during Jefferson's Administration? Mr. H. said he believed not. We were under no obligations to engage in every contest which arises in Europe. What Power in Europe, he asked, has a disposition to invade us? None. What danger menaces us from any quarter? None. Why then keep up an army to fight windmills? Are the double and triple alliances to be the order of the day, such as those of George the First? Mr. H. said he abhorred them, and we had no business with them. But the gentleman from Kentucky (Mr. CLAY) had said, instead of diminishing, he would have increased the Army. Was it possible that the gentleman had lost his old ideas on this subject? Was it necessary to the safety of this Republican Government to maintain large standing armies? Or was it, Mr. H. said, that the gentleman had snuffed the tainted gales from the plains of Waterloo, and was disposed to fight and to negotiate with every nation? During WASHINGTON's Administration the Army had never been as high as even eight thousand men; and there was less danger now than then. The Powers of Europe had as little regard to justice then as now. We were then weak, compared to what we are now, and more inviting to foreign invasion, as being an easier prey. When we have increased from three to eight millions, can we be in greater danger than we were then, when a smaller force was deemed sufficient? Every means of offence and defence have proportionately increased with our population. The importance and magnitude of the establishments in Europe have increased, it is said. In name they may, but they are not in effect as strong: we shall soon see the military Powers, drawn together by a common object, to put down Bonaparte, plunge their daggers in each other's bosom. Mr. H. said his hair did not stand on end at the glimmer of moonlight through the trees. Those fears which had been expressed by other gentlemen in debate might arise from minds a little distempered by too great a desire to preserve the nation. Mr. H. said he was opposed to a standing army on principle; and the more so, because all the train of bloodsuckers about it were to be sustained by taxes on the people. Down with the whole system! said he; down with it, like Lucifer, never to rise again! and let us depend on militia, well trained, well disciplined—on militia, happy at home; not a militia who are ground down by taxes—a militia, not like dogs and spaniels, that the more you chastise them the more they like you. Militia must be disciplined; but they will not fight without affection to their country, created by an attention on your part to their interests. There are two kinds of patriotism, Mr. H. said—the clamorous whip-syllabub patriotism—one rain will wash it all off; and the other, that of the man who reaps his own harvest, cuts his own grain, and uses it after it is cut; the man who has a fireside and farm of his own, who like the Scythian refuses to go from home to fight, but will fight till death if an invader comes to his father's tomb. Carthage had a standing army, and she fell. Rome had but a militia, and defended herself. The instant she established a standing army, disorder, confusion, and mobs, ensued, and she soon became, by means of her military champions, a prey to the veriest despots the world ever knew. These are the effects of standing armies, to maintain which here, the direct tax is to be retained. I have made these remarks with a view of showing that we ought to get rid of these taxes, even at the expense of this governmental favorite. If necessary, let us strangle it. Mr. H. said, however, he would not go the length of some gentlemen in their ideas of economy. He was in favor of a gradual increase of the Navy, one consistent with our means, and for all those expenditures which a liberal, not a profuse policy, will require.

Mr. H. proceeded to examine the merits of this tax, to show, that if it could at all be dispensed with, it ought to be put down. The money arising from the direct tax was the most expensive that ever came into the Treasury; it is put down as costing three hundred thousand dollars in the collection; but, Mr. H. said, he would venture to say that the actual cost of collection would be found to be not less than four or five hundred thousand dollars, what with your collectors, commissioners of the revenue, and a hundred other officers. Was it not important that contributions should not be levied in this inconvenient and expensive mode? If the money must be collected, why not find a way of loosing the purse-strings more conveniently? If money be collected by indirect taxes, the consumer has the option whether or not he will buy the articles so taxed, whether he will run his stills or not. He has an option, and this sweetens his feelings. But, when the proud, official, strutting, consequential character, the deputy collector, waits upon him with his saddlebags on his arm, and takes his bed from under him to pay the direct tax, he feels indignant, and wishes he had not been born in such a Government. Besides, the direct tax is that tax by which the State governments are and always must be supported. Is this mode of taxation selected in order to let the people know who protects them? Surely not. This was a tax, he said, hateful to the people, and subjecting them to innumerable frauds. The best half of the men employed in this business of collecting a few cents from one, a few from another, and so on, were scoundrels, and cheats, and would not stop at doubling the amount of the tax they ought to collect from a man who was not well enough informed to detect their roguery. Fortunately or unfortunately, Mr. H. said, it had been his duty as a professional man, to detect practices of this kind. These collectors, he said, were something like the man's son whose father told him to make money, honestly if he could, but to make money. Most of them cared but little how they made it. The direct tax, he said, is a costly, odious, and oppressive tax, which strengthened the arm of the Government, by oppressing the people. He had witnessed, with some regret, the rapid increase of Executive patronage; he had witnessed, with pain, the efforts to make the arm of the mighty stronger—to extend that Executive influence which had already swollen to a mighty torrent, carrying devastation before it. Instead of seeing the streams which fed this mighty river, increased—by what? this mammoth bank—by what more? by military academies, invalid corps, direct taxes, and all the energies of power; instead of seeing this, he wished to see the streams reduced, dried up as fast as they could, so that this river, instead of carrying destruction to every one coming in contact with it, should be confined within its banks, as in the time of General Washington—he wished to see it used in the good old way; and the good old way, believe him, was at last the best.

Mr. H. said, he had heard a great deal, since he came here, about what is called the national glory. What it meant precisely, he knew not. If the glory acquired in the late war was meant, he begged to distinguish Congress and the President from the sailors and the Army, who fought our battles. The latter, he said, had acquired glory, by land and sea, which would last until the history of these times should be no more. As to the President and Congress, said he, we had better say nothing about the glory they have got. I know several gentlemen in Congress who obtained in the war imperishable fame, who carry about them the honorable scars they obtained in war. But their merit does not attach to Congress. Congress met in October, 1811, to prepare for war; it was declared in June following—and their first troops, in a month after they went out, had to come back and beg for clothing from the ladies of Kentucky. How will Johnny Congress feel, when the pen of history tells this fact? When the pen of the historian narrates the disgrace of the affair at Bladensburg, how will the President and Secretary of State feel? How will the members of the Executive feel, when it is recorded that men, draughted in August in Kentucky, sent down in November, were drawn up on the west bank of the Mississippi river, without arms? It was something like a crop he once heard of on a plantation: the overseer had a share and a half, and every other hand had a share but Jim, and he had none—he was afraid that Johnny Congress would come out about the glory of the war, as Jim did in the crop. He was astonished to hear gentlemen talk about glory gained by the Government in the war Many of our soldiers and sailors had acquired glory, and more than one member of this House had distinguished himself in a manner to do them honor, and make their children proud of their name to the third or fourth generation. But the Government had gained none. We had not, he said, gained any one point for which we went to war, and we lost a part of our fisheries, part of our tonnage, &c., and this is the amount of our gain. He differed from gentlemen in their views of national honor and glory. It did not consist, he said, in a standing army, but in the reduction of the national debt, and the expenses of Government also, so as that every citizen should be enabled to enjoy the fruits of his industry, and be ready on occasion to defend his own fireside. It seems we are to have national glory by opening great military roads, from here to New Orleans—one in this direction and one in that. Whenever a farmer in the country, said Mr. H., purchases more than he can pay for, we suspect he is going to ruin, and that a commission of bankruptcy will soon issue against him. Whenever a Government lavishly disburses money, more than her income, it equally proves that the Government is going to ruin. The national debt of Great Britain has made a limited Government a despotic one. Establish a moneyed aristocracy, separate and distinct from the body of the people—which will be the effect of your system—and in the course of a few years the axe will be laid to the root of the tree of liberty, and the last stage of freedom in this world, and when it falls, it will fall with a mighty crash, never again to rise. Such will be the end of this mighty glory, these mighty prejudices and expenses. How can we pay off the national debt, if we give in to these projects of invalid corps, military academies, turnpike roads, canals, &c., which are to consume so much money? The national glory consists in the pristine principles of this Government, in the blessings of tranquillity and comfort at home, and peace with all foreign Powers. Mr. H. concluded his remarks, by observing that his remarks were not intended to give offence to the gentlemen who preceded him—his observations were directed to their arguments only, and not meant in disrespect to them.

Mr. CONNER, of Massachusetts, rose and said that the honorable gentleman from Kentucky, who had just sat down, (Mr. HARDIN,) had, in the course of his remarks, acknowledged that the Army had nobly fought and bled in defence of our country; that it had covered itself with glory; this would prevent him from noticing the acrimonious epithets which the gentleman had previously bestowed on that honorable and highly useful body of men, for whom he had the greatest respect, farther than to say, that he should leave the honorable gentleman to struggle with that sentiment of strong disapprobation, which such a course of proceeding was calculated to excite in that House, and in this nation.

Mr. C. said, that they were then in committee of the whole House on the state of the nation; that this involved in itself subjects of primary importance: our foreign relations; the propriety of augmenting the Navy; the quantum of military force to be retained; and, what was the substratum of military and naval force, taxation. The subject, indeed, admitted of a widely extended range, but he should only take a cursory, a rapid glance.

Mr. C. differed materially from opinions which he had heard advanced on that floor, with regard to abolishing internal taxation, reducing the Army, or dismantling any part of the Navy. He was for gradually increasing the Navy, and placing the Army in such a state of organization as would admit of its being suddenly enlarged in the event of danger and emergency. He was far from looking on the world as in a state of settled and permanent tranquillity. The subjugation of France, he said, had rendered our natural rival the most formidable Power, perhaps, the world had ever seen. History was reversed; Carthage had conquered Rome, and Hannibal had made his triumphal entry in her gates. We were now happily at peace with that nation; but he confessed, and he sincerely hoped he might be mistaken, that the best reflection he had been able to give that subject, the best observation he was capable of forming of the circumstances and character of the two nations, led him to distrust its durability. There was a political necessity of England's being at war; her agricultural interest was as clamorous for it as her military or naval; her financial system had been wound up to a state of such high excitement, that relapse would carry with it ruin. We were becoming a great commercial nation, a formidable maritime Power; and when, asked Mr. C., did England cease to view nations of that description with jealousy—with incessant, watchful, anxious solicitude and jealousy? When did she ever suffer as favorable opportunity of giving the fatal blow to the commerce of such Powers to pass by? Where were the navies of Spain, France, Holland, and Denmark? Who aimed the mortal blow at the commerce of these nations? Were we alone to be exempt from the effects of those passions and motives which were coeval with the fall of man, and had uniformly produced the same result in all nations and ages? Might not a secret cession of the Floridas, and a refusal to a peremptory demand of territory, be made a pretext of war? And yet honorable gentlemen talked as if it were in our power to perpetuate a state of peace. It had been said, that one nation could make war, but that it required two to make peace. Sir, said Mr. C., two nations can make peace, but it requires the will of many to prevent a state of war. It was true, that we had for several years enjoyed tranquillity, which resulted from the severe contest then carried on between the two great belligerents of Europe. The power at one time was so nicely balanced between these two nations, the efforts they exerted against each other were so incessant and tremendous, that they had neither leisure nor disposition to divert any portion of their hostility towards us; and consequently, we were permitted to reap the fruits of a rich commerce unmolested. These were pleasant hours, sir, said Mr. C. It was the May-morn of our political life; and the fallacy of hope is such, that we thought this serene sky was never to be overcast; that we were ever to be entertained with the dulcet strains of the pastoral pipe of peace. But the tempest of war soon brushed away these Arcadian images—the thunder of cannon interrupted this delicious repose. Peace had again returned; these Arcadian images were again revived; the poppy again hung heavy on our eye-lids. Under these circumstances, they were called upon by honorable gentlemen to reduce the Army. He thought that gentlemen who advocated this, must either believe that an army of ten thousand men was too large a force to garrison and defend a frontier of four thousand miles, or that an army was of itself totally useless and inefficient. He believed the former would hardly be contended for; he should therefore beg the indulgence of the House while he devoted a few minutes to the consideration of the comparative efficiency of regular troops and militia; on which subject, he believed, very erroneous impressions were generally prevalent in this country. Mr. C. indicated his surprise that such misconceptions should so generally prevail; he should have supposed that the experience of the Revolutionary war, and the war recently terminated—the experience of ages, and the solemn decision of General WASHINGTON, who said "if he were called upon to declare under oath whether militia had been most serviceable or prejudicial to the country, he should subscribe to the latter;" this accumulation of evidence, he thought, would have produced but one opinion on the subject. He did not deny that militia, under a different organization, should be relied on as a body of national guards; he did not deny that, individually, they were a finer body of men than those which constitute regular armies; but without that discipline, experience, and system—without that inurement to hardship and danger—without that artificial courage, which is a compound effect of habit, confidence, sympathy, and responsibility, and which in large bodies is much more uniform and phlegmatic than natural intrepidity—to say nothing of that military science of engineering, tactics, encamping, &c., which had occupied the attention of many of the greatest

men, from the days of the Romans down to the era of Napoleon Bonaparte, they were vastly less efficient.

The honorable gentleman from South Carolina, for whose abilities, Mr. C. said, he had the highest respect, on a former occasion, when the bill for establishing military academies was before the House, seemed to think that the cadets of those schools, by training the militia, for a short time, would render them equal to regular troops; and the honorable gentleman alluded to General Scott's brigade on the Niagara frontier, which he supposed to have consisted principally of recruits which had been but for a short time in service. He said that General Scott's brigade, and that of General Ripley, which co-operated with him—which brigade constituted the division of General Brown—had received a large accession of recruits a short time previous to the commencement of operations. But the regiments composing those brigades had been for two years in service, and by frequent engagements, and constant exposure to hardship and danger, had acquired, in a great measure, the discipline and firmness of veterans. Mr. C. said, that it was well known to military men, that when recruits are arranged to veteran skeletons of regiments, consisting of officers and staff, non-commissioned officers and staff, and but a small part of its complement of privates, they soon acquire the discipline and skill to which the honorable gentleman from South Carolina alluded. This, perhaps, could be better illustrated by an allusion to the human frame: the skeleton was the bones, the nerves, and the muscles; the recruits were the flesh and blood. If the former had acquired consistency and strength, the latter would impart health and vigor, though but of recent origin. He said, that, in his humble opinion, the interests of the country would have been much better consulted, and the expense would not have been materially greater, if the Military Peace Establishment had been organized on this principle. We should then, in the event of hostility, have been able to display a formidable column on any point, that would at once carry terror to the bosom of the enemy, and secure from depredation an extensive inland frontier. Mr. C. remarked, that he was far from being disposed to withhold from the Western militia that tribute to their valor which had been so universally paid them. No one held in higher estimation the patriotism with which they took the field, the patience with which they endured privation, and the intrepidity they exhibited in action. No one had a greater respect than himself for a people who, when pressed into war, are fitted by occupation, climate, and nature, for deeds of chivalry and daring enterprise. But he appealed to those honorable gentlemen from the West to know whether, if the discipline, subordination, and experience, of veteran armies, had been superadded to their valor and perseverance, Kentucky would have mourned so many of her sons cut off by surprise and massacre, and perished by disease? Whether, in fact, the same exertions, the same privations, would not have insured the reduction of Upper Canada, and carried conquest to the walls of Quebec? Mr. C. thought that very unnecessary, and groundless apprehensions were entertained in this country with regard to the danger of a Military Establishment. He denied that the military ever destroyed the liberties of its country; it was only when the liberty and virtue of a country were extinct that the military usurped power; it was only when the great foundations of Government and morals were broken up, when liberty was a sound and virtue a name; it was when contending factions had imbrued their hands in each other's blood, and when the Government became rotten to the heart; it was in this unhinged, this corrupt, this debased state of things alone, when the military would attempt to usurp the functions of Government. It was immaterial, he said, whether it was the head of an army, or the head of an armed faction, who should be guilty of this usurpation. If a military were not already in existence, one would be created for the occasion. He remarked that, perhaps, it would be more for the interests of the people, (if anything could be for the interests of the people,) under such circumstances, that they should settle down early into despotism, than wade through seas of blood, and arrive at last to the same result. Mr. C. asked, whether there were liberty and virtue in England when Cromwell drove out his canting and hypocritical Parliament? Whether there were liberty and virtue in France when Bonaparte clothed himself with Consular power? Had not, said Mr. C., as a preparatory step to this usurpation, angry factions previously embattled themselves against each other on its plains, and flitted away in succession, like the blood-stained spectres of Macbeth? Rome, he said, was a military and free nation for centuries; it had nearly all that time powerful armies in the field. But Rome, at last, by that inevitable process of decay, to which all nations, as well as individuals, are subject, became corrupt. It was a mere contest of faction; its liberty and virtue were no more; it was a struggle for power between Sylla and Marius; between Cæsar and Pompey; and it appeared of little consequence which should prevail. It is strange indeed, sir, said Mr. C., that we should harbor such dismal forebodings of an army, officered from among our own citizens, and at the beck and disposal of Government, and still view with listless apathy and unconcern the overgrown veteran army of a nation, by nature and circumstances inimical to us, and which could be borne to our shores on the wings of the wind. He said, by nature inimical to us—he meant that nature had placed the two nations in such geographical, political, and commercial relation as to produce that rivalry, of course enmity; otherwise, he believed, there was neither natural love nor enmity between nations. *Oderint dum metuant*, he said, was a bad maxim for an individual; it was that of a tyrant; but it was a very safe one for a Republic in its relations with foreign Powers.

Mr. C. observed, that he believed no one truth was better established in that unerring school of wisdom, experience, than that large masses of untutored levies, (individually heroes, if you please,) in an open country, without works, could be easily defeated and dispersed by one-third the number of veterans. How often had it been witnessed on the plains of India, that great armies, but without military skill, of fifty or a hundred thousand men, supported by a numerous artillery, had been totally routed and scattered by five or ten thousand veterans. And yet these natives of India, he said, these Sepoys, when officered and organized, were said to exhibit more dauntless bravery, more unyielding, vigorous, phlegmatic firmness, than the British veterans in that country. Which, then, asked Mr. C., is the soundest policy, to expose your territory to be ravaged, your cities to be pillaged and sacked, and permit rapine and conflagration to do their worst work, or to establish the foundation of such a military force as could, on emergency, be suddenly enlarged to prevent these evils—not as the honorable gentleman from Virginia said, to emblazon the glory of our country in blood, but to prevent the glory of the enemies of our country being emblazoned in the blood of our citizens? It was this glance at some of our foreign relations, his conviction of the necessity of preparation, the expediency of rapidly reducing the public debt, the ruinous impolicy of diminishing the Army, the necessity of augmenting the Navy, which would influence him in voting substantially for the taxes proposed by the honorable the chairman of the Committee of Ways and Means. Mr. C. said, he revered the precepts of WASHINGTON, not ostentatiously, but sincerely; that great man was never for prostrating the defences of the country, and permitting the wild beasts of the forest, or of Europe, to enter and satiate themselves in our beautiful pastures; he was for keeping up a regular, but not oppressive, system of taxation, and retaining a military and naval force proportioned to our means and the exigencies of the times. Mr. C. said, that in the course of the observations he had the honor to make on this floor, he had several times alluded to the prospect of collisions at some future time with a nation with whom we are now at peace. The minister of a monarch, sir, said Mr. C., would not find it necessary or politic to promulgate these opinions; but the people are *our* sovereign; we are *their* ministers; this hall is the cabinet chamber for consultation, and here we are bound freely to disclose our views and opinions, although we should be overheard by Europe.

When Mr. CONNER had concluded, at the suggestion of Mr. RANDOLPH, the Committee rose, and the House adjourned.

THURSDAY, January 25.

On motion of Mr. PARRIS, the Committee on the Judiciary were instructed to inquire into the expediency of providing by law for holding a circuit court of the United States, within and for the District of Maine.

On motion of Mr. GOLDSBOROUGH, the Committee of Ways and Means were instructed to inquire into the expediency of making provision by law, requiring the collectors of the United States taxes, or their deputies, to keep an office at the county town in each county, or to attend there one day in each week for the transaction of the business of their office.

On motion of Mr. McLean, of Ohio, the Committee of Claims were instructed to inquire into the expediency of making provision by law for paying into the treasury of the county of Hamilton, in the State of Ohio, the amount of damages sustained by the destruction of the court-house in Cincinnati, occasioned by fire, through the negligence of the troops of the United States, while occupying said building as barracks.

Mr. McL. presented a document in support of the claim presented by the foregoing resolution; which was referred to the Committee of Claims.

VALUATION OF REAL ESTATE, &c.

The Speaker laid before the House a letter from the Secretary of the Treasury, transmitting a statement of the valuations of lands, lots, and dwelling-houses, and of slaves, in the several States, made under the act of Congress of the 22d of July, 1813, in obedience to a resolution of the 22d instant; which were read, and ordered to lie on the table. The letter is as follows:

Treasury Department,
January 25, 1816.

Sir: In obedience to the resolution of the House of Representatives, of the 22d instant, I have the honor to transmit a statement of the amount of valuations of lands, lots, and dwelling-houses, and of slaves in the several States, made under the act of Congress of the 22d of July, 1813; so far as the same have been returned by the principal assessors to this Department.

I have the honor to be, yours, &c.
A. J. DALLAS.

The Honorable the Speaker
of the House of Representatives.

Statement of the amount of valuations of lands, lots, and dwelling-houses, and of slaves, in the several States, made under the act of Congress of the 22d of July, 1813, and returned by the principal assessors to the Treasury.

The States of New Jersey, Pennsylvania, Virginia, South Carolina, Georgia, Ohio, and Kentucky, assumed and paid their quotas of the tax, and no valuations, therefore, were made under the act of July 22, 1813, in those States.

Value of lands, lots, and dwelling-houses.

New Hampshire	$36,957,825
Massachusetts	149,253,514
Vermont	32,747,290
Rhode Island	21,567,020
Connecticut	86,546,841
New York*	265,224,963
Delaware†	14,218,950
Maryland	106,490,638
North Carolina‡	58,114,962
Tennessee§	28,748,986
Louisiana, one district, viz: the 2d	2,312,785

Value of slaves.

New Hampshire	
Massachusetts	
Vermont	
Rhode Island	
Connecticut	$3,192
New York*	842,162
Delaware†	142,519
Maryland	14,525,845
North Carolina‡	34,082,545
Tennessee§	9,662,925
Louisiana, one district, viz: the 2d‖	2,384,765

Total Valuation.

New Hampshire	$36,957,825
Massachusetts	149,253,514
Vermont	32,747,290
Rhode Island	21,567,020
Connecticut	86,550,033
New York*	266,067,145
Delaware†	14,361,469
Maryland	121,016,483
North Carolina‡	92,197,497
Tennessee§	38,411,911
Louisiana, one district, viz: the 2d‖	4,957,550

* The returns from the two districts (the 12th and 25th) of the valuations for the year 1814, have not been received. The valuations of these two districts for the year 1815, have been taken. In four districts (the 7th, 12th, 21st, and 25th) the valuations of slaves are not given distinctly from the valuations of lands, lots, and dwelling-houses.

† In one district (the 3d) the valuation of slaves is not given distinctly from the valuation of lands, lots, and dwelling-houses.

‡ In two districts (the 5th and 12th) the valuation of slaves is not given distinctly from the valuation of lands, lots, and dwelling-houses.

§ The returns from one district (the 2d) of the valuations for the year 1814, have not been received. The valuation of this district for 1815, as fixed by the board of principal assessors, has been taken. The valuations of slaves in two districts (the 3d and 4th) are not given distinctly from the valuation of lands, lots, and dwelling-houses.

‖ No returns for the year 1814 have been received from any of the districts, except the 2d, here given.

THE REVENUE.

The House again resolved itself into a Committee of the Whole, on the report of the Committee of the whole House in regard to the revenue.

The resolution respecting the direct tax being under consideration, together with Mr. Hardin's motion to declare it expedient to repeal the said tax—

Mr. Randolph rose and spoke on the subject nearly four hours. He had not concluded, when, being requested to give way for the purpose, the Committee rose, on motion of Mr. Ross. Mr. Randolph opposed the direct tax and the system of internal taxation generally.

FRIDAY, January 26.

Mr. Ward, of Massachusetts, presented a petition of the President and Fellows of Harvard College, in Cambridge, Massachusetts, praying

765   HISTORY OF CONGRESS.   766

JANUARY, 1816.   *Captain Morgan—Receipts and Expenditures.*   H. OF R.

that the duties, secured by the treasurer of the said college, to be paid on an invoice of books, designed for the use of that seminary, may be remitted; and that an act may be passed permitting the importation of books, by seminaries of learning, free of duty.—Referred to the Committee of Ways and Means.

Mr. SERGEANT presented a petition of sundry inhabitants of the counties of Montgomery, Chester, and Delaware, in Pennsylvania, praying for the establishment of a National Bank.—Referred to the Committee of the Whole on the bill to incorporate the Bank of the United States.

The following Message was received from the PRESIDENT OF THE UNITED STATES:

To the House of Representatives
of the United States:

In compliance with the resolution of the 24th inst., I transmit two letters from the Envoy Extraordinary and Minister Plenipotentiary of Spain to the Secretary of State, with his answer.   JAMES MADISON.
JANUARY 26, 1816.

Referred to the Committee on Foreign Affairs.

CAPTAIN MORGAN.

Mr. CHAPPELL reported a bill for the relief of the widow and minor children of Zacquille Morgan, late a captain in the Army of the United States; which was twice read, and committed.

The report is as follows:

That the petitioner states that her husband was a captain in the Army, and was engaged with his company in the defence of the City of Washington in August, 1814; that, by reason of the excessive heat of the weather, and the forced marches which he made to join the American forces before the battle at Bladensburg, and the exertions which he used to keep his company in order after the retreat of that day was ordered, he became completely exhausted, and fell dead in the road. She states that Captain Morgan left six small children, and prays that Congress will place her and her children on the same footing with the widows and orphans of those officers who died of wounds received in battle.

The material facts stated in the petition are supported by the testimony submitted, and show that although Captain Morgan did not die as gloriously as some other officers of our Army, yet he died in the service of his country, and, consequently, that this case is within the spirit of those provisions which have heretofore been made. Whether these provisions be viewed as mere inducements to tempt the citizen to engage in the service of his country, or as the charity of a grateful Government extended to the bereaved widow and orphan, or as both, they are no less applicable to this than the cases provided for. They think the relief prayed for should be granted, and for that purpose report a bill.

RECEIPTS AND EXPENDITURES.

The SPEAKER laid before the House a letter from the Secretary of the Treasury, transmitting statements of the receipts and expenditure of the Treasury, from the third day of March, 1789, to the third day of March, 1815, in obedience to a resolution of the 20th instant; which were read, and ordered to lie on the table. The letter is as follows:

TREASURY DEPARTMENT,
January 25, 1816.

SIR: In obedience to the resolution of the House of Representatives, of the 20th instant, I have the honor to lay before the House—

No. 1. An explanatory letter from the Register of the Treasury, accompanying the statements required by the resolution.

No. 2. A statement of the annual receipts and expenditures of the United States, from the 3d of March, 1789, to the 31st of March, 1815, exclusive of the moneys received from loans, foreign and domestic, and payments on account or the foreign and domestic debt, and on account of the Revolutionary Government, which are separately stated.

No. 3. Statements, first, of the moneys annually received from foreign and domestic loans; second, of the sums paid annually on account of the public debt; and third, of the whole amount paid annually on account of the Revolutionary Government from the commencement of the present Government.

I have the honor to be, yours, &c.
A. J. DALLAS.

Hon. HENRY CLAY,
Speaker of the House of Reps.

No. 1.

TREASURY DEPARTMENT,
Register's Office, January 25, 1816.

SIR: I have the honor to transmit a statement, formed in pursuance of a resolution of the House of Representatives of the United States, of the 20th instant, with accompanying documents, (A, B, C,) in relation to the receipts on account of foreign and domestic loans, and of the payments on account of the foreign and domestic debt, and of the payments in relation to the Revolutionary Government.

The receipts into the Treasury from imports and tonnage, have been - - - $222,530,374 56
Internal revenue - - - 9,015,342 24
Direct tax - - - 4,476,826 53
Postage of letters - - 747,388 40
Sales of public lands - - 8,658,869 38
Miscellaneous - - 1,590,001 68

              247,019,302 79

The receipts from foreign and domestic loans, (as per statement A,) amount to - - - 107,138,184 41

The sum total of receipts to 31st March, 1815, the latest period to which the Treasurer's account is settled at the Treasury, is - $354,157,487 20

The expenditures are stated, viz:

Pay and subsistence of the Army - - $86,270,562 85
Fortification of ports and harbors - - 4,374,805 26
Fabrication of cannon - - 263,611 54
Purchase of saltpetre - - 150,000 00
Additional arms - 300,000 00

Arming & equipping the militia - - -	1,100,000 00	
Detachment of militia	170,000 00	
Services of militia	2,000,000 00	
Services of volunteers - -	1,000,000 00	
		$97,628,979 65
Indian department—Holding treaties, &c. - -	878,313 68	
Trading houses -	459,726 98	
		1,338,040 66
		47,816,363 68
Naval Department - - -		
Foreign intercourse, exclusive of Barbary Powers, and including the sum of $6,361,000 paid under the convention with Great Britain, of the 8th of January, 1802, and with France, of the 30th of April, 1803 - - -	10,678,015 34	
Barbary Powers - - -	2,405,322 40	
Civil list - - - -	14,940,695 79	
Miscellaneous civil - - -	9,909,978 91	
To which, add the expenditures in relation to the payment of the interest and charges on the foreign loans, and principal of the foreign and domestic debt at the Treasury of the United States, and by their Commissioners abroad, as per statement B - - -	167,524,588 00	
And the expenditures on account of the Revolutionary Government, as per statement C - - -	316,268 70	
The sum total of expenditures from the 3d of March, 1789, to the 31st of March, 1815 - - -	352,560,193 13	
Which, with the balance in the Treasury, on the 31st of March, 1815, as settled at the Treasury -	1,597,294 07	
Make the sum total of receipts as before stated - - - -	$354,157,487 20	

It will be perceived that these statements are a continuation, in point of form, of those rendered to the House of Representatives of the United States, by the Secretary of the Treasury of the 11th of January, 1812, under a resolution of that House of the 24th of December, 1812, and embrace all receipts and payments, whether made at the Treasury, or by the commissioners of loans abroad, to the date of the latest settlement at the Treasury, of the accounts of the United States' Commissioners in London and Amsterdam.

I have the honor to be, very respectfully, yours, &c.
JOSEPH NOURSE, *Register.*
Hon. A. J. DALLAS,
    Secretary of the Treasury.

[The Tabular Statements, in detail, are omitted.]

THE REVENUE.

The House again resolved itself into a Committee of the Whole on the report of the Committee of Ways and Means upon the subject of revenue. The whole sitting of the Committee was occupied by Mr. RANDOLPH in continuation of his speech. He did not conclude before the Committee rose, and the House adjourned.

SATURDAY, January 27.

Another member, to wit, from New Jersey, THOMAS WARD, appeared, produced his credentials, was qualified, and took his seat.

Mr. PLEASANTS, from the Committee on Naval Affairs, reported a bill authorizing the payment of a sum of money to James Levins; which was read twice, and committed to a Committee of the whole House on Monday next.

Mr. JACKSON, from a select committee, by leave of the House, reported a bill authorizing Robert Lowe Stobie to obtain patents for certain inventions; which was read twice, and committed.

The SPEAKER laid before the House a letter from the Secretary of War, transmitting documents containing the information required by the resolution submitted by Mr. WRIGHT on the 22d instant, relative to the execution of the act fixing the Military Peace Establishment; which was read and referred to the Committee on Military Affairs.

THE REVENUE.

The House again resolved itself into a Committee of the Whole, on the report of the Committee of Ways and Means.

Mr. RANDOLPH concluded his speech, which he began on Thursday at about three o'clock; when the Committee rose, and the House adjourned.

MONDAY, January 29.

Mr. KING, of Massachusetts, presented a petition of Jabez Mowry, and others, citizens of the United States, stating that, upon the capture of Eastport by the British forces during the late war, a number of bonds given by them to the United States, to secure the duties on imported merchandise, fell into the hands of the British authorities; that suits have been commenced against some of them by the British Government at Halifax, and judgment rendered; that the cases are now pending before the higher courts in Great Britain; that some of them have been arrested and confined for three months at Halifax, and that others have been pursued by the British military force within the acknowledged limits of the United States, since the ratification of the Treaty of Peace; that the civil authorities of the United States have also commenced suits against them on said bonds; and praying the interposition of the Government of the United States between them and Great Britain; upon which they are prepared to pay the money into the Treasury of the United States.—Referred to Messrs. KING, of Massachusetts, CONNER, WHEATON, YATES, and BENNETT.

Mr. SERGEANT presented a petition of the merchants and traders in the city of Philadelphia, praying that the present rate of duties may con-

769 HISTORY OF CONGRESS. 770

JANUARY, 1816. *Money Lost by a Paymaster—Indemnity to Militia.* H. OF R.

tinue for such length of time as shall produce equal justice to all, or that a new tariff of duties may be established, to go into operation when the existing rate of duties shall cease.—Laid on the table.

Mr. CANNON presented a petition of William P. Lawrence, praying compensation for a negro slave, the property of the petitioner, who died of a disease contracted while attending a detachment of sick and disabled soldiers belonging to the Army of the United States.—Referred to the Committee of Claims.

Mr. LOWNDES, from the Committee of Ways and Means, reported a bill making appropriations for ordnance and ordnance stores for the year 1816; which was read twice, and committed to a Committee of the Whole.

Mr. ROBERTSON, from the Committee on the Public Lands, made a report on the petition of Samuel Dick, Asa Kitchell, and William Bruce, which was read; when Mr. R. reported a bill for the relief of Samuel Dick, William Bruce, and Asa Kitchell; which was read twice, and committed to a Committee of the Whole.

Mr. TUCKER, from the Committee for the District of Columbia, reported a bill making appropriation for enclosing and improving the public square near the Capitol; which was read twice, and committed to a Committee of the Whole.

Mr. TUCKER also reported a bill to incorporate the Columbian Insurance Company of Alexandria; which was read twice, and committed to a Committee of the Whole.

Mr. CANNON, after a pretty full explanation by him of the circumstances of this case, offered a resolution, which (having been modified on the suggestion of Mr. DESHA, to embrace the case generally of all militia who had been situated in the same manner as those of Tennessee, whom Mr. C. desired particularly to relieve) was agreed to in the following words:

Resolved, That the Committee on Military Affairs be instructed to inquire into the expediency of making provision by law for paying the different volunteers and militia corps, in the service of the United States during the late war with Great Britain, for the transportation of baggage, when such transportation was not furnished by the Government.

Mr. YANCEY, from the Committee of Claims, made a report on the petition of Manassah Minor, which was read; when Mr. Y. reported a bill for the relief of Manassah Minor; which was read twice, and committed to a Committee of the Whole.

MONEY LOST BY A PAYMASTER.

Mr. YANCEY also made a report on the petition of Zachariah Schoonmaker; which was read, and committed to a Committee of the whole House to-morrow.

The report is as follows:

That the petitioner was a Paymaster to the second regiment of volunteer militia of the State of New York, a part of which was stationed at Fort Richmond, on Staten Island, and a part at Sandy Hook, in the month of October, 1813; that, on the 8th day of that month,

14th CON. 1st SESS.—25

the petitioner received of the district Paymaster a check on the Bank of America for the sum of $9,000, which was paid him at the bank in three and ten dollar notes; that he paid to the troops stationed at Fort Richmond the sum of $4,159 95, and immediately proceeded to Sandy Hook, for the purpose of paying the troops at that place; that, before he left the fort, he had put the money which remained in his possession into a small trunk, which, for safe-keeping, he deposited in a large trunk, and kept the keys of the same himself. When he arrived at Sandy Hook he discovered that he had lost from his trunk the sum of $2,256, in which were included all the ten dollar notes and a part of the three dollar notes. Of that sum, $810, all in ten dollar notes, was afterwards found in a pile of sand in Fort Hudson; but the petitioner states that the balance, to wit, $1,436, he has entirely lost. The petitioner prays of Congress to be remunerated for the loss.

This case was presented at the second session of the last (thirteenth) Congress, and the committee were then of the opinion that the petitioner was not entitled to relief; [report 10th March, 1814, which was burnt at the destruction of the Capitol on the 24th August, 1814.] The principle has often been adopted, and which this committee are persuaded is correct, that, when a Paymaster has received money from the United States, to discharge a debt which the Government owes to its soldiers, and for which he receives an adequate compensation, he must be considered liable for the risk of the money, as well as its faithful and honest application. If the loss were produced by some inevitable accident, such as capture by an enemy, or some other unforeseen event, and which it would not be in the power of human diligence and wisdom to prevent or control, it would present a fit case for the equitable consideration and interference of Congress; but, in a case situated like the present, it is believed that sound policy and correct principles require that the party should abide by the contract he has made with the Government, and be held accountable for the money. The committee, therefore, recommend to the House the following resolution:

Resolved, That the prayer of the petitioner ought not to be granted.

INDEMNITY TO MILITIA.

Mr. YANCEY made a report on the petition of Daniel Gold, and others, militiamen, in the 20th brigade of Virginia militia, which was read; when Mr. Y. reported a bill for the relief of a company of the 20th brigade of Virginia militia, commanded by Captain Jonathan Walmsley; which was read twice, and committed to a Committee of the Whole.

The report is as follows:

That, in the year 1814, the petitioners served a tour of duty in the military service of the United States, at and near Norfolk, and, after having faithfully served out their time, obtained an honorable discharge for the same; that the funds which had been placed in the hands of the district Paymaster not being sufficient to discharge the amount of their pay, they received, at the time of their discharge, each, the sum of twenty dollars and twenty cents, and requested of Captain Jonathan Walmsley (who commanded the company to which they belonged) to settle and receive the balance of their pay from the Paymaster, and carry it to them in the county of Randolph, in the State of Virginia, where they resided. Captain Walmsley received of the

771   HISTORY OF CONGRESS.   772

H. of R.   *Post Office Department—The Revenue.*   January, 1816.

Paymaster at Norfolk a check on Robert Brent, Paymaster General, for the amount of the balance due to his men, and discounted it at that place at five per cent. On his way home, having taken a passage in the stage, he lodged at the Columbian hotel, in the city of Richmond, where his trunk was robbed of the money.

It appears to the committee, from the affidavits of John Mayoe, Lieutenant John Brown, and Captain Walmsley, that they all arrived at the hotel together, and lodged in the same room; that, after getting into the room, it was thought by them that the money which Captain Walmsley had in his pocket would be equally safe, and more conveniently kept in a trunk which belonged to Brown and Mayoe; that the money was accordingly placed in the trunk by Walmsley, in the presence of Brown and Mayoe, and the key of the trunk given to Walmsley. On the next morning after the money was deposited, upon unlocking the trunk for the purpose of taking it out, it was ascertained by all three of them that the money had been stolen.

In the room in which the trunk was, Mr. Mayoe lodged all night, and was at no time absent from the same, except a few minutes while at supper on that evening, and during that time he locked the door of the room upon starting to supper, and found it so locked upon his return to the same. The committee have the assurances of a member of the House of Representatives, that Walmsley, Brown, and Mayoe, are all men of good character.

The petitioners ask of Congress to be paid the balance of the money due them for their services.

In this case Walmsley may, perhaps, be considered the agent of the petitioners. Admitting that he is so to be considered, the question would arise in this case, whether they are to be bound by his acts, and receive the misfortune of his conduct. It is certainly a correct rule of justice that, in ordinary cases, the principal is bound by the acts of the agent; but the committee conceive this to be an exception to the general rule, the justice and policy of which they are willing to admit. In this case it was the duty of the Government, pointed out by one of its own laws, to have paid the militia for their services at the time and place of their discharge. In consequence, however, of circumstances not to be foreseen, and which must often occur in this country, especially in times of war, it was found inconvenient, on the part of the Government, to pay the militia at the time and place of their discharge. Not having done this, it seems to the committee reasonable and just, and not subversive of any correct principle of justice or policy, that, in this case, the Government should bear the risk of the money until it was paid over to the petitioners. They, therefore, report a bill for their relief.

POST OFFICE DEPARTMENT.

Mr. Ingham, from the Committee on the Post Office and Post Roads, made a report on the letter from the Postmaster General, of the 22d instant; which was read, and concurred in by the House, as follows:

The Committee of the Post Office and Post Roads, to whom was referred a letter addressed to the Speaker by the Postmaster General, requesting an investigation of the fiscal concerns of his Department, report: That they have had a conference with the Postmaster General on the subject of his letter, who states, that a rumor is in circulation with respect to the conduct of certain persons in his Department, which he considered was of such a nature as to require an investiga-

tion by a Committee of the House of Representatives. Your committee have ascertained that the rumor has proceeded from clerks in the General Post Office, and that it purports to indicate a suspicion, that some persons in that Department have been in the practice of selling draughts upon deputy postmasters for premiums, which have not been passed to the credit of the Department on the books. Your committee have not ascertained any fact to justify this rumor, but they consider it due to the character of the Post Office Department, as well as to the interest and policy of the Government, to comply with the request of the Postmaster General in recommending a more particular inquiry than would have been in their opinion compatible with the duties assigned to the Committee of Post Offices and Post Roads by the rules of the House. They, therefore, submit the following resolution:

Resolved, That a select committee be appointed, in conformity with the request of the Postmaster General, to investigate the conduct of the Post Office Department.

Messrs. Ingham, Barbour, Creighton, Cady, Tallmadge, Pickering, and Forney, were appointed the said committee.

THE REVENUE.

The House then again resolved itself into a Committee of the Whole on the Revenue subject. The question still under consideration was the proposition, by way of amendment, to repeal the direct tax.

Mr. McKee spoke in favor of this motion.

Mr. Parris, of Massachusetts, said:—I should not have risen in favor of the amendment proposed by the honorable member from Kentucky, had it not been for the unexpected opposition it met with from one of my honorable colleagues on yesterday; unexpected I say, sir, because, representing a people whose interests and sentiments are the same, I did not anticipate a difference in opinion on so important a subject. But, since I am so unfortunate as to differ from that honorable gentleman, with whom I usually act, it may be due to him, it certainly is to myself, that I should explain, in a few words, the reasons which will influence my vote.

I consider the object of the amendment to be a total repeal of the system of direct taxation upon the country; a total repeal of a measure obnoxious in itself, and to which this nation will never submit, unless under circumstances rendering it necessary for the purpose of defending its rights or protecting its liberties. Sir, when this tax was laid, such necessity was apparent; when it was increased its necessity was doubly so. What then was the situation of this country? Under what extreme pressure were these taxes submitted to? It is fresh in the recollection of every member of this House. Where, on the frontiers, were we not assailed? In the West, where were we not constantly alarmed by the depredations of the savages? In the North, where were we not threatened with immediate invasion? In the East, what part of our territory was in possession of the enemy? On the Atlantic, what coasts were not lighted by the flames of our ships; and I might ask, what was the internal situation of this country? An honorable member from Massachusetts, (Mr. HULBERT,) told us the other day, that the face of this nation had become pale. Sir, instead of a paleness being upon the face of the nation, the stupor, the coldness, and the inactivity of death were fast seizing upon some of its extreme members—a disease which threatened not so much the dissolution of the system, as the most fatal consequences to the parts disordered. Sir, under such circumstances, these taxes were submitted to. The people saw the necessity of placing in requisition the resources and energies of the nation, and of making a most powerful effort to save their country from the ravages of a vindictive enemy.

From the Administration that had declared war, not only by the consent, but at the imperative call of the people; from that Administration the same people would not withhold the means of its prosecution.

I ask gentlemen to recollect for what purpose these taxes were laid; I call upon them to consider the extreme circumstances under which they were laid, and I warn them of the consequences of continuing the system after that pressure and those circumstances are removed. If I believed this tax to be necessary for the purpose of defraying the expenses of the late war, if the faith of the Government could not be redeemed without it, or were it necessary to resuscitate the drooping credit of the nation, as odious as it is, as obnoxious as it is, as unequal as it is, it should have my warmest support, as should all other bills having the same object that might find their way to your table. Sir, in no section of this country have the people done more to aid the prosecution of the war, than in that which I have the honor particularly to represent. In none, have they been more ready to contribute the means or furnish the efficient force, and in no district of equal population are to be found more of those honorable but unfortunate testimonials which are the pride and the glory of the soldier. It is with peculiar satisfaction that I can assert, confidently assert, that the yeomanry of Maine are among the most firm supporters of your measures; and knowing them, as I do, respecting those with whom I have been intimate from my birth, I should hazard nothing in guaranteeing their future support. But, patriotic as they are, they do not expect that the taxes levied in consequence of the war will be continued as a system in peace. For what purpose do we want the product of this tax? To what use will we apply it? These are questions which the people have a right to ask us, and which we cannot avoid, but must answer. They pay the money, and of however little importance we may think the laying of this tax, believe me, sir, the farmer will not consider it so unimportant when he is paying it. Compare the receipts and expenditures as estimated by the Secretary of the Treasury in his official report, compare the same as estimated by the Committee of Ways and Means in their exhibit to the House, and granting those estimates to be perfectly correct, tell me if you can, where will be the deficiency. It will be

nowhere, there will be no deficiency; your ways and means will be sufficient, amply sufficient, without the direct tax, without the furniture tax, and without the taxes on manufactures, the long catalogue of which I hope never again to see incorporated in our statute book. Why will this tax be odious?—because, as was the case in 1798, it may be difficult to convince the people of its necessity. Like causes produce like effects. The fate of the unfortunate Administration of that day should be held up as a memento to every succeeding, and the rocks on which that foundered ought never to be obliterated from our political chart. Another reason why this mode of taxation is odious, is the great expense of its assessment and collection, and the number of officers employed in aiding its passage from the pocket of the citizen to the vaults of our Treasury. The people are unaccustomed to this mode of taxation; instead of rendering the valuation and paying the assessment to officers of their own choice, and belonging to their immediate neighborhood, they are called upon by men with whom they have no acquaintance, and in whose selection they have no voice. To this may be added, another reason for repealing this tax, which, although the last, is by no means the least important; I refer to the great inequality of its operation, not only among the several States, but among individuals of the same State, which I will attempt to prove. Sir, on examining the books in the office of the Secretary of the Treasury, it will be found, that taxable property of a given value in one State, pays more than double the amount of tax that is paid on property of an equal value in another, and that too in States where the Constitutional provisions relating to direct taxation, have a similar operation. Take for example, Massachusetts, Rhode Island, Connecticut, and Vermont. The average of the tax contemplated by the resolution now under debate, will be in Massachusetts twenty-one cents on each hundred dollars of taxable property; in Vermont it will be thirty cents; in Rhode Island but sixteen; and in Connecticut but thirteen. The result will be this, that laying the proposed tax according to the provisions of the Constitution, the State of Massachusetts at the above rate of twenty-one cents upon each hundred dollars of taxable property will pay three hundred and sixteen thousand dollars, when at the rate as paid by Rhode Island, her proportion would amount to but two hundred and forty-two thousand dollars, and as paid by Connecticut only to one hundred and ninety-seven thousand dollars. Against Vermont, the inequality will be still greater; the quota of that State will be ninety-eight thousand dollars, while the same amount of property in Connecticut will pay but forty-three thousand. This great inequality, which cannot be avoided without a violation of Constitutional principles, is to my mind a sufficient justification for advocating an entire repeal of the system.

But, I have another reason for supporting the amendment proposed by the honorable member from Kentucky. Unless driven to the last resort,

I would not tax the poor and the honest laborer who supports a numerous family by the cultivation of a few acres of our soil. Such rather merit the fostering protection of this Government. I could stand in the door of my humble dwelling, and point you to men possessing a few hundred dollars of property, who will pay more of this tax, than their neighbors who own so many thousands; and yet, for all the purposes of defence and protection, you will find the former the most spirited and effective. This I believe to be the fact throughout this nation. No, sir, if taxes we must have, let them be paid by the wealthy, by the man who rides in the coach, and not by him who passes for the footman; let them be laid upon the luxuries and superfluities of life, and not upon those articles of necessity, without which it cannot be supported. If the receipts of the ensuing year will meet the expenditures, and I am constrained to believe so from evidence derived from official sources, now lying on our tables, how can we justify to the people the continuance of this tax? It cannot be done, its repeal is expected, confidently expected.

In that section of the country in which I am more immediately acquainted, it has been with extreme difficulty that the farmer could procure the cash to discharge this tax; I say cash, sir, for we, there, have nothing of that circulating medium which the gentleman from Virginia (Mr. Randolph) denominates rags. Of the first tax of three millions, the whole has been paid; of the last tax of six millions, not a cent. Sir, I hope while our tax-gatherers are enforcing the collection of this tax, the like of which they have never known, we shall not be here preparing to follow them with another. Whatever may be the opinion entertained in this House or this nation of the disposition of that State, I feel myself not bound to refute it. I answer only for a part, for that people with whom I am immediately connected, a people who, I rejoice in the opportunity of assuring you, have not participated in that kind of loyalty for which their State has been so proverbial. I know them well, I know their attachment to your measures, an attachment which has been tried in the days of adversity and cannot fail to be respected in the days of prosperity. On this subject I know their wishes, their sentiments and their feelings, and in their behalf I call for a repeal of this tax.

Sir, much has been said in this debate about reducing the Army and dismantling the Navy; I confess myself not to be a favorite of large standing armies, they add nothing to the security of the citizen, little to that of the States. But why reduce the present Peace Establishment? it is not so large as to be dangerous in the hands of any Executive, nor so expensive as to be burdensome to the people. We have already dismissed from our service a host of officers, many of whom are equally brave, equally meritorious as those we have retained. Let us provide for those now in service, and while doing that forget not the claims of others who have served us with equal fidelity. The Navy—reduce the Navy!

no, sir, on that we depend not only for protection, but for negotiation; for the former more effectual than all our armies, for the latter more powerful than all our Ministers; instead of reducing I would increase the Navy; and while we have such men to command as grace the naval history of the late war, we have no cause to be apprehensive of the recurrence or the result of another.

Mr. Clay (Speaker) said the course had been pursued ever since he had had the honor of a seat on this floor, to select some subject during the early part of the session, on which, by a general understanding, gentlemen were allowed to indulge themselves in remarks on the existing state of public affairs. The practice was a very good one, he said, and there could be no occasion more proper than that of a proposition to lay a direct tax.

Those who have for fifteen years past administered the affairs of this Government, have conducted this nation to an honorable point of elevation, at which they may justly pause, challenge a retrospect, and invite attention to the bright field of prosperity which lies before us.

The great objects of the Committee of Finance in the report under consideration are, in the first place, to provide for the payment of the public debts, and in the second, to provide for the support of the Government, and the payment of such expenses as should be authorized by Congress. The greater part of the debt, Mr. C. admitted, had grown out of the late war; yet a considerable portion of it consisted of that contracted in the former war for Independence, and a portion of it perhaps of that which arose out of the wars with Tripoli and Algiers. Gentlemen had on this occasion, therefore, fairly a right to examine into the course of the Administration heretofore, to demonstrate the impolicy of those wars, and the injudiciousness of the public expenditures generally. In the cursory view which he should take of this subject, he must be allowed to say he should pay no particular attention to what had passed before in debate. An honorable colleague, (Mr. Hardin,) who spoke the other day, like another gentleman who preceded him in debate, had taken occasion to refer to his (Mr. C.'s) late absence from this country on public business; but, Mr. C. said, he trusted among the fruits of that absence were a greater respect for the institutions which distinguish this happy country, a greater confidence in them, and an increased disposition to cling to them. Yes, sir, said Mr. C., I was in the neighborhood of the battle of Waterloo, and some lessons I did derive from it; but they were lessons which satisfied me that national independence was only to be maintained by national resistance against foreign encroachments, by cherishing the interests of the people, and giving to the whole physical power of the country an interest in the preservation of the nation. I have been taught that lesson; that we should never lose sight of the possibility that a combination of despots, of men unfriendly to liberty, propagating what in their opinion constitutes the principle of legitimacy, might reach our happy land, and subject us to that tyranny and degradation which seems to be one of their objects in another country. The result of my reflections is the determination to aid with my vote in providing my country with all the means to protect its liberties, and guard them even from serious menace. Motives of delicacy, which the committee would be able to understand and appreciate, prevented him from noticing some of his colleague's (Mr. HARDIN's) remarks; but he would take the occasion to give him one admonition, that when he next favored the House with an exhibition of his talent for wit—with a display of those elegant implements, for his possession of which the gentleman from Virginia had so handsomely complimented him, that he would recollect that it is bought and not borrowed wit, which the adage recommends as best. With regard to the late war with Great Britain, history, in deciding upon the justice and policy of that war, will determine the question according to the state of things which existed when that war was declared. I gave a vote for the declaration of war, said Mr. C.—I exerted all the little influence and talents I could command to make the war. The war was made; it is terminated; and I declare, with perfect sincerity, if it had been permitted me to lift the veil of futurity, and to have foreseen the precise series of events which have occurred, my vote would have been unchanged. The policy of the war, as it regarded our state of preparation, must be determined with reference to the state of things at the time that war was declared. Mr. C. said he need not take up the time of the House in demonstrating that we had cause sufficient for war. We had been insulted, and outraged, and spoliated upon by almost all Europe—by Great Britain, by France, Spain, Denmark, Naples, and to cap the climax, by the little contemptible Power of Algiers. We had submitted too long and too much. We had become the scorn of foreign Powers, and the contempt of our own citizens. The question of the policy of declaring war at the particular time when it was commenced, is best determined, Mr. C. remarked, by applying to the enemy himself; and what said he? That of all the circumstances attending its declaration, none was so aggravating as that we should have selected the moment which, of all others, was most inconvenient to him; when he was struggling for self-existence in a last effort against the gigantic power of France. The question of the state of preparation for war at any time is a relative question—relative to our own means, the condition of the other Power, and the state of the world at the time of declaring it. We could not expect, for instance, that a war against Algiers would require the same means or extent of preparation as a war against Great Britain; and if it was to be waged against one of the primary Powers of Europe, at peace with all the rest of the world, and therefore all her force at command, it could not be commenced with so little preparation as if her whole force were employed in another quarter. It is not necessary again to repel, said

Mr. C., the stale, ridiculous, false story of French influence, originating in Great Britain and echoed here. I now contend—so I have always done—that we had a right to take advantage of the condition of the world at the time war was declared. If Great Britain were engaged in war, we had a right to act on the knowledge of the fact, that her means of annoyance, as to us, were diminished; and we had a right to obtain all the collateral aid we could from the operations of other Powers against her, without entering into those connexions which are forbidden by the genius of our Government. But, Mr. C. said, it was rather like disturbing the ashes of the dead, now to discuss the questions of the justice or expediency of the war. They were questions long since settled, and on which the public opinion was decisively made up in favor of the Administration.

He proceeded to examine the conditions of the peace and the fruits of the war—questions of more recent date, and more immediately applicable to the present discussion. The terms of the peace, Mr. C. said, must be determined by the same rule that was applicable to the declaration of war—that rule which was furnished by the state of the world at the time the peace was made. And, even if it were true that all the sanguine expectations which might have been formed at the time of the declaration of war were not realized by the terms of the subsequent peace, it did not follow that the war was improperly declared, or the peace dishonorable, unless the condition of the parties in relation to other Powers remained substantially the same throughout the struggle, and at the time of the termination of the war, as they were at the commencement of it. At the termination of the war, France was annihilated—blotted out of the map of Europe;—the vast power wielded by Bonaparte existed no longer. Let it be admitted that statesmen, in laying their course, are to look at probable events—that their conduct is to be examined with reference to the course of events which in all human probability might have been anticipated—and is there a man in this House in existence who can say, that on the 18th day of June, 1812, when the war was declared, it would have been anticipated that Great Britain would, by the circumstance of a general peace, resulting from the overthrow of a Power whose basements were supposed to be deeper laid, more ramified, and more extended, than those of any Power ever were before—be placed in the attitude in which she stood in December, 1814? Would any one say that the Government could have anticipated such a state of things, and ought to have been governed in its conduct accordingly? Great Britain, Russia, Germany, did not expect—not a Power in Europe believed—as late even as January, 1814, that, in the ensuing March, Bonaparte would abdicate, and the restoration of the Bourbons would follow. What then was the actual condition of Europe when peace was concluded? A perfect tranquillity reigned throughout; for, as late as the 1st of March, the idea of Napoleon reappearing in France was as little entertained as that of a man's coming from the moon to take upon himself the government of the country. In December, 1814, a profound and apparently permanent peace existed. Great Britain was left to dispose of the vast force—the accumulation of twenty-five years—the work of an immense system of finance and protracted war. She was at liberty to employ that undivided force against this country. Under such circumstances, it did not follow, Mr. C. said, according to the rules laid down, either that the war ought not to have been made, or that peace, on such terms, ought not to have been concluded.

What then, Mr. C. asked, were the terms of the peace? The regular Opposition in this country—the gentlemen on the other side of the House—had not come out to challenge an investigation of the terms of the peace, although they had several times given a sidewipe at the treaty on occasions with which it had no necessary connexion. It had been sometimes said that we had gained nothing by the war—that the fisheries were lost, &c. How, he asked, did this question of the fisheries really stand? By the first part of the third article of the Treaty of 1783, the right was recognised in the people of the United States to take fish of every kind on the Grand bank and on all the other banks of Newfoundland; also in the Gulf of St. Lawrence, and at all other places in the sea, where the inhabitants of both countries used at any time to fish. This right was a necessary incident to our sovereignty, although it is denied to some of the Powers of Europe. It was not contested at Ghent; it has never been drawn in question by Great Britain. But, by the same third article, it was further stipulated that the inhabitants of the United States shall have "liberty to 'take fish of every kind on such part of the coast ' of Newfoundland as British fishermen shall use, ' (but not to dry or cure the same on that island) ' and also on the coasts, bays, and creeks of all ' other of His Britannic Majesty's dominions in ' America; and that the American fishermen shall ' have liberty to dry and cure fish in any of the ' unsettled bays, harbors, and creeks, of Nova ' Scotia, Magdalen Island, and Labrador, so long ' as the same shall remain unsettled; but, so soon ' as the same or either of them shall be settled, it ' shall not be lawful for the said fishermen to dry ' or cure fish at such settlement, without a previ- ' ous agreement for that purpose with the inhab- ' itants, proprietors, or possessors, of the ground."

The British Commissioners, assuming that those liberties had expired by the war between the two countries, at an early period of the negotiation declared that they would not be revived without an equivalent. Whether the Treaty of 1783 does not form an exception to the general rule, according to which treaties are vacated by a war breaking out between the parties, is a question on which he did not mean to express an opinion. The first article of that treaty, by which the King of Great Britain acknowledges the sovereignty of the United States, certainly was not abrogated by the war; that all the other parts of the same instrument which define the limits, privileges, and lib-

erties, attaching to that sovereignty, were equally unaffected by the war, might be contended for with at least much plausibility. If we determined to offer them the equivalent required, the question was, what should it be? When the British Commissioners demanded, in their *projet*, a renewal to Great Britain of the right to the navigation of the Mississippi, secured by the Treaty of 1783, a bare majority of the American Commissioners offered to renew it, upon the condition that the liberties in question were renewed to us. He was not one of that majority. He would not trouble the Committee with his reasons for being opposed to the offer. A majority of his colleagues, actuated he believed by the best motives, made however the offer, and it was refused by the British Commissioners.

If the British interpretation of the Treaty of 1783 be correct, we have lost the liberties in question. What the value of them really is, he had not been able to meet with any two gentlemen who agreed. The great value of the whole mass of our fishery interests, as connected with our navigation and trade, was sufficiently demonstrated by the tonnage employed; but, what was the relative importance of these fisheries, there was great contrariety of statements. They were liberties to be exercised within a foreign jurisdiction, and some of them were liable to be destroyed by the contingency of settlement. He did not believe that much importance attached to such liberties. And, supposing them to be lost, we are perhaps sufficiently indemnified by the redemption of the British mortgage upon the navigation of the Mississippi. This great stream, on that supposition, is placed (where it ought to be) in the same independent condition with the Hudson, or any other river in the United States.

If, on the contrary, the opposite construction of the Treaty of 1783 be the true one, these liberties remain to us, and the right to the navigation of the Mississippi, as secured to Great Britain by that instrument, continues with her.

But, Mr. C. said, he was surprised to hear a gentleman from the Western country (Mr. Hardin) exclaim, that we had gained nothing by the war. Great Britain acquired, by the treaty negotiated by Mr. Jay, the right to trade with the Indians within our Territories. It was a right upon which she placed great value, and from the pursuit of which she did not desist without great reluctance. It had been exercised by her agents in a manner to excite the greatest sensibility in the Western country. This right was clearly lost by the war; for whatever may be the true opinion as to the Treaty of 1783, there can be no doubt that the stipulations of that of 1794 no longer exist.

It had been said, that the great object in the continuation of the war had been to secure our mariners against impressment, and that peace was made without accomplishing it. With regard to the Opposition, he presumed that they would not urge any such argument. For, if their opinion was to be inferred (though he hoped in this case it was not) from that of an influential and distinguished member of the Opposition, we had reason to believe that they did not think the British doctrines wrong on this subject. He alluded to a letter said to be written by a gentleman of great consideration, residing in an adjoining State, to a member of this House, in which the writer states that he conceives the British claim to be right, and expresses his hope that the President, however he might kick at it, would be compelled to swallow the bitter pill. If the peace had really given up the American doctrine, it would have been, according to that opinion, merely yielding to the force of the British right. In that view of the subject, the error of the Administration would have been in contending for too much in behalf of this country; for he presumed there was no doubt that, whether right or wrong, it would be an important principle gained to secure our seamen against British impressment. And he trusted in God that all future Administrations would rather err on the side of contending for too much than too little for America.

But Mr. C. was willing to admit that the conduct of the Administration ought to be tried by their own opinions, and not those of the Opposition. One of the great causes of the war, and of its continuance, was the practice of impressment exercised by Great Britain; and if this claim has been admitted, by necessary implication or express stipulation, the Administration has abandoned the rights of our seamen. It was with utter astonishment that he heard that it had been contended in this country, that because our right of exemption from the practice had not been expressly secured in the treaty, it was therefore given up! It was impossible that such an argument could be advanced on that floor. No member who regarded his reputation would, dared, advance such an argument here.

Had the war terminated, the practice continuing, he admitted that such might be a fair inference; and on some former occasion he had laid down the principle, which he thought correct, that if the United States did then make peace with Great Britain, the war in Europe continuing, and therefore she continuing the exercise of the practice, without any stipulation to secure us against its effects, the plain inference would be, that we had surrendered the right. But what was the fact? At the time of the conclusion of the Treaty of Peace, Great Britain had ceased the practice of impressment; she was not only at peace with all the Powers of Europe, but there was every prospect of a permanent and durable peace. The treaty being silent on the subject of impressment, the only plain rational result was, that neither party had conceded its rights, but they were left totally unaffected by it. Mr. C. said he recollected to have heard in the British House of Commons, whilst he was in Europe, the very reverse of the doctrine advanced here on this subject. The British Ministry were charged by a member of the Opposition with having surrendered their right of impressment, and the same course of reasoning was employed to prove it as he understood was employed in this country to prove our acquiescence in that practice. The argument was this: the war was made on the professed ground of resistance of the practice of impressment; the peace having been made without a recognition of the right by America, the treaty being silent on the subject, the inference was, that the British authorities had surrendered the right; that they had failed to secure it, and, having done so, had in effect yielded it. The member of the Opposition in England was just as wrong as any member of this House would be, who should contend that the right of impressment is surrendered to the British Government. The fact was, Mr. C. said, neither party had surrendered its rights; things remain as though the war had never been made; both parties are in possession of all the rights they had anterior to the war. Lest it might be deduced that his sentiments on the subject of impressment had undergone a change, he took the opportunity to say, that although he desired to preserve peace between Great Britain and the United States, and to maintain between them that good understanding calculated to promote the interest of each, yet, whenever Great Britain should give satisfactory evidence of her design to apply her doctrine of impressment as heretofore, he was, for one, ready to take up arms again to oppose her. The fact was, that the two nations had been placed in a state of hostility as to a practice growing out of the war in Europe. The war ceasing between Great Britain and the rest of Europe, left England and America engaged in a contest on an aggression which had also practically ceased. The question had then presented itself, whether the United States should be kept in war, to gain an abandonment of what had become a mere abstract principle, or looking at the results, and relying on the good sense and sound discretion of both countries, we should not recommend the termination of the war. When no practical evil could result from the suspension of hostilities, and there was no more than a possibility of the removal of the practice of impressment, I, as one of the mission, consented with sincere pleasure to the peace, satisfied that we gave up no right, sacrificed no honor, compromitted no important principle. He said, then, applying the rule of the actual state of things, as that by which to judge of the peace, there was nothing in the conditions or terms of the peace that was dishonorable, nothing for reproach, nothing for regret.

Gentlemen have complained that we had lost the islands in the Bay of Passamaquoddy. Have they examined into that question, and do they know the grounds on which it stands? Prior to the war we occupied Moose Island, the British Grand Menan. Each party claimed both islands. America, because they are within the limits of the United States, as defined by the Treaty of 1783; and Great Britain, because, as she alleges, they were in the exception contained in the second article of that treaty as to islands within the limits of the province of Nova Scotia. All the information which he had received concurred in representing Grand Menan as the most valuable

mensurate with the actual state of the country, should grow with its growth, and keep pace with its progress. Look at that map, (said he, pointing to the large map of the United States which hangs in the Hall of the House of Representatives;) at the vast extent of that country which stretches from the Lake of the Woods, in the Northwest, to the Bay of Fundy, in the East. Look at the vast extent of our maritime coast; recollect we have Indians and powerful nations conterminous on the whole frontier; and that we know not at what moment the savage enemy or Great Britain herself may seek to make war with us. Ought the force of the country to be graduated by the scale of our exposure, or are we to be uninfluenced by the increase of our liability to war? Have we forgotten that the power of France, as a counterpoise to that of Great Britain, is annihilated—gone; never to rise again, I believe, under the weak, unhappy, and imbecile race, who now sway her destinies? Any individual must, I think, come to the same conclusion with myself, who takes these considerations into view, and reflects on our growth, the state of our defence, the situation of the nations of the world, and above all, of that nation with whom we are most likely to come into collision; for it is in vain to conceal it, this country must have many a hard and desperate tug with Great Britain, let the two Governments be administered how and by whom they may. That man must be blind to the indications of the future, who cannot see that we are destined to have war after war with Great Britain, until, if one of the two nations be not crushed, all grounds of collision shall have ceased between us. I repeat, said Mr. C., if the condition of France were that of perfect repose, instead of that of a volcano ready to burst out again with a desolating eruption; if with Spain our differences were settled; if the dreadful war raging in South America were terminated; if the marines of all the Powers of Europe were resuscitated as they stood prior to the Revolution of France; if there was universal repose, and profound tranquillity among all the nations of the earth, considering the actual growth of our country, in his judgment, the force of ten thousand men would not be too great for its exigencies. Do gentlemen ask if I rely on the regular force entirely for the defence of the country? I answer, it is for garrisoning and keeping in order our fortifications, for the preservation of the national arms, for something like a safe depository of military science and skill, to which we may recur in time of danger, that I desire to maintain an adequate regular force. I know that in the hour of peril our great reliance must be on the whole physical force of the country, and that no detachment of it can be exclusively depended on. History proves that no nation not destitute of the military art, whose people were united in its defence, ever was conquered. It is true that in countries where standing armies have been entirely relied on the armies have been subdued, and the subjugation of the nation has been the consequence of it; but no example is to be found of a united people being conquered who possessed an adequate degree of military knowledge. Look at the Grecian Republics struggling successfully against the overwhelming force of Persia; look more recently at Spain. I have great confidence in the militia, and I would go with my honorable colleague, (Mr. McKee,) whose views I know are honest, hand in hand, in arming, disciplining, and rendering effective the militia; I am for providing the nation with every possible means of resistance. I ask my honorable colleague, after I have gone thus far with him, to go a step further with me, and let us retain the force we now have for the purposes I have already described. I ask gentlemen who propose to reduce the Army, if they have examined in detail the number and extent of the posts and garrisons on our maritime and interior frontier? If they have not gone through this process of reasoning, how shall we arrive at the result that we can reduce the Army with safety? There is not one of our forts adequately garrisoned at this moment; and there is nearly one-fourth of them that have not one solitary man. I said the other day, that I would rather vote for the augmentation than the reduction of the Army. When returning to my country from its foreign service, and looking at this question, it appeared to me that the maximum was 20,000, the minimum 10,000 of the force we ought to retain. And I again say, that rather than reduce I would vote to increase the present force.

A standing army, Mr. C. said, had been deemed necessary from the commencement of the Government to the present time. The question was only as to the quantum of force; and not whether it should exist. No man who regards his political reputation would place himself before the people on a proposition for its absolute disbandment. He admitted a question as to quantum might be carried so far as to rise into a question of principle. If we were to propose to retain an army of thirty or forty or fifty thousand men, then truly the question would present itself, whether our rights were not in some danger from such a standing army, whether reliance was to be placed altogether on a standing army or on that natural safe defence which, according to the habits of the country and the principles of our Government, is considered the bulwark of our liberties. But between five and ten thousand men, or any number under ten thousand, it could not be a question of principle; for, unless gentlemen were afraid of spectres, it was utterly impossible that any danger could be apprehended from ten thousand men, dispersed on a frontier of many thousand miles—here twenty or thirty, there an hundred, and the largest amount at Detroit, not exceeding a thin regiment. And, yet, brave gentlemen—gentlemen who are not alarmed at hobgoblins—who can intrepidly vote even against taxes, are alarmed by a force of this extent? What, he asked, was the amount of the Army in the time of Mr. Jefferson, a time, the orthodoxy of which had been so ostentatiously proclaimed? It was true, when that gentleman came into power, it was with a determination to retrench as far as practicable. Under the full influence of these notions, in 1802, the bold step of wholly disbanding the Army, never was thought of. The Military Peace Establishment was then fixed at about four thousand men. But, before Mr. Jefferson went out of power, what was done—that is, in April 1808? In addition to the then existing Peace Establishment, eight regiments, amounting to between five and six thousand men, were authorized, making a total force precisely equal to the present Peace Establishment. It was true that all this force had never been actually enlisted and embodied; that the recruiting service had been suspended; and that at the commencement of the war we had far from this number; and, Mr. C. said, we have not now actually ten thousand men, being at least two thousand deficient of that number. Mr. C. adverted to what had been said on this and other occasions of Mr. Jefferson's not having seized the favorable moment for war which was afforded by the attack on the Chesapeake. He had always entertained the opinion, he said, that Mr. Jefferson on that occasion took the correct, manly and frank course, in saying to the British Government—your officers have done this—it is an enormous aggression—do you approve the act, do you make it your cause or not? That Government did not sanction the act; it disclaimed it, and promptly too—and, although they for a long time withheld the due redress, it was ultimately tendered. If Mr. Jefferson had used his power to carry the country into a war at that period, it might have been supported by public opinion during the moment of fever, but it would soon abate, and the people would begin to ask, why this war had been made without understanding whether the British Government avowed the conduct of its officers, &c. If the threatening aspect of our relations with England had entered into the consideration which had caused the increase of the Army at that time, Mr. C. said, there were considerations equally strong at this time, with our augmented population, for retaining our present force. If, however, there were no threatenings from any quarter, if the relative force of European nations, and the general balance of power existing before the French revolution were restored; if South America had not made the attempt, in which he trusted in God she would succeed, to achieve her independence; if our affairs with Spain were settled, he would repeat, that ten thousand men would not be too great a force for the necessities of the country, and with a view to future emergencies.

He had taken the liberty the other day to make some observations which he might now repeat, as furnishing auxiliary considerations for adopting a course of prudence and precaution. He had then said, that our affairs with Spain were not settled, &c., that the Spanish Minister was reported to have made some inadmissible demands of our Government. The fact turned out, Mr. C. said, as he had presented it. It appeared that what was then rumor was now fact; and Spain had taken the ground not only that there must be a discussion of our title to that part of Louisiana

formerly called West Florida, (which it might be doubted whether it ought to take place,) but had required that we must surrender the territory first and discuss the right to it afterwards. Besides this unsettled state of our relations with Spain, he said, there were other rumors—and he wished to God we had the same means of ascertaining their correctness, as we had found of ascertaining the truth of the rumor just noticed—it was rumored that the Spanish province of Florida had been ceded, with all her pretensions, to Great Britain. Would gentlemen tell him, then, that this was a time when any statesman would pursue the hazardous policy of disarming entirely—of quietly smoking our pipes by our firesides, regardless of impending danger? It might be a palatable doctrine to some, but, he was persuaded, was condemned by the rules of conduct in private life, by those maxims of sound precaution by which individuals would regulate their private affairs. Mr. C. said, he did not here mean to take up the question in relation to South America. Still it was impossible not to see that, in the progress of things, we might be called on to decide the question whether we would or would not lend them our aid. This opinion he boldly declared—and he entertained it, not in any pursuit of vain glory, but from a deliberate conviction of its being conformable to the best interests of the country—that having a proper understanding with foreign Powers—that understanding which prudence and a just precaution recommended—it would undoubtedly be good policy to take part with the patriots of South America. He believed it could be shown that, on the strictest principles of public law, we have a right to take part with them, that it is our interest to take part with them, and that our interposition in their favor would be effectual. But he confessed, with infinite regret, that he saw a supineness on this interesting subject throughout the country, which left him almost without hope, that what he believed the correct policy of the country would be pursued. He considered the release of any part of America from the dominions of the Old World, as adding to the general security of the new. He could not contemplate the exertions of the people of South America, without wishing that they might triumph and nobly triumph. He believed the cause of humanity would be promoted by the interposition of any foreign Power which should terminate the contest between the friends and enemies of independence in that quarter, for a more bloody and cruel war never had been carried on since the days of Adam than that which is now raging in South America—in which not the least regard is paid to the laws of war, to the rights of capitulation, to the rights of prisoners, nor even to the rights of kindred. I do not, said Mr. C. offer these views expecting to influence the opinions of others; they are opinions of my own. But, on the question of general policy, whether or not we shall interfere in the war in South America, it may turn out that, whether we will or will not choose to interfere in their behalf, we shall be drawn into the

HISTORY OF CONGRESS.

The Revenue.

contest in the course of its progress. Among other demands by the Minister of Spain, is the exclusion of the flag of Buenos Ayres and other parts of South America from our ports. Our Government has taken a ground on this subject, of which I think no gentleman can disapprove—that all parties shall be admitted and hospitably treated in our ports, provided they conform to our laws while amongst us. What course Spain may take upon this subject, it was impossible now to say. Although I would not urge this as an argument for increasing our force, said Mr. C., I would place it among those considerations which ought to have weight with every enlightened mind in determining upon the propriety of its reduction. It is asserted that Great Britain has strengthened and is strengthening herself in the provinces adjoining us. Is this a moment when in prudence we ought to disarm? No, sir. Preserve your existing force. It would be extreme indiscretion to lessen it.

Mr. C. here made some observations to show that a reduction of the Army to from four to five thousand men, as had been suggested, would not occasion such a diminution of expense as to authorize the rejection of the report, or any essential alteration in the amount of revenue, which the system proposes to raise from internal taxes, and his colleague (Mr. McKee) appeared equally hostile to all of them. Having, however, shown that we cannot in safety reduce the Army, Mr. C. would leave the details of the report in the abler hands of the honorable chairman, (Mr. Lowndes,) who, he had no doubt, could demonstrate, that with all the retrenchments which had been recommended, the Government would be bankrupt in less time than three years, if most of these taxes were not continued. He would now hasten to that conclusion, at which the Committee could not regret more than he did, that he had not long since arrived.

As to the attitude in which this country should be placed, the duty of Congress could not be mistaken. My policy is to preserve the present force, naval and military; to provide for the augmentation of the Navy; and if the danger of war should increase, to increase the Army also. Arm the militia, and give it the most effective character of which it is susceptible. Provide in the most ample manner, and place in proper depots, all the munitions and instruments of war. Fortify and strengthen the weak and vulnerable points indicated by experience. Construct military roads and canals, particularly from the Miami of the Ohio to the Miami of Erie; from the Sciota to the Bay of Sandusky; from the Hudson to Ontario; that the facilities of transportation may exist of the men and means of the country to points where they may be wanted. I would employ on this object a part of the Army, which should also be employed on our line of frontier, territorial and maritime, in strengthening the works of defence. I would provide steam-batteries for the Mississippi, for Borgne and Pontchartrain, and for the Chesapeake, and for any part of the North or East where they might be

beneficially employed. In short, said Mr. C., I would act seriously, effectively act, on the principle, that in peace we ought to prepare for war—for I repeat, again and again, that in spite of all the prudence exerted by the Government, and the forbearance of others, the hour of trial will come. These halcyon days of peace, this calm will yield to the storm of war; and when that comes, I am for being prepared to breast it. Has not the Government been reproached for the want of preparation at the commencement of the late war? And yet the same gentlemen who utter these reproaches, instead of taking counsel from experience, would leave the country in an unprepared condition.

He would as earnestly commence the great work, too long delayed, of internal improvement. He desired to see a chain of turnpike roads and canals from Passamaquoddy to New Orleans, and other similar roads intersecting the mountains, to facilitate intercourse between all parts of the country, and to bind and connect us together. He would also effectually protect our manufactories. We had given at least an implied pledge to do so by the course of administration. He would afford them protection, not so much for the sake of the manufacturers themselves as for the general interest. We should thus have our wants supplied when foreign resources are cut off, and we should also lay the basis of a system of taxation, to be resorted to when the revenue from imports is stopped by war. Such, Mr. Chairman, is a rapid sketch of the policy which it seems to me it becomes us to pursue. It is for you now to decide whether we shall draw wisdom from the past, or, neglecting the lessons of recent experience, we shall go on headlong without foresight, meriting and receiving the reproaches of the community. I trust, sir, notwithstanding the unpromising appearances sometimes presenting themselves, during the present session, we shall yet do our duty. I appeal to the friends around me—with whom I have been associated for years in public life, who nobly, manfully vindicated the national character by a war, waged by a young people, unskilled in arms, single-handed, against a veteran Power; a war which the nation has emerged from covered with laurels. Let us now do something to ameliorate the internal condition of the country; let us show that objects of domestic no less than those of foreign policy receive our attention; let us fulfil the just expectations of the public, whose eyes are anxiously directed towards this session of Congress; let us, by a liberal and enlightened policy, entitle ourselves, upon our return home, to that best of all rewards, the grateful exclamation—"Well done thou good and faithful servant!"

When Mr. Clay had taken his seat—

Mr. Hopkinson rose and said: My participation in the counsels of the country is of such recent date, that I may feel astonishment at occurrences which excited no surprise in more experienced politicians. The course which the business now under discussion has taken appears to me to be a phenomenon in legislation. This Congress, sir, assembled after the conclusion of a war which had called for vast efforts and expenditures, and accumulated a very heavy debt. At the commencement of the session the usual committees for the arrangement of the public business were appointed, and among the rest, most prominent and most important, the Committee of Ways and Means. It was the duty of this committee to examine into the state of the finances of the nation, to make accurate estimates of its wants, a judicious examination of its means, and fairly and impartially to apply the one to the necessities of the other. The committee then appointed, in due time, and it is presumed on due consideration, made their report upon these high matters to the House, and the debate we are now engaged in arises out of that report. In the usual course of Parliamentary affairs, it was doubtless to have been expected, that the opposition, if any, to the estimates and means thus furnished by the avowed friends of the Administration, would have come from what I find is called "the Opposition." But no such thing. We, on this side of the House, sat patient and silent, prepared to take our share of the burden, and endure our portion of the suffering. As far as we can judge from the indications in our knowledge, the system then matured and delivered, would have, generally at least, been adopted and carried into operation—when, behold, the storm of opposition rises, not with the Opposition, but the declared friends and supporters of the Administration, and of those measures which have called for these extraordinary burdens and supplies! I should have supposed that these gentlemen would have been willing to forget local interests, to surrender subordinate opinions, and to unite heartily in the great work of paying the national debt, and providing for future expenditures. But, I beg it may be distinctly remembered that the first assault upon the reported system of finance, that assault which goes to its vitality, and opened a breach which others—still declared friends of the Administration—have widened, was made by the honorable gentleman from Kentucky, the Speaker of the House. A motion was made by that gentleman to reduce the land tax from three to two millions. This motion failed. Not disheartened by the defeat, he followed up the attempt by a blow infinitely more deadly to the whole scheme, by moving that the land tax should be an annual tax; while every other tax reported is perpetual, and the whole together declared to be a permanent system of taxation. In this the gentleman was successful, and so great a part as three millions of a permanent system, has assurance of existence but for a single year. If this unfortunate, and I may say ill-judged movement, shall throw the whole into confusion, and the Government is thereby embarrassed, the public faith impeached, and the public establishments pinched, let it be remembered whence these evils have flowed; let them be traced to their true source, the friends of the Administration, and not to the Opposition. When the honorable Speaker had made this first step, it was natural to expect that some other

gentleman, of the same side, should be ambitious to step before him, and accordingly we find that his colleague proposes to abolish altogether this odious land tax, and strike it out of the system; and, of course, to throw these three millions upon the shoulders of those who have been, or may be, kind enough to take the rest of the burden. Is this dealing fairly and equitably by all? But, sir, the cause of wonder does not stop here; the greater wonder is yet untold. No sooner does the honorable Speaker suggest his essential, his vital change in this system of finance, than the honorable chairman of the committee, by whom it was reported, surrenders it at discretion, without an effort to defend or a struggle to preserve it. Can it be expected that we, in opposition, however well disposed, can retain our confidence in a system thus solemnly reported, as the mature work of knowledge and deliberation, and thus abandoned as if the plaything of a child? I know not the reasons which have determined the honorable chairman to this course. His intelligence and candor oblige me to believe that he can give a satisfactory explanation of it, but until it is given I must pause in my confidence. For myself, sir, I assure you most seriously, that I took my seat here with a fixed intent to give all the aid in my power to extricate the country from her difficulties, and to provide for her future support; to place the resources of the nation fairly and liberally at the disposal of those whom the people have chosen to govern them, and to suffer no feelings of my own in relation to the Administration to interfere with the conscientious discharge of my duty as an American legislator. But how must I hesitate in the course which would bring me to these results, when I find those who are appointed to lead the way, and are presumed to have all the information necessary for the purpose, halting and receding in their steps, and uncertain whether the path lies in this or in that direction; in fact differing among themselves as to the measures to be pursued! While I would watch, with double scruple and care, the uses made of the public resources by an Administration not possessing my confidence, I could by no means feel justified in withholding those resources, and suffering the Government itself to fall into dissolution. I will not let my house go to decay, because I do not like the tenant.

On the subject of the motives, the policy, and the conduct of the war; the advantages and the glory of the peace; I had hoped to hear not a syllable within these walls, and certainly never intended to make them topics of discussion. I was willing to consider the war as an evil gone by, to be remembered no more as a source of irritation and reproach, and recurred to only for its lessons of wisdom and experience. I desired to look to the country in the actual situation in which we find her; to heal the deep wounds inflicted upon her; re-animate her powers, and restore her strength. My attention has not, therefore, been for a moment turned to the numerous considerations that belong to the questions of the war and the peace. But, sir, how has this moderation, for such I must call it, been received by the honorable Speaker, who has this moment sat down. He has gone into an elaborate and animated justification—nay, eulogium of the war, and a magnificent display of the glory and advantages of the peace. And, sir, not satisfied with this, he has said the Opposition, as he calls us, has not yet challenged either; and he challenges us to do so. Sir, I feel most fully the rashness of taking up this challenge on the instant, unarmed, unprepared, and without a moment's anticipation that I should be drawn into the contest. I will, however, venture upon it, taking the gentleman's own positions for my guide; and hoping to refute him on the very points and grounds he has chosen to place himself, in relation to the gains of the peace particularly. Let me, however, premise that this peace had, and has, my hearty approbation; and most grateful I am to those who made it. God forbid, that I should reproach a measure which I solemnly and conscientiously believe snatched my country from the brink of the gulf of ruin. The Federal Government was at the last gasp of existence. But six months longer, and it was no more. Yes, sir; trust me that but for this providential peace, you and I would not be here listening to proud declamations on the glory of the war; we should have heard nothing of a Congress at this time but as a thing that was; we should have had no profound plottings about a next President; no anxious longings for federal offices. The General Government would have dissolved into its original elements; its powers would have returned to the States from which it was derived, and they, doubtless, would have been fully competent to their own defence against any enemy. Does not everybody remember that all the great States, and, I believe, the small ones too, were preparing for this state of things, and organizing their own means for their own defence? When, therefore, I speak of our desperate condition, I speak only of the General Government, and not of the country, of which I never did despair, and never can. But, sir, as I believe that the strength, prosperity, and happiness of this country essentially depend upon the maintenance of the Federal Government, can I but be grateful for an event which has preserved it? This source of approbation, however, is obviously independent of the terms of this boasted treaty, in which I see none of the advantages so boasted of; and, indeed, no excellence but the redemption from evil.

The honorable Speaker has boldly and distinctly put the question, "What have we gained by the war?" and imposed upon himself the task of exhibiting and proving those mighty gains. But, to my astonishment, the whole of his argument was exerted to prove not what we have gained, for not an item of gain was produced, but what we have not lost. In what manner any gain is to be made out of this I cannot conjecture. To begin with the fisheries. The gentleman has told us that our right in them was held under the treaty of 1873; that in the late negotiation the British Commissioners contended that, by our war, we

had forfeited all the rights held under former treaties, and, among the rest, the use of these fisheries. I do not understand from the gentleman that our Commissioners assented to this doctrine, but rather that they made their objections to it. But, still, I cannot see how all this proves we have not lost the fisheries; and whether we lost them by the argument or the war, the only important fact remains unquestioned, that we have lost them. As our present inquiry, to which we are challenged, is into the gains of the war, it seems to me that the loss of the fisheries, however lost, cannot add much to the account of our gains. Thus a physician may give a most learned and unanswerable detail of the reasons why and how his patient died; but I have never heard that the argument restored him to life, or satisfied anybody that he was not dead. The honorable Speaker, however, has endeavored to comfort us for this gain, by reminding us that the same argument which deprived us of the fisheries took from the enemy the navigation of the river Mississippi, which he held under a former treaty. If this set-off were even of a sufficient value to compensate for our loss, (and one gentleman thinks it essentially more valuable,) I still cannot see how it could aid the main point of this discussion, which is, to display our gains by war, and to place the loss of the fisheries on the list. But, unfortunately for his comfort, the gentleman has been candid enough to inform us that our Commissioners actually offered to renew the Mississippi right to the British if they would renew our right to the fisheries. The offer was rejected, and proves, at least, that our Commissioners thought the fisheries worth the navigation of the river, and that the British Commissioners did not think that navigation worth the fisheries.

The next attempt made by the honorable gentleman, in displaying our gains by the war, was on the subject of the impressment of seamen—this great bone of contention. What is the argument to show that we have gained anything here? The gentleman sets out with alluding to a letter, which has appeared in the papers, and excited much clamor with some people, written by a distinguished gentleman in the Opposition, as the honorable Speaker describes him. Now, says the Speaker, the writer of this letter fully adopts and justifies the British doctrine on the subject of impressment; and if the gentlemen in the Opposition hold the same opinions, surely it is not for them to complain that the treaty has done nothing in relation to it. This is the great argument. Now, in the first place, I deny that it is fair to urge upon us, on this floor, the sentiments or opinions of a letter, by whomsoever it may have been written. I am not now called upon to express any opinion upon the principles held by the respectable writer of that letter; at present I protest against members on this floor being called upon to be judged by a document of that description. But that the honorable gentleman may have the full benefit of this circumstance, I will agree that the Opposition maintain the doctrines of that letter. What inference can be drawn from it, to prove that the treaty in question has gained anything on that subject? We have no right to complain—be it so—but is anything gained by this? Is the American seamen more secure than he was before, or the American doctrine better established? If, indeed, the gentlemen who went to war for this principle have changed their opinion of it; if they also agree with the writer of this letter on the subject, I admit their justification of a treaty, which it does not surrender, at least leaves it as it was, is full and complete; for, why should they ask a principle to be recognised in a treaty, which they are convinced is erroneous, and ought to be abandoned? But if, on the other hand, those gentlemen adhere to their old opinions; if they still deny the right to search our vessels for British sailors, and to take such as they find there; if, in short, they still hold the principles, the recognition of which was the declared cause and object of the war, then, indeed, I cannot see how a war or a treaty which has gained nothing on this point, can be considered either successful or glorious. Certainly we can reckon nothing here in our account of gains. But, we are told such a change took place in the affairs of Europe, as to stop the practice of impressment; and this is all we need be concerned about. If it be so, we owe it confessedly, not to the success of our war, or the skill of our treaty, but to a change in the affairs of Europe, over which we had no control, and for which we can honestly claim no credit. How, then, is it an item in the account of our gain by the war and the treaty? We should have had the same gain in the same way, and at the same time, if we had had neither the war nor the treaty.

But I must beg leave to correct the honorable gentleman in this part of his argument. A mere abstinence from the practice of impressment was not all the American Government asked and contended for; but an explicit relinquishment of the principle under which it was defended. Let me refer to the official declarations of the Cabinet, that the war would be in vain, without an express recognition of our principle; let me also refer to the speeches on the floor of Congress, of the honorable Speaker himself, in which, in the strongest language, he maintains the same ground. Besides, if a cessation of the practice was all that was required, why did an arrangement fail? Why was a treaty rejected, which would have prevented the abuse of the principle, and secured us from the dangers of the practice. At least, however, says the honorable Speaker, we are in statu quo, we stand as well on this subject, as we did before the war; we have given up nothing. To this, however, I cannot assent; and, if I did, I do not see how it would prove a gain by the war. How is the fact? Do we stand as strong on this point as we did before we took up arms for it? I think not; whatever may have been the strength of our claim before the war, it is weaker now. When a nation makes this last, this dread appeal, in support of an asserted right, and then concludes the war by a voluntary treaty without obtaining

the right, or any recognition of it, the right is weakened by the unsuccessful attempt, followed by a voluntary abandonment, if not of the right, at least, of any acknowledgement of it. I may liken it to the case of an individual, who brings suit for a debt he alleges to be due to him, or a piece of land he claims as his own. If, after the commencement of the trial, he prosecutes it not to the issue, but suffers a nonsuit, and gives up his suit, if not his cause, nobody will think as well of his right as before. The man who abandons the prosecution of an asserted right will excite much distrust of the right itself, and even of his own confidence in it. We do not, therefore, stand in statu quo, on the question of impressment.

The next subject of gain, introduced by the honorable gentleman as resulting from the joint operations of the war and the peace, is in relation to the islands in Passamaquoddy bay. We have lost nothing here, says he; we have merely agreed that each party shall hold in that bay what he might be possessed of at the date of the treaty; and the right be afterwards settled by Commissioners. Besides, says the honorable Speaker, we, the American negotiators, had every reason to believe that the valor and patriotism of Massachusetts would not only have rescued her own soil from the possession of the enemy, but have taken possession of the island of Grand Menan; and, in this case, we should have been the gainers by this arrangement; that, as to the first branch of this argument, we have lost nothing, because the right is not surrendered, but to be hereafter ascertained. Is it not undeniable, that we have, at least, lost the possession, which is transferred to the enemy until the right shall be determined; and all the advantages to be derived, even in the arbitration, by this possession? Has not a large portion of the citizens of the United States, in the meantime, been handed over to a new master and a new Government? and, more than all this, does anybody believe, but for this war, Great Britain would ever have troubled herself or us about those islands; or drawn into question the boundaries, as they have been received by both parties for so many years? In point of fact, therefore, in sober truth, we have, by this war and this treaty, lost the right, if hereafter it shall be decided against us; because, but for the war, it could never have been submitted to any question or decision. As to the expectations that were entertained by our Commissioners, of the conquest to be made by Massachusetts, I can see no just foundation for them. The arms and resources of all the United States being placed at the disposal of the General Government, whose duty it is to defend every State from invasion and conquest, the expectation would have been far more reasonable if it had been applied to the General Government, and not to the government of a State whose territory was occupied by the enemy. The expectation, however, apply it where you will, was disappointed; the possession of that portion of our country is lost; the right, at least, brought into unnecessary doubt and jeopardy; and, under these circumstances, I cannot reckon the result among the gains of the war.

But, leaving these matter of fact calculations, the honorable gentleman has expatiated upon a wider field of gain by the war, the glory that has been acquired. I do not exactly understand how those gentlemen who declared and produced the war, make out their claim to all the glory that was acquired by it. The war was made by the men in power—by the existing Administration, and I can trace none of the glory to their foresight, their wisdom, or their personal agency. The glory is due to the valor, the patriotism, the self-denial of our citizens, who met and repelled the dangers that surrounded them, and not to the Administration that brought them upon us; and, in many instances, perhaps a majority, the men who acquired this glory for their country were men utterly opposed to the war, to those who made it, and to the policy that produced it. Sir, I am not insensible of national glory; I hope I never shall be. It is the spring of national virtue, the source of high achievements; the people who disregard it are incapable of great actions, and unworthy of honor. But still I have never understood that the acquisition of glory is a legitimate cause of war, or an admitted justification of it, and therefore our glory cannot be taken as a gain of one of the objects of the war, which is the true point of inquiry now. In order that this blaze of glory may show the brighter by contrast, the honorable Speaker has painted in strong colors the degraded situation of our country, at the period of declaring war. Our character was sunk almost to infamy; we had become the scorn and contempt of all Europe, and there was no nation so pitiful and weak that it did not insult and tread upon us. If this be true, and I am not disposed to question it, let me ask the honorable gentleman who made it so? Washington raised the reputation of the United States to a pitch of the most envied honor, and left them covered with true glory. He is guiltless. In the hands of Mr. Adams it faded a little, but was not extinguished. Then followed Mr. Jefferson, with whom the honorable Speaker has informed us his friends came into power, and they have held it ever since, to what purpose, he has told us himself.

Thus, sir, I close the examination of the honorable gentleman's account of the gains of the war; and, be it as it is, I repeat that I heartily rejoice at the treaty he made for us; not because it is good in itself, but because it snatched us from infinitely greater evils. I have rashly ventured, on the instant, upon a reply to the argument of the gentleman, which deserved, and perhaps required, a much more deliberate and careful refutation.

Permit me now to offer a few observations on the subject of the tax immediately under consideration. I repeat my entire willingness to put the resources of the country fairly and justly, but with proper caution and accountability, at the disposal of those whom the people have chosen to trust with the administration of their affairs. It is better that unfit men should have the means necessary to govern, than that the Government should perish for want of means. I repeat, too, that if the Administration shall be drawn into any strait or difficulty for these supplies, it must not be charged on the Opposition. The first incision into the system of finance was made by the honorable Speaker himself. It has been followed up, and, as might have been expected, widened and deepened by other gentlemen, on the same side. For myself, sir, I came here to lay taxes. After so expensive a war, which destroyed all the ordinary sources of revenue, while it increased most enormously all the demands for money, it was to be expected that a system of taxation and revenue, and a pretty efficient one too, would be required. For my constituents, I am ready to grant it; and I doubt not of their approbation, provided it be formed with moderation, justice, and equality. Equality is the great essential principle of taxation. Men are not so apt to complain of quantum as of inequality. Now, in the nature of things, it is impossible that this equality can be obtained in any one tax, which necessarily must affect some of our citizens greatly, while it scarcely touches others. Equality can be produced only by a variety of taxes, judiciously applied and distributed, some of which draw upon one party of the community and some on another. Proceeding upon this principle, the Committee of Finance has reported a system comprehending a great variety of objects of revenue, and among the rest a tax upon land, amounting to three millions of dollars per annum. This tax I entirely approve of, because it is fair and just, inasmuch as, without it, many landholders in the interior will contribute but little, if anything, to the general wants; and because it is moderate, being not more than one quarter of one per cent. on the whole landed capital of the United States. But, sir, I object, most decidedly, to the modification in relation to the law introduced by the honorable Speaker, because it is unequal and unjust. If all the people of these States are equally bound for the payment of these debts, are equally bound to furnish the future supplies, why should any difference be made in the duration any more than the amount of the requisite supplies? Why should my constituents—I may say the citizens of Pennsylvania—be bound to contribute to the end, by the imposition of taxes, made perpetual, while the citizens of other States are to be exempted at the end of a year? The salt tax or stamp tax, the whiskey tax, and many others, which are perpetual, will press peculiarly on Pennsylvania, and are all perpetual; but the land tax, which reaches some of the States to the South and West, comparatively but little affected by the other taxes, shall be but for a year.

No, sir, let us embark fairly, and equally, and honestly together, in the same bark, and hold together for the whole voyage—let no one be landed and escape further duty and difficulty at the end of the first mile. If four men were united in a firm bond to pay a debt contracted for a common object, and to furnish supplies for common future interest, would it be tolerated that one should ask his companions to acquit him at the end of a year, and go on by themselves afterwards, not only to contribute their proportion, but make good his deficiency? And yet this is the precise effect of the amendment of the honorable Speaker to the report of the committee, which has made the land tax annual, while the other assessments are perpetual. Besides, this change breaks up the whole character of the report, which avows itself to be a permanent system. When, therefore, a most essential part of it, both as to principle and amount, is thus made annual, what becomes of the permanency of the system? As a ground of objection to this branch of revenue, we have heard a most violent philippic pronounced against tax gatherers—they are caterpillars; they are bloodsuckers; nay, one honorable gentleman has said, they are scoundrels. I cannot feel either the justice or policy of these attacks. In justice I do not know that they deserve it—I have no reason to believe they are more dishonest than other men exposed to the same temptations. He, through whose hands large sums of money, especially if it be public money, are continually flowing, and whose accountability is far from being rigid and precise, must be strongly armed in integrity if he never falls. But the remark applies no better in theory, and not here so often in practice, to tax gatherers, than other officers of the Government whose temptations are greater and whose accountability is less. As to the policy of this sort of abuse, I would submit it to honorable gentlemen to say whether it is wise or politic, to endeavor to bring the odium, and suspicion, and contempt of the people, upon a class of public officers, so useful and necessary to the very existence of the Government; that class of officers, too, which comes directly in contact with the people, and brings the Government into every man's house? In truth, this hostility to tax gatherers has neither justice nor policy to rest upon, but is founded on a natural aversion we all have to pay money on compulsion, and for benefits too remote to be immediately seen or felt. But, sir, I hope my political friends will pursue a more liberal course—I hope I shall never find any of them teaching the doctrine, that tax gatherers and libellers are the best reformers of a State.

Those gentlemen who oppose every internal tax, raise this clamor against tax gatherers; and of course would throw us altogether upon the foreign commerce of the country for our revenue—but is this any more satisfactory, even in this respect? Far from it—we must then listen to the assailants upon custom-house officers—we must hear of their insolence, their extortions, their frauds—the tax gatherer thrusts his hand into your pocket; and the custom-house officer ransacks your trunks and baggage—so that if charges of this sort, against the officers who must collect the revenue, are to be received in forming your system of taxation, the consequence is, that you will have no revenue at all. But, sir, armies,

navies, and taxes, have been placed, again and again, in dread array before us: Are you for armies, navies, and taxes, those instruments of despotic power—the destroyers of the liberties of the people; the greedy consumers of their earnings? Yes, sir, I am for armies, navies, and taxes; and I have no more idea of a Government without them, then I have of a living and moving body without flesh, or bones, or blood. But how am I for them? how regulated? to what extent? I am for an army which shall have in truth all the physical force it professes to have; and not for a lifeless, useless skeleton, covered with epaulets, and sashes, and sword knots: or, in other words, for an army of officers without soldiers; affording a wide field for Executive patronage and favor, but providing no substantial means of strength or defence for the country. If this abuse exists, as has been asserted, it is our duty to correct it. As to number, I would have it not so large as to be either dangerous to the liberty, or oppressive to the pockets of the people. It is our duty to take care of both these points, and we have it fully in our power to do so. The present establishment appears to me to offend in neither of these particulars; and not to be larger than is really required. As to the Navy—I would not have it disproportioned to our wants or strength; but sufficient for the defence of our coast at the commencement of a war, with a provision of means for an immediate enlargement when required. It should not be a monster, living on the bosom of the waters and devouring all the productions of the land; but large enough to maintain its high character on the most sudden emergency. As to taxes, they should neither grind the poor, nor be unjust to the rich; they should be fair and necessary; and, above all, be equally assessed upon those bound to contribute to the wants of the State. So much every Government has a right to exact from its citizens; and so much every good citizen will cheerfully afford to his Government. But the first principle in relation to the money concerns of a people, is a regular and inexorable accountability for its expenditure. Without this, no taxes will be sufficient to supply the demands of any Administration. I will conclude by explaining the course I shall take on the subject directly before the Committee. I will vote against the motion of the honorable member from Kentucky (Mr. Hardin) because it expunges a land tax altogether from the system of revenue—I shall also vote against the resolution of the Committee of Finance, as amended on the motion of the honorable Speaker, because it introduces inequality and uncertainty in the system, which ought to be and professes to be permanent; but am perfectly willing to maintain the resolution as reported by the Committee.

When Mr. H. concluded, on the suggestion of Mr. Troop, the resolution respecting the direct tax was ordered to be laid on the table, and the House proceeded to consider the following resolution, (the 8th,) as being more pressing in its nature:

Resolved, That it is expedient to repeal, from and after the 18th day of April next, the act entitled "An act to provide additional revenues for defraying the expenses of Government, and maintaining the public credit, by laying duties on various goods, wares, and merchandise, manufactured within the United States," passed on the 18th of January, 1815; and also the act, entitled "An act to provide additional revenues for defraying the expenses of Government, and maintaining the public credit, by laying a duty on gold, silver, and plated ware, and jewelry, and paste work, manufactured within the United States," passed on the 27th of February, 1815, from the same day.

Mr. Desha moved to strike out so much of the resolve as proposes to repeal the duties on manufactures of jewelry, &c.; which motion was, however, negatived, being opposed by Mr. Lowndes.

The resolution was finally agreed to, and referred to the Committee of Ways and Means, to bing in a bill accordingly.

Mr. Randolph (in consequence of what had fallen from Mr. Clay in debate) laid upon the table the following resolution:

Resolved, That it is expedient to reduce the Military Establishment of the United States.

The House then adjourned.

Tuesday, January 30.

Mr. McLean, of Kentucky, presented a memorial of the Legislature of the State of Kentucky, praying that a prompt and liberal provision may be made for the widows and orphans of militia and volunteers who have been killed in battle or died in the service of the United States.—Referred.

Mr. Nelson, of Virginia, from the Committee on the Judiciary, reported a bill authorizing the Judge of the circuit court for the District of Columbia to prepare a code of jurisprudence for the said District, which was read twice, and committed to a Committee of the Whole.

Mr. Nelson also reported a bill to alter and amend the law of costs; which was read twice, and ordered to be engrossed and read a third time.

Mr. Nelson also reported a bill to amend the act conferring certain powers on the Levy Court for the county of Washington in the District of Columbia, passed the first day of July, 1812, which was read twice, and committed to a Committee of the whole House to-morrow.

Mr. Robertson, from the Committee on the Public Lands, reported the bill from the Senate, "authorizing the sale of a lot of ground belonging to the United States situated in the town of Knoxville and State of Tennessee," without amendment, and the bill was committed to a Committee of the Whole.

Mr. Robertson also made an unfavorable report on the petition of the Legislature of the Indiana Territory, respecting a salt spring; which was read, and concurred in by the House.

Mr. Pleasants reported a bill concerning Pharaoh Farrow; which was read twice, and committed to a Committee of the Whole.

A message from the Senate informed the House that the Senate have passed bills of the following titles, to wit: "An act for the relief of Xaverio Nandi;" "An act to increase the pensions of Robert White and Jacob Wrighter;" and "An act for the relief of Edward Barry and George Hodge;" in which bills they ask the concurrence of this House.

CAPTAIN HENLEY.

Mr. Pleasants, from the Committee on Naval Affairs, made a report on the memorial of Captain John D. Henley; which was read, and the resolution therein contained was concurred in by the House. The report is as follows:

The memorialist presents that, during the invasion of Louisiana by the British forces in December, 1814, he commanded the schooner Caroline, belonging to the United States, then lying at New Orleans; that, on the landing of the enemy on the 23d of December, he was requested by the American General to fall down the river, and take a position on the enemy's flank; that, in compliance with said request, the schooner fell down the river to the required position, where they opened a destructive fire on the enemy, which was continued until the Americans were so closely engaged with the British that a continuance of it would have been destructive to them as well as the enemy; that a fire of hot shot was at length opened on the schooner, by which she was set on fire, and finally blown up; that the memorialist, with his officers and crew, escaped with difficulty with their lives, and were unable to save their property, consisting of their clothing, and the nautical books and instruments of the officers, which was entirely lost, and for which they pray a remuneration from Congress.

The committee think this one of the cases of loss to which military men, both in the land and naval service, are frequently exposed; that numerous cases of the kind occurred during the late war, and must occur during all wars; that they believe there is no precedent of remuneration by Government for such losses. They therefore recommend the following resolution:

Resolved, That the prayer of the memorialist ought not to be granted.

THE REVENUE.

The House then resolved itself into a Committee of the Whole, on the subject of the revenue—the question being on the proposition to repeal the direct tax.

Mr. Wright supported the abolition of the direct tax, and in a speech of considerable length, delivered his opinions on public affairs generally.

Mr. King, of Massachusetts, addressed the Chair as follows:

Mr. Chairman, the report under consideration contains that system of revenue, for the present and succeeding years, which the Committee of Ways and Means recommends for our adoption. It is founded substantially, as was to have been expected, upon the annual report of the Secretary of the Treasury, made to the House at an early day in the session. In that report he says, if the system of 1815 should be preserved entire, there would be a deficit, for 1816, of $3,484,269, but with the modifications which he submits the deficit will be $6,484,269; and he remarks, that "the 'unexecuted authority to borrow money and issue 'Treasury notes, already provided by the acts of 'Congress, is sufficient to enable the Treasury to

805   HISTORY OF CONGRESS.   806

JANUARY, 1816.   *The Revenue.*   H. OF R.

'meet the deficit in either of these modes, and 'consequently no further legislative aid appears 'at this time to be required;" observing further, "that the uniform experience of the Treasury 'evinces that the demands for a considerable por-'tion of the annual appropriation will not be 'made during the year.' If, then, sir, it can be shown to the House that the estimate of expenses for 1816 be too light, or that of the revenue too low, a proportionate deduction may be made from the taxes proposed to be levied. We fortunately have received from the Secretary a report supplementary to his annual report, whereby it appears he had estimated the revenue for 1816, receivable from the customs, too low by $3,348,897. If from this excess you deduct the net amount of the land tax proposed by the resolution under consideration to be laid, to wit, $2,700,000, and also the duty from postage, which it is intended to repeal, to wit, $400,000, there will still remain $248,897 to be carried to the surplus fund. From this view, then, it appears that the land tax is not necessary. I know very well that the Secretary informs us, in his supplementary report, that he could make a very good use of this excess; but, as he can do without it, I had rather oblige the people of this country, by lightening their burdens, than the Secretary.

Let us next take a view of the estimates of expense or appropriations for 1816. I mean, sir, of this pamphlet or letter from the Secretary of the Treasury, which I hold in my hand, containing the estimates of appropriations for the service of the year 1816; and I sincerely wish that I could hold it up to the view of the whole American people; nay, I wish that each householder in this nation had one; that, next to the sacred volume, he would peruse it, to see the infinite variety of objects and persons on whom their money is lavished with the utmost profusion. I believe the States would say to you, unless you curtail their enormous expenditures, unless you correct their gross abuses in your financial department, we must dissolve this copartnership; we cannot bear the load of this establishment; we pay too dear for nominal protection and equivocal benefits. Let us approach, then, this many-headed many-limbed monster, and see if we cannot reduce or lop off some of them. First under the annual, civil, diplomatic, and miscellaneous head:

Gross amount - - - - -	$1,800,000
Estimated amount - - - -	1,735,683
Excess in favor of the people of - -	64,317

which ought to be plucked as a brand from the burning.

Next deduct, from what is called the contingent or miscellaneous items - - $253,000

Still leaving $200,000 for these mysterious unaccounted for items; for, sir, you will please to remark, that the Secretary has, under each head, named each object and person requiring appropriation; then follows a contingent item, which is never accounted for and carrying under the different heads, from $200 to $300,000.

I would next propose to abolish the office of superintendent general of military supplies, saving - - - - 10,580

This office was an excrescence of the war, and ought to have fallen with it, or at least in one year thereafter. It cannot be necessary for your Peace Establishment; and even in war, two additional clerks in your War Department would have performed all the duty. It is now a mere sinecure.

I next propose to strike off all submissions, as they are called, except $30,000, say - 93,107

These submissions are humble requests, in behalf of the various persons employed in the offices, for an increase of their pay. The first which I see in this court calendar, is under the Department of State, it runs thus: " in consequence of the increased price of all the articles of living, the further sum of twenty-five per cent. is now respectfully submitted for the clerks of this office;" the same per cent. for the messenger of the Office of State; the same for the messenger of the Patent Office; notwithstanding the sum originally appropriated for clerks in this office is $11,340—being, the report says, " the amount appropriated for that object in 1815—including the fifteen per cent. annually allowed since 1800. I do not wish that insufficient salaries should be given to any one of your officers; no, sir, 'tis not economy. Give such compensation as will command the best talents, and those that are suitable to the various departments; dismiss from your offices all supernumeraries; retain or hire such officers as are able and willing to do their duty.

Next, under the head Medical and Hospital department, we are surprised with an item of - - - 50,000

For what! for purchasing horses for the artillery—Medical and Hospital department, indeed! unless, indeed, they are to follow the fate of some brave horses of which we have heard so much on this floor, and for which compensation is claimed, who died of wounds received in battle. You may remember, sir, when the subject of appropriation for the last year was before the House, a similar item for the purchase of horses was contained therein, and was objected to; and can the House believe that an annual appropriation of this amount can be necessary for our Peace Establishment? Better down with the establishment altogether than to tolerate the various abuses which have crept therein. Strike from the same head half the amount ($600,000) for fortifications - - 300,000

The remaining half will be sufficient to complete and keep them in repair.

From the enormous amount ($1,065,224) for ordnance, and ordnance stores, arsenals, &c., deduct - - 365,000

The remaining $700,000 is quite sufficient, especially if a proper use has been made of the sums before appropriated to these objects; unless, indeed, you intend immediately to involve us in the horrors and expense of another war.

The next head, "Brevet officers, commanding agreeably to the fourth section of an act of July 6, 1812," strike it off -
Besides, sir, the above act was passed after your declaration of war, and peculiarly related thereto; but two of your officers, and these major generals, commanding the western and southern military districts, can be considered as commanding. Do the people of this country know, that instead of two major generals retained by the act fixing the present Military Peace Establishment, that six major generals are now receiving the emoluments of that office; and that, instead of four brigadier generals, nine are actually receiving pay and rations as such; and that there are receiving pay, by brevet rank, seven colonels, eleven lieutenant colonels, forty-one majors, and twenty captains? Could it have been the intention that the commanding officer of a company, or of a battalion, should receive pay by brevet rank? These can be but two independent commands under the law referred to. Believe me, sir, the establishment is sufficiently expensive, without devising new ways and means to render it more so. I intended, too, sir, to have proposed to strike from the estimate, "officers provisionally retained, under the regulations of May 17, 1815," I suppose, for disbanding the Army; but, not being able to procure correct information respecting these provisional officers, they remain for the present. It is, sir, a fact which ought to strike with astonishment, that, under the law fixing your Military Peace Establishment, ten thousand men are actually attached to this establishment—twelve thousand nine hundred and eighty-two officers of various kinds, and privates, including the corps of engineers—a very decent standing army in time of peace, and at an annual expense of $6,112,159. Who are to pay this and other annual burdens, amounting in the whole to $13,778,649, without including anything for payment of the principal of the public debt, of at least $110,000,000? The people will know when they shall have paid all the taxes, direct and indirect, to which they are and will continue to be subjected by these enormous expenditures.

The last head I shall propose to strike off, at present, is that of "Bounties and Premiums"—

Bounties and premiums in time of peace, when more officers and men are pressing into your service than you know what to do with! Many, very many, other retrenchments might be named.

The above amount to - - - - $1,190,767

	84,784
	20,000

And, sir, rather than your land tax should be continued, and the other burdens proposed, I should say reduce your present Military Peace Establishment one-third; the annual estimated expense of it is $5,112,159; deduct the Indian department of $200,000, (for I would have you keep your faith with those Indians whom your wars have spared,) one-third of the balance is $1,450,791. The whole of these retrenchments will save to the country, annually, $2,634,458—a sum almost equal to the net amount of a land tax of $3,000,000. It would seem then, sir, that on either proceed of excess of revenue, or retrenchment of expense, the land tax is not necessary for 1816. Then, sir, as to the system of revenue for succeeding years, and for the extinguishment of the national debt, I prefer that of the Secretary of the Treasury, which proposes to add $2,000,000 only to the Sinking Fund, on the principle of that established in 1802—making the whole fund, annually applicable to the payment of the principal and interest of the public debt, $10,000,000. "At the commencement of the year 1817," the Secretary says, "it is estimated (too low, I think, by at least '$5 000,000) that the principal of the public debt 'will amount to $110,000,000, requiring the sum 'of $6,150,000 for the payment of its annual in-'terest;" apply the further sum of $3,850,000 to the reduction of the debt. These two last mentioned sums constitute the Sinking Fund of $10,000,000; "a sum," as the Secretary says, "sufficient, if strictly and regularly applied, with-'out interruption, upon a compound principle, to 'pay off the whole of the funded debt in a period 'less than eighteen years." This plan will be sufficiently burdensome; but if you adopt that proposed by the Committee. and increase your Sinking Fund to $13,150,000, and your annual expenditures to $22,778,669, to endeavor to extinguish the public debt in less than twelve years, you will be obliged to continue a system of internal taxation too grievous to be borne.[*]

But, sir, as to these accumulated taxes, to the land tax particularly, I have one objection, which is local in its nature—the inability of a large portion of my constituents, and of Maine, generally, to

[*] This imperfect view of our expenditures will give the people some idea of the pretended economy of the present Administration, and a faint idea of some of the impositions practised upon them. A comparative statement of all the money expended by the different Administrations, from the institution of the Federal Government, on the 4th March, 1789, to 31st December, 1815, will show more clearly the gross profusion, I should perhaps say corruption, of the present Administration:

Expenditures during the eight years of Washington	$15,639,429
Expenditures during the four years of Mr. Adams	21,269,351
Expenditures during the eight years of Mr. Jefferson	41,100,788
Expenditures during the seven years of Mr. Madison	198,695,366

Since the Administration of Washington, one-third

pay these taxes. Sir, I consider it the sacred duty of members to represent the situation of the different sections of the country from which they come. God forbid that I should not endeavor, however humbly, to do justice to those constituents, without distinction of party, who have done more than justice to me. This is the first wish of my heart, but I say it not to win their favor; on the contrary, I can with equal sincerity say, that if it be their wish that I should this moment retire from these walls, I should do it with infinitely more pleasure than I ever entered them. The tax of six millions, for the last year, has not yet been collected; the lists were not delivered to the collectors until this month. At this inclement season of the year, in a cold, inhospitable climate, when many of them find it difficult to procure the common necessaries of life—deprived of some of their accustomed modes of obtaining a living—a part of their fisheries and lumber trade gone—thus destitute, thus oppressed, they are called upon by your tax-gatherers. Sir, they cannot, they will not, in a time of peace, contibue to pay these oppressive taxes; they are bad citizens who do not attend to the wants of their households, to all the domestic charities. You must not be surprised, then, if they provide for the wants of their families before those of the Government. One of my honorable colleagues, (Mr. PARRIS,) who addressed you yesterday, gave you the same information, and other honorable gentlemen have affirmed the same of their constituents. The fact is undeniable; our citizens are impoverished by the war, with the exception of a few favored districts in the South and West, and a host of army contractors and agents of the Government, who have friends at court, and swarms of vermin generated in the corruption of the Administration.

But what is the real object of this overgrown, expensive, Military Establishment—of this burdensome system of duties and taxes? I think the honorable gentleman from Kentucky, (the SPEAKER,) in his eloquent speech yesterday, gave us a clue to it. War, war, is again to be the cry. And that honorable gentleman hesitated not to declare, that he considered it the true interest of this country to assist the patriots of South America; all his sympathies appear to be enlisted on their side;

of the increase of our expenditures may be ascribed to the increase of our country; one-third to folly and extravagance; and the other third to corruption. By the time Mr. Madison winds up his eight years, he will round off the expenditures, during his most pacific and auspicious reign, at $150,000,000; (for the probable demands on the Treasury for 1816, the Secretary informs us, will be, including arrearages, $42,884,269.) What use he has made of a part of this enormous sum, wrung from the hard earnings of the people, or snatched "from the mouth of labor," we can be informed by John Henry, and the numerous pecuniary friends, or rather harpies of the Administration, and of the late war, to use the expression of a celebrated author, as quoted by Mr. Randolph in debate, "whose equipages glide like meteors, and whose castles rise like exhalations."

nay, more, the haughty Spaniard is to be driven from Florida; he cannot brook the imperious demand of the Don. I would advise that honorable gentleman seriously to reflect on the consequences of the late war, which he had so great an agency in producing, before he involves us in another. How does the honorable gentleman work himself up into this war fever? Where did he take this contagion? Was it on the fields of Waterloo, which he informs us he visited, that he was inoculated with this military ardor? I should have thought the purport of that bloody field would have caused very different sensations—forty thousand human beings there, sunk to rest, caused by the mad ambition of a military despot! Still, the honorable gentleman cries, "glory, glory, I do love glory," with all the enthusiasm of a Parisian mob. What is the military glory of which he is enamored; is it "the baseless fabric of a vision," or is it founded on the blood of our citizens and the treasures of our country—on the misery and distress of human beings? Is he, indeed, again ready to "cry havoc, and let slip the dogs of war;" to devour thirty thousand more American citizens; to squander one hundred millions more of treasure, wrung from the hard earnings of industry, and the distress of our people? Is he, indeed, enamored of the fame to which an Alexander, a Cæsar, a mad Swede, or a Bonaparte, are damned? Is he to be the perpetual advocate for war? Does he delight in blood?

> "Curs'd is the man, and void of law and right,
> Unworthy property, unworthy light,
> Unfit for public rule, or private care;
> That wretch, that monster, who delights in war:
> Whose lust is murder, and whose horrid joy
> To tear his country, and his kind destroy."

And let him remember, sir—

> "That one murder makes a villain;
> Thousands a hero!"

But it seems that the honorable gentleman commiserates France; or rather his sympathies, I suppose, as in the case of South America, are enlisted on the side of the revolutionists of that country; writhing under the lash of the combined despots, as he calls them; and he feelingly tells us to beware of the fate of France. What, let me ask him, brought down on France, as if from Heaven, this merited chastisement? Was it not this same thirst for glory, which is consuming him—the same career of conquest to which he would urge the people of this country—a most righteous retribution, that the liberties of France, if such they can be called, should fall, as she has caused those of other nations to fall? 'Tis just they should have right for right, which they have hacked by the sword, from other nations; drop for drop of blood; life for life; till the same measure of suffering which they have meted to other nations should be meted back to them again, heaped up and running over.

The honorable Speaker has adverted to the horrid, as I call them, but glorious, as he calls them, scenes of the late war—its causes, conduct, conclusion, and consequences—and then deliberately asserts, that were it to do over again, that were we now debating, under the same circumstances in relation to this and other nations, whether or not war should be declared, his voice and his hand should again be raised in favor of it.

But a very different decision would be made by the people of this country; it may be sport to him, but it is death to them; it is their blood and their treasure which must be sacrificed in the contest. As to the principal cause of the war, impressment, the honorable gentleman says he cannot, nay, that he will not, hear the doctrine advanced on this floor, that sailors' rights have been surrendered by the peace. As to free trade, he is silent; the commercial treaty speaks volumes on this subject; but, sir, that honorable gentleman will hear—nay, shall hear, unless he leaves the Hall or stops his ears—that to him offensive doctrine, that he has by the Treaty of Peace abandoned the cause of the sailors, which he so pathetically plead on this floor before the war. Yes, sir, he was an able advocate for them here—how it was at Ghent, the treaty determines. There is no doctrine better settled than that the real grievances, or causes of war, not provided for in the Treaty of Peace, are surrendered and abandoned forever. But this part of the honorable Speaker's address has been so ably replied to by my honorable friend from Pennsylvania, (Mr. Hopkinson,) that nothing more is necessary to be said thereon. The honorable Speaker next attempts to count the gains, and estimate the glory of the war, but he should have remembered that war is a picture made up of light and shade—dark shades, indeed; and, while he was recounting the gallant deeds of our land and naval heroes, (I don't include the Constitutional Commander-in-Chief,) he should have remembered the misery, the distress of the inhabitants; he should have cast his eyes on the ruins of your capital; he should have recollected that he was accessary, before the fact, to this work of destruction; that he assisted in lighting the torch of war, which consumed the Capitol, burnt Havre, and more than burnt Hampton, and kindled a flame on the Northern frontier, which illumined that hemisphere, and desolated some of the fairest portions of New York.

Think not, sir, that I am insensible to the renown which individuals have acquired in this disastrous conflict, though I am not sensible that your Administration have acquired any. Your Jackson, sir, was borne on the bosom of the Mississippi to victory and triumph at Orleans; may his gallant exploits, while that noble river rolls its rich contribution to the ocean, be in like manner wafted down the stream of time, till it mingles with the ocean of eternity! The fame of your Hull will survive his Constitution, and I fear that of his country; and Perry's victory of the Lake will be *æra perennius;* your other heroes, sir, will live in the affections of a grateful country.

The honorable gentleman next goes from the gains of the war to the benefits of the peace; let us then examine, for a moment, the Treaty of Peace, and the famous convention with England.

But he here complains that gentlemen on this side of the House have not come out on this subject. How could he expect it? It was not till Saturday last we received the information on the subject, which was laid before the Senate; indeed it was not till yesterday, when the honorable Speaker favored the House with his explanation of the business, that we understood it in all its bearings. He first informs us why Moose Island was left in the possession of the enemy; why that should be the only point to which the *uti possidetis* should apply; that it was confidently expected, by the Commissioners at Ghent, that the patriotism of Massachusetts would not only rescue that island from the enemy, but would also acquire the island of Grand Menon, as he calls it, but which we, in plain Yankee, call Grand Menan—to which we have claim, the former lying "in the Bay of Passamaquoddy, which is part of the Bay of Fundy," and near the American coast, and the latter more remote in the Bay of Fundy. Sir, I will persuade myself that the honorable Speaker meant to do justice to the patriotism of Massachusetts—that never has been found wanting in the hour of peril and difficulty; nay, sir, it was never impeached, and I trust in God it never will be, while the blood of our ancestors, who have nobly fought the battles of our country, circulates in the veins of their posterity. But was this expectation rational? Would any patriotism, under the same disadvantages, have achieved these conquests? It was the memorable Summer of 1814—a period of distress and alarm—which saw the Capitol of our country, and the very tomb of Washington, in the possession of the enemy—numerous fleets of that enemy, full of sailors and marines, were blockading our ports, landing and harassing our people, and destroying their property. Maine, with a seacoast of nearly three hundred miles, was peculiarly exposed to the incursions and wandering parties of the enemy. Yes, sir, that extended coast was accessible at almost every point to the enemy. I remember well, sir, the attempts of that enemy within the district which I have the honor to represent; and remember well the ardor and patriotism of the brave militia manifested on these occasions. There was no distinction of party then, sir; the contest was, who should meet the enemy soonest and repel him from our soil. What protection was afforded us, in this hour of peril and alarm, by the General Government? Was her arm raised in our defence? Were her resources employed in our favor? Far, far from it! Nay, she mocked when our danger approached. She withdrew her soldiers; yes, the very soldiers which were recruited in the bosom of the parent, were, in an hour of peril, withdrawn from her support. For what? to perish—miserably to perish, in the swamps of Canada. Yes, sir, many of the bravest sons of New England, driven by a necessity of your creating into your ranks, have fallen by the sword, disease, and famine—the bones of thousands are now bleaching on the barren heights, or mouldering in the swamps of Canada—their fate less perhaps to be pitied than the weeping monuments of their departure—their miserable parents, orphans, and widows. Bow thy Heavens, O God! and come down with divine consolation to their souls. Under these circumstances, Castine and Moose Island were taken possession of by the enemy. Castine that could not be defended with a less force than 5,000 men, and Moose Island, which lies at the mercy of the mistress of the ocean. Under these circumstances, I repeat, was it to have been expected that the militia, in one part of the country, would leave that open to the attacks of the enemy, forsake their property, their families, their household gods, and cross rivers, and march through deserts, to repel this enemy? Sir, it would not have been accomplished; it ought not to have been expected, except from the general arm. But the honorable Speaker thinks they have provided in the Treaty of Peace sufficiently for these islands: they have submitted to two Commissioners whether Moose Island, whether Eastport, one of our own towns, belong to us or not; and if these Commissioners do not agree, they are to draw up a state of the case, which the two Governments may further submit, if they please, to some friendly nation. No, sir, I consider Moose Island given up, abandoned forever; this submission is a mere cloak to hide the gross nature of the bargain. Sir, it is surrendered in part consideration of the free, exclusive navigation of the Mississippi, and our shore fisheries are thrown into the bargain. Yes, sir, the interest of the East has been sacrificed to that of the West. Why did we not hear anything of these fisheries in the negotiations at Ghent and London? The honorable Speaker informs us, that a majority of his colleagues, against his opinion, were in favor of continuing to the British a limited navigation of the Mississippi, as an equivalent for the fisheries, and for these islands, too, I suppose, for I have no doubt Great Britain would have yielded both these objects for that right—anything said by the Commissioners at Ghent to the contrary notwithstanding. But the honorable gentleman has alleged, as a reason why the fisheries did not receive more attention, that gentlemen differed as to their value; some alleging the value of the shore fishery as equal to one-third of the whole fishery, bank and shore; while others deemed it worth little or nothing. Sir, we have an evidence in the treaty, that those unacquainted with them did value them at nothing; while those who did enjoy the privilege, considered them of the greatest importance, full one-third in value of the whole fishery. The citizens of Maine were in a peculiar manner, from its proximity to them, interested in this branch of the fisheries; it was almost their daily bread to them, because it afforded them the means of providing this daily bread.

But, sir, unfortunately for the people of Massachusetts, and of New England generally, the above are not the only occasions in which their interests have been sacrificed to those of the South and West. In the commercial convention, too, with Great Britain, our lumber, and other staples of our country, have been offered up as a sacrifice to the growers of cotton; indeed, sir, the convention itself, instead, as it purports, of offering a reciprocal liberty of commerce, is a mere contract between the growers of cotton, in this country, with its manufacturers in England. Think not that I repine at the prosperity of our brethren in the South and West; far from it—we only wish to enjoy those few benefits with them. Nor, sir, are you to suppose that I impeach the integrity of the Commissioners; I highly respect their talents—of the honorable Speaker in particular, who in this debate has given us so conspicuous a proof of his talents and his eloquence. I only regret, sir, that they had not been employed at Ghent and London, in some degree, in favor of New England. I assert again, sir, and am prepared to prove, that the staple of the North has, in this convention, been sacrificed to the South and West; that, contrary to the spirit of our Constitution, that "no preference shall be given by any regulation of commerce, or revenue, to the ports of one State over those of another," such preference has been given, by this convention, to the ports of the South. Either, sir, our Commissioners did not understand the navigation laws of Great Britain, particularly her colonial system, or they committed an unpardonable error in concluding this convention. It is indeed, sir, but an experiment for four years, and nothing but this limitation could reconcile me to it for a moment; and I sincerely wish, when the debate took place upon the treaty, we had possessed the information which the other branch did upon the subject; the debate would then have turned upon the merit and provisions of the treaty, instead of the limitation of the treaty-making power. The concession made by our Commissioners, that we had no equivalent to offer for a participation in the India trade, and the trade to the British West Indies, cannot be correct. Sir, we granted them everything, by throwing all our ports open to them, upon equal terms with our own citizens; besides, the East India trade carried its equivalent with it, in its intrinsic value and immense advantage to the British possessions there. Sir, the trade of this country is of the last importance to Great Britain; she had better throw open all her islands, and would do it, than be deprived of it. The importance of this West India trade to the northern part of this country, could not have been understood by our Commissioners; by the majority of them, at least, South of the Hudson, or, sir, had they in view to encourage the production of sugar, rum, and molasses, in the South? Whatever may be the motive, the trade is lost to us. Let us see, then, how our trade stands with the British territories in Europe under this convention. I will advert to a few items of an "An abstract of duties of Customs, paid in Great Britain in 1815," published by order of the Senate and House. First, the article of cotton, which, before the convention, paid three pence sterling per pound, now pays but a penny, whether imported in British or American ships, from foreign countries or British colonies, being a saving of two pence on each

The Revenue.

pound. In the year ending the 30th September, 1815, there was exported from the United States to the territories of Great Britain, in Europe, 42,973.465 pounds of cotton; this, at two pence per pound, is a saving to the growers of cotton, annually, of £374,778 17 06 sterling, or $1,664,-048; and, in the year ending on the 30th September, 1807, there was exported, as above, 59,180.211 pounds. making a saving to the South of $1,980,-687. Well may the honorable Speaker express, as he did yesterday, his surprise, that gentlemen from the West (alluding to Mr. McKEE and Mr. HARDIN) should ask, what have we gained by the war? They have, indeed, gained the exclusive navigation of the Mississippi, and a fair market for their cotton, at the expense of New England, her shore fishery, and her staple commodities. Let us now see how our unmanufactured wood stands in the market, in the territories of Great Britain, in Europe; premising that the duties were comparatively light in 1797, under Jay's Treaty, and large quantities of our timber and lumber found a ready and good market there, particularly at Liverpool, but now, sir, oak timber imported into Great Britain, under this convention, from the United States, will pay, on fifty cubic feet, £3 01 09, while the same, imported from the British colonies in America, which can only be in British ships, pay only 5s. 6½d., and nearly in the same proportion as to other timber, boards, masts, spars, &c.; a duty, sir, which amounts to a prohibition. Some of our lumber found its way into the British West Indies, by the way of St. Bartholomews, some ports in Cuba, and a few other places, subjected, however, to a loss of additional freight and insurance from island to island; our vessels received products in return, subject to the same expense. But a heavy duty has lately been laid in Jamaica, and the same will, doubtless, be done in other British islands, as it is a part of their rigid colonial system, on all lumber, and many other articles from the United States. The ports of the world, indeed, seem fast closing upon New England; and when our own Government neglects or sacrifices our best interests, we cannot expect that foreign nations will pay much attention to them.

And it is under these circumstances of sacrifice, hardship, and distress, you demand of us new sacrifices, and impose on us grievous burdens. You do, indeed, put our patriotism to a severe test. If you expect from us an equality of distribution, we demand of you in return an equality of benefits. You must do this people justice, or they will take justice into their own hands. They wish not for a dissolution of the Union, but at the same time they know that is not the worst, the most degraded situation to which freemen may be reduced; our freedom was purchased by the blood of our forefathers, and will be defended by that of their sons.

Much has been said in this debate respecting our standing army, or as it is now called, or disguised, our Military Peace Establishment—nominally of ten thousand men, really of more than twelve thousand, officers and men. Never did I expect,

sir, within your days or mine, to hear eulogies on this floor in favor of standing armies, but such has been the fact; an honorable colleague of mine, (Mr. CONNER,) whose urbanity and correct deportment are acknowledged by all, is an advocate for these armies; not, I am persuaded, sir, to an extent which would endanger the liberties of his country, but he thinks our chief dependence would be upon them; that, in the day of alarm and danger, our militia are not to be relied on. On the contrary, in the spirit of our Constitution I do consider a well regulated militia as the best security of a free State; it is the effectual defence of the nation. I should wish to see every citizen a soldier, but at the same time every soldier a citizen, and the military in complete subordination to the civil authority. But, sir, as this subject has already been noticed by the honorable gentleman from Virginia, (Mr. RANDOLPH,) and he intends to bring it immediately before the House on a motion to reduce the standing army, I will leave it, with confidence, in better hands. Since I have named that honorable gentleman, I should do injustice to my feelings, and to his merit, did I not notice the effort, the great effort, which for three days in succession he lately made on this floor, in favor of true Constitutional principles, with some exceptions, and the freedom of our country; the information communicated by him to this House, and this nation, is invaluable; he has given us the experience of a long and active political life; from the vast treasures of his mind he has brought forth things, old and new; he has laid open the folly, the corruption, the wickedness of Cabinets. What villain—high, low, rich, or poor—of importance to attract the attention of a gentleman, has he neglected to drag before an insulted people? To what merit, known to him, exerted in favor of his country, has he been insensible, or denied the meed of praise? Sir, the thanks of an humble individual are poor, indeed, but, such as they are, I most heartily tender them to him; were it in my power I would do it in behalf of this House, nay, in the name of the American people. However, sir, he will have what is of infinitely more importance to him, the approbation of his own conscience, and, I hope, of his God.

One word, at parting, with the honorable Speaker, and I have done; for what he and his political friends have done in relation to the war, its declaration, progress, and termination—they have a right, he says, to expect from the people of this country the divine benediction of " well done good and faithful servants; you have been faithful over a few things, I will make you rulers over many things." It is very true, indeed, sir, that the honorable gentleman and his friends have received even more than five talents of the people's money; but instead of even making that use of them which the servant did that received the one talent—dig in the earth and hide it—they have squandered away their Lord's money and run him in debt; are they not the wicked, slothful servants, and ought not the people to say—" cast ye the unprofitable servants into outer dark-men, there shall be weeping and gnashing of teeth?" And happy, thrice happy, will it be for that honorable gentleman and his friends in the Administration, if the righteous judge of all the earth shall not, for their political sins, add the awful sentence—"Depart from me ye cursed;" but I do humbly beseech his mercy, to redeem their immortal souls from that "everlasting fire, prepared for the devil and his angels."

When Mr. K. had concluded, the Committee rose, and the House adjourned.

WEDNESDAY, January 31.

The Committee of the whole House, to whom was committed the bill making appropriations for ordnance stores, was discharged from the further consideration thereof; and it was committed to the Committee of the Whole on the report of the Committee of Ways and Means upon the subject of revenue.

The bill from the Senate "for the relief of Xaverio Nandi," was read the first time.

The bill from the Senate " to increase the pensions of Robert White and Jacob Wrighter," was read twice, and committed to the Committee on Pensions and Revolutionary Claims.

The bill from the Senate "for the relief of Edward Barry and George Hodge," was read twice, and committed to the Committee on Naval Affairs.

An engrossed bill, entitled "An act to alter and amend the law of costs," was read the third time and passed.

A message from the Senate informed the House that the Senate have passed the bills from this House of the following titles : "An act to repeal so much of an act passed on the 23d of December, 1814, as imposes additional duties on postage ;" "An act to continue in force an act entitled 'An act for imposing additional duties upon all goods, wares, and merchandise, imported from any foreign port or place, and for other purposes ;' and "An act to continue in force certain acts laying duties on bank notes, refined sugars, and for other purposes ;" with amendments to the two latter. They have also adopted a resolution directing a copy of the documents printed by a resolve of Congress, on the 27th of December, 1813, to be transmitted to each of the Judges of the Supreme Court. In which amendments and resolution they ask the concurrence of this House.

The amendments to the said bills were read and concurred in by the House.

A Message was received from the President, transmitting a report of the Secretary of State, and sundry documents, respecting the transactions at Dartmoor, in April, 1815.—Laid on the table.

The resolution from the Senate " directing a copy of the documents printed by the resolve of Congress on the 27th of December, 1813, to be transmitted to each of the Judges of the Supreme Court," was read the first time.

MONEY LOST BY A COLLECTOR.

The SPEAKER laid before the House a report from the Secretary of the Treasury on the petition of Henry Malcolm; which was read and referred to the Committee of Ways and Means.

The report is as follows:

The House of Representatives having, by their order of the 17th of January, 1816, referred to the Secretary of the Treasury the petition of Henry Malcolm, with the documents accompanying the same, the Secretary has the honor to lay before the House the following report :

The petitioner, Henry Malcolm, was appointed the collector of the customs for the district of Hudson, in the State of New York, in the year 1795, when the district was established. It was his constant practice to remit the money which he received on account of duties in bank notes to the branch of the Bank of the United States in the city of New York, and no accident or loss occurred in consequence of this practice until the 28th of June, 1808. On that day the petitioner put under cover, addressed to the cashier of the Branch Bank, a sum of one thousand dollars in notes of the Bank of Columbia, in the city of Hudson, and delivered the packet to the postmaster of Hudson to be sent by the next mail. A letter of advice was at the same time forwarded to the cashier, which was duly received ; but the money was stolen on its way, and has never been received at the Branch Bank, or passed to the credit of the Treasury. The accounting officers have refused to credit the remittance in the settlement of the petitioner's account, and he prays to be relieved by the authority of Congress.

The facts thus stated are satisfactorily proven, and serve to exonerate the petitioner from every suspicion of fraud in the course of the transaction. To entitle him, however, to the relief which is solicited, it is necessary to show that the mode of making the remittance did not transgress the rule prescribed by the Treasury Department; and, in this respect, it appears, from documents on record as well as from those which accompany the petition, that two objections have heretofore been made ; 1st. That the remittance by mail was not authorized, or, if authorized, should have been guarded by cutting the bank notes in two parts, and sending the parts by successive mails. 2. That the remittance was made in the notes of the Bank of Columbia, instead of the notes of the Bank of the United States or its branches.

1st Objection. The Treasury circular, addressed to the collectors on the 14th of October, 1789, authorized the remittance of bank notes by the mail, but prescribed the mode of doing it, by requiring, among other things, that each note should be divided into two equal parts and endorsed by the collector ; one-half to be sent by one post, and the other half by the next post, with descriptive lists, to the Treasurer of the United States.

But the Treasury instruction, addressed to the petitioner on the 9th of June, 1796, soon after his appointment to office, required him, in general terms, " to remit, from time to time, whatever moneys should come into his hands in payment of duties, beyond the sum necessary for drawbacks, and to pay the expenses incident to his office, to the office of discount and deposite at New York, there to be placed to the credit of the Treasurer of the United States ;" and the Treasury instructions, addressed to the petitioner on the 9th of November, 1809, subsequent to the loss of the bank notes in question, directed him " to deposite in the Branch Bank, New York, the public moneys in his hands ; and, if the remittance be made in bank notes, he was directed to cut them, and postpone the transmission of the second halves until the receipt of those first sent was acknowledged."

The remittance of bank notes by mail appears, then, from this review, to have been authorized by the Treasury Department. The first instruction, prescribing a mode of remitting the notes in halves, referred to remittances to be made to the Treasurer of the United States at the Seat of Government, and it was issued before the Bank of the United States and its branches were established, as well as long before the establishment of the district of Hudson. The second instruction, which directed the petitioner to make his remittances to the Branch Bank at New York, is silent as to the mode of remitting the notes in halves; and the petitioner, considering this as the ruling instruction for his official conduct, after it had been received, uniformly made his remittances of bank notes to the Branch Bank, without severing the notes, from the date of the instruction the 9th June, 1796, until the date of the instruction of the 9th of November, 1809, without encountering, as is already stated, any other loss or accident than that which is the subject of his petition.

Under these circumstances, so peculiar as to preclude any danger from the precedent of a favorable decision in the present case, it is believed that the petitioner, exonerated as he is from all suspicion of fraud, may also be justly relieved from the imputation of wilful or gross negligence.

2d Objection. If the petitioner does not suffer by the force of the first objection, it is presumed that the second objection will not be allowed to prevail against the prayer of the petition. The kind of bank notes remitted would have become an important question if the Branch Bank refused to credit them as cash in the account of the Treasurer, or if the notes had been depreciated in value. But the question now arises on a loss which would have happened whether the notes remitted were issued by the Bank of the United States or by the Bank of Columbia.

It is proper to observe, however, that the amount of the notes of the United States and its branches in circulation at Hudson was not equal to the demand for bank notes; that the notes of the Bank of Columbia circulated at par with gold and silver; that they had been constantly received in payment of duties, and remitted to the cashier of the Branch Bank at New York, who had credited them uniformly as cash, in the account of the Treasurer; and, finally, that, in a letter dated the 23d of August, 1806, the cashier, while objecting to bank notes of a particular description, expressly adds that, "if any other than notes of the banks in New York are sent, those of the Hudson Bank would be most convenient; they pass equally well, and you could get large ones."

All which, including copies of the several Treasury instructions referred to, is respectfully submitted.

A. J. DALLAS,
Secretary of the Treasury.
Treasury Department, *Jan.* 28, 1816.

THE REVENUE.

The House again resolved itself into a Committee of the Whole, on the report of the Committee of Ways and Means, on the subject of revenue.

Mr. Reynolds, of Tennessee, addressed the Chair as follows:

Mr. Chairman, on my motion last evening the Committee were kind enough to rise, for which I tender them my thanks. I fear, sir, they will be ill rewarded at best, but more particularly now, when indisposed. It becomes, however, my imperious duty to address you on this occasion, because my honorable colleagues and myself differ as to the vote I am about to give on the resolution now under consideration. I regret the circumstance, because they are men with whom I delight to co-operate; many of them I have been long acquainted with, and in the late contest for our sacred rights, some of them not only paid the taxes imposed with cheerfulness, but rushed to the field of battle and participated in the glory of their countrymen; I hope, however, it is an honest difference of opinion.

I am in favor, sir, generally of the reduced system of taxation as proposed by the Committee of Finance, and the direct tax, so modified, to be continued for one year. Every one admits the necessity of a revenue to be raised by some mode of taxation. And it would be well for gentlemen now to reflect for a moment how far they have already gone on the ground of this necessity. A few days ago, sir, a very large majority of the House agreed to continue the double duties, and also to continue the salt tax. Now, sir, none of these taxes affect me at all; I do not pay one cent towards the war debt, or for the restoration of the public faith and credit of this nation, unless I dip pretty deeply with the merchant. Shall it be said, sir, that I would evade the payment of the just proportion of the debt incurred by the war; for there was not a man, woman, or child, in my district, who were not in favor of that measure? Yes, sir, we were advocates of the war, and no people on the continent of America contributed more largely in support of it, according to their numbers and wealth, than they did. They fought the battles of their country, and paid an enormous and oppressive tax without a murmur.

I have also, sir, fully appreciated the remark made by the honorable gentleman from Kentucky, (Mr. McKee,) whose good sense always makes him intelligible to every one. He admits that a direct tax is the most just and equitable, but, being opposed to all taxes, he wishes this one in particular to pass, because it reaches all classes of citizens, puts all on the alert to inquire into the necessity of such a tax; and if it is found totally unnecessary, they will, says the gentleman, soon bring their Representatives to an account. Sir, to place the question on this ground, I shall always be ready to answer to my constituents for any vote I may give in this House, with promptitude. If, however, Mr. Chairman, they have forgotten the cause of the war, hailed by them, too, as a new era of their independence; if they have already forgotten how bravely they participated in that glorious contest, in subduing a powerful savage nation, and secondly, the powerful aid they gave in defeating the veterans of Europe before New Orleans, and saving that city from their bloody grasp; if, I say, they have forgotten all these noble feelings, and those scenes of danger and of glory, and are now unwilling to support that Government that has brought them to a safe and honorable peace, then indeed I shall stand condemned before them, and be permitted to retire; but, sir, I shall retire with a conscience undisturbed. I am not, however, to be driven from a discharge of my duty by such threats. My conduct shall be judged of by a gallant and intelligent people, on whose magnanimity and justice I shall rest my defence.

I shall now proceed, sir, to a brief examination of the subject before the Committee, and also answer some of the arguments on the other side of the House. Taxation will always be unpleasant to a free people, unless you can show them that the tax is necessary, either to support the public faith and credit of the nation, or to vindicate its honor and promote the internal resources of the country; show them this, honestly and candidly point it out to them, and my word for it they will always pay cheerfully any reasonable tax imposed upon them. These incentives and those objects of American interest and honor are, in my opinion, in bright review before us. But why, sir, are we referred to the history of '98 as a case in point? Although the honorable gentleman from Virginia (Mr. RANDOLPH) has learnedly narrated the history of those times, and given you a luminous display of his political career, yet he has not thought proper, at least on this occasion, to show that they are at all analogous. Sir, what is the real history of that eventful period? It was this, sir, France was then struggling for her liberty against all the crowned heads of Europe, with England at their head, and strange to tell, but it is nevertheless the fact, that the then Administration of this country was also inclined to go with the royal corps to strangle and destroy the infant Republic of France, then in its cradle! The hue and cry was accordingly raised against France. British pirates and ships-of-war were capturing our merchantmen daily, without much noise having been made about it. The French pirates began to think they might as well participate in the plunder of American commerce as the British—they also captured some. Nothing now but war with the Directory of France would do. Taxes were imposed, and a large standing army was created. Now, sir, the people of this country knew that this pretext would not do. The American citizens had not forgotten the debt of gratitude they owed the people of France, for nobly aiding them in the sacred struggle for their independence; this was yet fresh in their minds. The nation, therefore, could not have been dragged into such a war. Besides, sir, your citizens knew that the Directory of France at that time had too much power to contend against at home, to send anything like a force to meet the American armies. Then, sir, it was not against the expenses of supporting an army your citizens complained; it was the mere pretext, without a just foundation; and against the extreme impolicy of waging such a war, the people of this country entered their solemn protest; and with these measures, together with the Sedition Law, fell the Administration that gave them birth.

Sir, what is now the situation of the country? We are not now to meet a debt created for the purpose of going to war. No, sir. It is a large and accumulated debt for being actually engaged in a state of war. No pretext here. It is in large round numbers. I shall not now stop and inquire whether it was a just or unjust war. It is sufficient for my purpose, that it was declared by the proper and Constitutional authorities of the empire, and we are now called upon to make ways and means for the discharge of the expense. Some gentlemen think that the customs arising from tonnage will be sufficient to extinguish the debt in eighteen or twenty years; others speak of borrowing money to pay the interest. The last expedient I cannot think it would be wise to adopt. A nation never can do well that has to borrow money in time of peace. Instead of diminishing the public debt it is adding more to it. As to the revenue arising from commerce I think well of it. But I really do not think it just that the consumer should literally pay the whole debt of the nation. Besides, sir, I do not view it now as altogether a certain revenue. It depends too much on the winds and tides, and the good understanding of those nations with whom we have intercourse. All may be dashed from us in a moment, and left in the forlorn situation we found ourselves in the year 1812, when war was declared, and not a cent in your Treasury,—indeed, upwards of a million short in meeting the current expenses of that year. Are gentlemen prepared to fall back to such a state of things? Will such a course enable us manfully to meet the crisis, at no great distance, I fear, will burst upon us?

But, sir, is it not known that the mercantile world is at this moment inundated with a vast importation on hand? Perhaps there has been within these ten months more goods imported than there may be for two years to come; and, looking at the present posture of affairs with the Old World, I consider this revenue too precarious to depend alone on it for the support of a great and growing nation, and particularly to pay off large war debts in due time. I am, sir, for finding out ways and means to discharge this debt in our own times, and not saddling posterity with it. You perceive from this sentiment, that I do not adopt the principle that "a public debt is a public blessing." The debts we incur, either by errors or judicious acts, let us provide for the payment of within a reasonable time. Let the heirs receive the inheritance without encumbrance, and the world will pronounce you wise and just.

Now, sir, what is the sum we have to provide for; the old and new debt amounts to nearly one hundred and twenty millions of dollars. From the Treasury report it appears that there will be demands on that Department for the sum of $42,884,269, comprehending the gross amount of the arrearages of the War Department, and for the whole of the floating debt for the year 1816. To meet this, the revenue that will probably accrue for that year, taking into view the reduction of the direct tax, and the abolition of some other duties, will amount to $39,400,000, leaving a deficit of more than three and a half millions of dollars. Thus, sir, stands the account. Notwithstanding this, it is right to abolish some of the taxes imposed by the last Congress, that were not only unproductive, but too oppressive on industry; but what was still more alarming, a tax on *knowledge.*

But, sir, there is another strong reason why we should continue the direct tax for one year at least. We do not, we cannot see now the full extent of the debts against the Government. Nearly two millions are to be paid in Tennessee to the brave militia and volunteers of that State. There is still a larger sum in Kentucky, and there are considerable demands from every State in the Union. Now, an appropriation of ten millions of dollars has been made; but can any one tell the sum that will be required to meet the provisions of those bills on your table, I trust will pass this session? One of them has already passed, providing for the pay of lost property during the late war, the sum entirely unknown. The bill establishing an additional military academy, and the bill for the relief of invalids and Revolutionary soldiers, if they pass, will require an additional sum, which at present is also unknown.

Can I then, sir, in conscience vote against the resolution, when the salvation of those measures, just in themselves, and necessary, depends much on the success of the system of revenue recommended by the Committee of Ways and Means?

Mr. Chairman, I shall vote against any reduction of the Army at present, or of the Navy; and I shall now beg leave to examine this subject for a moment. As it regards the Army, I do not conceive that ten thousand regulars can ever be dangerous to eight millions of freemen. The only question is, is it expedient and proper to keep up that number in time of peace? If we examine the affairs in Europe, we shall see all is not settled in that quarter. If you will look at the papers on your table, lately received from the Spanish Minister, you have the best reasons that can be offered why your present force should be retained. But of this Spanish demand I shall examine hereafter. I consider, sir, it a very great saving to the people to have at all times a competent force to be brought out on every emergency that may happen. The voice of experience will tell us that this will be the greatest gain. It never will do in any Government, and particularly in a free one, to have people called from their homes, from the pure air they inhale, and be cooped up in camps for two or three months waiting for the approach of the enemy, as was the case at the city of Norfolk and elsewhere during the late war. And what was the sad consequence? Thousands of the bravest and finest fellows in the world died with camp disease without ever seeing the enemy. And it is a fact, that more men during the war died of disease and sickness than by the sword.

And it will eternally be the case, where the yeomanry of the country, without discipline, be obliged to be encamped for any length of time. It is totally inconsistent with their habits and mode of living. Our militia, sir, are emphatically the bulwark of your liberties; but let your armies be so organized, either with regular troops or militia previously trained and disciplined, and somewhat inured to camp duties, or to wait for the enemy and give them the first onset, and then have your militia in full vigor from their homes brought into action, and they will always give you a good account of the enemies of your country.

Let the period of their call be for a very short time, and the moment it is out discharge them, and have others marching to the tented field if necessary. And I would also wish to see the Government in funds, always to pay the militia and soldiers the moment they are discharged. In this way you will always have brave, practical patriots, and good soldiers to defend you in times of danger. Sir, from the extensive frontier we have to guard, the numerous garrisons we have to take care of, and from the appearance of the times, I do humbly apprehend that ten thousand regulars will not be too many. And I warn the Government to see speedily that there are that number now in service. And in case of a deficiency I would have it immediately made up.

I need not, sir, say anything in praise of the Navy. It has established its fame by reports more loud and effectual than anything we can utter. It is fixed on a basis as solid and as durable as the adamantine rock. It would be vain to talk about it. I shall, therefore, be for a gradual increase of our navy. But not in such manner as would be felt by the people.

The present direct tax will not be oppressive upon the citizen. A man, for instance, who has real estate to the amount of $4,000, will not have to pay more than six or eight dollars per annum to his Government. The honest and industrious farmer, who has not a vast quantity of out lands, can never feel this tax—particularly when he reflects that he is contributing his share towards the honor, dignity, and credit of his own Government. But, sir, this tax may reach the great nabob and speculator, who have monopolized large tracts of country, and keep the same in the wild forest, to the great injury of the particular State in which it may lie, and also to the United States. Such pressure I shall not regret, if it becomes the means of inducing those gentlemen to bring their lands, or a part of them, into market, and receive a just equivalent from those citizens disposed to purchase, who will at once be adding new strength and wealth to the nation.

Permit me now, sir, briefly to notice some of the remarks that have fallen from my honorable friend from Maryland, (Mr. Wright,) and the honorable gentleman from Massachusetts, (Mr. King.) Indeed, sir, I merely intended to reply to my worthy friend from Maryland on yesterday, and to have confined myself to the single question before the Committee, until I heard the gentleman from Massachusetts (Mr. KING) last evening. He, sir, has lit the torch, which is now in full blaze, and will enable gentlemen to see the line distinctly drawn between us, and conduct them to their proper stand. I regret it much, sir; for I did felicitate myself on a very harmonious session. You could not perceive the first four or six weeks we sat here, any line of distinction, or any party feeling among us. Gentlemen from all sides of the House independently supported measures according to their best judgment, regardless of party. But unfortunately the mask is now thrown off. The gentleman from Massachusetts, however, must know that we shall not shrink from an investigation of the course the Administration has pursued, and to justify the war and the measures that were adopted.

It seems the honorable gentleman from Maryland (Mr. WRIGHT) is opposed to all taxation, and would have the Government rely on tonnage altogether. I believe, sir, the gentleman is sincere in his project, and it will do very well so far as it goes. But it is sufficiently evident that it is too small and too uncertain to meet the present exigencies of the Government. I listened to the gentleman's speech with much pleasure. It was to be sure learned, so much so, that I could not for my life comprehend all of it; particularly where he wishes that the Presidential election was over a month ago. Now, sir, what has this election to do with the question before us? I presume very little. As a member of this House, I conceive I have nothing to do with it. That great and important election is, I trust, to be left to better judges than the honorable gentleman and myself—to the people of the United States.

Much has been said about my honorable friend from Kentucky (Mr. CLAY) having snuffed the carnage at Waterloo. This has been repeated often. But the honorable gentleman from Massachusetts (Mr. KING) now says, he lit a torch there. Sir, the honorable gentleman certainly has, as he stated, learned a sad and melancholy lesson at the sight of that place. He saw the combination of a number of petty tyrants united to put down a great one. They have succeeded, and I lament the result. And it seems that my worthy friend is of opinion that France is down never to rise again. I differ with him in this sentiment. Sir, the blood of Marshal Ney is now seeking before high Heaven, calling aloud for vengeance, and it will fall most assuredly, sooner or later, on the heads of those who have perpetrated that foul deed. The honorable gentleman to whom I have so often referred has charged my honorable friend from Kentucky of having been necessary before the fact in burning your Capitol. Sir, that gentleman stands in need of no encomium from me. His eminent services to his country, and his undeviating patriotism, have forever endeared him to his countrymen. But as the honorable member from Massachusetts told you he looked much on the dark side of the picture, permit me again to draw your attention further to that gloomy side, and perhaps he will see

the true causes which led to the burning of the Capitol of this empire. He will observe, on that dark picture, a strong and violent opposition in this House against the war, of which the honorable gentleman took a distinguished part. Their eloquence, no doubt, had some effect on the people in those regions, but it had little in the West. When he contemplates this, let him take a view of the conduct of his own dear Governor Strong, who refused to obey the calls of the General Government, in times of peril and danger, in calling out the honest and brave yeomanry of Massachusetts in defence of their country. Let him, then, cast his eyes upon the Hartford Convention. When the honorable gentleman is tired with these scenes, I would then call his attention to the affair at Queenstown. Here he will witness the militia of New York contending, on Constitutional ground, and actually disputing the point, in sight of the enemy, whether it was right to kill a British soldier on this side of the line or on the other. These sad occurrences, during the war, led to some fatal disasters; and was it not for the bright side of the picture, which I will now present to him, they might have proved dangerous to the liberties of this country. I know the gentleman delights to contemplate this side occasionally, for he has more than once complimented my friend, the hero of New Orleans, for which I tender him my thanks. The honorable gentleman will perceive, that notwithstanding the apathy the British found in the people in this quarter, the moment they saw the Capitol of the empire in flames, their soil invaded by the modern barbarians of Europe, that moment they rose in their majesty. What is the fact? Sir, the very people who were panic-struck, running from the bloody plains of Bladensburg to Montgomery Courthouse, were found in a few weeks after with their neighbors manfully defending the city of Baltimore, meeting the British in open fight, and leaving their chief to bite the ground. Need I conduct the gentleman to the scene at New Orleans? Or remind him of the empty boasts of Cockburn that he would eat his Christmas dinner in that city? Sir, they expected this as a sure prize. Indeed I have been told that they were prepared to colonize that country. How great must have been their disappointment! The eighth of January will be remembered by them as long as they are a nation, and I hope in God it will be celebrated by us as an annual day of grand jubilee. They were beat and literally mowed down. Never, in the annals of warfare, was it yet known, such a prodigious slaughter on one side, and so little on the other. Sir, the hero Jackson was there. But, much as he is entitled to the just plaudits of his country, and the admiration of posterity, yet there is a youth of whom little has been said in this place, who ought to share largely in the glory of that day—I mean the bold and intrepid youth, General William Carroll, of Nashville. Sir, it is my firm belief, that it was him and the brave volunteers and militia from the State of Tennessee who saved your city from the grasp of the invading foe, and your country from ruin and disgrace. The event could not be otherwise, for we had Providence on our side. And this youth, who has the fire and genius of a Bonaparte, and the unerring firmness of a Jackson, never, I believe, in his short but glorious career, has once failed in any enterprise he has undertaken. I hope, therefore, without detaining the Committee with a particular review of the noble and glorious deeds of valor achieved by his own countrymen at the battles of Bridgewater and Chippewa, the honorable gentleman will be contented to let his gloomy side of the picture be eternally shaded by the brilliant and glorious deeds of the late war.

The gentleman wishes that every freeholder in the Union was furnished with a copy of the annual report of the Treasurer. Sir, I join him in this respect. And I shall certainly endeavor to make it known among my constituents. They will see more clearly from this very able report the absolute necessity of adopting the measure now under consideration. But the gentleman complains that our late Commissioners of Peace have not attended sufficiently to the interest of the fisheries in the treaty. Sir, if that treaty had not been signed at that juncture of time, I ask you in what situation would the gentleman's fisheries and his constituents be at this moment? Instead of attending to complaints of this kind, we would now be probably engaged in finding out new ways and means of taxation to support a powerful army, at the head of which General Jackson, I have no doubt, would have celebrated the first day of May (after his victory at Orleans) with the citizens of Quebec. I humbly conceive, therefore, that the honorable gentleman has no just grounds of complaint against the Commissioners for the treaty they did make. On the contrary he and his people owe them a debt of eternal gratitude, the chief of whom (Mr. BAYARD) I regret is no more! I was delighted the other day to hear the gentleman from Virginia (Mr. RANDOLPH) pronounce such an eloquent eulogium on the memory of that great man. Sir, it does honor to his heart to speak in such terms of his old and powerful antagonist, with whom he had to wield the sword of argument so often in this House. That great man, sir, was the pride and boast of the American name at home and abroad, although he was a Federalist. And as long as the eloquent, patriotic, and accomplished statesman is estimated among mankind, his name will be cherished and respected by the latest generation of his countrymen. Sir, I will not say with the honorable gentleman from Virginia, (Mr. RANDOLPH,) that he would give all the glory acquired in the late war to restore the life of the celebrated and much lamented Davies, of Kentucky, but this I will say, that to have met with the late and much esteemed Commissioner in this place now, to have an opportunity of returning to him my sincere acknowledgments for his friendship to me, certain I am that it would have been the greatest gratification I ever can enjoy on this side of the grave. I beg pardon, sir, for this digression; I should not have introduced the topic, however grateful to my feelings, had not the example of the honorable gentleman from Virginia (Mr. RANDOLPH) presented the opportunity. I return the Committee my sincere thanks for the polite attention with which I have been honored. I shall now hasten to a close.

The wish the honorable gentleman from Kentucky (Mr. CLAY) expressed, that New Spain could be free, has been much sneered at in this House. Sir, I am one who most cordially join him in that wish. And I hope that day is not very distant when that country shall be free and independent.

I have said, sir, that the people whom I have the honor of representing did not murmur about the payment of taxes. It is notorious they did not. But they complained of the inequality of your direct tax, and well and justly they might, Mr. Chairman. Many of them were paying fifty-six and sixty cents to the hundred while the people of the rich and opulent county of Davidson were paying not more than twenty cents. I shall further look into this matter during the present session, and see whether there cannot be a more effectual remedy applied than heretofore. I came here, Mr. Chairman, to support the just views and measures of an Administration whom I believe to be virtuous and upright, and while under this impression, I can never abandon a course which I most solemnly consider to be the best calculated to promote the interest, honor, and prosperity of this nation.

I ask again, sir, what is our situation with Spain at this moment? Look at the correspondence on your table between the Minister of that country and your Secretary of State and you will perceive the position assumed. What does the Spanish Minister demand, sir? Why, that you should give up part of your territory without discussion as a preliminary to future negotiation, and moreover that the raising of men in Tennessee and Kentucky to join the patriots in New Spain should be immediately prohibited. Sir, I would be the last man in this House to treat foreign Ministers with disrespect on this floor. But I must be permitted to assure the House and the nation that the information the gentleman has received as it respects the raising of men in the State of Tennessee is not correct, and I believe I might vouch for Kentucky also. Sir, the people of Tennessee are too patriotic to join in any crusade against the laws of the United States. They will not do it. But make it legal for them to co-operate with the patriots, and, my word for it, they will soon give you a good account of their enemies. Sir, as a strong proof of their attachment to their country, what was their conduct towards the celebrated Burr when he was among them endeavoring to raise men for some illegal purpose?—we cannot now call it treasonable;—the Chief Justice of the United States has settled that question. But, sir, he used all his eloquent address to procure men in that State, and I pray you how many followed him? I believe not more than twenty or thirty, and these were principally boys. And those very boys, so soon as they began to suspect his designs, instantly deserted him. Sir, you need have no apprehension of treason in that quarter. One word more, and I have done. What would gentlemen have contributed to have saved this country from the disgrace of Hull's surrender and the burning of yonder Capitol? Sir, for myself, I declare, in the presence of this House and my God, that I would rather see the little property I have scattered before the winds of Heaven than experience such another shock.

When Mr. R. had concluded, Mr. CALHOUN rose.

Mr. CALHOUN commenced his remarks by observing, that there were in the affairs of nations, not less than that of individuals, moments, on the proper use of which depended their fame, prosperity and duration. Such he conceived to be the present situation of this nation. Recently emerged from a war, we find ourselves in possession of a physical and moral power of great magnitude; and, impressed by the misfortunes which have resulted from the want of forecast heretofore, we are disposed to apply our means to the purposes most valuable to the country. He hoped that, in this interesting situation, we should be guided by the dictates of truth and wisdom only; that we should prefer the lasting happiness of our country to its present ease—its security to its pleasure—fair honor and reputation to inglorious and inactive repose.

We are now called on to determine what amount of revenue is necessary for this country in time of peace. This involves the additional question, What are the means which the true interests of this country demand? The principal expense of our Government grows out of measures necessary for its defence; and, in order to decide what those measures ought to be, it will be proper to inquire what ought to be our policy towards other nations, and what will probably be theirs towards us? He intentionally laid out of consideration the financial questions which some gentlemen had examined in the debate; and also the question of retrenchments, on which he would only remark that he hoped, whatever of economy entered into the measures of Congress, they would be divested of the character of parsimony.

Beginning with the policy of this country, it ought, he said, to correspond with the character of its political institutions. What, then, is their character? They rest on justice and reason. Those being the foundations of our Government, its policy ought to comport with them. It is the duty of all nations, especially of one whose institutions recognise no principle of force, but appeal to virtue for their strength, to act with justice and moderation—with moderation approaching to forbearance. In all possible conflicts with foreign Powers, our Government should be able to make it manifest to the world that it has justice on its side. We should always forbear, if possible, until all should be satisfied that when we take up arms it is not for the purpose of conquest, but to maintain our essential rights. Our Govern-

ment, however, is also founded on equality. It permits no man to exercise violence; it permits none to trample on the rights of his fellow-citizen with impunity. These maxims we should also carry into our intercourse with foreign nations; and, as we render justice to all, so we should be prepared to exact it from all. Our policy should not only be moderate and just, but as high-minded as it is moderate and just. This, said Mr. C., appears to me the true line of conduct. In the policy of nations, said he, there are two extremes: one extreme in which justice and moderation may sink into feebleness; another, in which that lofty spirit which ought to animate all nations, particularly free ones, may mount up to military violence. These extremes ought to be equally avoided; but, of the two, he considered the first far the most dangerous—far the most fatal. There were, he said, two splendid examples of nations which had ultimately sunk by military violence: the Romans in ancient time—the French in modern. But, how numerous were the instances of nations gradually sinking into nothingness through imbecility and apathy! They have not, indeed, struck the mind so forcibly as the instance just mentioned, because they have sunk ingloriously, without anything in their descent to excite either admiration or respect. I consider the extreme of weakness not only the most dangerous of itself, said Mr. C., but as that extreme to which the people of this country are peculiarly liable. The people are indeed high-minded, and therefore it may be thought my fears are unfounded. But, they are blessed with much happiness moral, political, and physical;—these operate on the dispositions and habits of this people, with something like the effects attributed to Southern climates: they dispose them to pleasure and inactivity, except in pursuit of wealth. I need not appeal to the past history of the country; to the indisposition of this people to war, from the commencement of the Government, arising from the nature of our habits, and the disposition to pursue those courses which contribute to swell our private fortunes. We incline, not only from the causes already mentioned, but from the nature of our foreign relations, to that feeble policy, which I consider as more dangerous than the other extreme. We have, it is true, dangers to apprehend from abroad, but they are far off, at the distance of three thousand miles, which prevents that continued dread which they would excite if in our neighborhood. Besides, we can have no foreign war which we should dread, or ought to fear to meet, but a war with England; but a war with her breaks in on the whole industry of the country, and affects all its private pursuits. On this account we prefer suffering very great wrongs from her, rather than to redress them by arms. The gentleman from Pennsylvania asked, if the country did forbear till it felt disgrace, whose fault was it? Not, he said, that of the administrations of Washington and Adams; for neither of them had left it so. A few words, said Mr. C., on this point. The fault was principally in neither of our several Administrations—in neither of the two great parties. It arose from the indisposition of the people to resort to arms, from the reason already assigned. It arose also from two incidental circumstances—the want of preparation, and the untried character of our Government in war. But, there were other circumstances connected with the party to which the gentleman belongs, which caused the country to forbear too long. That party took advantage of the indisposition of the people to an English war, and preached up the advantages of peace, when it had become ignominious, and until we had scarcely the ability to defend ourselves. The gentleman from Pennsylvania further said, if peace had not been made when it was, we should not have been here deliberating at this time. This assertion is an awful one, if true. If the nation was on the verge of ruin, the defects which brought it to that situation ought to be known, probed, and corrected, even if they rose out of the Constitution. But, Mr. C. said, it is an assertion that ought not to be lightly made. The effects are dangerous ; for what man hereafter, with such consequences before his eyes, would venture to propose a war? If such were the admitted fact, a future enemy would persist in war, expecting the country to sink before his efforts; his arms would be steeled, his exertions nerved against us. The position was, in every view, one of such dangerous bearing on the future relations of the country, that it ought not to be admitted without the strongest proof. What, said Mr. C., was the fact? What had been the progress of events for a few months preceding the termination of the war? At Baltimore, at Plattsburg, at New Orleans, the invaders had been signally defeated : a new spirit was diffused through the whole mass of the community. Can it be believed, then, that the Government was on the verge of dissolution? No, sir; it never stood firmer on its basis than at that moment. It was true, indeed, we labored under great difficulties; but it is an observation made by a statesman of great sagacity, (Edmund Burke,) when Pitt was anticipating the downfall of France, through her finances, that an instance is not to be found of a high-minded nation sinking under financial difficulties. And it would have been exemplified in our country, had the war continued. Men on all sides began to unite in defence of the country; parties in this House began to rally on this point; and, if the gentleman from Pennsylvania had been a member at that time, he also, from what he has said, would have taken that ground. The gentleman had taken a position on this point as erroneous as it was dangerous; and, Mr. C. said, he had thought proper thus to notice it.

As a proof, said Mr. C., that the situation of the country naturally inclines us to too much feebleness rather than too much violence, I refer to the fact, that there are, on this floor, men who are entirely opposed to armies, to navies, to every means of defence. Sir, if their politics prevail, the country will be disarmed, at the mercy of any foreign Power. On the other side, sir, there is no excess of military fervor, no party inclining to military despotism ; for, though a charge of such a disposition has been made by a gentleman in debate, it is without the shadow of foundation. What is the fact in regard to the Army? Does it bear out his assertion? Is it even proportionally larger now than it was in 1801 and 1802, the period which the gentleman considers as the standard of political perfection? It was then about four thousand men; it was larger in proportion than an army of ten thousand men would now be. The charge of a disposition to make this a military Government, exists only in the imaginations of gentlemen; it cannot be supported by facts; it is contrary to proof and to evidence.

Having dismissed this part of the subject, Mr. C. proceeded to consider another part of it, in his opinion, equally important, viz: What will be the probable policy of other nations? With the world at large, said he, we are now at peace. I know of no nation with which we shall probably come into collision, unless it be with Great Britain and Spain. With both of these nations we have considerable points of collision. I hope this country will maintain, in regard to both of them, the strictest justice ; but with both these nations there is a possibility, sooner or later, of our being engaged in war. As to Spain I will say nothing, because she is the inferior of the two, and those measures which apply to the superior Power, will include all the inferior. I shall consider our relations, then, with England only.

Peace now exists between the two countries. As to its duration I will give no opinion, except that I believe the peace will last the longer for the war which has just ended. Evidences have been furnished, during the war, of the capacity and character of this nation, which will make her indisposed to try her strength with us on slight grounds. But, what is the probable course of events respecting the further relations between the two countries? England is the most formidable Power in the world—she has the most numerous army and navy at her command. We, on the contrary, are the most growing nation on earth; most rapidly improving in those very particulars in which she excels. This question, then, presents itself: will the greater Power permit the less to attain its destined greatness by natural growth, or will she take measures to disturb it? Those who know the history of nations, will not believe that a rival will look unmoved on this prosperity. It has been said, that nations have heads, but no hearts. Every statesman, every one who loves his country, who wishes to maintain the dignity of that country, to see it attain the summit of greatness and prosperity, regards the progress of other nations with a jealous eye. The English statesmen have always so acted. I find no fault with them on that account, but rather to point it out as a principle which ought also to govern our conduct in regard to them. Will Great Britain permit us to go on in an uninterrupted march to the height of national greatness and prosperity? I fear not. But, admitting the councils on that side of the water to be governed by a degree of magnanimity and justice, the world has never experienced from them, and I am warranted in saying never will, may not some unforeseen collision involve you in hostilities with Great Britain? Gentlemen on the other side have said, that there are points of difference with that nation, (existing prior to the war,) which are yet unsettled. I grant it. If such, then, be the fact, does it not show that points of collision remain; that, whenever the same condition of the world that existed before the war shall recur, the same collisions will probably take place? If Great Britain sees the opportunity of enforcing the same doctrines we have already contested, will she not seize it? Admitting this country to maintain that policy which it ought; that its councils be governed by the most perfect justice and moderation, we yet see, said Mr. C., that, by a difference of views on essential points, the peace between the two nations is liable to be jeopardized. I am sure that future wars with England are not only possible, but I will say more, that they are highly probable—nay, that they will certainly take place. Future wars, I fear, with the honorable Speaker, future wars, long and bloody, will exist between this country and Great Britain—I lament it—but I will not close my eyes on future events—I will not betray the high trust reposed in me—I will speak what I believe to be true. You will have to encounter British jealousy and hostility in every shape, not immediately manifested by open force or violence, perhaps, but by indirect attempts to check your growth and prosperity. As far as they can, they will disgrace everything connected with you; her reviewers, paragraphists, and travellers, will assail you and your institutions, and no means will be left untried to bring you to contemn yourselves, and be contemned by others. I thank my God, they have not now the means of effecting it which they once had. No; the late war has given you a mode of feeling and thinking which forbids the acknowledgment of national inferiority, that first of political evils. Had we not encountered Great Britain, we should not have had the brilliant points to rest on which we now have. We, too, have now our heroes and illustrious actions. If Britain has her Wellington, we have our Jacksons, Browns, and Scotts. If she has her naval heroes, we have them not less renowned, for they have snatched the laurel from her brows. It is impossible that we can now be degraded by comparisons; I trust we are equally above corruption and intrigue; it only remains, then, to try the contest by force of arms.

Let us now, said Mr. C., consider the measures of preparation which sound policy dictates. First, then, as to extent, without reference to the kind: They ought to be graduated by a reference to the character and capacity of both countries. England excels in means all countries that now exist, or ever did exist; and has, besides, great moral resources—intelligent and renowned for masculine virtues. On our part our measures ought to correspond with that lofty policy which becomes

14th CON. 1st SESS.—27

freemen determined to defend our rights. Thus circumstanced on both sides, we ought to omit no preparation fairly in our means. Next, as to the species of preparation, which opens subjects of great extent and importance. The Navy most certainly, in any point of view, occupies the first place. It is the most safe, most effectual, and the cheapest mode of defence. For, let the fact be remembered, our navy costs less per man, including all the amount of extraordinary expenditures on the Lakes, than our army. This is an important fact, which ought to be fixed in the memory of the House; for, if that force be the most efficient and safe, which is at the same time the cheapest, on that should be our principal reliance. We have heard much of the danger of standing armies to our liberties—the objection cannot be made to the Navy. Generals, it must be acknowledged, have often advanced at the head of armies to imperial rank and power; but in what instance had an Admiral usurped on the liberties of his country? Put our strength in the Navy for foreign defence, and we shall certainly escape the whole catalogue of possible ills, painted by gentlemen on the other side. A naval power attacks that country, from whose hostility alone we have anything to dread, where she is most assailable, and defends this country where it is weakest. Where is Great Britain most vulnerable? In what point is she most accessible to attack? In her commerce—in her navigation? There she is not only exposed, but the blow is fatal. There is her strength; there is the secret of her power. Here, then, if ever it become necessary, you ought to strike? But where are you most exposed? On the Atlantic line—a line so long and so weak that you are peculiarly liable to be assailed in it. How is it to be defended? By a navy, and by a navy alone can it be efficiently defended. Let us look back to the time when the enemy was in possession of the whole line of the seacoast, moored in your rivers, and ready to assault you at every point. The facts are too recent to require to be painted. I will only generally state that your commerce was cut up; your specie circulation destroyed; your internal communication interrupted; your best and cheapest highway being entirely in possession of the enemy; your ports foreign, the one to the other; your Treasury exhausted in merely defensive preparations and militia requisitions; not knowing where you would be assailed, you had at the same moment to stand prepared at every point. A recurrence of this state of things, so oppressive to the country in the event of another war, could be prevented only by the establishment and maintenance of a sufficient naval force. Mr. C. said he had thought proper to press this point thus strongly, because, though it was generally assented to that the Navy ought to be increased, he found that assent too cold, and the approbation bestowed on it too negative in its character. It ought, it is said, to be gradually increased. If the Navy is to be increased at all, let its augmentation be dimited only by your ability to build, officer, and man. If it is the kind of force most safe, and at the same time the most efficient to guard against foreign invasion, or repel foreign aggression, you ought to put your whole force on the sea side. It is estimated that we have in our country eighty thousand sailors. This would enable us to man a considerable fleet, which, if well directed, would give us the habitual command on our coast—an object, in every point of view, so desirable. Not that we ought, hastily, without due preparation, under present circumstances, build a large number of vessels; but we ought to commence preparation, establish docks, collect timber and naval stores, and, as soon as the materials are prepared, we ought to commence building to the extent which I have mentioned. If anything can preserve the country in its most imminent dangers from abroad, it is this species of armament. If we desire to be free from future wars, as I hope we may, this is the only way to effect it. We shall have peace then, and what is of still higher moment, with perfect security.

In regard to our present Military Establishment, Mr. C. said, it was small enough. That point the honorable Speaker had fully demonstrated: it was not sufficiently large at present to occupy all our fortresses. Gentlemen had spoken in favor of the militia and against the army. In regard to the militia, said Mr. C., I would go as far as any gentleman, and considerably farther than those would who are so violently opposed to our small army. I would not only arm the militia, but I would extend their term of service, and make them efficient. To talk about the efficiency of militia called into service for six months only, is to impose on the people; it is to ruin them with false hopes. I know the danger of large standing armies, said Mr. C. I know the militia are the true force; that no nation can be safe at home and abroad which has not an efficient militia; but the time of service ought to be enlarged, to enable them to acquire a knowledge of the duties of the camp, to let the habits of civil life be broken. For though militia, freshly drawn from their homes, may, in a moment of enthusiasm, do great service, as at New Orleans; in general they are not calculated for service in the field, until time is allowed for them to acquire habits of discipline and subordination. Your defence ought to depend, on the land, on a regular draught from the body of the people. It is thus in time of war the business of recruiting will be dispensed with—a mode of defending the country every way uncongenial with our Republican institutions—uncertain, slow in its operation, and expensive; it draws from society its worse materials, introducing into our army, of necessity, all the severities which are exercised in that of the most despotic Government. Thus compounded, our army, in a great degree, lose that enthusiasm which citizen-soldiers, conscious of liberty, and fighting in defence of their country, have ever been animated. All free nations of antiquity intrusted the defence of the country, not to the dregs of society, but to the body of citizens; hence that heroism which modern times may admire but cannot equal. I know that I utter truths unpleasant to those who wish to enjoy liberty without making the efforts necessary to secure it. Her favor is never won by the cowardly, the vicious, or indolent. It has been said by some physicians that life is a forced state; the same may be said of freedom. It requires efforts; it presupposes mental and moral qualities of a high order to be generally diffused in the society where it exists. It mainly stands on the faithful discharge of two great duties which every citizen of proper age owes the Republic: a wise and virtuous exercise of the right of suffrage, and a prompt and brave defence of the country in the hour of danger. The first symptom of decay has ever appeared in the backward and negligent discharge of the latter duty. Those who are acquainted with the historians and orators of antiquity know the truth of this assertion. The least decay of patriotism, the least verging towards pleasure and luxury, will there immediately discover itself. Large standing and mercenary armies then become necessary; and those who are not willing to render the military service essential to the defence of their rights, soon find, as they ought to do, a master. It is the order of nature, and cannot be reversed. This would at once put an adequate force in your hands and render you secure. I cannot agree with those who think that we are free from danger, and need not prepare for it, because we have no nation in our immediate neighborhood to dread. Recollect that the nation with whom we have recently terminated a severe conflict, lives on the bosom of the deep; that, although three thousand miles of ocean intervene between us, she can attack you with as much facility as if she had but two hundred or two hundred and fifty miles over land to march. She is as near you as if she occupied Canada, instead of the islands of Great Britain. You have the power of assailing as well as being assailed; her provinces border on our territory; the dread of losing which, if you are prepared to attack them, will contribute to that peace which every honest man is anxious to maintain as long as possible with that country.

Mr. C. then proceeded to a point of less but yet of great importance—he meant the establishment of roads and opening canals in various parts of the country. Your country, said he, has certain points of feebleness and certain points of strength about it. Your feebleness should be removed, your strength improved. Your population is widely dispersed; though this is greatly advantageous in one respect, that of preventing the country from being permanently conquered, it imposes a great difficulty in defending your territory from invasion, because of the difficulty of transportation from one point to another of your widely extended frontier. We ought to contribute as much as possible to the formation of good military roads, not only on the score of general political economy, but to enable us on emergencies to collect the whole mass of our military means on the point menaced. The people are brave, great, and spirited; but they must be brought together in sufficient number and with a certain promptitude to enable them to act with effect. The importance of military roads was well known to the Romans: the remains of their roads exist to this day; some of them uninjured by the ravages of time. Let us make great permanent roads, not like the Romans, with views of subjecting and ruling provinces, but for the more honorable purposes of defence, and connecting more closely the interests of various sections of this great country. Let any one look at the vast cost of transportation during the war—much of which is chargeable to the want of good roads and canals—and he will not deny the vast importance of a due attention to this subject.

Mr. C. proceeded to another topic, the encouragement proper to be afforded to the industry of the country. In regard to the question how far manufactures ought to be fostered, Mr. C. said it was the duty of this country, as a means of defence, to encourage the domestic industry of the country; more especially, that part of it which provides the necessary materials for clothing and defence. Let us look at the nature of the war most likely to occur. England is in possession of the ocean. No man, however sanguine, can believe that we can deprive her soon of her predominance there. That control deprives us of the means of maintaining our Army and Navy cheaply clad. The question relating to manufactures must not depend on the abstract principle that industry, left to pursue its own course, will find in its own interest all the encouragement that is necessary. I lay the claims of the manufacturers entirely out of view, said Mr. C., but on general principles, without regard to their interest, a certain encouragement should be extended, at least, to our woollen and cotton manufactures.

There was another point of preparation which, Mr. C. said, ought not to be overlooked—the defence of our coast by means other than the Navy, on which we ought to rely mainly, but not entirely. The coast is our weak part, which ought to be rendered strong, if it be in our power to make it so. There are two points on our coast particularly weak, the mouths of the Mississippi, and the Chesapeake bay, which ought to be cautiously attended to; not, however, neglecting others. The Administration which leaves these two points, in another war, without fortification, ought to receive the execration of the country. Look at the facility afforded by the Chesapeake bay to maritime powers, in attacking us. If we estimate with it the margin of rivers navigable for vessels of war, it adds fourteen hundred miles, at least, to the line of our seacoast; and that of the worst character, for, when an enemy is there, it is without the fear of being driven from it. He has, besides, the power of assaulting two shores at the same time, and must be expected on both. Under such circumstances, no degree of expense would be too great for its defence. The whole margin of the bay is, besides, an extremely sickly one, and fatal to the militia of the upper country. How it is to be defended, military and naval men

will best judge, but I believe that steam frigates ought at least, to constitute a part of the means; the expense of which, however great, the people ought and would cheerfully bear.

There were other points, to which, Mr. C. said, he might call the attention of the Committee, but for the fear of fatiguing them. He would mention only his views in regard to our finance, as connected with preparatory measures. A war with Great Britain, said he, will immediately distress your finances, as far as your revenue depends on imports. It is impossible, during war, to prepare a system of internal revenue in time to meet the defect thus occasioned. Will Congress, then, leave the nation wholly dependent on foreign commerce for its revenues? This nation, Mr. C. said, was rapidly changing the character of its industry. When a nation is agricultural, depending for supply on foreign markets, its people may be taxed through its impost almost to the amount of its capacity. The nation was, however, rapidly becoming, to a considerable extent, a manufacturing nation. We find that exterior commerce (not including the coasting trade) is every day bearing less and less proportion to the entire wealth and strength of the nation. The financial resources of the nation will, therefore, daily become weaker and weaker, instead of growing with the nation's growth, if we do not resort to other objects than our foreign commerce for taxation. But, gentlemen say, the moral power of the nation ought not to be neglected, and that moral power is inconsistent with oppressive taxes on the people. It certainly is with oppressive taxes, but to make them so they must be both heavy and unnecessary. I agree, therefore, with gentlemen in their premises, but not in their conclusion, that, because an oppressive tax destroys the whole moral power of the country, there ought, therefore, to be no tax at all. Such a conclusion is certainly erroneous. Let us, said Mr. C., examine the question, whether a tax laid for the defence, security, and lasting prosperity of a country, is calculated to destroy the moral power of this country? If such be the fact, as indispensable as I believe these taxes to be, I will relinquish them; for, of all the powers of the Government, the power of a moral kind is the most to be cherished. We had better give up all our physical power than part with that. But, what is moral power? The zeal of the country, and the confidence in the administration of its Government. Will it be diminished by laying taxes wisely, necessarily, and moderately? If you suppose the people intelligent and virtuous, it cannot be admitted. But if a majority of them are ignorant and vicious, then it is probable a tax laid for the most judicious purpose may deprive you of their confidence. The people, I believe, are intelligent and virtuous. The wiser, then, you act, the less you yield to the temptation of ignoble and false security, the more you attract their confidence. The very existence of your Government proves their intelligence; for, let me say to this House, that, if one who knew nothing of this people were made acquainted with its

Government, and with the fact that it had sustained itself for thirty years, he would know at once that this was a most intelligent and virtuous people. Convince the people that measures are necessary and wise, and they will maintain them. Already they go far, very far, before this House in energy and public spirit. If ever measures of this description become unpopular, it will be by speeches here. Are any willing to lull the people into false security? Can they withdraw their eyes from facts menacing the prosperity, if not the existence of the nation? Are they willing to inspire them with sentiments injurious to their lasting peace and prosperity?

The subject is grave. It is connected with the happiness and existence of the country. I do most sincerely hope that this House are the real agents of the people. They are brought here, not to consult their ease and convenience, but their general defence and common welfare. Such is the language of the Constitution.

I have faithfully, in the discharge of the sacred trust reposed in me by those for whom I act, pointed out those measures which our situation and relation to the rest of the world render necessary for our security and lasting prosperity. They involve no doubt much expense; they require considerable sacrifices on the part of the people; but are they on that account to be rejected? We are called on to choose; on the one side is great ease it is true, but on the other the security of the country. We may dispense with the taxes; we may neglect every measure of precaution, and feel no immediate disaster; but in such a state of things what virtuous, what wise citizen, but what must look on the future with dread! I know of no situation so responsible, if properly considered, as ours. We are charged by Providence not only with the happiness of this great and rising people, but in a considerable degree with that of the human race. We have a Government of a new order, perfectly distinct from all which has ever preceded it. A Government founded on the rights of man, resting not on authority, not on prejudice, not on superstition, but reason. If it succeed, as fondly hoped by its founders, it will be the commencement of a new era in human affairs. All civilized Governments must in the course of time conform to its principles. Thus circumstanced, can you hesitate what course to choose? The road that wisdom points, leads it is true up the steep, but leads also to security and lasting glory. No nation, that wants the fortitude to tread it, ought ever to aspire to greatness. Such ought and will certainly sink into the list of those that have done nothing to be known or remembered. It is immutable; it is in the nature of things. The love of present ease and pleasure, indifference about the future, that fatal weakness of human nature, has never failed in individuals or nations to sink to disgrace and ruin. On the contrary, virtue and wisdom, which regard the future, which spurn the temptations of the moment, however rugged their path, end in happiness. Such are the universal sentiments of all wise writers, from the didactics of the philosophers to the fictions of the poets. They agree that pleasure is a flowery path leading off among groves and meadows, but ending in a gloomy and dreary wilderness; that it is the syren's voice, which he who listens to is ruined; that it is the cup of Circe, which he who drinks, is converted into a swine. This is the language of fiction, reason teaches the same. It is my wish to elevate the national sentiment to that which every just and virtuous mind possesses. No effort is needed here to impel us the opposite way; that also may be but too safely trusted to the frailities of our nature. This nation is in a situation similar to that which one of the most beautiful writers of antiquity paints Hercules in his youth: He represents the hero as retiring into the wilderness to deliberate on the course of life which he ought to choose. Two Goddesses approached him; one recommending to him a life of ease and pleasure; the other of labor and virtue. The hero adopted the counsel of the latter, and his fame and glory are known to the world. May this nation, the youthful Hercules, possessing his form and muscles, be inspired with similar sentiments and follow his example!

[Mr. RANDOLPH had spoken before in this debate, but the length of his first speech, which continued three days, and which it would take more than a week to write off from the reporter's brief notes, prevents its publication. The remarks which follow were in reply to Mr. CALHOUN.]

Mr. RANDOLPH said, as the gentleman from South Carolina (Mr. CALHOUN) had done him the honor to pay some attention to his previous remarks, he would show his respect for him by explaining in this way, after he had taken his seat, rather than in interrupting him whilst he was on the floor. The gentleman had, by his speech, much as (Mr. R. said) he had before respected his talents and principles, contributed in no small degree to increase the respect he entertained for his abilities, and integrity, and for the principles by which he was governed. I subscribe, continued Mr. R., in the abstract to his principles. I was not bred in the grovelling school he reprobates; I know the value of the moral power as well as the gentleman from South Carolina—and if I had been permitted by the state of my health, when on a former occasion I had exhausted my powers by an effort greater than I had supposed them capable of—if I had been permitted to continue my rambling discourse, the gentleman would have seen that I have the same contempt for grovelling, for all that is mean, popular, and eleemosynary, that any gentleman could have in this or any other assembly. I never have flattered the people, and so help me God I never will. I must say, in the abstract, I was pleased with the gentleman's speech, said Mr. R.—but I have long believed there was a tendency in the administration of this Government, in the system itself indeed, to consolidation, and the remarks made by the honorable gentleman from South Carolina have not tended to allay any fears I have entertained from that quarter. Make this a simple integral Government, said Mr. R., and I subscribe to the doctrines of the honorable gentleman; because they are drawn from the same fountain from which I have drawn my own principles. Mr. R. said he was glad to see that the gentleman had not raked in the kennels (he would say) of democracy, for the principles of which he had formed his political creed. But, Mr. R. said, ours is not an integral Government, but a Government of States confederated together. He put it to the Committee, to the gentleman himself, whether the honorable gentleman's principles (which he had demonstrated with an ability honorable to the State he represented, to the House, and to himself) did not go the destruction of the State governments. It was not, Mr. R. said, from the preference of present good to a little self-denial, that he opposed the system of the gentleman and his political friends. I say, Mr. R. repeated, that these doctrines go to prostrate the State governments at the feet of the General Government. If the warning voice of Patrick Henry had not apprized me long ago, the events of this day would have taught me that this Constitution does not comprise one people, but that there are two distinct characters in the people of this nation. Mr. R. said he had been led heretofore to question whether the fact was so; he now believed it as much as any article of his political creed. When speaking of the value of our form of Government, the gentleman might have added to his remarks, Mr. R. said, that whilst in its federative character it was good, as a consolidated Government it would be hateful; that there were features in the Constitution of the United States, beautiful in themselves when looked at with reference to the federative character of the Constitution, which were deformed and monstrous when looked at with reference to consolidation. The gentleman was too deeply read in Aristotle, too well versed in political lore, to deny the fact. Mr. R. said he must be permitted, he trusted in so doing he should not trespass on the patience of the Committee, to notice some of the prominent positions of the gentleman.

The gentleman had set out with observing, that the policy of this country ought to correspond with the character of our Government; that that character was distinguished by justice and reason, and that, as we are disposed to do justice to all nations with whom we have any relation whatever, we ought to be in a situation to exact it. Granted, said Mr. R. The gentleman also stated, that as moderation and forbearance had a tendency to degenerate into tameness and imbecility, so, too, a domineering spirit might end in a military despotism, and inferred that we were in more danger from an abyss of forbearance, than from any disposition to climb the precipices of ambition. There, said Mr. R., I differ from the honorable gentleman. He must give me leave to say, that there is in every Government, the form of which is free, a tendency to exactly the reverse; a tendency to domination—to ambition, not of dominion at home, but among its neighbors. Mr. R. said, he would not detain the Committee with illustrations of this

position. In popular Governments, he said, the popular passion was for glory, show, sensation, excitement. This it was that made Pericles, who ought to have been the benefactor of his country, the malefactor of Athens. I too, said Mr. R., like the gentleman, entertain a respect for the country from which both of us drew our blood; and, when I speak of the enormities committed by the British forces disgraceful to the country, enormities, the effects of which will never be got over, I speak of her troops and her Ministry. I cannot come to this House—I cannot go to the hustings, and pick up a little personal popularity at the expense of truth—of that respect which I, which every man descended from her loins, must bear for their great progenitors. We are to have frequent and bloody wars with England!—I believe it, said Mr. R.—I believe we are to have frequent and bloody wars with England, and that we must take means to guard against the danger. Sir, it was not one of the least objections I had to the late war—and I hope the gentleman will do me the justice to believe, that I am not disposed to rip up old wounds and make them bleed afresh—that it would lay the foundation of wars *in perpetuam*, between us and that country. The die is cast. The course is given to the ship, and she must hold it on; it is not for me, for you, sir, for a million of men to change it. The destiny is fixed. The die is set—a hue is given to public opinion on this side the Atlantic, confirmed, indelible; and a similar sentiment of hostility exists on the other side. Mr. R. said, he had in past days always expressed, because he had always felt astonishment at the prevalence of a spirit of hostility between two nations who had so few points of actual collision: but, he said, there was a wide difference between the state of things before and after a magazine explodes. The explosion had now taken place; and a state of things existed between this country and England, which puts it in the power of every demagogue who should wriggle himself into the Presidency, or into a seat on this floor, to light the torch of war between us and England. He knew it was impossible to avoid it. If means were to be taken to defend the Chesapeake, to defend New Orleans, to defend the whole coast of the United States, by means commensurate with the national ability, Mr. R. said, he would never go whining to his constituents, and tell them that they were not able to pay the taxes. They are able to pay taxes, said he. On whom do your impost duties bear? Upon whom bears the duty on coarse woollens, and linens, and blankets, upon salt, and all the necessities of life? On poor men and on slaveholders. When the time arrived, however, Mr. R. believed he could demonstrate that these taxes were unnecessary, even as regarded the gentleman's own plan of defence. Mr. R. was for yielding to the States these direct taxes, stamp duties, &c., when they are to be laid at all. They must be left to the States, or this consequence must follow, and it was because of that consequence that he dissented wholly from this system. The people would say, what! pay to the General

Government a land tax yearly, stamp taxes, taxes on this, that, and the other, and pay taxes on the same articles too to the State governments? Yes, would be answered;—and, speaking of the State to which he belonged, it might be added, that they had managed their finances as badly as those of the United States had been managed—they had gone on increasing their expenditures without as good a reason as the gentleman had assigned in regard to the expenses of this Government. The people will say, remarked Mr. R., as Patrick Henry told you they would sooner or later say, we cannot serve two masters—we cannot worship God and Mammon—we cannot have two Governments grinding us, when one would answer, &c. This was the point to which the argument of the gentleman from South Carolina necessarily led.

A standing army, it seemed to be admitted, was not what we wanted, but a naval force. Of what value, for instance, would be even a large military force, for the defence of the country on the shores of the Chesapeake alone, cut up as it was into an hundred (he was going to say a thousand) peninsulas—containing not, as the gentleman calculated, one thousand four hundred miles of seacoast, and that, as he had said, of the worst for us and the best for an enemy in the world, but comprising more seacoast than the whole sea-line of the United States. Mr. R. said he had taken the trouble, on a late occasion, to, make a calculation of the length of that coast for Virginia alone, in the presence of a gentleman from Massachusetts, who was of opinion that that State had a greater seacoast than Virginia; it appeared, on examination, that the seacoast of Virginia considerably more than doubled that of Massachusetts. He said, therefore, cut up as the country of the Chesapeake is, with bold and deep rivers, what figure would ten thousand men make in defending it, the enemy being in possession of the water? And if we had the command of the Chesapeake, what should we want with the men on shore? If we could beat our enemy out of that great sea—for it is a Mediterranean sea—we do not want the army *quoad* the Chesapeake.

Mr. R. said he understood the honorable gentleman to say that he would go into a great and immediate increase of our naval means, not by building ships out of green timber, but by providing everything necessary for a great marine. Will the honorable gentleman from South Carolina permit me, said Mr. R., to tell him—I do it with the most perfect respect—that with whatsoever sentiments he may go into this business, it becomes in the end nothing better than a great job? He may vote the money as a patriot, if he follows that vote through all the different ramifications of its execution, he will find it in insecure pockets, or given for rotten timber; he will find it by the right hand received from the Treasury by the navy agent of the Government, and he will find it paid with the left hand into the pocket of the same agent—that virtuous man will not let his left hand know what his right hand doeth.

The honorable gentleman would indeed effect a great object if he would establish a system of retrenchment and reform in the different departments. When I speak of them, said Mr. R., I do not allude to the particular men now in power—I fly at no such ignoble quarry—I allude to the habits of this Government. A man, inferior in point of ability to none in this country, said to me on a late occasion—a man too who rarely says that which he is not prepared to execute and do—that, let the money supposed to be in the possession of the different departments of the Government, be actually there, he would take two millions of dollars from the Treasury, a proportion of it from every fund, and would defy the Heads of the Departments to know, not who took the money, but whether any was gone. This is the present state of accountability, said Mr. R., and if the honorable gentleman from South Carolina, or his political friends, will give us a system of rigorous accountability, and prevent that system of plunder which has been going on for some time—as to the plunderers of the public, Mr. R. said, he met them on the avenue as familiarly as the lords in England are said to meet the blacklegs at the gaming table—he saw them rising from nothing by the stilts of fat contracts into sumptuous palaces;—if the gentleman from South Carolina would devise a rigorous system of accountability, it would give Mr. R. much better heart to vote with him. But he could not yield to the gentleman from South Carolina his views on the first principles of political wisdom, which he had imbibed at home at a time when that gentleman had scarcely ever turned his mind to politics at all—he meant those which respected the sovereignty of the States. If the gentleman took that key in his hand, Mr. R. said, he would unlock his political conduct. It was his policy, Mr. R. said, to stick to the States in contests arising between them and the General Government—to the people in all collisions between them and the Government, and between the popular branches and unpopular branch of the Government—he was wrong, however, he said, to call it unpopular; for, unfortunately, its popularity was that which gave to it an irresistible weight in this House and in this nation.

Sir, said Mr. R., the gentleman has met this question manfully. Shall I be pardoned if I say that the honorable gentleman handled the question in a way very different from that in which it was handled by the gentleman who preceded him? There is no more a popular than a royal road to mathematics. As the gentleman from South Carolina has presented the question to the House, they and the nation cannot have the slightest difficulty in deciding whether they will give up the States or not; whether they will in fact make this an elective monarchy. The question is, whether or not we are willing to become one great consolidated nation, under one form of law; whether the State governments are to be swept away; or whether we have *still* respect enough for those old respectable institutions to regard their integrity and preservation as a part of our policy? I, for one, said Mr. R., cling to them, because in clinging to them, I cling to my country; because I love my country as I do my immediate connexions; for the love of country is nothing more than the love of every man for his wife, child, or friend. I am not for a policy which must end in the destruction, and speedy destruction, too, of the whole of the State governments.

The gentleman had represented this country as contending with Great Britain for existence. Could the honorable gentleman, or any other man, Mr. R. asked, believe that we would ever have a contest with any nation for existence? No, said Mr. R., we hold our existence by charter from the great God who made this world; we hold it in contempt of Great Britain—I speak of our existence as a people politically free—I do not speak of civil freedom—I am addressing myself to one who understands these distinctions. We do not hold our right to physical being or political freedom by any tenure from Europe or any power of Europe; yet we hold our tenure of civil liberty by a precarious tie, which must be broken; for, from the disposition to follow the phantom of honor, or from another cause, this country is fairly embarked in a course of policy like that which is pursued by other governments in Europe. Finding weakness coming on him, Mr. R. said, though he had much to say, he would endeavor to gasp out another sentiment, and be done. It was this:

The gentleman from South Carolina had pointed to the consequences of a war with England, which grew out of a war with England alone, exposing the coasts of our own country, and even our firesides to destruction, threatening the ruin of our whole system of finance, the stagnation of commerce, the banishment of specie, and the complete bankruptcy of the country. Ought not these considerations, Mr. R. asked, to weigh, and to deeply weigh, on the minds of this House, and ought they not to have done before the war with that Power, the issue of which, according to the arguments of gentlemen themselves, only went to prove that we have the capacity to defend ourselves; that we could, to use a term which ought never to have been used on this floor, be kicked into a war. The view which the honorable gentleman took of this subject, said Mr. R., was single and complete. He would have roads, he said, but for military purposes; he would encourage manufactures, too, not for the reason—and I was very glad to hear it, for it is a reason which, in my opinion, would not weigh with any man of sense—not for the reason of the petitions of the manufacturers, but with a view to their military consequence! The honorable gentleman will do nothing but with a view to military effect. Are we, sir, to become a great naval Power, because, forsooth, an admiral was never saluted as an emperor? I too, sir, am an advocate for roads and canals; I too would like to see roads through the country, which might facilitate the march of armies; but

I see in this very feature of the gentleman's system the same danger to the State confederacies as I see, sir, in the whole speech of the honorable gentleman.

Mr. R. then took his seat, and Mr. ROSS spoke against the continuation of the tax, when, on motion of Mr. TUCKER, the House adjourned.

THURSDAY, February 1.

Mr. BROOKS presented the petition of Abigail O'Flyng, praying that land warrants may be issued to her for the services of her husband and three sons, as soldiers of the Army; which warrants are withheld because her said husband was "over age," her son Edmund "under age," and her sons Patrick and Elijah, in consequence of their gallant conduct, were promoted to commissioned officers, in which capacity one of them was killed in battle, and the other lately died, both without issue.—Referred to the Committee of Claims.

Mr. LOWNDES, from the Committee of Ways and Means, reported a bill to repeal the duties on certain articles manufactured within the United States; which was read twice, and committed to the Committee of the Whole on the report of the Committee of Ways and Means upon the subject of revenue.

On motion of Mr. INGHAM, the committee appointed on the 29th of January, to investigate the conduct of the General Post Office Department, were granted power to send for persons and papers.

The bill from the Senate "for the relief of Xaverio Nandi, was read the second time, and referred to the Committee of Commerce and Manufactures.

The resolution from the Senate "directing a copy of the documents printed by a resolve of Congress, on the 27th of December, 1813, to be transmitted to each of the Judges of the Supreme Court," was read the second and third time; and passed.

THE REVENUE.

The House, in Committee of the Whole, resumed the consideration of the revenue subject.

Mr. TUCKER spoke as follows:

Mr. Chairman, I should be without an apology for troubling the Committee with my remarks on the report of the Committee of Ways and Means, and in support of the propriety of retaining a part of the direct tax, if it was not afforded by the division which exists in the State which I have the honor, in part, to represent, in relation to that important subject. Thus circumstanced, however, I ask the attention of the Committee while I submit my views of the state of the nation, and of the imperious duty of retaining a vigorous system of finance in the present situation of our country. I beg the Committee, however, to be assured, that I do not intend to cover the ground which has been already so ably occupied by the gentleman from South Carolina, (Mr. CALHOUN.) I shall not venture to touch what he has treated, lest I should diminish the force of that impression, which his frank, manly, liberal, and comprehensive remarks, have left upon the minds of the Committee. His able and expanded view of the real policy of this nation, and the watchful sagacity of the gentleman from Virginia, ever on the alert in defence of his beloved State rights, have given an interesting character to the debate, well worthy of the important matter which it embraces. It is, indeed, an important debate; it is, indeed, an important question on which we are now to pronounce. It is the most interesting crisis which has for a long time engaged the feelings of the representatives of the nation. We are called upon at this moment, when events of a gloomy and an anxious period are fresh in our recollections, to decide whether we shall learn wisdom from the lessons of experience; or, closing our eyes upon the past, shall suffer our country to remain without money, without credit, without arms, without defence, without the means of rendering her rights respected abroad, or of making her character an object of veneration at home. A new era—an important epoch .has arrived in our national history. We have just emerged from a season of danger and turbulence; we have just been restored to the blessings of peace, after the difficulties and embarrassments of a war of three years; and we are now to decide whether we shall, in time, prepare for the hour of adversity, or content ourselves with permitting the country to remain without the means of protection, should a foreign enemy once more venture upon its invasion. On such an occasion it behooves us to act with more than usual calmness, and to divest ourselves of all pride of opinion before we pronounce an ultimate decision. It has been in vain, indeed, that during the war we have freely sacrificed our fortunes and our ease, and hazarded our lives in the field or in the camp, if, upon the termination of this arduous contest, we are not willing to perform the more difficult and more important duty of sacrificing our pride of opinion upon the altar of our country's good.

Looking then to the past, not with a design to draw from thence subjects of contention and irritation, but with the praiseworthy view suggested by the gentleman from Pennsylvania (Mr. SERGEANT) some time ago, of deriving lessons for the future; and what, let me ask, does it inculcate? The great, the important lesson, which all mankind must learn, of preparing in the moment of prosperity for the hour of peril At the commencement of the late war, what was our state of preparation? We were without the means of defence, without money, without credit. Troops were only to be raised at an immense expense; money could scarcely be commanded at ruinous usury. Defeat for a long time attended the arms of the United States, because we had entered upon the war without the necessary preparation. And though the glories of the latter part of the conflict have not only obliterated the disgraces of the first campaigns, but will forever emblazon the page of faithful history, yet no man can ever look back to the state of our affairs last winter, when, amidst the embarrassments of our Treasury, every patri-

otic bosom throbbed with an anxiety for the public weal, without resolving in his own heart to use his efforts, however feeble, to avoid a similar recurrence. And yet this is precisely, I conceive, the matter now in question: Shall we pay the debt now pressing upon the nation; shall we increase the essential power of the country by discharging its burden; shall we garrison our forts, improve our fortifications, preserve the military art, increase gradually the navy of the Union, and strengthen our means of defence? Or shall we sink again into languor and lethargy; relax our exertions, become a prey to our love of ease, and indulge our propensity to avoid the taxes necessary to pay off our debts, by leaving that debt as a burden upon our children? Here, then, is the important matter of this debate.

It has always seemed to me, Mr. Chairman, that the real question to be solved in relation to the policy of this country is, "How far we can, in 'time of peace, prepare for war; in time of prosperity prepare for adversity, without burdening 'improperly the industry of the nation, or repressing its energy by systems of taxation." It is, indeed, but analogous with the common maxims of prudence which govern the affairs of life. The man who, in the moment of success, in the full tide of prosperity and fortune, shall forget that the day of adversity may come upon him, and shall fail to provide against the storm, is unworthy of that gift of foresight which is the great prerogative of man. Nor does he deserve a seat in the great councils of a nation, who shall permit a timorous and .niggardly policy to frighten him from the observance of a great principle of political wisdom, enforced by authority of the wisest statesmen in every age. I need mention but one; I need only allude to the man whose name has been repeatedly introduced into this debate by the honorable gentleman from Virginia, (Mr. RANDOLPH.) I mean General WASHINGTON—*clarum atque venerabile nomen!*—a man, whose experience has transmitted to us the valuable lesson that I am thus feebly endeavoring to inculcate.

So strikingly, indeed, has the policy of preparing, in time of peace, the means of defence for the country in the event of war, been manifested by the occurrences of the last three years, that I may venture to pronounce that the great mass of the community would unhesitatingly retain the taxes, even in their present extent, rather than see our country unprotected, all military science disappearing, our forts falling into ruins, and our gallant navy rotting in our docks. Where is the man to be found, that would prefer the continuance of the present debt, the annual payment of its heavy interest, and transmission of the burden of the principal to our children, rather than bear for a while a tax, which, as I shall show, cannot operate oppressively? We know little of the people of this country, if we imagine such to be their temper. Those who have been so liberal of their lives are not disposed to refuse the aid of their fortunes, and, if necessity required, I have no doubt they would pay without a murmur the tax as it at present stands. But this we do not ask of them; we are willing to reduce it to one-half its present amount, and feel assured that our constituents will be entirely satisfied with such a reduction.

The report of the Committee of Ways and Means, which is under discussion, is founded upon that just, liberal, and wise policy, which it is our duty to pursue. It contemplates a revenue that will be adequate to the necessities of the nation, and which, at the same time, will not be burdensome to the people. It contemplates a revenue that will enable us to discharge the national debt in twelve or thirteen years; that will justify us in retaining the present military force for the purpose of garrisoning the forts of the United States, and permit us gradually to increase our navy—the glory and boast of the nation. I am not ashamed, Mr. Chairman, to speak of national glory. I love national glory (properly understood) as much as the honorable gentleman from South Carolina. I do not mean that false glory, which consists in foreign wars and foreign conquests; that false glory, which triumphs in the wretchedness of mankind, and waves the sword of desolation over prostrate millions; but I mean the glory of being able to protect our country and our rights from every invader. There is no national glory in suffering our coasts to be ravaged, and our capital reduced to ashes, because we have been backward in providing the means of their protection. There is no glory in a nation's submitting to every invasion of its rights, because it wants the spirit to defend them, or the liberality to pay for their defence. This is not national glory—it is national disgrace; and to avoid such ignominy for the future, I, on the part of my constituents, am content to retain a portion of the public burdens, for the laudable purposes contemplated by the Committee of Ways and Means.

This report has been very warmly attacked, and particularly in relation to that part of it which relates to the Army Establishment. At one time it is contended that the army is too large, at another it is said to be too small; it is at first pronounced not only to be dangerous, but even fatal to public liberty. It is then said to be too small; that it can afford no essential service to the nation, and that the real defence of this country is in the militia. Strange, indeed, that this force, which is too small to defend the land, should be able to enslave it; that an army, which is pronounced (and properly pronounced) to be inferior to the whole body of the militia, should be capable of overwhelming them. Strange, that a scattered body of about eight thousand men should be considered dangerous to seven millions of people.

To any reflecting mind, it must at once appear that there can be no danger to the liberty of the country from such an establishment; scattered over this immense continent, along a frontier in circumference six thousand miles; the mind must be visionary indeed, which dwells upon their existence with serious apprehension. The same consideration of the extensiveness of our frontier sufficiently evinces, that they are not too numerous

for the necessities of the nation. They are wanted for the purpose of garrisoning and preserving the forts, which it would be unpardonable extravagance to suffer to go to ruin, whilst they will always keep alive some knowledge of the military art, and form the basis of an army in the event of another war.

But it is contended, that the report of the Committee is anti-republican, because it recommends the retention of a standing army. Is it, then, what can with propriety be called a standing Army? If it be, had not even Mr. Jefferson a standing army? Did he disband the whole of the troops of the United States? Did he, and those who acted with him, consider it anti-republican to keep up as many regular troops as were necessary to garrison our forts and keep them in a proper state of repair? By no means!—Republican as they were, they did not consider a few men, scattered over our immense frontier, as endangering our liberties—they did not consider it improper to retain what the necessities of the nation required, and we ask no more. Shall it be said, that our present Army consisted of a greater number than Mr. Jefferson retained? I admit it: but our territory has greatly increased, our frontiers have been widely extended, our forts have become much more numerous; and as our population has well nigh doubled, we are in no more danger from eight thousand men now, than we were from half the number twelve years ago.

It has been remarked by the gentleman from Virginia, (Mr. RANDOLPH,) in opposition to the retaining of the present number of troops, that regular forces are not our implements of war, and that the militia is the natural defence of our country. Whilst I admit, to the fullest extent, the value of the militia; whilst I acknowledge that they are the great defence of the nation, and that to them we must ultimately look for the protection of the country, I cannot assent to the idea that regulars are unnecessary. Without entering into a view of their comparative merits; without endeavoring to enhance the one, and depress the other, I will venture to say that all experience establishes the necessity of some regular forces in a period of war. From the time of General WASHINGTON, whose opinions, in relation to the continentals and militia, cannot but be recollected, to the present day, no one has ventured to suggest the propriety or advantage of attempting to carry on a war with militia alone. The possession of both species of force has always been found necessary, and the use of regular troops during the last war was utterly indispensable. So must it be in every future war; and however valuable militia may be, regulars are necessary for the garrisoning the forts in time of peace, and for the most active and arduous operations during the war. If so, prudence requires that we should not dismiss them altogether, nor reduce the present establishment, which scarcely suffices for the necessary garrisons.

But the gentleman from Virginia, (Mr. RANDOLPH,) does not confine his objections to the Army, but contends that the general tendency of the system advocated by his opponents and by the gentleman from South Carolina in particular, is to strengthen the hands of the General Government and to overthrow the power of the States. He admits, indeed, that the policy recommended would be wise and salutary, if this was a National and not a Federative Government, but believes that if such a system be pursued, the federative principle will soon become annihilated. This, indeed, forms the strongest argument against State powers that I have ever yet heard advanced, since it supposes that for the preservation of these powers we must forego proper measures of defence, and a just, wise, and liberal system of policy. I cannot, therefore, admit the correctness of the suggestion, nor can I persuade myself that there is any foundation for this alarm about State rights. I will not detain the Committee by a detail of those arguments with which they must be familiar, establishing the position, that there is in our Government a greater tendency to anarchy among the members than tyranny in the head. Nor will I contend, that the State should have less, or the General Government more power. I am satisfied with the present distribution of power. I will mention only two instances which serve to establish, beyond contradiction, that the power of the States, under our present Constitution, is amply sufficient for their self-protection; the first of these was afforded a few days ago by the gentleman himself, when he reminded us, that about the year 1798, a personage now high in office, left his seat in this House for one on the floor of the State Legislature, and retired from the National Council, where his exertions were unsuccessful, to wield in another body the Democracy of Virginia. Whatever may be our opinions of this affair, gentlemen on the other side of the House will acknowledge that here was one instance of the successful efforts of a State to break down an Administration whose views it disapproved. Gentlemen on our side of the House will be equally satisfied with a more recent example. I mention this without any disposition to criminate, and with no wish to excite irritation. I allude to the course of events in some of the Eastern States during the late war; events which sufficiently demonstrate the powers of the States not only to protect themselves against encroachments of the General Government, but even to jar the whole political body, and retard the motion of this complicated machine.

For my own part, Mr. Chairman, I anticipate little danger to the States from the Federal Government, so long as we only exercise the powers fairly conferred on us by the Constitution. If an attack should be made upon State rights and privileges, the alarm will be sounded throughout the Union. The *esprit du corps* will animate the whole, and, should they unite, they have power, in different ways, to stop the wheels of Government. Even a refusal to elect their Senators would at once arrest its powers. So long as a State confines itself within its proper sphere, every other State will sympathize when it shall be attacked. It is only when it wanders beyond its orbit that it will meet neither countenance nor sympathy.

The natural course of events, Mr. Chairman, is also gradually lessening the capacity of the General Government to crush the States, or to circumscribe their Constitutional power. The continued and immense increase of our territory, the expansion of our population, the multiplication of the States, all tend to weaken the bands of the Federal, and to increase the security of the State powers. The extension of territory itself is a sure protection against consolidation. So far from this nation being disposed to slide into that system of Government, it may be confidently said, that it could not exist in such a form, for it is scarcely possible to conceive that the multifarious and complicated concerns of such an extended and various community, could be conducted by a single Legislature or superintended by a single Administration.

I have said that the extension of our territory and the multiplication of distant States increased the security of State power, and weakened the Federal band. All experience justifies the remark. Power is always weak when operating at a distance. Feebleness in its authority over distant Provinces is the immediate law of extended empire. The power of the Federal Government over remote States, in case of collision, must diminish with their distance. The lever is against it. Months must expire between an order and its execution, whilst the well-organized State Legislature can always act with promptitude and decision; and although I am by no means disposed to change their relative proportions of power, I confess I have less apprehension for the States than I have for the existence of the Confederacy. If there be anything, however, calculated to produce a subversion of the State governments and an increase of power in the Federal head, I am inclined to believe that a feeble exercise of the fair and unquestioned powers of the Federal Government, will give rise to that effect so much deprecated. If ever the moment shall arrive when, for want of a proper exertion of the Constitutional powers of this Government, the safety of the nation shall be in danger; when, for want of credit and resources, of military strength and of naval defence, the independence of our country shall be prostrate before the invader, then, indeed, will the existence of the State Governments be in jeopardy. Pressed from without, while all the elements are jarring within, to what resource will the people look for salvation? Will they suffer the Government to dissolve in its own weakness, and look for protection to the individual States? By no means; no one can be so sanguine as to believe that the States can, without union, successfully defend themselves. To union we shall still look, but to a stronger union; for, however indisposed we may be to consolidation and all its train of ills, there is nothing which we shall not be ready to encounter for national safety, for protection, for independence. The great object of every people, in the establishment of their Government, is self-protection. If their institutions do not afford it, they will fall into contempt with the people themselves, and the natural, the inevitable course of things will be to infuse into them greater vigor by a liberal extension of power. The very Constitution, under which we hold our seats in this House, strikingly evinces the justness of my position. Whence did it spring? From the debility of the Confederation. And whenever this Constitution shall be so feebly administered as to afford no protection against foreign aggression, when danger shall be at our doors, and confusion and distraction within; then, indeed, may we apprehend an effort to circumscribe, yet farther, the powers of the States, and increase, yet more, the powers of the Federal arm. From this wreck of elements a consolidation may grow, but it never can arise from a just exercise of the powers we now possess. As a lover of freedom, as an admirer of our happy Constitution, as a stickler for the rights of States, I pray you let us not bring our institutions into disrepute, and endanger the fabric of our Government, by leaving the nation without credit, without resources, without defence, without the means of protection. Let us rather use, with the moderation suggested by the committee, our unquestioned Constitutional powers, to preserve our nation from self-contempt, and to secure the inestimable blessings of national independence.

Having thus, Mr. Chairman, presented my view of the necessity of retaining our present military force, and replied to some of the prominent objections to that measure. I beg leave to say something in respect to the Navy. It is proposed that this important part of the defence of our country, should be gradually increased, until it shall be enabled to protect our coast from the ravages of every hostile naval power. I shall not attempt, Mr. Chairman, to blazon the praise of those whose achievements are their best eulogium, and whose glories have

> Stuck upon them as the sun
> In the grey vault of heaven:

But I will confine myself to the remark, that a navy affords to this nation, and particularly the State which I have the honor in part to represent, the best, the surest, the cheapest, defence. While, on the one hand, it can never endanger the liberties of the nation, whatever may be its extent, on the other, it forms the most complete protection for our very extensive and very exposed Atlantic frontier. Let the history of the last war teach us wisdom on this subject. With a superior navy, and a few thousand regulars, the enemy kept in continual alarm a coast of three thousand miles. The spot which they found protected, they avoided; the exposed and undefended, they ravaged unresistingly. Thousands of our militia have been called to the seaboard for its protection; millions of treasure have been consumed on that expensive system of defence, and many a gallant fellow has been the victim of disease, while the foe has confined his attack to vulnerable points, and has rarely assailed us where the yeomanry of our country were in in arms. It

is impossible that, without a navy, we ever should defend our coast, deeply indented, as it is, with large and navigable rivers, against the ravages of any naval power. The whole population and the whole wealth of the nation would not enable us to present, at every point, men in arms, sufficient to repel the foe; while, on the contrary, by means of a gradual increase of our Navy, a few years will see us masters of our own seas, and our soil will be protected from the pollution of an invading enemy. Is there not wisdom, then, in the measure? It is one which the interest of our country commands, and the general voice of our constituents requires at our hands.

I come next to the redemption of the public debt; one of the most important and interesting subjects presented to us by the Committee of Ways and Means. That debt has largely accumulated since the commencement of the war, and the committee have proposed to adopt at once a vigorous system of finance which will enable us to discharge the whole as rapidly as its redeemable character will admit. Who is there that can doubt the wisdom of such a policy? Who can doubt the propriety of the most vigorous exertions to get rid of a burden, which oppresses the nation in peace, and must paralyze her exertions when she is engaged in war? Who can hesitate to discharge the debt we have contracted instead of leaving it as a legacy to our children? In whatever point of view the subject is considered, it is of the utmost importance to this nation that the debt should be reduced as rapidly as possible. If we do not desire to pursue the fearful example of Great Britain; if we wish to avoid the continued accumulation of public burdens, we should not shrink from the duty which the present moment imposes. Whence is it that the British finances have become so involved? Whence is it that her debt has accumulated to a thousand millions? Because, after the termination of one war, she has never liquidated the additional debts it created before the expenses of another had commenced. Let us then take a lesson from her example. Let us rapidly discharge our debt, lest, as has once already happened to us, we should, before it is paid off, be involved in other wars that may infinitely increase it. Let us not flatter ourselves that we are now to have a never-ending peace. God forbid we should again have war. No man can be more averse to its horrors, none can be more forcibly impressed with the propriety of avoiding it, than I am. But peace does not depend on us alone. Any nation which may be disposed to involve us in hostility may do so, however contrary to our wishes; and we may think ourselves fortunate indeed if we shall enjoy the blessings of peace for the term of thirteen years, which is the period fixed on by the committee for the extinguishment of the debt. I do not, indeed, believe with the gentleman from Virginia, that Republics are prone to war, and still less that this nation has any such propensity. The history of this people—the peace of thirty years—acquits them of the charge. But there is a Power, of warlike disposition, with whom, from various causes, we may expect frequent and serious collisions. That Power is Great Britain. The gentleman from Virginia has admitted that other wars with that powerful people are not only probable but certain. It is one of the evil consequences, as he alleges, of the war from which we have emerged. "The bolt," he tells us, "has been shot," and we may now look for frequent wars and contentions. Be it so. Is it not then important that we should prepare for them, at least, by freeing our resources from the weight of debt by which they are encumbered? Shall we, with every prospect of frequent collision with a powerful nation, leave ourselves defenceless, and enter into another arduous conflict without money, without credit, and with an overwhelming debt? or shall we free ourselves from the burden, get rid of the heavy encumbrance of the interest, and if (which Heaven avert) new wars arise, be enabled to apply the resources of the nation to her defence, and to command the capital of her people for the supply of her coffers in the hour of her adversity? Of all the plans of the committee this is nearest my heart; of all the means of strengthening this nation, the best is, the emancipation of our finances from the burdens which oppress them. Our finances are, and must long continue, our weakest point. Do as we will, we shall always find it difficult enough to command resources in time of war. Let us not increase the difficulty. Let us endeavor to diminish it. If we enter into war under the pressure of debt, we shall find it difficult to borrow, both because our credit will not be so good, nor the amount of capital to be loaned so great, as if that debt had first been discharged; and if we lay taxes, those taxes must go to pay interest to the public creditor, instead of raising soldiers, procuring supplies and giving vigor and efficacy to our military operations. I trust, therefore, Mr. Chairman, that a just sense of these important considerations will urge us to adopt the vigorous system of the extinguishment of the debt, which has been proposed by the Committee of Finance.

But how shall we effect these desirable objects? How retain the necessary troops, make provision for our crippled officers, prepare for the gradual increase of the Navy, and secure the extinguishment of the debt which presses upon the nation? How—but by bearing the necessary taxes? Fortunately there never was a period at which the produce of the country, from one end of the continent to the other, commanded higher prices than now. Our prosperity is great, and our people are willing to pay something towards the important objects I have been contemplating. They will perceive that all the taxes have been reduced to about one-half their former amount, and those which were peculiarly oppressive or disagreeable have been entirely removed. I feel the fullest confidence that they will approve the measures which propose to retain a portion, rather than forego the advantages we have in view.

There remains but a few remarks in relation to the direct tax in particular, with which I shall trouble the Committee. It has been severely animadverted on, as unequal and oppressive. I cannot believe it. If indeed there be an inequality, I am surprised to hear the complaints from the quarter whence they have proceeded. If unequal, it must operate against those States where the nominal price of the land bears the greatest proportion to its real value. It must, therefore, be unfavorable to thickly settled States, and favorable to the people of the South and the West, whose population is more dispersed, and whose lands are not estimated at their intrinsic worth. But the inequality, if it existed, cannot be very important, since the tax itself is so light; amounting, in the State of Virginia, to only fourteen cents on one hundred dollars value, or about seven dollars on an estate worth five thousand. The people of these States are too intelligent to be led to regard a tax like this as odious and oppressive.

I know not, Mr. Chairman, whether it be in order to allude to the probable course which may be pursued in the other branch of the Legislature, (the Senate.) Let it be recollected that, by the law of the last session, the direct tax was rendered permanent, and it cannot now be removed without the consent of that branch. There is reason to suppose that if an entire repeal of the tax should pass this House, the Senate may reject it, and gentlemen will probably be left to the alternative of taking a permanent tax of six millions, or a tax for one year of three millions. If, then, they are averse to the direct tax, they ought to support the resolution upon your table, rather than encounter the still greater evil which will ensue from its rejection.

In tendering my thanks to the Committee for their polite attention to my lame and uninteresting remarks, I will conclude with expressing my earnest solicitude that we may pursue the path, on the present important occasion, that leads to the happiness and honor of our common country.

When Mr. T. had concluded—

Mr. Randolph moved that the Committee should rise, in order to take into consideration his proposition for reducing the Army, previous to deciding on the question now before the House.

This motion having been negatived—

Mr. Randolph rose, and delivered a speech of three hours on the opposite side of the general question from that taken by Mr. Calhoun and Mr. Tucker, to whom principally his speech was in reply. When he concluded, the Committee rose, reported progress, and obtained leave to sit again.

Mr. Randolph rose to make a motion respecting a discrepancy he had discovered between the account of the receipts and expenditures from the commencement of the Government, recently laid before the House, and that which was laid before Congress some years ago.

Before the motion was stated from the Chair, it was discovered there was not a quorum present; and the House adjourned.

FRIDAY, February 2.

Mr. ROBERTSON, from the Committee on the Public Lands, reported a bill for the relief of Charles Levan Trudeau; which was read twice, and committed to a Committee of the Whole.

Mr. RANDOLPH submitted the following resolution, which was read, and ordered to lie on the table:

Resolved, That the Secretary of the Treasury be required to lay before this House the cause of the difference in the annual amount of expenditures in relation to the Military and Naval Establishments, from the 4th March, 1789, to the end of the year 1809, as presented in the letter from the Secretary of the Treasury of April 3, 1810; and the annual amount of expenditures in relation to the same objects, as stated in a letter from the same Department, bearing date January 24, 1816.

The SPEAKER laid before the House a letter from the Commissioner of the General Land Office, transmitting a supplementary report of the land commissioners in the late Territory of New Orleans, now State of Louisiana; which were referred to the Committee on the Public Lands.

THE REVENUE.

The House then resolved itself into a Committee of the Whole, on the report of the Committee of Ways and Means.

A bill making appropriations for the Ordnance department—for ordnance stores, fortifications, &c.—was taken up, and the blank therein, on motion of Mr. LOWNDES, after some opposition from Messrs. WRIGHT, and KING of Massachusetts, was filled up with the sum of $1,650,224.

The resolution reported by the Committee of Ways and Means, and Mr. HARDIN's motion to amend the same, respecting the direct tax, next occupied the attention of the Committee of the Whole.

Mr. JOHNSON, of Kentucky, said he had many reasons, not only to justify, but to make it his duty, against his inclination, to trouble the Committee. First, the discussion had not been confined to the subject under consideration, but had been extended, as usual, to all subjects, foreign and domestic; secondly, the most direct attack had been made upon all the military subjects submitted to the Military Committee; all the measures reported by them, the invalid corps, military academies, &c., and particularly the reduction of the Army from ten thousand to six thousand. Mr. J. said, although he should confine himself principally to the military subject, he could not let the opportunity pass of saying a word in reply to some remarks which had been made in debate. The gentleman from South Carolina (Mr. CALHOUN) has expressed an opinion that our measures should be predicated upon a supposition that Great Britain was only separated from the United States as the Canadas and the Floridas. We often resort to the history of England, and to the opinions of her statesmen, for information on political subjects. If, on this occasion, we resort to the same sources, we shall discover that, from the views and sentiments of the most distin-

guished patriots, the British channel is of itself sufficient to make it the true policy of the British Government to act upon its insular situation—to abstain from interfering in the Continental system. The Court party maintained a different opinion, and succeeded in their policy, (except for short intervals,) the consequences of which have involved Great Britain in great difficulties and wars. Expenses have been incurred that would have raised a Chinese wall around the island. It must be left to conjecture what would have been the precise result of the opposite doctrine; but it is confidently believed that the English nation would have been at least as happy, as rich, and as free; that the poor would not have been more numerous; that the public debt would not have been more enormous; that the character of the nation would have been as distinguished for wisdom, science, and valor; that the taxes would not have been more burdensome; that liberty of conscience would not have been more limited. If the British channel could justify such a system, the separation of the United States from Europe and Great Britain left not a single doubt upon the mind. But this view of the subject does not depend upon reasoning and analogy, but upon matters of fact. Only suppose England and Ireland, with a population of two millions, annexed to Canada and separated from us by a mathematical line, length without breadth, a geographical boundary, governed by the Prince Regent and his Ministry, with their jealousy and hostility, and all the pecuniary resources of that absolute monarchy; would not every gentleman agree that our measures would have to be different from what they need to be now, in expense, in extent? In such event you would have forthwith to increase your Army and your Navy to an extent that would be very burdensome to the people. Mr. J. said he could not agree in the sentiments of the same worthy member, that a statesman should act upon possibility, and not upon probability, in measures of defence and precaution. This sentiment would lead us into great extravagance, such as could not be supported consistently with the enjoyment of that independence and liberty which our Constitution and Government would seem to hold out to us. We should not act upon any evidence less than probability. To prove the danger of this doctrine, we need only advert to the sentiment which grew out of it—for the gentleman treats with great severity the idea of increasing our Navy gradually. He is for going the whole length at this time. Now is the time, says the gentleman, and the only limit given is our power to man this Navy with our sailors and seamen, who are estimated at eighty thousand. The universal gallantry and good conduct of our Navy has produced a universal sentiment as to its efficiency, and a willingness to increase its power gradually, according to our means, until we have a pledge of a reasonable protection in case of war. Any measure, or any other sentiment, would have a direct tendency to prevent the growth of the Navy. A different course may be recommended from zeal and patriotism, but it will injure the cause is intended to promote.

The gentleman from Virginia (Mr. RANDOLPH) had discovered, previous to the declaration of war, a speck of war in the political horizon, and was alarmed. Mr. J. begged leave to call the attention of the worthy gentleman to a memorable example to be found in the pages of sacred writ, as to the consequences of submission, and bearing insults without resistance—reference was made to a book which abounded with examples, in religion, in morals, and in politics, and to which the gentleman from Virginia so often alluded with so much pleasure; when Moses brought the children of Israel in sight of the promised land, chosen men were sent down to view it; when they returned, such an account was given of the giants who possessed the land, that notwithstanding the influence of their great leader, the children of Israel refused positively to go down and possess themselves of their inheritance. The sons of Anak terrified them. This cowardice was the effect of submission to Egyptian bondage, for which God manifested his displeasure by dooming all the warriors to wander forty years in the wilderness and to die, until a new race of men should grow up who had never felt the heavy hand of oppression, and who willingly accomplished that which their fathers should have done.

It is now time to confine our attention to the reduction of the Army. This subject has given to the ingenuity of gentlemen a wide range; but the question does not admit of it. Points have been elaborately discussed that are not involved. There are many points in which we agree, and very few in which there is a difference of opinion. First, there is no disagreement as to the worth and character of the militia; nor is the relative merit of regular troops and militia involved in this debate. Such questions cannot be decided by mathematical certainty. Nor is it necessary; the merit of each is acknowledged; the efficiency of every kind of military force depends upon so many contingencies, the cause in which they are engaged, the term of service, the manner of fighting, the ground occupied, the officers commanding, that no particular case of panic or misfortune can change our opinion. For, in appealing to history, we should find memorable examples to support this idea, such as the defence of Thermopylæ, the battle of Marathon, composed of the population of Greece, and the battle of Cannæ, by what we call mercenary troops, or a regular army. The ancients had no very correct idea of a well-organized standing army, although Carthage and other kingdoms employed mercenary troops, while the citizens were exempt from military duty. For these troops, under trying circumstances, could not be relied on nor controlled. Thirdly, the subject of a standing army cannot be involved in this examination, although gentlemen have uniformly pressed the subject. No consideration can justify a standing army in time of peace. We may differ as to the amount of the Peace Establishment; there cannot be a diversity of sentiment among men who love liberty, independence, and a free country, as to standing armies. A standing army would be, in time of peace, inconsistent with the Constitution and our free institutions. We want no regular army to suppress insurrection, for none exists. In such an event the militia are subject to the call of the President. Nor to execute the laws, for the civil officers are all obeyed by the citizens; and if the citizens resist the execution of the laws, the marshal has the power of putting down any such resistance as is likely to arise in the United States. Nor to support the Administration of the Government; this depends upon the will of the people; upon the elective franchise. A standing army is dangerous to liberty. Rome depended upon the citizens, the militia of the country, four hundred and fifty years before the introduction of a mercenary force, which ultimately brought such calamity upon that great and mighty empire. Nor can it be forgotten that a standing army has been the most powerful instrument in the hands of power and usurpation. It has seldom failed of success. But notwithstanding the examples of ancient times, such as Philip of Macedon, and Cæsar, a regular army in modern times has been most mischievous and dangerous to liberty, on account of its perfect organization, subordination, and discipline; all the despotisms in the world are supported by this powerful instrument. All the Governments of Europe and all the tyrants of the day are supported by this means.

All must, therefore, agree, that in times of peace, and in the first moments of war, we must depend upon the population of the United States, well organized, classified, and the term of service extended. What has been said does not presuppose that we can dispense with all of our forces. All agree that we must keep a Peace Establishment, a small force, commensurate with certain objects and views, which will be mentioned. The first object is to garrison our forts on our wide-extended territorial frontier, and to maintain and keep in repair our fortifications on the seaboard and on the lakes; not only the existing fortifications and forts, but those to be erected. We should cast the eye around and view the great extent of this maritime and territorial exposure, and look at the number of our garrisons and our fortifications,—at Castine, Wiscasset, Portland, Portsmouth, Boston, New Bedford, Newport, New London, New York, Fort Mifflin, Fort McHenry, Fort Washington, Norfolk, Fort Johnson, in North Carolina, Charleston, Savannah, Fort Hawkins, Mobile, Fort St. Philippe, New Orleans, Natchez, St. Louis, Fort Clark, Fort Wayne, Chicago, Greenbay, Mackinac, Detroit, Fort Niagara, Sackett's Harbor, Plattsburg, Greenbush, and others about to be erected in such places as the late war has pointed out. To each garrison assign the nominal amount of one hundred men, which will not give more than seventy efficient men, and you have for this object alone a demand for five thousand.

2d. The second object will embrace such a distribution of force as will secure us on our frontier, from banditti, or marauding parties of Indians, or the insults and invasions of the subjects of Spain in Florida, and of Great Britain in Canada.

One thousand men should be placed somewhere on the Niagara or Northern frontier; one thousand in some healthy situation in Louisiana or the Mobile; one thousand in the neighborhood of Detroit, and one thousand in some eligible place on the Mississippi. This will amount to the whole military force of the United States except the corps of light artillery. Indeed, it is well known that an army of ten thousand men can never give us an efficient force of more than seven or eight thousand. To enforce my idea of this distribution, let us recollect the indignity and abuse offered to citizens of Detroit since the war, who were arrested and driven from Sandwich by the military, without any provocation; citizens of Detroit who had crossed the Straight for the common purposes of collecting debts, and for the purposes of commerce and trade. From actual returns, at this moment the Army of the United States is less than eight thousand men.

3d. There is another object for retaining this force, not less important than those which have been mentioned—the preservation of military knowledge; to have a rallying point in case of danger or war; to retain the knowledge we have acquired of camp duty, field evolutions and military discipline. This science cannot be taught in garrison, or with one hundred men—it requires at least a regiment.

It is believed that the people of the United States would be dissatisfied with a greater reduction of the Army. The country would be too insecure, and the militia subject to be called from their farms on every alarm. In relation to the direct tax—if the Committee will reduce it one-half, from $6,000,000 to $3,000,000, and limit its operation to one year, Mr. J. said, he would vote for it.

The direct tax is the most objectionable tax that can be collected, and, therefore, it should be limited to one year, that we may dispense with it as soon as possible. It is expensive in its collection, and burdensome in its operation. In time of war we must tax everything from necessity, but in time of peace we should be moderate in our taxes, and take hold of the luxuries of life and the rich, as much as possible; and after the present year, it is probable we may dispense with the direct tax, but it must be continued for the present, as we have a floating debt of $25,000,000 to pay off; and our national debt is upwards of $100,000,000. We have to pay for horses lost in the service of the United States, and other property; and we have to provide for the widow and the orphan of the officer and soldier who were killed in battle, or who died in the service; and these claims should be paid by every part of the United States, which can only be done by taking the money from the Treasury of the United States.

Much has been said respecting internal policy. On this subject there should be but one opinion.

Upon the subject of protecting manufactures by discriminating duties—this interest claims our first attention. It is as important as the independence of the nation; for how can any nation be independent without making its own necessaries of life? The voice of the nation has been distinctly heard upon this point, and all classes of men, with few exceptions, call for this protection. Independent of the importance of this subject in a national point of view, the manufactures of hemp, of cotton, of wool, and of everything else, have been the result, in a great measure, of the late war.

Citizens have turned their capital into domestic manufactures, not subject to the control of foreign nations; and this being the case, there is a moral obligation existing upon the Government to give reasonable protection to these people. Upon this subject the mind must expand, and take in the various climates and productions of the United States, and the various manufactories, and act upon a policy enlarged and liberal. Any other views would consider the States foreign to each other, and the people as strangers—a policy which does not become the American statesman. And in relation to roads and canals, which may open different channels of commerce, or which may facilitate military operations in future; we should all unite in this system of internal improvement. These are some of the fruitful sources of the prosperity of nations, with which we must encourage everything that will inculcate virtue, morality, patriotism, intelligence, and courage.

Mr. LOWNDES then addressed the Committee in defence of the report under consideration, and in reply to the objections urged against it in the course of the debate.

The question was then taken on Mr. HARDIN's motion to amend the resolution so as to declare it expedient to repeal the direct tax, and decided in the negative—for the amendment 69, against it 88.

At the request of Mr. HARDIN, the resolution was then laid on the table; and the Committee took up the bill to repeal the duties on certain domestic manufactures; which having been gone through, the Committee rose, reported progress, and obtained leave to sit again.

The House took up, successively, the bill making appropriations for the Ordnance department, agreeing to the amendment made therein by the Committee of the Whole; and the bill to repeal the duties on certain domestic manufactures.— The latter bill was so amended, on motion of Mr. SERGEANT, as to make the repeal take effect from the passage of the act, instead of the 18th April next. Both bills were ordered to a third reading. and the House adjourned.

SATURDAY, February 3.

An engrossed bill entitled "An act to repeal the duties on certain articles manufactured within the United Statess," was read the third time, and passed.

INDIAN DEPREDATIONS.

Mr. LATTIMORE, from the committee to whom were referred the memorial of the Legislature of the Mississippi Territory, and the petitions of sundry inhabitants of said Territory, relating to Indian depredations, made a report; which was read, and committed to a Committee of the Whole on Wednesday next.—The report is as follows:

The petitioners state that the inhabitants of the eastern section of the Mississippi Territory sustained, during the late war, very great losses of property, which was stolen or destroyed by the hostile Creek Indians, and, in some instances, taken from them by the troops in the service of the United States; and pray that reparation may be made to the sufferers out of the lands obtained from that nation of Indians by the Treaty of Peace.

Amongst the documents relating to this subject are statements (which are sworn to) of the losses sustained by one hundred and thirteen persons, which are estimated, in the whole, at $127,905. As these injuries were inflicted by the enemy, who have made, by a cession of territory, what the petitioners conceive to be ample compensation for all losses sustained as well as expenses incurred by their hostility, they seem to think that the sufferers in question are entitled to peculiar relief.

Your committee have examined the ground of this claim, but they find nothing to support it, either in the treaty with the Creeks or any other authentic document which they have been able to procure. If, therefore, relief shall be granted to these sufferers, it must, in the opinion of your committee, be done upon a general principle, which would be applicable to the cases of all who have suffered from similar causes in other parts of the United States. In giving this opinion, your committee have no disposition to impair the impression produced by the afflicting scenes through which the eastern inhabitants of the Mississippi Territory have passed, or to diminish whatever claim they may have to the humanity of the Government, in consideration of their present distress. But, whatever may be the merits of their claim on this score, your committee cannot perceive the propriety of any provision for their relief which shall not extend similar relief in all similar cases, and therefore submit the following resolution:

Resolved, That the prayer of the petitioners ought not to be granted.

THE REVENUE.

The House then resolved itself into a Committee of the Whole on the report of the Committee of Ways and Means, respecting the revenue; and after a short time spent therein, the Committee rose.

The House took up the report of the Committee of the Whole, on the proposition to reduce the annual direct tax to three millions. The amendment—agreed to on the suggestion of Mr. CLAY, in Committee of the Whole—to limit the tax to one year, so as to bring the question annually before the House, was concurred in by yeas and nays—for the amendment 109, against it 16, as follows:

YEAS—Messrs. Alexander, Atherton, Baer, Barbour, Bassett, Baylies, Bennett, Betts, Blount, Boss, Bradbury, Breckenridge, Brigham, Brooks, Brown, Bryan, Burnside, Burwell, Caldwell, Cannon, Chappell, Clarke of North Carolina, Clopton, Comstock, Conner, Crawford, Culpeper, Cuthbert, Darlington, Desha, Forsyth, Glasgow, Goldsborough, Goodwyn, Griffin, Hahn, Hale, Hardin, Hawes, Heister, Henderson, Herbert, Huger, Hungerford, Irwin of Pennsylvania, Jackson, Johnson of Virginia, Johnson of Kentucky, Kent, Kerr of Virginia, Lewis, Love, Lowndes, Lumpkin, Lyle, Lyon, Maclay, Mayrant, McKee, McLean of Kentucky, McLean of Ohio, Murfree, Nelson of Virginia, Newton, Noyes, Ormsby, Parris, Piper, Pitkin, Pleasants, Powell, Reed, Reynolds, Rice, Roane, Root, Ross, Ruggles, Savage, Sheffey, Smith of Virginia, Southard, Stanford, Stearns, Strong, Taggart, Tate, Taul, Taylor of South Carolina, Telfair, Thomas, Throop, Tucker, Vose, Wallace, Ward of Massachusetts, Ward of New York, Ward of New Jersey, Wheaton, Whiteside, Wilcox, Wilde, Williams, Willoughby, William Wilson, Woodward, Wright, Yancey, and Yates.

NAYS—Messrs. Birdsall, Birdseye, Gaston, Gold, Hammond, Hanson, Hopkinson, Jewett, Middleton, Mills, Milnor, Sergeant, Smith of Pennsylvania, Wendover, Wilkin, and Thomas Wilson.

Mr. HARDIN then renewed the motion, which he had made without success in the Committee of the Whole, to amend the resolution so as to declare it expedient to repeal immediately the direct tax, and thereon demanded the yeas and nays.

Mr. DESHA spoke a few words to correct a misapprehension of the reporter, from not being able to hear Mr. D. distinctly on a former day, when the motion was made to reduce the direct tax. He was desirous to reduce the direct tax, and to make it annual, but not to abolish it at present.

Mr. ROSS also rose for a similar purpose. He was now understood to say that he would not object to a direct tax, if necessary to defray the reasonable expenses of the Government; but, believing it might be dispensed with without detriment to the public interest, he should vote for its repeal.

Mr. STANFORD inveighed against the whole system of taxation in very severe terms, and in still more severe terms inveighed against the doctrines which, during the discussion, had been broached by certain ministerial members. Doctrines which, he said, if republican, must be republican after a new fashion—and if federal, were ultra-federal, and not at all of the old kind. It was not amiss at times to refer to first principles; he thought it would be well if the House would remember what they were, and what our freedom was, as understood by those who purchased it. The strongest feature in the character of our fathers, he said, was insurgency against taxes, and he recited the various insurrections which had taken place on that particular score, from the first opposition to British taxation, up to the present day. He then directed the attention of the House to certain injunctions which passed the Virginia Convention, when the Constitution was adopted, and which were annexed as amendments to the Constitution by a committee. These he said, enjoined that no standing army or body of regular troops should in time of peace be kept in the United States without the concurrence of two-thirds of both Houses of Congress. He read the provision from "the debates of the Virginia Convention"—and he read the names of those who formed that committee, and who made a constellation of patriots, such he said as had not since appeared in the United States. Among them were the names of Wythe, Matthew, Patrick Henry, George Mason, and Mr. Monroe. And yet gentlemen now advised the adoption of that very measure which those patriots solemnly interdicted. He observed, that when he first took a seat in that House he had on either side of him old Revolutionary men of high patriotic character. If he looked forward, he had them before him—if he looked back he saw them behind him. So that, being young at the time, he could not help feeling conscious that he was too green to sit among such personages. But now he looked in vain for them; they were gone, and had left very few like them—sorry indeed was he to say that they had not left their principles with their sons. Deeply did he regret to hear such doctrines as were now in vogue, from their successors—doctrines which they would not have dared at that time to avow. He admired the candor of Mr. CALHOUN—never indeed was candor more truly admirable—for that gentleman had unequivocally pronounced an execration upon all those who should not agree to erect fortifications immediately—forthwith ; and the venerable patriots whose names he had just read—to wit: Wythe, Matthew, Henry, Mason, and Monroe, were unquestionably objects of that execration, and so was Thomas Jefferson, and so were the best and greatest men this country had produced, for they purposely rejected fortifications, and chose to rely, for the country's defence, on the courage and hardihood of the people. But they were Republicans in heart—they had no wild notions about conquests, and national energy and military glory, and all that mischievous trumpery that entered so much into the character of gentlemen's policy in these new days. As to Mr. Jefferson, once the object of those gentlemen's admiration as well as the corner stone of their ascendency and elevation to power, he was sunk in their feelings—he was dead—nay, he was more than dead, for he and his principles were spurned by them. He, whose word was once bowed to by them as wisdom and law, was now condemned by them as a visionary theorist. Yes, that man who more than any man, except WASHINGTON, had been consecrated with the veneration and confidence of the public, and to whose popularity those very persons owed their situation in public trust, was now disregarded by them.

Mr. S. then read from a public journal of that period a paper written at the close of Jefferson's first term of Administration, in which the policy of his conduct was delineated, and from which it appeared that the pride of that policy and the glory of Mr. Jefferson was directly the reverse of that which seemed to animate our new politicians. The diminution of public expenses, the reduction of the Army, the abolition of internal taxes and the consequent discharge of five hundred officers—in a word, peace and economy—those were what Mr. Jefferson, and his friends, and his panegyrists

14th CON. 1st SESS.—28

maintained to be true national glory. If, not to follow the system now proposed, deserved execration, surely tenfold execration was due to those whose policy was such as that paper described.

Mr. S. then showed the folly of proposing to fortify our shores—they were too extensive to be fortified by anything but the arms of the people. Nor was there any call for it—even in the last war, what mischief did the British do along our seaboard, except that disgraceful affair to us the burning of Washington, that would justify such a system of extravagance? Along shore, they burned barns, and robbed hen-houses; and when negroes ran away to them, they took them—but they did nothing else; and he recommended to gentlemen the consideration that there was nothing they could do in their proposed system that would not be a reproach to their own past professions. They were actually taking a summerset over the heads of the Federalists and running on far before them. From the Administrations of WASHINGTON, or even of Mr. Adams, no examples could be adduced of their resorting to such energies as these. And for his part he did not understand what could be meant by building up armies on possibilities. We had nothing to fear—an ocean of three thousand miles rolled between Europe and our country—and there was no nation contiguous from which we could apprehend danger.

Mr. S. then read several passages from the report of the committee of the Virginia Assembly, drawn up by Mr. Madison as chairman of that committee, in which they expressed their alarm at the danger which the liberties of the country, incurred by Mr. Adams's raising an army, though he himself was now (in an universal peace too) for calling out a greater number—and deprecated the burdens on the people, at that time, though they amounted only to three dollars a head—while he now urged taxes that would amount to more than five dollars a head. And Mr. S. stated it as a circumstance characteristic of the views of those in power, as well as of the acquiescence of the people of this country under imposture, that, while in France they paid but five dollars, and in England but five and a half—we in this country paid rather more than five, taking all taxes together.

Mr. S. then read a passage from WASHINGTON's Farewell Address to the people of America. "Why," said the Father of his Country, " why ' forego the advantages of so peculiar a situation ? ' why quit our own, to stand upon foreign ground ? ' why, by interweaving our destiny with any part ' of Europe, entangle our peace and prosperity in ' the toils of European ambition, rivalship, inter-' est, humor, or caprice ?" We profess to be free, (said Mr. S.) and yet at every step we take we identify ourselves with monarchists. I am glad, however that gentlemen are so very frank and open in their avowals, and that they with so little disguise acknowledge their entire renunciation of their old principles.

Mr. BURNSIDE said he rose under great embarrassment to ask the indulgence of the House for a very few minutes.

A resolution has been reported by the Com-

867   HISTORY OF CONGRESS.   868

H. of R.   *The Revenue.*   February, 1816.

mittee of Ways and Means for laying a direct tax of three millions of dollars, and it was proposed to amend the resolution so as to declare it inexpedient to have a direct tax.

The proposition was plain and simple; but the discussion had involved not only the past, but the future policy of this Government. In the latter point of view, the question was extremely important and well worthy the most serious consideration of the National Legislature. His observations, he said, would be principally confined to the course and policy this Government should now pursue. Much had been said by the honorable gentleman from Virginia (Mr. Randolph) and others, in the course of this debate, about members being influenced by the patronage created by the Army, and the system of taxes contemplated by the Government. He did not feel the application of those observations to himself; he had no relatives to serve; his friends were in no other way connected with this Government than that of private citizens. There was not in the district which he had the honor to represent, one solitary citizen holding an office at this time in the Army of the United States. He did not mention these things at present in any other point of view, or with any other object, than to show that he was not influenced by any sordid motive, and if the policy he wished this Government to pursue was wrong, it arose from an error in judgment, and not from any personal or selfish feeling. His object solely was to secure the high and honorable standing of this happy country, and to continue this Government in a situation to preserve peace and to resist aggression. It had been fully demonstrated, in the course of this discussion, that to keep up the present Army of ten thousand men—to produce a gradual increase of the Navy—to put our fortifications in a proper state of defence, and to sink the national debt, this tax was necessary. Was this course of policy wrong? Ten thousand men were not more than sufficient for the garrison duty of this country. It was but the mere skeleton of an army. They would scarcely be sufficient for sentinels along our northern frontier. It was idle to talk about this number being dangerous to the liberties of this country. Gentlemen talk of five thousand under former Administrations—ten thousand was not more at this time than five thousand formerly, when we consider the vast increase of wealth, the extended territory of the country, and the great increase of population. He had no intention of making this nation a military Government; but if the Army was to be reduced, it must inevitably follow that many of the present important and necessary fortifications will fall into ruins. . He wished to avoid the situation many of them were in at the commencement of the late war. The militia most certainly are the great military bulwark of this nation; to them the country must look in all great struggles; but you cannot call them out to perform garrison duty in time of peace. It was a prodigious loss to the yeomen of the country, to be absent three or six months from their farms, their families,

and their homes; and it was infinitely more to their advantage to pay a small tax to support the necessary army. As to the national debt, he was extremely desirous to sink it as fast as possible; at the same time not to put any unnecessary burden upon the people. There was no honesty or political wisdom in leaving a large national debt upon our posterity, when a considerable part of it could be easily paid by ourselves. But look, said he, at the situation of your national enemy. There never was a period in the history of Great Britain when she possessed such a disposable force, and such powerful means of annoyance, as at the present time. France was humbled in the dust. She will probably withdraw her powerful army from France, and she might as well support that army in Canada as in England. Would gentlemen calculate on her magnanimity? We were her competitors in commerce, in manufactures, in the arts. She viewed us with jealousy and hatred; and he would ask gentlemen to point to a solitary instance in the history of that nation, where she was governed by any other motive than that of self-aggrandizement?

He should also be in favor of a very considerable increase of the Navy—not that he wished to see a great number of ships in immediate commission. He wished additional ships-of-war to be built—a large supply of necessary timber to be procured for the construction of others, and every kind of naval stores in the possession of the Government, so that ships could be immediately constructed, if the exigencies of the country required it. It would be well that fortifications should be erected and improved along our whole seaboard, as well as our northern boundary. The mouth of the Mississippi, the Chesapeake, and the Delaware, New York and Boston, should be fortified and strengthened, as well as many intermediate points. He would have the seaboard so strong that an enemy would meet with resistance at the threshold. We are charged by honorable gentlemen with changing our principles. He denied that the Republican party of this country had changed their principles. The situation of Europe had changed, and our measures should be calculated to meet that change. But a change of measures was not a change of principles. When a navy was formerly wished by some men in this country, it was not necessary to preserve our existence as a nation. It would have been burdensome, and we flourished without it. Great Britain had then use for her navy near herself. France, Spain, Holland, and Denmark, had considerable navies. She required nearly her whole force to watch her neighbors, and they watched each other; but now the navies of France, Spain, Holland, and Denmark, were either possessed by Great Britain, or had disappeared from the ocean. In short, a navy was not at that time wanted by this country. The present time was most favorable for the constructing ships-of-war for this rising and growing nation. We had the advantage of experience. We know the precise force of British ships-of-war of every class, and it would be the policy of this Government, in the construction of ships, to have each class superior to that of the British, so as to secure victory, should they ever come in contact.

But, suppose we have a surplus revenue over the expenditures contemplated by this Government at the present time, are there not ways and means of appropriating it to great national advantage? Are not national roads much wanted? Are not canals almost indispensably necessary? He believed it to be the interest of this Government to turn their attention particularly to these subjects.

It would be the interest of his constituents to pay a direct tax to assist in cutting a canal from the Chesapeake to the Delaware; and he had no doubt they would most cheerfully pay it for that object. If, then, this view of the policy to be pursued by this nation is correct, taxes are indispensably necessary, and, if necessary, the people were prepared to pay them. The people were enlightened and intelligent, and well understood the situation of their country, and would no doubt submit with cheerfulness to any moderate burdens that might be imposed. The direct tax was the most equal of all others that could be devised or levied on the people of the United States; it operated equally on the North and the South, the East and the West—every State paid in proportion to its population, and every citizen paid in proportion to the extent and value of his real property. No other tax could be devised that would unite those great advantages of equality. Gentlemen had called our attention to the situation of the country before the late war. It was painful to look at our humbled situation at that period. Our commerce was the sport and prey of nearly every nation in Europe. England and France, pretending to retaliate on each other, nearly swept our flag from the ocean. Little Denmark suffered her cruisers to capture our ships, and thought our commerce fair game; and even the Neapolitans could not resist the temptation, and came in for a small share of the spoil. It was impossible for this country to be in a more miserable and degraded situation.

But mark the contrast. See your present proud pre-eminence. Where is the Power in Europe that does not respect you—that dare commence the same system of spoliation and injustice?

The national character of this country stands pre-eminently high. You have acquired national glory, and where is the honorable-minded man that is not proud of the exalted situation of his country? It was his sincere and ardent wish to maintain this dignified and honorable character, this high and exalted situation, as the best pledge of peace and happiness.

My honorable colleague (Mr. HOPKINSON) has exercised the whole extent of his ingenuity to find out what we have lost by the war, and unfortunately for him and his friends he has hit upon the fisheries. He perceived that his colleague meant the right of drying fish on the islands in the possession of the British and on their main shore, not the right of fishing on the great bank. If the people of that part of our country had been blest with the spirit of the West; if they had not thrown immense difficulties in the way of the national arms, they would not have this trifling solitary matter to complain about. They may thank themselves, and the shameful policy and conduct they pursued, for their loss on this subject.

Mr. McKEE said that the question in itself, separate from the arguments which had been introduced upon it, was a very unimportant one; but the doctrines which some gentlemen had broached in discussing it, must produce the most weighty bad effects on the happiness and prosperity of the country. Thinking it probable that from this very discussion historians would hereafter commence their accounts of a new era in this country, he considered it his duty to give his vote in that way which was most likely to avert evil, and promote the interests of the country. Gentlemen talked of being guided to their new projects by experience, and had inferred, from the miscarriages in the conduct of Government, a defect in the Constitutional system; but, looking to facts, it was demonstrable that incapacity in the official departments of State was the true cause of those miscarriages. Gentlemen ought not to forget that while the Secretary at War was early furnished by Congress with everything that he required for carrying on the war, in the most unsparing manner, the recruiting officers were not furnished with the means of proceeding upon their duty till the succeeding May. Inefficiency in the administration of Government was no reason for resorting to a system subversive of the principles of that Government. But, gentlemen had said that times were changed; yes, they were—and they might have added that they themselves were changed along with the times; and their projects, if persisted in, would change every idea of Government established in America, to the pernicious doctrines which have for centuries prevailed in the Old World. The true policy of this country was to preserve the moral power of it—but the tendency of the schemes of those innovators was to destroy the moral power, and to create an apathy in the people. What, he asked, was the cause of our successes against the English in the late war? Why, they arose from the operation of a superior moral power upon the people; the Americans having fought for everything that was dear to them, while the English fought only for objects in which they were not at all personally interested. Without exception, all the events of history showed that those who were most conspicuous in deeds of arms, were those whose interest were most intermingled with the objects at stake. At the beginning of the French Revolution, it was the increase of the moral power arising from the objects they had in view, which enabled that people to perform such prodigies of valor as are recorded of them. The moral power was the best security, and the increase of the physical power diminished that security by dwindling the moral power. Mr. McK. differed entirely from Mr. CALHOUN's opinion, that an apathy prevailed in the people of America—or, if it did, it respected domestic dangers only; they had shown their alacrity to meet the British foe; and there was much more cause to fear their submitting to some home-bred despot, than their yielding to any foreign attack. As a proof of this, he remarked, that when the finances of the country were tottering in the late war—when Government were unable to devise how they should carry on another campaign, the people never once shrunk, or uttered a word of despondence. No—not a man of them. Where, then, did their hopes rest? Why, where it ought to rest—on their confidence in the moral power, and consequent exertions of the nation. This was the sole anchor on which they relied.

Mr. McKee then directed his argument to show that all the fiscal difficulties which had ensued were occasioned not by any indisposition in the people to meet the exigencies of the times, but by the impolicy and incapacity of Government as evinced in their restrictive system.

The course now projected and developed, filled Mr. McK., he owned, with fears that that great rock of our national safety, the moral power of the country, would be deserted and left uncherished, while the physical would be increased—and that the consequence would be the nation's driving headlong on the same road which led those of Europe into the gulf of ruin; and he desired the House to compare the words of Mr. Pitt, whose talents nevertheless he owned to be superior to those of any other man, with the doctrines now maintained here. Mr. McK., however, owned, that while he urged this, because he thought it his duty to do, he had no hope of its producing any effect, for he was convinced that there existed a pre-determination, against which reason would exert all its force in vain.

Mr. Wright again spoke against the taxes with great earnestness, and evident sincerity.

Mr. Gaston said, that he would be glad to repeal the direct tax, because he thought it oppressive, if he could reconcile it to his conceptions of the interest of the country to do so—but, considering that, with such a heavy debt as the country was pledged for, a vigorous system of finance was absolutely necessary, he was unwilling to decline his share of the responsibility, whatever it might be, annexed to granting the taxes for that purpose.

But while he thus voted for the taxes recommended by the Committee of Ways and Means, he thought himself entitled to state the purposes to which he conceived they ought to be applied—and this he would do in the words of Sir Fletcher Norton, who, when placed in a situation and in circumstances which laid his chief hopes at the mercy of the Crown, had the virtue, when presenting the civil list bill to the King of Great Britain, to tell him "it was hoped that what the Commons had given cheerfully His Majesty would spend wisely." In other words Mr. G. thought he had a right to demand, that with respect to the grants of the House, there should be not only wisdom in selecting the means, but economy observed in the application of them.

He would tell them that he did not vote this money for the prosecution of wild schemes of erratic chivalry. He did not vote it with a view to run in the race of glory, nor to divert the citizens of the Republic from the occupations of honest industry to military pursuits. He wished them to remain what they are. The only change he desired in them, was to be more industrious—but not in the military life.

Nor did he vote it for the purpose of enabling Government to run the brilliant career which gentlemen had proposed, of extensive improvements in military roads and canals. The Government, he observed, was confederated for certain general objects, and ought to leave those improvements to the municipal regulations of the particular States.

Nor did he vote for it because war was inevitable, as some gentlemen had insinuated. He did not coincide in opinion with those gentlemen who thought it was; and he thought there was much danger in giving indulgence to such sentiments; for, the moment one nation viewed another as a natural enemy, its conduct inevitably began to partake of that feeling, and endless causes of hostility would arise. But he would indulge the hope that the councils of both countries would be animated by a superior spirit—a spirit of magnanimity and mutual tolerance; and that the two families would not weaken their strength by groundless ineffectual struggles with each other.

In short, he voted with a view, in the first place, to a vigorous system of defence for the country, by permanent, safe and Constitutional means; not by armies, but by extending the Navy—and, in the next place, with a view to the payment of the national debt. That ought to be discharged, he said, as speedily as possible—for it hung like a mill-stone about the neck of the country, incapacitating it from vigorous exertion. This season of peace he observed, ought to be made use of for the purpose; the debt must be paid some time, and that being the case, the sooner it was paid the better; for, if an evil was to be encountered, it ought never to be postponed.

These, Mr. G. said, were the purposes for which he voted for this system of finance. He was the only one of the members from his State who took up that responsibility; and he did so with a thorough conviction that he was doing his duty;—but, doing it alone, he had a right to demand of gentlemen some little economy. Economy had ever been a principal ingredient in the ways and means of the greatest statesmen—and a favorite maxim of Burke's, which he would recommend to the consideration of the honorable gentlemen who conducted our financial concerns, was, *magnum est vectigal parsimonia.* By parsimony, in his construction of this maxim, he did not understand anything sordid, contracted or mean, but plainly this: "there is no revenue equal to a liberal and discreet economy."

And here, Mr. G. held up the report of the Treasury, and pointing to a particular sheet of it, said: It is melancholy to look at this balance sheet—it proves how deficient our Government has been in husbanding the resources of the country. If these balances are due, as no doubt they are, our Government is inexcusable in not compelling those concerned to render an account of them. There is not a department of Government whose accounts would be received, nor is there a voucher among them that would be admitted in a settlement between any gentleman and his overseer. This money which the House is now voting may also be prodigally squandered away, and to speak my mind, I very much fear that a great part of it will be so; yet I do not think that I should be justified in withholding it upon that presumption.

Mr. RANDOLPH rose, he said, not to repeat the trespass he had already so frequently, during the discussion of the revenue system, committed on the politeness of the House, but to redeem himself from an apparent inconsistency in the vote he was about to give—he rose, but to explain.

If Government required any other supplies than those already granted, and he was bound to decide between the raising of it by a direct tax, and by internal taxes, he would prefer the former—because he was convinced that the principle of internal taxation, if once let to slip out of the hands of the House, would be gone forever from their grasp.

He dissented from Mr. GASTON's doctrine about paying off the public debt; and he acknowledged with him, that the way to meet an enemy, was to confront him directly; but how true soever that might be in the case of a conflict between man and man, it was not true of a financial difficulty, and he put it to Mr. GASTON to say, whether there were not instances in which it would be madness to pay off a portion of a debt unnecessarily.

The honorable gentleman (Mr. GASTON) had spoken of economy, and said that he was cheered by the promise of the chairman of the Committee of Ways and Means that a system of accountability was about to be introduced; but he would tell both those gentlemen, that, to use the words of a rule in grammar, we should always find ourselves in *the future* in RUS—we should never be nearer than *about to be*. No, no—he knew those concerned better. There were too many interested in keeping up the disease, for any one who knew them, reasonably to hope for a cure. We are corrupted, said he, we are corrupted with our own money. The purchaser is here. About to have acountability, indeed! when the finger of contempt is pointed at any man who dares to speak of accounting. I have seen a man laughed at, for only talking of the corruption of the Executive Department.

He then stated, that it was his intention on Monday, or whenever the House meant to act upon the measure now under consideration, to demonstrate, not to mathematical, but to moral certainty, that there is money enough without this tax, to support the Government—not, indeed, to support its extravagance—not to support its *nepotism*—not to support its abuses—but to uphold it, in the situation in which it was wont to be upheld, before this general solution of morals, that has come upon us; as it was under JEFFERSON and WASHINGTON—to pay the interest of the public debt, and to redeem the principal as soon as it had ever been thought advisable to redeem it, before certain new financiers found it convenient to think otherwise. "*Timeo Danaos*," said he, I shrewdly suspect, that they have no just view in this violent haste, all at once to pay off the debts, which, till now, they were well enough satisfied to leave to the regular course of liquidation.

Mr. R. said that he was willing to support the Navy, and to increase it from time to time, to a degree commensurate with the necessities of the country—to put into the hands of every militiaman, at once, a musket and a bible—in order to arm him with moral and physical force. He would also keep the existing fortifications in repair; and I will demonstrate, said he, 'that, for all these purposes, there are now, ample funds—but, I will not, therefore, agree, that because the ordnance has undergone some dilapidations, a million of dollars shall be given—and that forthwith—to increase it; or that while some objects are left unprovided for, others shall be starved or neglected.

After specifying some particular points, upon which he intended to animadvert on Monday, he declared that he should not be as liberal as Mr. GASTON was, on this occasion; he would require security—an endorser. That gentleman, he said, was out in his reckoning, if he thought that Government could be brought to account, by any provisions they could make for the purpose; for his part, he would not give a pepper-corn for their accountability. Who is your auditor? Who is your comptroller?—he exclaimed. Do you expect any effectual control over an Administration, through the medium of men who hold their offices by its gift, and are dependent on its will and pleasure? Look at your accounts! They are such accounts as no court would receive from a guardian or executor—nor any man of common sense receive from any other person, unless it were in the case of a friend, to whom he might say, "I'll take your word for it." No, no—no account can be had from them, but one general, systematic prostration of law and morals."

You cannot go even through the avenues of this House, said he, without meeting the public despoilers, with faces dressed in smiles, and bodies bending into bows; but if you are known to look deeply into them—if you are suspected of keeping them steadily in your eye, and of searching them through—they look at you, just as the nightly robber looks at the honest mastiff, lying before the door which he wishes to break open. I know them—and the nation shall know them. I shall not be deterred by delicacy—or etiquette, as it is called—from putting home questions, on this floor; and, if those questions shall be sanctioned by the votes of this House, I will lay before you such a scene of collusion, corruption, and public robbery, as never was brought to light before, in any age or nation. I know what I shall

875   HISTORY OF CONGRESS.   876

H. of R.   *Petitions of R. M. Pomeroy and Colonel Schuyler.*   FEBRUARY, 1816.

have to pay for this, but I care not; had I consulted selfish policy or personal ease, I should never have left home. I know what it is to rouse the guilty host; I know what it was to have roused the Yazoo clan, but I despise them all. I know the price I am to pay for my duty—I know that the assassin of reputation already nibs his pen for me, but that shall not deter me from a proceeding which I owe to my country, which I owe to myself, which I owe to my God.

After a few words against the motion from Mr. WOODWARD, and an ineffectual effort of Mr. HARDIN, to procure an adjournment, with the view of submitting, on Monday, some propositions which, if agreed to, would obviate the necessity of the direct tax; the question was taken on the motion to repeal the tax entirely, and decided in the negative, as follows:

YEAS—Messrs. Atherton, Baer, Barbour, Baylies, Blount, Boss, Bradbury, Breckenridge, Brigham, Brown, Bryan, Cady, Cannon, Champion, Cilley, Clarke of North Carolina, Cooper, Culpeper, Davenport, Goldsborough, Hale, Hardin, Hawes, Heister, Henderson, Herbert, Hulbert, Hungerford, Jackson, Jewett, Kent, King of Massachusetts, King of North Carolina, Langdon, Law, Lewis, Love, Lovett, Lyon, Mason, McCoy, McKee, Mills, Moore of South Carolina, Moseley, Noyes, Parris, Pitkin, Powell, Randolph, Reed, Reynolds, Rice, Ruggles, Sergeant, Sharpe, Sheffey, Smith of Virginia, Stanford, Stearns, Strong, Sturges, Taggart, Tallmadge, Tate, Taul, Thomas, Voss, Ward of Massachusetts, Ward of New York, Wheaton, Wilcox, Williams, Wright, and Yancey —73.

NAYS—Messrs. Alexander, Baker, Bassett, Bateman, Bennett, Betts, Birdsall, Birdseye, Brooks, Burnside, Burwell, Caldwell, Calhoun, Chappell, Clark of Kentucky, Clendennin, Clopton, Comstock, Crawford, Creighton, Cuthbert, Darlington, Desha, Forney, Gaston, Glasgow, Gold, Goodwyn, Griffin, Grosvenor, Hahn, Hall, Hammond, Huger, Ingham, Irving of New York, Irwin, of Pennsylvania, Johnson of Kentucky, Kerr of Virginia, Lowndes, Lumpkin, Lyle, Maclay, Mayrant, McLean of Kentucky, McLean of Ohio, Middleton, Milnor, Nelson of Massachusetts, Nelson of Virginia, Newton, Ormsby, Pickens, Pickering, Piper, Pleasants, Reynolds, Roane, Robertson, Root, Ross, Sergeant, Savage, Schenck, Smith of Pennsylvania, Southard, Taylor of New York, Telfair, Throop, Tucker, Wallace, Ward of New Jersey, Wendover, Whiteside, Wilde, Wilkin, Willoughby, Thomas Wilson, William Wilson, Woodward, and Yates—81.

Mr. PICKENS then made a motion to amend the resolution for continuing a direct tax of three millions, so as to reduce the tax from three to two millions; but, before the question was taken, the House adjourned.

MONDAY, February 4.

Another member, to wit: from Maryland, SAMUEL SMITH, elected to supply the vacancy occasioned by the resignation of Nicholas R. Moore, appeared, produced his credentials, was qualified, and took his seat.

Mr. LOWNDES laid before the House a letter from the Secretary of War to the Committee of

Ways and Means, enclosing a detailed statement of the sums necessary for the Ordnance department for the year 1816. Ordered to lie on the table.

Mr. PLEASANTS, from the Committee on Naval Affairs, made a report on the petition of Captain Charles Stewart, late Commander of the frigate "Constitution," which was read; when Mr. P. reported a bill rewarding the officers and crew of the Constitution for the capture of the British sloop-of-war "Levant;" which was read twice, and committed to a Committee of the Whole.

The SPEAKER laid before the House a letter from the Governor of Ohio, announcing the unanimous rejection by the Legislature of that State, of the amendments proposed to the Constitution by the States of Massachusetts and Connecticut.

On motion of Mr. JOHNSON, of Kentucky,

Resolved, That the Committee on the subject of the Militia be instructed to inquire into the expediency of paying, for the term of six months, the officers and soldiers of the militia who were taken prisoners at Fort Meigs, in the late war, under the command of Colonel Dudley, who fell in battle on that occasion.

The motion of Mr. RANDOLPH to inquire into the causes of the variance in amount of the statements obtained from the Treasury in 1809, and at this time, in regard to the receipts and expenditures of the Government since the year 1789, was taken up and agreed to—no objection being made to it.

PETITION OF R. M. POMEROY.

Mr. YANCEY, from the Committee of Claims, made a report on the petition of Ralph M. Pomeroy; which was read, and the resolution therein contained was concurred in by the House.

The report is as follows:

That, on the 24th of November, 1812, and for some time previous thereto, the petitioner owned and occupied a dwelling-house in the village of Buffalo, in the State of New York; that, on the aforesaid day, a number of soldiers belonging to the United States Army came to his house, broke it open, destroyed his furniture, and set the House on fire and burnt it. The petitioner prays of Congress to be paid the value of his house and furniture.

It does not appear to the committee, from the *ex parte* evidence of the petitioner, what was the cause of such wanton and unlawful conduct on the part of the soldiery. However much it is to be deprecated in those who perpetrated the offence, yet it certainly has created no obligation, moral or legal, on the Government to pay for the injury. This principle has often been adopted, and is believed by the committee to be founded in a wise and just policy. They recommend to the House the following resolution:

Resolved, That the prayer of the petitioner ought not to be granted.

PETITION OF COLONEL SCHUYLER.

Mr. YANCEY made a report on the petition of Colonel Peter P. Schuyler; which was read, and the resolution therein contained was concurred in by the House. The report is as follows:

That, in 1812, the petitioner, late a Colonel in the thirteenth regiment of infantry, was assigned to the recruiting service, the head-quarters of which was in the city of New York; that he received from the Department of War, at several times, large sums of money for that purpose; that, in the month of August, 1812, he put into the post office, in the city of New York, two hundred dollars, enclosed in a letter addressed to Major Joseph L. Smith, then at Litchfield, Connecticut, for the recruiting service, and which Major Smith informed him did not reach him. The petitioner states that, upon a settlement of his accounts with the Department, that sum has not been allowed him, because he could not produce a receipt from Major Smith. He asks of Congress to be allowed the sum in the settlement of his accounts.

It does not appear to the committee that the money was transmitted to Major Smith by mail, by the order of the Department; and, unless special orders for that purpose had been given, they are of opinion that the risk of such transmission was with the petitioner, and therefore he is not entitled to relief. They recommend to the House the following resolution:

Resolved, That the prayer of the petitioner ought not to be granted.

COMMERCIAL RESTRICTIONS.

Mr. KING, of Massachusetts, presented for consideration the following resolution:

"*Resolved,* That the Committee on Foreign Relations be instructed to inquire into the expediency of excluding from the ports of the United States all foreign vessels, owned in, coming from, bound to, or touching at, any of His Britannic Majesty's possessions in the West Indies, and in the continent of North America, from which the vessels of the United States are excluded; and of prohibiting, or increasing the duties on, the importation in foreign vessels, of any articles the growth, produce, or manufacture, of such possessions."

Mr. K. said, he was induced to present this resolution, as well from information as to the state of the trade already alluded to, received before and since he left that part of the country which he had the honor to represent, as from his own conviction of the necessity of some legislative provision on the subject. It is, said Mr. K., by no means the object of this resolution, to revive an extensive, odious, restrictive system, or commercial warfare with Great Britain; but justly to retaliate upon her some of those embarrassments, which her rigid colonial system is at this moment inflicting upon us. When you turn your attention to that nation, you do see in operation one of the most rigid, exclusive colonial systems that ever was adopted by any nation; well digested and prepared, as to her interest, for the present state of commerce in the world. I will ask your attention to its effects on our country, with relation to the possessions mentioned in the resolution; for as to our commerce with her European territories, the fate of that has been determined for four years, by the commercial convention. It will be seen that Great Britain had, before the formation of the arrangement with us, secured to her subjects in North America every advantage in her power, by securing to them a ready market for every article which they could furnish, at a very low duty; while on the same

article, when imported in the vessels of the United States, or even British vessels from this country, a duty is imposed, amounting to a prohibition.

In relation, then, to this trade, all our vessels are permanently excluded from her islands and continental possessions in America. She did, indeed, for a time, offer one or two insignificant ports in the island of Bermuda, under great limitation, which we ought to have rejected with scorn. While the United States, on the contrary, threw all their ports open to British vessels of every description. She next selects from her stores such articles as are not important to her, and sends them to the United States; and also selects, in return, such articles as she cannot produce or do without; that is, she picks and culls our market, as a petty shopman does his wares; and we greedily receive whatever she is pleased to vouchsafe to us—a beggar, like us, devours the crumbs which fall from the rich man's table—we ought to spurn such a degraded, such a contemptible traffic. In regard, then, to the direct trade between the United States and the possessions named, the subjects of Great Britain are the only carriers; her ships from Great Britain may come to any of our ports with full freights of dry goods; with part of the proceeds purchase a load of lumber, stock, provisions, &c., (such I mean as they choose to admit in the islands,) sell it at their islands at great profit, take in a cargo of West India produce, and carry it to any part of Europe, giving them full freights in three distinct voyages. And a portion of our lumber, and pot and pearl ashes, will and does, by Champlain and other waters, find their way to the St. Lawrence, are bought up by the British capitalist at his own price, and sent to a most profitable market in Great Britain and the West Indies, giving employment to their ships and great profit to their merchants. The only way in which lumber, fish, flour, rice, &c., in our vessels, find a market in the British West Indies, is through some island belonging to some other foreign nation, less rigid than Great Britain in her colonial system; and in the same way we receive in our ships some of her products, all loaded with additional freight and insurance, for carriage among the islands. But of this, miserable as it was, we are in part deprived, or attempted to be, by an act of one of her colonial assemblies, made expressly against this country, and no doubt the same will be done in other islands. I allude to "An act laying a duty on certain goods, wares, and merchandise, imported into this island (Jamaica) from the United States of America, and other places," passed the 14th November, 1815, by which it is enacted, that, from the passing of that act, and during its continuance, there shall be levied and paid to His Majesty, &c., on all goods, wares, and merchandise, imported into that island "from any port or 'ports of the United States of America, or from 'any colony or plantation in America, belonging 'to, or under the dominion of any foreign Euro- 'pean sovereign, in a state of amity with His 'Majesty, the following duties, viz., among others— 'For every barrel of wheat flour, not weighing

' more than 196, net weight, thirteen shillings
' and four pence.
'For 100 pounds of rice, six shillings and eight
' pence.
'For every 1,000 shingles, or Boston chips, not
' more than twelve inches in length, six shillings
' and eight pence." (About three times the first
cost, being what we call common shipping shingles.)
"For every 1,000 shingles more than twelve
' inches inches in length, thirteen shillings and
' four pence;" (being more than the value in the
northern parts of this country.)
"For every 1,000 feet of white and yellow pine
' lumber of all descriptions, twenty shillings;"
(which is above half the original cost in this
country.)

Various other articles, on which specific duties
are imposed in the same proportion, and an ad
valorem duty of ten per cent. on all other articles
which they see fit to admit. And information
has been received that it is their intention, in relation to the article of plaster from Nova Scotia,
to impose an export duty on it of five dollars the
ton, (nearly its value in the Boston market,) when
landed East of New Haven, so that their vessels
may be the exclusive carriers to those States
where it is used. The operation of this system
in the North and East is such, that our lumber
trade to the West Indies has been nearly destroyed, and two-thirds of the vessels in that trade
thrown out of employ. I presume that nearly
one-third of all the tonnage of Maine (which, in
1814, not a very propitious year, amounted to
125,000) was formerly employed in the West
India trade. A large proportion of our vessels
have now become useless, and British vessels
have, in many cases, become our carriers.

The question then is, said Mr. K., whether we
shall aid Great Britain to enforce her colonial
system, exclusively for the benefit of her subjects,
or retaliate upon her some of the injuries which
we suffer from her navigation laws. It will be
in vain, and worse than in vain, that we freed
ourselves from former impositions and pretensions, if we must again be brought in subjection
to colonial servitude.

The whole trade of this country is too valuable
to be bartered away for a portion of that of any
nation. I cannot admit the doctrine, that we have
no equivalent to offer Great Britain for this trade;
it carries its equivalent with it, as she may and
ought to find it, in that immense traffic she enjoys
with this country. She appeared disposed, by
the treaty, to put the commerce of the two countries upon the most liberal ground of reciprocity.
Instead of that, we do not gain half the advantages which we yield to her, while she closes so
many of her ports against us. Whatever interest
Great Britain has to favor the colonial trade of
her subjects, we have none; nor ought we to aid
her in this semi-terrapin policy. If these colonists
suppose they can do without a trade, on the
ground of reciprocity with us, let us see, in return, if we cannot do without a trade with them;
one good effect, at least, will be produced; we

shall encourage the production of sugar, molasses, rum, &c., in our Southern States; and thus,
with the trade we shall enjoy with the colonial
possessions of other nations in the West Indies,
free our citizens from these colonial impositions.
Unless foreign nations are disposed to trade with
us on the ground of the most perfect reciprocity,
I would reject their commerce, and by every
means in our power encourage all articles, the
growth, produce, or manufacture of our country, &c.

Mr. FORSYTH thought the resolution too limited in its terms. He therefore suggested an
amendment, by inserting after the words "United States," the words "or laying additional duties on."

Mr. KING said, he had no kind of objection to
the amendment, which he therefore accepted as
a part of his motion.

Mr. BURWELL said, this was a proposition, it
appeared to him, of such importance, that the
House ought to act with much caution in respect
to it. If the United States undertook to countervail the British colonial policy, it was in vain to
suppose that it would not produce collision with
that nation. The subject of this proposition
would necessarily affect the consumers, and particularly the agriculturists of every part of the
country. The course of this nation, on this subject should depend much on the policy pursued
by the other nations of Europe in regard to those
colonies. It was perfectly evident, Mr. B. said,
that the effect of these measures of the British
Government must be to embarrass the intercourse
with her colonies, and enhance to the consumers
in the islands the price of every necessary of
life; if the policy of the other owners of islands in
the West Indies should be more liberal, Great Britain will lose the benefit of the trade she burdens so
heavily, and the evil will cure itself. England
has a right to regulate the trade to her colonies
as she pleases; and an attempt to coerce her to
change her policy in this respect would, he apprehended, ultimately prove the commencement of
a new commercial contest with England. He
was, therefore, desirous that no decision should
be made on this proposition, without mature consideration, and full information, particularly as
to the policy of the other Powers in Europe who
have colonies abroad.

Mr. KING spoke in reply, and in further support
of his motion. He said, he had intended to have
made this resolution more general, to countervail
the restrictions and impositions to which our trade,
with the colonial possessions of other foreign
nations, is subjected. But, as we yet had no opportunity of forming any new commercial arrangements with other foreign nations, I thought
it best, for the present, to omit them. Great
Britain too, of all nations in the world, is bound
to form with us the most liberal and reciprocal
commercial arrangements; I mean from the
amount and kind of trade which she enjoys with
us. She receives from us the raw material to
keep in motion a great proportion of her manufacturing industry and ingenuity, then sends a

large proportion back in its finished state, as to manufacture, to be consumed in this country. Mr. K. further said, it might be feared by some, that the retaliation proposed would deprive us of some necessary supplies. I think not, said he; it is for the interest of the islands to receive various products of this country, in exchange for their produce. It will be impossible to prevent a traffic of this kind, through the possessions in the West Indies of other European Powers; from these possessions, then, and our Southern States, an abundant supply can be afforded. Will it not lead to a war with Great Britain? Just commercial retaliation can never be a just cause of war. When Great Britain thinks it for her interest to have a war with this country, pretexts will not be wanting. We are not to be deterred from any just or necessary measure by any fear of this kind; it is quite sufficient for us, that the interest of our citizens and the honor and dignity of this nation demand it.

Mr. Wright said, he was surprised at any opposition being made to the adoption of a proposition to inquire into this highly interesting subject. He desired nothing more than reciprocity in our intercourse with Great Britain. But he was not to be deterred from countervailing her commercial regulations, by the fear of new collisions with her, and he hoped we should never let her transgress the rules of a just policy towards us, without attempting, by corresponding regulations, to bring her to a sense of justice. He would give her a *carte blanche,* to inscribe thereon what regulations she chose for her intercourse with us, provided they were exactly reciprocal. He was glad his honorable friend from the East had introduced this proposition, and he hoped it would be the means of bringing the question fully before the House. He would not supply her islands with a biscuit or a cigar, but on terms of reciprocity.

Mr. Lowndes said, he hoped the gentleman from Massachusetts would permit such a modification of his motion, as should include in the inquiry not only the policy of Great Britain, but of other nations. He could see no reason why the measures of France, Spain, and Holland, respecting the trade with their colonies, should not meet the same counteraction. He could not, however, see the subject in the serious aspect in which it had appeared to the gentleman from Virginia. He could not agree in the opinion that it would involve us in a serious commercial conflict with England, because it did not propose an abandonment of her commercial system. Some discriminating duties might be adopted, not by way of retaliation of those imposed by Great Britain, but to induce her, by considerations of reciprocity and mutual convenience, to abandon those regulations. The adoption by this country of a policy which would only burden with considerable duties the vessels of those countries which exclude our vessels, &c., would merely have the effect of inviting a change of their system. It would be merely offering them an inducement to reciprocity. He could see no reason, however,

why a distinction should be made in this proposition between Great Britain and other nations.

Mr. King professed his readiness to give the inquiry the utmost latitude although his object had been more limited; and was willing to accept any amendment proposed for that purpose.

Mr. Lowndes then moved to amend the resolve by striking out the words " of His Britannic Majesty."

Mr. Wilde said he did not rise for the purpose of opposing the motion of the honorable gentleman from Massachusetts (Mr. King.) He had no objection to consider the resolution, and he was in favor of the amendment proposed by the gentleman from South Carolina (Mr. Lowndes.) But as his friend and colleague, the chairman of the Committee of Foreign Relations (Mr. Forsyth) was not in the House at the time the honorable gentleman from Massachusetts (Mr. King) commenced his remarks, and therefore could not reply to some of them which he had not heard; Mr. W. thought it his duty to say a few words in answer to what had fallen from the honorable gentleman. He begged leave in the first place to recall to the remembrance of the House the fact that some days ago his friend, the chairman of the Committee of Foreign Relations, proposed certain amendments to the bill regulating the commerce of the United States with Great Britain according to the late convention, the object of which was to exclude vessels and goods not coming directly from the European territories of His Britannic Majesty, from the benefits of the act, agreeably to the fair and evident construction of the convention, as understood by both parties. These amendments were then rejected, although the effect of them was, to a certain extent, the same as the measures contemplated by the resolution of the gentleman from Massachusetts, and were rejected from a very fastidious delicacy about the construction of the treaty. Then it was contended that the terms of the treaty did not authorize us to say that British vessels coming from or touching at the West India islands or his Britannic Majesty's colonies in North America should be subjected to the payment of our discriminating duties. Now it is asked of us to increase those discriminating duties upon such vessels and their cargoes, on the ground that this species of trade is not at all within the provisions of the treaty. He would leave gentlemen to reconcile these different constructions of the same instrument as they could. To him it appeared there was no small share of inconsistency in such conduct. When the terms of the convention were to be found fault with—when those who made it were to be accused of sacrificing the interests of the country—then it meant one thing; when the interests of gentlemen's constituents required it, then it meant another. Mr. W. said, that on this subject it was also his duty to correct a mistake into which the honorable gentleman from Massachusetts had fallen—he called it a mistake, for as he was sincere himself he was willing to allow sincerity to all others; yet he certainly thought it strange that one so well informed as that honorable gentleman should have been misled upon such a subject. The honorable gentleman had stated to-day, and he had stated the same thing some days since in reference to the treaty, it might be taken as his deliberate opinion, that the interests of his part of the country were sacrificed in this convention to the interests of the cotton States—that the fisheries had been given up to preserve these interests—and that the grand object of the treaty seemed to be to secure to the Southern planters a saving upon their cotton, by the reduction of the British discriminating duties upon that article. Now, sir, I can assure the honorable gentleman that the Southern planter never felt the slightest inconvenience from the operation of those duties. He never got a cent less for his cotton—he only shipped it in British instead of American vessels, and the loss therefore fell upon the American shipowner, not on the agriculturist. Mr. W. said, he himself had received previous to his arrival at Washington various communications on this subject, but they all related to the owners of American tonnage and not to the planters of American produce. The argument which they all contained, was, not that our agriculture, but that our navigation would be ruined. Whom, sir, (said Mr. W.) would the ruin of our navigation most severely affect? Who own nine-tenths of the tonnage of the United States? Certainly the Eastern and Northern States. Mr. W. hoped it was unnecessary to say, that neither here nor elsewhere, had he been or would he ever be the advocate of local interests or the encourager of narrow and selfish jealousies, which had so long disturbed the repose and happiness of this Union. It was for this very reason that he had wished to correct the mistake of the gentleman from Massachusetts. Such statements go abroad and make injurious impressions; they induce our brethren of the East to believe that we of the South are hostile to their prosperity, destroyers of their commerce, in short, enemies and oppressors who have no community of feeling or of interest with them. It was very possible, Mr. W. said that his reply to this statement would have very little effect; most probably it would never reach the people of Massachusetts, whose prejudices, prejudices which had been purposely fomented, it was intended to remove. Still, however, he had felt it his duty to make it, in justice to the people whom he had the honor to represent, in justice to the Administration whom that people by choice supported, and for the sake of that union and harmony among the people of the United States, which all such mistaken views of public measures as that taken by the gentleman from Massachusetts had a tendency to destroy.

Mr. RANDOLPH said, we had just got out of a war with Great Britain, the foundation of which was laid some eight or nine years ago, by a resolution moved in this House at the instigation of commercial meetings in different seaport towns of the United States. He was not prepared now to say whether he was ready to recommence a system which might lead to the same practical and

disastrous results; but this he would say, that the House ought not to act on a subject of this importance without one day's previous notice. He therefore moved to lay the resolution on the table.

Mr. KING, of Massachusetts, said, he had no more desire for a new war with Great Britain than the honorable gentleman; nor had he more agency in the late war than that gentleman—nor did he he view his motion of that nature which could possibly lead to war, &c. He was proceeding to discuss its merits, when the SPEAKER reminded him the question was merely on postponement.

The question to lay the resolution on the table was decided in the affirmative.

THE REVENUE.

The House resumed the consideration of the proposition of the Committee of Ways and Means to continue the direct tax at three millions. Mr. PICKENS's motion to reduce the direct tax from three to two millions was negatived after a few observations from Mr. BRIGHAM and Mr. PICKENS. He then moved to reconsider the vote on repealing the tax. Mr. BARBOUR, in a neat and forcible speech, assigned the reasons why he was opposed to the continuance of this tax, because he believed it might be dispensed with without any detriment to the public interest. On motion of Mr. FORSYTH, Mr. LOWNDES assenting to it, the subject was ordered to lie on the table, to take up the following, the decision of which was considered to be more urgently demanded:

COMMERCE WITH GREAT BRITAIN.

The House then, on motion of Mr. FORSYTH, resolved itself into a Committee of the Whole, on the bill from the Senate, concerning the commercial convention with Great Britain.

On motion of Mr. FORSYTH, the bill was amended from its declaratory form by striking out the whole of the bill, and inserting in lieu thereof, in the very terms, the bill which passed this House several days ago, and was rejected in the Senate.

This motion Mr. FORSYTH supported by a speech, in which he compared the merits of the two bills, and condemned the Senate's bill as an interference with the judicial power, and also as an attempt to deprive this House of its just powers in relation to the origination of propositions affecting the public revenue.

The bill having been thus amended, was reported to the House; and the question being on the concurrence in the amendments made in Committee—

Mr. LYON spoke as follows:

Mr. Speaker, it was my intention to have observed the same silence on this question, as I have on all others, since I had the honor of a seat in this House. But being called, once more, to give my negative, I deem it my duty, in a very simple and brief manner, to adduce some of the reasons which influence my conduct. The subject is of great moment, not as involving the acceptance or rejection of this treaty, on which all are agreed, but as defining the powers of the different branches of this Government—fixing the limits prescribed by the Constitution. It has been in operation for more than twenty years; and are we yet ignorant of the duties assigned, and the bounds set to our authority.

While my mind is whirling in the vast circle generated by the debate on this question, I can fix on objects with sufficient distinctness to influence my decision. I am obliged to cast from my notice a multitude of subjects brought into view, as being wholly unconnected with the point in debate.

The precedents which have been adduced, are discarded, as arising from questions totally distinct from that now before us. Precedents are in themselves important. When well founded, they should have their full weight, and cannot fail strongly to influence the inquiring mind; but when drawn from subjects remote from those which they are designed to influence, they mislead the judgment, and produce the most erroneous conclusions.

We have been often referred to the ratification of the British Treaty in 1795; but the ground then taken was very different from that which has now been assumed. The Opposition, in the House of Representatives, then condemned the President for proclaiming the treaty before it had been submitted for their sanction. They demanded that the whole correspondence, in forming the treaty, should be laid before them, that they might judge of its merits, and determine on the propriety of confirming or rejecting. Nothing like this has been avowed on the present occasion. No censure has been attempted against the proclamation, no resolutions have been moved for documents. The question on which the House then decided, was an appropriation of money, which all agree that this treaty does not require. The cases are so totally different, that proceedings on the one, can form no example for measures on the other. I know well that resolutions were then passed expressive of the opinion of the House, that when a treaty embraces those subjects which are expressly by the Constitution placed under the power of Congress, the concurrence of the House of Representatives is necessary to its full operation. This resolution I however considered as the manœuvre of a rear guard, to cover a retreat—they found they had occupied untenable ground, and they wished to retire as safely and decently as possible—the deliberation on an appropriation only, and even then they dare not risk the responsibility of refusing it. The first question was then above what was now assumed, and the last below it—neither, therefore, afford a precedent for the present occasion.

Concerning the law of 1798, it has been said, that, in requiring bonds to be given by the commanders of private armed vessels, the stipulations of the British Treaty of 1794 were enacted. This, however, is a misconception of that law. It requires that these bonds shall secure the observance, not only of the British Treaty, but of all treaties. We had treaties then existing with Prussia, with Sweden, the States General, and some others. In some of these, there was no formal stipulation for bonds to be given. That with the States General, required sufficient caution to be given, but did not fix the amount of the penalty. The law joined all these in one system, required the bond, fixed the penalty, and enjoined the observance of those that required no bonds, as well of those that did. It was not a mere echo of the British Treaty, but embraced subjects far more extensive.

The Treaty with Spain provided that goods, landed in our ports in consequence of distress and to make repairs, should not be subject to duties, on being reladen. A law is said to have been passed, enacting this stipulation, for the sake of carrying it into effect. A recurrence to this act will show, that it was not a repetition of that clause of the treaty, but embraced a very different subject. On the face of the treaty the provision appears to be for goods reladen on board the same vessel, after being repaired. The law provides for the case wherein the vessel should be found not seaworthy, and the goods should be laden on board another vessel. It also requires, that as duties had been received, in the case of the Nancy, they should be refunded. That law was entirely different from the amendment proposed to the bill from the Senate. This merely enacts the stipulations of the treaty—that embraced a new subject. That was necessary—this must be wholly useless.

The law making appropriations for carrying into effect the Treaty with France, is said to mention the restoration of vessels, and we are told that the Berceau was given up under this law, and not by the authority of the treaty. But does that statute require that vessels shall be restored? It does not. No such enacting clause is to be found. The restoration was made under the authority of the treaty, or by no authority whatever. The act gives the form of law to no stipulation of the treaty, but appropriates a specific sum to fulfil that obligation which the treaty itself had created.

The act authorizing the President to take possession of Louisiana, has also been mentioned as an instance of authority being given to a treaty by law. But surely this is wide from the purpose for which it has been adduced. The law contemplates a very different mode from that expressed by the treaty. The treaty proposes possession to be taken by commissaries, the law authorizes the President to possess and hold, by a military force.

The law regulating duties and drawbacks, in Louisiana, is said to have been unnecessary, on the principle which opposes this amendment. If the treaty, it is said, was sufficient to make that country a part of the United States, then all our laws would take effect there of course, and those which contravened them would be repealed. Waiving here any question whether the Constitution would admit of that addition, it is admitted that the treaty had made Louisiana a part of the United States, as to all its privileges. A similar effect of a treaty has been lately witnessed, on our Eastern border. By the Treaty of Peace, without any law to echo or enact its provisions, a part of the citizens of the United States have been placed beyond the power and privileges of our laws. But the treaty did not place Louisiana under the benefit of our laws. It stipulated that this should be done at an early future time. This could be effected only by law. The treaty contemplated this law, not to give effect to what it had done, but to perform what it had not done. By the law regulating trade the treaty was partly fulfilled, and, by the admission of that country into the Union as a State, all its privileges were conferred.

That part of this law which secured privileges to French and Spanish vessels, trading from their respective countries to Louisiana, has been mentioned as enacting merely the provisions of the treaty. It is true both the treaty and the subsequent law gave this right, for twelve years, but, in one essential point, the law differs from the treaty. The commencement of this term was not fixed by the treaty, but by the law it is particularly defined.

The law providing for the punishment of crimes committed in the Indian territory, has been also noticed as enacting the stipulations of the treaties with certain tribes. It does more. It fixes the place and process of trial, and extends its provisions not only to the territories of those tribes, with whom we have stipulations, but to all others. It is not the response of any particular treaty, but enacts those rules concerning which every treaty is silent.

The honorable gentleman who moved this amendment, has just brought into view the act of 1799, respecting the inland trade with Canada, as enacting the stipulations of the Treaty of 1794. This, sir, was a general law imposing and regulating the collection of duties. It was not by law giving effect to a particular treaty, as is now contemplated, but an extensive system, made in conformity to all existing treaties. When we pass a general law, as we must do when we establish our new tariff, it will be proper to fix, specifically, the duty and tonnage to be paid both by the British and Americans. That this act is not a mere echo of the treaty, will be seen by referring to the section on the importation of furs. By the treaty those only are free from duty which are brought by land, or inland navigation, the law exempts those introduced in any direction.

In all these precedents there is not one which compares with the amendment now proposed. Not one of them is merely the re-enacting the stipulations of a treaty. In every instance the law which was passed secures that, for which the treaty did not provide. Not one of them throws any light on this question, and, therefore, all are to be rejected.

I also dismiss from my consideration the British practice which has been so often brought into view. In that country, the genius of the Gov-

ernment is so different from ours, that no analogy, applicable to this case, can be traced. There the people can have no influence in making or confirming treaties but through the medium of the Commons in Parliament. The treaty-making power is hereditary, in the creation and continuance of which the freemen have no voice; the House of Lords is also hereditary or created by the breath of the Monarch. In the King belongs the power of making war, and peace, and all other international regulations. The voice of the nation cannot be heard, except in the act of Parliament, enacting or refusing the necessary laws. Here the case is very different, the President is chosen, once in four years, almost immediately by the people. The Senators are the representatives of the States. They are selected for a longer period than the President or the Representatives, and consequently, are further removed from the effects of party influence and popular change. The power of making treaties is lodged in safe hands, by the Constitution, nor can we need the check from the Commons, which is so important in Britain.

On this question I am not to be influenced by that frightful display of consequences, which has so often been made. We are not inquiring what rule ought to have been prescribed, but what is the path actually delineated by the Constitution. Recurrence to consequences would be highly proper, were we establishing a new Constitution, or passing resolutions to amend that which we now have. Were such our present business, we might, with propriety, view consequences in all their inviting and frightful forms, and shape our decisions accordingly. We might then talk of our own fatherly care, and the dreaded usurpation of the other branches. We might paint to our imaginations, convulsions, insurrections, revolutions, and freedom prostrate. We might listen, to use the language of the gentleman from Virginia, to the voice from Heaven and the blast from Erebus. But with these, our present subject has no connexion. No consequences, however dreadful in anticipation, should induce us to overleap the bounds prescribed by the Constitution. We are to presume that these were all considered, by those who made it. If we have doubts, a motion to amend that fundamental instrument is always in order.

Rejecting, then, from my consideration the precedents, the appeal to British practice, and the list of consequences which have been adduced, the subject is presented distinctly and within very narrow limits. The people are the sovereign—from them all power is derived. They have a right to withhold it, to give it, and to prescribe to it, when given, what limits they please. The different branches of this Government have been created and are limited by their will; on assuming a national character they perceived that different kinds of laws would be needed; they saw the necessity of laws regulating their intercourse with other nations, and the importance that they should be the result of the wisdom of both nations concerned, securing the rights of

889   **HISTORY OF CONGRESS.**   890

FEBRUARY, 1816.   *Commerce with Great Britain.*   H. OF R.

each, and having the binding authority of international compacts. These laws are called treaties; they embrace all subjects in which different nations can have a legitimate and proper concern. Whatever does not directly and intimately affect the interest of the other nation, cannot be the subject of an international compact; it must be left for each nation to determine in its own way. We made a treaty with Great Britain, stipulating, for certain good reasons, to pay her a sum of money. The sum and the rate of exchange were of importance to both nations, and therefore proper subjects of treaty. But from what sources this money should be derived, whether from imposts, excise, the sale of public lands, loans, or direct taxes, was of no importance only to ourselves. This, therefore, could not be the subject of treaty stipulations, but was to be determined by ourselves alone. This, sir, is the true boundary to which treaties may come, but should proceed no further. The people also, saw the necessity of other laws, not international, but binding only within our own territory and its dependencies. These municipal regulations are of different kinds, some operating only on the members of this body, some only on those of the other, as the rules of each House; others binding on all the inhabitants of our country, as the objects to be obtained may require. The making of those laws the people have assigned to different hands, and have pointed out the manner in which that duty shall be performed. The making of treaties they have committed to the President of the United States, but have enjoined, that he shall perform his duty, by and with the advice and consent of two-thirds of the Senators who shall be present. The power of corresponding and agreeing with foreign nations, of reducing the articles to form, giving them the force of a compact and finally ratifying the same, is with the President only. The Senate have no part but that of advising and consenting. In making some of the other laws each House has entire and exclusive authority. The rules by them made, within their proper sphere, have as high authority as any laws of the United States can have. Of the other laws, those for raising revenue must commence, be embodied and matured in this House only. We alone can introduce a new system for replenishing our Treasury, or bring forward a new tax, or move for the alteration of an old one. On this subject the Senate has no power but to propose or concur with amendments. Other laws may originate either in this House or in the Senate, and may be revised, amended, adopted, or rejected by either. All general acts and resolutions, before they become laws, must be laid before the President for his approbation; nor can they have any authority without his consent, or their being again passed by two-thirds of each House. In making treaties the President consults, proposes, arranges, and forces the compact, and the Senate can only accept or reject. In passing laws the two Houses propose, arrange, amend, and enact, and the President has only the power of recommending and approving and disapproving. Thus particularly

have the people declared who shall make their different laws, and in what precise manner they shall be enacted. The code by which they have thus declared their sovereign will, is the Constitution, which they have made the supreme law, paramount to every other law, and the foundation of all the authority which this Government or any of its branches can use. In this distribution of power no right is given to this House to interfere with the treaty-making power. This is as exclusively given to the President, with the advice and consent of the Senate, as the making of our own rules is given to this House, or the enacting of laws, with the approbation of the President to the two Houses. The President and Senate with as much propriety may claim to ratify or reject the rules of this House as we can interfere with the confirmation of any treaty which they have made. We adopt rules and execute them by the admission, expulsion, or punishment of our members. Has the President or the Senate any right to control or say it shall not be, because they are a part of the law-making power? They are part of that power with respect to general laws, but over the laws of this body they have no control; and as little have we over those laws which are called treaties. It was a charge of the great WASHINGTON, "let nothing·be done by usurpations." The safety and life of this ·Government depend on each branch knowing and performing its particular duty. Should the President this day recommend a particular branch of revenue, should the Senate send us a bill to impose a tax for that purpose, how should we receive it? Should we not spurn it with indignation from our table? Should we not consider it a high encroachment upon our rights, an unwarrantable contempt of the Constitution? In the same light may they view our interference with the ratification of treaties. I am aware the 1st section of the Constitution declares that "all ' legislative powers therein granted shall be vested ' in a Congress, which shall consist of a Senate ' and House of Representatives." But attention to the different articles, will show that "all legislative powers," in that section, does not mean all the powers to be used in making laws. Powers to be so used, to say nothing here of the rules of the two Houses, are granted to the President, to a convention, and to the Legislatures of the different States. No act of the two Houses, can become a law till it has been presented to the President for his approbation. Articles of the Constitution become laws, when proposed by two-thirds of both Houses, or by a convention, and are ratified by the Legislatures of three-fourths of the several States. Powers to be used in making laws are lodged in different hands, besides those of Congress. "All legislative powers," in the first section, therefore, must mean, not all that are authorized to be employed in making laws, but such as are distinct from the other two branches of powers the Executive and the Judicial. An act may have all the authority which these legislative powers can give it, and yet not be a law; and that may be a law, and paramount to other laws, which these legislative powers have never enacted. Law is, whatever the Constitution has declared to be such. Legislative acts, made in pursuance of the Constitution, are laws, because the Constitution has so declared them. Conventional acts, duly ratified, are laws, because the Constitution has made them so. And Executive acts, called treaties, made under the authority of the United States, are equally laws; because the Constitution has given them that authority. Neither are laws merely because the legislative powers have passed them, but each are the supreme laws of the land, because they are so declared by that authority over which the legislative powers have no control.

Treaties, then, are laws, and as such, have operative force as other laws. They cannot repeal or set aside the Constitution; nor can this be done by any legislative acts. That they have equal grade with other laws, subordinate to the Constitution, is certain, from their being declared the supreme laws of the land; and from the judges in every State, and of the supreme and inferior courts of the United States, being bound by them. If they are laws, they have power to repeal prior, contravening laws; for it is absurd to suppose two conflicting laws, in equal force, at the same time. According to this interpretation of the Constitution, all its provisions perfectly harmonize; on any other, they are at variance with themselves.

If further reasons, in support of this opinion are demanded, I answer, it was the intention of the Convention which formed the Constitution to give this power to the President and Senate. They said "the President shall have power, by and with the advice and consent of the Senate, to make treaties," without mentioning this House, because they intended to exclude the Representatives from any share in making or confirming those laws. A proposition was made in that body that "no treaty should be valid, until it should be ratified by law." This restriction was rejected, and nothing more was required, to give a treaty its utmost validity, as a supreme law, than its ratification by the President, in conformity to the advice and consent of two-thirds of the Senate. It has, indeed, been said, that the makers of the Constitution are not its best interpreters. This is, in a degree, true, for we are not to be governed by what they intended, but by what they have declared. But when the interpretation appears to conform to the most natural meaning of the words, and the framers of the instrument assure us, that they used those words with intent to convey such meaning, and confirm their testimony by the record of their proceedings, we have the highest possible evidence that it is the true import.

The State conventions for ratifying the Constitution gave it that construction which is now contended for. In more than one it was made an objection, that as the Representatives were not to be consulted in forming treaties, the majority in the Senate ought to have been, not two-thirds of those present, but two-thirds of the whole num-

ber. It does not appear that, in a single instance, it was supposed that this House was to be consulted in the ratification of any treaty.

The same opinion appears to have been held by Congress, in all its sessions, down to the present time. Not one treaty in ten has had any law passed concerning it. Are these all yet invalid? Where laws have been passed, they have not been for enacting the provisions of the treaties, but for extending them, providing means for carrying them into effect, or fixing what they had left uncertain. No act like that now contemplated, a mere echo of the treaty, has ever become a law, or, until now, been reported to this House. Treaties embracing almost every subject, receiving foreigners as citizens, and yielding citizens to the control of foreigners; making goods contraband of war, or free; establishing boundaries, and regulating duties and tonnage have been carried into full effect, without any laws enacting their particular stipulations. Without legislative enactment they have set aside all laws interfering with them; they have been the rule by which the Executive has been guided, the judiciary has decided, and by which the most important national concerns have been conducted. Would this have been, if legislative interference had been necessary?

If treaties have not the authority of laws until their provisions have been enacted by Congress, we ought surely to pass those laws with that well-informed deliberation which their importance demands. A view of the instructions and correspondence, according to which the various concessions and arrangements were made, is as necessary for this House as for the Senate. But no such documents have accompanied any treaty, which has been laid before the House of Representatives. They have been called for but in one instance, and that call was positively refused by Washington himself, because the treaty had full authority without their decision. In this refusal, every succeeding Congress has acquiesced.

That a treaty has all the force of law, without the aid of Congress, was the decided opinion of President Washington, as was read by an honorable gentleman the other day. As a member of the Convention, and its President, he must have known the intention of that body, and finding it plainly expressed in the written Constitution, he uniformly declared this to be the true construction, and practiced accordingly, under the most solemn responsibility.

Mr. Jefferson also early embraced the same opinion. Of his decisions, when correct, I most cordially approve. In 1790 a treaty was made with the Indians of the Creek nation. They wished that the goods they should receive should be imported free from duties. The President submitted to the Heads of Department this question, whether a treaty with that nation would authorize the admission of those goods, without paying the duties. Mr. Jefferson, then Secretary of State, gave his opinion, that "a treaty made by the President, with the advice and consent of two-thirds of the Senate, was a law of the land, and would repeal past laws." In this opinion it is believed the whole Cabinet agreed. This was not a vapor of philosophy—a mere theoretic fancy—it was a solemn decision of an important question brought to the test of practice.

Mr. Madison appears also to be of the same opinion. The late Treaty of Peace contains many important stipulations. It cedes the present possession of territory, it authorizes Commissioners to establish our whole Eastern and Northern boundary, it submits to their decision the jurisdiction of tracts of much value and of great importance to our frontiers. On this he has acted; he is carrying its provisions into effect; he has commanded all officers, civil and military, faithfully to observe and fulfil it; he has appointed the Commissioners, and doubtless assigned them their pay, and given them their instructions. All this has been done without a legislative act, confirming the treaty or enacting any of its stipulations. He has called for no such act, and appears never to have deemed it necessary. Does he require a ratification of the treaty to be carried into effect by this amendment? What, sir, has he sent us? Take it from your table, look at it, examine it carefully. What is it? It is nothing more than a scrap of a newspaper. It purports to be nothing more than the copy of a proclamation, not of a treaty. Are we to ratify, confirm, give life and energy to this? Had he deemed our approbation necessary, his wishes would have been expressed in a very different manner. Before the Senate he laid the original official treaty. Such documents as were necessary to understand it, and the reasons why it was made, were also presented for their information. As nothing of these came to us, it is evident he contemplated the passage of no such bill as is contained in this amendment. He considers the treaty as being now in full force, and needing no aid from us. It is, however, said that this cannot be the opinion of the President, for he instructed Mr. Russell to stipulate "that the employment of British seamen should be prohibited by law." If he considered a treaty to be law, why engage, by a treaty, to make a law? The answer is at hand. The manner and the penalty of the prohibition are entirely municipal, and therefore could not be fixed by treaty. In the thing promised the other nation has a concern, but the manner of fulfilling the stipulation belongs wholly to ourselves, and must be determined by our legislative acts.

Where, then, it is gravely inquired, is the power of Congress to regulate trade? It is not certainly in this House, the Constitution has not placed it there, but in the two Houses of Congress. There it remains entire, notwithstanding the extent of the treaty-making power. Whatever regulations we make, with the concurrence of the Senate, and approbation of the President, or without its assent, under certain restrictions will be the laws of the land, and will repeal all prior conflicting laws, whether in the form of acts or treaties. But can the consent of the Sen-

ate be obtained to any bill in opposition to the provisions of the convention? We know it cannot. The power then contended for by the advocates of this amendment is not of regulating trade, but of embarrassing the regulations that are attempted. Not of introducing order, but confusion into all proceedings on that important concern. But is the power of regulating trade taken away, by the interpretation of the Constitution contended for, even in the case now before us? Not in the least? The treaty fixes only the equality of duties and tonnage, not the *quantum;* this is yet to be determined by law. We may reduce the rate of British vessels until they shall equal the American, or raise our own until they equal the foreign standard, or we may deviate from both, either by diminution or excess. A law thus regulating our trade with Great Britain will be necessary, and will doubtless be comprised in the bill for a new tariff, if not otherwise obtained. This law, when it shall be passed, will determine not the equality, which is already fixed by the treaty, as is proposed by this amendment, but the precise sum which is to be received from British subjects and from Americans.

It has often been inquired whether this House is bound to carry into effect such treaties as the President and Senate shall make? Most certainly. We are bound by all laws which are constitutionally enacted. If the treaty is so made as to become the law of the land, it binds this House, the other branches of the Government and every individual of the community. After the Government has been in operation for so many years, have we yet to learn that all laws, while they continue laws, are binding on all persons and all bodies? In some countries there are orders and individuals who are above the laws, but we have reason to be thankful that here there are no such privileged orders. Whatever is necessary to be done to give effect to a law by the President, by the Senate, by this House, by any officer or by any citizen, each is bound by that law to perform it. There is, there can be no exception. If we can obtain the necessary consent of the other branches, we can repeal a law, but until that repeal is effected, we are, and must be bound to observe it. Treaties may be repealed, or set aside for good reasons, as well as other laws, and a majority of the two Houses, with the approbation of the President, can at any time render them void. But, while they remain in force, this House is bound to obey them, and do every incumbent act to give them complete effect.

The late Treaty of Peace has been confirmed by no law enacting its stipulations. The President and Senate, however, have appointed the Commissioners, as agreed, to ascertain our Eastern and Northern boundary. One honorable gentleman has been taken from this House. They have probably made arrangements for the performance of their duties, and will soon enter upon them. When the arduous task is performed, shall we be under no obligations to make appropriations for their services? Can we plead we never ratified the treaty, and therefore we are not bound? The principle is too absurd to be admitted for a moment.

If it be so, says an honorable gentleman, the President and Senate, by the aid of a foreign Power, or even of a Chickasaw chief, may levy and repeal taxes. Not so; such monstrous consequences do not follow. The laying and repealing of taxes are municipal acts, with which foreign nations can have no proper concern. They cannot, therefore, be the subjects of treaty stipulations. Beside, all bills for raising revenue must originate in this House. They cannot be introduced, much less completed, by the President, nor Senate, nor by both united.

It has been, however, confidently asserted, that if such be the treaty-making power it may obtain a subsidy, and apply it for its own purposes. One gentleman has assured us that, by treaty, money to any amount may be placed in the hands of the Paymaster General, and thus wars, if not commenced, may be prolonged without legislative consent. But here, too, the Constitution has introduced an ample guard. If the subsidy be made to the United States, it must be paid into the Treasury, and cannot be drawn therefrom but by an appropriation passed in this House. If it be made to an individual officer it is expressly forbidden—"that no person holding any office of 'profit or trust, shall, without the consent of Con-'gress, accept of any present or emolument from 'any king, prince, or foreign State." A gentleman from Virginia has with much complacency inquired, which is most safe, to lodge this extensive power with the President and Senate only, or to require the consent of the popular branch, the more immediate representatives of the people? With leave from that gentleman, and from his known candor I am sure he will indulge me, I would somewhat vary the question. Would it not be more safe to disregard the Constitution than to obey it; to leap the bounds prescribed, than to keep within them? I might ask, also, would it not be more safe to extend our case not only to the Senate, but to the courts of justice? They may be ignorant or corrupt—juries may be led astray—would it not increase our safety for the representatives of the people to revise their proceedings; to make it more certain that the innocent shall be acquitted and the guilty condemned?

Is this, Mr. Speaker, the inquiry of the people? No; they have already declared, by the adoption of the Constitution, in whose hands they deem this concern most safely lodged. Their laws for raising revenue they have intrusted to us in the first place; their ordinary municipal regulations they have placed in our hands, in concurrence with the Senate and President, but the formation of their compacts with other nations they have committed exclusively to the President and Senate. It is this House that makes the inquiry. Flushed with self-approbation, we imagine ourselves not only immaculate, but impeccable. This, sir, is natural. It is no new language to

say, O that I were made judge in the land, and I would do justice. All that need to be said here is, the people in their wisdom have thought differently.

But what is this House, concerning which this inquiry of safety has been made? It is that body which, when the people, by their representatives, would have complained, has commanded silence; when they were proposing measures of relief, has denied the liberty of speech; when presenting amendments to burdensome laws, has refused to hear them; when attempting to plead their own cause, to use a favorite expression of a gentleman from Virginia, has put a gag in their mouth, lest a shriek should give the alarm. This is the body with whom it is imagined our treaty-making concerns might be intrusted with such perfect safety. Is it said this obnoxious rule is now to be laid aside? I ardently hope and confidently believe it will; but does not the fact of its having existed so long, in opposition to every correct principle and every right, but that of power in the minority, give us reason to fear it may return? The people, sir, have made a wise choice; they have placed *this* important power in the safest hands, as appears from abundant experience.

This bill has been called a disease; a disease, not dangerous from its nature, but from the treatment it has received. I, sir, would rather call this itch for power the disease. This leaping Constitutional bounds, this grasping at authority on every side, is a political disease, contagious, malignant, and extremely dangerous. Unless promptly checked, it will inevitably prove fatal. It has brought to the dust most of the free Governments which have been in the world; some by sudden revolutionary spasms, and some by more lingering, but not less certain decay. This disease, unless speedily cured, will prove fatal to us. Its symptoms are many; it indicates to be deeply seated in this House, the very vitals of our Government.

It is but a few hours, Mr. Speaker, since I had the honor of a seat on this floor. During this short space, within these walls, which should be sacred to liberty and Constitutional order, I have heard that, at which I am astonished, at which my soul has trembled. Authority, sovereign, uncontrolled, unbounded by any law, has been claimed for this House. On the one hand, the treaty-making power is denounced for pursuing the plainest directions of the Constitution, for not stooping to the high command which we are pleased to assume. On the other, the courts of justice are condemned for presuming to give preference to the Constitution over the laws which we have enacted. Though their power extends to "all cases in law and equity, arising under the Constitution and the laws;" yet, if they dare to decide against an act of ours, which opposes the Constitution, here it is declared usurpation—an abridgment of the sacred rights of the guardians of the people. Where, sir, will this thirst for power, this spurning at all restraint, lead us? Go but a little further, sir, and decrees of condemnation, and execution for treason will issue from your table. Go but a little further, sir, and your Sergeant-at-Arms will bring from his cell your prisoners, to the block or the stake. Yes, sir, take but a few steps more, and you plunge whence you never, never can return, but by blood, convulsion, and all the horrors of revolution.

When Mr. Lyon concluded, Mr. Forsyth briefly replied.

The question on concurring in the amendments which go to substitute the bill which first passed this House, in lieu of the Senate's bill, was then decided: For the amendments 81, against them 70, as follows:

Yeas—Messrs. Alexander, Archer, Baker, Barbour, Bassett, Bateman, Bennett, Birdseye, Blount, Brooks, Bryan, Burnside, Caldwell, Cannon, Clarke of North Carolina, Clendennin, Clopton, Comstock, Condict, Conner, Crawford, Creighton, Cuthbert, Darlington, Desha, Forsyth, Glasgow, Griffin, Hahn, Hall, Hawes, Henderson, Hungerford, Ingham, Irving of New York, Irwin of Pennsylvania, Jackson, Kerr of Virginia, King of Massachusetts, Lowndes, Lumpkin, Lyle, Maclay, Mayrant, McCoy, McLean of Kentucky, McLean of Ohio, Middleton, Newton, Parris, Pickens, Piper, Pleasants, Powell, Randolph, Roane, Robertson, Root, Ross, Savage, Schenck, Sharpe, Sheffey, Smith of Virginia, Southard, Taul, Taylor of New York, Taylor of South Carolina, Telfair, Tucker, Wallace, Ward of New Jersey, Wendover, Whiteside, Wilde, Wilkin, Williams, Willoughby, Thomas Wilson, William Wilson, and Yancey.

Nays—Messrs. Atherton, Baer, Bayliss, Betts, Boss, Bradbury, Breckenridge, Brigham, Brown, Cady, Calhoun, Champion, Chappell, Cilley, Cooper, Culpeper, Davenport, Forney, Gaston, Gold, Goldsborough, Grosvenor, Hale, Hanson, Hardin, Herbert, Hopkinson, Hugar, Jewett, Kent, King of North Carolina, Langdon, Law, Lewis, Love, Lovett, Lyon, Mason, Mills, Milnor, Moore of South Carolina, Moseley, Nelson of Massachusetts, Noyes, Ormsby, Pickering, Pitkin, Reed, Rice, Ruggles, Sergeant, Smith of Pennsylvania, Stanford, Stearns, Strong, Stuart, Sturges, Taggart, Tallmadge, Tate, Thomas, Throop, Vose, Ward of Massachusetts, Ward of New York, Wheaton, Wilcox, Woodward, Wright, and Yates.

The amendments were ordered to be engrossed and the bill read a third time to-morrow.

Tuesday, February 5.

Mr. Huger submitted the following resolution, which was read and ordered to lie on the table:

Resolved, That a select committee of —— members be appointed, to examine generally into the subject of unsettled balances due the United States, and especially into the annual statements laid before Congress by the Comptroller of the Treasury, in conformity to an act of the third of March, 1809, requiring that an annual statement should be laid before Congress of the accounts in the Treasury, War, and Navy Departments, which may have remained more than three years unsettled, or on which balances appear to have been due more than three years prior to the 30th September then last past; to investigate the causes which have given rise to such extensive unsettled balances; to recommend such measures as may in their opinion be most likely to bring defaulters to a speedy settlement of their accounts, and prevent, in time to

come, the recurrence and continuance of unsettled balances to so large and alarming an amount.

A message was received from the President of the United States respecting the lands in the Michigan Territory, designated by law towards satisfying the land bounties promised to the soldiers of the late army, &c.; which was referred to the Committee on the Public Lands.

The Speaker laid before the House a letter from the Secretary of the Treasury, transmitting a letter from the Register of the Treasury, and two statements in answer to the resolution submitted by Mr. Randolph on the second instant, and adopted by the House yesterday; which were ordered to lie on the table.

The bill from the Senate "concerning the convention to regulate the commerce between the United States and His Britannic Majesty," was read the third time as amended, and passed.

The House, on motion of Mr. King, resumed the consideration of the resolution submitted by him yesterday. He then withdrew his motion, and in lieu thereof laid on the table, for future consideration, the following:

Resolved, That the Committee of Foreign Relations be instructed to inquire into the expediency of excluding from the ports of the United States, or of increasing the duties on all foreign vessels owned in, coming from, bound to, or touching at, any of the possessions of any nation of Europe in the West Indies, and in the continent of America, from which the vessels of the United States are excluded, and of prohibiting or of increasing the duties on the importation in foreign vessels of any articles of the growth, produce, or manufacture of such possessions.

This motion lies on the table.

STAFF OF THE ARMY.

Mr. Johnson, of Kentucky, from the Committee on Military Affairs, reported a bill for organizing the general staff, and making further provision for the Army of the United States, which was read twice and committed to the Committee of the Whole on the bill making provision for an additional military academy.

Mr. Johnson also communicated the following document:

War Department, *Dec.* 27, 1815.

Sir: In replying to your letter of the 21st instant, inquiring into the expediency of providing by law for the staff appointments which have been provisionally retained, and for such others as the interest of the service may require, it is presumed that the intention of the Committee over whose deliberations you preside is to give to the Military Peace Establishment that organization which is necessary to secure to it all the efficiency which can be expected from its numerical force. The experience of the two first campaigns of the last war, which has furnished volumes of evidence upon this subject, has incontestably established not only the expediency, but the necessity of giving to the Military Establishment, in time of peace, the organization which it must have to render it efficient in a state of war.

It is believed also to be demonstrable, that a complete organization of the staff will contribute as much to the economy of the establishment as to its efficiency.

The stationary staff of a military establishment should be substantially the same in peace as in war, without reference to the number or distribution of the troops of which it is composed. It is, therefore, respectfully proposed that this branch of the general staff be organized in the manner following, viz:

One adjutant and inspector general, at Washington.
One quartermaster general, at Washington.
One paymaster general,   do.
One commissary general, at Philadelphia.
One apothecary general,   do

The organization of the division of staff should be regulated by the number of independent corps into which the military force is distributed. By general order of the 17th May last, the United States were divided into military divisions, commanded by generals, independent of each other, within their respective divisions. As nothing has occurred, since this distribution of the military force has been made, to change the opinion which was then entertained of its expediency, it is proposed to organize the division staff so that each division shall comprehend—

One adjutant general and two assistant adjutant generals;
One inspector general and two assistant inspector generals;
One quartermaster general and two deputy quartermasters general, with regimental quartermasters, as at present authorized;
Three judge advocates;
Two chaplains;
One deputy commissary general and two assistant commissaries of issues, four hospital surgeons, and eight hospital surgeons' mates, and as many post surgeons, with the pay and emoluments of hospital surgeons' mates, as the distribution of the forces into garrisons and posts may require, not exceeding twelve;
Four assistant apothecaries;
Two assistant deputy paymasters, with regimental paymasters, as now established.

It is not deemed necessary to change the organization of the corps of artillery, the corps of engineers, or the ordnance department, unless the committee should be disposed to increase the corps of engineers. Considering the qualifications of the officers of that corps, and the great utility which may be derived from transferring them into the line of the Army, when a sudden augmentation of the Military Establishment should become necessary at the approach of war, some increase of that scientific corps is respectfully submitted.

The act fixing the Military Peace Establishment has produced some inequalities in the pay and emoluments of the officers, which, owing to the particular circumstances under which that act was passed, it is probable were neither foreseen nor intended. One case of this nature is the allowance of forage to a major general of twenty dollars a month, whilst the adjutant general is allowed thirty. The allowance of a clerk to one of the major generals, and not to the other, must have proceeded from the same cause. The fact of these inequalities are mentioned here with a view to attract the attention of the committee to the pay and emoluments of the officers of the Army generally.

Should any explanations growing out of this communication be required, it will afford me great pleasure to give them, in writing or verbally, to the committee, whenever it shall suit their convenience.

I have the honor to be, respectfully, your very humble servant,   WM. H. CRAWFORD.

THE REVENUE.

The House resumed the consideration of the proposition of the Committee of Ways and Means to continue the direct tax of three millions another year.

Mr. PICKENS's motion to reconsider the vote on the question of repealing said tax being under consideration—

Messrs. LOWNDES, HANSON, and SERGEANT, spoke at length against this motion, and Messrs. STEARNS, ATHERTON, RANDOLPH, and PICKENS, in favor of it; the debate turning on the merits of the proposed direct tax, on general principles, at the present conjuncture of our affairs. Mr. TUCKER spoke briefly in explanation.

Mr. ATHERTON spoke as follows:

Mr. Speaker, if it appeared to me that a direct tax was necessary, either for the support of the public credit, or to meet any system of public expenditure, of which I could approve, it should not fall for the want of my support. But believing, as I do, that a direct tax is not wanted for either of those purposes, I shall use my vote and my endeavors to procure its repeal. This course I should take, even if I did not feel any particular hostility to a direct tax; for I should think it correct to avail myself of what I hope will be the prevailing disposition of the House, to effect an alleviation of the public burdens, where there seems the greatest probability of success. Yet there are gentlemen, no enemies to lessening those burdens, who will take no reduction, because they cannot procure it in taxes, which they esteem more objectionable. They are willing to sacrifice a general object to one of minor consequence. I shall act, sir, upon a different principle. I say retrench; and if I cannot have retrenchment when I would, I will take it when I can.

I presume, sir, there is no member of this House so little acquainted with the concerns and feelings of his constituents, as not to know that the direct tax is the most offensive of any on the long catalogue of taxation. This is not a sudden and impetuous disgust on the part of the people. It is of long standing; it has been uniform and universal. "Consideration, like an angel, has come;" yet the people are hostile to this tax. Upon every principle that binds a representative to his constituent, these circumstances are entitled to great weight and deep consideration in all parts of this House. By this repeal, we should diffuse a general joy throughout the great mass of the American population. It is certainly worthy our most serious deliberation, whether these universal impressions of the people upon this subject are not well founded.

During this discussion, various reasons have been assigned why the people do, and why they ought to, feel a peculiar jealousy against this mode of approaching their purses and property, on the part of the General Government—these reasons I shall not repeat. But, there are gentlemen here who profess to be attached to this tax, because they say it is an equal tax; others say, that if not equal, it has the happy power of making even the inequalities of the other taxes; that it bears with a light hand where other taxes press heavily, and that it bears with a heavy hand where other taxes press lightly. They, in short, represent it as a smoothing plane, that reduces to a perfect level the superficies of taxation, and that no system of taxation can be perfect without it. Others imagine that the States not holding slaves ought to cling to this mode of raising money as favorable to them—as the consideration which they receive for having consented to a diminished representation in this body. To these views, I wish to draw the consideration of the House. From a document that has been laid upon our tables, in pursuance of a resolution which I had the honor of moving the other day, and from some other sources of information, of the correctness of which I entertain no doubt, results follow not favorable to either of the positions above stated. No proposition can be more fallacious than that a tax is equal, because it is apportioned according to numbers. This pre-supposes an equality of property, which does not exist. If the rate per centum on a hundred dollars of valuation be not the same, the tax is unequal. How is this with us, next to the direct tax of six millions? Massachusetts pays forty-two cents on the hundred dollars of valuation; New Hampshire fifty-two cents, and Vermont sixty-two cents; while Connecticut pays only twenty-six cents, New York thirty cents, and Pennsylvania twenty-two cents. That is to say, New Hampshire pays twice as much as Connecticut, and Vermont twice as much as New York, and nearly three times as much as Pennsylvania. New York as easily pays its proportion of a direct tax of four millions as New Hampshire does its proportion of a direct tax of two millions. Vermont pays its proportion of a direct tax of six millions, when Pennsylvania only pays its proportion of two millions—that is, if the valuation of property be taken as the basis of taxation. These returns are in the office of the Secretary of the Treasury; the results are undeniable. Where, then, I ask, is the boasted equality of this tax, and how does it show its mercy to those States that pay an undue proportion of the other taxes? What States pay the tax on salt? Massachusetts, New Hampshire, and Vermont. What States pay the enormous duty on imported rum? Massachusetts, New Hampshire, and Vermont. What States are most severely oppressed with the land tax? The same. Nor do I find any relief from this picture, by observing how it operates on the slaveholding States. Maryland, for instance, pays twenty-five cents on the valuation of one hundred dollars; Virginia pays twenty-eight cents. But it may be said that this includes the valuation of their States. True, it does; but exclusive of their slaves the tax would only be increased four cents in Maryland, and perhaps six cents in Virginia, leaving them at about one-half what New Hampshire and Virginia pays. If, sir, any confidence is to be attached to these results, it follows—

1st. That a direct tax is oppressively unequal.

2d. That it does not restore the inequalities of the other taxes, but increases their unequal operation.

3d. That the States not holding slaves cannot discover in this mode of raising money anything favorable to them.

Indeed, sir, if they expected to receive, in direct taxation, as regulated by the Constitution, a compensation for having bartered a portion of their independence, they have been most grossly deceived. In the language of poor Richard, they have "paid too dear for the whistle." This tax is also particularly severe in its pressure upon those farmers who are in debt for their land, which is the case with a large portion of our young men, and upon those whose farms are only cultivated in part, when the labor goes to improving and enhancing the value of the farm, but not to the production of a crop. In such case it operates as a tax on industry, and not on income. The fluctuating state of the population of the United States is also another source of inequality. While some States have, since the last census, gained an additional population, sufficient to entitle them to two and three Representatives, other States have been nearly stationary; but the tax is levied according to the population of 1810, which varies materially from the present population, and weighs most heavily against those States that have so many other reasons to complain against this tax.

Besides, sir, I must confess that I feel strong objections against the apparatus and machinery which this tax requires. I accord most sincerely with the honorable member from Massachusetts, whose head is whitened with the frosts of seventy, but whose mind still blooms in the verdure of Spring, in a reply which he so happily made the other day, that "Executive influence had increased, was increasing, and ought to be diminished." As nearly as I can calculate, it takes a standing army of about three thousand retainers of the Government to assess and collect a direct tax in the United States. That is, about one man to every thousand dollars of tax, of which he takes from one to two hundred dollars. This is an army, in my opinion, quite too numerous for a Peace Establishment. I am for disbanding them, and for doing it so effectually that there shall be no excuse for retaining, breveting, or paying any portion of the staff provisionally. I cannot, sir, but indulge the hope that a revenue of thirty-six millions, exclusive of the direct tax, will satisfy the demands of the Government for the current year.

We are too, sir, at the close of a war which has not added to the resources of our country—of a war in which Canada has not been taken—of a war in which no rights have been secured to the merchant flag. Gentlemen do not seem to remember, that prior to this war, and as if preparatory to it, we were sweated to exhaustion by the empiricism of embargo, non-importation, and non-intercourse; that while we were suffering under the weakening influence of their prescriptions, there was administered to our unwilling throats the caustic bolus of war. The people, sir, do not expect to be followed up by a course o mercurials in the form of taxes. Your encour agements their expectations require; their condition will imperatively demand of you the adoption of a system of economy and retrenchment. Sir, like the gentleman from South Carolina, I would cultivate moral power. I would cherish that high and independent spirit which should make this people feel and know that they were superior to the people of every other country on earth, superior in intelligence, superior in mental resources, superior in civil and political privileges. But how would I do this? Not by causing them to doubt whether they possessed these privileges. Not by alienating their affections from the Government by exactions unreasonably severe. No, sir, I would cause them to know, that upon them you depended for the essential defence of the country; that you cherished their comforts and rejoiced at their blessings. Leave them something worth preserving, and they will preserve it by their valor and virtue. I would cause them ever to be more proud of their condition than of your establishments, however great, supported at their expense. Sir, I would not repudiate a Navy; I would support and increase it. But I would reject most promptly and decisively all those wild, magnificent projects of expense and military fame which seem to have seized the imaginations of some. They are of the most alarming import to the American people. I see in them an entire change of the policy of our ancestors; I see in them interminable wars—a great crop of military glory; but the subversion of the Constitution, and a system of unrelenting taxation, that will make this people the veriest slaves to the exactions of the General Government. Between the adoption of such a policy and the liberties of this country there is no Rubicon—it is already passed—the die is cast, and Cæsar is in hostile march to the Capitol.

At no period since the establishment of the independence of the United States has there been, in my opinion, a fairer prospect for the continuance of peace than at the present moment. Happy, thrice happy should we be, if we would learn justly to appreciate our own blessings. Yes, sir, never a fairer prospect for the continuance of peace, unless we destroy that prospect by the blasting mildew of our own folly and madness, Great Britain, sir, made a peace with you, at a time when all her other enemies were prostrated at her feet; when she was flushed with victory; when her army and navy were in the highest possible state of discipline and preparation; when her undivided force could have been directed against us. And, what is of more importance, she concluded a peace with you when it was universally believed in England that her forces were in possession of New Orleans. If, sir, she made peace with us under such circumstances, how heated with an unreasonable jealousy must be that imagination which can see in the relative situation of the two countries, an interest and a desire on her part to renew the contest. Spain must feel the deepest interest to preserve the relations of peace with this country. This she must continue to do so long as she has any claims

upon Mexico and South America. I hope we shall treat Spain with the most exemplary justice, but such is the crippled condition of that monarchy, and such her peculiar situation as respects the United States, that although we should treat her with the most direct and positive injustice, however she might complain, she would not push those complaints to the extremity of war. Whence then, sir, these alarms of war? Whence the necessity of great military preparations and expensive enterprises? Why is the war-whoop kept up? Why are ghosts and hobgoblins so adroitly moved back and forth before terrified imaginations? One gentleman imagines that he sees in the circumstance that our territory is limited by that of a neighboring Power, not only a speck of war, but a black threatening cloud of impending war. And so, sir, he would go on conquering and to conquer, till the limits of our empire shall be continuous with the continent we inhabit. Another gentleman is for directing our military prowess and resources to succor the cause of the oppressed in countries remote and foreign from our own. Let the oppressed of our own country ever find eloquent counsel here; but I hope never to see in this House any person in character of the orator of the human race. These are the patent munitions that have given rise to the standing armies, and oppressed even them, by which Europe has been bound in vassalage. Never may I see them introduced into the country of my birth; against such an abandonment of our good old principles—against the inception of such a policy I enter my most solemn protest. Again, sir, I say retrench. It is written there is a time for peace; we have had it. That there is a time for war; we have had that also. I hope the leaf is not torn from our political bible which says there is a time for retrenchment. If there be that time, it is now present with us. Let it not escape; it is a precious moment. In allusion again to what fell from the gentleman from South Carolina: Dash, yes, sir, dash the Circean cup from the mouth of sycophants, contractors, and office-seekers. Do not enervate the American Hercules by steeping him in the hot-bed of Executive patronage. The people are in no danger from the corruption of delicious draughts and inglorious ease. They are far, far enough removed from these evils. This disease does not attack the extremities of the body politic. It begins at the heart; it has there been manifested. Here, then, let gentlemen direct their caution, and not to the great mass of the American population, where there is no danger of the enemy. Moderate the car of State; cease, at least for a while, to whip and to goad the generous but almost breathless animal that draws the burden.

Mr. STEARNS spoke as follows:

Mr. Speaker, after the very full discussion which this subject has undergone in Committee of the Whole, I shall not long detain the House with the remarks I have to offer. Just beginning to take a share in its deliberations, I have been inclined rather to listen to the opinions and arguments of others than to obtrude upon them my own. I hope, sir, that I have not listened without profit. Not only the general principles, but the minute details of the report have been examined. Honorable gentlemen, with whose views I in the main coincide, have produced their estimates and calculations, and urged their reasoning with a conclusiveness and force which I might in vain desire to imitate. It only remains for me to explain, in as few words as I can, the grounds and reasons of the vote which I am about to give on this important question. For such I consider every question which relates to the burdens to be imposed upon our constituents.

It is not my purpose to inquire whether the necessity which we are told exists for these burdens might have been avoided. Whatever opinions I may have entertained of the impolicy and injustice of the war, from which we were so providentially rescued, peace, objectionable as its terms were to my mind, was by me hailed with gratitude, because it saved the country when on the brink of ruin. I will not, therefore, on this occasion, inquire, whether the avowed objects of the war have been obtained or abandoned, or whether the terms of peace were calculated, or were intended to be equally advantageous to all parts of this widely extended empire. Nor yet, sir, shall I ask a question, in which my constituents are, perhaps, more particularly interested, whether it was just or necessary to barter the fisheries or the territory of the East for an exclusive right and navigation at the West. These are subjects about which gentlemen on different sides of this House totally disagree; and I shall not attempt to accord the difference.

But, sir, honorable gentlemen on the other side have even gone out of their way to allude to the war, and its consequences; a subject which I expected, because I thought it would be their wisdom, they never would have wished to revive. If they have thought otherwise, if those who made the war, and those who concluded the peace, choose to describe the one as an act of manifest justice and necessity, and the other, as productive of incalculable honor and advantage, I must attribute it to the different meaning which words have in the mouths of patriots and politicians, from the common import of language, or set it down to the account of that partiality which every parent has towards its own offspring. They are, perhaps, not much more extravagant or farther from the truth than the crow in the fable, who dotingly called her young ones. "*little snow-white swans.*"

Sir, I have no inclination to indulge in irritating remark; but I am not bound to forbear to expose misrepresentation, and to repel unmerited reproach. When those who hurried the country into a dangerous war, without preparation, and without plan, and brought upon it accumulated disaster and disgrace—the monuments of which, even here, meet the reluctant eye at every turn—when such men attempt to throw upon the government and people of a respectable and patriotic State the blame and odium of suffering a small portion of territory, which the General Govern-

ment was bound to protect, to be occupied by the enemy;—and above all, sir, when they endeavor to conceal their nakedness and shame by snatching from the Navy and Army a share of that honor, or (if you please) that *glory*, which belongs exclusively to them—if my aid were needed, I would lend it to strip and expose the pilferer, and restore the stolen garment to its owner. But this has already been promptly done by my honorable friends on this side of the House, and my feeble help is not needed.

Sir, when the credit of the nation is languishing, I am willing to forbear the inquiry, how the burdens which are required became necessary: it is sufficient for me, if a manifest necessity exists. When that is the case, if I can be assured that they will be faithfully appropriated, I am not disposed to withhold the requisite supplies. If those who made the war refused to count the cost of it, I know that we and our constituents *must* count it; yes, sir, and *pay* it, too. And I am ready to vote all the taxes which, with reasonable regard to economy, may be necessary. I only require this one condition, that they be the least burdensome in their operation, and imposed equally, upon all parts of the country. On these terms, I will give my consent to a direct tax—a permanent one, if necessary.

But, sir, I consider that the honorable committee who gave shape and direction to the financial concerns of the Government in this House, require of us what is unreasonable. By the course which they have adopted, they compel us, in effect, to legislate *imperio ordine.* They would have us first vote immense revenues, and then look at the objects of appropriation and expenditure pointed out by the Government. I know very well that this course has the apology of precedent—too long established precedent among ourselves—and so have a great many other measures which tend to improvidence and profusion. Sir, it is so common, that it has almost become a trite observation that Governments always demand revenues commensurate to the utmost resources of their country; and I am sure, from melancholy experience, we are not to expect this Government to form an exception.

Will it be said that it is necessary, first, to grant the revenues, that we may know how to limit the expenditure? that, if we first maket he appropriations, we may go beyond the ability of the country? Sir, that is not the case. Exhausted as the country is, the people are yet able—more than that, they are willing—to bear every burden that, with reasonable economy in expenditure, may be necessary. Satisfy them that their money is fairly and prudently appropriated to pay the public creditors, and to defray only useful and necessary expenditures—that you do not demand these enormous sums to extend influence and patronage, but to restore the public credit—and nothing will be denied you which they ought to give or you to require.

Sir, it should always be remembered, that is not wisdom and prudence in a Government which would be folly and madness in an individual.

What course would the discreet merchant or tradesman or planter adopt, in the circumstances of this Government? He would first consider, what sum it would require for his necessary expenses and to perform his engagements and maintain his credit—how much might be saved by diminishing some expenditures and wholly retrenching others. And he would not mortgage the freehold until it became necessary, nor until he had at least endeavored to collect his debts, and ascertained the eventual deficiency. The builder, sir, first determines the necessary dimensions and figure and strength of the edifice, and then sets about providing the materials.

Mr. Speaker, we have had thrown upon our tables, this morning, a long and shameful list of balances, which have been due more than three years to one Department of the Government. A similar document from another Department we were favored with some days ago. I say *shameful*, sir, because, though the whole amount is enormous, and many of the items very large, it appears by these documents that none of the officers of the Government know who or where a great proportion of the debtors are. This race of unknown, unaccountable nondescripts, are the consumers or the scape-goats of no very small part of the revenues of this country. If these long lists of balances are something real and substantial, it is the duty of this House to make the proper use of information which some of them contain, and let those debts be made to furnish a part of the revenue required. But, if these are a mere phantom—if they are only form, and to all useful purposes no better than waste paper—let us know it, and let them never again encumber our tables.

But, sir, this is not all. From other documents and reports and letters laid before us, it appears, that within these three years, immense sums have been appropriated and furnished to the various Departments and officers of the Government, the disposition of which we and our constituents ought to be informed of, and which still remain unaccounted for. How much of it has been honestly applied to its legitimate object, God knows; but I will venture to affirm, that with respect to the disposition of thousands and hundreds of thousands of it, no one in this House or this nation will ever be informed. Do our constituents know this, or do they believe that all the money which has been taken from them has been faithfully and honestly expended? If they do, (blessed be the slumbers of honest, unsuspecting ignorance!) the pilferer and defaulter need not fear that my voice will be heard—that any effort of mine will rouse the deluded people of this land from their death-like sleep. And perhaps, if it were possible, it would be an offence of indiscreet friendship to discover to them those injuries and abuses which I might wish in vain to correct.

Sir, I wish not to indulge unreasonable jealousy and suspicion of any of those who are or have been intrusted with the disposition of the public money. We are assured by their friends, their dependents, and not very unfrequently even by themselves, that they are the best patriots and best men of the country. We are told that there is a perfect system of accountability, and that it is impossible public money should be purloined, or even misapplied. Granted, sir. The system, in theory, is most beautiful and perfect. We have Accountants and Comptrollers, and all the checks and balances of the most perfect machinery: we need only give ourselves the trouble to wind it up. How well the practice might formerly have corresponded with this fine theory, I cannot pretend to decide: at present, it seems to be quite at variance with it. It has grown old, and everything human is liable to deterioration and decay. Yes, sir, "there's the rub." The impelling force is wasted by *friction;* it is diminished by the continually increasing tendency to the great centre of attraction; and the whole force of the country will hardly keep it in motion. What, then, is the value of all our checks and balances? And where is the intrepid, or rather the rash and imprudent man, who would dare attempt to apply them? Who will venture to demand a voucher, or disallow a claim, when the consequence might be dismissal from office; to effect which, if necessary, perhaps, even the Head of the Government might be induced to lend his aid? When the struggle is between conscience and the loss of office—perhaps of bread—it does not require the gift of prophecy to foretell the event.

Sir, it is seriously asked, what ought to be done—what course should be pursued? In the answer, at least, there is no difficulty. Commence a reform; correct the abuses of office—those open, notorious abuses, which are so manifest that no man can wink so hard as not to see them;—institute an examination into the management and expenditure of public money; collect your debts; dismiss from office the speculator—yes, sir, and (if you can detect him) the *peculator* too—those wonder-working jugglers, who out of hundreds expend thousands, and grow rich; cherish and protect the honest, faithful public servant, who dares to do his duty, and brave the menaces *prava juventium;* abolish sinecure and unnecessary offices; create no new ones, for the purpose of extending influence and patronage; place the Navy and the Army upon a respectable, and (as far as is consistent with the interest and security of the country) upon an economical establishment. But, beware you do not excite and nourish a love of military glory and a thirst for conquest: it would be fatal to your liberty and national happiness. Abundance of military resources and preparation has a certain tendency to produce war, though the want of them may not always prevent it. The man who wears his pistols and his dirk is much more likely to get into collision with those whom he may meet, than the plain citizen who is without them.

Sir, I believe that when the errors in the estimates presented by the Committee of Ways and Means shall be corrected, and some moderate and reasonable deductions made, it will be found that remaining sources of revenue will yield even more than is demanded. Let it be first clearly

HISTORY OF CONGRESS.

The Revenue.

ascertained what amount is indispensable to support the Government, and maintain the credit of the nation, and then, if the ordinary sources prove insufficient, resort to the land. Impose a direct tax of three, or even four millions—a permanent one, if necessary. I have no instinctive dread of taxes. With the honorable gentleman from Pennsylvania, (Mr. HOPKINSON,) I will say, I came here to impose taxes, but to impose only necessary ones. And, until I have more satisfactory evidence than I now have that this tax is necessary—until I see some mistake or fallacy in the calculations and estimates of gentlemen opposed to this measure—I feel bound to withhold my consent from the imposition of this (as I deem it) unnecessary burden upon my constituents.

Mr. HANSON said he could not conceal the regret he felt at the additional evidence just given by the worthy gentlemen who preceded him, (Messrs. ATHERTON and STEARNS,) of a strong opposition by his political friends to the whole system under discussion. But, however much he might lament the diversity of opinion prevailing, and what he considered a departure from the soundest principles and wisest maxims of the party in concert with which he had always acted, yet his conscience and judgment left him no choice but to separate from most of his friends in the vote to be given. Even if he stood alone in the present question, he should consider himself as dishonoring his station, as unworthy the seat he occupied, if he surrendered his judgment or fled the question. Let the responsibility and the consequences be what they might, he would encounter them; preferring, as he hoped he ever should, the people's good to the people's favor. For one, he was free to declare his willingness to have permitted the question of supplies to be taken without debate. Having made up his mind to accept, in the main, the system reported by the Committee of Finance, he saw no object in provoking a discussion, which, if not exactly challenged by the Speaker, had certainly been provoked, as far as the introduction of irritating topics could provoke it. He was too well acquainted with Parliamentary etiquette to reply to the Speaker when he was not on the floor. Another opportunity could be embraced for that purpose. But as the House had seen fit to entertain a discussion in its most extended form, he saw no reason to regret the course the debate had taken. Indeed, a review of the remarks which fell from prominent gentlemen on the other side, afforded ample cause of congratulation and triumph to those who were bred in the school of Washington and Hamilton. By one gentleman, (Mr. Ross, of Pennsylvania,) the House had been favored with the confession that a morbid languor had seized the Government under Mr. Jefferson, as soon as the impetus given to it by the preceding Administrations ceased to be felt. A second honorable gentleman, from South Carolina, (Mr. CALHOUN,) whose manly frankness and independence deserve the highest commendation, had substantially admitted that all the embarrassments, difficulties, and disasters suffered by

the country, were ascribable to an unfortunate departure, by those who administered the Government, from those cardinal maxims and principles which constituted the system of Washington and the creed of his disciples. A third honorable gentleman, from Virginia, (Mr. TUCKER,) modestly, but eloquently, echoing the sentiments of his friend who had preceded him, pushed his admissions yet a key higher, and, acknowledging that the men in power had all along preceeded upon mistaken and false principles of Government, he adjured his friends around him to subdue their pride of opinion, to renounce and abandon their vicious system, which they had learnt in the school of adversity, and which could be productive of only disappointment, disgrace, and danger to the country. Though not claimed as an intentional, studied, panegyric upon the system of the minority, yet a more splendid eulogy could not be pronounced upon it, because it was praise, extorted by truth, from the mouth of an enemy. As such, I receive it, said Mr. H., though not without amazement, for that would be impossible; but I receive it as a just and noble tribute to the purity and wisdom of Federal counsels. What more unequivocal and conclusive proof could be required, that the principles and conduct of the minority were right, than the admission by the majority that they themselves were in the wrong? From my heart, Mr. Speaker, do I wish they had sooner become sensible of their errors. Pity, indeed, it is that their eyes had not been sooner opened; what suffering, how much distress, what sorrows, what agonizing spasms, how much disgrace, how much treasure, blood, and national character would have been saved to this much abused people. Had the conviction of the most obvious and solemn truths been earlier wrought in the minds of gentlemen, the saving to the nation would be incalculable, and many a black and dismal page of our history would have been most fair to view.

The honorable gentlemen not only profess themselves converts to the principles of Washington and Federalism, but to my great joy they are engaged in reducing them to practice. Let the nation rejoice, for it forms a new and glorious era in its affairs. Yes, sir, I recognise in the language and the actions of the gentlemen, the influence of Federal principles; and come from whom those principles may, no matter how presented, or in what form I find them, whether "vamped up," as one gentleman (Mr. RANDOLPH,) in the shape of Executive Messages, or assuming the more substantial and intelligible form of legislative acts. Though they come in the questionable shape of repairing the ravages of a war which the Opposition had deprecated and resisted, by all the Constitutional means they possessed, yet will I afford every proper aid to resuscitate and sustain the public credit, to retrieve the national character, and provide in the most ample manner for the future defence and security of the country. We warned you of the consequences of plunging the country into an unjust, unnecessary, and wicked war; we portrayed, with a faithful pencil, the black and midnight counsels which lurked at the bottom of the measure. Did we not caution you against the rashness of precipitating the country from a state of peace, unprepared, unqualified, and unprovided, into a fearful contest, with the most powerful nation the world ever saw? Who will deny it? Did we not clearly foresee and foretell the consequences of your obstinate refusal to provide a solid basis for the finances, by an adequate system of revenue; preferring, as you did, the precarious and desperate reliance upon loans to pay the interest of loans? We never ceased to admonish you of the result of such a war, commenced without armies and competent commanders; without an adequate marine, and sufficient fortifications; without revenue, or any of the warlike means of self-defence prepared, much less to dash beyond our borders in quest of conquest. True as I consider all this, it is no justification for holding back, now that we are invited, upon our own principles, to join in repairing acknowledged mischief; and, while we endeavor to remedy the evil effects of past political errors, to guard against future misfortune. Upon such terms, and for such professed objects, I unite with all my heart in the effort to staunch and heal the deep wounds inflicted upon the country. While I agree to grant all the means necessary to these ends, I shall not be unmindful of the danger of falling into the extreme, opposite to that of feebleness and imbecility, which led us to the brink of ruin. I need not say my back is turned upon every plan to disturb the repose of the country, by romantic schemes of future war and conquest, if such are now really entertained. My views extend not beyond the defence of the country, against any and every nation able to attack us. For this purpose, pursuing the advice of Washington, to be found in his last legacy to his children, and in almost every Message sent to Congress, I would rely upon the preparation for war to preserve peace. I would prefer the season of peace for providing the means of defence, by pushing forward the necessary preparations for war. Thus far would I go—at least to the utmost of our power—to restore the public credit, and place it upon a solid, permanent basis, enabling the Government to pay punctually the interest of the public debt, and gradually to extinguish the principal; which is "the true secret," says Hamilton, "of rendering public credit immortal." I would increase the navy as rapidly as the finances would allow; I would keep embodied troops sufficient to garrison all our fortifications at exposed positions; and, while they were preserved from decay, I would erect others at every vulnerable point. I would omit nothing, nor spare any expense, to place the United States in a posture of complete defence, as the best means of preventing war; and, should war unfortunately come, of abridging its evils.

On this subject, summoning to their aid the principles and maxims of Washington and Hamilton, the gentlemen already referred to on the other side have introduced them in debate with all the air of novelty, for which they have taken, and, strange to say, received credit as the inventors. Why sir, the first book put into the hands of those who were bred in the school of the illustrious men at its head, taught us all this. We read in the horn-book of Federal politics, that, in return for the protection the people receive from Government, the people must contribute to the support of Government; that the public credit must be maintained inviolate; the faith of the nation preserved without a stain. And upon the subject of defence and security, we are taught to consider no sacrifice too great, no burdens too heavy, to insure both, as the end of all Government. All these ideas, as old as the Federal party itself, with which the gentlemen have bespangled and embellished their orations, are borrowed from that system upon which the Federal Administrations constantly acted, and the writings of Washington and Hamilton, which will remain forever recorded, though the remnant of our archives be consigned to the flames kindled by another war.

Mr. H. said, in approving the policy now in contemplation, therefore, for the defence of the country, and the maintenance, against the world, of its just rights and dignity, we were only pursuing the advice of the immortal founder of the Republic. I cannot agree, said he, with the gentleman from North Carolina, (Mr. Gaston,) that our resorting to preparatory measures of defence will have a tendency to excite and cultivate a sentiment of hostility to England, which would ultimately grow into a national feeling of inveterate and deadly hatred, such as the British and French nations cherish against each other. In the very nature of our relations with that country, there will always exist a powerful impulse produced by natural causes, unfavorable to causeless enmity. Sprung from one ancestry, speaking the same language, our customs, manners, and domestic habits, nearly the same; they will tend to produce, on both sides, a sentiment adverse to hostility. I could wish to speak plainly, without reserve, leaving nothing to inference; for I have nothing to conceal, nothing to regret, nothing to retract. I consider it, then, the true policy of this Government to be frank, to be just, rigidly impartial, and friendly to Great Britain, cultivating assiduously, by all fair and manly means, the best possible understanding with her. But we should not forget that the state of things which made it wise and patriotic to pray fervently for her success, to overlook or bear with her wrongs, to strengthen her hands to the utmost of our power, for the combat with our enemy and the enemy of all nations, and to exult in her final triumph, we should not forget that this state of things is now at an end. Thank God, in his mercy and goodness, they are at an end; that the disturber of the repose of mankind, is hurled from his dizzy eminence, and delivered over to captivity, I trust, forever. Yes, sir, the state of things which once made hostility to England criminal and base, no longer exists, she is not now, as she then was, the world's sole defence against a colossal tyranny that bestrode it.

Is it too much to say, sir, (I knew I am imprudently venturing on ticklish ground,) is it too much to say that England is now mistress of the ascendant, and it will be a duty, henceforward, to be on our guard against her as a powerful nation, if not a natural and jealous rival, impelled by her interests, if not her best policy, to keep us down, and check our quick march to that high rank which, sooner or later, this people must take among the nations? Is it venturing too far to say, that the balance of power is now restored, or rather, that France, if not already, is in danger of being reduced too low, while her great rival is too much exalted? May I not venture a little further and say, with that rival, few who look into futurity can doubt, we must ultimately be called to contend for the liberty, if not the empire of the seas; for to that, I believe, it must at last come. Shall I be pardoned for advancing yet a step further, by saying that, for this great contest, we ought to begin to prepare, gradually, if preferred, but to begin to prepare, and never to relax our precautionary preparations until we are prepared; at the same time, however, always observing the most frank, friendly, and scrupulously just conduct towards her, while we equally bear in mind the necessity of so regulating our partiality as not to permit ourselves to be rendered blind to her policy? I repeat, the interesting and critical state of things which not only justified, but rendered patriotic, our sympathy and partiality for England, is past. Far from my wish or intention is it to deny that, before the tyrant was overthrown, I rejoiced in the success of England; I gloried in her triumphs; I triumphed whenever victory perched upon her banners; but, now, I regard her with no kinder feelings than France, or any other nation. She is not now fighting our battles, and those of the civilized world, against a despotic and overgrown Power, which threatened all; we should view her, therefore, as that nation we have most to fear, and with whom, as a maritime and commercial people, we are most likely to come in collision. In a word, Mr. Speaker, I mean to be understood as saying, it is the part of wisdom to make the best use of our means and the season of peace to prepare for the worst, while we hope and labor for the best, resolving to bear and forbear to the utmost, thinking few sacrifices, short of national honor, too great to preserve our pacific relations.

Such are my ideas, sir, upon the subject of preparation for defence, and the relation in which England and this country stand towards each other. I am not entering the course to run the race of popularity. Upon the usual terms of acquiring, and the common means of seeking it, I should despise myself if I had it in possession. If excused for referring to events of the last session of Congress, one object would be to show how I lost what little popularity I may have possessed. By the same motives and the same principles which I am now actuated, I was then actuated, and trust I shall ever be guided, the good of the country, not of self or of party. Meanly as I think and no man can hold a meaner opinion of

the capacity and honesty of the men who administer the Government, profligate and corrupt as I always considered, and still consider the motives of the authors of the late war, I never lost sight of principles which govern my conduct now. In all the vicissitudes of the war, the security and welfare of the country were at no time separate from my thoughts. True, I opposed the war with a zeal and constancy not to be denied, and as little to be repented of. Though selected for one of its first victims at home, no sooner did it change its aggressive for a defensive character, than I took the ground of granting the supplies asked for, and strengthening the arm of Government. I distinctly took the ground of recovering and restoring the public credit, of uniting for the purpose of defence, and until the danger had passed by to forget and forgive, unmindful of the past, and looking only to the future. This ground was promptly taken as soon as the memorable November despatches were communicated to the House, and it was steadily maintained by voting for the most odious taxes. This ground was taken at the most critical juncture in our annals, when all was confusion, dismay, and terror. Your Treasury publicly bankrupt, the Government had been put to flight, the Capitol reduced to ashes, the Army without pay, food, or clothing, and dying by hundreds, like sheep, of the rot. Though power seemed ready to drop into our hands, like fruit rotten-ripe, I was willing to overlook for a moment the necessity of a change of rulers, and to take a stand in opposition to the feelings of those who sent me here, and in the teeth of their known opinions, roused as they reasonably were, to the highest pitch of indignation against the authors of our danger. But the country was threatened with dismemberment and ruin, and I felt there was no choice but to assist in its salvation. My aid was certainly not solicited; perhaps it was not wanted; but I judged for myself in affording it, trifling as may have been the benefit derived from it.

Perhaps an apology is due to the House for detaining them a moment, by referring, after the manner of some gentlemen, to my own peculiar situation. If on this occasion guilty of what may be considered egotism, the best plea I can offer, is that it is my first transgression of the kind, and I will avail myself of the patience kindly manifested by the House to advert to the style of remark, upon that two parties, occasionally indulged by an honorable gentleman from Virginia (Mr. RANDOLPH) and his estimable friend (Mr. STANFORD.) My feelings are too kind and warm towards these gentlemen to harbor any resentment, though I cannot refrain from saying their allusions are sometimes too strong to pass without being repelled. Whatever, sir, may be the opinion of a third party in this House, who think that the other two like factions seek to make their country a prey, and are squabbling only about dividing the spoil, while they possess all the integrity and virtue, I shall forbear to institute a comparison of political honesty and consistency.

It is undoubtedly true, unfortunately for the country it is true, as more than once alluded to, the party now in the minority lost the power they once enjoyed. They lost it, if gentlemen please, first through indiscretion, but secondly, because they disdained resorting to the vile means of retaining power which others found successful in obtaining it. Nor can any one of us reproach ourselves for having at any time, under any delusion, sanctioned and given currency to principles which, fully put in practice, have reduced the country to the condition which all now unite in deploring. Most true, the people were to their cost seduced to discard us, but we have acted out of power as we did in power; we have heretofore maintained, and I trust will continue to maintain, the same steadiness and uniformity of conduct, the reverse of which is generally reducible to no principle but self interest, and often renders even integrity itself suspicious. I hold, that the principles of Federalism, *old* and *new*, as they have been denominated, are the same, having consistency at least to recommend them, and let who may be placed at the helm of Government, they must be the star and compass to steer by. Like the beams of the great luminary of the heavens, which bear on their bosom both light and general heat to earth, our principles are not the offspring of fleeting circumstances, which rise like the floating vapors to disappear again. Clinging to the right, spurning the expedient, we cleave to our principles, though found in the measures of our opponents. And why? because we look not to power and office, but to the country, to advance the good, the greatness and true glory of which has ever been, and now is, our sole aim. Who amongst this minority has not been ever ready to sacrifice his prejudices, his resentments, everything, upon the altar of his country? May I not say, love of country has ever been their mother feeling, the fountain of their principles, the mainspring of all their political actions?

Can it be supposed that we will now abandon our principles, and shift sides with the majority, because they have been driven to the necessity of adopting them? I will never disown and renounce the holy Scriptures though preached by a depraved minister of the Gospel? I will not reject good because proffered by an evil hand. If they have been taught by adversity the important lesson, that the country can only flourish and grow great by administering the Government upon our principles, shall we disown and renounce them? Never; I trust never. I sicken with disgust at the bare idea of taking up their old, exploded, discarded notions of false economy, the cheap defence of nations, gunboats, dry docks, and militia. No man in this House, shall I not say in this nation, has more cause to hold out to the last than I have, in a dead, decided opposition to all the measures of Government. God knows none have more cause to detest the war, and deprecate the doctrines disseminated and successfully put in practice at its commencement—doctrines which levelled at civil liberty itself the blow of death—doctrines sapping the foundation of Government and social order, and unhinging society—doctrines involving a complication of slavery and chains, misery and torture, an agony both of body and mind, and death with every horrible aggravation of its terrors and its pains. The torments of the cross and stake may equal them; he who is broken upon the wheel may suffer more, but the pains of the gallows, or the gloom of the dungeon, are mercy compared with the torments inflicted by the hellhounds of Jacobinism. All these do not influence my political conduct, nor prevent me from looking back with unclouded contentment of conscience, if not with pride and exultation, upon the course I have pursued from the beginning of the war down to the present hour.

A few words more, and any claim I may have had upon the politeness of the House is discharged. Gentlemen doubt the propriety of granting further means to the Administration until it is shown that former supplies have not been corruptly expended, and they see no reason to doubt that corruption will continue its depredations upon the public treasure. I have not a doubt it will, unless the majority unite in devising a system of checks and accountability in the Departments. To this I understand prominent gentlemen on the other side have freely pledged themselves. But allowing the utmost weight to this argument, drawn from the probable abuse of power, corruption has taken such deep root in the Government, and attained so rank a growth, I much fear, let who may administer the Government, it will not totally disappear. Corruption has taken so strong a hold upon the political system of this country that it can no more be cured than the leprosy of *Gehazy*, which was hereditary to all his posterity.

This argument of corruption, however, goes to the withholding of all means from the Government, which would soon terminate all our contests by bringing them to a violent end. Confidence must be placed somewhere; that kind of confidence, I mean, necessary to prevent the Government from stopping. There must be oil supplied or the lamp will expire. That confidence must be placed in the men whom the people, however mistakenly and blindly, have chosen to administer the Government. To them, therefore, must be intrusted the execution of the system which looks to the defence of the country, the extinguishment of the war debt, and the restoration of the public credit. I shall support the system of finance, I believe unanimously agreed to by the committee who reported it, trusting that the means it provides will be used in promoting the prosperity, the honor, and the security of the country.

The question on the motion to reconsider, essentially the question to repeal the tax altogether, was decided by yeas and nays—for the reconsideration 67, against it 86, as follows:

Yeas—Messrs. Atherton, Baer, Barbour, Baylies, Boss, Bradbury, Breckenridge, Brigham, Bryan, Burwell, Champion, Cilley, Clarke of North Carolina, Clayton, Cooper, Culpeper, Davenport, Forney, Goldsborough, Hale, Hardin, Hawes, Heister, Henderson, Hungerford, Jackson, Jewett, King of Massachusetts, King of North Carolina, Langdon, Law, Lewis, Love, Lyon, Mason, McCoy, McKee, Moore of South Carolina, Moseley, Noyes, Parris, Pitkin, Pickens, Powell, Randolph, Reed, Rice, Ruggles, Sharpe, Smith of Virginia, Stanford, Stearns, Strong, Stuart, Sturges, Taggart, Tallmadge, Taul, Thomas, Voss, Ward of Massachusetts, Ward of New York, Wheaton, Wilcox, Williams, Wright, and Yancey.

NAYS—Messrs. Alexander, Archer, Baker, Bassett, Bateman, Bennett, Betts, Birdsall, Birdseye, Brooks, Burnside, Caldwell, Calhoun, Chappell, Clark of Kentucky, Clendennin, Clopton, Comstock, Condict, Conner, Crawford, Creighton, Cuthbert, Darlington, Desha, Forsyth, Glasgow, Gold, Goodwyn, Griffin, Grosvenor, Hahn, Hall, Hammond, Hanson, Hopkinson, Huger, Ingham, Irving of New York, Irwin of Pennsylvania, Johnson of Kentucky, Kerr of Virginia, Lovett, Lowndes, Lumpkin, Lyle, Maclay, Mayrant, McLean of Kentucky, McLean, of Ohio, Middleton, Milnor, Nelson of Massachusetts, Nelson of Virginia, Newton, Ormsby, Pickering, Piper, Pleasants, Reynolds, Roane, Robertson, Root, Ross, Sergeant, Savage, Schenck, Sheffey, Smith of Pennsylvania, Smith of Maryland, Southard, Taylor of New York, Taylor of South Carolina, Telfair, Throop, Tucker, Wallace, Ward of New Jersey, Wendover, Whiteside, Wilde, Wilkin, Willoughby, Thomas Wilson, William Wilson, and Yates.

The resolution to continue the direct tax of three millions for one year was then agreed to, and referred to the Financial Committee to bring in a bill accordingly.

The House then proceeded, in Committee of the Whole, to consider the next proposition of the Committee of Ways and Means, viz: that which proposes the continuance of certain duties on distillation; when, on motion of Mr. WILLIAMS, of North Carolina, who considered this question too important to be decided without discussion, the Committee rose, reported progress, and the House adjourned.

WEDNESDAY, February 7.

Two other members, to wit, from New Hampshire, DANIEL WEBSTER, and from North Carolina, WELDON N. EDWARDS, (elected in the place of Nathaniel Macon, resigned,) appeared, produced their credentials, were qualified, and took their seats.

Mr. INGHAM presented petitions from sundry inhabitants of the State of Pennsylvania, praying that Congress will take into their consideration the manufacturing interest in the United States, and adopt such measures as will afford to the said interest the best security and protection.

Mr. RANDOLPH gave notice of his intention to move an inquiry into the constitutionality of the appointment of Peter B. Porter, late a member of this House, to the office of a Commissioner under the Treaty of Great Britain, he being at the time of his appointment a member of this House.

Mr. PLEASANTS, from the Naval Committee, reported amendments to the bill from the Senate, authorizing the appointment of Admirals, the object of which are to create one Vice Admiral and two Rear Admirals, instead of one Admiral and two Vice Admirals—a mere change of denomination. The bill and amendments were referred to a Committee of the Whole.

On motion of Mr. ROOT, the Committee of Ways and Means were instructed to inquire into the expediency of discharging Ebenezer Keeler and John Francis from their confinement in the county of Delaware, New York, at the suit of the United States.

Mr. MOSELEY, from the select committee, to whom was referred the petition of sundry inhabitants of the State of Connecticut, on behalf of the widow and children of Charles Dolph, deceased, reported a bill for the relief of the widow and children of said Dolph; which was twice read, and committed.

Mr. BASSETT, from the committee to whom was referred the memorial of Commodore John Rodgers, of the Navy, respecting a judgment obtained against him by John Donnell, of Baltimore, for the value of a vessel detained by a frigate belonging to a squadron under the command of Commodore R., reported a resolution for his relief.

This resolution, after some conversation on the form of the report, it being contended that it should have been by bill instead of resolution, was twice read, and referred to a Committee of the Whole.

COMMERCIAL RESTRICTIONS.

The House, on motion of Mr. KING, of Massachusetts, resumed the consideration of the following resolution, submitted by him yesterday:

Resolved, That the Committee on Foreign Relations be instructed to inquire into the expediency of excluding from the ports of the United States, or of increasing the duties on, all foreign vessels owned in, coming from, bound to, or touching at, any of the possessions of any nation of Europe in the West Indies, and on the continent of America, from which the vessels of the United States are excluded; and of prohibiting, or of increasing the duties on the importation in foreign vessels, of any articles the growth, produce, or manufacture of such possessions.

Mr. BRADBURY moved to amend the resolution of Mr. KING, by striking out the words, "excluding from the ports of the United States foreign vessels," so as to confine the inquiry to the expediency of increasing the tonnage duty, &c., only. He observed, in support of his motion, that he was not in the habit of obtruding his opinions and views of subjects upon the House; and, on this occasion, should have been silent, had not the subject under consideration presented itself to his mind in a different light from what it appeared to have done to the mind of his honorable colleague, (Mr. KING.) As we both represent a district of country in Maine, said Mr. B., whose commercial interests are precisely similar, their Representatives, it is fairly to be presumed, cannot have views or wishes hostile to those interests, however they may differ as to the methods most likely to advance them. I object to one of the phrases in the resolution, that which I have proposed to strike out; because, sir, it appears to me to be a renewal of the old, and to the people of that part of the country, odious restrictive system. The restrictive energies of this country have, in my judgment, had a fair experiment; and, as was observed on another occasion the other day, "been found wanting." In my humble opinion the true policy on this subject is regulation simply, and not exclusion. I believe more beneficial effects can be accomplished by the mild and clement sun of regulation, than by the fierce and rude winds of exclusion and prohibition. If the course, on this occasion, most congenial to my views could be adopted, it should be a simple direction to the Committee on Foreign Relations to inquire "Whether any measures ought to be 'adopted by Congress to regulate the intercourse 'between the United States and His Britannic 'Majesty's possessions in the West Indies, and on 'the continent of North America," agreeably to the power reserved in the second article of the treaty. But I am, nevertheless, willing to adopt the resolution of my colleague, if amended; that is, sir, I am willing to inquire, and if, on mature consideration it is thought best, to say, increase the tonnage duty on foreign vessels coming from ports and places from which our vessels are excluded. Increase also the additional per centage on the permanent rate of duties to a reasonable amount; at least commence only in this way, and reserve the severer measures of exclusion and prohibition, until the efficacy of this course is tried. I believe, sir, such a course is the safest and the wisest—more congenial to the wishes of mercantile men, and in my judgment to their true interests. The opposite course is, I fear, calculated to build up the British colonies at American expense. Prohibit intercourse in foreign vessels between the British West Indies and this country, and it operate as a bounty or encouragement to the colonies adjacent to us on this continent; to the export of lumber and bread stuff from those colonies. It is not difficult for a reflecting mind to trace this as the sure consequence of such a course of policy. It is, in my opinion, owing to the restrictive system, and its necessary consequence, the war, that we have now to deplore the loss of the valuable trade to the British West Indies. Prior to the war we enjoyed that commerce substantially as a permanent trade, though, in point of form, we held it by the uncertain tenure of a British proclamation of the colonial Governors, issued semi-annually, under an Order in Council. But the merchants could calculate, and did calculate on its continuance, for a long period prior to the war, with nearly as much certainty as if it was regulated by convention. To restore this trade is, indeed, all-important; but I am disposed to think it cannot be effected by measures merely compulsory. Prior to the war, also, we enjoyed a valuable commerce in plaster of paris; it was to a number of my constituents, while it continued, a source of wealth, and to the cultivators of land at the South served to fertilise and enrich their fields and plantations. It has been

enjoyed also since the peace until recently, and I know not that it is not still enjoyed. But reports are in circulation, as I perceive from newspapers, that our shipholders are by British regulations to be deprived of this branch of trade. It has been stated in the papers that the British have laid a duty of $5 per ton on all plaster of paris exported from the colonies in English bottoms, which shall be landed east of New Haven; the effect of which will inevitably be to exclude our vessels from this branch of commerce. Whether this information be correct, ought forthwith to be ascertained, and I trust the committee will instantly institute the necessary inquiry on this subject, by applying through the Executive to the British agent here, to ascertain whether any and what duties have been imposed on any merchandise, more especially this article. To preserve and restore branches of commerce to my constituents so valuable and important, is highly desirable; but, in our haste to do this, I hope no measure will be adopted calculated eventually to injure and defeat the object in view, or to become a source of future regret.

This motion was opposed by Mr. KING, of Massachusetts, on the grounds he took on originally proposing the resolution.

Mr. S. SMITH said, that he was adverse to the amendment; that he thought the resolution ought to go to the Committee of Foreign Relations, on the broad ground which it assumed; the committee would consider whether the object contemplated would be answered best by an exclusion or by laying extraordinary duties. He said, he had not made up his own mind as to which course would be best. The duties might operate as a charge on the consumer, unless they were such as would be prohibitory. The total exclusion of the importation of goods from such ports as the vessels of the United States were not permitted to enter and trade freely, for similar articles, might operate to induce the parties to meet at some port free for both, and there interchange their cargoes; for instance, at a Swedish or Danish island, to all which the ships of the United States were received as freely as their own vessels. He said, he would take a short view of the subject. The European Powers which had established colonies, had generally maintained the principles of an exclusive commerce thereto. This monopoly they claimed as a remuneration for the expense of their first establishment, and their future protection; and there appeared to be some reasons on their side. It behooved the United States to inquire whether they could not procure on equal terms, or nearly so, commodities similar to those produced by such colonies, from countries into which their own vessels were permitted to enter and trade freely. If such ports are open to them, then it becomes a duty of the United States to favor the importations therefrom, and to exclude those from the countries which will not permit our vessels to enter and trade on equal terms with their own; nor can any such country complain. It ought not to be a cause of commercial warfare by such nation. He said, he would take a view of the conduct of the nations possessing colonies which produced coffee and sugar. Spain had uniformly excluded from all her colonies the ships of other nations, unless when compelled to open the ports of Cuba, when at war with Great Britain, and since the French Revolution. During peace, she drew the flour necessary for Cuba, from the United States to Cadiz, where it was bought by the Commissary of the Indies, and by him sent to Cuba; at present the trade to Cuba is open as well for imports as for exports, but it cannot be expected to continue so. She has granted a free trade to her colony of Porto Rico, but confined to Spanish subjects or residents of the island, and in Spanish vessels only, intending, perhaps, to supply Cuba with flour through that island, as she may hereafter grant similar privileges to Cuba; the fact is, that this system is to the exclusion of the vessels of the United States.

Portugal prohibited all intercourse with her colonies of the Brazils until the King removed his Court. Since then the ports of that immense country are open. The Brazils produce an immense quantity of sugar, from whence a supply, equal perhaps to our wants, might be drawn; but the Brazils require very few of our products; the balance of trade with them would be greatly against the United States.

The Dutch have two free ports—St. Eustatia and Curacoa; they produce very little; their ports of Surinam, Essequibo, and Berbice have been partially opened to our trade. Molasses was permitted to be exported from thence in American bottoms; at present those ports are in possession of the British, who exclude our vessels.

France, I believe, admitted our vessels with fish, lumber, and pork. She excluded our flour, and permitted the export of molasses and taffia. She prohibited us from exporting sugar and coffee.

Great Britain excludes the entry of American vessels from her colonies, except when necessity compels their Governors to issue their proclamations; this has frequently happened during her war with France. Seldom in time of peace their supplies have been furnished from the United States, either in their own vessels direct, or from St. Jago de Cuba, where they come for our flour, or from St. Bartholomews, a Swedish island.

The Danes and Swedes have pursued a more liberal policy; they admit our vessels freely to their islands, and they might perhaps become entrepots where the vessels of both parties would meet and exchange cargoes. The Island of St. Croix produces sugar to a considerable amount. The State of Louisiana, and lately Georgia, produce sugar. With the supply they can furnish, and what may be drawn from Hispaniola, and other countries in the East and West Indies, (where our vessels are admitted,) I am inclined to think that ample supplies of colonial produce may be obtained. But, Mr. Speaker, the subject is one of great delicacy, and will require the serious attention of the committee before they report upon it. He was not prepared to say, that the present is the proper time to decide upon it;

however, he was willing to send the resolution to the committee. He was, however, prepared to say, that Congress ought to use every exertion to favor the navigation of the Eastern States—a navigation which gave us the seamen, by whose bravery the United States would, at no very distant day, be enabled to maintain an equality on the high seas with any nation now in existence.

The amendment was negatived without a division, and the resolution was then agreed to.

THE REVENUE.

The House resolved itself into a Committee of the Whole, on the subject of the report of the Committee of Ways and Means on the Revenue. The following resolution, reported by the committee being under consideration:

Resolved, That it is expedient to repeal an act, entitled "An act to provide additional revenues for defraying the expenses of Government, and maintaining the public credit, by laying duties on spirits distilled within the United States and Territories thereof, and by amending the act laying duties on licenses to distillers of spirituous liquors," passed on the 21st of December, 1814, excepting only the 16th, 18th, 19th, and 24th sections thereof, from and after the first day of April next, and from the same day to add 100 per cent. to the amount of the duty which all stills now subject to duty are liable to pay.

Mr. WILLIAMS, of North Carolina, moved to amend the same, so as to read as follows:

Resolved, That it is expedient to repeal the act, entitled "An act laying a duty on licenses to distillers of spirituous liquors, passed on the 24th of December, 1813;" also the act, entitled "An act laying a duty on spirits distilled within the United States," passed on the 21st of December, 1814, and that, in lieu thereof, an act be passed laying a duty of —— cents on each gallon of spirits distilled within the United States from the material of fruit, and of —— cents on each gallon distilled from the material of grain.

Mr. WILLIAMS spoke as follows:—Permit me to solicit the indulgence of the Committee, while I offer the reasons which have induced the motion just made. The amendment is submitted with diffidence; because I am sensible of that superior deference which is due to the judgment and measures of senior members in this House, and from my perfect acquiescence in a custom, which attributes to age, both in and out of this House, additional respect and consideration; I should certainly have forborne an attempt to obtrude upon your notice any of my remarks; but, sir, the interest of my constituents is as dear to them as any other portion of the community; and I should betray a culpable neglect of that interest, were I to remain silent when it is, as I think, about to be sacrificed.

I propose the amendment with diffidence again, because I am also sensible of that deference which is always due, and generally paid, to the Committee of Ways and Means. A course different from this, would hardly be practicable at any time, and frequently improper; for it is presumed the committee have examined the subjects referred to them, with a patience and scrutiny, which she

House would scarcely be adequate to undergo in its corporate and legislative capacity. They have free and familiar access to facts and opinions, which the House, from its very nature and its numbers, could not have; being a small body, they perform their business with a facility and despatch, which would be impracticable to a large legislative assembly. Hence, I apprehend, the custom of referring all subjects to the committee in the first instance; of receiving their reports when made, with great deference, and of allowing them to contain the best evidence which the nature of the case will admit.

By no means, sir, would I object to the custom of the House. On the contrary, I think it is generally the best course to be pursued with all committees, and particularly so with the present committee; for, so far as my acquaintance with that body will enable me to judge, I must say, that the selections were made with discernment as to the talents and promised zeal of the committee. But as the greatest judge or most profound lawyer may sometimes advance an erroneous opinion, so, I think, the committee, in this case, have misconceived the true interest of the country. If I should be so fortunate as to make this appear, the House, I know, will give their support to the amendment I have proposed.

It has, Mr. Chairman, been asserted by gentlemen, that it would be politic to impose a heavy duty, amounting in many cases almost to a prohibition, on the distilling of spirituous liquors, because it would tend to counteract that habit of intemperance which we sometimes see prevalent in the country. But if the argument has any force, I am unable to perceive it. To a certain extent, spirits are a necessary of life, to every extent in which they are used they will not be dispensed with. If not made at home, they will be imported from abroad. However much, therefore, morality may condemn the use of spirituous liquors, and however wise it might be to prevent, as much as possible, intemperance in that way, I do not yet understand that it is the object of Government to prohibit, entirely, the use or distillation of spirits. On the contrary, the object of Government, as I have understood it, is to raise a revenue, is to bring money into the Treasury.

It will be admitted, that stills are a fair object of taxation. Perhaps no species of property, owned by the citizen, can better sustain a tax, which is moderate and duly equalized; and while contributions are necessary to defray the expenses of Government, no one is able or more willing to furnish his proportionable part than the distiller. If it were consistent with the public engagements to abolish all other taxes except this, I should not object to the measure, merely because it would operate on those whom I represent. So far as I could ascertain the sentiments of my constituents, they did not expect, nor did they wish that the tax on stills, under existing circumstances of the country, should be entirely removed; they know we had a great debt to pay, and that money must be raised to support the credit of the nation. But, sir, they well know, and I myself also know, that

the duty proposed by the committee is impolitic; that it is excessive; and that it will thereby defeat its own object—the raising of the revenue.

By the law of 1813, the following duties were imposed, to- wit: for two weeks, nine cents per gallon on the capacity of the still; for one month, eighteen cents per gallon on the capacity of the still; and so on.

The most experienced distillers in the country where I live, and I speak in reference to that particularly, have estimated that this duty would have amounted to ten cents per gallon, if it had been imposed on the quantity made, instead of the capacity of the still; and moderate as it may seem, many persons stopped their distilleries; others worked them not more than half the time they would have done, if the law had not been passed. The revenue accruing under this law for the year 1814, as stated by the Secretary of the Treasury, amounted to $1,681,087. In 1814 a law was passed, imposing a duty of twenty cents on the gallon, in addition to that which had been laid on the capacity. If, therefore, the aggregate duty be estimated at thirty cents per gallon; and if it be supposed that the same number of stills were used, as under the former law, then there ought, in a direct proportion, to have accrued for the year 1815, the sum of $5,063,661. But the Secretary of the Treasury states the sum accruing for the year 1815, to be only $3,500,000.

If the aggregate duty be estimated at twenty-five cents per gallon, then there ought to have accrued, in the same proportion, for the year 1815, the sum of $4,202,777; consequently, in both cases there was a defalcation of revenue; in the first case, of more than $1,500,000; in the second, of more than $700,000.

But the idea may be placed in a still stronger point of view. The Secretary states the revenue accruing in 1814 for licenses on stills and boilers to be $1,681,067, as before mentioned. But in 1815, the revenue accruing from the same source amounted only to $1,000,000. This was owing, no doubt, to the imposition of the additional tax. Hence, then, it will appear, that more than one-third of the distillers must, in 1815, have ceased their operations altogether.

I am well aware, sir, that we have no very certain data on which to found our calculations in regard to this subject. But knowing, from my own observation, that a great stop was put to the business of distilling, by the additional duty imposed in 1814, I have submitted these calculations more for the purpose of exemplifying the manner in which a defalcation of the revenue was produced, than of offering anything like substantial or incontrovertible evidence. It is not by calculation that we are to ascertain whether or not a tax is oppressive, whether it operates on the people as a grievance. This must be collected from the people themselves, by being among them; by attending to their statements; and finally, by observing the difficulty with which the demands of Government are met. This, sir, is the most safe and best practical criterion by which to judge of the extent and operation of a tax. In the district I represent, many persons who carried on distillation, most extensively, put a total stop to their business, although there was a great surplus of grain, and a greater abundance of fruit than was ever known at any antecedent period. Sir, the fruit alone, in many parts of North Carolina, if it had been saved and converted into brandy, would, in my judgment, have yielded a greater revenue than has been yielded in that quarter by the distillation, both of grain and fruit, under the superadded and almost prohibitory duties of 1815.

The committee now propose to repeal the law imposing a duty on distilled spirits, and to double the duty on licenses to distillers. If the measure should be carried, the duty will amount to about twenty cents on each gallon. This cannot be a sufficient reduction of the tax. It is indeed alleviating the burdens imposed by the necessity of the war with a vengeance; for twenty cents, in time of peace, is as great a duty, as thirty cents in a state of war. In war, very few importations of foreign liquors can take place. The distillers of domestic spirits have then a monopoly of the market; whereas in time of peace they are obliged to struggle with competition from abroad. I appeal to the experimental knowledge of commercial gentlemen to support the truth of the position, and am confident that I shall not be answered in the negative. Besides, if you contemplate no greater reduction than that proposed by the committee, you conflict with the policy which our Government announced to the world it was ready to pursue. The President has recommended the propriety of encouraging domestic manufactures, either by laying a protecting duty on foreign importations, or by repealing that on domestic articles. Accordingly, we have found it proposed by the committee to repeal all the duties on domestic manufactures. Not only so, but to reduce the customs more than one-half; the direct tax to one-half; and to repeal entirely the duty on furniture, and some other articles; but the duty on domestic distilled spirits is proposed to be reduced not more than a third. Can it, I would ask, be just or reasonable, that all other duties should be greatly reduced, or entirely repealed, except that on domestic distilled spirits? Why should it not be encouraged, as well as the manufacture of any other article? It is as necessary, to give us complete independence of foreign nations, as any other kind of manufacture. I trust, sir, that the just, equal, and magnanimous spirit which induces us to alleviate the burdens of the war, will not, cannot fail to direct us on this occasion, to an enlightened and upright policy. Such a policy as our constituents, in every quarter, and of every profession, may expect at our hands.

In another point of view this tax is impolitic. If it does not, on account of its excess, prohibit the manufacture of domestic spirits, it will, at least, cause the people to look out for expedients to evade the law, and will, thereby, be injurious, not only to the revenue, but to the morals of the country. The arguments from all sides of the House, in favor of reducing the customs, were bottomed on the supposition that they would be evaded. The gentleman from Massachusetts, (Mr. PICKERING,) said, the other day, that but one of the excessive duties growing out of the war had been enforced. Our merchants knew not how to smuggle. Now, if the merchants were thus honest and upright before those burdens were laid on them, will not the same argument apply with equal force to the distiller? Excessive taxes will ever produce smuggling and evasion; but when moderate and equal, they never have that tendency. I have heard that distillers would, under the enormous duties of 1815, run their spirits to fourth proof; that they would return only this to the collector, and then bring it down with water to the usual strength of saleable spirits. Though this act could not be called a violation of the law, it may yet be an evasion of that duty which the Government expected to receive; whereas, if the duty had been less, the distillers would have run their spirits to the usual strength, have given an account of it to the collector, and would have paid on it a greater amount of revenue, than they did when the duty was so high as to make them think of evading it; nay, when they were almost compelled to evade it. There is, in fine, a certain point in the taxation of every object to which you may go, and beyond which you cannot go, with any hope of augmenting your revenue. If a tax shall have gone beyond that point, the people will see and feel that the hand of Government is upon them, and, by a species of reaction, natural and inevitable, they will either oppose or evade the pressure. That the tax on stills has been much too high, we have every reason to believe, from the smaller number employed, and the less quantity of spirits distilled than would have been if the duty had been moderate.

Thus far, sir, as to the amount of the tax. I think it, however, objectionable on the score of inequality in its operation. It may be laid down as a rule, as a principle the most consistent with our Government, that all taxes should be equal in their operation; but this tax will violate that rule, and operate with an extreme and inordinate pressure on particular sections of the country. In a grain-growing country, or one producing orchards, remotely situated from market, spirits may be called the staple commodity. It is, then, extremely unequal to impose a tax on this staple almost prohibitory of its production. You might, with as much propriety, lay an exorbitant duty on the tobacco of Virginia, or the cotton of South Carolina and Georgia, as on the whiskey produced in other sections of the country. But gentlemen have said it is impossible to devise a tax which will not operate unequally. That in order to remedy this you must impose various taxes; that as some will operate unequally on this, and some on that section of the country, it may be fairly concluded that a general equality will be the result. But if the argument is correct in principle, it is far from being supported by the practice of the House. The salt tax is continued, although it is the most improper of all objects of indirect taxation. On whom does it operate? Certainly on the interior of the country. A direct tax of three millions is to be continued, notwithstanding it also operates most oppressively on the interior. But the furniture tax, which operates on our seaboard and our towns, and which, therefore, according to the argument of gentlemen, is necessary to produce equality, is proposed to be repealed. If to these instances be added the still tax, that unequal pressure on the interior of the country of which we complain will be increased, and the grievance can be lessened only by reducing the tax.

Another objection as to the inequality of the tax grows out of the manner in which it is to be laid, to wit: on the capacity of the still, and not on the quantity of spirits distilled, by which the duty is oppressive in some parts, and is scarcely felt in others. Owing to a peculiar structure of the stills in a certain section of the country, the distillers can, in twenty-four hours, make seven or eight times the quantity they are enabled to make in other sections. By this means the former class have greatly the advantage over the latter, while the latter may have performed as much labor, and been at as great an expense as the former. Does it, then, seem right or just that not only the cotton and tobacco planter should have the advantage over the distiller, but that one distiller should have the advantage over another? For my part, I cannot think it is; on the contrary, it is evidently more just and proper that the duty should be on the quantity. Then, he who makes one hundred gallons per day, will pay ten times as much tax as he who makes only ten gallons per day; and certainly he should do so, because the expense of making a hundred gallons is not ten times as great as the expense of making only ten gallons. In a direct proportion, therefore, he is more able to pay ten times the tax. In confirmation of this, let me ask, what is the principle universally aimed at in the levying and collecting of all our taxes? It is, that each individual should contribute revenue to the Government, in proportion to his pecuniary means or ability to do so. Land, for instance, ten times more fertile and productive than other land, is required to pay ten times the tax. The product of the soil, in this case, constitutes the ability of the landholder to contribute to Government. Why, then, should not the same criterion be adopted in regard to the distiller, from the product of his still, and the sales of spirits which he makes, (and the one supposition necessarily includes the other,) we may as fairly judge of his ability as of the ability of the landholder. I should, therefore, hope that the House would subject stills to the operation of the same equal and impartial rules as other objects of taxation are subjected to; that they alone would not be an exception to the general principles observed in the system of revenue which is proposed to be adopted.

I am aware, sir, of the reasons which have suggested this mode to the committee. They have thought that it would prevent abuses and evasions

of the law; but I am unable to perceive the force of such argument. A man disposed to cheat the Government cannot be made honest and upright by the provisions and penalties of law, however circumspect and vindicatory they may be. The sanguinary code of Great Britain has not yet been, and never will be, sufficient to restrain offenders. A dishonest man, who enters his still for two weeks or one month, when the duty is on the capacity, can work it for six weeks or two months with nearly as much ease as he could practise the deception of running spirits to fourth proof and bringing it down with water; or, as he could commit the fraud of making two thousand gallons and returning only one thousand to the collector, when the duty was on the quantity distilled. I cannot, therefore, feel the force of the argument offered by the committee. On the contrary, I think it better to make laws so easy and agreeable to the people that no inducements to transgress them will be afforded, than to aim at preventing violations by rigorous enactments.

A tax on the capacity of the still is injurious in another respect. One great advantage always to be derived from distillation is the support of stock. Some men, of experience and economy, have estimated that for every five bushels of grain worked daily, thirty head of stock could be fed. Upon trial, this is found to be so great a benefit, that many distillers continue their operations more for the advantage of their stock than for the profits of their whiskey. When the duty is on the capacity, they are forced to use great and wasteful exertions, and of course they are deprived of considerable advantage in that way; whereas, when the duty is on the quantity distilled, they may operate at leisure, according as they find it to their interest; and at certain times, when the season does not suit, when it is too warm or too cold, they may stop altogether.

In short, sir, there is a repugnance in the mind of the community against employing their stills by the capacity. The people see that a certain duty imposed on the capacity, operates partially; that if applied to the gallon, it would be more convenient to them, and more profitable to the Government. An evidence of this has lately occurred in Virginia; a gentleman from that State has favored me with the sight of a communication received from the collector of the district he represents. It is stated in the communication, that of near seven hundred stills which had been entered on his books, not more than about sixty had taken licenses. This proves indisputably the point for which I contend, that there is a repugnance in the mind of the community against the tax in that mode. Is it not, therefore, the duty and the policy of the Legislature to make laws agreeable to the people, especially when those laws, formed and fashioned to the will of the people, are not likely to be less productive of revenue to the Government? It is the mode, and not so much the amount of taxation, that renders it at any time odious and unacceptable to the people. But gentlemen have said, that if you do not lay the tax on the capacity of the still, you must either subject the citizens to domiciliary visits, or require them to make returns upon oath of the quantity of spirits they have distilled. But will a duty on licenses wholly remedy the evil, if it is one, of which you have such fears? No, I apprehend not. How did you ascertain the capacity of stills under the law of 1813, if your officers did not visit the houses of citizens, or if the latter were not permitted to state the capacity on oath? It is a fact coming within my own knowledge, that under the law of 1813 domiciliary visits were made by the collectors or their deputies—the people did not complain of this, but of the inconvenience to which they were subjected in not being permitted to use their stills at leisure by the gallon. Contrast the two objections, that of domiciliary visits, and that of their convenience just alluded to, and my word for it the people will choose the former. These visits are not so frightful as gentlemen would imagine. The collector, when not the messenger of an oppressive law, will be received as a visiting acquaintance or friend, more than as a person to whom odium should attach.

But, sir, you have already acted on both the principles of which you are now so fearful. Under the laws of 1813 domiciliary visits were made; by the law of 1814, distillers were required to keep an account of the quantity of spirits they had distilled, and to verify or return the same upon oath. Why then should we at this time be so apprehensive of those which have heretofore been in use? For my own part, I see as much necessity for their continuance as for their original adoption.

But farther, sir, I should have no objection against allowing the citizens to make their returns by a simple statement or declaration—upon such statements you collect evidence for equalizing the direct tax. The assessors did not visit the houses of the citizens in one case out of twenty, and I have never heard of attempts to evade the law; on the contrary, there is a principle in human nature always to respect and reverence a confidence which has been liberally reposed. Laws which are tedious in detail, watchful and vindictive in their provisions, almost necessarily address themselves to the ingenuity of the evil-minded and excite a wish to evade them. Solon laid down the principle, that in order to prevent certain offences, it was better not to enact laws against them, because, as he maintained, those laws would only remind his fellow-citizens of the crimes which he had thus silently denounced and effectually prohibited. In like manner, sir, I would not remind our fellow-citizens of the possibility of swearing falsely by the multiplying oaths on every occasion—let us trust to their justice and their generosity. It is to be hoped, not indeed without assurance, that our confidence will not be misplaced. An individual who makes his return by a simple statement will feel that he is called upon by every noble principle of his nature to declare the truth—he will see that this Government has generously reposed in him a confidence, which his pride as a citizen,

and his conscience as a man, cannot fail to reciprocate fully and sincerely. Believe me, sir, that any man who, under such circumstances, would state falsely, would not be much too good to swear falsely or to violate any other law which you can possibly make. If, however, gentlemen should think it better to require returns to be made upon oath, I am willing to the measure. Only accommodate your laws to the convenience of the people, and I shall be satisfied. In doing which it may be considered a rule, liable to very few exceptions, that the same degree of rigor necessary to prevent violations of the law when the duty is imposed on the gallon, will also be necessary to prevent violations when the duty is on the capacity. If the latter mode of taxation should be preferred, your laws, I think, must be as rigorous, as circumspect, and as offensive to the people, in order to obstruct abuses and evasions, as if the former mode were to be adopted.

The last part of my proposition is, that there should be a distinction between the tax on the distillation of spirits from the material of fruit, and that on the distillation of spirits from the material of grain. This I should think requires no confirmation, as the propriety of it must be obvious. The reasons are: first, that grain is a necessary of life, and it may sometimes happen, even in the most plentiful country, that this article will be scarce—hence no one will doubt but that as little of it as possible should be consumed by distillation. If then the difference which I propose should be adopted, it will have a tendency to promote the distillation of less grain and more fruit.

In the second place, grain is a necessary of life; but when converted into spirits it becomes a luxury. Fruit, on the other hand, is not a necessary of life, and when distilled it is the converting of one luxury into another. It would then seem an object worthy of legislative attention, so to provide by law that an article of necessity should not be converted into a luxury, when it is practicable to produce the latter, by the conversion of one luxury into another.

In the third place, if grain is not distilled it is an article which may be preserved. It may be applied to the various purposes of life not necessary now to be mentioned; or if not used by the grower, it may always be disposed of for a value at least equivalent to the toil of producing it. Fruit, on the contrary, is an article which cannot be kept. If not distilled within a short and given time it will perish, and we lose so much of the produce of our lands and profits of our labor. In proportion then as fruit is more perishable than grain, in the same proportion let it be more practicable and easy to distil the former than the latter.

The propriety of the distinction, in the fourth place, appears to be enforced by a consideration of more weight than any yet mentioned. Who, sir, are the persons that generally distil brandy? Are they men of the greatest wealth, or the less opulent portion of the community? I answer that they are generally of the latter class—

men who live on poor lands and who derive much of their subsistence from the profit of their orchards. They are not cultivators of fertile lands producing rice, corn, or tobacco, but high, arid, and thin soils, which yield a greater profit from orchards than anything else in which they can be planted. Now, sir, if you make no difference in the duty, you confine or limit the business of distilling almost exclusively to one class of citizens. Those who distil whiskey are generally men somewhat advanced as to property, &c. They have such command of the products of the country that they can at any time purchase grain for their distilleries, whatever be the price or scarcity of the article, and can also at any time pay the tax to Government. Being possessed of wealth, they can shield themselves against any grievance or oppression to which by the operation of your laws they might otherwise be subjected. But with regard to fruit, although the rich have orchards, yet the poor have them also, and, when productive, the most indigent man in the community can have a little brandy to exchange for such articles of subsistence as he may want. By adopting then the distinction which I propose, you consult the interest, not of the wealthy or indigent alone, but of both together, whereas, when there is no distinction, you consult more the interest of the former and disparage that of the latter.

It has in the last place been laid down as the most correct principle of policy in a course of legislation, that the rights and interests of the poor should be the objects of chief concern; for this plain reason, that the rich can always take care of themselves. But, sir, as my proposition does not contemplate any partial or exclusive advantage to either, but a common benefit to both, I hope it will meet with the general support of the House.

Mr YANCEY made a speech of some length in support of Mr. WILLIAMS's motion; and against it Mr. INGHAM and Mr. BURNSIDE.

Mr. HARDIN preferred the amendment to the original proposition, though desiring a different modification.

Mr. WILLIAMS's motion was negatived by a large majority.

Mr. YANCEY successively moved two amendments, (having nearly the same object as that of Mr. WILLIAMS,) which were negatived, by majorities of 20 or 30 votes.

A motion was then made to strike out of the original resolution the words "one hundred," and in lieu thereof to insert "fifty," so as to reduce one-half the proposed addition to the capacity tax.

On motion of Mr. INGHAM the Committee rose, reported progress, and obtained leave to sit again.

THURSDAY, February 8.

Mr. CONDICT presented a petition of sundry manufacturers of woollen goods in the States of New Jersey, Pennsylvania, and Delaware, praying that such measures may be adopted by Con-

gress as will afford to them, and others engaged in similar manufactures, the security and encouragement necessary to a continuance of their labors.—Referred to the Committee on Commerce and Manufactures.

Mr. McLEAN, of Ohio, presented a resolution of the General Assembly of the State of Ohio, respecting the settlers on reserved lands within said State.—Referred to the Committee on the Public Lands.

Mr. YANCEY, from the Committee of Claims, reported a bill for the relief of Thomas B. Farish; which was read twice, and committed.

Mr. ROBERTSON reported a bill confirming pre-emption rights given on the purchase of lands, to certain settlers in the State of Louisiana, and Territories of Missouri and Illinois; which was read twice, and committed to a Committee of the Whole.

Mr. NELSON, of Virginia, from the Committee on the Judiciary, reported that it was inexpedient to grant the prayer of the petition, for the removal of the district court, of the District of Maine, from the place where it is now held.—Agreed to.

Mr. CANNON laid before the House a resolution of the Legislature of Tennessee, requesting that the collection of the direct tax of the present year may be delayed wholly, or in part, to the next or a subsequent year; and also a resolution rejecting the amendments proposed to the Constitution of the United States by the States of Massachusetts and Connecticut.

The SPEAKER laid before the House the annual report of the Commissioners of the Sinking Fund.

On motion of Mr. INGHAM, the Secretary of the Treasury was requested to lay before the House a statement of the valuation of lands, &c., under the direct tax.

A message from the Senate informed the House that the Senate have passed bills of the following titles, to wit: "An act providing for the settlement of certain accounts against the Library of Congress, and for establishing the salary of the Librarian;" and "An act concerning certain courts of the United States in the State of New York;" in which bills they ask the concurrence of this House.

THE REVENUE.

The House resumed the consideration of the report of the Committee of Ways and Means, on the revenue.

The proposition to amend the resolve respecting the whiskey tax, by reducing the proposed addition of 100 per cent. on the capacity of the still to 50 per cent., was further debated at much length; supported by Messrs. CANNON, TAUL, THROOP, ROSS, McKEE, and YANCEY.

Mr. TAUL observed, that he had not expected to have participated in the debate on the subject now before the House. He was admonished, by his want of parliamentary experience, to be silent. Instead of attempting to lecture others, he felt it to be his duty to receive from them the lessons of wisdom and experience. In adhering to the resolution thus formed he had already (he hoped) profited much. To no member of this House had he listened with more pleasure as well as profit, than the honorable gentleman from South Carolina, at the head of the Committee of Ways and Means. Though he had the highest confidence in the opinions and views of that gentleman, and the members composing the committee, he believed that on this particular subject they were in an error; and, believing so, he should be an unfaithful public servant, were he to be silent. Should the resolution as reported by the committee be adopted, serious injury will be inflicted upon the Western country generally, without a countervailing benefit to the revenue of the country.

We are in Committee of the Whole on the state of the nation; and when thus in committee, it seems to be the fashion for gentlemen to express their opinion of the past, as well as their views of the present, and what ought to be the future course of policy to be pursued in this nation.

I do not purpose following the example which has been set. I will only observe, that my opposition to the resolution of the Committee of Ways and Means, does not proceed from a want of confidence in the Administration. The Administration has had, and still has my confidence. It has received my support to the extent of my feeble abilities. This country has contracted a very considerable debt in asserting its just rights. The revenue of the country should be equal, in time of peace, to the demands against it. I for one am decidedly in favor of raising this revenue; but I may differ with other gentlemen, as to the proper subjects of taxation; and when we agree as to the subjects of taxation, we may differ as to the amount. Such is the case, as to the tax proposed on licenses to distillers. The amount recommended by the committee to be continued, is in my opinion too high. While I agree in the general with gentlemen on this side of the House, I must be permitted to enter my protest against some of the projects I have heard recommended.

The honorable member of the Committee of Ways and Means (Mr. INGHAM) to whom the defence of this branch of the report seems to have been committed, in the remarks made by him last evening, observed that he expected the members of this House to have communicated the local information which they possessed in relation to the particular subject now under consideration, I thank the gentleman, sir, for this remark. At the time of the adoption of the Constitution of the United States, one of the most prominent objections against it, was, that the people would not be sufficiently represented, particularly in laying taxes. Gentlemen may talk of voting and taking that course which their judgment dictates; but the first principles of political science teach me to look to the situation, the wants, the feelings, and wishes of the people I represent. Sir, it is impossible to arrive at any just conclusions in legislative deliberations without adhering to those principles.

If one of the foreign tourists or journalists who travel through your country for the purpose of abusing it, had been in your gallery last evening and heard gentlemen narrating the various shifts and devices which they had understood had been resorted to, to evade the particular tax in question, he would have been much gratified. He would have flattered himself that he had conclusive evidence of everything that had been said or written to the disadvantage of this country—that our patriotism was idle rant, nothing of reality about it. Sir, unwise revenue laws will be evaded in every country; it is no reproach upon the people. I have no idea, however, that evasions have taken place to the extent which gentlemen suppose. The article of spirits distilled from domestic materials was taxed beyond what it could bear; hence, and hence only, the law was partially evaded. The tax may not be too high in some parts of the United States, particularly when distillation is carried on on a large capital. The committee doubtless labor under the impression, that the article in all parts of the United States will bear the tax; otherwise I am confident they would not have recommended it. The local information sought for by the honorable member before alluded to (Mr. INGHAM) most readily will I impart. I have no hesitation in stating it as a fact, that the heavy tax on spirits had the effect to prostrate nine out of ten of the distillers in the district which I represent. It is impossible for the manufacturer to sell the article for as much money as will pay the tax. A neighbor of mine (a distiller) informed me, not many days previous to my leaving home, that he had on hand nearly the whole of the spirits manufactured last Winter and Spring. He had paid the tax without being able to sell for money as much as would pay the one-twentieth part of the tax. This is not the case of a single individual only—it is the case of many, if not most of the distillers. Indeed I was credibly informed, previous to my leaving home, that the largest distillery in the district would not go into operation again under the existing rate of duties. Levy the tax contemplated, and it is certain death to all the small distilleries; the consequence of which will be a loss of all the capital invested in those establishments: besides the great loss to the farmer in not being able to convert his surplus grain into a less bulky article for importation, and the advantage of his distilling to his stock or cattle.

It is said, that the distiller has no cause of complaint; that the tax is paid by the consumer. Sir, it is true, that such is the belief, the expectation of most gentlemen; and the tax is laid under that impression. The practical result, however, proves the incorrectness of the theory. It would be correct, I grant you, if the article could be sold.

It is also contended, that, inasmuch as it is an article of luxury, it is a fit subject for taxation. It is perhaps not necessary to controvert the policy of the tax on principle, since there seems such a general, I may say almost unanimous determination to continue it in some shape. It ought to be recollected, however, that it is an article of luxury used by the poor, by the yeomanry of the country, by the laborer.

The wealthy part of the country can afford to use a beverage of a different quality. Imported spirits and the juice of the grape are theirs. It has always been deemed politic to tax articles of luxury, not because they were such, but because they were used by those whose income was considerable, and of course were able and ought to pay.

The honorable member from Louisiana (Mr. Robertson) certainly misunderstood my friend from Tennessee, (Mr. Cannon,) who moved the amendment, or he would not have imputed to him his being influenced by narrow views. He seems to have understood the gentleman from Tennessee as opposing the tax, solely on the ground of its inequality. Sir, it is unequal, highly unequal, as the gentleman from Tennessee has, in my opinion, clearly demonstrated; and this inequality ought to have great influence; but the gentleman from Tennessee opposed it, as I do, on broader ground. It is not only unequal, it is oppressive, ruinous; tax the article too high, and you prohibit its manufacture. Your revenue of course must be lost.

I am decidedly of opinion, that an addition of 50 per centum on licenses to distillers, will produce nearly, if not quite as much as 100 per cent., and I believe it is as heavy a duty as the article will bear.

But the gentleman from Louisiana says, that the spirit manufactured in the Western country is exported to the Orleans market and sold there. That honorable and enlightened gentleman well knows that the Orleans market is a very precarious one; that spirits distilled from grain or fruit is a dull article in the market at that port, as is almost every other article, the produce of Ohio, Kentucky, Tennessee, &c. This must be the case for many years to come. Such is the vast extent of fertile country, watered by the tributary streams of the Mississippi, that the Orleans market is generally glutted.

I do not pretend to have anything like a correct knowledge of the average price of whiskey, brandy, &c., at that market, but I doubt very much if an exporter could get the first cost of the article. I am well convinced that the exportation of this article from Kentucky, since the increased duty was laid, has been considered a bad business.

Sir, this is a dull subject; the House cannot be entertained with anything that could be said. Our opinion on estimating the amount of duty proper to be levied must be governed by practical results; a detail of which is all I have attempted.

Mr. Throop said, that the interest his constituents had in the subject in debate, made it his duty to submit a few arguments to the consideration of the Committee. He lamented, that at a period when we were left calmly to consider and adopt such measures as would contribute to the wealth of the country, repair its finances, and restore its credit, the productions of the interior of the Northern States should be selected as the prey of a system of revenue, which, in every other respect, had his entire approbation and support. He approved of that system, not merely because it would enable the Government to keep up proper military and naval establishments, but because it would produce an extinguishment of a national debt in a short period of time. He should vote for the motion, and should have liked it better had it been to reduce the increase on the capacity of stills to twenty-five per cent., and would have been better pleased with the bill, had it proposed to leave the capacity-tax as it now stood. He should not vote this reduction because he was opposed to a tax on whiskey; he thought it as fit a subject of taxation as anything presented by the pursuits of the country. Our country at present affords but few subjects for internal taxation, and none which operate with exact equality. The tax on whiskey is paid by the consumer, and the consumption is so universal that he thought the tax would operate more equally than any other which had been selected. But while he was willing it should be taxed, all he asked was, that it should be reasonable, and not so heavy as to suppress the business, or distress the farmer. He spoke of the productions of the interior of the Northern States as the prey of the system, for these reasons: the world is now at peace, the inhabitants are relieved from that desolating warfare, which, for a long period of time, had depressed their resources; they would now return to their agricultural pursuits, and would make the earth yield sufficient of all the articles of provision for their own consumption, and that of their colonies. The produce of the interior of the Northern States is wheat, corn, and other grain, which go to market, either in their natural state, or as pork and beef. While war continued in Europe, a demand was created in that part of the world for these articles, and this demand raised the price of them sufficiently high to bear transportation. The interior of the Northern States derived their wealth from the sale of their surplus produce in this manner. But by the peace these resources were cut off; their productions will not bear transportation to other parts of the United States, where there is a deficit of those articles. What were these people to do? They cannot raise cotton, tobacco, and sugar, productions of the Southern States, which bear so high a price, and enrich the planter. Their climate will not admit of it; they must either sink into poverty, or turn their produce into a more portable as well as marketable form. This can only be done by making it into whiskey. A high tax upon whiskey would not tend very much to reduce the quantity which will be made, nor will it operate against the large distiller. On the contrary, the large distiller would profit by it. He would extend his business with immense profit, for, by driving the small distiller from the business, he would be enabled to regulate the price both of the article manufactured, and the material of which it is made. There are many persons engaged in that business of small capitals, say two or three thousand dollars, and many farmers who distil the surplus produce of their own farms. The small manufacturers and farmers were driven from the business by the heavy duties imposed during the war, and will not return to it, if we continue a heavy duty. The effect will be, by driving so many purchasers of grain from the market, to destroy competition, and particularly competition between credit and money, and to place the farmer in the power of those who continue the business; the latter will fix the market price of grain, and ask what they please for the liquor. The small distiller will be compelled to relinquish the business, because he cannot sell his production for money to meet the demands of the tax-gatherer, which will amount for stills in ordinary use, at the proposed rates of duty, to seven or eight hundred dollars. The manufacturer will be enriched, but the farmer will be impoverished. But it is said that a system of taxation is a system of compromise, and, therefore, it is necessary to lay a heavy duty on whiskey to equalize the other taxes to be imposed. He replied, that he did not understand how that reasoning applied to this case. The objection was not to a tax, but to an enormous and oppressive tax. But how was this tax to counterbalance or equalize other taxes? Do we not pay our proportion of the imposts? We certainly do so in the consumption of foreign articles. Do we not pay our share of the duty on refined sugar? We do. Do we not pay our share of the stamp duty? I think we do. We may not have as much business directly with banks as in some other parts of the country; but the returns of that source of revenue show that it is in the first place paid in the great mercantile places, probably by merchants; and there can be no doubt but it is added to the price of the goods those merchants sell. Do we not pay our part of the duty on sales at auction? We do; for this also is paid in the first place by merchants, who add what they pay to the price of their merchandise. Do we not pay our proportion of the salt tax? We do; and it needs no argument to show that we pay our proportion of the land tax. We pay our proportion of every other internal tax imposed, and have superadded to it the license to distillers.

But, sir, said Mr. T., there is another point of view in which the tax under consideration is very popular. It is said that the excessive use of ardent spirits is immoral. It is true, sir, that it is a vice, a deep-rooted vice; but it finds soil in the passions and propensities of man. I would gladly suppress it. But will you suppress it by imposing upon it a tax? No, sir. He who indulges in it knows that it leads directly to disease, poverty, and disgrace. If these are not sufficient restraints upon his appetite, vain will be the attempt to restrain him by increasing the price of the article. His inclinations will be indulged, and if he cannot find their gratification in the home production, he will seek the foreign. If, sir, it is intended seriously to suppress the vice, we set about it in the wrong way. It can be done only by prohibiting, under some penalties, the

manufacture or importation of liquors. It, then, becomes every nation to develope its own resources, and by judicious laws to bring into action every pursuit which will add to its wealth. While man will indulge his appetite for spirituous liquors, it becomes our Government to encourage its manufacture at home, as one of the sources of national wealth. From the experience we have already had, we can form our conclusions to what extent it may be made to supply the place of importations. It is not only used in the simple form of whiskey, but after going through the process of rectification, by which the essential oil and offensive taste is extracted, it is made into gin, and mixed with rum and brandy. It may be in some cases practised as fraud, but the habit of mixing is so universal, and well understood, that the merchant will sell you, as brandy and rum, the mixed liquors at a reduced price. It forms a liquor less prejudicial than the mixture of poisonous drugs we receive from abroad, and, when skilfully done, would require a nice palate to distinguish it from unmixed liquors. Should, then, this manufacture be properly encouraged, it would, ere long, almost wholly supersede the necessity of importing those liquors, and thus stop to enrich our own soil, that flood of wealth which issues from it, for the purpose of those articles. It remains to be considered how the amendment proposed will affect the revenue.

The Committee of Ways and Means propose to raise, by this duty, $2,400,000. If we look at the proceeds of this tax it will be seen, that during the year 1814, the licenses to distillers produced about $1,688,000. If the amendment prevails, and the returns of 1814 be considered a correct data to judge of its produce, it will yield to the revenue between $2,500,000 and $2,600,000, being a sum more than is required. He believed, however, that it would produce more. If the heavy war excise is taken off, many persons will engage in the business, and the want of a foreign market for produce will compel the farmers to have their grain manufactured. Hence, as the manufacture increases, the revenue will also increase. But, should the estimate of the proceeds of the present capacity duty be correct, that is to say $1,200,000, then the addition of fifty per cent., as proposed by the amendment, would produce $1,800,000, leaving a deficit of $600,000. He said he believed that deficit would be abundantly supplied from other sources of revenue. The public lands were estimated to produce one million, but it will be seen that the revenue received from that source during the year 1815, amounted to nearly two and a half millions; and he had no doubt, from the excellence of the lands the Government had for sale, and the immense emigration to the Western countries, that those lands would be much more productive to the revenue than they have ever been. But even should this fail, we have, after making all the appropriations contemplated, a surplus revenue of more than two millions, from which the deficit may be supplied. And he thought it would be better to do so, should we be compelled to it, than to suppress a very important manufacture of the country.

Messrs. ROBERTSON, LOWNDES, SMITH, of Maryland, and TAYLOR, of New York, opposed the motion. It was negatived by a very small majority.

Mr. McLEAN, of Kentucky, then moved to amend the resolve, so as to equalize the rate of a license to distil per week, month, &c., to the rate of the license per year; which motion was agreed to by a majority of twenty or thirty votes.

The main resolution, to repeal the duty on the quantity of spirits distilled, and to increase the duty on the capacity of the still 100 per cent, was then agreed to.

The next resolution was then taken up, as follows, viz:

Resolved, That it is expedient to repeal the act, entitled "An act to provide additional revenues for defraying the expenses of Government, and maintaining the public credit, by laying duties on household furniture, and on gold and silver watches," passed on the 18th of January, 1815.

Mr. JACKSON, of Virginia, Mr. SOUTHARD, and Mr. ROSS, opposed the agreement to this resolution, on the ground of the equity of the tax, and the practicability of amending it so as to defeat the evasion of it, and to make it more productive.

Mr. LOWNDES defended the resolve, on the ground of the unproductiveness of the tax, having been calculated to produce $1,200,000, and producing in fact, only $70,000; though willing to listen and accede to any definite proposition for rendering it efficient and productive.

Mr. FORSYTH moved to amend the resolve, by adding at the end thereof the words, "except so far as relates to the duty on gold and silver watches." This motion was negatived.

Mr. JACKSON, of Virginia, then moved to amend the resolve, so as to embrace the continuance of the duty on household furniture, &c., "and also to provide against the evasion of said law." This motion was negatived—66 to 68.

The resolve of the Committee of Ways and Means was then agreed to by the Committee—ayes 66.

The remaining resolution was then taken up, as follows:

Resolved, That it is expedient so to amend the rates of duties upon imported articles, after the 30th of June next, as that they shall be estimated to produce an amount equal to that which would be produced by an average addition of 42 per cent. to the permanent rates of duties.

Agreed to without a division.

The Committee then rose, and reported their proceedings to the House.

Mr. LOWNDES, from the Committee of Ways and Means, reported a bill to carry into effect the proposition respecting the direct tax, (adopted by the House the other day,) which bill was twice read, and committed.

And on motion, the House adjourned until to-morrow.

FRIDAY, February 9.

The bill from the Senate "providing for the settlement of certain accounts against the Library of Congress, and for establishing the salary of the Librarian," was read twice, and committed to a Committee of the Whole.

The bill from the Senate "concerning certain courts of the United States in the State of New York," was read twice, and referred to the Committee on the Judiciary.

Ordered, That the Committee of the whole House to whom is committed the bill for the relief of the Canadian refugees who joined the American army during the late war with Great Britain, be discharged from a farther consideration thereof, and that it be committed to the Committee of the whole House on the bill making provision for an additional military academy.

Mr. BURWELL, from the committee appointed on the petition of Dr. James Smith, reported a bill supplementary to "An act to encourage vaccination;" which was read twice, and committed to a Committee of the Whole.

Mr. KING, of Massachusetts, rose to make some observations in reply to some remarks from Mr. WILDE, which he had seen in the *National Intelligencer*, but which, not having distinctly heard, he had permitted to pass without reply, which he should not have done had he understood them. Mr. K. was proceeding to speak on this subject, when the Speaker reminded him that no debate could be permitted unless on some question before the House; in the justice of which Mr. K. acquiescing, waived his remarks until a fit occasion should offer for them.

Mr. WARD, of Massachusetts, offered for consideration the following resolutions:

Resolved, That all duties, imports, and excises, laid by Congress, ought not only to be laid uniformly throughout the United States, agreeably to the provision in the Constitution, but ought to be collected in all parts of the United States in the same currency, or in currencies equivalent in value.

Resolved, That the Secretary of the Treasury be instructed to receive, alone, in payment of duties, imposts, and excises, and debts due to the United States, gold, silver, and copper coin, Treasury notes, and the notes of such banks as pay specie for their bills, excepting in cases in which it is otherwise provided by law.

Mr. WARD briefly assigned his reasons for offering these propositions, which will be found concisely and clearly stated in the first of the above resolutions.

Mr. SMITH, of Maryland, rose to speak; but, on motion of Mr. TUCKER, the resolutions were laid on the table for the present.

INQUIRY RESPECTING OFFICE, &c.

Mr. RANDOLPH rose to make the motion of which he gave notice the day before yesterday, to inquire into the constitutionality of the late appointment of General P. B. Porter, not having got to the House in time to make it yesterday. It was not his purpose, he said, to amplify on this occasion at all. The House would recollect that

at the time he had submitted notice of this motion he had distinctly stated that it was not for him to pronounce whether the office in question had or had not been created during the time for which the late honorable member of this House from New York had been elected to serve. Some very obliging friend had been kind enough to hint to him that perhaps he had not pondered on the subject so well as he ought to have done before he introduced it to the House; that this office, under the authority of the United States, being created by the Treaty, was called into existence, although it remained vacant until lately, at the moment when the exchange of the ratifications of that treaty took place. This might or might not be, Mr. R. said; for, what was this argument but to assume (he would not say to beg) the very question concerning the treaty-making power which this House had already once decided in the negative, viz., that a treaty, without the intervention, instrumentality, without the aid of this House, is *ipso facto* the law of the land. Mr. R. said he should be extremely ashamed ever to venture so crude a motion in this House as this would have been, if he had not taken into consideration, and deep and mature consideration. too, the point which some were obliging enough to suppose he had overlooked, and civil enough to put him right in respect to it. If he understood the doctrines which he had heard, he did not say uttered, on this floor, in respect to the treaty-making power, this case of the honorable member from New York, who had recently vacated his seat in this House, came fully within the purview of the article in the Constitution of the United States; and he would go further, as special pleading was the order of the day, and say that if it did not come within its purview in this view of the subject, it nevertheless would in another. It did not follow, it was not logic, he said—it might be logic in Westminster Hall, but it was not in Parliament—that because the appointment in question did not come within the purview of this section for particular reasons, it might not for some other very substantial reason, which was not disclosed, but about which he had no concealment, as he had not, never had, and never would have, about public men or measures. After reading the following clause from the sixth section of the first article of the Constitution, viz: "No Senator or Repre-
'sentative shall, during the time for which he
' was elected, be appointed to any civil office un-
' der the authority of the United States, which
' shall have been created, or the emoluments
' whereof shall have been increased during such
' time"—Mr. R. moved

"That a committee be appointed to inquire whether the acceptance, by the Hon. Peter B. Porter, late a member of this House from the State of New York, of a civil office under the authority of the United States, does contravene the provisions of the sixth section of the first article of the Constitution of the United States."

Mr. FORSYTH suggested that the terms of this motion did not embrace the question which he

understood the gentleman to desire to place before the House—the acceptance of a civil office not being an offence against any provision of the Constitution of the United States. He should be pleased to see it modified so as to place the question distinctly before the House.

Mr. RANDOLPH said he had no objection to any modification which would attain his object. He bottomed himself, in proposing this inquiry, on facts which are on record, and which the House was presumed to know. Had not the gentleman vacated his seat in this House? Was he amenable to the order of the Speaker as a member of this House? How did his seat become vacated? By his acceptance of a civil office under the authority of the United States, which the gentleman from Georgia had said was no offence against the Constitution? No, said Mr. R., it is neither an offence against the Constitution, nor *contra bonos mores*, that I know; but there is a modification of the proposition which may make it contrary to the Constitution—the Committee are to try that question. Is there not an issue made up? The honorable gentleman has accepted an office; it is our duty to inquire whether the acceptance of. it be Constitutional or not, because, if unconstitutional, then it is the duty of this House to see that the breach is repaired, that the wrong is redressed. Mr. R. said he was not acquainted with the styles and titles of the gentleman in question; he had had a great many; with the old one he was acquainted, with the new one he was not. Mr. R. said he had no more doubt that this appointment was a breach of the Constitution than the acceptance of another office by a late member of this House, the office having been created and the salary fixed a few days before his term of service expired, was an evasion, and scandalous evasion, of the provision of the Constitution which he had just quoted.

Mr. FORSYTH having suggested a modification of the motion, declaring at the same time that he should not vote for the inquiry, Mr. RANDOLPH accepted it, so as to read as follows:

"*Resolved*, That a committee be appointed to inquire whether the acceptance, by the Hon. Peter B. Porter, of the office of Commissioner under the late Treaty of Ghent, is in contravention of the sixth section of the first article in the Constitution of the United States."

On suggestion of Mr. WRIGHT, the words "appointment and" were inserted before the word "acceptance."

The question having been stated on the adoption of the resolve—

Mr. FORSYTH rose and said, it was with much reluctance he opposed any motion, the object of which was inquiry into alleged abuses under Government. But the appointment of a committee on this occasion, appeared to him so totally unnecessary, that he was compelled to oppose it. If he had understood the gentleman from Virginia, his idea was, that the office had been created during the time for which the gentleman in question had been elected to serve in this House. But the person named in the resolve had been elected to serve from the 4th of March, 1815, to the 4th of March, 1817. The office which he had accepted, had existence prior to the 4th of March, 1815; or it is not yet created. Either it has no existence, or it existed from the day on which the ratifications of the Treaty of Peace were exchanged—the 18th February, 1815. If the office was created by the Treaty of Peace, the acceptance of it was certainly no violation of the letter or spirit of the Constitution. If it was necessary this House should act on the treaty before the office has being, then Peter B. Porter has accepted no office; the office he is said to have accepted having no existence. The gentleman from Virginia seems to suppose, said Mr. F., that the doctrines maintained by this House as to the treaty-making power, are adverse to the idea of the office having been created by the treaty. Not so, said Mr. F., those doctrines are perfectly consistent with the idea that this office was created by the convention. It is not pretended that Commissioners for any purpose of foreign intercourse, as regulated by treaty, may not be created by the President and Senate; on the contrary, according to my understanding, the office is correctly created by the President and Senate, and entirely within their power. The agreement between the two Governments that certain questions should be settled by Commissioners, required not the sanction of this House, further than it would become necessary for the House to make an appropriation to pay them for their services. If their services were to be compensated by any act of this House which Peter B. Porter had assisted in passing, there would be some evidence of a violation of the Constitution; that no such fact existed, nor any other that was sufficient to authorize this House to inquire into the subject.

Mr. RANDOLPH said, the honorable gentleman's dilemma, which he had so triumphantly presented to the House, carried on its horns no terrors for him. The honorable gentleman ought to be obliged to him, he said, for having, by timely notice of this motion, given him an opportunity to sharpen the horns of his dilemma. They reminded him, he said, of a circumstance attending the exhibition of the bull-fights of the Portuguese, in their ancient and better days—the horns of the animal turned out were covered with leather; they threatened, but wounded not; and that is the case, said he, with the horns with which the gentleman makes full butt at me. The gentleman had said, that the office to which the late member from New York was appointed, has been in existence from the 18th day of February last; or, because the House has not definitively acted on the treaty, the office itself is yet in embryo, ready to be called, but not yet springing into existence. Would the honorable gentleman from Georgia tell this House, and would he tell this nation that to appoint to an office not in existence, and to accept an office which has no existence, is no offence? On the contrary, Mr. R. said, if the office was not in existence, then the indecent hurry to reward a political partisan with some of the fruits of the war, which was concocted under his

auspices, called forth the decisive interference and correction of this House. So much for that horn of the dilemma—that horn, said he, I think is sawed off—the other will not remain on much longer. But this office was created by the treaty. Does it therefore follow, that it does not come within the purview of the part of the provision of the Constitution which I have read? There was not an instant of time from the creation of the office, be it created when it will, that the acceptor of the office was not a member of this House. Mr. R. here spoke of the precise time when the term of service of a new Congress commences—mathematically, at midnight of the 3d of March; politically, at that moment the index of the clock of the House, set backwards or forwards, to suit circumstances, pointed to twelve o'clock, &c. Was there a moment, he asked, from the creation of the office, supposing it to have been created under the treaty, in which that gentleman was not a member of this House? He would go farther—was not the acceptor of the office a member of the House pending the discussion of the question, whether the treaty should or should not be carried into effect by a vote of this House? [Mr. R. was here informed, that he was not.] I am mistaken, it appears, said he; I retract this inference—I do not say recant it; for I detest all sorts of canting, and particularly recanting. If the office had been created by the Treaty of Peace, Mr. R. said it did not follow that the honorable member was (if he might coin a word) appointable to that office? If the Constitution forbade the appointment of a member to an office, the salary of which was increased during the term for which he was elected, *a fortiori* the creation of the salary constitutes the same impediment. The gentleman from Georgia had told the House he deemed this inquiry wholly unnecessary. Mr. R. said, if he had understood the honorable gentleman's arguments during the discussion of the question lately decided by this House, respecting the treaty, he should have been led to believe, that of all the members of this body, he was that member to whom the necessity of such an inquiry would be obvious, and the propriety of it most readily acknowledged. Mr. R. said, he was not without expectations, knowing the honorable gentleman's lead in this House, that he would be a member of the committee, if raised, and would have an opportunity of showing much more satisfactorily than he had done this morning, of establishing, by facts and deductions too, that the appointment of Peter B. Porter was not a contravention of the Constitution. The inquiry would do very little harm, in any view. Mr. R. said that, for one, he was certainly not much pestered with committee business, and if the inquiry should devolve on him, he should endeavor to execute it to the best of his capacity—he certainly would present a report that would embrace all the facts; and he would endeavor to state even the law of the case as well as he could, in his hobbling way—not being even journeyman in the profession. If this inquiry was denied, Mr. R. said, he could easily come at his object in another way; he had only to lay a resolution on the table, that such an appointment was contrary to the provisions of the Constitution. But, if facts were wanted, a committee ought to be appointed to get them. We ought to reason from facts, and not to them. As to the legal question, Mr. R. said, he should not set much value on this particular clause of the Constitution, if it were not that it was a part of it, and his vote could not put it in or expunge it. He was no Constitution-monger or fancier—he took the Constitution, *ita scripta est*, as he found it. This clause was not, he repeated, of any value, as to its effect; it was about as good a fence around this House against the temptation of office, as the accountability at the Treasury was fence around it against the public robber. If you want mischievous stock on your farm or plantation, he said, you must keep bad fences; if you would have roguish hogs, cows, and horses, keep bad fences—those who would not otherwise have ventured to jump over a straw, will in that way soon learn to jump, as we say in the Southern country, over ten rails and a rider. As a fence round the purity of this House he said, this part of the Constitution was of little or no value—he considered it of none, and rather worse than none. The warnings of Patrick Henry and George Mason on this article of the Constitution were yet ringing in his ears. This clause, he said, was a stalking-horse, put into the Constitution, as if there was some guard set against the appointment of a member of the House by the Executive to office—some guard against the establishment of Executive influence over this body. There is none, said he. It is as good a defence as a fishing seine would be against a constant shower of rain. You may dart straws through it; and the honorable members from New York and Georgia have amused themselves with darting straws through it. It was so easy a thing, he said, to put new men in old offices, and old men in new, that the only thing that astonished him in this business was, the indecency of the appointment of such a man to such an office, in contravention of the Constitution—such a man, he said, for he had the honor of serving on the Committee of Foreign Relations with him during the session which ended in the declaration of war—the gentleman had been at that time chairman of the Committee of Foreign Relations—but he had vacated that office. Mr. R. said, he had nothing to do with that honorable gentleman, except in his public character as a member of this body—and, knowing the agency which he had had, at least at the eleventh hour—he returned to the war feast at the eleventh hour—knowing the agency he had had in bringing about the war, he was only astonished, when he considered how easy it was to get in, over, and around this provision of the Constitution, at the indelicacy with which it has been violated in this instance.

Mr. Forsyth said, he regretted that the gentleman from Virginia should have supposed he had come to the House with his horns sharpened to wound him. I had no such intention, said Mr. F.; whilst I continue a member of this House

with that honorable gentleman, all that I expect is to escape his horns. Mr. F. said, that he had no intention to say, that an appointment to an office not created, was no violation of the Constitution; but it was no violation of the particular section of the Constitution which the gentleman had quoted. The inquiry was limited in its object, and if I show to the satisfaction of the House, said Mr. F., that there was no violation of the particular article of the Constitution, whether the office was or was not created, my object is answered. The honorable gentleman had said enough to show that he was mistaken in the facts which had induced him to submit this motion. The gentleman seemed to suppose that the late member from New York had been a member of Congress at the time of the ratification of the Treaty of Peace; but he was not at any time a member of the last Congress, having become a member on the 4th day of March last, a day posterior to the creation of the office, if the office were at all created.   •

With respect to the observation respecting the selection of such a man, Mr. F. observed he would say nothing; the appointment was before the people, for them to approve or condemn, and he trusted their decision would not be influenced, or at all affected by the observations of the gentleman from Virginia. Of General Porter, Mr. F. said, he knew nothing, but as he knew him here; he would, he doubted not, as well discharge the duties of his office as any gentleman who could have been appointed.

[Mr. Randolph here explained. He had said nothing of the moral character of Mr. Porter. He had spoke of him as one of the agents in producing the war, and as being now rewarded by the fruits of the peace. He spoke of him and his appointment in that light only.]

Mr. F. said he knew not, as he had not been a member of the Twelfth Congress, how far he had an agency in producing that war. Such an agency would, in the eyes of the gentleman, be a crime—in his eyes, Mr. F. said, it was no crime; and he believed by the people generally it was not regarded as a criminal act. Mr. F. said he did not precisely understand the force of the gentleman's allusion to his having darted straws through the Constitution; so far as he understood the provisions of this Constitution, he had scrupulously obeyed its injunctions. He should do so with the same spirit of sincerity as the gentleman from Virginia, or any other gentleman. The gentleman from Virginia might have intended to intimate that the doctrines of Mr. F. were contradictory or inconsistent in regard to the construction of the Constitution; but to himself, Mr. F. said, it was sufficiently clear there was no contradiction between them; and the gentleman from Virginia must forgive me, said he, for preferring my own judgment in this respect to his.

Mr. Wright was desirous to see a spirit of scrutiny prevail, but he did not wish to see it unnecessarily exerted. The provision of the Constitution which had been quoted, he said, was intended to guard against the creation of office, and the increase of emolument, by members of Congress, for the benefit of themselves. This appointment, however, cannot come within the purview of this provision of the Constitution. Did the treaty create the office; and, if it did, was that the kind of office which the Constitution had contemplated? He contended not. The terms of the treaty did not create the right, he argued, but imposed the obligation to appoint those Commissioners. The office to which the late member of this House was appointed, he considered not a civil but a ministerial office, for the execution of international objects. The President did not derive from the treaty his authority to appoint these Commissioners, but from the Constitution. The office was made necessary by the treaty, but the obligation to make the appointment is imposed by the Constitution. The office was created by the Constitution; the necessity of the appointment was created by the treaty. But even the treaty was ratified before the acceptor of this office became a member of this House; and the emolument attached to it had been neither diminished nor increased whilst he was a member. Mr. W., therefore, expressed his hope that his honorable friend from Virginia, for whom he had a great respect, particularly on account of his investigating spirit, would withdraw his motion; and that, if it was not withdrawn, it would not be agreed to.

Mr. RANDOLPH said he did not set up for the model of the gentleman from Georgia, or any other gentleman; he was the keeper of no man's conscience, the arbiter of no man's opinions. The consistency of the gentleman's opinions was his own affair; but if they are what I consider inconsistent, said Mr. R., it is my affair, and I must retain my opinion, however reluctant to think so of his opinions, &c. If the gentleman from Maryland had succeeded in convincing him that the appointment in question was not an office, Mr. R. said, he should certainly withdraw his proposition; but he had not succeeded. The words of the Constitution are—"any civil office under the authority of the United States." If the appointment in question be not an office, he said he should like to know what an office is. What could the duty of Commissioners be resolved into, if it was not resoluble into an office? If it were not an office, he asked, what was it? *Officium*—it had every character of an office, filled by the regular Constitutional power, the acceptance of which was incompatible with a seat on this floor. The acceptor of the office was himself conscious he could not retain his seat on this floor; he would have been very glad, I have no doubt, said Mr. R.—I judge of other men by no unfair criterion—he would have been very glad to have held his seat—for I have seen nothing in the history of the gentleman which leads me to suppose he has any very violent objection to pluralities. Mr. R. then proceeded to reply to Mr. WRIGHT's argument, and appealed to the older members of the House—to the fathers in point of age—and particularly to the honorable gentleman from North Carolina, (Mr. STANFORD,) who, he

said, was the father of the House, as being the oldest member—he appealed to them for the doctrines laid down in 1793, and particularly by Mr. Gallatin, then a member from Pennsylvania, in respect to the power and discretion residing in the President and Senate as to the appointment of Ministers, &c., and stated more amply his argument in favor of the inquiry in this particular case.

Mr. GROSVENOR briefly examined this case. He did not incline to believe that the Constitutional objections to the appointment in question could be sustained. This appeared to be his general impression; but, as there were great doubts on the minds of some gentlemen, and he was not himself perfectly satisfied as to the question, the inquiry ought to be had. We ought never, said Mr. G., to permit the Executive to set his foot in this House without inquiry, nor even to suffer a suspicion to exist of his having done so.

Mr. FORSYTH spoke in explanation and reply to some incidental remarks by Mr. RANDOLPH when last up.

Mr. RANDOLPH explained in turn; and answered some of Mr. GROSVENOR's observations, &c.

Mr. GROSVENOR and Mr. WRIGHT further replied to Mr. RANDOLPH's observations on the construction of the Constitution; the first favoring, the other opposing the inquiry.

Mr. STANFORD advocated the inquiry, and quoted the records to show that the House had decided a violation of the spirit of the Constitution to be a sufficient ground for them to protest against the case in which it occurred. If he were, indeed, the *father* of the House, according to the figure used by Mr. RANDOLPH, he said he would advise its members to avoid the crumbs of office from the Executive, and to look to the People only, to whom they owed their appointments, as the source of honor, &c.

Mr. YATES, besides showing by argument the weakness of the grounds on which this motion was sustained, vindicated General Porter from any intimations or insinuations which had been thrown out unfavorable to him in the course of debate. He adverted to his high character and conduct, and particularly to his disinterestedness in supporting the late war, if he had contributed to it as was said; since, in so doing, he had devoted to certain destruction an immensely valuable property lying on the shores of the Niagara, which had since fallen a sacrifice, &c.

The question was then taken on Mr. RANDOLPH's motion, as modified, and agreed to—70 votes to 55.

Mr. RANDOLPH, Mr. GROSVENOR, Mr. FORSYTH, Mr. JACKSON, and Mr. YATES, were appointed the said committee.

THE REVENUE.

The House then resumed the consideration of the report of the Committee of the Whole on the remaining proposition of the Committee of Ways and Means.

The proposition respecting the duty on distillation (to repeal the duty on the quantity of spirits distilled, and to add one hundred per cent. to the present tax on the capacity of the still) first came up.

Mr. THROOP moved to amend the proposition by striking out one hundred and inserting fifty in lieu thereof, so as to reduce the additional capacity tax from one hundred to fifty per cent. on the existing duty.

This motion was decided without debate: For the amendment 74, against it 70, as follows:

YEAS—Messrs. Adgate, Alexander, Baer, Baker, Bassett, Bennett, Birdseye, Blount, Breckenridge, Brooks, Burnside, Burwell, Caldwell, Cannon, Clarke of North Carolina, Clark of Kentucky, Comstock, Crawford, Creighton, Culpeper, Darlington, Desha, Edwards, Glasgow, Goodwyn, Griffin, Hahn, Hardin, Hawes, Heister, Henderson, Hungerford, Jackson, Johnson of Kentucky, Kerr of Virginia, Love, Lumpkin, Lyle, Maclay, McCoy, McKee, McLean of Kentucky, McLean of Ohio, Moore of South Carolina, Ormsby, Parris, Pickens, Piper, Pleasants, Powell, Roane, Root, Ross, Savage, Schenck, Sharpe, Sheffey, Smith of Virginia, Southard, Stanford, Stuart, Taul, Thomas, Throop, Tucker, Wallace, Ward of New York, Whiteside, Williams, Willoughby, Thomas Wilson, William Wilson, Woodward, and Yancey.

NAYS—Messrs. Archer, Barbour, Bateman, Bayliss, Betts, Brigham, Brown, Cady, Calhoun, Chappell, Cilley, Clayton, Condict, Connen, Cuthbert, Davenport, Forney, Gaston, Gold, Goldsborough, Grosvenor, Hale, Hall, Hanson, Herbert, Huger, Hulbert, Ingham, Jewett, Kent, King of Massachusetts, King of North Carolina, Langdon, Law, Lovett, Lowndes, Lyon, Mason, Mayrant, Mills, Milnor, Moseley, Nelson of Massachusetts, Nelson of Virginia, Newton, Noyes, Pickering, Pitkin, Randolph, Rice, Robertson, Ruggles, Sergeant, Smith of Pennsylvania, Smith of Maryland, Stearns, Sturges, Taggart, Tallmadge, Taylor of New York, Taylor of South Carolina, Telfair, Vose, Ward of Massachusetts, Wheaton, Wilcox, Wilde, Wright and Yates.

So the amendment was agreed to.

Mr. GOLDSBOROUGH then moved further to amend the resolve so as to exempt from this addition to the capacity-tax on stills, such stills as shall be wholly employed in the distillation of spirits derived from fruit, herbs, and roots.

This motion was opposed by Mr. LOWNDES and Mr. ROSS, (by the latter on the ground of the impossibility of guarding the duty, thus modified, from evasion,) and was negatived, by yeas and nays—107 to 36—as follows:

YEAS—Messrs. Archer, Baer, Baker, Bennett, Bradbury, Bryan, Burwell, Clarke of North Carolina, Condict, Cooper, Crawford, Forney, Glasgow, Gold, Goldsborough, Hanson, Hawes, Herbert, Huger, Hungerford, Jackson, Johnson of Kentucky, Kerr of Virginia, King of North Carolina, Lewis, Maclay, McKee, Parris, Pickens, Piper, Pleasants, Roane, Stanford, Taylor of South Carolina, Williams, and Wright.

NAYS—Messrs. Adgate, Alexander, Barbour, Bassett, Bateman, Bayliss, Birdseye, Blount, Boss, Breckenridge, Brigham, Brooks, Brown, Burnside, Cady, Caldwell, Calhoun, Cannon, Chappell, Cilley, Clark of Kentucky, Clayton, Comstock, Creighton, Culpeper, Cuthbert, Darlington, Davenport, Desha, Findley, Forsyth, Gaston, Goodwyn, Griffin, Grosvenor, Hahn, Hale, Hall, Hardin, Heister, Henderson, Hulbert,

Ingham, Irving of New York, Jewett, Kent, King of Massachusetts, Langdon, Law, Love, Lovett, Lowndes, Lumpkin, Lyon, Mason, Mayrant, McCoy, McLean of Kentucky, McLean of Ohio, Mills, Milnor, Moore of South Carolina, Moseley, Nelson of Massachusetts, Nelson of Virginia, Newton, Ormsby, Pickering, Pitkin, Powell, Rice, Robertson, Root, Ross, Ruggles, Sergeant, Savage, Schenck, Sheffey, Smith of Pennsylvania, Smith of Maryland, Smith of Va., Southard, Stearns, Sturges, Taggart, Tallmadge, Taul, Taylor of New York, Telfair, Thomas, Throop, Vose, Wallace, Ward of Massachusetts, Ward of New York, Webster, Wheaton, Whiteside, Wilcox, Wilde, Wilkin, Willoughby, William Wilson, Woodward, Yancey, and Yates.

A motion was then made by Mr. THOMAS further to amend the said seventh resolution, by striking out all thereof after the word "expedient," and to insert as follows:

"To repeal the act entitled 'An act laying duties on licenses to distillers of spirituous liquors,' passed on the 24th of December, 1813; also the act entitled 'An act laying a duty on spirits distilled within the United States,' passed on the 21st of December, 1814, and that in lieu thereof, that all stills, boilers, and other instruments of machinery adapted to the distillation of spirits, be assessed and taxed in proportion to their assessed value, at a ratio corresponding with the tax paid in each of the States upon the hundred dollars' worth of lands and slaves."

And the question thereon being taken, it was determined in the negative.

Mr. KING, of Massachusetts, took the opportunity of pursuing the course of remarks indicated at the commencement of to-day's proceedings, in reply to Mr. WILDE's observations on Monday last, as reported in the *National Intelligencer*—to which Mr. WILDE replied at some length.

This debate lasted some time; and, when it terminated, the House adjourned without deciding the main question on the proposition of the Financial Committee.

SATURDAY, February 10.

Mr. YANCEY, from the Committee of Claims, reported a bill for the relief of Charles Todd; which was read twice, and committed to a Committee of the Whole.

Mr. POWELL, from the committee appointed on the petition of Thomas H. Boyle, made a report thereon, which was read; when Mr. P. presented a bill for the relief of Thomas H. Boyle; which was read, and committed to a Committee of the Whole.

The Committee on Military Affairs were discharged from a further consideration of the letter from the Secretary of War, transmitting information relative to the execution of the act fixing the Military Peace Establishment, and the said letter was ordered to lie on the table.

Mr. EASTON presented a resolution of the Legislature of the Territory of Missouri, respecting the leasing and working the lead mines belonging to the United States in said Territory; which was referred to the Committee on the Public Lands.

On motion of Mr. McKEE,

Resolved, That the President of the United States be requested to have laid before this House such of the accounts of James Thomas, late a Deputy Quartermaster General of the United States, as relate to purchases made, or expenses incurred, under any order of General Smyth, in the years 1812 and 1813, together with all the evidence relating to such accounts, and the manner in which the said accounts were settled, and the principles established in the settlement thereof.

Mr. McKEE and Mr. HERBERT were appointed a committee to present the said resolution to the President.

The SPEAKER laid before the House a report from the Secretary of War, on the memorial of William Tatham; which was read, and referred to the Committee on Military Affairs.

On motion of Mr. ROOT, the Committee on the Copper Coin were instructed to inquire into the expediency of increasing the alloy, or reducing the weight of the small silver coin of the United States.

THE REVENUE.

The House then resumed the consideration of the report of the Committee of Ways and Means, being the seventh resolution thereof, as amended by the Committee of the Whole, as follows:

Resolved, That it is expedient to repeal the act to provide additional revenues for defraying the expenses of Government and maintaining the public credit, by laying duties on spirits distilled within the United States and the Territories thereof, and by amending the act laying duties on licenses to distillers of spirituous liquors, passed on the 21st of December, 1814, excepting only the 16th, 18th, 19th, and 24th sections thereof, from and after the first day of April next, and from the same day to add fifty per centum to the amount of the duty which all stills, now subject to duty, are liable to pay; and that the act imposing duties on licenses to distillers be so amended, that licenses granted for periods of time less than a year, shall be paid for in proportion to the time for which they are granted.

On the adoption of this resolution, the question was decided in the affirmative, by yeas and nays, without further debate. For the resolution 105, against it, 37, as follows:

YEAS—Messrs. Alexander, Atherton, Baker, Barbour, Bassett, Baylies, Bennett, Betts, Birdsall, Birdseye, Blount, Boss, Breckenridge, Brigham, Bryan, Burnside, Burwell, Caldwell, Calhoun, Cannon, Cilley, Clarke of North Carolina, Clendennin, Comstock, Conner, Culpeper, Cuthbert, Darlington, Desha, Forney, Forsyth, Gaston, Gold, Goodwyn, Griffin, Hahn, Hammond, Hardin, Hawes, Heister, Henderson, Hulbert, Hungerford, Ingham, Jackson, Johnson of Kentucky, Kerr of Virginia, King of Massachusetts, King of North Carolina, Lewis, Love, Lowndes, Lumpkin, Lyle, Maclay, Mayrant, McCoy, McKee, McLean of Kentucky, Mills, Moore of South Carolina, Nelson of Virginia, Newton, Ormsby, Parris, Pickens, Pickering, Piper, Pleasants, Powell, Roane, Root, Ross, Ruggles, Sergeant, Savage, Schenck, Sheffey, Smith of Pennsylvania, Smith of Maryland, Smith of Virginia,

Southard, Stanford, Stearns, Stuart, Taul, Taylor of New York, Taylor of South Carolina, Telfair, Thomas, Throop, Tucker, Wallace, Ward of New York, Wendover, Wheaton, Whiteside, Wilde, Wilkin, Williams, Thomas Wilson, William Wilson, Woodward, Yancey, and Yates.

NAYS—Messrs. Baer, Bateman, Bradbury, Brown, Cady, Champion, Clayton, Condict, Davenport, Goldsborough, Grosvenor, Hale, Hopkinson, Huger, Irving of New York, Jewett, Kent, Langdon, Law, Lovett, Lyon, Mason, Milnor, Moseley, Nelson of Massachusetts, Noyes, Pitkin, Randolph, Reed, Rice, Strong, Taggart, Vose, Ward of Massachusetts, Ward of New Jersey, Wilcox, and Wright.

The House then proceeded to the consideration of the ninth resolution, reported by the Committee of Ways and Means, as follows:

Resolved, That it is expedient to repeal the act, entitled " An act to provide additional revenues for defraying the expenses of Government and maintaining the public credit, by laying duties on household furniture and gold and silver watches," passed on the 18th of January, 1815.

Mr. JACKSON of Virginia, moved to amend the resolution, so as to make it read as follows:

" *Resolved,* That it is expedient to continue the act laying duties on household furniture and gold and silver watches; and so to amend the said act as to insure the faithful execution thereof, and to guard against its violation, by specifying the articles liable to taxation, and the amount to be levied on each article, or by requiring a valuation to be made by the owner on both."

Mr. JACKSON said, he would submit his proposition with a few remarks, explanatory merely of his views. He would commence with answering the objections urged by the chairman of the Committee of Ways and Means—1st, as to the expense of assessing and collecting, which it was said would be disproportionate to the product of the tax. It being decided that the direct tax shall be continued, said Mr. J., it necessarily follows that you must keep up the assessors, as the valuations of land, &c., must be annual; otherwise a tax would be collected for a house that was consumed by fire, or a slave who had died. As to the States who would assume the direct tax, if that feature in the existing law were preserved, he thought we might adopt provisions similar to those to be found in the law imposing the carriage tax. The second objection was, that the law had been evaded, and might be again evaded. This argument applied to all the indirect taxes, and the answer given was, and it was a complete answer, that further provisions might be adopted to remedy this evil. It was true, the law had been shamefully evaded. The estimate of the Treasury was, that the furniture tax would produce $1,238,000, and the duty on watches $230.000. Yet, although the duty on watches was $225,000, which proves the extreme accuracy of the calculation made by that department, the furniture tax has only produced $75 000. He would guard against these frauds, either by requiring the valuation to be made by the owner on oath, or laying the duty on the specific articles of furniture;

these modes of taxing property were adopted by the State of Virginia, and had not been complained of. He would not allow of domiciliary visits, so justly odious to the people. The valuation or specification he proposed, should be made by the owner. This question he argued simply as a question of revenue; and he thought if so much money was requisite, as the Committee of Ways and Means contemplated, no subject of taxation was more fair and more just than this; indeed, all intelligent economists held that wealth, income, and luxury, were the fairest. These duties, proposed to be repealed, might be made to yield one-third of the amount of the direct tax, and authorize the reduction of that tax from three to two millions. The direct tax, as all direct taxes necessarily do, falls not upon the wealthy alone, but upon the extremely poor and middling classes of the people; it has no relation to income, for the lands may be cultivated and not appreciating in value; or, as is often the case, yielding a scanty subsistence to the humble owner.

Mr. J. estimated the number of families in the United States to be 1,000,000; one-tenth of these, he supposed, were liable to pay the tax, viz., 100,000; 50,000 he supposed owned furniture of the average value of $600; which, at three dollars each. as the law now is, would be $150,000

Twenty-five thousand persons would average one thousand dollars, at six	150,000
The remaining twenty-five thousand would average two thousand dollars, at seventeen	425,000
Which, with the product of the duty on watches of	225,000
Will yield a total sum of	$950,000

Which is equal to the proceeds of one-third of the direct tax—the whole being estimated to yield a net revenue of $2,700,000. When it was proposed to repeal the direct tax, we were met with the objection that it was pledged to the public creditor; yet those making that objection voted for the repeal of this duty, which is also pledged in the same language with the other. The pledge is only to supply an adequate revenue; and the revenue, independent of the proceeds of the land tax and the furniture tax, was adequate to all necessary purposes. He relied on the report of the Committee of Ways and Means for the proof of this assertion; they showed that, with the taxes recommended by them, we could increase the Sinking Fund to upwards of $13 000,000 per annum, and still have a surplus of $2,500,000 to appropriate to other objects. Although he wished to pay off the debt, he would not do it by giving another premium to those who, in the hour of difficulty, exacted twenty per cent. of us; and he contended, we could not employ a sinking fund to the amount recommended, without giving a premium to the holders of stock to part with it. Of the new debt, there fell due in

1825	$11,129.449
In 1826	26,607 958
In 1827	25 407.763

Amounting, in those three years, to - $63,145,170

How, then, he asked, could a fund of any amount, upon the principles of a sinking fund, extinguish such a debt in twelve years, say in 1827, unless by purchasing the stock long before it became payable by the contract? And that it would rise above its par value, when the redundant stock was withdrawn from the market, was undoubted. He recollected that, under the operation of the $8,000,000 sinking fund, the creditors prayed to be exempted from its operation; and it was only by declaring that the stock should cease to bear interest after the day it was payable, by allotment, that the commissioners were enabled to pay it off.

The same result will again be produced, unless we have war, and he conceived it the idlest fantasy that ever entered the heads of intelligent gentlemen, that we were to be soon involved in war; for his part, he had no faith in the probable necessity or disposition to wage a new war with any nation; he confided as well in their pacific temper as in our own; and our strength, with such dispositions, was a safe guarantee. Augment the Sinking Fund, as the Secretary of the Treasury proposed, to $10,000,000, and repeal the direct tax, and then there will be a surplus of more than $2,900,000. according to the estimates of the Committee of Ways and Means. But if we are to have the direct tax continued as part of a permanent system, he was for continuing the furniture tax, also, in order that the accumulated revenue would enable us to dispense with both together, at some early period, even though the other parts of the recommendation of the committee should be adopted. A system of taxation to be just must draw, from every part of the community, a sum in proportion to their wealth and income. Expenditure was, in general, the best evidence of income. This was a tax upon expenditure, and did not embrace the necessaries of life or domestic comfort; the articles excluded, and the extent of the exemption of such as are liable to valuation, rendered the duty inoperative upon those to whom the direct tax was oppressive; and this was the only internal tax that did bear upon the wealthy, in proportion to their ability. He concluded by saying, in his humble opinion, it was incorrect to urge, as an argument against a general proposition, objections applicable solely to the details. When the proposition was decided, it would be for its advocates to render the details unexceptionable; and on failure to do so, then, and not till then, was the argument admissible. As far as his observation extended, all the independent inhabitants of the towns possessed furniture of a kind and value falling within the provisions of the law; and he could not admit that they were so depraved as to violate it, when proper amendments were adopted.

Mr. LUMPKIN spoke as follows:

Mr. Speaker, I rise, sir, as an advocate for the amendment proposed by the honorable gentleman from Virginia, (Mr. JACKSON.) Since I took my seat in this House no vote of mine has been withheld from the support of the plan for raising revenue, submitted by the Secretary of the Treasury, except the proposed continuance of the duties on imported salt, and my object at that time was to supply the deficiency of revenue accruing upon that article, (which I considered as one of the first necessaries of life) by continuing the tax on watches and household furniture. In selecting objects or articles for taxation, I deem it to be a correct principle, that due regard should be given to wealth, luxury, and income; and the articles now proposed to be taxed are generally found in the possession of this class of citizens, and therefore are least affected by paying taxes. The agricultural part of your citizens, the planter and the farmer, are in many instances paying taxes upon very unproductive estates. The poor man who supports himself and family by the sweat of his face; the cultivator of the earth, has to pay a direct tax, when it is with difficulty, in many cases, that they can make a bare support for their families. While you are continuing taxes upon that part of society, on whom depends the best interests of this country, I will say more, on whom depends the stability of our republican institutions, shall we adopt a system of favoritism, in favor of the luxurious and wealthy, who have the largest income estates? I trust not, sir, I confess it excited my astonishment when I discovered that the Secretary of the Treasury had proposed a repeal of the watch and furniture tax. I was still more astonished, sir, when I found this recommendation had received the co-operation of the Committee of Ways and Means.

Sir, when the debate on the subject of revenue enlarged its course so as to lead to an investigation of the present state of the nation, I felt a desire to present my views to this honorable body. What prevented me from doing so, was, that the ground which I had marked out to take was completely occupied before a favorable opportunity presented itself for me to get the floor. Sir, it was occupied with such ability as to forbid any feeble attempt of mine to travel over the same ground. But, being a new member on this floor, I will use the present opportunity to state, that I differ with some gentlemen here who have expressed a want of confidence in those who administer the Government. The Administration has enjoyed my confidence and feeble support while I remained a private citizen, and becoming a member of this House has not changed my opinions. The principal difference between myself and the Administration has heretofore been, that instead of following, I have kept a little before the Administration. I was in favor of the late war with Great Britain, and wanted the declaration long before we got it; and after war was declared, I was in favor of energetic measures to support and prosecute the war before they were resorted to by the Government. The President of the United States, at the commencement of the present session, in performing his Constitutional duty, called the attention of Congress to many important national objects, which I have carefully examined, and which not only merit my general approbation, but which I consider of

so much importance to the country, that I regret that they have been so long permitted to slumber; and I consider the present moment peculiarly auspicious to their commencement. The plan of finance submitted by the Secretary of the Treasury, and the report of the Committee of Ways and Means, founded on that plan, have received my particular examination and consideration, and the result is, I feel it to be my duty to support that plan generally, but am bound to dissent on some points, one of which is, the tax now under consideration. The watch and furniture tax, under the existing law, has produced a revenue to the Government of $300,000, and it is admitted that the law has been very frequently evaded. I therefore conclude, by proper amendments to the law, it may be made a source of considerable and sure revenue. And, as I consider these articles very proper objects of taxation, I shall give my vote in favor of the amendment proposed by the gentleman from Virginia.

Mr. LOWNDES opposed the motion, and again explained the reasons which induced the Committee of Ways and Means to recommend the repeal of the tax, which recommendation he defended at some length, on its entire unproductiveness and vexatious character, as proved during the term it had been in operation.

On Mr. JACKSON's proposition, a debate took place of nearly two hours continuance, in which several gentlemen participated. Messrs. CONDICT, SOUTHARD, CANNON, WRIGHT, and BARBOUR, severally spoke in favor of the motion, and against the repeal of the tax; and Messrs. TAYLOR of New York, MILNOR, GASTON, and PICKERING, opposed the amendment and advocated the repeal. The ground occupied in the debate was not very extensive; a few prominent and obvious arguments, with some illustration, comprising the pith of the discussion. Those who advocated a repeal of the tax, did so, principally, on the ground of its failing to produce the anticipated revenue, its whole product amounting to about seventy-five thousand dollars, instead of upwards of a million, which had been calculated on; because, also, of its odious character which subjected every man's house to the intrusion of the collector, and to domiciliary visits, without sufficient object; because, after all, it would be evaded in many cases, and the odium of the tax be incurred, without affording a productive revenue, &c. Those opposed to repealing the tax, replied, that all taxes were, more or less, odious to the people; but this not particularly so; that its unproductiveness had arisen from evasions, and an unfaithful collection of the duty; that it was equitable, and, if repealed, would exempt a certain class of the community almost entirely from contributing to the public support; that it was a tax on wealth and luxury, and was necessary to equalize and perfect the system of revenue now in progress, &c.

The question on the motion to amend was taken by yeas and nays, and decided in the negative—yeas 64, nays 90, as follows:

YEAS—Messrs. Alexander, Baker, Barbour, Bateman, Bennett, Blount, Brooks, Bryan, Burwell, Caldwell, Calhoun, Cannon, Clarke of North Carolina, Clark of Kentucky, Comstock, Condict, Crawford, Darlington, Desha, Edwards, Goodwyn, Griffin Hall, Hardin, Hawes, Henderson, Huger, Hungerford. Irwin of Pennsylvania, Jackson, Johnson of Kentucky, Kerr of Virginia, King of North Carolina, Love, Lumpkin, Lyle, Lyon, Maclay, Maynant, McCoy, McKee, McLean of Kentucky, Nelson of Virginia, Ormsby, Pickens, Piper, Pleasants, Powell, Reane, Robertson, Ross, Sharpe, Smith of Virginia, Southard, Taul, Taylor of South Carolina, Telfair, Thomas, Tucker, Ward of New York, Williams, Willoughby, Wright, and Yancey.

NAYS—Messrs. Archer, Atherton, Baer, Bassett, Bayliss, Betts, Boss, Bradbury, Breckenridge, Brigham, Brown, Burnside, Cady, Champion, Chappell, Cilley, Clayton, Clendennin, Conner, Cooper, Creighton, Culpeper, Cuthbert, Davenport, Forney, Forsyth, Gaston, Gold, Goldsborough, Grosvenor, Hahn, Hale, Hammond, Hanson, Hopkinson, Hulbert, Ingham, Irving of New York, Jewett, Kent, King of Massachusetts, Langdon, Law, Lewis, Lovett, Lowndes, Mason, Middleton, Mills, Milnor, Moore of South Carolina, Moseley, Nelson of Massachusetts, Newton, Noyes, Parris, Pickering, Pitkin, Randolph, Reed, Rice, Root, Ruggles, Sergeant, Savage, Schenck, Sheffey, Smith of Pennsylvania, Smith of Maryland, Stanford, Stearns, Strong, Stuart, Sturges, Taggart, Taylor of New York, Throop, Voss, Ward of Massachusetts, Ward of New Jersey, Webster, Wendover, Wheaton, Wilcox, Wilde, Wilkin, Thomas Wilson, William Wilson, Woodward, and Yates.

The ninth resolution was then concurred in by the House, and, together with the seventh resolution, referred to the Committee of Ways and Means, with instructions to report a bill or bills conformably thereto.

The remainder of the orders of the day were then laid on the table, on motion of Mr. BASSETT, and the House went into Committee of the Whole on the resolution reported by a select committee for the relief of Commodore Rodgers. After some time spent on this subject, the Committee rose, and reported the resolution, which was ordered to be engrossed for a third reading ; and the House adjourned at half past four o'clock.

MONDAY, February 12.

Mr. ROBERTSON, from the Committee on the Public Lands, to whom were referred the petition of the Legislature of the Mississippi Territory, the petitions from sundry inhabitants of said Territory, and of Seth Hunt, upon the subject of British grants of lands lying in that Territory, made a report; which was read; when Mr. R. reported a bill for quieting and adjusting claims to lands in the Mississippi Territory; which was read twice, and committed to a Committee of the Whole.

Mr. NELSON, from the Committee on the Judiciary, reported the bill from the Senate "concerning certain courts of the United States in the State of New York," without amendment, and the bill was read a third time, and passed.

On motion of Mr. CADY, the Secretary of the Treasury was directed to report to this House what additions, if any, have been made to the funded public debt, and to the floating public debt, since the 30th day of September last.

Mr. PLEASANTS, from the Committee on Naval Affairs, reported a bill for the relief of Erastus Loomis; which was read twice, and committed to a Committee of the Whole.

On motion of Mr. CADY, the Committee of Ways and Means were instructed to inquire into the expediency of so amending the act entitled "An act to provide additional revenues for defraying the expenses of Government and maintaining the public credit, by duties on carriages, and the harness used therefor," that no duty shall be paid for any carriage usually employed in husbandry, or for the transportation of goods.

On motion of Mr. JENNINGS, the Commissioner of the General Land Office was directed to lay before this House a statement exhibiting the number of acres of land to which rights of pre-emption have been granted to individuals, in any of the States or Territories of the United States respectively; together with the probable difference in the amounts of moneys received for lands sold at public sale, and such amounts received for lands sold at private sale.

The engrossed resolution for the relief of Commodore John Rodgers, having been announced for a third reading, it was, on motion of Mr. BASSETT, recommitted to a select committee. Mr. B. from that select committee subsequently reported an amendment to the resolution; which was agreed to, and the resolve was ordered to a third reading.

The House resolved itself into a Committee of the Whole on the bill for reducing the direct tax on the United States to three millions, &c. No amendment being proposed to it, the Committee rose and reported the bill; which was laid on the table, on suggestion of Mr. ROOT, of New York, to give him time to prepare an amendment to the detail of the bill.

The resolution expressive of the sense of Congress of the gallantry of Captain James Biddle, the officers and crew of the Hornet ; and a similar resolution respecting Captain Charles Stewart, and the officers and crew of the Constitution, for their last victory, passed through a Committee of the Whole, and were severally ordered, *nem. con.*, to be engrossed, and read a third time.

The bill for rewarding the officers and crew of the Hornet for the capture and destruction of the British sloop-of-war Penguin, passed through a Committee of the Whole. The blank was filled with $25,000, being the amount allowed in former cases ; and the bill ordered to be engrossed for a third reading.

CANADIAN REFUGEES.

The House resolved itself into a Committee of the Whole, on the bill for the relief of certain refugees from the British Provinces during the late war.

Several papers were read respecting their merits and services, among which was a very strong testimony to their merits, &c., from General Porter, lately a member of this House.

This bill gave rise to a rather animated debate, in which the claim of the petitioners to indemnity or compensation was sustained by Messrs. THROOP, YATES, WRIGHT, GOLD, and JOHNSON, of Kentucky, and opposed by Messrs. HULBERT, WEBSTER, and STRONG.

This case has been fully presented to our readers in the shape of the petition of the committee on behalf of these sufferers. Their claim is precisely of a character with that for which ample provision was made at the close of the Revolutionary war. They were natives of this country, and, on the breaking out of the war, preferred ranging themselves under the banners of their native country, than that to which, for purposes of business, they had a temporary allegiance.

The opponents of the bill (which proposes to compensate the claimants' losses by donations of land) oppose it as rewarding treachery, as poisoning the fountains of morality, and use those general expressions of dislike, and even detestation, which such a bill is likely to call forth from those who view it in so odious a light.

The bill was not decided on; but, on motion of Mr. JOHNSON, laid on the table.

The Committee then proceeded to the consideration of another bill making further provision for the widows and orphans of those who fell in the late war.

The House was occupied on this subject until the usual hour of adjournment.

TUESDAY, February 13.

Mr. CALDWELL presented to the House a resolution adopted by the General Assembly of the State of Ohio, instructing their Senators, and requesting their Representatives in Congress, to use their endeavors to obtain the passage of an act of Congress providing for the organization, arming, and disciplining the militia, and for governing such parts of them as may be employed in the service of the United States; which was referred to the Committee on Military Affairs.

Mr. STEPHENSON presented a petition of the Legislature of the Territory of Illinois, praying that the powers granted to, and enjoyed by the Governor of that Territory, may be abridged.—Referred to the Committee on the Judiciary.

Mr. STEPHENSON presented another petition of the said Legislature, praying that the certificate of a Paymaster, given to certain companies of rangers lately raised in that Territory for military services, may be received in payment for public lands.—Referred to the Committee on Military Affairs.

Mr. MIDDLETON, from the committee to whom were referred the petition of Lewis Bringier, made a report, which was read; when Mr. M. reported a bill to enable the President of the United States to lease out or grant, for a term of years, mines of the precious metals, discovered upon the public lands; which was read twice, and committed to a Committee of the Whole.

A message from the Senate informed the House that the Senate disagree to the amendments of this House to their bill "concerning the convention to regulate the commerce between the territories of the United States and His Britannic Majesty." The Senate have passed a bill "authorizing a subscription for the printing of a second edition of the public documents;" and they have passed the bill "for the relief of William Morrissett," with an amendment; in which bill and amendment they ask the concurrence of this House.

The SPEAKER laid before the House a letter from the Secretary of the Treasury, accompanied with a tariff of duties proper to be laid and imposed on all goods, wares, and merchandise, imported into the United States from any foreign port or place; which were referred to the Committee of Ways and Means.—[See Appendix.]

The message of the Senate rejecting the amendments of this House to their bill concerning the Convention of Commerce, &c., was taken up, and, on motion of Mr. FORSYTH, the House determined to insist on its amendments, and to ask a conference thereon with the Senate.

The bill from the Senate, entitled "An act authorizing a subscription for the printing of a second edition of the public documents," was read twice, and committed to a Committee of the Whole.

The amendment of the Senate to the bill "for the relief of William Morrissett," was read and concurred in by the House.

An engrossed resolution, entitled "A resolution requesting the President to present medals to Captain James Biddle and the officers of the sloop-of-war Hornet," was read the third time, and passed unanimously.

An engrossed resolution, entitled "A resolution requesting the President to present medals to Captain Charles Stewart and the officers of the frigate Constitution," was read the third time, and passed unanimously.

An engrossed bill, entitled "An act rewarding the officers and crew of the sloop-of-war Hornet, for the capture and destruction of the sloop-of-war Penguin," was read the third time, and passed.

DOMESTIC MANUFACTURES.

Mr. NEWTON, from the Committee of Commerce and Manufactures, to whom were referred the several memorials and petitions of the manufacturers of cotton wool, made a report thereon; which was read, and ordered to lie on the table.

The report is as follows:

The Committee of Commerce and Manufactures, to whom were referred the memorials and petitions of the manufacturers of cotton wool, respectfully submit the following report:

The Committee were conscious that they had no ordinary duty to perform, when the House of Representatives referred to their consideration the memorials and petitions of the manufacturers of cotton wool. In obedience to the instructions of the House, they have given great attention to the subject, and beg leave to present the result of their deliberations.

They are not a little apprehensive that they have not succeeded in doing justice to a subject so intimately connected with the advancement and prosperity of agriculture and commerce—a subject which enlightened statesmen and philosophers have deemed not unworthy of their attention and consideration.

It is not the intention of the Committee to offer any theoretical opinions of their own, or of others. They are persuaded that a display of speculative opinions would not meet with approbation. From these views the Committee are disposed to state facts, and to make such observations only as shall be intimately connected with and warranted by them.

Prior to the years 1806 and 1807, establishments for manufacturing cotton wool had not been attempted but in a few instances, and on a limited scale. Their rise and progress are attributable to embarrassments to which commerce was subjected; which embarrassments originated in causes not within the control of human prudence.

While commerce flourished, the trade which had been carried on with the continent of Europe, with the East Indies, and with the colonies of Spain and France, enriched our enterprising merchants, the benefits of which were sensibly felt by the agriculturists, whose wealth and industry were increased and extended. When external commerce was suspended, the capitalists throughout the Union became solicitous to give activity to their capital. A portion of it, it is believed, was directed to the improvement of agriculture, and not an inconsiderable portion of it, as it appears, was likewise employed in erecting establishments for manufacturing cotton wool. To make this statement as satisfactory as possible—to give it all the certainty that it is susceptible of attaining, the following facts are respectfully submitted to the consideration of the House. They show the rapid progress which has been made in a few years, and evidently the ability to carry them on with certainty of success, should a just and liberal policy regard them as objects deserving encouragement:

In the year 1800, 500 bales of cotton were manufactured in manufacturing establishments.

In the year 1805, 1,000 bales of cotton were manufactured in manufacturing establishments.

In the year 1810, 10,000 bales of cotton were manufactured in manufacturing establishments.

In the year 1815, 90,000 bales of cotton were manufactured in manufacturing establishments.

This statement the Committee have no reason to doubt; nor have they any question as to the truth of the following succinct statement of the capital which is employed, of the labor which it commands, and of the products of that labor:

Capital - - - - - -	$40,000,000
Males employed, from the age of 17 and upwards - - - - -	10,000
Women and female children - -	66,000
Boys under 17 years of age -	24,000
Wages of one hundred thousand persons, averaging $150 each - - -	$15,000,000
Cotton wool manufactured, ninety thousand bales, amounting to -	£27,000,000
Number of yards of cotton, of various kinds - - - - -	81,000,000
Cost, per yard, averaging 30 cents -	$24,000,000

This rise and progress of such establishments can

excite no wonder. The inducements to industry in a free government are numerous and inviting. Effects are always in unison with their causes. The inducements consist in the certainty and security which every citizen enjoys of exercising exclusive dominion over the creations of his genius, and the products of his labor; in procuring from his native soil, at all times, with facility, the raw materials that are required, and in the liberal encouragement that will be accorded by agriculturists to those who, by their labor, keep up a constant and increasing demand for the produce of agriculture.

Every State will participate in those advantages. The resources of each will be explored, opened, and enlarged. Different sections of the nation will, according to their position, the climate, the population, the habits of the people, and the nature of the soil, strike into that line of industry which is best adapted to their interest and the good of the whole; an active and free intercourse, promoted and facilitated by roads and canals, will ensue; prejudices, which are generated by distance, and the want of inducements to approach each other and reciprocate benefits, will be removed; information will be extended; the Union will acquire strength and solidity, and the Constitution of the United States, and that of each State, will be regarded as fountains from which flow numerous streams of public and private prosperity.

Each government, moving in its appropriate orbit, performing with ability its separate functions, will be endeared to the hearts of a good and grateful people.

The States that are most disposed to manufactures, as regular occupations, will draw from the agricultural States all the raw materials which they want, and not an inconsiderable portion also of the necessaries of life; while the latter will, in addition to the benefits which they at present enjoy, always command, in peace or in war, at moderate prices, every species of manufacture that their wants may require. Should they be inclined to manufacture for themselves, they can do so with success, because they have all the means in their power to erect and to extend at pleasure manufacturing establishments. Our wants being supplied by our own ingenuity and industry, exportation of specie, to pay for foreign manufactures, will cease.

The value of American produce, at this time exported, will not enable the importers to pay for the foreign manufacture imported. Whenever the two accounts shall be fairly stated, the balance against the United States will be found many millions of dollars. Such is the state of things, that the change must be to the advantage of the United States. The precious metals will be attracted to them; the diffusion of which, in a regular and uniform current, through the great arteries and veins of the body politic, will give to each member health and vigor.

In proportion as the commerce of the United States depends on agriculture and manufactures as a common basis, will it increase and become independent of those revolutions and fluctuations, which the ambition and jealousy of foreign Governments are too apt to produce. Our navigation will be quickened; and supported as it will be by internal resources, never before at the command of any nation, will advance to the extent of those resources.

New channels of trade to enterprise, no less important than productive, are opening, which can be so cured only by a wise and prudent policy appreciating their advantage.

If want of foresight should neglect the cultivation and improvement of them, the opportune moment may be lost, perhaps, for centuries, and the energies of this nation be thereby prevented from developing themselves, and from making the boon which is proffered our own. By trading on our own capital, collisions with other nations, if they be not entirely done away, will be greatly diminished.

This natural order of things exhibits the commencement of a new epoch, which promises peace, security, and repose, by a firm and steady reliance on the produce of agriculture; on the treasures that are embosomed in the earth; on the genius and ingenuity of our manufacturers and mechanics; and on the intelligence and enterprise of our merchants.

The Government, possessing the intelligence and the art of improving the resources of the nation, will increase its efficient powers, and, enjoying the confidence of those whom it has made happy, will oppose to the assailant of the nation's rights the true, the only invincible ægis, the unity of will and strength. Causes producing war will be few. Should war take place, its calamitous consequences will be mitigated, and the expenses and burdens of such a state of things will fall with a weight less oppressive and injurious on the nation. The expenditures of the last war were greatly increased by a dependence on foreign supplies. The prices incident to such a dependence will always be high.

Had not our nascent manufacturing establishments increased the quantity of commodities at that time in demand, the expenditures would have been much greater, and consequences the most fatal and disastrous—alarming even in contemplation—would have been the fate of this nation. The experience of the past teaches a lesson never to be forgotten, and points emphatically to the remedy. A wise Government should heed its admonitions, or the independence of this nation will be exposed to " the shafts of fortune."

The committee, keeping in view the interests of the nation, cannot refrain from stating that cotton fabrics, imported from India, interfere not less with that encouragement to which agriculture is justly entitled, than they do with that which ought reasonably to be accorded to the manufacturers of cotton wool. The raw material of which they are made is the growth of India, and of a quality inferior to our own. The fabrics themselves, in point of duration and use, are likewise inferior to the substantial fabrics of American manufacture. Although the India cotton fabrics can be sold for a lower price than the American, yet, the difference in the texture is so much in favor of the American, that the latter may be safely considered as the cheapest.

The distance of most of the Western States from the ocean, the exuberant richness of the soil, and the variety of its products, forcibly impress the mind of the committee with a belief that all these causes conspire to encourage manufactures, and to give an impetus and direction to such a disposition. Although the Western States may be said to be *in the gristle*, in contemplation of that destiny to which they are hastening, yet the products of manufactures in those States are beyond every calculation that could reasonably be made; contrary to the opinion of many enlightened and virtuous men, who have supposed that the inducements of agriculture, and the superior advantages of

that life, would suppress any disposition to that sort of industry. But theories, how ingeniously soever they may be constructed,—how much soever they may be made to conform to the laws of symmetry and beauty—are no sooner brought into conflict with facts, than they fall into ruins. In viewing their fragments, the mind is irresistibly led to render the homage due to the genius and taste of the architects; but cannot refrain from regretting the waste, to no purpose, of superior intellects. The Western States prove the fallacy of such theories; they appear in their growth and expansion to be in advance of thought. While the political economist is drawing their portraits, their features change and enlarge with such rapidity that his pencil in vain endeavors to catch their expressions, and to fix their physiognomy.

It is to their advantage to manufacture, because, by decreasing the bulk of the articles, they at the same time increase their value by labor, bring them to market with less expense, and with the certainty of obtaining the best prices. Those States, understanding their interest, will not be diverted from its pursuit. In the encouragement of manufactures, they find a stimulus for agriculture.

The manufacturers of cotton, in making application to the National Government for encouragement, have been induced to do so for many reasons. They know that their establishments are new and in their infancy, and that they have to encounter a competition with foreign establishments, that have arrived at maturity, that are supported by a large capital, and that have from the Government every protection that can be required.

The American manufacturers expect to meet with all the embarrassments which a jealous and monopolizing spirit can suggest. The committee are sensible of the force of such considerations. They are convinced that old practices and maxims will not be abandoned to favor the United States. The foreign manufacturers and merchants will put in requisition all the powers of ingenuity; will practise whatever art can devise, and capital can accomplish, to prevent the American manufacturing establishments from taking root and flourishing in their rich and native soil. By the allowance of bounties and drawbacks, the foreign manufacturers and merchants will be furnished with additional means of carrying on the conflict, and of insuring success.

The American manufacturers have good reasons for their apprehensions—they have much at stake. They have a large capital employed, and are feelingly alive for its fate. Should the National Government not afford them protection, the dangers which invest and threaten them will destroy all their hopes, and will close their prospects of utility to their country. A reasonable encouragement will sustain and keep them erect; but if they fall, they fall never to rise again.

The foreign manufacturers and merchants know this; and will redouble with renovated zeal the stroke to prostrate them. They also know, that should the American manufacturing establishments fall, their mouldering piles—the visible ruins of a legislative breath—will warn all who shall tread in the same footsteps, of the doom, the inevitable destiny, of their establishments.

The National Government, in viewing the disastrous effects of a short-sighted policy, may relent; but what can relenting avail? Can it raise the dead to life! Can it give, for injuries inflicted, the reparation that is due! Industry, in every ramification of society, will feel the shock, and generations will, as they succeed each other, feel the effects of its undulations. Dissatisfaction will be visible everywhere, and the lost confidence and affections of the citizens will not be the least of the evils the Government will have to deplore. But, should the National Government, pursuing an enlightened and liberal policy, sustain and foster the manufacturing establishments, a few years would place them in a condition to bid defiance to foreign competition, and would enable them to increase the industry, wealth, and prosperity of the nation; and to afford to the Government, in times of difficulty and distress, whatever it may require to support public credit, while maintaining the rights of the nation.

Providence, in bountifully placing within our reach whatever can minister to happiness and comfort, indicates plainly to us our duty, and what we owe to ourselves. Our resources are abundant and inexhaustible.

The stand that Archimedes wanted, is given to the National and State Governments; and labor-saving machinery tenders the lever—the power of bringing those resources into use.

This power imparts incalculable advantages to a nation whose population is not full. The United States require the use of this power, because they do not abound in population. The diminution of manual labor, by means of machinery, in the cotton manufacture of Great Britain, was, in the year 1810, as two hundred to one. Our manufactures have already availed themselves of this power, and have profited by it. A little more experience in making machines, and in managing them with skill, will enable our manufacturers to supply more fabrics than are necessary for the home demand. Competition will make the prices of the articles low, and the extension of the cotton manufactories will produce that competition.

One striking and important advantage which labor-saving machines bestow is this, that in all their operations they require few men, as a reference to another part of this report will show. No apprehensions can, then, be seriously entertained, that agriculture will be in danger of having its efficient laborers withdrawn from its service. On the contrary, the manufacturing establishments, increasing the demand for raw materials, will give to agriculture new life and expansion.

The committee, after having with great deference and respect presented to the House this important subject, in various points of view, feel themselves constrained, before concluding the report, to offer a few observations, which they consider as being immediately connected with it, and not less so, with the present and future prosperity of this nation.

The prospects of an enlarged commerce are not flattering.

Every nation, in times of peace, will supply its own wants from its own resources, or from those of other nations.

When supplies are drawn from foreign countries, the intercourse which will ensue will furnish employment to the navigation only of the countries connected, by their reciprocal wants.

Our concern does not arise from, nor can it be increased by, the limitation which our navigation and trade will have prescribed to them, by the peace and apparent repose of Europe.

Our apprehensions arise from causes that cannot animate by their effects. Look wheresoever the eye can glance, and what are the objects that strike the vision? On the continent of Europe, industry, deprived of its motive and incitement, is paralyzed; the accumulated wealth of ages, seized by the hand of military despotism, is appropriated to, and squandered on objects of ambition; the order of things unsettled, and confidence between man and man annihilated. Every moment is looked for with tremulous, anxious, and increased solicitude; hope languishes, and commercial enterprise stiffens with fear. The political horizon appears to be calm, but many of no ordinary sagacity think they behold signs portentous of a violent tempest, which will again rage and desolate that devoted region. Should this prediction fail, no change for the better, under existing circumstances, can take place. Where despotism, military despotism, reigns, silence and fearful stillness must prevail.

Such is the prospect which continental Europe exhibits to the enterprise of American merchants. Can it be possible for them to find in that region sources which will supply them with more than seventeen millions of dollars, the balance due for British manufactures; this balance being over and above the value of all the exports to foreign countries from the United States. The view which is given to the dreary prospect of commercial advantages, accruing to the United States by an intercourse with continental Europe, is believed to be just. The statement made of the great balance in favor of Great Britain, due from the United States, is founded on matter of fact.

In the hands of Great Britain are gathered together and held many powers which they have not been accustomed hitherto to feel and to exercise. No improper motives are intended to be imputed to that Government. But does not experience teach a lesson that should never be forgotten, that Governments, like individuals, are apt "to feel power and forget right?" It is not inconsistent with national decorum to become circumspect and prudent. May not the Government of Great Britain be inclined, in analyzing the basis of her political power, to consider and regard the United States as her rival, and to indulge an improper jealousy—the enemy of peace and repose? Can it be politic, in any point of view, to make the United States dependent on any nation for supplies absolutely necessary for defence, or comfort, and for accommodation? Will not the strength, the political energies of this nation, be materially impaired, at any time, but fatally so in those of difficulty and distress, by such dependence? Do not the suggestions of wisdom plainly show that the security, the peace, and the happiness of this nation depend on opening and enlarging all our resources, and drawing from them whatever shall be required for public use or private accommodation? The committee, from the views which they have taken, consider the situation of manufacturing establishments to be perilous. Some have decreased, and others have suspended business. A liberal encouragement will put them again into operation with increased powers; but should it be withheld they will be prostrated. Thousands will be reduced to want and wretchedness. A capital of near sixty millions of dollars will become inactive, the greater part of which will be a dead loss to the manufacturers. Our improvidence may lead to fatal consequences. The Powers jealous of our growth and prosperity, will acquire the resources and strength which this Government neglects to improve. It requires no prophet to foretell the use that foreign Powers will make of them. The committee, from all the considerations which they have given to this subject, are deeply impressed with a conviction that the manufacturing establishments of cotton wool are of real utility to the agricultural interest, and that they contribute much to the prosperity of the Union. Under the influence of this conviction, the committee beg leave to tender respectfully, with this report, the following resolution:

Resolved, That, from and after the 30th day of June next, in lieu of the duties now authorized by law, there be laid, levied, and collected on cotton goods imported into the United States, and Territories thereof, from any foreign country whatever, —— per centum ad valorem, being not less than —— cents per square yard.

THE REVENUE.

The House took up the bill to reduce the amount of direct tax upon the United States and the District of Columbia, for the year 1816; and the same being amended, a motion was made by Mr. ATHERTON further to amend the said bill by striking out from the third line the words *so much of,* and from the eighth, ninth, and tenth lines, the following words: "*as lays a direct tax of six millions of dollars, for the year* 1816, *and for succeeding years ;*" and by adding to the end of the section the words following: "*Provided, nevertheless,* that the same shall be in force so far as may be necessary to complete the collection of the direct tax for the year 1815;" thereby proposing a total repeal of the act imposing a direct tax.

And the question thereon being taken, it was determined in the negative—yeas 65, nays 82, as follows:

YEAS—Messrs. Atherton, Baer, Barbour, Baylies, Boss, Bradbury, Breckenridge, Brigham, Brown, Bryan, Cady, Cannon, Champion, Cilley, Clarke of North Carolina, Clayton, Cooper, Culpeper, Edwards, Goldsborough, Hale, Hardin, Hawes, Heister, Herbert, Hungerford, Jackson, Jewett, King of Massachusetts, King of North Carolina, Law, Lewis, Love, Lyon, Mason, McCoy, McKee, Moore, Moseley, Noyes, Parris, Pickens, Pitkin, Reed, Rice, Sheffey, Smith of Virginia, Stanford, Stearns, Strong, Stuart, Sturges, Taggart, Tallmadge, Taul, Thomas, Vose, Ward of Massachusetts, Ward of New York, Webster, Wheaton, Wilcox, Wright, and Yancey.

NAYS—Messrs. Adgate, Alexander, Archer, Baker, Bateman, Bennett, Betts, Birdsall, Birdseye, Brooks, Burnside, Burwell, Caldwell, Calhoun, Chappell, Clark of Kentucky, Comstock, Condict, Conner, Crawford, Creighton, Cuthbert, Darlington, Desha, Forney, Forsyth, Gaston, Gold, Goodwyn, Griffin, Hahn, Hall, Hopkinson, Ingham, Irving of New York, Irwin of Pennsylvania, Johnson of Kentucky, Kent, Kerr of Virginia, Lovett, Lowndes, Lumpkin, Lyle, Maclay, Mayrant, McLean of Kentucky, McLean of Ohio, Middleton, Mills, Milnor, Nelson of Massachusetts, Newton, Ormsby, Pickering, Piper, Pleasants, Reynolds, Roane, Robertson, Root, Ross, Ruggles, Sergeant, Savage, Schenck, Smith of Pennsylvania, Smith of Maryland, Taylor of New York, Taylor of South Carolina, Telfair, Throop, Tucker, Wallace, Ward of New Jersey, Wendover, Whiteside, Wilde, Willoughby, Thomas Wilson, William Wilson, Woodward, and Yates.

Mr. PICKERING then moved further to amend the said bill by inserting in the second line of the second section, after the word "hereby," the word

"annually," and by striking out from the third and fourth lines the following words: "for the year one thousand eight hundred and sixteen ;" thereby proposing to render the direct tax a permanent, and not an annual one.

And the question thereon being taken, it was determined in the negative—yeas 20, nays 129, as follows:

YEAS—Messrs. Bateman, Birdseye, Gaston, Hopkinson, Ingham, Irving of New York, Jewett, Kent, Law, Lovett, Mills, Milnor, Nelson of Massachusetts, Pickering, Sergeant, Schenck, Smith of Pennsylvania, Taylor of New York, Wendover, and William Wilson.

NAYS—Messrs. Adgate, Alexander, Archer, Atherton, Baer, Baker, Barbour, Bassett, Baylies, Bennett, Betts, Birdsall, Boss, Bradbury, Breckenridge, Brigham, Brooks, Brown, Bryan, Burnside, Burwell, Cady, Caldwell, Calhoun, Cannon, Champion, Chappell, Cilley, Clarke of North Carolina, Clark of Kentucky, Comstock, Condict, Conner, Crawford, Creighton, Culpeper, Cuthbert, Darlington, Desha, Edwards, Forney, Forsyth, Gold, Goldsborough, Goodwyn, Griffin, Hahn, Hale, Hall, Hardin, Hawes, Heister, Herbert, Hulbert, Hungerford, Irwin of Pennsylvania, Jackson, Johnson of Kentucky, Kerr of Virginia, King of Massachusetts, King of North Carolina, Langdon, Lewis, Love, Lowndes, Lumpkin, Lyle, Lyon, Maclay, Mason, Mayrant, McCoy, McKee, McLean of Kentucky, McLean of Ohio, Moore, Moseley, Nelson of Virginia, Newton, Noyes, Ormsby, Parris, Pickens, Piper, Pitkin, Pleasants, Reynolds, Rice, Roane, Robertson, Root, Ross, Ruggles, Savage, Sharpe, Sheffey, Smith of Maryland, Smith of Virginia, Stanford, Stearns, Strong, Stuart, Sturges, Taggart, Tallmadge, Tate, Taul, Taylor of South Carolina, Telfair, Thomas, Throop, Townsend, Tucker, Vose, Wallace, Ward of Massachusetts, Ward of New York, Ward of New Jersey, Webster, Wheaton, Whiteside, Wilcox, Wilde, Williams, Willoughby, Woodward, Wright, Yancey, and Yates.

Mr. LYON then moved to strike out the second section of the bill; which motion was negatived.

A motion was made by Mr. MAYRANT to strike out the words "*three millions,*" the amount of the direct tax proposed to be levied, and in lieu thereof to insert "*two millions;*" and the question thereon being taken, it was determined in the negative—yeas 54, nays 96, as follows:

YEAS—Messrs. Alexander, Baer, Barbour, Bassett, Breckenridge, Brooks, Brown, Bryan, Burwell, Cannon, Clarke of North Carolina, Desha, Edwards, Forney, Goldsborough, Goodwyn, Hall, Hawes, Hulbert, Hungerford, Jackson, Johnson of Kentucky, King of Massachusetts, King of North Carolina, Lewis, Lyon, Mayrant, McCoy, McKee, McLean of Kentucky, Noyes, Ormsby, Parris, Pickens, Pitkin, Reynolds, Rice, Sharpe, Sheffey, Smith of Virginia, Stanford, Strong, Stuart, Sturges, Tate, Taul, Thomas, Vose, Webster, Wheaton, Wilcox, Williams, Wright, and Yancey.

NAYS—Messrs. Adgate, Archer, Atherton, Baker, Bateman, Baylies, Bennett, Betts, Birdsall, Birdseye, Boss, Bradbury, Brigham, Burnside, Cady, Caldwell, Calhoun, Champion, Chappell, Cilley, Clark of Kentucky, Clayton, Comstock, Condict, Conner, Crawford, Creighton, Culpeper, Cuthbert, Darlington, Forsyth, Gaston, Gold, Griffin, Grosvenor, Hahn, Hale, Herbert, Hopkinson, Ingham, Irving of New York,

Irwin of Pennsylvania, Jewett, Kent, Kerr of Virginia, Langdon, Law, Love, Lovett, Lowndes, Lumpkin, Lyle, Maclay, Mason, McLean of Ohio, Middleton, Mills, Milnor, Moore, Moseley, Nelson of Massachusetts, Nelson of Virginia, Newton, Pickering, Piper, Pleasants, Reed, Roane, Robertson, Root, Ross, Ruggles, Sergeant, Savage, Schenck, Smith of Pennsylvania, Smith of Maryland, Stearns, Taggart, Tallmadge, Taylor of New York, Taylor of South Carolina, Telfair, Throop, Townsend, Tucker, Wallace, Ward of New York, Ward of New Jersey, Wendover, Whiteside, Wilde, Willoughby, William Wilson, Woodward, and Yates.

Mr. McLEAN, of Ohio, moved an amendment, the object of which was, in case the States of Ohio or Louisiana should assume their quota of the direct tax, to authorize the Legislatures to collect their proportion of the same from the purchasers of public land from the Government, notwithstanding any provision in the contract between the United States and the States to the contrary. This motion was agreed to—ayes 82, noes 45.

A motion was made by Mr. TALLMADGE to add the following proviso to the second section thereof, to wit:

"*Provided*, That so much of the fortieth section of the aforesaid act, passed on the 9th of January, 1815, as authorizes any State to assume and pay its quota of the direct tax, is hereby repealed."

And the question being taken thereon, it was determined in the negative. The question was then put, Shall the bill be engrossed and read a third time? It passed in the affirmative—yeas 106, nays 46, as follows:

YEAS—Messrs. Adgate, Alexander, Archer, Atherton, Baker, Barbour, Bassett, Bennett, Betts, Birdsall, Birdseye, Blount, Breckenridge, Brooks, Burnside, Burwell, Cady, Caldwell, Calhoun, Cannon, Chappell, Clarke of North Carolina, Clark of Kentucky, Clayton, Clendennin, Comstock, Condict, Conner, Cooper, Crawford, Creighton, Culpeper, Cuthbert, Darlington, Desha, Edwards, Forney, Forsyth, Gaston, Gold, Goodwyn, Griffin, Hahn, Hall, Hawes, Henderson, Herbert, Hungerford, Ingham, Irving of New York, Irwin of Pennsylvania, Jackson, Johnson of Kentucky, Kent, Kerr of Pennsylvania, Lewis, Love, Lowndes, Lumpkin, Lyle, Lyon, Maclay, Mayrant, McKee, McLean of Kentucky, McLean of Ohio, Nelson of Virginia, Newton, Ormsby, Parris, Piper, Pitkin, Pleasants, Powell, Reynolds, Roane, Robertson, Root, Ross, Sergeant, Savage, Schenck, Sharpe, Sheffey, Smith of Maryland, Smith of Virginia, Southard, Taul, Taylor of New York, Taylor of South Carolina, Telfair, Thomas, Townsend, Tucker, Wallace, Ward of New York, Ward of New Jersey, Webster, Wendover, Whiteside, Wilde, Willoughby, William Wilson, Woodward, Yancey, and Yates.

NAYS—Messrs. Baer, Baylies, Boss, Bradbury, Brigham, Brown, Champion, Cilley, Davenport, Goldsborough, Grosvenor, Hale, Heister, Hopkinson, Hulbert, Jewett, King of Massachusetts, Langdon, Law, Lovett, Mason, McCoy, Mills, Moore of South Carolina, Moseley, Nelson of Massachusetts, Noyes, Pickering, Reed, Rice, Ruggles, Smith of Pennsylvania, Stanford, Stearns, Strong, Stuart, Sturges, Taggart, Tallmadge, Tate, Vose, Ward of Massachusetts, Wheaton, Wilcox, Williams, and Wright.

The bill was then ordered to be read a third time to-morrow.

ORDNANCE DEPARTMENT.

The House resumed the consideration of the bill making appropriations for the ordnance and ordnance stores for the year 1816.

The question being on agreeing with the Committee of the Whole, to fill up the blank, for this purpose, with $1,065,224—

Mr. WRIGHT opposed this amount, and proposed to substitute $500,000 in lieu thereof.

Mr. DESHA said, although he should vote against filling the blank with one million and sixty-five thousand dollars, he did believe that the sum of five hundred thousand dollars, as proposed by the gentleman from Maryland, was rather under the mark, and was in hopes that the gentleman would modify his motion from five to six hundred thousand dollars, which was sufficient to answer every purpose of enabling the Government to meet its engagements, to keep up and regularly progress in manufacturing arms of every description necessary to meet a state of war, let it occur when it would, as well as to finish the fortifications, arsenals, and magazines, already commenced, and construct some new ones. Mr. D. said, that a state of war was always a state of extreme expense; that he could not be charged with a want of liberality pending the late war, in refusing to grant men or money, or anything that was necessary to insure an energetic and vigorous prosecution of the war. He said that he had supported everything (independent of expense) that was calculated to nerve the national arm and give it vigor, knowing the people would not hesitate to submit to any privations in defence of their rights. They gave personal service cheerfully, and paid taxes willingly; and the war terminating happily and triumphantly, is more to be attributed to the valor and native energies of the American people than management; and I rejoice to think, that while this native energy exists in the American character, this country never can be subjugated, even by a combination of despots, independent of management, or who may be at the helm. The war is now over; it was happily terminated; he felt disposed to retrench, to curtail our expenses, and lighten the burdens of the people, who acted so meritoriously throughout the most trying difficulties. Enormous expenses necessarily result from a state of war, but now was the time, not only to retrench in our expenses, but to go on an economical scale. Although the people submitted without a murmur to heavy burdens to sustain a state of war, where their rights were involved, they will expect those burdens to be measurably removed in a time of peace; they will expect frugality from our hands instead of profusion, and they have a right to expect it.

Gentlemen tell you that one million and sixty-five thousand dollars is necessary to fulfil engagements entered into in relation to the Ordnance department. If this was the case I would not hesitate a moment to grant it. I hold punctuality to be essential in Governments as well as individuals. There is not a man in this House who would go greater lengths to preserve the character of the nation than I would, or prevent its honor from being compromitted; but if gentlemen would cast their eyes over the document that was this morning laid on their tables, they would discover this not to be the fact; they would discover that it requires only two hundred and ninety thousand dollars to meet the engagements in the Ordnance department. I am willing to give every facility to the Ordnance department, and if the one million and sixty-five thousand dollars, as contemplated, was to be appropriated for one year only, I should not hesitate about it; but it is intended, agreeable to the provisions of the bill, as an annual, a permanent regulation. As a permanent regulation, I think that six hundred thousand dollars would not only be an ample, but a liberal appropriation. It would not only enable Government to comply with its engagements, but finish the arsenals, magazines, and fortifications that have been commenced, and to construct new ones if it is found necessary. Mr. D. said, he had not as much confidence in fortifications for the defence of our extensive coast or frontiers as some gentlemen appeared to have; he depended more on the yeomanry of the country, under proper organization and discipline, to deter foreign Powers from encroaching on our rights, or making a descent on our territory, than batteries, fortifications, or even such a standing army as this country will ever be willing to keep up, while the people retain their present republican habits, which I hope will be while time lasts. Notwithstanding the good old doctrine of 1798, that a well organized militia is the bulwark of our safety and the sheet-anchor of our liberty, has been measurably exploded, and the predilection is so strong in favor of armies and expensive establishments, that it is almost unfashionable to mention militia, I have no hesitation in saying, that the militia, under a proper organization, is not only the cheapest, but the strongest and best walls, batteries, or fortifications, you can have for the defence of this country, as well as the most congenial with the nature of our Government and the habits of the people. I know that it is necessary to keep up a portion of regular forces to take care of our garrisons, and to keep them from dilapidating, as well as to keep our arms in repair. But I venture to say, without fear of contradiction, that our little Army, according to the number of forces, is the most expensive in the world. I have no doubt but it will cost the Government for the present year, independent of the million and sixty-five thousand dollars contemplated by this bill, for the Ordnance department, nearly five millions of dollars. What would it be if we were to lay aside our confidence in the militia, and increase the regular forces so as to amount to an adequate defence and strength in case of emergencies? Why, it would ultimately engulph this country in ruin—it would finally prostrate its liberties. It is presumed that a portion of the direct tax will have to be con-

tinued for one year, to meet the ordinary or extraordinary expense incurred by the late necessary but expensive war, and aid the Government in settling up claims for property lost while in the service. But if you continue to go on in this extravagant style, for expensive fortifications, expensive armies, expensive and extensive navies, (further than a moderate increase, providing gradually for the defence of our ports and harbors, to expel marauders from our waters, and give a reasonable protection to our commerce,) you will have to lay additional burdens on the people; you will have to increase your present taxes, resort to a new system, or involve the Government in a lasting national debt. But why do I talk of economy? The expression is unfashionable. Expensive establishments are the order of the day. It would seem that gentlemen have not taken into the account where the money is to come from to support such high notions. Gentlemen certainly have not reflected that it must ultimately come out of the pockets of the people. They will let them know, in language perhaps that will not be altogether pleasant, that both them and their extravagant projects must go down together. I hope it will not be considered offensive to say that in the districts we represent there are a number as capable of judging as ourselves. They will scrutinize our acts, and when they find that our hands bear heavy on them, they will apply the corrective. Mr. D. said he felicitated the gentleman from Georgia on his happy facility in attaching ridicule to everything said that did not comport with his ideas of propriety. He said he had attended closely to the specimen of eloquence the gentleman had favored the House with on this occasion, and, agreeable to his understanding of it, it was, in substance, simply this—that the Secretary of War had recommended the appropriation of one million and sixty-five thousand dollars for the Ordnance department, and it ought to be granted. Mr. D. said he had the highest opinion of the talents, capacity, integrity, and purity of intentions of that high and responsible officer, but he had too much confidence in his correct Republican principles to believe that the Secretary wished his recommendation to be binding where it did not convince the reason. As a representative of freemen, I certainly shall take the liberty of exercising my own judgment on this occasion, as well as all others that are laid before me for examination; and I do believe that we are going on in a degree of profusion not warranted by the occasion. I do believe that six hundred thousand dollars, as a permanent annual appropriation for the Ordnance department, is not only ample, but liberal, and that the blank in the bill ought not to be filled with one million and sixty-five thousand dollars.

On the question to concur in the amount reported by the Committee of the Whole, there arose a considerable debate; Mr. WRIGHT, Mr. GOLDSBOROUGH, and Mr. KING of Massachusetts opposing, and Mr. SMITH of Maryland, and Mr. FORSYTH, advocating this amount.

Mr. JOHNSON, of Kentucky, said, the appropriation formed a part of the general estimate for the War Department, and nothing but the urgency of the case had induced the Secretary of War to recommend the passage of a separate law previous to the general appropriation. Mr. J. said he could not have anticipated objections to the bill, after its objects had been submitted to the House.

Arsenals, magazines, military depots, ordnance stores of every description, and munitions of war, were considered as indispensable to the security of every nation, in peace as well as in war; and while reasonable objections might be urged as to many objects of expenditure, in this he thought there should be but one opinion, after the experience of the late war. The duty of the ordnance corps was very important to the nation, and the present provision was indispensable to their continued and successful operation, in collecting public property; in finishing the arsenals and magazines, which were in a state of progression, and the hands now employed in them; the operations of the public armories at Springfield and Harper's Ferry; the public and private cannon foundries, and manufactories of small arms. The corps of ordnance was composed, he said, generally of valuable officers, scientific and practical men, and the privates were mechanics, enlisted like other soldiers, such as gunsmiths, wheelwrights, blacksmiths, and carpenters, of various descriptions. A considerable sum was due to these laborers and others, employed in finishing these valuable works; money was due for the materials furnished, and he did not suppose that any gentleman would wish to leave these public works unfinished, to lose the money expended on them that others might be built; nor did he suppose any wished to dismiss these laborers, or dismiss this useful corps.

Besides the places where arsenals and magazines had been commenced, other sites had been fixed upon to commence and create others, that the United States might have their own military depots for their ordnance stores, cannon, muskets, rifles, powder, balls, fixed ammunition, camp equipage, and not be dependent upon private store-houses, as was the case during the late war, and cost the Government near $500,000; nor to let the property injure and ruin, after being purchased, for want of safekeeping. He stated that the positions for the arsenals and magazines in the different parts of the United States had been selected with a view to any future war. The position was secure and convenient; and in case of successful invasion, such would be the construction that the military depots could be defended by a company of men against a large force; the walls were to be cannon-proof, and eighteen feet high, and defendable on every side with artillery.

It is necessary that this should be the case, as some millions of property may be deposited at one of these military depots at the same time. But, independent of the vast sum of upwards of $400,000 paid in a war of less than three years for the want of these places of safer deposite,

the expenses of extra transportation of the munitions of war, and camp equipage, from one to other parts of the United States (increased expense) could not amount to less than a million of dollars, and to this it would be proper to add the incalculable consequences which did result on on many occasions for want of cannon, arms, ammunition, camp equipage, medical stores, &c. It is impossible to say what different results might have followed a well-digested and organized system of an ordnance office, some few years previous to the declaration of war.

But this appropriation is also to continue the operations of the armories, public and private, now engaged in the service of the United States; and it is to be presumed that gentlemen do not wish to diminish the present manufacture of arms, estimated at 30,000 stand annually; more especially as it is said, that at this moment the United States could not muster 80,000 stand of arms fit for use. The third object of the appropriation is to enable the Government to comply with contracts which they have made with individuals or companies, and to meet existing engagements, all of which originated during the late war, and with individuals who had failed in their contracts with the Government, and from advances made remained in debt to various amounts; and to secure these arrearages, contracts were renewed with these individuals, who have been compelled to give good security, rather than jeopardize that which was due to the United States by a tedious law suit; and in many cases the individual failed without any fault of his own, from the pressure of the times. Under these circumstances the Government pursued the wise course of securing such ordnance stores as could not be dispensed with. In concluding these remarks, Mr. J. said it was necessary to state, that in relation to arsenals, magazines, timber, &c., the appropriation at a subsequent period must be lessened, as these objects of expenditure will have been completed; and, indeed, as we increase our military stores the annual appropriation may diminish, but it will be indispensably necessary to make annual appropriations to a reasonable extent to manufacture arms, continue to improve the public armories, to purchase munitions of war, military stores, &c.

The letter from the Secretary of War gives the following estimate (with details) of the appropriation he deems necessary for the year:

For the United States Armory at Springfield	$165,793
For do. at Harper's Ferry	172,054
For erecting and completing arsenals, depots, &c., as prescribed	457,765
For timber to be seasoned	75,000
For coals, steel, iron, materials, &c.	79,000
For amount of existing contracts for articles to be delivered in 1816, viz:	
For gunpowder	93,000
Cannon and shot, shells, &c.	111,000
Muskets and rifles	89,000
Transportation of ordnance, &c.	23,000

It was on the one hand contended, the amount

of appropriation proposed was extravagant, under present circumstances entirely too large, and calculated unnecessarily to burden the people without adequate object. On the other hand, the advocates of the appropriation pointed to the items of the report, and supported the policy of authorizing the proposed expenditure on general principles of forecast and providence.

The question on concurring with the Committee was decided in the affirmative—yeas 92, nays 48, as follows:

YEAS—Messrs. Adgate, Alexander, Archer, Baker, Barbour, Bassett, Bateman, Betts, Birdsall, Birdseye, Blount, Brooks, Bryan, Burnside, Caldwell, Calhoun, Cannon, Chappell, Clark of Kentucky, Clendennin, Comstock, Condict, Crawford, Creighton, Cuthbert, Darlington, Edwards, Forney, Forsyth, Gold, Goodwyn, Griffin, Hahn, Hanson, Hardin, Hawes, Henderson, Hopkinson, Hulbert, Hungerford, Ingham, Irving of New York, Jackson, Johnson of Kentucky, Kerr of Virginia, King of North Carolina, Love, Lowndes, Lumpkin, Maclay, Mason, Mayrant, McLean of Kentucky, Middleton, Moore, Nelson of Virginia, Newton, Ormsby, Parris, Pickens, Piper, Pitkin, Pleasants, Reynolds, Roane, Robertson, Root, Ross, Sergeant, Savage, Sharpe, Smith of Maryland, Smith of Virginia, Southard, Taylor of New York, Taylor of South Carolina, Telfair, Thomas, Throop, Tucker, Wallace, Ward of New York, Ward of New Jersey, Wendover, Wilde, Wilkin, Williams, Willoughby, William Wilson, Woodward, Yancey, and Yates.

NAYS—Messrs. Atherton, Baylies, Boss, Bradbury, Breckenridge, Brigham, Brown, Champion, Cilley, Clayton, Cooper, Culpeper, Davenport, Desha, Goldsborough, Heister, Herbert, Jewett, Kent, King of Massachusetts, Langdon, Lewis, Lovett, Lyon, Mills, Milnor, Moseley, Nelson of Massachusetts, Noyes, Pickering, Reed, Rice, Ruggles, Sheffey, Smith of Pennsylvania, Stanford, Strong, Sturges, Taggart, Tallmadge, Tate, Vose, Ward of Massachusetts, Webster, Wheaton, Whiteside, Wilcox, and Wright.

The bill was ordered to be engrossed and read a third time to-morrow.

WEDNESDAY, February 14.

Mr. BRADBURY presented a petition of sundry merchants and inhabitants of Portland, in the District of Maine, complaining of the loss of their fisheries, the West India trade, and plaster trade; and suggesting the propriety of imposing extra duties on foreign vessels and merchandise imported in them, coming from places from which our vessels are excluded.—Referred to the Committee on Foreign Affairs.

Mr. RUGGLES presented a petition of a convention lately held in the county of Norfolk, in the State of Massachusetts, praying that the mails may not be opened or transported on Sundays.—Referred to the Committee on the Post Office and Post Roads.

Mr. HOPKINSON presented a petition of Lewis Enters and William Zeigler, praying the aid and patronage of Congress in carrying into execution a discovery which they have lately made, of producing light from the gas of stone coal.—Referred to Messrs. HOPKINSON, CONDICT, and HAWES.

Mr. EASTON presented sundry resolutions passed by the Legislature of the Territory of Missouri, upon the subject of land titles in said Territory.—Referred to the Committee on the Public Lands.

Mr. CHAPPELL, from the Committee on Pensions and Revolutionary Claims, reported the bill from the Senate, entitled "An act to increase the pensions of Robert White and Jacob Wrighter," with amendments; which were read, and the first thereof was disagreed to; when the said report and bill were ordered to lie on the table.

Mr. LOWNDES, from the Committee of Ways and Means, reported a bill for the relief of Henry Malcolm, which was read twice, and committed to a Committee of the whole House, on the bill for the relief of Edward Hallowell.

On motion of Mr. FORSYTH, the Naval Committee were instructed to inquire into the expediency of making provision for those American seamen, who were wounded, and for the widows and families of those who were killed, at Dartmoor Prison on the 6th of April, 1815.

On motion of Mr. STEPHENSON, the Committee on the Public Lands were instructed to inquire into the expediency of reporting a bill extending relief and certain permissions to the settlers on the public lands, embraced by the proclamation of the President of the United States, dated ——— day of ——— 1815, upon such reasonable conditions as will not prejudice the rights and interests of the United States, excepting such characters and settlers as may have used any violence, or made any resistance to the authority of the United States.

An engrossed bill, entitled "An act to reduce the amount of the direct tax upon the United States and the District of Columbia, for the year 1816," was read the third time. Mr. CADY moved to recommit the bill to a Committee of the whole House, and the question being taken thereon, it was determined in the negative; when the question was then taken on the passage of the bill, and passed in the affirmative.

The House resumed the consideration of the report of the Committee on Pensions and Revolutionary Claims, upon the bill from the Senate, "to increase the pensions of Robert White and Jacob Wrighter:" whereupon the said report and bill were recommitted to the said committee.

WEST INDIA TRADE.

Mr. BURWELL moved the following motion:

" *Resolved*, That the Secretary of the Treasury be directed to inform the House whether discriminating duties are, at this time, levied in ports of the United States, on British vessels arriving from the West Indies, and laden with West India produce."

Mr. BURWELL said, he should not offer many remarks, to show the propriety of this resolution; he was satisfied they would not be required. The petitions offered to the House had given much importance to the subject, and he was convinced they had taken a view of it not entirely correct. The petitioners seemed to state, that they have to struggle against the impediments thrown in their way by the British colonial policy, without any countervailing advantages, in our own ports. Unless he misunderstood the provisions of the late convention, an equality of tonnage duty and imposts upon the cargoes, had been confined to vessels coming from the British European possessions, and goods the product of those possessions; the existing laws, applicable to foreign trade and produce, were enforced against the British colonial trade. This seemed the natural construction, and he had little doubt the instructions from the Treasury Department to the collectors were conformable to it; if they are not, the House should be informed. According to existing laws, all vessels coming from the British West Indies, are subject, until the 30th of June, to ten per cent. discriminating duty in favor of American vessels, and the tonnage duty of two dollars laid by that act; after that period, to the same discrimination upon an advance upon the old duties of forty-two per cent. These, said Mr. B. are important advantages, and such as will operate favorably in competition with British navigation in our own ports. Should any other arrangements become necessary, they should be left with the treaty-making power, to which it naturally belonged, and it was fair to suppose it would receive the most proper attention. Under any view of the subject, the House should know officially the extent to which the laws in force operated, to estimate justly the additional provisions required by the state of that trade.

Mr. BRADBURY expressed his assent to the resolution, but wished it modified so as to embrace all the British colonies.

It was replied by Mr. BURWELL, that the amendment would be verbal and not substantial, as the operation of the convention on the existing revenue laws upon the British West India possessions, would equally apply to all their colonies.

The resolution was then agreed to.

ORDNANCE, &c.

An engrossed bill, entitled "An act making appropriations for ordnance and ordnance stores, was read the third time, and passed—yeas 107, nays 46, as follows:

YEAS—Messrs. Adgate, Alexander, Archer, Baker, Barbour, Bassett, Bateman, Bennett, Betts, Birdsall, Birdseye, Blount, Brooks, Bryan, Burnside, Burwell, Cady, Caldwell, Calhoun, Cannon, Clarke of North Carolina, Clark of Kentucky, Clendennin, Clopton, Comstock, Condict, Conner, Crawford, Creighton, Cuthbert, Darlington, Desha, Edwards, Forney, Forsyth, Gaston, Glasgow, Griffin, Grosvenor, Hahn, Hall, Hammond, Hanson, Hawes, Henderson, Hopkinson, Hulbert, Hungerford, Ingham, Irving of New York, Jackson, Johnson of Kentucky, Kerr of Virginia, King of North Carolina, Love, Lowndes, Lumpkin, Lyle, Maclay, Mason, Mayrant, McCoy, McKee, McLean of Kentucky, McLean of Ohio, Middleton, Moore, Newton, Ormsby, Parris, Piper, Pitkin, Pleasants, Powell, Reynolds, Roane, Robertson, Root, Ross, Sergeant, Savage, Schenck, Sharpe, Smith of Maryland, Smith of Virginia, Southard, Taul, Taylor of New York, Taylor of South Carolina, Telfair, Thomas, Throop, Townsend, Tucker, Wallace, Ward of New York, Ward of New Jersey, Wendover, Whiteside, Wilde,

Wilkin, Williams, Willoughby, Thomas Wilson, William Wilson, Woodward, and Yancey.

NAYS—Messrs. Atherton, Baer, Baylies, Boss, Bradbury, Breckenridge, Brigham, Champion, Cilley, Cooper, Culpeper, Davenport, Goldsborough, Hale, Jewett, Kent, King of Massachusetts, Langdon, Law, Lewis, Lovett, Lyon, Milnor, Moseley, Nelson of Massachusetts, Noyes, Pickering, Reed, Rice, Ruggles, Sheffey, Smith of Pennsylvania, Stanford, Stearns, Strong, Stuart, Sturges, Taggart, Tallmadge, Tate, Vose, Ward of Massachusetts, Webster, Wheaton, Wilcox, and Wright.

The House again resolved itself into a Committee of the Whole, on the bill to provide for the widows and orphans of the officers, non-commissioned officers, and privates of the volunteers and militia, who have been killed in battle, died in service, or of wounds received while in the service of the United States, during the late war.

The remainder of the day was occupied by the Committee in discussing various amendments to the details of the bill. Before the subject was finished, the usual hour of adjournment arrived—when the Committee rose, reported progress, and obtained leave to sit again.

THURSDAY, February 15.

Mr. LATTIMORE presented a petition of sundry members of the Legislative Council and House of Representatives of the Territory of Mississippi, praying that the members of the Convention proposed to be held in said Territory, to form a constitution, may be apportioned among the counties, according to the white population in each.— Referred to the Committee of the Whole, on the bill to enable the people of the Mississippi Territory to form a constitution and State government.

The SPEAKER presented a resolution of the Legislature of the Territory of Missouri, requesting that measures may be adopted, with respect to a certain tract of land in said Territory, claimed by the Shawanese and Delaware Indians.—Referred to the Secretary of State.

Mr. ROBERTSON, from the Committee on the Public Lands, made a report on the petition of the trustees of the Vincennes University, which was read, when, Mr. R. reported a bill confirming the titles of certain purchasers of land, who purchased from the Board of Trustees for the Vincennes University; which was read twice, and committed to a Committee of the Whole.

Mr. ROBERTSON also reported a bill relating to settlers on the lands of the United States; which was read twice, and committed to a Committee of the Whole.

Mr. CHAPPELL, from the Committee on Pensions and Revolutionary Claims, reported a bill for the relief of Young King, a Chief of the Seneca tribe of Indians; which was read twice, and committed to a Committee of the Whole.

Mr. CHAPPELL, from the Committee on Pensions and Revolutionary Claims, reported with amendments the bill from the Senate for the relief of Robert White, Jacob Wrighter, and others, soldiers in the late army. The House consumed some time in settling the amount of pension to be allowed the persons named, whose cases excited no little interest from having been severely wounded and entirely disabled in the late war; after which the amendments were ordered to be engrossed, and, with the bill, to be read a third time.

The Speaker laid before the House a letter from the Commissioner of the General Land Office, transmitting an estimate of the number of acres of land to which rights of pre-emption have been granted; also a statement of the difference in the amount of money received for lands sold at public and at private sale; which were referred to the Committee on the Public Lands.

The Speaker also laid before the House a letter from the Secretary of the Treasury, to which is annexed a statement of the valuation of lands, lots, and dwelling-houses, and slaves, made under the act laying a direct tax, in pursuance of the resolution of the 18th instant; which was read and ordered to lie on the table.

A message from the Senate informed the House that the Senate insist on their disagreement to the amendments, proposed by this House, to the bill "concerning the convention to regulate the commerce between the territories of the United States and His Britannic Majesty," and agree to the conference asked by this House, and have appointed managers on their part.

MILITARY SERVICES.

The House then resolved itself into a Committee of the Whole, on the bill making further provision for military services during the late war.

A motion made yesterday by Mr. Cannon, to strike out the 3d section of the bill, which provides a bounty of land to the deranged officers of the late army, still under consideration.

This motion produced a discussion which occupied nearly the remainder of the day.

Mr. Johnson, of Kentucky, said, he had expected some observations in favor of the bill from other members, and he had waited in that expectation until the question was about to be put to the Committee; but as objections had been made to some of the sections, he considered it his duty to submit some views for the consideration of those whose duty it was to decide upon the expediency of measures reported by the Military Committee for their sanction. Two leading objections have been made to the second section of the bill, which proposes a donation in land to the officers of the late army who were deranged by the consolidation of regiments during the war, and who were dismissed the service on the 15th of May, 1815, by the act reducing the army from sixty-two thousand to ten thousand men, after the termination of the war on the 17th of February, 1815. First, it is alleged that we have not embraced the soldiers as well as the officers. Every member in this House, and every citizen out of it, ought to know that we have already provided for the soldier of the regular army, both in land and in money; every soldier of the regular army, at his honorable discharge from the public service,

was entitled to either one hundred and sixty, or three hundred and twenty acres of land, and the retained bounty of twenty-four dollars, according to the terms of enlistment. In addition to this, the soldier was clothed and fed, received his eight dollars per month, a bounty of one hundred dollars, besides the retained bounty of twenty-four dollars; and in all such cases where the soldier dies in the service, whether by wounds, or disease, or accident, his heirs are entitled to the benefit of the provision to which he was entitled, although he might have died the next day after entering the service; and as some of these regular soldiers, under eighteen years and over forty-five, had not the right to the bounty land, we have in this bill intended to give them and their heirs the same provisions in land and money bounty; thus it was the very first care of the Military Committee to see the faithful soldier provided for in consequence of his faithful services. The faithful soldier deserved all this for his toil and suffering; and in case of wounds, to this add the provision of a pension for life. The land and bounty alone, to which the soldiers of the late war are entitled, will amount to at least ten million of acres. Under this view, can we reasonably oppose the provision of land and bounty to the officers, which will not amount to one million of acres, because we make no farther provision for the soldier? If that objection be a good one, why not offer an amendment to embrace the soldier? No such proposition has been made, because we must be governed by our capacity and not our inclinations; our bounty should be equally dispensed to the officer and soldier, and not extend to one aid and comfort and refuse it to the other; and if gentlemen oppose a measure of bounty where no provision has been made; a much greater opposition and more rational would have been made to a measure proposing relief where a liberal relief had been granted. Liberality, as well as justice, has its equal scales, and in a national point of view impartiality in one is as important as in the other. We must therefore consider this objection as cutting both ways, operating equally against the officer, as to the proposed bounty, and as to the soldier against any additional provision. The second objection arises from its limitation to the officers of the regular army; in other words, that the provision does not embrace the sea fencibles, the rangers, the militia, the twelve months and eighteen months' volunteers, who were engaged in the late war, who would amount to at least three hundred thousand men, which would require at least fifty millions of acres of land, which at two dollars would amount to one hundred million of dollars—a sum almost equal to the national debt now due of the Revolutionary war and of the late war. The Military Committee had a difficult task to perform. If their feelings and affections could have had the sole influence in their decision, the present provisions would have fallen far short of their wishes. In the discharge of the important duties which devolved upon them, they were compelled to consult, first, their own reason, judgment, and conscience; second, ondly, the feelings, the opinions, and wishes of Congress, as far as they could be ascertained; thirdly, the wishes, the feelings, the honorable sentiment of the nation, and the just expectations of the party concerned. It could not be forgotten, that at the last session of Congress a proposition like the present passed the House, after very warm opposition, and was finally rejected in the Senate; we had, therefore, to look at practicable results, which always fall short of what we would desire to do, and it was much to be regretted that it was not in the power of the committee to recommend more effectual measures of relief for the officer and soldier of every description. The capacity and condition of the country were also consulted and kept in mind—the various heavy demands against it, and the great amount of unliquidated claims which must be paid as soon as settled; thus limited in the discharge of gratitude to those who have served us so faithfully, it is to be lamented that we should be divided on the subject. We can easily ascertain the number of dismissed and deranged officers. Mr. JOHNSON said he had the official statement; about one hundred and seventy field and one thousand five hundred regimental officers had been dismissed. And because we could not extend to three hundred thousand men a bounty in land, was it a good argument against a bounty to these? Mr. J. said the people, or in other words, the militia, have never claimed such bounty; they have never expected such bounty; they would object to such a prodigal waste of public lands, which would be thrown into the market in such quantity as to lessen its market value to a cent, and millions of acres would fall into the hands of rich speculators.

Capital and fortune might be benefitted by such a course, but not the private soldier; and such serious encroachment upon the national domain would very much lessen the resources of revenue from the sale of public lands; the consequence of which would be additional taxation. The impracticability of the measure prevented a proposition of the kind, and the acquiescence of all in this sentiment is tested by a failure in any member to propose such amendments as will embrace these cases.

But, in the discussion of the subject, a comparison had been drawn between the militia and the regular army. Comparisons were often odious, and distinctions invidious. On this occasion there was no necessity for either, because the question of merit was not involved. If so, he would say that both had performed their duty faithfully, honorably, gallantly. The battles of Maguago, of Talapozie, of Chippewa, of Bridgewater, the defence of Fort Sandusky, the sortie from Fort Erie, and New Orleans, all proved thee qual and corresponding merit of the militia and regular army; several of which battles were as bloody and as well fought as the great battle of Zama, according to numbers, between two among the greatest Generals in the world—Hannibal and Scipio Africanus. The Roman legions were in part veterans; Hannibal had his mercenaries, al-though some were raw troops; Carthage being a commercial, rich nation, had no militia, but maintained a mercenary army; which army, at the close of the first Punic war, involved Carthage in a most bloody civil war for four years; in which Hamilcar, the father of Hannibal, at the head of the population of the country, totally defeated and destroyed it—a remarkable instance of the effect of union and zeal in a people who, without having been trained to arms, could subdue, conquer, and, indeed, annihilate the most powerful, disciplined, veteran army. And the cause of this war arose from the demands of the army after the termination of the first Punic war, and Carthage was not in a condition to comply with them. No such views have entered into the bosom of the American Army; no corps has ever given the least evidence of disaffection. A few individuals have clamored in the newspapers as to the reduction of the army, and particularly as to a failure in Congress to make some provision or donation which might discharge the debt of gratitude and justice. But this was the enjoyment of a right to express our sentiments, and in our country altogether harmless; and even this course was disapproved by a great majority of the army.

Mr. J. said, he did not, however, approve of such a course; it had a tendency to injure and create prejudice against a regular army, without a corresponding benefit. For he held as a fundamental principle in a free Government, that the reduction of an army should always be made without regard to the number of officers who wished to be retained; and, he said, he was for the reduction to ten thousand men; and he considered Congress entitled to more credit and merit in that act than would be given to them by the present generation. But, after having said this, he considered these principles as operating with double force on the Representatives of the people, to make some reasonable provision for those who have been dismissed the service of their country, and who have fought and bled for us. For, let it be recollected, that no regular army was ever actuated by the same pure motives of love of country, love of liberty, desire of honest fame, and also have contributed their just share in fixing upon a rock our independence, against which the wide billows of the tempestuous ocean may beat in vain. It has been truly said, that the militia did not expect bounty in land; of course, none has been offered; but there is a provision, for which the militia has called; they have demanded it of us, and we have complied with their wishes—have gratified their expectations—we have reported a provision to extend half-pay for five years to the widows and children of the rangers, sea-fencibles, twelve and eighteen months' volunteers, and the militia of the different States. This provision they expected, and this provision has been sanctioned; and at the end of five years, should that provision be considered inadequate, Congress has the power to extend it. This provision is not confined to the officers and soldiers who were killed in battle, died of wounds, but extended to all who may have died in service in any other way, and to those who may have died on their way home, after being dismissed the service. Without such a measure as this, the militia would not have been satisfied; with it, they cannot be dissatisfied. This very provision is doing more for the militia than the donation proposed to the dismissed officers; and this question might be left with safety to the people themselves—to the militia—and they would not hesitate to demonstrate their liberality, their honorable feelings. The people are generous, magnanimous, brave, and just. But, look to the extent of this provision in favor of the militia. It looks to every part of the nation, and embraces every part of our extended frontier. It contemplates every battle fought during the war, and it provides for sickness and disease.

The State of Ohio may look to Hull's surrender, the battle of Brownstown, &c.; Kentucky, to the Northwestern army, the river Raisin, the two sieges of Fort Meigs, Colonel Dudley's defeat, &c.; Virginia, to Hampton, Norfolk, &c.; Maryland, to Baltimore; New York, Pennsylvania, Vermont, to the Niagara, Plattsburg, &c.; Connecticut, to Stonington, &c.; Tennessee, to her various splendid victories over the Creeks, at New Orleans, &c.; and all other States, without going into detail, according to their sufferings and losses. Is this nothing? Is it nothing to Kentucky that you embrace the case of the widow of Colonel John Allen, whose worth was well known —as pure as a sun-beam—and who had left a name as imperishable as our liberties; the widow of the unfortunate Major Graves, whose memory was dear to his country; the widow of the gallant Hart, of the determined Hickman, and all those gallant sons of the West who died in their country's cause, leaving behind widows or children? As much as this is to Kentucky, so is it a just representation of the case of every other State, as to their losses.

The bill does not neglect the militia. Mr. J. said, no man could suppose he felt indifferent to the militia, whatever may be the merit of the militia. In time of war, it is important that the draughts should be as light as is consistent with the national security; and to make the draughts as light as possible, inducements must be held out to increase the regular army. The good of the people requires this imperiously. This also justified that bounty in land and money which was given to the regular soldier, and not to the militia. Of this we heard no complaint; and, although we made no promise to the officers of land bounty, the obligation is not lessened to do it, if we think they deserve it. It will have great influence in a future emergency. Nor is it any argument against it, that we could always get officers for our Army; but this presents an additional argument in its favor, provided patriotism be worth rewarding. Nor is it sufficient to say, that some do not deserve our bounty. It is enough that we know the fact that a great majority of the officers deserve more than we propose to give them by this bill.

As to the pay of the officers during the war, it

is generally admitted that, with the most rigid economy, they had to call upon their own funds, or upon paternal kindness, for pecuniary aid; and, as soon as an officer entered the regular army, he had to give up every other prospect—his pursuits, his family connexions. It did not happen to the same extent with those who entered for the term of six months. In reducing our army to 10,000, it was well known that efficient men, both in body and in mind, were generally retained; of course, those who had ruined a constitution by hard service; those who had served ten, fifteen, and twenty years, and advanced in life; the wounded officer wanting an eye, a leg, or an arm, were dismissed; such men have some claims upon their country. The memorable Congress of '83, which closed the Revolution, gave half-pay for life to the officers, or five years whole pay. This bill proposes only a donation in land. Much has been said upon the subject of preparing for war in time of peace. In a Republic large standing armies cannot be maintained, nor other expensive establishments; the means of preparation must be cheap, but effectual. If so, the bill under debate would be a strong measure of preparation; preparation which would give moral power, physical power, and intellectual power. Moral power, by such illustrious examples of honor, virtue, gratitude, and justice—physical, by uniting all hearts and all hands in support of a Government inspiring such confidence—intellectual, by extending the means of support and cultivation to the indigent and distressed. The true maxim in a Republic will ever remain—that the militia is the palladium of our rights, the ultimate reliance in the storms of adversity. With this maxim there is another principle no less correct, that the militia are valuable in the first moments of war, until regular troops can relieve them from garrison duty, long and distant campaigns; this was the universal sentiment of the people during the late war, and such will their sentiments continue to be; it is their interest that it should be so.

Mr. J. said, he had omitted one important consideration, which should have great influence in inducing Congress to extend this land bounty to the deranged and dismissed officers. The Army of the United States was constituted upon principles, and composed of materials, differing from the regular armies of ancient or modern times.

In looking into history we should find that the armies of Alexander, in the invasion of Asia; of Hannibal, in the invasion of Italy; of Cæsar, in the invasion of Gaul and Britain, and of all others, the mercenary troops were devoted to their leaders, and these leaders repaid their devotion by rapine, plunder, and often with the lands of the conquered country. But the troops of the United States were devoted to their country; no chieftain could influence them to turn their arms against it; nor do they expect to be paid for their devotion to their country by plunder—by sacking villages and towns. They receive no such reward; they are actuated by no such inducement; they have no such expectations; they receive no other compensation than that which they receive as ordinary pay by the laws of the United States; nor do they expect anything, except from our gratitude and justice. The reasonable expectations of such men ought not to be disappointed; it is a pity that more cannot be done for them.

The duties of the Military Committee have been increasing in number and in importance since the attack on the Chesapeake; however arduous and important those duties may have been at any time, they were not of more difficulty than those which have devolved upon the committee at the present session; and such will always be the case at the termination of a war. So various were the expectations of different classes of individuals; so various the duties resulting from the claims of those different classes; so difficult to discharge those great duties which look with discernment to the interests of the Commonwealth, and to that portion of it which has claims upon us. In this situation, the committee endeavored to embrace the cases of all who were entitled to consideration, without injury to the Republic. In this view of the subject we did not confine ourselves to the late war, but extended aid and comfort to the surviving officers and soldiers of the Revolution, who are unable to gain a livelihood by labor, and those of the late war who are so disabled as to be unable to maintain themselves. The committee reported a bill, for the purpose of organizing a corps of invalids; for the wounded, a pension; for the widows and orphans, half-pay for five years; for the dismissed and deranged officers, a bounty in land. These provisions, if carried into effect, will relieve much distress, alleviate much sorrow, bind up the broken hearted, and administer to them the healing balm of affection. The regular soldier has his money and land bounty—his widow and children the same provision in case of his death. For the officer and soldier of the regular army and militia, who have lost their vouchers by captivity or unavoidable accident, a provision is here recommended, giving equitable powers of adjustment to the War Department; and, as measures of precaution and efficiency, we have recommended a general and division staff, that will make our forces efficient in the field; and a Military Academy, to diffuse military instruction throughout the United States.

Mr. J. said, the formation of a national character was of great importance; every nation has a character of some sort—mixed or positive in its kind. A character for all the virtues—of liberality, of generosity, of magnanimity, of gratitude, of justice, of wisdom; or it may be positive, of the opposite qualities and attributes—of parsimony, of ingratitude, of injustice, of ignorance; or mixed, combining a part of the virtues that exalt, and part of the virtues that degrade the human character. On the present occasion it would be discovered that the provisions of the bill were neither prodigal, on the one hand, nor parsimonious on the other. In measures of State we should avoid extremes.

In concluding, Mr. J. said, he would not inquire whether we had promised to provide for the widow and orphan, or make donations to the officer; a tender father never stops to inquire whether he is bound by contract to aid and relieve a worthy son; nor does a man of noble feelings inquire whether he is bound by contract to extend the hand of assistance to a friend in distress. The Government contracted no legal obligation; it acted wisely in not doing it. It was wise to be free to act, as circumstances would warrant. This is no argument, however, against the bill. It will reflect more honor upon Congress to give where it is merited, without legal obligation. In the beginning of the war we did not know how the army would act; we have their conduct now before us, and we approve it. If individual cases should be selected, as has been done, to depreciate the claims of the army, it should be recollected that the same might be done of all associations of men; and it is to be regretted that we should indulge prejudices against men who have generally acted so well, and that jealousy should be excited between the army and militia. The praise of the army should not be considered as censure of the militia, nor well-earned praise of the militia, as lessening the claims of the army. With these views, the hope is indulged that the bill will pass without material amendment.

Mr. COMSTOCK said, this was a subject upon which much might be said on each side, by gentlemen of learning and eloquence. It is one, said he, on which my mind has labored with considerable anxiety. Possessing only very limited claims, sir, to either of these valuable accomplishments, I must content myself with glancing at some of the reasons which will influence my conduct upon this occasion.

Mr. C. said, I early imbibed a respect for the patriot soldier. He possesses qualities of mind which challenge and receive my admiration and esteem. Forsaking the hallowed shades of domestic happiness, he courts the danger, toils, and privations, incident to his profession. His best days are devoted to the service of his country. His health, his blood, and his life, are nobly sacrificed upon the altar of the public weal.

This respect, so early imbibed, has strengthened with succeeding years. I feel all its force in contemplating the officers of the late army; I believe, in general, they deserve well of their country; I rejoice that they merit, and receive, the meed of her applause. They have exhibited a degree of fortitude and intelligence not surpassed in any age or nation; and they have essentially contributed, under the auspices of Heaven, to the speedy, honorable, and beneficial issue of the conflict, from which the nation has recently emerged.

Mr. C. said it can scarcely be imagined that I am actuated in the vote I am about to give, by an apprehension that the late war was unjust or unnecessary; for although I have not been in the habit of presenting my views upon this subject in elaborate speeches, nevertheless, the votes I have uniformly given upon questions calculated to promote the military service, abundantly evince my ideas of the justice and propriety of the late war. While I lamented the imperious necessity which demanded its declaration, I conceived it forced upon us by the injustice and rapacity of the enemy. Hence, sir, I have ever deemed it my duty, as a member of this honorable body, to invigorate the national arm, by furnishing to the Government the means of humbling and vanquishing our foes; of vindicating the honor and interest of the nation, and of placing them upon a firm and stable foundation.

Mr. C. said, what induced the officers to enter the service? What multiplied the number of candidates for military office, to an extent beyond that which it was proper to gratify and employ? I answer, sir, patriotism, the love of fame, and the laudable desire of rendering benefit to the country. It has been said, that military glory is the pay of a soldier. Does justice require those donations? No sir. Has the Government failed to perform its engagements with the officers? Has it subjected itself to the imputation of bad faith? Sir, no such thing exists, no such pretension has been suggested; the Government has strictly adhered to the requisition of those laws in virtue of which they solicited and received their commissions. They have had an opportunity to manifest their love of country, and to render her honorable service in the exercise of their military talents. They have received pretty ample pecuniary compensation, (especially the superior officers,) and enjoy all the advantages of victory, with the respect and gratitude of the nation.

Mr. C. said, does sound policy demand these donations? I think not, sir. I am aware that we may be exhorted by honorable members to transport ourselves in imagination to a period when we may be again engaged in a conflict of arms with an enemy; a conflict similar in character to that through which we have lately passed in defence of our dearest rights; in defence of the very attributes of sovereignty. We may be told that, at a period so eventful, we may solicit in vain the heroes of the country to wear our commission, and to fight our battles. They will be deterred from entering our service, from the illiberality which the history of our conduct, in relation to the deranged officers, will disclose, should this section be rejected.

Sir, I do not believe that such a state of things will ever occur. Real vision, in my judgment, will never behold this fanciful picture. History will record that we have complied with every legal and moral obligation imposed on us in reference to these deranged officers. Have they been wounded? we inscribe their names, as invalid officers, on the roll of pensioners of the United States. Have officers been slain in battle? we grant a gratuity, for a term of years, to their legal representatives. Sir, without adverting to all the provisions upon this subject, suffice it to say, that history will proclaim the justice and munificence of the conduct of the Government in regard to the Army. Thus, sir, the period, I apprehend, will never arrive when men of military talents and heroic cast of character, in

sufficient numbers, cannot be found, proud to wear your uniform. courting your service, and ready to rally round the standard of the country in the hour of trial. An honorable sense of duty, and an ardent and long cherished attachment to those eternal principles of civil and religious liberty, guarantied to us by our excellent political institutions, will be among the powerful motives which will secure forever to the Government their best services and affection.

Mr. Chairman, invidious distinctions are involved in this section, to which I am opposed. It excludes from its benefits the most meritorious class of the Army. Those officers of the Army who are retained in service are not embraced by this provision; and yet it is fair to conclude that many of them have rendered more service to the country, and have stronger claims on her bounty than those who have been deranged.

At the reduction of the Army, when a selection of officers was made for the Peace Establishment, we may naturally conclude that regard was had, in some measure, to the respective merits of the officers composing the late army. Hence, sir, the imperfection of this system is manifest.

Mr. Chairman, what reason have we to discriminate in this way, between the regular and militia officers of the late army. Have not the latter displayed military genius and devotion to their country? Have they not rendered her signal services, and performed many noble and gallant achievements? They certainly have, sir; in this exists no difference of opinion. With what justice or propriety, then, can we withhold from them this boon? Sir, the names of these brave and patriotic officers thicken on my recollection. I could mention a Shelby, a Porter, and many others, if it were proper to name them in this place, equally deserving the benefits of this section, as the deranged officers of the regular army. Sir, the honorable chairman of the Military Committee has reminded us, that we grant land to privates, and asks, why we withhold it from officers? Sir, there is a great difference between the pecuniary compensation afforded a private, and an officer. Besides, by the terms of your contract with the private soldier, when he entered the service you promised him land; no such contract exists, no such promise was made in relation to the officers. The same gentleman, when speaking of the advantages extended to the militia, with a view to do away the imputation that the deranged officers of the regular army are the favored objects of our partiality, remarked, that we place the militia, when wounded, on the pension list. Sir, this privilege is common to militia and regulars; and, therefore, cannot be adduced to justify the distinction to which I have adverted.

But my estimable friend from Kentucky complains of our turning the deranged officers upon the world without the means of support. Sir, when the people have no business for their public servants to perform, when the necessity which induced their official elevation ceases to exist, it is just and proper they should retire to private life; of this practice no one can, of right, complain. We maintain no sinecures in this Republic. Mr. Chairman, from the best reflection I have been able to bestow upon the subject of this section, I am induced to believe it ought not to be adopted. If, however, it shall obtain, I hope its benefits will be confined to captains and subalterns. Thus, sir, I am constrained, from a sense of duty, to oppose, upon this occasion, the wishes of my honorable friend, the chairman of the Military Committee, with whom I am generally happy and proud to act in concert.

Mr. TAUL said: Though I am decidedly of opinion that the section of the bill proposed to be stricken out is impolitic, and of course ought not to pass, I confess that I distrust my own judgment, when it is different from that of any of the standing committees of the House. The members composing those committees are selected for their capacity and particular knowledge of the business to be referred to them. Those selections have been judiciously made. The standing committees have a double responsibility on them. Hence it is to be presumed that every measure, before it is reported to the House, undergoes a very nice scrutiny. Those committees have deservedly great weight in the investigation and decision of such questions as may have come before and been decided on by them. In opposing, therefore, any measure recommended by them, you have to encounter " fearful odds" indeed.

In addition to the support given to this measure by the Military Committee, it has also received the support of an honorable, highly respectable, enlightened, and consequently influential member from Maryland, (Mr. SMITH.)

In opposing the proposed donation of lands to the disbanded officers, I wish it to be distinctly understood that I have no idea of detracting from their merits. They stand high in my estimation. They have the richest reward in the nation's treasury—its thanks, its gratitude.

But, sir, is it to the regular army exclusively, or the officers commanding it, that you are indebted for the splendid victories achieved during the late war?—for your present high standing amongst the nations of the earth? Much, very much, Mr. Chairman, was performed by the militia; yes, the militia, that was once considered the bulwark of the nation; but which some gentlemen seem to consider, at this time, worse than nothing. It is not my intention to make any invidious comparisons; I shall not say that this was done by the militia, that by the regular army.

But I must be pardoned in directing your attention back to the Fall of 1813. What was the situation of this country then, and the state of the public mind and feelings of the people? Disaster had succeeded disaster in such rapid succession, that this nation was literally clad in mourning, was covered with sackcloth and ashes; every face was pale; the highest-minded and most sanguine in this nation was bowed down; nothing but the brilliant achievements of your gallant tars on the water prevented you from sinking into the lowest depths of despair and despondency. From what quarter did the first ray of hope beam upon you? From the Northwest—Kentucky's venerable chief, at the head of her volunteer militia, in the capture of the British Army under Proctor, and the dispersion of the Indians with the slaughter of their favorite leader, brought you relief. Despair and despondency disappeared like an unwelcome guest. Confidence and hope succeeded. Bonfires and illuminations in all parts of the United States evidenced the change produced by the gallant deeds of your militia. The honorable gentleman at the head of your Military Committee (Mr. JOHNSON) knows well their merits. He has commanded them; he has fought and bled with them. As the commander of a militia corps, he has rendered signal services to his country; and should the occasion require it, will doubtless do so again. It is unnecessary to enumerate instances of the gallant achievements of your militia. The plains of New Orleans will be a lasting monument to their fame, their worth and usefulness.

But, says an honorable gentleman from Massachusetts, (Mr. CONNER,) for whom I have the highest personal respect, General Washington pronounced during the war of the Revolution, that the militia under his command had been prejudicial, instead of serviceable, to the country, General Washington spoke of the heterogeneous, discordant, unorganized, and undisciplined militia of that day. His various communications to Congress during the time he administered the Government, will demonstrate that he considered the militia the nation's best, surest, and, I may say, only defence. His anxiety to have the militia properly organized, armed, and disciplined, is manifested in all his communications to Congress on the subject. The same honorable gentleman (Mr. CONNER) has referred us to the military operations in India, as an evidence of the correctness of the position which he has assumed. In that country he has informed you that an army of fifty or an hundred thousand men has been put to flight by a few thousand British troops. I must be permitted to flatter myself that the American militia are something superior to the Hindoo; if they are not, it is high time we were looking out for some other dependence than the militia. Sir, if your militia are not capable of defending themselves, of fighting their own battles—if they are not fit materials for soldiers, they are not fit for citizens; it is time they were subjects. Gentlemen seem to have misunderstood the ground of opposition to the proposed donation to the disbanded officer. Sir, it is not because your militia officers are not included; I will not say that the militia officer would not accept anything of the kind, which the Government, in the plenitude of its liberality, might bestow; but this much I will say, that he ought not.

Sir, if suffering is to be rewarded, you should begin with the non-commissioned officers and privates of the militia. Comparatively speaking, the situation of the officer during the late war was enviable, the situation of the soldier wretched, deplorable. I would not make a donation of land to the officer, without making a similar donation to the soldier; and I do not think either entitled to it. I doubt the right of the Congress of the United States to make such a disposition of the public lands. It has been too common a practice under almost all governments to reward a few at the expense of the many. Let us not, if possible, fall into this error. If we are to exercise our charity, let us find fit objects; for ill-directed or misplaced charity, is worse than no charity at all.

Hitherto the Congress of the United States has provided only for the widows and children of such officers as may have been killed in battle. The humane and laudable object of this bill is to make provision for the widows and children of such non-commissioned officers and privates as may have died in your service. It is worthy a great and magnanimous people. The best feelings of the human heart must be enlisted in their favor; I therefore regret that the proposed bounty to the disbanded officers should be ushered into this House in company with the claim of the widow and orphan. They stand on very different ground. It is contended that the disbanded officers were taken from lucrative professions, from profitable agricultural and commercial pursuits, that their business has been deranged and cannot be resumed to advantage. Sir, one, two, or three years' service will not disqualify a man for the pursuits of civil life. The disbanded officer who cannot resume his civil pursuits was unfit to be honored with a commission; the country is under no obligation to support him. The meritorious disbanded officer, in resuming business, will have considerable advantages over others in the same line of business; his military services will have enlisted the sympathies of the people on his side, and consequently command their friendship and support. Pass the section of the bill now under consideration, and, my word for it, your militia is disgusted, great violence will be done to public sentiment. It is considered in the light of a charitable donation; all who held commissions during the late war are included; the great mass of the community will not be able to perceive that because a young gentleman (worthy as he may be) may have worn epaulets for a few months or a year, that he is, therefore, an object of charity. Sir, he stands on very different ground from that of the superannuated, war-worn officer or soldier. This Government is founded (as I remarked on a former occasion) on the affections of the people; their feelings, their wishes must be consulted. It is no reproach to them that they would be opposed to the proposed grant of land to the officers. Select meritorious objects, and you will find no limit to the bounty, to the gratitude of this people. The Legislature of the State which I have the honor, in part, of representing on this floor, has forwarded us a memorial in behalf of the widow and orphan. As well as I recollect, it is stated to have passed both branches of the Legislature unanimously.

It has been observed, in the course of this debate, that the disbanded officers have acquired a great deal of military information; that by making this provision for them, they will be enabled to perfect their military education, and, in the event of another war, would make valuable officers. Perhaps I have not the same confidence in making good and valuable officers by education that some gentlemen have. You cannot make a military commander as you can make a cobbler. He must be formed by the plastic hand of nature herself. An honorable, ingenious, and enlightened gentleman from Massachusetts, (Mr. HULBERT,) some time since, in debate, on the bill to establish an additional Military Academy, (which he advocated with great zeal and ability,) embellished his speech and undertook to illustrate the position which he assumed, by quoting the old maxim, "That an army of hares commanded by a lion was superior to an army of lions commanded by a hare." Be it so. I should doubt making a lion of a hare by any course of education that could be taken. It requires a combination of rare qualities to make an able commander. Those qualities actual service alone can develope.

Much as our hopes were rested upon our old experienced officers at the period when war was declared, and for some time thereafter, our egregious disappointment will never be forgotten. Without intending a reflection upon any particular officer, it is with pain that I say that many of them at the trying moment were found wanting.

The distinguished heroes who shone with such resplendent lustre at the closing scene, and who "have filled the measure of their country's honor," were unthought of at the commencement of hostilities.

The resources of your country could, in my opinion, be better applied, than in the way contemplated by the section of the bill under consideration. Amongst other things your militia want arms—though they are, in my opinion, superior to any troops in the world, it is not to be disguised that they are in a most wretched situation. They know nothing of the musket and bayonet until they are called into service. For the first time those arms are put into their hands. They are dissatisfied with the musket, because they are acquainted with the rifle and know its efficacy. They should be habituated to the use of those arms on which they have to depend in battle. It takes some time to reconcile a militiaman to arms with which he was unacquainted, and which he has not been used to handling.

I shall vote for striking out the section; the rest of the bill I do most sincerely hope and trust will receive the unanimous support of the House.

Mr. EASTON said. he entertained the highest regard and respect for the honorable, the chairman and members of the Military Committee who reported the bill now under discussion, and if the honorable members of the committee had gone a little farther they would have been entitled to more of his respect.

I have heard, Mr. Chairman, said Mr. E., a great deal about national glory upon the floor of this House: I, too, love national glory—not only national glory, but also love national justice. He considered the present question, whether a donation of lands should be granted to the disbanded officers of the Army as altogether a question of policy. He had, at an early period in the session, offered a resolution instructing the committee on Military Affairs to inquire into the expediency of paying to the officers. non-commissioned officers, and privates, of the militia, army, and rangers, who served in the late war, interest on the sums due to them, from the time they ought to have been paid, until they should be paid. He understood it had been reported against; had the inquiry been as to its justice, instead of its expediency, he believed it could not have been reported against; he thought the nation should be just before it was bountiful. If the committee had reported in favor of the payment to the army and militia what was in truth due to them, and also in favor of granting a bounty in land to the officers and privates of the militia, we should then have had the question of justice, as well as policy, before us. He, for one, was not for giving donations to the disbanded officers, and withholding what was justly due to the militia. He thought such a measure was neither just nor politic. The officers of the army had sought, with great competition, to procure commissions in the service of the country, while many of the militia, some of whom were equally meritorious and would have made as good officers had they have been commissioned, have been forced into the service by a draught, others had volunteered, and greatly distinguished themselves in their country's cause.

Mr. E. said, he had heard, with great pleasure, glory in high-toned and very eloquent strains poured forth, and very properly bestowed upon Jackson, Brown, Scott, Ripley, Macomb, Gaines, Porter, Miller, and the long list of heroes who had helped to fight the battles of the country; they justly merited all that could be said in their praise, and he was not disposed to detract in the least from the merit, the praise, or the honor, to which they were so justly entitled; he would not pluck one solitary feather from their cap of fame. He would however ask, how was this glory acquired? Who acquired it for them? While he was not disposed to eulogise mortal man, he could not forbear to bring into view before the committee the merits of the militia. He recollected, when quite a youth, a respectable old lady from the neighborhood where he lived had made a visit into Vermont; on her return, she was asked how she liked the settlements and the people? She observed, smilingly, that they lived in log cabins in the woods, and at every house she saw more children than panes of glass in their windows. It is to these hardy sons of America that a portion of this glory ought to be ascribed. Who defeated the British at Sackett's Harbor? Who helped to gain the successive battles of Chippewa, Niagara, and Erie? The militia. Who defeated General Proctor's army at the Mo-

14th Con. 1st Sess.—32

ravian towns? The militia. Who terrified and beat a veteran army, greatly superior in number, at Plattsburg on the 18th of September, 1814, and gave military fame to Macomb? The Vermont and New York militia. Who expelled the British veteran foe from before New Orleans on the 8th of January, 1815, immortalized the hero Jackson, and crowned their country with everlasting glory? It was the brave and hardy sons of the West—the militia and volunteers. And what were these glorified Generals at the commencement of the war; they, most of them, were of the militia?

Sir, this is, or ought to be, a Government of equal rights—equal protection should be extended to all, and equal and exact justice measured out to all alike. How had the war borne in its operation upon the people of this nation? It would be found that certain portions of the people had made money during the war—Pittsburg, Carlisle, and other places in Pennsylvania; also, in certain parts of the State of New York, and other States to the South, had made money by the war, while the frontiers had suffered incalculable losses, whether that frontier was on the Atlantic or in the interior. The war had raged upon the Niagara frontier, upon the seacoast, and in the Northwest. On the Niagara frontier, the people had been plundered, and their houses burned by the enemy; many had lost everything they possessed. Portions of the seaboard had also been ravaged, and the inhabitants plundered of their property, and their persons violated; while, on the Northwest frontier, the people had been shot dead in their fields, their houses burned, property robbed, and many left without a cent to give support or succor to the agonizing widow and helpless orphan. And was this nation to give to the rich, to disbanded officers, to the aristocratic branch of the community, who sought with eagerness the honor of holding your commissions, and the truly unfortunate to remain wholly unprovided for? He wished not to be understood as being opposed to this donation; as a matter of policy to the officers, he thought it should be granted, but not until relief should be extended to such as had been ruined by the war; the militia and army paid what was due to them, and the like bounty in lands extended to the militia. Equal rights do not exist where justice is not measured out to all alike; individuals who have loaned to the Government, always have been paid interest; and what is the withholding from the militia, rangers, and others employed in your service, sums really due to them, but a forced loan? If you provide for these disbanded officers, why not make provision for the militia, the great bulwark of our liberty, the ark of our political safety? Does not sound policy dictate this course? To whom will you look, and to whom will posterity look, for the defence of the country, in case of another war, if it be not to the militia?

Let any member of this honorable Committee figure to himself the situation of a frontier-man, a ranger, in the war upon the Western frontier. He enlists, because his family, his country, liberty, and property, everything held dear and sacred, is endangered; he scorns to fly, he expects pay, because it is right, and he cannot serve without it. He goes in debt, supplies his own provision, horse, and clothing; he marches not into the open field to meet in broad day-light a civilized enemy, but, in the wide wilderness, to combat with the rifle, the tomahawk, and scalping-knife, leaving his defenceless family behind, at home, expecting every night to be slaughtered by the ruthless and relentless savage foe, who creep from their hiding places, make their attack in the dark, by surprise, and, unless successful, are off through the thicket with all the rapidity of the deer. The savage hunts the ranger as he would hunt the doe. Wet and cold are the days, and dismal are the nights he has spent in his country's cause. Peace is proclaimed—it brings glad tidings to every honest heart. The ranger and the militia-man return, they expect payment, everybody supposed they long since would have been paid, without it they cannot discharge their debts. Their certificates for pay more worthless than Philadelphia bills in New York, or New York bills in Philadelphia were, during the war. They must dispose of them at a discount, or the bailiff sells their property or confines them in prison. Similar has been the fate of many an honest husbandman. The militia of that portion of the country which he had the honor to represent, had defended the country before and during the whole war. We were without regular troops; it is true there were ten companies of rangers for three Territories, but those were taken from the militia of that country, and the few regular troops did little more than perform garrison duty. The country was greatly harassed during the whole war, and he could here give a long catalogue of barbarous and bloody murders committed, which he forebore to detain the Committee to relate.

The militia, the independent farmers of the West, when the colonization of the Western country was threatened by the British veteran forces at New Orleans, and hordes of blood-thirsty savages, headed by British myrmidons and emissaries, were pressing upon the settlements in the North, they, the people of the West, the father and the son, the aged and the infirm, rallied around the standard of their country, and did march, and would again march, at the point of the bayonet, to spill the last drop of blood sooner than the tyrant of the ocean, the destroyer of mankind, the spoiler of free trade, and the deadly enemy of all free Governments, should have gained a foothold in this happy land of liberty and equal rights.

The honorable chairman of the Committee on Military Affairs, (Mr. JOHNSON, of Kentucky,) says they have not neglected the militia, in his opinion, if I understood him right; and undertakes to prove this position, by stating that Congress have given a donation of land to the widows of the late John Allen, and Captains Hart and Hickman; that we have embraced the cases of widows and orphans. Certainly, providing for the widows and orphans of the deceased, is not providing for the militia themselves. Make liberal and generous provision for the militia; reward those whose interest it will be to rally around the standard of the country, and to meet the invasion of the enemy as they would trespassers upon their own personal concerns, and you will never be forced to resort to conscriptions.

On the contrary, if you grant extra bounties to such professional gentlemen as have given up the practice of the law, worth five thousand dollars a year; to commercial men who have quit their pursuits, worth ten thousand dollars a year, as stated by an honorable gentleman, and the exclusive advocates of disbanded officers, who, with such lucrative professions and employments, have a competency to return to; while you withhold relief to such as have been ruined by the war, and refuse to reward your militia, who have gained you most splendid victories, fought the battles of the country, preserved the honor of the nation—soldiers composed of farmers, American husbandmen, fresh from their fields, separated from their families, firesides, and homes, who, upon the sound of their country's alarm, have marched to its standard, and met the invasion of the mercenary enemies to the rights of man, to liberty, and a free Government; forced them to retire with great slaughter, and crowned this nation with immortal glory—withhold, I say, a reward to this meritorious class of the community—put them off with the honorable thanks of the nation—bestow bounties exclusively upon disbanded officers, and in all future contests, as in the late war, you will have officers by thousands, but few soldiers, to fight the battles of this beloved country.

Messrs. CANNON, ROSS, McKEE, and WILLIAMS, supported the motion, and opposed the grant of land to the disbanded officers. Messrs. SMITH of Maryland, JACKSON of Virginia, and WILDE, were adverse to the motion, and in favor of awarding the bounty proposed in the bill.

The motion to strike out the section was finally agreed to—ayes 74, nays 60.

On motion, of Mr. DESHA, the 2d section of the bill was so amended as to confine the land bounty to those soldiers, above forty-five and under eighteen years of age, who enlisted "for five years or during the war."

On motion, of Mr. JACKSON of Virginia, a new section was added to the bill for the purpose of guarding, as far as possible, the bounty from falling into the hands of speculators, by prohibiting the transfer of right thereto, until after the patent has issued.

The Committee then rose, reported progress, and obtained leave to sit again.

FRIDAY, February 16.

Mr. SERGEANT presented a petition of sundry inhabitants of Montgomery county, and of the Northern Liberties of the city of Philadelphia, in the State of Pennsylvania, praying that the mails may not be transported or opened on Sundays.

Mr. EASTON presented a resolution of the Legislature of the Territory of Missouri, requesting that some provision may be adopted to afford relief to settlers on public lands in that Territory, who have been ordered to remove therefrom by the proclamation of the President of the United States, of the 12th December, 1815.—Referred to the Committee of the Whole on the bill relating to settlers on the public lands.

Mr. JEWETT submitted the following resolution; which was read and ordered to lie on the table:

Resolved, That the President of the United States be requested to cause to be laid before this House, a statement of all expenses which have been incurred in the City of Washington, under the authority of the United States, for erecting edifices of any kind, and for repairing and ornamenting buildings of any kind, and for improving the streets and squares of the city, and for all other purposes of ornament and improvement, (excepting the navy yard and its buildings and improvements,) designating, as specifically as the nature of the case will admit, the years when the several expenditures were incurred, the purposes to which they were applied, and the funds out of which the same were paid or appropriated, distinguishing between such payments as were made out of the Treasury of the United States, and such as were made out of the proceeds of the sales of the public property within the District of Columbia, or out of other district funds, or donations received: and also a statement of the amount of the funds derived from the sale of lots, and other public property within the City of Washington, and of the probable value of the public property remaining on hand.

The bill from the Senate, entitled "An act to increase the pensions of Robert White, and Jacob Wrighter," was read the third time, as amended, and passed.

Ordered, That the title be "An act to increase the pensions of Robert White, Jacob Wrighter, John Young, and John Crampersey."

PETITION OF WILLIAM FLOOD.

Mr. YANCEY, from the Committee of Claims, made a report on the petition of William Flood, which was read; when Mr. Y. reported a bill for the relief of William Flood; which was read twice, and committed to a Committee of the Whole. The report is as follows:

That the petitioner owned and occupied a valuable dwelling-house, together with a valuable mill and other outhouses, on the west side of the river Mississippi, previous to the month of December, 1814; on the 27th of that month, the plantation of the petitioner was taken possession of by Brigadier General David B. Morgan, under an order from General Andrew Jackson, then commanding the United States troops in New Orleans and its vicinity, and the houses occupied by the officers and troops under his command. On the morning of the 8th of January, 1815, General Morgan was attacked by the enemy, forced from his position, and the houses of the petitioner, together with his mill and timber, at the same time destroyed by the enemy. It appears to the committee, from documents accompanying the petition, that the property was destroyed on account of its being occupied by the troops of the United States, and for the purpose of preventing barracks being again erected for the defence of New Orleans. No other buildings at that place, or in the neighborhood, were destroyed; and it was known to

the enemy that the mill of the petitioner had furnished the timber with which the batteries had been constructed.

The committee are of opinion that the petitioner is entitled to relief, and therefore report by bill.

PETITION OF EDMUND DANA.

Mr. YANCEY also made a report on the petition of Edmund Dana; which was read, and the resolution therein contained was concurred in by the House. The report is as follows:

That the petitioner states that, during the late war, he acted in the capacity of a clothing sutler to the different posts and regiments of the third military district; that he opened shop in the different garrisons for the sale of such articles of clothing as suited the convenience of the officers and soldiers; and that, having given credit to many of the soldiers for such articles as they purchased, he has lost many of his debts by the death and desertion of his debtors, and by some of the soldiers having been discharged on account of their being minors.

He asks of Congress to pass a law authorizing him to receive the wages which may be due from the Government to such deserters, deceased and discharged soldiers.

The committee are of opinion that he is entitled to no relief from Government. If he has made contracts with the officers or soldiers, he must look to them to comply with the same; the Government cannot interfere to settle such accounts. The committee recommend to the House the following resolution:

Resolved, That the prayer of the petitioner ought not to be granted.

MILITARY SERVICES.

The House then resolved itself into a Committee of the Whole, on the order of the day; and the Committee proceeded to consider the bill further to provide for military services during the late war.

Mr. BRADBURY offered the following amendment to the second section of the bill:

"That if any non-commissioned officer, musician, or private, of the regular Army, shall have died while in the service of the United States, leaving a widow, or, if no widow, a child or children under fourteen years of age, such widow, or, if no widow, such child or children shall be entitled to receive half the monthly pay to which the deceased was entitled at the time of his decease, for and during the term of five years, upon the same terms and conditions, and under the same rules, restrictions and conditions as are provided by law for the widows and children of non-commissioned officers, musicians, and privates, of the regular Army, who have been killed or died of wounds received in battle."

After a few remarks from Mr. BRADLEY, in support of his motion, and by Mr. DESHA and Mr. JOHNSON against it, the amendment was disagreed to; and Mr. JOHNSON moved to add the following to the second section of the bill:

And be it further enacted, That in case of the death of a soldier of the regular Army, the widow shall, in all cases, be considered as one of the heirs, with the child or children of said regular soldier; and in all such cases, the said widow shall have her election to take for herself and child or children the five years' half pay, in lieu of the land bounty and the three months' pay now allowed by law to the heirs and representatives of said decedent.

Before this proposition was decided on, a motion was made, and carried, to lay the bill on the table.

CANADIAN REFUGEES.

The Committee proceeded to the consideration of the bill for the relief of certain Canadian refugees who entered the American service during the late war. A motion was made by Mr. WEBSTER, when the bill was last under consideration, to strike out the first section, being the first question for decision.

On this motion a very animated, and, from the argument introduced, a very interesting debate took place. The bill was advocated with much zeal by Messrs. CUTHBERT, and ROBERTSON; and as warmly opposed by Mr. HULBERT.

The following is the substance of the remarks made by Mr. HULBERT, at different times, on this bill, while it was before a Committee of the Whole.

Mr. HULBERT said: I can never consent, Mr. Chairman, to give my vote in favor of the bill which is now under consideration. My cool and deliberate judgment, and all the feelings of my heart, are utterly opposed to it.

Without meaning to question, in the slightest degree, the purity of intention of any gentleman who has had an agency in reporting this bill, or has in any way given it his support, I must say, that I think it is founded on principles which are wholly inconsistent with the doctrines of morality, and the dictates of justice and sound policy.

Sir, what does this bill propose; what are its objects? Let me examine, in the first place, its most exceptionable and odious provision—I mean that which relates to those inhabitants of Canada, who, in the late war, owing allegiance to Great Britain, deserted to your standard, and fought against their own Government.

If you adopt this part of the bill, you sanction one of the foulest and most detestable crimes that can be perpetrated by a human being; a crime that strikes deep at the foundation of all Governments, and of civilized society—you sanction treason. Nay, you go a frightful distance beyond this; you embrace the traitor, and give him a rich reward for his crime.

Sir, a nation is styled a moral person; and I do think that we, as the Representatives of this nation, ought never to adopt any measure which, in our private capacity, we would not cordially approve. Surely we are not sent here to legislate against the dictates of our own consciences, and the best feelings of our hearts. Let me ask, then, is there a single person in this honorable committee who would, upon any consideration whatsoever, in private life, encourage and reward a villain for the commission of a base and infamous crime? No, sir. Then let us instantly condemn and reject the proposition before us. In principle it is perverse, in example it would be dangerous.

What is it that makes us admire those instances of conduct recorded in history, where the proffered assistance of treacherous men has been indignantly refused? Let me take a single and familiar instance. What is it that makes us admire the conduct of the Romans, in spurning the proposition of the physician of Pyrrhus, who offered to poison his master, and thereby free the Romans from a most powerful and dreaded enemy? It is that noble and exalted principle in our nature which inspires us, nay, which constrains us, to love great and generous actions wherever we find them. It is that self-same principle which ought, at this moment, irresistibly to impel us to stamp with abhorrence the bill now before the Committee.

It is one of the noblest traits in the character of Lord Thurlow, that, when he was Chancellor of England, he refused to dishonor the great seal of that nation by placing it to the grant of a pension to the infamous Arnold. And shall the seal of this enlightened and virtuous Republic be stamped upon this foul iniquity, this palpable treason? Shall traitors carry with them this high testimony of your approbation? Sir, while you extend your bounty to these faithless foreigners, you corrupt the hearts of your own people. You teach them that fidelity is no virtue, and that treason is no crime. What must they think of the political morality of that Government, which, in one law, denounces against its own citizens the awful punishment of death, for desertion, and in another law, in force at the same time, gives a high reward to the subjects of a foreign nation for having been guilty of the same crime? It does appear to me that such proceedings have a manifest tendency to confound all notions of right and wrong, and to annihilate the very distinctions between vice and virtue.

Gentlemen say they can find precedents in the history of our own Government, to justify this measure. Sir, precedents avail nothing against principle; they can never justify anything radically wrong. If it can be shown that you have heretofore done anything like that which is now proposed, I pray you to repeat of the sin you have done, and sin no more.

The honorable gentleman from New York, (Mr. TROOP,) has compared the case of these deserters to the glorious cause of the American Revolution. Need I vindicate your country against this unmerited charge? Shall I offer to show that the illustrious founders of your liberties were not deserters, were not traitors? No, I will not thus degrade them; I will leave their vindication to your own heart, to the hearts of the American people, and to impartial history.

Sir, the honorable Speaker, (Mr. CLAY,) in the fervor of his attachment to this bill, has pronounced a high eulogium on the character and conduct of the late Colonel Wilcox, commander of the corps of Canadian volunteers. He has praised in the highest strains of admiration the imputed virtues of this man, and has ranked him among the most exalted patriots of the earth. He has even censured, with no little severity, the opposers of this bill, who have dared in debate to name this deceased patriot—dared to disturb the ashes of the dead. Sir, let me remind the honorable Speaker, that Wilcox was first named by the friends of this bill, and that his alleged patriotism and devotedness to this country were stated in glowing terms, to influence the decision of this question. Could I believe that the history of this person is correctly understood, I would dwell no longer on the subject, for I war not with the dead. But I am confident that erroneous impressions have been made. I have reason to suspect that many members of this Committee do at this moment believe that he was a native citizen of this country, and that he returned to the United States to fight the battles of the land that gave him birth. It is my duty to put this matter right.

Colonel Wilcox was a native of Ireland—none the worse for that—I love an honest full-hearted Irishman. Having become discontented at home, he abandoned the land of his nativity, and, removing into Upper Canada, established his residence in Newark, where he became the editor of a newspaper, and was elected a member of the Parliament of that province. He was resident in Newark when the late war against Great Britain was declared. Did he then fly to your country, and espouse your cause? No, he took up arms against you. He fought for his King. He was a leader of Canadian militia at the battles of Queenstown and Fort George. His allegiance to his royal master held out until Fort George and Newark were subdued by your arms. Then, when the cause of your enemy was considered desperate, when it was confidently expected that all Canada would soon be in your possession, he deserted his friends, and joined your standard, his sword yet reeking with the blood of your citizens. Such was the man on whom this warm eulogium has been pronounced, and of whom the honorable Speaker was pleased to say, "if Wilcox was guilty of treason, then was your Washington a traitor." Surely the history of this person was not rightly understood. Sir, I admire the ingenuity of the honorable Speaker—I admire the warmth of his heart—but I regret that his torrent of feeling, his tempest of thought, should have been poured out in praise of such a person, and in support of such claims.

But the plea of retaliation is urged in favor of this bill. It is said that, during the late war, Great Britain attempted to seduce your citizens from their allegiance to your Government. Sir, this is a dangerous plea, and may lead to most disastrous consequences. It ought to be kept constantly in mind, that there is a wide difference between what an enemy may have a right to demand of you, and what your own conscience and the laws of morality may require. If an enemy has been guilty of wanton cruelty toward you— if he has practised seductive arts upon your citizens, or has in any way violated any of those rights which he ought to hold sacred, surely he cannot complain if his own weapons be turned against him. But are you justified, because the guilt of your enemy will not allow him to re-

proach you? Sir, this doctrine of retaliation has heretofore proved not a little unfortunate for you. It was the plea which our late enemy used as an excuse for the most unfeeling and barbarous conduct. Had it not been for this abominable doctrine, the people of Lewiston and Buffalo might still have been enjoying, in their own houses, the comforts and blessings of domestic life. And had it not been for this wicked doctrine, your once proud and magnificent Capitol might still have been standing, the pride and ornament of your country. Let no one suspect me of wishing to offer the slightest apology for the enemy, for desolating the villages I have named, or for burning the public buildings of this city. No, they were vandal deeds, and my soul detests them. But still more do I detest the odious principle of this bill. He who destroys palaces, and demolishes cities, does an infinitely less injury to the cause of humanity, than he who poisons the fountain of morality, and corrupts the human heart.

But, Mr. Chairman, let it for a moment be granted that we have an unquestionable right to adopt this measure, and that there is no objection to it in point of principle. Still we are bound to inquire, whether it would be politic. I contend that it would be directly the reverse. Pass this bill, sir, and it may hereafter bring wretchedness upon many of the people of this country. The tears of thousands may flow in consequence of the rash and impolitic act. Should we again be involved in war with Great Britain, do you believe that the enemy would forget, or would patiently bear this insult? No, it would kindle in his mind an unquenchable flame of resentment. It would provoke him to the most desperate acts of retaliation. Do you not shudder at the thought that he might excite Ethiopia to stretch forth a desolating hand over some parts of your territory? Even in that case, you could not complain. No, this bill would stare you in the face, and your mouth would be hermetically sealed. You seduced, and armed against your enemy, his own subjects; he, in return excites your slaves to treason and rebellion. Sir, I need not enumerate the calamities that would be consequent upon such a system of retaliation. Your own imagination already calls them up in dreadful array before you.

But we are reminded, that there is another description of persons, whose claims are included in the provisions of this bill. It is stated, that these men were native citizens of the United States; that, with a view to improve their condition, they removed to Canada before the late war, where they became owners of real estate; that, at the commencement of hostilities, they were compelled either to join the standard of that Government, or to fly from the territory of your enemy, and abandon their estates to confiscation; that they preferred the latter course, returned to this country, and joined your armies, in consequence of which their property was confiscated. And they now ask of you indemnification for the losses they have thus sustained.

Sir, admit all these facts, and yet what claims

have these refugees on your generosity, or your justice, beyond those of thousands who could be named? Why are they to be preferred to those good citizens, who have constantly remained within your territory, been undeviatingly faithful to your Government, and suffered, in consequence of the war, the severest losses? It is answered, that these refugees have rendered you peculiar and extraordinary services. In attempting to show this fact. the honorable gentleman from New York (Mr. Troup) has made a statement, which, instead of inclining me to support this bill, excites my indignation against it. He tells you that these refugees, having lived in Canada, became intimately acquainted with the country, and afterwards served as guides to conduct your armies and your scouting parties into different parts of the territory of your enemy. Yes, they did know the country; and how came they to know it? The generous proclamation of the Canadian Government had led them there. They had received lands of the Crown, almost without price. They had formally declared themselves British subjects, and had taken an oath of allegiance to the King. They remained under the protection of their adopted royal master, until his cause in Canada appeared hopeless. Then, forgetting his bounty, spurning the declaration they had made, and the oath they had taken, they fled to your country, and soon appeared leading your armies, and pointing their bayonets against their late neighbors and friends. Sir, every good feeling of my heart rebels against a claim founded on such conduct.

But it is asserted that the faith of the Government is pledged to make good these losses; that your commanders on the Canadian frontier made the pledge, and that you are bound to redeem it. And to put this matter beyond a doubt, the celebrated proclamation of General Hull is introduced. Sir, history speaks of a famous Grecian, who never laughed but once, and that was when he saw an ass mumbling a thistle. But sure I am that grave gentleman would have laughed at least once more, could he have read this proclamation, and seen it offered as high authority in the Grand Councils of this nation. Do not gentlemen know that the Government have constantly disowned this proclamation, and denied that they ever gave any authority or countenance to it? Have they not condemned to death its author? And does he not now live at the mercy of the President? But I care not whether this ludicrous thing was authorized or not. It does not contain a single word which favors the claims of these refugees. Let us look at that part, on which reliance has been placed. It is this: "In the name of my country, and by authority of my Government, I promise you protection to your persons, properties, and rights." This proclamation was addressed "to the peaceful and unoffending inhabitants of Canada;" they were assured that the General had "a force which would look down all opposition," and were told that they "should be treated as enemies, and should suffer all the calamities of war, if they took part with

their Government." It is perfectly manifest, that the object of this address was to prevent the people of Canada from joining the British standard; and it impliedly condemns the course which these refugees pursued. For they were cautioned to remain peaceful, and were promised protection if they did so; but they were not invited to join your armies, or to give any aid or assistance to your cause. Sir, General Hull promised no more to the Canadians, than all great generals engage on entering the territories of their enemy. Bonaparte, when he entered Russia, promised the people protection to their persons and property, if they would remain quiet, and take no part in the contest; and the allied generals made a like engagement to the people of France, when they lately marched into that kingdom.

When it was stated that your commanders on the Canadian line had encouraged these claimants to desert, what said my honorable friend, (Mr. Conner,) who had acted as the aid of General Dearborn? With the pride of a soldier, and the feelings of a high-minded man, he denied the assertion, and repelled the charge. He declared that such conduct would have been abhorrent to the mind of General Dearborn, and the officers under his command; that they disained to practise anything but open and honorable warfare.* Where, then, is the proof that Govern-

* The remarks of Mr. Hulbert, of Massachusetts, on the Canadian Volunteer bill, have been published in the Federal Republican. From this statement it might be inferred, as indisposition prevented Mr. Conner from giving his vote on that question, that he was opposed to the passage of the bill; on the contrary, it would have received his cheerful support. The honorable Mr. Throop, of New York, had referred to Colonel Preston's proclamation at Fort Erie, as authority that Major General Dearborn, then commanding on the Niagara frontier, had invited the inhabitants of Canada to join the American standard, or at least to leave the country.

Mr. Conner explained. He said, that at the time alluded to proclamations had become a byeword through the nation; they had become ridiculous. It was the intention of General Dearborn to effect what he attempted by the sword, and not by the pen; and had not a most severe illness entirely prevented his personal attention to the concerns of the army, at a time when it was most required, or had not a mere accident, which could not be so well expressed in any other terms, than "a strange fatality," prevented the enemy's destruction at Sandy Creek;—from a minute acquaintance with every particular of the transaction, he knew that General Chandler's arrangements at that point were judicious—his troops formed for battle at the time of attack, and his conduct gallant; as evidence of it, the enemy were completely routed, after having sustained three times the American loss;—had not these unfortunate circumstances intervened, he had no doubt that Upper Canada would have been conquered that campaign. Mr. C. said, that at the time General Dearborn took possession of Fort George, Colonel Preston had just arrived with his command at Fort Erie. The enemy at that post, having masked his retreat under a cannonade, abandoned and demol-

ment is under any particular engagement to these refugees? None has been produced, and none exists. Why, then, are they to be preferred to thousands of good honest people, who are daily supplicating us in vain for assistance?

Sir, while you are considering these claims, do you forget the people of Lewiston and Buffalo? Have you forgotten that you brought upon them an enemy, who in the spirit of revenge reduced their villages to ashes? Faithful to your cause, many of these brave and patriotic citizens were fighting the battles of your country, while their houses were in flames, and their wives and children, driven from their homes, were shivering in the storms of winter. Have you extended relief to these good people? No, they have pleaded in vain. You have left them to moisten with their tears the ashes of their dwellings. You have told them that you pitied them, but that justice did not require, and that policy forbad, that you should give them assistance. In like manner have you treated the inhabitants of Havre de Grace, and of other places desolated by the enemy. Sir, you have allowed nothing to the owners of cannon foundries, mills, and ropewalks, which were destroyed by the enemy, because such establishments were peculiarly calculated to assist you in the prosecution of the war. Let me remind you of the case of Jabez Hull, who lately came from Sackett's Harbor to this city, and attended here for weeks, asking for what he considered his just and honest dues. Among other injuries which he sustained in the late war, his dwelling-house was wantonly demolished by your own soldiers, and a part of the bricks converted into ovens for the use of the camp. Yet the Committee of Claims reported against his petition, on the ground that the Government was not bound to afford indemnification for such losses; and the honorable chairman of that committee (Mr. YANCEY) maintained the report by such irresistible arguments, that it was adopted by a large majority of the House, and the applicant returned to his family, disappointed and distressed. Sir, let us not forget a decision which has this day been made. The honorable gentleman from Louisiana (Mr. ROBERTSON) moved an amendment to this same bill, providing relief for all your citizens, who during the late war, without any fault of their own, lost property by the ravages of the enemy. Did you adopt this amendment? No, you instantly rejected it. I beseech you, then, to reject this bill. Let it not be said that these traitors, these refugees, are faring sumptuously at the national table, while your own citizens, who have constantly adhered to your Government, are left, like dogs, to pick up the crumbs that fall from the same table.

Sir, I do hope for the honor of the nation that this bill will not be passed into a law. I should consider it a foul stain, an indelible blot, on the annals of American legislation.

Mr. GROSVENOR denied the right of these men to compensation in any other character but as soldiers. He would not ask whether they were traitors or not; it was as soldiers they fought, and as soldiers ought to be rewarded; so ought our own citizens who fought also. As, however, they demanded more than as soldiers they could be entitled to, and grounded that demand on their particular merits, it became proper to inquire into the principles upon which they stood forward and made that claim; and those principles when examined would be found such as our nature was abhorrent of. Mr. G. then took a view of the case, not only in its political, but its moral aspect, in both of which the measure and the grounds taken for its defence were, he contended, entirely indefensible. How came it, he asked, that no proposition was made for compensation to our citizens whose property was ravaged, and who never left their country to become the subjects of a monarchy? He contrasted this intended benefaction; first, with the conduct of our Government to our native merchants who happened to be in England in pursuit of their business when the war broke out, and in hastening back again to their country, were pillaged by privateers let loose upon them by Government; and, secondly, with the total disregard exhibited by the Administration to the sufferings of the people of Havre de Grace. He animadverted upon the singularity of the fact, that a claim should be now set up and sustained upon the invitation held out by General Hull, in his proclamation to the people of Upper Canada, though that proclamation was formally disavowed by our Ministers at Ghent; and he put the question, why, if they rewarded those men as deserters, they did not reward all the other deserters that came over also?

ished his works. Colonel Preston took possession of them, and probably from the earnest solicitations of the inhabitants of Buffalo, who knew the wishes and feelings of the inhabitants of Canada, certainly not with the knowledge or by the authority of General Dearborn, he was induced to publish the proclamation alluded to. Mr. C. said, that Colonel Preston was undoubtedly actuated by the purest and most honorable motives. He knew that gentleman personally: there was not a more gallant and amiable officer in the army; one more loved and respected. No one regretted more than himself the severe wound, which would in a great measure deprive the country of his usefulness. But it was his duty to state, that the proclamation was not authorized or sanctioned by the Commanding General. Mr. C. said, he should vote for the passage of that bill. He believed that with one or two exceptions, the petitioners were natives of the United States, who had moved into Canada, and who wished to remain neutral during the contest. But, he said, a conscription was put in force in that peninsula of the most arbitrary nature; and a non-compliance with which was followed by the most sanguinary consequences; the petitioners were driven to the necessity of plunging their bayonets in the bosoms of their native countrymen or join the American cause, and, under these circumstances, he hoped there never would be an American who would not adopt the same alternative. He hoped that Congress would make an adequate compensation for the severe losses they had sustained, which was called for by every principle of justice and liberality.

Mr. CLAY replied to Mr. HULBERT and Mr.

Grosvenor, as did Mr. Wright. Mr. Hopkinson followed, supporting the motion of Mr. Webster, who supported his motion in a short but forcible speech.

Before the question was taken on the motion to strike out the section, the usual hour of adjournment had arrived; when the Committee rose, reported progress, and obtained leave to sit again.

REMAINS OF GENERAL WASHINGTON.

Mr. Huger rose, as the House was about to adjourn, and observed: That what he deemed a solemn duty obliged him to claim the indulgence of the House for a few moments. He had been detained by severe indisposition from attending his duties in that body since Saturday last, and, though better, he should not have ventured out to-day but for a piece of information which had accidentally reached him that morning. In glancing his eyes over the papers just brought him, he was struck by certain resolutions published in the *Richmond Enquirer,* from which it appeared that the Legislature of Virginia had, by an unanimous vote, authorized the Governor of the State to apply to the Honorable Bushrod Washington, to permit the remains of her beloved son, the late General George Washington, to be removed and interred near the capital of Virginia. His heart sunk within him, he confessed, on reading those resolutions, and recalling to mind the scenes he had once witnessed, and in which he had personally acted a part on the floor of that Congress, which represented the American nation, on the death of this great man. He had often since thought with astonishment, and more than regret, of the apathy of the American people on this subject. But, although he remembered with the most poignant grief the failure of his exertions, and the far more powerful exertions of some of the best and greatest men who were at that time members of Congress, to get something done worthy of the Father of his Country, and not unworthy of the American nation; yet he had not forgotten that the Sixth Congress had gone so far as to authorize the President of that day to write in behalf of the nation to Mrs. Washington, and to make of her a like request in regard to the remains of our beloved Washington. Neither had he forgotten the admirable and pathetic letter written by that lady, in which she grants their request. The remains of Washington then were pledged to the whole nation, and he trusted the time was at length come, when the honors sacredly due to them would be paid, as they ought long ago to have been, by the Representatives of the whole American people. He had himself been a member of that Congress, and one of those who had approved of the application made to Mrs. Washington. He had, moreover, been one of the committee (the only one now honored with a seat on this floor) to whom the subject had been referred, when it had last been before Congress. He did not, therefore, he trusted, assume too much to himself, when he ventured to think,

that it had in some degree devolved on him, as a sacred and solemn duty, to call the attention of Congress to this subject at the present time, and under the particular circumstances which he had noticed above. Accordingly, indisposed as he was, he had, without the loss of a single moment, hurried down to the House, and seized the first possible opportunity to offer the resolution he held in his hand. Before he read it to the Chair, he would be permitted to add, that he trusted no gentleman could possibly suppose he meant thereby to express any disapprobation in regard to the resolutions of the Legislature, or to evince the smallest disrespect to the State of Virginia. He was one of the last men in that House to do so. Virginia had been to him, in no small degree, a second *alma mater.* Though he first drew his breath in the capital of South Carolina, he had passed, during the Revolutionary war, several of his early years in the former State—being exiled from his native State, then in possession of the enemy. He had met everywhere, and from thousands in Virginia, hospitality, kindness, friendship, and he might with propriety add, parental affection and protection. It was impossible all this could ever be erased from his heart, and as he before observed, he had never ceased to regard Virginia as his second *alma mater.* But South Carolina was not less dear to him, nor could he forget her claims on the present occasion. She formed a portion, and he was bold to say an honorable portion of the great American nation. As such, she had her full interest in the pledge possessed, to the mortal remains of our Father and Chief. As a South Carolinian, therefore, and member of the American family, as well as from the peculiar circumstances connected with his personal situation, being an immediate Representative on the occasion before alluded to, and at the present time of the State of South Carolina, he felt himself imperiously bound to offer the following resolution to the House:

Resolved, That a committee be appointed to examine into the proceedings of a former Congress, on the lamented death of the late General Washington, and to take into consideration what further measures it may be expedient to adopt at the present time in relation to that sacred and interesting subject.

Before the resolution was disposed of, a motion was made to adjourn, and carried.

Saturday, February 17.

On motion of Mr. Cady, the Committee on the Public Lands were instructed to inquire into the expediency of authorizing the officers who are authorized to sell the public lands, to accept from the soldiers to whom land warrants have been or shall be granted, for their services in the late war, such land warrants in part payment for any lands which such soldiers may purchase for the purpose of cultivating the same.

On motion of Mr. Robertson, the Committee on Roads and Canals were instructed to inquire into the expediency of improving the roads between Duck River in the State of Tennessee, and

1009   HISTORY OF CONGRESS.   1010

FEBRUARY, 1816.   *Remains of Washington—Canadian Refugees,*   H. OF R.

Madisonville, in the Mississippi Territory, by the Cherokee agency; and also, that between Fort Hawkins in the State of Georgia and Fort Stoddart.

After some remarks by Mr. PITKIN, explanatory of his views, he offered the following resolution, which was agreed to:

Resolved, That the President of the United States be requested to cause to be laid before this House, information relative to the duties laid on articles imported from the United States into the British provinces of Canada, Nova Scotia, and New Brunswick, and the duties on articles exported to the United States from the said provinces; also relative to duties laid on goods, wares, and merchandise, imported into the British West India islands, or any of them, from the United States, or from colonies in America owned by other foreign European Powers; and information likewise as to the duties on *imports* and *exports,* to which vessels of the United States are subject in the ports of the British East Indies.

Mr. PITKIN and Mr. PARRIS were appointed a committee to present the said resolution to the President.

On motion of Mr. JEWETT, the House proceeded to consider the resolution submitted by him yesterday, and the same being again read, was agreed to by the House; and Mr. JEWETT and Mr. THOMAS were appointed a committee to present the said resolution to the President.

REMAINS OF GENERAL WASHINGTON.

On motion of Mr. HUGER, the House proceeded to consider the resolution submitted by him yesterday.

Mr. HUGER made a few remarks in support of the resolution, and called the attention of the House to the correspondence which took place long since between Congress and Mrs. Washington; and the pledge then given to the nation on this interesting subject.

Mr. ROOT, of New York, said he was unwilling for one to agree to the consideration of the resolution, but did not desire to make any remarks against it. He knew, he said, that it was considered political heresy to oppose anything plumed with the name of WASHINGTON, but on this occasion he should disregard that imputation. It had once been attempted to erect a mausoleum, an Egyptian pyramid to him, and he presumed such was the object of the resolution now offered. Such an enterprise he was unwilling to second; not because the fame and virtues of WASHINGTON had less effect on his mind than on others, but because he wished to protect that fame, which he revered. Mr. R. said this resolution declared the fame of WASHINGTON perishable, if a monument of marble be not erected to perpetuate it. Sir, his fame fills the four quarters of the globe, and will survive long after your marble has crumbled to dust. *Ære perennis*—his fame is more durable than brass or marble. Let his remains slumber on their native plantation; for my part, said Mr. R., I would rather his name should live in history than in marble. Erect a monument to him, and it may at some future day be exposed to the insults of an enemy. We have had one

enemy who would not respect an edifice erected to him, nor could his name protect it from destruction; but they cannot reach his fame—can never touch it. By this resolution too, some may be deprived of the exercise of their political devotion. We know that professing devotees who now come here, must make a pilgrimage to Mount Vernon to show their devotion. The expense likewise, said Mr. R., forms a serious objection to such a scheme, and every good and great man hereafter will have a claim to a similar honor. Let us not establish the precedent.

Mr. HUGER said in reply, that in one respect the gentleman was in an error; no expense was now proposed. He had endeavored so to word the resolution as to escape objection. He could not, he said, reconcile it to his mind, as a citizen of this country, longer to neglect those sacred remains. Whether that neglect was right or wrong, he had not said, nor did he intend now to pronounce; but this he could with propriety assert, that the United States are bound to act on the subject in some shape or other, and the object of the resolution was simply to call on them to say what they are willing to do. He was a member of that Congress which gave to the nation a solemn pledge on this subject, and he wished them now to decide whether that pledge was to be redeemed or relinquished. He had not thought of a mausoleum, nor indeed had he contemplated any particular object of that kind. But, because there may be some expense attending it, are Congress to do nothing in a case where they are so sacredly pledged? Sir, said Mr. H., we are called on to act on this subject—a great State has most solemnly called on us. The majority may say, "our father is dead, we are satisfied, let his remains rest;" but if such be the case, let Virginia at once have the honor and glory of providing for them. Unwilling as I am, that any State should possess the venerated remains of WASHINGTON; yet, if we decline it, let his native State do them honor. Nothing has been said by me about a mausoleum or a monument. All I ask is a decision in one way or other; to redeem or reject the pledge given—in that I surely ask nothing wrong.

The resolution was then modified and agreed to by the House as follows, and a committee of seven appointed on the part of this House:

Resolved, That a committee be appointed, to join such committee as may be appointed by the Senate, to examine into the proceedings of a former Congress on the lamented death of the late GEORGE WASHINGTON, and to take into consideration what farther measures it may be expedient to adopt at the present time in relation to that solemn and interesting subject.

Messrs. HUGER, SMITH, of Maryland, TALLMADGE, JACKSON, MOORE, CHAMPION, and CONNER, were appointed the committee on the part of this House.

CANADIAN VOLUNTEERS.

The House then resolved itself into a Committee of the Whole, on the bill for the relief of the Canadian volunteers; Mr. WEBSTER's motion to strike out the first section (to reject the bill) still under consideration.

The debate on this question was resumed and continued with unabated warmth, until near sunset. In this debate the bill was advocated by Messrs. COMSTOCK, ROOT, and ROBERTSON, and opposed by Messrs. HARDIN, SERGEANT, and GROSVENOR. Messrs. JEWETT, and KING, of Massachusetts, also spoke; though hostile to the bill in its present shape, if amended so as to include American citizens only, they would vote for it.

Mr. COMSTOCK spoke as follows: •

Mr. Chairman, perhaps prudence dictates me to be silent upon this occasion; but really, sir, I cannot, without doing violence to my feelings, submit to its suggestions.

After the ample and lucid discussion which this subject has received, I cannot have the vanity to suppose it in my power to present it in a more just or correct point of view. And indeed, sir, were I ever so competent, I have too much respect for this honorable body to wish to detain them at this late hour of the day. Coming from that State which the gentleman, upon whose petition the bill before us is predicated, contributed nobly and bravely to defend; yes, sir, coming from that town in which one of these petitioners formerly had the happiness to reside; possessing a knowledge of the fair and honorable character of some of these Canadian refugees, I must be permitted to express my anxious wish that the motion under consideration may be negatived, and that the bill may pass.

Sir, from private citizens, the former neighbors of him whose name appears first on the petition to which I have alluded, as well as from intelligent and respectable officers of the late army; from these unquestionable sources of information, I have derived a knowledge of his conduct and character. As a citizen, he is represented to be gentlemanly and virtuous; as a soldier, honorable and brave. If I am not much mistaken, he is the man who, at the battle of Queenstown, sought and found one of my wounded townsmen, secured him from savage ferocity, poured into his wounds the oil and the wine, and did all that lay in his power to meliorate his condition, and alleviate his sufferings.

With the history of a number of these unfortunate men I am somewhat acquainted; that history is highly creditable to them as citizens and as soldiers. One of your petitioners is respectable in a learned profession. I do not believe, sir, they merit the reproaches which have been lavished upon them by gentlemen with such unmerciful profusion. Mr. Chairman, what is their crime? Antecedent to the late war, when relations of peace and amity subsisted between the Government of Great Britain and this country, these men became adventurers in Canada; there they pursued honest private avocations, to better their fortunes, and to acquire a livelihood for themselves and families. Sir, there was no crime in this; it was perfectly lawful and commendable. We do not learn that, at this time, they were guilty, or even accused of any incendiary proceedings. On the contrary, every part of their conduct, from the best information, indi-

cated the industrious and peaceful citizen. Soon after the commencement of the late war, these petitioners were treated by the administration in Canada with suspicion and unkindness. Some of them, I understand, were arrested, restrained of their liberty, dragged from their families and business, and confined to the precincts of a prison. Deplorable, indeed, must have been their situation; their amiable and tender families deprived of earthly protection, left to mourn the absence of those whose cheering society and kind offices had conduced to supply the wants and alleviate the cares of life; society and kind offices rendered doubly dear and necessary in the stormy and distressing season of hostility. No specific charges, sir, were ever adduced to justify this violent procedure; it was obviously founded on a mere suspicion that these persons were attached to the eternal principles of virtuous liberty. After having endured this bondage and degradation for some time, the devoted objects of jealous and vindictive passion, they were liberated from confinement. Repeated solicitations were made by those oppressed persons for an explicit declaration of the charges against them, which were as often refused. They entertained the opinion that protection and allegiance are of reciprocal obligation. The Provincial Government having practised towards them a cruel and outrageous violation of law and justice, induced a conviction that they no longer owed it any allegiance. To remain in Canada promised nothing but wretchedness and destruction. Every prospect of enjoying happiness and prosperity in that province was annihilated. At this painful crisis, sir, their minds were naturally directed to their native country, whose inhabitants they recollected with fraternal affection; and whose political institutions, founded on the principles of reason and philosophy, invited their respect and admiration. A country, sir, where the human mind seems destined to receive the greatest development and expansion, morality its utmost refinement, and where I believe the undefiled religion of Jesus will be inculcated and embraced with divine power and constancy. Invited through the proclamations of your Generals, as well as from the spirit and tenor of the instructions of the Secretary of War, to Colonel Wilcox, the gallant and lamented leader of their corps, with promises of protection; they joined your standard from the noblest motives. They have fought by your side, assisted in sustaining your eagles on the shores of Canada, acquired laurels, but reduced themselves and families to poverty and distress.

Mr. Chairman, have they committed an unpardonable offence? Shall they find no asylum on this side the grave? Why are they the subjects of obloquy? Why treat them with "scoffs, and scorns, and contumelious taunts?"

Mr. Chairman, the principles of virtue are binding upon us at all times, and upon all occasions. They are of universal and eternal application; in private and public situations we are bound by their sanctions. It is not enough for us to deplore in mere expression the adversity of a friend; it is not enough for us to say to naked and hungry brethren, be ye clothed and fed. No, sir, it behooves us to evince the nature and degree of our sympathy; to demonstrate the sincerity of our professions, by stretching forth the hand of benevolence to alleviate their sufferings. Let us be just, if not generous, upon this occasion; let us evidence the honest sincerity of our attachment to those who revere the immutable principles of propriety upon which our Republic is predicated.

Mr. Chairman, these petitioners have been likened to assassins. Sir, I deny the justice of the comparison; they are humane and honorable men; they have not invaded the private sanctuary of the citizen to perpetrate foul deeds of cruelty and murder. They have not approached the enemy obliquely; but have met him boldly in front, in open and manly warfare.

We are asked why we would remunerate the losses of these petitioners, and refuse equal justice and liberality to our own citizens. Sir, these petitioners, in entering our service, hazarded more, and have lost more, than even our own citizens. Confiscation of real estate and the halter might have been their fate. The former they have suffered; they have lost all their property; had they been made prisoners, the latter evil, to which they exposed themselves by espousing the cause of the States, would most certainly have been inflicted upon them. But, sir, I would remunerate our citizens for all the losses resulting from the conflagration and ravages of the enemy during the late war.

We went to war for national wrongs and indignities; the war was a common cause; and the burdens and privations consequent upon its prosecution, ought to be, as far as practicable, mutually borne, as the advantages of its issue are universally enjoyed. Because a fellow-citizen has the misfortune to reside on the frontier, where he is exposed to the first onset of the war, and to the predatory incursions of the enemy, I would not leave him to sustain alone the destruction of his property. This is an evil in which every individual of the nation, in my apprehension, ought to participate. I think the people of the interior, whose local situation comparatively exempted them from the dangers and devastations of the war, ought to alleviate the sufferings of the inhabitants of the borders, with pecuniary assistance, by sharing equally with them their losses. Great and good men have admitted the justice of this principle, and we are abundantly able to carry it into execution.

Mr. Chairman, by granting these petitioners donations of land, you will promote the sale and enhance the value of those belonging to the United States. They will make roads, erect bridges, mills, &c., and form a society which must invite and encourage emigration into the western wilds. Besides, sir, should our pacific relations change and give place to war; should the savage warrior raise his tomahawk in the West, the men for whom this bill provides, possessing gratitude, attachment, and fidelity to the Government, with military talents and experience, will form a useful barrier against his sanguinary assaults.

When Mr. C. had concluded, several motions were made for the Committee to rise, to defer the question to another day, but without success.

The question to strike out the first section was at length put, about five o'clock, and decided in the negative; only twenty-five rising in favor of the motion.

The Committee then rose, reported progress, and the House adjourned.

MONDAY, February 19.

Mr. WARD, of Massachusetts, presented a petition of sundry merchants in the State of Massachusetts, stating, that in consequence of the occupation of Castine, in the district of Penobscot, by the British forces during the late war, they entered their goods at the port of Hamden, in said district, which was not established as a port of entry, in consequence of which the said goods have been seized and libelled by the revenue officers, and praying the interposition of Congress.—Referred to the Committee of Ways and Means.

Mr. KING, of Massachusetts, presented a petition of Joseph Cutts, setting forth that he paid to the collector of the port of York, in the District of Maine, the amount due by him on several custom-house bonds, and that the said collector has since absconded, and, having neglected to cancel the said bonds, he has been sued, and judgment recovered against him by the United States, and praying relief in the premises.—Referred to the Committee of Claims.

Mr. ROBERTSON presented a petition of sundry inhabitants of the State of Louisiana, praying a confirmation of all Spanish grants, warrants, and orders of survey, of lands lying within that part of the late district of West Florida embraced within the State of Louisiana, and which were issued prior to the taking possession of that country by the United States.—Referred to the Committee on the Public Lands.

Mr. EASTON presented a petition of the Legislature of the Territory of Missouri, stating that in the Winter of 1812 the frontier inhabitants, at the request of Governor Howard, erected forts along the extensive frontier of the Territory, furnished the same with arms and ammunition at their own expense, and defended the same, and praying a donation of lands as a compensation.—Referred to Mr. EASTON, Mr. MCLEAN of Kentucky, Mr. ALEXANDER, Mr. JEWETT, and Mr. VOSE.

Mr. YANCEY, from the Committee of Claims, made a report on the petition of Peter Audrain, which was read; when Mr. Y. reported a bill for the relief of Peter Audrain; which was read twice, and committed to a Committee of the Whole.

Mr. YANCEY also made a report on the bill from the Senate "for the relief of Edward Barry and George Hodge;" which was read, and, together with the bill, committed to a Committee of the Whole.

Mr. PLEASANTS, from the Committee on Naval

Affairs, to which has been referred the petitions of sundry persons who were wounded at Dartmoor prison, in England, reported a bill placing certain persons on the list of navy pensioners; which was read twice, and committed to a Committee of the whole House to-morrow.

Mr. PLEASANTS also reported a bill authorizing the payment of a sum of money to John T. Courtney and Samuel Harrison, or their legal representatives; which was read twice, and committed to a Committee of the Whole to-morrow.

The SPEAKER laid before the House a letter from the Secretary of the Treasury, enclosing his report made in obedience to a resolution of the 14th instant, respecting the duties paid on the tonnage of British vessels entering the ports of the United States, with cargoes from the British West Indies; which were read, and ordered to lie on the table.

On motion of Mr. WEBSTER, a committee was appointed to inquire into the state of the incorporated banks within the District of Columbia, so far as such inquiry may be consistent with the privileges of their respective charters; and also to inquire into the number of unincorporated banking associations which exist within the said District, and the rules and principles of such associations, and to ascertain as near as may be the amount of bills by them issued, their ability to redeem the same, and to make a report to this House.

Mr. WEBSTER, Mr. CALHOUN, Mr. PLEASANTS, Mr. DESHA, and Mr. YATES, were appointed a committee pursuant to the said resolution.

A message from the Senate informed the House that the Senate have passed the bill of this House, entitled "An act for the relief of John Redman Coxe," with an amendment, in which they desire the concurrence of this House.

PETITION OF TAYLOR AND McNEAL, &c.

The SPEAKER laid before the House a report from the Secretary of War, on the petition of Taylor and McNeal and others; which was read, and ordered to lie on the table.—The report is as follows:

WAR DEPARTMENT, *Feb. 16, 1816.*

SIR: In obedience to the order of the House of Representatives of the 6th instant, referring the petition of Taylor and McNeal and others to this Department, I have the honor to state:

That, in all cases where losses have been incurred by the application of private property to public purposes by military commanders, under circumstances which, in the opinion of the Executive, justified the act, indemnity is considered within the legitimate powers of the War Department.

Had the case of the petitioners been founded upon a proceeding purely military, under the principle here stated, satisfaction would have been made. It appears, however, that the application of private property to public purposes, in this case, has been made by a body of citizens, acting as a committee of vigilance, who, in that capacity, were not subject to the military orders of the Commanding General.

The claim for redress is not weakened by this circumstance; but the petitioners must obtain that re-

dress from the Legislature, which is competent to afford it.

Under an act of Congress bearing date the 16th of July, 1813, the sum of $250,000 was appropriated for the purpose of hiring or purchasing hulks to be sunk in such ports or harbor as should be menaced by the enemy. This appropriation was considered as forming a part of that for fortifications, and has been applied partly to its legitimate object, and the remainder, together with other sums under that head of appropriation, has been transferred to the head of subsistence, and exhausted upon that object.

A liberal construction of this act, did the fund yet exist, might embrace the case of the petitioners. An appropriation for this object is, therefore, indispensable, if relief is intended to be given.

I have the honor to be your most obedient and very humble servant,

WM. H. CRAWFORD.
Hon. HENRY CLAY,
   Speaker of the House of Reps.

CONTESTED ELECTION.

Mr. TAYLOR, of New York, from the Committee of Elections, made a report on the petition of Robert Porterfield, contesting the seat of William McCoy, one of the members of this House for the State of Virginia; which was referred to a Committee of the whole House on Monday next. The report is as follows:

That, at the last election in Virginia, the petitioner and sitting member were opposing candidates in the Congressional district composed of the counties of Augusta, Rockingham, Pendleton, and Bath. The whole number of votes given in the district were 2,378, of which 1,213 were returned for the sitting member, and 1,165 for the petitioner. One of the votes given for the sitting member was, by mistake, set down and returned for the petitioner; and three votes offered to be given for the sitting member were improperly rejected by the sheriff, and have been added to his poll by the committee. From these facts, it appears that the sitting member's majority amounts to fifty-three votes. But, of the votes given at the said election, 745 were objected against as illegal; of which 390 were given for the petitioner, and 355 for the sitting member. The committee have carefully investigated the titles upon which the said votes were given, and find that there are upon the polls of the petitioner 171, and of the sitting member 149 illegal votes. The difference between these numbers being added to the 53 votes above mentioned, gives to the sitting member a majority of 75 over the petitioner. The election in the said district commenced in the county of Pendleton on the 4th, and closed in the county of Augusta on the 24th day of April last. On the next day the petitioner caused a notice, in writing, to be served on the sitting member, communicating the intention of contesting his election. On the 22d day of May the petitioner served on the sitting member a list of votes, to the legality of which he objected; on the 9th of June the sitting member served a similar list on the petitioner, and invited him to a speedy commencement of the investigation. On the 22d of August the petitioner notified the sitting member of his intention to commence the investigation on the 4th of September then next, at the court-house in the county of Augusta, and to proceed with as little delay as circumstances would admit to the other counties in the district. On the last mentioned day the sitting member caused to be delivered to the petitioner a protest, in writing, against the legality of his proceedings, and declined attending accordingly. The petitioner proceeded to take testimony in support of his votes, pursuant to the notice. Upon these facts the sitting member contended that the committee ought not to receive the testimony so taken; first, because it had not been taken within the period limited for that purpose in contested elections for members of the General Assembly of the Commonwealth of Virginia; and second, because the delay of the petitioner in commencing the investigation for more than four months, was unreasonable, and ought not to be allowed.

The committee overruled these objections, and admitted the evidence.

Upon proceeding to a scrutiny of the votes in the county of Rockingham, the petitioner contended that the whole poll ought to be rejected.

1st. Because the election commenced in his absence.

2d. Because the four clerks or writers appointed by the sheriff to keep the poll were not sworn previous to the commencement of the voting, "that they would take the poll fairly and impartially;" but, on the next day after the election, examined and subscribed the poll; and made affidavit thereon, "that the same did contain a just and true account of all the votes taken at the said election, to the best of their knowledge and belief."

3d. Because the names of the voters were not written under the names of the candidates in separate columns, but in the same column, and the votes carried forward and marked under the names of the candidates for whom they respectively voted; and,

4th. Because great noise and confusion prevailed at the election, without any effectual attempt by the sheriff to prevent it.

The first and fourth of these objections were not supported by evidence; the second and third were overruled by the committee. In regard to the second objection, it was proved by the affidavit of two of the clerks who kept the poll, "that although they were not sworn before the voting commenced, yet they conducted their poll-book under the impression that they would be sworn after the polls were closed, and that this had been the most usual custom in the county of Rockingham." In regard to the third objection, it not only was proved that it had been usual to keep the poll in that manner in the county of Rockingham, but the poll in the county of Pendleton, where the election commenced, and in which the petitioner had a majority of the votes, was kept in the same manner, and was not impeached by either party. The errors specified in these objections, in the judgment of the committee, relate more to form than substance. It was not alleged or pretended that the final result had been in anywise varied in consequence of a deviation in these particulars from the letter of the law regulating elections.

In the course of the investigation, the sitting member applied to the committee for permission to avail himself of an agreement entered into between him and the petitioner at the election in the county of Pendleton, to the following effect: That votes should be admitted on title bonds for a sufficient quantity of land, accompanied with a possession of six months; that persons having a right to vote in one county, but happening to be at an election in another county of

the same district, might vote in such other county, and that votes of persons residing out of the district should not be admitted. The petitioner admitted such agreement to have been made, but contended that he was absolved from its obligation, because the sitting member had admitted the votes of two or more persons not residing within the limits of the Congressional district to be entered on his poll and counted among his votes. This allegation was denied by the sitting member.

The committee being of opinion that the agreement of the parties could not either diminish or enlarge the elective franchise as secured to the freeholders of the district, by the laws of the Commonwealth, decided,

1st. That the votes of the freeholders residing out of the district, but having competent estate and possessions within it, be held legal.

2d. That all votes not given in the county where the land upon which they were respectively given was situate, be rejected; and,

3d. That all votes given by virtue of title bonds, not conveying a legal freehold estate, be rejected.

The committee further decided,

1st. That all votes recorded on the poll lists should be presumed good, unless impeached by evidence.

2d. That certified copies of the commissioner's books or land lists should be read in evidence, and deemed satisfactory as to the qualification or disqualification of voters, unless corrected by other evidence;* and,

3d. That the affidavit of a voter taken before competent authority, in pursuance of regular and sufficient notice, should be read in evidence to prove his title to vote.

The committee deem it proper to report to the House these decisions, by which it has been regulated in conducting the investigation, and respectfully submit the following resolution:

"*Resolved,* That William McCoy is entitled to a seat in this House."

The Committee of Elections were discharged from the further consideration of the documents heretofore presented and referred to them in relation to the election of George Baer.—They were laid on the table.

COMMERCE WITH GREAT BRITAIN.

Mr. FORSYTH, from the managers on the part of this House, at the conference with the managers on the part of the Senate, upon the subject-matter of the disagreeing votes of the two Houses upon the bill, from the Senate, "concerning the convention to regulate the commerce between the territories of the United States and His Britannic Majesty," made a report, which was read; and ordered to lie on the table.—The report is as follows:

The committee appointed to confer with the committee of the Senate on the disagreeing votes of the two Houses, upon the bill concerning the convention to regulate the commerce between the United States and His Britannic Majesty; submit to the House a report of the result of their conference.

For the consideration of the committee of the Sen-

---

* In England, on the trial of contested elections, the poll-book is admitted in evidence; [See 1st Peckwell on Contested Elections, page 208; and 2d Peckwell, page 376.]

ate, they presented, in pursuance of the duty assigned to them, and for the reasons therein mentioned, a statement in writing, to the following effect:

"The committee appointed on the part of the House of Representatives to confer with a committee of the Senate, on the subject of the disagreement of the latter to certain amendments proposed by the House, to a bill from the Senate, entitled "A bill concerning the convention to regulate the commerce between the Territories of the United States and His Britannic Majesty," with a view to guard against misapprehension, to give greater precision to discussions of the conference, and to reduce, into as narrow a compass as possible, the points of difference between the two branches of the legislative body, have deemed it advisable to submit to the committee of the Senate, the reasons which have governed the House in its determinations, in the shape of a written communication.

"It is not to be concealed that the disagreement between the two Houses has originated in a question in relation to their respective Constitutional powers; but the committee of the House of Representatives is not without a hope that the diversity of opinion on this interesting and important question is not so material (at least in its operation upon the specific subject before the legislative body) as at first view it might appear. Without entering upon an extensive inquiry in relation to the treaty-making power, the committee will venture to define, as accurately as they can, the real line which at present divides the contending parties. It is of less importance to ascertain how far they have heretofore disagreed, or may hereafter differ, than to discover what it is precisely that now divides them.

"In the performance of this duty the committee of the House of Representatives are inclined to hope that it will sufficiently appear, that there is no irreconcilable difference between the two branches of the Legislature.

"They are persuaded that the House of Representatives does not assert the pretension that no treaty can be made without their assent; nor do they contend that in all cases legislative aid is indispensably necessary, either to give validity to a treaty, or to carry it into execution. On the contrary, they are believed to admit, that to some, nay many treaties, no legislative sanction is required, no legislative aid is necessary.

"On the other hand, the committee are not less satisfied that it is by no means the intention of the Senate to assert the treaty-making power to be in all cases independent of the legislative authority. So far from it, that they are believed to acknowledge the necessity of legislative enactment to carry into execution all treaties which contain stipulations requiring appropriations, or which might bind the nation to lay taxes, to raise armies, to support navies, to grant subsidies, to create States, or to cede territory; if indeed this power exists in the Government at all. In some or all of these cases, and probably in many others, it is conceived to be admitted, that the legislative body must act, in order to give effect and operation to a treaty; and if in any case it be necessary, it may confidently be asserted that there is no difference in principle between the Houses; the difference is only in the application of the principle. For if, as has been stated, the House of Representatives contend that their aid is only in some cases necessary, and if the Senate admit that in some cases it is necessary, the inference is irresistible, that the only question in each case that presents itself is, whether it be one of the cases in which legislative provision is requisite for preserving the national faith, or not.

"This appears to the committee to be by no means an unimportant point gained. Its influence upon the feelings with which the two bodies will naturally approach questions of this description may be of no trivial consequence; for, as every case, according to this course of reasoning, would appear to rest upon its own foundation, there is less danger of its being drawn into precedent, and therefore less occasion for solicitude in regard to it. It is a view of the subject therefore calculated to harmonize, and to enable us to yield at all times to the application of another principle which the committee deem of the utmost consideration on all such occasions.

"The committee allude to the principle which inculcates the propriety of always taking care, if we do err, to err on the safe side. Should Congress fail to legislate where legislation is necessary, either the public faith must be broken, or, to avoid that evil, the executive branch of the Government must be tempted to overstep the boundaries prescribed by the Constitution. If, on the contrary, Congress should legislate where legislation is not necessary, the act could only be drawn into precedent in a case precisely similar; because, upon the principle assumed, "that each rests upon its own circumstances," it never could serve as a precedent, save where those circumstances are the same. Nor is it indeed unimportant to mention that there is little danger of much respect being paid to precedents upon great Constitutional questions. Conscience will always burst the trammels of precedent, unless restrained by reason.

"The committee therefore believe that it is safer, in every doubtful case, to legislate, and by the joint act of the whole Congress, to give authority to the execution of the stipulations of a treaty by the Executive, than to leave a doubtful case, without the sanction of the Legislature, to tempt the Executive to overleap its proper bounds, or to endanger the public faith by a failure to perform the provisions of a treaty which has received a Constitutional ratification. The very case under discussion may furnish us with an instance. The Senate believe legislation unnecessary. The House regard it as indispensable. What is the opinion of the President? Should he believe a law necessary, and should no law pass, he would be reduced to the alternative of breaking the Constitution or the treaty. He must either set at naught the supreme law of the land, or jeopardize the national faith and the national peace.

"It is of importance, too, to consider that if the legislative body, from the considerations above suggested, should legislate in every doubtful case, there would in all cases be less danger of a former proceeding being drawn into precedent; so that the committee are sanguine in the belief, that while such a course is calculated to avoid difficulties, on the one hand, it has no tendency to increase them on the other.

"The committee perceive, with satisfaction, that on the present occasion the two Houses appear to have approximated in their opinions, and that, as far as can be discerned, the Senate are disposed to act upon the liberal principles that have been suggested. They allude to the passage of the bill in question by that

On the 3d of August, 1780, (the same year that Mr. Smith was referred to the loan office in Georgia,) $456,000, in bills on Paris, were prepared to pay interest on loan office certificates. On the same day Congress ordered the loan office of Georgia to be removed to some place of safety, as contiguous as possible to the State, until it could be re-established with convenience and safety; and that, until such office be so fixed, and public notice given thereof, the Treasurer of the United States be empowered to pay all interest due, &c., on certificates issued from that office, in the same manner that such interest is directed to be paid by the Commissioners of the Continental loan offices.

In obedience to this resolution of Congress, interest was paid by the Treasurer of the United States on these certificates, in bills of exchange, from 23d December, 1777, to the 23d December, 1781, who endorsed the same on the back of each certificate, in his own handwriting, and sanctioned the act by his official signature.

That these certificates belong to that class, the interest upon which was to be paid in bills of exchange, appears by a resolution of Congress of the 10th of September, 1777.

The committee further report, that these certificates were deposited in the office of the Auditor of the Treasury, pursuant to an act of Congress of the 12th of February, 1793, on the 18th day of April, 1794, and, consequently, are not barred by any law of limitation.

As far as the committee have been able to ascertain the fact, there appears to be but seventy-six of the description of certificates under consideration outstanding.

Whether the certificates of the residue of the $200,000, sent by Captain Medici, (amounting to $169,500,) were bought in by the loan officers of Georgia, or whether they have been returned and cancelled at the Treasury board, or funded, cannot be ascertained, as all the old papers relating to the settlement of accounts between the United States and Georgia were burnt in August, 1814, by the enemy.

By the report of 1795, it appears probable that the certificates were employed in the purchase of Indian goods for the State of Georgia. And from the certificate of Mr. Farrell, of the Auditor's office, it appears that that State, "in her accounts exhibited against the United States, got credit for various articles delivered out of a public store." It is, therefore, highly probable that these certificates were appropriated to furnish supplies for such public store.

It further appears to your committee, that repeated applications have been made by the holders of this description of public securities to Congress, and upon which no positive decision has been made. The subject, therefore, is fairly open for legislative interference.

In making up their opinion, the committee have considered the situation of the United States, and particularly that of the State of Georgia, at the time these certificates were issued. In 1776 South Carolina was invaded; in 1777 Georgia was subject to the predatory incursions of the enemy from East Florida, to prevent which they carried on an expedition against that country, under Major General Robert Howe, which proved unsuccessful; and in 1778 Georgia was invaded, and its capital taken. (Lee's Memoirs, 1 vol., pp. 68, 69, 70.)

When the committee reflect upon the general confusion and distress of that day; when they consider that the public safety required "that a great number of individuals be necessarily invested with the power of binding the public by their contracts;" and when it

14th CON. 1st SESS.—33

is not to be denied that "almost every officer of the army, whether in the Commissary's department or otherwise, in different stages of the war, had it in his power to contract debts legally or equitably binding upon the United States;" and when the committee give due weight to these facts, they do not hesitate to believe that the act of Governor Treutlen, in issuing these certificates, was known and sanctioned by Congress, which abundantly accounts for the conduct of the Treasurer (who issued them) in recognising their correctness and validity.

As the principal and a part of the interest due on these certificates have never been paid, and as no fraud is imputed, the committee consider the faith of the United States as solemnly pledged for their redemption or payment, and that the prayer of the petitioner ought to be granted.

They have therefore directed their chairman to ask for leave to bring in a bill for that purpose.

TREASURY DEPARTMENT,
March 28, 1792.

The Secretary of the Treasury, to whom was referred the petition of William Smith, of Baltimore town, in the State of Maryland, respectfully submits the following report:

The resolutions of the United States in Congress assembled, which respect the issuing of the certificates commonly called loan office certificates, make it necessary that they should be previously countersigned by certain officers denominated Commissioners of Loans, who were to be appointed under the authority of the particular States.

After diligent inquiry within the State of Georgia no evidence has been obtained, either of the appointment of E. Davies (the person by whom the certificates in question were countersigned) to the office of commissioner of loans for that State, or that he was ever known or reputed to have acted in that capacity. The reverse of this, indeed, appears from various communications to the Treasury; copies and extracts of which are contained in the schedule herewith transmitted. It is to be remarked, that E. Davies does not even style himself Commissioner of Loans; but, instead of this, adds to his signature the words, "by order of J. A. Treutlen, Governor of Georgia."

The certificates, however, are signed by the proper officer, and all such as have appeared are genuine; and interest, as alleged in the petition, has been paid upon them by the late Treasurer of the United States, as in other cases. A number of those certificates have been offered to the present commissioner of loans for the State of Georgia, to be subscribed pursuant to the act making provision for the debt of the United States, and, upon a reference to the Treasury by that officer, have been directed to be refused.

The reasons for this direction are substantially as follows:

The certificates in question having been irregularly issued, and without the requisites prescribed by the acts of Congress, were, of course, in the first instance, not obligatory upon the United States.

The subsequent payment of interest upon them by an Executive officer, without the sanction of any order or resolution of Congress, could not confer validity upon a claim originally destitute of it, though it might occasion hardship to individuals who, upon the credit of that payment, may have been induced to become possessors of those certificates for valuable consideration.

There are examples of the payment of interest, by the mistakes of public officers, upon counterfeit and forged certificates. It seems to be clear that such payments cannot render valid or obligatory certificates of that description; and yet a similar hardship to those which have been mentioned would attend those who may have afterwards become possessed of them for valuable consideration; nor does there occur any distinction between the effect of such payment in the one and in the other case.

Between individuals, the payment of interest by an agent, upon the presumed but not real obligation of his principal, either through mistake or otherwise, without special authority of the principal, could certainly give no new validity to such an obligation; and the same rules of right govern cases between the public and individuals.

These considerations were deemed conclusive against the admission of those certificates under the powers vested in the officers of the Treasury. It remains for the Legislature to decide how far these are considerations strong enough to induce a special interposition in their favor. In making this decision the following circumstances will, it is presumed, appear to deserve attention:

The present is not a case of mere informality; there is no evidence that the certificates were issued for any purpose of the United States. The contrary, indeed, is stated to be the fact.

Their amount is not positively ascertained; no account of the issues having ever been rendered, though there is no appearance of any considerable sums being afloat.

All which is respectfully submitted.

Extract of a letter from Richard Wyllxhyr, Commissioner of Loans for Georgia, to the Secretary of the Treasury.

May 17, 1791.

I have the honor of enclosing you the affidavit of Mr. John Wereat, Auditor of this State, respecting the late Edward Davies, who issued sundry loan office certificates without, I believe, any authority, as I can receive no answer from our Governor, to whom I wrote long since, on this subject. I have requested Mr. William Houston, who is gone to Augusta, to endeavor to find out by the public records whether Mr. Davies had any appointment or not.

Mr. O'Bryan, Mr. Wade, and Mr. Davies are all dead.

Georgia, *Chatham county:*

Personally appeared John Wereat, Auditor for the said State, who, after being duly sworn, said: That he well knew Edward Davies, Esq., formerly of the city of Savannah, in the said State; and, further, this deponent verily believes that the said Edward Davies never was at any time loan officer for the State aforesaid, as your deponent constantly resided here, and was well acquainted with all the officers of Government, *except when the British forces had possession of the country*; and further saith not.

JOHN WEREAT.

Sworn to this 16th day of May, 1791.
JOS. HABERSHAM, J. P.

Extract of a letter from the Commissioner of Loans for Georgia to the Secretary of the Treasury.

June 13, 1791.

I have, without success, applied a second time to the Governor to know by what authority Mr. Davies acted as loan officer. I am well assured he had none.

Extract of a letter from the Commissioner of Loans to William Simmons, Principal Clerk in the Auditor's Office.

August, 31, 1791.

Herewith you will receive thirty-three loan office certificates, which I have examined, and believe them genuine; the five last in the abstract, which were issued by Edward Davies, I do not, however, think should be received, for the reasons assigned in my former letter to the Secretary of the Treasury, and the late Auditor. I applied to Mr. Steick (the gentleman I mentioned in my letter to Mr. Wolcott, dated the 20th ultimo,) for a copy of the Order of Council, which he said he had. I now enclose you his answer; which you will please to show to the Secretary of the Treasury.

Samuel Steick to Richard Wyllxhyr.

Savannah, *August* 31, 1791.

Sir: Agreeably to your request, I made search among my papers for the order of the Executive of the year 1777, authorizing Edward Davies and Thomas Stone to make a purchase of goods from a Captain Farquhar, but cannot find it. As well as my recollection serves me, it was to the following effect: that they, the said commissioners, were directed to purchase, and pledge the faith of the State for the payment, either in indigo at the Carolina price, or in loan office certificates, which were then expected from Congress. The contract was concluded, and the goods delivered by Farquhar to Davies. When the loan office certificates arrived, the Governor paid Mr. Davies ten thousand pounds, or something near that sum, which it was expected would be paid to Farquhar or his agent; this was not done. Davies kept the goods and certificates, and did not before his death account with the State for either. These certificates can very easily be ascertained, as they are countersigned by Edward Davies, by direction of John Adam Treutlen, as Governor.

I am, &c.   SAMUEL STEICK.
Richard Wyllxhyr,
    Commissioner of Loans.

Treasury Department, *Jan* 9, 1816.

Sir: In answer to the inquiries contained in your letter of the 4th instant, relating to certain loan office certificates belonging to John Delafield, and referred to in his petition, a copy of which was enclosed in your letter, I have the honor to state:

1. That the certificates (if they are of the description supposed, as they are not sufficiently designated to render it certain) were not regularly issued from any loan office of the United States.

2. The interest for four years was paid on a part of them by Michael Hillegas, formerly Treasurer of the United States.

3. No certificates belonging, as far as appears from any papers accompanying them, to John Delafield, are in the Treasury. Forty-three certificates, correspond-

ing in amount with those referred to in his petition, and which were presented at the Treasury on the 18th of April, 1794, by Uriah Tracy, in behalf of Benjamin Tallmadge, are now in the Auditor's Office, and are supposed to be the certificates in question.

4. There are four other certificates, of the nominal amount of $400 each, of the same description, and presented in behalf of other persons, also remaining in the Auditor's Office.

5. The objections against funding the certificates are stated in the report of the Secretary of the Treasury of the 28th of March, 1792, on the petition of William Smith, of which a copy is enclosed.

I will only add that this subject has been repeatedly before Congress, and that no provision has hitherto been made for the payment, in any way, of the certificates issued under the circumstances of those in question.

I have the honor to be, &c.

A. J. DALLAS.

Hon. B. TALLMADGE, *Chairman, &c.*

TREASURY DEPARTMENT,
Register's Office, Feb. 5, 1816.

SIR: In reply to the queries you have done me the honor to propose:

1st. When were O'Bryan and Wade appointed loan officers for the State of Georgia?

Answer. To the best of my recollection, they were in office on the 10th May, 1779, when I first entered the Treasury Office as Assistant Auditor General, under an appointment by Congress. Before that period I have not any knowledge of them.

2d. What is the date of the first entry respecting those officers to be found in any books in your office?

Answer. An account was opened by my predecessor, William Gevott, in leger A, folio 214, entitled "—— Commissioners' loan office, State of Georgia, account current;" which account obtained a credit, March 18, 1778, by Joseph Clay, of $202,423. The blank left for their names was inserted by myself on debiting them, 4th September, 1780, with $12,000 to Thomas Smith, his account current.

3d. Are O'Bryan and Wade charged with the $200,000 alluded to in Mr. Wolcott's report?

Answer. They are charged with that sum on the 22d November, 1781; but it appears by the report of the Auditor of the Treasury, dated 19th January, 1795, that they were transmitted on the 24th September, 1777, when the record might have been made had Mr. Gevott been possessed of the voucher on which I afterwards made the record.

4th. Have they any credit, and to what amount?

Answer. They have credit for returned loan office certificates amounting to $402,000.

5th. In reply to the last query: Were the papers of the State of Georgia, on which a settlement was made by the United States with that State, burnt? They were burnt on the —— day of August, 1814, at the irruption of the late enemy.

I have the honor to be, &c.

JOSEPH NOURSE.

Hon. BENJAMIN TALLMADGE.

CANADIAN REFUGEES.

The House then went into Committee of the Whole, on the orders of the day. The bill to relieve certain Canadian volunteers in the late war being under consideration—

Mr. JOHNSON, of Kentucky, moved to amend the bill, so as to include in its provisions those refugees only who had been citizens of the United States previously to the late war; which motion was carried without a division.

Mr. ROBERTSON then moved a new section to the bill, embracing for relief or remuneration all our own citizens, whether on the maritime or territorial frontier, who suffered losses by the enemy during the late war.

Mr. HOPKINSON moved to amend the amendment, by incorporating the cases of those citizens who sustained loss by the British in the Revolutionary war.

Both the preceding motions, after a short discussion between the respective movers, were successively rejected; after which—

Mr. BARBOUR proposed, by way of amendment, an entire substitute to the bill, the object of which was, to allow to the volunteers in question a bounty of land, in proportion to the rank they held in our service, instead of graduating the bounty by the amount of their losses in Canada.

A debate ensued on this proposition, which, by branching a good deal into the merits of the case, and the deserts of the refugees, occupied nearly the remainder of the day. The advocates of the amendment were, Messrs. BARBOUR, HULBERT, TUCKER, and CADY; and its opponents, Messrs. JOHNSON, ALEXANDER, YATES, and CLAY.

The question was finally taken on the proposed amendment, and carried—ayes 77, noes 49.

Mr. FORSYTH moved to amend the bill, by expunging the discrimination, and extending its benefits to all the inhabitants of Canada who came over and took up arms for the United States.

This motion was opposed by Mr. GROSVENOR, and supported by Mr. FORSYTH; and disagreed to—ayes 49, noes 79.

The Committee then proceeded to fill up the blanks in the bill—to apportion the bounty—after which the Committee rose, reported the bill to the House, and the House adjourned.

TUESDAY, February 20.

Mr. SERGEANT presented a petition of George Helmbold, praying that the land bounty to which he was entitled for services as a soldier in the late Army may be given to him, which is withheld, because of his having been appointed a commissioned officer.

Mr. BASSETT submitted the following resolution, which was read and ordered to lie on the table:

Resolved, That the rules of this House be so amended as to admit, within the Hall, the Governor, for the time being, of any State in the Union, who may attend at the Seat of the General Government during the sessions of Congress, and who may choose to avail himself of such privilege.

A message from the Senate informed the House that the Senate have passed bills of the following titles, to wit: "An act for the relief of Lieutenant Colonel William Lawrence of the Army of the United States, and the officers, non-commissioned officers and privates composing the garrison of Fort Bowyer, in the year 1614;" and "An act to extend certain privileges, as therein mentioned, to Bernard Edme Verjon;" in which bills they ask the concurrence of this House.

Mr. MILLS submitted a resolution, which was read, as follows, viz:

Resolved, That the Secretary of War be directed to lay before this House a statement of the expenses incurred for the service of the militia called forth by the authority of the United States during the late war, and also a statement of the accounts which have been exhibited, and claims which have been made by the respective States for services rendered by the militia of said States, when called forth with or without such authority, designating such items of claim as have been rejected, in cases where the calls were made by the authority of the United States, and the grounds of such rejection; together with the sums which have been paid, and the accounts and claims which have been allowed therefor; designating for what services and to what States, respectively, such sums have been paid or accounts allowed.

Mr. FORSYTH moved to amend the said resolution by adding the following words:

"And if the claim of any State or States, for the services of the militia thereof, have been rejected or admitted, to state the ground of such rejection or admission."

The said resolution and amendment were ordered to lie on the table.

NATIONAL UNIVERSITY.

Mr. WILDE, from the committee appointed on that part of the President's Message, at the commencement of the session, which relates to a national seminary of learning within the District of Columbia, reported a bill for the establishment of a National University; which was read twice, and committed to a Committee of the Whole.

The bill is as follows:

A Bill for the establishment of a National University.

Be it enacted, by the Senate and House of Representatives of the United States of America in Congress assembled, That the President of the United States be, and he is hereby, authorized to cause to be erected, on such site within the District of Columbia as he shall select, the buildings necessary for a National University; and, for defraying the expense thereof, the sum of —— thousand dollars is hereby appropriated, to be paid out of any money in the Treasury of the United States not otherwise appropriated by law.

SEC. 2. *And be it further enacted,* That the President of the United States be, and he is hereby, authorized and required to cause to be surveyed and laid into building lots the whole, or such parts as he may think proper, of the ground reserved for the use of the United States, in the City of Washington; and to cause the same to be sold, at such times and places, and in such proportions, and under such regulations as he shall prescribe; and the proceeds thereof, after defraying the charges of survey and sale, to be invested in such stocks or public securities as shall by him be deemed most advisable; and the same, when so invested, and the dividends thereon arising, shall constitute a fund for the support of a National University.

SEC. 3. *And be it further enacted,* That the President of the United States be, and he is hereby, requested to cause to be prepared and laid before Congress, at its next session, a plan for the regulation and government of the said university.

CANADIAN REFUGEES.

The House then proceeded to the consideration of the report of the Committee of the Whole to the bill to compensate certain Canadian volunteers.

The amendment reported by the Committee of the Whole changed the original principle of the bill from compensation in proportion to loss of property in Canada, to remuneration according to rank in our service, agreeably to the following scale; to a colonel, 960 acres; a major, 800; a captain, 640; a subaltern, 480; and non-commissioned officers and privates, 320 acres each.

Mr. JACKSON, of Virginia, moved an amendment to the second section, to authorize the immediate location of the several bounties on any surveyed public lands in the Indiana Territory.

After some opposition to the motion by Mr. PICKERING, and reply by Mr. JOHNSON, of Kentucky, the amendment was agreed to without a division.

Some further amendment was made to the amendments of the Committee of the Whole; when

Mr. ALEXANDER said: I have to regret, Mr. Speaker, that I have taken any part in this discussion, as it necessarily invites, nay, impels me to support, and more explicitly to explain, the views which I had the honor to submit when in Committee of the Whole yesterday. My views of doing justice, sir, are guided and directed by the extent of the injury complained of, and submitted for my examination and decision.

The amendment which has been adopted in this bill, by the Committee of the Whole on yesterday, has wholly and entirely changed the original character and principle of this bill, by assuming (*pro hac*) a fact which is not true, and which cannot be justified by a true statement of the case of these Canadian refugees, as they are called. The assumed fact is this, sir; that these Canadian gentlemen are to be considered, by the principles of this amendment, as our own disbanded officers; for, the compensation in land proposed to them by this amendment is graduated by the very terms, and in the very language of the bill which had for its object a bounty in land to our own disbanded officers, as a reward to the soldier's merit, and which bill was, three days ago, rejected by a large majority, when in Committee of the Whole on that subject.

These Canadians have substantial merits, and ought to be relieved, on principle, for the losses sustained by them. and we ought to meet their case fairly, and decide it upon its own merits. They are either entitled to compensation for the losses sustained by them, or they are not entitled. If they are entitled, it is just, and honor compels you to relieve them to the extent of their loss, and that, too, on principle. Now, sir, for the principle of this amendment. By its provisions, some of these Canadians will get ten times more, perhaps, than ever they were worth in property, and some of them will get ten times less than the loss they have actually sustained. A private soldier may have been worth more than his colonel, major, or captain; yet his colonel will get nine hundred and sixty acres, his major eight hundred, his captain six hundred and forty acres, and himself but three hundred and twenty acres. Is this doing justice on principle? Away with such justice as this! it has no charms for me. I had like to have said it would be absurd—I will say it—and if it is not, *that word* ought not to have a place in the English language. It shall not; and I will insert in its place the word *ridiculous.* These Canadians are to be considered as our own disbanded officers, and to be rewarded as such for their gallant services—not indemnified for their losses—by the same scale, too, that our own officers have been proposed to be rewarded.

But, sir, I suppose our own officers are not equally meritorious, or that it would take a little more land to reward them. Sir, I fear this latter ground is the grand objection and secret which has rejected the bounty to your own disbanded officers. Sir, the Canadians ought to be indemnified, and our own officers rewarded; and although their cases are perfectly distinct in principle, yet they are both meritorious claims on your bounty. Humanity and every noble principle of our nature cry aloud in their favor. Sir, what do these Canadians ask of you? They do not ask a reward, they ask indemnity for losses sustained by them in consequence of having joined your standard in the late war.

Sir, the motion which I shall presently have the honor to submit, is intended to have the truth, and the real merits of the case of these Canadians laid before us, that we may meet their case fairly and manfully.

Sir, it is said that some of these Canadians have lost twenty thousand dollars? And pray, sir, is that the objection to our paying it. If it was an hundred thousand dollars, it is not the less just. Plead your poverty and your bankruptcy, but never deny your debt. I suspect that some of these Canadians have not lost twenty dollars in property. I am for paying each in proportion to his actual loss. I move, therefore, that this bill, as amended, be recommitted to the Committee on Military Affairs, with instructions to report to the House the facts which constitute the claims of these Canadian refugees.

Mr. BARBOUR opposed the commitment, and defended the principle substituted, on his motion, by the Committee of the whole House yesterday.

Mr. JOHNSON, of Kentucky, stated his reasons against recommitment, and for wishing the subject to be acted on in its present shape.

The question was taken on the motion to recommit, and decided in the negative.

On motion of Mr. JACKSON, of Virginia, the bill was so amended, as to exclude from the provisions of the bill such refugees as were enlisted, and to extend them only to volunteers.

Mr. JACKSON then renewed a motion previously made by Mr. HAMMOND, without success, to grant to those of the refugees who served as privates in the service, an additional allowance of three months pay; which motion was now agreed to.

Mr. NELSON, of Virginia, then stated his objections to the report of the Committee of the Whole, and to the bill in its present shape. He protested with zeal against giving preference to the refugees over such of our own citizens as had served in the late war, and who, on being disbanded, have been denied a similar bounty. He was, however, warmly in favor of remunerating, to a reasonable extent, the refugees in question, for their losses, sufferings and services; and preferred the principle of relief originally proposed.

Mr. WRIGHT spoke as follows:

Mr. Speaker, I am sorry to discover such an indisposition to remunerate the petitioners, who, by proclamation, were invited to join the American standard, being then subjects of Great Britain, resident in Canada. The honorable gentleman from Massachusetts says, that "it is immoral to encourage crime;" and he, therefore, is opposed to giving these gentlemen the amount of their losses by confiscation, which they have sustained by their confidence in the faith of this nation, pledged by that proclamation. Sir, in the abstract I admire the purity of the gentleman's principles, and was that question fairly before us, I should view the subject as he does. But that is not the question; but whether we shall fulfil the promises of the Government, in indemnifying these gentlemen for their losses sustained in joining the American standard, by the invitation of the Government. However we may admire the gentleman's principles in the abstract, yet, sir, practically, as in application to the case before us, I cannot but support the conduct of the Administration in their proclamation, and of course the claim of the gentlemen claiming under that proclamation. Sir, the *lex talionis* imposed that policy on this Administration. The British arts of seduction of the Indians and negroes to join their standard, and imbrue their hands in the blood of their fellow-citizens and masters, admit of no doubt; nay, sir, in time of peace, their attempts to seduce whole States from allegiance, through the agency of the noted Henry, has been fully proved, although he failed to effect the object of his demoralizing mission, owing to the unshaken fidelity of the citizens of that region, so pridefully called the cradle of the Revolution. I ask, with this evidence before the eyes of our Government, could they, in justice to the nation, forego this act of retaliation? I presume not. But, sir, if that act was in itself improper, it having been done by authority, and the United States having obtained the benefits, can it be possible that honorable men can deny to these gentlemen that remuneration which reason and justice entitled them to expect. A number of these gentlemen were natives of the United States, who, unwilling to imbrue their hands in the blood of their relatives and countrymen, under this proclamation joined the American standard; to these the objections do not so directly apply, but to me, that can make no distinction, because the measure of remuneration is not to be regulated by the limit of the proclamation, and as all were alike invited, so all are equally entitled to the same remuneration. In the war of the Revolution the native sons of America were all invited to join our standard; we considered all Americans as the American *natale solum*, and we considered these invitations to them to unite with us to defend America against foreign oppressions, as most justly growing out of the state of affairs in which we found ourselves at the commencement of the war—and I, therefore, shall most cordially vote for their relief, in the cases before us, which a just and wise policy induces the Government to adopt, and their devotion to this country, and their confidence in its pledged faith, induced them to embrace.

Mr. McLEAN, of Ohio, followed on the same side. He defended the character of the volunteers from the aspersions cast on them, and advocated the propriety of relieving them according to the principle first proposed, in preference to compensation according to rank.

Mr. KING, of Massachusetts, likewise opposed the report of the committee, and stated his reasons for discriminating between these persons and such of our private citizens as had suffered loss; and urged the superiority of the former plan of remuneration.

Mr. GROSVENOR replied to the argument of discrimination, advanced by Mr. KING, and disputed the existence of any difference in the cases of the suffering refugees and our own citizens; to whom—

Mr. INGHAM and Mr. NELSON successively replied.

Mr. SERGEANT spoke in reply to Mr. NELSON and others, and generally against any indemnification of the volunteers in question.

After an unsuccessful motion by Mr. HALL, to lay the bill on the table for the purpose of having it printed, and some explanatory remarks from Mr. INGHAM, the question on concurring in the report of the Committee of the Whole, (to apportion the bounty according to rank) was taken by yeas and nays, and decided in the affirmative—yeas 86, nays 48, as follows:

YEAS—Messrs. Adgate, Archer, Atherton, Bear, Barbour, Bassett, Bayliss, Bennett, Betts, Birdseye, Blount, Boss, Bradbury, Breckenridge, Brooks, Brown, Bryan, Cady, Champion, Chappell, Clark of Kentucky, Clendennin, Comstock, Cooper, Culpeper, Darlington, Davenport, Edwards, Gaston, Gold, Goodwyn, Griffin, Grosvenor, Hahn, Hammond, Hardin, Hawes, Heister, Hopkinson, Huger, Hulbert, Hungerford, Irving of New York, Jackson, Kent, Kerr of Virginia, Lewis, Lovett, Lyon, McCoy, McKee, Moseley, Newton, Noyes, Pickering, Piper, Pleasants, Reed, Sergeant, Savage, Schenck, Sheffey, Smith of Pennsylvania, Smith of Virginia, Stanford, Strong, Sturges, Tallmadge, Tate, Taul, Taylor of South Carolina, Telfair, Thomas, Townsend, Tucker, Voss, Wallace, Webster, Wheaton, Whiteside, Williams, Woodward, Wright, Yancey and Yates.

NAYS—Messrs. Alexander, Baker, Bateman, Birdsall, Burnside, Burwell, Calhoun, Cannon, Clarke of North Carolina, Clopton, Condict, Crawford, Creighton, Cuthbert, Desha, Goldsborough, Hale, Henderson, Ingham, Jewett, Johnson of Kentucky, King of Massachusetts, Langdon, Law, Lumpkin, Maclay, Mason, Mayrant, McLean of Kentucky, McLean of Ohio, Milnor, Moore, Nelson of Virginia, Ormsby, Powell, Roane, Root, Smith of Maryland, Southard, Taylor of New York, Throop, Ward of New York, Wendover, Wilcox, Wilkin, Willoughby, Thomas Wilson, and William Wilson.

Ordered, That the said bill be engrossed and read a third time to-morrow.

The bill, as originally committed to the Committee of the Whole, is as follows:

Be it enacted, by the Senate and House of Representatives of the United States of America in Congress assembled, That it shall be the duty of the Secretary of State, as soon as may be after the passage of this act, to appoint two commissioners to examine into and ascertain, in a summary way, the actual losses of real estate sustained by such persons as were, at the commencement of the late war between the United States and Great Britain, inhabitants of the province of Upper Canada; and who, during the said war, joined the armies of the United States, were slain, died in service, or continued therein until honorably discharged, and whose losses shall have been occasioned by their thus abandoning the British and joining the American cause.

SEC. 2. *And be it further enacted,* That it shall be the duty of the said commissioners to give notice for four weeks successively, in the newspapers printed in the villages of Buffalo and Batavia, in the State of New York, specifying the time when, and place where, they will meet, and requiring all persons interested to present their claims on the day specified in such notice; and the said commissioners shall meet, pursuant to their notice, on or before the —— day of —— next, at Williamsville, in the county of Niagara, and State of New York; and after having taken an oath, before some judicial officer of said State, faithfully and impartially to execute the duties enjoined on them by this act, shall proceed to inquire into the losses which the persons aforesaid sustained, for the cause aforesaid, respectively sustained. The said commissioners shall have power to administer oaths or affirmations to witnesses, and shall not take the evidence of any witness who shall not be sworn or affirmed by them; they shall adjourn from day to day, until they shall have completed the objects of their commission: *Provided, however,* That no claim for losses shall be received or examined by them, which shall not be presented to them within the space of —— weeks after they shall have convened pursuant to the said notice. And it shall be the further duty of the said commissioners, after they shall have completed the examination aforesaid, to report their proceedings to the Commissioner of the Land Office, together with a list of the persons who shall have satisfactorily established losses, and the amount of such losses respectively.

SEC. 3. *And be it further enacted,* That it shall be the duty of the said Commissioner of the Land Office to issue to each of the said persons a certificate of the amount of the losses established by him or her, under the provisions of this act; and in case of the death of any person, whose losses shall be established as aforesaid, then the said certificate shall be issued to his widow, or if no widow to the child or children of such deceased person; which certificate shall be received to the amount specified in it, but without interest, in any payment for the public lands which may hereafter be sold in the Territories of Indiana and Illinois: *Provided, however, and it is hereby expressly declared,* That the whole amount of certificates issued under this act shall not exceed the sum of —— thousand dollars; and in case the aggregate amount of losses reported by the said commissioners shall exceed the said sum of —— thousand dollars, then the certificate to be issued by the Commissioner of the Land Office to each claimant, shall not be for the whole amount of the loss sustained by him or her, but only for a sum proportioned to his or her actual loss, as the said sum of —— thousand dollars is to the aggregate of all the losses so reported.

SEC. 4. *And be it further enacted,* That each of the commissioners, to be appointed in pursuance of this act, shall receive, out of the Treasury of the United States, the sum of —— for each and every day he shall be employed in discharging the duties required of him by this act.

And as amended, it will read—

Be it enacted, by the Senate and House of Representatives of the United States of America in Congress assembled, That all such persons as had been citizens of the United States anterior to the late war, and were at its commencement inhabitants of the province of Canada, and who during the said war joined the armies of the United States as volunteers, and were slain, died in service, or continued therein till honorably discharged, shall be entitled to the following quantities of land, respectively, viz: Each colonel to nine hundred and sixty acres; each major to eight hundred acres; each captain to six hundred and forty acres; each subaltern officer to four hundred and eighty acres; each non-commissioned officer, musician, or private, to three hundred and twenty acres; and the bounties aforesaid shall extend to the medical and other staff, who shall rank according to their pay. And it shall be lawful for the said persons to locate their claims in quarter sections upon any of the unappropriated lands of the United States within the Indiana Territory, which shall have been surveyed prior to such location, with the exception of salt springs and lead mines therein, and of the quantities of land adjacent thereto, which may be reserved for the use of the same by the President of the United States, and the section number sixteen in every township to be granted to the inhabitants of such township for the use of public schools; which locations shall be subject to such regulations, as to priority of choice, and the manner of location, as the President of the United States shall prescribe.

SEC. 2. *And be it further enacted,* That the Secretary for the Department of War for the time being shall, from time to time, under such rules and regulations, as to evidence, as the President of the United States shall prescribe, issue to every person coming within the description aforesaid a warrant for such quantity of land as he may be entitled to by virtue of the aforesaid provision; and in case of the death of such person, then such warrant shall be issued to his widow, or if no widow, to his child or children.

SEC. 3. *And be it further enacted,* That the Treasurer of the United States be, and he is hereby, authorised and required to pay to each of the persons aforesaid three months additional pay, according to the rank they respectively held in the Army of the United States during the late war.

MILITARY SERVICES.

The House then proceeded to the other part of the report of the Committee of the Whole, being their amendments to the bill making further provision for military services during the late war.

After agreeing to the other amendments of the committee, the question was stated on concurring with the Committee of the Whole, in striking out the third section of the bill (which provided a bounty in land to the disbanded officers of the late army.)

Mr. NELSON, of Virginia, expressed a hope that those who had just voted a similar bounty to the Canadian refugees, would not deny it to our own officers.

Mr. TELFAIR and Mr. SMITH of Maryland opposed the report of the committee and advocated the bounty.

Mr. LUMPKIN spoke as follows:

Mr. Speaker, it is with diffidence, upon any occasion, that I rise to submit my views and opinions to this honorable body. And upon the present occasion my embarrassment is increased; because I rise in opposition to a measure emanating from a source which I highly respect. This measure has also received the sanction of the Military Committee, and the support of many other honorable gentlemen on this floor, amongst whom are most of my worthy colleagues. But upon this, as well as all other questions presented to this House for consideration, I feel myself bound to examine and investigate for myself, and then pursue that course which my own best judgment may dictate to be right. And upon due examination of this subject, the result has been, that I am constrained to conclude that it will be partial and impolitic to give the proposed donation in lands to the disbanded officers of the late Army of the United States. First, let us examine how these offices were created, and how those gentlemen came into them. The necessity of having a large number of military officers, grew out of the war in which this country has recently been engaged with a formidable enemy.

The various laws passed by Congress for raising armies, pointed out the number of officers necessary to command those armies; also the pay and subsistence that they should be entitled to receive for their services. And I presume they have received the full amount held out to them at the time they engaged in the service; and therefore, as has been admitted by my friend and colleague, as well as every other gentleman who has spoken on that side of the question, they have no just claims on the Government. But the appeal is made to the magnanimity and liberality of Congress. Sir, I admire liberality in Governments, as well as individuals. But I differ with some gentlemen in the selection of objects to bestow liberality upon. I have no disposition to bestow my charity or liberality where no necessity exists; I am not disposed to make my selection from the elevated ranks of life. I will now make the inquiry, how those officers came into office? They were not pressed into the service of their country, but in most cases were personally, or by their friends, applicants for the commands which they have held; indeed there was a great many more applicants than there were offices to bestow, which proves that it was not a very objectionable or disagreeable service, to the patriotic and gallant young gentlemen of this country. And it is a subject of regret that the best in every instance could not have been selected from the numerous candidates. But I do not intend to insinuate but that it was intended in every case to select those who were best qualified, but from the nature of the case it could not be done. Much has been said in regard to the pay of the officer and the soldier. It has been stated that the pay and bounty of the soldier was raised extravagantly high, because it was with difficulty that they could be procured; and that the pay of the officers was pared down as low as possible, because there was a great number ready to take commands. I admit that it was difficult to procure soldiers, and there was always a plenty ready to take commands. But I claim the attention of the House, while I examine what was the pay of the officers and the soldier, that we may be able to judge correctly on this subject. I find the pay of a major general (including forage and rations) to be two hundred and forty-five dollars per month; two thousand nine hundred and forty dollars per year, and more than eight dollars per day. A brigadier general, one hundred and thirty-two dollars per month, and fifteen hundred and eighty-four dollars per year. A colonel, ninety-three dollars per month, and eleven hundred and sixteen dollars per year. A major, sixty-four dollars per month, and seven hundred and eighty-eight dollars per year. A captain forty-three dollars per month, and five hundred and sixteen dollars per year; and thus gradually decreasing, down to the third lieutenant. The high pay of the soldier that has been so much dwelt upon, was during the war raised to eight dollars per month, and ninety-six dollars per year, besides his bounty in money and land. Since the conclusion of peace, his pay is reduced to five dollars per month.

I admit the assertion, that no country has rewarded or paid their soldiers higher than this. But, in its principles and form, our Government differs from all others, and I rejoice that it does; here we have no distinctions but such as arise from merit, from intrinsic worth of character; therefore there should not be so much difference between the pay of the officers and soldiers in this, as in other countries. If we were to pursue the example of the European nations, I know that we should forget the soldier, and make liberal provision for the officers. In Great Britain, if once an officer you are always so, at least their officers receive half pay for life. But in this country, if we adhere to the principles of our own Government, we ought to reward merit, not rank. Let us follow the example of the immortal Washington, the political Father of his Country. Examine his letters to the Marquis Lafayette and other friends, on his returning from the command of the American Army, at the close of the Revolutionary war. He felt himself eased from a load

of public care, and anticipated the pleasure of spending the remainder of his days as a private citizen, on the banks of the Potomac, in the practice of the domestic virtues. He asked of the Government no remuneration for his all-important services; and when his native State (Virginia) offered him donations, he declined accepting, and recommended that the fund proposed to be vested in him, should be applied to useful objects. Mr. Speaker let us follow the example of our Washington, and closely adhere to our own principles and form of Government. In ancient history I recollect reading of a nation, who received its laws immediately from, and was governed by the Supreme Ruler of the Universe; and while they were content with their good form of government they prospered, and were more blessed and happy than all the nations which surrounded them; but they became wicked and then dissatisfied, and asked for a king to rule over them; and the reason why they asked a king, was, that they might be like other nations. The request of this people was granted—a king was given to them—their pride was gratified; but in obtaining a king, they procured a curse, and not a blessing. I have no doubt but this nation has been equally blessed and protected by the guardian care of a kind and indulgent Providence; and I am confident that we do err, whenever we depart from the spirit and nature of our own republican institutions, and assimilate our laws or policy to those of other countries, whose forms of government essentially differ from ours in first principles.

I will now call the attention of the House to the provision proposed to be made to the officers, and the number proposed to be benefitted thereby. The chairman of the Military Committee informed the House the other day, that there was between fifteen hundred and two thousand disbanded officers to be provided for; and that the land proposed to be given to them was upwards of nine hundred thousand acres, nearly one million. And from the most accurate calculations which I have been able to make, I am inclined to the opinion that the number of officers and quantity of land are both estimated too low. But, in justice to the disorganized officers, permit me to say, that I entertain no doubt but many of them entered the service of their country from the most pure, upright, and patriotic motives, and that many of them have done honor to themselves and to the country for which they fought; they have gained an imperishable fame that is riveted in the hearts of the American people; a fame more durable than a marble monument. They are entitled to, and are daily receiving the honors and gratitude which their fellow-citizens have to bestow. Let us not tarnish their fame and merit by any act of ours, which will make those honorable men appear to posterity in the light of mercenaries.

But, sir, I am compelled to say, that many of those officers have no claim on their Government. There were many, who during the war were living in luxury and dissipation, spending their time in idleness and pleasure, at their recruiting stations, and frequently their conduct was such, that they were so little respected by the community where they were stationed, that they scarcely enlisted a man, and I have no doubt they injured the cause they were in honor bound to support. They were living upon the Government, without rendering the smallest benefit to it.

Delicacy and decorum forbid the mention of names, but is it not known to every gentleman on this floor, that there were officers of the regular army not worthy to be compared with many of our militia officers? And yet, nothing is said about donations of land for those brave, patriotic, volunteer militia officers, whose heroic deeds have immortalized and reeorded their names in the hearts of the American people.

Sir, it is known to you, it is known to every member of this House, that many of the militia officers have achieved far more honor in defending their country's rights, than many of those officers that we are now called upon to make provision for. I call upon gentlemen to say, if this is sound policy? If this is administering justice with an impartial hand? Sir, I cannot forget, and delicacy shall not prevent me from mentioning, the toils and services of the militia of that State which I have the honor in part to represent. But first, permit me to say, that from anything which I have seen, emanating from any department of the Government, it would appear, that the useful services of the Georgia militia, and the merit of the officers who commanded them, had not reached the War Department.

But, be this as it may, the intrepidity and bravery of the militia of the South will long be remembered by the people in that section of the country. Can I feel justified with myself to vote donations, indiscriminately, to the regular officers, some of whom have been worse than useless to the Government, while the arduous and important military services of Floyd, Newnan, Thomas, and many others who acted with them, are fresh in my recollection, and are passed over, entirely neglected? Sir, these men, not half supplied by the agents of the Government, at the head of a brave and patriotic militia, sought and found the savage foe in the wilderness, and carried terror into the heart of their country. And when attacked, and surrounded by a numerous host of yelling savages—and that in the awful solemnity of the night, without fortifications, breastworks, or shelter—every officer, every soldier, was immoveably firm to their duty, and the enemy put to flight with severe loss.

But such men as these are forgotten here. It is the officers of the regular army that must be provided for. It has been said, that the militia does not complain; and if the question now under consideration was submitted to the officers of the militia, they would be in favor of granting the proposed donations. Admit these statements to be true, and the answer is, to the praise of the militia be it spoken, that they have made no complaints; and to the officers who possess so much disinterested generosity as to grant to others that which is due to themselves. The donations proposed to be given are spoken of by gentlemen as a mere trifle. It has also been said, money is not asked for, it is lands, and that we have plenty of land, and it would be to the interest of the country to have it settled.

I will ask, if all the citizens of the United States are not interested in what is called Government land? And does not this land average to the Government, when sold, a revenue of at least two dollars per acre? Under existing laws which have been passed by Congress, for the disposition of public lands, it is obliged to bring two dollars per acre at least. If my statement be correct, we are in our liberality about to bestow donations in lands, equal in value to two millions of dollars, upon the disbanded officers of the late army. To a mind that estimates the necessity of economy in Governments as I do, this is no inconsiderable donation or gratuity. For my part I cannot reconcile it to my feelings, to vote a direct tax of three millions of dollars indiscriminately on the people, and then, in the next vote, give away two millions of their property, or money; for in reality I view it as the same thing. It is clear to my mind, that the pay and subsistence of the officer has been better than that of the soldier. And the part which the officer is required to act in performing his duty, is certainly the most pleasant and agreeable service. The situation of our soldiers during the late war, in many instances, has been a scene calculated to excite the compassion of the hardest heart. When we consider the hardships and dangers through which they have passed, upon a bare allowance of bread and beef, and their eight dollars per month, and contrast it with the pay of the officers, I trust the conclusion will be, that the liberality of the Government is not more pledged to the officers than to the soldiers, and that the obligation is as strong to many of the militia officers as to the regulars.

Mr. McKee made some remarks which could not be heard by the Reporter; and Mr. PICKERING, explained his reasons for voting in favor of the bounty to the Canadians, and yet against allowing the same to our officers.

Mr. CANNON said, he had not intended to say a single word on this subject, nor should he at this time have troubled the House with a single remark in addition to what he had submitted to the Committee of the whole House, a few days ago, when this subject was under consideration, had it not been for the arguments which had just fallen from the honorable gentleman from Maryland, (Mr. SMITH.) Sir, there is no member of this House, who has a higher regard, or feels more respect for that class of individuals who are to be benefitted by the passage of the section of the bill, which is now the subject of debate, than I have. I have not forgotten the important services many of them have rendered in defence of our country. They are entitled to, and will receive the gratitude and esteem of every virtuous citizen of this nation. They have covered themselves with glory that will last for ages to come—that could not, in the smallest degree, be increased or diminished by anything it is possible for me to say. But, sir, this question presents itself to me, in a different shape from that in which it seems to be viewed by the honorable gentleman from Maryland. I ask you, sir, if these officers, who have been discharged from the service of the United States, are the only persons in our country who are entitled to our respect, and the liberality of this nation? Does justice or policy require that we should select this particular class of men, as the only objects of our gratitude and our favor, while at the same time we turn our backs on a much larger number, composed of the citizen soldiers of our country, equally meritorious, who have served us with equal patriotism and equal firmness—the gallant heroes, who have defended our nation, our rights and our liberties, and have nobly supported, and borne our Government through all the most trying scenes of this war? I think it does not. In passing on this subject, Mr. Speaker, I consider that an unjust and improper distinction has been made between the disbanded officers of the regular army, and the citizens of our country, who have served us as soldiers; and to grant the donations of land contemplated by this section of the bill, to the disbanded officers of the regular army, and withhold an equal provision from others equally deserving the bounty of the Government, would, in my opinion, not only be making an unjust discrimination between the officers and soldiers of the regular army but also between the officers of the regular army and the officers of the volunteers and militia, who have rendered us equal service, as well as the soldier who has entered our service as a volunteer or militiaman, all of whom have served us, and that too in the most trying times of difficulty, danger and alarm; they have rendered important services to this nation—they have taken on themselves the humble though arduous duties of the soldier—they have calmly encountered the toils of the camp, and the dangers of the field of battle—they have been our noble and gallant defenders, and have driven from our soil and our shores those boasted hordes of British slaves, who have vainly attempted to lay prostrate our liberties—they have done their duty, their deeds are without a parallel in the pages of history—they have suffered, they have bled, and many of them have sacrificed their lives on the altar of our country's honor. And, sir, can it be possible that the members of this House have forgotten all these great sacrifices and important services? Is not the citizen, who has served us as a soldier, as much entitled to our consideration as the man who has served us as an officer; or are we to pass by them as unworthy of our notice, and make this partial provision for the disbanded officers? While I admit, Mr. Speaker, that many of the disbanded officers of the regular army have rendered important services to our country, I cannot forget that the citizens of our country have also rendered important services to us, during the late war; and though in a more humble and less conspicuous capacity, let us not forget them. Sir, it must be known to every person, that the place of an officer in any army, whether regular, militia, or volun-

teers, is by far better than that of a soldier. I am, therefore, opposed to rewarding the officers, and neglecting the soldiers. The difference between the pay and emoluments of your officers, and the pay and bounty of your soldiers is, in my opinion, already fully sufficient. Your officers received, perhaps, from two hundred and fifty, down to twenty-five or thirty dollars per month, while your soldier received but eight dollars per month, who encounters the most danger, and often performs the most arduous duty. I cannot agree with the honorable gentleman, that the officer's duty is so much harder than that of the soldier, although I feel the highest respect for the opinions of that gentleman. I yet believe the performance of the duties of the soldier equally as hard as that of the officer. Commissions in the regular service have been much sought after during the war, and the very persons for whom you are now about to provide donations of land, have already once been made the favorites of the nation. In getting those appointments, they have had the best places in your Army, and I might say, the best places in our country, during the war. Gentlemen may say what they please about it, but I know that, generally, the place of an officer in any army, whether regular, militia, or volunteer, is better, is enviable to that of a soldier, and why make this unjust and partial discrimination in favor of your disbanded officers?

The Government of the United States has held out to her citizens certain conditions and inducements to enter into the service; certain pay and emoluments to officers, and certain pay and bounties to soldiers; and it is known to every member of this House, that, on those conditions, you could have got more officers than you wanted, but not near so many soldiers as you wanted. This circumstance alone I would think sufficient to show clearly that the inducements given to your officers were by far greater than those given to your soldiers. But gentlemen, in the course of this debate, have contended that this land ought to be given to them, as an inducement to enter the service of our country again, in the event of another war. But, sir, I have no fears that there ever will be any difficulty found in this country to get officers for a regular army; the great difficulty is in getting soldiers. What, sir, has been the situation of our army during the late war? It has been a skeleton, an army of officers without soldiers, and, if additional inducements are given, I contend they should given to the soldier. For my part, I cannot see on what ground it can be shown, that the disbanded officers of the regular army are more entitled to this additional bounty or favor of the Government, than the citizens of our country are, who have served us in the humble capacity of soldiers; I cannot believe that the officer has any stronger claim on this Government than the soldier. Indeed, sir, I believe his claim is less strong than that of your citizen, who has served you in the humble place of a soldier. I have said before, sir, that I was opposed to the principle of rewarding officers, and neglecting our soldiers. Sir, can it be possible that the Congress of the United States will show by her acts such partiality in favor of any class of her citizens, while, at the same time, she neglects others equally meritorious? I hope they will not. The honorable gentleman from Kentucky, who is chairman of the committee who reported this bill, has, in the course of the debate on striking out this section, said something about national character. Sir, I am as anxious to preserve national character as that gentleman is, or any other member of this House. But, sir, I cannot agree that the adoption of this measure would add anything to our national character. I have a different view of this course; I believe the best way to preserve national character, is to act impartially on this subject, as well as all others that come before us, and to show by our acts that we have an equal regard for all who have rendered to us equal services. It has been contended by some gentlemen, in the course of the debate on this subject, that we ought to grant this land to the disbanded officers, on account of the sacrifices they have made in entering into our service. Sir, I admit many of them have made sacrifices in this way, but have the gentlemen forgotten that the citizens of our country generally have made sacrifices during this war, and many of them, perhaps, have made as great sacrifices, if not greater, than those who obtained commissions in the regular army? I should suppose our militia officers had made sacrifices in defending our country, and I know the volunteers have sacrificed much for the defence of our country; and, sir, the common citizens generally have made sacrifices in defending our country; many of them have sacrificed their all, and, however little it may have been, it was as dear to them as if they had much. What has been the situation of a poor man with a helpless family, entirely dependent on his labor and attention for comfort and support? I say, what has been his situation, when called to march eight hundred or a thousand miles from his home to defend his country? He has no alternative, he must go; and if retained in your service but six months, he loses his crop and he is ruined, and everything he has is sacrificed in defiance of our country; and are we now to forget all these sacrifices, except those alone which have been made by the gentlemen who were fortunate enough to obtain appointments in the regular service, and those alone we are now called on to provide for? No, sir; I hope we will pursue a different and more impartial course. But Mr. Speaker, the honorable gentleman from Maryland has said something about the great responsibility of officers, and contrasted their duties and services with that of our soldiers. Sir, I know that every officer has a share of responsibility attached to him in proportion to his grade; but is there no responsibility attached to the duties of a soldier? I ask you, sir who watches and guards the borders of your country against the sudden or midnight attack of the enemy—is it not your soldiers? and do you not require the soldier, when sentinel, to remain firm and watchful at his post, amidst the pelting storms of rains and snow?

And, sir, should he chance to grow weary with fatigue and slumber, what do you require of him? Why, sir, by the laws of your country, you require his life! And, yet, will gentlemen say he has no responsibility? I contend, the duty of a soldier has much responsibility attached it; he performs the drudgery of the camp, and makes the greatest sacrifice of his feelings and his liberty, while he is in your service; and the sufferings and danger to which he is exposed are not less even in the field of battle. Ask the gallant officer who has received the thanks of this House, and the applause of this nation, to whom he is indebted for his fame and his military glory, and he will tell you it is to the firmness and bravery of his soldiers as well as his officers. And to whom is this nation indebted for its defence, to the North, the South, the East, and the West? It is to the patriotism of our citizens, and their firmness in the different fields of battle. Sir, I feel the highest respect for every individual who has aided in the defence of our country; whether officer, soldier, or citizen, I feel grateful for their services; but I cannot agree to make what I believe to be an unjust discrimination, not only between one class of officers and others equally meritorious, but also between officers and soldiers generally. I think the gentlemen who have advocated this measure have began at the wrong end of the row. If I was called on to make the decision, which I would give donations of lands to first, the officers or soldiers, I should not hesitate to give it first to the soldier. And if the gentlemen will begin at the other end of the row, and provide for the soldiers first, I will go with them as far as any member of this House, but not until then. Therefore, I hope the amendment made to the bill, while, in Committee of the whole House, by striking out the third section, will be agreed to.

When Mr. C. had concluded, the House adjourned.

WEDNESDAY, February 21.

Mr. SMITH, of Maryland, submitted the following resolution:

Resolved, That the Committee of Ways and Means be instructed to inquire whether any, and, if any, what alterations are necessary to be made in the laws imposing duties on the tonnage of foreign vessels entering the ports of the United States.

After some remarks from Mr. SMITH, illustrative of his views, and the necessity of the resolution, it was adopted without opposition.

The following resolution, submitted yesterday by Mr. BASSETT, and modified at the suggestion of Mr. TAYLOR, of New York, so as to include the Governors of Territories, was considered and agreed to:

Resolved, That the rules of this House be so amended as to admit within the Hall the Governor, for the time being, of any State in the Union, or of any of the Territories thereof, who may attend at the Seat of the General Government during the sessions of Congress, and who may choose to avail himself of such privilege.

1047   HISTORY OF CONGRESS.   1048

H. of R.   *Canadian Refugees—Commerce with Great Britain.*   February, 1816.

On motion of Mr. Mills, the House took up the resolution submitted by him yesterday, and the same being again read, was agreed to, modified so as to read as follows:

Resolved, That the Secretary of War be directed to lay before this House a statement of the expenses incurred for the services of the militia called forth by the authority of the United States during the late war; and also a statement of the accounts which have been exhibited, and claims which have been made by the respective States, for services rendered by the militia of said States when called forth, with or without such authority, together with the sums which have been paid, and the accounts and claims which have been allowed therefor; and in case the claim of any State or States has been rejected or allowed, to state the grounds of such rejection or allowance, designating for what services, and to what States respectively, such sums have been paid or accounts allowed; and designating also such items of claim as have been rejected in cases where the calls were made by authority of the United States, and the grounds of such rejection.

On motion of Mr. McLean, of Kentucky, the Committee on Roads and Canals were instructed to inquire into the expediency of improving the navigation of the Saline creek, from its junction with the Ohio to the Saline Lick, in the Illinois Territory.

On motion of Mr. Wilde, the Committee on the Judiciary were instructed to inquire whether any, and what, more convenient arrangements can be made relative to the times and places of holding the Circuit Courts of the United States for the districts of Georgia and South Carolina.

On motion of Mr. Easton, the Committee on the Judiciary were instructed to inquire if any, and what, alterations are necessary to be made in the act entitled "An act providing for the government of the Territory of Missouri," approved June 4, 1812.

On motion of Mr. Creighton, the Committee on the Public Lands were instructed to inquire into the expediency of providing by law for the sale of the reservation of twelve miles square, at the foot of the rapids of the Miami of Lake Erie, and the reservation of two miles square at the lower rapids of Sandusky river, in the State of Ohio.

On motion of Mr. Nelson, of Virginia, the Committee on the Judiciary were instructed to inquire into the expediency of lending some aid or encouragement to the publication of Mr. Cranch's reports of cases decided in the Supreme Court of the United States during the last four or five years.

On motion of Mr. Sergeant, the Committee on the Judiciary were instructed to inquire and report whether any and what alterations and amendments are necessary to be made in the judicial system of the United States.

The amendment proposed by the Senate to the bill "for the relief of John Rodman Coxe," was read and concurred in by the House.

The bill from the Senate for the relief of Lieutenant Colonel William Lawrence, of the Army of the United States, and of the officers, non-commissioned officers and privates, composing the garrison of Fort Bowyer in the year 1814, was read twice, and referred to the Committee on Military Affairs.

The bill from the Senate "to extend certain privileges, as therein mentioned, to Bernard Edme Verjon," was read twice, and referred to Messrs. Jackson, Pitkin, and Smith, of Maryland.

CANADIAN REFUGEES.

The engrossed bill to compensate certain Canadian volunteers was read the third time, and put on its passage.

Mr. Williams stated succinctly why he had voted against an indiscriminate bounty to our own disbanded officers, and why he should likewise oppose the present bill.

Mr. Alexander stated why he should give a reluctant vote against a bill whose object he so heartily approved; but his objections were insuperable to the shape it had now assumed.

Mr. Gaston made a few remarks on the impropriety of opposing a measure because it did not exactly coincide with all our views; after which the question was taken on passing the bill, and decided in the affirmative—yeas 89, nays 54, as follows:

Yeas—Messrs. Adgate, Archer, Barbour, Bassett, Bennett, Betts, Birdsall, Blount, Brooks, Brown, Bryan, Burnside, Cady, Calhoun, Chappell, Cilley, Clarke of North Carolina, Clark of Kentucky, Clendennin, Comstock, Condict, Crawford, Creighton, Culpeper, Cuthbert, Darlington, Desha, Edwards, Forney, Forsyth, Gaston, Gold, Goodwyn, Griffin, Grosvenor, Hahn, Hammond, Hawes, Heister, Herbert, Huger, Hungerford, Ingham, Jackson, Jewett, Johnson of Kentucky, Kent, Kerr of Virginia, King of North Carolina, Lyle, Maclay, Mayrant, McCoy, McLean of Kentucky, McLean of Ohio, Newton, Ormsby, Parris, Piper, Pleasants, Powell, Robertson, Root, Sergeant, Savage, Schenck, Sharpe, Smith of Maryland, Smith of Virginia, Southard, Sturges, Taylor of New York, Taylor of South Carolina, Telfair, Townsend, Tucker, Wallace, Ward of New Jersey, Wendover, Whiteside, Wilde, Wilkin, Willoughby, Thomas Wilson, William Wilson, Woodward, Wright, Yancey, and Yates.

Nays—Messrs. Alexander, Baer, Baker, Bayliss, Boss, Bradbury, Breckenridge, Burwell, Cannon, Champion, Clayton, Cooper, Davenport, Goldsborough, Hale, Hall, Henderson, Hopkinson, Hulbert, King of Massachusetts, Langdon, Law, Lewis, Lovett, Lumpkin, Lyon, Mason, McKee, Mills, Moseley, Nelson of Massachusetts, Nelson of Virginia, Noyes, Pickens, Pickering, Pitkin, Reed, Rice, Roane, Ruggles, Sheffey, Stanford, Stearns, Strong, Tallmadge, Tate, Taul, Thomas, Vose, Ward of Massachusetts, Ward of New York, Wheaton, Wilcox, and Williams.

Ordered, That the title be "An act granting bounties in land and extra pay to certain Canadian volunteers," and that the Clerk carry the said bill to the Senate, and ask their concurrence therein.

COMMERCE WITH GREAT BRITAIN.

On motion of Mr. Forsyth, the House then proceeded to take up the report of the Managers on the part of this House, on the subject of the disagreeing votes of the two Houses, on the bill to carry into effect the Convention of Commerce with Great Britain. [This report embraces the whole ground taken by the conferees of this House, and those of the Senate. The form given to the bill by this House was substantially agreed to by the conferees, except the declaratory words in the enacting clause, which were insisted on by the conferees of the Senate, admitted by those of this House, and their acceptation recommended.]

Mr. KING, of Massachusetts rose, and expressed a wish, that the chairman of that committee would, on the part of that committee, favor the House with their views on the subject, particularly with the reasons which induced them to recommend the adoption of the amendments proposed, which, according to his impressions, tended to strengthen the pretensions set up by the other House, to weaken the force of the bill, and to add new strength to the convention; as the suspension of the acts of Congress was to be commensurate in point of duration with that convention, and to commence with it; that as to the declaratory part, of which the Senate were so tenacious, he deemed it of no further importance than as it showed the disposition of the Senate on this occasion, and as giving name and body to the power contended for. Did this question concern this House alone; were it merely a question of power or jurisdiction between the two Houses, though important in that view, he should not consider it in that serious point of light, of that high importance, which he now did. When the House is called upon to surrender a part of that power and those privileges confided them by the people, and guarantied by the Constitution, what, said he, is the claim of the Senate in this case? He would forbear to dwell upon the manner in which this bill, from the Senate, was forced upon the attention of this House. It was reported in Senate about a week after that which originated in this House; they well knew that there was a bill on the same subject pending in the House. The printed bill from the House, as usual, was upon their tables; the debate in the House had commenced; honorable gentlemen from the other branch had attended. Notwithstanding all this, and that it was a subject which particularly concerned their own powers, they thrust their bill in upon the House, while a gentleman was actually upon the floor debating the bill of the House upon the same subject. [The honorable SPEAKER here intimated to Mr. K. that he feared his language did not fully comport with that decorum which ought to be observed in speaking of the acts of the other branch.] Mr. K. inquired if he alluded to the word *thrust?* The honorable SPEAKER answered in the affirmative. Mr. K. said, he certainly should not have used that word if he could have found another which suited the occasion better. Such, he said, was the impression made on him at the time; and if he could be persuaded that no improper interference was intended on the part of the Senate, he would certainly take it back. But, said Mr. K., what is the claim

of the Senate upon this occasion?—to bind the United States in all cases upon which the treaty-making power may be exercised, contending that there is no limitation in the Constitution upon that power. In other words they claim the high, the dangerous power, to bind this country in all cases whatever; and this, in his opinion, they asserted by the present declaratory law. Such dangerous pretensions were resisted by our ancestors, and, as one of their descendants, he was disposed, in a Constitutional manner, to follow their example; and that it made no difference to him whether such pretensions were asserted by Kings, Lords, and Commons, or by a President and his Senate.

Mr. FORSYTH recapitulated the reasons which induced the committee to recommend the proposition to the House. He had viewed the declaratory words as mere surplusage, and not at all changing the character or impairing the force of the act.

Mr. CALHOUN moved that the report be laid on the table. His impression was, that the report was entirely negative, and recommended nothing decisive on the subject. At any rate, the House was just put in possession of the printed report, and being of a dubious character, some further time was necessary to a due consideration of the subject.

Mr. YANCEY supported the motion. He thought the report did yield the ground taken by this House; and, in his opinion, the House ought to stick or go through. He hoped, therefore, more time for reflection would be allowed.

Mr. TUCKER was willing the report should lie, for the present, on the table. He was confident, however, the House would find that nothing had been yielded by the committee; but, on the contrary, that the substantial rights of this House had been maintained.

The report was then laid on the table.

PROVISION FOR MILITARY SERVICES.

The House resumed the consideration of the report of the Committee of the Whole, on the bill making further provision for military services during the late war, and for other purposes.

The question recurred on concurring with the Committee of the Whole, in striking out the following section of the bill:

SEC. 3. *And be it further enacted,* That donations of land be granted to all the officers of the regular army who have been disbanded as supernumeraries, either in consolidating regiments or corps during the late war, or in reducing the army conformably to the act of March the third, one thousand eight hundred and fifteen, as follows, to wit: to each Major General one thousand two hundred and eighty acres; to each Brigadier General, one thousand one hundred and twenty acres; to each Colonel and Lieutenant Colonel, nine hundred and sixty acres; to each Major, eight hundred acres; to each Captain, six hundred and forty acres; to each subaltern, four hundred and eighty acres; and to officers of the medical and other staff, who have no rank, in proportion to their pay according to the scale aforesaid.

And the said question being taken, it passed in the affirmative—Yeas 77, nays 59, as follows:

Yeas—Messrs. Adgate, Archer, Atherton, Baer, Baylies, Betts, Boss, Bradbury, Breckenridge, Brown, Burwell, Cady, Cannon, Champion, Cilley, Clayton, Comstock, Cooper, Crawford, Culpeper, Davenport, Edwards, Gaston, Gold, Goldsborough, Hahn, Hale, Hall, Hammond, Heister, Henderson, Herbert, Jewett, Kent, King of Massachusetts, Langdon, Law, Lewis, Lovett, Lumpkin, Lyon, Mason, McKee, McLean of Kentucky, Mills, Milnor, Nelson of Massachusetts, Noyes, Pickering, Pitkin, Powell, Reed, Rice, Roane, Ruggles, Savage, Sheffey, Smith of Pennsylvania, Smith of Virginia, Southard, Stanford, Stearns, Strong, Sturges, Taggart, Tallmadge, Tate, Taylor of New York, Thomas, Townsend, Vose, Ward of Massachusetts, Ward of New York, Webster, Wheaton, Wilcox, and Williams.

Nays—Messrs. Alexander, Baker, Barbour, Bassett, Bennett, Birdsall, Brooks, Burnside, Calhoun, Chappell, Clark of Kentucky, Clendennin, Condict, Creighton, Cuthbert, Darlington, Forsyth, Goodwyn, Griffin, Grosvenor, Hawes, Huger, Hulbert, Hungerford, Ingham, Jackson, Johnson of Kentucky, Kerr of Virginia, King of North Carolina, Maclay, Mayrant, McCoy, McLean, of Ohio, Moore, Nelson of Virginia, Ormsby, Parris, Pickens, Piper, Pleasants, Robertson, Root, Schenck, Sharpe, Smith of Maryland, Taylor of South Carolina, Telfair, Tucker, Wallace, Ward of New Jersey, Wendover, Whiteside, Wilde, Wilkin, Willoughby, Thomas Wilson, William Wilson, Woodward, and Yancey.

So the House concurred with the Committee of the Whole in striking out the third section, and successively adopted the remainder of the amendments reported by the Committee.

Various motions were subsequently made to amend the bill, the most important of which was, by Mr. WILDE, to add a section, authorizing a bounty in land, according to rank, to such disbanded officers as had served one year, and who had been wounded, brevetted, or distinguished by any approving vote of Congress, &c.

The words "one year," were afterwards struck out, and motions successively made to fill the blank with ten, five, four, three, and two years, and eighteen and six months, but all in vain. Mr. W. then withdrew his amendment, with the view, as he said, of bringing the subject before the House in a form unconnected with the present bill.

The House had not got through the bill, when, about four o'clock, a motion was made and carried to adjourn.

Thursday, February 22.

Mr. INGHAM, from the Committee on the Post Office and Post Roads, reported a bill in addition to an act to regulate the Post Office Establishment; which was read twice, and committed to a Committee of the Whole.

Mr. NELSON, from the Committee on the Judiciary, reported a bill for the more convenient arrangement of the times and places of holding the circuit courts of the United States for the districts of South Carolina and Georgia; which was read twice, and committed to a Committee of the Whole.

Mr. ROBERTSON from the Committee on the Public Lands, made a report on the petition of Amos Spafford; which was read; when Mr. R. reported a bill granting to Amos Spafford the right of pre-emption; which was read twice, and committed to a Committee of the Whole.

Mr. HULBERT, from the committee appointed on the petition of Ann Gerry, by leave of the House, reported a bill authorizing payment to the widow of Elbridge Gerry, deceased, late Vice President of the United States, of half of such salary as would have been payable to him during the residue of the term for which he was elected, had he so long lived; which was read twice, and committed to a Committee of the Whole.

Mr. KING, of Massachusetts, from the Committee appointed on the petition of Jabez Maury, and others, made a report thereon; which was read; when Mr. K. reported a joint resolution to indemnify Jabez Maury, John W. C. Baxter, Samuel Wheeler, Jonathan Bartlett, Josiah Dana, and Aaron Hayden, and their sureties, against certain prosecutions under the authority of the British court of vice-admiralty; which was read twice, and committed to a Committee of the Whole.

On motion of Mr. MOORE, the Committee on the Judiciary were instructed to inquire into the propriety of providing by law to compel witnesses to attend, from one State to another State, to prosecute or give evidence in cases of felony or other high crimes.

Mr. EASTON submitted the following resolution:

Resolved, That it is expedient to grant donations of land to the disbanded officers of the late army of the United States who have been wounded in battle, and to the officers, non-commissioned officers, musicians, and privates of the militia, including volunteers and rangers, who have been wounded in battle during the late war, as follows, to wit: to each officer above the rank of colonel, —— acres; to each officer above the rank of captain and below the rank of brigadier general, —— acres; to the other commissioned officers, —— acres each; and to every non-commissioned officer, musician, and private 160 acres; and to the officers of the medical staff who have no rank, in proportion to their pay, according to the above scale, and that the Committee on Military Affairs are hereby directed to report a bill accordingly.

On the question to consider this resolution, it was determined in the negative.

Mr. HOPKINSON after suggesting that he regarded as one of the most inauspicious circumstances that appeared in the general aspect of public affairs, the voting of immense sums of money when a great portion of the members, frequently not fewer than sixty, were absent—submitted the following resolution, which was read and ordered to lie on the table:

Resolved, That the following rule be added to the standing rules of the House, to wit; "If any member shall be absent at the taking of the yeas and nays on any question, he shall be considered as absent from the service of the House for that day, unless he have leave or be sick, and therefore unable to attend."

UNSETTLED BALANCES.

Mr. HUGER said he had been so long out of Congress, and so lately become a member again, as yet not to have obtained that Parliamentary tact or feeling, which would enable him to judge whether the vote given a day or two ago, against taking up the resolution he had offered, on the subject of unsettled balances, had originated in a wish to yield a precedence to other business, or to give the go-by altogether to his resolution. He flattered himself, however, he would not allow himself to doubt, but that his motion to take up the resolution had been rejected for the last reason. Every gentleman who had turned his attention to these unsettled balances, and had only glanced his eye over the voluminous volumes in which they were contained, and which, year after year, and session after session, uselessly encumbered their tables, must feel a conviction, not only that there was great room, but in truth an urgent and imperious necessity, for inquiry and investigation in regard to them. This point admitted, it must also be admitted, that the present time was peculiarly favorable to such investigation. He had never witnessed, perhaps there never was a session since the existence of the Federal Government in which such general and reciprocal harmony, and such almost universal good humor prevailed in both branches of the Legislature. Party spirit, and party animosities, seemed to have disappeared—to have been banished from within these walls. What moment could be more auspicious, or better calculated for the consideration of subjects of this kind? He did not know how members could better dispose of their time, or in what they could more essentially serve their constituents and the public than by this investigation, and others of a similar nature.

The act requiring the annual publication of balances unsettled in the different departments, for three years previous, together with the names of those charged with such unsettled balances, had been passed by a Congress of which he was not a member. He could not, therefore, pretend to say what had been the particular objects in view when this measure was adopted. No doubt, however, that it was supposed likely to contribute in some way towards the settlement of outstanding accounts of the different departments. Perhaps it was thought that persons who might be, or had been, in the public service, and in the habit of handling public money, would feel some little delicacy, and be possibly deterred from allowing their accounts to remain so long unsettled, by the certainty of having their names thus brought before Congress, and thereby held up to the world. If such was the expectation, he was sorry to say it had, in a great measure, if not altogether, failed; for the most respectable names were to be found in the same columns with those who were probably real defaulters, and who thereby escaped, in a great degree, the opprobrium so richly their due. This was one among the many motives which induced him to wish an investigation of the subject. Another, was the amount of these balances. It was not a question in regard to hundreds or thousands, or tens of thousands. He could put his finger on unsettled, balances of hundreds of thousands—in some instances of more than half a million of dollars.

He begged leave, therefore, again to call up his resolution. And here he would resume his seat, but some gentleman near him suggested a call of the yeas and nays. For himself, he had no wish or intention to demand them. On the contrary, he did not want the yeas and nays called. His object was not to excite party feeling, nor to animadvert upon any Administration, nor upon any description of men. His real and *bona fide* object was to have the business fairly and fully investigated; to learn how it happened that such enormous balances remained so long unliquidated and unsettled, and to see whether measures could not be devised to remedy, or at least check the growth of what appeared to him, and he believed to every gentleman who heard him, a serious evil. The time, as before observed, was peculiarly favorable to such an investigation; so much so, that if the House thought with him, he would be disposed to have select committees appointed to examine into the expenditure, accounts, and mode of settlement in each and every department. He verily believed that Congress could not adopt a measure which would be more grateful to their constituents, and to the Chief Executive Magistrate himself, nor one more likely to have a beneficial operation, as well in correcting any possible abuses heretofore, as in promoting a correct administration of the public revenue in time to come.

Mr. H. observed, it had become the fashion of the day to quote Latin. He would ask leave to contribute his mite to the common stock, and offer a Latin sentence to their consideration. He said it was an old and trite maxim, familiar to everybody, and which he recollected to have heard often quoted, when a boy, by an old-fashioned master of arithmetic, under whom he had studied. It nevertheless appeared to him by no means unworthy of the attention of even that honorable body, nor altogether inapplicable to the matter under discussion. It was to the following effect:

"*Nullus tantus quæstus, quam quod habes parcere.*"

[At the last word Mr. H. hesitated somewhat, not being able to recall it immediately to mind; which excited considerable laughter. On recollection, however, he proceeded.]

Parcere, to economise, is the word, and a very significant and important word it was. At the moment, it had escaped his recollection; but this was not surprising, for it was a word not unfrequently forgotten by other honorable members in the House. No wonder, therefore, that the air of that hall, and an *esprit de corps*, had unexpectedly, and somewhat untowardly to be sure, affected his memory. He joined, however, with pleasure in the laugh, though at his own immediate expense. He did so the more willingly and readily, as he augured favorably to the success of

1055   HISTORY OF CONGRESS.   1056

H. of R.   *Petitions of W. P. Lawrence and E. Hamilton.*   February, 1816.

his resolution from the good humor the House was in.

But as he appeared to have failed in making his Latin quotation, he would, before he sat down, endeavor to present it in an English dress; his translation would be a free one, but he trusted he should be able to make himself perfectly intelligible to honorable gentlemen.

In vain do you continue a high duty on salt—increase that upon whiskey. In vain is your tax upon sugar—and your stamp-tax. In vain you lay a direct tax of three millions on the lands throughout the Union; equally in vain do you double your duties on foreign importations, and propose a new and exorbitant tariff. All—all is in vain, perfectly in vain; unless, after the resources of the nation are thus drawn into your coffers, you take special care that the treasure is not wasted, and provide proper and sufficient checks against the undue expenditure and disbursement of it.

Mr. Tucker made some observations, not distinctly heard, but which ended with a resolution to appoint a standing committee to superintend the expenditures of every particular department of Government.

Mr. Pickering moved that the resolution should be laid on the table. It was accordingly ordered.

DEATH OF MR. BRIGHAM.

Mr. Pickering then announced the death of his colleague Mr. Brigham, and moved that a committee should be appointed to superintend his funeral. A committee of seven was accordingly appointed for the purpose.

Mr. Pickering then moved that the House should, as a testimony of their respect for the deceased, wear a black crape on the left arm for a month, which was ordered. He then moved that the members of the House should attend the funeral at twelve o'clock to-morrow; and that a message should be sent to the Senate with information to that effect; which was all ordered.

The House then adjourned to Saturday.

Saturday, February 24.

Mr. Yancey reported a bill for the relief of Ephraim Shayler, which was read twice, and committed to a Committee of the Whole.

Mr. Pleasants, from the Committee on Naval Affairs, reported a bill for the gradual increase of the Navy of the United States, which was read twice and committed to a Committee of the Whole.

On motion of Mr. Tucker, the Committee on the Judiciary were instructed to inquire into the expediency of so amending the laws of the United States, as to allow an appeal from the decision of the several Territorial courts.

WILLIAM P. LAWRENCE.

Mr. Yancey, from the Committee of Claims, made a report on the petition of William P. Lawrence, which was read, and the resolution therein contained was concurred in by the House.

The report is as follows:

That the petitioner was a surgeon in the detachment of militia from Tennessee, called to the defence of New Orleans, in December, 1814; that, upon the return of the militia to Tennessee, in the month of March, 1815, the petitioner was ordered to be stationed at Bogue Chitto, in the State of Louisiana, with a number of men taken sick, on their return. The petitioner states that the disease of the soldiery became contagious, and, from the scarcity of servants to attend the sick, his own servant and slave was obliged to be employed as such; and that, while thus engaged in waiting on the sick, he took the disease and died. He asks of Congress to be paid his value.

The committee are of opinion he is not entitled to relief. If an officer of the Government thinks proper to take into his own service his slave in the capacity of servant, and receives the pay allowed for servants, instead of employing a freeman for that purpose, the United States should not be considered liable for his value in case of death or other loss to the owner.

It was the obvious and correct policy of the act of Congress, and it is evidently its intention, not to make the Government liable for the value of the servant, but to provide a sufficient compensation for his services.

The committee recommend the following resolution :

Resolved, That the prayer of the petitioner ought not to be allowed.

ELIZABETH HAMILTON.

Mr. Comstock, from the Committee on Pensions and Revolutionary Claims, made a report on the petition of Elizabeth Hamilton, which was read; when Mr. C. reported a bill for the relief of Elizabeth Hamilton, which was read twice, and committed to a Committee of the Whole. The report is as follows:

That it is stated by the petitioner that her late husband, Alexander Hamilton, was, as she is advised, justly entitled to five years' full pay (as commutation of half-pay during life) of a lieutenant colonel, in which capacity he served in the regular Army of the United States during the Revolutionary war.

That her husband never received the said pay to which he was so entitled; that if he ever relinquished his claim to said pay, of which an apprehension is expressed by the petitioner, it was from the delicate motive of divesting himself of all interest upon the subject of making provision for the disbanded officers of the Revolutionary army who served during the war, in which important business he was called on to act, as a member of Congress, in the year 1783; and that the present situation of the family of her lamented husband renders it desirable that they should receive that remuneration to which he was justly entitled from his country. This remuneration, therefore, the petitioner respectfully solicits.

The committee are not aware of any public record or document showing the time at which Colonel Hamilton resigned his commission in the Army. From the uniform tenor of various letters of distinguished officers of the Revolutionary army, addressed to the Honorable Richard M. Johnson, as chairman of the Committee of Claims, in the year 1810, as well as from a brevet commission dated the 28th of October, 1783, by which Lieutenant Colonel Alexander Hamilton was promoted to the rank of Colonel by brevet in the Army of the United States, the committee entertain the opinion that Colonel Hamilton served during the war, and that

1057   HISTORY OF CONGRESS.   1058

FEBRUARY, 1816.   Commerce with Great Britain.   H. OF R.

he never received either half-pay during life, or full pay for five years in lieu thereof as commutation, to which he was entitled by law.

Of any relinquishment of Colonel Hamilton to the claim now asked to be satisfied, the committee possess no knowledge, except that derived from the apprehension expressed in the petition to which they have already adverted, and from a written document signed A. H., importing to be a statement of the temporal concerns of Colonel Hamilton in which allusion is made to a note by him signed, addressed to the Secretary of War, relinquishing the claim in question. The committee would further remark that, should a probability exist that Colonel Hamilton may have relinquished his said claim, and notwithstanding it is barred by the statute of limitation, nevertheless, as the services have been rendered to the country, by which its happiness and prosperity have been promoted, they are of opinion that, to reject the claim under the peculiar circumstances by which it is characterized, would not comport with that honorable sense of justice and magnanimous policy which ought ever to distinguish the legislative proceedings of a virtuous and enlightened nation.

They have therefore prepared a bill granting the relief solicited in the premises.

COMMERCE WITH GREAT BRITAIN.

The House again took up the report of the conferees on the disagreeing votes of the two Houses on the amendment proposed by this House to the bill from the Senate "concerning the convention to regulate the commerce between the territories of the United States and His Britannic Majesty," and the modifications proposed by the said conferees being stated in the words following to wit:

That the House of Representatives recede from their amendment to strike out the words " and declared," contained in the enacting clause, and their other amendments to the bill from the Senate, and agree to the following amendments:

Line 2, of the engrossed bill, after word "act," strike out the words "or acts as is," and insert these words "as imposes a higher duty of tonnage or of impost on vessels, and articles imported in vessels of the United States."

Line 4, strike out the word " shall," and, after the word "be," insert the words "from and after the date of the ratification of the said convention, and during the continuance thereof."

The question was taken, Will the House recede from their amendments, and agree to the modification recommended by the conferees? it passed in the affirmative—yeas 100, nays 35, as follows :

YEAS—Messrs. Alexander, Archer, Atherton, Baker, Barbour, Bassett, Bateman, Baylies, Bennett, Birdsall, Birdseye, Blount, Boss, Bradbury, Breckenridge, Brown, Burnside, Cannon, Champion, Cilley, Clopton, Comstock, Condict, Conner, Creighton, Cuthbert, Darlington, Davenport, Forsyth, Glasgow, Goldsborough, Goodwyn, Griffin, Hahn, Hawes, Henderson, Herbert, Hopkinson, Ingham, Irving of New York, Jackson, Jewett, Johnson of Kentucky, Kent, Kerr of Virginia, Langdon, Law, Lewis, Lovett, Lowndes, Lumpkin, Lyle, Maclay, Mayrant, McCoy, McKee, McLean of Kentucky, McLean of Ohio, Middleton, Milnor, Moseley, Nelson of Virginia, Newton, Parris, Pickens, Pit-

14th CON. 1st SESS.—34

kin, Pleasants, Powell, Reed, Reynolds, Roane, Sergeant, Schenck, Smith of Pennsylvania, Smith of Maryland, Smith of Virginia, Southard, Stanford, Stearns, Strong, Stuart, Sturges, Taggart, Tallmadge, Taylor of New York, Taylor of South Carolina, Telfair, Townsend, Tucker, Vose, Wallace, Ward of Massachusetts, Wendover, Wheaton, Wilcox, Wilde, Williams, Willoughby, Thomas Wilson, and Yates.

NAYS—Messrs. Baer, Cady, Calhoun, Chappell, Clark of Kentucky, Cooper, Crawford, Desha, Edwards, Forney, Gaston, Hammond, Hanson, Heister, Huger, King of Massachusetts, Lyon, Mills, Moore, Nelson of Massachusetts, Ormsby, Pickering, Randolph, Robertson, Root, Sheffey, Thomas, Ward of New York, Whiteside, Wilkin, William Wilson, Woodward, Wright, and Yancey.

MILITARY SERVICES.

The House again resumed the consideration of the bill making further provision for military services during the late war and for other purposes, which occupied the remainder of the sitting.

Several amendments were successively offered to the bill, most of them verbal, and involving no principle—some of which were agreed to, and others rejected. Among the former was an amendment adopted, on motion of Mr. CANNON, to include the cases of those persons who shall have died after their return home, of wounds, &c. received in service. Among the rejected amendments was one offered by Mr. BIRDSEYE, to grant the allowance provided in the bill, to the father or mother, where there be no widow or child left by the decedent.

After several unsuccessful motions to lay the bill on the table and have it printed as amended, and to adjourn—

The bill was finally ordered, with the amendments, to be engrossed and read a third time.

MONDAY, February 26.

Mr. SMITH, of Maryland, presented a petition of John M. Forbes, late Consul of the United States at Hamburg, praying that the Secretary of State may be authorized to admit and pay such part of his claim for loss of exchange, interest, and other incidental charges, as may be found equitably due to him, on account of his expenditures for the relief and protection of destitute and distressed American seamen in European ports.—Referred to Messrs. SMITH, IRVING, of New York, and PITKIN.

Mr. BARBOUR presented a petition of Thomas Mallory, praying compensation for the time he was sick, while on a tour of militia duty, and for remuneration of his expenses while sick and returning to his place of residence.—Referred to the Committee of Claims.

Mr. TUCKER presented a petition of the Mayor, Alderman, and Common Council of the City of Washington, praying that the said city may be established as a port of entry.—Referred to the Committee of Commerce and Manufactures.

Mr. FORSYTH, from the Committee on Foreign Relations, reported a bill supplementary to the act passed on the 30th of March, 1802, to regulate trade and intercourse with the Indian tribes, and to preserve peace on the frontiers; which was read twice and committed to a Committee of the Whole.

An engrossed bill, entitled "An act making further provision for military services during the late war, and for other purposes," was read the third time and passed.

BOUNTY FOR MILITARY SERVICES.

Mr. Yancey from the Committee of Claims, made a report on the petition of Abigail O'Flyng, which was read; when Mr. Y. reported a bill for the relief of Patrick O'Flyng, Abigail O'Flyng, and Edmund O'Flyng; which was read twice and committed to a Committee of the whole House to-morrow.

The report is as follows:

That Abigail O'Flyng is the wife of Patrick O'Flyng, of the town of Batavia, in the State of New York. During the late war Patrick O'Flyng, and three of his sons, Patrick, Temple E., and Edmund O'Flyng, enlisted as soldiers in the army of the United States. The father continued in the service until the 28th of June, 1815, and was then honorably discharged; Edmund O'Flyng, the youngest son, on account of distinguished good conduct and bravery, was discharged from the service, and obtained a cadet's appointment in the Military Academy at West Point; Patrick O'Flyng, on account of his brave and meritorious conduct, was promoted to the appointment of a lieutenancy, and Temple E. O'Flyng to that of ensign. Patrick led the forlorn of the first brigade, under the command of General Miller, in the sortie at Fort Erie; and of the twenty-four men whom he commanded, twenty were killed or wounded. Since the termination of the war he has died, without wife or child. Temple E. O'Flyng, on that memorable occasion, equally distinguished himself; he received a wound, of which he died the next day, leaving no wife or child.

The petitioner states that her husband, being old and infirm, is unable to attend to his business, and that she has made application to the War Department for the bounty land of her husband and sons, and has received for answer that her husband, Patrick O'Flyng, being above forty-five, and her youngest son, Edmund, being under eighteen, at the time of their enlistment, the act of Congress does not authorize the department to issue warrants for the land; and that, in consequence of the promotion of her other two sons, Patrick and Temple, to appointments in the Army, they are not entitled to their bounty lands.

The committee entertain no doubt that the construction of the act of Congress, given to it by the department, is correct; but they, at the same time, entertain no doubt of the equitable and just claim of the petitioner and her husband. Notwithstanding the father was above forty-five, and the youngest son under eighteen, they performed services, as soldiers, important and valuable to their country, and highly honorable to themselves and their family.

The committee are also of opinion that the claim of the petitioner and her husband, for the bounty land of Lieutenant and Ensign O'Flyng, is equally meritorious and just. It cannot possibly be the policy of the Government to withhold the bounty land of a soldier because he has distinguished himself by his bravery and good conduct so as to merit and receive an appointment in the Army.

The committee are of opinion that the persons interested are entitled to relief, and therefore report by bill.

Mr. Yancey also made a report on the petition of Thomas Ap Catesby Jones, a Lieutenant in the Navy; which was read; when Mr. Y. reported a bill for the relief of Thomas Ap Catesby Jones; which was read twice and committed to a Committee of the Whole.

NATIONAL BANK.

The House having resolved itself into a Committee of the Whole, Mr. Nelson, of Virginia, in the Chair, on that subject, the bill having been read, establishing a National Bank, with a capital of thirty-five millions of dollars—

Mr. Calhoun rose to explain his views of a subject so interesting to the Republic, and so necessary to be correctly understood, as that of the bill now before the Committee. He proposed at this time only to discuss general principles, without reference to details. He was aware, he said, that principle and detail might be united, but he should at present keep them distinct. He did not propose to comprehend in this discussion the power of Congress to grant bank charters, nor the question whether the general tendency of banks was favorable or unfavorable to the liberty and prosperity of the country; nor the question whether a National Bank would be favorable to the operations of the Government. To discuss these questions, he conceived, would be an useless consumption of time. The Constitutional question had been already so freely and frequently discussed, that all had made up their mind on it. The question whether banks were favorable to public liberty and prosperity, was one purely speculative. The fact of the existence of banks, and their incorporation with the commercial concerns and industry of the nation, proved that inquiry to come too late. The only question was, on this hand, under what modifications were banks most useful, and whether the United States ought or ought not to exercise the power to establish a bank. As to the question whether a National Bank would be favorable to the administration of the finances of the Government, it was one on which there was so little doubt, that gentlemen would excuse him if he did not enter into it. Leaving all these questions then, Mr. C. said, he proposed to examine the cause and state of the disorders of the national currency, and the question whether it was in the power of Congress, by establishing a National Bank, to remove those disorders. This, he observed, was a question of novelty and vital importance—a question which greatly affected the character and prosperity of the country.

As to the state of the currency of the nation, Mr. C. proceeded to remark that it was extremely depreciated, and in degrees varying according to the different sections of the country, all would assent. That this state of the currency was a stain on public and private credit, and injurious to the morals of the community, was so clear a position as to require no proof. There were, however, other considerations arising from the state of the currency not so distinctly felt, nor so generally assented to. The state of our circulating medium was, he said, opposed to the principles of the Federal Constitution. The power was given to Congress by that instrument in express terms to regulate the currency of the United States. In point of fact, he said, that power, though given to Congress, is not in their hands. The power is exercised by banking institutions, no longer responsible for the correctness with which they manage it. Gold and silver have disappeared entirely; there is no money but paper money, and that money is beyond the control of Congress. No one, he said, who referred to the Constitution, could doubt that the money of the United States was intended to be placed entirely under the control of Congress. The only object the framers of the Constitution could have in view in giving to Congress the power "to coin money, regulate the value thereof and of foreign coin," must have been to give a steadiness and fixed value to the currency of the United States. The state of things at the time of the adoption of the Constitution, afforded Mr. C. an argument in support of his construction. There then existed, he said, a depreciated paper currency, which could only be regulated and made uniform by giving a power for that purpose to the General Government. The States could not do it. He argued, therefore, taking into view the prohibition against the States issuing bills of credit, that there was a strong presumption this power was intended to be exclusively given to Congress. Mr. C. acknowledged there was no provision in the Constitution by which States were prohibited from creating the banks which now exercised this power; but, he said, banks were then but little known; there was but one, the Bank of North America, with a capital of only four hundred thousand dollars; and the universal opinion was, that bank notes represented gold and silver, and that there could be no necessity to prohibit banking institutions under this impression, because their notes always represented gold and silver, and they could not be multiplied beyond the demands of the country. Mr. C. drew the distinction between banks of deposite and banks of discount, the latter of which were then but little understood, and their abuse not conceived until demonstrated by recent experience. No man, he remarked, in the Convention, much talent and wisdom as it contained, could possibly have foreseen the course of these institutions; that they would have multiplied from one to two hundred and sixty; from a capital of four hundred thousand dollars to one of eighty millions; from being consistent with the provisions of the Constitution, and the exclusive right of Congress to regulate the currency, that they would be directly opposed to it; that so far from their credit depending on their punctuality in redeeming their bills with specie, they might go on, *ad infinitum*, in violation of their contract, without a dollar in their vaults. There had, indeed, Mr. C. said, been an extraordinary revolution in the currency of the country. By a sort of under-current, the power of Congress to regulate the money of the country had caved in, and upon its ruin had sprung up those institutions which now exercised the right of making money for and in the United States—for gold and silver are not the only money, but whatever is the medium of purchase and sale, in which bank paper alone was now employed, and had, therefore, become the money of the country. A change, great and wonderful, has taken place, said he, which divests you of your rights, and turns you back to the condition of the Revolutionary war, in which every State issued bills of credit, which were made a legal tender and were of various value.

This, then, Mr. C. said, was the evil. We have in lieu of gold and silver a paper medium, unequally but generally depreciated, which affects the trade and industry of the nation; which paralyzes the national arm; which sullies the faith, both public and private, of the United States; a paper no longer resting on gold and silver as its basis. We have indeed laws regulating the currency of foreign coin, but they are under present circumstances a mockery of legislation, because there is no coin in circulation. The right of making money—an attribute of sovereign power, a sacred and important right—was exercised by two hundred and sixty banks, scattered over every part of the United States, not responsible to any power whatever for their issues of paper. The next and great inquiry was, he said, how this evil was to be remedied. Restore, said he, these institutions to their original use; cause them to give up their usurped power; cause them to return to their legitimate office of places of discount and deposite; let them be no longer mere paper machines; restore the state of things which existed anterior to 1813, which was consistent with the just policy and interests of the country; cause them to fulfil their contracts, to respect their broken faith, resolve that everywhere there shall be an uniform value to the national currency, your Constitutional control will then prevail.

How, then, he proceeded to examine, was the desirable end to be attained? What difficulties stand in the way? The reason why the banks could not now comply with their contract was that conduct which in private life frequently produces the same effect. It was owing to the prodigality of their engagements without means to fulfil them; to their issuing more paper than they could possibly redeem with specie. In the United States, according to the best estimation, there was not in the vaults of all the banks more than fifteen millions of specie, with a capital amounting to about eighty-two millions of dollars; hence the cause of the depreciation of bank notes—the excess of paper in circulation beyond that of specie in their vaults. This excess was visible to the eye, and almost audible to the ear; so familiar was the fact that this paper was emphatically called *trash* or *rags*. According to estimation, also, he said there were in circulation at the same date, within the United States, two hundred millions of dollars of bank notes, credits, and bank paper, in one shape or other. Supposing thirty millions of these to be in possession of the banks themselves, there were perhaps one hundred and seventy millions actually in circulation, or on which the banks draw interest. The proportion between the demand and supply which regulates the price of everything, regulates also the value of this paper. In proportion as the issue is excessive, it depreciates in value; and no wonder, when, since 1810 or 1811, the amount of paper in circulation had increased from eighty or ninety to two hundred millions. Mr. C. here examined the opinion entertained by some gentlemen that bank paper had not depreciated, but that gold and silver had depreciated, a position he denied by arguments founded on the portability of gold and silver which would equalize their value in every part of the United States, and on the facts, that gold and silver coin had increased in quantity instead of diminishing, and that the exchange with Great Britain had been (at gold and silver value) for some time past in favor of the United States. Yet, he said, gold and silver were leaving our shores. In fact, we have degraded the metallic currency; we have treated it with indignity, it leaves us, and seeks an asylum on foreign shores. Let it become the basis of bank transactions, and it will revisit us. Having established, as he conceived, in the course of his remarks, that the excess of paper issues was the true and only cause of depreciation of our paper currency, Mr. C. turned his attention to the manner in which that excess had been produced. It was intimately connected with the suspension of specie payments; they stood as cause and effect; first, the excessive issues caused the suspension of specie payments, and advantage had been taken of that suspension to issue still greater floods of it. The banks had undertaken to do a new business, uncongenial with the nature of such institutions; they undertook to make long loans to Government, not as brokers, but as stockholders—a practice wholly inconsistent with the system of specie payments. After showing the difference between the ordinary business of a bank in discounts, and the making loans for twelve years, Mr. C. said, indisputably the latter practice was a great and leading cause of the suspension of specie payments. Of this species of property (public stock) the banks in the United States held on the 30th day of September last about eighteen and a half millions, and a nearly equal amount of Treasury notes, besides stock for long loans made to the State governments, amounting, altogether, to within a small amount of forty millions, being a large proportion of their actual capital. This, he said, was the great cause of the suspension of specie payments. Had the banks (he now discussed the question) the capacity to resume specie payment? If they have the disposition, he said, they may resume specie payments. The banks are not insolvent, he said; they never were more solvent. If so, the term itself implies that,

if time be allowed them, they may before long be in a condition to resume payment of specie. If the banks would regularly and consentaneously begin to dispose of their stock, to call in their notes for the Treasury notes they have, and moderately curtail their private discounts; if they would act in concert in this manner, they might resume specie payments. If they were to withdraw by the sale of a part only of their stock and Treasury notes, twenty-five millions of their notes from circulation, the rest would be depreciated to par, or nearly, and they would still have fifteen millions of stock disposable to send to Europe for specie, &c. With thirty millions of dollars in their banks, and so much of their paper withdrawn from circulation, they would be in a condition to resume payments in specie. The only difficulty, that of producing concert, was one which it belonged to Congress to surmount. The indisposition of the banks, from motives of interest, obviously growing out of the vast profits most of them have lately realized, by which the stockholders have realized from 12 to 20 per cent. on their stock, would be, he showed, the greatest obstacle. What, he asked, was a bank? An institution, under present uses, to make money. What was the instinct of such an institution? Gain, gain; nothing but gain; and they would not willingly relinquish their gain from the present state of things, which was profitable to them, acting as they did without restraint, and without hazard. Those who believed that the present state of things would ever cure itself, Mr. C. said, must believe what is impossible; banks must change their nature, lay aside their instinct, before they will aid in doing what it is not their interest to do. By this process of reasoning, he came to the conclusion that it rested with Congress to make them return to specie payments by making it their interest to do so. This introduced the subject of the National Bank.

A National Bank, he said, paying specie itself, would have a tendency to make specie payments general, as well by its influence as by its example. It will be the interest of the National Bank to produce this state of things, because otherwise its operations will be greatly circumscribed, as it must pay out specie or National Bank notes; for he presumed one of the first rules of such a bank would be to take the notes of no bank which did not pay in gold and silver. A National Bank of thirty-five millions, with the aid of those banks which are at once ready to pay specie, would produce a powerful effect all over the Union. Further, a National Bank would enable the Government to resort to measures which would make it unprofitable to banks to continue the violation of their contracts, and advantageous to the observation of them. The leading measures of this character would be to strip the banks refusing to pay specie of all the profits arising from the business of the Government, to prohibit deposites with them, and to refuse to receive their notes in payment of dues to the Government. How far such measures would be efficacious in producing a return to specie payments, he was unable to say; but it was as far as he would be willing to go at the present session. If they persisted in refusing to resume payments in specie, Congress must resort to measures of a deeper tone, which they had in their power.

The restoration of specie payments, Mr. C. argued, would remove the embarrassments on the industry of the country, and the stains from its public and private faith. It remained to see whether this House, without whose aid it was in vain to expect success in this object, would have the fortitude to apply the remedy. If this was not the proper remedy, he hoped it would be shown by the proposition of a proper substitute, and not opposed by vague and general declamation against banks. The disease, he said, was deep; it affected public opinion, and whatever affects public opinion touches the vitals of the Government. Hereafter, he said, Congress would never stand in the same relation to this measure in which they now did. The disease arose in time of war; the war had subsided, but left the disease, which it was now in the power of Congress to eradicate; but, if they did not now exercise the power, they would become abettors of a state of things which was of vital consequence to public morality, as he showed by various illustrations. He called upon the House, as guardians of the public weal, of the health of the body politic which depended on the public morals, to interpose against a state of things which was inconsistent with either. He appealed to the House, too, as the guardians of public faith and private faith. In what manner, he asked, were the public contracts fulfilled? In gold and silver, in which the Government had stipulated to pay? No; in paper issued by these institutions; in paper greatly depreciated; in paper depreciated from five to twenty per cent. below the currency in which the Government had contracted to pay, &c. He added another argument: the inequality of taxation in consequence of the state of the circulating medium, which, notwithstanding the taxes were paid with strict regard to the Constitutional provision for their equality, made the people in one section of the Union pay perhaps one-fifth more of the same tax than those in another. The Constitution having given Congress the power to remedy these evils, they were, he contended, deeply responsible for their continuance.

The evil he desired to remedy, Mr. C. said, was a deep one; almost incurable, because connected with public opinion, over which banks have a great control; they have, in a great measure, a control over the press. For proof of which, he referred to the fact that the present wretched state of the circulating medium had scarcely been denounced by a single paper within the United States. The derangement of a circulating medium, he said, was a joint thrown out of its socket; let it remain for a short time in that state, and the sinews will be so knit that it cannot be replaced; apply the remedy soon, and it is an

operation easy, though painful. The evil grows, whilst the resistance to it becomes weak; and, unless checked at once, will become irresistible. Mr. C. concluded by observing, that he could have said much more on this important subject, but he knew how difficult it was to gain the attention of the House to long addresses.

Mr. RANDOLPH, in explaining an allusion which Mr. CALHOUN had made to a remark of his on a former occasion, said that he had listened to the honorable gentleman with pleasure; he was glad to see a cause so important in hands so able. He promised the honorable gentleman, though he might not agree in his mode of remedying the evil, he would go with him in the application of any adequate remedy to an evil which he regarded as most enormous.

Mr. WARD, of Massachusetts, acknowledged the correctness of the representation of the existing evil, for which he appeared to think the remedy was near at hand and more simple in its application than the establishment of a National Bank, viz: by refusing to receive the notes of those banks, which do not pay specie, in dues to the Government. But for an alliance, which he considered disgraceful to the country and unjust to individuals, between the Secretary of the Treasury and the banks which refused to pay specie, the evil never would have existed. If Congress adopted the measure which he (Mr. W.) proposed, those banks must go down and public credit rise. Why not resort at first to the obvious expedient, and then proceed to the consideration of the less argent question of establishing a National Bank? The banks, who it was now agreed had engaged in a business for which they were not calculated, having received a sufficient bonus for the loans they made to Government, and made handsome profits by it, had no claim on Government to protect them in their refusal to pay specie. Mr. W. rose not to propose any amendment to the bill, but to express his entire coincidence in the gentleman's opinion that a great evil exists, which Congress had the power to remedy; and, if the remedy were not immediately applied, on them would be the responsibility and the blame.

Mr. SERGEANT moved to amend the first section of the bill by striking out the words "thirty-five," and inserting "twenty," as the amount of the capital of the bank. He did not intend, he said, to go into a general consideration of the principle of the bill, or of the motion now submitted by him. He made the motion on the ground of the facts and arguments just delivered by the gentleman from South Carolina, (Mr. CALHOUN.) From the quantity of paper stated to be in circulation, he thought the calculation fair that the amount proposed to be added to the existing bank capital was larger than necessary, and entered into some calculations to support the propriety of his motion.

Mr. CALHOUN hoped the motion would not prevail, and replied briefly to the calculations of Mr. SERGEANT. The necessity of a larger capital consisted, he said, in the important functions to be performed by the National Bank. The desirable point was to fix the capital so large as to prevent undue profit, and so as to prevent a loss to the stockholders. Perhaps a bank of twenty millions might afford a fair profit, but the great business it would have to perform made a larger capital necessary.

Mr. Pitkin supported the motion to reduce the capital. He thought the banking capital of the country already too great, and offered a few calculations to prove the position. In 1805, 1806, and 1807, said he, when the commerce of the country was very great, our banking capital did not exceed fifty or sixty millions; and yet, in those times, no complaint was heard of the deficiency of capital. If not more than that amount was wanted, then, is it possible that one hundred and thirty or one hundred and forty millions can be necessary at this time? Mr. P. declared himself in favor of a National Bank, if it could be established on good principles, such as would restore the old state of things when bank notes were paid with specie. If, however, the bill passed with its present capital, it would in his opinion increase the evil instead of proving a remedy. Such a capital was not necessary, either, for the purposes wanted. As to loans, no bank could make long loans without stopping the payment of specie and destroying the circulating medium; and to support the assertion, he quoted the fate of various banks in Europe. A large capital for that purpose, therefore, was unnecessary. Loans, he said, must be made by individuals; it cannot be done by banks, without ruin; and a large capital was not necessary, therefore, to enable the Government to obtain from the bank all the aid it could or ought properly to receive. Nor would a large capital, he said, restore the old state of things—that must be done by the co-operation of the large banks in the cities; the specie has got into those banks, and there it will remain until they resume the payment of it. Mr. P. said, likewise, he was unwilling to place fifty millions of money in the hands of any set of men in this country. They would use it oppressively; the old Bank of the United States had done so, and so would this. Such a power would enable them to wield the destinies of this nation. For this strong reason, Mr. P. said, as well as the others he had stated, he was in favor of reducing the capital; and, to allow more time to reflect on this important feature of the bill, he moved that the Committee rise.

After a few remarks by Mr. Calhoun, on what had fallen from Mr. Pitkin, the Committee rose, reported progress, and obtained leave to sit again.

Tuesday, February 27.

Mr. King, of Massachusetts, presented petitions from the merchants in the towns of York and Castine, in the District of Maine, complaining of the monopolizing policy of the British Government, in securing to the vessels of that nation the exclusive right to trade between the United States and the British West Indies, and North American possessions, as well as to the fisheries;

and praying that such measures may be adopted as will counteract the said policy, and tend to the admission of American vessels in the trade aforesaid.—Referred to the Committee on Foreign Relations.

Mr. Sergeant presented a petition of the American Convention for promoting the abolition of Slavery, stating their belief that the act prohibiting the importation of slaves is evaded in the southern part of the Union, and praying that the provisions of the said act may be strengthened, and its penalties increased; and that measures may be adopted to prevent the frequent practices of kidnapping free negroes.—Referred to Messrs. Sergeant, Taylor of South Carolina, Wright, Wilde, and Cady.

Mr. Nelson, from the Committee on the Judiciary, reported a bill to establish an uniform system of bankruptcy throughout the United States; which was read twice, and committed to a Committee of the Whole.

Mr. Robertson, from the Committee on the Public Lands, reported on the expediency of selling forfeited lands in the Jeffersonville district, which was read; when Mr. R. reported a bill to authorize the sale of lands forfeited to the United States, in the district of Jeffersonville, at the land office in said district; which was read twice, and committed to a Committee of the Whole.

Mr. Robertson also reported a bill providing for the sale of the tract of land at the British fort at the Miami of the Lake, and at the foot of the Rapids, and for other purposes; which was read twice, and committed to a Committee of the Whole.

Mr. Robertson also reported a bill providing for the sale of the tract of land at the lower rapids of Sandusky river; which was read twice, and committed to a Committee of the Whole.

On motion of Mr. Forsyth, the Committee of Commerce and Manufactures were instructed to inquire into the expediency of passing an act declaring the consent of Congress to an act of the Legislature of Georgia, passed on the 12th of December, 1804, establishing the fees of the harbor master and health officer of the ports of Savannah and St. Mary's.

On motion of Mr. Creighton, the Committee on the Public Lands were instructed to inquire into the expediency of providing by law for the sale of the lands of the United States within that tract of country in the State of Ohio heretofore set apart and reserved for satisfying the claims of refugees from the British Provinces of Canada and Nova Scotia.

Mr. Johnson, of Kentucky, from the Committee on Military Affairs, reported on the following subjects of inquiry, &c., referred to that committee. 1st. That it is inexpedient at this time to make additional provision by law for military transportation. 2. That no provision is necessary to be made for paying certain corps of volunteers in Maine, the President being already fully empowered by existing laws to do so. 3d. That it is inexpedient to assume the payment of interest on unpaid sums which may have been due for military services. 4th. That no further provision is necessary at this time for printing and distributing the militia and military laws and articles of war. 5th. Unfavorable reports on the petitions of Isidore Remensin and Christopher Colles. The above reports were ordered to lie on the table.

UNSETTLED ACCOUNTS.

Mr. HUGER called up the resolution submitted a few days ago by him, to inquire into the manner of keeping certain public accounts, and into the amount and cause of the great balances now standing against individuals, on the books of the Comptroller, &c.

Mr. ROBERTSON made some remarks to enforce the propriety of the inquiry. He had no doubt there was great defalcation and abuse in the public accounts, and hoped the inquiry would be effectually followed up. He adverted to the remissness which he believed to exist in some of the salary officers in the Government, in relation to the settlement of the public accounts. In some instances, he said, the accounting officers had raised accounts against those who had none with the Government, with no other effect than to screen villains who depredate on the public treasure. That there were swindlers and defaulters among the public agents, that there were men who fattened on the spoils of Government, he had no doubt, and the best way to screen them was to foist into their company the names of those whom they know to be of a different character.

Mr. CONDICT approved the principle embraced in the resolution, but asked the mover, Mr HUGER, whether the inquiry did not belong to the Committee on Public Expenditure, and referred to the standing rule of the House, which requires them to superintend the expenditures of money in the different Departments, and report whether disbursements have been made agreeably to law, &c.

That committee, he said, most probably had already progressed in the inquiry, and if so, he thought it would not be prudent at so late a day in the session, to take it from them and place it in other hands. These balances, he said, had at a former session been referred to the Committee of Ways and Means, upon a resolution moved by himself, instructing that committee to inquire and report, what further legal provisions were necessary to enforce payment, and prevent future delinquencies. A gentleman from Virginia, in the last session of the 12th Congress, instituted an inquiry through a committee, in the hope, as he expressed it, "that if they could not destroy the mammoth, the great beast of the forest, they might at least be able to poison the rats." This rat-catching committee, as it had been facetiously termed, after spending much time and labor, in turning over the cart-loads of documents and papers thrown upon them to stifle the inquiry, made a report at the close of the session, and there it ended. Such an inquiry, said Mr. C., to be productive of any beneficial result to the nation,

should be divided and subdivided among different committees, giving to each a distinct object, to be pursued minutely in all its intricate winding, and in that way only, in his opinion, could the errors be remedied. Such a course, he should be glad to see pursued at an early period of the session. For these reasons, he should prefer the method proposed by another gentleman, (Mr. TUCKER,) which by distributing the investigation, and dividing the labors, would best promote the public interest.

Mr. HUGER replied to Mr. CONDICT, and offered some further remarks to obviate the objections urged against the inquiry. He believed the object he had in view was practicable, and that great good would grow out of it. For one, he would be willing, should he be selected, to devote his utmost exertions and labor to an end so important; not that he expected to expose or detect defaulters—for he knew not that there was a single one—but for the satisfaction and benefit to be derived from such a report. One of the objects also of the inquiry was to aid the public officers and facilitate their operation, &c.

After a few words more by Mr. CONDICT, the resolution was agreed to, as follows:

Resolved, That a select committee of five members be appointed to examine, generally, into the subject of unsettled balances due the United States, and especially into the annual statements, laid before Congress by the Comptroller of the Treasury, in conformity to an act of the 3d of March, 1809, requiring that annual statements should be laid before Congress, of the accounts in the Treasury, War, and Navy Departments, which may have remained more than three years unsettled, or on which balances appear to have been due more than three years, prior to the 30th September, then last past; to investigate the causes which have given rise to such unsettled balances; to recommend such measures as may, in their opinion, be most likely to bring defaulters to a speedy settlement of their accounts, and prevent, in time to come, the recurrence and continuance of unsettled balances to such an amount.

Mr. HUGER, Mr. BARBOUR, Mr. CONDICT, Mr. LYON, and Mr. FORNEY, were appointed a committee pursuant to the said resolution.

NATIONAL BANK.

The House went into Committee of the Whole on the Bank bill. Mr. SERGEANT'S motion to reduce the proposed capital from thirty-five to twenty millions being under consideration—

Mr. SMITH, of Maryland, rose to express his views of the subject generally, as well as on the particular point under consideration. He appeared to coincide in opinion with Mr. CALHOUN, that the establishment of a Bank of the United States would contribute better than any other measure to the restoration of a general medium of circulation of uniform value. He was afraid that it was the only remedy. Perhaps he should not agree with the gentleman in some of his positions, particularly as respected the conduct and state of the banks. It might be prudent on the part of Congress, he remarked, to let down these institutions as gently as they could, and do everything to enable them to meet their engagements by specie payments on some future day. With some modification of the plan proposed by this bill, he thought the establishment of a National Bank would effectually contribute to that object. The banks pending the war were the pillars of the nation, on which and through whose instrumentality the Government was enabled to raise money and men to carry on the war, not only by their direct loans, but by enabling individuals to make loans to the Government. Now, that we could do without them, they had been called caterpillars. He would not call those caterpillars now, who, in war, had been the pillars of the Government. The information of the gentleman in relation to the state of the banks might be very good, but it did not coincide with the information or impressions of Mr. S., who took a different view of it. He thought that, as far as he had information, the banks had not issued more notes than, from the amount of their capitals, they had a fair right to do. Adverting to Mr. C.'s statement of the number of the banks, (he wished there were not so many,) and of their capital, he differed from the view which estimated the amount on which they draw interest, at an hundred and seventy millions. But deducting from this amount the loans, &c., estimated at forty millions, an hundred and thirty millions would remain, at the estimated amount on which the banks draw interest, with a capital of eighty-two millions. Was this too much? With much less could the banks pay bank expenses, and make a reasonable dividend? But, might not the gentleman have been mistaken, even in this estimate? Mr. S. thought he was, and supported this impression by a reference to such documents on the subject as were within his reach. He referred to the document on the table, showing the state of the chartered banks within the District of Columbia. He was rather inclined to believe that these banks had gone a little further than most of the banks of the United States in their issues, the cause of which might be traced to the large loans to the Government. The amount of the capital paid in by all these banks was $3,321,600; the bills and notes discounted $4,860,031. Was this too large a business on their capital? These banks, than which perhaps no banks in the Union had done larger business, had not discounted more than fifty per cent. beyond the amount of their capital paid in. As to the amount of paper which the gentleman estimated to be in circulation, Mr. S. differed widely from him. Instead of two hundred millions of dollars of paper being in circulation on a capital of eighty-two millions, he doubted whether the amount was half that of the capital of the banks, say forty-one millions of dollars. He had some acquaintance with the operations of banks from his practice in them. Some banks could put out more paper than others from their particular situation; but, in general, banks did not issue paper to more than half the amount of their capital. The notes of the banks of this District were more depreciated than

any others, and if the depreciation was in fact owing to excessive issues, it might be presumed that they had issued more largely than banks generally. These banks had notes in circulation to the amount of $2,094,000; a greater proportion of notes to their capital than banks generally have in circulation; but only three-fifths of the amount of the capital paid in. There were not now in circulation, Mr. S. verily believed, as many bank notes, properly so called, as there were prior to the stoppage of specie payments. Banks everywhere were endeavoring to draw in their notes. Mr. S. concluded on this point, that, as the banks had demonstrably not been prodigal in the issue of their paper, its depreciation was not owing to the excess of issue. This brought Mr. S. to another point of Mr. CALHOUN's speech, in which they concurred in opinion. To the long loans, he agreed, in a great measure, might be attributed the depreciation of the paper of this city, of Baltimore, Philadelphia, and of New York. But he was not disposed to censure the banks for having made those loans. On the contrary, said he, they aided you in times of need. I give them credit for it. I would nurse them and bring them back to the same healthy state as before they reduced themselves to serve you. At the same time Mr. S. said he agreed that it was the duty of the banks to resume specie payments so soon as it was possible to do it without loss. If they did not do it, they ought to be compelled to do it; and through the instrumentality of a Bank of the United States, the Government might be able to coerce them. The loans made to the Government had been principally confined to the country between the Hudson and the Potomac; a small amount only had been obtained north and south of these limits. The notes obtained by the Treasury by way of loan, were disbursed in other quarters of the country than that in which they were obtained. They had been thrown back upon the banks, and specie demanded for them; with which demand, made in large quantities, the banks found themselves unable to comply. The gentleman had given his opinion how the evil might be remedied. This remedy, Mr. S. went on to observe, he was one of those who had pressed on the directors of the banks of the city he had the honor to represent. All the banks had to do, he said, was to send their millions of stock to the eastward and southward, sell their stock, and thus change the balance of exchange and trade in their favor. When they should do that, the cause of the depreciation of their paper being removed, Mr. S. said we should hear no more of it. In less than three months, those States which now had the advantage of the exchange would be the debtor States. The difference in exchange was little more than nominal, very little specie being paid in any part of the country. Where bank notes were nominally at par, the banks did very little or no business, and had comparatively no notes out. If merchants negotiated with those banks, they did not receive or pay them specie, but paper. Mr. S. coincided in Mr. C.'s view, that if all the banks agreed to resume specie payments, they might do it. But he would use no coercion now to hasten the period, but suffer them to do it peaceably and quietly, and therefore safely.

Adverting to the observation in debate yesterday respecting an alliance between the Secretary of the Treasury and the banks, which had prevented Treasury notes from becoming a circulating medium, &c., Mr. S. vindicated the conduct of the Treasury. Could the Secretary do otherwise, he asked, than receive the public dues in the currency of the country where they were collected? The Secretary had further undertaken (Mr. S. doubted whether that officer had not in this gone too far) to say that the paper of those banks which did not receive Treasury notes and issue them again, should not be received in payment of debts due to the Government.

Gentlemen were mistaken, Mr. S. said, if they supposed they could make Treasury notes a circulating medium—experience had proved it. Referring to the value of Treasury notes, depreciated gradually in their progress from this District to Boston, he remarked that, although they were six per cent. above par at Baltimore, they were not there as valuable as the note of a merchant at New York. It would, it was true, be a great convenience if Government could issue a paper of this sort, which would serve as a circulating medium, but it could not; whatever paper was put out of that sort, would become an article of merchandise, to be bought and sold. The community was now accustomed to bank notes, and partial to them; and their place could not be supplied by Government paper.

As to the motion now under consideration to reduce the capital, Mr. S. said, he had not expected it from a gentleman from Pennsylvania, and particularly not from the gentleman who made it. Reverting to the period of the establishment of the Bank of the United States, he said, ten millions bore a larger proportion to the uses and demands of that day, than thirty-five millions did to those of this. The price of everything was then very low—commerce in its infancy, the shipping of the United States extremely and almost incredibly limited, &c. It was impossible that any man could suppose that a bank of the same amount could now perform the functions which the Bank of the United States then performed, particularly, since the Government had spread taxes over the whole surface of the country, and made the aid of this institution more extensively necessary. With a reduced capital, Mr. S. said, the operations of the bank would be so circumscribed, that it would afford but little aid to merchants. He was not, indeed, very tenacious, he said, about four or five millions of capital, more or less, but he did not think thirty-five millions at all too much.

Mr. S. said he was not entirely satisfied with the plan of the bank, proposed by the committee; but might not the plan be so modified as to meet the views of a large majority of the House? He could find but few gentlemen, he said, who, in conversation, did not appear favorable to the establishment of a bank. Some preferred a plan less complex than the present; some were hostile to the control of the Government in it, in which, perhaps, they were right. Others were hostile to Treasury notes forming any part of the capital; in which, Mr. S. said, he concurred. Where was the difficulty in yielding those minor points, for the sake of obtaining a general concurrence in favor of the bill? Other features were objected to—the power to authorize suspension of payments in specie, &c.—these he would also give up, rather than they should defeat the bill altogether. As to the question, when the specie payments of the bank should commence, Mr. S. said, according to the proposed mode of payment, it would not be very soon. To remedy this objection, he proposed that, for the seven millions of Treasury notes to be paid in on account of the United States, there should be substituted a stock to be created for the purpose, bearing an interest of five per cent. per annum, which would leave a gain to the United States (the bank dividing eight per cent.) of three per cent. per annum on that amount; which would, by its accumulation and proper application, in the course of twenty years, absorb the whole of that stock, and operate as a bonus to the United States to that amount. He also showed, by calculation, that the United States, in this mode, by merely advancing their credit, might absorb twelve millions of the war debt; which he believed would be no unpalatable thing to the people, nor unwise in the Government. Further, Mr. S. said, he wished to see the bank go immediately into operation, that, while he lived, he might derive some advantage from it. He would therefore wish to see the whole of the specie part of the stock paid in within a given number of months. With seven millions of dollars in its vaults, the bank would have neither fear nor trembling in commencing specie operations; they would have time to send their stock to Europe for sale, or make such other arrangements as, in their opinion, might be proper. The specie thus paid in, would not drain the State banks, but would be imported, for the purpose, from Europe and elsewhere. In the meantime, he said, until all the specie payments were made to the bank, he did not think it would do any harm if the bank were to commence its operations without specie, but with an assurance in its charter, of payment of specie at a particular day. Such an assurance would make the bank notes equally good, in his eyes at least, as gold and silver. With these views of the subject, Mr. S. concluded his practical speech.

Mr. SERGEANT spoke as follows:

Mr. Chairman, the honorable member from Maryland (Mr. SMITH) has expressed his surprise that this motion should be made by a member from Pennsylvania, and still more that it should have been made by a member from Philadelphia, meaning, it would seem, to express his surprise that a member from Philadelphia should be willing to give up the great influence and advantage that city would derive from being the seat of such a bank. He (Mr. S.) should have supposed that gentleman had been long enough in public life to believe that a member of this House might sometimes lose sight of a personal or local advantage, when a measure of great national importance and concern is under consideration. So he considered the present bill.

He made this motion, he said, principally for two reasons. First, because it appeared to him, from the statements made by the chairman of the committee who reported the bill, that the capital proposed by the bill (thirty-five millions) is larger than is necessary; and, in the next place, to give gentlemen an opportunity fully to explain their views on this very interesting subject. He held it to be a sound rule in legislation to abstain from acting until you are satisfied that what you are about to do is right. If you have doubts—if the effect of the measure proposed is involved in uncertainty—if you do not clearly see your way—it is wise to hesitate, to pause, and to consider. This subject, particularly, deserved the most deliberate and careful consideration. It was not, he said, an ordinary act of legislation which Congress might at their pleasure repeal, if upon trial it should be found inconvenient or mischievous, which would be constantly under their control from session to session, to modify, to alter, to abrogate. The proposed act of legislation was to continue in force for twenty years'; there would be no power within that period to repeal it. It was, besides, to create a vast machine of incalculable force, the direction of whose momentum was to be placed in the hands of they knew not whom. Within a very few years past, a similar but less extensive question arose upon the application to renew the charter of the late Bank of the United States. It agitated the nation from one extreme to the other. The agitation was strongly felt in this House—the memory of it was too recent to be forgotten. By some of those who opposed the renewal, it was asserted that Congress had no Constitutional power to grant a charter of incorporation to a bank; by others, that the powers of that corporation had been exercised in a manner that was unjust, oppressive, and dangerous to the people. Without at all yielding to either of these opinions, the impression of which could not be so soon worn out, he must be allowed to say that the mere fact of their having been very seriously and very generally inculcated, gave to the subject under consideration peculiar importance. If, as gentlemen then alleged, it was believed that great injury had been done by that bank, they, at least, ought to be very cautious in adopting the present plan, which had certainly, in every respect, a much more formidable aspect, and which was so little understood that the best informed and most intelligent of its advocates did not seem to agree even as to essential points. The two gentlemen who had discussed the matter, differed in some very important particulars; they did not even seem to agree whether it was to be, in effect, a specie bank or a paper bank. He protested, he said, most seriously against this sort of legislation,

which proceeded without distinctly settling principles, and left everything to hazard. He protested against establishing a great National Bank upon the apparent basis of specie, without something approaching to a certainty that it would be able to pay in specie, against its professing to pay specie, with a considerable risk of its being obliged in a short time to break its faith, and in that way aggravate the malady it was intended to cure. The question, he said, ought first to be decided, whether we were to have a specie bank or paper bank. That being decided, then proceed upon a plain, simple, intelligible plan, in conformity with the decision. The plan proposed was complicated and unintelligible. The capital was to be composed of United States stock, of Treasury notes, and a small proportion of specie. The specie was to be paid in instalments, and there could be no doubt that the bank would never receive from its subscribers a greater quantity of specie than the first instalment. With a nominal capital, then, of thirty-five millions of dollars, and so small a proportion of specie, with what greater propriety could it be called a specie bank, than the Bank of Pennsylvania, for instance? That bank, having a capital of two million five hundred thousand dollars, possesses one million eight hundred thousand dollars of United States stock, and upwards of four hundred thousand dollars in specie. Yet that was a bank that did not pay specie. He admitted that the Bank of Pennsylvania had discounted to a large amount, that it had large deposites, and that it had paper in circulation; in one word, that it was in full operation as a bank. But was not the proposed bank, if the bill then under discussion should become a law, to go into operation, and to go into operation upon the common principles of banking? Would not the stockholders and the directors be governed by what was termed "commercial instinct?" Would they not be desirous of making profit and making dividends? Was there in this bill any peculiar restraint to prevent them from trading to excess? The obligation to pay in specie was no restriction, no effectual restriction, for the State banks were compellable by law to pay their notes with specie, and as far therefore as any legal restraints could guard them, they were safe.

If the suspension of specie payments, on the excessive issue of bank paper, he said, were the cause of the evils that were complained of, and the State banks deserved to be censured for producing them; if we were to adopt the theory in its full extent, that traces every existing mischief in the circulation to one or both these causes, what is the lesson we ought to derive from this consideration? The State banks—he meant the principal ones—up to the period of the capture of Washington, continued to pay specie. If that circumstance was to be regarded as a proper test of their conduct, they were till then without blame; they might be considered, at least with the exception of the loans to Government, as having conducted their business upon fair principles. Of those loans, he would say nothing further than that he did not think that they, a constituent part of the Government, could justly censure them; they were necessary to the Government, they were necessary for the purposes of defence, and, in some instances, the banks were compelled into them by the force of public sentiment. In truth, without the aid of the banks afforded to the Government, either by direct loans or through the medium of loans to States and individuals, the exertions of the country must have been arrested—the Government would have been at a stand for want of money. These banks, therefore, have a meritorious claim to the public consideration. But if specie payments, in other words, the capacity to meet all the probable demands for specie, be the just criterion, what was the state of the matter then? It has been thought a safe rule in banking, and it had been, he believed, adopted as a rule, that a bank might safely lend, and was prudent in lending, to the amount that in ordinary, in the usual course of its business, judging from experience, would not expose it to demands greater than it was able to meet. This rule, founded upon experience in ordinary times, was adapted to that state of things from which it was deduced—to ordinary times and ordinary circumstances—when an extraordinary emergency arose, producing extraordinary and urgent and unexpected demands for specie, the rule would fail, and any general rule would fail. That, he said, was the true state of the matter; immediately upon the capture of Washington, a general alarm was spread throughout the country, every possible danger was apprehended. Indeed, the fears and anxiety of that moment were not confined within the limits even of possibility. A run upon the banks for specie was the consequence. It is not material to inquire why that run was made; want of confidence was the immediate cause of it. Would the proposed bank, he asked, be more securely guarded, or less exposed to similar difficulties. Would it not, with a view to the interest of its stockholders, be governed by similar principles? Nay, was there not a chance, under existing circumstances, that it would, almost at its outset, be involved in the same difficulties that have thus, gradually, and by the occurrence of extraordinary circumstances fallen upon the State banks? Was it certain that it would be able to pay specie? And, if it should not, would it not deserve a much severer censure, would it not, with its immense capital and power, inflict upon the community much greater evils than the State banks were supposed to have occasioned? Would it not be infinitely disgraceful, that, professing to pay specie, it would be obliged at the very commencement of its operations to dishonor its bills, to violate its engagements at the moment of entering into them?

When the Bank of the United States was established in 1791, the difficulties experienced, and which it was intended to aid in removing, were of an opposite character; the bank started with entirely different views. In 1791, the object was to increase the active or productive capital of the

country, which was then deficient; there was not a sufficient circulation. The evil now complained of is an excess of circulation, and the remedy is to be the same in the one disease as in the other. The same remedy that was employed to increase a deficient circulation is to be applied for reducing a circulation that is said to be excessive. There was a wide distinction between the evils that were then supposed to exist, and those now complained of. It is not very easy to see how the surcharged circulation is to be removed by throwing in the additional quantity of paper that is to be issued by this bank.

The late Bank of the United States went into operation with a capital of ten millions of dollars; it had but ten millions of capital through all the period of its existence. This capital, he presumed, was found to be sufficient. The present scheme proposed a capital of thirty-five millions, with a power to increase it to fifty millions. So great an enlargement of capital, at so short a distance of time as four years from the expiration of the former charter, imposed it as a duty upon those who advocated the bill to show, distinctly, why so large a capital was necessary. Let us, said he, examine the data for a moment, that have been furnished by gentlemen who maintain its necessity. Our commercial transactions, says one, have increased in the proportion of five to one since the establishment of the Bank of the United States. Money, says another, is but of half the value it then was. Supposing both these statements to be correct, gentlemen had entirely lost sight of a most material consideration, which ought to enter into the estimate, and without which their estimate could not possibly be correct. In the year 1791 there were but three banks in the United States; their capitals did not altogether exceed three millions of dollars, and probably did not amount to so much. Now, there were stated to be two hundred and sixty-two banks, and their aggregate capital was said to exceed eighty millions of dollars. If, therefore, our trade had increased in the proportion of five to one, and money is but half the value, the bank capital of the country had increased in a still greater proportion; it was probably at this time more than twenty times as great as it was in 1791. It was perfectly evident, upon the gentleman's own grounds, that, for commercial purposes, no additional bank capital was necessary, much less such an enormous capital as was proposed by the bill. The amount of capital, indeed, was upon these grounds sufficient of itself to supersede all the State banks.

That such an amount of capital was necessary for the purpose of supplying an uniform medium of circulation, or how it was to restore the depreciated paper of the country to its value, gentlemen had equally failed to establish. They ought to have shown us, first, what amount of that kind of circulation was necessary, and how it was to operate, then we might endeavor to ascertain what amount a given capital was capable of supplying. If he understood correctly the statement made by the chairman of the committee who reported the bill, he had himself shown that his object did not require so large a capital, nor anything like it. That statement would show that not even twenty millions were requisite. The banks now in existence, he stated, now draw an interest upon about one hundred and seventy millions, of which about forty millions are in public stock. If, as he had stated, they would draw in ten per cent. upon that amount, say seventeen millions, or at the utmost twenty-five millions, which they might do by a sale of their stock, their paper would recover a par (specie) value. Without entering at all into an examination of the correctness of this statement, either as to the matter of fact or the hypothesis, it was sufficient to remark that in substance it amounted to this: The excess of circulation, which has caused the depreciation of bank paper, is some where between seventeen and twenty-five millions. Let us, said Mr. S., admit this to be true, can it then be necessary, in order to effect a reduction to that extent of between seventeen and twenty-five millions, can it be necessary to put in operation a bank of thirty-five millions? It would, of course, be governed by the same commercial instinct that had been ascribed to the other banks; it would extend its business for the purposes of profit, and would endeavor to create a circulation in the same proportion to its capital. How was the circulation, thus to be created, to operate? It must, he said, either displace the circulation of the existing banks, to a much greater extent than was supposed by the statement to be necessary, or it must be added to that circulation, and in either way it would be injurious. In the one case, its effect upon the State banks was too evident to require elucidation—in the other, it would only aggravate existing evils by increasing the supposed excess.

He repeated, there was nothing in the bill to save this bank from the same extremity of difficulty—from bankruptcy, if gentlemen choose so to term it, which the existing banks had endured. He did not mean, however, to join in unqualified censure of the State banks, much less did he mean to censure them for the loans which the Government, and the public sentiment had in some instances urged them to make, to a greater extent, perhaps, than they ought to have done, and which ought not to be indiscrimately attributed to interest and cupidity. Neither would he insist upon their adopting, at once, measures injurious to themselves, and to all who were in any way concerned with them. These institutions had become connected, very extensively, with the business and the interests of the community. There could be no pressure upon them, that would not press with still greater severity upon the people in a great variety of ways. Give them a reasonable time, he said, if they will not make a fair effort, then coerce them. But he was extremely unwilling to resort to a very doubtful experiment, which, if it did not succeed as you wished, would have a tendency to aggravate the evil.

If the State banks deserved to be charged

with having violated their engagements, how did the Government stand in that respect? Let the Government set the example of redeeming its plighted faith. Was the public creditor in Philadelphia paid his interest during the war in gold and silver? No. In the notes even of the banks in Philadelphia? It was a notorious fact, that one quarter's interest, he believed, that which accrued the first of January, 1815, was paid, in part, in Baltimore paper, which at that very time was depreciated five or six per cent. below the paper of Philadelphia. Should it be said the Government could not procure gold and silver? Neither could the banks procure it. Should it be said, the Government could not procure Philadelphia paper? They might have obtained it by paying, as they ought to have done, the difference in value between the Baltimore paper and the Philadelphia paper. But they did not do so. They threw the loss arising from the difference upon the public creditor in Philadelphia, and a part of the loss fell upon the banks in Philadelphia, who were the holders of public debt. When we are considering the conduct of the banks, said he, we ought also to consider whether justice has been done to them. But, further, did not the Government in that transaction, assist in producing the excessive issue of paper now complained of, by forcing the depreciated Baltimore notes upon the creditors in Philadelphia? Could they be ignorant, that paper which required to be so forced, must be excessive? With such an example of the Government, countenancing and assisting excessive issues, it would not have been at all surprising if the banks had even gone much further than they did go.

With regard to the present times, he said, it appeared to him the Treasury had the complete command of payments. Let the Treasury begin the work, and the payment to the public creditor go hand in hand with the demand upon the public debtors. It cannot be done at once, but if the Government had the power, by the use of means so simple, to restore uniformity, how much better and safer would it be to employ that power, than to put in operation the great machine contemplated by this bill, which, once in motion, would be beyond their control, whatever might be its effects.

He did not, he said, feel inclined to grope in the dark upon a measure of so much magnitude, and so doubtful a nature. He could not consent to commit such important interests upon the issue of a mere experiment, especially when he saw, that for the avowed purpose of bringing about the payment of specie, it proposed to throw into circulation a large quantity of paper, which he perceived from the state of existing establishments, formed and conducted upon the same principles, and possessing the same materials, could not be redeemed with specie; and when, of course, he was warranted in believing that under similar circumstances, if they should again occur, it must be involved in precisely the same difficulties.

There was another point about which, he said, there ought to be an explicit understanding.

Was this to be a commercial bank, or a Government bank? He did not intend at present to consider the propriety of the Government's interference in the management of the bank by appointing directors and president; but he could conceive no reason why the Government should become a partner in any such scheme.

If there was to be a bank at all, it was necessary first to decide, whether it is to be a specie bank, or a paper bank. If it is to be a specie bank, he could not consent to any bill for that purpose, unless it contained such provisions as would afford a reasonable certainty that it would at all times be able to pay specie; not a mere bank of deposite, for at this time of day we could not expect men to embark in anything so limited and unproductive; but if it is to commence its operations as a specie bank, and afterwards be obliged to suspend the payment of specie, when its notes shall have gone extensively into circulation, it will produce in a still greater degree all the consequences, so strongly described, which have followed the suspension by the State institutions. I should very much prefer a plan more simple and intelligible. The basis of it should be, that the bank should enter into no engagements which there was a doubt of its ability to fulfil. A bank note in its usual form, imports an engagement to pay specie, and if the bank cannot or will not pay specie for it when demanded, the contract is violated. The bank should, therefore, be prohibited from issuing such notes to a greater amount than it actually possessed specie to pay. There should be no risk of breaking its faith. If it had but five millions of specie, notes should not be issued to a greater amount. But if a larger quantity of paper were necessary, it should be of a different form and character, importing upon the face of it no engagement to pay in specie; certificates of credit, for instance, receivable in payments to the bank and the Government; their final redemption secured by stock, or whatever else might be deemed an adequate security. Such paper, if it went into circulation, would go into circulation fairly, and with a perfect understanding of its nature. There would be no mistake about it, nor any danger of its dishonor. Every engagement would be complied with. Prior to the month of August 1814, it was not supposed that the banks had not been conducted with prudence, according to the usual rules of banking; there was no depreciation of their paper; their notes were in the ordinary acceptation of the terms specie notes. The very instant, however, a state of things arose to create alarm, or when, from whatever cause, their notes came in upon them in unusual quantities, they were unable to proceed in specie payments. This bank being put in operation upon the same principles, must run the same course, unless its managers should practice a degree of self-denial without example, and which it would be vain to expect. In every point of view, it appears to me, that if this bill is to pass, the capital of twenty millions will be amply sufficient for every purpose which the supporters of it have in view.

Mr. RANDOLPH rose to ask two questions; one, of the gentleman from South Carolina, the other of the gentleman from Maryland. First, how the paper to be created by this bank will correct the vitiated state of our currency? and, secondly, how bank notes can answer the purposes of a circulating medium better than Treasury notes? Though no stickler for Treasury notes, Mr. R. intimated his opinion that they were, in time of peace, a better substitute for gold and silver than any paper he had heard yet submitted. Mr. R. added some incidental observations, amongst which was the remark, that he was sorry to see the apathy, the listlessness, on this subject; on a question which, if it passed, would perhaps be the most important decided since the establishment of the Constitution; and that, though he agreed fully as to the extent of the existing evil, the remedy had been totally mistaken, &c.

Mr. SMITH said, in reply, that the gentleman from Pennsylvania and himself only differed in premises, not in their conclusions; and then answered, at some length, the arguments of Mr. SERGEANT. Banks, to obtain a fair profit, he said, must discount to fifty per cent. more than the amount of their capital; but he would be willing they should not be allowed to issue paper to an amount beyond one-half their capital. He had stated that the banks of Columbia, at this time, had not more than two-fifths of their capital paid out in notes, and the old Bank of the United States, at no period, had out more than ten millions of notes; and this bank, unless it should sell its stock, could only do business to the extent of the cash in its vaults. Mr. S. protested against the attempt at dexterity which was imputed to him by Mr. RANDOLPH. He had distinctly stated his opinions, and argued fairly; he had asserted that the notes of this bank would be everywhere better than Treasury notes; but it was on the presumption that the bank would redeem its issues with specie; and he repeated, that if the bank be compelled to pay specie in a short time, as he was sure it would, then its notes would be greatly preferable to Treasury notes, whether at Boston or New Orleans.

Mr. WARD, of Massachusetts, hoped the amendment would prevail. He acknowledged that, in the progressive state of this country, it was not very important whether the capital was thirty-five or twenty millions; the latter amount could be used with nearly as much effect for any mischievous purpose as the former; that sum would be quite sufficient to influence the destinies of this nation. But he preferred the smaller sum, because he believed that amount large enough for every commercial purpose. During the existence of the old Bank of the United States, a period of very great commercial activity, that institution answered all the demands of the country; and he was confident that twenty millions now, in addition to the local capital, was enough. Mr. W. defended the Boston banks from the charge of deception, in promising to pay specie without doing so. They had not, he said, broken their faith to the public, and any man could there

1083   HISTORY OF CONGRESS.   1084

H. of R.   *National Bank.*   February, 1816.

obtain specie whenever he presented one of their notes for payment. If this bank is to pay specie, said Mr. W., I admit that it will be very useful; but if it does not, its notes will be much below the value of Treasury notes, and will not answer any good purpose. He quoted the price of Treasury notes at different places, and detailed the reasons for their unequal value; and such, he said, would be the condition of the notes of a National Bank, unless bottomed and conducted on a specie capital. To expect a paper of unequal value to answer the purposes of a general medium, would be as bad, he said, as to expect pieces of cloth of different lengths to cover an equal space of ground in every part of the country. Mr. W. believed that nothing but mismanagement had caused the inequality in the value of Treasury notes. These notes were a common paper, emanating from the trustees of the people, to whom all the people were more or less indebted, and this paper could only have been depreciated by misconduct; which opinion he entered into some details to prove.

This bank, it was asserted, would remedy the great evil now existing in our depreciated currency. If the gentleman from Maryland (Mr. SMITH) were to lay down before him a machine, and tell him it would fly, the gentleman would pardon him for saying he could not credit it, until he showed some means which would enable it to do so. So it was, he said, with the bank now under consideration. He deprecated the present state of things as much as any one, and hoped an adequate remedy would be provided. The United States, he said, lost at present, by the depreciated currency, more per annum than the whole amount derived from the direct tax in the large State of Maryland. Such an evil called loudly for a remedy, and he hoped one would be applied; but a bank on the plan now proposed would disappoint its advocates, and fail to cure the evil. That this cure would be complete he did not, however, expect from any plan—some inconvenience would attend any remedy; it was to be expected, like the amputation of a limb to preserve life. In reply to an assertion made in the course of the debate, Mr. W. denied that the banks had loaned the Government from any other motives than those of gain. Their turn had been served, he said, and in devising the plan of a National Bank he should not be influenced by any strong regard for their interest. But the present question was on reducing the amount of capital; and he concluded by saying that, as the larger sum would increase the means of doing mischief, and the smaller would be sufficient for every useful purpose, he should vote to reduce it to twenty millions.

Mr. WRIGHT made a few remarks against the amendment. In former times a capital of ten millions was found necessary, and the increased demands of the country would certainly require now the amount proposed by the bill. He declined giving at present, he said, any opinion on the measure itself; but if a bank was to be created, it ought not to be less than thirty-five millions.

Mr. TUCKER said, that, before the question was taken, he would offer a few remarks on the propriety of rejecting the proposition of the gentleman from Pennsylvania, and of retaining the amount of capital which formed a constituent part of the plan of the committee that reported the bill. He would not enter into the general question at this time; he would waive all inquiries, for the present, into the constitutionality of the scheme, and into the policy of establishing an institution such as was in contemplation. By the amendment proposed, he considered it to be admitted that a bank was necessary, and that a considerable capital would be required to effect the important, the essential purposes which had induced the Committee of Finance to submit to the House a measure of so much magnitude for their adoption. The question immediately before the House, and to which he should therefore strictly confine himself, is not whether this institution shall be erected, but whether the capital proposed be too great to accomplish its object.

In this inquiry, said Mr. T., I shall not dwell upon the danger of the bank as a great political engine, because I am inclined to believe with an honorable gentleman from Virginia, that, in this point of view, there is very little difference between a bank with a capital of twenty millions, and one with a capital of thirty-five millions. If the bank can be used, and shall be used as an engine of oppression, the smaller sum would have little to recommend it in preference to the larger. We should scarcely discern the difference between the pressure of the two, distributed, as the capital must be, through all the States of the continent. If, then, gentlemen are averse to a bank with thirty-five millions of capital, because they conceive it dangerous to the liberties of the country, are they serious in declaring that they are in favor of such an institution with a capital of twenty millions? Have they shown any reason for the opinion that the latter will not be injurious, if the former will prove destructive; or are we to understand the proposition as indicative of a disposition hostile to the institution altogether, and not merely hostile to the bill before you, because of the exorbitant capital proposed? I hope not. Gentlemen assure us that they are favorable to the establishment of a bank with such a capital, and on such principles as are consistent with the general welfare, and I am willing to place all proper confidence in their sincerity. I must suppose, therefore, that they rest their objections to the amount of the capital on other grounds than that which has been suggested, since that would be equally fatal to every such institution, whose capital was at all calculated to effect the ends of the establishment.

The question as to the proper extent of the capital, must mainly depend on the result of an inquiry as to the probability of a bank of thirty-five millions carrying on its business profitably to the stockholders. If the proposed bank can readily find employment for the whole of the proposed capital, there can be no reason for diminishing it, with a view to the profits of those concerned.

That such will be the case must readily be admitted, when we refer to acknowledged facts, and apply them to the situation in which this institution will be placed. Of the amount of thirty-five millions, twenty-eight millions will consist of United States' stock, carrying an interest of six per cent., and thus, of itself, affording employment for so much of the capital; the residue of seven millions, distributed throughout the Union, cannot fail to find employment. Facts within our knowledge furnish the best test on this subject. We have been told, in the course of the debate, that when the old Bank of the United States was established, there was only one other bank in existence whose capital did not exceed $400,000. Since that time the number of banks has increased to upwards of two hundred and fifty, and the bank capital to more than eighty-two millions. Does not this fact prove the readiness with which bank capital can find employment among us? Does it not prove that, in this new country, which is every day opening to the population new occupations for capital—in agriculture, commerce, and manufactures—there is no difficulty in disposing of real or fictitious capital, in stimulating the active industry of the nation? Is it not, indeed, in strict conformity with the doctrines of all political economists, and with the experience of every practical man, that, in all new and growing countries, the great difficulty is not to find employment for capital, but to supply the demand for it? Is not our comparatively high interest itself an evidence that, notwithstanding the immense increase of capital, the demand has kept pace with the increase? If, as has been justly contended, the rate of interest is governed by the proportion between the demand for capital and the supply, the rate of interest here proves that capital has not yet equalled that proportion to the demand which exists in other countries. The argument, then, which has been advanced in debate, that we cannot require so large a capital, because that of Great Britain is not as great, is not entitled to much consideration, for the reasons I have mentioned. New countries always require a greater capital, in proportion to their actual wealth and population, than old ones, because the field for its employment is always more extended in the former than in the latter. And if the question as to the expediency of establishing new banks, depended only on the probability of their finding employment for their capital, none could doubt the propriety of the measure. We have, indeed, on this subject, a test which rarely errs. Mercantile men are aware that additional capital can be employed in banking, with great advantage to the bankers. They form a class of our population which is proverbially said to understand its pecuniary interests, and to make accurate calculations of profit. These and others are everywhere engaged in the effort to establish new banks. In New York, as I have understood, it is contemplated to put into activity an additional bank capital of fourteen millions. In the State which I have the honor to represent, efforts have been lately made to establish fifteen new banks, with a capital, I presume, of about seven millions. Do not these things prove that there is a fair prospect of profit; and that, however we may differ as to the policy of increasing those establishments, there is no ground for supposing they will find difficulty in employing their capital? If so, I think we may reasonably suppose that the Bank of the United States (of whose capital twenty-eight millions will be at once actively employed) can readily find occupation for the residue.

Another important subject of inquiry, in relation to the extent of the capital of the proposed bank, is connected with a supposed probable increase of the circulating medium, or of the bank notes in circulation. It has been contended by the gentleman from Pennsylvania, (Mr. SERGEANT,) that the establishment of this bank would increase, instead of diminishing, the evil which the Chairman of the Committee of Finance has so ably inveighed against. That evil is the surcharged state of the circulation; and the idea seems to have been entertained, that the issues of the United States Bank will further "surcharge it."

If this argument be correct, it would be fatal to a bank of twenty millions; nay, to every bank that can now be established. Will the gentleman then urge it, when he professes his friendly disposition to the establishment of a bank with a smaller capital? It is, however, I conceive, an argument at variance with acknowledged facts. It is not true, that a superabundant paper medium can be forced into circulation, so long as specie redemptions are preserved. Bank notes cannot go out, unless they are wanted, so long as the banks redeem them when demanded. It is an aphorism among political economists, that it is impossible to surcharge the circulation whilst specie is the basis of that circulation. The truth is self-evident, and has been happily illustrated by the celebrated author of the Wealth of Nations, who has remarked, that the channel of circulation can only contain a certain quantity, and if more be attempted to be poured into it, it will flow back upon its source. I am ready to admit, that unlimited and blind confidence in banking institutions may sometimes enable them to overdeal; but I need not stop to show that no such blind confidence now exists, or is likely to prevail.

The danger of a surcharged circulation, when specie redemption shall have been resumed, seems then to be visionary. The Bank of the United States will either be unable to send its notes into circulation, or it will drive in a part of the notes of the State banks. That the former will not be difficult, every day's experience demonstrates. Every bank that is established, soon finds means to push out as much paper as its business requires. Why, therefore, should we believe for a moment, that the Bank of the United States, whose paper will be desirable for so many reasons, will find that an insuperable barrier, which is so easily surmounted by others? If, as has been shown, it can lend its capital, its borrowers will circulate its paper, and the natural effect will be to diminish in proportion to the circulation of the paper of the State banks. But this effect will be produced without an injury to them. It is an error to suppose that the business of a bank is always measured by the quantity of its paper in circulation. It rarely happens that any bank has notes in circulation equal to the amount of its actual capital; and it is notorious, that they sometimes draw interest upon twice the amount of the paper which they have afloat. Having risen, without preparation, merely to reply to some of the arguments that have been used by gentlemen, I am unprovided with the estimate lately published of the state of the Philadelphia banks. If I am not mistaken, the amount of notes discounted, Government stock, &c., on which they drew interest, was nearly three times as great as their notes in circulation. I have before me a statement of the banks of this District, whose issues have been generally deemed more excessive than those of any other place. From this I find, that whilst their actual capital somewhat exceeds the sum of $3,000,000, their notes in circulation are only $2,094,000; and whilst the same institutions have lent out in discounted notes and Government stock $6,280,000, their notes in circulation have not exceeded $2,095,000; which is about one-third of the sum on which they are making a profit. Here, then, we have decisive evidence of what every man at all acquainted with banking transactions must know, that the profits of banks cannot fairly be measured by the amount of their notes in circulation. The same statement furnishes still more decisive evidence. While the Bank of Columbia has lent to Government and to individuals much more than twice the amount of their capital, to wit, about $1,900,000, it has in circulation only $336,800, or about one-sixth of the amount of its loans; whereas the Union Bank, for instance, has lent to Government and individuals much less than twice the amount of its capital, to wit, only $736,900, and has in circulation more than $427,000, largely upwards of one-half the amount of its loans; from which it is evident that the Bank of Columbia, whilst it has the smallest amount in circulation, has proportionably the largest capital at interest, and is, of course, making the largest profit.

These statements, are furnished, not as affording a test of the comparative merits of these institutions, but merely to establish what I think they unequivocally prove, that the profits of banks bear no direct ratio to the amount of their notes in circulation, and that it is not fair to conclude that the United States Bank will injure the State banks generally, by reducing the amount of their circulating paper.

I must not, however, be understood to contend that the establishment of the United States Bank, if its effects are to re-establish the specie basis for our circulation, will not reduce the profits of any of the banks. It doubtless will and ought to reduce the profits of those which have over dealt. Those profits have been too large just so far as the banks have been guilty of overdealing. They ought to be corrected, but it will be the resuming

of the payment of specie through the operation of the United States Bank, which will correct them. If this bank were to go into operation on any other than a specie basis, the issue of its notes would not affect the profits of the State banks. It is not then the competition of their notes for the circulation, but the necessity of specie payments that will compel them to curtail their discounts and reduce their profits. This is as it should be; the effect upon the State banks will be wholesome and salutary. Whilst the profits of some are reduced, those of others will be increased by the operation of a National Bank upon the national currency. Whilst some must curtail their business, to meet the demands of specie, others, which are now restrained, because specie redemption is confined to themselves, will be once more enabled to enlarge their business to its accustomed extent. Gentlemen from the Eastern States, I should imagine, are therefore peculiarly interested in the measure, because it is so eminently calculated to reproduce that equalization of profits among the banks which has for some time been suspended, much to their disadvantage.

It will be observed that I have throughout proceeded upon the idea that this bank is always to redeem its paper with specie. A specie basis is the only true foundation of all banking. Any other will be found delusive and destructive. The committee therefore had taken a precaution which seemed to have escaped the observation of the gentleman from Pennsylvania (Mr. SERGEANT.) That gentleman has asked what greater security we have for the payment of specie by this bank than by others? I answer, that it is a condition of their charter. It is expressly provided by that charter that they shall not at any time suspend specie payments without authority so to do. If they do, their charter is violated—it is void. For my own part, as a member of the committee who reported this bill, I was disposed " to make assurance doubly sure, and take a bond of fate," by an express provision that the charter should be void if they suspended specie payment. Professional gentlemen, however, on the committee, and among others, if I mistake not, the able gentleman from Pennsylvania, (Mr. HOPKINSON,) believed such a clause unimportant, because it was necessarily implied in the condition attached to the charter by the provisions of the bill. It is then an essential part of the system that the bank should redeem its notes in specie. I would never give my vote to any bank of another character. We have then in this bank an assurance of specie payment not afforded by others, except perhaps by those of the Eastern States. Of this much we are assured, that as soon as it ceases to be a specie bank, it ceases to exist, so that we are in no danger of encountering the evil which the gentleman appears to apprehend.

But the same gentleman appears to suppose that the contemplated bank will be enabled to pay specie because the Bank of Pennsylvania, having its capital in specie and United States stock, in equal proportions with those proposed by this bill, finds itself without the power of meeting its engagements. I cannot admit the analogy contended for. Though the proportion of specie to stock may be the same, yet the amount of specie capital in this bank will be so much greater as to add to its capacity to keep its notes in circulation. But this is not the only reason. The Bank of Pennsylvania has already in circulation a vast deal of paper, with only a small amount of specie in their vaults. Were they to commence specie payments, their notes would return upon them for payment, to the imminent danger of the bank, unless they should previously adopt the precautionary measures in their power. But the Bank of the United States, when it goes into operation, will have its $1,400,000 of specie, without a note in circulation. In issuing their paper they will be governed by circumstances, and should it return upon them too rapidly for specie they will at once lessen the quantity thrown into circulation. There is then all the difference between the situation of the two banks that may reasonably be expected between two concerns, one of which is just commencing business, while the other is deeply involved, and supposed to be unable to meet the just demands of its creditors. Thus we see, that whilst the Bank of Pennsylvania is neither bound to pay specie by the conditions of its charter, nor able at once to redeem its notes, the Bank of the United States will be able and obliged to make gold and silver the basis of its circulation.

Mr. TUCKER concluded his remarks by shortly recapitulating the grounds which he had attempted to maintain. He had endeavored to show that a capital of thirty-five millions would readily find employment; that the proposed bank would not still farther surcharge the circulation, as had been contended; that the establishment of the Bank of the United States would not injure the State banks, though he admitted the resuming of specie payments would necessarily reduce the profits of some of them; and that this bank would be bound by its charter, and enabled by its funds, to rest its circulation upon the solid foundation of a specie basis. He hoped therefore the amendment proposed would be rejected.

WEDNESDAY, February 28.

A message from the Senate informed the House that the Senate have passed a bill " concerning field officers of the militia ;" also a bill " for the relief of Jacob Babbitt and John Dennis ;" in which they ask the concurrence of this House.

Mr. JOHNSON, of Kentucky, from the Committee on Military Affairs, reported the bill from the Senate "for the relief of Lieutenant Colonel William Lawrence, of the Army of the United States, and of the officers, non-commissioned officers, and privates, composing the garrison of Fort Bowyer, in the year 1814," without amendment; and the bill was ordered to be read a third time to-morrow.

Mr. JOHNSON, of Kentucky, from the committee to whom was referred the bill from the Senate, "relative to evidence in cases of naturali-

zation," reported the same with amendments; which were read and concurred in by the House, and the bill was ordered to be read the third time to-morrow.

On motion of Mr. PARRIS, the President of the United States was requested to cause to be laid before this House a statement of the number of impressed American seamen confined in Dartmoor prison ; the number surrendered, given up, or taken from on board of British vessels captured during the late war; together with their places of residence, respectively.

Mr. PARRIS and Mr. TATE were appointed a committee to present the said resolution to the President.

Mr. CONDICT submitted the following resolution, which was read :

Resolved, That, for the residue of the session, after the first day of March next, the stated hour of meeting of this House shall be 10 o'clock in the morning.

Mr. NELSON, of Virginia, moved to amend the said resolution by adding thereto the following :

And the hour of adjournment, five in the afternoon of each day.

Whereupon, the said resolution and amendment were ordered to lie on the table.

PUBLIC EXPENDITURES.

Mr. TUCKER submitted the following proposition to amend the standing rules and orders of the House ; which was read and ordered to lie on the table :

Resolved, That the following standing committees be appointed to serve during the present Congress, and that hereafter, at the commencement of the first session in each Congress, like committees shall be appointed, whose duties shall continue until the first session of the ensuing Congress :

A Committee on so much of the Public Accounts and Expenditures as relate to the Department of State.

A Committee on so much of the Public Accounts and Expenditures as relate to the Treasury Department.

A Committee on so much of the Public Accounts and Expenditures as relate to the Department of War.

A Committee on so much of the Public Accounts and Expenditures as relate to the Department of the Navy.

A Committee on so much of the Public Accounts and Expenditures as relate to the Post Office ; and

A Committee on so much of the Public Accounts and Expenditures as relate to the Public Buildings.

The said committees shall consist of three members each, and shall at all times have leave to meet during the session of the House.

It shall be the duty of the committees to examine into the state of the accounts and expenditures, respectively submitted to them, and to inquire and report particularly—

Whether the expenditures of the respective Departments are justified by law ;

Whether the claims from time to time satisfied and discharged by the respective Departments are supported by sufficient vouchers, establishing their justness both as to their character and amount ;

Whether such claims have been discharged out of

the funds appropriated therefor, and whether all moneys have been disbursed in conformity with appropriation laws; and

Whether any and what provisions are necessary to be adopted to provide more perfectly for the proper application of the public moneys, and to secure the Government from demands unjust in their character or extravagant in their amounts.

And it shall moreover be the duty of the said committees to report, from time to time, whether any and what retrenchments can be made in the expenditures of the several Departments, without detriment to the public service; whether any and what 'abuses at any time exist in the failure to enforce the payment of moneys which may be due to the United States from public defaulters or others, and to report, from time to time, such provisions and arrangements as may be necessary to add to the economy of the several Departments and the accountability of their officers.

NATIONAL BANK.

The House went into Committee of the Whole on the Bank bill. Mr. SERGEANT's motion to reduce the proposed capital to twenty-five millions being yet under consideration.

Mr. WEBSTER first addressed the House. He regretted the manner in which this debate had been commenced on a detached feature of the bill, and not a question affecting the principle; and expressed his fears that a week or two would be lost in the discussion of this question, to no purpose, inasmuch as it might ultimately end in the rejection of this bill. He proceeded to reply to the arguments of the advocates of the bill. It was a mistaken idea, he said, which he had heard uttered on this subject, that we were about to reform the national currency. No nation had a better currency, he said, than the United States; there was no nation which had guarded its currency with more care; for the framers of the Constitution, and those who enacted the early statutes on this subject, were hard-money men; they had felt, and therefore duly appreciated the evils of a paper medium; they therefore sedulously guarded the currency of the United States from debasement. The legal currency of the United States was gold and silver coin. This was a subject in regard to which Congress had run into no folly.

What, then, he asked, was the present evil? Having a perfectly sound national currency—and the Government have no power, in fact, to make anything else current but gold and silver—there had grown up in different States a currency of paper issued by banks, setting out with the promise to pay gold and silver, which they had been wholly unable to redeem. The consequence was, that there was a mass of paper afloat, of perhaps fifty millions, which sustained no immediate relation to the legal currency of the country—a paper which will not enable any man to pay money he owes to his neighbor, or his debts to the Government. The banks had issued more money than they could redeem, and the evil was severely felt. Mr. W. declined occupying the time of the House to prove that there was a depreciation of the paper in circulation; the legal standard of value was gold and silver; the relation of paper to it proved

its state, and the rate of its depreciation. Gold and silver currency, he said, was the law of the land at home, and the law of the world abroad; there could, in the present state of the world, be no other currency. In consequence of the immense paper issues having banished specie from circulation, the Government had been obliged, in direct violation of existing statutes, to receive the amount of their taxes in something which was not recognised by law as the money of the country, and which was, in fact, greatly depreciated. This was the evil.

As to the conduct of the banks, Mr. W. said he would not examine whether the great advances they had made to the Government during the war were right or wrong in them, or whether it was right or wrong in the Government to accept them; but since the peace, he contended, their conduct had been wholly unjustifiable, as also had that of the Treasury in relation to them. It had been supposed the banks would have immediately sold out the stocks, with which they had no business, and have fulfilled their engagements; but public expectation had in this respect been disappointed. When this happened, Mr. W. continued, the Government ought, by the use of the means in its power, to have compelled the banks to return to their specie payments. In his opinion, Mr. W. said, any remedy now to be applied to this evil, must be applied to the depreciated mass of paper itself; it must be some measure which would give heat and life to this mortified mass of the body politic. The evil was not to be remedied by introducing a new paper circulation; there could be no such thing, he showed by a variety of illustrations, as two media in circulation, the one credited and the other discredited. All bank paper, he argued, derives its credit solely from its relation to gold and silver; and there was no remedy for the state of depreciation of the paper currency but the resumption of specie payments. If all the property of the United States was pledged for the redemption of these fifty millions of paper, it would not thereby be brought up to par; or, if it did, that would happen which had never yet happened in any other country. An issue of Treasury notes, he added, would have no better effect than the establishment of a new bank paper. He illustrated this general position by referring to a period anterior to the time of the reformation of the coin of England, when the existing coin had been much debased by clipping, &c., which had created much alarm. An attempt had been made to correct the currency thus vitiated, by throwing a quantity of sound coin into circulation with the debased; the result was, that the sound coin disappeared, was hoarded up, because more valuable than that of the same nominal value which was in general circulation.

The establishment of a National Bank not being in his opinion the proper remedy, he proceeded to examine what is. The solvency of the banks was not questioned. There could be no doubt, he said, if the banks would unite in the object, they might in three weeks resume the payment of specie, and render the adoption of any measure by this House wholly unnecessary. The banks, he said, were making extravagant profits out of the present state of things, which ought to be curtailed. He referred, for illustration of this point, to the state of the Bank of Pennsylvania, as exhibited in the return to the Legislature of that State, which with a capital of $2,500,000 had done a discount business of $4,138,000, at the same time that it held $1,811,000 of United States stock; so that, without taking into account a mass of Treasury notes, real estate, &c., that bank was receiving interest on six and a half millions—nearly three times the amount of its capital. This he considered an extraordinary fact. That bank had been pronounced by the Legislature to be in "a flourishing state." It was so to the stockholders in the bank, he doubted not; but how was it to those who were affected by the depreciation of it—to the man who comes into an office for life, and relinquishes all his prospects and profits for a fixed salary, not to be diminished during his continuance in office; to the poor pensioner whose wounds received in his country's service are yet bleeding?

These banks not emanating from Congress what engine were Congress to use for remedying the existing evil? Their only legitimate power, he said, was to interdict the paper of such banks as do not pay specie from being received at the custom-house. With a receipt of forty millions a year, Mr. W. said, if the Government was faithful to itself and to the interests of the people, they could control the evil; it was their duty to make the effort; they should have made it long ago, and they ought now to make it. The evil grows every day worse by indulgence. If Congress did not now make a stand, and stop the current whilst they might, would they, when the current grew stronger and stronger, hereafter do it? If this Congress should adjourn without attempting a remedy, he said, it would desert its duty.

If this bank were calculated to do good at all, Mr. W. contended, it was only as an agent of the revenue officers of the Government. As a bank establishment for ordinary banking purposes, what would be its operation? If this were to be a specie bank, it would go into operation at Philadelphia; would promise but little, but would perform all its promises; independent of its connexion with the Government, it would not be able to get its notes into circulation; nobody would borrow of it; it would operate merely as a bank of deposite. All its transactions would be confined to the negotiation of paper for merchants, to enable them to anticipate for a short time so much of their income as was necessary to pay their bonds for duties on importations; and so far, but no farther, it would have a positive good operation. But, as a measure to supply a remedy for the disorders of our currency, Mr. W. argued, this bank would be of no efficacy; because, if he were not mistaken in his views, its bills would have but a very limited circulation.

As to the evil of the present state of things, Mr. W. admitted it in its fullest extent. If he was not mistaken, there were some millions in the Treasury of paper, which were nearly worthless, and were now wholly useless to the Government, by which an actual loss of considerable amount must certainly be sustained by the Treasury. This was an evil which, he said, ought to be met at once, because it would grow greater by indulgence. In the end, the taxes must be paid in the legal money of the country, and the sooner that was brought about the better. Such was the operation of the present state of the circulating medium, he proceeded to show, that the duties laid by the United States were at a rate ten per cent. higher in Boston than in Baltimore, and in Baltimore higher than in Washington, &c. If Congress were to pass forty statutes on the subject, he said, they would not make the law more conclusive than it now was, that nothing should be received in payment of duties to the Government but specie; and yet, no regard was paid to the imperative injunctions of the law in this respect. The whole strength of the Government, he was of opinion, ought to be put forth to compel the payment of the duties and taxes to Government in the legal currency of the country.

In regard to the plan of this proposed bank, Mr. W. said he would consent to no bank which to all intents and purposes was not a specie bank; and in that view he was in favor of the proposed amendment. He expressed some alarm at the stock feature of the bank, which would enable and might induce the existing bank corporations to come forward and take up the whole stock of this National Bank. He should be glad to see a bank established, he observed, in the course of his remarks on this point, which would command the solid capital of the country. There were men, he said, of wealth and standing, who would embark their funds in a bank constituted on commercial specie principles, but who would not associate in such an institution with the stockholders in the country, any more than a good currency would associate with a bad one. A National Bank, he said, ought to be regarded, not as the power to rectify the present state of the currency, but as a means to aid the Government in the exercise of its power in this respect. He concluded his remarks, by saying that the power of the Government must be exercised in some way, and that speedily, or evils would result, the extent of which he would not attempt to describe.

Mr. CUTHBERT followed in opposition to the proposed amendment, though, he remarked, there were few of the positions of the gentleman from New Hampshire in which he did not concur, without agreeing with him, however, in his results. In reply to his objection to the stock feature of the bank, as forming an obstacle to its paying specie, Mr. C. argued that it would have a contrary effect. Thus: that to become and remain a specie bank, the institution must be slow in its operations, and the directors and stockholders be content with small gains on their capital; that the interest they would draw, of six per cent. on the stock part of their capital, would aid them in this course, and induce them to be satisfied with less gains in the way of discounts,

&c. In opposition to the proposal to reduce the capital of the bank, he took for his groundwork two facts which would not be questioned. First, that this is a growing nation in population, resources, wealth, and commerce. Secondly, that there is, from the nature of things, an absolute uncertainty as to the quantity of capital which may be required, and the extent of the business which may be done by a National Bank. He argued, from these positions, that the bank ought to have the power of contracting or expanding itself to the wants of the country; and if the business of the country required a larger amount of discount than would be made on the twenty millions, that the operations of the bank ought not to be cramped. In this nation, growing in population, enterprise, and wealth, where all those uses of society which require active capital and a general circulating medium were every day rapidly multiplying and extending, he would not place narrow limits on the useful agency of this bank. He compared such a course to placing a case of iron on the swelling muscles and growing energies of a vigorous youth. It was much better, he concluded, to have a capital larger than necessary, than one much too small. Mr. C. next proceeded to examine the utility of a National Bank as compared with the State banks, in promoting exchanges, remittances, and transfers by Government and individuals. He stated their various operations in a plain and intelligible manner; and, from his facts on this subject, drew the conclusion that a National Bank only could efficaciously promote the exchange of moneys and commodities—that internal commerce which serves to knit together and fertilize every section of the country. A National Bank he compared to the ocean of commerce, which bears on its bosom the freights of all regions, from one to the other; the State banks to the rivers, which are the channels of communication within their particular, limited sphere. In reply to the argument that the evil of the redundancy, and depreciation of the present paper circulation would not be corrected by throwing other paper into circulation, he said that the National Bank, instead of increasing the quantum of paper, would substitute other paper in lieu of a portion of that now in circulation, and by this operation, the remainder would be brought up to a specie value. A further argument he urged in favor of a large capital was this: that a bank of twenty millions would issue as much paper as a bank of thirty-five millions, as the issue would be limited by the demands of society; but with a large capital there would be greater security to individuals. The difference between the two capitals would be the difference between two merchants carrying on the same commercial speculations, the one with a large, and the other with a small capital; the creditors of the first having undoubtedly better security than those of the last, &c. On these, and other grounds, Mr. C. opposed the amendment.

Mr. HOPKINSON addressed the Chair as follows:

Mr. Chairman: I came to this Congress strongly impressed with the expediency of establishing a National Bank, and with the conviction that it would certainly be done. I presumed that this impression was so general throughout the United States, that but little discussion would be necessary to attain the object. My personal feelings and dispositions were strongly in favor of the measure; and I believe the general, nay, almost the universal, wishes of my immediate constituents, notwithstanding the insinuations about their interest in the State banks, were of the same kind. Not, sir, that I believe a National Bank absolutely indispensable to restore the distracted state of our currency, for I believe this may be effected by other means; but because I believe a bank, established on fair and proper principles, would be a powerful agent in producing this most desirable reformation; because it would afford many essential accommodations to the administration of our revenue, and be, at the same time, of general utility to the community. Under these impressions, I had trusted that some scheme would have been presented to us, plainly calculated to answer these desirable ends, entirely free from known and important objections, and framed on principles not likely to excite discontent and opposition in those, at least, who favor the general design. At the last session of Congress, the subject was examined and discussed with great minuteness; theories of various kinds were proposed, examined, and rejected; new projects were weighed, and found wanting. After all these fruitless attempts to find something new and better than the past, I hoped we should now have abandoned such endeavors, and turned our sober attention to the lessons of experience to be found in the construction and conduct of the late Bank of the United States. No public institution ever conducted its affairs with more general and deserved satisfaction, or closed them, with more integrity and honor. Taking that for our guide, with such enlargements and alterations as the changes that have taken place in the condition of the country would point out and require, we might have erected a fabric unexceptionable to every man not hostile to every and any establishment of the kind. This course, however, has not been pursued. We have a system proposed to us abounding with new ingredients, many of which are known to be absolutely inadmissible in the judgment of many of the best friends of a National Bank. To me this is, truly, a serious disappointment, and I am sincerely sorry it is not in my power to give my feeble support to the plan offered. I do not propose, at this time, to take a general view of the whole system; and regret that it comes before us in detached parts. It would have been much more satisfactory to have examined the whole together, and seen how the various parts bear upon each other. The question now, however, is on the motion for reducing the capital from thirty-five to twenty millions. To this question, and such matters as have been connected with it by those who have opposed the motion, I shall confine my observations.

Before I proceed, may I be permitted to hold

out a caution to the Committee—it is this: not to be too hasty in adopting any plan. We are suffering under great evils, and a state of suffering is not favorable to safe deliberation; impatient under the anguish of the disease, we are too apt to seize upon anything that is proposed as a remedy, without a due examination into its probable effects and consequences. This impatience under misfortune is a great source of increased evil, both in private and public affairs. We feel the suffering as existing and known, and adopt the remedy merely because it promises a change, without duly examining if it may not be for the worse. In struggling to shake off one difficulty, we plunge into a greater—to imagine that nothing but some great and single effort can extricate us, when perhaps we ought to have trusted to slow and gradual means of redress, and exercised our patience until they had time to operate. To sit quietly under suffering, to be doing nothing for a painful disease, requires great strength of understanding and discretion, and yet it is generally better to do nothing when we are uncertain what we should do. Thus, a trader meets with some unexpected loss. Instead of waiting to repair it by slow and certain means, he makes some great endeavor; he plunges in some speculation, he borrows to the extent of his credit; and in a short time finds himself in irretrievable ruin. The privations, the injuries, and the demands of the late war, necessarily deranged all the concerns of the country; and especially its pecuniary concerns—public and private institutions of every kind were shaken to their centre; public credit was almost demolished, and private credit greatly impaired. It is idle, sir, to expect that evils so broad and deep are to be rooted out in an hour; that on the name of peace, everything is to be restored to health and regularity, and we are no longer to remember that we have suffered. The shock was tremendous; its vibrations cannot instantly cease. Such evils must require gradual remedies. I have, sir, much faith in the *vis medicatrix*, in the political as well as the natural body; when the general health of both is sound. Our nation is young and vigorous; her resources vast and increasing; her powers of healing incalculable. Why then should we be driven to rash expedients, in mere despair, when we have such means of restoration if we will but give them time to operate. Impatience, rashness, error, and repentance, are the children of despair. I make these remarks, sir, not to prevent every fair and deliberate endeavor to remove existing and serious evils; nor to induce the members of this House to sit with folded arms in listless indifference, waiting for time and chance to relieve us. I would merely guard against too much despondency, or a belief that it is better for us to do anything, than to do nothing.

The question now for consideration is the amount of capital proper for a National Bank, supposing everything else in the bill to be as it should be. I regret that the examination of the scheme must be made in detached parts—a general view of the whole would have been much more satisfactory, even for the fair estimate and understanding of each particular provision. I shall, however, confine my remarks to the precise question. The honorable Chairman, by whom this bill was reported, has portrayed, in powerful and appropriate colors, the extent and pressure of the evils under which the country labors, in consequence of the distracted state of its currency. He has not been so full and explicit in showing how the remedy he proposes is to meet and remove the disease; reserving himself, probably, on this head, until the provisions of this bill shall come under examination—this however, is really the important inquiry now. In confining my remarks to the proposed amount of capital, I would not be understood to mean that there are not other provisions in the bill much more exceptionable in my opinion than this, and to which I shall offer my objections as they arise. One honorable gentleman has said, that he cannot discern any difference between having the capital at twenty or thirty-five millions. Does he see any difference between thirty-five and fifty, or between fifty and an hundred, and so on? If the amount of the capital of a bank is a mere nominal, unimportant feature in its character and operations, then, indeed, it is useless to dispute about it; but if the difference between any two sums is of importance, it must be found between the sums of twenty and thirty-five millions. Without adverting to the diminution of profits by the extent of the capital, which is a matter for the subscribers and stockholders to look to; is it not indisputable, that the power of a bank over similar institutions, and generally over the moneyed concerns of a country depends much on the strength of its capital? The extent of its business; the amount of its issues; its power to do good, and its power to do mischief; its means to monopolize, to oppress, to ruin, are all regulated, in a great degree, by the capital, and influence and interest which it commands. It is so in other affairs as well as banks; great capitalists, in commerce, in manufactures, in everything, overshadow and overpower smaller ones, and drive them out of the market; though with equal honesty and equal industry. Are not our manufacturers this moment complaining they cannot stand against the great manufacturing capitalists of Great Britain, and praying for assistance and support in the unequal contest? The capital of this bank, therefore, especially if the whole machine is to be wielded by the arm of the Government, is of great importance, and ought to be fixed with great caution and deliberation. Just so much should be afforded as is consistent with its fair, legitimate objects; and not inconsistent with other interests in the community entitled to our protection and regard. What are the circumstances and considerations to which we should appeal in deciding this question? We should look, sir, to the uses expected from this bank; the object to be attained by its establishment; and grant a capital sufficient for those uses and objects and no more. In the nature of the thing, no very exact rule or measure can be obtained;

but a very fair and reasonable estimate may be made. Let me ask, then, what are the objects we have in view in establishing a National Bank? To accommodate the Government in the business of its revenue, and to afford to the community the usual benefits of such institutions. It is also presumed that a National Bank will have the power of regulating and equalizing our currency in the different States. This, however, is a matter distinct from the question of capital. We come then directly to the real question: Is a capital of thirty-five millions necessary, either for the accommodation of the Government or the business of the community? I hold it, sir, to be clear that the Government can lawfully require of us a National Bank for no other purposes than as an instrument of finance; a necessary accommodation in collecting and disbursing revenue, receiving and paying debts, and facilitating loans. Beyond this the Constitution does not warrant it; nor have the friends of the old bank ever contended for anything beyond this. If a bank is to be raised as an instrument of power in the hands of our rulers, of whatever party denomination; if it is to be a source of speculation and profit; a field for the exercise of patronage and appointment, it is a direct and dangerous violation of the Constitution. With such objects the Government have nothing to do; nor should it have any connexion with a bank, or derive any advantage from it merely and solely as an instrument of finance. If, indeed, other benefits flow incidentally and necessarily from it, they may not be rejected; but they should form no part of the original design, nor should any measure or principle be introduced into the system for the direct purpose of obtaining such objects. It is true that the Government subscribed a fifth part of the stock of the late bank; but it should be remembered, that this was deemed necessary not only to create a necessary confidence in the institution with the public, which was then much more shy of banks than it has since been, but also to furnish the amount of capital required; which probably could not have been done without this aid from the Government, the wealth of the country being then inconsiderable in proportion to its present amount.

It is then incumbent on those gentlemen who insist on this immense capital to show how it is required for the business of the Government. I cannot conceive it. The Bank of the United States, with a capital of ten millions, was able to furnish all the financial assistance required, to the very hour of its destruction, without the least difficulty or embarrassment, either to itself or the Administration. It was able to do much more than this; to grant large loans to the Government, and no defect was ever discovered in the amount of capital for all these purposes; or, in other words, for all the purposes which could be lawfully required of it. If more than these are to be required, it shall never be with my sanction. I desire not to see the Government entering into partnerships with its citizens in commercial or stock speculations; entering into the market and trafficking on the exchange. Much less would I see it maintaining its power, encouraging and rewarding its friends, and overthrowing its adversaries by the patronage, the influence, and the vengeance of a vast and uncontrollable moneyed institution. Inasmuch, therefore, as no attempt has been made to show that the capital now demanded for this bank is necessary to the fiscal operations of the Government, nor that the substitute proposed is not amply sufficient for these purposes, I dismiss this part of the subject; and inquire whether the wants of the community call for this immense addition to its banking capital.

A bank is useful to the community by exciting and aiding the industry of the country with loans of money; by furnishing a circulating medium more convenient in many respects than gold and silver; by greatly enlarging the active capital of the country; and by providing commodious, cheap, and safe means of making payments and remittances to the most distant places. Do we want thirty-five millions more than we now have in banks, for these objects? I think not; and I will endeavor to prove it. Permit me again to take you back to the experience of the past for the premises from which I would reason for the present. When the Bank of the United States was established, in the year 1791, there were in the United States but three other banks; one in Philadelphia, one in New York, and one in Boston. I do not know what was the capital of each; but presume when I say that the whole did not exceed four millions, I give them enough. These then, with the Bank of the United States, gave a banking capital of fourteen millions; and were found, for a time, amply sufficient for all the wants both of the Government and the community. To obviate the consequences which flow from these facts, we are told of the vast additions to the business and wealth of this country; of the extension of our commerce; the improvements in our agriculture; the growth of our manufactures, the increase of our population. All this is true, and no man rejoices in this unparalleled prosperity more than I do. But before we suffer ourselves to be hurried away by this captivating picture of our own greatness and importance, we must take into the calculation some other facts and changes, and give them a fair consideration and influence before we pass upon the result. If at this time, as in 1791, there were in these United States, but the three banks then existing, and we were about to establish a national bank, the argument would be most fair and unanswerable. But how is this matter? If the business and population of the country have increased, has not your banking capital increased in a full proportion? In 1791 the capital of this description was $14,000,000; and in 1816 we are told by the Secretary of the Treasury it is eighty-five millions. Is there nothing in this to meet and destroy the whole force of the argument drawn from increase of our wants? To this enormous addition to the banking capital, must be added the equally enormous increase of the general wealth of the country; of the wealth of individuals, which is as useful and efficient in carrying on its business, and employing its industry, as the capitals of banks. If we look to Great Britain for information on this subject, how do we find it? The capital of the Bank of England is about fifteen millions of pounds sterling; there may have been some addition since that estimate was made. The notes issued by this bank prior to the stoppage of specie payments in 1797, did not exceed eleven millions; and the country banks are estimated to have issued about as much; it is true that these issues have increased since specie has ceased to circulate, but probably not beyond the amount of the specie withdrawn; the whole business then of that Kingdom, its commercial, agricultural, and manufacturing concerns, have been transacted with less bank capital than we are now told is requisite for us. To meet the force of this comparison, it is urged that this is a new and a growing country, and therefore calls for more accommodation of this sort than an old and settled one—making every just allowance for this difference, still it can scarcely be seriously contended that, whatever our prospects may be, and I rejoice in their brightness and extent, our business in the various walks of enterprise and industry now is, or for a long time can be, as vast and wide as that of Great Britain. It should be remembered, too, that the period of our prosperity and increase has been her's also—her commerce and manufactures, and I believe her agriculture also, have been in a rapid progress of increase and improvement for the last twenty years. It cannot be, then, that this country demands a banking capital of one hundred and twenty millions, while that is sufficiently accommodated with a much smaller amount.

But we are asked, where is the danger of this capital? We might ask, where is the necessity; its usefulness? But, sir, the dangers are obvious; as an engine, almost irresistible, of State power and corruption, it is appalling; its influence will pervade every corner of the Union; its power will be felt wherever it may choose to strike; every great moneyed power is an efficient power, and, of course, always attended with some danger. It overshadows and destroys the growth of humbler efforts, it may exact a submission to its will; it may punish a disobedience—in the hands of the Government these dangers increase an hundred fold. But, sir, the principal danger I would call your attention to is this, that which may fall upon and crush the State banks. These banks, whatever may have been thought and said to the contrary, are entitled, fully entitled, to our care and consideration; the interest of a great portion of the community is deeply embarked in them; its industry and enterprise mainly depend upon them, and it would be an outrage of injustice and impolicy to overthrow or injure them. Eighty-five millions of capital, with all its dependencies, is not a trifle to be sported with, or blown away by vague denunciations and unexamined charges. The great body of our fellow-citizens, whose property and prospects are embarked in these institutions; the numerous widows and orphans who have in-

vested their all in their stock; the great mass of industry and labor which depends upon them for assistance, are matters of the most serious concern, and we are bound to look well to the consequences before we do anything that may injure and destroy them.[*]

Permit me, in this place, sir, to notice the charges which have been urged against these State banks with so much acrimony. I must first, however, distinctly state, that I mean not to include in my defence, that miserable litter of forty-two, which came forth from the Pennsylvania Legislature at one monstrous birth. They crawled into a sickly existence; and spread themselves over the land, like so many vipers; poisoning the atmosphere, and killing the soil. Speculation became an epidemic, which corrupted and destroyed the morals and the industry of the country. It followed the farmer into his field, and he sold it; the mechanic into his shop, and he pledged it. Even the daily laborer cast away his spade and his hoe in scorn, and determined no longer to rely on the labor of his hands for his bread. Every man, from the highest to the lowest, was to become rich by the magic of these wonderful banks—the lamp of Aladdin was placed in every county, and each man, woman, and child, expected to have the rubbing of it in their turn. The Governor of Pennsylvania endeavored to check this madness with the whole force of his Constitutional power—he put himself manfully against it, but all in vain; he was overwhelmed with the torrent of private speculation and legislative fraud. I say, sir, legislative fraud, because it is a fact indisputable, that when that Legislature passed a single act incorporating forty-two banks, no one of the whole batch could have obtained a majority for itself—what was it then but a system of bargaining and selling; of conspiracy and combination, to do a great mischief by common consent, when a small part of the same mischief would have received no countenance or support!

To return to the State banks, properly so called, what is the great reproach that has been so severely visited upon them? The stopping of specie payments. Before we decide upon the justice of their condemnation, on this account, we should, with a proper calmness and impartiality, inquire into the causes which led to it, and the necessity which demanded it. The cause of this unfortunate measure has been found by some in the loans made by these banks to the Government, which are declared to be unwarranted in their amount, and ruinous in the length of the credit. Others charge the misfortune to the excessive issues of notes, which, if true, is in a great degree the consequence of the former. I do not believe that these causes, either separately or together, have produced or

---

[*] That the National Bank is expected and intended to hold a command over the State banks cannot be questioned, when we find the Secretary of the Treasury in his report on this subject, distinctly avowing it, and calculating on the combined force of the Treasury and the Bank to direct and control the operations and conduct of the State institutions.

could have produced the result attributed to them, without the pressure of other circumstances to which the evil ought truly to be traced, and which would have produced precisely the same results, had there been no loans, and no issues in consequence of them. Whatever, however, may have been the effects of these loans to the Government, they hardly afford a fair subject of reproach here; and we are bound at least to mitigate the crime, (if you will call it so,) by a consideration of the circumstances under which it was committed. The enemy was upon you to the North and to the South; the defence of the country languished for the means of support; the public Treasury was exhausted, and the citizen refused his further aid to replenish it. Everything looked to ruin for want of money. In this condition of the country, the banks were applied to for assistance. Every inducement that could be suggested was addressed to their interest, their fears, and their patriotism. The Secretary of the Treasury condescended to present himself in person at the board of the directors, imploring (I may say) their compassion. From without they were pressed and assailed by the public sentiment—always powerful, and sometimes irresistible;—and had they not yielded to solicitations and circumstances like these, they must have taken upon themselves the consequences, however disastrous, that may have followed a refusal. I do not, sir, exclude from the inducements a hope or prospect of profit from these Treasury bargains and negotiations. This may fairly and honorably have entered into the consideration. So much for these loans, which, after all, were not the cause of suspending specie payments; that must have been done just when it was done, had no loans been made.

As to the allegation of excessive issues, where is the proof of this charge? Who has shown what was the amount of notes in circulation at the time of the suspension, or that it was greater than usual? I understand the fact was not so; and if it were, the proof should be made by those who maintain the charge. We have lately obtained some important information on this point from the highest source of authority. An examination has been made, under the authority of the Legislature of Pennsylvania, into the condition of those banks in Philadelphia which have made the largest loans to the Government, and which, therefore, must show in the strongest manner, the consequences of these loans, or their issues. What has been the result? The notes of the whole do not average one-third of the capital of the whole. In some they are less, in others something more. Are these excessive issues? May not any bank, honestly and fairly, and discreetly too, issue notes to one-third of the amount of its capital. I know of no system of banking which proceeds on the calculation of a smaller issue. It is not here, then, that we shall find the true cause of a suspension of specie payments; nor will it be found in a real scarcity of coin. It is probably true that large quantities of specie were withdrawn from the country in the purchase of English bills; and, perhaps, in direct remittances,

tempted by the extravagant price it bore in Great Britain. But enough was left, and now remains, to do all the banking business in ordinary times and circumstances. The honorable chairman of the committee has stated, and I doubt not he speaks from correct and official information, that, in June last, there was, in the different banks in the United States, the sum of fifteen millions of dollars in gold and silver. Now, this amount is assuredly sufficient for the specie business of their capital of eighty-five millions, in ordinary times, and in the full enjoyment of the public confidence. When to this sum you add the deposites of specie which have been withdrawn by the loss of that confidence, and which will be returned to the vaults of the bank on its restoration, I think it is demonstrated that it is not for the want of specie in the country that the banks cannot pay it. It is well known that when paper is in good credit, no large payments are made in specie. It is thought burdensome to pay or to receive them, and a bank is therefore required only to keep specie enough to answer trifling demands, and supply change for the small business of the community. The usual estimate has been about one-fifth the amount of the capital; and no bank would be thought delinquent, much less insolvent, because it could not pay all its notes on any sudden demand. No bank of discount and deposite ever did, or ever could do this. What then was the cause—what is the justification of the stoppage of these banks?

In my opinion it was the gloomy and calamitous condition of our public affairs, which destroyed the public confidence not only in the banks, but in every public institution in the country; a dark and desponding uncertainty hung over us, and every hour seemed big with our fate. The credit of the Government was demolished; it could pay neither paper nor silver. The ruin of the country, the breaking up of the Government would of course have broken up all the moneyed institutions, and indeed all our public institutions of every description. In such a state of things, it is obvious that every man would be eager to seize upon something that would hold its value in all times, under any circumstances, and in all places. What was the note of the best bank worth at such a period? Gold and silver could alone be called wealth—could alone be relied upon to procure the necessaries of life; of course every man that had a deposite in a bank ran to withdraw it in gold and silver; every man who held a note demanded its payment in solid coin. It is an undoubted fact that such was the run upon the Philadelphia banks that had they kept their vaults open for twenty-four hours longer than they did, not a doit would have been left in them. It will be remembered that these things took place just before the burning of Washington, and when a just apprehension was universal that Philadelphia would be the next object of attack. But the Eastern banks did not resort to this desperate measure. Sir, the Eastern part of the United States had not connected itself, and in truth was not, from its situation and other circumstances, so closely and inseparably connected with the fate of the General Government as we were. They had not the same cause for alarm and precaution. In my judgment, then, sir, it was neither the excessive issues of paper, which at this time does not exceed from forty to fifty millions in the whole United States, nor any real scarcity of the precious metals, that has compelled our banks to adopt the measure so much complained of; but the loss of public confidence, arising not from the misconduct of the banks, but the uncertain and disastrous aspect of our national affairs.

But I am asked, if this is the case, why have not these banks, on the returning days of peace, prosperity, and confidence, resumed the payments of their debts; and why do they not sell their stock to enable them to do so? I will answer. They must do both these things, and they can do them, but they must have a reasonable time and indulgence. The derangement of systems so complicated and extensive cannot be removed in an instant. The ability of the banks to do their business as formerly, must wait for the restoration of their former confidence; the public alarm must have time to subside; the troubled waters to become smooth again—these things are all gradual and slow in their operations; and by attempting to force them, we shall but defeat their success. As to the stock held by the banks upon which they are drawing interest, while they neither pay the principal nor interest of their own debts, and by which they are enabled to make such enormous dividends. I say, without hesitation, they must sell, but not too suddenly. It is said that, in stocks, Treasury notes, and State loans, the banks are creditors of the public to the amount of forty millions. Now, what would be the effect of throwing all this suddenly in the market? Where would the purchasers be found, and where would these institutions get specie for it to enable them to pay their debts in specie? Still the banks must begin the work of reformation. I hope they have; if not, they must and may be made to do it. Could I suspect them of holding their stock for the mere object of profit, while they refuse payment of their debts, I would consign them to contempt and destruction.

Mr. SHARPE next addressed the Chair on this subject, expressing in the outset his regret that the attack on this bank had been on its details, instead of its principle. Mr. S. explained his views of the difference between the aspect of this question at this time, and that which it presented at the last winter, when it had been so long fruitlessly agitated. The principal object of the advocates of a National Bank at the last session, was to afford to the Government the facility of obtaining occasional loans to carry on the operations of the Government, &c., and to sustain the public credit; the object at present was of a different character—to remedy the evil of a vitiated currency, which had lately been much exaggerated, and which demanded a remedy. Mr. S. here examined the operation of this depreciation on the revenues of Government, which, he clear-

ly showed, were most injuriously affected by it. The Government sustained a clear loss of large amount—a loss which must be made up by taxes levied on the industry and labor of the community; and who gained by it? Those whose duty it is to remedy the evil. It is the owners of bank stock who derive the benefit from the depreciation of their own paper. All acknowledged the extent of the evil, and the necessity of a remedy, though they differed as to the nature of the remedy.

In reply to the argument of Mr. WEBSTER, that the remedy for the evil was in the power of the Secretary of the Treasury, by requiring payment of the dues to Government in specie, Mr. S. said the gentleman had not demonstrated that there was specie enough in the country for the purposes of the payment of the revenue to the Treasury, nor that the banks have not the means ultimately to force the Treasury to take their paper in payments to the Government. The disposition was not wanting in the officer at the head of that Department to apply the remedy, if it were in his power; but, Mr. S. said, an act of Congress could apply an adequate remedy. If that now proposed was the proper measure, let it be adopted; if a better can be proposed, let it be shown. He was not, he added, so opinionated as to assert that this was the only remedy; but a National Bank was a measure tried and understood, and he therefore preferred it; if it should not succeed, he would support any other measure adequate to the object in view.

In reply to Mr. HOPKINSON's reference to the old Bank of the United States, as an institution whose wisdom had been tested by experience, Mr. S. said he could not see the force of the wide distinction the gentleman had drawn between the plan of that bank and of this. He compared these features, and showed that their dissimilarity was not such as to change their principle. This, he said, was intended to be a specie bank, gradually put in operation, and by its business, connected with the measures of the Government, to introduce a general resumption of specie payments and circulation. In regard to the State banking institutions, Mr. S. avowed as strong an attachment to their interest and prosperity as the gentleman from Pennsylvania; but his attachment to them as individuals must be regulated by the correctness of their conduct. If they abandoned the path of probity and duty, he must renounce his attachment to them unless they showed a disposition to return to it. In regard to the means alleged to have been employed to obtain loans from these banks, when they yielded to the solicitations of the Treasury, Mr. S. said, they took care to get the best bargain they could out of its necessities; in addition to the just interest of six per cent. they got a premium of somewhere about twenty per cent. for their friendly loans to the Government. To prove that they had made a good business of it, he said that there was not one of those banks but could sell out its stock for specie, and make a handsome profit on the whole transaction, besides the advantages they have already derived; but, he said, they did not want to do it; they had rather keep their stock bearing interest, and issue paper on it, &c.

As to the idea of danger to the Government from a bank of thirty-five millions, he said it was fanciful. How far could a bank be dangerous to the Government? When banking was a monopoly in the hands of a Government, or of a few individuals; and then only. Competition, he said, destroyed monopoly, and destroyed the danger from such an institution; and it could not be argued that there was not now competition enough to deprive such an institution as this of the character of an engine dangerous to the liberties of the country. A bank, he said, might be more profitable to the stockholders with a capital of twenty millions; but it would be more useful to the community with a larger capital, &c. Having offered these and other views of the subject, he concluded by expressing his hope that this bill would pass with very little alteration of its present provisions.

Mr. Calhoun then rose, and in an energetic manner vindicated the bill, and his views of it, from the attack which had been made on them. He said no man in the House would reprobate more than him the establishment of a bank which was not a specie bank. A bank not to pay specie, he said, would be an instrument of deception; it would have no character or feature of a bank; he should regard it with disgust and abhorrence. This bank, he asserted in reply to contrary assertions, if established, would be a specie bank. He professed himself ready to remedy any defects which should be pointed out; but he hoped the Committee would not be influenced to destroy its essential features by such vague arguments as had been urged against them. This was to be a specie bank, or he would have nothing to do with it. He called upon gentlemen not to give way to objections to the details of the bill, made by those who were altogether inimical to the establishment of any bank; their arguments, he intimated, ought to be received with suspicion, because their view of the subject might be supposed to be warped by their hostility to the project altogether. Mr. C. then spoke at length in explanation and reply to those gentlemen who had preceded him in the debate. In regard to the estimation of paper in circulation, &c., he took occasion to say, that he and Mr. Smith had not widely differed in opinion on that head, when they came to understand terms. Mr. C. said he had not specified the particular items in his estimate of the amount of bank issues and transactions; his object had been merely to show, without descending to particulars, that the banks had over traded. He referred, for illustration, to the Bank of Washington, reputed a prudent bank, which on a capital of $350,000, what with stock and discounts to individuals, drew interest on $800,000. His object, he said, when up before, was to prove that the banks generally had done a business which would authorize them to divide at the enormous rate of fourteen and an half per cent. on their capital paid in, &c.

Mr. Sergeant spoke at some length in explanation of his views.

Mr. Pitkin followed in support of the motion to reduce the capital of the bank, declaring himself decidedly friendly to the incorporation of a bank of something like moderate capital, on true commercial and practical principles, but on no other.

The question on reducing the capital to twenty millions was finally taken, and decided in the negative—yeas 49, nays 74. The Committee then rose, and the House adjourned.

Tuesday, February 29.

Mr. Hopkinson presented a petition of a committee on behalf of the surviving officers of the Pennsylvania line of the Revolutionary army, praying for further compensation for the services of said officers.

Mr. Hopkinson also presented petitions of sundry inhabitants of Pennsylvania, praying that the claims of the officers and soldiers of the Revolutionary army may be again taken into consideration, and that additional allowances may be made to them.—Referred to the Committee on Pensions and Revolutionary Claims.

Mr. Nelson, from the Committee on the Judiciary, made a report on the petition of the Legislature of the Territory of Illinois, respecting the powers of their Governor; which was read, and the resolution therein contained was concurred in by the House, as follows:

Resolved, That it is inexpedient to grant the prayer of the petition.

On motion of Mr. Hanson,

Resolved, That the President of the United States be and he is hereby requested to cause to be laid before this House a statement of the cases in which he has employed or caused to be employed counsel to assist the Attorney General in prosecuting causes in the Supreme Court of the United States, in behalf of the United States; stating as nearly as may be the amount of property in dispute in each case, the names of the counsel so employed, the period of employing them, and the compensation granted to them in each case; also the manner of making such compensation, and the fund out of which the same was paid.

Mr. Hanson and Mr. Darlington were appointed a committee to present the foregoing resolution to the President.

The bill from the Senate "concerning field officers of the militia," was read twice, and committed to a Committee of the Whole House on Monday next.

The bill from the Senate "for the relief of Jacob Babbitt and John Dennis," was read twice, and committed to the Committee of Commerce and Manufactures.

The bill from the Senate " relating to evidence in cases of naturalization," was read the third time as amended, and being on its passage, it was ordered to lie on the table.

The bill from the Senate "for the relief of

Lieutenant Colonel William Lawrence, of the Army of the United States, and the officers, non-commissioned officers, and privates, composing the garrison of Fort Bowyer, in the year 1814," was read the third time, and passed.

NATIONAL CURRENCY.

Mr. WARD, of Massachusetts, moved that the House proceed to consider the resolutions submitted by him some days ago, in the following words:

Resolved, That all duties, imposts, and excises, laid by Congress, ought not only to be laid uniformly throughout the United States, agreeably to the provision in the Constitution, but ought to be collected in all parts of the United States in the same currency, or in currencies equivalent in value.

Resolved, That the Secretary of the Treasury be instructed to receive alone in payment of duties, imposts, excises, and debts, due to the United States, gold, silver, and copper coin, Treasury notes, and the notes of such banks as pay specie for their bills, excepting in cases in which is is otherwise provided by law.

And, on the question of consideration, he demanded the yeas and nays.

The House agreed to consider the resolutions—yeas 52, nays 49: and the question being stated on adopting the resolutions—

Mr. CALHOUN moved to refer the resolutions to the Committee on the National Currency, which, he said, already had the subject under consideration.

This motion was opposed by Mr. WARD at some length, who thought the resolution spoke for itself, and could be decided on by the House without the aid of a committee; that the reference would also be productive of delay, in regard to measures which he regarded as of great urgency, as well as of necessity.

Mr. WRIGHT supported the reference, and replied briefly to the remarks of Mr. WARD.

After some further discussion, the resolutions were referred as moved by Mr. CALHOUN—ayes 62, nays 49.

THE NATIONAL BANK.

The House then again resolved itself into a Committee of the Whole on the National Bank.

On motion of Mr. CADY, with the assent of Mr. CALHOUN, the bill was amended by striking out so much thereof as gives to Congress the privilege, hereafter, of extending the capital of the bank from *thirty-five* to *fifty* millions.

Mr. CADY moved to amend the bill by striking out so much thereof as authorizes a subscription by the Government of seven millions to the capital stock of the bank, and supported his motion by a number of observations. He contended that no advantage would accrue to the United States from the possession of this interest in the Bank. The money to pay for this stock, he said, would cost the United States more than any profit they could derive from it—that is, by the expense attending its collection; all the funds of the Government accruing sooner or later from taxation on the people; and would, besides, render necessary the imposition of additional taxes to meet it. It would be like an individual's taking up money at 18 per cent. (which he estimated as the cost of collection, &c.) to put into this bank. The seven millions of money, he added, would contribute more to the wealth and improvement of the country—would produce in the end a better interest to the United States, by suffering it to remain in the hands of the people—than it could possibly do by being invested in the stock of this bank. But it had been intimated that a stock might be created, bearing 5 or 6 per cent. interest, for the purpose of paying the proportion of the United States' subscription to the bank, the bank interest on which would redeem it in time. Though this idea was plausible, Mr. C. argued it was not solid. The United States must ultimately pay the stock; and as to the income or profit to the Government from the bank, it would be much more simple to compel it to pay such a sum annually to the Treasury, without the circuitous process of taking stock in it, &c. He suggested other modes by which the bank could be made to contribute to the general wealth, without the Government's becoming a stockholder, &c.

Mr. CALHOUN opposed the motion, so decidedly, that he said he should consider the success of it as tantamount to a decision to strike out the first section of the bill. He showed by his statement of the operation of vesting this stock in the bank (which by the bill is to be done in certain annual proportions) that there would be a clear gain to the Government of at least 2 per cent. per annum —being the difference between the interest the Government pays on the stock and the interest it would receive on its bank shares.

Mr. RANDOLPH supported the motion, and availed himself of the occasion of his rising to enter largely into the subject, in a speech of considerable length. His general views follow: He said he should vote for this motion, because one of his chief objections—one of them, he repeated—was the concern which it was proposed to give to the United States in this bank. He referred to the sale by the Secretary of the Treasury, some years ago, of the shares belonging to the Bank of the United States, and stated the reasons of his approving that step; but, he added, that it was a strong argument against the feature of the bank bill, now under discussion, that, whenever there should be in this country a necessitous and profligate administration of the Government, that bank stock would be laid hold of by the first *Squanderfield* at the head of the Treasury, as the means of filling its empty coffers. But, if there was no objection to this feature stronger than that it would afford provision for the first rainy day, it might not be considered so very important. He argued, however, that it was eternally true, that nothing but the precious metals, or paper bottomed on them, could answer as the currency of any nation or any age, notwithstanding the fanciful theories that great payments could only be made by credits and paper. How, he asked, on this point, were the mighty armies of the ancient world paid off? Certainly not in paper or bank credits. He expressed his fears lest gentlemen had got some of their ideas on these subjects from the wretched pamphlets under which the British and American press had groaned on the subject of a circulating medium. He said he had himself once turned projector, and sketched the plan of a bank, of which it was a feature that the Government should have a concern it; but he became convinced of the fallacy of his views; he found his project would not answer. His objection to the agency of the Government in a bank was therefore, he said, of no recent date, but one long since formed. The objection was vital; that it would be an engine of irresistible power in the hands of any Administration; that it would be in politics and finance what the celebrated proposition of Archimedes was in physics—a place, the fulcrum from which, at the will of the Executive, the whole nation could be hurled to destruction, or managed in any way, at his will and discretion.

This bill, in the view of Mr. R., presented two distinct questions: the one frigidly and rigorously a mere matter of calculation; the other, involving some very important political considerations. In regard to the present depreciation of paper, he did not appear to agree with those who thought the establishment of the National Bank would not aid in the reformation of it. If he were to go into the causes which produced the present state of things, he said, he should never end. As to the share the banks themselves had in producing it, he regarded the dividends they had made, since its commencement, as conclusive proof. The present time, Mr. R. went on to remark, was in his view one of the most disastrous he had ever witnessed in the Republic, and this bill proved it. The proposal to establish this great bank he described as a crutch, and, as far as he understood it, it was a broken one: it would tend, instead of remedying the evil, to aggravate it. The evil of the times, he said, was a spirit engendered in this Republic, fatal to Republican principles, fatal to Republican virtue; a spirit to live by any means but those of honest industry; a spirit of profusion—in other words, the spirit of Catiline himself, *alieni avidus, sui profusus*—a spirit of expediency, not only in public but private life; the system of Diddler in the farce, living any way and well—wearing an expensive coat, and drinking the finest wines, at anybody's expense. This bank, he imagined (he was far from ascribing to the gentleman from South Carolina any such views) was to a certain extent a modification of the same system. Connected, as it was to be, with the Government, whenever it went into operation, a scene would be exhibited on the great theatre of the United States, at the contemplation of which he shuddered. If we mean to transmit our institutions unimpaired to posterity, if some now living wish to continue to live under the same institutions by which they are now ruled—and, with all its evils, real or imaginary, he presumed no man would question that we live under the easiest Government on the globe—we must put bounds to the spirit which seeks wealth by every path but the plain and regular path of honest industry

and honest fame. This was one of the grounds on which he was hostile to this bill.

Alluding to Mr. WEBSTER's observation respecting the laws fixing the currency of the United States, he said, it was very true they were clear and peremptory in their provisions. If the existing laws did not compel men to pay their debts, the establishment of a bank would not. Let us not disguise the fact, said he, pursuing his remarks on what he described as the evil of the times; we think we are living in the better times of the Republic, we deceive ourselves; we are almost in the days of Sylla and Marius; yes, we have almost got down to the time of Jugurtha. It was unpleasant, he said, to put one's self in array against a great leading interest in a community, be they a knot of land speculators, paper jobbers, or what not; but, he said, every man you meet in this House or out of it, with some rare exceptions, which only served to prove the rule, was either a stockholder, president, cashier, clerk, or doorkeeper, runner, engraver, paper-maker, or mechanic in some other way to a bank. The gentleman from Pennsylvania, he said, might dismiss his fears for the State banks, with their one hundred and seventy millions of paper on eighty-two millions of capital. However great the evil of their conduct might be, he asked, in the course of his illustrations, who was to bell the cat—who was to take the bull by the horns? You might as well attack Gibraltar with a pocket pistol as to attempt to punish them. There were very few, he said, who dared to speak truth to this mammoth; the banks were so linked together with the business of the world, that there were very few men exempt from their influence. The true secret is, said he, the banks are creditors as well as debtors; and if we were merely debtors to them for the paper in our pockets, they would soon, like Morris and Nicholson, go to jail (figuratively speaking) for having issued more paper than they were able to pay when presented to them. A man had their note, he said, for fifty dollars perhaps in his pocket, for which he wants fifty Spanish milled dollars; but they have his note for five thousand in their possession, and laugh at his demand. We are tied hand and foot, Mr. R. said, and bound to conciliate this great mammoth, which is set up to worship in this Christian land—we are bound to propitiate it, &c. Thus, he said, whilst our Government denounces hierarchy, will permit no privileged order for conducting the service of the only true God, whilst it denounces nobility, &c., has a privileged order of new men grows up, the pressure of whose foot he at this moment felt on his neck. If anything could reconcile him to this monstrous alliance between the bank and the Government, he could, if the object could be attained of compelling these banks to fulfil their engagements, almost find in his heart to go with the gentleman in voting for it.

Mr. R. proceeded to a minute examination of the state of the paper currency, and its various phases, recently and in earlier times. The stuff uttered on all hands, and absolutely got by rote by the haberdashers' boys behind the counters in the shops, that the paper now in circulation would buy anything you want as well as gold and silver, was answered, he said, by saying, that you want to buy silver with it. He examined, in detail, the present mode of banking, which, he said, goes to demoralize society; it was as much swindling to issue notes with intent not to pay, as it was burglary to break open a house. If they were unable to pay, the banks were bankrupts; if able to pay, and would not, they were fraudulent bankrupts, &c. But, he said, a man might as well go to Constantinople to preach Christianity, as to get up here and preach against banks. He despaired, he said, almost, of remedying the evil they cause, when he saw so many men of respectability directors, stockholders, debtors of the banks. To pass this bill, he said, would be like getting rid of the rats by setting fire to the house; whether any other remedy could be devised, he did not now undertake to pronounce. The banks, he said, had lost all shame, and exemplified a beautiful and very just observation of one of the finest writers, that men banded together in a common cause, will collectively do that at which every individual of the combination would spurn. This observation had been applied to the enormities committed and connived at by the British East India Company, and would equally apply to the modern system of banking; but still more to the spirit of party, &c., on which Mr. R. digressed at some length.

He then resumed the consideration of the history of bank paper in this country, and stated the fact that, not many years ago, the New England paper had been at almost as great a discount here, as the paper of this part of the country now was there; and that even in New England the notes of some of the banks were not current within their own States, except at a discount. As to establishing this bank to prevent a variation in the rate of exchange of bank paper, he said, you might as well expect to prevent a variation of the wind; you might, said he, as well pass an act of Congress (for which, if it would be of any effect, he should certainly vote) to prevent the northwest wind from blowing in our teeth as we go from the House to our lodgings. After a minute discussion of the causes and rates of the difference of exchange in the paper of various banks, Mr. R. concluded his remarks by pledging himself to agree to any adequate means to cure the great evil, that were consistent with the administration of the Government, in such a manner as to conduce to the happiness of the people, and the reformation of the public morals.

Mr. WARD defended the Massachusetts banking institutions from imputations, which he thought a part of Mr. R.'s remarks on the currency calculated to cast on their correct management.

Mr. SMITH, of Maryland, then rose, and addressed the House at considerable length in opposition to the motion before the House, and in reply to Mr. CADY, Mr. RANDOLPH, and other gentlemen. He explained, by ample illustrations, the preference which a note of the National Bank

would have over the notes of other banks, and even over Treasury notes bearing interest, and the manner in which it would guard itself from a run for specie, &c., by a combination of individuals or other banks. In regard to the direction and management of fiscal affairs, he said, the late Secretary of the Treasury, (meaning Mr. Gallatin,) who went into that Department with as many prejudices as any man could well entertain, thought all was wrong there, and he was the very person to set all right. He had examined the subject day and night, and, after all his examination, he had not found a single iota of Mr. Hamilton's system which it was necessary to alter, &c. By this anecdote, Mr. S. illustrated the advantage of practice over theory. He made many remarks, to show the operation which made Treasury notes generally more valuable than the notes of any bank not paying specie, and less valuable than the notes of any bank which does pay specie; and, he said, if this were not to be a specie bank, he should not have been found in favor of it. The depreciation of paper, he said, was not wholly owing to the suspension of specie payments, as he proved by a reference to the difference of exchange between Baltimore and New York, in both of which places specie was not paid by the banks, and yet the exchange was 9½ per cent. against Baltimore, &c. This was owing to the balance of trade being thrown against them during the war, the Chesapeake having been almost wholly shut up, whilst Baltimore vessels put into the port of New York, with their cargoes and prizes, &c. He did not wish the Government to pay any money into this bank, but stock to be created, &c., respecting which he did not know; but he should move an amendment, and also to expedite the payment of the specie portion of the subscription by individuals to the bank, for, without three-fourths of the proposed amount of specie in its vaults, the bank would not dare to issue a note.

Mr. CADY again spoke in support of his motion, and in reply to the objections against it. When he concluded the Committee rose.

FRIDAY, March 1.

Mr. TELFAIR presented a petition of James E. Houstoun, brother and guardian of Moosman Houstoun, late a Lieutenant Colonel in the Army of the United States, and who, while in that incapacity, became deranged in his mind, praying that some measure may be adopted for the support of his said brother.—Referred to the Committee on Military Affairs.

Mr. YANCEY made a report on the petitions of Thomas Farrar, William Young, and William Moseley; which was read; when Mr. Y. reported a bill for the relief of Thomas Farrar, William Young, and William Moseley; which was read twice and committed to a Committee of the Whole.

On motion of Mr. SMITH, of Maryland, the Secretary of War was directed to lay before this House an estimate of the damages sustained by the vessels sunk in the entrance of the port of Baltimore, by order of the Commanding General, to prevent the enemy from passing Fort McHenry.

The bill in addition to the act establishing the Post Office Establishment, passed through a Committee of the Whole, and was reported to the House.

DISTRICT OF COLUMBIA.

On motion of Mr. Goldsborough—

Resolved, That the Committee on the District of Columbia be instructed to inquire by what authority and for what object the digging of the ground on Capitol square has been commenced, and into the propriety of putting a stop to it.

[Mr. G. had reference in his resolution to some operations commenced on the public square for making bricks.]

After some remarks to show the great evils resulting to the community from the influx of unauthorized notes purporting to be issued by banks which no one knew, and which in some cases were palpable frauds, unsupported by any ability to pay them, Mr. G. moved the following resolution, which was agreed to:

Resolved, That the committee appointed to inquire into the state of the several banks in the District of Columbia be instructed to inquire into the expediency of prohibiting, within the said District, the circulation of notes issued by any private banking association, whether existing within the District or elsewhere, and of restraining the formation of such private banking associations in future.

TRAFFIC IN SLAVES.

Mr. Randolph then rose and said that it was his purpose to move for instructions to the Committee of the said District upon a subject of infinitely more importance in every point of view than those to which Mr. Goldsborough had adverted. He expressed a wish that some other gentleman had undertaken the business; but as no one had thought proper to awaken the House to a sense of their concern in it, or to point the finger of scorn at it, he would take upon him the office to do it, and to call upon the House to put a stop to proceedings at that moment carried on under their very noses; proceedings that were a crying sin before God and man; a practice which, he said, was not surpassed for abomination in any part of the earth; for in no part of it, not even excepting the rivers on the coast of Africa, was there so great and so infamous a slave market as in the metropolis, in the very Seat of Government of this nation, which prided itself on freedom. Before he proceeded further, he fenced himself in against all suspicion of unduly interfering in the very delicate subject of the relation between the slave and his owner, and to that end he reminded the House that where a bill was brought in some years before to prevent the prosecution of the African slave trade, he had voted against it, because it professed a principle against which it was the duty of every man of the southern or slaveholding States to set his face; for it assumed a prerogative to interfere in the right of property between the master and

his slave. On account of that opposition he had been calumniously and falsely held up, as one of the advocates of the most nefarious, the most disgraceful, and most infernal traffic that has ever stained the annals of the human race. Upon another occasion, too, when a member of that House had taken upon him the lien between slave and master, he had raised his voice against him. He had never directly or indirectly acquiesced in the weak and wailing plans of those who, by way of relieving the unfortunate African, would throw the States into danger; he would never weaken the form of the contract between the owner and his slave, and he would never deny that the citizens of other States coming into the slaveholding States might exercise the right of ownership over the slaves they might purchase; but it was not necessary to that exercise that this city should be made a depot of slaves, who were bought either from cruel masters or kidnapped; and of those who were kidnapped, he said there were two kinds—slaves stolen from their masters, and free persons stolen, as he might say, from themselves. It was not necessary that we should have, here in the very streets of our new metropolis, a depot for this nefarious traffic—in comparison with which the traffic from Africa to Charleston or Jamaica was mercy, was virtue. Indeed there could be no comparison rationally instituted between taking those savages from their native wilds and tearing the civilized informed negro, habituated to cultivated life, from his master, his friends, his wife, his children, or his parents. As to the right of passing through the place, as ordinary occasions might require, it was unquestionable; but there was a great difference between that and making the District a depot for a systematic slave market—an assemblage of prisons where the unfortunate beings, reluctant, no doubt, to be torn from their connexions, and the affections of their lives, were incarcerated and chained down, and thence driven in fetters like beasts, to be paid for like cattle. Mr. R. therefore moved that the Committee of the District of Columbia should be instructed to inquire into the inhuman and illegal traffic in slaves carried on in the District, and to devise some speedy means to put a stop to it.

Mr. Tucker (chairman of that committee) suggested that it would be better to have it referred to the committee some time since appointed to form a system of laws for the District.

Mr. Randolph expressed his regret that the honorable gentleman seemed disposed to decline the task, and offered himself to take his share in the enterprise. The object of the resolution, he said, was a more coercive police. He knew that the demands for cotton, tobacco, and latterly of sugar, created a demand for slaves, and we had a description of people here like those described by Mungo Park, (only that they are not so humane or so honest,) white traders, who make this their depot, and sell human beings; and to verify this charge, and show the audacious villainy of their proceedings, he dwelt upon these words of an advertisement of a sale of negroes—"*No objection to* TRADERS *bidding*." The increase in the price was the temptation for which their base, hard-hearted masters sold out of their families the negroes who had been raised among them. That very day he had heard a horrible fact from a respectable gentleman as he came to the House, which he would relate. A poor negro, by hard work and saving of his allowances, had laid by money enough to buy the freedom of his wife and child, and had paid it from time to time into the hands of his master, but the poor fellow died. The transaction was an affair of honor with the master, and the day after the poor fellow's death, the woman and child were sold. One fact like this spoke volumes. He repeated, that if the honorable chairman of the Committee of the District of Columbia refused to take upon him the inquiry into this rank offence, he (Mr. R.) would himself be among these people. He declared that he was lately mortified at being told by a foreigner of high rank, "You call this the land of liberty, and every day that passes things are done in it at which the despotisms of Europe would be horrorstruck and disgusted."

Mr. WRIGHT said the laws were sufficient to take cognizance of this business, and said that there was worse slavery practised in Europe, [Alluding to pressing in the navy of England.]

Mr. GOLDSBOROUGH expressed his satisfaction at this affair being brought before the House. He had himself more than once met more than a dozen of those unhappy wretches marching in droves through the street. He met them even in the avenue, and it was a notorious fact that this was the channel of transmission for them. Speaking of laws was useless. When the evils were seen to exist, and were not prevented, it was a proof that the laws were of no value, or were not executed.

Mr. HOPKINSON had no idea of Congress taking such care about matters of inferior consideration, while such flagitious, and, to the nation, disgraceful deeds of guilt were suffered to be perpetrated under its very eye and with its knowledge. He suggested that as Mr. RANDOLPH had, to his own great honor, offered his co-operation, it would be best to appoint a select committee for the purpose, and moved for one accordingly.

Mr. TUCKER declared that the honorable gentleman (Mr. R.) had misunderstood him, and that he was no less willing than himself to co-operate in the measure, and concurred in Mr. HOPKINSON'S opinion, that a select committee would be best.

The resolution passed is as follows:

Resolved, That a committee be appointed to inquire into the existence of an inhuman and illegal traffic in slaves carried on in and through the District of Columbia, and to report whether any, and what, measures are necessary for putting a stop to the same.

Messrs. RANDOLPH, HOPKINSON, GOLDSBOROUGH, MAYRANT, and KERR, were appointed the said committee.

NATIONAL BANK.

The House again resolved itself into a Committee of the Whole on the National Bank bill. The motion to strike out so much of the first section as allows Government to subscribe for seventy thousand shares of the stock, being still under consideration—

Mr. WRIGHT opposed the amendment at some length. He was sorry to see a plan which promised such great benefit to the country in the present deranged state of its currency, endangered by the present motion. If the motion prevailed, he should be compelled, he said, to vote against the bill, much as he was in favor of establishing a bank. He wished to see the bank possessed in part by the Government and partly by the citizens, because the stock of it would be extremely profitable. The Government ought to have an interest in the bank, as they would thereby be informed of all the plans which might be at any time entertained by the directors of so powerful an institution. He was not afraid, however, to trust our citizens; nor ought they to be suspicious of the Government; and the participation of the Government could not, he conceived, be productive of injury or mischief. Mr. W. adverted to the assertion that such an institution would realize the imagined lever of Archimedes, with which the world might be moved. He wished it did possess that mighty power, and it could be brought to bear on the rotten and corrupt Governments of Europe. We have, he said, given to that portion of the world examples of liberty, of valor on the sea and on the land, and he should be glad if, by any power, we could crush the despotisms which oppress it, &c. He said he was surprised at the objections made by gentlemen from the East to establish this bank on so large a proportion of the public stock, as the effect would be to raise that stock immediately to par, &c.

Mr. JEWETT, in reply, said, the gentleman who had just sat down had exorcised the House in the outset, and had threatened it with voting against the bill if it did not suit him. He would not follow the example of that gentleman. He would not go to Europe to put down Governments, to light flames, and put out fires; but he would state a few matters of fact. This question affected the interest of every State and town in the country. It was of great magnitude; it would either restore the credit of our currency, or make it worse than it is already; and to illustrate his opinion on this important subject, he would state a case in point. Some ten or fifteen years ago, he said, there was a certain State (Vermont) which had no bank; but there were banks in adjoining States which afforded much profit; and the people of the State thought they might as well grow rich by banking as their neighbors. They supposed, if the limited means and numbers of private banks could make money, that the extended means of a State would make an institution still more profitable; that it would drive out the paper of other banks, facilitate the operations of the State, &c., as had been argued in favor of the bank now proposed. A State bank was accordingly established on a small specie capital, and paper to a large amount issued, which they thought would never be returned for payment. What was the consequence? The paper of other banks, it was true, disappeared; but it was because of the suspicion which attached to the State paper. The machine, if it might be called so, went on badly; it was attributed to bad management of its concerns; and attempts were made to remedy the defects, but in vain. The paper depreciated from six to ten, and from ten to fifteen per cent.; and finally, by the juggle, the people of the State lost, how much he was not certain, but a great amount he knew. So it would be, he said, with the plan now contemplated, if not amended; and if the objections to it were not obviated, he should be compelled to vote against the bill, although he was strongly in favor of a bank on proper principles. If passed in its present shape, it would entail evils on the country, which money could not compensate, &c.

Mr. Ross advocated the motion to amend the bill. He did not believe, as had been argued, that a participation in the bank would strengthen the arm of the Government, or be very profitable. If, however, the arm of Government was to be strengthened by weakening that of the citizens, and uniting with a privileged aristocracy, he was decidedly opposed to it. He did not wish the Government to become partners in such a privileged order. If the reasons for retaining the principle in the bill were correct, he thought the proportion allowed too small. If Government was to derive this great profit from the participation, its share was not great enough. It had been said that the influence of one bank (the Manhattan) could have prevented the election of Mr. Jefferson to the Presidency; if that bank had been under Executive control, he believed its power would have been exerted. This was a proof of the danger of giving Government a great influence in such institutions. He was opposed to the plan chiefly from his objections to joining a moneyed aristocracy, and his fears that it might operate injuriously to the liberties of the country, &c.

Mr. GOLDSBOROUGH made a few remarks on the motion. If the provision was inserted as an apology for the appointment of the five directors by the Government, then he was opposed to it; but if it would be as profitable as was predicted, and would enable us to dispense with some of the existing internal taxes, he should be glad to vote for it. A good bank, Mr. G. said, would be very serviceable; and he should vote against the motion because he could not see that any harm would arise from the nation participating in a pecuniary establishment, &c.

The question was then taken on striking out the provision, and decided in the negative, as follows: For the amendment 38, against it 61.

The Committee of the Whole proceeded with the consideration of the rest of the bill. After the adoption of some verbal amendments—

Mr. WRIGHT moved to substitute Washington city for Philadelphia, as the place to which to return the books, &c., (to place the bank at Washington.) Mr. W. said, having a strong desire that the bill should pass, and knowing some to feel a delicacy in supporting it, from Constitutional scruples, he thought it better to fix the bank where there could be no objections on that score, and where also its operations would be facilitated. Washington is the seat of Government of the nation, and here, he said, it would be under the eye of the Government, where there would be less danger from so great a moneyed aristocracy, and the national interest would be better guarded than at any other place. Mr. W. said it was not his purpose to anticipate objections to his motion; but the principal one he knew to be, that a sufficient number of persons could not be found at Washington qualified for directors. The force of this objection he denied in the extent to which it was urged. In the city and neighboring country, he was convinced that there would be found abundant talents for managing the concerns of the bank. The people of this District, moreover, deserved highly of the Government. They had, in time of need, done as much or more, in proportion to numbers, to aid the country, than any other section of the Union. Mr. W. adverted to the source whence the bill originated, and insinuated that much of the ground for recommending Philadelphia must be attributed to the partiality of those who had named that city in the bill; and concluded by saying that the motive for fixing the old Bank of the United States at Philadelphia was the same that ought now to place the present bank here, to wit, that it is the seat of Government.

Mr. ROBERTSON said he coincided with the gentleman in some of his views. He could see no strong reason for preferring Philadelphia; because, if the object was to select a city on account of its commerce, Philadelphia was not the most commercial place; and if that reason carried the bank from the Seat of Government, the same reason would prevent its being located at Philadelphia. But Mr. R. said he had another reason for disapproving the place, mentioned in the bill—he was unwilling to impose upon Philadelphia an institution so obnoxious to the Representatives from that city, all of whom were so decidedly hostile to the bank. However, he said, he should not vote for the motion, because, as a place of greater commerce, he preferred Philadelphia to Washington.

At the suggestion of Mr. CALHOUN, who thought the motion had better be offered on a subsequent stage of the bill, Mr. WRIGHT withdrew his amendment for the present.

On motion of Mr. WEBSTER, the bill was amended by inserting a clause making foreign coins receivable for subscriptions at their real ascertained value, and not according to the rate fixed by the former act of Congress, which was admitted to be incorrect, particularly in the value placed on Spanish gold coins.

Mr. SMITH, of Maryland, adverting to the insinuation which had been thrown out, that the bank was not intended to be, and could not be, a specie bank; and repeating that he, for one, had in view a bank of no other kind—to insure to it that character therefore, and remove the doubts now entertained by others—he moved to strike out the word *five* (the amount of the second payment, required in specie) with the intention of moving to substitute a larger sum. He thought it better to enable the bank to do, as soon as practicable, a liberal business, and at the same time lessen the chance of drawing out, by any run on it, the specie at first paid in, &c.

Mr. CALHOUN had not much objection to the motion; though he thought the bank could certainly do safely a business to the amount of the first specie payment; and if a greater business was offered to them, they would have it in their power to increase their specie at pleasure. His only objection to enlarging the first cash instalment was, that it might have the effect to draw the specie out of the existing banks.

Mr. SMITH's motion to strike out the word *five* was carried, and he then moved to fill the blank with the word *fifteen*, and to strike out altogether the last payment of ten dollars in specie, which was to have been made at eighteen months from the day of subscription;—which was also agreed to—ayes 56, noes 44.

Mr. ROOT said the section under their consideration was the essential part of the contemplated institution, as it contained its constituent or vital parts; and proceeded to enumerate the various stocks receivable in subscription, the rates fixed for them by the bill; the price paid for them by the lenders to the Government, and the profits now about to be given to those lenders, by raising the stocks to par—thus granting a bounty to those men. The same reasons did not exist, he said, for such a measure at present, as existed at the last session. Then, the credit of the Government was weak; now it was strong. He would not deny that the leaders to the Government might have been actuated by patriotic motives; but that was no reason for granting to them anything more than was bargained for—and he proceeded to show that by allowing the Commissioners of the Sinking Fund to buy up this stock, instead of permitting it to be subscribed in the bank at the rates prescribed by the bill, the Government would save about two millions in its redemption, &c. For these and other reasons adduced, he moved to amend the bill by fixing the rate at which the six per cent. stock shall be received in subscription to the bank at ninety per cent. instead of par.

Mr. CALHOUN objected to the motion. Its obvious effect, if not its object, he said, was to increase the bonus. If the stocks are depreciated, said Mr. C., it is not the fault of the holders of it, but of the Government itself, and it would be improper in the Government to take advantage of this depreciation. The measure would also have an injurious influence on the subscriptions to the bank, without answering any good purpose, and he, therefore hoped the motion would not prevail.

Mr. ROOT said in reply, that those who boasted so much of having loaned their money to the

Government, only gave their depreciated notes, and received in return the notes of the Government, by which they made a great profit, and that was all their merit, &c.

Mr. GOLDSBOROUGH made a few remarks on the motion. He thought it questionable whether a Government ought to fix on its own stock a manifest depreciation, and in this instance, it would be an act of very great injustice, and a violation of public faith; because, in the next clause, it was provided, that the stock shoud be redeemed and liquidated at the rates at which it was paid in to the bank, &c.

Mr. ROSS thought the circumstance deprecated by the gentleman last up, existed already; which opinion he supported by a few arguments. The whole system of this bill, he said, was an encouragement to stock-jobbers, and was of the same character as the measure which once benefitted the speculators at the expense of the Revolutionary soldier, by funding their certificates, &c.

The question was then taken on the motion of Mr. ROOT, and negatived—only seven or eight gentlemen rising in favor of it.

The Committee then rose, reported progress and obtained leave to sit again.

SATURDAY, March 2.

The SPEAKER laid before the House a letter from the Secretary of the Treasury, transmitting a report and statement of additions which have been made, since the 30th September last, to the funded and floating debts of the United States; which was read, and ordered to lie on the table.

Mr. WRIGHT, from the committee on that part of the President's Message which relates to an arrangement of the militia expenses, incurred by the States without the sanction of the General Government, reported a bill for the payment of the militia in the case therein mentioned; which was read twice, and committed to a Committee of the Whole.

On motion of Mr. HALL,

Resolved, That the Committee on the National Currency be directed to inquire into the expediency of compelling the banks in the different States, after the first day of November next, to resume specie payments, by increasing the duty on stamps, or in any other manner which may be best calculated to produce the desired effect.

A message from the Senate informed the House that the Senate have passed the bill "to reduce the amount of the direct tax upon the United States and the District of Columbia, for the year 1816," with amendments; they have also passed a bill "for the relief of Richard Mitchill," in which amendments and bill they ask the concurrence of this House.

POST OFFICE BILL.

The House then proceeded to the report of the Committee of the Whole, on the bill in addition to the act regulating the Post Office Establishment. The report being gone through, many amendments were successively offered to the bill, which produced much discussion.

The bill having been amended, on motion of Mr. Wright, so as to allow to members of Congress the privilege of franking letters during the recess, the same power was attempted to be obtained for the Chaplain; which motion was supported by Mr. Wright, and opposed by Mr. Pickering, and then negatived—yeas 5.

Mr. Tallmadge moved the following amendment as section 4.:

And be it further enacted, That no mail shall be transported on the Sabbath; nor shall any post office be opened for the receipt or delivery of letters, packets, or newspapers, on the Lord's day; any law or usage to the contrary notwithstanding.

Mr. T. said, when he recollected the numerous petitions which had been presented to Congress from all parts of the United States, at the present session, he had hoped that, when the Committee on the Post Office and Post Roads made their report, they would have noticed this subject with particular attention. He said he was fortified in this hope, from the consideration that the subject was not a new one; it had been presented again and again, by various classes of the community, without respect to party, praying for the interposition of the National Legislature to prevent the transportation and opening of the mail on the Sabbath, but in this he was disappointed.

He was, moreover, aware that great difficulties were to be surmounted, and strong prejudices overcome, to effect the objects he had in view. The worst passions of the human heart would be brought into exercise when their stronghold should thus be attacked. The plea of necessity, and very possibly even of duty, would be urged to continue a practice which had too long been a reproach to our legislative code, and exposed our country to the judgments of Heaven.

Mr. T. said, the argument he proposed to offer to the House, in support of his amendment, was of a twofold nature. It had for its basis the unequivocal command of the Supreme legislator, and it was fraught with blessings to mankind.

It would be needless, said Mr. T., if not indecorous, to prove the Divine institution of the Sabbath day. In this enlightened age, and in a Christian country, it is presumed that such a task would be useless. I will only take occasion, said he, to remark, that in the decalogue this precept is given with a solemn sanction, and with great clearness and precision; nor does there appear to be any dispensing power left to human wisdom, but that which may be derived from works of necessity and mercy.

As to the advantages resulting from a due observance of this sacred precept, they are numerous and great. The cessation of labor through one day out of seven, serves greatly to relieve and refresh both man and beast, and thus to fit them more effectually to perform the duties of the ensuing week. But the solemn duties of public worship, which are more immediately enjoined on this holy day, are by no means to be dispensed with. In the sanctuary of the Lord, and from the lips of the priest, are the people to expect lessons of pure morality and virtue.

The history of the world, in every age, exhibits indubitable evidence, that where the Sabbath has been revered, and the worship of the Supreme Being attended with reverence and devotion, then public prosperity and private happiness have been most abundantly enjoyed. In ancient history, the Jews afford the most incontrovertible evidence of this truth. While under the immediate direction of the Supreme lawgiver, they were commanded to observe the Sabbath day and keep it holy; to worship the great Jehovah in their solemn assemblies, and wholly to abstain from servile labor. To the observance of these duties manifold blessings were promised; and, on their neglect, the heaviest judgments were denounced. And who is so ignorant as not to know that, so long as they remained faithful to their covenant obligations and obedient to their God, (and no duty was more pointedly enjoined than a due observance of the Sabbath,) they were the most prosperous and happy nation on the earth; but when they declined in their duty, and forgot their vows; when they neglected to keep the Sabbath day holy, according to the Divine command, and the consequent practice of idol worship supplanted that of the living and true God, they became uneasy under the restraints of the law. He fulfilled his righteous judgments, by giving them up to be destroyed. And where are they now as a nation, and what has become of their beautiful temple and their glory? Nay, further, Mr. Speaker, I venture to assert that there is not a nation on earth, where the great Jehovah is not respected by a due observance of the Sabbath, that the people can be said to be either prosperous or happy.

On a former occasion, when this subject was before Congress, I recollect that a prominent objection against granting the relief prayed for, was, that the nation was in a state of war, and that it became indispensable that every facility should be afforded to communication as well as transportation. Happily for this country this heavy judgment has been removed, and we are now at peace with all the world. A more favorable time may probably never occur to retrieve our national character, and wipe this foul reproach from our system. Let it not be said that our laws, relating to the Post Office, do not absolutely require that the Sabbath should be broken to carry them into effect. If evils exist which the Legislature can only remedy, and they omit to correct them, they must be deemed responsible for all their consequences.

I am aware, however, Mr. Speaker, that objections will be made to the amendment now proposed, by men of pleasure and amusement, by men of business, and by those who are burdened with the cares of State. The pleasure of hearing from friends; of receiving and communicating the earliest news; and of promoting worldly profits, will be deemed by many insuperable objections to the proposition which I have now submitted. But, sir, to every objection of this sort, it is enough for me to find what is the rule of duty. If the sanction of the Supreme lawgiver can be clearly discovered claiming the Sabbath for himself, and prohibiting worldly amusements and employments, our duty is clear, and the neglect of it is criminal. In that case we may not confer with flesh and blood; we are not left to consult our own pleasure and advantage; but we are bound to obey, and to trust the providence of God to provide for us in some other way. "Thus saith the Lord," is calculated to silence every objection, and lay the whole race of Adam at his footstool.

I beg leave further to remark, that if the mails are permitted freely to pass on the Sabbath, and the post offices to be opened for the delivery of letters and newspapers, the former will probably increase to disturb the worship of our solemn assemblies, while the latter may become, in some places, receptacles for those devoted to noise and riot. Sir, I wish to see this evil remedied before it has progressed so far as almost to defy the salutary restraints of municipal law; I wish to see the Sabbath rescued from violation and reproach.

In offering the present amendment, I hope no one will impute to me motives derived from selfishness or popularity. I am fully aware that the predominant passions of the human heart are all against me, and, having nearly closed my political life, I have nothing to hope for or expect from popular applause. I am always ambitious to obtain the approbation of the virtuous and the good; and, whether this attempt shall succeed or not, I ask no more of this honorable House than a belief that I have offered this amendment from a solemn conviction of duty, and that the best interests of our country demand such a measure at our hands. I have only one request further to make, which is, that the yeas and nays may be granted on the final decision of this question.

Mr. T.'s motion gave rise to a debate of considerable length, involving the arguments, pro and con. It was opposed by Mr. INGHAM, (chairman of the Post Office Committee,) because the subject of the motion was specially referred to that committee, on which they would very soon make a report, when the propriety of the measure might be argued. The motion was also opposed by Messrs. PICKERING, MILLS, of Massachusetts, JACKSON, HALL, and WRIGHT, for this and other reasons.

The motion was finally decided in the negative—yeas 35, nays 100, as follows:

YEAS—Messrs. Baylies, Brown, Champion, Comstock, Culpeper, Davenport, Hulbert, Jewett, Kent, Langdon, Law, Lovett, Lyle, Lyon, Maclay, Marsh, Milnor, Nelson of Massachusetts, Nelson of Virginia, Noyes, Pitkin, Reed, Rice, Southard, Stearns, Strong, Sturges, Taggart, Tallmadge, Vose, Ward of Massachusetts, Whiteside, Wilcox, Wilkin, and Wright.

NAYS—Messrs. Adgate, Alexander, Archer, Baker, Barbour, Bassett, Bateman, Birdsall, Blount, Boss, Breckenridge, Brooks, Burnside, Cady, Calhoun, Cannon, Chappell, Cilley, Clarke of North Carolina, Clayton, Clendennin, Condict, Conner, Cooper, Crawford, Creighton, Cuthbert, Darlington, Desha, Edwards, Forney, Forsyth, Gaston, Goldsborough, Goodwyn, Griffin, Grosvenor, Hale, Hall, Hammond, Hanson, Hardin, Hawes, Henderson, Herbert, Hopkinson, Hungerford, Ingham, Jackson, Johnson of Virginia,

Johnson of Kentucky, Kerr of Virginia, King of North Carolina, Lowndes, Lumpkin, Mason, Mayrant, McCoy, McKee, McLean of Kentucky, McLean of Ohio, Middleton, Mills, Moore, Newton, Ormsby, Parris, Pickens, Pickering, Piper, Powell, Randolph, Reynolds, Robertson, Root, Sergeant, Savage, Schenck, Sharpe, Sheffey, Smith of Pennsylvania, Smith of Maryland, Smith of Virginia, Stanford, Taul, Taylor, of New York, Taylor of South Carolina, Telfair, Thomas, Throop, Tucker, Wallace, Ward of New York, Ward of New Jersey, Wilde, Williams, Thomas Wilson, Woodward, Yancey, and Yates.

The House then, on motion of Mr. HALL, for reasons which he stated, agreed to reconsider the amendment which gives to the members of Congress the privilege of franking during the recess.

In the debate which ensued on this subject, the privilege of franking during the recess was advocated by Messrs. RANDOLPH, WRIGHT, GROSVENOR, and CULPEPER; and opposed by Messrs. HALL, COMSTOCK, and PICKERING. The debate was of a miscellaneous character, desultory but rather interesting. The principal argument against granting the privilege was, that it created at their homes, in private life, an odious and unjust distinction from other citizens, in favor of members of Congress. To this it was replied, besides the arguments obviously favoring the amendment, that this privilege was not comparable in magnitude to that of exemption from militia service already existing by law, and which no one would propose to abrogate, &c.

The amendment going to allow this privilege to members of Congress, was at length agreed to —yeas 74, nays 62, as follows:

YEAS—Messrs. Adgate, Atherton, Bateman, Baylies, Betts, Birdseye, Blount, Boss, Breckenridge, Burnside, Cady, Calhoun, Champion, Chappell, Cilley, Clarke of North Carolina, Condict, Conner, Cooper, Creighton, Culpeper, Gaston, Grosvenor, Hammond, Hanson, Hardin, Henderson, Hopkinson, Hulbert, Ingham, Jackson, Jewett, Johnson of Kentucky, King of North Carolina, Langdon, Law, Lewis, Love, Lovett, Lowndes, Marsh, Mason, Mayrant, McKee, McLean of Ohio, Middleton, Mills, Milnor, Newton, Noyes, Parris, Powell, Randolph, Reed, Reynolds, Robertson, Sergeant, Schenck, Sharp, Sheffey, Smith of Pennsylvania, Smith of Maryland, Sturges, Taggart, Taylor of New York, Taylor of South Carolina, Thomas, Throop, Ward of Massachusetts, Wilkin, Thomas Wilson, Wright Yancey, and Yates.

NAYS—Messrs. Archer, Baker, Barbour, Bassett, Bennett, Brooks, Clayton, Comstock, Crawford, Cuthbert, Darlington, Davenport, Desha, Edwards, Forney, Forsyth, Goldsborough, Goodwyn, Griffin, Hale, Hall, Hawes, Herbert, Hungerford, Johnson of Virginia, Kent, Kerr of Virginia, Lumpkin, Lyle, Lyon, Maclay, McCoy, McLean of Kentucky, Moore, Nelson of Virginia, Pickens, Pickering, Piper, Pitkin, Root, Savage, Smith of Virginia, Southard, Stanford, Stearns, Strong, Tallmadge, Taul, Telfair, Townsend, Tucker, Vose, Wallace, Ward of New York, Ward of New Jersey, Whiteside, Wilcox, Wilde, Williams, Willoughby, William Wilson, and Woodward.

Mr. GOLDSBOROUGH moved to insert in the bill the following section, as the fifth thereof, viz:

SEC. 5. *And be it further enacted,* That vessels

whose business is confined to bays and rivers, and to ports and places between which no regular and direct mail is carried by water, shall be excepted from the operation of the fourth and fifth sections of the act passed at the last session of Congress, entitled "An act in addition to an act regulating the Post Office Establishment."

And the question thereon being taken, it passed in the negative.

Several other amendments were proposed to the bill, which being rejected, the bill was ordered to be engrossed and read a third time on Monday next.

MONDAY, March 4.

Mr. SMITH, of Maryland, from the committee appointed on the petition of John M. Forbes, reported a bill for the relief of John M. Forbes; which was read twice and ordered to be engrossed and read the third time to-day, which was subsequently done, and the bill passed.

The bill in addition to the act to establish the Post Office Department was announced for a third reading, but recommitted to the Post Office Committee, for the purpose of receiving some trivial amendment.

The bill from the Senate for the relief of Richard Mitchell was twice read, and committed.

Mr. RANDOLPH, on the part of the committee appointed to inquire into the illegal traffic of slaves carried on through this District, asked and obtained authority to send for persons and papers relative to the inquiry.

COMPENSATION OF MEMBERS, &c.

Mr. JOHNSON, of Kentucky, said he considered it his duty to make a proposition to the House, the object of which was the despatch of public business, a more punctual attendance of the members of Congress to their duty, and to shorten the sessions of Congress, by changing the compensation of the members from six dollars per day into a gross sum for each session, and by other regulations connected with the subject, having the same tendency; and to deduct the compensation of members in proportion to their absence from the House during the session. The public business has been so protracted, that at the close of three months, no member could yet see, with any certainty, the termination of the session. This delay may be ascribed to a variety of causes: such as the accumulation of business after a war; the variety of sentiment on every subject; but to no cause could we ascribe so much the delay of business, as to the constant and never-ending debate on every subject that came before Congress for decision. On subjects of importance, difficulty, and complication, discussion was necessary and proper; and on such occasions it should always be indulged, without restraint, until the subject was thoroughly understood. In speaking of the proceedings of the House, he did not wish to be considered as casting censure upon any member; he spoke of the House as a body; he spoke of evils which were apparent to all, and it was the duty of all to put

an end to them. He could speak more freely of the necessity of reform in the proceedings of the House, because he did not pretend to inculpate himself less than others; on minor subjects, on detail, as to phraseology, and all amendments to bills and reports, it was the bounden duty of members to have confidence in each other, and not presume any to be unprepared to act. On the contrary, it should be admitted, as a matter of fact, that each member could judge for himself, and correctly, upon hearing the proposition made; and if any difficulty should exist as to matters of fact, a single inquiry of those whose duty it had been to examine them, would be all that should be required, in the way of conversation, and not in set speeches. In any such cases it would be a poor compliment to the capacity or attention of any member to suppose tedious examination necessary. Indeed we are very much mistaken if we presume that the silent members of the House (and they compose a majority) think less than those who speak most. Those who said but little were generally masters of the subject, understanding the principles and the *details* of a bill before it was acted upon. The House had adopted a rule that no member should speak more than twice on the same question. It was easy to evade the rule, by varying the question, and, indeed, the rule was nominal, for leave was always granted, when asked. The cry for the question was a kind of disorder that had no influence, because it was the duty of the Speaker, at all times, to suppress it, if a member was on the floor speaking. The inattention of the House to members speaking, had no greater influence, as it was not uncommon to see an interesting speaker occupying the floor, with an able speech, with a half dozen friends around him, listening, more out of courtesy, than a desire to have any doubts removed in relation to the subject. It is well known to the House that for several years past, particularly during the war, there was a universal disgust, clamor, and censure throughout the nation at our much talking and little action. The people had much reason on their side in this disgust, but they were not exactly acquainted with all the difficulties we had to encounter. It is, however, high time that Congress should be redeemed from imputations which have lessened very much the confidence of the people. It is also well known that daily and hourly we hear the entreaties of claimants, urging us to act upon their petition, until the applicants in many cases have to return home upon the bounty of friends, and continue to attend Congress many years, without a decision of their cases; and in most instances their claims were of the most meritorious character. To these inducements, Mr. J. said, a rule existed, known by the name of the previous question—a rule which would never be enforced but in the most extreme necessity; but, if it could be enforced, it would be effectual. But even in war, when we had such strong reason for it, very few members could be brought even to call it, and, when demanded, very seldom supported by the House;

and, if supported there, certain members to whom the rule was obnoxious, would call the ayes and noes, and put every obstacle in the way of progressing. From the experience of the House on this subject, all would agree that the previous question, however proper to be in the hands of a majority of the House, was a dead letter in time of peace. There must be some remedy for this evil, and what is so effectual as to give a gross sum of money by which members will be made attentive to business, and not adjourn any day at four o'clock, when such a course of conduct would be to deprive them of an adequate compensation, &c.; on the other hand to take away the imputation on members of remaining in session for the per diem; and it will hold out the inducement of a higher reward, in proportion to the industry of the House. Without this remedy Congress would, after a while, have to sit all the year, which would ultimately drive every man from Congress whose time was valuable to himself and family, and who was not wealthy enough to make such a sacrifice of time. In a few years, riches and not patriotism would rule the nation; whatever we have, let it be by the session and not by the day. We can do in three months what we fail to do in ten under the present arrangement. As soon as the Spring opens what do we witness? The farmer wishes to return to his family and farm; the mechanic to his shop; the lawyer to his courts; applications are daily made for leave of absence, until we are left with a bare quorum, and sometimes not that; we have to send for members, and those who stay are injured, and some ruined, and ultimately quit Congress from necessity.

The session should be reduced to three, and not extended to six months. In such a case its sacrifice would not be so great. If inquiry should be made in this stage of the business, what compensation should be given as a gross sum of money to each member, the answer would be easy: such a compensation as will not cost the United States one cent more, but by our industry might be more to us; give a member of Congress what you give to your Doorkeeper, your Sergeant-at-Arms, and it will be better than the present system. Nothing extravagant, nothing prodigal; a compensation received by a good clerk in one of the departments would be sufficient: give what we may, the compensation should be in a gross sum, and not a compensation by the day. Mr. J. said the effect of this change would produce three results: 1st. It would lessen the duration of the session; 2d. It would give the members greater compensation if they acted with industry; 3d. It would save money to the nation, by lessening the contingent expenses of the House in fuel, stationery, and attendance, which was now very great. But it may be asked, should a gross sum operate upon members of Congress to be more industrious, as it would upon the day laborer, and he who worked by the job? Mr. J. said he had no doubt on the subject, and it was no disgrace to members to say that they could be operated upon like other men. In a Government like ours, we

should avoid extravagance, so we should extreme parsimony. In relation to the Representatives of a free people, he thought they should be actuated from patriotic, and not sordid motives; and a reasonable compensation was all they should have. But a member of Congress who represents thirty-five thousand free men would feel himself degraded, and so would the people, if such was the reward as to drive from Congress all but the rich and the favored few. Mr. J. then moved the following resolution:

Resolved, That a committee be appointed to inquire into the expediency of changing the present mode of compensation to the members of Congress into a gross sum for each session; and to report such other provisions as may have a tendency to the despatch of public business, and to compel the punctual attendance of members of Congress during the session.

Mr. RANDOLPH expressed his hope the resolve would be adopted, and carried into complete effect. In moving it, he said, the gentleman from Kentucky had acted with a manliness which became his character; with a frankness and independence which deserves not only the thanks of this body, but the approbation of the nation. The situation in which members of Congress were placed, growing out of the manner in which they were compensated for their public services, was, he said, disgraceful to them individually, as well as a great public detriment. Was it wonderful, he asked, that they should be considered by the people at large in the light of day laborers, who work here for something less than a dollar an hour; for something more perhaps than you have to pay a man for sawing wood? He premised, with a solemn assurance of his sincerity in the declaration, that his opinion was now, and always had been, that the members of this and the other branch of the Government ought to receive no pay at all. This, he said, he knew to be an unpopular sentiment, but he sincerely entertained it. But, if the members were to receive pay, he would have them paid like gentlemen; because members of Congress ought to be gentlemen—they ought to be, and he trusted they were, in principle—not merely in their exterior, but in their high sense of honor, in a character which scorns, which spurns, to do that which is mean and base. In this point of view, Mr. R. said, he was decidedly in favor of the proposition of the gentleman from Kentucky. Mr. R. here took a discursive view of the course and origin of the Committee of Accounts, and of an attempt on the part of the Senate some years ago to establish a difference in the rates of payment between members of the Senate and the other House. A member of Congress, he went on to say, was as much entitled to his pay for the day he does not attend as for the day he does attend: it was not to be presumed, because he was not in his seat, that he was idle. His business, he said, was not merely to come here to write and frank so many letters, read so many newspapers, and stitch together so many documents as he daily finds on his table; to adjourn whenever the index of the clock pointed to four o'clock, and pass the remainder of the four and twenty hours in a perfect abstraction of mind and body from labor and exertion. No, Mr. R. said, even Sunday shone no Sabbath day for him; and yet, his account with the public for his services when a member heretofore, to this day remained unsettled, because he could not undertake to say to the Committee of Accounts how many days he had been absent, &c. This is a sort of economy he condemned—would they think of subtracting from the compensation of the head of a Department so much for every day he did not go to his office? A member of Congress, if he deserved to come at all, Mr. R. said, had no compensation for his services in the miserable pittance which the Government now allows, &c. He hoped this motion would pass, and that another reform would take place in the mode of doing business in the House; that was, by allowing days for business in the House, and leaving other days for doing business out of the House, &c. The present system might do, said he, for mercenary soldiers, for day laborers; but not for men of our time of life and of our state. With respect to devising any mode of forcing the attendance of members, he was afraid no better could be devised than that which exists; the compulsory process, stopping wages, &c., treating the members of this House like livery servants, would not do. Mr. R. concluded his remarks by saying he had sometimes reflected with pain on the gradual depreciation of the value of a seat in this House, since he first had the honor of a seat in it. Members then made no sacrifices of the dignity of their station, and of their own personal dignity. If they had not possessed native dignity, they acquired it from their stations; they felt themselves the Representatives each of thirty thousand souls. They thought it beneath them in those days, he said, to truckle to the great or to the small vulgar; to curry favor even with great officers of State, either foreign or domestic; much less with printers of journals, newspapers, &c.

Mr. STANFORD rose to enter his protest against any increase of the compensation of members of Congress; against offering such emoluments as would induce men of abilities to prefer offices and stations under the General Government to those under the State Governments. He would diminish rather than increase the compensation of the members of this House. He was willing to change the mode of compensation, but not in any way so as to increase it. The depreciation of money was, he said, a great and just complaint; but any change contemplating an increase of the compensation of the members, he thought, would be a change essentially to the mischief of principle. He was willing to change the mode of compensation; because in such a change there might be both economy and advantage.

Mr. RANDOLPH again rose. He said that whenever he differed from the gentleman last up, he doubted the correctness of his own judgment, so great reliance had he on that of that honorable gentleman. The resolution before the House did not speak of increase at all, but of a change in the mode of compensation. And, he asked, ought it

not to be changed? Was it not an allegation every day presented to their eyes in the public prints, that the sessions of Congress were protracted for the convenience of some members who saved four dollars a day out of six? Mr. R. said he could conceive nothing worse than giving pay not adequate to the support of a member of this House, as he ought to live, and yet very adequate to the support, and profit too, of a man who lives as a member of this House ought not to live. This was the very surest mode that could be fixed on to make them tools of the Executive. He did not mean to speak of the present members, but he knew, he said, that in old times there were members who did live as members ought not to live, and there were members who laid up a very considerable sum by the end of the session, which they carried home with them in round eagles and half eagles, and not in rags. Ambition, "the infirmity of noble minds," might bring a man here, he said, but he seldom served long, because a proper regard to his private affairs would not authorize him to do so. The consequence had been, he added, that young men, not destitute of capacity, certainly, nor, perhaps, of education, but of anything that constitutes statesmen, had stept into the chair of this House, to the heads of committees; and to their genius, if you will, but nothing like wisdom, are the destinies of this nation committed; and by the time they form some tolerable notion of the affairs of Government, they, too, are obliged to go home, and their place is supplied by another brood, equally callow and unfledged. If the State governments did not pay their officers properly, Mr. R. said he had no objection to offer such compensation to their men of talents as should compel the State governments to loose their niggard purse-strings. In speaking of Legislatures, Mr. R. said, we see, about November, about the time the fogs set in, men enough assembled in the various Legislatures, General and State, to make a regiment; then the legislative maggot begins to bite; then exists the rage to make new, and repeal old laws. He said he should not think we should find ourselves at all worse off if no law of a general nature had been passed by either General or State governments for ten or twelve years last past. Like Mr. Jefferson, he said, he was averse to too much regulation—averse to making the extreme medicine of the Constitution our daily food. He referred to the depreciation of paper as being a standing violation of the Constitution, (where it provides that the compensation of judges shall not be diminished during their continuance in office,) and intimated that an attempt had been lately made to induce the Chief Justice (Marshall) to accept his salary in the paper of this District, &c. The salaries of the officers of the Government were notoriously scanty; and though he would rather see the salary a disgrace to the man, than the man a disgrace to the office, he would give the public servants such salaries as would enable them to live without the imputation of dishonor. For, he asked, what man can live here on five thousand dollars a year? He may breathe on it.

But who can keep a family, rent a house, furnish it, keep an equipage, give and receive entertainments on that annual amount? A five-penny bit would be just as adequate to that purpose, both being notoriously incompetent. A man so situated may have no patrimonial estate; he may be *sui fortuna faber*—have sprung from the Lord knows where, and be without resources. If he lives as he ought in his station, the imputation is, that he wants money, and must have it, and that he has the means of coming at it directly or indirectly. If he had no other object, he said, in increasing the compensation of the members, if he could thereby compel the State governments to rescue their officers from the situation in which they were placed, he would do it. We have a right, said he, to go into market and bid against them. When we want a lawyer in an important case, do we go to him who will do our business for fifteen shillings, or to the Emmetts, the Tazewells, the Pinkneys, the Wickhams? When our personal interest is concerned we apply to master workmen, not to those who will job for us at six dollars a day.

Mr. WEBSTER said, the resolution presenting no question but that of inquiry, in that view he should concur in it. There was, he said, something radically defective in the present system of legislation. No Legislature in the world, he believed, however various its concerns, or extensive its sphere, sat as long as this, notwithstanding that its sphere of operation was so greatly contracted by the intervention of eighteen distinct Legislatures. The system does not compel, on the part of members, that attention which the nature of their public business requires. He referred to the letters and papers on the desks of the members every day. They ought to have none of them. When a man came into this House, he ought to leave on the threshold every feeling and thought but what was connected with the public service. Private letters and private conversation ought not to be permitted to encroach on the unity of his object. If, in any way, the attention of the House could be fixed on the speaker, Mr. W. said there would be an end to long speeches; for he defied any man to address any assembly of this sort, and address them long, if that attention was fixed on him. They would cease to speak when they ceased to have anything to say on anything or subject under debate. Mr. W. maintained that, under proper regulations, a session of two months in a year was perfectly adequate to the ordinary business of legislation. He expressed no opinion whether the compensation of members should be increased or diminished; but he was willing to inquire whether the mode of compensation could not be beneficially changed.

Mr. STANFORD said he had no idea of opposing this motion for inquiry when up before, but had merely risen to protest against any increase of compensation. The inquiry he thought proper. He believed such a change might be devised as would economize both the time and the funds of the nation.

The resolution was then agreed to without opposition; and Messrs. JOHNSON, of Kentucky, WEBSTER, PITKIN, JACKSON, GROSVENOR, YATES, McLEAN, of Ohio, were appointed the committee.

DIRECT TAX.

The amendment of the Senate to the bill to reduce the direct tax on the United States to three millions, and continue the same one year, was taken up for consideration.

The amendment made by the Senate was merely to provide, that where a State shall assume the payment of its quota of the direct tax and shall fail to pay it, then the Secretary of the Treasury shall direct the United States officers to proceed to assess and collect the same.

Mr. STANFORD moved to amend the amendment by placing in the President of the United States a discretionary power to suspend the assessment in the cases referred to, if in his opinion it should be found expedient.

This motion was opposed by Mr. RANDOLPH and Mr. JACKSON, and rejected without a voice in its favor.

Mr. HANSON, then, after stating his objections to the bill because it had not been modified in the Senate, as he hoped, into the form of a permanent tax, in which shape only it could be extensively useful to the nation, moved (with a view to repeal the direct tax in toto) to postpone this bill indefinitely, and thereon demanded the yeas and nays.

The motion was decided in the negative, without debate, as follows:

YEAS—Messrs. Atherton, Baylies, Boss, Bradbury, Brown, Champion, Goldsborough, Grosvenor, Hale, Hanson, Hopkinson, Jewett, King of Massachusetts, Langdon, Lewis, Lyon, Marsh, Mason, Noyes, Pickering, Pitkin, Randolph, Reed, Smith of Pennsylvania, Strong, Sturges, Tallmadge, Tate, Vose, Webster, Wheaton, and Wilcox—32.

NAYS—Messrs. Adgate, Alexander, Baker, Barbour, Bassett, Bateman, Bennett, Betts, Blount, Breckenridge, Brooks, Burnside, Cady, Calhoun, Cannon, Chappell, Cilley, Clarke of North Carolina, Clark of Kentucky, Clayton, Clopton, Comstock, Condict, Conner, Cooper, Crawford, Creighton, Culpeper, Cuthbert, Darlington, Davenport, Desha, Edwards, Forney, Forsyth, Gaston, Goodwyn, Griffin, Hall, Hammond, Hardin, Hawes, Henderson, Huger, Hulbert, Hungerford, Ingham, Irving of New York, Jackson, Johnson of Virginia, Johnson of Kentucky, Kent, Kerr of Virginia, King of North Carolina, Lowndes, Lumpkin, Lyle, Maclay, Mayrant, McCoy, McKee, McLean, of Kentucky, McLean of Ohio, Middleton, Milnor, Moore, Nelson of Massachusetts, Nelson of Virginia, Newton, Ormsby, Parris, Piper, Powell, Robertson, Root, Ross, Savage, Sharpe, Sheffey, Smith of Maryland, Smith of Virginia, Southard, Stanford, Taggart, Taul, Taylor, of New York, Telfair, Thomas, Townsend, Tucker, Wallace, Ward, of New York, Ward of New Jersey, Wendover, Whiteside, Wilde, Williams, Willoughby, Thomas Wilson, William Wilson, and Woodward—101.

Mr. RANDOLPH then, after disclaiming any disposition to embarrass or delay the public business by the motion, moved to postpone the subject until to-morrow, but subsequently withdrew his motion to make way for one by Mr. GASTON.

Mr. Gaston moved that the bill, as it was returned from the Senate, should be recommitted to the Committee of Ways and Means. Notwithstanding he was in favor of the land tax, as necessary to preserve the public faith, and to perfect the system of taxation, and had hoped that the other branch of the Legislature would have been able to restore the bill to its original character; yet, as the system had been broken up by the limitation of the tax to one year, and believing the revenue would eventually be reduced to the actual expenditures of the country, he wished the whole subject again referred to the committee which originally reported it, with a view to attempt the entire repeal of the tax.

Mr. Lowndes thought the motion entirely irregular, inasmuch as it was properly impracticable to recommit a bill whose provisions had been assented to by both branches of the Legislature. He submitted it to the gentleman himself, as well as the Speaker, whether such a course was proper after the bill had reached its present stage; and if any amendment, which could be proposed by the Committee of Ways and Means, would be in order after the principle had been fully acted on by both Houses.

Mr. Gaston, in reply, said it was perfectly immaterial whether any amendment could be acted on or not. The motion was made to try whether a majority of the House was willing to repeal the tax altogether, or keep it on as a permanent tax; there would be no difficulty in finding a way of carrying their decision into effect.

Mr. Sheffey avowed himself in favor of a total repeal of the tax, but could not see how that object could be effected by recommitting the bill; because the committee could report no amendment which could with propriety be acted on. Both Houses have agreed that a tax of three millions shall be imposed, and a committee of one House could not now properly recommend a repeal of it. Besides, the question had just been tried to postpone the bill indefinitely, and rejected by a large majority.

Mr. Goldsborough likewise desired a repeal of the direct tax, if it could be done consistently with the obligations of the Government. There were various modes, he said, by which the object could be yet effected, and amongst them the motion to recommit was perfectly regular; for if the Committee of Ways and Means should, on reconsideration, think the tax was unnecessary, they could report such propositions as would effect a repeal.

Mr. Hardin had been in favor of an entire repeal of the land tax; but, not being able to get that, had favored the smallest amount proposed. He could say with confidence, that three-fourths of the Senators who voted against the tax, did so because it was not made permanent; and if we lose this bill, said he, I am afraid we shall be saddled with a tax of six millions. Who made the present motion? A gentleman in favor of a permanent direct tax. This excited his suspicions; and fearing that the repeal of the tax could not be now effected, he should vote against the mo-

tion to recommit the bill. In fact, he considered the motion not in order; but, if the gentleman would propose to effect the repeal in any other way, he would go with him.

Mr. Gaston again explained his view in making the motion, which was simply to try the disposition of the House; but as those who were in favor of repeal were averse to his motion, he would withdraw it.

Mr. Randolph then renewed his motion to lay the bill on the table until to-morrow; which was decided in the negative—ayes 62, nays 67.

Mr. Randolph then rose, and among other general remarks said, there was no question more susceptible of proof than that this tax of three millions was not wanted for any purpose of finance; and had no doubt it would be allowed, although insisted on now, to terminate with the next session. If, however, it was determined to raise the amount contemplated, he trusted the House would not persist in the present mode; although, Mr. R. said, he preferred the land tax, when necessary, to any other internal tax. But, much as he was opposed to loans, he would rather authorize the Government to borrow these three millions than vex the people with such a tax for one year only. After some further remarks on the impropriety of the present policy of the majority in regard to large expenditures, &c., he moved that the bill be laid on the table; that measures might be taken in concert with the Senate for a total repeal of the direct tax.

This motion was decided in the negative—ayes 63, nays 67.

The House then agreed to the amendment of the Senate. The bill is therefore passed.

NATIONAL BANK.

The House resolved itself into a Committee of the Whole on the bill to incorporate the subscribers to the National Bank.

Mr. Smith, of Maryland, moved to strike out of the sixth section the words "Treasury notes," as forming a constituent part of the Government subscriptions to the bank, the effect of which amendment would be to limit the mode of payment of the subscription to stock and specie.

The motion was supported by Mr. Smith, assented to by Mr. Calhoun, and opposed by Mr. Hopkinson; and then agreed to without a division.

Mr. Smith then moved further to amend the same section by making the amount of the shares reserved to the Government receivable in stock bearing an interest of five instead of six per cent., with the view also of providing subsequently that the whole subscription of the Government shall be made on the 1st of January, 1817, instead of being paid in instalments, at distant dates.

After some objection on the part of Mr. Webster, the motion was agreed to—ayes 63, noes 40.

The bill was subsequently amended so as to make its provisions correspond with the preceding amendments.

After the adoption of some other amendments, involving no principle—

Mr. PITKIN moved to strike out of the tenth section so much as gives to the President and Senate the power of appointing five directors of the bank.

This motion was supported by Messrs. PITKIN, WARD of Massachusetts, HOPKINSON, McKEE, HUGER, SHEFFEY, ROSS, and GROSVENOR; and opposed by Messrs. SMITH of Maryland, CALHOUN, TUCKER, and ROBERTSON.

The reporter can only generalize the argument. On the one hand, it was said this control over the bank would be an engine in the hands of the Government which might be used in a manner dangerous to the best interests of the country; that this feature would be pernicious to the interests of the bank, which would be best managed without the interference of the Government; that the reservation of this power would be of no advantage to the Government, (except that it would tend to increase Executive patronage, already much too extensive,) as every necessary investigation could be made into the state of the institution, without the aid of this power; that the Government would have quite as much influence over the bank as it ought to have, without this power being given to it; that the principle would be most odious to moneyed men, and of such an inquisitorial character as would deter many of our most respectable citizens from embarking in the institution, &c. On the other hand, it was contended by gentlemen in favor of retaining the provision, that it was necessary as well to guard the public interest, as to secure a just administration of the affairs of the bank as regarded the public, that a proportion of the direction should be appointed by the Government; that it was certainly not unfair that the Government should stand on a footing with the individual stockholders, by having a share in the direction of the bank; that such a feature existed in the charters of many State banking institutions, and was not abused as far as was known; that this power could not be dangerous either to the bank of the nation, as the twenty directors appointed by the individuals would always be competent to control the five appointed by the Government; some State banks were cited, in which the State possessed an entire control, from which no disadvantage had been realized; and as the selection by the Government in this case would certainly be made with a reference to the wealth and respectability of the persons chosen, no abuse ought to be anticipated, any more than it could succeed if attempted.

Before deciding the question, the Committee rose, and obtained leave to sit again.

TUESDAY, March 5.

Mr. WARD, of Massachusetts, presented a petition of sundry merchants of Boston, interested as owners and shippers in certain vessels which have sailed since the peace for British ports in the East Indies, praying that the provisions of the proposed new tariff duties, as regards the importation of cotton goods from India may not be extended to such goods as may arrive under orders sent out in said vessels, or that such provisions may be adopted as will protect them against the evils of which they complain.—Referred to the Committee of Ways and Means.

Mr. MILNOR presented a petition of U. P. Levy, praying a remuneration of expenses incurred by him in prosecuting and bringing to justice a band of pirates.

Mr. MIDDLETON presented a petition of John Philip Wilhemi, a citizen of the United States, praying permission to import from the West Indies a number of negro slaves, the property of the petitioner.—Referred to the Committee of Commerce and Manufactures.

Mr. EASTON presented a petition of John P. Maxwell and Hugh H. Maxwell, praying to be permitted to inherit a landed estate of which their uncle died possessed, leaving no other heirs in America, which they are prevented from doing because they were not citizens of the United States at the time of the death of their said uncle, although they were in the United States and gave notice of their intention to become citizens thereof previous to that event.—Referred to the Committee on Public Lands.

Mr. HOPKINSON, from a select committee, reported a bill for the relief of Bible Societies in the United States; (exempting from duty all plates, &c. imported for such societies;) which was twice read and committed.

On motion of Mr. EASTON, the Committee on the Public Lands were instructed to inquire into the expediency of providing by law for the appointment of a surveyor of lands of the United States, for the Territories of Illinois and Missouri.

On motion of Mr. GOLDSBOROUGH, the Secretary of the Treasury was directed to lay before this House a statement, showing the valuation of real property and slaves, in the city of Baltimore, and in each county of the State of Maryland, the quota or amount of direct tax apportioned to the said city and each of the said counties, and the rate of tax on the one hundred dollars assessed property, agreeably to the valuation and apportionment made under the act entitled "An act for the assessment and collection of direct taxes and internal duties," passed July 22, 1813, and the act entitled "An act to lay and collect a direct tax within the United States," passed August 2d, 1813; and a similar statement of the valuation, apportionment, and rate of tax under the act entitled "An act to provide additional revenues for defraying the expenses of Government and maintaining the public credit, by laying a direct tax upon the United States, and to provide for assessing and collecting the same," passed on the 9th of January, 1815; so as to exhibit a comparative view of the valuation, apportionment, and rate of tax in the said city and each of the said counties, under the several acts above-mentioned; also, the names of the principal assessors within the said State for the year 1815, and the counties embraced within their respective districts, and such further statement of the transactions of the board of principal assessors within the said State, as reported to the Treasury Department, as will show what changes, if any, have been made by them in the relative valuation of property in any of the said counties, and the principles on which they have proceeded in performing the duties required of them by the act last above-mentioned.

A message from the Senate informed the House that the Senate have passed the bill "making appropriations for ordnance and ordnance stores for the year 1816," with amendments; and they have passed a bill "for the relief of Edward Wilson; also, a bill "to increase the pension of William Munday;" in which amendments and bill they ask the concurrence of this House.

The bill from the Senate "for the relief of Edward Wilson," was read twice and referred to the Committee on the Public Lands.

The bill from the Senate "to increase the pension of William Munday," was read twice and committed to a Committee of the Whole.

The House took up the amendments proposed by the Senate to the bill "making appropriations for ordnance and ordnance stores, for the year 1816," which were read and referred to the Committee of Ways and Means.

NATIONAL BANK.

The House then again resolved itself into a Committee of the Whole, on the National Bank bill; the question to strike out the provision giving to the President and Senate the power of appointing five of the directors, being still under consideration.

On this question the debate was resumed and continued to a late hour, before the decision took place. The gentlemen who supported the amendment were Messrs. GASTON and PICKERING; and those who opposed it, were Messrs. WILDE, TELFAIR, WRIGHT, CLAY, CALHOUN, and FORSYTH. The ground taken was substantially the same as that already stated, but illustrated and enforced by various arguments, which gave much interest to the debate.

In the course of the day an amendment was adopted, on motion of Mr. CONDICT, to confine the selection of directors to be made by the President and Senate, to persons holding stock in the bank.

On motion of Mr. SMITH of Maryland, an amendment was also adopted, to prevent more than three of the directors appointed by the President and Senate from being taken from any one State.

The main question was at length taken, about 4 o'clock, on Mr. PITKIN's motion to exclude the Government from the appointment of any of the directors, and decided in the negative—for the amendment 64, against it 79.

The Committee then rose, reported progress, and obtained leave to sit again.

The following are the only remarks which we have been enabled to find on the above question.

Mr. FORSYTH said, he was one of those who was unfortunate enough to attach great importance to that part of the plan of the bank which was intended to be altered by the motion of the gentleman from Connecticut. At the last session

of Congress he had in vain endeavored to convince the members composing it, of the necessity of retaining such an influence over the management of the institution. The honorable gentleman from North Carolina (Mr. GASTON) had suggested, that the opposition to the amendment proposed came from the Treasury Department, or from the Executive. He begged leave to assure him, that the recommendation or opinion of the Department, or of the President, was not the foundation of his belief of the necessity of this measure. Although he did not expect to satisfy others who differed with him, of the incorrectness of their views of the subject, he did hope to be able to show at least plausible reasons in favor of his own. At the last session of Congress he had the honor to advocate, with a zeal arising from a thorough conviction of the necessity of the measure, the establishment of a bank differing from the present, because it imposed an obligation to make a large loan to Government. He had to regret that the ability with which that duty was discharged was not equal to his zeal, and still more, that his exertions were not crowned with success. It would have produced at least one good effect—this discussion would have been avoided, and the time occupied in it might have been usefully employed on a different subject. This plan failed, for causes which it was unnecessary to trace, and its failure was rendered comparatively unimportant by the restoration of peace. He did not believe, with some gentlemen, that this measure was now necessary. The necessity for it had ceased. It was no longer essential, but it was both politic and prudent to adopt it. If it fails, no dangerous consequences will result from its failure. He should survive the shock, although this bill should follow its predecessor to the tomb. The body politic was obstructed by a diseased circulation, but time would furnish a healing remedy, although the application of this panacea should be rejected by the State physicians. Mr. F. said, he did not wish to be understood as recommending the establishment of any bank as prudent and politic; it was not a bank, but a bank of a peculiar character which was required. We had banks enough already; they rose like mushrooms from every hotbed in the country; it was not a moneyed bank only—a bank exclusively regulated by the moneyed interest, and governed by the jealousy, avarice, or factious views of moneyed men, capable of being made the instrument of artful and designing combinations, to cramp your resources, and destroy your capacity to make either permanent or temporary loans—it must be a bank having a national character, regulated by the national interest, and under the influence of the national councils. If it was not of this character, its failure or success was indifferent to him. It seemed to be admitted on all hands, that we ought to have an interest in the proposed institution. It was admitted, too, that we ought to have an influence, and the dispute was between a direct influence by the appointment of directors, or an indirect influence by the operation of the revenue system. It would not be difficult to demonstrate, that an indirect influence would be altogether insufficient. Your seven millions of interest in the capital gives you no power, unless it is coupled with the authority to appoint a portion of the directors. This, it is said, must not be given, because you have ample influence by means of your revenue system. What difference will be produced by the establishment of this new plan? Will your direct influence over it be greater than over the State institutions? You may withhold your deposites; so you may from the State banks; you may refuse to receive its paper in payment of taxes or imposts; you may refuse the paper of the State banks; you may tax either at your pleasure. After this plan is perfected, the annulment of the charter is for twenty years as completely beyond your authority as the annihilation of the State banks. The sole difference is, that at the end of twenty years the Bank of the United States will be dependent on you for a renewal of its charter, while the State banks look only to the State Legislatures. Your power, then, over the present banks is equally great with your power over the one proposed. An honorable gentleman from New York (Mr. GROSVENOR) has told you, and truly told you, that when you threaten the State banks they laugh at your threats—when you menace them, they menace you in turn. If a mere local institution cannot be beneficially controlled by your indirect influence, how can you expect to affect an institution extending through the whole community, which combines the great moneyed capital of all the States into one solid column of power? It seems, however, to be imagined, a direct control is unnecessary. The keen magnetic sense of the directors will always induce them to pursue their own interest, and their interest will always produce a compliance with the reasonable wishes of the Government. This sense was too magnetic for Mr. F.'s taste; it pointed with unerring polarity to self, and the general interest, when in conflict with self-interest, did not produce even a vibration of the needle. Besides, there was such a thing as the sacrifice of pecuniary to political interest or party policy. This institution might, in the course of time, fall into the hands of men who would think it immoral and criminal to loan their money for the necessary purposes of Government. What would be the situation of the country in such an event, at a time when this institution furnished the great mass of the medium of circulation? It was to guard against such an event an immediate interest in the direction was necessary; there was a greater probability of finding eight reasonable and virtuous men out of twenty, than thirteen out of twenty-five. Mr. F. regretted that the number of directors to be appointed by Government was not greater; and also the amendment which prevented the President from appointing more than three at the seat of the mother bank; but he supposed he must be satisfied with it as it stood, as there was little hope of obtaining more. It was objected, however, that moneyed men would not like the introduction of this direct

influence. This was perfectly natural. Moneyed men have no objection to manage your funds for their benefit, but have no desire to admit your influence in the management of theirs. But will the introduction of this principle prevent the subscription of the capital from being filled? No gentleman had or would venture to predict such an effect. They will no doubt make wry faces, but the bitter pill would be swallowed if it was well gilded. Arguments had been urged against this part of the plan, founded upon the supposition that improper appointments would be made. The President and Senate had not the same information to enable them to choose proper directors. Stockholders were better judges of the necessary qualifications of directors. Corrupt men would solicit and procure these appointments for improper purposes. Great injury would result to the bank from their success. They would procure for themselves and friends accommodations to which they were not entitled. A slight examination of these arguments would show their fallacy. Intelligence and integrity were the qualifications required in directors. The same ability existed to ascertain who possessed them, for this as for all other offices. The President and Senate can command or procure the most accurate information of the character of persons who are thought of for these appointments, from every source to which it may be necessary to apply. Is it not passing strange that a man, who has raked up money from every kennel into which he may have dipped his fingers, is, from that circumstance, a better judge of the proper person for a director than the President and Senate; that a stupid fellow, who has blundered into a fortune in New Orleans or Providence, should be able to procure better information of the character and circumstances of individuals than the President residing at Washington, and the Senators coming from the several States. These men, however, who intend to swindle the bank, will worm themselves into the good graces of the President, and receive the appointment. After their appointment, paper will be discounted having their names upon it, which ought not to be discounted, because the extreme delicacy of the other directors will not permit them to object to it. This morbid delicacy, too, is to be found in persons chosen by the keen-sighted individual stockholders, who are the best judges of the persons competent to manage their concerns. Such is the argument. It supposes folly in the President and Senate who make the appointments; corruption in the persons seeking to be appointed; and stupidity and criminality in the other directors, in permitting this folly and corruption of the choosers and the chosen to injure the institution.

Mr. F. asked, what advantages could be derived from this institution if this amendment prevails, which could not be produced through the agency of the State banks? It is admitted that the great object of this bill, the restoration of specie payments, might be effected by a rigorous system of measures against the State institutions. Mr. F. said, he did not feel that indignation against the State banks for stopping the payment of specie, which had been expressed by others. His indignation had been so thoroughly exhausted upon the smugglers of English goods, and the cash dealers in British Government bills for the use of the Canadian army, that he had none left for the banks who had loaned their notes to their own Government, who, in consequence of an extraordinary emission of their paper, had been under the necessity of dishonoring it. He was not, however, the apologist of the banks for withholding specie payments since the restoration of peace. It was, however, certain, that no one bank could, without ruin, resume the payment of specie. The resumption must be simultaneous. He had no objection to any system which should induce the banks to perform their obligations in this regard to the community; but he protested against the cruelty and injustice of any rigorous measures which should compel them immediately either to sell their Government stocks or to curtail their discounts. It was saying to these banks, you have loaned us too much of your paper; you have made too much money out of the General Government; your paper has, indeed, performed the trifling service of carrying us triumphantly through a dangerous conflict, but we are not now in want of a further accommodation; you must take in your paper; you must sell your stock; you must disgorge your gains; you must resume your specie payments. And what will be the consequence of all this? They are forced to sell their stock; it goes into market, and its price is depressed. Are you in a situation to buy—to take advantage of this disgorging of their unrighteous gains? Far from it; you cannot be benefitted—you cannot enter as a competitor into the market. And who are the gainers by this system of rigor? The hard-money men, who withhold their money in the hour of your necessity and peril; who combined together for the purpose of defeating your loans. Mr. F. begged the House, if these banks were to be punished, to wait until the Government, who had been the sufferer, should be prepared to take advantage of their punishment. At all events, to be so cautious in their castigation, that, in punishing puny, petty speculation, they do not reward the vilest of all gamblers, those who staked their money against the safety of your empire; who sought to destroy you by cramping your resources; who sought to beggar the country, that an Administration might be ruined.

Mr. TELFAIR observed, that the great cause of difference of opinion on this question, seemed to arise from a misapprehension of those who advocated the amendment, as to the primary objects for which this institution is designed. Gentlemen argue as though the moving cause for the establishment of a National Bank was the interest of the individuals who may become subscribers, and that the Government has but one interest, and that is, the attainment of the highest possible bonus.

In this view of the subject, I must be permitted totally to differ from those who are disposed to deprive the Government of all participation in its direction. Did I deem it practicable to manage such an institution without greater liabilities to corruption of its principles, I should most decidedly prefer one whose stock was exclusively the property of the nation. But it requires no great political sagacity, and but ordinary experience to ascertain, that those institutions which derive their principle of action from private interest, are more active in pursuit of their object, more vigilant in the detection of error, and more likely to prosper, than those which derive their impulse from the spirit of patriotism, and have in contemplation solely the public good. Private interest is ever more active, more vigilant, more pervading, more alive to its object, than national; which is more sluggish, because its direction is towards remote or general good, less quicksighted, because its instinct is not so strong.

This institution is designed not merely to fulfil the ordinary purposes of banks of discount; it aspires to great national objects; it contemplates a restoration of the legitimate currency of the country; its end is to give an uniform and valuable medium to the whole empire; its design is to facilitate the fiscal operations of the Treasury Department. It is, in one word, to restore to this Government the rightful and Constitutional control over the national medium, which is vested in every civilized Government, and which was intended to be vested in the Congress of the United States, when to it was assigned the supervisorship of the Mint establishment. These are the primary and essential objects of its creation; from the attainment of these great objects, certainly, benefits flow to every class of the community; but exclusive benefits are designed by none, save so much as may be deemed necessary to the obtention of these ends, and conformable to these results.

According to these views, then, the interest of the stockholders is not to be considered as holding a priority of station to that of the Government; on the contrary, the institution is to be looked upon as the property of the nation, and that individuals for political considerations, viz., because their aid will facilitate, or, if you please, is necessary to participate in its immediate profits—that characterizes the schemes of individual pursuit—that while its capacities and controlling power be national, its impulse, its life and animation, shall be private interest. But private interest, unrestrained, naturally produces much mischief. I have admitted that a bank, exclusively managed by the Government, would be exposed to a corruption of its principle; and with so many facts to support me, while casting an eye upon the numberless banks around, I certainly shall not be charged with overweening suspicion, when asserting that banks, too exclusively managed by stockholders, are liable to become instruments of public evil from the invitations of self-interest.

The true policy in the creation of a bank, then, is to give it a double character—to combine in it the elements of public and private interest—but to secure to the former a control over the latter; for the Government which creates this institution is responsible for its fulfilment of the great objects of its creation; and it is wiser to use means of precaution, than to rest upon ultimate means of severe correction. But the gentleman from North Carolina, (Mr. GASTON,) who has certainly spoken with ability on this subject, is satisfied with the incidental powers and benefits which the Government would derive from this bank. And this brings me to two objections which have been urged—first, an indiscriminate dread is felt of the influence of the Government over this institution, provided it participates in its direction. In what way, let me ask, can the influence of the Government be injurious? Is it presumable that the influence of the Government would induce the bank to loan individuals who were incapable of repaying the debt? Can it be believed that the Government would ever descend, by its influence over the bank, to benefit one class of individuals by loans, while it oppresses another by refusing to extend these benefits? Or can it be imagined that the Government, which is so deeply interested in preserving an uniform and valuable currency, would, in ordinary circumstances, induce the bank to make over issues, and thereby cause a depreciation of its paper? I presume not; these are apprehensions too fantastic to be ascribed to men of sense; they are absurdities too great for them to ascribe to a Government as enlightened as ours; but if they mean that the Government, under the pressure of trying emergencies, may by their influence induce loans from the bank, which prudence in ordinary times would forbid them to make, I shall not deny the probability, but must be permitted to answer there are, or may be periods during a nation's travail, when exertions of such means would be attended with less evil than a want of money; and as this objection has reference to an extreme case, I an willing to await the crisis. But their second objection, which is not a little inconsistent with the first, is, that the President will appoint ignorant, inefficient, and needy directors. What weight, then, could these directors possess? But let us approach this objection a little nearer, and look it in the face. Why is the presumption indulged, that the President will be thus injudicious? Has he not the same respectable class of merchants from whom to make his selection as the stockholders have? Is it reasonable to suppose that any President would be willing thus to commit his fame and reputation; and, if such a one could be found, is there no reliance to be put upon the vigilance of the Senate? But the gentleman from North Carolina thinks that the Government is never safe in trusting its money concerns in the hands of an individual. How then, Mr. Chairman, is any nation to transact its financial concerns—does our Government not daily trust individuals with its money? Is it not obliged to do so? And if in this case it did not trust directors appointed by itself, would it not be obliged exclusively to trust those appointed by the stockholders? If the gentleman's argument is carried a little further, it would recommend the system of farming the revenue as pursued in France, in-

stead of appointing our own officers to collect it. Our policy, in collecting the dues of the Government, has been, to couple the interest of the officer with our own; he derives a profit or per ceptage upon the money collected, and hence the stimulus superadded to that of a sense of duty. The interest of this bank should be made subservient to the interest of the public, of the people; and hence I wish for some control in its direction.

Mr. GASTON supported the amendment. He concurred with the Chairman of the Committee of Finance in the opinion that the evils which arose from the irregular and depreciated state of the currency called for a remedy—he agreed with him that they affected the industry, morals, the probity, and the public faith of the country—and he added, that there was another evil which no less imperiously demanded the attention of Government, since from it arose the greatest facility of committing frauds upon the revenue. He stated that we had in fact three kinds of currency; one worse than another; and in all of which disbursements were made and the same voucher retained, be the payment made in which currency it might; for an illustration of this he referred to a particular part of the report of the Secretary of the Treasury, which stated that Government had made $33,000 by the difference on depreciated paper. He would not, he said, inquire here whether such a transaction was, or was not honorable to Government, nor should he have mentioned it, but to show that a sum of no less an amount than $33,000 might have been placed in the Treasury, or disposed of in any other manner; and to remind the House that they were unfaithful guardians of the public finances, if they did not take better care that they were better attended to. He agreed with the chairman that the banks ought to be compelled to make payments in specie, but he did not see how that object was to be effected by this bill; yet he thought that a bank formed on correct principles would greatly facilitate. Well constituted, he conceived that a bank would be useful; while badly constituted, he was convinced it would be productive of mischief. As to the capital already fixed upon, he thought it much larger than was necessary; but if that were the only evil it would not be insuperable. The next point of consideration to that of the capital of the bank, was the government of it; and this led him to the question before the House, viz: whether the President and Senate should or should not be empowered to appoint five of the directors. On this subject he would say, that it was incumbent on those who supported the affirmative, to prove its expediency. He had listened to all that had been said upon it, and he heard nothing which appeared to him anything like a sound reason for those appointments being confided to Government. Government, he observed, stood in two relations to the banks, the first of them being as Government merely, and what were the interests it had, as such in the bank? Why that, by its means, a safe and easy transmission would be made of the revenue. And on that head, that is as to the custody, the receipt, the guardianship, and the transmission of the revenue, he affirmed that those were sufficiently well secured. In a word, he thought that by the bill, Government in those respects possessed all the power it ought to desire; but it had far more important interests as guardians of the welfare of the nation, which it was to protect, by taking care that the bank should not degenerate into a paper-making machine, that no persons should be intrusted with its direction that would be likely to abuse it, and that it should be governed by men of skill and integrity. The question then that naturally presented itself was, which would be most likely to make fit appointments, Government or the stockholders of the bank? And the answer to that question was, that, as a cold sense of duty could never stand in competition with a strong sense of interest and fear, the stockholders, whose own interests were deeply involved, would be the most likely. Such directors as they would appoint, would be men versed in the business of money dealing, and well known to be such by them before they were selected; while from the necessity of his situation the President could have no accurate knowledge of such kind of dealings or of men qualified for them, and must trust to the information of others for his election. From that would arise a great evil, namely, that the directors would be appointed, not for their capabilities for the banking trade, but for their political service, past, or to come. If the directors were appointed by the stockholders, they would do right; but if by the President, who could hope that, should the emergencies of the State require a large draft from the banks, they could be able, or would be willing to resist his demand. If there was no positive irresistible reason given for it, therefore, why vest the President with that power? Public confidence, he said, was essential to the success of the bank, and without it that institution could not effect any of the purposes of its establishment. What then, he asked, must be the effect of appointing the directors in the way proposed? Were Government solely to appoint the directors, no man would say that there was a stockholder in the United States who would venture his money in the bank. If Government appointed a majority of them, it would be nearly the same; and exactly in proportion as Government had any hand in the appointments of those officers, the credit of the bank would be impaired. Another objection made by Mr. G. was, the increase of patronage created by these appointments. He said he was no vulgar declaimer against patronage; he had no dread of the ordinary exercise of the President's patronage in the cases of high officers—the judges, for instance, of offices of State—but he was averse to the President's patronage over that kind of office to which little or no salary was annexed, and which could only be rendered profitable by a dexterous management of the facilities it afforded, of employing undue influence. Who would accept such offices? Certainly none but those who know how to make an adroit use of the opportu-

nities they afforded. Here Mr. G. adverted to the disposition expressed by the chairman of the Committee of Finance, to meet the opponents of the bill half way, in a spirit of compromise; he had, he said, agreed to, and acted upon that proposal. There was three leading subjects of controversy belonging to the bill; the capital of the bank, the government of it, and the mode of its operations. One of those had been yielded up, he said, but if the other two were to go in direct violation of his opinions and principles, he would not agree to the compromise. If the gentlemen who were interested in carrying those points, should think that they saw their way clearly, with them be the responsibility!—but for himself, he considered the present amendment a *sine qua non*, without which he could not give his vote for the bill.

Mr. Pickering spoke in favour of it, and supported his observations with the authority of Hamilton; respecting which he reminded the House of what was said a few days ago, on that floor, by Mr. Smith. That gentleman related that when Mr. Gallatin came into the Treasury office, he resolved if possible to detect some errors in the system established by that profound statesman and financier, the first Secretary of the Treasury, General Hamilton; but, after having studied and exhausted much labor and ingenuity in examining and devising the means, he could not with all his natural astutia make a single change for the better in the original system of finance. Such was Hamilton, whose opinions Mr. P. now read from one of his reports, to this effect; namely, that banks could be beneficial only under the direction of private individuals, but never under that of Governments. If the President and Senate owned the stock themselves, the arguments drawn from the right of holding stock might apply, but it was not so; they had but a slight interest in it, and that merely a public one. Needy men would get, through sycophants, recommended for the appointments without regard to their qualifications, so that an honest Government would be glad to get rid of the importunities it would occasion.

Mr. Clay considered the arguments employed against this part of the bill as very strange. The evil complained of, he said, was that two hundred banks—that is, two hundred and sixty strong powers—were in action without any possible control from Government, or any hope of being stopped except by indirect exertion. Was it proper that they should continue to be uncontrolled? And was it come to this, that the Government could not be trusted with the appointment of five officers, who had no salary? He insisted, that the proposed bank was a power over which Government ought to retain a salutary influence; not only that indirect influence which gentlemen were willing to allow it, but the direct influence imparted by the appointment of those five officers. It ought to have a direct active power, since, possessing one-fifth of the capital, there would always be a sum of from fifteen to twenty millions of its deposites continually in the coffers of the banks. And yet gentlemen said it would be better to place the appointment in the hands of individuals.

Mr. GASTON spoke in answer to some things said by Mr. CLAY, and was replied to by that gentleman to whom he again rejoined.

WEDNESDAY, March 6.

Mr. NEWTON, from the Committee on Commerce and Manufactures, to which were referred the memorials and petitions of the manufacturers of wool, made a report thereon, which was read, and ordered to lie on the table.

Mr. INGHAM, from the Committee on Post Offices and Post Roads, reported the bill in addition to the act regulating the Post Office Establishment, with amendments, amongst which was a variation of the privilege of franking during recess, voted to members of Congress recently, so as to make the privilege read, "from the commencement of Congress, and until thirty days thereafter."

Mr. ROOT spoke against the report of the committee, and moved to amend it so as to restore the privilege to its former footing, that is, "during each session, and for twenty days thereafter."

The question on Mr. ROOT's motion was decided in the negative—yeas 47, nays 53.

After some remarks by Mr. CONDICT, the report of the committee was agreed to, and the bill was ordered to be engrossed for a third reading.

Mr. NELSON, from the Committee on the Judiciary, reported a bill to alter certain parts of the act providing for the government of the Territory of Missouri; which was read twice, and committed to a Committee of the Whole.

Mr. LOWNDES, from the Committee of Ways and Means, made a report on the petitions from the following named persons, to wit: John Kauffett and Michael Hengst, Jacob Reily, and Michael S. Van der Cook; which was read, and committed to the Committee of the Whole on the report of the Committee of Ways and Means of the 2d instant.

Mr. LOWNDES, from the Committee of Ways and Means, reported a bill directing the discharge of Ebenezer Keeler and John Francis from imprisonment; which was read twice, and committed to the Committee of the Whole on the bill for the relief of Edward Hallowell.

Mr. LOWNDES also reported a bill directing the discharge of Moses Lewis from imprisonment, which was read twice, and committed to the Committee of the Whole last mentioned.

Mr. LOWNDES also reported a bill for the remission of certain duties on the importation of books for the use of Harvard College; which was read twice, and committed to the Committee of the Whole last mentioned.

Mr. LOWNDES also reported a bill for the relief of Robert Kid; which was read twice, and committed to the Committee of the Whole last mentioned.

Mr. LOWNDES reported the agreement of the Committee of Ways and Means to the amendments proposed by the Senate to the bill, "making appropriations for ordnance and ordnance stores, for the year 1816." and the bill and amendments were ordered to lie on the table.

Mr. SERGEANT, from the committee, appointed on the 4th instant, on the petition of Andrew Kurtz, reported a bill authorizing and requiring the Secretary of State to issue letters patent to Andrew Kurtz; which was read twice, and ordered to be engrossed and read a third time tomorrow.

Mr. JOHNSON, of Kentucky, from the committee appointed on that subject, reported a bill to change the mode of compensation to the members of Congress. [Instead of the six dollars per diem, to allow the gross sum of $1,500 per session to each member.] And the bill was twice read and committed.

Mr. JACKSON, of Virginia, moved,

"That a committee be appointed to suggest to the architect of the Capitol such alterations in the Representatives Chamber therein, as may best provide for the accommodation of the Representatives."

Mr. PICKERING suggested a modification of the resolution, so as to include in its object the improvement of the Hall of the Supreme Court; which was received by the mover of the resolution, and agreed to, and a committee for that appointed accordingly. Messrs. JACKSON, PICKERING, RANDOLPH, MCKEE, and PITKIN, were appointed the committee.

AMENDMENT TO THE CONSTITUTION.

Mr. PICKERING submitted the following proposition of amendment to the Constitution of the United States, which was read, and committed to the Committee of the whole House on the state of the Union:

Resolved, by the Senate and House of Representatives of the United States of America in Congress assembled, two-thirds of both Houses concurring, That the following be proposed to the Legislatures of the several States as an amendment to the Constitution of the United States; which, when ratified by the Legislatures of three-fourths of the several States, shall be valid, to all intents and purposes, as a part of the said Constitution, to wit:

That, for the purpose of choosing representatives in the Congress of the United States, each State shall, by its Legislature, be divided into a number of districts equal to the number of Representatives to which such State may be entitled.

Those districts shall be formed of contiguous territory, and contain, as nearly as may be, an equal number of inhabitants entitled by the Constitution to be represented. In each district the qualified voters shall elect one representative, and no more.

That, for the purpose of appointing electors of President and Vice President of the United States, each State shall, by its Legislature, be divided into a number of districts equal to the number of electors to which each State shall be entitled. Those districts shall be composed of contiguous territory, and contain, as nearly as may be, an equal number of inhabitants entitled by the Constitution to representation. In each district, the persons qualified to vote for representatives shall appoint one elector, and no more. The electors, when convened, shall have power, in case of any of those appointed as above prescribed shall fail to attend for the purposes of their said appointment, on the day prescribed for giving their votes for President of the United States, to appoint another, or others, to act in the place of him or them so failing to attend.

Neither the districts for choosing representatives, nor those for appointing electors, shall be altered in any State until a census, and apportionment of Representatives under it, subsequent to the division of the State into districts, shall be made. The division of the States into districts, hereby provided for, shall take place immediately after this amendment shall be adopted and ratified as a part of the Constitution of the United States; and successively, immediately afterwards, whenever a census and apportionment of Representatives under it shall be made. The division of such State into districts for the purposes both of choosing representatives and of appointing electors, shall be altered agreeably to the provisions of this amendment, and on no other occasion.

THE NATIONAL BANK.

The House then again resolved itself into a Committee of the Whole, on the bill to incorporate the subscribers to the National Bank.

Mr. SMITH, of Maryland, moved to amend the tenth section, so as to allow the choice of President of the Bank to be made from *any* of the Directors, and not to confine the selection of that officer to one of the Directors appointed by the President and Senate. Mr. S. made a few remarks in justification of his motion.

Mr. CALHOUN had no objection to the amendment. He thought the clause proposed to be amended not necessary to give the Government a due control over the concerns of the bank; and that it would still retain as much influence as would serve every beneficial purpose.

Mr. ROBERTSON condemned the motion. He thought it would diminish too greatly the power which it was necessary the Government should have over the Bank. He did not want merely a great money machine, but an institution of a national character; and, therefore, could not consent to part with, one after another, all the features of the bill which gave the Government a proper and necessary control over the bank. He adverted to the liberality which had been manifested by the chairman who reported the bill, (Mr. CALHOUN,) and thought the principle of accommodation might be carried too far. He admonished gentlemen to remember the painter who flattered everybody and pleased nobody. His fate would be that of the bill, if this spirit of concession was carried too far; and he could not, for one, be so far governed by it as to give up those powers which were necessary to the salutary management of the bank, and without which it would not be worth having.

Mr. ROSS could see no reason why the President of the bank should not be selected from the whole twenty-five directors, if it was the object to get the best man. If the President and Senate appoint a director, the most proper for the office, he would doubtless be elected. But, if not, why exclude the fittest character? It would have

been just as well to confine the selection of President of the United States to one State, though it might not contain a person as well qualified as one in another State. Mr. R. called the attention of the House to the importance of the office and duties of the President of the Bank, and the absolute necessity of selecting the director best qualified. Such a course was congenial with our political institutions, although he believed the bank itself was by no means congenial with the Constitution, being, as he viewed it, a moneyed aristocracy. He condemned the policy of giving so much additional strength to the Executive arm. Alexander Hamilton himself, in the zenith of his influence, would not have dared to propose such a grant of power to the President as the control and regulation of a great moneyed institution. Mr. R. concluded by saying he thought it would be much safer to adopt the amendment, and withhold from the Executive so important a power, &c.

Mr. CALHOUN rose to make a remark or two in reply to his friend (Mr. ROBERTSON.) He almost despaired of the passage of the bill, after some of the indications which he had witnessed, and began to doubt whether any bill would pass at all on the subject. For himself, Mr. C. said, his anxiety for the measure was not extreme; but as long as there was a lingering hope of its success, he should omit no effort to make it an efficient remedy for the evils of the present currency. If, after making it suit, as far as possible, the taste of every one, gentlemen determined to oppose it, it was time for them to look out for some other remedy. Mr. C. said, he felt deeply the evil of the disordered state of our currency, and the necessity of a cure. In devising that cure, difficulties were to be expected. The direction of the bank he knew had been made a *sine qua non* by some gentlemen on one side of the House, and he was sorry to find it was one also with some on the other. It was a fate peculiar to great measures to fail in their details. The obstinacy of gentlemen in matters of what they deemed principle, was honorable to them, but he feared it would be fatal to the bill. He lamented it; the disorders were so deep, so great, that justice to the country called for a remedy at the hands of the Government. If gentlemen would seriously consider the character, and power, and nature of the evil—two hundred and sixty banks issuing almost as many millions of depreciated paper—they must see the necessity of co-operating in the measure of relief. The necessity for union was great and urgent, for the disease was almost incurable; it was a leprosy on the body politic, &c.

The question was then taken on Mr. SMITH's motion, and carried—ayes 80, nays 46.

After some further amendment, affecting no principle—

Mr. RANDOLPH moved to add the word *native* in the clause which limits the choice of directors to citizens of the United States; which motion was agreed to without debate—ayes 68.

After the Committee had proceeded to the clause, which provides for the appointment of directors for the Branch Banks, which clause likewise restricted the choice to citizens of the United States—

Mr. JEWETT moved that the word *native* be inserted also in that clause, so as to limit the appointment to native citizens.

Mr. CALHOUN objected to the amendment. It was the first time, he said, that any attempt had been made in this country to discriminate between native and naturalized citizens. The Constitution recognised no such distinction, except in the eligibility to the highest office in the Government, and he could see no reason for introducing on this occasion so odious and unprecedented a distinction.

Mr. RANDOLPH said it was indisputably true that it was to our system of naturalization laws the United States owed that spirit of faction by which they had been torn for the last twenty years, and along with it the war out of which the country had just emerged. He spoke from the information of statesmen inferior to none in this or any other country, that the system of granting protections to foreign seamen was one of the chief causes of the war with Great Britain, which system had grown out of our naturalization laws. Much had been said, and he dared to say much more would be now said, and much more be written on this subject, for it was a melancholy truth, that the press was in the hands of those very people who had long taken upon them to dictate to the American people, and to tell them who ought to be their President, who their Vice-President, and who their Representatives, and to direct them in their most essential concerns. He was aware, therefore, that the press would be at work, and that much would be said and much printed about what he was now saying; but that had no terror for him. How long the country would endure this foreign yoke, in its most odious and disgusting form, he could not tell; but this he would say, that if we were to be dictated to, and ruled by foreigners, he would much rather be ruled by a British Parliament than by British subjects here. Should he be told that those men fought in the war of the Revolution, he would answer that those who did so were not included by him in the class he adverted to. That was a civil war, and they and we were, at its commencement, alike British subjects. Native Britons, therefore, then taking arms on our side, gave them the same rights as those who were born in this country, and his motion could be easily modified so as to provide for any that might be of that description; but no such modification, he was sure, would be found necessary, for this plain reason. Where were the soldiers of the Revolution who were not natives? They were either already retired, or else retiring to that great reckoning where discounts were not allowed. If the honorable gentleman would point his finger to any such kind of person now living, he would agree to his being made an exception to the amendment. It was time, Mr. R. said, that the American people should have a character of their own; and where would they

find it? In New England and in Virginia only, because they were a homogeneous race—a peculiar people. They never yet appointed foreigners to sit in that House for them, or to fill their high offices. In both States this was their policy; it was not found in, nor was it owing to, their paper constitutions; but what was better, it was interwoven in the frame of their thoughts and sentiments, in their steady habits, in their principles from the cradle—a much more solid security than could be found in any abracadabra, which constitution mongers could scrawl upon paper. It might be indiscreet in him to say it, for, to say the truth, he had as little of that rascally virtue prudence,* he apprehended, as any man, and could as little conceal what he felt as affect what he did not feel. He knew it was not the way for him to conciliate the manufacturing body, yet he would say that he wished, with all his heart, that his bootmaker, his hatter, and other manufacturers, would rather stay in Great Britain, under their own laws, than come here to make laws for us, and leave it to us to import our covering. We must have our clothing homemade, said he, but I would much rather have my workmen home-made, and import my clothing. Was it best, he demanded, to have our own unpolluted Republic peopled with its own pure native Republicans, or erect another Sheffield, another Manchester, and another Birmingham, upon the banks of the Schuylkill, the Delaware, and the Brandywine, or have a host of Luddites amongst us, wretches from whom every vestige of the human creation seemed to be effaced? Would they wish to have their elections on that floor decided by a rabble? What, he asked, was the cause of the ruin of old Rome? Why, their opening their gates and letting in the rabble of the whole world to be her legislators. If, said he, you wish to preserve among your fellow-citizens that exalted sense of freedom which gave birth to the Revolution—if you wish to keep alive among them the spirit of '76—you must endeavor to stop this flood of foreign emigration. You must teach the people of Europe that if they do come here, all they must hope to receive is protection; but that they must have no share in our Government. From such men a temporary party may receive precarious aid, but the country cannot be safe, nor the people happy, where they are introduced into Government, or meddle with public concerns in any great degree. Let them then take away their spinning jennies—let them carry off their principles and their machinery back again to Europe, and leave our Republic to its repose. I dread those men; I have a horror, a loathing of a paper machine, and a manufacturing aristocracy; I would protect commerce, but I dislike and contemn manufacturing. Can you be defended by a rabble of manufacturers? No, you cannot depend upon them; they would leave you to be sacked. It would be as rational for any man who really valued his coun-

---

* The only virtue, says Goldsmith, that is left us at three-score.

try, to bring in a bill for the encouragement of a breed of wolves. I never see a merino sheep without its occurring to me that we are about to be the tributaries of the most timid, weak, inefficient animal on the face of the earth. Among our home manufactures, I wish gentlemen would attend to that of human bodies, and not keep foreigners for the purpose of making their clothing at home, when they could import to so much more advantage from abroad. This, he said, was a favorable time to make a stand against this evil, and if not this session, he hoped that in the next there would be a revival of the naturalization laws. He was not partial to the French, but if we were to have emigrants, he wished them to be of that people. Not the birds of Newgate or Kilmainham, nor the rabble of British manufacturing towns. He preferred the French, because they would be a distinct people among us, and not as the subjects of Great Britain, who, from the similarity of their language and manners, identified themselves at once with our people, and brought their principles into our councils.

Mr. WRIGHT said: Mr. Chairman, I cannot be silent when an amendment is proposed to insert the word *native*, so that none but natives can be directors of this bank. Sir, it is a libel on the Constitution, on that WASHINGTON who recommended its adoption. It would exclude Alexander Hamilton, was he alive, from being a director, who so pre-eminently distinguished himself in the promotion of that Constitution. Look, sir, at that picture. See the bleeding Montgomery weltering in his gore, and sacrificing his life on the altar of American liberty, and then say whether such men ought to be excluded. Sir, the members of the Senate and House of Representatives who may be naturalized citizens—nay, a foreigner, who was here at the adoption of the Constitution, might be a President of the United States; but, if this amendment obtains, he could not be a director of this bank!

The question was taken on Mr. JEWETT's motion, and lost, without a division.

Mr. SMITH, of Maryland, then moved to strike out that part of the seventeenth section, which gives the President of the United States power, during the recess of Congress, on the application of the stockholders, to authorize the bank to suspend the payment of specie.

Mr. CALHOUN, after admitting the propriety of the motion, said he had no objection to extend it to the whole proviso of the section, so as to deprive Congress, as well as the President, of the power to suspend specie payments.

Mr. FORSYTH opposed this proposition, and Mr. RANDOLPH supported it; after which, the Committee rose, reported progress, and obtained leave to sit again.

The House then went into Committee of the Whole on the report of the Committee of Ways and Means, on the amendments of the Senate to the bill making appropriations for the Ordnance department. The Senate's amendments were agreed to by the Committee of the Whole, when it rose; and the House adjourned.

THURSDAY, March 7.

Mr. ROBERTSON, from the Committee on the Public Lands, reported a bill further extending the time for issuing and locating military land warrants; which was read twice, and committed to a Committee of the Whole.

On motion of Mr. CRAWFORD,

Resolved, That the Secretary of the Treasury be directed to lay before this House a statement, showing the valuation of real property and slaves in the city of Philadelphia, and in each county of the State of Pennsylvania, the quota or amount of direct tax apportioned to the said city and each of the said counties, and the rate of tax on the one hundred dollars of assessed property, agreeably to the valuation and apportionment made under the act entitled "An act for the assessment and collection of direct taxes and internal duties," passed July 22, 1813, and the act entitled "An act to lay and collect a direct tax within the United States," passed August 2d, 1813; and a similar statement of the valuation, apportionment, and rate of tax under the act entitled "An act to provide additional revenues for defraying the expenses of Government and maintaining the public credit, by laying a direct tax upon the United States, and to provide for assessing and collecting the same," passed on the 9th day of January, 1815; so as to exhibit a comparative view of the valuation, apportionment, and rate of tax in the said city, and each of the said counties, under the several acts abovementioned; also, the names of the principal assessors within the said State, for the year 1816, and the counties embraced within their respective districts, and such further statement of the transactions of the board of principal assessors within the said State, as reported to the Treasury Department, as will show what changes, if any, have been made by them in the relative valuation of property in any of the said counties, and the principles on which they have proceeded in performing the duties required of them by the act last abovementioned.

On motion of Mr. MARSH,

Resolved, That the Secretary of the Treasury lay before this House a statement of the accounts exhibited, and of the expenditures in the prosecution of offences against the United States, in the courts thereof, in the districts of Connecticut, Massachusetts, New Hampshire, Vermont, and New York, respectively, from the year 1808, to the year 1815, inclusive of both; also, a statement of the fines and penalties paid into the Treasury of the United States, from those districts, during that period; exhibiting the names and number of the indictments, informations, and suits which have been instituted for such offences, and distinguishing those in which there have been convictions, from those in which there have been acquittals.

An engrossed bill, entitled "An act authorizing and directing the Secretary of State to grant letters patent to Andrew Kurtz," was read the third time and passed.

An engrossed bill, entitled "An act in addition

to an act regulating the Post Office Establishment," was read the third time and passed.

NATIONAL BANK

The House then again resolved itself into a Committee of the Whole, on the National Bank bill—the motion to strike out the proviso which gives to Congress the power of authorizing the bank, on application of the stockholders, to suspend the payment of specie, being still under consideration.

Mr. RANDOLPH supported the amendment, and reprobated the remarks of the honorable gentleman (Mr. FORSYTH) who opposed it as the most extraordinary he had ever heard. Was that gentleman yet to learn, he asked, that Congress sat under a delegated power, by which they were authorized to do that only which was found specified in their charter, the Constitution? The power to violate contracts between individuals was not one of those granted to Congress and enumerated in the Constitution, and yet that was the amount of the gentleman's argument. Nor could he conceive a case in which their power could extend to impair a contract. If the competency to suspend payment was to be vested in either of them, he would rather trust it to the President than to that House, because nothing was so shameless as a popular assembly. No crime had ever been committed that popular assemblies had not countenanced. He declared that it was astonishing and afflicting to him to hear principles which he had ever been taught to consider monstrous and preposterous, openly and with the greatest indifference promulgated in that House—for what less than monstrous and preposterous was it to insist that Government had a right to make paper a legal tender?

Mr. WEBSTER said he should be sorry if such notions as those of Mr. FORSYTH were to grow into general belief. The language of the Constitution was, he said, that all that was not delegated was reserved. If the power in question therefore was not delegated, it did not exist. He urged the impolicy of retaining the clause, on the grounds that it would defeat the object of the bill, by adding to the depreciation of bank paper. If the power to suspend specie payments were known to exist by authority, individuals holding it would, on the slightest grounds, suspect that it was intended, and press upon the bank for their money. In short, the ingenuity of man could not devise a thing more tending to bring about the evil for which the bill is presumed to be a cure.

Mr. CLAY (Speaker) agreed that the retention of the clause was unnecessary, and said that he would no more make a provision for the suspension of specie payments in a bank, than in forming a government he would provide for a revolution. Either case could arise but from an extraordinary convulsion not likely to occur, and which, if it ever did arise, would bring its own remedy time enough along with it. Providing for it according to Mr. FORSYTH's notion was not only unnecessary but would be pernicious—it would be like calling in a physician to a sick person, and mingling with his prescriptions materials to increase the disease. Were such a power ready at hand to be administered when necessity should require, the bank, whose interest it would be to suspend specie payments, would soon contrive to make that necessity. He therefore concurred in the amendment; which after some observations from Mr. SHARPE, was carried by a very large majority.

Some other amendments were also made to the bill; when at length the Committee, having got through the bill, rose, reported progress and had leave to sit again.

COMPENSATION OF MEMBERS.

The House then went into Committee of the Whole, on the bill to alter the compensation allowed to the members of Congress.

Mr. JOHNSON said, he thought no diversity of opinion could arise on this bill but as to the sum which it proposed to allow the members per annum. If members of Congress were satisfied to adopt a smaller sum, he avowed himself willing to meet them, though he had no doubt the sum mentioned was as low as it ought to be, and was less than the salary received by twenty-eight clerks employed by the Government. Mr. J. also defended the propriety of the proposed mode of compensation over the per diem allowance, and concluded with a few statements to show, that the trifling addition to the pay would be nothing in comparison with the despatch of public business, which would be the effect of the change.

Mr. RANDOLPH coincided fully with Mr. JOHNSON in his views of the proposed change; and in order to divest the measure of its only odious consideration, he moved to amend the bill by suspending its operation until the 4th of March next, so as not to take effect during the present Congress. Mr. R. declared his conviction, however, that the object would not be fully attained by the change. Are not members, said he, obliged to be wakened up to vote; roused up to hear the question? Do they not keep the House from adjourning because they have not finished a letter, or sent off the last newspaper? The debates of the House are swelled to their great length by inattention of members; and to remedy it, we must get rid of this bookbinder's shop. The House, he said, was not exactly like a Dover court, where they were all speakers; but here there is one speaker and no listener.

Mr. JOHNSON was opposed to the amendment. He thought if the bill was necessary at all, it was as proper for the present Congress as a future one. However, he would not refuse his support to the bill, if the motion should be adopted. Congress, he said, had always to act for themselves on this subject, and he was averse to the postponement.

Mr. RANDOLPH said, for himself he would prefer the bill as it stood; but it was to satisfy any overtender consciences, that he proposed the amendment. For his part, he was not afraid of the thing called popularity; to vote to himself one thousand five hundred dollars—for what? For coming here and living as in a boarding school, or a monastery, &c. There was no profession scarcely by which a man could not earn one thousand five hundred dollars in six months, and do it much more pleasantly too than by coming here. Mr. R. concluded by repeating, that the object of his amendment was intended merely as a quietus to over-tender consciences.

Mr. GROSVENOR said, to decide on the amendment, it was only necessary to inquire, whether this measure was at all proper. If it be necessary, is it not so at this, as the next session? On what principle, he asked, was it necessary to postpone the effect of the bill? It would be viewed only as a little attempt to evade the imputation of regarding their own particular interests; and he was decidedly opposed to it.

Mr. HUGER assured the House, he had never risen to address them with more reluctance, or less satisfaction to himself, than on the present occasion. He had waited to the last moment, and until the question was on the point of being taken, in the hope that some other gentleman would undertake the unpleasant task, (for an unpleasant task it certainly was,) of rising in opposition to a measure, evidently so popular and so well received. Providence in its beneficence, had blessed him with independence, and somewhat more, perhaps, of the good things of this life, than had fallen to the lot of several of those he addressed. He was sensible, that under such circumstances, opposition to the proposed increase of pay might not come with the best possible grace from him; and be most sincerely wished that it had devolved upon any other gentleman, rather than on himself. He had waited, however, as before observed, to the last moment, but no one evinced the least disposition to rise in opposition to the bill. He did not, therefore, think himself so bound down, hand and feet, by the above consideration, or by the feelings of delicacy arising out of it, as to be absolutely precluded from expressing his dislike to a measure, which he disapproved of most decidedly, and in all its bearings; nor under any moral obligation to let it pass *sub silentio,* and without the most trifling attempt being made to stop its progress. He should, without further preface, throw himself on the candor and indulgence of the House. And whilst he cheerfully acknowledged the merits of the honorable gentleman from Kentucky (Mr. JOHNSON) who had so greatly distinguished himself in other fields, and a kind of warfare rather more glorious than that for which he had been, on the present occasion, extolled in such glowing language; he flattered himself, that he might at least hope and calculate upon the pardon and forgiveness of gentlemen, if he ventured, in like manner, to come forward with some little independence, and oppose a measure, evidently so popular within the walls of the Chamber, and which received such kind, and to all appearance, such general welcome.

Mr. H. repeated that he was decidedly opposed to the bill in all its bearings and provisions; to the increase of pay it proposed, (especially at the present time and under existing circumstances,) and still more to the manner in which that increase was to be brought about. Nothing could

be further from his wish or intention than to attribute improper motives to the worthy chairman, or any other honorable gentleman of the committee by whom the bill had been introduced. But he must be permitted to say that the bill, so far as he comprehended its scope and tenor, presented itself to his understanding in a very questionable shape. It wore too much the appearance of disguise and concealment. If there really was such evident necessity for an increase in the pay of members of Congress, why not grant it in the good old way of a per diem. If six dollars a day were not adequate to meet their reasonable expenses, and afford them a comfortable subsistence at the Seat of Government, let the rate be augmented to eight, ten, or twelve dollars, or to whatever sum might be deemed sufficient. But let this be done in such a manner as that their constituents might at a glance, understand what had been done, and have an opportunity of making a fair comparison between the present allowance, and what it was now proposed to raise it to. By changing the per diem, or daily allowance, into a salary, or gross sum, a concealment of the increase of pay was, he would not say sought or intended, yet it certainly was effected. What number of persons abroad, he asked, would comprehend the full effect of the change, or possess proper data upon which to make a correct estimate and comparison between the present daily allowance and that which was contemplated? Even in that House there was great difference of opinion on the subject. The chairman of the committee stated it, including an average of extra sessions, at between nine and ten dollars. He contended they were not likely to have, for some years to come, any extra session. Yet the very fact that there might or might not be extra sessions, was almost conclusive argument of itself in favor of the old mode of a per diem, and against the proposed change of it into a fixed salary and gross sum. At all events there was not the most distant prospect of an extra session, neither had there been one during the Constitutional term of the present Congress. He was strictly correct, therefore, and fully authorized in estimating the addition of pay which would actually be received by the present members, at an increase of from one hundred to one hundred and fifty per cent., or at an average of at least fourteen dollars a day, besides the annual travelling allowance of six dollars every twenty miles. Indeed, this was so obviously the case, that he had heard it in conversation, candidly acknowledged, that the mode adopted of giving an annual salary instead of a per diem, was the only one which could render the thing palatable, and make it go down with the people. And this very observation and acknowledgment had been by no means one of the smallest inducements with him to turn his attention particularly to the subject, and rise in opposition to the bill.

But even granting it to be expedient to increase their pay for the future, it was, in every possible view, incorrect and unbecoming to give the bill a retrospective operation. When the members of this Congress were elected they well knew they would be entitled to six dollars a day, and no more. They accepted their seats under this express condition. But if the bill passed, each member would receive fifteen hundred dollars for the year ending on the 4th of March, which was already elapsed, and during which they had barely been in session three months. Thus, instead of $180 a month, or $540 for three months, to which they were now entitled, and which many had already drawn, the members would receive $1,500 each, while the President *pro tem.* of the Senate, and the Speaker of the House of Representatives, instead of $1,080, to which they would be entitled as the law now stood, would each receive $3,000; the members a per diem at the rate of about seventeen dollars per day, exclusively of the usual allowance for travelling expenses; the President *pro tem.* of the Senate, and the Speaker of the House of Representatives a per diem of rather upward thirty-three dollars, likewise exclusive of the usual allowance of travelling expenses. The President *pro tem.*, and the Senate, and the Speaker, and House of Representatives of the Fourteenth Congress, would consequently receive a gratuity, (for a gratuity, concealed as it might be, it certainly was,) over and above their usual per diem, at the close of a bloody and expensive war, out of the public coffers, to the amount of about $200,000 for their services the three months last past, during which they had literally, and to the best of his recollection, done nothing else but make appropriations, and lay taxes. Yet honorable gentlemen had spoken of this gratuity and augmentation of pay they were about to vote to themselves, as a mere pittance, which the liberality of their constituents would confirm without a second thought on the subject; nay, several had gone so far as to say, if the committee had erred, it was rather in fixing upon a sum too small, than in recommending one too large. He thought very differently. And though he had as much confidence in the liberality of those whom he immediately represented, as any other gentleman could have in that of his immediate constituents, yet when he recollected how liberally taxes had been laid on them already during the present Congress, and the high tariff of duties on foreign importations about to be added to these, by way of bounty to domestic manufactures, he could not find it in his conscience to draw upon their liberality for a gratuity, and an addition to his pay at such a moment, and under such circumstances.

Were there no other objections then to the bill, this extravagant retrospective operation would be a sufficient inducement with him to vote against it. But he had a still stronger, and, in his opinion, unanswerable objection to the bill, on account of the proposed change in the mode of compensation, and the novelty of converting members of the Legislature into salary officers. They were said, indeed, to be mere day laborers, and that it was beneath their dignity to receive a stipend, as though they were mere hewers of wood and drawers of water. He saw [no force in the observation. They were in fact, and in truth, day laborers, and must, from the nature of their services, continue such. Their predecessors had been so, and had received for upwards of thirty years a per diem, in proportion to their daily services. Yet, it was the first time he had ever heard a whisper as to its baneful influence on their dignity, or that the receipt of a per diem had affected, one way or the other, the standing or respectability of the members of Congress.

Not only their dignity, however, was all of a sudden found to be lessened by the old mode of compensation, but members, it seems likewise to be most unexpectedly discovered, received less than clerks in many of the offices, or those employed to copy their own proceedings; and, it was triumphantly demanded, whether members of that honorable body were not worthy of at least as much compensation as mere quill-drivers. He really did not expect such an argument (well enough adapted, perhaps, to a newspaper paragraph) would have been seriously urged in that House. He would ask in return, whether the question had been fairly stated, or whether there was any point of comparison between a clerk who earned his daily bread by personal labor and his skill in figures and penmanship, and a member who was elevated to a seat in that august body; to whose care was committed the destinies of this great and rising Republic. He put it to gentlemen themselves to say, whether it was indeed with a view of making a livelihood, or upon the principle of obtaining compensation for their services, that they sought or accepted of the high, dignified, and responsible situation of a Representative of the people. He was confident that gentlemen, one and all, would spurn at the suggestion. Indeed, the honorable gentleman from Virginia, (Mr. RANDOLPH,) who was one of the most zealous supporters of the bill, had given the most decided negative to any such idea, and the strongest argument in favor of the principle he advocated, when he stated it to be his sober and well-digested opinion, that the members of Congress should not be allowed any pay whatever.

On this point, however, he had the misfortune likewise to differ from that gentleman; and he well remembered, at a former period, and as a member of a former Congress, when "economy and republican frugality and simplicity" were as much the cry and watchword of the day, as are at this time "dignity, and living like gentlemen," he well remembered he had resisted most strenuously a proposal to reduce the pay of members of Congress to three or four dollars a day. He had done so from motives and principles not dissimilar to those which actuated him at present in opposing an increase of pay.

He had always understood that the object of giving a *per diem* to members, either of the State or National Legislatures, was not by way of a compensation for their services, still less to remunerate them for sacrifices of pecuniary or personal advantages of any kind. No; the real object was to enable individuals, whose private means would not enable them to attend the sessions of the respective Legislatures, to meet the moderate and reasonable expenses to which they must necessarily be subjected by their attendance on them, and to the end that the country might not be altogether deprived of the services of men in narrow circumstances, from their inability to suffice to this extra expense. Hence, and in the same spirit, a moderate and reasonable allowance was made for travelling expenses—not at such a rate, however, as would be required by the nabob of the South, whom the gentleman from Massachusetts (Mr. King) describes, and who, he tells us—with all the gravity and dignity he possesses in no eminent a degree, and which so well becomes the occasion—cannot get along without his carriage and two horses, and two black servants, and two dogs, but such as would enable a decent and respectable individual to transport himself comfortably and conveniently from his place of residence to the Seat of Government.

Such, beyond all doubt, was the principle upon which pay has heretofore been given to members of the State and National Legislatures. This was the correct medium between the two extremes of refusing to pay their reasonable expenses, or of giving salaries sufficiently large to compensate members of the respective Legislatures for the loss of time, the sacrifices they made of individual comfort, and the diversion of their talents and industry from their usual avocations; by the first alternative, depriving the country altogether of the services of persons in narrow circumstances, and throwing the Government entirely into the hands of the rich; by the latter, attempting to do that which, if carried into execution, would bankrupt the nation. It was, in fact, not to be expected nor calculated upon, that the best and first-rate talents of the country could or would be drawn out, in common and peaceable times, by any salary which might be offered; far less by such an annual stipend as that proposed. In moments of great crisis—on occasions of imminent danger and national exigency—the *amor patriæ* —the genial impulse of great minds would force such men to come forward and take a part in the public councils. But, to expect such a sacrifice of private pursuits, and individual enjoyment and emolument on their part, in ordinary times, was out of the question. He more than doubted, indeed, whether any salary, the most sanguine friends of the bill could prevail on themselves to propose, would insure a more respectable representation than that which composed the present Congress.

The point at issue, then, it would seem, between the gentleman and himself, was, that they proposed to remunerate members for their services and sacrifices; whilst he, according to the principle heretofore acted upon, thought it most expedient to confine the pay to such an amount as would defray their necessary and reasonable expenses, coming to, attending on, and returning from, the National Legislature. Take either horn of the dilemma, and he was equally opposed to the bill. He contended that it was perfectly farcical to talk of drawing out the first-rate talents and characters by such a salary as fifteen hundred dollars. On the contrary, this sum, when fixed and certain, was about sufficient to tempt the cupidity and excite the avarice of the second or third rate county court lawyer, the idle and noisy demagogue, or the lowest grade of political brawlers, who haunted the taverns and tippling houses, and stunned the ears of the peaceable citizens with their devotion to republicanism, their love of the people, and their exclusive patriotism.

Here the question presented itself, and he would examine whether the old *per diem* of six dollars was or was not sufficient to meet the reasonable and necessary expenses of a member whilst attending to his official duties. He would candidly acknowledge that money had depreciated; that living was (nominally at least) higher; that the pecuniary resources of a member, arising from his pay, were not as great or as favorable to him as they had been in former and better times. But this was not to last forever. In the meantime, it was equally felt by all those in any way connected or concerned with the General Government—the public creditor, the old soldier, the disbanded officer—indeed, by every portion of the community, even in their private concerns and capacity. He saw no reason, therefore, why the members of Congress should separate themselves from all other classes of that community, and make use of their official station to escape from the pressure of an evil common to all, and one for which it would better become them, and it was their bounden duty, to endeavor to find an efficient remedy. He moreover contended, the depreciation notwithstanding, that a member could live conveniently, comfortably, abundantly—ay, and like a gentleman, too, if *this* was to be the criterion, upon the present *per diem*. He could prove it, he thought, beyond all contradiction, by figures. Take, for example, the expenditure of a week in Washington, at the highest rate, and for what he should presume to be an ample establishment, even for a gentleman: boarding and lodging, (the highest charge he had heard of,) fifteen dollars, a servant four, two horses eight. He did not include the two dogs of the honorable gentleman from Massachusetts, as this necessary appendage to the dignity of a member was unknown to himself or either of his colleagues, and must belong, he presumed, exclusively to Virginia and the other large States. The above three items amount to twenty-seven dollars, which, deducted from twelve dollars, the gross amount of a week's pay, at six dollars *per diem*, would leave a balance of fifteen dollars per week for extra expenses, including Madeira, which the veteran member from Maryland (Mr. Wright) seemed to think had likewise become indispensable to the dignity of a gentleman who had in these days a seat in Congress. And on this point, at least, he candidly acknowledged, and was happy to find, that his feelings were somewhat in unison with his old Congressional friend and acquaintance; though he had, nevertheless, some doubts whether the member who had made a late dinner or his supper with brown bread and a tumbler of genuine cider, would not find himself on the following morning fully as adequate to perform the duties of a legislator, as the one who had feasted sumptuously with the best white loaf, or enjoyed his bottle, even of the deservedly far-famed old *lath* of Alexandria.

The gentleman from Virginia (Mr. RANDOLPH) had said it was immoral, *contra bonos mores,* to oblige members to live, for the want of means, so many months separated from their families. There was point and pith in this, as there usually were in the remarks of that gentleman. He perfectly acquiesced in the truth and justice of it; but, before it could have any weight with him in making up his mind on the present question, he must be convinced that the proposed augmentation would remedy, or at least have a considerable tendency to remedy, the evil. From his own knowledge, he was convinced it could and would not. He was confident that the contemplated addition to the old per diem would not enable gentlemen, who had not other and private means of their own, to bring their wives and children with them; nor did he believe that one additional family would spend their Winter at Washington in consequence of it. The only effect of this increased compensation would be, that the expensive habits and inclinations of one portion of the members would be encouraged and excited, whilst others, who were more saving and economical, would carry heavier purses home with them.

Another argument had been advanced, which likewise carried with it some appearance of plausibility. It was said this addition of pay would lessen the anxiety and necessity for Executive favors and appointments, and that Executive influence and control in and over that body would be thereby diminished. He was convinced, however, it would have a contrary tendency. The moment a seat in Congress was regarded as a money job, or members were induced to change their habits, and live beyond their regular means, by a temporary addition to them, they would imbibe expensive notions and inclinations. Their wants would increase; their families, as well as themselves, would be disposed to ape the follies and extravagances of the rich contractor, unprincipled speculator, and every other description of moneyed men, or of men without money, who lived by means of their wits, and at the expense of the industrious classes of the community. Dependence must be the natural and unavoidable consequence. An overweening anxiety and irresistible necessity of obtaining Executive favors and patronage, *per fas aut nefas,* must as certainly follow. Moderation, frugality, and economy were the only safeguards to the independence and integrity of men in public life. It was not only in direct opposition to the most sacred maxim of morality, thus to lead them into temptation; but the doctrine of the present day, and that preached up on the present occasion, which went to persuade members that it was necessary to live in a style beyond what was decent, respectable, and comfortable, and to entice them into expenses and a kind of living beyond what they were accustomed to, or had the private means of keeping up at home, was contrary to the soundest dictates of common sense, and dangerous in the extreme. By doing so, they must become needy and craving, and be placed precisely in that situation most likely to render them subservient to, and then perhaps reluctant, yet not less implicit tools of, that branch of the Government which could alone supply their immediate and most pressing wants, and hold out to them in expectation a rich harvest and ample share of the loaves and fishes at its disposal.

But it was contended by the chairman of the committee, that this increase of pay, and change of the per diem into a salary, would shorten the sessions of Congress, put an end to long speeches—in a word, be the panacea or cure-all to every evil. Such might be the case in part, particularly as relates to the shortening of the sessions of that body. He more than doubted, nevertheless, if it was so, whether such an alternative was altogether desirable. The honorable chairman appeared to him not to have examined, with his usual sagacity, both sides before he had made up his mind on the question. Upon his own data, it would seem evident, on the one hand, that an augmentation of pay could not be necessary; for his arguments went to show, that the present six dollars per diem tempted members to make long speeches, and spin out the session—to the end that they might reap the greater emolument by remaining here and obtaining a greater number of days' pay. It followed, of necessity, that the old and present allowance was found experimentally to be not only sufficient, but highly desirable. On the other hand, if the per diem was changed into a salary, and that salary increased, in order to shorten the sessions and put down long speeches, might there not (deducing the same probable effects from the same efficient causes) be with justice serious apprehensions entertained lest the members should, in time to come, be induced to shorten the sessions too much, and hurry over the public business somewhat unadvisedly, and before it was properly and sufficiently matured? This was perhaps too often the case, even at this time, and under existing circumstances.

What, then, was to be expected, according to the data given, from a measure the necessary operation of which was to place the interest of the individual in direct opposition to his duty, and to render his emolument greater or less, in exact proportion to the shortness of the period he devoted to his public duties, and remained in this, as it was said, most expensive city. Now, though he was by no means fond of too much regulation, yet he confessed he saw no very great inconvenience or danger likely to accrue to the Republic from too much discussion. For his own part, he would rather be condemned to listen to fifty long and tedious speeches than contribute, *sub silentio,* to the passage of one bad law, or be obliged to vote for a measure he had not heard explained or did not comprehend.

1167   **HISTORY OF CONGRESS.**   1168

H. of R.   *Compensation of Members.*   March, 1816.

There was another aspect in which this subject presented itself to him as of vital importance, and as affording cause for serious alarm. He was perfectly satisfied, in his own mind, that no measure could be devised which would increase, so enormously and fearfully, the influence of the executive over the legislative branch of the Government, or throw the latter so completely under the control of the former as this salary system. Not only the sessions would thereby be injuriously shortened, but business would be hurried through any how and every how. Congress would meet for little else than to lay taxes and make appropriations. Laws would be passed as they were sent ready drawn up from the several departments, and measures, kindly and previously matured by the industry and superior wisdom of the Executive, would be adopted, right or wrong, with little if any discussion. He entreated gentlemen to take this view of the subject, before they made up their minds on the question, and to postpone the bill at least till the next session, and until they had gone home and consulted with their constituents in regard to it. He could not, for his own part at least, but regard this change of the per diem into a salary, or gross sum, as a dangerous innovation, and one likely to be attended with the worst consequences.

Our Government had been described with some humor, and not less justice, perhaps, as a species of *logocracy*. It was in fact and in essence very much of one. It could not get along without considerable discussion. The people ought and would know, what were the motives which led to this or that measure, or why one law was passed, and another rejected. Now, he knew of no mode by which this information could be obtained by them more conveniently or satisfactorily, than through the debates in Congress, and the speeches of their Representatives. He was disposed, therefore, to view this *cacoethes loquendi*, which some gentlemen (who possessed it in no trifling degree themselves) complained so much of, with some little indulgence. There was, indeed, at times, irksome, tedious and most ridiculous speeches made in that House. But gentlemen enjoyed a privilege which they had very generally, and not very unfrequently availed themselves of during the present session—the privilege of not listening to such speeches; whilst the good people abroad read them, or read them not, according as the subject, or speaker, or any other circumstance, excited their curiosity, or attracted their attention.

These few observations, he hoped, would tend to reconcile the worthy gentleman from Kentucky, a little, to the inconvenience of long speeches, and would also, he trusted, plead in some measure his own apology for the length of time he had encroached upon their patience. He should not have indulged himself to such an extent, but that the active opposition to the bill appeared to devolve almost exclusively upon himself, whilst the first talents in the House had been brought forward in support of it. He would further observe that in the ground he had taken, he thought himself supported by the spirit, if not

the letter of that article of the Constitution, which prohibited a Senator or Representative from being appointed to any civil office under the United States, that had been created, or the emoluments of which were increased during the time for which he had been elected. Certain he was that in South Carolina, his native State, and the one he had the honor, in part, to represent, no act to increase the compensation of the members of the Legislature could take effect till after a new election; nor did the provisions of any such act go into operation, except in favor of those who were chosen to serve in a succeeding Legislature. He had long, therefore, been accustomed to regard this as the true and the most decorous, as well as the most correct principle, and he should not, he trusted, be accused of presumption if he ventured to recommend it to that House, as a precedent which it would well become them to imitate.

Before he sat down, Mr. H. said he would add, that he was perfectly aware, the stand he had made in opposition to an increase and change of the per diem into a salary, (indeed it had been more than insinuated in the course of the debate,) would be attributed to a desire of obtaining popularity, and an anticipation of the popular edict it would probably have out of doors. He would not say that such feelings might not have had some influence on his mind and conduct; for he pretended not to be less fallible than those around him. But he could with justice, and in sober truth aver, that he was opposed upon principle to the measure, and more especially to the change of the per diem into a fixed salary; a system that, he was perfectly satisfied, would augment most enormously the power of Executive influence, which no one, he believed, would deny had increased, was increasing, and would be, if it was not already, placed by this new system beyond all control. Besides, convenient as he acknowledged such an addition to his pay would be to himself, at the present time, as well as to other gentlemen, yet when he recalled to mind the heavy taxes which had been or must be laid; the exorbitant tariff of duties on foreign importations, likely to be adopted; the large and unprecedented (at least in time of profound peace) appropriations they were called upon to make; the number of veterans who had lately been disbanded, and thrown penniless upon the world; the debt which had been incurred, and partially funded; the large outstanding demands not yet liquidated—in a word, when he passed in review these and similar matters, it did seem to him that the proposed measure was wrong, and most obviously ill-timed. He at least could not reconcile it to himself; and, though sneered and laughed at by more than one honorable gentleman, for so expressing himself he would repeat, he should be ashamed to return home and acknowledge that, under such circumstances, and at the close of so bloody and expensive a war, he had voted for, or even neglected to oppose an increase of pay to himself and to those who, like himself, represented the good people of these United States on that floor, and consequently held the purse-strings of the nation at their disposal.

Mr. H. concluded by repeating, he did not think the sessions long. The House was sometimes vexed with the *cacoethes loquendi*, but the consequence was, that measures had a fair and deliberate consideration. It was necessary, he thought, the community should rightly understand the acts of Congress; and one of the advantages of this speechification, was, that the people would be well informed, and our measures be well matured. Long speaking, he contended, was no such great evil as had been asserted; he would rather have ten days speaking than one law; for many laws were an evil. Mr. H. said that the Abbe Sicard, so celebrated for teaching the deaf and dumb, had lately published that there was a nation in North America who had no language at all, but did everything by signs. He was friendly to debate because he himself felt its good effects, for he now entertained very different opinions on some subjects from those he brought here. Ours, he said, was a *logocracy*; it was in vain to deny it, and we ought to act in the spirit of the Government, &c. Mr. H. adverted to the charge of folding newspapers, &c., and said it was no worse than the practice of lounging about the House as some did. He concluded by declaring it his opinion that instead of diminishing the sessions, he thought it would be better to make them longer; and as to the pay, he thought the honor of the station was sufficient to bring gentlemen to Congress, without any influence from pecuniary considerations.

Mr. RANDOLPH said, in reply to Mr. HUGER, that he agreed with him in just one half of one of his propositions, which was that speeches did no harm. In his opinion they were like old women's physic, they did neither good nor harm. The gentleman (Mr. HUGER) thought no pay ought to be allowed, because gentlemen ought to come here for honor; if that is the case, many, said Mr. R., come for what they do not get. Many of the clerks, it had been said, received more than the members of Congress—yet, Mr. R. said, there was no clerk who ever drudged harder than he did; in proof of which, he briefly detailed the course of labor and study he imposed on himself whilst here in the public service. Mr. R. denied that the members could live comfortably on six dollars a day now, whatever might have been the case when the pay was first fixed. He adverted also to the salaries of some other officers of the Government, particularly the Chief Justice, who was put off with a scanty pittance. The pay at first fixed for those officers was something like a decent compensation, but now pitiful and disgraceful. The gentleman (Mr. HUGER) must pardon me, said Mr. R., if I think his arguments are better calculated for what is called on this side of the river *stump*, than for this Committee, &c.

Mr. JOHNSON, of Kentucky, said he wished this measure correctly and properly understood, that the people might judge of its merits. He never concealed from his constituents his senti-

ments on political subjects, and although it was a measure in which every member was concerned individually, he never, on any occasion, consulted more the honor, the happiness, the rights, the independence of his constituents and his country, than in proposing a change in the mode of compensation to members of Congress.

He had been a member of Congress for eight years, in times of trial and difficulty, when the rights of the nation had been violated, when storms menaced its peace and tranquillity, and when a severe and sanguinary war threatened the very basis of our independence. During all this period, he had discovered imminent danger to the Republic in the councils of the nation, in the very councils to which the American people looked for wisdom and direction—the Congress of the United States. We wanted energy and decision of character to take wise and strong measures. The people called for despatch of business, and we answered them with long speeches. We were many times upon the point of taking the most important questions; and when it was expected that some great measure would be decided, a motion for adjournment was carried. In this way, from day to day, from week to week, and from month to month, a long session was spun out, the six dollars per day pocketted, and little or nothing done to relieve our distresses. When, under this state of things, the people, driven almost to despair, poured upon us their anathemas, every member could go home and tell his constituents that he himself was innocent, and that the fault of indecision and delay rested entirely with others. It was impossible for the people to ascertain who attended to his duty or who neglected it. The members, in this respect, evaded their responsibility, because invisible to their constituents. Although we might patrol the streets, or vote for an adjournment at three o'clock, or even at an earlier hour, the people remained ignorant of our delinquency.

Mr. J. said he wished every man to be responsible for his conduct to the people, the legitimate fountain of power and authority. He said he wished his constituents were collected, and after hearing the subject discussed, could decide on this occasion. They were a wise people, a patriotic people, a well-judging people, who valued independence, liberty, and honor more than a few cents, or dollars, or pounds. Although he did not wish to say anything of his own attendance, it was known to his friends that he lost no time during sessions of Congress, and he never voted to adjourn when the House could progress with business. So much for the change of the mode of compensation. But one objection has been made, which was that Congress might hurry business, and not well mature it. There was no danger of any such thing. Business of importance would always be thoroughly investigated; and as to matters of less difficulty, of course, they would be easily understood; and not only so, but the mode of doing business precluded the idea of too much despatch. What was that mode? A subject was introduced by resolution or by communication from the President, or head of a department, or by petition. In either case, the subject was referred to a committee of seven members, who investigated and reported, for or against the measure; the report was committed to the whole House of 182 members in committee, printed, and taken up at some future day, when it was read twice over, discussed by sections, and then reported to the House. If, after this investigation, it was approved by the House, it was ordered to a third reading, and engrossed, subject to the inspection of an engrossing committee. It was then read over a third time to the House before it was finally decided. If it passed the House, it was sent to the Senate, where the same routine was pursued, after which it was enrolled and inspected by a joint committee of both Houses, and ultimately examined and approved by the President. So much as to the only objection made to the mode.

Let us now attend to the other branch of the argument, the amount of compensation. On this subject Mr. J. said he felt much less anxious than on the other. He wanted a certain sum given for the year, whether it amounted to one dollar per day, or to ten; and, as to himself individually, he did not care whether the sum was one thousand five hundred dollars, or half that sum; that was with the House to determine. He was aiming at a reform in the proceedings of Congress—a reform which must take place now or at some other period, or the country would one day be endangered, and the rights of the people invaded. Every member who has voted against this measure has declared the present compensation inadequate. Some of them have said we should have nine, others ten, and others twelve dollars per day. Mr. J. said he would not vote for one cent in addition to the per diem. It would be an inducement to protract the sessions, till they would become perpetual, and that would be the final result of raising the wages by the day. But if members would vote for the change, and thereby shorten the sessions, and not only shorten the sessions, but despatch and transact all the public business, then, he said, he was willing to vote for a liberal compensation—a compensation which would induce members to remain in their seats, which would, in some degree, indemnify them for the sacrifices of happiness and property, which any man of business must make, who serves his country as a Representative.

Mr. J. said he would vote for no sum which, in his opinion, would ultimately cost the people of the United States one cent more than the present system. He asked, then, whether the sum proposed would be too great? and whether such a sum would ultimately cost the Government more? Mr. J. said he had looked back into the various sessions since the beginning of the Government—at the various contingent expenses of each session, and he had no doubt but that under the proposed compensation money would be saved to the nation. In this pecuniary point of view, the nation would be the gainer. 1st. By dispensing with extra sessions of Congress, which never

ought to take place in the United States, but which are becoming common. Every extra session would cost the Government at least from $120,000 to $150,000 more than the per diem in mileage and contingencies. But let it be recollected that in case of an extra session, which we may suppose necessary in some extreme case, no member will have anything more in consequence of it. It may be asked, what would you do in any emergencies, such as those which have produced extra sessions? In such cases, the call of Congress some four or five weeks previous to the time of adjournment, would always answer the purpose, as in the case of the attack upon the Chesapeake.

Connected with the whole system of expense, therefore, the public will save money; and if that be the case, no patriot will think the compensation too great to be paid for the representative of his choice.

But let us confine our view to the compensation, abstracted from the foregoing considerations. Members cannot consider this as a great augmentation. Indeed none can think so, compared with what we get. Nine months sessions will give each member, at six dollars per day, one thousand six hundred and twenty dollars. Mr. J. said, he had himself received at one session, one thousand five hundred dollars at six dollars per day; and he was convinced, that in a very little time, the wealthy would unite with another class of men, and have either perpetual sessions, or sessions that would bring to each member at least one thousand five hundred dollars. This, he said, demonstrated the propriety of having a fixed sum, beyond which we could not go; that if we wasted our time, it would be at our own expense. Suppose, said he, we were to continue our eight months sessions, what enormous contingent expenses should we incur? At our last session, our contingent expenses amounted to $50,000, or thereabout. Despatch of business would prevent this. In a session of three months, the contingent expenses ought not, nor would they be, more than about $20,000, a saving of $30,000 in each session of six months. Indeed, with the rules of reform which this measure must introduce, instead of $50,000, the amount heretofore expended for printing, stationery, fuel, attendants, and other contingencies, the whole ought not to exceed $15,000 for the contingent expenses of a session. But Congress have not only had a session which gave each member $1,560; it is in our power, (and I fear the time is not far distant when we shall avail ourselves of it,) to remain in session till each member will draw $2,000 from the Treasury. In this point of view, it is necessary to limit that power. But there are many other weighty reasons why this compensation is not too great.

1st. It will unite patriotism and interest to secure the attendance and industry of members.

2d. It will enable a man of merit, though poor, as well as the man of wealth, to come to Congress, if elected by the people, which is no trifling consideration. This is the only free and happy Government on the earth. Other nations are groaning under the yoke of despotism. Privileged orders are established—a nobility to riot upon the spoils of the people. Here all are on an equality, and eligible to office. The people, on the day of election, look to merit, not to riches. They ask for the qualities of the candidates. They inquire into their political sentiments, their personal integrity and talents, and they decide accordingly. These persons may have families to support, dependent upon their business or profession, which, if neglected, will subject them to suffering. It is then the duty of the people to afford them such compensation as will justify their engagement to serve them, that the country may not be subject to the dominion of the idle and profligate, or of such as are born to princely fortunes, while the most meritorious are driven, by a sense of that duty which they owe to their families, from public employment. Mr. J. said, he advocated the amount, not on his own individual account. In his present situation, he felt little interest as to the amount. He was, nevertheless, willing to receive it, because he did not think it too great. It was after all a poor compensation. His main object was, to shorten sessions, and despatch business, for he would rather serve three months for nothing, than six months in each year for six dollars per day. The sacrifice was, in breaking in upon all the avocations of the farmer, the mechanic, the lawyer, the merchant, &c., which began generally, and always demanded special attention, in the Spring.

3d. The rights and honor of the nation will be preserved by a despatch of public business, and by acting with more promptness upon petitions and other claims during the session in which they are presented, and not continue them from session to session for ten years, as has been done in many cases of just claims, when the amount has been exhausted by the expenses of attendance. Such a course is incompatible with the dignity of a magnanimous nation—there must be a reform.

But admit for a moment, that the United States would be charged with a few thousand dollars more, what is that compared with the effects of such a measure? No more than a grain of sand upon the seashore to a mountain. It is well known that six dollars a day was given twenty-five years ago, which was more, compared with expenses now, than three times the amount would be at present. This compensation may so remain for twenty years to come, because many are afraid to do right upon a subject of so much delicacy, for fear the wicked may misrepresent, and the motives of members may be misunderstood. But, delicate as this subject is, it ought to be borne in mind, that no other branch of the Government has power to touch it. Members may be accused of sordid views and selfish motives—but, Mr. J. said, he was willing to be judged by his constituents as to motives and views. He was not afraid on this point—they would not judge him harshly. They were a different people, they would take the whole of his conduct together, and he considered he had never served his

country more than by advocating the measure now under debate.

Mr. CLAY took the opportunity afforded him by the Committee of the Whole, to yield his support to the bill, and at once to commit himself in its favor. As to the amendment to defer the commencement of its operation until the next Congress, he would remark, that, in his judgment, there was more propriety in the law ending than in beginning there. It was more respectful to our successors to leave them free to determine what was the just measure of indemnity for their expenses than for us to prescribe the rule for them. We can best judge for ourselves. With regard to the supposed indelicacy of our fixing upon our own compensations, let the Constitution, let the necessity of the case, be reproached for that, not us. Mr. C. said his own personal experience determined him in voting for the bill. He had attended Congress, sometimes without his family, and at others with a part of it; and although his compensation, while he had enjoyed the honor of presiding in this House, was double that of other members, he declared, with the utmost sincerity, that he had never been able to make both ends meet at the termination of Congress.

The honorable gentleman from South Carolina (Mr. HUGER) tells us he was born to opulence. He ought to recollect that few in this House have had the same good fortune. Would he reserve the seats here for the well born and the rich alone? And yet they must be confined to them, unless such an allowance is made as will enable the poor and the middling classes to come here. Mr. C. thought the rate of compensation ought to be such at least as that ruin should not attend a long service in this House. And yet how many are driven out of it by their inability to sustain the expenses and losses incident to the situation! This had been particularly the case from the State to which he had the honor of belonging. And he regretted to find that this cause was still operating, and was about to deprive the House and the country of the valuable services of several of his colleagues. Mr. C. thought the compensation ought to effect more; it ought to guaranty the independence of the members of this House against the influence of the Executive branch. How was the fact in another country? There the members of the Legislature received no stipend; and the consequence was, that it was filled with pensioners, placemen, and the creatures of the Ministry. The laborer is worthy of his hire; and if you do not give him the wages of honesty, it is to be apprehended the wages of corruption may, in process of time, come to be sought. He should give his most decided vote for the bill.

Mr. JOHNSON, of Virginia, said, he should vote for the amendment—not from any motive of popularity—he disclaimed so unworthy an influence. Adverting to the reason advanced by the mover of the amendment, Mr. J. said he generally found, that those who attributed improper motives to others, would, if they took a glance at the mirror, find those motives reflected from their own bosoms. He admitted the pay was too low, and ought to be augmented; the pitiful sum of six dollars might induce a lounging lout to come here. but he was convinced it would be inadequate of itself to bring any gentleman here. Although this was his opinion, he thought the amendment proper, and should vote for it.

Mr. Robertson said a few words in support of the bill, which he thought was proper, simply because the present pay was not enough; and as to popularity, he knew his vote would arrive at home about the time of his election, and he wished to give his constituents the opportunity of deciding on his conduct.

Mr. Barbour said that he should vote for the amendment, and disclaimed any influence but that which was correct and proper. The six dollars now allowed, if taken as a salary, he said, was not enough; but, if as an allowance to support members of Congress while here on the public business, was insufficient for many, though he himself could live comfortably on that sum. He disclaimed any concealments, and was the last to impute an impure motive to others. He supposed, therefore, gentlemen were governed by correct motives in supporting this bill, and claimed for himself the same allowance. He knew it was a delicate matter to act for self; there was an inextinguishable feeling in such a case, which nature had implanted in us, and he was aware that in acting on it, the greatest purity could not escape suspicion. Like Cæsar's wife, not wishing even to be suspected of improper views in this case, he should vote for the amendment. He avowed his desire of that popularity which attended good actions—not that which was got without merit, and lost without a fault. He should, therefore, vote for the motion.

Mr. Jackson said, it was unnecessary to say anything with regard to the real object of the bill; that was unquestionable; and he was extremely pleased that there was no diversity on the subject, because he did not wish to see the time when the places here should be filled solely by men of fortune; neither did he desire to witness the reverse, when members of this House should be liable to Executive influence on account of their needy circumstances. With regard to discrimination, Congress had heretofore passed laws giving themselves compensation, as well while here as for mileage, travelling expenses; to prove which, he quoted the acts of Congress of 1795. The amendment, Mr. J. said, was useless, because one branch of the Legislature was indissoluble, and to postpone the act until it would cease to affect any of the present members, might be to put it off for fifty years. If it be right in relation to ourselves, said Mr. J., it must be right in relation to the Senate also; and if not so to them, cannot be to us. Mr. J. said, he was not deterred from supporting this measure by any fear of the effect it would produce at home. The people had once before borne him out in a similar course, when he had voted for an increase of compensation in the Legislature of Virginia, and he was not afraid to encounter the same responsibility now.

Mr. Huger entered into some explanations in reply to Mr. Randolph, and added a few more remarks in opposition to the bill.

Mr. Pickering said, if the present compensation was inadequate, let it be augmented. He was in favor of the bill for many reasons. It would certainly despatch the public business and save the public money. The depreciation of money had been more than fifty, some thought seventy-five per cent.; and if, as had been said, the compensation was originally fixed on democratic principles, it ought now to be increased to what would equal the value of what six dollars were when that sum was fixed. If the change is proper, said Mr. P., shall we adopt a self-denying ordinance, and say we will not give to ourselves what we are willing to give to our successors? After some remarks on an alteration in the mode of doing business which Mr. P. thought would be useful, if the bill passed, he concluded by saying that, as to that rascally prudence which had been mentioned on a former day by Mr. Randolph, he was as destitute of it as anybody. He had never in his life taken time to think whether an act would make him popular or otherwise, and he should disregard such a consideration on this occasion.

Mr. Randolph declared that he had such an aversion to the bare name of self-denying ordinances, that since his motion had been so denominated, he was induced to withdraw it; which he did accordingly.

Mr. Stanford then said that there were some in this House who had believed that the Constitution prohibited Congress from increasing its own pay; and, as he was averse to augmenting it, he renewed the motion just withdrawn by Mr. Randolph, to refer the operation of the act to the next session of Congress.

The question was then taken on the motion, and negatived by a large majority.

The Committee of the Whole having risen and reported the bill to the House—

Mr. Stanford renewed the motion just rejected, and made a subsequent motion to leave the sum in the bill blank; both of which were successively negatived.

Mr. Burnside moved to reduce the proposed salary to one thousand one hundred dollars; which was also lost.

Mr. Taylor, of New York, then moved to strike out "one thousand five hundred," and insert "one thousand dollars," as the salary.

Mr. Root rose to express his opinion of the scheme, as it might be called, proposed by the bill. It was intended, he was informed, to cure a great evil, and that evil was the length of the sessions; and as it was wrong to apply the previous question, the evil must be cured by an annual salary. This object, he said, bore no relation to the present compensation; and, therefore, it was to advance the pay in disguise. It was argued that the pay was inadequate, and that the members staid here to increase it, thereby protracting the sessions; and that an annual salary must be allowed to remedy this evil. These reasons were inexplicable to him. He had no objection that members of Congress should receive an adequate compensation for their services; but that would depend on their mode of living. If six dollars were not enough, meet the question fairly, and not in this disguised manner. He believed the increased privilege of franking and continuing the mileage allowance, would virtually make the proposed compensation twelve dollars per day. Mr. R. said he was bred a democrat, and never could tolerate anything like aristocracy. He, therefore, rejected the distinctions which had been claimed for members of Congress on account of the dignity of their stations, and their not being day-laborers, &c. Some of them, he said, might be more honest than day-laborers, but take mankind in the gross, and you will find honesty and intrinsic merit pretty generally distributed through the different classes of society.

The bill was then ordered to a third reading by a large majority.

FRIDAY, March 8.

Mr. CREIGHTON presented a resolution of the General Assembly of the State of Ohio, requesting that power may be vested in that State to sell as much of reserved land in the county of Jackson, in said State, as may be necessary for laying out a town thereon.—Referred to the Committee on Public Lands.

A message from the Senate informed the House that the Senate have passed a bill, " relative to settlers on the lands of the United States ;" also, a bill in " addition to an act, entitled 'An act in relation to the Navy Pension Fund ;" in which bills they ask the concurrence of this House.

Mr. YANCEY made a report on the petition of Joseph Wilson, which was read ; when Mr. Y. reported a bill for the relief of Joseph Wilson ; which was read twice, and committed to a Committee of the Whole.

Mr. YANCEY also made a report on the petition of Gustavus Loomis, which was read ; when Mr. Y. reported a bill for the relief of Gustavus Loomis, which was read twice, and ordered to be engrossed and read a third time to-morrow.

Mr. YANCEY also made a report on the petition of Paul D. Butler, which was read ; when Mr. Y. reported a bill for the relief of Paul D. Butler, which was read twice, and committed to a Committee of the Whole.

Mr. ROBERTSON, from the Committee on the Public Lands, made a report on the petition of Gabriel Winter, which was read ; when Mr. R. reported a bill confirming certain lands in the county of Arkansas, in the Missouri Territory, to the heirs of Elisha Winter, deceased, to the heirs of William Winter, deceased, and to Gabriel Winter, which was read twice, and committed to a Committee of the Whole.

The bill from the Senate " relating to settlers on the lands of the United States," was read twice, and referred to the Committee on the Public Lands.

INCREASE OF THE RATES OF PENSION.

Mr. CHAPPELL, from the Committee on Pensions and Revolutionary Claims, who were instructed by a resolution of the 28th of December last to inquire into the expediency of increasing certain pensions, made a report thereon, which was read ; when Mr. C. reported a bill to increase the pensions of invalids in certain cases, for the relief of invalids of the militia, and for the appointment of pension agents in those States and Territories in which there is no commissioner of loans ; which was read twice, and committed to a Committee of the Whole. The report is as follows:

The Committee on Pensions and Revolutionary Claims, to whom was referred the resolution of the House of Representatives of the 28th of December last, directing an inquiry into the expediency of increasing the rate of pensions to officers and soldiers disabled in the service of the United States during the late war with Great Britain ; and also into the expediency of amending the law relative to the proof required from officers and privates in the militia to establish their claim to a pension, report :

That the pension now allowed to a non-commissioned officer or soldier for the greatest disability is five dollars per month, and to the commissioned officers the half of their monthly pay ; making the highest pension, per month,

Of an ensign amount to - - - -	$10 00
Of a third lieutenant - - - -	11 50
Of a second lieutenant - - - -	12 50
Of a first lieutenant - - - -	15 00
Of a captain - - - - -	20 00
Of a major - - - - -	25 00
Of a lieutenant colonel - - -	30 00

That for all disabilities less than total, the pension is proportionably less ; and that the half-pay of a lieutenant colonel is the highest pension which any officer can receive.

In the investigation of this subject the committee have been necessarily led to consider the time when the present rates of pensions were established, and to contrast the then prices of the articles which constitute the necessaries of life with the present. The difference is manifest ; and the result is, that what was then considered a competent provision now falls far short of the object. Sixty dollars per annum is the pension allowed a soldier for the greatest disability. This, under the change which has taken place in the prices of articles, the committee deem insufficient to enable him to support himself plentifully and comfortably. They think that whatever sum the Government may allow, should have, at least, this end in view. It seems to be the object of all Governments—it is certainly the peculiar duty of this, dictated alike by a just regard to sound policy and the injunctions of humanity.

The same absolute necessity may not exist to increase the pensions of the officers, because it is possible they may, with the present rates, live free from actual want ; but as there is a difference in their grade and responsibility, in their pay whilst in service, and the pensions which have been allowed, not only in this, but in other Governments, the committee deem it improper to depart from these rules ; they think some regard should be paid to the conditions of men, and that, as far as can, consistently with policy, they should be placed in circumstances of relative ease and comfort.

The resolution instructs them to inquire into the expediency of increasing the pensions of the officers and soldiers disabled in the late war with Great Britain only. In doing this, they have unavoidably been obliged to consider the cases of all persons who have been disabled whilst in the military service of this Government, and they have not been able to discover any difference in their claims, They think no distinction should be allowed to exist, but that whatever provisions are made should relate equally to all invalids.

The committee are in favor of a partial increase of pensions; but as it may be satisfactory to the House to see the effect of this increase on the Treasury, they have ascertained the number of pensioners now on the list, what number are officers, and what privates, distinguishing those of both denominations who were of the Revolutionary army, and the amount of pensions at present paid, and find there is paid annually the sum of $119,624 05 for that object; that there are 165 officers, and 1,572 non-commissioned officers and soldiers of the Revolutionary army, and 52 officers, and 391 non-commissioned officers and soldiers who have become disabled since the Revolution, making an aggregate of 237 officers and 1,963 non-commissioned officers and privates, and a total of 2,200 pensioners.

The above statement extends to as late a date as the 4th of January last. Since that time it is probable many applications have been made to the War Department for pensions; and there are, also, from the best judgment the committee can form from the papers now before them, from 80 to 100 cases which will be added to the number during the present session. What number springing out of the late war remains to be presented cannot be stated. The committee, however, deem it proper to observe that the Revolutionary cases, compose the great mass of those already on the list which, from the course of nature, cannot very long remain a charge on the Government. The very circumstance of the advanced age of most of the pensioners, and the consequent diminution of their ability to add much by their personal exertions to their own support, seems to strengthen their claim to an increase of pensions. The pensions now allowed to captains, and those above that rank, the committee think are sufficient to discharge the obligations of gratitude and duty which the Government owe them, and to place them not only above actual want, but in tolerable comfort. They, therefore, do not deem it necessary to increase their pensions; but as this is not the case with the other officers and soldiers, they deem it proper to recommend to the House to increase their pensions so as to allow to them the following sums, per month, in lieu of those to which they are now entitled, viz:

To a first lieutenant	- $17 00
To a second lieutenant	- 15 00
To a third lieutenant	- 14 00
To an ensign	- 13 00
To each private	- 8 00

For the highest degree of disability, and for all less degrees, a sum proportionably less. The effect of this would be an increase of sixty per cent. on the pensions of the soldiers, and about an average increase of twenty-one per cent. on the pensions of the officers, and would require about the sum of $200,000 per annum.

The committee do not deem it necessary to recommend any alterations in the laws relating to the proof necessary to place the officers and soldiers of the militia on the pension list, other than to put them on the same footing in that regard with the officers and soldiers of the regular army. The rules at present prescribed for that purpose are not more rigid than is necessary to guard with sufficient care against frauds on the Government, and, as these rules have been long established, they are known to the public in some degree, and will be acted on; whereas, if new ones were established, they would, perhaps, only tend to confuse without benefiting the applicant. To effect the above object, they report a bill.

COMPENSATION OF MEMBERS.

The engrossed bill to change the mode of compensation to the members of Congress, was read the third time, and the question stated, "Shall the bill pass?"

Mr. WRIGHT said, intending to vote for the increase of the compensation to members, I shall vote for this bill to effect that object, so necessary to preserve a republican representation in Congress of honest, independent, and honorable men; and, although I might prefer the mere increase of the daily wages, without converting it into an annual compensation, yet, sir, I am satisfied with the act of a majority in the change, and bound to admit that the strong reasons assigned by the friends of that measure are entitled to great weight, and satisfactorily justified by the provision of the bill to deduct a rateable proportion of the salary for every day's absence from Congress, during its sessions. Sir, the denunciation in the public prints of the dilatory proceedings of Congress, and the long speeches of its members, for the purpose of prolonging the sessions, and increasing the compensation of its members, was as devoid of truth, as it was offensive to the honorable feelings of the Representatives of the people. And it is a well-known fact, that many of the most valuable members of Congress, balancing between the painful separation from their families and the great expense beyond the means of men of moderate fortunes to sustain, had retired, and many more had contemplated it. It may not be extraordinary to find men of wealth, such as the honorable gentleman, (Mr. HUGER,) opposed to the increase of the compensation. It is by such means, Mr. Speaker, that the men of wealth, who alone possess the funds to support them here, will by this indirectly work out men of moderate fortunes, and thereby lead to the most dangerous consequences; as the Government, once in the hands exclusively of the wealthy, would render insecure the rights of the common people, and endanger the happiness of the Republic. Sir, the devotion of Congress to their duty at the last session—having omitted to sit but one Saturday during the session, and having sat every day till near night; and, sir, the like conduct during this session, having practised the same assiduity when sitting on the six-dollar compensation—must satisfy every one of the wickedness of the said denunciation, so offensive to us all; and that, when our time is our own, and the compensation graduated by our diligence, that it will insure it by the strongest ties—the interest of the individuals—and that the public business will more expeditiously be performed, and the other expenses of the session decreased equal to the augmentation of the compensation to the members; so that the public will profit by the change. Sir, I, as a Representative of Maryland, feel no difficulty as to my vote on this subject. Indeed, sir, I feel in a certain degree instructed on the subject. Sir, prior to the adoption of the present Constitution, under the Confederation, the States fixed the compensation of their respective members of Congress, and paid their own members. Then, sir, the State of Maryland, gave her members of Congress eight dollars per day for their services, and paid the same in gold or silver. So that Congress, from the establishment of the present compensation, were in the receipt of two dollars per day less than the State of Maryland by her law gave her members for the same services upwards of thirty years ago, and when that compensation would purchase double what it would at this time of any of the articles necessary for the comfort or accommodation of the members. Again, sir, the compensation of a member of the Legislature of Maryland, at the time eight dollars was allowed to a member of Congress, was not more than two dollars; but now, sir, the sum of four dollars is the compensation allowed by the State of Maryland to the members of the State Legislature, as I understand. Thus sir, I show what was the former compensation to the members of Congress, and to the members of the State Legislature; and I show that that Legislature has doubled the compensation to its members, which I might surely consider as instruction to increase the compensation of members of Congress in the same ratio, which would greatly exceed the compensation proposed by the bill now under consideration to be given to the members, and I have no doubt would justify me with my constituents, who know the sacrifices I have made on the altar of the Republic; many of whom, I am sure, would be glad to see me in official receipt of twenty-five thousand dollars, and can never be induced to find fault with my vote. I, sir, shall not be governed by popular motives in opposing this measure, as the purest principles of distributive justice command it; nor shall I suffer the affectation of delicacy to overrule my judgment, in this case, because I am interested. If it is right, it *ought* to be done; if it ought to be done, it *must* be done by Congress, who alone can do it. Nor, sir, can I feel a propriety in giving it a prospective operation, in exclusion of the present Congress. If it is proper as to them, it is surely proper as to ourselves; and a moment's reflection shows that most of the same members will be re-elected, so that the veil of delicacy would be too thin to conceal the views of members to provide for themselves, though in future.

Sir, what would be the feelings of honorable men towards the highly honorable mover of this bill, (Mr. JOHNSON, of Kentucky,) who slew Tecumseh with his own hands; who came up here covered with wounds and glory, with his favorite war-horse, and his more favorite servant—his attendant in the army, his nurse and necessary assistant;—being unable to do anything for himself at the close of the session; being obliged to sell his war-horse or his servant to close his accounts, or to have recourse to his private funds to clear him out? That this may not be considered an exaggerated account, let any gentleman with two horses and a servant try the case by one week's residence at Crawford's at Georgetown, where many members reside, or Mr. Gadsby's in Baltimore, and live in the style of a gentleman, and he will give unequivocal proof of the reality of such an alternative.

Sir, if we go back to those times when the Legislature of Maryland fixed the compensation of eight dollars to members of Congress, and two dollars to the State Legislature, you will find them halcyon days, when for that compensation they lived like gentlemen, and enjoyed a glass of generous wine, which cannot be afforded at this time for the present compensation.

Mr. Speaker, I hope this bill will pass, and that honorable gentlemen who consider it unjust to put their hands into the public Treasury for themselves will be excused from taking this increased compensation, particularly when it might subject them to the unkind remark that the receiver was as bad as the thief.

Mr. HUGER again rose in opposition to the bill, and argued to prove that the proposed change was in effect an increase of compensation of one hundred and fifty per cent., which, under the present circumstances of the Government, while encumbered with an immense public debt, he decidedly condemned. Mr. H. closed a long speech, by moving to postpone the bill to December next, of course to reject it.

Mr. GROSVENOR replied to Mr. HUGER, and advocated the bill. The Constitution, he said, had provided that Congress should fix its own compensation, and he was opposed to postponement. He maintained that the pay was inadequate to the comfortable subsistence of the members; and it never was intended that they should come here to live on hominy and molasses in hovels, but to live like gentlemen. He wished not to put the seats in Congress up to the lowest bidder, but to induce those best qualified to fill them; and would make such a compensation as would enable the poorest man to come here. The reverse of this, he said, would be anti-republican, and tend to bring those only of wealth.

Mr. RANDOLPH said he was sorry to see the time and talents of his friend (Mr. GROSVENOR) misapplied, in answering the objections of the gentleman, (Mr. HUGER,) and was surprised at the gentleman (Mr. HUGER) persisting in his course, after the good advice he had taken the liberty of giving him yesterday, though he could not say that he had followed it himself. Mr. R. said he now began to descry, through the fog of debate, the latitude of the gentleman's arguments—the speeches were perhaps intended to meet his constituents. He scouted the idea of plastering over a vote for the taxes by saving this miserable pepper corn to the Treasury. The gentleman had advised us to go home and consult our constituents. Consult them for what? For four-pence-half-penny? Instead of receiving instructions from his constituents on this subject, Mr. R. said he should instruct them. He was an enemy, he said, to that self-denying principle which had given rise to the great military usurpation in England, which in the revolution was one of the chief agents in the hands of that hypocritical demagogue—a man whose talents almost redeemed his vices—commonly called Oliver Cromwell. Mr. R. adverted to the salaries of other officers of our Government, of whom even many clerks and doorkeepers received more than the members of Congress, and said that Congress was the only branch of the Government whose compensation had not been increased; so that they could at least say they had not began with themselves. This, said he, we have let alone until the gentleman from Kentucky, (Mr. JOHNSON,) with a gallantry that belongs to him, flung himself into the breach to repair it or perish in it. Another argument in favor of a liberal salary was, that it is the only way to counteract Executive influence in this House—not the necessary and proper influence—by placing every member above the temptation of office, &c. Mr. R. said his only objection to the bill was that it had not made the compensation $2,500, instead of $1,500; then a man might come here with a prospect of something like the comforts of home. At present all the charities of life were broken by it; wife, children, and family were all abandoned. He would also advert, though it was a subject of some delicacy, to the demoralizing effect of being separated from home for six months in the year. *Nullius jurare in verba magistri;* he hoped the gentleman (Mr. HUGER) would pardon him for quoting Latin in that House. Mr. R. concluded by saying that the honorable gentleman (Mr. HUGER) had greatly mistaken the powers of his logic and eloquence if he supposed the bill could be overturned by them.

Mr. CALHOUN said, so far as this bill proposed to increase the compensation to members, he was in favor of it, because he thought the present pay very inadequate to the dignity of the station, and far short of the time, labor, and sacrifice required. He thought $1,500 would be found not sufficient, and would prefer, on the ground of a due compensation, as well as regard to principle, $2,500. He said on principle, for in the fixing the pay of members heretofore, it had not been sufficiently attended to. Our extent, population, and wealth made a strong Executive necessary; and we accordingly find the framers of our Constitution have made that the preponderating part of our Government. It constitutes a branch of the Legislature, and has besides the whole patronage of Government, while the other branches have naked power only, without patronage or influence. He did not complain of any undue influence of Executive power now; he wished not to be so understood, as he was speaking solely in relation to the Constitutional powers of the President. The best and wisest men in this country have always thought his power so great as to render it ultimately dangerous. What then is to be done? To weaken it, would be to weaken the country; perhaps to endanger it. The only safe control is in the character, experience, and intelligence of this House. Whenever this House is properly composed, when it contains a sufficient number of men of ability, experience, and integrity, it of necessity will give direction to public affairs; but a weak and inexperienced House necessarily falls under Executive control. The increased pay is calculated to draw men of abilities into this House; and, what is of equal importance, to keep them here until they are matured by experience. What is the usual fact? Young men of genius, without property, for in four instances in five, such is the case with genius, are elected; being tempted into public service by the honorable desire of acquiring distinction in the service of the country; they remain here until they have acquired some experience, and begin to be useful to the country; but are finally compelled to return to private life from the inadequacy of the pay. It is a great public misfortune; it is highly injurious to the proceedings of this House. Ever since he had known the body, there had been no want of talent; but the want of experience had often been felt. If we are wise, we will, as far as possible, attract and secure ability and integrity in the public service. Providence intended them, as the best gift to the nation, for that purpose; and any people, as they use or neglect them, flourish or decay. Another view of this subject, connected with the great extent of our Republic, made it expedient. A majority of the members come from three to eight hundred miles. In serving the country, they are not only obliged to be absent a great part of the year from their families; but what is almost equally distressing, to be absent a great distance. We serve at the expense of the best sympathies of our nature; we are far removed from the centre of that system of social feelings, which at once constitutes the solace and ornament of our nature. The best dispositions are the most sensible to this sacrifice; and are by it most likely to be driven out of the councils of the nation. We serve at things ought to be counteracted as far as possible; the condition of a member ought to be made more desirable than at present; he ought at least to be able to have his family about him, which he cannot, at the present pay, without ruin, unless he be a man of property. For these reasons he thought the measure a wise one, and to be highly republican. It had for a long time been felt to be necessary. It was worthy of the disinterested gallantry of the member who had introduced it.

Mr. KING, of Massachusetts, was in favor of the bill, because it would shorten the sessions of Congress. If the measure was necessary at all, he asked if it was not as necessary for the present as a future Congress? For one, he was not afraid to trust himself in making compensation; besides, he said, the country had extended and increased many millions in population; and the weight and responsibility of the members had increased in proportion; those of the Speaker in a double proportion. Mr. K. said he knew not the sentiments of his constituents on this subject, nor was he bound to know them; but he was not afraid to say, that they ought never to send a person to Congress who deserved not this sum; and if their present Representatives did not, they would have an opportunity to correct the procedure. He maintained that the Representative of thirty-five thousand high-minded people ought to have enough to live as such a man ought to live. Gentlemen had boasted of their wealth, and perhaps thought that a little cider and brown bread would do for such as had no resources beyond their pay. Mr. K. was in favor of the yeas and nays, that the gentleman might have an opportunity, if he believed he had not earned his pay, to put it on record, and let his constituents know it. Some of us, said Mr. K., are poor men; we cannot keep here, to follow us about, two or three servants, two or three horses, and two or three dogs; but we desire to live as befits our station, without loss, &c.

Mr. ROSS said, from the arguments of those in favor of the bill, it would appear, that it required more firmness to act on this than on any other question. Mr. R. defended himself from the opprobrious epithets which had been heaped on those who were too cowardly to vote for this bill. He was not satisfied that the bill would be attended with the beneficial effects predicted to this House, and to the public business. He could not expect more talents than were assembled in the present Congress, which had not been excelled since the first. They did not come here for pay; he whose mind ran on the grovelling idea of his pay, would here feel the same sordid sentiments, and would be looking for further promotion. Mr. R. thought the consequence of giving a large salary would be to prompt adventurers to get into this House, while the man of intelligence, worthy of serving, would find employment in his avocations at home. He, therefore, saw this measure in a very different light. As to the Speaker's salary, that was fixed higher, because of his duties in the House, and because it was supposed he ought to become better acquainted with the members, that he might know which were fit for the various situations, and to acquire that knowledge, it was necessary he should entertain them; but since Jupiter Tonans (alluding to the former Speaker, Mr. DAYTON,) took the Chair, the practice of giving dinners had ceased, it being thought that he could distinguish by intuition the qualifications of members. Mr. R. concluded some further remarks, by demanding the yeas and nays.

Mr. RANDOLPH rose to explain.—It might be inferred perhaps, from what he had said, that he thought the Speaker of the House and President of the Senate received enough. I should, said Mr. R., have liked the bill better if it had given them five thousand dollars each; they were great officers of the State; they might be President of

14th CON. 1st SESS.—38

the United States. The miserable creature who was generally appointed Vice President, was selected merely because he was totally unfit for the Presidency; but he begged pardon of the House, as the office was now vacant: but the Speaker of this House was much more proper for President of the United States than the character who was usually Vice President. The Speaker, he thought, ought be enabled to take a house and reside here, as a great officer should do. Mr. R. replied further to Mr. HUGER's arguments; and concluded by saying, he did not think those who opposed the bill so violently, ought to accept the additional compensation; for his part, he would as soon be caught with his hands in a gentleman's pocket, as receiving the pay after saying so much against it.

Mr. HOPKINSON thought the gentleman (Mr. JOHNSON) who had begun this warfare, was entitled to the support of all who approved the bill, and for that it was he rose. The principle being conceded that the Representatives are entitled to compensation, the question was, what ought that compensation to be? On this question, Mr. H. said, he would meet gentlemen on fair grounds; not those of popularity. The rule proper in deciding this question was, justice to ourselves, not extravagance. If on the one hand, we do not come here to make money, how can the country expect us to come to make sacrifices? The truth is, we ought to be allowed to come here without any great sacrifice, and every one be enabled to live in the style that he does at home. He spoke what all hearts would acknowledge, that the comforts of home and family were superior to what could be found here. The intervals between the daily sessions were spent in gloomy and solitary meditation, or in dissipation. This, he said, would not be the case, if we were enabled to bring a part at least of our families with us. He thought men ought not to be driven from their seats here for want of suitable support. There were, at the present session, eighty new members in this House. Such great changes must produce a fluctuation of councils and of system. Legislation, said Mr. H., requires experience as well as any other avocation; as well might a man attempt the lawyer without reading or learning. He maintained, that the compensation, as fixed by the former Congress, was greater than what was now proposed. Six dollars a day was even then expected to be something more than sufficient for the expenses of the members. It was reasonable that their expenses should be less at that time than they are now. Mr. H. thought if they consulted what was strictly and justly due to themselves, the bill would and ought to pass.

Mr. TUCKER said, that as the yeas and nays were called on the passage of the bill, he felt it his duty to state, in a few words, the reasons which induced him to vote against it in committee and would lead him to adhere to that vote. He did so because he did not wish to shrink from a candid expression of his opinion. He believed with many others that the pay of members of Congress ought to be such as to enable, not the rich only, but men of merit, (however moderate their circumstances) to take a seat in this House. It was the true Republican principle; for otherwise the Government would degenerate into an aristocracy. But though such were his opinions on this subject, without deciding whether a per diem allowance or annual compensation were preferable, he could not vote for any bill which gave additional compensation to himself. He had been elected under the expectation of receiving six dollars per day for his services; he could not think himself justified in increasing it. Gentlemen had termed this a *squeamish* delicacy. He had from his childhood been taught on all occasions of this kind that it was safest to err on the side of delicacy. He should therefore vote in the negative, though he would have had no objection to an increase of the allowance to members if its operation were postponed to a future Congress.

Mr. GASTON opposed the bill, not because he thought the pay too high—he believed it not high enough—but because it contemplated a mode radically wrong. He thought the services of members ought to be paid for according to those services, and not by an annual salary. To enforce this opinion, Mr. G. used various arguments. He did not believe the country would be benefitted by facilitating legislation; even if it were true that the bill would produce that effect; which he did not believe; because no Congress, as a body, could ever have protracted the session, and remained here, for the sordid motive supposed. The comforts of home would hasten them away if nothing else. In North Carolina, said Mr. G., from an ill-judged parsimony, the members were not allowed sufficient compensation to defray their expenses, and the effect was that the public business was hurried through improperly. He denied that the compensation of members by an annual stipend would accord with the genius of our Government; and advocated the per diem mode, as preferable in every view which he could take of the subject.

Mr. YANCEY said he would vote with his colleague, (Mr. GASTON,) but for a very different reason. He thought the compensation, and had always thought it, inadequate. A member ought to have enough to compensate him for his services to his constituents and country. If the motion made yesterday to postpone the operation of the bill to the next Congress had prevailed, he would have been willing to vote for two thousand dollars instead of fifteen hundred. He was not afraid of despatching public business too fast, and he believed the proposed measure would produce that effect more than the previous question. Fix a salary, said he, and remove all obstacles to attention in the House, and business would be greatly facilitated. Mr. Y. repeated that, if not applied to the present Congress, he would support the bill, convinced that it was proper. He repelled the possible imputation of voting from an over-nice conscience—he imputed to none the desire to run after an unworthy popularity, and he should not incur such a suspicion himself.

Mr. CULPEPER said, that believing with his colleague (Mr. YANCEY) that the measure was

right, he should vote for it now; because if not applied to the present Congress, he did not know that it would ever do any good. He thought its immediate operation was the best part of the plan, and he should therefore vote for it.

Mr. SHARPE wished publicly to express his gratitude to his friend and colleague (Mr. JOHNSON of Kentucky) for bringing forward the proposition; and he was willing to go even further. The Constitution had provided that the compensation of Congress should be fixed by law, and if this measure was right, as had been conceded, was it proper to postpone its application to a succeeding Congress? One word, he said, as to the propriety of the compensation. If gentlemen wished to arrive at civilization it was not by imitating savage life. The American people ought to be known by another principle, and be distinguished as well for dignity of character, liberality, and civilization, as for the wisdom of their political institutions. The same solicitude ought to be felt in legislation to cherish talent, and to employ it, as in other branches of the Government.

The question was then put, on the passage of the bill, and decided in the affirmative—ayes 81, noes 67, as follows:

YEAS—Messrs. Alexander, Atherton, Baylies, Betts, Birdsall, Bradbury, Breckenridge, Brown, Calhoun, Champion, Chappell, Chipman, Clarke of North Carolina, Clark of Kentucky, Clayton, Clendennin, Condict, Conner, Creighton, Culpeper, Davenport, Gold, Grosvenor, Hardin, Henderson, Hopkinson, Hulbert, Irving of New York, Jackson, Jewett, Johnson of Kentucky, Kent, Kerr of Virginia, King of Massachusetts, King of North Carolina, Law, Lovett, Marsh, Maynard, McLean of Kentucky, McLean of Ohio, Middleton, Milnor, Moore, Moseley, Nelson of Massachusetts, Newton, Noyes, Ormsby, Parris, Pickens, Pickering, Pitkin, Randolph, Reed, Robertson, Sergeant, Savage, Sharpe, Sheffey, Smith of Pennsylvania, Smith of Maryland, Stearns, Sturges, Taggart, Tallmadge, Tate, Taul, Taylor of South Carolina, Thomas, Throop, Ward of Massachusetts, Ward of New York, Webster, Wendover, Wheaton, Thomas Wilson, Woodward, Wright, and Yates.

NAYS—Messrs. Adgate, Baer, Barbour, Bassett, Bateman, Bennett, Blount, Boss, Burnside, Cannon, Cilley, Clopton, Comstock, Crawford, Crocheron, Cuthbert, Darlington, Desha, Edwards, Forney, Forsyth, Gaston, Glasgow, Goldsborough, Goodwyn, Griffin, Hale, Hall, Hammond, Hawes, Herbert, Huger, Hungerford, Ingham, Johnson of Virginia, Langdon, Lewis, Love, Lowndes, Lumpkin, Lyle, Lyon, Maclay, Mason, McCoy, Piper, Root, Ross, Smith of Virginia, Southard, Stanford, Strong, Taylor of New York, Telfair, Townsend, Tucker, Vose, Wallace, Ward of New Jersey, Whiteside, Wilcox, Wilde, Wilkin, Williams, Willoughby, William Wilson, and Yancey.

SATURDAY, March 9.

Mr. LOWNDES, from the Committee of Ways and Means, reported a bill to repeal the act entitled "An act to provide additional revenues for defraying the expenses of Government and maintaining the public credit, by laying duties on household furniture, and on gold and silver watches;" which was read twice, and committed to the

Committee of the Whole on the report of the Committee of Ways and Means upon the subject of revenue.

Mr. LOWNDES also reported a bill to abolish the existing duties on spirits distilled within the United States, and to lay other duties in lieu of those at present imposed on licenses to distillers of spirituous liquors; which was read twice and committed to the Committee of the Whole last mentioned.

On motion of Mr. INGHAM, the Secretary of the Treasury was directed to report to the next session of Congress whether any, and, if any, what alterations are necessary to equalize the duty on the capacity of stills, boilers, and other implements used in distillation.

On motion of Mr. LOWNDES, the Committee of Ways and Means were instructed to inquire into the expediency of exempting from the payment of duties, the carriage of His Excellency Mr. Gore, Governor of the British Province of Upper Canada, who landed at New York and passed through the State of New York, in the month of August or September last, on his way to his Government.

The bill from the Senate "in addition to the act entitled 'An act concerning the Navy Pension Fund,'" was read twice and referred to the Committee on Naval Affairs.

Mr. JACKSON, from the committee to whom was referred the bill from the Senate "to extend certain privileges as therein mentioned to Bernard Edme Verjon," reported the same with amendments; which were read and agreed to, and ordered to be engrossed, and the bill read the third time on Monday next.

An engrossed bill, entitled "An act for the relief of Gustavus Loomis," was read the third time and passed.

NATIONAL BANK.

The intervening orders of the day were postponed, and the House resolved itself into a Committee of the Whole, on the National Bank bill.

Mr. CADY offered an amendment to prevent the establishment of more than one branch of the bank in any one State.

The motion was opposed by Messrs. CALHOUN, BRADBURY, and WRIGHT; and supported by Messrs. CADY and CULPEPER; and then negatived without a division.

After some unimportant amendment, and the bill having been gone through, the question was stated on the Committee's rising and reporting it to the House, when Mr. CLAY rose and delivered at length his sentiments in favor of the bill, its principle and details.

A desultory debate followed, between Mr. JACKSON, Mr. CLAY, and Mr. RANDOLPH, on one or two points of Mr. CLAY's arguments—Mr. RANDOLPH touching incidentally on the bill itself.

After which, the Committee rose and reported progress.

[The speech delivered on this occasion, by Mr. CLAY, appears not to have been reported, and, of course, cannot be inserted as uttered in the House; but,

after the return of Mr. C. to Kentucky, he made an address to his constituents, in which he gave the substance of it, as follows:]

On one subject, that of the Bank of the United States, to which, at the late session of Congress, he gave his humble support, Mr. CLAY felt particularly anxious to explain the grounds on which he had acted. This explanation, if not due to his own character, the State and the district to which he belonged had a right to demand. It would have been unnecessary if his observations, addressed to the House of Representatives pending the measure, had been published; but they were not published, and why they were not published he was unadvised.

When he was a member of the Senate of the United States, he was induced to oppose the renewal of the charter to the old Bank of the United States, by three general considerations: The first was, that he was instructed to oppose it by the Legislature of the State. What were the reasons that operated with the Legislature, in giving the instruction, he did not know. He had understood from members of that body, at the time it was given, that a clause, declaring that Congress had no power to grant the charter, was stricken out; from which it might be inferred, either that the Legislature did not believe a bank to be unconstitutional, or that it had formed no opinion on that point. This inference derives additional strength from the fact, that, although the two late Senators from this State, as well as the present Senators, voted for a National Bank, the Legislature, which must have been well apprized that such a measure was in contemplation, did not again interpose, either to protest against the measure itself, or to censure the conduct of those Senators. From this silence, on the part of a body which has ever fixed a watchful eye upon the proceedings of the General Government, he had a right to believe that the Legislature of Kentucky saw, without dissatisfaction, the proposal to establish a National Bank; and that its opposition to the former one was upon grounds of expediency, applicable to that corporation alone, or no longer existing. But when, at the last session, the question came up as to the establishment of a National Bank, being a member of the House of Representatives, the point of inquiry with him was, not so much what was the opinion of the Legislature, although, undoubtedly, the opinion of a body so respectable would have great weight with him under any circumstances, as what were the sentiments of his immediate constituents. These he believed to be in favor of such an institution, from the following circumstances: In the first place, his predecessor (Mr. HAWKINS) voted for a National Bank, without the slightest murmur of discontent. Secondly, during the last Fall, when he was in his district, he conversed freely with many of his constituents upon that subject, then the most common topic of conversation, and all, without a single exception, as far as he recollected, agreed that it was a desirable, if not the only efficient remedy for the alarming evils in the currency of the country.

And, lastly, during the session he received many letters from his constituents, prior to the passage of the bill, all of which concurred, he believed, without a solitary exception, in advising the measure. So far, then, from being instructed by his district to oppose the bank, he had what was perhaps, tantamount to an instruction to support it—the acquiescence of his constituents in the vote of their former Representative, and the communications, oral and written, of the opinions of them in favor of a bank.

The next consideration which induced him to oppose the renewal of the old charter, was, that he believed the corporation had, during a portion of the period of its existence, abused its powers, and had sought to subserve the views of a political party. Instances of its oppression, for that purpose, were asserted to have occurred at Philadelphia and at Charleston; and, although denied in Congress by the friends of the institution, during the discussions on the application for the renewal of the charter, they were, in his judgment, satisfactorily made out. This oppression, indeed, was admitted in the House of Representatives, in the debate on the present bank, by a distinguished member of that party which had so warmly espoused the renewal of the old charter. It may be said, what security is there that the new bank will not imitate this example of oppression? He answered, the fate of the old bank—warning all similar institutions to shun politics, with which they ought not to have any concern; the existence of abundant competition, arising from the great multiplication of banks, and the precautions which are to be found in the details of the present bill.

A third consideration upon which he acted in 1811 was, that, as the power to create a corporation, such as was proposed to be continued, was not specifically granted in the Constitution, and did not then appear to him to be necessary to carry into effect any of the powers which were specifically granted, Congress was not authorized to continue the bank. The Constitution, he said, contained powers delegated and prohibitory—powers expressed and constructive. It vests in Congress all powers necessary to give effect to enumerated powers; all that may be necessary to put into motion and activity the machine of Government which it constructs. The powers that may be so necessary, are deducible by construction; they are not defined in the Constitution; they are, from their nature, indefinable. When the question is in relation to one of these powers, the point of inquiry should be, is its exertion necessary to carry into effect any of the enumerated powers and objects of the General Government? With regard to the degree of necessity, various rules have been, at different times, laid down; but, perhaps, at last there is no other than a sound and honest judgment exercised under the checks and control which belong to the Constitution and the people.

The constructive powers being auxiliary to the specifically granted powers, and depending for their sanction and existence upon a necessity to give effect to the latter, which necessity is to be sought for and ascertained by a sound and honest discretion, it is manifest that this necessity may not be perceived, at one time, under one state of things, when it is perceived, at another time, under a different state of things. The Constitution, it is true, never changes—it is always the same; but the force of circumstances, and the lights of experience, may evolve to the fallible persons charged with its administration, the fitness and necessity of a particular exercise of constructive power to-day, which they did not see at a former period.

Mr. C. proceeded to remark, that, when the application was made to renew the old charter of the Bank of the United States, such an institution did not appear to him to be so necessary to the fulfilment of many of the objects specifically enumerated in the Constitution, as to justify Congress in assuming, by construction, a power to establish it; it was supported mainly upon the ground that it was indispensable to the Treasury operations. But the local institutions in the several States were, at that time, in prosperous existence, confided in by the community, having a confidence in each other, and maintaining an intercourse and connexion the most intimate. Many of them were actually employed by the Treasury, to aid that Department in a part of its fiscal arrangements; and they appeared to him to be fully capable of affording to it all the facility that it ought to desire in all of them. They superseded, in his judgment, the necessity of a national institution. But how stood the case in 1816, when he was called upon again to examine the power of the General Government to incorporate a National Bank? A total change of circumstances was presented—events of the utmost magnitude had intervened.

A general suspension of specie payments had taken place, and this had led to a train of consequences of the most alarming nature. He beheld, dispersed over the immense extent of the United States, about three hundred banking institutions, enjoying, in different degrees, the confidence of the public, shaken as to them all, under no direct control of the General Government, and subject to no actual responsibility to the State authorities. These institutions were emitting the actual currency of the United States; a currency consisting of a paper, on which they neither paid interest nor principal, whilst it was exchanged for the paper of the community, on which both were paid. He saw these institutions, in fact, exercising, what had been considered at all times, and in all countries, one of the highest attributes of sovereignty—the regulation of the current medium of the country. They were no longer competent to assist the Treasury, in either of the great operations of collection, deposite, or distribution of the public revenues. In fact, the paper which they emitted, and which the Treasury, from the force of events, found itself constrained to receive, was constantly obstructing the operations of that Department; for it would accumulate where it was not wanted, and could not be used where it was wanted for the purposes of Government, without a ruinous and arbitrary brokerage. Every man who paid or received from the Government, paid or received as much less than he ought to have done, as was the difference between the medium in which the payment was effected and specie. Taxes were no longer uniform. In New England, where specie payments have not been suspended, the people were called upon to pay larger contributions than where they were suspended. In Kentucky, as much more was paid by the people in their taxes, than was paid, for example, in the State of Ohio, as Kentucky paper was worth more than Ohio paper.

It appeared to Mr. C. that, in this condition of things, the General Government could depend no longer upon these local institutions, multiplied and multiplying daily; coming into existence by the breath of eighteen State sovereignties, some of which, by a single act of volition, had created twenty or thirty at a time. Even if the resumption of specie payments could have been anticipated, the General Government remaining passive, it did not seem to him that the General Government ought longer to depend upon these local institutions exclusively for aid in its operations; but he did not believe it could be justly so anticipated. It was not the interest of all of them, that the renewal should take place of specie payments; and yet, without concert between all, or most of them, it could not be effected. With regard to those disposed to return to a regular state of things, great difficulties might arise as to the time of its commencement.

Considering, then, that the state of the currency was such, that no thinking man could contemplate it without the most serious alarm; that it threatened general distress, if it did not ultimately lead to convulsion and subversion of the Government, it appeared to him to be the duty of Congress to apply a remedy, if a remedy could be devised. A National Bank, with other auxiliary measures, was proposed as that remedy. Mr. C. said, he determined to examine the question, with as little prejudice as possible arising from his former opinion; he knew that the safest course to him, if he pursued a cold, calculating prudence, was to adhere to that opinion, right or wrong. He was perfectly aware that, if he changed, or seemed to change it, he should expose himself to some censure; but, looking at the subject with the light shed upon it by events happening since the commencement of the war, he could no longer doubt. A bank appeared to him not only necessary, but indispensably necessary, in connexion with another measure, to remedy the evils of which all were but too sensible. He preferred, to the suggestions of the pride of consistency, the evident interests of the community, and determined to throw himself upon their candor and justice. That which appeared to him, in 1811, under the state of things then existing, not to be necessary to the General Government, seemed now to be necessary, under the present state of things. Had he then foreseen what now exists,

and no objection had laid against the renewal of the charter, other than that derived from the Constitution, he should have voted for the renewal.

Other provisions of the Constitution but little noticed, if noticed at all, on the discussions in Congress in 1811, would seem to urge that body to exert all its powers to restore to a sound state the money of the country. That instrument confers upon Congress the power to coin money, and to regulate the value of foreign coins; and the States are prohibited to coin money, to emit bills of credit, or to make anything but gold and silver coin a tender in payment of debts. The plain inference is, that the subject of the general currency was intended to be submitted exclusively to the General Government. In point of fact, however, the regulation of the general currency is in the hands of the State Governments, or, which is the same thing, of the banks created by them. Their paper has every quality of money, except that of being made a tender, and even this is imparted to it by some States, in the law, by which a creditor must receive it, or submit to a ruinous suspension of the payment of his debt. It was incumbent upon Congress to recover the control which it had lost over the general currency; the remedy called for was one of caution and moderation, but of firmness. Whether a remedy directly acting upon the banks, and their paper thrown into circulation, was in the power of the General Government or not, neither Congress nor the community were prepared for the application of such a remedy; an indirect remedy, of a milder character, seemed to be furnished by a National Bank. Going into operation with the powerful aid of the Treasury of the United States, he believed it would be highly instrumental in the renewal of specie payments. Coupled with the other measure adopted by Congress for that object, he believed the remedy effectual. The local banks must follow the example which the National Bank would set them, of redeeming their notes by the payment of specie, or their notes will be discredited and put down.

If the Constitution, then, warranted the establishment of a bank, other considerations besides those already mentioned strongly urged it. The want of a general medium is everywhere felt; exchange varies continually, not only between different parts of the Union, but between different parts of the same city. If the paper of a National Bank were not redeemed in specie, it would be much better than the current paper; since, although its value, in comparison with specie, might fluctuate, it would afford an uniform standard.

If political power be incidental to banking operations, there ought, perhaps, to be in the General Government some counterpoise to that which is exerted by the States. Such a counterpoise might not, indeed, be so necessary, if the States exercised the power to incorporate banks equally, or in proportion to their respective populations. But that is not the case. A single State has a banking capital equivalent, or nearly so, to one fifth of the whole banking capital of the United States. Four States combined have the major part of the

1195   HISTORY OF CONGRESS.   1196

H. of R.   *Thomas Kemp—Memorial of General Harrison.*   MARCH, 1816.

banking capital of the United States. In the event of any convulsion, in which the distribution of banking institutions might be important, it may be urged that the mischief would not be alleviated by the creation of a National Bank, since its location must be within one of the States. But, in this respect, the location of the bank is extremely favorable, being in one of the middle States, not likely, from its position, as well as its loyalty, to concur in any scheme for subverting the Government; and a sufficient security against such contingency is to be found in the distribution of branches in different States, acting and reacting upon the parent institution, and upon each other.

MONDAY, March 11.

On motion of Mr. WEBSTER,

Resolved, That it is expedient to provide by law for making the gold coins of England, France, Portugal, and Spain, and the crowns of France, parts of the legal currency of the United States, at rates corresponding with the intrinsic value of such coins, respectively, and that the Committee on the National Currency be instructed to prepare and report a bill accordingly.

A message from the Senate informed the House that the Senate have passed a bill "further supplementary to the act, entitled 'An act providing for the indemnification of certain claimants of public lands in the Mississippi Territory.'"

The said bill was read twice, and committed to the Committee on Public Lands.

The SPEAKER laid before the House two communications from the President of the United States, one transmitting the amount of expenses incurred for public buildings, &c., in Washington; and the other a statement of the militia of the United States, according to the latest returns at the Naval Department.

The bill from the Senate "to extend certain privileges, as therein mentioned, to Bernard Edme Verjon," was read the third time as amended, and passed.

Mr. YANCEY, from the Committee of Claims made a report on the petition of Captain John T. Wirt, which was read; when Mr. Y. reported a bill for the relief of John T. Wirt; which was read twice, and ordered to be engrossed and read a third time to-morrow.

Mr. YANCEY also made a report on the petition of Richard Ridgely, Edward Pugh, and Charles W. Hanson, which was read; when Mr. Y. reported a bill for the relief of Richard Ridgely, and others; which was read twice, and committed to a Committee of the Whole.

Mr. YANCEY also made a report in pursuance of the resolution of the House, of the 25th January, 1816, which was read; when Mr. Y. reported a bill authorizing payment for the county courthouse of Hamilton in the State of Ohio; which was read twice, and committed to a Committee of the Whole.

The report is as follows:

That, in the month of February, 1814, a detachment of the troops of the United States, under the command of Captain Thomas Ramsay, occupied as barracks the county court-house of Hamilton, in the town of Cincinnati, by permission of the sheriff of the county, there being at that time no other house which they could procure, and the weather being so cold and severe as to require good quarters. It satisfactorily appears to the committee, that, while the court-house was thus occupied, from some uncontrollable accident, fire was communicated to the house, and it was consumed.

The house having been thus in the occupation of the United States, and, in consequence of that, consumed by accident, which no one whose duty it might have been to take care of it could control, it is the opinion of the Committee that the damage sustained in consequence thereof should be paid to the county, to enable them to rebuild the house. They therefore report by bill.

PETITION OF THOMAS KEMP.

Mr. YANCEY also made a report on the petition of Thomas Kemp; which was read and ordered to lie on the table.

The report is as follows:

That, early in the year 1813, the petitioner entered into a contract with the Navy Department to build two sloops-of-war, "the Erie and Ontario," at Baltimore. The sum which was agreed, on the part of the Government, to be given for the vessels was then considered by the petitioner to be adequate to cover the expenses of materials and labor, and afford a sufficient compensation for the undertaking; but he states that, in consequence of the British naval force which soon after came into the Chesapeake, the materials out of which the vessels were built cost him a much larger sum than they otherwise would have done, and that he has sustained a loss of six thousand three hundred and twenty-three dollars, which he prays may be paid him.

In making this contract, there can be no doubt that the petitioner considered he had taken sufficient care of himself; and if it had turned out, upon the completion of the contract, that he had made, beyond a reasonable compensation for his labor, care, and expenses, the sum of money in question, it could not have been expected by the Government that he should have refunded that sum. The contract should be reciprocal. All that can be expected by the Government is, that it should fairly and honestly comply with its engagements. If it should be fortunate enough sometimes to make a profitable contract, it will only by that means supply a deficiency often produced by bad ones. The Committee are of opinion that the petitioner is not entitled to relief, and therefore recommend to the House the following resolution:

Resolved, That the prayer of the petitioner ought not to be granted.

MEMORIAL OF GENERAL HARRISON.

The SPEAKER laid before the House a letter from General William H. Harrison, soliciting an inquiry into the expenditure of public money within the 8th military district, while under his command; which was read.

On a proposition of Mr. McLEAN to refer the letter to a select committee, a short discussion arose, in which Mr. HALL and Mr. WRIGHT supported the propriety of laying it on the table, on the ground that it would be impossible now for a committee to discharge such a duty faithfully; and Mr. McLEAN maintained his own motion. After which the letter was referred to the Committee on Public Expenditures. The letter is as follows:

NORTH BEND, (OHIO,) *Dec.* 20, 1815.

SIR: I should apologise for this intrusion upon the time of the House of Representatives, if I considered the subject upon which I address them exclusively of a private and personal nature. Although the investigation I solicit is of the utmost importance to myself, it will, I conceive, be readily admitted, that both the national honor and interests are deeply concerned in the result. My object is to obtain an inquiry into the expenditure of public money within the eighth military district whilst under my command, and particularly whatever relates to the supplies of provision by the special commissaries of the United States, and under the contract of Messrs. Orr and Greely. My reasons for making this application, and the particular claim I conceive myself to have upon the indulgence of the House of Representatives, are most respectfully submitted to them through you, sir, in the following statement:

Shortly after the adjournment of Congress, in 1814, I was informed that the honorable Mr. FISK, the chairman of a committee which had been appointed to inquire into some complaints of the army contractors, had declared to one of the Western delegation that documents had been submitted to that committee which were deeply injurious to my public character. I immediately addressed a letter to Mr. FISK, of Vermont, demanding an explanation of this declaration. From the answer of this gentleman, I learned that I had mistaken him for another of the same name, a representative from the State of New York, and who was the chairman of the committee alluded to. To the latter, at the commencement of the last session of Congress, a similar letter was sent. In his answer he denied having used the expressions concerning me which had been attributed to him, but admitted that he had formed an opinion not very favorable to me from the statements which had been made to the committee, supported by authentic documents, chiefly my own letters, all showing a wonderful inconsistency in the orders given to the contractors for supplying the Army with provisions. Being perfectly convinced that these documents were very artful mutilations of my letters to the contractors and the Secretary of War, I transmitted to Mr. FISK, through the honorable Mr. HAWKINS, of Kentucky, all the original letters and papers in my possession relating to the subject of the supplies I had demanded of Orr and Greely. These papers were accompanied by an explanatory statement from me, and a request to Mr. HAWKINS to bring the affair before Congress, should he deem it necessary to the vindication of my character. It was not until very late in the session that Mr. FISK could spare a moment from his public duties to devote to my affair. In the answer, however, with which he honored me, he was pleased to express much satisfaction at the information contained in my memoir, and to add, that "if the documents (which accompanied it) had been exhibited to the committee of investigation they would, he was persuaded, have made an impression upon the minds of that committee different from that produced by the imperfect information which was received." That a committee should have thought proper to investigate

the conduct of a general officer commanding an army without his knowing it, and to suffer their minds to receive unfavorable impressions concerning him, upon the imperfect information furnished by his enemies, is, I am persuaded, a novel procedure with the Representatives of the people, who are the guardians of their rights and privileges. I am confident, however, that the committee acted from no previous hostility to me, and I attribute their conduct to inadvertency produced by the pressure of important business at that momentous period of our affairs. It is nevertheless certain, that these impressions of the committee have been communicated to others, and malice and hatred have given them currency in a considerable portion of the Union. To resist this torrent of calumny, I have no alternative but to solicit an investigation. If the granting of this favor is beyond the merits of an officer who has spent the greatest portion of his life in the service of the public, it will be accorded to the claims of the nation, and to the vindication of the honor and character of the country. The annals of the late war will not record the treachery of a second Arnold, but they will give to posterity an instance of military crime scarcely less detestable than that foul blot in our Revolutionary history. If another officer of high rank and trust can be truly charged with a crime so disgraceful as that of peculating upon the funds of his army, it will in the estimation of the world detract largely from the blaze of renown with which the achievements of Brown and Jackson have encircled the nation; and I humbly conceive, that no pains should be spared to ascertain the guilt or innocence of the individual accused. Under the circumstances in which the country was placed in the late war, the diversion of the public funds to individual purposes would have been equally fatal with treason, and merits punishment as severe. For myself, I was well aware that the Treasury could scarcely answer the weighty demands which were made upon it by the Military Department; and knowing, as I well did, the heroic valor of our countrymen, in common with every patriot, I believed that America had no cause of alarm but from the inadequacy of her fiscal arrangements. To some it may appear idle to speak of punishing a man for a military crime who no longer holds a military commission. The right of the Government to do this, however, is in my opinion incontrovertible. The principle being as well settled as any other in relation to the proceedings and jurisdiction of courts martial, which are derived from the "custom of war." It was the practice of all the ancient Republics, and in England, from whence we derive our military as well as our civil common law; the precedent was established in the case of Lord George Sackville, who, for alleged misconduct at the battle of Minden, was brought before a military tribunal and cashiered long after his resignation had been accepted. If, in the inquiry I solicit, anything should appear to create a doubt as to the purity of my conduct in the command of the army that was intrusted to me, let a court martial decide my fate. I promise most solemnly to admit its jurisdiction and abide its decision.

I make this application to the House of Representatives with the fullest confidence that it will not be rejected. It is the only reward I claim for a long course of laborious and faithful service. The greater the latitude which is given to the inquiry, the better shall I like it; and I most respectfully request that it may embrace the following points: Whether any supplies were ever demanded by me of the contractors, Orr and Greely, which were not called for by the state of the army, and warranted by the conditions of their contract. Whether any injustice was done to the said Orr and Greely, by any order given by me to the purchasing or special commissaries of the Army. Whether there is reason to believe that any sentiment of hostility existed in my mind towards the said contractors, and which operated injuriously to their interests, either by forcing them to do what was unnecessary, or withholding from them anything that they had a right to claim. Whether there is any reason to believe that any connexion (other than that which the relations of our commissions necessarily produced) existed between myself and any of the staff officers of the Army. And, generally, whatever relates to the expenditure of public money for the support of the Northwestern army, as far as I may have been concerned.

These points will embrace everything that any but a military tribunal is competent to decide. The inquiry will, I trust, produce a perfect conviction that the measures which were adopted were those alone by which the subsistence of the Army could have been ascertained.

I have forwarded to the Representative of the district in which I live, a number of original documents, with an explanatory statement. These, together with the testimony of Colonel Morrison, late quartermaster general, and Mr. Piatt, late purchasing commissary, both of whom will be at the Seat of Government, will furnish every information necessary to my vindication.

With the highest consideration, I have the honor to be, sir, your humble servant,

WM. HENRY HARRISON,
Late Major General in the U. S. Army.

Honorable Speaker
of the House of Representatives.

ALLEGED DEFALCATION.

The Speaker laid before the House a letter from William Simmons, late Accountant of the War Department, stating certain defalcations and misapplications of public moneys by Colonel James Thomas, late a Quartermaster General in the Army; also certain alleged improper reductions by the Treasury officers, of the amount due by Colonel Thomas to the Government; and a belief that all was not fair, which had prevented the prompt communication of the information called for by the House from the President on the tenth ultimo.

Mr. McKee moved that the letter be referred to a select committee, with power to send for persons and papers.

This motion produced a debate of considerable scope and duration. Mr. Forsyth moved that the letter he laid on the table, in which he was supported by Messrs. Wright, Smith of Maryland, and Alexander; and opposed by Messrs. McKee, Sheffey, Stanford, Grosvenor, Pitkin, and Hulbert.

The debate was confined chiefly to the character and motives of Mr. Simmons, the character of Colonel Thomas, &c. It was argued in favor of laying the letter on the table, that information on this subject had already been called for from the proper Department by a resolution of this House, which was hourly expected, and then could be properly acted on; that the letter itself was couched in indecorous and insolent terms, and was not entitled to any respect; that it was improper to countenance individuals in bringing their private quarrels and venting their spleen before Congress; that from the character of the writer his statement ought not to be received as true on his single evidence; and the reference to a committee of such statements so introduced would invite a repetition of such communications; and that the power to send for persons and papers was too great to be lightly granted, &c.

In favor of referring the letter to a select committee, for the purpose of inquiry, it was argued—that every person who came before the House on a public concern, was entitled to a hearing; that an inquiry at a former session had disclosed fraud in the individual accused by Mr. Simmons, and gave color to the charges now made in the letter; that everything calculated to awaken the attention of the House to a subject so important was salutary and ought to be listened to; that the letter contained nothing offensive to decorum; that the character of Mr. Simmons merited no disrespect, and that the character of Colonel Thomas himself required the reference, &c.

On these points the debate was very diffuse; and after it had continued about two hours,

On motion of Mr. McKee, a resolution was agreed to, creating a committee of five members to inquire into the state of the accounts rendered and settled by James Thomas, late a Deputy Quartermaster, and also to examine all accounts connected therewith, and that said committee have power to send for persons and papers.

Mr. McKee, Mr. Sheffey, Mr. Hall, Mr. Goldsborough, and Mr. Savage, were appointed the said committee.

NATIONAL BANK.

The House then resumed the consideration of the Bank bill.

The House successively concurred in the amendments of the Committee of the Whole, without objection, until it reached that which substituted the sum of fifteen dollars as the second cash instalment to the bank, instead of five.

Mr. Calhoun repeated the objections that he made in the committee to this amendment, and moved that the House disagree thereto, with the view hereafter of making the sum ten dollars.

After a few remarks from Mr. Smith of Maryland, in justification of the amendment; it was agreed to by the House.

The House then proceeded to that amendment of the committee which restrained the Government from appointing more than three of the directors from any one State.

This amendment was objected to in a few words by Mr. Telfair, and opposed also by Mr. Robertson at some length, who wished the clause restored to its original state.

After a few remarks from Mr. Smith of Maryland, in favor of the amendment, it was concurred in.

The next amendment considered, was that which added the word "native" to a clause of the bill, and thereby excluded from the direction naturalized citizens.

Mr. CALHOUN opposed the adoption of this amendment, on the ground formerly stated; and Mr. RANDOLPH again advocated it in a short speech; when

The decision of the committee was reversed, and the word "native" rejected—ayes 44, noes 67.

On motion of Mr. WEBSTER, the bill was then so amended, after a short discussion, in which Mr. SMITH of Maryland opposed the motion, as to make it equally compulsory and penal on the bank to pay its deposites in specie, as its notes or bills.

When the House arrived at the amendment providing sanctions for compelling the bank to perform its engagements—

Mr. WRIGHT made a motion substantially to strike out the clause which makes the charter forfeitable, in case of the non-payment of specie, and thereby leave only the penalty of paying ten per cent. on their notes if not so paid.

A debate commenced on this motion, which continued until near 5 o'clock, without a decision, when the House adjourned.

TUESDAY, March 12.

Mr. CLOPTON presented a petition of sundry inhabitants of the city of Richmond, in Virginia, praying that, if the National Bank should be established, a branch thereof may be fixed in the said city.—Laid on the table.

Mr. LOWNDES, from the Committee of Ways and Means, reported a bill to regulate the duties on imports and tonnage and to provide suitable buildings for transacting the business of the customs; which was read twice, and committed to the Committee upon the subject of Revenue.

Mr. ROBERTSON, from the Committee on Public Lands, reported the bill from the Senate, "relating to settlers on the public lands, without amendment;" and the bill was committed to a Committee of the Whole to-morrow.

On motion of Mr. TAYLOR, of New York, the Committee of Ways and Means were instructed to inquire into the expediency of making provision by law for the renewal of defaced Treasury notes.

On motion of Mr. COMSTOCK, the Committee on Pensions and Revolutionary Claims were instructed to inquire into the propriety of augmenting the pensions allowed by law to those private soldiers who have suffered the amputation of either of their arms or legs, by reason of wounds received in the service during the late war.

The SPEAKER laid before the House a report from the Secretary of War, in obedience to the resolution of the House, of the 21st ultimo, respecting the settlement of the claims of several of the States to reimbursement of moneys expended by them in calling out and supporting militia without the sanction of the General Government; which was read, and ordered to lie on the table.

An engrossed bill, entitled "An act for the re-

lief of John T. Wirt," was read the third time and passed.

A message from the Senate informed the House that the Senate have passed a bill "providing for the publication of the decisions of the Supreme Court of the United States;" also a bill "concerning the Library of Congress;" in which bills they ask the concurrence of this House.

NATIONAL BANK.

The House proceeded to the order of the day, being the report of the Committee of the Whole, on the National Bank bill. The motion to strike out that part of an amendment reported by the Committee, which makes the charter forfeitable for non-payment of its notes in specie, being still under consideration—

Mr. CALHOUN supported the motion to amend the amendment. It was with much reluctance, Mr. C. said, that he opposed any provision which the House had deemed necessary to perfect the bill; but in the present instance he was compelled to make an objection. The fundamental character of this bank was, that it should pay its notes in gold or silver coin, and a sufficient penalty was provided to effect that end. It is a good rule in law, said Mr. C., that where you attach a separate penalty to a particular violation of a law, you weaken the general penalty; and, as he thought the general penalty would attach in the case without this special provision, which would, therefore, weaken the general sanctions of the bill, he hoped it would be stricken out.

The motion to amend the amendment was agreed to without a division.

Mr. RANDOLPH then moved to amend the amendment of the Committee, by making the interest demandable on the notes of the bank, in case of refusal to pay specie, twenty per cent. instead of ten.

Mr. CALHOUN repeated the reluctance with which he objected to any motion which, in the opinion of the gentleman who made it, would improve the bill; but he thought that even the propriety of ten per cent. contemplated by the bill was very questionable, as he doubted whether that provision might not produce combinations against the bank, which were so anxiously guarded against. Every man acquainted with the subject knows, that no bank can at all times possess the means of meeting a general run upon it; and he submitted it to the House, whether such a provision as was now proposed would not be dangerous to the institution, by inviting a run upon it, and thereby producing a suspension of payment. He admitted that it was all-important to the benefit anticipated from the bank, that it should pay its notes, at all times, in specie; and he thought that end already secured by other sanctions sufficiently guarded. This bank, said Mr. C., is no more than a part of the commercial community in which it is established, and any embarrassment of the bank must press also on the whole commercial community; that community would be the first to give way in such a case, and this would produce a run on the bank, and compel the stoppage of payment. If the amendment would produce a greater certainty of specie payments, it might be proper; but believing that it might defeat its own object, and produce that which it was intended to guard against, he thought it dangerous.

Mr. WARD, of Massachusetts, was in favor of the amendment. He thought Mr. CALHOUN had overrated the mischiefs which might possibly ensue from its adoption. Mr. W. believed that no person would resort to the penalty, unless where the bank might exceed a temporary refusal to pay its notes. If the bank declined payment for a short time only, there was no person who would peremptorily go to law for the penalty, and there was no danger of the combination predicted. It was his opinion that the provision would be beneficial to the bank, by the character it would give it as a specie bank, the superior consequence which it would of course possess throughout the country, and the great business it would consequently be enabled to do.

Mr. RANDOLPH said, the argument of the gentleman from South Carolina, (Mr. CALHOUN,) was a very powerful objection to the principle of the bill, but none against the amendment; it was an argument which he had been keeping in reserve for another stage of the bill. He had no objection to take fifteen per cent. as the penalty, but he preferred twenty for another reason. The flagitious conduct of the banks for some time back, had proven that they could make ten per cent. more than their fair profits; and his object was to make the damages surpass any profits the bank could make by refusing to pay specie. We ought, he said, to remember certain surplusses which the banks on particular occasions distributed, in addition to the declared dividends, and it was proper in this case to guard against speculation of this kind. All banking institutions were alike in their desire to swell their profits to the greatest extent, howsoever correct and virtuous the directors might be in their private characters; and he would guard against every public robber of every grade, whether he be a Governor General of India or a Bagshot highwayman. He would put it out of the power of this bank to commit frauds on the community, without ruin to itself. Let the penalty be ample, said Mr. R.; make the bank a good one, and there is no danger of their being unable always to pay specie.

The question on making the penalty twenty instead of ten per cent. was then negatived.

The House then proceeded with the remaining amendments of the Committee of the Whole; the consideration and decision on which having been completed—

Mr. CALHOUN moved to amend the bill, by fixing the amount of the second cash payment at $10 instead of $5, as it stood in the bill. This being agreed to, and some other minor motions being disposed of—

Mr. WEBSTER moved to amend the clause which declares that the bank may sue and be sued "in all courts whatsoever," by designating the State courts.

Mr. HALL asked, if it would be not better, before this motion was acted on, to inquire a little whether Congress have the power to grant jurisdiction to the State courts, which, in some cases, they had refused to exercise, he thought properly, and the constitutionality of which was very doubtful.

Mr. WEBSTER said, the question was an important one; but this was not the first time Congress had legislated on it, though the courts of Virginia had resisted their jurisdiction. Without, however, discussing the question at present, Mr. W. said, the bill was just as objectionable as it stood, because it gave the bank the power to appear in "all courts whatsoever."

After some further discussion between Messrs. CALHOUN, WRIGHT, WILDE, and GROSVENOR, on the propriety of granting jurisdiction to the State courts specifically, the question was taken, and the amendment adopted.

Mr. ROOT then renewed the motion he had unsuccessfully made in Committee of the Whole, to reduce the rate at which six per cent. stock is to be received in subscriptions to the bank, from par to ninety per cent. Mr. R. repeated briefly his reasons for the motion, and Mr. CALHOUN his objections to it; when, after some remarks in support of it by Mr. ROSS, the question was taken, and decided in the negative—yeas 34, nays 106, as follows:

YEAS—Messrs. Adgate, Baker, Bennett, Betts, Birdsall, Brooks, Burnside, Caldwell, Chappell, Clopton, Comstock, Crawford, Crocheron, Darlington, Desha, Hahn, Hall, Hammond, Hawes, Lyle, Mayrant, McLean of Ohio, Root, Ross, Savage, Smith of Virginia, Southard, Stanford, Throop, Townsend, Wallace, Ward of New York, Whiteside, and Williams.

NAYS—Messrs. Alexander, Atherton, Baer, Barbour, Bassett, Blount, Boss, Bradbury, Breckenridge, Cady, Calhoun, Cannon, Champion, Cilley, Clarke of North Carolina, Clark of Kentucky, Clendennin, Condict, Conner, Cooper, Creighton, Culpeper, Cuthbert, Davenport, Edwards, Forney, Gaston, Gholson, Gold, Goldsborough, Griffin, Grosvenor, Hale, Hanson, Hardin, Henderson, Herbert, Hopkinson, Hulbert, Hungerford, Ingham, Irving of New York, Jewett, Johnson of Virginia, Kent, Kerr of Virginia, King of Massachusetts, King of North Carolina, Langdon, Law, Lewis, Love, Lovett, Lowndes, Lumpkin, Lyon, Marsh, Mason, McCoy, McKee, McLean of Kentucky, Middleton, Milnor, Moore, Moseley, Murfree, Nelson of Massachusetts, Newton, Noyes, Ormsby, Pickering, Piper, Pitkin, Reed, Robertson, Ruggles, Sergeant, Sharpe, Smith of Pennsylvania, Smith of Maryland, Stearns, Strong, Sturges, Taggart, Tallmadge, Tate, Taylor of New York, Taylor of South Carolina, Telfair, Thomas, Voss, Ward of Massachusetts, Webster, Wendover, Wheaton, Wilcox, Wilde, Wilkin, Thomas Wilson, William Wilson, Woodward, Wright, Yancey, and Yates.

Mr. HALL then moved a new section to the bill, the object of which was to apply the bonus arising to the Government from the incorporation of the bank to the internal improvement of the country; and to avoid any contention about the part of the country in which to commence the work, Mr. H. said he would leave that to the decision of a future Congress. The bonus, he thought, would afford from year to year as much as could be easily employed, and by the end of twenty years, when the charter would expire, the proceeds would have accomplished every object of improvement which would be proper for the General Government to attempt.

Mr. CALHOUN declared his approbation of the object, but feared the adoption of the amendment might drive off some who would otherwise support the bill. Unfortunately for us, he said, there was not a unanimous feeling in favor of internal improvement, some believing this not the proper time to commence that work; and such a provision might deprive the bill of some friends, which at present was the main object of his solicitude.

Mr. HALL thought this the most proper moment for commencing the great work of internal improvement; but if he thought his amendment would draw off any support from the bill, he would not urge it. He believed, however, it would produce a different effect, and would gain friends for the bill, who otherwise would not vote for it. His principal reason for wishing to provide for his object in this bill, was that it would then be sanctioned by a charter, and not revocable, &c.

Mr. GROSVENOR had no objection to the application of the bonus in the way proposed, but he disapproved of providing for the object in this bill. Government might hereafter wish, for various reasons, to get rid of its stock in the bank, but it would be precluded from doing so, if this amendment was adopted. There was no good reason for attaching it to this bill, because if a majority of the House were, as he hoped they were, friendly to internal improvements, they could act on the subject separately.

Mr. WRIGHT and Mr. WILDE successively offered some remarks in favor of the motion.

The amendment was rejected by a considerable majority.

Mr. CONDICT proposed to amend the bill by substituting "New York" for "Philadelphia," in the clause which fixed the location of the bank. It was, Mr. C. remarked, unnecessary to say anything as to the considerations which ought to prevail in fixing a bank for commercial purposes. He would merely remark, that in addition to the superior commerce of New York, the bank in that city would serve the financial purposes of the Government, as well as it could at Philadelphia. In the latter city he believed, moreover, there was already a plenty of bank capital.

Mr. CALHOUN observed that this was a question on which, he presumed, all had made up their minds; and it would be superfluous to say anything on it. He hoped, however, the motion would not prevail. The old Bank of the United States was established at Philadelphia, and he would prefer that city for the present institution.

Mr. ROBERTSON said that Mr. CALHOUN's reason for preferring Philadelphia, if it had any weight at all, operated against himself; for the old bank having been fixed in Philadelphia, was

an argument for placing this bank in some other city, that the benefits might not be given to one place alone; besides, if the bank was taken from the Seat of Government, to place it in a more commercial situation, it ought to be fixed in that city which was most commercial. But he had another objection in this case to Philadelphia, and, with him, the strongest one; this was, the hostility of the Representatives of that city to the bank itself. He would not consent to impose upon a place an institution which was so odious to them, &c.

Mr. WRIGHT also spoke in favor of the motion, and incidentally urged the high claims of Baltimore and of Washington city.

Mr. COMSTOCK argued in favor of New York, as possessing superior commercial advantages, and the propriety of selecting that city for a bank intended to aid commercial activity.

The motion to strike out Philadelphia and insert New York was then decided in the affirmative: For the motion 70, against it 64.

Mr. ATHERTON, with a view to restrain attempts to speculate in the stock of the bank, by persons subscribing for more than they could pay for, and selling it afterwards at an advanced price, and to make all the subscriptions *bona fide* ones, moved substantially to amend the bill by providing that in apportioning the shares, no subscription should be reduced as long as there was on the list a larger subscription.

After a few words from Mr. SMITH, of Maryland, who thought the provision would be ineffectual and was unnecessary, the amendment was adopted—ayes 67, noes 43.

Mr. MAYRANT offered a new section to the bill, the object of which was to allow the five directors appointed by the Government each a salary of —— dollars, and to prevent their obtaining any loan or accommodation from the bank.

In support of his proposition, Mr. M. spoke at some length. He adverted to the immense funds of the Government which would pass through this bank, amounting annually to the sum of twenty-five millions, exclusive of the stock owned therein by the Government. We were entering into partnership, he said, with persons unknown to us, and about to place in their hands the immense revenues of the country. It was indispensable, therefore, that the Government should not only have a strong influence in the bank, but its directors ought to be made independent, and, as far as possible, placed beyond the temptation of betraying their trusts; he would make them indeed as independent as the judges. Mr. M. quoted examples from many countries in Europe to prove the necessity of giving the Government greater influence in the bank, which, in none of the instances he cited, had ever been injurious to the prosperity of those institutions.

Mr. CALHOUN replied that his colleague's object could not be effected by his amendment; because, if the directors were precluded from borrowing from the bank, directly, they could borrow in the name and through the medium of some friend. Mr. C. remarked, further, that the salary offered must be very large to induce a commercial man of any standing to forego the benefits of the bank.

Mr. MAYRANT thought a salary of three thousand dollars would be a sufficient inducement to men well qualified for the direction, to relinquish the privilege of borrowing from the bank. After some further observations, in answer to Mr. CALHOUN,

Mr. MAYRANT'S motion to amend the bill was negatived, without a division.

The only remaining motion, meriting particular notice, was by Mr. ATHERTON, who moved that the rate at which the 3 per cent. stock shall be received for subscription, shall be reduced from 65 to 50 per cent.

Some debate ensued on this motion, which had not concluded, when the House adjourned.

WEDNESDAY, March 13.

Mr. CHAPPELL, from the Committee on Pensions and Revolutionary Claims, made a report on the petition of Sarah Easton and Dorothy Storer, which was read; when Mr. C. reported a bill for the relief of Sarah Easton and Dorothy Storer; which was read twice, and committed to a Committee of the Whole.

Mr. SERGEANT, from the Committee on the Judiciary, reported a bill further to extend the judicial system of the United States; which was read twice, and committed to a Committee of the Whole.

The bill from the Senate, "concerning the Library of Congress," was read twice, and committed to a Committee of the Whole.

The bill from the Senate, "providing for the publication of the decisions of the Supreme Court of the United States," was read twice, and referred to the Committee on the Judiciary.

A message from the Senate informed the House that the Senate have passed a bill "for the relief of George Rossier, and others," in which they ask the concurrence of this House.

NATIONAL BANK.

The House took up the National Bank bill. Mr. ATHERTON'S motion to make the rate of subscribing the three per cent. stock "fifty" instead of "sixty-five," per cent. being still under consideration, this motion was negatived; and Mr. A. subsequently moved to receive the three per cent. at "sixty" instead of "sixty-five" per cent., which was also negatived—88 to 55.

Mr. CLENDENNIN moved to reconsider the vote of yesterday, which fixed the principal bank at the city of New York. This motion produced a debate of some length and considerable animation. Messrs. SMITH, of Maryland, and WRIGHT spoke in favor of the reconsideration, and incidentally urged the claims of Baltimore to the possession of the mother bank. Messrs. HOPKINSON, SERGEANT, CALHOUN, PICKERING, ROSS, and INGHAM, likewise advocated the reconsideration, and the claims of Philadelphia; those who spoke against the reconsideration, and of course in favor

of New York, were Messrs. CONDICT, SOUTHARD, ROOT, TAYLOR, of New York, ROBERTSON, GROSVENOR, GOLD, and HULBERT.

The question was finally decided in the affirmative—yeas 81, nays 65, as follows:

YEAS—Messrs. Baer, Baker, Barbour, Bassett, Bateman, Blount, Breckenridge, Burnside, Calhoun, Chappell, Cilley, Clayton, Clendennin, Cooper, Crawford, Creighton, Cuthbert, Darlington, Desha, Forney, Forsyth, Gholson, Goldsborough, Goodwyn, Griffin, Hahn, Hale, Hanson, Hawes, Herbert, Hopkinson, Huger, Hungerford, Ingham, Jewett, Kerr of Virginia, King of North Carolina, Lewis, Love, Lowndes, Lumpkin, Lyle, Maclay, Mayrant, McCoy, McKee, McLean of Kentucky, McLean of Ohio, Middleton, Milnor, Moore, Nelson of Va., Newton, Pickens, Pickering, Pinkney, Piper, Randolph, Ross, Sergeant, Sharpe, Smith of Pennsylvania, Smith of Maryland, Smith of Va., Stanford, Taggart, Tate, Taul, Taylor of South Carolina, Telfair, Tucker, Voss, Wallace, Whiteside, Wilcox, Wilde, Thomas Wilson, William Wilson, Woodward, Wright, and Yancey.

NAYS—Messrs. Adgate, Atherton, Betts, Birdsall, Boss, Bradbury, Brown, Cady, Caldwell, Cannon, Champion, Clarke of North Carolina, Clark of Kentucky, Clopton, Comstock, Condict, Conner, Crocheron, Culpeper, Davenport, Edwards, Gaston, Gold, Grosvenor, Hammond, Hardin, Henderson, Hulbert, Irving of New York, Johnson of Virginia, Kent, Langdon, Law, Lovett, Lyon, Marsh, Mason, Moseley, Murfree, Nelson of Massachusetts, Noyes, Ormsby, Pitkin, Reed, Robertson, Root, Ruggles, Savage, Southard, Stearns, Strong, Sturges, Tallmadge, Taylor of New York, Thomas, Throop, Townsend, Ward of Massachusetts, Ward of New York, Wendover, Wheaton, Wilkin, Williams, Willoughby, and Yates.

Mr. WRIGHT made an unsuccessful motion to substitute Baltimore. And the House then struck out "New York," and replaced "Philadelphia."

Mr. ROOT, after observing that the State of New York possessed a considerable portion of United States three per cent. stock, and wishing, as the Legislature of that State was now in session, if so disposed, to subscribe that stock in the bank, moved to insert the word "States," in the clause permitting companies or corporations to subscribe; which motion was agreed to.

Mr. WRIGHT moved to restore to Congress the power of increasing the capital of the bank to forty-five millions—[the clause which granted to Congress the power of increasing the capital to fifty millions was stricken out, it will be recollected, in Committee of the Whole.] Mr. W. supported his motion with a variety of remarks on the impropriety of tying up the hands of the Government for twenty years, and prohibiting it by charter from legislating according to the growth of our population, the wants of the country, &c. He concluded by requiring the yeas and nays, which were refused; and then his proposition to amend the bill was rejected, only nine or ten rising in its favor.

Some other motions, not requiring particular mention, being disposed of—

Mr. McLEAN, of Kentucky, rose to renew a motion which he had made without success in Committee of the Whole, and which he should not again offer, if he did not conceive that his former attempt was decided under an incorrect view of the subject. Mr. McL. then moved a clause to the bill to prohibit the establishment of a branch of the bank in any State, unless such branch should be accepted by a law of the State. Mr. McL. supported his proposition at some length; showing, by facts, the injury which might result to some States extensively interested in their own banks, by forcing a branch of the National Bank upon them. This was the case in Kentucky, where the State owned a great portion of the stock of the State Bank, which was very prosperous, and its stocks very profitable; and, Mr. McL. said, he was unwilling to put it in the power of any twenty-five men to impose upon that State, without its consent, an institution which might be extremely prejudicial to its interests.

Mr. CALHOUN replied briefly, that this motion appeared to involve an inquiry into the Constitutional power of Congress to establish banks in the States. This was a question which he had wished to avoid on the present occasion, and he should decline saying anything on it. When the necessity arose for discussing the question, he should be prepared to meet it.

Mr. McLEAN's motion was negatived.

Mr. PITKIN then proposed to amend the bill, by striking out entirely the provision which gives the President and Senate the power of appointing five of the directors, and thereby leaving the whole direction to be chosen by the corporation. Mr. P. went into a general investigation of this question, the arguments on which were so fully given when before the Committee. In support of his motion he said, that, with all the interest of the Government in the old Bank of the United States, it appointed none of the directors, yet there was no complaint ever heard of the public concerns being mismanaged by that bank. If there was no necessity for exercising the power in that bank, he argued there was none for it in the present one. Neither the safekeeping of its deposites, nor the care of its interest in the bank, required the Government to possess the power, because there would necessarily always be a close connexion between the bank and the Government, produced by the strongest of motives—interest. If the power, then, was not necessary for any useful purpose, he would not willingly risk any danger from the possibility of the power being converted into an engine of oppression in the hands of the Government. He argued, that it was probable but few directors would be appointed in Philadelphia by the stockholders; that seven being sufficient to do business, and the Government directors being always on the spot, they might frequently constitute a majority of the board, and be able to wield the bank as they pleased. No man, he was confident, would embark his money in a banking concern when one of the partners had the absolute appointment of one-fifth of the directors. Mr. P. concluded by declaring that, if the provision objected to was not stricken out, he should be compelled to vote against the bill.

Mr. CALHOUN rose, not to argue the motion, because it had been fully discussed in Committee, but only to express his regret at the determination declared by Mr. PITKIN. He was aware that great difference of opinion existed on this subject, and that great difficulties must be encountered in maturing its details; but he had began to hope, from the concessions which had been made, that gentlemen would reconcile their various views, and that the bill would survive the conflicting opinions under which it started. It was, therefore, he regretted to hear Mr. PITKIN declare the direction a *sine qua non* with him.

After a few words by Mr. PITKIN, stating that he had invariably declared in conversation that this feature was with him a *sine qua non*, the question was decided in the negative—yeas 54, nays 91, as follows:

YEAS—Messrs. Atherton, Baer, Boss, Bradbury, Breckenridge, Brown, Cady, Champion, Clayton, Cooper, Culpeper, Davenport, Gaston, Gold, Goldsborough, Grosvenor, Hale, Hanson, Herbert, Hopkinson, Huger, Hulbert, Jewett, Kent, Langdon, Law, Lewis, Lovett, Lyon, Marsh, Mason, McKee, Milnor, Moseley, Nelson of Massachusetts, Noyes, Pickering, Pitkin, Randolph, Reed, Ruggles, Sergeant, Smith of Pennsylvania, Stanford, Stearns, Strong, Sturges, Taggart, Tallmadge, Tate, Vose, Ward of Massachusetts, Wheaton, and Wilcox.

NAYS—Messrs. Adgate, Alexander, Baker, Barbour, Bassett, Bateman, Betts, Birdsall, Blount, Burnside, Caldwell, Calhoun, Cannon, Chappell, Clarke of North Carolina, Clark of Kentucky, Clendennin, Clopton, Comstock, Condict, Conner, Crawford, Creighton, Crocheron, Cuthbert, Darlington, Desha, Edwards, Forney, Forsyth, Gholson, Goodwyn, Griffin, Hahn, Hall, Hammond, Hardin, Hawes, Henderson, Hungerford, Ingham, Irving of New York, Jackson, Johnson of Virginia, Kerr of Virginia, Love, Lowndes, Lumpkin, Lyle, Maclay, Mayrant, McCoy, McLean of Kentucky, McLean of Ohio, Middleton, Moore, Murfree, Newton, Ormsby, Pickens, Pinkney, Piper, Robertson, Root, Savage, Sharpe, Smith of Maryland, Smith of Virginia, Southard, Taul, Taylor of New York, Taylor of South Carolina, Telfair, Thomas, Throop, Townsend, Tucker, Wallace, Ward of New York, Ward of New Jersey, Wendover, Whiteside, Wilde, Wilkins, Williams, Willoughby, Thomas Wilson, William Wilson, Woodward, Wright, Yancey, and Yates.

Mr. PITKIN then made a motion to reduce the capital of the bank from thirty-five to twenty millions of dollars.

This motion was decided, without debate, in the negative.

Mr. GOLDSBOROUGH, after a few remarks, moved an amendment to provide that if the Government should at any time sell or relinquish its stock in the bank, it should then cease to have the appointment of any part of the directors; which motion was also negatived.

After rejecting various other propositions to amend the bill, among which was the motion of Mr. WEBSTER to increase the value of the shares to four hundred dollars, and diminish the number to 87,500, the question was taken on ordering the bill to be engrossed, and read a third time, and decided in the affirmative—yeas 82, nays 61, as follows:

Yeas—Messrs. Adgate, Alexander, Atherton, Baer, Bateman, Betts, Bess, Bradbury, Brown, Calhoun, Cannon, Champion, Chappell, Cilley, Clarke of North Carolina, Clark of Kentucky, Clendennin, Comstock, Condict, Conner, Creighton, Crocheron, Cuthbert, Edwards, Forney, Forsyth, Ghelson, Grosvenor, Hawes, Henderson, Huger, Halbert, Hungerford, Ingham, Irving of New York, Jackson, Jewett, Kerr of Virginia, King of North Carolina, Langdon, Love, Lowndes, Lumpkin, Maclay, Mason, McCoy, McKee, Middleton, Moore, Moseley, Murfree, Nelson of Massachusetts, Noyes, Pickens, Pinkney, Piper, Robertson, Sharpe, Smith of Maryland, Smith of Virginia, Southard, Sturges, Taul, Taylor of New York, Taylor of South Carolina, Telfair, Thomas, Throop, Townsend, Tucker, Ward of New Jersey, Wendover, Wheaton, Wilde, Wilkins, Williams, Willoughby, William Wilson, Woodward, Wright, Yancey, and Yates.

Nays—Messrs. Baker, Barbour, Bassett, Blount, Breckenridge, Burnside, Cady, Caldwell, Clayton, Clopton, Cooper, Crawford, Culpeper, Darlington, Davenport, Desha, Gaston, Gold, Goldsborough, Goodwyn, Hahn, Hale, Hall, Hanson, Hardin, Herbert, Hopkinson, Johnson of Virginia, Kent, Law, Lewis, Lovett, Lyle, Lyon, Marsh, Maynard, McLean of Kentucky, McLean of Ohio, Milnor, Newton, Ormsby, Pickering, Pitkin, Randolph, Reed, Root, Ross, Ruggles, Sergeant, Savage, Smith of Pennsylvania, Stanford, Stearns, Strong, Tallmadge, Vose, Wallace, Ward of Massachusetts, Webster, Whiteside, and Wilson.

The Speaker laid before the House two Messages from the President of the United States, one enclosing the documents respecting the public accounts of Colonel James Thomas, called for by the House; and the other a report respecting the Cumberland road; which being severally referred, the House adjourned.

Thursday, March 14.

Mr. McLean, of Ohio, presented a resolution of the General Assembly of the State of Ohio, requesting that measures may be taken for defining the legal exposition of the conflicting claims to an exclusive use of the late improvements on steamboat navigation, and whether recent improvements made to a discovery that has long been in use can entitle the discoverer to the benefit of a patent agreeably to the Constitution of the United States.—Referred to the Committee on the Judiciary.

Mr. Creighton, from the Committee on the Public Lands, reported a bill for the relief of William Crawford and Frederick Bates; which was read twice, and committed to a Committee of the Whole to-morrow.

Mr. Sergeant, from the Committee on the Judiciary, reported a bill for altering the times of holding the circuit and district courts of the district of Vermont; which was read twice, and ordered to be engrossed, and read a third time to-morrow.

Mr. Middleton, from the Committee on Naval Affairs, reported the bill from the Senate "in addition to an act in relation to the navy pension fund," without amendment; and the bill was committed to a Committee of the Whole.

The Speaker laid before the House a supplemental report of the Secretary of War, in relation to invalid pensions; which was referred to the Committee on Pensions and Revolutionary Claims.

The bill from the Senate "for the relief of George Rossier, and others," was read twice, and committed to the Committee of Ways and Means.

MONUMENT TO WASHINGTON.

Mr. Huger, from the joint committee appointed on the 16th ultimo, respecting the remains of the late General George Washington, made a report containing joint resolutions providing for the erection of a monument to commemorate the virtues of George Washington; which were read, and referred to a Committee of the whole House on Saturday next. The report is as follows:

That they have carefully and attentively examined into the subject referred to them, and submit to the consideration of their respective Houses the following resolutions:

Resolved, by the Senate and House of Representatives of the United States of America in Congress assembled, That, in pursuance of the resolution of Congress of the 24th of December, 1799, a marble monument be erected by the United States to commemorate the military, political, and private virtues of George Washington.

That the receptacle for his remains be prepared in the foundation of the Capitol, and that the monument be placed over the same, and in the centre of the great hall of the Capitol.

That, on the four sides of the monument, he be represented—

As the defender of his country against the French and Indians in the war before the Revolution.

As the protector of her rights against British invasion, and the Captain of her Armies in the war of independence.

As the first President of the United States wisely administering the public affairs during eight years of peace, other nations being engaged in war.

As a private citizen voluntarily retired from public office, and engaged in the employments of agriculture.

And be it further resolved, That the President of the United States be, and is hereby, authorized to take measures to carry the foregoing resolution into execution.

NATIONAL BANK.

The bill to incorporate the subscribers to the Bank of the United States, was read a third time; and the question stated on the passage of the bill.

Mr. Webster rose to oppose it, declaring that he had long held, and still continued to hold, the opinion that a bank formed upon proper principles would be good for the country, and as a proof of his sincerity, he expressed his wish that the House, by agreeing to strike out the objectionable part of the bill, would justify him in agreeing to the present one. He said, he had two objections to the bill, the first, the unnecessary magnitude of the capital; the other, the vesting Government with the appointment of five of the directors. Of the first, he said, that it was unprecedented; such a capital had never in any country been given to any bank, and he considered that alone as sufficient cause for rejecting the bill, unless its advocates could demonstrate that it was necessary. Besides, the object of the bill being to restore the currency of the country to a proper condition, the remedy necessary was not one to work far hence; it must be speedy, for which this capital would not answer, as it was to come in, only in reversion; it was unalienable, either this year or in the next: and he challenged gentlemen to show that the magnitude of the capital had any necessary connexion with the great object of the bill. Besides, he contended that great danger was to be apprehended from a large capital. He reminded the House that the very gentlemen who were the advocates of this capital, were the same who opposed the old United States Bank, upon the grounds that it would introduce great foreign influence; and insisted that Jay's Treaty was carried by it. Yet the capital of that bank was ten millions only—how then could they now insist upon a capital of thirty-five millions? If there there was danger in one, there was, of course, great danger in the other. The worst feature in this capital he considered to be its connexion with the influence given to Government over the direction of the bank; and to throw a light upon his intention, he said, that if any means could be adopted to take security against that undue influence, he would even now vote for the bill. That, to be useful, a bank must be independent of Government, had long been a maxim—in our own country that maxim was first established by the report of Hamilton, and was ratified by Washington, and the existence and conduct of the United States Bank for twenty-five years confirmed and proved the correctness of the opinion. What, he asked, could be the object of the provision? Gentlemen said it was not to control the bank—and in saying so, he contended that they gave up the argument; for, as to all necessary knowledge of the transactions of the bank that was sufficiently provided for by another provision of the bill. But if not for the purpose of exercising an undue influence in Government over the directors, he asked, what could they want it for. Mr. W. spoke at considerable length.

Mr. Grosvenor supported the bill, and insisted that the power of appointing directors could not give to Government the influence which Mr. Webster apprehended. Whatever influence those directors created could only be exercised by being backed with the deposites of Government—take away those deposites and the directors were nothing—for they had no control but by the influence of the deposites. As to the amount of capital he never thought it an objection; for, in order to encounter the obnoxious banks, it would be necessary for the National Bank to have a proud and commanding capital; and if it were true, as Mr. Webster himself had said, that more of active capital than seven millions could not be

brought into use, the rest would be inoperative and harmless. For his own part Mr. G. should not be afraid of a capital of a hundred millions; for he should deprecate as much as Mr. Webster a real Government bank, because it would not answer the object for which this was intended—for which purpose it must be entirely independent; and he endeavored to prove, by the state of the New York banks, that the Government having a share in the direction was perfectly innocuous.

Mr. Holmes spoke in favor of the bill.

Mr. Cady spoke as follows:

Mr. Speaker: It has been said, that the greatest evil with which our country is now afflicted, arises from the conduct of the State banks in refusing to pay their debts; and that the hope of gain will deter them for ever resuming a correct course of conduct, unless the Government shall compel them to redeem their bills in specie. And sir, the friends of the bill upon your table insist that it will furnish a remedy for the evil which threatens ruin to our country; that it is absolutely necessary that that bill should become a law in order to enable the Government to coerce the State banks to alter their conduct. But, sir, what security have we that this great National Bank with a capital of thirty-five millions of dollars will, if incorporated, be an engine in the hands of the Government, by which the State banks can be chastised for their past transgressions, and hereafter be constrained to pursue a different course? What security have we that the National Bank will not pursue the same conduct of which we complain in the State banks? It has been truly said, that they are governed by motives of interest, and will never voluntarily redeem their bills. Will not the National Bank be governed by the same motives; will it not pursue that course which promises the greatest profit? Can you hope sir, that the magnitude of its capital will make it honest? It would be as reasonable to calculate that the ferocity of a lion would be decreased as his size was increased. What, sir, are the provisions incorporated in that bill, by which the instinct of the National Bank is to be controlled and the bank compelled to pay its notes? There is but one single provision calculated to have that effect, but what may be found in the charter of every bank in the Union; and that provision, considering the city in which the bank is to be placed, furnishes no security that the National Bank will be more punctual in paying its debts than the State banks. The provision to which I allude is this, that the bank is made liable to pay an interest of twelve per cent. per annum on such of its bills as shall be presented for payment, and payment be refused. What, sir, would be thought of this provision, had it also provided that any person who should prosecute the bank should pay his own costs, which will amount to more than the interest of twelve per cent.? Sir, the provision would be considered useless, it would be deemed a mockery. Yet such is the provision in effect; because this bank can only be sued in the State of Pennsylvania, where the plaintiff must pay all, or nearly all, his own costs. Had the bank been placed in New York, where defendents are obliged to pay the costs of compelling them to do justice, the amount of such costs, and the twelve per cent. interest, would have some influence in inducing the bank to pay its debts. But being placed in Philadelphia the bank will feel protected against its creditors; it will know that no one of its creditors, for any ordinary sum, can prosecute without submitting to a loss. Sir, the bills of this bank are to be circulated in every part of the United States, and no person who resides out of the State of Pennsylvania would think of prosecuting the bank, while he could dispose of its bills for any reasonable discount. We have then no security that the National Bank, if incorporated, will pay its notes, but the probability is, that it will at once adopt the practice of the State banks, and thus render the evils of which we complain almost incurable.

The Secretary of the Treasury in his annual report to us, expressly states in relation to a national currency, as follows: "It is nevertheless 'with the State banks that the measure for restor-'ing the national currency, of gold and silver, 'must originate; for, until their issues of paper 'be reduced, their specie capitals be reinstated, and 'their specie operations be commenced, there will 'be neither room, nor employment, nor safety for 'the introduction of the precious metals."

It is then the avowed and deliberate opinion of the Secretary of the Treasury, who controls the financial concerns of this country, that this National Bank cannot go into operation and circulate the precious metals with safety, till the State banks resume specie payments. And yet gentlemen on this floor tell us that this National Bank can and must go into operation in order to compel the State banks to pay specie. How can the opinion of the learned Secretary and the declarations of these honorable gentlemen be reconciled? His opinion is, that the diseased state of the national currency must be cured before the National Bank can safely go into operation. They insist that it must go into operation in order to produce that cure. How, sir, is this National Bank either to flatter or compel the State banks to pay specie? To be of any service in this great work of reformation, it must, contrary to the opinion of the Secretary of the Treasury, go into operation surrounded by banks which do not and will not pay specie. It must be able to issue its bills and redeem them with specie. But, sir, from whence is this National Bank to obtain its specie capital of seven millions of dollars? We have been told that in June last all the banks in the United States had but fifteen millions of dollars in specie. From whence, I again ask, is the National Bank to get its specie capital? Can it draw that capital from South America or from Europe? No, sir; its specie capital must be drawn from the vaults of the existing banks, or from the pockets of its individuals. If the vaults of the State banks are to be drained to supply the National Bank with its specie capital, how is that mea-

sure to enable them to redeem their bills in specie? If the patient be debilitated and bled to fainting, would you not suspect the sanity of the physician who should insist that more bleeding was necessary, and was the only means of restoring to the patient a full pulse and strength? Sir, the directors of the State banks have wisdom enough to perceive that this great national engine, created to chastise them, will not soon be able to inflict a blow, unless they impart to it strength by giving it their specie. Pass the bill, then, upon your table, and you furnish the State banks with an apology for keeping their vaults shut, to prevent their specie from giving strength to the National Bank. There is, therefore, no hope that the banks which have hitherto refused to pay specie will soon resume such payments. No; self-preservation will dictate to them a different course. But, sir, there are other grounds on which I object to the bill under consideration. This bill gives to the National Bank a power to establish branches, without limit as to number, in every part of the United States. This appears to me an unnecessary and dangerous power. If we at first give to this bank the power to establish one branch in each State, it is enough to answer all the purposes of Government in the collection and distribution of its revenue. If experience shall show that the interests of the country require that this bank should have the power to establish more than one branch in any one State, Congress can hereafter grant to banks that power; but to grant to the bank at this time the power to establish as many branches as its interests may within twenty years dictate, is extremely unwise. No man can foresee the changes which may take place, and the improvements which may be made in this country in the next twenty years. Should this bank ever sell the Government stock, which at first is to form three-fourths of its capital, so as to have in its vaults a specie capital of thirty-five millions of dollars, it will then be able to control all the moneyed operations in this country; its interests and its avarice will dictate to it the establishment of branches in every commercial town in the United States, where banking capital can be used to advantage. I am unwilling this or any other bank should have this power over the State of New York; that State once had the misfortune to have within its bosom a bank claiming such a power. That State, sir, contains many commercial towns in which banking may be carried on profitably; and towns of that character will probably be very much increased, both in number and importance, during the time this bank is to exist; and I will not aid in giving to any class of men who already have accumulated sufficient wealth to become the proprietors of the National Bank, the power for the succeeding twenty years to establish a bank in every commercial town in the State of New York. No, sir, the citizens of that State ought to enjoy all the profits of all the banks within it, other than such as may be necessary to answer the fair purposes of the General Government. When the General Government claims more than this for its favorite bankers, the claim is unreasonable and ought not to be sanctioned.

There is another provision in this bill to which I am opposed. It is that, sir, which gives to the President and Senate of the United States power to appoint five of the directors of the bank. The effect of that provision will be to deter prudent, cautious capitalists from investing their funds in this bank; such men choose to manage their own business in their own way, or to have it managed by agents chosen by themselves, and will not very willingly subject their money to the control or interference of governmental agents. Suppose, sir, we were passing a law to sell a valuable tobacco plantation, but should reserve to the Government the right of appointing the overseer of that plantation: What prudent, cautious capitalist would purchase the plantation thus offered for sale? No man in his senses would make the purchase. Would it be said that the President of the United States, with the aid of the Senate, could not appoint a fit overseer for a tobacco plantation? Certainly, for he is as competent to make such appointment as to appoint the directors of a bank. Yet, sir, no prudent planter would purchase your plantation, unless he was at liberty to appoint the overseer. So, few cautious men will purchase stock in a bank in which the Government are, in any manner, to have an influence in the direction. Men, however, of daring enterprise, who are now loaded with Government stock, may take stock in the proposed bank, under an expectation that they can sell bank stock to more profit than they can sell the stock they now have. In the hands of such men, I do not believe a National Bank will be a national blessing.

Mr. CLOPTON said, that he did not intend to detain the House; it was utterly out of his power to do so, if he were ever so willing; the situation of his health would not admit of it: but that he rose merely to enter his protest, in as solemn a manner as he was able, against the doctrine advanced by the gentleman from Maryland (Mr. WRIGHT)—a doctrine which, he believed, had diffused itself extensively among members of this House—that is, that acts of Congress, and the execution of them, determined and settled the Constitutional question as to the right of future legislation upon the objects of those acts, so that when the subject-matter of any former act, which had been regularly executed, should be proposed to this Legislature as the object of a new act, the question whether it be Constitutional or not, was precluded from any further examination, and the Legislature bound to consider the act as authorized by the Constitution. This doctrine he abhorred, and took this occasion to enter his most solemn protest against it.

Sir, said Mr. C., I have been long a member of the House of Representatives. I was a member of it at the gloomiest period of Federal times, and have been during the whole course of the Republican Administration since; and I must say that of all the pernicious doctrines I have ever heard 14th CON. 1st SESS.—39

advanced, this, in my view, is one of the most pernicious.

Are gentlemen, said he, whose fancies are tickled with this new idea, apprized of what may be the consequence of deciding and settling Constitutional questions by this standard? Do they not see that a few acts of Congress, affecting the great essential principles of personal liberty and personal property, might destroy everything valuable in the Constitution? We have, said he, already witnessed evil times, and evil times may again occur (I wish they may not be fast approaching) when such acts may be passed. According to this doctrine, the freedom of the press is already gone, for, by this doctrine, you declare that you have a right to revive the Sedition act whenever you please. That act had all the public recognitions spoken of as sanctioning and confirming the validity of the bank act. It was enacted in due form of legislation, carried fully into execution, as a valid law of the land, by judges and by juries, on many grievous and oppressive prosecutions; some of its victims heavily fined, and subjected to long and severe imprisonment; while the whole community submitted to the progress of its operation; and, though a large proportion of the people in some sections of the Union denounced it with expressions of abhorrence, at the same time as large a proportion, perhaps, in some other sections, made no objection to it. Thus it continued in force and operation until the expiration of the term for which it was enacted.

I have said, sir, observed Mr. C., and I feel myself justified in making the declaration, that, according to this doctrine, the freedom of the press is already gone; for, if this doctrine be correct, the Constitutional authority of Congress to revive the Sedition act, or pass a similar one, is established, and the free use of the press is every moment at the mercy of the Legislature. The right no longer exists, if the use can be taken away or restrained, *ad libitum*, by an act of the Legislature, and if that act is authorized by the Constitution. But, sir, continued he, the doctrine is not correct—it is grossly incorrect—it is an horrible political heresy. It is equally incorrect, equally heretical, applied to this bill.

The consequence of the establishment of such a doctrine as this, said Mr. C., would be that the Constitution itself, the supreme rule, by which all Legislatures acting under it should be governed, and which they are sworn to support, in making their laws, would, in a process of time, be superseded and rendered altogether a dead letter by a series of the acts of those Legislatures; nor would it require that the series be a very long one. What a monstrous doctrine! be exclaimed. He felt himself totally unable to denounce it in terms any way adequate to its enormity. He lamented this inability, this want of physical power to expose it in such a manner as, he believed, it ought to be exposed. Still more did he lament his unfortunate situation, from the circumstance that it had prevented him from entering into a general argument against the bill before them. He had wished to present to the House his views, extensively, on this important subject; but he found himself unable to sustain the fatigue of going through one-twentieth part of the remarks he wished to make; the few he had made in protesting against the shocking, destructive doctrine, just alluded to, had almost entirely exhausted him, and nearly deprived him of the power of respiration.

Messrs. STANFORD, HANSON, and PICKERING, also spoke against the bill, and Mr. CALHOUN concluded the debate by a few remarks in favor of it.

The question was loudly called for during the latter part of the sitting; and, being taken at a late hour, the vote on the passage of the bill was—yeas 80, nays 71, as follows:

YEAS—Messrs. Adgate, Alexander, Atherton, Baer, Betts, Boss, Bradbury, Brown, Calhoun, Cannon, Champion, Chappell, Clarke of N. C., Clark of Ky., Clendennin, Comstock, Condict, Conner, Creighton, Orocheron, Cuthbert, Edwards, Forney, Forsyth, Gholson, Griffin, Grosvenor, Hawes, Henderson, Huger, Hulbert, Hungerford, Ingham, Irving of New York, Jackson, Jewett, Karr of Va., King of N. C., Love, Lowndes, Lumpkin, Maclay, Mason, McCoy, McKee, Middleton, Moore, Moseley, Murfree, Nelson of Massachusetts, Parris, Pickens, Pinkney, Piper, Robertson, Sharpe, Smith of Maryland, Smith of Virginia, Southard, Taul, Taylor of New York, Taylor of South Carolina, Telfair, Thomas, Throop, Townsend, Tucker, Ward of New Jersey, Wendover, Wheaton, Wilde, Wilkin, Williams, Willoughby, Thomas Wilson, William Wilson, Woodward, Wright, Yancey, and Yates.

NAYS—Messrs. Baker, Barbour, Bassett, Bennett, Birdsall, Blount, Breckenridge, Burnside, Burwell, Cady, Caldwell, Cilley, Clayton, Clopton, Cooper, Crawford, Culpeper, Darlington, Davenport, Desha, Gaston, Gold, Goldsborough, Goodwyn, Hahn, Hale, Hall, Hanson, Hardin, Herbert, Hopkinson, Johnson of Virginia, Kent, Langdon, Law, Lewis, Lovett, Lyle, Lyon, Marsh, Mayrant, McLean of Kentucky, McLean of Ohio, Milnor, Newton, Noyes, Ormsby, Pickering, Pitkin, Randolph, Reed, Root, Ross, Ruggles, Sergeant, Savage, Sheffey, Smith of Pennsylvania, Stanford, Stearns, Strong, Sturges, Taggart, Tallmadge, Vose, Wallace, Ward of Massachusetts, Ward of New York, Webster, Whiteside, and Wilcox.

FRIDAY, March 15.

Mr. LOWNDES, from the Committee of Ways and Means, reported a bill making appropriations for the support of Government for the year 1816; which was read twice, and committed to the Committee of the Whole.

Mr. YANCEY, from the Committee of Claims, made a report on the petition of R. S. Reed and D. Dubbins; which was read; when Mr. Y. reported a bill for the relief of Rufus S. Reed and Daniel Dubbins; which was read twice, and committed to a Committee of the Whole.

Mr. NEWTON, from the Committee of Commerce and Manufactures, reported a bill for the relief of David Coffin, Samuel and William Rodman, and Samuel Rodman, junior; which

was read twice, and committed to a Committee of the Whole.

An engrossed bill, entitled "An act to alter the times of holding the circuit courts of the United States for the district of Vermont," was read the third time, and passed.

The House took up the resolution submitted on the 28th ultimo, by Mr. CONDICT, and the amendment proposed thereto by Mr. NELSON, of Virginia; whereupon, Mr. NELSON withdrew his said amendment.

Mr. CONDICT then modified his said resolution so as to read—

"*Resolved,* That for the residue of the session the stated hour of meeting of this House shall be ten o'clock in the morning."

On the question to agree to the resolution, it was determined in the negative.

The bill for the relief of John Delafield occupied much time in Committee of the Whole, and the Committee having risen, was refused leave to sit again. The bill lies on the table.

The bill making further provision for settling the claims to lands in the Territory of Illinois, was considered, and ordered to be engrossed for a third reading.

The bill for the relief of certain claimants to lands in the district of Vincennes, was also considered, and engrossed for a third reading.

The House resolved itself into a Committee of the Whole on the bill for the relief of John T. David. The bill was reported without amendment, and ordered to lie on the table.

The House resolved itself into a Committee of the Whole on the bill for the relief of Erastus Loomis. The bill was reported without amendment, and ordered to be engrossed, and read a third time to-morrow.

SATURDAY, March 16.

On motion of Mr. FORNEY, a select committee of five members was appointed to inquire into the expediency of increasing the salary of the Clerk of the House of Representatives. Messrs. FORNEY, PITKIN, CLARK of Kentucky, GASTON, and JACKSON, were appointed the said committee.

An engrossed bill, entitled "An act for the relief of Erastus Loomis," was read the third time, and passed.

An engrossed bill, entitled "An act making further provision for settling claims to land in the Territory of Illinois," was read a third time, and ordered to lie on the table.

An engrossed bill, entitled "An act for the relief of certain claimants to lands in the district of Vincennes," was read the third time, and passed.

The House took up the bill from the Senate "relative to evidence in cases of naturalization;" Whereupon the said bill was again read as amended, and passed by the House.

MISSISSIPPI LAND CLAIMS.

The House then went into Committee of the Whole on the bill providing for quieting and adjusting certain claims in the Mississippi Territory.

A motion made by Mr. STRONG, to strike out the first section, produced a good deal of debate on the merits of the bill; from which we extract the following substantial view of the question. After the Treaty of 1783, that is, in 1795, when the United States took possession of the Mississippi country, they found certain settlers on lands who had settled under Spanish grants, issued when Spain was possessed of the country—the United States, without demanding any equivalent therefor, relinquished to those settlers all the right acquired by the Treaty of 1783, but without warranting them in the title; subsequently, however, certain persons holding patents under the British Government set up a claim to these lands, as having the elder title; and the actual settlers, those holding under the Spanish grants, petitioned the United States to examine and decide the claims of the British grantees, and if it be adjudged that they have the stronger title, that their claims may be satisfied by an equivalent grant of public land elsewhere. The bill reported by the Committee on the Public Lands, to whom the petition was referred, and now under consideration, provides that the Secretary of State, the Attorney General, and the Commissioner of the General Land Office be authorized to examine the disputed claims, and decide thereon according to law, as soon as the claims to 140,000 acres have been filed for decision; that if the claim of the British grantee should in any case be confirmed, the Commissioner of the Land Office shall issue his certificate for the amount thereof, which certificate shall be a final satisfaction of his claim, and shall be received in payment for any of the public lands of the United States, at the rate of two dollars per acre for every acre of the certificate; that no claim shall be filed under this act which has been barred by any former law; and that the decision of the Commissioners shall be final and conclusive.

The motion to strike out the first section being a vital one, gave rise to the debate above mentioned, in which Messrs. STRONG, WRIGHT, FORSYTH, JACKSON, and ROSS, supported the motion, and of course opposed the bill; and Messrs. ROBERTSON, McKEE, JOHNSON, CLARK of Kentucky, PICKERING, LATTIMORE, and HOPKINSON, spoke against striking out the section; Mr. CLAY, also, on a subsequent question, advocated the bill.

The question was finally determined against striking out the section; and, after some further unsuccessful attempts to amend the bill, the Committee rose, reported progress, and the House adjourned.

MONDAY, March 18.

Mr. LOWNDES, from the Committee of Ways and Means, reported a bill supplementary to the act to provide additional revenues for defraying the expenses of Government and maintaining the public credit, by laying a direct tax upon the United States, and to provide for assessing and collecting the same; which was read twice, and committed to the Committee of the Whole upon the subject of revenue.

Mr. LOWNDES, from the same committee, also reported a bill for the distribution of $100,000 among the captors of the Algerine vessels captured and restored to the Dey of Algiers; which was read twice, and committed to the Committee of the Whole on the bill for the relief of Edward Hallowell.

Mr. NEWTON, from the Committee of Commerce and Manufactures, reported a bill authorizing the Comptroller of the Treasury to cancel certain export bonds executed by Casper C. Schott; which was read twice, and committed to a Committee of the Whole.

Mr. NELSON, of Virginia, from the Committee on the Judiciary, reported the bill from the Senate "providing for the publication of the decisions of the Supreme Court of the United States," without amendment, and the bill was committed to a Committee of the Whole.

The SPEAKER laid before the House a letter from the Secretary of the Treasury, transmitting statements of the valuation of lands, dwelling houses, and slaves, in the State of Maryland, in obedience to the resolution of the House of the fifth instant; which were ordered to lie on the table.

A message from the Senate informed the House that the Senate have passed a bill "respecting the late officers and crew of the sloop-of-war Wasp," and a bill "to limit the right of appeal from the circuit court of the United States for the District of Columbia," in which they ask the concurrence of this House.

MISSISSIPPI LAND CLAIMS.

The House then again resolved itself into a Committee of the Whole on the bill for quieting and adjusting certain claims to lands in the Mississippi Territory.

After some time spent in discussing various amendments to the details, and, incidentally, the principle of the bill, the Committee rose, and reported it to the House.

The debate was resumed in the House, as well on the object of the bill as its details, in which Messrs. CALHOUN, JACKSON, ROSS, and STEARNS, spoke in opposition, and Messrs. ROBERTSON, JOHNSON of Kentucky, LATTIMORE, McKEE, and EASTON, in favor of it.

In the course of the debate, on motion of Mr. JACKSON, an amendment was adopted to confine the certificates, in case the titles of the claimants be established, to the purchase of lands in the Mississippi Territory; in other words, to exclude the claimants from purchasing, with their certificates, public lands in any other than the Mississippi Territory.

The question was then taken on engrossing the bill for a third reading, and decided in the negative—yeas 43, nays 84, as follows:

YEAS—Messrs. Bassett, Bateman, Breckenridge, Brooks, Clark of Kentucky, Conner, Creighton, Culpaper, Cuthbert, Darlington, Davenport, Forney, Gold, Hahn, Hardin, Henderson, Hopkinson, Huger, Johnson of Kentucky, Kent, Love, Levett, Lyon, Marsh, McKee, McLean of Kentucky, Middleton, Milnor, Moore, Moseley, Nelson of Virginia, Ormsby, Pickering, Powell, Reynolds, Robertson, Sharpe, Sheffey, Taggart, Taul, Vose, Wilcox, and Willoughby.

NAYS—Messrs. Adgate, Alexander, Atherton, Baer, Barbour, Betts, Blount, Boss, Brown, Bryan, Burwell, Cady, Caldwell, Calhoun, Cannon, Champion, Chappell, Clarke of North Carolina, Clayton, Clendennin, Clopton, Condict, Cooper, Crawford, Crocheron, Desha, Edwards, Forsyth, Goldsborough, Goodwyn, Hale, Hall, Hammond, Hawes, Hulbert, Hungerford, Ingham, Jackson, Jewett, Johnson of Virginia, Kerr of Virginia, King of North Carolina, Langdon, Law, Lewis, Lowndes, Lumpkin, Lyle, Mason, Mayrant, McCoy, McLean of Ohio, Murfree, Nelson of Massachusetts, Newton, Noyes, Parris, Pickens, Piper, Reed, Ross, Savage, Smith of Virginia, Southard, Stanford, Stearns, Strong, Sturges, Taylor of New York, Taylor of South Carolina, Telfair, Thomas, Townsend, Tucker, Wallace, Ward of Massachusetts, Ward of New York, Ward of New Jersey, Webster, Wendover, Whiteside, Wilde, Wilkins, and Thomas Wilson.

TAX ON STILLS.

The House then, on motion of Mr. LOWNDES, resolved itself into a Committee of the Whole, on the bill to abolish the existing duties on spirits distilled within the United States, and to lay other duties on distillation in lieu thereof.

The bill proposes to change the duty from a tax on the product to a tax on the capacity of the still, and to reduce the existing duties fifty per cent. The principle of the bill, the amount of duty, &c., were discussed at large, and fully reported, when the subject was before the House in the shape of a resolution, reported by the Committee of Ways and Means.

On motion of Mr. LOWNDES, the bill was so amended as to defer the expiration of the existing duties to the 30th of June next, instead of the 30th of March, as proposed by the bill.

After accepting some amendments to conform the bill to the preceding, and adopting some others of an unimportant character—

Mr. LOWNDES proposed an amendment to the bill, the object of which was to add one hundred per cent. to the amount of the present duty on the capacity of the still on licenses for one year, and to make the price of licenses for short periods bear the same proportion as the duty imposed on the license for a year.

This motion produced considerable discussion, in which Messrs. LOWNDES and TAYLOR, of New York, supported the amendment, and Messrs. HARDIN, JOHNSON of Kentucky, TUCKER, and ROSS opposed it. It was finally agreed to—ayes 64, noes 54.

On motion of Mr. ROSS, the bill was amended, by striking out the proviso which remitted to stills wholly employed in distilling from roots, half the duties to which they would otherwise be subjected.

After some further amendment, not affecting any principle, the Committee rose, reported progress, and obtained leave to sit again.

TUESDAY, March 19.

Mr. ROBERTSON presented a petition of the Legislature of the State of Louisiana, praying that a light-house may be erected at the mouth of the Mississippi river.—Referred to the Committee of Commerce and Manufactures.

Mr. ROBERTSON, from the Committee on the Public Lands, to whom the subject was referred, reported that it is inexpedient so to alter the existing laws, as to authorize the acceptance of soldiers' warrants in payment for lands purchased at the respective land offices of the United States; which was read and agreed to by the House.

Mr. ROBERTSON, from the same committee, reported a bill providing for the sale of certain lands in the State of Ohio, formerly set apart for refugees from Canada and Nova Scotia; which was read twice, and committed to a Committee of the Whole.

On motion of Mr. BASSETT, a committee was appointed by this House to join such committee as may be appointed by the Senate, to consider and report what business will demand the attention of Congress prior to an adjournment; and also when such adjournment may probably take place.

The bill from the Senate "to limit the right of appeal from the Circuit Court of the United States for the District of Columbia," was read twice, and referred to the Committee on the Judiciary.

The bill from the Senate "respecting the late officers and crew of the sloop-of-war Wasp," was read twice, and committed to the Committee on Naval Affairs.

The House took into consideration the engrossed bill entitled "An act making further provision for settling claims to land in the Territory of Illinois," and the said bill having been read the third time, the question was taken, "Shall the bill pass?" and determined in the affirmative.

A message from the Senate informed the House that the Senate have passed the bill "to authorize the payment for property lost, captured, or destroyed, while in the military service of the United States," with amendments. They have also passed a bill "further extending the time for issuing and locating military land warrants, and for other purposes." In which amendments and bill they ask the concurrence of this House.

TAX ON STILLS.

The House again resolved itself into a Committee of the Whole, Mr. BASSETT in the Chair, on the bill to change the existing duties on distillation.

Mr. HARDIN, after adverting to the distance of many parts of the country from market, particularly the people of Kentucky, who were obliged generally to carry the product of their stills to Natchez and New Orleans, and the considerable time which must consequently elapse before they could receive any returns to enable them to discharge the duties imposed on their manufacture, moved to extend to eight months the credit of six months allowed by the bill to those whose license exceeds twenty dollars.

Mr. CLAY said, he was in favor of the motion. He avowed himself decidedly friendly to a duty on distillation, so long as any part of the existing public debt remained unpaid; but, in imposing this duty, he wished to see every proper indulgence extended to those on whom the tax was laid. To show the necessity of the proposed amendment, he adduced an instance in one of his own constituents, who had paid in duties to the Government the sum of $3,000, before he had received a single cent in return from the sale of his manufacture. The situation of the Western distillers, he said, demanded an extension of the proposed credit; they were obliged to seek a market at Natchez or New Orleans, and thence, perhaps, to ascend the Red and other rivers to Natchitoches or elsewhere. Sound policy and justice to those concerned required, therefore, the alteration proposed by his colleague; from whom he differed only in the extension of the credit moved for. Mr. C. said he would prefer twelve months, believing that term to be necessary to meet the cases already stated. A credit of two years was allowed in the duties on the India trade, and the voyages performed by the Western people in seeking a market, almost equalled those to the Indies. Mr. C. then (Mr. HARDIN having previously withdrawn his motion) moved to insert twelve instead of six months.

Mr. SMITH, of Maryland, concurred in the views of the gentleman who supported the proposed alteration, but he would prefer nine months, conceiving that term sufficient for every fair purpose. He thought every facility and encouragement ought to be given to distillation, which he believed would, in time, become a very great source of revenue, as the farmers would find it more and more their interest to carry their surplus grain to the great distilleries, and barter it for whiskey, &c. He wished also to encourage the manufacturer of that article, because he believed it the least pernicious of the ardent spirits generally used.

Mr. LOWNDES rose to state the motives which influenced the Committee of Ways and Means in fixing the period of credit at six months. It was deemed by the committee a sufficient time to allow the manufacturer to receive his returns, yet not enough to endanger the public revenue by too long a credit. But whilst he stated these views of the committee, he was obliged to concur in the arguments which had been advanced in favor of an extension of the term. He thought, however, that twelve months was rather a longer credit than necessary, and that nine months would be enough to enable the most remote manufacturers to make payment from the proceeds of their manufacture, and still not endanger the revenue by too long a credit.

After a few words from Mr. HARDIN in support of the motion, the question was taken thereon, and carried—yeas 76.

Mr. H. moved to strike out the clause which prohibits the collector from entering a distillery except in the day time; which motion was also agreed to.

The bill contained a provision that all persons taking out a license on which the duty should amount to $20, should be required to pay the same down, and should be allowed a discount thereon, at the rate of eight per cent. per annum. This discount Mr. SMITH, of Maryland, moved to increase to ten per cent.; which motion, after some discussion, was negatived.

After some other unsuccessful motions—

Mr. TAUL moved to strike out, entirely, the provision which required all duties for license under $20 to be paid down in money; which motion he supported by a few remarks.

The motion was opposed by Mr. LOWNDES, who said it was very questionable whether the sum required by the bill to be paid down, was not too small. The motion was negatived.

Mr. CONDICT then offered the following proviso to the 4th section:

"That stills employed solely in distilling fruit, shall not be subjected to the payment of more than three-fourths of the duties required in other cases; and in those cases where the pomace is fermented and distilled, without having been first separated from the liquor by the press, not more than two-thirds shall be exacted."

This motion produced some desultory debate, and was finally negatived.

Mr. PICKENS, after a few remarks in support of the motion, moved a new section to the bill, providing that the owner or user of any still employed wholly in distilling from fruit, have the option of taking out license, either on the capacity agreeably to this act, or on the product at —— cents per gallon.

Mr. P. offered this amendment principally on account of the short time which those who distilled only from fruit were able to use their stills, which he thought entitled them to the privilege he proposed.

His motion was, however, negatived without a division.

The Committee then rose and reported the bill and amendments, and the House proceeded to consider the report.

The House agreed successively, without objection, to the several amendments reported by the Committee, until it came to that adopted yesterday, on motion of Mr. LOWNDES, to increase the duty on licenses for one year one hundred per cent., and to graduate the price of licenses for shorter periods in proportion to these for one year.

On concurring in this amendment the yeas and nays were demanded, and the question decided—yeas 66, nays 62, as follows:

YEAS—Messrs. Adgate, Atherton, Barbour, Bassett, Brown, Calhoun, Champion, Chappell, Cilley, Clayton, Condict, Cooper, Crocheron, Cuthbert, Darlington, Forney, Gaston, Gold, Hale, Hall, Hawes, Herbert, Hopkinson, Huger, Hulbert, Ingham, Irving of New York, Jewett, Kent, Langdon, Law, Lewis, Lovett, Lowndes, Lumpkin, Lyon, Marsh, Mason, Mayrant, Middleton, Milnor, Moseley, Nelson of Massachusetts, Nelson of Virginia, Pickering, Pinkney, Pitkin, Reed, Smith of Maryland, Stearns, Sturges, Taggart, Tallmadge, Taylor of New York, Telfair,

Townsend, Tucker, Voss, Ward of Massachusetts, Ward of New Jersey, Webster, Wendover, Wilcox, Wilde, Willoughby, and Yates.

NAYS—Messrs. Alexander, Baer, Baker, Bennett, Betts, Blount, Breckenridge, Bryan, Burwell, Caldwell, Cannon, Clarke of North Carolina, Clark of Kentucky, Clendennin, Comstock, Crawford, Creighton, Culpeper, Desha, Edwards, Goldsborough, Hahn, Hardin, Henderson, Hungerford, Jackson, Johnson of Virginia, Johnson of Kentucky, Kerr of Virginia, King of North Carolina, Love, Lyle, Maclay, McCoy, McKee, McLean of Kentucky, Moore, Murfree, Newton, Ormsby, Parris, Pickens, Piper, Powell, Reynolds, Roane, Root, Ross, Savage, Sharpe, Shaffey, Smith of Virginia, Southard, Stanford, Taul, Taylor of North Carolina, Thomas, Throop, Wallace, Ward of New York, Whiteside, and William Wilson.

Mr. PARRIS then moved to restore the proviso in the fourth section, which had yesterday been stricken out in Committee of the Whole, and which was in the following words, viz: "*Provided*, That there shall be paid upon each still employed wholly in the distillation of roots, but one-half the rates of duties abovementioned, according to the capacity of such still."

Mr. P. stated that, upon retaining this provision, would entirely depend whether the distillers in the District of Maine could work their stills. He assured the House that his constituents were materially interested in having it retained, for without it distillation from roots, particularly in that section of the country, must be entirely suspended; that it was the only liquor distilled in his district, and he believed nearly the only liquor consumed; with the farmers he was sure it was.

The question was then taken on concurring with the Committee in striking out the proviso, and decided against concurrence, by the casting vote of the Speaker. So the proviso was retained.

Mr. CONDICT renewed the motion he made this day in Committee, with some modifications, and supported it with zeal; but his exertions were ineffectual.

Mr. PICKENS then moved to add a new section to the bill; the object of which was to retain the option allowed in the last act in case of small distillers, whereby a duty might be paid of —— cents on the spirits distilled, or the proposed tax on the capacity, at the option of the owner.

This varied from the motion he had made in Committee of the Whole, as that extended the alternative to all stills used in distillation from fruit only. Embracing in some measure the same principle as his former motion, he would not, he said, consume time in repeating his former arguments. The option proposed would afford great convenience to the farmers of the interior country, many of whom owned small distilleries, which it was only an object for them to use occasionally, and which would in many cases not be used at all, if compelled to be entered for a given period. The returns of the duties since the last act went into operation, prove how much preference had been given, in the State he represented, to paying the duty on the spirit; as

he had before observed, nearly ten times as much was collected in that State under this alternative, as that on the capacity-tax. He had heard of no evasions of the law in that case, and thought it wise to consult the convenience and the habits of the people in the mode of levying burdens when there could be no public loss.

The motion was then negatived.

Mr. P. felt a reluctance in further troubling the House after the unwelcome reception of his former motions for amendment; he, however, thought it his duty to make another essay to attain in some proportion the objects of his former amendment.

He then moved the same amendment as the last, limiting it to the distillation of *fruits.*

This motion was also negatived.

No other amendment being offered, the bill was ordered to be engrossed, as amended, and read a third time.

WEDNESDAY, March 20.

Mr. TUCKER, from the Committee for the District of Columbia, reported a bill to prevent the circulation of unchartered bank notes, in the District of Columbia; which was read twice and committed to a Committee of the Whole.

[This bill does not operate on the notes of any unchartered bank already established, and the penalties for circulating the notes prohibited are not to attach to the passer of the notes, but to the institution which shall issue them.]

Mr. TUCKER also reported a bill making an appropriation for completing the centre building of the Capitol; which was read twice, and committed to the Committee of the Whole on the bill making an appropriation for enclosing and improving the Capitol square.

Mr. TUCKER also reported a bill to appropriate the marriage license tax within Washington county in the District of Columbia; which was read twice, and committed to a Committee of the Whole.

Mr. WARD, of New Jersey, from a select committee, made a report on the petition of Andrew Law; which was read: when, Mr. W. reported a bill to extend the patent granted to Andrew Law for an improvement in the mode of printing music; which was read twice, and committed to a Committee of the Whole.

Mr. MIDDLETON, from the Committee on Naval Affairs, made a report on the petition of Samuel Travis, and others, which was read; when, Mr. R. reported a bill allowing pay to certain persons made prisoners with the revenue cutter Surveyor; which was read twice, and committed to a Committee of the Whole.

The amendments proposed by the Senate to the bill "to authorize the payment for property lost, captured, or destroyed, by the enemy, while in the service of the United States," were read, and referred to the Committee of Claims.

Mr. CLARK, of Kentucky, from the Committee on the Classification and Organization of the Militia, reported a bill for organizing, classing, and arming the militia, and for calling them forth to execute the laws of the Union, suppress insurrections, and repel invasions, and to repeal the laws heretofore passed for those purposes; which was read twice, and committed to a Committee of the Whole.

Mr. STEARNS submitted the following resolution to amend the rules and orders of the House; which was read, and ordered to lie on the table:

Resolved, That the following be added to the standing rules of the House, viz:

There shall be a standing committee, consisting of —— members, to be called "the Committee of the Revision of Bills."

It shall be the duty of the said committee carefully to examine all bills which may be reported, before they are introduced into the House, to make verbal or technical alterations, or take the same into a new draught, if they shall think proper. But they shall not change the principles or provisions of any bill without the consent of the committee who shall have reported the same.

The bill from the Senate "further extending the time for issuing and locating military land warrants, and for other purposes," was read twice, and committed to the Committee on the Public Lands.

NATIONAL CURRENCY.

Mr. CALHOUN, from the Committee on National Currency, reported a bill to regulate the currency within the United States of the gold coins of Great Britain, Portugal, France, and Spain, and the crowns of France and five franc pieces of Napoleon; which was read twice, and committed to a Committee of the Whole.

Mr. CALHOUN also laid before the House the following letter from the Secretary of the Treasury:

TREASURY DEPARTMENT, *March* 19, 1816.

SIR: I have the honor to acknowledge the receipt of your letter dated the 15th instant, making the following inquiries on behalf of the Committee on the National Currency:

1st. "Is it practicable or expedient, at present, to collect the dues of Government in gold, silver, and copper coins, Treasury notes, and notes of such banks as pay specie for their bills?"

2d. "If this be not practicable or expedient, at present, when ought an act directing the dues of Government to be so paid, to go into effect, and what ought to be the provisions of such an act?"

3d. "Would it be expedient, after the 1st of November next, or at any other time, to increase the duties on stamps on the notes of such banks as do not pay in specie?"

4th. "Are there any other measures that it would be expedient to resort to for that purpose?"

As a brief consideration of the general subject of your letter will afford the best foundation for specific answers to the questions which have been proposed, I pray the indulgence of the committee in the adoption of that course.

When the banks, during the Summer of 1814, suspended the payment of their notes in coin, the Treasury notes which had been issued, were manifestly incompetent, both in amount and credit, to constitute a substitute for the metallic currency. A declaration, therefore, at that time, that the Government would only accept, in payment of the revenue, gold and silver, Treasury notes or bank notes payable on demand in coin, would have been equivalent to a denial of the means for paying the duties and taxes, at the very crisis that rendered indispensable a strict enforcement of the obligation to pay them. Nor could such a declaration have been properly applied to the loans which the necessities of the Treasury required. A subscription in coin was not to be expected; a subscription in Treasury notes could not yield any active aid for general purposes; and consequently a subscription in the local currencies of the several States must have been contemplated as the chief resource for procuring the public supplies, as well as for discharging the public engagements. Under a sense, therefore, of the necessity which seems, for a time, to have reconciled the whole nation to the suspension of payments in coin, the Treasury continued to receive bank notes, in satisfaction of every public claim and demand; and Congress, after a session of six months, adjourned on the 3d of March, 1815, without intimating any objection, or making any provision, upon the subject.

The same state of things continued throughout the year 1815. In the annual estimates communicated to Congress, at the commencement of the present session, it was stated, that the aggregate amount which would probably be realized and received at the Treasury during 1815, from revenue and loans, might be placed at the sum of about $30,400,000. But the gross amount of Treasury notes issued and unredeemed in 1815, could not be averaged higher than $16,000,000; and the amount in actual circulation must be taken at a much less sum; for, whenever and wherever the Treasury notes rose to par, and above par, they were, for obvious reasons, withheld from the ordinary uses in exchange. Nor was it in the power of the Treasury to augment the issue of Treasury notes beyond the immediate demand for fiscal purposes. Treasury notes have not hitherto been regarded by the law as a substitute for the national currency, and the authority to issue them is only granted, as an auxiliary for supplying the occasional deficiencies of the revenue. In the New England States alone, the banks still professed to pay their notes upon demand in gold and silver; but, in fact, the issues of bank notes in that quarter have proved inadequate to meet the wants of the community; and the revenue is almost entirely collected in Treasury notes, which have been purchased at a considerable discount. It is certain, therefore, that neither Treasury notes, nor circulating coin, nor the notes of banks paying in coin, could furnish, in 1815, a sufficient medium, to satisfy the amount of the duties, taxes, and loans, for the year. But, it is important here to add, that while the interior of the country was as destitute of a currency of coin, as the cities and towns upon the Atlantic, the Treasury note medium was, in effect, monopolized by the commercial cities; and the local banks furnished all the means which the planter or the farmer could collect for the payment of his rent or his tax.

During the year 1815, the effects of the late war upon public and private credit were still felt; and the extraordinary event, which involved Europe in a new conflict, threatened a continuance of the drain upon our gold and silver; to be augmented, according to a general apprehension, by the force of an unfavorable balance of trade. Under such circumstances, the restoration of the national currency of coin could not cease to be desirable; but it must become more difficult in the accomplishment. The alternative issue of the measure deserved, therefore, the most serious consideration; and it was to be determined, not only upon views of fiscal interest and accommodation, but upon principles of national policy and justice. The consequence of rejecting bank notes, which were not paid on demand in coin, (if such payments were not thereby rendered general) must have been to put at hazard the collection of the revenue, in point of time and in point of product; to deteriorate (if not to destroy) the only adequate medium of exchange, adopted by the common consent of the nation, in a case of extreme necessity; and, in short, to shake the very foundations of private property. The powers of the Treasury Department were granted, for purposes contemplated by the Legislature in making the grant; but it is not believed, that a case attended with circumstances so extraordinary, embracing interests so extensive, and involving consequences so important, was at any time anticipated by the Legislature; or that it could be properly subjected to any other than the legislative agency. Having, therefore, made several ineffectual attempts to relieve the public embarrassments, it was deemed the duty of the department to repose, with confidence, upon the wisdom and authority of Congress, for the application of a remedy suited to the malady of the times.

The period has arrived when such a remedy may be safely and surely applied. The opinion expressed in the Treasury report of the 6th of December last, is still however entertained, that the currency in coin cannot at once be restored; that it can only be restored through a gradual reduction of the amount, attended by an amelioration of the value of the existing paper medium, and that the measure of reform must originate with the State banks. It has been said, indeed, that those institutions have already begun the salutary work; that the amount of their discounts has been reduced; that the issues of their paper have been restricted; and that preparations are made for converting their capital of public stock into the mere legitimate capital of gold and silver. Public confidence must naturally follow these just and judicious arrangements; but the interposition of the Government will still be required, to secure a successful result.

It must at all times be a delicate task to exact the payment of duties and taxes in gold and silver, before the Treasury is prepared, independent of any contingency, to give an assurance that the public creditors shall be paid in the same or an equivalent medium. If, however, a National Bank be now established, this assurance may be confidently given; and it is believed that the apprehension will prove unfounded, which suggests that the issue of bank paper will be increased, and consequently will depreciate by the operation of such an institution. A demand for the paper of the National Bank may diminish the demand for the paper of the State banks, but, after the restoration of the currency in coin, the whole issue of bank paper will be regulated by the whole demand; and the proportion of the issue to be enjoyed by the National Bank and the State banks, respectively, will be the subject of a fair competition, without affecting the public interests or convenience. If, therefore, the State banks have resumed the payment of their notes in coin, before the National Bank shall be organized, there will be no hazard of disappointment in promising a similar

payment to the public creditors; but even if that be not the case, the hazard will be slight, considering all the legislative precautions which it is proposed to adopt. Added to the metallic capital of the National Bank, the deposites of the revenue, collected in gold and silver, must be a sufficient basis for a circulation of coin; as the uses for the paper of the bank, extending throughout the nation, will be constant as well as uniform.

Under these general impressions I have the honor to submit the specific answers to your inquiries, in the following form:

1. That it be made by law the duty of the Secretary of the Treasury to give public notice that, from and after the 31st day of December next, it will not be lawful to receive in payment to the United States, anything but gold, silver, and copper coins, constituting the lawful national currency; provided, that the Secretary of the Treasury may, as heretofore, authorize and allow the receipt of the notes of such banks as may pay their notes, on demand, in the lawful money of the United States.

2. That, from and after the same day, it shall not be lawful for the Secretary of the Treasury to authorize or allow deposites of the revenue to be made, or to be continued, in any bank which shall not pay its notes, when demanded, in the lawful money of the United States.

3. That, from and after the same day, it shall be the duty of the Secretary of the Treasury to take legal measures for obtaining payment, in the lawful money of the United States, of all notes or sums on deposite, belonging to the United States, issued by, or deposited in, any bank which shall not then pay its notes and deposites, on demand, in the lawful money of the United States.

4. That, from and after the same day, the notes of banks and bankers shall be charged with a graduated stamp duty, advanced at least two hundred per cent. upon the present duty, without the privilege of commutation; saving, in that respect, all existing contracts: *Provided*, That if any banks or bankers shall, on or before the 1st day of November next, notify the Secretary of the Treasury that their notes will be paid in coin, upon demand, after the 31st of December; and if it be proved to his satisfaction that, after that day, payment was so made, then, with respect to such banks or bankers, the rate of duty and the privilege of commutation shall remain as now established by law.

Although the success of these measures is not in any degree doubted, it may be proper to add, that if it ever shall become necessary to increase their force, provision might be made, under the Constitutional power of Congress, to subject all banks and bankers, failing to pay their notes, according to the terms of the contract, to a seizure of their estates and effects, for the benefit of their creditors, as in a case of legal bankruptcy.

I cannot conclude this letter, without an expression of some solicitude, at the present situation of the Treasury. The State banks have ceased to afford any accommodation for the transfer of its funds. The revenue is paid (as already stated) in Treasury notes, where Treasury notes are below par; and the public engagements can only be satisfactorily discharged in Treasury notes, which are immediately funded at seven per cent. Where Treasury notes are above par, the local accumulation of bank credits is beyond the local demands, and the excess cannot be used elsewhere. Discontent and speculation are abroad; and all the

1233   **HISTORY OF CONGRESS.**   1234

MARCH, 1816.   *Duty on Stills—Tariff—Military Staff.*   H. OF R.

estimates of the amount of the funded debt, created since the commencement of the late war, will probably fail, unless the wisdom of Congress shall effectually provide for the early restoration of an uniform National Currency.

I have the honor to be, &c.

A. J. DALLAS.

Hon. J. C. CALHOUN, *Chairman, &c.*

TAX ON STILLS.

An engrossed bill, entitled "An act to abolish the existing duties on spirits distilled within the United States, and to lay other duties in lieu of those at present imposed on licenses to distillers of spirituous liquors," was read the third time; and on the question, Shall this bill pass? it passed in the affirmative—yeas 118, nays 13, as follows:

YEAS—Messrs. Adgate, Alexander, Archer, Atherton, Baker, Bassett, Bateman, Bennett, Betts, Birdsall, Blount, Boss, Bradbury, Brooks, Brown, Bryan, Cady, Calhoun, Champion, Chappell, Cilley, Clarke of N. Carolina, Clark of Kentucky, Clayton, Clendennin, Comstock, Condict, Conner, Cooper, Crawford, Crocheron, Cuthbert, Darlington, Davenport, Desha, Edwards, Forney, Gaston, Gholson, Gold, Goodwyn, Grosvenor, Hahn, Hale, Hall, Hammond, Hardin, Hawes, Henderson, Herbert, Hopkinson, Huger, Ingham, Irving of New York, Jewett, Johnson of Kentucky, Kent, Kerr of Virginia, King of North Carolina, Langdon, Law, Lewis, Love, Lowndes, Lumpkin, Lyon, Maclay, Marsh, Mason, Mayrant, McCoy, McLean of Kentucky, McLean of Ohio, Middleton, Milnor, Moore, Moseley, Nelson of Massachusetts, Nelson of Virginia, Parris, Pickens, Pickering, Piper, Powell, Reed, Robertson, Root, Ross, Ruggles, Savage, Smith of Maryland, Smith of Va., Southard, Stearns, Strong, Sturges, Taggart, Tate, Teal, Taylor of New York, Taylor of S. Carolina, Telfair, Throop, Townsend, Tucker, Wallace, Ward of New York, Ward of New Jersey, Webster, Wendover, Whiteside, Wilcox, Wilde, Wilkin, Willoughby, William Wilson, Yates.

NAYS—Messrs. Baer, Breckenridge, Burwell, Culpeper, Goldsborough, Hungerford, Johnson of Virginia, McKee, Newton, Randolph, Roane, Stanford, Vose.

LIQUIDATION OF CLAIMS.

The bill to provide for the adjustment of certain accounts, in which papers or vouchers have been lost, was withdrawn from the Committee of the Whole, to whom it had been referred; and the House proceeded to consider the bill.

After a good deal of discussion on the principle as well as the details of the bill (to which sundry amendments were offered)—in which Messrs. JOHNSON of Kentucky, LOWNDES, PARRIS, GOLD, and others, supported the bill; and Messrs. PITKIN, HUGER, HOPKINSON, and others, opposed it—the bill was ordered to be engrossed for a third reading.

The House then, on motion of Mr. LOWNDES, went into a Committee of the Whole on the bill to repeal the duties on household furniture, and on gold and silver watches; to which no amendment being offered, the Committee proceeded to take up the bill to regulate

THE TARIFF;

which, having been read through, and taken up by sections—

Mr. STRONG proposed to amend the bill by striking out the clause which imposes a duty of 25 per cent. ad valorem on imported woollen and cotton manufactures of all descriptions, and to substitute a provision imposing a tax of 33½ per cent. on manufactures of cotton, and 28 per cent. on those of wool.

This motion involving the question to what extent domestic fabrics shall be encouraged by protecting duties on foreign manufactures—

Mr. STRONG supported his motion, and the expediency of making the duty on the imported articles higher than was proposed by the bill.

Mr. LOWNDES rose and replied to Mr. STRONG on the question of extending the duty, taking a clear and comprehensive view of the subject of protecting duties generally; supporting the system proposed by the bill, and stating the motives which induced the Committee of Ways and Means to report a smaller duty on the articles named, than was recommended by the Secretary of the Treasury, &c.

Mr. SMITH, of Maryland, commenced some remarks on the subject, but not anticipating that the question would be put to-day, and wishing to refer to some notes not by him, he moved that the Committee rise.

The Committee then rose, reported the bill to repeal the tax on furniture and watches—which was ordered to be engrossed for a third reading—and obtained leave to sit again on the bill to regulate the tariff of duties.

THE MILITARY STAFF.

The House, on motion of Mr. JOHNSON, of Kentucky, resolved itself into a Committee of the Whole on the bill to organize a general staff for the Army.

Mr. JOHNSON then entered into a detailed comparative view of the staff proposed by the bill with that which existed during the war, to show that the Military Committee had not recommended an extravagant staff, or one greater in proportion to the number of men retained on the Peace Establishment than was allowed and found necessary during the war.

Mr. SMITH, of Maryland, followed Mr. JOHNSON in support of the general object of the bill, but regretted there was not a greater proportion of officers allowed for the Quartermaster's department, the value and necessity of whose services he enforced by a few remarks.

The Committee then proceeded in the consideration of the bill, and adopted several minor amendments at the suggestion of Mr. JOHNSON, of Kentucky.

A motion was made by Mr. TAYLOR, of New York, to strike from the bill the clause which provides for the retention of certain staff officers who had been provisionally retained by the President of the United States since the time of reducing the Army to the Peace Establishment. Mr. T. thought this clause interfered with the Constitutional power of the President and Senate to fill offices. Although the officers alluded to had been in the service, and had been passed on by the President and Senate, they were now to all intents private citizens, and this bill would legislate them into office again without allowing the President to act in the case. Mr. T. declared that his motion arose from no want of respect for the characters of the gentlemen referred to in the bill.

Mr. JOHNSON, of Kentucky, said he thought, instead of the bill legislating those persons into office, the motion would legislate them out of office, and he was opposed to the latter legislation as much as to the former. He denied that they were reduced to the rank of private citizens, and asserted that they had been constantly in service. After some further remarks by Mr. J. to prove the impropriety of carrying those officers again before the Senate, and to establish the propriety of the clause as it stood in the bill—

Mr. HULBERT said he would not sanction the clause if he thought it susceptible of the construction given to it by Mr. TAYLOR; but the President and Senate had already done their duty, and as those officers were now in office, and had been so ever since their appointment, he could see no reason for going through the process again, or troubling the Senate to repeat its former decision, &c.

After a few words from Mr. PICKERING against the proposition—

Mr. TAYLOR's motion was decided in the negative.

The Committee having gone through the Staff bill, proceeded, on motion of Mr. JOHNSON, to take up the bill to establish an additional military academy; which having been read—

Mr. PICKERING said it had occurred to him that provisions might be incorporated into this bill which would make it much more useful, by extending it to naval as well as military young men; and as West Point would, in his opinion, be a proper situation for the instruction of both, he had prepared a substitute for the present bill, which with permission he would read.

Mr. P. then offered, as an amendment to the bill, a substitute, embracing in detail the view substantially stated by him; which was received without objection, and subsequently the House ordered it to be printed.

No other motion being made, the Committee rose, and reported the bills with their several amendments; and

The House proceeded to consider the amendments to the general staff bill; which were successively agreed to.

An ineffectual motion was made by Mr. BETTS to reduce the number of judge advocates proposed from three to one.

Mr. JOHNSON had made an unsuccessful motion, in Committee, to add a section to the bill authorizing the President of the United States to employ five thousand dollars in the purchase of certain military charts and surveys owned by William Tatham.

Mr. NELSON, of Virginia, now renewed this motion, which he supported with zeal and feeling, on the ground of the Revolutionary services of Colonel Tatham, and the value of the charts and maps which it was proposed to purchase for the use of the nation.

The motion was supported also by Mr. CONDICT, and opposed by Mr. HALL, and carried—yeas 48, nays 44.

The bill was then ordered to be engrossed, and the House adjourned.

THURSDAY, March 21.

Mr. ROBERTSON, from the Committee on the Public Lands, made a report; which was read, and the resolution therein contained was concurred in by the House, as follows:

Resolved, That it is inexpedient at this time to establish a land office for the sale of public lands at the town of Arkansas, in the Territory of Missouri, or at the town of Jackson, in the county of Cape Girardeau, in the same Territory.

Mr. NELSON, from the Committee on the Judiciary, reported the bill from the Senate "to limit the right of appeal from the circuit court of the United States for the District of Columbia," with an amendment; which was read, and agreed to by the House; and the said amendment was ordered to be engrossed, and the bill read a third time to-morrow.

On motion of Mr. SMITH, of Maryland, the Secretary of War was directed to inform this House what course has been pursued by the War Department as to the payment of interest in cases where bills have been drawn on the Department for money actually received by a public agent, and which bills it was not in the power of the Secretary to pay for want of funds.

On motion of Mr. FORSYTH, the Committee of Ways and Means were instructed to inquire into the expediency of increasing the annual allowance to Ministers of the United States to foreign nations, and of allowing annual salaries to the Consuls of the United States at foreign ports.

An engrossed bill, entitled "An act to repeal the act entitled 'An act to provide additional revenues for defraying the expenses of Government and maintaining the public credit, by laying duties on household furniture and on gold and silver watches,'" was read the third time, and passed.

An engrossed bill, entitled "An act for the liquidation of certain claims, and for other purposes," was read a third time, and passed.

MILITARY STAFF.

The engrossed bill to organize a general staff for the Army, was read the third time.

Mr. TAYLOR, of New York, after repeating his objections to that clause of the bill which provides for retaining certain officers (deemed by him not to be in service) without the further sanction of the President and Senate, and the necessity he was therefore under of voting against a bill whose objects he approved, if the clause was not modified—and for the purpose of having the bill made conformable to his views on this point, he moved that it be recommitted to the Military Committee.

Messrs. HALL, ROOT, and HARDIN, respectively

supported the recommitment on the ground of objection to the section of the bill, yesterday adopted, to appropriate five thousand dollars for the purchase of military maps and charts.

Mr. Nelson, of Virginia, opposed the recommitment, and supported that provision of the bill which was the ground of the latter objection, which turned entirely on the merits of Colonel Tatham, the owner of the maps which it was contemplated to purchase, and the value of the charts, &c.

The motion to recommit the bill was agreed to.

THE TARIFF.

The House again resolved itself into a Committee of the Whole, on the bill to regulate the duties on imports, &c.

Mr. Strong withdrew the motion he made yesterday to increase the duty on imported cottons and woollens; and

Mr. Clay then moved to amend the bill by increasing the duty on imported cottons from twenty-five to thirty-three and a third per cent. Mr. C. made this motion, he said, to try the sense of the House as to the extent to which it was willing to go in protecting domestic manufactures—assuming that there was no difference of opinion on the propriety of such protection, but only on the degree to which encouragement should be carried. He proceeded to advocate a thorough and decided protection by ample duties, and supported his motion at some length.

Mr. Smith, of Maryland, replied to Mr. Clay, and argued against increasing the duty beyond the amount recommended in the bill. Mr. S. took a very wide view of the subject; discussing separately and fully the effect which would be produced by the proposed duties on commerce, on manufactures, on agriculture, and on the revenue, and stating incidentally some objections to the bill, and to the recommendations of the Secretary of the Treasury. He was in favor of protecting domestic fabrics, but differed from Mr. Clay as to the extent of that protection.

Mr. Lowndes followed in reply to Mr. Clay, and in reply also to Mr. Smith's objections to the report of the Committee of Ways and Means. He entered into an ample and particular defence of the system reported on the subject by the committee; when the question on Mr. Clay's motion was decided in the negative—ayes 51, nays 43.

Mr. Pickering then, with the view of substituting an ad valorem duty, moved to strike out that clause of the first section which provides that all cotton cloths, (except nankeens,) the original cost of which at the place whence imported shall be less than twenty-five cents per square yard, shall be taken to have cost twenty-five cents per square yard, and shall be charged with duty accordingly.

This motion gave rise to further debate, in which the expediency of protecting duties and their extent were discussed at much length. It was supported by the mover, and opposed by Messrs. Lowndes, Strong, and Taylor, and negatived—only eight or ten rising in its favor.

Mr. Clay then renewed his motion in a modified shape, by proposing to extend the duty on cotton goods to thirty per cent. in lieu of twenty-five.

Mr. C. advocated this motion still more at length than the first—replying to many of Mr. Smith's arguments, and entering largely into the general question of the expediency of affording protection to our own manufactures.

Mr. Robertson replied to Mr. Clay, and answered generally the objections which had been urged by Mr. C. and others to the report of the Committee of Ways and Means, which he defended as proposing a just and ample protection to domestic manufactures.

After Mr. R. concluded, the Committee rose, obtained leave to sit again, and the House adjourned.

Friday, March 22.

Mr. Bassett submitted the following resolutions:

Resolved, That a Naval Academy be established at Washington, to consist of —— professors and teachers, at which all the midshipmen in the service of the United States shall be instructed, when not in actual service. That the Secretary of the Navy be required to adjust a proper plan, to select a proper site, to cause a just estimate of the expense, and report thereon in the first week of the next session of Congress.

Resolved, That an able teacher be provided for each seventy-four and forty-four in commission, whose salary shall be —— dollars. There shall be allotted to each ship, as above, a double portion at least of midshipmen, and their time shall be equally divided between ship duty and study. No midshipman shall be allotted to any of the smaller vessels until he has been two years at least in service.

Resolved, That —— number of apprentices be entered annually to the United States, to be maintained, and instructed in naval architecture, draughting, drawing, all the branches of mathematics, geometry, and navigation.* Their instruction to close with two years service at sea, as carpenter, in a vessel of the United States.

After a few remarks from Mr. Bassett, in which he quoted the examples of various European countries, in support of his motion, the resolutions were agreed to.

On motion of Mr. Ormsby, the Committee of Ways and Means were instructed to inquire into the expediency of increasing the compensation now allowed by law to the collectors of the internal revenue of the United States.

The Speaker laid before the House a report of the Secretary of the Treasury, respecting the valuation of lands, lots, dwelling-house, and slaves, in Pennsylvania, made in obedience to the resolution of the House of the 7th instant, which was ordered to lie on the table.

Mr. Burwell, from the Committee of Ways and Means, reported a bill making appropriations for the support of the Military Establishment of the United States, for the year 1816; which was read and committed to the Committee of the Whole upon the subject of revenue.

Mr. NELSON, of Virginia, from the Committee on the Judiciary, reported a bill concerning John P. Maxwell and Hugh H. Maxwell; which was read twice, and committed to a Committee of the Whole.

Mr. JOHNSON, of Kentucky, from the Military Committee, reported the bill organizing a general staff, with an amendment [striking out the last section, containing the appropriation of five thousand dollars for the purchase of military charts, &c.]

After a short discussion on the propriety of the amendment, and the supposed value of the charts referred to, &c., the amendment was agreed to by the House, and the bill was ordered to be engrossed for a third reading.

The House, on motion of Mr. FORSYTH, resolved itself into a Committee of the Whole, on the bill concerning settlers on the public lands, which passed through the Committee, was reported to the House without amendment, and ordered to be engrossed for a third reading.

The bill from the Senate, to limit the right of appeal from the Circuit Court of the District of Columbia, was read a third time, and passed.

The bill authorizing a subscription to a second edition of the public documents by T. B. Wait & Co., passed through a Committee of the Whole, and was ordered for a third reading.

THE TARIFF.

The House then again resolved itself into a Committee of the Whole, on the bill to regulate the tariff of duties—Mr. CLAY's motion to increase the duty on imported cotton cloths to thirty per cent. being still under consideration.

Mr. INGHAM said, he had risen yesterday for the purpose of replying to some observations that were made by the gentleman from Louisiana. (Mr. ROBERTSON.) and also the chairman of the Committee of Ways and Means, (Mr. LOWNDES)—he had not intended then to occupy much of the time of the Committee, and he should not abuse the indulgence he had received by doing it now. Having been a member of the committee who reported the bill, and having had the misfortune to be in the minority when some very important principles had been decided by that committee, which he hoped would not now be the case, he thought it his duty to submit some of the views that had occurred to him in the course of the discussion.

It was not his intention to go at large into the discussion of the policy of the Government, in encouraging manufactures, but he should endeavor to confine himself to a consideration of the objections that had been urged against the motion before the House, which he had understood, by the general course of the arguments, to be—

1st. That the amount of duty proposed was incompatible with the fiscal policy of the Government.

2d. That the high duties on imported cotton and woollen goods will injure the navigating interests of the United States.

3d. That we ought to confine our protection of manufactures exclusively to articles of indispensable necessity in time of war, and to articles of first necessity in time of peace.

As respects the revenue question, Mr. I. said, he had not expected to have seen the discussion assume this direction, because the great principle involved in this bill was not a revenue proposition. Congress had already provided by law for all the revenues demanded by the exigencies of the Government, and the only relation this bill could have to the revenue was, the general limit of the aggregate of the duties to be imposed. Its great primary object was to make such a modification of duties upon the various articles of importation, as would give the necessary and proper protection and support to the agriculture, manufactures, and commerce of the country. The revenue is only an incidental consideration, and it ought not to have any influence in the decision upon the proposition before the Committee. With a view then, to these great objects, is it not most obviously the policy of the Government to insure to its agriculture the advantage of a home market, that cannot be affected by the caprice and vexatious impositions of foreign nations? The principal raw materials used in our manufactories have become great staples of the country, the value of which would be greatly increased by a demand for them at home, as well as many other articles, that cannot now find a market anywhere else. Mr. I. said, he did not intend to pursue the argument on this part of the subject; it was only necessary to mention it, the intelligence of the House would supply the omission. But the manufacturing interests are vitally concerned in the fate of this bill and its details. It is believed that not less than $100,000,000 have been invested in manufactures, in the course of the last eight or ten years, and these furnish, in times of prosperity, profitable employment to many thousands of persons who could procure subsistence in no other way; they consume vast quantities of the products of the country, and create a demand for raw materials which are imported from abroad, to an extent not easily believed by those who have no practical acquaintance with the facts; they supply substantial and valuable fabrics for the convenience and comfort of the people, which they can pay for with their surplus products, and contribute to the completion of by their own labor. The revenue question must, therefore, be regarded as a minor consideration, even if it had been shown (which it has not) that the proposed duty would yield either too much or too little revenue. Mr. I. said, he considered this bill as involving a great principle of national policy; not a mere contrivance to collect taxes from the people in the easiest way, without their knowing it, but a measure intended and calculated to increase their comfort, happiness, and wealth, and of course their disposition and ability to pay whatsoever the exigencies of the Government may require, and as a necessary consequence to increase and perpetuate the security, the peace, and especially the independence of the nation. Mr. I. said, he felt himself altogether incompetent to do anything like justice to this great and interesting subject; but he regretted this the less, because he knew it would be discussed by those who could not be indulged with a similar excuse. But it has been said, that the promotion of manufactures would tend to injure our navigation and commerce, though he had not heard any attempt to prove the allegation. What, said Mr. I., was the present condition of our navigation? Totally excluded from the British West Indies, and the carrying trade we formerly had divided among the Powers of Europe—this must continue as long as they remain at peace. In addition to this, it may be remarked that, but for the late treaty, we could not have carried our own cotton to its principal market. Many of the products of the Middle States can find no market abroad. And do gentlemen suppose that our navigation can be preserved by encouraging the importation of cotton and woollen goods, which, in many States, we have not the means of paying for, the balance of trade being already most decidedly against us. This employment for our navigation has already failed, and it is worse than illusory to rely upon it. We must seek for some more certain employment for our shipping, that cannot be affected by the navigation acts of other nations. This can only be found in our coasting trade, which must increase with our population, and will be especially promoted by every pursuit that increases the intercourse between the States on our maritime frontier; and it is the only trade exclusively our own. Do not manufactures, in an especial manner, contribute to this object; particularly that of cotton, the raw material being produced in one extreme, and the fabrics made in the other; tending also to bind the States by the indissoluble bonds of interest and mutual dependence? Another source of employment for our navigation is the trade with South America, which must essentially depend upon the success of our manufactures. We shall require from thence a great variety of raw materials, and the profit we make by working them will enable us to purchase European goods with which to pay for them. Many articles that we make, have already found a vent in that country, and this trade must increase with the increase of American manufactures, and will depend almost exclusively upon their success. But it has been said, the East India trade will be destroyed, and hence our navigation diminished in that branch of our commerce. The honorable gentleman from Maryland, (to whom, Mr. I. said, he always listened with pleasure, and never without receiving valuable instruction,) had assumed rather too strongly the fact that the East India trade would be destroyed by the proposed duty on cotton goods. Although he had no hesitation to say that, if we must be reduced to the alternative of abandoning our manufactures or the East India trade, the latter ought to give way, because it is the least valuable to the nation; for if, according to the gentleman's estimate, forty ships are employed in it, and its continuance depends upon the importation of muslins for domestic consumption, we shall find the trade rather an unprofitable one in the present state of the world. The average cargo of an India ship is one thousand bales of eighteen hundred yards each—one million eight hundred thousand yards for each ship, and seventy-two million yards for forty ships. These goods will require eighteen million pounds of cotton, which are exclusively of foreign growth, and the cost of the goods, at nine cents a yard, will be $6,480,000, which we cannot pay for in the products of the country. Such is the state of that trade, and unless some protection is afforded against the introduction of these fabrics, our manufactures must sink. There is no nation in Europe that pretends to compete with the manufacturers of India; and their goods are often sold in the United States, by regular sale, for less than they could be woven for here. Where cotton can be bought for four pence a pound, and men work for four pence a day, it is in vain for us to think of rivalling them in the cheapness of their fabrics. The protection asked for, is not, therefore, an unreasonable one, nor will it destroy the India trade. We import various other articles from India; silks, spices, drugs, dyes, &c.; and the China trade is not affected by the bill. Besides, the re-exportation of the India goods can be effected as well as heretofore, and no part of the trade can be sensibly affected by the minimum price fixed for the charge of duties, except that which is employed in importing coarse muslins for consumption. But the trade to India is almost exclusively a cash trade, and can only be carried on by the profit of our trade with other countries. Commerce between nations resembles traffic between individuals, and by this assimilation many of its supposed mysteries will vanish. A farmer who barters with a merchant, and furnishes him no more products than the amount of merchandise received, will have neither cash nor credits with which to make purchases from a cash merchant, however cheap he may offer his goods; we must, therefore, trade, in the first instance, with nations who will purchase our products, and it is not very material what the price is, provided it bears the same relation to the goods sold and bought. If we desire a profit from this trade, the balance can be employed in purchasing merchandise from India; but we have no such balance now in our favor, nor is it likely that we shall have, until we determine to buy up and manufacture more for ourselves. But it is urged that our encouragement to domestic manufactures ought to be confined to fabrics of necessity, in time of war, and especially articles of the first necessity.

Mr. I. said, this doctrine had always appeared to him as a plausible theory, not founded in sound policy; nor did he think it would bear the test of reason and experience. As to articles of necessity in time of war, it would not be possible for any two persons in the nation entirely to agree what were, and what were not, articles of necessity in time of war; almost everything we import from abroad was esteemed in some degree necessary to our comfort; but it would not be pretended that we ought to impose heavy duties to encourage

1243   HISTORY OF CONGRESS.   1244

H. of R.   *The Tariff.*   March, 1816.

the growth of products or the manufacturing of fabrics, which neither our climate nor the pursuits of the people had given any indications of our abilities to produce; for instance, it will not avail us to lay a heavy duty on coffee, when our climate will not permit the propagation of the plant; nor would it be policy to impose heavy duties on fabrics which the people of the United States have neither indicated the ability nor the disposition to manufacture. The rule laid down by the honorable gentleman then fails, and this proves that our policy ought not to be governed by it. But there is another principle that will not fail, viz: That we ought to promote every species of internal industry which the inclinations, the habits, and interest of the people, as well as the soil, climate, and general conditions of the country indicate, as likely to succeed, and most especially those pursuits which experience has shown we can succeed in. And as to articles of first necessity, the same difficulty exists. The great object of the Government ought to be to promote the prosperity and happiness of the people, because it surely promotes in some degree its own prosperity and durability. Its policy in relation to manufactures, must be a great national policy—it ought not to be limited by any fastidious calculations of sheer necessity. It cannot be an adequate object for this Government to provide, by protecting duties, for the manufacturing of a few coarse goods to cover mendicants; but if the doctrine be, that we ought to secure the domestic manufacture of clothing for the poor generally, and that therefore high duties should be imposed on coarse muslins, &c., Mr. I. said, he could see no reason why a poor man should be taxed, in order to induce him to wear a home-made shirt, that did not apply with more force to justify a duty that would induce a rich man to wear a home-made coat. But this doctrine about first necessity is fallacious; its design seems to be to limit the manufacturing industry of this country by an artificial distinction that has no existence in reality; the only rule that admits of no exception, is that which has been already laid down. It is the province and almost an essential quality of arbitrary and despotic Governments, to force industry out of its natural and proper channels, or to cramp it by monopolies; but it is the duty of a Republican Government, having a due regard to the interest and happiness of the people, to encourage every pursuit (not morally wrong) in which the conditions of the country and the inclinations and capacity of the people may authorize a reasonable prospect of success. Mr. I. said, he could not be driven from this policy by the denunciations of gentlemen against (what they have been pleased to call) *regulation*. The word that has often been used before in this House for the same purpose, but it appeared to him that it had lost its original signification, and had become a cabalistic term, that was always at hand to oppose every measure against which other more cogent arguments could not be found. Do gentlemen mean that there shall be no regulation? If they do, why not avow their doctrine in its extent, and propose

at once to unloose the bonds of the social compact, which are but regulations? Unfetter men from the regulations of Government, resolve society into its primitive elements, and let us mingle with the savage of the forest—this would be the effect of yielding to this cabalistic denunciation of regulation. But they do not mean to carry their doctrine thus far—and therefore the only question to be considered is: Do we propose to regulate too much? Their doctrine is to let industry pursue its natural channels; ours is to follow and support the industry of the country, and to straighten and clear away the obstructions from the channels it has chosen to flow in—we would be justified in doing much more, but the bill before us is based upon this principle. When a farmer desires to irrigate his grounds, he diverts a stream of water from its natural channel, and by continued regulation spreads its fertilizing influence over the most sterile spots; and so also the manufacturer—he throws a dam across a stream and diverts it by a new channel to his factory, which is put in motion by its power; this is also regulation—and surely none will pretend that it would be better to permit these valuable streams to find their way through zigzag natural channels to the ocean, than to be thus employed for the comfort and happiness of man. This cabalistic denunciation might as well be directed against such purposes as against manufactures. It is evident that these facts require a long series of practical operation before the experience and skill necessary to enable our workmen to compete with those of the Old World can be attained. The circumstances of the country for several years past, have given a new direction to a great portion of our capital and our industry—much skill has been acquired; our manufacturers have demonstrated, that they can succeed with a little aid from the Government to protect them against extraordinary pressure; they desire to have some advantages over foreigners in the home market, and this policy, which has become an axiom with all other Governments, is denounced as a ruinous regulation.

The honorable gentleman from Louisiana has also complained of the partiality of the report of the Secretary of the Treasury, and the bill under consideration—that it is calculated to favor the manufactures of the Northern and Middle States more than those of the South. But he has not given any instance of this partiality, except that of the proposed duty on sugar; and it would not be difficult to show that he had been most unfortunate in the selection of this case. The Secretary of the Treasury had proposed two and a half cents a pound on brown sugar, which is not less than 36 per cent. ad valorem upon the average cost of the article in the West Indies—in the East Indies, much more. The gentleman complains of 30 per cent. on cotton goods as exorbitant and partial, while 36 per cent. on sugar is considered by him no protection at all; but, in order to escape from the dilemma, he says that two and a half cents was the old duty, and that it was laid for revenue. If he can prove that a duty imposed for revenue has no effect in encouraging the domestic production of sugar, his argument is entitled to some weight; but, until then, he will permit us to deny the partiality of the report to the Northern section of the Union, in this particular. But, what says the bill, which he also complains of? It proposes a duty of four cents a pound on sugar, which is more than 36 per cent. ad valorem on the cost of the article; and yet it is complained of by the gentleman from Louisiana as partial. It is indeed partial, but the partiality is in his favor; and it was extremely unfortunate for *him*, at least, to object to the proposed duty on cotton goods upon this ground. Mr. I said, he had no objection to give a liberal encouragement to the production of sugar; he rejoiced to find that it could be produced in such quanities, and would give employment to a very considerable tonnage in its transportation; but, unless there was some disposition for reciprocity, it could not be expected that so high a duty would be voted for.

There is, said Mr. I., another circumstance in this case which ought to be understood. The chairman of the Committee of Ways and Means had informed the House that the increased specific duties, in consequence of the alteration made by the committee on sugars, from two and a half to four cents, would require but 20 per cent. on cottons and woollens to make up the necessary revenue, required. He did not, however, take into his account the various reductions made by the committee on coffee, copper sheets, &c., which there was very little doubt would be quite equal to the increased duty on sugar. Suppose it to be, however, as the gentleman has stated, then the Committee of Ways and Means have granted a *protecting* duty of 56 per cent. on sugar, and procuring therefrom the necessary revenue, they used this as a pretext to reduce cottons and woollens to 20 per cent. Mr. I. said he was present in the Committee of Ways and Means when this argument was used, but he was struck dumb with astonishment when the motion succeeded. It was, however, too glaringly inconsistent and palpably wrong to be persisted in, and therefore it was that the Committee of Ways and Means, upon reconsideration, substituted the 25 per cent., which was reported in the bill. But he did not think the 25 per cent. sufficient protection, nor that it would be the cheapest production for American manufactures. The higher duties you impose, the more powerful the stimulus, and the sooner we have a supply and a competition at home. This ought to be our object, and the effect would more than compensate for all the difference of price for a few years, which was no more than as a dust in the balance, if we consider the great national objects to be attained by fostering and promoting internal industry and skill in domestic manufactures. But, Mr. I said, he would not enter into that part of the discussion—the field was unlimited—but he would admonish gentlemen not to be too parsimonious in their encouragement to their great interests. He had heard a demand from various quarters for estimates and calculations to show the precise amount of duty

that would enable the American manufacturer to come into the market upon equal terms with the importer. Such demands are in their nature unreasonable and unfair, because it must be obvious that they could not be answered with any kind of certainty; but, more especially, because the amount that would be sufficient to protect an establishment in the best perfection, with the best skill of the country, and the most perfect system of economy, would be utterly inadequate to protect the establishments that are in their infancy, which constitute by far the greatest portion of manufactories in the United States. But there are difficulties, independently of mere cost, to be overcome by the American manufacturer. The European fabrics made of the same material have the advantage in appearance, though not in durability, which gain them a preference; and th prejudice of the country against domestic fa —yes, the prejudice of the country—the mere kind of prejudice that pervades a portion of this House—pervades a portion of the United States. It was a fact, said Mr. I., that the paper used by the members of this House to enclose their newspapers in, had the water-mark of the British Crown upon it, though the paper was made in the District of Columbia! The manufacturer could not have done this to gratify any attachment to Crowns—he found it his interest thus to disguise his paper. Similar artifices had been practised in other branches, particularly the manufacture of powder. The best powder made in the United States—or perhaps the world—could not a few years ago be sold without the British mark upon the kegs. These deceptions had succeeded, because prejudice and ignorance are mostly, if not always, associated; but they prove the power of this pernicious prejudice, and he thought it was the bounden duty of Congress to protect the industry of the country from such discouragements. If there be a great portion of people in this country who prefer to have everything that is foreign, when they cannot tell the difference but from the mark, they ought to pay for it; and the American artisan has a strong claim upon his Government for protection against this unnatural prejudice.

Mr. I. said he had trespassed upon the patience of the Committee longer than he had intended; he would only add, we had now acquired a degree of skill in many of the arts, that, if cherished and improved, would be a source of inexhaustible wealth to the nation; neglect it, and it is lost for centuries—perhaps forever. The success of this bill determines this great question. The history of Europe, especially of Spain and France, in the early part of the last century, sufficiently proves the fact, that, when the arts fall by the folly or negligence of the Government, they are not easily revived.—"There is a tide in the affairs" of nations as well as "of men, which, taken at the flood, leads on to fortune." This is that critical moment: permit it but to pass by, and a similar opportunity to perpetuate the prosperity and happiness of this country may not, and probably will not, present again for ages to come.

Mr. Lowndes again entered into a particular defence of the report of the committee, and the degree of encouragement which the bill proposed giving to our manufacturing establishments, and replied, in detail, to the arguments of Messrs. Ingham and Clay.

Mr. Clay followed in support of his motion, and in reply to the gentlemen who had spoken in opposition to it.

Messrs. Gold and Hulbert also successively advocated the amendment, and the expediency of extending an indubitable encouragement and security to our manufacturing citizens.

The question was then taken on Mr. Clay's motion to increase the duty on cottons to thirty per cent. and carried—ayes 68, noes 61.

Mr. Clay then moved so to amend the bill as to class hempen and sail cloths (including cotton bagging) with those of woollen, so that if the duty on the latter should be hereafter increased, as he wished, to twenty-eight per cent, it would be also on the former articles, and if not, the duty thereon would still be raised to twenty-five per cent., the same as the duty on woollens.

After some remarks explanatory of his motives for offering the amendment, Mr. Clay withdrew it, at the request of Mr. Smith, of Maryland, who said he had intended to propose a specific increased duty on a certain species of imported hempen cloth, and would co-operate in Mr. C.'s object, if allowed to vary it in some degree.

Mr. Smith then proceeded with some additional remarks on particular features of the bill, involving commercial questions, which he discussed in that minute and technical manner which his practical acquaintance with the subject renders peculiar to him.

In the course of his remarks, Mr. S. submitted the following statements:

British Goods.

One yard cotton, valued at - - - - 25 cts.
Add ten per cent. - - - - - - 2.50c.

                27.50c.

Duty of 25 per cent. on 27.50 is - - - 7c.
Insurance, freight, transport to Liverpool, packages, and agent's commission, seven and a half per cent. on twenty cents, the average value of cotton, low-priced goods - - - 1½c.
Average gain to the importer of twelve and a half per cent. on a cost of twenty cents - 2½c.

On a cost of twenty cents - - - 11c.

The manufacturer will then have an advantage over the importer of eleven cents per yard on an article which costs in England only twenty cents, and of course he will have that bounty given to him.

At 33⅓ per cent. the duty alone will be nine cents and a fraction, on cotton goods, which, on an average, cost twenty cents per yard in Manchester, and will cost the retailer thirteen cents per yard in addition to the prime cost.

An assortment of India goods, such as generally compose the cargoes imported into the United States, cost on an average nine cents per yard.

Cotton goods (most what they will less) are charged in the bill as if they cost per yard twenty-five cents.

Add twenty per cent. to make the supposed value on arrival in the United States, five cents duty per yard.

The duty of twenty-five per cent. is charged on thirty cents, which, at twenty-five per cent. is - 7½c.
Freight, &c. - - - 14 per cent.
Insurance - - - 8
Cost of specie - - - 5
Eighteen months' interest   9

        36 per cent. on 9 cents 3¼c.

Cents per yard - - - - 10¾c.
Add merchants' profit, twenty per cent. on nine cents. - - - - - - 2 c.

           12¾c.

Say 12¾ cents in favor of the manufacturers on an article which cost nine cents.

A view of the actual cost of cotton goods imported from Great Britain.

Suppose a trunk of cotton goods to cost in Great Britain - - - - £100 00
To make the ad valorem - - - 10 00

        £110 00

The duty of 25 per ct. ad valorem is charged on £110, and will be - - - 27 10
Insurance, freight, commission, and other charges, will, on an average, be - 7 10
Average gain expected by the importer - 13 10

        £147 10

Every £100 sterling, the bona fide cost in England, will cost the retailer £147 10; or 47½ per cent. in favor of the American manufacturer, besides the difference in the price of the raw materials.

When Mr. S. concluded, the Committee rose, and obtained leave to sit again.

Saturday, March 23.

Mr. Robertson, from the Committee on the Public Lands, reported a bill to provide for the appointment of a surveyor of the public lands for the Territories of Illinois and Missouri; which was read twice, and committed to a Committee of the Whole.

Mr. Robertson also reported a bill for the confirmation of certain claims to land in the western district of the State of Louisiana; which was read twice, and committed to a Committee of the whole House on Monday next.

Mr. R., from the same committee, reported the bill from the Senate "further supplementary to the act entitled 'An act providing for the indemnification of certain claimants of public land in the Mississippi Territory,'" without amendment, and the bill was committed to a Committee of the Whole.

Mr. Robertson also reported a bill supplementary to the act entitled "An act for the final adjustment of land-titles in the State of Louis-

1249   HISTORY OF CONGRESS.   1250

March, 1816.   *Staff of the Army—The Cumberland Road.*   H. of R.

iana and Territory of Missouri," which was read twice, and committed to a Committee of the Whole.

Mr. R. also reported the bill from the Senate "for the relief of Edward Wilson," with amendments; which were read, and together with the bill committed to a Committee of the Whole.

Mr. Forney, from the committee appointed on that subject, reported a bill to increase the compensation of the Clerk of the House of Representatives, (to $3,000,) which was twice read, and committed.

On motion of Mr. Pleasants, the House went into Committee of the Whole on the bill to place the surviving sufferers at Dartmoor prison on the Navy pension list; which was reported to the House with an amendment (making the pensions commence on the 6th of April, 1815, the day on which the Dartmoor massacre took place) and the bill. as amended, was ordered to be engrossed for a third reading.

The bill from the Senate, entitled "An act authorizing a subscription for the printing of a second edition of the public documents," was read the third time and passed.

The bill from the Senate, entitled "An act relating to settlers on the lands of the United States," was read the third time and passed.

ALLOWANCE OF INTEREST.

The Speaker laid before the House a report from the Secretary of War, in obedience to the resolution of the 21st instant, respecting the allowance of interest on charges against the War Department; which was read and ordered to lie on the table.

The letter is as follows:

Department of War, *March 23, 1816.*

Sir : In obedience to the resolution of the House of Representatives of the 21st instant, I have the honor to state that the general usage of the War Department has been to pay no interest upon any demand whatever, without regard to its origin.

During the latter part of the year 1814, and through the whole of 1815, the Department, being unable to discharge the multiplied and extensive demands which were made upon it, in some instances authorized different officers employed in disbursing the public money, and various contractors, to obtain money upon a loan; and, in some instances, where their bills were presented and remained unpaid for the want of funds, assurances were given to the banks that interest would be paid upon them if they were taken up by them. In all such cases, interest has been paid. Interest has also been allowed upon bills drawn by contractors pursuant to their contracts, which have been protested for the want of funds. This is the only case in which it has been allowed, except upon special agreement to that effect. No distinction has been made between bills drawn for money actually received by a public agent and for debts contracted by such agent in the course of his official duty.

I have the honor to be your most obedient and very humble servant,

WM. H. CRAWFORD.

Hon. Henry Clay, *Speaker:*

STAFF OF THE ARMY.

The engrossed bill to organize a general staff for the Army, was read the third time.

An inquiry made by Mr. Hardin into the necessity of one of the officers named in the bill, (the Commissary General of Purchases,) the nature of his duties, &c., produced a short discussion on that point.

Messrs. Grosvenor and Pickering argued that the duties of the Commissary General and those of the Superintendent General of Purchases, were in fact the same; that one of the offices was useless, and ought to be abolished, &c.

Mr. Johnson, of Kentucky, explained the various duties of the officers referred to, the dissimilar character of their duties, their separate responsibilities, and the necessity of both to form a complete staff, &c.

The yeas and nays being demanded by Mr. Davenport, the question on the passage of the bill was decided in the affirmative—yeas 96, nays 22, as follows :

Yeas—Messrs. Adgate, Archer, Bateman, Bennett, Betts, Birdsall, Boss, Bradbury, Breckenridge, Brooks, Brown, Bryan, Burwell, Caldwell, Calhoun, Champion, Chappell, Clarke of North Carolina, Clark of Kentucky, Clayton, Clendennin, Comstock, Condict, Crawford, Crocheron, Cuthbert, Darlington, Desha, Edwards, Forsyth, Gaston, Gold, Goodwyn, Griffin, Grosvenor, Hahn, Hall, Hammond, Heister, Henderson, Hopkinson, Huger, Hungerford, Irving of New York, Jackson, Johnson of Virginia, Johnson of Kentucky, Kerr of Virginia, King of North Carolina, Lowndes, Lumpkin, Lyle, Maclay, Mayrant, McCoy, McLean of Kentucky, McLean of Ohio, Middleton, Moore, Nelson of Massachusetts, Nelson of Virginia, Newton, Pickens, Pickering, Pleasants, Powell, Reynolds, Roane, Robertson, Ross, Ruggles, Savage, Smith of Maryland, Southard, Strong, Sturges, Tate, Taul, Taylor of South Carolina, Telfair, Throop, Townsend, Tucker, Wallace, Ward of Massachusetts, Ward of New York, Ward of New Jersey, Webster, Wendover, Whiteside, Wilcox, Wilde, Wilkin, Willoughby, William Wilson, and Yates.

Nays—Messrs. Atherton, Cady, Cilley, Cooper, Culpeper, Davenport, Hale, Hardin, Jewett, Kent, Langdon, Law, Lewis, Lyon, Marsh, Mason, Milnor, Noyes, Stanford, Stearns, Vose, and Wheaton.

CUMBERLAND ROAD.

Mr. Jackson, from the committee to whom was referred the Message of the President of the United States, of the 12th instant, containing a statement of proceedings in relation to the execution of the act to regulate the laying out and making a road from Cumberland, in the State of Maryland, to the State of Ohio, made a report thereon ; which was read, and committed to the Committee of the whole House on the bill making appropriations for the support of Government for the year 1816. The report is as follows:

That they have attentively considered the subject confided to them, and respectfully submit to the House, the following facts and observations : It appears by an act of Congress, passed on the 1st of May, 1802, entitled "An act to enable the people of the eastern division of the Territory northwest of the river Ohio to form a constitution and State government, and for the admission of such State into the Union, on an equal footing with the original States, and for other purposes," that on condition that the Convention of the said State would provide by an ordinance, irrevocable without the consent of the United States, that each tract of land sold by Congress, after the 30th of June next, ensuing, shall be, and remain exempt from any tax laid by order or under authority of the State, whether for State, county, township, or any other purpose whatever, for the term of five years from and after the day of sale: the United States among other stipulations agreed to apply one-twentieth part of the net proceeds arising from the sale of said lands, from and after the said 30th of June, to the laying out and making public roads, leading from the navigable waters emptying into the Atlantic, to the Ohio, to the said State, and through the same; such roads laid out under the authority of Congress, with the consent of the several States through which the same shall pass. It further appears that these conditions were accepted by the State of Ohio, on the 29th of November in the same year, subject, as regards the road fund, to a modification which provides that three per cent. of the net proceeds arising from the sales aforesaid should be subject to the control of the Legislature of that State, and be applied to the making roads within the same. It also appears by an act passed on the 3d of March, 1803, that this modification received the sanction of Congress; and that in pursuance of this compact a law was passed on the 28th of March, 1806, authorizing the President of the United States to appoint commissioners to lay out a road from Cumberland, or a point in its vicinity, to the river Ohio; and, on their report, to pursue such measures as in his opinion were proper, to obtain from the States through which the road was laid out their consent to its location and completion.

It further appears to the committee that the location crossing portions of the States of Maryland, Pennsylvania, and Virginia, applications were made to their respective Legislatures, and permission was given by each, to open and establish the said road.

By the report of the Secretary of the Treasury referred to the committee, it appears that of the appropriations heretofore made towards completing this road, and amounting in the whole to the sum of $410,000 00 There have been expended $285,786 60 Carried to the surplus fund 22,679 75
    —————— 306,486 35
Leaving a balance on the 27th of February, 1816, of - - - - - 101,513 65 applicable to that object. And that a further appropriation of $300,000 is recommended by that report to complete the road to Brownsville on the Monongahela river; to cover the expenses of a survey from thence by Washington and Alexandria to Wheeling, and to make the road at and from Wheeling to the one hundred and thirteenth mile tree, a distance of about twelve miles.

It also appears, by the letter of the superintendent of the road to the Secretary of the Treasury, that frequent abuses are committed on the road, such as throwing down the walls, digging away the banks, &c. and he suggests that measures ought to be promptly adopted to prevent, and to punish these outrages.

This investigation suggested to the committee two points of inquiry, to which their attention has been directed. First, the necessity of protecting the work already completed against lawless violence; and, secondly, the propriety of making an ample appropriation for advancing its progress to completion, in order that the benefits it promises may soon be realized.

In considering the first point, although it appears that the Secretary of the Treasury, in his letter communicated at the last session, doubts the authority of Congress to pass any laws for punishing the offenders, the committee do not perceive any defect of jurisdiction. Without controverting the opinion that the Constitution does not, in virtue of any grant of power conferred by that instrument, authorize Congress to open roads and canals in any State, it seems to be admitted by all, that if a compact be made with a State, for which the nation receives an equivalent, as in this case, whereby it is agreed that a road shall be opened by the Government of the Union, and the States through which the road passes grant the right to make it, that the performance of such compact is not in contravention of that construction; as it is believed that the exercise of such power has in no instance been doubted, notwithstanding the repeated acts of legislation for a period of thirteen years. The permission of the States having been given, it follows as a necessary consequence, that all the powers obviously necessary and proper to carry the grant into complete effect and preserve it inviolable have been conferred also. A different construction would render the consent a nullity, and exempt from punishment, as well the individuals who resisted the execution of the work, as those that afterwards destroyed it.

If the right to punish these offences belongs to the National Government, it may be effected without the passage of any law, by indictment or information in the courts of the United States; or by enacting statutory provisions fixing the penalties. It being a fundamental right of the judiciary inherent in every Government to punish all offences, against the laws passed in pursuance of a delegated power, independently of express legislative sanctions. Although the committee deem it proper to make this explicit assertion of a right which it may become necessary to exercise on some future occasion, in case of a peremptory refusal by a State to pass any law upon the subject, yet as they believe no such disposition exists in relation to the road in question, and the prosecutions under State laws may be most effectual in preventing the practices complained of, because of the distances to the places where the respective Federal courts are held, they abstain from recommending, at this time, the passage of any law upon that subject.

In regard to the second branch of the inquiry, viz: the amount of appropriation proper to be made at the present session, it appears to the committee, that although the fund chargeable with the reimbursement of expenditures has been anticipated, it is growing more productive every year and will be eventually adequate to defray the expenses of completing the road.

If Congress persevere with becoming spirit in this great public work, we shall soon see one of the best roads in the world over the chains of mountains which separate the western from the Atlantic waters, and which, but a few years since, were supposed to present insurmountable obstacles to a safe and easy intercourse. The committee learn, with much satisfaction, that the State of Maryland is engaged in extending the turnpike road that reaches from Baltimore to Boonesborough, on to Fort Cumberland; and, in all probability, it will be completed before the national road from that point to the Ohio is finished.

It is not intended to expatiate at large upon the moral, political, and physical advantages of this road to the nation. They doubtless entered fully into the contemplation of the Congress by whom the original law was passed; time and experience have given the fulness of their sanctions to the wisdom of their decision; and it is alike a source of surprise and regret to the committee, that the work has been suffered, with the ample means possessed by the Government, to linger for a period of more than nine years. A vigorous prosecution of it now can alone, in any degree, repair the past neglect; and, in the estimation of the committee, no subject is more deserving the favor of Congress. They are aware of the opinion entertained by some that the Western country already holds out sufficient lures to the inhabitants of the Atlantic States to migrate thither, and that it is impolitic to contribute to their increase, which will be the effect, as it is supposed, of giving facilities to such removal. The error of this reasoning is proved by the infallible test of experience, applied to the past and present population of the States and Territories west of the mountains. The emigrant removes with intention to reside for life in his new habitation; and when he determines upon such removal, he bestows but little attention upon the inquiry whether the road on which he has to travel is a very good one, or in the condition of the principal State roads now used. This policy, therefore, although it cannot prevent him from going to the West, may, and, if persisted in, soon will materially affect his future connexions with the Eastern country in all the ramifications of a mutually profitable trade and intercourse. The natural advantages of a water over a land communication for the purposes of transporting all articles of merchandise, will not be denied by any; and trade will always seek that channel which affords it the fairest prospects of realising its legitimate profits. Whenever, therefore, land and water communication are found to possess a fair competition with each other in any country, the improvements on both must be equal to prevent the monopoly of either.

The navigation of the Mississippi and Ohio rivers, by steamboats, is now in its infancy; its success is no longer doubtful, and it is increasing with a rapidity corresponding to that success. During the last years the sugar and cotton of Louisiana were brought up by the water to Pittsburg, and, in consequence of the extraordinary demand, were transported thence in wagons to the Atlantic cities, and sold at prices affording a profit to the owner. With the great advantages of steam navigation, unless the roads across the mountains are much improved, the merchants of the Western country will cease to purchase goods from the importers at New York, Philadelphia, Baltimore, &c., and New Orleans will soon become the sole emporium of their trade.

This result never can be produced if a due attention be paid to the improvement of the means of internal communication. The rivers that take their rise in the mountains may be made navigable. In various sections of the country, the portage between them can be diminished to an inconsiderable distance, and roads passing over the entire route will present an option to the merchants as to the mode of transportation. Their connexions have been formed for a considerable period. These have begotten confidence, and a mutuality of interests which bind the parties to a future intercourse, and which will not be changed unless for a positive and unequivocal benefit.

But the advantages of an intimate commercial connexion, though addressed to the interest of the parties, are not the most important. Good roads have an influence over physical impossibilities. By diminishing the natural impediments, they bring places and their inhabitants nigher to each other. They increase the value of lands, and the fruits of the earth in remote situations, and by enlarging the sphere of supply, prevent those sudden fluctuations of prices, alike prejudicial to the grower and consumer. They promote a free intercourse among the citizens of remote places, by which unfounded prejudices and animosities are dissipated, local and sectional feelings are destroyed, and a nationality of character, so desirable to be encouraged, is universally inculcated.

The road, which is the subject of the particular inquiry of the committee, has additional recommendations. It leads as far as Washington, Pennsylvania, in a direct line from the Seat of Government to the important frontier of the United States on the Upper Lakes; and if, as the committee suppose, it be the true policy of the nation to have a direct military communication for the entire distance, a road can be extended from Washington, and passing, as it will, through a large extent of public lands, inducements will be held out to the Western settlers to purchase them, and by a rapid increase of the population, the necessity of keeping up a considerable military force in that quarter will be diminished, if not entirely superseded.

These constitute a part of the reasons which have induced the committee to recommend an appropriation of three hundred thousand dollars at this time, and therefore they submit the following resolution:

Resolved, That the bill entitled "an act making appropriations for the support of Government for the year 1816," be amended in the —— line by inserting the following paragraph:

"For making the road from Cumberland, in the State of Maryland, to the State of Ohio, to be repaid out of the five per cent. fund reserved for that purpose, $300,000."

ATTORNEY GENERAL.

The following Message was received from the PRESIDENT OF THE UNITED STATES:

I transmit to the House of Representatives a report from the Secretary of the Treasury, complying with their resolution of the 29th of February last.

JAMES MADISON.
MARCH 22, 1816.

TREASURY DEPARTMENT, March 21, 1816.

The Secretary of the Treasury, to whom the President of the United States referred the resolution of the 29th of February, 1816, requesting that there be laid before the House of Representatives "a statement of the cases in which he has employed, or caused to be employed, counsel to assist the Attorney General prosecuting causes in the Supreme Court of the United States; stating, as nearly as may be, the amount of the property in dispute in each case, the names of the counsel so employed, the period of employing them, and the compensation granted to them in each case; also the manner of making such compensation, and the fund out of which the same was paid," has the honor to present the following report:

That it appears to have been the practice of the Government to employ counsel to assist the Attorney General, and also the district attorneys, in cases of great importance, either as to the principle or as to the value involved in the controversy. Thus, for example, so early as the February term, 1796, of the Supreme Court, Alexander Hamilton received a fee of $500 to assist the Attorney General in maintaining the affirmative upon the question respecting the Constitutionality of the carriage tax; and Alexander Campbell and Jared Ingersoll, counsel, maintaining the negative, received a fee of $233 33, under an agreement that, for the purpose of obtaining a final decision, the United States should pay all the expenses incident to the transfer of the cause from the circuit court to the Supreme Court.

That on the 24th of March, 1804, in obedience to a resolution of the House of Representatives of the 2d of the same month, the Secretary of the Treasury presented a statement "of all the moneys which, since the establishment of the present Government, had been paid at the Treasury of the United States as fees to assistant counsel, and for legal advice in the business of the United States, in which were distinguished the several sums, when paid, for what services, and to whom paid respectively," amounting, in the whole, to the sum of $5,022 16.

That the statement hereunto annexed, marked A, contains a like specification of all the moneys paid, or payable, at the Treasury of the United States, from the 24th of March, 1804, until the present time, for the employment of counsel to assist, or to represent, the Attorney General in causes depending in the Supreme Court of the United States, amounting, in the whole, to the sum of $4,540.

That this Department does not possess the means of stating the amount of the property in dispute, in each case, in which assistant counsel has been employed in the Supreme Court; but it is confidently believed, from general information, that in every such case, either the value of the property was great, or the principle of the controversy was important; or the employment of assistant counsel in the cases of sickness, or other casualties, was essential to the public interests, as will more particularly appear by the notes accompanying statement A.

That the manner of making the compensation to the assistant counsel has uniformly been by issuing the warrants of the Secretary of the Treasury, founded upon the official settlement of the Comptroller and Auditor; and by paying the amount, either out of the appropriation, annually passed by Congress, "for the discharge of such miscellaneous claims against the United States, not otherwise provided for, as shall have been admitted in due course of settlement at the Treasury;" or out of the appropriations annually made "for the discharge of such demands against the United States, on account of the civil department, not otherwise provided for, as shall have been admitted in due course of settlement at the Treasury."

All which is respectfully submitted.

A. J. DALLAS,
Secretary of the Treasury.

STATEMENT A.

March 19, 1805.—Alexander James Dallas was employed to assist the Attorney General in the Supreme Court, upon the argument of the case of the United States *vs.* the assignees of Blight, a bankrupt, for which he received a compensation of - - - - $500

Note.—In this case, the claim of a general priority for the satisfaction of debts due to the United States, occurred. The amount in dispute was considerable, but the principle involved was of much more importance. The Attorney General being indisposed, the assistant counsel argued the case alone.

January 1, 1813.—Alexander James Dallas was employed to assist the Attorney General in the case of the French Government schooner Balou, (formerly the Exchange,) and generally in the business of the United States, at February term, 1812, for which he received a compensation of - - - 1,200

Note.—The Balou was a public armed vessel of France, attached in the port of Philadelphia by persons claiming her as their property. The case involved the important question whether such an attachment would lie; and on the remonstrance of the Minister of France, the President directed it to be brought before the Supreme Court. Mr. Pinkney, the Attorney General, being recently appointed, requested also some general assistance in the business of the term, to prevent delay. Mr. Dallas argued the case of the Exchange, and ten other cases.

May 14, 1808.—Walter Jones was employed to assist the Attorney General in the Supreme Court, upon the argument of the case of the United States *vs.* the schooner Betsey and Charlotte, William Yeaton, claimant, for which he received a compensation of - 200

February 7, 1814.—William Pinkney, having resigned the office of Attorney General, was employed as counsel to argue the cases of the United States depending in the Supreme Court at February term, 1814, for which he received a compensation of - - 1,000

Note.—Mr. Pinkney's resignation, though previously intimated, was not received until the term had commenced; and Mr. Rush, who was appointed his successor, could not take the oath of office, under his commission dated the 10th of February, 1814, until the 12th of the same month. In accepting his appointment, it was explicitly understood that he did not undertake to argue the causes of the United States during the current term, as it would have been impracticable to read the records, and to make the necessary preparation. It was, therefore, an alternative, either to postpone the public business until the next term, or to engage the services of Mr. Pinkney, who had a previous knowledge of the records. He was accordingly engaged, and he procured decisions in many important cases, besides giving a general attention to the interests of the United States throughout the term. Mr. Pinkney's compensation has not been paid at the Treasury, but has been credited in his account as Minister at the Court of London.

November 14, 1814.—John Law was employed to prepare the statements of the cases depending before the Supreme Court at February term, 1814, for which he received a compensation of - - - 440

Note.—Mr. Pinkney having only undertaken

to discharge the duty of counsel, it was necessary to engage Mr. Law's services in the Solicitor's business.

February —, 1815.—Walter Jones was employed, on account of the extreme indisposition of the Attorney General, to transact the business of the United States in the Supreme Court at February term, 1815, and a compensation has been authorized, but not yet paid, of - - - - - - - 1,000

                   $4,340

THE TARIFF.

The House then again resolved itself into a Committee of the Whole on the bill to regulate the tariff of duties.

Mr. BETTS made a motion to strike out the words *ad valorem*, in the clause fixing the duty on woollens and cottons; which was negatived, ayes 40, noes 65.

Mr. WEBSTER submitted a motion to alter the tariff proposed on cottons, by laying a maximum duty of thirty per cent. for two years, and then gradually reducing it to —— per cent. Mr. W. offered several arguments in support of his motion, but, at the suggestion of Mr. LOWNDES, he withdrew it, for the present, to wait some information which would enable the House to act more understandingly on the subject.

Mr. WARD, of Massachusetts, moved an amendment, the object of which, substantially, was to defer the operation of the duties on India cottons, proposed by the bill, to January next. He offered this motion to protect the merchants engaged in the India trade from the ruin which would inevitably be inflicted on them by the duties proposed if laid suddenly, after merchants had goods on their way home or ordered, and without sufficient notice to enable them to frame their measures accordingly.

Mr. LOWNDES opposed the motion. If the duty was necessary at all to secure our manufacturers, it was necessary to commence its operation without delay; and he thought the gentleman would find that more mischief would ensue to the manufacturing interest from the delay he proposed than would be prevented to the mercantile class from its adoption.

Mr. HULBERT was also hostile to the motion. It was said that the bill would ruin the India merchants; he wished the merchants all possible success and happiness, but he wished well also to the manufacturers; and to save them from ruin it was necessary to act promptly. This is the moment, said Mr. H.—the physician is not wanted after the patient is dead; and if the manufacturers are suffered now to go down, it will be impossible hereafter to resuscitate them. He hoped at least that his colleague would for the present withdraw his motion, for the reason stated on Mr. WEBSTER'S.

Mr. WARD supported his motion, and replied to the objections which had been made to it. It was not his object to ruin, nor would it ruin, any part of the community—but to save a valuable class of citizens from destruction. He argued that the time asked for would not be so injurious to the manufacturers as was predicted; because they would be able to get on very well under the double duties that would still be in force; but the merchants he alluded to had no relief at all.

After some remarks by Mr. PICKERING, on the impropriety of producing a prohibition of a particular trade by high duties which it was wrong to do by a direct interdiction, Mr. WARD, for the present, withdrew his motion.

Mr. MILNOR moved to strike out the proposed duty of five cents per bushel on coal; which motion, however, he subsequently withdrew.

Mr. SMITH, of Maryland, then, with the view of encouraging and protecting the great quantity of machinery erected in different parts of the country for rolling and slitting iron, and encouraging that manufacture, and showing by several statements that the proposed duty was an insufficient protection—moved to increase the duty on the imported iron sheets, rod and bolts, from one hundred and fifty cents to two hundred and fifty cents per hundred weight.

The motion was supported by Messrs. IRVING of New York, ROOT, and CONDICT, and carried without a division.

Mr. SMITH then moved to increase the duty on lump and loaf sugar to eighteen cents per pound—believing that the manufactories of the article now established in the United States were fully able to supply the whole country, and the duty proposed by the bill being in his opinion insufficient to protect those establishments from a successful foreign competition.

Mr. SMITH afterwards gave way to Mr. HUGER, who wished to reduce the duty of four cents per pound on brown sugar; believing that no protection was necessary to encourage the manufacture of that article, by which large fortunes were now making, and which it was unnecessary to encourage by taxing the community for that purpose. Mr. H. then moved to strike out the proposed duty of four cents, with the view, if successful, of filling the blank with two and an half cents.

Mr. ROBERTSON said: I rise Mr. Chairman, to oppose the motion of the gentleman from South Carolina. Before, however, I enter on my reply, I beg leave to make a few observations of a general nature, but strictly applicable to the question under consideration.

I think I am founded in saying, that the proposition of the Secretary of the Treasury, now brought forward by the gentleman from South Carolina, has resulted from inattention or forgetfulness; it can be traced to no other source; it can be executed on no other ground; for it is at war with every principle he has laid down, and violates the whole system which he professes to approve. I will not repeat his principles or his plans; they are before the eyes of every gentleman in the House. I content myself with saying again, that his plan of reduction in regard to the duty on sugar, is a clear and manifest violation of his own principles, and at war with the whole system.

The State of Louisiana, Mr. Chairman, from its happy climate and fertile soil, is competent to furnish the United States with all the sugar they may require; but that this may be done with certainty and within a short time, some encouragement is indispensable. Is any manufacture more important to the nation? Is there one which may be aided by a tax on its foreign competition with less injustice to the community, or with greater advantage to the revenue? Gentlemen call it an agricultural product; is that sufficient to render it an object of prejudice? Have our manufacturers already, by their combinations, succeeded in placing their employment on higher ground than that of the agriculturist? But, say gentlemen, why not hold out encouragement to the manufacturer of flour, to the growers of rice, tobacco, wheat, &c.? Is it possible that an argument of this kind can have any weight; is it seriously urged? Let me ask gentlemen, if tobacco, rice, and wheat, were interfered with by foreign importation, whether they would not see the propriety of giving that aid, by which we should be enabled to raise these important products within our own country? Would it not be wise to do so? Would not a dependence on foreign supply for these essential articles, be fatal to our happiness and prosperity? And let them ask themselves if the cane were the favorite culture of their State, whether they would not see the propriety of sustaining it against the rival efforts of a foreign country?

In the decision of this question, the interests of Louisiana are not alone concerned. Is it not important that in time of war we should be furnished with this valuable article? Let the situation of the country, little more than a year ago, answer the question. The States of the Union may hereafter not only be supplied with sugar from a sister State, but supplied at a cheap rate; the steamboat navigation of the Mississippi and its various waters will produce this effect. The high price during the war grew simply out of the want of transportation; this state of things will never again occur.

In times of peace the distant and extensive trade with New Orleans will give employment to our maritime industry; thus substituting a trade with one of the States of the Union, for that with the West Indies, and which we already have lost. Whilst an exclusion of all other foreign manufactures, however beneficial to our international prosperity, destroys a commerce, if in no other point of view desirable, important to navigation, let us take care, that while we promote manufactures, we do not so far annihilate commerce as to destroy maritime industry, and thus cut off the right arm of the nation. Commerce, considered in regard to America, is maritime strength; render useless the merchant, and you may save yourself the expense of building vessels of war. In the hour of battle they will be without seamen. The planter of Louisiana offers you a valuable manufacture, an extensive com-

merce, and an increased revenue; but the cotton manufacturer, who destroys your voyages to the East Indies, offers you none other in return. Our intercourse with foreign nations can never be entirely cut off; it will be always sufficient to breed dispute, and produce war. Let it be also sufficient, if it plunge us into war, to carry us through it with success and honor; to this end maritime force is necessary.

The duty paid on imported sugars, if taken from the pocket of the consumer, augments the public Treasury, because, although it affects the price, it will not in the same degree affect the quantity imported; whereas the duty laid on imported cottons, by excluding them entirely, is added to the price of the domestic manufacture, taken out of the pocket of the consumer, and put into that of the manufacturer; thus, in the one case, we pay a tax to the public, in the other, to individuals. Gentleman have indulged themselves in the most extravagant misrepresentations in regard to the wealth of the planters of Louisiana; whence they have received their information, I know not. They have probably formed their opinions from the false and ridiculous statements which we have seen of the great profits of the cultivation in Georgia; and a gentleman from South Carolina tells us that his constituents are running into the business with the utmost alacrity. This may be so, but I beg leave to tell the gentleman, that after a very little while, they will run with redoubled alacrity out of it; it will not answer. The sugar planters of Louisiana are not so enormously rich as gentlemen affect to believe; I know some who have been ruined; many who have done nothing more than hold their own; a few, and these generally with all the advantages of commencing with large capitals, independent, if you please, rich. But the same may be said of our cotton planters and our merchants. There is nothing, as yet, which very advantageously distinguishes the cultivation of the cane. I believe the planters stand in need of the protecting care of Government; in their behalf I ask it. I have no personal interest. I am not a sugar maker, and from present prospects I believe I never shall be. I have not brought my private feeling into operation on this question. I wish it were the case that no pecuniary consideration could ever be seen to shape or decide our political course.

In regard to every article mentioned in the tariff, one excepted, the people of Louisiana are the purchasers and consumers; they are to be heavily taxed to augment the wealth of other parts of the country; they are willing to make the sacrifice—but they ask in return reciprocal sacrifices; they ask protection to their single manufacture—to that employment in which more capital is embarked, in relation to the State, than in any other in any State in the Union, in regard to its wealth and resources. I suppose the capital thus employed amounts to nearly $90,000,-000, one-third of the agricultural and manufacturing wealth of the nation. Does any manufacture, in any other State, bear as great a proportion to its wealth?

1261   HISTORY OF CONGRESS.   1262

March, 1816.   *The Tariff.*   H. of R.

The motion of the gentleman has a most important bearing on the revenue of the nation, as well as on the prosperity of Louisiana; if it succeed, it will strike off about $900,000 from the receipts of the Treasury. Does the gentleman propose to make up the loss by additional taxes on other articles? On what can it be laid with more propriety? No idea is entertained of increasing the direct tax, and augmented duties on any other subject will amount to a total prohibition or invite extensive smuggling; if the article be bulky, it will not be imported, if it be otherwise, it will be surreptitiously introduced—in either event, no benefit accrues to the customs.

My friend from South Carolina, the chairman of the Committee of Ways and Means, who, I hesitate not to say, is better acquainted with the fiscal concerns of the nation than any member of this House, has recommended the duty which I now advocate; he tells you explicitly, it is required by the necessities of the Government. Impartial and intelligent as he is, he has not said as much in regard to any other tax; he has not supported high duties on cotton and woollen goods, because no benefit would result to the public from laying them; they would, as they will, cease to be imported, or be smuggled; and the benefit to the nation, if either of these should occur, cannot be easily perceived; no danger of this kind is to be apprehended in respect to sugar, it is too bulky to be smuggled, and too necessary to the community to be dispensed with.

I fear, Mr. Chairman, that an interest is springing up before which every other is to be prostrated; the mere manufacturer is to be preferred; whether he be a manufacturer of the raw material, produced by our own country, or that of other States, is not to be asked—whatever injury be done to the revenue, whatever ruin be brought on maritime industry, however much the agriculturist suffer, the manufacturer must and will be encouraged. Does the manufacturer of wool want encouragement, foreign cloth is shut out, the value of the duties given up, and the competition, so beneficial to the consumer, is destroyed; does the farmer ask to be protected in raising sheep, so as to furnish the raw material, the necessary duty on foreign wool is denied, because it is convenient and profitable to the manufacturer to purchase wool as cheap as possible, whether it be foreign or native. Apply the same examination to other subjects—does the sugar refiner ask it, foreign refined sugar is excluded from the market by enormous duties; does the grower of the raw material solicit protection, it is denied, because it is convenient and profitable to the refiner to obtain the raw material as cheap as possible. I will detain the House no longer. I have endeavored to show that it is as important to the interests of the nation to protect the cultivation of the cane and the manufacture of sugar, as any other manufacture whatever; that, by so doing, in opposition to what will occur from augmenting the duties on imported goods generally, you encourage the commerce and naviga-

tion and add to the revenues of the nation. I hope the motion will not prevail.

Mr. Huger acknowledged that the statements he had just heard had done away much of his objection to the duty proposed in the bill, and if the gentleman from Louisiana could convince him that the cultivators of sugar could not go on safely without the duty, he would not press his motion further; but he apprehended the gentleman had been in some measure influenced by his feelings, and, not being a grower himself, might be misled by an imperfect acquaintance with this subject.

Mr. Robertson replied at some length to Mr. Huger, in support of his previous statement; after whom

Mr. Lowndes made a few remarks on the same side. He argued that the manufacture of sugar demanded encouragement as strongly as any other, and that he thought the duty proposed by the bill was even too low, being a very small increase on the specific duty; and it was as necessary for the purpose of revenue as the protection of the article.

Mr. Sheffey said, he was in favor of the motion. He objected to a high duty being laid for the purpose of revenue, because it would press too heavily on the poorer classes. Sugar had become an article of necessity, and was used almost as much by the poor as the rich; it was taxing the poor, therefore, to impose a heavy duty on it. As to the necessity of protecting the article, the increase of the culture for several years was a sufficient argument that it was profitable, and needed no protection. Self-interest, he said, was eagle-eyed, and would pursue only what was productive of profit. Mr. S. resorted to a variety of other arguments to show that two and an half cents would be an ample duty on the article, either for protection or revenue.

Mr. Calhoun made a few remarks against the motion. He dwelt on the great importance of the article, and the expediency of encouraging its production in our own country, by which our supplies would be so much more certain; and he enforced particularly the necessity of encouraging all those articles at home, for which we now depended on the West Indies, to which the trade was so precarious that a proclamation from the Governor of an island might any moment cut it off.

Several other gentlemen entered into this debate, whose remarks cannot be given in the above condensed manner. Mr. Wilde opposed the motion, and Messrs. Milnor, Pickering, and Pitkin, advocated it.

The question on striking out the sum of four cents was then taken, and carried—ayes 62, noes 55.

Mr. Pitkin moved to fill the blank with three cents.

Mr. Forsyth proposed to fill it with five cents, and spoke some time in support of a high duty on the article; which, he said, would be cultivated very extensively in Georgia, if proper encouragement were given to it by the Government.

Mr. F. protested also with warmth against the injustice of taxing the South to support the manufacturers of the East, and yet denying to the South any security for their manufactures in return.

Mr. ROBERTSON also advocated this motion, and Mr. PITKIN opposed it; when

The question on five cents was negatived.

Mr. CLAY then moved to fill the blank with three cents and a half, but hoped some gentleman would propose to restore four cents; in favor of which Mr. C. argued at some length.

Mr. GASTON spoke a short time in opposition to the proposed duty; and earnestly entreated the House to consider those unfortunate manufacturing States, which were burdened on the one hand to encourage the manufactures of the East, and taxed on the other to protect the products of the South, &c.

After an ineffectual attempt by Mr. WOODWARD to obtain a reconsideration of the question on striking out, with the view of moving to restore four cents; his reasons for which he briefly stated,

The question on filling the blank with three and a half cents, was carried—ayes 64, noes 58.

The Committee then rose, reported progress, and obtained leave to sit again.

And on motion, the House adjourned until Monday.

MONDAY, March 25.

Mr. IRVING presented a petition of Jacob Barker, of the city of New York, praying that certain suits instituted against the endorsers of certain bills of exchange drawn by him on his agents in London, in the Kingdom of Great Britain, during the late war with that country, (which were sold to the Government of the United States and were returned protested in consequence of the British Government having prohibited its subjects from trading in the United States stock, upon which the said bills were bottomed,) may be discontinued upon their returning the purchase money given for the said bills, together with interest and all the costs which have accrued thereon.—The petition was referred to the Committee of Ways and Means.

Mr. PLEASANTS, from the Committee on Naval Affairs, to whom was referred the bill from the Senate "respecting the late officers and crew of the sloop-of-war Wasp," reported the same without amendment, and the bill was committed to a Committee of the Whole.

An engrossed bill entitled "An act placing certain persons on the list of Navy pensioners," [wounded at Dartmoor prison] was read the third time and passed.

A message from the Senate informed the House that the Senate have passed a bill "for the relief of John Holkar, formerly Consul General of France to the United States;" also, a bill "for the relief of the Baltimore and Massachusetts Bible Societies;" in which bills they ask the concurrence of this House.

BANKS IN THE DISTRICT OF COLUMBIA.

Mr. TUCKER, from the Committee on the District of Columbia, to whom was referred the petitions of sundry banking associations in said District, praying for charters, made a detailed report thereon, favorable to the prayer of the petitioners, on their complying with certain conditions; which was ordered to lie on the table, and be printed.

The report is as follows:

The committee have participated in that deep and general concern to which the unauthorized establishment of banking associations throughout the country has given rise. They will forbear to dilate upon the incalculable evils which inevitably flow from suffering any association of individuals, who choose to engage in such pursuit, to pour into the circulation of the country a flood of bank paper at their discretion. The general sentiment has been so perfectly settled on this subject, and has been so entirely justified by the lessons of a dear bought experience, that your committee have chosen rather to avoid unprofitable speculations, and to act at once upon the subject, by the introduction of a bill, which has already been reported, for the suppression of the notes of the unchartered banks. The provisions of that bill (however harsh they may appear) are believed by your committee to be essentially necessary to effect the great and important end which they have in view, in common, as they believe, with other members of the Congress of the United States. They have recommended the punishment of the persons engaged in banking, and of the officers of such institutions, rather than a general penalty on the circulation of the notes of unchartered banks, because the experience of an adjoining State has sufficiently demonstrated that provisions of the latter description cannot be carried into execution. A large proportion of society becoming implicated in the offence, it becomes impossible to enforce the provisions of the law, however wise in its views, and salutary in its design.

But whilst your committee unhesitatingly recommend the prohibition of the establishment of new banks, the maturest reflection has convinced them, that the existing state of things absolutely requires those which have gone into operation within the District without charters, to be incorporated, and suffered to continue an employment of their capital, which was legitimate when their associations were formed. In presenting their views on this subject, your committee will ask attention to the following considerations:

1. What are the evils that can fairly be anticipated from chartering the unincorporated banks?
2. What are the evils which are likely to ensue from arresting them in the course of their business?
3. What are the public advantages that may be derived from their incorporation?

It is of material consequence, in determining the first of these questions, to observe, that it is proposed by the committee to make the resumption of specie payments by the banks an essential condition of the charters, and to prohibit the suspension of specie redemption, under the penalty of forfeiting their privileges as a corporation. With such a provision, they indulge the hope that no evil of sufficient magnitude can fairly be apprehended from incorporating the banking companies now in operation.

An opinion has been entertained by some, that the amount of bank capital in the District far exceeds its wants, and that it is better to limit it by putting down a part of the existing unchartered banks, if not the whole. It is believed that this opinion is founded on a misapprehension of the amount of capital in the District, and is also contradicted by facts which admit not of controversion.

The actual bank capital of the District of Columbia is as follows:

Actual capital of the chartered banks, appearing from a printed statement before the House	$3,331,597
Proposed capital of six unchartered banks, which it is contemplated to incorporate, each $500,000	3,000,000
	$6,331,597

The actual capital of the six unchartered banks does not amount, it is believed, to more than two millions at the present time, and the sum of five hundred thousand dollars has been fixed on as the amount of the capital of each, because it is probable the demand for bank capital may increase before the expiration of the proposed charters, and because the provisions of the National Bank bill prohibit the granting of any others.

This capital of five millions three hundred thousand dollars, is not confined in its active operations, and its beneficial effects, to the population of the three towns in the District, amounting to about twenty thousand souls. Even if it were, it is believed it would not exceed the proportion of bank capital in Baltimore to the population of that city. But when we take into the estimate the extensive and rich country on the shores of the Potomac, and even of the Shenandoah, stretching up nearly two hundred miles West and Southwest into Virginia, whose produce chiefly centres in this District, and whose prosperity is, in some measure, dependent on the command of capital here, we may venture to doubt the accuracy of that opinion which pronounces the banking capital too large. A single fact ought to place this matter beyond doubt. It is the fact, that there is no difficulty in the employment of the capital. That capital cannot, it is believed, be justly pronounced to be too large, which, so far from exceeding the demand for capital, does not even now meet the extent of that demand. It is notorious, that the banks of this District are even now unable to discount all the paper which is offered them by men of unquestionable solvency, of the highest respectability, and engaged in the most laudable and lucrative employments; and though this incapacity proceeds, in some measure, from the absorption by Government stock of a part of their capital, yet that circumstance is neither supposed to be of sufficient importance to vary materially the position assumed, nor ought it indeed to be taken into the estimate.

The only evil it is supposed that can be plausibly assigned as likely to flow from the chartering of the unincorporated banks, is that which may be supposed to arise from a surcharged circulation of their paper. So long as banks continue their operations without redeeming their notes in specie, this is a well grounded apprehension. The love of gain—one of the most powerful instincts of the human heart—without the salutary check of specie redemption, will always tempt banking associations to overtrade. But the necessity of paying specie for their notes when demanded, affords an ample check to that propensity, at least in the present state of our public affairs. The committee will not intrude upon the House a disquisition, on a proposition so plain as to be at present almost received

as an axiom, that an excessive issue of notes will furnish its own check, if banks redeem with punctuality the notes they send into circulation. And as the principle of specie redemption is the foundation of this report, it is believed that no evil will ensue from the adoption of the measure recommended by them.

2. The evils which are likely to ensue from suppressing the chartered banks already in operation, are, on the other hand, believed to be great and manifest.

Your committee are not in possession of any statement of the concerns of the several banks, from which it can be accurately known what amount has been discounted or lent by the unincorporated associations to individuals. The committee appointed by order of the House to make an investigation into their situation, will probably furnish correct information on the subject. It appears, however, from a statement of one of the banks, that they have discounted, on an actual capital of only $249,050 in money, to the amount of $489,000; and if the discounts of the other unchartered banks bear a like proportion to their capitals, we may fairly conclude that there is an amount of between three and four millions of dollars discounted by them at the present time. The effect upon the mercantile class, and upon society in general, of a suppression of these institutions, may then easily be conceived. The suppression, whether immediate, or even at a period somewhat remote, must compel those institutions immediately to commence a heavy and ruinous curtail of their discounts, perhaps an immediate payment of the whole of the debts due to them. These debts, amounting to perhaps four millions, form most probably nearly one-half of the money lent by all the banks in the District, chartered as well as unchartered. A demand of payment of a sum bearing so large a proportion to the mercantile capital of the towns of Georgetown, Washington, and Alexandria, must inevitably produce the most serious distress among all the debtors of the banks, and among all the debtors of those debtors, and thus extend throughout every ramification of society. Bankruptcy and ruin to individuals here, loss and embarrassments to those connected with them in trade, or their creditors elsewhere, and a paralysis of the commerce and active industry of this District, must be the inevitable consequence; and those to whom the Constitution has left no other protection than the Legislature of the nation, will find themselves prostrated by the hand to which alone they can look for support.

It is not here that the evil will stop. The suppression of the unchartered banks, and the consequent annihilation of so much capital, or the withdrawing so large an amount as two or three millions of dollars from the active capital of the country, must, of course, produce a visible effect upon the prices of the produce brought to this market; and whilst it thus indirectly injures the agriculturist, will drive him to seek in some other more distant and less convenient market, that fair price for the returns of his labor, which the distresses and limited capital of this District will prevent his receiving here. To whatever side we turn, there seems to your committee to be mischief and ruin to individuals, and to the District, in the suppression of the unchartered banks of the District. Nor will the chartered institutions be able to afford relief. Notwithstanding the allegation that there is too much capital in the District, it is believed that the chartered banks have discounted as far as they think it prudent to go, and are daily refusing the offer of good paper for discount.

For these reasons, and for others, (which they forbear to press lest this report, although extended beyond their expectations, should become unreasonably voluminous,) your committee earnestly recommend that the unchartered banks of the District should not be suppressed. They trust it will also be perceived that a mere postponement of the period when they shall cease, will not avoid the evils which have been contemplated.

3. Your committee next proceed to state very succinctly what are the public advantages that may be derived from the incorporation of the unincorporated banks of the District. These will be found in the effectual aid which will be afforded by those institutions, in promoting public works connected with the prosperity of the District, of the greatest utility and importance.

The committee will not enlarge upon the subject of public improvement in roads and navigation, from a conviction that every member of the National Legislature is sufficiently impressed with their importance. They will only mention the public works to which the banks will contribute an essential and salutary aid.

The navigation of the Potomac and Shenandoah rivers, which extend two hundred miles into the interior, passing through a fertile and rapidly improving country, has long been an object of the greatest interest, as affecting not only the wealth and convenience of the States of Maryland and Virginia, and the commerce and prosperity of their people, but as intimately connected with the general welfare of this District, whose interests are confided to the guardianship of the National Legislature. Individual exertion has done much towards opening that navigation, and at the present moment a great effort is making to complete what has so long been slowly in progress. Even now, however, some aid is required to prevent a failure of this important object; and this aid the banks of the District are willing to afford. It is proposed that the banks, when chartered, should advance or loan to the Potomac and Shenandoah companies, at moderate interest, two per centum of the amount of their capitals, and it is understood that the banks readily accede to this proposition, and to the other conditions here after mentioned. Those other conditions relate to the aid to be afforded by the banks for the completion and construction of certain turnpike roads terminating in the District, and leading to the upper and fertile part of the country. These roads are as follows:

The road from Georgetown to Fredericktown.

That from Washington to Montgomery court-house.

The road from Georgetown to Snicker's Gap, passing through Leesburg.

The road from Snicker's Gap to Winchester.

The road leading from Alexandria to Thornton's Gap. And,

The road from Winchester to Cumberland.

It is contemplated to appropriate ten per cent. of the capital of the banks in the District to these roads; and it is believed that, when united to individual subscriptions, the aid of the banks will be sufficient to effectuate these desirable objects. Should these important ends be obtained, there will then be afforded an admirable water carriage for the produce of a very wealthy portion of the community to this commodious market, whilst, at the same time, roads will be opened, communicating both through Frederick and Winchester, with the great national road leading through the Western States.

Your committee cannot forego the expression of a hope, that we shall not permit this favorable opportunity for effecting a great national work to pass by unimproved; they, therefore, respectfully submit the following resolution:

Resolved, That it is expedient to incorporate the following banking associations within the District of Columbia; that is to say: The Farmers and Mechanics' Bank of Georgetown; the Central Bank of Washington and Georgetown; the Bank of the Metropolis; the Patriotic Bank; the Union Bank of Alexandria; the Merchants' Bank of Alexandria; and the Franklin Bank of Alexandria.

THE TARIFF.

The House then again resolved itself into a Committee of the Whole on the bill to regulate the tariff of duties on imports.

Mr. SMITH, of Maryland, renewed the motion he made, and afterwards withdrew, on Saturday, to increase the duty on lump sugar to twelve cents, and on loaf to fifteen cents per pound; which, after some objections by Mr. PICKERING, and reply by Mr. SMITH, was decided in the affirmative—ayes 56.

Mr. SOUTHARD proposed to increase the duty on gunpowder from six to ten cents per pound, which he supported on the ground of the ability of existing manufactories in the United States to supply the whole country, and the expediency of even prohibiting, by high duties, the importation of an article which it was so much our true policy to encourage the manufacture of at home.

After a few words from Mr. LOWNDES in reply, explanatory of the views of the Committee in fixing the duty at six cents, which was deemed fully adequate to protect the domestic manufacture, the motion was negatived.

Mr. RUGGLES moved to strike out the duty proposed by the bill, of one cent per pound on imported tallow, which he advocated in a short speech.

After some discussion, in which Mr. SMITH opposed and Mr. STEARNS favored the motion, it was lost without a division.

Mr. REED moved to reduce the duty on cocoa from four to two cents per pound; which amendment was also rejected—ayes 43, noes 55.

Mr. RUGGLES moved to include copper sheets in the list of copper articles, on which the duty of four cents per pound is laid by the bill.

This motion was supported by the mover, Mr. MILNOR, Mr. STEARNS, and Mr. WEBSTER, and opposed by Mr. LOWNDES; and ultimately negatived, without a division.

Mr. RUGGLES then moved to incorporate in the bill a duty of two cents per pound on copper sheets; which was also negatived.

Mr. SMITH, after some explanatory observations, and with the view of encouraging our own shipping by every means, moved to charge teas imported in foreign ships from China the higher duties charged in the bill on teas imported "from other countries than China," and thus to secure the China trade to the American shipping, as had been the case under the former law.—His motion obtained.

Mr. HOPKINSON, after observing that the proposed duty on lead was greater than that on shot, and presuming it an inadvertency on the part of the Committee of Ways and Means, moved to raise the duty of one cent on lead in bars, &c., to two cents per pound; which was agreed to without objection.

Mr. INGHAM moved an amendment, the object of which was to change the ad valorem duty on iron and steel wire of twenty-two per cent., to a specific duty of five cents per pound on wire under No. 18, and of nine cents per pound on that of No. 18.

After a few words from Messrs. IRVING, of New York, WARD, of Massachusetts, and PICKERING, to show the impropriety of the proposed change of duty, and by Messrs. INGHAM and MILNOR in support of the amendment, the motion was agreed to.

Mr. HALE, on account of the high freight which imported bar iron had to pay, and the consequent impropriety of a high duty on that article, moved to reduce the duty from seventy-five to fifty cents per cwt. on iron in bars and bolts.

Mr. CONDICT opposed the motion because of the opposite fact, that bar iron generally paid no freight, and was brought from Europe chiefly as ballast, and submitted some statements to support his views of the subject.

Mr. HALE replied; after which the motion was negatived—ayes 31.

Mr. IRVING, of New York, proposed, for reasons which he stated, to amend the bill, by changing the duty on clocks and parts of clocks from seven and a half per cent. ad valorem to twenty-two per cent. ad valorem, and to include parts of watches in the duty of seven and a half per cent. on watches imported entire; which motion was agreed to without a division.

Mr. IRVING also proposed to change the duty of seven and a half per cent. on cotton laces to twenty-two per cent., and include lace veils, shawls, &c., in the articles liable to the duty of seven and a half per cent.; which was also agreed to, *nem. con.*

Mr. INGHAM moved to add the following clause to the paragraph which fixes the duties on woollen and cotton goods: "on cotton yarn or thread, the same; provided, that all unbleached and uncolored cotton yarn or thread, the original cost of which shall be less than sixty cents per pound, shall be deemed and taken to have cost sixty cents per pound, and shall be charged with duty accordingly; and all bleached or colored yarn, the original cost of which shall have been less than seventy-five cents per pound, shall be taken and deemed to have cost seventy-five cents per pound, and shall be charged with duty accordingly."

The motion was supported by the mover, and in a few remarks by Messrs. SMITH, CLAY, MILNOR, and STRONG, and also by Mr. WHEATON, (who entered into a general investigation of the question of protection of manufactures, and his reasons for favoring a decided and effectual protection,) and opposed by Messrs. LOWNDES and TUCKER; when the amendment was agreed to.

On motion of Mr. ROBERTSON, the words "on grain" were stricken out of the clause fixing the duty on imported spirits; so as to embrace all spirits, whether made of grain, molasses, or other material, within the highest rate of duties specified in the bill on spirits.

Mr. MILNOR moved, after some introductory remarks, to strike out the proposed duty on tin plates, of one dollar and fifty cents per box of one hundred square feet, for the purpose of substituting a lower duty.

Mr. LOWNDES offered a few arguments in support of the duty proposed by the bill, and in opposition to the amendment; after which the motion was negatived.

Mr. MILNOR moved to reduce the duty on tin, by changing the duty of one dollar and fifty cents from boxes of one hundred to boxes of two hundred and eighteen square feet; which motion was also rejected.

Mr. WEBSTER then renewed the motion which he offered and withdrew on Saturday, to strike out the duty proposed by the bill to be imposed on imported cottons, and to substitute the following: "For two years next ensuing the 30th day 'of June next, a duty of thirty per centum ad 'valorem; for two years, to commence at the 'termination of the two years last aforesaid, a 'duty of twenty-five per centum ad valorem; and 'after the expiration of the two years last aforesaid, a duty of twenty per cent. ad valorem."

Mr. CLAY moved to amend the amendment by changing the word two, in the first line, to three; the word two, in the second instance, to one; and to conform the remainder of the amendment accordingly. We all know, said Mr. C., that now is the time for encouragement, and that the domestic manufacturer has to struggle more at the end of a war, and at that moment the greater aid is necessary to support him against foreign competition. If the amendment he offered prevailed, four years would still reduce the duty to the minimum proposed by the original motion, and would give to our own manufactures an adequate protection at the time of the greatest difficulty.

Mr. LOWNDES assented to the motion. He rejoiced to see gentlemen who had manifested the strongest friendship for the manufacturing interest the advocates of a proposition which would, in prospect, produce a return of correct principles. Satisfied that twenty-five and even twenty per cent. was a sufficient protection to the manufactures in question, he would, nevertheless, support the proposed motion, though not perfectly correct in his opinion, persuaded that it would eventually produce the state of things which he thought most desirable.

Mr. ROOT believed the proposition now under consideration was worse than any other which had been offered on the subject. He was opposed to the graduation, by which the manufacturing establishments would be sustained for two years, and then left to their fate. If twenty per cent. was a sufficient protection, as had been stated, by this amendment a bounty of ten per cent. would be given to the manufactories already established, and in effect would be a monopoly to them. He was in favor of encouraging the erection of others, which could not be effected under the advantage of the powerful competition which the amendment would give to the existing establishments.

Mr. HULBERT said if the amendment was modified as proposed by Mr. CLAY's motion, he should be in favor of it. Since the amendment was offered on Saturday, he had consulted with gentlemen acquainted with the subject, and had been informed that the manufacturers would be satisfied with the encouragement which the amendment would afford to them; and if the minimum was retained, he was decidedly in favor of the motion.

Mr. WEBSTER observed that he had conversed with those well informed on the subject, and had understood that the manufacturers would be satisfied with a duty of 30 per cent. for one year; but he had proposed two years, for the purpose of meeting the views of those who advocated a greater degree of encouragement.

Mr. HULBERT said the individual consulted by the gentleman, though intelligent and honorable, was a manufacturer of large capital, and could better stand under the operation of the amendment than many others whose means were limited, and who had not got well established.

Mr. WARD, of Massachusetts, wished it distinctly understood that he was in favor of encouraging manufactures; and his object was to give a substantial and permanent support to them, and not a bounty for a short time, which would temporarily discourage foreign importation altogether. It was said by some that foreign goods ought to be excluded, because the country was so completely stocked with them now as to contain enough for two years' consumption. He asked if this course would not be a bounty on those already imported, by allowing the holders of them to put on 30 per cent? This would be promoting the interest of the merchants, and while he desired to protect them against injury, he wished not to give one part of them a bounty, to the exclusion of the other; and asked if consequences would not result from the course proposed, which were not contemplated?

Mr. WEBSTER said the question was, how far the country was bound to support those institutions. He was not prepared to say that the Government was bound to adopt a permanent protection, or one which would exclude those goods already in the country. From the course pursued by the Government for some years back, the community had a right to expect relief from the danger to which the sudden change of circumstances exposed our manufactures; but Government had a right to say whether that relief should be permanent or not, and to reduce the protecting duties if it thought proper. But Mr. W. said he was opposed to a changing and fluctuating policy, and the object of his motion was to impose a duty so moderate as to insure its permanency and be still an adequate one.

Mr. CALHOUN hoped the amendment to the amendment would not prevail. He believed the mode proposed by the original motion was correct, and that the permanent duty of 20 per cent. was an ample protection; he believed the policy of the country required protection to our manufacturing establishments, and he hoped it would be adopted in the way proposed by the amendment.

Mr. PITKIN said, in forming his opinions on this subject, he would not be influenced by the statements of those who had large manufactories already established. He wished to act on a large national scale; not to give a monopoly to those now in existence, but to enable others to embark in the business of manufacturing. Under this amendment a man could not get his buildings erected in the two years proposed, and the time offered would be of no use to them at all. Mr. P. supported Mr. CLAY's modification, and argued at some length in favor of the policy of holding out encouragement to additional establishments.

Mr. WEBSTER repeated that his object was to protect the manufacturers permanently. He asked gentlemen to recollect that even under the duty of 20 per cent., the minimum of his proposition, the India cottons would be forever excluded; the India trade, he said, was at an end. He contended further, that manufacturing establishments could now be erected at less than two-thirds the cost of those which were first commenced in the country.

Mr. CLAY said the object of protecting manufactures was, that we might eventually get articles of necessity made as cheap at home as they could be imported, and thereby to produce an independence of foreign countries. In three years, he said, we could judge of the ability of our establishments to furnish these articles as cheap as they were obtained from abroad, and could then legislate with the lights of experience. He believed that three years would be sufficient to place our manufacturers on this desirable footing, and others would not hesitate to enter into the business, because they would look to that liberal and enlarged policy which they might anticipate from the Government at a future period.

Mr. SMITH, of Maryland, did not believe that 20 per cent. was at this time an adequate duty on cotton goods, but that it would give an advantage to the American manufacturer of 50 per cent. over the British manufacturer in cotton goods.

Mr. ROSS believed that 20 per cent. was an encouragement amply sufficient; and replied at some length to those who maintained that the Government was pledged to afford a high protection to manufactures, and against the rage for fostering them to the exclusion of every other pursuit. He desired the independence of the people as well as national independence, and wished not to see one class of the community enslaved by another; to illustrate which, he introduced the situation of China, where the government was completely independent, and yet the people all slaves. If the extravagant duties proposed were not necessary for revenue, he said, he could see no strong necessity for them. The failure of certain manufacturers was no reason for them, because some individuals of all professions were unfortunate in the best times, and no sympathy was felt for the merchants who failed. Adverting to a remark that some manufactories were worked in Kentucky by slaves, Mr. R. said all manufactories were conducted with slaves, because the occupation had a tendency to degrade and debase the human mind. It was, he argued, a vain attempt to carry manufactures to such extent in this country, while there were so many inducements to seek an independent support by agriculture, and other beneficial pursuits. The only kind of manufactures he wished to see flourish, were those conducted in families; any other would prove destructive to the liberties of this Republic, by combinations effecting a revolution in this House and in the Government. There was already great necessity for a strong country party to withstand the manufacturing and commercial parties here.

Mr. CLAY's motion was negatived—ayes 47, noes 61; and Mr. WEBSTER's amendment was agreed to by a large majority.

The Committee then rose, and obtained leave to sit again.

TUESDAY, March 26.

On motion of Mr. JENNINGS, the Committee on Public Expenditures were instructed to inquire into the state of the accounts connected with the superintendency of Indian affairs for the Territory of Indiana, and the manner in which the said superintendency has been discharged.

Mr. JENNINGS, in proposing the above motion, observed that he wished to state to the House, that each of the Governors of the Territories of the United States, at least of the Territories northwest of the river Ohio, were likewise superintendents of Indian affairs, for and within their respective Territories. That it would be difficult to ascertain the mischief which might accrue by reason of any neglect, or other malfeasance in relation to the duties of such superintendencies. That he had long been of opinion that malconduct had taken place in the superintendency for the Territory of Indiana. Mr. J. said, that the laws of the United States had long since prohibited any superintendent from being concerned in merchandising; though he had no hesitation in stating, that the late superintendent for the Territory of Indiana had been concerned in trade while acting as such, and that he had purchased goods for the use of the Indians, on account of the United States, from the concern in which he was a partner. Mr. J. said, that he did not intend to make any allusion to the present Governor of Indiana—he alluded particularly to a former Governor, late a Major General of the Army of the United States. He hoped the inquiry would be instituted.

On motion of Mr. BRYAN, the Committee on Military Affairs were instructed to inquire into the expediency of providing by law for the payment of such articles of military clothing as may be due soldiers discharged from the Army of the United States.

On motion of Mr. TUCKER, a committee was appointed to inquire into the expediency of providing by law for the turnpiking a road from the town of Winchester, in Virginia, to Cumberland, so as to unite with the great western turnpike road.—Messrs. TUCKER, PIPER, LEWIS, BASS, and LYLE, were appointed the said committee.

The bill from the Senate "for the relief of the Baltimore and Massachusetts Bible Societies," was read twice and committed to a Committee of the Whole.

The bill from the Senate "for the relief of John Holkar, formerly Consul General of France to the United States," was read and committed to the Committee of Ways and Means.

THE TARIFF.

The House then again resolved itself into a Committee of the Whole on the bill to regulate the tariff of duties on imports.

Mr. LOWNDES offered the following amendment to the clause fixing the duty of twenty-five per cent. on woollens: "Excepting blankets, and woollen rugs, shall be levied, collected, and paid until the 30th of June, 1818, and after that day twenty per cent. on the said articles."

Mr. LOWNDES observed that he believed the manufacture of woollens, and particularly of blankets, required a decided present encouragement; and after receiving that support, his amendment would produce the reduction of the duties to that correct standard which only ought to be encouraged and looked to.

Mr. INGHAM favored a duty of twenty-five per cent. for three years, and a duty of twenty-two per cent. for one year; but he was willing to take the amendment with simply substituting the year 1819 for 1818, and moved so to modify it.

Mr. HULBERT hoped Mr. INGHAM's amendment would be accepted by the mover of this proposition, and offered a few reasons in support of it.

Mr. LOWNDES repeated some of the reasons which induced him to prefer his own proposition.

Mr. HUGER argued some time in opposition to extravagant duties, the consequence of which would be to tax the community to give a monopoly to a few large manufacturers. He was also opposed to legislating for the next Congress; though willing to lay an adequate protection during the present Congress, he desired to leave the next to act for themselves, and impose such duties as to them should seem proper.

Mr. INGHAM replied, and offered some additional reasons in favor of the motion as he wished to modify it. Mr. HUGER rejoined.

Mr. LOWNDES entered into a more comprehensive investigation of the question, defending his proposition, and replying to the gentleman who had opposed it.

Mr. INGHAM's modification was then agreed to—ayes 63; and the question recurred on the amendment as amended.

Mr. ROOT opposed it at some length; and likewise the adoption of a policy which, in his opinion, would encourage the most odious of all monopolies.

On motion of Mr. STEARNS, the words "woollen stuffs" were added to the amendment, being accepted by Mr. LOWNDES.

And the original proposition was agreed to as amended.

Mr. FORSYTH offered the following proviso to follow the amendment:

"*Provided,* That all woollen cloths, or cloths of which wool is the material of chief value, the original cost of which, at the place whence imported, shall be less than four shillings sterling per square yard, shall be subject to no higher duty than fifteen per cent. ad valorem."

Mr. SMITH opposed the motion, and submitted some statements to show that its adoption would be extremely injurious to the revenue.

The motion was also opposed by Mr. LOWNDES and Mr. HULBERT, and was supported by Mr. HUGER. Mr. CUTHBERT also said a few words on the subject, advocating moderation in a duty which would fall with peculiar force on the poor. The question was then taken, and decided in the negative, without a division.

Mr. WARD, of Massachusetts, offered the following proviso to the clause respecting the duty on cotton goods imported from India, &c.:

"*Provided further,* That nothing in this act shall be so construed as to subject any goods of the description last mentioned, which may be imported directly from beyond the Cape of Good Hope, which shall arrive in the United States before the 1st day of January next, to any other or higher duty than would be imposed upon them, should they arrive in the United States before the 30th day of June next."

Mr. WARD supported his motion by a variety of arguments, and at considerable length; and was replied to by Mr. HULBERT, who was answered by Mr. WARD. Mr. SMITH indirectly argued against the motion, believing that the amendment would cover but a very small number of voyages, &c. Mr. CLAY likewise spoke against the amendment, and against legislating on every voyage which might be thought to suffer hardship from the policy of the Government, and also in reply to Mr. WARD's arguments. Mr. MASON spoke some time in opposition to the motion, and Mr. WARD again in favor of it. Mr. PICKERING made a few remarks in favor of relieving the merchants now engaged in the trade, and in danger of ruin by the bill. Mr. SHEFFEY supported the amendment; arguing that the duty on India imports was from 113 to 150 per cent. on the cost, and that a system which required such enormous protection was unnatural and oppressive on the great body of the community. Mr. PICKERING explained, and Mr. MASON rejoined; when, after a very long discussion, almost entirely of a commercial character, the question was taken on the amendment, and lost—ayes 32.

Mr. ROBERTSON moved to amend the clause of the bill fixing the duty on *books,* so as to confine the duty to books printed in the English language; observing that the heavy duty on books

in the English language was obviously necessary, because they could be reprinted in our own country; but that the same reason did not operate on books in other languages, as we had to depend almost wholly for them on Europe, and their importation ought not to be restricted, as we were not yet in the habit of republishing them.

Mr. LOWNDES said, in reply, that one reason for the duty in the bill, was that the duty of twenty per cent. was supposed by the committee sufficient to enable the reprinting to advantage of books of any language in this country.

Mr. PICKERING remarked that books on the dead and other languages, were not altogether from Europe, as they were now printed in different parts of the country.

Mr. GROSVENOR agreed, in part, with Mr. ROBERTSON; but those who read books in other languages were able to pay for them; that there was no reason for the discrimination, and that he would prefer striking out the duty altogether, as in his view it would answer no valuable purpose.

Mr. INGHAM argued, that as printing establishments were extremely costly, those who embark in the publishing of books ought to be encouraged; that they would be thereby able to circulate many more books in the community, and that he looked on them as among the most valuable establishments in the country.

Mr. GROSVENOR replied, and contended that if the duty was not necessary for revenue, it was not so for protection.

Mr. ROBERTSON varied his motion so as to embrace the whole duty on printed books. He agreed with Mr. GROSVENOR in his views, and wished not to retard the improvement of the country, because it might diminish in a little way the profits of some of the mechanical employments.

The motion was carried—ayes 48, noes 45.

Mr. SMITH then made a motion he had promised some days ago, the object of which was to take off the ad valorem duty of twenty per cent. on Russia and Holland duck, and to lay a specific duty of $2 50 per piece on the former, and $3 per piece on the latter; which motion was agreed to *nem. con.*

On motion of Mr. BETTS, the bill was amended by adding *gold leaf* to the articles on which a duty of fifteen per cent. is laid.

Mr. McKEE moved to strike out the words three cents from the duty on lead ground in oil, with the view of inserting a larger sum; which was supported by Mr. JOHNSON, of Kentucky, and Mr. CLAY, who stated that the article was already manufactured, and of a better quality than the imported article, amply sufficient for the consumption of the country, and that the great possessions of the Government in lead mines was an additional reason for laying a high duty on the imported article.

After a few remarks on the subject by Messrs. LOWNDES, SMITH, and IRVING, to show that the present sum would be a sufficient protection, the motion was negatived—49 to 43.

Mr. CLAY then moved that the duty be increased from three to four cents per pound on red or white lead ground in oil; which motion was carried—ayes 48, noes 43.

On motion of Mr. PITKIN, the bill was so amended as to extend the duty on *teas* to those which may be imported from any other place than China, east of the Cape of Good Hope.

The Committee then rose, and obtained leave to sit again.

WEDNESDAY, March 27.

Mr. ROBERTSON, from the Committee on the Public Lands, to whom was referred the bill from the Senate "further extending the time for issuing and locating military land warrants," reported the same without amendment, and the bill was committed to the Committee of the Whole on the bill of this House, upon the same subject.

Mr. ROBERTSON, from the Committee on Public Lands, to whom was referred the Message of the President of the United States of the 20th of January last, recommending the ratification of certain donations of land made by the friendly Creek Indians to General Andrew Jackson, Colonel Benjamin Hawkins, and others, made a report thereon; which was read and committed to a Committee of the whole House on Monday next.

Mr. YANCEY made a report on the petition of the President and Directors of the Washington Bridge Company; which was read; when Mr. Y. reported a bill for the relief of the President and Directors of the Washington Bridge Company; which was read twice and committed to a Committee of the Whole.

Mr. FORSYTH, after some introductory observations, in support of his object, offered the following resolution:

Resolved, That the Committee for the District of Columbia be instructed to report a bill to incorporate the subscribers to the Female Orphan Asylum of the City of Washington, and to vest in them the fee simple title to four of the public lots in the City of Washington, to promote the benevolent objects of the said institution.

The question on proceeding to consider the resolution, was decided in the negative—ayes 44.

DAY OF ADJOURNMENT.

Mr. BASSETT, from the joint committee appointed on that subject, made a report on the probable business which the two Houses have to act on during the present session, and recommending that the President of the Senate and Speaker of the House of Representatives be authorized to close the session on the —— day of April next.

Mr. HARDIN moved that the blank be filled up with Monday, the 22d of April.

Mr. JACKSON moved Saturday, the 20th, being opposed to legislating on the Sabbath, except in case of great emergency, and one day would make but little difference.

Mr. SMITH, of Maryland, asked if gentlemen were serious in their motions, and declared it as his opinion that the necessary business could not be completed sooner than the 22d of May. If we hurry off, said he, and leave the public business unfinished, the alteration we have made in the mode of our compensation, will prove a very bad one, &c.

Mr. MILNOR offered some reasons to show the impropriety of fixing on the day at present, and moved that the report lie on the table; which was agreed to.

The report lies on the table accordingly.

SEIZURE BY A COLLECTOR.

Mr. LOWNDES, from the Committee of Ways and Means, reported a bill for the relief of David Gelston and Peter A. Schenck; which was read twice and committed to the Committee of the Whole on the bill for the relief of Edward Hallowell.

Mr. L. also communicated the following document:

TREASURY DEPARTMENT, *Feb.* 19, 1816.

SIR: It is my duty to lay before the Committee of Ways and Means a request for an appropriation to pay the amount of judgment recovered by Gould Hoyt against David Gelston, the collector, and Peter A. Schenck, the surveyor of the port of New York, under the following circumstances:

Information having been received in July, 1810, from the French Minister, as well as from various official sources, that a ship called the "American Eagle" was arming and equipping as a vessel of war in the port of New York, for the use of Petion, one of the chiefs of the island of St. Domingo, the collector and surveyor of the port were instructed by the Secretary of the Treasury, acting with the authority of the President, to seize the ship for adjudication, under the act of the 5th of June, 1794. The seizure was accordingly made, but, upon trial, (after a delay of more than two years,) a decree of restitution was pronounced. Mr. Hoyt, the alleged owner of the ship, then instituted an action against Messrs. Gelston and Schenck, to recover damages, and has, in fact, obtained a verdict for $107,369 43, upon which judgment has been rendered by the Supreme Court of the State of New York.

The case involving a construction of an act of Congress upon questions highly interesting to the United States in their relation to foreign Powers, the attorney for the district of New York was instructed to aid in the defence of the suit, and to take the proper measures to obtain the judgment of the Supreme Court of the United States, should the decision of the State court render it necessary. Accordingly, the case has been removed by writ of error into the highest court of law in the State of New York, with a view to its being brought finally before the Supreme Court. It has, however, been represented by the counsel of the defendants that the expense of prosecuting the writ of error will be great, and that the probability of reversing the judgment is slight. It becomes necessary, therefore, to provide for the event of a final judgment in favor of the plaintiff.

In explanation of the facts thus generally stated, I have the honor to transmit the following documents:

1. A copy of the report made by this Department to the Senate on the 13th February, 1815, in which the circumstances that led to the seizure of the ship "American Eagle" are particularly stated.

2. A transcript from the record in the case of Hoyt *vs.* Gelston and Schenck.

3. The correspondence with Mr. Gelston and his counsel relating to the suit.

4. A letter from Albert Gallatin, Esq., who was Secretary of the Treasury at the time of the seizure of the "American Eagle," explanatory of the facts and principles on which the seizure was directed.

From the whole, it will satisfactorily appear—

That the instructions for seizing the "American Eagle" were founded upon official information of an illicit design in her equipment, upon a sense of public duty, and upon a fair and reasonable construction of the law :

That the seizure was made by the collector and surveyor, in the course of their official duty, under the official instructions of the Treasury Department :

And that an indemnity is due from the Government to the collector and surveyor, by providing for the payment of the damages which have been awarded against them.

If, therefore, the Committee of Ways and Means concur in this view of the subject, I respectfully ask their direction to insert in the general bill of annual appropriations (which is now preparing) an item "for discharging the judgment obtained in the Supreme Court of the State of New York, by Gould Hoyt against David Gelston and Peter A. Schenck, in an action of trespass for seizing the ship "American Eagle," under instructions from the Treasury Department, a sum not exceeding $112,000."

I have the honor to be, very respectfully, sir, your most obedient servant,

A. J. DALLAS.

Hon. W. Lowndes,
Chairman Committee Ways and Means.

POST OFFICE DEPARTMENT.

Mr. Ingham, from the committee appointed on the 29th January, at the request of the Postmaster General, to investigate the conduct of the Post Office Department, made a detailed report of said investigation, accompanied by the evidence submitted to the committee by the various witnesses who appeared before it. The report and documents were committed to a Committee of the Whole, and ordered to be printed.—The report is as follows:

The committee appointed to investigate the conduct of the General Post Office Department, make report :

That they have used their utmost endeavors to ascertain every fact that appeared to be material to a full understanding of the conduct of the officers of that Department. As the inquiry originated in a request of the Postmaster General, the committee, in the first place, addressed to him a letter, requesting to be informed of the reasons of his application to Congress, and also that he would give them such information as appeared to be calculated to facilitate the investigation. The Postmaster General stated, in his answer, that the application was induced by a rumor that some person or persons of the Department had sold drafts for money due to the General Post Office for premiums, which had been converted to their private use.

The committee, therefore, proceeded to inquire into the truth of the rumor, by the examination of every person who seemed likely to have any knowledge of the fact ; but, in the examination of some of the clerks in the General Post Office, various suggestions were made of improper transactions in the Department, other than those to which their attention had been

drawn by the Postmaster General. The investigation has therefore assumed a very extensive scope, and has consequently occupied more time than could have been anticipated, at its commencement. This delay has also been increased by circumstances arising out of the nature of the inquiry. As no person appeared to make any specific charges, the committee had no alternative but to abandon their undertaking, or listen to rumors and the hearsays of some of the witnesses to prove the facts. They made choice of the latter course, and have examined every person who was either suggested to them, or appeared as likely to possess any information on the subjects of their inquiry.

The charges arising out of the suggestions of the witnesses, and which, from the various communications they made to the committee, it appeared to be the desire of some of them most especially to establish, are as follows :

1. That certain persons in the General Post Office, and particularly Abraham Bradley, jr., Assistant Postmaster General, had sold post office drafts and checks, and applied the premium to his private use.

2. That an erasure had been made in the cash-book of the General Post Office, and an erroneous entry found thereon.

3. That private accounts were improperly kept with individuals on the books of the post office.

4. That Phineas Bradley had been concerned in a contract for carrying the mail, that was improperly obtained.

5. That P. Bradley had received corrupting presents from mail contractors.

6. That P. Bradley and Abraham Bradley, jr., had made use of post office money, in purchasing depreciated bank notes, for which they received a premium, and applied it to their private use.

7. That bank notes which were better than the paper of the District of Columbia, and a Treasury note, had been returned to postmasters, by order of Abraham Bradley, jr.

8. That the Washington and Union Bank and certain individuals had profited by the sale of post office drafts.

9. That a contract for carrying the mail from Washington to Fredericksburg had been superseded by order of the Postmaster General, before it expired, and about double the amount given for the same service.

An examination of the subjoined testimony and documents will enable the House to determine how far the charges, or either of them, have been sustained. The committee have, however, no hesitation in expressing their opinion on them severally.

1. With respect to the first charge, in relation to Abraham Bradley, jr., there is no evidence whatever to induce a suspicion that he has sold post office drafts or checks for a premium ; nor does it appear that any other person in the General Post Office has sold post office drafts or checks for a premium, other than drafts obtained for their own salaries, except in the case of H. H. Edwards, who bought a post office draft on Boston, for District of Columbia paper, and disposed of it by an agent in New York, (as "he presumes,") for a premium.

The committee have not relied upon negative testimony to disprove this charge, but have attentively examined the books of the Union Bank containing the accounts with the General Post Office, as well as the private accounts of Abraham Bradley, jr., and Phineas Bradley, with that bank, and have satisfactorily ascertained that no credits have been given to them, or any other person in the General Post Office, for premium on drafts or checks; they have also ascertained, that the premiums for post office drafts and checks sold by the bank, have been entered in the profit and loss account thereof. It therefore conclusively follows, that these premiums have accrued to the bank, and to none other.

2. It appears that a draft in favor of Elisha Riggs is charged in the cash book of the General Post Office, as sold to the Union Bank, the words *Union Bank* being apparently written on an erasure. But from an examination of the books of the Union Bank, the committee ascertained, that the General Post Office had credit for this draft thereon, and therefore, the draft having been actually sold to, and negotiated by the Union Bank and not Elisha Riggs, they do not perceive any impropriety in the entry, and still less have they been able to discover any improper purpose to be effected by the alterations on the cash book.

3. It appears to have been the practice of the Assistant Postmaster General, A. Bradley, jr., to open an account with certain individuals, partly of a public and partly of a private nature; there were cases in which members of Congress have, by means of the agency of Abraham Bradley, jr., transferred funds from one part of the United States to another part, or have received money for some of their constituents, who were contractors for carrying the mail, by which their names became entered on the books; no advantages accrued to any person by the transaction other than that of the accommodation in transferring an inconsiderable fund from one place to another. It may be observed that the post office offered peculiar facilities in this particular, and has frequently been resorted to by members of Congress and others for this purpose, but their names do not appear in an open account on the books, except when the drafts exchanged did not exactly balance at the time of exchange.

The only account of this nature which is ascertained to remain open on the books was made in December, 1800, where there is a balance in favor of the General Post Office of three hundred and twenty dollars, due from General H. Lee, of Virginia.

4. It appears that Phineas Bradley, a clerk in the General Post Office, has been concerned in carrying the mail, and that he owned somewhat more than one eighteenth of a line of stages which carried the mail from Baltimore to Georgetown and Alexandria for $2,800 a year. Whatever may be the opinion of the committee as to the strict propriety of the mode in which a compromise was effected in this case between rival contractors, it is but proper to add, that Mr. Bradley had no legal agency in influencing the decision upon the contract, nor could he have had any other agency in it, unless a corrupt disposition is presumed on the part of the then Postmaster General, who was consulted before the contract took effect as to the propriety of his being concerned in it; but there is no circumstance in the case to authorize such a presumption.

5. There is no evidence which, in the opinion of the committee, can justify the imputations in this charge.

6. It appears that bank notes to a small amount have been sold by Abraham Bradley, jr., and P. Bradley, previous to the general depreciation of bank paper, for which they received a premium. The evidence does not prove that they made use of public money for this purpose; but so far as a fact of this kind could be

14th CON. 1st SESS.—41

ascertained from circumstances, it proves the transaction to have been a private one.

7. It appears that a Treasury note of one hundred dollars, and bank notes to a small amount, which were supposed to be better than the money of the District of Columbia, have been returned to postmasters; this transaction, so far as it regards the bank notes returned, is in conformity with an order of the Postmaster General to his deputies. The only reason alleged for returning the Treasury note is, that it might have been purchased at a discount by the postmaster who remitted it.

8. The committee have ascertained that drafts to the amount of $121,346 46 have been disposed of to the Union Bank; and to the amount of $4,000 to the Washington Bank, and to the amount of $15,348 25 to individuals who were not public creditors since the 1st of October, 1814, the commencement of the general depreciation of bank paper. Those drafts appear to have been exchanged at par, and, except in a few cases, for the paper of the District of Columbia. It is evident, from the rate of exchange during this period between the District of Columbia and most of the places upon which these drafts were drawn, that the purchasers must have derived an advantage other than that of a mere transfer of their funds. It has not been in the power of the committee to ascertain the value of these drafts in the paper of the District of Columbia, having no means of determining, at the several dates, the respective rates of exchange; nor did this appear to them very material, as the amount of profit which accrued to the purchasers could have but little influence upon the principle which must determine the propriety of the measure. With respect to the banks, it is stated that a small proportion of these drafts were sold for premiums, some having been exchanged for specie, and others used for the payment of debts due to other banks.

It cannot, however, be of any importance (if the drafts were essentially more valuable than the District of Columbia paper) whether they were employed in the payment of debts, sold for specie, or for bank notes of this District with a premium for the difference of value; the principle is the same in either case, and whatever may be the amount of advantage to the individuals or the banks in this transaction, resulting from the difference of exchange, the same will be the amount of disadvantage to the Government. It does not however appear that any change has taken place in the practice of the General Post Office Department, in this respect, for a series of years; and as the operation complained of is evidently the effect of an existing arrangement under a change of the circumstances of the circulating medium, it is not to be presumed that the practice has arisen out of a design to promote private interests, or to prejudice the interests of the Government. The committee are however decidedly of opinion, that the advantage arising from the difference of exchange as to all the moneys that are due to the Treasury ought to accrue exclusively to the Government; but as the Postmaster General has expressed a willingness to pay over these balances in any way that may best accommodate the Treasury Department, the evil admits of a very simple remedy.

9. The facts stated in this charge are admitted to be correct, and the letter of the Postmaster General contains a satisfactory explanation of the reasons for altering the terms of the contract in question; whether too much was eventually given for the service, under the

changes required by the Postmaster General, is a subject not in the power of the committee to decide; nor would they be justified in presuming any misconduct in a transaction that appears to have been so fairly conducted.

The committee subjoin to this report the substance of all the testimony which appeared to them in any degree material to the inquiry, also sundry communications made in writing, and beg leave to offer the following resolution, viz:

Resolved, That the committee appointed to investigate the conduct of the General Post Office Department be discharged from the further consideration of the subject referred to them.

[Accompanying this report is an abstract of the evidence given before the committee, and some written statements made in answer to its queries. These documents, being voluminous, are omitted.]

THE TARIFF.

The House then again resolved itself into a Committee of the Whole, on the bill to regulate the duties on imports.

Mr. LYON, after some remarks to show the oppressiveness of the proposed duty on salt on the people of his part of the country, and the general impolicy and odiousness of a heavy tax on that article, moved to strike out the duty of twenty cents per bushel on salt.

Mr. LOWNDES, without following the gentleman in the discussion of the general question, hoped the House would not now reverse its former decision on this subject, and reject the duty.

The motion was then negatived by a large majority.

Mr. INGHAM moved, for reasons which he offered, that the duty of six cents per pound on imported gunpowder, be raised to eight cents; which was assented to by Mr. LOWNDES, and agreed to by the House.

Mr. WARD, of Massachusetts, after remarking on the difficulty of discriminating between London Particular and market wines, and the ease of evading the difference of duty, moved to abolish the discrimination, and make the duty on each ninety cents per gallon.

Mr. SMITH gave a particular statement of the different wines of Madeira, their qualities, &c.; declaring his belief that the duty proposed on wine was so high as to endanger the revenue therefrom, and showing, by various illustrations, that a moderate duty was more productive to the Government, by preventing smuggling.

Mr. MILNOR argued in favor of the discriminating duty, and adduced some facts in support thereof.

Mr. WARD replied, that his objection was not to the expediency of discriminating, but its impracticability, &c.; after which

Mr. SMITH observed, in addition, that the high duties might operate as an encouragement to the brewing of wine at home, because thirty gallons of good cider, thirty of sherry, ten of Malaga, and ten of good Madeira, would make wine which would pass anywhere for Madeira; and, as we

were greatly encouraging some manufactures, he said, ironically, gentlemen might think that it would be proper to encourage this.

The amendment was then agreed to—ayes 65.

Mr. ROBERTSON, after observing that claret was not a luxury alone in some parts of the country; but, from the nature of the climate, an absolute necessary to the health of the people in that section of the Union which he represented, moved to strike out the duty on certain kinds of wine named in the bill, with the view of establishing a lower duty.

Mr. SMITH, in the course of some remarks, said he wished to retain the highest duty on Spanish and Portuguese wines, for political reasons; in those countries, our flour being subjected to a duty of two dollars per barrel, and he wished to induce our citizens to go elsewhere in search of foreign wines, &c.

Mr. HARDIN spoke against the motion, and in favor of high duties on luxuries, such as he considered claret wine, particularly at a time when we were taxing the indispensable articles of life; and remarked, incidentally, that if the Louisianans could not obtain wine, they could obtain an abundant supply of whiskey from Kentucky in lieu of it.

Mr. ROBERTSON repeated that claret, in the part of the country referred to, was not only necessary to the health, but to the morals, of the people. They were a sober people, he said, and it was to save them from the whiskey offered by the gentleman from Kentucky that he wished to reduce the duty on claret. The liquid fire of alcohol would, in so warm a climate, be poison to them, and its use be more pernicious than arsenic.

Mr. CLAY said he was in favor of the motion, because of the cheapness of the article at the places whence it was imported; but he was sorry his friend from Louisiana had declared war against the whiskey of the West; and regretted, if such was the fact, that the taste of the people of Louisiana was so bad as to prefer bad claret to good whiskey.

Mr. SMITH then—Mr. ROBERTSON having withdrawn his motion for that purpose—moved to reduce the duty on claret wine in casks, from twenty-five to fifteen cents per gallon; which was negatived—ayes 44.

Mr. BURNSIDE moved to increase the duty on imported iron in bars, &c., from seventy-five to one hundred and twenty-five cents per hundred weight, which he advocated by a speech of some length.

The motion was opposed by Messrs. HALE, PICKERING, SMITH, of Maryland, LOWNDES, GROSVENOR, HARDIN, CUTHBERT, and IRVING, and advocated by Messrs. REYNOLDS and CONDICT; the last named gentleman concluding by moving to raise the duty to one hundred and fifty cents per hundred weight.

After a very extended discussion of the question, in which it was argued on one side that our iron factories required additional encouragement and protection; and, on the other, that it was already a profitable pursuit, by which large fortunes were made; that if it could not now do without so high a protection, it would always require it; that the duty in the bill was three times the former duty, under which iron factories were established to great advantage—

The amendment was rejected—five or six only rising in favor of the motion.

Mr. STRONG then moved to reduce the duty on imported iron, from seventy-five to fifty cents per hundred weight.

This motion was supported by Mr. ROSS, who wished that the ambassadors from the cotton factories had at once made a treaty with the Committee of Ways and Means, which the House might have swallowed, and have left the other manufactories to themselves, and not be burdening the people in every possible way, under the plea of protection. The motion was advocated also by Mr. WEBSTER, chiefly on the ground of the great navigation the iron importations employed to the Baltic.

It being suggested that this motion had been already decided a few days ago, Mr. STRONG varied it, by moving to reduce the duty to thirty-seven and a half cents per hundred weight, which was negatived—ayes 45.

Mr. WEBSTER then moved to reduce the duty to forty-five cents per hundred weight.

This motion was opposed by Mr. BURNSIDE, and advocated by Messrs. WEBSTER and HALE, and carried—ayes 62, noes 43.

Mr. BETTS moved to strike out the duty of five cents per bushel on coal, with the view of inserting the article in the second section, among those which are to be admitted free of duty; in support of which a memorial from the Common Council of New York was read.

The motion was opposed with much earnestness by Mr. PLEASANTS, who adduced various arguments in support of the duty, and of encouraging the home production of the article.

The motion was negatived without a division.

Mr. PLEASANTS then moved to add one cent more to the duty on the imported coal, and make it six instead of five cents per bushel.

This motion was opposed by Mr. IRVING, at some length, as one which would fall with peculiar and unequal severity on the poorer classes of citizens in the Atlantic towns; as a partial and unjust tax, &c.; and he argued against the impolicy of legislating in this sectional and special manner.

Mr. CLAY also made a few remarks on the subject, saying that he supposed it was a substitute for a motion which Mr. PLEASANTS had previously made and withdrawn, (to make the imported bushel an *even* and not a *heaped* one,) and as he could not shave the bushel down to a level, he wished to put a cent on the top of it. Mr. C. asked his friend from Virginia, coming as he did from the South, used to cheerful coal fires, to recollect the shivering condition of those of the North, &c., who had to import their coal.

Mr. PLEASANTS said he did not expect, by his motion, to excite so much seriousness on the one hand, or so much pleasantry on the other, and then proceeded to defend the propriety of his motion, in reply to Mr. IRVING; after which, the amendment was negatived—ayes 46, noes 63.

Mr. CONDICT then moved to reduce the duty to three cents per bushel; which was negatived by a large majority.

Mr. IRVING moved the following clause to the first section :

"That in all cases where an *ad valorem* duty shall be charged, it shall be calculated on the net cost of the article, (exclusive of packages, commissions, and all charges,) and on the usual addition, established by law, of twenty per cent. on all merchandise imported from places beyond the Cape of Good Hope, and of ten per cent. on articles imported from all other places."

This amendment, after a short discussion, was adopted, without a division.

The Committee then proceeded to the second section of the bill, which enumerates the articles to be admitted free of duty.

Mr. FORSYTH moved to strike out " burr stones unwrought," with the view of subjecting them to a duty, on the ground that Georgia could supply all the wants of the country in this article of the best quality, and that it ought to be encouraged, &c.

The motion was opposed by Messrs. GROSVENOR and MILNOR, and supported by Messrs. FORSYTH and WILDE, and negatived.

The Committee then rose, and obtained leave to sit again.

THURSDAY, March 28.

Mr. CHIPMAN, from the select committee appointed on the 27th December last, reported a bill for the relief of John H. Peaslee, Nathan B. Haswell, and Russell Jones; which was read twice, and committed to the Committee of the Whole on the bill for the relief of Edward Hallowell.

A message from the Senate informed the House that the Senate have passed "An act in addition to the act to regulate the late Post Office Establishment," with amendments, in which they ask the concurrence of this House.

The amendments were read, and referred to the Committee on the Post Office and Post Roads.

The SPEAKER laid before the House a supplemental report of the Secretary of War, of applications to be placed on the list of invalid pensioners; which was referred to the Committee of Pensions and Revolutionary Claims.

Mr. HARDIN moved a resolution fixing the future hour of meeting during the session, at ten instead of eleven o'clock.

The resolution was opposed by Mr. HULBERT, and supported by Mr. HARDIN, and adopted by a considerable majority.

THE TARIFF.

The House then again resolved itself into a Committee of the Whole, on the bill for the regulation of the duties on imports and tonnage.

Mr. MIDDLETON moved so to amend the second section as to admit maps, charts, and drawings, free of duty; which motion was agreed to.

On suggestion of Mr. STEARNS, and assented to by Mr. LOWNDES, chemical apparatus was also included in the free articles, when imported for incorporated societies.

Mr. REED, after some introductory observations, moved to strike out "olive oil in casks" from the free articles, for the purpose of subjecting it to duty. It was his opinion that spermaceti oil was a good substitute, and that its manufacture ought to be encouraged.

After some opposition from Messrs. STRONG and HULBERT—the motion was lost.

Considerable conversation then took place on the subject of a proposed duty on the importation of foreign unmanufactured wool; but no decision took place on the subject, the motion respecting it being waived for the present.

Mr. WILDE moved some amendments in the phraseology of the second section, which were agreed to.

On motion of Mr. ATHERTON, gold and silver coin were added to bullion in the list of free articles,

On taking up the 3d section, which imposes 12½ per cent. on all articles imported after the 30th June next, in ships or vessels not of the United States,

Mr. SMITH moved that 10 per cent. be substituted for 12½. That rate, he said, had been the uniform duty from the commencement of the Government to this time; and he further wished to impose as moderate a duty as we could, because of the number of our citizens residing in the Hanse Towns, &c., and carrying on an extensive trade with us.

Mr. PITKIN supported the motion, also, in a few remarks; and the amendment was then agreed to, without objection.

Mr. SMITH moved to reduce the amount to be deducted from the duties on articles exported, with the benefit of drawback, from 5 per cent., as proposed by the bill, to 2½ per cent.

On this motion a short discussion ensued, after which, the amendment was adopted by a large majority.

Mr. SMITH moved further to amend this section, by reducing the proposed deduction on spirits exported with the benefit of drawback.

The motion was opposed by Messrs. LOWNDES and PICKERING, and negatived.

Mr. LOWNDES moved the following proviso to the enumeration of the articles entitled to drawback:

"*Provided, however,* That piece goods imported in ships or vessels of the United States from India, which shall have sailed before the passing of this act, and shall arrive between the 30th of June 1816, and the 30th of June 1817, may be re-exported with the benefit of drawback, and without any deduction from the amount of duties secured or paid, at any time within twelve months from the time of importation."

The proviso was offered without the periods stated above, but the blanks were filled up, and the amendment finally adopted in the form stated.

Mr. IRVING moved the following as an additional section to the bill:

"That after the 29th of June next, in all cases of entry of merchandise for the benefit of drawback, the time of twenty days shall be allowed from the date of the entry, for giving the exportation bonds for the same: *Provided,* That the exporter shall, in every other particular, comply with the regulations and formalities heretofore established for entries of exportation for the benefit of drawback."

The amendment was adopted without opposition as the 5th section of the bill.

On motion of Mr. EDWARDS, a clause was added to the bill empowering the President to purchase as well as erect houses for the use of the customs.

On motion of Mr. ATHERTON a section was added to make more positive and unequivocal the repeal of former acts respecting discriminating duties, interfering with the provisions of this bill.

Mr. MILNOR proposed to take from the President the application of the fund called "warehouse money," and vest it in the Secretary of the Treasury, under the direction of Congress.

This motion was negatived by a large majority.

Mr. CADY then moved to strike out the whole section providing a fund from drawbacks, &c., for the erection of custom-houses.

This motion was agreed to without a division.

Mr. INGHAM moved a long amendment, the object of which was to reduce the number of grades of ad valorem duty, and transfer the articles falling under the rate of twenty per cent. to other classes—which was agreed to.

On motion of Mr. INGHAM the duty on unmanufactured wool was fixed at 7½ cents ad valorem—ayes 63.

Mr. ROBERTSON, after some explanatory observations, in which he adverted to the decision of the committee on this subject a day or two ago moved to strike out the exception in favor of books imported for the use of incorporated societies, &c., so as to make the importation of books entirely free; a duty on which, he argued, was unnecessary for the purpose of encouragement to the American publisher, &c., and would create only a greater competition amongst the printers here.

The motion was opposed by Messrs. INGHAM and LYON, the latter of whom maintained that the encouragement was necessary for the business here; that very few books were published in the United States in the foreign languages; that our printing was greatly inferior to that of England; that until very lately we had not republished any of the standard works, &c., and that a duty on foreign imported books was necessary to improve the business of book-making in this country.

The motion was then negatived.

Mr. GOLDSBOROUGH moved a new section, to limit the operation of the act to the term of four years.

This motion was opposed by Messrs. SMITH and HULBERT, on the ground of the injurious effect on commerce as well as manufactures which the constant apprehension of change would produce, and it was advocated by the mover, who said if the act passed without limitation it would be still liable to repeal at any time by a majority of Congress, and present protection he had understood was all that the manufacturers wanted, &c. After which the amendment was rejected, by a large majority.

The Committee then rose, and reported the bill and amendments, which were ordered to lie on the table and be printed.

DIRECT TAX.

The House then went into Committee of the Whole, on the bill supplementary to the act laying a direct tax.

Mr. GOLDSBOROUGH moved that the assessors should be compelled to attend two full days in each county in their several districts, instead of one day; which motion was negatived without a division.

Mr. NELSON, of Virginia, moved to strike out the proviso which makes the seller of a slave, after the purchaser has entered such slave as his property, responsible for the tax as well as the purchaser; which motion was agreed to.

After some ineffectual attempts to amend the bill, Mr. McLEAN, of Kentucky, offered an amendment, the object of which was to compel the assessors to attend at each court-house in their respective districts, as well when the counties exceed six, as when they do not; which was agreed to without objection.

The Committee then rose and reported the bill as amended. The House concurred in the amendments, and the bill, as amended, was ordered to be engrossed for a third reading.

The Committee of Ways and Means obtained leave to sit to-morrow during the session of the House; and then the House adjourned.

FRIDAY, March 29.

Mr. MILNOR presented the petition of the managers of the Pennsylvania Hospital, praying that the property of said hospital may be exempted from the payment of the direct tax; which was referred to the Committee of Ways and Means.

Mr. YANCEY, from the Committee of Claims, reported, with amendments, the amendments of the Senate to the bill authorizing payment for property lost, captured, or destroyed by the enemy, while in the public service; which were ordered to lie on the table.

The House went into Committee of the Whole on the bill supplementary to the act for defining the duties of the judges of the Territory of Illinois. The bill received a verbal amendment in committee, was reported to the House, and ordered to be engrossed and read a third time.

The House resolved itself into a Committee of the Whole on the bill to authorize the President to lease out the United States saline on the Wabash river; which was reported to the House with some unimportant amendments, and the bill, as amended, was ordered to be engrossed for a third reading.

The House went into Committee of the Whole on the bill for the relief of Benjamin and John Tyler, of New Hampshire. The Committee rose, reported progress, was refused leave to sit again; and the bill was laid on the table.

The remaining orders of the day were suspended, on motion of Mr. NELSON of Virginia; and Mr. N. then submitted the following resolution:

Resolved, That a committee be appointed to inquire into the official conduct of Matthias B. Tallmadge, one of the District Judges of the State of New York, and to report their opinion whether the said Matthias B. Tallmadge has so acted in his judicial capacity as to require the interposition of the Constitutional power of this House; and that the said committee be authorized to send for persons, papers, and record.

The resolution was adopted without objection, and a committee of seven appointed accordingly.— Messrs. NELSON of Virginia, GROSVENOR, BUTTE, GOLDSBOROUGH, YANCEY, WILKIN, and LAW, were appointed the said committee.

The bill for the relief of Edward Hallowell; the bill for the relief of Henry Malcolm; the bill for the relief of Edward Keeler and John Francis; the bill for the relief of Moses Lewis; the bill to remit certain duties on books imported for Harvard College; the bill for the relief of Robert Kidd; and the bill allowing 100,000 dollars to the captors of certain Algerine vessels, severally passed through a Committee of the Whole, and (with the exception of the last named, which was ordered to lie for the present on the table,) were ordered to be engrossed and read a third time.

MISSISSIPPI TERRITORY.

The bill for the relief of certain purchasers of public lands in the Mississippi Territory, also passed through a Committee of the Whole, and was reported to the House with an immaterial amendment, which was agreed to.

Mr. HALL then moved the following as a new section to the bill: "That, from and after this 'day, the sum of money due the State of Georgia, under the articles of agreement and cession, 'shall bear an interest of six per cent. per annum, 'until paid."

This motion was objected to by Mr. ROBERTSON, who could see no reason or justice in the amendment; and supported by Mr. HALL, who said if the United States chose to grant gratuitous indulgence to their debtors, it was no reason why they should delay the payment of their debts without giving interest, &c.

The amendment was rejected by a large majority.

Mr. FORSYTH then offered an amendment to the bill, in the following words: "That the in-'terest due, and which shall become due, from 'the persons entitled to the benefits of this act, 'shall be paid to the State of Georgia, in addition 'to the sum due by the articles of cession and 'agreement for the purchase of the Mississippi 'Territory."

This motion was supported by the mover, and opposed by Mr. ROBERTSON, and negatived; and

1291   HISTORY OF CONGRESS.   1292

H. or R.   *Previous Question—Salary of District Judge.*   MARCH, 1816.

then the bill was ordered to be engrossed for a third reading.

REMISSION OF DUTIES.

The bill remitting the duties to Harvard College was, on motion of Mr. CLAY, amended in the Committee of the Whole, by including in the bill the remission of duties on the carriage of Governor Gore, of Upper Canada, who landed at New York in 1815, and passed through part of the United States to his Government.

It was inquired by Mr. FORSYTH, who conceived the remission of the duty an act of courtesy only, what the practice of the British Government was in such cases: that if the courtesy was not usual with that Government, he should be unwilling to extend it in the present instance.

It was replied by Mr. CLAY that, though his motion was founded in strict justice, it not being within the contemplation of the law to exact duties on a carriage which was not to be used in the country, the courtesy was usual in England, and on the continent of Europe.

Mr. HOPKINSON stated a fact, also, in which the duties accruing in Great Britain on certain paintings intended for the Pennsylvania Hospital were remitted, on the ground that they were for the general encouragement of the arts, and for a public institution.

The amendment was agreed to in committee, and concurred in unanimously by the House.

THE PREVIOUS QUESTION.

The SPEAKER proceeded to announce, severally, the orders of the day. On calling the report of the Committee on the Standing Rules and Orders of the House, which was under discussion some weeks ago,

Mr. STANFORD moved that the House resolve itself into a Committee of the Whole on the said order.

Mr. BASSETT moved that the order be indefinitely postponed.

Mr. STANFORD said, so far as it was the object of the House to get clear of the discussion of the previous question, it might be well enough to postpone indefinitely; but the motion itself he considered as opening the whole discussion. He considered the rule unconstitutional, and oppressive upon a minority of this House; that it always called up the worst feelings in the House, and he thought the present a propitious time to get clear of it. But, he was as anxious as any other gentleman to bring the session to a close, and would therefore content himself with asking the ayes and noes upon the question; which were ordered.

Mr. JACKSON expressed his wish that the gentleman from Virginia (Mr. BASSETT) would withdraw his motion.

Mr. TUCKER united in that request; not from an indisposition to express an opinion on the subject of the rule relating to the previous question, which it was the object of the mover of the order of the day to bring under consideration. He had always believed the rule an essential rule, however cautious the House should be in the exercise of it. But he was averse to this mode of acting on the question, preferring to meet it directly, and if the motion for postponement was persisted in he should vote against it.

Mr. BASSETT replied that he could not withdraw the motion. Gentlemen must perceive that it was now too late to take up the subject and go into a long debate—that subjects of a more pressing nature called for the attention of the House in order to bring the session to a close; and if the gentleman from North Carolina (Mr. STANFORD) wished to go into a discussion, he had it in his power, by a resolution to that effect.

Mr. STANFORD said that the gentleman, (Mr. B.,) and the House, knew there were other previous questions besides the main one. If he made the motion the gentleman spoke of, then followed the question of consideration, and the House had it in their power to evade the discussion at will. The other gentleman, from Virginia, (Mr. TUCKER,) declares that he thinks the rule a necessary and proper one, and ought, at times, to be resorted to. If, said Mr. S., the rule be a proper one—say a Constitutional one—then it was fair to use it upon one subject, as well as another, upon all subjects before the House; then we might be made a dumb Legislature complete; or we might be carried through a whole session in that way. He would forbear, however, as the ayes and noes were called, and it would be seen who were for, and who against the tyranny of this rule.

On taking the yeas and nays, it was discovered that a quorum had not voted—the ayes being 56, the noes 34.

Mr. STANFORD and Mr. BASSETT then successively withdrew their motions.

SALARY OF NEW YORK DISTRICT JUDGE.

The House then resolved itself into a Committee of the Whole on the bill to allow additional compensation to the District Judge of the Southern District of the State of New York, for performing the judicial duties in both districts in the State.

This bill gave rise to some discussion, not on the propriety of allowing the compensation proposed, but on the expediency of adopting some course by which the Judge of the Northern district (Judge Tallmadge) should be compelled either to perform his official duties, or to resign; and not be permitted to hold a sinecure office.

Mr. CLAY thought it would be better to meet the question fairly at once, by inquiring into the conduct of the offending Judge, than to get round it by allowing extra compensation to the Judge who performs the duty of both.

Mr. NELSON said that the inquiry had not devolved on the Judiciary Committee, nor had they conceived it their duty to enter into an examination of the conduct of the Judge of the Northern district; but they had incidentally become acquainted with his improper conduct; and Mr. N. said he believed he ought to be turned out of office. That consideration, however, ought not to throw any impediment in the way of this bill, because a former law had enjoined on the Southern Judge (Van Ness) to perform those extra duties, if necessary, and he ought to be compensated therefor.

Mr. STANFORD had some doubt as to the constitutionality of voting a temporary increase of salary to a Judge. He doubted whether, if the compensation was allowed, it could with propriety afterwards be reduced; and for the purpose of entering into the inquiry of a general increase of salary to the Judges, he moved that the Committee rise.

Mr. BETTS remarked that Judge Tallmadge was incapacitated by bodily infirmity from performing his official duties, and that he had not received the salary for some time, &c.; to which it was replied by Mr. GROSVENOR and others that that fact was immaterial, as the Judge had a claim to the salary and could at any time demand and receive it.

The necessity of an inquiry into the neglect of Judge Tallmadge, was also urged by Mr. GROSVENOR and Mr. HOPKINSON.

The Committee then rose, ayes 53, noes 51, obtained leave to sit again, and the bill was laid on the table.

INDIANA AND MISSISSIPPI.

The House then resolved itself into a Committee of the Whole, on the bill to enable the people of Indiana Territory to form a Constitution and State government and be admitted in the Union on the footing of the original States.

The bill received a variety of amendments in its details, and having been gone through,

The Committee proceeded to take up the bill to enable the people of the Mississippi Territory to form a Constitution and State government, and be admitted into the Union on an equal footing with the original States.

After adopting various amendments and rejecting others, the discussion of which consumed considerable time, the bill was got through.

The Committee rose and reported the two bills with their amendments to the House.

The amendments reported to the first were successively agreed to, and the bill, as amended, was ordered to be engrossed for a third reading.

The amendments reported to the Mississippi bill were also agreed to, with the exception of one adopted by the Committee, on the motion of Mr. JOHNSON, reserving to the Congress the power of hereafter altering the boundary of the new State. This amendment was widely discussed, and finally disagreed to; after which, the bill was ordered to be engrossed, as amended, for a third reading; and the House adjourned.

SATURDAY, March 30.

Mr. LOWNDES, from the Committee of Ways and Means, reported a bill making appropriations for the support of the Navy of the United States for the year 1816; which was read twice and committed to the Committee of the Whole on the report of the Committee of Ways and Means upon the subject of revenue.

Mr. L. also reported a bill continuing the salaries of certain officers of Government; which was read twice and committed to the Committee of the Whole last mentioned.

Mr. L. also reported a bill to fix the commissions of the collectors of the direct tax and internal duties, and to revive and continue in force "an act further to provide for the collection of duties on imports and tonnage;" which was read twice and also committed to the Committee of the Whole last mentioned.

Mr. INGHAM, from the Committee on the Post Office and Post Roads, reported a bill to establish post roads; which was read twice and committed to a Committee of the Whole.

A message from the Senate informed the House that an omission has taken place in engrossing the amendments made by the Senate to the bill "in addition to an act to regulate the Post Office Establishment," and to request the House to return the said bill and amendments to the Senate, with a view that the said omission may be supplied.

Ordered, That the Committee on the Post Office and Post Roads be discharged from a consideration of the bill and amendments aforesaid, and that the Clerk carry the same to the Senate.

On motion of Mr. JACKSON, a committee was appointed to inquire into the expediency of providing, by law, for making an artificial road from Washington, in Pennsylvania, through Charlestown, on the Ohio river, to the Sandusky river, at or near Fort Stephenson. Messrs. JACKSON, ROSS, LEWIS, LYLE, and PICKERING, were appointed the said committee.

Mr. HOPKINSON, after some introductory observations, in which he animadverted on the inconvenience and expense of the present mode of doing business, by which all bills, &c., which are not finally consummated at one session, are commenced at a following session *de novo;* also the additional expense to the parties who are brought here session after session on the same business, the repeated trouble to the House, &c., &c., for the purpose of remedying these evils, he submitted the following resolution:

Resolved, That the Committee upon the Rules and Regulations of the House be instructed to inquire into the expediency of making, in conjunction with the Senate, the following alterations in the mode of transacting the public business of Congress, to wit: That the standing committees appointed at the commencement of any Congress shall not be dissolved at the end of the session at which they were appointed; that, on the adjournment of Congress, the unfinished business, to wit, bills, resolutions, and reports of committees shall remain over to the next session of the same Congress, in the same situation as they were at the time of adjournment.

The resolution for the present was, with the consent of the mover, laid on the table.

On motion of Mr. LOWNDES, the Committee of Commerce and Manufactures were instructed to inquire into the expediency of making an appropriation for preserving Little Gull Island, in Long Island Sound, near New London, from the encroachments of the sea.

The bill from the Senate " to authorize the Legislature of the State of Ohio to sell certain part of a tract of land reserved for the use of that State" was read twice and referred to the Committee on the Public Lands.

The bill from the Senate " establishing a port of delivery at the town of Bayou St. John" was read twice and referred to the Committee of Commerce and Manufactures.

The bill from the Senate " to authorize the President of the United States to alter the road cut from the foot of the rapids of the river Miami, of Lake Erie, to the western line of the Connecticut reserve," was read twice and committed to a Committee of the Whole.

Engrossed bills of the following titles, to wit:

An act supplementary to the act to provide additional revenues for defraying the expenses of Government and maintaining the public credit by laying a direct tax upon the United States, and providing for assessing and collecting the same;

An act for the relief of certain purchasers of public lands in the Mississippi Territory;

An act authorizing the President of the United States to lease the saline near the Wabash river, for a term not exceeding seven years;

An act for the relief of Edward Hallowell;

An act supplementary to the act entitled "An act regulating and defining the duties of the judges of the Territory of Illinois, and for vesting in the courts of the Territory of Indiana a jurisdiction in chancery cases arising in the said Territory;

An act for the relief of Henry Malcolm;

An act directing the discharge of Edward Keeler and John Francis from imprisonment;

An act directing the discharge of Moses Lewis from imprisonment;

An act for the relief of Robert Kidd;

Were severally read the third time and passed by the House.

An engrossed bill for the remission of certain duties on the importation of books for the use of Harvard College, was read the third time and passed.

Ordered, That the bill be "An act for the remission of certain duties on the importation of books for the use of Harvard College, and on the carriage and personal baggage of his Excellency W. Gore, Governor of the British province of Upper Canada."

CASE OF SHIP ALLEGANY.

Mr. STANFORD, from the Committee of Claims, reported a bill for the relief of the house of Bowie & Kurtz, and others; which was read twice and committed to a Committee of the Whole.

Mr. STANFORD also made the following report in the case:

That Richard Forrest, as agent for the Department of State, chartered the ship Allegany, Captain Evelith, of the house of Bowie, Kurtz, and others, of Georgetown, to take out a cargo to the Dey of Algiers, in fulfilment of our treaty with the Regency. The charter party was entered into on the 30th day of January, 1812, and stipulated the time of receiving the cargo on board in the United States, and the time of its delivery at Algiers, the amount of freight, where and how it should be paid, and all the terms of the voyage, in the most precise and formal manner, binding the memorialists, with their ship, her freight and appurtenances, to the true and faithful performance of the same, under the penal sum of twelve thousand dollars, lawful money of the United States.

After the public cargo, however, was taken on board, room was found in the cabin and other parts of the ship to admit a further shipment of coffee and spices, and the privilege of such an adventure was accorded to the owners, on their private account, in consideration of their agreeing to receive in the United States the portion of their freight which the Government was otherwise bound to pay them at Algiers, which was accordingly accepted and agreed to.

Thus chartered and loaded, the Allegany sailed on her destined voyage, but was soon arrested by the embargo which preceded the declaration of war, and could not proceed until a special act was passed by Congress to permit the departure of vessels in the public service. When released, she proceeded and arrived at Algiers in good time, and, in all respects, conformably to contract. The cargo was consigned to Colonel T. Lear, the Consul General of the United States near the Dey and Regency of Algiers.

He states, in his communication to the Government on this subject, that the Dey and his officers at first appeared well pleased with the arrival of the Allegany; that the articles on board were at the time much needed; and that on the 20th of July (the third day after the arrival of the ship) the Minister of the Marine sent off a lighter, and actually received from on board the ship a considerable quantity of plank and spars, and proceeded to the landing place of the Marine.

Until now, everything appeared to be going on well, when, of a sudden, the temper and conduct of the Dey assumed the reverse aspect. He at once affects to be disappointed in the quantity of gunpowder and cables which had been sent to him; directs the lighter to be sent back to the ship with the plank and spars received, and at the same time sends a peremptory order " that the Allegany should depart from Algiers in three days, and take with her our Consul General, and all other citizens of the United States then at Algiers."

Against this violent proceeding remonstrances were made by Colonel Lear, but all was in vain—no argument availed anything. Instead of relaxing, he went still further, and demanded a cash payment of $27,000, which he insisted, according to the Mahometan year, was the balance due upon his annuities. Our Consul contended that $15,837 was all that was due, and that the cargo of the Allegany, if received, was more than sufficient to discharge it. But the Dey refused to have anything to do with the cargo, or to suffer it to be sold at Algiers. He did, however, extend the time two days longer for the departure of the ship, and then repeated his mandate that if, within the time, " the demanded balance was not paid into his treasury, and the ship did not depart, with the Consul, his family, and all the other Americans on board, he would detain them in slavery, confiscate the ship and cargo, and declare war against the United States."

Under this unpleasant alternative, Colonel Lear determined to raise the money, if possible, and depart accordingly. The house of Bacri was the only one where he could obtain the money for a bill on Gibraltar, and he drew one on John Salvino, Consul of the United States at that place, giving Bacri to understand that he bottomed the credit and redemption of the bill on the cargo of the Allegany, so far as it would go, who expressed his confidence in the pledge, and advanced the money; and the ship was then early on the morning of the 25th of July, within the prescribed time, carried by an Algerine captain and crew out of the port, whence she proceeded to Gibraltar.

Captain Evelith, of the Allegany, yielding to the necessity of the case, states in his protest that he should abandon the ship to the United States, and consider her as in their service and at their risk, but would navigate her under Colonel Lear's control and direction. Colonel Lear admits that, although he does not recollect any formal abandonment of the ship, Captain Evelith did submit her to his destination and control, and that he directed her to Gibraltar, a place from whence he could better serve the interests of the United States in sending out information of the events at Algiers to our different Consuls in the Mediterranean, in disposing of the Allegany's cargo, and providing to meet the bill which he had drawn on that place.

The committee have thus given as brief a view of the case of the Allegany as the history of the case would admit. Considering that she was chartered by the Government, and performed the stipulated voyage to their entire satisfaction; that she was then, by the arbitrary power of the Dey, compelled, not chartered, into their further service, and that, too, to save their citizens and their property from Algerine seizure; sent upon a new voyage, as opposed to the interests of the owners as it was contrary to the instructions given to their commander; that she was thus diverted from her proper destination, and thrown into the hands of a different enemy, where she was seized and ultimately condemned, ship and cargo, to the serious disadvantage and loss of the memorialists—the committee are impressed with the justice of their claim, and are of opinion that they are entitled to indemnity in this case, when they reflect that the Government has awarded relief in similar cases recollected, and particularly in the cases of the Anna Maria, of New York, and the Resource, of Baltimore, vessels employed in the same service, and suffered in like manner by the arbitrary conduct of some one or other of the Barbary Powers.

They therefore beg leave to report a bill for the relief of the memorialists in the present case.

COMMITTEES ON PUBLIC EXPENDITURES.

Mr. TUCKER called up for consideration the resolutions he submitted some weeks ago respecting the appointment, at the commencement of each session, of additional standing committees for the investigation of the public expenditures.

Mr. SMITH, of Maryland, did not believe that much good could flow out of the measure. There were already, he said, an accountant of the War and an accountant of the Navy Departments, and a comptroller over them, and now we are to appoint committees of Congress over the whole, to inspect accounts after the money has been paid away. Furthermore, he thought it would be impracticable for the committees to act efficiently unless they sat all the year. Mr. S. said he remembered that a gentleman of this House (Mr. RANDOLPH) once moved a similar investigation into what was called the Augean stable; the inquiry was ordered; the gentleman went into it; five thousand dollars were spent in printing documents, &c., and, after all, there was not even a resolution or any other proceeding predicated on the examination.

The motion was advocated by Messrs. TUCKER, DESHA, STANFORD, WRIGHT, and LOWNDES, by whom it was argued that the experience of other States, particularly Virginia, proved the utility of such committees; that they were also found extremely beneficial and useful in England; that clamors and suspicions had gone abroad, and though they might not be well founded, still they rendered the inquiry necessary; that if anything was wrong in the public accounts, the Government ought to know it and the evil be corrected; that if the committees only entered into a general, and not a minute and detailed investigation of those accounts, much good would still result from it, as it would tend to correct frauds, or errors, if any; that it was the duty of this branch of the Government to inspect the money concerns, and see that they were correctly and faithfully conducted.

The resolutions were then agreed to in the following form:

Resolved, That the following standing committees be appointed to serve during the present Congress, and that hereafter, at the commencement of the first session in each Congress, like committees shall be appointed, whose duties shall continue until the first session of the ensuing Congress:

1. A committee on so much of the Public Accounts and Expenditures as relate to the Department of State.

2. A committee on so much of the Public Accounts and Expenditures as relate to the Treasury Department.

3. A committee on so much of the Accounts and Expenditures as relate to the Department of War.

4. A committee on so much of the Public Accounts and Expenditures as relate to the Department of the Navy.

5. A committee on so much of the Public Accounts and Expenditures as relate to the Post Office; and

6. A committee on so much of the Public Accounts and Expenditures as relate to the Public Buildings.

The said committees shall consist of three members each.

It shall be the duty of the committees to examine into the state of the accounts and expenditures respectively submitted to them, and to inquire and report, particularly,

Whether the expenditures of the respective Departments are justified by law;

Whether the claims, from time to time satisfied and discharged by the respective Departments, are supported by sufficient vouchers, establishing their justness both as to their character and amount;

Whether such claims have been discharged out of funds appropriated therefor, and whether all moneys have been disbursed in conformity with appropriation laws; and

Whether any and what provisions are necessary to be adopted to provide more perfectly for the proper application of the public moneys, and to secure the

Government from demands unjust in their character or extravagant in their amount.

And it shall be, moreover, the duty of the said committees to report, from time to time, whether any and what retrenchments can be made in the expenditures of the several Departments without detriment to the public service; whether any and what abuses at any time exist in the failure to enforce the payment of moneys which may be due to the United States from public defaulters, or others, and to report, from time to time, such provisions and arrangements as may be necessary to add to the economy of the several Departments and the accountability of their officers.

Messrs. YATES, MASON, and EDWARDS, were appointed a committee pursuant to the first rule.

Messrs. SMITH, of Maryland, HULBERT, and HAHN, were appointed a committee pursuant to the second rule.

Messrs. ROOT, FORNEY, and SHEFFEY, were appointed a committee pursuant to the third rule.

Messrs. ARCHER, LUMPKIN, and HUGER, were appointed a committee pursuant to the fourth rule.

Messrs. CANNON, PARRIS, and MILNOR, were appointed a committee pursuant to the fifth rule.

Messrs. CONDICT, DARLINGTON, and REED, were appointed a committee pursuant to the sixth rule.

LOST AND CAPTURED PROPERTY, &c.

The House then proceeded to consider the amendments of the Senate to the bill from this House, to authorize the payment for property lost, captured, or destroyed by the enemy while in the public service.

One of the Senate's amendments was the addition of a clause providing for the payment of the forty cents per day stipulated to be paid for certain horses which were afterwards lost, as well as the value of each horse. The Committee of Claims, to whom the Senate's amendments were referred, recommended the disagreement to this amendment. This recommendation to disagree was the question first considered.

The Senate's amendment was strenuously advocated by Messrs. JOHNSON, of Kentucky, DESHA, McLEAN, of Kentucky, HARDIN, JACKSON, McKEE, and SHARPE, who supported the justice of allowing the 40 per cent. per day first stipulated, together with the value of the horse lost. The adverse side was taken by Messrs. YANCEY, CULPEPER, and STEARNS, who denied the justice of the remuneration to the extent contended for. The debate on this question occupied much time, taking the course through which it extended when the subject was originally brought before the House.

The question was finally decided against the recommendation of the Committee of Claims, and in favor of the Senate's amendment—68 to 50.

Mr. ROANE proposed to add the following clause to the cases in the bill in which payment is to be made by the Government: " When any produce or merchandise with which any wagon, cart, boat, or sleigh, impressed into the service of the United States was laden, shall have been lost or consumed in consequence of such impressment."

After some objections to the amendment by Mr. YANCEY, and reply by Mr. ROANE, the motion was negatived.

Various other unsuccessful amendments were offered to the amendments of the Senate; after which the latter were concurred in by the House.

INDIANA TERRITORY.

An engrossed bill, entitled "An act to enable the people of the Indiana Territory to form a constitution and State government, and for the admission of such State into the Union on an equal footing with the original States," was read the third time, and on the question, Shall this bill pass? it passed in the affirmative—yeas 108, nays 3, as follows:

YEAS—Messrs. Adgate, Archer, Baker, Barbour, Bassett, Bateman, Bennett, Betts, Boss, Bradbury, Breckenridge, Brooks, Bryan, Burnside, Cady, Caldwell, Chappell, Clarke of North Carolina, Clayton, Clendennin, Condict, Cooper, Crawford, Creighton, Crocheron, Culpeper, Cuthbert, Darlington, Davenport, Desha, Edwards, Forsyth, Gold, Goodwyn, Griffin, Hahn, Hall, Hammond, Hardin, Hawes, Heister, Henderson, Huger, Hulbert, Hungerford, Irving of New York, Jackson, Johnson of Virginia, Johnson of Kentucky, Kent, Kerr of Virginia, King of North Carolina, Langdon, Love, Lovett, Lumpkin, Lyle, Lyon, Maclay, Marsh, McCoy, McKee, McLean, of Kentucky, Milnor, Nelson of Massachusetts, Nelson of Virginia, Newton, Parris, Pickens, Pickering, Piper, Pitkin, Pleasants, Powell, Reynolds, Roane, Root, Ross, Ruggles, Savage, Schenck, Sharpe, Smith of Maryland, Smith of Virginia, Stanford, Strong, Sturges, Taggart, Taul, Telfair, Throop, Townsend, Tucker, Vose, Wallace, Ward, of Massachusetts, Ward of New Jersey, Wendover, Whiteside, Wilcox, Wilde, Wilkin, Willoughby, William Wilson, Woodward, Wright, Yancey, and Yates.

NAYS—Messrs. Goldsborough, Lewis, and Randolph.

MISSISSIPPI TERRITORY.

An engrossed bill, entitled "An act to enable the Mississippi Territory to form a constitution and State government, and for the admission of such State into the Union on an equal footing with the original States," was read the third time.

A short debate took place, arising from some objections made to the bill by Mr. STANFORD, who was opposed to it because it contained no provision for the future division of the Territory, which he thought entirely too large, considered in relation to the other States, and in time would be too powerful if it continued an undivided State; and he wished the bill might be recommitted for amendment in that particular.

Mr. STANFORD was replied to by Messrs. LATTIMORE and HARDIN, who argued that the Territory, it was believed, had a sufficient population to entitle it to a State constitution; at any rate it would the next session have enough to demand admission into the Union, and it was as well to grant that now, with a good grace, which in so short a time Congress would be unable to refuse;

that if the Territory be now divided, it would be twenty years before the half of it would be able to ask a State government; that from the immense quantities of barrens unfit for cultivation, and the great quantity of Indian lands it contained, it would be a very long time before its population would, if ever, exceed that of any other State; that it was good policy to encourage by every means the population of that section of the country, to be able promptly to repel an enemy where attacks would very probably be made; that it was an older Territory than Indiana, in whose favor a bill had just passed, with scarcely a dissenting voice.

Mr. JOHNSON, of Kentucky, also opposed the recommitment and advocated the passage of the bill, though he was decidedly of opinion that Congress ought to retain the power of altering the boundary of the new State hereafter, if they should deem the alteration necessary; but the House having yesterday decided against such a reservation, he thought it wrong to impede the passage of the bill.

Mr. J. supported his opinions by a variety of arguments; after which the bill passed, by yeas and nays—for the passage 70, against it 53, as follows:

YEAS—Messrs. Adgate, Archer, Barbour, Bassett, Bateman, Betts, Brooks, Bryan, Chappell, Clarke of North Carolina, Clendennin, Condict, Crawford, Creighton, Crocheron, Darlington, Desha, Forsyth, Goodwyn, Hahn, Hall, Hammond, Hardin, Henderson, Hungerford, Ingham, Irving of New York, Jackson, Johnson of Virginia, Johnson of Kentucky, Kerr of Virginia, King of North Carolina, Love, Lumpkin, Lyle, Lyon, Maclay, Mayrant, McCoy, McKee, McLean of Kentucky, Moore, Nelson of Virginia, Newton, Parris, Pickens, Piper, Pleasants, Powell, Reynolds, Root, Ross, Savage, Schenck, Sharpe, Smith of Maryland, Smith of Virginia, Taul, Throop, Wallace, Wendover, Whiteside, Wilde, Wilkin, Willoughby, William Wilson, Woodward, Wright, Yancey, and Yates.

NAYS—Messrs. Alexander, Baer, Baker, Boss, Bradbury, Breckenridge, Brown, Burnside, Chipman, Cilley, Clayton, Cooper, Culpeper, Cuthbert, Davenport, Edwards, Gaston, Gold, Goldsborough, Griffin, Hale, Hawes, Heister, Hopkinson, Hulbert, Jewett, Kent, Langdon, Law, Lewis, Lovett, Marsh, Milnor, Moseley, Nelson of Massachusetts, Pickering, Pitkin, Randolph, Roane, Ruggles, Southard, Stanford, Stearns, Strong, Sturges, Taggart, Telfair, Tucker, Vose, Ward of Massachusetts, Ward of New Jersey, Webster, and Wilcox.

MONDAY, April 1.

Mr. EASTON presented a petition of sundry inhabitants of the Territory of Missouri, praying to be incorporated as a commercial company, for the purposes of trade and intercourse with the Indian tribes.—Referred to Messrs. EASTON, McKEE, THOMAS WILSON, CADY, ATHERTON, CLENDENNIN, and POWELL.

Mr. LOWNDES, from the Committee of Ways and Means, reported a bill for the relief of certain owners of goods entered at Hampden, in the District of Maine; which was read twice, and committed to the Committee of the Whole on the bill for the relief of David Gelston and Peter A. Schenck.

Mr. LOWNDES, from the same committee, reported the bill from the Senate "for the relief of Richard Mitchell," without amendment; and the bill was ordered to be read a third time to-morrow.

The SPEAKER laid before the House a letter from the Treasurer of the United States, transmitting his annual accounts of receipts and payments at the Treasury for the year ending October 1, 1815; which was ordered to lie on the table.

The SPEAKER laid before the House a report from the Secretary of the Navy on the petition of John McCauley, prize agent of the officers and crew of the brig Vixen; which was read and referred to the Committee on Naval Affairs.

The SPEAKER laid before the House a letter from the Secretary of the Treasury, transmitting his report in obedience to a resolution of the House of the 9th ultimo, relative to expenses incurred in prosecutions on behalf of the United States in the States of New Hampshire, Massachusetts, Connecticut, Vermont, and New York; which were ordered to lie on the table.

A message from the Senate informed the House that the Senate have passed a bill "to reward the officers and crew of the United States frigate Constitution," in which they ask the concurrence of this House. The Senate also returned to this House the bill "in addition to an act to regulate the Post Office Establishment," with the amendments of the Senate corrected.

The House then resolved itself into a Committee of the Whole, on the bill to increase the pensions of certain invalid pensioners. No amendment being offered, the Committee rose, reported a bill to the House; and it was then ordered to be engrossed for a third reading.

REPORTS FROM COMMITTEES.

Mr. YANCEY, from the Committee of Claims made a report on the petition of Asher Palmer, which was read; when Mr. Y. reported a bill for the relief of Asher Palmer; which was read twice, and committed to a Committee of the Whole.

Mr. YANCEY also made a report on the petition of the supervisors of Clinton county, in the State of New York, which was read; when Mr. Y. reported a bill for the relief of the supervisors of the county of Clinton, in the State of New York; which was read twice, and committed to the Committee of the Whole last appointed.

The report is as follows:

That, in the month of September, 1814, when the British forces invaded the United States on the frontier of the State of New York, they took possession of a part of the village of Plattsburg, and sought a cover from the American artillery at the fort near the village, from a number of houses belonging to individuals, and the court-house of the county of Clinton. In order to uncover and dislodge the enemy, General Macomb, who at that time commanded the American troops at that place, considered it prudent and proper to fire hot shot into the houses for the purpose of destroying them Among the number thus destroyed was the court-house of Clinton. The petitioners, on behalf of the county, pray that Congress will pay the value of the house.

The facts in the petition having been satisfactorily established, and it appearing to the committee that the property was destroyed for public good, they are of opinion that the petitioners are entitled to relief, and therefore report by bill.

Mr. YANCEY also made a report on the petition of John Crosby and John Crosby, junior, which was read; when Mr. Y. reported a bill for the relief of John Crosby and John Crosby, junior, which was read twice, and committed to the Committee of the Whole.

The report is as follows:

That, in the month of August, 1814, the United States frigate Adams, commanded by Captain Charles Morris, arrived at Hampden, in the county of Hancock and State of Massachusetts, and was moored at the wharf of the petitioners. The Adams remained at the wharf until the 3d day of September following, when a British naval force appeared and attacked her. Captain Morris, after having bravely defended his ship for a considerable time against a much superior force, considered it prudent, under all circumstances, to set fire to the ship and blow her up, to prevent her falling into the possession of the enemy. The fire which was thus applied to the ship communicated itself to the wharf and storehouse of the petitioners, and they were consumed, together with their stock of goods on hand. They pray that Congress would pay them the value of their property destroyed.

The committee are of opinion that the injury which the petitioners have sustained, being immediately consequential of a justifiable and prudent act of an officer of the Government, they are entitled to relief, and therefore report by bill.

Mr. YANCEY also made a report on the petition of Taylor & McNeal, Evans & McNeal, and Henry & John McCleister, which was read; when Mr. Y. reported a bill for the relief of Taylor & McNeal, Evans & McNeal, and Henry & John McCleister; which was read twice and committed to the Committee of the Whole last mentioned.

Mr. MIDDLETON, from the select committee appointed on the 10th of January last on the petition of James H. McCulloch, made a report thereon; which was read, and committed to a Committee of the Whole to-morrow.

The report is as follows:

The said petitioner states, that he entered upon the office of collector of the port of Baltimore early in the year 1808, with a prospect, indeed, of difficulties and labors arising from the peculiar situation of the country at that time, but under an assurance of receiving adequate compensation for his services. That such an expectation was reasonable, may be inferred from the universal practice of this Government, which has ever been to provide fixed salaries where other profits are either inadequate or forbidden. The petitioner was confirmed in this his belief, from the circumstance of the House of Representatives having, in that particular juncture of affairs, under the impression that the

emoluments of the officers of the customs would be lessened by the embargo acts, directed the Secretary of the Treasury to report his opinion of the cases where a temporary increase of salary might be necessary. In obedience to this resolve, the then Secretary addressed a circular to the officers of the customs, under date of April 28, 1808, giving instructions respecting the embargo act, and calling upon the said officers to make returns of their emoluments, in order that he might make his report in conformity to the views of Congress.

That the emoluments of the petitioner, as collector of the port of Baltimore, have not been by any means adequate to the services he performed within the period alluded to, appears from his statement that in 1808 he seemed to receive $72, but actually sunk $428, on account of a salary to a clerk paid by himself; in the year 1809 he received $589; in the year 1810 he received $512; in 1814 he paid $980 for performing the public service, while the support of his family each year amounted to $2,000; the result is, that in these four years he received from the public $673, and expended in the maintenance of a frugal family $8,000, and in the support of a custom-house for the public $980. His account at the Treasury will establish the correctness of what is here stated. The intervening years were more profitable, but below the common receipts of the office and the limit of the law.

The committee, having duly considered the foregoing statement, are of opinion that the compensation allowed by law to James H. McCulloch, collector of the customs at Baltimore, having been taken away by the operation of other laws enacted for the public benefit, he has an undoubted claim upon the public justice to provide an equivalent; and inasmuch as the committee believe that there exist other similar cases of hardship, arising from the non-productive state of the revenue derived from impost during the embargo and non-intercourse laws, with a view to embrace such cases, they recommend the following resolution:

Resolved, by the Senate and House of Representatives, That the President of the United States be authorized to allow an extra compensation, for a limited time, to those officers of the customs whose emoluments were diminished below a reasonable salary during the restrictive system.

GENERAL APPROPRIATION BILL.

The House, on motion of Mr. LOWNDES, resolved itself into a Committee of the Whole, on the bill making appropriations for the support of Government for the year 1816.

In filling up the blank in the bill, left for the appropriation for the payment of the members of Congress, some debate arose as to the manner of drawing this compensation. The act lately passed to alter the mode of compensating the members of Congress, declares that they shall receive an "annual" salary of one thousand five hundred dollars; and in a subsequent clause, provides that the compensation shall be "certified and made in the manner heretofore provided by law;" the custom under the former law was to pay the members from time to time, as the services were rendered.

Mr. L. in obedience to instructions from the Committee of Ways and Means, and in accordance with what he understood to be the construction given to the act by the Attorney General, moved to fill the blank with a sum sufficient to defray the compensation for the year ending on the 4th of March, 1816, and making no provision for the services which would intervene between that period and the end of the next session.

This construction of the act was disputed by Mr. CLAY, the Speaker. He thought that the members, whenever they could exhibit evidence of the rendition of services, had a fair claim for a due proportion of the annual salary. Such had been the practice heretofore; and if the rule laid down by the Attorney General were adopted, a member who happened to come into Congress after the 4th of March, would receive nothing until the next March. Against the inconvenience and hardships of this construction, Mr. C. argued at some length; and for the purpose of making an appropriation out of which to compensate the members for the remainder of this session, and part of the next, moved to fill the blank with a sum adequate to meet that object. Mr. C. added, that as the public interest would be unaffected by this decision, let either construction of the act be adopted, he saw no objection to pursuing the course he proposed, without however allowing any member to draw so much of the salary as would bring him at any time in debt to the Government.

Mr. JOHNSON, of Kentucky, differed both from the Speaker and the Attorney General in this, that the compensation given to members was intended to embrace a whole session, long or short; but as it made no difference to the United States, and that construction had been given, he should acquiesce, and vote for the appropriation, provided an amendment which he had drawn up should be adopted, which did not interfere with the construction given, and was indispensable to do justice to the Government, and to certain members who had not attended the whole session; which amendment was intended to make a deduction from the compensation of members for absence, in the proportion that absence bore to the whole days of the session.

Mr. JACKSON explained the views of the select committee, when they originally reported in favor of changing the mode of compensation; and concurred in the construction given by Mr. CLAY.

Mr. SMITH, of Maryland, also concurred in the construction of the law given to it by the Speaker. According to the other interpretation of it, if the members were called here to an extra session, they would be obliged to bring money in their pockets to defray their expenses, as they would receive no compensation until the end of the year.

Mr. GASTON thought it not of much importance which construction was adopted; but stated the reasons that induced him to believe the construction given by the Attorney General the true one. Mr. G. compared the terms of the several acts on this subject to establish what he believed the proper construction, and to show that Mr. CLAY's could not be sustained.

Mr. WRIGHT thought it entirely unnecessary to dispute about the construction of the late law.

Congress had voted to its members a certain annual compensation, which might be viewed in the light of a contingent fund, and it was perfectly competent for Congress to direct in what way, and in what proportions, that compensation should be drawn.

The Committee then agreed to the amendment proposed by Mr. CLAY, and filled the blank in the bill accordingly.

With the exception of some objections made by Mr. JEWETT to an appropriation for additional clerks for one of the departments, the Committee met with no difficulty in its progress through the bill, until Mr. JACKSON moved to insert a clause appropriating $300,000, out of the fund set apart for that purpose, for carrying on the great western road from Cumberland to Ohio.

This amendment was earnestly opposed by Mr. GASTON, on the ground that it was improper to introduce into an ordinary bill an appropriation for an object which had not been authorized by a previous act. In support of his position Mr. G. cited a recent course pursued by the Committee of Ways and Means, who, although aware of the necessity of protecting an island whereon an important light-house was placed (Gull Island) from the encroachments of the sea, did not think it proper to resort to the slovenly mode of inserting an appropriation for that purpose in the bill now under consideration, but instructed its chairman to move that the Committee of Commerce and Manufactures be previously directed to inquire into the propriety of the expenditure, and to report thereon. Mr. G. said the checks upon the disbursement of the Government were already few enough, and they ought not to be further diminished by this House.

Messrs. JACKSON, CLAY, RANDOLPH, SMITH, WRIGHT, and GOLDSBOROUGH, respectively, advocated the amendment. The three gentlemen first named being particularly zealous in its support. It was argued that the appropriation moved for was extremely interesting to the Western States, and more important to the people of every section of the country than any other item in the bill, if the Union of the States was to be, as all expected it to be, the means of public happiness, prosperity, and safety. That the appropriation was required from a fund already set apart for the work by a solemn compact; that if this House could be called on to appropriate money to carry into effect a convention with a foreign Government, it could surely make an appropriation to execute a contract with the States, a double compact, too, it being between the General Government, and the States of Ohio, Pennsylvania, and Virginia, as they were all parties to it; that the appropriation was, furthermore, sanctioned by former laws directing the work to be prosecuted, and that nothing was wanting to fulfil the law but the present appropriation of money, for which there were several precedents; that the single State of Maryland had undertaken to complete, in five years, a road from Baltimore to the point at which the Cumberland road commenced, and that it would be derogatory to the character

1311   HISTORY OF CONGRESS.   1312

H. or R.   *General Appropriation Bill—The Tariff.*   APRIL, 1816.

ing it to them. He thought it was proper to confine the privilege strictly to the session, or to extend it to the recess also.

Mr. REYNOLDS was also in favor of retaining the privilege. An important reason for it was, the resolution this very day adopted, to make the standing committees permanent during the whole Congress, which would involve them in correspondence on public business.

Mr. JACKSON spoke a short time against the amendment. He thought it important that communication should be kept up during the recess, between the members and their constituents. In this case, said he, we should not be presenting petitions on the last day of the session, if a free channel of communication could be kept open. In every point of view, without going over the elevated, the dignified ground on which this question stood, it ought to be maintained by the House.

Mr. WRIGHT and Mr. GROSVENOR also made some remarks in favor of the privilege; after which the question was decided in favor of concurring with the Senate—yeas 80, nays 51, as follows:

YEAS—Messrs. Adgate, Alexander, Archer, Atherton, Baker, Barbour, Bassett, Bennett, Betts, Bradbury, Brooks, Burnside, Caldwell, Cilley, Comstock, Conner, Crawford, Creighton, Crocheron, Cuthbert, Darlington, Davenport, Desha, Edwards, Forney, Forsyth, Gold, Goldsborough, Griffin, Hahn, Hale, Hall, Hardin, Hawes, Heister, Herbert, Hungerford, Jewett, Johnson of Virginia, Kent, Kerr of Virginia, Langdon, Lumpkin, Lyle, Maclay, McCoy, McLean of Kentucky, Milnor, Nelson of Massachusetts, Nelson of Virginia, Ormsby, Parris, Pickens, Pickering, Piper, Pitkin, Pleasants, Reed, Roane, Root, Ross, Savage, Smith of Va., Southard, Stanford, Stearns, Taul, Telfair, Throop, Townsend, Wallace, Ward of New York, Wendover, Wheaton, Whiteside, Wilcox, Wilde, Willoughby, William Wilson, and Woodward.

NAYS—Messrs. Baer, Boss, Breckenridge, Brown, Calhoun, Champion, Chappell, Clarke of North Carolina, Clendennin, Culpeper, Gaston, Grosvenor, Hammond, Henderson, Hopkinson, Hulbert, Ingham, Jackson, Johnson of Kentucky, King of North Carolina, Law, Lewis, Lovett, Lowndes, Lyon, Marsh, Mason, Mayrant, McKee, Middleton, Moore, Moseley, Newton, Pinkney, Powell, Randolph, Reynolds, Ruggles, Sergeant, Schenck, Sharpe, Sturges, Taggart, Tate, Vose, Webster, Wilkin, Thos. Wilson, Wright, Yancey, and Yates.

The residue of the said amendments were then concurred in by the House.

GENERAL APPROPRIATION BILL.

The House then proceeded to consider the report of the Committee of the Whole, on the bill making appropriations for the support of Government, for the year 1816.

The original bill contained an appropriation of twenty-five per cent. in addition to the salaries heretofore allowed to the clerks of the several departments. This increase of compensation was stricken out by the Committee of the Whole, and, on the question of concurring in the amendment—

Mr. CULPEPER said, he felt some objection to the indiscriminate rejection of the addition first proposed. He adverted to the great depreciation of money, the increased price of necessaries, &c., as a reason for believing that an additional allowance was in some cases necessary. Mr. C. thought that every man who devoted himself to the public service ought to be comfortably supported; he believed a few did already receive a compensation sufficiently high, the salaries of some being $2,000, and he would not, therefore, lay on the twenty-five per cent. indiscriminately; but, he said, there were individuals in the public service who were not decently maintained, and to such he wished an increase. Mr. C. thought a maximum might with reason and propriety be established, which no salary of a clerk should exceed, and by which others might be graduated.

When Mr. C. concluded, the amendment was concurred in by the House, without a dissenting voice.

The House agreed successively to the remaining amendments of the Committee; and then ordered the bill to be engrossed for a third reading.

THE TARIFF.

On motion of Mr. LOWNDES the House proceeded to consider the report of the Committee of the Whole, on the bill to regulate the duties on imports.

The question on agreeing to the amendment of the Committee, to reduce the duty on unmanufactured wool, from 15 to 7½ per cent. ad valorem, being put—

Mr. ROOT opposed the amendment, and made some remarks on the impolicy of leaving the country open to foreign competition, in an article which it was so important to encourage the domestic increase of. He hoped the House would not agree to the amendment reported by the Committee, and demanded the yeas and nays on the question.

The amendment was then agreed to—yeas 73, nays 42, as follows:

YEAS—Messrs. Alexander, Archer, Baer, Bassett, Baylies, Bennett, Boss, Bradbury, Breckenridge, Calhoun, Champion, Cilley, Clayton, Conner, Cooper, Crawford, Creighton, Culpeper, Cuthbert, Davenport, Edwards, Forney, Gaston, Gold, Grosvenor, Hahn, Hale, Hardin, Hopkinson, Hulbert, Hungerford, Ingham, Kent, Law, Lewis, Love, Maclay, Marsh, Mason, McKee, McLean of Kentucky, Middleton, Milnor, Moseley, Nelson of Massachusetts, Newton, Pickering, Pinkney, Piper, Pitkin, Pleasants, Randolph, Reed, Ross, Ruggles, Sergeant, Schenck, Stanford, Stearns, Sturges, Tate, Throop, Vose, Wallace, Ward of New Jersey, Ward of New York, Webster, Wendover, Wheaton, William Wilson, Woodward, Yancey, and Yates.

NAYS—Messrs. Adgate, Atherton, Baker, Barbour, Bateman, Brooks, Brown, Bryan, Burnside, Caldwell, Chappell, Clarke of North Carolina, Comstock, Crocheron, Darlington, Desha, Forsyth, Goldsborough, Griffin, Hall, Hammond, Hawes, Heister, Herbert, Jewett, Johnson, of Virginia, Johnson of Kentucky, Kerr of Virginia, King of North Carolina, Langdon, Lowndes, Lumpkin, Lyle, Lyon, Mayrant, McCoy, Moore, Murfree, Nelson of Virginia, Noyes, Ormsby, Parris, Pickens, Powell, Reynolds, Roane, Root, Savage, Sharpe, Smith of Maryland, Smith of Virginia, Southard, Taul, Taylor of South Carolina, Telfair, Townsend, Whiteside, Wilcox, Wilde, Wilkin, Willoughby, and Wright.

Mr. FORSYTH then moved to strike out the whole of the amendment adopted by the Committee, to graduate the duty on imported cottons, (by laying a duty of thirty per cent., for two years, from the 30th of June, of twenty-five per cent. for two years thereafter, and then of twenty per cent.,) except the last named sum; in other words, to reduce the duty on cottons to twenty per cent. from June next.

This motion, involving the general question of the degree of protection proper to be afforded to domestic manufactures—

Mr. GASTON rose and delivered his opinions in opposition to the policy of burdening the community by an extravagant duty on imports, for the purpose of encouraging domestic manufactures. Mr. G. spoke about an hour.

Mr. CUTHBERT followed on the same side of the question, in a speech of about the same length; when the question was decided in the negative—yeas 65, nays 69, as follows:

YEAS—Messrs. Archer, Baer, Barbour, Bassett, Breckenridge, Bryan, Caldwell, Champion, Cilley, Clarke of North Carolina, Clayton, Culpeper, Cuthbert, Edwards, Forney, Forsyth, Gaston, Goldsborough, Hale, Hall, Hardin, Heister, Henderson, Herbert, Huger, Hungerford, Jewett, Johnson of Virginia, Kerr of Virginia, Lewis, Love, Lovett, Lowndes, Lyon, McCoy, McKee, Middleton, Moore, Moseley, Murfree, Nelson of Massachusetts, Nelson of Virginia, Noyes, Pickens, Pickering, Pleasants, Randolph, Roane, Root, Ross, Smith of Virginia, Stanford, Stearns, Sturges, Tate, Taylor of North Carolina, Telfair, Thomas, Vose, Ward of Massachusetts, Wilcox, Wilde, Woodward, Wright, and Yancey.

NAYS—Messrs. Adgate, Alexander, Atherton, Bateman, Baylies, Bennett, Betts, Birdsall, Boss, Brooks, Calhoun, Chappell, Comstock, Crawford, Creighton, Crocheron, Darlington, Davenport, Desha, Gold, Griffin, Hahn, Hammond, Hawes, Hopkinson, Hulbert, Ingham, Johnson of Ky., Kent, Langdon, Lyle, Maclay, Marsh, Mason, Mayrant, McLean of Kentucky, Milnor, Newton, Ormsby, Parris, Pinkney, Piper, Pitkin, Powell, Reed, Reynolds, Ruggles, Sergeant, Savage, Schenck, Sharpe, Smith of Maryland, Southard, Taggart, Taul, Throop, Townsend, Wallace, Ward of New York, Ward of New Jersey, Wendover, Willoughby, and Thomas Wilson.

Mr. WRIGHT then, after declaring his belief that many members had voted on the question, who, from being interested in its decision, were of right excluded by a decision of the House, submitted the following proposition, which was read:

"That no member, being a proprietor, or having any share in any factory of cotton or cotton yarn, was, by the rules of this House, entitled to vote on the question fixing the duty on the importation of articles of cotton imported into America."

Before the question was put on this resolution, a motion was made to adjourn, and carried.

14th CON. 1st SESS.—42

WEDNESDAY, April 3.

Mr. CREIGHTON, from the Committee on the Public Lands, to whom was referred the bill from the Senate, "to authorize the Legislature of the State of Ohio to sell a certain part of a tract of land reserved for the use of that State," reported the same without amendment; and the bill was committed to the Committee of the Whole, on the bill to authorize the sale of lands forfeited to the United States, in the district of Jeffersonville, at the land office in said district.

Mr. EASTON, from the committee to whom was referred, on the 19th of February last, the petition of the Legislature of the Territory of Missouri, made a report thereon, which was read, when Mr. E. presented a bill for the relief of certain frontier inhabitants of the Territory of Missouri; which was read twice, and committed to a Committee of the Whole.

On motion of Mr. SAVAGE, the Committee on the Judiciary were instructed to inquire into the expediency of annexing the county of Rensselaer, in the State of New York, to the northern district of said State.

On motion of Mr. JOHNSON, of Kentucky, the Committee on Pensions and Revolutionary Claims were instructed to inquire into the expediency of increasing the pension of George Shannon.

Engrossed bills of the following titles, to wit: "An act to increase the pensions of invalids in certain cases; for the relief of invalids of the militia; and for the appointment of pension agents in those States where there is no commissioner of loans," and "An act making appropriations for the support of Government for the year 1816," were read the third time and passed.

A message from the Senate informed the House that the Senate have passed "An act to incorporate the subscribers to the Bank of the United States," with amendments. The Senate have also passed a bill "supplementary to an act, entitled, 'An act to incorporate a company for making certain turnpike roads in the District of Columbia;'" in which amendments and bill they ask the concurrence of this House.

THE TARIFF.

The House then took up the unfinished business of yesterday, being the bill to regulate the duties on imports—Mr. WRIGHT's motion, to exclude from voting all members concerned in manufacturing, being still under consideration.

Mr. SMITH, of Maryland, expressed his regret that his colleague had offered the resolution, and made one or two remarks on its impropriety; after which,

The resolution was withdrawn by the mover, and the question then recurred on Mr. FORSYTH's motion, so to amend the amendment of the committee respecting the duty on imported cottons, as to substitute a duty thereon of twenty per cent. ad valorem from the 30th of June next.

Mr. WRIGHT proposed to modify this amendment, by making the duty twenty-one per cent., which he thought was an ample protection, and with which the manufacturers ought to be satisfied.

Mr. Smith objected to this modification, because it varied in so small a degree from the original motion. He had hoped that some gentleman would propose to return to the twenty-five per cent. reported by the Committtee of Ways and Means, which he would prefer as a permanent protection.

Mr. Hardin moved still further to amend the original motion by making the duty twenty-five per cent. for two years after June, and twenty per cent. thereafter; which Mr. Wright accepted as a modification of his motion.

Mr. Mason then spoke at considerable length on the general question of protection, giving a summary history of the rise of cotton manufactures in this country, and adducing various statements and calculations to prove the necessity of a high duty in order to sustain the existing manufactures.

Mr. Hopkinson remarked, that the arguments submitted by Mr. Mason were so conclusive on his mind of the necessity of a liberal protection, that they had decided him to vote for Mr. Hardin's amendment.

Mr. Pickering argued a short time against an extravagant duty, as unnecessary for a reasonable protection, not believing that the existing manufactures required a duty of twenty-five per cent. for two years; after which, the question on Mr. Hardin's motion was decided in the affirmative—yeas 84, nay 60, as follows:

Yeas—Messrs. Archer, Atherton, Baer, Barbour, Bassett, Bradbury, Breckenridge, Burnside, Champion, Chappell, Cilley, Clarke of North Carolina, Clayton, Culpeper, Cuthbert, Edwards, Forney, Forsyth, Gaston, Goldsborough, Goodwyn, Grosvenor, Hale, Hall, Hanson, Hardin, Hawes, Heister, Henderson, Herbert, Hopkinson, Huger, Hungerford, Jewett, Johnson of Va., Kent, Kerr of Virginia, King of North Carolina, Langdon, Law, Lewis, Love, Lovett, Lowndes, Lumpkin, Lyon, McCoy, McKee, Middleton, Moore, Moseley, Nelson of Mississippi, Nelson of Virginia, Noyes, Pickens, Pickering, Pinkney, Pleasants, Randolph, Reed, Roane, Root, Ross, Ruggles, Sheffey, Smith of Maryland, Smith of Virginia, Stearns, Stuart, Sturges, Taggart, Tate, Taylor of South Carolina, Telfair, Thomas, Vose, Ward of Massachusetts, Webster, Whiteside, Wilcox, Wilde, Woodward, Wright, and Yancey.

Nays—Messrs. Adgate, Alexander, Baker, Bateman, Baylies, Bennett, Betts, Birdsall, Boss, Brooks, Calhoun, Chipman, Clendennin, Comstock, Conner, Crawford, Creighton, Crocheron, Darlington, Davenport, Desha, Glasgow, Gold, Griffin, Hahn, Hulbert, Ingham, Irwin of Pennsylvania, Jackson, Johnson of Kentucky, Lyle, Maclay, Marsh, Mason, Mayrant, McLean, Milnor, Newton, Parris, Piper, Pitkin, Powell, Reynolds, Sergeant, Savage, Schenck, Sharpe, Southard, Strong, Taul, Throop, Townsend, Wallace, Ward of New York, Wendover, Wheaton, Wilkin, Willoughby, William Wilson, and Yates.

Mr. Mason then moved further to amend the amendment by striking out the minimum duty of twenty per cent. and the limitation to the twenty-five per cent., as reported originally by the Committee of Ways and Means.

Mr. Hardin opposed this motion, and wished he could ascertain what gentlemen really wanted. They first voted for thirty per cent. for two years, then for twenty-five, for the same period; and he had no doubt they would next be very willing to accept twenty per cent. Their policy seemed to be to get all they could and keep what they got.

Mr. Hulbert replied to Mr. Hardin, denying any impropriety in the course adopted by the friends of the manufacturers; showing that they had asked no further protection than the Secretary of the Treasury, after long inquiry, made by the order of Congress, and mature preparation, had recommended as a proper and necessary encouragement; that the House have decided against the thirty-three per cent. reported in the tariff of the Secretary, they wished only now to bring back the duty to what was reported by the Committee of Ways and Means.

The motion made by Mr. Mason, and the question of concurring or disagreeing with the Committee of the Whole, being the same, Mr. Mason withdrew his amendment, and the question recurred on agreeing with the Committee of the whole House in their amendment, as amended by Mr. Hardin's motion.

On this question there was much desultory debate; a few only of the gentlemen who participated entering into the general subject.

Mr. Grosvenor spoke in favor of the graduated duty. He argued, that as it had been admitted on all hands that present protection only was necessary to the manufacturers, and as they had acknowledged that twenty-five per cent. was sufficient for that purpose, it was of course too high for a permanent duty, and he was opposed to it.

Mr. Gaston replied to some previous remarks of Mr. Hulbert, and stated a fact, that a majority of the Committee of Ways and Means were at first in favor of twenty per cent. only until the day of the report, when a compromise had taken place with the gentlemen who wish a higher duty, and twenty-five per cent. was reported in the bill.

Mr. Telfair spoke as follows: On the subject of impost I hold it a sound general rule that no other or higher duties should be laid than are both necessary and proper for the purposes of revenue. To attempt more, necessarily increases the inducements to smuggling; and if the encouragement of manufactures be the object, it is, in effect, to plunge on the wide ocean of uncertainty, guided by factitious lights, emanating from the selfishness alone of those who tender them, and which never can be relied upon for the purposes of wise legislation.

I will not deny but that, in the imposition of duties for the purposes of revenue, it is wise so to select your objects that while the original intent is secured, the interest of the manufacturer may be regarded as an incidental consideration. But what is the character of the measure before you? Instead of contemplating the protection and encouragement of manufactures as secondary or collateral, it refers to them as the primary and essential cause of legislation; instead of the ben-

also flowing to them being considered merely as some alleviation of burdens, made necessary by the wants of the Government, their encouragement has, in the whole course of the discussion, been placed in the foreground, and admitted to be the principal object for which so enormous a tax is laid upon the people of this country—a tax, the proceeds of which, so far as it means protection, are never to enter the coffers of the nation, but, by a species of magic, transferred from the hands of the consumer into those of the manufacturer—paid by the people indeed, but not for the purposes of Government.

The support of this bill rests upon two considerations. First, it is urged that the course of measures pursued by Government for some time previous to, as well as during the war, had the tendency of a pledge of support. This suggestion involves a principle of more importance than at the first glance will appear. Is it to be held that, if the Government in the pursuit of some important object, either the establishment of its rights, or the avenging its wrongs, shall pursue a course of measures, the indirect and undesigned tendency of which shall be to foster any particular species of industry, that thence it derives a claim to future encouragement and protection, even at the expense of all others? To what an infinite order of pledges would such a system give rise? Scarcely a single variation can be made in the ordinary policy of the nation but must engender an obligation of this kind. A change from peace to war necessarily injures the immediate interests of commerce and agriculture; a return of peace alike injures those institutions which grow up amid the circumstances of war. Is the nation, after all these changes and effects, to hold itself as bound to compensate the losses of those who may have suffered? I presume this will not be urged. But I may be told that the manufacturing class constitutes so small a portion of the community, that, while public policy requires it, they may be sustained by less injury to the others and less expense to the Government, and therefore they should be upheld. Sir, I deem it unsafe to legislate for particular interests. Did not the interest of the merchant and the planter suffer under those very causes which cherished the manufacturer? While the latter was accumulating wealth, were not the former consuming their capital? And because they now begin to derive a profit, is it wise and just in us to rob them of it by increasing the expenses of articles of consumption, merely to contribute such a bounty to the manufacturer as will enable him to derive something like his accustomed profits? And upon what evidence are you about to award the protection asked for? You are told by the persons interested, that, without some aid from the Government, it would be impossible for them to sustain the shock of foreign importations which threatens to overwhelm them. They exhibit to you no particular statements, but in general call for duties, almost amounting to prohibition, of the articles upon which they are laid. You are not advised of the expenses they have

incurred in founding their establishments; of the price of labor to be employed in supporting them; of the costs of the raw material; of the profit which they are in the habit of enjoying, or which may be necessary for them to outlive the storm. But, in your munificence, you are about to allow, by way of bounty, five per cent. more than is required for revenue upon cottons and woollens, which is as much as the duties during the war, and one hundred per cent. more than those prior to the war. In words you are called upon for protection, but what are the ideas involved in this phrase? Why, that the planter of this country, who consumes the article manufactured, shall be made to pay the difference between the wages of labor in the factory and field, together with the difference of profit which superior skill in the foreign manufacturer gives over the manufacturer of this country. In one word, all articles are made dear to the consumer, whether of foreign or domestic fabrication, merely that the manufacturer may derive a profit upon his capital. Now, let me ask, said Mr. T., is the agriculture of this country in a condition sufficiently thriving to make this sacrifice? Are its profits and improvements such as to enable it to spare the amount required? Is the Government prepared to say that, after an expensive war which has embarrassed its finances, or the people, after the privations incident upon it, to admit, that it is wise to grant such a donation with no better evidence of its necessity, and no better proofs of its efficacy and policy than the testimony adduced? But the agriculturist in Europe—and if we commence the system of protection and favoritism, the agriculturist here—will be continually influenced by the selfish doctrines of this class of men, which have so often succeeded in inducing him to believe that their, and not his, was the public interest. Their policy is, and ever has been, to diminish competition, while they extended the sphere of their own market. Hence, every suggestion flowing from this class of the community, whatever be the individual integrity of character of its members, should be examined with scrupulousness and even suspicion.

The amount of surplus duty has been fairly, and has been truly, estimated at five millions of dollars; for, in estimating the sacrifices made by the people of this country, it is but just to add the amount laid beyond the requisitions of the revenue to the deficit which will arise from its operation as a prohibition to importations—for the latter must be made up by other objects of taxation; and, therefore, so much of the land, as well as other taxes as may be necessary to make up this deficit, may, and ought to be taken into the estimate which attempts to appreciate the bounty which the people have to pay, in order to satisfy the cupidity of a few manufacturers, and to give trial to the theory of a few politicians.

But the second consideration, and that which is most relied on, arises from the policy of other nations, and promises a more permanent security to the independence of this people. Imposing, indeed, is such a ground of argument; and if the independence of this nation either required or could be guarantied by this bill, abhorrent indeed would be all opposition to it; but, believing, as I do, that the liberties of this people, and the independence of this Government, rest on a basis too firmly laid in their very genius and nature to require such protection, for one I will not consent to adopt the measure proposed. After having advanced in prosperity and improvement far beyond the march of any other nation on the globe, in the same period of time, you are now called upon to reject the admonitions of experience, and adopt a part of the very policy which, with reference to the people of Europe, is congenial, because it denotes the absence of all ideas of self-government. You are about to abjure that principle which was peculiarly your own, and the offspring of freedom, of leaving industry free to its own pursuit and regulation, and to assume to yourself the capacity and right of judging and dictating that labor which is wisest and best for the people of this country. The extent of territory, the exuberance of our soil, the genius of our people, the principles of our political institutions, have in their combination decreed, as by a law of nature, that, for years to come, the citizens of America shall obtain their subsistence by agriculture and commerce. And we, in our wisdom, would fain issue a counter order, to withdraw industry from its natural and accustomed channels, and, by our laws, force into a state of prematurity the manufacturing enterprise of this country. But we are told it would be idle, weak, and absurd in us, while all the powers of Europe are devising plans for the encouragement of manufactures, to let them stagnate for want of national aid. To this I answer, that such are the profits and enjoyments flowing from labor in the ordinary pursuits of life with us, that you cannot draw off the citizen and tempt him to a new and less active pursuit, without robbing from the national wealth a considerable portion which is thrown in to make up his profits. Is not, then, the productive labor of the country thereby diminished? Has not a great portion of it been thrown away, unless some great benefit is derived from this new direction of industry? And is the policy of other Governments to be urged as sufficient justification? It must be borne in mind, that the circumstances of our country are totally different from those of Europe; there, a crowded population causes it to be an object of real national importance to discover means of employment for the many hands which would otherwise encumber society. With us, however, the case is widely different. Here, every hand would find ample employment in tilling the earth; and the calls of society are sufficient, without bounty, to give occupation to such as prefer other employments to those of agriculture. And every occupation which requires the aid of bounty, contains within itself a proof that it is not productive of national wealth, though it may be of national glory. I must protest against the habit of resorting to the regulations of other governments, as rules by which to quadrate our own. Because the Governments of the Old World have resorted

to this mode of facilitating the collection of taxes by creating protuberances upon the body politic, are we to be influenced by their examples? Because monopolies have for ages become familiarized to them, are we to disregard the evidence in favor of an unshackled pursuit of our own interest, and in despite of the warning voice of these very nations, which attests the ruinous effects of such a policy upon every principle held sacred by the friends of freedom, are we to give aid to a favorite class of the community by a tax upon the rest? Like the State banks, sir, these manufactures grew up while a state of war gave a feverish heat to our political atmosphere, because the temporary wants of the people and the Government, and the sluggish state of trade, required them. The return of peace has diminished the demand for the paper of the one and the fabrics of the other; they may both be said to have depreciated in their relative value. The depreciation of bank paper, it is to be hoped, will be arrested in its progress, the combination of these moneyed monopolists broken as to all capacity for harm, by the establishment of a bank, governed in part by ourselves, and by other ulterior measures in contemplation. But, when the different manufacturing States may have deemed it wise to follow the example of Great Britain, and incorporate the different manufacturing establishments, grant them exclusive privileges, prop them by by-laws, and regard them as favorites, how, I ask, are you to control the mighty combination to which such a policy would give rise, for they can concert as well as the State banks? Will you, in such event, open the flood-gates, and let in the ocean of foreign goods threatening to overwhelm them? Certainly not; and yet this would be the only corrective left you.

Sir, while these establishments grow as other branches of industry have done, I shall feel for them no hostility; on the contrary, my preference would be given to articles manufactured by them; but their interest once identified with that of the Government, and I do fear them.

It has been remarked, that the arts flourish in the society of each other; not so, however, in their infancy, while both are attempted to be encouraged at the same time, do the manufactures and the navy spring up. For all the protection given to the former is a deduction from the support of the latter.

But my friend from South Carolina (Mr. CALHOUN) reproaches us with a disposition to relapse into a state of ease—a generality of expression not easily definable. Is the doctrine which leaves industry to those pursuits which formed the heroes of New Orleans, braced their muscles and fired their souls, which developed a power to contest for the trident of the ocean, evincive of a disposition to countenance a course of ease? If ease and aversion to too much regulation on the part of Government mean the same thing, I am disposed to see it indulged for the benefit of this nation. If the contrary of ease means the state in which all Europe is concerned, then am I the more anxious to retain to this people that state of ease which defies too much regulation.

HISTORY OF CONGRESS.

The Tariff.

Mr. GOLD.—The situation of the district which I have the honor to represent in this House, the numerous petitions which have been committed to me by my constituents, to be presented to the House for relief, under pressing embarrassments, make it my duty to address the House on this occasion.

It is not, Mr. Speaker, a distinct class of manufacturers who have petitioned Congress for relief, but almost all classes, and principally the farmers, have embarked in the manufacture of woollen and cotton, and now pray at your hands the protection of their interests, put in so great jeopardy.

It is proper, I should state, after the example of some who have preceded me in debate, that I too have a concern in those manufactures.

Let not any honorable gentleman be alarmed by the apprehension that a general system of manufactures is about to be introduced; that this country is now to attempt the manufacture of the almost endless list of goods contained in the importer's invoice; no, sir, that is not the question, but simply, will you uphold the present manufactures of woollen and cotton, against the inundation of foreign fabrics, co-operating with the unexampled price of cotton, to their destruction?

The manufactures in question are, in the language of the President of the United States, who has in his Message so strongly recommended them to the protection of Congress, of primary want or necessity; they are indispensable to the community, and whenever the country shall be involved in war with Great Britain (from whom we receive our supplies, and with whom the relations of peace and trade are greatly exposed to interruption) the same disgraceful scenes of smuggling, fraud, and perjuries, will be reacted This event is inevitable; there is no other resort; if the country does not furnish the goods, they will be procured from abroad. It is no light consideration, that our country supplies the raw material of both wool and cotton, while the whole of the former and about half of the latter, which enters into the manufacture of imported goods, are of foreign growth, and much of the cotton of an inferior quality.

Arkwright's machinery has produced a revolution in the manufacture of cotton; the invention is so excellent, the effect in saving labor so immense, that five or six men are sufficient for the management of a factory of two thousand spindles, spinning one hundred thousand pounds of twist or yarn yearly; the other hands are mere children, whose labor is of little use in any other branch of industry. The nation which does not avail itself of this machinery, and pays another nation for fabrics produced by it, sacrifices, in the situation the United States are now placed, the entire value of the abridged labor saved by the machinery. It is a maxim of political economy, laid down by Sir James Stewart, that "a nation ought to restrain, by duty on importation, that which may be produced at home, and to manufacture as much as possible of the raw material."

The same writer says, that a *new manufacture*

cannot be established without encouragement, without restraint on importation; old establishments in possession of the ground, in possession of capital, (a most important consideration,) in possession of extended machinery, with all the fruits of experience in skill and economy, actuated by a *jealousy* against rival establishments, rising into competition, which never sleeps, never did cease, in any age or country, to exert their undivided force upon these rival establishments, and for a time to make sacrifices in the sale of their goods. The Government itself, not unfrequently lends itself by bounties on exports, to such unhallowed designs upon the manufactures of other nations; where these nations have, as is the case of the United States, been long the great customers and consumers of the fabrics of such Government. Is this mere declamation, or is the charge supported by facts, attested by the most respectable writers on political economy?

"Combinations by those engaged in a particular branch of business in one country to frustrate the first efforts to introduce it into another, by temporary sacrifices, recompensed, perhaps, by extraordinary indemnifications of the Government of such country, are believed to have existed, and are not to be regarded as destitute of probability. The existence or assurance of aid from the Government of the country, in which the business is to be introduced, may be essential to fortify adventurers against the dread of such combinations, to defeat their effects if formed, and to prevent their being formed, by demonstrating that they must in the end prove fruitless."

This is the language of Secretary Hamilton, one of the brightest stars in our political hemisphere, in his report to the House of Representatives, on manufactures, in the year 1791. He further says, in the same report—

"It is well known (and particular examples in the course of this report will be cited) that certain nations grant bounties on the exportation of particular commodities, to enable their own workmen to undersell and supplant all competitors in the country to which those commodities are sent."

The enlightened Secretary stands fully supported in his opinions by the annals of the Board of Trade of Great Britain, and in the correspondence of the Provincial Governors in America with that Board, (as recorded by Anderson on Commerce) for above half a century. The great Earl of Chatham, the least hostile of the British Ministry to America, in his speech in the House of Lords on the address to the King in 1770, (2d vol. of his life, p. 92,) declares his great alarm for the manufacturing interests of Great Britain, at the first efforts at manufactures in America. The same alarm was manifested at the non-importation associations of the American Colonies under the stamp act of 1765, and those associations forced from the Ministry the repeal of that darling measure.

Mr. Brougham, a distinguished British writer, in his "inquiry," published in 1803, states, that "the mere hat manufactory of Massachusetts was an object of jealousy to the British Legislature." He further states, that "statutes were passed in the reign of George the 2d, prohibiting the erection of furnaces, &c. in America."

An honorable member of this House from Connecticut, in his invaluable treatise on "Statistics," recently published, pages 5, 8, and 9, has given a just description of the continuing hostile policy of Great Britain to American manufactures.

Upon what other principle, sir, can it be, that hitherto double duties have added nothing to the price of cottons in the market?

I beg leave, sir, now to refer to the Parliamentary history of the interesting events which led to the entire exclusion of India cotton fabrics from consumption in Great Britain. In this we shall find a picture of our own times, the same causes occurring to oppress manufactures, and a remedy much more severe for the evil is now proposed. I refer, sir, to the 6th vol. page 877 and 941, of Anderson's Commerce, continued by Combe, under the year 1787. From this history the following facts appear:

That Arkwright's machinery, then recently invented, had produced a revolution in the cotton manufacture.

That such are the difficulties attending the establishment of new manufactures, that, had India cottons continued to be imported it would have destroyed the cotton manufacture of Great Britain.

That the East India Company actually reduced the prices of their goods above 20 per cent., for the purpose of underselling and ruining the British manufacture.

This same East India Company is now raising the same weapon against the American manufactures, aided in this by Great Britain, which that Company wielded against the British in 1787, and the effect in prostrating them is as certain. If the British factories could not stand against the East India importation, how is it possible that the American can?

The present ruinous state of our cotton factories, and that many of them are wholly suspended, others partially, must be known to many members of this House, who have no concern in the establishments. He who listens to and acts upon suggestions to the contrary, will hereafter experience deep regret.

I proceed to notice some objections to encouraging manufactures. It is said, that "industry ought to be left free to its own course." Now, sir, this is true or false, according to circumstances. Like most maxims, it is to be received with qualifications and exceptions. If other nations adopt the rule, it is generally true; but if a nation like Great Britain shall swell her negotiations on manufactures and commerce into a system—into volumes—secured by severe penalties, assuming to manufacture for the world, and excluding the manufactures of all the world; if this great policy is pursued with a steady eye from century to century, by which a wealth and power is acquired that no nation of so small territory ever attained, does the maxim apply?

So severe was the regulation in Great Britain, that cloth of foreign wool was by statute, in the reign of Henry II., required to be burned. All

attempts to transfer her artisans or the instruments of manufacture to other nations are severely punished. At times a bounty is given on the export of goods, as well as on the import of the raw material. As to India cotton fabrics, the admission for consumption is prohibited in France, Holland, and other European Governments, as well as by Great Britain.

Agriculture is certainly the great and favorite theatre of industry in the United States, and, so long as our surplus products can find a good foreign market, it should be the first object. But, how is this fact? With the exception of a period of war, no such market is found, and the grain of our country raised beyond consumption must rot in the granary. Lord Sheffield, in his *American Commerce*, (page 20,) states that there never was a good market for American flour and wheat for more than three or four years. Though Europe is not recovered from the shock of war, yet Great Britain is now giving a bounty on the export of grain. .Where can the United States now look for a market for her grain equal to that at home?

No friend of his country can look at the enormous importation of goods into the United States, the past year, without concern. The British accounts give thirty millions sterling (above one hundred and thirty millions of dollars) as the amount of her export of goods to the United States, while our whole export to Great Britain is twenty-one millions only. Is it possible to see such a course of trade in any other light than as most ruinous to the country? "If the balance of trade be against a nation, it is her interest to put a stop to it," is the language of Sir James Stewart. To ascertain the exact balance of trade is always difficult, but it is manifest that the United States cannot continue this present course of trade with Great Britain half a dozen years without ruinous consequences. The trade of the United States with Great Britain has always been, in the opinion of both countries, as against the United States; but the balance against the United States was reimbursed by the favorable trade with the West Indies and other ports, which are now in a great degree closed on us. The British Government appears at length to have adopted a new course of policy, strongly recommended by Mr. Anderson, the commercial advocate of her American provinces, who published his book in 1814. By this policy the United States are to be excluded from the commerce of the British West Indies, and resort is to be had to the Canadas and New Brunswick for supplies for the West Indies. Hence, very heavy duties are laid on the admission of cargoes in American ships, and our commerce is to be hedged in on every side.

The importation of cotton goods into the United States from British possessions has been much greater than is generally supposed. In each of the years 1806 and 1807, it was, from England, nineteen millions of dollars; from Scotland and Calcutta, about five millions. During the last year the importation must have been nearly double this amount.

It is further objected, that our manufacturers will extort extravagant prices, and the prices during the last year are referred to in support of the objection. Is this charge against manufacturers just? Does not every member of this Committee know that the charge applies equally against all classes during the late war? Did not the merchant who had cloths on hand profit equally by the times? Did he not impose 100 per cent. profit on his peace importation? Was not the settled order of things unhinged by the war, and did not all classes exact the most extravagant prices? If the manufacture of cottons were a mystery, confined to a few, there might be foundation for the objection; but, the fact is, the manufacture is simple—machine makers greatly multiplied—and the manufacture is now actually spread over more than half of the United States. It began in the East, has spread to the West, and has now actually passed the mountains. Instead of concert to raise prices, competition and the spirit of underselling prevail to such an extent, that sales are often made without a profit.

Justice to different portions of the Union, and the harmony of the whole, require the encouragement of manufactures.

While the South has, from the export of her cotton and tobacco alone, received about thirty millions the last year, the Northern and Middle States, having no such great staples, must of necessity turn their attention to manufacturing, or become greatly impoverished, to the injury of the whole. The relinquishment of the port duties by the Northern and Middle States, to the amount of nearly three-fourths of the customs, by the adoption of the Constitution, creates an equitable claim to such an adjustment of the duties as shall favor and protect the interests of those States.

The amount of duties now proposed on cottons and woollens will be found, on examination, to be less than the average of the specific duties. The reason of the former low duties on woollens and cottons will be found in the consideration that at that time the manufacture had not been in any degree established in the United States. Had the manufacture been established to the extent it is now, instead of the lowest, a much higher rate of duties would have been imposed.

Mr. INGHAM spoke in reply to the statements and arguments offered by Mr. GASTON yesterday.

Mr. MASON again advocated a high duty, and moved to strike out the limitation of two years to the twenty-five per cent. and insert four years. This motion was negatived—ayes 67, noes 72.

Mr. SMITH, of Maryland, then proposed to make the limit of the twenty-five per cent. duty three years, instead of two.

This motion was carried, ayes 79, noes 71—and then the amendment of the Committee of the Whole, as amended, (twenty-five per cent. for three years, and twenty per cent. thereafter,) was agreed to by a large majority.

The House then proceeded with the remaining amendments of the Committee of the Whole.

On the question of agreeing with the committee on reducing the duty on imported iron from seventy-five to 45 cents per one hundred weight, Mr. BURNSIDE demanded the yeas and nays, and the amendment was concurred in—for the amendment 89, against it 51, as follows:

YEAS—Messrs. Alexander, Archer, Atherton, Barbour, Baylies, Boss, Bradbury, Breckenridge, Bryan, Caldwell, Champion, Chappell, Chipman, Cilley, Clarke of North Carolina, Clayton, Cooper, Crawford, Creighton, Culpeper, Cuthbert, Davenport Edwards, Forney, Forsyth, Gaston, Goldsborough, Goodwyn, Grosvenor, Hale, Hall, Hanson, Herbert, Huger, Hulbert, Hungerford, Jewett, Johnson of Virginia, Kent, Kerr of Virginia, King of North Carolina, Langdon, Law, Lewis, Love, Lovett, Lowndes, Lumpkin, Lyon, Marsh, McCoy, McKee, Middleton, Moore, Moseley, Murfree, Nelson of Massachusetts, Nelson of Virginia, Newton, Noyes, Pickens, Pickering, Pitkin, Pleasants, Randolph, Reed, Roane, Ross, Ruggles, Savage, Sheffey, Smith of Maryland, Smith of Virginia, Stearns, Strong, Stuart, Sturges, Taylor of South Carolina, Telfair, Thomas, Throop, Vose, Ward of Massachusetts, Webster, Wheaton, Wilcox, Woodward, Wright, and Yancey—89.

NAYS—Messrs. Adgate, Baer, Baker, Bassett, Bateman, Bennett, Birdsall, Brooks, Burnside, Calhoun, Clendennin, Comstock, Crocheron, Darlington, Desha, Glasgow, Gold, Griffin, Hahn, Hammond, Hardin, Hawes, Hopkinson, Ingham, Jackson, Johnson of Kentucky, Lyle, Maclay, Mason, Mayrant, McLean of Kentucky, Milnor, Ormsby, Parris, Piper, Sergeant, Schenck, Sharpe, Southard, Taggart, Townsend, Wallace, Ward of New York, Ward of New Jersey, Wendover, Whiteside, Wilkin, Willoughby, Thos. Wilson, William Wilson, and Yates—51.

In the progress of the House through the other amendments of the Committee, Mr. HOPKINSON made an unsuccessful motion to raise the duty on shot to three cents per pound. The duty originally was one cent, and raised by the Committee to two cents.

The House disagreed to the amendment respecting lead, dry or ground in oil, &c., and restored the duty to three cents per pound.

Mr. STEARNS moved that the amendment of the Committee which reduced the duty on brown sugar to three and a half cents per pound be amended, by further reducing the duty to two cents per pound. This motion was decided, by yeas and nays, in the affirmative—for the amendment 86, against it 56, as follows:

YEAS—Messrs. Baer, Bateman, Baylies, Bennett, Birdsall, Boss, Bradbury, Brooks, Burnside, Champion, Chappell, Cilley, Clarke of N. Carolina, Clayton, Clendennin, Comstock, Cooper, Crawford, Crocheron, Culpeper, Darlington, Davenport, Edwards, Forney, Gaston, Glasgow, Goldsborough, Goodwyn, Grosvenor, Hahn, Hale, Heister, Herbert, Hopkinson, Huger, Hungerford, Jewett, Kent, Kerr of Virginia, King of North Carolina, Langdon, Law, Lewis, Love, Lovett, Maclay, Marsh, McKee, Milnor, Moseley, Nelson of Massachusetts, Nelson of Virginia, Noyes, Parris, Pickering, Piper, Pitkin, Pleasants, Randolph, Reed, Roane, Ross, Ruggles, Sergeant, Savage, Sheffey, Smith of Virginia, Southard, Stearns, Sturges, Taggart, Townsend, Vose, Wallace, Ward of Massachusetts, Ward of New York, Webster, Wendover, Whiteside, Wilcox, Wilkin, Willoughby, William Wilson, Woodward, Wright, and Yancey—86.

NAYS—Messrs. Adgate, Alexander, Archer, Atherton, Baker, Barbour, Bassett, Betts, Caldwell, Calhoun, Chipman, Conner, Creighton, Cuthbert, Desha, Forsyth, Gold, Griffin, Hall, Hammond, Hardin, Hawes, Henderson, Hulbert, Ingham, Jackson, Johnson of Virg'a, Johnson of Kentucky, Lowndes, Lumpkin, Lyle, Lyon, Mason, Mayrant, McCoy, McLean of Kentucky, Middleton, Moore, Newton, Ormsby, Pickens, Pinkney, Powell, Reynolds, Root, Schenck, Sharpe, Smith of Maryland, Strong, Taul, Taylor of South Carolina, Telfair, Thomas, Wilde, Thomas Wilson, and Yates—56.

And the amendment of the Committee, as amended, was agreed to without a division.

The duty on lump sugar, on motion of Mr. SMITH of Maryland, was then reduced to ten cents per pound, instead of twelve, as reported by the Committee of the Whole.

The House disagreed to the amendment of the Committee in the duty on wine, and restored it to one dollar per gallon on London particular Madeira, and eighty cents per gallon on all other Madeira.

A motion was made by Mr. PICKERING, so to amend the proviso adopted by the Committee respecting India cottons, as to admit all importations from India, within one year after the 30th June next, on their paying 25 per cent. on the cost of the goods in India, with the addition of the usual 20 per cent.; in other words, to reduce the amount to the old double duty.

Mr. P. advocated his motion at some length, and was supported with zeal by Mr. WARD, of Massachusetts, who argued that it would be unjust to ruin one class of citizens to benefit another, which would be the effect, if those merchants who had sent out orders to India were subjected to the heavy duty reported by the Committee.

Before the question on this amendment was taken, a motion was made and carried to adjourn.

THURSDAY, April 4.

Mr. NEWTON, from the Committee of Commerce and Manufactures, reported a bill declaring the assent of Congress to acts of the State of South Carolina, authorizing the City Council of Charleston to impose and collect a duty on the tonnage of vessels from foreign ports; which was read twice, and committed to a Committee of the Whole on the report of the Committee of Ways and Means upon the subject of revenue.

The bill from the Senate, "supplementary to an act, entitled 'An act to incorporate a company for making certain turnpike roads within the District of Columbia,'" was read twice, and committed to the Committee for the District of Columbia.

NATIONAL BANK.

The House took up for consideration the amendments of the Senate to the bill to incorporate the subscribers to the Bank of the United States. After the amendments had been read—

Mr. CALHOUN observed, that he had examined the amendments; that they were not important; and hoped the question would be put on them generally.

Mr. RANDOLPH objected to so sudden a decision on the amendments; at so early an hour, too, when the House was thin, and before they had been printed. He moved that the consideration of the amendments be postponed until to-morrow.

This motion, after some further conversation between Messrs. CALHOUN and RANDOLPH, was agreed to—ayes 60, noes 55.

THE TARIFF.

The House resumed the consideration of the report of the Committee of the Whole, on the bill to regulate the duties on imports—Mr. PICKERING's motion to reduce the proposed duty on India cottons, to the rate of the present double duties, for one year from June next, being still under consideration.

Mr. PICKERING modified his motion by substituting the 1st of March for the 30th of June, 1817, as the period within which vessels arriving, and which sailed from the United States before the 1st of February last, are to be allowed the benefit of the amendment.

Mr. P. added some remarks to those he offered yesterday in support of his motion, and in explanation of the difference of opinion on the subject between gentlemen from the Eastern States.

Mr. MASON spoke a short time in opposition to the amendment.

Mr. SMITH, of Maryland, read a letter on the subject from certain merchants in New York, and offered some commercial explanations, without pointedly opposing, though not in favor of the amendment.

Mr. RANDOLPH made some general remarks on the trade affected by the proposed amendment, and on the inconsistency of the policy formerly and now pursued on the subject of commerce. He declared his unwillingness to sacrifice the *bona fide* American merchants to what he called the mushroom interest which had sprung into favor; and argued, at some length, and with some invective, against the object of the bill, which he characterized as a scheme of public robbery; and concluded his remarks by moving the indefinite postponement of the whole subject.

After some conversation on the subject, Mr. RANDOLPH withdrew his motion, with the declaration, that it had been made upon mature reflection, and that he should offer it at another stage of the business.

Mr. WEBSTER advocated Mr. PICKERING's amendment, as an act of strict justice to those who had embarked in the India trade before the policy of the Government on the subject of manufactures had disclosed itself, and before they had any reason to expect so great and sudden a change in that policy, and argued to show that its adoption would not injure the manufacturing interest, as the goods now ordered would, in any event, arrive in the country, and, being selected particularly for this market, must be consumed here, no matter at what loss to the importer.

Mr. TELFAIR opposed the amendment; protesting against taxing the community one day to foster the interest of the manufacturers, and on the next to secure to the mercantile class a high profit, and against legislating for particular cases instead of on a general and national scale.

Mr. WRIGHT argued a short time on the same side.

Mr. INGHAM, though very friendly to the manufacturers, thought the amendment fair and reasonable, and such a one as ought to be adopted.

Mr. HULBERT, also, though very friendly to the manufacturers, concurred in opinion with Mr. INGHAM, and thought the amendment ought to prevail.

Mr. PITKIN supported the amendment on the same grounds.

Mr. PICKERING replied to the argument of Mr. TELFAIR, and argued further in support of his amendment.

Mr. HOPKINSON supported the amendment at some length, on the ground of justice to the merchants concerned, declaring that it was giving them no more than, under similar circumstances, would be granted to them by an enemy; which point he supported by various arguments and illustrations.

The question on the amendment was then decided in the affirmative by a large majority; the word "nineteen" being substituted therein in lieu of "twenty-five," on motion of Mr. CHAMPION, and the amendment was adopted in the following words:

"*Provided*, That cotton piece-goods of India, imported in ships or vessels of the United States, which shall have sailed from the United States before the first day of February last, and shall arrive therein between the 30th of June, 1816, and the first of March, 1817, (the original cost of which cotton piece-goods, at the place whence imported, shall have been less than twenty-five cents per square yard) shall be admitted to entry, subject only to a duty of 33½ per cent. on the cost of the said cotton piece-goods in India, and on the usual addition of twenty per cent. on that cost."

The remaining amendments reported to the bill by the Committee of the Whole having been successively concurred in—

Mr. RANDOLPH moved to strike out so much of the proviso of the second section as fixes the minimum price of cotton goods (except nankeens directly from China) at twenty-five cents per square yard.

Mr. R. then entered into a pretty wide discussion of his motion, avowing his willingness to encourage, as far as was proper, those manufactures of cloths conducted in the families of our citizens, and argued against the propriety of promoting the manufacturing establishments to the extent, and in the manner proposed by the bill, and against laying up eight thousand tons of shipping now employed in the East India trade, and levying an immense tax on one portion of the community to put money into the pockets of another.

Mr. CALHOUN.—The debate heretofore on this subject, has been on the degree of protection which ought to be afforded to our cotton and woollen manufactures; all professing to be friendly to

those infant establishments, and to be willing to extend to them adequate encouragement. The present motion assumes a new aspect. It is introduced professedly on the ground that manufactures ought not to receive any encouragement, and will, in its operation, leave our cotton establishments exposed to the competition of the cotton goods of the East Indies, which, it is acknowledged on all sides, they are not capable of meeting with success, without the proviso proposed to be stricken out by the motion now under discussion. Until the debate assumed this new form, he had determined to be silent; participating, as he largely did, in that general anxiety which is felt, after so long and laborious a session, to return to the bosom of our families. But on a subject of such vital importance, touching, as it does, the security and permanent prosperity of our country, he hoped that the House would indulge him in a few observations. He regretted much his want of preparation—he meant not a verbal preparation, for he had ever despised such, but that due and mature meditation and arrangement of thought, which the House is entitled to on the part of those who occupy any portion of their time. But whatever his arguments might want on that account in weight, he hoped might be made up in the disinterestedness of his situation. He was no manufacturer; he was not from that portion of our country supposed to be peculiarly interested. Coming, as he did, from the South, having, in common with his immediate constituents, no interest but in the cultivation of the soil, in selling its products high, and buying cheap the wants and conveniencies of life, no motive could be attributed to him but such as were disinterested.

He had asserted, that the subject before them was connected with the security of the country. It would, doubtless, by some be considered a rash assertion, but he conceived it to be susceptible of the clearest proof, and he hoped, with due attention, to establish it to the satisfaction of the House.

The security of a country mainly depends on its spirit and its means; and the latter principally on its moneyed resources. Modified as the industry of this country now is, combined with our peculiar situation, and want of a naval ascendency, whenever we have the misfortune to be involved in a war with a nation dominant on the ocean, and it is almost only with such we can at present be, the moneyed resources of the country, to a great extent, must fail. He took it for granted, that it was the duty of this body to adopt those measures of prudent foresight which the event of war made necessary. We cannot, he presumed, be indifferent to dangers from abroad, unless, indeed, the House is prepared to indulge in the phantom of eternal peace, which seemed to possess the dream of some of its members. Could such a state exist, no foresight or fortitude would be necessary to conduct the affairs of the Republic; but as it is the mere illusion of the imagination—as every people, who ever has or ever will exist, are subjected to the vicissitudes of peace and war, it must ever be considered as the plain dictate of wisdom, in peace to prepare for war. What, then, let us consider, constitute the resources of this country, and what are the effects of war on them? Commerce and agriculture, till lately, almost the only, still constitute the principal sources of our wealth. So long as these remain uninterrupted, the country prospers; but war, as we are now circumstanced, is equally destructive to both. They both depend on foreign markets, and our country is placed, as it regards them, in a situation strictly insular; a wide ocean rolls between. Our commerce neither is or can be protected by the present means of the country. What, then, are the effects of a war with a maritime Power—with England? Our commerce annihilated, spreading individual misery, and producing national poverty; our agriculture cut off from its accustomed markets, the surplus product of the farmer perishes on his hands; and he ceases to produce, because he cannot sell. His resources are dried up, while his expenses are greatly increased; as all manufactured articles, the necessaries as well as the conveniencies of life, rise to an extravagant price. The recent war fell with peculiar pressure on the growers of cotton and tobacco, and other great staples of the country; and the same state of things will recur in the event of another, unless prevented by the foresight of this body. If the mere statement of facts did not carry conviction to any mind, as he conceived it is calculated to do, additional arguments might be drawn from the general nature of wealth. Neither agriculture, manufactures, nor commerce, taken separately, is the cause of wealth; it flows from the three combined, and cannot exist without each. The wealth of any single nation, or any individual, it is true, may not immediately depend on the three, but such wealth always presupposes their existence. He viewed the words in the most enlarged sense. Without commerce, industry would have no stimulus; without manufactures, it would be without the means of production; and without agriculture, neither of the others can subsist. When separated entirely and permanently, they perish. War in this country produces, to a great extent, that effect; and hence the great embarrassments which follow in its train. The failure of the wealth and resources of the nation necessarily involved the ruin of its finances and its currency. It is admitted, by the most strenuous advocates on the other side, that no country ought to be dependent on another for its means of defence; that, at least, our musket and bayonet, our cannon and ball, ought to be of domestic manufacture. But what, he asked, is more necessary to the defence of a country than its currency and finance? Circumstanced as our country is, can these stand the shock of war? Behold the effect of the late war on them! When our manufactures are grown to a certain perfection, as they soon will under the fostering care of Government, we will no longer experience these evils. The farmer will find a ready market for his surplus produce; and, what is almost of equal consequence, a certain and cheap supply of all his wants. His prosperity

will diffuse itself to every class in the community; and instead of that languor of industry, and individual distress now incident to a state of war, and suspended commerce, the wealth and vigor of the community will not be materially impaired. The arm of Government will be nerved, and taxes in the hour of danger, when essential to the independence of the nation, may be greatly increased; loans, so uncertain and hazardous, may be less relied on; thus situated, the storm may beat without, but within all will be quiet and safe. To give perfection to this state of things, it will be necessary to add, as soon as possible, a system of internal improvements, and at least such an extension of our navy as will prevent the cutting off our coasting trade. The advantage of each is so striking, as not to require illustration, especially after the experience of the recent war. It is thus the resources of this Government and people would be placed beyond the power of a foreign war materially to impair. But it may be said, that the derangement then experienced resulted, not from the cause assigned, but from the errors or the weakness of the Government. He admitted that many financial blunders were committed, for the subject was new to us; that the taxes were not laid sufficiently early, or to as great an extent as they ought to have been; and that the loans were in some instances injudiciously made; but he ventured to affirm, that had the greatest foresight and fortitude been exerted, the embarrassment would have been still very great; and that even under the best management, the total derangement which was actually felt would not have been postponed eighteen months, had the war so long continued. How could it be otherwise? A war, such as this country was then involved in, in a great measure dries up the resources of individuals, as he had already proved; and the resources of the Government are no more than the aggregate of the surplus incomes of individuals, called into action by a system of taxation. It is certainly a great political evil, incident to the character of the industry of this country, that, however prosperous our situation when at peace, with uninterrupted commerce, and nothing then could exceed it, the moment that we were involved in war the whole is reversed. When resources are most needed; when indispensable to maintain the honor, yes, the very existence of the nation, then they desert us. Our currency is also sure to experience the shock, and becomes so deranged, as to prevent us from calling out fairly whatever of means is left to the country. The result of a war in the present state of our naval power, is the blockade of our seacoast, and consequent destruction of our trade. The wants and habits of the country, founded on the use of foreign articles, must be gratified; importation to a certain extent continues, through the policy of the enemy, or unlawful traffic; the exportation of our bulky articles is prevented, too; the specie of the country is drawn to pay the balance perpetually accumulating against us; and the final result is a total derangement of our currency.

To this distressing state of things there were two remedies, and only two; one in our power immediately, the other requiring much time and exertion; but both constituting, in his opinion, the essential policy of this country; he meant the Navy, and domestic manufactures. By the former, we could open the way to our markets; by the latter, we bring them from beyond the ocean, and naturalize them. Had we the means of attaining an immediate naval ascendency, he acknowledged that the policy recommended by this bill would be very questionable; but as this is not the fact—as it is a period remote, with any exertion, and will be probably more so, from that relaxation of exertion, so natural in peace, when necessity is not felt, it became the duty of this House to resort, to a considerable extent, at least as far as is proposed, to the only remaining remedy. But to this it has been objected, that the country is not prepared, and that the result of our premature exertion would be to bring distress on it, without effecting the intended object. Were it so, however urgent the reasons in its favor, we ought to desist, as it is folly to oppose the laws of necessity. But he could not for a moment yield to the assertion; on the contrary, he firmly believed that the country is prepared, even to maturity, for the introduction of manufactures. We have abundance of resources, and things naturally tend at this moment in that direction. A prosperous commerce has poured an immense amount of commercial capital into this country. This capital has, until lately, found occupation in commerce; but that state of the world which transferred it to this country, and gave it active employment, has passed away, never to return. Where shall we now find full employment for our prodigious amount of tonnage; where markets for the numerous and abundant products of our country? This great body of active capital, which for the moment has found sufficient employment in supplying our markets, exhausted by the war, and measures preceding it, must find a new direction; it will not be idle. What channel can it take but that of manufactures? This, if things continue as they are, will be its direction. It will introduce a new era in our affairs, in many respects highly advantageous, and ought to be countenanced by the Government. Besides, we have already surmounted the greatest difficulty that has ever been found in undertakings of this kind. The cotton and woollen manufactures are not to be introduced—they are already introduced to a great extent; freeing us entirely from the hazards, and, in a great measure, the sacrifices experienced in giving the capital of the country a new direction. The restrictive measures and the war, though not intended for that purpose, have, by the necessary operation of things, turned a large amount of capital to this new branch of industry. He had often heard it said, both in and out of Congress, that this effect alone would indemnify the country for all of its losses. So high was this tone of feeling, when the want of these establishments were practically felt, that he remem-

bered, during the war, when some question was agitated respecting the introduction of foreign goods, that many then opposed it on the ground of injuring our manufactures. He then said that war alone furnished sufficient stimulus, and perhaps too much, as it would make their growth unnaturally rapid; but, that on the return of peace, it would then be time to show our affection for them. He at that time did not expect an apathy and aversion to the extent which is now seen. But it will no doubt be said, if they are so far established, and if the situation of the country is so favorable to their growth, where is the necessity of affording them protection? It is to put them beyond the reach of contingency. Besides, capital is not yet, and cannot, for some time, be adjusted to the new state of things. There is, in fact, from the operation of temporary causes, a great pressure on these establishments. They had extended so rapidly during the late war, that many, he feared, were without the requisite surplus capital or skill to meet the present crisis. Should such prove to be the fact, it would give a back set, and might, to a great extent, endanger their ultimate success. Should the present owners be ruined, and the workmen dispersed and turn to other pursuits, the country would sustain a great loss. Such would, no doubt, be the fact to a considerable extent, if not protected. Besides, circumstances, if we act with wisdom, are favorable to attract to our country much skill and industry. The country in Europe having the most skilful workmen is beaten up. It is to us, if wisely used, more valuable than the repeal of the Edict of Nantz was to England. She had the prudence to profit by it; let us not discover less political sagacity. Afford to ingenuity and industry immediate and ample protection, and they will not fail to give a preference to this free and happy country.

It has been objected to this bill, that it will injure our marine, and consequently impair our naval strength. How far it is fairly liable to this charge, he was not prepared to say. He hoped and believed it would not, at least to any alarming extent, have that effect immediately; and he firmly believed that its lasting operation would be highly beneficial to our commerce. The trade to the East Indies would certainly be much affected; but it was stated in debate that the whole of that trade employed but six hundred sailors. But whatever might be the loss in this, or other branches of our foreign commerce, he trusted it would be amply compensated in our coasting trade—a branch of navigation wholly in our own hands. It has at all times employed a great amount of tonnage, something more, he believed, than one-third of the whole; nor is it liable to the imputation thrown out by a member from North Carolina, (Mr. GASTON,) that it produced inferior sailors. It required long and dangerous voyages; and, if his information was correct, no branch of trade made better or more skilful seamen. The fact that it is wholly in our own hands is a very important one, while every branch of our foreign trade must suffer from competition with other nations. Other objections, of a political character, were made to the encouragement of manufactures. It is said they destroy the moral and physical power of the people. This might formerly have been true to a considerable extent, before the perfection of machinery, and when the success of the manufactures depended on the minute subdivision of labor. At that time it required a large portion of the population of a country to be engaged in them; and every minute subdivision of labor is undoubtedly unfavorable to the intellect; but the great perfection of machinery has in a considerable degree obviated these objections. In fact it has been stated that the manufacturing districts in England furnish the greatest number of recruits to her army, and that, as soldiers, they are not materially inferior to the rest of her population. It has been further asserted that manufactures are the fruitful cause of pauperism, and England has been referred to as furnishing conclusive evidence of its truth. For his part, he could perceive no such tendency in them, but the exact contrary, as they furnished new stimulus and means of subsistence to the laboring classes of the community. We ought not to look to the cotton and woollen establishments of Great Britain for the prodigious numbers of poor with which her population was disgraced. Causes much more efficient exist. Her poor laws, and statutes regulating the price of labor, with heavy taxes, were the real causes. But if it must be so; if the mere fact that England manufactured more than any other country, explained the cause of her having more beggars, it is just as reasonable to refer her courage, spirit, and all her masculine virtues, in which she excels all other nations, with a single exception—he meant our own—in which we might without vanity challenge a pre-eminence. Another objection had been made, which he must acknowledge was better founded, that capital employed in manufacturing produced a greater dependence on the part of the employed, than in commerce, navigation, or agriculture. It is certainly an evil, and to be regretted; but he did not think it a decisive objection to the system, especially when it had incidental political advantages which, in his opinion, more than counterpoised it. It produced an interest strictly American, as much so as agriculture; in which it had the decided advantage of commerce or navigation. The country will from this derive much advantage. Again, it is calculated to bind together more closely our widely-spread Republic. It will greatly increase our mutual dependence and intercourse; and will, as a necessary consequence, excite an increased attention to internal improvement—a subject every way so intimately connected with the ultimate attainment of national strength, and the perfection of our political institutions. He regarded the fact that it would make the parts adhere more closely; that it would form a new and most powerful cement, far outweighing any political objections that might be urged against the system. In his opinion the liberty and the union of the country were inseparably united. That as the destruction of the latter would most certainly involve the former, so its maintenance will with equal certainty preserve it. He did not speak lightly. He had often and long revolved it in his mind, and he had critically examined into the causes that destroyed the liberty of other States. There are none that apply to us, or apply with a force to alarm. The basis of our Republic is too broad, and its structure too strong to be shaken by them. Its extension and organization will be found to afford effectual security against their operation; but let it be deeply impressed on the heart of this House and country, that while they guarded against the old, they exposed us to a new and terrible danger—disunion. This single word comprehended almost the sum of our political dangers; and against it we ought to be perpetually guarded.

Mr. Cuthbert answered briefly some of Mr. Calhoun's arguments.

Mr. Randolph entered into a more particular reply to Mr. Calhoun, and further arguments in support of his opinions.

Mr. Gaston also spoke some time in reply to Mr. Calhoun, and in support of the opinions and statements he advanced on the subject on a former occasion.

Mr. Newton, in a speech of about two hours, advocated the bill and the protection therein proposed to our manufactures, entering into a full discussion of the general question of promoting domestic fabrics.

Mr. Hale moved to modify the motion by reducing the minimum price specifically to fifteen cents per square yard.

This motion was decided in the negative—ayes 66, noes 72; and the question recurred on Mr. Randolph's motion to strike out the minimum price altogether.

Mr. Wilde rose, about 4 o'clock, and submitted his views on the subject, in opposition to the bill. He had proceeded about an hour, when Mr. Randolph withdrew his amendment, believing, from the decision on Mr. Hale's motion, that the House would not go still further and agree to his amendment.

Mr. Wilde then, for the purpose of accommodating the bill to his views, and to enable him to vote for it, moved an amendment, substantially, to substitute an *ad valorem* duty of twenty per cent. on woollen and cotton goods, and then resumed the thread of his speech in opposition to higher duties. Mr. W. concluded his remarks about half past 5 o'clock.

Mr. Mason made a few remarks in reply, when

The question on Mr. Wilde's proposition was decided in the negative—yeas 51, nays 76, as follows:

Yeas—Messrs. Archer, Barbour, Bassett, Bradbury, Brown, Bryan, Champion, Clarke of North Carolina, Culpeper, Cuthbert, Edwards, Forsyth, Gaston, Goldsborough, Goodwyn, Hale, Hardin, Heister, Herbert, Huger, Hungerford, Johnson of Virginia, Kerr of Virginia, King of North Carolina, Love, Lovett, Lowndes, Lumpkin, Lyon, Middleton, Moore, Moseley, Murfree, Nelson of Virginia, Noyes, Pickens, Pickering, Pleasants, Randolph, Roane, Root, Ross, Smith of Virginia, Tate, Taylor of So. Carolina, Telfair, Thomas, Vose, Wilcox, Wilde, and Yancey.

NAYS—Messrs. Adgate, Alexander, Atherton, Baker, Bateman, Bennett, Betts, Birdsall, Boss, Brooks, Cady, Calhoun, Chappell, Chipman, Clendennin, Comstock, Conner, Crawford, Creighton, Crocheron, Darlington, Davenport, Desha, Gold, Griffin, Hahn, Hammond, Hawes, Henderson, Hopkinson, Hulbert, Ingham, Irwin of Pennsylvania, Jackson, Johnson of Kentucky, Kent, Langdon, Lyle, Maclay, Marsh, Mason, Mayrant, McCoy, McLean of Kentucky, Milnor, Newton, Ormsby, Parris, Piper, Pitkin, Powell, Ruggles, Sergeant, Savage, Schenck, Sharpe, Smith of Pennsylvania, Smith of Maryland, Southard, Strong, Sturges, Taul, Throop, Townsend, Ward of New York, Ward of New Jersey, Wendover, Wheaton, Whiteside, Wilkin, Willoughby, Thomas Wilson, William Wilson, Woodward, Wright, and Yates.

Mr. Ross then moved further to amend the said bill, by striking out from the fifty-sixth line of the first section (being the first line of the fifth clause) the word "thirty," and to insert "twenty;" when the House adjourned.

FRIDAY, April 5.

On motion of Mr. BETTS, the Committee on the Judiciary were instructed to inquire into the expediency of establishing an uniform mode of trial and punishment for all crimes and offences properly cognizable by the courts of the United States.

NATIONAL BANK.

Mr. CALHOUN moved that the House proceed to consider the amendments of the Senate to the National Bank bill. On putting the question, however, it was found that a quorum of members were not present.

Mr. RANDOLPH, with the view of producing a more punctual attendance hereafter, moved that the House adjourn.—Negatived.

A quorum soon after appearing, Mr. RANDOLPH moved that the rule for convening at 10 o'clock, be rescinded, that the hour of 11 might be again adopted; which was also disagreed to.—Ayes 40.

The House then, by a vote of 55 to 45 agreed to consider the amendments of the Senate to the bank bill.

Mr. MILNOR, because of the thinness of the House and the importance of the subject; further, because he understood that the Committee on the National Currency were on the point of reporting a very important bill, which might materially affect the decision on the bank question, &c., moved that the consideration thereof be postponed to Monday next.

Mr. CALHOUN hoped the motion would not prevail. The reasons for it he did not think sufficient; the House was as full as usual; and the bill alluded to as on the eve of being reported by the committee, presupposed the existence of a National Bank, and the committee had determined not to report it pending the passage of the Bank bill.

After some further conversation between Messrs. CALHOUN and MILNOR, in which the latter gentleman insisted on the propriety of first being in possession of the report referred to, the motion to postpone the subject to Monday, was negatived—ayes 43, noes 66.

After the amendments of the Senate were read, Mr. RANDOLPH moved that the bill and amendments be indefinitely postponed, avowedly for the purpose of destroying the bill. Mr. R. supported his motion, by adverting to the small number of members present, and the impropriety of passing, by a screwed-up, strained, and costive majority, so important a measure, at the end of a session, when the members were worn down and exhausted by a daily and long attention to business; a measure, which, in a time of war and of great public emergency, could not be forced through the House; a measure so deeply involving the future welfare, and which was to give a color and character to the future destiny of this country; a measure which, if it and another, (the tariff) should pass into laws, the present session would be looked back to as the most disastrous since the commencement of the Republic; and which, much as he deprecated war, he would prefer war itself to either of them. Mr. R. then proceeded to argue against the bill as unconstitutional, inexpedient, and dangerous.

Mr. CALHOUN said, it certainly could not be expected of him to enter into so untimely and unnecessary a discussion of the general question. The bill had been before the House three weeks, when it was maturely considered; it was sent to the Senate; and now comes back with a few unimportant amendments, on which the House had to pass. It was unfair to say, that the bill was urged through the House improperly; and the gentleman was mistaken also in stating, that a bank bill could not be passed at the last session; it was notorious that a bill to establish a National Bank did pass at the last session, and was rejected by the President of the United States.

Mr. GROSVENOR did not know what the gentleman meant by a hard-screwed majority. He would venture to say that the House had advanced on this subject with as much deliberation and calmness as they ever did on any public matter whatever; the bill was not pressed through improperly. The pressure talked of by the gentleman was in fact directly the other way. With two hundred State institutions bearing down on the members of this House, it required something more than common firmness, it required boldness to urge the bill. This influence would every day become stronger, and if the subject was deferred to the next session its passage would be impossible. He had never since he came to Congress known a bill passed with more ample discussion; the gentleman from Virginia had himself taken a part, an able part in it. It was not smuggled through the House; a fair majority had passed it, and he was convinced, from information he received, that if the people themselves could be consulted, there would be ten to one in favor of it. Mr. G. answered some of Mr. RANDOLPH's objections to the principles of the bill; declaring his difference from that gentleman on the Constitutional question; and his belief of its necessity to the safety of the country. The Constitutional question had been long since put to sleep by the repeated decisions of all the proper authorities, after mature reflection, and ought never again to be revived.

Mr. RANDOLPH replied to Mr. GROSVENOR, and enforced his Constitutional objections to the bill, in which he was borne out by the decision of Congress in refusing to renew the charter of the old bank, which decision was grounded on the want of Constitutional power. He adverted also, in support of his opinion, to the instructions from the Legislatures of Virginia and Kentucky, to their Senators, to vote against the old bank; which instructions were given on the ground of that institution being unconstitutional. Mr. R. declared himself the holder of no stock whatever, except live stock, and had determined never to own any; but if this bill passed, he would not only be a stockholder to the utmost of his power, but would advise every man, over whom he had any influence, to do the same, because it was the creation of a great privileged order of the most hateful kind to his feelings, and because he would rather be the master than the slave. If he must have a master, let him be one with epaulettes, something that he could fear and respect, something that he could look up to—but not a master with a quill behind his ear.

Mr. WEBSTER said this was a subject on which a great change of opinion had taken place on both sides of the House; and animadverted on what he called a compromise of principle on a great moneyed institution; and the desertion, not only of principles but of friends, which had characterized the proceedings on this bill. He then spoke some time against the bill, which he pointedly condemned, on account of the participation of the Government in its direction and management. If, said he, instead of the little scraps of amendments which were very well as far as they went, but very trifling, and only served to cover the view and deformity of the scheme, the Senate had returned the bill healthy, in all the beauty of the original institution, it would have passed through the House swifter than the current of the Potomac.

Mr. HULBERT replied to Mr. WEBSTER, in defence of the bill and of the course he had pursued in relation to it. He disavowed any compromise of opinion either in the principle or the details of the bill. He had sought the best lights to guide him in deciding on this bill; he had listened to the gentleman from New Hampshire as one who would, if any could, point out its defects and convince him of its danger; but the only objection he heard from that gentleman was the Government direction. That objection, Mr. H. said, was not with him a strong one; and he was free to say that if he had the power of legislating at his will he would hesitate before he gave any class of men the control of an institution of thirty-five millions of dollars, without reserving to the Government a strong check on them. Mr. H. protested with warmth against the proscription

which had been denounced against those who did not on this subject go with the majority of that party in the House opposed to the Administration. He disclaimed any such influence over his public conduct; he came here to act according to his own sincere convictions, and should despise himself if he could submit to act as this or that side of the House pointed its finger. Mr. H. concluded by declaring his support of the bank bill to be disinterested; he expected to hold not a cent's worth of its stock, as he was not able so to do—but the bank he believed would be a great benefit to the country.

Mr. WRIGHT said he was one of those who had aided in putting down the old bank, and was sure that, a thousand years after he was buried, his vote on that occasion would be a monumental proof of his worth and his regard for the best interests of his country. He opposed it on the ground of inexpediency as well as unconstitutionality; but the Supreme Judicial tribunal had decided on its constitutionality by often recognising it as a party, and it was now too late to insist on the objection. Mr. W. argued some time in favor of the bill; and, adverting to Mr. RANDOLPH's epithet that the bank was a scheme of public robbery, and his declared intention to hold as much of its stock as he could, Mr. W. said his friend from Virginia ought to recollect that the receiver was always considered as bad as the thief.

Mr. HARDIN next delivered at length his views of the question; objecting to the plan of the bank as embraced in this bill, on Constitutional grounds as well as from a belief of its inexpediency. He was a member of the Kentucky Legislature at the time, and was one of those who had instructed its Senators to vote against the old bank because of its unconstitutionality, and his opinion remained unchanged, though he perceived some of those who had acted with him in the case alluded to, had changed their opinion and were now supporters of the bank.

Mr. SHARPE spoke in reply to the remarks of Mr. HARDIN, respecting the instructions from the Kentucky Legislature, and justified his opinions on the subject of the bank.

Mr. SOUTHARD made a few remarks, principally to show that it was not on the ground of unconstitutionality that Congress had refused to renew the charter of the old bank, and that it had been recognised by the courts.

Mr. GROSVENOR replied to the observations of Mr. WEBSTER in a decided manner. He denied the right of that gentleman to lecture other members of the House for the course which their duty prescribed to them. As to the changes of principle, of which the gentleman had spoken, Mr. G. said he did not mean to inquire whether the gentlemen on the other side of the House had acted consistently; but this he knew, that last year the gentleman had been proud to shake hands with them in relation to a bank, &c. The gentleman had spoken of another change of principle, alluding to gentlemen from this side of the House, who voted for the present bill. In reply to this remark, Mr. G. said, in the first place, he had something of that old puritanical principle in him, which objected to being drilled in to vote in this or that manner, on whatever any gentleman chose to call a question of principle. Why did the gentleman call the power of appointment of five directors given to the Government, a question of principle? The question is, whether one-fifth of the direction gives the Government a control over the bank? I say no, said Mr. G.—the gentleman says yes, and saying so, this must be a question of principle. That, Mr. G. said, appeared to be the course of the gentleman's argument—the force of which he denied. He showed, that in the State banks in New York, (not undertaking to say how it might be in New Hampshire,) such features had been incorporated, even whilst General Hamilton was in the full vigor of his life and influence, and it was done by his party too, &c. The gentleman has said this control would be a lever in the hands of the Government. It was a straw, Mr. G. said, instead of a lever, and could not move an eagle, much less five-and-thirty millions of dollars. When, even on this side of the House, did this feature become a question of principle? Mr. G. went on to show, that he had objected to the feature in question, and endeavored to procure it to be expunged; but he never considered it, nor had it been debated, but as a question of detail. All legislation, he proceeded to argue, was founded in the idea of mutual compromise of modifications of details; and this clause, now so much objected to, could produce no possible injury to the people or to the Government. When and where did this clause grow into a principle? He could tell, he said, the way it travelled, and where it became a principle—not in the open face of day—he would not, however, here relate its history. It had not been a principle with him, and never should be. Mr. G. went on to say, that he had never heard a wish expressed from any side of the House, that the Government should have an absolute control over the operations of the bank, &c. When the discussion on this bill had been first opened, Mr. G. said, he had heard an able and eloquent speech of the gentleman from New Hampshire, on the subject; and that very speech, in which the evils of the present system were fully depicted, had convinced him of the expediency of the establishment of this bank, as better calculated than anything else to remedy the evil. The gentleman had concluded that address with saying, that if Congress rose without providing a proper remedy, they would deserve the execration of the nation. Mr. G. said he believed it; and believing, as he had fully delivered his opinion the other day, that there was no remedy but the bill on the table, he should certainly vote for it. Mr. G. made other remarks to show the correctness of this conclusion, and ending by saying that in the course he was obliged to take, nothing grieved him so much as the necessity of differing on an important question from men whom he had been in the habit of respecting as oracles, and with whom it was generally his pride and pleasure to act.

Mr. WEBSTER, in replying to Mr. GROSVENOR,

disclaimed any intention to dictate, &c. In regard to the feature of the bill which was the subject of discussion, Mr. W. said, he considered it a matter of principle, but attributed that opinion to the gentleman from New York no further than he had assumed the charge of a departure from principle to apply to himself. What is the matter of principle in this case? That control and influence over a great banking institution should not be possessed by the Government. The degree of that influence was not material—the principle remaining the same, be the influence more or less extensive. That principle was violated by this bill, which, he went on to say, could not be fairly compared with similar features in small banks in the State Governments. But, he added, every bank so constructed in the United States had failed to answer the purposes for which it was instituted, and was at this moment in the daily habitual violation of its engagements. Could it be doubted, Mr. W. said, that with this capital, and this power over it, the Government could bring any man into terms, and make the banks act as they pleased? Gentlemen had done him honor in quoting his opinions in support of part of the bill; but he asked, if it was fair to quote a part of his opinions as authority, and abuse him for the rest? Mr. W. expressed the pleasure he had enjoyed in travelling with his friends here. If, in journeying with a friend, on a road pleasant and smooth, through verdant fields, they should arrive at a part rough and disagreeable; if they should encounter gloom, and darkness should overtake him; if then his friend chose to abandon him, and seek a road more agreeable, let him not, said he, complain, if I continue on the old one. To complain of him, Mr. W. said, the gentleman might as well complain of the fifty-nine others with whom he acted. The gentleman reminded him of the anecdote of the eleven obstinate jurors, and related a case, in which one juror informed the judge that there would be no difficulty in making up a verdict, if it were not for the other eleven, who were the most obstinate fellows he ever met with, and that he himself was the only candid and liberal man of the whole twelve. Mr. W. said he had shaken hands with the gentleman last session on this subject; if they had changed their opinions, they had not made the world the wiser for them. Mr. W. said, though young, he found that he possessed antiquated notions; and that, to be useful, he ought to have been with generations that had gone by.

Mr. HULBERT said, until the gentleman could show himself divested of the frailties of human nature, he ought not to complain that a part only of his opinions were quoted. Mr. H. reminded the gentleman of an authority with which he doubtless was well acquainted; the learned Coke, having finished his great and elaborate commentary on law—a work which would be the admiration of all ages—concludes it by advising his readers not to believe that all which he finds in that book to be law, for there was much of it that was not law. Mr. H. said, if he had had any doubts on this bill, his friend from New York

(Mr. Grosvenor) had made a speech which perfectly satisfied him of the excellence of the bank. The gentleman from New Hampshire (Mr. Webster) had at first made the amount of capital an all-important, a fatal error; soon afterwards he came into the House, and declared that the government of the bank was a *sine qua non*, and for that would compromise his other objections. [Mr Webster here denied that he had said so.] I do not, said Mr. H., pretend to repeat the gentleman's words, but I appeal to this honorable House, if the gentleman did not say that the government of the bank was a *sine qua non* with him, and, if that was given up, he would support the bill. I do not censure that declaration, said Mr. H.; the great charter under which we sit here, is the work of compromise; the South suffered itself to be taxed by the North, for its slave population; the spirit of compromise and concession pervades the whole instrument. What the gentleman meant by green fields, smooth roads, separation, &c., Mr. H. said he could not tell; but if he meant to attribute to him any improper influence, he disdained the insinuation; while he lived he would act on solid and independent principles. He came here first in a time of war, and, being a young member, expected to find the party to which he was proud to belong, as the saying is, sticking together; but he was surprised to find that gentleman often voting on this side and the other. Mr. H. said he would not part with friends, unless they thrust him off; but he would prefer parting with friends to parting with his conscience.

Mr. McKee spoke in support of the bill; and asked the gentleman from New Hampshire, notwithstanding he would to-morrow oppose the suspension of the writ of habeas corpus, or any other unconstitutional measure, yet, if a case might not arise in which its suspension would be proper, and he consent to it? Mr. McK. argued, that there now existed a similar necessity for this bank. The Constitution had made it the duty of Congress to regulate the national currency, and remedy evils therein; and the proper inquiry now was, whether this bank was a proper measure to carry the Constitutional power into effect in this emergency? For this inquiry there was the most rational ground. No Treasury regulation would remedy the evil; the banks would laugh at any such regulation. Mr. McK. said he had voted for the old bank; that he had survived the storm in which his vote had involved him; experience had justified his conduct; and he hoped still to survive, should another storm succeed his present course.

Mr. Sheffey said, he was not scrupulous as to the power of the Government to establish this bank; but he did not admit that what was unconstitutional to-day would not be so to-morrow; that instrument was fixed and eternal, and could not be got over. The suspension of the writ of habeas corpus was dependent on a fact, which, if it occurred, the suspension would be proper; but, if not, it was unauthorized. Mr. S. said he had voted for renewing the old bank, because he

thought it was necessary; and if he could be convinced that this bank would realize the expectation of its friends, he would give up his objections. But, without any disparagement to his friends, and notwithstanding the great talents of the gentleman (Mr. Calhoun) who led the business, Mr. S. said the question had not been properly met and discussed. When they came to show how the promised remedy was to be produced, they dealt in generals; they did not demonstrate their assertions; it was here they failed, and would fail. Mr. S. then argued at some length, to show that the bank would not answer the purpose of correcting the evils in the currency, and that the expectation was visionary and delusive.

The question was then taken, and decided against postponement—yeas 67, nays 91, as follows:

Yeas—Messrs. Baker, Barbour, Bassett, Bennett, Birdsall, Breckenridge, Burnside, Cady, Caldwell, Cilley, Clayton, Clopton, Cooper, Crawford, Culpeper, Darlington, Davenport, Desha, Glasgow, Goldsborough, Goodwyn, Hahn, Hale, Hammond, Hanson, Hardin, Heister, Herbert, Hopkinson, Johnson of Virginia, Johnson of Kentucky, Kent, Langdon, Law, Lewis, Lovett, Lyle, Lyon, Marsh, Mayrant, McLean of Kentucky, Milnor, Newton, Noyes, Pickering, Pitkin, Randolph, Reed, Roane, Root, Ross, Ruggles, Sergeant, Savage, Sheffey, Smith of Pennsylvania, Stearns, Strong, Stuart, Sturges, Taggart, Vose, Wallace, Ward of Massachusetts, Webster, Whiteside, and Wilcox.

Nays—Messrs. Adgate, Alexander, Archer, Atherton, Baer, Bateman, Betts, Boss, Bradbury, Brooks, Brown, Bryan, Calhoun, Cannon, Champion, Chappell, Chipman, Clarke of North Carolina, Clendennin, Comstock, Condict, Conner, Creighton, Crocheron, Cuthbert, Edwards, Forney, Forsyth, Gaston, Gholson, Gold, Griffin, Grosvenor, Hawes, Henderson, Huger, Hulbert, Hungerford, Ingham, Irwin of Pennsylvania, Jackson, Jewett, Kerr of Virginia, King of North Carolina, Love, Lowndes, Lumpkin, Maclay, Mason, McCoy, McKee, Middleton, Moore, Moseley, Murfree, Nelson of Massachusetts, Nelson of Virginia, Ormsby, Parris, Pickens, Piper, Pleasants, Powell, Reynolds, Robertson, Schenck, Sharpe, Smith of Maryland, Smith of Virginia, Southard, Tate, Taul, Taylor of South Carolina, Telfair, Thomas, Throop, Townsend, Tucker, Ward of New York, Ward of New Jersey, Wendover, Wheaton, Wilde, Wilkin, Willoughby, Thomas Wilson, William Wilson, Woodward, Wright, Yancey, and Yates.

The amendments of the Senate were then, after some ineffectual attempts to amend them, concurred in, and the House adjourned.

Saturday, April 6.

Mr. Lowndes, from the Committee of Ways and Means, reported a bill to increase the compensation now allowed by law to inspectors, measurers, weighers, and gaugers, employed in the collection of the customs; which was read twice, and committed to the Committee of the whole House on the report of the Committee of Ways and Means, upon the subject of revenue.

Mr. Robertson, from the Committee on the Public Lands, reported a bill for the relief of Joseph S. Newell; which was read twice, and committed to a Committee of the Whole.

Ordered, That the Committee for the District of Columbia be discharged from a further consideration of the bill from the Senate, supplementary to the act to incorporate a company for making certain turnpike roads in the District of Columbia, and that it be referred to Mr. HERBERT, Mr. CALDWELL, Mr. LEWIS, Mr. ORMSBY, and Mr. PIPER.

A message from the Senate informed the House that the Senate have passed a bill "for the benefit of the widow and children of Robert Fulton, deceased;" also, a bill "to establish a system of navigation for the United States," in which they ask the concurrence of this House.

SPECIE PAYMENTS.

Mr. CALHOUN from the Committee on a National Currency, reported a bill for the more effectual collection of revenue in the lawful money of the United States, which was twice read and committed. The bill is as follows:

A bill for the more effectual collection of the public revenue, in the lawful money of the United States.

Be it enacted, &c., That it shall be the duty of the Secretary of the Treasury, as soon as conveniently may be after the passing of this act, to give public notice, in any one or more of the papers published in each and every State or Territory of the United States, that, from and after the thirty-first day of December next, the payment of duties, taxes, debts, and generally of all sums of money whatsoever, which have then accrued and become payable, or which shall thereafter accrue and become payable to the United States, or to any public officer, agent or other person, for their use, will be demanded in the gold, silver and copper coins of the United States, or in such foreign coins as have been or shall be made current by law. And from and after the said thirty-first day of December next, it shall not be lawful for any public officer, agent or other person whomsoever, employed in the collection or receipt of the revenue, or other public money whatsoever, to accept or allow payment of any such duties, taxes, debts or sums of money whatsoever, in any other medium than in the said coins, or in Treasury notes: *Provided, always*, That it shall be lawful for the Secretary of the Treasury to authorise and permit, as heretofore, the notes of any bank or bankers which are payable and paid on demand in the said coins, to be accepted and allowed in all payments to the United States.

SEC. 2. *And be it further enacted*, That, from and after the said thirty-first day of December next, the Secretary of the Treasury shall not authorise or permit any public money to be deposited, or to continue to be deposited with any bank or bankers, whose notes are not payable and paid on demand in the said coins of the United States, or in foreign coins made current by law as aforesaid. And from and after the said thirty-first day of December, all public moneys shall be deposited in such secure place, in the States and Territories respectively, as the Secretary of the Treasury, with the approbation of the President of the United States, shall designate and appoint.

SEC. 3. *And be it further enacted*, That, from and after the said thirty-first day of December next, it shall be the duty of the Secretary of the Treasury to cause

legal measures to be taken for enforcing a lawful payment of all sums of money due to the United States, on account of bank notes or deposites, from any bank or bankers, whose notes are not then payable and paid on demand in the said coins of the United States, or in foreign coins made current by law as aforesaid.

SEC. 4. *And be it further enacted*, That, from and after the said thirty-first day December next, upon any promissory notes, or notes payable either to bearer or to order, issued by any of the banks or corporations who issue and discount notes, bonds or obligations, either incorporated or not incorporated, which now are or hereafter shall be established in the United States or Territories thereof, there shall be levied, collected and paid the several stamp duties following—

If not exceeding one dollar, ten cents.

If above one dollar, and not exceeding two dollars, twenty cents.

If above two dollars and not exceeding three dollars, thirty cents.

If above three dollars and not exceeding five dollars, fifty cents.

If above five dollars and not exceeding ten dollars, one dollar.

If above ten dollars and not exceeding twenty dollars, two dollars.

If above twenty dollars and not exceeding fifty dollars, five dollars.

If above fifty dollars and not exceeding one hundred dollars, ten dollars.

If above one hundred dollars and not exceeding five hundred dollars, fifty dollars.

If above five hundred dollars, one hundred dollars.

And in relation to the stamp duties herein and hereby imposed, there shall not be allowed any annual or other composition or commutation, but the same shall be specifically collected for and upon the stamps affixed to the notes hereby charged therewith, saving the rights of all persons under existing contracts. And it shall be the duty of the Commissioner of the Revenue to cause to be provided so many marks and stamps, differing from each other, as shall correspond with the several rates of duty aforesaid; but each stamp shall express, among other things, the following words at length, in distinct and legible characters: "Not a specie note." And all the provisions of the act entitled, "An act for laying duties on notes of banks," &c., passed on the second of August, one thousand eight hundred and thirteen, and of the supplements thereto, passed on the tenth of December, one thousand eight hundred and fourteen, shall be applied to the stamp duties imposed by this act, as fully as if the same were herein recited and re-enacted, except so far as respects the rates of duty and an annual composition in lieu of the stamp duties. *Provided always, nevertheless*, That if any banks or bankers shall, on or before the first day of November next, certify to the Secretary of the Treasury that their notes will be payable and paid in coin as aforesaid, upon demand, after the thirty-first day of December next, and if it appear to his satisfaction that payment is to be made, then, with respect to such banks and bankers, the rate of duty and the privilege of composition and commutation shall remain in all respects as if this act had not been passed.

THE TARIFF.

The House proceeded to consider the bill regulating the duties on imports and tonnage: when The amendment proposed by Mr. ROSS, and

1347   HISTORY OF CONGRESS.   1348

H. of R.   *The Tariff.*   April, 1816.

depending on the 4th instant, was modified by the mover, and agreed to by the House.

A motion was made by Mr. ROBERTSON to recommit the bill to a Committee of the whole House.—Negatived.

A motion was made by Mr. HUGER further to amend the bill by inserting, at the end of the 34th line of the 1st section of the printed bill, the following proviso:

"*Provided,* That woollen cloths, or cloths of which wool is the material of chief value, the original cost of which at the place whence exported shall not exceed three shillings sterling per square yard, shall be charged with no higher duty than twelve and a half per centum ad valorem; but such cloths, to be entitled to the advantage of this provision, shall be imported in separate and distinct packages, which shall contain no cloth, the prime cost of which, at the place whence exported, shall exceed three shillings sterling per square yard."

And the question being taken on agreeing to the said proviso, it was determined in the negative—yeas 51, nays 85, as follows:

YEAS—Messrs. Archer, Baer, Barbour, Breckenridge, Bryan, Burnside, Chappell, Clarke of North Carolina, Clayton, Clopton, Cooper, Culpeper, Edwards, Forney, Forsyth, Gaston, Gold, Goldsborough, Goodwyn, Grosvenor, Hale, Huger, Hungerford, Johnson of Virginia, Kerr of Virginia, Law, Lewis, Love, Lovett, McKee, Middleton, Moore, Murfree, Nelson of Massachusetts, Nelson of Virginia, Pickens, Pleasants, Randolph, Roane, Robertson, Sheffey, Smith of Maryland, Smith of Virginia, Stuart, Taylor of South Carolina, Telfair, Vose, Wilde, Williams, Wright, and Yancey.

NAYS—Messrs. Adgate, Alexander, Atherton, Baker, Bassett, Bateman, Baylies, Bennett, Birdsall, Boss, Bradbury, Brooks, Cady, Calhoun, Champion, Cilley, Clendennin, Comstock, Conner, Crawford, Creighton, Crocheron, Cuthbert, Darlington, Davenport, Desha, Glasgow, Griffin, Hahn, Hammond, Hardin, Hawes, Hopkinson, Hulbert, Ingham, Jewett, Johnson of Kentucky, Kent, Langdon, Lowndes, Lumpkin, Lyle, Lyon, Maclay, Marsh, Mayrant, McCoy, McLean of Kentucky, Milnor, Moseley, Newton, Noyes, Parris, Pickering, Piper, Pitkin, Reynolds, Ruggles, Sergeant, Savage, Schenck, Sharpe, Smith of Pennsylvania, Southard, Stearns, Strong, Sturges, Taggart, Taul, Thomas, Throop, Townsend, Tucker, Ward of Massachusetts, Ward of New York, Wendover, Wheaton, Whiteside, Wilcox, Wilkin, Willoughby, Thomas Wilson, William Wilson, Woodward, and Yates.

A motion was then made by Mr. HUGER to strike out the word "*five,*" contained in the 30th line of the first section, so as to reduce the duty on woollen manufactures from twenty-five per centum ad valorem, to twenty per centum ad valorem. And the question being taken thereon, it was determined in the negative—yeas 52, nays 84, as follows:

YEAS—Messrs. Archer, Baer, Barbour, Breckenridge, Bryan, Burnside, Champion, Clarke of North Carolina, Clopton, Culpeper, Cuthbert, Edwards, Forney, Forsyth, Gaston, Goldsborough, Goodwyn, Hale, Hardin, Huger, Hungerford, Johnson of Virginia, Kerr of Virginia, King of North Carolina, Law, Lewis, Love, Lovett, Lowndes, Lumpkin, McKee, Middleton,

Moore, Murfree, Nelson of Massachusetts, Nelson of Virginia, Pleasants, Randolph, Roane, Roberts, Root, Smith of Virginia, Sturges, Telfair, Thomas, Vose, Wilcox, Wilde, Williams, Woodward, Wright, and Yancey.

NAYS—Messrs. Adgate, Alexander, Atherton, Baker, Bateman, Baylies, Bennett, Birdsall, Boss, Bradbury, Brooks, Brown, Cady, Calhoun, Cannon, Chipman, Cilley, Clayton, Clendennin, Comstock, Conner, Cooper, Crawford, Creighton, Crocheron, Darlington, Davenport, Desha, Glasgow, Gold, Griffin, Hahn, Hammond, Hawes, Hopkinson, Hulbert, Ingham, Jewett, Johnson of Kentucky, Kent, Langdon, Lyle, Lyon, Maclay, Marsh, Mason, Mayrant, McCoy, McLean of Kentucky, Milnor, Newton, Ormsby, Parris, Pickering, Piper, Pitkin, Powell, Reynolds, Ruggles, Sergeant, Savage, Schenck, Sharpe, Smith of Pennsylvania, Smith of Maryland, Southard, Stearns, Strong, Taggart, Taul, Throop, Townsend, Tucker, Ward of Massachusetts, Ward of New York, Wendover, Wheaton, Whiteside, Wilkin, Willoughby, Thomas Wilson, William Wilson, and Yates.

A motion was made by Mr. WARD, of Massachusetts, to reduce the duty on hemp from one dollar and fifty cents per hundred weight, to one dollar per hundred weight. And the question being taken, it was determined in the negative.

A motion was then made by Mr. TUCKER further to amend the said bill, by striking out from the first section thereof the following words:

"*Provided,* That all cotton cloths, or cloths of which cotton is the material of chief value, (excepting nankeens imported directly from China,) the original cost of which at the place whence imported shall be less than twenty-five cents per square yard, shall be taken and deemed to have cost twenty-five cents per square yard, and shall be charged with duty accordingly, and on cotton yarn or thread the same."

And the question being taken thereon, it was determined in the negative—yeas 51, nays 83, as follows:

YEAS—Messrs. Baer, Barbour, Bassett, Bryan, Burnside, Champion, Clarke of North Carolina, Culpeper, Cuthbert, Edwards, Forsyth, Gaston, Goldsborough, Goodwyn, Hale, Hardin, Hahn, Henderson, Huger, Hungerford, Johnson of Virginia, Kerr of Virginia, King of North Carolina, Law, Lewis, Love, Lovett, Lumpkin, Lyon, McKee, Moore, Nelson of Massachusetts, Nelson of Virginia, Pickens, Pleasants, Randolph, Roane, Robertson, Roos, Sheffey, Smith of Virginia, Taylor of South Carolina, Telfair, Thomas, Tucker, Vose, Wilde, Williams, Wright, and Yancey.

NAYS—Messrs. Adgate, Alexander, Archer, Atherton, Baker, Bateman, Bennett, Betts, Birdsall, Boss, Bradbury, Brooks, Brown, Cady, Calhoun, Chappell, Chipman, Cilley, Clendennin, Comstock, Crawford, Creighton, Crocheron, Darlington, Davenport, Desha, Glasgow, Gold, Griffin, Grosvenor, Hahn, Hammond, Hawes, Hopkinson, Hulbert, Ingham, Jackson, Jewett, Johnson of Kentucky, Kent, Langdon, Lowndes, Maclay, Marsh, Mason, Mayrant, McCoy, McLean of Kentucky, Middleton, Milnor, Newton, Ormsby, Parris, Piper, Pitkin, Powell, Reynolds, Root, Ruggles, Sergeant, Savage, Schenck, Sharpe, Smith of Pennsylvania, Smith of Maryland, Southard, Strong, Taul, Throop, Townsend, Wallace, Ward of New York, Ward of New Jersey, Wendover, Wheaton, Whiteside,

Wilkin, Willoughby, Thomas Wilson, William Wilson, Woodward, and Yates.

The bill was then further amended, and ordered to be engrossed and read a third time on Monday next.

MONDAY, April 8.

Mr. LOWNDES, from the Committee of Ways and Means, to whom was referred the bill from the Senate "for the relief of John Holkar, formerly Consul General of France to the United States," reported the same without amendment, and the bill was committed to a Committee of the Whole.

Mr. NELSON, of Virginia, from the committee appointed to inquire into the official conduct of Judge Tallmadge, made a report; which was read, and the resolution therein contained was concurred in by the House, as follows:

Resolved, That the Senate of the United States be requested to permit the attendance of the Hon. Nathan Sanford, a member of their body, before the committee of the House of Representatives appointed to inquire into the official conduct of Judge Tallmadge, to be examined touching the subjects contained in the preceding report relative to the alleged misconduct of Judge Tallmadge in his office, as one of the judges of the district court for the State of New York.

Ordered, That the several committees of the whole House to whom are committed the various bills and reports originating with the Committee of Claims, be discharged from the further consideration thereof; and that they be committed to the Committee of the Whole on the bill for the relief of William Hamon.

On motion of Mr. PLEASANTS, a committee was appointed to inquire into the expediency of passing a law giving the assent of Congress to an act of the General Assembly of Virginia, passed at their last session, entitled "An act incorporating a company for the purpose of improving the navigation of James River from Warwick to Rockett's Landing," and that they have leave to report by bill or otherwise.—Mr. PLEASANTS, Mr. BRECKENRIDGE, and Mr. CLOPTON, were appointed the committee.

On motion of Mr. ROOT, the Secretary of the Treasury was instructed to lay before this House a statement of all the loans made to the Government by the several banks since the 1st of March, 1812, designating at what times and on what terms such loans were made.

The SPEAKER laid before the House a letter from the Commissioner of the General Land Office, transmitting a copy of a report of the commissioners for settling claims to land in the Western district of the State of Louisiana; which was referred to the Committee on the Public Lands.

On motion of Mr. NEWTON,

Resolved, That the Secretary of the Treasury be, and he is hereby, required to report to the House of Representatives of the United States, at the next session of Congress, whether any, and if any, what alterations or modifications are necessary to be made in the laws establishing ports of entry and delivery; and what new regulations, if any, are required for the government of the same; and also whether ports of entry are not multiplied beyond the number which policy prescribes for the safe collection of the revenue.

Ordered, That the Committee of Commerce and Manufactures be discharged from a further consideration of the several petitions and resolutions referred to them during the present session respecting the establishment of ports of entry and delivery, and that they be referred to the Secretary of the Treasury.

The bill from the Senate "for the benefit of the widow and children of Robert Fulton, deceased," was read twice, and committed to Mr. GROSVENOR, Mr. TUCKER, Mr. SERGEANT, Mr. SHARPE, Mr. CREIGHTON, Mr. CONNER, and Mr. CALHOUN.

The bill from the Senate "to establish a system of navigation for the United States," was read twice, and committed to the Committee on Foreign Relations.

Ordered, That the Committee of the Whole, to whom is committed the bill for the more convenient arrangement of the times and places of holding the circuit courts of the United States for the districts of South Carolina and Georgia, be discharged from a further consideration of the same, and that the bill be engrossed, and read a third time to-morrow.

THE TARIFF.

The engrossed bill to regulate the duties on imports and tonnage, was read the third time; and the question stated, "Shall the bill pass?"

Mr. RANDOLPH moved that the bill be postponed to December next. In making this motion, Mr. R. said, he was not actuated by the usual motives of similar motions. It proceeded from a belief that the subject had not been properly and maturely prepared by the Secretary of the Treasury. He wished the subject postponed to the next session, that the system might be printed collaterally with the present duties, that every member might take it home and consult his constituents—those whose opinions he ought to respect. The bill, Mr. R. said, had been precipitated through the House, and the discussion on it showed a strange and mysterious connexion between this measure and one (the bank bill) which had just passed, and was now beyond the control of this House. Another reason for referring the subject to the next session was, he said, the material injury it would produce on the revenue if adopted now; and at this time the Secretary of the Treasury ought strictly to guard against any deficit in the revenue. He thought the reasons for postponement were imperious.

Mr. SMITH, of Maryland, opposed the motion for postponement. Among other arguments, in reply to Mr. RANDOLPH, he said it was extremely necessary to adopt at once some permanent system on which commercial men, as well as others, might rely with confidence. If the tariff were not passed, the commercial community would have to look to the next session, without knowing how to shape their conduct, or form their calculations, uncertain of the policy which might be then adopted.

Mr. LOWNDES also offered some remarks in reply to Mr. RANDOLPH, and against postponing the bill. He denied the charge of precipitation in the Secretary of the Treasury in making his report; and referred to the circular letters long since sent to various quarters in search of information, to show that the Secretary had not acted prematurely, and that measures were long ago taken to obtain all possible light on the subject. Mr. L. admitted that there were particular features in the bill about the passage of which he was not anxious; but in a system so extensive there must be particular parts on which members could not agree. As a whole, however, he had no doubt it would be beneficial to the revenue, &c., and to the general interests of the country.

Mr. CALHOUN had no intention of entering in a discussion of the motion; but he wished merely to reply to the, insinuation of a mysterious connexion between this bill, and that to establish the bank. He denied any improper or unfair understanding, and could challenge the House to support the charge. In fact, Mr. C. said, the most zealous friends of the bank were generally unfriendly to this tariff; and the warmest friends of either could not be found on the same side.

After some further conversation between Mr. RANDOLPH and Mr. CALHOUN, the question was taken by yeas and nays, on the postponement, and decided in the negative—yeas 47, nays 95, as follows:

YEAS—Messrs. Baer, Breckenridge, Bryan, Burnside, Champion, Clarke of North Carolina, Clopton, Culpeper, Edwards, Forney, Forsyth, Goldsborough, Hale, Hall, Hardin, Herbert, Huger, Hungerford, Kerr of Virginia, Law, Lewis, Love, Lovett, Lyon, McKee, Murfree, Nelson of Va., Pickens, Pickering, Randolph, Reynolds, Roane, Robertson, Root, Sheffey, Smith of Va., Stuart, Tate, Taylor of South Carolina, Telfair, Thomas, Vose, Wilcox, Wilde, Williams, Wright, and Yancey.

NAYS—Messrs. Adgate, Alexander, Archer, Atherton, Baker, Barbour, Bassett, Bateman, Baylies, Bennett, Betts, Birdsall, Boss, Bradbury, Brooks, Cady, Caldwell, Calhoun, Cannon, Chappell, Chipman, Clayton, Clendennin, Comstock, Conner, Cooper, Crawford, Creighton, Crocheron, Cuthbert, Darlington, Davenport, Desha, Glasgow, Gold, Griffin, Grosvenor, Hahn, Hammond, Hawes, Henderson, Hopkinson, Ingham, Irwin of Pennsylvania, Jackson, Jewett, Johnson of Virginia, Johnson of Kentucky, Kent, Langdon, Lowndes, Lumpkin, Lyle, Maclay, Marsh, Mason, Mayrant, McCoy, McLean of Kentucky, Middleton, Milnor, Moore, Newton, Ormsby, Parris, Piper, Pitkin, Pleasants, Powell, Ruggles, Sergeant, Savage, Schenck, Sharpe, Smith of Pennsylvania, Smith of Maryland, Southard, Strong, Sturges, Taggart, Taul, Throop, Townsend, Tucker, Ward of New York, Ward of New Jersey, Wendover, Wheaton, Whiteside, Wilkin, Willoughby, Thomas Wilson, William Wilson, Woodward, and Yates.

The question then recurred on the passage of the bill; when

Mr. RANDOLPH rose and spoke nearly three hours in opposition to the bill, and generally against the policy of encouraging manufacturing establishments at all, especially against the propriety of affording a high bounty by taxing the community.

Mr. WRIGHT also spoke some time against the bill; as also did

Mr. TELFAIR, who opposed the bill in a speech of half an hour; when the question on the passage of the bill was taken, and decided in the affirmative—yeas 88, nays 54, as follows:

YEAS—Messrs. Adgate, Alexander, Archer, Atherton, Baker, Barbour, Bassett, Bateman, Baylies, Bennett, Betts, Birdsall, Boss, Brooks, Brown, Cady, Caldwell, Calhoun, Cannon, Chipman, Clendennin, Comstock, Crawford, Creighton, Crocheron, Cuthbert, Darlington, Davenport, Desha, Glasgow, Gold, Grosvenor, Hahn, Hall, Hammond, Hawes, Henderson, Hopkinson, Ingham, Irwin of Pennsylvania, Jewett, Johnson of Kentucky, Kent, Langdon, Lowndes, Lumpkin, Lyle, Maclay, Marsh, Mason, Mayrant, McCoy, McLean of Kentucky, Milnor, Newton, Noyes, Ormsby, Parris, Piper, Pitkin, Pleasants, Powell, Ruggles, Sergeant, Savage, Schenck, Sharpe, Smith of Pennsylvania, Smith of Maryland, Southard, Strong, Taggart, Taul, Throop, Townsend, Tucker, Wallace, Ward of New York, Ward of New Jersey, Wendover, Wheaton, Whiteside, Wilkin, Willoughby, Thos. Wilson, William Wilson, Woodward, and Yates.

NAYS—Messrs. Baer, Bradbury, Breckenridge, Bryan, Burnside, Champion, Clarke of North Carolina, Clopton, Culpeper, Edwards, Forney, Forsyth, Gaston, Goldsborough, Goodwyn, Hale, Hardin, Heister, Herbert, Huger, Hungerford, Johnson of Virginia, Kerr of Virginia, Law, Lewis, Love, Lovett, Lyon, Moore, Murfree, Nelson of Massachusetts, Nelson of Virginia, Pickens, Pickering, Randolph, Reynolds, Robertson, Roane, Root, Ross, Sheffey, Smith of Virginia, Stearns, Stuart, Tate, Taylor of South Carolina, Telfair, Thomas, Vose, Wilcox, Wilde, Williams, Wright, and Yancey.

On motion of Mr. JOHNSON, of Kentucky, the House then took up the resolution fixing the period of adjournment.

After some conversation on the propriety of various days which were named, and the inexpediency of fixing at this time on any day for adjournment, a motion to postpone the resolution until Monday was made and carried.

TUESDAY April 9.

Mr. ROBERTSON, from the Committee on the Public Lands, reported a bill to authorize the survey of two millions of acres of the public lands, in lieu of that quantity heretofore authorized to be surveyed in the Territory of Michigan, as military bounty lands; which was read twice and committed to a Committee of the Whole.

Mr. PLEASANTS, from a select committee, reported a bill declaring the assent of Congress to an act of the Legislature of Virginia to incorporate a company to improve the navigation of James river; which was twice read and committed to a Committee of the Whole House, passed forthwith through the committee, and was ordered to be engrossed for a third reading.

Mr. HOPKINSON, from the joint committee appointed on the subject of regulating the proceedings of Congress, reported two resolutions providing that the business of all kinds which may remain unfinished at the close of the present session, shall be taken up at the next session at the precise point to which it shall have progressed during the present session; which resolutions were laid on the table.

An engrossed bill, entitled "An act for the more convenient arrangement of the times and places of holding the Circuit Courts of the United States for the districts of South Carolina and Georgia," was read the third time and passed.

The following bills passed through a Committee of the Whole, were reported to the House, and severally ordered to be engrossed for a third reading, to wit: The bill to fix the commissions of the collectors of the direct tax and internal duties, &c.; a bill to increase the compensation now allowed to gaugers, weighers, inspectors, &c., employed in the customs; a bill declaring the consent of Congress to an act of the State of South Carolina, authorizing the city of Charleston to lay a certain duty on vessels from foreign ports; and a bill for the relief of the widow and children of Captain Z. Morgan.

The House resolved itself into a Committee of the Whole on the bill to authorize the settlement and payment of certain claims for the services of the militia; and after some time spent therein, the Committee rose, reported progress, and had leave to sit again.

The House resolved itself into a Committee of the Whole on the bill for the relief of William Hamon, and on the several subjects thereto committed; and after some time spent therein, the Committee rose and reported the bill for the relief of William Hamon; the bill for the relief of Charles Ross and Samuel Breck, surviving executors of John Ross, deceased; the bill for the relief of Thomas Farrar, William Young, and William Moseley; the bill for the relief of Joseph Wilson; the bill for the relief of Paul D. Butler; the bill to authorize payment for the county court-house of Hamilton, in the State of Ohio; the bill for the relief of Rufus S. Reed and Daniel Dobbins; the bill for the relief of Thomas Ap Catesby Jones; the bill for the relief of Joseph Wheaton; the bill for the relief of Manasseh Minor; the bill for the relief of William Flood; the bill for the relief of the president and directors of the Washington Bridge Company; the bill for the relief of Asher Palmer; the bill for the relief of the supervisors of the county of Clinton, in the State of New York; the bill for the relief of John Crosby and John Crosby, jr.; the bill for the relief of Ephraim Shayler; the bill for the relief of Taylor & McNeal, Evans & McNeal, and Henry & John McCleister; the bill for the relief of Charles Todd; the bill for the relief of Thomas B. Farish; the bill for the relief of Peter Audrain, without

amendment; the bill for the relief of a company of the 20th brigade of Virginia militia, commanded by Captain Jonathan Wamsley; and the bill for the relief of Patrick O'Flyng, and Abigail and Edmund O'Flyng, with an amendment to each; and their agreement to the report of the Committee of Claims on the bill from the Senate, entitled "An act for the relief of Edward Barry and George Hodge."

Ordered, That the Committee of the Whole House have leave to sit again upon the residue of the said order.

The amendments to the bill " for the relief of a company of the 20th brigade of Virginia militia, commanded by Captain Jonathan Wamsley," and to that "for the relief of Patrick O'Flyng, and Abigail and Edmund O'Flyng," were read and concurred in by the House, and the said bills ordered to be severally engrossed and read a third time to-morrow.

The bill for the relief of Thomas Farrar and others was amended at the Clerk's table, and, together with the several other bills to which the Committee of the Whole have reported their assent as aforesaid, were ordered to be severally engrossed, and read a third time to-morrow.

Ordered, That the bill from the Senate " for the relief of Edward Barry and George Hodge," with the report thereupon, lie upon the table.

A message from the Senate informed the House that the Senate have passed the bill " for the relief of the heirs of George Nebinger," with an amendment, in which they ask the concurrence of this House.

The House resolved itself into a Committee of the Whole on the bill for the relief of David Gelston and Peter A. Schenck, and on the several bills thereto committed; and after some time spent therein, the Committee rose and reported the bill for the relief of certain owners of goods entered at Hampden, in the district of Maine, with an amendment; which was read and concurred in by the House, and the bill ordered to be engrossed and read a third time to-morrow.

The House resolved itself into a Committee of the Whole on the report of the Committee on the Public Lands on the petition of Thomas Carr; and after some time spent therein, the Committee rose and reported progress, and had leave to sit again.

The House resolved itself into a Committee of the Whole on the bill from the Senate "to authorize the President of the United States to alter the road laid out from the foot of the rapids of the river Miami of Lake Erie to the western line of the Connecticut reserve; and after some time spent therein, the bill was reported without amendment, and ordered to be read a third time to-morrow.

The House resolved itself into a Committee of the Whole on the bill to authorize the sale of lands forfeited to the United States in the district of Jeffersonville, at the land office in said district; and on the bill from the Senate, to authorize the Legislature of the State of Ohio to sell a certain part of a tract of land reserved for the use of that State; and after some time spent therein, the bills were reported without amendment.

Ordered, That the first mentioned bill be engrossed, and, together with the bill from the Senate, read a third time to-morrow.

The House resolved itself into a Committee of the Whole on the bill providing for the sale of a tract of land at the British fort at the Miami of Lake Erie, at the foot of the rapids, and for other purposes; and after some time spent therein, the bill was reported without amendment, and ordered to be engrossed and read a third time on Friday next.

The House resolved itself into a Committee of the Whole on the bill providing for the sale of the tract of land at the Lower Rapids of Sandusky river; and after some time spent therein, the bill was reported without amendment, and ordered to be engrossed, and read a third time on Friday next.

The House resolved itself into a Committee of the Whole on the resolution directing the Secretary of State to compile and print, biennially, a register of the civil, military, and naval officers of the United States; and after some time spent therein, the resolution was reported without amendment, and ordered to be engrossed and read a third time to-morrow.

This House resolved itself into a Committee of the Whole on the bill for the payment of the militia in the case therein mentioned; and after some time spent therein, the bill was reported without amendment.

The said bill was then amended, and ordered to be engrossed, and read a third time on Thursday next.

DEATH OF MR. STANFORD.

Mr. GASTON announced the death of RICHARD STANFORD, a member of this House, from the State of North Carolina: whereupon,

Resolved, unanimously, That a committee be appointed to take order for superintending the funeral of Richard Stanford, deceased, late a Representative from the State of North Carolina.

And Messrs. GASTON, YANCEY, CULPEPER, FORNEY, PICKENS, CLARKE, and EDWARDS, were appointed the said committee.

Resolved, That the members of this House will testify their respect for the memory of Richard Stanford, late one of their body, by wearing crape on the left arm for one month.

Resolved, unanimously, That the members of this House will attend the funeral of the late Richard Stanford, to-morrow, at 12 o'clock.

Ordered, That a message be sent to the Senate to notify them of the death of RICHARD STANFORD, late a member of this House, and that his funeral will take place to-morrow at 12 o'clock.

Ordered, That when the House adjourns, it will adjourn until the day after to-morrow.

THURSDAY, April 11.

Mr. CALDWELL presented a petition of sundry inhabitants of Steubenville, in the State of Ohio,

praying that a public road may be laid out and made from Washington, in Pennsylvania, to the head of Sandusky bay, in the State of Ohio.—Referred to the committee appointed upon the same subject on the 30th ultimo.

Mr. NEWTON, from the Committee of Commerce and Manufactures, reported a bill making appropriations for rebuilding light-houses, and for completing the plan of lighting them according to the improvements of Winslow Lewis; for placing beacons and buoys; for the preservation of Little Gull Island; and for surveying the coast of the United States;—which was read twice, and committed to the Committee of the Whole on the report of the Committee of Ways and Means on the subject of revenue.

Mr. NEWTON also reported the bill from the Senate "for the relief of Xaverio Nandi," without amendment; and the bill was committed to the Committee of the Whole on the bill for the relief of Richard Ridgeley and others.

Mr. WILCOX, from the Committee on Pensions and Revolutionary Claims, reported a bill concerning invalid pensioners; which was read twice, and committed to a Committee of the Whole on Monday next.

Mr. HERBERT, from the committee to whom was referred the bill from the Senate "supplementary to an act, entitled 'An act to incorporate a company for making certain turnpike roads within the District of Columbia,'" reported the same without amendment; and the bill was ordered to be read a third time to-day.

On motion of Mr. JOHNSON, of Kentucky, a committee was appointed to inquire into the expediency of continuing in force the law in relation to Indian trade.—Mr. JOHNSON of Kentucky, Mr. JACKSON, Mr. ALEXANDER, Mr. LYON, and Mr. BAYLIES, were appointed the committee.

The amendment proposed by the Senate to the bill "for the relief of the heirs of George Nebinger," was read, and referred to the Committee on Pensions and Revolutionary Claims.

The bill to reward with one hundred thousand dollars the captors of certain Algerine vessels was called up by Mr. FORSYTH, on whose motion it was amended by striking out the words "in consideration of the valor and promptitude with which the capture was effected;" and the bill was then ordered to be engrossed for a third reading.

The bill reported by the Currency Committee to compel specie payments, was, on motion of Mr. CALHOUN, recommitted to the select committee, for the purpose of making some amendment in its details.

In moving the recommitment, Mr. C. remarked that the modification intended to expunge a feature [the high duties] in the bill, which, if retained, would probably require more discussion than, at this late period, the House would be willing to devote to it; and that it would, perhaps, be better not to agitate the question during the present session.

Ordered, That the Committee of the Whole be discharged from the further consideration of the bill for the more effectual collection of the public revenue in the lawful money of the United States, and that it be recommitted to the Committee upon the subject of an Uniform National Currency.

Engrossed bills of the following titles, viz:

An act to fix the commissions of the collectors of the direct tax and internal duties, and to revive and continue in force "An act further to provide for the collection of duties on imports and tonnage;"

An act to increase the compensations now allowed by law to inspectors, measurers, weighers, and gaugers, employed in the collection of the customs;

An act declaring the consent of Congress to acts of the State of South Carolina, authorizing the City Council of Charleston to impose and collect a duty on the tonnage of vessels from foreign ports; and to acts of the State of Georgia, authorizing the imposition and collection of a duty on the tonnage of vessels in the ports of Savannah and St. Mary's;

An act declaring the assent of Congress to an act of the General Assembly of Virginia, therein mentioned;

An act for the relief of the widow and orphan children of Zacquille Morgan, late a captain in the United States' Army;

An act for the relief of William Hamon;

An act for the relief of Charles Ross and Samuel Brock, surviving executors of Charles Ross, deceased;

An act for the relief of Thomas Farrar, William Young, William Moseley, and William Leach;

An act for the relief of Joseph Wilson;

An act for the relief of Paul D. Butler;

An act authorizing the payment for the court-house of Hamilton county, in the State of Ohio;

An act for the relief of Rufus S. Reed and Daniel Dobbins;

An act for the relief of Joseph Wheaton;

An act for the relief of Manasseh Miner;

An act for the relief of Thomas Ap Catesby Jones;

An act for the relief of William Flood;

An act for the relief of the President and Directors of the Washington Bridge Company;

An act for the relief of Asher Palmer;

An act for the relief of the supervisors of Clinton county, in the State of New York;

An act for the relief of John Crosby and John Crosby, jr.

An act for the relief of Ephraim Shayler;

An act for the relief of Taylor & McNeal, Evans & McNeal, and Henry and John McLeister;

An act for the relief of Charles Todd:

An act for the relief of Thomas B. Parish;

An act for the relief of Peter Audrain;

An act for the relief of a company of non-commissioned officers and privates, of the 20th brigade of Virginia militia, commanded by Captain Jonathan Wamsley:

An act for the relief of Patrick O'Flyng and Abigail O'Flyng and Edmund O'Flyng;

An act to authorize the sale of lands forfeited to the United States, in the district of Jeffersonville, at the land office in said district;

An act for the payment of militia claims, in the cases therein mentioned; and

An act for the relief of certain owners of goods entered at Hampden, in the District of Maine; were severally read the third time and passed.

A joint resolution requiring the Secretary of State to compile and print, once in every two years, a register of all officers and agents, civil, military, and naval, in the service of the United States, was read the third time and passed.

The bills from the Senate, entitled "An act to authorize the President of the United States to alter the road laid out from the foot of the rapids of the river Miami, of Lake Erie, to the western line of the Connecticut Reserve;" "An act to authorize the Legislature of the State of Ohio, to sell a certain part of a tract of land, reserved for the use of said State;" and "An act supplementary to an act to incorporate a company for making certain turnpike roads in the District of Columbia," were severally read the third time and passed.

The House resolved itself into a Committee of the Whole on the bill for the relief of the Bible Societies of the United States; and after some time spent therein, the bill was reported with amendments, which were read and concurred in by the House, and the bill ordered to be engrossed, and read a third time to-morrow.

The House resolved itself into a Committee of the Whole on the bill to alter certain parts of the act providing for the government of the Territory of Missouri; and after some time spent therein the bill was reported without amendment, and the bill was ordered to be engrossed, and read a third time to-morrow.

The House resolved itself into a Committee of the Whole on the bill from the Senate "to increase the pension of William Munday;" and after some time spent therein, the bill was reported with an amendment, which was read and concurred in by the House, and the bill ordered to be read a third time to-morrow.

The House resolved itself into a Committee of the Whole on the bill of this House, further extending the time for issuing and locating military land warrants, and for other purposes; and on the bill from the Senate, farther extending the time for issuing and locating military land warrants, and for other purposes; and after some time spent therein, the bill from the Senate was reported without amendment.

Ordered, That the said bill from the Senate be read a third time to-morrow, and that the bill of this House lie on the table.

The House resolved itself into a Committee of the Whole on the bill concerning Sarah Easton and Dorothy Storer; and after some time spent therein, the Committee rose and reported progress, and asked leave to sit again, which was refused, and the bill was ordered to lie on the table.

The House resolved itself into a Committee of the Whole on the bill for the relief of Moses Turner; and after some time spent therein, the bill was reported with amendments, and ordered to lie on the table.

The House resolved itself into a Committee of the Whole on the bill confirming certain lands in the county of Arkansas, in the Missouri Territory, to the heirs of Elisha Winter, deceased, to the heirs of William Winter, deceased, and to Gabriel Winter; and after some time spent therein, the bill was reported without amendment, and ordered to be engrossed, and read a third time to-morrow.

The House resolved itself into a Committee of the Whole on the bill for the relief of William Crawford and Frederick Bates; and after some time spent therein, the bill was reported with an amendment, which was read and concurred in by the House, and the bill ordered to be engrossed, and read a third time to-morrow.

The House resolved itself into a Committee of the Whole on the bill for the relief of the heirs of Alexander Roxburgh, deceased, and on the petition of Maria S. Tyson; and after some time spent therein, the bill was reported with amendments, which were read and concurred in by the House; and it was ordered that the said bill be engrossed and read a third time to-morrow, and that the Committee of the Whole be discharged from further considering the petition of Maria S. Tyson, and that it be referred to the Committee on Pensions and Revolutionary Claims.

A message from the Senate informed the House that the Senate have passed the bill "making appropriations for the support of Government for the year 1816," with amendments, in which they ask the concurrence of this House. The Senate have passed a bill "concerning the entry of vessels at the port of Middletown," and a resolution "for printing the laws relative to naturalization," in which bill and resolution they ask the concurrence of this House.

The following Message was received from the PRESIDENT OF THE UNITED STATES:

To the Senate and House of Representatives of the United States:

With a view to the more convenient arrangement of the important and growing business connected with the grant of exclusive rights to inventors and authors, I recommend the establishment of a distinct office within the Department of State, to be charged therewith, under a Director, with a salary adequate to his services, and with the privilege of franking communications by mail from and to the office. I recommend, also, that further restraints be imposed on the issues of patents to wrongful claimants, and further guards provided against fraudulent exactions of fees by persons possessed of patents.

JAMES MADISON.

APRIL 11, 1816.

The Message was read and ordered to lie on the table.

The House resolved itself into a Committee of the Whole on the bill from the Senate "in addition to an act, entitled 'An act in relation to the Navy Pension Fund;'" and after some time spent therein, the bill was reported without amendment, and read a third time and passed.

The House resolved itself into a Committee of the Whole on the bill from the Senate "confirming to the Navigation Company of New Orleans the use and possession of a lot in the said city; and after some time spent therein, the bill was reported without amendment, and ordered to be read a third time to-morrow.

The House resolved itself into a Committee of the Whole on the bill authorizing the payment of a sum of money to James Levins; also, on the report of the Committee on Naval Affairs on the petition of John Rodgers, and others, and on the petition of Joseph Stewart, and others; and after some time spent therein, the bill was reported with an amendment; also, the agreement of the Committee of the Whole in the resolution submitted in the said report.

The amendment to the said bill was concurred in by the House, and it was ordered to be engrossed and read a third time to-morrow.

The resolution submitted in the report aforesaid was concurred in by the House, as follows:

Resolved, That the prayer of the petition of John Rodgers, and others, is reasonable and ought to be granted.

Ordered, That the Committee on Naval Affairs prepare and report a bill in pursuance of the said resolution, and that the Committee of the Whole be discharged from a further consideration of the petition of the aforesaid Joseph Stewart, and others, and that it be referred to the said Committee on Naval Affairs.

The House resolved itself into a Committee of the Whole on the bill for the relief of Samuel Dick, William Bruce, and Asa Kitchell; and after some time spent therein, the bill was reported without amendment, and ordered to be engrossed and read a third time to-morrow.

The House went into Committee of the Whole, on the bill making an appropriation for the improvement of the Capitol Square. The blank was filled, on motion of Mr. TUCKER, with the sum of $30,000; and Mr. CLAY made a few remarks in support of the object of the bill; when the Committee reported the bill and amendments to the House.

The amendment and the bill itself were opposed by Messrs. WRIGHT and NELSON, the former of whom moved to lay it on the table; and were advocated by Messrs. TUCKER, CALHOUN, JACKSON, and ROBERTSON. Mr. WRIGHT's motion was negatived; and he then demanded the yeas and nays on the question of engrossing the bill, which were refused by the House; and the bill was finally ordered to be engrossed for a third reading to-morrow.

The amendments proposed by the Senate to the bill "making appropriations for the support of Government for the year 1816," were read and committed to a Committee of the whole House on the report of the Committee of Ways and Means upon the subject of revenue.

FRIDAY, April 12.

Mr. NEWTON, from the Committee of Commerce and Manufactures, reported a bill for the relief of Isaac Lawrence and others, merchants, of New York; which was read twice, and committed to a Committee of the Whole.

Mr. NEWTON from the same committee, to whom was referred the bill from the Senate "for the relief of Jacob Babbitt and John Dennis," reported the same without amendment, and the bill was committed to the Committee of the Whole on the report of the Committee of Ways and Means upon the petitions of Elisha Talbot and others.

Mr. WRIGHT, from the Committee on the Judiciary, reported a bill concerning the owners, officers, and crew of the late privateer Roger; which was read twice, and committed to a Committee of the Whole to-day.

Ordered, That the Committee on Naval Affairs be discharged from so much of the petition of Captain David Porter, as has been referred to them, and that he have leave to withdraw the same, with the accompanying documents.

Mr. CALHOUN, from the Committee on an Uniform National Currency, reported, in a modified shape, the bill to provide for the collecting the revenue in the legal currency. The amendment made by the committee to the bill, consists in striking out the 3d section, which imposed a stamp duty of ten per cent. on the notes of those banks which shall not pay specie on the 31st of December next, leaving only the provision which excludes such notes from being received in payment of debts due the United States. The bill was committed to a Committee of the Whole.

On motion of Mr. GROSVENOR, the Committee appointed on the subject of an Uniform National Currency were instructed to inquire in the expediency of prohibiting, by law, the exportation of bullion and specie from the United States for a limited period, and that they report thereon to this House.

On motion of Mr. JENNINGS, a committee was appointed to inquire what amendments, if any, are necessary to the act, entitled "An act granting bounties in land, and extra pay, to certain Canadian volunteers," with leave to report by bill or otherwise.—Messrs. JENNINGS, YATES, and BARBOUR, were appointed the said committee.

Ordered, That the bill providing an additional compensation to the District Judge of the Southern District of New York, with the amendment depending thereto, be committed to a Committee of the Whole to-day.

The engrossed bill making an appropriation for graduating, enclosing, and improving the Capitol Square, was read the third time, and the question on its passage stated. This question gave rise to a short debate, in which Messrs. SMITH of Maryland, TUCKER, REYNOLDS, and CUTHBERT, advocated the bill; and Messrs. ROOT, HARDIN, WRIGHT, PICKERING, and WEBSTER, opposed it. The last named gentleman moved to lay the bill on the table, which motion finally prevailed—ayes 65, noes 51; and the bill lies on the table accordingly.

An engrossed bill confirming certain lands in the county of Arkansas, in the Territory of Missouri, to the heirs of Elisha Winter, deceased, to the heirs of William Winter, deceased, and to Gabriel Winter, was read the third time, and ordered to lie on the table.

Engrossed bills of the following titles, to wit:

An act providing for the sale of the tract of land at the British fort, at the Miami of the Lake, at the foot of the rapids; and for other purposes;

An act providing for the sale of the land at the lower rapids of Sandusky river;

An act providing for the distribution of one hundred thousand dollars among the captors of the Algerine vessels, captured and restored to the Dey of Algiers;

An act to alter certain parts of the act providing for the government of the Territory of Missouri;

An act for the relief of Samuel Dick, William Bruce, and Asa Kitchell;

An act for the relief of the heirs of Alexander Roxburgh, deceased;

An act for the relief of William Crawford, Frederick Bates, and William Garrard; and

An act authorising the payment of a sum of money to James Levins; were severally read the third time, and passed.

An engrossed bill for the relief of the Bible Societies of the United States, was read the third time and passed.

Ordered, That the title be "An act for the free importation of stereotype plates, and to encourage the printing and gratuitous distribution of the Scriptures, by the Bible Societies within the United States."

Bills from the Senate of the following titles, to wit:

An act to increase the pension of William Munday, was read the third third time as amended; and

An act further extending the time for issuing and locating military land warrants; and for other purposes; and

An act confirming to the Navigation Company of New Orleans, the use and possession of a lot in the said city; were severally read the third time and passed.

The bill from the Senate concerning the entry of vessels at the port of Middletown, was read twice, and committed to a Committee of the Whole.

The resolution from the Senate "for the printing the laws relative to naturalization," was read three times, and passed.

The House resolved itself into a Committee of the Whole, on the bill from the Senate "authorizing the sale of a lot of ground belonging to the United States, situated in the town of Knoxville, in the State of Tennessee;" and, after some time spent therein, the bill was reported without amendment, and ordered to be read a third time to-morrow.

The House resolved itself into a Committee of the Whole, on the bill concerning Pharaoh Farrow, and others; and, after some time spent therein, the bill was reported without amendment, and ordered to be engrossed, and read a third time to-morrow.

The House resolved itself into a Committee of the Whole, on the bill for the relief of Charles Leveaux Trudeau; and, after some time spent therein, the bill was reported without amendment, and ordered to be engrossed, and read a third time to-morrow.

The House resolved itself into a Committee of the Whole, on the bill to reward the officers and crew of the United States frigate Constitution, for the capture of the British sloop-of-war Levant; and, after some time spent therein, the bill was reported without amendment, and ordered to be engrossed, and read a third time to-morrow.

The House resolved itself into a Committee of the Whole, on the bill from the Senate "providing for the settlement of certain accounts against the Library of Congress, and for establishing the salary of the Librarian;" and, after some time spent therein, the bill was reported with an amendment; which was concurred in by the House, and the bill was ordered to be read a third time to-morrow.

The House resolved itself into a Committee of the Whole, on the bill for the relief of Thomas H. Boyle; and, after some time spent therein, the bill was reported with an amendment; which was concurred in by the House, and the bill ordered to be engrossed, and read a third time to-morrow.

The House resolved itself into a Committee of the Whole, on the bill for the relief of the widow and children of Charles Dolph, deceased; and, after some time spent therein, the bill was reported with an amendment; which was concurred in by the House, and the bill ordered to be engrossed, and read a third time to-morrow.

The House resolved itself into a Committee of the Whole, on the bill authorizing the Comptroller of the Treasury to cancel certain export bonds executed by Casper C. Schalt; and, after some time spent therein, the bill was reported without amendment, and ordered to be engrossed, and read a third time to-morrow.

Ordered, That the Committee of the Whole be discharged from the further consideration of the bill relating to settlers on the lands of the United States, and that it be indefinitely postponed.

A message from the Senate informed the House that the Senate have disagreed to the amendments proposed by this House to the bill from the Senate, "to increase the pension of William Munday;" and they have receded from their fifth amendment to the bill of this House, "making appropriations for the support of Government for the year 1816."

The House resolved itself into a Committee of the Whole, on the bill confirming the titles of certain purchasers of land, who purchased from the Board of Trustees of the Vincennes University; and, after some time spent therein, the bill was reported with an amendment; which was concurred in by the House, and the bill ordered to be engrossed, and read a third time to-morrow.

The House resolved itself into a Committee of the Whole, on the bill for the relief of Young King, a Chief of the Seneca tribe of Indians;

and, after some time spent therein, the bill was reported with amendments; which were concurred in by the House, and the bill ordered to be engrossed, and read a third time to-morrow.

The House resolved itself into a Committee of the Whole, on the bill authorizing the payment of a sum of money to John T. Courtney and Samuel Harrison, or their legal representatives; and, after some time spent therein, the bill was reported without amendment, and ordered to be engrossed, and read a third time to-morrow.

The House resolved itself into a Committee of the Whole, on the bill granting to Amos Spafford the right of pre-emption; and, after some time spent therein, the bill was reported without amendment, and ordered to be engrossed, and read a third time to morrow.

The House then proceeded to the orders of the day. On calling the bill to authorize the appointment of Admirals in the naval service, Mr. PLEASANTS moved that the House go into Committee of the Whole on that bill; which motion was negatived—ayes 38, noes 54.

The bill to establish a National University was also called up by Mr. WILDE, but the House refused to consider it by a large majority.

GENERAL APPROPRIATION BILL.

The House resolved itself into a Committee of the Whole, on the amendments reported by the Senate to the bill making appropriations for the support of Government for the year 1816; and, after some time spent therein, the bill was reported, with the agreement of the Committee to the said amendments, with an amendment to the last; which was read, and concurred in by the House.

The first, second, third, and fourth, of the said amendments of the Senate, were then concurred in by the House.

The question was then taken to concur with the Senate in their fifth amendment, amended to read as follows:

SEC. 2. *And be it further enacted*, That, for the present year, there shall be allowed to the clerks employed in the different offices, and to the principal and engrossing clerks in the offices of the Secretary of the Senate and the Clerk of the House of Representatives, the following additional compensation, that is to say: to all clerks who receive salaries, respectively, not exceeding $800, an addition of twenty-five per cent. to such salary; to those above $800, and not exceeding $1,250, twenty per cent.; to those above $1,250, and not exceeding $1,600, fifteen per cent.; and to those above $1,600, and not exceeding $2,000, ten per cent.; and, moreover, an additional sum of twenty per cent. shall be allowed to the messengers and assistants, respectively; and, for the purposes mentioned in this section, the sum of $28,036 be, and the same is hereby, appropriated.

And the question being taken thereon, it was determined in the negative—yeas 56, nays 65, as follows:

YEAS—Messrs. Adgate, Alexander, Baker, Betts, Boss, Breckenridge, Champion, Clarke of North Carolina, Clark of Kentucky, Clendennin, Conner, Creighton, Culpeper, Cuthbert, Davenport, Desha, Forney,

Forsyth, Gold, Griffin, Greevenor, Hammond, Hanson, Hopkinson, Huger, Hungerford, Irwin of Pennsylvania, Jackson, Law, Lovett, Lowndes, Mayrant, McLean of Kentucky, McLean of Ohio, Middleton, Milnor, Moseley, Murfree, Newton, Ormsby, Pickens, Pickering, Piper, Pleasants, Powell, Reynolds, Savage, Schenck, Smith of Maryland, Sturges, Taggart, Telfair, Tucker, Vose, Ward of Massachusetts, Wendover, Thomas Wilson, and Wright.

NAYS—Messrs. Archer, Barbour, Bassett, Baylies, Bennett, Brooks, Brown, Burnside, Cady, Caldwell, Calhoun, Cannon, Clayton, Clopton, Comstock, Condict, Cooper, Crawford, Crocheron, Darlington, Edwards, Gaston, Glasgow, Hahn, Hale, Hall, Hardin, Hawes, Heister, Jewett, Johnson of Virginia, Kerr of Virginia, Langdon, Lumpkin, Lyle, Lyon, Macley, Marsh, McCoy, McKee, Moore, Nelson of Virginia, Noyes, Parris, Reed, Roane, Root, Ruggles, Sharpe, Smith of Pennsylvania, Smith of Virginia, Southard, Taul, Townsend, Wallace, Ward of New York, Wheaton, Whiteside, Wilcox, Wilde, Williams, Willoughby, and Yancey.

SATURDAY, April 13.

The SPEAKER laid before the House a letter, addressed to him by James Thomas, respecting his accounts, and the charges exhibited against him on account of his conduct as Quartermaster General in the armies of the United States. It was referred to the select committee appointed on the 11th ultimo, on the accounts of the said James Thomas.

Mr. McLEAN, of Ohio, presented a petition of sundry inhabitants of Cincinnati, and its vicinity, in the State of Ohio, praying that some provision may be made for the support of Colonel Zebulon Pike, the father of the late General Pike, whom the petitioners represent to be in reduced circumstances.—Referred to the Committee on Pensions and Revolutionary Claims.

Mr. CALHOUN, from the Committee on National Currency, who were instructed to inquire into the expediency of prohibiting, for a limited time, the exportation of bullion and specie, reported a resolution, that it is inexpedient, at the present time, to make the prohibition; which was read, and ordered to lie on the table.

Mr. FORSYTH, from the Committee on Foreign Affairs, to whom was referred the bill from the Senate "to establish a system of navigation for the United States," reported the same without amendment, and the bill was committed to a Committee of the Whole.

The SPEAKER laid before the House a letter from the Secretary of the Treasury, accompanied with a statement of the loans made to the Government by the several banks within the United States since 1st March, 1812; which were ordered to lie on the table.

Ordered, That the bill making an appropriation for enclosing and improving the public square near the Capitol, be recommitted to a Committee of the Whole to-day.

The House proceeded to reconsider their amendment, proposed to the bill from the Senate, "to increase the pension of William Munday," to which the Senate have disagreed; whereupon, it was resolved that this House recede from their said amendment.

Engrossed bills of the following titles, to wit:

An act concerning Pharaoh Farrow, and others;

An act for the relief of Charles Levaux Trudeau;

An act rewarding the officers and crew of the frigate Constitution, for the capture of the British sloop-of-war Levant;

An act for the relief of the widow and children of Charles Dolph, deceased;

An act for the relief of Thomas H. Boyle;

An act for the relief of Young King, a Chief of the Seneca tribe of Indians;

An act confirming the titles of certain purchasers of lands, who purchased from the Board of Trustees of the Vincennes University;

An act authorizing the payment of a sum of money to John T. Courtney and Samuel Harrison, or their legal representatives;

An act granting Amos Spafford the right of pre-emption;

An act authorizing the Comptroller of the Treasury to cancel certain export bonds executed by Casper C. Schult; were severally read the third time, and passed.

Bills of the Senate, of the following titles, to wit:

An act authorizing the sale of a lot of ground belonging to the United States, situated in the town of Knoxville, and State of Tennessee;

An act providing for the settlement of certain accounts against the Library of Congress, and for establishing the salary of the Librarian, as amended; were severally read the third time, and passed.

The title of the latter bill was amended, by inserting, after the word Congress, these words: "for extending the privilege of using the books therein."

The House resolved itself into a Committee of the Whole, on the joint resolution to indemnify Jabez Mowry, and others; and, after some time spent therein, the resolution was reported, with an amendment; which was concurred in by the House, and the resolution ordered to be engrossed, and read a third time to-day.

The House resolved itself into a Committee of the Whole, on the bill for the relief of Elizabeth Hamilton; and, on the question of ordering the bill to be engrossed for a third reading—

Mr. ROOT spoke at considerable length, and with much zeal against the bill; and moved that it be recommitted to the Committee of Pensions, that they might supervise their report; which motion was disagreed to.

The bill was advocated by Messrs. WRIGHT, JOHNSON, of Kentucky, COMSTOCK, and PICKERING, in support of which various documents were read, and further opposed by Mr. ROOT; after which, the question on engrossing the bill for a third reading, was carried by a large majority.

The House resolved itself into a Committee of the Whole, on the bill, supplementary to the act passed on the 30th day of March, 1802, to regu-

ions, as he preferred the naval defence, but of that kind whose utility and management we were well acquainted with.

Mr. MIDDLETON's motion to insert four instead of three steam frigates, was negatived by a large majority.

Mr. WEBSTER then moved to amend the bill by striking out the words directing two of the batteries to be stationed in the Chesapeake and the other at New Orleans, so as to leave their application to the direction of the President.

Mr. ROBERTSON could not consent to the amendment. The great distance of New Orleans from the Seat of Government and from other parts of the United States, required a constant defence there; it ought not to be left to an uncertain protection. From the Chesapeake and other parts they could make known their wants immediately, and obtain, in case of emergency, prompt aid from the Government, backed also by a numerous representation here. A steam frigate might possibly move from New York to Philadelphia, but he believed it impracticable to navigate the coast with them to New Orleans; a voyage to which, from any of the other cities, was so difficult and dangerous as one across the Atlantic. It was therefore necessary to have one built and stationed there. The President might not deem a frigate so necessary for the Mississippi as he (Mr. R.) did, and he wished to legislate on it to put his object beyond accident or anything else. The Legislature of Louisiana had considered it so important that they had instructed their representatives in Congress to use their best exertions to obtain one for the waters of that State. He repeated that a place so important, so weak and so distant, ought to have a certain and assured protection. However much may have been stated in theory that steam vessels could navigate the ocean, still it remained untried and questionable. He wanted no confidence in the Executive; but the best way, he said, to get business done is do do it ourselves; and he wished, therefore, to secure the defence of New Orleans by a legislative provision.

Mr. CLAY felt the same desire for the defence of New Orleans as his friend from Louisiana; but he must surely be struck, said Mr. C., with the impropriety of directing one steam frigate to be stationed at this place and one at another, &c. We may confidently rely, he said, on the President of the United States for the prudent application of the public force; a contrary course would imply a suspicion of an improper employment of the force by the Executive, which he was certain the Naval Committee did not mean.

Mr. PICKERING had no objection to the amendment. The President of the United States, having here near him a board of experienced naval officers, would be always ready to act on the business with the best advice. He agreed with Mr. FORSYTH, that instead of additional steam batteries, we had better have more seventy-fours, which can move with facility from one point to another. Steam frigates might be peculiarly proper for Charleston and New Orleans, and he

was willing to have two for those places, but more he could not approve.

Mr. PLEASANTS said, that the Naval Committee had taken advice of those best qualified to afford it, and they had sanctioned the course reported in the bill. He thought there was no impropriety in expressing by law where certain engines of defence should be employed. They were floating batteries, and it was no less proper to say they should be placed at particular points, than to direct by law the erection of a land battery at this or that place. Mr. P. adverted to the course pursued by the late enemy, whose first attempts were in the Chesapeake, which he took possession of, and of course of all its extensive waters. Mr. P. also referred to the wide scope which the Chesapeake afforded to the operations of an enemy; the immense trouble and expense required to defend its shores and those of its tributary waters; and to enforce the necessity of providing for it now a particular and adequate defence, by which the expense might be avoided of calling out a double force at so many points to repel an enemy when he came. Though he should vote against the amendment, Mr. P. said he felt every confidence in the Executive, and should acquiesce in the amendment with pleasure, if the House accepted it.

Mr. WEBSTER said if the President of the United States be the Commander-in-Chief of the Naval force, it was certainly improper to take out of his hands the direction of it. He considered the steam frigates strictly a part of that force, and there was an impropriety in not leaving it to his control. The law authorizing the one built at New York did not fix it there permanently; and to do so in this case he thought unnecessary as well as improper, believing that those frigates could, as had been asserted by experienced persons, be moved from one place to another, as the exigency might demand.

Mr. WEBSTER's motion was then agreed to by a large majority, and the bill, as amended, ordered to a third reading *nem. con.*

MONDAY, April 15.

Mr. YANCEY, from the Committee of Claims, made a report on the petition of Thomas Miller and Stephen Baker; which was read; when Mr. Y. reported a bill for the relief of Thomas Miller and Stephen Baker; which was read twice, and committed to the Committee of the Whole on the bill for the relief of Bowie and Kurtz, and others.

Ordered, That the Committee of Claims be discharged from a further consideration of the several petitions, and other matters referred to them during the present session, and upon which they have not reported to the House.

Mr. ROBERTSON, from the Committee on the Public Lands, to which have been referred the several petitions from inhabitants of the State of Louisiana and the Mississippi Territory, in relation to the decisions of the Boards of Commissioners on their claims to land, made a report thereon; which was read; when Mr. R. reported a bill to establish a Board of Commissioners to decide finally on claims to land in Louisiana and the Mississippi Territory; which was read twice, and, together with the report, ordered to lie on the table.

Mr. LOWNDES, from the Committee of Ways and Means, reported a bill increasing the compensation of Public Ministers (to $12,000;) which was read twice, and committed to the Committee of the Whole on the report of the Committee of Ways and Means upon the subject of revenue.

Mr. LOWNDES also reported a bill for reducing the duties on licenses to retailers of wines, spirituous liquors, and foreign merchandise; which was read twice, and committed to the Committee of the Whole last mentioned.

Mr. NEWTON, from the Committee of Commerce and Manufactures, reported a bill to authorize the building of three light-houses, viz: one on Race Point; one on Point Gammon; and one on the island of Petite Manon, in the State of Massachusetts; which was read twice, and committed to the Committee of the Whole on the report of the Committee of Ways and Means upon the subject of revenue.

Mr. CREIGHTON, from the Committee on Roads and Canals, reported a bill to authorize the surveying and making a road in the Illinois Territory; which was read twice, and committed to a Committee of the Whole.

Mr. CREIGHTON also reported a bill making an appropriation for repairing the road from Duck River, in the State of Tennessee, to Madisonville, in the Mississippi Territory, and between Fort Hawkins, in the State of Georgia, and Fort Stoddard; which was read twice, and committed to a Committee of the Whole.

Mr. PLEASANTS, from the Committee on Naval Affairs, to whom was referred the bill from the Senate "to reward the officers and crew of the United States frigate Constitution," made a report thereon; which was read, and, together with the bill, ordered to lie on the table.

Mr. JENNINGS, from the committee appointed on the 12th instant, reported a bill supplemental to an act entitled "An act granting bounties in land and extra pay to certain Canadian volunteers;" which was read twice, and ordered to be engrossed and read a third time to-morrow.

The amendment proposed by the Senate to the bill "to abolish the existing duties on spirits distilled within the United States, and to lay other duties in lieu of these at present imposed on licenses to distillers of spirituous liquors," was read and concurred in by the House.

The amendments proposed by the Senate to the bill "to enable the people of the Indiana Territory to form a constitution and State government, and for the admission of such State into the Union on an equal footing with the original States," were read and concurred in by the House.

The House proceeded to consider the report of the joint committee appointed to examine the business depending before the two Houses, to ascertain what portion required to be acted on at the present session, and when it will be expedient to close the same; whereupon the House came to the following resolution:

Resolved, That the President of the Senate, and Speaker of the House of Representatives be authorized to close this session, by the adjournment of their respective Houses on Saturday, the 20th day of April, instant.

An engrossed resolution, entitled "A resolution to indemnify Jabez Mowry and others," was read the third time, and passed.

Engrossed bills of the following titles, to wit:

An act supplementary to the act passed on the 30th day of March, 1802, to regulate trade and intercourse with the Indian tribes, and to preserve peace on the frontiers;

An act for the gradual increase of the Navy of the United States; and

An act providing for the sale of certain lands in the State of Ohio formerly set apart for refugees from Canada and Nova Scotia; were severally read the third time, and passed.

A message from the Senate informed the House that the Senate have passed the bill "supplementary to the act to provide additional revenues for defraying the expenses of Government and maintaining the public credit, by laying a direct tax upon the United States, and to provide for assessing and collecting the same," with amendments; in which they ask the concurrence of this House.

The House proceeded to consider the resolutions recommended by the joint committee appointed to inquire into the expediency of making certain alterations in the mode of transacting the business of Congress; and the said resolutions being again read, the further consideration thereof was postponed until to-morrow.

On motion of Mr. BETTS, the Secretary of the Treasury was directed to lay before Congress, at the commencement of the next session, (as fully as the same can be made,) a statement of the amount of loan-office and final settlement certificates, issued under the authority of the Continental Congress, and now outstanding, unsatisfied; designating such as are barred by statutes of limitation only, and such as remain unsettled for other reasons.

The House resolved itself into a Committee of the Whole on the bill regulating the currency within the United States of the gold coins of Great Britain, France, Portugal, and Spain, and the crowns of France, and five-franc pieces of Napoleon; and after some time spent therein, the bill was reported with amendments; which were concurred in by the House, and the bill was ordered to be engrossed, and read a third time to-morrow.

The House resolved itself into a Committee of the Whole on the bill concerning John P. Maxwell and Hugh H. Maxwell; and after some time spent therein, the bill was reported without amendment, and ordered to be engrossed, and read a third time to-morrow.

The House resolved itself into a Committee

of the Whole on the bill to provide for the appointment of a surveyor of the public lands in the Territories of Illinois and Missouri; and after some time spent therein, reported it with an amendment; which was concurred in by the House, and the bill ordered to be engrossed, and read a third time to-morrow.

The House resolved itself into a Committee of the Whole on the bill supplementary to the act entitled "An act for the final adjustment of land titles in the State of Louisiana and Territory of Missouri;" and after some time spent therein the Committee rose, reported progress, and had leave to sit again.

The House resolved itself into a Committee of the Whole on the bill for the confirmation of claims to land in the western district of Louisiana; and after some time spent therein, the bill was reported with amendments; which were concurred in by the House, and the bill was ordered to be engrossed, and read a third time to-morrow.

The House resolved itself into a Committee of the Whole on the bill fixing the compensation of the Clerk of the House of Representatives; and after some time spent therein, the bill was reported with amendments; which were concurred in by the House, and the bill ordered to be engrossed, and read a third time to-morrow.

The House resolved itself into a Committee of the Whole on the bill from the Senate "for the relief of Edward Wilson," and after some time spent therein, the bill was reported with amendments; which were concurred in by the House, and the bill was ordered to be read a third time to-morrow.

The House resolved itself into a Committee of the Whole on the bill from the Senate "further supplementary to the act entitled 'An act providing for the indemnification of certain claimants of public lands in the Mississippi Territory;" and after some time spent therein, the bill was reported with amendments; which were concurred in by the House, and the bill was ordered to be read a third time to-morrow.

The House resolved itself into a Committee of the Whole on the bill from the Senate "respecting the late officers and crew of the sloop-of-war Wasp;" and after some time spent therein, the bill was reported with amendments; which were concurred in by the House, and the bill ordered to be read a third time to-morrow.

The House resolved itself into a Committee of the Whole on the bill from the Senate "for the relief of the Baltimore and Massachusetts Bible Societies;" and after some time spent therein, the bill was reported without amendment, and ordered to be read a third time to-morrow.

The House resolved itself into a Committee of the Whole on the bill to establish post roads; and after some time spent therein, the bill was reported with amendments; which were concurred in by the House.

The said bill was further amended, and ordered to be engrossed, and read a third time to-morrow.

ELIZABETH HAMILTON.

An engrossed bill, entitled "An act for the relief of Elizabeth Hamilton," was read the third time; and, on the question, "Shall this bill pass?" it passed in the affirmative—yeas 84, nays 30, as follows:

YEAS—Messrs. Atherton, Bassett, Boss, Breckenridge, Brown, Cady, Caldwell, Calhoun, Champion, Chappell, Chipman, Cilley, Clark of Kentucky, Clayton, Conner, Cooper, Creighton, Culpeper, Cuthbert, Darlington, Davenport, Forney, Gold, Goldsborough, Hale, Hardin, Henderson, Hopkinson, Hungerford, Ingham, Irwin of Pennsylvania, Jackson, Jewett, Johnson of Virginia, Kent, Kerr of Virginia, King of Massachusetts, King of North Carolina, Langdon, Law, Lowndes, Lyon, Marsh, Mason, McKee, McLean of Kentucky, McLean of Ohio, Middleton, Moseley, Murfree, Nelson of Massachusetts, Nelson of Virginia, Newton, Noyes, Pickens, Pickering, Pitkin, Pleasants, Powell, Ruggles, Savage, Schenck, Sharpe, Sheffey, Smith of Pennsylvania, Smith of Md., Stearns, Sturges, Taggart, Tate, Throop, Tucker, Vose, Ward of Massachusetts, Ward of New York, Webster, Wendover, Wheaton, Wilcox, Wilde, Wilkin, Williams, Wright, and Yates.

NAYS—Messrs. Alexander, Baker, Barbour, Bennett, Betts, Brooks, Clendennin, Clopton, Condict, Crawford, Crocheron, Desha, Edwards, Glasgow, Griffin, Hahn, Lyle, Mackay, McCoy, Moore, Parris, Roane, Robertson, Root, Smith of Virginia, Southard, Telfair, Townsend, Willoughby, and Woodward.

Tuesday, April 16.

Mr. YANCEY, from the Committee of Claims, made a report on the petition of Samuel Manac; which was read; when Mr. Y. reported a bill for the relief of Samuel Manac; which was read twice and committed to a Committee of the Whole on the bill for the relief of Bowie and Kurtz and others.

Mr. ARCHER, from the Committee on Expenditures in the Navy Department, made a report; which was read and ordered to lie on the table.

Mr. FORSYTH, from the Committee on Foreign Relations, made a report on the various petitions respecting the plaster trade, and the trade of the British West Indies, recommending that no importations be permitted from British colonies in America, or the British West India islands, but in American vessels. The report was ordered to lie on the table.

Mr. JOHNSON, of Kentucky, from the Committee on Military Affairs, reported a bill for the liquidation of certain claims, and for other purposes; which was read twice and ordered to lie on the table.

The amendments reported by the Committee of the Whole on the 11th instant, to the bill for the relief of Moses Turner, were taken up, and concurred in by the House, and the bill ordered to be engrossed, and read a third time to-morrow.

The amendments proposed by the Senate to the bill "supplementary to the act to provide additional revenues for defraying the expenses of Government and maintaining the public credit, by laying a direct tax upon the United States, and

1377　　　　　　HISTORY OF CONGRESS.　　　　　　1378

April, 1816.　　　　　Clerk of the House—Compensation to Collectors.　　　　　H. of R.

to provide for assessing and collecting the same," were read, and referred to the Committee of Ways and Means.

Engrossed bills of the following titles, to wit: An act supplemental to an act entitled "An act granting bounties in land and extra pay to certain Canadian volunteers;"

An act regulating the currency within the United States of the gold and silver coins of Great Britain, France, Portugal, and Spain, and the crowns of France and five franc pieces;

An act concerning John P. Maxwell and Hugh H. Maxwell;

An act for the appointment of a surveyor of the public lands in the Territories of Illinois and Missouri;

An act for the confirmation of claims to land in the western district of Louisiana; and

An act to establish post roads; were severally read the third time, and passed.

Bills of the Senate of the following titles, to wit:

An act for the relief of the Baltimore and Massachusetts Bible Societies;

An act further supplementary to the act entitled "An act providing for the indemnification of certain claimants of the public lands in Mississippi Territory, as amended;"

An act respecting the late officers and crew of the sloop-of-war Wasp, as amended; and

An act for the relief of Edward Wilson, as amended; were severally read the third time, and passed.

The House resolved itself into a Committee of the Whole on the report of the Committee of Ways and Means upon the subject of revenue, and upon the several bills thereto committed; and after some time spent therein, the committee rose and reported the bill making appropriations for rebuilding light-houses, and for completing the plan of lighting them on the plan of Winslow Lewis; for placing beacons and buoys; for preservation of Little Gull Island, and for surveying the coast of the United States; and the bill to authorize the building of three light-houses, viz: one on Race Point, one on Point Gammon, and one on the island of Petite Manon, in the State of Massachusetts; with amendments to each. The amendments were concurred in by the House, and the bill ordered to be engrossed, and read a third time to-morrow.

The House resolved itself into a Committee of the Whole on the bill from the Senate "for the relief of Richard Mitchell;" and after some time spent therein, the bill was reported without amendment, and ordered to be read a third time to-morrow.

The House resolved itself into a Committee of the Whole on the bill for the relief of Bowie and Kurtz, and others, and upon the several subjects thereto committed; and after some time spent therein, the Committee rose and reported the bill for the relief of Thomas Miller and Stephen Baker, and the bill for the relief of Samuel Manac, and the bill from the Senate " for the relief of Xaverio Naudi," without amendment.

14th Con. 1st Sess.—44

The question was then taken, Shall the bill for the relief of Thomas Miller and Stephen Baker be engrossed and read a third time? and it was determined in the negative—54 to 48. And so the said bill was rejected.

The bill for the relief of Samuel Manac was ordered to be engrossed, and, together with the bill for the relief of Xaverio Naudi, read a third time to-morrow.

The House refused, by a large majority, to consider the bill confirming to General Jackson, Colonel Hawkins, &c. certain lands bestowed on them by the Creek Indians in the late treaty.

CLERK OF THE HOUSE.

The engrossed bill to increase the salary of the Clerk of the House, and the compensation of the subordinate clerks twenty per cent. for extra duty in bringing up old arrears of business, was read the third time.

Mr. Hardin opposed the bill, with some warmth, and demanded the yeas and nays on its passage. It was advocated by Mr. Hopkinson and Mr. McKee, and passed—yeas 64, nays 51, as follows:

Yeas—Messrs. Alexander, Atherton, Baer, Bassett, Betts, Boss, Calhoun, Champion, Cilley, Clark of Kentucky, Clayton, Conner, Creighton, Cuthbert, Edwards, Gaston, Gold, Grosvenor, Hammond, Henderson, Hopkinson, Huger, Jewett, Johnson of Virginia, Johnson of Kentucky, Law, Love, Lovett, Lowndes, Mayrant, McKee, McLean of Kentucky, McLean of Ohio, Middleton, Moore, Nelson of Massachusetts, Nelson of Virginia, Newton, Pickens, Pickering, Pinkney, Pleasants, Powell, Reynolds, Ruggles, Savage, Schenck, Sharpe, Sheffey, Smith of Pennsylvania, Smith of Maryland, Stearns, Stuart, Sturges, Taggart, Telfair, Tucker, Vose, Ward of Mississippi, Webster, Wendover, Wilkin, Woodward, and Wright.

Nays—Messrs. Archer, Baker, Barbour, Bateman, Bennett, Brooks, Bryan, Cannon, Clendennin, Clopton, Comstock, Crocheron, Darlington, Forsyth, Griffin, Hahn, Hale, Hardin, Hawes, Heister, Hungerford, Kent, Kerr of Virginia, King of North Carolina, Langdon, Lumpkin, Lyle, Lyon, Maclay, Marsh, McCoy, Milnor, Parris, Piper, Roane, Robertson, Root, Smith of Virginia, Southard, Taul, Throop, Wallace, Ward of New York, Whiteside, Wilcox, Wilde, Williams, Willoughby, Thomas Wilson, William Wilson, and Yancey.

COMPENSATION OF COLLECTORS.

The House went into a Committee of the Whole on the joint resolution for the relief of James H. McCulloch, Collector of the port of Baltimore, allowing an extra compensation to him and other collectors, whose emoluments were materially reduced by the operation of the restrictive system. The resolution is as follows:

Resolved, &c. That the President of the United States be authorized to allow an extra compensation for a limited time to those officers of the customs whose emoluments were diminished below a reasonable salary during the restrictive system.

The resolution gave rise to a short debate, peculiarly interesting, from the brief but eloquent narrative given by Mr. Pinkney of the gallantry of Mr. McCulloch, who, though nearly eighty

1379   HISTORY OF CONGRESS.   1380

H. of R.   *Proceedings.*   April, 1816.

years of age, and exempted by years and by office from the toils of military service, yet shouldered his musket when the British approached Baltimore in 1814, entered the ranks as a private soldier, and was the foremost to meet the enemy at North Point, where he received a wound which renders him a cripple for life.

The resolution was also supported by Mr. SMITH, and Mr. WRIGHT; and opposed by Mr. SHEFFEY and Mr. GROSVENOR, not from any want of regard for the character and conduct of the petitioner; but on the ground of the inexpediency of making good the reduced emoluments of the collectors, who took their office with a foreknowledge of its precarious profits, and because it was in that character alone Mr. McCulloch appeared before the House for relief.

The resolution was reported to the House without amendment, and laid on the table.

The House resolved itself into a Committee of the whole House on the bill to authorize the survey of two millions of acres of the public lands, in lieu of that quantity heretofore authorized to be surveyed, in the Territory of Michigan, as military bounty lands; and after some time spent therein, the bill was reported without amendment. The bill was then amended at the Clerk's table, and the House adjourned.

WEDNESDAY, April 17.

Mr. PLEASANTS, from the Committee on Naval Affairs reported a bill appropriating the sum of two thousand five hundred dollars to Captain Stewart and crew, of the Syren, for a capture during the war with Tripoli; which was read twice, and committed to the Committee of the Whole to-day.

Mr. PLEASANTS also reported a bill authorizing the payment of a sum of money to John Rodgers, and others; which was read twice, and committed to the last mentioned Committee of the Whole.

Mr. PLEASANTS also reported a bill authorizing payment of a sum of money to Joseph Stewart, and others; which was read twice, and also committed to the last mentioned Committee of the Whole.

Mr. JOHNSON, of Kentucky, from the Committee on Military Affairs, reported a bill providing for cases of lost military land warrants, and discharges for faithful services; which was read twice, and ordered to be engrossed and read a third time to-morrow.

Ordered, That the Committee on Foreign Affairs be discharged from a further consideration of the resolution of the 7th of February last, relative to the trade between the United States and the British West India islands.

Mr. NELSON, from the committee appointed to inquire into the official conduct of Judge Tallmadge, made a report; which was read, and the resolution therein contained was concurred in by the House, as follows:

Resolved, That all further proceedings in relation to the inquiry into the official conduct of Matthias B. Tallmadge, be postponed until the next session of Congress.

On motion of Mr. STEPHENSON, the Committee on the Public Lands were instructed to inquire into the expediency of establishing an office for the disposal of the public lands at Edwardsville, Madison county, Illinois Territory.

On motion of Mr. EASTON, the Secretary of the Treasury was requested to procure all the information he may be enabled to obtain, in relation to the lead mines of the United States, in the counties of Washington and St. Genevieve, in the Missouri Territory, and report the same, at the next session of Congress, to this House.

The Message received yesterday from the PRESIDENT OF THE UNITED STATES, communicating copies of a Convention concluded between the United States and the Cherokee Indians, on the second day of March last, was referred to the Committee on Foreign Affairs.

Engrossed bills of the following titles to wit:

An act making appropriations for rebuilding light-houses, and for completing the plan of lighting them, according to the improvement of Winslow Lewis; for placing beacons and buoys; for the preservation of Little Gull Island; and for surveying the coast of the United States;

An act to authorize the building of three lighthouses, viz: one on Race Point, one on Point Gammon, and one on the island of Petite Manon, in the State of Massachusetts;

An act for the relief of Samuel Manac; and

An act for the relief of Moses Turner; were severally read the third time and passed.

Bills from the Senate, of the following titles, to wit:

An act for the relief of Xaverio Naudi; and

An act for the relief of Richard Mitchell; were severally read the third time, and passed.

The bill, under discussion yesterday, when the House adjourned, to authorize the survey of two millions of acres of public land in lieu of that quantity ordered to be surveyed in Michigan Territory, was, on motion, laid on the table.

The bills concerning field officers of the militia, and the bill for the relief of David Coffin, David and William Rodman, and Samuel Rodman, jr.; passed through Committees of the whole House, and were ordered to a third reading.

The bill authorizing the Potomac Company to acquire certain lands by purchase, and dispose of water rights, was indefinitely postponed.

The House resolved itself into a Committee of the Whole on the bill to allow the crew of the privateer Roger the legal bounty on thirty-seven prisoners captured in a British vessel, after the treaty was ratified, but within the time allowed for the continuance of hostilities in the latitude where the capture was made.

A motion, made by Mr. SMITH, of Maryland, to make the provisions of the bill general, and embrace all similar captures, produced some debate, and was finally negatived.

The bill was reported to the House, and ordered to a third reading.

1381   HISTORY OF CONGRESS.   1382

APRIL, 1816.   *Petition of John McCauley—Specie Payments.*   H. OF R.

PETITION OF JOHN McCAULEY.

Mr. PLEASANTS, from the Committee on Naval Affairs, to whom was referred the petition of John McCauley, prize agent for the officers and crew of the brig Vixen, during the war with the Regency of Tripoli, with the report of the Secretary of the Navy, made a report thereon; which was read, and the resolution therein contained was concurred in by the House. The report is as follows:

The Committee on Naval Affairs, to whom was referred the report of the Secretary of the Navy on the petition of John McCauley, prize agent, report:

That they have considered the report of the Secretary of the Navy, together with the opinion of the Attorney General on the case of the Madonna Catapoliana, captured by the Syren for a breach of the blockade of the port of Tripoli in the war carried on by the United States against that Power. The Attorney General gives it as his opinion that the subject is a proper one for the consideration of Congress, as he does not think it different in principle from the case of the Algerine vessels taken in the late war against that Power, and restored at the Treaty of Peace, and for which the captors have been compensated by a bill which has passed this House. The Algerine vessels were taken in open war from an enemy; the Madonna Catapoliana was taken from a neutral and friendly Power for a breach of blockade, and restored without having ever been carried before a court of admiralty. The committee think it would be carrying the principle too far to say that a vessel, belonging to a friendly and neutral Power, captured for breach of blockade, and restored to the neutral by the commander of the blockading squadron, without the case having been decided on by a court of admiralty, [should oblige the Government] to pay to the captors the supposed value of such prize. They therefore recommend to the House the following resolution:

Resolved, That it is inexpedient to grant the prayer of the said petition, and that the petitioners have leave to withdraw their petition and documents.

NAVY DEPARTMENT, *March* 29, 1816.

SIR: I have the honor, in obedience to an order of the House of Representatives of the 5th of February last, to transmit to you, to be laid before them, the petition of John McCauley, with the papers connected therewith, and a copy of the opinion of the Attorney General of the United States, to whom I referred the points of law which the subject involved. Should Congress decide, in conformity with the opinion of the Attorney General, to grant the amount of the original valuation of the brig Transfer, a special appropriation will be necessary for that object. It will remain for Congress to judge of the principle and policy which led to the restoration of the ship Madonna Catapoliana without a judicial appeal, and how far the case is analogous to the late transactions with Algiers.

All which is respectfully submitted.

I have the honor to be, very respectfully, sir, your obedient servant,   B. W. CROWNINSHIELD.

The honorable the SPEAKER
     of the House of Representatives.

WASHINGTON, *March* 27, 1816.

SIR: I have examined the papers transmitted to me with your letter of the 12th of last month, and have now the honor to submit, according to your request, the following opinions upon the cases which they present:

1st. It appears that the brig Transfer was captured off Tripoli for a breach of blockade on the 17th of March, 1804, by a part of the squadron under the command of Commodore Preble; that she was regularly condemned as a prize of war; and that she was taken by the Commodore at a valuation of $6,000, and placed in the service of the United States, where she co-operated as a cruiser with the squadron afterwards said in the course of its subsequent belligerent operations. Under such a state of facts, I do not think that the captors are divested of their prize interest. They are entitled to it at the hands of the Government, which thus became the purchaser of the prize. Considering this interest as a vested one on their part, I can see no objection to a payment of the amount by the Navy Department, provided there be any existing appropriation of money to cover such payment. I also think that the portion of the prize to which the United States are entitled should, as in other cases, be applied to the use of the navy pension fund, as directed by the ninth section of the act of Congress of the 23d April, 1800.

2d. In regard to the ship Madonna Catapoliana, captured by a part of the same squadron off Tripoli, on the 23d March, 1804, and restored to the former owners by the authority of the Commodore, before any condemnation or judicial proceedings had, it would seem alike equitable that the captors should be reimbursed. I forbear, at this time, the expression of any more direct opinion upon this case, the power of Congress being fully competent to act upon it, as in the case now before that body of the Algerine vessels lately surrendered, from which the present is not, in principle, distinguishable.

I pray you, sir, to receive as an apology for this late answer to your letter, that, when it was received, and for some weeks afterwards, my constant public engagements at the Supreme Court of the United States prevented an attention to other subjects.

With great respect, I have the honor to be, &c.,
     RICHARD RUSH.

Hon. B. W. CROWNINSHIELD,
     Secretary of the Navy.

SPECIE PAYMENTS.

The House then resolved itself into a Committee of the Whole, on the bill providing for the collection of debts due to the Government in the lawful money of the country—in other words, to compel the banks to resume the payment of specie.

Mr. CALHOUN took a succinct view of the bill, and recapitulated briefly the evils which demanded this measure.

Mr. SMITH, of Maryland, said he felt great difficulty on this subject; but, to make the measure as unexceptionable as possible, he moved to insert the 1st of March next, instead of the 31st of December, as the day on which the act should commence its operation. In the present situation of the currency of the country, he observed, no specie being paid anywhere, except in the New England States, if indeed there be, the measure may be attended with great inconvenience to the Treasury, and also to the interior of the country, if the banks are compelled in a short time to pay in coin. In considering the present state of the banks, it may be doubted whether it can be done. In the large cities it would be attended with great difficulty, and with stagnation of business, because no man will make engagements on credit; every one will be cautious in making contracts to pay at a future day. The banks must, in a great degree, stop their discounts; their stoppage will paralyze those around them; to what extent he could not say, but that it would be great, Mr. S. argued, from the result of the late attempt in Virginia, where the banks, by similar coercion, lessened their discounts greatly, in consequence of which flour had fallen to five dollars a barrel. Will you, he asked, be able to collect your taxes there? He apprehended not. Mr. S. said, he had never been able, with all his practice and experience, to understand the subject of money fully. He had a hope, however, that, if extended to March, with the aid of the Bank of the United States, this measure might succeed. The bank would contain a great part of the hoarded treasure of the country; after the three first instalments were got in, with importations from abroad, the bank would be able to pay specie. They will postpone going into operation until they are thus prepared; and that would not be until the 1st of January. This made it necessary, he thought, for the time in this bill to be extended to March, which would soften the measure and make it less dangerous. But what would be done in the interior, Mr. S. said, he did not know. The Secretary of the Treasury would, doubtless, make the change as easy as possible by Treasury regulations; but as the present officer, it was understood, would not continue, he could not tell what would be the effect; he feared much from the measure. He hoped it would likewise be aided somewhat by the tariff, which would lessen the extent of the India trade, which, of course, would not consume so much of the specie of the country. Mr. S. cited some fiscal transactions in Baltimore to support his opinion, that the Secretary of the Treasury would do everything in his power to lessen the pressure, and enable the State banks to enter into the proposed measure without great pressure on the Treasury or on the country, but did not believe the bill would be beneficial or proper, unless the time was extended beyond the day proposed; and he hoped, therefore, his amendment would be adopted.

Mr. Hopkinson said, make this measure as they would, still it must inevitably be very oppressive. But all had agreed it was wrong to let things go on in their present course, and that Congress should devise a remedy for them. In considering this question, the time, he said, was of much consequence. In any great change in the community, time was necessary to enable them to meet it. In the present it was not, in his opinion, necessary, to fix any precise period; but a better rule, he thought, might be adopted. Mr. H. presumed, the State banks should commence paying specie at the same time the United States Bank should begin; because, said he, if you compel the State banks to open their vaults and give out their coin, it will all be drawn from them, and they cannot continue to redeem their notes with specie. On the other hand, if the United States Bank commences before the State banks do, the same evil will result to it; because two banks cannot exist at the same time, one paying specie, and the other not. Mr. H. said, he could wish, therefore, that the State institutions should start fair with the Bank of the United States, and instead of fixing a time at all in the bill, which might prove too soon or too late, he hoped it would be modified so as to say, from and after the time at which the Bank of the United States should commence its operations. [This proposition being decided not to be at this time in order, no question was taken on it.]

Mr. Ward, of Massachusetts, was opposed to Mr. Smith's motion, and to any extension of the period whatever; because it would be injurious to the United States, and unjust to particular parts of the Union. The Constitution, he said, required that the duties to Government should be levied in an uniform and impartial manner, and such a provision would make the Constitutional injunction null and void; for where would be the difference, Mr. W. inquired, between directly and expressly allowing a difference, in collecting the revenues, to some parts of the country, and passing a law which would indirectly create such a difference? In some sections of the country the State bank notes are as good as specie; in others they are greatly depreciated. Could it be right that one section of the United States should be bound to pay in gold or silver, or in paper superior to that in other parts? They had been told of the bad consequences which would ensue from adjourning without applying a remedy to the disordered state of our currency—the proposed measure, he thought, would put it out of their power to do anything. He could not understand the subject as other gentlemen did; he thought it would be better to let the State banks alone; if they choose to pay or not to pay specie, still let them alone, if they can get on—we, said Mr. W., have nothing to do with them at all; but it is due to ourselves to refuse their notes when they do not pay specie. There was no mystery in this business, any more than in transactions with individuals. If they do not pay specie let their notes go out of circulation, or let the United States refuse to take them. It had been said, the Government could not get on, could not collect its duties in particular parts of the country, without the aid of this measure;—this opinion he thought erroneous—the Government would find no difficulty in the case. Suppose there was not a dollar of specie or coin in the United States, could not the Government still get on in its negotiations with the community without resorting to any measure like this? It had been stated in the course of the session, that the premiums received for difference between Treasury notes and depreciated notes amounted to $30,000—could it be right, he asked, for individuals to be defrauded in this way? Suppose the Government were to say, that Treasury notes should be received for taxes, &c.—the people everywhere owed Government, and the citizens would very cheerfully take them. Why could not the Government issue Treasury notes, then, and direct that no other paper should be received in the public dues? They would soon circulate everywhere, and be had without difficulty. He thought the operation would be easy and highly expedient, and it ought not to be delayed. If the depreciated bank notes would then answer the common purposes of marketing, &c., let them be used—when they cease to be useful they will go out of circulation. Mr. W. repeated, that it was partial and wrong to exact the taxes in one part of the country in gold or silver, or what was equal to specie, and receive in other parts a depreciated paper. The banks in Boston had never ceased to pay when demanded of them; and they had persevered in it, too, without any aid from the Government. He recapitulated a few arguments against the amendment, and concluded with the opinion, that it would be better to make the bill take effect from and after its passsage.

Mr. TUCKER said, he rose to express his dissent to the proposition of the gentleman from Maryland (Mr. SMITH.) As one of the committee which had reported the bill, he had conceived the first of January to be upon the whole the most proper period to commence the operation of the provisions contemplated by that committee. He hoped the House would coincide in their opinion; he hoped we should not now shrink from the adoption of measures which were intimately connected with and formed a part of that system of which the bank bill was a principal feature. The evils under which this nation was laboring had long been of serious and threatening magnitude. The currency of the country was in a state of disorder and embarrassment which had been too often strongly depicted, and was too generally and seriously felt to require any farther comment from him. In the strong language of the gentleman from South Carolina, the disease was deep-rooted, and it required the most rigorous remedies to produce a cure. Nothing but a sense of the absolute necessity of the strongest measures to restore soundness to the circulating medium, had induced the assent of Congress to the establishment of a National Bank. It was now to be seen whether we would follow up that important measure by others which were necessary to give it complete efficacy, and which had always been contemplated by its friends as intimately and essentially connected with its success. He hoped the Committee would not be unmindful of the change this bill had undergone since it was first reported to the House, and that it would be recollected that everything of a harsh and penal character had been erased from it. It had been recommitted on the motion of the chairman of the committee, with a view to an amendment, in which the select committee had concurred. They had stricken out the clause imposing an increased duty upon the notes of such banks as refused to redeem their notes in specie, not from any hesitation as to the ultimate propriety of adopting such provisions,

but from a hope that measures less energetic might effect the great object they had in view. Should these fail, he believed there was a very general sentiment in the House favorable to the adoption at a future period of the vigorous means which at first had been reported by the committee. At present, however, the House was not called upon to decide upon that proposition. The measure now proposed, and to which their assent is asked, is one so palpably correct, so manifestly right and proper, that he had hoped it would have met with no opposition. What is proposed? Merely that the officers of the United States should not receive the duties and other sums payable to the Government in the depreciated paper of those banks which will not redeem their notes and fairly discharge their debts. Can such a measure be disapproved? Shall not the United States, who lay the taxes, have the privilege of prescribing the medium in which they shall be paid? Shall the nation alone be the sufferer by a tender law? Shall the humblest citizen in the community have a right to refuse to receive of his debtor the depreciated and worthless paper which is in circulation, and shall the nation be compelled to submit to such a payment? By no means. Justice to the nation, justice to the various parts of this Confederacy, justice to public creditors require that the revenues should be paid in a sound and undepreciated currency. The system at present existing, operates with peculiar hardship on some particular sections of the Union, and on some particular seaport towns. In the present state of things, the duties and taxes not only fall much more heavily upon those portions of the Union where the paper is least depreciated, but another consequence fatal to their interest is produced. Their seaport towns will be materially injured. The importing merchant in Norfolk, who can pay the duties on his cargo in Baltimore in paper worth twelve per cent. less than that of Norfolk, will find it to his interest to enter at Baltimore—pay the duties there and send his goods coastwise to Norfolk. He had heard from one of the most intelligent men in Virginia, lately from Norfolk, that things were already taking that course. The gentleman from Maryland could inform us whether it was really the case. For his own part he believed it, not only because of the source whence the information had been derived, but because it was the natural course of things. Twelve per cent. difference upon the amounts of duties on a large importation would, he presumed, justify the course of business to which he alluded. Its effect cannot be misconceived. It must tend to accumulate capital where the duties can be paid low, and to draw it from those ports where they were high. Thus by a strange injustice making, in effect, a distinction in favor of those who least deserve peculiar encouragement, whilst at the same time the amount and perhaps the security of the revenue may be considerably impaired. He, for one, was anxious to put an end to this state of things.

The Northern and the Southern States were equally liable to be sufferers from a situation of affairs calculated chiefly to benefit Baltimore, Philadelphia, and perhaps New York; and it was therefore necessary to adopt, as promptly as prudence would permit, a measure which would restore a just equality between the various sections of the Union. He would not dilate further on the general principles upon which he believed the proposed measure to be justified, but confine himself to the question raised by the motion of the gentleman from Maryland. That gentleman, on whose judgment the greatest reliance might be placed, had in the course of his remarks informed us that the Bank of the United States would most probably be in operation by the first of January. If so, and he had no doubt of the correctness of the opinion, upon what principles could the proposal to postpone the operation of the bill under consideration be justified? If, for two months after the United States Bank goes into operation, we permit the State banks to go on without paying specie—if we suffer them to continue the places of deposite of our revenue; if we give a credit to their depreciated paper by permitting it to be received in the collection of the revenue, shall we do justice to the bank we have lately chartered—shall we derive to the nation the benefit we anticipated from its establishment? Far from it. The inevitable effect will be, either to postpone the operations of the new bank till March, or, if it commences business, to expose it to the demands of the State banks, which collect its paper and draw out its specie, whilst on their part they will refuse to redeem their own notes with the same good faith. Moreover, the present inequality in the payment of duties will continue, as the duties in the Middle States will still be paid in their depreciated paper. And what good end was to be effected by the postponement? A little more time is asked. What use has been made of the past—what is likely to be made of the future, which cannot equally be effected by fixing on the first of January? The gentleman told the House very truly, that specie would be necessarily imported. Is there not time for these importations? If an effort was to be made to increase the quantity of coin in the country by importation, he believed that it would easily be effected by the Fall arrivals; and that no additional advantage would in this point of view accrue from extending the period during the Winter months of January and February. As, therefore, he was opposed to the continuation of the mischief from which we now suffer, and as he could see no necessity for the delay, he was decidedly opposed to it. He apprehended, seriously apprehended, that every day would add to the difficulty of effecting the desirable object of returning to a specie circulation. The banks now in existence—opposed from motives of self-interest to specie redemption—were almost too strong for the legislative arm. They formed a colossal power which it was difficult to resist. We already felt how arduous was the undertaking to control them, and to resist their influence. The longer we delay, the more seriously is that influence to be apprehended.

Mr. T. said, that he should consider it better to pass no law on the subject, than to extend the period mentioned in the bill. It would furnish an irresistible argument against the Secretary of the Treasury, should he after the first of January refuse to receive the paper of banks which do not redeem their notes. It would then be said, that Congress, by passing this bill (as proposed to be amended) had impliedly authorized the payment of the revenues in depreciated paper to the first of March. With such a construction in their favor, it is scarcely probable that the Secretary of the Treasury, who has been already compelled to yield to the force of circumstances in receiving their paper, will be able to withstand the torrent; and to insist, as he ought to do after the commencement of the operations of the Bank of the United States, on receiving the revenues in something better than a paper currency, which is not convertible into anything but paper.

Mr. T. said, he had no doubt that the State banks could prepare for the resumption of specie payments by the first of January. Though they have unquestionably overtraded, and probably cannot at this time redeem their paper, yet they have ample funds to effect the object if they would set seriously about it. The measure proposed will compel them to do so. If we let them alone they will never do it. They cannot do it without concert; there never will be that concert. If, instead of pressing their dealers, that their outcries may influence the measures of the Legislative body and prevent this necessary measure, they would curtail their discounts with moderation; if they would sell their stock, the price of which will be so much enhanced by the increased demand for it in payments of subscriptions to the National Bank;—if, after having for several years made immense dividends while the profits of every other class of society were reduced to nothing by the operation of the war, they would declare no dividend till they were enabled to pay their debts, he had no doubt they might in six months resume the payment of specie, without ruin or even material distress to the mass of society. It was a course which honesty and justice required—which the welfare of the nation demanded, and which we must enforce.

It had been intimated that there would be great difficulty in collecting the taxes for want of a medium. But the direct tax which will be payable before March next will be paid by January, so that the people of the interior will not be affected by this act, and as to those of the seaports, if they have the depreciated paper, they can always command what will pay their taxes, if they are willing to allow a fair discount. Upon the whole, Mr. T. had no doubt that it was necessary to give effect to this measure at as early a period as possible, and he was persuaded that the first of January would not be found too remote. He should therefore vote against the amendment.

Mr. SMITH having varied his motion from the first of March to the first of February—

Mr. INGHAM said, he would prefer the first of March to the first of February. It had been suggested that the State banks ought to be compelled to pay specie at the same time the National Bank commenced its operations; but it had not been shown at what time that bank could commence; he presumed neither the Secretary of the Treasury nor the Committee had calculated the National Bank to go into operation by the 31st of December. He perceived that the letter of the Secretary, by its date, was written before the Bank bill was passed; the time for opening the books had been protracted one month, and also the time for taking the subscriptions, making near two months longer than was contemplated at the time the letter was written. He presumed, therefore, that the first of March would be as early as the bank could be put into operation; and as this measure had been relied on to give facility to the State banks in resuming specie payments, this effect could not be produced if the State banks were compelled to pay specie before the United States Bank commenced its operation; but it would be better to protract the period somewhat beyond the time, than to attempt to coerce them before. The State banks had difficulties to encounter in resuming specie payments, which the United States Bank will not be exposed to; the former have contracted debts by issuing their notes in large quantities—the latter has no debts to pay; it will commence with caution; specie will circulate to a limited extent, and confidence will be gradually restored. The State banks having taken proper measures for that purpose, will feel the effect of this confidence, and the difficulty will be essentially diminished. The object of restoring the currency is a very desirable one, and whatever Congress do, they ought to do it with effect, avoiding all unnecessary pressure; but, taking a reasonable and practicable course, there will not be the same motive to relax the measure; and, having demanded nothing more than is reasonable, they will not be importuned for a suspension of the law at the next session, as was now the case in the State of Virginia, which had adopted a similar measure. If the time was protracted as proposed, Congress would be able to resist, with more fortitude and effect, the influence that would assail them, and the great object more effectually secured, than if the shortest period was adopted.

Mr. Robertson said, it was true the State of Virginia had passed a law to compel specie payments; but the Legislature might be quickly called together, and he should not be surprised if, by the very influence of the banks, the clamor was, in that State, excited and kept up for the purpose of forcing a repeal of the law, and enabling them to continue their very profitable business. The clamor in Virginia for a call of the Legislature being, as he believed, factitious, and produced, indirectly, by the banks themselves, ought not to deter Congress from adopting proper measures to enforce the payment of specie. He believed this the last opportunity which would occur for years to act efficiently on the subject, and he trusted it would not be neglected.

Mr. Calhoun hoped the motion to insert the first of February would not prevail. He added a few remarks to those he submitted when he first introduced the bill; and adverting to the effect of the Virginia enforcing act, observed, that an attempt to compel specie payments in a particular State, when all the surrounding banks did not so pay, was a very different thing from a general regulation, which would operate on every part of the country alike. He had all along believed no single State could safely resume the payment of specie—could not meet the consequent curtailment of discounts; but this did not prove that specie payments were impracticable, if resumed contemporaneously throughout the country. Mr. C. felt very anxious for the fate of this measure; he strongly suspected the banks did not mean voluntarily to resume specie payments, though it was in their power to import specie from abroad. He spoke boldly on the subject; he did not believe the banks sincere in their declarations, and if there was the least giving back here, the object would be lost. He hoped there would be such a vote on the bill, as would give assurance that Congress was determined to compel the restoration of a sound currency. To this end, Mr. C. believed, the last of December would afford the banks ample time; but he would not be tenacious on the subject, if the House thought otherwise.

Mr. Grosvenor said, for himself, he would have preferred the bill in its original shape, to compel the payment of specie. He objected to the proposed amendment, not that a month or two was anything in the result, but that it was important, as it would affect ulterior measures of the Government. He hoped the time would be fixed as early in the next session as possible, that no difficulty might ensue from any pressure on Congress by the banking interest. Such pressure might be anticipated at the next session, and it might be too great to be resisted, if not now provided for.

Mr. Smith, of Maryland, again rose in support of his motion. He wished eight weeks allowed for the United States Bank to commence its operations, that the pressure might be taken off the State banks; without this, merchants would not be able to pay their bonds at the customhouses, and there would be a general shock to business throughout the community. Mr. S. declared that, if the 31st of December were retained, he should be obliged to vote against the bill. His anxiety to make the measure easy to the banks arose from no interested feeling—he owned not a cent's worth of bank stock. He believed the banks were making arrangements to meet the crisis, and that they would be able and willing to resume specie payments in a reasonable time. The banks of Baltimore had now less notes out than those of Boston; and he himself had purchased one hundred thousand silver dollars at five per cent. only. Mr. S. thought a little indulgence to the banks on this subject would produce much good, and that too much hardship would do great harm. He was averse to any attempt to force the banks to do what it was impracticable for them to perform immediately. In reply to Mr.

Ward's remark, that the banks of Boston had persevered in paying specie without any aid from Government, Mr. S. said, that these banks never gave any aid to the Government, except in one instance, and that was the reason they were sometimes censured in this House.

Mr. Sheffey was opposed to this amendment. Every day, he said, which the measure was delayed, would make it more difficult, and the evil would daily become worse and worse. He was in favor of strong measures, and of the shortest time, and was afraid this bill would prove too weak to effect the object in view; but, mild as it was, he was willing to take it, and hoped the session would not be suffered to slip over without something being done. Instead of extending the time, he would prefer the first of November, by which day the banks would be able to sell their Government stock, and be prepared for the change.

Mr. Grosvenor, in reply to Mr. Smith, said, there was no law to compel the United States Bank to commence its operations on the first of January; and begged to know if that bank was not to have some protection against the cupidity of the State banks? He would give the State banks a fair and proper time to prepare, on condition that they honestly intended to return to specie payments, and would use all means to do it; and instead of crushing and convulsing the commercial community to every extent, would sacrifice a few per cent. of their Government stock. Would any man tell him they could not sell that stock? They could, if not at par, at something below it. The secret is, said Mr. G., the banks study their own interest solely, and make as much as they can, without considering or regarding the country; in some instances their profits were between fifteen and eighteen per cent. And how did they pay for the stock which they hold? Why, in this very depreciated paper. There was a most powerful reason for not putting off this measure; he did not believe it would be effectual if delayed; it was too weak, and Congress would, at the next session, be beset with the whole weight of the banking influence. It would be deferring the remedy forever; but rather than submit to the disorder, and fasten on the country a paper system, he would amputate the rotten part; rather than submit to the evils which would ensue from such a course, he would, if he had the power, bury them in the earth, and give life to institutions of a sound, healthy, and useful constitution. But, so long as he believed the banks sincere, he would not put them down; he would resort to lenient measures first, and trusted they would be effectual.

Mr. Smith, of Maryland, had already said that this subject was one of extreme difficulty; that Government intermeddling with subjects of such delicacy, might involve the country in ruin and destroy many unoffending individuals; that Virginia had passed a law to compel her banks to pay specie on the 15th of November. The result was as might have been expected, and such as ought to cause a doubt, and induce the committee to apprehend consequences of the most se-

rious kind. The bill forbids the Treasury to receive in payment the notes of banks which shall not pay specie after the 31st of December next—that is, it exacts of the banks to do what, he feared, would be found impracticable. The injury will not be to the banks alone; it will fall principally on those who do business with them. A merchant's bond becomes due at the custom-house, he has the amount in one of the State banks, (who do not pay specie,) a check on such bank will not pay his bond; the bank will say, we have not the specie, we cannot aid you. What is he to do? He cannot pay, and his bond will remain unpaid; his credit will be destroyed at the custom-house, and he must (until his bond is paid) pay ready money for all goods that he may thereafter import. He cannot pay, and his goods will be put in the public warehouse, sold at auction for the duties, and ruin and bankruptcy will follow in many instances. He did not know whether a postponement until the 1st of February would cure the evil. He thought that if the time was fixed at the 1st of March it would greatly lessen the danger which was apprehended. Mr. S. then said, that if the Bank of the United States went into operation on the 1st of January, the merchants would offer good notes to that bank or one of its branches for the amount of their bonds, which would be discounted and enable them to pay; that by this means a pressure would be taken from the State banks, and he had a hope, that with forbearance on the part of the Treasury towards those banks which held the public funds, and by sales of United States stock, the banks in the great cities would be enabled to pay specie after the 1st of March. Confidence (which was the all-important) would be restored by two months' paying of specie by the United States Bank; and the State banks, being then better prepared, would make the attempt to recommence specie payments, he hoped, without much danger. But in this opinion he differed with almost all the merchants in Baltimore. They thought specie payments by the banks at so short a day impossible. He again would assert that it was not excessive issues of paper, or excessive discounts to merchants, that occasioned what was called depreciation; that he had seen the balance sheet of two banks of Baltimore, by which it appeared that neither their discounts nor their notes in circulation were equal to what they were in 1812. Yet the notes were not equal in value to those of the Bank of Pennsylvania, whose issues and discounts it had been shown had been excessive. In one of our largest banks, he would state, that its discounts did not exceed its actual capital more than ninety thousand; that its notes in circulation amounted to little more than one-third of its capital; that it had 6 per cent. stock of the United States to an amount nearly equal to the whole it owed for deposites by individuals and by the Treasury; that the deposite of the Treasury in that bank was so small that it fully showed that no loss had arisen to the Government by the receiving of Baltimore paper in payment, and that the Treasury had been able to pay in such paper for the interest of the stock and its debts without loss to the Treasury. Mr. S. further said that the difference of value between Baltimore and Virginia paper had, in a great measure, been owing to the Treasury having (last Spring) drawn from the Baltimore banks $750,000, which were sent to Richmond to pay the debt due to Virginia by the United States. That so large a sum could not fail to have an effect on the exchange between those States. That the bank he had alluded to had lately sold stock in Richmond, and withdrawn their own notes, which, with other banks doing the same, and with the course of trade with the interior of Virginia, would, he hoped, soon lessen the balance that had been against Baltimore; that he had, on a former occasion, shown how the balance of trade had arisen against Baltimore, and in favor of the States to the Eastward; that the exchange had fallen, he believed, since Congress had met, with Boston. He said that it would perhaps not be proper for him to give a view of the Boston banks, but this, he hoped, he might be permitted to say, that if the drain of their specie progressed as it had done between June and January last, they would be in a pitiable situation. Connecticut, he said, would feel the operation of the bill; her banks were called specie banks, but they paid no specie—their business was done, he believed, in New York bank notes; thus, when they discounted merchants' notes, they contracted that they were neither to pay specie nor their own notes; they were to pay in the notes of the banks of New York. He said that it was believed that the banks of New York had as much, if not more, notes in circulation, in proportion to their capital, than those of Baltimore; yet their paper was 8 per cent. better, both paying in notes, and neither in specie. It had been represented to him that some of the banks of the interior of New York have issued their notes to an excess, and yet their notes were better in the market than those of Baltimore; which did not prove a depreciation, but that the balance of trade was greatly against Baltimore and in favor of New York, a circumstance that will cure itself in a few months perhaps.

The gentleman from Massachusetts (Mr. WARD) had pressed this subject with great zeal. He had said that the State he represented paid more real value to Government for public dues than any other State. The gentleman is mistaken. Last Spring they paid much less; for dollars were then purchased in Baltimore at 5 per cent., Treasury notes at par; at which time the merchants of Boston paid their bonds in Treasury notes, which, he believed, they purchased at 15 per cent. below par; at this time they paid in Treasury notes which cost 8 per cent. below par. They have, therefore, on the average, paid their public dues on at least equal terms with those of Baltimore. The same gentleman has said that the merchants and banks of Boston had received no aid from Government. Was it no aid when they were enabled to pay the public dues in

Treasury notes, which on an average of the year saved them 10 per cent.? If, however, the merchants, or the banks of Boston, received no aid from Government, the gentleman ought to recollect that they refused all aid to the Government when the banks and merchants in the Middle States contributed to the support of Government to the extent of their means. Mr. S. concluded by saying that he could not vote for the bill without an extension of time.

The question was taken on Mr. SMITH's motion, and negatived—ayes 48.

Mr. SHARPE moved to revive and incorporate in the bill, the fourth section originally reported, but subsequently withdrawn by the Committee of Finance, laying a high stamp duty, about ten per cent. on the notes of all banks failing to pay specie from and after the 31st of December next.

Mr. SHARPE said, he was induced to propose this amendment, partly from the arguments of gentlemen who had opposed the bill. He was sorry that the committee who reported the bill consented to strike out this section; and in listening attentively to the arguments against the other provisions of the bill, he was still more clearly convinced of the importance and necessity of this section. What, said Mr. S., are the arguments that have been used against this bill? Not a justification of the banks that had violated their contracts, for them they cannot venture to justify; but that this is a measure that will operate most severely upon the people, and the banks will save themselves, if required to pay specie, by refusing to discount, and by calling in their paper which is in circulation; and that will distress the whole community, particularly the mercantile interest, who have large accommodations. Under these circumstances, the people will not have money to pay their taxes. As you reduce the circulating medium, you will reduce the price of produce, lessen the value of land and labor, and produce a stagnation of all kinds of business.

If these arguments, said Mr. S., are entitled to weight, they establish one of two facts, either that the banks are never to resume specie payments, and we must tolerate them in that course of dealing; or that, if we are to compel them to resume specie payments, our measures should be made to operate on them directly, (which is the very thing intended by this amendment,) and not indirectly, which will be felt by the community as well as by the banks. He would ask gentlemen if the first was admissible in principle, or if they had the most distant idea that every little banking company throughout the Union was to give a circulating medium to the country; and that Congress, who have to establish the current coin of the nation, shall not control them?

Many of the State banks, he was convinced, would be prepared at any day Congress should appoint, to resume specie payments, but they cannot commence while others are suffered to do business without paying specie; it must be simultaneous in every part of the nation, or those banks that attempt to do a specie business cannot discount or make any profits, while those banks that do not pay specie will do all the business and make all the profits; the notes of banks that pay specie will be scarce as specie itself, while the notes of other banks will occupy all the avenues of circulation. This was evidenced by the fact: those banks which pay nothing for their paper, are dividing a profit of from twelve to fifteen per cent., while the banks in New England that pay specie divide only from three to four per cent. You acknowledge this fact, said Mr. S., when you state that if the banks are compelled to pay specie, they will make no dividends this year. This accounts for their unwillingness to pay specie; it is not expected that moneyed institutions, whose only instinct is gain, will be willing voluntarily to give up exorbitant profits. During the war they had an apology for stopping payment: they had loaned largely to Government, and were unable to sell their stock without loss; this some gentleman say was patriotism, for which they are entitled to our greatest indulgence. I must acknowledge for one, said Mr. S., that my gratitude is not as great as it would have been for their patriotism, if they had loaned their money at a profit of from six to eight, instead of from fifteen to twenty per cent. I recollect their patriotism was very fairly measured by the profit they made, and if they loaned us their paper they made us pay for it. I do not complain of this, it was fair; they had a right, as money dealers, to make the best bargain they could, and they did so. It is our duty to comply with our contract; when we have done that, we owe them nothing, no, not even gratitude. There was nothing gratuitous in their favors; we bought them, and we will pay for them. During the war the defalcation of the banks was tolerated from necessity, and on the return of peace no immediate steps were taken against them; we were then induced to believe, they would resume payment in six or eight months, at the farthest; it is now above fourteen months, and we are told they are less prepared to pay specie than they were at the close of the war; that the balance of trade has been against us, and the money has been all exported. This bill proposes to give near one year longer, and yet we are told this is not sufficient time, and that the whole country is to be distressed by the measure. Those moneyed institutions, said Mr. S., will always think it too soon; they will never be prepared for paying specie; fourteen months has found them less prepared than at the close of the war; one or two years more and they will persuade you the measure is wholly impracticable. Whenever an attempt is made to compel them, as individual citizens are compelled, to pay their contracts, they will commence curtailing their discounts, and produce such pressure on the community as will excite a strong interest in their favor, and it will be found impracticable to pass an efficient measure on the subject. This course of theirs is conclusive to my mind, said Mr. S., that they do not intend resuming specie payments; for, if they did, they have the means in their power without the least oppression to the community. What was

the principal reason for their stopping specie payments? It was owing to their permanent loans to Government, of greater amounts than they could pay; that stock, which many of the banks got at a reduced price, can now be sold in the market at a profit of from five to fifteen per cent.; they have only to convert it into money and they are prepared to resume specie payments at once. They are not willing to do this, because it is not their interest; they can make more profit by issuing notes they never mean to pay. Their opposition to this bill was full evidence of that fact. This bill, Mr. S. said, without the proposed amendment, is an indulgence, not a coercion; it gives till the first of next January, before the Secretary of the Treasury is directed to refuse the paper of all banks in payment of the revenue, unless they pay gold or silver for their notes. Without this bill, the Secretary has a right to refuse their paper, or indeed he has no right to receive it at all, and may issue his order to-morrow, directing it not to be received. Yet we are told that such an order, issued on the first of January next, will be ruinous. Shall any other rule of morality, said Mr. S., govern the transactions of those corporations than is applied to the contracts of individuals? If an individual refuses to fulfil his contract, it is held disreputable, and he is prosecuted and made to pay costs and damages; executions are levied on his property, and it is sold at any price it will bring; his wife and children are turned out of house and home upon the world's cold charity, and be thrown into prison. When these banks have done the same act, and even refuse to pay interest on their debt, where they fail to pay the principal, they are held to be free from censure or reproach. My sentiments of justice, said Mr. S., are not so pliant as to consider the conduct of a community of men in any different point of view from the conduct of an individual; numbers divide responsibility, but the act is the same; there is no good reason why they who will post the name of one of their customers as dishonored if he does not meet his contract to a day, shall be allowed to violate theirs with impunity. It is indispensable, they must pay their debts honestly, or it is our duty, said Mr. S., to compel them to do it; and if this measure is not adequate, we must resort to a bankrupt law, and sell all their effects. Legislators who will tolerate this violation of contracts can have but little regard for the morality of the country.

The delinquency of the banks, said Mr. S., is a species of speculation upon the whole community; it is nothing less than taxing the whole nation. Where paper is issued at a value from which it depreciates, the whole amount of depreciation is a clear loss to the community, and is the same as paying the tax to that amount. Say that the banks who do not pay specie have issued ten millions of dollars at par, in the course of one year that sum depreciates ten per cent.—one million is the loss to the community, and is the same as if the money had not depreciated, and they had paid one million in taxes. The evil does not rest here, said Mr. S., but it is a fraud upon the revenue, and consequently upon all the Government creditors. The taxes are paid in an inferior currency, and the Government has to pay the same to its officers, and that is paying them less than what is due them. As the depreciation is not uniform, the revenue is unequally paid by different sections of the Union, according to the difference of value of the several kinds of papers in which it is paid. Say the depreciation of Baltimore paper is twelve per cent., and Boston three per cent., the people of Baltimore pay nine per cent. less in taxes and imposts than those of Boston. By paying nine per cent. less on their imposts they can afford to sell their goods lower, and in that manner engross the custom of the interior country which depends on the seaport towns for its goods. Hence it is not only the interest of the banks that their paper should depreciate, but it is the interest of importing cities that they lighten their dues to Government. This, said Mr. S., is an evil of no small magnitude; it is taking deep root in society, and entwines itself with all the large moneyed interests of the community. Had it not been for this disease of the circulating medium, would Congress, he said, have been induced to charter a National Bank? Was it not as a remedy for this evil that the bank was mainly intended? And was not that remedy to be effected by the National Bank's being compelled to pay specie for its notes and giving a currency of an uniform value and at all times equal to gold and silver? If this was the object, it will never be accomplished, said Mr. S., so long as our revenue is allowed to be collected in an inferior paper; no man will pay in the paper of most value when the other will do as well, and he can make ten or twelve per cent. in the exchange. I also view this measure, said Mr. S., as necessary to aid and protect your National Bank when it goes into operation. If these banks are not compelled to resume specie payments, they will have it in their power to purchase the bills of the National Bank and draw all the money out of its vaults, and compel it to stop payment or quit business. That we have the right to impose this additional tax on them, said Mr. S., I have no doubt—that it is good policy to impose it is equally obvious; otherwise we are to suffer them to give a depreciated circulating medium to the country, to the prejudice of our revenue, and to the injury of commerce. These are some of the considerations, said Mr. S., that induced me to move this amendment; and I hope they will induce the Committee to adopt it; and if this bill shall not then be sufficient to produce the desired effect, at the next session of Congress it is to be hoped measures more efficient will be resorted to.

Mr. BARBOUR said, that, as the section now proposed (by Mr. SHARPE) to be introduced as an amendment, had been stricken from the bill by the committee which reported it, he had not expected that it would have been offered again; but, as it was brought forward, he would offer to the Committee a few ideas which had suggested themselves to him upon the spur of the occasion, for the purpose of showing that the proposed amendment ought not to be adopted. He said that he was fully sensible of the evil under which the country labored, in consequence of the depreciation and varying value of the circulating medium; that he was as desirous as any member of the Committee to apply a proper remedy, but he was desirous also to be duly careful, both as to the character and extent of that remedy, and particularly that one should not be applied which was worse than the evil which it was intended to cure. In the first place, then, it behooved the Committee to consider well whether they had the right to enact such a provision. He did not mean to affirm that they had not the right, but he thought it somewhat questionable.

The section now offered proposed to impose an enormous stamp duty, with a proviso that it should be mitigated in relation to such banks as should by a given day make payment of their notes in specie. The object evidently was not to raise a revenue, but to operate as a penalty for the purpose of enforcing another object—namely, specie payments. It was in its character of penalty that he thought the doubt resided.

These institutions have been incorporated by the States, whose power so to do has not been called into question. If then the Governments which created them be willing, under imperious circumstances, to dispense them from the necessity of specie payments, he asked if it would not be going very far for the Committee to say that they should incur a heavy penalty for not doing that from which they were absolved by the power creating them? But, he said that it was not necessary to press that point, inasmuch as there were considerations of expediency, which seemed to him sufficient to reject the provision.

If, he said, a direct appeal to the interest of the State banks be a sufficient motive to induce them to pay specie, then he thought that the bill, without the proposed amendment, contained provisions of a character strong enough to produce the desired effect. These provisions were, first, a withdrawal of all the deposites of Government from such banks as should not pay specie by the 1st of January, 1817; secondly, that the notes of such banks should not be receivable in taxes and debts to the Government. If, notwithstanding these provisions, the banks should not pay specie, he thought it fair to infer that the reason would be an inability to do so; and he asked, whether a severe penalty, imposed upon institutions for not doing that which they might be unable to do, would not be an act of harsh legislation?

Let us examine, said he, the extent of this penalty: a single example will suffice to show it. The amendment proposed a stamp duty of fifty dollars upon every note above one hundred dollars, and not exceeding five hundred dollars. Now, no person could say, with certainty, that the banks would be able to resume specie payments by the 1st of January, 1817. Some gentlemen thought that they would, others that they would not be able to do so. The effect of this provision, then, would be to put an entire stop to the operation of all those banks which might be thus unable; because, to continue business under such stamp duties would be altogether out of the question. Such is the effect which this provision might have upon the banks themselves. Let us now inquire, for a moment, what might be its operation upon the circulating medium of the country, and consequently upon the interests of the community.

It seems to be agreed on all hands that the banks have not, at this time, anything like specie enough. It has been stated by the chairman of the Committee on National Currency, that the quantity in the banks amounted to about fifteen millions of dollars, while it is probable that the paper in circulation is near seventy millions. It will be borne in mind, also, that of the quantity which we have already, much too small, a considerable portion must be drawn, if not from the State banks, from the stock in the country, to supply the demand of the National Bank. It is said, however, that the banks have stock, by a sale of which they can procure it. Not to mention the difficulty that there might be in converting so much stock in so short time into specie, let it be remembered that, of the two hundred and sixty banks in the United States, a very large number of them have either none or very little stock. The only means, then, by which the banks could enable themselves to take up their notes with cash would be by curtailing their discounts and dealings in their debts. A moderate and well-regulated system of curtailment was not to be objected to. Such a one the present provisions were calculated to produce; but there was great reason to fear, if this provision should be adopted, that, under the terror of such an enormous penalty, the banks would be driven into so large and severe a curtailment, that it would produce a most distressing pressure upon their customers, and, through them, inflict the deepest wounds upon the community at large. The effect of curtailment resulted from this circumstance, that as bank paper had filled up the channel of circulation to the exclusion of specie, every operation of this sort necessarily diminished, to an extent equal to its amount, the quantity of circulating medium, or currency of the country, out of which alone the amount of succeeding curtailments could be paid. If this process were conducted with moderation, although inconvenience must, to a certain degree, be the inevitable result, yet the very circumstance of its moderation would make it *tolerable*; but if, on the contrary, it were violent in its operation, such a great and sudden drain of the circulating medium would be produced as would make it intolerable.

The whole subject seemed to him to be reducible to this single proposition, either the banks will or will not be able to pay specie at the time required. He hoped they would be able. If they should, then the provisions already in the bill, addressed themselves sufficiently to the interest of the banks to make them pay it. If they should not, then the proposed tax or penalty, call it by what name you please, would be as unjust and oppressive in its principle as it would be ruinous in its consequences. He should therefore vote against the amendment.

Mr. Hopkinson was also opposed to the motion made by Mr. Sharpe, and thought the House could not pursue that course one step further. He was decidedly of opinion that the power proposed by the amendment could not be constitutionally exercised; and this opinion, he said, was not ideal. The stamp duty proposed to be laid on the notes of the delinquent banks had been called a tax; but was it not a fact that this duty was to be contingent, that it compelled the State banks to pay so much money unless they performed a certain act? Was this of the nature of a tax? Mr. H. said it was a penalty on the banks; a penalty inflicted without the decision or sanction of a court of justice. Such a procedure could by no means be considered in the light of a tax, from which it differed most essentially. A tax was unconditional, imperative, and impartial; the duty proposed, as had been remarked, was penal, contingent, and operated as a punishment upon the banks. Mr. H. denied that any such power could be derived from the Constitution, in which no such right existed. It would also be a violation of contract with those institutions, many of which had paid large sums of money for their charters; and was it for any power to alter or infringe the conditions of those charters? Mr. H. believed the proposed measure so unwarrantable, so obviously wrong, he thought the House could not hesitate in rejecting it, and trusted it would not prevail.

Mr. Grosvenor replied to Mr. Hopkinson. He had not one doubt of the right of Congress to exercise this power. Not a principle, he said, existed in this bill which had not been involved in every stamp act ever passed by the Government. Mr. G. argued at some length, and declared that not a doubt existed in his mind as to the right. The justice and expediency of the clause, he said, was another question. The object in view was to enforce, as soon as practicable, the resumption of specie payments. Now, Mr. G. said, he was willing to refrain from any measure of a strong character for the present; he was willing to give ample time and opportunity for the banks, by their own operations, to heal the disorder. He would now take the bill as it stood, although he considered it as a measure of little efficacy or consequence. Mr. G. said, he had great hopes that the banks, by prudent measures, by selling their Government stock as soon as possible, and thus diminishing their paper and increasing their specie, would make such progress towards a state of health as to render any further proceedings unnecessary. If, however, the contrary should happen; if from any motives no proper efforts should be made to remedy the present disordered state of their paper, he would not hesitate to say that it would be the duty of Congress to resort to all strong and effective measures within their power, to compel the banks to perform their duty to their country and to their fellow-citizens. He was, however as he before said, for waiting; for giving the banks full time; and therefore hoped Mr. SHARPE would not press his motion to a decision, but allow the bill to pass in its present shape.

Mr. CLAY said a few words on the same side. He was averse to so rigorous an act at present; he wished first to adopt softer measures and see whether the banks would resume the payment of specie. If they did not, Mr. C. pledged himself to go with gentlemen hereafter in any measures to coerce the banks into their duty. He hoped, however, his friend (Mr. SHARPE) would not, at this time, urge his motion.

Mr. SHARPE, after observing that though all his friends seemed to regard his motion favorably, in principle, yet appearing to think it improper at present, he would not now press it without their support, and accordingly withdrew it.

After an ineffectual attempt by Mr. GOLDSBOR-OUGH to carry an amendment—

Mr. WARD, of Massachusetts, moved to carry the act into operation on the 1st of May next, instead of the 31st December.—Negatived by a large majority.

Mr. WARD moved, also, an amendment providing a graduated scale of value, by which the notes of certain banks would be received in payment; which motion was also negatived.

The Committee then rose and reported the bill without amendment; when Mr. WEBSTER suggesting an amendment which he deemed necessary, but not having prepared it, and the hour being late, a motion was made to adjourn, and carried.

THURSDAY, April 18.

The SPEAKER presented a petition of the messengers attached to the several offices in the Departments of State, Treasury, War, and Navy, and the office of the Board of Navy Commissioners, respectively praying an increase of compensation.—Laid on the table.

The SPEAKER laid before the House a letter from WILLIAM PINKNEY, resigning his seat as a member of this House from the State of Maryland, having accepted the appointment of Minister Plenipotentiary of the United States at the Court of St. Petersburg, in Russia.

Mr. LOWNDES, from the Committee of Ways and Means, reported a bill for the relief of George T. Ross, Daniel T. Patterson, and the officers and men lately under their command; which was read twice, and committed to the Committee of the Whole on the bill for the relief of David Gelston and Peter A. Schenck.

Mr. LOWNDES also reported a bill to allow drawback of duties on spirits distilled and sugar refined within the United States; which was read twice, and committed to the Committee of the Whole on the report of the Committee of Ways and Means upon the subject of revenue.

Mr. TUCKER, from the Committee on the District of Columbia, reported a bill to enable the levy court of the county of Alexandria to lay a tax for the purpose of defraying the expense of

erecting a jail and court-house; which was read twice, and ordered to be engrossed, and read a third time to-morrow.

Mr. ROBERTSON, from the Committee on the Public Lands, reported a bill to establish a land district in the Illinois Territory, north of the district of Kaskaskia; which was read twice, and ordered to be engrossed, and read a third time to-day.

Engrossed bills of the following titles, to wit:

An act for the relief of David Coffin, Samuel and William Rodman, and Samuel Rodman, jr.;

An act providing for cases of lost military land warrants, and discharges for faithful services; were severally read the third time, and passed.

The bill from the Senate "concerning field officers of the militia," was read the third time, and passed.

The House proceeded to consider the bill to authorize the survey of two millions of acres of the public lands, in lieu of that quantity heretofore authorized to be surveyed in the Territory of Michigan, as military bounty land; and the said bill being further amended, was ordered to be engrossed, and read a third time to-morrow.

An engrossed bill, entitled "An act to establish a land office in the Illinois Territory, north of the district of Kaskaskia," was read the third time, and passed.

The bill providing an additional compensation, for extra services, to the Judge of the Southern District of the State of New York, passed through a Committee of the Whole, and was ordered to a third reading.

The bill from the Senate concerning the entry of vessels at the port of Middletown, and the bill concerning pre-emption rights in Louisiana, Missouri, and Illinois, severally passed through Committees of the Whole; and the committee on the former obtained leave to sit again. The latter bill was ordered to lie on the table.

The House went into a Committee of the Whole on the bill to provide a system of navigation for the United States.

The bill having been read through, and no amendment being offered, the Committee rose, and reported it without amendment; when

Mr. FORSYTH intimating that he wished to offer some amendments which the lateness of the hour did not this day permit, moved to lay the bill on the table until to-morrow; which was agreed to.

The SPEAKER laid before the House a letter from the President of the United States enclosing a report from the Secretary of State, in pursuance of a request of the House, of 17th February last, exhibiting a table of the duties imposed on American articles in the British possessions of Canada and Nova Scotia; which letter, &c., were ordered to lie on the table and be printed.

AMENDMENTS TO THE CONSTITUTION.

Mr. PLEASANTS, one of the Representatives from the State of Virginia, laid before the House the following communications; which were read, and ordered to lie on the table:

The Legislatures of Connecticut and Massachusetts having proposed the following as amendments to the Constitution of the United States:

1st. Representatives and direct taxes shall be apportioned among the several States, which may be included within this Union, according to their respective numbers of free persons, including those bound to serve for a term of years, and excluding Indians not taxed, and all other persons.

2d. No new State shall be admitted into the Union by Congress, in virtue of the power granted by the Constitution, without the concurrence of two-thirds of both Houses.

3d. Congress shall not have power to lay any embargo on the ships or vessels of the United States, in the ports or harbors thereof, for more than sixty days.

4th. Congress shall not have power, without the concurrence of two-thirds of both Houses, to interdict the commercial intercourse between the United States and any foreign nation, or the dependencies thereof.

5th. Congress shall not make or declare war, or authorize acts of hostility against any foreign nation, without the concurrence of two-thirds of both Houses, except such acts of hostility in defence of the Territories of the United States, when actually invaded.

6th. No person who shall hereafter be naturalized shall be eligible as a member of the Senate or House of Representatives of the United States, nor capable of holding any civil office under the authority of the United States.

7th. The same person shall not be elected President of the United States a second time; nor shall the President be elected from the same State two terms in succession.

Resolved, By the Senate and House of Delegates of the Commonwealth of Virginia, that it is inexpedient to adopt the amendments aforesaid.

Resolved, also, That the Governor be, and he is hereby, requested to transmit copies of the aforesaid resolution to each of the Senators and Representatives of this State in Congress, and to the Executive of each State of the United States, with a request that the same be laid before their respective Legislatures.

Agreed to by the House of Delegates, February 13, 1816.   WM. MUNFORD, C. H. D.

February 16, 1816—Agreed to by the Senate.
     THEO. HANSFORD, C. S.

The Legislature of North Carolina having proposed the following as an amendment to the Constitution of the United States:

That, for the purpose of choosing Representatives in the Congress of the United States, each State shall, by its Legislature, be divided into a number of districts equal to the number of Representatives to which each State may be entitled.

Those districts shall be formed of contiguous territory, and contain, as nearly as may be, an equal number of inhabitants entitled by the Constitution to be represented. In each district the qualified voters shall elect one Representative, and no more.

That, for the purpose of appointing Electors of President and Vice President of the United States, each State shall, by its Legislature, be divided into a number of districts equal to the number of Electors to which each State may be entitled. Those districts shall be composed of contiguous territory, and contain, as nearly as may be, an equal number of inhabitants entitled by the Constitution to representation. In each district the persons qualified to vote for Representatives shall appoint one Elector, and no more. The Electors, when convened, shall have power, in case any of those appointed as above prescribed, shall fail to attend, for the purposes of their said appointment, on the day prescribed for giving their votes for President and Vice President of the United States, to appoint another, or others, to act in the place of him or them so failing to attend.

Neither the districts for choosing Representatives, nor those appointing Electors, shall be altered in any State, until a census, and apportionment of Representatives under it, made subsequent to the division of the State into districts, shall change the number of Representatives and Electors to which such State may be entitled. The division of States into districts hereby provided for shall take place immediately after this amendment shall be adopted and ratified as part of the Constitution of the United States, and successively afterwards, whenever, by a census, and apportionment of Representatives under it, the number of Representatives and of Electors to which any State may be entitled shall be changed. The division of such State into districts for the purposes both of choosing Representatives and of appointing Electors shall be altered agreeably to the provisions of this amendment, and on no other occasion.

Resolved, by the General Assembly of Virginia, that it is expedient to adopt the said amendment.

Resolved, also, That the Governor be, and he is hereby, requested to forward to the Executive of each of the States in the Union, and to each of our Senators and Representatives in Congress, a copy of the above preamble and resolution; and that our said Representatives be requested to use such means as to them may seem expedient to cause the amendment aforesaid to be proposed by Congress to the Legislatures of the several States in the Union for their adoption.

February 28, 1816—Agreed to by both Houses of the General Assembly.
     WM. MUNFORD, C. H. D.

PRIVATEER ROGER.

The engrossed bill to allow the privateer *Roger* the bounty for certain British prisoners, was read the third time.

Some debate again ensued on the propriety of awarding this bounty. Messrs. GASTON, LYON, and CADY, opposed the bill, mainly on the ground, that all prisoners were, and of right ought to be, free from the ratification of the treaty, agreeably to the terms thereof, and the usages of nations; that the prisoners were not desired by the United States after the war had terminated; and that there was in law or equity no title to the bounty on the part of the claimants, &c. The claim of the captors was advocated by Messrs. SHEFFEY, NELSON, and WRIGHT, who rested their support on the stipulations of the treaty, and our own law encouraging the capture of enemy seamen, by offering a bounty therefor; arguing, from the condemnation of the vessel, &c., that the capture was legal, and that the prisoners were as good prize as the vessel itself, which has been awarded to the captors. The debate took a wide scope, embracing points of the law of nations, the law of prize, &c.

The question on the passage of the bill was decided in the affirmative—yeas 63, nays 52, as follows:

YEAS—Messrs. Adgate, Archer, Bassett, Bateman, Betts, Bess, Breeks, Caldwell, Calhoun, Chipman, Clopton, Conner, Crawford, Crocheron, Darlington, Forney, Forsyth, Griffin, Hahn, Huger, Hungerford, Johnson of Virginia, Johnson of Kentucky, Kerr of Virginia, Love, Maclay, Mason, Mayrant, McCoy, McLean of Kentucky, Moore, Murfree, Nelson of Virginia, Newton, Ormsby, Piper, Pleasants, Reynolds, Roane, Robertson, Root, Savage, Schenck, Sharpe, Sheffey, Smith of Maryland, Smith of Virginia, Southard, Taul, Telfair, Townsend, Wallace, Webster, Wendover, Wilde, Wilkin, Williams, Willoughby, Thomas Wilson, William Wilson, Woodward, Wright, and Yates.

NAYS—Messrs. Atherton, Barbour, Baylies, Bennett, Birdsall, Bradbury, Breckenridge, Brown, Cady, Chappell, Cilley, Clarke of North Carolina, Clayton, Glendennin, Culpeper, Cuthbert, Davenport, Desha, Edwards, Gaston, Goldsborough, Grosvenor, Heister, Henderson, Herbert, Ingham, Irwin of Pennsylvania, Jewett, Kent, Langdon, Lovett, Lumpkin, Lyle, Lyon, Marsh, Milnor, Nelson of Massachusetts, Parris, Pickens, Pickering, Ruggles, Stearns, Strong, Sturges, Tate, Tucker, Ward of Massachusetts, Ward of New York, Wheaton, Whiteside, Wilcox, and Yancey.

SPECIE PAYMENTS.

The unfinished business of yesterday, the bill providing for collecting the debts due to the United States in the lawful money of the country, being called by the Speaker.

Mr. CALHOUN stated that it was the wish of several gentlemen that the bill should be laid on the table until to-morrow, it being in contemplation to offer a section to authorize such an issue of Treasury notes as would supply the deficiency of the circulating medium which might be produced by the banks calling in their notes, and providing a relief for the community under the pressure which would consequently ensue. He, therefore, moved to lay the bill, for the present, on the table; which motion was agreed to.

CAPITOL SQUARE.

The House then resolved itself into a Committee of the Whole on the bill making an appropriation for graduating, enclosing, and improving the Capitol Square.

Mr. TUCKER moved an additional section to the bill, providing for the appointment of one Commissioner of the Public Buildings, instead of the three now in commission, and repealing the authority under which they were appointed; and vesting in him the application of the present appropriation, the superintendence of the improvements of the square, &c., with a salary of $3,000 per annum.

After considerable debate, in which Mr. NELSON opposed the motion, and Messrs. TUCKER, CLAY, WEBSTER, and PICKERING advocated it, the amendment was adopted.

Mr. INGHAM moved to postpone the operation of the bill to the 1st of June, which was negatived; and Mr. TUCKER proposed to increase the compensation of the Commissioner to $2,500 which was also negatived.

Mr. WILDE moved to incorporate a provision in the bill to authorize the President of the United States to cause to be sold certain lots, the property of the United States, within the City; the proceeds of the sale to constitute a fund, the interest of which to go to the support of a National University; which motion he supported at some length, urging the propriety of such policy as tended to foster and benefit the City, and censuring that hostile spirit, which, after Congress had determined to make it the permanent Seat of the Government, yet withheld any aid in its improvement, and left it to languish in a state which made it odious to those who were brought here on the public business, &c.

Mr. WEBSTER suggested the impropriety of connecting the proposition with the present bill, which it might endanger without being itself successful, &c.; after which Mr. WILDE withdrew his motion.

The Committee then rose and reported the bill and amendments to the House; and the latter were further amended, on motion of Mr. TUCKER, by inserting a clause to prohibit the Commissioner, while serving as such, from holding or exercising any other office.

Mr. TUCKER then renewed his motion to increase the compensation of the Commissioner, but without success.

The amendments of the Committee, as amended, were concurred in by the House, and the question put on ordering the bill to a third reading; when

Mr. WRIGHT moved to strike out so much of the first section as provided the appropriation for improving the Capitol Square.

The motion was opposed by Mr. WEBSTER, and Mr. WRIGHT replied, and asked for the yeas and nays on the question, which were refused by the House; after which the motion was rejected. The bill was then ordered to be engrossed for a third reading to-morrow.

After refusing to take up one or two bills which were called up, the House adjourned.

FRIDAY, April 19.

Mr. WARD, of Massachusetts, presented a petition of the Trustees of Phillips's Academy, in Andover, in the State of Massachusetts, praying that the duties imposed on several invoices of books imported for the use of the said Academy may be remitted, and that they may be permitted to import other books free of duty.—Referred to the Committee of Ways and Means.

Mr. WILKIN, from the Committee on Foreign Affairs, reported a bill making appropriations for carrying into effect a treaty between the United States and the Cherokee nation of Indians, concluded at Washington on the 22d day of March, 1816; which was read twice, and committed to a Committee of the Whole.

On motion of Mr. ROBERTSON,

Resolved, That the Committee on the Public Lands be, and they are hereby, directed to inquire into the expediency of authorizing the President

of the United States to cause to be printed ——
copies of the book entitled "Laws, Treaties, and
other Documents, having operation and respect to
the Public Lands, collected and arranged pursuant to an act of Congress, passed April 27, 1810."

The House went into a Committee of the
Whole on the report of the Committee of Elections, in the case of the election of Wm. McCoy,
a member from Virginia, whose seat is contested
by Robert Porterfield. The Committee of the
Whole concurred in the report of the Committee
of Elections, that Mr. McCoy is entitled to his
seat; and the House agreed in the concurrence.
So that the sitting member is confirmed in his
seat as a Representative from the Commonwealth
of Virginia.

Ordered, That the Committee of the Whole
be discharged from a further consideration of the
report of the Committee of Claims on the petition of Zachariah Schoonmaker, and that it lie
on the table.

An engrossed bill making an appropriation for
enclosing and improving the public square near
the Capitol, was read the third time, and passed.

Ordered, That the title be "An act making an
appropriation for enclosing and improving the
public square near the Capitol, and for the
office of Commissioners of the Public Buildings,
and of Superintendent, and for the appointment
of one Commissioner for the Public Buildings."

Engrossed bills of the following titles, to wit:

An act to authorize the survey of two millions
of acres of the public lands, in lieu of that quantity heretofore authorized to be surveyed in the
Territory of Michigan, as military bounty land;

An act providing an additional compensation
to the district judge of the southern district of
New York;

An act to enable the Levy Court of the county
of Alexandria to lay a tax for the purpose of defraying the expense of erecting a jail and court-
house; were severally read the third time, and
passed.

The bill making an appropriation for repairing
the road from Duck river, in the State of Tennessee, to Madisonville, in the Mississippi Territory, and between Fort Hawkins, in the State of
Georgia, and Fort Stoddart, passed through a
Committee of the Whole, and was ordered to be
engrossed for a third reading.

The following bills passed through Committees of the Whole, and were ordered to be engrossed, and read a third time to-morrow:

The bill appropriating the sum of $2,500 for
the purpose therein mentioned. [This money is
to be distributed as prize money to Captain C.
Stewart, the officers and crew of the United
States schooner Syren, being the appraised value
of a vessel captured by the said vessel for a breach
of the blockade of Tripoli, during the war with
that nation in 1804.]

A bill authorizing the payment of a sum of
money to John Rogers, and others. [This money,
$300, to be given to these persons, of Connecti-
cut, for their gallantry and good conduct in capturing a midshipman and two seamen of the Brit-

ish navy, and as compensation for the value of
said prisoners to the United States.]

The bill authorizing the payment of a sum of
money to Joseph Stewart, and others. [This
money, $1,800, to be given to Stewart and his as-
sociates, in the same terms as the above, for the
capture of a lieutenant, a midshipman, and a
number of seamen and marines.] This bill was
also amended, so as to include the case of John
Woodward and Mathew Guy, for a capture made
in the waters of St. Mary's county, Maryland.

The bill for the relief of Joseph S. Newell. [A
land case.]

The House, on motion of Mr. CANNON, took
up, in Committee of the Whole, the report of a
committee unfavorable to the petition of the heirs
of Absalom Tatom; but, on the suggestion of Mr.
CLAY, the Committee rose and dismissed the subject, on the ground that it was useless to consider
a subject like this, because, even if the report was
reversed, a bill on the subject could not possibly
be finally acted on the present session.

On motion of Mr. TUCKER, the Committee of
the Whole was discharged from the further consideration of the bill to incorporate the Columbia
Insurance Company of Alexandria; and Mr. T.
then moved that the bill be engrossed, and read a
third time to-morrow. On motion of Mr. WEB-
STER, the bill was ordered to lie on the table.

The following bills next passed under consideration, and were ordered to be engrossed for a third
reading to-morrow:

A bill authorizing the formation of a code of
jurisprudence for the District of Columbia. [Di-
recting the Judges of the District of Columbia to
form and report to Congress, for their adoption or
modification, &c., a code of jurisprudence, both
civil and criminal; and allowing to the judges,
for this service, a compensation of five hundred
dollars each.]

The bill concerning vaccination. [This bill
proposes to compel the agent for vaccination to
furnish, free of expense, to applicants by mail,
true and genuine vaccine matter, with instructions for using the same.] Much discussion took
place as to the amount of annual compensation to the agent who now is, or hereafter may
be appointed. It was ultimately, on motion of
Mr. PLEASANTS, fixed at $1,500.

Mr. HUGER made an unsuccessful motion to
suspend the intervening orders, and take up the
resolution respecting the remains of General
WASHINGTON.

Mr. JOHNSON, of Kentucky, after a few prefatory remarks, moved the following resolutions,
which were successively agreed to:

Resolved, That the Secretary of War be requested
to report to the House, at an early day of the next session of Congress, a system for the organization and
discipline of the Militia, best calculated, in his opinion,
to promote the efficiency of that force when called into
the public service.

Resolved, That the Secretary of War be requested
to report, if there be any, and if any, what modification or alteration is necessary in relation to the various
branches of the War Department, for the faithful exe-

cution of their duties; and to suggest any plan which, in his opinion, will promote the public interest and despatch of business, by responsibility of officers, and economy in the execution of the various duties of the War Department.

The bill concerning pre-emption rights to lands in Louisiana, Missouri, and Illinois; the bill to authorize the surveying and making a road in the Territory of Illinois; and the bill allowing pay to persons made prisoners with the revenue cutter Surveyor; severally passed through Committees of the Whole, and were ordered to a third reading.

The bill to organize, class, and arm the militia, &c., and the bill supplemental to the act for the final adjustment of land titles in Louisiana, were postponed indefinitely.

PORTS OF ENTRY.

The bill from the Senate, to provide for the entry of vessels at the port of Middletown, Connecticut, was taken up in Committee of the Whole.

Mr. NEWTON suggested the propriety of letting this bill take the same course as similar propositions brought before the House at this session; all of which, on the recommendation of the Committee of Commerce and Manufactures, had been referred to the Secretary of the Treasury, to make a general report thereon at the next session.

Mr. MOSELEY replied to Mr. NEWTON, and submitted some reasons in favor of the bill.

Mr. CLARKE, of North Carolina, moved to include in the bill the port of Plymouth, in North Carolina; the petition from which place had been referred, with others, to the Secretary of the Treasury, as mentioned by Mr. NEWTON. Mr. C. briefly supported his motion, in which he spoke against legislating partially on this subject; after which the amendment was agreed to without objection.

The bill was then reported to the House as amended, and ordered to a third reading.

LICENSES—PAY OF MINISTERS.

The House went into a Committee of the Whole, on the bill to reduce the duty on licenses to retailers of spirits, foreign merchandise, &c.

Mr. PICKENS moved that the bill be amended, by inserting a proviso, that no retailer of imported salt, whose stock does not exceed one hundred dollars, shall be compelled to take out license.

The motion was supported by the mover and by Mr. WILLIAMS, and agreed to; after which, the Committee of the Whole proceeded to consider the bill from the Senate, to increase the compensation of our Ministers resident at the Courts of London, Paris, and St. Petersburg, to the sum of $12,000, instead of the present allowance of $9,000 per annum.

Mr. ROBERTSON moved to reduce the sum in the bill to $9,000, so as to leave the salary at its present amount. Mr. R. supported his motion by a number of remarks, to show that the present salary, with the outfit, was sufficient to maintain our Ministers at any of the European Courts, in

a style consistent with their comfort, respectability, and dignity. The motion was opposed by Messrs. SMITH, of Maryland, LOWNDES, GROSVENOR, WRIGHT and PICKERING, who maintained the reverse of Mr. ROBERTSON'S opinions, and argued that the present salary was entirely inadequate to support our Ministers abroad, particularly at the courts named, in a manner suitable to the Representatives of the nation, or in such a style as was common and necessary in Europe to their respectability; and that it was necessary to allow an adequate compensation, to induce men of talents to leave their professions at home to go abroad in the public service, &c. Both sides of the question were argued at considerable length, and a variety of facts and illustrations introduced in support of the opinions urged.

The question was finally decided against Mr. ROBERTSON'S motion; after which the Committee rose, and reported their amendment to the bill first considered, which was concurred in, and the bill ordered to a third reading.

The second bill being reported without amendment, the question on engrossing it was stated; but before it was put, a motion to adjourn prevailed.

MONDAY, April 22.

The Committee of Commerce and Manufactures were discharged from a further consideration of the bill from the Senate, "establishing a port of delivery at the town of Bayou St. John," and the bill was ordered to be read a third time.

Mr. CHAPPELL, from the Committee on Pensions and Revolutionary Claims, to whom was referred the amendment proposed by the Senate to the bill "for the relief of the heirs of George Nebinger, deceased," reported the same with amendments; which were read, and, together with the said amendments of the Senate committed to a Committee of the Whole to day.

Mr. ROBERTSON, from the Committee on the Public Lands, reported a bill providing for reprinting the collection of land laws; which was read twice, and committed to a Committee of the Whole.

A message from the Senate informed the House that the Senate have passed the bill "to regulate the duties on imports and tonnage," with amendments, in which they ask the concurrence of this House.

Mr. PLEASANTS, from the Naval Committee, reported a bill to fix the Peace Establishment of the Marine Corps [reducing it to one thousand non-commissioned officers and privates;] which was twice read and committed.

A message from the Senate informed the House that the Senate have passed the bill "for organizing the General Staff, and making further provision for the Army of the United States," with amendments. The Senate have passed a bill "to increase the compensation of the superintendents of the manufactories of arms at Springfield and Harper's Ferry," and a bill "concerning the annual sum appropriated for arming and equipping the militia ;" in which amendments and bills they ask the concurrence of this House.

The amendments proposed by the Senate to the bill " to regulate the duties on imports and tonnage" were read, and referred to the Committee of Ways and Means.

The amendment proposed by the Senate to the bill " for organizing the General Staff, and making further provision for the Army of the United States" was read, and concurred in by the House.

Mr. GROSVENOR, from the select committee to whom was referred the bill from the Senate "for the benefit of the widow and children of Robert Fulton, deceased," reported the same, with amendments; which were read, and, together with the bill, committed to a Committee of the Whole to-morrow.

The bill from the Senate " to increase the compensation of the superintendents of the manufactories of arms at Springfield and Harper's Ferry" was read twice, and committed to a Committee of the Whole.

The bill from the Senate " concerning the annual sum appropriated for arming and equipping the militia," was read twice, and committed to a Committee of the Whole.

Engrossed bills of the following titles, to wit:

An act making appropriations for repairing certain roads therein mentioned;

An act for the relief of Joseph S. Newell ;

An act appropriating the sum of two thousand five hundred dollars for the purpose therein mentioned ;

An act authorizing the payment of a sum of money to John Rodgers and others ;

An act authorizing the payment of a sum of money to Joseph Stewart and others ;

An act authorizing the judges of the circuit court for the District of Columbia to prepare a code of jurisprudence for the said District ;

An act concerning pre-emption rights given in the purchase of lands to certain settlers in the State of Louisiana, and in the Territories of Missouri and Illinois ;

An act allowing pay to certain persons made prisoners with the revenue cutter "Surveyor ;"

An act to authorize the surveying and marking a road in the Territory of Illinois ; and

An act for reducing the duties on licenses to retailers of wines, spirituous liquors, and foreign merchandise ; were severally read the third time, and passed.

The bill from the Senate "establishing a port of delivery at the town of Bayou St. John," was read the third time, and passed.

The bill from the Senate "concerning the entry of vessels at the port of Middletown," was read the third time as amended, and passed.

Ordered, That the title be "An act concerning the entry of vessels at the ports of Middletown and Plymouth."

The engrossed bill respecting vaccination. This bill was laid on the table, on motion of Mr. SOUTHARD,; who stated, in making the motion, that a member of the committee which reported the bill, who was at present absent from indisposi-

tion, had received important information from the vaccine agent, and also from officers of the Army and Navy ; and had in consequence prepared some amendments which he wished to make to the bill to introduce vaccination into the Army and Navy ; to give time for this, Mr. S. asked that the bill might lie on the table a day or two.

Ordered, That the Committee of the Whole be discharged from a further consideration of the bill to provide for the widows and orphans of volunteers and militia who have been killed or died of wounds, and from the report of the select committee appointed to revise the rules and orders of the House; and that the said bill and report be postponed indefinitely.

The House went into Committee of the Whole on the bill for the relief of David Gelston, Collector, and P. A. Schenck, Naval Officer of the port of New York; to indemnify them $100,000 damages recovered against them by Gould Hoyt, and others, for the seizure of a vessel, which afterwards proved to be not authorized by law.

This bill also produced some debate. It was opposed by Mr. SHEFFEY, on the ground that the seizure was made without probable cause, otherwise damages would not have been awarded by the court; that where an officer thus acts he does so on his own responsibility, and ought not to be indemnified therefor by the Government. The bill was advocated by Mr. LOWNDES at some length, on the ground, generally, that the private property of an officer ought not to be held responsible for acts committed in the discharge of his public duty, acting according to his best judgment. The discussion embraced various considerations arising out of the trial of the case before the circuit court.

The Committee then took up the bill for the relief of George T. Ross and Com. D. T. Patterson* and their officers and men, [granting them $50,000 a moiety of the value of the vessels, &c. captured by them from the pirates of Barrataria.]

The bills were reported to the House without amendment. The former, on motion of Mr. TUCKER, was laid on the table, and the latter ordered to a third reading.

The Committee of the Whole to whom was committed the report of the Committee on the Public Lands on the petition of Thomas Carr, the bill for the relief of Bowie and Kurtz, and others, and the bill to establish an uniform system of bankruptcy, were discharged from a further consideration thereof, and the said report and bills were postponed indefinitely.

DIRECT TAX.

The House took up for consideration the amendments made by the Senate to the bill from this House, to regulate the assessment of the direct tax, &c., one of which was the addition of a section directing a revision of the assessment and valuation of property in the State of Delaware. The amendment, it appeared, was predicated on a petition of the Legislature of that State, growing out of the alleged injustice of the board of principal assessors, who altered the valuation of property made and reported by the assistant asses-

1413   HISTORY OF CONGRESS.   1414

APRIL, 1816.   *Specie Payments—Salaries of Ministers.*   H. OF R.

sors in different counties, so as to produce a very unequal and unjust apportionment of the direct tax among the counties of the State. The Committee of Ways and Means, to whom the amendment had been referred, recommended a disagreement thereto; and the question was on concurring with the committee. The amendment produced a good deal of debate, in which Messrs. CLAYTON, WRIGHT, SHEFFEY, WARD of Massachusetts, and GASTON, supported, and Messrs. LOWNDES and INGHAM opposed the adoption of the amendment. By the advocates of the amendment, it was urged that the conduct of the board of assessors was partial, unauthorized, unjust, and oppressive, and required the revision provided by the new section. The amendment was opposed on the ground that the proper business of the board was to supervise and equalize the valuations of the assistant assessors; that although they had not acted conformably to the letter of the law, still the result of their decision was the same as if they had proceeded in strict accordance with the law, and that it was an error in form only; and that if this amendment were agreed to, it would open a door to endless applications for the revision of assessments, &c. To establish the above points, a variety of arguments and illustrations were used, which protracted the debate to a considerable length. The report of the Committee of Ways and Means was finally disagreed to by a decided majority, and the amendment of the Senate concurred in.

SPECIE PAYMENTS.

The House proceeded to take up the bill to provide for collecting the public revenues in the lawful money of the country—(to enforce the payment of specie.)

Mr. CALHOUN moved to amend the bill by adding several additional sections, authorizing the issue of —— millions of Treasury notes, not to bear interest or be fundable, to be received in all dues to the United States, providing the usual penalties for counterfeiting, &c.

The amendments were ordered to be printed, and the bill was recommitted to a Committee of the Whole, for the purpose of considering the amendments; it being decided by the Speaker that it was necessary to take that course.

In answer to some inquiries by Mr. GROSVENOR, Mr. CALHOUN stated it as his intention to move to fill up the blank with fifteen millions, as the amount of Treasury notes to be issued.

SALARIES OF MINISTERS.

The House then took up the unfinished business of Friday—being the bill from the Senate to increase the salaries of our Ministers at the Courts of St. Petersburg, Paris, and London, [to twelve thousand dollars per annum;] which bill had passed through a Committee of the Whole; and the question now was, whether it should be engrossed and read a third time. This question was decided in the negative—yeas 36, nays 67, as follows:

YEAS—Messrs. Archer, Atherton, Baer, Betts, Breck-

enridge, Calhoun, Chappell, Cuthbert, Forney, Gaston, Grosvenor, Ingham, Johnson of Virginia, King of North Carolina, Love, Lovett, Lowndes, Lyon, Mayrant, Murfree, Nelson of Massachusetts, Nelson of Virginia, Newton, Pickering, Pleasants, Savage, Schenck, Sheffey, Smith of Maryland, Taggart, Ward of Massachusetts, Wilkin, Thomas Wilson, Woodward, Wright, and Yancey.

NAYS—Messrs. Adgate, Alexander, Barbour, Bennett, Birdsall, Boss, Bradbury, Brooks, Brown, Bryan, Cady, Cannon, Champion, Chipman, Cilley, Clopton, Crawford, Crocheron, Culpeper, Darlington, Davenport, Desha, Edwards, Glasgow, Hahn, Hale, Hanson, Hardin, Hawes, Heister, Herbert, Hungerford, Irwin of Pennsylvania, Langdon, Law, Lewis, Lumpkin, Lyle, Marsh, Mason, McCoy, McLean of Kentucky, Milnor, Noyes, Ormsby, Pitkin, Reed, Reynolds, Roane, Robertson, Root, Ruggles, Southard, Stearns, Strong, Stuart, Sturges, Tate, Taul, Telfair, Tucker, Vose, Wallace, Whiteside, Wilcox, Williams, and Willoughby.

And so the said bill was rejected.

TUESDAY, April 23.

Mr. NELSON, from the committee to whom the subject was referred, on the 23d of January last, reported a joint resolution requesting the President of the United States to cause further observations to be made with a view of ascertaining the longitude of the Capitol, in the City of Washington; which was read twice and ordered to be engrossed, and read a third time to-morrow.

Ordered, That the Committee of the Whole, to whom is committed the bill to amend the act confirming certain powers of the Levy Court of the county of Washington, in the District of Columbia, passed on the 1st of July, 1812; the bill making an appropriation for completing the centre building of the Capitol; the bill further to extend the judicial system of the United States; and the bill from the Senate "authorizing the appointment of Admirals;" be discharged from a further consideration thereof, and that the said bills be postponed indefinitely.

A message from the Senate informed the House that the Senate have passed the bill "making further provision for settling claims to land in the Territory of Illinois;" also the bill "supplemental to the act entitled an act regulating and defining the duties of the judges of the Territory of Illinois and for vesting in the courts of the Territory of Indiana a jurisdiction in chancery cases arising in the said Territory;" also the bill "for the relief of Joseph Wilson;" also the bill "for the relief of the President and Directors of the Washington Bridge Company," with amendments to each, in which they ask the concurrence of this House;

They have passed a bill "for the relief of the legal representatives of Ignace Chalmet Delino, deceased;" also, a bill "authorizing the sale of lots owned by the United States in the city of New Orleans, and for other purposes;" also, a bill "for settling the compensation of the commissioner, clerk, and translator of the Board for Land Claims in the eastern and western district of the Territory of Orleans, now State of Louisiana;" and a bill "for adjusting the claims to land and establishing a land office for the district of lands lying east of the Mississippi river and island of New Orleans; in which said bills they ask the concurrence of this House.

Mr. LOWNDES, from the Committee of Ways and Means, to whom was referred the amendments proposed by the Senate to the bill "to regulate the duties on imports and tonnage," reported the agreement of the committee to the said amendments.

Ordered, That the said amendments be committed to the Committee of the Whole House on the bill for the more effectual collection of the revenue in the lawful money of the United States.

The House went into Committee of the Whole on the annual provision for invalid pensioners. The details of this bill, embracing additional cases of pension, the increase of former ones, and the various propositions made to insert other cases, with the discussion of the claims, as usual, occupied much time. The bill was finally reported to the House, the numerous amendments were again considered and disposed of, and the bill ordered to a third reading.

SPECIE PAYMENTS.

On motion of Mr. CALHOUN, the House resolved itself into a Committee of the Whole, on the bill to provide for the more effectual collection of the public revenue in the lawful money of the country—to enforce the payment of specie.

The amendments offered yesterday by Mr. CALHOUN were read, the first section of which provides, substantially, for the issue of Treasury notes to the amount of —— dollars, of such convenient denominations as the Secretary of the Treasury shall direct; transferrable by delivery; not to bear interest; not to be fundable; to be received everywhere in dues to the United States, and may be re-issued from time to time.

The second, third, and fourth sections provide for the preparing, signing, and issuing the Treasury notes, for paying the expense thereof, and the usual penalties for counterfeiting them.

The fifth section provides, that the Secretary of the Treasury shall issue said notes upon loan to the Bank of the United States, or any State bank applying therefor, on such terms as he shall deem necessary, having regard to the circumstances of each case, and the security of the United States, at a rate of interest not less than —— per cent. per annum; but not to loan to any State bank more than a moiety of their capital paid in these loans; to be reimbursable in three equal annual instalments, computed from the date of the respective loans, and be paid for as they become due in the legal coin, or in Treasury notes. [The *moiety,* on motion of Mr. SMITH, was subsequently converted into *one-fourth.*]

The fifth section authorizes the Secretary of the Treasury to issue said notes at their par value to individuals, companies, or corporations, and receive in payment therefor the United States'

stocks; but the amount sold for funded debt not to exceed [five] millions; the notes so sold to be taken out of the annual appropriations for the Sinking Fund, and the funded debt thus acquired to be transferred to the Commissioners of the Sinking Fund, and by them applied as the law directs, with other funded debt.

The seventh section makes it the duty of the Secretary of the Treasury, annually, to withdraw from circulation and to cancel a portion of said Treasury notes, equal to one-third of the whole amount issued.

The eighth section of the amendments provides that the future issues of Treasury notes, under the act of February 24, 1815, shall not exceed the sum of five millions of dollars.

The amendments having been read—

Mr. CALHOUN moved to fill the blank in the first section with "fifteen" millions; and then, in a speech of some length, stated to the Committee the benefits which were anticipated from the proposed issue of Treasury notes; the aid and relief they would afford to the community, under the pressure which would unavoidably be produced by the banks in the necessary curtailment of their discounts, the withdrawal of their notes from circulation, &c., preparatory to the resumption of specie payments, which the bill would enforce. It was his opinion that the bill would be effectual in producing the payment of specie, without the aid of this feature; but there were others who doubted whether the restoration could be well or safely effected without it; and he wished to afford every facility and relief that could be with propriety given, as well to the banks as to the community.

Mr. ROBERTSON followed in opposition to the amendment, against which he argued at some length. He objected to it chiefly on the ground that it would form an unfortunate and hazardous connexion between the Government and the State banks; extending the indirect influence of the banks, which had been often complained of, to a direct influence; and, instead of compelling the banks to sell their public stock and meet their engagements, would increase their means of resisting the measures to coerce them into the payment of specie.

Mr. CADY spoke against the amendment. It would be reloaning the public funds at five per cent., while the Government of the United States was borrowing at seven; would be collecting the revenues of the Government in its own paper only, and defeating the object of laying taxes; that it would tend to depress our stocks in Europe; that it would be better to give credit to those indebted to the Government at six per cent. a year; that no bank would borrow these notes which meant to pay for them, as it would be giving five per cent. for notes to lend out to its customers; and that the issue of fifteen millions, if they could be kept in circulation, would drive specie out of the country instead of drawing it thither.

Mr. BARBOUR replied to Mr. ROBERTSON, and defended the amendment on the ground of the great assistance it would afford to the community in meeting the state of things which must take place under the pressure inevitably created by the banks in returning to specie payments; his desire to resort to mild means; its accustoming the people to give credit to paper issued under the authority of Government; its embracing and assisting those banks possessing no public stock.

Mr. TUCKER moved to fill the blank with "*ten*" millions.

Mr. CALHOUN replied to the arguments against the amendment. He had no idea the banks would resume specie payments willingly; they would go into it only because they would see inevitable ruin in refusing; but as they would be compelled to embrace the measure, he wished to give them ample means.

Mr. CUTHBERT made some remarks in favor of the larger sum. Fifteen millions might be used for other purposes than in loaning to the banks; it might be applied to the purchase of stocks, to loans to individuals.

The motion to fill the blank with "fifteen" was lost—ayes 55, noes 59.

Mr. TUCKER then, for the present, withdrew his motion.

The question on agreeing to the first section as an amendment, still in blank, was carried—ayes 59, noes 58.

Mr. TUCKER renewed his motion to fill the blank with "ten" millions.

Mr. WEBSTER stated some objections to the provision in its present shape. He should have no unwillingness to authorize an issue of Treasury notes in another way; to make them payable to the public creditors, he thought, would be preferable to the manner contemplated.

Mr. NEWTON moved the sum of "thirteen."

Mr. GROSVENOR then rose and stated his objections to the proposed issue of Treasury notes, which he viewed as the first attempt yet made to create a paper currency for the country. In this light Mr. G. discussed the subject at much length, arguing against an experiment so dangerous in principle, and which universal experience proved would always end in a depreciated currency, however feasible it might appear in time of peace and tranquillity. When he concluded—

The question of filling the blank with "thirteen" was negatived—ayes 66, noes 62; and the question recurred on the sum of "ten" millions.

Mr. CUTHBERT then replied to Mr. GROSVENOR, and to the arguments grounded on the presumption that this measure was to be a permanent one, and contending that, as the Government had, by long usage, given credit to the present paper, making it in fact the currency of the country, it would be wrong suddenly to discredit this paper and destroy its value in the community without supplying the country with something as a substitute. He viewed the proposition under discussion as one which would produce the happiest consequences.

The question was then taken on filling the blank with "ten," and carried—ayes 66.

Mr. WEBSTER moved to strike out of the fifth section the words "to the Bank of the United States;" which, after some discussion, was agreed to.

Mr. SMITH, of Maryland, moved to fix the amount of interest to be required of the banks at *three* per cent. per annum; and supported his motion at some length, entering somewhat into the general question of the expediency of the measure.

Mr. CALHOUN moved to fill the blank with *five* per cent., and replied at still greater length than before to Messrs. GROSVENOR, ROBERTSON, and others, who had spoken in opposition.

Mr. ROBERTSON moved *six* per centum, and added some remarks in support of the opinions he had advanced.

After some further discussion, the motion to fill the blank with *six* per centum was carried—ayes 55, noes 52.

Mr. SHEFFEY moved an amendment, which would confine the loan of these Treasury notes to such banks only as hold no stock of the United States. Negatived—ayes 45.

The eighth section was then agreed to—58 to 51.

Mr. HALL then proposed to amend the bill by reviving and adding thereto the former fourth section, which imposed a high stamp duty on the notes of the banks not paying specie on the day specified; which motion Mr. H. made some remarks in favor of—stating his object to be to give the solvent banks an opportunity of paying specie, and of putting down those that could not pay; which could only be done by the provision he proposed to renew.

Mr. TUCKER agreed with Mr. HALL in some degree; and proposed to modify the amendment by making it an uniform stamp duty of ten per cent. on all notes issued by the delinquent banks.

Mr. ROOT spoke against the motion to renew the section, and disputed the power of Congress, under the Constitution, to adopt such a measure, which was of the nature of a penalty, and intended as a punishment that could not constitutionally be inflicted on the banks.

Mr. RANDOLPH also opposed the adoption of this section, to which nothing similar could be found in the code of any nation under the sun. He argued against the measure at some length, and condemned it as anti-republican and dangerous—as adding to the power and patronage of the Secretary of the Treasury, already too great, a discretion dangerous in the extreme, and in effect making his will the measure of taxation.

Before the motion was decided, the Committee rose, reported progress, and was refused leave to sit again, leaving the bill in the House.

WEDNESDAY, April 24.

Mr. HUGER from the committee appointed by a resolution of the 27th of February last, to examine generally into the subject of unsettled balances, made a report; which was read and ordered to lie on the table; when Mr. H. reported a bill to establish the office of Accountant in the Department of State; which was read twice and ordered to lie on the table.

Mr. Root, from the Committee on Expenditures in the War Department, reported a bill supplementary to the several acts organizing the office of Accountant of the Department of War; which was read twice, and committed to a Committee of the Whole.

Mr. Nelson, from the committee to whom was referred the Message of the President of the United States, respecting the Patent Office, reported a bill establishing the Patent Office, providing the means of further encouragement to "authors and inventors," and guarding more effectually against frauds and impositions by patentees; which was read twice and committed to a Committee of the Whole.

The amendment proposed by the Senate to the bill "supplemental to the act, entitled "An act regulating and defining the duties of the judges of the Territory of Illinois, and for vesting in the courts of the Territory of Indiana a jurisdiction in chancery cases arising in the said Territory," was read and disagreed to by the House.

The amendment proposed by the Senate to the bill "for the relief of the President and Directors of the Washington Bridge Company," was read; whereupon, ordered that this House concur in the said amendment.

The amendments proposed by the Senate to the bill "making further provision for settling claims to lands in the Territory of Illinois," were read and concurred in by the House.

The amendment proposed by the Senate to the bill "for the relief of Joseph Wilson," was read and concurred in by the House.

The bill from the Senate for adjusting the claims to land, and establishing a land office for the districts of lands lying east of the Mississippi River and island of New Orleans," was read twice and committed to a Committee of the Whole.

The bill from the Senate "authorizing the sale of lots owned by the United States in the city of New Orleans, and for other purposes," was read twice and ordered to lie on the table.

The bill from the Senate "for settling the compensation of the commissioners, clerk, and translator of the Board for Land Claims in the eastern and western district of the Territory of Orleans, now State of Louisiana," was read twice and committed to a Committee of the Whole.

Engrossed bills of the following titles: An act concerning invalid pensioners; an act for the relief of George T. Ross, Daniel T. Patterson, and the officers and men under their command; were severally read the third time and passed.

An engrossed resolution "requesting the President of the United States to cause further observations to be made with a view of ascertaining the longitude of the Capitol in the City of Washington," was read the third time and passed.

A message from the Senate informed the House that the Senate have passed bills of the following titles, to wit: "An act authorizing payment for the court-house of Hamilton in the State of Ohio;" "An act making appropriation for the support of the Military Establishment of the United States for the year 1816;" and "An act for the relief of the supervisors of the county of Clinton, in the State of New York," with amendments, in which they ask the concurrence of this House.

The bill from the Senate "for the relief of the legal representatives of Ignace Chalmet Delino, deceased," was read twice and committed to a Committee of the Whole.

QUARTERMASTER'S ACCOUNTS.

Mr. McKee, from the committee appointed to inquire into the accounts rendered and settled of James Thomas, a deputy quartermaster general in the Army of the United States, and to examine into the accounts connected therewith, made a report, embracing a statement of facts and many documents, but expressing no opinion on the subject, and recommending a more mature examination into the matter at the next session; which report was ordered to lie, and be printed.

The report is as follows:

The committee appointed to inquire into the state of the accounts (rendered and settled) of James Thomas, a deputy quartermaster general of the United States, and also to examine all accounts connected therewith, report:

That the committee have examined the subject referred to them with as much care as a due attention to the current business of the House would permit. When the papers were referred to the committee, it was understood that James Thomas was in the Western country, and a letter was addressed to him at Pittsburg, informing him that a committee was appointed to examine and report on his accounts.

James Thomas arrived in this city on the 13th instant, and made application to the committee to postpone a report on his case to the next session of Congress; the reasons assigned in support of this application are fully disclosed in the papers herewith submitted to the House as a part of this report, from which it will appear that the committee had neither time nor the means of pronouncing on the character of the transaction, or the conduct of James Thomas, without wholly disregarding the statements made by him to the committee.

So far, therefore, as James Thomas is concerned, the committee recommend a postponement of the case to the next session of Congress, so that the case may then undergo a more mature examination than can now be given to it.

The settlement made in this case by the accounting officers of the Government seems to require examination; the settlement was made on the papers and documents now before the committee, and on that evidence alone the settlement, and the principle on which it was made, must stand the test of examination.

Without designing to express any opinion in relation to James Thomas, the committee submit to the House the following statement of the case, as it seems to have been presented to the accounting officers of the Government for settlement, as well as the several occurrences which happened in the progress of the settlement.

On the 22d day of November, 1812, General Smyth, commanding on the Niagara frontier, ordered James

Thomas, deputy quartermaster general, to purchase immediately, and deposite at or near Buffalo, flour for five thousand troops for two months, besides the current issues; and Michael T. Simpson immediately thereafter proceeded to purchase flour from the country people, and in effecting the purchase he represented himself as the agent of James Thomas, and entered into a contract in that character. Said Simpson procured, in the vicinity of Batavia and Caledonia, about 1,500 barrels of flour, at or near the average price of $9 per barrel at those places, as it appears from the depositions and certificates of the persons from whom it was obtained.

On the 12th day of December, 1812, Michael T. Simpson charges the United States $29,155 for 2,305 barrels of flour delivered at Caledonia and Batavia, $738 87 commission for purchasing the same, and $3,520 for transporting 680 barrels of flour from Caledonia to Buffalo. Between the 12th of December, 1812, and the 28th of June, 1813, Michael T. Simpson charges the United States for a variety of articles of army supplies, amounting, inclusive of the bill of the 12th of December, 1812, to the sum of $61,192 15½; and James Thomas obtains Simpson's receipts for this sum in nine separate bills and receipts, which he renders as evidence of disbursement made by him on public account.

The late Accountant of the War Department, to whom the accounts were rendered, regarding Michael T. Simpson as a citizen of the country, who had possessed himself of the articles sold to James Thomas with his own funds or credit, and at his own risk, in the ordinary course of business, considered his receipts as good evidence of disbursement. But it was discovered to the satisfaction of the late Accountant of the War Department, before the account was finally settled, that Michael T. Simpson was not a citizen of that part of the country, but merely a wayfaring person seeking employment, and that he had not become possessed of the property sold to the public in the ordinary course of business, or at his own risk, but that he had purchased the same by means of the public funds in the hands of James Thomas. It was also discovered that the flour was charged to the United States at a rate much higher than its actual cost. The late Accountant of the War Department therefore ordered the amount of Michael T. Simpson's receipts (except a part of the receipt for $10,510 25) to be taken from the credits of James Thomas, and suspended until the receipts of those persons from whom the articles were actually purchased should be produced as evidence of the disbursement as well as the cost of the articles. This suspension seems to have been made on the principle that M. T. Simpson was the agent of J. Thomas, and that he was enabled to make the purchases aforesaid from the public funds in his hands. After this decision was made known, the copy of a letter from James Thomas to Michael T. Simpson of the 25th of November, 1812, and Simpson's answers of the 28th of November, and 4th of December, 1812, were filed in the handwriting of James Thomas, with the intention of establishing thereby the existence of a contract between Michael T. Simpson and James Thomas in regard to the flour purchased by said Simpson. This evidence was deemed by the late Accountant insufficient to authorize a change of the decision made; and the account was closed, leaving a balance due to the United States by James Thomas of $133,087 84. From this decision James Thomas appealed to the accounting officers of the Treasury Department, and the accounts were sent to the Treasury Department by Peter Hagner, the acting Accountant, by whom they were closed on the 14th day of July, 1814, for re-examination and final adjustment, where they were examined by the Auditor of the Treasury, and $2,411 80 of the suspended items admitted to the credit of James Thomas, leaving a balance due by him to the United States of $130,-676 04. The principles settled by the Accountant of the War Department were not changed by the admission aforesaid. The accounts were reported to the late Comptroller of the Treasury on the 8th day of August, 1814, by the Auditor. It appears that the accounts were examined by the late Comptroller, and that he did not alter the balance, or change the principles settled at the War Department; he was, in the opinion of the committee, prevented from deciding finally on the case by a protest filed in his office by James Thomas on the 13th of August, 1814, alleging, amongst other things, that his accounts, since they were rendered to the Accountant of the War Department, had been mutilated and robbed of documents and vouchers belonging thereto. The committee deem it proper to state that this charge of mutilation and robbery is not supported by any evidence yet disclosed.

On the 5th day of April, 1815, James Thomas requested the present Comptroller of the Treasury to permit him to withdraw his appeal, and to submit his case again to the present Accountant of the War Department, together with evidence not before rendered in support of the suspended items in his account. This request was granted, and the accounts were sent to the present Accountant of the War Department on the 6th day of April, 1815. James Thomas filed with the Accountant of the War Department copies of several letters and certificates, which are on the files, relating to the suspended items, and supposed to contain evidence of a contract between Michael T. Simpson and James Thomas as to the flour, and the prices thereof. With regard to these letters and certificates, the committee have sought in vain for the originals, which are not now to be found in the public offices, and the copies obtained by the committee are extracts taken from a pamphlet written by James Thomas in defiance of himself.

The Accountant of the War Department restated the account, and admitted the suspended items, for payments made to Michael T. Simpson, to the credit of James Thomas, on the following grounds: 1st. The charge for 2,305 barrels of flour, commission, and transportation, was admitted, because, in the opinion of the Accountant, the evidence aforesaid establishes a contract between Simpson and Thomas for the flour at a specified price. 2d. The residue of the suspended items are admitted to the credit of James Thomas, except $201 10, charged as commission, because it does not appear that Michael T. Simpson, was the acknowledged agent of James Thomas.

The foregoing is, in substance, a correct statement of the settlement of the accounts of James Thomas, and the principles established in the settlement. So far only as relates to the disbursements made by Michael T. Simpson, there are many accounts settled on principles which seem to the committee objectionable, but which must now be admitted. Without entering at all into the question whether or not the copies of letters and certificates filed establish a contract between James Thomas and Michael T. Simpson, the committee will only say that, if the evidence is considered authentic, and sufficient to prove the existence of a contract, it is certainly competent also to prove that Michael T. Simpson misrepresented the state of the market, with a view to his advantage and the public injury. But the committee cannot regard any contract made by a public agent charged with providing supplies for the public, however formal, which is fulfilled by means of the public funds in his hands, in any other light than as a badge of fraud. If such contracts are countenanced and drawn into practice, it must supersede the necessity as well as the propriety of requiring any public agent to render receipts (from those persons who have the articles wanted for public use, procured by their industry, with their own funds, and at their own risk) as evidence of price and payment, because this rule imposes much labor on honest agents, without affording any barrier against fraud and dishonesty. For what is more easy of accomplishment than for a public agent, inclined to defraud the public, to enter into a formal contract with a friend (whose moral feelings suit the occasion) to deliver property suited to the public wants, at a specific price, exceeding the market price, and then, by means of the public funds in his hands, to enable his friend to fulfil the contract for their mutual benefit? Cases may be supposed, and may occur in practice, where contracts made by a public agent to furnish supplies, with the aid of the public funds, which it is the agent's duty to furnish, may be right; but those possible cases must be accompanied with peculiar circumstances, and on those circumstances their justification must rest.

It cannot be doubted that Michael T. Simpson purchased the 2,205 barrels of flour with the aid of the public funds in the hands of James Thomas; and it is worthy of remark that there is no conflict between the depositions filed by Mr. Porter and the copies of certificates furnished by James Thomas: they relate to different parcels of flour—the first are specific as to quantity and price, the latter are general.

The committee, therefore, cannot but regard the principle on which the suspended item for $32,403 87 was allowed as erroneous, and destructive of all accountability. The principle on which the residue of the suspended items were allowed seems to the committee to be equally or more objectionable.

It is evident that the supplies were purchased by means of the public funds in the hands of James Thomas, and intended for the public use, to which they were alone suited. No man in the right use of his reason would have possessed himself of the articles in the prosecution of any ordinary business; and to consider Mr. Simpson unconnected in some way with the public officer is absurd, especially after he had charged a commission on part of his purchases. The receipts of those persons who were the original owners of the property, or who have acquired it at their own risk, is the only good evidence of price and payment, and, in the opinion of the committee, ought, in all ordinary cases, to be required as evidence of disbursement.

WASHINGTON, *April* 12, 1816.

SIR: I learn that a committee has been appointed by the House of Representatives to examine my accounts with the United States, in consequence of allegations made by William Simmons, late Accountant of the War Department, that fraudulent charges to a considerable amount had been made by me, and allowed,

under the special directions of the officers of the Treasury.

As these accounts had already been before a committee of Congress on the representations of this person, and as they had been referred by that committee to the accounting officers of the Treasury for settlement, and had been settled accordingly, I might have expected that such allegations would not have been repeated, at least until the legal tribunals of the country had decided on my complaints for similar calumnies propagated by him, with so much boldness and industry, by means of the public press.

Conscious, however, that my conduct has been in all respects honorable, I can have no objection to any inquiry, however rigid; on the contrary, I am happy to have any opportunity to bring these accusations to the test of truth. I hope the result will set them forever at rest; for, so highly do I value the good opinion of the community, that even the consciousness of rectitude does not render me indifferent to aspersions which strike at my reputation. I trust, however, that the inquiry will be complete, and I am sure it is foreign from the wish of any member of your honorable body to decide on a question which, through life, will affect the character of one of their fellow-citizens, without a full and fair investigation. I ask, therefore, to go before the committee, to know the specific act of criminality with which I am charged, and to be allowed the means which justice demands of substantiating my innocence.

In order that the true situation in which I stand towards the public, whether as debtor or creditor, may be known, I ask, further, that the whole of my claims connected with the discharge of my public duties may be placed before the view of the committee; these are contained in the letters and accounts presented by me to the War Department in the months of December and February last. It will then be seen that, so far from having profited by fraud and imposition on the public, I am, after seven years of active military duty, a sufferer through arduous and laborious exertions in the public service.

I have the honor to be, sir, your obedient servant,
         JAMES THOMAS.

The Hon. the SPEAKER
   of the House of Representatives.

WASHINGTON CITY, *April* 15, 1816.

SIR: You have applied to the committee to whom your accounts have been referred for a postponement of any decision or report thereon until the next session of Congress, on the general ground that time or opportunity has not been afforded you to procure testimony, explaining such parts of your accounts as seem to be mysterious, and rebutting the evidence tending to charge the accounts with unfairness or fraud. That the committee may have the means of deciding on your application, I am instructed by them to state to you the cases in your accounts most liable to exception, and to request you to say, in answer, whether you can (if time be allowed you) obtain evidence to explain and remove the mystery in which the cases are involved.

1st. The depositions on file (which are numbered progressively from 1 to 16, with the exception of No. 10, which is not with the documents referred to the committee, and Nos 12 and 13, which relate to your defence,) go to prove that Michael T. Simpson purchased nearly fifteen hundred barrels of flour, at a price averaging about $8 78 per barrel; that those purchases were made before the 12th of December, 1812; and Michael T. Simpson, in effecting those purchases, represented himself as your agent, and purchased with the aid of the public money or credit, and not on his own money or credit, or at his risk.

2d. On the 12th day of December, 1812, Michael T. Simpson renders an account against the United States for $32,403 87, composed of the following items, to wit: 2,305 barrels of flour, $29,155; commission, $728, 87; and $2,520 for transporting 630 barrels of flour from Caledonia to Buffalo, making an average price of $13 54 per barrel, including commission, and excluding the transportation; and $4 per barrel for transportation from Caledonia to Buffalo, when it appears by document No. 16 that transportation was offered to you from Caledonia to Buffalo for any quantity of flour at $2 per barrel.

3d. You have introduced copies of letters purporting to have been written by Michael T. Simpson to you, and dated the 26th of November, the 4th, the 7th, and 12th of December, 1812, and your answer of the 6th of December, 1812, as evidence of a contract with Mr. Simpson. The original letters are not with the papers referred to the committee, who have been unable to obtain them from the War or Treasury Department. The copies of the letters of the 28th of November and 4th of December, 1812, are in your handwriting: can the original letters be produced?

4th. Michael T. Simpson purchased other articles, to wit, corn, hay, oats, &c., amounting, inclusive of his flour account, to $61,192; and it is alleged, but not yet in proof, that one of the articles, to wit, the corn, was purchased by him for much less than the prices charged by him.

5th. You have produced two receipts from Daniel Mowry, one for $509 60, dated 5th of December, 1812, and one for $382 20, dated the 20th of December, 1812; and it appears, by reference to the settlement made by the wagonmaster of General Tannahill's brigade of Pennsylvania militia, that Daniel Mowry was attached to the said brigade as a teamster, and was paid by the public at the rate of $4 per day up to the 20th of December, 1812; and from a letter written by General Tannehill, and addressed to the late Accountant of the War Department, the correctness of the whole transaction may be questioned.

6th. You charge the United States with $276, paid to Michael T. Simpson for the hire of three large wagons from the 9th to the 31st of March, both days inclusive, and $216, as paid to said Simpson for the hire of three large teams from the 1st to the 18th of April, 1813, both days inclusive; and by Morgan Lewis's letter to you of the 2d of March, 1813, in answer to a letter acknowledged to have been received from you of the 24th of the preceding month, it appears that the same teams were purchased by you at $1,715, in February, 1813, from Michael T. Simpson.

7th. In the settlement of your accounts, you protested against the late Comptroller of the Treasury proceeding to a decision on your accounts, because, as you state in your protest, your papers are irregularly rendered, were mutilated, and robbed of part of the documents. This charge made by you is not supported by evidence, or accompanied by any specification of the documents alleged to have been mutilated or taken away.

You will say whether or not a postponement to the next session of Congress will enable you to introduce evidence explaining these points, and specify what evidence you expect to be able to procure in explanation of each point. Your most obedient servant,

SAMUEL McKEE.

JAMES THOMAS, Esq.

WASHINGTON, *April* 17, 1816.

SIR: In answer to your letter of the 15th instant, I have to state to you that if, from the partial testimony which may be before the committee, or from the misrepresentations of those who are interested in calumniating me, the transactions to which you have referred should be involved in any mystery, I can produce abundant evidence to remove it. But, as all my papers relating to those transactions are now in the District of Maine, (the place of my residence,) whither they were sent on the final adjustment of my accounts with the Government, and as it may be necessary to call persons who were on the spot and acquainted with the facts to give information on such points as may appear doubtful, it is impossible that a full investigation can be had during the present session of Congress. I pledge myself, however, if time and opportunity be allowed me, to disprove completely every charge of fraud or unfairness which may be alleged or insinuated against me.

With respect to the original letters for which you inquire, I have to inform you that I can prove them to have been exhibited at the offices of the Accountant of the War Department and the Comptroller of the Treasury. Indeed, no copies were produced by me, of which the originals were not also exhibited. But, if the originals in question cannot now be found, I can prove satisfactorily the correctness of the copies. On this occasion, it may be proper to call your attention to the fact, that, since the calumnies against me have been abroad, my accusers and others interested have had notice to all the papers relating to my accounts, &c., in the Register's office.

The complaint to which you allude, as having been made by me to the late Comptroller of the Treasury, of the mutilation of my accounts, I can substantiate.

Your letter contains, I presume, all the subjects on which the committee require any evidence or explanation. But, as Mr. Simmons has endeavored to give the impression that his decision on my accounts was sanctioned by the Treasury, I do most unequivocally deny that my accounts were, as he asserts, ever finally settled by the late officers of the Treasury on any appeal from me, or that any balance was struck against me by them. On the contrary, my accounts remained open, in consequence of the suspensions made by Mr. Simmons, until they were finally settled by his successor, whose decision was confirmed by the Comptroller.

I have already told you that, when I first heard of the appointment of your committee, I was at Pittsburg, on my way from the Lakes to this city, on business connected with the contract in which I was engaged with the Government for subsisting the troops, &c., in the Michigan country, and which requires my speedy return. Since my arrival, I have lost no time in presenting myself before you, and making such representations as appeared necessary. And it remains for the committee to determine whether they will proceed at once in the inquiry with the imperfect evidence which can now be had, or will defer it until all the testimony which the case admits may be laid before them.

I am, sir, your obedient servant,

JAMES THOMAS.

WASHINGTON CITY, *April* 18, 1816.

SIR: Your letter of the 17th instant was this morning laid before the committee to whom your accounts have been referred, and I am instructed by the committee to request you to inform the committee whether or not you have any papers or other evidence relating to the points stated in my letter of the 15th instant which has not been produced to the War or Treasury Department, and, if you have, then I have to request you to state specifically what that evidence is.

From your answer to my letter of the 15th instant, you pledge yourself to prove the mutilation of your accounts, and the robbery committed on them in part, as stated in your protest filed with the late Comptroller of the Treasury. You also state that the original letters which passed between you and Michael T. Simpson were filed with the accounting officers of the War and Treasury Department. As the evidence relating to these points must be in the city, the committee will hear any testimony you may think proper to introduce to them this evening at six o'clock, in their committee room, where you will attend.

Your most obedient,

SAMUEL McKEE.

N. B. Will you return to me the original letter to you of the 15th instant, and this letter also, as I have not time to copy them?

S. McKEE.

JAMES THOMAS, Esq.

———

Interrogatories stated to James Thomas by the committee to whom his accounts were referred, on his application for a postponement of a decision by the committee to the next session of Congress.

Question 1. If time is allowed you, do you believe you can show that the 2,205 barrels of flour delivered to you by Michael T. Simpson at Caledonia and Batavia did actually cost said Simpson, delivered at the places aforesaid, more than $8 78 per barrel, and that the cost to Simpson was near or about the prices charged by said Simpson; and do you expect to establish the facts aforesaid by the receipts or testimony of the persons from whom Simpson made the purchase of the flour?

Answer by James Thomas. I expect to show that much of it was delivered at Caledonia and Batavia to me, by Michael T. Simpson, at or near the price which it cost him delivered at Caledonia and Batavia; and I expect to prove these facts by the testimony of persons from whom said Simpson purchased the flour, and that the transaction was a fair one.

Question 2. Can you show that the rate of $4 per barrel, charged for transporting 630 barrels of flour from Caledonia to Buffalo, was not higher than the usual price at the time it was effected?

Answer. I can.

Question 3. Can you show that the teams purchased from Michael T. Simpson were actually and *bona fide* purchased by you on the 19th day of April, 1813, and not on the 24th of February, as it would seem they were by the letter of Morgan Lewis of the 2d of March, 1813?

Answer. I can show that the teams were actually and *bona fide* purchased on the 19th of April, 1813, and not before that time, when I paid for them.

Question 4. Can you make it appear that the account rendered by Michael T. Simpson for hay, oats, corn, and other articles delivered to you, cost him the prices which he charges the United States for the same; and which is paid by you; and that the prices of the said articles, at the time of their delivery to you, were reasonable?

Answer. I can make it appear that the articles mentioned were delivered at or near the cost to said Simpson, and that the prices charged for them were reasonable.

Question 5. Can you account for the public property so purchased and paid for?

Answer. I can, with correctness and ease.

Question 6. Can you make it appear that the money receipted for by Daniel Mowry, was actually paid to him for services performed by him?

Answer. I can make it appear that I employed teams of Philip and Daniel Mowry to transport the flour mentioned in the receipt, and that the service was performed; and the receipt is itself the evidence of payment. And with regard to Mowry's receiving pay at the same time from the United States, I can only say I knew nothing of the fact.

JAMES THOMAS.

WASHINGTON, *April* 20, 1816.

———

Requisition for twelve pieces of muslin and ten gallons of brandy for the use of the general hospital.

12 pieces muslin.   (Duplicate.)
10 gallons brandy.

GENERAL HOSPITAL, BURLINGTON, VT.,
September, 11, 1814.

SIR: The sick and wounded are hourly coming in from Plattsburg, and I am destitute of bandages to dress their wounds, and of funds to purchase. Although this request may be out of the ordinary course of application, you would render an indispensable service by furnishing the above articles.

HENRY HUNTT,
Hospital Surgeon.

Col. JAMES THOMAS,
Quartermaster General.

BURLINGTON, VT., *Sept.* 12, 1814.

Received the within twelve pieces of muslin and ten gallons of brandy, for the use of general hospital.

HENRY HUNTT,
Hospital Surgeon.

The United States, to Nathan B. Haswell.		DR.
1814. For 10 pieces India cotton, at $5	-	-$50 00
For 2 pieces India cotton, at $6	-	12 00
For 10 gallons Cognac brandy, at $3	-	30 00
		$92 00

BURLINGTON, *Sept.* 10, 1814.

Received of James Thomas, Colonel and Quartermaster General, ninety-two dollars, in full for the above account, having signed duplicate receipts therefor.

SPECIE PAYMENTS.

The House then took up the report of the Committee of the Whole on the bill providing for the more effectual collection of the public revenues in the lawful money of the country.

Mr. CALHOUN withdrew the amendment which he proposed to the bill for the issue of Treasury notes.

Mr. BRADBURY then offered the following proviso, to come in at the end of the first section; which was adopted by the House by a large majority:

"*Provided, nevertheless,* That nothing in this act contained shall be construed as an indemnity or justification to any officer or agent of the Government, for any negligence or misconduct in the past or future collections and receipts of public moneys."

A motion was then made by Mr. WARD, of Massachusets, further to amend the same, by inserting the following section:

"*And be it further enacted,* That in all cases in which the revenue of the United States, in any section thereof, shall be received in the bills of any State, which bills at the time of receiving them are of less value than their nominal sum in Treasury notes, it shall be the duty of the officer who receives said bills to require the person who pays the same, to make a discount thereon, equal to such difference in value; and it shall be the duty of such officer to render his account under oath, as to the amount of such discount."

This section, after much discussion, was rejected by yeas and nays—yeas 10, nays 100, as follows:

YEAS—Messrs. Hale, Hanson, King of North Carolina, Marsh, Mason, Nelson of Massachusetts, Noyes, Stearns, Strong, and Ward of Massachusetts.

NAYS—Messrs. Adgate, Alexander, Archer, Atherton, Baer, Barbour, Bateman, Bennett, Betts, Bradbury, Breckenridge, Brooks, Bryan, Cady, Caldwell, Calhoun, Chappell, Cilley, Clayton, Clendennin, Clopton, Condict, Cooper, Crawford, Creighton, Crocheron, Culpeper, Cuthbert, Darlington, Davenport, Desha, Edwards, Forney, Gaston, Glasgow, Goldsborough, Griffin, Grosvenor, Hahn, Hall, Hardin, Hawes, Heister, Henderson, Herbert, Huger, Hungerford, Ingham, Irwin of Pennsylvania, Johnson of Virginia, Kent, Langdon, Law, Lewis, Love, Lovett, Lumpkin, Lyle, Lyon, Mayrant, McCoy, McLean of Kentucky, Milnor, Moseley, Murfree, Nelson of Virginia, Newton, Parris, Pickering, Pitkin, Pleasants, Randolph, Reed, Roane, Robertson, Root, Ruggles, Savage, Schenck, Sheffey, Smith of Maryland, Southard, Stuart, Taylor of South Carolina, Telfair, Throop, Tucker, Vose, Wallace, Ward of New York, Whiteside, Wilcox, Wilkin, Williams, Willoughby, Thomas Wilson, William Wilson, Woodward, Wright, and Yates.

A motion was then made, by Mr. MASON, further to amend the said bill by inserting therein the following section:

"*And be it further enacted,* That, to establish uniformity in the payment of duties and taxes within the United States, the Secretary of the Treasury shall forthwith cause to be published, in one or more newspapers in each State and Territory, a list of all the banks within the United States, the notes of which are thereafter to be received in their respective districts in payment of duties, taxes, and other debts due to the United States; and any debtor of the United States may, until the said 31st day of December next, at his election, pay the amount of any duties, taxes, or other debts due and payable to the United States in Treasury notes, or in the notes of any of the said banks until notice shall be given from the Treasury Department that such notes are not received in discharge of any debts due to the United States within the districts where such banks are respectively situated: *Provided,*

nevertheless, That no collector, or other officer or receiver of moneys due to the United States, shall receive, in payment of any duty, tax, bond, obligation, or other demand, which, according to the terms thereof, or the provisions of law, shall not be due and payable before the said 31st day of December next, the notes of any bank or banker which, at the time of such payment, shall not be payable and paid on demand in current gold and silver coin."

And the question thereon being taken, it was determined in the negative—yeas 32, nays 88, as follows:

YEAS—Messrs. Atherton, Boss, Breckenridge, Brown, Bryan, Cady, Chipman, Cilley, Culpeper, Forney, Gaston, Hale, Jewett, Langdon, Lyon, Marsh, Mason, Murfree, Nelson of Massachusetts, Noyes, Parris, Pickering, Pitkin, Reed, Root, Ruggles, Stearns, Strong, Vose, Ward of Massachusetts, Webster, and Wilcox.

NAYS—Messrs. Adgate, Alexander, Archer, Baer, Barbour, Bassett, Bateman, Bennett, Betts, Bradbury, Brooks, Caldwell, Calhoun, Champion, Clayton, Clendennin, Clopton, Cooper, Crawford, Creighton, Crocheron, Cuthbert, Darlington, Davenport, Desha, Edwards, Goldsborough, Griffin, Grosvenor, Hahn, Hall, Hardin, Hawes, Heister, Henderson, Herbert, Huger, Hungerford, Ingham, Irwin of Pennsylvania, Johnson of Virginia, Johnson of Kentucky, Kent, King of North Carolina, Law, Lewis, Love, Lovett, Lumpkin, Lyle, Mayrant, McCoy, McLean of Kentucky, Middleton, Milnor, Moseley, Nelson of Virginia, Newton, Ormsby, Pickens, Pleasants, Powell, Randolph, Reynolds, Roane, Robertson, Savage, Schenck, Sharpe, Smith of Maryland, Southard, Stuart, Sturges, Taylor of South Carolina, Telfair, Throop, Tucker, Wallace, Ward of New York, Whiteside, Wilkin, Williams, Willoughby, Thomas Wilson, William Wilson, Woodward, Wright, and Yates.

A motion was then made, by Mr. HARDIN, that the said bill be postponed indefinitely; which, after a good deal of debate, was determined in the negative—yeas 44, nays 64, as follows:

YEAS—Messrs. Adgate, Archer, Baer, Bennett, Betts, Brooks, Clayton, Clopton, Cooper, Crawford, Crocheron, Culpeper, Darlington, Forney, Gaston, Hahn, Hardin, Irwin of Pennsylvania, Law, Lewis, Lovett, Lyle, Lyon, Mason, Milnor, Murfree, Newton, Randolph, Roane, Root, Savage, Sheffey, Smith of Maryland, Southard, Throop, Wallace, Ward of Massachusetts, Whiteside, Wilkin, Williams, Willoughby, William Wilson, Wright, and Yates.

NAYS—Messrs. Alexander, Atherton, Barbour, Bassett, Bateman, Boss, Bradbury, Bryan, Cady, Caldwell, Calhoun, Champion, Chipman, Cilley, Clendennin, Creighton, Cuthbert, Desha, Edwards, Griffin, Grosvenor, Hale, Hall, Heister, Huger, Hungerford, Ingham, Jewett, Johnson, of Virginia, Johnson of Kentucky, Kent, King of North Carolina, Langdon, Love, Lumpkin, Marsh, Mayrant, McCoy, McLean of Kentucky, Middleton, Moseley, Nelson of Massachusetts, Ormsby, Parris, Pickering, Pitkin, Pleasants, Reed, Reynolds, Robertson, Ruggles, Schenck, Sharpe, Strong, Sturges, Taylor of South Carolina, Telfair, Tucker, Vose, Ward of New York, Webster, Wilcox, Thomas Wilson, and Woodward.

Mr. HALL then moved to recommit the bill to a Committee of the Whole.—Rejected.

Mr. REYNOLDS then moved that the House reconsider their vote which adopted the amendment proposed by Mr. BRADBURY.—Rejected by a large majority.

Mr. INGHAM then moved further to amend the said bill, by striking out "31st day of December next," and to insert "31st day of January next," as the time after which the payment of duties, taxes, debts, &c., owing to the United States will be demanded in specie made current by law, or in Treasury notes. The amendment was negatived without a division.

The question was then taken on engrossing the bill for a third reading, and was decided as follows: For engrossing 57, against 46.

THURSDAY, April 25.

Mr. ROOT, from the committee appointed on the 19th of January last, upon the subject of the copper and small silver coin of the United States, made a report; which was read, and the resolution therein contained was concurred in by the House, as follows:

Resolved, That it is inexpedient to reduce the weight or fineness of the copper and small silver coins of the United States.

Mr. EASTON, from the committee to whom was referred on the 1st instant, the petition of sundry inhabitants of the Territory of Missouri, relating to Indian trade. made a report thereon; which was read, and ordered to lie on the table.

The amendment proposed by the Senate to the bill "making appropriations for the support of the Military Establishment of the United States for the year 1816," was read, and committed to a Committee of the whole House to-day.

The amendment proposed by the Senate to the bill "authorizing the payment for the court-house of Hamilton, in the State of Ohio," was read, and concurred in by the House.

The amendment proposed by the Senate to the bill "for the relief of the supervisors of the county of Clinton, in the State of New York," was read, and concurred in by the House.

A message from the Senate informed the House that the Senate have passed bills from this House of the following titles, to wit:

An act for the relief of Charles Ross, and Samuel Breck, surviving executors of John Ross, deceased;

An act for the relief of Manasseh Minor;

An act to fix the commissions of the collectors of the direct tax and internal duties, and to revive and continue in force "An act further to provide for the collection of duties on imports and tonnage;"

An act for the relief of Paul D. Butler;

An act for the relief of Thomas Farrar, William Young, William Moseley, and William Leach;

An act for the relief of Charles Levaux Tradeau; and

An act for the relief of William Crawford, Frederick Bates, and William Garrard; with amendments, in which they ask the concurrence of this House.

The amendments proposed by the Senate to the bills, entitled.

An act for the relief of Charles Ross, and Samuel Breck, surviving executors of John Ross, deceased;

An act for the relief of Charles Levaux Tradeau;

An act for the relief of Thomas Farrar, William Young, William Moseley, and William Leach;

An act for the relief of Paul D. Butler;

An act to fix the commissions of the collectors of the direct tax and internal duties, and to revive and continue in force an act further to provide for the collection of duties on imports and tonnage; were read, and severally concurred in by the House.

The amendments proposed by the Senate to the bill for the relief of William Crawford, Frederick Bates, and William Garrard," were read, and committed to a Committee of the Whole to-morrow.

The amendment proposed by the Senate to the bill, entitled "An act for the relief of Manasseh Minor," was read, and committed to a Committee of the Whole to-morrow.

SPECIE PAYMENTS.

The engrossed bill providing for the more effectual collection of the public revenues in the lawful money of the country, was read the third time, and the question stated, "Shall the bill pass?"

Mr. WRIGHT rose and spoke as follows: Mr. Speaker, before this bill shall be put on its passage, and placed beyond the reach of the real guardians of the people, I must claim the indulgence of the House while I do detect and expose its direful operation and effect on the American people—that people who have so lately crowned themselves with laurels and covered the nation with glory. Sir, I will show that it is fraught with partiality, with ingratitude, with injustice, and with cruelty; and, if passed into a law, and attempted to be enforced, may lead to the most serious and dangerous consequences. Sir, it was but a short time ago when this nation was coerced into a bloody foreign war to avenge her wrongs, and contemporaneously threatened with a serious domestic insurrection, having for its object the severance of this Union; when the patriotism of every American was in requisition; and when the banks were invoked by their patriotism to lend their money (the sinews of war) to save the sinking credit of their bleeding country. And, sir, can we ever efface from recollection the promptitude with which the friendly banks advanced their moneys on loan to the nation, so as to greatly afflict and derange their own concerns; whereby the sinews of war were supplied, the drooping spirits of an exhausted Treasury raised, a patriot Army and Navy fed and clothed, and a glorious war brought to a glorious conclusion by the instrumentality of these friendly banks and the noble exertions of the American people. Nor, sir, can we forget the conduct of the Opposition in the East to prevent the Eastern banks from lending their money, nor its effect. And although, sir, it is an unquestionable fact that in the proportion that these friendly banks extended their loans to the nation, in the same ratio they paralyzed their own means to resume specie payments, and in the same ratio they are now to be sacrificed on the altar of ingratitude; while the Eastern banks withheld their money from the nation, and retained all their means to continue or resume specie payments, and whose friends on this floor are now goading the Administration on this subject, and endeavoring to wreak their vengeance (by the passage of this bill) on the friendly banks for saving the sinking credit of the nation, which the Eastern banks, by withholding their loans endeavored to destroy.

Sir, do not we discover the hand and spirit of persecution in this business? And can we be at a loss, with this evidence before our eyes, to discover the cause? or so far lull to sleep our patriotism and magnanimity as to become accomplices in the fell and unkind stroke meditated at these friendly banks?

Sir, I cannot, in justice to the banks of Maryland, withhold the prideful remark that her banks advanced more money to the United States than the banks of any other State in the Union; nor can withhold my utmost exertions to protect these banks from the injury which the adoption of this bill will inevitably impose.

Sir, that this bill is fraught with partiality can any man hesitate for a moment to affirm, when he observes the different bearing it will have on the banks that did, and did not, loan their money, to resume specie payments; and when the fact is not only well known, but admitted, that, in the ratio of their loans, their powers to resume specie payments are arrested? I have also charged this bill with being fraught with ingratitude. Sir, we all recollect the glow of approbation which filled the patriot's bosom at the time of these loans. The awful crisis was averted by the loans ascribed to the patriotism of these banks, which a traiterous Eastern pen endeavored in vain to arrest, and that gloom that the exhausted state of the Treasury imposed on patriots was entirely dispelled. And can an American friendly to the liberties of his country say that to join the Eastern persecution of these friendly banks in the passage of this bill would not be the blackest ingratitude to those banks? But, however Republics may have been famed for ingratitude, I trust the American Republic will not, on this occasion, suffer the foul stain to pollute her fair fame. I have thus shown that this bill, as it related to the banks, was partial and ungrateful. I will now show, that, as it relates both to the banks and the people, that this bill is both unjust and cruel.

Sir, it is a fact of record that these friendly banks were obliged to suspend specie payments to avoid the whole specie of the country being drained into the hands of our enemies, whose agents were everywhere to be found occupied in that business; and that, however perilous it was to the credit of these institutions, necessity, grow-

ing out of the war, beyond their control, compelled the directors of those banks to the measure, which was not only approved by every patriot in America, but by the Government itself. Nor were the Eastern banks, who did not suspend specie payments, freed from the suspicion of being actuated by motives the very reverse of those which induced the friendly banks to suspend specie payments. Sir, from the moment the banks suspended specie payments there was a general understanding that in all the moneyed transactions of this country, the bank paper was to be paid and received in fulfilment of the contracts, although it was well known that specie would not be paid on demand, agreeably to the express tenor of the notes, and there was a certainty that a depreciation would ensue. The contracts of the citizens were made and executed understandingly in this paper, by universal consent, and the price of the article bought and sold was knowingly and intentionally valued by this new standard, so that let the positive letter of the law be even admitted to compel the payment of specie as the only current money, yet, where by universal consent its circulation was suspended, that could not be the case, *Conventio vincit leges.* "The agreement of the party makes the law;" and it would be unjust to compel a man whose agreement was made after the suspension of specie payments, and with an understanding that it was to be paid in bank paper, to compel the payment in specie.

Sir, it is a fact that, from the well known small quantity of specie in circulation in this country, it is impossible for the banks to assume the payment at this time; and every commercial man knows, that, while the balance of trade is against us, the specie of foreign countries cannot be expected to return to America. If, then, from the small quantity of specie in this country, and the state of our commerce, it is impossible to resume the payment of specie for the necessary quantity of circulating medium for the purposes of the nation, I ask, would it not be as farcical to attempt to coerce it, as it would be to demand of a farrier to extract a certain quantity of blood from a dead horse, when all his blood was congealed in his veins? But, Mr. Speaker, when I record the fact, that there is now in the hands of the people upwards of fifty millions of bank paper, and that the very paper that was loaned by the banks to the Government, and by the Government paid to the people for their supplies for the army and navy, and for their military services, whether that paper ought not to be received in payment for their public dues; and I humbly ask, if the Government pass the bank paper into the hands of the people, purporting to be redeemable on demand in specie, whether the Government are not thereby virtual endorsers, and equitably bound to see the engagement performed, or to take back the note, as much as if it was counterfeit, and give them a good note for it, unless, as I allege, there was a mutual understanding that bank paper was the medium of the contract, and that, too, without its being redeemable in specie on demand. Sir, I ask if a farmer, being executed for his taxes after

Specie Payments.

tendering his money thus received from the Government to the amount of his taxes, was, by replevin, to bring this subject fairly before a court and jury, and the jury were specially to find the facts, that he did tender this money to the amount of his taxes, and had brought the same into court, whether the court would not adjudge him discharged? Yes, sir, the court would so decide; and I very much incline to believe, that if the Secretary of the Treasury, with the champions of this bill, were charged with the collection of the public dues in specie under such circumstances, they would find themselves in an unpleasant box, and that people who had achieved their independence by deposing a foreign tyrant, would not submit to be despoiled of their property so unjustly by domestic oppression.

Sir, when Congress passed the Revenue laws, and imposed the six million and three million land tax, did they contemplate the payment of specie? No; they knew the people had it not, and of course could not pay it. When they borrowed the money from the banks, and compelled all the public creditors to receive it for their debts, can it be possible they intended to refuse taking it back again from the people for their taxes? I cannot conceive the Government capable of such political immorality. Does any man doubt that Congress intended these taxes being paid in bank paper? Nay, has not the conduct of the Secretary, whose administration of the Treasury Department has been so conspicuous for its intelligence and firmness, sealed this construction of the law, by taking the bank paper in discharge for these taxes? Yes, sir; and honorable men have been found on this floor, who have insinuated that the Secretary of the Treasury ought to be impeached for receiving the taxes in bank notes. I have differed so materially from these gentlemen, that I have no hesitation in declaring, that, if he had exacted these taxes in specie, he ought, and probably would have been impeached, when it was well known that Congress, when they imposed these taxes, intended them to be paid in bank paper. The Secretary, no doubt, by the letter of the Constitution, might have considered nothing but specie current money, and to have exacted specie, had it depended solely on the Constitution; but when he knew, by all the circumstances of the case, that the taxes were laid, and intended to be paid in bank paper, he had too great a respect for the principles and policy of the Government, and too much patriotism, to have done an act that would have convulsed this Government to its centre, and probably have shaken the Chief Magistrate from his seat; and I advise gentlemen to be upon their guard in the passage of this bill, lest they sour the nation, and disappoint the well-founded hopes of the contemplated successor to the Presidential Chair. Sir, if this bill shall pass into a law, and impose the payment of taxes and public dues in specie, it will, no doubt, have the same effect on the contracts of citizen and citizen, and introduce discord and confusion, and probably destruction to thousands; for every man must know the extreme dis-

tress of the people would labor under, if they were compelled to pay their debts in specie at this time. And I warn gentlemen how they introduce such a state of things, as too serious and dangerous to be attempted, and awful in the extreme, as they were produced by the war, and not by any fault of the people. Gentlemen will excuse me in reminding them of the contests in Rome, between the patricians and plebeians, about the payment of their debts in a time of great difficulty, and the awful crisis produced thereby; it being no less than the appointment of the first Dictator in Rome, who was clothed with absolute despotic power, and who, to appease the plebeians, suspended the collection of the debts due to the patricians for a limited time. I ask, if the advocates of this bill were pressed even for their board in specie, how they could comply with their contracts? Nay, sir, I unhesitatingly declare, that if the boarding-houses were to refuse to board the members but for specie, it would force the members to abandon their seats. This single consideration ought to satisfy every man, that the bank paper was the money contemplated to be paid and received, and induce him to move with caution, and not impose impossibilities on the people. Sir, can we so soon forget what is due to that people, whose star-spangled banners have illumined both hemispheres, and whose stripes have humbled the British Lion, and compelled him to give up our impressed seamen, and subdued the proud Turk, and compelled him to give up our enslaved citizens, and reduced to practice the Eastern *gasconade,* (for they voted against the Algerine war,) "millions for defence, but not a cent for tribute;" and while the echoing of our conquering cannon at Chippewa, at Plattsburg, at Baltimore, and at New Orleans, is yet hanging on the ear, and while they recollect their victories by sea and land had so raised the American character, that, without the aid of the star and garter, a certificate of American citizenship is a passport into the highest circles of Europe? And yet there are gentlemen on this floor, who would compel the Secretary of the Treasury to play the Dictator, not like the Roman Dictator, with a power to relieve the distresses of the people, but by coercing him to exact the revenue and taxes in specie, to the destruction of the American people.

Indeed, sir, in order to carry this monstrous bill, I discover the most unnatural connexion between gentlemen on this floor. We see those who advocated the United States Bank, upon the principle that the nation had seven millions of its stock, (netting three per cent. revenue,) and the appointment of five of its directors to guard the nation against any improper influence, and who voted against the old bank because seven-eighths of its stock was British, and gave to the foreign stockholders eight per cent., uniting with the Eastern gentlemen, (whose ports had been exempt from British blockades, to the extent represented by the Hartford Convention,) and who voted against the present United States Bank expressly because the United States had any part of the stock, or the appointment of any of its directors, and who voted to continue the old bank charter, when seven-eighths of its capital was the property of British stockholders. And Congress are now pressed by this extraordinary union to sanction this monstrous measure, fraught, as I trust I have proved, with partiality, with ingratitude, with injustice, and with cruelty. Sir, I have endeavored to do my duty to this nation on this occasion; and I confidently hope that this House will reject this bill, and prove themselves to be what they have been justly esteemed, the honest guardians of the interest, the happiness, and the prosperity of the American people.

Mr. Root followed on the same side, in a speech of about half an hour.

Mr. Telfair made a few remarks in reply to Mr. Root.

Mr. Grosvenor answered the opponents of the bill, and spoke some time in its support.

Mr. Randolph replied to Mr. Grosvenor, and opposed the passage of the bill.

Mr. Grosvenor rejoined, and added some further arguments in favor of the bill.

Mr. Calhoun also replied to Mr. Randolph, and offered some considerations in favor of the bill.

Mr. Robertson explained the reasons why he should vote for the bill, and made some remarks in reply to other gentlemen.

Mr. Webster also submitted his reasons for wishing the bill to pass.

Mr. Randolph again spoke about an hour in opposition to the bill, and in reply to its advocates.

Mr. Wright also opposed the bill in a second speech.

Mr. Gaston submitted his reasons in opposition to the bill; after which the question on its passage was decided in the negative—yeas 59, nays 60, as follows:

Yeas—Messrs. Alexander, Atherton, Bassett, Bateman, Boss, Bradbury, Brown, Cady, Calhoun, Champion, Chipman, Cilley, Condict, Conner, Creighton, Cuthbert, Desha, Edwards, Griffin, Grosvenor, Hale, Hawes, Huger, Hungerford, Johnson of Kentucky, Kent, Love, Lowndes, Lumpkin, Marsh, Mayrant, McCoy, McLean, of Kentucky, Middleton, Nelson of Massachusetts, Noyes, Ormsby, Parris, Pickering, Pitkin, Pleasants, Reed, Reynolds, Robertson, Ruggles, Schenck, Sharpe, Sheffey, Stearns, Sturges, Taggart, Taylor of South Carolina, Telfair, Tucker, Vose, Ward of New York, Webster, Wilcox, and Woodward.

Nays—Messrs. Adgate, Archer, Baer, Bennett, Betts, Birdsall, Breckenridge, Brooks, Bryan, Caldwell, Clayton, Clopton, Cooper, Crawford, Crocheron, Culpeper, Darlington, Davenport, Forney, Gaston, Glasgow, Hahn, Hall, Hardin, Heister, Henderson, Herbert, Ingham, Johnson of Virginia, King of North Carolina, Langdon, Law, Lewis, Lovett, Lyle, Lyon, Milnor, Murfree, Newton, Pickens, Powell, Randolph, Roane, Root, Savage, Smith of Maryland, Southard, Stuart, Tate, Throop, Wallace, Ward, of Massachusetts, Whiteside, Wilkin, Williams, Willoughby, William Wilson, Thomas Wilson, Wright, and Yates.

So the bill was rejected.

THE TARIFF.

The House went into a Committee of the Whole on the amendments of the Senate to the bill to regulate the duties on imposts and tonnage. The amendments were successively agreed to by the Committee, and reported to the House.

Mr. Randolph made an ineffectual motion to postpone the decision on the report until to-morrow, believing the amendments too important to be acted on without more mature consideration.

Mr. R. opposed subsequently, at some length, the Senate's proposition to increase the duty on imported sugar from $2\frac{1}{2}$ to 3 cents per pound, which he deemed not only oppressive on the people, but highly improper as coming from the Senate, whose right he disputed, according to the spirit of the Constitution, thus in effect to assess a tax on the people, and demanded the yeas and nays on the question of concurrence.

Mr. Robertson made a few remarks in reply, and in favor of the amendment.

After some further conversation between Mr. Randolph and Mr. Robertson, the amendment was concurred in by the following vote: For the amendment 54, against it 48, as follows:

Yeas—Messrs. Adgate, Alexander, Archer, Atherton, Bassett, Bateman, Betts, Brooks, Cady, Caldwell, Calhoun, Chipman, Condict, Crawford, Creighton, Crocheron, Cuthbert, Darlington, Desha, Griffin, Hall, Hardin, Hawes, Henderson, Ingham, Johnson of Virginia, Johnson of Kentucky, Lowndes, Lumpkin, Lyle, Mason, Mayrant, McKee, McLean of Kentucky, Middleton, Newton, Ormsby, Pleasants, Powell, Reynolds, Robertson, Root, Savage, Schenck, Sharpe, Smith of Maryland, Southard, Taylor of South Carolina, Telfair, Tucker, Ward of New York, Wilkin, Thomas Wilson, and William Wilson.

Nays—Messrs. Baer, Bennett, Boss, Bradbury, Breckenridge, Champion, Cilley, Clayton, Clopton, Cooper, Culpeper, Davenport, Edwards, Gaston, Goldsborough, Hahn, Hale, Heister, Huger, Hungerford, Kent, Law, Lewis, Love, Lovett, Lyon, Marsh, Milnor, Moseley, Nelson of Massachusetts, Parris, Pickens, Pickering, Pitkin, Randolph, Reed, Roane, Ruggles, Sheffey, Stearns, Vose, Ward of Massachusetts, Webster, Whiteside, Wilcox, Williams, Woodward, and Wright.

The residue of the said amendments were then read, and concurred in by the House.

Friday, April 26.

The bill to allow a drawback of duties on spirits distilled and sugar refined within the United States, passed through a Committee of the Whole, and was ordered to a third reading.

The bill to carry into effect the treaty with the Cherokee Indians; the bill for settling the compensation of the commissioners, &c., of land claims in Louisiana; the bill for adjustment of certain land claims in Louisiana, &c.; and the bill for the relief of Manasseh Minor; successively passed through a Committee of the Whole, and were severally ordered to a third reading.

The bill fixing the peace establishment of the Marine Corps was indefinitely postponed, on motion of Mr. Pleasants, who remarked, that it had been ascertained that the Secretary of the Navy had already placed the corps on the establishment contemplated by the bill; and further, that it was believed the corps might be made still more efficient than as it was at present constituted, if organized differently from what was contemplated by the bill.

The bill respecting the patent rights of the representatives of Robert Fulton, deceased, was also, on motion of Mr. Culpeper, indefinitely postponed.

A message from the Senate informed the House that the Senate have passed bills of this House of the following titles, to wit:

An act for the gradual increase of the Navy of the United States; an act authorizing the Judges of the Circuit Court for the District of Columbia to prepare a code of jurisprudence for the said District; an act concerning the owners, officers, and crew of the privateer Roger; an act making an appropriation for enclosing and improving the public square near the Capitol; and to abolish the office of Commissioners of the Public Buildings, and of Superintendent, and for the appointment of one Commissioner for the Public Buildings; an act for the relief of Peter Audrain; an act for the relief of David Coffin, Samuel and William Rodman, and Samuel Rodman, jun.; an act for the confirmation of certain claims to land in the Western district in the State of Louisiana; an act to provide for the appointment of a surveyor of the public lands in the Territories of Illinois and Missouri; an act to establish post roads; an act fixing the compensation of the Secretary of the Senate and Clerk of the House of Representatives, and making a temporary provision for the clerks employed in their offices, with amendments. The Senate have also passed the resolution "to indemnify Jabez Mowry, and others," with amendments; and they have passed the bill "to increase the salary of the Register of the Treasury, and to allow him a compensation for his agency in countersigning and issuing Treasury notes;" and a resolution, "authorizing the President of the United States to employ a skilful assistant in the Corps of Engineers;" in all of which amendments, together with the said last mentioned bill and resolution, they ask the concurrence of this House.

The House went into a Committee of the Whole, on the bill from the Senate, entitled "An act to increase the compensation of the Superintendents of the manufactories of arms at Springfield and Harper's Ferry." The bill was reported without amendment, and ordered to be read a third time to-day.

The House went into a Committee of the Whole, on the bill supplementary to the several acts organizing the office of Accountant of the Department of War; and, after some time spent therein, the bill was reported with amendments; which were concurred in by the House, and the bill ordered to be engrossed, and read a third time to-morrow.

The House went into a Committee of the Whole, on the amendments proposed by the Sen-

ate to the bill from this House, entitled "An act for the relief of William Crawford, Frederick Bates, and William Garrard;" and, after some time spent therein, the Committee reported their concurrence in the said amendments; which were concurred in by the House.

The House then went into a Committee of the Whole, on the amendments proposed by the Senate to the bill from this House, entitled "An act making appropriations for the support of the Military Establishment of the United States, for the year 1816;" and, after some time spent therein, the Committee reported their concurrence in the said amendment; which was concurred in by the House.

COLLECTION OF THE REVENUE.

Mr. Webster rose, and submitted the following resolutions:

Resolved, by the Senate and House of Representatives of the United States of America in Congress assembled, That, all duties, taxes, imposts, and excises, laid or imposed by Government, ought, by the provisions of the Constitution, to be uniform throughout the United States; and that no preference ought to be given or allowed by any regulation of commerce or revenue, to the ports of one State over those of another.

And resolved further, That the revenues of the United States ought to be collected and received in the legal currency of the United States, or in Treasury notes, or in the notes of the Bank of the United States, as by law provided and declared.

And resolved further, That the Secretary of the Treasury be, and he is hereby, required and directed to adopt such measures as he may deem necessary, to cause, as soon as may be, all duties, taxes, debts, or sums of money accruing or becoming payable to the United States, to be collected and paid in the legal currency of the United States, or Treasury notes, or notes of the Bank of the United States as aforesaid; and that from and after the 1st day of February next no such duties, taxes, debts, or sums of money accruing or becoming payable to the United States as aforesaid, ought to be collected or received otherwise than in the legal currency of the United States, or Treasury notes, or notes of the Bank of the United States, as aforesaid.

Mr. Webster said, that he had felt it to be his duty to call the attention of the House once more to the subject of the collection of the revenue, and to present the resolutions which had been submitted. He had been the more inclined to do this from an apprehension that the rejection, yesterday, of the bill which had been introduced, might be construed into an abandonment, on the part of the House, of all hope of remedying the existing evil. He had had, it was true, some objections against proceeding by way of bill; because the case was not one in which the law was deficient, but one in which the execution of the law was deficient. The great object, however, was to obtain a decision of this and the other House, that the present mode of receiving the revenue should not be continued, and as this might be substantially effected by the bill, he had hoped that it might pass. This hope had been disap-

1441   HISTORY OF CONGRESS.   1442

April, 1816.   Collection of the Revenue.   H. of R.

pointed. The bill had been rejected. The House had put its negative upon the only proposition which had been submitted to it, for correcting a state of things, which everybody knows to exist, in plain violation of the Constitution, and in open defiance of the written letter of the law. For one, he could never consent to adjourn, leaving this implied sanction of the House upon all that had taken place, and all that might hereafter take place. He hoped not to hear again that there was not now time to act on this question. If other gentlemen considered the question as important as he did, they would not forbear to act upon it from any desire, however strong, to bring the session to an early close.

The situation of the country, said Mr. W., in regard to the collection of its revenues, is most deplorable. With a perfectly sound legal currency, the national revenues are not collected in this currency, but in paper of various sorts, and various degrees of value. The origin and progress of this evil are distinctly known, but it is not easy to see its duration or its future extent, if an adequate remedy be not soon found. Before the war, the business of the country was conducted principally by means of the paper of the different State banks. As these were in good credit, and paid their notes in gold and silver on demand, no great evil was experienced from the circulation of their paper. Not being, however, a part of the legal money of the country, it could not, by law, be received in the payment of duties, taxes or other debts to Government. But being payable, and hitherto regularly paid, on demand, the collectors and agents of Government had generally received it as cash; it had been deposited as cash in the banks which received the deposites of Government, and from them it had been drawn as cash, and paid off to creditors of the public.

During the war, this state of things changed. Many of the banks had been induced to make loans to a very great amount to Government. These loans were made by an issue of their own bills. This proceeding threw into circulation an immense quantity of bank paper, in no degree corresponding with the mercantile business of the country, and resting on nothing for its payment and redemption but the Government stocks, which were holden by the banks. The consequence immediately followed, which it would be imputing a great degree of blindness both to the Government and to the banks to suggest that they had not foreseen. The excess of paper which was found everywhere, created alarm. Demands began to be made on the banks, and they all stopped payment. No contrivance to get money, without inconvenience to the people, ever had a shorter course of experiment, or a more unequivocal termination. The depreciation of bank notes was the necessary consequence of a neglect or refusal on the part of those who issued them to pay them. It took place immediately, and has continued, with occasional fluctuation in the degree of depression, to the present moment. What still further increases the evil is, that this bank paper being the issue of very many different in-

14th Con. 1st Sess.—46

stitutions, situated in different parts of the country, and possessing different degrees of credit, the depreciation has not been, and is not now, uniform throughout the United States. It is not the same at Baltimore as at Philadelphia; nor the same at Philadelphia as at New York. In New England the banks have not stopped payment in specie, and of course their paper has not been depressed at all. But the notes of banks which have ceased to pay specie, have, nevertheless, been, and still are, received for duties and taxes, in the places where such banks exist. The consequence of all this is, that the people of the United States pay their duties and taxes in currencies of different values in different places. In other words, taxes and duties are higher in some places than they are in others, by as much as the value of gold and silver is greater than the value of the several descriptions of bank paper which are received by Government. This difference, in relation to the paper of the District in which we now are, is twenty-five per cent.; taxes and duties, therefore, collected in Massachusetts, are one quarter higher than the taxes and duties which are collected, by virtue of the same laws, in the District of Columbia.

By the Constitution of the Government, it is certain that all duties, taxes, and excises, ought to be uniform throughout the United States; and that no preference should be given, by any regulation of commerce or revenue, to the ports of one State over those of another. This Constitutional provision, it is obvious, is flagrantly violated. Duties and taxes are not uniform. They are higher in some places than in others. A citizen of New England pays his tax in gold and silver, or their equivalent. From his hand the collector will not receive, and is instructed by Government not to receive, the notes of the banks which do not pay their notes on demand, and which notes he could obtain twenty or twenty-five per cent. cheaper than that which is demanded of him. Yet a citizen of the Middle States pays his taxes in these notes at par. Can a greater injustice than this be conceived? Can Constitutional provisions be disregarded in a more essential point? Commercial preferences also are given, which, if they could be continued, would be sufficient to annihilate the commerce of some cities and some States, while they would extremely promote the others. The importing merchant at Boston pays the duties upon his goods, either in specie or cash notes, which are at least twenty per cent., or in Treasury notes, which are ten per cent. more valuable than the notes which are paid for duties, at par, by the importing merchant at Baltimore. Surely this is not to be endured. Such monstrous inequality and injustice are not to be tolerated. Since the commencement of this course of things, it can be shown, that the people of the Northern States have paid a million of dollars more than their just proportion of the public burdens. A similar inequality, though somewhat less in degree, has fallen upon the States south of the Potomac, in which the paper in circulation, although not equivalent to specie, is yet of higher value than the bank notes of this District, Maryland, and the Middle States.

But it is not merely the inequality and injustice of this system, if system it may be called—if not rather the want of all system—which call for reform. It throws the whole revenue into derangement, and endless confusion. It prevents the possibility of order, method, or certainty, in the public receipts or disbursements. This mass of depressed paper, thrown out at first in loans to accommodate Government, has done little less than to embarrass and distress Government. It can hardly be said to circulate, but it lies in the channel of circulation, and chokes it up by its bulk and its sluggishness. In a great portion of the country, the dues to Government are not paid, or are paid badly; and in an equal portion of the country the public creditors are not paid, or are paid badly.

It is quite clear, that, by the statute, all duties and taxes are required to be paid in the legal money of the United States, or in Treasury notes, agreeably to recent provisions. It is just as clear, that the law has been disregarded, and that the notes of banks of an hundred different descriptions, and almost as many different values, have been received, and still are received where the statute requires legal money or Treasury notes to be paid.

In these circumstances, I cannot persuade myself that Congress will adjourn without attempting something by way of remedy. In my opinion, no greater evil has threatened us. Nothing can more endanger, either the existence and preservation of the public revenue, or the security of private property, than the consequences which are to be apprehended from the present course of things, if they be not arrested by a timely and an effectual interference. Let gentlemen consider what will probably happen, if Congress should rise without the adoption of any measure on the subject.

Virginia, having passed a law for compelling the banks in that State to limit the circulation of their paper and resume specie payments by the Autumn, will, doubtless, repeal it. The States further to the South will probably fall into a similar relaxation, for it is hardly to be expected that they will have firmness and perseverance enough to persist in their present most prudent and commendable course, without the countenance of the General Government.

If, in addition to these events, an abandonment of the wholesome system which has thus far prevailed in the Northern States, or any relaxation of that system, should take place, the Government is in danger of falling into a condition from which it can hardly be expected to extricate itself for twenty years, if indeed it shall ever be able to extricate itself, and if that state of things, instead of being changed by the Government, shall not change the Government.

It is our business to foresee this danger, and to avoid it. There are some political evils which are seen as soon as they are dangerous, and which alarm at once as well as the people as the Govern-

ment. Wars and invasions, therefore, are not always the most certain destroyers of national prosperity. They come in no questionable shape. They announce their own approach, and the general safety is preserved by the general alarm. Not so with the evils of a debased coin, a depreciated paper currency, or a depressed and falling public credit. No so with the plausible and insidious mischief of a paper money system. These insinuate themselves in the shape of facilities, accommodation, and relief. They hold out the most fallacious hope of an easier payment of debts, and a lighter burden of taxation. It is easy for a portion of the people to imagine that Government may properly continue to receive depreciated paper, because they have received it, and because it is more convenient to obtain it than to obtain other paper, or specie. But on these subjects it is, that Government ought to exercise its own peculiar wisdom and caution. It is supposed to possess, on subjects of this nature, somewhat more of foresight than has fallen to the lot of individuals. It is bound to foresee the evil before every man feels it, and to take all necessary measures to guard against it, although they may be measures attended with some difficulty and not without temporary inconvenience. In my humble judgment the evil demands the immediate attention of Congress. It is not certain, and in my opinion not probable, that it will ever cure itself. It is more likely to grow by indulgence, while the remedy which must in the end be applied, will become less efficacious by delay.

The only power which the General Government possesses of restraining the issues of the State banks, is to refuse their notes in the receipts of the Treasury. This power it can exercise now, or at least it can provide now for exercising in reasonable time, because the currency of some part of the country is yet sound, and the evil is not universal. If it should become universal, who, that hesitates now, will then propose any adequate means of relief? If a measure, like the bill of yesterday, or the resolutions of to-day, can hardly pass here now, what hope is there that any efficient measure will be adopted hereafter?

The conduct of the Treasury Department in receiving the notes of the banks, after they had suspended payment, might or might not have been excused by the necessity of the case. That is not now the subject of inquiry. I wish such inquiry had been instituted. It ought to have been; it is of dangerous consequence to permit plain omissions to execute the law to pass off, under any circumstances, without inquiry. It would probably be easier to prove that the Treasury must have continued to receive such notes, or that all payments to Government would have been suspended, than it would be to justify the previous negotiation of great loans at the banks, which was a voluntary transaction, induced by no particular necessity, and which is nevertheless, beyond doubt, the principal cause of their present condition. But I have expressed my belief on more than one occasion, and I now repeat the

1445　　　　　　　　HISTORY OF CONGRESS.　　　　　　　　1446

April, 1816.　　　　　　Collection of the Revenue.　　　　　　H. of R.

opinion, that it was the duty, and in the power of the Secretary of the Treasury, on the return of peace, to have returned to the legal and proper mode of collecting the revenue. The paper of the banks rose, on that occasion, almost to an equality with specie; that was the favorable moment. The banks in which the public money was deposited ought to have been induced to lead the way, by the sale of their Government stocks, and other measures calculated to bring about, moderately and gradually, but regularly and certainly, a restoration of the former and only safe state of things. It can hardly be doubted, that the influence of the Treasury could have effected all this. If not, it could have withdrawn the deposites and the countenance of Government from institutions, which, against all rule and propriety, were holding great sums in Government stocks, and making enormous profits from the circulation of their own dishonored paper. That which was most wanted, was the designation of a time, for the corresponding operation of banks in different places. This could have been made by the Head of the Treasury, better than by anybody or everybody else. But the occasion was suffered to pass by unimproved, and the credit of the banks soon fell again, when it was found they used none of the means which the opportunity gave themselves for enabling them to fulfil their engagements.

As to any power of compulsion to be exercised over the State banks, they are not subject to the direct control of the General Government. It is for the State authorities which created them to decide, whether they have acted according to their charters, and, if not, what shall be the remedy for their irregularities. But, from such of them as continued to receive the deposite of public money, Government had a right to expect that they would conduct their concerns according to the safe and well known principles which should properly govern such institutions. And this Government has in all cases a right to protect its own revenues, and to guard them against defalcation by bad or depreciated paper. It is bound also to collect its taxes of the people on a uniform system. These rights and these duties are too important to be surrendered to the accommodation of any particular interest or temporary purpose.

The resolutions before the House take no notice of the State banks. They express neither praise nor censure of them. They neither commend them for their patriotism in the loans made to Government, nor propose to tax them for their neglect or refusal to pay their debts. They assume no power of interfering with these institutions. They say not one word about compelling them to resume their payments; they leave that to the consideration of the banks themselves, or of those who have a right to call them to account for any misconduct in that respect. But the resolutions declare that taxes ought to be equal; that preferences ought not to be given; that the revenues of the country ought not to be diminished in amount, nor hazarded altogether by the receipt of varying and uncertain paper; and that the present state of things, in which all these un-

constitutional, illegal, and dangerous ingredients are mixed, ought not to exist.

It has been said that these resolutions may be construed into a justification of the past conduct of the Treasury Department. Such an objection has been anticipated. It was made, in my opinion, with much more justice to the bill rejected yesterday, and a provision was accordingly subsequently introduced into that bill to exclude such an inference. This is certainly not the time to express any justification or approbation of the conduct of that Department on this subject, and I trust these resolutions do not imply it. Nor do the resolutions propose to express any censure. A sufficient reason for declining to do either is, that the facts are not sufficiently known. What loss has actually happened, what amount (it is said to be large) may be now in the Treasury, in notes which will not now pass, or under what circumstances these were received, is not now sufficiently ascertained.

But before these resolutions are rejected, on the ground that they may shield the Treasury Department from responsibility, it ought to be clearly shown that they are capable of receiving such a construction. The mere passing of any resolution cannot have that effect. A declaration of what ought to be done, does not necessarily imply any sanction of what has been done. It may sometimes imply the contrary. These resolutions cannot be made to imply any more than this, that the financial affairs of the country are in such a condition that the revenue cannot be instantly collected in legal currency. This they do imply, and this I suppose almost all admit to be true. An instantaneous execution of the law, without warning or notice, could, in my opinion, produce nothing, in a portion of the country, but an entire suspension of payments.

But to whose fault it is owing that the affairs of the country are reduced to this condition, they do not declare. They do not prevent, or in any degree embarrass, future inquiry on that subject. They speak to the fact, that the finances are deranged. They say also that reformation, though it must be gradual, ought to be immediately begun, and to be carried to perfection in the shortest time practicable. They cannot, by any fair construction, be made to express the approbation of Congress on the past conduct of any high officer of Government; and if the time shall ever come, when this House shall deem investigation necessary, it must be a case of very unpromising aspect, and of most fearful issue, which shall afford no other hope of escape than by setting up these resolutions by way of bar to an inquiry.

Nor is it any objection to this measure that inquiry has not first been had. Two duties may be supposed to have rested on the House: the one, to inquire into the origin of the evil, if it needed inquiry, and the other to find and apply a remedy. Because one of these duties has not hitherto been discharged, is no reason why the other should be longer neglected. While we are deciding which to do first, the time of the session is going by us, and neither may be done. In the mean time public mischiefs, of unknown magnitude and incalculable duration, threaten the country. I see no equivalent, no consolation, no mitigation, for these evils, in the future responsibility of departments. Let gentlemen show me any responsibility which will not be a name and a mockery. If, when we meet here again, it shall be found that all the barriers which have hitherto, in any degree, restrained the emissions of a mere paper money of the worst sort have given way, and that the floods have broken in upon us and come over us; if it shall be found that the revenues have failed—that the public credit, now a little propped and supported by a state of peace and commerce, has again tottered and fallen to the ground, and that all the operations of Government are at a stand, what then will be the value of the responsibility of departments? How great then the value of inquiry, when the evil is past prevention—when officers may have gone out of place, and when, indeed, the whole Administration will necessarily be dissolving, by the expiration of the term for which the Chief Executive Magistrate was chosen!

I cannot consent to take the chance of the greatest public mischiefs upon a reliance on any such responsibility. The stakes are too unequal.

As to the opinion advanced by some, that the object of the resolution cannot, in any way, be answered—that the revenues cannot be collected, otherwise than as they are now, in the paper of any and every banking association which chooses to issue paper, it cannot for a moment be admitted. This would be at once giving up the Government; for what is Government without revenue, and what is a revenue that is gathered together in the varying, fluctuating, discredited, depreciated, and still falling promissory notes of two or three hundred distinct, and, as to this Government, irresponsible banking companies? If it cannot collect its revenues in a better manner than this, it must cease to be a Government. The thing therefore is to be done; at any rate it is to be attempted. That it will be accomplished by the Treasury Department, without the interference of Congress, I have no belief. If from that source no reformation came, when reformation was easy, it is not now to be expected. Especially after the vote of yesterday, those whose interest it is to continue the present state of things, will arm themselves with the authority of Congress. They will justify themselves by the decision of this House. They will say, and say truly, that this House, having taken up the subject and discussed it, has not thought fit so much as to declare that it is expedient ever to relieve the country or its revenues from a paper money system. Whoever believes that the Treasury Department will oppose this tide, aided, as it will be, by strong feeling and great interest, has more faith in that Department than has fallen to my lot. It is the duty of this House to interfere with its own authority. Having taxed the people with no light hand, it is now its duty to take care that the people do not sustain these burdens in vain. The taxes are not borne without feeling. They

will not be borne without complaint, if, by mismanagement in collection, their utility to Government should be lost, and they should get into the Treasury at last only in discredited and useless paper.

A bank of thirty-five millions has been created for the professed purpose of correcting the evils of our circulation, and facilitating the receipts and expenditures of Government. I am not so sanguine in the hope of great benefit from this measure as others are. But the Treasury is also authorized to issue twenty-five millions of Treasury notes, eighteen or twenty millions of which remain yet to be issued, and which are also allowed by law to be received for duties and taxes. In addition to these is the coin which is in the country, and which is sure to come forth into circulation whenever there is a demand for it. These means, if wisely and skilfully administered, are sufficient to prevent any particular pressure or great inconvenience, in returning to the legal mode of collecting the revenue. It is true it may be easier for the people in the States in which a depreciated paper exists to pay their taxes in such paper, than in the legal currency or Treasury notes, because they can get it cheaper. But this is only saying that it is easier to pay a small tax than to pay a larger one, or that money costs more than that which is less valuable than money: a proposition not to be disputed. But a medium of payment, convenient for the people and safe for the Government, will be furnished, and may everywhere be obtained for a reasonable price. This is all that can justly be expected of Congress. Having provided this, they ought to require all parts of the country to conform to the same measure of justice. If taxes be not necessary, they should not be laid. If laid, they ought to be collected without preference or partiality.

But while some gentlemen oppose the resolutions because they fix a day too near, others think they fix a day too distant. In my own judgment, it is not so material what the time is, as it is to fix a time. The great object is to settle the question, that our legal currency is to be preserved, and that we are not about to embark on the ocean of paper money. The State banks, if they consult their own interest, or the interest of the community, will dispose of their Government stocks, and prepare themselves to redeem their paper and fulfil their contracts. If they should not adopt this course, there will be time for the people to be informed that the paper of such institutions will not answer the demands of Government, and that duties and taxes must be paid in the manner provided by law.

I cannot say, indeed, that this measure will certainly produce the desired end. It may fail. Its success, as is obvious, must essentially depend on the course pursued by the Treasury Department. But its tendency, I think, must be to produce good. It will, I hope, be a proof that Congress is not regardless of its duty. It will be evidence that this great subject has not passed without notice. It will record our determination to resist the introduction of a most destructive

1449　　　　　　　　　'HISTORY OF CONGRESS.　　　　　　1450

APRIL, 1816.　　　　　　Collection of the Revenue.　　　　　H. OF R.

and miserable policy into our system, and if there be any sanction or authority in the Constitution and the law; if there be any regard for justice and equality; if there be any care for the national revenue, or any concern for the public interest, let gentlemen consider whether they will relinquish their seats here, before this or some other measure be adopted.

When Mr. W. had concluded, Mr. LEWIS moved that the resolutions be indefinitely postponed.

A debate of much length and no little warmth followed, occupying, in a great degree, the ground taken on the bill on the same subject, which was yesterday rejected—the friends of the resolutions urging the necessity of some legislative act in a matter so deeply interesting to the public weal; the alarming consequences which might and probably would follow from adjourning, without doing something on the subject; and the fact that there was a majority yesterday in favor of the bill, but accidentally absent when the question was decided: and the opponents of the measure protesting against it, as well from its objectionable nature as against attempting it, when there were so few members remaining; and after the question had been decided by the House, in the rejection of the bill yesterday. The gentlemen who spoke against the resolutions, were Messrs. CALHOUN, GROSVENOR, ALEXANDER, MOSELEY, PICKERING, LYON, CULPEPER, GOLDSBOROUGH, HARDIN, and SHEFFEY; those who opposed the resolutions were Messrs. LEWIS, SMITH, of Maryland, and WRIGHT.

At the close of the debate, Mr. LEWIS withdrew his motion for postponement.

Mr. WEBSTER, after observing that it was in compliance with the wishes of gentlemen friendly to the general object of the resolutions, but averse to the adoption of the two first, withdrew those two.

Mr. CALHOUN proposed to amend the remaining resolution by extending its provisions to the notes of all banks which should, at the time specified therein, pay their notes in specie on demand.

Mr. WEBSTER saw no necessity for this amendment, and it would be better, he thought, to leave it for a Treasury regulation. It might happen that a bank, pretending to pay specie, might send its notes to a great distance, where, if they were offered in payment, it would be impossible to ascertain whether they were redeemable with specie or not.

Mr. CALHOUN agreed that it was not necessary, because the Treasury had already exercised the power, and it might very well be left with the Secretary still; but he had offered the amendment to meet the wishes of other gentlemen. As, however, it was objected to, he would not press it, and therefore withdrew it.

Mr. SMITH, of Maryland, moved to strike out the "first of February," and insert the "first of March." Negatived—ayes 52, noes 53.

Mr. PICKENS, after some introductory remarks, offered the following amendment:

"All banks and banking institutions, whose notes

may have been received in the collection of taxes or other dues in behalf of the United States to pay the same notes in gold or silver, or in Treasury notes of the Bank of the United States."

The amendment was opposed by Messrs. EDWARDS, CALHOUN, and MILNOR, and supported at some length by Mr. PICKENS, and negatived by a large majority.

On motion of Mr. PITKIN, who remarked that a few days would be of much importance to the banks in preparing for the payment of their notes, the "twentieth" was inserted instead of the first of February.

Mr. WRIGHT moved the following clause after the word "declared," in the eleventh line of the third resolution:

"Or any notes of any banks which have been or which shall hereafter be paid by the United States for any debt due, or demand by the said United States."

Mr. EDWARDS had no objection to the amendment, if the mover would designate the mode by which the notes paid away by the Government could be identified. Without that, the amendment would be useless.

Mr. WRIGHT replied, that it would be very easy to ascertain the notes so paid by marking them in a way to be identified, and that that difficulty could be readily obviated. He asked for the yeas and nays on the question, which were refused; and the amendment was rejected almost unanimously.

Mr. GOLDSBOROUGH then moved to insert the following words after the word "necessary," in the fourth line of the third resolution, so as to read

"Such measures as he may deem necessary, to pay all claims against the United States in legal money, or such Treasury notes as may hereafter be acceptable to the parties having such claims against the United States."

This motion produced a good deal of discussion, in which Messrs. INGHAM, PITKIN, CADY, and WEBSTER, opposed the amendment; and Messrs. GOLDSBOROUGH and WRIGHT advocated it. Mr. W. demanded the yeas and nays on the question, which were again refused; and the amendment was negatived without a division.

The question on ordering the resolution to be engrossed and read a third time, was decided in the affirmative—yeas 79, nays 35, as follows:

YEAS—Messrs. Adgate, Alexander, Atherton, Bær, Bassett, Bdm, Bradbury, Breckenridge, Brown, Cady, Calhoun, Champion, Chappell, Chipman, Cilley, Condict, Creighton, Culpeper, Cuthbert, Davenport, Edwards, Forney, Gaston, Goldsborough, Griffin, Grosvenor, Hale, Hardin, Hawes, Henderson, Herbert, Huger, Hungerford, Ingham, Johnson of Virginia, Johnson of Kentucky, Kent, Langdon, Love, Lovett, Lowndes, Lumpkin, Lyon, Marsh, Mayrant, McKee, McLean of Kentucky, Middleton, Moseley, Nelson of Massachusetts, Nelson of Virginia, Newton, Noyes, Ormsby, Parris, Pickering, Pitkin, Pleasants, Reed, Reynolds, Ruggles, Schenck, Sharpe, Sheffey, Smith of Maryland, Stearns, Strong, Stuart, Sturges, Taggart, Taul, Taylor of South Carolina, Telfair, Voss, Ward of New York, Webster, Wilcox, Willoughby, and Woodward.

Nays—Messrs. Archer, Bennett, Betts, Birdsall, Brooks, Bryan, Caldwell, Clayton, Clendennin, Clopton, Cooper, Crawford, Darlington, Hahn, Hall, Heister, Irwin of Pennsylvania, Lewis, Lyle, Milnor, Pickens, Roane, Root, Savage, Southard, Tate, Throop, Ward of Massachusetts, Whiteside, Wilkin, Williams, Thomas Wilson, William Wilson, Wright, and Yates.

The resolution was ordered to be read a third time to-day, and was forthwith read a third time and passed—yeas 71, nays 34, as follows:

Yeas—Messrs. Adgate, Alexander, Baer, Boss, Bradbury, Breckenridge, Brown, Cady, Calhoun, Champion, Chappell, Cilley, Condict, Creighton, Culpeper, Cuthbert, Davenport, Edwards, Forney, Gaston, Goldsborough, Grosvenor, Hale, Hawes, Henderson, Herbert, Huger, Hungerford, Ingham, Johnson of Virginia, Johnson of Kentucky, Kent, Langdon, Love, Lovett, Lowndes, Lumpkin, Lyon, Marsh, Mayrant, McKee, McLean of Kentucky, Middleton, Moseley, Nelson of Virginia, Newton, Noyes, Ormsby, Pickering, Pitkin, Pleasants, Reed, Reynolds, Ruggles, Schenck, Sharpe, Sheffey, Smith of Maryland, Stearns, Strong, Stuart, Sturges, Taggart, Taul, Taylor of South Carolina, Telfair, Tucker, Vose, Webster, Wilcox, and Willoughby.

Nays—Messrs. Archer, Bennett, Birdsall, Brooks, Bryan, Caldwell, Clayton, Clendennin, Clopton, Crawford, Darlington, Hahn, Hall, Heister, Irwin of Pa., Lewis, Lyle, Milnor, Pickens, Randolph, Roane, Root, Savage, Southard, Tate, Throop, Ward of Massachusetts, Whiteside, Wilkin, Williams, Thomas Wilson, William Wilson, Wright, and Yates.

Ordered, That the title be "a resolution relative to the more effectual collection of the public revenue."

SATURDAY, April 27.

Ordered, That the Committee on the Public Lands be discharged from a further consideration of the several petitions and documents referred to them, and upon which they have not reported, and that the said petitions and documents lie on the table.

Mr. ROBERTSON submitted the following proposition to amend the Standing Rules and Orders of the House; which was read, and ordered to lie on the table.

Resolved, That, at the commencement of any future session of Congress, a standing committee be appointed, consisting of seven members, to be denominated "the Committee on Private Land Claims," whose duty it shall be to take into consideration all private claims to land which may be referred to them, or shall or may come in question, and to report their opinion thereupon, together with such propositions for relief therein, as to them shall seem expedient.

Ordered, That the Committee on Pensions and Revolutionary Claims be discharged from a further consideration of the several petitions to them referred, and upon which they have not reported, and that the said petitions lie on the table.

Ordered, That the Committee on the Judiciary be discharged from a further consideration of the several subjects to them referred, and upon which they have not reported, and that the same be laid on the table.

The SPEAKER laid before the House a letter

from the Comptroller of the Treasury, enclosing sundry documents explanatory, and in justification of the conduct of that branch of the Department in the settlement of the accounts of Colonel James Thomas, late a Deputy Quartermaster General in the Army of the United States; which was read, and ordered to lie on the table.

The bill from the Senate, "to increase the salary of the Register of the Treasury, and to allow him compensation for his agency in countersigning and issuing Treasury notes," was read twice, and committed to a Committee of the Whole.

The resolution from the Senate, "authorizing the President of the United States to employ a skilful assistant in the Corps of Engineers," was read twice, and ordered to be read a third time to-day. The resolution was read a third time accordingly, and passed.

The amendments proposed by the Senate to the bill "concerning the owners, officers, and crew of the late privateer Roger," were read, and concurred in by the House.

The amendments proposed by the Senate to the bill, "making an appropriation for enclosing and improving the public square near the Capitol," and to abolish the office of Commissioners of the Public Buildings, and of Superintendent, and for the appointment of one Commissioner for the Public Buildings, being under consideration, a motion was made by Mr. CHAPPELL, that the said bill and amendments be postponed indefinitely.

This motion was supported by Mr. CHAPPELL, and opposed by Mr. GROSVENOR and Mr. CALHOUN, and negatived almost unanimously. The said amendments were then concurred in by the House.

The amendments proposed by the Senate to the bill to establish post roads were read and concurred in, except the third amendment, which was disagreed to by the House.

The amendments proposed by the Senate to the bill "fixing the compensation of the Secretary of the Senate and the Clerk of the House of Representatives, and making a temporary provision for the clerks employed in their offices," were read, and disagreed to by the House.

The amendments proposed by the Senate to the bill "for the confirmation of claims to land in the western district of Louisiana," were read, and concurred in by the House.

The amendments proposed by the Senate to the bill "for the appointment of a surveyor of the public lands in the Territories of Illinois and Missouri," were read, and concurred in by the House.

The amendments proposed by the Senate to the resolution "to indemnify Jabez Mowry and others," were read, and concurred in by the House.

The amendment proposed by the Senate to the bill "for the relief of David Coffin, Samuel and William Rodman. and Samuel Rodman, jr." was read, and concurred in by the House.

The amendment proposed by the Senate to the bill "for the relief of Peter Audrain," was read, and committed to a Committee of the Whole to-day.

The amendments proposed by the Senate to the bill "for the gradual increase of the Navy of the United States," were read, and concurred in by the House.

The amendments proposed by the Senate to the bill "authorizing the Judges of the Circuit Court of the District of Columbia to prepare a code of jurisprudence for the said District," were read, and concurred in by the House.

An engrossed bill, entitled "An act to allow drawbacks of duties on spirits distilled and sugar refined within the United States," was read the third time, and passed.

The bill from the Senate "to increase the compensation of the superintendents of the manufactories of arms at Springfield and Harper's Ferry," was read the third time, and passed.

The bill from the Senate "for settling the compensation of the commissioners, clerk, and translator, of the board of land claims, in the Eastern and Western districts of the Territory of Orleans, now State of Louisiana," was read the third time, and passed.

A message from the Senate informed the House that the Senate have passed the resolution fixing the time for an adjournment of the present session of Congress, with an amendment, in which they ask the concurrence of this House; and they insist on their amendments to the bill "fixing the compensation of the Secretary of the Senate and the Clerk of the House of Representatives, and making a temporary provision for the clerks in their offices."

An engrossed bill, entitled "An act making appropriations for carrying into effect the treaty between the United States and the Cherokee nation of Indians, concluded at Washington the 22d day of March, 1816," was read the third time, and passed.

An engrossed bill, "supplementary to the several acts organizing the office of Accountant of the War Department," was read the third time, and passed.

Ordered, That the title be "An act supplementary to an act making alterations in the Treasury and War Departments, passed the 8th day of May, 1792."

The amendment proposed by the Senate to the resolution fixing the time for an adjournment of the present session of Congress, was read, and is as follows: Strike out " Saturday the 20th," and insert " Tuesday the 30th."

Resolved, That this House agree to the said amendment.

The House again proceeded to consider the amendments proposed by the Senate to the bill "fixing the compensation of the Secretary of the Senate and the Clerk of the House of Representatives, and making a temporary provision for the clerks in their offices." Whereupon,

Resolved, That this House insist on their disagreement to the first and third, and do recede from their disagreement to the second of the said amendments.

Ordered, That the Committee of the Whole be discharged from a further consideration of the bill to authorize the settlement of certain claims for the services of the militia, and that the said bill be postponed indefinitely.

Ordered, That the engrossed bill supplementary to the act to encourage vaccination, be committed to a Committee of the Whole to-day.

Ordered, That the Committee of the Whole be discharged from a further consideration of the report of the Committee on the Public Lands, to whom was referred the President's Message of the 20th January last, recommending the ratification of certain donations of land made by the friendly Creek Indians to General Andrew Jackson, Colonel Benjamin Hawkins, and others, and that the said report be postponed indefinitely.

The House resolved itself into a Committee of the Whole on the bill from the Senate "for the relief of John Holkar, formerly Consul General of France to the United States; and after some time spent therein, the bill was reported without amendment.

A motion was made by Mr. Chappell that the bill be postponed indefinitely; which was negatived, and the bill was ordered to be read a third time to-day. The bill was then read a third time accordingly and passed.

Ordered, That when the House adjourns, it adjourn to meet again on Monday next, at 11 o'clock.

Ordered, That the Committee of the Whole, to whom is committed, the bill to authorize the President of the United States to lease out public lands containing mines of the precious metals, and the bill to establish a National University, be discharged from a further consideration thereof, and that the said bills be postponed indefinitely.

Ordered, That the Committee of the Whole be discharged from a further consideration of the bill authorizing payment to the widow of Elbridge Gerry, deceased, late Vice President of the United States, of half of such salary as would have been payable to him during the residue of the term for which he was elected, had he so long lived; the bill to prevent the circulation of unchartered bank notes in the District of Columbia; the bill to extend the patent granted to Andrew Law for an improvement in printing music; the bill to appropriate the marriage license tax within the county of Washington, in the District of Columbia; the bill providing for reprinting the collection of land laws; the report of the Committee of Ways and Means, upon the petition of Elisha Talbott, and others; and of the report of the Committee of Ways and Means upon the subject of revenue and that the said bills and reports be postponed indefinitely.

The House resolved itself into a Committee of the Whole on the bill from the Senate "concerning the annual sum appropriated for arming and equipping the militia;" and after some time spent therein, the bill was reported without amendment, and ordered to be read a third time to-day. It was accordingly read the third time and passed.

The House resolved itself into a Committee of the Whole on the bill to establish the office of Accountant in the Department of State; and after some time spent therein, the bill was reported with an amendment, and ordered to be postponed indefinitely.

Ordered, That the Committee of the Whole be discharged from a further consideration of the bill establishing the Patent Office; providing the means of further encouragement to "authors and inventors," and guarding more effectually against frauds and impositions by patentees; and that the said bill be postponed indefinitely.

A message from the Senate informed the House that the Senate further insist on their first and third amendments to the bill "fixing the compensation of the Secretary of the Senate and Clerk of the House of Representatives, and making a temporary provision for the clerks employed in their offices," and ask a conference upon the subject-matter of the disagreeing votes of the two Houses upon the said amendment, to which conference they have appointed managers on their part.

The House proceeded to consider the said message: whereupon,

Resolved, That this House further insist on their disagreeing to the said first and third amendments, and agree to the conference asked by the Senate.

Ordered, That the Committee of the Whole be discharged from a further consideration of the bill from the Senate "for the relief of the legal representatives of Ignace Chalmet Delino, deceased," and that the said bill be postponed indefinitely.

Ordered, That the Committee of the Whole be discharged from a further consideration of the bill from the Senate "for adjusting the claims to land and establishing a land office for the districts of lands lying east of the Mississippi river and island of New Orleans," and that the said bill be postponed indefinitely.

VACCINATION.

The House resolved itself into a Committee of the Whole on the bill supplementary to an act to encourage vaccination.

Mr. Condict introduced an amendment, enjoining it as a duty on the Secretaries of the War and Navy Departments, to cause all the soldiers and seamen forthwith to be vaccinated, who should not furnish proof of having had small pox, or the vaccine disease. In support of this motion, Mr. C. stated, that the small pox broke out among the crew of the Guerriere at Naples; twelve had the disease, four of whom died. During the same cruise, a case of small pox occurred on board the Congress frigate on the 9th of October, 1815, the infection having probably been received at Malaga, which place the ship left the 25th September. The crew was mustered on the 17th and eighty-five persons inoculated, of whom sixty-seven had the disease. From these facts, Mr. C. presumed the House would see the utility of the proposed amendment.

The amendment was agreed to; as well as one offered also by Mr. C. to extend the duration of the act to *seven* instead of *three* years.

The amendments were reported to the House; when Mr. Hardin moved the indefinite postponement of the bill. After some debate, this motion was negatived by a large majority; and the House adjourned.

Monday, April 29.

Ordered, That the Committee of Ways and Means be discharged from a further consideration of the several subjects to them referred, and upon which they have not reported.

The House proceeded to consider the resolution submitted by Mr. Robertson, on the 27th instant, proposing an amendment to the standing rules and orders of the House, which being again read, was amended, and agreed to by the House, as follows:

Resolved, That at the commencement of each future session of Congress, a standing committee be appointed, consisting of five members, to be denominated "the Committee on Private Land Claims," whose duty it shall be to take into consideration all claims to land, which may be referred to them, or shall, or may come in question, and to report their opinion thereupon, together with such propositions for relief therein, as to them shall seem expedient.

On motion of Mr. Thomas Wilson,

Ordered, That the Committee on Public Expenditures be discharged from a further consideration of the letter and documents of General William Henry Harrison, and that the same, together with the communications and documents presented to the committee, on the same subject, be referred to the Secretary of War, and that he be instructed to report thereon to this House at their next session.

A message from the Senate informed the House that the Senate have passed the bill of this House "to allow drawback of duties on spirits distilled and sugar refined within the United States," with an amendment, in which they ask the concurrence of this House. The Senate have passed a bill, entitled "An act fixing the compensation of the Chaplains of Congress," in which bill they ask the concurrence of this House. And they insist upon their first and third amendments to the bill from this House, fixing the compensation of the Secretary of the Senate, and the Clerk of the House of Representatives, and making a temporary provision for the clerks employed in their offices, with the amendment recommended by the Managers at the conference on that subject.

Mr. Hardin, from the Managers at the conference on the disagreeing votes of the two Houses, upon the bill fixing the compensation of the Secretary of the Senate, and Clerk of the House of Representatives, and making a temporary provision for the clerks employed in their offices, reported that the conferees recommended—

"That the House of Representatives recede from their disagreement to the first and third amendments, and that the bill be further amended by inserting after the word 'effect,' in the last line thereof, the following words: 'And continue in force for two years.'"

The House then proceeded to consider the said report and amendment; whereupon,

Resolved, That this House recede from their disagreement to the said first and third amendments, with the amendment to the bill recommended by the conferees.

The amendment proposed by the Senate to the bill "to allow drawback of duties on spirits distilled and sugar refined within the United States," was read, and committed to a Committee of the Whole to-day.

The bill from the Senate "fixing the compensation of the Chaplains of Congress," was read the first and second time, and committed to the Committee of the Whole last appointed.

Ordered, That the Committee of the Whole to whom is committed the bill for the relief of John H. Peaslee, Nathan B. Haswell, and Russell Jones; and the bill from the Senate "concerning the library of Congress, be discharged from a further consideration thereof, and that the said bills be postponed indefinitely.

The SPEAKER laid before the House a letter from the President of the United States, communicating certain information called for respecting the number of American prisoners at Dartmoor, which had been impressed, &c.; which, with the documents, was ordered to be printed.

The bill supplementary to the act to encourage vaccination, which was under consideration at the time of adjournment on Saturday, was taken up.

A motion was made that the bill be indefinitely postponed.

The postponement was supported by Mr. WEBSTER and Mr. PICKERING on various grounds, unconnected with any view of obstructing the dissemination of the vaccine matter; the want of time to deliberate on the provisions of the bill; the doubt whether Congress could constitutionally appropriate money for such purposes, &c. The postponement was opposed by Messrs. WRIGHT and CONDICT, who replied to the gentlemen above named; after which the motion was agreed to; and the bill indefinitely postponed—ayes 49, noes 48.

The bill to increase the salary of the Register of the Treasury, [from $2,400 to $3,000,] and to compensate him for signing Treasury notes, passed through a Committee of the whole House, in which the allowance for signing Treasury notes, was, on motion of Mr. LOWNDES, stricken out. The House concurred in the amendment; and ordered the bill to a third reading; which was subsequently read a third time, and passed.

The House resolved itself into a Committee of the Whole on the amendment proposed by the Senate "to the bill for the relief of Peter Audrain;" and after some time spent therein, the Committee reported their agreement to the amendment.—The amendment was then concurred in by the House.

The House resolved itself into a Committee of the Whole on the amendment proposed by the Senate to the bill "to allow drawback of duties on spirits distilled and sugar refined within the

United States;" and on the bill from the Senate "fixing the compensation of the Chaplains of Congress;" and after some time spent therein, the Committee reported their agreement to the said amendment, as also the said bill without amendment.—The amendment was then concurred in by the House.

Ordered, That the bill "fixing the compensation of the Chaplains of Congress," be read a third time to-day. The bill was accordingly read the third time, and passed.

Ordered, That the Committee of the whole House to whom is committed the bills from the Senate, "for the relief Jacob Babbitt and John Dennis," and "providing for the publication of the decisions of the Supreme Court of the United States;" the bill "for the relief of Isaac Lawrence and others, merchants of New York;" and the report of the select committee respecting the remains of the late General George WASHINGTON, be discharged from a further consideration thereof, and that the said bills and report be postponed indefinitely.

Mr. PICKERING submitted the following proposition of amendment to the standing rules and orders of the House; which was read and ordered to lie on the table:

Resolved, That the following be added to the rules and orders of the House:

1. All standing committees, except the Committee of Ways and Means, shall consist each of five members, and no member shall be put on more than one standing committee at the same time.

2. Of the journals of the House printed from day to day while Congress is in session, ten copies only shall be delivered in sheets, and these shall be in the custody of the Clerk.

3. Daily, while the House is in session, the post office attached to it shall be and continue shut,

POST OFFICE INVESTIGATION.

Mr. CULPEPER, after expressing his desire that the House would go into consideration of the subject, and pronounce some opinion upon it, moved that the Committee of the Whole be discharged from the consideration of the report of the committee of investigation into the fiscal affairs of the General Post Office, that the same might be brought at once before the House.

Mr. ROOT suggested the propriety of referring the subject to the President of the United States, who would investigate the report, the evidence, &c., and do justice to the parties concerned.

Mr. CULPEPER opposed this course. The Postmaster General had asked of the House the investigation, which had in part been acted on, and it was the duty of the House to prosecute the inquiry. It was his misfortune to know a great deal of this affair, and he wished it taken up in this House, that it might be amply developed and fully acted on.

Mr. McKEE made a few remarks on the propriety of taking up the subject, unconnected with the merits of the case. He adverted to a fact which had come to his knowledge—the dismissal of some of the clerks from the Post Office; and he should be glad to learn whether that had been done in consequence of any facts they had disclosed, or whether it appeared to the committee that those men possessed any evidence which their dismissal might be intended to prevent.

Mr. WRIGHT.—Mr. Speaker, I am not a little surprised at the present effort of the honorable gentleman from North Carolina (Mr. CULPEPER) to bring up the report of the committee on the General Post Office, after the honorable chairman of that committee has gone home with leave, and a week after this House has sent their resolution to the Senate to adjourn—especially when it is a fact of notoriety, that the honorable chairman of that committee had made several abortive efforts to take up that report. There must be some secret spring to this untimely attempt to take up a subject of so much moment. Mr. Speaker, the manner that this subject was brought before this House, so highly honorable to the head of that Department, tests the feelings of that highly honorable officer, that the character of that office should not only be pure, but unsuspected. He therefore sought the investigation, which has eventuated in the report of the committee of the evidence of the facts, which will show that they were not of an order to induce an unkind suspicion of any impurity in any of the officers in the establishment, unless in the malcontents, who, by their indirections and false clamors, have evinced a disposition to undermine their superiors, and thereby gain a grade for themselves—but who, by this timely inquiry, have been disappointed, and, for their false clamor, have been themselves removed. I heard with pleasure the remarks of the honorable Messrs. CREIGHTON, PICKERING, and FORNEY, members of the committee, going all lengths to testify their sense of the correct conduct of the officers complained of. They charge Mr. Bradley with being a contractor to carry the mail by a contract with the Postmaster-General, Mr. Granger, although Mr. Bradley declined such a copartnership, but by the express approbation of Mr. Granger. They charge that, after that contract was closed, the compensation was greatly increased by an additional article, but on inquiry it is found that the same additional article of compensation contained an extension of the route beyond the additional compensation. They charge, also, that Mr. Bradley caused the moneys paid into the Post Office, to be deposited in a bank, to which he had been chosen president. Sir, the honorable selection of that gentleman to be the president of a bank, is strong evidence of the integrity of his character; and, sir, if the money of the public were necessarily to be deposited in some bank for safe-keeping, and for the facility of disbursement, can any man be of opinion that they would not be as safe there, under the double responsibility of the officer who was to direct the deposites, as well as the disbursements? And, sir, if any profit could arise to the officer at the head of the bank, can it be an objection with any honorable man, that he should be excluded from that benefit, *because* he was high in the confidence of the nation, where, it is well known, he had long been a perfect drudger? And, sir, it is well

known that the Post Office deposites were always made in that bank, and long before the selection of Mr. Bradley to be the president—and would any man feel disposed to remove the deposites, because Mr. Bradley was put at the head of that bank?

Mr. GROSVENOR thought, if the Postmaster General, after asking the investigation, had discharged clerks with a view to prevent the remainder of the clerks from giving testimony, it was a high contempt of this House, and deserved its severe animadversion. He did not know such was the fact—he had no evidence of it but common report.

Mr. JOHNSON, of Kentucky, said, that this was a subject in the estimation of the member from North Carolina (Mr. CULPEPER) sufficiently important to arrest all other business before the House. It is a little astonishing, said Mr. J., that a member, impressed with this importance, and which he would not deny, should make such a motion one day only previous to the close of the session, when the House had before it a great number of bills, which it was indispensable to be acted upon; not only this, but to make the motion the day the chairman had left Congress, and not the chairman only, but other members—one from Virginia, (Mr. BARBOUR,) who was anxious to have the subject before the House, but which the House, on several occasions, had refused, or neglected if you will, to take into consideration. Mr. J. said, he was equally anxious that the subject should be investigated; yes, thoroughly investigated; for he never had been placed in a situation where he was afraid to accuse or acquit any person, if it became *his* duty to do so. To meet the wishes of the gentleman from North Carolina, he said, he would vote to rescind the joint resolution of adjournment, if the proposition was made; for no member could believe that justice could be done to either party, in so short a time, if the subject was so important. Mr. J. said, that he was very glad to find that the honorable mover knew so much. Did he know more than the committee of investigation? If so, how? Did the committee refuse testimony, or did they suppress any important fact? Mr. J. wished to ask each member of the committee on this subject, and he wanted to know if the committee agreed to the report unanimously, or was the committee divided? These were inquiries he should make; and if the member from North Carolina knew more than the committee, he would inquire from what source he obtained his information, and why such information was withheld from the committee? But at this time these inquiries could not be made of all the committee, because one-half had left the city.

If this matter was not brought forward, whose fault was it? It was in the power of any member to make a motion at any time, that would have involved the discussion of the merits of the report. Those very members were to blame, who were dissatisfied with the course the chairman pursued in calling up the report, when the Speaker read the order of the day on that subject; for to his knowledge the chairman had called it twice, and on neither occasion would the House take up the subject—and he presumed because the more pressing concerns of the nation were before the House. If that was the reason, or whatever reason, it is impossible, said Mr. J., that justice can be done to the parties concerned, at this time; nor could members express their sentiments, which he was desirous to do, at the close of the session. This view alone would prevent him from voting to take up the subject now. Some observations had been made in relation to three of the clerks being dismissed. Mr. J. said, if the necessity existed for such dismissal, he regretted that necessity. If they were dismissed without necessity, he would still more regret the circumstance, because, deserved or not, the dismissed clerks would, no doubt, feel it in relation to their avocations. But, Mr. J. said, who was the judge on this occasion? Who had the power of appointing clerks in the various Executive offices, from the foundation of the Government? Was it Congress, or the Heads of Departments? Would it be proper for Congress to appoint the various clerks? If so, they would then have the right to dismiss. Have we ever had an inquiry into the causes of the dismissal of any officer of the Government by the Executive, or the dismissal of any clerk by the Head of a Department? He believed no such case could be adduced; of course, Mr. J. said, whether he considered these clerks worthy of confidence or not, he was not the judge of their continuance in employment; it was the Postmaster General. But, say gentlemen, shall clerks be turned out for giving evidence in an inquiry into the conduct of the Department to which they belong? Mr. J. said no, they should not be turned out for speaking the truth—but if they made false accusations, it was with the Head of the Department to judge of their conduct, and retain them or dismiss them, as he thought proper. In saying this, Mr. J. did not intend to give any opinion on the case, because the Speaker considered it out of order; but he wanted that opportunity, whenever time would admit—nor did he wish to say anything to injure the dismissed clerks. He did not know them; he wished their condition could have been otherwise—he had no feeling of hostility to them. But it had been said that these clerks had been dismissed while the investigation was progressing, and because they had made the accusations. Mr. J. said, the fact was otherwise, as to the pendency of the investigation. It was a fact that the investigation was closed previously to their dismissal; after their dismissal he understood the clerks were indignant, and requested to be brought before the committee again; they were brought forward, and also had access to the Post Office books, and the use of other witnesses, and he understood that the additional testimony had been taken and reported by the committee, and was now before the House.

In relation to the dismissal of clerks, this was the principle the House would adopt, that is to say—the House would inquire whether any imposition had been practised to make them conceal or suppress the truth. If a bribe, or any reward should be offered to a clerk, or any other witness, to conceal the truth, or suggest a falsehood, such act being proven, would be sufficient to consign such officers to infamy and to dismissal; or the fact that a clerk was threatened with dismissal, if he told the truth—such a charge, from respectable authority, would demand examination. He should vote for a standing committee in the recess, or during the session, either, to make inquiries; but no such fact had been proven, and no such suggestion had been made.

It had been stated that the clerks told the committee that they understood they were to be dismissed, and when dismissed that it had been on account of giving evidence, but it could not be on account of any fact to which they made oath; because, with all their testimony, they had proved nothing that they stated they could prove. So says the report; and now we ask if the committee suppressed any fact? If not, then no charge has been proven. Mr. J. said, that while he would at every hazard maintain his independence as a representative, he would as obstinately oppose any interference with Executive duties. Indeed, said Mr. J., the dismissal of the clerks was the very course to make them prove everything that could be proven; and we see, from the statements of members of the committee, that it had the effect of a request on the part of the dismissed clerks to be heard again; they were heard again as to the investigation—therefore, the dismissal could not have been with a view to prevent them from giving all the information in their power; and with all that additional incentive not one charge had been proven, unless a committee of seven members have been wanting in their duty. Nor had he heard a suggestion from any of the committee, that any of the charges had been proven. There was one subject upon which he also wished to express his views—as to the deposites of the Post Office, and the regulation of its fiscal concerns. But that was not now in order, and he should say no more.

Mr. PICKERING said, the gentleman from New York (Mr. GROSVENOR) considered the removal of those clerks of the General Post Office who had appeared as accusers in relation to the conduct of that Department, while that conduct was under investigation by the orders of this House, as a contempt of the House. On the fact assumed by the gentleman, his observation must be admitted to be correct. But before their removal those clerks had been themselves examined, and the committee had for a long time and very patiently listened to the statements, and summoned before them every person within their reach whom the clerks or any of them represented as able to give any testimony in support of the suggestions. Towards the close of the investigation, those clerks discovered no abatement of zeal, in hunting for persons who had exchanged any bank notes with the persons accused. But most or all of these cases occurred prior to the difference in value of the notes of different banks; and for very small sums, as twenty to fifty, and once for a hundred dollars. These exchanges appear to have been made to accommodate persons in this District, by giving them District notes or those current in the District in exchange for notes of distant banks. But it did not appear that these exchanges were ever made with public money.

But whatever may be the just construction of the conduct of the Post Office Department, said Mr. P., in dismissing the accusing clerks—they, or some of them, must certainly be deemed to have acted in contempt of this House; while the investigation was going on, and he believed almost from its commencement, partial and inflammatory statements were furnished to the editors of one or more newspapers, which were republished by others, calculated to make improper and unfounded impressions on the minds of all who read them. And those statements, from their nature, must be presumed to have been made by those clerks, or some of them.

Mr. GROSVENOR, in reply to Mr. JOHNSON said, if the rule was once established that they could not inquire into such transactions, every officer of the Government would set them at defiance, and might do injustice with impunity. He acknowledged he knew of no fact or evidence of improper conduct in this affair; but the gentleman himself had by his arguments proved the necessity of resisting conduct such as had been mentioned respecting the clerks. Did not the House see it was holding a threat over the heads of the remaining clerks to prevent them from giving testimony? If it was a fact, it would require the interference of the House. Admit, said Mr. G., that you have no right to interfere with the discretion of the Heads of Departments unless they touch our privileges, still this is a case requiring the interference of Congress.

Mr. CREIGHTON said, notwithstanding the absence of the chairman and two of the members of the select committee, as a member of that committee he should be gratified that the Committee of the Whole should be discharged from the further consideration of the report, that the subject might be brought before the House for full examination; but would have been better pleased if the House had indulged the chairman in the call made by him a few days since to go into Committee of the Whole on the report, as more time for discussion would have been afforded. The committee had a laborious task to perform; their sittings were long and frequent, and many witnesses were examined. He believed all the clerks in the General Post Office were examined; the books and papers stated by any of the witnesses as containing evidence relating to the inquiry were produced and submitted to the clerks calling for the same, to improve as evidence; the names of many individuals were furnished by the clerks as witnesses, and in every instance they were summoned and carefully examined. After the examination was closed three clerks in the General Post Office were dismissed, as they afterwards informed the committee, and requested to be again heard. The committee, anxious to afford the fullest opportunity, convened and heard the statements they had to make, and at their instance summoned several witnesses, who attended and testified before them. The books of the Post Office were again produced, on the suggestion of one of the clerks, which he said contained important testimony, from which no testimony was submitted to the committee that had not been previously examined. A full and fair opportunity was afforded to all persons, whether in the character of accusers or witnesses; and the result had been presented to the House. He should vote for the motion of the gentleman from North Carolina, and even at this late period of the session hoped the report would be taken up and acted on by the House.

Mr. FORSEY said, believing that the merit of this report was not now properly under consideration, he should only state in answer to the inquiries made by the honorable gentleman from Kentucky, (Mr. McKEE,) that the committee were not in possession of any facts relative to the dismissal of the clerks in the Post Office, except what were given by the clerks themselves. The committee did not think it their duty to enter into an investigation of the motives governing the Postmaster General in dismissing these clerks, as he undoubtedly had the power to do in that case as he should think proper. Had the committee discovered any undue influence or tampering with the witnesses, it was probable they would then have thought it their duty to have gone into a more particular examination of the matter. During this investigation, two of the principal clerks in that Department stated to the committee that they were denied access to the books of the office, by which they could be enabled to support the charges. In consequence of this statement, the books thought necessary were demanded by the committee; the evidence resulting from their investigation is before the House. But it is an undeniable fact, that, a short time after the commencement of this investigation, these clerks stated that they were removed from the duties they used to perform, and reduced to do the lowest drudgery in the office. While up, Mr. F. felt it his duty to state, that he was fully in possession of the sentiments of the honorable gentleman from Virginia, (Mr. BARBOUR,) a member of this committee, now absent, in relation to this report—which Mr. F. had been requested to state when this subject should be taken up.

Mr. HALL was decidedly of opinion with Mr. GROSVENOR, not that the amount was of consequence, but on principle. If the alleged conduct respecting the clerks was tolerated, you take away all inquiry into the conduct of the Heads of Departments. He knew not that the fact was so had been suggested; but shall we suffer men, said Mr. H. to be discharged from their public employment because they were expected to give evidence of improper conduct? He repeated, he knew not that the fact was so; but if it was, he would redress it. He inquired whether a certain piece of evidence in his hands respecting the sale of a draft had been submitted to the committee.

Mr. CREIGHTON stated in reply, that the circumstance referred to had been the subject of investigation, during the examination of other testimony. on oath.

Mr. CULPEPER's motion was then agreed to; and, on motion of Mr. GROSVENOR, the report was laid on the table.

TUESDAY, April 30.

Mr. RANDOLPH presented the petition of sundry inhabitants of Charlotte county, in the State of Virginia, praying that the mails may not be transmitted or opened on Sundays.—Laid on the table.

Mr. RANDOLPH, from the committee appointed on the first of March last, to inquire into an illegal traffic in slaves, carried on through the medium of this District; by persons in different States, reported various testimony collected by the committee, in the course of their investigation of the subject; but without other report of facts or opinions. The documents containing the testimony, were ordered to lie on the table.

A message from the Senate informed the House that the Senate have passed the bill from this House entitled, "an act concerning invalid pensioners," and the "resolution relative to the more effectual collection of the public revenue," with amendments to each. They have passed a bill "making further appropriations for the year 1816." In which bill and amendments they request the concurrence of this House.

The bill from the Senate, entitled "An act making further appropriations for the year 1816," was read twice and committed to a Committee of the Whole.

The House then went into a Committee of the Whole on the said bill; and after some time spent therein, the bill was reported with an amendment, which was read and concurred in by the House, and the amendment ordered to be engrossed, and the bill, as amended, read a third time to-day. The bill was then read the third time and passed.

The House then took up the amendments of the Senate to the invalid pension bill, striking out the pensions to various persons inserted in the bill by this House. The consideration of these amendments produced a good deal of discussion on the merits of particular cases. The amendments were all finally agreed to.

The House proceeded to consider the amendments proposed by the Senate to the resolution relative to the more effectual collection of the public revenue, which were concurred in by the House.—Ayes 68, noes 23.

A message from the Senate informed the House that they have passed a resolution "proposing the appointment of a joint committee to wait on the President of the United States, and inform him of the approaching recess of Congress; and have appointed a committee on their part."

On motion of Mr. NELSON, of Virginia,

Resolved, That the sum of fifty dollars, each, be paid out of the contingent fund of this House, to John Oswald Dunn, Elextius Spalding, Manly A. Beach, George Thomas, Samuel Stewart, William Papcost, and George Cooper, the attendants of this House, for their faithful services during the present session.

On motion of Mr. NELSON, of Virginia,

Resolved, That the sum of one hundred dollars be paid to James Claxton, out of the contingent funds of this House, for his services in the post office of this House; and fifty dollars to James Barron, out of the same fund, as an attendant.

The House took up the resolution from the Senate, "for the appointment of a joint committee to wait on the President of the United States, and inform him of the intended recess of Congress;" which being read, was concurred in by the House, and Messrs. CRAWFORD and REED were appointed a committee conformably thereto on the part of this House.

A message from the Senate notified the House that the Senate, having completed the legislative business before them, are about to adjourn.

Mr. CRAWFORD, from the joint committee appointed to wait on the President, reported that they had performed that duty, and that the President had informed them he had no further communication to make.

The SPEAKER then rose and addressed the House with some brief but cordial valedictory expressions; after which he adjourned the House *sine die.*

APPENDIX

TO THE HISTORY OF THE FOURTEENTH CONGRESS.

[FIRST SESSION.]

COMPRISING THE MOST IMPORTANT DOCUMENTS ORIGINATING DURING THAT CONGRESS, AND THE PUBLIC ACTS PASSED BY IT.

SPAIN.—PROHIBITION OF ILLEGAL EXPEDITIONS IN THE UNITED STATES.

A PROCLAMATION,

By the President of the United States of America.

Whereas information has been received that sundry persons, citizens of the United States, or residents within the same, and especially within the State of Louisiana, are conspiring together to begin and set on foot, provide, and prepare the means for a military expedition or enterprise against the dominions of Spain, with which the United States are happily at peace; that, for this purpose, they are collecting arms, military stores, provisions, vessels, and other means; and deceiving and seducing honest and well-meaning citizens to engage in their unlawful enterprises; or organizing, officering, and arming themselves for the same, contrary to the laws in such cases made and provided: I have, therefore, thought fit to issue this my proclamation, warning and enjoining all faithful citizens who have been led, without due knowledge or consideration, to participate in the said unlawful enterprises, to withdraw from the same without delay; and commanding all persons whatsoever engaged or concerned in the same to cease all further proceedings therein, as they will answer the contrary at their peril. And I hereby enjoin and require all officers, civil and military, of the United States, or of any of the States or Territories, all judges, justices, and other officers of the peace. all military officers of the army or navy of the United States, and officers of the militia, to be vigilant, each within his respective department, and according to his functions, in searching out and bringing to punishment all persons engaged or concerned in such enterprises; in seizing and detaining, subject to the disposition of the law, all arms, military stores, vessels, or other means provided or providing for the same; and, in general, in preventing the carrying on such expedition or enterprise, by all the lawful means within their power: and I require all good and faithful citizens and others, within the United States, to be aiding and assisting herein; and especially in the discovery, apprehension, and bringing to justice of all such offenders; in preventing the execution of their unlawful combinations or designs; and in giving information against them to the proper authorities.

In testimony whereof, I have caused the seal of the United States of America to be affixed to these presents, and signed the same with my hand. Done at the City
[L. S.] of Washington, the first day of September, in the year of our Lord one thousand eight hundred and fifteen, and of the independence of the said United States of America the fortieth.

JAMES MADISON.

By the President:

JAMES MONROE, *Secretary of State.*

ALGIERS.

[Communicated to the Senate, December 6, 1815.]

To the Senate of the United States:

I lay before the Senate, for their consideration and advice, as to a ratification, a Treaty of Peace with the Dey of Algiers, concluded on the 30th day of June, 1815; with a letter relating to the same from the American Commissioners to the Secretary of State.

JAMES MADISON.

WASHINGTON, *Dec.* 6, 1815.

Treaty of Peace and Amity concluded between the United States of America and His Highness Omar Bashaw, Dey of Algiers.

ARTICLE 1. There shall be, from the conclusion of this treaty, a firm, inviolable, and universal peace and friendship between the President and citizens of the United States of America, on the one part, and the Dey and subjects of the Regency of Algiers in Barbary, on the other, made by the free consent of both parties, and on the terms of the most favored nations: and if either party shall, hereafter, grant to any other nation any particular favor or privilege in navi-

Relations with Algiers.

gation or commerce, it shall immediately become common to the other party—freely, when it is freely granted to such other nations; but when the grant is conditional, it shall be at the option of the contracting parties to accept, alter, or reject such conditions, in such manner as shall be most conducive to their respective interests.

ART. 2. It is distinctly understood between the contracting parties, that no tribute, either as biennial presents, or under any form or name whatever, shall ever be required by the Dey and Regency of Algiers, from the United States of America, on any pretext whatever.

ART. 3. The Dey of Algiers shall cause to be immediately delivered up to the American squadron now off Algiers all the American citizens now in his possession, amounting to ten, more or less; and all the subjects of the Dey of Algiers now in possession of the United States, amounting to five hundred, more or less, shall be delivered up to him; the United States, according to the usages of civilized nations, requiring no ransom for the excess of prisoners in their favor.

ART. 4. A just and full compensation shall be made by the Dey of Algiers to such citizens of the United States as have been captured and detained by Algerine cruisers, or who have been forced to abandon their property in Algiers, in violation of the twenty-second article of the Treaty of Peace and Amity concluded between the United States and the Dey of Algiers on the 5th of September, 1795.

And it is agreed between the contracting parties, that, in lieu of the above, the Dey of Algiers shall cause to be delivered, forthwith, into the hands of the American Consul residing at Algiers, the whole of a quantity of bales of cotton left by the late Consul General of the United States in the public magazines in Algiers; and that he shall pay into the hands of the said Consul the sum of ten thousand Spanish dollars.

ART. 5. If any goods belonging to any nation with which either of the parties are at war should be loaded on board vessels belonging to the other party, they shall pass free and unmolested, and no attempts shall be made to take or detain them.

ART. 6. If any citizens or subjects, with their effects, belonging to either party, shall be found on board a prize vessel taken from an enemy by the other party, such citizens or subjects shall be liberated immediately; and in no case, or on any pretence whatever, shall any American citizen be kept in captivity or confinement, or the property of any American citizen found on board of any vessel belonging to any other nation with which Algiers may be at war be detained from its lawful owners, after the exhibition of sufficient proofs of American citizenship and of American property by the Consul of the United States residing at Algiers.

ART. 7. Proper passports shall immediately be given to the vessels of both the contracting parties, on condition that the vessels of war belonging to the Regency of Algiers, on meeting with

merchant vessels belonging to the citizens of the United States of America, shall not be permitted to visit them with more than two persons besides the rowers; these only shall be permitted to go on board, without first obtaining leave from the commander of said vessel, who shall compare the passport, and immediately permit said vessel to proceed on her voyage; and should any of the subjects of Algiers insult or molest the commander, or any other person, on board a vessel so visited, or plunder any of the property contained in her, on complaint being made by the Consul of the United States residing in Algiers, and on his producing sufficient proof to substantiate the fact, the commander or rais of said Algerine ship or vessel of war, as well as the offenders, shall be punished in the most exemplary manner.

All vessels of war belonging to the United States of America, on meeting a cruiser belonging to the Regency of Algiers, or having seen her passports and certificates from the Consul of the United States residing in Algiers, shall permit her to proceed on her cruise unmolested, and without detention. No passports shall be granted by either party to any vessel but such as are absolutely the property of citizens or subjects of the said contracting parties, on any pretence whatever.

ART. 8. A citizen or subject of either of the contracting parties having bought a prize vessel condemned by the other party, or by any other nation, the certificate of condemnation and bill of sale shall be a sufficient passport for such vessel for six months, which, considering the distance between the two countries, is no more than a reasonable time for her to procure proper passports.

ART. 9. Vessels of either of the contracting parties, putting into the ports of the other, and having need of provisions or other supplies, shall be furnished at the market price; and if any such vessel should so put in from a distance at sea, and have occasion to repair, she shall be at liberty to land and re-embark her cargo, without paying any customs or duty whatever; but in no case shall she be compelled to land her cargo.

ART. 10. Should a vessel of either of the contracting parties be cast on shore within the territories of the other, all proper assistance shall be given to her crew; no pillage shall be allowed; the property shall remain at the disposal of the owners; and, if reshipped on board of any vessel for exportation, no customs or duties whatever shall be required to be paid thereon; and the crew shall be protected and succored, until they can be sent to their own country.

ART. 11. If a vessel of either of the contracting parties shall be attacked by an enemy within cannon-shot of the forts of the other, she shall be protected as much as possible. If she be in port, she shall not be seized or attacked, when it is in the power of the other party to protect her; and when she proceeds to sea, no enemy shall be permitted to pursue her from the same port within twenty-four hours after her departure.

Relations with Algiers.

ART. 12. The commerce between the United States of America and the Regency of Algiers, the protections to be given to merchants, masters of vessels, and seamen, the reciprocal rights of establishing Consuls in each country, and the privileges, immunities, and jurisdictions to be enjoyed by such Consuls, are declared to be on the same footing, in every respect, with the most favored nations, respectively.

ART. 13. The Consul of the United States of America shall not be responsible for the debts contracted by citizens of his own nation, unless he previously gives written obligations so to do.

ART. 14. On a vessel or vessels of war belonging to the United States anchoring before the city of Algiers, the Consul is to inform the Dey of her arrival, when she shall receive the salutes which are, by treaty or custom, given to the ships-of-war of the most favored nations on similar occasions, and which shall be returned, gun for gun; and if, after such arrival, so announced, any Christians, whatsoever, captives in Algiers, make their escape and take refuge on board any of the ships-of-war, they shall not be required back again; nor shall the Consul of the United States or commanders of said ships be required to pay anything for the said Christians.

ART. 15. As the Government of the United States of America has, in itself, no character of enmity against the laws, religion, or tranquillity of any nation; and as the said States have never entered into any voluntary war, or act of hostility, except in defence of their just rights on the high seas, it is declared by the contracting parties, that no pretext arising from religious opinions shall ever produce an interruption of the harmony existing between the two nations; and the Consuls and agents of both nations shall have liberty to celebrate the rites of their respective religions in their own houses.

The Consuls, respectively, shall have liberty and personal security given them to travel within the territories of each other, both by land and sea; and shall not be prevented from going on board any vessels they may think proper to visit; they shall likewise have liberty to appoint their own dragoman and broker.

ART. 16. In case of any dispute arising from the violation of any of the articles of this treaty, no appeal shall be made to arms, nor shall war be declared, on any pretext whatever; but, if the Consul residing at the place where the dispute shall happen shall not be able to settle the same, the Government of that country shall state their grievance in writing, and transmit the same to the Government of the other; and the period of three months shall be allowed for answers to be returned, during which time no act of hostility shall be permitted by either party; and, in case the grievances are not redressed, and a war should be the event, the Consuls and citizens or subjects of both parties, respectively, shall be permitted to embark with their effects unmolested, on board of what vessel or vessels they shall think proper reasonable time being allowed for that purpose.

ART. 17. If, in the course of events, a war

should break out between the two nations, the prisoners captured by either party shall not be made slaves; they shall not be forced to hard labor, or other confinement than such as may be necessary to secure their safekeeping, and shall be exchanged rank for rank; and it is agreed that prisoners shall be exchanged in twelve months after their capture; and the exchange may be effected by any private individual legally authorized by either of the parties.

ART. 18. If any of the Barbary States, or other Powers at war with the United States, shall capture any American vessel and send her into any port of the Regency of Algiers, they shall not be permitted to sell her, but shall be forced to depart the port on procuring the requisite supply of provisions; but the vessels of war of the United States, with any prizes they may capture from their enemies, shall have liberty to frequent the ports of Algiers for refreshments of any kinds, and to sell such prizes in the said ports, without any other customs or duties than such as are customary on ordinary commercial importations.

ART. 19. If any of the citizens of the United States, or any persons under their protection, shall have any disputes with each other, the Consul shall decide between the parties; and whenever the Consul shall require any aid or assistance from the Government of Algiers to enforce his decision, it shall be immediately granted to him; and if any disputes shall arise between any citizens of the United States, and the citizens or subjects of any other nation having a Consul or agent in Algiers, such disputes shall be settled by the Consuls or agents of the respective nations; and any disputes or suits at law that may take place between any citizens of the United States, and the subjects of the Regency of Algiers, shall be decided by the Dey in person, and no other.

ART. 20. If a citizen of the United States should kill, wound, or strike a subject of Algiers; or, on the contrary, a subject of Algiers should kill, wound, or strike a citizen of the United States, the law of the country shall take place, and equal justice shall be rendered, the Consul assisting at the trial; but the sentence of punishment against an American citizen shall not be greater or more severe than it would be against a Turk in the same predicament. And if any delinquent should make his escape, the Consul shall not be responsible for him, in any manner whatever.

ART. 21. The Consul of the United States of America shall not be required to pay any customs or duties whatever on anything he imports from a foreign country for the use of his house and family.

ART. 22. Should any of the citizens of the United States of America die within the limits of the Regency of Algiers, the Dey and his subjects shall not interfere with the property of the deceased, but it shall be under the immediate direction of the Consul, unless otherwise disposed of by will. Should there be no Consul, the effects shall be deposited in the hands of some person worthy of trust, until the party shall appear who has a right to demand them, when he shall render an account of the property; neither shall the Dey nor his subjects give hindrance in the execution of any will that may appear.

ON BOARD THE U. S. SHIP GUERRIERE,
July 6, 1815.

I certify the foregoing to be a true copy of a treaty of peace negotiated by Commodore Decatur and myself with the Regency of Algiers, and signed by the Dey of that Regency on the 30th June, 1815.

WILLIAM SHALER.

UNITED STATES SHIP GUERRIERE,
BAY OF ALGIERS, *July 4, 1815.*

SIR: We have the honor to refer you to the official reports of Commodore Decatur to the Navy Department, for an account of the operations of this squadron previous to our arrival off Algiers, on the 28th ultimo.

Having received information that the Algerine squadron had been at sea for a considerable time longer than that to which their cruisers usually extend, and that a despatch-boat had been sent from Gibraltar to Algiers to inform them of our arrival in the Mediterranean, we thought that they might have made a harbor where they would be in safety. We, therefore, while they were in this state of uncertainty, believed it a proper moment to deliver the President's letter, agreeably to our instructions. Accordingly, on the 29th ultimo, a flag of truce was hoisted on board the Guerriere, with the Swedish flag at the main. A boat came off about noon, with Mr. Norderling, Consul of Sweden, and the captain of the port, who confirmed the intelligence we had before received, and to whom we communicated information of the capture of their frigate and brig. The impression made by these events was visible and deep. We were requested by the captain of the port (Mr. Norderling declaring he was not authorized to act) to state the conditions on which we would make peace; to which we replied by giving the letter of the President to the Dey, and by a note from us to him; a copy of which (No. 1) we have the honor to transmit herewith. The captain of the port then requested that hostilities should cease pending the negotiation, and that persons authorized to treat should go on shore; he and Mr. Norderling both affirming that the Minister of Marine had pledged himself for our security and return to our ships when we pleased. Both these propositions were rejected, and they were explicitly informed that the negotiation must be carried on on board the fleet, and that hostilities, as far as they respected vessels, could not cease. They then returned on shore. On the following day the same persons returned, and informed us that they were commissioned by the Dey to treat with us on the proposed basis, and their anxiety appeared extreme to conclude the peace immediately. We then brought forward the model of a treaty, which we declared would not be departed from in substance; at the same time declaring that, although the United States would never stipulate for paying tribute under any form whatever, yet, that they were a magnanimous and generous nation, who would, upon the presentation of Consuls, do what was customary with other great nations in their friendly intercourse with Algiers. The treaty was then examined, and they were of opinion that it would not be agreed to in its present form, and particularly requested that the article requiring the restitution of the property they had captured, and which had been distributed, might be expunged; alleging that such a demand had never before been made upon Algiers. To this it was answered that the claim was just, and would be adhered to. They then asked whether, if the treaty should be signed by the Dey, we would engage to restore the captured vessels? which we refused. They then represented that it was not the present Dey who had declared the war, which they acknowledged to be unjust; conceding that they were wholly in the wrong, and had no excuse whatever; requesting, however, that we would take the case of the Dey into consideration, and, upon his agreeing to terms with us, more favorable than had ever been made with any other nation, to restore the ships, which they stated would be of little or no value to us, but would be of great importance to him, as they would satisfy the people with the conditions of the peace we were going to conclude with him.

We consulted upon this question, and determined that, considering the state of those vessels, the sums that would be required to fit them for a passage to the United States, and the *little* probability of selling them in *this part of the world*, we would make a compliment of them to His Highness in the state they then were; the Commodore engaging to furnish them with an escort to this port. This, however, would depend upon their signing the treaty as presented to them, and could not appear as an article of it, but must be considered as a favor conferred on the Dey by the United States.

They then requested a truce, to deliberate upon the terms of the proposed treaty, which was refused; they even pleaded for three hours. The reply was, "not a minute; if your squadron appears in sight before the treaty is actually signed by the Dey, and the prisoners sent off, ours would capture them." It was finally agreed that hostilities should cease when we perceived their boat coming off with a white flag hoisted, the Swedish Consul pledging his word of honor not to hoist it unless the treaty was signed, and the prisoners in the boat. They returned on shore, and, although the distance was full five miles, they came back within three hours, with the treaty signed as we had concluded it, and the prisoners.

During the interval of their absence a corvette appeared in sight, which would have been captured if they had been detained one hour longer.

The treaty has since been drawn out anew, translated by them, and duly executed by the Dey; which we have the honor to transmit herewith.

Mr. Shaler has since been on shore, and the cotton and money mentioned in the fourth article have been given up to him. They now show every disposition to maintain a sincere peace with us, which is, doubtless, owing to the dread of our arms; and we take this occasion to remark that, in our opinion, the only secure guaranty we can have for the maintenance of the peace just concluded with these people is, the presence in the Mediterranean of a respectable naval force.

As this treaty appears to us to secure every interest within the contemplation of the Government, and as it really places the United States on higher grounds than any other nation, we have no hesitation, on our part, in fulfilling such of its provisions as are within our power, in the firm belief that it will receive the ratification of the President and Senate.

We have the honor to be, with great respect, sir, your obedient servants,

STEPHEN DECATUR,
WILLIAM SHALER.
Hon. JAMES MONROE,
    Secretary of State.

No. 1.

The American Commissioners to the Dey of Algiers.

The undersigned have the honor to inform His Highness the Dey of Algiers that they have been appointed by the President of the United States of America Commissioners Plenipotentiary to treat of peace with his Highness; and that, pursuant to their instructions, they are ready to open a negotiation for the restoration of peace and harmony between the two countries, on terms just and honorable to both parties; and they feel it incumbent on them to state, explicitly, to His Highness, that they are instructed to treat upon no other principle than that of perfect equality, and on the terms of the most favored nations; no stipulation for paying any tribute to Algiers, under any form whatever, will be agreed to.

The undersigned have the honor to transmit, herewith, a letter from the President of the United States, and they avail themselves of this occasion to assure His Highness of their high consideration and profound respect.

STEPHEN DECATUR,
WILLIAM SHALER.

COMMERCIAL CONVENTION WITH GREAT BRITAIN.

[Communicated to the Senate, December 6, 1815.]

To the Senate of the United States:

I lay before the Senate, for their consideration and advice, as to a ratification, a Convention to regulate the commerce between the United States and Great Britain, signed by their respective Plen-

ipotentiaries on the 3d of July last, with letters relating to the same, from the American Plenipotentiaries to the Secretary of State; and also the declaration with which it is the intention of the British Government to accompany the exchange of the ratifications of the Convention.

JAMES MADISON.
WASHINGTON, *Dec.* 6, 1815.

A Convention to regulate the Commerce between the Territories of the United States and His Britannic Majesty.

The United States of America and His Britannic Majesty, being desirous, by a convention, to regulate the commerce and navigation between their respective countries, territories, and people, in such manner as to render the same reciprocally beneficial and satisfactory, have respectively named Plenipotentiaries, and given them full powers to treat of and conclude such convention: that is to say, the President of the United States, by and with the advice and consent of the Senate thereof, hath appointed for their Plenipotentiaries John Quincy Adams, Henry Clay, and Albert Gallatin, citizens of the United States; and His Royal Highness the Prince Regent, acting in the name and on the behalf of His Majesty, has named for his Plenipotentiaries the Right Honorable Frederick John Robinson, Vice President of the Committee of Privy Council for Trade and Plantations, Joint Paymaster of His Majesty's Forces, and a member of the Imperial Parliament; Henry Goulburn, Esq., a member of the Imperial Parliament, and Under Secretary of State; and William Adams, Esq., Doctor of Civil Laws: and the said Plenipotentiaries, having mutually produced and shown their said full powers, and exchanged copies of the same, have agreed on and concluded the following articles, viz:

ART. 1. There shall be, between the territories of the United States of America and all the territories of His Britannic Majesty in Europe, a reciprocal liberty of commerce. The inhabitants of the two countries, respectively, shall have liberty freely and securely to come with their ships and cargoes to all such places, ports, and rivers in the territories aforesaid, to which other foreigners are permitted to come, to enter into the same, and to remain and reside in any parts of the said territories, respectively; also to hire and occupy houses and warehouses for the purposes of their commerce; and, generally, the merchants and traders of each nation, respectively, shall enjoy the most complete protection and security for their commerce, but subject always to the laws and statutes of the two countries, respectively.

ART. 2. No higher or other duties shall be imposed on the importation into the United States of any articles the growth, produce, or manufacture of His Britannic Majesty's territories in Europe, and no higher or other duties shall be imposed on the importation into the territories of His Britannic Majesty in Europe of any articles the growth, produce, or manufacture of the Uni-

Commercial Convention with Great Britain.

ted States, than are, or shall be, payable on the like articles, being the growth, produce, or manufacture of any other foreign country; nor shall any higher or other duties or charges be imposed in either of the two countries, on the exportation of any articles to the United States, or to His Britannic Majesty's territories in Europe, respectively, than such as are payable on the exportation of the like articles to any other foreign country; nor shall any prohibition be imposed on the exportation or importation of any articles the growth, produce, or manufacture of the United States, or of His Britannic Majesty's territories in Europe, to or from the said territories of His Britannic Majesty in Europe, or to or from the said United States, which shall not equally extend to all other nations.

No higher or other duties or charges shall be imposed in any of the ports of the United States, on British vessels, than those payable in the same ports by vessels of the United States; nor in the ports of any of His Britannic Majesty's territories in Europe on vessels of the United States, than shall be payable in the same ports on British vessels.

The same duties shall be paid on the importation into the United States of any articles the growth, produce, or manufacture of His Britannic Majesty's territories in Europe, whether such importation shall be in vessels of the United States or in British vessels; and the same duties shall be paid on the importation, into the ports of any of His Britannic Majesty's territories in Europe, of any article the growth, produce, or manufacture of the United States, whether such importation shall be in British vessels or vessels of the United States.

The same duties shall be paid, and the same bounties allowed, on the exportation of any articles the growth, produce, or manufacture of His Britannic Majesty's territories in Europe, to the United States, whether such exportation shall be in vessels of the United States or in British vessels; and the same duties shall be paid, and the same bounties allowed, on the exportation of any articles the growth, produce, or manufacture of the United States, to His Britannic Majesty's territories in Europe, whether such exportation shall be in British vessels or in vessels of the United States.

It is further agreed, that, in all cases where drawbacks, are, or may be, allowed upon the re-exportation of any goods the growth, produce, or manufacture, of either country, respectively, the amount of the said drawbacks shall be the same, whether the said goods shall have been originally imported in a British or an American vessel. But when such re-exportation shall take place from the United States in a British vessel, or from the territories of His Britannic Majesty in Europe in an American vessel, to any other foreign nation, the two contracting parties reserve to themselves, respectively, the right of regulating or diminishing, in such case, the amount of the said drawbacks.

The intercourse between the United States and His Britannic Majesty's possessions in the West Indies and on the continent of North America shall not be affected by any of the provisions of this article, but each party shall remain in the complete possession of its rights with respect to such an intercourse.

ART. 3. His Britannic Majesty agrees that the vessels of the United States of America shall be admitted, and hospitably received at the principal settlements of the British dominions in the East Indies, viz: Calcutta, Madras, Bombay, and Prince of Wales's island; and that the citizens of the said United States may freely carry on trade between the said principal settlements and the said United States, in all articles of which the importation and exportation, respectively, to and from the said territories, shall not be entirely prohibited: *Provided, only,* That it shall not be lawful for them, in any time of war between the British Government and any State or Power whatever, to export from the said territories, without the special permission of the *British* Government, any military stores, or naval stores, or rice. The citizens of the United States shall pay for their vessels, when admitted, no higher or other duty or charge than shall be payable on the vessels of the most favored European nations; and they shall pay no higher or other duties or charges on the importation or exportation of the cargoes of the said vessels than shall be payable on the same articles when imported or exported in the vessels of the most favored European nations. But it is expressly agreed that the vessels of the United States shall not carry any articles from the said principal settlements to any port or place, except to some port or place in the United States of America, where the same shall be unladen.

It is also understood that the permission granted by this article is not intended to allow the vessels of the United States to carry on any part of the coasting trade of the said British territories; but the vessels of the United States, having in the first instance proceeded to one of the said principal settlements of the British dominions in the East Indies, and then going with their original cargoes, or part thereof, from one of the said principal settlements to another, shall not be considered as carrying on the coasting trade.

The vessels of the United States may also touch for refreshment, but not for commerce, in the course of their voyage to or from the British territories in India, or to or from the dominions of the Emperor of China, at the Cape of Good Hope, the island of St. Helena, or such other places as may be in the possession of Great Britain, in the African or Indian seas; it being well understood that, in all that regards this article, the citizens of the United States shall be subject in all respects to the laws and regulations of the British Government from time to time established.

ART. 4. It shall be free for each of the two contracting parties, respectively, to appoint Consuls for the protection of trade in the dominions and territories of the other party; but, before any

Commercial Convention with Great Britain.

Consul shall act as such, he shall, in the usual form, be approved and admitted by the Government to which he is sent; and it is hereby declared, that in case of illegal or improper conduct towards the laws or Government of the country to which he is sent, such Consul may either be punished according to law, if the laws will reach the case, or be sent back; the offended Government assigning to the other the reasons for the same.

It is hereby declared, that either of the contracting parties may except from the residence of Consuls such particular places as such party shall judge fit to be excepted.

ART. 5. This convention, when the same shall have been duly ratified by the President of the United States, by and with the advice and consent of their Senate, and by His Britannic Majesty, and the respective ratifications mutually exchanged, shall be binding and obligatory on the United States and His Majesty for four years from the date of its signature; and the ratifications shall be exchanged in six months from this time, or sooner, if possible.

Done at London, this third day of July, in the year one thousand eight hundred and fifteen.

JOHN QUINCY ADAMS,
HENRY CLAY,
ALBERT GALLATIN,
FREDERICK J. ROBINSON,
HENRY GOULBURN,
WILLIAM ADAMS.

Extract of a letter from the American Commissioners, Messrs. Clay and Gallatin, to the Secretary of State, dated

LONDON, *May* 18, 1815.

Having had reason to believe that the British Government had abstained from answering the communication of the joint commission from Ghent of the —— day of December, 1814, until they received official information of the American ratification of the Treaty of Peace, we thought it advisable, soon after that event was known to us, to repair to this city, in order that we might ascertain the disposition of this Government as to the commercial intercourse between the two countries.

Shortly after our arrival here, we were invited by Lord Castlereagh to an interview with him. A minute of the substance of the conversation which took place on that occasion, as drawn up and agreed to by the parties, is enclosed. We communicated to Mr. Goulburn, the next day, our answer upon the three subjects to which the conversation related.

In the interview with Lord Castlereagh, he had stated that four or five days might be necessary on their part to prepare for the proposed conversation. Nearly three weeks having elapsed without hearing further on the subject, we took what appeared to us a fit occasion to intimate our intention of leaving London. A few days after, we received an invitation from the Vice President of the Board of Trade, Mr. Robinson,

to call at his office on the 11th instant. We accordingly attended, and were received by him and Messrs. Goulburn and Adams, two of the British Commissioners who had negotiated the Treaty of Ghent.

They opened the conversation by adverting to what had led to this interview, and professed themselves to be ready to receive any propositions we might choose to make. We observed, that in the treaties which America had heretofore made (particularly with this country) regulating commercial intercourse, there were generally comprised two subjects : one, which respected commercial regulations, applicable to a state of peace as well as of war; the other, which respected the rights and duties of the parties, one being at war and the other remaining at peace. Accordingly, our Government had instructed us to bring forward both those subjects.

As to the commercial intercourse, without at this time going into details, or minor points, which it might be necessary in the progress of the negotiation to adjust, we would content ourselves, in this unofficial conversation, with touching on the most important topics which it seemed to us desirable to discuss and arrange. These were, that the two countries should respectively be placed on the footing of the nation the most favored; that, in the trade between America and the British European dominions, all discriminating duties on tonnage and on merchandise, either imported or exported, should be abolished; that the trade between America and the British West Indies should be regulated, and placed on some more permanent basis than the occasional acts of the colonial authorities; that the nature and kind of intercourse between America and the adjoining British provinces should be defined and provided for; and that the trade with the British India possessions should be opened to America on liberal principles.

In regard to the discriminating duties, we remarked, that a proposition to abolish them first came from Great Britain, and a provision to that effect was inserted in the unratified treaty of 1806. Congress had taken up the matter at their last session, and passed an act, which we explained. We thought it desirable that they should be abolished, in order to prevent those collisions, and that system of commercial warfare, in which the two countries would probably be involved by an adherence to them. As an example, we mentioned the great extra duty to which, as we understood, the article of cotton was liable by the British laws, when imported in foreign vessels, and which, if persisted in, would certainly be met by some countervailing regulations.

With respect to the trade to British India, we observed, that we had no equivalent to offer for it; that it was for Great Britain to consider whether a commerce, consisting as it did almost entirely in the exchange of our specie for India produce, was not of a nature to deserve the most liberal encouragement; but that we had rather enter into no stipulation on the subject than be restricted to a direct intercourse, as had been proposed by the unratified treaty, both on the outward and return voyage.

On the other subject, (the rights and duties of the parties, one being at war and the other in a condition of peace,) we proceeded to remark, that whilst a prospect of a long European peace appeared to exist, as was the case when the Treaty of Ghent was concluded, it was less important to provide for questions arising under this head. But it was impossible to shut our eyes to the demonstrations everywhere making of a new war, which, if it should assume a maritime character, might again menace the harmony and good understanding between the two countries. It was desirable, therefore, to anticipate and provide for the evil. The first and most important point was that of impressment. Great Britain had always professed a willingness to receive and consider any proposition which America should be disposed to make on that subject. It would, perhaps, be unprofitable at this time to go into a discussion of the right; as to which we would merely remark, that it was impossible that there could be a stronger conviction on the part of Great Britain that it was with her, than there was on the part of America that it was on her side. It was better to look to some practical arrangement, by which, without concession of right by either party, the mischiefs complained of on both sides might be prevented. To this end the attention of our Government had been turned. We believed that Great Britain had never heretofore contended that the American Government was bound to prohibit the merchants of the United States from employing foreign seamen, any more than it was bound to forbid their shipping contraband articles. America was, however, now willing to take upon herself such an obligation, and to exclude British seamen from her merchant service; and we believed such exclusion might be as effectually executed as our revenue laws. Here we called their attention to the act which Congress had passed on that subject, and to the message of the President to that body towards the close of its last session. Upon the supposition that the exclusion of British seamen should be absolute and entire, there would no longer exist any ground for the claim of impressment, and, of course, no objection to its abandonment. We stated that, besides the motive which existed with our Government of guarding against collision with Great Britain, another powerful one operated—that of encouraging our native seamen, and of not being obliged to rely on the uncertain supply of foreigners. To this system, as a substitute for that of impressment, it did not appear to us that Great Britain could object, unless it was thought to be impracticable in its execution. We had no doubt ourselves that, even admitting that there might be, as in cases of smuggling, occasional instances of evasion of the system of exclusion, it would nevertheless be, upon the whole, much more favorable in its result to Great Britain. This system would apply to and operate upon every American vessel; whilst that of impressment reached only the cases of those vessels with which it accidentally came in contact. We were aware of the difficulties which had heretofore opposed a satisfactory arrangement on this subject. Still, it was one of such vital importance, so tending to bring the two countries into collision, that it was impossible it should receive a consideration too earnest and too anxious.

The next point which it seemed to us important to settle was, the trade of America with the colonies of the enemies of Great Britain. Towards the end of the last European war, questions growing out of that trade had been terminated by the conquest of those colonies by Great Britain; but many of them having been restored at the peace, the disputes which heretofore existed might again arise. The former arrangements on this subject might, with some modifications, serve as a basis.

We then stated that we did not intend, in this preliminary and unofficial conversation, to discuss the other points belonging to this branch of the subject. A definition of blockades was desirable, and could not, it seemed, be attended with much difficulty, as we believed that there was no real difference between the two countries with respect to the abstract principle; but we apprehended that the disputes which might hereafter take place on that subject would arise almost exclusively from questions of fact, which no previous definition could prevent.

As, in the event of war, Great Britain might desire to know the disposition of our Government on the subject of privateers and prizes, we would only now say that the principle which might be adopted with respect to Great Britain, whether of admission or exclusion, must equally and impartially apply to all the parties to the war.

These were all the topics noticed by us, and we enforced and illustrated them by various other observations.

The British gentlemen, professing not to have expected those points to be brought forward which applied to a belligerent state of one of the parties, expressed a wish to know whether, in our view, the two subjects were inseparable, and whether we could not come to an agreement on those topics which were probably less difficult to be adjusted, leaving the others for further consideration and future arrangement? We replied, that, heretofore, they had always been blended together by our Government, and that we intended to bring them all up for consideration; that, at present, however, we only presented them for consideration, as it would be premature, at this time, to make any of them a *sine qua non;* and that whether a treaty omitting some of them would be acceptable, must depend on its general tenor, and upon the extent and importance of the subjects which might be comprehended in the arrangement.

They proceeded to remark that some of the subjects had been always found to involve ex-

Commercial Convention with Great Britain.

treme difficulty, particularly that of impressment; that Great Britain was certainly prepared, at all times, to receive and to consider any proposition that America might be disposed to make in relation to it; but one of the gentlemen remarked that, from the deep interest which was felt by Great Britain in it, she must view with great jealousy (by which, he said, he meant vigilance) any such proposition; that the inquiry which they had just made as to our willingness to separate the two subjects proceeded from a wish to ascertain whether it were likely that any practical result could be speedily obtained, if they entered upon the negotiation at this time.

On the subject of discriminating duties, mentioned by us, they said their Government would receive favorably the proposition for a mutual abolition of them. As to the trade with India, their Government was not at all disposed to shut us out from it. In regard to the trade to the West Indies, considering the difficulties which had heretofore presented themselves in placing it, by treaty, upon a footing satisfactory to both parties, they feared it would not now be practicable to enter into any stipulation respecting it which should meet the views of the two countries.

The interview terminated by their stating that they would report to the Cabinet the substance of what had passed between us, and by their pledging themselves to do all in their power to afford us an early answer.

On the 16th instant, having been again invited by the Vice President of the Board of Trade to call at his office, we accordingly attended, and were received by the same gentlemen. They stated that they had reported to the Cabinet what had passed at the last interview, and were now prepared to give us an answer on the several topics to which the conversation related; in doing this, they would observe the order which had been marked out by us.

1st. On the commercial intercourse between the two countries, they were authorized to state that their Government was ready to treat with us on the footing of the most favored nation, and was also willing to enter into any arrangement by which all discriminating duties on importations and tonnage should be mutually done away. They were willing to admit us to the enjoyment of the trade with British India, unclogged by the restriction on the outward voyage contained in the unratified treaty, but must still insist on that contained in the treaty of 1794, on the return voyage. Considering that we had no equivalent to offer, except what was to be found in the trade itself, they would expect, for this concession, a spirit of accommodation on our side in other parts of the commercial arrangement—the fur trade, or some other.

The trade with the British West Indies, they stated, had always been a subject of great difficulty, and their Government was not prepared to make any change in that colonial policy to which they had so long adhered; but they would

hope that this would not form any obstacle to the negotiation.

With respect to the trade with their North American possessions, they were ready to receive and discuss any propositions we might have to offer, with an anxious desire to place it on a footing mutually satisfactory.

2dly. On those subjects which related to a state in which one of the parties should be at war and the other in peace, it was not necessary to disguise that they had been always attended with great difficulties. Still they were willing, in a spirit of amity and with candor, to receive and to discuss any propositions we might offer.

With regard to blockades, they could not think it necessary to enter into any treaty definition of them, as the questions which might hereafter arise on that subject, according to our own statement, would relate rather to the fact than to the principle, on which the two Governments seemed to agree. Indeed, they thought that such a definition might tend to weaken, as implying a doubt of the correctness of the principle.

In relation to the trade with enemies' colonies, besides the intrinsic difficulty of the question, as heretofore experienced in all attempts to arrange it, there was another, arising out of their want of information as to whether France had adopted any, and what, system of colonial policy, since the restoration of her colonies. It might be that she had opened their trade to foreign nations in peace as well as in war; in which case, the questions that had heretofore existed could not be agitated again.

Impressment had, they continued, of all this class of subjects, been found most difficult to arrange. They were aware how important it was considered in both countries, and how, in both, it touched public sensibility. As heretofore, they were now ready to receive and consider any proposition our Government might make respecting it; and, even without any treaty stipulation, their Government was now anxiously engaged in devising means to prevent the abuses of which we complain. If the law which we had mentioned at the last interview should be effectual in its object, it would doubtless do away a great motive which they had for impressment. Still they were bound to consider, with the most vigilant attention, any proposition for the abandonment of what they must consider a right essential to their safety. That law did not, however, as they understood, settle the question who were to be considered as British subjects—a question on which the two countries might not be able to come to an understanding.

With regard to our ideas respecting privateers and prizes, they were certainly fair and unexceptionable.

As they had hinted at some accommodation in the fur trade, or in other parts of the commercial arrangement, for their supposed concession respecting the India trade, we thought the occasion suitable for stating that we were positively instructed not to consent to the renewal of the trade between British subjects and the Indians within our territories. We stated that the disposition of our Government on this subject did not proceed from commercial, but political considerations. They did not insist upon it, nor seem to think that the determination of our Government would prevent an arrangement of the Canada trade. One of them inquired whether we expected, in like manner, to be excluded from the trade with the Indians in their territories? To which we replied, certainly.

We explained the law for the exclusion of foreign seamen from our service, and mentioned that the naturalization of seamen would be almost altogether prevented, in future, by the necessity of a continued residence of five years. We stated that we were authorized to enter into stipulations that would forbid the employment of such British seamen as might, under our laws, be hereafter naturalized ; but that we could not do it with respect to those who were already naturalized. We had thought that, as to them, an exception might be made, permitting, on both sides, the voluntary employment of such seamen, natives of one country, as might have heretofore been naturalized under the laws of the other country. We added, that the number of British seamen already naturalized, which could constitute, as it appeared to us, the only difficulty in an arrangement, was very inconsiderable. Doctor Adams concurred in opinion that there were not many.

We made some further explanations, and finally told them that, considering the dispositions which we had been happy to meet with in them, we would now say, that we would enter upon the negotiation ; reserving to ourselves, however, the right, as our powers were several as well as joint, to withdraw from it if circumstances should make it eligible to do so, and to leave Mr. Adams, whom we daily expected, to conclude it.

The interview closed by their undertaking to provide themselves immediately with the necessary powers to proceed in the negotiation, and by an assurance that they would continue to do all in their power to bring it to a speedy and successful issue.

Extract of a minute of a conversation which took place at Lord Castlereagh's, between his Lordship and Messrs. Clay and Gallatin, April 16, 1815.

Lord Castlereagh then called the attention of the American Commissioners to a communication made by them at Ghent, relative to their power to treat on the commercial intercourse between the two countries. He said, before he gave an answer to that communication, he should be glad, if it were agreeable to the American Commissioners, that there should be an unofficial conversation between them and the British Commissioners who negotiated the Treaty of Peace, together with Mr. Robinson, whom he would associate with them for that purpose, to ascertain if it were likely that some general principles could be agreed upon to form the basis of a treaty of commerce. He should prefer that this conversation, like that which he understood had taken place in the former negotiation between Lords Holland and Auckland, and Messrs. Monroe and Pinkney, should be free from official forms; and thought such a course best calculated to ascertain if it were likely that the two Governments could come to any practical result on this interesting subject.

It was observed by one of the American Commissioners, that such a conversation would be on terms of inequality, (the American Commissioners being invested with powers, and the other gentlemen having none,) unless it was understood not only that it should be considered as entirely unofficial, but that the same gentlemen should afterwards be commissioned to conclude a treaty, if it were thought that one could be formed. Lord Castlereagh remarked, in reply, that such was certainly his intention.

The conversation ended in an understanding that the American Commissioners would consult together upon the three topics mentioned by Lord Castlereagh, and communicate on the following day to Mr. Goulbourn the result of their deliberations.

The American Plenipotentiaries to the Secretary of State.

LONDON, July 3, 1815.

SIR: We have the honor to transmit a convention for regulating the commercial intercourse between the United States and Great Britain, which we concluded this day with the British Plenipotentiaries.

Messrs. Clay and Gallatin's despatch of the 18th May last has informed you of the preliminary steps taken by them on that subject. Mr. Adams arrived in London on the 24th of May, and on the 5th of June we were invited by Messrs. Robinson, Goulburn, and Adams, to meet them on the 7th. At this conference, after a mutual exhibition of our powers, and some general observations, we delivered to them our project of a commercial convention, a copy of which (marked No. 1) is herewith enclosed. They promised to take it into immediate consideration, and on the 9th informed us that they would prepare and transmit to us a contre-projet.

Believing that there was no prospect of an immediate arrangement on the subject of seamen, and knowing that without it no treaty defining the rights and duties of belligerents and neutrals was admissible, we excluded all that related to that branch of the subject from our projet, and confined it to objects purely commercial.

We took the third article of the Treaty of 1794, respecting the intercourse with Canada, as the basis of the corresponding article: omitting, according to our instructions, whatever related to the Indian trade. In drawing the other articles, we were principally guided by the unratified Treaty of 1806 ; by the instructions given in relation to it by the Secretary of State, in his despatch of May 20, 1807 ; and by the act of Congress of the 3d March last, for abolishing all discriminating duties. From the previous explicit declarations of the British Plenipotentiaries, we deemed it useless to offer any article on the subject of the intercourse with the West India islands, and only inserted a clause to prevent the application to that intercourse of the provisions contemplated by the convention.

On the 16th the British Plenipotentiaries addressed to us a note, enclosing their contre-projet, (marked No. 2,) and on the 17th we transmitted our answer, (marked No. 3.) The whole subject was discussed at large in conferences held on the 19th and 21st. The British Plenipotentiaries, in a note of the 10th, (marked No. 4,) stated the substance of their answer to ours of the 17th. In the conference of the 21st we delivered the additional clause to the second article of the contre-projet, (marked No. 5,) and afterwards, on the same day, we transmitted our note, marked No. 6.

It will be perceived, by these notes, that we had come to an understanding as to the intercourse between the United States and the British territories in Europe, and that we disagreed on three points—the intercourse with Canada ; placing, generally, both countries on the footing of the most favored nations ; and the intercourse with the British East Indies.

On the first point, the British Plenipotentiaries persisted in refusing to admit that the citizens of the United States should have the right to take their produce down the river St. Lawrence to Montreal, and down the river Chambly (or Sorel) to the St. Lawrence ; and, without that permission, the article was useless to us, and unequal in its practical operation. The provision that the importation of our produce into Canada should not be prohibited, unless the prohibition extended generally to all similar articles, afforded us no security, as no similar articles are imported into Canada from any other foreign country ; whilst the corresponding provision respecting the importation into the United States, through Canada, of the produce and manufactures of Great Britain, effectually prevented us from prohibiting such an importation, since this could not be done without extending the prohibition to the importation of all similar articles, either of British or other growth or manufacture, into the Atlantic ports of the United States.

The article for placing, respectively, the two countries on the footing of the most favored nation, limited, as was insisted on by the British Plenipotentiaries, to the intercourse between the United States and the European territories of Great Britain, was unnecessary, since all that appeared desirable on that subject was secured by the second article ; and a provision of that nature, unless offering some obvious advantage, was deemed embarrassing, on account of the difficulties attached to its execution.

With this view of the two subjects, and finding that to arrange them in a satisfactory manner was impracticable, we proposed, in our note of the 21st, to omit altogether the articles relating to them.

On the subject of the intercourse with India,

the British Plenipotentiaries, contrary to the impression made in the unofficial conversations on Messrs. Clay and Gallatin, insisted, on our official conferences, that our admission to that trade was, on the part of Great Britain, a concession altogether gratuitous, and for which, particularly as to the privilege of indirect outward voyages, she ultimately expected an equivalent ; whilst we strenuously contended that an equivalent was found in the trade itself, which was highly beneficial to India, or, at all events, considering the nature of the commercial intercourse generally between the two countries, in the other provisions of the convention. On the same ground, we urged our claim to be placed in India on the same footing, at least, as the most favored nations ; to which it was replied that they made a distinction between those nations which had possessions there and those which had none. The refusal not being altogether explicit, we renewed our proposal to that effect in our note.

The British Plenipotentiaries, in a note of the 23d, (marked No. 7,) acceded to our proposal to omit the third and fifth articles, and refusing that on the subject of Indians, offered to omit the article altogether, and to sign a convention embracing only the provisions respecting the intercourse between the United States and the British territories in Europe.

This proposal we rejected in our note of the 24th, (marked No. 8.) But in order to meet, if practicable, the views of the British Government, and to avoid making any distinction between the East India trade and the other branches of commercial intercourse, we proposed to limit the duration of the whole convention to four years ; and we offered, as an alternative, an arrangement for the sole purpose of abolishing the discriminating duties, in conformity with the act of Congress of the last session.

In a note of the 26th, (marked No. 9,) the British Plenipotentiaries informed us that they found it necessary to refer our last proposals to their Government ; and by their note of the 29th, (marked No. 10.) they accepted our offer of a convention embracing the East India article, and limited to four years, to be calculated from the date of its signature. We replied to this in a note dated 30th June, (and marked No. 11,) and on the same day arranged, in a conference, the details of the convention.

We beg leave to add, that the same restriction which confines our vessels to the principal ports of India is, except in special cases, imposed by the act of Parliament on British subjects ; and that, besides the discrimination in the export duty from England, the difference on the import duty on the article of cotton had, by a late act of Parliament, been increased to two-pence sterling per pound in favor of every species imported in British vessels, and even of Brazil cotton imported in Portuguese vessels.

We have the honor to be, respectfully, &c.
JOHN QUINCY ADAMS,
H. CLAY,
ALBERT GALLATIN.

No. 1.

Projet of the American Ministers.

ART. 1. There shall be between the territories of the United States and all the dominions of His Britannic Majesty in Europe, a reciprocal and perfect liberty of commerce and navigation. The people and inhabitants of the two countries, respectively, shall have liberty, freely and securely, and without hindrance and molestation, to come with their ships and cargoes to the lands, countries, cities, ports, places, and rivers within the territories and dominions aforesaid, to enter into the same, to resort there, and to remain and reside there without any limitation of time; also, to hire and possess houses and warehouses, for the purposes of their commerce; and, generally, the merchants and traders on each side shall enjoy the most complete protection and security for their commerce, but subject always, as to what respects this article, to the laws and statutes of the two countries, respectively.

ART. 2. No other or higher duties shall be imposed on the importation into the United States of any articles the growth, produce, or manufacture, of the dominions of His Britannic Majesty in Europe, nor on the importation into His Britannic Majesty's dominions in Europe of any article the growth, produce, or manufacture, of the United States, than are or shall be payable on the like articles being of the growth, produce, or manufacture, of any other foreign country. Nor shall any higher duties or charges be imposed, in either of the two countries, on the exportation of any articles to the United States, or to His Britannic Majesty's dominions in Europe, respectively, than such as are payable on the exportation of the like articles to every other foreign country; nor shall any prohibition be imposed on the exportation or importation of any articles the growth, produce, or manufacture, of the United States, or of His Britannic Majesty's dominions in Europe, to or from the said States or the said dominions, which shall not equally extend to all other nations. No other or higher duties or charges shall be imposed, in any of the ports of the United States, on British vessels, (such only excepted as may be bound from or to British possessions to which vessels of the United States are not permanently admitted,) than shall be payable in the said ports by vessels of the United States; nor in the ports of any of his Britannic Majesty's dominions in Europe, on the vessels of the United States, than are or shall be payable in the said ports by British vessels. The same duties of exportation and importation, and also the same drawbacks and bounties, shall be respectively paid and allowed in either country than on all articles the produce, growth, or manufacture, of the United States or of His Britannic Majesty's dominions in Europe, whether such exportation or importation be in vessels of the United States or in British vessels.

ART. 3. His Britannic Majesty agrees that the vessels of the United States shall be admitted, and hospitably received, in all the seaports and harbors of the British dominions in the East In-

dies; and that the citizens of the said States may freely carry on a trade with the said territories, in all articles of which the importation or exportation respectively to or from the said territories shall not be entirely prohibited: *Provided, only,* That it shall not be lawful for them, in any time of war between the British Government and any other Power or State whatever, to export from the said territories, without the special permission of the British Government there, any military or naval stores, or rice.

The citizens of the United States shall pay for their vessels, when admitted into the said ports, no other or higher duty or charge than shall be payable on British vessels in the ports of the United States; and they shall pay no other or higher duties or charges on the importation or exportation of the cargoes of the said vessels than shall be payable on the same articles when imported or exported in British vessels. But it is expressly agreed that the vessels of the United States shall not carry any of the articles exported by them from the said British territories to any port or place, except to some port or place in America, where the same shall be unladen; or to some port or place, or ports or places in China, or in the Indian seas, whence the said vessels shall proceed, as aforesaid, to some port or place in America, and there unlade the whole of the articles exported, in the manner abovementioned, from the aforesaid British territories; and such regulations shall be adopted by both parties as shall from time to time be found necessary to enforce the due and faithful observance of this stipulation. It is also understood that the permission granted by this article is not to extend to allow the vessels of the United States to carry on any part of the coasting trade of the said *British* territories, without the special permission of the British Government there; but the vessels going from one port to another of the said *territories*, for the sole purposes either of discharging their original cargoes, or part thereof, or of completing their return cargoes, are not to be considered as carrying on the coasting trade. Neither is this article to be construed to allow the citizens of the United States to settle or reside within the said territories, or to go into the interior parts thereof, without the permission of the British Government established there; and if any transgressions shall be attempted against the regulations of the British Government in this respect, the observance of the same shall and may be enforced against the citizens of America, in the same manner as against British subjects or others transgressing the same rule. And the citizens of the United States, whenever they arrive in any port or harbor in the said territories, or if they should be permitted, in manner aforesaid, to go to any other place therein, shall always be subject to the laws, government, and jurisdiction, of whatsoever nature, established in such harbor, port, or place, according as the same may be. The vessels of the United States may also touch for refreshment at the island of St. Helena, or at such other ports or places as may be in the possession of Great

Britain in the African or Indian seas, but subject in all respects to such regulations as the British Government may from time to time establish there.

ART. 4. The navigation of all the lakes, rivers, and water communications, the middle of which is the boundary between the United States and His Britannic Majesty's dominions on the continent of North America, shall, at all times, be free to the citizens of the United States and to His Majesty's subjects. The said citizens and subjects may freely carry on trade and commerce with each other, and, for that purpose, pass and repass by land or inland navigation, into the respective territories of the two parties on the said continent; and no higher or other tolls, or rates of ferriage, than what are or shall be payable by natives, shall be demanded on either side. All goods or merchandise, whose importation into the United States shall not be wholly prohibited, may freely, for the purposes of the commerce abovementioned, be carried into the same, in the manner aforesaid, by His Majesty's subjects; and such goods and merchandise shall be subject to no higher or other duties than would be payable by citizens of the United States, on the importation of the same in American vessels into the Atlantic ports of the said United States; and, in like manner, all goods and merchandise, whose importation into His Majesty's said territories in America shall not be entirely prohibited, may freely, for the purposes of commerce abovementioned, be carried into the same, in the manner aforesaid, by the citizens of the United States; and such goods and merchandise shall be subject to no higher or other duties than would be payable by His Majesty's subjects on the importation of the same from Europe into the said territories. All goods not prohibited to be imported from the said territories, respectively, may, in like manner, be carried out of the same by the two parties. No duty of importation or exportation shall be levied by either party on peltries or furs which may be brought, in the manner aforesaid, by land or inland navigation, from the said territories of one party into the said territories of the other party.

ART. 5. It shall be free for each of the two contracting parties, respectively, to appoint consuls for the protection of trade, and agents for the protection of seamen, to reside in the dominions and territories of the other party; and the said consuls and agents shall enjoy the liberties and rights which belong to them by reason of their functions. But before any consul or agent aforesaid shall act as such, he shall be, in the usual form, approved and admitted by the party to whom he is sent; and it is hereby declared to be lawful and proper, that, in case of illegal or improper conduct towards the laws or Government, a consul or agent aforesaid may either be punished according to law, if the laws will reach the case, or be dismissed, or even sent back; the offended Government assigning to the other the reasons for the same.

ART. 6. It being the intention of the high con-

tracting parties, that the people of their respective dominions shall be placed on the footing of the most favored nation, it is agreed, that in case either party shall hereafter grant any additional advantage in navigation or trade to any other nation, the citizens or subjects of the other party shall fully participate therein ; freely, where it is freely granted to such other nation, or yielding the same compensation where the grant is made for some equivalent.

No. 2.

The British Plenipotentiaries to the American Plenipotentiaries.

BOARD OF TRADE, *June* 16, 1815.

The undersigned have the honor to transmit to the Plenipotentiaries of the United States a contre-projet for the arrangement of the commercial intercourse between the two countries. The American Plenipotentiaries will observe, that the article respecting the British East Indies is not proposed to be included in the body of the Treaty, but in a separate article, and more limited in point of duration, than would be suitable to the arrangements of the Treaty itself. The undersigned, nevertheless, flatter themselves that the American Plenipotentiaries will see in the proposed article for the East India intercourse, a proof of the liberal and conciliatory disposition with which the British Government is disposed to act upon the subject.

It will be recollected that at one of the unofficial conferences, and, subsequently, at the first official conference held with the American Plenipotentiaries, the undersigned stated, by order of their Government, that if the power of going from the United States to the British dominions in the East Indies by an indirect course were conceded, Great Britain must be considered as entitled to some equivalent for the concession, and that the fur trade was pointed out by the undersigned as capable of furnishing that equivalent.

The American Plenipotentiaries having stated that their instructions did not permit them to grant, by stipulation, any commercial intercourse between His Majesty's subjects and the Indians residing within the acknowledged boundaries of the United States, and not having suggested any other means of finding an equivalent, the undersigned would have been fully justified in tendering a contre-project which wholly omitted the concession in question. But His Majesty's Government, anxious to renew the commercial relations of the two countries, in the true spirit of peace and harmony, has authorized the undersigned to offer a separate article, by which the indirect voyage from the United States to the British East Indies will be permitted, without equivalent; for the space of two years, in the confident hope that, during that period, the American Government will be enabled to propose such an equivalent as may induce Great Britain to make that permission commensurate with the general duration of the treaty.

The undersigned will be happy to have the

honor of seeing the American Plenipotentiaries on any day which may suit their convenience, and request them to accept the assurance of their high consideration.

F. ROBINSON,
HENRY GOULBURN,
WILLIAM ADAMS.

Contre-projet of the British Commissioners.

ARTICLE 1. There shall be, between all the territories of His Britannic Majesty in Europe, and the territories of the United States of America, a reciprocal liberty of commerce. The inhabitants of the two countries, respectively, shall have liberty fully and securely to come with their ships and cargoes to all such places, ports, and rivers in the territories aforesaid, to which other foreigners are permitted to come; to enter into the same, and remain and reside in any parts of the said territories, respectively; also to hire and occupy warehouses for the purposes of their commerce; and, generally, the merchants and traders of each nation, respectively, shall enjoy the most complete protection and security for their commerce, but subject always to the laws and statutes of the two countries, respectively.

ART. 2. No other or higher duties shall be imposed on the importation into the territories of His Britannic Majesty in Europe, of any articles the growth, produce, or manufacture of the United States; and no other or higher duties shall be imposed on the importation into the United States of any articles the growth, produce, or manufacture of his Britannic Majesty's territories in Europe, than are or shall be payable on the like articles being the growth, produce, or manufacture of any other foreign country; nor shall any other or higher duties or charges be imposed in either of the two countries on the exportation of any articles to His Britannic Majesty's territories in Europe, or to the United States, respectively, than such as are payable on the exportation of the like articles to any other foreign country; nor shall any prohibition be imposed upon the exportation or importation of any article the growth, produce, or manufacture of His Britannic Majesty's territories in Europe, or of the United States, to or from the said territories of His Britannic Majesty in Europe, or to or from the said United States, which shall not extend to all other nations. No other or higher duties or charges shall be imposed in the ports of any of His Britannic Majesty's territories in Europe on the vessels of the United States, than shall be payable on British vessels; nor in any of the ports of the United States on British vessels, than those payable in the same ports by vessels of the United States.

ART. 3. The navigation of all lakes, rivers, and water communications, the middle of which is or may be the boundary between His Britannic Majesty's territories on the continent of North America, and the United States, shall, with the exceptions hereinafter mentioned, at all times be free to His Majesty's subjects and the citizens of the United States. The inhabitants of His Britannic Majesty's territories in North America, and the citizens and subjects of the United States, may freely carry on trade and commerce by land or inland navigation, as aforesaid, with goods and merchandise the growth, produce, or manufacture of the British territories in Europe or North America, or of the United States, respectively, within the territories of the two parties, respectively, on the said continent, (the country within the limits of the Hudson's Bay Company only excepted;) and no other or higher duties or tolls, or rates of ferriage, or portage, than what are or shall be payable by natives, respectively, shall be taken or demanded on either side. All goods or merchandise, whose importation into the United States shall not be wholly prohibited, may fully, for the purposes of the commerce abovementioned, be carried into the said United States, in the manner aforesaid, by His Britannic Majesty's subjects; and the said goods and merchandise shall be subject to no higher or other duties than would be payable by citizens of the United States on the importation of the same in American vessels into the Atlantic ports of the United States. And, in like manner, all goods and merchandise the growth, produce, or manufacture of the United States, whose importation into His Majesty's said territories in America shall not be entirely prohibited, may fully, for the purposes of the commerce abovementioned, be carried into the same by land, or by means of such lakes, rivers, and water communications as abovementioned, by the citizens of the United States; and such goods and merchandise shall be subject to no other or higher duty than would be payable by His Majesty's subjects on the importation of the same from Europe into the said territories. No duty shall be levied by either party on peltries or furs which may be brought in the manner aforesaid by land or inland navigation, from the said territories of the other; but tolls, or rates of ferriage, or portage, may be demanded and taken in manner abovementioned on such peltries or furs.

It is hereby declared, that nothing in this article contained, as to the navigation of rivers, lakes, or water communications, shall extend to give a right of navigation upon or within the same, in those parts where the middle is not the boundary between His Britannic Majesty's territories and the United States of America.

ART. 4. It shall be free for each of the two contracting parties to appoint consuls for the protection of trade, to reside in the dominions and territories of the other party; but, before any consul shall act as such, he shall, in the usual form, be approved and admitted by the Government to which he is sent. And it is hereby declared that, in case of illegal or improper conduct towards the laws or Government of the country to which he is sent, such consul may either be punished according to law, if the laws will reach the case, or be sent back, the offended Government assigning to the other the reasons for the same.

It is hereby declared, that either of the contracting parties may except from the residence of

Commercial Convention with Great Britain.

consuls, such particular places as such party shall judge proper to be so excepted.

ART. 5. It being the intention of the contracting parties that the inhabitants of His Britannic Majesty's territories in Europe, and the inhabitants of the United States, shall, in respect to commerce between the said territories, be placed on the footing of the most favored nations, it is agreed, that in case either of the contracting parties shall hereafter grant any additional advantages in commerce or navigation to any European nation as to the importation or exportation to or from such other European nation and His Britannic Majesty's territories in Europe, or to or from such European nation and the territories of the United States, the citizens and subjects of the other contracting party shall likewise enjoy the same, freely, where it has been freely granted to such other European nation; and, where conditionally granted, on the same terms and conditions on which such advantage shall have been granted, or on terms and conditions which may be afterwards agreed upon as equivalent thereto by the contracting parties.

FIRST SEPARATE ARTICLE.

His Britannic Majesty agrees that the vessels of the United States shall be admitted and hospitably received at the principal settlements of the British dominions in the East Indies, *videlicet*, Calcutta, Madras, Bombay, and the Prince of Wales's island; and that the citizens of the said United States may fully carry on trade between the said principal settlements and the said United States, in all articles of which the importation and exportation, respectively, to and from the said territories, shall not be entirely prohibited: *Provided, only,* That it shall not be lawful for them, in any time of war between the British Government and any Power or State whatever, to export from the said territories, without the special permission of the British Government, any military stores, or naval stores, or rice. The citizens of the United States shall pay for their vessels, when admitted, no other or higher duty or charge than shall be payable on the vessels of the most favored European nations; and they shall pay no other or higher duties or charges on the importation or exportation of the cargoes of the said vessels, than shall be payable on the same articles when imported or exported in the vessels of the most favored European nation.

But it is expressly agreed, that the vessels of the United States shall not carry any articles from the said principal settlements to any port or place, except to some port or place in the United States of America, where the same shall be unladen.

It is also understood, that the permission granted by this article is not to extend to allow the vessels of the United States to carry on any of the coasting trade of the said British territories; but the vessels of the United States having, in the first instance, proceeded to one of the said principal settlements of the British dominions in the East Indies, and then going with their original cargoes, or part thereof, from one of the said principal settlements to another, shall not be considered as carrying on the coasting trade.

The vessels of the United States may also touch for refreshment, but not for commerce, in the course of their voyage to or from the British territories in India, at the Cape of Good Hope, the island of St. Helena, or such other places as may be in the possession of Great Britain in the African or Indian seas; it being well understood that, in all that regards this article, the citizens of the United States shall be subject in all respects to the laws and regulations of the British Government from time to time established.

SECOND SEPARATE ARTICLE.

It is hereby agreed and declared, that the first separate article of the present treaty shall be limited in its duration to the period of two years from the date of the exchange of the ratifications of the said treaty.

No. 3.

The American to the British Plenipotentiaries.

HARLEY STREET, *June* 17, 1815.

The undersigned have the honor to acknowledge the receipt of the note of His Britannic Majesty's Plenipotentiaries of the 16th instant, enclosing their contre-projet for the arrangement of the commercial intercourse between the two countries.

Anxious to ascertain, with as little delay as possible, whether there be any probability that such an arrangement can now be concluded as shall be satisfactory to both parties, the undersigned will not at this time enter into a discussion of the subject, and, leaving minor points for subsequent consideration, will only propose the following alterations in the contre-projet of His Britannic Majesty's Plenipotentiaries, viz:

ART. 2.—1st. To reinstate the clause in the projet of the undersigned which provided that the same duties, drawbacks, and bounties should be paid and allowed in either country, on the importation or exportation of articles the produce, growth, or manufacture of His Britannic Majesty's territories in Europe, or of the United States.

2d. To reinstate the clause in the projet of the undersigned which excepted from the provision to equalize tonnage duties British vessels bound to or from British possessions to which vessels of the United States were not permanently admitted; or to introduce a new article, providing that neither the intercourse between the United States and His Britannic Majesty's possessions in the West Indies, nor that by sea between the said States and His Britannic Majesty's possessions in North America, shall be affected by any article in the treaty, but that each party shall remain in the complete possession of its rights, in respect to such an intercourse.

ART. 3. To reinstate, in substance, the article proposed on that subject by the undersigned, so that the commerce by land or inland navigation, sanctioned by the article, be confined to that which may be carried on between the citizens of

Commercial Convention with Great Britain.

the United States and His Britannic Majesty's subjects; and so as not to preclude the citizens of the United States from carrying articles of the growth, produce, or manufacture of the said States down the river St. Lawrence, as far at least as Montreal, and down the waters of Lake Champlain, as far at least as the St. Lawrence; or, if no satisfactory arrangement can at present be formed on this subject, to omit the article altogether.

Art. 5. To place, generally, each nation on the footing of the most favored nation, without restricting that privilege, as relates to the citizens of the United States, to the commerce with His Britannic Majesty's territories in Europe.

Second separate article to be omitted.

The undersigned will have the honor to wait on His Britannic Majesty's Plenipotentiaries on Monday, the 19th instant, at two o'clock, at the Office of Trade, when the undersigned hope they will be able to communicate to them their final determination on the proposed alterations.

The undersigned request His Britannic Majesty's Plenipotentiaries to accept the assurances of their distinguished consideration.

JOHN QUINCY ADAMS,
HENRY CLAY,
ALBERT GALLATIN.

The Right Hon. F. J. ROBINSON, H. GOULBURN, and Dr. WILLIAM ADAMS.

No. 4.

The British to the American Plenipotentiaries.

BOARD OF TRADE, *June* 20, 1815.

In compliance with the request of the American Plenipotentiaries, the undersigned have the honor to communicate to them, in writing, the substance of the observations which were made on the part of the British Plenipotentiaries, in the conference of yesterday, upon the different points referred to in the note of the American Plenipotentiaries of the 17th instant.

Upon the first point, relating to a part of the second article of the contre-projet of the undersigned, the British Plenipotentiaries stated it to be the intention of their Government to agree not only to a mutual equalization of such duties as may be properly called tonnage duties, but also of all duties upon the importation of goods the growth, produce, or manufacture of the two countries, respectively, whether imported in British or in American ships; they stated, further, their readiness to accede to a similar and mutual equalization of bounties payable upon the above articles. Upon the subject of drawbacks, they represented that the clause, as proposed by the American Plenipotentiaries, appeared to give to the vessels of the United States which might be engaged in the general re-exportation of American produce from this country to all other parts of the world an advantage equal to that enjoyed by British ships; and that this privilege went beyond the general principle of an article which was confined to the trade between the two countries, respectively. They expressed a wish to receive from the American Plenipotentiaries a more precise explanation of their views upon this point.

Upon the second point referred to in the note of the American Plenipotentiaries, the undersigned expressed their readiness to agree to a clause which should contain the latter alternative suggested by the American Plenipotentiaries.

Upon the third article, relating to the intercourse between Canada and the United States, the undersigned disclaimed any intention of obtaining, by any interpretation of the words of the article as they had proposed it, a right to an intercourse with the Indians residing within the acknowledged limits of the United States, which the American Plenipotentiaries had already stated that their instructions forbade them to concede. And they expressed their readiness to agree to the insertion of such words as would clear up any doubt which might exist upon the subject.

As to the navigation of the river St. Lawrence as far as Montreal, and that of the waters flowing from Lake Champlain to that river, the undersigned stated themselves not to be authorized to stipulate the concession of that indulgence in the way proposed by the American Plenipotentiaries. The undersigned likewise stated their objections to extending Article 5 beyond the intercourse between the United States and His Britannic Majesty's dominions in Europe.

In regard to the two separate articles of the contre-projet, the undersigned stated that they had no authority to grant the first, unless accompanied by a limitation in point of time; and when the American Plenipotentiaries proposed, as a substitute for that article, one which should give the United States the same privileges as the most favored European nations in their intercourse with the British possessions in that quarter, the undersigned, while they admitted that, in some respects, it stood upon different grounds from an article which should grant the indirect voyage to the East Indies, without any equivalent or limitation in point of time, did not feel themselves authorized to hold out any expectation that this new suggestion could be acceded to by Great Britain.

The undersigned request the American Plenipotentiaries to accept the assurances of their high consideration.

F. ROBINSON,
HENRY GOULBURN,
WILLIAM ADAMS.

No. 5.

Second sketch of article for equalizing duties.

The same duties shall be paid on the importation into the ports of any of His Britannic Majesty's territories in Europe of any articles the growth, produce, or manufacture of the United States, and the same drawbacks shall be allowed on the re-exportation thereof, whether such importation shall be in vessels of the United States or in British vessels; and the same duties shall be paid on the importation into the United States

Commercial Convention with Great Britain.

of any articles the growth, produce, or manufacture of His Britannic Majesty's territories in Europe, and the same drawbacks shall be allowed on the re-exportation thereof, whether such importation shall be in vessels of the United States or in British vessels. The same duties shall be paid, and the same bounties allowed, on the exportation of any articles the growth, produce, or manufacture of the United States to His Britannic Majesty's territories in Europe, whether such exportation shall be in vessels of the United States or in British vessels; and the same duties shall be paid, and the same bounties allowed, on the exportation of any articles the growth, produce, or manufacture of His Britannic Majesty's territories in Europe to the United States, whether such exportation shall be in vessels of the United States or in British vessels.

No. 6.

The American to the British Plenipotentiaries.

HARLEY STREET, *June* 21, 1815.

The undersigned have the honor to acknowledge the receipt of the note of the British Plenipotentiaries dated the 20th instant, communicating the substance of the observations which they had made in the conference of the 19th, upon the different points referred to in the note of the undersigned of the 17th instant.

The views of the undersigned, with respect to the second article, being precisely the same with those stated by the British Plenipotentiaries, there will be no difficulty in framing a clause embracing the objects contemplated by both parties, and which shall be free from ambiguity.

The explanation given by the British Plenipotentiaries upon that part of the third article which the undersigned apprehended might be liable to a construction, in reference to the Indian trade, not intended by either party, is perfectly satisfactory. But they regret that they cannot accede to the alterations proposed in other respects by the British Plenipotentiaries to the article which had been offered by the undersigned, particularly as they affect the privilege of inland navigation by the river St. Lawrence and by the waters flowing from Lake Champlain; nor have they found it practicable to frame any article compatible with the different views entertained by the two parties respecting the intercourse between the United States and Canada. They, therefore, recur to the proposal made in their note of the 17th instant, to omit that article altogether, that proposal not having been noticed in the note of the British Plenipotentiaries of the 20th instant.

They make the same offer as to the fifth article of the contre-projet.

And, thirdly, they hereby renew the proposal made verbally in the conference of the 19th inst., to substitute, for the two separate articles, one placing the United States, in their intercourse with the British possessions in India, on the footing of the most favored European nation.

The undersigned request to be made acquainted with the determination of the British Plenipotentiaries on those three propositions.

The undersigned tender again to the British Plenipotentiaries assurances of their distinguished consideration.

JOHN QUINCY ADAMS,
HENRY CLAY,
ALBERT GALLATIN.

The Right Hon. F. ROBINSON, H. GOULBURN, and Dr. WILLIAM ADAMS.

No. 7.

The British to the American Plenipotentiaries.

BOARD OF TRADE, *June* 23, 1815.

The undersigned have the honor to acknowledge the receipt of the note of the American Plenipotentiaries of the 21st instant, and are happy to find that no difficulty exists on either side as to the second article. Upon the subject of the third article, the undersigned regret to learn that the American Plenipotentiaries have not found it practicable to frame any article compatible with the different views entertained by the two parties respecting the intercourse between Canada and the United States; and as the undersigned are equally unable to accede to the proposition made on the part of the United States respecting the navigation of waters lying exclusively within the territories of His Britannic Majesty, they accede to the proposal of omitting the article altogether. They have also no objection to the omission of the fifth article.

In regard to the trade with the British East Indies, the undersigned are not authorized to substitute, for the two separate articles which they had proposed, one which shall put the intercourse of the United States in that quarter upon the footing of the most favored European nation, inasmuch as it would have the practical effect of granting, in another shape, that which the undersigned are instructed to withhold, unless accompanied by a greater limitation of time than they would think it expedient to apply to the other arrangements of the treaty. If, however, the American Plenipotentiaries adhere to their objection to the substance of the two separate articles, as proposed on the part of Great Britain, the undersigned are ready to omit altogether any article upon the subject of the East Indies.

The undersigned are nevertheless disposed to consider the arrangements of the second article (as agreed upon, or understood,) to be of sufficient importance to the mutual interests of Great Britain and the United States, particularly in the common object of securing a free commercial intercourse between the two countries, to induce them readily to sign a treaty or convention for that single purpose, independent of the other points to which the negotiation has referred.

The undersigned are happy, upon this occasion, to renew to the American Plenipotentiaries the assurances of their high consideration.

F. J. ROBINSON.
WILLIAM ADAMS.

To the AMERICAN PLENIPOTENTIARIES.

Commercial Convention with Great Britain.

No. 8.

The American to the British Plenipotentiaries.

HARLEY STREET, *June* 24, 1815.

The undersigned have the honor to acknowledge the receipt of the note of the British Plenipotentiaries of the 23d instant, expressing their assent to the proposal of omitting the third and fifth articles of the contre-projet. To the proposal of omitting, also, altogether, any article upon the subject of the East Indies, and of signing an arrangement embracing all the provisions contained in the second article, the undersigned do not feel themselves authorized to accede. But they offer to sign a convention embracing that article entire, and the first separate article, the whole of which convention shall be limited to the term of four years from the date of the exchange of the ratifications; or they will agree to a convention for the sole purpose of abolishing all discriminating duties on American and British vessels, and their cargoes, in the intercourse between the United States and His Britannic Majesty's territories in Europe, in the manner contemplated by the second article, and as explained and mutually agreed on in the conferences on that subject, omitting all the other provisions contained in the same article, and which had for object to place the two countries, respectively, on the footing of the most favored nation.

The undersigned request the British Plenipotentiaries to accept the assurances of their distinguished consideration.

JOHN QUINCY ADAMS,
HENRY CLAY,
ALBERT GALLATIN.

The Right Hon. F. J. ROBINSON, H. GOULBURN, and Dr. WILLIAM ADAMS.

No 9.

The British to the American Plenipotentiaries.

BOARD OF TRADE, *June* 26, 1815.

The undersigned have the honor to acknowledge the receipt of the note of the American Plenipotentiaries of the 24th instant, in which they offer to sign a convention embracing the second article entire, and the first separate article, the whole convention to be limited to the term of four years from the date of the exchange of the ratifications; or to agree to a convention for the sole purpose of abolishing all discriminating duties on American and British vessels, and their cargoes, in the intercourse between the United States and the British territories in Europe, omitting all the other provisions contained in the same article, and which had for object to place the two countries, respectively, on the footing of the most favored nation.

As neither of these proposals were contemplated in the instructions with which the undersigned were originally furnished, and which were framed with a view to a less limited arrangement, they have felt themselves under the necessity of referring the last note of the American Plenipotentiaries to the consideration of their Government,

and will not fail to communicate the result of that reference as soon as they shall be enabled to do so.

The undersigned are happy to avail themselves of this opportunity of renewing to the American Plenipotentiaries the assurances of their high consideration.

F. J. ROBINSON,
HENRY GOULBURN,
WILLIAM ADAMS.

No. 10.

The British to the American Plenipotentiaries.

BOARD OF TRADE, *June* 29, 1815.

In reference to the note which the undersigned had the honor to address to the American Plenipotentiaries on the 26th instant, they are now instructed to acquaint them that the British Government is ready to agree to a convention for four years, (to be calculated from the date of its signature,) which shall contain the whole of the second article, as proposed by the undersigned, and as explained and mutually agreed upon in their several conferences; and also the first article, relating to the East Indies, as proposed on the part of Great Britain, (the latter article also to be in force for four years from the same date.) The undersigned, in making this communication to the American Plenipotentiaries, feel it to be their duty to state, in the most explicit manner, that although, in the earnest desire of promoting a good understanding between the two countries, the British Government has, at the present time, forborne to insist on making in the body of the treaty any marked distinction between its concession in regard to the East Indies, and its other concessions, for which a stipulated equivalent is obtained, yet that it still considers itself as granting to the United States a privilege, to the East Indies, for which it is entitled to require an equivalent; and the undersigned must, therefore, be distinctly understood as reserving to His Majesty's Government, in any future negotiations, the clear right either of withholding this privilege altogether, after the expiration of four years, or of renewing the grant of it for such equivalents, or subject to such modification, as expediency may seem to require at the time of such future negotiation.

The undersigned request to have the honor of seeing the American Plenipotentiaries on Friday next, the 30th instant, at two o'clock, at the Board of Trade; and avail themselves of this opportunity of again offering the assurances of their high consideration.

F. J. ROBINSON,
HENRY GOULBURN.
WILLIAM ADAMS.

No. 11.

The American to the British Plenipotentiaries.

HARLEY STREET, *June* 30, 1815.

The undersigned have had the honor to receive the note of the British Plenipotentiaries, dated the 29th instant, and stating the terms on which their Government is ready to agree to a convention on the subject of the commercial intercourse between the United States and Great Britain.

The undersigned have already, in the conferences which they had the honor to hold with the British Plenipotentiaries, expressed their opinion that the proposed convention, taken altogether, was founded on principles of reciprocity, was equally advantageous to both parties, and contained in itself a fair equivalent for every presumed concession made by either party; but both Governments will undoubtedly have a clear right, after the expiration of four years, of refusing to renew, or of subjecting to modifications, any of the stipulations now agreed on which may appear to either party injurious, or requiring some further equivalent. The same earnest desire of promoting a good understanding between the two countries, which has been expressed on the part of Great Britain, has induced the undersigned to agree to a convention more limited both as to its objects and duration than they had contemplated, with a hope that, in the mean time, its deficiencies may be supplied, and such other provisions may be adopted, as will conduce to mutual convenience, and tend to strengthen the relations of amity and friendship happily restored between the two countries.

The undersigned will have the honor to meet the British Plenipotentiaries this day, and feel pleasure in renewing the assurances of their high consideration.

JOHN QUINCY ADAMS,
H. CLAY,
ALBERT GALLATIN.

The Right Hon. F. J. ROBINSON, H. GOULBURN, Esq., and Dr. W. ADAMS.

The undersigned, His Britannic Majesty's Chargé des Affaires in the United States, has the honor to acquaint the American Secretary of State, for the information of the President, that he has received His Royal Highness the Prince Regent's ratification, in the name and on the behalf of His Majesty, of the commercial Convention between the two countries, signed at London on the 3d of July; and that he has been authorized and is ready to proceed to the exchange, whenever the ratification on the part of the United States shall have taken place.

In communicating this intelligence, the undersigned has received the Prince Regent's commands, at the same time, to transmit to the Government of the United States the accompanying declaration, explanatory of the intentions of His Majesty's Government in so far as regards the intercourse of vessels belonging to the United States with the island of St. Helena; the existing circumstances of the world having rendered it necessary that that island should, for the present, be excepted from the ports of refreshment enumerated in the third article of the said convention.

The undersigned avails himself of this opportunity of requesting the American Secretary of

State to accept the assurance of his high consideration.

A. ST. JOHN BAKER.

DECLARATION.

The undersigned, His Britannic Majesty's Chargé des Affaires in the United States of America, is commanded by His Royal Highness the Prince Regent, acting in the name and on the behalf of His Majesty, to explain and declare, upon the exchange of the ratifications of the convention concluded at London on the 3d of July of the present year, for regulating the commerce and navigation between the two countries, that, in consequence of events which have happened in Europe subsequent to the signature of the convention aforesaid, it has been deemed expedient, and determined, in conjunction with the allied Sovereigns, that St. Helena shall be the place allotted for the future residence of General Napoleon Bonaparte, under such regulations as may be necessary for the perfect security of his person; and it has been resolved, for that purpose, that all ships and vessels whatever, as well British ships and vessels as others, excepting only ships belonging the East India Company, shall be excluded from all communication with or approach to that island.

It has, therefore, become impossible to comply with so much of the third article of the treaty as relates to the liberty of touching for refreshment at the island of St. Helena; and the ratifications of the said treaty will be exchanged under the explicit declaration and understanding that the vessels of the United States cannot be allowed to touch at or hold any communication whatever with the said island, so long as the said island shall continue to be the place of residence of the said Napoleon Bonaparte.

A. ST. JOHN BAKER.

WASHINGTON, *November* 24, 1815.

MASSACRE AT DARTMOOR PRISON.

[Communicated to the House, January 31, 1816.]

To the House of Representatives :

I transmit a report of the Secretary of State, complying with a resolution of the 4th instant.

JAMES MADISON.

WASHINGTON, *Jan.* 31, 1816.

DEPARTMENT OF STATE, *Jan.* 31, 1816.

The resolution of the House of Representatives of the 4th instant, requesting the President to cause to be laid before the House (if in his opinion it will not be inconsistent with the public welfare) any authentic information he may have received, or communications which may have passed between this Government and the Government of Great Britain, in relation to the transactions at Dartmoor prison, in the month of April last, as far as the American prisoners of war there confined were affected by such transactions, having been referred to the Secretary of State, he has the honor to submit to the President the accompanying papers, marked A, B, and C, as containing all the information in this Department called for by the resolution, or immediately connected with it.

All which is respectfully submitted.

JAMES MONROE.

List of papers in packet marked A.

Extract of a minute of a conversation which took place at Lord Castlereagh's, between his lordship and Messrs. Clay and Gallatin, on the 16th of April, 1815.

Extract of a letter from Messrs. Clay and Gallatin to Mr. Beasley, dated the 18th of April, 1815.

Letter of Mr. Charles King to Mr. Adams, dated Plymouth, 26th April, 1815.

Report of Messrs. Larpent and King, upon the occurrence at Dartmoor prison, dated 25th of April, 1815.

Letter of Lord Castlereagh to Messrs. Clay and Gallatin, dated 22d of May, 1815.

Letters of Messrs. Clay and Gallatin to Lord Castlereagh. dated 24th of May, 1815.

Extract of a letter from Mr. Adams to the Secretary of State, dated 23d of June, 1815.

Letter of Mr. Baker, His Britannic Majesty's Chargé des Affaires. to the Secretary of State, dated August 3, 1815.

Letter of the Secretary of State to Mr. Baker, dated December 11, 1815.

A.

Extract of a minute of a conversation which took place at Lord Castlereagh's, between his Lordship and Messrs. Clay and Gallatin, on the 16th of April, 1815.

Lord Castlereagh began by adverting to the unfortunate event which had taken place at Dartmoor, and proposed that, as a statement of the transaction had been received from the American prisoners differing very materially in fact from an inquiry instituted by the port admiral, some means should be devised of procuring information as to the real state of the case; in order either, on the one hand, to satisfy the United States that the lives of their citizens, however unfortunately, had not been wantonly sacrificed, or, on the other, to enable the British Government to punish their civil and military officers, if they should be found to have resorted to measures of extreme severity without necessity, or with too much precipitation. He therefore proposed that one of the American Commissioners should proceed to Dartmoor, with one of the gentlemen with whom they had negotiated at Ghent, and, after examining the persons concerned, and such other evidence as might be thought necessary, should make a joint report upon the facts of the case; that as neither Government could have any wish beyond that of clearing up a transaction which might, if left unexplained, as it now stood, upon *ex parte* statements, create much irritation between the two countries, so the

British Government had no desire to screen any person whose conduct might have been improper or precipitate.

The American Commissioners, agreeing to the principles of Lord Castlereagh's proposition, so far as related to the advantage of having a joint report upon the facts of the case, entertained doubts whether they could, with propriety, take such a duty upon themselves; and suggested that Mr. Beasley, from the situation which he held in this country, appeared to them better qualified for the task. Lord Castlereagh replied, that it was only from a desire of giving to any report which might be made the sanction of the highest authority, that he had suggested the employment of the Commissioners themselves; and, deeming it of the most essential importance to satisfy the public in both countries on this subject, he was induced to prefer his original proposition; but that he must, of course, leave it to the American Commissioners to decide whether Mr. Beasley was better fitted for this service; and that, upon receiving the result of their consideration of the subject, the Government would appoint some person properly qualified to meet the American gentleman who might be so selected; such person being either one of the late British Commissioners at Ghent, or a commissioner of the transport board, according as the American Commissioners might decide upon going themselves or sending Mr. Beasley. Lord Castlereagh then entered upon the immediate release of the American prisoners of war detained in this country. After stating the inconvenience of retaining in confinement men who had a right, under a treaty of peace, to be liberated, he requested information as to whether Mr. Beasley was proceeding in the measures which he understood to have been taken for conveying them back to America.

The American Commissioners stated that Mr. Beasley had certainly taken up some transports, on his own responsibility, previous to the receipt of instructions from America; but the American Government considered the restoration of prisoners to imply their reconveyance to their own country by the Power detaining them; and the American Commissioners did not know whether Mr. Beasley had either authority or funds for continuing the service which he had, on his own view of the subject, commenced.

Lord Castlereagh stated that he saw no objection to adopting some such measure as that which had been adopted in America, and proposed that each party should defray half the expense of conveying the prisoners from this country to America, leaving the ultimate construction of the treaty for future arrangements. But he remarked, that the article on which the doubt had arisen being founded on principles of perfect reciprocity, it appeared to him scarcely consonant with those principles, that the only expense to be defrayed by the United States should be that of conveying the British prisoners from the United States to Bermuda or Halifax, while Great Britain should have not only to convey to America the American prisoners now in this country, but also to bring home from colonies nearly as distant as the United States all her own prisoners.

Extract of a letter from H. Clay and Albert Gallatin, Esquires, to Mr. Beasley.

LONDON, *April* 18, 1815.

At the request of Lord Castlereagh, we have had interviews with him and Mr. Goulburn, on the subjects of the transportation of the American prisoners now in this country to the United States, and of the late unfortunate event at the depot at Dartmoor.

On the latter subject, as a statement of the transaction has been received from the American prisoners differing very materially in fact from that which had resulted from an inquiry instituted by the port admiral, it has been thought advisable that some means should be devised of procuring information as to the real state of the case, in order, on the one hand, to show that there had not been any wanton or improper sacrifice of the lives of American citizens, or, on the other, to enable the British Government to punish their civil and military officers, if it should appear that they have resorted to measures of extreme severity, without necessity, or with too much precipitation.

Lord Castlereagh proposed that the inquiry should be a joint one, conducted by a commissioner selected by each Government; and we have thought such an inquiry most likely to produce an impartial and satisfactory result.

We presume that you will have too much occupation on the first subject, and the other incidental duties of your office, to attend to this inquiry in person. On that supposition, we have stated to the British Government that we should recommend to you the selection of Charles King, Esq., as a fit person to conduct it in behalf of the American Government. If Mr. King will undertake the business, he will forthwith proceed to Dartmoor, and, in conjunction with the British Commissioner, who may be appointed on the occasion, will examine the persons concerned, and such other evidence as may be thought necessary, and make a joint report upon the facts of the case to J. Q. Adams, Esq., Minister Plenipotentiary of the United States at this Court, and to the British Government.

The mode of executing this service must be left to the discretion of Mr. King and his colleague. If they can agree upon a narration of the facts, after having heard the evidence, it will be better than reporting the whole mass of testimony in detail, which they may, perhaps, find it necessary to do, if they cannot come to such an agreement.

We are, &c.

H. CLAY.
ALBERT GALLATIN.

R. G. BEASLEY, Esq., &c.

Mr. Charles King to Mr. Adams.

PLYMOUTH, *April* 26, 1815.

SIR: In pursuance of instructions received from Messrs. Clay and Gallatin, I have the honor to transmit to you the report prepared by Mr. Larpent and myself, on behalf of our respective Governments, in relation to the unfortunate transaction at Dartmoor prison of war, on the 6th of the present month. Considering it of much importance that the report, whatever it might be, should go forth under our joint signatures, I have forborne to press some of the points which it involves as far as otherwise I might have done; and it therefore may not be improper, in this letter, to enter into some little explanation of such parts of the report. Although it does appear that a part of the prisoners were, on that evening, in such a state and under such circumstances as to have justified, in the view which the commander of the depot could not but take of it, the intervention of the military force, and even in a strict sense the first use of fire-arms, yet I cannot but express it as my settled opinion, that, by a conduct a little more temporising, this dreadful alternative of firing upon the unarmed prisoners might have been avoided. Yet, as this opinion has been the result of subsequent examination, and after having acquired a knowledge of the comparatively harmless state of the prisoners, it may be but fair to consider whether, in such a moment of confusion and alarm as that appears to have been, the officer commanding could have fairly estimated his danger, or have measured out with precision the extent and nature of the force necessary to guard against it. But when the firing became general, as it afterwards appears to have done, and caught with electric rapidity from the square to the platforms, there is no plea nor shadow of excuse for it, except in the personal exasperation of the soldiery; nor for the more deliberate (and, therefore, more unjustifiable) firing which took place into three of the prisons, Nos. 1, 3, and 4, but more particularly into No. 3, after the prisoners had retired into them, and there was no longer any pretence of apprehension as to their escape. Upon this ground, as you, sir, will perceive by the report, Mr. Larpent and myself had no difference in opinion; and I am fully persuaded that my own regret was not greater than his, at perceiving how hopeless would be the attempt to trace to any individual of the military those outrageous proceedings.

As to whether the order to fire came from Captain Shortland, I yet confess myself unable to form any satisfactory opinion, though, perhaps, the bias of my mind is that he did give such an order. But his anxiety and exertions to stop it, after it had continued some little time, are fully proved; and his general conduct, previous to this occurrence, as far as he could with any propriety enter into such details, appears to have been characterized by great fairness, and even kindness, in the relation which he stood towards the prisoners.

On the subject of any complaints existing against their own Government by the prisoners, it was invariably answered, to several distinct questions put by me on that head, that none whatsoever existed, or had been expressed by them, although they confessed themselves to entertain some animosity against Mr. Beasley, to whom

Massacre at Dartmoor Prison.

they attribute their detention in this country; with what justice, you, sir, will be better able to judge. They made no complaint whatsoever as to their provisions, and general mode of living and treatment in the prison.

I have transmitted to Mr. Beasley a list of the killed and wounded on this melancholy occasion, with a request that he would forward it to the United States for the information of their friends at home; and I am pleased to have it in my power to say that the wounded are, for the most part, doing well.

I have also enclosed to Mr. Beasley the notes taken by me of the evidence adduced before us, with a request that he would have them fairly copied, as also a copy of the depositions taken before the coroner, and desired him to submit them to you when in order.

I cannot conclude, sir, without expressing my high sense of the impartiality and manly fairness with which this inquiry has been conducted on the part of Mr. Larpent, nor without mentioning that every facility was afforded to us in its prosecution, as well by the military officers commanding here and at the prison, as by the magistrates of the vicinity. I have the honor to be, sir, &c.

            CHARLES KING.

To his Excellency J. Q. ADAMS, &c.

Report of Messrs. Larpent and King upon the occurrence at Dartmoor Prison.

        PLYMOUTH, *April 26, 1815.*

We, the undersigned Commissioners, appointed on behalf of our respective Governments to inquire into and report upon the unfortunate occurrence of the 6th of April instant, at Dartmoor prison, having carefully perused the proceedings of the several courts of inquiry instituted immediately after that event, by the orders of Admiral Sir John T. Duckworth and Major General Brown, respectively, as well as the depositions taken at the coroner's inquest, upon the bodies of the prisoners who lost their lives upon that melancholy occasion; upon which inquest the jury found a verdict of "justifiable homicide," proceeded immediately to the examination, upon oath, in the presence of one or more of the magistrates of the vicinity, of all the witnesses, both American and English, who offered themselves for the purpose, or who could be discovered as likely to afford any material information on the subject, as well those who had been previously examined before the coroner as otherwise, to the number, in the whole, of above eighty. We further proceeded to a minute examination of the prison, for the purpose of clearing up some points which, upon the evidence alone were scarcely intelligible; obtaining from the prisoners, and from the officers of the depot, all the necessary assistance and explanation; and premising that we have been, from necessity, compelled to draw many of our conclusions from statements and evidence highly contradictory. We do now make, upon the whole of the proceedings, the following report:

During the period which has elapsed since the arrival in this country of the account of the ratification of the Treaty of Ghent, an increased degree of restlessness and impatience of confinement appears to have prevailed amongst the American prisoners at Dartmoor, which, though not exhibited in the shape of any violent excesses, has been principally indicated by threats of breaking out, if not soon released. On the 4th of this month, in particular, only two days previous to the event the subject of this inquiry, a large body of the prisoners rushed into the market square, from whence by the regulations of the prison they are excluded, demanding bread instead of biscuit, which had on that day been issued by the officers of the depot. Their demand, however, having been then almost immediately complied with, they returned to their own yards; and the employment of force, on that occasion, became unnecessary.

On the evening of the 6th, about six o'clock, it was clearly proved to us that a breach or hole had been made in one of the prison walls, sufficient for a full-sized man to pass, and that others had been commenced in the course of the day, near the spot, though never completed; that a number of the prisoners were over the railing, erected to prevent them from communicating with the sentinels on the walls, which was of course forbidden by the regulations of the prison; and that, in the space between the railing and those walls, they were tearing up pieces of turf, and wantonly pelting each other in a noisy and disorderly manner; that a much more considerable number of the prisoners were collected together at that time in one of their yards, near the place where the breach was effected; and that, although such collection of prisoners was not unusual at other times, (the gambling tables being commonly kept in that part of the yard,) yet, when connected with the circumstances of the breach, and the time of the day, which was after the horn (the signal for the prisoners to retire to their respective prisons) had ceased to sound, it became a natural and just ground of alarm to those who had charge of the depot.

It was also in evidence that, in the building formerly the petty officers' prison, but now the guard barrack, which stands in the yard, to which the hole in the wall would serve as a communication, a part of the arms of the guard who were off duty were usually kept in the racks; and though there was no evidence that this was, in any respect, the motive which induced the prisoners to make the opening in the wall, or even that they were ever acquainted with the fact, it naturally became at least a further cause for suspicion and alarm, and an additional reason for precaution.

Upon these grounds, Captain Shortland appears to us to have been justified in giving the order (which about this time he seems to have given) to sound the alarm-bell, the usual signal for collecting the officers of the depot, and putting the military on the alert. However reasonable and justifiable this was as a measure of precaution, the effects produced thereby in the prisons (but which could not have been intended) were most unfortunate, and deeply to be regretted. A considerable number of prisoners in the yards where no disturbance existed before, and who were either already within their respective prisons, or quietly retiring as usual towards them, immediately upon sound of the bell rushed back from curiosity, as it appears, towards the gates where, by that time, the crowd had assembled; and many who were at the time absent from their yards, were also, from the plan of the prison, compelled, in order to reach their own homes, to pass by the same spot. And thus, that which was merely a measure of precaution, in its operation increased the evil it was intended to prevent.

Almost at the same instant that the alarm-bell rang, (but whether before or subsequent is, upon the evidence, doubtful, though Captain Shortland states it as one of his further reasons for causing it to ring,) some one or more of the prisoners broke the iron chain which was the only fastening of No. 1 gate, leading into the market square, by means of an iron bar; and a very considerable number of the prisoners immediately rushed towards that gate, and many of them began to press forward, as fast as the opening would permit, into the square.

There was no direct proof before us of previous concert or preparation on the part of the prisoners, and no evidence of their intention or disposition to effect their escape on this occasion, excepting that which arose by inference from the whole of the above detailed circumstances connected together.

The natural and almost irresistible inference to be drawn, however, from the conduct of the prisoners, by Captain Shortland and the military was, that an intention on the part of the prisoners to escape was on the point of being carried into execution, and it was at least certain that they were, by force, passing beyond the limits prescribed to them, at a time when they ought to have been quietly going in for the night.

It was also in evidence that the outer gates of the market square were usually opened about this time to let the bread-wagon pass and repass to the store, although, at the period in question, they were in fact closed.

Under these circumstances, and with these impressions necessarily operating upon his mind, and the knowledge that, if the prisoners once penetrated through the square, the power of escape was almost to a certainty afforded to them, if they should be so disposed, Captain Shortland, in the first instance, proceeded down the square, towards the prisoners, having ordered a part of the different guards, to the number of about fifty only at first, (though they were increased afterwards,) to follow him. For some time both he and Doctor Magrath endeavored, by quiet means and persuasion, to induce the prisoners to retire to their own yards, explaining to them the fatal consequences which must ensue if they refused, as the military would, in that case, be necessarily compelled to employ force. The guard was, by

this time, formed in the rear of Captain Shortland, about two-thirds of the way down the square: the latter is about one hundred feet broad, and the guards extended nearly all across. Captain Shortland, finding that persuasion was in vain, and that, although some were induced by it to make an effort to retire, others pressed on in considerable numbers, at last ordered about fifteen file of the guard, nearly in front of the gate which had been forced, to charge the prisoners back to their own yards.

The prisoners were in some places so near the military that one of the soldiers stated he could not come fairly to the charge, and the military were unwilling to act as against an enemy. Some of the prisoners, also, were unwilling and reluctant to retire, and some pushing and struggling ensued between the parties, arising partly from intention, but mainly from the pressure of those behind preventing those in front from getting back. After some little time, however, this charge appears to have been so far effective, and that with little or no injury to the prisoners, as to have driven them, for the most part, quite down out the square, with the exception of a small number, who continued their resistance about No. 1 gate.

A great crowd still remained collected after this in the passage between the square and the prisoners' yards, and in the part of these yards in the vicinity of the gates. This assemblage still refused to withdraw, and, according to most of the English witnesses, and some of the American, was making a noise, hallowing, insulting, and provoking, and daring the military to fire; and, according to the evidence of several of the soldiers and some others, was pelting the military with large stones, by which some of them were actually struck. This circumstance is, however, denied by many of the American witnesses; and some of the English, upon having the question put to them, stated that they saw no stones thrown previously to the firing, although their situation at the time was such as to enable them to see most of the proceedings in the square.

Under these circumstances the firing commenced. With regard to any order having been given to fire, the evidence is very contradictory; several of the Americans swear, very positively, that Captain Shortland gave that order; but the manner in which, from the confusion of the moment, they describe this part of the transaction, is so different in its details, that it is difficult to reconcile their testimony. Many of the soldiers and other English witnesses, heard the word given by some one; but no one of them can swear it was by Captain Shortland, or by any one in particular; and some, amongst whom is the officer commanding the guard, think, if Captain Shortland had given such an order, that they must have heard it, which they did not. In addition to this, Captain Shortland denies the fact; and from the situation in which he appears to have been placed at the time, even according to the American witnesses, in front of the soldiers, it may appear somewhat improbable that he should then have given such an order. But, however it may remain a matter of doubt whether the firing first began in the square by order, or was a spontaneous act of the soldiers themselves, it seems clear that it was continued and renewed both there and elsewhere without orders; and that on the platforms, and in several places about the prison, it was certainly commenced without any authority.

The fact of an order having been given at first, provided the firing was, under the existing circumstances, justifiable, does not appear very material in any other point of view than as showing a want of discipline and self-possession in the troops, if they should have fired without orders.

With regard to the above important consideration of "whether the firing was justifiable or not," we are of opinion, under all the circumstances of the case, from the apprehension which the soldiers might fairly entertain, owing to the number and conduct of the prisoners, that this firing, to a certain extent, was justifiable in a military point of view, in order to intimidate the prisoners, and compel them thereby to desist from all acts of violence, and retire, as they were ordered, from a situation in which the responsibility of the agent and military could not permit them with safety to remain.

From the fact of the crowd being so close, and the firing, at first, being attended with very little injury, it appears probable that a large proportion of the muskets were as stated by one or two of the witnesses, levelled over the heads of the prisoners; a circumstance, in some respects, to be lamented, as it induced them to cry out "blank cartridges," and merely irritated and encouraged them to renew their insults to the soldiery, which produced a repetition of the firing in a manner much more destructive.

The firing in the square having continued for some time, by which several of the prisoners sustained injuries, the greater part of them appear to have been running back with the utmost confusion and precipitation to their respective prisons, and the cause for further firing seems, at this period, to have ceased. It appears, accordingly, that Captain Shortland was in the market square exerting himself and giving orders to that effect, and that Lieutenant Fortye had succeeded in stopping the fire on his part of the guard.

Under these circumstances, it is very difficult to find any justification for the further renewal and continuance of the firing, which certainly took place both in the prison yards and elsewhere, though we have some evidence of subsequent provocation given to the military, and resistance to the turnkeys in shutting the prisons, and of stones being thrown out from within the prison doors.

The subsequent firing appears rather to have arisen from the state of individual irritation and exasperation on the part of the soldiers who followed the prisoners into their yards, and from the absence of nearly all the officers, who might have restrained it, as well as from the great difficulty of putting an end to the firing when once commenced under such circumstances. Captain

Shortland was, from this time, busily occupied with the turnkeys in the square, receiving and taking care of the wounded. Ensign White remained with his guard at the breach, and Lieutenants Avelyne and Fortye, the only other subalterns known to have been present, continued in the square with the main bodies of their respective guards.

The time of the day, which was the officers' dinner hour, will, in some measure, explain this, as it caused the absence of every officer from the prison whose presence was not indispensable there. And this circumstance, which has been urged as an argument to prove the intention of the prisoners to take this opportunity to escape, tended to increase the confusion, and to prevent those greater exertions being made which might, perhaps, have obviated at least a portion of the mischief which ensued. At the time that the firing was going on in the square a cross fire was kept up from several of the platforms on the walls round the prison, where the sentries stand, by straggling parties of soldiers, who ran up there for that purpose. As far as this fire was directed to disperse the men assembled round the breach, (for which purpose it was most effectual,) it seems to stand upon the same ground as that in the first instance in the square. But that part which, it is positively sworn, was directed against straggling parties of prisoners running about the yards and endeavoring to enter the few doors which the turnkeys, according to their usual practice, had left open, does seem, as stated, to have been wholly without object or excuse, and to have been a wanton attack upon the lives of defenceless, and, at that time, unoffending individuals.

In the same, or even in more severe terms, we must remark upon what was proved as to the firing into the doorways of the prison, more particularly into that of No. 3 prison, at a time when the men were in crowds at the entrance.

From the position of the prison and of the door, and from the marks of the balls, which were pointed out to us, as well as from the evidence, it was clear this firing must have proceeded from soldiers a very few feet from the door-way; and though it was certainly sworn that the prisoners were at the time of part of the firing, at least, continuing to insult, and occasionally to throw stones at the soldiers, and that they were standing in the way of and impeding the turnkey who was there for the purpose of closing the door, yet still there was nothing stated which could, in our view, at all justify such excessive harsh and severe treatment of helpless and unarmed prisoners, when all idea of escape was at an end.

Under these impressions, we used every endeavor to ascertain if there was the least prospect of identifying any of the soldiers who had been guilty of the particular outrages here alluded to, or of tracing any particular death at that time to the firing of any particular individual, but without success; and all hopes of bringing the offenders to punishment would seem to be at an end.

In conclusion, we, the undersigned, have only to add, that whilst we lament, as we do most

Massacre at Dartmoor Prison.

deeply, the unfortunate transaction which has been the subject of this inquiry, we find ourselves totally unable to suggest any steps to be taken as to those parts of it which seem most to call for redress and punishment.

CHARLES KING,
FRS. SEYMOUR LARPENT.

Lord Castlereagh to Messrs. Clay and Gallatin.

FOREIGN OFFICE, *May* 22, 1815.

GENTLEMEN: I lost no time in laying before the Prince Regent the report made by Mr. Larpent and Mr. King, respectively appointed on the part of His Majesty's Government and that of the United States of America, to inquire into the circumstances of the late unfortunate occurrence at Dartmoor prison.

His Royal Highness has commanded me to express, through you, to the Government of America, how deeply he laments the consequences of this unhappy affair.

If any thing can tend to relieve the distress which His Royal Highness feels on this occasion, it is the consideration that the conduct of the soldiers was not actuated by any spirit of animosity against the prisoners, and that the inactivity of the officers may be attributed rather to the inexperience of militia forces, than to any want of zeal or inclination to afford that liberal protection which is ever due to prisoners of war.

But His Royal Highness has observed, at the same time, with sincere regret, that although the firing of the troops upon the prisoners may have been justified at the commencement, by the turbulent conduct of the latter, yet, that as the extent of the calamity must be ascribed to a want of steadiness in the troops, and of exertion in the officers, calling for the most severe animadversion, His Royal Highness has been pleased to direct the commander-in-chief to address to the commanding officer of the Somerset militia his disapprobation of the conduct of the troops, which, it is trusted, will make a due impression on the minds of the officers and men who were engaged in this unfortunate transaction.

As an additional proof of the sentiments which animate the Prince Regent on this occasion, I am further commanded to express His Royal Highness's desire to make a compensation to the widows and families of the sufferers; and I have to request that you, gentlemen, would make this known to your Government, inviting them, at the same time, to co-operate with His Majesty's Chargé des Affaires in the United States in investigating the respective claims, for the purpose of fulfilling His Royal Highness's benevolent intentions upon this painful occasion.

I request that you will accept the assurance of the distinguished consideration with which I have the honor to be, &c.

CASTLEREAGH.

To H. CLAY, and A. GALLATIN, Esqs.
American Commissioners.

Copy of a letter from Messrs. Clay and Gallatin to Lord Castlereagh.

HANOVER STREET, HANOVER SQUARE,
May 24, 1815.

MY LORD: We have the honor to acknowledge the receipt of your Lordship's official note of the 22d instant. Having, as we have already informed your Lordship, no powers on the subject to which it refers, we will lose no time in transmitting it to our Government. We will also place in the possession of the American Minister near His Britannic Majesty's Government (whose arrival here we daily expect) a copy of your Lordship's note, together with a statement of what had previously passed respecting the unfortunate event at Dartmoor.

We have the opportunity of tendering, &c.

H. CLAY,
ALBERT GALLATIN.

The Rt. Hon. VISCOUNT CASTLEREAGH.

Extract of a letter from Mr. Adams to the Secretary of State, dated

JUNE 23, 1815.

He (Lord Castlereagh) then mentioned the late occurrence at Dartmoor prison, and the measures which had been taken, by agreement, between him and Messrs. Clay and Gallatin on that occasion. I said I had received a copy of the report made by Mr. King and Mr. Larpent, after their examination into the transaction, and of the written depositions that had been taken, as well on that examination as previously, at the coroner's inquest; that, after what had been done, I considered the procedure as so far terminated that I was not aware of any further steps to be taken by me until I should receive the instructions of my Government on the case. From the general impression made on my mind from the evidence that I had perused, I regretted that a regular trial of Captain Shortland had not been ordered, and I thought it probable that such would be the opinion of my Government. He said that undoubtedly there were cases in which a trial was the best remedy to be resorted to, but there were others in which it was the worst; that a trial, the result of which would be an acquittal, would place the whole affair in a more unpleasant situation than it would be without it; that the evidence was extremely contradictory; that it had been found impossible to trace to any individual the most unjustifiable part of the firing; and that Captain Shortland denied having given the order to fire. I admitted that the evidence was contradictory, but said that from the impression of the whole mass of it upon me, I could not doubt either that Captain Shortland gave the order to fire, or that, under the circumstances of the case, it was unnecessary. It was true, the result of a trial might be an acquittal; but as it was the regular remedy for a case of this description, the substitution of any other was susceptible of strong objections, and left the officer apparently justified, when I could not but consider his conduct as altogether unjustifiable.

Massacre at Dartmoor Prison.

Mr. Baker, His Britannic Majesty's Chargé des Affaires, to the Secretary of State,

PHILADELPHIA, *Aug.* 3, 1815.

SIR: In a communication made by Viscount Castlereagh, His Majesty's principal Secretary of State for Foreign Affairs, to Messrs. Clay and Gallatin, on the 20th of last May, relative to the unfortunate occurrence at Dartmoor prison, his Lordship expressed to those gentlemen, by the command of His Royal Highness the Prince Regent, how deeply His Royal Highness lamented the consequences of that unhappy affair, and that, if anything could have alleviated the distress which His Royal Highness felt on that occasion, it was the consideration that the conduct of the soldiers was to be attributed rather to the inexperience of a militia force, than to any want of zeal or inclination to afford that liberal protection which is ever due to prisoners of war. His Lordship likewise informed them that, although the firing appeared to have been justified at its commencement, by the turbulent conduct of the prisoners, yet, that as the extent of the calamity was to be ascribed to a want of steadiness in the troops, and of exertion in the officers, calling for the most severe animadversion, His Royal Highness has been pleased to direct the commander-in-chief to address to the commanding officer of the Somerset militia his disapprobation of the conduct of the troops, so that a due impression might be made on the minds of the officers and men engaged in that unfortunate transaction.

As an additional proof of the sentiments which animated the Prince Regent on this painful occasion, his Lordship was also further commanded to express to Messrs. Clay and Gallatin His Royal Highness's desire to make a compensation to the widows and families of the sufferers.

In reiterating these sentiments on the part of His Majesty's Government, for the information of the President of the United States, I have the honor to acquaint you, that I have been directed to concert with the American Government the most efficient means of carrying into execution these benevolent intentions of His Royal Highness the Prince Regent, and shall be ready, with a view of expediting the arrangements to be made, to proceed without delay to Washington, for the purpose of communicating with you personally on the subject, should it suit your convenience to meet me there. I beg leave, at the same time, to suggest, as a necessary preliminary to any measures which may be adopted, that information should be procured from the different States with respect to the families of the sufferers, and any other circumstances which may facilitate the completion of the arrangements alluded to.

I have the honor to be, &c.

———

The Secretary of State to A. St. John Baker, Esq., His Britannic Majesty's Chargé des Affaires.

DEPARTMENT OF STATE,

WASHINGTON, *Dec.* 11, 1815.

SIR: I have had the honor to receive your letter of the 3d of August, communicating a propo-

sition of your Government to make provision for the widows and families of the sufferers in the much-to-be-lamented occurrence at Dartmoor.

It is painful to touch on this unfortunate event, from the deep distress it has caused to the whole American people. This repugnance is increased by the consideration that our Governments, though penetrated with regret, do not agree in sentiment respecting the conduct of the parties engaged in it.

Whilst the President declines accepting the provisions contemplated by His Royal Highness the Prince Regent, he nevertheless does full justice to the motives which dictated it.

I have the honor to be, &c.

JAMES MONROE.

ANTHONY ST. JOHN BAKER, Esq. &c.

———

B.

DEVON, *to wit:*

Informations of witnesses severally taken and acknowledged on behalf of our Sovereign Lord the King, touching the death of John Haywood, at the prison of war at Dartmoor, in the parish of Lidford, in the county of Devon, the eighth day of April, in the fifty-fifth year of the reign of our Sovereign Lord King George III., before Joseph Whiteford, gentleman, one of the coroners of his said Majesty for the said county, on an inquisition then and there taken on view of the body of the said John Haywood, then and there lying dead, as follows:

Thomas Edwards, a private soldier in His Majesty's first regiment of Somerset militia, on his oath, saith: That he is stationed with the said regiment at the barracks at Dartmoor, adjoining the prison of war there; that, on Thursday last, the sixth day of this present month of April, he was on the guard called the West piquet guard, and, at the hour of half-past six in the evening, was fixed as sentinel in what is called the barrack yard, which is situated within the walls of the prison, but the yard allotted to the prisoners is separated from the barrack yard by a stone wall; that about the hour of seven in the evening of same day, he (this informant) was near his post, when he heard a noise, as if some persons on the other side of the wall were attempting to undermine it; whereupon he went to that part of the wall from whence the noise proceeded, and, on looking at the wall, he perceived that the mortar between the stones was moving, at the height of between three and four feet from the ground; whereupon this informant immediately went to the corner of a building which is called the cook-house, and alarmed the sentinel nearest to this informant on the wall, and desired him to order the piquet out; that this informant then returned to the spot where he had seen the mortar moving, and by this time there was a hole made through the wall large enough for this informant to put his musket and bayonet through, and, on looking through the hole in the wall, he saw a great number of the prisoners, he believes to the number of three or four hundred, assembled to-

Massacre at Dartmoor Prison.

gether near the hole in the wall; and he thinks that there were altogether upwards of one thousand assembled nearly around the same place; that this informant spoke to the prisoners through the wall, and ordered them off several times, but many of the prisoners declared that they would not go, and they still continued beating against the wall; and this informant observed that one of the prisoners had an iron bar in his hand, with which he was tearing down the wall, and the prisoners within the prison were at this time hallooing and making a great noise; that the prisoners continued beating against the wall until they had made a hole in it large enough for the largest man in the prison to pass through, when this informant cocked his musket and presented it to the prisoners, threatening to fire at them unless they desisted; when the prisoners abused this informant, asked him why he did not fire, and said he was afraid to do so, and they still continued tearing down the wall of the prison; that shortly after the piquet guard came to this informant's assistance, and then this informant left that part of the wall and went to his post; that Lieutenant White, of the same regiment, commanded the piquet guard, and this informant heard him order the prisoners to go from the wall, but they refused to do so, and still continued tearing down the wall; that some of the men of the piquet guard threatened to fire at the prisoners, but Lieutenant White told them that they should not fire, and remained in the barrack yard with his party, where the hole was; that, about half-past seven o'clock, whilst this informant was at his post, he heard the report of several muskets in the direction of the market place, but did not leave his post; and at this time the prisoners were still beating against the wall on the inside, at several different places, but after many muskets had been discharged they quitted the wall; that this informant remained at his post until he was relieved at half-past eight o'clock, and during this time no musket was fired in the barrack yard; and after this informant was relieved he did not hear the report of any muskets, and the firing had entirely ceased; and this informant further saith, that he was not within the walls of the prison, and did not see any musket discharged, but only heard the report of them.

THOMAS EDWARDS.

Sworn before me,
JOSEPH WHITEFORD, *Coroner.*

Samuel White, a lieutenant in His Majesty's regiment of first Somerset militia, on his oath, saith: That, on Thursday last, the 6th day of the present month, (April,) he (this informant) had the west guard of the prison of war at Dartmoor, and about half past six o'clock in the evening he was in the guard room, when, in consequence of some information he received, he ordered out the guard, and proceeded with it to the barrack yard, which adjoins that part of the prison distinguished by No. 7, and is separated therefrom by a stone wall; that Charles Edwards, now present, was then a sentinel in the barrack yard, and at his post,

and at the distance of about fifteen yards from the post where he was the sentinel, he (this informant) observed a hole in the wall which separated the barrack yard from the prison, large enough for a man of any size to come through; that at this time there were a great number of prisoners within the wall near the hole, and several of them tearing down the wall, and he particularly noticed two of the prisoners with iron bars in their hands, removing the stones from the wall; that this informant spoke to the prisoners repeatedly, and desired them to desist from what they were about, and told them that, unless they did, the whole of the military would be called out, and obliged to commit violence to compel them to desist: but the prisoners still continued tearing down the wall, and repeated volleys of turf and stones were thrown through the opening the prisoners had made in the wall, and over it, at this informant and the guard; and this informant was struck by some of the mortar and stones taken from the wall, and thrown at him by the prisoners, and several of the men complained of having been also struck with the stones thrown; that this informant did not see Captain Shortland, the agent for the prisoners of war, in the barrack yard, after this informant came; that when this informant spoke to the prisoners who were about the wall, they abused this informant and the guard, declared they would not leave the spot, and said *"fire, fire!"* that the prisoners within the walls of the prison were, throughout, in a state of disturbance, and whilst some of them were tearing down the wall, the rest were huzzaing and making a great noise, and at this time it was about the hour in the evening when the prisoners are usually locked up in their different prisons; that he (this informant) had been in the barrack yard about fifteen minutes when he heard the prisoners huzzaing and making a great noise adjoining the yard where the market is held, which is the principal entrance to the prison, and at the same time he heard the alarm bell ring, and the drum beat to arms, and immediately after he heard the report of a single musket, which proceeded as in a direction from the prison gates leading into the market place, and this informant then proceeded towards the market place, to ascertain by whose orders the firing had commenced, leaving the piquet guard under the care of the sergeants; and in his way to the market place he heard several other muskets discharged in the same direction as the former, whereupon he immediately returned to his guard, without going to the market place, and still found the prisoners tearing down the wall between the prison and the barrack yard, endeavoring to widen the breach; that the prisoners continued tearing down the wall, when some muskets were fired from the walls by the sentinels towards the place where the breach was; whereupon the number of prisoners near the breach lessened considerably, many running towards their respective prisons, and others towards the principal gate; that some of the prisoners attempted to force their way through the breach, when he (this informant) or-

Massacre at Dartmoor Prison.

dered the guard to charge, and warned the prisoners against the consequences that would follow; that this informant was at this time at the breach in the wall, and part of his body was through, to see what was passing within the walls, and he then observed that the principal rush of the prisoners was towards the main gate, leading to the market place; and just at this moment he (this informant) heard a volley of musketry discharged in the market place, and immediately after the prisoners began to retreat; and shortly after, this informant saw the guard, and the rest of the soldiers who were not on guard, pass on the inside of the prison wall, opposite the breach, and they were drawn up in front of the prison No. 7, and Major Jolliff was persuading the prisoners to go to their prisons, but many of them remained at the prison door, abusing the military; that after a considerable effort on the part of the guard, the prisoners were driven into No. 7 prison, and the door locked; that at the time this informant heard the volley of musketry in the market place, or immediately after, there were several muskets fired from the different platforms where the sentinels were placed, but the firing ceased instantly after the soldiers entered the prison yard; that this informant remained with the guard until half-past eight o'clock at night, when everything was reported to be quiet, when, by order of the field officer, the guard was returned to the guard-room; that there was not a musket discharged in the barrack yard, and he (this informant) saw no person killed or wounded; that when this informant saw the prisoners rush towards the gates, they were in a very riotous, disorderly state, and they appeared to this informant as if determined to force their passage through the gateway; that the soldiers on guard are directed to refrain from any communication with the prisoners, to prevent the prisoners from getting over the iron railing within the walls of the prison, and likewise to prevent the prisoners from tearing down or undermining the walls; that in case the prisoners do not desist from such practices when spoken to, the guard is to be alarmed, but the sentinels are ordered not to fire unless in cases of absolute necessity, or where a prisoner or prisoners is or are in the act of escaping from the prison; that on the 4th day of April instant this informant was also on the guard, and the prisoners were then very disorderly, and refused to obey the commands, insomuch that the guards were turned out, the alarm-bell rung, and the drums beat to arms; and at this time, which was about seven o'clock in the evening, the prisoners had forced the gates of the prison, and had the possession of the whole of the market place, and their demand was then for bread instead of biscuit, which this informant understood had been offered them instead of bread, there being much biscuit in store; but on the 6th day of April instant he did not hear the prisoners assign any cause for their conduct. And this informant further saith, that on the 7th day of April instant he attended Admiral Sir Josias Rowley and Captain Schornberg to the walls of the prison, and heard the Admiral speak to the prisoners from the platform at the main gates, opposite the prison No. 7, and requested to know their grievances, and why the breaches had been made in the wall, and the gates forced; when one of the prisoners, whom this informant understood to be one of the committee, said, in reply to the Admiral, that there was no cause of complaint, and that the breach made in the wall was to get a ball which had been thrown over the wall by some of the boys; that the prisoner said that the chain at the gates was not sufficiently strong, and the press at the gates was so strong, that the gates were forced open, and one or two hundred rushed out, but that there was no intention to escape; that when this informant saw the prisoners breaking down the wall on the 6th day of April, instant, the persons employed about it were all men, and they were all the time abusing the military; and during the time this informant was in the barrack yard, no person asked for a ball, or said a ball had been thrown over the wall.

SAM. WHITE,
Lieut. 1st Somerset reg't militia.

Sworn before me,
Jos. WHITEFORD, *Coroner.*

John Mitchell, one of the clerks in the office of Thomas George Shortland, Esq., the agent for prisoners of war at Dartmoor, in the parish of Lidford, in the county of Devon, on his oath, saith: That, on Thursday, the sixth day of April instant, about a quarter before seven in the evening, he (this informant) was in his own room, the duty of the day having been finished, except receiving the evening report, when one of the turnkeys, called Richard Arnold, came to this informant's room, and, in consequence of information which he gave, this informant walked towards the south guard, accompanied by Mr. John Bennett, store clerk at the prison, and observed the officer of the guard on the platform; and this informant went on the platform, and saw a great number of prisoners between the iron railing within the walls of the prison and the wall of the military way, which is a place where the prisoners are not permitted to go, and the prisoners were throwing peat and other light articles; that this informant then went to the guard room, where there was a report that a breach had been made by the prisoners in the hospital wall, where he immediately went, but saw no appearance of breach there. That he then returned to the lodge, and, finding that the west guard were not at their post, he went to the north guard and requested the sergeant to assemble his guard, and they followed this informant to the station of the west guard; that this informant then went to the front of the principal entrance to the prison, and saw Captain Shortland in the front of the prison, and the gate of the prison nearest to the hospital was open, and the prisoners were coming through the gates of the prison, towards the upper gates, in a body, at a quick pace, making a great noise, and using the word "keeno," which this informant has frequently heard the prisoners use when they were bent on anything; that Captain Shortland ad

Massacre at Dartmoor Prison.

vanced towards the prisoners, calling on the guard to follow, form, and be steady, and directed them to keep possession of the market square; that this informant followed Captain Shortland, keeping between him and the military, and this informant heard Captain Shortland desire the prisoners to return quietly to their prisons, for fear of any unpleasant consequences, and he repeatedly urged the prisoners to return to their prison, but they still continued advancing, speaking in a riotous manner, and making a great noise; and at this moment he (this informant) also saw the surgeon, Dr. Magrath, speaking to the prisoners, and he heard him persuade the prisoners to return; that, at this time, he (this informant) observed a large body of prisoners assembled at the other gate, or the opposite side of the market place, and proceeded towards this gate with an intention of observing their conduct minutely, but, on hearing a noise on his left, he turned round and observed the prisoners were much further up the square, more numerous, and part of the guards had charged their bayonets towards the prisoners to force them down, and almost at the same moment he (this informant) heard the report of a musket discharged, and the sound came from where the guard were charged to force the prisoners down, but this informant did not see any person fall; that he (this informant) ran and got in the rear of the military, and almost instantly a discharge of musketry took place from the guards who were forcing the prisoners down, and shortly after he heard various discharges of musketry from different parts of the prison; that he (this informant) did not hear any person give orders to fire; that several muskets were fired in the market square, but what number he cannot say, and, immediately after the firing had ceased, he heard Captain Shortland call for turnkeys to take up the wounded; that this informant made his way through the military with some of the turnkeys, and the first person he saw was a black man lying on the ground, on his face, apparently dead; and there was another man wounded in the square, and sitting in the sentry box, but this informant did not notice any other; that there was then an outcry from the military for the key of the gate which leads to Nos. 5 and 7 prisons, and this informant went and procured a turnkey, who brought the key and opened the gate; and, after some of the military has passed in, this informant went inside the gate, and there saw a white man lying on the ground, also apparently dead; and at this time this informant heard the report of several single muskets, at different parts of the prison, apparently as if from the walls, and, considering it unsafe, he retired behind the military, and went again to the lodge, where he remained until there was a call for turnkeys to shut up the prison, when he procured the necessary turnkeys and sent them down, and then went towards the military himself, and, at Captain Shortland's request, went to ascertain the number of prisoners who had been sent up, and afterwards, by order of Captain Shortland, went to the surgery ward of the hospital to receive the wounded and ascer-

tain their number, and whilst there he received thirty-four prisoners, who were wounded, and one dead man was also brought to the hospital by mistake; that this informant remained there until he was sent for by Captain Shortland to report the number; that, at the time the first musket was fired, he thinks that there were about five hundred prisoners in the market square, and the foremost of them were behaving in a very riotous and disorderly manner, quite disrespectful to Captain Shortland, and without appearing to pay the least attention to what Captain Shortland or Dr. Magrath were saying, and though requested to retire they continued to advance, and seemed to this informant as if determined to force their way to the upper gates, which were then opened to permit the bread-wagon to go out; that, since the 26th day of March last, there has been much dissatisfaction among the prisoners in the prison towards Mr. Beasley, the American agent, whom the prisoners understood was appointed to send them home; and, on the 4th day of April instant, about seven o'clock in the evening, the prisoners got open the gates leading to the market square, and came up and occupied the square until about ten o'clock, when they retired to their respective prisons; that this informant went to the gates and spoke to some of the prisoners, and also went inside amongst them, and asked what they came up for, when they replied it was because they had had no bread that day; that the transport board had permitted the contractor to issue biscuit, of which he had a store, for his contract, and it was arranged by Captain Shortland that they were to have it only one day in a week, and the prisoners had been offered their rations of biscuit, which was one pound of biscuit instead of one pound and a half of soft bread, but they had refused to accept it throughout the day, but remained quiet till the evening; that, on the 5th day of April instant, soft bread had been issued to the prisoners as usual, and Captain Shortland had, on the 5th, communicated to the committee for the prisoners that he did not intend to issue any biscuit without further directions from the board; that this informant did not observe anything thrown by the prisoners at the military on the evening of the 6th, and did not see the prisoners armed with any offensive weapons; that if the prisoners had forced their way to the upper gate of the market square, there would have been no obstacle to their getting out of the prison, as all the gates were open; that about a quarter of an hour previous to this informant seeing the prisoners coming in a body through the gate, the usual horn, the signal for their retiring to their respective prisons, had been blown, and continued to blow nearly the whole of the time.

JOHN MITCHELL.

Sworn before me,
  Jos. Whiteford, *Coroner.*

Richard Arnold, one of the turnkeys of the prison of war at Dartmoor, on his oath, saith: That on the 6th day of April instant he (this informant) was stationed at the lower gate in the market square, adjoining to the wall of the military hospital; that just before seven o'clock in the evening this informant went on the platform in the front of the gates of the prison leading into the market square, when he saw a great number of prisoners between the iron railing and the military wall which separates the military way from the prison, and went and reported the circumstance to Mr. Mitchell, and from thence went to Mr. Holmden, the clerk of the agent at the prison, and then this informant returned towards the lodge, and there met Mr. Holmden with a guard, and he went into the prison with them to turn the prisoners from between the railing and the wall, and this informant went to the lower gate again; that, just as this informant got to the gate, he heard a sentinel call from the barrack yard to a sentinel on the platform near the market square, that the prisoners were breaking a hole through the barrack wall, and desiring him to call the guard; that this informant immediately went to the west guard and called them, and when the guard was turned out Captain Shortland came through the lodge, and went with the guard to the barrack yard, and this informant went there also, after having called the north and south guard to be in readiness if they were wanted; that on coming into the barrack yard he observed a hole in the wall on the south side of the cook room, large enough for a man to creep through, and he saw a great number of prisoners through the hole in the wall, who were abusing the soldiers and the captain; that this informant then returned to the market square, leaving Captain Shortland in the barrack yard, and the horn was then sounding for the prisoners to turn into their respective prisons, when he observed a large body of prisoners collected between the iron railing in the front of the prisons, and they were attempting to force the gates, which were locked and secured by an iron chain, and were very riotous; that this informant went away to call the guard, and met Captain Shortland at the upper gate; that the guard was outside by the guard house, drawn out, and Captain Shortland called to them to follow him, and this informant returned with him, and by this time the prisoners had forced the gate, and many hundreds had assembled in the market square; that Captain Shortland desired the soldiers to draw up, be steady, and keep their ground, and the soldiers formed just across the square; that this informant saw Captain Shortland go up in front of the military, and heard him desire the prisoners to go in, or otherwise he should be obliged to use means which he should be very sorry for; that the prisoners were very riotous, calling out "keeno, keeno," several times, and advanced instead of retiring, when some of the soldiers came to a charge, and this informant made the best of his way to get in their rear, and just after he got in the rear he heard a single musket, and soon after he heard several muskets discharged, but the muskets were at first elevated so high that he does not think a single shot touched either of the prisoners, and then he observed that many of the

prisoners had got a great way in the yard, when some of them called out "Fire, you buggers, you have no shot in your pieces or guns;" when the military fired again, and this informant heard a cry amongst the prisoners, and almost immediately he heard Captain Shortland call for the turnkeys to help the wounded away; that this informant saw one man dead in the gateway of prison No. 7, and saw several men carried towards the hospital wounded, but he does not know any of them; that this informant did not hear any person give orders to fire; that he was near to Captain Shortland when the firing first began, and, if Captain Shortland had given any orders to fire, he thinks he must have heard them; that between the first discharge and the second the prisoners had retreated from the market square towards the prison, but had made a stand when the second firing commenced; that he did not see the prisoners armed with any offensive weapons, nor did he see them throw any stones at the military; that the same evening, after the prisoners were locked up, he went into the prison yard, and saw several places in the wall where the stones had been taken out, but there was only one hole entirely through the wall.

RICHARD ARNOLD.

Sworn before me,
  JOSEPH WHITEFORD, *Coroner.*

Stephen Hall, one of the turnkeys at the prison of war at Dartmoor, on his oath, saith: That on the 6th day of April instant, about a quarter before seven o'clock in the evening, he went into the market square, and went to the lower gate, when he saw some of the prisoners come over in a body from the wall which separates the barrack yard from the prison, and they came to the gate next to the hospital, and forced the gate open, and went up towards the market square; that this informant was close by Captain Shortland in the square, and heard the captain desire them to go back, but they said they would not; that there were some soldiers at this time formed in the market square, and when the prisoners refused to retire they came to a charge, and then this informant went to the rear, when he heard a single musket fire; and at this time he had not heard any person give orders to fire, nor did he hear any such orders given afterwards; that after the musket was fired he went towards the lodge, and heard several muskets fired, and shortly after he heard the captain call for the turnkeys to bring up the wounded, when this informant went down and assisted in taking up two wounded men, one of them in the market square and the other in the prison, and he also picked up one man dead in the market square, but he does not know the man; that when this informant saw the prisoners coming across the yard towards the gate, they were behaving in a very riotous manner, and this informant observed that they had some iron bars, and he thinks that three of the men had an iron bar each; that he did not see either of the men attempt to strike with them, and he did not see either of the prisoners throw anything towards

Massacre at Dartmoor Prison.

the military; that this informant heard the alarm bell ring just before he saw the prisoners come across the prison and force the gate; that after they had forced the gate this informant persuaded the prisoners to go back, but they refused to do so; that they made no complaints whatever in this informant's hearing; that on the 7th day of April instant, he was at the lower gate, when he heard some persons who were walking between the railing, and they were talking about a black man that was killed; and this informant heard the prisoners say, if the black man had not been killed he would have killed Captain Shortland, and that he had a knife in his pocket prepared to stab him; that there was no person present with this informant at the time he heard this conversation, and he does not know the prisoners who were talking together.

STEPHEN HALL.

Sworn before me,
JOSEPH WHITEFORD, *Coroner.*

Richard Cephus, an American prisoner of war, on his oath, saith: That he hath this day seen the bodies of several men lying dead at the dead-house in the hospital at Dartmoor, and amongst them he saw the body of John Haywood, a black man; that John Haywood was in prison No. 4, with this informant, and on Thursday last, about half past five in the evening, he went to the privy adjoining to prison No. 4, and had not been there above a few minutes when he heard a firing of musketry as from the market square and the ramparts around the prison; that at first there was a single musket which he heard the report of, and immediately after several volleys were fired; that about six o'clock he came out of the privy and then saw John Haywood going down to go out of the prison, and asked him where he was going; he said he was going out to see what the firing was about, and parted from this informant; that this informant went back to the privy, and about ten minutes after he heard that Haywood was dead, but did not see him till this day; that this informant was not out in the prison yard from four o'clock in the afternoon of the 6th day of April instant until the following day about half past eight in the morning.

RICHARD CEPHUS, his X mark.

Sworn before me,
JOSEPH WHITEFORD, *Coroner.*

George Magrath, surgeon at the hospital at the prison of war at Dartmoor, on his oath, saith: That, on the 6th day of April instant, about ten minutes before seven o'clock in the evening, whilst sitting in his own house, he heard the alarm bell ring on the outside of the prison, and immediately ran out, and, on arriving at that part of the military way which fronts the market square, he saw a line of soldiers drawn up on the outside of the square fronting the outer gate; that, on looking into the square, he observed a considerable body of the prisoners advancing up the square, and, having understood that the prisoners were breaking out, this informant, with as much haste as he could, advanced towards them;

as soon as this informant got amongst them, he began to exhort them to return quietly into the prison, and told them that he feared any attempt of that kind (meaning an attempt to escape) would be attended with serious consequences; that many of the prisoners told this informant that they were kept an unnecessary length of time in prison after they considered themselves as free, or some words to that effect; that this informant observed to them that their detention appeared to be entirely the fault of their own agent, Mr. Beasley; and several of those whom this informant had addressed, appearing to be sensible of the truth of what this informant had advanced, went back and retired towards the gate leading into the prison from the market square; that this informant continued to address himself to others, and, whilst expostulating with them, this informant saw the soldiers march down the square and form in a line fronting the prisoners, about the middle of the square, and, during this time, greater numbers of the prisoners were pressing up through the gate; and whilst this informant was still using language to those whom he addressed, calculated to induce them to return into prison, he heard a voice (but whose it was this informant did not know) ordering the soldiers to charge; that, at this time, Captain Shortland was near to this informant, and he appeared to be employing the same means as he (this informant) was to induce the prisoners to return to the prison; that, on hearing the word "charge" given, he looked round, (for his back was then to the soldiers, and his face towards the prison,) and found himself on the point of the soldiers' bayonets, who were close to him; that he (this informant) was driven a considerable way, at the point of the bayonet, with the prisoners, when he found it necessary to make some attempt to extricate himself, and succeeded in getting round the left wing, which rested on the wall which separates the market square from the hospital, and, whilst this informant was endeavoring to get round, the firing commenced; at first he heard two or three muskets, but afterwards the discharges became more frequent, and almost amounted to a volley; that as soon as this informant had extricated himself, being apprehensive that his assistance might be required, in consequence of the firing, he went to make preparation for the purpose; that this informant went to his own house and carried some instruments to the receiving room of the hospital, where he awaited the arrival of some wounded men, but he did not see any of those who were killed on the spot until this morning; that this informant has this day examined the body of a black man, stated to be called John Haywood, and found that the ball had entered a little posterior to the acremien of the left shoulder; passing obliquely upwards, it made its egress about the middle of the right side of the neck, and, in the judgment of this informant, he died of that wound, which appeared to have been inflicted by a musket ball; that this informant, at the time the order was given to charge, was in warm conversation with the prisoners, and, therefore, cannot take upon himself to say who gave the order, but this informant heard no person give an order to fire; that there was a great deal of confusion among the prisoners, and, therefore, he cannot speak to the general conduct of the prisoners; but those to whom this informant spoke appeared disposed to listen to him, and many receded towards the gate amongst those with whom this informant had been conversing; that the number of the prisoners that were assembled in the market square he cannot say, or even form an estimate, but there was a considerable crowd together, and, during the time this informant was in conversation with the men, they were pressing forward in a body; that, as the whole of this informant's attention was engrossed with a few to whom this informant addressed himself, he cannot take upon himself to give any opinion as to the necessity of coercion; but this informant is of opinion that the prisoners ought not to have been in that situation at so late an hour in the evening; that there was a great clamor of voice, and a general murmur among the prisoners, but this informant did not observe them proceed to any acts of violence before he came away; that, after he came away, and in going to his own house, and from thence to the hospital, he heard the discharge of musketry; and this informant's attention was not attracted to it above two or three minutes, but whether it continued beyond that time he cannot say.

GEORGE MAGRATH.

Sworn before me,
JOSEPH WHITEFORD, *Coroner.*

John Odiorne, a citizen of the United States of America, on his oath, saith: That he has been at the prison of war at Dartmoor ever since the 29th day of September last: that, on Thursday last, the 6th day of April instant, a little after six o'clock in the evening, he was at the store in market square, standing by the door, and the wagon with the bread for the prisoners was partly unladen, when this informant heard some person talking loud at the gate at the upper end, and went around the wagon to see who it was, and saw Captain Shortland advancing into the yard, and he was giving his orders to the turnkeys at the lodge in a loud voice; and Richard Arnold spoke to him, and told him something about the wall, when Captain Shortland said, "Damn you, why did not you tell me about it before? ring the bell; call the guards out:" that the guard immediately followed Captain Shortland into the yard, when he ordered them to form across the yard, about two-thirds of the way down; that there were not soldiers enough to stretch across the yard, and they formed with their right on the southern wall, leaving some distance between their left and the northern wall: that Captain Shortland used some harsh expressions to the guard, and bade them form on the northern wall, for that was the place where the prisoners were coming; and just as Captain Shortland gave the orders, this inform-ant saw the prisoners force the gate No. 1, which

adjoins the hospital wall; and before this time this informant had not seen a single prisoner in the market square, except those who were employed with him: that there could not have been a body of men in the square without the informant's seeing them, as at this time he was on the steps, at the store, which is about ten feet high, and commands a complete view of the square; that, after the prisoners had advanced to the distance of between twenty-five and thirty feet, Captain Shortland then ordered the men to charge upon them, and the soldiers charged upon the prisoners, when they retreated into the yard, leaving one man behind, who appeared to this inform-ant to have fallen down, and a soldier was standing over him with a bayonet, threatening to stab him if he did not get up; and the man on the ground appeared to be drunk, but this informant could not hear what he said; that, after the prisoners had retreated within the prison, this inform-ant saw an officer put his hand to the gate which opened against the hospital wall, as this inform-ant thought to shut the gate; but instead of shutting it he retreated to the soldiers, at a little distance from the gate, when he heard an order given to fire by Captain Shortland, as the informant supposed, for he was looking directly at him; that the order was not instantly complied with as soon as a musket might have been fired; but in a few seconds a musket was fired by a person at the right of Captain Shortland, a few paces in advance of the others, and immediately after two muskets were fired to the left of Captain Short-land, by the hospital wall, after that there was a general discharge; and immediately after the general discharge a party of soldiers marched to No. 1 yard, through the gate, and fired a volley, and then wheeled about and returned into the square; and after the soldiers had returned into the square, and formed into a line, the officer ordered them to fire, and immediately the whole line across the square fired into the yard; after which the line broke up and advanced into the yard, and this informant could not see any further, but he heard the report of guns in the yard; that, soon after, this informant saw a prisoner coming out of the yard, bringing a prisoner on his back, and a corporal or sergeant spoke to the man, abused him, called him a coward, and said, "this comes of your keeno:" that this informant spoke to the sergeant or corporal, and abused him for having spoken so to the wounded man; but by the advice of Mr. John Arnold he went into the store, and remained there all night: that, about forty minutes, or forty-five, before he saw Captain Shortland, he was in No. 7 prison yard, and he did not perceive there was anything the matter; there was a great crowd round the gambling tables, as usual, but he was not near the place where this informant has seen the holes mended in the wall: that he saw a small hole in the wall the day before, about six or seven inches in depth, and, on inquiring what it was done for, some person said it was done to make quoits with: that this informant never heard that the hole was made for boys to go out and fetch their balls. And this informant further saith that he did not see Dr. Magrath in the square addressing the prisoners, nor did he see him either go in or out.

JOHN ODIORNE.

Sworn before me,
    Jos. Whitford, *Coroner.*

Addison Holmes, a citizen of the United States of America, on his oath, saith: That on Thursday, the 6th day of this present month of April, between the hours of five and six o'clock in the evening, he was at the lower part of the yard of the prison No. 3, and, understanding that a hole had been broken through the wall in the prison No. 7, by the boys, to get at their balls, he was going to see it; and hearing the alarm-bell rung, he went into the market square, having found the gate open, and there were about a dozen prisoners in the square, and a great many more followed after him; he was going up to see what the alarm-bell was rung for, when he saw the troops entering the outer gate of the square, and Captain Shortland was with them: that, as the troops came through the gate, they were paraded across the square; and this informant saw Dr. Magrath at the left of the troops, talking to about a dozen of the prisoners, advising them to go down to the prison quietly; and some of them turned and went towards the gate, but others were talking with him still: that at this time there was a considerable body of prisoners in the rear: that Captain Shortland was in front of the troops, and about the middle of them, speaking to one man, who wanted to say something to him; but it appeared that the captain would have no conversation with him, and pushed him from him twice, when the man turned about and was going down slowly: that the captain then turned round and ordered the troops to charge their bayonets, twice; but they did not do so until they were ordered by one of their own officers, and then the troops charged their bayonets and the prisoners were forced on before them, and Dr. Magrath, being in front, stepped in between two bayonets, and got to the rear: that this informant stepped aside, and got between two sentry boxes, and the troops passed him; and by this time the prisoners were forced to the gate, had got inside the prison, and shut the gate after them; but Captain Shortland, who was in front of the troops, shoved the gate open, and this informant, thinking it was a good opportunity for him to get in, pushed on between two men, and then saw that Captain Shortland had hold of a musket, and immediately that musket was discharged; but whether Captain Shortland pulled the trigger or not, this informant does not know; and immediately after, there was firing at the left: that Captain Shortland had ordered the troops to fire before he took hold of the musket, but he was not obeyed, and then took hold of the musket, and he believes the soldier had hold of it at the same time: that just after the firing at the left, as he (this informant) was passing between two men, one of whom had discharged his

musket, this man was hauling his musket back to stab this informant, and before he drew it past this informant, he (this informant) unshipped the bayonet and threw it on the ground, and then pushed off the bayonet on the left with his arm, and got in round the gate, when the soldiers immediately fired another round, and he saw a man fall: that this informant stopped a few minutes, and the soldiers fired several rounds, and this informant went round the prison No. 1, to the prison No. 3, and the soldiers were firing from the walls up the prison: that this informant got into the prison No. 3, when two rounds were fired into the prison door, which killed one man and wounded another; but who it was that was killed he does not know: that directly after this the prison doors were shut, and he heard no more of it: that he cannot say what was doing in the yard of prison No. 7, as he was not there; but the prisoners in the yard of prison No. 3 were walking the yard quietly, it being just before the time of turning in when he heard the alarm-bell.

ADDISON HOLMES.

Sworn before me,
    Jos. Whitford, *Coroner.*

John Arnold, steward of the prisoners in health at the prison of war at Dartmoor, on his oath, saith: That on Thursday, the 6th day of April instant, about seven o'clock in the evening, he was at the door of the contractor's store in the market square, receiving bread from a wagon into the store, and John Odiorne, an American prisoner, was with him, when suddenly he heard a great noise at the bottom of the square, and some persons were saying that the prisoners were pulling down the barrack wall, and the soldiers were running through the military way, as this informant supposed, to get their arms; and almost immediately after the alarm-bell was rung, and the drums beat to arms, and the horns sounded; that, soon after, this informant saw a great body of prisoners between the railing and the market square, and some prisoners were in the market square; that just about this time, he (this informant) saw Dr. Magrath and Mr. McFarlane, the surgeons, go down the market square, and, just after, Captain Shortland also came into the market square, and the soldiers marched in with their officers; that this informant ordered the wagon away, not thinking it safe to let it remain, as the prisoners were at this time very riotous; and just as this informant had ordered the wagon away, the prisoners burst open the gate next the hospital and rushed in the market square, in a very large body, and at this time the outer gates were all open to permit the wagon to pass; and this informant believed, at the time, that the prisoners, taking advantage of the circumstance, were endeavoring to effect their escape; that the soldiers were formed across the square, and the prisoners had advanced in a body, in a riotous manner, calling out "keeno," close to the soldiers, within musket length, or thereabout, when the soldiers immediately charged upon the prisoners, but this informant did not hear any order to

Massacre at Dartmoor Prison.

charge given, and this informant thinks that, from the noise made by the prisoners, it was impossible to hear any word of command; that the soldiers drove the prisoners at the point of their bayonets within the gates of the prison, whereupon the prisoners turned their faces towards the soldiers, still continuing assembled together in a large body, and began to throw stones at the soldiers, and, from the appearance of the size of the stones, he (this informant) has no doubt but that some of them were five or six pounds in weight; that the prisoners threw a great number of stones, and continued doing so for about two minutes, when this informant saw one of the muskets from the soldiers discharged towards the prison yard, and within a minute afterwards he saw the whole party fire their muskets, and it appeared to this informant that the muskets were elevated above the prisoners; that there was a large body of the prisoners assembled in the three yards in front of the gate, and stones were throwing in all directions towards the military, when this informant saw the soldiers fire their muskets towards the prisoners; and, about this time, he saw Dr. Magrath and Mr. McFarlane run up the market square, and soon after he saw a man brought up wounded; that this informant was standing on the steps of the store all the time before alluded to, and could distinctly see what was passing, except when the soldiers were involved in the smoke; that Odiorne and six or seven American prisoners were standing on the steps of the store, and they all saw the prisoners throwing stones at the soldiers; and this informant remarked to them, that, if the prisoners continued to assault the soldiers so, some of them would be shot; that this informant never heard Captain Shortland give any directions to the soldiers to fire, and he was so near to Odiorne that if orders had been given which he might have heard, he (this informant) must have heard also, as he has as quick an ear as most people; and this informant further saith, that the firing was very irregular, and it did not seem like firing in obedience to orders; and this informant further saith, that it appeared to him the soldiers were in danger from the stones thrown at them by the prisoners.

JOHN ARNOLD.

Sworn before me,
    Jos. Whiteford, *Coroner.*

William Gifford, a private soldier in His Majesty's first regiment of Somerset militia, on his oath, saith: That on Thursday, the 6th day of this present month of April, about half-past six o'clock in the evening, he (this informant) was posted as sentinel in the market place, at the gate adjoining the hospital wall; that about half an hour after this informant had been posted, he heard the prisoners huzzaing in the yard of prison No. 7, and soon after the west guard, to which this informant belonged, was called for; that this informant then saw a prisoner come from No. 7 yard, with an iron bar in his hand, and a great number of prisoners were following him, and the prisoner who had the bar broke the

lock of the gate, where this informant was sentinel, with it, and the prisoners rushed out as fast as they could come, crying out "keeno;" whereupon the alarm-bell was rung, and part of the north guard came into the market square, and Captain Shortland was with them; that the soldiers formed on the left side, where the crowd of prisoners was forcing up, there not being enough to form across the yard; that Captain Shortland spoke to the prisoners and ordered them back, but they did not go, and at this time they were so close to the military that they could be touched by the bayonet; that Captain Shortland ordered the soldiers to charge, which they did, and forced the prisoners almost to the prison gate, but they would not go into the prison yard, and stood fast at the gate; that the prisoners then began to throw stones at the soldiers, and this informant saw several of the men's caps knocked off with the stones; that the prisoners were very riotous, huzzaing and throwing a great number of stones or bricks at the soldiers, when this informant heard the word "fire" given by some person, but whom he does not know; that this informant immediately heard a discharge of musketry, and saw that the muskets were presented in the air; that the prisoners still continued huzzaing and throwing stones at the military, when the soldiers began to fire towards the prisoners, and this informant afterwards saw two men, like prisoners, lying in the market place apparently dead, one on the right side of the guard, and the other on the left; that the soldiers then went into the different prison yards to turn the prisoners in, and this informant heard some firing in the yards; that Major Jolliff had the command of the first Somerset regiment of militia, but he was not present when the first firing commenced; and this informant further saith, that the stones thrown at the soldiers were large enough to have killed some of them, and the stones were thrown so thick that it appeared to this informant the soldiers were in great danger; that this informant did not discharge his musket at all; that this informant was near to Captain Shortland when the prisoners were forced to the prison gate, and he never saw Captain Shortland with a musket in his hand, or attempt to take a musket; if he had, he (this informant) thinks that it was impossible for him not to have seen it; that he never heard Captain Shortland give any orders to fire, and this informant was so near to him that he thinks he must have heard him if he had given any such orders; that whilst the prisoners were huzzaing, many continued calling out "murder the rascal," by which this informant understood they meant Captain Shortland—and this was before any firing took place; and this informant further saith, that he did not hear or see a musket discharged on the evening of the 6th day of April instant before the prisoners began to throw stones.

WM. GIFFORD, his X mark.

Sworn before me,
    Jos. Whiteford, *Coroner.*

James Groves, a private soldier in the first regiment of Somerset militia, on his oath, saith: That he was placed as sentinel in the barrack yard at Dartmoor prison, on the 6th day of April instant, and was relieved by Thomas Edwards at half-past six o'clock in the evening; that about five o'clock in the evening a ball was thrown over the wall close by the old cook room, which is now the armorer's shop, and the armorer was there at the door at the time, and he caught up the ball and threw it over the wall into the prison again; that this informant saw no other ball whilst he was on sentry, and no person whatever called to this informant to throw over any ball; that just at the time the armorer was about to throw the ball over, some person from the prison called out "throw the ball over," but after the ball was thrown over, this informant heard no further call; that whilst this informant remained on sentry, he did not hear any attack upon the wall, and saw no breach whatever therein.

JAMES GROVES, his X mark.

Sworn before me,
    Jos. WHITEFORD, *Coroner.*

David Spencer Warren, a citizen of the United States of America, on his oath, saith: That on Thursday last, the 6th day of April instant, in the evening, about half an hour before the usual time of turning in the prisoners, he heard the alarm-bell, and went up to the gate of the yard of the prison No. 1, and when he arrived there he saw a number of prisoners in the market square, and a number of soldiers were in the square, and Captain Shortland was at the head of one party of them, and he was forming a line across the yard, which after he had done, he told them to charge; that the soldiers did charge on the prisoners, who ran back into the prison yard, and Captain Shortland and the soldiers followed them to the gate, and as the prisoners got inside the gate they flung one of them to; that Captain Shortland ordered one of the soldiers to fire, and immediately there was a soldier with his musket turned to the right, and Captain Shortland caught hold of the musket and pointed it towards a man that stood by the gate, and said "God damn you, fire;" that directly after this a fire of musketry became general; that this informant went through No. 1 prison and into No. 3, and was in prison No. 3 when the soldiers fired into the prison No. 3; and there was a man called Smith, a shipmate of this informant, wounded, and he also saw a man fall on the inside of the prison, but whether he was killed or wounded this informant cannot say; that this informant did not see any of the officers with the soldiers when Captain Shortland gave the order to fire; that after the firing began he saw some stones, he believes two or three, thrown by the prisoners over the wall into the square—he saw one of them about as big as his fist; that this informant did not observe whether the muskets were elevated at the first firing, but he did not see any man fall, and therefore he remarked to some of the prisoners that he thought

14th Con. 1st Sess.—49

they were blank cartridges; that this informant was not in the yard of No. 7.

DAVID S. WARREN.

Sworn before me,
    Jos. WHITEFORD, *Coroner.*

James Greenlaw, a citizen of the United States of America, on his oath, saith: That on Thursday, the 6th day of April instant, he was in No. 3 yard, near the door of the prison, when he heard the alarm bell ring; that he went from thence towards the railing, at the entrance into the market square, and saw some prisoners in the market square, and at the same time he saw the troops coming through the market gate, with Captain Shortland at their head, and saw him form the men in one line extending across the square, and he then ordered them to charge; whereupon the prisoners retreated into the prison yard, when this informant heard Captain Shortland give orders for the soldiers to fire upon the prisoners; and thereupon this informant ran into No. 4 yard for shelter, and as this informant turned to go back again he saw two black men, whom he did not know, fall; that as soon as this informant thought the firing had ceased, he ran up towards the grating to speak to Captain Shortland, and asked if he would allow him to speak to him, when Captain Shortland said "No, you damned rascal!" whereupon two soldier officers put their swords through the iron railing towards this informant, and one soldier pricked him with his bayonet; that this informant then retreated into No. 3 yard, and he then heard two distinct volleys, and the soldiers shortly afterwards came into No. 3 yard, when he retreated into No. 3 prison, and sat down inside to assist in dressing a wounded man, and a moment after this he heard two distinct volleys fired into the prison, which killed one man and severely wounded another; that this informant did not see any stones thrown from the prison into the square until the firing had commenced, and then he saw two stones thrown over the wall from No. 4 prison; that this informant was not in No. 7 prison yard.

JAMES GREENLAW.

Sworn before me,
    Jos. WHITEFORD, *Coroner.*

Thomas Burgess Mott, a citizen of the United States of America, on his oath, saith: That on the 6th day of April instant, this informant was in prison No. 5, when some persons came to him, as being one of the committee for the prisoners, and, in consequence of the information they gave, he procured some assistance, and was going out of the door of the prison to go towards a wall which he understood some men and boys were breaking, to prevent it; and just as he came to the door of the prison he heard a fire of musketry, as from the gateway of the market square, and met a crowd of prisoners retiring to their prisons, apparently in great confusion; when most of the people had passed, he met a man between No. 5 and No. 6 prisons, who was wounded and bleeding very much, and the man leaned on this informant, and he was proceeding towards the gateway to take him to the surgeon, but the fire of musketry and balls came so thick that he stepped forward a step or two to request permission to take the wounded man away, but he believes he was not heard; that he then turned to the back of No. 5 cook house, out of the way of the fire, where several others were standing, and they had not opened a fire from the ramparts of the lower wall which commanded the lower door of No. 5 prison; but as this informant and the others turned from the place to go into the prison, a fire of musketry was discharged towards the only door which was open of No. 5 prison, and shortly after this informant saw two men in the prison dead, but he does not know their names himself, or where they were killed, and he saw also several others wounded.

            THOS. B. MOTT.

Sworn before me,
     Jos. WHITEFORD, *Coroner.*

Enoch Burnham, a citizen of the United States on his oath, saith: That on Thursday, the 6th day of April instant, about half-past six o'clock in the evening, he went to the railing of the market place, and remained there about half an hour, when he saw a crowd of the prisoners making a noise, but the principal part of them were youngsters, full of mischief, and they came, some of them, between the two railings, and he saw seven or eight go into the market square, but there was no great body there; that at this time he saw some soldiers come down the square, and Captain Shortland with them, and the soldiers charged upon the prisoners, who retreated into No. 1 prison yard, without making any resistance; that this informant remained at the gate when the military began to fire, and at this time there was no crowd of prisoners within the gate—there might have been forty or fifty men; that when the firing commenced he retreated into the prison yard, and lay down by the wall, and the prisoners who were about the gate also retreated; that this informant lay by the wall about five or seven minutes, when this informant went up by the barrack wall, towards where there was a hole, and the soldiers then began to fire from the ramparts of the south wall, when he went to No. 7 prison, and got as far as the steps, when a heavy firing again commenced from the wall, and this informant lay down, to save his life, for about four or five minutes, and then got into the prison, and was going through to go to his own prison, and had got to the steps, when the firing commenced from the platform next to the south corner; whereupon he retreated into No. 7 again, and went into the north end, and saw one prisoner in the yard who appeared to be wounded, and he ran back against the wall, and he saw several soldiers raise their muskets and fire at him, and he fell immediately, but this informant does not know who the man was; that this informant saw the wounded man lift up his hands towards the soldiers before they fired; that this informant did not see any stones thrown, but he heard some of the youngsters

speak about throwing stones; that he did not hear the word to fire given, and he was near the gratings; when the military first began to fire they were at some distance from the gratings.

            ENOCH BURNHAM.

Sworn before me,
     Jos. WHITEFORD, *Coroner.*

Robert Holmden, first clerk to Captain Shortland at the prison of war at Dartmoor, on his oath, saith: That on Thursday, the 6th day of April instant, Richard Arnold, the turnkey, reported to this informant that the prisoners had got over the iron railing, near the south guard; whereupon he (this informant) went to an officer on the ramparts, and from him understood that a guard was going in to turn them out, and, on returning to the entrance gate, he met the guard going down; that there was also a rumor that a hole had been broken in the hospital wall; whereupon he went and reported it to Captain Shortland, who came out of the house, and went with this informant to the entrance gate, when they understood the hole was in the barrack wall, and Captain Shortland, with Sergeant Manning and some soldiers, went to the barrack yard, and found that a hole large enough for a person to creep through had been made; that Captain Shortland cautioned some prisoners who were looking through the aperture in the wall, and recommended them to retire, but they remained there; and a guard was left at the breach, and Captain Shortland and this informant returned to the entrance gate, and had not been there long when it was reported to Captain Shortland that the prisoners had forced one of the lower iron gates; whereupon Captain Shortland ordered the alarm-bell to be rung; and as soon as the guards could be collected, he went with them into the market square; and at this time he (this informant) saw a great number of prisoners coming up the north side of the yard in a riotous and disorderly state; that after a short time had elapsed, he (this informant) heard one shot fired, which was followed by several others; that he did not go down among the prisoners, or see what took place there.

            ROBERT HOLMDEN.

Sworn before me,
     Jos. WHITEFORD, *Coroner.*

Homer Hull, a citizen of the United States of America, on his oath, saith: That he is in the prison No. 3; that on the 6th day of April instant, he (this informant) was walking in the lower part of the prison yard No. 7, about six o'clock in the evening, when, in consequence of a report he heard in the prison, he observed some drunken men breaking down the wall which separates the barrack yard from No. 7 yard; and one of the soldiers called from the wall at the corner of the barrack yard, and said, "Go in, men; they are going to charge upon you." That this informant went away towards the prison No. 3, and had to go out of No. 7 yard, near the market square, when he saw some drunken men, about half a dozen in number, at the gate leading

Massacre at Dartmoor Prison.

into the market square, attempting to force it; one of them had a small iron bolt in his hand, and they succeeded in getting the gate open; that the man who forced the gate went a few yards into the square before any followed him, and then some others went in; that just at the time the gate was forced open, he saw some soldiers come into the market square at the upper gate, and Captain Shortland was with them; and at this time this informant thinks there were about sixty men in the square; that the soldiers marched about two-thirds of the way down, when Captain Shortland gave the soldiers orders to charge, and the soldiers accordingly charged, when the prisoners retreated into the prisons, and one of them shut to the gates; and the soldiers marched down a little further, when Captain Shortland ordered them to fire; that this informant went to his own prison, and tried to get in, but the crowd was so great that he could not succeed; that he tried at other prisons, but could not get in, and *there succeeded;*[*] that the alarm bell had not been rung when the soldier first ordered them to go into their prisons; that this informant heard the alarm-bell ring just after the man ordered them to go into their prisons; that he did not see any stones thrown before the musketry began to be discharged, but afterwards he saw a stone thrown from the prison yard towards the square.

HOMER HULL.

Sworn before me,
Jos. WHITEFORD, *Coroner.*

Robert McFarlane, assistant surgeon at the prison of war at Dartmoor, on his oath, saith: That on Thursday, the 6th day of this present month of April, about seven o'clock in the evening, or rather afterwards, he was at the outer gate of the prison, when he heard the alarm-bell ring, and immediately went to the lodge, and seeing the guard drawn up in line in front of the guard house, he observed Captain Shortland walking by himself from the barrack yard towards the guard; that this informant turned round and looked down the market yard, and saw a multitude of prisoners proceeding up the square; whereupon he went down with Dr. Magrath, who came just at this moment, and began to reason with a number of prisoners there on the unnecessary steps they were taking; that some of them seemed to pay attention to what this informant said, and turned aside towards the prison, but others said they were not prisoners of war, and that they were determined to be out—one of whom had a stick behind his back, in his hand; that this informant saw Captain Shortland reasoning with a number of them to go back into the prisons, but they used very abusive language towards him, and this was in front of the guard; that this informant had taken two by the shoulders, and was insisting upon their going back; and, on looking back, the guard had charged, and this informant with great difficulty got himself extricated from between the bayonets; that by the

* So in the original.

time this informant got to the rear of the guard a single musket was fired, and immediately after several others; that this informant heard no order given to fire; that Captain Shortland was at the south end of the guard, and this informant thinks if he had given orders to fire he must have heard it; that at the time the first musket was fired, nearly one-third of the market square was filled with the prisoners, making a great noise in a very riotous and disorderly manner, and stones were throwing by the prisoners from all quarters, and one large stone fell about a yard from this informant; that immediately after the firing commenced, and this informant had got to the rear, he went away to the hospital; that from the number and size of the stones which were thrown, if he (this informant) had been obliged to remain on the spot where the soldiers were, he should have apprehended great danger to his person.

ROB. McFARLANE.

Sworn before me,
Jos. WHITEFORD, *Coroner.*

John Tozer, one of the turnkeys at the prison, on his oath, saith: That on Thursday, the 6th day of April instant, about seven o'clock in the evening, the turnkeys were called into the market square, and he found that it was to take up some dead and wounded prisoners; that he went to the lower market gate, and just inside the gate he took up a black man dead, and assisted in carrying him to the bathing place in the hospital; that the man appeared to be about thirty; but this informant should not know him again.

JOHN TOZER.

Sworn before me,
Jos. WHITEFORD, *Coroner.*

Joseph Manning, sergeant in the first Somerset regiment of militia, on his oath, saith: That on Thursday, the 6th day of this present month of April, about seven o'clock in the evening, he was in the military way when he saw Captain Shortland, and reported to him that the prisoners had made a hole in the wall leading to the barracks, and he went with this informant, an officer, and some other persons, to see it; that this informant kept before Captain Shortland, and went away to the breach first, and saw the prisoners pulling the wall, and he desired them to desist, but they gave him abusive language, and he then took a musket and threatened to fire at them if they would not leave off, and they then drew back a little; that Lieutenant Avelyn interfered, and put his head in the breach, telling them if they did not desist the consequences would be serious; Captain Shortland then inquired for Major Jolliff, and, by Captain Shortland's directions, this informant went to call Major Jolliff, and met him between the south guard and the barracks, when he ordered the troops to be formed, and put himself at the head of the grenadiers, and before Major Jolliff had gone ten yards from the south guard gate the firing commenced; that this informant, by Major Jolliff's orders, remained behind, to assist in form-

Massacre at Dartmoor Prison.

ing the regiment; that it was impossible for Major Jolliff to give orders to fire, as he was not near the spot where the firing first began.

JOS. MANNING,
Sergeant 1st Somerset regiment.

Sworn before me,
Jos. WHITEFORD, *Coroner.*

Examination at the Guildhall of Plymouth, on Friday, the 21st of April, 1815.

Present, John Hawker, Esq., one of the magistrates of the county of Devon.

John Rust, one of the committee of the American prisoners at Dartmoor, being sworn, says: The report made of the occurrence of the 6th instant, signed by me, was from the evidence of other persons. About six o'clock in the evening I came from the place where I was taking supper, and persuaded the prisoners to leave the breach; they did go away towards the square previous to the commencement of the firing. At the time I went to the breach the horn had not sounded; it sounded but a few minutes before the firing. I heard the alarm-bell ring before the firing took place; the firing continued at intervals about fifteen minutes. After the firing commenced, I went round the southeast part of prison No. 7, and went in at the southeast door. I saw nothing of the firing in the market square.

John T. Trowbridge, one of the committee, being sworn, says: I made no part of the report from my own knowledge, but I was one of them employed in taking depositions. I was walking about the southeast part of No. 7, near the breach in the wall, which, when I saw it, was about large enough for my body to pass through; about thirty persons were round it; did not know what it was made for; understood it was to get a ball. I remained in the prison yard, seeing the soldiers collect on the platforms. I saw nothing of what was passing in the square. I understood that the soldiers desired the prisoners to go in before the firing took place; the prisoners were not riotous. I heard the alarm-bell ring and the drum beat to arms before the firing; I heard no tumult in the market square before it began; I should have heard it, had there been any, from the place I was in. I do not believe there were many prisoners in the square; it was the alarm-bell which collected the prisoners, at least it made them go out of prisons Nos. 5 and 7. The firing lasted, in a straggling manner, from fifteen to twenty minutes; there were three or four volleys from the market square. I heard no order to fire after the firing from the square; there was firing from the platforms on the wall, from which it continued while the prisoners were endeavoring to get into their prisons; there was firing at No. 5 while they were entering.

James Boggs, one of the committee, being sworn, says: I made no part of the report from my own knowledge. I went into the northeast door of No. 3 before the firing. I understood that there was a man killed in that prison, but I did not state it from my own knowledge.

Amos Wheeler, sergeant of the north guard, being sworn, says: I was with the guard on the evening of the 6th; another sergeant was with me; assembled the guard by order, I believe, of Captain Shortland's clerk; had orders to march to the west guard house. On arriving, was ordered by the clerk to order arms; remained about ten minutes, and was then ordered by Captain Shortland to march to the market square; the officer of the guard was not then with it; our force was thirty-eight, besides two corporals; about five or six of another guard went into the square about the same time; the west guard was employed at the breach; there were not many prisoners in the market square when our guard entered. The alarm-bell had rung before we marched. When we entered, the prisoners were endeavoring to burst the gates below; cannot say whether the alarm-bell preceded the bursting of the gates; when they had succeeded in bursting them, there was a great rush towards the soldiers; their number kept increasing, until the space between the iron railings was quite full. They threw stones at the soldiers before there was any firing; they were not armed with anything that I saw; they appeared in the square nearly at the same time as my guard; they made the greatest push towards our left flank, where the guard was weakest; I was on the left flank; the prisoners were desired to go back, but they did not; they pressed on, and made a greater resistance against us. Then Captain Shortland ordered the soldiers to bring their muskets down to the charge, but, not advancing upon the prisoners, it appeared to have no effect upon them. I believe Captain Shortland was in front of the guard at this time, desiring the prisoners *to go* back. I saw none of the prisoners wresting the arms from the soldiers; I saw none of them attempt to seize the arms. The guard pressed to the left, to keep from being turned, by which I was thrown in the rear. Many more soldiers came from different parts before the firing commenced; I heard no order to fire, nor do I know how it began; did not hear any of the prisoners challenging the soldiers to fire; at this time there might be about two hundred prisoners in the square; they were much more numerous than the guard. I did not see the officer of the guard at this time. The firing was in an independent manner, three or four muskets being discharged at a time. After the firing commenced, the prisoners began to retire towards their prisons. I did not hear any cheering among them, or see them rally after the fire; think I must have heard it, had there been any cheering. I do not think that the prisoners could have been made to retire without firing; the soldiers might, by killing them with the bayonet, have dispersed them. I did not go into the prison yard. I did not hear of any firing of my guard after the prisoners had retreated.

John Saunders, private in the first regiment of Somerset militia, one of the north guard, being sworn, says: I was with the first party of soldiers that marched into the market square; at that time the gate was broken open; the prisoners were coming through in a crowd as fast as they possibly could; the alarm-bell rung at the time we reached the west guard house; the officer of the guard was with us, I believe; I believe it was he who ordered us into the square. The west guard was marched in nearly about the same time; fifteen file were told off on the left, whom Captain Shortland, after some time of discourse with the prisoners to make them retire, ordered to charge; with some difficulty we got the prisoners back to the gates; some of them were retiring through the gates. I do not know that any injury was done to them until after they were inside the gates; had, till this, heard no firing. The square was nearly clear of prisoners before the firing; they did not return into the square, but threw some stones through the rails. I heard the word "fire" given, but do not know by whom. There were no prisoners in the market square when the first shots were fired. The prisoners had the command of the gates, so as to open them when they thought proper. I fired my musket. The prisoners closed the gates after them, which we opened, and we received orders from the commanding officer to charge the men to their prisons. No muskets were fired in compelling them to their prisons. Just before the firing, the prisoners were throwing stones, and insulting the soldiers, calling out to them to fire. Saw no prisoners attempting to wrest the arms from the soldiers. Several shots were fired into prison No. 3; they were fired into the doorway; they were fired by two or three soldiers. I heard no order given for this fire, and had heard none to cease firing; there was much disturbance among the prisoners going in, and a stone was thrown out, which I saw myself. The turnkey was then near the soldiers, close to the door, and was endeavoring to shut it; the prisoners were willing to go in, and the turnkey could not close it; they stood at the door, challenging the soldiers, and offering to fight them if they would lay down their pieces; this was before the firing into the door; it was locked up immediately after the fire; do not think I could say rightly who the soldiers were that fired into the prison.

William Smith, private of the first Somerset militia, being sworn, says: I was on the north guard on the evening of the 6th of April. I marched into the market square with the guard. As we were going into the square, the prisoners were coming through the gates in a violent manner; the alarm-bell rang before we entered the square, while we were at the west guard house. I was one of the fifteen file ordered to charge; the prisoners fell back when we came down to the charge, but, after a little while, advanced again. The prisoners fell back to the gates, and had partly gone through before the firing began; I heard no order to fire; do not know the soldier who fired the first musket; was not near him; the prisoners had not come back upon our left when the firing began, and after the charge, but they were throwing stones, (one of which fell about a yard from me,) and were abusing the

soldiers, daring them to come on. The firing was in an independent manner, one after another, till nearly all the guard had fired, and then they loaded again; no order was given to fire; do not know of any soldier having fired into any of the prisons; do not know how long the firing lasted. After the prisoners had returned into their yards, we went into them, to see if there were any stragglers about. When I went into the yard, did not hear any firing from sentinels on the walls.

John Tutt, private, being sworn, says: I was on the north guard the night of the disturbance; the alarm-bell rang when I was at the west guard house, before I entered the market square; about forty or fifty prisoners had burst into the square, through the gate next the hospital, when we marched in. I was one of the fifteen file ordered to charge; cannot say exactly who ordered us to charge, but think it was Captain Shortland's voice. The prisoners were so close to me that I had not room to come down to the charge, and drove them back to get room. We advanced upon them at the charge. While charging, a stone, of seven or eight pounds weight, knocked off my cap, I stooped to pick it up; was not knocked down, but somewhat stunned, and the plate of my cap was bruised; the firing began directly; the prisoners resisted greatly while we were charging; they resisted up to the time we fired. I think there were about one hundred prisoners in the square when the firing began; after they were driven back, there was much firing into the prisons; saw one soldier firing into prison No. 1; the prisoners were throwing out stones at the time; they were all nearly in when the firing into No. 1 took place, but some were still pushing in at the doorway; the turnkey was endeavoring to get near the door, but was not in front, in consequence of the stones thrown out; I heard no order for the firing in the square; it commenced while I was picking up my cap; saw no more than one shot fired into No. 1.

William Rowles, private, one of the north guard, being sworn, says: I was one of the fifteen file told off in order to charge. Captain Shortland gave the order to charge. I could come down to the charge, and did so; and those near me advanced at the charge upon the prisoners, who would not retire at first, even when the point of the bayonet touched their clothes. We advanced on them about eight or ten yards down towards the gate. A great many of them retired through the gate before there was any firing; they aggravated the soldiers by insulting and abusive language, and dared them to fire. I heard an order to fire, but do not know from whom. When the firing began, the prisoners were rushing again through the gate, into the square, and throwing stones over the platform. I suppose there were twenty times more prisoners in the market square than soldiers before the firing. I entered the prison yard, saw a soldier level his musket into prison No. 3, who was then about five or six yards from the door; many prisoners stood at the door in a resolute manner, and would not let the turnkey shut it; the doorway was as full it could as hold; they threw out great stones, as big as my head. I heard no order to the soldier to fire into No. 3; saw no officer there at this time. I was telling the prisoners to go into the prison, when one of them endeavored to wrest the bayonet from my musket, but I drew it back in time to save it; this was before the firing into the doorway. I believe that there was no more than one shot fired into No. 3; after it was fired, the prisoners went back, and allowed the turnkey to shut the door.

John Hamlet, private, one of the north guard, being sworn, says: I was the right hand man of fifteen file told off to charge; I heard the order given to charge by Captain Shortland; I immediately came down to the charge, having room enough; we advanced a short distance; we could not advance far, owing to the prisoners being so near; they did not retire very fast; cannot exactly say how many prisoners there were in the square when we began to charge, but suppose there might be a hundred; we used all possible means to make them retire, but some were so obstinate that they advanced even to the points of the bayonets; others, however, retreated; they were very abusive, and throwing stones; many dared us to fire. I was struck with a stone in advancing, on my right knee, which nearly knocked me down, and I very narrowly escaped another blow on my head. I received the blow after the firing commenced; our charge with the bayonet made some few of them retire through the gates; the greater part, indeed, retired through the gates, and remained on the other side throwing stones. Before the firing, and after the charge, some returned back through the gates, and advanced; some advanced even after the first fire; they shouted and cheered while advancing, which was intended to animate others to persevere like themselves; numbers of the first muskets fired were elevated in the air, some were elevated to the centre, I did not see any one fall on the first fire; the firing was not in volleys. I followed into the prison yards; did not see any firing into the prisons; after the firing had been kept up for some considerable time, the prisoners retreated. I heard an order to fire given before any firing took place, but do not know by whom. I do not think the prisoners could have been driven back without firing, unless great slaughter had been made of them by the bayonet. I cannot positively assert whether there was any firing on our right besides that by ourselves.

John Williams, sergeant, being sworn, says: I was on the south guard the night of the disturbance; our guard entered the market square after the north guard, and formed to its right; our number was about forty; it consisted of fifty-one, but had several sentries out. The firing had not commenced when we formed upon the north guard; it began about ten minutes or a quarter of an hour after we had formed; we were formed just about the time the north guard charged; when we formed, there were about one hundred prisoners in the square. I think they were more

numerous than the soldiers; the line of soldiers almost occupied the breadth of the square, but there were not enough to form it completely across; there was an opening between our guard and the north; the prisoners did not fall back for some considerable time after the charge; they were throwing stones through and over the rails, and abusing the soldiers, when the firing began; I heard no order to fire; our officers never ordered us to fire; our guard, seeing the state the prisoners were in, and the north guard fire, began firing of their own accord, but not in volleys, and then the reports made prevented us hearing what was going on; the north guard fired first; at the first fire the prisoners ran back through the gateway, but afterwards many returned again to the gate, but did not advance through on us; heard cheering, and did not know whether they would not come out on us. I did not go into the prison yard, nor did any of our guard; our officer kept us in line till the prisoners were all locked up. I do not suppose the prisoners would have gone back without firing, because they did not appear to retire even when the bayonets were quite close to them. I heard the firing for some minutes after the prisoners had retired through the gate.

John Tewfort Jolliff, major commanding, being sworn, handed in a statement, of which the following is a copy:

APRIL 7, 1815.

Yesterday evening, between the hours of six and seven o'clock, soon after the officers' dinner, the mess waiter came into the mess room, and said that the American prisoners had broken out of the prison, and were attempting their escape. I immediately ordered the troops composing the garrison to fall in at the alarm-post. Whilst the troops were forming I heard several shots fired, upon which I immediately took the grenadiers, and proceeded to the west guard, supposing that the prisoners were actually coming down the military way (as it is called) in great bodies. Upon my arrival at the west guard, several of the troops were formed in the market place, and had fired some shots. I immediately called out to them to cease firing; and finding that the prisoners still refused to go into their prisons, I took a party of grenadiers, and went into two of the prison yards, and told the prisoners to go into their prisons, which they very reluctantly did. Several stones were thrown at the military, and two at myself, one of which came very near me. The military fired a few shots at the prisoners in the yard, in consequence of their throwing stones and refusing to go into the prison, but the firing was without my orders, and I conceive took place owing to the military being so exasperated. As soon as the prisoners were all gone into their different prisons, and properly secured, I returned to the barracks, having ordered the guards to be reinforced, and the troops to be ready to fall in at a moment's notice. It appears that they had selected the hour of the officers' dinner to begin their operations, supposing we should not be ready.

J. T. JOLLIFF,
Major 1st Somerset militia.

Understanding that evidence has been produced to prove that a bugle sounded the signal to fire, I beg leave to observe, that I was first apprized of this circumstance after my return from Dartmoor. I never gave, as commanding officer, any order, directly or indirectly, to that effect, nor did I hear previously any report that such a circumstance had taken place.

J. T. JOLLIFF,
Major 1st Somerset militia.

He further says: There was no general order that when the soldiers on sentry heard one of them fire, they should consider it an order to fire also; but I suppose they might so consider it. One man fired into one of the prisons, which arose, as I believe, from exasperation, on being struck by a stone thrown by of the prisoners. I did not see any one put his musket into the door to fire. Several shots were fired in the prison yards, but entirely without any command.

George Pitt, sergeant, being sworn, says: I was with Major Jolliff among the grenadiers in the prison yard, and he used all the means in his power to prevent the firing. I heard him crying out to the men to cease firing.

Henry Burgoyne, private, being sworn, says: I was on the platform at the bottom of the market square. A prisoner came with an iron bar, who, upon hearing a shout from the prisoners at the breach, when a piece fell out of the wall, which I heard, broke the gate open immediately, by striking off the lock, and the prisoners rushed through; and when we left the platform they pressed very much upon us; they were as thick as they could be; the alarm bell was ringing about this time; the yard where the break was, was as full of prisoners as it could be. I belonged to the west guard. I did not see any prisoners wresting the arms from the guard. I could not see the breach on account of a projection of the wall, but heard the bar at work; they were quite thick down to the prison, waiting, I suppose, till the breach was made; the horn had sounded as usual for them to go in, but, instead of going in as they usually did very quietly, they came out; they pressed on us so much that we were forced to fall back; after we came to the charge they would not retire, and, being unwilling to stab, we were forced to give back. I heard an order to fire, but do not know who gave it. I did not observe how the first muskets were levelled.

Edward Jackson, private of the Derby militia, being sworn, says: I was on the platform 18 and 19, between prisons Nos. 5 and 6. I think there had been two volleys in the market square before the men on this platform fired; myself and another sentry were posted on the platform; we had not fired before some soldiers came up on the platform; I never fired; it was the men who came up; I cannot say whether the sentry fired; they fired into the yard up towards the gate; there were a great many prisoners at the upper part of the yard; I did not see any firing into the prisons. There was one or two officers on the platform; no order was given to fire on my platform;

to the best of my recollection, I think I heard a command "to commence firing from the right." The prisoners were all in a great body, near the gates at the top of the yard, when the firing commenced, and, after the firing, they retreated to their prisons. When I was placed sentinel, several prisoners were inside the palisades clodding one another; some soldiers charged them out of it; there were two rounds of firing from my platform; there were about twenty soldiers on it, but cannot say exactly; it was full of them; I could not see the breach; I saw no tumult in the yard before the firing in the square, except the clodding; I cannot say I heard the alarm bell ring.

Adjourned till to-morrow.

———

Examination at Dartmoor prison of war, on Saturday, the 22d April, 1815.

Present, Paul Treby Treby, Esq., one of the magistrates for the county of Devon.

Thomas Burgess Mott, one of the committee of American prisoners, sworn: (A letter had been handed in by Captain Shortland, signed in this witness's hand, and addressed to Captain Shortland, requesting his release, and stating that "although he had been called on by the respectable part of the prisoners to inquire into the cause of the late unfortunate affair, neither his depositions nor conduct appeared to shew that he would wish to lay the blame to Captain Shortland, but on the contrary, for which he had since been insulted by those men that were and had been the occasion of the late unfortunate affair.") There never has been, to my knowledge, any concerted plan among the American prisoners at this prison to break out. I have never been insulted by any of the men supposed to be ringleaders in the late affair, but, on the contrary, the prisoners think I was doing everything in my power for their benefit. The letter handed in by Captain Shortland was written for me by another prisoner, to get me clear in any way; it was not signed by me; I told him I would give him a pound if he got me released; it was written without design to injure anybody, and merely to get me clear, as my term of release was not near; I never read the letter; I was one of the committee who made the report to Mr. Beasley; some part of it was from my own knowledge, and some part of it from the testimony of others. I saw a crowd where the hole was, but did not think it was occasioned by anything but gambling, till I was called upon by the prisoners to go and make them desist from the hole. When I was in the yard of Nos. 5 and 7, and when the firing into it from the platform took place, there was no tumult; there were then but few persons in it; I was not in the market square; I think the making of the hole was merely through mischief, but not at all to get out, for I do not think twenty would have wanted to go out if the gates had been open; I do not know particularly of any subject of complaint shortly before the affair; I do not know of any one who complained before Admiral Rowley of the American Government; I was present the whole time; I do not know of any particular uneasiness among the prisoners at present, or any cause of complaint of their treatment; they are a little impatient to be sent home; there has been frequent little vexatious interruptions to the market, &c., on slight grounds; I did not see any one shot, though some fell close by me; I did not hear the horn sound before the firing.

Walter Colton, one of the committee, being sworn, says: None of the report was made from my own knowledge, but entirely from examinations. I am confident there was no disposition on the part of the prisoners to break out; had there been, I should certainly have known it, because I was in the constant habit of going through the prisons, having much business with the prisoners as one of their committee. It is impossible but it must have been known had there been any. Had the gates been thrown open, not more than a hundred would have gone out: those who chose could have got away on the 4th. The first I heard of the disturbance was the firing; I was then in No. 3; did not hear the horn; it is not generally heard inside; there was great irritation against Captain Shortland before the disturbance; this was owing to acts of barbarity on his part. I speak from my own knowledge. Instead of doing things to make them comfortable, he did quite the contrary. He has kept two prisons, the best and most comfortable, shut, when it was in his power to have opened them; the prisoners remonstrated against this, but it produced no effect, while they were turned into prisons open at top, and floating with water two or three inches deep; this was No. 2. There was a plan formed in No. 6, one of the best and most commodious prisons, two several times, to dig out, which was both times discovered by Captain Shortland, and on the second occasion the prisoners were turned into No. 2; they were, however, only kept there two nights, and then returned to No. 6; I call this an act of barbarity. Captain Shortland never returned any answer to our application to go into the empty prisons; I know of no statement of complaint against the American Government, previous to the late affair; there have been often complaints of neglect against Mr. Beasley, but not against the American Government. Another act of Captain Shortland was: about the time of the attempt to dig out, there were some bars broken in one of the prisons, in consequence of which, and the digging out, I suppose, one-third of our provisions was stopped for ten days. I know not what it was for, unless for this and the digging out. Captain Shortland frequently stopped our provisions in the same way, without giving any reason. There has been no particular uneasiness among the prisoners to get out, since the account of the ratification of the treaty, and I know of no acts of violence among them in consequence; they were only anxious to be sent home, and expressed their opinions about it.

William Hobart, one of the committee, being sworn, says: Some part of the report was made from my own knowledge, but not much; I was in the lower part of the yard Nos. 1 and 3 when the alarm-bell rang; I had not heard the horn sound to go in when the alarm-bell rang; I expect I should have heard it; it can *generally* be heard all over the yard; when I heard the bell I walked up to the railing next the market square to see what occasioned the alarm; when I got within a few yards of the railing, saw the soldiers coming into the market square. I think there must have been four or five hundred soldiers in the square before the firing began; there were many there, and others marching in and forming; I heard no orders to fire; the prisoners were coming up, as I was, to see what was the matter; I returned immediately to my own prison. There were two volleys fired into a prison, into No. 3; most of the prisoners were retreating after the first volley; I had been in about five minutes before the firing; was on the second floor; did not see the soldiers who fired, but heard the report; and when I came down, saw marks of balls within; there were no stones thrown from the second floor; should have known it, as I was *walking* with some others. There were *several lines* of soldiers drawn across the square; a *few prisoners* were at the bottom of it then, but they were not so numerous as the soldiers; I am fully confident there was no intention to break out. I heard no shouting or threats against Captain Shortland when the firing commenced. The prisoners did not cheer in the yard I was in, nor in the market square, while I was present. Captain Shortland has behaved in a very tyrannical manner towards the prisoners; he stopped the market for ten days for a very trivial occurrence, and part of the provisions for the same length of time; do not think there was any intention among the prisoners to revenge themselves on Captain Shortland; there has been some irritation against Mr. Beasley lately, because they thought he was somewhat dilatory in preparing cartels, but there were none whatever against the American Government; there was a report that vessels of war would come from America to take prisoners, but even when first started it did not gain much credit; the upper stories of Nos. 3 and 4 have been unfit for the men to live in, very open, and sometimes afloat with rain.

William B. Orne, one of the committee, being sworn, says: I saw a little of the affair stated in the report, but the principal part was from the examination of others. I was walking between No. 7 and the barrack wall; did not observe that many prisoners were there; they are always so numerous in the yard, that one might not observe whether there was a crowd or not; I heard no bar breaking the wall; went into my own yard, Nos. 1 and 3; the prisoners were almost all in. I heard the alarm-bell, upon which I walked up to the railings, and saw the soldiers firing on the prisoners; could not tell the number of the soldiers, but the yard appeared to be full; it appeared to me, from the number of muskets I heard, that the whole regiment must have fired several volleys. I went behind the cook house, and heard the balls flying in all directions; the prisoners ran up to the railings from curiosity; was not

Massacre at Dartmoor Prison.

near enough to hear an order to fire; after firing a few volleys, they opened the gates, and charged the prisoners in the yard, and, after they were in their prisons, they fired in; I heard that shots were fired into No. 3—into the door; saw no stones thrown out of No. 3; saw only one stone thrown into the square; the firing appeared to me to last fifteen or twenty minutes. I heard a noise among the prisoners, but no particular shouting or cheering; saw the greater part of the prisoners run; after the first fire, every man secured himself as well as he could; there appeared no interval in the firing; it continued all the while, until the soldiers opened the gates and went into the yard. I knew of no intention whatever among the prisoners to break out; we were then daily expecting cartels.

Niel McKinnon, prisoner, being sworn, says: I was in the yard No. 7 before the alarm-bell rang. I saw some men making a breach in the wall. At first, there were only three or four, but afterwards they increased to about twenty or twenty-five, standing round. I can ascribe this conduct to nothing but mere wantonness; can ascribe it to no other motive. I staid till the hole was made, and they began to throw things at the sentry. I saw the sentry put his bayonet through as a warning; he desired them several times to go away. I belong to another prison. I came to the gate. I heard the alarm-bell ring before I came. I saw a turnkey looking in the direction of the breach, and, expecting that the military would be called out, I went to gate No. 4. I remained there a considerable time, until the troops were drawn up in line; they then charged. I could see into the market square. I saw the prisoners between the railings, and the soldiers in front of No. 4 gate. My attention was engrossed by what was before me, and I did not observe how many there were to my right at No. 1 gate. I heard an order given to charge and fire, but do not know by whom. At this time the prisoners were daring the military, but not expecting they really would hurt them. Cannot say I saw any stones thrown. I saw the first fire, but did not observe the elevation of the muskets. The prisoners retreated after the first fire, but I heard them shouting and rallying—cheering each other—and I think I heard them again dare the soldiers to fire. I heard several say they thought they were blank cartridges; I gave it as my opinion. I went down towards my prison, and was told on the way that Haywood was killed. I went to see, and saw a black man lying within the inner gate of No. 4. I then went up to the gate to speak to Captain Shortland. The turnkey let me through, and I told Captain Shortland that a man was killed, and begged him to make the firing cease, and not to be wasting the lives of the prisoners. He told me to go to my prison. I spoke to the officer apparently commanding the guard to the same purport, who said there should be a truce if the prisoners would go to their prisons. Captain Shortland knew me personally. I was going to No. 1 gate, and saw several persons at the door of the receiving house, with two or three wounded

men. One of these persons was drunk, and abused the soldiers, who did not appear to attend to him so much as they might, had he been sober. I went down to No. 4 yard. While going down the yard, a volley was fired into it by the soldiers in the market square. There were many prisoners then in the yard. I did not see more than one line of military in the square; it was two deep, and extended almost across. Was going up the yard, when I met a party of military with an officer, driving along four or five prisoners. I went up to the officer, (who I understood afterwards was Major Jolliff,) and remonstrated with him on the harsh treatment the prisoners were receiving. He put his fist in my face, and swore "by God, they would not trifled with any longer by us," (the prisoners.) I was then driven with the rest into No. 4, the sergeant having his halbert close to one of the prisoners, and the soldiers their bayonets charged. I entered the prison with my face to the soldiers, until I was so far that I thought I was safe, when I turned my back, and at that moment a musket was fired close to me, which wounded a little boy, who screamed and dropped down; he died the next day. There were no stones thrown out when the shot was fired, nor any insulting language used towards the soldiers. The prisoners were crowding round the door, not being able to get in fast enough, but there was no tumult among them. Heard no order to fire the shot. I heard the report near me. The doors were then locked up. I have not the least belief that there was any concert or intention among the prisoners to break out. I did not know the arms were kept in the barrack yard, nor do I believe it was generally known among the prisoners. I think the breach and the breaking of the gate were only acts of wantonness, like throwing turf at each other. There was a good understanding between the prisoners and the soldiers, particularly the Derby militia; they used to be of assistance to them when the markets were stopped. The Somerset regiment was not up to so much as the Derby. I think the sentries were removed from the yard to prevent communication with the prisoners, not through any fear of them. If there had been any concert, they would have made some preparations; but there did not appear any among them, as the gambling tables were not removed from where they usually were. I have since seen some who broke the wall, who have expressed sorrow for what they had done, from the consequences resulting from it, but declared they had no intention to escape.

Francis Joseph and *Henry Allen*, the two remaining of the committee, knew nothing of their own knowledge, and were, therefore, not examined.

John G. Gatchell, prisoner, being sworn, says: I belong to No. 7 prison. On the 6th of April, between six and seven in the afternoon, while walking in that yard, I heard a report that some boys were making a hole in the wall. Being in the yard abreast of the market square, I saw Captain Shortland coming down the market square at the head of a party of soldiers; they were formed in a line, and began to fire immediately. I did not see any prisoners then in the square; a few were between me and the railings. I could have seen any who might have been in the square. I saw no charge of the bayonet. I heard an order to fire, but do not know by whom; at the first volley one man fell about four yards from me. I went to him, and asked what was the matter; he said he was wounded in the breast, but I did not believe it, thinking it impossible, till I felt it. I called assistance, and was trying to get him to the receiving house, when Captain Shortland entered No. 7 gate with two soldiers, and said something which induced the two others to run away and leave the wounded man with me; upon which, Captain Shortland, seeing I did not run, said, "Kill the damned rascal;" the soldiers charged on me, and a bayonet pierced my clothes and skin, going in about a quarter of an inch. I was then forced to leave the wounded man and run, when a soldier followed me; and Captain Shortland, urging him on, repeated several times "Kill the damned rascal." While running on I was pricked three times, and should have been killed, but, stepping aside, the bayonet ran under my arm; and the soldier, with the force of the thrust, fell on his knees, by which means I escaped into the prison. There are four doors to No. 7 prison; all but one were shut, which one was exposed to the fire; all the prisoners were crowding to one door; the door left open was the one which was usually so; but the doors were shut, I think, sooner than usual, and the prisoners were trying to get in at the shut doors; the prisoners being pursued by the soldiers, all crowded to one door, one over the other, and, being unable to get in fast enough, were wounded by the bayonets of the soldiers pressing behind. While getting in No. 7, I saw Captain Shortland running down the yard towards No. 5 with the soldiers, and heard him order them to fire; am quite sure I heard him order them to fire; he was facing me at the time; was running towards No. 5, and ordering them to fire as they ran, which they did; cannot positively say he had arms in his hands when coming down the yard. I did not see that the soldiers hesitated to fire when ordered; they did fire. Never had any personal altercation or difficulty with Captain Shortland; never spoke to him, nor been spoken to by him. Do not think there was any intention to break out. The firing in the yard was after that in the market square; two soldiers came in the gate abreast of Captain Shortland, but many followed him—thirty or forty, perhaps. After the soldiers were in the yard, those on the ramparts did not fire. There were about forty or fifty shots by those in the yard. While the prisoners were running to No. 7, they were cut off by a cross-fire from the ramparts; (he pointed to the place where he was wounded in the back,) was told by others my wound was a quarter of an inch deep; it swelled up considerably, and was very sore, as was the case with all three wounds; was never under any of the surgeons or surgeons' mates.

Andrew Davis, prisoner, being sworn, says: I belong to No. 3 prison. I was at the bottom of No. 3 yard on the evening of the 6th, just before, counting in time, the horn had sounded. On the first report of muskets, the prisoners said they were blank cartridges. I went up to No. 1 gate. When I got there, five or six men were bringing a man who appeared to be badly wounded into the market square; they had brought him inside the inner gate next the square. I heard Captain Shortland order them to let go the wounded man. One of them remonstrated against it, and Captain Shortland struck him with his fist. The man then went outside of the gate into the passage between the two gates, and said to Captain Shortland, "You'll recollect you have struck me twice, and I'll have satisfaction for it." Captain Shortland told him to go into the prison, or he would order the men to fire on him. I then went down to No. 1 prison, and saw no more. The soldiers were drawn up in the square when the wounded man was there, and Captain Shortland in front of them. It was about ten minutes or a quarter of an hour after the firing began that the above transaction took place. One or two volleys were fired after that.

John Odiorne, prisoner being sworn: (His evidence before the coroner being read to him, said he had no correction to make in it, other than it was possible that there might have been some few prisoners in the square, but there were no numbers of them, previously to the drawing up of the soldiers in the square.) I stood on the steps at the cook-house in the market square. I could see the whole of what was passing in the square. The gate was burst about the same moment the soldiers were firing obliquely to the left, after they were drawn up in line. The prisoners rushed in immediately, but not violently. I heard an order to fire, which was from Captain Shortland, as near as I can judge of any man who had his back to me: it was in Captain Shortland's voice. He was about one hundred feet from me. I am as positive as I can be under such circumstances that the order came from him. Captain Shortland appeared to be in a great passion when entering the square: he looked very red, and spoke loud. I am confident there was no disposition to break out. There was very little interval of time between the marching of the soldiers into the square and the sounding of the horn for turning in; the horn was first; the alarm-bell rang nearly at the same time that the soldiers entered the square. The prisoners generally conceived that there was a tardiness in Mr. Beasley's fitting out ships, and there was discontent among them against him, but no complaint against the American or British Governments.

Gerard Smith, prisoner, being sworn, says: I was in the market square with Captain Odiorne, who requested me to stay, after the horn was sounded, till the wagon was unloaded. I told him my prison would be shut, as the horn had sounded, and I would be shut out, and I thought I had better go. I did stay several minutes longer. Seeing the prisoners nearly all in, I said I must

Massacre at Dartmoor Prison.

go. I saw Arnold coming up the square, and saw also Captain Shortland by himself close to the wagon. The captain asked Arnold whether the prisoners were all in. Arnold said, "Sir, they have got two holes in the wall." Captain said, "Damn you, why did you not let me know that before?—go and ring the bell." I turned from Odiorne, bade him good night, and went down to the gates, which were all closed, and I was obliged to get over the railing. When I got over, I saw no tumult among the prisoners. One man told me that some boys had taken some stones out of the wall, and wondered what it could be for. "I do not know," said I, "but I suppose it is through mischief."

Robert Johnson, prisoner, being sworn, says: I know Gatchell; I was at the gate No. 7 when Capt. Shortland spoke to him; I ran directly up to the gate from No. 5; at the first firing a wounded man lay about five or six yards from the gate, on the prison side; Gatchell and two or three others came up to take him, as I suppose, to the receiving house; when he got into the passage between the railings, Captain Shortland came in with two or three soldiers, and told them to go back, or he would kill them; the soldiers followed; in rushing in, Captain Shortland stumbled over the wounded man; Gatchell did not go away immediately; Captain Shortland ordered the soldiers to charge on him; one did charge on him, and another on me; I then made my escape into the prison; I am quite sure Captain Shortland ordered the soldiers to charge; this was after the firing in the market square. At the first fire I was in my berth; had no idea that there would be any disturbance, or that the military were firing with ball. I heard no abusive language from Captain Shortland.

James N. Bushfield, prisoner, being sworn, says: I was present all the time the breach was being made, but was not one of those who did make it; I had no idea it was for the purpose of making their escape, but supposed it was through mere mischief; there were about twenty or twenty-five prisoners round it; they began in the morning; I was there when the sentinel told them to go away, or he would fire; they set up a laugh, and drew back after he put his bayonet through the hole, forming a circle of fifteen or twenty-five feet from the wall; at that time there were not more than twenty-five or thirty people, but afterwards they ran from all quarters to see the hole, hearing the others at it laughing; they knew nothing of it before; I went towards the gate when I heard the first fire, which I supposed was with blank cartridges, until I heard the balls whistle; do not suppose a man in the yard knew there were arms in the barrack yard.

Adjourned until to-morrow, 8 o'clock.

DARTMOOR, *Sunday, April* 23, 1815.

Met, pursuant to adjournment, at 8 o'clock.
Present: Paul Treby Treby, Esq., one of the magistrates for the county of Devon.
William Clements, prisoner, being sworn, says:

I was most of the evening at prison No. 1, and towards the close of the evening was going to my own prison, No. 7; I saw about twenty or thirty prisoners gathered round the wall of No. 7, and considered they were gambling; going up to it, saw dirt about a breach in the wall, and then several took up stones and threw them at it, in order to force it through. I went down the yard, and came up again, at which time they were still throwing against the breach; they made a hole; I then saw Captain Shortland come up to it with some soldiers on the other side; he spoke though the hole, asking what they did it for; a number answered they had nothing to do with it, and some said they dug it for amusement; Captain Shortland said, if they did not disperse, he would be obliged to fire upon them; he then went away; they then dispersed and some who were digging went into their prisons; I heard no insulting language to Captain Shortland; the hole was then large enough for a man to get through; saw none attempt to get through; I considered the digging of the hole was merely through mischief; a number of small places had been dug in the wall in the course of the day; a great many prisoners were in the yard No. 7—more, perhaps, than usual, it being so fine an evening; I went towards my own prison, and found all the doors but one shut; I heard a great noise at the top of the yard, and went towards the gates; heard many cry out "keeno;" *keeno* is said among the prisoners when anything falls, even in the prison; many cry it out when they do not know what is the matter; I suppose there were about forty or fifty soldiers then in the market square, drawn up on one side; the prisoners were going through at No. 1 gate; the soldiers came down to the charge, and then drew back; the prisoners were not so numerous as the soldiers; I suppose there might be thirty prisoners in the square; they made no opposition; some of them appeared to be in liquor; the prisoners are not permitted to be in the market square; the gates were locked; when the prisoners were driven through the gate, the soldiers fired; they fired into No. 1 gate. I heard no order to fire; was not in a situation to hear it; the soldiers fired right into the gates; did not observe how the muskets were levelled the first fire; I considered they fired with blank cartridges first; this was into No. 1 gate, and there were only a few shots, but afterwards a volley; I saw a man fall at No. 1 gate, when I, with others, attempted to remove him, when another volley was fired in; put him behind the wall; he said he was wounded in the breast; we put our hands there, but felt nothing; he soon died, and then we found the ball had entered his head. At the time of the first fire I heard no abuse from the prisoners, nor saw any stones thrown during the whole time; there was some turf inside the square, which I thought had been brought in by the people who had the liberty of the square; after the first fire the prisoners did not rally or cheer, but were eager to get into their prisons; I cannot say why so many of the prisoners were out at the time; I did not hear the

Massacre at Dartmoor Prison.

alarm bell; a number of prisoners knew nothing of it till they heard the reports of the muskets; saw an officer with the soldiers; the officer was the first man who entered No. 7 yard; it was not Captain Shortland; I saw Captain Shortland in the yard, but whether it was he or the other officer who first came in I do not know; I saw an officer having hold of a prisoner by the collar, and strike him with a sword once or twice; he made no attempt to stab him; I then went into No. 7, and saw nothing more. There was no particular uneasiness among the prisoners, at not being released, only talking about it, and saying they thought it hard; but they were as obedient to the orders and regulations of the prison as before the account of the ratification.

John Hubbard, prisoner, being sworn, says: I was carrying a wounded man to the hospital; Captain Shortland came up to me, (I was then about half way up the market square;) he ordered me to drop the man; I told him I should not, for he was a dead man, and I wanted to take him to the hospital; he gave me a crack on the neck with his fist, and ordered the soldiers to charge on us; I then went back directly, as the soldiers were running towards me, and ran in; they did not follow us any distance; they halted as soon as we ran; when I got in I called to Captain Shortland, and told him, "You will recollect, sir, you struck me, if you are brought to account for this;" he said, "he would strike my damned heart if he had me there;" I am sure of this; I did not threaten him that I would have satisfaction of him. I do not know any of the men who were with me, helping to take the dead man; there were about four or five; the soldiers at this time were drawn up across the square; there had been much firing before this; I saw the soldiers fire into No. 3, after the prisoners were in; I was standing close to the door; I belong to that prison, and mess close to the door; there were eighteen or twenty soldiers at the door, but do not know whether they all fired; I saw the muskets levelled; seven or eight shots struck the stairs, and some went to the other side of the prison; at this time there were five or six prisoners going in at the door; one got wounded on the step; I did not see any stones thrown out, but heard afterwards there was one thrown out.

Homer Hull.—(His evidence before the coroner being read to him, he said it was correct.) I am sure I heard Captain Shortland give orders to fire; I was then about thirty or forty feet from him, near gate No. 4, under the platform; he was then facing me; the first fire was a volley; there were no straggling guns preceded the volley; they fired immediately after they got the word; there was no hesitation. I do not think there were more than three or four prisoners in the market square, in front of the soldiers, at the time of the first fire; they had retreated through the gate, and shut it after them.

James Reeves, prisoner, being sworn, says: I belong to prison No. 1. I was rather groggy that evening. I saw a mulatto man, who was groggy, break the chain which fastened the gate No. 1,

with a bar like a crowbar; the bar was flat and thick, something like a chisel, about two feet long; the alarm bell was ringing at the time he was breaking the chain, before the gate was broken open. I suppose there were as many as fifty persons around the gate; the pressure they made parted the gate sooner. As soon as the gate was open, a great many rushed through into the square; there were about twelve or thirteen; there were a great many between the two railings; they were all hallooing and making a noise. I went out into the square; I was tipsy, or I suppose I should not have done it. I saw the soldiers coming down; they charged upon us immediately, and I then went back directly. I was pricked. I lost my hat, and went to pick it up, when I was pricked again. I went back with my face to them; some turned their backs; but I stood a little more upon going back than I should have done had I been sober. I received two pricks in the breast, and two in the arm. We shut the gate as soon as we could. Captain Shortland was abreast of the gate No. 1, in front of the soldiers. I am pretty sure he was in front of them. I heard him sing out "fire" twice; heard him order both to charge and fire; can swear I heard him order to fire twice; think Captain Shortland was in front of the soldiers; cannot say how he escaped being shot more than myself. I heard no shouting among the prisoners after the firing. After we were inside No. 1 prison, I watched an opportunity, being mad at being pricked, and flung a stone myself out at the soldiers; the soldiers had fired into the prison before I did so. I saw no stones thrown, nor heard any abuse after the charge and before the firing; but, after the firing, the prisoners ran into the yard, and sung out "fire, and be damned," and dared them. I cried out "fire, and be damned," which I did because I was mad at being pricked for nothing, as I thought. Mr. Magrath, the surgeon, spoke to us, and desired us to go back; he said, if any blame was to be attributed to anybody that we were not sent home, it was not owing to Captain Shortland or the English Government, but to Mr. Beasley. Some did go back in consequence, and if I had been sober I should probably have done so too. This was before any soldiers were in the square.

William Mitchell, prisoner, being sworn, says: I belonged to No. 1; was walking in the yard, as were a great many more, it being very fine; did not know anything particular was going on. I saw Nichols, the turnkey, running down, and a great many prisoners with him singing out "keeno;" they ran out of curiosity, to see what was the matter; I did not know what was the matter. About this time I heard first a single musket, and afterwards a volley, and then more. I asked what was the matter? And was told some boys had made a hole in the wall of No. 7 yard. I said, "what do they fire here for?" I went and helped to shut the inner gate of No. 1, and said we had no business with soldiers there. There were not above thirty prisoners there at that time. The soldiers came in. I saw two officers, and spoke

Massacre at Dartmoor Prison.

to one, and asked him why he fired upon people who made no resistance? He told me he had been through the hole in the wall himself. Captain Shortland told the prisoners to go to their prisons. The soldiers came in, charged them to their prisons, and wounded several. I did not hear the horn or the alarm bell. The prisoners do not usually go in when the horn first sounds, till the turnkeys come down and tell them to turn in; they first go and lock three doors, and afterwards the fourth and last.

George Challacumb, being sworn, says: I am a carter, belonging to the prison establishment. I went to Plymouth on the 6th of April with a letter; I overtook a man named Roberts on the road, who had been released from prison that morning; he told me his name was Roberts. I entered into conversation with him; he said he was glad he was released, for he thought that in a few days an attempt would be made to break out of prison. I asked him how it would be done? He said there was talk among the ringleaders that it should be at the time the bread wagons went in, when the iron gates were open, and he feared the consequences would be very great; he said that Slater and Jack Crandall were ringleaders of the whole. I did not mention this at Plymouth. It was ten o'clock at night when I returned, and then the affair at the prison had happened. Next morning I told the chief clerk, Mr. Holmden, what I had heard, and advised him not to keep both gates open at once. (There are on the books two such names as Slater and Crandall.)

Lot Davis, prisoner, of No. 5 prison, being sworn, says: I was walking about half way between the hole and the gate. The cook-house of No. 6 was, I thought, the only safe place from the firing; I tried to get into No. 5, but could not, and remained in the cook-house until next morning. I heard scattering guns firing after the prisoners were all running away, as if fired at single persons crossing the yard.

Samuel Best, turnkey, being sworn, says: On opening the door from the railing towards the receiving house, on the morning of the 5th April, about half-past seven o'clock, a prisoner said to me, "Well, turnkey, how did you like the keeno yesterday?" I told him I did not know anything of it, having been away; but, from what I heard, they had acted very improperly; he said, "damn you, in a quarter of an hour we can have all the bloody walls down." I turned round, and the conversation ended. No other prisoners joined in these expressions; several were round, waiting to go into the receiving house. On the 6th inst., in the evening, when all was quiet after the affray, Mr. Mercer, who assisted in the dispensary, said he hoped the prisoners would not attempt anything again; I replied, it would be quite madness, as they were unarmed, and hoped they would be reconciled. He said it might be different if they were to make another attempt, as they would not be taken by surprise again; and intimated, as I understood, that they had upwards of three hundred pistols and five hundred files, which I under-

stood were sharp and fastened on pieces of wood, and enough gunpowder to blow up the walls. I heard the next day a prisoner say, on the other side of the wall, if they could have got one hundred muskets, they would have been better pleased, or would have done better, or something to that effect.

David Spence Warren, prisoner, being sworn. (His evidence before the coroner was read to him, and he said it was all true, and that he had nothing to correct.) I was within seven or eight feet of Captain Shortland when I heard him give orders to fire; I was inside my own prison-yard, and Captain Shortland was close to the gate; that was the first firing I heard; there had been none before. Soldiers had broken up their line when Captain Shortland led them into the prison yard. Captain Shortland was at the head of them, in front of them all, when I heard him tell the men to fire. They did not fire the first time he said "fire;" it was about a minute afterwards before they fired. He said "fire" three times; the last time he caught hold of a musket, and turned it towards a man standing opposite him, saying, "God damn you, fire." I cannot swear that that musket was fired. The firing commenced at first by one musket, then two, and afterwards a general fire. I am sure the firing did not begin by a volley. I am sure what I state is true. There had been no firing before I saw Captain Shortland take hold of the musket; I had heard none. I saw no prisoners have hold of this musket at the time. Captain Shortland, when he told them to fire, was in front; one soldier beside him. They might have fired at his side, or over him, without hurting him.

Richard Walker, private in the Derby militia, being sworn, says: I was one of the south guard on the evening of the 6th; I was in the market square when the firing began, on the right of the north guard; when it began, there was not a prisoner in the square; when the soldiers charged there were a great many in; cannot say how many. They went back to their own yard directly; was formed nearly on a line with the north guard. After the charge the prisoners returned to the gate, and tried to force it; they made a great noise, and used very abusive language; they did not come back into the market square. I heard no order to fire; first one musket was fired; it was by a sentry posted at the bottom of the square, in consequence of the prisoners abusing him. I saw this; I cannot say I saw the prisoners take hold of his musket. I saw them throw no stones before, but after it was fired they did; one hit me on the arm. I might not have seen it had the prisoners caught hold of his musket. It might be two minutes before there was firing again. As soon as the prisoners threw stones, there was more firing. They fired several together, but not in a volley. Do not recollect I heard any order to fire. Heard several call out "fire," and supposed it might be the prisoners who were calling out. I heard the word "fire" repeated, but do not know by whom. I was close enough to hear the prisoners call out. Saw Captain Shortland come down, break through the guard, and order them to cease firing; this was very soon after the firing began. He called out to the prisoners, "For God's sake, men, go in, go in." The soldiers did the same. Captain Shortland came down the square from behind the line, broke through the guard, and ordered them to cease firing. I did not know where he was before the firing.

William Ward, private in the Derby militia, being sworn, says: I was not in the market square when the firing began; I came up just after. Captain Shortland, after it had continued some time, came up, and ordered the soldiers to cease firing; they immediately ceased. He said to the prisoners, "For God's sake, all of you go in;" the whole of the soldiers said the same. The prisoners ran up to the gates after that with a stronger force than before, making a great noise, but not insulting the soldiers. Saw no stones thrown. When Captain Shortland gave orders to cease firing, they did so immediately; afterwards the prisoners came up in large bodies; there was more firing; I did not see any prisoners come into the square after that. I do not know who ordered the firing afterwards; I heard Captain Shortland order the soldiers to cease firing; he ran from behind the line to the front, and held up both his hands, saying, "For God's sake, cease firing."

William Norris, turnkey, being sworn, says: I was not in the market square before the firing ceased. I came into the front yard, and was told by a turnkey in the lodge that the prisoners had made a breach. I ran to it, and some soldiers came to relieve the sentry at the hole. The prisoners were abusing him, and daring him to fire, saying his orders were not to fire. I saw Captain Shortland at the breach; he said the prisoners must have some bad intention. He came round by the military way to the front of the gate, and ordered me to ring the alarm bell, which I did; he was then in front of the upper gate, between it and the lodge; this was previous to any knowledge of the bursting the gate. When I had rung the alarm bell, I went to the military way; one musket was fired first, and afterwards there was a general fire; after which Captain Shortland and some officers called for the turnkeys; I ran through the line; he told me to take a wounded man to the hospital, which I and two others did. I returned to the market square; he ordered me to take another; he was dead. I took him to the burying house. The wounded man was brought out of No. 1; the dead man I found in the square. I was afterwards employed in carrying away the wounded.

John Rodd, turnkey, being sworn, says: I blew the horn for locking up, on the evening of the 6th; blow it always for about a quarter of an hour; I did so that evening; I went down afterwards to lock up No. 4 prison; while at the doors of it, I heard the alarm-bell ring; as soon as the prisoners hear the horn, they generally begin to go in; they did so that night; they were going into No. 4 quite fast; they rushed out

again, up to the gates, to see what was the matter; they ran up the yard; I cried out that night, as I went down the yard, "Turn in, turn in; the alarm-bell is rung to assemble all the department." I came back into market square, and when I got there, there was a firing, and a cry for the turnkeys; I came, and assisted to carry the wounded men to the hospital.

Daniel Nicholls, turnkey, being sworn, says: I was in prison yard No. 1, to lock the doors; the horn had done sounding before; before I came to the first door to lock up, the alarm-bell rang; the prisoners were going in just as usual; but, when the alarm-bell rang, they called out to know what was the matter, and thronged so much to the door that I could not shut it; I proceeded towards the gate, but, before I reached it, the firing commenced; I was about half-way up the yard when it began; hearing a ball whizzing by me, I returned to the end of the prison, and waited some time, till, seeing the lamplighter get over the wall by his ladder, I thought it a good opportunity for me to get over also, and did so; I came round to the market square; Captain Shortland was calling for turnkeys, and I went to assist in carrying the wounded to the hospital; the firing had ceased in the market square when I reached it; I heard much firing afterwards in the prison yard; when I came to lock up the second time, the prisoners threw a stone at me from No. 1, and the sentry then fired in at the door; I do not know who the sentry was; they shoved the door to, and would then open it again, and throw out stones, before I could fasten it; I cannot say whether the door was open when the sentry fired.

David Pitmore, turnkey, being sworn, says: The first I heard of the affair was a call for the guard; I went to the lodge, when Captain Shortland ordered the alarm-bell to be rung; I staid at the top of the yard till I heard a call for the turnkeys, and I then assisted in carrying away the wounded men; was at the lodge before the alarm-bell rang; I saw the soldiers charging the prisoners back; they drove them out under the platform; saw the first firing; several prisoners rushed into the square before the charge; I do not think there were any in the square before the alarm-bell rang; afterwards a gate was open, and they were coming through.

John French, turnkey of prison No. 3, being sworn, says: I was going to lock up as usual on the evening of the sixth, after the horn had sounded; I was in the yard; the prisoners were going in very quietly; had locked one door, and then heard the alarm-bell; the prisoners asked what was the matter; I said I did not know; I continued locking up, and locked three doors; this went on till the firing began; I stood at the end of the prison, and then got over the wall by the lamplighter's ladder; I did not see the prisoners come out of No. 3 after the firing began; came round to the market square; the firing was then over there; after assisting to carry the wounded to the hospital, I went to lock up No. 3; the soldiers fired in the door of that prison; I told the prisoners to go in; they were in the doorway, and I touched them slightly with my hand, telling them to go in and let me shut the door, or the soldiers would fire; one of the soldiers touched one with his bayonet, and advised the same, or they should fire; one man told him he might fire and be damned; immediately an order was given to fire by somebody behind—whether by an officer or non-commissioned officer, I do not know, and several muskets were fired into the open door, (I cannot say how many,) upon which I saw some prisoners drop; do not know who ordered to fire; sentries said to them, "If you do not go in we must fire on you;" they said "Fire and be damned;" I believe only one said so; there were many soldiers about the door; cannot say whether the soldiers could have driven them back by their bayonets, without firing, so as to have enabled me to shut the door; the soldiers were about eight feet from the door when they fired; I was in front, and got back as quick as I could, and bent down as they fired.

James Carley, turnkey, being sworn, says: I came to the front of the iron gate in the military walk; saw Captain Shortland coming from the barracks with soldiers; he made a halt at the blacksmith's shop; I saw prisoners rushing towards the gate No. 1, between the two railings; they sang out "keeno;" I ordered out the bread wagon, then in the market square; I opened the gate for the purpose; as soon as the wagon was out I heard a bar knock against No. 1 gate; I called out to Captain Shortland that the prisoners were breaking out; he went down with the military with both his hands in his breeches pockets; the prisoners were rushing out, but I could not see how many there were, the military being between them and me. I staid till I heard a cry for the turnkeys; went down to assist in carrying the wounded; I saw a charge, but do not know whether it made the prisoners go back.

Samuel Morgan, turnkey of No. 7, being sworn, says: After the horn had sounded I was in Nos. 5 and 7 yards, going to lock up. No door was locked when the alarm-bell rang. When I first went into the yard there was a great crowd of prisoners round a hole in the wall; as I passed by they sang out "keeno," and they and others in the yard ran towards the railings, near the market square; about this time there were nearly seven or eight hundred prisoners in the yard; many belonged to other yards; I took no notice. When I got to the cook house the bell rang; they asked me what was the matter; I said I did not know; I passed on, and when I had shut one door I heard a firing; the prisoners seemed to retreat then. I got over the railings into the military way by the lamplighter's ladder. There were then three doors of the prison open. I saw no stones thrown by the prisoners, being at the lower part of the yard, where there was no tumult. I came round to the market square when the firing was over; only a few muskets were fired afterwards; but did not see any while I was in the military walk. I saw the sentries fire from the ramparts. I then helped to carry away the wounded, seeing others do so. After looking up prison No. 7, which I did without difficulty, I went to No. 1, to shut up, and, when putting one of the doors to, stones were thrown out; I was struck by one on the breast, and by one on the chin; I was pulling the inside door to; no muskets were fired into it then.

William Wakelin, turnkey of No. 5, being sworn, says: I had locked three doors of No. 5, when I heard a great noise, and the word "keeno" several times. On entering the prison yard there was a great body of prisoners between prison No. 7 and the barrack wall, round where the hole was; there were not more than usual round the railing. As usual, some prisoners were going in, and some kept coming out: there was nothing unusual in their manner at the bottom of the yard. I was coming up towards where the noise was, when a bullet hissed by close to me. I then ran towards the ramparts to get out of the way. I got over the wall by the lamplighter's ladder; then I came round to the market square, where I saw the soldiers drawn up in ranks. I went down, and heard Captain Shortland call out for the turnkeys. I assisted to carry the wounded. The prisoners brought a wounded man from No. 1, and insisted on carrying him up themselves; Captain Shortland ordered them to go back, but, as they refused, he put out his hand, and pushed one of them, without using violence; they would not go, and the soldiers were obliged to charge on them; one man pulled open his clothes, and challenged them to fire; Captain Shortland pushed him, but it was not with violence. This man was very turbulent; his name is James Reeves. Afterwards I went to lock up No. 5; then all was quiet, and the prisoners were all away from the door.

Richard Arnold, turnkey, being sworn: (His evidence before the coroner was read to him, and he said it was all perfectly correct.) Captain Shortland, at the time of the first fire, was in front of the line of soldiers, and it was almost impossible for him, had they fired a volley, to escape death himself. He was persuading the prisoners to go back when I told Captain Shortland they were making a hole in the wall; he told me to call the guard, but did not use any oath, nor did he blame me for not telling him of it before.

John Arnold, steward at the contractor's store for the prisoners in health, being sworn. (His evidence before the coroner was read to him, and he said it was correct, and that he had nothing material to add to it.)

Stephen Hall, turnkey, being sworn: (His evidence before the coroner was read to him, and he said it was correct.) One of the iron bars mentioned therein was bent; the bars appeared to him to be some of those from the railings.

John Tozer, being sworn. (His evidence before the coroner was read to him, and he said it was correct, and that he had nothing to add to it.)

Massacre at Dartmoor Prison.

Henry Wroe, plumber and glazier at the prison establishment, being sworn, says: I saw the sentry at the breach charge down his musket, and several stones thrown at him, while he kept telling the prisoners he must fire. I was then on the south guard platform. I went to the platform, at the foot of the market square, and saw about six or seven hundred prisoners at the hole; and presently they sung out "keeno," and ran towards the railing; they rushed in under the platform. Seeing this, I left the platform, and was going up the market square; before I was half-way up I heard them knocking the chain of No. 1 gate, which soon burst open, and a great number (I cannot say how many, but suppose about five or six hundred) rushed into the square. I did not see Captain Shortland or the soldiers come into the square. The prisoners had broken the lock before they came in; it was done before I left the square; the alarm-bell rang after I left it. Being called again, he said: he does remember to have told Captain Shortland that the gate was burst; Captain Shortland was then in the military walk, near the turnkeys' lodge, standing alone, without the guard; he did not hear him give any order in consequence. It might be a minute or so before Captain Shortland went into the square.

John Mitchell, clerk to Captain Shortland, being sworn: (His evidence before the coroner was read to him, and he said that it was correct, and he had only to add as follows:)

While I was on the platform observing the prisoners throwing peat at each other, as I stated in the deposition, between the wall and the iron railings, I observed a great body of prisoners round the place where the breach was, but they were so numerous that I could not see what was doing. When I went with the turnkeys to remove the wounded, I observed Captain Shortland exerting himself as much as a man could do for them, and in having them conveyed to the hospital; he desired me to procure turnkeys to remove a wounded man who was sitting in a sentry box, and desired me to exert myself as much as possible in having the wounded removed; the cry of the military for the keys Nos. 5 and 7 was from those who had not been active, and appeared to me to proceed from anxiety to secure the prisoners, not from any vindictiveness: this party did not fire while I was in the yard with them; they called for the keys for the purpose of shutting up the prisoners.

Robert Holmden, first clerk to Captain Shortland, being sworn: (His evidence before the coroner was read to him, and he said it was correct.) I saw a great body of prisoners at the breach; the prisoners had broken the gate of No. 1, next the market square, before the alarm-bell rang; I was with Captain Shortland when the report of it was made to him; it was made by Henry Rowe; whereupon Captain Shortland, who was a great deal agitated, said, "Where are the guards? where shall we get help?" and I advised ringing the alarm-bell, which was done.

Robert McFarlane, assistant surgeon, being sworn. (His evidence before the coroner being read to him, he said it was all correct.)

John Bennett, store clerk, being sworn, says: I was at the breach; the prisoners were using very abusive language. I saw no stones thrown. I proceeded down the military walk; I was very near Captain Shortland, near the blacksmith's shop in the military way; several people reported to Captain Shortland that the prisoners were forcing the gate, and he then ordered the alarm-bell to be rung; he went into the square with the guard; I heard Captain Shortland tell the prisoners in the market square to go back to their different prisons, and say how sorry he should be to use force; he remonstrated with them; this seemed to have no other effect than to produce the most infamous language from them; some minutes after a musket went off, and soon after many others; I was then so near Captain Shortland that I am sure I should have heard it had he given orders to fire, but I did not, nor did I hear an order from anybody. I did not see the charge. I heard Captain Shortland order the soldiers to advance. Captain Shortland said, in my hearing: "My good fellows, go to your different prisons, or the military must do their duty." I suppose the prisoners in the square must have exceeded some hundreds when Captain Shortland went in with the guards.

George Magrath, surgeon of the hospital, being sworn: (His evidence before the coroner was read to him, and he said he had nothing to add to it, but felt it his duty to say:)

As some imputation of inebriety has been made against Captain Shortland, I think it justice to say, that, having observed him on the evening of the 6th, no man could be more free from it; and from my acquaintance with him, and with his general habits in his family, I do not think any man can be more abstemious. I should consider it equally incumbent on me, as imputations of barbarity have been made against him, to say, that, whenever I had occasion, as often happened, to make representations to him of any arrangement calculated for the health and comfort of the prisoners, he has always adopted it with great alacrity, and shown every disposition to do everything for their welfare.

George Holland, bugler of the Derby militia, being sworn, says: I recollect sounding the bugle on the evening of the 6th, in consequence of the prisoners breaking the wall; several officers of the Somerset passing backwards and forwards in the military way said the prisoners were breaking down the wall, and were breaking out of the gates and getting out, and every person would be killed, and told me on that account to sound a fire on the bugle, which I did; before this, a considerable time, there had been firing, and I am sure not four men would have known anything about the sounds of the bugle if they were asked now.

Adjourned until to-morrow at 8 o'clock.

Massacre at Dartmoor Prison.

DARTMOOR PRISON OF WAR,
Monday, April 24, 1815.
Met, pursuant to adjournment, at 8 o'clock.
Present: Paul Treby Treby, Esq.
John Collard, sergeant in the first Somerset militia, being sworn, says: I was on the north guard, commanded, on the evening of the 6th, by Lieutenant Avelyn. Some one belonging to the department came and told me to call out my guard, saying, "Fall in your guard as soon as possible, and march it up to the west yard," and that that guard was going to the barrack yard where the breach was. I fell in the guard, and marched them up opposite the west guard, where I halted them; was not there long before Captain Shortland came up; he ordered me to take the guard to the market square and form it across; had seen nothing before this of what had passed. On entering the market square, I heard a chain rattle at gate No. 1, on the left hand side. I formed the guard across the square; the guard was at the west guard-house before the alarm-bell rang; it rang a little at first, stopped, and then I heard Captain Shortland order it to be rung again. This was before we went into the square; it was not rung again till we were going in. I observed two or three prisoners come out of gate No. 1, from the prison yard, just as I entered the market-gate; a greater number had entered before the guard formed; whilst it was forming I ordered the two sentries in front of the railings at the bottom, and the two on the platform above, to leave their posts and join the guard; they were all that were at those situations. As soon as they heard me thus order, the prisoners began to cry out "keeno," and rushed into the square in as great numbers as they possibly could, through the gate which had been broken. By the time I had formed my guard they came up in great numbers, close to us, on our left flank; the guard gave way on the left, where it was weakest, and where the prisoners made the greatest efforts to pass; the soldiers were then at the shoulder, when the guard gave way. Captain Shortland ordered it to charge; he told off about fifteen file himself, whom he ordered to charge; repeated it two or three times before they did; they endeavored to drive them back, but did not charge the same as they would an enemy; if they had they must have killed scores of them, as every bayonet would have told; they tried to drive them back without committing murder; the right of the guard did not charge; we drove them back about half the ground they had gained in the square. I was in the rear of the charging party; only the fifteen file told off charged in this way at first; the prisoners then began to throw stones at us in great numbers from within the railings and from the market square; there were some scores still in the market square; they were hurraing at the same time. An order was then given to fire on them; I heard the word given to fire by some one; I think the word given was in my rear; we were in great confusion; I was then in the rear of the soldiers; the prisoners were crying out "fire;" I could not then see Captain Shortland; I did not look out for him; I had

something else to think of when the order to fire was given; two or three men fired; immediately they obeyed the order; one musket was discharged first, and one or two very soon after. When these were discharged I did not see any man killed, or any one hurt among the prisoners; I think the soldiers fired over their heads; then some prisoner or prisoners said, "You buggers, why do you not fire? you have nothing but blank cartridges." Afterwards the firing became general, and the prisoners were driven into the yard. I heard no word of command for the second firing; the firing was not in a volley, but in small numbers at a time. There was no general return of the prisoners from the yard after the firing had taken place; they could not stand the firing; they could not come without being murdered, the whole of them; they did not rally after the firing became general. I do not know how long the firing continued; but after it had gone on some time the prisoners dispersed into their yards; then Captain Shortland ordered the firing to cease. I am sure he did. He put up his hands, and said "cease firing," giving it as a word of command; it then ceased generally in the market place. As soon as possible a party of soldiers was ordered into the prison yards to turn the prisoners into their different prisons. I know nothing of what happened afterwards in the prison yard, as I remained in the square with the rest of the guard. I afterwards heard some firing in the yard, but paid no attention to it. I think the firing must have ceased from the ramparts soon after, otherwise some of our soldiers in the yard must have been shot. The general tenor of the prisoners' conduct was riotous. Many of our men were much hurt by the stones thrown, but not so as to be disabled from doing duty. I am satisfied, in my own mind, that, without the firing, the prisoners could not have been driven back. Had we charged on them like an enemy, we must have killed a great number; every bayonet must have killed one or more prisoners, they being so thick. The number of soldiers in the square, at the first firing, was about fifty-four, exclusive of sergeants; our guard was about thirty-eight, and there were about fourteen of the west guard. I cannot say how many came in afterwards. The whole regiment assembled as soon as possible after the alarm; no officer gave orders to cease firing before Captain Shortland; had there been such an order, it would have been obeyed.

Stephen Lopthorn, private in the first Somerset militia, being sworn, says: I was on the north guard on the evening of the 6th; went into the market square with it; when I first went in I saw two or three prisoners in the square near No. 1 gate; about one hundred and fifty came in afterwards, while we were forming; they pressed up very near the military; some of the military were ordered to charge, which was done; some prisoners went back in consequence, but others were coming through the gate upon us. Before the firing began they had never been entirely driven out of the square. I heard an order given to fire, but do not know who gave it; it came from the right in front; I was on the left. I did not see Captain Shortland at this time; I cannot say whose voice it was; am not sure whether it was from the prisoners or the military. The firing began immediately from about the centre; it did not begin by one musket, but by several together. When the firing began, I was at the charge; two prisoners seized my bayonet, and tried to twist it off; I do not know who they were. I told them to let go; they said they would not, adding, "fire, and be damned." I got myself in danger, and was obliged to fire to get my musket released; I did so; but there were upwards of twenty fired before mine; saw a great quantity of stones thrown before my firing; while we were at the charge the prisoners threw them till the last; one man stooped to pick up his cap, which, I believe, had been knocked off by a stone; this was before any firing. I do not think the prisoners would have been driven back without firing; as they continued pressing on, Captain Shortland was persuading them to retire, but they would not, saying they were not prisoners of war. I heard Major Jolliff give orders to cease firing before they were driven into the prison yard, and before the firing ceased in the market square. I think he did so as soon as he came down; he was not there at first. Stones were thrown, and the firing continued in consequence after this order. I also heard several voices say "cease firing," but cannot say whether they came from the military or from the prisoners.

William Gifford, private in the Somerset militia, being sworn: (His evidence before the coroner was read to him, and he said it was all correct.)

I heard Captain Shortland say "cease firing," about a few minutes after it began; he put his hand up by way of signal, and said so; I do not know who gave the word to fire; I did not see where Captain Shortland was when the order was given to fire; I think he had just gone towards the left, and the word appeared to me to come from the right, therefore I think it could not have been he who gave it; I did not hear first one musket discharged; the firing at first must have been in the air, otherwise there must have been more prisoners hurt. Captain Shortland was running up and down when the word was given to fire; I heard no order given by any body else than Captain Shortland to cease firing; I do not know that it would have ceased had orders been given; the prisoners were throwing stones and bricks continually; the firing ceased for a few minutes, after Captain Shortland had ordered it to cease; the conduct of the prisoners was such that it made us afraid, from the stones thrown; and I do not think they could have been driven back without the firing. Had orders been given by anybody else to cease firing, it might not have been heard, from the noise.

John Soathern, private in the Derby militia, being sworn, says: I was one of the south guard on the evening of the 6th; was one of those formed across the square on the right of the north

guard; I saw the prisoners charged down nearly to the railings; our guard charged down to the railings after the north guard. We went close to the railings; my bayonet touched them; when we got there, the prisoners began throwing stones; we stepped back a few paces, being so near the railings; one stone struck me on the right side; it almost knocked me down; I should have fallen had not a man kept me up; just then the firing commenced; after some time of firing Captain Shortland came in front, and said, holding his hands up, "For God's sake, men, cease firing—cease firing." He went near to the railings; I and several others called to him, "Come back, it is almost dusk;" he said "You know me, men; do cease firing;" but several muskets were discharged after this. Captain Shortland was not near me when it commenced; I did not see him; the order to fire was given at the left, and it passed through the ranks one after another, saying "fire, fire," but there was so much noise and shouting by the prisoners, that it is impossible for me to say who gave the word; I believe I was the sixth or seventh file from the right; I remained in the market square; I do not know what passed in the prison yard; I heard no officer before Captain Shortland say "cease firing;" but a few seconds afterwards some officers did. I did not see any prisoners in the market square when the firing began, but they were behind the railings under the platform, throwing stones; I could not see about gate No. 1, there being sentry boxes between.

Lieutenant Avelyn, of the first Somerset militia, being sworn, says: I commanded the north guard on the evening of the 6th; I came into the market square with Captain Shortland; the prisoners had burst No. 1 gate, and were rushing through in a great crowd when we went in, so that I thought the whole of them were coming out; Captain Shortland went forward to speak to them. I heard him saying "My good fellows, do go back;" I did hear him say that, but the prisoners were making so much noise that I could not distinguish much of what he said; he also called to me not to suffer the prisoners to come too near my guard; they were then pressing forward in a very threatening manner; the guard was formed across the square, about the middle; my guard was then about thirty-eight men, and there were some others; the prisoners were so pressing on my guard, that many on the left fell back several paces, in order that they might not come too near them; they were then not close up to the wall, but I made them form close up afterwards; the left of my guard charged, and I was with them, driving the prisoners back; they did not charge by my order, nor did I hear Captain Shortland order it; I considered myself under Capt. Shortland's orders; had I been alone, I certainly would have charged the prisoners long before, or rather have fired, conceiving it to be necessary from the threatening manner of the prisoners, and the great body of them which was coming up, and could soon have surrounded my guard. They were not quite driven out of the square by the charge; it

Massacre at Dartmoor Prison.

was during this charge that I heard the first musket fired; I could not see where it was fired from, not being near enough, and being so much engaged in driving the prisoners back; it was, I think, to my right; at the first there was a single shot, and almost instantly after several others were fired; I heard no distinct order to fire; many of the prisoners were crying out to fire, and defying the soldiers; I was very near Captain Shortland at the time, and think I should have heard him had he given the order; I heard no distinct order at first, or at any time, to fire; Captain Shortland was then near gate No. 1, to the left, in front of the soldiers, and it would have been madness in him to have given the order in that situation. I was in front when the firing commenced, and retired into the rear for my own safety; the prisoners retreated on the firing taking place; I gave orders to cease firing after some time; my guard then ceased, and I went to the front of the men; I did not hear anybody else give orders to cease firing before myself, neither Major Jolliff nor Captain Shortland; the noise was so great that I could not hear; I am certain, had any one man by chance fired, the irritation of the soldiers, from the stones thrown at them previously, was then so great that almost the whole of them would have followed; the prisoners did not appear to care for the bayonet, and I do not think, from the state they were in, they could have been driven back without firing. The charge was not made with violence, as against an enemy; the prisoners were struggling with the soldiers; many defied them; but others said they could not go back, as the press was so great; I remained in the market square; did not go into the prison yard; I kept my guard with me; one prisoner, after the firing was over, came up, opened his clothes, and dared the soldiers to fire; I do not think the prisoners generally were intoxicated, but resolute. I do not think any man could have behaved like Captain Shortland who was intoxicated, and I think he behaved with courage and humanity.

Ensign Samuel White, of the first Somerset militia, being sworn: (His evidence before the coroner was read to him, and he said he had nothing to add or alter.) I do not know of any order to the soldiers on the ramparts to fire, but suppose they took it up from the others; I suppose there might have been about half a dozen of my guard in the market square; there was no firing through the breach.

Lieutenant Fortye, one of the first Somerset militia, being sworn, says: I had the command of the south guard on the evening of the 6th; I went into the square with my guard after the north was in, and formed on their right; they were already formed and in the act of firing when I arrived; that guard was then about fifteen or twenty feet from the iron railings; there were no prisoners in the square between my guard and the railings; could not see to the left, on account of the north guard; my guard took up the firing from others without any orders, immediately after they had formed in support of the north guard;

as soon as we formed I ordered the firing to cease; as soon as it could possibly be restrained, I stopped it; it ceased almost immediately; I saw nobody else endeavor to stop the firing before; as soon as the prisoners had retired to their yards, my guard ordered their arms, remained where they were, and I remained with them; I cannot, therefore, speak to anything that took place afterwards.

James Greenlaw, late second officer of the Prince de Neufchatel, American prisoner, being sworn: (His evidence before the coroner was read to him, and he said it was all correct.) I was between the two railings under the platform when I heard Captain Shortland give the order to fire; I saw him then at the head of the troops, about the centre of the yard, close in front of them; when I heard the word to fire, I retreated into yard No. 4; had just got inside the gate when it began; it began immediately by a volley, not by a single musket; I am sure it began by a volley; I do not know how Captain Shortland escaped; I suppose he knew how to take care of himself, and that his own men would not fire on him; he appeared to me to be standing close to the soldiers; I saw no stones thrown before the firing began; I do not know that I could have seen them; the prisoners were trying to get into No. 3 quietly, when the soldiers fired into it; I did not see any resistance among them. (This prisoner has a midshipman's warrant in the United States Navy, and a furlough.)

John Slater, citizen of the United States, being sworn, says: I do not know an American prisoner named Roberts; I have been confined here above six months; I know of no concert among the prisoners to break out by force, only attempts of individuals to escape at different times; I was at the gate No. 7; I was passing between Nos. 6 and 7 with two more men, when a party of five soldiers, I think, crossed at the further end of the prison from us; one man named Washington fell, but whether from the firing of this party, or from the ramparts, I do not know; he fell against me and knocked me down; I got up and ran away to my own prison, No. 5; there were only three prisoners on the spot where he was shot; the shot went through his temple.

Enoch Burnham, citizen of the United States, being sworn. (His evidence before the coroner was read to him, and he said it was all correct, and that he had nothing to add to it.)

Alexander Marshall, citizen of the United States, being sworn, says: I belong to prison No. 1; there were not more than fifty prisoners in the square when the soldiers charged; they charged as upon an enemy; they began firing, and I ran to No. 1 gate to get to my prison, but was nearly ten minutes before I could, on account of the press of the prisoners; there were about four hundred soldiers in the market square.

Cornelius Rowe, citizen of the United States, being sworn, says: I belong to No. 1 prison; I went to the breach; those about it told me it was made to get back a ball; they afterwards ran towards the gate. No. 7, saying it was to shut it against the military; I saw the military come down the square, and heard Captain Shortland order them to charge; at which time there were about forty or fifty prisoners in the square; I made towards my prison, and just as I got into the yard there was a firing, and the prisoners were rushing as fast as possible to their own prisons; they shut the gate behind them; there were about one hundred and fifty soldiers in the square.

William Dewetter, citizen of the United States, being sworn, says: I ran towards the gate to see what was the matter; on arriving, I saw the soldiers charge; I turned round, and just as I got inside the inner gate shots were fired; one grazed the side of my head, which made me giddy, and turned me round two or three times; I saw a prisoner named Mann fall; went to him and took him up; the balls flew about so thick that if there was one I suppose there were one thousand.

Thomas Tindale, citizen of the United States, being sworn, says: I was under the platform; saw the soldiers coming down the market square, and heard Captain Shortland give orders to fire; he was then about the centre, and in front of the soldiers; he had on a blue coat, but without epaulettes; he had a drawn sword in his hand; he gave orders twice to fire; I was not ten steps from him when I heard him; I heard every word he said; I saw him plainly; the firing commenced by one musket first, then two, and afterwards a whole volley; the firing began when Captain Shortland gave the word the second time; I heard Captain Shortland tell the soldiers to fire low; he was then still in front of the soldiers; I believe he was standing before the muzzles of the foremost muskets; the soldiers were formed two deep; when the balls began to fly thick, I escaped into No. 3, and saw no more of what passed afterwards; when I heard the order to fire, I was about the middle of gate No. 4; the soldiers charged up to the railings, and then fell back four or five paces, when Captain Shortland gave the order to fire.

John C. Rowles, citizen of the United States, being sworn, says: I saw forty or fifty prisoners in the market square when the soldiers were drawn up.

Thomas George Shortland, captain royal navy, commanding at the depot, being sworn, says: On the evening of the 6th April, a little before seven o'clock, Mr. Holmden, first clerk, came to my house and informed me there was a disposition of the prisoners to be riotous, as they had got between the railings and wall of No. 7 yard, and there were a number of people collected in No. 7 yard; in consequence, I walked down to the upper gates: on coming there, I was informed the prison barrack wall had been breached. I went to that yard and saw a large hole, and the military guarding it under an officer whom I since knew to be Lieutenant Avelyn; on getting to the breach I observed the prisoners using an iron bar to enlarge it. I remonstrated, and told them it was the prison barrack yard, and that it would be dangerous for them to attempt to force

it; the prisoners shouted, and threw stones through the breach, and still continued at times to enlarge it. I then heard some one say, "They are breaching the wall above the cook house in the prison barrack yard," and nearly at the same time there was a call out that they were forcing the lower gates, while I was still in the lower barrack yard. I immediately left the yard, and Lieutenant Avelyn followed me, leaving the breach with a party and a sergeant; when I arrived at the blacksmith's shop, I saw a rush of prisoners between the iron rails under the platform; the gate was at this time forced, and the prisoners were without the gates, in the market square, where they were not allowed to be; seeing this, and having in my mind the breach in the barrack wall, and the reported breach above the cook house; bearing this in mind, with the reported threats that had been constantly told me that the prisoners would liberate themselves on or before the 10th April, I ordered the alarm-bell to be rung: at this time part of the west guard, which is called the piquet, had gone round to turn the prisoners out of the railway in No. 7 yard, and another part of the same piquet was in the prison barrack yard; so that the force was reduced to the north guard only. Lieutenant Avelyn formed that guard and marched down into the market square. I preceded them, and about half-way down the guard formed in a line, this keeping their left close to the hospital wall; at time I should suppose there were from four to five hundred prisoners in the market square. I was perfectly unarmed, and went down to remonstrate with them, using all the persuasions in my power to make them return to their prisons, stating that the military guard was formed above them, and it was dangerous to attempt to use force. I was, at this time, about six paces in front of the guard; the prisoners kept still pressing up, and pressing me on the military; they appeared to want to get round the left of the military, keeping close to the hospital wall. At this time I looked back, and said, "For God's sake, soldiers, keep your ground;" bearing in mind that there was not a single soldier above them so prevent escape through the outer gates; almost immediately, about twelve or fifteen soldiers charged down towards No. 1, towards the hospital gates, about five or six paces, and they returned into line again. I was still at this time in front, and had gone forward again, urging the prisoners, who had retreated, when a discharge of musketry took place; while I was in that position, being to the right of the centre of the guard, and not near the hospital wall, a musket ball grazed my temple in that discharge, when I retreated into line with the soldiers; the prisoners retreated and advanced again, and about this time Major Jolliff came down. There was a call of "wounded men" from the prisoners, upon which I called to the turnkeys to assist in passing the wounded through the line of military, as they would not allow the prisoners to pass with them. While this was doing, there was another discharge both to my right and left. Those near me did not fire at this time, as, whenever I could, I had requested them to desist; the turnkeys came down, (this was after the second discharge,) and I was busily employed with Mr. Mitchell in directing the removal of the wounded up to the hospital. I can say nothing more of discharges of muskets in the market square. I only observed two discharges there. I heard some from the prison yards and from the ramparts. I was in the market square the whole time till the firing ceased, when Major Jolliff came down to the market square. I gave myself no further thoughts to the military, my whole mind being occupied in directing assistance to the wounded. I repeatedly said to the prisoners, "For God's sake, go to your prisons," previously to the firing, and between the discharges; for, being between the soldiers and them, I was warned by some of the former to keep clear of their fire, otherwise I should be shot. After the firing had ceased, and I got the receiving house door open to receive the wounded, I went into the north prison yard to see the prisoners shut up; the turnkey (Nicholls) of No. 1 had got them all in, but the door was not secured, but which was soon effected by the military without firing. All the troops were marched out before I saw anything more: I was in my undress uniform, and was perfectly unarmed. I never did give an order to fire; and in support of this I can say, I stated in my official letter to General Brown, that Major Jolliff gave the orders to fire, conceiving he had done so, from seeing the major appear at that moment. Indeed, in a former conversation with General Brown, in the presence of Major Gladding, being asked whether, if an attempt were made to resist the authority of the depot, I should order the military to fire, I told General Brown, as well as the major, that I did not think myself authorized to command the military to fire, because it was their duty to do it when they thought it necessary. I do not recollect a suspension of the ringing of the bell and then commencing again; it was a continual ringing. I ordered it in consequence of seeing that the prisoners had broken through the breach in the wall and the other reported breach. I did not hear any order to fire; it must be understood that I was with the prisoners, who were making a great noise, hurraing and rioting at the time.

The two best prisons (as the prisoners call them) are the two smallest, and I do not conceive them to be the best, as the others are the most roomy, and have been put in a state of repair since the release of the French prisoners; those two (which are Nos. 9 and 6) have not. Being smaller, we keep one of them for a receiving prison for any draughts of prisoners who may come in of a sudden wet and fatigued; the other, when Doctor Baird, inspector of hospitals, was down, he requested might be reserved for particular cases of contagion, as a sort of quarantine receiving house for newly arrived prisoners, to prevent contagion spreading; the prisoners have been distributed nearly according to the directions of Doctor Baird, (he having power to alter the

distribution on his visits.) The provisions of all the prisoners were stopped by the transport board's direction, for undermining the prisons. I remonstrated with them that the innocent would suffer with the guilty; but they replied that it must be so, as in all general transactions of the kind. I was not out of the market square until all the firing had ceased; I was not in No. 7 yard until an hour after the whole was over. Gatchell's statement, about my running down that yard, is not true. I recollect a man coming up the market square with a wounded man, and after being told to go away he would not, and I gave him a push; he said that I must recollect I had struck him, but I made him no answer. Taking into consideration the apparent temper and resolution of the prisoners, and my remonstrances having no effect, I do not think they could have been driven back without firing; without the firing, I think they might have forced the guard, which they were in the attempt to do; if that guard had been forced, the depot would have been lost. On all occasions when the market was stopped, or any measure of the kind was taken, it was reported to the Transport Board, along with the reasons for it, and they sometimes directed the stoppage to be continued. I am in the habit of reporting it after it is done. (Captain Shortland read the copy of a letter to the Transport Board, dated 14th February, 1815: it states, that, in consequence of the escape of Simon Hayes, who had been directed by the board to be kept in close confinement in the Cachot, and his taking refuge among the prisoners, and the disorderly conduct of the prisoners in not allowing the lamplighters to do their duty, he had stopped the market; and he read their answer, dated 16th February, approving of the measure in consequence of the reasons he stated.) The market has not been stopped more than twice. The first time was on the 24th October, 1814, on account of the prisoners not permitting themselves to be counted out of their prisons in the morning, which was necessary to ascertain if there was any escape. In a letter of the 27th, the board approved of the measure. In consequence of this, and the riotous conduct of the prisoners, Captain Shortland stated several arrangements he had made since he came to the depot for the welfare of the prisoners; among others, the following. On one occasion, when orders had been sent to remove the stoves from the prison, on account of the health of the prisoners, he wrote a very strong letter to the board, urging that they might be retained, as they were very instrumental to the comfort of the prisoners. All the letters from prisoners to himself he opened and answered, and he keeps a clerk for the mere purpose of keeping accounts of moneys received for the prisoners.

He dates the commencement of the antipathy of the prisoners to him from the time when he got the Transport Board to prosecute some men for tattooing others; and states, that till that he was on good terms with them, going down at all times among them, as he used among the French prisoners.

Massacre at Dartmoor Prison.

Deposition of John C. Clement.

I sailed from New York the 9th January, 1813, on board the brig Star, Captain Reed, for Bordeaux, and was captured on the 9th February following, in the Bay of Biscay, by His Britannic Majesty's ship Superb, (74,) Honorable Sir Charles Paget, commander. Went into Basque Roads, where, with other prisoners, I was put on board the Warspite, (74,) Captain Sir Henry Blackwood; proceeded in her to Plymouth, (England,) and on 19th March was sent on board the Hector, prison ship. On the 2d April, two hundred and fifty of us, American seamen, were marched to Dartmoor prison, where we were stowed in among nine or ten thousand French prisoners, who were in a filthy, dirty condition. During our confinement, Shortland, the keeper, repeatedly stopped our markets for several days at a time, without any provocation, or giving any reasons for this conduct, and our provisions were repeatedly short, not having our full allowance issued us. Shortland attempted several times to give us bad bread and provisions, and was guilty of many acts tending to irritate us, and render our situation very uncomfortable. On the 5th of April last, particularly, he gave orders to the contractors to serve us bad bread, which the prisoners would not receive, and, at the usual hour of closing the prisons, the turnkeys came to shut us in for the night; but we proceeded in a body to the market square, where an officer of the guard, on our representations to him, (Shortland then being absent to Plymouth,) advised us to return to our prisons, and he would have the bread sent us; which was done, and we retired to rest about twelve at night.

On the 6th of April, (the following day,) at 6 P. M., while a number of American prisoners were playing ball in yard No. 7, where a small hole, the size of a large pane of glass, sufficiently large to admit a boy or small man to pass through, had been made by some person or persons for the purpose of obtaining the ball when it flew over the wall into a large yard enclosed by high walls, (wherein the soldiers were stationed in the barracks:) at 6 P. M., as before mentioned, Captain Shortland, the keeper, entered the gate of No. 1, with 250 or 300 soldiers, armed with muskets and bayonets, the alarm-bell ringing at the same time, when he (Shortland) ordered one of the soldiers to fire at the prisoners in yard No. 1 : the soldier not willingly obeying, he snatched a musket from one of them, and shot a prisoner. The soldiers then commenced firing on the prisoners, who were then sallying out of their prisons to learn the cause of the firing; the soldiers continuing at the same time to re-load and fire on them. Four or five soldiers proceeded at this time also to the extremity of the yard in pursuit of the flying prisoners, and, as they cried for quarters, they replied, "No quarter shall be given you, you damned Yankee rascals," or similar words, and instantly shot the flying prisoners. Shortland and the soldiers then proceeded to prison No. 3, (No. 2 being empty and closed,) where they fired through the windows and doors on the prisoners inside, and shot through the heart one man while in the act of drinking a can of beer, and wounded another as he was endeavoring to escape up stairs; they then proceeded to yard No. 4, where the second lieutenant, snatching a musket out of a soldier's hand, shot a boy; soldiers firing at the same time into the prison, through the doors and windows. After having received a reinforcement of soldiers they proceeded to yard No. 7, where they commenced an indiscriminate fire on the prisoners while they were flying to escape into their prisons. On this day there were seven prisoners killed on the spot, and thirty-eight wounded, three of whom died two days after.

On the 7th of April a coroner's inquest was held, composed of American prisoners, (the officers of the prison being present, all save Captain Shortland,) when a verdict of "wilful murder" was brought in. On the 8th the coroner's inquest was held, composed of a number of neighboring farmers, who returned a verdict of "justifiable homicide." On the 9th, Admiral Rowley and a British post captain arrived at the prison from Plymouth, by direction of the Transport Board, to inquire of the prisoners into the transaction. During our confinement the American agent (Beasley) did not give us, say from the 2d April, 1813, to March, 1814, the 6s. 8d. sterling per month, as well as the suit of clothes allowed us annually by our Government, which money and clothes the prisoners have never received; and when I, with two hundred and fifty others, were released from prison, there were likewise a shirt, pair of shoes, and 6s. 8d. due us, which we never received. The prisoners had applied to Beasley repeatedly for what was due them, but received no satisfaction.

He never visited the prisons but once during two years and upwards I was there. The two hundred and fifty prisoners (and among them myself) were released from prison on the 20th of April last, and proceeded to Plymouth, and were put on board the cartel Maria Christiana, and arrived at New York on 5th of June, 1815. I did not know, nor did I hear of a plot or scheme of escape out of prison, as alleged by Shortland, in justification of his attack on us of the 6th April; on the contrary, it is my firm belief, if the gates had been thrown open to us at this time, none of us would have sallied forth to escape, because, being most of us destitute of money, (the agent having withheld our pay;) numbers of us miserably clothed, and without shoes, (also withheld from us;) numbers having walked, when released from prison, barefoot to Plymouth; through fear also of being arrested and closely confined, or, what was more probable, impressed into the British service, at a time when there was a very hot impressment going on in England; because having also heard, some weeks previous, of peace having taken place between Great Britain and America, which would release us from prison.

I know of no cause or reason that can justify the unprovoked attack upon us by Shortland and the soldiery, but do verily believe that the thing was wantonly, wickedly, and maliciously premeditated by Shortland and his officers, to spill the

Massacre at Dartmoor Prison.

blood and destroy a number of unarmed, defenceless American seamen.

Everything I have stated, I do, to the best of my recollection, believe to be, without the least exaggeration, strictly true.

JOHN C. CLEMENT.

Affirmed before　　　JOHN GEYER,
　　　　　　An Alderman of Philadelphia.

JUNE 19, 1815.

———

List of papers in packet marked C.

Extracts of a letter from the Commissary General of Prisoners to R. G. Beasley, Esq., American agent for prisoners of war in England, dated March 6, 1815.

Letter of the Commissary General of Prisoners to George Barton, Esq., dated March 6, 1815.

Table of provisions to be allowed to prisoners of war, whether American or British, on board of vessels transporting them.

Letter from R. G. Beasley to the Commissary General of Prisoners, dated April 13, 1815.

Letter of Alexander McLeay to R. G. Beasley, dated Transport Office, April 10, 1815.

Letter of J. P. Morier to R. G. Beasley, dated Foreign Office, April 11, 1815.

Letter of J. W. Croker to J. P. Morier, dated Admiralty Office, April 10, 1815.

Letter from R. G. Beasley to the Commissary General of Prisoners, dated April 15, 1815.

Report of the Committee of the American prisoners confined at Dartmoor, dated April 7, 1815.

Letter of R. G. Beasley to the Commissary General of Prisoners, dated April 18, 1815.

List of prisoners wounded on the evening of the 6th April, 1815, signed by George Magrath, surgeon.

A return of American prisoners of war who were killed and wounded in an attempt to force the military guard at Dartmoor prison on the evening of the 6th April, 1815, signed "Thomas George Shortland, agent; George Magrath, surgeon."

Letter of Alexander McLeay to R. G. Beasley, dated Transport Office, April 19, 1815.

Letter of R. G. Beasley to the Commissary General of Prisoners, dated April 30, 1815.

Extract of a letter from R. G. Beasley to the Commissary General of Prisoners, dated October 10, 1815.

Letter of R. G. Beasley to Alexander McLeay, dated January 1, 1815.

Letter of Alexander McLeay to R. G. Beasley, dated Transport Office, January 21, 1815.

Letter of R. G. Beasley to Alexander McLeay, dated March 15, 1815.

Letter of Alexander McLeay to R. G. Beasley, dated Transport Office, March 15, 1815.

Extract of a letter from R. G. Beasley to the committee of American prisoners of war at Dartmoor, dated March 22, 1815.

Letter of R. G. Beaslay to the American prisoners of war at Ashburton, dated March 23, 1815

Letter of R. G. Beasley to Captain Shortland, dated March 25, 1815.

Letter of R. G. Beasley to Dr. George Magrath, surgeon of Dartmoor prison, dated March 31, 1815.

Letter of R. G. Beasley to the committee of American prisoners of war at Dartmoor, dated March 31, 1815.

C

Extracts of a letter from the Commissary General of Prisoners to Reuben G. Beasley, Esq., American Agent for Prisoners in England, dated

MARCH 6, 1815.

I have received your letters of November 17th, December 21st and 31st last, by the British sloop of war Favorite. I could write you nothing definitive by the return of that vessel, in relation to the arrangements to be made in England for the restoration of our prisoners held there, as I could not, until after the time her despatches left the Seat of Government of the United States, come to an understanding with Mr. Baker, Chargé des Affaires for His Britannic Majesty, as to the terms and manner of restoring the prisoners on both sides under the treaty.

I now enclose you a correspondence begun on the 22d February, and concluded on the 28th, on that subject; by this you will perceive the construction which is given here in relation to this point, and that Mr. Baker has declined in any way to commit his Government; and that, in order to produce as little expense and delay as possible to either Government in the operation, I have given him the election of several propositions, (after he declined to proceed on the principle which I had presumed to exist, and which in his letter of the 23d February he appears to admit;) that each party should restore to the country from which taken the prisoners held by it; and that the proposition he has accepted embraced the transportation of all the prisoners, British and American, at English or American stations in this quarter, at the expense, in the first instance, of this Government; the accounts to be adjusted hereafter, according to justice and the terms of the treaty between the two Governments. Preparations are now actually going on for the immediate removal and transportation of all the British prisoners we now hold in this country; in numbers probably about 3,590, military and maritime.

The question, you will remark, as to the restoration of American prisoners in England, is left open. You are requested, immediately on the reception of this letter, to communicate the correspondence with Mr. Baker to the proper authority of the British Government, to show what is doing here in relation to the delivery and receipt of prisoners of both countries, and to state that the liberal proposition, of taking upon ourselves the transportation both of British and American prisoners, and to make the requisite advances for this purpose, was offered in that spirit of amity which it was deemed, on the happy return of peace between the two nations, to belong to the case; to insure the most speedy relief to the unfortunate men held in durance by either; and to lessen the expense as much as possible to both Governments; and with an express reservation of the construction of the treaty, as given here without commitment of the principle contended for by us, that is, that each party should pay the expense of the transportation and delivery of the prisoners held by it; that the operation will be performed in the most economical manner practicable; and accurate lists of prisoners and accounts kept for the final adjustment of an account between the two Governments. And you will require of the British Government to transport and deliver all the American prisoners now in England, or elsewhere, not embraced in the arrangement with Mr. Baker, in the most speedy and convenient manner. If this is consented to, (as I trust it will,) you will ask to be permitted to make the same kind of interference which has been afforded here to the British agents, as by the enclosed copy of a letter to Mr. Barton (delegated by Mr. Baker) of the 6th instant.

You will request that the same rations be allowed to our prisoners which are supplied on board ships to the British prisoners about to be transported from this country, and that a sufficiency of sound stores be laid in to supply them for ninety days; and you will apply for permission to place on board each transport an agent on whom you can rely, who shall have power to inspect the stores and accommodations, and see that the prisoners are regularly and properly supplied. Persons proper for these agencies may, no doubt, be found among the American masters and mates, now prisoners in England, to whom it will be right to make some reasonable compensation for their trouble—say 30 or 40 dollars per month; and you will instruct each in writing, and direct them to make report, on their arrival, to this office. You will require, also, that the British Government put a surgeon on board each vessel, supplied with a proper quantity of medicine and medical stores, as has been done here.

In the embarcation and distribution, as to the ports of delivery here, you will have examined carefully all the lists; endeavor, as much as possible, so to assort the prisoners as that each may be placed, as far as is conveniently practicable, nearest his home, or, more properly speaking, to the port from which he sailed; and, for this purpose, you will designate for the destination of the transports four of our principal ports along the coast; that is to say, Boston, New York, Norfolk, and Charleston. I have named those near the ocean as being most of access, and less liable, on that account, to objection. To prevent complaint, it will be proper, with as few exceptions as possible, to send those prisoners first who have been longest in captivity. There is no other rule that carries so much justice with it; and it is naturally to be expected that, after such long and severe confinement, the anxiety of our unfortunate citizens, so held, to be released, will be very great; and preferences out of turn will be viewed with great jealousy and discontent.

It remains to point out to you what is to be done, should the British Government, under all the circumstances stated, refuse to restore to us our prisoners in England at its expense. After making all proper efforts on this point, and with as little delay as possible, should you fail, there will be nothing left (having first protested in a respectful but firm manner against such refusal, should it happen, and giving notice that an accurate account will be kept of all expenditures made by us, in this part of the transaction, for future adjustment under the terms of the treaty) but to take the most speedy and effectual measures of transporting them, at the expense of this Government, in the first instance at least, to the United States.

I have been particular in my instructions in this letter in endeavoring to anticipate alternatives, and to put you fully in possession of my ideas on all the points that occur to me at present, in order that you may be prepared to proceed, immediately on its reception, in some one course, without a moment's delay. The operation you will have to perform, whatever course be taken, is one of much consequence in every view; important to the Government, in affording the most speedy relief possible to our countrymen placed in the hands of its late enemy by the fate of war; highly interesting to these unfortunate men, whose anxiety to return to their country and friends must increase with the knowledge of the end of the war, and the expectation that nothing but forms and want of opportunity now retard their departure; and of great consideration to the commercial interest of the United States, to have restored to it so many valuable seamen with as little delay as possible.

Your zeal and activity are, therefore, fully counted on, to do all that may depend on you to conduct this business to the best advantage, in all its bearings, and with the requisite economy.

I particularly recommend that you do not permit the interchange of sentiments, in negotiation with the British Government, as to the mode and expense of transportation, to be spun out. It will be expected that it will be prompt in deciding on the course it may determine to take in that matter. You will be readily able to show the necessity of an immediate decision.

From the Commissary General of Prisoners to George Barton, Esq.

OFFICE COMM'RY GEN. OF PRISONERS,
Washington, March 6, 1815.

SIR: Having been referred to you by Anthony St. John Baker, Esq., Chargé des Affaires of His Britannic Majesty in the United States, in relation to the steps necessary to be taken to carry into execution the restoration of the prisoners of war, American and British, held in the United States, Canada, Nova Scotia, and the West Indies, according to the understanding which has taken place between him and myself, (of the nature of which you are apprized,) I have the honor to inform you that orders, some days ago, have been given for the immediate march of all the

Massacre at Dartmoor Prison.

British prisoners captured on land or the lakes to the frontiers of Canada, to be delivered at or near Odletown, and for the immediate embarcation, in commodious vessels, of all the maritime prisoners held at New York, Providence, Rhode Island, Salem, and at any port east of Salem, (comprising all the prisoners, indeed, held at or east of New York,) for Halifax. These will be transported in the public cartel ships Perseverance and Analostan, and an additional private transport ordered to be taken up at Salem. All the prisoners held at New York or Providence will be sent from Providence in the Perseverance or Analostan, whichever is first ready; and those at Salem, or east of it, or at any intermediate port, will be sent in the other public ship, and in the private ship from Salem. The British prisoners at Philadelphia have been ordered this day to be removed to New York, where they will be embarked in the frigate John Adams, armed *en flute*, for Bermuda. Those who were held in the waters of the Chesapeake have been ordered to be delivered on board the British public ships now in those waters, by an understanding had with the senior officer, (Captain Clavell, of the frigate Orlando,) and, it is presumed, have been by this time received by him. All those in North or South Carolina, or Georgia, will be, as soon as practicable, embarked from Wilmington, Charleston, and Savannah, for Bermuda, in public ships or private transports. As soon as the vessels are designated, which will be in a few days, you will be informed. Orders have been sent to the marshal of Orleans to collect and deliver, forthwith, all the British prisoners in that State, and the adjoining Territories, to the British officer commanding in those waters; and it is presumed they will reach him time enough to dispose of them before your public ships withdraw from that quarter. All these arrangements have been made, or are now in train, as I believe, according to the detail settled in different conversations between you and myself. If there is anything in what I have stated different from your understanding of it, I shall be glad, as far as is in my power, to conform to it.

I have given particular orders that the British prisoners be not put in such numbers on board the vessels transporting them as to crowd them improperly, and am willing, if you think proper, that this shall be regulated by a certain number of men per ton. I have directed that sound and wholesome provisions, and plenty of water, be laid in for them, and served out on the passage in rations, as by the enclosed table; that a surgeon be allotted to each ship, provided with a proper quantity of medical and hospital stores; and I have directed the agents of this office, at the ports from which the prisoners are to be embarked, to make provision on board each ship for the accommodation of an agent, to be put on board by you, if you think proper to do so, to superintend the treatment and accommodation of the prisoners, and to inspect the quantity and quality of the provisions issued to them on the passage; and the masters of the respective ships

will be instructed to respect such agents on your part in the performance of the duties assigned them.

In conformity with the request made in your letter of the 25th February, I have directed the marshal of North Carolina, and all the other marshals of the different States having charge of British prisoners, to release all the British prisoners, officers in their districts, respectively, whether of public or private service, who may not choose to wait the sailing of the cartels, and to permit them to leave the country at their option and expense.

I have ordered that all the British maritime prisoners be held and subsisted, as heretofore, at the several depots, until they are regularly embarked. If it be your wish, however, that any portion of these, other than those you have already designated for that purpose, should be discharged in the United States, it shall be done.

I have the honor to be, &c.

               J. MASON.

GEORGE BARTON, Esq.

Table of provisions to be allowed to prisoners, whether American or British, on board of vessels transporting them.

Days	Allowance for each person.		
Sunday	1 lb. beef,	1 lb. bread,	½ lb. potatoes.
Monday	1 lb. beef,	1 lb. bread,	½ lb. potatoes.
Tuesday	1 lb. pork,	1 lb. bread,	½ pint peas.
Wednesday	1 lb. beef,	1 lb. bread,	½ lb. potatoes.
Thursday	1 lb. beef,	1 lb. bread,	½ lb. potatoes.
Friday	1 lb. pork,	1 lb. bread,	½ pint peas.
Saturday	1 lb. beef,	1 lb. bread,	½ lb. potatoes.

1 gill of vinegar per week.
3 quarts of water per day.

RECAPITULATION.

Beef	-	-	-	5 pounds per man per week.
Pork	-	-	-	2 do. do. do.
Bread	-	-	-	7 do. do. do.
Potatoes	-	-	-	2½ do. do. do.
Peas	-	-	-	1 pint do. do.
Vinegar	-	-	-	1 gill do. do.
Water	-	-	-	21 quarts do. do.

OFFICE OF COMM'RY GEN. OF PRISONERS.

               J. MASON.

From R. G. Beasley to the Commissary General of Prisoners.

            LONDON, April 13, 1815.

SIR: I had the honor to receive yesterday your letters of the 15th January, 6th, (two,) and 8th of March. I shall avail myself of the earliest occasion to notice their contents. In the mean time, I have to inform you that I have communicated to the Transport Board the correspondence between yourself and Mr. Baker on the subject of the restoration of prisoners, and have called on them to undertake the transportation to the United States of our prisoners in this country. Prior, however, to the receipt of your letter on this subject, I had engaged in this port nine ships for the conveyance of our prisoners, several of which have sailed for Plymouth to take them on board. I, in the first instance, endeavored to engage vessels at Portsmouth and Plymouth; but the turn of affairs in France having induced this Government to take up transports for the conveyance of troops, I could obtain none in those ports.

It is with extreme regret I have to state, that on the 6th instant the guard of the depot at Dartmoor, by order of the agent, fired on the American prisoners, killed five, and wounded thirty-four. I transmit, herewith, two reports of this unfortunate affair, (one from the Transport Board, and one from the Admiralty Office, through the Foreign Office.)

By the latter you will perceive that the prisoners are accused of having attempted to liberate themselves by force, and are stated to have been urged to this by the impression they were under that their own Government had neglected to provide means for their early conveyance home.

As the prisoners have been constantly informed of the exertions made by me for their release, and as on this occasion I had written twice to let them know the number of vessels taken up for their conveyance home, and the time they might be expected at Plymouth, it is difficult to believe, under such circumstances, that this is really the cause of this melancholy occurrence. I shall, therefore, inquire most minutely into all the circumstances attending it, and shall communicate the result to you, as also the names of those who have been killed and wounded.

I am, sir, your obedient servant,
R. G. BEASLEY.

The Hon. JOHN MASON, &c.

From Alexander McLeay to R. G. Beasley.

TRANSPORT OFFICE, *April* 10, 1815.

SIR : I am directed by the Commissioners for the transport service, &c. to acquaint you, that, by a letter this day received from Captain Shortland, the agent for prisoners of war at Dartmoor prison, it appears that on the 6th instant the American prisoners confined at that depot made a breach in the prison wall, and attempted to liberate themselves, by making a violent attack on the guard; and that it became indispensably necessary, in order to quell the revolt, for the guard to fire upon them; in consequence of which five of the prisoners were killed and thirty-three were wounded.

I am further directed to observe, that it is much to be lamented that the extreme impatience of these unfortunate men to be discharged, at a time that measures were in a train for their liberation, should have produced such melancholy consequences. I am, &c.

ALEX. McLEAY, *Secretary.*

R. G. BEASLEY, Esq.

From J. P. Morier to R. G. Beasley.

FOREIGN OFFICE, *April* 11, 1815.

SIR : I lose no time in transmitting to you the copy of a letter which I have received from Mr. Crocker, of the Admiralty, giving a circumstan-

tial account of the alarming riot which broke out on the 6th instant amongst the American prisoners of war confined at Dartmoor, and of the measures which it became necessary to pursue for the purpose of restoring order; and I am *directed* by Lord Castlereagh to request that you *will take* an early opportunity of forwarding this statement of the unfortunate event to your Government.

I have the honor to be, sir, your most obedient humble servant,
J. P. MORIER.

R. G. BEASLEY, Esq.

From J. W. Croker to J. P. Morier.

ADMIRALTY OFFICE, *April* 10, 1815.

SIR: My Lords Commissioners of the Admiralty think it right to acquaint Lord Castlereagh that, on the evening of the 6th instant, a very alarming riot broke out among the American prisoners of war confined at Dartmoor. The rioters, it appears, endeavored to overpower the guard, to force the prison, and had actually seized the arms of some of the soldiers, and made a breach in the walls of the depot, when the guard found itself obliged to have recourse to their fire-arms, and five of the rioters were killed and thirty-three wounded; after which the tumult subsided, and the depot was placed in a state of tranquillity and security.

Admiral Sir J. T. Duckworth, Commander-in-Chief at Plymouth, having received information of this unfortunate event, lost no time in directing Rear-Admiral Sir Josias Rowley, Bart. and K. B., and Captain Shornberg, the two senior officers at that port, to proceed to Dartmoor, and to inquire into the circumstances. Those officers accordingly repaired to the depot, where they found, on examination of the officers of the depot, and all the American prisoners who were called before them, that the circumstances of the riot were as before stated, and that no excuse could be assigned for the conduct of the prisoners but their impatience to be released; and the Americans unanimously declared that their complaint of delay was not against the British Government, but against their own, which ought to have sent means for their early conveyance home; and, in replies to distinct questions to that effect, they declared they had no ground of complaint whatsoever.

Their Lordships think it right to add, that, on the 15th of last month, they directed the Transport Board to take measures for carrying the article of the treaty for the release of American prisoners into effect; and again, on the 30th ultimo, I was directed to write to know what steps had been taken under these directions; and the Transport Board answered, in their letter of the next day, that they had communicated with Mr. Beasley, the American agent, on the subject, who had acquainted them that he had already provided some transports, and was employed in procuring others, for the conveyance of the prisoners to America.

It will be for Lord Castlereagh to judge whether

it may not be proper to make a communication on this subject to the American Government.

I am, &c.　　　　　J. W. CROKER.

J. P. MORIER, Esq.

From R. G. Beasley to the Commissary General of Prisoners.

LONDON, April 15, 1815.

SIR: I enclose a copy of the report of the committee of our prisoners on the lamentable transaction of the 6th instant, which I communicated to you on the 13th, with a statement from the Admiralty office on that subject.

I have transmitted a copy of the report of the committee to Lord Castlereagh, as also affidavits of three prisoners, who were in the prison at the time, and have since arrived in town.

As soon as I can obtain a list of the names of the unfortunate sufferers, it shall be transmitted to you.

I have the honor to be, &c.

R. G. BEASLEY.

The Hon. JOHN MASON, &c.

From the Committee appointed to investigate the circumstances attending the massacre at Dartmoor:

We, the undersigned, being each severally sworn on the Holy Evangelists of Almighty God, for the investigation of the circumstances attending the late massacre, and having heard the depositions of a great number of witnesses, from our own personal knowledge, and from the depositions given in as aforesaid, report as follows:

That, on the 6th of April, about six o'clock in the evening, when the prisoners were all quiet in their respective yards, (it being about the usual time for turning in for the night,) and the greater part of the prisoners being then in the prisons, the alarm bell was rung. Many of the prisoners ran up to the market square to learn the occasion of the alarm. There were then drawn up in the square several hundred soldiers, with Captain Shortland (the agent) at their head; it was likewise observed, at the same time, that additional numbers of soldiers were posting themselves round the walls of the prison yard. One of them observed to the prisoners that they had better go into their prisons, for they would be charged upon directly. This, of course, occasioned considerable alarm among them; in this moment of uncertainty they were running in different directions, inquiring of each other what was the cause of the alarm—some towards their respective prisons, and some towards the market square; when about one hundred were collected in the market square, Captain Shortland ordered the soldiers to charge upon them, which orders the soldiers were reluctant in obeying, as the prisoners were using no violence; but, on the orders being repeated, they made a charge, and the prisoners retreated out of the square into their respective prison yards, and shut the gates after them. Captain Shortland

himself opened the gates, and ordered the soldiers to fire in among the prisoners, who were all retreating in different directions towards their respective prisons. It appears there was some hesitation in the minds of the officers, whether or not it was proper to fire upon the prisoners in that situation; on which Shortland seized a musket out of the hands of a soldier, which he fired. Immediately after, the firing became general, and many of the prisoners were either killed or wounded; the remainder were endeavoring to get into the prisons, when, going towards the lower doors, the soldiers on the walls commenced firing on them from that quarter, which killed some, and wounded others; after much difficulty, (all the doors being closed in the interim but one in each prison,) the survivors succeeded in gaining the prisons. Immediately after which, parties of soldiers came to the doors of Nos. 3 and 4 prisons, and fired several volleys into them through the windows and doors, which killed one man in each prison, and wounded severely several others.

It likewise appears that the preceding butchery was followed up with a disposition of peculiar inveteracy and barbarity. One man, who had been severely wounded in No. 7 yard, and, being unable to make his way to the prison, was come up with by the soldiers, whom he implored for mercy, but in vain; *five* of the hardened wretches immediately levelled their pieces at him, and shot him dead! The soldiers who were posted on the walls manifested equal cruelty, by keeping up a constant fire on every prisoner they could see in the yard endeavoring to get into the prisons, when the numbers were very few, and when not the least shadow of resistance could be made or expected. Some of them had got into No. 6 prison cook-house, which was pointed out by the soldiers on the walls to those who were marching in from the square; they immediately went up and fired into the same, which wounded several. One of the prisoners ran out, with the intention of gaining his prison, but was killed before he reached the door.

On an impartial consideration of all the circumstances of the case, we are induced to believe it was a premeditated scheme in the mind of Captain Shortland, for reasons which we will now proceed to give. As an elucidation of its origin, we will recur back to an event which happened some days previous. Captain Shortland was at the time absent at Plymouth, but, before going, he ordered the contractor or his clerk to serve out one pound of indifferent hard bread, instead of one pound and a half of soft bread, their usual allowance. This the prisoners refused to receive. They waited all day, in expectation of their usual allowance being served out; but at sunset, finding this would not be the case, they burst open the lower gates, and went up to the store, demanding to have their bread. The officers of the garrison, on being alarmed, and informed of the reasons of this proceeding, observed that it was no more than right the prisoners should have their usual allowance, and strongly reprobated the conduct of Captain Shortland in withholding it from them. They were accordingly served with their bread, and quietly returned to their prisons. This circumstance, with the censures that were thrown on his conduct, reached the ears of Shortland on his return home, and he must then have determined on the diabolical plan of seizing the first slight pretext to turn in the military to butcher the prisoners, for the gratification of his malice and revenge. It unfortunately happened, that in the afternoon of the 6th of April some boys, who were playing ball in No. 7 yard, knocked their ball over into the barrack yard, and, on the sentry in that yard refusing to throw it back again, they picked a hole through the wall to get in after it. This afforded Shortland his wished-for pretext, and he took his measures accordingly. He had all the garrison drawn up in the military walk, additional numbers posted on the walls, and everything ready prepared before the alarm bell was rung. This he naturally concluded would draw the attention of a great number of prisoners towards the gate, to learn the cause of the alarm, while the turnkeys were despatched into the yards to lock all the doors but one of each prison, to prevent the prisoners retreating out of the way before he had sufficiently wreaked his vengeance.

What adds peculiar weight to the belief of its being a premeditated massacre, are—

Firstly. The sanguinary disposition manifested on every occasion by Shortland; he having, prior to this time, ordered the soldiers to fire into the prisons, through the windows, upon unarmed prisoners asleep in their hammocks, on account of a light having been seen in the prisons; which barbarous act was repeated several nights successively; that murder was not committed was owing to an overruling Providence alone, for the balls were picked up in the prisons, where they passed through the hammocks of men then asleep in them; he having ordered the soldiers to fire upon the prisoners in the yard of No. 7 prison, because they would not deliver up to him a man who had made his escape from the Cachot, which order the commanding officer of the soldiers refused to obey; and, generally, he having seized on every slight pretext to injure the prisoners, by his stopping the marketing for ten days repeatedly, and once a third part of their provisions for the same length of time.

Secondly. He having been heard to say, when the boys had picked the hole in the wall, and some time before the alarm bell rung, and while all the prisoners were quiet in their respective yards, as usual, "I'll fix the damned rascals directly."

Thirdly. His having all the soldiers on their posts, and the garrison fully prepared, before the alarm bell was rung. It could not, of course, then be done to assemble the soldiers, but to alarm the prisoners and create confusion among them.

Fourthly. The soldiers on the wall, previous to the alarm bell being rung, informing the prisoners that they would be charged upon directly.

Fifthly. The turnkeys going into the yard and closing all the doors but one in each prison, whilst the attention of the prisoners was attracted by the alarm bell. This was done about fifteen minutes

sooner than usual, and without informing the prisoners it was time to shut up. It was ever the invariable practice of the turnkeys, (from which they never deviated before that night,) when coming into the yards to shut up, to halloo to the prisoners so loud as to be heard all over the yards, "turn in, turn in;" while on that night it was done so secretly, that not one man in a hundred knew they were shut; and, in particular, their shutting the door of No. 7, which the prisoners usually go in and out at, (and which was formerly always the last one closed,) and leaving one open in the other end of the prison, which was exposed to a cross-fire from the soldiers on the walls, and which the prisoners had to pass in gaining the prison.

It appears to us that the foregoing reasons sufficiently warrant the conclusions we have drawn therefrom. We likewise believe, from the depositions of men who were eye-witnesses of a part of Shortland's conduct on the evening of the 6th April, that he was intoxicated with liquor at the time, from his brutality in beating a prisoner who was then supporting another severely wounded; from the blackguard and abusive language he made use of; and from his having frequently been seen in the same state. His being drunk was, of course, the means of inflaming his bitter enmity against the prisoners, and no doubt was the principal cause of the indiscriminate butchery, and of no quarter being shown.

We here solemnly aver, there was no preconcerted plan to attempt breaking out. There cannot be produced the least shadow of a reason or inducement for that intention, the prisoners daily expecting to be released, and to embark on board cartels for their own native country; and we solemnly assert, likewise, that there was no intention of resisting, in any manner, the authority of the government of this depot.

[Signed by the Committee.]

N. B. Seven were killed, thirty dangerously and thirty slightly wounded, making a total of sixty-seven killed and wounded.

Dartmoor Prison, *April* 7, 1815.

We hereby certify this to be a true copy of the original report:

William B. Bond,	William Hobart,
James Boggs,	James Adams,
Francis Joseph,	John T. Trowbridge,
John Rust,	Henry Allen,
Walter Colton,	Thomas B. Mott,
	Committee.

R. G. Beasley to the Commissary General of Prisoners.

London, *April* 18, 1815.

Sir: I had the honor to transmit, on the 13th and 15th instant, two reports on the unfortunate transaction of the 6th instant at Dartmoor prison —the one by the British authorities, and the other by a committee of our prisoners. The latter I lost no time in laying before this Government; and, on the receipt of it, Lord Castlereagh sought an interview with Mr. Clay and Mr. Gallatin, at which it was agreed that each party should appoint a commissioner to investigate the circumstances. If it had suited the convenience of Mr. Clay or Mr. Gallatin to have undertaken it, one of the British Commissioners who signed the Treaty of Ghent would have been appointed to act with him; but as neither of these gentlemen could go, and as my presence here could not be dispensed with at present, they advised me to apply to Mr. Charles King, of New York, who has readily undertaken to act, although it interferes in some degree with his private affairs.

Mr. King left town last evening for Dartmoor, with a Mr. Larpent, who is to act with him.

The result of the investigation shall be transmitted to you as soon as received; in the meantime, I am happy to have it in my power to state that every disposition has been manifested to do what is due to the occasion.

I transmit, herewith, a list of the unfortunate sufferers in this affair.

I also enclose a copy of a letter which I have just received from the Transport Board, relative to the proposals I made, on the receipt of your letter of the 6th ultimo, for sending home our prisoners.

It is proper that I should here remark, that, at the interview which took place between Lord Castlereagh and Messrs. Clay and Gallatin, his Lordship proposed this arrangement, and that these gentlemen advised me to agree to it.

I have the honor to be, &c.

R. G. BEASLEY.

The Hon. JOHN MASON, &c.

List of prisoners wounded on the evening of the 6th April, 1815.

Thomas Smith, amputated thigh.

Philip Ford, punctured wound of the back, and punctured wound of the belly.

John Gray, amputated arm.

Robert Willet, (tawney,) amputated thigh.

James Bell, bayonet wound of the thigh.

Thomas Findlay, gunshot wound through the thigh and testicle; the ball entered the hip, and passed out the fore part of the thigh, and through the testicle.

William Leverage, lacerated hand and amputated thumb.

Joseph Bezreck, (alias Masick,) gunshot wound of the thigh, through which the ball passed.

John Willett, (black,) fractured jaw, lacerated hip, complicated with a shattered state of the upper jaw.

James Esdaile, gunshot wound of the hip.

Henry Montcalm, gunshot wound of the left knee.

Frederick (or John) Howard, gunshot wound of the leg, through which the ball passed.

William Penn, (black,) gunshot wound of the thigh.

Robert Fittez, gunshot wound of the penis.

Cornelius Garrison, gunshot wound of the thigh. The ball passed through the limb.

James Turnball, amputated arm.

Edward Whittlebanks, bayonet wound of the

back, producing paralysis of the sphincture ani et urini, with paralysis of the lower extremities.

Stephen Phipps, bayonet wounds of the abdomen and thigh.

James Wells, gunshot fracture sacrum and crista iliæ, and gunshot fracture of both bones of the left arm.

Caleb Codding, gunshot wound of the leg.

Edward Gardner, gunshot fracture of the left arm.

Jacob Davis, gunshot wound of the thigh. The ball passed through the thigh.

John Hagabets, gunshot wound of the hip.

Peter Wilson, gunshot fracture of the hand. The ball passed through the palm of the hand.

John Perry, gunshot wound of the shoulder.

John Peach, gunshot wound of the thigh. The ball passed through the thigh.

John Roberts, (black,) gunshot wound of the thigh.

John Guie, amputated thigh.

Ephraim Lincoln, gunshot wound of the knee. Discharged cured 23d April, 1815.

John Wilson, bayonet wound. Discharged cured 12th April, 1815.

William Blake, bayonet wound. Discharged cured 12th April, 1815.

* Thomas Jackson, (black,) gunshot wound of the abdomen. He died early in the morning of the 7th.

* James Campbell, gunshot fracture, with depression of the whole of the frontal bone, orbital ridge, and nasal bones. He died on the morning of the 8th.   GEORGE MAGRATH.

Description of death wounds inflicted on the evening of April 6, 1815.

John Haywood, (black.) The ball entered a little posterior to the acromien of the left shoulder, and, passing obliquely upwards, made its egress about the middle of the right side of the neck.

Thomas Jackson. The ball entered the left side of the belly, nearly in a line with the navel, and made its egress a little below the false ribs in the opposite side; a large portion of the intestinal canal protruded through the wound made by the ingress of the ball. He languished until 8 o'clock on the morning of the 7th, when he died.

John Washington. The ball entered at the squamous process of the left temporal bone, and, passing through the head, made its exit a little below the crucial ridge of the occipital bone.

James Mann. The ball entered at the inferior angle of the left scapula, and lodged under the integument of the right pectoral muscle. In its course, it passed through the inferior margin of the right and left lobes of the lungs.

Joseph Toker Johnson. The ball entered at the inferior angle of the left scapula, penetrated the heart, and, passing through both lobes of the lungs, made its egress at the right axilla.

William Leveridge. The ball entered about the middle of the left arm, through which it passed, and, penetrating the corresponding side,

* These names are included in the list of deaths.

Massacre at Dartmoor Prison.

betwixt the second and third ribs, passing through the left lobe of the lungs, the mediastinum, and over the right lobe, lodged betwixt the fifth and sixth ribs.

James Campbell. The ball entered at the outer angle of the right eye, and in its course it fractured and depressed the greater part of the frontal bone, fractured the nasal bones, and made its egress above the orbital ridge of the left eye. He languished until the morning of the 8th, when he died.   GEORGE MAGRATH.

A return of American prisoners of war who were killed and wounded in an attempt to force the military guard on the evening of the 6th of April, 1815.

Current number.	Number on general entry book.	Names.	Quality.	Ship.	Whether man of war, merchant vessel, or privateer.
		KILLED.			
1	4,834	Wm. Leveridge,	Seaman,	Enterprise, prize to Saratoga, -	Privateer.
	970	James Mann,	Do.	Siroc, - - - -	Letter of marque.
	3,194	John Haywood,	Do.	Gave himself up from H. M. ship Scipion.	
	1,347	Jos. T. Johnson,	Do.	Paul Jones, - - - -	Privateer.
5	3,936	John Washington,	Do.	Rolla, - - - -	Merchant vessel.
		WOUNDED.			
1	6,520	*Thomas Jackson,	Boy,	Gave himself up from H. M. ship Prontes.	
	2,647	†James Campbell,	Seaman,	Volontaire.	
	5,769	John Guier,	Do.	Rambler, - - - -	Merchant vessel.
	1,733	William Penn,	Do.	Despatch; impressed at London,	Merchant vessel.
5	5,003	Cornel's Garrison,	Do.	Invincible, - - - -	Letter of marque.
	3,614	H. Montcalm,	Do.	Hornby, prize to Gov. Tompkins,	Privateer.
	1,965	Robert Willet,	Do.	H. M. ship Andromache.	
	5,326	John Peach,	Do.	Enterprise, - - - -	Privateer.
	3,148	Ed. Whittlebanks,	Do.	H. M. ship Royal William.	
10	1,981	James Turnbull,	Boy,	Elbridge Gerry, - - -	Privateer.
	3,652	James Wells,	Seaman,	Thorn, - - - -	Privateer.
	1,236	Philip Ford,	Do.	H. M. ship Sultan, - -	
	685	James Bell,	Do.	Joel Barlow, - - -	Merchant vessel.
	94	John Gray,	Do.	St. Martin's Planter, - -	Merchant vessel.
15	426	Wm. Leverage,	Do.	Magdelene, - - - -	Merchant vessel.
	1,034	Edward Gardner,	Do.	Joseph, - - - -	Merchant vessel.
	1,545	Stephen Phipps,	Do.	Zebra, - - - -	Letter of marque.
	486	John Roberts,	Do.	Two Brothers; impressed at Cork,	Letter of marque.
	1,640	Thomas Smith,	Do.	Paul Jones, - - - -	Privateer.
20	1,819	Caleb Codding,	Do.	H. M. ship Swiftsure.	
	5,015	Jacob Davis,	Do.	Charlotte, prize to Mammoth, -	Privateer.
	2,013	James Esdaile,	Do.	Governor Tompkins, - -	Privateer.
	380	Peter Wilson,	Do.	Virginia Planter, - -	Merchant vessel.
	2,884	†William Blake,	Do.	H. M. ship Repulse.	
25	338	John Hagabeta,	2d mate,	Good Friends, - - -	Merchant vessel.
	4,153	Ephraim Lincoln,	Seaman,	Argus, - - - -	Merchant vessel.
	4,493	Thomas Findlay,	Do.	Enterprise - - -	Privateer.
	4,109	John Howard,	Do.	Flash, - - - -	Privateer.
	1,236	Joseph Masick,	Do.	H. M. ship Furieux.	
30	6,133	Robert Fittes,	Do.	Grand Turk, - - -	Privateer.
	1,812	John Willett,	Do.	H. M. ship Rosario.	
	3,060	John Perry,	Do.	H. M. ship Tiger.	
33	2,662	‡John Wilson,	Do.	H. M. ship Fortune.	

TH. GEO. SHORTLAND, *Agent.*
GEO. MAGRATH, *Surgeon.*

* Dangerously; died April 7, 1815.   ‡ Discharged cured April 12, 1815.
† Dangerously; died April 8, 1815. § Discharged cured April 12, 1815.

Massacre at Dartmoor Prison.

From Alexander McLeay to R. G. Beasley.

TRANSPORT OFFICE, *April* 19, 1815.

SIR: I am directed by the Commissioners for the transport service, &c., to acquaint you that the Lords Commissioners of the Admiralty have, by their order of yesterday's date, been pleased to signify the consent of his Majesty's Government that the expense of conveying the American prisoners of war from this country to America should be shared by the two Governments, leaving the interpretation of the article in the late Treaty of Peace upon this subject for future explanation; and that the board are accordingly about to take measures for providing vessels for the conveyance of the remainder of the prisoners, understanding that the vessels already engaged by you are calculated to convey about three thousand men. I am, sir, &c.,

ALEXANDER McLEAY.

R. G. BEASLEY, Esq.

From R. G. Beasley to the Commissary General of Prisoners.

LONDON, *April* 30, 1815.

SIR: In my letter of the 19th instant I informed you of the measures which had been adopted here in consequence of the late unfortunate event at Dartmoor prison.

I have now the honor to transmit the copy of a letter addressed to me by Mr. Clay and Mr. Gallatin, relative to that occurrence, and to the transportation of the American prisoners in this country to the United States.

In the absence of Mr. Adams, it becomes my duty to communicate, for the information of our Government, the result of the investigation at Dartmoor. I enclose a copy of the joint report of the Commissioners appointed for that purpose; also a letter from Mr. King to Mr. Adams, and of a list of the killed and wounded on that melancholy occasion.

I shall leave to Mr. Adams any further steps which he may deem it proper to take in this business. I cannot, however, forbear to notice here the erroneous impression of the prisoners, that their detention so long has been owing to me. You are aware, sir, of my constant exertions during the war to effect their liberation. Immediately on the signing of the Treaty of Peace at Ghent, I received my instructions on that subject, proposing, as a condition, that all the prisoners who might be delivered over to me by the British Government should be considered as prisoners of war, and not at liberty to serve until regularly exchanged, in the event of the treaty not being ratified by the President. This proposition was declined, and in a peremptory manner. On the receipt of the intelligence of the ratification from America, I lost not a moment in requesting the release of the prisoners, according to the terms of the treaty; and the number of vessels which I had hired, as mentioned in my letter of the 13th instant, and which are now on their voyage to the United States, will show that the necessary steps were taken to provide for their immediate transportation to their country. The prisoners also, were informed of these measures, and of the exertions which had been made from the commencement to return them to their homes with the least possible delay. Therefore, whatever may have been their uneasiness under confinement, and whatever hostile feelings they may have had towards me, as noticed in the report and in Mr. King's letter, I may say, with confidence, that I could not prevent the one, nor have I deserved the other.

I have the honor to be, &c.,

R. G. BEASLEY.

HON. JOHN MASON, &c.

Extracts of a letter from R. G. Beasley, Esq., Agent for American Prisoners of War in England, to the Commissary General of Prisoners, dated

OCTOBER 10, 1815.

"In compliance with the request contained in that of the 5th August, [the Commissary General's letter,] I transmit, herewith, copies of my correspondence with the Transport Board on the subject of the general release of American prisoners in this country on the conclusion of the treaty at Ghent, and on the receipt of the President's ratification; also, copies and extracts of letters informing the prisoners of the measures taken for their release, preceding the occurrence at Dartmoor of the 6th April.

"It was always my practice before requesting, by written communication, the release of prisoners, to urge the measure in person; and this repeatedly, until either it was granted, or there appeared not any hope of success; and then my letter followed, for the purpose of reducing the negotiation to a more official form. This practice I pursued upon the conclusion of the treaty at Ghent, when my request was refused; and again on the receipt of the ratification of the President, when the release was agreed upon. Upon these occasions I, of course, availed myself of every circumstance which I conceived calculated to accomplish the object I had in view; and I frequently found the board concurring with me upon points which, when submitted to the Admiralty, were rejected." "One of my letters, informing the prisoners of the measures taken for their release, was addressed to those on parole at Ashburton, which is about sixteen miles distant from Dartmoor, and with whom the prisoners at this place were in constant correspondence. I have to observe, further, that when inquiry as to the probable time of release was made at my office by friends of prisoners, which at that time was very frequently the case, they were always requested, when writing to them, to desire the information to be made as public in the prison as possible."

From R. G. Beasley to Alexander McLeay.

HARLEY STREET, *Jan.* 18, 1815.

SIR: A treaty of peace having been concluded at Ghent between Great Britain and the United

Massacre at Dartmoor Prison.

States, I am induced, by a desire to shorten the sufferings of the American prisoners in this country, to address the board relative to them. I do this with the more confidence of its being favorably received, as I am persuaded that this wish is equally entertained by the British Government.

I have, therefore, to request that a certain number of prisoners may be released, as soon as I may be able to procure proper conveyances for them to the United States, under the condition that they shall be subject to exchange should the treaty not be ratified by the President of the United States. I am, &c.

R. G. BEASLEY.

A. McLEAY, Esq., *Transport Office.*

From Alexander McLeay to R. G. Beasley.

TRANSPORT OFFICE, *Jan. 21, 1815.*

SIR: Having received, and laid before the Commissioners for the transport service, &c., your letter of the 18th instant, proposing, under the circumstances therein stated, that a certain number of American prisoners of war may be permitted to return to the United States, I have it in command to acquaint you that the same has been referred to the consideration of the Lords Commissioners of the Admiralty, and that their Lordships have, in reply, been pleased to signify that they do not think proper to accede to your proposition. I am, &c.

A. McLEAY, *Secretary.*

From R. G. Beasley to Alexander McLeay.

HARLEY STREET, *March 15, 1815.*

SIR: The Treaty of Ghent having been ratified by the Governments of the United States and this country, and peace being thus happily restored between the two nations, I beg to inquire whether there is any objection to deliver over to me the prisoners detained in this country, as soon as I can provide for their conveyance?

I am, &c.   R. G. BEASLEY.

A. McLEAY, Esq., *Transport Office.*

From Alexander McLeay to R. G. Beasley.

TRANSPORT OFFICE, *March 15, 1815.*

SIR: I have received, and laid before the Commissioners of the transport service, &c., your letter of the 15th instant, requesting to be informed, under the circumstances therein stated, whether there be any objection to deliver over to you the Americans now detained as prisoners of war in this country, upon your providing vessels for their conveyance to the United States.

In reply, I am directed to acquaint you that the board are ready to embark all the prisoners in question, upon your providing vessels at Plymouth for their conveyance; it being understood that all the debts contracted by them in this country must previously be paid.

I am, &c.,

A. McLEAY, *Secretary.*

R. G. BEASLEY, Esq.

Extract of a letter from R. G. Beasley, addressed to the Committee of American Prisoners of War at Dartmoor.

LONDON, *March 22, 1815.*

" Three cartels are now preparing here, with all expedition, for the conveyance of the prisoners to the United States."

R. G. Beasley to American Prisoners of War at Ashburton.

AGENCY FOR AM. PRISONERS OF WAR,

London, *March 24, 1815.*

GENTLEMEN: I have to inform you, that the Treaty of Peace having been ratified by the President, the release of the prisoners of war will commence without delay.

Although I have not as yet received any instructions from our Government, I have engaged, and am fitting out, four vessels for their conveyance, to proceed to Plymouth to receive them, and shall use every despatch in sending them to the United States.

I am, &c.   R. G. BEASLEY.

Extract of a letter from R. G. Beasley to Captain T. G. Shortland, Agent for Prisoners of War at Dartmoor.

LONDON, *March 25, 1815.*

" I have engaged four vessels for cartels, which are fitting out with all despatch. They will sail, I hope, in five or six days for Plymouth, to receive prisoners. Their tonnage, together, is about 1,600 tons."

From R. G. Beasley to Dr. Magrath.

LONDON, *March 31, 1815.*

SIR: I have received your letter of the 29th instant, acquainting me with your opinion of the complaints of Mr. Proctor and Mr. Robinson, now in Dartmoor hospital. In return, I beg to inform you that these two prisoners shall be sent home in the first cartel, which will, I expect, sail from this place to-morrow for Plymouth.

I am, &c.   R. G. BEASLEY.

GEORGE MAGRATH, Esq., *Surgeon, &c.*

From R. G. Beasley to the Committee of American Prisoners of War.

AGENCY FOR AM. PRISONERS OF WAR,

London, *March 31, 1815.*

GENTLEMEN: It appearing by several letters which I have received from Dartmoor, that the prisoners have taken up an idea that any who may have the means of proceeding to the United States would, on application, receive a free discharge, I request that you will make it known throughout the prison that such is not the fact.

There must be other and better reasons to induce me to consent to their release in this manner, at this time. The situation of Europe, under the prospect of another war, multiplies the risk of impressment. I have taken measures to have

State of the Finances.

them all released and sent home by cartels with as little delay as possible, where they are much wanted, and where wages are very high.

I am, &c.   R. G. BEASLEY.

STATE OF THE FINANCES.

[Communicated to the Senate, December 8, 1815.]

TREASURY DEPARTMENT, *Dec.* 6, 1815.

In obedience to the acts entitled, respectively, "An act to establish the Treasury Department," and "An act supplementary to the act entitled an act to establish the Treasury Department," the Secretary of the Treasury has the honor to lay before Congress the following report:

I. A cursory review of the financial operations of the Government, in reference to the recent state of war.

II. A view of the finances for 1815, with estimates of the public revenue and expenditures for 1816.

III. Propositions for the improvement and management of the revenue, and for the support of public credit.

I. *A cursory review of the financial operations of the Government in reference to the recent state of war.*

In order to introduce to the consideration of Congress, with advantage, the measures which will be respectfully suggested, for replacing the finances of the United States upon the basis of a Peace Establishment, a review of the financial operations of the Government, in reference to the recent state of war, appears to be a necessary preliminary.

The restrictive system, which commenced in the year 1807, greatly diminished the product of the public revenue; but it was not until the crisis involved an actual declaration of war, that the augmentation in the expenses of the Government became obvious and important. With the occasional aid of temporary loans the ordinary receipts of the Treasury had exceeded the ordinary expenditures, even during the period of a suspended commerce; and a report from this Department, presenting the estimates for the year 1812, seems to have given the first intimation that the portion of extraordinary expenses, to be incurred for the military and naval service, on account of the then existing state of the country, would raise the demands upon the Treasury to a considerable amount beyond the estimated product of the current revenue. The ordinary disbursements for the year ending on the 30th of September, 1811, were stated as amounting to the sum of $13,052,657 73; and the ordinary receipts, for the same year, were stated as amounting to the sum of $13,541,446 37, independent of a temporary loan raised in 1810, and repaid in 1811, as well as of the balances in the Treasury at the commencement and the close of the year. But the estimates for the year 1812 required, on

14th CON. 1st SESS.—51

account of the current expenses, the sum of $9,400,000.

For the Civil and Diplomatic
departments - - - - $1,260,000
For the Military Department, (including the militia, the Indian department, the charge of arsenals, army, and ordnance, &c.) - - - 3,415,000
For the Naval Department - 2,500,000
And for the interest on the public debt - - - - 2,225,000
                         $9,400,000

And the subsisting revenue to meet these expenses was estimated at $8,200,000, proceeding—
From the customs - - - 7,500,000
From the sale of public lands - 600,000
And from miscellaneous payments - - - - 100,000
                         8,200,000

Leaving a deficit, for which it was proposed to provide by a loan, amounting to the sum of - - - - - - $1,200,000

Such were the limited objects of expense, and such the limited means of supply, at the commencement of the year in which war was declared. An increase of the expense, and a diminution of the supply, must have been anticipated as the inevitable consequences of that event; but the Government reposed with confidence, for all the requisite support, upon the untried resources of the nation, in credit, in capital, and in industry. The confidence was justly reposed; yet it may, perhaps, be considered as a subject for regret, and it certainly furnishes a lesson of practical policy, that there existed no system by which the internal resources of the country could be brought at once into action, when the resources of its external commerce became incompetent to answer the exigencies of the times.

The existence of such a system would, probably, have invigorated the early movements of the war; might have preserved the public credit unimpaired; and would have rendered the pecuniary contributions of the people more equal as well as more effective. But, owing to the want of such a system, a sudden and almost an exclusive resort to the public credit was necessarily adopted as the chief instrument of finance. The nature of the instrument employed was soon developed; and it was found that public credit could only be durably maintained upon the broad foundations of public revenue.

On the opening of the session of Congress in November, 1811, the legislative attention was devoted to the organization of the Military and Naval Department upon the enlarged scale of the War Establishment; so that the appropriations for this purpose far exceed, in a short time, the estimates and the resources of the Treasury, as they have been already described. Ways and means were, therefore, provided to meet the extraordinary demands thus created; but they were deriv-

State of the Finances.

ed exclusively from the operations of foreign commerce and public credit.

1. The Mediterranean fund was at first continued until the 4th of March, 1813, and afterwards until March, 1815, when it became extinct, affording an additional duty of two and a half per cent. *ad valorem* on all imported goods paying duties *ad valorem*; and a discriminating duty of ten per cent. upon that additional duty, in respect to all goods imported in vessels not of the United States.

2. There were imposed an additional duty of one hundred per cent. upon the permanent duties on goods imported into the United States, from any foreign place, a discriminating duty of ten per cent. upon that additional duty, in respect to all goods imported in vessels not of the United States; and an additional duty of one dollar and fifty cents per ton (the previous duty being at the rate of fifty cents per ton) upon all vessels belonging wholly or in part to the subjects of foreign Powers. But the continuance of the set being limited to the expiration of one year after the conclusion of the peace, those additional duties will cease on the 17th of February, 1816.

3. An authority was given to raise, by loan, a sum not exceeding $11,000,000, and to create stock for the amount, bearing interest, not exceeding the rate of six per cent. per annum, and reimbursable at any time after the expiration of twelve years, from the 1st of January, 1813. The payment of the interest, and the redemption or the purchase of this stock, are charged upon the Sinking Fund.

4. And an authority was given to issue Treasury notes for a sum not exceeding $5,000,000, bearing interest at the rate of five and a half per cent. per annum, and reimbursable at such places, respectively, as should be expressed on the face of the notes, one year after the day on which the same shall have been issued. The notes were declared to be receivable in payment of all duties and taxes laid by the United States, and all public lands sold by their authority; and the payment of interest, and the redemption or the purchase of these notes were charged, like the funded debt, upon the Sinking Fund.

The effect of the additional ways and means provided by Congress, from time to time, during the late war, may readily be traced. From the report, dated the 1st of December, 1812, it appears that the actual receipts into the Treasury, during the year ending on the 30th of September, 1812, including a portion of the loan, and the issue of Treasury notes, amounted to the sum of $16,782,159 40; (almost double the amount of the previous estimate;) and that the actual disbursement for the same year amounted to the sum of $18,368,325 7, (which was, also, almost double the amount of the previous estimate,) independent of the balances in the Treasury at the commencement and the close of the year. But the estimates for the year 1813 required, on account of the accumulating expenditures, a sum of $31,925,000.

For the Civil and Diplomatic Departments	$1,500,000	
For the Military Department	17,000,000	
For the Naval Department	4,925,060	
And for the interest and reimbursement of the principal of the public debt	8,500,000	
		$31,925,000
And the subsisting revenue to meet these expenditures was estimated at the sum of $12,000,000, proceeding—		
From the customs	11,500,000	
From the sales of public lands, &c.	500,000	
		12,000,000
Leaving a deficit, for which it was proposed to provide, first by the outstanding balances of the authorised loan and issue of Treasury notes, and second by a new authority to borrow, and to issue Treasury notes to the amount of		$19,925,000

During the session of Congress, which commenced in November, 1812, and closed on the 3d of March, 1813, the appropriations for the Army, the Navy, and other branches of the public service, were considerably augmented; but, without adverting to the imposition of a small duty upon imported iron-wire, no new source of revenue was then opened, but additional aid was extended to the Treasury by authorizing a repetition of the appeal to public credit.

1. An authority was given to raise, by loan, a sum not exceeding $16,000,000, and to create stock for the amount, bearing interest not exceeding the rate of six per cent. per annum, and reimbursable at any time after the expiration of twelve years, from the 1st of January, 1814. The payment of the interest, and the redemption or purchase of this stock, are charged upon the Sinking Fund.

2. And an authority was given to issue Treasury notes for a sum not exceeding $5,000,000, absolutely, with a provisional authority to issue an additional sum of $5,000,000, to be deemed and held to be a part of the loan of $16,000,000, authorized as above stated to be raised. The notes were to bear interest at the rate of five and two-fifths per cent. per annum, to be reimbursable at such places, respectively, as should be expressed on the face of them, one year after the day on which they should be issued; to be receivable in payment of all duties and taxes laid by the United States, and all public lands sold by their authority; and the payment of the interest, and the redemption or purchase of these notes were charged, like the funded debt, upon the Sinking Fund.

The necessities of the Treasury becoming, however, more urgent, and the reliance on the public credit becoming more hazardous, Congress determined, at a special session, which commenced in May, 1813, to lay the foundation of a system of internal revenue; selecting, in particular, those subjects of taxation which were recommended by the experience of a former period, and computing

State of the Finances.

their general product at the sum of $5,000,000. The continuance of these taxes being limited, at first, to one year after the termination of the war, they acquired the denomination of the "war taxes;" but, by subsequent laws, almost all the existing revenues are pledged, with the faith of the United States, to provide for the payment of the expenses of Government, for the punctual payment of the public debt, principal and interest, according to the contracts; and for creating an adequate sinking fund, gradually to reduce, and eventually to extinguish, the public debt; until those purposes shall be accomplished, or until Congress shall provide and substitute, by law, for the same purposes, other duties, which shall be equally productive. In the session of May, 1813—

1. A direct tax of $3,000,000 was laid upon the United States and apportioned to the States respectively for the year 1814, and it was afterwards subjected to the general pledge above stated.

2. A duty of four cents per pound was laid upon all sugar refined within the United States. The continuance of the duty was limited to one year after the war; and, as the general pledge has not been applied to it, the duty will cease on the 17th of February, 1816.

3. A duty was laid upon all carriages, for the conveyance of passengers, kept by any person for his own use, or to be let out for hire, or for the conveyance of passengers; which was graduated according to the denomination of the carriage, from the yearly sum of $20, to the yearly sum of $2. The continuance of this duty was originally limited to the war; but the general pledge has been applied to it, with some modifications in the mode of laying and collecting the duty.

4. A duty was imposed on licenses to distillers of spirituous liquors, which was graduated according to the capacity of the still, the time of employing it, and the materials consumed. The continuance of this duty was originally limited to the war; but the general pledge has been applied to it, with considerable modifications in the principles and provisions of the law.

5. A duty was laid on sales, at auction, of merchandise, and of ships and vessels, at the rate of one per cent. of the purchase money of goods, and of twenty-five cents for every hundred dollars of the purchase money of ships and vessels. The continuance of this duty was originally limited to the war; but the general pledge has been applied to it, with a considerable addition to the amount, and a modification of the provisions of the law.

6. A duty was laid on licenses to retailers of wines, spirituous liquors, and foreign merchandise, graduated according to the place of retailing, and the nature of the article retailed. The continuance of this duty was originally limited to the war; but the general pledge has been applied to it.

7. A duty was laid on notes of banks, and bankers; on bonds, obligations, or promissory notes, discounted by banks or bankers; and on foreign or inland bills of exchange, above $50, and having

one or more endorsers; graduated according to the nominal amount of the instrument. The continuance of this duty was limited to one year after the war; and as the general pledge has not been applied to it, the duty will cease on the 17th of February, 1816.

But besides the direct tax and the internal duties, there were added to the resources of the Treasury, during the session of May, 1813—

8. A duty of twenty cents per bushel upon all salt imported from any foreign place into the United States, which, being limited to the war, and not being included in the general pledge, will cease on the 17th of February, 1816.

9. And an authority to raise, by loan, a sum not exceeding $7,500,000, and to create stock for the amount, reimbursable at any time after the expiration of twelve years from the 1st of January, 1814. The rate of interest was not limited by the law; but it was provided, that no certificate of stock should be sold at a rate less than eighty-eight per cent., or $88, in money, for $100 in stock. The payment of the interest, and the redemption or the purchase of this stock, are charged upon the Sinking Fund.

The sources of the revenue thus opened in 1813, could not, however, be expected to aid the Treasury until 1814; and, accordingly, in the annual report from this department, dated the 8th January, 1814, neither the direct tax, nor the internal duties, will be found as an item of the actual receipts into the Treasury, during the year ending the 30th of September, 1813. The amount of those receipts was stated in the proceeds of the customs of the sales of public lands, &c., at $13,568,042 43, and in the proceeds of loans and Treasury notes at $23,976,912 50, making together $39,907,607 62; and the actual disbursements of the same period were stated at $32,928,855 19, independent of the balances in the Treasury at the commencement and the close of the year. But the estimates for the year 1814 required a sum of $45,350,000.

For civil, diplomatic, and miscellaneous expenses	$1,700,000
For the payment of interest on the old and new debt, and the instalments of the principal of the old debt	12,300,000
For the Military Establishment	24,550,000
For the Naval Establishment	6,900,000
	45,350,000

And the subsisting revenue to meet these expenditures was estimated at the sum of $14,370,000, proceeding—

From the customs and sales of public lands	$6,600,000
From the internal duties and direct tax	3,500,000
From a balance of loans and Treasury notes	4,270,000
	14,370,000

Leaving a deficit, for which it was proposed to provide, 1st, by a part of the balance in the Treasury, and, 2d, by loans and Treasury notes, amounting to 30,980,000

State of the Finances.

For the deficit thus approaching the sum of $40,000,000, the only provision made during the session, which commenced in December, 1813, rested again upon the public credit.

1. An authority was given to issue Treasury notes for a sum not exceeding $5,000,000, absolutely; with a provisional authority to issue an additional sum of $5,000,000, to be deemed and held to be a part of any loan which might be authorized during the session. The notes were to bear interest at the rate of five and two-fifths per cent. per annum; to be reimbursable at such places respectively, as should be expressed on the face of them, one year after the day on which they should be issued; to be receivable in payment of all duties and taxes laid by the United States, and all public lands sold by their authority; and the payment of the interest, and the redemption, or purchase of these notes, were charged, like the funded debt, upon the Sinking Fund.

2. And an authority was given to raise, by loan, a sum not exceeding $25,000,000, and to create stock for the amount, reimbursable at any time after the expiration of twelve years from the last day of December, 1814. Neither the rate of the interest, nor the price of the stock, was limited; and the payment of the interest, and the redemption or the purchase of the stock, are charged upon the Sinking Fund.

The embarrassments of the Treasury, after the adjournment of Congress in the year 1814, became extreme. It appears that the disbursements, during the first half of that year, had amounted to the sum of $19,693,781 27.

For the civil, diplomatic, and miscellaneous expenses	- - -	$1,444,762 60
For the Military Department	- - -	11,210,238 00
For the Naval Department	- - -	4,012,199 90
For the public debt	-	3,026,580 77
		$19,693,781 27
And the balance of the appropriations for the same objects of expenditure required, during the other half of the same year, was stated at the sum of	-	27,576,391 19
		47,270,172 46

But the actual receipts into the Treasury, during the first half of the year 1814, had amounted to $19,219,946 33, proceeding—

From the customs	-	4,162,066 25
From the sale of public lands, (including those in the Mississippi Territory, the proceeds of which are payable to the State of Georgia,)	- - -	540,065 68
From the internal duties and direct tax	-	2,189,272 40
From postage and incidental receipts	-	166,744 00
From loans	-	9,679,676 00
From Treasury notes	-	2,426,100 00
		19,219,946 33

And it was estimated that there would be received from the same sources of revenue, (including loans and Treasury notes to the amount of $8,320,000,) during the other half of the same year, the sum of - 13,160,000 00

	32,379,946 33
To this amount add the balance of the cash in the Treasury on the 1st of July, 1814 - - - -	4,732,639 22
And the estimated aggregate of the funds to meet the demands on the Treasury to the close of the year 1814, was the sum of - - -	37,103,585 55

Leaving a deficit for the service of 1814, after absorbing all the cash of the Treasury, amounting to the sum of $10,167,586 91

To supply this deficit of $10,167,586 91, to provide an additional sum for the contingencies of the year, and to accelerate the fiscal measures, which were essential to the prosecution of the war in 1815, the interposition of the Legislature was deemed indispensable. The plan of finance, which was predicated upon the theory of defraying the extraordinary expenses of the war by successive loans, had already become inoperative. The product of the revenues had ceased to furnish an amount equal to the expenditure of the former Peace Establishment, with an addition of the interest upon the debt contracted on account of the war. And the sudden suspension of specie payments at the principal banks established in the different States, (however it may be excused, or justified, by the apparent necessity of the case,) had exposed the Government, as well as private citizens, to all the inconveniences of a variable currency, devoid, alike, of national authority and of national circulation. The Treasury could no longer transfer its funds from place to place; and it became, of course, impracticable to maintain the accustomed punctuality in the payment of the public engagements.

Under these circumstances, the Congress was convened by the special call of the President, in September, 1814, when the citizens of every occupation and pursuit seemed eager to second the legislative efforts to replenish an exhausted Treasury, and to renovate the public credit. Commerce continued to contribute, perhaps, to the extent of its capacity. Agriculture, though suffering the want for a vent for some of its important staples, was every where prepared for the requisite exertion. Domestic manufactures, which had scarcely surmounted the first struggle for existence, yielded to the patriotic impulse; and the capital of individuals, in all its variety of form, offered a ready tribute to relieve the necessities of the country. Thus, during the session which commenced in September, 1814, and closed on the 3d of March, 1815—

1. The following internal duties were increased

in their amount; the duties were rendered permanent, and the general pledge was applied to them:

(1.) The direct tax was raised to an annual sum of $6,000,000, and it was extended to the District of Columbia.

(2.) The duty on carriages was raised, and a duty on the harness was added.

(3.) The duty on licenses to distillers of spirituous liquors was continued, and a duty on the spirits distilled was added.

(4.) The duties on sales at auction, and on licenses to retail wines, spirituous liquors, and foreign merchandise, were raised.

(5.) The rates of postage were raised fifty per cent.

2. The following new duties were permanently laid, and the general pledge was applied to them. But it was, at the same time, declared, that so long as the duties imposed on the articles of domestic manufacture should continue to be laid, the duties then payable on the like description of goods imported into the United States, should not be discontinued or diminished.

(1.) Duties on various articles, manufactured or made for sale within the United States or their Territories, as specified in the annexed table, marked B.

(2.) Duties on articles in use, to wit:

On household furniture, the value in any one family (with certain exceptions) exceeding $200 in money, according to a scale graduated from $1 on a value of $400, to $100 on a value of $9,000.

On every gold watch kept for use, $2.

On every silver watch kept for use, $1.

But, besides establishing these further sources of revenue, (and others were contemplated at the period when the Treaty of Ghent was announced,) Congress sought to confer upon the Treasury the means of anticipating the collection of the duties, of recovering the punctuality of its payments, and of inviting the co-operation of the moneyed institutions and moneyed men of the United States, in plans for restoring a uniform and national currency. With these views various measures were sanctioned.

1. An authority was given to raise, by loan, a sum not exceeding $3,000,000, (particularly destined to provide for the expenditures of the last quarter of the year 1814,) and to create stock for the amount, reimbursable at any time after the 31st of December, 1814. No limitation was prescribed as to the rate of interest, or the price of the stock, but it was declared that, in payment of subscriptions to this loan or to loans authorized by any other act of Congress, it should be lawful to receive Treasury notes becoming due on or before the 1st of January, 1815, at their par value, together with the interest accrued.

The payment of the interest, and the redemption, or the purchase of the stock to be thus created, were charged upon the Sinking Fund, but the act contained these further assurances, 1st. That, in addition to the annual sum of $8,000,000, heretofore appropriated to the Sinking Fund, adequate and permanent funds should be provided and appropriated during that session of Congress, for the payment of the interest and the reimbursement of the principal of the stock; and, 2d, that an adequate and permanent sinking fund gradually to reduce, and eventually to extinguish the public debt contracted during the war, should also be established during the same session of Congress.

2. An authority was given to anticipate the collection and receipt of the duties on licenses to distillers of spirituous liquors, and on distilled spirits, by obtaining a loan upon the pledge of the duties to an amount not exceeding $6,000,000, and at a rate of interest not exceeding six per cent. per annum. And a similar authority was given to raise a like sum, at the same rate, by the pledge of the direct tax.

3. An authority was given to issue Treasury notes for so much of the sums authorized to be borrowed under the acts of the 24th of March, and the 15th of November, 1814, as had not been borrowed, or otherwise employed in the issue of Treasury notes; provided, that the whole amount should not exceed the sum of $7,500,000. And, by the same act, an authority was also given to issue a further sum of $3,000,000, to supply a deficiency in the appropriations for the expenses of the War Department. The Treasury notes, issued under these authorities, were in all respects similar to the prior issues of Treasury notes, except that the payment of the interest, and the reimbursement of the principal, were not, as heretofore, charged upon the Sinking Fund, but upon any money in the Treasury not otherwise appropriated.

4. An authority was given to issue and re-issue Treasury notes for a sum not exceeding $25,000,000, upon principles essentially different from the prior issues.

(1.) These Treasury notes might be of any denomination. If they were of a denomination less than $100, they were to be payable to the bearer, to be transferable by delivery, and to bear no interest. This denomination has acquired the designation of "Small Treasury Notes." If they were of the denomination of $100 or upwards, they might conform to the foregoing description, or they were to be payable to order, to be transferable by endorsement, and to bear interest at the rate of 5 2-5 per cent. per annum. This denomination (of which only notes for $100, bearing interest, have been issued) has acquired the designation of "Treasury notes of the new emission."

(2.) The principal and interest of these Treasury notes are not payable at any particular time, but the notes are everywhere receivable in all payments to the United States.

(3.) The holders of "small Treasury notes" may exchange them, at pleasure, in sums not less than $100, for certificates of funded stock, bearing interest at seven per cent. per annum, from the first day of the calendar month next ensuing that in which the notes shall be presented to the Treasury of the United States, or to a commissioner of loans, for the purpose of exchange.

State of the Finances.

(4.) The holders of "Treasury notes of the new emission" may exchange them, at pleasure. in sums not less than $100, for certificates of funded stock, bearing interest at six per cent. per annum, from the first day of the calender month next ensuing that in which they shall be presented to the Treasury of the United States, or a commissioner of loans.

(5.) The stock, thus created by the exchange of Treasury notes of either denomination, is reimbursable at any time after the 31st of December, 1824, and it is charged upon such funds as had been, or should be, established by law for the payment and reimbursement of the funded public debt contracted since the declaration of war.

5. An authority was given to raise, by loan, a sum not exceeding $18,452,800, and to create stock for the amount, reimbursable at any time after the expiration of twelve years from the last day of December, 1815. Neither the rate of interest nor the price of the stock was limited; but it was declared that there might be received in payment of subscriptions to the loan, such Treasury notes as were actually issued before the passing of the act, and which were made by law a charge on the Sinking Fund. And the payment of the interest, and the reimbursement on the purchase of the principal of the stock are charged upon the Sinking Fund.

6. It was declared that any holder of any Treasury note issued, or authorized to be issued, under any laws previously passed, might convert them into certificates of funded debt, bearing an interest of six per cent. per annum.

7. And it was declared that it should be lawful for the Secretary of the Treasury to cause to be paid the interest upon Treasury notes which have become due and remain unpaid, as well with respect to the time elapsed before they became due, as with respect to the time that shall elapse after they become due; and, until funds shall be assigned for the payment of the said Treasury notes, and notice thereof shall be given.

The progress of expenditure and of revenue for the entire period of the war is thus developed, and, independent of the balance of the appropriations for the year 1814, which is transferred to the accounts for the year 1815, the subject may be reduced to the following general abstract:

The actual receipts of the Treasury.

In 1812, they amounted to the sum of $22,639,032 76
From revenue - - $9,801,132 76
From loans - - - 10,002,400 00
From Treasury notes, 2,835,500 00

In 1813, they amounted to the sum of 40,524,844 95
From revenue - - $14,340,709 95
From loans - - - 20,089,635 00
From Treasury notes, 6,094,500 00

In 1814, they amounted to the sum of $34,878,432 25
From revenue - - $11,500,606 25
From loans - - - 15,080,546 00
From Treasury notes, 8,297,280 00

The aggregate amount of the receipts into the Treasury, for the three years of war, being the sum of $98,042,309 96

The actual disbursements of the Treasury.

In 1812, they amounted to the sum of $22,279,121 15
For the civil, diplomatic, and miscellaneous expenses of Government $1,791,360 31
For the military service, (including the Indian Department,) 12,078,773 24
For the naval service, 3,959,365 15
For the public debt, 4,649,622 45

In 1813, they amounted to the sum of 39,190,520 26
For the civil, diplomatic, and miscellaneous expenses of Government $1,833,308 80
For the military service, (including the Indian Department, &c.) - 19,802,468 02
For the naval service, 6,446,600 10
For the public debt, 11,108,123 44

In 1814, they amounted to the sum of 38,547,915 62
For the civil, diplomatic, and miscellaneous expenses of Government $2,337,897 13
For the military service, (including the Indian Department, &c.,) - 20,510,328 00
For the naval service, 7,312,699 90
For the public debt, 8,386,990 59

         $100,017,557 13

But, as the receipts of the Treasury for the year 1815 are derived principally from the war revenue and resources, and as its expenditures arise, also, principally from the arrearages of the war demands, it is proper to comprise them, as far as they are ascertained, in the following supplemental statement:

1. The gross receipts of the Treasury for 1812, 1813, and 1814, amounted, as above stated, to the sum of $98,042,309 96
The receipts of the Treasury for 1815, to the 30th of September last, cannot be precisely stated, as the accounts to that time are not yet actually made up; but they are estimated to have amounted to the sum of   39,372,000 00
From revenue - $12,400,000 00
From loans - 11,034,000 00
From Treasury notes, 15,938,000 00

         $39,372,000 00

State of the Finances.

The aggregate of the receipts of the Treasury from the 1st of January, 1812, to the 30th of September, 1815, being the sum of - $137,414,209 96

2. The gross disbursements of the Treasury for 1812, 1813, and 1814, amounted, as above stated, to the sum of - - - $100,017,557 13
The disbursements of the Treasury for 1815, to the 30th of September last, amounted to the sum of - 33,686,323 18
For the civil, diplomatic, and miscellaneous expenses - $2,537,000 00
For the military service, &c. - 15,190,144 71
For the naval service, &c. - - 7,050,000 25
For the public debt - 8,909,178 22
$33,686,323 18

The aggregate of the disbursements of the Treasury from the 1st of January, 1812, to the 30th of September, 1815, being the sum of - $133,703,680 31

It will be natural here to inquire into the general effects of the war upon the public debt of the United States; and the annexed table, marked C, exhibits a detailed statement of the unsatisfied amount, on the 1st day of January, annually, from the year 1791 to the year 1815, both inclusive. The subject, however, may be placed distinctly in the following point of view, upon estimates referring to the date of the 30th of September, 1815:

Of the Public Debt.

2. The amount of the funded debt contracted before the late war, which remained unsatisfied on the 30th of September, 1815, may be stated at the sum of $39,135,484 96, to wit:

(1.) In old six per cent. stock, the nominal amount being - $17,350,871 39
And the amount reimbursed being - 13,467,587 00

Balance due on the 30th of September, 1815 - - - 3,783,284 39
(2.) In deferred six per cent. stock, the nominal amount being - 9,358,320 85
And the amount reimbursed being - 4,152,543 93

Balance due on the 30th of September, 1815 - - - 5,205,776 42
(3.) In three per cent. stock - 16,158,177 43
(4.) In exchanged six per cent. stock, under the act of 1812 - 2,984,746 72
(5.) In six per cent. stock of 1796 - 80,000 00
(6.) In Louisiana six per cent. stock 10,923,500 00

Balance on the 30th of September, 1815, of the whole of the public debt contracted before the war - - - - $39,135,484 96

2. The amount of the funded debt contracted on account of the late war, on the 30th of September, 1815, may be stated at the sum of $63,144,972 50, to wit:

(1.) In six per cent. stock of 1812, (the $11,000,000 loan,) authorized by the act of the 4th of March, 1812, obtained at par, and not reimbursable before the year 1825 - - - 7,860,500 00
(2.) In six per cent. stock of 1813, (the $16,000,000 loan,) authorized by the act of the 8th of February, 1813, obtained at the rate of $88 in cash for $100 in stock, and not reimbursable before the year 1826 - - - 18,109,377 43
(3.) In six per cent. stock of 1813, (the $7,500,000 loan,) authorized by the act of the 2d of August, 1813, obtained at the rate of $88 25 in money for $100 in stock, and not reimbursable before the year 1826 - - 8,498,581 95
(4.) In six per cent. stock of 1814, (which arose from loans in parts of a sum of $25,000,000, called the $10,000,000 loan and the $6,000,000 loan,) authorized by the act of the 24th of March, 1814, obtained at different rates, and not reimbursable before 1827, to wit:
$12,292,888 90, at 80 per cent. stock 15,366,111 21
140,810 00, at 85 per cent. do. - 165,658 82
43,222 22, at 90½ per cent. do. - 47,657 79
74,590 75, at 90½ per cent. do. - 82,420 72

12,551,511 67.
(5.) In six per cent. stock of 1815, (the $12,000,000 loan,) authorized by the act of the 3d of March, 1815, obtained at different rates, payable in Treasury notes, or in cash, and not reimbursable before 1827, to wit:
$7,924,219 59, at 95 per cent. stock - 8,341,283 77
1,047,846 90, at 96½ per cent. do. - 1,085,851 08
32,978 49, at 97 per cent. do. - 33,998 44
275,000 00, at 98 per cent. do. - 280,612 24
4,000 00, at par do. - 4,000 00
(6.) In seven per cent. stock of 1815, created by funding Treasury notes not bearing interest, issued part at par, and part upon an advance, under the act of the 24th of February, 1815, and not reimbursable until 1825 - - - - 3,268,949 00

Estimated amount of the whole of the funded public debt in reference to the late war - - - - 63,144,972 50

3. The amount of the floating debt contracted since the commencement of the late war, calculated to the 30th of September, 1815, may be stated at the sum of $17,355,101, to wit:

State of the Finances.

(1.) The aggregate of Treasury notes issued under the authority of the several acts of Congress passed prior to the act of the 24th of February, 1815, amounted to the sum of $20,201,600 00, to wit:

Payable in the year 1814, but unpaid	2,799,200 00	
Payable in the year 1815, but unpaid	7,847,280 00	
Payable in the year 1816, but unpaid	$2,772,720 00	
Payable also in 1816, (issued under the special authority of the act of the 26th of December, 1814,) but unpaid	8,318,400 00	
	21,737,600 00	
Deduct the amount reimbursed in 1815, at Philadelphia, Baltimore, Washington, Charleston and Savannah)	1,536,000 00	
		20,201,600 00

Of this aggregate there has been subscribed in principal and interest to the loan of 1815, about the sum of   4,531,587 06
From which deducting an average estimate of near one year's interest, about the sum of   216,587 06

There will remain for the amount of principal subscribed to the loan, about the sum of   4,315,000 00
And it is estimated that there has been paid on account of duties and taxes to the collectors of the customs, the internal duties, and the direct tax, about the sum of   1,200,000 00
       5,515,000 00

Outstanding amount of Treasury notes bearing interest at 5 2-5 per cent. per annum, about the sum of   14,686,600 00

(2.) The aggregate of small Treasury notes issued and reissued under the act of the 24th February, 1815, amounts to about the sum of   4,142,850 00
Of this aggregate there has been funded for seven per cent. stock, included in the foregoing statement of the funded public debt, about the sum of   3,268,949 00
And there has been paid on account of duties and taxes, about the sum of   50,000 00
       3,318,949 00

Outstanding small Treasury notes, about the sum of $823,901 00

(3.) The aggregate of Treasury notes of the new emission, issued under the act of the 24th February, 1815, amounts to about the sum of   694,800 00

Leaving the amount of floating public debt, in Treasury notes, on the 1st of October, 1815, about the sum of   16,205,101 00

But to this amount of the public floating debt, in Treasury notes, there must be added the following temporary loans, to wit:

(1.) A temporary loan, made by the State Bank of Boston in 1812, payable the 15th and 31st of December, 1814, but unpaid	500,000 00	
(2.) A temporary loan, made by the Cumberland Bank in 1812, payable the 15th of November, 1817	50,000 00	
(3.) A temporary loan, made by the Bank of the State of South Carolina, in 1814, payable the 1st of December, 1815	50,000 00	
(4.) A temporary loan, made by the Mechanics' Bank of New York, in 1815, payable when demanded	200,000 00	
(5.) A temporary loan, made by the State of New York, payable in the year 1817	350,000 00	
		1,150,000 00

Making the aggregate amount of the floating public debt about the sum of   17,355,101 00

RECAPITULATION.

1. The amount of the unsatisfied funded public debt, contracted before the war, on the 30th of September, 1815, was the sum of $39,135,484 96

2. The amount of the funded public debt contracted, in reference to the late war, on the same day, the sum of   63,144,972 86

3. The amount of the floating public debt, contracted since the war, was, on the same day, the sum of 17,355,101 00

Total of the ascertained amount of
the public debt created since the
war, to the 30th of September,
1815 - - - - - - $80,500,073 50

Total amount of the national debt on
the 30th of September, 1815 - - 119,635,558 46

It is proper to remark, that the aggregate of the national debt thus stated to the 30th of September, 1815, is subject to considerable changes and additions. The floating debt in Treasury notes is convertible, at the pleasure of the creditors, into funded debt; and, independent of a direct application of the current revenue to discharge the Treasury notes, as well as the temporary loans, there must be a great, though gradual reduction of the floating debt, by the payments made in Treasury notes, for duties, taxes, and public lands. There are, indeed, some claims know to exist for loans, supplies, and services, during the late war, which have not been liquidated, or are not embraced by existing appropriations; and doubtless there are other legal and equitable claims which have not yet been brought into view, in any form, at the accounting departments, but which may eventually receive the sanction of Congress. It is not, however, within the scope of any estimate hitherto made, to state the probable addition to the funded debt, under all circumstances, at more than $7,000,000, which would consequently place the aggregate of the funded debt, created in consequence of the war, at a sum not much exceeding $70,000,000. But it may be important to recollect, that the war debt has not been entirely incurred for objects limited to the continuance of the war; and that the military and naval establishments in particular have derived durable advantages from the expenditures of the Treasury.

For the payment of the interest, and the reimbursement or gradual extinguishment of the national debt, the resources of the Treasury are abundant, although the state of the circulating medium (which will be more particularly considered hereafter) has rendered it impracticable to obtain at all times, upon reasonable terms, the local currency of some of the places appointed for the discharge of the public engagements. These resources depend upon the Sinking Fund, connected with the faith of the United States, which is pledged to supply from the existing, or from other subjects of revenue, the deficiencies of that fund.

The Sinking Fund.

The public debt amounted, on the 1st of January, 1791, to the sum of $75,463,476 52, and it consisted—

Of the foreign debt - - - $12,612,821 92
Of the domestic debt - - - 62,650,654 60

75,463,476 52

The foreign debt experienced various changes in form and in amount. From 1792 to 1795 it rose above the amount stated for 1791, but from that period it was gradually reduced; and on the 1st of January, 1801, it stood at the sum of $10,419,000. From the year 1801, however, the annual reduction was more rapid; and in the year 1810 the foreign debt became extinct.

The domestic debt has also experienced various changes in form and amount. It was originally stipulated that it should be subject to redemption by payments, not exceeding in one year, on account both of principal and interest, the proportion of eight dollars upon one hundred dollars of the stock; and when the Sinking Fund was constituted and organized, provision was made for effecting the payments in that proportion, until the whole debt should be extinguished by dividends payable on the last days of March, June, and September, in each year, at the rate of one and a half per cent, and, on the last day of December, in each year, at the rate of three and a half per cent. upon the original capital. During the first period of about ten years, from 1791, until the 1st of January, 1801, the amount of the domestic debt never fell below the sum which has been stated; and in 1801 it stood at about the sum of $72,619,050 80. The augmentation, created on account of the purchase of Louisiana, (amounting to $15,000,000,) raised the capital of the domestic debt, in 1804, to the sum of $80,691,120 88; but from that period there was a considerable annual diminution of the amount, until it was reduced on the 30th of September, 1815, to the already specified sum of $39,135,484 96.

The Sinking Fund, by whose operations these beneficial effects have been produced, may be regarded as coeval with the organization of the present Government; but it has undergone many important modifications.

1. The early appropriations of the revenue were confined to the payment of the interest and instalments of the foreign debt, and to the payment of the interest of the domestic debt; but so early as the 4th of August, 1790, the proceeds of the sales of the public lands in the Western territory were permanently and exclusively appropriated and pledged towards sinking and discharging the debts for which the United States were then holden. The annexed table, D, will exhibit a statement of the quantity of the public lands which have been annually sold, and of the proceeds of the sales, as far as can be now ascertained.

2. In the year 1792, however, commissioners were designated and authorized to purchase the public debt at its market price, not exceeding the par value, and the interest of the debt purchased, together with the surplus of certain other appropriations, was assigned for that purpose. When the annual amount of the fund thus created should be equal to two per cent. on the six per cent. stock, it was directed to be first applied to the redemption of that stock, according to the right reserved, and then to the purchase, at its market price, of any other public stock.

3. In the year 1795 "the Sinking Fund" was

established by name; its resources were vested in the same commissioners, and its operations were subjected to their direction and management. The duty of the commissioners, independent of temporary objects, consisted in applying the Sinking Fund, 1st, to the payment of the six per cent. stock, at the stipulated rate of eight per cent. per annum; 2d, to the payment of the deferred stock after the year 1801, according to the same stipulation; and, 3d, if any surplus remained, towards the further and final redemption of the public debt, of every denomination. For the accomplishment of these purposes there were permanently appropriated and pledged, in addition to the other moneys constituting the Sinking Fund, and the interest of the amount of the purchased or redeemed debt, 1st, a sufficient sum arising yearly, and every year, from the duties on imports and tonnage, and the duty on domestic distilled spirits and stills, as might be rightfully paid of the principal of the six per cent. stock, commencing on the 1st of January, 1802. 2d. The dividends on the public shares in the Bank of the United States; but the shares were sold in 1796 and 1802, under an authority given in 1795. 3d. The net proceeds of the sales of public lands in the Western territory. 4th. Moneys received into the Treasury on account of old debts. 5th. The surpluses of revenue beyond the amount of the appropriations.

4. Such was the outline of the Sinking Fund, when, on the 6th of April, 1802, the internal duties were repealed; and, on the 29th of April, 1802, a new and additional provision was made for the redemption of the public debt. Thus, an annual sum of $7,300,000 was permanently appropriated and vested in the Commissioners of the Sinking Fund, to be produced, 1st, by the moneys (other than the surpluses of revenue) which then constituted the fund, or should arise to it by virtue of any previous provisions. 2d. By the sums annually required to discharge the interest and charges of the public debt; and, 3dly. By so much of the duties on merchandise and tonnage as would be necessary, together with the preceding resources, to complete the annual investment of $7,300,000. The act not only placed the reimbursement of the principal, but also the payment on account of interest and charges of the public debt, under the superintendence of the commissioners; making it their duty to cause the fund to be applied in payment, 1st, of such sums as by virtue of any acts they had previously been directed to pay; 2d, of such sums as may be annually wanted to discharge the interest and charges accruing on any other part of the then debt of the United States; 3d, of such sums as may be annually required to discharge any instalment of the principal of the then debt; and 4th, as to any surplus, to apply it towards the further and final redemption, by payment or purchase of the then debt. The act of the 10th of November, 1803, having created six per cent. stock to the amount of $11,250,000, in pursuance of the convention for the purchase of Louisiana, added an annual sum of $700,000 to the Sinking

Fund, to be paid out of the duties on merchandise and tonnage, and to be applied by the commissioners to the payment of the public debt, including the Louisiana stock, in the manner above stated. It may be added, that the interest on the Louisiana stock is payable in Europe; but the principal is reimbursable at the Treasury of the United States, in four annual instalments, commencing in 1818.

It is obvious that a sinking fund of $8,000,000 (independent of the general pledges in prior laws) was ample for the payment of the interest and the principal of the public debt, amounting only to the sum of $36,000,000, extinguishing the six per cent. stock in 1818, the deferred stock in 1824, and the Louisiana stock in 1822, as fast as the terms of the contracts and the policy of Government would permit. The general operation of the fund, indeed, has been shown; but it is proper more particularly to add, that, on the 1st of January, 1815, there had been transferred to the credit of the commissioners, in the books of the Treasury, an amount of public debt equal to the sum of $33,873,463 96, of the following denominations, to wit:

1.—Foreign Debt.

Three per cent. stock,	$8,300,000 00
Four and a half per cent. stock	820,000 00
Four per cent. stock	3,180,000 00
	$12,300,000 00

2.—Domestic Debt.

Six per cent. stock	1,946,026 92
Three per cent. stock	698,555 41
Deferred six per cent. stock	1,965,179 82
Eight per cent. stock	6,462,500 00
Exchanged six per cent. stock	6,394,051 12
Commuted six per cent. stock	1,559,850 70
Four and a half per cent. stock	176,000 00
Five and a half per cent. stock	1,848,900 00
Navy six per cent. stock	711,700 00
Louisiana six per cent. stock	326,500 00
Six per cent. stock of 1812	394,200 00
	21,673,463 96
	$33,873,463 96

But the charges upon the Sinking Fund have accumulated, in consequence of the late war, to an amount which it has not the capacity to defray; while its operations, in other respects, have been obstructed by the temporary failure of the revenue arising from duties on merchandise and tonnage, and the protracted embarrassments of the circulating medium: thus,

1. The annual appropriation for the Sinking Fund amounts to $8,000,000, and consists at present—

State of the Finances.

(1.) Of the interest on such parts of the public debt as have been reimbursed or paid off, (which, however, is itself derived from the customs,) estimated on the 30th of September, 1815, at the sum of - - - - - $1,968,577 64

(2.) Of the net proceeds of the sales of the public lands, exclusive of lands sold in the Mississippi Territory, (which as yet belong to the State of Georgia,) estimated annually at the sum of - - - - - 800,000 00

(3.) Of the proceeds of duties on imports and tonnage, to complete the annual investments, estimated at the sum of - - - - - 5,230,422 36

$8,000,000 00

2. The annual charge upon the Sinking Fund estimated for 1816, will amount probably to the sum of $14,524,200.

On account of the interest and the instalments of the old debt, the sum of $3,460,000 00

On account of the interest of the new debt, computed on a capital of $70,000,000, about the sum of - 4,200,000 00

On account of the principal and interest of the Treasury notes, issued under the act of the 30th of June, 1812, the 25th of February, 1813, and the 4th of March, 1814, (after allowing for the amount reimbursed, subscribed to the loan, and paid for duties,) about the sum of - - 6,864,200 00

$14,524,200 00

Deficit in the amount of the Sinking Fund, compared with the charges upon it, estimated for 1816 - $6,524,200 00

From this view of the financial operations of the Government the Secretary of the Treasury, with every sentiment of deference and respect, presents the following general conclusions for the consideration of Congress:

1. That the existing revenue of the United States arises, 1st, from duties on imported merchandise, and the tonnage of vessels; 2d, internal duties, including the direct tax upon lands, houses, and slaves; and, 3d, the proceeds of the sales of public lands; but some of these duties and taxes are permanently imposed, and some are limited in their duration.

2. That the following duties or taxes are either partially or wholly limited in their duration: 1. The duties on merchandise and tonnage will be reduced one-half on the 17th of February, 1816, except such as are imposed on goods of the like description with the articles of domestic manufacture, on which duties have been laid, and included in the general pledge. 2. The new duty on salt; the duty on sugar refined within the United States; and the stamp duty on bank notes, promissory notes discounted, and on bills of exchange, are not included in the general

pledge, and will wholly cease on the 17th of February, 1816.

3. That the following duties or taxes are not limited in their duration, and are included in the general pledge: 1. The direct tax upon lands, houses, and slaves. 2. The duties upon licenses to distillers of spirituous liquors and upon the liquors distilled. 3. The duty upon licenses to retailers of wines, spirituous liquors, and foreign merchandise. 4. The duty upon sales at auction. 5. The duty upon carriages and harness. 6. The duties upon household furniture and watches. 7. The duties on articles manufactured or made for sale within the United States. 8. The rate of postage.

4. That the faith of the United States, and the revenue arising from the duties and taxes, which are not limited in their duration, are pledged for the punctual payment of the public debt, principal and interest, according to the terms of the contracts respectively; and, for creating an adequate sinking fund, gradually to reduce, and eventually to extinguish the debt. But this pledge will be satisfied by the substitution of other adequate duties or taxes; and the increase in the proceeds of the duties on merchandise, subsequent to the pledge, affords an advantageous opportunity of making such substitution in respect to the more inconvenient and burdensome portion of the internal duties.

5. That the establishment of a revenue system, which shall not be exclusively dependent upon the supplies of foreign commerce, appears, at this juncture, to claim particular attention.

II.—*A view of the finances for 1815, with estimates of the public revenue and expenses for 1816.*

At the close of the last session of Congress the demands upon the Treasury were interesting in their nature, as well as great in their amount. Exclusively of the ordinary expenses of the Government, they consisted of demands for the payment of the army, preparatory to its reduction to the Peace Establishment, with other very heavy arrearages and disbursements in the War and Navy Departments; for the payment of the dividends on the funded debt, and of the arrearages, as well as the accruing claims on account of the Treasury note debt; and for the payment of the Louisiana dividends, with other considerable debts contracted in Europe in consequence of the late war.

The efficiency of the means which were possessed for the liquidation of these demands depended upon circumstances beyond the control of the Government. The balance of money in the Treasury consisted of bank credits, lying chiefly in the southern and western sections of the Union. The revenue proceeding from the provision made prior to the last session of Congress was, comparatively, of small amount. The revenue proceeding from the provision made during that session could not be available for a great portion of the present year; and, in both instances, the revenue was payable in Treasury notes, or it assumed the form of bank credits, at the respective places of collection. The only remaining resources for immediate use were an additional issue of Treasury notes, and a loan; but the successful employment of these resources was rendered for some time doubtful, by the peculiar situation of the credit and currency of the nation.

The suspension of specie payments throughout the greater portion of the United States, and the consequent cessation of the interchange of bank notes and bank credits, between the institutions of the different States, had deprived the Treasury of all the facilities of transferring its funds from place to place; and a proposition which was made, at an early period, to the principal banks of the commercial cities, on the line of the Atlantic, with a view, in some degree, to restore those facilities, could not be effected, for the want of a concurrence in the requisite number of banks. Hence it has happened (and the duration of the evil is without any positive limitation) that, however adequate the public revenue may be, in its general product, to discharge the public engagements, it becomes totally inadequate in the process of its application, since the possession of public funds in one part no longer affords the evidence of a fiscal capacity to discharge a public debt in any other part of the Union.

From the suspension of specie payments, and from various other causes, real or imaginary, differences in the rate of exchange arose between the several States, and even between the several districts in the same State; and the embarrassments of the Treasury were more and more increased, since Congress had not sanctioned any allowance on account of the rate of exchange; and the amount of the legislative appropriations was the same, wherever the legislative objects were to be effected. But the Treasury notes partook of the inequalities of the exchange in the transactions of individuals, although the Treasury could only issue them at their par value. The public stock, created in consideration of a loan, also partook of the inequalities of the exchange, although to the Government the value of the stock created, and the obligation of the debt to be discharged, were the same, wherever the subscription to the loan might be made.

Thus, notwithstanding the ample revenue provided and permanently pledged for the payment of the public creditor, and, notwithstanding the auspicious influence of peace upon the resources of the nation, the market price of the Treasury notes, and of the public stock, was everywhere far below its par or true value, for a considerable period after the adjournment of Congress; vibrating, however, with a change of place, from the rate of 75 to the rate of 90 per cent. Payments in bank paper were universally preferred, during that period, to payments in the paper of the Government; and it was a natural consequence that wherever the Treasury failed in procuring a local currency, it failed also in making a stipulated payment.

Under these extraordinary and perplexing circumstances, the great effort of the Treasury was, 1st. To provide promptly and effectually for all urgent demands, at the proper place of payment, and to the requisite amount of funds. 2d. To overcome the difficulties of the circulating medium, as far as it was practicable, so that no creditor should receive more, and no debtor pay less, in effective value, on the same account, than every other creditor, or every other debtor. And, 3d. To avoid any unreasonable sacrifice of the public property, particularly when it must also be attended with a sacrifice of the public credit. It was not expected that this effort would everywhere produce the same satisfaction, and the same results; but the belief is entertained that it has been successful in the attainment of its objects, to the extent of a just anticipation.

Of the uses of the Treasury Notes.

The Treasury notes, which were issued under acts passed prior to the 24th of February, 1815, were, for the most part a denomination *too high* to serve as a current medium of exchange, and it was soon ascertained that the small Treasury notes, fundable at an interest of 7 per cent., though of a convenient denomination for common use, would be converted into stock almost as soon as they were issued. With respect to the first description, therefore, the issue has not been restrained; but with respect to the second description, the issue has been generally limited to cases of peculiar urgency; such as the payment of the army, preparatory to its reduction; the payment of the dividends on the public debt where the local currency could not be obtained; and the payment of an inconsiderable amount of miscellaneous claims, apparently entitled to distinction.

The annexed table, marked E, contains a statement of the amount of the small Treasury notes which had been issued on the 30th of September, 1815, from which it appears,

1. That there had been issued, for the payment of the army, the sum of - - - - - $1,465,069
2. That there had been issued, for the payment of the dividends of the public debt, the sum of - - - - - - 1,203,100
3. That there had been issued, for sundry miscellaneous claims, the sum of - 109,881
4. That there has been sold at an advance (producing $32,167 64,) for the purpose of raising funds to meet the general engagements of the Treasury, a sum of - 1,365,000

                            $4,143,850

Of the Loan

The act of the 3d March, 1815, authorized a loan for a sum not exceeding $18,452,800. It was made lawful to accept, in payment of subscriptions, such Treasury notes as had been charged on the Sinking Fund; and a commission, not exceeding one quarter of one per cent., was allowed for selling the certificates of stock, or procuring subscriptions to the loan. Under this authority the annexed notice, marked F., dated the 10th of March, 1815, was published, opening a loan for

State of the Finances.

the sum of $12,000,000, with a view, 1st, to absorb a portion of the Treasury note debt; 2d, to obtain funds for paying the unsubscribed arrearages of that debt; and, the 3d, to aid the Treasury with a supply of the local currencies of different places, in some proportion to the probable amout of the local demands.

The offers to subscribe to the loan prior to the 19th of April, 1815, placed (as it were proper to place) money and Treasury notes upon the same footing; but the offers varied essentially in the terms and conditions that were annexed to them; and, in point of fact, no direct offer was made to subscribe at a higher rate than 89 per cent, while some of the offers were made at a rate even lower than 75 per cent, Upon this experiment, therefore, it was seen at once that the new situation of the Treasury required a new course of proceeding, and that neither the justice due to the equal rights of the public creditor, nor a fair estimate of the value of the public property, nor an honorable regard for the public credit, would permit the loan to assume the shape and character of a scramble, subservient to the speculations, which create what is called a market price, and shifting in every town and village of every State, according to the arbitrary variations of what is called the difference of exchange.

In this view of the subject all the offers of subscriptions to the loan, made in the first instance, were declined; but it was declared, at the same time, that offers at the rate of 95 per cent. would be accepted. The rate thus proposed was adopted upon a consideration of the value of the stock, of the equitable as well as legal claim of the holders of Treasury notes, and of the real condition of the public credit. The object of the loan being (as already stated) to absorb a portion of the Treasury note debt, and to acquire a sufficiency of local currency for local purposes, the price of the stock at the Treasury was, of course, independent of the daily up and down prices of the various stock markets in the Union, and could only be effected by the progress towards the attainment of those objects. Thus, while the wants of the Treasury were sufficiently supplied, offers to subscribe were freely accepted. and the parties were sometimes authorized and invited to increase the amount of their offers; but, where local funds had so accumulated as to approach the probable amout of the local demands, the price of the stock was raised at the Treasury; and when the accumulation was deemed adequate to the whole amount of the local demands, the loan was closed.

The policy of the course pursued at the Treasury was soon demonstrated. Offers of subscription to the loan, at the rate of 95 per cent., payable in Treasury notes or in money, were presented to a large amount soon after the rule of the Treasury was declared; and the annexed table, marked G, will exhibit the progressive and actual state of all the subscriptions to the 30th of September last.

In the District of Columbia the money subscriptions (including the subscription of certain liquidated claims upon the Treasury) were, suc-

cessively, at 95, 96½, 97, and 98 per cent., and finally at par. In the city of Baltimore the money subscriptions have been at 95 and 96½ per cent. In the city of Philadelphia the money subscriptions have been entirely at 95 per cent. The price was raised at the Treasury from 95 to 98 per cent. on the 18th of June, (subject, of course, to all unexecuted subscriptions previously accepted or authorized,) and since that time considerable offers have been received at 95 and 96 per cent., but none have been received at the increased rate of 98 per cent. The subscriptions, payable in Treasury notes, have been made in all places at the same rate of 95 per cent. A general abstract of the state of the loan may, therefore, be reduced to the following form:

In the District of Columbia the subscriptions have amounted—

1. In money, to the sum of $2,282,037 38		
2. In Treasury notes, to	257,276 65	
		2,539,314 03

In Baltimore the subscriptions have amounted—

1. In money, to -	- $1,994,818 50	
2. In Treasury notes, to	608,661 90	
		2,603,480 40

In Philadelphia the subscriptions amounted—

1. In money, to -	$1,845,000 00	
2. In Treasury notes, to -	1,260,568 69	
		3,105,568 69

In New York the subscriptions have amounted—

1. In money, to -	- 601 44	
2. In Treasury notes, to	858,371 61	
		858,973 05

In Rhode Island the subscriptions have amounted, in Treasury notes, to -	132,020 69
In Massachusetts the subscriptions have amounted, in Treasury notes, to -	97,201 33
In New Hampshire the subscriptions have amounted, in Treasury notes, to -	52,386 20
In North Carolina the subscriptions have amounted, in Treasury notes, to -	95,000 00
	$9,284,044 38

Having thus absorbed a portion of the Treasury note debt, and deeming the Treasury to be possessed of a sufficient supply of the local currency of the places at which the Treasury notes, unsubscribed and in arrears, were payable by law, except in the cities of New York and Boston, the Secretary of the Treasury proceeded to assign funds for the payment of the Treasury notes, and to give notice thereof in the form of the annexed copies, (marked, respectively, H and I,) in pursuance of the act of Congress, passed on the 3d of March, 1815. As a sufficient supply of the local currencies of Boston and New York had not been obtained, the overture was made in the same notice to discharge the Treasury notes payable in those cities, and in arrears, by accepting them in subscription to the loan, at the rate of 95 per cent., by exchanging them for other Treasury notes, in which the interest due should be inclu-

State of the Finances.

1. Treasury notes bearing interest:

Under the act of March
4, 1814 - - - $2,772,720
Under the act of Dec. 26,
1814 - - - - 8,318,400
Under the act of February 24, 1815 - - 694,600

Per statement annexed,
marked L - - $11,785,720

2. Small Treasury notes not
bearing interest, under act
of February 24, 1815.—
Amount issued and re-
issued, per statement an-
nexed, marked E - 4,152,850

$15,938,570

Amt. estimated to be issued
and re-issued, from Oct. 1
to December 31, 1815 - 1,000,000

16,938,570 00

Making the total amount estimated to
be actually received into the Treasury during the year 1815 - $48,849,613 01

The application of the moneys actually received into the Treasury, during the year 1815, will be as follows: To the 30th September the payments have amounted to the following sums nearly;—the accounts not being yet made up, the precise amount cannot be given.

For civil, diplomatic, and miscellaneous
expenses - - - - $2,587,000 00
For military service - - - 15,190,144 71
For naval service - - - 7,650,000 25
For public debt, (exclusive of the sum
of $300,000, repaid by the Commissioner of Loans for Georgia) - 8,909,178 22

$33,686,323 18

During the fourth quarter of the year
the payments are estimated to amount
to the following sums, viz:
For civil, diplomatic, and miscellaneous expenses - $500,000
For naval service - 1,500,000
For public debt to the 1st of
January, 1816, inclusive - 3,000,000

5,000,000 00

Making together - - - $38,686,323 18
As the receipts into the Treasury during the year have been estimated at 48,849,613 01

The sum left in the Treasury at the end
of the year will be - - - $10,163,289 83

And will consist principally of Treasury notes, paid on account of the revenue and of loans.

Of the estimates of the Public Revenue and Expenditures for 1816.

In the consideration of this subject, it is proper to premise, that the revenue of 1816 must be charged with the payment of a considerable amount of the unliquidated debts incurred during the war; and, consequently, that the proportions of revenue and expenditure for that year cannot be reduced by the scale of a Peace Establishment. The arrearages in the War and Navy Departments are, generally, the outstanding balance of the floating public debt, including Treasury notes and temporary loans, and must be satisfied before a permanent and uniform arrangement of the finances can be effected; but it is believed that the period of a single year will be sufficient for that purpose.

It is also proper to premise, that, although the estimates of the demands on the Treasury for 1816 may be satisfactorily made, there is no settled ground upon which estimates of the ways and means can be confidently formed. The entire system of external and internal taxation must necessarily be revised during the present session of Congress, and the sources as well as the product of the public revenue can only be ascertained from the result of the legislative deliberations. In order however to obviate this difficulty, as far as it is practicable, distinct statements *will* be presented for 1816—1. Of the probable demands of the Treasury; 2. Of the revenue, *estimated* according to the laws now in force; and, 3. Of the revenue, estimated according to the modifications, which will be respectfully submitted.

1. *Of the probable demands on the Treasury.*

The amount of civil, diplomatic, and miscellaneous expenses, is estimated at the
sum of - - - - $1,800,000
The amount of military expenses is estimated at the sum of - - 14,549,246
For the Military Establishment of 1816 - - - $5,112,159
For the arrearages of 1815,
beyond the amount of the
appropriations - - - 9,437,087

Making together - $14,549,246

The amount of the naval expenses (supposing them to be reduced, on the Peace Establishment, to one-half the amount appropriated for 1815, and adding the annual appropriation of $200,000 for the purchase of timber) is estimated at the sum of - - - - - 2,716,510
The amount of the payments required on account of the public debt is estimated at the sum of - - - - - 23,818,513

$42,884,269

For the interest and annual reimbursement of the principal of the funded debt
prior to the war - - - 3,460,800
For the interest on the funded debt created since the war, estimated on a capital of $70,000,000 - - - 4,200,000
For the balance of principal and interest on Treasury notes of every denomination now due or payable in 1815 and 1816, or estimated to be paid in those years, by being received for duties

and taxes, as set forth in the
annexed table, marked L - 15,456,513
For the amount of temporary
leans due to the State Bank
of Boston, ($500,000,) and
the Mechanics' Bank of
New York, ($200,000) - 700,000

  Making together - **$23,816,513**

From this aggregate of the demands for 1816, the charges
of a temporary nature being
deducted, to wit: deduct the
amount of the arrearages
for the military services of
1815 - - - - **$9,437,087**
And the amount of the floating debt to be liquidated in
1816 - - - 16,158,513
          25,595,600

There will remain as the probable annual
expenditure of the Peace Establishment, independent of any addition to
the Sinking Fund, the sum of • -$17,288,669

2. *Of the revenue for 1816, estimated according to
the laws now in force.*

By the laws now in force the revenue arising
from customs, during the year 1816, will be affected in the following manner: The present
rates of duties continue until the 18th of February, 1816, when the duty on salt imported will
cease, and the rates of duties on merchandise of
every description, imported in American vessels,
will fall to one-half of the existing amount, with
the exception of certain manufactured articles,
being of the same kinds as the manufactured articles on which internal duties have been imposed;
the duties on the imported articles continuing at
the existing rates, so long as the existing internal
duties shall be continued upon the corresponding
articles of domestic manufacture. On the 18th
of February the extra duties on merchandise imported in foreign vessels, which is now 15½ per
cent. on the amount of the duty in American
vessels, will fall to 10 per cent. on that amount,
and the tonnage duty on foreign vessels, which
is now $2 per ton, will fall to fifty cents per ton.
The extra duty is, also, liable to be affected by
the operation of the act for abolishing all discriminating duties upon a basis of natural reciprocity.

By the laws now in force the revenue arising
from internal duties will be affected in the following manner: The duties on bank notes, on notes
discounted by banks, and bills of exchange,
(commonly called the stamp duties,) and the
duty on refined sugar, will cease on the 18th of
February, 1816. All the other internal duties,
together with the direct tax, and the increased
rates of postage, will continue.

Under these circumstances the revenue which
will accrue to the United States, during the year
1816, is estimated as follows:

From customs - - - - $13,600,000
 internal duties - - - 7,000,000
 direct tax, (net produce to the Treasury) - - - - 5,600,000
 sales of public lands - - - 1,000,000
 postage and incidental receipts - 400,000
          $27,000,000

The sums actually receivable into the Trea-
ury, during the year, are estimated as follows:
From customs - - - - $20,000,000
 internal duties - - - 6,500,000
 direct tax, including arrears of 1815 8,500,000
 the sales of public lands - - 1,000,000
 postage and incidental receipts - 400,000
          $36,400,000

If to this be added the probable amount
of money in the Treasury, at the commencement of the year 1816, which
may be estimated, exclusive of Trea-
ury notes paid in, previously to that
time, on account of revenue and of
loans, at the sum of - - - - 3,000,000

The effective ways and means of 1816
will produce, in the whole, the sum of $9,400,000
But as the demands upon the Treasury,
for the same year, will amount, as
above stated, to - - - - 42,884,269

There will be left a deficit, to be supplied
by means other than the revenue, of
the sum of - - - - - **$3,484,269**

3. *Of the revenue for 1816, estimated according to the
modifications which will be respectfully submitted.*

From the review of the financial measures of
the Government, in reference to the recent state
of war, which constitutes the first part of the
present report, it appears that the almost entire
failure of the customs, or duties on importations,
and the increasing necessities of the Treasury,
rendered it necessary to seek for pecuniary supplies in a system of internal duties; but both in
respect to the subjects of taxation, and to the
amount of the several taxes, the return of peace
has always been contemplated as a period for
revision and relief. In the fulfilment of that
policy, a reduction of the direct tax; a discontinuance of taxes which, upon trial, have proved
unproductive as well as inconvenient; and, above
all, the exoneration of domestic manufactures
from every charge that can obstruct or retard
their progress, seem to be the objects that particularly invite the legislative attention. There
will still remain, however, a sufficient scope for
the operation of a permanent system of internal
duties upon those principles of national policy
which have already been respectfully suggested.

As an equivalent for the diminution of the
revenue, by the contemplated abolition or reduction of some of the duties and taxes, and in observance of the public faith which is pledged, in
the case of such abolition or reduction, to provide
and substitute other duties and taxes equally pro-

State of the Finances.

ductive, it is intended respectfully to recommend a continuance of the duty on imported salt, and a competent addition to the permanent rates of the duties on merchandise imported. In the general tariff which has been directed by a resolution of the House of Representatives to be prepared, and which will be submitted to Congress as soon as the materials for forming it can be digested and arranged, the subject will be more distinctly, as well as more satisfactorily, presented; but, as it is not probable that this measure can be so matured as to go into operation on the 18th of February next, it becomes necessary to suggest the expediency of continuing the present rates of duties until the 30th of June, when the new rates, with all the necessary details to give effect to the system, may be introduced, and sufficient notice be given to the merchants, to regulate their commercial operations accordingly.

In relation, then, to the internal duties, it is intended respectfully to recommend that the duties imposed at the last session of Congress, on various articles manufactured within the United States, shall be abolished on the 18th day of April next, which will complete the year, commencing from the time the duties went into operation; that the duty imposed during the last session of Congress, on spirits distilled within the United States, shall be abolished on the 30th day of June next, but that, at the same time, there be added 100 per cent. on the rate of the duty which had been charged on licenses to distillers of spirituous liquors in the year 1813; that the duty on household furniture, and on gold and silver watches, be abolished on the 31st day of March next; that the additional duty imposed during the last session of Congress, on licenses to retail wines, spirituous liquors, and foreign merchandise, be abolished on the 31st day of December, 1816; and that the duties on refined sugar, and the stamp duties, be continued; and, finally, in relation to the direct tax, it is intended respectfully to recommend that, on the 31st day of March next, it be reduced to one-half of its present amount; that is, to the annual amount of $3,000,000.

The subtraction from the revenue by these changes and reductions in the direct tax, and the internal duties, is estimated at the annual sum of $7,000,000. But the substitutes for supplying the equivalent amount are estimated to produce, 1st, from the increase of the duty on licenses to distillers, and the continuance of the stamp duties, and duties on refined sugar, the annual sum of $1,500,000; 2d, from the continuance of the duty on imported salt, the annual sum of $500,000; and, 3d, from an increase upon the permanent rates of duties on the importation of foreign merchandise, the annual sum of $5,000,000.

The full effect of the alterations which have been stated will not be developed until some time after the year 1816; but if they be adopted, the state of the revenue for that year, in the two views of which it is susceptible—1st, of revenue accruing during the year, and, 2odly, of money receivable into the Treasury during the year, may be estimated as follows:

1. The revenue which will accrue in 1816 may be estimated—

From customs - - - -	$17,000,000
From internal duties - - - -	4,500,000
From direct tax, (net product to the Treasury)	2,700,000
From sales of public lands - - -	1,000,000
From postage and incidental receipts	400,000
	$25,600,000

2. The moneys which will be actually receivable into the Treasury, from revenue, in 1815, may be estimated—

From the customs - - - -	$21,000,000
From internal duties - - - -	5,000,000
From direct tax, including arrears of 1815	6,000,000
From sales of public lands - - -	1,000,000
From postage and incidental receipts -	400,000
	$33,400,000

If to the sum thus estimated to be receivable into the Treasury, from the revenue, during the year 1816 - - - -	$33,400,000
There be added the money which will probably be in the Treasury at the beginning of the year - - - -	3,000,000
The aggregate will be the sum of -	36,400,000
And the demands being estimated, as above, at - - - - -	42,884,269
There will be left a deficit of - - -	6,484,269

It is here, however, to be recollected, that the estimate of the demands on the Treasury comprehends the gross amount of the arrearages of the War Department, and a provision for the whole of the floating *public debt*; and although, for the purposes of a *legislative appropriation*, the aggregate of the expenditures to be *authorized* for the year 1816 is necessarily made the basis of the official estimates, yet the uniform experience of the Treasury evinces that the demands for a considerable portion of the annual appropriation will not be made during the year.

It may also be observed, that to raise a revenue by the imposition, or even by the continuance, of taxes, adequate to the immediate discharge of every unliquidated demand upon the Treasury, at the close of an expensive war, seems hardly to be necessary under the present circumstances of the country. The product of the revenue arranged in the manner which has been stated, may be estimated, after the year 1816, at an annual amount, nearly four millions greater than the sum required for the interest on the public debt, and for the probable expenses of the Peace Establishment. If the public debt, therefore, were increased in the year 1816, by a sum equal to the whole amount of the deficit as above stated, an equivalent reduction would be effected in less than two years. The unexecuted authority to borrow money, and to issue Treasury notes, already provided by the acts of Congress, is sufficient to enable the Treasury to meet the deficit in either of these modes, and consequently no further legislative aid (except, perhaps, in the modification of the issues of Treasury notes) appears at this time to be required.

III.—*Propositions for the improvement and management of the revenue, and for the support of public credit.*

The propositions which are now to be respectfully submitted, relate: 1. To the revenue. 2. To the Sinking Fund. 3. To the national circulating medium.

1. *Propositions relating to the revenue.*

The changes contemplated in the revenue, on the estimates of a Peace Establishment, having been already stated as the intended objects of recommendation, it is only now necessary to submit to the consideration of Congress the measures requiring their sanction for carrying the plan into effect.

First. It is respectfully proposed that the act of the 1st of July, 1812, imposing an additional duty of 100 per cent. upon the permanent duties on goods, wares, and merchandise imported into the United States from any foreign port or place, and the act of the 29th of July, 1813, imposing a duty upon imported salt, be continued in force until the 30th day of June, 1816.

Second. It is respectfully proposed that the act of the 24th of July, 1813, imposing a duty on sugar refined within the United States, and the act of the 2d of August, 1813, imposing a duty on bank notes, notes discounted, and bills of exchange, be continued by law, in force, without limitation, but with proper amendments to render the collection of the duties more equal and more certain; and that the act of the 15th of December, 1814, imposing duties on carriages and the harness therefor; and that so much of the act of the 23d of December, 1814, as relates to the duties on sales at auction, and to the increasing of the rates of postage, be allowed to remain in force.

Third. It is respectfully proposed that there be a reduction or modification in the following taxes and duties:

1. That the direct tax be reduced from six millions to three millions of dollars, for the year 1816, and for each succeeding year.

2. That the duties on distilled spirits be discontinued after the 30th day of June, 1816; and that the duty on licenses to distillers be raised on that day to double the amount fixed by the act of the 24th of July, 1813.

3. That the duties on licenses to retailers of wines, spirituous liquors, and foreign merchandise, be reduced to the rates of the year 1813, with proper regard to the periods when licenses commence and expire.

Fourth. It is respectfully proposed that the act of the 18th of January, 1815, and the act of the 27th of February, 1815, imposing duties on various articles manufactured, or made for sale within the United States, and the act of the 18th of January, 1815, imposing duties on household furniture and watches, be absolutely and entirely repealed.

Fifth. It is respectfully proposed that the act of the 3d of March, 1815, further to provide for the collection of the duties on imports and tonnage, and the act of the 3d of March, 1815, to fix the compensations, and increase the responsibility of the collectors of the direct tax and internal duties, and for other purposes connected with the collection thereof, so far as it relates to the compensation of the collectors of the direct tax and internal duties, be continued in force without limitation.

2. *Proposition relating to the Sinking Fund.*

The Sinking Fund, as it is at present constituted, amounts to the annual sum of - - **$8,000,000**

It is charged, in the first instance with the payment of the interest, and the annual reimbursement of the principal of the old funded debt, which will require for 1816, and each of the two ensuing years, the sum of - - - **$3,460,000**

And it is charged with the payment of the interest, and the eventual reimbursement of the principal of the new funded debt; the interest, computed on a capital of $70,000,000, will require for the year 1816, and each subsequent year, the sum of - - - **4,200,000**

The total present charge on the Sinking Fund, on account of the funded debt, being the annual sum of - **$7,660,000**

In 1818 the fund will be released from the annual charge of $1,380,000, accruing upon the old six per cent. stock, as the stock will then be paid and extinguished; but in the same year it will be subjected to a charge of $3,000,000, for the first instalment of the principal of the Louisiana stock, which will then become payable. In each of the two succeeding years a similar sum will be payable; and, in the year 1821, such sum will be payable as may be necessary to complete the reimbursement of that stock, and which is estimated at $1,923,500.

The Sinking Fund is also, at present, charged with the payment of the principal and interest of the Treasury notes issued under the act of the 4th of March, 1814, and of prior acts, and of certain temporary loans obtained under the loan acts of 1812, and of subsequent years. The several acts charging these payments on the Sinking Fund have directed that such sums, in addition to the annual appropriation of $8,000,000, should be taken from any moneys in the Treasury not otherwise appropriated, as should be necessary to meet and satisfy the demand. The temporary loans and Treasury notes will, therefore, be probably paid or absorbed in 1817; and it is deemed unnecessary, for the present purpose, to include them in the consideration of the form and extent which it is proposed to give to the Sinking Fund in that year.

In 1803, when the Sinking Fund was established on its present footing, the principal of the public debt was about $86,000,000, and the inter est annually payable upon it about $4,500,000. At that time there was assigned to the Sinking Fund, out of the public revenue, $8,000,000, of which about $3,500,000 were annually applicable to the reduction of the principal of $36,000,000.

At the commencement of the year 1817 it is estimated that the principal of the funded debt will amount to $110,000,000, requiring the sum of $6,150,000 for the payment of its annual interest. If a sum applicable to the reduction of the principal of the debt were now to be assigned, bearing the same proportion to that principal which the sum assigned in 1804 then bore to the principal, it would amount to about $4,350,000. When it is added, therefore, to the sum of $6,150,000, which is necessary for the payment of the interest, there would be required for the amount now to be set apart, to constitute the Sinking Fund, the sum of $10,500,000 per annum. It is proposed, however, to carry the amount only to the sum of $10,000,000, which will allow about $3,850,000 as applicable to the reduction of the principal of the debt; a sum sufficient, if strictly and regularly applied without interruption, upon a compound principle, to pay off the whole of the funded debt in a period less than eighteen years.

Upon these grounds, then, the Secretary of the Treasury respectfully submits the following proposition:

That, in the year 1817, and annually in every subsequent year, there be appropriated the sum of $10,000,000, in addition to the sum of $3,000,000 now annually appropriated for the payment of the interest and principal of the public debt; that the payment of this additional sum be made out of the proceeds of the revenue derived from the customs, the sales of the public lands, and the internal duties, or from either of them, available after the payment of the sums for which they are now respectively pledged or appropriated; and that the said additional sum of $3,000,000 annually be payable to the Commissioners of the Sinking Fund, to be applied by them in the same manner as the moneys which they are now entitled by law to receive; that is to say, 1st, to the payment of the interest on the public funded debt; 2ndly, to the reimbursement of the principal, from time to time, as the same, or any portion of it, shall become reimbursable, according to the terms of the contracts by which it has been created; and, 3dly, after having answered these purposes, if there shall remain a surplus at their disposal, to the purchase of such parts of the public funded debt as shall appear to them to be most for the advantage of the United States, in the manner prescribed by law, and at a rate not exceeding the par value.

3. *Proposition relating to the National circulating medium.*

The delicacy of this subject is only equalled by its importance. In presenting it, therefore, to the consideration of Congress, there is occasion for an implicit reliance upon the legislative indulgence.

By the Constitution of the United States, Congress is expressly vested with the power to coin money, to regulate the value of the domestic and foreign coins in circulation, and, as a necessary implication from positive provisions, to emit bills of credit; while it is declared by the same instrument, that "no State shall coin money, or emit bills of credit." Under this Constitutional authority the money of the United States has been established, by law, consisting of coins made with gold, silver, or copper. All foreign gold and silver coins, at specified rates, were placed, in the first instance, upon the same footing with the coins of the United States, but they ceased (with the exception of Spanish milled dollars, and parts of such dollars) to be a legal tender for the payment of debts and demands in the year 1809.

The Constitutional authority to emit bills of credit has also been exercised in a qualified and limited manner. During the existence of the Bank of the United States the bills or notes of the corporation were declared, by law, to be receivable in all payments to the United States; and the Treasury notes, which have been since issued for the services of the late war, have been endowed with the same quality. But Congress has never recognised, by law, the notes of any other corporation; nor has it ever authorized an issue of bills of credit to serve as a legal currency. The acceptance of the notes of banks, which are not established by the Federal authority, in payments to the United States, has been properly left to the vigilance and discretion of the Executive Department; while the circulation of the Treasury notes, employed either to borrow money, or to discharge debts, depends entirely (as it ought to depend) upon the option of the lenders and creditors to receive them.

The Constitutional and legal foundation of the monetary system of the United States is thus distinctly seen, and the power of the Federal Government to institute and regulate it, whether the circulating medium consist of coin or of bills of credit, must, in its general policy, as well as in the terms of its investment, be deemed an exclusive power. It is true, that a system depending upon the agency of the precious metals will be affected by the various circumstances which diminish their quantity, or deteriorate their quality. The coin of a State sometimes vanishes under the influence of political alarms; sometimes in consequence of the explosion of mercantile speculations, and sometimes by the drain of an unfavorable course of trade. But whenever the emergency occurs that demands a change of system, it seems necessarily to follow that the authority, which was alone competent to establish the national coin, is alone competent to create a national substitute. It has happened, however, that the coin of the United States has ceased to be the circulating medium of exchange, and that no substitute has hitherto been provided by the national authority. During the last year the principal banks, established south and west of New England, resolved that they would no longer issue coin in payment of their notes, or of the drafts of their customers, for money received upon deposite. In this act the Government of the United States had no participation, and yet the immediate effect of the act was to supersede the only legal currency of the nation. By this act, although no State can constitutionally emit bills of credit, corporations, erected by the several States, have been enabled to circulate a paper medium, subject to many of the practical inconveniences of the prohibited bills of credit.

It is not intended, upon this occasion, to condemn, generally, the suspension of specie payments; for appearances indicated an approaching crisis, which would, probably, have imposed it as a measure of necessity, if it had not been adopted as a measure of precaution. But the danger which originally induced, and perhaps justified, the conduct of the banks, has passed away, and the continuance of the suspension of specie payments must be ascribed to a new series of causes. The public credit and resources are no longer impaired by the doubts and agitations excited during the war by the practices of an enemy, or by the inroads of an illicit commerce; yet the resumption of specie payments is still prevented, either by the reduced state of the national stock of the precious metals, or by the apprehension of a further reduction to meet the balances of foreign trade, or by the redundant issues of bank paper. The probable direction and duration of these latter causes constitute, therefore, the existing subject for consideration. While they continue to operate, singly or combined, the authority of the States individually, or the agency of the State institutions, cannot afford a remedy commensurate with the evil; and a recurrence to the national authority is indispensable for the restoration of a national currency.

In the selection of the means for the accomplishment of this important object, it may be asked, 1st. Whether it be practicable to renew the circulation of the gold and silver coins? 2d. Whether the State banks can be successfully employed to furnish a uniform currency? 3dly. Whether a National Bank can be employed more advantageously than the State banks for the same purpose? And, 4thly. Whether the Government can itself supply and maintain a paper medium of exchange, of permanent and uniform value throughout the United States?

1. As the United States do not possess mines of gold or silver, the supply of those metals must, in a time of scarcity, be derived from foreign commerce. If the balance of foreign commerce be unfavorable, the supply will not be obtained incidentally, as in the case of the returns for a surplus of American exports, but must be the subject of a direct purchase. The purchase of bullion is, however, a common operation of commerce, and depends, like other operations, upon the inducements to import the article.

The inducements to import bullion arise, as in other cases, from its being cheap abroad, or from its being dear at home. Notwithstanding the commotions in South America, as well as in Europe, there is no reason to believe that the quantity of the precious metals is now (more than at any former period) insufficient for the demand throughout the commercial and civilized world. The price may be higher in some countries than in others; and it may be different in the same country, at different times; but, generally, the European stock of gold and silver has been abundant, even during the protracted war which has afflicted the nations of Europe.

The purchase of bullion in foreign markets upon reasonable terms is then deemed practicable, nor can its importation into the United States fail eventually to be profitable. The actual price of gold and silver in the American market would in itself afford for some time an ample premium, although the fall in the price must of course be proportionate to the increase of the quantity. But it is within the scope of a wise policy to create additional demands for coin, and in that way to multiply the inducements to import and retain the metals of which it is composed. For instance, the excessive issue of bank paper has usurped the place of the national money, and, under such circumstances gold and silver will always continue to be treated as an article of merchandise; but it is hoped that the issue of bank paper will be soon reduced to its just share in the circulating medium of the country, and consequently that the coin of the United States will resume its legitimate capacity and character. Again, the Treasury, yielding from necessity to the general impulse, has hitherto consented to receive bank paper in the payment of duties and taxes; but the period approaches when it will probably become a duty to exact the payment either in Treasury notes, or in gold and silver coin—the lawful money of the United States. Again, the institutions which shall be deemed proper, in order to remove existing inconveniences, and to restore the national currency, may be so organized as to engage the interest and enterprise of individuals in providing the means to establish them. And, finally, such regulations may be imposed upon the exportation of gold and silver as will serve in future to fix and retain the quantity required for domestic uses.

But it is further believed that the national stock of the precious metals is not so reduced as to render the operation of reinstating their agency in the national currency either difficult or protracted. The quantity actually possessed by the country is considerable; and the resuscitation of the public confidence in bank paper, or in other substitutes for coin, seems alone to be wanting to render it equal to the accustomed contribution for a circulating medium. In other countries, as well as in the United States, the effect of an excessive issue of paper money, to banish the precious metals, has been seen; and, under circumstances much more disadvantageous than the present, the effect of public confidence in national institutions, to call the precious metals to their uses in exchange, has also been experienced.

Even, however, if it were practicable, it has sometimes been questioned whether it would be politic again to employ gold and silver for the purposes of a national currency. It was long and universally supposed that, to maintain a paper medium without depreciation, the certainty of being able to convert it into coin was indispensable; nor can the experiment which has given rise to a contrary doctrine be deemed complete or conclusive. But, whatever may be the issue of that experiment elsewhere, a difference in the structure of the Government, in the physical as well as the political situation of the country, and in the various departments of industry, seem to deprive it of any important influence, as a precedent for the imitation of the United States.

In offering these general remarks to the consideration of Congress it is not intended to convey an opinion that the circulation of the gold and silver coins can at once be renewed. Upon motives of public convenience the gradual attainment of that object is alone contemplated; but a strong, though respectful, solicitude is felt that the measures adopted by the Legislature should invariably tend to its attainment.

2d. Of the services rendered to the Government by some of the State banks during the late war, and of the liberality by which some of them are actuated in their intercourse with the Treasury, justice requires an explicit acknowledgment. It is a fact, however, incontestably proved, that those institutions cannot, at this time, be successfully employed to furnish a uniform national currency. The failure of one attempt to associate them with that view has already been stated. Another attempt, by their agency in circulating Treasury notes, to overcome the inequalities of the exchange, has only been partially successful. And a plan recently proposed, with the design to curtail the issues of bank notes, to fix the public confidence in the administration of the affairs of the banks, and to give to each bank a legitimate share in the circulation, is not likely to receive the general sanction of the banks. The truth is, that the charter restrictions of some of the banks, the mutual relation and dependence of the banks of the same State, and even of the banks of different States, and the duty which the directors of each bank conceive they owe to their immediate constituents, upon points of security or emolument, interpose an insuperable obstacle to any voluntary arrangement, upon national considerations alone, for the establishment of a national medium through the agency of the State banks. It is, nevertheless, with the State banks that the measures for restoring the national currency of gold and silver must originate; for, until their issues of paper be reduced, their specie capitals be reinstated, and their specie operations be commenced, there will be neither room, nor employment, nor safety, for the introduction of the precious metals. The policy and the interest of the State banks must, therefore, be engaged in the great fiscal work, by all the means which the Treasury can employ, or the legislative wisdom shall provide.

3d. The establishment of a National Bank is regarded as the best, and, perhaps, the only adequate resource to relieve the country and the Government from the present embarrassments. Authorized to issue notes, which will be received in all payments to the United States, the circulation of its issues will be co-extensive with the Union, and there will exist a constant demand, bearing a just proportion to the annual amount of the duties and taxes to be collected, independent of the general circulation for commercial and social purposes. A National Bank will, therefore, possess the means and the opportunity of supplying a circulating medium of equal use and value in every State, and in every district of every State. Established by the authority of the Government of the United States, accredited by the Government to the whole amount of its notes in circulation, and intrusted as the depository of the Government with all the accumulations of the public treasure, the National Bank, independent of its immediate capital, will enjoy every recommendation which can merit and secure the confidence of the public. Organized upon principles of responsibility, but of independence, the National Bank will be retained within its legitimate sphere of action, without just apprehension from the misconduct of its directors, or from the encroachments of the Government. Eminent in its resources, been to raise money in anticipation its resources, and in its example, the National Bank will conciliate, aid, and lead, the State banks in all that is necessary for the restoration of credit, public and private. And acting upon a compound capital, partly of stock, and partly of gold and silver, the National Bank will be the ready instrument to enhance the value of the public securities, and to restore the currency of the national coin.

4th. The power of the Government to supply and maintain a paper medium of exchange will not be questioned; but, for the introduction of that medium, there must be an adequate motive. The sole motive for issuing Treasury notes has, hitherto, been to raise money in anticipation of the revenue. The revenue, however, will probably become, in the course of the year 1816. and continue afterwards, sufficient to discharge all the debts, and to defray all the expenses of the Government; and, consequently, there will exist no motive to issue the paper of the Government as an instrument of credit.

It will not be deemed an adequate object for an issue of the paper of the Government, merely that it may be exchanged for the paper of the banks, since the Treasury will be abundantly supplied with bank paper by the collection of the revenue; and the Government cannot be expected to render itself a general debtor, in order to become the special creditor of the State banks.

The co-operation of the Government with the National Bank, in the introduction of a national currency, may, however, be advantageously employed by issues of Treasury notes, so long as they shall be required for the public service.

Upon the whole, the state of the national currency, and other important considerations connected with the operations of the Treasury, render it a duty respectfully to propose—

That a National Bank be established at the

Prohibition of the Importation of Coarse Cotton Fabrics.

city of Philadelphia, having power to erect branches elsewhere, and that the capital of the bank (being of a competent amount) consist of three-fourths of the public stock, and one-fourth of gold and silver.

All which is respectfully submitted.

A. J. DALLAS,
Secretary of the Treasury.

[The tabular statements accompanying the report being voluminous, are necessarily omitted.]

PROHIBITION OF THE IMPORTATION OF COARSE COTTON FABRICS.

[Communicated to the Senate, December 13, 1815.]

To the honorable the Senate and House of Representatives of the United States of America in Congress assembled:

The petition of the undersigned citizens of the United States, concerned in the manufacturing of cotton fabrics, in behalf of themselves and others interested in similar establishments, respectfully showeth: That, during the late season of domestic pressure, arising in a measure from the interruption of the foreign commerce of the country, your petitioners, together with numerous others, citizens of the United States, undertook, and after a considerable expenditure of money and of labor, have at length partially succeeded in the erecting and putting into operation extensive works employed in the manufacturing of cotton goods. That large sums of money have been expended by your petitioners and others upon these objects. That, by means of these exertions, and of the commodities furnished from these sources, the pressure of the late war upon the great body of the community was considerably alleviated. That, from the difficulties inseparable from the establishment of new branches of manufacture; the scarcity of persons properly qualified to superintend their operation; the enormous compensation demanded by those whose skill and experience were requisite, and the high price of labor throughout the country, your petitioners have not as yet been remunerated for the heavy expenses which they have incurred, while the prospect which is just opening of a free and unrestricted importation of the same articles of foreign manufacture, threaten to deprive them of every expectation of a reasonable profit, and, at one blow, to crush the establishments themselves, and to sink the capital which has been invested in them.

Your petitioners, under these circumstances of impending ruin, respectfully entreat the interposition of your honorable bodies, to preserve them and the country from these disastrous and fatal results; and more particularly is it the wish of your petitioners to suggest the propriety and expediency of effecting this desirable object by imposing an absolute or virtual prohibition upon the importation of foreign cotton fabrics of a coarse texture.

Your petitioners will not at this moment venture to encroach upon the time of your honorable bodies by entering into a minute and elaborate argument to substantiate their claims to the attention of Government, or to prove the proposed measure reconcilable with the permanent and solid interests of the community at large; but they beg leave, respectfully, to submit a few prominent facts and leading arguments bearing upon the question:

The establishments for the manufacturing of various articles of cotton, which have already been erected in the United States, are at this moment extensive, and capable of affording a supply nearly or quite commensurate with the demand for domestic consumption.

They have afforded the means of employment to thousands of poor women and children, for whom the ordinary business of agriculture supplies no opportunities for earning a livelihood, educating them in habits of honest industry, and giving additional encouragement to labor and to population.

They have also supplied at moderate prices the necessary demands of the country and the Government, during the recent interruption of our foreign trade.

They have assisted the Southern agriculturist by the consumption of some portion of that superfluous produce which was deprived of its ordinary vent in the demands of foreign nations.

The articles which your petitioners humbly suggest may be subjected to large additional duties, or an absolute prohibition, are chiefly the production of countries lying beyond the Cape of Good Hope.

They are manufactured in a large proportion of cotton of foreign growth, and thus interfere with and discourage a primary object of our own agriculture.

They are not paid for with articles of domestic production, but occasion a continual and wasteful drain of specie of the country.

They are made of a very inferior material, and are manufactured in a manner which make them a mere deception on the consumer. Nearly all Europe have legislated against them; several of which nations have not a single spindle in their dominions, but on the grounds of their little real usefulness, and as sapping the industry of the country; and by thus prohibiting or restricting their introduction, urge the people to seek a better substitute.

They pay an *ad valorem* duty, and add but a small amount to the resources of the Treasury.

They afford employment to but a few tons of our shipping, and will, in all probability, be hereafter introduced in the ships, or through the medium of a rival nation.[*]

* June 24, 1815, arrived at New York the English ship Princess Charlotte, Turnbull, from Calcutta, Madras, the Cape of Good Hope, and fifty-five days from St. Helena, with nine hundred bags of sugar, indigo, spices, saltpetre, pepper, and nearly six hundred tons of piece goods, (selected for this market.)

Prohibition of the Importation of Coarse Cotton Fabrics.

It is by admitting those goods that England will not herself admit for home consumption, that we encourage her to make conquests in India, by thus making them valuable to her.

Their free introduction will prove the necessary ruin of our own establishments, and the total loss of the immense capital now invested in them.

Your petitioners are aware that the measures which they have respectfully suggested may seem to militate against one of the fundamental principles of political economy, as laid down by the ablest writers on the subject, viz: that trade should, as far is practicable, be left free and unrestrained; and that heavy imposts or prohibitions upon foreign commodities, with a view of encouraging their domestic production, are usually inimical to the general interests of the community, and productive of injurious results. Your petitioners, without impugning the soundness of this doctrine in theory, would respectfully suggest that it is an abstract speculation, requiring, when reduced to practice, numerous and important exceptions from its literal import, and always dependent upon two bases essential to its accuracy, and which, from the operation of human passions, can rarely be calculated upon. First, that the rule is universally adopted and acted upon as a principle of policy, regulating the practice of all those foreign nations with whom we have commercial dealings. Secondly, that the freedom of commerce shall never be interrupted by a recurrence to hostilities, or embarrassed by the watchful jealousy of foreign rivals. Unless these circumstances fortunately concur, it will not unfrequently happen that the strict adherence to the letter of the rule will operate as a manifest violation of the principle upon which it is founded, and which it is designed to express.

When the jealousy, the policy, or the ignorance, of other nations have occasioned the adoption of special exceptions among themselves, the equal regard to every branch of industry which it was the intention of the doctrine to preserve unimpaired, as well as a wise regard to our own interests, will frequently require that these partial and injurious aberrations should be met and counteracted by corresponding deviations on our part from its original strictness. If, in order to obtain or preserve a permanent monopoly of certain branches of trade, one nation vexes and harasses every rival that can interfere with this favorite object of policy, the ordinary dictates of prudence

Six hundred tons, at the large allowance of four ounces to the yard, will make about five million of yards; at an average sale of twenty-five cents per yard, is $1,200,000; thus one single ship, and she a foreign ship, draws from the stock of industry of the United States $1,200,000 that might have remained with the common stock of industry of the country, and literally put out at compound interest for the benefit of the country generally: whereas it will now be drawn from us never again to appear, and our own poor women and children, not capable otherwise of earning their living, thrown back upon the community for support.

would require that these attempts should be resisted, and their injurious consequences to ourselves be averted. It is an undisputed fact, that every nation with whom the United States have or can expect to have commercial intercourse have studiously sought by artificial means to secure some peculiar advantage, or to guard against some apprehended evil, by occasionally favoring certain branches of commerce and certain articles of manufacture. Recently there has appeared no disposition among them to adopt more liberal principles of policy. The Prince of Orange, the intimate ally of England, without a spindle in his dominions, has, since the peace in Europe, prohibited the importation of cotton twist and the coarser cotton goods; all cotton goods that shall not have cost thirty cents per square yard, and all cotton colored goods that shall not have cost thirty-six cents per square yard. France has, more than six years since, prohibited all cotton yarn and all cotton goods from beyond the Cape of Good Hope. England does not admit an article for home use that has the appearance of being manufactured, but gives a bounty to the exporter of her own manufactured cottons. Whether their example may be adduced as a proof that the results of experience sometimes militate against the deductions of speculative theory, or whether the United States are not required, by a wise attention to their own interests, to provide against the inconveniences to which they have thus been subjected by the policy of other nations, your petitioners would humbly submit to the consideration of your honorable bodies.

The frequent interruptions to which even the freest commerce is exposed opens a still more fruitful source of argument in favor of your petitioners. While nations are subjected to have their foreign trade embarrassed or impeded in its operations by the hostile aggressions of those over whose measures they have no control, it would deserve another name than philosophical wisdom to permit an adherence to a technical rule of theoretical politics to interfere with, or prevent a watchful attention to their own vital interests. The evident tendency of an unrestrained trade is to create a mutual and equal dependency among nations, and to preserve among them the relations of peace by withdrawing from all every inducement to war. So far as one country receives the superfluous productions which minister to its artificial wants or luxurious habits from another, this effect will be produced, and the dependence that is created must be reciprocal. But when we rely upon a foreign market for commodities of universal and necessary consumption, we receive only the superfluous productions which they can spare, and subject ourselves to an absolute dependence upon their caprices or passions, in which we may be compelled to submit to indignity and oppression, or to draw upon ourselves the most grievous sufferings, and, perhaps, utter ruin, by resisting their ungenerous and galling outrages. Every nation, therefore, whose government has been administered with sagacity and wisdom, and whose natural resources did not interpose insurmountable barriers to the attempt, has labored, unremittingly, to place those objects upon which they depended for subsistence or defence beyond the reach of accident or war, by encouraging their domestic production at every expense, and at every sacrifice.

Your petitioners would respectfully submit that the domestic manufacture of cotton goods comes within this last mentioned exception in two ways. The cultivation of this article, as a product of agriculture, is an object of primary importance to a large and wealthy section of the country; and the consumption of the coarser cotton fabrics extends so equally and universally, as to include every family within the territories of the United States. Unless the domestic manufacturing establishments can afford a partial vent for the productions of the Southern agriculturist, and afford an adequate supply for the extensive demands of a population of eight millions of people, any sudden interruption of our foreign commerce must be productive of the most disastrous consequences to all the growers and all the consumers of the article in question; and should this interruption prove permanent, or even be protracted to a period not exceeding the ordinary continuance of modern wars, may eventuate in the utter ruin of many, and the extreme distress of all. The growers of cotton must lose, or change their crops; the consumers must pay enormous prices for articles of daily and universal use, or have recourse to those wretched expedients, the use of which is ever generated by necessity.

Nor will these evils be prevented, or even in any considerable degree alleviated, by domestic establishments in a season of calamity, created for the emergency, and perishing with the circumstances, which gave them birth. Manufactories are erected at an enormous expense of capital; and time, industry, and experience are required for their effectual operation. The ephemeral attempts to which a severe pressure would give rise must be of uncertain duration; and monstrous as well as immediate profits will be wrung from the distress of others, to afford some remuneration for the risk that has been incurred. Articles of necessary consumption will be subjected to the most enormous variations in their price, and extravagant and casual profits will take the place of the moderate and reasonable returns of a safe and certain trade.

Your petitioners would respectfully submit that the injurious consequences which they have thus briefly sketched, can be effectually provided against, only by a liberal encouragement of the domestic manufactures, by an absolute or virtual prohibition, during a period of peace, of foreign commodities of the same description; and they would beg leave further to suggest that the present season affords a happy opportunity for the interposition of Congress to prevent these evils, and to protect those whose individual and unassisted exertions have hitherto tended to avert or alleviate them.

It cannot have escaped the attention of your honorable bodies that it would be the obvious interest of the European nations, and consistent with those maxims of policy by which their measures have ever been guided, and to which they are at this moment giving additional efficacy, to crush the infant, and as yet immature, establishments in this country, which threaten at no distant period of time to interfere with their own profits, and to place us above a dependence which it has ever been their anxious wish to extend and strengthen. By pouring in upon us, during the present year, a flood of goods, at reduced prices, this result would in all probability, be accomplished, and there is too much reason to apprehend that their respective Governments would shrink from no pecuniary assistance to further the mercenary views of individual cupidity. If these rivals be once crushed to the earth, even by a large temporary sacrifice, it will be in their power effectually to prevent their second growth, and thus to hold a complete control over our consumers and our planters, by regulating, according to their own discretion, the price of the raw production and the manufactured commodity in our markets, and thus to perpetuate a dependence which their monopolizing predilections are but too prone to abuse to our detriment.

Your petitioners would farther respectfully submit to the consideration of your honorable bodies, that, at this period of general pacification throughout Europe, every nation will become the carrier of its own articles of production and consumption; that a large portion of our accustomed commerce must necessarily perish, and the means of discharging the enormous balance in favor of England will soon be exhausted by a total drain of our specie from the country, already at a premium of fifteen per cent. Under these circumstances the encouragement of the domestic manufactures of the coarser goods would tend much to prevent the embarrassments likely to ensue from this aspect of affairs, and to relieve the country from these threatening evils.

The manufacturing establishments in this country have now attained a degree of importance, and embrace so great a variety of interests, as to entitle them to some portion of the liberal patronage of Government. Commerce, agriculture, and manufactures, have become intimately connected, and, if duly and proportionably encouraged, will mutually assist and support each other. The natural advantages of the country have opened to its citizens a broad and even road to prosperity and greatness. To harmonize the various interests of the whole, and to complete the great circle of national grandeur, manufactories are essentially necessary. The advantageous sites for the erection of suitable works which every district supplies, render it emphatically an object of national importance; by the purity of manners, and the intelligence which eminently characterize our citizens; the wholesome jealousy with which all monopolizing institutions are regarded, and the salutary superintendence of a vigilant and impartial administration of the laws, promise to secure us for ages against those evils of which politicians

Protection to Manufacturers.

and moralists have considered them to be productive.

Your petitioners would beg leave to call the attention of your honorable bodies to some of those interests which would be protected by the measure proposed, and to some of the consequences of which it would be productive.

The growers of cotton would be presented with a convenient market for a large portion of their produce, not subject to the fluctuations of political events, nor controlled by the cupidity of foreign traders, certain in its demand, and enlarging with the increasing consumption and abilities of the country.

The consumers would be assured of a never-failing supply of well-wrought fabrics, daily improving in quality and diminishing in price, and unaffected by the interference, the jealousy, or the hostility of foreign nations.

The country would preserve the whole amount of capital already invested in these establishments, be no longer subjected to the uncertainties of foreign trade for an important article of necessary consumption, enlarge and increase the objects of industry, affording new encouragements to her population and emigration to our country of foreign artists, and relieve herself from the pressure of a serious balance against her in her foreign trade.

To the Government would be secured the means of clothing its troops under every emergency, and a new, certain, productive, and increasing source of revenue during a season of war.

The internal and coasting trade, and the communication between the different and remote sections of the country would be substituted for an inconsiderable and injurious branch of foreign commerce, harmonizing their conflicting and jarring interests, and strengthening the bonds of mutual dependance.

These considerations your petitioners would beg leave to press upon the serious attention of your honorable bodies in support of the measure they have proposed, relying implicitly upon the patriotism and wisdom of Congress for the adoption of some means of relief and encouragement.

And your petitioners, as in duty bound, will ever pray, &c.

JOHN R. WATROUS, *and others.*

PROTECTION TO MANUFACTURERS.

—

[Communicated to the Senate, December 22, 1815.]

To the honorable the Senate and House of Representatives of the United States of America in Congress assembled:

The petition of the undersigned citizens of the United States, being a committee appointed by, and acting for and in behalf of the cotton manufacturers residing in Providence and its vicinity, respectfully showeth: That, in consequence of the interruption of commerce, and relying on the favorable disposition uniformly manifested by the Government of the United States towards domestic manufactures, your petitioners have, at a great expense of money and labor, erected and put into operation extensive works for manufacturing cotton goods. Most of the establishments for this object have been completed within a few years, and, owing to the numerous and unavoidable difficulties always attendant on the introduction of new branches of business, and the embarrassments arising from the situation of the foreign relations of the country, the proprietors have, hitherto, been prevented from reaping the reasonable profits which they calculated to obtain. During the continuance of the late war, in addition to the ordinary expenses and difficulties of prosecuting the business, they had also to struggle against the enormous advances in the price of almost every article they used, together with the trouble, cost, and delay, which accrued from the necessity of transporting by land the raw material, and every other commodity required for the supply of the manufactories, and for the support and maintenance of the people employed therein. The same burdensome expense and disadvantage were also experienced in conveying the goods, when finished, to distant markets for sale. But while your petitioners have had to lament that the circumstances of the times did not permit them to realize the profits which they had a right to expect, they had the satisfaction to perceive that the nation was deriving great and important benefits from their labors, receiving, from the skill and industry of our own citizens, vast supplies of useful and necessary commodities, at moderate prices, calculated for universal consumption, and at a period when they could not be obtained from abroad; and that employment and the means of earning a comfortable livelihood were at the same time extended to thousands of poor people, dependent on their labor alone for support, and who must otherwise have been reduced to a state of misery and want.

The event has also fully proved, in the opinion of your petitioners, that, by due encouragement on the part of Government to domestic manufactures, there may be insured to the country, from this source alone, an abundant and regular supply of the most essential and important kinds of cotton goods, at fair prices, and independent of foreign nations.

Your petitioners would now respectfully represent that, in addition to the accumulated embarrassments and losses under which they have labored, the pressure of which has been so great, during the last year, as to induce many of the manufacturers to contract their business, and some to suspend it entirely, the free and unrestricted admission at present allowed into the United States, of cotton fabrics of foreign production, not only extinguishes the hope of a reasonable profit in future from the manufacture of similar goods at home, but threatens the speedy destruction of the establishments already erected for that purpose, and the loss of the immense capital invested in them. They, therefore, earnestly entreat the interposition of your honorable

Protection to Manufacturers.

body, to preserve them from impending ruin. They are the more encouraged in this application, as they conceive the time propitious for Government to extend its fostering care to the manufactures of the country, and are convinced that the request accords with the general feelings and wishes of the people, and with the best interests of the nation.

As an eligible mode of effecting the object in view, your petitioners would respectfully submit to the consideration of Congress the expediency of prohibiting, by law, the importation of all cotton goods, (nankeens excepted,) the production of countries beyond the Cape of Good Hope, and of augmenting the duty on those of a coarse texture imported from other parts of the world.

It is well known that the cotton fabrics of India are made from very inferior stock, and that they are so badly manufactured as to be of little intrinsic value, compared with the substantial and durable manufactures of our own country ; and it is believed that almost every nation of Europe has found it expedient to discourage their use, by subjecting them to very heavy duties, or have prohibited their importation entirely ; and it is deserving of particular observation that their consumption is interdicted in England, although they are the production of her own colonies. It is also a weighty consideration that, being made wholly of a material of foreign growth, so far as their introduction is permitted, they operate to deprive our own citizens, engaged in the cultivation of cotton, of their best and surest market, and thus injuriously affect one of our most important branches of agriculture.

In order to show the extent and importance of the cotton manufacture in the United States, your petitioners beg leave respectfully to state that it has been satisfactorily ascertained that in the small district alone comprised within a circle of thirty miles from Providence, there are not less than one hundred and forty manufactories, containing, in actual operation, more than 130,000 spindles, and capable of holding a much larger number, few of them having yet received their full complement of machinery. The quantity of cotton which, in their present state, they spin in a year, may be computed at 29,000 bales, which, when manufactured into cloth of the descriptions commonly made, will produce 27,840,000 yards, the weaving of which, at the average price of eight cents, amounts to $2,227,200, and the total value of the cloth will exceed $6,000,000. To complete the manufacture from the raw material, until the goods are fit for market, it is estimated would afford steady and constant employment to 26,000 persons. But the benefits resulting from this vast amount of labor are much more extensively diffused than if the whole were done by people constantly engaged in the business, a considerable portion of it being performed by those who are partially occupied in other pursuits, particularly the weaving, which is almost wholly executed at the farm-houses throughout the country, few of which are to be found not supplied with looms.

In this estimate are not intended to be included the numerous classes of persons engaged in occupations indirectly connected with and dependent upon the manufacture, such as those employed in furnishing the various kinds of machinery used in the works, in supplying the people with provisions and other necessaries and conveniences, in transporting goods to and from the manufactories, together with those engaged in the coasting trade, in bringing the raw material and other commodities required for the use of the establishments, and in conveying the manufactures to market.

From this cursory view of the subject a faint representation is exhibited how intimately the cotton manufacture, although but in its infancy, is united and blended with almost every other occupation ; thus creating an interest, in a greater or less degree, in all classes for its maintenance and success, and involving in its destruction very disastrous consequences to the whole body of the community.

Your petitioners know of no description of persons who are not, either directly or indirectly, benefited by this branch of manufacture, except a few capitalists engaged in the trade to India, a commerce affording employment for comparatively but few of our ships and mariners, far less, it is humbly conceived, than would be necessary to carry on the coasting trade arising from the manufacture at home of the same quantity of goods imported from thence. Nor does it afford a market for a single article of our own production, but operates as a continual and destructive drain of the specie of the country, the scarcity of which is at this moment most severely felt. It may be also worthy of remark that the augmentation of the revenue arising from the increased consumption of indigo and other articles used in dying, and the various commodities and materials required in the erection of the works, and in the different processes of the manufacture, many of which are subjected to heavy duties, would, it is humbly believed, nearly, if not entirely, remunerate the Treasury for the loss occasioned by the interdiction proposed.

Your petitioners are aware that it has been a favorite maxim with some, that commerce should be left free and unrestrained; and, while they are far from being disposed to controvert its correctness as a general rule, subject, like all others, according to circumstances, to particular exceptions and modifications, they beg leave respectfully to suggest that they believe it far safer, and more agreeable to the dictates of political wisdom, to follow in the beaten tract of successful experience, rather than to pursue a course of policy not sanctioned by the practice of any other commercial or manufacturing people, and resting solely on opinion and theory for its support. All those nations which have carried commerce and manufactures to the greatest extent, have judged it expedient to protect their citizens against foreign competition. No Government has been more vigilant and rigid in this particular than that of England—a policy which it has steadily pursued

Protection to the Sugar Planters of Louisiana.

for ages, and which has been crowned with unexampled success. While the same principles continue to be persevered in by other nations, a contrary practice on the part of the United States would subject us to a species of colonial dependence, rendering us at once the victim of our own liberality and a prey to foreign cupidity and caprice.

Your petitioners would endeavor to avoid encroaching upon the time of your honorable body, by the repetition of arguments of a general nature, which have been often urged, and which must readily occur to every reflecting mind; but deeming the subject of primary importance in a national point of view, and deeply affecting their individual interests, they persuade themselves it will not be considered obtrusive, succinctly to enumerate some of the particular and immediate advantages, which they conceive the country would derive from the extension of the patronage of Government to the manufacture in question.

It would insure a constant and competent supply, at reasonable prices, of articles wanted for general and daily consumption, not liable to be interrupted by the hostility or injustice of foreign nations.

The internal and coasting trade, which has always been considered as the most advantageous to a nation, and worthy of a high degree of public encouragement, would be thereby promoted and extended; and, by the mutual interchange of commodities between the remote sections of our extensive country, would have a salutary and powerful tendency to bind and link together the various parts in the bonds of reciprocal dependance and friendship.

By a portion of our population being engaged in manufactures a market would be created at home for the productions of agriculture, not subject to be destroyed or materially injured by the enmity or jealousies of foreign Governments. This consideration is of the more importance in the present state of the world, when a general pacification has taken place between the nations of Europe, which promises to be of long duration, and forbids the expectation that the productions of the United States will continue to command such high prices abroad as during the last twenty years, while those nations were engaged in the most destructive and sanguinary wars.

A sure and regular demand would be produced for a considerable portion of the cotton raised in the United States, continually augmenting with the means of manufacturing it, and the increasing consumption of the goods.

It would enlarge the field of useful industry and enterprise, and, by multiplying the sources of wealth and the means of subsistence, would encourage population and the emigation to our country of foreign artists and others, bringing with them the latest improvements in manufactures and the mechanic arts. The vast capital already invested in these establishments would be preserved, and, by its active and successful employment, would continue to contribute largely to the riches and prosperity of the nation.

Your petitioners would further respectfully suggest that the cotton fabrics of India usually imported into the United States, being of a coarse texture and cheaply made, their prime cost is very inconsiderable, and paying only an *ad valorem* duty, they afford but a small income to the Treasury; and the loss incurred by their exclusion might, it is humbly conceived, in a great degree, if not wholly, be restored, by increasing the duty on the coarser kinds of cotton goods imported from other parts of the world.

They, therefore, pray your honorable body to take their case into your serious consideration, and that a law may be passed prohibiting the importation of all cotton goods, (nankeens excepted,) the production of places beyond the Cape of Good Hope, and laying such duty on those of a coarse texture, imported from other countries, as shall give to your petitioners the necessary protection and relief, and as Congress in their wisdom may deem expedient.

And, as in duty bound, will ever pray,

James Burrill, jr.   Philip Allen,
Daniel Lyman,   Abr'm Wilkinson,
Thomas Burgess,   Amasa Mason,
Timothy Greene,   Samuel Ames,
Seth Wheaton,   John S. Dexter,
George Jackson,   Samuel W. Greene,
James Rhodes,   Jos. T. Franklin,
                       Committee.

PROTECTION TO THE SUGAR PLANTERS OF LOUISIANA.

[Communicated to the House, January 5, 1815.]

To the honorable the Senate and House of Representatives of the United States in Congress assembled:

The memorial of the sugar planters, citizens of the State of Louisiana, respectfully represents:—That there is, perhaps, no culture more important and advantageous to the United States than that of the sugar cane, the produce of which, though at first ranked among the luxuries of life, has, from its universal use, become an article of the first necessity. Before the acquisition of Louisiana, vast sums of money were lost to the United States in the purchase of sugar, rum, and molasses, made in the East and West Indies, from whence alone those commodities were obtained. In time of war supplies from thence are precarious, and the consumer would be either entirely deprived of those necessary articles, or could obtain them only at extravagant rates. It is, then, obviously the interest of the United States to encourage the cultivation of the cane, and to secure to themselves the advantages which Louisiana offers in this particular. Whilst its citizens rejoice in the means which nature has placed within their reach, of supplying the wants of the other States of the Union, they have at the same time to lament that their ability to effect it will depend on the fostering aid of the General Government.

Beyond all others, the culture of the cane is

attended with difficulties. It requires enormous capitals. The lands that produce it are dear, large gangs of slaves, and laboring animals are required, immense edifices are to be erected, mills, and expensive utensils are to be obtained; add to those the costly and unceasing labor that is required in forming, and keeping up the works that are necessary to prevent the overflowing of the mighty stream that borders those lands, the numerous canals for draining them, and without which they would not be susceptible of cultivation; so that after a fortune has been consumed, and often distressing debts incurred, years on years elapse before the most fortunate and successful reap the reward of their expenditures and toils. It is true, in a propitious season this culture affords greater profit than any other, but numerous and dreadful are the accidents that often blast the hopes of the planter. The climate is subject to hurricanes, the ravages of which not only destroys the crop in the ground, and often the expectation of the one ensuing it, but levels to the ground the buildings which had been erected at such an immense cost. Those are evils which sugar planters every where experience; but there are others, which are the peculiar scourge of those of Louisiana—an early frost prevents the maturity of the cane, and greatly injures its yield; a warm day, in the season of making sugar, occasioning it to ferment, sours the juice, and destroys the labor of the year; the coldness of the climate, and destructive attacks of worms, to which the cane is subject, requires it to be frequently replanted, and is a serious drawback on the planter, as the growth of one acre is only sufficient to plant four; the same cause also often destroys the cane intended for plants, and blasts his hopes of the ensuing crop. At times high winds, or the negligence of an individual, causing a break in the dike that retains the river, the water rushing down, sweeps buildings, crop, and animals before it, and spreading on all sides carries irresistible ruin with it. Such inundations, by covering the fields with a poor, sandy sediment, often renders them for many years useless, and they are not unfrequent. With such serious evils to contend with, it cannot be expected that the planter of Louisiana can, without some encouragement from the Government, stand in competition with those who rear the plant in its congenial climate; yet it is impossible for him successfully to attend to any other branch of agriculture. Indigo, cotton, tobacco, and sugar, are the only kinds of produce which have as yet been considered as suitable to the country. About thirty years ago the raising of indigo absolutely ceasing to afford the means of subsistence to the cultivator, tobacco, and afterwards, cotton were resorted to; but experience has shown the impossibility of standing in competition with the States of Virginia, Maryland, and Kentucky, with regard to tobacco, from whence our supplies for consumption are at present received, and those of Georgia, the Carolinas, Tennessee, and the Mississippi Territory, in that of cotton. The planters of Louisiana, therefore, hope that the liberal views of Congress will in-

duce that honorable body to come to their aid. As part of the American family they believe it suffices for them to make known their wants to the common parent, to have every proper relief extended to them. But they address it with more confidence, from the conviction that the interests of the Union loudly demand that this distant State should be assisted in securing to herself, and, consequently, to the nation, the vast advantages which its climate and situation promise. With the encouragement of Congress she would in a few years be able to supply her sister States with sugar, rum, and molasses, and will in return consume a considerable portion of their produce and manufactures. Political considerations require also that this distant and frontier State should be strengthened, and its population augmented; let, then, the only kind of agriculture for which nature intended her, which she alone of all the States is capable of producing, and which is at the same time so essentially necessary to all, be fostered and encouraged.

We, therefore, humbly entreat your honorable body that the same sound policy which has hitherto invariably excited the General Government to protect the growing manufactures of our country, and, consequently, made us in many branches completely independent of foreign nations, may be extended to the cultivators of the cane, and that the duties laid during the war on foreign sugar, rum, and molasses, be made permanent by law.   BERNARD MARIGNY,
                        and others.

New Orleans, Louisiana, 1815.

MILITARY AND NAVAL EXPENDITURES.

[Communicated to the House, February 5, 1816.]
                     Treasury Department, *Feb.* 5, 1816.

Sir: In obedience to a resolution of the House of Representatives, passed yesterday, I have the honor to transmit a letter from the Register of the Treasury, and the statements which accompany it, viz:

(A.) A comparative statement between the annual amount of the expenditure for the Military Establishment of the United States, as rendered by the Treasury Department, under a resolution of the House of Representatives of the United States, of the 20th of January, 1816, and the statement thereof furnished under the resolution of the House, of the 31st of March, 1810.

(B.) A comparative statement between the annual amount of the expenditure for the Navy of the United States, as rendered by the Treasury Department, under a resolution of the House of Representatives of the United States, of the 20th of January, 1816, and the statement thereof furnished under the resolution of the House, of the 31st of March, 1810.

I have the honor to be, &c.
                                   A. J. DALLAS.
Hon. Henry Clay, *Speaker, &c.*

Military and Naval Expenditures.

TREASURY DEPARTMENT, REGISTER'S OFFICE, *February* 5, 1816.

SIR: I have the honor to transmit papers A and B, being comparative statements between the annual amount of the expenditures of the Military and Naval Establishments as rendered by the Treasury Department, under a resolution of the House of Representatives of the United States of the 20th of January, 1816, and the statement thereof furnished under the resolution of the House, of the 31st March, 1810. I have the honor to be, &c.

JOSEPH NOURSE.

Hon. ALEXANDER J. DALLAS, *Secretary of the Treasury.*

(A.)

A comparative statement between the annual amount of the expenditures for the Military Establishment of the United States, as rendered by the Treasury Department, under a resolution of the House of Representatives of the United States, of the 20th of January, 1816, and the statement thereof furnished under the resolution of the House, of the 31st of March, 1810.

Years.	Amount as exhibited under resolution of Mar. 30, 1810.	Expenditures out of appropriations for War Department, in relation to Indian Department, other than treaties and trading-houses.	Amount as exhibited under resolution of Jan. 20, 1816.	A repayment.	Indian expenditure.
1791	$632,804 03	–	$632,804 03		
1792	1,103,038 47	–	1,100,702 09	$2,336 38	
1793	1,132,443 91	–	1,130,249 08		$2,194 63
1794	2,589,097 59	$50,000 00	2,609,097 59		
1795	2,423,385 81	58,524 32	2,480,910 13		
1796	1,246,237 82	13,996 02	1,260,263 84		
1797	1,002,299 04	37,103 62	1,039,402 66		
1798	1,939,692 39	69,829 91	2,009,522 30		
1799	2,405,669 17	61,277 81	2,466,946 98		
1800	2,517,409 99	43,468 78	2,560,878 77		
1801	1,600,944 08	72,000 00	1,672,944 08		
1802	1,179,148 25	42,000 00	1,221,148 25		
1803	822,055 85	60,000 00	882,055 85		
1804	875,923 93	63,000 00	938,923 93		
1805	712,781 28	55,500 00	768,281 28		
1806	1,224,355 38	159,200 00	1,383,555 38		
1807	1,288,685 91	100,600 00	1,389,285 91		
1808	2,900,834 40	140,600 00	3,041,434 40		
1809	3,345,772 17	125,000 00	3,470,772 17		
	30,941,669 47	$1,152,040 46 (a)	$32,069,178 72	$2,336 38	$2,194 63

Amount of expenditures as exhibited under the resolution of 31st March, 1810 - - - $30,941,669 47
Deduct the repayment of $2,336 38 as above, and the sum of $2,194 63 as Indian expenditure - - - - - - - - - - - - - - - - 4,531 21

                              30,937,138 26

To which expenditures out of the appropriations for the War Department, in relation to Indian Department, other than the expenditures exhibited for treaties with the Indians, and trading-houses - - - - - - - - - - - - - - - - 1,152,040 46

As above - - - - - - - - - - - - - - - - $32,089,178 72

(a) This amount, with the annual subdivisions, was formed by the Register, by estimate, for the purpose of excluding the payments which had been made by the purveyors of public supplies, contractors, and other persons who had expended public moneys in the purchase of Indian goods, rations, or supplies, which might apply to the Indian Department, and which had been made from moneys charged and exhibited in the annual printed public accounts as advanced for the Military Establishment.

These annual amounts, ascertained from the best materials to which access could be had, were deducted from the total amount of the annual actual expenditures, with a view to conform, as nearly as possible, with the resolution of the House, of the 31st March, 1810, by excluding the expenditures on account of the Indian Department.

TREASURY DEPARTMENT, REGISTER'S OFFICE, *February* 6, 1816.

JOSEPH NOURSE, *Register.*

State of the Sinking Fund.

(B.)

A comparative statement between the annual amount of the expenditure for the Navy of the United States, as rendered by the Treasury Department, under a resolution of the House of Representatives of the United States, of the 20th January, 1816, and the statement thereof, furnished under the resolution of the House, of the 31st of March, 1810.

Years.	Amount as exhibited under the resolution of 20th January, 1816, excluding expenditure for marine hospital.	Marine hospital expenditure.	Revenue cutter excluded in statement of the 31st March, 1810.	Total amount exhibited under resolution of March 31, 1810, in which the marine hospital was included.
1791	$570 00	–	$570 00	
1792	53 02	–	53 02	
1793				
1794	61,406 97	–		$61,406 97
1795	410,562 03	–		410,562 03
1796	274,784 04	–	–	274,784 04
1797	382,631 89	–		382,631 89
1798	1,381,347 76	–		1,381,347 76
1799	2,858,081 84	–		2,858,081 84
1800	3,448,716 03	–		3,448,716 03
1801	2,111,424 00	–		2,111,424 00
1802	915,561 87	$250 00	–	915,811 87
1803	1,215,230 53	31,087 36	–	1,246,317 89
1804	1,189,832 75	84,027 50	–	1,273,800 25
1805	1,597,500 00	–		1,597,500 00
1806	1,649,641 44	–		1,649,641 44
1807	1,722,064 47	–	–	1,722,064 47
1808	1,884,067 80	–	–	1,884,067 80
1809	2,437,758 80	–	–	2,437,758 80
	$23,531,237 24	$115,364 86	$623 02	$23,645,979 08

Amount of expenditures as exhibited under the resolution of 20th January 1816 -   . $23,531,237 24

And the marine hospital expenditure   - - - - - - - - - 115,364 86

                                            23,646,602 10

From which deduct expenditure for revenue cutter   - . - - - - - 623 02

     As above   - - - . - . - - - - - 23,645,979 08

TREASURY DEPARTMENT, REGISTER'S OFFICE, *February* 5, 1816.

                        JOSEPH NOURSE, *Register.*

SINKING FUND.

[Communicated to the Senate, February 7, 1816.]

WASHINGTON, *February* 7, 1816.

The Commissioners of the Sinking Fund respectfully report to Congress as follows:

That the measures which have been authorized by the board, subsequent to their last report of the 6th of February, 1815, so far as the same have been completed, are fully detailed in the report of the Secretary of the Treasury to this board, dated the 6th day of the present month, and in the statements therein referred to, which are herewith transmitted, and prayed to be received as part of this report.

      J. GAILLARD, *Pres't Senate pro. tem.*
      J. MARSHALL, *Chief Justice U. S.*
      J. MONROE, *Sec'ry of State.*
      A. J. DALLAS, *Sec'ry of Treasury.*

TREASURY DEPARTMENT, *Feb.* 6, 1816.

The Secretary of the Treasury respectfully reports to the Commissioners of the Sinking Fund:

That the balance of moneys advanced on account of the public debt, remaining unexpended at the end of the year 1813, and applicable to payments falling due after that year, which balance amounted to $761,205 75

Together with the sums disbursed from the Treasury during the year 1814, on account of the principal and interest of the public debt, which sums amounted to - - - - 8,386,880 59

Together with a further sum arising from profit in exchange on remittances from America to Europe during the year 1814, amounting to - . - 19,837 61

And amounting together to - $9,167,913 95

Have been accounted for in the following manner viz:

There was repaid into the Treasury during the year 1814, on account of the principal of moneys heretofore advanced for the payment of the public debt, the sum of - - - - - $286,336 65

The sums actually applied during the year 1814 to the payment of the principal and interest of the public debt, amounted, to the sum of $8,940,074 08, viz:

In reimbursement of the principal of the public debt - - $4,283,692 34
On account of the interest and charges on the same - - - 4,656,381 74
                     $8,940,074 08

But of this sum there was short provided, consisting of unclaimed dividends on the public debt, not demanded or applied for by the proprietors - - - 58,496 79
                     8,881,577 30
                     $9,167,913 95

That, during the year 1815, the following disbursements were made out of the Treasury on account of the principal and interest of the public debt, viz:

On account of the interest and reimbursement of the funded domestic debt - - - $6,373,847 73
On account of the principal and interest of the registered debt - - 6 49
On account of the principal and interest of temporary loans, viz: reimbursement of principal $1,800,000 00
Payment of interest - - 69,230 07
                     1,869,230 07
On account of principal and interest of Treasury notes - - - 3,872,706 95
On account of the interest on Louisiana stock payable in Europe - 724,136 11

Amounting together to the sum of $12,839,929 35

Which disbursements were made out of the following funds, viz:

I. From the balance of the annual appropriation of eight millions of dollars for the year 1814, remaining unexpended at the end of that year, which balance amounted, as stated in the last annual report to - - - - - $341,710 17

II. From the funds constituting the annual appropriation of eight millions of dollars for the year 1815, viz:
From the fund arising from the interest on the debt transferred to the Commissioners of the Sinking Fund, as per statement I - $1,969,577 64
From the fund arising from the net proceeds of the sales of public lands - 1,200,000 00
From proceeds of duties on goods, wares, and

merchandise imported, and on the tonnage of vessels - $4,839,422 24
                     $8,008,999 00

III. From the proceeds of the duties on goods, wares, and merchandise imported, and on the tonnage of vessels, and from the proceeds of the direct tax and internal duties in advance, and on account of the annual appropriation of eight millions of dollars for the year 1816 - - - 4,496,219 18
                     12,838,929 35

That the aforesaid sum of twelve millions eight hundred and thirty-nine thousand nine hundred and twenty-nine dollars and thirty-five cents will be accounted for in the next annual report, in conformity with the accounts which shall have been rendered to this Department.

That, in the meantime, the manner in which the said sum has been applied is estimated as follows, viz:

There is estimated to have been applied to the payment of the deficiency of the provision at the end of the year 1814, as above stated, the sum of 58,496 79
There was paid for loss on exchange on remittances from America to Europe, during the year 1815, the sum of - 53,868 17
There is estimated to have been applied during the year 1816 to the reimbursement of the principal of the public debt - - $7,094,016 48
And to the payment of interest on the same 5,606,966 02
                     12,640,981 50

And there is estimated to have been left unapplied at the end of the year 1815, a sum applicable to payments on account of the public debt during the year 1816, of - - - - 87,412 90
                     $12,839,929 35

That the temporary loans, which became payable during the year 1815 were paid, but the two instalments amounting to $500,000, which became payable to the State bank, Boston, in the month of December, 1814, and which were not then paid from the inability of the Treasury to apply the moneys within its control to that object, owing to the disordered state of the public currency.

That, during the year 1815, and on the 1st day of January, 1816, Treasury notes charged upon the Sinking Fund fell due amounting to $7,747,280. It was not within the power of the Treasury to make provision for the payment of any part of these notes, or of those which had fallen due, and had not been paid in the preceding year, (with the exception of such as were applied by their holders to the payment of duties and taxes,) until the 1st of July, 1815, when provision was made, and public notice thereof given for the reimbursement of such Treasury notes as had previously to that time become payable at Baltimore and Washington. The same provision was made on the 1st of August for those previously payable

Protection to the Manufacturers of Cotton Fabrics.

at Philadelphia ; on the 1st of September for those previously payable at Savannah ; and on the days when they respectively become payable, for those reimbursable at all other places, with the exception of New York and Boston ; at neither of which places have funds yet been obtained to an extent sufficient to meet the payment of the Treasury notes reimbursable at those two places respectively. The annexed statement marked L, shows the time when, and the places at which, all the Treasury notes reimbursable in the year 1815, and on the 1st of January, 1816, became payable.

A statement, marked H, is annexed, which exhibits the whole amount of stock transferred to the Commissioners of the Sinking Fund, and standing to their credit on the books of the Treasury on the last day of December, 1815.

All which is respectfully submitted by
    A. J. DALLAS, *Sec'ry Treasury.*

[The tabular statements are omitted.]

PROTECTION TO THE MANUFACTURERS OF COTTON FABRICS.

[Communicated to the House, February 13, 1816.]

Mr. NEWTON, from the Committee of Commerce and Manufactures, to whom was referred the memorials and petitions of the manufacturers of cotton wool, submitted the following report:

The committee were conscious that they had no ordinary duty to perform, when the House of Representatives referred to their consideration the memorials and petitions of the manufacturers of cotton wool. In obedience to the instructions of the House they have given great attention to the subject, and beg leave to present the result of their deliberations.

They are not a little apprehensive that they have not succeeded in doing justice to a subject so intimately connected with the advancement and prosperity of agriculture and commerce ; a subject which enlightened statesmen and philosophers have deemed not unworthy of their attention and consideration.

It is not the intention of the committee to offer any theoretical opinions of their own or of others; they are persuaded that a display of speculative opinions would not meet with approbation. From these views the committee are disposed to state facts, and to make such observations only as shall be intimately connected with, and warranted by them.

Prior to the years 1806 and 1807, establishments for manufacturing cotton wool had not been attempted, but in a few instances, and on a limited scale. Their rise and progress are attributable .to embarrassments, to which commerce was subjected, which embarrassments originated in causes not within the control of human prudence.

While commerce flourished, the trade which had been carried on with the continent of Europe, with the East Indies, and with the colonies

of Spain and France, enriched our enterprising merchants ; the benefits of which were sensibly felt by the agriculturists, whose wealth and industry were increased and extended. When external commerce was suspended the capitalists throughout the Union became solicitous to give activity to their capital. A portion of it, it is believed, was directed to the improvement of agriculture ; and not an inconsiderable portion of it, as it appears, was likewise employed in erecting establishments for manufacturing of cotton wool.

To make this statement as satisfactory as possible, to give it all the certainty that it is susceptible of attaining, the following facts are respectfully submitted to the consideration of the House. They show the rapid progress which has been made in a few years, and, evidently, the ability to carry them on with certainty of success, should a just and liberal policy regard them as objects deserving encouragement :

In the year 1800, 500 bales of cotton were manufactured in manufacturing establishments; in 1805, 1,000 ; in 1810, 10,000 ; and in 1815, 90,000.

This statement the committee have no reason to doubt; nor have they any to question the truth of the following succinct statement of the capital which is employed, of the labor which it commands, and of the products of that labor:

Capital - - - - - -	$40,000,000
Males employed from the age of 17 and upwards - - - - -	10,000
Women and female children - - -	66,000
Boys under 17 years of age - - -	24,000
Wages of 100,000 persons, averaging $150 each - - - - - -	$15,000,000
Cotton wool manufactured, 90,000 bales, amounting to - - - - lbs.	27,000,000
Number of yards of cotton of various kinds - - - - -	81,000,000
Cost per yard, averaging 30 cents -	$24,300,000

The rise and progress of such establishments can excite no wonder. The inducements to industry, in a free Government, are numerous and inviting. Effects are always in unison with their causes. The inducements consist in the certainty and security, which every citizen enjoys, of exercising exclusive dominion over the creations of his genius, and the products of his labor ; in procuring from his native soil, at all times, with facility, the raw materials that are required ; and in the liberal encouragement that will be accorded by agriculturists to those who, by their labor, keep up a constant and increasing demand for the produce of agriculture.

Every State will participate in those advantages ; the resources of each will be explored, opened, and enlarged. Different sections of the Union will, according to their position, the climate, the population, the habits of the people, and the nature of the soil, strike into that line of industry which is best adapted to their interest and the good of the whole ; an active and free intercourse, promoted and facilitated by roads and canals, will ensue ; prejudices, which are generated by distance, and the want of inducements to approach each other and reciprocate benefits, will be removed; information will be extended; the Union will acquire strength and solidity; and the Constitution of the United States, and that of each State, will be regarded as fountains, from which flow numerous streams of public and private prosperity.

Each Government, moving in its appropriate orbit, performing with ability its separate functions, will be endeared to the hearts of a good and grateful people.

The States that are most disposed to manufactures as regular occupations, will draw from the agricultural States all the raw materials which they want, and not an inconsiderable portion, also, of the necessaries of life; while the latter will, in addition to the benefits which they at present enjoy, always command, in peace or in war, at moderate prices, every species of manufacture that their wants may require. Should they be inclined to manufacture for themselves, they can do so with success, because they have all the means in their power to erect and to extend, at pleasure, manufacturing establishments. Our wants being supplied by our own ingenuity and industry, exportation of specie to pay for foreign manufactures will cease.

The value of American produce at this time exported will not enable the importers to pay for the foreign manufactures imported. Whenever the two accounts shall be fairly stated, the balance against the United States will be found to be many millions of dollars. Such is the state of things that the change must be to the advantage of the United States. The precious metals will be attracted to them, the diffusion of which, in a regular and uniform current through the great arteries and veins of the body politic, will give to each member health and vigor.

In proportion as the commerce of the United States depends on agriculture and manufactures, as a common basis, will it increase, and become independent of those revolutions and fluctuations, which the ambition and jealousy of foreign Governments are too apt to produce. Our navigation will be quickened, and, supported as it will be by internal resources never before at the command of any nation, will advance to the extent of those resources.

New channels of trade, to enterprise no less important than productive, are opening, which can be secured only by a wise and prudent policy appreciating their advantage.

If want of foresight should neglect the cultivation and improvement of them, the opportune moment may be lost, perhaps, for centuries, and the energies of this nation be, thereby, prevented from developing themselves, and from making the boon which is proffered our own.

By trading on our own capital, collisions with other nations, if they be not entirely done away, will be greatly diminished.

This natural order of things exhibits the commencement of a new epoch, which promises peace, security, and repose, by a firm and steady reliance on the produce of agriculture, on the treasures that are embosomed in the earth, on the genius and ingenuity of our manufacturers and mechanics, and on the intelligence and enterprise of our merchants.

The Government, possessing the intelligence and the art of improving the resources of the nation, will increase its efficient powers, and, enjoying the confidence of those whom it has made happy, will oppose to the assailant of the nation's rights, the true, the only invincible ægis—the unity of will and strength.

Causes producing war will be few; should war take place its calamitous consequences will be mitigated, and the expenses and burdens of such a state of things will fall with a weight less oppressive and injurious on the nation. The expenditures of the last war were greatly increased by a dependence on foreign supplies; the prices incident to such a dependence will always be high.

Had not our nascent manufacturing establishments increased the quantity of commodities, at that time in demand, the expenditures would have been much greater, and consequences the most fatal and disastrous, alarming even in contemplation, would have been the fate of this nation. The experience of the past teaches a lesson never to be forgotten, and points emphatically to the remedy. A wise Government should heed its admonitions, or the independence of this nation will be exposed to " the shafts of fortune."

The committee, keeping in view the interest of the nation, cannot refrain from stating that cotton fabrics imported from India, interfere not less with that encouragement to which agriculture is justly entitled, than they do with that which ought reasonably to be accorded to the manufacturers of cotton wool. The raw material of which they are made is the growth of India, and of a quality inferior to our own.

The fabrics themselves, in point of duration and use, are likewise inferior to the substantial fabrics of American manufacture. Although the India cotton fabrics can be sold for a lower price than the American, yet the difference in the texture is so much in favor of the American, that the latter may be safely considered as the cheapest.

The distance of most of the Western States from the ocean, the exuberant richness of the soil, and the variety of its products, forcibly impress the mind of the committee with a belief that all these causes conspire to encourage manufactures, and to give an impetus and direction to such a disposition. Although the Western States may be said to be in the gristle, in contemplation of that destiny to which they are hastening, yet the products of manufactures in those States are beyond every calculation that could reasonably be made; contrary to the opinion of many enlightened and virtuous men, who have supposed that the inducement to agriculture, and the superior advantages of that life, would suppress any disposition of that sort of industry. But theories, how ingeniously soever they may be constructed, how much soever they may be made to conform to the laws of symmetry and beauty, are no sooner

Protection to the Manufacturers of Cotton Fabrics.

brought into conflict with facts, than they fall into ruins. In viewing their fragments the mind is irresistibly led to render the homage due to the genius and taste of the architects, but cannot refrain from regretting the waste, to no purpose, of superior intellects. The Western States prove the fallacy of such theories; they appear in their growth and expansion to be in advance of thought; while the political economist is drawing their portraits, their features change and enlarge, with such rapidity, that his pencil in vain endeavors to catch their expression, and to fix their physiognomy.

It is to their advantage to manufacture, because, by decreasing the bulk of the articles, they at the same time increase their value by labor, bring them to market with less expense, and with the certainty of obtaining the best prices.

Those States understanding their interest will not be diverted from its pursuit. In the encouragement of manufactures they find a stimulus for agriculture.

The manufacturers of cotton, in making application to the National Government for encouragement, have been induced to do so for many reasons. They know that their establishments are new and in their infancy, and that they have to encounter a competition with foreign establishments that have arrived at maturity, that are supported by a large capital, and that have from the Government every protection that can be required.

The American manufacturers expect to meet with all the embarrassments which jealous and monopolizing policy can suggest. The committee are sensible of the force of such considerations. They are convinced that old practices and maxims will not be abandoned to favor the United States. The foreign manufacturers and merchants will put in requisition all the powers of ingenuity; will practice whatever art can devise, and capital can accomplish, to prevent the American manufacturing establishments from striking root and flourishing in their rich and native soil. By the allowance of bounties and drawbacks, the foreign manufacturers and merchants will be furnished with additional means of carrying on the conflict, and of insuring success.

The American manufacturers have good reasons for all their apprehensions; they have much at stake; they have a large capital employed, and are feelingly alive to its fate. Should the National Government not afford them protection, the dangers which invest and threaten them will destroy all their hopes, and will close their prospects of utility to their country. A reasonable encouragement will sustain and keep them erect; but, if they fall, they fall never to rise again.

The foreign manufacturers and merchants know this, and will redouble with renovated zeal the stroke to prostrate them. They also know that, should the American manufacturing establishments fall, their mouldering piles, the visible ruins of a legislative breath, will warn all who shall tread in the same footsteps, of the doom, the inevitable destiny of their establishments.

The National Government, in viewing the disastrous effects of a short-sighted policy, may relent, but what can relenting avail? Can it raise the dead to life? Can it give for injuries inflicted the reparation that is due? Industry, in every ramification of society, will feel the shock, and generations will, as they succeed each other, feel the effects of its undulations. Dissatisfaction will be visible everywhere, and the lost confidence and affections of the citizens will not be the least of the evils the Government will have to deplore. But should the National Government, pursuing an enlightened and liberal policy, sustain and foster the manufacturing establishments, a few years would place them in a condition to bid defiance to foreign competition, and would enable them to increase the industry, wealth, and prosperity of the nation, and to afford to the Government, in times of difficulty and distress, whatever it may require to support public credit, while maintaining the rights of the nation.

Providence, in bountifully placing within our reach whatever can administer to happiness and comfort, indicates plainly to us our duty, and what we owe to ourselves. Our resources are abundant and inexhaustible.

The stand that Archimedes wanted is given to the National and State governments, and labor-saving machinery tenders the lever—the power of bringing those resources into use.

This power imparts incalculable advantages to a nation whose population is not full. The United States require the use of this power, because they do not abound in population. The diminution of manual labor, by means of machinery, in cotton manufacture in Great Britain was, in the year 1810, as two hundred to one.

Our manufacturers have already availed themselves of this power, and have profited by it. A little more experience in making machines, and in managing them with skill, will enable our manufacturers to supply more fabrics than are necessary for the home demand.

Competition will make the prices of the articles low, and the extension of the cotton manufactories will produce that competition.

One striking and important advantage which labor-saving machines bestow is this, that in all their operations they require few men, as a reference to another part of this report will show. No apprehensions can then be seriously entertained that agriculture will be in danger of having its efficient laborers withdrawn from its service. On the contrary, the manufacturing establishments increasing the demand for raw materials will give to agriculture new life and expansion.

The committee, after having, with great deference and respect, presented to this House this important subject, in various points of view, feel themselves constrained, before concluding this report, to offer a few more observations, which they consider as being immediately connected with it, and not less so with the present and future prosperity of this nation.

Protection to the Manufacturers of Cotton Fabrics.

The prospects of an enlarged commerce are not flattering.

Every nation, in times of peace, will supply its own wants from its own resources, or from those of other nations.

When supplies are drawn from foreign countries, the intercourse which will ensue will furnish employment to the navigation only of the countries connected by their reciprocal wants.

Our concern does not arise from, nor can it be increased by, the limitation which our navigation and trade will have prescribed to them, by the peace and apparent repose in Europe.

Our apprehensions arise from causes that cannot animate by their effects. Look wheresoever the eye can glance, and what are the objects that strike the vision? On the continent of Europe industry, deprived of its motive and incitement, is paralyzed; the accumulated wealth of ages, seized by the hand of military despotism, is appropriated to and squandered on objects of ambition; the order of things unsettled, and confidence between man and man annihilated. Every moment is looked for with tremulous, anxious, and increased solicitude; hope languishes, and commercial enterprise stiffens with fear. The political horizon appears to be calm, but many, of no ordinary sagacity, think they behold signs portentous of a change—the indications of a violent tempest which will again rage and desolate that devoted region.

Should this prediction fail, no change for the better, under existing circumstances, can take place. Where despotism, military despotism, reigns, silence and fearful stillness must prevail. Such is the prospect which continental Europe exhibits to the enterprise of American merchants.

Can it be possible for them to find in that region sources which will supply them with more than $17,000,000, the balance due for British manufactures imported? this balance being over and above the value of all the exports to foreign countries from the United States. The view which is given of the dreary prospect of commercial advantages accruing to the United States by an intercourse with continental Europe is believed to be just. The statement made of the great balance in favor of Great Britain, due from the United States, is founded on matter of fact.

In the hands of Great Britain are gathered together, and held many powers, which they have not been accustomed hitherto to feel and to exercise.

No improper motives are intended to be imputed to that Government; but does not experience teach a lesson that should never be forgotten—that Governments, like individuals, are too apt to feel power and forget right?" It is not inconsistent with national decorum to become circumspect and prudent. May not the Government of Great Britain be inclined, in analyzing the basis of her political power, to consider and regard the United States as her rival, and to indulge an improper jealousy—the enemy of peace and repose?

Can it be politic, in any point of view, to mak

the United States dependent on any nation for supplies absolutely necessary for defence, for comfort, and for accommodation?

Will not the strength, the political energies of this nation be materially impaired, at any *time*, but fatally so in those of difficulty and distress, by such dependence?

Do not the suggestions of wisdom plainly show that the security, the peace, and the happiness of this nation depend on opening and enlarging all our resources, and drawing from them whatever shall be required for public use or private accommodation?

The committee, from the views which they have taken, consider the situation of the manufacturing establishments to be perilous. Some have decreased, and others have suspended business. A liberal encouragement will put them again into operation, with increased powers; but, should it be withheld, they will be prostrated. Thousands will be reduced to want and wretchedness. A capital of near $60,000,000 will become inactive, the greater part of which will be a dead loss to the manufacturers. Our improvidence may lead to fatal consequences; the Powers jealous of our growth and prosperity will acquire the resources and strength which this Government neglects to improve. It requires no prophet to foretell the use that foreign Powers will make of them.

The committee, from all the considerations which they have given to this subject, are deeply impressed with a conviction that the manufacturing establishments of cotton wool are of real utility to the agricultural interest, and that they contribute much to the prosperity of the Union.

Under the influence of this conviction the committee beg leave to tender, respectfully, with this report, the following resolution:

Resolved, That, from and after the 30th day of June next, in lieu of the *duties* now authorized by law, there be laid, levied, and collected, on cotton goods imported into the United States, and the Territories thereof, from any foreign country whatever, —— per centum *ad valorem*, being not less then —— cents per square yard.

The number of cotton spindles supposed to be now employed, or ready to be employed, in the United States, are 550,000; but, upon sure grounds, may be stated at 500,000. The capital necessary to carry on the manufacture, including the stock of cotton wool, the yarn in the hands of weavers, the cloth in the hands of the agents, or sold at a credit of six months, added to the real estate, buildings, and machinery, is estimated at seventy-five dollars per spindle, which, on 500,000 spindles, amounts to $37,500,000.

The number of persons employed constantly and steadily may be stated at one hundred those of whom not more than one-ninth, or, perhaps, one-tenth are able-bodied men; the rest are infirm, feeble men, or women and children. The manufacture must, also, give incidental employment to a much greater number of persons, in weaving and otherwise, whose ordinary employment is agriculture, and who devote to the manufacture those hours of Winter and bad weather, when the labors of the farm are suspended.

After calculating the cost of the raw material, the labor, interest of money at 6 per cent., insurance, repairs, and other charges, we are of opinion that a duty of at least ten cents on the square yard is necessary for the protection of the American manufacture, and that an ad valorem duty of even 40 or 50 per cent. on the India goods, on account of the lowness of the first cost, would not give the requisite encouragement. It may not be improper here to state that an increase of the duties upon cotton goods, generally, though it might diminish the importation of such goods as we make, would, on the whole, not diminish the receipts of the Treasury, because the increased receipts from such goods as we do not manufacture would counterbalance the loss on such as we do.

With the machinery already erected, the cotton manufacturers can supply the United States with about ninety millions of yards of cotton cloth annually. These consist chiefly of ginghams, plaids, bed-ticks, stripes, checks, sheetings, shirtings, and in part of canvass and velvets and other cut stuffs.

At present the coarse shirtings made from yarn No. 12, will bring about 23 cents in New York, at which price they cannot be afforded : the same article has been sold at 33 to 35 cents. The price must necessarily be regulated by the price of cotton wool which during the war was very high at the North, and since the war has been high everywhere.

The principal markets are the cities of New York, Philadelphia, and Baltimore, and, in a less degree, Charleston and Savannah : from these cities they are spread over the South and West.

Of the number of spindles now in operation, very few were effectually at work before the war. Such establishments have as yet reaped no profit whatever. Had the whole number been in complete operation before the war, the home competition would have reduced the prices much lower than they were; but the greater number produced no effect till about the conclusion of the war.

We are unable to state, with any exactness, the amount or value of cotton goods imported into the United States in different years; but, to show of how much importance this trade is to Great Britain, we would state that between a quarter and a third of all the exports of British produce and manufacture during the years 1806 and 1807—say £11,417,834, on an average of the two years—were made to the United States. In the same years, the real value of cotton goods exported to the United States from Great Britain (exclusive of Scotland) was, on an average of the two years, £4,393,449, and of woollen goods, £4,591,437—being $19,000,000 of cotton, and $20,000,000 of woollen.

It is proper to add, that there is now one manufactory of cut fustians and velvets at Hudson, and another about to begin at Frankfort, and that these goods require a duty higher than we have proposed for other goods. They cost more—say

from 14*d*. to 30*d*. per yard of 18 inches width—and therefore will require a duty of 30 cents per square yard for such as cost 23*d*. and under, and 36 cents for such as cost more.

TARIFF OF DUTIES ON IMPORTS.

—

[Communicated to the House, February 13, 1816.]

TREASURY DEPARTMENT, *Feb.* 12, 1816.

SIR: In obedience to the resolution of the House of Representatives of the 23d of February, 1815, I have the honor to transmit a report on the subject of a general tariff of duties proper to be imposed on imported goods, wares, and merchandise.

I have the honor to be, &c.

A. J. DALLAS.

Hon. SPEAKER *of the House of Reps.*

On the 23d February, 1815, the House of Representatives "*Resolved*, That the Secretary of the Treasury be directed to report to Congress, at their next session, a general tariff of duties proper to be imposed upon goods, wares, and merchandise," and, in obedience to that resolution, the Secretary of the Treasury has now the honor to lay before Congress the following report, comprehending—

I. A view of the tariff of the United States, and its incidents upon the Peace Establishment.

II. A statement of the general principles for reforming the tariff of the United States, including the means of enforcement.

III. A general tariff proposed for the consideration of Congress.

I. *A view of the Tariff of the United States, and its incidents upon the Peace Establishment.*

By an act of Congress, passed on the 1st July, 1812, the permanent duties previously imposed by law upon goods imported into the United States from foreign places were doubled ; an addition of 10 per cent. was made to the double duties upon goods imported in vessels not of the United States; and vessels belonging wholly or in part to the subjects of foreign Powers, entering the United States, were charged with an additional tonnage duty of $1 50 per ton. This act was limited in its continuance to the period of one year after the peace with Great Britain, and it expires of course on the 17th of February, 1816. The act (with all its supplements) imposing an additional duty, commonly called the "Mediterranean Fund," of 2½ per cent. ad valorem on all imported goods paying duties ad valorem, and a discriminating duty of 10 per cent upon that additional duty, in respect to all goods imported in vessels not of the United States, had expired on the 3d March, 1815.

Considering the subject, therefore, upon the foundation on which it is placed by the extinction of the Mediterranean Fund, and by the restoration of peace, the annexed table (marked A) exhibits the general tariff of the United States, resulting from the successive acts of Congress imposing, augmenting, and modifying the duties

Tariff of Duties on Imports.

upon imported merchandise, compared with the rates of duties proposed for the new tariff; and it is susceptible of the discrimination marked in the table No. 1, comprising the articles charged with specific duties; No. 2, comprising the articles charged with duties ad valorem, at the several rates of 12½ per cent., 15 per cent., and 20 per cent.; and No. 3, comprising the articles that are free from duty.

It is another important view of the subject, connected with the details of the table A, that the rate of duty upon the tonnage of vessels of the United States, and of the duties upon the goods which they import, is less than upon the tonnage of other vessels, and of their cargoes. Thus:

1. *As to the duty on tonnage.*

Ships or vessels of the United States entering from any foreign port or place, or carrying goods from one district to another district, are charged at the rate, per ton of - - - - 6 cts.

Ships or vessels built within the United States, but belonging wholly or in part to the subjects of foreign Powers, entering from a foreign place or port, are charged at the rate, per ton, of - - 30 do.

Ships or vessels of every other description entering from a foreign port or place, carrying goods from one district to another district within the United States, are charged at the rate, per ton, of - 50 do.

And it may be properly here added that ships and vessels not of the United States, or not wholly owned by American citizens, entering the ports of the United States, are charged by law with the duty called "light money," at the rate, per ton, of - - - - 50 do.

2. *As to the duty on goods imported.*

The discriminating duty imposed by law on goods imported in vessels of the United States is not made a direct charge upon the goods as specified in the table A, but it is charged generally upon the rate of duty imposed on the like goods, when imported in vessels of the United States; and it is uniformly an addition of 10 per cent. upon the American rate of duty, whether that be specific or ad valorem.

The discriminating duty is to be considered, however, in connexion with the treaties and acts of Congress which have subjected it to temporary or permanent modifications. Thus, 1. The Louisiana Convention suspended the discriminating duties for a period of twelve years, (which will expire on the 6th March, 1816,) in relation to French and Spanish vessels and cargoes arriving within the ceded Territory. 2. The convention to regulate the commerce between the territories of the United States and His Britannic Majesty will suspend the discriminating duties in relation to British vessels and cargoes arriving within the United States from the British territories in Europe, for a period of four years, commencing on the 3d July, 1815. And, 3. The act of the 3d March, 1815, has authorized the aboli-

tion of the discriminating duties in relation to every foreign nation which shall abolish such of its discriminating and countervailing duties as are disadvantageous to the United States.

The duty on tonnage is payable at the *time of* entry; but, before the product of the duties on goods imported reaches the public Treasury, the collection is affected by the credit which the law allows to the importer, and the amount is liable to a reduction, by the allowance of drawbacks and bounties, as well as by the expense of collection.

1st. *As to the credit for duties on goods imported.*

On the produce of the West Indies, (salt excepted,) and on goods imported by sea from all foreign ports and islands lying north of the equator, and situated on the eastern shores of America, it is three months for one-half, and six months for the other half.

On salt it is nine months.

On Madeira, and all other wines, it is twelve months.

On goods imported from Europe, (other than wines, salt, and teas,) it is eight months for one-third, ten months for one-third, and twelve months for one-third.

On goods (other than wines, salt, and teas) imported from any other place than Europe and the West Indies, it is six months for one-half, nine months for one-fourth, and twelve months for one-fourth.

On teas imported from China or Europe it is conditionally, upon deposites, two years, subject, as intermediate sales may be effected, to payment at four months, eight months, or twelve months, according to the amount of sales, respectively.

2d. *As to the drawback of duties on goods exported.*

The general provision of the law allows a drawback of the duties on goods imported into the United States, provided they amount to fifty dollars, if the goods be exported within twelve calendar months after the importation to any foreign port or place other than the dominions of any foreign State immediately adjoining to the United States. This local limitation has been modified, however, so as to authorize an exportation, with the benefit of the drawback, from Louisiana to any port or place situated to the southward thereof.

To the general provision of the law for the allowance of drawback there are some exceptions: 1st. The additional duty of ten per cent. imposed upon goods imported in vessels not of the United States, is not the subject of drawback. 2dly. The right of exportation for the benefit of drawback is not allowed in the case of foreign dried and pickled fish, and other salted provisions, fish oil, or playing cards. 3dly. The rate of a half cent per gallon on spirits, with two and a half per cent. on the duties, and the rate of three and a half per cent. on the amount of the duties on all other goods imported, is to be retained, when they are exported for the benefit of drawback, as an indemnification for the expense accrued concerning them.

Tariff of Duties on Imports.

3d. *As to the allowance of bounties on exports.*

The act of the 29th of July, 1813, (which will expire on the 17th of February, 1816,) when it imposed a duty of twenty cents per bushel upon imported salt, allowed a bounty upon all exported pickled fish of the fisheries of the United States, at the rate of twenty cents per barrel, provided the fish were wholly cured with foreign salt, on which a duty had been paid or secured. The same act authorizes an annual allowance to the owners and crews of American vessels and boats employed in the fisheries, graduated according to the tonnage.

The act of the 24th of July, 1813, (which will also expire on the 17th of February, 1816,) when it imposed a duty of four cents per pound upon all sugars refined within the United States, authorized a drawback, in the nature of a bounty, upon all such of the sugar so refined, as should be exported from the United States to any foreign port or place.

4th. *As to the expense of the collection of duties on imports.*

The successful collection of the duties on imports, before the introduction of the restrictive system, depended more upon the integrity of the commercial community than upon the rigor of the laws, or an expensive vigilance at the custom-house. It is not to be denied or disregarded, however, that soon after that event the spirit of illicit commerce was kindled, that it spread during the late war, and that, with every just reliance upon the honor of the American merchant, measures of great energy have become necessary for the protection of the fair trader, as well as for the security of the revenue. Hitherto the average annual expense of collection may be stated at nearly four per cent. upon the annual product (exclusive of the fees paid by individuals, which may be estimated at one per cent. more) during a season of open and prosperous commerce; and it is believed that the effect of an increased expenditure in the employment of the means which are necessary to prevent and detect offences against the laws, will so augment the product of the duty, as to afford a certain and ample equivalent for the original advance.

The operation of the tariff, exhibited in table A, with the incidents which have been stated, may be concisely viewed with reference to two periods in the commerce of the United States : 1st. Before the introduction of the restrictive system, from 1804 to 1807, both years inclusive; and, 2d, after the introduction of the restrictive system, from 1808 to 1811, both years inclusive. Thus—

	During the four years, from 1804 to 1807, both inclusive.	During the four years, from 1808 to 1811, both inclusive.
The average annual gross product of duties on merchandise imported	$24,236,091 51	$12,423,774 09
The average annual amount of debentures issued for drawback on merchandise imported - - - -	8,714,073 50	2,755,802 25
The average annual amount of bounties and allowances - - -	192,700 37	53,036 23
The average annual product of duties on merchandise imported, after deducting drawbacks, bounties, &c.	15,319,317 64	9,615,135 61
The average annual product of the ad valorem duties, including the Mediterranean fund, after deducting ditto - - - -	6,536,975 89	4,316,329 43
The average annual product of the Mediterranean fund, after deducting ditto - - - -	968,066 36	692,399 36
The average annual product of the specific duties, after deducting do.	8,365,737 10	5,073,278 80
The average annual product of the three and a half per cent. retained on drawback - - - - - -	318,917 06	100,203 75
The average annual product of the additional duty of ten per cent. in merchandise imported in foreign vessels	197,687 59	125,233 63
The average annual product of duties on merchandise imported in American vessels, after deducting drawbacks, &c. -	13,144,754 18	8,236,575 88
The average annual product of duties on merchandise imported in foreign vessels - - - -	2,174,563 46	1,378,559 93
The average annual product of duties on tonnage - - -	160,660 50	169,135 90
The average annual product of light-money - - -	51,869 90	32,165 42
The average annual expenses on collection - - -	564,813 88	479,633 12

Tariff of Duties on Imports.

II. *A statement of the general principles for reforming the tariff of the United States, including the means of enforcement.*

The tariff which has been thus generally reviewed originated in the year 1790, soon after the organization of the Federal Government. Notwithstanding the various alterations to which it was subjected during the long period of American neutrality, it certainly has not been left in a state adapted to the present epoch. The peace of Europe will give a new course and character to the commerce of the world; and the condition of the United States is essentially changed in population, in wealth, in the employment of labor and capital, in the demand of luxuries, or of necessaries for consumption, and in the native resources to supply the demand. These considerations forcibly recommend the measure of revision and reform which is now contemplated; the task, however, is not more important in its object than difficult in the performance. The means of information are scattered and imperfect. Many conflicting interests and prejudices are to be reconciled; and, in the unsettled state of commerce, much of any plan connected with its operations must unavoidably rest upon hypothesis, and be tested by future experiment. In every effort, therefore, to diminish the force of these obstacles, an ulterior reliance upon the wisdom of the Legislature has been respectfully indulged.

In framing the propositions which this report will submit to the consideration of Congress for the establishment of a general tariff, three great objects have been principally regarded: 1st. The object of raising, by duties on imports and tonnage, the proportion of public revenue which must be drawn from that source. 2d. The object of conciliating the various national interests, which arise from the pursuits of agriculture, manufactures, trade, and navigation; and, 3d. The object of rendering the collection of the duties convenient, equal, and certain.

1. The report which the Committee of Ways and Means presented to the House of Representatives on the 9th day of January, 1816, furnishes a foundation to estimate, with sufficient precision, for the present purpose, the proportion of the public revenue to be annually raised through the medium of the customs.

It is there stated that the amount of the annual demands of the Peace Establishment may be placed at the sum of - - - - - $15,778,069

But to this sum it is now proper to add this general amount which is appropriated for the payment of the principal of the public debt, estimated at $1,850,000

The difference between the Treasury estimate for the naval service, made upon conjectural ground, and the subsequent statement of the Secr'y of the Navy, made upon official documents, to wit:

The Secretary of the Navy's statement, after adding the sum of $200,000, annually appropriated for three years for the purchase of timber, being - - $3,838,071

The Treasury estimate being - 2,716,510

The difference being - - - 1,121,561

And the amount which is proposed by the Committee of Ways and Means to add to the Sinking Fund, (raising it from $8,000,000 to $13,150,000) - - - 5,150,000

                 8,121,561

                 $23,900,230

The annual revenue to be raised for the service of Government, may then be stated in round numbers at the sum of $24,000,000, independent of any provision for public institutions and public improvements; such as the President has recommended to the patronage of the Legislature; such as the patriotism of Congress may, from time to time, be induced to sanction; and such as will at once enlighten, enrich, and adorn the nation.

Upon the general principles of public policy, developed in the report of the Committee of Ways and Means, the supply for all the expenses of Government will be derived, in part, from internal duties and taxes, but principally from duties on imports.

Stating, therefore, the amount of demand for revenue at - - - - - - - $24,000,000

It has been proposed to supply annually, from internal duties and taxes, and from the sales of public lands, the sum of $6,925,000; that is to say, from the direct tax on lands, houses, and slaves, the sum of - - - $3,700,000

From the duty on stills the sum of - - - 1,200,000

From the duty on stamps the sum of - 400,000

From the duty on refined sugar the sum of - 150,000

From the duty on carriages the sum of - 175,000

From licenses to retailers, (a tax proposed to be modified) the sum of - 900,000

From the duties on sales at auction the sum of - 400,000

From the sales of public lands the sum of - 1,000,000

                 6,925,000

And the reliance for the residue of the supply must be of course upon the customs, to the amount of - - - $17,075,000

It is here to be considered, that the report of the Committee of Ways and Means contemplates the abolition, or the reduction of duties or taxes heretofore pledged "to provide for the payment of the expenses of Government, for the punctual

Tariff of Duties on Imports.

payment of the public debt, and for creating a Sinking Fund," to an amount not less than $7,064,340: that is to say—

To abolish the duties on furniture and watches, on domestic manufactures, and on distilled spirits, in amount about · - - - - $2,864,340

To abolish the additional duty on postage, in amount about - - - - - 300,000

And to take from the direct tax, in net amount, about - - - - - 3,900,000

                                                    $7,064,340

And for supplying this sum of $7,064,340, in observance of the plighted faith of the Government, it has been proposed to make an addition to the customs, equal to an average rate of forty-two per cent. upon the products of the duties imposed prior to the act of the 1st of July, 1812, by which the impost was doubled (as already stated) during the continuance of the late war.

If, then, the average annual product of the single duties on imports and tonnage may be estimated (and it cannot be prudently estimated higher) at the sum of - - - - - - - $12,000,000

The addition of forty-two per cent. upon that amount will yield a sum of - - 5,040,000

And will give, for the amount to be produced by the customs - - - $17,040,000

2d. The social compact is formed on the basis of a surrender of a part of the natural rights of individuals, for the security and benefit of the whole society. The Federal compact is formed on the basis of a surrender of a part of the political rights of each State, for the benefit and security of the whole Confederation. Hence, in the attempt "to conciliate the various national interests which arise from the pursuits of agriculture, manufactures, trade, and navigation," it is necessary to recollect that the common object of the nation will not invariably correspond with the separate objects of individuals, or of their professions, nor with the local objects of the respective States, or of the industry of their inhabitants.

Under the beneficent dispensations of Providence, the territory of the United States produces almost all the natural fruits of the earth; and, pursuing the subdivision of which labor is susceptible, the citizens of the United States are engaged in the cultivation of almost every art, and every science, within the scope of human knowledge. But the fruits produced, although they are the fruits of the nation, are not the same in every State; and the labor employed, although it be the labor of the nation, is employed upon very different materials, with very different results in the principal sections of the Union.

From these considerations are derived the principles of general policy by which the national character is formed, and the national interests are maintained. The interests of agriculture require a free and constant access to a market for its staples, and a ready supply of all the articles of use and consumption on reasonable terms; but

the national interest may require the establishment of a domestic in preference to a foreign market, and the employment of domestic in preference to foreign labor, in furnishing the necessary supplies. And, again, the interests of foreign commerce flourish most when foreign commerce is the only medium to convey the natural products of the country to a market, and to provide for all the wants of the people in the fabrics of the manufacturer and the artist; but the national interest may require (contemplating equally the state of peace and the state of war) that the people should be as independent in the resources of their subsistence as in the operations of their Government. It must, however, be the aim of every just system of political economy to secure the national interest with as little prejudice as possible to the peculiar interests of agriculture and of commerce.

There are few, if any, governments which do not regard the establishment of domestic manufactures as a chief object of public policy. The United States have always so regarded it. In the earliest acts of Congress, which were passed after the adoption of the present Constitution, the obligation of providing, by duties on imports, for the discharge of the public debts, is expressly connected with the policy of encouraging and protecting manufactures. In the year 1790 the Secretary of the Treasury was directed by the House of Representatives to take the subject of manufactures into consideration, with a view particularly to report upon "the means of promoting such as would render the United States independent of foreign nations for military and other essential supplies." In the year 1810 the Legislature again manifested a marked solicitude to ascertain the progress of the national independence in manufactures, by combining the business of the census with an inquiry into the state of the several manufacturing establishments and manufactures within the several districts, territories, and divisions of the United States. But it was emphatically during the period of the restrictive system and of the war, that the importance of domestic manufactures became conspicuous to the nation, and made a lasting impression upon the mind of every statesman and of every patriot. The weapons and munitions of war, the necessaries of clothing, and the comforts of living, were at first but scantily provided. The American market seemed, for a while, to be converted into a scene of gambling and extortion; and it was not the least of the evils generated by the unequal state of the supply and the demand, that an illicit traffic with the enemy, by land and by water, was corruptly and systematically prosecuted from the commencement to the termination of hostilities.

From these circumstances of suffering and mortification have sprung, however, the means of future safety and independence. It has been thought that, with respect to industry applied to manufactures as well as with respect to industry applied to commerce, individuals should be left to pursue their own course untouched by the

hand of Government, either to impel or to restrain. Without examining how far this opinion
is sanctioned by experience, it is sufficient upon
the present occasion to observe that the American manufactures, particularly those which have
been introduced during the restrictive system and
the war, owe their existence exclusively to the
capital, the skill, the enterprise, and the industry
of private citizens. The demands of the country, while the acquisition of supplies from foreign
nations was either prohibited or impracticable,
may have afforded a sufficient inducement for
this investment of capital, and this application of
labor; but the inducement, in its necessary extent, must fail when the day of competition returns. Upon that change in the condition of the
country, the preservation of the manufactures
which private citizens, under favorable auspices,
have constituted the property of the nation, becomes a consideration of general policy, to be
resolved, by a recollection of past embarrassments, by the certainty of an increased difficulty
of reinstating, upon any emergency, the manufactures which shall be allowed to perish and
pass away, and by a just sense of the influence of
domestic manufactures upon the wealth, power,
and independence of the Government.

The object to be encouraged and protected
merits, in its intrinsic value, as well as in its general influence, the attention of the Legislature.
From the peace of 1783, until the year 1808, the
march of domestic manufactures was slow but
steady. It has since been bold, rapid, and firm;
until, at the present period, considering the circumstances of time and pressure, it has reached
a station of unexampled prosperity. The attempt, however, to obtain detailed and accurate
information upon the subject has only been successful in a very limited degree; and, consequently, the result must be presented to the view
of Congress rather as an outline and an estimate
than as a complete and demonstrative statement
of facts. With this understanding the American
manufactures may be satisfactorily divided into
three principal classes, allowing for such diver-
sities of shade as will sometimes seem to render
the classification of particular manufactures
doubtful or arbitrary:

First class. Manufactures which are firmly
and permanently established, and which wholly,
or almost wholly, supply the demand for domestic use and consumption.

Second class. Manufactures which, being recently or partially established, do not at present
supply the demand for domestic use and consumption, but which, with proper cultivation,
are capable of being matured to the whole extent
of the demand.

Third class. Manufactures which are so slightly cultivated as to leave the demand of the country wholly, or almost wholly, dependent upon
foreign sources for a supply.

1st class. In the first class it is believed the
following articles may be embraced:

Cabinet wares and all manufactures of wood.
Carriages of all descriptions.

Cables and cordage.
Hats of wool, fur, leather, chip, or straw, and
straw bonnets.
Iron castings, fire and side-arms, cannon, mus-
kets, pistols.
Window glass.
Leather, and all manufactures of leather, in-
cluding saddles, bridles, and harness.
Paper of every description; blank books.
Printing types.

2d class. In the second class it is believed the
following articles may be embraced:
Cotton goods of the coarser kinds.
Woollen goods of the coarser kinds generally,
and some of the finer kinds.
Metal buttons.
Plated wares.
Iron manufactures of the larger kinds; shovels,
spades, axes, hoes, scythes, &c.; nails, large and
small.
Pewter, tin, copper, and brass manufactures.
Alum, copperas.
Spirits, beer, ale, and porter.

3d class. In the third class it is believed the
following articles may be embraced:
Cotton manufactures of the finer kinds; muslins, nankeens, chintzes, stained and printed cot-
tons of all descriptions.
Linen of all descriptions, linen cambrics, lawns.
Hempen cloths, sailcloth, Russian and German linens.
Silk goods of all descriptions.
Woollen goods of many descriptions; worsted
goods of all kinds, stuffs, camblets, blankets, car-
pets and carpeting.
Hosiery of all descriptions, including knit or
woven gloves.
Hardware and ironmongery, excepting the
large articles, cutlery, pins, needles.
China ware, earthen ware, porcelain.
Glass of all descriptions, except window glass
and phials.

The matured state of the *first class* of manufactures relieves the task of forming a tariff, with
respect to them, from any important difficulty.
Duties might be freely imposed upon the importation of similar articles, amounting wholly, or
nearly, to a prohibition, without endangering a
scarcity in the supply, while the competition
among the domestic manufacturers alone would
sufficiently protect the consumer from exorbitant
prices, graduating the rates of the market generally by the standard of a fair profit upon the capital and labor employed. It is true, however, on
the other hand, that, by imposing low *duties* upon
the imported articles, importation would be encouraged, and the revenue increased; but, without adding to the comfort, or deducting from the
expense of the consumer, the consumption of the
domestic manufacture would, in an equal degree, be diminished by that operation, and the
manufacture itself might be entirely supplanted.
It is, therefore, a question between the gain of the
revenue and the loss of the manufacture, *to be*
decided upon principles of national policy. *Under*
the circumstances of an abundant market the im-

Tariff of Duties on Imports.

terest of the consumer must stand indifferent, whether the price of any article be paid for the benefit of the manufacturer, or of the importer; but a wise Government will surely deem it better to sacrifice a portion of its revenue, than to sacrifice those institutions which private enterprise and wealth have connected with public prosperity and independence.

The *second class* of manufactures presents considerations of the most interesting, and not of the least embarrassing nature, in the formation of a tariff. Some remarks have already been made upon the danger which at present threatens those manufactures, as well as upon the policy of rendering them permanently beneficial to the nation; for it is respectfully thought to be in the power of the Legislature, by a well-timed and well-directed patronage, to place them, within a very limited period, upon the footing on which the manufactures included in the first class have been so happily placed, by the lapse of a few years, and the perseverance of a comparatively few individuals. The means of promoting this great object are various, but it appears to have been the early and continued practice and policy of the Government to afford encouragement to domestic products and manufactures, rather by the imposition of protecting duties than by the grant of bounties and premiums; and, indeed, it is in that course alone that the subject properly falls within the scope of the present report. Although some indulgence will always be required, for any attempt so to realize the national independence in the department of manufactures, the sacrifice cannot be either great or lasting. The inconveniences of the day will be amply compensated by future advantages. The agriculturist, whose produce and whose flocks depend for their value upon the fluctuations of a foreign market, will have no occasion eventually to regret the opportunity of a ready sale for his wool or his cotton in his own neighborhood; and it will soon be understood that the success of the American manufacture, which tends to diminish the profit (often the excessive profit) of the importer, does not necessarily add to the price of the article in the hands of the consumer.

Assuming, therefore, the ground, that the manufactures of the second class will be fostered by the legislative care, the amount of the protecting duties, and the mode of imposing them, in order to be effectual, become important considerations. It must be agreed, upon all hands, that the amount of the duties should be such as will enable the manufacturer to meet the importer in the American market upon equal terms of profit and loss, and that the mode of imposing the duties should be such as to secure the resulting competition from the influence of clandestine or illicit practices. There still, however, remains a diversity of opinion as to the amount which will be competent, and as to the mode which will be efficient; and the aim of this report will be to strike the medium which appears to be best established from all the information that has been collected.

The *third class* of manufactures does not require further attention, at this time, than to adjust the rate of duty to the amount of revenue which it is necessary to draw from them. They have not yet been the objects of American capital, industry, and enterprise, to any important degree; and the present policy of the Government is directed to protect, and not to create, manufactures.

There is, however, a distinct view of the subject which ought not to be omitted. Where the demand for raw materials, or manufactured articles in any of the departments of domestic industry, is wholly, or almost wholly, dependent upon the supply from foreign nations, the access to the American market should be easy, if not entirely free. Acting upon this principle it will be proper, above all, to respect the interests of ship-building and navigation at a period when the equalization of the duties upon tonnage and merchandise, by the operation of acts of Congress and treaties, will probably give rise to an interesting competition between foreign vessels and vessels of the United States. The shipping interest and the manufacturing interest must, however, be reconciled; and, consulting the best interests, the following suggestions are respectfully offered:

1. Imported iron cables, anchors, and bar iron; cables, cordage, hemp, packthread, twine, and seines; sheet copper, copper nails, and lead; so far as they enter essentially into the construction and equipment of ships, and are not supplied by the American manufacturer, ought to be lightly taxed.

2. The case of foreign vessels employed in bringing to the United States goods that are not the growth or manufacture of the country to which the vessels belong, may furnish a proper field for legislative regulations.

3. The case of goods imported from countries which, by law, confine the carriage of such goods to their own vessels, respectively, will also furnish a proper field for similar regulations.

The principles involved in the proposition for a new tariff, in relation to the protection of domestic manufactures, being thus presented for consideration, the more general principles of the system remain to be briefly stated, in relation to the production of the revenue. Thus:

1. Articles intended as the source of revenue should never be so heavily charged with duties as to prevent importation, or much to diminish it.

2. Articles should never be so heavily charged with duties as to create a temptation to smuggle.

3. Articles of great size and weight, of comparatively small value, are difficult to be smuggled; and, other things being equal, they may be charged with higher duties.

4. Articles of small size and great value are easily smuggled, and must be charged with low duties, to destroy the otherwise fatal temptation to evade the law.

5. Articles imported to a great amount should rather be charged with specific duties upon their weight and measure, in order to guard against

Tariff of Duties on Imports.

evasions and frauds, than with ad valorem duties on their value.

The difficulty of carrying the last mentioned rule into practice has been found almost insurmountable. It has been already intimated that, in the classification of manufactures, there were several articles, differently classed, which can scarcely be distinguished from each other, and which could not be separately described with such distinctness and precision as is requisite in a tariff to mark the line of discrimination for different rates of specific duties. In the cotton and woollen manufactures of the United States, for instance, there are several kinds of goods extensively produced, whose names are arbitrary, and continually changing, and whose texture and quality are so various, and so easily altered or disguised, as to elude the vigilance and skill of the custom-house. For this reason, and considering, also, that the ascertainment of duties by the original cost of the goods, according to their weight and measure, is sometimes a source of vexation to the importer, leading, perhaps, to great corruption in the execution of the law, the precedent of the existing tariff has been generally pursued, which subjects all goods, (for example, all cotton and woollen goods,) whether fine or coarse, and whether they are, or are not, of the kinds manufactured in the United States, to one common rate of duty. A general description designates the article, renders the imposition of the duty uniform and certain at all ports of entry, and effectually guards against mistake or evasion.

Upon the principles and with the views, thus stated, the proposition for the new tariff has been formed. The variations from the tariff of permanent single duties consist principally in the following points:

1. The rates of the duties ad valorem are changed in number from three to eight. The increase of the number will not, it is thought, be attended with any disadvantage, and it will, at least, afford a better means of ascertaining, hereafter, the value of articles of different descriptions which are now blended in one class, as well as the amount of the duties collected from each description. The amount of the duties ad valorem is also changed from 12½, 15, and 20 per cent. to 7½, 15, 20, 22, 25, 30, 33⅓, and 35 per cent.

2. The rates of the specific duties are generally increased upon the amount of the permanent single rates, averaging, with the increase of the rates of duties ad valorem, an aggregate of about 42 per cent. upon the aggregate product of the customs, estimated at about $12,000,000 per annum.

3. The following articles, heretofore free, are charged with duties, to wit:

Alum, per cwt. - - - - - $2 00
Copperas, per cwt. - - - - - 1 50
Copper, in sheets, rods, bolts, or nails, per pound - - - - - - 04
Gum Arabic, and gum Senegal, ad valorem, 7½ per cent.

Mahogany, per cubic foot - - - - 12
Tin plates per box of 100 square feet - 1 50
Woods for dying—
  Brazil, Braziletto, Camwood, per ton - 6 00
  Fustic, logwood, per ton - - - 3 00
  Nicaragua, per ton - - - - 8 00
Wire brass, ad valorem, 22 per cent.

4. The following articles, heretofore subject to an ad valorem duty, are charged with a specific duty, to wit:
Iron, in bars or bolts, per cwt. 75 and 150 cents.

5. The following articles, heretofore subject to specific duties, are charged with duties ad valorem ; because the product of the specific duties has been so inconsiderable as to render it useless to distinguish them from the mass of articles charged with duties ad valorem, to wit:

Woollen or cotton cards, former duty per dozen - - - - - - - $0 50
Glauber salts, former duty per cwt. - 2 00
Hair powder former duty per lb. - - 04
Lime, former duty per cask of 60 gallons 50
Malt, former duty per bushel - - - 10
Ochre, yellow, dry, former duty per lb. 01
Ochre, in oil, former duty per lb - - 01½
Pewter, plates and dishes, former duty per lb. - - - - - - 04
Starch, former duty per lb. - - - 03
Spanish brown, former duty per lb. - 01
Quicksilver, former duty per lb. - - 06

3. The means of enforcing the tariff.

The means of enforcing the collection of the duties on imports, or, in other words, the means of preventing or detecting frauds upon the revenue, require a prompt, energetic, and steady attention. The remedies to be provided for the existing defects should be particularly applied: 1st. To guard against smuggling, by the clandestine introduction of merchandise, without report, entry, or permit; 2d. To guard against smuggling, in the case of duties ad valorem, by fraudulent entries of merchandise upon fictitious invoices; 3d. To guard against smuggling, in the case of specific duties, by fraudulent entries of merchandise upon false statements of the weight, or the measure; and, 4th. To guard against smuggling, by clandestinely relanding merchandise exported with the benefit of drawback, or by fraudulently obtaining debentures for duties on merchandise exported in cases that are not entitled to the benefit. The details necessary to give effect to a system embracing these objects must unavoidably be postponed until the sense of Congress shall be ascertained ; but it is proper, at this time, to bring distinctly into view the essential features of the system. In addition, therefore, to the provisions contained in the laws which now regulate the collection of duties on imports and tonnage, the following propositions are respectfully suggested :

1. That a competent judicial authority be provided to take cognizance of all suits, prosecutions, informations, and libels, for debts, fines, penalties, and forfeitures, arising and accruing under the laws of the United States ; a provis-

ion rendered indispensable by late decisions of some of the State courts declining such cognizance, in certain cases.

2. That a more competent provision be made for the employment of custom-house officers, cutters, and barges.

3. That an adequate fund be created and set apart for the creation of custom-houses, warehouses, and stores, at the principal ports of entry; a fund to be created, first, by retaining an additional amount of the duties, in cases of exportation for the benefit of drawback; and, secondly, by imposing a small duty, to be called "warehouse money," upon every permit for unlading merchandise.

4. That provision be made to enforce more effectually the duty of reporting and entering vessels, and exhibiting manifests of their cargoes, upon their arrival in any port of the United States; and to abolish the privilege of making port entries.

5. That provision be made to guard more effectually against imposition, under pretence that vessels arrive in distress, that goods are damaged, and that invoices are lost.

6. That provision be made to place all the avenues to the cargoes of the vessels, before unlading, under the seal of the custom-house, and to keep the same more effectually in the charge of the inspectors while unlading.

7. That provision be made that all invoices upon which entries may be effected, shall be endorsed by the American Consul, by a notary public, or by some other trustworthy agent or officer, to be designated, by law, at the place of exportation, certifying the merchandise to be priced "at the then current market price;" that entries shall only be permitted upon invoices so endorsed; and that the invoices shall be conspicuously stamped with the seal of the custom-house at the time of entry.

8. That provision be made authorizing the collectors, in all cases of suspicion, to add to the invoice price of the merchandise ten per cent. beyond the addition now prescribed; and, if the importer refuse to pay duties on that amount, then either to take the merchandise on account of the United States, at the additional price, or to permit an entry upon the original invoice.

9. That provision be made that in all cases the custom-house officers shall send merchandise imported to the public stores for examination; and that they shall be there compared with the invoice, identified as to the kind and quality, ascertained as to the weight and measure, and estimated as to the value.

10. That provision be made requiring from the person who offers to enter merchandise, a declaration whether he acts as owner, consignee, or agent, and whether he has been instructed, after entry, to hold the merchandise to the order of the shipper; in which last mentioned case, the collector may be authorized to suspend the entry, until the shipper, or the person having an order from him, appears to make it.

11. That provision be made requiring the seal of the custom-house to be stamped upon all the original packages, &c., of merchandise entered for exportation, with the benefit of drawback, which shall remain entire at the time of exportation, and which shall be certified by the Consul, or other proper person, to remain entire at the foreign place of landing, in order to discharge the debenture bond.

12. That provision be made more effectually to secure the revenue from fraud and imposition, in the transportation of merchandise from district to district, and generally in carrying on the coasting trade.

13. That provision be made more effectually to secure the revenue from fraud and imposition, in making out invoices in the money of foreign countries, particularly of such countries as employ a paper currency.

But, while these suggestions are offered to guard the collection of the revenue, and to secure to the manufacturer the full benefit of the protecting duties, it must be recollected that there are some provisions in the existing laws which require to be modified in behalf of the merchant. For instance:

1. The time allowed by law to complete the export entries, for the benefit of drawback, is only ten days; and, if not completed within that time, the whole amount of the drawback is forfeited. The period should be extended, and the penalty for non-compliance should be reduced.

2. The right to export merchandise, with the benefit of drawback, ceases at the expiration of a year. The period might, without injury to the revenue, be enlarged.

3. The period allowed for making a return of damaged goods, with a view to a correspondent abatement of the duties, is limited to ten days; and the importer is sometimes charged with the whole duties on perishable articles, under the present restrictions, after the articles have perished, or are greatly decayed. A discretion should be confided to the proper officer, to make a proper abatement of the duties in both cases, upon satisfactory proof of their existence.

III. A general tariff proposed for the consideration of Congress.

Upon the policy and principles which have been stated, the following tariff, in reference to duties, drawbacks, and bounties, has been formed:

TARIFF.

1st. A schedule of the articles to be imported into the United States free of duty.

All articles imported for the use of the United States; philosophical apparatus, instruments, or books, specially imported for the use of any incorporated society, for philosophical or literary purposes, and for the use of any seminary of learning; specimens in natural history, mineralogy, botany, and anatomical preparations, models of machinery, and other inventions; wearing apparel, and other personal baggage in actual use; and the implements, or tools of trade, of persons arriving in the United States; regulus

Tariff of Duties on Imports.

of antimony ; bark of the cork tree unmanufactured; animals imported for breed ; burr stones, unwrought ; bullion ; clay, unwrought; copper imported in any shape for the use of the Mint; copper and brass, in pigs or bars ; tin, in pigs or bars ; old copper and brass, and old pewter; furs, undressed, of all kinds; raw hides and skins; lapis calaminaris ; plaster of Paris; rags, of any kind of cloth; wool, and wood, unmanufactured, except mahogany and dye-wood; zinc, tutenague, or spelter; olive oil, in casks, to be used in manufactures.

2d. A schedule of articles to be charged with duties ad valorem.

At seven and a half per centum.—Dying drugs, and materials for composing them, not subject to other rates of duty; gum arabic ; gum senegal.

Jewelry ; gold and silver watches and clocks, or parts of either, and of the frames of clocks, of whatever materials made ; gold and silver lace ; embroidery and epaulettes; precious stones, and pearls of all kinds, set or not set; Bristol stones or paste work ; and all articles composed chiefly of gold, silver, pearl, and precious stones.

Laces of thread, silk, or cotton.

At fifteen per centum.—All articles not free, and not subject to any other rate of duty.

At twenty per centum.—Linens of all descriptions, linen cambrics, lawns; hempen cloth, sailcloth, Russian and German linens; stockings and gloves of thread or silk; silks, satins, and all articles of which silk is the material of chief value.

At twenty-two per centum.—All articles manufactured from brass, copper, iron, steel, pewter, lead or tin, or of which these metals, or either of them, is the material of chief value; brass and iron wire; cutlery, pins, needles, buttons, and buckles of all kinds; gilt, plated, and japanned wares of all kinds ; cannon, muskets, fire arms, and side arms.

At twenty-eight per centum.—Woollen manufactures of all descriptions, and of which wool is the material of chief value.

At thirty per centum.—China ware, earthen ware, stone ware, porcelain and glass manufacture; bonnets and caps for women, fans, feathers, ornaments for head dresses, artificial flowers, millinery of all sorts; hats or caps of wool, fur, leather, chip, straw, or silk; cosmetics, washes, balsams, perfumes; painted floor cloths, mats of grass or flags; salad oils, pickles, capers, olives, mustard, comfits or sweetmeats preserved in sugar or brandy, wafers.

At thirty-three and one-third per centum.—Cotton manufactures of all descriptions, or of which cotton is the material of chief value ; provided that all cotton cloths, or cloths of which cotton is the chief material of value, (excepting nankeens imported directly from China,) the original cost of which, at the place whence imported, shall be less than twenty-five cents per square yard, shall be taken and deemed to have cost twenty-five cents per square yard, and shall be charged with duty accordingly.

At thirty-five per centum.—Cabinet wares, and

all manufactures of wood; carriages of all descriptions, and parts thereof; leather, and all manufactures of leather, or of which leather is the material of chief value; saddles, bridles, harness; paper of every description ; paper hangings, blank books, pasteboard, parchment, vellum, printed books, brushes, canes, walking sticks, whips; printing types; clothing ready made.

3d. A schedule of articles to be charged with specific duties.

Ale, beer, and porter, bottles, per gal.	$0 20
imported otherwise than in bottles, per gal.	10
Alum, per cwt.	2 00
Almonds per lb.	3
Bottles, black glass quart, per gross	1 44
Boots, per pair	2 00
Bristles, per lb.	3
Playing cards, per pack	30
Cables and cordage, tarred, per lb.	3
Cables untarred, yarns, twine, pack-thread, seines, per lb.	4
Candles of tallow, per lb.	3
Candles of wax or spermaceti, per lb.	4
Chinese cassia, per lb.	6
Cinnamon, per lb.	25
Cloves, per lb.	25
Cheese, per lb.	9
Chocolate, per lb.	9
Cocoa, per lb.	6
Coal, per bushel	8
Copperas, per cwt.	1 50
Copper, in sheets, rods, bolts, or nails, composition spikes, bolts, or nails, per lb.	4
Coffee, per lb.	6
Cotton, per lb.	3
Currants, per lb.	3
Figs, per lb.	3
Fish, foreign caught, per quintal	1 00
mackerel, per bbl.	1 50
salmon, per bbl.	2 00
all other pickled, per bbl.	1 00
Glass, window, not above 8 by 10 in. per 100 sq. ft.	2 50
not above 10 by 12 inches, per 100 sq. ft.	2 75
above 10 by 12, per 100 sq. ft.	3 25
Glue, per lb.	5
Gunpowder, per lb.	6
Hemp, per cwt.	1 50
Iron, in bars, or bolts, excepting rolled iron, per cwt.	0 75
in sheets, rods, or hoops, rolled iron in bars, or bolts, and anchors, per cwt.	1 50
Indigo, per lb.	15
Lead, in pigs, bars or sheets, per lb.	1
red or white, dry or ground in oil, per lb.	3
Mahogany, per cubic ft.	12
Mace, per lb.	1 00
Molasses, per gal.	5
Nails, per lb.	3
Nutmegs, per lb.	60
Pepper, per lb.	8
Pimento, per lb.	6
Plums and prunes, per lb.	3
Raisins in jars and boxes, and muscatel, per lb.	3
all other, per lb.	2
Salt, per bushel of 56 lbs.	20
Steel, per cwt.	1 00
Segars, per M.	2 50

Tariff of Duties on Imports.

Spirits from grain, to wit:

1st proof, per gal.	$0 42
2d proof, per gal.	45
3d proof, per gal.	48
4th proof, per gal.	52
5th proof, per gal.	60
above 5th proof per gal.	75

From other materials, to wit:

1st and 2d proof, per gal.	38
3d proof, per gal.	42
4th proof, per gal.	48
5th proof, per gal.	57
above 5th proof. per gal.	70
Shoes and slippers of silk, per pair	40
of leather, per pair	30
for children, per pair	20
Spikes, per lb.	2
Soap, per lb.	3
Sugar, brown, per lb.	2½
white clayed, or powdered, per lb.	4
lump, per lb.	9
loaf, per lb.	12
candy, per lb.	12
Snuff, per lb.	12
Tallow, per lb.	1

Tea, from China direct, to wit:

Bohea, per lb.	10
Souchong, and other black, per lb.	25
Imperial, gunpowder, and gomee, per lb.	50
Hyson and young hyson, per lb.	40
Hyson skin, and other green, per lb.	28

From any other place to wit:

Bohea, per lb.	14
Souchong, and other black, per lb.	34
Imperial, gunpowder, and gomee, per lb.	68
Hyson and young hyson, per lb.	56
Hyson skin, and other green, per lb.	38
Tin plates, per box of 100 square feet	1 50
Tobacco, manufactured, other than snuff and segars, per lb.	10

Woods, dying, viz:

Brazil wood, brazilletto, red wood, or camwood, per ton	6 00
Fustic and logwood, per ton	3 00
Nicaragua, per ton	8 00
Whiting, per lb.	1
Umbrellas or parasols of silk, each	2 00
of other materials, each	1 00
Frames or sticks for umbrellas or parasols, each	75

Wine, to wit:

Malmsey Madeira, and London particular, per gal.	1 00
other Madeira, per gal.	80
Burgundy, Champagne, Rhenish and Tokay per gal.	75
Sherry and St. Lucar, per gal.	60
Claret and other wines not enumerated, when imported in bottles or cases, per gal.	70
Lisbon, Oporto, and other wines of Portugal and Sicily, per gal.	50
Teneriffe, Fayal, and other wines of the western islands, per gal.	40
All other wines when imported otherwise than in case and bottle, per gal.	25

Alien duty.

There shall be charged an additional duty of twelve and a half per cent. upon all goods imported in vessels not of the United States, with the exception of goods imported in foreign vessels, which are specially entitled by treaty, or acts of Congress, to be entered upon payment of the domestic duty.

The additional alien duty of twelve and a half per cent. shall not be the subject of drawback in cases of exportation.

Tonnage duty and light money.

Ships or vessels of the United States, entered from any foreign port or place, or carrying goods from one district to another district, shall pay per ton	6 cents.
Ships or vessels built within the United States, but belonging wholly or in part to the subjects of foreign Powers, entering from a foreign port or place, shall pay per ton	30 "
Ships or vessels, of every other description, entering from a foreign place or port, or carrying goods from one district to another within the United States, shall pay per ton	50 "
Ships or vessels not of the United States, or not wholly owned by American citizens, entering the ports of the United States, shall pay for "light money" per ton	50 "

But the additional duty upon tonnage, and the light money imposed upon foreign vessels, are not to be exacted in the case of foreign vessels specially entitled by treaty or acts of Congress to an entry upon domestic duties and charges only.

Warehouse money.

To constitute a fund for erecting and maintaining custom-houses, warehouses, and stores,

1. There shall be paid for every permit to unlade goods, twenty-five cents.

2. There shall be retained upon the amount of the duties of goods exported, for the benefit of drawbacks, (except spirits,) five per cent.

3. There shall be retained in the case of spirits exported, for the benefit of drawback, two cents per gallon, and also three per cent. on the amount of the duties.

A separate account shall be kept at the custom-house of the money collected for this fund; and the amount shall be expended, from time to time, under such directions as the President of the United States shall approve and authorize.

Drawbacks and bounties.

There shall be allowed a drawback of the duties on goods imported into the United States, if the goods be exported within twelve months after the time of importation, subject to the following exceptions and provisions:

1. There shall not be an allowance of drawback in the case of goods imported in foreign vessels from any of the dominions or colonies of any foreign Power to which the vessels of the United States are not permitted to trade.

2. There shall not be an allowance of drawback for the additional duty of twelve and a half per cent. imposed on goods imported in vessels not of the United States.

Tariff of Duties on Imports.

3. There shall not be an allowance of drawback in the case of foreign dried and pickled fish and other salted provisions, fish oil, or playing cards.

4. There shall be retained upon the amount of the duties of goods exported for the benefit of drawback, (except spirits,) five per cent.

5. There shall be retained in the case of spirits exported, for the benefit of drawback, two cents per gallon, and also three per cent. on the amount of the duties.

6. The present bounties, allowances, and drawbacks, shall be continued in the case of exporting pickled fish, of the fisheries of the United States; in the case of American vessels employed in the fisheries; and in the case of exporting sugar refined within the United States.

These provisions respecting drawbacks must, however, be conformed to the privileges specially allowed to foreigners by treaty, or by acts of Congress.

It only remains, in the performance of the task prescribed by the House of Representatives, to give a succinct statement of the probable product of the duties upon imports, according to the proposed tariff.

The annual product of the single duties has been estimated at $12,000,000; and of this sum, the

specific duties produced about	$7,200,000
The duties *ad valorem* produced about	4,800,000
	12,000,000
But the amount proposed to be raised by the new tariff being	17,000,000
Such additions must be made to the old tariff as will produce	$5,000,000

The additions to the old tariff are made, first upon the specific duties; and, secondly, upon the duties *ad valorem;* and the estimated amount of the additions may be thus stated:

First. Of the additions to the specific duties.

Principal articles.	Former duty.	Proposed duty.	Former average product.	Estimat'd product of additional duty.
Coffee - - - -	5 cents -	6 cents - - - -	$527,000	$120,000
Hemp - - - -	100 cents -	150 cents - - -	108,000	50,000
Pepper - - - -	6 cents -	8 cents - - -	36,000	12,000
Spirits - - - -	Sundry rates -	Average increase of 50 per cent.	1,992,000	300,000
Sugar, white, clayed, &c. -	3 cents -	4 cents - - -	195,000	60,000
Teas - - - -	Sundry rates -	Average increase of 33⅓ per cent.	780,000	250,000
Wines - - - -	Sundry rates -	Average increase of 60 per cent.	600,000	350,000
Sundry small articles	- - -	- - - -	—	may 50,000
Total additional amount estimated to be derived from specific duties - -	- - -	- - -	—	$1,200,000

Second. Of the additions to the duties ad valorem.

Principal articles.	Former rate of duty.	Proposed rate of duty.	Proposed increase of the former rate.
All articles not free and not subjected to any other rate of duty - - - -	12½ per cent. -	15 per cent. -	20 per cent.
Linen, hempen cloths, silks, satins -	12½ per cent. -	20 per cent. -	60 per cent.
Hardware, cutlery, arms, and manufactures of metals - - - -	12½ and 15 per ct.	22 per cent. -	46⅔ and 70 per cent.
Woollens - - - -	19½ per cent. -	28 per cent. -	19½ per cent.
Cottons - - - - -	12½ per cent. -	33⅓ per cent. -	166⅔ per cent.
Porcelain, earthenware, hats, bonnets, perfumery, floor cloths, pickles, comfits -	15 per cent. -	30 per cent. -	100 per cent.
Glass, other than window glass - -	20 per cent. -	30 per cent. -	50 per cent.
Brushes, canes, whips, clothing ready made - - - - -	12½ per cent. -	35 per cent. -	180 per cent.
Paper, cabinet wares, leather and its manufactures - - - - -	15 per cent. -	35 per cent. -	133⅓ per cent.
Carriages - - - - -	20 per cent. -	35 per cent. -	75 per cent.

Report on the Public Debt.

It is not practicable to ascertain the amount of revenue heretofore produced by each of the classes of goods specified in the last table; but it is sufficiently known that some of them produced little, while the product of others was proportionably great. Taking the whole, however, together, it is estimated that the proposed increase of duty is equal to one hundred per cent. upon the aggregate amount of the former *ad valorem* duties. But the effects to be expected from the increased duties on woollen and cotton goods, from the diminution of the alien duties under treaties or acts of Congress, and from other considerations involved in the new system, will not permit a higher estimate of the aggregate product of the increased rates of the *ad valorem* duties than the rate of seventy-five or eighty per cent. upon the former product.

Assuming, then, an advance of eighty per cent. upon $4,800,000, (the aggregate product of the duties *ad valorem*, as above stated,) the sum will be - - - - - $3,840,000
And adding to this sum the amount produced as above stated by the increase of the specific duties - - 1,200,000

There will be produced, to complete the amount of additional revenue required, a sum of - • - $5,040,000

All which is respectfully submitted.
             A. J. DALLAS,
             Secretary of the Treasury.
TREASURY DEPARTMENT,
        February 12, 1816.

[The tabular statements are omitted.]

PUBLIC DEBT.

[COMMUNICATED TO THE HOUSE, MARCH 2, 1816.]

Treasury Department, February 28, 1816.

In obedience to the resolution of the 12th of February, 1816, inquiring " what additions, if any, have been made to the funded public debt, and to the floating public debt, since the 30th day of September last," the Secretary of the Treasury has the honor to lay before the House of Representatives the following report :

I. That, by the annual report upon the state of the finances of the United States, presented on the 6th December, 1816, it appears that the balance of the whole of the public funded debt, contracted before the war, amounted, on the 30th of September, 1815, to the sum of - - $39,135,484 96
That, on the 1st of January, 1816, there was reimbursed of the principal of that debt (besides the payment of the interest) the sum of - - - - - - 799,652 38
And that, at this time, the balance of the whole of the public debt contracted before the war amounts to the sum of - - - - - - - - - 38,335,832 58

II. That, by the annual report, it also appears, that the estimated amount of the whole of funded public debt, in reference to the late war, was, on the 30th of September, 1815, the sum of - - - - - - - - - - - - $63,144,972 50
That, to this amount, there have been added the following items, since the 30th of September, 1815:

1. In six per cent. stock of 1814, at the rate of $100 in stock for $80 in money, to pay the city of Charleston, according to the contract, for a loan made during the late war - - - - - - - - - - - - - - $204,889 23
2. In six per cent. stock of 1814, in lieu of Treasury notes funded at ninety-five per cent., and which so far operates to reduce the amount of the floating debt due on the 30th of September, 1815 - - 2,206,954 21
3. In six per cent. stock, in lieu of Treasury notes funded at par, and which so far operates to reduce the amount of the floating debt due on the 30th September, 1815 - - - - - - - 2,057 00
4. In seven per cent stock, in lieu of small Treasury notes funded at par, estimated at - - - - - - - - - - - 2,815,871 00

Amount of the addition, since the 30th of September, 1815, to the public funded debt contracted in reference to the war - - - - - - - - 5,229,772 44

Estimated amount of the whole of the public funded debt on the 12th of February, 1816, contracted in reference to the late war - - • - - - - $68,374,764 94

III. That by the annual report, it also appears that the amount of the floating public debt on the 30th of September, 1815, was - - - - - - - $17,355,101 00

14th CON. 1st SESS.—54

Report on the Public Debt.

To this sum there have been added, between the 30th of September, 1815, and 12th of February, 1816, the following items:

1. There have been issued and reissued small Treasury notes, amounting, as is estimated, to the sum of - - - - - - - - - $3,471,537 00
2. There have been issued Treasury notes bearing interest at five and two-fifths per cent., the sum of - - - - - - - 2,704,600 00

                                         6,176,137 00

3. There have been obtained temporary loans from sundry banks in the District of Columbia, under the act of the 13th of February, 1815, providing for the reconstruction of the public buildings at Washington - - - - - - 180,000 00

                                         $23,631,238 00

But the floating debt has been diminished during the same period in the following manner:

1. By the subscription of Treasury notes to the six per cent. loan, as above stated, at the rate of $100 in stock for $95 in principal and interest of Treasury notes. Stock having been issued to the amount of $2,206,955 21, produced a reimbursement of Treasury notes amounting to - - - - - - $2,096,607 53

But of this sum there was included an estimate, in the sum of $4,315,000, stated as thus reimbursed in the annual report, the sum of $1,153,412 94, contracts for sundry sums uncertain in their amount, having been made, but not completed at that time, and which, therefore, is now deducted - - - - - - - 1,153,412 94

                                         $943,194 59

2. By funding Treasury notes at par for six per cent. stock, as above stated - - - - - - - - - - - $2,057 00
3. By funding small Treasury notes for seven per cent. stock, as above stated - - - - - - - - - 2,815,871 00
4. By the payment in Treasury notes of duties and taxes, estimated to have amounted, in Treasury notes bearing interest, to the sum of - - - - - - - - $2,650,000
In small Treasury notes, to the sum of - - - 50,000

                                   2,700,000 00

5. By the repayment of temporary loans, viz: To the Bank of the State of South Carolina - - - - - 50,000
To the Mechanics' Bank, New York - - - - 200,000

                                 250,000 00

                                         6,711,122 59

Estimated amount of the whole of the floating debt, on the 12th of February, 1816 $16,920,115 41

IV. That, from the preceding estimates, it appears that, on the 12th of Feb'y, 1816, the aggregate amount of the public debt was the sum of $123,630,692 93, consisting of the following items:

1. Funded public debt before the war - - - - - - $38,335,832 58
2. Funded public debt contracted since the war - - - - - 68,374,744 94
3. Floating public debt outstanding - - - - - - - 16,920,115 41

                                         $123,630,692 93

That the aggregate amount of the public debt on the 30th September, 1815, was the sum of - - - - - - - - - - - - 119,635,558 46

And that the aggregate addition since 30th of September, 1815, is - - - - $3,995,134 47

All which is respectfully submitted.

                              A. J. DALLAS, *Secretary of the Treasury.*

Protection to Manufacturers of Woollen Fabrics.

PROTECTION TO MANUFACTURERS OF WOOLLEN FABRICS.

[Communicated to the House, March 6, 1816.]

Mr. NEWTON, from the Committee of Commerce and Manufactures, to which were referred the memorials and petitions of the manufacturers of wool, submitted the following report:

The committee, having given this subject all the consideration that its importance merits, beg leave to present, with due respect to the House, the result of their investigations.

The correctness of the following estimate the committee are no way disposed to question:

Amount of capital supposed to be invested in buildings, machinery, &c. - - - -	$12,000,000
Value of raw material consumed annually - -	$7,000,000
Increase of value by manufacturing - -	12,000,000
Value of woollen goods manufactured annually - -	19,000,000
Number of per- } constantly 50,000 sons employed } occasionally 50,000	100,000

The committee having in a report presented to the House on the 13th of February last, on the memorials and petitions of the manufacturers of cotton, expressed their opinion on the policy of fostering manufacturing establishments, consider themselves relieved from the necessity of repeating the same arguments. Every reason then urged for sustaining the cotton manufacturing establishments applies with equal force in favor of the woollen. The committee, influenced by the same reasons, feel themselves bound to accord the same justice to the manufacturers of wool.

The following resolution is, therefore, with due respect submitted to the House:

Resolved, That, from and after the 30th day June next, in lieu of the duties now authorized by law, there be laid, levied, and collected on woollen goods imported into the United States and Territories thereof, from any foreign country whatever, —— per centum *ad valorem*.

To the honorable the chairman and members of the Committee of Commerce and Manufactures.

GENTLEMEN : Being informed that you are preparing to submit to Congress a report on the subject of manufactures, as connected with the national prosperity of the country, we, the subscribers, respectfully submit the following remarks respecting the capital employed in the woollen business in the United States, the number of persons employed, the quantity of wool consumed, and the aggregate amount of all the woollen cloth now manufactured.

At this time there are in the State of Connecticut alone twenty-five establishments for the manufacture of woollen cloths, employing twelve hundred persons, and as many more indirectly who do not immediately appertain to the establishment. The capital already invested therein amounts to four hundred and fifty thousand dollars; and they are capable of making, and probably do manufacture annually, equal in amount to three hundred and seventy-five thousand yards of narrow, or one hundred and twenty-five thousand yards of broadcloths. Besides this quantity made at the establishments, it is calculated there are five hundred thousand yards made annually in families and dressed in the country clothiers' shops; part of which is regularly sold to the country stores; doing away, thus far, their former practice of supplying themselves with British goods of a similar description. The value of all the woollen cloths thus manufactured, at the lowest estimate, is about $1,500,000, making a home market for a staple of nine hundred thousand pounds of wool, or the produce of four hundred thousand sheep. With regard to the whole quantity of woollen goods manufactured in the United States we cannot at present speak with precision; but, from the best information obtained there is at this time annually manufactured in all the States to the amount of $19,000,000, requiring a capital, in buildings and machinery, of $12,000,000, and employing fifty thousand persons immediately in the business, and as many more indirectly. With that encouragement which we deem it the policy of the Government to bestow on this branch of our industry, the quantity of woollens manufactured in this country would be doubled in four years, and nearly sufficient to supply the whole demand of the United States.

When it is considered that the woollen manufacture is now making a home market for an important staple of our country, equal in value to $7,000,000; that the product of its industry, equal to $19,000,000, is a great gain of national wealth, in giving employment to various kinds of labor, at the same time preventing foreigners from drawing great resources from us in the sale of their manufactures; that it produces an interest in the country that, under all circumstances, is an American interest; the policy of giving it the necessary support becomes obvious to every unprejudiced mind. At the same time that it is aiding and encouraging agriculture in consuming her productions, it is in no degree taking from her the labor necessary to carry on her operations. A great proportion of the woollen manufacture is done by the assistance of labor-saving machinery, which is almost exclusively superintended by women and children, and the infirm, who would otherwise be wholly destitute of employment; whereas they are now able to maintain themselves. The manual labor employed is of that class who, from their previous habits and occupations in life, are wholly unfitted for agricultural pursuits; and who, if not thus employed would, in most instances, be a burden on society. Among this description are to be numbered many valuable foreigners who are daily arriving among us in needy and indigent circumstances, and whose only employment has been in the manufacturing business at home. In the exchange between the different States of the manufactured goods, and

Protection to Manufacturers of Woollen Fabrics.

of the raw materials, and in the growing wants of many foreign articles, as dye stuffs, &c., the commerce of our country, particularly the coasting trade, is equally benefited with our agriculture.

If the woollen manufacture does not languish for want of necessary support from Government at this time, there cannot be a doubt but in the course of a very few years we shall be able to supply the whole demand of the United States, and at a lower rate than our manufacture can be imported from abroad. Great Britain excludes all woollen goods, nor suffers a yard of cloth to be exported except in a finished state. It is not now a question with her manufacturers who shall sell at highest prices, but, who can manufacture the cheapest; and this competition has enabled her to undersell all the nations in Europe. The same encouragement to the business in this country will produce a like competition, and enable us, eventually, to undersell her even in foreign markets. The amount of woollen cloths now imported into the United States is supposed to be about ——

The quantity now manufactured is about $19,-000,000 in value. It is a business susceptible of an increase of twenty-five or thirty per cent. annually; so that, in the course of five years at least, we may be able to clothe ourselves independent of any foreign nation, and give a new stimulus to agriculture which is now languishing from the necessity of depending upon a precarious foreign market for most of her important productions.

We remain, gentlemen, very respectfully, your obedient humble servants,

ARTHUR W. MAGILL,
WM. YOUNG.

My actual experience being principally in the cotton manufacture, my entire belief in the correctness of the preceding statement is founded on my knowledge of the gentlemen who have signed it; I, therefore, cheerfully add my name.

ISAAC BRIGGS.

SUMMARY.

Permanent capital in buildings and machinery		$12,000,000
Annual value of raw material, manufactured		7,000,000
Value of cloths annually manufactured		19,000,000
Increase of value by manufacturing		12,000,000
Number of persons employed		
Directly	50,000	
Incidentally	50,000	
	100,000	

This manufacture is capable of an increase in the ratio of twenty-five to thirty per cent. per annum.

To the honorable the Senate and House of Representatives of the United States of America, in Congress assembled:

The memorial and petition of the subscribers, manufacturers of woollen articles in the States of New Jersey, Pennsylvania, and Delaware, on behalf of themselves and others engaged in similar manufactures in the said States, respectfully showeth: That your memorialists are impelled by the situation of their manufacture, and the effects which may be produced upon it by the contemplated measures of Congress, respectfully, to offer their sentiments, and to point out those circumstances in which they conceive their interests and that of the public are so united as to merit the most serious attention of the National Legislature.

Your memorialists beg leave to remind Congress that, from the first settlement of the country, domestic manufactures have formed an important feature of its industry; these, founded on the genius of its inhabitants, and the arts they brought or have acquired from Europe, have introduced and established many of the most useful manufactures, among which none is more conspicuous than that of woollen; this has not only increased as fast as the agriculture of the country supplied the raw material, but whenever any circumstances have given it further encouragement, it has shown itself sufficiently founded in the wants and ability of the country to go beyond this, and to rise in a very material degree to its support. Such was the case during the stamp act and the Revolutionary war, when the woollen manufacture became greatly extended; but the raw material, the population and general ability of the country were then all too feeble to give it a decided permanent establishment, so that, upon the renewal of intercourse with foreign nations, it sunk again under a competition with their manufactures, until within the last five years, when many circumstances have arisen, and particularly two, viz: the introduction of sheep, and the separation from Europe by the war, which have given to the manufacture such a basis, that its complete establishment in the country is no longer doubtful.

The introduction of sheep, and particularly of the merino breed, gave to the country at once an agricultural object, which every State in Europe had been striving to realize, but without an immediate demand for the wool it would not have been realized here, at least at the time and to the extent which has been done, for while it furnished the raw material, it was the immediate manufacture which afforded the price and demand for that material, and occasioned its present extension and establishments.

It is notorious that, during the period referred to, a great number of the citizens of these States have devoted themselves both to the breed of sheep, and the woollen manufactures; that vast capitals have been expended, and large establishments every where diffused through the States, which have supplied the public wants, and shows themselves capable of great future extension, so that altogether a national object has been erected, uniting the features of agriculture and commerce in so eminent a degree as conspicuously to demand the attention of the Government in all those acts which are directed to its national economy.

Protection to Manufacturers of Woollen Fabrics.

Your memorialists beg leave to state that, upon the introduction of the merino breed of sheep, the prices which the manufacturers afforded for their wool were high beyond that of every other country; so that the encouragement it received was precisely such as the infant arts almost always require on their introduction, and other countries have been obliged to give by legislative provision: accordingly, the breed of sheep has been permanently fixed and diffused over the soil of the United States without any other aid. At present the prices which the manufacturers allow are still higher than those abroad, although wool is now much dearer in Europe than the usual level of peace prices, chiefly owing to the demand for manufactures to be sent here.

It is thus that the import of our clothing operates with the double disadvantage: first, of keeping up the raw material of Europe by manufacturing it for our use; and, secondly, depressing that material here by impairing the manufactures of our own; in both cases the agricultural object is effected through the manufacture, and in the proportion as that is encouraged abroad, so both are depressed at home.

It is vain to pretend that the breed of sheep can be maintained in these States by an export of the wool; even the present prices in Europe will not admit of it; and if they decline, as they unquestionably will, under a peace establishment, it is out of the question. In the year 1800 the average price of British wool was less than twenty cents per pound, which, after the expense of export, could in no way support the growth of it here; at this moment the prices of wool are higher here than abroad, and, if the manufacture is supported, they will probably always remain so, since the charges of export and import give them a material support. Besides this, it is by manufactures actually existing on the spot where the wool is grown, that it receives its surest encouragement. These furnish an immediate market, and teach the agriculturist all the improvements in quality, by which excellence is obtained; of this the whole history of the material furnishes a proof. It was by the refined manufactures of the Arabs in Spain, that the fleeces of that country received those improvements, which the laws of the Mesta now barely support; and the present variety and goodness of the British wool has been obtained by its manufactures. No doubt, therefore, can exist as to the fact that it is through the medium of the manufacture that the growth of the wool can be improved, or even maintained, in these States.

Our manufacturers have already furnished a large quantity of superfine cloths, of coarse cloths, and many new articles peculiarly suited to our climate. In their infancy they could scarcely be expected to furnish all that the country demanded, or to obtain the perfect excellence of nations who had manufactured them for ages. But it is notorious, that the quantity was rapidly becoming sufficient for our consumption, and that a large proportion of our cloths were equal to the best in Europe. What deficiencies existed would have

soon yielded to existing skill; and one object was obtained with certainty, viz: that of giving the country a large amount of substantial clothing, with every moderate degree of excellence, and inferior only to articles of refined luxury.

On this head your memorialists beg leave to remark that, although the importation of foreign manufactures comprises a great number of most useful articles essential to the wants of the country, yet a large proportion of it consists of those which are more alluring by their fashion than their use. The wealth of Europe encourages these at home, and a constant supply of them is required by its luxury and the state of its arts, which are better rewarded by these refined inventions than the more useful ones. Here, without railing against the introduction of elegance, and even a moderate degree of luxury itself, it is certain that our own manufactures are depreciated more by the novelty and fashion of foreign articles than by those which are the most useful; and that a very great proportion of our wealth goes abroad for the allurements which foreigners present to us. While, therefore, we can supply ourselves with articles sufficient for every moderate degree of gratification, it is consistent with the practice of the wisest nations, and the soundest principles of political economy, that they should be encouraged; and that foreign articles which interfere with them should be made the objects of revenue by Government, which those who use them ought to pay.

Almost every nation has now adopted the system of making its revenue laws the organ of protection to its arts; and this system having been already used in these States, a universal conviction prevails that Congress will make it one of the bases of the new tariff of duties. Your memorialists are, therefore, impressed with the belief that it must be desirable to Congress to obtain correct information of what precise duties the interests of the manufacturers demand, and it is their sincere desire to furnish such information as to that in which they are engaged.

Upon this head your memorialists beg leave to remark that they do not wish for a rate of duties which may injure any other department of industry, or give an excessive encouragement to their own; their sole object is such as will prevent their individual ruin, and maintain the manufacturing establishments of the country. It is certain that a considerable duty is necessary for this purpose, and there are some circumstances which may enable us to fix it with tolerable precision. Under the old duties, previous to the war, there was not encouragement enough to introduce the woollen manufacture, so that it appears certain that these duties would not now maintain it. Under the present duties it has languished, and in a considerable degree declined since the peace; yet there is reason to hope that when the shock first given by foreign import subsides, they may be maintained with a moderate, though certainly not with a great profit to the manufacturer. There are two circumstances which prevent a more precise opinion on this

Protection to Manufacturers of Woollen Fabrics.

subject; first, the almost certain decline of the prices abroad; and the next, the excessive importation of the present year, which has lowered prices here beyond their fair or accurate value. The last of these is accidental, though it may often occur again, and the best checks for it exists in considerable duties. Of the former, the extent cannot yet be ascertained; it is certain, however, that future improvement in the state of the manufacture here is less to be looked for than discouragement; so that, without any speculative calculations upon what may occur, but taking what we know as our guide, it seems certain that the present duties may maintain the manufactures of the country, but that unquestionably nothing less will do it.

Your memorialists might urge a great number of facts and further reasoning to show the propriety of fixing the duties at the rate they have mentioned, or even higher, but they are not desirous unnecessarily to swell this memorial into a trespass upon the attention of Congress. It appears proper, however, that, in expressing their sentiments as to their own manufacture, they should also express those they feel for others, and particularly the two great objects of agriculture and commerce. It is certain that all the three great divisions of labor ought to receive the patronage and support they require without partiality, and they trust the wisdom of Congress will always afford it when necessary.

Your memorialists, however, cannot but remark that the agriculture and commerce of these States already rest upon a basis which does not appear easily impaired; the agriculture, directed to objects in universal demand for the most necessary wants of mankind, derives from these wants the surest support, and whenever the introduction of new objects of cultivation, or the support of the old require legislative aid, they ought, and will, doubtless, receive it; in the same manner the carriage of our vast produce gives a support to our commerce equally permanent. The two united afford a solid aid to each other; the agriculture by furnishing the means, and commerce, by exploring the sources of supply. It is thus that both possess a foundation which, aided by a just protection of our rights, and by those favorable regulations which it has always been the object of Congress to make, presents at once a stimulus and support to the existing agriculture of our country which will extend it over all our soil.

But manufactures advance with a feebler step; those which are matured to the highest excellence often depend, in their infancy, upon individual exertion, and they have a peculiar species of competitors in the population, the skill, and long experience of other nations, above all, in the jealousy with which each nation watches its own arts; their whole history, therefore, is a record that, in the introduction of them into any nation, there is a period when public aid is essential, and that they cannot be introduced without it. In every State they furnish the greatest resources of commerce, as may be seen by the vast carriage

required by manufactured articles. This sort of aid has already been given to the commerce of the United States by their manufactures: a great portion of our agricultural produce is already doubled in value before it leaves us, and is carried to other nations in a shape which still more enhances it. Our flour, for instance, would not be applied to the supply of many countries without manufacture, and the produce of our minerals and forests requires this sort of conversion, often, to give them value at all; but, beyond the resource thus furnished to commerce, the supply of our wants at home, and the independence of the country are objects of still greater importance. In this way our wealth is increased by saving it, the genius of our citizens awakened, their industry rewarded, and the value of every portion of labor enhanced at home, instead of encouraging the agriculture, commerce, and manufacturing skill of other nations.

Your memorialists feel no doubt that the applications of other manufacturers will receive the same attention from Congress as their own, and especially that of the cotton manufacturers; leaving these, then, to what they can urge with more propriety for themselves, they cannot but remark that the cotton manufacture bids fair to supply so large a portion of our clothing, as to free that of wool from the fears which might be entertained as to its inability to furnish a sufficient supply for the country. It is certain that our resources for the cotton manufacture are unbounded, and that, in our climate, it will furnish a vast portion of our clothing; the extension of the growth of wool and its manufacture, therefore, are such as to leave no reasonable doubt but that, under proper encouragement, it will, at no very distant period, supply all our remaining wants, and especially those articles for which wool is essential.

Your memorialists cannot conceive that, at this period, any friend to this country would draw distinctions between its various establishments unfavorable to either. Speculative theories derived from other countries or other ages can rarely be applied, with justice, to our own; but if these theories are indulged they can only be drawn from abuses or a state of society different from what we enjoy. The manufactures abroad may be considered as of two distinct kinds; the one consisting of great commercial establishments, to which the whole mass of society is devoted; the other those of a more confined character, which run hand in hand with agriculture, and afford a useful aid to commerce, without becoming its sole support. The latter exists throughout all the continent of Europe, and nourishes every other application of labor; the former exists chiefly in Great Britain, from whence we derive some of the most useful, and all the injurious ideas of manufactures. Her institutions, however, are derived from her peculiar situation; abounding in minerals, and with a soil incapable of sustaining her inhabitants, she is compelled to an unbounded scope of manufactures to sustain her commerce, and to feed her

Protection to Manufacturers of Woollen Fabrics.

people. In these, however, it is from momentary abuses in some of her manufactures alone, that injurious impressions of them are derived; for if we examine them all, with proper discrimination, we shall find that the far greater part of them, and particularly her woollen manufacture, comprises the most free and comfortable portion of her population; this character applies to every State of the Continent. France and Germany have, for ages, carried on large manufactures, without the least injury to their people, or their agriculture; and the history of Europe will prove that manufactures have been, in every age, the nurseries of its freedom and prosperity. To their existence liberty is essential; for to raise or to buy the raw materials, to sell their productions, or to pursue their inventions and skill, requires that freedom from restraint which first compelled the feudal lords of Europe to emancipate their artists, while they chained their agricultural subjects to the soil. From hence the cities of Italy first rose into free States, and the progress of the useful arts nourished the Reformation, and gave to the cities of Germany and Flanders, to Geneva, and to Nismes, a portion of liberty which no other part of Europe possessed.

Your memorialists cannot ask for an encouragement injurious to any portion of their fellow-citizens, or the interests of their country. The mass of labor here, as elsewhere, is comprised in the three great divisions of agriculture, commerce, and manufactures; but these are so connected that benefit bestowed on one must extend to all. Under a free constitution and equal laws, the children of the State justly ask the same patronage, to whichever object they direct their industry. Our population has now risen to a large amount, and a considerable portion of it is comprised in our cities and towns; these are necessary to nourish the more diffused districts of agriculture, by furnishing them with markets, and supplying those wants for which a combination of labor is required; hence their application to manufactures is at once natural and essential. Besides these, our numerous streams of water, our minerals, our woods, and our tillage, all invite to the employment of manufacturing skill. In this the choice will always be best determined by the most necessary wants of the country; and what we ask is, not to direct or give to manufactures an unnatural aid, but to protect them from foreign injury. For a long period, it is none but the most necessary which can be reared, and while our vast territory, and the unbounded scope it offers for agricultural labor will, perhaps, forever prevent the introduction of any other, the settlement of that territory itself will proceed with the surer step, as we become independent in our resources.

There are two facts of considerable importance, which your memorialists believe may be fully established: first, that the import of foreign goods in most years, and particularly in the present one, already exceeds the value we can pay by our exports. This circumstance is in a great degree similar to what occurred upon the peace of 1783, when the country was so inundated with foreign articles that the manufactures were destroyed, and our citizens torn to pieces for many years to pay for them. The late wars in Europe by presenting new and extraordinary objects of commerce to us, retrieved our embarrassments, and threw into the country a mass of wealth which overpaid the deficiency of our proper exports; but these extraordinary objects are not to be expected in peace, when the balance against us must again increase, unless we can prevent it by our domestic economy.

The other fact is, that the manufactures of the country, altogether, have become so important that the carriage of raw materials from abroad, (chiefly of kinds we do not produce at all, or not in sufficient quantities,) actually exceeds, in point of tonnage, that which is employed in manufactured articles; and if, to the tonnage thus employed abroad, we add that which conveys our raw materials and manufactures coastwise, we shall find that they already support a most important part of our commerce, of that kind which we can secure and extend in peace, and which is of all others the most interesting to the country, viz: the increase and employment of our ships and seamen, to whom freights are the proper objects of employment, and it will be at once perceived how much these are increased by the import of such articles as hemp, iron, copper, lead, brimstone, and the like, over fine and costly manufactures.

Your memorialists are sensible that very erroneous ideas have prevailed as to the profit yielded by the woollen manufacture, which has been considered as very great during the war. In order to counteract this opinion, which is incorrect, your memorialists state that when the manufacture was begun, just before the war, washed merino wool was at less than one dollar per pound, but that, during the war, it rose to three dollars, so that the wool in a yard of cloth cost at least six dollars, and the materials for finishing it and workmanship were equally high; it was these, therefore, and not the profit, that enhanced the price of cloth; and they prove that the manufacture was actually instituted at the risk of the manufacturer himself, but that the profit was largely shared with the agriculturist and other laborers of the country; besides which, it is certain the profit, whatever it was, came at a fortunate period to introduce the manufacture and supply the country; nor has it been employed long enough to give either a reward or fair experiment to the introducers of it; since the period has been so short that a great part of it has necessarily been taken up in forming the establishments, at great cost, and they are always known to be least productive for the first few years. At present, the manufacturer here can afford to make a piece of cloth at about the same price as it may be imported for, that is, at eight dollars per yard; but he cannot make it here for what it can be made in England, because the materials and workmanship are both much higher here; nor is the cost of carriage and old duties enough to pay the difference. It absolutely requires the whole of the present duties, as they now exist, and these cannot be considered as high when it is seen that they are to comprise all the manufacturer's profit, and protect him from all his disadvantages, especially the following: first, the higher prices he pays here for the wool, the machinery, and the workmanship; second, the probable depression of wool and cloth abroad; thirdly, the enormous import sold here below their cost; and, lastly, the prejudice of the country in favor of foreign fabrics.

Your memorialists cannot but conclude by expressing their conviction that the absolute fate of their manufacture depends on the determination of Congress, and with it the fate of a great number of citizens who have engaged in it; that they entered into it under the encouragement given by the late war, is correct, as without encouragement from some source no important institution would ever be begun; but it is certain that neither now, nor upon any future occasion, could the citizens of the United States be supposed to embark in such undertakings, where the private hazard is always great, solely upon the precariousness of public measures; to look forward, therefore, to the public patronage when they might require it, was, as it ever will be, a reasonable resource, upon which every man who engages in such undertakings must depend. It is, then, with confidence that they now rely upon the measures of Congress for that protection which is essential to them, and with them to the woollen manufacture and growth of wool in the United States; and they respectfully pray that Congress, taking the premises into its most serious consideration, will grant the protection they require, by continuing at least the present duties upon all woollen articles of foreign manufacture imported into the United States.

WM. R. RODMAN, *and others.*

COMPENSATION OF OFFICERS OF THE CUSTOMS.

[Communicated to the House, March 21, 1816.]

TREASURY DEPARTMENT,
March 21, 1816.

SIR: The petitions hereinafter mentioned have been referred to this Department at different times:

1. The petition of the inspectors of the customs of the port of Philadelphia, praying an increase of their compensation.

2. The petitions of the inspectors and weighers of the customs at New York, with a similar prayer.

3. The petition of the inspectors of the customs at Baltimore, with a similar prayer.

By the act of the 2d of March, 1799, (vol. 4,) the compensation of an inspector was fixed at a sum not exceeding two dollars for every day that he should be actually employed in aid of the customs, to be paid by the collector out of the revenue, and charged to the United States, according to the amount produced, at certain rates, regulated by the quantity, and the kind of the articles measured, weighed, or gauged. It is believed that the compensation of this class of officers has seldom exceeded at any place the average of two dollars for each day; and that, at many places, it falls much below that sum.

It is obvious that the effective value of the compensation, which was allowed in 1799, has been greatly reduced in consequence of the enhanced price of every article of subsistence and comfort. The service of the inspector has, also, become much more severe and important than it was at that period. The compensation of the weighers, measurers, and gaugers, might be considered as increasing with the increase of their business; but, in truth, the effect of the increase of business must be the employment of a greater number of those officers, and, consequently, the compensation of each will probably remain stationary.

Under every view of the subject I am impressed with the justice and policy of granting the prayer of the petitioners, by advancing their present compensation at the rate of fifty per cent.

I have the honor to be, very respectfully, sir, your most obedient servant,

A. J. DALLAS.

Hon. WILLIAM LOWNDES.

WASHINGTON, *March* 8, 1816.

DEAR SIR: Some weeks ago petitions from the weighers and inspectors of the customs, belonging to the port of New York, were presented to Congress, praying for an augmentation of salary. This petition was referred to the Committee of Ways and Means, who, I have understood, have laid it before you. I feel impressed with the necessity of granting some relief to the petitioners, and I have, therefore, taken the liberty to address you on the subject.

The officers of the customs in the city of New York are a very reputable class of men, many of them old Revolutionary officers; many of them persons who once were in comfortable, and even elevated circumstances, and who, owing to adverse fortune, have had to take refuge, in advanced life, in the scanty shelter from want that the *per diem* of a custom-house officer affords; and all of them, as far as my knowledge extends, possess the character of being upright and exemplary. They are remarked for their official integrity: so much so, that I have never heard a lisp of such a thing as corruption having been found among them.

The salary now given them, of two dollars per day, was established about eighteen years ago when it was probably quite sufficient; but everything has so enhanced since that day that one thousand two hundred and fifty dollars will not go as far now as seven hundred and thirty dollars did then. No small tenement, of any decent appearance is to be obtained at present under two hundred and fifty dollars. The fuel to support one fire will cost eighty dollars. A solitary ser-

Remission of Forfeitures.

vant eighty more. Here is four hundred and ten dollars of the seven hundred and thirty gone for three items. The fact is, I have ascertained, to my perfect conviction, that these men are in a deplorable situation. Some of them have families of five, six, and I know of one who has nine children. They are perplexed with small debts, contracted through poverty, for the absolute wants of their families; and many of them are becoming shabby in their appearance. I have been told by one that to school his children was out of the question, for he could not afford them shoes in the Winter. Many of them have grown gray in the employ, and most of them have been so long engaged that they have either lost the knowledge of all other business, or have lost the means of helping themselves to a change; and are too necessitous to throw up this "half a loaf" for the uncertain hope of getting into better bread.

I ought to mention, also, that in consequence of the double duties, there has been a necessity for increase of vigilance; and this has compelled the officers, by the direction of their superiors, to watch by night as well as by day; so that they have, of late, lost two nights' sleep in a week. This has made their duty peculiarly hard. From all these circumstances and facts I cannot refrain from saying that I think equity and common humanity dictate that they should be relieved.

Setting aside their own personal claims, good policy must imperiously require that their situation should be comfortable. These men, thus perplexed and needy, are, indirectly, the collectors of the revenue, which, in New York, under the expected tariff, will amount to nothing short of eight millions of dollars per annum. Ought not the guardians of this amount of impost to be kept decently alive? You must agree with me, sir, that starvation is no great friend of honesty; and the question becomes a serious one, whether, while all the means of life are amply at hand, starving men will not be apt, even at the expense of integrity, to help themselves! Men are best kept honest by not being led into temptation. Should they at once get corrupted, and the frauds that are common all over Europe and elsewhere, become familiar here, it is impossible to calculate the amount of injury the revenue may sustain.

We certainly ought to augment the salaries of these officers at the same moment that we augment the duties. One hundred thousand dollars, and, perhaps, a smaller sum divided annually among the petty officers of the customs, in addition to their present salaries, may be the means of saving one million per annum to the public income. Something of this kind, most unquestionably, must be done; the good of the community at large demands it, and if it be neglected, the alternative is inevitable; either our inspectors of the customs will become dishonest, or quit the employ in order that dishonest men may take their places.

You will pardon the freedom with which I have addressed you, and believe me, with sincere regard, dear sir, &c.,   WM. IRVING.

The Hon. A. J. DALLAS.

SENATE CHAMBER, *March* 19, 1816.

SIR: Several respectable individuals of New York, whose business gives them a particular knowledge of the duties of the Inspectors of the customs, have signified their opinion that an increase of the compensation of these officers was expedient, and that the public interest would be secured and promoted by such increase.

I take the liberty of uniting in this opinion, and of communicating the same to you, on the information that the subject has been referred for your consideration and report.

I am, sir, with great respect, your obedient servant,

               RUFUS KING.

A. J. DALLAS, Esq.,
   Secretary of the Treasury.

REMISSION OF FORFEITURES.

[Communicated to the House, March 22, 1816.]

TREASURY DEPARTMENT,
             March 22, 1816.

SIR: The petition of "sundry merchants of Massachusetts," which was transmitted in your letter of the 24th ultimo, with a request from the Committee of Ways and Means for "any information on the subject of the petition, or any opinion in regard to the claim of the petitioners that it was thought proper to communicate," has been duly considered, in connexion, as well with the documents that accompanied it, as with other documents in this Department upon the same subject, and I have now the honor to communicate the result.

Towards the close of the year 1814 great quantities of goods, of British manufacture, amounting, probably, in the aggregate value, to more than a million of dollars, were admitted to entry at Hampton, in the district of Penobscot, and the duties upon them were paid or secured at the time of the entry. The goods, or a considerable proportion of them, on their way to Boston, from Hampden, were afterwards seized as forfeited, under various laws; some of them were libelled in the district court of Massachusetts, and others in the district court of Maine; and, upon the trial of one of the libels in Massachusetts, with an agreement that the fate of that case should, generally, be binding on all the other cases, the jury gave a verdict in favor of the claimants, under the direction of the court. To that direction, however, a bill of exceptions was tendered, and, upon a writ of error, the judgment of the district court was reversed, and a new trial ordered to be had at the bar of the circuit court.

In this state of the legal proceedings, the petitioners, who are the claimants of the goods, apply to Congress to be relieved from the alleged forfeiture, for the reasons which are assigned in the petition; and, upon the whole, two questions arise for consideration; 1st, whether the claimants are the *bona fide* owners of the goods, and became so

Remission of Forfeitures.

in a lawful manner ; 2d, whether the importation and entry of the goods at Hampton were, under all circumstances, lawful. To pave the way for the decision of the committee, on these questions, a more particular statement of the facts, which are involved in the case, becomes proper and necessary.

The general facts of the case.

The British Government having declared, during the late war, a general blockade of the whole coast of the United States, the American Government on —— of ——, issued a proclamation, protesting against the extravagance of the measure, and offering to neutral traders an assurance of all the protection it could give. Upon the same principle and policy letters were, on particular occasions, written from the Treasury Department to the collectors of the customs, authorizing the protection and encouragement of neutral commerce ; and, on the 4th of April, 1814, the non-intercourse laws had been repealed so as to admit, generally, the importation of goods of British growth, produce, or manufacture, and to allow neutral vessels to trade between the United States and Great Britain and Ireland, and the colonies or dependencies of Great Britain. But neither the President's proclamation, nor the Treasury correspondence, nor the repealing act, were designed to sanction a merely colorable neutrality, covering the property of the enemy, involving an unlawful intercourse between the citizens and the enemies of the United States, and violating the positive sanctions of the laws enacted for the security of the public revenue.

On the 1st of September, 1814, a British military and naval force took possession of Castine, the port of entry for the district of Penobscot, and claimed, by proclamations and military orders, the sovereignty and jurisdiction of all the territory east of the bay and river Penobscot. The actual possession and occupancy of the British troops did not extend over the territory claimed ; and, in particular, it is to be observed that, although the town of Orrington, which was neither a port of delivery nor of entry, situated on the east side of the Penobscot, was probably once visited, during the month of November, 1814, by a small detachment, "it never had attempted to surrender to the British arms," as Judge Story judicially declared, in delivering the judgment of the circuit court, "and it always continued to assert and claim its American rights and privileges, and to obey the laws of the United States." When the British forces took possession of Castine the collector of Penobscot removed his office to Hampden, (which was a port of delivery for vessels of the United States only, and was not a port of entry for any vessels,) situated on the west side of the Penobscot, nearly opposite to Orrington.

The appearances of an illicit traffic between the inhabitants of the west and the military occupants of the east side of the bay and river Penobscot were soon displayed, and strong representations were made to the Government upon the subject. It was not found practicable, however,

in this quarter, any more than at Passamaquoddy, to prevent the intercourse. Supplies were sent in abundance to the enemy ; and goods, almost without stint, were imported into the United States from his possession, either clandestinely, or in vessels assuming a neutral flag. The goods claimed by the petitioners were brought from Orrington to Hampden in the latter mode. The petitioners do not, either in the allegations of their petition, or in the documents accompanying it, furnish the means of making a discrimination in the merit of their cases ; but, on the contrary, as they all united in an agreement to be bound in the decision of one case, and as they unite in one application to Congress upon the same general statement, it must be presumed that the cases are not susceptible of any important distinction. They will, therefore, be embraced without discrimination, in the narrative of the transaction, which the petition places upon a footing of a fair and open neutral trade ; as to the owner and character of the vessel employed ; as to the owners of the goods imported, and as to the course of the trade.

1st. As to the owner and the character of the vessel employed.

In delivering the judgment of the circuit court, Judge Story states that the goods claimed by the petitioners "were found at Orrington, in the month of November, 1814, and were then shipped on board of a small sloop, called the Christina, commanded by a Mr. William P. Unger, and transferred to Hampden, where they were admitted to an entry by the collector of the district, as foreign goods imported in a foreign vessel, &c.; that the sloop was American built, and was, until the 14th of October, 1814, enrolled and licensed for the coasting trade, in the district of Penobscot, by the name of the Union ; that, on that day, she was sold to Mr. Unger, the master, who called himself a Swedish subject, although it was in proof that he had for several years domiciled in the United States ; and that, at the time of transporting the goods, the sloop was navigating under a pass from Mr. Soderstrom, the Swedish Consul, dated the 14th of the same October, recognising her as entitled to the benefit of the Swedish flag ; but her crew, with the exception of the master, were all Americans."

The character of Unger and the Christina, thus described by the judge, is also to be traced in the depositions and documents accompanying the petition.

It is stated by Charles Tibbet, the deputy collector of Penobscot, "that he had known the Christina by the name of Union, prior to the arrival at Hampden, for several years; that he did not recollect where she was built, but she was originally an American vessel; that her last owners were Samuel Bartlett and another person, both of Buckstown ; that she continued to be their property until October last, at which time, according to a bill of sale, she appeared to have been transferred to Mr. Unger ; that he had known Mr. Unger about three months ; had heard Unger say he was married ; had a wife at the Southward.

Remission of Forfeitures.

&c.; that he did not know where Unger resided for the last three years, but he had heard him say that he had sailed from the Southward and Westward; that Unger occasionally then resided at Hampden; that he was at Castine about the end of September, 1814, where he saw Unger, who told him that he had goods on hand which he wished to introduce into the United States, stating that he was a neutral subject, asking him if he could import the goods in a neutral vessel, and whether such a vessel would be admitted to an entry on application being made; and that he told Unger he thought there would be no difficulty if it were a regular vessel," &c.

It is stated by Samuel Bartlett, (who proves to have been the owner of the Union, on the 14th of October, 1814, the date of the alleged bill of sale to Unger,) that, in the month of October, 1814, Unger informed him that he was a naturalized and Swedish subject, and had, with other neutrals, a large quantity of goods at Castine, then in the possession of the British, which he wished to ship into the United States; and applied to him to go to Hampden, in order to learn, from the collector, whether he felt himself authorized, by the laws of the United States, to enter goods in a neutral vessel with consular papers at Hampden; that he went accordingly, and Mr. Hook, the collector, being absent, Mr. Tibbet, his deputy, informed him that he would enter all goods which came in that way, and thought there would be no kind of difficulty in so doing; that he observed, that he wished Tibbet to be sure he was right, for it was of great importance to his employer; that he returned immediately to Castine, and gave information to Unger of Tibbet's answer, and Unger a few days after sent the sloop Christina to Orrington," &c.

It is stated by Joseph Lee, "that, in the months of November and December, 1814, he was employed by Unger, master and owner of the Swedish sloop Christina, to do the necessary writing, &c.; that he prepared the master's manifests and owner's entry of several cargoes of foreign goods, which were shipped on board of the said sloop at Orrington and Buckstown, and imported into and delivered at Hampden and Frankfort; that he was knowing to Unger's purchasing large quantities of foreign goods of British merchants at St. John's and Halifax, which were transported to Orrington, and imported and delivered at Hampden; and that he verily believed that Unger was, what he said he was, a native of Bohemia, and a naturalized Swede; that John Nyman was a native Swede; and that Constantino Lefrio was a native Spaniard."

It is stated by Edward W. Bradshaw, "that, in the month of November, 1814, while acting as Swedish vice-consul, under the authority of Richard Soderstrom, Esq., he went to Hampden, in the county of Hancock, in the district of Maine, for the purpose of examining the papers of the Swedish sloop Christina, whereof Unger was master and owner; on examination he found her papers to be original ones, and that Captain Unger was entitled to all the privileges of a natural-

ized citizen of Sweden; that he could not say where he was born, but believed he was born in Denmark, and had a Swedish burgher's brief."

It is stated, generally in the thirteen manifests of the successive cargoes imported in the sloop Christina from Orrington to Hampden and Frankfort, that Peter W. Unger is master and owner of the vessel, and that he is a burgher of St. Bartholomew.

Upon the evidence thus recited, in relation to the owner of the vessel, it appears that, on the 14th of October, 1814, the alleged Swedish sloop Christina, owned by Unger, a naturalized Swede, was the American licensed sloop Union, owned by Samuel Bartlett and another person, citizens of the United States; that Unger (as Judge Story says) had been for several years domiciled in the United States; but that, on the 14th of October, 1814, with a view to the transportation of goods from Orrington to Hampden, the vessel assumed a neutral flag, and Unger obtained a certificate and pass from the Swedish consul, recognising him as a naturalized Swede.

2d.—*As to the owners of the goods imported.*

It appears from the thirteen manifests which have been already referred to, that all the goods imported in the Christina were entered at Hampden from Orrington, between the 29th of October and the 22d of December, 1814, both days inclusive; that the only shippers of the goods were W. P. Unger, S. J. M. Peillon, John Lyman, and Lefrio, and that the goods were consigned to order, to Unger, to Nyman, to Lefrio, to Herrick, and to Crosby, respectively. The only bill of sale exhibited with the petition, purports to be one from John Nyman to Mr. Arthur Tappan, dated Hampden, the 3d of December, 1814, for goods to the amount of $58,962 70. It is stated that the goods had been bought by Nyman of "James Chapman, on the 13th of November, 1814;" that "the advance was twenty per cent., it being understood that the said Tappan is to pay the duties on the above goods when they become due;" and it concludes with a receipt in these words: "December 5. Received payment, by draft, on John Tappan, of Boston, payable in sixty days from date. John Nyman." The signature to the receipt is the subject of a deposition by Timothy Rogers, who says, "that he has seen the said Nyman write his name, and had no doubt but that the signature of John Nyman to the annexed bill of sale to Anthony Tappan, dated December 3, 1814, &c., is the proper handwriting of the said Nyman, and that the deponent spoke of this fact as from his best recollection, having never seen Nyman write but once."

The real ownership of the great quantity of goods imported, appears, therefore, to be referred, without explanation, by the petitioners to Unger, to Nyman, to Lefrio, and to Peillon.

Of Unger, and his competency to be owner of a great portion of the goods, the facts already stated are all that can be traced.

Of Nyman, and of his competency to be the owner of a great portion of the goods, it is stated by Timothy Rogers, "that John Nyman arrived at Gloucester in May, 1814, master of the schooner Magdalena, and applied to the deponent to enter his vessel, and to transact his business. That the vessel and cargo, from papers, appeared to be the property of Nyman, and the cargo was consigned to the deponent, as his agent or commission merchant. That the deponent followed his instructions in the management and disposal of it; and that he acted, in all respects, as owner, the deponent knowing no one else as owner." The manifest of the Magdalena's cargo is exhibited. It is further stated by John S. Trott, that Nyman is a Swede, a man of integrity and credit in trade; and Mr. Soderstrom, the Consul General of Sweden, as well as Mr. Blagge, the Swedish Consul for Massachusetts, states that Nyman is a Swede.

Of Lefrio, and his competency to be the owner of the goods imported in his name, all that occurs is a statement by Joseph Lee, that Lefrio is a Spaniard, and that it appears by the invoices that he was an owner of some of the goods.

Of Peillon there is no trace in the documents accompanying the petition, except his name occurs in the manifests. Peillon has, however, filed a petition for a remission of the forfeiture incurred, in which he claims a part of the goods in his own right as a neutral Frenchman, and admits that his goods were transported from Castine to Orrington by land, alleging such course to have been necessary, in order to avoid the British blockade.

3d.—*As to the course of the trade.*

It is sometimes alleged that the goods were purchased in Halifax, and sometimes that they were purchased at Castine; but how or when they were deposited at Orrington, does not appear upon the documents accompanying the petition; nor, indeed, did the fact appear (as Judge Story states) in the evidence before the circuit court.

To these general views of the case it is proper to add that, on the 25th October, 1814, four days previously to the first entry of the Christina at Hampden, a letter was written to Josiah Hook, by John Tappan, agent, and Edmund Munroe, agent, in which they inquire as follows: "We are desired to ascertain from you if a neutral vessel, with neutral papers, and with a cargo owned by a neutral subject, will be admitted to an entry in the district of Penobscot, say in Hampden or Bangor, if such a one should arrive without a clearance," &c. Mr. Hook answered that "he would admit a vessel to an entry, of the description mentioned, at either Hampden or Bangor, and that he should afford every facility that the law would authorize to encourage fair trade." An application was also made by Mr. Tappan to Mr. Blake, the district attorney, for an opinion on the legality of the course contemplated by the above inquiry. Mr. Blake's answer branches into a number of points, but, in substance, it confirms the opinion given by Mr. Hook.

For whom Messrs. Tappan and Munroe acted as agents, in their application to the collector and district attorney, does not appear. Mr. Tibbet states that "he does not know whether any part of the goods was the property of Mr. Unger, nor does he know to whom the said goods did belong. That the duties were secured, and is part paid by Thomas W. Storrow, of Boston, John Crosby, jun., of Hampden, and Hartwell Williams, of Augusta, all of them American citizens. That he does not know by whom the goods were transported to Boston, but that the certificates intended to accompany them were delivered by him to Mr. Storrow.

Having thus examined the documents accompanying the petition, without referring, except generally, to the contemporaneous information received at the Treasury Department, it is proper to bring into view the material allegations of the petitioners in point of fact, (not already brought into view by the foregoing statement,) that they may be compared with the evidence. They are the following:

1. That the petitioners were, respectively, purchasers of goods imported into the *district* of Penobscot, since the 1st of October, 1814, by *divers* persons, subjects of Powers in amity with the United States, being neutrals, not domiciliated in the United States, nor in the United Kingdom of Great Britain and Ireland, nor in any of the colonies, provinces, dependencies, or possessions thereof.

2. That, after the repeal of the non-importation and non-intercourse laws, goods were imported by neutrals from British possessions into the district of Passamaquoddy, were admitted to an entry, and there sold to American merchants, without prohibition, seizure, or detention; and, after the capture of Eastport, the custom-house was removed to Lubec, where similar entries and sales were allowed.

3. That the collector of Penobscot, or his deputy, "on application being made by sundry neutral merchants," to ascertain whether *goods* of British manufacture, but the property of neutrals, could be admitted to entry at Hampden, as well from Castine as from other places in the actual possession of the British, answered in the affirmative; and, in consequence thereof, such importations were made.

4. That thereupon the petitioners purchased, bona fide, a considerable quantity of the goods so imported, after they were entered and landed, at an advance, and paid for them, at the *terms* of purchase, by drafts and bills on different *places* abroad, and in the United States.

5. That, on the trial of the libel in the district court, it was admitted on the part of the United States, and of the officer who made the seizure, that, at the time of the importation, the goods were the property of neutral subjects, not domiciled in the United States, nor in any of the British dominions, and were imported in a vessel admitted by the collector to be a neutral vessel.

6. That Orrington was deemed by the collector either a British possession, from which neutrals might trade to the United States, or a place at which the goods might be landed, as in a case

of necessity, under the twenty-seventh section of the collection law, (vol. 4,) without incurring the penalties and forfeitures of the act interdicting to neutrals a participation in the coasting trade of the United States.

Upon the whole, the question recurs, 1st. Whether the petitioners are the bona fide owners of the goods claimed, and became so in a lawful manner? And, 2d. Whether the importation and entry of the goods at Hampden were, under all circumstances, lawful?

The consideration of these questions is submitted, respectfully, to the Committee of Ways and Means, upon the following propositions:

1. That if the vessel, master, and other persons employed were, in fact, neutral, and not the instruments of a contrivance, to evade the law of war, as well as the municipal law; and if the goods, when landed and entered at Hampden, were, bona fide, the property of neutrals, and not the property of an enemy, or of citizens having purchased them from the enemy, the first question may be answered in the affirmative. But if there be a doubt upon the subject, the petitioners may be allowed time to produce further evidence before Congress, or they may be referred to the decision on the trial, which has been ordered at the bar of the circuit court.

2. That, if the first question be answered in the affirmative, the legal answer to the second question, arising upon the strict law of the case, may be superseded by an exercise of the legislative authority. It will then be unnecessary to decide upon the lawfulness of establishing a port of entry at Hampden; and upon the lawfulness of the importation and deposite of the goods at Orrington; and upon the unlawfulness of the trade between Hampden and Orrington, upon the waters of the United States, under a neutral flag, and with an unlicensed vessel.

I have the honor to be, &c.

              A. J. DALLAS.

Hon. WM. LOWNDES,
   Chairman Com. Ways and Means.

UNSETTLED BALANCES.

[Communicated to the House, April 24, 1816.]

Mr. HUGER, from the committee appointed by a resolution of the 27th February last, to examine generally into the subject of unsettled balances, submitted the following report:

At an early period after their appointment the committee proceeded to turn their attention to the subject submitted to them. Although prepared to meet many difficulties, in the proposed investigation of unsettled balances, they had by no means anticipated that these difficulties would have been so serious, or to the extent they have experienced. They found themselves advancing into a labyrinth, the intricacies of which increased at every step they progressed. Little versed in the laws under which they were established, and

still less in the rules, regulations, and modes of proceeding adopted by the different departments, it became necessary that they should, in the first instance, endeavor to obtain some information on these points; and having no particular clue to guide them in making an investigation, the labor, zeal, and attention they were able to devote to this or that particular object of research not unfrequently turned out to have been unnecessary, or of little or no avail. The want of time, arising from their other official duties, the fast approaching period of the adjournment, and more than all, the measure wisely adopted by the House, of appointing distinct standing committees to examine hereafter into each respective department, have therefore induced the committee to suspend, at least for the present session, any further attempt to investigate the details of particular balances, and rather to confine themselves to a general view of the subject of the causes which have given rise to so many unsettled balances, and of the provisions which presented themselves as likely to remedy, or at least check the evil, and which it might be deemed expedient to submit to the consideration of the House.

It will be recollected that, at its commencement and first establishment under the new Constitution, large and extensive powers and duties devolved upon the General Government, which had been previously vested in the several States. They had, of course, to enter upon a wide and unexplored field of action, and wise and efficient as the regulations and measures adopted for the collection of the revenue in the first instance no doubt were, it was impossible to anticipate all the difficulties or mal-practices which would necessarily arise under an administration of the affairs of this growing country, co extensive with the Union. Hence, various inconveniences were, in progress of time, experienced, and among others unsettled balances and defalcations in other branches of the public revenue, but more especially among the collectors, and in the customs, began at an early period to be experienced and complained of. Occasional checks and amendments were devised and adopted, as experience showed the necessity of them; but it is believed that there is great room for improvement, and that a general revisal of the organization of the several departments in regard to the management of their fiscal concerns, with additional checks in the collection and expenditures of the public moneys, is most desirable and requisite. On the propriety, therefore, of offering a resolution directing the Secretary of the Treasury to prepare and submit at the next session of Congress some such general and improved system, the committee feel confident that they are supported by the opinion of all those connected or acquainted with the actual state of the several departments.

In the meantime they feel authorized, not only by what has fallen under their own observation, but by the concurrent approbation of all those whom they have consulted, and in particular by that of the Comptroller, and of the Secretary of State himself, to recommend that provision be

Unsettled Balances.

immediately made for establishing the office of accountant in the Department of State. The business of that, as well as of most other of the departments, has greatly increased within a few years, and is likely to continue to increase. There is, moreover, a great mass of unsettled accounts in the Department of State; nor is it easy to anticipate, under the present organization, when they can be finally acted upon and settled. Its transactions embrace a wide and most extensive field, and it is impossible that the high officer of this branch of the Government, upon whom the whole burden now devolves, can pay the proper and requisite attention to all the little minutiæ of the office, and to the increased, increasing, and various pecuniary transactions with agents in every habitable country with which the United States have had, or may have, intercourse or political relations. To all who have attended to the subject the necessity is, indeed, evident; for, having such a subordinate officer, whose immediate duty it will be to bring up the business at this time so much in arrear, to retain precedents, and thereby establish greater system and uniformity in the final adjustment of different accounts, and to bring all those who have transacted or may hereafter transact business, and have accounts with the Department, to frequent and regular settlements. On the other hand, it would seem not less expedient to oblige all foreign Ministers and public agents to send in a regular and semi-annual account current, with the usual and necessary vouchers of all their money transactions with and on account of the Government. This appears to have been heretofore left very much to the individual himself to do or not, as he judged proper; and instances are not wanting of those in high and responsible situations who have never furnished any account whatever of their expenditure, or of the moneys which have passed through their hands. From these considerations, the committee have deemed it incumbent on them to report a bill for the establishment of the office of accountant, and directing regular accounts to be rendered by foreign Ministers and agents, which, if time permit the House to act upon during the present session, it is believed will save the United States many thousand dollars.

With respect to the unsettled balances, (the subject more immediately submitted to their consideration,) which are, by law, annually submitted to the House and published, they may be divided into three separate and distinct classes, viz:

1st. Balances of a doubtful or equitable nature.

2d. Balances on accounts not finally liquidated or acted upon.

3d. Balances liquidated, acted upon, and evidently due to the United States.

The first class includes such of the balances as the departments may not have been able, under existing laws and circumstances, or have felt a difficulty, and perhaps even a delicacy, in acting finally upon. These are not very numerous, but they relate, in several instances, to characters and persons who have held the highest offices under the Government; some of them are, moreover, of long standing, and not likely ever to be finally adjusted under the existing state of things. It appears therefore to the committee, both expedient and desirable that some mode should be adopted for disposing of them, or some tribunal established which might pass them in review, and decide finally upon them, or report them, with their opinions in each respective case, to the House for their further examination and ultimate decision in regard to them.

The second class embraces that description of balances which appears upon accounts, from whatever cause, not finally settled at the several departments. This sometimes happens in cases where further time is allowed for procuring vouchers, or bringing forward additional charges or pretensions to which the individual believes himself, or affects to be entitled. On other occasions unsettled balances are published in obedience to the laws, where the accounts are still in a course of liquidation, and where there is, in fact, no balance actually due, but the balance published as such is what appears to be due at the end of three years on the face of the account, and as far as it has been liquidated. In some instances, it would seem that unliquidated and unsettled balances are published, in cases even where the individual has been ready and prepared to settle finally his accounts, but for want of time, or from doubts in regard to some undecided points, or from some other cause, proceeding not from him, but the Department, a final settlement has not taken place.

The necessary publication of some of these unsettled balances, in the manner pointed out by the existing provisions of the law, is perhaps to be regretted; for, whilst defaulters and those guilty of peculation deserve to be thus published and made known, it tends greatly to diminish the odium and contempt which they would experience, that their names should be coupled to, and appear with, those who are less culpable, or perhaps in nowise defaulters. Nor can it fail to be peculiarly painful and aggravating to the feelings of honest and honorable men to find themselves in such company, and held up to the public under at least the appearance of having committed like frauds upon the Government.

It would seem, indeed, that no account ought to remain unliquidated and unsettled after a lapse of three years. Yet as this may, and has happened, the committee are of opinion that the Comptroller ought to have the discretionary power of distinguishing cases of this kind, as well as those which fall under the first class, from the general mass of unsettled balances, and to present them in a separate and special report, stating the circumstances of each, and the course, where necessary, he would recommend to be pursued in regard to them.

It might, perhaps, be likewise proper to render it a part of the duty of the several departments to keep a regular annual account in the name of each and all of the salary officers, and of any other persons, whose accounts might at all times be satisfactorily stated without recourse to the indi-

Unsettled Balances.

vidual for vouchers. And it seems evidently proper, on the other hand, that each and every person having money transactions with the Government should be bound to render at least semi-annual accounts, and, where possible, to make an annual settlement in full of all receipts and expenditures of public moneys which have passed through their hands, or under their management.

To the third, last, and most important class of unsettled balances, belong those of all real defaulters, who either acknowledge themselves to be such, or are found to be so upon a final settlement of their accounts. It is much to be regretted that this class of defaulters should be so numerous, and in some instances for considerable sums; nor is it less to be regretted that the names are found among them of persons of high standing and consideration in society.

The committee, although for reasons already mentioned they have declined entering into a strict and detailed examination of the accounts of each individual, or bringing any of them forward at the present time, have devoted considerable attention to, and taken into serious consideration, this class of cases, with a view of devising means to lessen the number already existing, and prevent, as far as possible, if not altogether, the recurrence of them in time to come. A hope that the greater experience, and better practical information of the Secretary of the Treasury would enable him to come to their aid in promoting these desirable objects is, likewise, one of their principal inducements for recommending a call upon him to submit a new and revised financial system to Congress at their next session; and, though they are aware that the advanced period of the present session will necessarily prevent any measure on the subject from being brought to maturity at this time, yet the committee deem it not amiss to suggest, for the consideration of the House, the following provisions as likely to contribute, in some degree, to prevent such large defalcations in the future receipts and expenditure of the public revenues as are found on the face of many of the unsettled balances. In this view the committee respectfully propose:

That the Comptroller and Secretary of the Treasury be authorized to review and examine such cases of doubt, equity, or difficulty, in regard to the unsettled balances, as fall under the description of the first or second class specified in this report, and to dispose of them, either by adopting some equitable mode of bringing them to a final settlement, or by specially reporting them, with their opinions in regard to each particular case, to the House, for their further examination and ultimate decision in regard to them.

That the district attorneys, or others, employed on behalf of the United States, be required to make an annual and detailed report to the Comptroller, by him to be laid before Congress, of their proceedings in regard to public defaulters, in their respective districts.

That the Heads of the several Departments be required to specify, in their annual reports to Congress, the names of the persons to whom ad-

vances of the public moneys, or with whom contracts have been made, the amount of the sums advanced, and the objects for which they were advanced; also, the names of their sureties, and the amount for which the several sureties are respectively liable.

That all collectors of the customs, and all other receivers of the taxes, duties, or other public moneys whatsoever, be required to pay over weekly, or as frequently as the Secretary of the Treasury may direct, to the Bank (or branch bank) of the United States, when established and in operation, or to such other bank in the town or neighborhood in which they reside, as the Secretary of the Treasury may fix on or approve of, all moneys which they may have collected or received; provided, in the opinion of the Secretary of the Treasury, their vicinity to such bank, and other circumstances, render it convenient and proper to be done.

That all persons whatever, having pecuniary transactions with the Government, be bound to furnish quarterly, or at least semi-annual accounts, and, where the nature of the case permits, be brought to an annual settlement in full.

That all balances found on settlement to be due the Government, which are not paid up in the course of three months, be forthwith, and without favor or distinction, put into suit; leaving to the Comptroller, however, the authority to make such exceptions to the general rule as he may, in his discretion, deem necessary and expedient; but, in every case where the suit is postponed the Comptroller shall report, at the next session of Congress, the inducements to, and reasons for, such postponement.

That all judgments obtained against defaulters be rigidly enforced, unless otherwise directed by the Comptroller, who shall report, at the ensuing session of Congress, all such cases, and the reasons for granting further indulgence.

That no defaulter, against whom a balance upon settlement of his accounts may be found, be qualified to receive an appointment to any office of trust or profit under the United States, or to obtain any contract from the Government, until such balance be paid up and finally settled.

That the pay and emoluments of all public officers and agents, as far as it can constitutionally be done, be retained and appropriated to the discharge of any balance found upon settlement to be due by them, until such balances be finally paid and satisfied.

The committee further submit, and recommend for the adoption of the House, the bill accompanying this report, to establish the office of Accountant in the Department of State, together with the following resolution:

Resolved, That the Secretary of the Treasury be required, and he is hereby directed, to report, at an early period of the next session, whether any, and, if any, what modifications or amendments may be advisable in the present organization of the several Departments, and especially in regard to their pecuniary concerns; and to submit such general plan or revised system for

Unsettled Balances.

their future regulation and management, as may in his opinion, be likely to promote economy, and responsibility in the receipt and expenditure of the public moneys, despatch in the public business, and the public interest in general.

HOUSE OF REPRESENTATIVES,
March 9, 1816.

SIR: I am directed by the committee appointed to "examine generally into the subject of unsettled balances due the United States," to communicate for your consideration certain points or matters, concerning which they wish to receive information in detail, and to request that you will return as early and as full an answer, in regard to each of them, as circumstances may permit. The most prominent of these are as follows:

How, and with what checks, are accounts received and settled at the respective Departments?

What are the nature and description of the accounts in particular received from the Department of State, and what are the conditions and regulations governing their settlement?

Are there any defects in the laws establishing the respective Departments, in relation to the mode of adjusting and settling their accounts respectively; and, if there be any such defects, what provisions suggest themselves by way of remedy?

In the settlement of accounts is priority given at pleasure; or, are they taken up in rotation, and according to certain fixed rules?

Is the period, at which ascertained balances are sued, fixed; or, is there any rule, or principle, according to which all unsettled balances are indiscriminately sued; or are suits directed and postponed, at pleasure, by the Comptroller? In the latter case upon what principles are suits upon ascertained balances commenced or deferred?

To what are the large outstanding balances to be principally or generally attributed?

Do any further checks, penalties, or changes in the management of the several Departments suggest themselves as likely to remedy, or at least lessen, the evils complained of, in regard to such numerous and large unsettled balances, or to facilitate and render more speedy and easy the settlement of accounts in all or either of the Departments?

Are the officers receiving salaries, the agents of, and contractors with the Government, obliged by any law or penalty to render in their accounts quarterly, annually, or at any specified period; or do they render them in at pleasure?

Are the same unsettled balances, which appear on the first or any subsequent annual report, continued to be published in each subsequent annual report, unless finally settled?

It has been complained of that officers and other persons, having accounts to settle with the several Departments, are frequently delayed, sometimes detained at the Seat of Government an unreasonable length of time, at an enormous and ruinous expense. If these complaints be not altogether groundless, does this detention arise from the want of clerks, &c.; or does any mode suggest itself, which would secure a greater facility, and an earlier examination and settlement of their accounts to persons so attending at the Seat of Government?

Is there any other mode of recovering balances due the United States than by suit at law, or any penalty attached by law or custom to defaulters? For example: when considerable balances appear due by individuals for three years and upwards, is it customary, or anything like a fixed principle, to suspend them from farther public agencies, or to refuse to make further contracts with them?

In general, any information or suggestion which may be deemed useful, or likely to throw light on this subject, either as to the past, or in relation to measures hereafter to be recommended, is requested.

With sentiments of great respect, &c.,
BENJAMIN HUGER, *Chairman.*

Jos. ANDERSON, Esq.,
Comptroller of the Treasury.

TREASURY DEPARTMENT,
Comptroller's Office, March 14, 1816.

SIR: Your letter, dated the 9th instant, as chairman of the committee appointed to "examine generally into the subject of unsettled balances due the United States," I had the honor to receive upon the 11th, and I take leave to present my answers to your several questions in the order following:

"How, and with what checks, are accounts received and settled at the offices of the respective Departments?"

"What are the nature and description of the accounts in particular received from the Department of State, and what are the conditions and regulations governing their settlement?"

At the Treasury Department, accounts which exclusively belong thereto are received by the Comptroller, the Auditor, Commissioner of the Land Office, and Commissioner of the Revenue; all of which, except those belonging to the Land Office, are placed in possession of the Auditor, who states them, and examines and reports them to the Comptroller, who revises and finally decides upon them. The accounts received by the Commissioner of the General Land Office are such only as properly appertain to that department of the Treasury; and they are stated and examined by that officer in the manner accounts are stated and examined by the Auditor, and are reported to the Comptroller, who finally decides upon them. When these accounts are thus acted upon by the Comptroller, they are sent to the office of the Register of the Treasury to be recorded, and the accounts remain under the care of the Register of the Treasury. This mode of settlement comprehends all the checks that belong to the whole accounts of the Treasury Department.

Unsettled Balances.

Department of State. The accounts received from the Department of State, by the accounting officers of the Treasury, are those of Ministers, Consuls, special agents, messengers, and generally all such as relate to foreign intercourse, and other pecuniary concerns of that Department. Since the year 1801, the settlement of these accounts, agreeably to an arrangement then made by the Comptroller, has devolved upon the accounting officers of the Treasury, under the direction of the Secretary of State; that is, the Secretary of State states the nature and time of service of the persons employed, the allowance to be made for contingent and other expenses, and, in cases where the law is silent, the compensation to be received. All the requisite information being possessed by the Secretary, he decides on the principles of settlement, and the officers of the Treasury have little more to do than to arrange and give form to the account, to make the necessary calculations, and to see that the party is charged with all advances or payments on account ascertained to have been made to him.

The accounts of the War and Navy Departments are (or should be) rendered by their respective agents, contractors, &c., according to forms and rules prescribed by the accountants of those Departments: when received, they are settled without any immediate check. The sums admitted to the credit of individuals for supplies, services, &c., are entered in the accountants' books to the debit of the general account of expenditure to which they belong; each of these general accounts is closed at the end of the quarter by passing its amount to the debit of the United States, and they, of course, form the debtor side of the quarterly account which the accountant transmits, with all his settlements and vouchers, for revision at the Treasury. If any errors are discovered, the accountant is advised of them, in order that he may make the necessary corrections in his book, and hold the parties accountable. In the revision, thus made, consists nearly all the control which the accounting officers of the Treasury possess over the accounts of those Departments.

It may be proper to observe that, whenever an account is settled by either of the accountants of the War or Navy Department, and a balance is found due from the United States, a warrant is issued by the Secretary of the Department, countersigned by the accountant, and the money received by the party. Many items are admitted in the accounts, under rules, regulations, and ordinances of the Departments, over which the accounting officers of the Treasury do not consider themselves as having any control; and, when it is considered what a length of time must necessarily elapse, in consequence of the immense accumulation of accounts which now have to pass the accounting officers of the Treasury, before any control can be exercised, the effects of its utility must be very limited.

"In the settlement of accounts is priority given at pleasure; or are they taken up in rotation, and according to certain fixed rules?"

At the Treasury there are no fixed rules as to the time of taking up accounts for settlement. They are, however, generally taken up according to the time at which they are rendered; and, if the necessary vouchers accompany them, they are finally acted upon. If vouchers be wanting the party is advised thereof by letter, and the account suspended until the vouchers be supplied; though it is sometimes found necessary to settle the account, as far as the vouchers furnished will enable the accounting officers to do so, and suspend the items, not vouched, until vouchers are supplied.

"Is the period at which ascertained balances are sued, fixed; or is there any rule or principle according to which all unsettled balances are indiscriminately sued; or are suits directed and postponed at pleasure by the Comptroller? In the latter case, upon what principles are suits upon ascertained balances commenced or deferred?"

There is no period fixed at which ascertained balances are sued for; sometimes suits are instituted immediately upon the balance being ascertained, according to what may be the circumstance of the case. In important cases the Secretary of the Treasury is always consulted. In minor cases the Comptroller has heretofore been governed by his sound discretion, which has been regulated by the advice and information of the several district attorneys of the United States within whose district the debtors might reside. This mode has been deemed expedient, because more correct and proper information was to be expected from them than could be had by any other means; but information has been sought and sometimes obtained through other channels, and in many cases we have not been able to find out where the debtor lives; this is one reason why a number of suits have not been brought against defaulters. Suits are sometimes continued upon the special recommendation of the district attorneys, with a view of obtaining better security where the debt is doubtful; and, upon that condition, allowing further time for payment, and upon some occasions where the debt is secure, and the vigorous prosecution of the suit would ruin the party, indulgence is given.

"To what are the large outstanding balances to be generally or principally attributed?"

By a law passed on the 3d day of March, 1809, it is made the duty of the Comptroller to lay an annual statement before Congress of the accounts in the Treasury, War, and Navy Departments, which may have remained more than three years unsettled, or on which balances appear to have been due more than three years prior to the 30th of September then last past. In consequence of this law all the balances found due, according to its provisions, were reported, and the names of the persons upon the annual list which have been submitted, have all been retained on the respective reports, the Comptroller not conceiving himself authorized to discontinue the names of any person, except in case where the accounts have been paid, or finally settled,

Unsettled Balances.

which have been but few. The increase of these annual lists may be attributed to the delays of persons claiming credits, furnishing the necessary vouchers to establish such credits as will be seen in numerous cases remarked on the list of balances; to the tediousness of the legal proceedings, to returns of balances against officers of the Government for moneys advanced, many of whom reside abroad, and whose accounts are unavoidably continued open for more than three years.

It is, however, believed that, in many cases, nothing is really and justly due from those apparent debtors, some of whom were salary officers who have not rendered their accounts, and have been charged with the money they have received upon drafts made on account of salary.

"Are the officers receiving salaries the agents of, and contractors with, the Government, obliged, by any law, or under any penalty, to render in their accounts quarterly, annually, or at any specified period, or do they render them in at pleasure?"

The several laws, which establish the salaries of the officers of Government, authorized the compensation to be paid at the Treasury of the United States in quarterly payments; and although there is no positive law which obliges any salary officer to render his account quarterly, or at any particular period, the law, making the salary payable quarterly, implies that the account ought to be rendered accordingly, and this, I learn, has been the constant understanding at the Treasury since its organization. The salary officers at the Seat of Government render accounts quarter yearly for themselves, and the agents of salary officers render quarterly accounts for them. On the adjustment of which accounts, by the accounting officers of the Treasury, the amount found due is passed to the credit of the party, and a warrant is drawn on the Treasurer of the United States, and the warrant itself is debited to the officer in whose favor it was issued.

Officers who have an annual salary, and, in addition thereto, receive fees, perquisites, and emoluments, render their salary accounts quarterly with their accounts of fees, perquisites, emoluments, and expenditures; collectors of the customs quarterly, under a penalty of $1,000, to be recovered by suit; and collectors, naval officers, and surveyors, render their accounts of emoluments and expenditures annually under a penalty of $500. Collectors of direct taxes and internal duties render their accounts quarterly under the forfeiture of their official bond, and judgment to be entered thereon at the return term, on motion in open court by the attorney. From the recent establishment of the internal duties no penalty has yet occurred. The Receivers of Public Moneys, on the sale of lands, are required, by law, to render their accounts quarterly.

The agents of the United States render their accounts quarterly, such as agents of the marine hospitals, for the payments of invalid pensioners, light-houses, &c.

The contractors with Government render their accounts agreeably to the time and terms specified in their respective contracts, or according to the rules and regulations which may be established in the different offices where the contracts are made.

"It has been complained of that officers and other persons having accounts to settle with the several Departments are frequently delayed, and sometimes detained at the Seat of Government an unreasonable length of time at an enormous and ruinous expense. If these complaints be not altogether groundless, does this detention arise from the want of clerks, &c., or does any mode suggest itself which would secure a greater facility and an earlier examination and settlement of their accounts to persons so attending at the Seat of Government?"

I am warranted in stating that, as a general rule, no officer nor other person, having accounts to settle at the Treasury Department, who have personally attended, with proper vouchers, have been detained longer than was absolutely necessary for their accounts to be fairly examined, and pass the usual forms of settlement.

The accounts of the principal assessors have not been acted upon as promptly as other accounts. The several laws establishing the internal revenue, and the instructions given by the Secretary of the Treasury upon these laws, have both been so differently construed by the respective principal assessors, and their accounts differing considerably from the view entertained at this office of the allowance to which they are entitled, that more than usual time is required to examine them, and compare the several changes and respective statements which have been made, with the laws and instructions under which they acted. A number of these accounts have also been necessarily suspended for want of proper vouchers, the assessors advised thereof, and the defects stated according to the established practice of the office.

The accounts of the General Land Office are greatly in arrears; some of them remain unsettled from seven to ten years. These accounts are intricate, and generally very large; from ten to fifteen days is required for the best accounting clerks to examine one of them.

Additional clerks have been asked for by several of the Departments, as will be seen in the estimate which was presented to Congress by the Secretary of the Treasury.

"Is there any other mode of recovering balances due the United States than by suit at law, or any penalty attached by law or custom to defaulters? For example, when considerable balances appear due by individuals for three years and upwards, is it customary, or anything like a fixed principle, to suspend them from further public agencies, or to refuse to make further contracts with them until the old balances are settled up?"

The general mode is by suit; but summary process is authorized in the cases of collectors of direct tax and internal duties. The Comptroller of the Treasury is authorized, by law, immediately upon a delinquency happening in this case, to issue a warrant of distress against the delinquent collector and his sureties. When a public agent becomes a real defaulter, or where it appears that he is likely to become so to any considerable amount, the practice has been to remove him. Contracts are seldom or never made with defaulters who have old balances against them. I know of no law, however, upon this subject.

"Are there any defects in the laws establishing the respective Departments, and do any further checks, penalties, or changes in the management of the several Departments, suggest themselves as likely to remedy, or at least lessen the evils complained of in regard to such numerous and large unsettled balances, or to facilitate and render more speedy and easy the settlement of accounts in all or either of the Departments?"

The several questions here propounded embrace so extensive a field that I cannot, within the short time allowed by the call of the committee, answer them satisfactorily.

The honorable committee well know that, at the time the present system of accounting was formed, the revenue arising from the customs was very limited; there were no internal taxes. The Military Establishment was very small, and there was not then any Navy Department or General Land Office, and the Post Office accounts were comparatively few, and, of course, the accounts which had to pass the accounting officers of the Treasury were but few, and these small, in comparison with those which now have to pass the form of revision. I, therefore, conceive, from the immense increase of the business of the several Departments, that a considerable modification, and some extension of the present system of accounting would be required to facilitate the settlement of accounts, and to render the necessary checks in the several Departments more prompt and efficient.

To present a view commensurate to the object which appears to be contemplated by the committee, would require time and deliberation.

The Comptroller, therefore, respectfully suggests to the committee, whether their views could not be better attained by requiring some officer of the Government to prepare a report upon this subject, to be laid before Congress at an early day of their next session.

I am, with great respect, &c.
                    JOSEPH ANDERSON.
Hon. Benjamin Huger,
  Chairman Com. of Unsettled Balances.

COMPENSATION TO MINISTERS AND CONSULS.
—
[Communicated to the House, April 15, 1816.]
DEPARTMENT OF STATE, *April 5, 1816.*

Sir: I have had the honor to receive your letter of the 28th of March, with a copy of a resolution of the House of Representatives, instructing the Committee of Ways and Means to inquire into the expediency of increasing the annual allowance to the Ministers of the United States in foreign countries, and of allowing salaries to the Consuls of the United States in foreign ports, and requesting such information or opinion on the subject as I may be able to communicate.

Considering it my duty to communicate all the information in the possession of the Department, or within its reach, on any public subject before the House, which may be desired by the committee, I have to add that, in performing that duty, I shall always be happy to give, without reserve, such opinion as I may have formed on the subject.

On the first part of the resolution, relating to the expediency of increasing the compensation of our Ministers in foreign countries, there is but one opinion among all those who have had the best opportunities of acquiring correct information, which is, that the present allowance is altogether inadequate. In this opinion, especially in respect to the principal Courts, I fully concur. Representations to this effect having been made by several of our Ministers, I annex a copy of their communications on the subject; well satisfied I am that great losses have been sustained by those who remained any considerable time abroad.

The members of the diplomatic corps at the several Courts of Europe live much in the same style. Their household establishment, equipage, number of their servants, expenses in attending Court, of intercourse with each other, and of hospitality, are, in the most material circumstances, similar. The habits and propensities of particular members of the corps may increase these expenses considerably; but no degree of economy can reduce them below a certain grade. From the nature of our Government, something may be spared to our Ministers in what regards style or mere ostentatious display, but in nothing else. All the other heavy items are as applicable to them as to the Ministers of other Powers.

Presuming that a view of the compensation allowed by the Powers of Europe to their representatives at foreign Courts may serve to give an idea of the expense of living there in that character, I have annexed a statement of it, as far as it has come within my knowledge.

Having stated the facts which are essential in this case, it is not necessary, and might be improper, for me to communicate any opinion as to the degree of augmentation which ought to be made to the salaries of our Ministers in foreign countries. With a knowledge of the facts, every member of the committee is as competent to judge of the proper augmentation as I can be. The United States constitute a distinguished member of the great community of nations. Their citizens, favored by many important circumstances, particularly by the great excellence of their Government, enjoy in the highest degree all the blessings which can be derived from the social compact. It is our duty to perpetuate these blessings, and, with that view, to fortify

Compensation to Ministers and Consuls.

ourselves at every point where danger of any kind menaces. Is it necessary that the United States should be represented with foreign Powers? That has long ceased to be a question. Shall they maintain a proper station there. not assuming, but dignified, such as the general expectation and common opinion of mankind have given them? That has never been a question. The character of the country, if not its rank, is in some degree affected by that which is maintained by its Ministers abroad. Their utility in all the great objects of their mission is essentially dependent on it. A Minister can be useful only by filling his place with credit in the diplomatic corps, and in the corresponding circle of society in the country in which he resides, which is the best in every country. By taking the proper ground, if he possesses the necessary qualifications, and is furnished with adequate means, he will become acquainted with all that passes, and from the highest and most authentic sources. Inspiring confidence by reposing it in those who deserve it, and by an honorable deportment in other respects, he will have much influence, especially in what relates to his own country. Deprive him of the necessary means to sustain this ground, separate him from the circle to which he belongs, and he is reduced to a cipher. He may collect intelligence from adventurers and spies, but it will be of comparatively little value; and, in other respects, he had as well not be there.

On the other part of the resolution—the propriety of allowing salaries to our Consuls in foreign ports—I have to state that it is deemed advisable to make such allowance, limited, in the commencement, to certain countries, and to the metropolis of each. On several of the Governments of Europe our citizens have claims to a considerable amount still to settle. In many of the ports of each Power we have, almost at all times, destitute seamen, discharged either from our own merchant vessels, or from those of other nations into which they had entered. Neither of these interests will be duly attended to without a special agent, with an adequate compensation. A Consul is the fittest person to perform these duties; and, under the superintendence of the Minister, whose business is to settle principles, he may with propriety be charged with them. Our citizens have claims on Great Britain, France, Spain, Denmark, the Netherlands, Sweden, and Naples; and we have often destitute seamen in the ports of most of those countries, especially Great Britain. These duties must be executed with some department of their respective Governments near which our agents must reside. It is therefore proposed to allow salaries at this time to our Consuls at London, Paris, Madrid, Amsterdam, Copenhagen, and Stockholm, at which places the fees of office and profits of trade do not afford them a support. As special reasons operate in favor of the allowance to these places, it is thought advisable to confine it to them, without deciding, at this time, on the policy of a general change of the system. That turns on other considerations, many of which are

suggested in Mr. Crawford's letter. The duties which it is proposed to vest in these Consuls being of a general nature, and, in regard to seamen, coextensive with the European dominions of each Power, it may be useful to give to their consular functions a corresponding extent. Such an extension of the consular authority in an agent residing at the metropolis of the country to which he is appointed, and paid by his Government, would, it is presumed, be found advantageous to our commerce. It would certainly make them more adequate to the other duties which it is proposed to assign them. It may likewise be observed, in favor of the proposed allowance. that the experiment on this scale would afford useful light as to the policy of a general change of the system, when that subject is entered on.

I have the honor to be, with great respect, sir, your most obedient servant,

             JAMES MONROE.

Hon. WILLIAM LOWNDES,
    Chairman Committee Ways and Means.

Great Britain allows to an Ambassador—

At Paris	£10,000	
A house estimated at	1,000	
An outfit	5,000	
		£16,000
At Vienna, St. Petersburg, and Madrid	10,000	
In lieu of a house	1,000	
Outfit	5,000	
		16,000
At Constantinople and the Hague	9,000	
At the first a house is found		
At the Hague, an allowance of	1,000	
Outfit, half the salary	4,500	
		14,500
At Berlin and Lisbon	8,000	
A house	1,000	
Outfit	4,000	
		12,000
Envoy Extraordinary and Minister Plenipotentiary to the United States of America	6,000	
Outfit	3,000	
House	600	
		9,600
Naples, same as the United States. Stockholm, Munich, and Copenhagen, each	5,000	
Outfit, half the salary	2,500	
House	500	
		8,000

At Madrid, when I was there in 1805, the compensation to the French Ambassador was, I understood, a salary of 45,000 crowns; that to the Portuguese, 25,000.

It is understood that the salaries allowed by the Emperors of Russia and Austria, and by the King of Spain, are of the same grade; and that those of Prussia, Denmark, Sweden, and Holland, though lower than are given by the principal Powers, are higher than those given by the United States. A distinction is made between the salaries of Ambassadors and Envoys Extraordinary and Ministers Plenipotentiary; to the principal

Compensation to Ministers and Consuls.

Courts Ambassadors are, for the most part, sent by the great Powers, and not Envoys Extraordinary and Ministers Plenipotentiary.

WASHINGTON, *April* 5, 1816.

SIR: I have the honor to acknowledge the receipt of your letter of the 3d instant, enclosing the resolution of the House of Representatives, instructing the Committee of Ways and Means to inquire into the expediency of increasing the annual allowance of Ministers of the United States at foreign Courts, and allowing annual salaries to the Consuls of the United States at foreign ports. In reply to your request for the communication of such information on that subject as my late residence abroad will enable me to furnish, I have the honor to state that, from my own experience, I am convinced that a considerable increase to the present allowance to our Ministers at London and Paris is highly expedient. From every circumstance which has come to my knowledge, the Court of St. Petersburg ought to be embraced by the proposed measure. The enclosed extract of a letter from Mr. Erving will show the propriety of extending the measure to the Court of Spain.

Annexed is a statement of the salaries of foreign Ministers at the different Courts of Europe as far as they have come within my knowledge.

The propriety of allowing annual salaries to the Consuls of the United States presents a question of more difficult solution. At present, the inducement to seek the appointment of Consul is the advantage which it confers in the prosecution of foreign trade. American Consuls are generally able to enter into partnership with the most respectable mercantile houses in the ports where they reside, without bringing anything into the firm except those advantages. It is manifest, therefore, that the strongest temptation will be presented to render their official acts subservient to the commercial interests of their foreign partners. It is more than probable that many of the abuses which were known to exist during the late European war, in relation to American papers, and which were seized as the pretext for the unprincipled spoliations committed by the belligerents upon American commerce, originated from this source. This view of the subject presents some inducement to allow American Consuls annual salaries, and for prohibiting them from all participation in trade. But the salary must be considerable, or it will be no equivalent for the restriction which ought to be imposed upon them. The commerce of the United States is now prosecuted in almost every part of the world. The number of Consuls necessary for the protection of this commerce would, with competent salaries, involve a very great annual expense. To allow salaries to none but the Consuls of the capitals of each maritime State would not remove the evil, because, in many cases, the capital is not the principal trading city of the country; and even where it is, there are, in every case, other trading cities in the same State where abuses may be committed to the same extent. To reduce the number of Consuls, and to compel vessels, whether American or foreign, to have their papers authenticated by them, in order to obtain admittance into an American port, would present a temptation to foreign nations to make the same regulation with regard to American ports, which might give to the ports of one State an advantage over those of another; but this regulation would be no radical remedy of the evil intended to be removed. The prosecution of commerce under surreptitious papers is carried on most securely in ports which are not much frequented. It is generally carried on between the ports of foreign States, and not between foreign ports and those of the United States. These abuses will occur more extensively in time of European wars than in peace, and will not fail to produce great embarrassments to the fair and legitimate commerce of the United States.

There is, however, some reason to believe that the appointment of a Consul General to each of the principal commercial States, with a competent salary, invested with power to superintend the conduct of the other Consuls, and to make general regulations for their Government, subject to the sanction of the President, might be found beneficial. Residing at the capital, and carrying on an active correspondence with the different ports of the country, abuses would be more likely to be discovered and corrected than at present. If it shall be deemed expedient to give them annual salaries, a fund might be created by levying a small tonnage duty upon all American vessels which enter foreign ports. Where the duty collected in a port exceeds the salary, the surplus might be paid over to another Consul in the same State, where there was a deficiency.

This mode of compensation might be adopted, whether salaries are allowed or not; and there is but little doubt that it would be received as an equivalent for the right of carrying on trade. In this case, a minimum ought to be fixed. The surplus might be applied in aid of those whose emoluments were the most below that maximum.

I have the honor to be, &c.

WM. H. CRAWFORD.

Hon. JAMES MONROE, *Secr'y of State.*

Minister of France in the United States, 15,000 crowns.

The same to the third rate Powers in Europe.

To the secondary Powers in Europe, 25,000 crowns.

Ambassadors to the latter Courts, 50,000 crowns.

Ministers Plenipotentiary to the principal European Courts, viz: London, Vienna, St. Petersburg, and Constantinople, the same as Ambassadors at the secondary Court.

Under the Emperor, Ambassadors at the latter Courts were not limited in their expense.

English Ambassadors at Paris, £10,000.

English Ambassadors at Lisbon, £8,000.

Extract of a letter from George W. Erving to the Hon. William H. Crawford.

" The raising" of the salary there [St. Peters-

Compensation to Ministers and Consuls.

burg,] would, I presume, be very proper, whoever might go; the including London and Paris in this liberal arrangement may also be proper; but why do they exclude Madrid? It is true that nobody has made any noise about the dearness of living at Madrid, for nobody has been there for ten years but myself, and, before my time, raising salaries was never contemplated as possible. In a great many points of view, Madrid may be considered as the most important mission; it is at this time the most difficult and laborious, and has the greatest and most delicate responsibility belonging to it; ought it in that view to be placed on a footing with Holland, Naples, Sweden, and Brazil? As to expense, I would undertake to prove that it is at least twenty-five per cent. dearer than London or Paris. The causes of this difference are evident; almost everything of superior excellence must be brought from France or England; no one attempts to live upon what is to be found in Spain; from the nature of society there, the *corps diplomatique* is necessarily crowded in upon itself; it makes its own society. This occasions a perpetual round of diplomatic dinners and entertainments, which are not to be avoided; for the same reason, all foreigners of distinction who arrive there are in some sort, as at Constantinople, dependent upon their Ministers for society; they are regularly introduced to such member of the *corps diplomatique*, and must be as regularly invited, &c. These, to say nothing of the change of residence, augment the expenses of a Minister terribly; in fine, he cannot retire—he must be always *in evidence*; and the more splendid, because he has to compete as it were with the grandees. Add to all these solid considerations, that it is a place, in every view, of *mal-aisé*, and, as I have found it heretofore, it may be again a post of personal danger. I do not write to the Secretary of State or the President on this matter, because I have made a general rule of never pressing upon them money considerations.

From the Hon. H. Clay to the Secretary of State.
     WASHINGTON, *April, 5, 1816.*

SIR: I have the honor to acknowledge the receipt of your letter of the 3d instant.

During my residence in Europe, my place of abode was so frequently changed, and it having been, moreover, principally at provincial towns, that I am not able to furnish much information on the subject of your letter, derived from my own personal experience. I was in London rather more than three months, and, expensive as I had previously understood that city to be, I found it in that respect greatly exceeding all my anticipations: and yet I kept no house, and was certainly not extravagant in my personal expenses.

My opinion of the style in which an American Minister ought to live is, that avoiding the meanness which provokes ridicule, and the ostentation which challenges observation, it should be one of neat simplicity, regulated by the habits of society in the country where he resides, and admitting

of the return of civilities and the dispensation to our respectable countrymen of expected hospitality. I believe the present salary wholly inadequate to sustain the expenses of such a style of living at most, if not all, the foreign *Courts* at which we have Ministers.

I can communicate to you no information of the salaries allowed by other Powers to their Ministers at foreign Courts, nor as to the propriety of allowing salaries to our Consuls.

I am, sir, with great respect, &c.
                 H. CLAY.

The Hon. JAMES MONROE.

Extract of a letter from Mr Barlow to the Secretary of State, dated
         PARIS, *Nov. 21, 1811.*

I need not tell you how necessary it is to raise the salary if you do not mean either to ruin your Minister or injure your affairs. A man in this situation must either spend double his salary, or keep himself excluded entirely from society and from his duty. I naturally and habitually love simplicity, and have an aversion to luxury; but my duty requires that, in this respect, I should give up my own taste. I am determined, while I stay, to do my duty; and, to do this, I must spend at least fifteen (probably eighteen) thousand dollars a year. In this way I cannot stand it long, and you cannot expect to find many men in our country who are at once willing and able to do it, and who are fit for the place.

Pardon the frankness with which I speak on a subject on which I may appear more selfish than I really am, for I feel myself impelled to it by a sense of duty, and I am not without hopes that you will likewise feel it a part of your duty to use your influence to set this matter right.

Extracts from Mr. Adams's letters to the Secretary of State
         LONDON, *July 31, 1815.*

It is needless to say to you, or to any person having been in the same capacity here, that the annual salary of an American Minister is insufficient to support a man with a family—I say not in the style of high official rank, but in the decency becoming a private gentleman.

         SEPTEMBER 30, 1815.

An experience of the expense of living here for upwards of four months even under all the privations to which I have submitted, has confirmed me in the desire to be recalled as early in the Spring as the President may find it convenient to replace me, if, upon the construction of the law, the Legislature should refuse an appropriation for the outfit.

         JANUARY 9, 1816.

With every expedient of economy that I find possible, I am living at an expense which, at the end of two years from my arrival in this country, would more than absorb the whole salary for those two years, even with the allowance for the outfit.

A very few years' residence here must involve my own affairs beyond all power of redemption.

Extracts of a letter from Mr. Adams to the Secretary of State.

JANUARY 4, 1816.

It is very desirable that some general revision of the consular establishments should be made, and some regular system concerning them be sanctioned by law. For the port of London a provision for the compensation of the Consul must be made, or the office must be given to some wealthy merchant established in the city, to whom it may be acceptable for the facilities of business which he may derive from it. Colonel Aspinwall cannot hold it long without a salary, or without a commercial establishment connected with it, and upon which alone he must rely for support.

In one of his late letters to me, (a copy of which has been transmitted to you,) Mr. Beasley expresses the conviction that the provision made by the laws of the United States for the relief of indigent and destitute seamen in foreign ports is liable to great abuse. The late and present excessive numbers of persons claiming the benefit of it, both at London and Liverpool, afford confirmations of that opinion; but, on the other hand, it is obvious that, with the increase of our commerce and navigation, the casualties incident to them must have proportionably multiplied. The opportunities and the chances of imposition must also be much greater, and require more caution to be guarded against in England than in any other country; and I believe it will be uniformly found, in a time of general European peace, that the duty of affording relief to the objects of this class really entitled to it, and that of discriminating between them and the impostors who would prey upon the fund allotted to this honorable purpose, will be the most arduous and important obligation of an American Consul. * * * Mr. Bourne, the Consul at Amsterdam, has also lately written to me on the same subject, and complains of similar charges. His claims for particular compensation to himself for his long services there, have been often made known to the Government.

The direct commerce between the United States and the port of London is comparatively small. The number of American vessels which come to it is inconsiderable. The official emoluments from year's end to year's end will not pay office rent and the wages of a single clerk. If the support and and reconveyance to the United States of destitute seamen be made the duty of the Consul, some provision for the payment of the necessary expenses of this service must be made.

MILITIA CLAIMS.

[Communicated to the House, March 12, 1816.]

DEPARTMENT OF WAR, *March* 7, 1816.

SIR:. In obedience to the resolution of the House of Representatives of the 21st ultimo, I have the honor to transmit the enclosed documents.

In addition to the sum advanced to the State of Virginia by the Paymaster General, the sum of four hundred thousand dollars has been paid to that State, for expenses incurred by the employment of the militia in its defence. The claims of that State have been admitted on the ground that the Governor of Virginia was invested with discretionary power, by the War Department, to call forth the militia in such numbers as the emergency should require, and that the force actually employed was, at that time, not believed by the Secretary of War to be excessive. It is now believed that the number of militia kept in service, when compared with that called into the field by the President for the defence of Baltimore, against the same hostile force, which could be brought to act against the capital of Virginia from various points, was not beyond what the emergency required. The force here referred to, and the expense intended to be sanctioned, are those which the letter of the Commissioners, and the statement of the Adjutant General of that State, herewith enclosed, exhibit. The claims of North Carolina and Rhode Island have been sanctioned, because they are founded upon expenses actually incurred upon militia called out under the authority of the United States, or had received the sanction of that authority after they were called into service. The claims exhibited by Delaware and New Hampshire have been suspended until evidence shall be produced to show that the emergency was such as to require the service without waiting the intervention of the Executive authority of the Union.

The State of New York has exhibited claims for arms and ammunition furnished the militia, or captured by the enemy in our military depots; and also for additional pay allowed their militia when in the public service. The claims of Virginia embrace items of the former, and that of New Hampshire of the latter character. No decision has been made upon these claims; but it is believed that the powers of the Department do not extend to their liquidation and admission, without further legal provision for that purpose.

It is believed that no other State has presented any specific claim for money expended upon militia service during the war; but it is proper to state, that in the correspondence between the Governor of Massachusetts and the Secretary of War, it was distinctly declared, that reimbursement would not be made of any expenses incurred upon militia called into service by State authority, with the declared intention of excluding the authority of the United States over such militia force.

Time and reflection, so far from having changed the opinion then formed, have tended only to strengthen and confirm it. The several States have a right, in time of war, to raise and maintain regular troops: more strongly have they the right to employ their militia in military operations, where it can be done without infringing the rights of the National Executive over the same force. But it never can be admitted, that expenses incurred by raising and supporting regular troops can be a charge against the nation; and it is equally clear, that expenses incurred upon militia service, under State authority, with the declared intention of directing and controlling that force to the exclusion of the authority, can form no such charge. No claims of this nature will be recognised by the Executive branch of the Government, unless provision shall be made by law for that purpose.

I have the honor to be, your most obedient, and very humble servant,

WM. H. CRAWFORD.

Hon. Henry Clay, *Speaker.*

DEPARTMENT OF WAR,
Accountant's Office, Feb. 29, 1816.

Sir: I have the honor to state, in relation to the resolution of the honorable the House of Representatives directing the Secretary of War to lay before the House,

1st. A statement of the expenses incurred for the services of the militia called forth by authority of the United States during the late war.

2d. Statement of the accounts which have been exhibited, and claims which have been made, by the respective States for services rendered by the militia of said States, when called forth with or without such authority, together with the sums which have been paid, and the accounts and claims which have been allowed therefor, and in case the claims of any State or States have been rejected or allowed, to state the grounds of such rejection or allowance, designating for what services, and to what States respectively such sums have been paid, or accounts allowed, and designating also such items of claims as have been rejected in the cases where the calls were made by authority of the United States, and the grounds of such rejection.

That, in regard to the first clause of the resolution, the accounts of expenditures during the war have not been kept in a manner to designate what amount has been expended for militia, distinct from the regular army. According to the directions contained in the act of the 3d March, 1809, "further to amend the several acts for the establishment and regulation of the Treasury, War, and Navy Departments," accounts of expenditures are kept, under each specific appropriation made for militia, after the year 1812; the whole expenses of the Military Establishment, including militia, having been included in the same appropriation, the expenditures have been made, and the accounts kept correspondently with the appropriations.

As it regards the other sections of the resolutions, I have to state that claims have been exhibited to this office by the States of Pennsylvania, Virginia, and North Carolina, Delaware and New Hampshire.

The amount claimed by the State of Virginia is $1,029,319 95.

The amount claimed by the State of Pennsylvania is $268,556 82.

The amount claimed by the State of North Carolina is $56,513 29¼.

The amount claimed by the State of Delaware is $30,619 79.

The amount claimed by the State of New Hampshire is $64,552 20.

These claims have not yet been acted upon definitively in this office, that part which relates to services referring itself in the first instance to the Paymaster of the Army, whose duty it is to discharge all claims in relation to the pay of the militia, and thereafter report them to this office, which has not yet taken place. What portion of these claims have been sanctioned by proper authority can only be ascertained on settlement.

It is not recollected that any claims of the respective States have been presented at this office, which have been rejected or allowed, and consequently no information can be furnished by me, in relation to that part of the resolution.

I have the honor to be, very respectfully, sir, your obedient servant,

TOBIAS LEAR.

The Hon. W. H. CRAWFORD.

ARMY PAY OFFICE,
Washington City, Feb. 27, 1816.

The Paymaster of the Army, to whom has been referred the resolution passed in the House of Representatives on the 21st ultimo, has the honor to report:

That sufficient data to enable him to ascertain, with a due degree of precision, the amount of "expenses incurred for the services of the militia called forth, by authority of the United States, during the late war," are not within his reach.

That from the immethodical manner in which the services have, on some occasions, been performed, many claims doubtless exist that have not yet made their appearance in a *specific form ;* some detachments have been called *into* service and discharged therefrom without ever having been mustered, whilst the muster-rolls of others are so very imperfect as to render it utterly impossible to act on them and make payments.

That many claims are paid, the accounts of which have, in company with those of the regular army, been rendered to this office, and are in a due course of examination and final settlement; but, from their great magnitude, and from the laborious task this office necessarily has to perform, more time and more labor will be required to get through with the whole.

The many claims, to a vast amount, are new in actual train of adjustment and payment, throughout the whole country, from appropriations made during the present session of Congress.

That the manner in which the appropriations have, for a few years past, been made by Congress, did not require a separate and distinct account of expenditures upon militia to be kept from those of the regular army; and indeed, if it had been required, the nature of the service,

Militia Claims.

particularly during a state of war, would have rendered it extremely difficult, if not totally impracticable.

It is to be understood that the foregoing statement relates to such services of militia only, as have been performed in virtue of orders issued by the Executive of the United States, or being performed without those orders, have been recognised by that authority, and payments sanctioned accordingly.

That so far as relates to expenditures by States themselves upon their own militia, independent of the sanction or authority of the General Government, the Paymaster of the Army is in possession of no official information. It is true, however, that two claims partly of this character have, not long since, been presented here, and advances, by special direction of the honorable the Secretary of War, have been made by me upon them: one to the State of Virginia, of two hundred thousand dollars, and another to the State of Rhode Island, of not quite twenty-two thousand dollars; but then these services were, as I understood, recognised by the United States, so that they partook but in part of the nature of those alluded to, namely, that they have been paid from the funds of those States, respectively, which, when the services were thus recognised, the United States were bound to reimburse.

Respectfully,
ROBERT BRENT, *Paymaster.*

Hon. WILLIAM H. CRAWFORD,
Secretary of War,

WASHINGTON, D. C., *Jan.* 14, 1815.

SIR: This note has been delayed by the expectation of some explanatory documents from Richmond. We have now the honor of submitting to you the grounds on which we expect the President's sanction to the calls of militia which were made by the Governor of Virginia for the defence of Richmond in August and September, 1814; being the only calls, as we understand, of the propriety of which a doubt is entertained, in the Department of War.

It is to be remembered that Richmond is assailable by the channels both of York and James rivers, within eight and forty hours after the enemy's squadron shall have entered our Capes. Arnold, during the Revolutionary war, had that city in flames, within twenty-four hours after the first notice of his approach. Hence the utter impracticability of announcing the approach to the President, and receiving his instructions in time to call forth the militia to an effectual defense. The enemy could have entered Richmond before an express could return from Washington. Hence it is obvious, that against a maritime enemy, like Great Britain, a place so situated is defensible in only one or two modes, either by keeping a standing force before it, equal to any force which the enemy could lend to the assault, or by vesting the Executive of the State with the discretionary power of calling forth the militia in such numbers as to meet the particular emergency, what-

soever it might be. The latter course was adopted by the President of the United States in relation to Richmond. We do not say that any instruction to this effect was given to the Governor of Virginia previously to the calls in the month of August; but the letters of the Secretary of War to the Governor of Virginia immediately thereafter, and indeed almost contemporaneously, do, in the most explicit manner, ratify that course of action; and a subsequent ratification, we understand, is equal to a prior command. Thus, in the Secretary's letter of the 31st of August, (herewith, numbered 1,) written after the destruction of Washington, he announces the descent of the enemy's barges down the Patuxent, and the reason given for the communication is, because it might have a bearing on the Governor's arrangements for his section of the country; but what those arrangements were to be, instead of being defined, is left exclusively to the discretion of the Governor. The same gentleman, in his letter of the next day, (September 1, No. 2,) apprizes the Governor that Richmond was known to be one of the enemy's objects, and closes his letter with these emphatic words: "Be on your guard, prepared at every point, and in all circumstances, to repel the invaders." In what light is it possible to construe these words, but as a clear and explicit recognition of the principle that the General Government placed the defence of the State of Virginia and its metropolis at the discretion of its Governor? The letter, of which we have just quoted an extract, was followed by the President's proclamation of the 3d of September, calling, in terms which no American bosom could resist, upon all officers, civil and military, and upon the nation, to rise to arms, and exterminate the ferocious and sanguinary invaders.

The effect of such a proclamation on such a State as Virginia will be easily conceived by you, sir, when you come to re-peruse the terms of the proclamation and bear in mind the character of the State which you so well know. The shock was electric and universal. The commonwealth rose en masse. Her mountains, fields, and forests, poured forth their armed multitudes, who rushed from all directions to surround and cover their metropolis from British outrage and pollution, and chastise the insolence which had just triumphed over Washington. It was, no doubt, the presence of this numerous concourse at Richmond, or upon their march to it from the country, which has produced the impression that the Governor had made an indiscreet use of the power of defence with which he was intrusted. But this is not the fact. The concourse of which we have spoken forms no part of the charge which we now have against the United States. They were not kept in arms. Their services were not accepted. It was, indeed, with infinite difficulty, and infinite address on the part of the Governor, and with the most painful reluctance, and even tears of regret on theirs, that the generous impulse which had brought them together could be so far repressed as that they could be prevailed upon to return to their homes, and trust the defence and honor of the State to the troops which the Governor had already embodied. But they did return; the sense of duty and order, which forms a no less honorable part of their character than their ardor of patriotism, prevailing over every consideration of personal feeling.

The next direction which the Governor received from the Department of War, was the Secretary's letter, herewith, (No. 3,) of the 6th of September, announcing that the enemy had received a reinforcement at the mouth of Patuxent, that the united squadrons were descending the bay, that Richmond was one of their objects, and repeating again the solemn injunction, "be prepared to meet the enemy." Thus, in every instance, the Governor of Virginia is thrown by the General Government upon his own energies and own judgment, without any notification of the enemy's strength, or the quantum of resistance which it would be expedient for him to call into the field.

To meet the advance guard, as it may be called, of the same enemy, the President of the United States, acting with the advice of his council, had made a call in the month of June or July, unless we are misinformed, of fifteen thousand men. To meet the united squadrons at Baltimore, we are advised that from eighteen to twenty thousand men were called to the defence of that place. To meet the same enemy, at the same crisis, the Governor of Virginia had never in the field more than between eleven and twelve thousand men.

We hand you, herewith, the several general orders calling out troops on the occasion of the first approach of the enemy within our Capes, as also after the fall of Washington, numbered 4, 5, and 6, and submit it with confidence to your judgment, whether these calls can be considered as indiscreet. Whether you take the standard of the call for Washington, or that for Baltimore; or consider the accessibility of Richmond, by the channels either of York or James river, and the consequent necessity of guarding, with equal strength, both those avenues of approach—of guarding them, too, with raw militia against veteran and highly disciplined troops, inured to victory;—it seems very clear that those calls, if censurable at all, are rather censurable for their moderation than their excess.

To these documents, we will add only a letter from the Secretary of War, of the 21st September, written with a full knowledge of all our preparations, and when they were at the highest; in which letter, so far is he from censuring the magnitude of those preparations, that he is considered thereby as having approved and sanctioned them. If this construction be right, there will be no occasion, we trust, of giving you any further trouble on this branch of the claims of Virginia for reimbursement.

We are, sir, very respectfully, &c.

WILLIAM WIRT,
JOHN CHEW.

Hon. Wm. H. Crawford,
   Secretary of War.

Statement of the number and positions of the Troops embodied by the Executive of Virginia, and actually in the field about the middle of September, 1814.

Names of commanding officers.	Aggregate of cavalry.	Aggregate of artillery.	Aggregate of riflemen & infan'y.	Total number.	Station.
Maj. Gen. John Pegram -		76	1,254	1,330	The vicinity of Petersburg.
Same -			366	366	Fort Powhatan.
Col. Thomas M. Randolph		60	413	573	Wereonish Church.
Colonel Moses Green		118	243	360	Charles City Court-house.
Brig. Gen. John H. Cocke		77	2,337	2,414	Camp Carter.
Brig. Gen. Chamberlayne -			919	919	Bottom's Bridge.
Brig. Gen. Breckenridge -			1,760	1,760	Camp Mitchell.
Brig. Gen. Leftwick -			1,831	1,934	Camp Mims.
Colonel Ambler -		103	892	892	City of Richmond.
Major Woodford -	650			650	Some of these cavalry were on vidette duty, and the others were distributed among the several corps of the army.
Aggregate, &c. -	650	634	9,418	10,697	

It is difficult to ascertain the number of the troops on any given day previous to the 15th of September. Many of them were discharged immediately upon their arrival, and before they were organized upon any regular plan, or reports could be received from them. This was particularly the case with the cavalry. Of this species of force it was found that the Governor's proclamation and the general orders of the 26th of August had brought into the field a larger proportion than was necessary; consequently, on the 12th of September, seventeen troops were discharged, of which eight were volunteers, and the residue draughts.

Captain Prosser's troop of cavalry was called into service on the 26th August, and performed vidette duty between Richmond and Washington City until the 10th of September, when it was discharged.

Colonel Boykin took the field on the 29th of August, with about eight hundred men, and con-

Militia Claims.

tinued in service until the 13th September. He was stationed at Cabin point, on James river.

The foregoing statement and remarks relate to the measures adopted by the Executive of Virginia for the defence of Richmond, Petersburg, and the shores of York and James river, together with such points of our maritime frontier as could be protected by that force; due regard being had to the safety of the Metropolis.

The situation of the other exposed parts of Virginia will be seen by an examination of the letters from the commanding officers in those parts.

G. W. GOOCH, Adj. Gen., Va.

No. 1.

WAR DEPARTMENT, *Aug.* 31, 1814.

SIR: We have this moment received information, the correctness of which is not doubted, that the enemy evacuated Nottingham yesterday, at 10 o'clock. The barges moved down about 4 o'clock. It is believed that they embarked from Benedict last evening and this morning. I give this notice for your information as early as possible, as it may have a bearing on your arrangements for the defence of your section of the country.

I have the honor to be your Excellency's most obedient servant,   JAMES MONROE.

His Ex'cy, J. BARBOUR,
     Governor of Virginia, Richmond.

No. 2.

WAR DEPARTMENT, *Sept.* 1, 1814.

SIR: The enemy have embarked on board their vessels on the Patuxent, and will, as I presume, in execution of their desolating system, proceed immediately to some other of our principal towns. Richmond is known to be one on which they have fixed their attention; Norfolk and Baltimore are others. Against which they will move, in the first instance, will probably not be known, until they land their men in a marked direction towards it.

Be on your guard, prepared at every point, and in all circumstances, to repel the invaders.

I have the honor to be your obedient servant,   JAMES MONROE.

The GOVERNOR *of the*
     State of Virginia, Richmond.

A copy of the original.

G. W. GOOCH, Adj. Gen., Va.

No. 2.

DEPARTMENT OF WAR, *Sept.* 6, 1814.

SIR: I am sorry to inform you that the enemy's squadron has passed our battery, at the White House, on the Potomac river. It was impossible to collect such a number of heavy pieces, in the present state of affairs here, as to prevent it.

The fleet which had descended the Patuxent, with the troops on board, lately employed against this city, and a reinforcement since received, which

had paused at the mouth of that river, on account, as was supposed, of the detention of this squadron, descended the bay yesterday, either for the Potomac or some other object lower down the bay. As it doubtless will immediately know that the squadron has passed our battery, it may proceed to such other object; which must be, I presume, if it has one in the bay, either Norfolk or Richmond.

I hasten to give you this intelligence, that you may be prepared to meet the enemy, should they present themselves at either place.

I have the honor to be, respectfully, sir, your obedient servant,   JAMES MONROE.

His Ex'cy the GOVERNOR OF VIRGINIA.

No. 4.

DEPARTMENT OF WAR, *Sept.* 19, 1814.

SIR: The enemy has passed down the bay, out of sight, below Annapolis. It may be presumed that they will attack either Richmond or Norfolk.

The force collected near Richmond is, I trust, fully adequate to its defence.

Norfolk, General Porter writes me, is not so well prepared. Cannot some additional force be thrown in to its aid? I fear the reinforcement from North Carolina will not arrive there in time.

I have the honor to be, very respectfully, sir, your obedient servant

JAMES MONROE.

His Ex'cy the GOVERNOR OF VIRGINIA.

WAR DEPARTMENT, *Oct.* 6, 1814.

SIR: For the expenditure attending the militia who have been called into the service of the United States by this Department, or the commander of the military district No. 5, the United States are regularly chargeable.

For any advances made by the State of Virginia, for the support of such troops, reimbursement is of course due.

No call of the militia, except in the modes above stated, is obligatory on the United States. In the case under consideration, it is true, that the call made by the Executive of the State was notified to this Government, with a request that the militia might be taken into the service of the United States. This, however, does not remove the objection to the right in a State, at its discretion, to subject the United States to such expenses.

The President is aware that the predatory incursions of the enemy, and the menace of a more serious attack on the principal cities along our seaboard, made an extra call of militia, in certain cases, necessary. Whether the troops which were called into service by the Executive of Virginia, for the defence of Richmond, are more than were necessary for the purpose, is a question which could not be immediately decided: it will be attended to as soon as circumstances will admit. In making the decision, regard must be had to just principles, taking into view similar claims of other States.

For the present, I am authorized to state that

Claim for Prize Money.

one hundred thousand dollars will be advanced to the Executive, on account of money paid by it in support of the troops in the service of the United States, in the first instance, and the balance on account of the other claims alluded to, which are hereafter to be adjusted.

On the proposition to take the militia now assembled for the defence of Richmond into the service of the United States, I have to state that it will be acceded to as to four thousand of these troops, provided the Executive of the State should be of opinion that they may be, in the present less menacing posture of the enemy, spared from their present service, to be employed between this and Baltimore, in lieu of a like number lately called from the State for that purpose.

I have the honor to be, very respectfully, sir, your obedient servant,

                          JAMES MONROE.

Hon. CHARLES EVERETT.

CLAIM FOR PRIZE MONEY.

[Communicated to the Senate, December 28, 1815.]

                  WASHINGTON, *Dec.* 20, 1815.

SIR: In support of the petition presented to the honorable the Senate of the United States, and referred to their honorable Naval Committee, praying remuneration to those interested, for the captures made by the late United States brig Argus, under the command of my late brother William H. Allen. I have the honor to present, herewith, a letter from Benjamin Homans, Esq., of the Navy Department, to me, with a chart of the track of the Argus, and a list of the vessels she captured, &c., and the documents that were found on board those vessels.

The chart shows the course of the Argus from L'Orient, up the western coast of Ireland, into the river Shannon, and thence round into St. George's Channel, where she was captured. The red letters on the list of vessels indicate the time and place of their capture on the chart.

It appears, upon examination, that no invoices were found on board the captured vessels; those appertaining to the vessels bound coastwise were probably sent overland by mail; but I am unable to account for the absence of the others; the bills of lading that were signed were probably likewise sent by mail; and the bills of lading and custom-house documents herewith, are the only or chief means by which an estimate of the value of the cargoes can be formed. Lieutenant Watson, of the Argus, on his return from England to this country, delivered at the Navy Department a report respecting the value, &c., of these vessels and their cargoes, which he estimated at about three millions of dollars, as will be seen by referring to the letter from Mr. Homans. I cannot find this report, and Lieutenant Watson is absent from this country. His means of ascertaining their value from the officers of the captured vessels, and while in England, were much greater than the papers presented herewith alone afford; but, unwilling to overrate the amount, and in order to make adequate allowance for such an error, should there be any in this report, I have thought best to state the sum in the petition at five hundred thousand dollars less than is expressed *in his* report.

I made application at the Navy Department for the log-book of the Argus, which, perhaps, contains some information of importance on the subject, but it has not yet been found; as soon as it is discovered, I shall beg leave to add the evidence it may afford to that presented now.

Some of the vessels taken were very valuable, and among them were those from the West Indies. The cargo of the Bedford alone (with Irish linen, &c., from Dublin for London) would have brought in this country nearly one million of dollars.

I have not been able to ascertain of what kind or quality were the goods chiefly composing the cargo of the brigantine Ann; but they were most probably linen manufactures, and, if fine, were very valuable. I have written to ascertain their character from Dennison, the Purser of the Argus, who is at Baltimore. The schooner Matilda and ship Betsey were the vessels recaptured by the enemy.

The schooner Salamanca, captured on the passage from this country to France, was an armed Government vessel, as her papers show; and the principle upon which awards have already been made for the destruction of the national vessels of the enemy, applies fully to her. And what prevents the application of the same principle where the commerce of the enemy has been destroyed? As having reduced the actual power of the enemy, the capture of a few of their national vessels cannot be considered of much importance, their whole number being so great, and the means of replacing those that *were lost* so extensive, it can only be *justly prized as having lessened* the *naval reputation of the enemy while it increased* our own, and raised the glory of the *nation.* Aside from this last consideration, the demolition of the enemy's instruments of annoyance gives claim to no greater reward than the destruction of the means by which those instruments are obtained. A nation cannot long support a war from which the means are taken that enabled her to operate against an enemy; but leave her the means, and she will always be armed, being at all times able to replace her losses. To attack the commerce of the enemy was, therefore, the best mode of wounding her, and upon that conviction were the orders to my brother predicated; in which the honorable Secretary of the Navy observes, "in no way can the enemy be made to feel our hostility so effectually, as by annoying and destroying his commerce, fisheries, and coasting trade; this would carry the war home to their direct feelings and interests, and would produce an astonishing sensation." And the sequel demonstrated that hostility in that form was far more dreadful and destructive to her interests than any other which it could assume.

In another view, the claim of the subject to

Claim for Prize Money.

consideration is at least as strong. A law of the United States gives to captors the moiety of their captures; and I believe the position is correct, that the property in them vests the moment they are captured. But the power to convert such property before condemnation is not possessed either by the United States or the captors; and the United States have no greater authority to dispose of it, either before or after condemnation, than is enjoyed by the captors. My late brother was, therefore, compelled by his orders to destroy what actually belonged in part to himself and his crew; and the Executive authority having exercised the power of directing the disposal of those captures in a way that deprived the captors of their property in them, they have, it is humbly conceived, a just claim upon the United States for indemnity. There is something accruing, under existing laws, for the guns and men captured, but the amount is very small.

The continued loss of sleep, together with the excessive fatigue consequent upon such a rapid succession of captures, and the extreme watchfulness necessary in so exposed a situation, disabled the Argus from making so great a resistance to her more powerful enemy as she might otherwise have done. And although victory hung no laurels over the tombs of those who fell, nor on the brows of the survivors, their misfortune has not sullied the fame of our arms, nor diminished their title to the remembrance of their country.

With the strongest conviction of the justice and liberal sentiments of the honorable gentlemen of the Senate, to whose consideration this subject has been referred, I shall look with confident hope to a favorable result.

I have the honor to be, with great respect, sir, your obedient humble servant,

      THOMAS J. ALLEN,
         Attorney and agent.
The Hon. CHARLES TAIT,
    Chairman Com. on Naval Affairs.

NAVY DEPARTMENT, *Dec.* 13, 1815.

SIR: I have the honor to transmit to the Naval Committee of the Senate, in compliance with your request of the 8th instant, the several papers herewith, marked A and B. The papers marked A contain a list of all the merchant vessels captured by the public armed ships of the United States during the late war, and subsequently destroyed at sea in obedience to the orders of this Department to that effect.

The papers marked B contain the orders, and extracts from such parts of orders, to the commanders of the ships and vessels of war under which the vessels captured were destroyed at sea.

Those captured vessels which were sent to the United States, and arrived safely, are not included, nor those which were manned for the United States, or friendly ports in Europe, and afterwards recaptured, with a number of others which were liberated as cartels; the list being exclusively confined to the captured vessels destroyed, as far as the journals and reports have been made to this Department by the several commanding officers.

I have the honor to be, very respectfully, sir, your obedient servant,
      B. W. CROWNINSHIELD.
The Hon. CHARLES TAIT,
    Chairman Naval Com. of Senate.

A.

Statement of all the vessels, other than vessels of war, which were taken and destroyed by the Navy of the United States, during the late war with Great Britain.

By the frigate Essex—Brig Hero, August 2, 1812; brig Mary, August 9, 1812; schooner Elizabeth, December, 1812; ship Greenwich, May 28, 1813; ship Hector, May 28, 1813; ship Catherine, May 28, 1813.

By the frigate Constitution—Brig Lady Warren, August 11, 1812; brig Adeona, August 12, 1812; schooner Phœnix, February 18, 1814; brig Catharine, February 19, 1814; brig Lord Nelson, December 24, 1814.

By the frigate President—Brig Traveller, July 2, 1812; brig Duchess of Portland, July 4, 1812; brig Jean and Ann, July 12, 1813; brig Daphne, July 18, 1813; brig Alert, July 29, 1813; ship Wanderer, January 5, 1814; ship Edward, January 9, 1814; schooner Jonathan, January 9, 1814.

By the corvette Adams—Schooner Prince Regent, January 29, 1814; schooner Industry, February 9, 1814; schooner Nayntim Fairy, March 4, 1814; brig Mentor, June 24, 1814; brig Mary, June 28, 1814; schooner Favorite, July 28, 1814; ship Paris, August 7, 1814; schooner Maria, August 16, 1814.

By the frigate Chesapeake—Brig Liverpool Hero, January 14, 1813.

By the sloop-of-war Wasp—Barque Neptune, June 2, 1814; brig William, June 13, 1814; brig Pallas, June 18, 1814; ship Orange Boven, June 26, 1814; brig Regulator, July 4, 1814; schooner Jenny, July 6, 1814; brig Lettice, August 30, 1814; brig Bon Accord, August 31, 1814; brig Mary, September 1, 1814; brig Three Brothers, September 12, 1814; brig Bacchus, September 14, 1814.

By the sloop-of-war Peacock—Brig Sea Flower, June 17, 1814; brig Stranger, July 5, 1814; sloop Fortitude, July 5, 1814; brig Venus, July 5, 1814; sloop Leith Packet, August 1, 1814; sloop William and Ann, August 2, 1814; sloop Peggy and Jane, August 3, 1814; barque William, August 14, 1814; brig Bellona, August 21, 1814; brig Triton, August 23, 1814; brig Duck, September 2, 1814; ship Mary, October 12, 1814; ship Union, June 13, 1814; ship Brie de Mar, June 29, 1814.

By the brig Siren—Ship Barton, May, 1814; brig Adventurer, May, 1814.

By the sloop-of-war Hornet—Brig Resolution, February 4, 1813.

By the brigs Rattlesnake and Enterprise—Brig Rambler, February 7, 1814.

Claim for Prize Money.

By the sloop-of-war Frolic—Brig Little Fox, March 17, 1814; schooner ———, April 3, 1814.

By the brig Rattlesnake—Brig John, June 10, 1814; brig Crown Prince, June 22, 1814.

By the brig Argus—Schooner Salamanca, brig Richard, brig Fowey, sloop Lady Frances, brig Alliance, ship Barbadoes, ship Mariner, sloop John and Thomas, sloop Dinah and Betsey, brig Ann, ship'defiance, brig Baltic, and brig Bedford. The precise time of capture of these vessels is not known; it, however, occurred about the beginning of August, 1813.

RECAPITULATION.

Essex - - - - -	6
Constitution - - - -	5
President - - - -	8
Corvette Adams - - -	8
Chesapeake - - - -	1
Wasp - - - -	11
Peacock - - - -	14
Siren - - - -	2
Rattlesnake and Enterprise -	1
Frolic - - - -	2
Rattlesnake - - - -	2
Argus - - - -	13
Hornet - - - -	1
Total - -	74

NAVY DEPARTMENT, *June* 5, 1813.

SIR: When the honorable Mr. Crawford, Minister Plenipotentiary from the United States to France, is ready for departure, you will receive him and his suite on board, and proceed, with the first favorable opportunity, to sea, directing your course, without deviating for any other object, to the first port in France. In all probability you will find Brest or L'Orient the easiest of access; but should you have an opportunity of landing the Minister, on any part of the coast of France, you may thereby avoid much risk in attempting to enter a port before which you may find a hostile squadron. But in whatever way you may effect the first object of your destination, you will then proceed upon a cruise against the commerce and light cruisers of the enemy, which you will capture and destroy in all cases; unless their value and qualities shall render it morally certain that they may reach a safe and not distant port. Indeed, in the present state of the enemy's force, there are very few cases that would justify the manning of a prize; because, the chances of reaching a safe port are infinitely against the attempt, and the weakening the crew of the Argus might expose you to an unequal contest with the enemy.

It is exceedingly desirable that the enemy should be made to feel the effects of our hostility, and of his barbarous system of warfare; and in no way can we so effectually accomplish that object, as by annoying and destroying his commerce, fisheries, and coasting trade. The latter is of the utmost importance, and is much more exposed to the attack of such a vessel as the Ar-

gus, than is generally understood. This would carry the war home directly to their feelings and interests, and produce an astonishing sensation.

For this purpose, the cruising ground from the entrance of the British channel to Cape *Clear*, down the coast of Ireland, across to, and along the northeast coast of England, would employ a month or six weeks to great advantage. The coasting fleets on this track are immensely valuable; and you would also be in the way of their West India homeward fleet, and of those to and from Spain, Portugal and the Mediterranean. When you are prepared to leave this ground, you may pass round the northwest of Ireland, towards Fair Island passage, in the track of the Archangel fleets, returning home in August and September.

When it shall be absolutely necessary to return home, you will pursue such route as may best promote the objects of your cruise, and endeavor to make some Eastern port; perhaps Portsmouth may be as easy of access, and as convenient, in other respects, as any other.

On your arrival in France you will, with the aid of Mr. Crawford, be better able to form an opinion of the expediency of attempting to send prizes into France, or of touching there to replenish your stores in order to protract your cruise.

Your own disposition, and the amiable character of the Minister, insure to him the kindest attention on your part; and I am persuaded that you will derive the most ample gratification from such an intercourse. Your talents and honorable services are deeply impressed upon this Department, and will not cease to excite its attention.

Wishing you a prosperous and honorable cruise, I am, very respectfully, your obedient servant,

WM. JONES.

Lieutenant WM. H. ALLEN,
   Commanding U. S. brig Argus.

Extract of a letter from the Secretary of the Navy to Captain Charles Stewart, commanding the United States' frigate Constitution, dated September 19, 1813.

The commerce of the enemy is the most vulnerable point we can attack, and its destruction the main object; and to this end all your efforts should be directed. Therefore, unless your prizes shall be very valuable, and near a friendly port, it will be imprudent, and worse than useless, to attempt to send them in; the chances of recapture are excessively great; the crew, and the safety of the ship under your command, would be diminished and endangered, as well as your own fame, and the national honor, by hazarding a battle after the reduction of your officers and crew by manning prizes. In every point of view, it will be proper to destroy what you capture; except valuable and compact articles, that may be transhipped.

This system gives to one ship the force of many; and, by granting to prisoners a cartel, as sufficient numbers accumulate, our account on that head will be increased to our credit, and not only facilitate the exchange, but insure better

Claim for Prize Money.

treatment to our unfortunate countrymen who are, or may be, captured by the enemy.

Extract of a letter from the Secretary of the Navy to Master Commandant George Parker, commanding the United States' brig Siren, dated December 8, 1813.

Your own observation must have proved to you how precarious and uncertain is the prospect of getting prizes into a friendly port; and that the manning of a few prizes will soon terminate your cruise, and diminish your force so as to jeopardise the safety of the Siren, and your own reputation, by a chance conflict with an enemy, nominally your equal, but fully manned. With every patriotic officer private motives will yield to considerations of public good; and as the great object and end of our public force is to harass and distress the enemy, and as the most effectual annoyance is the destruction of his trade and commerce, it ought to be the ruling principle of action with every commander.

A single cruiser, if ever so successful, can man but a few prizes, and every prize is a serious diminution of her force; but a single cruiser, destroying every captured vessel, has the capacity of continuing, in full vigor, her destructive power so long as her provisions and stores can be replenished, either from friendly ports or from the vessels captured.

Thus has a single cruiser, upon the destructive plan, the power, perhaps, of twenty, acting upon pecuniary views alone; and thus may the employment of our small force, in some degree, compensate for the great inequality compared with that of the enemy. Considered even in a pecuniary point of view, the chances of the safe arrival of the prize are so few, and of recapture by the enemy, so many, that motives of interest alone are sufficient; but when we consider that it is, in all probability, consigning the prize crew to a loathsome prison, in the hands of a perfidious and cruel enemy, every just motive will combine to urge the destruction, rather than the manning, of every prize.

The American people and Government have given abundant proof that they are deficient neither in gratitude nor generosity. I, therefore, strenuously urge and order the destruction of every captured vessel and cargo, unless so near to a friendly port as to leave little doubt of safe arrival, or that the merchandise shall be so valuable and compact as to admit of transhipment, without injury to the vessel under your command, or to the public service.

Extract of a letter from the Secretary of the Navy to Master Commandant John Orde Creighton, having under his command the United States' brigs Rattlesnake and Enterprise, Lieutenant Commandant James Renshaw, dated December 22, 1813.

The great object, however, is the destruction of the commerce of the enemy, and bringing into port the prisoners, in order to exchange against our unfortunate countrymen who may fall into his

hands. You will, therefore, man no prize, unless the value, place of capture, and other favorable circumstances, shall render her safe arrival morally certain. As the ransoming of British vessels is prohibited by a statute, and the ransom bonds declared void, you will not agree to the ransoming of any prize. The enemy has also, in violation of his own agreement, and of good faith, refused to recognise cartels granted at sea; you will, therefore, grant no cartel, nor liberate any prisoners, unless under circumstances of extreme and unavoidable necessity.

Be assured, sir, that the confidence of our country cannot be enhanced by any new achievements of our gallant Navy; it is now entire, and the services of an officer will now be estimated by the extent of the injury he may inflict upon the vital interest of the enemy in the destruction of his commerce.

[Instructions, the same as the preceding to Captain Creighton, were given, January 6, 1814, to Master Commandant Joseph Bainbridge, commanding the United States' sloop of war Frolic.]

Extract of a letter from the Secretary of the Navy to Master Commandant Lewis Warrington, commanding the United States' sloop-of-war Peacock, dated FEBRUARY 26, 1814.

You will therefore, sir, unless in some extraordinary cases that shall clearly warrant an exception, destroy all you capture; and by thus retaining your crew, and continuing your cruise, your services may be enhanced tenfold. The service you may render your country will be estimated by the extent of the injury you may inflict upon its implacable enemy; and this will be best accomplished in the annoyance and destruction of its commerce, from which no other object should be suffered to divert your attention for a moment. With this view, as well as from the rational and obvious policy opposed to this practice, I have it in command from the President, strictly to prohibit the giving or accepting, directly or indirectly, a challenge to combat ship to ship.

Extract of a letter from the Secretary of the Navy to Master Commandant Johnson Blakely, commanding the United States' sloop-of-war Wasp, dated MARCH 3, 1814,

If the qualities of the Wasp are such as I feel confident they will prove to be, you cannot fail to make a brilliant and productive cruise. Your own sound judgment and observation will sufficiently demonstrate to you, how extremely precarious and injurious is the attempt to send in a prize, unless taken very near a friendly port, and under the most favorable circumstances. A failure of success places our unfortunate seamen in the hands of the enemy, diminishes your means of achieving honor to yourself and glory to your country, curtails your cruise, and subjects you to the unequal attack of a foe, nominally your equal, but fully manned. Hence, it is evident, that policy, interest, and duty, combine to dictate the destruction of all captures, with the above exceptions. It is a great object with the enemy to capture and detain in prison, our seamen; and this can only be counteracted by capturing and bringing into port an equal number; this is an object of great national importance; the releasing at sea on parole, though practised by all civilized nations, is utterly disregarded by our enemy.

[Instructions relative to the disposition of captures, the same as the preceding, were given, March 16, 1814, to Master Commandant Charles D. Ridgely, commanding the United States' sloop of war Erie.]

Extract of a letter from the Secretary of the Navy to Captain Charles Stewart, commanding the United States' frigate Constitution, dated

NOVEMBER 29, 1814.

Having, on former occasions, urged the superior policy and advantage of destroying the captures you may make, in preference to the hazardous attempt to send them in, unless in the vicinity of a friendly port, and in the case of very valuable and fleet sailing prizes, I need not now dwell upon that subject.

Daily experience, and the grievous complaints of the merchants of Great Britain, sufficiently attest the efficacy of the system. Should you touch at any friendly port for succors, you will observe the strictest economy, and put to sea again with the least possible delay. The general instructions you have from time to time, received from this Department, and your own experience, will supersede the necessity of further details, and, in the event of any casualty, or occurrence, which, in your judgment, may render a deviation from these instructions indispensable to the public interest, you will act accordingly, still adhering, as near as may be, to their general spirit and intention.

[Instructions, similar to the preceding, were given, 30th November, 1814, to Captain Charles Morris, commanding the United States' frigate Congress.]

Extract of a letter from the Secretary of the Navy to Captain David Porter, commanding a squadron of small vessels at New York, dated

NOVEMBER 30, 1814.

Having already given to you the necessary instructions for procuring, arming, equipping, and manning, the five vessels destined for your command, you will, as soon as the squadron shall be ready for sea, proceed upon a cruise in the West Indies, where you will employ your force, either collectively or separately, in annoying and destroying the commerce of the enemy, which the nature of your force, seconded by your judgment and enterprise, will, I trust, enable you to execute, as well in his harbors as at sea, and upon a scale so extensive as to make him participate deeply in the evils which he has inflicted upon our prosperity.

[Instructions similar to the preceding to Captain Porter, were given the same day, November 30, 1814, to Captain Oliver H. Perry, commanding another squadron of small vessels.]

CAPTURE OF THE PENGUIN.

[Communicated to the House, December 31, 1815.]

NAVY DEPARTMENT, Dec. 21, 1815.

SIR: In compliance with your request, in behalf of the honorable Committee upon Naval Affairs, I have the honor to transmit to you, herewith, copies of letters from Captain James Biddle, of the United States ship Hornet, dated March 25th, and April 8th, 1815, addressed to Commodore Stephen Decatur, as commander of the squadron destined to cruise in the Indian seas; which contain all the information in the possession of this Department relative to the capture of the British sloop of war Penguin.

I have the honor to be, with the highest respect, your most obedient servant,

B. W. CROWNINSHIELD.

Hon. JAMES PLEASANTS, JUN.,
Chairman Naval Committee.

UNITED STATES' SLOOP HORNET,
Off Tristan D'Acunha, March 25, 1815.

SIR: I have the honor to inform you that, on the morning of the 23d instant, at half past ten, when about to anchor off the north end of the island of Tristan d'Acunha, a sail was seen to the southward and eastward, steering to the westward, the wind fresh from S. S. W. In a few minutes, she passed on to the westward, so that we could not see her for the land. I immediately made sail to the eastward, and shortly after, getting sight again, perceived her to be up before the wind; I hove to for her to come down to us. When she had approached near, I filled the maintopsail, and continued to yaw the ship, while she continued to come down, veering, occasionally, to prevent her passing under our stern. At forty minutes past one, P. M., being nearly within musket shot distance, she hauled her wind on the starboard tack, hoisted English colors, and fired a gun. We immediately luffed to, hoisted our ensign, and gave the enemy a broadside. The action being thus commenced, a quick and well directed fire was kept up from this ship, the enemy gradually drifting nearer to us, when, at fifty-nine minutes past one, he bore up, apparently to run us on board. As soon as I perceived he would certainly fall on board, I called the boarders, so as to be ready to repel any attempt to board us. At the instant, every officer and man repaired to the quarter deck, where the two vessels were coming in contact, and eagerly pressed me to permit them to board the enemy; but this I would not permit, as it was evident, from the commencement of the action, that our fire was greatly superior both in quickness and in effect. The enemy's bowsprit came in between our main and mizzen rigging, on our starboard side, affording him an opportunity to board us, if such was his design; but no attempt was made. There was a considerable swell on, and as the sea lifted us ahead, the enemy's bowsprit carried away our mizzen shrouds, stern davits, and spanker boom, and he hung upon our larboard quarter. At this moment, an officer, who was afterwards recognised to be Mr. McDonald, the first lieutenant, and the then commanding officer, called out that they had surrendered. I directed the marines and musketry men to cease firing, and, while on the taffrail, asking if they had surrendered, I received a wound in the neck. The enemy just then got clear of us, and his foremast and bowsprit being both gone, and perceiving us veering to give him a fresh broadside, he again called out that he had surrendered. It was with difficulty I could restrain my crew from firing into him again, as he had certainly fired into us after he had surrendered. From the firing of the first gun to the last time the enemy cried out he had surrendered, was exactly twenty-two minutes by the watch. She proved to be His Britannic Majesty's brig Penguin, mounting sixteen thirty-two pound carronades, two long twelves, a twelve pound carronade on the topgallant forecastle, with swivels on the capstern, and in the tops. She had a spare port forward, so as to fight both her long guns of a side. She sailed from England in September last. She was shorter upon deck than this ship by two feet, but she had a greater length of keel, greater breadth of beam, thicker sides, and higher bulwarks, than this ship, and was, in all respects, a remarkably fine vessel of her class. The enemy acknowledge a complement of one hundred and thirty-two, twelve of them supernumerary marines from the Medway seventy-four, received on board in consequence of their being ordered to cruise for the American privateer Young Wasp. They acknowledge, also, a loss of fourteen killed, and twenty-eight wounded; but Mr. Mayo, who was in charge of the prize, assures me that the number of killed was certainly greater. Among the killed are Captain Dickinson, who fell at the close of the action, and the boatswain; among the wounded are the second lieutenant, purser, and two midshipmen. Each of the midshipmen lost a leg. We received on board, in all, one hundred and eighteen prisoners, four of whom have since died of their wounds. Having removed the prisoners, and taken on board such provisions and stores as would be useful to us, I scuttled the Penguin this morning before daylight, and she went down. As she was completely riddled by our shot, her foremast and bowsprit both gone, and her mainmast so crippled as to be incapable of being secured, it seemed unadvisable, at this distance from home, to attempt sending her to the United States.

This ship did not receive a single round shot in her hull, nor any material wound in her spars; the rigging and sails were very much cut; but, having bent a new suit of sails, and knotted and secured our rigging, we are now completely ready, in all respects, for any service. We were eight men short of complement, and had nine upon the sick list the morning of the action.

Enclosed is a list of killed and wounded. I lament to state that Lieutenant Conner is wounded dangerously; I feel great solicitude on his account, as he is an officer of much promise, and his loss would be a serious loss to the service.

It is a most pleasing part of my duty to acquaint you that the conduct of Lieutenants Conner and Newton, Mr. Mayo, acting lieutenant, Lieutenant Brownlow, of the marines, Sailing-master Romney, and the other officers, seamen, and marines, I have the honor to command, was, in the highest degree, creditable to them, and calls for my warmest recommendation. I cannot, indeed, do justice to their merits. The satisfaction which was diffused throughout the ship, when it was ascertained that the stranger was an enemy's sloop-of-war, and the alacrity with which every one repaired to quarters, fully assured me that their conduct in action would be marked with coolness and intrepidity.

I have the honor to be your obedient servant,

J. BIDDLE.

Commodore DECATUR.

NAVAL OPERATIONS AGAINST THE BARBARY POWERS IN 1815.

[Communicated to the Senate, January 11, 1816.]

Mr. TAIT, from the Committee on Naval Affairs, communicated the following documents, relative to the operation of the squadron under the command of Commodore Decatur against the Barbary Powers:

U. S. SHIP GUERRIERE,
Off Carthagena, June 19, 1815.

SIR: I have the honor to inform you that on the 17th instant, off Cape de Gat, the squadron fell in with and captured an Algerine frigate of forty-six guns, and between four and five hundred men, commanded by Rais Hammida, who bore the title of Admiral. She struck her flag after a running fight of twenty-five minutes. The Admiral was killed at the commencement of the action. After the Guerriere (who from her favorable position was enabled to bring the enemy to close action) had fired two broadsides, they, with the exception of a few musketeers, ran below. The Guerriere had four men wounded by musket shot, which is the only injury done by the enemy in this affair. It is with pain I have to communicate to you that one of our main deck guns burst in the first discharge, by which accident five men were killed and thirty badly wounded and burnt. This gun was only doubly shotted; and permit me to state, that, unless some more effectual mode is adopted in proving our guns, I fear the frequency of such accidents will be injurious to the service, beyond the loss of men occasioned thereby. The steadiness of our men adjoining the bursting gun was worthy of admiration. Although many of them were much burnt and wounded, it did not occasion a pause in their fire. We have four hundred and six prisoners, including the wounded. The prisoners state about thirty were killed and thrown overboard.

Their squadron is said to be cruising in our vicinity; five days ago they were off this place. Unless I obtain some further intelligence of them by to-morrow, I shall proceed to the port of Algiers in the hope of intercepting their return. For the present I have determined to send the prize into Carthagena.

The enclosed is a return of the wounded by the enemy, as also those who were killed and wounded by the bursting of the gun.

I have the honor to be, very respectfully, sir, your obedient servant,

STEPHEN DECATUR.

Hon. B. W. CROWNINSHIELD,
Secretary of the Navy.

U. S. SHIP GUERRIERE,
Off Cape Palos, June 20, 1815.

SIR: I have the honor to inform you that, on the 19th instant, off Cape Palos, the squadron under my command captured an Algerine brig of twenty-two guns and one hundred and eighty men. After a chase of three hours, she run into shoal water, where I did not think it advisable to follow with our large ships, but despatched the Epervier, Spark, Torch, and Spitfire, to whom she surrendered after a short resistance. Twenty-three men were found dead on board. We received from her eighty prisoners, the residue of her crew having left her in boats; many of them must have been killed by the fire of our vessels, and one of the boats was sunk. None of our vessels sustained any damage, nor was there a man killed or wounded. This brig is larger than the Epervier, was built in Algiers five years ago by a Spanish constructer, the same who built the frigate captured on the 17th instant, and is perfectly sound.

I have the honor to be, very respectfully, sir, your obedient servant,

STEPHEN DECATUR.

Hon. B. W. CROWNINSHIELD,
Secretary of the Navy.

U. S. SHIP GUERRIERE,
Bay of Algiers, July 5, 1815.

SIR: I have the honor to inform you of the proceedings of this squadron subsequent to the date of my letter of the 20th ultimo. Having put the greater part of our prisoners on board the captured brig, I sent her into Carthagena, and made sail for Algiers, where we arrived on the 28th. Finding the Algerine squadron to be still out, and knowing that they had been at sea a longer period than usual, and that a despatch boat had been sent to Algiers to inform them of our arrival in the Mediterranean, I thought it probable that they would seek shelter in some neutral port. It seemed, therefore, a favorable moment to deliver a letter from the President to the Dey, pursuant to instructions from the Department of State, which would afford them an opportunity to open a negotiation, if they thought fit. A negotiation was accordingly opened, and a Treaty of Peace was dictated by us, and finally concluded in twenty-four hours, in the manner related in the despatch of Mr. Shaler and myself to the Secretary of State.

This treaty, possessing all the favorable features of those which have been concluded with the most favored nations, and other advantages conceded to us only, I flatter myself will be considered honorable to the United States, particularly when we compare the small force employed on this occasion with the formidable expeditions which have often, and without success, been sent against Algiers. It has been dictated at the mouth of the cannon, has been conceded to the losses which Algiers has sustained, and to the dread of still greater evils apprehended; and I beg leave to express to you my opinion, that the presence of a respectable naval force in this sea will be the only certain guarantee for its observance.

Having concluded the treaty, I have, in conformity with your instructions to dispose of such vessels we might capture as would be unsafe to send home in such manner as would seem to me most expedient, restored them, in their present state, to the Dey of Algiers. This was earnestly requested by the Dey, as it would satisfy his people with the conditions of the peace; and it was determined by Mr. Shaler and myself, that, considering the state of those vessels, the great expense which would be incurred by fitting them for a voyage to the United States, and the little probability of selling them in that part of the world, it would be expedient to grant the request.

I have appointed Captain Downes, of the Epervier, to the Guerriere, and Lieutenant Shubrick, first of the Guerriere, to the Epervier, which brig I have determined to send home with the despatches. These arrangements, I trust, will meet the approbation of the Government. The ten American prisoners who were confined in Algiers have been delivered up, and I have given them a passage in the despatch vessel.

I shall now proceed with the squadron to Tunis, and thence to Tripoli. At the latter place, I understand, there exists some difficulty between our Consul and the Regency; of what nature I am not particularly informed.

I have charged Captain Lewis with the delivery of the despatches to the Government, and the flags taken from the Algerine Admiral and brig. He is an officer of great merit, and whom I beg leave strongly to recommend to the notice of Government.

I have the honor to be, very respectfully, your most obedient servant,

STEPHEN DECATUR.

Hon. B. W. CROWNINSHIELD,
Secretary of the Navy.

UNITED STATES' SHIP GUERRIERE,
Bay of Tunis, July 31, 1815.

SIR: I have the honor to inform you, upon my arrival at this anchorage, I was made acquainted with the following transactions, which had taken place here during our late war with Great Britain: Two prizes, which had been taken by the Abellino privateer, and sent into this port, were taken possession of by a British vessel of war

Naval Operations against the Barbary Powers.

while lying within the protection of the Bey of Tunis.

The Consul having communicated to me the information of this violation of our Treaty with Tunis, I demanded satisfaction from the Bey. After some hesitation, and proposing a delay of payment for one year, my demand was acceded to, and the money, amounting to forty-six thousand dollars, was paid into the hands of the consul, Mr. Noah, agent for the privateer.

Of the papers I have the honor to transmit herewith, No. 1 is a copy of the Consul's letter to me, No. 2 is a copy of my letter to the Prime Minister of the Bey, and No. 3 is a copy of the Consul's acknowledgment of the receipt of the money.

I shall proceed immediately for Tripoli, and will give you early information of the further proceedings of this squadron. The Bey of Tunis has now lying in this harbor, nearly ready for sea, three frigates and several smaller vessels of war.

I have the honor be, with great respect, sir, your most obedient servant,

STEPHEN DECATUR.

Hon. B. W. CROWNINSHIELD,
    Secretary of the Navy.

No. 1.

U. S. CONSULATE, TUNIS,
    July 25, 1815.

SIR: On or about the 21st of February, two American prizes, while at anchor, and within the immediate protection of His Excellency the Bey of Tunis, were forcibly seized and taken possession of by the boats of His Britannic Majesty's brig Lyra, Dowell O'Reily, Esq., commander, and sent to Malta. In order to afford the just and necessary protection to American property, to cause our rights and the existing Treaty to be respected, I have deemed it my duty to claim of the Bey of Tunis the value of said prizes.

His Excellency, though sensible of the violation of the neutrality of his port, and the loss sustained in the illegal capture of the American property when within his waters, still waives the settlement of this claim, and is desirous to procrastinate the arrangement to a length of time which will deprive the owners of the benefit of their labor and danger. Under these circumstances, I do myself the honor to solicit from you such co-operation, in enforcing the respect due to our rights and treaties, as you may deem proper to afford. With great respect, &c.,

M. M. NOAH.

Com. S. DECATUR, *Commander, &c.*

P. S. In the disposal of the cargo of one of the English prizes, an intrigue was set on foot and prosecuted by a company of merchants, under the sanction and protection of the Prince Sidi Mustapha, by which the owners have been defrauded of a considerable sum of money. For the satisfactory adjustment of this claim, some interference appears equally necessary.

M. M. NOAH.

No. 2.

U. S. SHIP GUERRIERE,
    Bay of Tunis, July 26, 1815.

SIR: I have the honor to enclose to your Excellency a despatch from the Department of State of the United States, by which you will perceive the friendly disposition of my Government towards the Bey and Regency of Tunis. When that despatch was written, it was believed that an equally friendly disposition existed on the part of Tunis. With surprise I understood, on my arrival in the Mediterranean, that the treaty existing between the two countries had been violated on the part of Tunis; first, by permitting two vessels, which had been captured by an American vessel, to be taken out of the port of Tunis by a British cruiser; and secondly, by sanctioning a company of Jew merchants, subjects of Tunis, in taking the property of an American citizen at their own price, and much below its real value.

In consequence of this information, as soon as we had obtained justice from Algiers for their aggressions, I hastened to this port, with the power and disposition to exact from this Regency an observance of our treaty. I now require immediate restitution of the property or of its value. Your Excellency will perceive the necessity of the earliest attention to this communication, and of making known to me the decision of His Excellency the Bey with the least possible delay.

I have the honor to be, with great consideration, your Excellency's most obedient servant,

STEPHEN DECATUR,
    Commander, &c.

To the PRIME MINISTER
of His Excellency the Bey of Tunis.

No. 3.

CONSULATE OF THE UNITED STATES
OF AMERICA, AT TUNIS.

To all whom it may concern:

Whereas, on the 17th and 21st days of February, 1815, the English schooner Dunster Castle, and the English brig Charlotte, the former laden with oil and fish, the latter with currants and fustic, were sent into the harbor of Tunis, having been captured by the American private armed brig Abellino, William F. Wyer, commander; the said prizes, when within the waters and under the immediate protection of His Excellency the Bey of Tunis, were taken possession of and sent to Malta, by His Britannic Majesty's brig Lyra, Dowell O'Reily, Esq. commander, then at anchor in the said harbor of Tunis. That application was made to His Excellency the Bey of Tunis for payment for said vessels, amounting to forty-six thousand Spanish dollars, according to their just and regular valuation. His Excellency the Bey of Tunis having ascertained fully and satisfactorily, that the beforementioned vessels, being American property, were within his waters illegally and forcibly carried away, and being sensible of the necessity of causing his rights to be respected, did order that payment should be made for said vessels according to their valuation.

Now, therefore, I, the undersigned, Consul of the United States of America for the city and Kingdom of Tunis, and agent for the concerned, do hereby make known and certify, that the payment of said vessels according to their valuation, say forty-six thousand Spanish dollars, has been received from His Excellency the Bey of Tunis; who, by these presents, is acquitted from all claim against him on account of said prizes.

Given under my hand and seal of office, at Tunis, this 30th day of July, 1815, and [L. S.] in the fortieth year of the American independence. M. M. NOAH.

I do hereby certify, that the sum of forty-six thousand Spanish dollars has been paid for the two prizes as above stated, to the American Consul; and that the United States has no further claim on His Excellency the Bey of Tunis for these vessels. S. DECATUR, *Commander, &c.*

U. S. SHIP GUERRIERE,
Messina, August 31, 1815.

SIR: I have the honor to inform you that, immediately after the date of my last communication, I proceeded to Tripoli. Upon my arrival off that place, I received from our Consul a letter, a copy of which (No. 1,) is herewith transmitted. In consequence of the information contained in this letter, I deemed it necessary to demand justice from the Bashaw. The enclosure (No. 2) is a copy of my note to the Prime Minister of Tripoli. On the next day the Governor of the city of Tripoli came on board the Guerriere to treat in behalf of the Bashaw. He objected to the amount claimed by us, but finally agreed to our demands. The money, amounting to the sum of twenty-five thousand dollars, has been paid into the hands of the Consul, who is agent for the privateer. The Bashaw also delivered up to me ten captives, two of them Danes, and the others Neapolitans.

I have the honor to enclose the letter of the Consul, informing me of the conclusion of this affair. During the progress of our negotiations with the States of Barbary, now brought to a conclusion, there has appeared a disposition, on the part of each of them, to grant as far we were disposed to demand. Any attempt to conciliate them, except through the influence of their fears, I should expect to be vain. It is only by the display of naval power that their depredations can be restrained. I trust the successful result of our small expedition, so honorable to our country, will induce other nations to follow the example; in which case, the Barbary States will be compelled to abandon their piratical system. I shall now proceed with the squadron to Carthagena, at which place I hope to find the relief squadron from America.

I have the honor to be, with great respect, sir, yours, &c., STEPHEN DECATUR.
Hon. B. W. CROWNINSHIELD,
Secretary of the Navy.

No. 1.

U. S. CONSULATE AT TRIPOLI,
August 6, 1815.

SIR: I have the pleasure of now laying before you all the documents relative to the unlawfully seizing, in the port of Tripoli, and under the guns of the forts, two American prizes, captured by the Abellino, and taken out by the English brig Paulina. I have fully addressed the United States Government on this affair, and hope you have come fully prepared to demand and obtain ample satisfaction.

It is a case attended with such a flagrant violation of the United States' Treaty with this Regency, and our neutral rights, that it calls for the most prompt and energetic conduct on the part of the United States, which will not only convince this Power, but all others, that our rights and privileges cannot be invaded with impunity. If, however, the Bashaw, contrary to my opinion, should refuse us that satisfaction we are justly entitled to, it is my determination to leave the Regency by this occasion.

I shall have the pleasure of seeing you, and will detail more fully the events as they have taken place. In the interim, I have the honor, &c., RICHARD B. JONES.
Com. STEPHEN DECATUR,
On board the U. S. frigate Guerriere.

No. 2.

U. S. SHIP GUERRIERE,
Off Tripoli, August 6, 1815.

SIR: I have been officially informed that the Bashaw of Tripoli has permitted a British sloop-of-war, pending hostilities between that nation and the United States, to take from out of his harbor, and from under the guns of his castle, two American prizes, and refused protection to an American cruiser lying within his waters, in direct violation of the treaty which existed between our two nations. As soon as I had settled with Algiers for her aggressions, and with Tunis for a similar outrage to the one now complained of, I hastened to this place with a part of the squadron under my command.

With ample power to take satisfaction for the violation of our treaty above stated, I only follow the invariable rule of my Government, in first making a demand of justice. I have, therefore, to inform your Excellency that I require that immediate restitution be made of the value of the vessels taken from the harbor of Tripoli as before stated, and also compensation for the loss occasioned by the detention of the American cruiser, in violation of the treaty. Your Excellency will perceive the necessity of making known to me the determination of His Excellency the Bashaw, in relation to the above demands, with the least possible delay.

I have the honor to be, with great consideration, your Excellency's most obedient servant,
STEPHEN DECATUR.
His Exc'y the PRIME MINISTER
of His Exc'y the Bashaw of Tripoli.

TRIPOLI, *August* 9, 1815.

SIR: Permit me to congratulate you on the honorable adjustment of all differences which have existed between the United States and this Regency. This arrangement may not only be considered as just and honorable for the United States, but also as highly advantageous to the interest of our citizens. I have no doubt this lesson will long serve to keep in the remembrance of the Bashaw the power, justice, and humanity of the United States. To your dignified, firm, and manly conduct throughout this affair, the United States are indebted for the standing we now have ; and, as the representative of our country here, permit me to offer the sincere homage of respect, esteem, and regard, with which I have the honor to be, &c.

RICHARD B. JONES.

Commodore STEPHEN DECATUR,
Commander-in-Chief, &c.

UNITED STATES' SHIP GUERRIERE,
Naples Sept. 8, 1815.

SIR: I have the honor to inform your Excellency that in my late negotiation with the Bashaw of Tripoli, I demanded and obtained the release of eight Neapolitan captives, subjects of His Majesty the King of the Two Sicilies. These I have landed at Messina. It affords me great pleasure to have had it in my power, by this small service, to evince to His Majesty the grateful sense entertained by my Government of the aid formerly rendered to us by His Majesty during our war with Tripoli.

With great respect and consideration, I have the honor to be, &c.

STEPHEN DECATUR.

His Ex'cy the MARQUIS CIRCELLO,
Secretary of State, &c.

NAPLES, *September* 12, 1815.

SIR: Having laid before the King, my master, the papers which you have directed me, dated the 8th instant, in which you were pleased to acquaint me that, in your last negotiation with the Bey of Tripoli, you had freed from the slavery of that Regency eight subjects of His Majesty, whom you had also set on shore at Messina : His Majesty has ordered me to acknowledge this peculiar favor, as the act of your generosity, which you have been pleased to call a return for the trifling assistance which the squadron of your nation formerly received from his Royal Government during the war with Tripoli.

In doing myself the pleasure of manifesting this sentiment of my King, and of assuring you, in his name, that the brave American nation will always find in His Majesty's ports the best reception, I beg you will receive the assurance of my most distinguished consideration.

MARQUIS CIRCELLO,
Secretary of State, &c.

Com. DECATUR, *Commander, &c.*

ESTIMATES FOR BUILDING AND EQUIPPING SHIPS.

[Communicated to the Senate, Jan. 16 and 29, 1816.]
NAVY DEPARTMENT, *Jan* 13, 1816.

SIR: In compliance with the request of the honorable Committee of the Senate upon Naval Affairs, communicated by your letter of the 8th instant, I have the honor to enclose to you, herewith, the several estimates, in detail, marked A, B, and C.

By these estimates, it appears that the cost of

building a seventy-four gunship would be	$217,412
Equipping a seventy-four gunship would be	167,450
Building and equipping a seventy-four	$384,862

That the cost of building a forty-four would be	$153,475
Equipping a forty-four would be	114,925
Building and equipping a forty-four	$268,400

That the cost of building a sloop-of-war would be	$46,298
Equipping a sloop-of-war would be	36,930
Building and equipping a sloop-of-war	$83,223

It hence results that the expense which would be incurred in building and equipping one seventy-four, two forty-fours, and two sloops-of-war, would be as follows :

A seventy-four gunship	$384,862
A forty-four costs $268,400, therefore, two forty-fours would cost	536,800
A sloop-of-war costs $82,223, therefore, two would cost	164,446
Total cost of building and equipping one seventy-four, two forty-fours, and two sloops-of-war, would be	$1,086,108

In these estimates I have been aided by the practical knowledge and experience of the Commissioners of the Navy Board, who availed themselves of the calculations of scientific ship-builders, and the information derived from recent investigations and inquiries of the market price of the materials, and various articles of equipment.

The estimates are as correct as the fluctuating prices of labor and materials will admit, and sufficiently so to found the data upon for the amount of the contemplated annual increase of the Navy ; but, so far as the calculations are conjectural, it is presumed that they may exceed the actual expenditure from five to ten per cent.

All which is respectfully submitted.

B. W. CROWNINSHIELD.

Hon. CHARLES TAIT,
Chairman Naval Committee.

Estimates for Building and Equipping Ships.

A.

Estimate of the expense of building and equipping a seventy-four gunship.

22,000 feet of live oak, at $1 50	$35,200
120,000 feet of white oak and yellow pine, at 30 cents	36,000
24,000 lbs. of copper bolts, at 40 cts.	9,600
38,560 lbs. of sheathing copper and nails, at 45 cts.	18,752
106 tons, 212,000 lbs. of iron, at 6 cts.	12,780
13,500 lbs. of lead, at 10 cts.	1,350
Labor of carpenters, and mast-making	85,000
Labor of joiners, including stuff	8,000
Blacksmiths' work	12,780
Plumber's bill	1,350
Turner's bill	900
Carver's bill	700
Hull and spars complete	$217,412
Blockmaker's bill, including gun carriages and everything furnished by him	$8,500
Sailmaker's bill, two suits	28,300
Ropemaker's bill, 120 tons, at 13 cts. par lb.	31,200
Tanner's bill	750
Painter's bill	2,500
Cooper's bill	5,500
Boat-builder's bill	1,700
Ordnance, 54 thirty-two pounders, and 22 thirty-two pound carronades	30,000
6,000 thirty-two pound shot	9,000
1,500 thirty-two pound grape	3,500
300 barrels powder, at 45 cents	13,500
4,000 cylinders, at 50 cents	2,000
200 muskets, at $15	3,000
200 battle-axes, at $1 50	300
200 pikes, at $1 50	300
200 pairs of pistols, at $10	2,000
200 sabres, at $3	600
Colors and signals	1,200
Anchors	4,800
200 tons kentledge, at $40	8,000
Camboose	1,800
Rigger's bill, forty men, at $15 per month for four months	2,400
Charts, compasses, books, mathematical instruments, &c.	1,600
Contingencies	5,000
Equipment	167,450
Hull and spars complete	217,412
Building and equipment	$384,862

B.

Estimate of the expense of building and equipping a forty-four gun frigate of the first class.

14,400 feet of live oak, at $1 50	$21,600
85,000 feet white oak and yellow pine, at 30 cts.	25,500
20,000 lbs. copper bolts, at 40 cts.	8,000
27,500 lbs. copper sheathing and nails, at 45 cents	12,375
75 tons, 150,000 lbs. of iron, at 6 cts.	9,000
11,500 lbs. of lead, at 10 cts.	1,150
Labor of carpenters and mast-makers	60,600
Labor of joiners, including stuff	5,000

Blacksmiths' work	9,000
Plumber's bill	1,150
Turner's bill	700
Carver's bill	600
Hull and spars complete	$153,475
Blockmaker's bill, including gun carriages and everything furnished by him	$5,700
Sailmaker's bill, two suits	18,875
Ropemaker's bill, 100 tons, at 13 cts. per lb.	26,000
Tanner's bill	650
Painter's bill	1,500
Cooper's bill	4,200
Boat-builder's bill	1,200
Ordnance, 32 twenty-four pounders, and 20 forty-two pound carronades	16,500
3,000 round shot	3,680
1,000 grape	2,500
190 barrels of powder, at 45 cents	8,550
2,000 cylinders, at 50 cts.	1,000
150 muskets, at $15	2,250
150 battle-axes, at $1 50	225
150 pikes, at $1 50	225
150 pairs of pistols, at $10	1,500
150 sabres, at $3	450
Colors and signals	1,000
Anchors	3,800
Kentledge, 120 tons, at $40	4,800
Camboose	1,500
Rigger's bill, 36 men for 4 months, at $15 per month	2,000
Charts and mathematical instruments, &c.	800
Contingencies	4,000
Equipment	114,925
Hull and spars	153,475
Building and equipment	$268,400

C.

Estimate of the expense of building and equipping a sloop-of-war of the first class.

5,500 feet of live oak, at $1 30	$7,150
22,000 feet white oak and yellow pine, at 30 cents	6,600
6,000 lbs. of copper bolts and spikes, at 40 cents	2,400
7,875 lbs. of sheathing copper, and nails, at 45 cents	3,543
25 tons, 50,000 lbs. of iron, at 6 cts.	3,000
5,000 lbs. of lead, at 10 cts.	500
Labor of carpenters and mast-makers	18,000
Labor of joiners, including stuff	1,100
Blacksmiths' work	3,000
Plumber's work	500
Turner's bill	300
Carver's bill	200
Hull and spars complete	$46,293
Blockmaker's bill, including gun carriages and everything furnished by him	2,000 00
Sailmaker's bill, 2 suits	5,200 00
Ropemaker's bill	7,100 00
Tanner's bill	250 00
Painter's bill	600 00
Cooper's bill	1,180 00

Estimates for Building and Equipping Ships.

Boat-builder's bill - - -	700 00	Hull and spars - - - -	$46,293	
Ordnance, 20 thirty-two pound carronades,		Equipment - - - - -	35,930	
and two long twelve pounders	4,800 00			
Ordnance stores, 1,600 lbs. shot -	1,550 00	Building and equipment - -	$82,223	
45 bbls. powder, at 45 cents	1,845 00			
1,000 cylinders, at 40 cents	400 00			
75 muskets, at $15 - " -	1,125 00			
75 battle-axes, at $1 50 - " -	112 50			
75 pikes, at $1 50 - . -	112 50			
75 pairs of pistols, at $10 -	750 00			
75 sabres, at $3 - " -	225 00			
Colors and signals - - -	550 00			
Anchors - - - -	1,100 00			
Kentledge, 55 tons, at $40 -	2,260 00			
Camboose - - - -	800 00			
Rigger's bill, 20 men for 3 months, at $15				
per month - - -	900 00			
Charts, mathematical instruments, &c.	450 00			
Contingencies - - - -	2,000 00			
Equipment - - - -	$35,930 00			

[Communicated to the Senate, January 29, 1816.]

NAVY DEPARTMENT, *Jan.* 27, 1816.

SIR: In compliance with the request of the Committee of the Senate on Naval Affairs, communicated by your letter of the 23d, I have the honor to transmit to you for their information, the papers herewith marked A, B, C; which contain the estimates of expense necessary to keep in service, for one year, a seventy-four, a forty-four, and a twenty-two gun ship, respectively; each having a full complement of men and officers, and provisions for twelve months.

I have the honor to be, &c.,

B. W. CROWNINSHIELD.

HON. CHARLES TAIT.

A.

Estimate of the annual expense of a seventy-four gun ship.—January, 1816.

RANK.	PAY AND SUBSISTENCE.		
	Pay per month.	Rations estimated with pay.	Amount of Pay.
1 Captain - - - - - - - -	$100	7	$1,200 00
6 Lieutenants - - - - - -	40	12	2,880 00
1 Surgeon - - - - - - -	50	1	600 00
1 Chaplain - - - - - - -	40	1	480 00
1 Purser - - - - - - - -	40	1	480 00
3 Surgeon's mates - - - - -	30	3	1,080 00
2 Masters - - - - - - -	40	2	960 00
1 Boatswain - - - - - -	20	1	240 00
1 Gunner - - - - - - -	20	1	240 00
1 Carpenter - - - - - -	20	1	240 00
1 Sailmaker - - - - - -	20	1	240 00
3 Master's mates - - - - -	20	-	720 00
20 Midshipmen - - - - - -	19	-	4,560 00
1 Schoolmaster - - - - - -	25	-	300 00
1 Captain's clerk - , - - -	25	-	300 00
6 Boatswain's mates			
3 Gunner's mates			
2 Carpenter's mates } 12 - - - -	19	-	2,736 00
1 Sailmaker's mate			
1 Armorer			
1 Cooper			
1 Steward			
1 Master-at-Arms			
1 Coxswain			
1 Boatswain's yeoman			
1 Gunner's yeoman } 29 - - - -	18	-	6,264 00
1 Carpenter's yeoman			
10 Quarter gunners			
8 Quartermasters			
2 Ship's corporals			
1 Cook			
85 31 rations per day make 11,315 per annum, at 25 cts.	-	-	2,828 75
200 Able seamen - - - - - - -	12	-	26,800 00
300 Ordinary seamen and boys - - -	10	-	36,000 00
———			
585 Pay and subsistence of the Navy - -	-	-	$91,148 75

Estimates for Building and Equipping Ships.

ESTIMATE A—Continued.

RANK.	PAY AND SUBSISTENCE.		Amount of Pay.
	Pay per month.	Rations estimated with pay.	
1 Captain of marines - - - - - - -	$40	2	$480 00
1 First lieutenant - - - - - -	30	2	360 00
1 Second lieutenant - - - - - -	25	1	300 00
3 Sergeants - - - - - - -	9	—	324 00
3 Corporals - - - - - - -	8	—	288 00
2 Musicians - - - - - - -	7	—	168 00
60 Privates - - - - - - -	6	—	4,320 00
656 5 rations per day make 1,825 per annum, at 25 cts.	—	—	456 25
Pay and subsistence of marines - - - -	—	—	6,696 25
Pay and subsistence of navy officers, seamen, and marines - - - - - - - - -	—	—	$97,845 00

Provisions.

597 barrels of beef, at $17 50 - - - - - - -	$10,447 50
512 barrels of pork, at $21 50 - - - - -	11,008 00
171 barrels of flour, at $10 - - - - -	1,710 00
16,056 pounds of suet, at 20 cents - - - -	3,211 20
209,364 pounds of bread, at 6 cents - - -	12,555 84
13,170 pounds of cheese, at 20 cents - - -	2,634 00
4,264 pounds of butter, at 25 cents - - -	1,066 00
483 bushels of peas, at $1 20 - - -	692 20
34,112 pounds of rice, at 5 cents - - -	1,705 60
2,133 gallons of molasses, at $1 - - -	2,133 00
2,133 gallons of vinegar, at 25 cents - - -	533 00
14,934 gallons of spirit, at $1 - - - -	14,934 00
Provisions for 656 persons - - - - -	$62,510 04

Clothing for Marines.

3 Sergeant's suits, at $26 - - - -	$78 00
65 Corporals', musicians' and privates' suits, at $24 - - -	1,560 00
6 Pairs of shoulder knots, at $1 50 - - -	9 00
68 Caps, plumes, bands, and eagles, at $2 - - -	136 00
68 Stocks, at 20 cents - - - -	13 60
272 Pairs of shoes, at $1 37½ - - -	374 00
68 Blankets, at $5 - - - -	340 00
6 Watch coats, at $15 - - -	90 00
Clothing - - - - - - - -	$2,600 60

Military Stores for Marines.

68 Knapsacks, at $1 - - - - - - -	$68 00
68 Brushes and prickers, at 25 cents - - - -	17 00
Military stores - - - - - -	$85 00

Recapitulation and General Estimate.

Pay and subsistence of the Navy - - - - - - -	$91,148 75
Pay and subsistence of marines - - - -	6,696 25
Provisions - - - - - - - - -	62,510 04
Clothing of marines - - - - - -	2,600 60
Military stores for marines - - - - -	85 00
Hospital stores and medicines - - - -	1,600 00
Contingencies, wear and tear, &c. - - - -	25,000 00
Whole annual expense of a seventy-four - - - -	$189,740 64

B.

Estimate of the annual expense of a forty-four gun ship.—January, 1816.

RANK.	PAY AND SUBSISTENCE.		Amount of Pay.
	Pay per month.	Rations estimated with pay.	
1 Captain	$100	7	$1,200 00
6 Lieutenants	40	12	2,880 00
1 Surgeon	50	1	600 00
1 Chaplain	40	1	480 00
1 Purser	40	1	480 00
2 Surgeon's mates	20	2	720 00
1 Master	40	1	480 00
1 Boatswain 1 Gunner 1 Carpenter 1 Sailmaker } 4	20	4	960 00
2 Master's mates	20	-	480 00
20 Midshipmen	19	-	4,560 00
1 Captain's clerk	25	-	300 00
2 Boatswain's mates 1 Gunner's mate 1 Carpenter's mate 1 Sailmaker's mate } 5	19	-	1,140 00
1 Armorer 1 Cooper 1 Steward 1 Master-at-Arms 1 Coxswain 1 Boatswain yeoman 1 Gunner's do. 1 Carpenter's do. 10 Quarter gunners 8 Quartermasters 1 Ship's corporal 1 Cook } 28	18	-	6,048 00
150 Able seamen	12	-	21,600 00
170 Ordinary seamen and boys	10	-	20,400 00
29 rations per day make 10,585 per annum, at 25 cts.	-	-	2,646 25
Pay and subsistence of the Navy	-	-	$64,974 25
1 First lieutenant of marines	30	2	360 00
1 Second lieutenant	25	1	300 00
3 Sergeants	9	-	324 00
2 Corporals	8	-	192 00
2 Musicians	7	-	168 00
48 Privates	6	-	3,456 00
480			
3 rations per day make 1,095 per annum, at 25 cents	-	-	273 75
Pay and subsistence of marines	-	-	5,073 75
Pay and subsistence of navy officers, seamen, and marines	-	-	$70,048 00

Estimates for Building and Equipping Ships.

Provisions.

410 barrels of beef, at $17 50	$7,175 00
351 barrels of pork, at $21 50	7,546 00
118 barrels of flour, at $10	1,180 00
11,700 pounds suet, at 20 cents per pound	2,340 00
9,000 pounds cheese, at 20 cents	1,800 00
143,550 pounds bread, at 6 cents	8,613 00
2,985 pounds butter, at 25 cents	746 25
374 bushels peas, at $1	486 20
23,400 pounds rice, at 5 cents	1,170 00
1,462½ gallons molasses, at $1 per gallon	1,462 50
1,462½ gallons vinegar, at 25 cents	365 63
10,237½ gallons spirit, at $1	10,237 50
Provisions	$43,122 00

Clothing for Marines.

3 Sergeant's suits, at $26	$78 00
52 Corporals, musicians, and privates' suits, at $24	1,248 00
5 Pairs shoulder knots, at $1 50	7 50
55 Cap plumes, bands, and eagles, at $2	110 00
55 Stocks, at 20 cents	12 00
55 Blankets, at $5	275 00
220 Pairs shoes, at $1 37½	302 50
6 Watch coats, at $15	90 00
Clothing	$2,123 00

Military Stores for Marines.

55 Knapsacks, at $1	$55 00
55 Brushes and prickers, at 25 cents	13 75
Military stores	$68 75

Recapitulation of general estimate.

Pay and subsistence of the Navy	$64,374 25
Pay and subsistence of marines	5,673 75
Provisions	43,122 08
Clothing of marines	2,122 00
Military stores	68 75
Hospital stores and medicines	1,350 00
Contingencies, wear and tear, &c.	17,500 00
Whole annual expense of a forty-four	$134,210 83

Estimates for Building and Equipping Ships.

C.

Estimate of the annual expense of a sloop-of-war of the first class.—January, 1816.

RANK.	PAY AND SUBSISTENCE.		
	Pay per month.	Rations estimated with pay.	Amount of pay.
1 Captain	$75	5	$900 00
3 Lieutenants	40	6	1,440 00
1 Purser	40	1	480 00
1 Surgeon	50	1	600 00
2 Surgeon's mates	30	2	720 00
1 Sailing-master	40	1	480 00
1 Boatswain	20	1	240 00
1 Gunner	20	1	240 00
1 Sailmaker	20	1	240 00
1 Carpenter	20	1	240 00
3 Master's mates	20	-	720 00
10 Midshipmen	19	-	2,280 00
1 Captain's clerk	25	-	300 00
2 Boatswain's mates			
1 Gunner's mate	19	-	912 00
1 Carpenter's mate			
1 Coxswain			
2 Yeomen			
6 Quarter-gunners			
4 Quartermasters			
1 Armorer	18	-	3,888 00
1 Steward			
1 Cooper			
1 Master-at-arms			
1 Cook			
60 Able seamen	12	-	8,640 00
48 Ordinary seamen and boys	10	-	5,760 00
20 rations per day make 7,300 per annum at 25 cents	-	-	1,825 00
Pay and subsistence of the Navy	-	-	$29,905 00
1 Second Lieutenant of Marines	25	1	300 00
1 Sergeant	9	-	108 00
2 Corporals	8	-	192 00
2 Musicians	7	-	168 00
21 Privates	6	-	1,512 00
1 ration per day makes 365 per annum, at 25 cents	-	-	91 25
Pay and subsistence of marines	-	-	2,371 25
Pay and subsistence of Navy officers, seamen, and marines	-	-	$32,276 25

Provisions.

167 barrels of beef, at $17 50	-	$2,922 50
144 barrels of pork, at $21 50	-	3,096 00
48 barrels of flour, at $10	-	480 00
4,504 pounds of suet, at 20 cents	-	900 80
58,696 pounds of bread, at 6 cents	-	3,521 76
3,680 pounds of cheese, at 20 cents	-	736 00
1,196 pounds of butter, at 25 cents	-	299 00
150 bushels of peas, at $1 30	-	195 00
9,568 pounds of rice, at 5 cents	-	478 40
598 gallons of molasses, at $1	-	598 00
598 gallons of vinegar, at 25 cents	-	149 50
4,186 gallons of spirit, at $1	-	4,186 00
Provisions for one hundred and eighty-four persons	-	$17,562 96

Captors of the British Ship of War Levant.

Clothing for Marines.

1 Sergeant's suit - - - -	$26 00
25 Corporals, musicians, and privates' suits, at $24 - - - -	600 00
3 pairs of shoulder knots, at $1 50 -	4 50
26 caps, plumes, bands, and eagles, at $2	52 00
26 stocks, at 20 cents - - - , -	5 20
26 blankets, at $5 - - - -	130 00
104 pairs of shoes, at $1 37½ -	143 00
2 watch coats, at $15 - - -	30 00
	$990 70

Military Stores for Marines.

26 knapsacks, at $1 - - - -	$26 00
26 brushes and prickers, at 25 cents -	6 50
	$32 50

Recapitulation and general estimate.

Pay and subsistence of the Navy -	$29,905 00
Pay and subsistence of marines -	3,371 25
Provisions - - - - -	17,562 96
Clothing of marines - - -	990 70
Military stores for marines - -	32 50
Hospital stores and medicines - -	900 00
Contingencies, wear and tear, &c. -	7,500 00
	$59,162 41

CAPTORS OF THE BRITISH SHIP-OF-WAR LEVANT REWARDED.
—

[Communicated to the House, February 5, 1816.]

Mr. PLEASANTS made the following report: The Committee on Naval Affairs, to whom was referred the petition of Captain Charles Stewart, late commander of the frigate Constitution, praying to be paid the value of the Levant, a British ship-of-war captured by the Constitution in her late cruise, and taken by force out of the harbor of Port Praya, a neutral port, by a squadron of British ships, have had the said petition under consideration, and make the following report: The petitioner states that, on the 20th of February 1815, with the frigate Constitution under his command, whilst cruising in the neighborhood of the island of Madeira, he fell in with two British ships of war, the Cyane mounting thirty-four guns, and the Levant mounting twenty-one; that the Constitution brought the two ships to action, and captured both after a conflict of forty minutes; that having taken possession of her prizes the Constitution proceeded on her cruise, and on the 10th of March anchored with her prizes in Port Praya in St. Jago, one of the Cape de Verd islands belonging to Portugal; that, on the next day, March the 11th, whilst lying in the said port, they discovered a squadron of ships, which ultimately proved to be British, consisting of three sail, two of sixty-eight and one of fifty guns, commanded by Sir George Collier; that the Constitution with her prizes immediately got under way, and with much difficulty escaped the enemy, who had approached very near, under cover of a thick fog, before they were discovered; that the Constitution and Cyane got off without being brought to action by so superior a force, and the Levant, which had moved in a direction to divide the attention of the enemy, being pursued, was enabled to get back into Port Praya, and anchored close under the batteries, thinking the enemy would respect the neutrality of the port; that in that situation she was attacked and taken possession of by the enemy, without any attempt on the part of the Portuguese to prevent the outrage.

The petitioner asks of Congress to pay to the officers and crew of the Constitution the value of the Levant, she having been captured by them on the high seas, and forcibly taken from a neutral port by the enemy.

The committee are of opinion that the petitioners have not a right to demand of the United States the value of the said prize. Though the Government have a right to demand of the Portuguese Government compensation for the outrage committed in one of their ports, and if compensation is made, the amount ought to be paid to the captors, yet, in the many and great losses sustained by our citizens during the late war in Europe by the violation of their neutral rights, it has not been the practice of the Government to make compensation for such losses. Were it to be done in this case, the captors would be placed in a more eligible situation than if the outrage had not been committed; in that case they would have had to encounter the ordinary dangers of the sea in bringing their prize into port; and also the hazard of recapture by the enemy. But proceeding on the principle acted on by Congress in other cases which occurred during the late war, of making some compensation for the gallantry and good conduct of the officers and men, where they did not succeed in getting their prizes into port, and such gallantry and good conduct having been signally displayed in this action, the proper tribunals having determined that the force of the enemy was superior, the committee taking the case of the Frolic captured by the Wasp, and recaptured by the enemy, as a proper criterion, the force of the Levant being about equal to that of the Frolic, and the compensation made being twenty-five thousand dollars, recommend the passage of an act authorizing the payment of that sum to the officers and crew of the Constitution, to be deducted from the value of the Levant, provided the Government succeed in obtaining such value from the Portuguese Government. For this purpose they herewith report a bill.

To the honorable the Senate and House of Representatives of the United States of America, in Congress assembled. The petition of the subscriber respectfully showeth:

PHILADELPHIA, *December 22*, 1815.

That, on the 29th day of February, 1815, the United States frigate Constitution, then under his command, did, in pursuance of the orders of

Capture of the British Ship of War Levant.

the late honorable Secretary of the Navy, William Jones, overtake on the high seas, about sixty leagues from the island of Madeira. His Britannic Majesty's ships of war the Cyane, of thirty-four guns, commanded by Captain Gordon Falcon, and the Levant, of twenty-one guns, commanded by Captain the honorable George Douglas, both post captains in the navy of Great Britain, and did there bring to action, engage with, and capture the said two ships of war, the Cyane and Levant, after a sharp conflict of forty minutes; and that your petitioner did take possession of the two prizes aforesaid, and proceed in the frigate Constitution with them to the island of St. Jago, one of the Cape de Verds, in the possession of the troops and subjects of the Prince Regent of Portugal, with whom we were at peace, and from whom there had issued a declaration of neutrality when the war between the United States and Great Britain was made known to him; that your petitioner, having come to anchor with the Constitution, and the above named prizes, in Port Praya, in the aforesaid island of St. Jago, on the 10th day of March, 1815, discovered, on the following day, (while preparations were making by your petitioner to divest himself of his prisoners, by sending them on parole to Barbadoes agreeable to his instructions,) off the port, a squadron of three ships of war, belonging to the King of Great Britain, commanded by his officers generally, and under the command of the honorable Sir George Collier particularly, consisting of the Leander of sixty-eight guns, Newcastle of sixty-eight guns, and Acasta of fifty guns; that the said squadron by means of, and covered by, a thick fog, approached the ship Constitution and her two prizes within three miles before they were discovered, which near approach left no time for your petitioner to hesitate or deliberate on the situation of your good ship the Constitution and her two prizes, but obliged him, for the security of that valuable vessel intrusted to his care, to get under weigh and rescue her from the probable grasp of the enemy, which your petitioner did, taking with him the two prize ships aforesaid, that they might be used according to circumstances, and for the purpose of saving the Constitution: all of which was done according to the best skill and judgment of your petitioner; and your precious ship the Constitution returned in safety to the port of Boston.

And your petitioner begs leave to state, to your honorable body, that while they were in the act of getting under weigh in the harbor of Port Praya, the flag of the Prince Regent of Portugal was hoisted on two several forts, and a fire opened from their batteries upon the Constitution and her two prizes; several shot from them passing both over and striking near the bends of the Constitution; that after your petitioner had derived all the advantages he could from his prizes aforesaid, the Levant returned into the harbor of Port Praya, and came to anchor close to the batteries thereof, where she was soon after attacked by the aforesaid squadron, under the command of the aforesaid Sir George Collier, and forcibly taken

possession of by them and carried from out of the harbor of Port Praya aforesaid, without the troops, garrison, or subjects of the Prince Regent of Portugal making any resistance or hindrance whatever, as they were in duty bound to do within the harbors and neutral waters of the Prince Regent of Portugal.

Your petitioner, therefore, for and in behalf of himself, the gallant officers, and crew of the frigate Constitution under his command, and in consideration of their being so unlawfully and unjustly robbed and deprived of the usual advantages that would accrue to them, for their gallantry in engaging and subduing the aforesaid two ships-of-war belonging to the King of Great Britain; humbly beg your honorable body will take this their case into consideration; and that you will be pleased to grant to them the value of the said ship Levant, of which they have been deprived as above stated; and your petitioner will ever pray, &c.

CHARLES STEWART,
Late commander of frigate Constitution.

NAVY DEPARTMENT, *January* 5, 1816.

SIR: In compliance with the instructions of the honorable Committee upon Naval Affairs, communicated by your letter of the 29th ultimo, I have the honor to enclose to you papers No. 1 to 6; which contain all the information in the possession of this Department relative to the capture of the British vessels of war Cyane and Levant, by the United States' frigate Constitution, under the command of Captain Charles Stewart, of the United States' Navy.

I have the honor to be, very respectfully, your obedient servant,

B. W. CROWNINSHIELD.
Hon. JAMES PLEASANTS, Jun.
Chairman Com. on Naval Affairs.

No. 1.

U. S. FRIGATE CONSTITUTION, *May,* 1815.

SIR: On the 20th of February last, the island of Madeira bearing about west-southwest, distant sixty leagues, we fell in with His Britannic Majesty's two ships of war the Cyane and the Levant, and brought them to action about 6 o'clock in the evening; both of which, after a spirited engagement of forty minutes, surrendered to the ship under my command.

Considering the advantages derived by the enemy, from a divided and more active force, as also their superiority in the weight and number of their guns, I deem the speedy and decisive result of this action the strongest assurance which can be given to Government that all under my command did their duty, and gallantly supported the reputation of American seamen.

Enclosed you will receive the minutes of the action, and a list of the killed and wounded on board this ship; also, enclosed, you will receive, for your information, a statement of the actual force of the enemy, and the number of killed and wounded on board their ships as near as could be ascertained.

I have the honor to be, &c.

CHARLES STEWART.

Hon. B. W. CROWNINSHIELD,
Secretary of the Navy.

No. 2.

Minutes of the chase of the United States frigate Constitution, by an English squadron of three ships, from out the harbor of Port Praya, island of St. Jago.

Commences with fresh breezes and foggy weather; at five minutes past 12, discovered a large ship through the fog, standing in for Port Praya; at eight minutes past 12, discovered two other large ships astern of her, also standing in for the port. From their general appearance, supposed them to be one of the enemy's squadrons, and, from the little respect hitherto paid by them to neutral waters, I deemed it most prudent to put to sea. The signal was made to the Cyane and Levant to get under weigh; at twelve after meridian, with our topsail set, we cut our cable and got under weigh, (when the Portuguese opened a fire on us from several of their batteries on shore;) the prize ships followed our motions, and stood out of the harbor of Port Praya close under East point, passing the enemy's squadron about gunshot to windward of them. Crossed our top-gallant yards and set foresail, mainsail, spanker, flying jib, and top-gallant sails. The enemy seeing us under weigh, tacked ship, and made all sail in chase of us. As far as we could judge of their rates from the thickness of the weather, supposed them two ships-of-the-line, and one frigate. At half past meridian, cut away the boats towing astern, first cutter and gig; at 1 P. M. found our sailing about equal with the ship on our quarter, but the frigate luffing, gaining our wake, and rather dropping astern of us; finding the Cyane dropping astern and to leeward, and the frigate gaining on her fast, I found it impossible to save her if she continued on the same course, without having the Constitution brought to action by their whole force; I made the signal at ten minutes past 1 P. M. to her to tack ship, which was complied with. This manœuvre, I conceived, would detach one of the enemy's ships in pursuit of her, while, at the same time, from her position, she would be enabled to reach the anchorage at Port Praya before the detached ships could come up with her; but, if they did not tack after her, it would afford her an opportunity to double their rear, and make her escape before the wind. They all continued in full chase of the Levant and this ship; the ship on our lee quarter firing by divisions broadsides; her shot falling short of us. At 3 P. M. by our having dropped the Levant considerably, her situation became (from the position of the enemy's frigate) similar to the Cyane, it became necessary to separate also from the Levant, or risk this ship being brought to action to cover her. I made the signal at five minutes past 3 for her to

tack, which was complied with; at twelve minutes past three, the whole of the enemy's squadron tacked in pursuit of the Levant, and gave up the pursuit of this ship. This sacrifice of the Levant became necessary for the preservation of the Constitution. Sailingmaster Hixon, midshipman Varnum, one boatswain's mate, and twelve men, were absent on duty in the fifth cutter, to bring the cartel brig under our stern.

No. 3.

Minutes of the action between the United States frigate Constitution, and His Majesty's ships Cyane and Levant, on the 20th February, 1815.

Commences with light breezes from the eastward and cloudy weather; at 1, discovered a sail two points on the larboard bow; hauled up and made sail in chase; at quarter past 1, made the sail to be a ship; at three-quarters past 1, discovered another sail ahead; made them out at 2 P. M. to be both ships, standing close hauled with their starboard tacks on board. At 4 P. M. the weathermost ship made signals, and bore up for her consort, then about ten miles to leeward; we bore up after her, and set lower topmast, topgallant, and royal studding sails in chase; at half past 4, carried away our main royal mast; took in the sails and got another prepared. At 5 P. M. commenced firing on the chase, from our two larboard bow guns; our shot falling short, ceased firing; at half past 5, finding it impossible to prevent their junction, cleared ship for action, then about four miles from the two ships; at forty minutes after 5, they passed within hail of each other, and hauled by the wind on the starboard tack, hauled up their courses, and prepared to receive us; at forty-five minutes past 5, they made all sail close hauled by the wind, in hopes of getting to windward of us; at fifty-five minutes past 5, finding themselves disappointed in their object, and we were closing with them fast, they shortened sail, and formed on a line of wind about half a cable's length from each other. At 6 P. M., having them under command of our battery, hoisted our colors, which was answered by both ships hoisting English ensigns. At five minutes past 6, ranged up on the starboard side of the sternmost ship about three hundred yards distant, and commenced the action by broadsides, both ships returning our fire with great spirit for about fifteen minutes; then the fire of the enemy beginning to slacken, and the great column of smoke collected under our lee induced us to cease our fire to ascertain their positions and conditions; and in about three minutes, the smoke clearing away, we found ourselves abreast of the headmost ship, the sternmost ship luffing up for our larboard quarter; we poured a broadside into the headmost ship, and then braced aback our main and mizzen topsails, and backed astern under cover of the smoke, abreast the sternmost ship; when the action was continued with spirit and considerable effect until thirty-five minutes past 6, when the enemy's fire again slackened, and we discovered the headmost bearing up;

Capture of the British Ship of War Levant.

filled our topsails, shot ahead, and gave her two stern rakes; we then discovered the sternmost ship wearing also, wore ship immediately after her, and gave her a stern rake, she luffing too on our starboard bows, and giving us her larboard broadside; we ranged up on her larboard quarter within hail, and was about to give her our starboard broadside, when she struck her colors, fired a lee gun, and yielded. At fifty minutes past 6, took possession of His Majesty's ship Cyane, Captain Gordon Falcon, mounting thirty-four guns. At 8 P. M. filled away after her consort, which was still in sight to leeward; at half past 8, found her standing towards us, with her starboard tack close hauled, with topgallant sails set, and colors flying; at fifty minutes past eight, ranged close along side to windward of her, on opposite tacks, and exchanged broadsides, wore immediately under her stern and raked her with a broadside, she then crowded all sail, and endeavored to escape by running; hauled on board our tacks, set spanker and flying jib in chase; at half past 9, commenced firing on her from our starboard bow chaser, gave her several shot, which cut her spars and rigging considerably; at 10 P. M., finding they could not escape, fired a gun, struck her colors, and yielded. We immediately took possession of His Majesty's ship Levant, Hon. Captain George Douglas, mounting twenty-one guns. At 1 A. M. the damages of our rigging were repaired, sails shifted, and the ship in fighting condition.

No. 4.—*General Orders.*

U. S. FRIGATE CONSTITUTION,
February 23, 1815.

Captain Stewart takes the first opportunity of returning his thanks to the officers, seamen, ordinary seamen, and marines of this ship, for their gallantry, order, and discipline, displayed by all under his command on the night of the 20th instant, while engaged with His Majesty's late ships Cyane and Levant, and congratulates them on the glorious result of their exertions; a result which could not have been produced against so superior a force, commanded by distinguished officers, without the energy and order so conspicuously exhibited by all on that occasion. We were not only outnumbered in guns and weight of metal by the enemy, but had also to contend with a more active class of vessels, and a divided force, which gave to them every advantage. Be assured that the laurels you have acquired for yourselves will never fade, and that the share of glory you have given to your country will be hailed by your fellow-citizens with the greatest satisfaction, and posterity, in beholding the trophies gained by your gallant predecessors in victory, shall view with grateful sensations the two which you have added to their number.

You will accept his thanks for the promptness with which you repaired the damages and secured the three ships, and he assures you that it will not be least among your merits, when it is known, that in one hour after a contest so severe, your own ship was ready to fight another action, and your prizes enabled to make sail.

The excellent example hitherto shown by our naval victors in their respect towards the persons and property of a subdued enemy, he trusts, will not be deviated from by any under his command; surely, there can be none among you who can be desirous of tarnishing so much of your well-earned glory, as to hesitate between the choice of being scornfully pointed at as a plunderer, or to perceive the finger of satisfaction selecting you as a hero. If, therefore, any of you have unwarily possessed yourselves improperly of either public or private property, he commands you to give it immediately to the commanding officer. You surely cannot wish to bring disgrace on your commander or your officers, whom you have so gallantly supported.

It is much to be regretted, that on occasions like the present, the commander is not permitted to see with his own eyes the distinguished merits of each officer, that he might thank them individually for their exertions, but as all must have done their duty well to produce such decisive effect, he begs they will receive his thanks collectively. He tenders to the officers commanding the gundeck, forecastle, and quarterdeck divisions, his thanks for the steady and incessant fire kept up by their batteries, the vivacity of which nothing could surpass. To Captain Henderson and Lieutenant Freeman, commanding the marines, he owes his grateful thanks for the lively and well-directed fire kept up by the detachment under their command. He thanks Mr. Hixon, and the officers stationed on the forecastle and tops, for their steady attention to orders, and the promptness with which they replaced everything important that was shot away. To Mr. Pottinger, and the officers superintending the magazines and passages, he gives his thanks for the facility with which every essential was furnished the batteries from their departments. To Doctor Kearney, and his assistants in the cockpit, he feels great obligations for their humanity and skill in relieving and assisting the wounded. Captain Stewart begs Lieutenant Ballard to accept his thanks for the prompt assistance he gave him in all the operations and manœuvres of the ship, for the alacrity with which every order was attended to, and the promptness with which they were executed, and he assures him that the gallantry and good conduct displayed by him on that occasion will make a lasting impression on his gratitude. To Mr. Humphreys, commanding the flag-guard, and the officers attached to him as aids, he gives his thanks, and assures them that he is highly satisfied with their gallantry and support.

No. 5.

U. S. FRIGATE CONSTITUTION,
Off New York, May 18, 1815.

SIR: Agreeably to an act of Congress, I have the pleasure to transmit to you the flags of His

Public Acts of Congress.

An Act to repeal so much of an act, passed on the twenty-third day of December, one thousand eight hundred and fourteen, as imposes additional duties on postage.

Be it enacted, &c., That, from and after the thirty-first day of March next, so much of the act, entitled "An act to provide additional revenues for defraying the expenses of Government and maintaining the public credit, by duties on sales at auction, and on licenses to retail wines, spirit-uous liquors, and foreign merchandise, and for increasing the rates of postage," passed the twenty-third day of December, one thousand eight hundred and fourteen, as imposes additional duties on postage, be, and the same is hereby, repealed.

Approved, February 1, 1816.

An Act continuing in force certain acts laying duties on bank notes, refined sugars, and for other purposes.

Be it enacted, &c., That the act, entitled "An act laying duties on notes of banks, bankers, and certain companies; on notes, bonds, and obligations, discounted by banks, bankers, and certain companies; and on bills of exchange of certain descriptions," passed the second day of August, one thousand eight hundred and thirteen, and the act supplementary to said act, passed the tenth day of December, one thousand eight hundred and fourteen, and the act, entitled "An act laying duties on sugar refined within the United States," passed the twenty-fourth day of July, one thou-sand eight hundred and thirteen, shall be, and the same are hereby, continued in force; anything in the said acts in anywise to the contrary not-withstanding.

Approved, February 1, 1816.

An Act to continue in force the act, entitled "An act for imposing additional duties upon all goods, wares, and merchandise, imported from any foreign port or place, and for other purposes.

Be it enacted, &c., That the additional duties upon goods, wares, and merchandise, imported into the United States, and upon the tonnage of vessels, imposed by the act, entitled "An act for imposing additional duties upon all goods, wares, and merchandise, imported from any foreign port or place, and for other purposes," passed on the first day of July, in the year one thousand eight hundred and twelve, shall continue to be laid, levied, and collected in the mode therein pre-scribed, subject in all respects to the same regula-tions and provisions, and with the like fines, pen-alties, forfeitures, and remedies for breaches of the law, as are now provided by law, until the thir-tieth day of June next, anything in the said act to the contrary thereof in anywise notwithstand-ing.

Sec. 2. *And be it further enacted*, That, from and after the said thirtieth day of June next, there shall be laid, levied, and collected, in the manner and under the regulations and allowances now prescribed by law, for the collection and draw-back of duties on foreign goods, wares, and mer-chandise, an additional duty of forty-two per cent. on the duties which shall then exist on foreign goods, wares, and merchandise, until a new tariff of duties shall be established by law.

Sec. 3. *And be it further enacted*, That nothing in this act contained shall be so construed as to contravene any provision of any commercial treaty, or convention, concluded between the United States and any foreign Power or State; nor so as to impair, or in anywise affect the pro-visions of the act, entitled "An act to repeal so much of the several acts imposing duties on the tonnage of ships and vessels, and on goods, wares, and merchandise, imported into the United States, as imposes a discriminating duty on tonnage be-tween foreign vessels and vessels of the United States, and between goods imported into the United States in foreign vessels and in vessels of the United States," passed on the third day of March, in the year one thousand eight hundred and fifteen.

Approved, February 5, 1816.

An Act to continue in force "An act entitled an act laying a duty on imported salt, granting a bounty on pickled fish exported, and allowances to certain vessels employed in the fisheries."

Be it enacted, &c., That the act, entitled "An act laying a duty on imported salt, granting a bounty on pickled fish exported, and allowances to certain vessels employed in the fisheries," passed on the twenty-ninth day of July, in the year one thousand eight hundred and thirteen, shall be, and the same is hereby, continued in force, any-thing in the said act to the contrary thereof in anywise notwithstanding.

Approved, February 9, 1816.

An Act concerning certain Courts of the United States in the State of New York.

Be it enacted, &c., That no legal proceedings whatever in the courts of the United States, for the northern district of New York, shall be dis-continued, abated, impaired, or affected, by reason that the last terms of the district court for the said northern district, appointed to be held at Utica and Canandaigua were not held, but that every proceeding whatever shall be in the same state, and have the same force and effect, as if the said terms had been duly held.

Approved, February 15, 1816.

An Act to increase the pensions of Robert White, Ja-cob Wrighter, John Young, and John Crampersey.

Be it enacted, &c., That there be, and hereby is, granted to Robert White, of Reading, in the State of Vermont, who, in the defence of Fort Erie, lost both his arms by a cannon shot, in lieu of the pension to which he is now entitled by law, a pension of forty dollars per month, to commence on the fifth day of March, one thousand eight hundred and fifteen; to Jacob Wrighter, of the city of Trenton, in the State of New Jersey, who lost his right arm and right leg at the capture of

Little York, in Upper Canada, in lieu of the pension to which he is now entitled by law, a pension of thirty dollars per month, to commence on the tenth day of May, one thousand eight hundred and fifteen; to John Young, of the town of Boston, and State of Massachusetts, who lost both arms at French Creek, in descending the river St. Lawrence, by a cannon ball, in lieu of the pension to which he is now entitled by law, a pension of forty dollars per month, to commence from the thirtieth day of April, one thousand eight hundred and fifteen; and to John Cramper-sey, of the town of Beverly, and State of Massachusetts, who lost both arms in the late war with Great Britain, in lieu of the pension to which he is now entitled by law, a pension of forty dollars per month, to commence from the fifteenth day of November, one thousand eight hundred and fourteen; and the Secretary of War is hereby directed to place the said Robert White, Jacob Wrighter, John Young, and John Crampersey, on the pension list accordingly.

Approved, February 22, 1816.

An Act to repeal the duties on certain articles manufactured within the United States.

Be it enacted, &c., That the act, entitled "An act to provide additional revenues for defraying the expenses of Government, and maintaining the public credit, by laying duties on various goods, wares, and merchandise, manufactured within the United States," passed the eighteenth of January, one thousand eight hundred and fifteen, and also the act, entitled "An act to provide additional revenue for defraying the expenses of Government, and maintaining the public credit, by laying a duty on gold, silver, and plated ware, and jewelry, and paste work, manufactured within the United States," passed on the twenty-seventh of February, one thousand eight hundred and fifteen, be, and the same are hereby repealed: Provided, That for the recovery and receipt of such duties as have accrued, and remain outstanding, and for the recovery and distribution of fines, penalties, and forfeitures, and the remission thereof, which have been incurred in relation to any duty which shall have heretofore accrued, the provisions of the aforesaid acts shall remain in full force and virtue.

Approved, February 22, 1816.

An Act for the relief of John Redman Coxe.

Be it enacted, &c., That the duties which have been secured to be paid by John Redman Coxe to the United States, on the importation into the same of a philosophical apparatus, and of a collection of mineral substances, to be used by him as professor of chemistry in the University of Pennsylvania, be, and the same are hereby, remitted, on sufficient proof being made, to the Comptroller of the Treasury, that the articles abovementioned have been imported by the said Coxe, to be used for the purposes aforementioned.

Approved, February 26, 1816.

An Act rewarding the officers and crew of the sloop-of-war Hornet, for the capture and destruction of the British sloop-of-war Penguin.

Be it enacted, &c., That the President of the United States be, and he is hereby, authorized to have distributed, as prize money, to Captain James Biddle, of the sloop-of-war Hornet, his officers, and crew, the sum of twenty-five thousand dollars, for the capture and destruction of the British sloop-of-war Penguin; and that the sum of twenty-five thousand dollars, out of any money in the Treasury not otherwise appropriated, be, and the same is hereby, appropriated, for the purpose aforesaid.

Approved, February 28, 1816.

An Act concerning the Convention to regulate the commerce between the territories of the United States and His Britannic Majesty.

Be it enacted, &c., That so much of any act as imposes a higher duty of tonnage, or of impost, on vessels and articles imported in vessels of Great Britain, than on vessels and articles imported in vessels of the United States, contrary to the provisions of the convention between the United States and His Britannic Majesty, the ratifications whereof were mutually exchanged the twenty-second day of December, one thousand eight hundred and fifteen, be, from and after the date of the ratification of the said convention, and during the continuance thereof, deemed and taken to be of no force or effect.

Approved, March 1, 1816.

An Act to reduce the amount of direct tax upon the United States, and the District of Columbia, for the year one thousand eight hundred and sixteen; and to repeal in part the act, entitled "An act to provide additional revenue for defraying the expenses of Government, and maintaining the public credit, by laying a direct tax upon the United States, and to provide for assessing and collecting the same;" and also the act, entitled "An act to provide additional revenue for defraying the expenses of Government, and maintaining the public credit, by laying a direct tax upon the District of Columbia."

Be it enacted, &c., That so much of the act entitled "An act to provide additional revenues for defraying the expenses of Government, and maintaining the public credit, by laying a direct tax upon the United States, and to provide for assessing and collecting the same," passed on the ninth of January, one thousand eight hundred and fifteen, as lays a direct tax of six millions of dollars for the year one thousand eight hundred and sixteen, and for succeeding years, be, and the same is hereby, repealed.

Sec. 2. And be it further enacted, That a direct tax of three millions of dollars be, and the same is hereby, laid upon the United States, for the year one thousand eight hundred and sixteen, and apportioned to the States respectively, in the manner, and according to the sums prescribed by the first section of an act, entitled "An act to lay and collect a direct tax within the United States,"

Public Acts of Congress.

and all the provisions of the act, entitled "An act to provide additional revenues for defraying the expenses of Government, and maintaining the public credit, by laying a direct tax upon the United States, and to provide for assessing and collecting the same," passed on the ninth of January, one thousand eight hundred and fifteen, except so far as the same have been varied by subsequent acts, and excepting the first section of the said act, shall be held to apply to the assessment and collection of the direct tax of three millions of dollars, hereby laid upon the United States.

SEC. 3. *And be it further enacted,* That so much of the act, entitled "An act to provide additional revenue for defraying the expenses of Government, and maintaining the public credit, by laying a direct tax upon the District of Columbia," passed the twenty-seventh of February, in the year one thousand eight hundred and fifteen, as lays a direct tax of nineteen thousand nine hundred and ninety-eight dollars and forty cents, upon the said District, for the year one thousand eight hundred and sixteen, and for succeeding years, be, and the same is hereby, repealed.

SEC. 4. *And be it further enacted,* That a direct tax of nine thousand nine hundred and ninety-nine dollars and twenty cents be, and the same is hereby, laid upon the District of Columbia, for the year one thousand eight hundred and sixteen, and all the provisions of the act, entitled "An act to provide additional revenues for defraying the expenses of Government, and maintaining the public credit, by laying a direct tax upon the District of Columbia," passed on the twenty-seventh day of February, in the year one thousand eight hundred and fifteen, except so far as the same have been varied by subsequent acts, shall be held to apply to the assessment and collection of the direct tax which is hereinbefore laid upon the said District.

SEC. 5. *And be it further enacted,* That whenever the Secretary of the Treasury shall be duly advised of the assumption by any State of the payment of its quota of the said direct tax, he shall give directions to the assessors of such State to suspend the further execution of their respective offices in relation to this act: *Provided,* That if any State, so assuming the payment of its quota of said direct tax, shall fail to pay the same at the time fixed upon for such payment, the Secretary of the Treasury shall instruct the assessors of said State to proceed in the execution of their respective duties, in relation to this act.

SEC. 6. *And be it further enacted,* That if either the States of Ohio or Louisiana shall pay its quota of the direct tax according to the provisions of the act, entitled "An act to provide additional revenues for defraying the expenses of Government, and maintaining the public credit, by laying a direct tax upon the United States, and to provide for assessing and collecting the same," the Legislature thereof shall be, and they are hereby, authorized and empowered to collect of all the purchasers of public lands under any law of the United States, a just and equal propor-

tion of the quota of said States respectively, the compact between the United States and the said States to the contrary notwithstanding.
Approved, March 5, 1816.

An Act granting bounties in lands and extra pay to certain Canadian volunteers.

Be it enacted, &c., That all such persons as had been citizens of the United States anterior to the late war, and were at its commencement inhabitants of the province of Canada, and who, during the said war, joined the armies of the United States as volunteers, and were slain, died in service, or continued therein till honorably discharged, shall be entitled to the following quantities of land respectively, viz: Each colonel nine hundred and sixty acres; each major to eight hundred acres; each captain six hundred and forty acres; each subaltern officer to four hundred and eighty acres; each non-commissioned officer, musician, or private, to three hundred and twenty acres; and the bounties aforesaid shall extend to the medical and other staff, who shall rank according to their pay. And it shall be lawful for the said persons to locate their claims in quarter sections, upon any of the unappropriated lands of the United States, within the Indiana Territory, which shall have been surveyed prior to such location, with the exception of salt springs and lead mines therein, and of the quantities of land adjacent thereto which may be reserved for the use of the same, by the President of the United States, and the section number sixteen in every township, to be granted to the inhabitants of such township for the use of public schools; which locations shall be subject to such regulations, as to priority of choice, and the manner of location, as the President of the United States shall prescribe.

SEC. 2. *And be it further enacted,* That the Secretary for the Department of War, for the time being, shall, from time to time, under such rules and regulations as to evidence as the President of the United States shall prescribe, issue to every person coming within the description aforesaid, a warrant for such quantity of land as he may be entitled to by virtue of the aforesaid provision; and in case of the death of such person, then such warrant shall be issued to his widow, or, if no widow, to his child or children.

SEC. 3. *And be it further enacted,* That the Treasurer of the United States be, and he is hereby, authorized and required to pay to each of the persons aforesaid three months additional pay, according to the rank they respectively held in the Army of the United States during the late war.

Approved, March 5, 1816.

An Act making appropriations for ordnance and ordnance stores, for the year one thousand eight hundred and sixteen.

Be it enacted, &c., That for the expense of ordnance and ordnance stores, including arsenals, magazines, and armories, for the year one thou-

and eight hundred and sixteen, the following sums be, and the same are hereby, respectively appropriated, that is to say: for armories, three hundred and thirty-seven thousand eight hundred and forty-eight dollars twenty-five cents; for arsenals, three hundred and eighty-three thousand dollars; for timber for mounting cannon, seventy-five thousand dollars; for coals, iron, and steel, seventy-nine thousand dollars; for contracts for gunpowder, ninety-three thousand dollars; for contracts for cannon, shot, and shells, one hundred and eleven thousand dollars; in part of the annual sum of two hundred thousand dollars, appropriated for the purpose of providing arms and military equipments for the militia, eighty-nine thousand dollars.

Sec. 2. *And be it further enacted*, That the several appropriations hereinbefore made shall be paid out of any moneys in the Treasury not otherwise appropriated.

Approved, March 18, 1816.

An Act to change the mode of compensation to the members of the Senate and House of Representatives, and the Delegates from Territories.

Be it enacted, &c., That, instead of the daily compensation now allowed by law, there shall be paid annually to the Senators, Representatives, and Delegates from Territories, of this and every future Congress of the United States, the following sums, respectively: that is to say, to the President of the Senate, pro tempore, when there is no Vice President, and to the Speaker of the House of Representatives, three thousand dollars each; to each Senator, member of the House of Representatives, other than the Speaker and Delegates, the sum of fifteen hundred dollars: *Provided, nevertheless*, That in case any Senator, Representative, or Delegate, shall not attend in his place at the day on which Congress shall convene, or shall absent himself before the close of the session, a deduction shall be made from the sum which would otherwise be allowed to him, in proportion to the time of his absence, saving to the cases of sickness the same provisions as are established by existing laws. And the aforesaid allowance shall be certified and paid in the same manner as the daily compensation to members of Congress has heretofore been.

Approved, March 19, 1816.

An Act to alter the times of holding the Circuit and District Courts of the United States, for the District of Vermont.

Be it enacted, &c., That the circuit court of the United States within and for the district of Vermont, instead of the first day of May, shall hereafter be holden on the twenty-first day of May, and the district court of the United States, within and for the said district, instead of the seventh day of May, shall hereafter be holden on the twenty-seventh day of May, at the place now fixed by law for holding the said courts.

Sec. 2. *And be it further enacted*, That all indictments, informations, suits, or actions and pro-

ceedings of every kind, whether of a civil or criminal nature, now pending in the said courts, respectively, shall have day in court and be proceeded in, heard, tried, and determined on the days herein appointed for holding the said courts respectively, in the same manner as they might, and ought to have been done, had the said courts been holden, respectively, on the first and seventh days of May, as heretofore directed by law.

Sec. 3. *And be it further enacted*, That all writs, suits, actions, recognizances, or other proceedings which are or shall be instituted, sued, commenced, had, or taken to the said circuit court to have been holden as heretofore on the first day of May next, or to the said district court to have been holden as heretofore on the seventh day of May next, shall be returnable to, entered in, heard, tried, and have day in court in each of the said courts, respectively, to be holden at the times hereinbefore directed, in the same manner as might and ought to have been done, had the said courts been holden, respectively, on the first and seventh days of May, as heretofore directed by law.

Sec. 4. *And be it further enacted*, That, if at any time hereafter, the day or days prescribed by this act for holding either of the said courts shall be a Sunday, such court shall commence and be holden on the following day.

Approved, March 22, 1816.

An Act relative to evidence in cases of Naturalization.

Be it enacted, &c., That the certificate of report and registry, required as evidence of the time of arrival in the United States, according to the second section of the act of the fourteenth of April, one thousand eight hundred and two, entitled "An act to establish an uniform rule of naturalization, and to repeal the act heretofore passed on this subject; and also a certificate from the proper clerk or prothonotary, of the declaration of intention, made before a court of record, and required as the first condition, according to the first section of said act, shall be exhibited by every alien, on his application to be admitted a citizen of the United States, in pursuance of said act, who shall have arrived within the limits and under the jurisdiction of the United States since the eighteenth day of June, one thousand eight hundred and twelve, and shall each be recited at full length in the record of the court admitting such alien; otherwise he shall not be deemed to have complied with the conditions requisite for becoming a citizen of the United States; and any pretended admission of an alien, who shall have arrived within the limits and under the jurisdiction of the United States, since the said eighteenth day of June, one thousand eight hundred and twelve, to be a citizen after the promulgation of this act, without such recital of each certificate at full length, shall be of no validity or effect under the act aforesaid.

Sec. 2. *Provided, and be it enacted*, That nothing herein contained shall be construed to exclude from admission to citizenship any free white person who was residing within the limits and under the jurisdiction of the United States at any time between the eighteenth day of June, one thousand seven hundred and ninety-eight, and the fourteenth day of April, one thousand eight hundred and two, and who, having continued to reside therein without having made any declaration of intention before a court of record, as aforesaid, may be entitled to become a citizen of the United States according to the act of the twenty-sixth of March, one thousand eight hundred and four, entitled "An act, in addition to an act, entitled ' An act to establish an uniform rule of naturalization, and to repeal the act heretofore passed on that subject." Whenever any person without a certificate of such declaration of intention, as aforesaid, shall make application to be admitted a citizen of the United States, it shall be proved to the satisfaction of the court that the applicant was residing within the limits and under the jurisdiction of the United States, before the fourteenth day of April, one thousand eight hundred and two, and has continued to reside within the same, or he shall not be so admitted. And the residence of the applicant within the limits and under the jurisdiction of the United States for at least five years immediately preceding the time of such application shall be proved by the oath or affirmation of citizens of the United States; which citizens shall be named in the record as witnesses. And such continued residence within the limits and under the jurisdiction of the United States, when satisfactorily proved, and the place or places where the applicant has resided for at least five years, as aforesaid, shall be stated and set forth, together with the names of such citizens in the record of the court admitting the applicant: otherwise the same shall not entitle him to be considered and deemed a citizen of the United States.

Approved, March 22, 1816.

An Act authorizing a subscription for the printing of a second edition of the Public Documents.

Be it enacted, &c., That the Secretary of State be, and he is hereby, authorized to subscribe for and receive, for the use and disposal of Congress, five hundred copies of the second and improved edition of State papers and public documents, proposed to be printed by T. B. Wait and Sons; the said edition to be comprised in nine volumes; and the aforesaid copies to be delivered, in strong leather binding, at the Department of State, at the rate of two dollars and a quarter for each volume.

Sec. 2. *And be it further enacted,* That the Secretary of State be, and is hereby, authorized, on the delivery, as aforesaid, of five hundred copies of the first volume of the said edition, to pay for the same at the rate aforesaid; and in like manner to pay for the same number of each succeeding volume, when delivered as aforesaid; and the sum of ten thousand one hundred and twenty-five dollars is hereby appropriated for the purpose aforesaid, to be paid out of any money in the Treasury not otherwise appropriated.

Approved, March 25, 1816.

An Act relating to settlers on the lands of the United States.

Be it enacted, &c., That any person or persons who, before the first day of February, one thousand eight hundred and sixteen, had taken possession of, occupied or made a settlement on any lands ceded or secured to the United States, by any treaty made with a foreign nation, or by a cession from any State to the United States, which lands had not been previously sold, ceded, or released, by the United States, or the claim to which lands had not been previously recognised or confirmed by the United States, and who, at the time of passing this act, does or do actually inhabit and reside on such lands, may, at any time prior to the first day of September next, apply to the proper register or recorder, as the case may be, of the land office established for the disposal, registering or recording of such lands; and where there is no register or recorder, to the marshal, or to such person or persons as may be, by the registers, recorders, or marshals, respectively, appointed for the purpose of receiving such applications, stating the tract or tracts of land thus occupied, settled, and inhabited, by such applicant or applicants, and requesting permission to continue thereon; and it shall thereupon be lawful for such register, recorder, or marshal, respectively, to permit, in conformity with such instructions as may be given by the Secretary of the Treasury, with the approbation of the President of the United States, for that purpose, such applicant or applicants to remain on such tract or tracts of land, provided the same shall at that time remain unsold by the United States, not exceeding three hundred and twenty acres for each applicant, as tenants at will, on such terms and conditions as shall prevent any waste or damage on such lands, and on the express condition that such applicant or applicants shall, whenever such tract or tracts of land may be sold or ceded by the United States, or whenever, from any other cause, be or they may be required, under the authority of the United States, so to do, give quiet possession of such tract or tracts of land to the purchaser or purchasers, or to remove altogether from the land, as the case may be: *Provided, however,* That such permission shall not be granted to any such applicant unless he shall previously sign a declaration, stating that he does not lay any claim to such tract or tracts of land, and that he does not occupy the same by virtue of any claim, or pretended claim, derived or pretended to be derived, from any other person or persons: *And provided also,* That in all cases where the tract of land applied for includes either a lead mine or salt spring, no permission to work the same shall be granted without the approbation of the President of the United States.

Sec. 2. *And be it further enacted,* That all the applications made and permissions granted, by virtue of the preceding section, shall be duly entered on books to be kept for that purpose by the registers, recorders, and marshals, aforesaid, respectively; and they shall be entitled to receive from the party, for each application, fifty cents, and for each permission, one dollar.

Approved, March 25, 1816.

An Act placing certain persons on the list of Navy Pensioners.

Be it enacted, &c., That the Secretary of the Navy be, and he is hereby, authorized and required to place on the list of navy pensioners those persons who were wounded at Dartmoor prison, in England, in the month of April, one thousand eight hundred and fifteen ; also, the widows and children of such as were killed, or who died in consequence of wounds received there ; and that, in the allowance of pensions to persons aforesaid, the regulations established by law, in relation to the placing persons on the list of navy pensioners, be observed.

Sec. 2. *And be it further enacted,* That this act shall be construed to take effect from the sixth day of April, in the year one thousand eight hundred and fifteen.

Approved, April 2, 1816.

An Act to limit the right of appeal from the Circuit Court of the United States, for the District of Columbia.

Be it enacted, &c., That no cause shall hereafter be removed from the circuit court of the United States for the District of Columbia to the Supreme Court of the United States, by appeal or writ of error, unless the matter in dispute in such cause shall be of the value of one thousand dollars or upwards, exclusive of costs.

Sec. 2. *Provided always, and be it further enacted,* That when any person or persons, body politic or corporate, shall think him, her, or themselves, aggrieved by any final judgment, order, or decree of the said circuit court, where the matter in dispute, exclusive of costs, shall be of the value of one hundred dollars, and of less value than one thousand dollars, and shall have prayed an appeal, or shall desire to sue out a writ of error to the Supreme Court of the United States, such person or persons, body politic or corporate, may exhibit a petition, in writing, accompanied by a copy of the proceedings complained of, and an assignment of the errors relied on, to any judge of the said Supreme Court, who, if he should be of opinion that such errors, or any of them, involve questions of law of such extensive interest and operation as to render the final decision of them by the said Supreme Court desirable, may thereupon, at his discretion, and upon the terms and conditions prescribed by law, by his order, to be directed to the clerk of the county in which the proceedings shall have been had, direct such appeal to be allowed, or writ of error to be issued ; which shall be done accordingly.

Sec. 3. *And be it further enacted,* That when any appeal or writ of error shall have been directed in the manner prescribed by the second section of this act, and the order of the judge of the Supreme Court aforesaid thereon, shall have been filed in the office of the clerk of the proper county, within thirty days after the end of the term at which the judgment, order, or decree, to by affected by such writ of error or appeal, shall have been rendered or made, such writ of error or appeal shall operate as a supersedeas of all proceedings under such judgment, order, or decree.

Approved, April 2, 1816.

An Act to authorize the payment for property lost, captured, or destroyed by the enemy, while in the military service of the United States, and for other purposes.

Be it enacted, &c., That any volunteer, or draughted militiaman, whether of cavalry, mounted riflemen, or infantry, who, in the late war between the United States and Great Britain, has sustained damage by the loss of any horse which has been killed in battle, or which has died in consequence of a wound therein received, or in consequence of failure on the part of the United States to furnish such horse with sufficient forage, while in the military service of the United States, shall be allowed and paid the value thereof.

Sec. 2. *And be it further enacted,* That any person, whether of cavalry, mounted militia, or volunteers, who, in the late war aforesaid, has sustained damage by the loss of a horse, in consequence of the owner being dismounted, or separated and detached from the same, by order of the commanding officer, or in consequence of the rider being killed or wounded in battle, shall be allowed and paid the value of such horse at the time he was received into the public service.

Sec. 3. *And be it further enacted,* That any person who, in the late war aforesaid, has sustained damage by the loss, capture, or destruction, by an enemy, of any horse, mule, ox, wagon, cart, boat, sleigh, or harness, while such was in the military service of the United States, either by impressment or contract, except in cases where the risk to which the property would be exposed was agreed to be incurred by the owner, if it shall appear that such loss, capture, or destruction, was without any fault or negligence on the part of the owner ; and any person who, during the time aforesaid, has sustained damage by the death of any such horse, mule, or ox, in consequence of failure on the part of the United States to furnish the same with sufficient forage, while in the service aforesaid, shall be allowed and paid the value thereof.

Sec. 4. *And be it further enacted,* That any person who, in the time aforesaid, has acted in the military service of the United States as a volunteer or draughted militiaman, and who has furnished himself with arms and military accoutrements, and has sustained damage by the capture or destruction of the same, without any fault or negligence on his part, shall be allowed and paid the value thereof.

Public Acts of Congress.

Sec. 5. *And be it further enacted,* That where any property has been impressed, or taken by public authority, for the use or subsistence of the Army, during the late war, and the same shall have been destroyed, lost, or consumed, the owner of such property shall be paid the value thereof, deducting therefrom the amount which has been paid, or may be claimed, for the use and risk for the same, while in the service aforesaid.

Sec. 6. *And be it further enacted,* That nothing in this act contained shall be so construed as to enable the owner of any such property, or his legal representatives, to receive compensation for such loss or damage as abovementioned, where the owner of such property, or his legal representatives, may have recovered or received satisfaction for such loss from the persons who may have taken or impressed such property into the public service; and that every person claiming such compensation shall, at the time of receiving the same, release all claims he may have against the officer or person who may have impressed, taken, or used, such property in the public service; and that, in all cases where the owner of such property, or his legal representative, may have recovered or received satisfaction for such loss or injury, from the person who shall so have taken such property into the public service, the said officer or person, who shall so have paid such loss or damage, shall be entitled to receive the compensation provided by this act for such loss or damage.

Sec. 7. *And be it further enacted,* That the Accountant of the War Department, in adjusting and settling the accounts of the different paymasters, is hereby authorized to allow to the officers of volunteer cavalry, who furnished their own horses while in public service, at the rate of forty cents per day for each horse so furnished, which any such officer was entitled by law to keep in such service, agreeably to the rank of such officer.

Sec. 8. *And be it further enacted,* That when any officer, noncommissioned officer, or private, in the cavalry service, as aforesaid, having lost the horse or horses, which may have been taken by him into the said service, has received from the United States another horse or horses, in lieu, or in part payment, for the horse or horses so previously lost as aforesaid, such officer, noncommissioned officer, or private, shall be entitled to receive the allowance of forty cents per day for the use and risk of the horse on which he may have been so remounted.

Sec. 9. *And be it further enacted,* That any person who, in the time aforesaid, has sustained damage by the destruction of his or her house or building by the enemy, while the same was occupied as a military deposite, under the authority of an officer or agent of the United States, shall be allowed and paid the amount of such damage: *Provided,* It shall appear that such occupation was the cause of its destruction.

Sec. 10. *And be it further enacted,* That the loss or destruction, as aforesaid, as well as the value, of such property shall be ascertained by the best evidence which the nature of the case will admit of, and which may be in the power of the party to produce; and the amount thereof, when established and ascertained, according to the provisions of this act, shall be paid to the sufferer or sufferers, out of any money in the Treasury, not otherwise appropriated.

Sec. 11. *And be it further enacted,* That, for the more speedy execution of the provisions of this act, the President of the United States, by and with the consent of the Senate, is hereby authorized to appoint one commissioner, whose duty it shall be to decide upon all cases arising under this act; and who, in the discharge of his duties, shall be subject to such rules and regulations as shall be prescribed by the President of the United States. Such commissioner shall receive, as compensation for his services, at the rate of two thousand dollars per annum, for the time he shall be actually employed, which shall not exceed two years, to be computed from and after the passage of this act. All official communications to and from the commissioner appointed under this act shall be free of postage.

Sec. 12. *And be it further enacted,* That the said commissioner, so to be appointed, before he enters upon the duties of his office, shall take the following oath, to wit: "I, A B, do solemnly swear, that I will well and truly, according to the best of my abilities, discharge the duties of commissioner under an act of Congress, entitled 'An act to authorize the payment for property lost, captured, or destroyed, by the enemy, while in the military service of the United States, and for other purposes;' so help me God." Upon which he shall proceed to appoint a clerk; and shall proceed, with all practicable despatch, to establish, under the direction, or with the assent, of the President of the United States, such rules, as well in regard to the receipt of applications of claimants to compensation for losses provided for by this act, as the species and degree of evidence, the manner in which such evidence shall be taken and authenticated, as shall, in his opinion, be the best calculated to attain the objects of this act; paying a due regard, in the establishment of such regulations, as well to the claims of individual justice as to the interest of the United States: which rules and regulations shall, upon his adoption, be published for eight weeks, successively, in the newspapers in the several States and Territories in which the laws of the United States are published.

Sec. 13. *And be it further enacted,* That the said commissioner shall, in all cases in which the claim to compensation or indemnity shall exceed the sum of two hundred dollars, award a commission to some one or more discreet commissioner, in the vicinity of where the witnesses are stated to reside, accompanied by interrogatories to be propounded to such witnesses, which said commission, when executed, shall be returned, together with the examinations to be taken in virtue thereof, by mail, free of postage, to the office of the said commissioner.

Sec. 14. *And be it further enacted,* That, in all adjudications of the said commissioner upon the claims abovementioned, whether such judgment be in favor of, or adverse to, the claim of the applicant, the same shall be entered by his clerk in a book to be provided for that purpose. And when such judgment shall be in favor of such claim, shall entitle the claimant, or his legal representative, upon the production of a copy of such judgment, duly certified by the clerk of said commissioner, to payment of the amount thereof at the Treasury of the United States.

SEC. 15. *And be it further enacted*, That no claim authorized by this act shall be allowed or paid, unless the same shall be exhibited within two years from the passing thereof.

Approved, April 9, 1816.

An Act to repeal the act, entitled "An act to provide additional revenues for defraying the expenses of Government and maintaining the public credit, by laying duties on household furniture and on gold and silver watches."

Be it enacted, &c., That so much of the act, entitled "An act to provide additional revenue for defraying the expenses of Government and maintaining the public credit, by laying duties on household furniture and on gold and silver watches," as lays a duty on household furniture, and on watches kept for use, in the year one thousand eight hundred and sixteen, and in succeeding years, shall be, and the same is hereby, repealed.

Approved, April 9, 1816.

An Act for the remission of certain duties on the importation of books for the use of Harvard College, and on the carriage and personal baggage of his Excellency William Gore, Governor of the British province of Upper Canada.

Be it enacted, &c., That all duties due and payable to the United States on an invoice of books belonging to Harvard College, in Cambridge, Massachusetts, imported into Boston, in the year one thousand eight hundred and fifteen, be, and the same are hereby, remitted.

SEC. 2. *And be it further enacted*, That all duties due and payable to the United States on the carriage and personal baggage of his Excellency William Gore, Governor of the British province of Upper Canada, imported into New York, in the year one thousand eight hundred and fifteen, be, and the same are hereby, remitted.

Approved, April 9, 1816.

An Act in addition to an act to regulate the Post Office Establishment.

Be it enacted, &c., That, from and after the first day of May next, the following rates of postage be charged upon all letters and packets, (except such as are now excepted by law,) conveyed by the posts of the United States, viz:

For every letter composed of a single sheet of paper, conveyed not exceeding thirty miles, six cents; over thirty and not exceeding eighty, ten cents; over eighty and not exceeding one hundred and fifty, twelve and a half cents; over one hundred and fifty and not exceeding four hundred, eighteen and a half cents; over four hundred miles, twenty-five cents; and for every double letter, or letter composed of two pieces of paper, double those rates; and for every triple letter, or one composed of three pieces of paper, triple those rates; and for every packet composed of four or more pieces of paper, or one or more other articles, and weighing one ounce avoirdupois, quadruple those rates: and in that proportion for all greater weights: *Provided*, That no packets of letters conveyed by the water mails shall be charged with more than quadruple postage, unless the same shall contain more than four distinct letters.

No postmaster shall be obliged to receive, to be conveyed by the mail, any packet which shall weigh more than three pounds; and the postage marked on any letter or packet, and charged in the post bill which may accompany the same, shall be conclusive evidence, in favor of the postmaster who delivers the same, of the lawful postage thereon, unless such letter or packet shall be opened in presence of the postmaster or his clerk.

Every four folio pages, or eight quarto pages, or sixteen octavo pages, of a pamphlet or magazine, shall be considered a sheet, and the surplus pages of any pamphlet or magazine shall also be considered a sheet; and the Journals of the Legislatures of the several States, not being stitched or bound, shall be liable to the same postage as pamphlets. Any memorandum which shall be written on a newspaper, or other printed paper, and transmitted by mail, shall be charged letter postage; and any person who shall deposite such memorandum in any office for the purpose of defrauding the revenue, shall forfeit, for every such offence, the sum of five dollars.

SEC. 2. *And be it further enacted*, That the Postmaster General be, and he is hereby, authorized to allow to each postmaster such commission on the postages by him collected, as shall be adequate to his services: *Provided*, That his commission shall not exceed the following several rates on the amount received in one quarter; that is to say:

On a sum not exceeding one hundred dollars, thirty per cent.

On any sum over and above the first hundred dollars, and not exceeding four hundred dollars, twenty-five per cent.

On any sum over and above the first four hundred dollars, and not exceeding two thousand four hundred dollars, twenty per cent.

On any sum over and above the first two thousand four hundred dollars, eight per cent.

Except to the postmasters who may be employed in receiving and despatching foreign mails, whose compensation may be augmented not exceeding twenty-five dollars in one quarter; and excepting to the postmasters at offices where the mail is regularly to arrive between the hours of nine o'clock at night and five in the morning, whose commission, on the first hundred dollars collected in one quarter, may be increased to a sum not exceeding fifty per cent.

The Postmaster General may allow to the postmasters, respectively, a commission of fifty per cent. on the moneys arising from the postage of newspapers, magazines, and pamphlets; and to the postmaster whose compensation shall not exceed five hundred dollars in one quarter, two cents for every free letter delivered out of the office, excepting such as are for the postmaster himself; and each postmaster who shall be required to keep a register of the arrival and departure of the mails, shall be allowed ten cents for each monthly return which he makes thereof to the General Post Office.

The Postmaster General may allow to the postmaster at New Orleans, at the rate of eight hundred dollars, and to the postmaster at Warrenton, in North Carolina, at the rate of two hundred dollars, and to the postmaster at Wheeling, in Virginia, at the rate of two hundred dollars a year, in addition to their ordinary commissions. The Postmaster General is hereby authorized to allow to the postmaster at the City of Washington, in addition to the allowance made by this act for postage collected, and for free letters received by him for delivery, a commission of five per centum on the amount of mails distributed at his office: *Provided, nevertheless,* That the whole annual emoluments of the said postmaster, including the extra compensation heretofore allowed to him by law, shall always be subject to the restriction imposed by the fortieth section of the act of Congress approved the thirtieth of April, one thousand eight hundred and ten, to which this act is in addition.

SEC. 3. *And be it further enacted,* That letters and packets to and from any member of the Senate, or member or delegate of the House of Representatives of the United States, the Secretary of the Senate, and Clerk of the House of Representatives, shall be conveyed free of postage, for thirty days previous to each session of Congress, and for thirty days after the termination thereof: *Provided always,* That no letter or packet shall exceed two ounces in weight, and in case of excess of weight, that excess alone shall be paid for.

SEC. 4. *And be it further enacted,* That the eleventh and twenty-eighth sections of the act, entitled "An act regulating the Post Office Establishment," approved April thirtieth, one thousand eight hundred and ten, and the first and second sections of the act, entitled "An act in addition to the act regulating the Post Office Establishment," approved February twenty-seventh, one thousand eight hundred and fifteen, and the fourth and fifth sections of the same, except such parts as relate to steamboats, their masters, or managers, and persons employed on board the same, be, and the same are hereby, repealed.

SEC. 5. *And be it further enacted,* That this act shall take effect from and after the thirty-first day of March, one thousand eight hundred and sixteen.

Approved, April 9, 1816.

An Act to incorporate the subscribers to the Bank of the United States.

Be it enacted, &c., That a bank of the United States of America shall be established, with a capital of thirty-five millions of dollars, divided into three hundred and fifty thousand shares, of one hundred dollars each share. Seventy thousand shares, amounting to the sum of seven millions of dollars, part of the capital of the said bank, shall be subscribed and paid for by the United States, in the manner hereinafter specified; and two hundred and eighty thousand shares, amounting to the sum of twenty-eight millions of dollars, shall be subscribed and paid for by individuals, companies, or corporations, in the manner hereinafter specified.

SEC. 2. *And be it further enacted,* That subscriptions for the sum of twenty-eight millions of dollars, towards constituting the capital of the said bank, shall be opened on the first Monday in July next, at the following places: that is to say, at Portland, in the District of Maine; at Portsmouth, in the State of New Hampshire; at Boston, in the State of Massachusetts; at Providence, in the State of Rhode Island; at Middletown, in the State of Connecticut; at Burlington, in the State of Vermont; at New York in the State of New York; at New Brunswick, in the State of New Jersey; at Philadelphia, in the State of Pennsylvania; at Wilmington, in the State of Delaware; at Baltimore, in the State of Maryland; at Richmond, in the State of Virginia; at Lexington, in the State of Kentucky; at Cincinnati, in the State of Ohio; at Raleigh, in the State of North Carolina; at Nashville, in the State of Tennessee; at Charleston, in the State of South Carolina; at Augusta, in the State of Georgia; at New Orleans, in the State of Louisiana; and at Washington, in the District of Columbia. And the said subscriptions shall be opened under the superintendence of five commissioners at Philadelphia, and of three commissioners at each of the other places aforesaid, to be appointed by the President of the United States, who is hereby authorised to make such appointments, and shall continue open every day, from the time of opening the same, between the hours of ten o'clock in the forenoon and four o'clock in the afternoon, for the term of twenty days, exclusive of Sundays, when the same shall be closed, and immediately thereafter the commissioners, or any two of them, at the respective places aforesaid, shall cause two transcripts or copies of such subscriptions to be made, one of which they shall send to the Secretary of the Treasury, one they shall retain, and the original they shall transmit, within seven days from the closing of the subscriptions as aforesaid, to the commissioners at Philadelphia aforesaid. And on the receipt of the said original subscriptions, or of either of the said copies thereof, if the original be lost, mislaid, or detained, the commissioners at Philadelphia aforesaid, or a majority of them, shall immediately thereafter convene, and proceed to take an account of the said subscriptions. And if more than the amount of twenty-eight millions of dollars shall have been subscribed, then the said last mentioned commissioners shall deduct the amount of such excess from the largest subscriptions, in such manner as that no subscription shall be reduced in amount, while any one remains larger: *Provided,* That if the subscriptions taken at either of the places aforesaid shall not exceed three thousand shares, there shall be no reduction of such subscriptions, nor shall, in any case, the subscriptions taken at either of the places aforesaid be reduced below that amount. And in case the aggregate amount of the said subscriptions shall exceed twenty-eight millions of dollars, the said last mentioned commissioners, after having apportioned the same as aforesaid, shall cause lists of the said apportioned subscriptions to be made out, including in each list the apportioned subscription for the place where the original subscription was made, one of which lists they shall transmit to the commissioners or one of them, under whose superintendence such subscriptions were originally made, that the subscribers may thereby ascertain the number of shares to them respectively apportioned as aforesaid. And in case the aggregate amount of the said subscriptions made during the period aforesaid, at all the places aforesaid, shall not amount to twenty-eight millions of dollars, the subscriptions to complete the said sum shall be and remain open at Philadelphia aforesaid, under the superintendence of the commissioners appointed for that place; and the subscriptions may be then made by any individual, company, or corporation, for any number of shares, not exceeding, in the whole, the amount required to complete the said sum of twenty-eight millions of dollars.

SEC. 3. *And be it further enacted,* That it shall be lawful for any individual, company, corporation, or State, when the subscriptions shall be opened as hereinbefore directed, to subscribe for any number of shares of the capital of the said bank, not exceeding three thousand shares, and the sums so subscribed shall be payable, and paid, in the manner following: that is to say, seven millions of dollars thereof in gold or silver coin of the United States, or in gold coin of Spain, or the dominions of Spain, at the rate of one hundred cents for every twenty-eight grains and sixty hundredths of a grain of the actual weight thereof, or in other foreign gold or silver coin at the several rates prescribed by the first section of an act regulating the currency of foreign coins in the United States, passed tenth day of April, one thousand eight hundred and six, and twenty-one millions of dollars thereof in like gold or silver coin, or in the funded debt of the United States contracted at the time of the subscriptions respectively. And the payments made in the funded debt of the United States, shall be paid and received at the following rates: that is to say, the funded debt bearing an interest of six per centum per annum, at the nominal or par value thereof; the funded debt bearing an interest of three per centum per annum, at the rate of sixty-five dollars for every sum of one hundred dollars of the nominal amount thereof; and the funded debt

bearing an interest of seven per centum per annum, at the rate of one hundred and six dollars and fifty-one cents, for every sum of one hundred dollars of the nominal amount thereof; together with the amount of the interest accrued on the said several denominations of funded debt, to be computed and allowed to the time of subscribing the same to the capital of the said bank as aforesaid. And the payments of the said subscriptions shall be made and completed by the subscribers, at the times and in the manner following: that is to say, at the time of subscribing there shall be paid five dollars on each share, in gold or silver coin as aforesaid, and twenty-five dollars more in coin as aforesaid, or in funded debt as aforesaid; at the expiration of six calendar months after the time of subscribing, there shall be paid the further sum of ten dollars on each share, in gold or silver coin as aforesaid, and twenty-five dollars more in coin as aforesaid, or in funded debt as aforesaid; at the expiration of twelve calendar months from the time of subscribing, there shall be paid the further sum of ten dollars, on each share, in gold or silver coin as aforesaid, and twenty-five dollars more, in coin as aforesaid, or in funded debt as aforesaid.

SEC. 4. *And be it further enacted,* That, at the time of subscribing to the capital of the said bank as aforesaid, each and every subscriber shall deliver to the commissioners, at the place of subscribing, as well the amount of their subscriptions respectively in coin as aforesaid, as the certificates of funded debt, for the funded debt proportions of their respective subscriptions, together with a power of attorney, authorizing the said commissioners, or a majority of them, to transfer the said stock, in due form of law to "the president, directors, and company, of the Bank of the United States," as soon as the said bank shall be organized. *Provided always,* That if, in consequence of the apportionment of the shares in the capital of the said bank among the subscribers, in the case, and in the manner, hereinbefore provided, any subscriber shall have delivered to the commissioners, at the time of subscribing, a greater amount of gold or silver coin and funded debt than shall be necessary to complete the payments for the share or shares to such subscribers, apportioned as aforesaid, the commissioners shall only retain so much of the said gold or silver coin, and funded debt, as shall be necessary to complete such payments, and shall, forthwith, return the surplus thereof, on application for the same to the subscribers lawfully entitled thereto. And the commissioners, respectively, shall deposite the gold and silver coin, and certificates of public debt by them respectively received as aforesaid from the subscribers to the capital of the said bank, in some place of secure and safe keeping, so that the same may and shall be specially delivered and transferred, as the same were by them respectively received, to the president, directors, and company, of the Bank of the United States, or to their order, as soon as shall be required after the organization of the said bank. And the said commissioners appointed to superintend the subscriptions to the capital of the said bank as aforesaid, shall receive a reasonable compensation for their services respectively, and shall be allowed all reasonable charges and expenses incurred in the execution of their trust, to be paid by the president, directors, and company, of the bank, out of the funds thereof.

SEC. 5. *And be it further enacted,* That it shall be lawful for the United States to pay and redeem the funded debt subscribed to the capital of the said bank, at the rates aforesaid, in such sums, and at such times, as shall be deemed expedient, anything in any act or acts of Congress to the contrary thereof notwithstanding. And it shall also be lawful for the president, directors, and company, of the said bank, to sell and transfer for gold and silver coin, or bullion, the funded debt subscribed to the capital of the said bank as aforesaid: *Provided always,* That they shall not sell more thereof than the sum of two millions of dollars in any one year; nor sell any part thereof at any time within the United States, without previously giving notice of their intention to the Secretary of the Treasury, and offering the same to the United States for the period of fifteen days, at least, at the current price, not exceeding the rates aforesaid.

SEC. 6. *And be it further enacted,* That, at the opening of subscription to the capital stock of the said bank, the Secretary of the Treasury shall subscribe, or cause to be subscribed, on behalf of the United States, the said number of seventy thousand shares, amounting to seven millions of dollars as aforesaid, to be paid in gold or silver coin, or in stock of the United States, bearing interest at the rate of five per centum per annum; and if payment thereof or of any part thereof, be made in public stock, bearing interest as aforesaid, the said interest shall be payable quarterly, to commence from the time of making such payment on account of the said subscription, and the principal of the said stock shall be redeemable in any sums, and at any periods, which the Government shall deem fit. And the Secretary of the Treasury shall cause the certificates of such public stock to be prepared, and made in the usual form, and shall pay and deliver the same to the president, directors, and company, of the said bank on the first day of January, one thousand eight hundred and seventeen, which said stock it shall be lawful for the said president, directors, and company, to sell and transfer for gold and silver coin or bullion at their discretion: *Provided,* They shall not sell more than two millions of dollars thereof in any one year.

SEC. 7. *And be it further enacted,* That the subscribers to the said Bank of the United States of America, their successors and assigns, shall be, and are hereby, created a corporation and body politic, by the name and style of "The president, directors, and company, of the Bank of the United States," and shall so continue until the third day of March, in the year one thousand eight hundred and thirty-six, and by that name shall be, and are hereby, made able and capable, in law, to have, purchase, receive, possess, enjoy, and re-

tain, to them and their successors, lands, rents, tenements, hereditaments, goods, chattels, and effects, of whatsoever kind, nature, and quality, to an amount not exceeding, in the whole, fifty-five millions of dollars, including the amount of the capital stock aforesaid; and the same to sell, grant, demise, alien or dispose of; to sue and be sued, plead and be impleaded, answer and be answered, defend and be defended, in all State courts having competent jurisdiction, and in any circuit court of the United States: and also to make, have, and use, a common seal, and the same to break, alter, and renew, at their pleasure: and also to ordain, establish, and put in execution, such by-laws, and ordinances, and regulations, as they shall deem necessary and convenient for the government of the said corporation, not being contrary to the constitution thereof, or to the laws of the United States; and generally to do and execute all and singular the acts, matters, and things, which to them it shall or may appertain to do; subject, nevertheless, to the rules, regulations, restrictions, limitations, and provisions, hereinafter prescribed and declared.

SEC. 8. *And be it further enacted,* That, for the management of the affairs of the said corporation, there shall be twenty-five directors, five of whom, being stockholders, shall be annually appointed by the President of the United States, by and with the advice and consent of the Senate, not more than three of whom shall be residents of any one State; and twenty of whom shall be annually elected at the banking-house in the city of Philadelphia, on the first Monday of January, in each year, by the qualified stockholders of the capital of the said bank other than the United States, and by a plurality of votes then and there actually given, according to the scale of voting hereinafter prescribed: *Provided always,* That no person, being a director in the Bank of the United States, or any of its branches, shall be a director of any other bank; and should any such director act as a director in any other bank, it shall forthwith vacate his appointment in the direction of the Bank of the United States. And the directors, so duly appointed and elected, shall be capable of serving, by virtue of such appointment and choice, from the first Monday in the month of January of each year, until the end and expiration of the first Monday in the month of January of the year next ensuing the time of each annual election to be held by the stockholders as aforesaid. And the board of directors, annually, at the first meeting after their election in each and every year, shall proceed to elect one of the directors to be president of the corporation, who shall hold the said office during the same period for which the directors are appointed and elected as aforesaid: *Provided also,* That the first appointment and election of the directors and president of the said bank shall be at the time and for the period hereinafter declared: *And provided also,* That in case it should at any time happen that an appointment or election of directors, or an election of the president of the said bank, should not be so made as to take effect on any day when, in pursuance of this act, they ought to take effect, the said corporation shall not, for that cause, be deemed to be dissolved; but it shall be lawful at any other time to make such appointments, and to hold such elections, (as the case may be,) and the manner of holding the elections shall be regulated by the by-laws and ordinances of the said corporation: and until such appointments or elections be made, the directors and president of the said bank, for the time being, shall continue in office: *And provided also*, That in case of the death, resignation, or removal, of the president of the said corporation, the directors shall proceed to elect another president from the directors as aforesaid: and in case of the death, resignation, or absence from the United States, or removal of a director from office, the vacancy shall be supplied by the President of the United States, or by the stockholders, as the case may be. But the President of the United States alone shall have power to remove any of the directors appointed by him as aforesaid.

Sec. 9. *And be it further enacted*, That as soon as the sum of eight millions four hundred thousand dollars in gold and silver coin, and in the public debt, shall have been actually received on account of the subscriptions to the capital of the said bank (exclusively of the subscription aforesaid, on the part of the United States) notice thereof shall be given by the persons under whose superintendence the subscriptions shall have been made at the city of Philadelphia, in at least two newspapers printed in each of the places (if so many be printed in such places respectively) where subscriptions shall have been made, and the said persons shall, at the same time, and in like manner, notify a time and place within the said city of Philadelphia, at the distance of at least thirty days from the time of such notification, for proceeding to the election of twenty directors as aforesaid, and it shall be lawful for such election to be then and there made. And the President of the United States is hereby authorized, during the present session of Congress, to nominate, and, by and with the advice and consent of the Senate, to appoint, five directors of the said bank, though not stockholders, anything in the provisions of this act to the contrary notwithstanding; and the persons who shall be elected and appointed as aforesaid, shall be the first directors of the said bank, and shall proceed to elect one of the directors to be president of the said bank; and the directors and president of the said bank, so appointed and elected as aforesaid, shall be capable of serving in their respective office, by virtue thereof, until the end and expiration of the first Monday of the month of January next ensuing the said appointments and elections, and they shall then and thenceforth commence, and continue the operations of the said bank, at the city of Philadelphia.

Sec. 10. *And be it further enacted*, That the directors, for the time being, shall have power to appoint such officers, clerks, and servants, under them, as shall be necessary for executing the business of the said corporation, and to allow them such compensation for their services, respectively, as shall be reasonable; and shall be capable of exercising such other powers and authorities for the well governing and ordering of the officers of the said corporation as shall be prescribed, fixed, and determined, by the laws, regulations, and ordinances, of the same.

Sec. 11. *And be it further enacted*, That the following rules, restrictions, limitations, and provisions, shall form and be fundamental articles of the constitution of the said corporation, to wit:

1. The number of votes to which the stockholders shall be entitled, in voting for directors, shall be according to the number of shares he, she, or they, respectively, shall hold, in the proportions following, that is to say, for one share and not more than two shares, one vote; for every two shares above two, and not exceeding ten, one vote; for every four shares above ten, and not exceeding thirty, one vote; for every six shares above thirty, and not exceeding sixty, one vote; for every eight shares above sixty, and not exceeding one hundred, one vote; and for every ten shares above one hundred, one vote; but no person, copartnership, or body politic, shall be entitled to a greater number than thirty votes; and after the first election, no share or shares shall confer a right of voting, which shall not have been holden three calendar months previous to the day of election. And stockholders actually resident within the United States, and none other, may vote in elections by proxy.

2. Not more than three-fourths of the directors elected by the stockholders, and not more than four-fifths of the directors appointed by the President of the United States, who shall be in office at the time of an annual election, shall be elected or appointed for the next succeeding year; and no director shall hold his office more than three years out of four in succession; but the director who shall be the president at the time of an election may always be reappointed or re-elected, as the case may be.

3. None but a stockholder, resident citizen of the United States, shall be a director; nor shall a director be entitled to any emolument; but the directors may make such compensation to the president, for his extraordinary attendance at the bank, as shall appear to them reasonable.

4. Not less than seven directors shall constitute a board for the transaction of business, of whom the president shall always be one, except in case of sickness or necessary absence; in which case his place may be supplied by any other director whom he, by writing, under his hand, shall depute for that purpose. And the director so deputed may do and transact all the necessary business, belonging to the office of the president of the said corporation, during the continuance of the sickness or necessary absence of the president.

5. A number of stockholders, not less than sixty, who, together, shall be proprietors of one thousand shares or upwards, shall have power at any time to call a general meeting of the stockholders, for purposes relative to the institution,

giving at least ten weeks' notice in two public newspapers of the place where the bank is seated, and specifying in such notice the object or objects of such meeting.

6. Each cashier or treasurer, before he enters upon the duties of his office, shall be required to give bond, with two or more sureties, to the satisfaction of the directors, in a sum not less than fifty thousand dollars, with a condition for his good behaviour, and the faithful performance of his duties to the corporation.

7. The lands, tenements, and hereditaments, which it shall be lawful for the said corporation to hold, shall be only such as shall be requisite for its immediate accommodation in relation to the convenient transacting of its business, and such as shall have been *bona fide* mortgaged to it by way of security, or conveyed to it in satisfaction of debts previously contracted in the course of its dealings, or purchased at sales, upon judgments which shall have been obtained for such debts.

8. The total amount of debts which the said corporation shall at any time owe, whether by bond, bill, note, or other contract, over and above the debt or debts due for money deposited in the bank, shall not exceed the sum of thirty-five millions of dollars, unless the contracting of any greater debt shall have been previously authorized by law of the United States. In case of excess, the directors under whose administration it shall happen, shall be liable for the same in their natural and private capacities; and an action of debt may in such case be brought against them, or any of them, their or any of their heirs, executors, or administrators, in any court of record of the United States, or either of them, by any creditor or creditors of the said corporation, and may be prosecuted to judgment and execution, any condition, covenant, or agreement to the contrary notwithstanding. But this provision shall not be construed to exempt the said corporation or the lands, tenements, goods, or chattels of the same from being also liable for, and chargeable with, the said excess. Such of the said directors, who may have been absent when the said excess was contracted or created, or who may have dissented from the resolution or act whereby the same was so contracted or created, may respectively exonerate themselves from being so liable, by forthwith giving notice of the fact, and of their absence or dissent, to the President of the United States, and to the stockholders, at a general meeting, which they shall have power to call for that purpose.

9. The said corporation shall not, directly or indirectly, deal or trade in anything except bills of exchange, gold or silver bullion, or in the sale of goods really and truly pledged for money lent and not redeemed in due time, or goods which shall be the proceeds of its lands. It shall not be at liberty to purchase any public debt whatsoever, nor shall it take more than at the rate of six per centum per annum for or upon its loans or discounts.

10. No loan shall be made by the said corpora-

tion, for the use or on account of the Government of the United States, to an amount exceeding five hundred thousand dollars, or of any particular State, to an amount exceeding fifty thousand dollars, or of any foreign Prince or State, unless previously authorized by a law of the United States.

11. The stock of the said corporation shall be assignable and transferrable, according to such rules as shall be instituted in that behalf, by the laws and ordinances of the same.

12. The bills, obligatory and of credit, under the seal of the said corporation, which shall be made to any person or persons, shall be assignable by endorsement thereupon, under the hand or hands of such person or persons, and his, her or their executors or administrators, and his, her or their assignee or assignees, and so as absolutely to transfer and vest the property thereof in each and every assignee or assignees successively, and to enable such assignee or assignees, and his, her or their executors or administrators, to maintain an action thereupon in his, her or their own name or names: *Provided,* That said corporation shall not make any bill obligatory, or of credit, or other obligation under its seal for the payment of a sum less than five thousand dollars. And the bills or notes which may be issued by order of the said corporation, signed by the president, and countersigned by the principal cashier or treasurer thereof, promising the payment of money to any person or persons, his, her or their order, or to bearer, although not under the seal of the said corporation, shall be binding and obligatory upon the same, in like manner, and with like force and effect, as upon any private person or persons. if issued by him, her or them, in his, her or their private or natural capacity or capacities, and shall be assignable and negotiable in like manner as if they were so issued by such private person or persons; that is to say, those which shall be payable to any person or persons, his, her or their order, shall be assignable by endorsement, in like manner, and with the like effect as foreign bills of exchange now are; and those which are payable to bearer shall be assignable and negotiable by delivery only: *Provided,* That all bills or notes, so to be issued by said corporation, shall be made payable on demand, other than bills or notes for the payment of a sum not less than one hundred dollars each, and payable to the order of some person or persons, which bills or notes it shall be lawful for said corporation to make payable at any time not exceeding sixty days from the date thereof.

13. Half-yearly dividends shall be made of so much of the profits of the bank as shall appear to the directors advisable; and once in every three years the directors shall lay before the stockholders, at a general meeting, for their information. an exact and particular statement of the debts which shall have remained unpaid after the expiration of the original credit, for a period of treble the term of that credit, and of the surplus of the profits, if any, after deducting losses and dividends. If there shall be a failure in the pay-

ment of any part of any sum subscribed to the capital of the said bank, by any person, copartnership or body politic, the party failing shall lose the benefit of any dividend which may have accrued prior to the time for making such payment, and during the delay of the same.

14. The directors of the said corporation shall establish a competent office of discount and deposite in the District of Columbia, whenever any law of the United States shall require such an establishment; also one such office of discount and deposite in any State in which two thousand shares shall have been subscribed or may be held, whenever, upon application of the Legislature of such State, Congress may, by law, require the same: *Provided,* the directors aforesaid shall not be bound to establish such office before the whole of the capital of the bank shall have been paid up. And it shall be lawful for the directors of the said corporation to establish offices of discount and deposite, wheresoever they shall think fit, within the United States or the Territories thereof, and to commit the management of the said offices, and the business thereof, respectively, to such persons, and under such regulations, as they shall deem proper, not being contrary to law or the constitution of the bank. Or, instead of establishing such offices, it shall be lawful for the directors of the said corporation, from time to time, to employ any other bank or banks, to be first approved by the Secretary of the Treasury, at any place or places that they may deem safe and proper, to manage and transact the business proposed as aforesaid, other than for the purposes of discount, to be managed and transacted by such offices, under such agreements, and subject to such regulations, as they shall deem just and proper. Not more than thirteen, nor less than seven managers or directors, of every office established as aforesaid, shall be annually appointed by the directors of the bank, to serve one year; they shall choose a president from their own number; each of them shall be a citizen of the United States, and a resident of the State, Territory, or district, wherein such office is established; and not more than three-fourths of the said managers or directors, in office at the time of an annual appointment, shall be reappointed for the next succeeding year; and no director shall hold his office more than three years out of four, in succession; but the president may be always reappointed.

15. The officer at the head of the Treasury Department of the United States shall be furnished, from time to time, as often as he may require, not exceeding once a week, with statements of the amount of the capital stock of the said corporation and of the debts due to the same; of the moneys deposited therein; of the notes in circulation, and of the specie in hand; and shall have a right to inspect such general accounts in the books of the bank as shall relate to the said statement: *Provided,* That this shall not be construed to imply a right of inspecting the account of any private individual or individuals with the bank.

16. No stockholder, unless he be a citizen of the United States, shall vote in the choice of directors.

17. No note shall be issued of less amount than five dollars.

SEC. 12. *And be it further enacted,* That if the said corporation, or any person or persons, for or to the use of the same, shall deal or trade in buying or selling goods, wares, merchandise, or commodities whatsoever, contrary to the provisions of this act, all and every person and persons by whom any order or direction for so dealing or trading shall have been given; and all and every person and persons who shall have been concerned as parties or agents therein, shall forfeit and lose treble the value of the goods, wares, merchandise, and commodities in which such dealing and trade shall have been. one-half thereof to the use of the informer, and the other half thereof to the use of the United States, to be recovered in any action of law with costs of suit.

SEC. 13. *And be it further enacted,* That if the said corporation shall advance or lend any sum of money for the use or on account of the Government of the United States, to an amount exceeding five hundred thousand dollars; or of any particular State, to an amount exceeding fifty thousand dollars; or of any foreign Prince or State, (unless previously authorized thereto by a law of the United States,) all and every person and persons, by and with whose order, agreement, consent, approbation, and connivance, such unlawful advance or loan shall have been made, upon conviction thereof shall forfeit and pay, for every such offence, treble the value or amount of the sum or sums which have been so unlawfully advanced or lent; one-fifth thereof to the use of the informer, and the residue thereof to the use of the United States.

SEC. 14. *And be it further enacted,* That the bills or notes of the said corporation originally made payable, or which shall have become payable on demand, shall be receivable in all payments to the United States, unless otherwise directed by act of Congress.

SEC. 15. *And be it further enacted,* That during the continuance of this act, and whenever required by the Secretary of the Treasury, the said corporation shall give the necessary facilities for transferring the public funds from place to place, within the United States, or the Territories thereof, and for distributing the same in payment of the public creditors, without charging commissions or claiming allowance on account of difference in exchange, and shall also do and perform the several and respective duties of the Commissioners of Loans for the several States, or of any one or more of them, whenever required by law.

SEC. 16. *And be it further enacted,* That the deposites of the money of the United States, in places in which the said bank and branches thereof may be established, shall be made in said bank or branches thereof, unless the Secretary of the Treasury shall at any time otherwise order and direct; in which case the Secretary of the Treasury shall immediately lay before Congress, if in session, and if not, immediately after the commencement of the next session, the reasons of such order or direction.

Sec. 17. *And be it further enacted,* That the said corporation shall not at any time suspend or refuse payment in gold and silver, of any of its notes, bills, or obligations; nor of any moneys received upon deposite in said bank, or in any of its offices of discount and deposite. And if the said corporation shall at any time refuse or neglect to pay on demand any bill, note or obligation issued by the corporation, according to the contract, promise, or undertaking therein expressed; or shall neglect or refuse to pay on demand any moneys received in said bank, or in any of its offices aforesaid, on deposite, to the person or persons entitled to receive the same, then, and in every such case, the holder of any such note, bill, or obligation, or the person or persons entitled to demand and receive such moneys as aforesaid, shall respectively be entitled to receive and recover interest on the said bills, notes, obligations, or moneys, until the same shall be fully paid and satisfied, at the rate of twelve per centum per annum from the time of such demand as aforesaid: *Provided,* That Congress may at any time hereafter enact laws enforcing and regulating the recovery of the amount of the notes, bills, obligations, or other debts, of which payment shall have been refused as aforesaid, with the rate of interest abovementioned, vesting jurisdiction for that purpose in any courts, either of law or equity, of the courts of the United States, or Territories thereof, or of the several States, as they may deem expedient.

Sec. 18. *And be it further enacted,* That if any person shall falsely make, forge or counterfeit, or cause or procure to be falsely made, forged or counterfeited, or willingly aid or assist in falsely making, forging or counterfeiting any bill or note in imitation of or purporting to be a bill or note issued by order of the president, directors, and company of the said bank, or any order or check on the said bank or corporation, or any cashier thereof; or shall falsely alter, or cause or procure to be falsely altered, or willingly aid or assist in falsely altering any bill or note issued by order of the president, directors, and company of the said bank, or any order or check on the said bank or corporation, or any cashier thereof; or shall pass, utter or publish, or attempt to pass utter or publish as true, any false, forged, or counterfeited bill or note, purporting to be a bill or note issued by order of the president, directors, and company of the said bank, or any false, forged, or counterfeited order or check upon the said bank or corporation, or any cashier thereof, knowing the same to be falsely forged or counterfeited; or shall pass, utter or publish, or attempt to pass, utter or publish, as true, any falsely altered bill or note issued by order of the president, directors, and company of the said bank, or any falsely altered order or check on the said bank or corporation, or any cashier thereof, know-

ing the same to be falsely altered with intention to defraud the said corporation or any other body politic or person; or shall sell, utter or deliver, or cause to be sold, uttered or delivered, any forged or counterfeit note or bill in imitation, or purporting to be a bill or note issued by order of the president and directors of the said bank, knowing the same to be false, forged, or counterfeited; every such person shall be deemed and adjudged guilty of felony, and, being thereof convicted by due course of law, shall be sentenced to be imprisoned and kept to labor for not less than three years, nor more than ten years, or shall be imprisoned not exceeding ten years, and fined not exceeding five thousand dollars: *Provided,* That nothing herein contained shall be construed to deprive the courts of the individual States of a jurisdiction under the laws of the several States, over any offence declared punishable by this act.

Sec. 19. *And be it further enacted,* That if any person shall make or engrave, or cause, or procure to be made or engraved, or shall have in his custody or possession, any metallic plate, engraved after the similitude of any plate from which any notes or bills, issued by the said corporation, shall have been printed, with intent to use such plate, or to cause, or suffer the same to be used in forging or counterfeiting any of the notes or bills issued by said corporation; or shall have in his custody or possession, any blank note or notes, bill or bills, engraved and printed after the similitude of any notes or bills issued by said corporation, with intent to use such blanks, or cause, or suffer the same to be used in forging or counterfeiting any of the notes or bills issued by the said corporation; or shall have in his custody or possession, any paper adapted to the making of bank notes or bills, and similar to the paper upon which any notes or bills of the said corporation shall have been issued, with intent to use such paper, or cause, or suffer the same to be used in forging or counterfeiting any of the notes or bills issued by the said corporation, every such person, being thereof convicted, by due course of law, shall be sentenced to be imprisoned, and kept to hard labor, for a term not exceeding five years, or shall be imprisoned for a term not exceeding five years, and fined in a sum not exceeding one thousand dollars.

Sec. 20. *And be it further enacted,* That in consideration of the exclusive privileges and benefits conferred by this act upon the said bank, the president, directors, and company thereof, shall pay to the United States, out of the corporate funds thereof, the sum of one million and five hundred thousand dollars, in three equal payments; that is to say: five hundred thousand dollars at the expiration of two years; five hundred thousand dollars at the expiration of three years; and five hundred thousand dollars at the expiration of four years after the said bank shall be organized, and commence its operations in the manner hereinbefore provided.

Sec. 21. *And be it further enacted,* That no other bank shall be established by any future law of the United States during the continuance of the corporation hereby created, for which the faith of the United States is hereby pledged: *Provided,* Congress may renew existing charters for banks in the District of Columbia, not increasing the capital thereof, and may also establish any other bank or banks in said District, with capitals not exceeding, in the whole, six millions of dollars, if they shall deem it expedient. And, notwithstanding the expiration of the term for which the said corporation is created, it shall be lawful to use the corporate name, style, and capacity, for the purpose of suits for the final settlement and liquidation of the affairs and accounts of the corporation, and for the sale and disposition of their estate, real, personal, and mixed; but not for any other purpose, or in any other manner whatsoever, nor for a period exceeding two years after the expiration of the said term of incorporation.

Sec. 22. *And be it further enacted,* That if the subscriptions and payments to said bank shall not be made and completed so as to enable the same to commence its operations, or if the said bank shall not commence its operations on or before the first Monday in April next, then, and in that case, Congress may, at any time, within twelve months thereafter, declare, by law, this act null and void.

Sec. 23. *And be it further enacted,* That it shall, at all times, be lawful for a committee of either House of Congress, appointed for that purpose, to inspect the books, and to examine into the proceedings of the corporation hereby created, and to report whether the provisions of this charter have been, by the same, violated or not; and whenever any committee, as aforesaid, shall find and report, or the President of the United States shall have reason to believe that the charter has been violated, it may be lawful for Congress to direct, or the President to order a *scire facias* to be sued out of the circuit court of the district of Pennsylvania, in the name of the United States, (which shall be executed upon the president of the corporation for the time being, at least fifteen days before the commencement of the term of said court,) calling on the said corporation to show cause wherefore the charter, hereby granted, shall not be declared forfeited; and it shall be lawful for the said court, upon the return of the said *scire facias,* to examine into the truth of the alleged violation, and if such violation be made to appear, then to pronounce and adjudge that the said charter is forfeited and annulled: *Provided, however,* Every issue of fact which may be joined between the United States and the corporation aforesaid, shall be tried by jury. And it shall be lawful for the court aforesaid to require the production of such of the books of the corporation as it may deem necessary for the ascertainment of the controverted facts; and the final judgment of the court aforesaid, shall be examinable in the Supreme Court of the United States, by writ of error, and may be there reversed or affirmed, according to the usages of law.

Approved, April 10, 1816.

14th Con. 1st Sess.—58

An Act making appropriations for the support of Government, for the year one thousand eight hundred and sixteen.

Be it enacted, &c., That, for the expenditure of the civil list in the present year, including the contingent expenses of the several departments and offices; for the compensation of the several loan officers and their clerks, and for books and stationery for the same; for the payment of annuities and grants; for the support of the Mint Establishment; for the expenses of intercourse with foreign nations; for the support of lighthouses, beacons, buoys, and public piers; for surveying the coast of the United States; for making the Cumberland road; for ascertaining the titles to lands in Louisiana; for providing certificates of registry and lists of crews; and for satisfying certain miscellaneous claims, the following sums be, and the same are hereby, respectively appropriated, that is to say:

For compensation granted by law to the members of the Senate and House of Representatives, their officers, and attendants, five hundred and ninety-five thousand two hundred and fifty dollars, and the deduction to be made on account of the absence of members or delegates for any part of the present session, shall be in the proportion which the days of their absence respectively bear to the whole number of the days of the session.

For the expense of firewood, stationery, printing, and all other contingent expenses of the two Houses of Congress, forty-seven thousand dollars.

For the expenses of the Library of Congress, including the librarian's allowance for the year one thousand eight hundred and sixteen, eight hundred dollars.

For compensation to the President of the United States, twenty-five thousand dollars.

For rent and repairs of the tenement occupied by the President of the United States since August, one thousand eight hundred and fourteen, three thousand five hundred and fifty dollars.

For compensation to the Secretary of State, five thousand dollars.

For compensation to the clerks employed in the Department of State, being the sum appropriated for the service of the year one thousand eight hundred and fifteen, eleven thousand three hundred and fifty dollars and fifty cents.

For compensation to the messenger in said Department and in the Patent Office, six hundred and sixty dollars.

For the incidental and contingent expenses of the said Department, including the expense of printing and distributing ten thousand four hundred copies of the laws of the first session of the Fourteenth Congress, and printing the laws in newspapers, sixteen thousand nine hundred and thirty dollars.

For compensation to the Secretary of the Treasury, five thousand dollars.

For compensation to the clerks employed in the office of the Secretary of the Treasury, being the sum appropriated for the service of the year one thousand eight hundred and fifteen, ten thousand four hundred and thirty-three dollars and twenty-eight cents.

For compensation to the messenger and assistant messenger in the office of the Secretary of the Treasury, seven hundred and ten dollars.

For expense of translating foreign languages, allowance to the person employed in transmitting passports and sea letters, and for stationery and printing in the office of the Secretary of the Treasury, one thousand one hundred dollars.

For defraying the expenses of issuing Treasury notes, a sum not exceeding thirty thousand dollars.

For stating and printing the public accounts, for the years one thousand eight hundred and fifteen, and one thousand eight hundred and sixteen, two thousand four hundred dollars.

For compensation to the Comptroller of the Treasury, three thousand five hundred dollars.

For compensation to the clerks employed in the office of the Comptroller of the Treasury, being the sum appropriated for the service of the year one thousand eight hundred and fifteen, thirteen thousand three hundred and sixteen dollars and five cents.

For compensation to the messenger in said office, four hundred and ten dollars.

For compensation to additional clerks to be employed in the office of the Comptroller of the Treasury, two thousand two hundred dollars.

For expense of stationery, printing, and contingent expenses in the Comptroller's office, eight hundred dollars.

For compensation to the Auditor of the Treasury, three thousand dollars.

For compensation to the clerks employed in the Auditor's office, being the sum appropriated for the service of the year one thousand eight hundred and fifteen, ten thousand one hundred and thirty-two dollars and sixty-five cents, and the further sum of two thousand five hundred dollars.

For compensation to the messenger in said office, four hundred and ten dollars.

For compensation to additional clerks to be employed in the office of the Auditor, four thousand dollars.

For expense of stationery, printing, and contingent expenses in the Auditor's office, eight hundred dollars.

For compensation to the Treasurer, three thousand dollars.

For compensation to the clerks employed in the Treasurer's office, being the sum appropriated for the service of the year one thousand eight hundred and fifteen, four thousand two hundred and forty dollars and four cents.

For compensation to the messenger in said office, four hundred and ten dollars.

For compensation to additional clerks to be employed in the Treasurer's office, one thousand two hundred dollars.

For expenses of stationery, printing, and contingent expenses in the Treasurer's office, eight hundred dollars.

For compensation to the Commissioner of the General Land Office, three thousand dollars.

For compensation to the clerks employed in the office of the Commissioner of the General Land Office, ten thousand two hundred and fifty dollars.

For compensation to the messenger in said office, four hundred and ten dollars.

For stationery, printing, and contingent expenses in the General Land Office, including vellum for land patents, three thousand seven hundred dollars.

For arrears of compensation due to the chief clerk in the office of the said Commissioner, three hundred and twelve dollars and fifty cents.

For compensation to the Commissioner of the Revenue, three thousand dollars.

For compensation to the clerks employed in the office of the Commissioner of the Revenue, being the sum appropriated for the service of the year one thousand eight hundred and fifteen, nine thousand dollars.

For compensation to the messenger in said office, four hundred and ten dollars.

For stationery, printing, and contingent expenses, including the paper, printing and stamping of licenses, in the office of said Commissioner, three thousand two hundred dollars.

For compensation to the Register of the Treasury, two thousand four hundred dollars.

For compensation to the clerks employed in the office of the Register of the Treasury, being the sum appropriated for the service of the year one thousand eight hundred and fifteen, sixteen thousand two hundred and twenty-eight dollars and thirty-two cents.

For compensation to the messenger in said office, four hundred and ten dollars.

For compensation to additional clerks to be employed in the office of the Register of the Treasury, eight hundred dollars.

For expense of stationery, including books for the public stocks, printing the public accounts, and other contingent expenses of the Register's office, two thousand eight hundred and ninety dollars.

For fuel and other contingent expenses of the Treasury Department, including rent of the buildings now occupied by the department, expense of removing the records during the late war, transporting the same to the building preparing for them, cost of furniture for the offices, cases for the fire proof, and compensation to a superintendent and two watchmen employed for the security of the Treasury buildings, fifteen thousand dollars.

For the purchase of books, maps, and charts, for the Treasury Department, one thousand dollars.

For compensation to the Secretary to the Commissioners of the Sinking Fund, two hundred and fifty dollars.

For cost of vellum for patents for military bounty lands, printing them, and record books and wheels for military bounty lottery, in the office of the Commissioner of the General Land Office, seventeen thousand three hundred dollars.

For compensation to two clerks to be employed in the said office, to write and record the patents, seventeen hundred dollars.

For compensation to the Secretary of War, four thousand five hundred dollars.

For compensation to the clerks employed in the office of the Secretary of War, being the sum appropriated for the service of the year one thousand eight hundred and fifteen, fifteen thousand two hundred and thirty dollars.

For compensation to the messenger and his assistants in said office, seven hundred and ten dollars.

For expense of fuel, stationery, printing, and other contingent expenses in the office of the Secretary of War, three thousand dollars.

For compensation to the Accountant of the War Department, two thousand dollars.

For compensation to the clerks employed in the office of the Accountant of the War Department, being the sum appropriated for the service of the year one thousand eight hundred and fifteen, fourteen thousand seven hundred and seventy-five dollars.

For compensation to the messenger in said office, four hundred and ten dollars.

For compensation for additional clerks, to be employed in the the office of the Accountant of the War Department, six thousand five hundred dollars.

For expense of fuel, stationery, printing, and other contingent expenses in said office, two thousand dollars.

For compensation to the Paymaster of the Army, two thousand dollars.

For compensation to the clerks employed in the Paymaster's office, being the sum appropriated for the service of the year one thousand eight hundred and fifteen, thirteen thousand three hundred dollars.

For additional compensation of fifteen per cent. to the clerks employed in said office, on the sum hereinbefore appropriated, one thousand nine hundred and ninety-five dollars.

For compensation to the messenger in said office, four hundred and ten dollars.

For expense of fuel, stationery, printing, and other contingent expenses of the office of the Paymaster, two thousand dollars.

For compensation to the Superintendent General of Military Supplies, three thousand dollars.

For compensation to the clerks employed in the office of the Superintendent General of Military Supplies, being the sum appropriated for the service of the year one thousand eight hundred and fifteen, seven thousand dollars.

For compensation to the messenger in said office, four hundred and ten dollars.

For expenses of fuel, stationery, printing, and other contingent expenses in the office of the Superintendent General of Military Supplies, six hundred dollars.

For compensation to the Commissary General of Purchases, three thousand dollars.

For compensation to the clerks employed in the office of the said Commissary, being the sum appropriated for the service of the year one thousand eight hundred and fifteen, two thousand eight hundred dollars.

For contingent expenses in the said office of Commissary General of Purchases, nine hundred and thirty dollars.

For compensation to the clerks in the Adjutant and Inspector General's office, one thousand eight hundred dollars.

For compensation to the Secretary of the Navy, four thousand five hundred dollars.

For compensation to the clerks employed in the office of the Secretary of the Navy, being the sum appropriated for the service of the year one thousand eight hundred and fifteen, seven thousand two hundred and thirty-five dollars.

For compensation to the messenger in said office, four hundred and ten dollars.

For expense of fuel, stationery, printing, and other contingent expenses in said office, two thousand five hundred dollars.

For compensation to the Accountant of the Navy, two thousand dollars.

For compensation to the clerks employed in the office of the Accountant of the Navy, being the sum appropriated for the service of the year one thousand eight hundred and fifteen, twelve thousand two hundred dollars.

For compensation to the messenger in said office, four hundred and ten dollars.

For compensation to additional clerks to be employed in the office of said Accountant, two thousand five hundred dollars.

For contingent expenses of the office of said Accountant, one thousand two hundred and fifty dollars.

For compensation of the Commissioners of the Navy Board, ten thousand five hundred dollars.

For compensation to the Secretary of the Navy Board, two thousand dollars.

For compensation of the clerks employed in the office of the Navy Board, including the sum of two hundred and fifty dollars for the service of the preceding year, two thousand five hundred dollars.

For compensation of the messenger, including the sum of three hundred and seven dollars and fifty cents for the service of the preceding year, seven hundred and seventeen dollars fifty cents.

For the contingent expenses of the Navy Board, including the sum of one thousand five hundred dollars for the service of the preceding year, four thousand dollars.

For compensation to the Postmaster General, three thousand dollars.

For compensation to the Assistant Postmaster General, one thousand seven hundred dollars.

For compensation to the Second Assistant Postmaster General, one thousand six hundred dollars.

For compensation to the clerks employed in the General Post Office, being the amount appropriated for the service of the year one thousand eight hundred and fifteen, fifteen thousand one hundred dollars.

For compensation to additional clerks, four thousand two hundred and five dollars.

Public Acts of Congress.

For deficiency in appropriation for clerk hire for the year one thousand eight hundred and fifteen, nine hundred and thirty-five dollars.

For compensation to the messenger and assistant messenger, six hundred and sixty dollars.

For contingent expenses of the General Post Office, three thousand six hundred dollars.

For compensation to the several Commissioners of Loans, and for allowance to certain Commissioners of Loans in lieu of clerk hire, fourteen thousand five hundred and fifty dollars.

For compensation to the clerks of sundry Commissioners of Loans, and to defray the authorised expenses of the several loan officers, thirteen thousand seven hundred dollars.

For compensation to the Surveyor General and his clerks, four thousand one hundred dollars.

For compensation to the Surveyor of lands south of Tennessee, and his clerks, and for the contingent expenses of his office, three thousand two hundred dollars.

For compensation to the officers and clerks of the Mint, nine thousand six hundred dollars.

For wages to persons employed in the different operations of the Mint, including the sum of six hundred dollars allowed to an assistant engraver, five thousand dollars.

For repairs of furnaces, cost of iron and machinery, rents, and other contingent expenses of the Mint, two thousand four hundred and eighty dollars.

For allowance for wastage in the gold and silver coinage, one thousand five hundred dollars.

For the purchase of copper to coin into cents, fifteen thousand dollars.

For compensation to the Governor, Judges, and Secretary of the Indiana Territory, six thousand six hundred dollars.

For stationery, office rent, and other contingent expenses of said Territory, three hundred and fifty dollars.

For compensation to the Governor, Judges, and Secretary of the Mississippi Territory, nine thousand dollars.

For stationery, office rent, and other contingent expenses of said Territory, three hundred and fifty dollars.

For compensation to the Governor, Judges, and Secretary of the Missouri Territory, seven thousand eight hundred dollars.

For stationery, office rent, and other contingent expenses of said Territory, three hundred and fifty dollars.

For compensation to the Governor, Judges, and Secretary of the Michigan Territory, six thousand six hundred dollars.

For stationery, office rent, and other contingent expenses of said Territory, three hundred and fifty dollars.

For compensation to the Governor, Judges, and Secretary of the Illinois Territory, six thousand six hundred dollars.

For stationery, office rent, and other contingent expenses of said Territory, three hundred and fifty dollars.

For defraying the expenses incurred by print-

ing the laws of said Territory, one thousand one hundred and seventy-six dollars and twenty-five cents.

For the discharge of such demands against the United States on account of the civil department, not otherwise provided for, as shall have been admitted in due course of settlement, at the Treasury, two thousand dollars.

For compensation granted by law to the Chief Justice, the Associate Judges, and District Judges of the United States, including the Chief Justice and Associate Judges of the District of Columbia, sixty thousand dollars.

For compensation to the Attorney General of the United States, three thousand dollars.

For the compensation of sundry District Attorneys and Marshals, as granted by law, including those in the several Territories, seven thousand eight hundred and fifty dollars.

For defraying the expenses of the Supreme, Circuit, and District Courts of the United States, including the District of Columbia, and of jurors and witnesses, in aid of the funds arising from fines, penalties, and forfeitures, and for defraying the expenses of prosecutions for offences against the United States, and for the safekeeping of prisoners, forty thousand dollars.

For the payment of sundry pensions granted by the late Government, eight hundred and sixty dollars.

For the payment of the annual allowance to the invalid pensioners of the United States, one hundred and twenty thousand dollars.

For making the road from Cumberland, in the State of Maryland, to the State of Ohio, three hundred thousand dollars, to be repaid out of the fund reserved for laying out and making roads to the State of Ohio, by virtue of the seventh section of an act, passed on the thirtieth of April, one thousand eight hundred and two, entitled "An act to enable the people of the eastern division of the territory northwest of the river Ohio to form a constitution and State government, and for the admission of such State into the Union, on an equal footing with the original States, and for other purposes."

For the maintenance and support of lighthouses, beacons, buoys, and public piers, stakeages of channels, bars, and shoals, including the purchase and transportation of oil, keepers' salaries, repairs and improvements, and contingent expenses, ninety-seven thousand four hundred and sixty-four dollars.

To replace the amount heretofore appropriated for defraying the expense of surveying the coasts of the United States, which was carried to the surplus fund on the thirty-first of December, one thousand eight hundred and fourteen, twenty-nine thousand seven hundred and twenty dollars and fifty-seven cents.

For defraying the expense of ascertaining and adjusting land titles in Louisiana, five thousand dollars.

For defraying the expense of surveying the public lands within the several Territories of the United States, including the expense of surveys of private claims in Louisiana; for ascertaining the boundaries of the State of Ohio; of surveying the township lines in the Creek purchase, and of the salaries of two principal deputies in the State of Louisiana, one hundred and sixty-three thousand four hundred dollars.

For defraying the expense of printing certificates of registry and other documents for vessels, five thousand seven hundred and fifty dollars.

For the discharge of such miscellaneous claims against the United States, not otherwise provided for, as shall have been admitted in due course of settlement at the Treasury, four thousand dollars.

For the salaries, allowances, and contingent expenses of Ministers to foreign nations, and of secretaries of legation, one hundred and fourteen thousand dollars.

For the contingent expenses of intercourse between the United States and foreign nations, fifty thousand dollars.

For the expenses necessary during the present year for carrying into effect the fourth, sixth, and seventh articles of the Treaty of Peace concluded with His Britannic Majesty at Ghent, on the twenty-fourth December, one thousand eight hundred and fourteen, including the compensation of the Commissioners appointed under those articles, twenty-three thousand three hundred and thirty-two dollars.

For the salaries of the agents of claims on account of captures at London, Paris, and Copenhagen, at two thousand dollars each, six thousand dollars.

For replacing the sum of twenty-five thousand dollars, heretofore appropriated and carried to the surplus fund in the year one thousand eight hundred and fifteen, for objects in relation to the intercourse with the Barbary States, twenty-five thousand dollars.

For making good a deficiency in the appropriation of last year for the intercourse with foreign nations, arising from the difference in the exchange in transmitting the money to Europe, and in the drafts of Ministers and agents there upon bankers, and to meet similar expenses the present year, fifty thousand dollars.

To replace the sum of two thousand dollars, being part of an appropriation of five thousand dollars, appropriated by an act of the third of March, one thousand eight hundred and eleven, to discharge claims on account of depredations committed by the Osage Indians, and since carried to the surplus fund, two thousand dollars.

For the expenses of intercourse with the Barbary Powers, forty-seven thousand dollars.

For the relief of distressed American seamen for the present year, and to make good a deficiency in the preceding year, fifty thousand dollars.

SEC. 2. *And be it further enacted,* That the several appropriations hereinbefore made, shall be paid and discharged out of the fund of six hundred thousand dollars, reserved by the act making provision for the debt of the United States, and out of any moneys in the Treasury not otherwise appropriated.

Approved, April 16, 1816.

An Act providing for the settlement of certain accounts against the Library of Congress, for extending the privileges of using the books therein, and for establishing the salary of the Librarian.

Be it enacted, &c., That the accounting officers of the Treasury be, and they are hereby, authorized and required to investigate and settle the accounts against the Library of Congress, exhibited by George Waterston, Daniel Rapine, and William Elliott; and the amount thereof, which shall be deemed equitable, shall be paid out of any moneys in the Treasury not otherwise appropriated.

SEC. 2. *And be it further enacted,* That there shall be allowed to the Librarian, for attending said Library, an annual salary of one thousand dollars, payable quarterly, at the Treasury of the United States, to commence and take effect from and after the twenty-first day of March, one thousand eight hundred and fifteen.

SEC. 3. *And be it further enacted,* That the privilege of using the books in the Library shall be extended to the Attorney General of the United States and the members of the diplomatic corps, on the same terms and conditions as it is enjoyed by the Judges of the Supreme Court.

Approved, April 16, 1816.

An Act supplementary to an act, entitled "An act to incorporate a company for making certain turnpike roads within the District of Columbia."

Be it enacted, &c., That the company for making certain turnpike roads in the District of Columbia, established by an act of Congress passed on the twentieth day of April, one thousand eight hundred and ten, be authorized and empowered to open and make a turnpike road, at their own risk and expense, from the Eastern Branch bridge, to meet a road to be opened and made under the authority of the State of Maryland, from Edward H. Calvert's mill, in Prince George's county, to the line of the District of Columbia.

SEC. 2. *And be it further enacted,* That the said company may demand and receive the same tolls as are allowed for a like distance by the act to which this is a supplement, and shall possess and enjoy the same rights and privileges, and be subject to the same limitations, pains, and penalties, as are prescribed, enjoined, and directed by the aforesaid act, and an act in addition thereto, passed on the twenty-fifth day of April, one thousand eight hundred and ten.

Approved, April 16, 1816.

An Act confirming to the Navigation Company of New Orleans the use and possession of a lot in the said city.

Be it enacted, &c., That all the right and claim of the United States to the title, possession, and occupancy of a lot of ground of three hundred feet front on Rampart street, in the city of New Orleans, by six hundred feet in depth, on a line with St. Peter street, on which was erected the former hospital of charity in the said city be, and the same is hereby, vested in the Navigation Company of New Orleans: *Provided,* That nothing in this act contained shall affect the claim or claims of any individual or individuals, if any such there be.

Approved, April 16, 1816.

An Act further extending the time for issuing and locating military land warrants, and for other purposes.

Be it enacted, &c., That the Secretary of War be authorized to issue military land warrants to such persons as have or shall, before the first day of March, one thousand eight hundred and eighteen, produce to him satisfactory evidence of the validity of their claims; which warrants, with those heretofore issued, and not yet satisfied, shall and may be located in the name of the holders or proprietors thereof, prior to the first day of October, one thousand eight hundred and eighteen, on any unlocated parts of the fifty quarter townships, and the fractional quarter townships, reserved by law for original holders of military land warrants. And patents shall be granted for the land located under this act, in the same manner as is directed by former acts for granting military lands.

Sec. 2. *And be it further enacted,* That, at the expiration of the term limited by this act, for the location of the military land warrants aforesaid, it shall be the duty of the Commissioner of the General Land Office to transmit to the Surveyor General a list of all the lots of land within the fifty quarter townships and fractional quarter townships, which shall at that time remain unlocated; and the Surveyor General shall prepare and transmit to the registers of the land office at Chilicothe and Zanesville, respectively, general plats of the aforesaid unlocated lots, which lots shall, after the first day of March, one thousand eight hundred and nineteen, be offered for sale at the land offices in the districts in which they are situated, in the same manner, on the same terms and conditions, in every respect, as other public lands are offered at private sale, in the same districts.

Approved, April 16, 1816.

An Act to increase the pension of William Munday.

Be it enacted, &c., That there be, and hereby is, granted to William Munday, of the city of Baltimore, who lost both his arms in an attack on the enemy at St. Leonard's creek, on the twenty-eighth day of June, in the year one thousand eight hundred and fourteen, in lieu of the pension to which he is now entitled by law, a pension of twenty dollars per month, to be paid out of the navy pension fund.

Approved, April 16, 1816.

An Act authorizing the sale of a lot of ground, belonging to the United States, situated in the town of Knoxville and State of Tennessee.

Be it enacted, &c., That the President of the United States be, and he is hereby, authorized to cause to be sold, at public sale, a lot of ground belonging to the United States, situated in the town of Knoxville and State of Tennessee, ten days' notice being first given in the Knoxville Gazette, of the time and place of sale.

Sec. 2. *And be it further enacted,* That, on the receipt of the money arising from said sale, the President of the United States is hereby authorized to make or cause to be made a title or titles to the purchaser or purchasers of said lot.

Approved, April 16, 1816.

An Act for the relief of certain claimants to land in the district of Vincennes.

Be it enacted, &c., That the several persons whose claims were confirmed by the act of Congress, entitled "An act confirming certain claims to land in the district of Vincennes, and for other purposes," approved the third day of March, one thousand eight hundred and seven; and the act, entitled "An act confirming certain claims to land in the district of Vincennes," approved the thirteenth day of February, one thousand eight hundred and thirteen, which having been located cannot be surveyed agreeably to law, or which having been located have, in the opinion of the register of the land office, for the said district, been removed by the surveys of prior locations, from the spot intended to be occupied, are hereby authorized to enter their locations with the register of the land office at Vincennes, on any part of the tract set apart for that purpose in the said district, by virtue of the act, entitled "An act respecting claims to lands in the Indiana Territory and State of Ohio," and in conformity to the provisions of this act.

Approved, April 16, 1816.

An Act to authorize the President of the United States to alter the road laid out from the foot of the rapids of the river Miami of Lake Erie to the western line of the Connecticut reserve.

Be it enacted, &c., That the President of the United States be, and is hereby, authorized to cause to be made, in such manner as he may deem most proper, an alteration in the road laid out under authority of an act, entitled "An act to authorize the surveying and making of certain roads in the State of Ohio, as contemplated by the treaty of Brownstown, in the Territory of Michigan," so that the said road may pass through the United States' reservation at Lower Sandusky, or north thereof, not exceeding three miles.

Sec. 2. *And be it further enacted,* That the necessary expenses which shall be incurred in altering the said road shall be paid out of the moneys appropriated for the surveying of the public lands of the United States.

Approved, April 16, 1816.

An Act to authorize the Legislature of the State of Ohio to sell a certain tract of land, reserved for the use of that State.

Be it enacted, &c., That the Legislature of the State of Ohio shall be, and they are hereby, authorized and empowered to cause to be selected and sold, in such manner and on such terms and conditions as they may by law direct, any one section not exceeding the quantity of six hundred and forty acres of the tract of land of six miles square, reserved for the benefit of that State, at the Scioto salt springs: *Provided,* That the section so selected shall not include the said salt springs, and that the money arising from the sale of the aforesaid section shall be applied to the erection of a court-house, or other public buildings, thereon, for the use of the county of Jackson, in said State; and whenever the selection and sale of the said section of land shall have been made, and the same shall be duly certified to the Commissioner of the General Land Office, a patent shall be granted by the President of the United States, for the said section, in trust to such person or persons as the Legislature of the State shall have appointed and authorized to sell and execute titles to the purchasers of the land aforesaid.

Approved, April 16, 1816.

An Act making further provision for military services during the late war, and for other purposes.

Be it enacted, &c., That when any officer or private soldier of the militia, including rangers, sea fencibles, and volunteers, or any non-commissioned officer, musician, or private, enlisted for either of the terms of one year or eighteen months, or any commissioned officer of the regular army, shall have died while in the service of the United States during the late war, or in returning to his place of residence, after being mustered out of service, or who shall have died at any time thereafter, in consequence of wounds received whilst in the service, and shall have left a widow, or, if no widow, a child or children, under sixteen years of age, such widow, or, if no widow, such child or children, shall be entitled to receive half the monthly pay to which the deceased was entitled at the time of his death, for and during the term of five years; and in case of death or intermarriage of such widow, before the expiration of said five years, the half pay for the remainder of the time shall go to the child or children of said decedent. *Provided always,* That the Secretary of War shall adopt such forms of evidence, in applications under this act, as the President of the United States may prescribe. *Provided also,* That the officers and private soldiers of the militia, as aforesaid, who have been disabled by wounds or otherwise, while in the service of the United States in the discharge of their duty during the late war, shall be placed on the list of pensioners, in the same manner as the officers of the regular army, under such forms of evidence as the President of the United States may prescribe. *Provided also,* That the provisions of this act shall not extend to any person embraced in the provision of an act, entitled "An act to provide for the widows and orphans of the militia slain, and for militia disabled in the service of the United States," passed

the second day of August, one thousand eight hundred and thirteen.

SEC. 2. *And be it further enacted,* That when any non-commissioned officer, musician, or private soldier of the regular army of the United States shall have been killed in battle, or have died of wounds or disease, while in the service of the United States, during the late war, and have left a child or children under sixteen years of age, it shall be lawful for the guardian of such child or children, within one year from the passing of this act, to relinquish the bounty land to which such non-commissioned officer, musician, or private soldier, had he survived the war, would have been entitled; and, in lieu thereof, to receive half the monthly pay to which such deceased person was entitled at the time of his death, for and during the term of five years, to be computed from and after the seventeenth day of February, one thousand eight hundred and fifteen, the payment thereof to be made when and where other military pensions are or shall be paid; and where a warrant for the military bounty land aforesaid shall have been issued to or for the use of the child or children of any such deceased non-commissioned officer, musician, or private soldier, such child or children, or either of them, being under sixteen years of age, it shall be lawful for the guardian of such minor or minors to surrender and deliver such warrant, into the office for the Department of War, within one year from the passing of this act; of which surrender and delivery the Secretary of that Department shall give notice to the Secretary of the Treasury, who shall thereupon give the requisite orders for the payment of the half pay hereby provided for.

SEC. 3. *And be it further enacted,* That all soldiers who have been enlisted to serve for five years, or during the war, and were above the age of forty-five, or under the age of eighteen years, who have faithfully served during the late war, and have been regularly discharged, and the representatives of such soldiers as shall have died whilst in the service of the United States, and all soldiers who have been enlisted, and have faithfully served during the late war, until they have been promoted to the rank of commissioned officers, who, if they had served during the war under their enlistment, and been regularly discharged, would have been entitled to a bounty in land, shall be entitled to one hundred and sixty or three hundred and twenty acres of land, according to the term of enlistment; the warrants and patents to issue in the same manner as in the case of soldiers enlisted of proper age, and discharged under similar circumstances.

SEC. 4. *And be it further enacted,* That, for the purpose of carrying the provisions of this act into effect, and other acts giving bounty lands to soldiers of the regular army, the President of the United States is hereby authorized to cause to be surveyed and laid off, in one or more surveys, two millions of acres, not otherwise appropriated, in addition to the appropriations of lands by the act of May the sixth, one thousand eight hundred and twelve, for designating, surveying, and grant-giving at least ten weeks' notice in two public newspapers of the place where the bank is seated, and specifying in such notice the object or objects of such meeting.

6. Each cashier or treasurer, before he enters upon the duties of his office, shall be required to give bond, with two or more sureties, to the satisfaction of the directors, in a sum not less than fifty thousand dollars, with a condition for his good behaviour, and the faithful performance of his duties to the corporation.

7. The lands, tenements, and hereditaments, which it shall be lawful for the said corporation to hold, shall be only such as shall be requisite for its immediate accommodation in relation to the convenient transacting of its business, and such as shall have been *bonâ fide* mortgaged to it by way of security, or conveyed to it in satisfaction of debts previously contracted in the course of its dealings, or purchased at sales, upon judgments which shall have been obtained for such debts.

8. The total amount of debts which the said corporation shall at any time owe, whether by bond, bill, note, or other contract, over and above the debt or debts due for money deposited in the bank, shall not exceed the sum of thirty-five millions of dollars, unless the contracting of any greater debt shall have been previously authorized by law of the United States. In case of excess, the directors under whose administration it shall happen, shall be liable for the same in their natural and private capacities; and an action of debt may in such case be brought against them, or any of them, their or any of their heirs, executors, or administrators, in any court of record of the United States, or either of them, by any creditor or creditors of the said corporation, and may be prosecuted to judgment and execution, any condition, covenant, or agreement to the contrary notwithstanding. But this provision shall not be construed to exempt the said corporation or the lands, tenements, goods, or chattels of the same from being also liable for, and chargeable with, the said excess. Such of the said directors, who may have been absent when the said excess was contracted or created, or who may have dissented from the resolution or act whereby the same was so contracted or created, may respectively exonerate themselves from being so liable, by forthwith giving notice of the fact, and of their absence or dissent, to the President of the United States, and to the stockholders, at a general meeting, which they shall have power to call for that purpose.

9. The said corporation shall not, directly or indirectly, deal or trade in anything except bills of exchange, gold or silver bullion, or in the sale of goods really and truly pledged for money lent and not redeemed in due time, or goods which shall be the proceeds of its lands. It shall not be at liberty to purchase any public debt whatsoever, nor shall it take more than at the rate of six per centum per annum for or upon its loans or discounts.

10. No loan shall be made by the said corpora-tion, for the use or on account of the Government of the United States, to an amount exceeding five hundred thousand dollars, or of any particular State, to an amount exceeding fifty thousand dollars, or of any foreign Prince or State, unless previously authorized by a law of the United States.

11. The stock of the said corporation shall be assignable and transferrable, according to such rules as shall be instituted in that behalf, by the laws and ordinances of the same.

12. The bills, obligatory and of credit, under the seal of the said corporation, which shall be made to any person or persons, shall be assignable by endorsement thereupon, under the hand or hands of such person or persons, and his, her or their executors or administrators, and his, her or their assignee or assignees, and so as absolutely to transfer and vest the property thereof in each and every assignee or assignees successively, and to enable such assignee or assignees, and his, her or their executors or administrators, to maintain an action thereupon in his, her or their own name or names: *Provided,* That said corporation shall not make any bill obligatory, or of credit, or other obligation under its seal for the payment of a sum less than five thousand dollars. And the bills or notes which may be issued by order of the said corporation, signed by the president, and countersigned by the principal cashier or treasurer thereof, promising the payment of money to any person or persons, his, her or their order, or to bearer, although not under the seal of the said corporation, shall be binding and obligatory upon the same, in like manner, and with like force and effect, as upon any private person or persons, if issued by him, her or them, in his, her or their private or natural capacity or capacities, and shall be assignable and negotiable in like manner as if they were so issued by such private person or persons; that is to say, those which shall be payable to any person or persons, his, her or their order, shall be assignable by endorsement, in like manner, and with the like effect as foreign bills of exchange now are; and those which are payable to bearer shall be assignable and negotiable by delivery only: *Provided,* That all bills or notes, so to be issued by said corporation, shall be made payable on demand, other than bills or notes for the payment of a sum not less than one hundred dollars each, and payable to the order of some person or persons, which bills or notes it shall be lawful for said corporation to make payable at any time not exceeding sixty days from the date thereof.

13. Half-yearly dividends shall be made of so much of the profits of the bank as shall appear to the directors advisable; and once in every three years the directors shall lay before the stockholders, at a general meeting, for their information, an exact and particular statement of the debts which shall have remained unpaid after the expiration of the original credit, for a period of treble the term of that credit, and of the surplus of the profits, if any, after deducting losses and dividends. If there shall be a failure in the pay-

ment of any part of any sum subscribed to the capital of the said bank, by any person, copartnership or body politic, the party failing shall lose the benefit of any dividend which may have accrued prior to the time for making such payment, and during the delay of the same.

14. The directors of the said corporation shall establish a competent office of discount and deposite in the District of Columbia, whenever any law of the United States shall require such an establishment; also one such office of discount and deposite in any State in which two thousand shares shall have been subscribed or may be held, whenever, upon application of the Legislature of such State, Congress may, by law, require the same: *Provided,* the directors aforesaid shall not be bound to establish such office before the whole of the capital of the bank shall have been paid up. And it shall be lawful for the directors of the said corporation to establish offices of discount and deposite, wheresoever they shall think fit, within the United States or the Territories thereof, and to commit the management of the said offices, and the business thereof, respectively, to such persons, and under such regulations, as they shall deem proper, not being contrary to law or the constitution of the bank. Or, instead of establishing such offices, it shall be lawful for the directors of the said corporation, from time to time, to employ any other bank or banks, to be first approved by the Secretary of the Treasury, at any place or places that they may deem safe and proper, to manage and transact the business proposed as aforesaid, other than for the purposes of discount, to be managed and transacted by such offices, under such agreements, and subject to such regulations, as they shall deem just and proper. Not more than thirteen, nor less than seven managers or directors, of every office established as aforesaid, shall be annually appointed by the directors of the bank, to serve one year; they shall choose a president from their own number; each of them shall be a citizen of the United States, and a resident of the State, Territory, or district, wherein such office is established; and not more than three-fourths of the said managers or directors, in office at the time of an annual appointment, shall be reappointed for the next succeeding year; and no director shall hold his office more than three years out of four, in succession; but the president may be always reappointed.

15. The officer at the head of the Treasury Department of the United States shall be furnished, from time to time, as often as he may require, not exceeding once a week, with statements of the amount of the capital stock of the said corporation and of the debts due to the same; of the moneys deposited therein; of the notes in circulation, and of the specie in hand; and shall have a right to inspect such general accounts in the books of the bank as shall relate to the said statement: *Provided,* That this shall not be construed to imply a right of inspecting the account of any private individual or individuals with the bank.

16. No stockholder, unless he be a citizen of the United States, shall vote in the choice of directors.

17. No note shall be issued of less amount than five dollars.

Sec. 12. *And be it further enacted,* That if the said corporation, or any person or persons, for or to the use of the same, shall deal or trade in buying or selling goods, wares, merchandise, or commodities whatsoever, contrary to the provisions of this act, all and every person and persons by whom any order or direction for so dealing or trading shall have been given; and all and every person and persons who shall have been concerned as parties or agents therein, shall forfeit and lose treble the value of the goods, wares, merchandise, and commodities in which such dealing and trade shall have been, one-half thereof to the use of the informer, and the other half thereof to the use of the United States, to be recovered in any action of law with costs of suit.

Sec. 13. *And be it further enacted,* That if the said corporation shall advance or lend any sum of money for the use or on account of the Government of the United States, to an amount exceeding five hundred thousand dollars; or of any particular State, to an amount exceeding fifty thousand dollars; or of any foreign Prince or State, (unless previously authorized thereto by a law of the United States,) all and every person and persons, by and with whose order, agreement, consent, approbation, and connivance, such unlawful advance or loan shall have been made, upon conviction thereof shall forfeit and pay, for every such offence, treble the value or amount of the sum or sums which have been so unlawfully advanced or lent; one-fifth thereof to the use of the informer, and the residue thereof to the use of the United States.

Sec. 14. *And be it further enacted,* That the bills or notes of the said corporation originally made payable, or which shall have become payable on demand, shall be receivable in all payments to the United States, unless otherwise directed by act of Congress.

Sec. 15. *And be it further enacted,* That during the continuance of this act, and whenever required by the Secretary of the Treasury, the said corporation shall give the necessary facilities for transferring the public funds from place to place, within the United States, or the Territories thereof, and for distributing the same in payment of the public creditors, without charging commissions or claiming allowance on account of difference in exchange, and shall also do and perform the several and respective duties of the Commissioners of Loans for the several States, or of any one or more of them, whenever required by law.

Sec. 16. *And be it further enacted,* That the deposites of the money of the United States, in places in which the said bank and branches thereof may be established, shall be made in said bank or branches thereof, unless the Secretary of the Treasury shall at any time otherwise order and

commission, on the first hundred dollars collected in one quarter, may be increased to a sum not exceeding fifty per cent.

The Postmaster General may allow to the postmasters, respectively, a commission of fifty per cent. on the moneys arising from the postage of newspapers, magazines, and pamphlets; and to the postmaster whose compensation shall not exceed five hundred dollars in one quarter, two cents for every free letter delivered out of the office, excepting such as are for the postmaster himself; and each postmaster who shall be required to keep a register of the arrival and departure of the mails, shall be allowed ten cents for each monthly return which he makes thereof to the General Post Office.

The Postmaster General may allow to the postmaster at New Orleans, at the rate of eight hundred dollars, and to the postmaster at Warrenton, in North Carolina, at the rate of two hundred dollars, and to the postmaster at Wheeling, in Virginia, at the rate of two hundred dollars a year, in addition to their ordinary commissions. The Postmaster General is hereby authorized to allow to the postmaster at the City of Washington, in addition to the allowance made by this act for postage collected, and for free letters received by him for delivery, a commission of five per centum on the amount of mails distributed at his office: *Provided, nevertheless,* That the whole annual emoluments of the said postmaster, including the extra compensation heretofore allowed to him by law, shall always be subject to the restriction imposed by the fortieth section of the act of Congress approved the thirtieth of April, one thousand eight hundred and ten, to which this act is in addition.

SEC. 3. *And be it further enacted,* That letters and packets to and from any member of the Senate, or member or delegate of the House of Representatives of the United States, the Secretary of the Senate, and Clerk of the House of Representatives, shall be conveyed free of postage, for thirty days previous to each session of Congress, and for thirty days after the termination thereof: *Provided always,* That no letter or packet shall exceed two ounces in weight, and in case of excess of weight, that excess alone shall be paid for.

SEC. 4. *And be it further enacted,* That the eleventh and twenty-eighth sections of the act, entitled "An act regulating the Post Office Establishment," approved April thirtieth, one thousand eight hundred and ten, and the first and second sections of the act, entitled "An act in addition to the act regulating the Post Office Establishment," approved February twenty-seventh, one thousand eight hundred and fifteen, and the fourth and fifth sections of the same, except such parts as relate to steamboats, their masters, or managers, and persons employed on board the same, be, and the same are hereby, repealed.

SEC. 5. *And be it further enacted,* That this act shall take effect from and after the thirty-first day of March, one thousand eight hundred and sixteen.

Approved, April 9, 1816.

An Act to incorporate the subscribers to the Bank of the United States.

Be it enacted, &c., That a bank of the United States of America shall be established, with a capital of thirty-five millions of dollars, divided into three hundred and fifty thousand shares, of one hundred dollars each share. Seventy thousand shares, amounting to the sum of seven millions of dollars, part of the capital of the said bank, shall be subscribed and paid for by the United States, in the manner hereinafter specified; and two hundred and eighty thousand shares, amounting to the sum of twenty-eight millions of dollars, shall be subscribed and paid for by individuals, companies, or corporations, in the manner hereinafter specified.

SEC. 2. *And be it further enacted,* That subscriptions for the sum of twenty-eight millions of dollars, towards constituting the capital of the said bank, shall be opened on the first Monday in July next, at the following places: that is to say, at Portland, in the District of Maine; at Portsmouth, in the State of New Hampshire; at Boston, in the State of Massachusetts; at Providence, in the State of Rhode Island; at Middletown, in the State of Connecticut; at Burlington, in the State of Vermont; at New York in the State of New York; at New Brunswick, in the State of New Jersey; at Philadelphia, in the State of Pennsylvania; at Wilmington, in the State of Delaware; at Baltimore, in the State of Maryland; at Richmond, in the State of Virginia; at Lexington, in the State of Kentucky; at Cincinnati, in the State of Ohio; at Raleigh, in the State of North Carolina; at Nashville, in the State of Tennessee; at Charleston, in the State of South Carolina; at Augusta, in the State of Georgia; at New Orleans, in the State of Louisiana; and at Washington, in the District of Columbia. And the said subscriptions shall be opened under the superintendence of five commissioners at Philadelphia, and of three commissioners at each of the other places aforesaid, to be appointed by the President of the United States, who is hereby authorized to make such appointments, and shall continue open every day, from the time of opening the same, between the hours of ten o'clock in the forenoon and four o'clock in the afternoon, for the term of twenty days, exclusive of Sundays, when the same shall be closed, and immediately thereafter the commissioners, or any two of them, at the respective places aforesaid, shall cause two transcripts or copies of such subscriptions to be made, one of which they shall send to the Secretary of the Treasury, one they shall retain, and the original they shall transmit, within seven days from the closing of the subscriptions as aforesaid, to the commissioners at Philadelphia aforesaid. And on the receipt of the said original subscriptions, or of either of the said copies thereof, if the original be lost, mislaid, or detained, the commissioners at Philadelphia aforesaid, or a majority of them, shall immediately thereafter convene, and proceed to take an account of the said subscriptions. And if more than the amount of twenty-eight millions of dollars shall have been subscribed, then the said last mentioned commissioners shall deduct the amount of such excess from the largest subscriptions, in such manner as that no subscription shall be reduced in amount, while any one remains larger: *Provided,* That if the subscriptions taken at either of the places aforesaid shall not exceed three thousand shares, there shall be no reduction of such subscriptions, nor shall, in any case, the subscriptions taken at either of the places aforesaid be reduced below that amount. And in case the aggregate amount of the said subscriptions shall exceed twenty-eight millions of dollars, the said last mentioned commissioners, after having apportioned the same as aforesaid, shall cause lists of the said apportioned subscriptions to be made out, including in each list the apportioned subscription for the place where the original subscription was made, one of which lists they shall transmit to the commissioners or one of them, under whose superintendence such subscriptions were originally made, that the subscribers may thereby ascertain the number of shares to them respectively apportioned as aforesaid. And in case the aggregate amount of the said subscriptions made during the period aforesaid, at all the places aforesaid, shall not amount to twenty-eight millions of dollars, the subscriptions to complete the said sum shall be and remain open at Philadelphia aforesaid, under the superintendence of the commissioners appointed for that place; and the subscriptions may be then made by any individual, company, or corporation, for any number of shares, not exceeding, in the whole, the amount required to complete the said sum of twenty-eight millions of dollars.

Sec. 3. *And be it further enacted,* That it shall be lawful for any individual, company, corporation, or State, when the subscriptions shall be opened as hereinbefore directed, to subscribe for any number of shares of the capital of the said bank, not exceeding three thousand shares, and the sums so subscribed shall be payable, and paid, in the manner following: that is to say, seven millions of dollars thereof in gold or silver coin of the United States, or in gold coin of Spain, or the dominions of Spain, at the rate of one hundred dred cents for every twenty-eight grains and sixty hundredths of a grain of the actual weight thereof, or in other foreign gold or silver coin at the several rates prescribed by the first section of an act regulating the currency of foreign coins in the United States, passed tenth day of April, one thousand eight hundred and six, and twenty-one millions of dollars thereof in like gold or silver coin, or in the funded debt of the United States contracted at the time of the subscriptions respectively. And the payments made in the funded debt of the United States, shall be paid and received at the following rates: that is to say, the funded debt bearing an interest of six per centum per annum, at the nominal or par value thereof; the funded debt bearing an interest of three per centum per annum, at the rate of sixty-five dollars for every sum of one hundred dollars of the nominal amount thereof; and the funded debt

bearing an interest of seven per centum per annum, at the rate of one hundred and six dollars and fifty-one cents, for every sum of one hundred dollars of the nominal amount thereof; together with the amount of the interest accrued on the said several denominations of funded debt, to be computed and allowed to the time of subscribing the same to the capital of the said bank as aforesaid. And the payments of the said subscriptions shall be made and completed by the subscribers, respectively, at the times and in the manner following: that is to say, at the time of subscribing there shall be paid five dollars on each share, in gold or silver coin as aforesaid, and twenty-five dollars more in coin as aforesaid, or in funded debt as aforesaid; at the expiration of six calendar months after the time of subscribing, there shall be paid the further sum of ten dollars on each share, in gold or silver coin as aforesaid, and twenty-five dollars more in coin as aforesaid, or in funded debt as aforesaid; at the expiration of twelve calendar months from the time of subscribing, there shall be paid the further sum of ten dollars, on each share, in gold or silver coin as aforesaid, and twenty-five dollars more, in coin as aforesaid, or in funded debt as aforesaid.

Sec. 4. *And be it further enacted,* That, at the time of subscribing to the capital of the said bank as aforesaid, each and every subscriber shall deliver to the commissioners, at the place of subscribing, as well the amount of their subscriptions respectively in coin as aforesaid, as the certificates of funded debt, for the funded debt proportions of their respective subscriptions, together with a power of attorney, authorizing the said commissioners, or a majority of them, to transfer the said stock, in due form of law to "the president, directors, and company, of the Bank of the United States," as soon as the said bank shall be organized. *Provided always,* That if, in consequence of the apportionment of the shares in the capital of the said bank among the subscribers, in the case, and in the manner, hereinbefore provided, any subscriber shall have delivered to the commissioners, at the time of subscribing, a greater amount of gold or silver coin and funded debt than shall be necessary to complete the payments for the share or shares to such subscribers, apportioned as aforesaid, the commissioners shall only retain so much of the said gold or silver coin, and funded debt, as shall be necessary to complete such payments, and shall, forthwith, return the surplus thereof, on application for the same to the subscribers lawfully entitled thereto. And the commissioners, respectively, shall deposite the gold and silver coin, and certificates of public debt by them respectively received as aforesaid from the subscribers to the capital of the said bank, in some place of secure and safe keeping, so that the same may and shall be specially delivered and transferred, as the same were by them respectively received, to the president, directors, and company, of the Bank of the United States, or to their order, as soon as shall be required after the organization of the said bank. And the said commissioners appointed to superintend the subscrip-

Public Acts of Congress.

tions to the capital of the said bank as aforesaid, shall receive a reasonable compensation for their services respectively, and shall be allowed all reasonable charges and expenses incurred in the execution of their trust, to be paid by the president, directors, and company, of the bank, out of the funds thereof.

Sec. 5. *And be it further enacted*, That it shall be lawful for the United States to pay and redeem the funded debt subscribed to the capital of the said bank, at the rates aforesaid, in such sums, and at such times, as shall be deemed expedient, anything in any act or acts of Congress to the contrary thereof notwithstanding. And it shall also be lawful for the president, directors, and company, of the said bank, to sell and transfer for gold and silver coin, or bullion, the funded debt subscribed to the capital of the said bank as aforesaid: *Provided always*, That they shall not sell more thereof than the sum of two millions of dollars in any one year; nor sell any part thereof at any time within the United States, without previously giving notice of their intention to the Secretary of the Treasury, and offering the same to the United States for the period of fifteen days, at least, at the current price, not exceeding the rates aforesaid.

Sec. 6. *And be it further enacted*, That, at the opening of subscription to the capital stock of the said bank, the Secretary of the Treasury shall subscribe, or cause to be subscribed, on behalf of the United States, the said number of seventy thousand shares, amounting to seven millions of dollars as aforesaid, to be paid in gold or silver coin, or in stock of the United States, bearing interest at the rate of five per centum per annum; and if payment thereof or of any part thereof, be made in public stock, bearing interest as aforesaid, the said interest shall be payable quarterly, to commence from the time of making such payment on account of the said subscription, and the principal of the said stock shall be redeemable in any sums, and at any periods, which the Government shall deem fit. And the Secretary of the Treasury shall cause the certificates of such public stock to be prepared, and made in the usual form, and shall pay and deliver the same to the president, directors, and company, of the said bank on the first day of January, one thousand eight hundred and seventeen, which said stock it shall be lawful for the said president, directors, and company, to sell and transfer for gold and silver coin or bullion at their discretion: *Provided*, They shall not sell more than two millions of dollars thereof in any one year.

Sec. 7. *And be it further enacted*, That the subscribers to the said Bank of the United States of America, their successors and assigns, shall be, and are hereby, created a corporation and body politic, by the name and style of " The president, directors, and company, of the Bank of the United States," and shall so continue until the third day of March, in the year one thousand eight hundred and thirty-six, and by that name shall be, and are hereby, made able and capable, in law, to have, purchase, receive, possess, enjoy, and re-

tain, to them and their successors, lands, rents, tenements, hereditaments, goods, chattels, and effects, of whatsoever kind, nature, and quality, to an amount not exceeding, in the whole, fifty-five millions of dollars, including the amount of the capital stock aforesaid; and the same to sell, grant, demise, alien or dispose of; to sue and be sued, plead and be impleaded, answer and be answered, defend and be defended, in all State courts having competent jurisdiction, and in any circuit court of the United States: and also to make, have, and use, a common seal, and the same to break, alter, and renew, at their pleasure: and also to ordain, establish, and put in execution, such by-laws, and ordinances, and regulations, as they shall deem necessary and convenient for the government of the said corporation, not being contrary to the constitution thereof, or to the laws of the United States; and generally to do and execute all and singular the acts, matters, and things, which to them it shall or may appertain to do; subject, nevertheless, to the *rules*, regulations, restrictions, limitations, and provisions, hereinafter prescribed and declared.

Sec. 8. *And be it further enacted*, That, for the management of the affairs of the said corporation, there shall be twenty-five directors, five of whom, being stockholders, shall be annually appointed by the President of the United States, by and with the advice and consent of the Senate, not more than three of whom shall be residents of any one State; and twenty of whom shall be annually elected at the banking-house in the city of Philadelphia, on the first Monday of January, in each year, by the qualified stockholders of the capital of the said bank other than the United States, and by a plurality of votes then and there actually given, according to the scale of voting hereinafter prescribed: *Provided always*, That no person, being a director in the Bank of the United States, or any of its branches, shall be a director of any other bank ; and should any such director act as a director in any other bank, it shall forthwith vacate his appointment in the direction of the Bank of the United States. And the directors, so duly appointed and elected, shall be capable of serving, by virtue of such appointment and choice, from the first Monday in the month of January of each year, until the end and expiration of the first Monday in the month of January of the year next ensuing the time of each annual election to be held by the stockholders as aforesaid. And the board of *directors*, annually, at the first meeting after their *election* in each and every year, shall proceed *to elect* one of the directors to be president of the corporation, who shall hold the said office during the same period for which the directors are appointed and elected as aforesaid: *Provided also*, That the first appointment and election of the directors and president of the said bank shall be at the time and for the period hereinafter declared: *And provided also*, That in case it should at any time happen that an appointment or election of directors, or an election of the president of the said bank, should not be so made as to take effect on any day when, in pursuance of this act, they ought to take effect, the said corporation shall not, for that cause, be deemed to be dissolved; but it shall be lawful at any other time to make such appointments, and to hold such elections, (as the case may be,) and the manner of holding the elections shall be regulated by the by-laws and ordinances of the said corporation: and until such appointments or elections be made, the directors and president of the said bank, for the time being, shall continue in office : *And provided also,* That in case of the death, resignation, or removal, of the president of the said corporation, the directors shall proceed to elect another president from the directors as aforesaid : and in case of the death, resignation, or absence from the United States, or removal of a director from office, the vacancy shall be supplied by the President of the United States, or by the stockholders, as the case may be. But the President of the United States alone shall have power to remove any of the directors appointed by him as aforesaid.

SEC. 9. *And be it further enacted,* That as soon as the sum of eight millions four hundred thousand dollars in gold and silver coin, and in the public debt, shall have been actually received on account of the subscriptions to the capital of the said bank (exclusively of the subscription aforesaid, on the part of the United States) notice thereof shall be given by the persons under whose superintendence the subscriptions shall have been made at the city of Philadelphia, in at least two newspapers printed in each of the places (if so many be printed in such places respectively) where subscriptions shall have been made, and the said persons shall, at the same time, and in like manner, notify a time and place within the said city of Philadelphia, at the distance of at least thirty days from the time of such notification, for proceeding to the election of twenty directors as aforesaid, and it shall be lawful for such election to be then and there made. And the President of the United States is hereby authorized, during the present session of Congress, to nominate, and, by and with the advice and consent of the Senate, to appoint, five directors of the said bank, though not stockholders, anything in the provisions of this act to the contrary notwithstanding; and the persons who shall be elected and appointed as aforesaid, shall be the first directors of the said bank, and shall proceed to elect one of the directors to be president of the said bank; and the directors and president of the said bank, so appointed and elected as aforesaid, shall be capable of serving in their respective office, by virtue thereof, until the end and expiration of the first Monday of the month of January next ensuing the said appointments and elections, and they shall then and thenceforth commence, and continue the operations of the said bank, at the city of Philadelphia.

SEC. 10. *And be it further enacted,* That the directors, for the time being, shall have power to appoint such officers, clerks, and servants, under them, as shall be necessary for executing the business of the said corporation, and to allow them such compensation for their services, respectively, as shall be reasonable ; and shall be capable of exercising such other powers and authorities for the well governing and ordering of the officers of the said corporation as shall be prescribed, fixed, and determined, by the laws, regulations, and ordinances, of the same.

SEC. 11. *And be it further enacted,* That the following rules, restrictions, limitations, and provisions, shall form and be fundamental articles of the constitution of the said corporation, to wit :

1. The number of votes to which the stockholders shall be entitled, in voting for directors, shall be according to the number of shares he, she, or they, respectively, shall hold, in the proportions following, that is to say, for one share and not more than two shares, one vote ; for every two shares above two, and not exceeding ten, one vote ; for every four shares above ten, and not exceeding thirty, one vote ; for every six shares above thirty, and not exceeding sixty, one vote ; for every eight shares above sixty, and not exceeding one hundred, one vote ; and for every ten shares above one hundred, one vote ; but no person, copartnership, or body politic, shall be entitled to a greater number than thirty votes; and after the first election, no share or shares shall confer a right of voting, which shall not have been holden three calendar months previous to the day of election. And stockholders actually resident within the United States, and none other, may vote in elections by proxy.

2. Not more than three-fourths of the directors elected by the stockholders, and not more than four-fifths of the directors appointed by the President of the United States, who shall be in office at the time of an annual election, shall be elected or appointed for the next succeeding year ; and no director shall hold his office more than three years out of four in succession ; but the director who shall be the president at the time of an election may always be reappointed or re-elected, as the case may be.

3. None but a stockholder, resident citizen of the United States, shall be a director ; nor shall a director be entitled to any emolument ;- but the directors may make such compensation to the president, for his extraordinary attendance at the bank, as shall appear to them reasonable.

4. Not less than seven directors shall constitute a board for the transaction of business, of whom the president shall always be one, except in case of sickness or necessary absence ; in which case his place may be supplied by any other director whom he, by writing, under his hand, shall depute for that purpose. And the director so deputed may do and transact all the necessary business, belonging to the office of the president of the said corporation, during the continuance of the sickness or necessary absence of the president.

5. A number of stockholders, not less than sixty, who, together, shall be proprietors of one thousand shares or upwards, shall have power at any time to call a general meeting of the stockholders, for purposes relative to the institution,

direct; in which case the Secretary of the Treasury shall immediately lay before Congress, if in session, and if not, immediately after the commencement of the next session, the reasons of such order or direction.

Sec. 17. *And be it further enacted*, That the said corporation shall not at any time suspend or refuse payment in gold and silver, of any of its notes, bills, or obligations; nor of any moneys received upon deposite in said bank, or in any of its offices of discount and deposite. And if the said corporation shall at any time refuse or neglect to pay on demand any bill, note or obligation issued by the corporation, according to the contract, promise, or undertaking therein expressed; or shall neglect or refuse to pay on demand any moneys received in said bank, or in any of its offices aforesaid, on deposite, to the person or persons entitled to receive the same, then, and in every such case, the holder of any such note, bill, or obligation, or the person or persons entitled to demand and receive such moneys as aforesaid, shall respectively be entitled to receive and recover interest on the said bills, notes, obligations, or moneys, until the same shall be fully paid and satisfied, at the rate of twelve per centum per annum from the time of such demand as aforesaid : *Provided*, That Congress may at any time hereafter enact laws enforcing and regulating the recovery of the amount of the notes, bills, obligations, or other debts, of which payment shall have been refused as aforesaid, with the rate of interest abovementioned, vesting jurisdiction for that purpose in any courts, either of law or equity, of the courts of the United States, or Territories thereof, or of the several States, as they may deem expedient.

Sec. 18. *And be it further enacted*, That if any person shall falsely make, forge or counterfeit, or cause or procure to be falsely made, forged or counterfeited, or willingly aid or assist in falsely making, forging or counterfeiting any bill or note in imitation of or purporting to be a bill or note issued by order of the president, directors, and company of the said bank, or any order or check on the said bank or corporation, or any cashier thereof; or shall falsely alter, or cause or procure to be falsely altered, or willingly aid or assist in falsely altering any bill or note issued by order of the president, directors, and company of the said bank, or any order or check on the said bank or corporation, or any cashier thereof; or shall pass, utter or publish, or attempt to pass utter or publish as true, any false, forged, or counterfeited bill or note, purporting to be a bill or note issued by order of the president, directors, and company of the said bank, or any false, forged, or counterfeited order or check upon the said bank or corporation, or any cashier thereof, knowing the same to be falsely forged or counterfeited; or shall pass, utter or publish, or attempt to pass, utter or publish, as true, any falsely altered bill or note issued by order of the president, directors, and company of the said bank, or any falsely altered order or check on the said bank or corporation, or any cashier thereof, know-

ing the same to be falsely altered with intention to defraud the said corporation or any other body politic or person; or shall sell, utter or deliver, or cause to be sold, uttered or delivered, any forged or counterfeit note or bill in imitation, or purporting to be a bill or note issued by order of the president and directors of the said bank, knowing the same to be false, forged, or counterfeited; every such person shall be deemed and adjudged guilty of felony, and, being thereof convicted by due course of law, shall be sentenced to be imprisoned and kept to labor for not less than three years, nor more than ten years, or shall be imprisoned not exceeding ten years, and fined not exceeding five thousand dollars: *Provided*, That nothing herein contained shall be construed to deprive the courts of the individual States of i jurisdiction under the laws of the several States, over any offence declared punishable by this act.

Sec. 19. *And be it further enacted*, That if any person shall make or engrave, or cause, or procure to be made or engraved, or shall have in his custody or possession, any metallic plate, engraved after the similitude of any plate from which any notes or bills, issued by the said corporation, shall have been printed, with intent to use such plate, or to cause, or suffer the same to be used in forging or counterfeiting any of the notes or bills issued by said corporation; or shall have in his custody or possession, any blank note or notes, bill or bills, engraved and printed after the similitude of any notes or bills issued by said corporation, with intent to use such blanks, or cause, or suffer the same to be used in forging or counterfeiting any of the notes or bills issued by the said corporation; or shall have in his custody or possession, any paper adapted to the making of bank notes or bills, and similar to the paper upon which any notes or bills of the said corporation shall have been issued, with intent to use such paper, or cause, or suffer the same to be used in forging or counterfeiting any of the notes or bills issued by the said corporation, every such person, being thereof convicted, by due course of law, shall be sentenced to be imprisoned and kept to hard labor, for a term not exceeding five years, or shall be imprisoned for a term not exceeding five years, and fined in a sum not exceeding one thousand dollars.

Sec. 20. *And be it further enacted*, That in consideration of the exclusive privileges and benefits conferred by this act upon the said bank, the president, directors, and company thereof, shall pay to the United States, out of the corporate funds thereof, the sum of one million and five hundred thousand dollars, in three equal payments; that is to say: five hundred thousand dollars at the expiration of two years; five hundred thousand dollars at the expiration of three years; and five hundred thousand dollars at the expiration of four years after the said bank shall be organized, and commence its operations in the manner hereinbefore provided.

Sec. 21. *And be it further enacted*, That no other bank shall be established by any future law of the United States during the continuance of the corporation hereby created, for which the faith of the United States is hereby pledged: *Provided*, Congress may renew existing charters for banks in the District of Columbia, not increasing the capital thereof, and may also establish any other bank or banks in said District, with capitals not exceeding, in the whole, six millions of dollars, if they shall deem it expedient. And, notwithstanding the expiration of the term for which the said corporation is created, it shall be lawful to use the corporate name, style, and capacity, for the purpose of suits for the final settlement and liquidation of the affairs and accounts of the corporation, and for the sale and disposition of their estate, real, personal, and mixed; but not for any other purpose, or in any other manner whatsoever, nor for a period exceeding two years after the expiration of the said term of incorporation.

Sec. 22. *And be it further enacted*, That if the subscriptions and payments to said bank shall not be made and completed so as to enable the same to commence its operations, or if the said bank shall not commence its operations on or before the first Monday in April next, then, and in that case, Congress may, at any time, within twelve months thereafter, declare, by law, this act null and void.

Sec. 23. *And be it further enacted*, That it shall, at all times, be lawful for a committee of either House of Congress, appointed for that purpose, to inspect the books, and to examine into the proceedings of the corporation hereby created, and to report whether the provisions of this charter have been, by the same, violated or not; and whenever any committee, as aforesaid, shall find and report, or the President of the United States shall have reason to believe that the charter has been violated, it may be lawful for Congress to direct, or the President to order a *scire facias* to be sued out of the circuit court of the district of Pennsylvania, in the name of the United States, (which shall be executed upon the president of the corporation for the time being, at least fifteen days before the commencement of the term of said court,) calling on the said corporation to show cause wherefore the charter, hereby granted, shall not be declared forfeited; and it shall be lawful for the said court, upon the return of the said *scire facias*, to examine into the truth of the alleged violation, and if such violation be made to appear, then to pronounce and adjudge that the said charter is forfeited and annulled: *Provided, however*, Every issue of fact which may be joined between the United States and the corporation aforesaid, shall be tried by jury. And it shall be lawful for the court aforesaid to require the production of such of the books of the corporation as it may deem necessary for the ascertainment of the controverted facts; and the final judgment of the court aforesaid, shall be examinable in the Supreme Court of the United States, by writ of error, and may be there reversed or affirmed, according to the usages of law.

Approved, April 10, 1816.

An Act making appropriations for the support of Government, for the year one thousand eight hundred and sixteen.

Be it enacted, &c., That, for the expenditure of the civil list in the present year, including the contingent expenses of the several departments and offices; for the compensation of the several loan officers and their clerks, and for books and stationery for the same; for the payment of annuities and grants; for the support of the Mint Establishment; for the expenses of intercourse with foreign nations; for the support of lighthouses, beacons, buoys, and public piers; for surveying the coast of the United States; for making the Cumberland road; for ascertaining the titles to lands in Louisiana; for providing certificates of registry and lists of crews; and for satisfying certain miscellaneous claims, the following sums be, and the same are hereby, respectively appropriated, that is to say:

For compensation granted by law to the members of the Senate and House of Representatives, their officers, and attendants, five hundred and ninety-five thousand two hundred and fifty dollars, and the deduction to be made on account of the absence of members or delegates for any part of the present session, shall be in the proportion which the days of their absence respectively bear to the whole number of the days of the session.

For the expense of firewood, stationery, printing, and all other contingent expenses of the two Houses of Congress, forty-seven thousand dollars.

For the expenses of the Library of Congress, including the librarian's allowance for the year one thousand eight hundred and sixteen, eight hundred dollars.

For compensation to the President of the United States, twenty-five thousand dollars.

For rent and repairs of the tenement occupied by the President of the United States since August, one thousand eight hundred and fourteen, three thousand five hundred and fifty dollars.

For compensation to the Secretary of State, five thousand dollars.

For compensation to the clerks employed in the Department of State, being the sum appropriated for the service of the year one thousand eight hundred and fifteen, eleven thousand three hundred and fifty dollars and fifty cents.

For compensation to the messenger in said Department and in the Patent Office, six hundred and sixty dollars.

For the incidental and contingent expenses of the said Department, including the expense of printing and distributing ten thousand four hundred copies of the laws of the first session of the Fourteenth Congress, and printing the laws in newspapers, sixteen thousand nine hundred and thirty dollars.

For compensation to the Secretary of the Treasury, five thousand dollars.

For compensation to the clerks employed in the office of the Secretary of the Treasury, being the sum appropriated for the service of the year one thousand eight hundred and fifteen, ten thousand four hundred and thirty-three dollars and twenty-eight cents.

For compensation to the messenger and assistant messenger in the office of the Secretary of the Treasury, seven hundred and ten dollars.

For expense of translating foreign languages, allowance to the person employed in transmitting passports and sea letters, and for stationery and printing in the office of the Secretary of the Treasury, one thousand one hundred dollars.

For defraying the expenses of issuing Treasury notes, a sum not exceeding thirty thousand dollars.

For stating and printing the public accounts, for the years one thousand eight hundred and fifteen, and one thousand eight hundred and sixteen, two thousand four hundred dollars.

For compensation to the Comptroller of the Treasury, three thousand five hundred dollars.

For compensation to the clerks employed in the office of the Comptroller of the Treasury, being the sum appropriated for the service of the year one thousand eight hundred and fifteen, thirteen thousand three hundred and sixteen dollars and five cents.

For compensation to the messenger in said office, four hundred and ten dollars.

For compensation to additional clerks to be employed in the office of the Comptroller of the Treasury, two thousand two hundred dollars.

For expense of stationery, printing, and contingent expenses in the Comptroller's office, eight hundred dollars.

For compensation to the Auditor of the Treasury, three thousand dollars.

For compensation to the clerks employed in the Auditor's office, being the sum appropriated for the service of the year one thousand eight hundred and fifteen, ten thousand one hundred and thirty-two dollars and sixty-five cents, and the further sum of two thousand five hundred dollars.

For compensation to the messenger in said office, four hundred and ten dollars.

For compensation to additional clerks to be employed in the office of the Auditor, four thousand dollars.

For expense of stationery, printing, and contingent expenses in the Auditor's office, eight hundred dollars.

For compensation to the Treasurer, three thousand dollars.

For compensation to the clerks employed in the Treasurer's office, being the sum appropriated for the service of the year one thousand eight hundred and fifteen, four thousand two hundred and forty dollars and four cents.

For compensation to the messenger in said office, four hundred and ten dollars.

For compensation to additional clerks to be employed in the Treasurer's office, one thousand two hundred dollars.

For expenses of stationery, printing, and contingent expenses in the Treasurer's office, eight hundred dollars.

For compensation to the Commissioner of the General Land Office, three thousand dollars.

For compensation to the clerks employed in the office of the Commissioner of the General Land Office, ten thousand two hundred and fifty dollars.

For compensation to the messenger in said office, four hundred and ten dollars.

For stationery, printing, and contingent expenses in the General Land Office, including vellum for land patents, three thousand seven hundred dollars.

For arrears of compensation due to the chief clerk in the office of the said Commissioner, three hundred and twelve dollars and fifty cents.

For compensation to the Commissioner of the Revenue, three thousand dollars.

For compensation to the clerks employed in the office of the Commissioner of the Revenue, being the sum appropriated for the service of the year one thousand eight hundred and fifteen, nine thousand dollars.

For compensation to the messenger in said office, four hundred and ten dollars.

For stationery, printing, and contingent expenses, including the paper, printing and stamping of licenses, in the office of said Commissioner, three thousand two hundred dollars.

For compensation to the Register of the Treasury, two thousand four hundred dollars.

For compensation to the clerks employed in the office of the Register of the Treasury, being the sum appropriated for the service of the year one thousand eight hundred and fifteen, sixteen thousand two hundred and twenty-eight dollars and thirty-two cents.

For compensation to the messenger in said office, four hundred and ten dollars.

For compensation to additional clerks to be employed in the office of the Register of the Treasury, eight hundred dollars.

For expense of stationery, including books for the public stocks, printing the public accounts, and other contingent expenses of the Register's office, two thousand eight hundred and ninety dollars.

For fuel and other contingent expenses of the Treasury Department, including rent of the buildings now occupied by the department, expense of removing the records during the late war, transporting the same to the building preparing for them, cost of furniture for the offices, cases for the fire proof, and compensation to a superintendent and two watchmen employed for the security of the Treasury buildings, fifteen thousand dollars.

For the purchase of books, maps, and charts, for the Treasury Department, one thousand dollars.

For compensation to the Secretary to the Commissioners of the Sinking Fund, two hundred and fifty dollars.

For cost of vellum for patents for military bounty lands, printing them, and record books and wheels for military bounty lottery, in the office of the Commissioner of the General Land Office, seventeen thousand three hundred dollars.

For compensation to two clerks to be employed in the said office, to write and record the patents, seventeen hundred dollars.

For compensation to the Secretary of War, four thousand five hundred dollars.

For compensation to the clerks employed in the office of the Secretary of War, being the sum appropriated for the service of the year one thousand eight hundred and fifteen, fifteen thousand two hundred and thirty dollars.

For compensation to the messenger and his assistants in said office, seven hundred and ten dollars.

For expense of fuel, stationery, printing, and other contingent expenses in the office of the Secretary of War, three thousand dollars.

For compensation to the Accountant of the War Department, two thousand dollars.

For compensation to the clerks employed in the office of the Accountant of the War Department, being the sum appropriated for the service of the year one thousand eight hundred and fifteen, fourteen thousand seven hundred and seventy-five dollars.

For compensation to the messenger in said office, four hundred and ten dollars.

For compensation for additional clerks, to be employed in the office of the Accountant of the War Department, six thousand five hundred dollars.

For expense of fuel, stationery, printing, and other contingent expenses in said office, two thousand dollars.

For compensation to the Paymaster of the Army, two thousand dollars.

For compensation to the clerks employed in the Paymaster's office, being the sum appropriated for the service of the year one thousand eight hundred and fifteen, thirteen thousand three hundred dollars.

For additional compensation of fifteen per cent. to the clerks employed in said office, on the sum hereinbefore appropriated, one thousand nine hundred and ninety-five dollars.

For compensation to the messenger in said office, four hundred and ten dollars.

For expense of fuel, stationery, printing, and other contingent expenses of the office of the Paymaster, two thousand dollars.

For compensation to the Superintendent General of Military Supplies, three thousand dollars.

For compensation to the clerks employed in the office of the Superintendent General of Military Supplies, being the sum appropriated for the service of the year one thousand eight hundred and fifteen, seven thousand dollars.

For compensation to the messenger in said office, four hundred and ten dollars.

For expenses of fuel, stationery, printing, and other contingent expenses in the office of the Superintendent General of Military Supplies, six hundred dollars.

For compensation to the Commissary General of Purchases, three thousand dollars.

For compensation to the clerks employed in the office of the said Commissary, being the sum appropriated for the service of the year one thou-

sand eight hundred and fifteen, two thousand eight hundred dollars.

For contingent expenses in the said office of Commissary General of Purchases, nine hundred and thirty dollars.

For compensation to the clerks in the Adjutant and Inspector General's office, one thousand eight hundred dollars.

For compensation to the Secretary of the Navy, four thousand five hundred dollars.

For compensation to the clerks employed in the office of the Secretary of the Navy, being the sum appropriated for the service of the year one thousand eight hundred and fifteen, seven thousand and thirty-five dollars.

For compensation to the messenger in said office, four hundred and ten dollars.

For expense of fuel, stationery, printing, and other contingent expenses in said office, two thousand five hundred dollars.

For compensation to the Accountant of the Navy, two thousand dollars.

For compensation to the clerks employed in the office of the Accountant of the Navy, being the sum appropriated for the service of the year one thousand eight hundred and fifteen, twelve thousand two hundred dollars.

For compensation to the messenger in said office, four hundred and ten dollars.

For compensation to additional clerks to be employed in the office of said Accountant, two thousand five hundred dollars.

For contingent expenses of the office of said Accountant, one thousand two hundred and fifty dollars.

For compensation of the Commissioners of the Navy Board, ten thousand five hundred dollars.

For compensation to the Secretary of the Navy Board, two thousand dollars.

For compensation of the clerks employed in the office of the Navy Board, including the sum of two hundred and fifty dollars for the service of the preceding year, two thousand five hundred dollars.

For compensation of the messenger, including the sum of three hundred and seven dollars and fifty cents for the service of the preceding year, seven hundred and seventeen dollars fifty cents.

For the contingent expenses of the Navy Board, including the sum of one thousand five hundred dollars for the service of the preceding year, four thousand dollars.

For compensation to the Postmaster General, three thousand dollars.

For compensation to the Assistant Postmaster General, one thousand seven hundred dollars.

For compensation to the Second Assistant Postmaster General, one thousand six hundred dollars.

For compensation to the clerks employed in the General Post Office, being the amount appropriated for the service of the year one thousand eight hundred and fifteen, fifteen thousand one hundred dollars.

For compensation to additional clerks, four thousand two hundred and five dollars.

Public Acts of Congress.

For deficiency in appropriation for clerk hire for the year one thousand eight hundred and fifteen, nine hundred and thirty-five dollars.

For compensation to the messenger and assistant messenger, six hundred and sixty dollars.

For contingent expenses of the General Post Office, three thousand six hundred dollars.

For compensation to the several Commissioners of Loans, and for allowance to certain Commissioners of Loans in lieu of clerk hire, fourteen thousand five hundred and fifty dollars.

For compensation to the clerks of sundry Commissioners of Loans, and to defray the authorized expenses of the several loan officers, thirteen thousand seven hundred dollars.

For compensation to the Surveyor General and his clerks, four thousand one hundred dollars.

For compensation to the Surveyor of lands south of Tennessee, and his clerks, and for the contingent expenses of his office, three thousand two hundred dollars.

For compensation to the officers and clerks of the Mint, nine thousand six hundred dollars.

For wages to persons employed in the different operations of the Mint, including the sum of six hundred dollars allowed to an assistant engraver, five thousand dollars.

For repairs of furnaces, cost of iron and machinery, rents, and other contingent expenses of the Mint, two thousand four hundred and eighty dollars.

For allowance for wastage in the gold and silver coinage, one thousand five hundred dollars.

For the purchase of copper to coin into cents, fifteen thousand dollars.

For compensation to the Governor, Judges, and Secretary of the Indiana Territory, six thousand six hundred dollars.

For stationery, office rent, and other contingent expenses of said Territory, three hundred and fifty dollars.

For compensation to the Governor, Judges, and Secretary of the Mississippi Territory, nine thousand dollars.

For stationery, office rent, and other contingent expenses of said Territory, three hundred and fifty dollars.

For compensation to the Governor, Judges, and Secretary of the Missouri Territory, seven thousand eight hundred dollars.

For stationery, office rent, and other contingent expenses of said Territory, three hundred and fifty dollars.

For compensation to the Governor, Judges, and Secretary of the Michigan Territory, six thousand six hundred dollars.

For stationery, office rent, and other contingent expenses of said Territory, three hundred and fifty dollars.

For compensation to the Governor, Judges, and Secretary of the Illinois Territory, six thousand six hundred dollars.

For stationery, office rent, and other contingent expenses of said Territory, three hundred and fifty dollars.

For defraying the expenses incurred by print-ing the laws of said Territory, one thousand one hundred and seventy-six dollars and twenty-five cents.

For the discharge of such demands against the United States on account of the civil department, not otherwise provided for, as shall have been admitted in due course of settlement, at the Treasury, two thousand dollars.

For compensation granted by law to the Chief Justice, the Associate Judges, and District Judges of the United States, including the Chief Justice and Associate Judges of the District of Columbia, sixty thousand dollars.

For compensation to the Attorney General of the United States, three thousand dollars.

For the compensation of sundry District Attorneys and Marshals, as granted by law, including those in the several Territories, seven thousand eight hundred and fifty dollars.

For defraying the expenses of the Supreme, Circuit, and District Courts of the United States, including the District of Columbia, and of jurors and witnesses, in aid of the funds arising from fines, penalties, and forfeitures, and for defraying the expenses of prosecutions for offences against the United States, and for the safekeeping of prisoners, forty thousand dollars.

For the payment of sundry pensions granted by the late Government, eight hundred and sixty dollars.

For the payment of the annual allowance to the invalid pensioners of the United States, one hundred and twenty thousand dollars.

For making the road from Cumberland, in the State of Maryland, to the State of Ohio, three hundred thousand dollars, to be repaid out of the fund reserved for laying out and making roads to the State of Ohio, by virtue of the seventh section of an act, passed on the thirtieth of April, one thousand eight hundred and two, entitled "An act to enable the people of the eastern division of the territory northwest of the river Ohio to form a constitution and State government, and for the admission of such State into the Union, on an equal footing with the original States, and for other purposes."

For the maintenance and support of lighthouses, beacons, buoys, and public piers, stakeages of channels, bars, and shoals, including the purchase and transportation of oil, keepers' salaries, repairs and improvements, and contingent expenses, ninety-seven thousand four hundred and sixty-four dollars.

To replace the amount heretofore appropriated for defraying the expense of surveying the coasts of the United States, which was carried to the surplus fund on the thirty-first of December, one thousand eight hundred and fourteen, twenty-nine thousand seven hundred and twenty dollars and fifty-seven cents.

For defraying the expense of ascertaining and adjusting land titles in Louisiana, five thousand dollars.

For defraying the expense of surveying the public lands within the several Territories of the United States, including the expense of surveys of private claims in Louisiana; for ascertaining the boundaries of the State of Ohio; of surveying the township lines in the Creek purchase, and of the salaries of two principal deputies in the State of Louisiana, one hundred and sixty-three thousand four hundred dollars.

For defraying the expense of printing certificates of registry and other documents for vessels, five thousand seven hundred and fifty dollars.

For the discharge of such miscellaneous claims against the United States, not otherwise provided for, as shall have been admitted in due course of settlement at the Treasury, four thousand dollars.

For the salaries, allowances, and contingent expenses of Ministers to foreign nations, and of secretaries of legation, one hundred and fourteen thousand dollars.

For the contingent expenses of intercourse between the United States and foreign nations, fifty thousand dollars.

For the expenses necessary during the present year for carrying into effect the fourth, sixth, and seventh articles of the Treaty of Peace concluded with His Britannic Majesty at Ghent, on the twenty-fourth December, one thousand eight hundred and fourteen, including the compensation of the Commissioners appointed under those articles, twenty-three thousand three hundred and thirty-two dollars.

For the salaries of the agents of claims on account of captures at London, Paris, and Copenhagen, at two thousand dollars each, six thousand dollars.

For replacing the sum of twenty-five thousand dollars, heretofore appropriated and carried to the surplus fund in the year one thousand eight hundred and fifteen, for objects in relation to the intercourse with the Barbary States, twenty-five thousand dollars.

For making good a deficiency in the appropriation of last year for the intercourse with foreign nations, arising from the difference in the exchange in transmitting the money to Europe, and in the drafts of Ministers and agents there upon bankers, and to meet similar expenses the present year, fifty thousand dollars.

To replace the sum of two thousand dollars, being part of an appropriation of five thousand dollars, appropriated by an act of the third of March, one thousand eight hundred and eleven, to discharge claims on account of depredations committed by the Osage Indians, and since carried to the surplus fund, two thousand dollars.

For the expenses of intercourse with the Barbary Powers, forty-seven thousand dollars.

For the relief of distressed American seamen for the present year, and to make good a deficiency in the preceding year, fifty thousand dollars.

Sec. 2. *And be it further enacted,* That the several appropriations hereinbefore made, shall be paid and discharged out of the fund of six hundred thousand dollars, reserved by the act making provision for the debt of the United States, and out of any moneys in the Treasury not otherwise appropriated.

Approved, April 16, 1816.

An Act providing for the settlement of certain accounts against the Library of Congress, for extending the privileges of using the books therein, and for establishing the salary of the Librarian.

Be it enacted, &c., That the accounting officers of the Treasury be, and they are hereby, authorized and required to investigate and settle the accounts against the Library of Congress, exhibited by George Waterston, Daniel Rapine, and William Elliott; and the amount thereof, which shall be deemed equitable, shall be paid out of any moneys in the Treasury not otherwise appropriated.

Sec. 2. *And be it further enacted,* That there shall be allowed to the Librarian, for attending said Library, an annual salary of one thousand dollars, payable quarterly, at the Treasury of the United States, to commence and take effect from and after the twenty-first day of March, one thousand eight hundred and fifteen.

Sec. 3. *And be it further enacted,* That the privilege of using the books in the Library shall be extended to the Attorney General of the United States and the members of the diplomatic corps, on the same terms and conditions as it is enjoyed by the Judges of the Supreme Court.

Approved, April 16, 1816.

An Act supplementary to an act, entitled "An act to incorporate a company for making certain turnpike roads within the District of Columbia."

Be it enacted, &c., That the company for making certain turnpike roads in the District of Columbia, established by an act of Congress passed on the twentieth day of April, one thousand eight hundred and ten, be authorized and empowered to open and make a turnpike road, at their own risk and expense, from the Eastern Branch bridge, to meet a road to be opened and made under the authority of the State of Maryland, from Edward H. Calvert's mill, in Prince George's county, to the line of the District of Columbia.

Sec. 2. *And be it further enacted,* That the said company may demand and receive the same tolls as are allowed for a like distance by the act to which this is a supplement, and shall possess and enjoy the same rights and privileges, and be subject to the same limitations, pains, and penalties, as are prescribed, enjoined, and directed by the aforesaid act, and an act in addition thereto, passed on the twenty-fifth day of April, one thousand eight hundred and ten.

Approved, April 16, 1816.

An Act confirming to the Navigation Company of New Orleans the use and possession of a lot in the said city.

Be it enacted, &c., That all the right and claim of the United States to the title, possession, and occupancy of a lot of ground of three hundred feet front on Rampart street, in the city of New Orleans, by six hundred feet in depth, on a line with St. Peter street, on which was erected the former hospital of charity in the said city be, and the same is hereby, vested in the Navigation Com-

Public Acts of Congress.

pany of New Orleans: *Provided*, That nothing in this act contained shall affect the claim or claims of any individual or individuals, if any such there be.
Approved, April 16, 1816.

An Act further extending the time for issuing and locating military land warrants, and for other purposes.

Be it enacted, &c., That the Secretary of War be authorized to issue military land warrants to such persons as have or shall, before the first day of March, one thousand eight hundred and eighteen, produce to him satisfactory evidence of the validity of their claims; which warrants, with those heretofore issued, and not yet satisfied, shall and may be located in the name of the holders or proprietors thereof, prior to the first day of October, one thousand eight hundred and eighteen, on any unlocated parts of the fifty quarter townships, and the fractional quarter townships, reserved by law for original holders of military land warrants. And patents shall be granted for the land located under this act, in the same manner as is directed by former acts for granting military lands.

SEC. 2. *And be it further enacted*, That, at the expiration of the term limited by this act, for the location of the military land warrants aforesaid, it shall be the duty of the Commissioner of the General Land Office to transmit to the Surveyor General a list of all the lots of land within the fifty quarter townships and fractional quarter townships, which shall at that time remain unlocated; and the Surveyor General shall prepare and transmit to the registers of the land office at Chilicothe and Zanesville, respectively, general plats of the aforesaid unlocated lots, which lots shall, after the first day of March, one thousand eight hundred and nineteen, be offered for sale at the land offices in the districts in which they are situated, in the same manner, on the same terms and conditions, in every respect, as other public lands are offered at private sale, in the same districts.
Approved, April 16, 1816.

An Act to increase the pension of William Munday.

Be it enacted, &c., That there be, and hereby is, granted to William Munday, of the city of Baltimore, who lost both his arms in an attack on the enemy at St. Leonard's creek, on the twenty-eighth day of June, in the year one thousand eight hundred and fourteen, in lieu of the pension to which he is now entitled by law, a pension of twenty dollars per month, to be paid out of the navy pension fund.
Approved, April 16, 1816.

An Act authorizing the sale of a lot of ground, belonging to the United States, situated in the town of Knoxville and State of Tennessee.

Be it enacted, &c., That the President of the United States be, and he is hereby, authorized to cause to be sold, at public sale, a lot of ground belonging to the United States, situated in the

town of Knoxville and State of Tennessee, ten days' notice being first given in the Knoxville Gazette, of the time and place of sale.
SEC. 2. *And be it further enacted*, That, on the receipt of the money arising from said sale, the President of the United States is hereby authorized to make or cause to be made a title or titles to the purchaser or purchasers of said lot.
Approved, April 16, 1816.

An Act for the relief of certain claimants to land in the district of Vincennes.

Be it enacted, &c., That the several persons whose claims were confirmed by the act of Congress, entitled "An act confirming certain claims to land in the district of Vincennes, and for other purposes," approved the third day of March, one thousand eight hundred and seven; and the act, entitled "An act confirming certain claims to land in the district of Vincennes," approved the thirteenth day of February, one thousand eight hundred and thirteen, which having been located cannot be surveyed agreeably to law, or which having been located have, in the opinion of the register of the land office, for the said district, been removed by the surveys of prior locations, from the spot intended to be occupied, are hereby authorized to enter their locations with the register of the land office at Vincennes, on any part of the tract set apart for that purpose in the said district, by virtue of the act, entitled "An act respecting claims to lands in the Indiana Territory and State of Ohio," and in conformity to the provisions of this act.
Approved, April 16, 1816.

An Act to authorize the President of the United States to alter the road laid out from the foot of the rapids of the river Miami of Lake Erie to the western line of the Connecticut reserve.

Be it enacted, &c., That the President of the United States be, and is hereby, authorized to cause to be made, in such manner as he may deem most proper, an alteration in the road laid out under authority of an act, entitled "An act to authorize the surveying and making of certain roads in the State of Ohio, as contemplated by the treaty of Brownstown, in the Territory of Michigan," so that the said road may pass through the United States' reservation at Lower Sandusky, or north thereof, not exceeding three miles.
SEC. 2. *And be it further enacted*, That the necessary expenses which shall be incurred in altering the said road shall be paid out of the moneys appropriated for the surveying of the public lands of the United States.
Approved, April 16, 1816.

An Act to authorize the Legislature of the State of Ohio to sell a certain tract of land, reserved for the use of that State.

Be it enacted, &c., That the Legislature of the State of Ohio shall be, and they are hereby, authorized and empowered to cause to be selected and sold, in such manner and on such terms and conditions as they may by law direct, any one section not exceeding the quantity of six hundred and forty acres of the tract of land of six miles square, reserved for the benefit of that State, at the Scioto salt springs: *Provided*, That the section so selected shall not include the said salt springs, and that the money arising from the sale of the aforesaid section shall be applied to the erection of a court-house, or other public buildings, thereon, for the use of the county of Jackson, in said State; and whenever the selection and sale of the said section of land shall have been made, and the same shall be duly certified to the Commissioner of the General Land Office, a patent shall be granted by the President of the United States, for the said section, in trust to such person or persons as the Legislature of the State shall have appointed and authorized to sell and execute titles to the purchasers of the land aforesaid.

Approved, April 16, 1816.

An Act making further provision for military services during the late war, and for other purposes.

Be it enacted, &c., That when any officer or private soldier of the militia, including rangers, sea fencibles, and volunteers, or any non-commissioned officer, musician, or private, enlisted for either of the terms of one year or eighteen months, or any commissioned officer of the regular army, shall have died while in the service of the United States during the late war, or in returning to his place of residence, after being mustered out of service, or who shall have died at any time thereafter, in consequence of wounds received whilst in the service, and shall have left a widow, or, if no widow, a child or children, under sixteen years of age, such widow, or, if no widow, such child or children, shall be entitled to receive half the monthly pay to which the deceased was entitled at the time of his death, for and during the term of five years; and in case of death or intermarriage of such widow, before the expiration of said five years, the half pay for the remainder of the time shall go to the child or children of said decedent. *Provided always*, That the Secretary of War shall adopt such forms of evidence, in applications under this act, as the President of the United States may prescribe. *Provided also*, That the officers and private soldiers of the militia, as aforesaid, who have been disabled by wounds or otherwise, while in the service of the United States in the discharge of their duty during the late war, shall be placed on the list of pensioners, in the same manner as the officers of the regular army, under such forms of evidence as the President of the United States may prescribe. *Provided also*, That the provisions of this act shall not extend to any person embraced in the provision of an act, entitled "An act to provide for the widows and orphans of the militia slain, and for militia disabled in the service of the United States," passed

the second day of August, one thousand eight hundred and thirteen.

SEC. 2. *And be it further enacted*, That when any non-commissioned officer, musician, or private soldier of the regular army of the United States shall have been killed in battle, or have died of wounds or disease, while in the service of the United States, during the late war, and have left a child or children under sixteen years of age, it shall be lawful for the guardian of such child or children, within one year from the passing of this act, to relinquish the bounty land to which such non-commissioned officer, musician, or private soldier, had he survived the war, would have been entitled; and, in lieu thereof, to receive half the monthly pay to which such deceased person was entitled at the time of his death, for and during the term of five years, to be computed from and after the seventeenth day of February, one thousand eight hundred and fifteen, the payment thereof to be made when and where other military pensions are or shall be paid; and where a warrant for the military bounty land aforesaid shall have been issued to or for the use of the child or children of any such deceased non-commissioned officer, musician, or private soldier, such child or children, or either of them, being under sixteen years of age, it shall be lawful for the guardian of such minor or minors to surrender and deliver such warrant, into the office for the Department of War, within one year from the passing of this act; of which surrender and delivery the Secretary of that Department shall give notice to the Secretary of the Treasury, who shall thereupon give the requisite orders for the payment of the half pay hereby provided for.

SEC. 3. *And be it further enacted*, That all soldiers who have been enlisted to serve for five years, or during the war, and were above the age of forty-five, or under the age of eighteen years, who have faithfully served during the late war, and have been regularly discharged, and the representatives of such soldiers as shall have died whilst in the service of the United States, and all soldiers who have been enlisted, and have faithfully served during the late war, until they have been promoted to the rank of commissioned officers, who, if they had served during the war under their enlistment, and been regularly discharged, would have been entitled to a bounty in land, shall be entitled to one hundred and sixty or three hundred and twenty acres of land, according to the term of enlistment; the warrants and patents to issue in the same manner as in the case of soldiers enlisted of proper age, and discharged under similar circumstances.

SEC. 4 *And be it further enacted*, That, for the purpose of carrying the provisions of this act into effect, and other acts giving bounty lands to soldiers of the regular army, the President of the United States is hereby authorized to cause to be surveyed and laid off, in one or more surveys, two millions of acres, not otherwise appropriated, in addition to the appropriations of lands by the act of May the sixth, one thousand eight hundred and twelve, for designating, surveying, and granting military bounty lands according to the provisions of said act.

Sec. 5. *And be it further enacted,* That no transfer of land, granted in virtue of this or any other law, giving bounties of land to the non-commissioned officers, musicians, and privates, enlisted during the late war, shall be valid, unless the contract or agreement therefor, or letter of attorney, giving power to sell or convey, shall have been executed after the patents shall be issued and delivered to the persons entitled thereto.

Approved, April 16, 1816.

An Act in addition to the act, entitled "An act in relation to the Navy Pension Fund."

Be it enacted, &c., That in all cases of prizes captured by the public armed ships of the United States, which shall be sold under the order of the proper prize court, by interlocutory or final decree, it shall be the duty of the marshal of the United States, making the sale, to pay the proceeds thereof into the registry of the proper court, within thirty days after such sale shall be made and closed; and, immediately upon the payment into the registry of the proceeds as aforesaid, it shall be the duty of the clerk of the court to deposite the same in some bank, to be designated by the judge or judges, of the court, subject to the order and distribution of the court as in other cases; and when the said prizes shall have been duly condemned, it shall be the duty of the court to direct the share of such prizes belonging to the United States to be forthwith carried in the account with such bank, to the credit of the Treasurer of the United States, on account of the navy pension fund; and copies of the certificate of such deposite and credit shall be thereupon transmitted to the Treasurer of the United States and to the Secretary of the Navy, as soon as may be, by the clerk of such court; and the share of such prizes belonging to the captors, deposited as aforesaid, shall be paid over to the parties entitled, or to their authorized agent or agents, upon the order of the proper court in term, or of the judge or judges of such court in vacation.

Sec. 2. *And be it further enacted,* That it shall be the duty of the marshals of the several districts of the United States, and of the clerks of the respective courts of the United States, to state and settle their respective accounts in all cases of prizes captured as aforesaid, specifying therein all costs and charges taxed, claimed, and paid by them, and to submit the same to the proper court, having cognizance thereof, for examination and allowance, within sixty days after a final adjudication of such causes, unless a different time shall be assigned by such court; and thereupon such courts in term, or any judge thereof in vacation, may proceed summarily to hear, examine, and allow the same accounts; and, after such allowance, one copy of the same accounts shall be filed among the records of the court, and another copy shall be transmitted by the clerk of the court to the Secretary of the Navy, within thirty days after the allowance thereof.

Sec. 3. *And be it further enacted,* That it shall be the duty of the district attorneys of the respective districts of the United States to transmit to the Secretary of the Navy a statement of all prizes captured as aforesaid, which shall be libelled, condemned, or restored, at each term of the district and circuit courts, within their respective districts, as soon as may be after the conclusion of each term, and to accompany such list with a schedule and invoice of the various articles composing the cargoes of such prizes.

Sec. 4. *And be it further enacted,* That the respective courts of the United States, before whom a libel against any prizes captured as aforesaid shall be pending, or by whom a decree of condemnation and distribution of such prizes shall have been awarded, shall have full power and authority, in the exercise of their admiralty and maritime jurisdiction, to issue a monition, and other proper process, to compel the marshal and clerk to perform and obey the requisitions of this act; and upon the complaint of the United States, or any person interested in the premises, summarily to hear and examine the same, and to make such award, order, and decree therein, as to justice and law shall appertain. And if the marshal or clerk shall wilfully refuse, or unreasonably neglect, to perform and obey any of the requisitions of this act, the party so refusing or neglecting shall further forfeit and pay to the United States the sum of five hundred dollars for every such refusal or neglect.

Sec. 5. *And be it further enacted,* That there shall be allowed to the Accountant of the Navy Department, for his extra services in collecting, stating, and settling the accounts of prize money belonging to the navy pension fund, the annual sum of three hundred dollars, to be paid quarter-yearly out of the navy pension fund.

Sec. 6. *And be it further enacted,* That whenever sales of prizes captured as aforesaid have been made before the passing of this act, and the proceeds thereof have not been paid into the registry of the proper court, or finally distributed under its order, it shall be the duty of the marshal who made the sale, within six calendar months from the passing of this act, or such shorter reasonable time as may be assigned by the court, or the judge or judges thereof, to pay into the registry of the court the proceeds of such sale, with a written account of the costs and charges attending the same, and to submit the same account for examination and allowance to the court, or the judge or judges thereof; and, in like manner, it shall be the duty of the respective clerks of the district courts, within six calendar months from the passing of this act, or such shorter reasonable time as may be assigned by the proper court, or the judge or judges thereof, to present to such court, or the judge or judges thereof, for examination and allowance, a particular account of their fees and charges, in all cases of prizes captured as aforesaid, where such account has not been already presented and allowed; and after such account shall be examined and allowed, it shall be filed among the records of the court, and a copy thereof, duly attested, shall be transmitted by the clerk of the court to the Secretary of the Navy; and if any marshal or clerk shall neglect or refuse to perform the duties herein required, he may be proceeded against in the proper court, in the manner provided in the fourth section of this act.

SEC. 7. *And be it further enacted,* That in cases where the allowance of the half monthly pay, which may now be granted by law to officers, seamen, and marines, disabled in the service of the United States, shall, in the opinion of the commissioners of the navy pension fund, from the nature and extent of the disability, and the situation of the party disabled, be inadequate to his necessary subsistence, the said commissioners shall be, and hereby are, authorized, in their discretion, to increase such allowance to any sum not exceeding the full amount of the monthly pay to which the party so disabled was by law entitled in the said service.

Approved, April 16, 1816.

An Act to enable the people of the Indiana Territory to form a constitution and State government, and for the admission of such State into the Union on an equal footing with the original States.

Be it enacted, &c., That the inhabitants of the Territory of Indiana be, and they are hereby, authorized to form for themselves a constitution and State government, and to assume such name as they shall deem proper; and the said State, when formed, shall be admitted into the Union upon the same footing with the original States, in all respects whatever.

SEC. 2. *And be it further enacted,* That the said State shall consist of all the territory included within the following boundaries, to wit: bounded on the east by the meridian line which forms the western boundary of the State of Ohio; on the south by the river Ohio, from the mouth of the Great Miami river to the mouth of the river Wabash; on the west by a line drawn along the middle of the Wabash from its mouth, to a point where a due north line, drawn from the town of Vincennes, would last touch the northwestern shore of the said river; and from thence, by a due north line, until the same shall intersect an east and west line, drawn through a point ten miles north of the southern extreme of Lake Michigan; on the north by the said east and west line, until the same shall intersect the first mentioned meridian line which forms the western boundary of the State of Ohio: *Provided,* That the convention hereinafter provided for, when formed, shall ratify the boundaries aforesaid; otherwise they shall be and remain as now prescribed by the ordinance for the government of the territory northwest of the river Ohio: *Provided, also,* That the said State shall have concurrent jurisdiction on the river Wabash, with the State to be formed west thereof, so far as the said river shall form a common boundary to both.

SEC. 3. *And be it further enacted,* That all male citizens of the United States, who shall have arrived at the age of twenty-one years, and resided within the said Territory at least one year previous to the day of the election, and shall have paid a county or territorial tax; and all persons having in other respects the legal qualifications to vote for representatives in the General Assembly of the said Territory, be, and they are hereby, authorized to choose representatives to form a convention, who shall be apportioned amongst the several counties within the said Territory, according to the apportionment made by the Legislature thereof at their last session, to wit: from the county of Wayne, four representatives; from the county of Franklin, five representatives; from the county of Dearborn, three representatives; from the county of Switzerland, one representative; from the county of Jefferson, three representatives; from the county of Clark, five representatives; from the county of Harrison, five representatives; from the county of Washington, five representatives; from the county of Knox, five representatives; from the county of Gibson, four representatives; from the county of Posey, one representative; from the county of Warrick, one representative; and from the county of Perry, one representative. And the election for the representatives aforesaid shall be holden on the second Monday of May, one thousand eight hundred and sixteen, throughout the several counties in the said Territory, and shall be conducted in the same manner, and under the same penalties, as prescribed by the laws of said Territory, regulating elections therein for members of the House of Representatives.

SEC. 4. *And be it further enacted,* That the members of the convention thus duly elected be, and they are hereby, authorized to meet at the seat of the government of the said Territory, on the second Monday of June next; which convention, when met, shall first determine, by a majority of the whole number elected, whether it be or be not expedient, at that time, to form a constitution and State government for the people within the said Territory; and, if it be determined to be expedient, the convention shall be, and hereby are, authorized to form a constitution and State government; or, if it be deemed more expedient, the said convention shall provide by ordinance for electing representatives to form a constitution or frame of government; which said representatives shall be chosen in such manner, and in such proportion, and shall meet at such time and place as shall be prescribed by the said ordinance, and shall then form, for the people of said Territory, a constitution and State government: *Provided,* That the same, whenever formed, shall be republican, and not repugnant to those articles of the ordinance of the thirteenth of July, one thousand seven hundred and eighty-seven, which are declared to be irrevocable between the original States and the people and States of the Territory northwest of the river Ohio; excepting so much of said articles as relate to the boundaries of the States therein to be formed.

SEC. 5. *And be it further enacted,* That, until the next general census shall be taken, the said

Public Acts of Congress.

State shall be entitled to one representative in the House of Representatives of the United States.

Sec. 6. *And be it further enacted,* That the following propositions be, and the same are hereby, offered to the convention of the said Territory of Indiana, when formed, for their free acceptance or rejection, which, if accepted by the convention, shall be obligatory upon the United States.

First. That the section numbered sixteen in every township, and, when such section has been sold, granted, or disposed of, other lands equivalent thereto, and most contiguous to the same, shall be granted to the inhabitants of such township, for the use of schools.

Second. That all salt springs within the said Territory, and the lands reserved for the use of the same, together with such other lands as may, by the President of the United States, be deemed necessary and proper for working the said salt springs, not exceeding, in the whole, the quantity contained in thirty-six entire sections shall be granted to the said State, for the use of the people of the said State, the same to be used under such terms, conditions, and regulations, as the Legislature of the said State shall direct; provided the said Legislature shall never sell nor lease the same for a longer period than ten years at any one time.

Third. That five per cent. of the net proceeds of the lands lying within the said Territory, and which shall be sold by Congress from and after the first day of December next, after deducting all expenses incident to the same, shall be reserved for making public roads and canals, of which three-fifths shall be applied to those objects within the said State, under the direction of the Legislature thereof, and two-fifths to the making of a road or roads leading to the said State, under the direction of Congress.

Fourth. That one entire township, which shall be designated by the President of the United States, in addition to the one heretofore reserved for that purpose, shall be reserved for the use of a seminary of learning, and vested in the Legislature of the said State, to be appropriated solely to the use of such seminary by the said Legislature.

Fifth. That four sections of land be, and the same are hereby, granted to the said State, for the purpose of fixing their seat of government thereon; which four sections shall, under the direction of the Legislature of said State, be located, at any time, in such township and range as the Legislature aforesaid may select, on such lands as may hereafter be acquired by the United States from the Indian tribes within the said Territory: *Provided,* That such locations shall be made prior to the public sales of the lands of the United States surrounding such location : *And provided always,* That the five foregoing propositions herein offered, are on the condition that the convention of the said State shall provide, by an ordinance irrevocable, without the consent of the United States, that every and each tract of land

sold by the United States, from and after the first day of December next, shall be and remain exempt from any tax laid by order, or under any authority of the State, whether for State, county, or township, or any other purpose whatever, for the term of five years, from and after the day of sale.

Approved, April 19, 1816.

An Act to abolish the existing duties on spirits distilled within the United States, and to lay other duties, in lieu of those at present imposed, on licenses to distillers of spirituous liquors.

Be it enacted, &c., That, from and after the thirtieth day of June next, the act entitled "An act to provide additional revenues for defraying the expenses of Government, and maintaining the public credit, by laying duties on spirits distilled within the United States and Territories thereof, and by amending the act laying duties on licenses to distillers of spirituous liquors, passed the twenty-first day of December, one thousand eight hundred and fourteen, shall cease and determine, excepting in so much as the same is applicable to the duty payable for licenses for stills or boilers granted previously to the first day of July next: *Provided,* That the provisions of the aforesaid act shall remain in full force and virtue, so far as the same may relate to the rendering of accounts of spirits distilled previous to the first day of July next, and to the collection and recovery of all duties laid by the said act, that may have accrued previous thereto, and which shall then remain outstanding, and for the recovery, distribution, and remission of fines, penalties, and forfeitures, which may be incurred in relation to the said duties.

Sec. 2. *And be it further enacted,* That every person who, after the thirtieth day of June next, shall be the owner of any still or stills, or other implements in lieu of stills, used for the purpose of distilling spirituous liquors, or who shall have such still or stills, or implements as aforesaid under his superintendence, either as agent for the owner or on his own account, and for which a license extending beyond said day shall not have been previously obtained, and every person who, having such license, shall, after its expiration, use or intend to use any still or stills, or implements as aforesaid, either as owner, agent, or otherwise, shall, before he shall so begin to use such still or stills, or other implements in lieu thereof, for the purpose of distilling spirituous liquors, apply for and obtain from the collector appointed by virtue of the act, entitled "An act for the assessment and collection of direct taxes and internal duties," for the collection district in which such person resides, (or to the deputy of such collector duly authorized,) a license for using the said still or stills, or other implements as aforesaid; which licenses respectively shall be granted at the option of the proprietor or possessor of such still or stills, for any or either of the terms mentioned in this act, upon the payment in money, by such proprietor or possessor, of the duties payable on the said license or licenses, according to the provisions of this act, if the said duty upon such still or stills, or other implements, when added together, if there be more than one still or other implement for distilling spirits, shall not exceed twenty dollars; and if they shall exceed twenty dollars, on such proprietor or possessor executing and delivering to the collector, or to his deputy as aforesaid, a bond with two or more sureties, to the satisfaction of such collector or deputy, conditioned for the payment of said duties at the end of twelve months after the expiration of the term for which such license or licenses respectively shall have been granted. And the said bond shall be taken in the name of the United States of America, and in such form as shall be prescribed by the Treasury Department. And if any person shall, after the said thirtieth day of June next, use or cause to be used any still or stills, or other implements as aforesaid, in distilling spirituous liquors; or shall be the owner of, or have under his superintendence, either as agent or otherwise, any still or stills, or other implements as aforesaid, which shall after the said day have been used as aforesaid, without having a license therefor as aforesaid, continuing in force for the whole time during which the said still or stills, or implements as aforesaid shall have been thus used, or who shall keep, during any period for which a license has been granted to such person, any still or boiler, or other implement liable to duty in their fixtures, in a situation for use, without having first obtained a license for the same, agreeably to the provisions of this act, every such person shall forfeit and pay the sum of one hundred dollars, together with double the amount of duties which would have been payable for the term during which such still or stills, or implements as aforesaid, shall be thus used, or kept in a situation for use as aforesaid, had the said still or stills, or implements aforesaid, been entered according to the provisions of this act; to be recovered with costs of suit.

Sec. 3. *And be it further enacted,* That if any person shall keep in or about his distillery any beer or other liquor, prepared from grain, for the purpose of distillation, for more than eight days, during any time for which such person shall not have obtained a license for distillation, he shall forfeit and pay the sum of one hundred dollars for every such offence.

Sec. 4. *And be it further enacted,* That the licenses aforesaid shall and may be granted for and during the following terms or periods, and on the securing of payment, as aforesaid, of the duties undermentioned, namely:

For a still or stills employed in distilling spirits from domestic materials, for a license for the employment thereof, for and during the term of one week, four and a half cents for each gallon of the capacity of every such still, including the head thereof; for a license for and during the term of two weeks, nine cents for each gallon of its capacity as aforesaid; for a license for and during the term of one month, eighteen cents for each gallon of its capacity as aforesaid; for a license for and during the term of two months,

thirty-six cents for each gallon of its capacity as aforesaid; for a license for and during the term of three months, fifty-four cents for each gallon of its capacity as aforesaid; for a license for and during the term of four months, seventy-two cents for each gallon of its capacity as aforesaid; for a license for five months, ninety cents for each gallon of its capacity as aforesaid; for a license for and during the term of six months, one hundred and eight cents for each gallon of its capacity as aforesaid; for a license for one year, two hundred and sixteen cents for each gallon of its capacity as aforesaid: *Provided,* That there shall be paid upon each still employed wholly in the distillation of roots, but one-half the rates of duties abovementioned, according to the capacity of such still.

For a still or stills employed in distilling spirits from foreign materials, for a license for the employment thereof for and during the term of one month, twenty-three cents for each gallon of the capacity of every such still, including the head thereof; for a license for and during the term of two months, forty-six cents for each gallon of its capacity as aforesaid; for a license for and during the term of three months, sixty-eight cents for each gallon of its capacity as aforesaid; for a license for and during the term of four months, ninety cents for each gallon of its capacity as aforesaid; for a license for and during the term of six months, one hundred and thirty-five cents for each gallon of its capacity as aforesaid; for a license for and during the term of eight months, one hundred and eighty cents for each gallon of its capacity as aforesaid; for a license for one year, two hundred and seventy cents for each gallon of its capacity as aforesaid.

And for every boiler, however constructed, employed for the purpose of generating steam in those distilleries where wooden or other vessels are used instead of metal stills, and the action of steam is substituted for the immediate application of fire to the materials from which the spirituous liquors are distilled, for a license for the employment thereof, double the amount on each gallon of the capacity of the said boiler, including the head thereof, which would be payable for the said license, if granted for the same term, and for the employment on the same materials of a still or stills to the contents of which, being the materials from whence the spirituous liquors are drawn, an immediate application of fire, during the process of distillation, is made.

Sec. 5. *And be it further enacted,* That it shall be the duty of the collectors, within their respective districts, to grant licenses for distilling, which licenses shall be marked with a mark denoting the rate of duty thereupon, and shall be signed by the commissioner of the revenue, and being countersigned by the collector, who shall issue the same, or cause the same to be issued, shall be granted to any person who shall desire the same, upon application in writing, and upon payment, or securing of payment as aforesaid, of the sum or duty payable by this act, upon each license requested.

Sec. 6. *And be it further enacted,* That the application, in writing, to be made by any person applying for a license for distilling as aforesaid, shall state the place or places of distilling, the number and contents of the still or stills, boiler or boilers, and whether intended to distil spirituous liquors from foreign or domestic materials. And no person having obtained a license in one collection district shall be required to take out an additional license in another district for the same still within the period of the first license. And every person making a false statement in either of the said particulars, or who shall distil spirituous liquors from materials other than those stated in the application aforesaid, as well as the owner or superintendent of any distillery, still or stills, with respect to which such false statement shall have been made, or which shall be thus unlawfully employed, shall forfeit and pay the sum of one hundred and fifty dollars, to be recovered with costs of suit.

Sec. 7. *And be it further enacted,* That every such collector, or his deputy duly authorized under his hand and seal, shall be authorized to enter, at any time, any distillery, or place where any still, boiler, or other vessel used in distillation are kept or used within his collection district, for the purpose of inspecting, examining, or measuring the same, and the other vessels therein. And every owner of such distillery, stills, or boilers, or other vessels, or person having the care, superintendence, or management of the same, who shall refuse to admit such officer as aforesaid, or to suffer him to inspect, examine, or measure the same, shall, for every such refusal, forfeit and pay the sum of five hundred dollars.

Sec. 8. *And be it further enacted,* That, in cases in which a' license for stills or boilers may have been granted for their employment, according to the present rates of duty, for a period extending beyond the thirteenth day of June, one thousand eight hundred and sixteen, the person to whom the same may have been granted or transferred shall, on or before the said day, pay, or secure the payment, in manner aforesaid, of a sum equal to such proportion of the additional duty hereby imposed on licenses for stills and boilers as said period bears to that for which the said license was granted; the payment of which sum shall be endorsed by the collector on said license. And if any still or boiler shall, after the said thirteenth day of June, be employed in distilling spirituous liquors without the additional duty having been previously paid or secured as aforesaid, the owner, agent, or superintendent thereof shall forfeit and pay the sum of one hundred dollars, together with double the amount of the said additional duties.

Sec. 9. *And be it further enacted,* That all the provisions of this act shall be deemed to apply to any still or boiler, or other vessel, used in distillation, which shall be employed in the rectification of spirituous liquors.

Sec. 10. *And be it further enacted,* That any license heretofore or hereafter granted for employing a still, boiler, or other vessel, in distilling spirits from foreign materials, shall authorize the distilling spirits from domestic materials also.

Sec. 11. *And be it further enacted,* That a deduction at the rate of eight per centum shall be made for the duty payable for a license to distil spirituous liquors, on the payment thereof at the time of obtaining the same, whether the same be payable on a credit or not, according to the provisions of this act.

Sec. 12. *And be it further enacted,* That, in future, it shall be lawful for the distiller or distillers of domestic spirits, and all persons from whose materials such spirits shall be distilled, to sell without a license, by retail, any quantity thereof, not less than one gallon.

Sec. 13. *And be it further enacted,* That the several provisions of "An act making further provision for the collection of internal duties, and for the appointment and compensation of assessors," passed on the second day of August, one thousand eight hundred and thirteen, shall, and are, hereby declared to apply in full force to the duties laid by, and to be collected under, this act, the same as if such duties and this act were recognised therein; which said duties shall be collected by the same collectors, in the same manner, for the same commissions, and under the same directions, as are thereby established in relation to the other internal duties: and all the obligations, duties, and penalties, thereby imposed upon collectors, are hereby imposed upon the collectors of the duties laid by this act.

Sec. 14. *And be it further enacted,* That it shall be the duty of the collectors aforesaid, in their respective districts, and they are hereby authorized to collect the duties imposed by this act, and to prosecute for the recovery of the same, and for the recovery of any sum or sums which may be forfeited by virtue of this act. And all fines, penalties, and forfeitures, which shall be incurred by force of this act, shall and may be sued for and recovered in the name of the United States by bill, plaint, information, or action of debt, one moiety thereof to the use of the United States, and the other moiety thereof to the use of the person who, if a collector, shall first discover, if other than a collector, shall first inform of the cause, matter, or thing, whereby any such fine, penalty, or forfeiture, shall have been incurred, unless the breach of this act, for which such fine, penalty, or forfeiture, may be incurred, cannot be established without the testimony of such collector or other informant, in which case the whole of such fine, penalty, or forfeiture, shall be to the use of the United States.

Approved, April 19, 1816.

An Act for the relief of the Baltimore and Massachusetts Bible Societies.

Be it enacted, &c., That all the duties due and payable to the United States, on a set of stereotype plates, owned by the Baltimore Bible Society, imported from London to Philadelphia, in the year one thousand eight hundred and fifteen, on board the ship Electra; and from London to Baltimore in the same year, on board the ship Joseph, be, and the same are hereby, remitted.

SEC. 2. *And be it further enacted,* That the Comptroller of the Treasury be, and he is hereby, authorised to direct a debenture to be issued to the Massachusetts Bible Society, for a drawback of duties upon an invoice of bibles exported from the port of Boston, on board the brigantine Panther, in the year one thousand eight hundred and fifteen : *Provided however,* That the said Society shall produce satisfactory evidence to the said Comptroller, as the law directs, that the invoice aforesaid has been landed in some foreign port or place.

Approved, April 20, 1816.

An Act, further supplementary to the act, entitled "An act providing for the indemnification of certain claimants of public lands in the Mississippi Territory.

Be it enacted, &c., .That every person or persons claiming public lands in the Mississippi Territory, under the act or pretended act of the State of Georgia, passed January the seventh, one thousand seven hundred and ninety-five, who have not duly released their claims to the United States, so as to entitle them to the indemnification provided by the act of Congress, passed the thirty-first day of March, one thousand eight hundred and fourteen, entitled "An act providing for the indemnification of certain claimants of public lands in the Mississippi Territory," and the acts supplementary thereto, shall be allowed further time to execute and file with the commissioners appointed to decide on such claims, good and sufficient legal releases of their claim; as by said acts are required, until the first Monday of March next. And the commissioners aforesaid are hereby authorized and empowered to decide on such claims, and to adjudge to every such claimant or claimants the proportion of indemnification to which he or they may be respectively entitled.

SEC. 2. *And be it further enacted,* That the commissioners aforesaid shall be, and they are hereby authorized, in all cases where they shall direct suits to be commenced for the recovery of money fraudulently withdrawn from the treasury of Georgia, to transmit to the counsel or attorney appointed to institute and conduct such suits or prosecutions, all original papers or documents in their possession, that may furnish evidence to sustain the same.

SEC. 3. *And be it further enacted,* That there shall be allowed and paid, out of the Treasury of the United States, to each of the said commissioners and their secretary, the further sum of one thousand dollars, as a compensation for the additional services required by this act.

Approved, April 20, 1816.

An Act concerning field officers of the Militia.

Be it enacted, &c., That, from and after the first day of May next, instead of one lieutenant colonel commandant to each regiment, and one major to each battalion of the militia, as is provided by the act entitled "An act more effectually to provide for the national defence, by establishing a uniform militia throughout the United States," approved May the eighth, one thousand seven hundred and ninety-two, there shall be one colonel, one lieutenant colonel, and one major to each regiment of the militia, consisting of two battalions. Where there shall be only one battalion, it shall be commanded by a major. *Provided,* That nothing contained herein shall be construed to annul any commission in the militia which may be in force, as granted by the authority of any State or Territory, in pursuance of the act herein recited, and bearing date prior to the said first day of May next.

Approved, April 20, 1816.

An Act respecting the late officers and crew of the sloop-of-war Wasp.

Whereas, there is reason to apprehend that the sloop-of-war Wasp, an armed ship of the United States, and lately commanded by Captain Johnston Blakely, is lost :

Be it enacted, &c., That there be allowed and paid to the representatives of Captain Johnston Blakely, and of each of the officers and crew aforesaid, as is hereinafter directed, twelve months wages ; and that there be paid to the aforesaid representatives, and to the survivors of said officers and crew, if such there be, the sum of fifty thousand dollars, to be distributed as prize money for the capture and destruction, by said sloop-of-war, of the British armed vessels Reindeer and Avon.

SEC. 2. *And be it further enacted,* That the distribution of said wages and compensation shall be as follows, viz : one-third to the widow, and two-thirds parts to the children of the deceased ; and in case there be no child, the whole to the widow ; and if there be no widow, then to the child or children ; and if there be neither widow nor child, then to the parent or parents ; and if there be no parent, then to the brothers and sisters ; and if there be neither brother nor sister, then such share or shares, not claimed as aforesaid, shall be and remain part of the navy pension fund ; and the sums aforesaid shall be paid out of any moneys in the Treasury, not otherwise appropriated : *Provided,* That in all cases in which there shall be only one child, the widow shall have an equal share with the child.

SEC. 3. *And be it further enacted,* That the Secretary of the Navy be, and he hereby is, authorized and required to appoint a prize agent, whose duty it shall be to disburse the moneys aforesaid, or to refund any balance thereof, under such rules or regulations as the said Secretary may prescribe ; and that all moneys not claimed by virtue of this act, within two years from the day when said sums shall be put at the disposal of the said prize agent, shall be deemed and held a part of the navy pension fund.

Approved, April 20, 1816.

Public Acts of Congress.

For contingent expenses, including freight, transportation, and recruiting expenses, three hundred thousand dollars.

For pay and subsistence of the marine corps, one hundred and forty-one thousand, one hundred and seventy-two dollars.

For clothing for the same, thirty-four thousand one hundred and sixty-six dollars.

For military stores for the same, one thousand one hundred and eighty-eight dollars.

For contingent expenses for the same, fourteen thousand five hundred dollars.

Sec. 2. *And be it further enacted*, That the several appropriations, hereinbefore made, shall be paid out of moneys in the Treasury not otherwise appropriated.

Approved, April 24, 1816.

An Act for the more convenient arrangement of the times and places of holding the Circuit Courts of the United States, for the districts of South Carolina and Georgia.

Be it enacted, &c., That, from and after the first day of June next, the circuit courts in and for the sixth circuit of the United States shall be held at the following times and places, and no others; that is to say, for the district of Georgia, at Savannah, on the fourteenth day of December, in every year, and at Milledgeville, on the sixth day of May in every year; for the district of South Carolina, at Charleston, on the twentieth day of November in every year, and at Columbia on the twentieth day of April in every year; and the circuit courts for the said districts respectively, or the circuit judge of the said sixth circuit is authorized and required to make all such rules and orders as may be necessary to carry into effect the change in time and place of holding the said courts, according to the true intent and meaning of this act.

Approved, April 24, 1816.

An Act for the relief of certain purchasers of public lands in the Mississippi Territory.

Be it enacted, &c., That every person who, since the first day of April, one thousand eight hundred and eleven, and prior to the eighteenth day of June, one thousand eight hundred and twelve, had purchased any tract or tracts of public land in the Mississippi Territory, not exceeding in the whole six hundred and forty acres, unless the tract purchased be a fractional section or sections, or fractional sections classed with an entire section, and whose lands have not already been actually sold or reverted to the United States for non-payment of part of the purchase money, shall be allowed the further time of two years and eight months from and after the expiration of the present period already given by law for completing the payment of the said purchase money; which further term of two years and eight months shall be allowed only on the condition, that all arrears of interest on the purchase money shall have been paid on or before the time shall have expired for

completing the payment of the purchase money: *Provided,* That in all cases in which the time for completing the payment of the purchase money may have expired, or shall expire, before the first day of July next, the interest may be paid on or before that day. But in case of failure in paying either the arrears, or the residue of principal with the accruing interest, as is herein provided, the tract of land shall forthwith be advertised and offered for sale, in the same manner; and on the same terms, as is directed by law in case of lands not paid for within the limited term, and shall revert in like manner, if the sum due, with interest, be not at such sale bidden and paid. And in cases where any tract or tracts of land is said Territory, not exceeding in the whole, six hundred and forty acres, unless the tract be a fractional section or sections, or fractional sections classed with an entire section have, since the first day of October last, reverted to the United States, for default of payment, the original purchaser may again enter the same tract or tracts at the price at which such tract or tracts were *originally* sold; and all moneys which such original purchaser may have paid shall be replaced to his credit by the receiver of public moneys for the district in which the land may lie, and such re-purchasers shall be allowed the same benefits of the extension of the time of payment created by this act, as though no such reversion had occurred: *Provided,* That such original purchaser shall make to the proper officer such application for such re-entry as is required by law for the entry of lands on or before the first day of July next, and that the land so reverted shall not have then been previously resold.

Approved, April 24, 1816.

An Act supplementary to an act, entitled "An act granting bounties in lands and extra pay to certain Canadian volunteers."

Be it enacted, &c., That instead of the Treasurer of the United States, as is prescribed by the third section of the act to which this is a supplement, the Paymaster of the Army of the United States be, and he is hereby, authorized and required to pay to each of the persons described in the act above recited, according to the provisions thereof, three months' pay in addition to that to which they may have been previously entitled, according to the rank they respectively held in the Army of the United States during the late war.

Approved, April 26, 1816.

An Act declaring the assent of Congress to an act of the General Assembly of the State of Virginia.

Be it enacted, &c., That the assent of Congress is hereby given and declared to an act of the General Assembly of Virginia, entitled "An act incorporating a company for the purpose of improving the navigation of James river from Warwick to Rocketts's landing," which act was passed on the twenty-second day of February, in the year one thousand eight hundred and sixteen.

Approved, April 26, 1816.

An Act rewarding the officers and crew of the Constitution, for the capture of the British sloop-of-war Levant.

Be it enacted, &c., That the President of the United States be, and he hereby is, authorized to have distributed as prize money, to Captain Chas. Stewart, late of the frigate Constitution, his officers and crew, the sum of twenty-five thousand dollars, for the capture of the British sloop-of-war Levant; and that the sum of twenty-five thousand dollars, out of any money in the Treasury not otherwise appropriated, be, and the same is hereby, appropriated for the purpose aforesaid.

Approved, April 26, 1816.

An Act authorizing the payment of a sum of money to John T. Courtnay and Samuel Harrison, or their legal representatives.

Be it enacted, &c., That the Secretary of the Treasury be, and he is hereby, authorized and required to pay to John T. Courtnay and Samuel Harrison, citizens of Virginia, or if either of both of them be dead, then to their legal representatives, the sum of three hundred and seventy-five dollars, to be equally divided between them; which sum is paid them in consequence of their exertions in saving from being destroyed by fire, the gunboat schooner Asp, belonging to the United States, when she was set on fire and left burning by the enemy, after having been taken by them in an action in the month of July, one thousand eight hundred and thirteen, in the river Potomac.

Approved, April 26, 1816.

An Act establishing a port of delivery at the town of the Bayou St. John.

Be it enacted, &c., That the town of the Bayou St. John, in the State of Louisiana, be a port of delivery; that a surveyor shall be appointed to reside at said port; that all ships and vessels bound to said port shall, after proceeding thereto, and making report and entry, at the port of New Orleans, within the time limited by law, be permitted to unlade their cargoes at the said town of the Bayou St. John, or at the basin of the canal of Carondelet, adjoining the city of New Orleans, under the rules and regulations prescribed by law.

SEC. 2. *And be it further enacted,* That so much of the sixth section of the act of Congress, passed on the twenty-fourth day of February, one thousand eight hundred and four, entitled "An act for laying and collecting duties on imports and tonnage, within the territories ceded to the United States by the treaty of the thirtieth of April, one thousand eight hundred and three, between the United States and the French Republic, and for other purposes," as is contrary to this act, is hereby repealed.

Approved, April 26, 1816.

An Act supplementary to the act to provide additional revenues for defraying the expenses of Government and maintaining the public credit, by laying a direct tax upon the United States, and to provide for assessing and collecting the same.

Be it enacted, &c., That, in regard to the direct tax imposed by the act of Congress, passed the fifth of March, one thousand eight hundred and sixteen, and to any other direct tax that may be hereafter imposed, the enumerations, valuations, and assessments first made, or to be made, in virtue of the "Act to provide additional revenues for defraying the expenses of Government and maintaining the public credit, by laying a direct tax upon the United States, and to provide for assessing and collecting the same," passed the ninth of January, one thousand eight hundred and fifteen, shall remain unchanged, except insomuch as the respective amounts of tax may be affected by the augmentation or diminution of the aggregate tax laid, or to be laid, and the property so enumerated, valued, and assessed, shall continue liable, with such qualification, to the taxes so assessed, subject only to the changes hereinafter provided for, and to those that may arise from the correction of errors, as authorized by the last recited act.

SEC. 2. *And be it further enacted,* That the changes to be made in the said enumerations, valuations, and assessments, and in the subsequent revisions thereof, shall be relative to the first day of June in the present year, and in every subsequent year in which a direct tax may be imposed, shall be effected by the principal assessors, without the employment of assistant assessors, and shall extend to the supplying omissions of assessable property, to the transfers of real estate and slaves, to the changes of residents and non-residents, to the burning or destruction of houses or other fixed improvements of real estate, to the exemption of property that may have ceased to be assessable, and to the assessment of property that may have ceased to be exempted from assessment, to such other cases as the Secretary of the Treasury may find it necessary in the furtherance of justice specially to authorize, and to the birth or death of slaves, or their running away, or otherwise becoming useless: *Provided,* That changes in the last case shall be solely where the tax standing chargeable to any person for slaves would be diminished by the valuation on the said first day of June of all those then owned by such person, excepting those obtained by transfer, in which case the reduction in the valuation shall be equal to the difference between the amount of the original and existing valuation.

SEC. 3. *And be it further enacted,* That it shall be the duty of each of the principal assessors, within fifteen days from the first of June, to attend in person, or in case of his sickness, by a deputy to be appointed by him, at six several places within his district most convenient to the inhabitants, the court-houses being of the number, except where they exceed six, and then at each court-house within the district, for one full day at each place, for the purpose of receiving any information as to the changes as aforesaid, which may have taken place since the preceding assessment or revision, which information shall be given in writing under the signature of the person whose tax may be affected thereby; of which attendance, and the object thereof, the said principal assessor shall, on or before the fifteenth day of May preceding, cause notice to be given, which notice shall be inserted three times weekly in all the newspapers published within his district, and in handbills, to be posted up at all the court-houses therein; causing, at the same time and in the same mode, notice to be given that he will attend to hear appeals relative to any such changes at the times and places herein specified therefor.

Sec. 4. *And be it further enacted,* That each of the said principal assessors shall, within ten days after the said fifteen days, according to the information so received, or to any other information satisfactory to him, revise the general lists for his district, and note in a supplementary form such changes as shall appear to him to have occurred; and shall, within the said term of ten days, make out a distinct statement of each change, which shall include the name of the person so liable to tax, and the valuation of the property, and shall either cause the same to be delivered to such person, or to be put in the mail, addressed to him or her, and directed to the post office nearest to his or her abode, agreeably to the best information of the said principal assessor, with a notification of the times and places of hearing any appeals that may be made, as hereinafter provided for: *Provided,* That no such notice need be given to persons not residing within the district.

Sec. 5. *And be it further enacted,* That it shall be the duty of the said principal assessor to attend at the several places aforesaid within his district, within fifteen days from the expiration of the ten days aforesaid, for at least one day at each court-house, for the purpose of receiving any appeals that may be made in writing as to the changes aforesaid, which changes shall be open to the inspection of any person who may apply to inspect the same.

Sec. 6. *And be it further enacted,* That the changes aforesaid shall be made in the following manner, and according to the following principles, in addition to those hereinbefore stated, that is to say:

In all cases that relate to real estate, and to the transfer of slaves, other than is herein specially provided for, the rate at which the same were or would have been valued under the act aforesaid, passed the ninth of January, one thousand eight hundred and fifteen, shall, as near as may be, be maintained; excepting where a partial alienation of real estate shall occur, in which case the original tax shall be apportioned among the several parts according to their existing value.

In all other cases relative to slaves, the valuation shall be made according to their existing value.

In cases in which real property shall have been

once sold for taxes, and purchased on behalf of the United States, such property shall, notwithstanding, continue to be entered on the general lists, and the tax lists, in the name of the original proprietor, until the period allowed for the redemption thereof shall have expired, after which, unless redeemed, it shall be stricken therefrom; but after being so purchased it shall not, while it remains unredeemed, be again sold for any other direct tax; and, during such period, the redemption thereof shall only be effected on the payment of all the taxes, additions, and charges due thereon, the same as if it still continued the property of the original owner, and as if it had been sold for each accruing tax; and the collectors shall, on rendering the proper accounts, be credited for the amount of taxes on property thus continuing unredeemed.

Any person becoming the owner of a slave by transfer to him from a district other than that in which he resides, shall, at the time and place prescribed by the third section of this act, furnish the principal assessor with a statement, specifying the sex and age of such slave, who shall be valued according to his or her existing value; and any such person who shall neglect to furnish a statement, shall forfeit and pay a sum not exceeding ten dollars; one half thereof for the use of the United States, and the other half for the use of the informer. And where a transfer of a slave shall be made by a person residing within one district to a person residing in another, which shall become known to the principal assessor of the former district, he shall forthwith advise, through the mail, the principal assessor of the latter district thereof, who shall, in case the statement aforesaid shall not have been rendered as aforesaid, institute a prosecution against the person to whom the transfer has been made for the said penalty.

In all cases the individual statements of changes shall be made out in such a manner as may be directed by the principal assessor, and shall, in their form, be as similar as practicable to the lists taken at the preceding assessment.

Sec. 7. *And be it further enacted,* That, for the purpose of insuring a correct execution of the objects aforesaid, the principal assessors shall take and pursue all other lawful measures, by the examination of records, the entry on the premises, or by any other satisfactory proof, which they shall consider necessary.

Sec. 8. *And be it further enacted,* That, within thirty days after the expiration of the time allotted as aforesaid to the hearing of appeals, it shall be the duty of the principal assessor in each district to revise, agreeably to his decision and the information he may possess, the enumerations and valuations aforesaid, correcting the same agreeably to the changes aforesaid, and to make out a complete corrected list of all the enumerations and valuations in his district, agreeable to the form prescribed by the act aforesaid, passed the ninth of January, one thousand eight hundred and fifteen, which the said principal assessor shall sign and preserve among his official papers; and further to make out and deliver to the collector, within the same time, agreeably to the twenty-first section of the said act, the tax lists therein designated, made to conform to such changes; whereupon the respective steps required by the provisions of the said act, not incompatible with those prescribed by this act, shall be pursued.

Sec. 9. *And be it further enacted,* That so much of the thirty-ninth section of the act aforesaid, passed the ninth of January, one thousand eight hundred and fifteen, as respects the time within which transfers and changes of property shall be ascertained, and the making out and delivery of the lists thereof, be, and the same are hereby, repealed.

Sec. 10. *And be it further enacted,* That in case any circumstance shall prevent a compliance, in point of time, with the foregoing provisions, the steps required shall nevertheless be taken thereafter; in which event the same notices shall be given, and the same terms of time be allotted to the performance of the several duties that would have been requisite had no such failure existed.

Sec. 11. *And be it further enacted,* That the duties aforesaid, required of the principal assessors, and the compensation for the performance thereof, shall be confined to those States which shall not have assumed the payment of the direct tax laid in any year, or, having assumed, shall not have duly paid the same.

Sec. 12. *And be it further enacted,* That in default of the performance of the duties enjoined by this act on any principal assessor, he shall forfeit and pay, for the use of the United States, a sum not exceeding five hundred dollars, to be sued for and recovered in the name of the United States in any court having competent jurisdiction.

Sec. 13. *And be it further enacted,* That all letters to and from the principal assessors, relative to their official duties, shall be transmitted free of postage. And any principal assessor who shall put his frank on any other letter, shall forfeit and pay the sum of ten dollars, the whole of which shall be for the use of the person who shall give information thereof.

Sec. 14. *And be it further enacted,* That in lieu of the compensations heretofore allowed to the principal assessors, they shall respectively receive, for every year in which a direct tax shall be laid, a salary of two hundred dollars, and three dollars for every hundred taxable persons contained in the tax lists delivered to the collectors, together with an allowance for their necessary and reasonable charges for books and stationery used in the execution of their duties, which said duties shall be considered as embracing the correction of errors, as authorized by law. And the President of the United States shall be, and he is hereby, authorized to augment, in cases where he shall deem it necessary, the foregoing compensations: *Provided,* That there shall not be allowed to any one principal assessor, in any such year, more than two hundred dollars, in addition to his fixed compensation: *And provided,* That

the whole extra amount thus allowed shall not exceed in such year ten thousand dollars. And for the purpose of carrying this act into effect, there is hereby appropriated, in each year in which a direct tax shall be laid, a sum of one hundred thousand dollars, to be paid out of any money in the Treasury, not otherwise appropriated: *Provided,* That any other existing appropriation for the said purposes be, and the same is hereby, repealed.

Sec. 15. *And be it further enacted,* That in lieu of the time now fixed by law for the commencement of the collection of the direct tax, it shall be in each district immediately subsequent to the day on which the tax lists shall be delivered to the collector thereof.

Sec. 16. *And be it further enacted,* That in all cases in which a tax shall be charged for slaves, the real estate of the person charged therewith may be sold therefor, in the same manner as for a tax due thereon; but no slaves sold for taxes shall be purchased on behalf of the United States.

Sec. 17. *And be it further enacted,* That it shall be lawful for the Secretary of the Treasury to assign to the commissioner of the revenue the duty of superintending the assessor's valuations and assessments, under the laws imposing a direct tax, as well as the collection of the tax, subject to his directions and control, according to the powers vested in him by law.

Sec. 18. *And be it further enacted,* That the foregoing provisions shall apply to any direct tax imposed or to be imposed upon the District of Columbia, and shall be and remain in force, anything in any former act or acts to the contrary notwithstanding.

Sec. 19. *Provided always, and be it further enacted,* That the equalization and apportionment of the direct tax made in the year eighteen hundred and fifteen by the board of principal assessors for the State of Delaware, in virtue of the before recited act, entitled "An act to provide additional revenues for defraying the expenses of Government and maintaining the public credit, by laying a direct tax upon the United States, and to provide for the assessing and collecting the same," shall not be in force or have any effect as it relates to that State's quota of the direct tax imposed by the act of Congress, passed the fifth day of March, one thousand eight hundred and sixteen, or that shall be imposed by any subsequent act of Congress; and it shall be the duty of the said board of principal assessors again to convene in general meeting on the first Monday in June next, at Dover, in the said State, and then and there diligently and carefully reconsider and re-examine the several lists of valuation for the direct tax for the said State, for the year one thousand eight hundred and fourteen, and they shall have power to revise, alter, readjust, and equalize the several lists of valuation aforesaid for the counties of the said State respectively, by adding thereto or deducting therefrom such a rate per centum, as shall render the valuation of the said counties relatively equal according to the present actual ready money value of the property assessed and contained in the said lists of valuation; and shall thereupon apportion to each county in the said State a quota of the tax bearing the same proportion to the whole direct tax imposed on the State as the aggregate valuation of each county bears to the aggregate valuation of the State; and the valuation, equalization, and apportionment so made by the board of principal assessors aforesaid, shall be in full force and operation, and remain unchanged, subject only to the exceptions contained in the first section of this act; and the said board of principal assessors shall, within twenty days after their meeting, as hereinbefore directed, complete the said revision, equalization, and apportionment, and shall record the same, and in all respects, not herein otherwise directed, shall conform to the provisions contained in the act in this section first above recited.

Approved, April 26, 1816.

An Act for the relief of a company of the twentieth brigade of Virginia militia, commanded by Captain Jonathan Wamsly.

Be it enacted, &c., That the accounting officers of the War Department be, and they are hereby, authorized and directed to audit and settle the claims of such of the commissioned officers, noncommissioned officers, musicians, and privates of the Virginia militia, lately under the command of Captain Jonathan Wamsly, while in the service of the United States, as served a tour of duty at Norfolk, and to allow them, in the settlement thereof, the amount of their pay while in the service of the United States, which was drawn in their behalf by the said Captain Wamsly, after their discharge from service, and not paid over to them.

Sec. 2. *And be it further enacted,* That the amount of the said claims shall be paid out of any money in the Treasury not otherwise appropriated.

Approved, April 26, 1816.

An Act for the relief of the Supervisors of the county of Clinton, in the State of New York.

Be it enacted, &c., That the commissioner to be appointed by virtue of the act, entitled "An act to authorize the payment for property lost, captured or destroyed by the enemy while in the military service of the United States, and for other purposes," passed April ninth, one thousand eight hundred and sixteen be, and he is hereby, authorized and directed to audit and settle the claim of the supervisors of the county of Clinton, in the State of New York, for the destruction of the court-house of the said county, by order of General Alexander Macomb, by ascertaining, or causing to be ascertained, the value thereof, in the manner and form prescribed by the provisions of the aforesaid act.

Sec. 2. *And be it further enacted,* That the amount thereof, when so ascertained, shall be paid to the said supervisors for the benefit of the

county of Clinton, out of any money in the Treasury not otherwise appropriated.

Approved, April 26, 1816.

An Act authorising the payment of a sum of money to James Levins.

Be it enacted, &c., That the Secretary of the Treasury be, and he is hereby, authorized and required to pay, out of any money in the Treasury not otherwise appropriated, the sum of five hundred dollars, to James Levins, of South Carolina, or to his legal representative, which sum of five hundred dollars is paid to him as an evidence of the sense entertained by Congress of his valor and good conduct, in having recaptured, alone and unassisted, the schooner Santee, together with a midshipman and four seamen of the British navy, which prisoners were delivered to the marshal of the district of South Carolina, and also as compensation for the prisoners so taken.

Approved, April 26, 1816.

An Act for the relief of the widow and children of Charles Dolph, deceased.

Be it enacted, &c., That the Secretary of the Treasury be, and he is hereby, directed to pay to the widow of Charles Dolph, deceased, late of Saybrook, in the State of Connecticut, the sum of five hundred dollars, for the use of herself and the children of the said Dolph, (who was killed during the late war with Great Britain, in an engagement between a party of volunteers raised in said town of Saybrook, and the crew of a British privateer called the Rover,) in consideration of the capture of five British prisoners on that occasion, which prisoners were delivered over to the marshal of the United States for the district of Connecticut.

Sec. 2. *And be it further enacted,* That the money herein granted be paid out of any moneys in the Treasury not otherwise appropriated.

Approved, April 26, 1816.

An Act to increase the compensations now allowed by law to Inspectors, Measurers, Weighers, and Gaugers, employed in the collection of the customs.

Be it enacted, &c., That an addition of fifty per cent. upon the sums allowed as compensation to inspectors, or persons acting as occasional inspectors, employed in aid of the customs, and to the measurers, weighers, or gaugers, by the act, entitled "An act to establish the compensations of officers employed in the collection of the duties on imposts and tonnage, and for other purposes," passed on the second of March, one thousand seven hundred and ninety-nine, be, and the same is hereby, allowed to the said inspectors, measurers, weighers, or gaugers, to be ascertained, certified and paid, under the regulations prescribed in the abovementioned act.

Approved, April 26, 1816.

An Act for the relief of Young King, a chief of the Seneca tribe of Indians.

Be it enacted, &c., That the Secretary for the

Public Acts of Congress.

Department of War be, and he is hereby, authorized and required, to cause to be paid to Young King, a chief of the Seneca tribe of Indians, quarter yearly, the sum of fifty dollars, amounting to the sum of two hundred dollars per annum, during the term of his natural life, as a compensation for the brave and meritorious services which he rendered the United States in the late war with Great Britain, and as a provision for the wound and disability which he received in the performance of those services.

Sec. 2. *And be it further enacted,* That the said sum be paid out of any money in the Treasury not otherwise appropriated.

Approved, April 26, 1816.

An Act authorizing the payment for the Court-House of Hamilton, in the State of Ohio.

Be it enacted, &c., That the commissioner to be appointed by virtue of the act, entitled "An act to authorize the payment for property lost, captured, or destroyed by the enemy, while in the military service of the United States, and for other purposes," passed the ninth of April, one thousand eight hundred and sixteen, be, and he is hereby, authorized and directed to audit and settle the claim of the county of Hamilton, in the State of Ohio, for the destruction by fire of the county court-house while occupied by the troops of the United States, by ascertaining, or causing to be ascertained, the value thereof, in the manner and form prescribed by the aforesaid act.

Sec. 2. *And be it further enacted,* That the amount thereof, when so ascertained, shall be paid to the proper authority, out of any money in the Treasury not otherwise appropriated.

Approved, April 26, 1816.

An Act for the relief of John Crosby and John Crosby, junior.

Be it enacted, &c., That the proper accounting officers of the Navy Department be, and they are hereby, authorized and directed to audit and settle the claim of John Crosby and John Crosby, junior, on account of the destruction by fire of their store-house, goods, and wharf, in the town of Hampden, in the State of Massachusetts, and to allow them, in the settlement thereof, the value of the said property destroyed as aforesaid.

Sec. 2. *And be it further enacted,* That the amount thereof, when so ascertained, shall be paid to the said John Crosby and John Crosby, junior, out of any money in the Treasury not otherwise appropriated.

Approved, April 26, 1816.

An Act for the relief of the President and Directors of the Washington Bridge Company.

Be it enacted, &c., That the commissioner to be appointed by virtue of the act, entitled "An act to authorize the payment for property lost, captured, or destroyed by the enemy, while in the military service of the United States, and for other purposes," passed April ninth, one thou-

sand eight hundred and sixteen, be, and he is hereby, authorized and directed to audit and settle the claim of the president and directors of the Washington Bridge Company, for the injury done to the southwestern end of the said bridge by order of the Government, or any of its authorized agents, in August, one thousand eight hundred and fourteen, by ascertaining, or causing to be ascertained, the value thereof, in the manner and form prescribed by the provisions of the aforesaid act.

Sec. 2. *And be it further enacted,* That the amount thereof, when so ascertained, shall be paid to the said president and directors, out of any money in the Treasury not otherwise appropriated.

Approved, April 26, 1816.

An Act making further provision for settling claims to land in the Territory of Illinois.

Be it enacted, &c., That every person, and the legal representatives of every person, who, before the fifth day of February, one thousand eight hundred and thirteen, settled on and improved any tract of land reserved for the use of schools or seminaries of learning, and who, had not the same been reserved, would have had the right of pre-emption within the tract of country set apart by the third section of the act of the sixteenth day of April, one thousand eight hundred and fourteen, entitled "An act confirming certain claims to land in the Illinois Territory, and providing for their location," to satisfy the unlocated claims to land in said Territory, shall be, and they hereby are, authorized and allowed, until the first day of October, one thousand eight hundred and sixteen, to enter the same, for purchase, with the register and receiver of public moneys of the land office at Kaskaskia ; and it shall be the duty of the register and receiver to enter the same for purchase, according to the provisions of this and the said recited act : *Provided,* That such person or persons shall not have entered, in right of pre-emption, other lands in lieu thereof, in virtue of the third section of an act to amend the aforesaid act, passed the twenty-seventh day of February, one thousand eight hundred and fifteen.

Sec. 2. *And be it further enacted,* That the register and receiver of public money shall have power, and they are hereby authorized, to select any other vacant and unappropriated lands within the tract set apart to satisfy confirmed claims as aforesaid, in lieu of such of the lands formerly reserved for a seminary of learning, and for the support of schools, as have been appropriated in satisfaction of ancient grants or confirmed improvement claims, or as shall be entered in right of pre-emption, according to the provisions of the preceding section of this act: *Provided,* That the lands thus to be selected shall be taken as near adjacent to those in lieu of which they are selected as an equal quantity of land of like quality can be obtained, and shall be reserved and appropriated for the same purpose.

Sec. 3. *And be it further enacted,* That the

provisions of the second section of an act passed the twenty-seventh day of February, one thousand eight hundred and fifteen, respecting the settlers on the fractional sections and quarter sections within the aforesaid reserved tract, shall extend to all other settlers on the fractional sections or quarter sections within the Kaskaskia district.

SEC. 4. *And be it further enacted,* That all the claims filed in the name of the original claimants, or their heirs, not exceeding four hundred acres, contained in a list transmitted to the Commissioner of the General Land Office, by Michael Jones, register, and S. Bond, receiver of public moneys of the land office for the district of Kaskaskia, bearing date the twenty-ninth day of March, one thousand eight hundred and fifteen, be, and they hereby are, confirmed to the original claimants or their heirs: *Provided,* That the said claims, hereby confirmed, be, and they hereby are, deemed and taken to be unlocated claims, and they shall not in any wise defeat or interfere with locations made in virtue of other authorized claims on lands improved by the said claimants or others.

SEC. 5. *And be it further enacted,* That the claimants whose claims are confirmed by virtue of the fourth section of this act, and all others lawfully holding confirmed unlocated claims for lands within the tract reserved by the before recited act of the sixteenth day of April, one thousand eight hundred and fourteen, be allowed until the first day of October, one thousand eight hundred and sixteen, to register the same; and the said claims shall be receivable in payment for public lands within the said reserved tract, conformably with the provisions of the last above-mentioned act, and of the present act, any time prior to the first day of October, one thousand eight hundred and sixteen.

SEC. 6. *And be it further enacted,* That all persons, or their legal representatives, entitled to the right of pre-emption of lands within the boundary specified in the before-recited act of the sixteenth day of April, one thousand eight hundred and fourteen, which lands have not been surveyed under the authority of the United States, shall be, and they hereby are, allowed a further time for making their entries with the register of the land office, until the lands upon which they have respectively settled and improved shall be surveyed by the United States, and until the expiration of six months next thereafter.

SEC. 7. *And be it further enacted,* That every person, and the legal representative of every person, whose claim to a tract of land within the Illinois Territory is confirmed by this or any former act, and who has not previously obtained a patent for the same from the Governor either of the territory northwest of the Ohio, or of the Indiana Territory, shall, whenever his claim shall have been located and surveyed, be entitled to receive from the register of the land office at Kaskaskia a certificate, stating that the claimant is entitled to receive a patent for such tract of land by virtue of this act, for which certificate the register shall receive one dollar; and which certificate shall entitle the party to a patent for the said tract, which shall issue in like manner as is provided by law for lands purchased of the United States.

Approved, April 26, 1816.

An Act providing for the sale of the tract of land at the lower rapids of Sandusky river.

Be it enacted, &c., That no much of the tract of land of two miles square, at the lower rapids of Sandusky river, ceded by the Wyandots, Delawares, Shawanoes, Ottawas, Chippewas, Pottawatimies, Miamis, Eel River, Weeas, Kickapoos, Piankashaws, and Kaskaskias tribes of Indians to the United States, by the Treaty of Greenville, of the third of August, one thousand seven hundred and ninety-five, shall, under the direction of the Surveyor General, be laid off into town lots, streets, and avenues, and into out-lots, in such manner, and of such dimensions, as he may judge proper: *Provided,* The tract so to be laid off shall not exceed the quantity of land contained in one entire section, nor the town lots one-quarter of an acre each. When the survey of the lots shall be completed, a plat thereof shall be returned to the Surveyor General, on which the town lots and out-lots shall respectively be designated by progressive numbers, who shall cause two copies to be made, one to be transmitted, with a copy of the field notes, to the Commissioner of the General Land Office, and the other to the register of the land office at Wooster.

SEC. 2. *And be it further enacted,* That, previously to the disposal at public sale of the before-mentioned tract of land, the Surveyor General shall, and he is hereby directed to resurvey and mark the exterior lines of the said tract, conformably to the survey made in the year one thousand eight hundred and seven, by virtue of the act of the third of March, one thousand eight hundred and five, and also to cause divisional lines to be run through each fractional section, and of the adjoining quarter section, so that each subdivision having one front on the river may contain, as nearly as may be, eighty acres each. And in like manner to cause the large island, lying in the west half of section number one, to be surveyed, and the same to be divided into two equal parts: *Provided,* That, in running the subdivisional lines, no interference shall be made affecting the selection or location hereafter to be made under the direction of the Secretary of War: *Provided, also,* That in no case shall the subdivisional lines be so run, as to extend to or embrace the bed of the river, which shall be deemed, and is hereby declared to be, a public highway: *And provided, also,* That the whole expense of resurveying and marking the exterior lines of the said cession, and running and marking the subdivisional lines of the fractional and quarter sections lying adjacent to the river, shall not exceed three dollars for every mile actually surveyed, resurveyed, and marked, by virtue of this and the preceding section.

SEC. 3. *And be it further enacted,* That all the

Public Acts of Congress.

land contained within the aforesaid cession of two miles square, shall, with the exception of as many town lots and out-lots, as in the opinion of the Secretary of the Treasury may be necessary to reserve for the support of schools within the same, and with exception also of the salt springs and land reserved for the use of the same, be offered for sale to the highest bidder at Wooster, in the State of Ohio, under the direction of the register and receiver of the land office, and on such day or days as shall, by a public proclamation of the President of the United States, be designated for that purpose. The sale for the divided quarter sections, fractional sections, and of the town lots and out-lots, shall remain open at Wooster for seven days, and no longer. The divided quarter-sections and fractional sections shall not be sold for less than two dollars an acre; the in-lots for less than twenty dollars each, nor any out-lot for less than at the rate of five dollars per acre; and shall, in every other respect, be sold on the same terms and conditions as have been or may be provided by law for the lands sold north of the river Ohio, and above the mouth of Kentucky river. All the land, other than what is excepted as above-mentioned, remaining unsold at the closing of the public sales, may be disposed of at private sale by the register of the land office at Wooster, agreeably to the provisions of this act, and, in the same manner, under the same regulations and conditions as are or may be provided by law for the sale of the public lands of the United States north of the river Ohio, and above the mouth of Kentucky river; and patents shall be obtained for all lands granted or sold within the said cession, in the same manner, and on the same terms as are or may be provided by law for land sold in the State of Ohio. The superintendents of the public sales directed by this section, shall receive four dollars each for each day's attendance on the said sales.

Approved, April 26, 1816.

An Act continuing the salaries of certain officers of Government.

Be it enacted, &c., That the annual compensations of the different officers enumerated in the act passed the twentieth day of February, one thousand eight hundred and four, entitled "An act continuing, for a limited time, the salaries of the officers of Government therein mentioned," shall be continued as if the said act had not expired, or contained any provision for limiting its continuance.

Approved, April 27, 1816.

An Act for the payment of the militia, in the case therein mentioned.

Be it enacted, &c., That the detachment of the militia of Kentucky, under the command of Col. Dudley, for the term of six months, who were captured at Fort Meigs, and paroled, be paid for the said term of six months; and that the proper officers of the War Department liquidate and pay their claims, in the same manner that the claims of the regular troops of the United States would be liquidated and paid in like cases.

Approved, April 27, 1816.

An Act allowing pay to certain persons made prisoners with the revenue cutter "Surveyor."

Be it enacted, &c., That the Secretary of the Treasury be, and he is hereby, authorized to settle the accounts for pay of the boatswain, gunner, cook, and ten mariners, captured on board the revenue cutter Surveyor, during the late war with Great Britain, up to the period of their release and return from captivity, and to pay the amount to them, or their legal representatives, out of any moneys in the Treasury, not otherwise appropriated; and the Secretary of the Treasury is hereby authorized to settle with Samuel Traverse, late master of the cutter Surveyor, and pay him up to the seventeenth day of May, one thousand eight hundred and fourteen.

Approved, April 27, 1816.

An Act to regulate the duties on imports and tonnage.

Be it enacted, &c., That, from and after the thirtieth day of June, one thousand eight hundred and sixteen, the duties heretofore laid by law on goods, wares, and merchandise, imported into the United States, shall cease and determine, and there shall be levied, and collected, and paid, the several duties hereinafter mentioned, that is to say:

First. A duty of seven and a half per centum ad valorem, on all dying drugs and materials for composing dyes, not subject to other rates of duty; gum arabic, gum senegal, saltpetre; jewelry, gold, silver, and other watches, and parts of watches; gold and silver lace, embroidery, and epauletts; precious stones and pearls of all kinds, set or not set; Bristol stones or paste work, and all articles composed wholly or chiefly of gold, silver, pearl, and precious stones; and laces, lace veils, lace shawls, or shades, of thread or silk.

Second. A duty of fifteen per centum ad valorem on gold leaf, and on all articles free, and not subject to any other rate of duty.

Third. A duty of twenty per centum ad valorem on hempen cloth or sail cloth, (except Russian and German linens, Russia and Holland duck,) stockings, of wool or cotton; printing types; all articles manufactured from brass, copper, iron, steel, pewter, lead, or tin, or of which these materials, or either of them, is the material of chief value; brass wire, cutlery, pins, needles, buttons, button moulds, and buckles of all kinds; gilt, plated, and japanned wares of all kinds; cannon, muskets, firearms, and sidearms; Prussian blue, china-ware, earthen-ware, and stone-ware, porcelain and glass manufactures, other than window glass and black glass quart bottles.

A duty of twenty-five per centum ad valorem, on woollen manufactures of all descriptions, or of which wool is the material of chief value excepting blankets, woollen rugs, and worsted or stuff goods, shall be levied, collected and paid, from and after the thirtieth day of June next,

Public Acts of Congress.

until the thirtieth day of June, one thousand eight hundred and nineteen, and after that day, twenty per centum on the said articles; and on cotton manufactures of all descriptions, or of which cotton is the material of chief value, and on cotton twist, yarn or thread, as follows, viz: for three years next ensuing the thirtieth day of June next, a duty of twenty-five per centum ad valorem; and after the expiration of the three years aforesaid, a duty of twenty per centum ad valorem: *Provided*, That all cotton cloths, or cloths of which cotton is the material of chief value, (excepting nankeens, imported directly from China,) the original cost of which at the place whence imported, with the addition of twenty per centum, if imported from the Cape of Good Hope, or from places beyond it, and of ten per cent. if imported from any other place, shall be less than twenty-five cents per square yard, with such addition, be taken and deemed to have cost twenty-five cents per square yard, and shall be charged with duty accordingly: *Provided also*, That all unbleached and uncolored cotton twist, yarn or thread, the original cost of which shall be less than sixty cents per pound, shall be deemed and taken to have cost sixty cents per pound, and shall be charged with duty accordingly; and all bleached or colored yarn, the original cost of which shall have been less than seventy-five cents per pound, shall be taken and deemed to have cost seventy-five cents per pound, and shall be charged with duty accordingly: *And provided further*, That cotton piece goods imported in ships or vessels of the United States which shall have sailed from the United States before the passage of this act, and shall arrive therein between the thirtieth day of June, one thousand eight hundred and sixteen, and the first day of June, one thousand eight hundred and seventeen, the original cost of which cotton piece goods, at the place whence imported, shall have been less than twenty-five cents per square yard, shall be admitted to entry, subject only to a duty of thirty-three and a third per centum on the cost of the said cotton piece goods in India, and on the usual addition of twenty per centum on that cost.

Fifth. A duty of thirty per centum ad valorem on umbrellas, parasols, of whatever materials made, and sticks or frames for umbrellas or parasols; bonnets and caps for women, fans, feathers, ornaments for head dresses, artificial flowers, millinery of all sorts; hats or caps of wool, fur, leather, chip, straw or silk; cosmetics, washes, balsams, perfumes; painted floor cloths; mats, of grass or flags; salad oil, pickles, capers, olives, mustard, comfits or sweetmeats, preserved in sugar or brandy; wafers, cabinet wares, and all manufactures of wood; carriages of all descriptions, and parts thereof; leather, and all manufactures of leather, or of which leather is the material of chief value; saddles, bridles, harness; paper of every description, paste-board, paper hangings, blank books, parchment, vellum; brushes, canes, walking sticks, whips; and clothing ready made. And in all cases where an ad valorem duty shall be charged, it shall be calculated on the net cost of the article at the place whence imported, (inclusive of packages, commissions and all charges,) with the usual addition established by law, of twenty per cent. on all merchandise imported from places beyond the Cape of Good Hope, and of ten per centum on articles imported from all other places.

Sixth. The following duties, severally and specifically: on ale, beer, and porter, in bottles, fifteen cents per gallon; on ale, beer, and porter, imported otherwise than in bottles, ten cents per gallon; on alum, one dollar per hundred weight; on almonds, three cents per pound; on black glass quart bottles, one hundred and forty-four cents per gross; on boots, one dollar and fifty cents per pair; on bristles, three cents per pound; on playing cards, thirty cents per pack; on tarred cables and cordage, three cents per pound; on untarred cordage, yarns, twine, packthread, and seines, four cents per pound; on tallow candles three cents per pound; on wax and spermaceti candles, six cents per pound; on Chinese cassia, six cents per pound; on cinnamon, twenty-five cents per pound; on cloves, twenty-five cents per pound; on cheese, nine cents per pound; on chocolate, three cents per pound; on cocoa, two cents per pound; on coal, five cents per heaped bushel; on copperas, one dollar per hundred weight; on copper rods, bolts, spikes or nails, and composition rods, bolts, spikes or nails, four cents per pound; on coffee, five cents per pound; on cotton, three cents per pound; on currants, three cents per pound; on figs, three cents per pound; on foreign caught fish, one dollar per quintal; on mackerel, one dollar and fifty cents per barrel; on salmon, two dollars per barrel, and on all other pickled fish, one dollar per barrel; on window glass, not above eight inches by ten inches in size, two dollars and fifty cents per hundred square feet; on the same, not above ten inches by twelve inches in size, two dollars and seventy-five cents per hundred square feet; on the same, if above ten inches by twelve inches in size, three dollars and twenty-five cents per hundred square feet; on glue, five cents per pound; on gunpowder, eight cents per pound; on hemp, one dollar and fifty cents per hundred weight; on iron or steel wire, not exceeding number eighteen, five cents per pound, and over number eighteen, nine cents per pound; on iron, in bars and bolts, excepting iron manufactured by rolling, forty-five cents per hundred weight; on iron in sheets, rods and hoops, two dollars and fifty cents per hundred weight, and in bars or bolts, when manufactured by rolling, and on anchors, one dollar and fifty cents per hundred weight; on indigo, fifteen cents per pound; on lead, in pigs, bars or sheets, one cent per pound; on shot manufactured of lead, two cents per pound; on red and white lead, dry or ground in oil, three cents per pound; on mace, one dollar per pound; on molasses, five cents per gallon; on nails, three cents per pound; on nutmegs, sixty cents per pound; on pepper, eight cents per pound; on pimento, six cents per pound; on plums and prunes, three cents per pound; on muscatel raisins, and raisins in jars and boxes,

Public Acts of Congress.

three cents per pound; on all other raisins, two cents per pound; on salt, twenty cents per bushel of fifty-six pounds; on ochre, dry, one cent per pound, in oil, one and a half cents per pound; on steel, one dollar per hundred weight; on segars, two dollars and fifty cents per thousand; on spirits, from grain, of first proof, forty-two cents per gallon; of second proof, forty-five cents per gallon; of third proof, forty-eight cents per gallon; of fourth proof, fifty-two cents per gallon; of fifth proof, sixty cents per gallon; above fifth proof, seventy-five cents per gallon; on spirits from other materials than grain, of first and second proof, thirty-eight cents per gallon; of third proof, forty-two cents per gallon; of fourth proof, forty-eight cents per gallon; of fifth proof, fifty-seven cents per gallon; above fifth proof, seventy cents per gallon; on shoes and slippers of silk, thirty cents per pair; on shoes and slippers of leather, twenty-five cents per pair; on shoes and slippers for children, fifteen cents per pair; on spikes, two cents per pound; on soap, three cents per pound; on brown sugar, three cents per pound; on white clayed or powdered sugar, four cents per pound; on lump sugar, ten cents per pound; on loaf sugar and on sugar candy, twelve cents per pound; on snuff, twelve cents per pound; on tallow, one cent per pound; on tea, from China, in ships or vessels of the United States, as follows, viz: bohea, twelve cents per pound; souchong and other black, twenty-five cents per pound; imperial, gunpowder, and gomee, fifty cents per pound; hyson and young hyson, forty cents per pound; hyson skin and other green, twenty-eight cents per pound; on teas, from any other place, or in any other than ships or vessels of the United States, as follows, viz: bohea, fourteen cents per pound; souchong and other black, thirty-four cents per pound; imperial, gunpowder, and gomee, sixty-eight cents per pound; hyson and young hyson, fifty-six cents per pound; hyson skin and other green, thirty-eight cents per pound; on manufactured tobacco, other than snuff and segars, ten cents per pound; on whiting and Paris white, one cent per pound; on wine, as follows, viz: on Madeira, Burgundy, Champaign, Rhenish and Tokay, one dollar per gallon; on Sherry and St. Lucar, sixty cents per gallon; on other wine, not enumerated, when imported in bottles or cases, seventy cents per gallon; on Lisbon, Oporto, and on other wines of Portugal, and those of Sicily, fifty cents per gallon; on Teneriffe, Fayal, and other wines of the western islands, forty cents per gallon; on all other wines, when imported otherwise than in cases and bottles, twenty-five cents per gallon; on Russia duck, (not exceeding fifty-two archeens each piece,) two dollars; on ravens duck, (not exceeding fifty-two archeens each piece,) one dollar and twenty-five cents; on Holland duck, (not exceeding fifty-two archeens each piece,) two dollars and fifty cents; on spermaceti oil, of foreign fishing, twenty-five cents per gallon; on whale and other fish oil, of foreign fishing, fifteen cents per gallon; and on olive oil in casks, at twenty-five cents per gallon.

SEC. 2. *And be it further enacted,* That the following articles shall be imported into the United States free of duties; that is to say, all articles imported for the use of the United States; philosophical apparatus, instruments, books, maps, charts, statues, busts, casts, paintings, drawings, engravings, specimens of sculpture, cabinets of coins, gems, medals, and all other collections of antiquities, statuary, modelling, painting, drawing, etching, or engraving, specially imported by order and for the use of any society incorporated for philosophical or literary purposes, or for the encouragement of the fine arts, or by order, and for the use of any seminary of learning; specimens in natural history, mineralogy, botany, and anatomical preparations, models of machinery and other inventions, plants, and trees; wearing apparel and other personal baggage in actual use, and the implements or tools of trade of persons arriving in the United States; regulus of antimony, bark of the cork tree, unmanufactured; animals imported for breed; burr stones, unwrought; gold coin, silver coin, and bullion; clay; unwrought copper, imported in any shape for the use of the Mint; copper and brass, in pigs, bars, or plates, suited to the sheathing of ships; old copper and brass, and old pewter, fit only to be remanufactured; tin, in pigs or bars; furs, undressed, of all kinds; raw hides and skins; lapis calaminaris; plaster of Paris; rags of any kind of cloth; sulphur or brimstone; barilla; Brazil wood, brazilletto, red wood, camwood, fustic, logwood, Nicaragua, and other dye woods; wood, unmanufactured, of any kind; zinc, teutenague, or spelter.

SEC. 3. *And be it further enacted,* That an addition of ten per centum shall be made to the several rates of duties above specified and imposed, in respect to all goods, wares, and merchandise, on the importation of which in American or foreign vessels a specific discrimination has not been herein already made, which, after the said thirtieth day of June, one thousand eight hundred and sixteen shall be imported in ships or vessels not of the United States: *Provided,* That this additional duty shall not apply to goods, wares, and merchandise imported in ships or vessels not of the United States, entitled by treaty, or by any act or acts of Congress, to be entered in the ports of the United States, on the payment of the same duties as are paid on goods, wares, and merchandise, imported in ships or vessels of the United States.

SEC. 4. *And be it further enacted,* That there shall be allowed a drawback of the duties, by this act imposed, on goods, wares, and merchandise imported into the United States, upon the exportation thereof within the time, and in the manner prescribed by the existing laws, subject to the following provisions, that is to say: that there shall not be an allowance of the drawback of duties in the case of goods imported in foreign vessels from any of the dominions, colonies, or possessions of any foreign Power, to and with which the vessels of the United States are not permitted to go and trade; that there shall not be an allowance of the drawback of duties for the amount of the additional duties by this act imposed on goods imported in vessels not of the United States; that there shall not be an allowance of the drawback in case of foreign dried and pickled fish, and other salted provisions, fish oil, or playing cards; that there shall be deducted and retained from the amount of the duties on goods exported, with the benefit of drawback, (other than spirits,) two and a half per centum; and that there shall be retained in the case of spirits exported with the benefit of drawback, two cents per gallon upon the quantity of spirits, and also three per centum on the amount of duties payable on the importation thereof. But, nevertheless, the provisions of this act shall not be deemed in any wise to impair any rights and privileges which have been or may be acquired by any foreign nation, under the laws and treaties of the United States, upon the subject of exporting goods from the United States, with a benefit of the drawback of the duties payable upon the importation thereof.

Sec. 5. *And be it further enacted*, That after the thirtieth day of June next, in all cases of entry of merchandise for the benefit of drawback, the time of twenty days shall be allowed from the date of the entry for giving the exportation bonds for the same: *Provided*, That the exporter shall, in every other particular, comply with the regulations and formalities heretofore established for entries of exportation for the benefit of drawback.

Sec. 6. *And be it further enacted*, That the duty on the tonnage of vessels, and the bounties, advances, and drawbacks, in the case of exporting pickled fish, of the fisheries of the United States, in the case of American vessels employed in the fisheries, and in the case of exporting sugar, refined within the United States, shall be and continue the same as the existing law provides. *Provided always*, That this provision shall not be deemed in anywise to impair any rights and privileges, which have been, or may be acquired by any foreign nation, under the laws and treaties of the United States, relative to the duty of tonnage on vessels.

Sec. 7. *And be it further enacted*, That the existing laws shall extend to, and be in force for the collection of the duties imposed by this act, on goods, wares, and merchandise, imported into the United States; and for the recovery, collection, distribution, and remission of all fines, penalties, and forfeitures; and for the allowance of the drawbacks and bounties by this act authorized, as fully and effectually as if every regulation, restriction, penalty, forfeiture, provision, clause, matter, and thing, in the existing laws contained, had been inserted in, and re-enacted by this act. And that all acts, and parts of acts, which are contrary to this act, and no more, shall be, and the same are hereby, repealed.

Sec. 8. *And be it further enacted*, That the act passed the third day of March, one thousand eight hundred and fifteen, entitled "An act to repeal so much of the several acts imposing duties on the tonnage of ships and vessels, and on goods, wares, and merchandise, imported into the United States, as imposes a discriminating duty on tonnage between foreign vessels and vessels of the United States," shall apply and be in full force as to the discriminating duties established by this act on the tonnage of foreign vessels, and the goods, wares, and merchandise therein imported.

Approved, April 27, 1816.

An Act for the relief of certain owners of goods, entered at Hampden, in the district of Maine.

Be it enacted, &c., That on the trial of any information, libel, or other suit for the forfeiture or condemnation of goods and merchandise, which between the twenty-fifth day of October, and the thirty-first day of December, in the year one thousand eight hundred and fourteen, were entered at Hampden, in the district of Maine, and have been since seized as imported or entered contrary to law, all claims to forfeiture and condemnation be, and hereby are released, arising from want of lawful authority, to enter and deliver said goods at Hampden, or from the illegality of importing the said goods into Orrington, or depositing them there, or from the illegality of trading between Orrington and Hampden, in a neutral vessel not licensed for the coasting trade. *Provided*, That the claimants of the goods and merchandise so entered as aforesaid shall pay and satisfy all the reasonable expenses and charges attending the seizure and keeping thereof, and all the expenses, costs, and charges of prosecuting the informations, libels, and suits instituted against the same, to be taxed by the court in which final judgments shall be rendered against the respective claimants, whether the final judgments shall be in favor of the claimants respectively or against them.

Approved, April 27, 1816.

An Act to fix the commissions of the collectors of the direct tax and internal duties, and to revive and continue in force "An act further to provide for the collection of duties on imports and tonnage."

Be it enacted, &c., That the collectors of the direct tax and internal duties shall be allowed, in lieu of the commissions allowed by any existing law, in each calendar year, the following commissions upon moneys accounted for and paid by them into the Treasury, from and after the thirty-first day of December, one thousand eight hundred and fifteen—that is to say: Six per centum upon all sums until the same shall amount to forty thousand dollars; three per centum upon all sums above forty thousand, until the same shall amount to one hundred thousand dollars; and two per centum upon all sums above one hundred thousand dollars: *Provided*, That the entire amount of commissions allowed during such year in any collection district shall not, exclusive of the commission allowed to the collectors designated by the Secretary of the Treasury to receive the lists of taxes due on the property of non-residents, exceed five thousand dollars: *And, provided,* That the said allowance exceeding five thousand dollars shall be made only in the calendar years in which the collector shall have receipted for the lists of taxes.

Sec. 2. *And be it further enacted,* That all the provisions of the act "to fix the compensations and increase the responsibility of the collectors of the direct tax and internal duties, and for other purposes, connected with the collection thereof," passed the third of March, one thousand eight hundred and fifteen, excepting those contained in the first section thereof, be, and the same are hereby, continued in force.

Sec. 3. *And be it further enacted,* That the act, entitled "An act to provide further for the collection of duties on imports and tonnage, passed on the third day of March, one thousand eight hundred and fifteen, be, and the same is hereby, revived and made of force until the end of the next session of Congress, and no longer.

Approved, April 27, 1816.

An Act making appropriations for repairing certain roads therein described.

Be it enacted, &c., That the sum of ten thousand dollars be, and the same is hereby, appropriated, and payable out of any moneys in the Treasury not otherwise appropriated, for the purpose of repairing and keeping in repair the road between Columbia, on Duck river, in the State of Tennessee, and Madisonville, in the State of Louisiana, by the Choctaw agency; and also the road between Fort Hawkins, in the State of Georgia, and Fort Stoddart; under the direction of the Secretary of War.

Approved, April 27, 1816.

An Act authorizing the payment of a sum of money to John Rogers and others.

Be it enacted, &c., That the Secretary of the Treasury be, and he is hereby, authorized and required to pay, out of any money in the Treasury not otherwise appropriated, the sum of three hundred dollars to John Rogers, William C. Burdick, Joshua Hall, and Jeremiah Chapman, of New London, in the State of Connecticut; which money is paid to them for their valor and good conduct, in capturing a midshipman and two seamen of the British navy, and as compensation for the said prisoners.

Approved, April 27, 1816.

An Act confirming the titles of certain purchasers of land who purchased from the Board of Trustees of the Vincennes University.

Be it enacted, &c., That the several persons who purchased land in township numbered two, south of range numbered eleven west, in the district of Vincennes, from the Board of Trustees for the Vincennes University, which was incorporated by an act of the Legislature of the Indiana Territory, entitled "An act to incorporate a University in the Indiana Territory," passed the twenty-ninth day of November, one thousand eight hundred and six, be, and they are hereby, confirmed in their titles in fee simple, respectively.

Approved, April 27, 1816.

An Act providing for the distribution of one hundred thousand dollars among the captors of the Algerine vessels captured and restored to the Dey of Algiers.

Be it enacted, &c., That the sum of one hundred thousand dollars be, and the same is hereby, appropriated, to be paid out of any moneys in the Treasury, not otherwise appropriated, and distributed in the same proportions and under the same regulations as prize-money is now by law directed to be distributed, among the captors of the Algerine vessels, captured by the American squadron, under the command of Commodore Decatur, and afterwards restored to the Dey of Algiers.

Approved, April 27, 1816.

An Act making appropriations for rebuilding light-houses, and for completing the plan of lighting them, according to the improvements of Winslow Lewis, for placing beacons and buoys, for preserving Little Gull Island, and for surveying the coast of the United States.

Be it enacted, &c., That the sums hereinafter mentioned be, and the same are hereby, appropriated for the following purposes, to wit: For rebuilding the light-house on Point Jedith, Rhode Island, seven thousand five hundred dollars. For completing the fitting up of all the light-houses with Winslow Lewis's improvements, in addition to the sums heretofore appropriated for that purpose, sixteen thousand dollars. For the construction of works deemed necessary for the preservation of Little Gull island, thirty thousand dollars. For rebuilding the light-house on New Point Comfort, Virginia, seven thousand dollars. For rebuilding the light-house on Baker's island, Massachusetts, four thousand dollars. For the following objects, being the balances of former appropriations for the same purposes, carried to surplus fund: For erecting light-houses at the mouth of the Mississippi, and at or near the pitch of Cape Lookout, North Carolina, thirty-four thousand nine hundred and ninety-five dollars. For rebuilding a light-house at Naushawn island, near Tarpaulin Cove, Massachusetts, two thousand four hundred and seventy-five dollars. For erecting a beacon and placing buoys near the entrance of Savannah river, two thousand four hundred and ninety-four dollars and eighty-five cents. For placing buoys and beacons at or near the entrance of the harbor of Beverly, Massachusetts, three hundred and forty-one dollars and ninety-five cents. For erecting two lights on Lake Erie, to wit: at or near Bird island, and on or near Presque Isle, one thousand five hundred and ninety dollars. For placing beacons and buoys on Georgetown bar, and in Winyaw Bay, South Carolina, one thousand five hundred dollars. For rebuilding the Baldhead light-house

Public Acts of Congress.

in North Carolina, fifteen thousand dollars. For defraying the expense of surveying the coast of the United States, fifty-four thousand seven hundred and twenty dollars and fifty-seven cents. For repairing piers in the harbor of Newburyport, Massachusetts, a sum not exceeding seven hundred dollars : *Provided,* That the jurisdiction of the site where such piers are erected shall be first ceded to the United States.

Approved, April 27, 1816.

An Act to authorise the building of three light-houses, viz: one on Race Point, one on Point Gammon, and one on the island of Petite Manon, in the State of Massachusetts.

Be it enacted, &c., That as soon as a cession shall be made by the State of Massachusetts to the United States, of the jurisdiction over the land sufficient for the purpose, the Secretary of the Treasury shall be, and he is hereby, authorized to provide, by contract, to be approved by the President of the United States, for building three light-houses, viz: one on Race Point, one on Point Gammon, in the town of Yarmouth, and one on the island called Petite Manon, near Naraguages river, in the State of Massachusetts; and to furnish the same with all necessary supplies, and also to agree for the salaries or wages of the persons who shall be appointed by the President for the superintendence and care of the same; and the President shall be authorized to make the said appointments.

SEC. 2. *And be it further enacted,* That the sum of eight thousand dollars be, and the same is hereby, appropriated, out of any moneys in the Treasury not otherwise appropriated, for the purposes aforesaid, and also for purchasing such lots of land as shall be required for the erection of the said light-houses, and other buildings necessarily connected therewith.

SEC. 3. *And be it further enacted,* That the Secretary of the Treasury be, and he is hereby, authorized to cause the light of Scituate light-house to be extinguished, should the extinguishment thereof be deemed expedient for the safety of the navigation on that coast.

Approved, April 27, 1816.

An Act to authorize the sale of lands forfeited to the United States, in the district of Jeffersonville, at the land office in said district.

Be it enacted, &c., That the register and receiver of the land office for the district of Jeffersonville be, and they are hereby, authorized to expose to public sale, to the highest bidder, at the land office aforesaid, any tract or tracts of land which may hereafter become forfeited to the United States for non-payment, under such terms and conditions as are, or may be, prescribed by law.

SEC. 2. *And be it further enacted,* That so much of any former act of Congress as requires the register and receiver of the district aforesaid to expose to public sale, at the court-house of the county in which the said land office is established,

any tract or tracts of land which may become forfeited to the United States for non-payment, be, and the same is hereby, repealed.

Approved, April 27, 1816.

An Act for the relief of George T. Ross, Daniel T. Patterson, and the officers and men lately under their command.

Be it enacted, &c., That so much of the net proceeds of the forfeitures and penalties, not exceeding fifty thousand dollars, as has accrued to the United States by the condemnation and sale of the vessels and their cargoes, which were taken near the island of Barrataria, on the western coast of Louisiana, on the sixteenth day of September, one thousand eight hundred and fourteen, by a land and naval force, under the command of Colonel George T. Ross and Captain Daniel T. Patterson, and which were condemned and sold by order of the district court of the United States for the Orleans district, for violation of laws of the United States, be, and the same are hereby, given up and relinquished in favor of the said George T. Ross and Daniel T. Patterson, the amount of the said net proceeds of the said sales, not exceeding fifty thousand dollars, out of any money in the Treasury not otherwise appropriated, to be distributed among the land and naval forces employed in the capture of the said vessels, in such proportions, and under such regulations, as the Secretaries of the War and Navy, with the approbation of the President, shall prescribe and determine.

Approved, April 27, 1816.

An Act providing for cases of lost military land warrants, and discharges for faithful service.

Be it enacted, &c., That when any soldier of the regular army having obtained a military land warrant shall have lost, or shall hereafter lose the same, or the said warrant shall have been or may be by accident destroyed, every such soldier shall, upon proof thereof, to the satisfaction of the Secretary of War, be entitled to a patent, in like manner as if the said warrant was produced.

SEC. 2. *And be it further enacted,* That in all cases of discharges from the military service of the United States of any soldier of the regular army, when it shall appear to the satisfaction of the Secretary of War that a certificate of faithful services has been omitted, by the neglect of the discharging officer, by misconstruction of the law, or by any other neglect or casualty, such omission shall not prevent the issuing of the warrant and patent as in other cases. And when it shall be proven, as aforesaid, that any soldier of the regular army has lost his discharge and certificate of faithful service, the Secretary of War shall cause such papers to be furnished such soldier of the regular army as will entitle him to his land warrant and patent: *Provided,* Such measure be justified by the time of his enlistment, the period of service, and the report of some officer of the corps to which he was attached.

Approved, April 27, 1816.

Public Acts of Congress.

An Act for the relief of Thomas Farrer, William Young, William Moseley, and William Leech.

Be it enacted, &c., That the Secretary of the Treasury be, and he is hereby, authorized and directed to settle the claims of Thomas Farrer, William Young, William Moseley, and William Leech, assistant marshals, appointed to take the census, and an account of the manufactures in South Carolina, in the year one thousand eight hundred and ten, and to allow them, in the settlement thereof, such compensation as may be adequate to the services which they performed in the capacity aforesaid.

SEC. 2. *And be it further enacted,* That the amount thereof, when so ascertained, shall be paid to the said Thomas Farrer, William Young, William Moseley, and William Leech, out of any money in the Treasury not otherwise appropriated.—Approved, April 27, 1816.

An Act providing an additional compensation to the district judge of the southern district of New York.

Be it enacted, &c., That there be paid to the district judge of the southern district of the State of New York, out of any moneys in the Treasury not otherwise appropriated, the sum of one thousand five hundred dollars, for a compensation for his services in holding the courts of the United States, in the northern district of said State.

Approved, April 27, 1816.

An Act to enable the Levy Court of the county of Alexandria to lay a tax for the purpose of defraying the expense of erecting a jail and court-house.

Be it enacted, &c., That it shall and may be lawful for the levy court of the county of Alexandria, in the District of Columbia, to raise, by a tax upon the taxable inhabitants of the said county, a sum sufficient to defray the expense of building a jail and court-house, for the said county, which sum shall be appropriated to the erection of such buildings accordingly, under the direction of the said court.

Approved, April 27, 1816.

An Act to authorize the surveying and making a road in the Territory of Illinois.

Be it enacted, &c., That the President of the United States be, and he is hereby, authorized to appoint three commissioners, who shall explore, survey, and mark in the most eligible course, a road from Shawanee town, on the Ohio river, to the United States saline, and to Kaskaskia, in the Illinois Territory; and said commissioners shall make out accurate plats of such surveys, accompanied with field notes, and certify and transmit the same to the President of the United States, who, if he approves of said survey, shall cause the plats thereof to be deposited in the office of the Treasury of the United States, and the said road shall be considered as established and accepted.

SEC. 2. *And be it further enacted,* That the said road shall be opened and made under the direction of the President of the United States, in such manner as he shall direct.

SEC. 3. *And be it further enacted,* That the said commissioners shall each be entitled to receive three dollars, and their assistants one dollar and fifty cents, for each and every day which they shall be necessarily employed in the exploring, surveying, and marking said road; and for the purpose of compensating the aforesaid commissioners and their assistants, and opening and marking said road, there shall be, and hereby is, appropriated the sum of eight thousand dollars, to be paid out of any moneys in the Treasury not otherwise appropriated.

Approved, April 27, 1816.

An Act for the relief of Taylor and McNeal, Evans and McNeal, and Henry and John McCleester.

Be it enacted, &c., That the proper accounting officers of the War Department be, and they are hereby, authorized and directed to audit and settle the claim of Taylor and McNeal, Evans and McNeal, and Henry and John McCleester, for the use of their scows, applied under the authority of the United States, for the purpose of making a temporary bridge over the basin at Baltimore, in the month of September, one thousand eight hundred and fourteen, and to allow them, in the settlement thereof, such compensation as may be reasonable and just for the use aforesaid.

SEC. 2. *And be it further enacted,* That the amount thereof, when so ascertained, shall be paid to the said Taylor and McNeal, Evans and McNeal, and Henry and John McCleester, out of any money in the Treasury not otherwise appropriated.

Approved, April 27, 1816.

An Act providing for the sale of the tract of land, at the British fort at the Miami of the Lake, at the foot of the Rapids, and for other purposes.

Be it enacted, &c., That so much of the tract of land of twelve miles square, at the "British fort of the Miami of the Lake, at the foot of the Rapids," ceded by the Wyandots, Delawares, Shawanoes, Ottawas, Chippewas, Patawatamies, Miamis, Eel River, Weeas, Kickapoos, Piankashaws, and Kaskaskias tribes of Indians, to the United States, by the treaty of Greenville, of the third of August, one thousand seven hundred and ninety-five, shall, under the direction of the Surveyor General, be laid off into town lots, streets, and avenues, and into out lots, in such manner, and of such dimensions, as he may judge proper: *Provided,* The tract so to be laid off shall not exceed the quantity of land contained in two entire sections, nor the town lots one-quarter of an acre each. When the survey of the lots shall be completed, a plat thereof shall be returned to the Surveyor General, on which town lots and out lots shall, respectively, be designated, by progressive numbers, who shall cause two copies to be made, one to be transmitted, with a copy of the field notes, to the Commissioner of the General Land Office, and the other to the register of the land office at Wooster.

SEC. 2. *And be it further enacted,* That, previously to the disposal at public sale of the before mentioned tract of land, the Surveyor General shall, and he is hereby directed to resurvey, and mark the exterior lines of the said tract, conformably to the survey made in December, one thousand eight hundred and five, by virtue of the act of the third of March, one thousand eight hundred and five, and also to cause divisional lines to be run through each section and fractional section binding on the said river, so that each subdivision may contain, as nearly as may be, one hundred and sixty acres each. And in like manner to cause the "Great island," lying at the foot of the rapids, in the said river, to be surveyed, and by lines, running north and south, to divide the same, as nearly as may be, into six equal parts; that is to say, that part of the said island, described in the survey of the said cession, as lying in township number three, in four parts; and that part of the said island lying in township number four, into two parts: *Provided,* That in running the subdivisional lines no interference shall be made affecting or impairing the rights of persons to whom letters patent have been granted for land lying within the limits of the said twelve miles square, nor affecting the selection or location hereafter to be made under the direction of the Secretary of War, for military purposes: *Provided also,* That in no case, shall the subdivisional lines be so run as to extend to, or embrace the bed of the river, which shall be deemed, and is hereby declared to be, a public highway: *And provided also,* That the whole expense of resurveying and marking the exterior lines of the said cession and of the subdivisional lines of the sections, lying adjacent to the river, shall not exceed three dollars for every mile actually surveyed, re-surveyed, and marked, by virtue of this and the preceding section.

SEC. 3. *And be it further enacted,* That all the land contained within the aforesaid cession of twelve miles square, not excepted by virtue of any section of this act, shall, with the exception of number sixteen, which shall be reserved in each township, for the support of schools within the same, and with the exception also of the salt springs and land reserved for the use of the same, be offered for sale to the highest bidder, at Wooster, in the State of Ohio, under the direction of the register and receiver of the land office, and on such day or days as shall, by a public proclamation of the President of the United States, be designated for that purpose. The sale for the quarter sections, fractional quarter sections, and of the town lots and out lots, shall remain open at Wooster, for seven days and no longer. The quarter sections, and fractional quarter sections, shall not be sold for less than two dollars an acre; the in lots for less than twenty dollars each, nor any out lots for less than at the rate of five dollars per acre; and shall, in every other respect, be sold on the same terms and conditions as have been or may be, by law, provided for the lands sold

north of the Ohio river, and above the mouth of Kentucky river. All the lands other than the reserved sections and those excepted as above mentioned, remaining unsold at the closing of the public sales, may be disposed of at private sale, by the register of the land office at Wooster, agreeably to the provisions of this act, and in the same manner, under the same regulations and conditions, as are or may be provided by law for the sale of the lands of the United States north of the Ohio river, and above the mouth of Kentucky river. And patents may be obtained for all lands granted or sold within the said cession, in the same manner, and on the same terms, as are or may be provided by law for land sold in the State of Ohio. The superintendents of the public sales directed by this section, shall receive four dollars each, for each day's attendance on the said sale.

Approved, April 27, 1816.

An Act for the relief of Charles Ross and Samuel Breck, surviving executors of John Ross, deceased.

Be it enacted, &c., That the commissioner to be appointed by virtue of an act of Congress, passed at the present session, entitled "An act to authorize the payment for property lost, captured, or destroyed by the enemy, while in the military service of the United States, and for other purposes," be, and he is hereby, authorized to audit and settle the claim of Charles Ross and Samuel Breck, surviving executors of John Ross, deceased, by ascertaining or causing to be ascertained, in the manner prescribed in the aforesaid act, the amount of damages which they have sustained, in consequence of the occupation, by the troops of the United States, of Point Petre, in the State of Georgia, in the loss of the rent of the farm attached thereto, the destruction of the buildings, and of the wood, and other fuel thereon.

SEC. 2. *And be it further enacted,* That the amount thereof, when so ascertained, shall be paid to the said Charles Ross and Samuel Breck, executors aforesaid, out of any money in the Treasury not otherwise appropriated.

Approved, April 27, 1816.

An Act concerning the annual sum appropriated for arming and equipping the militia.

Be it enacted, &c., That the annual sum of two hundred thousand dollars, as appropriated for the purpose of providing arms and military equipments for the militia, either by purchase or manufacture, according to the act of the twenty-third of April, one thousand eight hundred and eight, entitled "An act making provision for arming and equipping the whole body of the militia of the United States," shall be paid, for each year, respectively, out of any moneys in the Treasury not otherwise appropriated.

SEC. 2. *And be it further enacted,* That the sum appropriated, to be paid as aforesaid, shall be applied for the purpose, and according to the intention specified in said act, without being liable at any time to be carried to the account of the surplus fund. And nothing in the act of the third of

March, one thousand eight hundred and nine, entitled "An act further to amend the several acts for the establishment and regulation of the Treasury, War, and Navy Departments," shall be construed to authorize the transferring of the sum annually appropriated as aforesaid, or any portion thereof, to any other branch of expenditure.

Approved, April 29, 1816.

An Act for the relief of Menassah Miner and Isaac Denison.

Be it enacted. &c., That the proper accounting officers of the Treasury Department be, and they are hereby, authorized and directed to pay to Menassah Miner the sum of three hundred and three dollars and seventy-four cents, and to Isaac Denison the sum of two hundred and fifty-five dollars and ninety-two cents, out of any money in the Treasury, not otherwise appropriated, for services rendered and expenses incurred by said Menassah in providing for his son John Miner, and for like services and expenditures rendered and incurred by Isaac Denison in providing for his son Frederick Denison, while they were diseased by wounds received by them in the service of the United States in defence of Stonington Point, in the year one thousand eight hundred and fourteen.

Approved, April 29, 1816.

An Act for reducing the licenses to retailers of wines, spirituous liquors, and foreign merchandise.

Be it enacted, &c., That, from and after the thirty-first day of December next, the additional duties laid on licenses to retailers of wines, spirituous liquors and foreign merchandise, by the third section of the act, entitled "An act to provide additional revenues for defraying the expenses of Government and maintaining the public credit, by laying duties on sales at auction, and on licenses to retail wines, spirituous liquors, and foreign merchandise, and for increasing the rates of postage," passed on the twenty-third day of December, one thousand eight hundred and fourteen, shall cease and determine; and in case of any application for a license to retail, between the thirtieth day of June and the first day of January next, a license therefor shall, agreeably to the present rates of duty, be granted, to expire on the thirty-first of December next, on paying to the collector a sum which shall bear the same proportion to the duty for a year by the existing rates as the time for which the license may be granted shall bear to a year; and for neglect or failure to obtain such license, the same penalty shall be incurred, to be recovered in like manner as for the neglect or failure to obtain a license under the act, entitled "An act laying duties on licenses to retailers of wines, spirituous liquors, and foreign merchandise," passed on the second of August, one thousand eight hundred and thirteen : Provided, That after the first day of January next, no retailer of imported salt alone, whose stock in trade shall not exceed one hundred dollars, shall be compelled

to take out a license for retailing the same, nor be liable to any penalty or forfeiture for failing to do so.

Approved, April 29, 1816.

An Act regulating the currency, within the United States, of the gold coins of Great Britain, France, Portugal, and Spain, and the crowns of France, and five franc pieces.

Be it enacted, &c., That, from the passage of this act, and for three years thereafter, and no longer, the following gold and silver coins shall pass current as money within the United States, and be a legal tender for the payment of all debts and demands, at the several and respective rates following, and not otherwise, videlicit : the gold coins of Great Britain and Portugal, of their present standard, at the rate of one hundred cents for every seventy-seven grains, or eighty-eight cents and eight-ninths per pennyweight ; the gold coins of France, of their present standard, at the rate of one hundred cents for every twenty-seven and a half grains, or eighty-seven and a quarter cents per pennyweight ; the gold coins of Spain, at the rate of one hundred cents for every twenty-eight and a half grains, or eighty-four cents per pennyweight ; the crowns of France, at the rate of one hundred and seventeen cents and six-tenths, per ounce, or one hundred and ten cents for each crown weighing eighteen pennyweights and seventeen grains ; the five franc pieces, at the rate of one hundred and sixteen cents per ounce, or ninety-three cents and three mills for each five franc piece, weighing sixteen pennyweights and two grains.

Sec. 2. And be it further enacted, That it shall be the duty of the Secretary of the Treasury to cause assays of the foregoing gold and silver coins, made current by this act, to be had at the Mint of the United States, at least once in every year ; and to make report of the result thereof to Congress.

Approved, April 29, 1816.

An Act for the gradual increase of the Navy of the United States.

Be it enacted, &c., That, for the gradual increase of the Navy of the United States, the sum of one million of dollars per annum, for eight years, is hereby appropriated, including the sum of two hundred thousand dollars per annum, for three years, or the unexpended balance thereof, appropriated by an act approved on the third day of March, one thousand eight hundred and fifteen, entitled "An act concerning the Naval establishment."

Sec. 2. And be it further enacted, That the President of the United States be, and he is hereby authorized, to cause to be built nine ships, to rate not less than seventy-four guns each, and twelve ships, to rate not less than forty-four guns each, including one seventy-four and three forty-four gun ships, authorized to be built by an act bearing date on the second day of January, one

Public Acts of Congress.

thousand eight hundred and thirteen, entitled "An act to increase the Navy of the United States ;" and, in carrying this act into effect, the President shall be, and he is hereby authorized, as soon as the timber and other necessary materials are procured, and the timber properly seasoned, to cause the said ships to be built and equipped ; or, if in his judgment, it will more conduce to the public interest, he may cause the said ships to be framed and remain on the stocks, and kept in the best state of preservation, to be prepared for service in the shortest time practicable, when the public exigency may require them.

SEC. 3. *And be it further enacted,* That, for the defence of the ports and harbors of the United States, the President shall be, and he is hereby, authorized to cause to be procured the steam engines, and all the imperishable materials necessary for building and equipping three steam batteries, on the most approved plan, and best calculated for the waters in which they are to act; and such materials shall be secured in the best manner, to insure the completing such batteries in the shortest time practicable, when they, or either of them, in the opinion of the President, may be required for the public service ; and the President is further authorized to cause to be completed and kept in the best state of preservation, the block ship now on the stocks, near New Orleans.

SEC. 4. *And be it further enacted,* That the moneys appropriated by this act shall not be transferred to any other object of expenditure, nor shall any part thereof be carried to the fund denominated " the surplus fund."

Approved, April 29, 1816.

An Act supplementary to an act making alterations in the Treasury and War Departments, passed the eighth day of May, 1792.

Be it enacted, &c., That there shall be appointed by the President of the United States, by and with the advice and consent of the Senate, an additional Accountant of the Department of War, whose duty it shall be to adjust and settle all the accounts in that Department existing at the conclusion of the late war and are now unsettled. In the execution of this duty he shall conform to the regulations which govern the Accountant of the War Department, and shall receive the same compensation for his services and be entitled to the same privileges of franking.

SEC. 2. *And be it further enacted,* That for defraying the expenses of clerks to be employed under his direction, and for the payment of his salary, the sum of eight thousand eight hundred and seven dollars is hereby appropriated, out of any money in the Treasury not otherwise appropriated.

SEC. 3. *And be it further enacted,* That this act shall continue in force for one year from the passing thereof, and to the end of the next session of Congress thereafter, and no longer.

Approved, April 29, 1816.

An Act to establish a land district in Illinois Territory, north of the district of Kaskaskia.

Be it enacted, &c., That so much of the public lands of the United States, heretofore included within the land district of Kaskaskia, and *lying* north of the base line in Illinois Territory, shall form a new land district, for the disposal of the said lands, and for which purpose a land office shall be established at Edwardsville, Madison county, under the direction of the register of the land office and receiver of public moneys to be appointed for that purpose, who shall reside at the place, give security in the same manner and in the same sums, and whose compensation, emoluments, duties and authority shall, in every respect, be the same in relation to the lands which shall be disposed of at their office, as are or may be by law provided in relation to the registers and receivers of public moneys in the several offices, established for the disposal of the lands of the United States northwest of the river Ohio.

SEC. 2. *And be it further enacted,* That the said lands shall be disposed of in the same manner, and on the same terms and conditions, as are or may be provided by law for the sale of public lands in the district of Kaskaskia ; provided that no tract of land, excepted from the sale by virtue of any former act, shall be sold by virtue of this act.

Approved, April 29, 1816.

An Act to increase the compensation of the superintendents of the manufactories of arms, at Springfield and Harper's Ferry.

Be it enacted, &c., That in addition to the pay and rations, as at present fixed, of the superintendents of the manufactories of arms, at Springfield and Harper's Ferry, they shall receive thirty dollars per month, and one ration per day.

Approved, April 29, 1816.

An Act authorising the Judges of the Circuit Court, and the Attorney for the District of Columbia, to prepare a code of jurisprudence for the said District

Be it enacted, &c., That the judges of the circuit court, and the attorney of the District of Columbia, be, and they are hereby, authorized to prepare and digest a code of jurisprudence, both civil and criminal, for the said District, to be hereafter submitted to the Congress of the United States, to be modified, altered, or adopted, as to them shall seem proper.

SEC. 2. *And be it further enacted,* That the sum of one thousand five hundred dollars be, and the same is hereby, appropriated, to be paid to the said judges and the attorney aforesaid, as a compensation for their services in this respect, out of any money in the Treasury, not otherwise appropriated.

Approved, April 29, 1816.

An Act authorizing payment for prisoners captured by private armed vessels.

Be it enacted, &c., That the Secretary of the Treasury be, and he is hereby, authorized and required to settle and pay unto the owners, officers, and crews of private armed vessels, the bounty allowed by law for the prisoners captured and brought into port, and delivered to the agent of the United States, captured on board any British vessel after the exchange of the ratifications of the treaty of peace between the United States and Great Britain, but before the said treaty took effect in the latitude wherein the capture was made; and the Secretary of the Treasury is hereby authorized to pay the aforesaid claims out of any moneys in the Treasury, not otherwise appropriated.

Approved, April 29, 1816.

An Act for settling the compensation of the commissioners, clerk, and translator of the board for land claims in the eastern and western district for the Territory of Orleans, now State of Louisiana.

Be it enacted, &c., That the proper accounting officers of the Treasury, in settling the accounts for compensation to the commissioners, the clerk and translator of the board for adjusting the titles and claims to lands in the eastern and western district of the Territory of Orleans, now State of Louisiana, shall allow to them, respectively, for the time they were actually employed in discharge of the duties aforesaid, at the rate of the following annual compensation: to each of the commissioners, two thousand dollars; to the clerk, one thousand five hundred dollars; and to the translator, one thousand dollars; which allowance shall commence, for the commissioners, clerk, and translator for the eastern district, on the first of July, one thousand eight hundred and nine, and continue until the first day of May, one thousand eight hundred and eleven, and for the commissioners, clerk, and translator for the western district, on the first day of January, one thousand eight hundred and eleven, and continue until the eleventh day of May, one thousand eight hundred and fifteen, and shall include the moneys they may have received, or are entitled to, according to the existing laws, and shall be in full for all service rendered by them in relation to the lands within the said district.

Approved, April 29, 1816.

An Act making an appropriation for enclosing and improving the public square near the Capitol; and to abolish the office of Commissioners of the Public Buildings, and of Superintendent, and for the appointment of one Commissioner of the Public Buildings.

Be it enacted, &c., That a sum not exceeding thirty thousand dollars be, and the same is hereby, appropriated, to be applied under the direction of the President of the United States, to enclosing and improving the public square, east of the Capitol, which sum shall be paid out of any money in the Treasury, not otherwise appropriated.

SEC. 2. *And be it further enacted,* That so much of any act or acts as authorizes the appointment of three commissioners, for the superintendence of the public buildings, be, and the

same is hereby, repealed; and in lieu of the said commissioners, there shall be appointed, by the President of the United States, by and with the advice and consent of the Senate, one Commissioner, who shall hold no other office under the authority of the United States, and who shall perform all the duties with which the said three commissioners were charged, and whose duty it shall also be to contract for, and superintend the enclosing and improvements of the public square, under the direction of the President of the United States.

SEC. 3. *And be it further enacted,* That there shall be allowed to the said Commissioner a salary of two thousand dollars, to be paid quarterly, out of any moneys in the Treasury not otherwise appropriated.

SEC. 4. *And be it further enacted,* That it shall be the duty of such persons as may have been appointed to superintend the repairing of the public buildings, to deliver up unto the Commissioner who shall be appointed in virtue of this act, all plans, draughts, books, records, accounts, contracts, bonds, obligations, securities, and other evidence of debt in their possession, which belong to their offices.

SEC. 5. *And be it further enacted,* That, from and after the third day of March next, the office of superintendent, established by act of Congress of first May, one thousand eight hundred and two, shall cease, and thereafter the duties of said office shall be performed by the Commissioner to be appointed by virtue of this act; and to whom the superintendent shall deliver all documents, securities, books, and papers, relating to said office; and from and after the third day of March next, the Commissioner aforesaid shall be vested with all the powers and perform all the duties conferred upon the superintendent aforesaid.

SEC. 6. *And be it further enacted,* That the President of the United States be, and hereby is, authorized and empowered, in repairing the public buildings in the City of Washington, to make such alterations in the plans thereof, respectively, as he shall judge proper, for the better accommodation of the two Houses of Congress, the President of the United States, and the various departments of the Government, or any of them.

Approved, April 29, 1816.

An Act to provide for the appointment of a surveyor of the public lands in the Territories of Illinois and Missouri.

Be it enacted, &c., That a surveyor of the lands of the United States in the Territories of Illinois and Missouri shall be appointed, whose duty it shall be to engage a sufficient number of skilful surveyors as his deputies, and to cause so much of the land abovementioned as the President of the United States shall direct, and to which the titles of the Indian tribes have been extinguished, to be surveyed and divided in the manner, and to do and perform all such other acts in relation to such lands, as the Surveyor General is authorized and directed to do, in relation to the same, or the lands lying northwest of the river Ohio: and it shall also be the duty of the surveyor to cause to be surveyed the lands in the said Territories, the claims to which have been, or hereafter may be, confirmed by any act of Congress, which have not already been surveyed according to law; and generally to do and perform all and singular the duties required by law to be performed by the principal deputy surveyor for the Territory of Missouri; and shall transmit to the registers of the land offices within the said Territories, respectively, general and particular plats of all the lands surveyed, or to be surveyed, and shall also forward copies of said plats to the Commissioner of the General Land Office; fix the compensation of the deputy surveyors, chain carriers and axemen: *Provided,* That the whole expense of surveying and marking the lines shall not exceed three dollars for every mile that shall be run, surveyed, and marked.

Sec. 2. *And be it further enacted,* That the surveyor of the lands of the United States, appointed in pursuance of this act, shall be allowed an annual compensation of one thousand dollars, and shall be entitled to receive from individuals the following fees: that is to say, for recording the surveys executed by any of the deputies, at the rate of twenty-five cents for every mile of the boundary line of such survey, and for a certified copy of a plat of a survey in his office twenty-five cents, and that all the plats of surveys, and all other papers and documents pertaining, or which did pertain to the office of the Surveyor General under the Spanish Government within the limits of the Territory of Missouri, or to the office of principal deputy surveyor for said Territory, or pertaining to the office of Surveyor General, or to any office heretofore established or authorized for the purpose of executing or recording surveys of lands within the limits of the Territories of Missouri and Illinois, shall be delivered to the surveyors of the lands of the United States, authorized to be appointed by this act; and any plat of survey duly certified by the said surveyor shall be admitted as evidence in any of the courts of the United States or Territories thereof.

Sec. 3. *And be it further enacted,* That so much of the act entitled "An act extending the powers of the Surveyor General to the Territory of Louisiana, and for other purposes," passed February twenty-eighth, one thousand eight hundred and six, as provides for the appointment of a principal deputy surveyor, and so much of any act of Congress heretofore passed, as is repugnant to, or inconsistent with, any provision of this act, be, and the same is hereby, repealed.

Approved, April 29, 1816.

An Act making appropriations for carrying into effect a treaty between the United States and the Cherokee tribe of Indians, concluded at Washington, on the twenty-second day of March, one thousand eight hundred and sixteen.

Be it enacted, &c., That, for the purpose of carrying into effect, a treaty between the United States and the Cherokee nation of Indians, concluded and signed at Washington, on the twenty-second day of March, one thousand eight hundred and sixteen, the sum of twenty-eight thousand six hundred dollars be, and the same is hereby, appropriated, to be paid out of any money in the Treasury not otherwise appropriated.

Approved, April 29, 1816.

An Act providing for the sale of certain lands in the State of Ohio, formerly set apart for refugees in Canada and Nova Scotia.

Be it enacted, &c., That such part of the tract of land which was set apart for refugees from Canada and Nova Scotia, by the act of Congress, passed the eighteenth day of February, one thousand eight hundred and one, entitled "An act regulating the grants of land appropriated for the refugees from the British provinces of Canada and Nova Scotia," which has not been located by the said refugees, shall be attached to, and made a part of the land district of Chillicothe; and the said unlocated land shall be offered for sale to the highest bidder, under the direction of the register of the land office and of the receiver of public moneys for the said district, at Chillicothe, on such day as shall, by proclamation of the President of the United States, be designated for that purpose; the sale shall remain open six days, and no longer; the lands shall not be sold for less than two dollars an acre, and shall in every other respect be sold in tracts of the same size, and on the same terms and conditions as have been or may be provided for lands in the said district. All the said unlocated land, remaining unsold at the close of the public sales, may be disposed of at private sale by the register of the said land office, in the same manner, under the same regulations, for the same price, and on the same terms as are or may be provided by law for the sale of lands in the said district; and patents shall be obtained in the same manner, and on the same terms, as for other public lands in the said district.

Sec. 2. *And be it further enacted,* That the superintendents of the public sales directed by this act shall each receive four dollars a day for each day's attendance on the said sales.

Approved, April 29, 1816.

An Act supplemental to the act, entitled "An act regulating and defining the duties of the Judges of the Territory of Illinois," and for vesting in the courts of the Territory of Indiana a jurisdiction in chancery cases, arising in the said Territory.

Be it enacted, &c., That when a new county shall be established in the Territory of Illinois, by the Legislature thereof, such new county shall be attached to the judicial circuit from which the largest portion thereof is taken; and it shall be the duty of the judges allotted to such circuit, in pursuance of the act to which this is a supplement, to hold courts in such new county twice in each year, at such time and place as the Legislature of the Territory may designate.

Public Acts of Congress.

SEC. 2. *And be it further enacted,* That when any judge in the said Territory shall be unable to hold the courts within the circuit to which he is allotted, by reason of any disability, it shall be the duty of the judge allotted to the circuit nearest thereto, to hold the courts in such circuit, until the disability of the judge allotted to the circuit shall be removed, or (in case of the death or resignation of a judge) until a successor is appointed.

SEC. 3. *And be it further enacted,* That the judge of any circuit within the said Territory shall have power to appoint a clerk to each court within his court, (circuit,) and to fill any vacancy occasioned by the death or resignation of the clerk.

SEC. 4. *And be it further enacted,* That when any person charged with felony shall be committed to prison, in any county within the Territory aforesaid, it shall be lawful for the Governor of the Territory to issue his writ, directed to the judge allotted to the circuit including the county where such accused person may be committed, commanding him to hold a court of oyer and terminer, for the trial of the accused; and it shall be the duty of the judge to whom such writ is directed, to hold the court at the court-house of the county at such time as may be specified in such writ; and all process issued, or proceedings had before the writ shall be issued, shall be returned to the said court of oyer and terminer.

SEC. 5. *And be it further enacted,* That this act, and the act to which this is supplemental, shall be and remain in force until the end of the next session of the Legislature of the said Territory, and no longer; and the Legislature of the said Territory shall have power and authority to make laws in all cases, for the good government of the Territory aforesaid, not repugnant to the principles and articles of the ordinances, and to organize the courts of the said Territory, and prescribe the times and places of their session.

SEC. 6. *And be it further enacted,* That the General Court of the Territory of Indiana be, and it is hereby, authorized and empowered to exercise chancery powers as well as a common law jurisdiction, under such regulations as the Legislature of said Territory may prescribe.

Approved, April 29, 1816.

An Act to alter certain parts of the act providing for the government of the Territory of Missouri.

Be it enacted, &c., That the electors of the Territory of Missouri, entitled to vote for members of the House of Representatives of the Territory, at the time of electing the representatives to the General Assembly, shall in each county in said Territory elect one member of the legislative council to serve for two years and no longer, qualified according to the provisions of the fifth section of the "Act providing for the government of the Territory of Missouri, passed June fourth, one thousand eight hundred and twelve, a majority of whom shall be a quorum, and shall possess the same powers as are granted to the legislative council by the said recited act: and in case of vacancy of a member of the legislative council, by resignation or otherwise, the Governor of the Territory shall issue a writ to the county to elect another person to serve the residue of the term.

SEC. 2. *And be it further enacted,* That so much of the eighth section of the said recited act as requires the General Assembly of said Territory to meet once in each year be repealed, and the said General Assembly shall meet once in every other year at St. Louis, and such meeting shall be on the first Monday in December, unless they shall by law appoint a different day: *Provided,* That the Governor for the time being shall have authority by proclamation to convene the General Assembly whenever he shall deem the interest of the Territory may require it.

SEC. 3. *And be it further enacted,* That the General Assembly of the said Territory shall be, and are hereby, authorized to require the judges of the superior court of the said Territory to hold superior and circuit courts, to appoint the times and places of holding the same, and under such rules and regulations as the General Assembly may in that behalf prescribe; the circuit courts shall be composed of one of the said judges, and shall have jurisdiction in all criminal cases, and exclusive original jurisdiction in all those which are capital, and original jurisdiction in all civil cases of the value of one hundred dollars, and the superior and circuit courts shall possess and exercise chancery powers as well as common law jurisdiction in all civil cases: *Provided,* That there shall be an appeal in matters of law and equity, in all cases, from the circuit courts to the superior court of the said Territory.

SEC. 4. *And be it further enacted,* That such part of the said recited acts as is repugnant to, or inconsistent with the provisions of this act, be, and the same is hereby, repealed.

Approved, April 29, 1816.

An Act for the relief of William Crawford, Frederick Bates, William Garrard, and Thomas B. Robertson.

Be it enacted, &c., That the proper accounting officers of the Treasury be, and they are hereby, authorized and required to allow and pay to William Crawford, commissioner of land claims east of Pearl river, the sum of five hundred dollars, for carrying his report upon land claims to the General Land Office, at the city of Washington.

SEC. 2. *And be it further enacted,* That the accounting officers of the Treasury be, and they are hereby, authorized and required to allow and pay to Frederick Bates, recorder of land titles for the Territory of Missouri, the sum of five hundred dollars, for carrying his report upon land claims to the General Land Office, at the city of Washington.

SEC. 3. *And be it further enacted,* That the accounting officers of the Treasury be, and they are hereby, authorized and required to allow and pay to William Garrard, commissioner of land claims for the western district of the State of Louisiana, and to Thomas Bolling Robertson, commissioner of land claims for the eastern district of Louisiana, the sum of five hundred dollars each, for carrying the reports upon land claims to the General Land Office, at the city of Washington.

SEC. 4. *And be it further enacted*, That a sum not exceeding two thousand dollars be, and the same is hereby, appropriated, for the purposes aforesaid, out of any moneys in the Treasury not otherwise appropriated.

Approved, April 29, 1816.

An Act to indemnify Jabez Mowry and others.

Be it enacted, &c., That upon the payment by Jabez Mowry, John W. C. Baxter, Samuel Wheeler, Jonathan Bartlett, Josiah Dana, and Aaron Hayden, citizens of the United States, of certain bonds now in suit in the district court of Maine, given by them to the United States, for duties on goods imported into the district of Passamaquoddy, amounting to the sum of sixty-five thousand five hundred and eight dollars and seventeen cents, which bonds, on the capture of Eastport, on the eleventh day of July, one thousand eight hundred and fourteen, fell into the hands of the enemy, and were afterwards, by the vice admiralty court of Nova Scotia, decreed forfeit, and the amount thereof ordered to be distributed among the captors, and attachments issued against the principals and sureties in said bonds, to compel the payment thereof, the United States will indemnify the principals and sureties in said bonds, and save them harmless against the loss thereof, and for the expenses already incurred by them in consequence of said loss; which expenses shall be ascertained by the accounting officers of the Treasury, and paid out of any moneys therein, not otherwise appropriated.

Approved, April 29, 1816.

An Act for the relief of John Holkar, formerly Consul General of France, to the United States.

Be it enacted, &c., That the accounting officers of the Treasury Department be, and they hereby are, authorized and directed to settle the account of John Holkar, formerly Consul General of France to the United States, for thirty-seven loan-office certificates, amounting to twenty-one thousand seven hundred dollars nominal, that is to say: three hundred dollars thereof issued from the loan office of New Hampshire; seven thousand nine hundred dollars thereof issued from the loan office of Massachusetts; eight hundred dollars thereof issued from the loan office of Rhode Island; twelve hundred dollars thereof issued from the loan office of New York; and eleven thousand five hundred dollars thereof issued from the loan office of Georgia; all of which had been signed by Francis Hopkinson, Treasurer of Loans, and countersigned by the loan officers of the States respectively, and which were destroyed by fire in the consulate office at Philadelphia, on the second day of January, in the year one thousand seven hundred and eighty; and that the specie value thereof, being five thousand eight hundred and three dollars, thirty-five nineteenths, be paid, with interest thereon, at six per cent, from the third day of July, one thousand seven hundred and seventy-eight, being the mean date of interest on the same, as examined and stated in the office of the Auditor of the Treasury, on the twenty-fifth day of October, one thousand seven hundred and ninety-four, to the said John Holkar, out of any moneys in the Treasury not otherwise appropriated, upon the said John Holkar giving a bond of indemnity, to the satisfaction of the Comptroller of the Treasury of the United States.

Approved, April 29, 1816.

An Act for the confirmation of certain claims to land in the western district of the State of Louisiana, and in the Territory of Missouri.

Whereas, by the eighth section of the act of third March, one thousand eight hundred and seven, it is required that the commissioners for ascertaining and adjusting the titles and claims to land in the then Territories of Orleans and Louisiana, should arrange their reports into three general classes, the second of which classes should contain claims which, though not embraced by the provisions of the several acts of Congress, ought nevertheless, in the opinion of the commissioners, to be confirmed, in conformity with the laws, usages, and customs of the Spanish Government: And whereas the commissioners, in and for the western district of the State of Louisiana, formerly Territory of Orleans, in their several reports of the sixteenth of October, one thousand eight hundred and twelve, fourth of December, one thousand eight hundred and twelve, ninth of March, one thousand eight hundred and thirteen, sixth of April, one thousand eight hundred and fifteen, first of May, one thousand eight hundred and fifteen, and fourth of May, one thousand eight hundred and fifteen, have formed this second class, recommending the claims which it embraces for confirmation, and have designated the same by letter B, and the register of the land office and receiver of public moneys, acting as commissioners for adjusting the titles and claims to land in the said district, in their report, dated the thirtieth day of December, one thousand eight hundred and fifteen, under the act giving further time for registering claims to land in the western district of the Territory of Orleans, passed the tenth day of March, one thousand eight hundred and twelve, the "Act giving farther time for registering claims to land in the eastern and western districts of the Territory of Orleans," passed the twenty-seventh day of February, one thousand eight hundred and thirteen, and the act of the twelfth day of April, one thousand eight hundred and fourteen, have arranged the claims into the following classes, to wit: one, two, three, four, five, six, seven, eight, nine, ten, eleven: Therefore,

Public Acts of Congress.

Be it enacted, &c., That the claims marked B and described in the several classes in the above-mentioned reports of the commissioners for the western district of the State of Louisiana, formerly Territory of Orleans, and recommended by them for confirmation, be, and the same are hereby, confirmed : *Provided, nevertheless,* That under no one claim shall any person or persons be entitled, under this act, to more than the quantity contained in a league square.

SEC. 2. *And be it further enacted,* That all claims embraced in the reports of the recorder of land titles, acting as commissioner for ascertaining and adjusting the titles and claims to land in the Territory of Missouri, dated November first, one thousand eight hundred and fifteen, and February second, one thousand eight hundred and sixteen, where the decision of the said commissioner is in favor of the claimants, shall be, and the same are hereby, confirmed, to wit : confirmations of village claims, under the act of Congress of the thirteenth day of June, one thousand eight hundred and twelve; grants of the late board of commissioners, appointed for ascertaining and adjusting the titles and claims to land in the Territory of Missouri, extended by virtue of the fourth section of the act of the third of March, one thousand eight hundred and thirteen; grants and confirmations under the several acts of Congress, commencing with the act of the thirteenth day of June, one thousand eight hundred and twelve.

SEC. 3. *And be it further enacted,* That in all cases not provided for by law for patent certificates to issue, every person, and the legal representative of every person, whose claim to a tract of land is confirmed by this or any former act, and who has not already obtained a patent certificate for the same, shall, whenever his claim shall have been located and surveyed according to law, be entitled to receive from the register of the land office at Opelousas, in the State of Louisiana, or from the recorder of land titles in the Territory of Missouri, as the case may be, a certificate, stating that the claimant is entitled to a patent for such tract of land, by virtue of this act ; for which certificate the officer issuing the same shall receive one dollar, and the certificate shall entitle the party to a patent for the tract of land, which shall issue in like manner as is provided by law for patents to issue for lands purchased of the United States.

Approved, April 29, 1816.

An Act making appropriations for the support of the Military Establishment of the United States, for the year one thousand eight hundred and sixteen.

Be it enacted, &c., That, for defraying the expenses of the Military Establishment of the United States, for the year one thousand eight hundred and sixteen, for the Indian department, for fortifications, for the expenses of the public buildings at West Point, and for the purchase of maps, plans, books, and instruments, for the Military Academy at said place, the following sums be, and the same are hereby, respectively appropri-

ated, that is to say : For the pay of the Army of the United States, one million one hundred ninety-six thousand four hundred and ninety-six dollars. For subsistence, one million forty-three thousand three hundred and fifty-five dollars. For forage for officers, twenty-five thousand six hundred and ninety-two dollars. For bounties and premiums, fifty-six thousand dollars. For clothing, three hundred and fifty thousand dollars. For the medical and hospital department, one hundred thousand dollars. For the quartermaster's department, three hundred and fifty thousand dollars. For fortifications, eight hundred and thirty-eight thousand dollars. For contingencies, one hundred and fifty thousand dollars. For the Indian department, two hundred thousand dollars. For the purchase of horses for the artillery, fifty thousand dollars. For the purchase of maps, plans, books, and instruments, for the War Office, twenty-five hundred dollars. For the erection of buildings at West Point, including arrearages, one hundred fifteen thousand eight hundred dollars. For the purchase of maps, plans, books, and instruments, for the Military Academy, twenty-two thousand one hundred and seventy-one dollars. For defraying the expenses incurred by calling out the militia during the late war, in addition to the sums heretofore appropriated by law to that object, one million two hundred and fifty thousand dollars. For the payment of damages sustained by the ships and vessels sunk at the entrance of the port of Baltimore, to prevent the ships of the enemy from passing the fort and entering the harbor, fifteen thousand one hundred eighty-eight dollars and fifty cents, being part of the amount of an appropriation of two hundred fifty thousand dollars, heretofore made, and by the President of the United States transferred to other objects.

SEC. 2. *And be it further enacted,* That the several sums specifically appropriated by this act, shall be paid out of any moneys in the Treasury not otherwise appropriated.

Approved, April 29, 1816.

An Act authorizing the payment of a sum of money to Joseph Stewart, and others.

Be it enacted, &c., That the Secretary of the Treasury be, and he is hereby, authorized and required to pay to Joseph Stewart, and his associates, of Dorchester county, in the State of Maryland, or to their legal representatives, the sum of one thousand eight hundred dollars, out of any money in the Treasury not otherwise appropriated ; which money is paid to them for their gallantry and good conduct in capturing, during the late war, a tender belonging to the Dauntless, British ship-of-war, and taking eighteen prisoners, to wit : one lieutenant, one midshipman, thirteen seamen, and three marines, and as compensation for the prisoners so taken.

SEC. 2. *And be it further enacted,* That any claim which the United States may have to the said captured vessel and property shall be, and the same is hereby, released to the said captors.

Sec. 3. *And be it further enacted*, That the Secretary of the Treasury be, and he is hereby, authorized and required to pay, out of any money in the Treasury not otherwise appropriated, the sum of five hundred dollars, in equal proportions, to Matthew Guy and John Woodward, of Prince William county, in Virginia, and Samuel Jennison and Wilfred Drury, of St. Mary's county, in Maryland, or to their legal representatives; which is paid to them as an evidence of the sense entertained of their valor and good conduct in capturing a boat belonging to the enemy, in Clement's bay, in Potomac river, in December, one thousand eight hundred and fourteen; making prisoners of the crew, consisting of a midshipman and four seamen, with their arms; and also as compensation for the prisoners so taken and delivered to the proper officers of the United States.

Approved, April 29, 1816.

An Act concerning pre-emption rights given in the purchase of lands to certain settlers in the State of Louisiana, and in the Territories of Missouri and Illinois.

Be it enacted, &c., That any person, and the legal representatives of any person, entitled to a preference in becoming the purchaser, from the United States, of a tract of land at private sale, in the State of Louisiana, and in the Territories of Missouri and Illinois, according to the provisions of the act, entitled "An act giving the right of pre-emption, in the purchase of lands, to certain settlers in the Illinois Territory," passed February fifth, one thousand eight hundred and thirteen, and the fifth section of the "Act for the final adjustment of land titles in the State of Louisiana, and Territory of Missouri," passed April twelfth, one thousand eight hundred and fourteen, who is settled on a fraction of a section or fractional quarter-section, containing less than one hundred and sixty acres, shall have the privilege of purchasing one or more adjoining fractional quarter-sections, or the adjoining quarter section, including their improvements, or the fraction improved by them, at their option; and the provisions of the said recited acts are hereby made applicable to them, so far as they are consistent with the provisions of this act.

Sec. 2. *And be it further enacted,* That in cases where two or more persons, entitled to the right of pre-emption, shall be settled upon one quarter or fractional quarter section of land, each person shall be authorized to purchase one or more quarter sections, or fractional quarter sections, of the section or fractional section of land upon which they are so settled; and the section or fractional section upon which such persons are settled shall be equally divided between them, in such manner as the register and receiver, within whose district such land lies, shall determine and direct, so as to secure, as far as may be practicable, to every such person their improvements respectively; and where the improvement of such person shall be upon two or more quarter sections, such person shall be entitled to purchase the quarter sections upon which his improvement shall be.

Approved, April 29, 1816.

An Act declaring the consent of Congress to acts of the State of South Carolina, authorizing the City Council of Charleston to impose and collect a duty on the tonnage of vessels from foreign ports; and to acts of the State of Georgia, authorizing the imposition and collection of a duty on the tonnage of vessels in the ports of Savannah and St. Mary's.

Be it enacted, &c., That the consent of Congress be, and is hereby, granted and declared to the operation of any act of the General Assembly of the State of South Carolina, now in existence, or which may hereafter be passed, so far as the same extends, or may extend, to authorize the City Council of Charleston, to impose and levy a duty, not exceeding ten cents per ton, on all ships and vessels of the United States, which shall arrive and be entered in the port of Charleston, from any foreign port or place, for the purpose of providing a fund for the temporary relief and maintenance of sick or disabled men in the marine hospital of the said port of Charleston.

Sec. 2. *And be it further enacted,* That the collector of the port of Charleston be, and he is hereby, authorized to collect the duties imposed or authorized to be imposed by this act, and to pay the same to such persons as shall be authorized to receive the same by the City Council of Charleston.

Sec. 3. *And be it further enacted,* That the consent of Congress be, and is hereby, granted and declared to the operation of any act of the General Assembly of the State of Georgia, now in existence, or which may hereafter be passed, so far as the same extends, or may extend, to authorize the levying and collecting a tonnage duty, not exceeding two cents per ton upon coasting vessels, and four cents per ton upon vessels from foreign ports, arriving at and entering the ports of Savannah and St. Mary's, for the purpose of providing a fund for the payment of the fees of the harbor master and health officer of those ports respectively: *Provided,* the said acts shall not contain provisions inconsistent with the operation of any law of the United States made in execution of existing treaties.

Sec. 4. *And be it further enacted,* That this act shall be in force for five years, and from thence to the end of the next session of Congress thereafter, and no longer.

Approved, April 29, 1816.

An Act to authorize the survey of two millions of acres of the public lands, in lieu of that quantity heretofore authorized to be surveyed, in the Territory of Michigan, as military bounty lands.

Be it enacted, &c., That so much of the "Act to provide for designating, surveying, and granting the military bounty lands," approved the sixth day of May, one thousand eight hundred and twelve; as authorizes the President of the United

States to cause to be surveyed two millions of acres of the lands of the United States, in the Territory of Michigan, for the purpose of satisfying the bounties of land promised to the non-commissioned officers and soldiers of the United States be, and the same is hereby, repealed; and in lieu of the said two millions of acres of land, the President of the United States be, and he is hereby, authorized to cause to be surveyed, of the lands of the United States fit for cultivation, not otherwise appropriated, and to which the Indian title is extinguished, one million five hundred thousand acres, in the Illinois Territory, and five hundred thousand acres, in the Missouri Territory, north of the river Missouri; the said lands shall be divided into townships, and subdivided into sections and quarter sections, (each quarter section to contain, as near as possible, one hundred and sixty acres,) in the manner prescribed by law for surveying and subdividing the other lands of the United States; and the lands thus surveyed, with the exception of the salt springs and lead mines therein, and of the quantities of land adjacent thereto as may be reserved for the use of the same by the President of the United States, and the section number sixteen in every township, to be granted to the inhabitants of such township for the use of public schools, shall, according to the provisions of the above recited act, be set apart for the purpose of satisfying the bounties of land promised to the non-commissioned officers and soldiers of the late Army of the United States, their heirs and legal representatives, by the act entitled "An act for completing the existing Military Establishment, approved the twenty-fourth day of December, one thousand eight hundred and eleven, and by the act entitled "An act to raise an additional military force," approved the eleventh day of January, one thousand eight hundred and twelve.

SEC. 2. *And be it further enacted,* That every person in whose favor any warrant for military land bounty is issued, shall be, and is hereby, authorized to draw by lot one of the quarter sections surveyed by virtue of this act, and shall obtain a patent therefor, in the same manner, in every respect, as is or shall be provided by law for patents to issue for other military land bounties, or as is provided by the act first above recited for patents to issue for such lands.

Approved, April 29, 1816.

An Act supplementary to the act passed the thirtieth of March, one thousand eight hundred and two, to regulate trade and intercourse with the Indian tribes, and to preserve peace on the frontiers.

Be it enacted, &c., That licenses to trade with the Indians within the territorial limits of the United States shall not be granted to any but citizens of the United States, unless by the express direction of the President of the United States, and upon such terms and conditions as the public interest may, in his opinion, require.

SEC. 2. *And be it further enacted,* That all goods, wares, and merchandise, carried by a for-

eigner into the lands to which the Indian title has not been extinguished, for the purpose of being used in the Indian trade; and all articles of peltry, of provisions, or of any other kind purchased by foreigners from Indians, or tribes of Indians, contrary to the provisions of this act, shall be, and the same are hereby, forfeited, one-half thereof to the use of the informer, and the remainder to the United States : *Provided,* That the goods, wares, and merchandise are seized prior to their sale to an Indian, or Indian tribe, and the articles purchased are seized before they are removed beyond the limits of the United States.

SEC. 3. *And be it further enacted,* That if a foreigner go into any country which is allotted or secured by treaty to either of the Indian tribes within the territorial limits of the United States, or to which the Indian title has not been extinguished, without a passport first had and obtained from the Governor of one of the States or Territories of the United States, adjoining the country into which he may go, or the officer of the troops of the United States, commanding at the nearest post on the frontiers, or such other person as the President of the United States may from time to time authorize to grant the same, he shall, on conviction thereof, pay a fine of not less than fifty or more than one thousand dollars; or be imprisoned not less than one month, or more than twelve months, at the discretion of the court.

SEC. 4. *And be it further enacted,* That trials for offences against this act shall be had in the courts of the United States of the territory in which the person accused may be arrested, or in the circuit court of the United States, of the district into which he may be first carried, after his arrest.

SEC. 5. *And be it further enacted,* That each and every person charged with a violation of the second section of this act shall, if arrested, be indicted and tried in one of the courts aforesaid, and that the conviction of the accused shall authorize the court to cause the goods intended to be sold to, and articles purchased from the Indians, belonging to him, or taken in his possession, to be sold, one-half to the use of the informer, and the other to the use of the United States. But if goods intended to be sold, or articles purchased from the Indians contrary to the provisions of this act, should be seized, and the owner or person in possession of them should make his escape, or from any other cause cannot be brought to trial, it shall and may be lawful for the United States Attorney of the Territory in which they may be seized, or the District Attorney of the United States, of the district into which they may have been first carried after they are seized, to proceed against the said goods intended to be sold to, or articles purchased from the Indians, in the manner directed to be observed in the case of goods, wares, or merchandise brought into the United States in violation of the revenue laws.

SEC. 6. *And be it further enacted,* That the President of the United States be, and he hereby is, authorized to use the military force of the United States whenever it may be necessary to carry into effect this act, as far as it relates to seizure of goods to be sold to, or articles already purchased from the Indians, or to the arrest of persons charged with violating its provisions.

Approved, April 29, 1816.

An Act to increase the salary of the Register of the Treasury.

Be it enacted, &c., That there be allowed and paid to the Register of the Treasury, for his annual salary, from the first of January, one thousand eight hundred and sixteen, the sum of three thousand dollars.

Approved, April 30, 1816.

An Act concerning Invalid Pensioners.

Be it enacted, &c., That the Secretary of War be, and he is hereby, directed to place the following named persons on the pension list of invalid pensioners of the United States, who shall be entitled to and receive pensions according to the rates, and commencing at the times herein mentioned, that is to say:

John Huie, at the rate of twenty dollars per month, to commence on the twenty-seventh of December, eighteen hundred and fifteen.

Erastus Desbrow, at the rate of six dollars per month, to commence on the eighteenth of November, eighteen hundred and fifteen.

John B. Williams, at the rate of six dollars per month, to commence on the twelfth of September, eighteen hundred and fifteen.

Ptolemy Sheldon, at the rate of eight dollars per month, to commence on the ninth of June, eighteen hundred and fifteen.

Humphrey Webster, at the rate of seventeen dollars per month, to commence on the first of June, eighteen hundred and fifteen.

Asa Glazier, at the rate of four dollars per month, to commence on the twenty-sixth of January, eighteen hundred and sixteen.

Joseph Westcott, at the rate of six dollars and sixty-seven cents per month, to commence on the sixth of January, eighteen hundred and sixteen.

Alston Fort, at the rate of eight dollars per month, to commence on the sixteenth of September, eighteen hundred and fourteen.

Luther Gregory, at the rate of four dollars per month, to commence on the twenty-second of February, eighteen hundred and sixteen.

Henry Parks, at the rate of eight dollars per month, to commence on the twenty-second of February, eighteen hundred and sixteen.

Lemuel Hewlit, at the rate of four dollars per month, to commence on the twelfth of January, eighteen hundred and sixteen.

Peter Mills, at the rate of eight dollars per month, to commence on the fifth of January, eighteen hundred and thirteen.

Bethuel Goodrich, junior, at the rate of four dollars per month, to commence on the eighteenth of November, eighteen hundred and fifteen.

William Vineyard, at the rate of four dollars per month, to commence on the second of November, eighteen hundred and fifteen.

Aaron Stewart, at the rate of four dollars per month, to commence on the fourth of October, eighteen hundred and fifteen.

Michael McDermott, at the rate of eight dollars per month, to commence on the twenty-fifth of March, eighteen hundred and fourteen.

William Bowyer, at the rate of eight dollars per month, to commence on the tenth of October, eighteen hundred and fifteen.

Samuel Jacaway, at the rate of four dollars per month, to commence on the ninth of January, eighteen hundred and fifteen.

Joseph S. Van Driesen, at the rate of eight dollars per month, to commence on the fourth of March, eighteen hundred and thirteen.

Jacob Kendelsperyer, at the rate of four dollars per month, to commence on the seventeenth of November, eighteen hundred and fourteen.

Thomas Fugate, at the rate of eight dollars per month, to commence on the thirty-first of May, eighteen hundred and fourteen.

Cornelius Williams, at the rate of four dollars per month, to commence on the eighteenth of December, eighteen hundred and fifteen.

John B. Fuller, at the rate of eight dollars per month, to commence on the twenty-eighth of November, eighteen hundred and fifteen.

Michael Chapu, at the rate of four dollars per month, to commence on the fifth of February, eighteen hundred and sixteen.

Joseph Henderson, at the rate of eight dollars and fifty cents per month, to commence on the twenty-fourth of December, eighteen hundred and fourteen.

John Pidgeon, at the rate of four dollars per month, to commence on the eighth of February, eighteen hundred and sixteen.

George Fitzsimmons, at the rate of four dollars per month, to commence on the first of June, eighteen hundred and fifteen.

Jesse Beach, at the rate of twenty dollars per month, to commence on the third of January, eighteen hundred and sixteen.

Daniel Stagg, at the rate of eight dollars per month, to commence on the twenty-sixth of February, eighteen hundred and sixteen.

Daniel Bailey, at the rate of four dollars per month, to commence on the eighteenth of December, eighteen hundred and fifteen.

Calvin Barnes, at the rate of four dollars per month, to commence on the fourteenth of February, eighteen hundred and sixteen.

Noble Morse, at the rate of eight dollars per month, to commence on the thirty-first of October, eighteen hundred and fifteen.

David McCracken, junior, at the rate of eight dollars per month, to commence on the ninth of February, eighteen hundred and sixteen.

John Patterson, at the rate of four dollars per month, to commence on the twenty-ninth of December, eighteen hundred and fifteen.

Thomas Baldwin, at the rate of eight dollars per month, to commence on the sixth of June, eighteen hundred and fifteen.

Public Acts of Congress.

Zenas Hastings, at the rate of eight dollars per month, to commence on the twenty-ninth of November, eighteen hundred and fifteen.

James Nowell, at the rate of eight dollars per month, to commence on the fifth of April, eighteen hundred and eleven.

Charles Hagin, at the rate of eight dollars per month, to commence on the eighth of November, eighteen hundred and fifteen.

Joseph Foster, at the rate of eight dollars per month, to commence on the tenth of October, eighteen hundred and fifteen.

Levie Frisbie, at the rate of eight dollars per month, to commence on the ninth of November, eighteen hundred and fifteen.

Joseph Gillett, at the rate of seventeen dollars per month, to commence on the eighteenth of April, eighteen hundred and fifteen.

Samuel Truby, at the rate of eight dollars per month, to commence on the ninth of September, eighteen hundred and fifteen.

David Hawkins, at the rate of eight dollars per month, to commence on the seventeenth of November, eighteen hundred and fifteen.

Philip Ulmer, at the rate of fifteen dollars per month, to commence on the twenty-second of January, eighteen hundred and sixteen.

John Hamilton, at the rate of ten dollars per month, to commence on the fifth day of February, eighteen hundred and fifteen.

Nathaniel Thompson, at the rate of four dollars per month, to commence on the sixteenth of June, eighteen hundred and fifteen.

John Downs, at the rate of four dollars per month, to commence on the twenty-second of March, eighteen hundred and sixteen.

John Fenton, at the rate of four dollars per month, to commence on the sixth of February, eighteen hundred and sixteen.

William Collins, at the rate of four dollars per month, to commence on the eighteenth of January, one thousand eight hundred and sixteen.

James Allen, at the rate of four dollars per month, to commence on the third of May, one thousand eight hundred and fifteen.

William Richardson, at the rate of four dollars per month, to commence on the twelfth of April, one thousand eight hundred and fifteen.

James Devouriz, at the rate of eight dollars per month, to commence on the eighth of July, one thousand eight hundred and fifteen.

Nathaniel Clark, at the rate of six dollars per month, to commence on the twentieth of February, one thousand eight hundred and fifteen.

John Haskell, at the rate of eight dollars per month, to commence on the eleventh of December, one thousand eight hundred and fifteen.

James Nourse, at the rate of four dollars per month, to commence on the seventeenth of November, one thousand eight hundred and fifteen.

John McNulty, at the rate of eight dollars per month, to commence on the twelfth of June, one thousand eight hundred and fifteen.

Joseph Kerr, at the rate of four dollars per month, to commence on the twenty-third of October, one thousand eight hundred and fifteen.

James Guthrie, at the rate of four dollars per month, to commence on the twenty-seventh of September, one thousand eight hundred and fifteen.

Stephen M. Conger, at the rate of four dollars per month, to commence on the seventeenth of October, one thousand eight hundred and fifteen.

Socrates Swift, at the rate of eight dollars per month, to commence on the eighteenth of March, one thousand eight hundred and fifteen.

Nathan Lockwood, at the rate of four dollars per month, to commence on the first of December, one thousand eight hundred and fifteen.

Samuel Gurnee, at the rate of eight dollars per month, to commence on the sixth of March, one thousand eight hundred and sixteen.

Emory Lowman, at the rate of eight dollars per month, to commence on the sixteenth of June, one thousand eight hundred and fifteen.

John McMillan, at the rate of fifteen dollars per month, to commence on the twenty-third of August, one thousand eight hundred and fifteen.

Reuben Goolsby, at the rate of four dollars per month, to commence on the first of April, one thousand eight hundred and sixteen.

William Rhodes, at the rate of four dollars per month, to commence on the third of November, one thousand eight hundred and fourteen.

Daniel Ruminer, at the rate of six dollars per month, to commence on the fourth of July, one thousand eight hundred and fifteen.

Beverly Williams, at the rate of twenty dollars per month, to commence on the twenty-fourth of September, one thousand eight hundred and fifteen.

James Shaw, at the rate of eight dollars per month, to commence on the fifth of September, one thousand eight hundred and fifteen.

Edmund Borum, at the rate of eight dollars per month, to commence on the twenty-first of August, one thousand eight hundred and fifteen.

Matthew Williams, at the rate of six dollars per month, to commence on the eleventh of July, one thousand eight hundred and fifteen.

William L. Sypert, at the rate of four dollars per month, to commence on the twenty-fourth of August, one thousand eight hundred and fifteen.

Samuel Scott, at the rate of eight dollars per month, to commence on the twenty-seventh of May, one thousand eight hundred and fifteen.

David Hubbard, at the rate of four dollars per month, to commence on the seventeenth of June, one thousand eight hundred and fifteen.

Hugh Hays, at the rate of four dollars per month, to commence on the fourth of July, one thousand eight hundred and fifteen.

William Dennie, at the rate of six dollars per month, to commence on the sixteenth of September, one thousand eight hundred and fifteen.

John Bruce, at the rate of six dollars per month, to commence on the sixteenth of September, one thousand eight hundred and fifteen.

George Sleeker, at the rate of six dollars per month, to commence on the twenty-third of August, one thousand eight hundred and fifteen.

Robert C. Davis, at the rate of six dollars per

Public Acts of Congress.

month, to commence on the fifteenth of September, one thousand eight hundred and fifteen.

Bracket Davison, at the rate of six dollars per month, to commence on the seventeenth of December, one thousand eight hundred and fifteen.

W. I. Shumate, at the rate of fourteen dollars per month, to commence on the twenty-seventh of July, one thousand eight hundred and fifteen.

Alexander M. Gray, at the rate of eight dollars per month, to commence on the twenty-seventh of July, one thousand eight hundred and fifteen.

John Patterson, at the rate of four dollars per month, to commence on the eighteenth of September, one thousand eight hundred and fifteen.

Paul Bonnel, at the rate of four dollars per month, to commence on the twenty-ninth of January, one thousand eight hundred and sixteen.

Daniel Hannah, at the rate of four dollars per month, to commence on the twenty-eighth of February, one thousand eight hundred and sixteen.

Joshua Mercer, at the rate of four dollars per month, to commence on the twenty-seventh of March, one thousand eight hundred and sixteen.

Samuel Schoonover, at the rate of eight dollars per month, to commence on the eighteenth of March, one thousand eight hundred and sixteen.

Alston Cook, at the rate of eight dollars per month, to commence on the twenty-sixth of October, one thousand eight hundred and fourteen.

John Chittim, at the rate of six dollars per month, to commence on the first of January, one thousand eight hundred and fifteen.

Abraham Johnson, at the rate of five dollars and thirty-three cents and one third of a cent per month, to commence on the eleventh of February, one thousand eight hundred and sixteen.

Thomas Gadd, at the rate of four dollars per month, to commence on the eleventh of July, one thousand eight hundred and fourteen.

William O'Neal, at the rate of four dollars per month, to commence the fifteenth day of February, one thousand eight hundred and sixteen.

Thomas Edmondson, at the rate of four dollars per month, to commence the twenty-seventh day of May, one thousand eight hundred and fifteen.

Josiah B. Pachard, at the rate of eight dollars per month, to commence on the twenty-second day of January, one thousand eight hundred and sixteen.

John Q. Talbotts, at the rate of four dollars per month to commence on the fifth day of April, one thousand eight hundred and fifteen.

James Jackson, at the rate of four dollars per month, to commence on the twenty-first of August, one thousand eight hundred and fifteen.

Jean Du Peron, at the rate of eight dollars per month, to commence on the twenty-eighth of December, one thousand eight hundred and fourteen.

John Lamb, at the rate of eight dollars per month, to commence on the first of April, one thousand eight hundred and sixteen.

Sec. 2. *And be it further enacted*, That the pensions of the following named persons, already placed on the pension list of the United States, be increased to the sums herein respectively annexed to their names; the said increase to commence at the times herein mentioned, and to be in lieu of the pensions they at present receive, that is to say:

Nero Hawley, at the rate of eight dollars per month, to commence on the thirtieth of October, one thousand eight hundred and fifteen.

Nathan Hawley, at the rate of eight dollars per month, to commence on the thirtieth of October, one thousand eight hundred and fifteen.

James Porter, at the rate of four dollars per month, to commence on the twenty-second of January, one thousand eight hundred and sixteen.

John Durell, at the rate of eight dollars per month, to commence on the twenty-ninth of June, one thousand eight hundred and fifteen.

James White, at the rate of eight dollars per month, to commence on the twenty-seventh of May, one thousand eight hundred and fifteen.

David Scott, at the rate of twenty dollars per month, to commence on the eighteenth of May, one thousand eight hundred and fourteen.

Hugh Barnes, at the rate of twenty dollars per month, to commence on the fourth of March, one thousand eight hundred and sixteen.

Edmund Stevenson, at the rate of eight dollars per month, to commence on the first of April, one thousand eight hundred and sixteen: *Provided*, That nothing in this act shall be construed as to allow any pensioners any other pension than is herein provided, or any higher rate of pension than has heretofore been allowed to him, or to others similarly situated, for any time previous to the passage of an act, entitled, "An act, to increase pensions of invalids in certain cases, for the relief of invalids of the militia, and for the appointment of pension agents, in those States, where there are no commissioner of loans."

Approved, April 30, 1816.

An Act fixing the compensation of the Secretary of the Senate, and Clerk of the House of Representatives, and making provision for the clerks employed in their offices.

Be it enacted, &c., That in lieu of the compensation heretofore allowed by law to the Secretary of the Senate, and Clerk of the House of Representatives of the United States, they shall severally receive the sum of three thousand dollars annually, payable quarterly, as heretofore.

Sec. 2. *And be it further enacted*, That so much of any act heretofore passed, providing any compensation, salary, or perquisites, of any nature or kind whatever, to the said Secretary and Clerk, shall be, and the same is hereby, repealed.

Sec. 3. *And be it further enacted*, That there be allowed to the principal and engrossing clerks of the Senate and of the House of Representatives, an addition of twenty per centum on the compensations to which they are at present entitled by law. This act shall take effect and continue in force for two years from and after the first day of January, one thousand eight hundred and sixteen.

Approved, April 30, 1816.

An Act fixing the compensation of the Chaplains of Congress.

Be it enacted, &c., That the Chaplains of Congress shall be allowed and paid five hundred dollars per annum, each, as a compensation for their services, to commence with the present session of Congress, any law to the contrary notwithstanding.

Approved, April 30, 1816.

An Act to establish Post Roads.

Be it enacted, &c., That the following post roads be, and the same are hereby, discontinued: that is to say,

From Portland, by Windham, Raymond, Bridgeton, Lovell, Waterford, Norway, Paris, Buckfield, Sumner, Hartford, Livermore, Turner, Poland, New Gloucester, and Hebron Academy, to Paris, in Maine.

From Waterford, by Norway, Rumford, and Bethel, in Maine.

From Maryland, to Milford, in New York.

From Delhi to Meredith, in New York.

From Onondaga, by Tully, Preble, and Homer, to Cortland court-house, in New York.

From Montgomery court-house, by Tatnall court-house, and Barrington, to Darien in Georgia.

From Abington, by Russell court-house, and Mockinson Gap, to Abingdon, in Virginia.

From Rogersville, Tennessee, by Lee court-house, Virginia, to Cumberland Gap, in Tennessee.

From Huntington, by the north road, to Smithtown, in New York.

From Buckstown, by Frankfort, Hampden, Bangor, and No. 1, to Orrington; also the route from Prospect, by Mount Ephraim, to Frankfort, in Maine.

From Plymouth, by New Hampton, Meredith, Gilmanton, Northwood, Nottingham, and Durham, to Portsmouth in New Hampshire.

From Greersburg, Pennsylvania, to New Lisbon, in Ohio.

From Barfields, by Port's Ferry to Johnson's Ferry, on Lynch's Creek, in South Carolina.

From Ports' Ferry to Conwayborough, South Carolina.

From Carthage to Lebanon, in Tennessee.

From Windsor to Williamston, in North Carolina.

From Triadelphia to Ellicott's Mills.

From Galway to Broadalbin.

From Centreville to Leesburg.

From Taunton to Weymouth, in Massachusetts.

From Canton to Goshen, in Connecticut.

SEC. 2. *And be it further enacted,* That the following be established as post roads, viz:

In Maine.—From Lowell to Fryburg.

From Portland, by Poland, Hebron, Norway, Paris, Buckfield, Sumner, Hartford, Livermore, Turner, Minot, New Gloucester, and Hebron Academy, to Paris.

From Norridgewalk, by Starks and Industry, to Farmington.

From Portland, by Windham, Raymond, Bridgetown, Lovell, Waterford, Norway, Paris, Rumford, Bethel, and Albany, to Waterford.

From Machias to Hagg's Point, in Lubeck.

From Belfast, by Mount Ephraim, Frankfort, Hampden, and Bangor, to Edington.

From Augusta, by Brown's Corner and Harlem, to Palermo.

From Orrington to Brewer.

From Canaan, by Palmyra, Newport, Crosleytown, and Carmel, to Hampden.

In New Hampshire.—From Plymouth, by Campton, Thornton, Peeling, and Lincoln, to Franconia.

From Portsmouth, by Dover, Madbury, Barrington, Barnstead, Gilmanton, Meredith, and New Hampton, to Plymouth.

In Vermont.—From Grand Isle to Alburg.

From Hyde Park, by Morristown and Stow, to Waterbury.

From Rutland, by Parkerstown, Pittsfield, to Stockbridge.

From Newbury, on the Passumpsic turnpike, by Barnet, St. Johnsbury, Lyndon, Sheffield, and Barton, to Derby.

From Colraine, Massachusetts, by Halifax and Whitingham, to Wilmington.

That the post road from Monkton to Hinesburg, pass through Starksborough.

In Massachusetts.—From Northampton, by Williamsburg, Goshen, Plainfield, and Savoy, to Adams.

From Worcester, by Milbury, Northbridge, and Uxbridge, to Smithfield, in Rhode Island.

From New Bedford, by Bridgewater, to Boston.

That the mail from Northampton to Worcester, pass through Paxton.

From the south parish of Bridgewater, by the west and north parishes of Bridgewater, Randolph, and Milton, to Boston.

In Connecticut.—From Middletown to Killingworth.

From Hartford, through Canton, Torringford, Torrington, Goshen, and Cornwall, to Sharon.

In New York.—From Essex, by Westport, Moriah, Crown Point, Ticonderoga, Hague, and Bolton, to Fort George, in Caldwell.

From Williamstown, Oneida county, by Richland, Ellisbury, and Henderson's, to Sackett's Harbor, in Jefferson county.

From Richfield, by Plainfield, Brookfield, and Hamilton, to Skaneateles.

From Catharinetown, by Reading, to Benton.

From Manlius, by Pompey east, and Pompey west, Hill, Tully, Preble, and Homer, to Cortlandt court-house.

From Whitehall, (to intersect the post road from Albany to Middlebury, Vermont, at Granville, to Pawlett,) in Vermont.

From Sullivan, by Camillus, Brutus, and Mentz, to Junius.

From Auburn, by Mentz, Cato, and Wolcott, to Sodus bay.

From Maryland, by Otego and Milford, to Hamburg, post office in Unadilla.

From Stamford, by Roseville, to Delhi.

From Genoa to Auburn.

From Oswego, by Hannibal and Sterling, to Cato.

From Whitesborough, along the new road to the east end of Oneida lake, to Camden.

From Brownsville to Cape Vincent.

From Saratoga Springs, by Palmertown and Moreau, to Sandy Hill.

From Canandaigua, by Rochester, and thence along the ridge road, to Lewistown.

From Owego, by Spencer court-house, in Tioga county, Dutch and Johnson's settlements, to Catharinetown.

From Geneva, by Phelps and Lyons, to Sodus.

From Westport, by Elizabeth and Keene, to Jay.

From Newburg, by Pleasant Valley, to New Paltz.

From Batavia, by Middlebury, to Warsaw.

From Goshen, by Minisink and Amity, to Warwick.

From Goshen, by Philipsburg, Middletown, Mount Hope, Deer Park, and Carpenter's Point, to post office in Montague, in New Jersey.

From Huntington, by Dixhill's, to Smithtown.

From Hudson, by Kinderhook Landing, Castleton, and Schodack Landing, to Greenbush.

From Hudson to Lebanon.

From Sagg Harbor to Easthampton.

In New Jersey.—From New Brunswick, by Boundbrook, Middlebrook, Somerville, White-House, Hunt's Mills, and Bloomsbury, to Easton, in Pennsylvania.

From Pittstown, in the county of Hunterdon, by Bloomsbury, Stewartsville, to Harmony, in the county of Sussex.

From Jobstown, in the county of Burlington, to Egypt, in the county of Monmouth.

In Pennsylvania.—From Meadville, by forks of Oil Creek, Warren, and outlet of Chetaugua lake to Mayville, in New York.

From Seller's tavern to Doylestown.

From Sunbury, by New Berlin, Union county, and Middleburg, to Lewistown.

From Lewisburg, by Loyal-sock Gap, to Williamsport.

From Bellefont, by Birmingham and Burgess Gap to Ebensburg.

From Downingstown, by Brandywine Manor, Waynesburg, Carnarvon, Ephrata, Elizabeth, Cornwall, and Hamelstown, to Harrisburg.

From Beavertown to New Lisbon, in Ohio.

From Gettysburg, by Oxford and Berwick, to York.

From Bedford, by Johnstown to Indiana.

In Ohio.—From Waynesville, by Bellebook, to Xenia.

From Hamilton, by Oxford, to Bath, in Franklin county, Indiana Territory.

From Gallipolis to Aurora; from West Union to Ripley.

From West Union, by Hillsborough and Wilmington, to Xenia.

From Steubenville, by Salem, Millersburg, and Hamburg, to Canton.

From Salem, by Canfield, Austintown, Warren, Braceville, Sharon, Nelson, Hiram, Mantua, and Aurora, to Newberry.

From Gallipolis, by Sciota Salt Works, to Chillicothe.

From Avery, by Jessup, to Ridgeville, to intersect the post route from Cleveland to Detroit at Rocky river.

In Indiana Territory.—From Brookville, by Bath, to Salisbury.

From Valonia, by Brownstown, to New Natchez, in Jackson county.

From Vincennes to Emmerson's mills, in Knox county.

That the post road from Vincennes to Shawnestown pass through Harmony, in Gibson county.

In Illinois Territory.—From Shawnestown, by White court-house and Edward court-house to Vincennes, in Indiana Territory.

In Missouri Territory.—From St. Louis, by Potosi and Lawrence court-house, to Arkansas.

From St. Charles, by Murphey's, in St. Johns settlement, to Fort Cooper or Howard court-house.

In Maryland.—From Triadelphia, by Damascus, to Newmarket.

From Hagerstown to McConnelstown, a Pennsylvania.

From Upper Marlborough to McGruder's tavern, in Prince George's county.

In Virginia.—From Cabin Point, by J. Edmund's, Baileysburg, Urquarhart's store, and C. Bower's, to South Quay.

From Wythe court-house, by Tazewell court-house, Russell court-house, Scott court-house, and Lee court-house, to Cumberland Gap, in Tennessee.

From Brown's store to Dickenson's store, Franklin county.

From Winchester, by Cedar creek, Trout run, and Lost river, to Mooresfields.

From Pittsylvania court-house, by B. Wadkin's store, and Island Ford, Smith's river, to Rockingham court-house, in North Carolina.

From Wythe court-house to Giles court-house.

From New Canton to Columbia.

From Aldie to Leesburg.

From Aldie to Battletown.

In Kentucky.—From Washington, by Mayville, to Xenia, in Ohio.

From Columbia to Greensburg.

From Great Crossings, by Sanders' mills and New Fredericksburg, to Vevay, in Indiana Territory.

From Washington, by Newtown, Marysville, and Cynthiana, to Georgetown.

From Middletown to Brunerstown.

From Glasgow, by Hartsville, to Lebanon, in Tennessee.

In North Carolina.—From Tarborough, by Staunton's bridge, Snowhill, and Kingston, to Duplin court-house.

From Murfreesborough, by Windsor, to Plymouth.

From Charlotte, by Harrisburg, Pine Hill, Alexander's, Landford, and Lewisville, to Chester court-house, in South Carolina.

In South Carolina.—From Chesterfield court-house, by Lawry's mills and Pickett's store, to Wadesborough, in North Carolina.

From Greenville court-house to Spartanburg.

From Barfield's, by Marion court-house, or Gilesborough, and Godfrey's ferry, to Johnson's ferry, on Lynch's creek.

From Conwayborough, by Gallivant's ferry, to Marion court-house.

From Conwayborough to Smithfield, in North Carolina.

From Chester court-house to Louisville.

In Georgia.—From Jefferson to Hurricane Shoals.

From Montgomery court-house, by Blackmore's and Hardin's to Riceborough.

In Tennessee.—From Nashville, by Murfreesborough, Stone Fort, and Winchester, in Tennessee, Lowry's, Van's Old Place, and Blackburn's, to Athens, in Georgia.

From Lebanon, by Williamsburg and Hilham, to Monroe.

From Sparta, by Liberty and Lebanon, to Nashville.

From Bean's station, by Stiffey's mill, to Iron Works of Mossy creek, thence to Danbridge.

From Marysville, by Morgantown, to Tellico block-house.

From Port Royal to John Hunt's, in Robertson's county.

That the post road from Jonesborough to Greenville pass through Leesburg and Brownsburg.

In the Mississippi Territory.—From Franklin court-house to Liberty, Amity court-house.

Approved, April 30, 1816.

An Act to allow drawback of duties on spirits distilled and sugar refined within the United States, and for other purposes.

Be it enacted, &c., That a drawback of six cents for every gallon of spirits, not below first proof, distilled within the United States, or the Territories thereof, shall be allowed on all such spirits as shall be exported to any foreign port or place, other than the dominions of any foreign State immediately adjoining to the United States, adding to the allowance upon every gallon of such spirits so distilled from molasses, four cents; which allowances shall be made without deduction: *Provided,* That the quantity so exported shall amount to one hundred and fifty gallons at the least, to entitle an exporter thereof to drawback, and that no drawback shall be allowed whenever any of the said spirits shall be exported otherwise than in vessels not less than thirty tons burden.

SEC. 2. *And be it further enacted,* That, in order to entitle the exporter or exporters to the benefit of drawback allowed by this act on such spirits so distilled, the vessels or casks containing the same shall be branded or otherwise marked, in durable characters, with progressive numbers, with the name of the owner, the quantity thereof, to be ascertained by actual gauging, and the proof thereof. And the exporter of such spirits shall, moreover, previous to putting or lading the same on board of any ship or vessel for exportation, give six hours' notice at least to the collector of the customs for the district from which the same are about to be exported of his or her intention to export the same; and shall make entry in writing of the particulars thereof, and of the casks or vessels containing the same, and of their respective marks, numbers, and contents, and of the place or places where deposited, and of the port or place to which, and ship or vessel in which they or either of them shall be so intended to be exported; and the form of the said entry shall be as follows: Entry of domestic spirits, intended to be exported by [here insert the name or names,] on board of the [insert the denomination and name of the vessel,] whereof [insert the name of the master] is master, for [insert the port or place to which destined,] for the benefit of drawback.

Marks.	Numbers.	Casks and contents.	Gauge.

And the said collector shall, in writing, direct the surveyor or other inspecting officer to inspect, or cause to be inspected, the spirits so notified for exportation; and if they shall be found to correspond fully with the notice concerning the same, and shall be so certified by the said surveyor, or other inspecting officer, the said collector, together with the naval officer, if any there be, shall grant a permit for lading the same, on board of the ship or vessel named in such notice and entry as aforesaid; which lading shall be performed under the superintendence of the officer by whom the same shall have been so inspected; and the said exporter or exporters shall likewise make oath that the said spirits, so notified for exportation, and laden on board such ship or vessel, previous to the clearance thereof, or within twenty days after such clearance, are truly intended to be exported to the place whereof notice shall have been given, and are not intended to be relanded within the United States or the Territories thereof.

SEC. 3. *And be it further enacted,* That, for all distilled spirits which shall be exported to any foreign port or place, and which shall be entitled to the benefit of drawback, in virtue of this act, the exporter or exporters shall be entitled to receive from the collector of the customs for such district a debenture or debentures, assignable by delivery and endorsement, for the amount of the drawback to which such spirits are entitled, which shall be received in payment of direct taxes and internal duties in the collection district in which the same shall be granted: *Provided, always,* That the collector aforesaid may refuse to grant such debenture or debentures, in case it shall appear to him that any error has arisen, or any fraud has been committed; and in case of such refusal, if the debenture or debentures claimed shall exceed one hundred dollars, it shall be the

Public Acts of Congress.

duty of the said collector to represent the case to the Comptroller of the Treasury, who shall determine whether such debenture or debentures shall be granted or not. *And provided further,* That in no case of an exportation of spirits entitled to drawback, in virtue of this act, shall a debenture or debentures issue, unless the exporter or exporters shall, before the clearance of the ship or vessel in which the spirits were laden for exportation, or within twenty days after such clearance, make oath or affirmation that the said spirits notified for exportation as aforesaid, and laden on board such ship or vessel, are truly intended to be exported to the place whereof notice shall have been given, and are not intended to be relanded within the United States; and shall moreover give bond, with one or more sureties, to the satisfaction of the collector, in a sum equal to double the amount of the sum for which such exporter may be entitled to claim a debenture, conditioned that the said spirits, or any part thereof, shall not be relanded in any port or place within the limits of the United States, and that the exporter or exporters shall produce, within the time limited, the proof and certificates required, of the said spirits having been delivered without the limits aforesaid.

Sec. 4. *And be it further enacted,* That the said bond shall be drawn, as near as may be, in the same form, and may be discharged in the same manner, as are, or may be prescribed by law in relation to cases where drawback is allowed on the exportation of merchandise imported into the United States, and the like penalties shall be incurred, and proceedings had, whether in regard to officers of the United States or other persons, and the same fees be allowed in cases relative to drawback on domestic distilled spirits, as in cases relative to drawback on foreign spirits; and the form of the said bond, and of the other documents, oaths, and affirmations, not herein inserted, shall be prescribed by the Treasury Department.

Sec. 5. *And be it further enacted,* That in all cases in which drawback shall be claimed for spirits made out of molasses, an oath or affirmation shall be made by two reputable persons one of whom shall not be the exporter, that, according to their belief, the said spirits were distilled from molasses of foreign production; which oath or affirmation, in case the collector of the customs shall not be satisfied therewith, shall be supported by the certificate of a reputable distiller to the same effect.

Sec. 6. *And be it further enacted,* That in addition to the duty at present authorized to be drawn back on sugar refined within the United States, and exported therefrom, there may hereafter be drawn back on such refined sugar, when made out of sugar imported into the United States, the further sum of four cents per pound without deduction, which shall be allowed under the same provisions with the duty now permitted to be drawn back; and furthermore, on the express condition that the person exporting the same shall swear, or affirm that the same, according to his belief, was made out of sugar imported from a foreign port or place; which oath or affirmation,

in case the collector of the customs shall not be satisfied therewith, shall be supported by the certificate of a reputable refiner of sugar to the same effect, and that the drawback on wined sugar heretofore imported, be allowed, subject to the regulations applicable to the drawback of duties on other imported articles.

Sec. 7. *And be it further enacted,* That if any principal or assistant collector of the internal revenue, or collector of the customs, or other officer, shall neglect to perform the duties enjoined upon him by this act, he shall, on conviction thereof forfeit and pay a sum not less than one hundred dollars, nor more than five hundred dollars.

Sec. 8. *And be it further enacted,* That the sum of two hundred and fifty thousand dollars be, and the same is hereby, appropriated, to be paid out of any moneys in the Treasury, not otherwise appropriated, to be applied by the Secretary of the Treasury, under the direction of the President of the United States, in the hire, purchase, or building of custom-houses, ware-houses, and stores, for the purposes of collecting and securing the revenue at such places, and in such manner as he shall deem most expedient.—Approved, April 29, 1816.

An Act making further appropriations for the year one thousand eight hundred and sixteen.

Be it enacted, &c., That the sum of ten thousand dollars be, and the same is hereby, appropriated for compensation to the commissioner appointed under an act, entitled "An act to authorize the payment for property lost, captured, or destroyed by the enemy, while in the military service of the United States, and for other purposes" and the further sum of one thousand dollars for compensation to the clerk, authorized by the act aforesaid; for the expense incurred by the board of commissioners appointed under the act providing for the indemnification of certain claimants of public lands in the Mississippi Territory, seven hundred dollars; and for additional compensation to the commissioners aforesaid, and their secretary, four thousand dollars; and for expenses of engraving, printing, and preparing certificates issued, and to be issued, by the commissioners, three thousand dollars; for the expense for clerks employed by the Board of Navy Commissioners seven hundred and fifty dollars; in addition to the former appropriation; for the payment of pensions, an additional sum of one hundred and fifty thousand dollars; and for the payment of a clerk in the secretary's office of the Mississippi Territory, employed by the Governor of that Territory from the first of April to the first of August, one thousand eight hundred and fifteen, two hundred dollars; to be paid out of any money in the Treasury not otherwise appropriated.—Approved, April 30, 1816.

Resolutions directing a copy of the documents printed by a resolve of Congress, of the 27th of December, 1813, to be transmitted to each of the Judges of the Supreme Court.

Resolved, &c., That of the two hundred copies

Public Acts of Congress.

of the documents ordered to be printed by a resolve of the Senate and House of Representatives of the twenty-seventh of December, one thousand eight hundred and thirteen, the Secretary of State be, and he is hereby, authorized to take one copy for each of the Judges of the Supreme Court of the United States, to be transmitted to said judges, according to the provision of the act of Congress of the eighteenth of April, one thousand eight hundred and fourteen.

Approved, February 6, 1816.

Resolution, to indemnify the sureties of Commodore John Rodgers.

Resolved, &c., That under the peculiar circumstances of the case, of an appeal taken by Commodore John Rodgers, from a decree of the United States circuit court for the district of Massachusetts, affirming that of the district court for the said district, to the Supreme Court of the United States, in the case wherein John Donnel of Baltimore was libellant, and the said John Rodgers and John Smith were respondents, the United States will indemnify and save harmless any person who may become sureties for the said John Rodgers, in a bond to respond the final judgment of the Supreme Court on the said appeal : *Provided,* That this interposition on the part of the United States shall not be considered as involving them in any other engagement or responsibility, than to indemnify and save harmless the said sureties from eventual loss, on account of such suretyship.

Approved, February 15, 1816.

Resolution, requesting the President to present medals to Captain Stewart and the officers of the frigate Constitution.

Resolved, &c., That the President of the United States be, and he is hereby, requested to present to Captain Charles Stewart, of the frigate Constitution, a gold medal, with suitable emblems and devices, and a silver medal, with suitable emblems and devices, to each commissioned officer of the said frigate, in testimony of the high sense entertained by Congress of the gallantry, good conduct, and services of Captain Stewart, his officers and crew, in the capture of the British vessels of war, the Cyane and the Levant, after a brave and skilful combat.

Approved, February 22, 1816.

Resolution, requesting the President to present medals to Captain James Biddle, and the officers of the sloop-of-war Hornet.

Resolved, &c., That the President of the United States be, and he is hereby, requested to present to Captain Jas. Biddle, of the sloop-of-war Hornet, a gold medal, with suitable emblems and devices, and a silver medal, with suitable emblems and devices, to each commissioned officer of the said sloop-of-war, in testimony of the high sense entertained by Congress of the gallantry, good conduct and services of Captain Biddle, his officers

and crew, in capturing the British sloop-of-war Penguin, after a brave and skilful combat.

Approved, February 22, 1816.

Resolution, for printing the laws relative to naturalization.

Resolved, &c., That the Secretary of State be authorized and directed to cause to be printed four thousand copies of the laws now in force on the subject of naturalization. And, of the copies which may be so provided, two shall be sent to each marshal of a judicial district of the United States, two to the clerk or prothonotary for each court of the United States, or of a particular State, which may, by law, admit persons to be naturalized, and two to each collector of the customs. The remaining copies, after reserving such as the President of the United States may deem proper for the use of the Executive departments, shall be placed in the Library of Congress.

Approved, April 16, 1816.

Resolution, requiring the Secretary of State to compile and print, once in every two years, a register of all officers and agents, civil, military, and naval, in the service of the United States.

Resolved, &c., That, once in two years, a register, containing correct lists of all the officers and agents, civil, military, and naval, in the service of the United States, made up to the last day of September of each year in which a new Congress is to assemble, be compiled and printed under the direction of the Secretary for the Department of State. And to enable him to form such register, he, for his own department, and the heads of the other departments, respectively, shall, in due time, cause such lists as aforesaid, of all officers and agents, in their respective departments, including clerks, cadets, and midshipmen, to be made and lodged in the office of the Department of State. And the said lists, shall exhibit the amount of compensation, pay, and emoluments allowed to each officer, agent, clerk, cadet, and midshipman, the State or county in which he was born, and where employed.

2. *Resolved,* That the Secretary of the Navy subjoin to the list of the persons employed in his department, the names, force, and condition of all the ships and vessels belonging to the United States, and when and where built.

3. *Resolved,* That five hundred copies of the said register be printed ; and that on the first Monday in January in each year, when a new Congress shall be assembled, there be delivered to the President, the Vice President, each head of a department, each member of the Senate and House of Representatives of the United States, one copy of such register ; and to the Secretary of the Senate, and Clerk of the House of Representatives, each, ten copies, for the use of the respective houses ; that twenty-five copies shall be deposited in the Library of the United States, at the Seat of Government, to be used like other books in that library, and that the residue of the

Public Acts of Congress.

said copies be disposed of in such manner as Congress shall from time to time direct.

4. *Resolved,* That, for the information of the present Congress, such register as aforesaid be prepared and distributed as aforesaid, on the first day of its next session.

Approved, April 27, 1816. .

———

A resolution relative to the more effectual collection of the public revenue.

Resolved, &c., That the Secretary of the Treasury be, and he hereby is, required and directed to adopt such measures as he may deem necessary to cause, as soon as may be, all duties, taxes, debts, or sums of money, accruing or becoming payable to the United States, to be collected and paid in the legal currency of the United States, or Treasury notes, or notes of the Bank of the United States as by law provided and declared, or in notes of banks which are payable and paid on demand in the said legal currency of the United States, and that from and after the twentieth day of February next, no such duties, taxes, debts, or sums of money accruing or becoming payable to the United States as aforesaid, ought to be collected or received otherwise than in the legal currency of the United States, or Treasury notes, or notes of the Bank of the United States, or in notes of banks which are payable and paid on demand in the said legal currency of the United States.

Approved, April 30, 1816.

———

Resolution, authorizing the President of the United States to employ a skilful assistant in the corps of engineers.

Resolved, &c., That the President of the United States be, and he is hereby, authorized to employ, in addition to the corps of engineers as now established, a skilful assistant, whose compensation shall be such as the President of the United States shall think proper, not exceeding the allowance to the chief officer of that corps.

Approved, April 30, 1816.

INDEX

TO THE PROCEEDINGS AND DEBATES OF THE FIRST SESSION OF THE FOURTEENTH CONGRESS.—SENATE.

Senate Proceedings and Debates.

Senate Proceedings and Debates.

Senate Proceedings and Debates.

Senate Proceedings and Debates.

Senate Proceedings and Debates.

Senate Proceedings and Debates.

Senate Proceedings and Debates.

Senate Proceedings and Debates.

Senate Proceedings and Debates.

Senate Proceedings and Debates.

Senate Proceedings and Debates.

Senate Proceedings and Debates.

Q.

R.

Senate Proceedings and Debates.

Senate Proceedings and Debates.

House Proceedings and Debates.

HOUSE OF REPRESENTATIVES AND APPENDIX.

House Proceedings and Debates.

House Proceedings and Debates.

House Proceedings and Debates.

House Proceedings and Debates.

House Proceedings and Debates.

House Proceedings and Debates.

House Proceedings and Debates.

House Proceedings and Debates.

House Proceedings and Debates.

House Proceedings and Debates.

House Proceedings and Debates.

House Proceedings and Debates.

House Proceedings and Debates.

House Proceedings and Debates.

House Proceedings and Debates.

House Proceedings and Debates.

House Proceedings and Debates.

PUBLIC ACTS AND RESOLUTIONS.

Public Acts and Resolutions.

Public Acts and Resolutions.

Lightning Source UK Ltd.
Milton Keynes UK
UKHW010925261118
332983UK00012B/1443/P